ROTHMANS FOOTBALL YEARBOOK 1990-91

EDITOR: JACK ROLLIN

QUEEN ANNE PRESS
MACDONALD & CO
LONDON and SYDNEY

A *Queen Anne Press* BOOK

© Rothmans Publications Ltd 1990

First published in Great Britain in 1990 by
Queen Anne Press, a division of
Macdonald & Co (Publishers) Ltd
Orbit House
London EC4A 1AR

A member of Maxwell Macmillan Pergamon Publishing Corporation

Cover photographs: Liverpool crowd (*Colorsport*)
FIFA World Cup (*All-Sport*)

Other photographic acknowledgements
All-Sport Photographic Ltd: Page 904
Action Images/USPA: Pages 53; 763, 773, 774
Associated Sports Photography: Pages 788, 883
Colorsport: Pages 8, 9, 11, 54, 651, 678, 898
Bob Thomas: Pages 613, 624, 824, 901

British Library Cataloguing in Publication Data
Rothmans football yearbook.—1990–91
1. Association football – Serials
796.334'05

ISBN 0-356-17912-5
ISBN 0 356 17911-7 Pbk

Typeset, printed and bound in Great Britain by
BPCC Hazell Books
Aylesbury, Bucks, England
Member of BPCC Ltd.

CONTENTS

EUROPEAN FOOTBALL

NON-LEAGUE FOOTBALL

INFORMATION AND RECORDS

INTRODUCTION

The 21st edition of *Rothmans Football Yearbook* has full coverage of the 1990 World Cup including matches in the qualifying tournament and finals in Italy. As last year every one of the 92 Football League clubs has a full page photograph of the 1989–90 squad and there are again six pages devoted to each team with extended information including the result of the club's first game in the Football League with line-up and scorers which should be of interest to readers. There are special articles on Sport and the Law and the Football Trust and looking ahead there are the fixtures for the 1992 European Championship. With England back in Europe, there are also the draws for the various European cup competitions.

All international matches involving the four home countries and the Republic of Ireland are also dealt with, together with coverage of Welsh and Northern Irish League football. More familiar items are a list of transfers during the season, important addresses and Football League managers for each League club over the years.

The Editor would like to thank Maurice Golesworthy for historical notes on the clubs and the diary, as well as Alan Elliott for the Scottish section. Thanks are also due to Melanie Georgi, whose painstaking and conscientious reading of the proofs has been of invaluable assistance in the preparation of the book as well as editorial assistance from Mavis Suckling.

The Editor would also like to pay tribute to the various organisations who have helped to make this edition complete, especially Mike Foster of the Football League, Mike McNamara of The Football Association, and the secretaries of all the Football League and Scottish League clubs for their kind co-operation. The ready availability of Football League secretary David Dent and his staff to answer queries was as usual most appreciated, and thanks are due in equal measure to Jim Farry, until recently the Scottish Football League secretary, and his staff.

ACKNOWLEDGEMENTS

The Editor would like to express his appreciation of the following individuals and organisations for their co-operation: Glynis Firth, Sandra Whiteside, Sheila Murphy, Lorna Parnell, Debbie Birch and Andrew Whittaker (all from The Football League), David Barber and Steve Clark (The Football Association), David C. Thompson of The Scottish Football League, Bernard Turner and David Cartwright (FA of Wales), Alan Dick, Malcolm Brodie, C. S. Allatt and Peter Hughes (English Schools FA), W. P. Goss (AFA), Ken Scott for GM Vauxhall Conference information, C. Ashridge, Rev. Nigel Sands, Edward Grayson, Andy Howland, Don Aldridge and former *Rothmans Football Yearbook* editor Peter Dunk.

Finally, thanks to Celia Kent, Publishing Director at Queen Anne Press, for her support and encouragement during the year, and to Lisa Burgess and Stephanie Bennett (Celia Kent's assistants), not forgetting Ian McFarlane and the staff at BPCC Hazell Books for their enthusiasm and commitment in the production of this book. This was much appreciated in the final stages.

EDITORIAL

In some strange way, finishing a creditable fourth in a largely discredited 1990 World Cup tournament, gave England a prestige it might not have achieved had it succeeded in winning the trophy. After a wretched start followed by incredible good fortune, the team played its most convincing football and unquestionably displayed such excellent conduct on the field of play that it clinched a place for English clubs back into Europe.

History will probably reflect that the 14th World Cup was best forgotten about and winning it might well have detracted from the performance of its victors. Losing out in the semi-finals on penalty kicks was a particularly sad way to leave the tournament, but as long as National Associations are prepared to support this kind of lottery, such an unsatisfactory method of determining a winner is inevitable.

One can only shudder at the game's administrators who are prepared for the spectacle of a team completing an entire World Cup final tournament without scoring a goal during normal or extra time, yet winning the trophy on penalties. But not only is this farcical in the World Cup, it has no place in the game at all and we must all take responsibility for allowing it to develop.

Highly trained professional footballers are expected to cope with the agonies of missing a penalty kick, but the effect on youngsters learning the game is crucial. How many lads even before their teenage years are still being branded as failures because they were the ones who caused their team to lose a cup game in this manner. Yet almost any other alternative would be preferable. Taking into account the number of corners would be a fairer method; it was even used in Scotland during the last war for cup games. It might even encourage attacking play if that is not too naïve a thought. Sudden death would also provide an exciting climax.

Not even FIFA are even suggesting by their attitude to goalkeepers facing penalty kicks that it is anything to do with the laws of the game. At least one team won through its shoot-out because the goalkeeper not only moved before the kick was taken as they all do, but was even off his line. It is high time the practice was buried.

So Bobby Robson departed as England's manager with his head held higher than he probably expected. He has been succeeded by Graham Taylor, an enthusiastic lover of the game who will find himself put under the intense pressure by the media that aged his predecessor. He understands the fine line between winning and losing. He came close to leading Aston Villa into relegation only the season before they finished runners-up.

Taylor's former club have made a bold move and an interesting choice as his successor in the manager of Czechslovakia, Dr. Jozef Venglos who becomes the first foreigner in charge of a First Division team in this country. Once it was that coaches from these shores spread their knowledge around the world to lasting effect.

There are many encouraging signs in the game now, but hooliganism is still around, kept in check by massive police presence and the day when all supporters can be trusted to enjoy their football without being segregated is far, far away.

Another annoying situation in the game today is the amount of time-wasting which is indulged in by passing back to the goalkeeper and the subsequent delay while the ball is dribbled around the penalty area, since any challenge on him is apparently considered worthy of nothing less than the death penalty . . . When Gary Crosby headed the ball out of the outstretched hand of Andy Dibble and scored a cheecky goal, one would have thought that it had been a hanging offence, judging by the furore it caused.

There will be those who will claim that this sharp practice did not bring any lasting reward in the League for Forest who had beaten Manchester City 1-0 as a result of this enterprise. Forest did not win again for eight games. That was a far-fetched explanation but surely over-protection of goalkeepers has also been carried to a farcical degree.

The transfer market was buoyant in 1989. There were fourteen £1 million-plus moves during the year affecting English clubs. Professional staffs are showing an increase which is clearly a reflection of the rise in attendances during the last four years. Capacity at grounds is shrinking and will pose problems.

Yet in the hot summer of 1990 we were coldly reminded of the gulf which exists between rich and poor. On 30 July Rumbelows agreed to sponsor the League Cup for £5 million over four years following the collapse of a deal with National Power. The following day Aldershot, £490,000 in debt, were wound up in the high court. The last Football League club to be forced to withdraw was Accrington Stanley in 1962. Then in early August the Football League clubs decided to revert to a 22 club First Division and gradually admit two more clubs to the competition overall making it 94 and immediately put themselves on a collision course with the FA.

JACK ROLLIN

Rothmans Football Awards

Selecting any representative team which is not required to prove itself on the field of play is a tempting exercise, but one inevitably leading to controversy. The wider the choice simply makes the task far more difficult, thus a World Cup team over the lifetime of *Rothmans Football Yearbook* covers six competitions.

Even with one tournament, the number of alternatives is amazing. Take the 1990 final series as an example. The number of various teams selected by interested parties confirms just how difficult it is to find any measure of consistency throughout the selections.

The West German magazine *Kicker* chose the following as its best team: Conejo (Costa Rica); Baresi (Italy), Bergomi (Italy), Buchwald (West Germany), Kohler (West Germany), Gascoigne (England), Matthaus (West Germany), Scifo (Belgium), Brehme (West Germany), Schillaci (Italy), Milla (Cameroon).

Arguably the most controversial selection in this team is the goalkeeper. While the last line of defence generally emerged as the department which provided as many outstanding players as the next, the claims of others like Claudio Taffarel (Brazil), Jan Stejskal (Czechoslovakia) and even West Germany's own Bodo Illgner might easily have been more popular elsewhere.

But imagine the problems confronting anyone wrestling with the 1970, 1974, 1978, 1982, 1986 and 1990 finals! From the outset, since the team will not be faced with any opposition on the field – merely criticism off it – it will be able to respond theoretically to its indvidual talent. But restricting selection to players who have appeared in a World Cup final tournament, means there can be no consideration for a player of the calibre of George Best of Northern Ireland.

The prime consideration in choosing the team was to provide one which reflected entertainment value as well as expertise. At the same time it had to be a viable proposition from a playing point of view with the accent on attacking skills. Whatever arguments might be put forward about the composition of the eleven and the five substitutes provided, there can be no doubt that they have established themselves at some period over the last 20 years as world class players.

Naturally players appearing in more than one final series have the edge. Thus Diego Maradona vintage 1990 might not have made the grade compared with the 1986 version. Even in the choice of manager there is an added problem. Franz Beckenbauer might easily qualify for the team as a player or as its coach, West Germany having finished runners-up in 1986 and winners four years later.

Ultimately the choice of manager goes to Helmut Schoen the German who was Beckenbauer's predecessor. His team is one of talented players and he has the extra advantage of a bench of substitutes who have their own claims to be included from the outset of any similar representative team.

Another interesting point: the selection contains three West German managers. In addition to Schoen and Beckenbauer already mentioned, there is Berti Vogts who has taken over from Beckenbauer as his country's national team manager following the 1990 tournament.

Selecting a captain for the team would be another difficult task with at least half a dozen candidates for the role. But again with a German manager it would be more appropriate to have Beckenbauer with the armband. Naturally there will be claims that Schoen and 'Kaiser Franz' did not always see eye to eye with each other, but some healthy exchange of views could provide added stimulation!

One of the biggest problems facing this all-star team would be the question of free-kicks. Just which one of several players could be called upon to take them, but then there is sufficient skill for a variety of options and they could share them out. Moreover, if they were called upon to display their talents, there seems little doubt that they would have plenty of opportunity to show their paces in all aspects of the game.

THE BEST WORLD CUP PLAYERS OF THE LAST 20 YEARS

THE ROTHMANS ALLSTARS SQUAD

1982–1986–1990

GIACINTO
FACCHETTI
(*Italy*)

FRANZ
BECKENBAUER
(*West Germany*)

Manager: HELMUT SCHOEN

GORDON BANKS
(*England*)

1970–1974–1978

BERTI VOGTS
(*West Germany*)

BOBBY MOORE
(*England*)

9

PELE
(Brazil)

OSSIE ARDILES
(Argentina)

MICHEL PLATINI
(France)

JOHAN CRUYFF
(Holland)

Substitutes:

GERD MULLER
(West Germany)

DIEGO MARADONA
(Argentina)

DANIEL
PASSARELLA
(Argentina)

KARL-HEINZ
RUMMENIGGE
(West Germany)

ZICO
(Brazil)

RUDI KROL
(Holland)

DINO ZOFF
(Italy)

1990 WORLD CUP

FINAL TOURNAMENT IN ITALY

The 14th World Cup ended in a disgraceful final with West Germany beating a nine man Argentina with a late controversial penalty. Much of what had gone before had been eminently forgettable. There were fewer goals than ever, more players sent off, infrequent moments of excitement and little in the way of inventive football from the supposed cream of the world's professional talent. But attendances were up on 1986 and there was a huge television audience.

The competition actually began with one team finishing with nine men, Argentina the holders being humiliated by a depleted Cameroon, the surprise team of the entire tournament who lacked only discipline and experience. They were unquestionably the most attractive team in the finals, reminiscent of Brazil. Before the matches began, Holland's Ruud Gullit had been asked to name his World Cup winners. He replied 'Cameroon'.

They failed only against England, but not before they led 2-1 and with more wisdom might easily have put the game beyond their opponents before conceding one penalty needlessly and another as a result of poor covering. Moreover they had four regular players out through suspension in this game.

In Roger Milla they had almost the best forward in the tournament. Despite being 38 years old and in semi-retirement playing on the island of Reunion for St Pierre, he was the master of the ball at his feet. Only the ebullient little Sicillian Salvatore Schillaci was better. He came off the substitutes bench to save Italy in their opening game with Austria and emerged as the top scorer with six goals. Nicknamed Toto, this former tyre repairer had played only one season in the First Division with Juventus. In the Wizard of Oz, Dorothy's dog was also called Toto, but Schillaci was over the moon rather than over the rainbow. Alas he was unable to steer Italy to the final pot of gold.

The Italians were technically the most gifted team, but they lacked finish and fell short of what was required in the last third of the field. The Germans were the strongest physically and with Italy emerged from the group games as the most likely finalists. England and the Republic of Ireland began their challenge with a typical encounter in which the ball probably needed to be carried off on a stretcher – as Tommy Docherty would say.

But England then had more than their share of luck in the second round against Belgium, who twice hit the woodwork. With Paul Gascoigne seeming to be everywhere despite his obvious lack of pace and lacking the experience to know when to release the ball, he provided excellent footwork, free-kicks and corners and along with Mark Wright, Des Walker and Gary Lineker was among England's outstanding players. In the semi-final with West Germany they had their best match of the tournament and one which ended in the unsatisfactory method of penalty kicks. Italy also failed in the same manner against Argentina, who had looked a pale shadow of their Diego Maradona-inspired victory four years earlier. Maradona himself managed one defence splitting pass of note and had one shot at goal in the entire competition. His distributive contribution led to Claudio Caniggia scoring the goal against the run of play which eliminated Brazil and his effort from a free-kick against Italy went harmlessly wide. Otherwise Argentina were pretty dreadful and fortunate to reach the final. But it was not difficult to get through as there were many other poor teams.

Holland were the biggest disappointments. Their big four of Marco Van Basten, Ruud Gullit, Ronald Koeman and Frank Rijkaard let them down badly. There was no spirit in the side as the players clearly did not relish Leo Beenhakker as coach, having wanted Johan Cruyff to take over. There was some excuse for Gullit, out with injury over a year, but none for Van Basten who scarcely had a kick, Koeman was off form and Rijkaard disgraced himself by getting sent off for spitting twice at Rudi Voller of West Germany.

The Germans tried their usual play-acting when fouled and intimidated most of the referees. But Lothar Matthaus often looked a powerhouse in midfield and Andreas Brehme supplied an endless stream of crosses from his famous left foot. He also converted the penalty in the final. In general many teams were let down by the players who should have done better.

Uruguay, in better discipline, were well organised in defence but poorly served by Enzo Francescoli and Ruben Sosa up front. Spain were as inconsistent as ever and Emilio Butragueno was anonymous. The Soviet Union were lethargic in the opening game with Rumania who were full value for their victory, but improved afterwards and were hit by a couple of refereeing decisions against Argentina which cost them a place in the next round. Maradona showed he had added a new dimension to his handling prowess, by stopping the ball in his own penalty area, an action which went unnoticed and the Soviets had a player sent off rather harshly.

Austria played their best football before the tournament started, Yugoslavia recovered from losing 4-1 to West Germany to finally sink in another penalty competition, Scotland committed suicide in the first game with Costa Rica and left themselves with too much to do. Sweden failed to do as well as expected and Colombia were fitful. The Colombian goalkeeper Rene Higuita, famed for his upfield sorties, was finally caught out attempting a sleight of foot against Milla.

Brazil lacked courage up front, but still managed to give the impression of a team capable of doing something better. Czechoslovakia did quite well until upset by the Germans and Egypt looked good in defence with Hany Ramzy outstanding. South Korea, the United Arab Emirates and the USA were not expected to shine, though the Americans showed some ability to learn and made the Italians look quite ordinary against them.

Individual players to enhance their reputations included Gheorghe Hagi (Rumania), Enzo Scifo (Belgium), Dragan Stojkovic (Yugoslavia) and had Caniggia not stupidly handled the gall to get himself banned from the final, who knows, Argentina as pathetic as they were might have repeated the scoreline of the 1986 final against West Germany. The Irish gave everything and enjoyed themselves.

England won the Fair Play award. They deserved that at least. Peter Shilton ended his international career on 125 caps, but was caught off his line when the Germans scored with a wicked deflection from a free-kick and dithered about to be dispossessed in the third place play-off with Italy. But then the game can be cruel. Stuart Pearce and Chris Waddle had the misfortune to fail from the penalty spot.

Refereeing left much to be desired. Those officials running the line had difficulty in understanding the off-side law. Now FIFA have announced through the International Football Association Board that a player will no longer be considered off-side if he is level with the second last opponent or with the last two opponents. This merely transfers the problem from one side of a fine line to another. Far better for them to outlaw off-side from all dead ball situations bringing free-kicks into line with corners, throw-ins etc.

Officials often had trouble in keeping up with the game. Clearly standards of fitness are not what they should have been. Most onlookers could see that they often made up their minds about a tackle upon the reaction of the victim. But surely refereeing is not about awarding Oscars for acting?

Television coverage has also plumbed the depths. Action replays *ad nauseum* are cutting into play. Commentaries are grating and opinions of studio experts of a banal nature. But then what can one expect if the standard of play is the same?

The Germans attacked ceaselessly in the first half of the final without the necessary guile to score. In the second half the Argentines clearly hung on for penalty kicks and the game which had begun badly fell away even more. Pedro Monzon became the first player to be sent off in a World Cup final and near the end Gustavo Dezotti became the second. This was after Roberto Sensini was adjudged to have brought down Rudi Voller. Andreas Brehme converted from the spot past Sergio Goycochea who had stood in for Nery Pumpido who had broken his leg in Argentina's second game.

Thus West Germany joined Brazil and Italy as teams who have won the cup three times. Manager Franz Beckenbauer became the first man to captain and manage a World Cup winning team.

If the coaches of the world cannot improve on this spectacle, the game faces a worrying future. If they blame the players for the spectacle then clearly talent is drying up as fast as the global warming effect. But perhaps hope lies in the situation facing the Cameroon. Their Soviet manager could speak no French and had difficulty communicating his instructions to the players. Eventually perhaps the way forward is to encourage individual talent not stifle it with systems – or coaches.

West Germany's Andreas Brehme beats Argentina's keeper Sergio Goycochea from the penalty spot to give West Germany their third World Cup final victory. (Colorsport)

FINAL TOURNAMENT IN ITALY

First Round
Group A
9 June, Rome, 72,303
Italy (0) 1 *(Schillaci 77)*
Austria (0) 0
Italy: Zenga; Maldini, Ferri, Baresi, Bergomi, De Napoli, Ancelotti (De Agostini 46), Donadoni, Giannini, Carnevale (Schillaci 74), Vialli.
Austria: Lindenberger; Russ, Streiter, Pecl, Aigner, Artner (Zsak 61), Herzog, Schottel, Linzmaier (Hortnagl 70), Ogris, Polster.
Referee: Wright (Brazil).

10 June, Florence, 33,266
Czechoslovakia (2) 5 *(Skuhravy 25, 78, Bilek 39 (pen), Hasek 50, Luhovy 90).*
USA (0) 1 *(Caligiuri 61)*
Czechoslovakia: Stejskal; Hasek, Kocian, Kadlec, Straka, Moravcik (Weiss 84), Chovanec, Kubik, Bilek, Knoflicek (Luhovy 79), Skuhravy.
USA: Meola; Armstrong, Stollmeyer (Balboa 65), Windischmann, Trittschuh, Caligiuru, Ramos, Harkes, Wynalda*, Vermes, Murray (Sullivan 80).
Referee: Rothlisberger (Switzerland).

14 June, Rome, 73,423
Italy (1) 1 *(Giannini 11)*
USA (0) 0
Italy: Zenga; Bergomi, Ferri, Baresi, Maldini, De Napoli, Berti, Giannini, Donadoni, Carnevale (Schillaci 50), Vialli.
USA: Meola; Armstrong, Windischmann, Doyle, Banks (Stollmeyer 80), Ramos, Balboa, Caligiuri, Harkes, Vermes, Murray (Sullivan 82).
Referee: Codesal (Mexico).

15 June, Florence, 38,962
Austria (0) 0
Czechoslovakia (0) 1 *(Bilek 30 (pen))*
Austria: Lindenberger; Russ (Ogris 46), Aigner, Pecl, Pfeffer, Hortnagl, Zsak, Schottel (Streiter 82), Herzog, Rodax, Polster.
Czechoslovakia: Stejskal; Hasek, Kadlec, Kocian, Nemecek, Moravcik, Chovanec (Bielik 31), Kubik, Bilek, Skuhravy, Knoflicek (Weiss 81).
Referee: Smith (Scotland).

19 June, Rome, 73,303
Italy (1) 2 *(Schillaci 9, Baggio 77)*
Czechoslovakia (0) 0
*Italy:*Zenga; Bergomi, Ferri, Baresi, Maldini, Donadoni (De Agostini 50), De Napoli (Vierchowod 66), Giannini, Berti, Baggio, Schillaci.
Czechoslovakia: Stejskal; Hasek, Kadlec, Kinier, Nemecek (Bielik 46), Moravcik, Chovanec, Weiss (Griga 58), Bilek, Skuhravy, Knoflicek.
Referee: Quiniou (France).

19 June, Florence, 34,857
Austria (0) 2 *(Ogris 51, Rodax 63)*
USA (0) 1 *(Murray 82)*
Austria: Lindenberger; Streiter, Aigner, Pecl, Pfeffer, Artner*, Zsak, Herzog, Rodax (Glatzmeyer 85), Polster (Reisinger 46), Ogris.
USA: Meola; Doyle, Windischmann, Banks (Wynalda 55), Armstrong, Caligiuri (Bliss 70), Harkes, Ramos, Balboa, Murray, Vermes.
Referee: Al-Sharif (Egypt).

	P	W	D	L	F	A	Pts
Italy	3	3	0	0	4	0	6
Czechoslovakia	3	2	0	1	6	3	4
Austria	3	1	0	2	2	3	2
USA	3	0	0	3	2	8	0

Group B
8 June, Milan 73,780
Argentina (0) 0
Cameroon (0) 1 *(Omam-Biyik 65)*
Argentina: Pumpido; Ruggeri (Caniggia 46), Fabbri, Simon, Lorenzo, Batista, Sensini (Calderon 69), Balbo, Basualdo, Burruchaga, Maradona.

Cameroon: Nkono; Tataw, Ebwelle, Massing*, Ndip, Kunde, Mbouh, Kana-Biyik*, Mfede (Libih 65), Makanaky (Milla 82), Omam-Biyik.
Referee: Vautrot (France)

9 June, Bari, 42,960
USSR (0) 0
Rumania (1) 2 *(Lacatus 40, 54 (pen))*
USSR: Dasayev; Kuznetsov, Khidiatulin, Gorlukovich, Rats, Aleinikov, Bessonov, Litovchenko (Yaremchuk 65), Zavarov, Protasov, Dobrovolski (Borodyuk 71).
Rumania: Lung; Rednic, Andone, Poescu, Klein, Rotariu, Timofte, Sabau, Lupescu, Lacatus (Dumitrescu 86), Raducioiu (Balint 79).
Referee: Cardellino (Uruguay).

13 June, Naples, 55,759
Argentina (1) 2 *(Troglio 27, Burruchaga 79)*
USSR (0) 0
Argentina: Pumpido (Goycochea 9); Monzon (Lorenzo 78), Serrizuela, Simon, Olarticoechea, Batista, Basualdo, Burruchaga, Troglio, Maradona, Caniggia.
USSR: Uvarov; Bessonov*, Kuznetsov, Khidiatulin, Gorlukovich, Zygmantovich, Aleinikov, Shalimov, Zavarov (Lyuti 85), Dobrovolski, Protasov (Litovchenko 75).
Referee: Fredricksson (Sweden).

14 June, Bari, 38,687
Cameroon (0) 2 *(Milla 76, 86)*
Rumania (0) 1 *(Balint 88)*
Cameroon: Nkono; Tataw, Onana, Ndip, Ebwelle, Kunde (Pagal 68), Mbouh, Mfede, Maboang (Milla 58), Makanaky, Omam-Biyik.
Rumania: Lung; Rednic, Andone, Popescu, Klein, Rotariu, Sabau, Timofte, Hagi (Dumitrescu 55), Raducioiu (Balint 79), Lacatus.
Referee: Silva (Chile).

18 June, Naples, 52,733
Argentina (0) 1 *(Monzon 61)*
Rumania (0) 1 *(Balint 67)*
Argentina: Goycochea; Simon, Serrizuela, Monzon, Troglio (Giusti 53), Batista, Burruchaga (Dezotti 60), Basualdo, Olarticoechea, Maradona, Caniggia.
Rumania: Lung; Rednic, Andone, Popescu, Klein, Rotariu, Sabau (Mateut 82), Lupescu, Hagi, Lacatus, Balint (Lupu 72).
Referee: Valente (Portugal).

18 June, Bari, 37,307
USSR (2) 4 *(Protasov 20, Zygmantovich 29, Zavarov 52, Dobrovolski 63)*
Cameroon (0) 0.
USSR: Uvarov; Khidiatulin, Kuznetzov, Demianenko, Gorlukovich, Aleinikov, Litovchenko (Yaremchuk 72), Zygmantovich, Shalimov (Zavarov 46), Protasov, Dobrovolski.
Cameroon: Nkono; Onana, Ebwelle, Kunde (Milla 34), Tataw, Ndip, Kana-Biyik, Mbouh, Mfede, Makanaky (Pagal 58), Omam-Biyik.
Referee: Wright (Brazil).

	P	W	D	L	F	A	Pts
Cameroon	3	2	0	1	3	5	4
Rumania	3	1	1	1	4	3	3
Argentina	3	1	1	1	3	2	3
USSR	3	1	0	2	4	4	2

Group C
10 June, Turin, 62,628
Brazil (1) 2 *(Careca 40, 62)*
Sweden (0) 1 *(Brolin 78)*
Brazil: Taffarel; Mauro Galvao, Mozer, Ricardo Gomes, Jorginho, Branco, Dunga, Alemao, Valdo (Silas 83), Muller, Careca.
Sweden: Ravelli; Nilsson R, Larsson P, Ljung (Stromberg 70), Limpar, Thern, Schwarz, Ingesson, Nilsson J, Brolin, Magnusson (Pettersson 46).
Referee: Lanese (Italy).

11 June, Genoa, 30,867
Costa Rica (0) 1 *(Cayasso 49)*
Scotland (0) 0
Costa Rica: Conejo; Chavarria, Flores, Marchena, Montero, Chavez, Gonzalez, Gomez, Ramirez, Jara (Medford 85), Cayasso.
Scotland: Leighton; Gough (McKimmie 46), McPherson, McLeish, Malpas, McStay, Aitken, McCall, Bett (McCoist 74), Johnston, McInally.
Referee: Lousta (Argentina).

16 June, Turin, 58,007
Brazil (1) 1 *(Muller 32)*
Costa Rica (0) 0
Brazil: Taffarel; Mauro Galvao, Jorginho, Mozer, Ricardo Gomes, Branco, Dunga, Alemao, Valdo (Silas 86), Careca (Bebeto 83), Muller.
Costa Rica: Conejo; Flores, Chavarria, Marchena, Gonzalez, Montero, Chavez, Gomez, Ramirez, Jara (Myers 72), Cayasso (Guimares 78).
Referee: Jouini (Tunisia).

16 June, Genoa, 31,823
Scotland (1) 2 *(McCall 10, Johnston 83 (pen))*
Sweden (0) 1 *(Stromberg 85)*
Scotland: Leighton; McPherson, Levein, McLeish, Malpas, Aitken, MacLeod, McCall, Fleck (McCoist 84), Durie (McStay 74), Johnston.
Sweden: Ravelli; Nilsson R, Larsson P (Stromberg 74), Hysen, Schwarz, Ingesson, Thern, Limpar, Nilsson J, Brolin, Pettersson (Ekstrom 65).
Referee: Maciel (Paraguay).

20 June, Turin, 62,502
Brazil (0) 1 *(Muller 81)*
Scotland (0) 0
Brazil: Taffarel; Jorginho, Mauro Galvao, Ricardo Rocha, Ricardo Gomes, Branco, Alemao, Dunga, Valdo, Careca, Romario (Muller 66).
Scotland: Leighton; McKimmie, McPherson, Aitken, McLeish, Malpas, McCall, McStay, MacLeod (Gillespie 39), Johnston, McCoist (Fleck 77).
Referee: Kohl (Austria).

20 June, Genoa, 30,223
Costa Rica (0) 2 *(Flores 75, Medford 87)*
Sweden (1) 1 *(Ekstrom 32)*
Costa Rica: Conejo; Marchena, Flores, Gonzalez, Montero, Chavarria, Gomez (Medford 62), Chaves, Cayasso, Ramirez, Jara.
Sweden: Ravelli; Nilsson R, Larsson P, Hysen, Schwarz, Pettersson, Stromberg (Engqvist 81), Ingesson, Nilsson J, Ekstrom, Brolin (Gren 34).
Referee: Petrovic (Yugoslavia).

	P	W	D	L	F	A	Pts
Brazil	3	3	0	0	4	1	6
Costa Rica	3	2	0	1	3	2	4
Scotland	3	1	0	2	2	3	2
Sweden	3	0	0	3	3	6	0

GROUP D

9 June, Bologna, 30,791
Colombia (0) 2 *(Redin 50, Valderrama 87)*
UAE (0) 0
Colombia: Higuita; Escobar, Gildardo Gomez, Herrera, Perea, Gabriel Gomez, Valderrama, Redin, Alvarez, Rincon, Iguaran (Estrada 75).
UAE: Faraj; Mubarak KG, Abdulrahman I, Abdulrahman E (Sultan 74), Mohamed Y, Juma'a, Abdullah Moh, Abbas, Mubarak N, Mubarak K (Bilal 58), Talyani.
Referee: Courtney (England).

10 June, Milan, 74,765
Yugoslavia (0) 1 *(Jozic 55)*
West Germany (2) 4 *(Matthaus 29, 63, Klinsmann 40, Voller 70)*
Yugoslavia: Ivkovic, Vulic, Hadzibegic, Jozic, Spasic, Katanec, Baljic, Susic (Brnovic 59), Savicevic (Prosinecki 56), Stojkovic, Vujovic.
West Germany: Illgner; Reuter, Berthold, Augenthaler, Brehme, Buchwald, Matthaus, Bein (Moller 74), Hassler (Littbarski 74), Klinsmann, Voller.
Referee: Mikkelsen (Denmark).

14 June, Bologna, 32,257
Yugoslavia (0) 1 *(Jozic 73)*
Colombia (0) 0
Yugoslavia: Ivkovic; Stanojkovic, Spasic, Hadzibegic, Jozic, Brnovic, Susic, Katanec (Jarni 46), Stojkovic, Sabanadzovic, Vujovic (Pancev 54).
Colombia: Higuita; Herrera, Perea, Gildardo Gomez, Escobar, Gabriel Gomez, Alvarez, Valderrama, Redin (Estrada 79), Rincon (Hernandez 67), Iguaran.
Referee: Agnolin (Italy).

15 June, Milan, 71,167
West Germany (2) 5 *(Voller 35, 76, Klinsmann 37, Matthaus 47, Bein 58)*
UAE (0) 1 *(Mubarak K 46)*
West Germany: Illgner; Reuter, Buchwald, Augenthaler, Brehme, Berthold (Littbarski 46), Matthaus, Hassler, Bein, Klinsmann (Riedle 72), Voller.
UAE: Faraj; Abdulrahman E, Mubarak KG, Mohamed Y, Abdulrahman I (Al Haddad 86), Abdullah Moh, Juma'a, Mubarak N, Mubarak K (Hussain 82), Abbas, Talyani.
Referee: Spirin (USSR).

19 June, Milan, 72,510
West Germany (0) 1 *(Littbarski 88)*
Colombia (0) 1 *(Rincon 90)*
West Germany: Ilgner; Reuter, Buchwald, Augenthaler, Pflugler, Berthold, Matthaus, Hassler (Thon 88), Bein (Littbarski 46), Klinsmann, Voller.
Colombia: Higuita; Herrera, Escobar, Perea, Gildardo Gomez, Gabriel Gomez, Alvarez, Estrada, Valderrama, Rincon, Fajardo.
Referee: Snoddy (N. Ireland).

19 June, Bologna, 27,833
Yugoslavia (2) 4 *(Susic 4, Pancev 8, 46, Prosinecki 90)*
UAE (1) 1 *(Juma'a 21)*
Yugoslavia: Ivkovic; Stanojkovic, Spasic, Hadzibegic, Jozic, Brnovic, Susic, Stojkovic, Sabanadzovic (Prosinecki 78), Pancev, Vujovic (Vulic 63).
UAE: Faraj; Mubarak KG, Abdulrahman I, Abdulrahman E (Al Haddad, Juma'a (Mubarak FK 46), Abdullah Moh, Abbas, Mubarak N (Sultan 34), Mubarak I*, Talyani.
Referee: Takada (Japan).

	P	W	D	L	F	A	Pts
West Germany	3	2	1	0	10	3	5
Yugoslavia	3	2	0	1	6	5	4
Colombia	3	1	1	1	3	2	3
UAE	3	0	0	3	2	11	0

Group E

12 June, Verona, 32,486
Belgium (0) 2 *(De Gryse 52, Dewolf 64)*
South Korea (0) 0
Belgium: Preud'homme; Gerets, Clijsters, Demol, Dewolf, Emmers, Van der Elst, Scifo, Versavel, De Gryse, Van der Linden (Ceulemans 46).
South Korea: Choi In-Young, Choi Kang-Hee, Chung Yong Hwan, Hong Myung-Bo, Park Kyung-Joon, Gu Sang-Bum, Lee Young-Jin (Cho Min-Kook 46), Noh Soon-Jin (Lee Tae-Hoo 62), Choi Soon-Ho, Hwang Seon-Hong, Kim Joo-Sung.
Referee: Mauro (USA).

13 June, Udine, 35,713
Spain (0) 0
Uruguay (0) 0
Spain: Zubizarreta; Chendo, Sanchis, Andrinua, Jimenez, Martin Vazquez, Roberto, Villaroya (Gorriz 79), Michel, Manolo (Rafa Paz), Butragueno.
Uruguay: Alvez; Herrera, Gutierrez, De Leon, Dominguez, Ruben Pereira (Correa 64), Perdomo, Paz, Alzamendi (Aguilera 64), Francescoli, Sosa.
Referee: Kohl (Austria).

17 June, Udine, 32,733
Spain (1) 3 *(Michel 23, 61, 81)*
South Korea (1) 1 *(Hwang Kwan-Bo 43)*
Spain: Zubizarreta; Chendo, Andrinua, Sanchis, Gorriz, Michel, Villaroya, Roberto (Bakero 81), Martin Vazquez, Butragueno (Fernando 76), Julio Salinas.

South Korea: Choi In-Young; Park Kyung-Joon (Chung Jong-Soo 68), Choi Kang-Hee, Hong Myung-Bo, Yoon Deuk-Yeo, Hwang Kwan-Bo, Chung Hae-Won (Noh Soo-Jin 52), Kim Joo-Sung, Gu Sang-Bum, Byun Byung-Joo, Choi Soon-Ho.
Referee: Guerrero (Ecuador).

17 June, Verona, 33,759
Belgium (2) 3 *(Clijsters 15, Scifo 22, Ceulemans 47)*
Uruguay (0) 1 *(Bengoechea 72)*
Belgium: Preud'homme; Gerets*, Grun, Clijsters (Emmers 46), Demol, Dewolf, Versavel (Vervoort 73), Van der Elst, Scifo, De Gryse, Ceulemans.
Uruguay: Alvez; Herrera, Gutierrez, De Leon, Dominguez, Ostolaza (Bengoechea 63), Perdomo, Paz, Alzamendi (Aguilera 63), Francescoli, Sosa.
Referee: Kirschen (East Germany).

21 June, Verona, 39,950
Spain (2) 2 *(Michel 26 (pen), Gorriz 38)*
Belgium (1) 1 *(Vervoort 29)*
Spain: Zubizarreta; Chendo, Sanchis, Andriuna, Villaroya, Gorriz, Michel, Roberto, Martin Vazquez, Butragueno (Alcorta 83), Julio Salinas (Pardeza 88).
Belgium: Preud'homme; Staelens (Van der Linden 79), Albert, Demol, Dewolf, Van der Elst, Emmers (Plovie 31), Vervoort, Scifo, De Gryse, Ceulemans.
Referee: Loustau (Argentina).

21 June, Udine, 29,039
Uruguay (0) 1 *(Fonseca 90)*
South Korea (0) 0
Uruguay: Alvez; Gutierrez, De Leon, Herrera, Dominguez, Perdomo, Ostolaza (Aguilera 46), Francescoli, Paz, Martines, Sosa (Fonseca 62).
South Korea: Choi In-Young; Park Kyung-Joon, Choi Kang-Hee, Chung Jong-Soo, Hong Myung-Bo, Yoon Deuk-Yeo*, Hwang Kwan-Bo (Chung Hae-Won 77), Lee Heung-Sil, Kim Joo-Sung (Hwang Seon-Hong 42), Byun Byung Joo, Choi Soon-Ho.
Referee: Lanese (Italy).

	P	W	D	L	F	A	Pts
Spain	3	2	1	0	5	2	6
Belgium	3	2	0	1	6	3	4
Uruguay	3	1	1	1	2	3	3
South Korea	3	0	0	3	1	6	0

Group F
11 June, Cagliari, 35,238
England (1) 1 *(Lineker 8)*
Rep of Ireland (0) 1 *(Sheedy 72)*
England: Shilton; Stevens, Walker, Pearce, Robson, Beardsley (McMahon 69), Gascoigne, Waddle, Barnes, Lineker (Bull 83).
Rep of Ireland: Bonner; Morris, McCarthy, Moran, Staunton, McGrath, Houghton, Sheedy, Aldridge (McLoughlin 64), Townsend, Cascarino.
Referee: Schmidhuber (West Germany).

12 June, Palermo, 33,288
Egypt (0) 1 *(Abdelghani 82 (pen))*
Holland (0) 1 *(Kieft 58)*
Egypt: Shoubeir; Hassan I, Yaken, Ramzi H, Yassine, Youssef, Ramzi A (Abdel Rahmane 68), Hassan H, Abdelhamid (Tolba 68), Abdelghani, Abdou.
Holland: Van Breukelen; Van Aerle, Rutjes, Koeman R, Van Tiggelen, Vanenburg (Kieft 46), Wouters, Rijkaard, Koeman E (Witschge 69), Van Basten, Gullit.
Referee: Aladren (Spain).

16 June, Cagliari, 35,267
England (0) 0
Holland (0) 0
England: Shilton; Parker, Walker, Wright, Butcher, Pearce, Robson (Platt 65), Waddle (Bull 59), Gascoigne, Barnes, Lineker.
Holland: Van Breukelen; Van Aerle, Rijkaard, Koeman R, Van Tiggelen, Wouters, Gullit, Witschge, Van't Schip (Kieft 74), Gillhaus, Van Basten.
Referee: Petrovic (Yugoslavia).

17 June, Palermo, 33,288
Egypt (0) 0
Rep of Ireland (0) 0
Egypt: Shoubeir; Hassan I, Yaken, Ramzi H, Yassine, Abdelghani, Orabi, Tolba (Abou Seid 59), Youssef, Abdou (Abdelhamid 76), Hassan H.
Rep of Ireland: Bonner; Morris, McCarthy, Moran, Staunton, McGrath, Houghton, Townsend, Sheedy, Aldridge (McLoughlin 84), Cascarino (Quinn 84).
Referee: Van Langehove (Belgium).

21 June, Cagliari, 34,959
England (0) 1 *(Wright 58)*
Egypt (0) 0
England: Shilton; Parker, Wright, Walker, Pearce, Waddle (Platt 86), McMahon, Gascoigne, Barnes, Lineker, Bull (Beardsley 84).
Egypt: Shoubeir; Hassan I, Yaken, Ramzi H, Yassine, Youssef, Abdelghani, Abdou (Soliman 81), Ramzi A, Abdelhamid (Adbel Rahmane 81), Hassan H.
Referee: Rothlisberger (Switzerland).

21 June, Palermo, 33,288
Rep of Ireland (0) 1 *(Quinn 71)*
Holland (1) 1 *(Gullit 10)*
Rep of Ireland: Bonner; Morris, McCarthy, Moran, Staunton, McGrath, Houghton, Townsend, Sheedy (Whelan 61), Aldridge (Cascarino 61), Quinn.
Holland: Van Breukelen; Van Aerle, Rijkaard, Koeman R, Van Tiggelen, Wouters, Witschge (Fraser 59), Van Basten, Gullit, Gillhaus, Kieft (Van Loen 78).
Referee: Vautrot (France).

	P	W	D	L	F	A	Pts
England	3	1	2	0	2	1	4
Rep of Ireland	3	0	3	0	2	2	3
Holland	3	0	3	0	2	2	3
Egypt	3	0	2	1	1	2	2

Second Round
23 June, Naples, 50,026
Cameroon (0) 2 *(Milla 106, 109)*
Colombia (0) 1 *(Redin 117)* aet
Cameroon: Nkono; Tataw, Ndip, Onana, Ebwelle, Kana-Biyik, Mbouh, Maboang, Mfede (Milla 54), Omam-Biyik, Makanaky (Djonkep 68).
Colombia: Higuita; Herrera, Perea, Escobar, Gildardo Gomez, Alvarez, Gabriel Gomez (Redin 79), Rincon, Fajardo (Iguaran 100), Valderrama, Estrada.
Referee: Lanese (Italy).

23 June, Bari, 47,673
Czechoslovakia (1) 4 *(Skuhravy 11, 63, 82, Kubik 76)*
Costa Rica (0) 1 *(Gonzalez 55)*
Czechoslovakia: Stejskal; Hasek, Kadlec, Kocian, Straka, Moravcik, Chovanec, Kubik, Bilek, Skuhravy, Knoflicek.
Costa Rica: Barrantes; Chavarria (Guimaraes 67), Marchena, Flores, Montero, Chavez, Ramirez, Gonzalez, Obando (Medford 46), Cayasso, Jara.
Referee: Kirschen (East Germany).

24 June, Turin, 61,381
Argentina (0) 1 *(Caniggia 80)*
Brazil (0) 0
Argentina: Goycochea; Basualdo, Monzon, Simon, Ruggeri, Olarticoechea, Giusti, Burruchaga, Maradona, Troglio (Calderon 62), Caniggia.
Brazil: Taffarel; Jorginho, Ricardo Rocha, Ricardo Gomes*, Mauro Galvao (Renato 85), Branco, Alemao (Silas 85), Dunga, Valdo, Careca, Muller.
Referee: Quiniou (France).

24 June, Milan, 74,559
West Germany (0) 2 *(Klinsmann 51, Brehme 85)*
Holland (0) 1 *(Koeman R 88 (pen))*
West Germany: Illgner; Reuter, Kohler, Augenthaler, Brehme, Buchwald, Berthold, Matthaus, Littbarski, Voller*, Klinsmann (Riedle 79).
Holland: Van Breukelen; Van Aerle (Kieft 56), Koeman R, Van Tiggelen, Wouters, Rijkaard*, Witschge (Gillhaus 79), Winter, Gullit, Van Basten, Van't Schip.
Referee: Loustau (Argentina).

25 June, Genoa, 31,818
Rep of Ireland (0) 0
Rumania (0) 0 aet
Rep of Ireland: Bonner; Morris, McCarthy, Moran, Staunton (O'Leary 93), Houghton, McGrath, Townsend, Sheedy, Quinn, Aldridge (Cascarino 21).
Rumania: Lung; Rednic, Andone, Popescu, Klein, Rotariu, Lupescu, Sabau (Timofte 97), Hagi, Raducioiu (Lupu 64), Balint.
Referee: Wright (Brazil).
Republic of Ireland won 5-4 on penalties.

25 June, Rome, 73,303
Italy (0) 2 *(Schillaci 67, Serena 85)*
Uruguay (0) 0
Italy: Zenga; Bergomi, Ferri, Baresi, Maldini, De Agostini, De Napoli, Berti (Serena 52), Giannini, Schillaci, Baggio (Vierchowod 80).
Uruguay: Alvez; Saldana, Gutierrez, De Leon, Dominguez, Ostolaza (Alzamendi 80), Perdomo, Francescoli, Ruben Pereira, Aguilera (Sosa 55, Fonseca.
Referee: Courtney (England).

26 June, Verona, 35,500
Spain (0) 1 *(Julio Salinas 83)*
Yugoslavia (0) 2 *(Stojkovic 77, 92)* aet
Spain: Zubizarreta; Chendo, Gorriz, Andrinua (Jimenez 50), Sanchis, Villaroya, Martin Vazquez, Roberto, Michel, Butragueno (Rafa Paz 78), Julio Salinas.
Yugoslavia: Ivkovic; Sabanadzovic, Spasic, Brnovic, Katanec (Vulic 78), Hadzibegic, Jozic, Susic, Stojkovic, Pancev (Savicevic 56), Vujovic.
Referee: Schmidhuber (West Germany).

26 June, Bologna, 34,520
England (0) 1 *(Platt 119)*
Belgium (0) 0 aet
England: Shilton; Parker, Butcher, Wright, Walker, Pearce, Waddle, Gascoigne, McMahon (Platt 71), Barnes (Bull 74), Lineker.
Belgium: Preud'homme; Gerets, Grun, Demol, Clijsters, Dewolf, Van der Elst, Scifo, Versavel (Vervoort 107), Ceulemans, De Gryse (Claesen 64).
Referee: Mikkelsen (Denmark).

Quarter-finals
30 June, Florence, 38,971
Yugoslavia (0) 0
Argentina (0) 0 aet
Yugoslavia: Ivkovic; Hadzibegic, Spasic, Brnovic, Vulic, Sabanadzovic*, Jozic, Susic (Savicevic 62), Prosinecki, Stojkovic, Vujovic.
Argentina: Goycochea; Simon, Ruggeri, Serrizuela, Basualdo, Olarticoechea (Troglio 52), Giusti, Burruchaga, Calderon (Dezotti 85), Caniggia, Maradona.
Referee: Rothlisberger (West Germany).
Argentina won 3-2 on penalties.

30 June, Rome, 73,303
Rep of Ireland (0) 0
Italy (1) 1 *(Schillaci 37)*
Rep of Ireland: Bonner; Morris, McCarthy, Moran, Staunton, McGrath, Houghton, Townsend, Sheedy, Quinn (Cascarino 52), Aldridge (Sheridan 77).
Italy: Zenga; Bergomi, Ferri, Baresi, Maldini, De Agostini, Donadoni, De Napoli, Giannini (Ancelotti 62), Baggio (Serena 70), Schillaci.
Referee: Valente (Portugal).

1 July, Milan, 73,347
Czechoslovakia (0) 0
West Germany (1) 1 *(Matthaus 24 (pen))*
Czechoslovakia: Stejskal; Hasek, Straka, Kocian, Kadlec, Moravcik*, Chovanec, Bilek (Nemecek 68), Kubik (Griga 79), Skuhravy, Knoflicek.

West Germany: Illgnerr; Berthold, Kohler, Augenthaler, Brehme, Buchwald, Matthaus, Bein (Moller 83), Littbarski, Riedle, Klinsmann.
Referee: Kohl (Austria).

1 July, Naples, 55,205
Cameroon (0) 2 *(Kunde 63 (pen), Ekeke 67)*
England (1) 3 *(Platt 25, Lineker 82, 104 (both pens))* aet
Cameroon: Nkono; Tataw, Massing, Kunde, Edwelle, Maboang (Milla 46), Libih, Pagal, Makanaky, Mfede (Ekeke 62), Omam-Biyik.
England: Shilton; Parker, Butcher (Steven 74), Wright, Walker, Pearce, Waddle, Platt, Gascoigne, Barnes (Beardsley 46), Lineker.
Referee: Codesal (Mexico).

Semi-finals
3 July, Naples, 59,978
Argentina (0) 1 *(Caniggia 67)*
Italy (1) 1 *(Schillaci 17)* aet
Argentina: Goycochea; Simon, Ruggeri, Serrizuela, Giusti*, Calderon (Troglio 46), Burruchaga, Basualdo (Batista 99), Olarticoechea, Caniggia, Maradona.
Italy: Zenga; Bergomi, Baresi, Ferri, De Napoli, De Agostini, Donadoni, Maldini, Giannini (Baggio 73), Schillaci, Vialli (Serena 70).
Referee: Vautrot (France).
Argentina won 4-3 on penalties.

4 July, Turin, 62,628
West Germany (0) 1 *(Brehme 59)*
England (0) 1 *(Lineker 80)* aet
West Germany: Illgner; Berthold, Augenthaler, Buchwald, Kohler Hassler (Reuter 67), Matthaus, Thon, Brehme, Klinsmann, Voller (Riedle 38).
England: Shilton; Parker, Butcher (Steven 70), Wright, Walker, Pearce, Platt, Gascoigne, Waddle, Beardsley, Lineker.
Referee: Wright (Brazil).
West Germany won 4-3 on penalties.

Match for third place
7 July, Bari, 51,426
Italy (0) 2 *(Baggio 70, Schillaci 84 (pen))*
England (0) 1 *(Platt 80)*
Italy: Zenga; Bergomi, Baresi, Ferrara, Maldini, Vierchowod, De Agostini (Berti 67), Ancelotti, Giannini (Ferri 89), Baggio, Schillaci.
England: Shilton; Stevens, Wright (Waddle 72), Parker, Walker, Dorigo, Steven, Platt, McMahon (Webb 72), Beardsley, Lineker.
Referee: Quiniou (France).

Final
8 July, Rome, 73,603
West Germany (0) 1 *(Brehme 84 (pen))*
Argentina (0) 0
West Germany: Illgner; Berthold (Reuter 73), Kohler, Augenthaler, Buchwald, Brehme, Littbarski, Hassler, Matthaus, Voller, Klinsmann.
Argentina: Goycochea; Lorenzo, Serrizuela, Sensini, Ruggeri (Monzon 46*), Simon, Basualdo, Burruchaga (Calderon 53), Maradona, Troglio, Dezotti*.
Referee: Codesal (Mexico).
* denotes players sent off.
In the 1990 finals there were 164 bookings, 16 dismissals (170 players had been cautioned but six of those who were subsequently sent off had their sending-off recorded, not the booking).
Top scorer: Schillaci (Italy) 6 goals.

Continued on page 633

1990 FIFA WORLD CUP

EUROPE

Group 1 *(Denmark, Bulgaria, Rumania, Greece)*

19 October, Sofia, 52,000

Bulgaria (1) 1 *(Kolev 31)*
Rumania (1) 3 *(Mateut 25, Camataru 79, 89)*

Bulgaria: Mikhailov; Nikolov, Rankov, Vasev (Kiryakov 55), Iliev, Stoichkov, Sadkov, Yordanov, Getov, Alexandrov (Kolev 30), Penev.
Rumania: Lung; Iovan, Andone, Belodedici, Rotariu, Mateut (Klein 55), Sabau, Hagi, Popescu, Lacatus (Vaiscovici 66), Camataru.

19 October, Athens, 45,000

Greece (1) 1 *(Mitropoulos 41)*
Denmark (0) 1 *(Povlsen 56)*

Greece: Talikariadis; Hatziathanassiu, Manolas, Mavridis, Kolomitrousis, Skartados (Karapialis 74), Tsalouhidis, Bonovas, Mitropoulos (Georgamlis 56), Saravakos, Anastopoulos.
Denmark: Schmeichel; Heintze, Nielsen I, Olsen L, Sivebaek (Kristensen 46), Bartram, Helt, Jensen J, Povlsen, Laudrup, Brylle (Elstrup 75).

2 November, Copenhagen, 34,600

Denmark (1) 1 *(Elstrup 8)*
Bulgaria (1) 1 *(Sadkov 38)*

Denmark: Schmeichel; Olsen L, Sivebaek, Nielsen K, Kristensen, Heintze (Brylle 76), Helt (Bartram 65), Jensen J, Laudrup, Elstrup, Povlsen.
Bulgaria: Valov; Iliev, Kiryakov, Dochev, Ivanov, Penev, Sadkov, Kirov, Yordanov (Rakov 86), Stoichkov (Balkov 88), Bezinski.

2 November, Bucharest, 22,500

Rumania (2) 3 *(Mateut 26, Hagi 40 (pen), Sabau 84)*
Greece (0) 0

Rumania: Lung; Iovan, Belodedici, Andone, Ungureanu, Popescu, Hagi, Sabau (Klein 85), Mateut, Lacatus (Vaiscovici 77), Camataru.
Greece: Talikariadis; Hatziathanassiu, Kolomitroussis, Manolas, Mavridis, Tsalouhidis, Saravakos, Bonovas, Anastopoulos, Mitropoulos (Kutulas 46), Tsiantakis (Nioblias 68).

26 April, Athens, 30,000

Greece (0) 0
Rumania (0) 0

Greece: Economopoulos; Apostolakis, Hatziathanasiu, Manolas, Mavridis, Tsalouhidis, Saravakos, Papadopoulos (Bonovas 65), Samaras, Savidis, Tsiantakis.
Rumania: Lung; Iovan, Bumbescu, Klein, Rednic, Mateut, Popescu, Sabau, Camataru (Vaiscovici 89), Hagi, Lupescu (Dumitrescu 78).

26 April, Sofia, 45,000

Bulgaria (0) 0
Denmark (1) 2 *(Povlsen 41, Laudrup B 89)*

Bulgaria: Valov (Donev 55); Kiryakov, Dochev, Bezinski, Iliev, Rakov, Kirov, Sadkov (Simeonov 46), Stoichkov, Mikhtarski, Getov.
Denmark: Schmeichel; Heintze, Nielsen K, Olsen L, Sivebaek, Larsen J, Olsen M (Vilfort 74), Jensen J (Helt 84), Bartram, Povlsen, Laudrup B.

17 May, Copenhagen, 38,500

Denmark (1) 7 *(Laudrup B 24, Bartram 47, Nielsen K 55, Povlsen 56, Vilfort 79, Andersen H 85, Laudrup M 89 (pen))*
Greece (1) 1 *(Samaras 39)*

Denmark: Schmeichel; Sivebaek (Vilfort 30), Olsen L, Nielsen K, Larsen J, Bartram (Andersen H), Olsen M, Jensen J, Laudrup M, Povlsen, Laudrup B.
Greece: Economopoulos; Hatziathanasiu, Mavridis, Manolas, Apostolakis, Tsalouhidis, Tsiantakis, Mitropoulos (Kalitzakis 50), Papadopoulos, Saravakos, Samaras.

17 May, Bucharest, 20,000

Rumania (1) 1 *(Popescu 35)*
Bulgaria (0) 0

Rumania: Stelea; Iovan, Bumbescu, Rednic (Balint 64), Mateut, Sabau (Dumitrescu 85), Popescu, Rotariu, Hagi, Lacatus, Camataru.
Bulgaria: Valov (Donev 46); Dochev, Ivanov, Vasev, Mladenov D, Tinchev, Kostadinov E, Stoichkov, Mladenov S, Bakalov, Balekov.

11 October, Varna, 15,000

Bulgaria (0) 4 *(Ivanov 72, Bankov 76, Iskrenov 79, Stoichkov 88)*
Greece (0) 0

Bulgaria: Valov; Dimitrov, Ivanov, Tinchev, Bankov, Yordanov (Lechkov 84), Kostadinov (Penev 65), Stoichkov, Balakov, Georgiev, Iskrenov.
Greece: Pietsis; Kutulas, Hatzithanasiu, Vakalopoulos, Mavridis, Papaioannou, Saravakos, Stamatis (Noblias 65), Dimitriadis, Sandakis, Kofidis.

11 October, Copenhagen, 45,000

Denmark (2) 3 *(Neilsen K 4, Laudrup B 26, Povlsen 85)*
Rumania (0) 0

Denmark: Schmeichel; Sivebaek, Nielsen K, Olsen L, Nielsen I, Bartram, Jensen, Heintze, Povlsen, Laudrup M, Laudrup B.
Rumania: Lung; Iovan, Klein, Rednic, Mateut, Andone, Rotariu, Sabau (Lupu 68), Camataru, Hagi, Popescu.

15 November, Athens, 2500

Greece (0) 1 *(Noblias 49)*

Bulgaria (0) 0

Greece: Papadopoulos; Karageorghiu, Mustakidis, Manolas, Deliyannis, Papadopoulos D (Alexiu 75), Borbokis, Vutiritsas, Samaras (Stamatis 29), Noblias, Marangos.
Bulgaria: Valov; Dimitrov, Ivanov, Tinchev, Dochev (Stoyanov 81), Bankov, Yanchez, Stoichkov, Balakov, Yordanov, Iskrenov (Kostadinov 75).

15 November, Bucharest, 30,000

Rumania (2) 3 *(Balint 25, 61, Sabau 38)*

Denmark (1) 1 *(Povlsen)*

Rumania: Lung; Petrescu (Ungureanu 85), Iovan, Andone, Rotariu, Hagi, Sabau, Popescu, Lupu (Mateut 78), Lacatus, Balint.
Denmark: Schmeichel; Sivebaek (Elstrup 72), Olsen L, Nielsen K, Nielsen I, Jensen J, Laudrup M, Lerby, Bartram, Povlsen, Laudrup B.

Final table	P	W	D	L	F	A	Pts
Rumania	6	4	1	1	10	5	9
Denmark	6	3	2	1	15	6	8
Greece	6	1	2	3	3	15	4
Bulgaria	6	1	1	4	6	8	3

Rumania qualified

Group 2 *(England, Poland, Sweden, Albania)*

19 October, Wembley, 65,628

England (0) 0

Sweden (0) 0

England: Shilton; Stevens, Pearce, Webb, Adams (Walker 64), Butcher, Robson, Beardsley, Waddle, Lineker, Barnes (Cottee 79).
Sweden: Ravelli; Nilsson R (Schiller 77), Hysen, Larsson P, Ljung, Thern, Stromberg, Prytz, Nilsson J, Holmqvist (Ekstrom 63), Pettersson.

19 October, Chorzow, 30,000

Poland (0) 1 *(Warzycha K 78)*

Albania (0) 0

Poland: Wandzik; Warzycha R, Wojcicki, Lukasik, Wdowczyk, Matsik (Ziober 46), Warzycha K, Urban, Furtok (Komornicki 73), Rudy, Smolarek.
Albania: Mersini; Alimehmeti, Josa, Hodja, Gega, Iera, Shehu (Stoia 70), Lekbello, Millo, Minga, Demollari.

5 November, Tirana, 11,500

Albania (1) 1 *(Shehu 33)*

Sweden (0) 2 *(Holmqvist 68, Ekstrom 71)*

Albania: Mersini; Alimehmeti, Hodja, Lekbello, Stoia, Josa, Gega, Demollari, Millo, Shehu, Minga.
Sweden: Ravelli; Nilsson R, Larsson P, Hysen, Ljung, Thern, Prytz (Holmqvist 66), Stromberg, Nilsson J, Pettersson, Ekstrom.

8 March, Tirana, 30,000

Albania (0) 0

England (1) 2 *(Barnes 16, Robson 63)*

Albania: Mersini; Zmijani, Josa, Hodja, Gega, Jera, Shehu, Lekbello, Millo (Majaci 75), Minga, Demollari.
England: Shilton; Stevens, Pearce, Webb, Walker, Butcher, Robson, Rocastle, Waddle (Beardsley 79), Lineker (Smith 79), Barnes.

26 April, Wembley, 60,602

England (2) 5 *(Lineker 5, Beardsley 12, 64, Waddle 72, Gascoigne 88)*

Albania (0) 0

England: Shilton; Stevens (Parker 77), Pearce, Webb, Walker, Butcher, Robson, Rocastle (Gascoigne 67), Beardsley, Lineker, Waddle.
Albania: Nallbani; Zmijani, Bubeqi, Hodja, Gega, Jera, Shehu, Lekbello, Millo, Hasanpapa (Noga 31), Demollari.

7 May, Stockholm, 35,021

Sweden (0) 2 *(Ljung 76, Larsson N 89)*

Poland (0) 1 *(Tarasiewicz 86)*

Sweden: Ravelli T; Nilsson R, Lonn (Ravelli A 80), Ljung, Schiller, Limpar, Prytz, Thern, Nilsson J (Larsson N 58), Ekstrom, Magnusson.
Poland: Bako; Soczynski, Lukasik, Wojcicki, Wdowczyk (Tarasiewicz 15), Prusik, Matysik, Urban, Dziekanowski (Kosecki 60), Furtok, Warzycha K.

3 June, Wembley, 69,203

England (1) 3 *(Lineker 24, Barnes 69, Webb 82)*

Poland (0) 0

England: Shilton; Stevens, Pearce, Webb, Walker, Butcher, Robson, Waddle (Rocastle 75), Beardsley (Smith 75), Lineker, Barnes.
Poland: Bako; Wijas, Wojcicki, Wdowczyk, Lukasik, Matysik, Prusik, Urban (Tarasiewicz 70), Furtok, Warzycha K, Lesniak (Kosecki 58).

6 September, Stockholm, 38,588

Sweden (0) 0

England (0) 0

Sweden: Ravelli T; Nilsson R, Hysen, Larsson P, Ljung, Engqvist, Thern, Ingesson (Stromberg 72), Nilsson J (Limpar 77), Ekstrom, Magnusson.
England: Shilton; Stevens, Pearce, Walker, Butcher, McMahon, Waddle, Webb (Gascoigne 72), Beardsley, Lineker, Barnes (Rocastle 76).

8 October, Stockholm, 32,423

Sweden (1) 3 *(Magnusson 20, Ingesson 55, Engqvist 89)*

Albania (1) 1 *(Kushta 8 (pen))*

Sweden: Ravelli T; Nilsson R, Hysen, Larsson P, Ljung, Gren (Engqvist), Ingesson, Thern, Limpar, Ekstrom (Lindqvist 82), Magnusson.
Albania: Mersini; Hodja, Zmijani, Lekbello (Noga 75), Taho, Jera, Josa, Gega (Arberi 87), Demollari, Millo, Kushta.

11 October, Chorzow, 30,000

Poland (0) 0
England (0) 0

Poland: Bako; Czachowski, Kaczmarek, Wdowczyk, Warzycha R, Nawrocki, Tarasiewicz, Ziober, Kosecki, Dziekanowski, Warzycha K (Furtok 57).
England: Shilton; Stevens, Pearce, Walker, Butcher, McMahon, Robson, Rocastle, Beardsley, Lineker, Waddle.

25 October, Chorzow, 12,000

Poland (0) 0
Sweden (1) 2 *(Larsson P (pen) 34, Ekstrom 60)*

Poland: Bako; Czachowski, Kaczmarek, Warzycha R (Kubicki 67), Wdowczyk, Nawrocki (Gora 82), Tarasiewicz, Ziober, Kosecki, Dziekanowski, Warzycha K.
Sweden: Ravelli T; Nilsson R, Hysen, Larsson P, Ljung, Engqvist, Thern, Ingesson (Larsson N 72), Nilsson J, Ekstrom (Lindqvist 82), Magnusson.

15 November, Tirana, 10,000

Albania (0) 1 *(Kushta 63)*
Poland (1) 2 *(Tarasiewicz 45, Ziober 84)*

Albania: Nailbani; Zmijani, Hodja, Xhumba, Iljadhi, Josa (Arberi 60), Demollari, Pano (Kepa 74), Jera, Kushta, Bubeqi.
Poland: Bako; Kubicki, Czachowski, Wdowczyk, Kaczmarek, Warzycha R, Tarasiewicz, Kosecki, Szewczyk, Dziekanowski (Warzycha K 36), Ziober.

Final table	P	W	D	L	F	A	Pts
Sweden	6	4	2	0	9	3	10
England	6	3	3	0	10	0	9
Poland	6	2	1	3	4	8	5
Albania	6	0	0	6	3	15	0

Sweden and England qualified

Group 3 *(USSR, East Germany, Austria, Iceland, Turkey)*

31 August, Reykjavik, 8300

Iceland (1) 1 *(Gretarsson 11)*
USSR (0) 1 *(Litovchenko 75)*

Iceland: Sigurdsson; Bergsson, Saevar Jonsson, Edvaldsson, Thordarsson, Gislason, Ormslev, Siggi Jonsson, Sigurvinsson, Gudjohnsen, Gretarsson (Torfasson G 82).
USSR: Dasayev; Bessonov (Dobrovolski 65), Khidiatulin, Kuznetsov, Demianenko, Aleinikov, Litovchenko, Zavarov, Rats, Protasov, Mikhailichenko.

12 October, Istanbul, 25,680

Turkey (0) 1 *(Onal 73)*
Iceland (0) 1 *(Torfasson O 62)*

Turkey: Fatih; Recep (Feyyaz 57), Semih, Cuneyt, Mucahit, Gokhan G, Oguz, Ridvan, Onal, Tanju, Savas K.
Iceland: Fridriksson; Gislason, Edvaldsson, Arnthorsson (Askelsson 79), Bergsson, Siggi Jonsson, Margeirsson, Torfasson O, Torfasson G, Gudjohnsen, Thordarsson.

19 October, East Berlin, 12,000

East Germany (1) 2 *(Thom 34, 88)*
Iceland (0) 0

East Germany: Weissflog; Kreer, Schossler, Stahmann, Lindner, Doschner, Raab, Ernst, Stubner (Sammer 34), Kirsten, Thom.
Iceland: Sigurdsson; Saevar Jonsson, Bergsson, Edvaldsson, Gislason, Thordarsson, Torfasson O, Gudjohnsen, Sigurvinsson, Gretarsson, Torfasson G (Margeirsson 77).

19 October, Kiev, 100,000

USSR (0) 2 *(Mikhailichenko 47, Zavarov 69)*
Austria (0) 0

USSR: Dasayev; Ivanauskas (Gorlukovich), Khidiatulin, Zigmantovich, Demianenko, Aleinikov, Litovchenko, Zavarov, Rats, Mikhailichenko, Protasov (Savichev 83).
Austria: Lindenberger; Russ, Degeorgi, Pfeffer, Weber H, Zsak, Keglevits, Artner, Polster, Hormann (Herzog 63), Willfurth.

2 November, Vienna, 25,000

Austria (2) 3 *(Polster 38, Herzog 42, 54)*
Turkey (0) 2 *(Feyyaz 61, Tanju 81)*

Austria: Lindenberger; Weber G, Russ, Pfeffer, Artner, Willfurth (Pacult 55), Prohaska, Herzog (Glatzmayer 68), Degeorgi, Ogris, Polster.
Turkey: Fatih; Cuneyt, Recep, Gokhan G (Savas K), Semih, Mustafa, Unal, Oguz, Gokhan K, Ridvan, Feyyaz (Tanju).

30 November, Istanbul, 39,000

Turkey (1) 3 *(Tanju 23, 63, Oguz 69)*
East Germany (0) 1 *(Thom 75)*

Turkey: Fatih; Recep, Semih, Cuneyt, Gokhan G, Onal, Ugur, Ridvan, Oguz (Hassan 88), Tanju (Metin 78), Feyyaz.
East Germany: Weissflog; Kreer (Schossler 66), Stahmann, Lindner, Doschner, Pilz, Stubner, Steinmann, Kirsten, Ernst (Doll 46), Thom.

12 April, Magdeburg, 23,000

East Germany (0) 0
Turkey (1) 2 *(Tanju 21, Ridvan 88)*

East Germany: Muller; Hauptmann, Rohde, Trautmann, Lindner, Stubner (Wuckel 64), Sammer, Pilz (Doll 19), Kirsten, Minge, Thom.
Turkey: Engin; Recep, Cuneyt, Gokhan B, Semih, Yusuf, Ugur (Erdal 65), Oguz (Gokhan G 80), Unal, Ridvan, Tanju.

26 April, Kiev, 100,000

USSR (3) 3 *(Dobrovolski 3, Litovchenko 22, Protasov 40)*
East Germany (0) 0

USSR: Dasayev; Luzhny, Gorlukovich, Kuznetsov, Dobrovolski (Savichev 75), Aleinikov (Kulkov 80), Litovchenko, Mikhailichenko, Protasov, Rats, Zavarov.
East Germany: Weissflog; Hauptmann (Mertz 46), Lieberam, Kohler, Trautmann, Doschner, Sammer, Wosz, Scholz (Kirsten 55), Doll, Thom.

10 May, Istanbul, 42,500

Turkey (0) 0

USSR (1) 1 *(Mikhailichenko 40)*

Turkey: Engin; Recep, Cuneyt, Gokhan B, Semih, Yusuf, Ugur (Hasan Vezir 46) (Feyyez 60), Unal, Mustafa, Ridvan, Tanju.
USSR: Dasayev; Luzhny, Gorlukovich, Kuznetsov, Aleinikov (Ketaschvili 89), Rats, Mikhailichenko, Litovchenko, Zavarov, Protasov (Borodyuk 86), Dobrovolski.

20 May, Leipzig, 22,000

East Germany (0) 1 *(Kirsten 86)*

Austria (1) 1 *(Polster 3)*

East Germany: Weissflog; Stahmann, Lindner, Trautmann (Doll 46), Kreer, Rohde, Stubner, Sammer (Weidemann 68), Steinmann, Kirsten, Thom.
Austria: Lindenberger; Weber G, Russ, Pfeffer, Pecl, Rodax (Ogris 68), Prohaska, Zsak, Artner, Herzog (Stoger 60), Polster.

31 May, Moscow, 50,000

USSR (0) 1 *(Dobrovolski 62)*

Iceland (0) 1 *(Askelsson 86)*

USSR: Dasayev; Luzhny, Gorlukovich, Kuznetsov, Rats, Aleinikov, Bessonov (Ketaschvili 82), Dobrovolski, Litovchenko, Protasov (Savichev 82), Zavarov.
Iceland: Sigurdsson; Edvaldsson, Jonsson A, Bergsson, Gislason, Siggi Jonsson, Thordarsson, Torfason O (Kristiansson 82), Arnthorsson, Gretarsson, Torfason G (Askelsson 69).

14 June, Reykjavik, 15,000

Iceland (0) 0

Austria (0) 0

Iceland: Sigurdsson; Edvaldsson, Bergsson, Gislason (Thorkelsson 65), Siggi Jonsson, Thordarsson, Saevar Jonsson, Arnthorsson, Sigurvinsson, Gretarsson, Torfason G.
Austria: Lindenberger; Pecl, Weber, Pfeffer, Hortnagl (Herzog 36), Russ, Zsak, Artner, Prohaska, Polster, Rodax (Ogris 46).

23 August, Salzburg, 18,000

Austria (0) 2 *(Pfeifenberger 47, Szak 62)*

Iceland (0) 1 *(Margeirsson 48)*

Austria: Lindenberger; Weber, Russ, Peci (Streiter 30), Pfeffer, Linzmaier, Zsak, Herzog (Hortnagi 59), Rodax, Pfeiffenberger, Ogris A.
Iceland: Sigurdsson; Bergsson, Saevar Jonsson, Jonsson A, Gislasson, Thordarsson O, Margeirsson (Torfasson O 80), Arnthorsson (Kristinsson 70), Siggi Jonsson, Torfasson G, Gretarsson.

6 September, Reykjavik, 7124

Iceland (0) 0

East Germany (0) 3 *(Sammer 55, Ernst 63, Doll 65)*

Iceland: Fridriksson; Gislasson, Jonsson A, Torfasson O, Thorkelsson, Saevar Jonsson, Bergsson, Torfasson G, Gretarsson, Sigurvinsson, Gudjohnsen (Margeirsson 59).

East Germany: Heyne; Kreer, Steinmann, Lindner, Doschner, Sammer, Stubner, Reich, Kirsten, Ernst (Steinmann 76), Doll.

6 September, Vienna, 62,500

Austria (0) 0

USSR (0) 0

Austria: Lindenberger; Weber, Russ, Pfeffer, Streiter, Linzmaier, Artner, Zsak, Herzog (Hortnagi 78), Ogris A (Rodax 65), Polster.
USSR: Chanov; Khidiatulin, Gorlukovich, Kuznetsov, Bessonov, Mikhailichenko, Cherenkov (Aleinikov 78), Litovchenko, Zavarov, Dobrovolski, Protasov.

20 September, Reykjavik, 3500

Iceland (0) 2 *(Petursson 56, 72)*

Turkey (0) 1 *(Feyyaz 85)*

Iceland: Sigurdsson; Thordarsson, Bergsson, Gislasson, Oddsson, Orlygsson, Gudjohnsen, Kristinsson, Sigurvinsson, Gretarsson (Margeirsson 71), Petursson.
Turkey: Engin; Gokhan K, Recep, Cuneyt, Semih, Yusuf (Feyyaz 66), Ugur (Mustafa Yucedag 48), Oguz, Unal, Hasan Vesir, Hakan.

8 October, Karl-Marx-Stadt, 15,900

East Germany (0) 2 *(Thom 80, Sammer 82)*

USSR (0) 1 *(Litovchenko 74)*

East Germany: Heyne; Kreer, Stahmann, Lindner, Doschner, Steinmann (Weidemann 88), Stubner, Ernst (Doll 74), Sammer, Kirsten, Thom.
USSR: Chanov; Bessonov, Khidiatulin, Kuznetsov, Kotovchenko, Zavarov, Mikhailichanko, Dobrovolski, Gorlukovich, Protasov, Aleinikov.

25 October, Istanbul, 40,000

Turkey (1) 3 *(Ridvan 12, 52, Feyyaz 60)*

Austria (0) 0

Turkey: Engin; Riza, Semih, Cuneyt, Gokhan K, Unal, Ugur (Tanju 76), Ridvan, Mustafa, Oguz, Feyyaz (Metin Tecimer 87).
Austria: Lindenberger; Russ, Streiter, Pfeffer, Weber, Zsak, Ogris A, Linzmaier, Polster, Herzog (Glatzmayer 57), Artner (Rodax 46).

15 November, Vienna, 65,000

Austria (2) 3 *(Polster 2, 23 (pen), 61)*

East Germany (0) 0

Austria: Lindenberger; Aigner, Peci, Pfeffer, Artner, Keglevits, Linzmaier, Zsak, Hortnagi, Ogris A (Herzog 76, Pfeifenberger 83), Polster.
East Germany: Heyne; Stahmann, Kreer, Lindner, Schossler, Doschner (Doll 43), Stubner, Sammer (Weidemann 78), Steinmann, Kirsten, Thom.

15 November, Simferopol, 30,000

USSR (0) 2 *(Protasov 68, 79)*

Turkey (0) 0

USSR: Dasayev; Luzhny (Rats 46), Khidiatulin, Zigmantovich, Gorlukovich, Yaremchum, Mikhailichanko, Litovchenko, Zavarov, Protasov, Dobrovolski (Cherenkov 46).

Turkey: Engin; Recep, Kemal, Semih, Gokhan K,
Mustafa (Metin 46), Oguz, Hakan (Tanju 77), Riza,
Ridvan, Feyyaz.

Final table	P	W	D	L	F	A	Pts
USSR	8	4	3	1	11	4	11
Austria	8	3	3	2	9	9	9
Turkey	8	3	1	4	12	10	7
East Germany	8	3	1	4	9	13	7
Iceland	8	1	4	3	6	11	6

USSR and Austria qualified

Group 4 *(West Germany, Holland, Wales, Finland)*

31 August, Helsinki, 31,693

Finland (0) 0

West Germany (2) 4 *(Voller 6, 15, Matthaus 52, Riedle 86)*

Finland: Laukkanen; Europaeus, Hannikainen (Lipponen 43), Lahtinen, Petaja, Myyry, Pekonen, Ukkonen (Alatensio 62), Hjelm, Rantanen, Paatelainen.
West Germany: Illgner; Brehme, Gortz, Kohler, Fach, Buchwald (Rolff 26), Littbarski, Hassler, Voller, Matthaus, Eckstein (Riedle 75).

14 September, Amsterdam, 58,000

Holland (0) 1 *(Gullit 82)*

Wales (0) 0

Holland: Van Breukelen; Van Aerle, Rijkaard, Koeman R, Van Tiggelen, Vanenburg (Kieft 66), Wouters, Koeman E, Kruzen, Gullit, Van Basten.
Wales: Southall; Hall, Blackmore, Williams, Knill, Davies, Horne, Nicholas, Rush, Hughes (Saunders 76), Aizlewood.

19 October, Swansea, 9603

Wales (2) 2 *(Saunders (pen) 16, Lahtinen (og) 40)*

Finland (2) 2 *(Ukkonen 8, Paatelainen 45)*

Wales: Southall; Hall (Bowen 59), Blackmore, Nicholas, Van Den Hauwe, Ratcliffe, Horne, Saunders, Rush, Hughes, Pascoe.
Finland: Huttunen; Pekonen, Lahtinen, Europaeus, Kanerva, Myyry (Lipponen 86), Holmgren, Ukkonen, Petaja (Rantanen 61), Paatelainen, Hjelm.

19 October, Munich, 73,000

West Germany (0) 0

Holland (0) 0

West Germany: Illgner; Fach, Kohler, Buchwald, Berthold, Hassler, Matthaus, Thon, Brehme, Klinsmann (Mill 67), Voller.
Holland: Van Breukelen; Van Tiggelen, Koeman R, Rijkaard, Vanenburg, Van Aerle (Winter 20), Wouters, Koeman E, Silooy, Van Basten, Bosman.

26 April, Rotterdam, 53,000

Holland (0) 1 *(Van Basten 87)*

West Germany (0) 1 *(Riedle 68)*

Holland: Hiele; Van Aerle, Van Tiggelen, Koeman R, Rijkaard, Hofkens (Rutjes 84), Vanenburg, Koeman E, Van Basten, Winter, Huistra (Eykelkamp 75).
West Germany: Illgner; Berthold, Brehme, Kohler (Rolff 75), Reuter, Buchwald, Riedle, Moller, Voller (Klinsmann 33), Matthaus, Hassler.

31 May, Cardiff, 25,000

Wales (0) 0

West Germany (0) 0

Wales: Southall; Phillips, Blackmore (Bowen 82), Ratcliffe, Aizlewood, Nicholas, Saunders, Horne, Rush, Hughes, Williams (Pascoe 82).
West Germany: Illgner; Berthold, Reinhardt, Buchwald, Reuter, Fach, Hassler, Moller, Brehme, Riedle (Klinsmann 77), Voller.

31 May, Helsinki, 48,000

Finland (0) 0

Holland (0) 1 *(Kieft 87)*

Finland: Laukkanen; Kanerva, Europaeus, Heikkinen, Ikalainen, Holmgren, Ukkonen (Tornvall 68), Hjelm (Petaja 83), Lipponen, Paatelainen, Myyry.
Holland: Van Breukelen; Koeman R, Van Tiggelen, Rutjes, Van Aerle, Vanenburg (Huistra 83), Rijkaard, Koeman E, Ellerman (Gullit 66), Van Basten, Kieft.

6 September, Helsinki, 7480

Finland (0) 1 *(Lipponen 50)*

Wales (0) 0

Finland: Laukkanen; Lahtinen, Heikkinen, Europaeus, Holmgren, Tarkkio, Ukkonen (Tauriainen 82), Ikalainen, Paatelainen (Tornvall 65), Lipponen, Myyry.
Wales: Southall; Blackmore, Phillips, Nicholas (Maguire 88), Aizlewood, Ratcliffe, Saunders, Williams (Bowen 80), Rush, Hughes, Davies.

4 October, Dortmund, 40,000

West Germany (1) 6 *(Moller 12, 80, Littbarski 46, Klinsmann 52, Voller 62, Matthaus 85 (pen))*

Finland (0) 1 *(Lipponen 75)*

West Germany: Illgner; Reiter, Brehme, Buchwald, Augenthaler, Hassler (Bein 46), Littbarski, Moller (Mill 81), Voller, Matthaus, Klinsmann.
Finland: Laukkanen; Lahtinen, Heikkinen, Europaeus, Holmgren, Tarkkio, Ukkonen, Ikalainen (Hjelm 71), Myyry, Paatelainen (Lius 62), Lipponen.

11 October, Wrexham, 9025

Wales (0) 1 *(Bowen 89)*

Holland (1) 2 *(Rutjes 13, Bosman 79)*

Wales: Southall; Blackmore, Bowen, Nicholas, Hopkins, Maguire, Saunders, Phillips, Roberts (Jones 64), Williams (Pascoe 85), Allen.
Holland: Van Breukelen; Van Aerle, Rutjes, Koeman R, Koot, Wouters, Van't Schip, Hofkens, Kieft, Rijkaard (Bosman 46), Rob Witschge (Van Basten 71).

15 November, Rotterdam, 49,500

Holland (0) 3 *(Bosman 57, Koeman E 62, Koeman R 69 (pen))*

Finland (0) 0

Holland: Van Breukelen; Van Aerle, Koeman R, Rijkaard, Van Tiggelen, Van't Schip (Rob Witschge 78), Wouters, Koeman E (Hofkens 68), Ellerman, Bosman, Van Basten.

Finland: Laukkanen; Kanerva, Holmgren, Europaeus, Heikkinen, Ikalainen, Myyry, Ukkonen (Tauriainen 56), Tarkkio (Petaja 75), Lipponen, Paatelainen.

15 November, Cologne, 60,000

West Germany (1) 2 *(Voller 27, Hassler 48)*

Wales (1) 1 *(Allen 11)*

West Germany: Illgner; Augenthaler (Reinhardt A 46), Reuter, Buchwald, Brehme, Hassler, Dorfner, Moller (Bein 82), Littbarski, Klinsmann, Voller.
Wales: Southall; Bowen (Horne 65), Aizlewood, Phillips, Blackmore, Saunders, Melville (Pascoe 80), Nicholas, Hughes, Allen, Maguire.

Final table	P	W	D	L	F	A	Pts
Holland	6	4	2	0	8	2	10
West Germany	6	3	3	0	13	3	9
Finland	6	1	1	4	4	16	3
Wales	6	0	2	4	4	8	2

Holland and West Germany qualified

Group 5 *(France, Scotland, Yugoslavia, Norway, Cyprus)*

14 September, Oslo, 22,769

Norway (1) 1 *(Fjortoft 44)*

Scotland (1) 2 *(McStay 14, Johnston 62)*

Norway: Thorstvedt; Henriksen, Johnsen, Bratseth, Giske, Osvold, Brandhaug, Loken, Sorloth, Sundby (Berg 2, Jakobsen 84), Fjortoft.
Scotland: Leighton; Nicol, Malpas, Gillespie, McLeish, Miller, Aitken (Durrant 55), McStay, Johnston, McClair, Gallacher.

28 September, Paris, 25,000

France (0) 1 *(Papin 84 (pen))*

Norway (0) 0

France: Bats; Amoros, Boli (Kastendeuch 63), Casoni, Sonor, Sauzee, Bravo, Dib, Passi (Paille 76), Papin, Xuereb.
Norway: Thorstvedt; Henriksen (Halle), Johnsen, Kojedal, Giske, Osvold (Gulbrandsen 81), Brandhaug, Bratseth, Berg, Sorloth, Jakobsen.

19 October, Hampden Park, 42,771

Scotland (1) 1 *(Johnston 17)*

Yugoslavia (1) 1 *(Katanec 36)*

Scotland: Goram; Gough, Malpas, Nicol, McLeish, Miller, Aitken (Speedie 70), McStay, Johnston, McClair, Bett (McCoist 55).
Yugoslavia: Ivkovic; Stanojkovic, Spasic (Sabanadzovic 83), Jozic, Hadzibegic, Radanovic, Stojkovic, Katanec, Cvetkovic (Jankovic M 89), Bazdarevic, Zlatko Vujovic.

22 October, Nicosia, 3000

Cyprus (0) 1 *(Pittas (pen) 78)*

France (1) 1 *(Xuereb 44)*

Cyprus: Pantzarias; Christodolu, Stavru, Miamiliotis, Pittas, Petsas, Yiangudakis, Nikolau, Kantilos, Savva, Christofi (Ioannu 77).
France: Bats; Sonor, Casoni, Boli, Amoros, Bravo (Paille 80), Dib, Sauzee, Passi (Vercruysse 72), Papin, Xuereb.

2 November, Limassol, 7767

Cyprus (0) 0

Norway (0) 3 *(Sorloth 56, 78, Osvold 89)*

Cyprus: Pantzarias; Pittas, Miamiliotis, Christodolu (Kastanis 25), Stavrou, Yiangudakis, Kantilos (Koliandris 31), Savva, Savvides, Nikolau, Christofi.
Norway: Thorstvedt; Lokken, Kojedal, Bratseth, Halle, Osvold, Brandhaug, Halvorsen, Gulbrandsen, Sorloth, Agdestein.

19 November, Belgrade, 16,000

Yugoslavia (1) 3 *(Spasic 11, Susic 76, Stojkovic 82)*

France (1) 2 *(Perez 3, Sauzee 68)*

Yugoslavia: Ivkovic; Stanojkovic, Spasic (Juric 55), Hadzibegic, Jozic, Stojkovic, Susic, Bazdarevic, Katanec, Cvetkovic (Savicevic 70), Zlatko Vujovic.
France: Bats; Roche, Boli, Kastendeuch, Amoros, Ferreri (Papin 78), Dib, Sauzee, Tigana, Paille, Perez (Bravo 69).

11 December, Rijeka, 9000

Yugoslavia (3) 4 *(Savicevic 13, 33, 82, Hadzibegic 44 (pen))*

Cyprus (0) 0

Yugoslavia: Ivkovic; Stanojkovic, Spasic (Juric 46), Brnovic, Hadzibegic, Josic, Stojkovic, Susic, Savicevic, Bazdarevic, Zlatko Vujovic.
Cyprus: Pantzarias; Antonionios, Pittas, Papacoats, Stavrou, Yiangudakis, Savva, Nikolau, Christodolu (Kastanas 65), Ioannu (Petsas 77), Tsingis.

8 February, Limassol, 25,000

Cyprus (1) 2 *(Koliandris 14, Ioannu 47)*

Scotland (1) 3 *(Johnston 9, Gough 54, 96 – injury time)*

Cyprus: Pantzarias, Pittas, Miamiliotis, Christodolu, Socratous, Yiangudakis, Koliandris, Savva (Petsas 36), Savvides, Nikolau, Ioannu.
Scotland: Leighton; Gough, Malpas, Aitken, McLeish, Narey, Nicol (Ferguson I 9), McStay, McClair, Speedie (McInally 68), Johnston.

8 March, Hampden Park, 65,204

Scotland (1) 2 *(Johnston 28, 52)*

France (0) 0

Scotland: Leighton; Gough, Malpas, Aitken, McLeish, Gillespie, Nicol, McStay, McCoist (McClair 69), Ferguson (Strachan 56), Johnston.
France: Bats; Amoros, Silvestre, Sonor, Battiston, Sauzee, Durand (Paille 57), Laurey, Papin, Blanc, Xuereb (Perez 70).

26 April, Hampden Park, 50,081

Scotland (1) 2 *(Johnston 26, McCoist 63)*

Cyprus (0) 1 *(Nicolau 62)*

Scotland: Leighton; Gough, Malpas, Aitken, McLeish, McPherson, Nevin (Nicholas 74), McStay, Johnston, McCoist, Durie (Speedie 59).
Cyprus: Charitou; Castanas, Pittas (Elia 64), Christodolou, Michael, Yiangudakis, Petsas, Nicolau, Savvides, Ioannou Y, Kollandris.

29 April, Paris, 39,469

France (0) 0

Yugoslavia (0) 0

France: Bats; Amoros, Sonor, Boli, Battison, Sauzee, Xuereb (Deschamps 76), Durand (Cocard 46), Paille, Blanc, Perez.
Yugoslavia: Ivkovic; Stanojkovic, Spasic, Katanec, Hadzibegic, Josic, Zoran Vujovic, Susic, Bazdarevic, Stojkovic, Zlatko Vujovic (Brnovic 85).

21 May, Oslo, 10,273

Norway (3) 3 *(Osvold 17, Sorloth 34, Bratseth 35)*

Cyprus (1) 1 *(Kollandris 44)*

Norway: Thorstvedt; Halle, Kojedal, Bratseth, Giske, Lokken, Serkh (Gulbrandsen 82), Osvold, Jakobsen, Sorloth (Agdestein 61), Fjortoft.
Cyprus: Charitou; Kastanas, Pittas, Christodolou, Socratous, Yiangudakis, Kollandris (Andrelis 69), Nicolau, Savvides (Orfanides 87), Petsas, Ioannou.

14 June, Oslo, 22,740

Norway (0) 1 *(Fjortoft 90)*

Yugoslavia (1) 2 *(Stojkovic 22, Zlatko Vujovic 88)*

Norway: Ole By Rise; Halle, Bratseth, Kojedal, Giske, Lokken, Berg (Gulbrandsen 83), Osvold, Jakobsen, Sorloth (Agdestein 63), Fjortoft.
Yugoslavia: Ivkovic; Spasic, Stanojkovic, Jozic, Katanec, Hadzibegic, Zoran Vujovic, Susic (Vujavic 73), Bazdarevic, Stojkovic, Zlatko Vujovic.

5 September, Oslo, 8564

Norway (0) 1 *(Bratseth 84)*

France (1) 1 *(Papin 40 (pen))*

Norway: Thorstvedt; Halle, Kojedal, Bratseth, Bjornebye, Lokken, Brandhaug (Berg 75), Ahlsen, Jakobsen JI, Jorn Andersen, Fjortoft (Agdestein 75).
France: Bats; Amoros, Di Meco, Le Roux (Silvestre 55), Sauzee, Pardo, Deschamps, Perez, Papin, Ferreri (Blanc 75), Cantona.

6 September, Zagreb, 42,500

Yugoslavia (0) 3 *(Katanec 52, Nicol (og) 58, Gillespie og 59)*

Scotland (1) 1 *(Durie 37)*

Yugoslavia: Ivkovic; Spasic, Baljic, Katanec, Hadzibegic, Brnovic, Susic, Bazdarevic, Jakovljevic (Savicevic 73), Stojkovic, Zlatko Vujovic.
Scotland: Leighton; Gillespie, Malpas, Aitken, McLeish, Miller, Nicol, McStay, McCoist, MacLeod, Durie (McInally 68).

11 October, Sarajevo, 30,000

Yugoslavia (1) 1 *(Hadzibegic 44 (pen))*

Norway (0) 0

Yugoslavia: Ivkovic; Spasic, Baljic, Brnovic, Hadzibegic, Jozic, Stojkovic, Bazdarevic, Susic, Jakovljevic (Stanojkovic 84), Zlatko Vujovic.
Norway: Thorstvedt; Halle, Kojedal, Bratseth, Bjornebye, Lokken, Brandhaug, Ahlsen, Jakobsen, Jorn Andersen (Sorloth 70), Fjortoft.

11 October, Paris, 25,000

France (1) 3 *(Deschamps 25, Cantona 61, Nicol (og) 89)*

Scotland (0) 0

France: Bats; Silvestre, Le Roux (Casoni 46), Sauzee, Di Meco, Durand, Pardo, Deschamps, Ferreri, Cantona, Perez (Bravo 81).
Scotland: Leighton; Nicol, Gough, McLeish, Malpas, Aitken, Strachan (McInally 64), McStay, MacLeod (Bett 75), McCoist, Johnston.

28 October, Athens, 5000

Cyprus (1) 1 *(Pittas 38 (pen))*

Yugoslavia (1) 2 *(Stanojkovic 5, Pancev 49)*

Cyprus: Kouis; Pittas, Kostadinou, Scoratous, Yiangudakis, Koliandris, Miamiliotis, Petsas (Tsingis 69), Kastanas, Nikolau, Ioannu (Agas 84).
Yugoslavia: Omerovic; Stanojkovic, Marovic, Brnovic, Vulic, Spasic, Prosinecki (Mijakovic 70), Savicevic, Pancev, Stojkovic, Skoro.

15 November, Hampden Park, 70,000

Scotland (1) 1 *(McCoist 44)*

Norway (0) 1 *(Johnsen 89)*

Scotland: Leighton; McPherson, Malpas, Aitken, McLeish, Miller (MacLeod 66), Johnston, McStay, McCoist, Bett, Cooper (McClair 74).
Norway: Thorstvedt; Hansen H, Bratseth, Kojedal (Halvorsen 83), Johnsen, Gulbrandsen, Bjornebye, Ahlsen, Skammelsrud (Bohinen 58), Sorloth, Fjortoft.

18 November, Toulouse, 34,687 *(including 15,450 children admitted free)*

France (1) 2 *(Deschamps 25, Blanc 75)*

Cyprus (0) 0

France: Bats; Amoros, Silvestre, Casoni, Sauzee, Ferreri, Pardo, Deschamps, Perez (Blanc 17), Papin, Cantona.
Cyprus: Charitou; Kastanas, Pittas, Christodolu, Socratous, Constantinou, Nikolau, Christofi, Savva, Koliandris, Ioannu.

Final table	P	W	D	L	F	A	Pts
Yugoslavia	8	6	2	0	16	6	14
Scotland	8	4	2	2	12	12	10
France	8	3	3	2	10	7	9
Norway	8	2	2	4	10	9	6
Cyprus	8	0	1	7	6	20	1

Yugoslavia and Scotland qualified

Group 6 *(Spain, Hungary, Northern Ireland, Eire, Malta)*

21 May, Belfast, 9000

Northern Ireland (3) 3 *(Quinn 14, Penney 23, Clarke 25)*

Malta (0) 0

Northern Ireland: McKnight; Donaghy, Worthington, McClelland, McDonald, O'Neill, Penney (McNally 81), Wilson D, Clarke, Quinn, Dennison (Black).
Malta: Cluett; Camilleri E (Refalo 46), Azzopardi, Galea, Brincat, Buttigieg, Busuttil, Scerri, Carabott, Scicluna, Di Giorgio (Caruana 60).

14 September, Belfast, 19,873

Northern Ireland (0) 0

Eire (0) 0

Northern Ireland: McKnight; Donaghy (Rogan), Worthington, McClelland, McDonald, O'Neill, Penney, Wilson D, Clarke, Quinn, Black.
Eire: Peyton; Morris, Hughton, McGrath, McCarthy, Moran, Houghton, Whelan, Aldridge, Cascarino, Sheedy.

19 October, Budapest, 18,000

Hungary (0) 1 *(Vincze 84)*

Northern Ireland (0) 0

Hungary: Disztl P; Sallai, Nagy, Sass, Meszoly (Dajka 46), Garaba, Kiprich, Kozma, Bognar, Detari, Hajszan (Vincze 81).
Northern Ireland: McKnight; Rogan, Worthington, McClelland, McDonald, Donaghy, Dennison, Wilson D, Clarke (Quinn 81), O'Neill (Wilson K 58), Black.

16 November, Seville, 50,000

Spain (0) 2 *(Manolo 52, Butragueno 66)*

Eire (0) 0

Spain: Zubizarreta; Quique Flores (Solana 84), Jimenez, Andrinua, Sanchis, Gorriz, Michel, Roberto, Martin Vazquez, Manolo (Ramon 67), Butragueno.
Eire: Bonner; Morris, McCarthy, Staunton, O'Leary, Moran, Houghton, Sheridan (O'Brien 82), Aldridge (Quinn 65), Cascarino, Galvin.

11 December, Valletta, 12,000

Malta (0) 2 *(Busuttil 46, 90)*

Hungary (1) 2 *(Vincze 5, Kiprich 56)*

Malta: Cluett; Camilleri E (Saliba 53), Azzopardi, Galea, Camilleri S, (Vella S 70), Busuttil, Vella R, Carabott, Gregory, De Giorgio, Woods.
Hungary: Disztl P; Kozma, Disztl L, Keller, Kekesi, Csuhay, Kiprich (Pinter 85), Kovacs, Czucsansky, Vincze (Fischer 70), Balog.

21 December, Seville, 70,000

Spain (1) 4 *(Rogan (og) 30, Butragueno 55, Michel 60 (pen), Roberto (64)*

Northern Ireland (0) 0

Spain: Zubizarreta; Quique Flores, Jimenez, Andrinua, Gorriz, Roberto, Manolo (Julio Salinas 78), Michel, Butragueno, Martin Vazquez, Beguiristain (Serna 65).
Northern Ireland: McKnight; Rogan, Worthington, McCreery (Quinn 54), McDonald, McClelland, Donaghy (O'Neill 72), Penney, Clarke, Wilson K, Black.

22 January, Valletta, 23,000

Malta (0) 0

Spain (1) 2 *(Michel (pen) 16, Beguiristain 51)*

Malta: Cluett; Camilleri S (Camilleri E 55), Galea, Buttigieg, Azzopardi, Brincat (Scerri 46), Vella R, Gregory, Carabott, De Giorgio, Busuttil.
Spain: Zubizarreta; Quique Flores, Sanchis, Andrinua, Jimenez, Michel, Roberto, Martin Vazquez, Manolo, Butragueno (Gorriz 76), Beguiristain (Eusebio 66).

8 February, Belfast, 20,000

Northern Ireland (0) 0

Spain (1) 2 *(Andrinua 3, Manolo 84)*

Northern Ireland: McKnight; Ramsey, Rogan, Donaghy, McClelland, Wilson D (Clarke 68), Dennison (O'Neill 63), Sanchez, Quinn, Wilson K, Black.
Spain: Zubizarreta; Chendo (Eusebio 44), Jimenez, Andrinua, Serna, Gorriz, Bakero (Manolo 75), Michel, Butragueno, Roberto, Martin Vazquez.

8 March, Budapest, 20,000

Hungary (0) 0

Eire (0) 0

Hungary: Disztl P; Kozma, Disztl L, Bognar Z, Sass, Kovacs E, Detari, Hajszan, Gregor (Boda 77), Kiprich, Meszaros (Bognar G 46).
Eire: Bonner; Morris, Hughton, McGrath, McCarthy, Moran, Whelan, Houghton, Aldridge (Brady 80), Cascarino (Quinn 80), Sheedy.

23 March, Seville, 50,000

Spain (1) 4 *(Michel 38, 68 (pen), Manolo 71, 80)*

Malta (0) 0

Spain: Zubizarreta; Quique Sanchez, Jimenez, Andrinua, Roberto, Sanchis, Michel, Butragueno, Martin Vazquez (Eusebio 68), Beguiristain (Eloy 68), Manolo.
Malta: Cluett; Camilleri E, Azzopardi A (Cauchi 30), Buttigieg, Galea, Vella R, De Giorgio, Scerri C, Carabott, Gregory, Busuttil.

12 April, Budapest, 15,000

Hungary (0) 1 *(Boda 49)*

Malta (1) 1 *(Busuttil 7)*

Hungary: Disztl P; Kozma (Kiprich 57), Keller, Disztl L, Kovacs E, Bognar Z, Boda, Bognar G, Sass (Fischer 46), Detari, Hajszan.
Malta: Cluett; Camilleri E, Azzopardi A, Galea, Cauchi (Vella S 46), Buttigieg, Busuttil, Vella R, Carabott, Scerri, Gregory.

26 April, Valletta, 15,000

Malta (0) 0

Northern Ireland (0) 2 *(Clarke 55, O'Neill 73)*

Malta: Cluett; Buttigieg, Camilleri E, Cauchi (Vella S 62), Galea, De Giorgio, Scerri, Vella R, Busuttil, Gregory, Carabott (Delia 78).
Northern Ireland: Wright; Donaghy, Worthington (Rogan 86), McCreery, McClelland, Dennison, Wilson D, Quinn, Clarke, Sanchez (O'Neill 70), Wilson K.

26 April, Dublin, 49,160

Eire (1) 1 *(Michel (og) 15)*

Spain (0) 0

Eire: Bonner; Hughton, Staunton, McCarthy, Moran, Whelan, McGrath, Houghton, Stapleton (Townsend 69), Cascarino, Sheedy.
Spain: Zubizarreta; Quique Sanchez (Eusebio 69), Jimenez, Serna, Sanchis, Gorriz, Manolo, Michel, Butragueno (Julio Salinas 70), Roberto, Martin Vazquez.

28 May, Dublin, 49,000

Eire (1) 2 *(Houghton 32, Moran 55)*

Malta (0) 0

Eire: Bonner; Hughton, Staunton, O'Leary, Moran, Whelan, McGrath, Houghton (Townsend 70), Stapleton (Aldridge 27), Cascarino, Sheedy.
Malta: Cluett; Camilleri E, Azzopardi (Carabott 65), Galea, Vella S, Buttigieg, Busuttil, Vella R, Scerri, De Giorgio, Gregory.

4 June, Dublin, 49,000

Eire (1) 2 *(McGrath 33, Cascarino 80)*

Hungary (0) 0

Eire: Bonner; Hughton, Staunton, O'Leary, McGrath (Morris 80), Moran, Houghton, Townsend, Aldridge (Brady 74), Cascarino, Sheedy.
Hungary: Disztl P; Bognar Z, Fitos, Disztl L, Garaba, Kozma, Meszaros (Vincze 71), Detari, Czehi (Bognar G 66), Keller, Boda.

6 September, Belfast, 8000

Northern Ireland (0) 1 *(Whiteside 89)*

Hungary (2) 2 *(Kovacs K 13, Bognar G 44)*

Northern Ireland: Wright; Fleming, Worthington, Rogan, McDonald, McCreery, Wilson D, Quinn (O'Neill M 64), Clarke, Whiteside, Black.
Hungary: Disztl P; Sallai, Keller, Disztl L, Kovacs E, Limperger, Bognar G (Istvan 84), Sass, Fischer (Bognar Z 89), Detari, Kovacs K.

11 October, Budapest, 40,000

Hungary (1) 2 *(Pinter 38, 82)*

Spain (2) 2 *(Julio Salinas 30, Michel 35)*

Hungary: Disztl P; Sallai, Keller (Lovasz 71), Pinter, Bognar Z, Roth (Kozma 46), Bognar G, Detari, Vincze, Kovacs K, Kiprich.
Spain: Zubizarreta; Chendo, Sanchis, Andrinua, Jimenez, Roberto, Michel, Martin Vazquez, Villaroya, Manolo (Hierro 84), Julio Salinas (Pardeza 67).

11 October, Dublin, 48,500

Eire (1) 3 *(Whelan 42, Cascarino 48, Houghton 57)*

Northern Ireland (0) 0

Eire: Bonner; Morris, Staunton (O'Leary 77), McCarthy, Moran, Whelan, Townsend, Houghton, Aldridge, Cascarino, Sheedy.
Northern Ireland: Dunlop; Fleming, Worthington, Donaghy, McDonald, McCreery (O'Neill C 72), Wilson D, O'Neill M (Wilson K 80), Clarke, Whiteside, Dennison.

15 November, Seville, 20,000

Spain (3) 4 *(Manolo 7, Butragueno 24, Juanito 40, Fernando 63)*

Hungary (0) 0

Spain: Zubizarreta; Chendo, Sanchis, Milla, Jimenez, Michel (Eusebio 65), Juanito, Fernando, Manolo (Julio Salinas 65), Butragueno, Villaroya.
Hungary: Disztl P; Simon, Pinter, Keller, Bognar Z, Kovacs E, Bognar G, (Szalma 62), Kovacs K, Fischer (Bacsi 62), Szekeres, Kozma.

15 November, Valletta, 25,000

Malta (0) 0

Eire (1) 2 *(Aldridge 31, 68 (pen))*

Malta: Cini; Vella S, Azzopardi (Suda 68), Galea, Scerri, Buttigieg, Busuttil, Zerafa (Zarb 68), Carabott, De Giorgio, Gregory.
Eire: Bonner; McGrath, Moran (Morris 26), Staunton, O'Leary, Houghton, Sheedy, Townsend, Whelan, Aldridge, Cascarino.

Final table

	P	W	D	L	F	A	Pts
Spain	8	6	1	1	20	3	13
Eire	8	5	2	1	10	2	12
Hungary	8	2	4	2	8	12	8
Northern Ireland	8	2	1	5	6	12	5
Malta	8	0	2	6	3	18	2

Spain and Eire qualified

Group 7 *(Belgium, Portugal, Czechoslovakia, Switzerland, Luxembourg)*

21 September, Luxembourg, 2500

Luxembourg (0) 1 *(Langers 80)*

Switzerland (3) 4 *(Sutter A 15 sec, Turkyilmaz 21 (pen), 53, Sutter B 28)*

Luxembourg: Van Rijswijk; Meunier, Bossi, Weis, Petry, Girres (Scuto 63), Hellers, Jeitz, Scholten, Langers, Krings (Morocutti 73).
Switzerland: Corminboeuf; Geiger, Tschuppert, Martin Weber, Mottiez, Andermatt (Lei-Ravello 70), Hermann, Favre, Sutter B, Turkyilmaz, Sutter A (Bonvin 79).

19 October, Brussels, 14,450

Belgium (1) 1 *(Vervoort 30)*

Switzerland (0) 0

Belgium: Bodart; Grun, Clijsters, Demol, Versavel, Emmers, Van der Elst F, Scifo, Vervoort, Ceulemans, Nilis (Severeyns 76).
Switzerland: Corminboeuf; Mottiez, Geiger, Weber, Schallibaum, Andermatt (Bonvin 76), Hermann, Favre, Zuffi, Sutter B, Turkyilmaz.

18 October, Esch-sur-Alzette, 2500

Luxembourg (0) 0

Czechoslovakia (2) 2 *(Hasek 25, Chovanec 35)*

Luxembourg: Van Rijswijk; Meunier, Scheuer, Petry, Bossi, Jeitz (Girres 82), Hellers, Weis, Scholten, Langers, Krings (Morocutti 61).
Czechoslovakia: Stejskal; Bielik, Kadlec, Hasek, Bilek, Nemecek, Fieber, Chovanec, Griga (Danek 81), Skuhravy, Weiss (Hyravy 75).

16 November, Bratislava, 48,000

Czechoslovakia (0) 0

Belgium (0) 0

Czechoslovakia: Stejskal; Bielik, Nemecek (Danek 87), Chovanec, Kadlec, Vlk, Weiss (Moravcik 80), Hasek, Bilek, Griga, Luhovy.
Belgium: Preud'homme; Demol, Gerets, Grun, Albert, Dewolf, Emmers, Veyt, Van der Elst F, Scifo (Van den Linden 75), Christiaens (Nilis 82).

16 November, Oporto, 29,000

Portugal (1) 1 *(Gomes 31)*

Luxembourg (0) 0

Portugal: Silvino; Jaime, Sobrinho, Morato, Alvaro, Rui Barros, Vitor Paneira, Nunes, Futre, Jordao (Jaime Magalhaes 46), Gomes.
Luxembourg: Van Rijswijk; Meunier, Scheuer, Petry, Bossi, Girres, Jeitz, Weis, Scholten (Thome 82), Krings (Malget 60), Langers.

15 February, Lisbon, 70,000

Portugal (0) 1 *(Paneira 53)*

Belgium (0) 1 *(Gerets 83)*

Portugal: Silvino; Joao Pinto, Oliveira, Sobrinho, Veloso, Nunes, Vitor Paneira (Cesar Brito 86), Sousa, Rui Barros, Futre (Pacheco 61), Semedo.
Belgium: Preud'homme; Gerets, Grun, De Wolf, Versavel, Emmers, Demol (Van der Linden 77), Scifo, Van der Elst, Ceulemans, De Gryse.

26 April, Lisbon, 15,000

Portugal (0) 3 *(Joao Pinto 48, Frederico 56, Vitor Paneira 69)*

Switzerland (0) 1 *(Zuffi 64)*

Portugal: Silvano; Joao Pinto, Sobrinho, Frederico (Oliveira 87), Veloso, Nunes, Andre, Vitor Paneira, Rui Barros, Sousa (Jorge Silva 46), Cesar Brito.
Switzerland: Brunner; Mottiez, Birrel (Ryf 73), Weber M, Koller, Marini, Sutter B, Hermann, Favre, Zuffi, Sutter A (Turkyilmaz 86).

29 April, Brussels, 21,000

Belgium (1) 2 *(De Gryse 29, 77)*

Czechoslovakia (1) 1 *(Luhovy 41)*

Belgium: Preud'homme; Gerets, Demol, Grun, Albert, Versavel, Van der Elst F, Emmers, Ceulemans, De Gryse, Nilis (Van der Linden 65).
Czechoslovakia: Stejskal; Bilek (Weiss 85), Chovanec, Kocain, Straka, Kadlec, Moravcik, Vik (Nemecek 83), Hasek, Griga, Luhovy.

9 May, Prague, 16,350

Czechoslovakia (1) 4 *(Griga 6, Skuhravy 76, 84, Bilek 81)*

Luxembourg (0) 0

Czechoslovakia: Stejskal; Bilek, Kadlec (Bielik 46), Hasek, Kocian, Nemecek (Weiss 71), Straka, Chovanec, Griga, Skuhravy, Moravcik.
Luxembourg: Van Rijswijk; Meunier, Scheuer, Petry, Bossi, Girres, Birsens, Weis, Jeitz (Salbene 76), Hellers, Krings (Malget 89).

7 June, Berne, 30,000

Switzerland (0) 0

Czechoslovakia (1) 1 *(Skuhravy 21)*

Switzerland: Brunner; Koller, Marini, Schepull, Weber, Hermann, Sutter R (Turkyilmaz 58), Geiger, Sutter A, Sutter B (Zuffi 71), Halter.
Czechoslovakia: Stejskal; Bielik, Kadlec, Kocian, Straka, Hasek, Chovanec (Nemecek 83), Moravcik, Bilek, Griga,Skuhravy (Danek 56).

1 June, Lille, 10,000

Luxembourg (0) 0

Belgium (1) 5 *(Van der Linden 13, 52, 62 (pen), 90, Vervoort 64)*

Luxembourg: Van Rijswijk; Meunier, Scheuer, Petry, Bossi, Girres, Birsens, Jeitz (Salbene 75), Scholten (Malget 83), Langers, Krings.
Belgium: Preud'homme; Gerets, Sanders, Versavel, Van der Elst F (Scifo 73), Emmers, Demol, Vervoort, De Gryse, Van der Linden, Ceulemans.

6 September, Brussels, 28,250

Belgium (1) 3 *(Ceulemans 34, Van der Linden 59, 69)*

Portugal (0) 0

Belgium: Preud'homme; Gerets, Grun, Demol, De Wolf, Emmers, Franky Van der Elst, Versavel, De Gryse, Ceulemans, Van der Linden (Nilis 86).
Portugal: Silvino; Joao Pinto, Sobrinho, Venancio, Veloso, Carlos Xavier, Vitor Paneira (Rui Aguas 60), Rui Barros, Cesar Brito, Futre, Andre.

20 September, Neuchatel, 16,500

Switzerland (1) 1 *(Turkyilmaz 28 (pen))*

Portugal (0) 2 *(Futre 74 (pen), Rui Aguas 77)*

Switzerland: Brunner; Rey, Weber, Baumann, Geiger, Piffaretti, Favre (Herr 78), Hermann, Chapuisat, Beat Sutter (Zuffi 69), Turkyilmaz.
Portugal: Silvino; Vitor Paneira (Sobrinho 89), Joao Pinto, Frederico, Venancio, Veloso, Andrea, Adelino Nunes, Jaime Magalhaes (Rui Aguas 44), Rui Barros, Futre.

6 October, Prague, 28,000

Czechoslovakia (1) 2 *(Bilek 11 (pen), 82)*

Portugal (0) 1 *(Rui Aguas 74)*

Czechoslovakia: Stejskal; Straka, Kadlec, Hasek, Kocian, Cabala (Nemecek 70), Bilek, Chovanec, Griga, Skuhravy, Moravcik (Kinier 89).
Portugal: Silvino; Frederico, Joao Pinto, Venancio, Veloso, Nunes (Lima 71), Sobrinho (Vitor Paneira 27), Rui Barros, Rui Aguas, Futre, Andre.

11 October, Basle, 5000

Switzerland (0) 2 *(Knup 50, Turkyilmaz 60)*

Belgium (0) 2 *(De Gryse 58, Geiger (og) 73)*

Switzerland: Brunner; Geiger, Piffaretti, Herr, Baumann, Koller, Hermann, Bickel, Douglas (Knup 46), Turkyilmaz, Chapuisat (Hottiger 80).
Belgium: Preud'homme; Demol, Gerets, Clijsters, Franky Van der Elst, Versavel, Emmers (Scifo 46), Vervoort, De Gryse, Ceulemans, Van der Linden.

11 October, Saarbrucken, 15,000

Luxembourg (0) 0

Portugal (1) 3 *(Rui Aguas 43, 53, Rui Barros 72)*

Luxembourg: Van Rijswijk; Bossi, Weiss, Birsens, Girres, Groff (Jeitz 70), Salbene, Langers, Malget, Hallers, Reiter (Scholten 58).
Portugal: Silvino; Joao Pinto, Venancio, Frederico, Fonseca (Pedro Xavier 33), Vitor Paneira, Nunes (Jaime Magalhaes 64), Veloso, Rui Barros, Rui Aguas, Lima.

25 October, Prague, 33,000

Czechoslovakia (1) 3 *(Skuhravy 17, Bilek 86, Moravcik 88)*

Switzerland (0) 0

Czechoslovakia: Stejskal; Straka, Kocian, Kadlec (Nemecek 60), Bilek, Weiss (Hyravy 73), Hasek, Chovanec, Moravcik, Luhovy, Skuhravy.
Switzerland: Brunner; Weber, Geiger, Herr, Baumann, Piffaretti (Andermatt 55), Hermann, Koller (Lorenz 70), Heldmann, Turkyilmaz, Bonvin.

25 October, Brussels, 20,000

Belgium (0) 1 *(Versavel 86)*

Luxembourg (0) 1 *(Hellers 88)*

Belgium: Preud'homme; Grun, Clijsters, Broeckart, Versavel, Emmers (Nilis 76), Van der Elst, Boffin (Claesen 76), De Gryse, Scifo, Ceulemans.
Luxembourg: Van Rijswijk; Bossi, Scheuer (Scholten 82), Weiss, Birsens, Girres, Hellers, Salbene (Jeitz 75), Groff, Langers, Malget.

15 November, Lisbon, 50,000

Portugal (0) 0

Czechoslovakia (0) 0

Portugal: Silvino; Joao Pinto (Vitor Paneira 46), Venancio, Frederico, Veloso, Jorge Ferreira, Pacheco, Sousa, Rui Barros, Cesar Brito (Pedro Xavier 80), Rui Aguas.
Czechoslovakia: Stejskal; Kocian, Straka, Kadlec, Nemecek, Bilek, Hasek, Chovanec, Moravcik (Kiniek 88), Skuhravy, Luhovy (Weiss 87).

15 November, St Gallen, 2500

Switzerland (0) 2 *(Bonvin 54, Turkyilmaz 62)*

Luxembourg (1) 1 *(Malget 14)*

Switzerland: Brunner; Geiger, Marini, Herr, Baumann, Koller, Heldmann (Schepull 59), Hermann, A Sutter (Bonvin 46), Turkyilmaz, Knup.
Luxembourg: Van Rijswijk; Bossi, Birsens, Weis, Scheuer, Girres, Ellers, Salbene, Groff, Malget (Scholten 83), Morocutti.

Final table	P	W	D	L	F	A	Pts
Belgium	8	4	4	0	15	5	12
Czechoslovakia	8	5	2	1	13	3	12
Portugal	8	4	2	2	11	8	10
Switzerland	8	2	1	5	10	14	5
Luxembourg	8	0	1	7	3	22	1

Belgium and Czechoslovakia qualified

ASIA

First Round

Group 1
6.1.89   Qatar (1) 1 Jordan (0) 0
6.1.89   Oman (1) 1 Iraq (1) 1
13.1.89 Oman (0) 0 Qatar (0) 0
13.1.89 Jordan (0) 0 Iraq (0) 1
20.1.89 Jordan (2) 2 Oman (0) 0
20.1.89 Qatar (0) 1 Iraq (0) 0
27.1.89 Jordan (0) 1 Qatar (0) 1
27.1.89 Iraq (1) 3 Oman (0) 1
3.2.89   Qatar (1) 3 Oman (0) 0
3.2.89   Iraq (2) 4 Jordan (0) 0
10.2.89 Oman (0) 0 Jordan (0) 2
10.2.89 Iraq (1) 2 Qatar (1) 2

Group 2 *(Bahrain withdrew)*
10.3.89 Yemen AR (0) 0 Syria (1) 1
15.3.89 Saudi Arabia (2) 5 Syria (1) 4
20.3.89 Yemen AR (0) 0 Saudi Arabia (0) 1
25.3.89 Syria (1) 2 Yemen AR (0) 0
30.3.89 Syria (0) 0 Saudi Arabia (0) 0
5.4.89   Saudi Arabia (1) 1 Yemen AR (0) 0

Group 3 *(Yemen PDR withdrew)*
6.1.89   Pakistan (0) 0 Kuwait (0) 1
13.1.89 Kuwait (1) 3 UAE (0) 2
20.1.89 UAE (2) 5 Pakistan (0) 0
27.1.89 Kuwait (1) 2 Pakistan (0) 0
3.2.89   UAE (0) 1 Kuwait (0) 0
10.2.89 Pakistan (0) 1 UAE (3) 4

Group 4 *(India withdrew)*
23.5.89 Malaysia (0) 2 Nepal (0) 0
23.5.89 Singapore (0) 0 Korea Rep (2) 3
25.5.89 Malaysia (0) 1 Singapore (0) 0
25.5.89 Nepal (0) 0 Korea Rep (5) 9
27.5.89 Singapore (2) 3 Nepal (0) 0
27.5.89 Korea Rep (1) 3 Malaysia (0) 0
3.6.89   Singapore (2) 2 Malaysia (1) 2
3.6.89   Korea Rep (3) 4 Nepal (0) 0
5.6.89   Malaysia (0) 0 Korea Rep (0) 3
5.6.89   Nepal (0) 0 Singapore (4) 7
7.6.89   Singapore (0) 0 Korea Rep (1) 3
7.6.89   Malaysia (1) 3 Nepal (0) 0

Group 5
19.2.89 Thailand (0) 1 Bangladesh (0) 0
23.2.89 China (0) 2 Bangladesh (0) 0
23.2.89 Thailand (0) 0 Iran (2) 3
27.2.89 Bangladesh (0) 1 Iran (1) 2
28.2.89 Thailand (0) 0 China (0) 3
4.3.89   Bangladesh (0) 0 China (1) 2
8.3.89   Bangladesh (2) 3 Thailand (0) 1
17.3.89 Iran (0) 1 Bangladesh (0) 0
30.5.89 Iran (2) 3 Thailand (0) 0
15.7.89 China (0) 2 Iran (0)
22.7.89 Iran (2) 3 China (0) 0
29.7.89 China 2 Thailand 0

Group 6
21.5.89 Indonesia (0) 0 Korea DPR (0) 0
22.5.89 Hong Kong (0) 0 Japan (0) 0
27.5.89 Hong Kong (0) 1 Korea DPR (2) 2
28.5.89 Indonesia (0) 0 Japan (0) 0
4.6.89   Hong Kong (1) 1 Indonesia (0) 1
4.6.89   Japan (0) 2 Korea DPR (0) 1
11.6.89 Japan (4) 5 Indonesia (0) 0
18.6.89 Japan (0) 0 Hong Kong (0) 0
25.6.89 Indonesia (0) 3 Hong Kong (1) 2
25.6.89 Korea DPR (1) 2 Japan (0) 0
2.7.89   Korea DPR (2) 4 Hong Kong (1) 1
9.7.89   Korea DPR 2 Indonesia 1

Second Round *(in Singapore)*
12.10.89 UAE (0) 0 Korea DPR (0) 0
12.10.89 China (0) 2 Saudi Arabia (1) 1
13.10.89 Korea Rep (0) 0 Qatar (0) 0
16.10.89 Qatar (0) 1 Saudi Arabia (1) 1
16.10.89 Korea Rep (1) 1 Korea DPR (0) 0
17.10.89 China (0) 1 UAE (0) 2
20.10.89 China (0) 0 Korea Rep (0) 1
20.10.89 Korea DPR (2) 2 Qatar (0) 0
21.10.89 Saudi Arabia (0) 0 UAE (0) 0
24.10.89 UAE (1) 1 Qatar (1) 1
24.10.89 Korea DPR (0) 0 China (0) 1
25.10.89 Saudi Arabia (0) 0 Korea Rep (1) 2
28.10.89 UAE (1) 1 Korea Rep (1) 1
28.10.89 Saudi Arabia (1) 2 Korea DPR (0) 0
28.10.89 Qatar (0) 2 China (0) 1

AFRICA

First Round

Group 1

7.8.88   Angola (0) 0 Sudan (0) 0
11.11.88   Sudan (1) 1 Angola (0) 2
    Lesotho withdrew; Zimbabwe walked over
    Zambia walked over; Rwanda withdrew
16.7.88   Uganda (0) 1 Malawi (0) 0
30.7.88   Malawi (2) 3 Uganda (0) 1

Group 2

3.6.88   Libya (3) 3 Burkina Faso (0) 0
3.7.88   Burkina Faso (0) 2 Libya (0) 0
7.8.88   Ghana (0) 0 Liberia (0) 0
21.8.88   Liberia (1) 2 Ghana (0) 0
5.8.88   Tunisia (2) 5 Guinea (0) 0
21.8.88   Guinea (1) 3 Tunisia (0) 0
    Togo withdrew; Gabon walked over

Second Round

Group A

6.1.89   Algeria (2) 3 Zimbabwe (0) 0
8.1.89   Ivory Coast (0) 1 Libya (0) 0
20.1.89   Libya v Algeria; *Libya refused to play on*
    the grounds that a state of war existed with
    the USA. Algeria were awarded the game
    2-0. Libya withdrew.
22.1.89   Zimbabwe (0) 0 Ivory Coast (0) 0
11.6.89   Ivory Coast (0) 0 Algeria (0) 0
25.6.89   Zimbabwe (0) 1 Algeria (1) 2

Group B

6.1.89   Egypt (2) 2 Liberia (0) 0
7.1.89   Kenya (0) 1 Malawi (1) 1
21.1.89   Malawi (0) 1 Egypt (0) 1
22.1.89   Liberia (0) 0 Kenya (0) 0
10.6.89   Kenya (0) 0 Egypt (0) 0
11.6.89   Liberia (0) 1 Malawi (0) 0
24.6.89   Malawi (0) 1 Kenya (0) 0
25.6.89   Liberia (1) 1 Egypt (0) 0

Group C

7.1.89   Nigeria (1) 1 Gabon (0) 0
8.1.89   Cameroon (0) 1 Angola (1) 1
22.1.89   Gabon (1) 1 Cameroon (2) 3
22.1.89   Angola (1) 2 Nigeria (0) 0
10.6.89   Nigeria (1) 2 Cameroon (0) 0
11.6.89   Angola (2) 2 Gabon (0) 0
25.6.89   Angola (1) 1 Cameroon (0) 2
25.6.89   Gabon (2) 2 Nigeria (0) 1

Group D

8.1.89   Morocco (1) 1 Zambia (0) 0
8.1.89   Zaire (2) 3 Tunisia (1) 1
22.1.89   Tunisia (2) 2 Morocco (1) 1
22.1.89   Zambia (2) 4 Zaire (1) 2
11.6.89   Zaire (0) 0 Morocco (0) 0
11.6.89   Zambia (0) 1 Tunisia (0) 0
25.6.89   Tunisia (0) 1 Zaire (0) 0
25.6.89   Zambia (1) 2 Morocco (0) 1

Third Round

8.10.89   Algeria (0) 0 Egypt (0) 0
17.11.89   Egypt (1) 1 Algeria (0) 0
8.10.89   Cameroon (0) 2 Tunisia (0) 0
19.11.89   Tunisia (0) 0 Cameroon (1) 1

OCEANIA

First Round

11.12.88   Chinese Taipei (0) 0 New Zealand (2) 4
15.12.88   New Zealand (3) 4 Chinese Taipei (0) 1
    (both matches played in New Zealand)
26.11.88   Fiji (0) 1 Australia (0) 0
3.12.88   Australia (2) 5 Fiji (0) 1

Second Round

5.3.89   Israel (1) 1 New Zealand (0) 0
12.3.89   Australia (2) 4 New Zealand (0) 1
19.3.89   Israel (0) 1 Australia (0) 1
2.4.89   New Zealand (2) 2 Australia (0) 0
9.4.89   New Zealand (2) 2 Israel (2) 2
16.4.89   Australia (0) 1 Israel (1) 1

Israel qualified for matches against the winner of South American Group 2.

CONCACAF

First Round

17.4.88   Guyana (0) 0 Trinidad/Tobago (2) 4
8.5.88   Trinidad/Tobago (1) 1 Guyana (0) 0
30.4.88   Cuba (0) 0 Guatemala (1) 1
15.5.88   Guatemala (0) 1 Cuba (1) 1
12.5.88   Jamaica (1) 1 Puerto Rico (0) 0
29.5.88   Puerto Rico (0) 1 Jamaica (1) 2
19.6.88   Antigua (0) 0 Netherlands Antilles (0) 1
29.7.88   Netherlands Antilles (0) 0 Antigua (1) 1
    (Netherlands Antilles won 3-1 on penalties
    after extra time)
17.7.88   Costa Rica (1) 1 Panama (1) 1
31.7.88   Panama (0) 0 Costa Rica (1) 2

Second Round

1.10.88   Netherlands Antilles (0) 0 El Salvador (0) 1
16.10.88   El Salvador (2) 5 Netherlands Antilles (0) 0
24.7.88   Jamaica (0) 0 USA (0) 0
13.8.88   USA (1) 5 Jamaica (0) 1
30.10.88   Trinidad/Tobago (0) 0 Honduras (0) 0
13.11.88   Honduras (1) 1 Trinidad/Tobago (0) 1
    Costa Rica walked over; Mexico disqualified
    for playing over-age players in youth
    tournament
9.10.88   Guatemala (1) 1 Canada (0) 0
15.10.88   Canada (0) 3 Guatemala (2) 2

Third Round

19.3.89   Guatemala (1) 1 Costa Rica (0) 0
2.4.89   Costa Rica (1) 2 Guatemala (0) 1
16.4.89   Costa Rica (1) 1 USA (0) 0
30.4.89   USA (0) 1 Costa Rica (0) 0
13.5.89   USA (0) 1 Trinidad/Tobago (0) 1
28.5.89   Trinidad/Tobago (0) 1 Costa Rica (0) 1
11.6.89   Costa Rica (*) 1 Trinidad/Tobago (*) 0
30.7.89   Trinidad/Tobago (0) 2 El Salvador (0) 0
13.8.89   El Salvador (0) 0 Trinidad/Tobago (0) 0
20.8.89   Guatemala (0) 0 Trinidad/Tobago (0) 1
3.9.89   Trinidad/Tobago (1) 2 Guatemala (1) 1
17.9.89   El Salvador (0) 0 USA (0) 1
8.10.89   Guatemala (0) 0 USA (0) 0
5.11.89   USA (0) 0 El Salvador (0) 0
19.11.89   Trinidad/Tobago (0) 0 USA (0) 1

Guatemala v El Salvador and El Salvador v Guatemala not played due to deterioration of political situation in El Salvador.

SOUTH AMERICA

Group 1

20 August, La Paz, 50,000

Bolivia (1) 2 *(Melgar 44 (pen), Ramallo 53)*
Peru (1) 1 *(Del Solar 43)*
Bolivia: Galarza; Fontana, Martinez, Perez, Soria,
Borja, Melgar, Takeo (Sanchez 46), Romero, Pena
(Roca 75), Ramallo.
Peru: Purizaga; Olivares (Manassero 46), Olaechea,
Requena, Carranza, Suarez, Reinoso, Del Solar,
Valencia, Navarro (Rey Munoz 46), Hirano.

27 August, Lima, 45,000

Peru (0) 0
Uruguay (0) 2 *(Sosa 46, Alzamendi 69)*
Peru: Purizaga; Carranza, Arteaga, Requena, Oli-
vares (Manassero 73), Del Solar, Reinoso, Uribe,
Dall'Orso, Hirano, Navarro.
Uruguay: Pereyra; Herrera, Guiterrez, De Leon,
Dominquez, Ostolaza (Correa 80), Perdomo, Paz
(Bengoechea 75), Alzamendi, Francescoli, Sosa.

3 September, La Paz, 52,000

Bolivia (1) 2 *(Dominguez (og) 38, Pena 47)*
Uruguay (0) 1 *(Sosa 49)*
Bolivia: Galarza; Martinez, Fontana, Ferrufino,
Perez, Borja, Soria, Romero, Melgar, Ramallo, Pena
(Sanchez 61).
Uruguay: Pereyra; Herrera (Bengoechea 82), Gutier-
rez, De Leon, Dominguez, Perdomo, Ostolaza, Paz,
Alzamendi, Francescoli, Sosa.

10 September, Lima, 9500

Peru (0) 1 *(Gonzalez 53)*
Bolivia (1) 2 *(Ramallo 44, Sanchez 76)*
Peru: Purizaga; Arteaga, Requena, Del Solar, Oli-
vares, Reinoso, Reyna (Yanez 46), Manassero
(Torres 46), Rey Munoz, Gonzalez, Hirano.
Bolivia: Truco; Montano, Martinez, Vargas, Fon-
tana, Soria, Ferrufino, Melgar, Romero (Sanchez 59),
Crisaldo, Ramallo.

17 September, Montevideo, 70,000

Uruguay (2) 2 *(Sosa 31, Francescoli 38)*
Bolivia (0) 0
Uruguay: Pereyra; Herrera, Gutierrez, De Leon,
Dominguez, Ostolaza, Perdomo (Correa 78), Paz
(Bengoechea 66), Alzamendi, Francescoli, Sosa.
Bolivia: Truco; Fontana, Vargas, Ferrufino, Marti-
nez, Montano (Sanchez 46), Borja, Villegas, Melgar,
Romero (Pena 46), Ramallo.

24 September, Montevideo, 60,000

Uruguay (1) 2 *(Sosa 43, 57)*
Peru (0) 0
Uruguay: Pereyra; Herrera, Gutierrez, De Leon,
Dominguez, Ostolaza, Correa, Bengoechea, Alza-
mendi, Paz, Sosa.

Peru: Purizaga; Guido, Sanjinez, Requena, Arteaga,
Yanez (Manassero 62), Del Solar, Reinoso, Carranza, Gonzalez, Hirano (Bazalar 54).

Final table	P	W	D	L	F	A	Pts
Uruguay	4	3	0	1	7	2	6
Bolivia	4	3	0	1	6	5	6
Peru	4	0	0	4	2	8	0

Uruguay qualified

Group 2

20 August, Barranquilla, 60,000

Colombia (1) 2 *(Iguaran 32, 72)*
Ecuador (0) 0
Colombia: Higuita; Wilson Perez, Escobar, Perea,
Villa, Ricardo Perez, Alvarez, Redin, Valderrama C,
Uzurriaga (Hernandez 55), Iguaran (Fajardo 80).
Ecuador: Morales; Izquierdo, Quinonez, Macias,
Capurro, Fajardo, Aguinaga, Rosero, Cuvi (Marsetti
77, Aviles, Benitez (Tenorio 57).

27 August, Asuncion, 50,000

Paraguay (0) 2 *(Javier Ferreira 58, Chilavert 90 (pen))*
Colombia (0) 1 *(Iguaran 87)*
Paraguay: Chilavert; Caceres, Zabala, Delgado,
Torales, Romerito (Javier Ferreira 50), Guasch,
Nunes, Neffa, Hicks (Buenaventura Ferreira 73),
Mendoza.
Colombia: Higuita; Wilson Perez, Perea, Escobar,
Hoyos, Alvarez, Ricardo Perez (Hernandez 67), Val-
derrama C, Redin, Iguaran, Galeano (Uzurriaga 55).

3 September, Guayaquil, 40,000

Ecuador (0) 0
Colombia (0) 0
Ecuador: Morales; Izquierdo, Quinteros, Quinonez,
Capurro, Aguinaga, Rosero (Benitez 65), Fajardo,
Cuvi (Verduga 72), Tenorio, Aviles.
Colombia: Higuita; Hoyos, Perea, Escobar, Wilson
Perez, Fajardo (Uzurriaga 82), Gomez, Ricardo
Perez, Valderrama C, Iguaran, Hernandez (Galeano
87).

10 September, Asuncion, 60,000

Paraguay (1) 2 *(Cabanas 36, Javier Ferreira 67)*
Ecuador (0) 1 *(Aviles 84)*
Paraguay: Chilavert; Caceres, Delgado, Zabala,
Torales, Guasch, Nunes, Javier Ferreira, Hicks
(Buenaventura Ferreira 58), Cabanas, Neffa
(Romero 62).
Ecuador: Morales; Bravo, Quinteros, Quinonez,
Capurro, Rosero (Cuvi), Fajardo, Aguinaga (Benitez
62), Munoz, Aviles, Guerrero.

17 September, Barranquilla, 60,000

Colombia (0) 2 *(Iguaran 55, Hernandez 66)*
Paraguay (1) 1 *(Mendoza 44)*
Colombia: Higuita; Wilson Perez, Perea, Escobar,
Villa, Alvarez, Gomez (Fajardo 46), Redin, Valder-
rama C (Uzuriaga 46), Iguaran, Hernandez.
Paraguay: Fernandez; Caceres, Delgado, Zabala,
Torales, Romero, Guasch, Nunes (Cabellero 63),
Palacios (Neffa 25), Buenaventura Ferreira,
Mendoza.

24 September, Asuncion, 16,000

Ecuador (1) 3 *(Aguinaga 26, Marsetti 71, Aviles 82)*

Paraguay (1) 1 *(Neffa 18)*

Ecuador: Mendoza; Bravo, Quinonez, Macias, Capurro, Fajardo, Marsetti (Veduga), Aguinaga, Munoz, Aviles, Guerrero (Tenorio).
Paraguay: Fernandez; Caceres (Guasch 75), Delgado, Zabala, Torales, Nunez, Canete (Hicks 67), Neffa, Buenaventura Ferreira, Cabanas, Mendoza.

Final table	P	W	D	L	F	A	Pts
Colombia	4	2	1	1	5	3	5
Paraguay	4	2	0	2	6	7	4
Ecuador	4	1	1	2	4	5	3

Colombia qualified

Group 3

30 July, Caracas, 20,000

Venezuela (0) 0

Brazil (1) 4 *(Branco 5, Romario 65, Bebeto 79, 81)*

Venezuela: Baena; Pacheco, Morovic, Acosta, Betancourt, Cavallo, Rivas, Anor (Carrero), Maldonaldo, Febles (Arreaza), Fernandez.
Brazil: Taffarel; Mazinho, Ricardo, Mauro Galvao, Aldair, Branco (Josimar), Dunga, Bebeto, Valdo, Romario, Careca (Silas).

6 August, Caracas, 25,000

Venezuela (0) 1 *(Fernandez 65)*

Chile (2) 3 *(Aravena 5, 34, Zamorano 71)*

Venezuela: Baena; Paz, Acosta, Betancourt (Anor), Cavallo, Fevles (Fernandez), Maldonaldo, Rivas, Torres, Carrero, Gallardo.
Chile: Rojas; Hisis, Gonzalez, Astengo, Puebla, Pizzaro, Ormeno, Aravena, Basay (Zamorano), Rubio, Yanez.

13 August, Santiago, 65,000

Chile (0) 1 *(Basay 91)*

Brazil (0) 1 *(Gonzales (og) 63)*

Chile: Rojas; Hisis, Gonzalez, Astengo, Puebla, Pizarro, Ormeno, Aravena, Zamorano (Letelier 87), Rubio (Basay 58), Yanez.
Brazil: Taffarel; Mazinho (Andre Cruz 77), Mauro Galvao, Aldair, Ricardo, Dunga, Branco (Jorginho 9), Silas, Valdo, Romario, Bebeto.

20 August, Sao Paulo, 106,000

Brazil (4) 6 *(Careca 9, 16, 78, 86, Silas 36, Acosta (og) 39)*

Venezuela (0) 0

Brazil: Taffarel; Ricardo II, Mauro Galvao, Ricardo I, Jorginho, Silas, Dunga (Alemao 65), Valdo (Tita 68), Branco, Careca, Bebeto.

Venezuela: Baena; Torres, Acosta, Paz, Pacheco, Rivas, Caballo, Carrero, Maldonaldo, Gallardo (Febles 71), Ariaza (Marazona 63).

27 August, Mendoza (Argentina), 20,000

Chile (3) 5 *(Letelier 14, 34, 68, Yanez 43, Vera 84)*

Venezuela (0) 0

Chile: Rojas; Hisis, Astengo (Contreras 46), Gonzalez, Puebla, Pizarro, Vera, Aravena, Yanez (Covarrubias 76), Letelier, Basay.
Venezuela: Gomez; Torres, Paz, Morovic, Cavallo, Carrero, Acosta (Gallardo 58), Lopez, Maldonaldo, Fernandez (Febles 50), Arreaza.

3 September, Rio de Janeiro, 141,072

Brazil (0) 1 *(Careca 49)*

Chile (0) 0

Brazil: Taffarel; Mauro Galvao, Aldair, Ricardo, Jorginho, Dunga, Silas, Valdo, Branco, Bebeto, Careca.
Chile: Rojas; Reyes, Gonzalez, Astengo, Puebla, Pizarro, Hisis, Vera, Aravena, Yanez, Letelier.
match abandoned after 65 minutes; Brazil awarded game 2-0

Final table	P	W	D	L	F	A	Pts
Brazil	4	3	1	0	13	1	7
Chile	4	2	1	1	9	4	5
Venezuela	4	0	0	4	1	18	0

Brazil qualified

Play-off between winner of Group 2 and winner of Oceania/Israel.

15 October, Barranquilla, 50,000

Colombia (0) 1 *(Uzurriaga 73)*

Israel (0) 0

Colombia: Higuita; Wilson Perez, Escobar, Perea, Villa, Alvarez, Valderrama C, Fajardo, Redin (Uzurriaga 46), Iguaran, Ruben Hernandez.
Israel: Ginzburg; Alon, Amar, Avi Cohen, Barda, Klinger, Sinai, Tikva (Pizanti 55), Davidi, Ohana (Levin 75), Rosenthal.

30 October, Tel Aviv, 50,000

Israel (0) 0

Colombia (0) 0

Israel: Ginzburg; Avi Cohen, Amar, Alon, Schmueli (Pizanti 46), Davidi, Klinger, Sinai, Tikva, Rosenthal, Levin (Ohana 50).
Colombia: Higuita; Wilson Perez, Escobar, Mendoza, Villa, Alvarez (Gomez), Valderrama C, Redin (Uzurriaga 46), Fajardo, Iguaran, Hernandez.

MILESTONES DIARY 1989–90

July 1989

1   The recently rejected idea of putting the **FA Cup** up for **sponsorship**, has been revived mainly to obtain funds for improving grounds in the wake of the **Hillsborough** disaster. The **FA** want **£2m** a year plus a **£15m** interest-free loan to be repaid at the end of five years. **Everton's Trevor Steven** finally completes his **£1m** move to **Glasgow Rangers** by signing a three-year contract. After four months with the Glasgow club, **Mel Sterland** is set to return to the Football League with **Leeds United** in a **£600,000** transfer.

3   **Swindon** manager **Lou Macari** accepts the job as only the **sixth manager** of **West Ham United**. There is a move to **lift the ban** on selling **alcohol** on **Football League grounds**. **Millwall** chairman **Reg Burr** is among those who believe this will cut down the number of drunk and ensure that fans arrive earlier. **Celtic** sign Englishman **Paul Elliott** for **£600,000** from the Italian club **Pisa**. He formerly played for Charlton, Luton and Aston Villa. **Doncaster Rovers** appoint **Billy Bremner** manager. He **previously** managed the club from **1978 to 1985**.

4   **Manchester City** sign **Ian Bishop** from **Bournemouth** in a **£700, 000** overall deal which includes **Paul Moulden** joining **Bournemouth**.

6   **Wigan**'s caretaker-manager **Bryan Hamilton** is appointed **chief executive**. There will be no "manager" as Hamilton will run day to day affairs as well as assisting in the coaching and team selection.

7   **Chris Waddle** agrees to move from **Spurs** to big-spending French club **Olympique Marseille** for a new British record fee of **£4.5m**. He will earn over **£30,000** per match. **Clive Allen** returns from **Bordeaux** to join **Manchester City** in a **£1m** move. **Coventry** price unsettled **England U-21** international **Steve Sedgley** at **£850,000**, plus **£150,000** when he gets his **first full England Cap**.

10   **Graeme Souness** shocks Scottish football by breaking with **Rangers' Protestant** tradition and signing **Roman Catholic Mo Johnston** for **£1½m**. The fact that only last month his return transfer to **Celtic** from **Nantes** fell through makes this latest move even more controversial.

11   **Aston Villa** sign **6ft** Danish defender **Kent Nielsen** from **Brondby** for **£500,000**.

12   The **Glasgow Rangers** accounts reveal that manager **Souness** was paid **£200,000** last year. **Don Howe** leaves his coaching post with **Wimbledon** to become assistant manager to **Trevor Francis** at QPR.

13   **Manchester Uniter** are angry that **Swedish** star **Glenn Hysen** has chosen to join **Liverpool** from **Fiorentina** in a deal costing **£650,000**. **West Ham** manager **Macari** prices unsettled midfielder **Paul Ince** at **£2m**.

14   West Bromwich Albion's board stop their manager **Brian Talbot** from signing **Bernard McNally** from **Shrewsbury** because they will have to gamble on what fee the tribunal may decide. **Spurs** complete the signing of Coventry midfield player **Sedgley** for **£850,000**.

15   **Laurie Cunningham**, the first black man to play for England, is **killed** in a **car crash** in Madrid.

16   **Brazil** beat **Uruguay 1–0** to win the **South American Championship** which is their first trophy since the **1970 World Cup**. There was a crowd of **170,000** at the **Maracana Stadium** in **Rio**.

19   **Ossie Ardiles** takes over as the new **Swindon** manager with a two-year contract and says he will continue to play. **West Bromwich** will go ahead with the signing of **Shrewsbury**'s Northern Ireland international **McNally** providing they accept the transfer tribunal's valuation. They have offered **£250,000** while **Shrewsbury** value the player at **£750,000**.

21   A transfer tribunal record fee of **£1.5m** is fixed on **Neil Webb**'s move from **Nottingham Forest** to **Manchester United**.

22   **Johnston** scores a **hat-trick** on his debut for **Rangers** but it is only in a pre-season friendly behind closed doors at **Airdrie** which **Rangers** win **6-0**. Brazilian **Mirandinha** will not be returning to **Newcastle** next season and has agreed to rejoin his former club **Palmeiras**.

24   **FIFA** fine **Johnston £3,000** for changing his mind about joining **Celtic**. The offence is "unsportsmanlike behaviour." They also **fine Sweden's Stefan Rehn** for joining **Everton** having allegedly agreed to sign for Swiss club **Neuchatel Xamax**. **Derby** give manager **Arthur Cox** a five-year contract worth over **£500,000**. **Manchester United**'s Republic of Ireland centre-half **Paul McGrath** joins **Aston Villa** in **£400,000** transfer and agrees a new Villa record wage of **£2,000-a-week**. Figures published today show that last season **West Ham** paid the **biggest police bill** of any Football League club – **£131,000** and had the worst record of **656** arrests and **ejections** at their ground. **Colchester** had the best record – no arrests. The **FA** recommend **automatic life bans** for serious **assaults** on match **officials**. This is in response to an appeal from the **Referees' Association** to help stop referees from leaving the game. The **Football League** announce **increased attendances** for the third successive season – **18,464,192** in 1988-89.

25   **Norman Whiteside** passes his **Everton** medical and will join them from **Manchester United** for **£600,000** plus a further **£150,000** after a certain number of appearances.

26   Following consideration of the **Hillsborough** disaster **FIFA** decide that all **World Cup** spectators must be **seated** commencing with the **qualifying** games for **1994**. This means that **Scotland** for one will have to move their games from **Hampden** where there are only **11,375** seats as against standing room for **61,780**. 'High risk' matches in domestic **League** and **Cup** games could also come under this ruling after **1992**. **Everton** top **£3m** in summer spending when the transfer tribunal order them to pay **£750,000** for **Martin Keown** from **Aston Villa**. **Nottingham Forest** agree to sign Republic of Ireland international **John Sheridan** from **Leeds United** for **£650,000**.

28   The **Scottish FA** settle a sponsorship deal for the **Scottish Cup** with brewers **Tennents Caledonian** for **£2.5m**. There will also be **£350,000** for competing clubs in each of the next four years. **Derby** will **re-erect** their **fences** at the visitors' end before the start of the new season.

29 There is widespread relief in Scottish football as **Mo Johnston**, **Rangers** controversial Catholic signing, is cheered on and off the field at **Airdrie** where the **Rangers** win **3-1**.

30 **Arsenal** beat **Liverpool 1-0** to win the final of the **Makita International** Football Festival at **Wembley** for the second year running. The **Gunners** had earlier beaten **Porto 1-0** while **Liverpool** beat **Dynamo Kiev 2-0**.

August

4 **Lord Justice Taylor**'s interim report on the **Hillsborough** disaster is generally welcomed and clubs promise prompt action on his call for **better policing**; improved **medical facilities**, and **emergency exit** gates in fencing. Justice Taylor has **still to decide** whether to recommend the lifting of the **alcohol** ban on grounds. **Adrian Heath**, disillusioned with his career in Spain is transferred from **Espanol** to **Aston Villa** for **£350,000**. His wages will be halved. The **FA** fine **Portsmouth £5,000** for their poor **disciplinary** record. Other clubs fined lesser amounts include **Leeds United**, **WBA.**, **Southampton** and **Stockport**.

5 A deal between a **Scottish sponsorship** company and the **Soviet Union** of **Trade Union Sports Society** is likely to cut away red tape which has prevented the transfer of more Russian footballers to the West. Negotiations are in progress for staging the **FA Cup semi-finals** at **Wembley**.

6 Worries about a boycott of **Rangers** because of the signing of Catholic **Mo Johnston** are dispelled as a crowd of over **41,000** see them beat **Tottenham Hotspur 1-0** with the only goal being scored by the latest English import **Trevor Steven**.

7 The **Football Grounds Improvement Trust** hand over **£4m** to bigger clubs with an average attendance of over **10,000** to help them instal more seating.

8 **Arsenal**'s accounts show a profit of over **£1m** on last season with manager **George Graham** receiving over **£200,000**.

10 The transfer **tribunal** order **Chelsea** to pay **£635,000** for **Alan Dickens** from **West Ham** plus 20% of any future transfer profit.

11 The **Football League** elect **Blackburn chairman**, **Bill Fox**, as their new president. He announces that **Gordon Taylor**, secretary of the **Professional Footballers' Association**, will take over as **chief executive** by the end of **September**. At the same meeting **artificial pitches** are **outlawed** in the top two divisions commencing with season **1991–92**. Clubs promoted to the **Second Division** with **artificial pitches** will have **three seasons** to change back to **grass**. **Referees** and **linesmen** will get a pay rise to **£100** and **£50** respectively.

12 In the **Charity Shield Liverpool** beat **Arsenal 1-0** in a hard fought encounter. In the **Scottish League**, **Celtic** are off to a good start winning **3-1** at **Hearts** with **Tommy Coyne** netting a **hat-trick**, but **Rangers** go down **1-0** to **St. Mirren** at Ibrox with goalkeeper **Chris Woods** injuring a shoulder as the winner is scored and taking no further part.

13 There is a row brewing in the **Football League** management committee over the appointment of players' union boss **Gordon Taylor** as the League's chief executive. He is being brought in alongside new president **Bill Fox** on a joint ticket.

14 The **PFA** say they will **not release** Taylor to become chief executive of the Football League and it now seems **unlikely** that he will take over this new job in September.

15 **Barclays Bank** sign a new **three-year contract** sponsoring the **Football League** for another **£7m** and extending their sponsorship to **six years**. **Charlton** fill the gap in their defence left by the recent transfer of **Peter Shirtliff** by signing **Joe McLaughlin** from **Chelsea** for **£600,000**. The transfer tribunal decide that **Newcastle** must pay **Portsmouth £680,000** for striker **Mick Quinn** for whom **£850,000** had been asked.

18 **Millionaire** property tycoon **Michael Knighton** agrees to buy **Manchester United**. He is paying **£20m** and pledging another **£10m** to rebuild the **Stretford End**. He will be **buying out** the club's major shareholder **Martin Edwards**.

19 With **safety** in mind, at least **two matches** kick-off **late** at the start of the new **Football League** season to allow a crush of latecomers to gain entry. **Wimbledon**'s kick-off with **Chelsea** is **delayed 15** minutes. In the First Division, **Manchester United** slam **Arsenal 4-1** while relegated **Newcastle** beat **Leeds 5-2** with **Quinn** scoring **four goals**. **West Ham** lose their **£1.2m** striker **Frank McAvennie** with a **broken leg** in their **1-1** draw at **Stoke**. There are **no away** wins in the **Fourth Division**. **Peterborough** make this their **13th consecutive season** without defeat in their opening game by beating newcomers **Maidstone 1-0**. In Scotland goalless **Rangers** lose again, this time **2-0** at **Hibs**.

21 **Luton** agree the signing of **Denmark**'s **Lars Elstrup** in a deal related to number of appearances which could cost them **£900,000**.

23 **Spurs** sign **Everton** defender **Pat Van Den Hauwe** for **£575,000**. **West Ham** sign **Martin Allen** who is relieved to leave **QPR** in **£675,000** transfer. **Falkirk** have **three** players **sent off** as they are beaten **4-1** at home to **Hearts** in the **Skol Cup** Third Round.

24 **Arsenal** give manager **George Graham** a **five-year contract** guaranteeing him **£1m**. **Manchester United** at last look like signing Young England midfielder **Paul Ince** from **West Ham** in a deal which could cost them **£2m** depending on the player's number of appearances.

26 After only three games there is no League club with a 100% record. **Sheffield Wednesday** have **yet to score** and are decisively beaten **4-0** by **Chelsea**. The **Derby-Manchester United** game is **delayed** for **25 minutes** because of hooliganism and overcrowding. There is a hectic tussle at **Bournemouth** where the home side beat **Hull 5-4** in the Second Division. **Tickets** for the Old Firm match at **Celtic Park** are worth more than their weight in gold as fans pack the stadium to see **Mo Johnston** return in **Rangers**' colours. The player seemed overawed by the occasion and failed to score in a **1-1** draw leaving **Rangers** as the only Premier League club **without a win** after only three games.

28 **Manchester United** break the **transfer record** between two British clubs by agreeing a fee of **£2.3m** for **Middlesbrough**'s **Gary Pallister**. However, the signing of **Paul Ince** from **West Ham** for another

£2m is postponed after the player fails a medical with a "pelvic problem." **Cardiff City**'s manager **Frank Burrows** returns to **Portsmouth** as assistant to **John Gregory**. **Portsmouth** sacked Burrows in **1982**.

29 The transfer tribunal price **Trevor Steven** at £1,525,000 in his summer move from **Everton** to **Rangers**. This is a **tribunal record fee** but nearly £1m below Everton's asking price. **Chelsea**'s **unbeaten record** goes in a surprise 3-0 defeat at **Charlton**. **Aldershot**'s 6-2 extra time **victory** over **Peterborough** takes them into the **Second Round** of the **Littlewoods' Cup** for the **first time** in the last **five seasons**.

30 A **last-minute goal** by **Dave Smith** gives **Coventry** a 2-1 home win over **Manchester City** and puts them on **top** of the **First Division** for the first time in their history. A **Harley Street specialist** gives **Paul Ince** the all-clear. Holders **Rangers** are through to the semi-finals of the **Scottish League Cup** with a 3-0 win at **Hamilton**.

31 **Cardiff City** appoint **Len Ashurst** manager. **Peterborough** dismiss manager **Mick Jones** following their 6-2 Littlewoods' **Cup** defeat at **Aldershot**.

September

2 Because of next week's **World Cup** Qualifying ties there are **no top division** games in either the **Football** or **Scottish Leagues**. **Bristol Rovers** and **Lincoln City**, leaders of the **Third** and **Fourth Division** respectively, are the only two clubs with **100% records** after only **three games**. In Scotland, only First Division leaders **St. Johnstone** have a 100% record after four games.

6 **England** play a **goalless draw** in **Sweden** which may be enough to see them through to the World Cup finals, although in theory they need a **point** in **Poland** next month to make certain. **Terry Butcher** was England's **hero** continuing to play a fine captain's game after having **10 stitches** inserted into a **cut head** during the interval. **Neil Webb** suffers an **Achilles tendon injury** which could keep him out of the **Manchester United** team for most of this season. **Scotland** still need a point to qualify following their 3-1 defeat in **Yugoslavia** where **Gordon Durie** had given them the lead. **Wales** have no chance of reaching the finals following a disappointing 1-0 defeat in **Finland**, while **Northern Ireland** are also prevented from qualifying losing 2-1 at home to **Hungary**. In a friendly, **Frank Stapleton** scores his **19th** goal for the **Republic of Ireland** to equal his **country**'s **scoring record** in a 1-1 home draw with **West Germany**. **Peterborough** appoint **Mark Lawrenson** manager.

7 Despite **efforts** by the new **Football League** president **Bill Fox** to appoint **Taylor** as **chief executive** a meeting of the **Management Committee** decide that Taylor must first be interviewed for the post.

8 **Fear** of **crowd trouble** forces the FA to call off **England**'s friendly with **Holland** in Rotterdam.

9 **Millwall** are back on **top** of the **First Division** after beating **Coventry City** 4-1 at The Den. They are one of only **three sides** still unbeaten in the **First Division**, the others being **Norwich** and **Liverpool**. Fourth Division **Lincoln** maintain their **100% record** by winning 3-0 at **Torquay** who suffered their fifth defeat in a row. **Celtic**'s first defeat of the season is 1-0 at **St. Mirren** where **one player** from **each** side is sent off.

10 **Brazil** go through to the World Cup finals when **FIFA** award them a win over **Chile** for the game abandoned when the **Chileans** walked off after their **goalkeeper** had been **hit** by a **flare**.

11 **Southampton** ask **£2.5m** for **Danny Wallace** wanted by **Manchester United** who are offering about half that amount.

12 **Liverpool** thrash newly-promoted **Crystal Palace** 9-0 which is the **biggest First Division victory** since Fulham beat **Ipswich** 10-1 in December 1963. **John Aldridge** was among the scorers and now moves to **Spanish First Division** club **Real Sociedad** for £1.1m with a three-year contract which will earn him £1m. In First Round, First leg matches **Celtic** go down 2-1 away to **Partizan Belgrade** in the **Cup Winners Cup** while **Hibernian** beat **Videoton** 1-0 at home in the **UEFA Cup**.

13 **Manchester United** at last complete the signing of **Ince** at £800,000 plus £5,000 for each game in which he plays and also agree to sign **Wallace** from **Southampton**. These transfers will bring their spending to around £13m in under **three years**. **Bayern Munich** give the expensive **Rangers** team a lesson in a 3-1 victory in **Glasgow** in the **European Cup**, while in the **UEFA Cup Aberdeen** beat **Rapid Vienna** 2-1 at **Pittodrie**. **Swansea** lose 3-2 to **Panathinaikos** in **Greece** where their fans cause trouble and a number are arrested.

15 **Stockport** punish **Hartlepool** 6-0 with **Brett Angell** getting **four** goals.

16 **Coventry** goalkeeper **Steve Ogrizovic** misses today's game with a **shoulder injury** ending a run of **344 consecutive appearances** spanning **seven years**, but his replacement **Keith Waugh** keeps a clean sheet as **Coventry** beat **Luton** 1-0 and move up into third place behind **Everton** and **Liverpool**. **Manchester United** enjoy their **biggest win** for three years beating **Millwall** 5-1 at **Old Trafford**, but **Tottenham** are jeered by their fans as they go down 4-1 at home to **Chelsea** from whom **Kerry Dixon** scores one and lays on the other three. After five games, **Hartlepool** are the **only** League side **without a point**. **Herts** head the Scottish Premier Division after a 3-1 victory at **Motherwell** with both sides having a player **sent off**. **Rangers** also had a player **sent off** and again fail to win, being held to a 2-2 draw by **Dundee** who equalise in the last minutes at **Ibrox**.

18 **Michael Knighton** has not yet completed his **£20m** purchase of **Manchester United**. The Football hierarchy have ignored calls from **Swansea** for their return with Greek team **Panathinaikos** to be **switched** to a **neutral** venue. There are **fears** of a riot after **10 Swansea** fans were jailed following fights in an **Athens** bar after the first leg. **Barnsley** manager **Allan Clarke** is fined **£3,000** by the FA for his **critical** comments in a newspaper about midfielder **Vinny Jones**.

19 **Rangers** reach the **Skol League Cup final** for the **fourth year** in succession with an easy **5-0** win over **Dunfermline** at Hampden.

20 Third from bottom in the Fourth Division, **Aldershot** add to **Sheffield Wednesday**'s misery by holding them to a **goalless draw** in the Littlewoods' Cup at **Hillsborough**. **Aberdeen** beat **Celtic** 1-0 to reach the **Skol final** for the **third successive year**. Their **winner** is scored by new signing **Ian**

Cameron. **Michael Knighton**'s bid to takeover **Manchester United** rolls on. It is reported that he has overcome the loss of his two biggest backers, but **Glasgow Rangers** chief **David Murray** has stepped in to help by introducing Knighton to his Scottish bankers and other friends. Meanwhile newcomer **Paul Ince** scores twice as **United** win **3-2** at **Portsmouth** in their **Littlewoods' Cup** tie.

23 **Two goals** by **Ian Rush** bring his total to **23** in **24** League and Cup **Merseyside** derbies as **Liverpool** win **3-1** at **Goodison**. **Norwich** the only other unbeaten First Division side draw **2-2** with **Spurs** at Carrow Road. **Manchester City**'s **5-1** victory over **Manchester United** is their **biggest win** against their local rivals for **nearly 64 years** and their first in a run of nine League derbies. In the Third Division, **Reading** highlight **Swansea's** weakness after the Welsh club's skipper **Andy Melville** limps off by going on to win **6-1** at the Vetch Field. **QPR** player-manager **Trevor Francis** plays his first full League game for nearly nine months and scores a **hat-trick** in his side's **3-1** win at Villa Park. As **Celtic** are held to a **1-1** draw by **Motherwell**, **Aberdeen** take over the lead in the Scottish League with a **2-0** win at **St. Mirren**.

24 Meeting in the League for the first time in five seasons, **Sunderland** and **Newcastle** play out a goalless draw in front of a crowd of **29,499**, **Sunderland**'s biggest League gate for over six years.

25 The **UEFA Cup** game between Ajax and **FK Austria** is abandoned with **22 minutes** of extra time remaining after **Ajax** fans riot as the visitors take a **2-1** lead.

26 **Hibernian** produce their best form and win through to the **Second Round** of the **UEFA Cup** with a **3-0** win and 4-0 on aggregate over **Videoton** in Hungary. **Three players are sent off** and another **two booked** as **Swindon** beat **Plymouth Argyle 3-0** in the Second Division. **Gillingham** not only score their first home goals of the season but **beat top-of-the-table Southend 5-0** in the Fourth Division.

27 **Rangers** are out of the **European Cup** after a **goalless draw** with **Bayern Munich** in Germany. **Butcher** missed an easy scoring **chance** after only **90 seconds** choosing to pass rather than shoot. **Celtic** beat **Partizan Belgrade 5-4** after extra time in the **Cup Winners' Cup** with Polish striker **Dariusz Dziekanowski** scoring **four** of their goals, but **Partizan** go through on away goals with the score **6-6** on aggregate. In the same competition, **Swansea** are out **6-5** on aggregate after drawing **3-3** with **Panathinaikos**. **Aberdeen** are knocked out of the **UEFA Cup** by **Rapid Vienna** on **away goals** but **Dundee United** are through to the next round after an **aggregate win** of **5-1** over **Glentoran**.

29 **Swansea** chairman **Doug Sharpe**, who saved the club from closure in a **£450,000** takeover deal, **threatens to quit** after criticism of his **support** for the club's fans who were convicted of **hooliganism** in Greece. **Tranmere Rovers** beat **Bristol City 6-0** to take over the lead in the Third Division from **Bristol Rovers**.

30 There are as many as **seven** individual **hat-tricks** in the **Football League** and **Scottish League**. **Gary Lineker** strikes form with a **hat-trick** in **Tottenham**'s **3-2** home win over **QPR** – his first goals at White Hart Lane since his **£1.5m** transfer from **Barcelona**. At the top of the Second Division, **Sheffield United** stretch this season's **unbeaten** run to **nine games** with a **1-1** draw at **Sunderland** after the home side had scored in the first minute. **Hartlepool** really are in a bad way; they go down **6-0** at home to **Doncaster Rovers** for whom **Lee Turnbull** gets a **hat-trick**. **Rangers** scrape a home win over **Herts** with a single goal from **Mo Johnston**. In the Scottish First Division, **Falkirk** beat **Albion Rovers 6-0** with **Alex Rae** scoring **four** goals.

October

1 **Coventry City**, one of the First Division's lowest scoring sides so far this season, sign **Glasgow Rangers'** striker **Kevin Drinkell** in **£800,000** transfer. He had been a great success with **Rangers** but has been sidelined since the arrival of **Johnston**.

2 After only one win in their first eight games of the season, **Torquay United**'s manager **Cyril Knowles resigns**.

3 Bottom-of-the-First-Division **Sheffield Wednesday** emphasise the difference in class between them and **Aldershot** by winning **8-0** on the Fourth Division club's ground in the return leg of their **Littlewoods' Cup** tie. This makes a **mockery** of the goalless draw in the first leg at Sheffield. **Steve Whitton** got **four** goals and **Dalian Atkinson three**. This was a **record away win** in the League Cup and Wednesday's first away victory of the season. In the same competition **Arsenal** win **6-1** at **Plymouth**, 8-1 on aggregate with **Michael Thomas** scoring a **hat-trick**.

4 **Michael Knighton**'s takeover of **Manchester United** hits the headlines again as he is reported to be trying to **sell off** a large part and has turned down the **financial package** offered by **Scottish bankers**. There are **three hat-tricks** in the **Littlewoods' Cup ties – John Thomas** in West Bromwich's **5-3** extra time win at **Bradford**; **Dean Saunders** in **Derby**'s **5-0** home victory over **Cambridge United**, and **Steve Staunton**, who came on in the second half as substitute for the injured **Ian Rush**, in **Liverpool**'s **3-0** win at **Wigan**. The **Inland Revenue** are reported to be investigating 'golden handshakes' involving **Norwich City** and **Dave Watson** (transferred to **Everton**), **Steve Bruce** (to **Manchester United**), **Chris Woods** and **Kevin Drinkell** (to **Glasgow Rangers**). **Irish FA** president **Harry Cavan**, 73, announces that he will retire as the **British vice-president** of FIFA after the **Congress** in Rome this summer.

5 **Manchester United** directors express their **grave concern** over reports about **Michael Knighton**'s company **MK Trafford Holdings**, which has an option to buy the majority shareholding of United's chief executive **Martin Edwards** for £20m. **Forty-eight** days have passed since **Kinghton** first announced that he was **buying United**. UEFA ban Ajax from **European** competitions for the **next two seasons** in which they may qualify. This follows their **fans' behaviour** at last week's tie with **FK Austria**.

6 The **Manchester United saga continues** with suggestions that **Knighton** may relinquish his option to buy **Edward**'s majority shareholding. Many now believe that the **club's reputation** has **suffered** through the public dealing surrounding a move which was first announced on **August 18**.

7 There are **no top games** in **England** or **Scotland** because of next week's **World Cup** Qualifying

matches, but **Sheffield United** open up their lead in the **Second Division** with a **2-1 win** at **Wolver-hampton**. In the Third Division, **Rotherham** striker **Bobby Williamson** gets his second **hat-trick** in eight days as his side beats **Birmingham 5-1**. At the bottom of the League, **Hartlepool** gain their **first win** of the season beating **Scunthorpe United 3-2**, while **Forfar Athletic** achieve the **same distinction** in the **Scottish League** winning **2-0** away to **Albion Rovers**. This leaves **Stoke, Hull** and **Wigan** as the only clubs **without a victory** in either the **Football** or **Scottish Leagues**. In the **GM Vauxhall Conference, Darlington** are fighting their way back to the **Football League** having been **undefeated** in their **first 11 games**. Their **attendances** show a **44%** increase on last season. Plans to **modernise Hampden Park**have now been overshadowed by the announcement of a scheme to build a brand new **60,000 all-seater** multi-purpose sports centre in an area of **120 acres**.

8   It is reported that the **Manchester United** board are ready to quit *en bloc* if **Knighton** completes his takeover.

9   The **High Court** action by **Manchester United** chairman **Martin Edwards** bringing an injunction against **Knighton** restraining him from publicising **potential investors** is adjourned as the two declare a truce. **Knighton** is now expected to **complete the deal** within the **next two days**.

10   **England** beat **Poland 3-1** in the **UEFA U-21** championship with **Steve Bull** scoring **twice**.

11   **England** earn their place in this summer's World Cup finals with a **goalless draw** in **Poland**, thanks largely to four brilliant saves by **40-year-old Peter Shilton**. **Republic of Ireland** are on the brink of **qualifying** needing only **one point** from next month's game in **Malta** to be certain after beating **Northern Ireland 3-0** in front of a **45,800** crowd at **Landsowne Road**. They might easily have doubled their score. **Scotland** also need **at least a point** from their last game with **Norway** at **Hampden** following their **3-0** defeat in **France** where they showed lack of domination in midfield. **Wales**, already out of the finals, are beaten **2-1** at **Wrexham** by **Holland**. **Knighton** ends the **Manchester United** takeover marathon by accepting a place on the board for a mere **£20,000**. In withdrawing his **£20m** bid he has realised that the uproar created and the board's threat to resign are too much to overcome.

14   Former **Manchester United** manager **Ron Atkinson** takes his bottom-of-the-table **Sheffield Wednesday** side to Old Trafford to force a **goalless draw** and add to the home club's trauma of the past couple of months. **United** are now only **four places** off the **bottom** of the First Division. **Spurs** gain their first away win of the season **3-1** against **Charlton Athletic**. Using a 4-2-4 formation, **Southampton** win **4-1** at **QPR**. **Manchester City's 4-0** defeat at **Arsenal** means that they have failed to score in over 10½ hours of League football on this ground. **Southend United** extend their lead at the top of the Fourth Division with a **3-0** win at **Hereford** their eighth victory in 10 games. **Scottish League** leaders **Celtic** make hard work of beating bottom club **Dundee 3-1** at Dens Park. **Hungarian** international **Istvan Kozma** scores a **hat-trick** as **Dunfermline** beat **St. Mirren 5-1**.

15   **Liverpool** hold on to the lead in the First Division after winning **2-1** at **Wimbledon**, but there are rumours about their manager **Kenny Dalglish** moving to **Glasgow Rangers**. **Celtic** are to spend **£30m** on turning Parkhead into an **all-seater** stadium. Work will be completed by **1993**.

16   It is re-affirmed that **Fulham** will be leaving **Craven Cottage** to the developers at the **end of this season** although they have not yet found an alternative venue. **Millwall** is floated as a **public company** on the **Stock Exchange**.

17   **Stoke** gain their first Second Division victory of the season in their 12th game beating **WBA 2-1** on the day that **Alan Ball** takes up his new job as their coach. **Wolves'** strikers **Andy Mutch** (in 50 seconds) and **Steve Bull** score in their **2-0** home win over **Port Vale** – Bull's ninth goal in his last seven games. **Portsmouth** fight back from 3-1 down at home to **Leeds** to **force a draw** with two goals by **Guy Whittingham** in the last two minutes. In their **UEFA Cup** tie **Dundee United** lose **4-0** to **Antwerp** in Belgium, their worst-ever defeat in Europe. Work begins this week, on **Yeovil Town's new £3m** ground at nearby **Houndstone**. It should be ready for next season.

18   **Hibernian** are unable to make use of their home advantage and are held to a **goalless draw** by **FC Liege** in the **UEFA Cup**. **Spurs** gain their **first** League victory over **Arsenal** in a run of **seven games**, winning **2-1** at **White Hart Lane**. The gate receipts of **£300,000** at this game are a new **League record** for the ground. **West Ham** give a dazzling display in beating **Sunderland 5-0** at Upton Park. **Justin Fashanu** hopes to **return** to League football after an absence of nearly **four years** and signs a month's contract with **Manchester City**. The big striker had a trial at **Maine Road** a year ago and has since had a season in **North American** football. He last played in the League for **Brighton** before **knee trouble** forced him out.

19   The FA fine **Wimbledon** manager **Bobby Gould £750** plus costs for a dressing-room outburst with a **referee**. The **Football League** have so far been unable to persuade any clubs to volunteer for a dummy run before the **Government** scheme of **identity cards** must be introduced.

21   **Everton** move into **top** position with a **3-0** victory over **Arsenal** who had won their last three League visits to Goodison. **Liverpool** suffer their first defeat of the season **4-1** at **Southampton**. This was their heaviest defeat at **The Dell** since their initial League visit in 1960. After equalling **Leeds United's** record run of four away First Division games without conceding a goal, **Norwich City** crash **4-1** at **Luton** where **Steve Williams** was outstanding. **Manchester United** recapture some lost form with a **4-1** victory at **Coventry. Hull City**, who draw **1-1** at **WBA**, are left as the only side without a League win this season as **Wigan** beat **Walsall 3-0**. **Bristol Rovers** go to the top of Division Three scoring **three goals** in the last 10 minutes of their **4-2** win over **Northampton**. At the top of the Fourth Division, **Southend United** suffer their first home defeat of the season **1-0** to struggling newcomers **Maidstone United**. A total of **seven players** are **sent off** in today's Football League games. **Celtic** make it six games without defeat at the top of the Scottish League by beating **Hearts 2-1** with a **Tommy Coyne** winner in the **89th minute**.

22   **Rangers** and **Aberdeen** appear in the Skol Cup Final for the **third season** in **succession** and the **Dons** are victorious by **2-1**, this being their first-ever win over Rangers in the League Cup Final. **Paul**

Mason gets the most vital goal in extra time. **Aston Villa** continue to climb the table, with a **2-1** win at **Manchester City**, but Skipper **Stuart Gray** is **sent off** along with City's **Trevor Morley**. The explosion of two **home-made bombs** injures **19 people** at the Dutch First Division game between **Ajax** and **Feyenoord**. Five fans were arrested.

23   Third Division **Tranmere** knockout First Division **Millwall 3-2** in the Third Round of the **Littlewoods' Cup**. After only **three wins** in 12 games, **Reading** sack manager **Ian Branfoot**.

24   **Brian Clough** is about to sign another **two-year contract** with **Nottingham Forest** said to be worth **£300,000**.

25   **Sweden**'s **2-0** win in **Poland** give them top place in their World Cup Qualifying group with **England** finishing second. This **lessens** the chance of **England** being among the **six seeded** for the finals. **Liverpool** go out of the **Littlewoods'** Cup beaten **1-0** by arch rivals **Arsenal** at Highbury. In the same competition, **Gary Lineker** scores his **eighth goal in seven** matches as **Spurs** beat **Manchester United 3-0** at Old Trafford to add to manager **Alex Ferguson**'s worries. However, **Spurs** defender **Terry Fenwick** breaks his **left leg**. **Oldham** striker **Frankie Bunn** breaks the Football League Cup (Littlewoods' Cup) record by scoring **six** in his side's **7-0** thrashing of **Scarborough**. **Chilean** goalkeeper **Roberto Rojas** is banned for life from International competition by **FIFA** after **faking injury** in the **World Cup** qualifying game with **Brazil** on September 3.

27   **West Ham** fine **Mark Ward** two week's wages for missing the club coach to their Littlewoods' Cup game at **Villa Park**.

28   **Gale-force winds** cause **problems** at many of today's matches. The **Portsmouth-Ipswich** game is interrupted, while games at **Torquay** and **Swindon** are postponed. **Aston Villa** make it **four wins** in a row by beating **Crystal Palace 2-1** and move up to seventh place. **David Platt** scores both of **Villa's** goals. Only three points separate the top eight clubs in the First Division where only **Wimbledon** can win away. They beat bottom club **Sheffield Wednesday** with a goal by **Terry Gibson**. **Manchester City** earn their first away point of the season in a **1-1** draw at **Chelsea** thanks to a spectacular 30-yard equaliser by **Clive Allen** two minutes from time. Losing **2-0** at home to **Brighton**, **Hull City** make it **25 games without a win**. After their dismal start to the season, **Rangers** continue to climb the table with a **3-0** home win over **Hibernian** – their biggest win against **Hibs** in a run of 12 League games.

29   **Liverpool** return to the **top** of the First Division with **John Barnes** scoring their only goal against **Spurs** at Anfield.

30   Bottom-of-the-Second Division, **Hull City** sack manager **Colin Appleton** and **chairman Don Robinson** is replaced by property developer **Richard Chetham**.

31   The **Football League** appoint **Arthur Sandford** as their new **£90,000** a year **chief executive**. Currently chief executive of **Nottinghamshire County Council**, and a former first-class referee, his appointment is a **shock** to the majority who still expected **PFA** secretary **Gordon Taylor** to get the job. Now that the **Football Spectators Bill** has passed through the House of Commons, **Derby County** agree to run a pilot scheme for the **Controversial identity card**. The deadline for their introduction is now **November 1990**. **Hibernian** and **Dundee United** are both knocked out of the **UEFA Cup** by **FC Liege** and **Antwerp** respectively. **Hibs** took **Liege** to extra time before the Belgians scored the winner. **Everton** sign **Peter Beagrie** from **Stoke City** for **£750,000**, taking this season's spending to nearly **£4m**. Struggling **Watford** make it **seven** League games **without a win** as they go down **1-0** at **Ipswich**. **Watford** skipper **Glenn Roeder** concedes two penalties, the first of which is saved before **Neil Thompson** converts the second. **Dixie McNeil** resigns after 4½ years as **manager** of **Wrexham** who are currently four places off the bottom of the League.

November

1   Rumours of a rift between **Rangers** manager **Graeme Souness** and chief executive **Alan Montgomery** end as Montgomery leaves Ibrox to take up another position in club owner **David Murray**'s business empire. This also **ends earlier speculation** about **Liverpool** manager **Kenny Dalglish** moving to **Rangers**. Following threats and poison-pen letters badly shaken **John Smart** resigns as chairman of bottom club **Hartlepool** and takes his **£100,000** with him, **Rolan Boyes**, **Labour MP**, is acting as chairman. **Wimbledon** celebrate their centenary. Knocked out of the **Littlewoods' Cup** in a **1-0** home defeat by **WBA** last week, **Newcastle** now go to the Hawthorns and beat the **Albion 5-1** in the Second Division. **Norwich** striker **Robert Fleck** has his third knee operation in nine months and is out of the game for at least four weeks. **Real Madrid** are out of the European Cup (2-1 on aggregate) after losing **1-0** at home to **AC Milan**. **Partick Thistle** manager **John Lambie** resigns.

2   **Exeter City** teenager **Chris Vinnicombe** is transferred to **Glasgow Rangers** in a deal which could be worth up to **£500,000** depending on the player's first team progress. He is the **16th Englishman** signed by **Graeme Souness** for **Rangers**. **Charlie Nicholas** hands in a transfer request at **Aberdeen**. **Ron Atkinson** manager of bottom First Division club **Sheffield Wednesday**, signs **Republic of Ireland** midfielder **John Sheridan** from Nottingham Forest for **£500,000** and left back Phil King from Oxford United for **£400,000**. Sheridan had played only one game for Forest since his £650,000 move from Leeds last summer. The **FA of Wales** decide **not to play** any more internationals at either **Swansea** or **Wrexham** but restrict these matches to **Cardiff**.

3   **Partick Thistle** appoint player-coach **Sandy Clark** as manager.

4   **Norwich** lose **4-3** at **Arsenal** after leading 2-0 but the game will be remembered for the **disgraceful scenes** which followed **Arsenal**'s **injury-time penalty winner** when almost all the players are involved in a melee which brought **police** onto the field. Surprisingly **Referee George Tyson** said that he would not be taking any action, but it is certain that a report will be called for as the scenes are witnessed on **TV**. It was **Arsenal**'s first home defeat of the season. **David O'Leary** breaks a **club record** with his **622nd** first-team appearance. **Cyrille Regis** gets his first goal of the season to give **Coventry City** their **first-ever win** at Anfield after **23 League visits**. **Ron Atkinson**'s dip into the transfer market

pays off as **Sheffield Wednesday** win **1-0** at **Nottingham Forest** although the winner was a sliced clearance by **Terry Wilson** into his own goal. **Swindon** add to **Stoke City**'s misery by slamming them **6-0**. **Rangers** return to the **top** of the Scottish League for the first time this season after beating **Celtic 1-0**, their winner coming from former **Celt**, **Mo Johnston two minutes** from time. There are three contenders for **Scotland**'s new national stadium. **Queen's Park** are determined to modernise **Hampden** while there are plans for a new stadium at **Renfrew** as well as in **Lanarkshire**.

5   **Aston Villa** produce one of the most surprising results of the season by beating **Everton 6-2** at Villa Park. The Villa were leading **6-0** with only eight minutes to play. This is **Villa's record score** against **Everton**.

6   **FA** chief executive **Graham Kelly** announces that both **Arsenal** and **Norwich City** are to face charges concerning the incident at the end of their recent **First Division** game when **police** came onto the field. The **Scottish FA** confirm **35-year-old Jim Farry** as their new secretary to succeed **Ernie Walker** who retires in April. **Farry** has been **Scottish Fooball League** secretary for **10 years**. **Chelsea** are another club chosen to try out the **identity card scheme**. **Scarborough**, fifth from bottom in the League, sack manager **Colin Morris**.

7   Yet another manager is sacked. **Mick Mills** leaves struggling **Stoke City** and **Alan Ball**, appointed coach only three weeks ago, takes over as caretaker manager. **Hartlepool** take another beating, this time going down **7-1** at **York** in the Preliminary Round of the **Leyland Daf Cup**.

8   After seven defeats in their last nine games, **Barnsley** manager **Allan Clarke** is sacked. Club **chairman Geoff Buckle** also resigns. Coach **Eric Winstanley** is caretaker. **Hull City** appoint **Stan Ternent** as their **third manager** of **1989**. The **Scottish Football League** name **Peter Donald** to succeed **Jim Farry** as secretary. He has been Farry's assistant at the Scottish League. **Pele** may run for **President** of **Brazil** in **1994**. **Sky Television** offer the **Foobtall League £4.5m** over four years to screen live matches in the **Zenith Data Systems Cup** (previously the Simod Cup) and the **Leyland Daf Cup** (previously the Sherpa Van Trophy etc.)

9   Promotion-chasing **Bristol Rovers** agree to sell their leading scorer **Gary Penrice** to **Watford** for **£500,000**, but manager **Gerry Francis** will have to have his arm twisted before he will also part with goalkeeper **Nigel Martyn** for whom **Crystal Palace** are offering **£1m**. UEFA fine **Real Madrid £80,000** for **crowd trouble** in the Champions' Cup game with **AG Milan**.

11   **Chelsea** pull off the best win of the day by beating **Everton 1-0** at Goodison and hold on to the **top place**, while **Liverpool** suffer their fourth defeat in five games going down **3-2** at QPR. **Derby** hit **Manchester City** for six without reply. It is **City's biggest defeat** for over **30 years**. Managerless **Barnsley** go down **7-0** at West Brom where **Don Goodman** scores a hat-trick. At the foot of the Second Division, **Hull City** gain their first win of the season **3-2** at **Bradford**. **Hartlepool** suffer another pasting, this time **6-1** at **Aldershot**. In the Scottish Premier Division's only game, **Hearts** go top after beating **Dundee 6-3** taking a two-goal lead after only three minutes.

12   **Gerry Pallister**, **Manchester United**'s British record **£2.3m** transfer from **Middlesbrough**, scores the only goal of his side's victory over **Nottingham Forest**. It was the first time since **1971** that United had beaten **Forest** in **successive** League games at **Old Trafford**.

13   the **FA** commence an investigation into allegations that Swindon chairman **Brian Hillier** bet that his club would lose a Cup tie at **Newcastle** last year. Veteran midfielder **Ray Wilkins** agrees to join **QPR** from **Glasgow Rangers**. **Arsenal** players are in the spotlight again as **Paul Merson** and **Steve Bould** are alleged to have behaved in a rowdy manner at a dinner to celebrate their League championship. **Derby** are planning to become the third League club after **Spurs** and **Millwall** to go public.

14   **Nigel Martyn** becomes England's most expensive goalkeeper as he leaves Bristol Rovers for **Crystal Palace** in a **£1m** transfer. Rovers' manager **Gerry Francis** is quoted as saying "we are selling him on the cheap." **Palace** will have to pay an extra **£100,000** if the 22-year-old Martyn is **capped**. Former **Everton** boss **Howard Kendall** leaves **Athletic Bilbao** by mutual agreement with a final pay-off of **£125,000** following the club's three defeats in six days. **Aberdeen** sign PSV Eindhoven striker **Hans Gilhaus** for a club record **£650,000**. This should enable unsettled **Charlie Nicholas** to leave. **Chelsea**'s assistant manager **Ian Porterfield** takes over at **Reading**.

15   **John Aldridge** scores both of the **Republic of Ireland**'s goals in a **2-0** World Cup qualifying victory in **Malta** to put them into the finals. **Scotland** clinch their place in the finals in front of a sell-out crowd of **63,987** despite being only able to **draw** with **Norway** at Hampden. The visitors equalised with almost the last kick of the game. **Wales** take the lead through **Malcolm Allen** but are beaten **2-1** by **West Germany** who go through to the finals. In a friendly with **Italy** resulting in a goalless draw, **England** prove their defence is up to standard but still leave doubt about the ability of their attack to score goals despite plenty of chances in this game at **Wembley**. The **cross-bar** over one of the goals at **Fratton Park** was found to be too low by **Danish** referee **Jan Dangaard** before the start of last Tuesday's **England** v **Czechoslovakia youth international** and had to be raised about an inch. Reports that it was more were **denied** by embarrassed **Portsmouth** officials. Unsettled by barracking fans at Aston Villa, **Nigel Callaghan** hoped for **£500,000** transfer to **Middlesbrough** falls through.

16   The **Football Spectators Bill** which includes the need for **ID** cards receives the **Royal Assent**. The **FA** revive the **England Travel Club** which was first launched in **1980** in a bid to control hooliganism.

17   Talks between **Ipswich** and **Justin Fashanu** who is trying to make a come-back are reported to have collapsed because the player was seeking a **£300,000** signing-on fee. Instead, he joins **West Ham** on a **month's trial**. **Malcolm Allison** quits as manager of struggling GM Vauxhall Conference club **Fisher Athletic**. The **FA** cancel this season's **England v Scotland** game in the **Rous Cup** choosing to invite **Argentine** and **Uruguay** to take part.

18   Improved **Manchester United** make it four wins out of five beating **Luton 3-1** at Kenilworth Road. **Coventry** have now made **16 League visits** to Villa Park **without a win** after going down **4-1**, a victory which places the **Villa** in third place behind **Arsenal** and **Chelsea**. In the FA Cup First Round two League clubs are knocked out by non-League opposition – **Southend** going down **1-0** at **Aylesbury**

and **Scarborough** losing by the same score at home to **Whitley Bay**. Having hit a bad patch **Celtic** are beaten **1-0** by **Dundee United** at Parkhead despite having more of the play. **Rangers** extend their current undefeated run at Dens Park to six League games by beating **Dundee 2-0**.

19 With **John Barnes** playing in the middle of the attack and opening the scoring, **Liverpool** win **2-1** at **Millwall**. In the **FA Cup Fulham** fight back from two goals down to draw **2-2** at **Bath**. The **USA** reach the **World Cup** finals for the second time after beating **Trinidad and Tobago 1-0**.

20 The **FA** will be investigating an allegation made by former player **Ernie Hunt** in a newspaper article that he paid players from other clubs to help **Coventry**'s fight to avoid relegation in the 1970s. Former **West Ham** manager **John Lyall** is appointed technical co-ordinator to **Tottenham Hotspur**. **Scarborough** appoint **Ray McHale** manager in succession to **Colin Morris**. **Iain Munro** is appointed co-manager of **Dunfermline** and **Billy Lamont** will return to his former job as manager of **Falkirk**.

22 **Oldham** knock **Arsenal** out of the **Littlewoods' Cup** with a **3-1** win on their artificial pitch at Boundary Park where they have been **undefeated** in a run of **23 matches**. **Everton** beaten **1-0** by **Nottingham Forest** in the same competition, dispute the winning goal which came from a free-kick given against **Neville Southall** and was scored by **Lee Chapman** six minutes from time. A **brawl** involving **17 men** marred the **Littlewoods' Cup** game between **West Ham** and **Wimbledon**. **West Ham** skipper **Julian Dicks** is **sent off** but 10-man West Ham win with a goal by **Martin Allen** in the 81st minute.

23 FA chief executive **Graham Kelly** criticises managers who turn a **blind eye** to **bad behaviour** by their players. The **FA fine Aston Villa**'s Republic of Ireland star **Paul McGrath** a record **£8,500** for comments he made about **Manchester United** manager **Alex Ferguson** in a newspaper article. **Stoke** confirm **Alan Ball** as manager with a contract until **June 1991**.

24 The **Italian League** fine **Diego Maradona £14,250** for **criticising** his club and returning late from the summer break. Rival managers **John Bird (York City)** and **Ray McHale (Scarborough)** are sent off after an incident during the Yorkshire derby which **York** won **3-1**. **Wimbledon** appoint **Brian Flynn** manager. Near the relegation zone, **Crystal Palace** agree to pay **Newcastle £650,000** for **Andy Thorn**.

25 **Southampton**, enjoying their best run for six years and the First Division's **top goalscorers**, beat **Luton 6-3**. **Aston Villa** make it seven wins in a run of eight League games with a **2-0** victory at **Wimbledon**. **Everton**'s **1-0** defeat at **Nottingham Forest** is their eighth consecutive League visit to the City ground without finding the net. In the Second Division, **Blackburn Rovers** win a nine-goal battle with **West Ham 5-4**. The Hammers were **5-1** down early in the second half. A first-half **hat-trick** by **Charlie Nicholas** enables **Aberdeen** to beat **St. Mirren 5-0** and stay top of the Scottish League. **Morton** make in nine draws in a run of **10 games** finishing **0-0** at home to **Hamilton**.

26 In an ever-changing First Division leadership, **Liverpool** are back at the top after beating nearest rivals **Arsenal 2-1** at Anfield.

27 After calling both clubs' top brass to a hearing the **FA fine Norwich £50,000** and **Arsenal £20,000** for the brawl at Highbury on **November 4** which was described as "30 seconds of madness." The **FA** also charge three managers with bringing the game into disrepute following scuffles in last week's games. They are **Colin Harvey (Everton)**, **Ray McHale (Scarborough)** and **John Bird (York)**. After a good deal of bitterness, **QPR** sack manager **Trevor Francis**. **Bobby Moncur**, manager of bottom-of-the-League **Hartlepool** resigns. **Reading** end Bristol Rovers' 16-match unbeaten run with a **1-0** victory in their FA Cup First Round replay at Twerton Park.

28 **Don Howe** is placed temporarily in charge of team affairs at **QPR** as a continental style coach and is likely to get this job on a permanent basis after a three weeks trial. **York** fine manager **John Bird** following the incident involving **Scarborough** manager **Roy McHale** when they were ordered from the dug-out by Referee **Jim Parker** last Friday. FA chairman **Bert Millichip** confirms that they will, if necessary, back referees by persuading the **League** to **deduct points** for bad behaviour.

30 **Scotland** officially withdraw from the **Rous Cup**.

December

2 **Aston Villa** are level on points with **Liverpool** at the **top** of the First Division after beating **Nottingham Forest 2-1** at Villa Park – Villa's eighth win in nine League games. Following a rejection by **Joe Royle** to fill their managership vacancy (he prefers to stay with **Oldham**), **Manchester City** crash **4-1** at home to **Liverpool**. **Chelsea** suffer their first defeat in a run of **29 home games** losing **5-2** to **Wimbledon**. The **Second Division**'s **top crowd** so far this season, **31,715**, see **Leeds United** beat **Newcastle 1-0** at Elland Road. Despite selling two of their best players recently for **£1.5m Bristol Rovers** open up a four-point lead in the Third Division after winning **2-1** at **Walsall**. **Aberdeen** go down **1-0** to **Celtic** (a 64th minute penalty by **Andy Walker**) their first defeat in a run of eight League visits to Parkhead.

3 **Arsenal** are back in second place after beating **Manchester United 1-0** in a **disappointing TV** game at Highbury. **Elton John** is selling his interest in **Watford** for a sum which could be as much as **£3m**. The new owners will be leisure company **Wrightson Enterprises** who will loan the club around **£3m**.

4 **Rangers** manager **Graeme Souness** is reported by the **police** to the Scottish FA following an incident in the tunnel involving **Hearts** captain **Dave McPherson** at the end of **Rangers 2-1** win at Tynecastle. **Souness** is complaining about players who **cheat** to get opponents into trouble. **FIFA** confirm that they are considering changing the **offside law** so that a player **standing level** with the **defending side**'s last outfield player will remain onside.

5 During one of the liveliest **AGM**'s in the club's history a large number of **Manchester United** shareholders call for **Martin Edwards**' resignation. He says he is ready to make a **quick sale** at **£30m**.

6 **Howard Kendall** becomes **Manchester City**'s sixth manager in nine years after agreeing a **three-year deal** that is not far short of **£500,000**. The club have apparently agreed to **release** him if the **England** managership is offered to him. Media mogul **Rupert Murdoch** is reported to be interested in buying **Manchester United** so that he can feature them on his **Sky TV** channel.

7   **England** are **seeded** for the **World Cup** which means that they will play all of their group matches at **Cagliari** on the island of **Sardinia** and so go a long way to solving hooliganism problems. **Spain** **complain** that they should have been seeded before **England**. An advertisement in the *Financial Times* offering a **controlling interest** in **A First Division club** sparks speculation as to that club's identity. **Derby County** deny that it is them.

8   There is fresh speculation that **Wolves** could be up for sale **three years** after being **saved** from **bankruptcy**.

9   The **World Cup** draw brings **England**, **Republic of Ireland**, **Holland** and **Egypt** together in the same group. This raises fresh fears of crowd trouble between **English** and **Dutch** fans. With **Liverpool** held to a **1-1** draw by **Aston Villa** at Anfield, **Arsenal** go two points clear at the **top** with a **1-0** win at **Coventry**. **Manchester United** manager **Alex Ferguson** is heavily barracked after his side's **2-1** home defeat by **Crystal Palace** – the Londoners' first away win of the season. **Leeds United** takeover the lead in the Second Division following their **2-0** win at **Middlesbrough**. In a low scoring **FA Cup** Second Round, **Whitley Bay** cause the biggest shock by beating **Preston 2-0**. **Aberdeen** and **Rangers** both win to remain level on points at the top of the Scottish League.

10 **Sheffield United** return to the top of the Second Division with a **2-0** victory at **Swindon** but lose striker **Peter Duffield** with a broken leg.

11 **Roy Wegerle** signs for **QPR** in **£1m** transfer from **Luton**. He hopes to play for the **USA** in the World Cup after his citizenship papers are sorted out.

12 **Paul Gascoigne** is star of the **England B 2-1** win over **Yugoslavia B** at Millwall where the visitors' goal scored from a free kick by **Mladen Mladenovic** is one of the most powerful **35-yard shots** seen for a long time. It is now reported that **Martin Edwards** is expected to sell **Manchester United** to **Amer Midani**, the club's second largest shareholder, before Christmas for around **£22m**. **Bobby Robson** wants **Wegerle** to hold off on his decision to play for the **USA** as the player could quality for **England**. After winning their **FA Cup replay 1-0** at **Gloucester City**, some **Cardiff City** supporters vandalise part of the stadium and there are three arrests.

13 **Bryan Robson** scores one of the fastest goals ever seen at Wembley when he opens **England**'s scoring in **38 seconds** against **Yugoslavia**. He also **scores England's other goal** in a 2-1 victory. **Edwards** denies reports of a pre-Christmas deal to sell his interest in **Manchester United**. **Charlton**'s proposed return to **The Valley** next year now looks doubtful following unacceptable demands by the **local council**. **Wegerle**, QPR's **£1m striker**, rejects the chance to play for **England** and will stand by his promise to play for the **United States**. **Gloucester City** are expected to send **Cardiff City** a bill for **£2,000** to cover the damage to their ground by Cardiff supporters in their **FA Cup replay**.

15 **England** manager **Bobby Robson**'s apparent lack of confidence in the skilful **Tottenham Hotspur** star **Paul Gascoigne** is now a major point of debate. **Spurs** manager **Terry Venables** joins in by backing to the hilt the player's character and commitment. Negotiations between **Edwards** and **Midani** over the purchase of **Manchester United** are broken off.

16 **Liverpool** without **John Barnes** thoroughly outplay **Chelsea** at Stamford Bridge and win **5-2**, but **Arsenal** hold on to top position with a **3-2** home win over defensive-minded **Luton** who have now suffered eight defeats in a row at Highbury. The ultimate local derby is played at **Selhurst Park** where **Crystal Palace** are the "visitors" and **Charlton** the "home" side for the first time since **Charlton moved in** four years ago. **Crystal Palace** emerge as **2-1 "away"** winners. In the Second Division, **Watford** beat **Bradford 7-2**. They were **5-0** up at the **interval**. **Six Football League** games are **postponed** but in **Scotland** there are no away wins as the **severe winter conditions** cause the postponement of **13 League games** with another abandoned.

17 **AC Milan** win soccer's **World Club Championship** (officially the **Toyoto Cup**) in **Tokyo**, the only goal being scored two minutes from the end of extra time by **Alberigo Evani**. **West Bromwich** miss **two penalties** inside a minute in a 2-1 home defeat by **Swindon**. **Justin Fashanu** leaves **West Ham** after a month's trial.

19 **Wimbledon** and **West Ham** are each **fined £20,000** for their **Littlewoods' Cup** fracas and the **FA** send out a reminder to all clubs that they **reserve** the **right** to **expel clubs** from their Cup competition. **Arsenal** win the **unofficial British club championship** by beating **Rangers 2-1** at Ibrox. The match was relayed live to Highbury.

20 With a profit of **£3.5m**, **Arsenal** manager **George Graham** is expected to make signings before the end of the tax year in **April**. **Jock Wallace**, who was appointed a director of **Colchester United** last week, decides to give up the management of the club and coach **Steve Foley** is now caretaker manager.

21 **Diego Maradona** makes a statement suggesting that the **World Cup** draw was fixed. **Birmingham City** anger shareholders by having their **AGM** at Manchester commencing at **9am**. **Rodney Wallace** rejects a **5-year contract** to remain with **Southampton**. He still has 18 months of his existing contract to run. **Reading** at last beat **Welling 2-1** in the **FA Cup** Second Round third replay (**seven hours**) both goals being scored by **Steve Moran**.

23 Most footballers get a Saturday off and in the only Football League game **Manchester United** give one of their best displays of the season to force a **goalless draw** with **Liverpool** at Anfield. **Derek Ferguson** and **Ian McColl** have both been fined two week's wages and banned from **Ibrox** for the same period for a breach of the Rangers club **discipline**.

26 In a **bad-tempered 2-2** draw between **Crystal Palace** and **Chelsea**, in which Chelsea substitute **Graeme Le Saux** scores his side's equaliser in injury time, a **policeman** runs onto the pitch and brings down a **Chelsea** fan before he can reach referee **Alf Buksh**. **Arsenal** lose the League leadership because of a **1-0** defeat at **Southampton** where **Rodney Wallace** volleys the winner. **Liverpool** are **leaders** again after a **1-0** home win over **Charlton**. **Aston Villa** retain third place by beating a sad **Manchester United 3-0** before a crowd of **41,247** which creates a new receipts record for **Villa Park**. Second Division leaders **Leeds** draw **2-2** with nearest rivals **Sheffield United** in an exciting Yorkshire

derby. Bottom club **Hartlepool** gain only their third win of the season but it is a **4-1** thrashing of **Scarborough**.

28   In a **£1m** part-exchange deal. **Howard Kendal** signs winger **Mark Ward** for **Manchester City** from **West Ham** while **Ian Bishop** and **Trevor Morley** join the Hammers. **FIFA** are taking no action against **Maradona** for his alleged remarks about the **World Cup** draw.

29   In the **New Year Honours England** skipper **Bryan Robson** gets an **OBE** while **Liverpool** chairman **John Smith** (also chairman of the Sports Council 1985–88) is **knighted**. **£2m** in debt, **Derby County** sell **Paul Goddard** to **Millwall** for **£800,000**.

30   **Aston Villa** prove they are genuine title contenders by beating champions **Arsenal 2-1** at Villa Park, the Gunners only scoring in last two minutes. A group of **Arsenal** players remain on the field to **remonstrate** with the **referee** and a **linesman** over a goal which they believed to be offside and are ushered away by assistant manager **Theo Foley**. **Liverpool** open up a four-point lead by beating **Charlton 1-0** with a goal by **John Barnes**. **Brian Clough's 1,000th match** as a manager sees **Nottingham Forest** dazzle **Spurs 3-2** at White Hart Lane. **Wolves** become the second club after **Aston Villa** to score **6,000** Football League goals – **Keith Downing** scoring their first in a **3-1** win over **Bournemouth**. **Exeter City**'s **Darren Rowbotham** is the League's top scorer with a total of **22** after getting both his side's goals in their **2-1** win at **Southend**. Veteran **Davie Cooper** scores both of **Motherwell**'s goals in a fighting come-back to gain a **2-2** draw at home to **Aberdeen**. This helps his former club **Rangers** to hold on to the leadership after a disappointing **goalless draw** at **Hibernian**. In the Scottish First Division, **Albion Rovers** beat **Partick Thistle 5-4** with a hat-trick on either side – **Colin Cougan** for the **Rovers** and **John Flood** for **Partick**.

January

1   In the New Year's Day matches **Paul Gascoigne** cracks a bone in an arm as **Spurs** force a **goalless draw** at **Coventry**. Leaders **Liverpool** also draw – **2-2** at **Nottingham Forest** but third placed **Arsenal** easily beat **Crystal Palace 4-1**. After defeating **Arsenal 2-1** on Saturday, **Villa** prove themselves to be genuine title contenders by winning **3-0** at **Chelsea**, their **11th victory** in their last **14 games**. After **13 games** without defeat, **Ipswich Town** go down **5-0** at **Port Vale**. **Steve Bull scores all** of his side's goals as **Wolves** win **4-1** at **Newcastle**. So tight is it at the foot of the Third Division that **Brentford's 4-0** win over **Walsall** takes them from **bottom** to **19th**. The Fourth Division's biggest crowd **8,154** see leaders **Exeter City** win their Devon Derby game **3-0** at home to **Torquay United**.

2   **Nigel Spackman** scores his first goal for **Rangers** since **£500,000** move from **QPR** and it is enough to give his side victory in the Old Firm game at **Parkhead**. **Aberdeen** keep in touch with **Rangers** at the top of the table by thrashing **Dundee 5-2** at Pittodrie. **Chelsea ban** the **sale** of provocative **World Cup T-shirts** showing English hooligans storming off a boat shouting **'We came, We Saw, We conquered'**. They were being sold in the Stamford Bridge shop run by a franchise holder independent of the club. **Mick Mills** is appointed manager of **Colchester United**.

3   **Luton Town** part company with manager **Ray Harford** 'by mutual consent', while **Portsmouth** sack manager **John Gregory** after a run of **nine Second Division** games with only **two victories**. Gregory had held this job for 50 weeks. Harford's assistant **Terry Mancini** is caretaker-manager. **FIFA** announce a 30% increase in money paid to countries in the World Cup Finals which means that those who do not progress beyond the group stage can expect to receive over **£1m**. each. **Chelsea chairman Ken Bates** reaffirms the club's ban on **BBC television cameras** at Stamford Bridge for Saturday's **F.A Cup tie** with **Crewe**.

4   The **FA** are apparently not too concerned about Chelsea's BBC TV ban but chief executive **Graham Kelly** says that they might have to **take action** if the ban takes place in the **quarter** or **semi-finals**.

5   The **FA** have charged **West Ham** manager **Lou Macari** and **Swindon Town** chairman **Brian Hillier** in connection with unauthorised betting. This is alleged to have taken place when Macari was in charge at Swindon when a **bet** was made that Swindon would **lose their tie** at **Newcastle**. A special **FA** commission will hear the case. **Shrewsbury Town** sack manager **Ian McNeill**.

6   **Coventry City** (FA Cup winners two years ago and beaten last season by non-League **Sutton United**) are knocked out of the third round **1-0** at **Northampton**. **Norwich City** gain a **1-1** draw at **Exeter** but only after the Devonians had taken the lead through **Darren Rowbotham** with his **24th goal** of the season. Both goals were scored in the last five minutes. **Chelsea** are held to a 1-1 draw by **Crewe** at Stamford Bridge where the home team is booed off the field. The only First Division sides beaten are **Wimbledon** who go down **1-0** at **West Bromwich**, and **Luton** beaten **4-1** at **Brighton**. **Swansea** deserve their replay after a **goalless draw** with **Liverpool** at Vetch Field, but **West Ham** are beaten **1-0** at **Torquay** where teenage substitute **Paul Hirons** gets the winner. Following their poor start to the season, **Rangers** have now gone **eight games without defeat** and continue to lead the table following a **2-0** home win over nearest rivals **Aberdeen** who concentrated on defence. In a **Scottish Cup** second round replay **Brechin City** beat **Elgin City 8-0** with **Paul Ritchie** and **Gordon Lees** each getting a hat-trick.

7   A goal by local product **Mark Robins** gives **Manchester United** a **1-0** third round FA Cup victory at **Nottingham Forest**.

8   **Cardiff City** have been robbed of the record takings from Saturday's cup tie with **QPR** amounting to over **£50,000**. Thieves got into their offices and broke open the safe. The **FA** continue in their determination to **protect referees** from abusive managers by fining another five with **Everton** boss **Colin Harvey** getting the biggest fine of **£1500** for criticising referee **George Tyson** after the Littlewoods' Cup tie with **Nottingham Forest**. **York Manager John Bird** and **Scarborough**'s **Ray McHale** are banned from the touchline for three months for aiming punches at each other at the end of their recent match.

9   **Swansea City** suffer a club record **8-0** defeat in their third round replay at **Liverpool** for whom **Ian Rush** gets another hat-trick. A group of **businessmen** are planning to form a football club in **Dublin**

and apply for membership of the **Scottish League**. The **Football League** are hoping to stage their end-of-season promotion and relegation play-off finals at Wembley. **Bristol Rovers**, who share **Bath City's** ground, are seeking permission to build a new 12,000-seater stadium closer to Bristol. Much travelled **Lee Chapman** joins promotion-chasing **Leeds United** from **Nottingham Forest** in £400,000 transfer.

10   **Five** more **First Division clubs** win through the third round replays but another is eliminated – **Derby** beaten **3-2** at home by Second Division **Port Vale**. **Everton** are again held to a draw by **Middlesbrough**, this time **1-1** at Goodison. **Cambridge United** are shocked by the resignation of **manager Chris Turner** so soon after earning a fourth round home tie with either **Manchester City** or **Millwall**. However, he wants to continue as general manager. **Newcastle United** pay **Celtic** **£500,000** for Scotland captain **Roy Aitken**.

11   **Everton** Grant unhappy **£2m.** striker **Tony Cottee** his request for a trasnfer but there is no rush to sign him at **£1.5m. Luton sack caretaker-manager Terry Mancini** just when he was expecting to be confirmed as the new manager. The club appoint reserve coach **Jim Ryan** to succeed **Ray Harford** who left eight days ago. The club's chairman **Brian Cole** also resigns. **Littlewoods** decide to **end** their **League Cup** sponsorship after five years. Having themselves already **fined four** of the **players** involved, **Arsenal** are not to be punished by the FA for the incident at the end of their game at **Villa Park** on 30 December.

12   The **92 Football League club chairmen** each receive a letter from the Football League demanding that they use their inflence to **improve discipline** among their managers and players following the recent frightening trend.

13   **Aston Villa** draw level on points with **Liverpool** at the top of the table following their **fourth win** in a row – a **2-0** victory at **Charlton** which pushes the Londoners closer to relegation. **Luton's** new manager **Jim Ryan** watches his side shock **Liverpool** at Anfield with a **2-2** draw. **Derby** complete their first League double over **Manchester United** for 60 years with a **2-1** victory at Old Trafford. **Newcastle** beat **Leicester 5-4** in a hectic game at St. James' Park after trailing 4-2. In the **Bury v Preston** Third Division game the opposing goalkeepers are brothers and sons of former Preston goalkeeper **Alan Kelly**. **Alan junior** keeps for **Preston** and **Gary** for **Bury who lose 2-1**. Bristol City takeover from **Notts County** as Third Division leaders after winning **4-0** at **Birmingham**. **Wigan Athletic** register their first away win of the season **2-1** at**Rotherham**. Allegations of illegal payments to players add to the worry at **Swindon Town** where club secretary **Dave King** has been dismissed and promises to reveal all.

15   **Brian Clough** apologises to **Manchester United** for the panning he gave the club in the **Saint and Greavsie Show** recently, a move which may save him from more trouble with the **FA**.

17   **Everton** win their **FA Cup** third round, second replay, against **Middlesbrough** with a **solitary goal** by **Norman Whiteside** a little over a minute from full-time. **Sunderland's skipper**, **Gary Bennett**, and **Coventry's** Scottish international, **Dave Speedie**, are sent off for fighting in their **Littlewoods' Cup**, fifth round, goalless draw at Roker Park.

18   **Brian Clough** completes half of his transfer bid of nearly **£2m.** by signing **Barnsley's David Currie** for **£750,000**. His other target, **Gary McAllistesr**, decides to remain with **Leicester City** until the end of the season. **Phil Starbuck** has joined **Barnsley** as part of the deal and **Lee Glover** also joins the Oakwell club on loan. Former **England** striker **Trevor Francis** and ex-**Manchester United** defender **Kevin Moran** (just returned from Spain) are signed free by **Sheffield Wednesday**. The **Scottish League reject** newcomers **Dublin City's** application to join them. The **Football League** postpone naming the new **League Cup sponsors** when it's discovered that the company is **South African** owned. South Africa are **banned** by **FIFA**.

20   **Southampton's** climb up the table is halted in an entertaining **2-1** defeat at **Aston Villa** who still share top position on points with **Liverpool**. Depression deepens for **Charlton Athletic** who lose **3-1** at **Chelsea**. They have now gone **11 First Division** games **without a win** and are **six points adrift** at the foot of the table. Nearly 10,000 fans are locked out at Highbury where **Arsenal** beat **Spurs 1-0** with a goal from **Tony Adams** in front of a crowd of **46,133** the **biggest League gate** of the season. **Crystal Palace** lose **Ian Wright** with a fractured leg as they go down 2-0 at home to **Liverpool**. **Leeds United** goalkeeper **Mervyn Day** celebrates his **600th League game** by **saving a penalty** in a win over Stoke. This is **Day's 19th season** in the League. In the third round of the **Scottish (Tennents) Cup**, **Motherwell** beat **Clyde 7-0** with seven different goalscorers. **Celtic** leave it until six minutes from time to get the winner in a **2-1** victory at **Forfar** who are bottom of the First Division.

21   **Robert Fleck** gets both goals in **Norwich City's 2-0** win over **Manchester United** who have now gone **10 League games without a win.**

22   **Leeds United** sell displaced striker **Ian Baird** to **Middlesbrough** for **£500,000** and want **Everton's** **Graeme Sharp**. Recently dismissed as manager of **Portsmouth**, **John Gregory** joins struggling **Plymouth Argyle** as a player. **Elton John's** second attempt to sell his 93% interest in **Watford** collapses. The deal would have been with London-based leisure company **Wrighton Enterprises**. In a **Scottish Cup** third round replay **Dundee United** beat **Dundee 1-0**. This was the fourth successive season they have eliminated their close rivals from this competition. **Swindon Town** chairman **Brian Hillier** admits that a bet was laid for his team to lose a Cup tie at Newcastle.

23   **Frank Burrows** will manage **Portsmouth** until the end of the season when the situation will be reviewed.

24   In the **Littlewoods' Cup**, fifth round, **Oldham Athletic** shock **Southampton** by drawing **2-2** at the Dell with **Andy Ritchie** levelling the scores in injury time. **Coventry** destroy **Sunderland 5-0** in a fifth round replay with **Steve Livingstone** netting **four times**. **Sunderland** were handicapped by the sending off of **Gary Owers** just before the interval. In another replay hyped up as a grudge match between rival manager **Brian Clough** and **Terry Venables**, **Forest win 3-2** at **White Hart Lane** after **Spurs** had scored first in 53 seconds. **St. Mirren** win their **first Scottish Cup** tie for **three years**

beating **Ayr United 2-1** despite being reduced to 10 men with striker **Gudmunder Torfason** sent off.

25 It now seems likely that **Prime Minister Margaret Thatcher** will accept **Lord Justice Taylor's** condemnation of the **Government's ID card scheme** on the basis that it will increase crushes outside of grounds. **Coventry City** break their club record trasnfer pay-out by signing **Dundee United** winger **Kevin Gallacher** for **£900,000**. The **Scottish FA** follow the pattern set by the **English FA** in punishing managers for dissent with **referees**, by fining **six managers** and other club officials. **Aberdeen manager**, **Alex Smith**, **Celtic** assistant **Tommy Craig** and youth coach **Gordon Neely** are each fined **£1,000** and **banned** from touchlines for **12 months**. **Three others** are fined a total of £800.

27 In the **FA Cup fourth round**, **Aston Villa** emphasise their superiority over Second Division **Port Vale** by thrashing them **6-0** at **Villa Park**. First Division **Millwall** are held to a **1-1** draw by **Cambridge United** at the Den and **Arsenal** can only draw **0-0** at home to **QPR** who defend so competently. **Rochdale** reach the **fifth round** for the first time in their history by beating **Northampton Town 3-0**. **Rangers** consolidate their lead in the Premier Division with a **1-0 victory** at Dunfermline and goalkeeper **Chris Woods' sixth successive League game without conceding a goal**.

28 **Manchester United** scrape a **1-0** win at **Hereford** in their FA Cup fourth round tie thanks to a goal by **Clayton Blackmore** six minutes from time, and **Norwich** hold **Liverpool** to a **goalless draw**. **Everton** win their tie **2-1** at **Sheffield Wednesday** thanks to two goals from **Norman Whiteside** and a **faultless** display by **goalkeeper Neville Southall**. **Everton** will now make their **eighth consecutive appearance** in the fifth round.

29 The publication today of **Lord Justice Taylor's** report on the safety of football grounds, which has followed the **Hillsborough** disaster, could mean costs of over **£130m.** to implement the new requirements. A new **Football Licensing Authority** will be created under the terms of the **Football Spectators Act** and stadiums are to be all-seater by **August 1999**, with **First** and **Second Division** clubs having only until **August 1994**. The **Government** accepted that the **ID scheme** should be **shelved**.

30 **Football League** clubs are naturally shocked at having to provide **all-seater stadiums** within the next five years and fear is expressed that many of the smaller clubs will be forced out of the game. The football hierarchy is asking why the **Government helps horse racing** but refuses to help **football**. **Millwall** are eliminated from the FA Cup **1-0** in their replayed tie at **Cambridge United** as centre-back **Dave Thompson** catches goalkeeping hero **Keith Branagan** off-guard with a wild pass-back four minutes from the end of extra time. **John Docherty** left **Millwall's new £800,000** striker **Paul Goddard** on the substitutes bench.

31 Never sent off or booked in more than **30 years** as a player, **Sir Stanley Matthews** gives his name to a new trophy which will be presented to the club, team or individual who most embodies Matthews' **sporting qualities**. **Greenwich Council** reject **Charlton Athletic's plans to resurrect their old ground at The Valley**. **Arsenal** go out of the FA Cup beaten **2-0** in the replayed tie at **QPR** but **Liverpool** and **Newcastle** are through to the fifth round. **Oldham Athletic** win their **Littlewoods' Cup** fifth round replay **2-0** with **Southampton**.

February

1 **Michel Platini**, **manager** of the **French team**, is supposed to have expressed interest in **Guernsey-born** striker **Matthew Le Tissier**, **Southampton's** top-scorer, who has yet to be picked by **Bobby Robson** but could qualify for any of the home countries as well as **France**.

2 The draw for the **1992** European Championship is made in **Sweden** and **England** are again grouped with the **Republic of Ireland** for the third consecutive major competition. The others in the same group are **Poland** and **Turkey**. **Scotland** are in Group 2 with **Rumania**, **Bulgaria**, **Switzerland** and **San Marino**. The **FA** have failed to persuade the other home countries to join them in a team to compete in the **Olympic Games**. The other associations believe that such a **Great Britain** team would jeopardise the continuation of fielding separate teams in other international competitions. **France's** reported interest in **Matthew Le Tissier** has spurred **England** manager **Bobby Robson** into guaranteeing the player a future with **England**. **Graham Taylor** who was threatened with the sack at **Villa Park** not so long ago is named **Barclay's Manager of the Month** for a **record-breaking third time in succession**.

3 **Liverpool** complete their first League double over **Everton** for seven years by winning the **142nd Merseyside derby 2-1** with **Peter Beardsley** getting the winner from a **penalty**. In other derbies, **Manchester United** draw **1-1** with the **City** and **Port Vale** and **Stoke** play out a **goalless draw**. **Steve Livingstone** scores for **Coventry** against **Chelsea** after only **27 seconds** at Highfield Road and an own goal by **Kevin McAllister** puts Coventry further ahead two minutes later but **Chelsea** fight back and only **lose** by the **odd goal in five**. Seventeen Football League games are **postponed** and there are only two away wins – **Notts County 2-1** at **Rotherham** and **Wolves** by a **solitary goal** at **Plymouth**. **Rangers** make it **20 home Premier Division wins** in a row by beating **Dundee United 3-1**. **Ally McCoist** equals **Derek Johnstone's post-war club** record with his **131st goal**.

4 **Spurs** take a big jump up the table with a **4-0** home win over **Norwich** thanks to a hat-trick from **Gary Lineker**. **Swindon** move into third position after beating Second Division leaders **Leeds United 3-2**.

6 Having won only **one** of their last **15 Second Division** games **Plymouth Argyle** sack manager **Ken Brown** who joined them in June 1988. Former **Portsmouth** manager **John Gregory**, who was recently signed as a **player** by Brown, takes charges on a **temporary** basis. There is a takeover at **Bradford City** where chairman **Jack Tordoff** sells his **80% holding** for **£800,000** and new **chairman David Simpson** offers the team a luxury holiday if they avoid the drop into the Third Division. **Norwich** manager **Dave Stringer** wins his fight to keep midfield star **Ian Crook** after it had been agreed by his chairman to sell him to **Coventry City** for **£750,000**.

7   **Bristol Rovers'** manager **Gerry Francis** and winger **Paul Nixon** are alleged to have had a punch-up which resulted in them both being taken to **West Drayton** police station. The alleged incident took place when the team coach stopped at the **Post House Hotel, Heathrow**, en route from their victory at **Brentford**. The **Football League** decide that this season's **play-offs** will take place at **Wembley** over the Bank Holiday weekend **May 26-28**.

8   With veteran goalkeeper **Phil Parkes** troubled with arthritic knees, **West Ham** sign Czechoslovakian international goalkeeper **Ludek Miklosko** from **Banik Ostrava** for **£300,000**.

9   **UEFA** announce that only **four foreigners** will be permitted in **any team** entering their **club competitions** from next season. Moreover, **Scottish, Welsh** and **Irish** players will be classed as **foreigners** in English club teams etc. Any player signed before **3 May 1988** will be exempt from this ban for a transitional period. **Cambridge United** decide not to keep former team manager **Chris Turner** as **general manager**. Fearing clashes between rival fans in **Sardinia** the local **World Cup** organising committee have ordered the **Republic of Ireland** team to move from the hotel they have booked. These are sad days for **Birmingham City** beaten **5-1** at **Tranmere** in the Third Division.

10 **Tottenham** establish themselves in fifth position with a **2-1** win at **Chelsea** – Lineker scoring in the last minute, while **Southampton** slip to eighth place after losing **3-1** at **Crystal Palace**. **Liverpool** have Swedish international defender **Glenn Hysen** sent off in a goalless draw at **Norwich** but retain the lead by one point over **Aston Villa** who register their sixth League win in a row by beating **Sheffield Wednesday 1-0**. **Manchester United** end their run of **11 League matches without a win** (one short of the club record) with a **2-1** victory at relegation bound **Millwall**. Near the bottom of the Fourth division, **Hartlepool** beat promotion-chasing **Stockport 5-0** with **Paul Baker** scoring four. **Hartlepool** had **lost 6-0** at **Stockport** in September. **Celtic's 1-1** draw with **Hibernian** means that they have now **dropped more home points** than in any season since **1964-65**. A **£175,000** signing **Owen Coyle** scores a **hat-trick** in his **debut** for top-of-the-table **Airdrie** as they beat **Ayr United 6-0** in the Scottish First Division.

12 The **Scottish FA** agree to pay each player a bonus of around **£30,500** if they win the **World Cup** this summer. If they reach the **last 12** they will receive £10,500 with the **non-playing** members of the squad getting **£2,475**. The FA give their verdict on the **Swindon betting affair**. Chairman **Brian Hillier** receives a **six-month's suspension** from any involvement in football; the club is fined **£7,500** and their manager at the time, **Lou Macari**, is fined £1,000 and censured for his minor part in what is termed 'a foolhardy misdemeanour.'

13 **John Docherty**, the manager who steered **Millwall** into the First division is **sacked** together with assistant **Frank McLintock**. The Club has **won only one of their last 18** First Division games. The Third Division game at **Preston** is halted for **35 minutes** while fans demonstrate against the club's poor record and call for **manager John McGrath's resignation**. They eventually lose **3-0** to **Leyton Orient**.

14 **Lou Macari** suffers another blow as his **West Ham** side are slammed **6-0** at **Oldham** in the Littlewoods **Cup** semi-final first leg. Chief scout **Bob Pearson** is appointed **manager** of **Millwall**. **John McGrath** succumbs to pressure from the fans and **quits as manager** of Preson North End. **Les Chapman** takes charge in a temporary capacity.

15 The **Scottish League** advise **Stirling Albion** that they will **not be allowed** to continue playing on their **synthetic pitch** after next season. It is the only one in the Scottish League.

16 **Liverpool** and **Everton** are reported to be considering **abandoning** their **respective grounds** and sharing a new **super stadium** to be built on the outskirts of the city.

17 In the **fifth round** of the **FA Cup**, **Aston Villa** stay on track for a League and Cup double by winning **2-0** at West Bromwich, their **16th League and Cup game** without defeat. **Liverpool** have little trouble in beating **Southampton 3-0**, but **Crystal Palace** make hard work of winning **1-0** against **Rochdale**. In the First Division, **Arsenal** fail to close up on the leaders by going down **1-0** at **Sheffield Wednesday** where the winner is an own goal by **Steve Bould** only **15 seconds** after the kick-off. **Preston** are pushed closer to the Fourth Division suffering a 6-0 beating at **Reading**. **Rangers** drop their **first point** at Ibrox since mid-September being held to a **goalless draw** draw by **Hearts**.

18 In **FA Cup ties**, **Manchester United** pull off a **3-2 win** at Newcastle while two other relegation threatened sides – **Barnsley** and **Blackpool** – draw with higher placed opposition, – **Barnsley 2-2** at **Sheffield United** and **Blackpool** holding **QPR** to a similar score at **Bloomfield Road**. In the Second Division, **West Ham** draw **2-2** at **Swindon** where their manager **Lou Macari** fails to put in an appearance. There are reports that **UEFA** are considering the formation of a new **European Super League** rumoured to include **Liverpool**, **Arsenal** and **Rangers**.

19 **West Ham United** confirm that manager **Lou Macari** resigned yestesrday. He was only the **sixth man** to hold this position in **nearly 90 years**.

20 Unable to get his place in **Aston Villa's** successful League side **£360,000** summer signing **Adrian Heath** joins his former **Everton** manager Howard Kendall at **Manchester City** for **£300,000**.

21 **Aston Villa** go **top** of the League for the **first time** in **nine years** by winning **2-0** at **Tottenham** with goals by **Ian Ormondroyd** and **David Platt**. All four of the **FA Cup fifth round replays** end in **draws**. Arguably the most notable is **Second Division Oldham Athletic's 1-1** draw at **Everton** although the home side had **Norman Whiteside sent off** early in the second half.

22 Following the **£18m.** deal between the **FA** and **BSB** satellite television it is announced that there will be **FA Cup ties** on Saturday nights next season.

23 The **Spanish Football Federation** formally submit a plan to **UEFA** to change all three European competitions from knockout to League. **West Ham** appoint former long-service player **Billy Bonds** as manager. He only gave up playing **18 months ago** at the age of **42**.

24 **Wimbledon** produce one of the biggest shocks of the season by beating League leaders **Aston Villa 3-0** at Villa Park with **John Fashanu** scoring twice. **Oldham Athletic** make it **34** home games without defeat by beating **Ipswich Town 4-1**. **Preston** beat fellow stragglers **Cardiff City 4-0** in the Third

Division with a **hat-trick** by **Steve Harper**. The **Scottish programme is again hit by the weather** but **Aberdeen**, **Hearts** and **Hibernian** are through to the Cup quarter-finals. **Charlie Nicholas** gets **Aberdeen's** winner against **Morton** after the First Division side had taken the lead.

25 **Nottingham Forest** play a defensive game to force a **goalless draw** at **Coventry City** and win through to the final of the **Littlewoods' Cup 2-1** on aggregate. **Celtic** beat **Rangers 1-0** in a hectic game at **Parkhead** to reach the **quarter-finals** of the **Scottish Cup** with a 44th minute goal by **Tommy Coyne**. Six players are booked. **Spurs** are fined **£500** and ordered to pay a similar amount in compensation to **Tranmere Rovers** for late payment of share of receipts for their Littlewoods' Cup game.

27 **Cambridge United** beat **Bristol City 5-1** in the **FA Cup fifth round replay** and so become the first Fourth Division side to reach the **FA Cup semi-finals** for 14 years.

28 **Stirling Albion** win their **Scottish Cup** fourth round tie with non-League **Inverness Caley 6-2**.

March

3 **Arsenal** beaten **2-0** at **QPR** have scored only once in their last seven matches and slip to fourth in the table. **Luton Town** score their **first goal** in over 11½ hours of League football but go down **4-1** at **Manchester City**. **Manchester City** are beaten by one of the most controversial goals of the season as **Nottingham Forest's Gary Crosby** nips in to head the ball out of **goalkeeper Andy Dibble's right hand** and fire into the net. **Russian Sergei Gotsmanov** scores in his first full game for **Brighton** as they **draw 1-1** with Oldham. **Plymouth Argyle's new manager David Kemp** sees his side end a 14-match run without a win by beating **Sunderland 3-0** at Home Park. Third Division leaders **Bristol City** halt **Chester's 13-match unbeaten home run** with a 3-0 victory – Bob Taylor getting a **hat-trick**. Not to be outshone, **Bristol Rovers** beat **Wigan Athletic 6-1** with a hat-trick by new signing **Carl Saunders**. This was Rovers' first six in the League since **December 1973**. Fourth Division leaders **Carlisle United** go down **2-0** at **Southend** where **two Carlisle players are sent off** while five from **Carlisle** and **two home players** are booked. **Hearts** record for the first season in which they have registered four Premier Division wins over **Motherwell** by beating them **2-0** at Tynecastle.

5 Following discussions with **Manchester United chairman Martin Edwards** Iraqi-born businessman **Sam Hashimi** decides to buy **Sheffield United** for **£5 million** and hopes to complete the transaction by June. **Partick Thistle** re-appoint **John Lambie** as manager four months after he left to take charge of **Hamilton Academical** for a second spell.

6 Without an away win in the Second Division this season, **Bradford City** prove no match for **Swindon** who beat them **3-1** scoring all of their goals in a shattering **four-minute spell** at the County Ground. **Tranmere Rovers** take over at the top of the Third Division by beating leaders **Bristol City 3-1** at Ashton Gate. Following another dressing room row with manager **Bruce Rioch**, **Middlesbrough** ban former England striker **Peter Davenport** from their stadium and training ground for two weeks.

7 With a **6-0** advantage, **Oldham Athletic** reach the **Littlewoods' Cup Final** despite losing their semi-final second leg **3-0** at West Ham. After more than **8½ hours without a goal**, **Arsenal** get back into the championship race by beating **Nottingham Forest 3-0** at Highbury. **Bradford City sack manager Terry Yorath**.

8 Each of the 22 members of **England's World Cup squad** will receive a **bonus** of around **£70,000** if they win the trophy.

9 **Middlesbrough** sack **Bruce Rioch**, the manager who steered the club out of their **1986 liquidation crisis** and back into the **First Division** before relegation last season. His assistant **Colin Todd** takes over.

10 **Oldham Athletic** continue the most exciting season in their history by winning their **FA Cup fifth round** (second replay) with Everton **2-1**. **Everton** rejected, **Ian Marshall**, gets the winner with a **penalty** in **extra time**. Fourth Division **Cambridge City's** remarkable **FA Cup run ends** in defeat by a **solitary goal** at home to **Crystal Palace** in their sixth round tie. Second Division leaders **Leeds United** stage an amazing fight-back at **Oxford** where they are **2-0 down** at the interval **but win 4-2**. Yet more **Scottish** matches are **postponed** owing to the weather but promotion-chasing **St. Johnstone win 5-2** at **Albion Rovers** with **four** in the last **nine minutes**.

11 **QPR** fight back from **2-1** down to draw **2-2** with **Liverpool** in a highly entertaining **FA Cup sixth round tie**, while a goal by **Brian McClair** is enough to see **Manchester United** through against **Sheffield United**.

13 Another manager bites the dust as **Swansea City** sack **Ian Evans** after just over a year in the job.

14 **Aston Villa's** bid for a **League and Cup double is shattered** in a **3-0** sixth round FA Cup defeat on **Oldham Athletic's** plastic pitch. **Liverpool** march closer to yet another Wembley visit by beating **QPR 1-0** in their **sixth round replay** with Peter Beardsley netting the winner in under five minutes.

15 After much thought, **Millwall's Tony Cascarino** agrees to join **Aston Villa** in a club record **£1.5 million** transfer. **Swansea City** recall **Terry Yorath** as manager 13 months after he walked out on the club to take over at **Bradford City**. **Coventry's** spending in six months passes the **£2m.** mark as they sign Crewe defender **Paul Edwards** for **£410,000**. **Manchester City** agree to buy Irish International striker **Niall Quinn** from Arsenal for £700,000. The purchase of **Sheffield United** is developing into a saga similar to the **Manchester United** debacle. Since the announcement that **Iraqi-born** businessman **Sam Hashimi** was buying there have been two counter bids. **Manager Dave Bassett** is one of many people unhappy with the situation and is reported as saying that there should have been no announcement until the deal was completed. **Colin Addison** returns to Spanish football as manager of **Cadiz**. He was sacked last season by **Atletico Madrid**.

17 A total of **nine players** are **sent off** in the Football League programme. **Aston Villa** are back on the League championship tracks again following their **FA Cup dismissal** and **win 1-0** at Derby with a goal by substitute **Ian Ormondroyd**. Only the brilliance of **Peter Shilton** prevents record signing **Tony Cascarino** from scoring on his **Villa** debut. **Charlton Athletic** score their **first goal in four games**

but **Nottingham Forest** make it a 1-1 draw and **Charlton** remain rooted to the bottom of the First Division. **John Bumstead** celebrates his **300th apperance** for **Chelsea** by scoring the **goal** which halts **Arsenal's** run of 16 matches without defeat at **Highbury**. This was only **Chelsea's second win** at Highbury in a run of **12 League visits**. There are no changes top or bottom of the Second and Third Divisions but **Exeter City** return to the top of Division Four after beating **Peterborough 2-0**. However, they lose leading scorer **Darran Rowbotham** with a **serious knee injury** which may keep him **out of the game** for **at least six months**. **Aberdeen** and **Dundee United** are through to the semi-finals of the **Scottish Cup** but Second Division **Stirling** draw **1-1** at First Division **Clydebank** and **Celtic** are held to a **goalless draw** at **Dunfermline**.

18 **Liverpool** gain only their second victory in a run of **17 League visits** to **Old Trafford** where **John Barnes** stars in a **2-0** win by scoring both goals. **Millionaire Sir Jack Hayward** wants to buy **Wolves** from **Gallaghers** the builders and the ground owners **Wolverhampton Council**.

19 **Liverpool** manager **Kenny Dalglish** and **Scotland** managerAndy Roxburgh are in open conflict over the latter's decision to drop **Steve Nicol** and **Gary Gillespie** from next week's game with **Argentina**. Roxburgh has given preference to those who were available for the previous game in **Genoa** and is annoyed at players being constantly unavailable to play for Scotland. **Walsall sack manager John Barnwell** after only **one win** in their **last 22** Third Division **games**.

20 Unexpected boost from **Government** in Budget: **Reduction** in **Betting duty** on Football Pools from **42½% to 40%** to help finance implementation of **Lord Justice Taylor**'s recommendation towards **all-seater stadia**. **Managers** continue to **tumble**: the latest is **Steve Harrison** who has been at **Watford** for a little over two years. However, there are still men brave enough to take on difficult jobs as **John Docherty** is appointed **manager** of **Bradford City** who seem doomed to relegation from the Second Division. **Bristol City** return to the top of the Third Division as **Bob Taylor** gets his **second League hat-trick** of the season in a **5-0** win at **Swansea**.

21 **Celtic** win through to the semi-finals of the **Scottish Cup**, beating **Dunfermline 3-0**, but in the other replay the "home" side **Stirling Albion** are beaten **1-0** by **Clydebank**. As in the previous round **Stirling** were prevented by the **Scottish FA** from playing this **Cup** tie on their **plastic pitch**. Following **five defeats** in a row, **Bill Ayre** resigns as manager of **Halifax Town**. **Bradford City** welcome new manager **John Docherty** by beating **Newcastle United 3-2**.

22 Although **England** manager **Bobby Robson** has expressed the wish to retain his job for another four years there is speculation that he will only be allowed to do so **if England win the World Cup**. **Arsenal** want to buy **Dave Seaman** from **QPR** for a new British record transfer fee for a goalkeeper of £1.3m. but QPR want Arsenal's **John Lukic** on loan for the remainder of this season and Lukic is reported as reluctant to move. Biggest fee of those successfully completed on the last day for transfers is **£250,000** by **Portsmouth** for former England international **Gary Stevens** from **Tottenham**.

23 **FIFA** tell representatives of the **24 World Cup** finalists at a meeting in Zurich that **referees** must rule out tackling from behind and that disproportionate or unnecessary force should result in automatic sending-off.

24 **Crystal Palace** beat League leaders **Aston Villa** with a debut goal by **Garry Thompson** a former Villa player. **Charlton Athletic** get off the bottom of the **First Division** with a shock **2-1 win** at **Coventry**. **Arsenal's 3-1** win at **Derby** was their first League victory on this ground in **15 visits**. **Leeds United** increase their lead to one of **10 points ahead** of **Sheffield United** in the Second Division by beating **Portsmouth 2-0** – their **22nd consecutive home League game** without defeat. **Exeter City**, the only other League side unbeaten at home this season, hammer **Rochdale 5-0** with central defender **Jim McNichol** getting a **hat-trick**. A shock for **Rangers** as they suffer their **first home defeat** in the **Premier League** this season. **Hibernian** are the winners with a single goal from **Keith Houchen**.

25 **Tony Dorigo** scores with a spectacular free-kick from 25 yards to give **Chelsea** the winner against **Middlesbrough** in the final of the **Zenith Data Systems Cup** in front of a crowd of over **76,000** at **Wembley** but the game is generally unentertaining.

27 **Norway** score two goals in a four-minute spell to come from behind and beat **Northern Ireland 3-2** at Windsor Park. In **B internationals** the **Republic of Ireland** shock **England's** rising stars by beating them **4-1** at **Cork**, while **Scotland** draw 0-0 with **Yugoslavia** in a dull game at **Motherwell**.

28 **Gary Lineker** scores his **30th international goal** to give **England** a **1-0** victory over **Brazil** at **Wembley**. Only **Bobby Charlton** and **Jimmy Greaves** have scored more. **Republic of Ireland** beat **Wales 1-0** with **Bernie Slaven** getting this first-ever winner against **Wales**. **Scotland's Stewart McKimmie** scores with a spectacular shot to give them the winner against world champions **Argentina**. The Welsh team is **robbed** of money and other valuables as **thieves** break into their dressing room. **FIFA** now agree to allow the **Republic of Ireland** to use a World Cup base near the England party in **Sardinia**. **Oldham Athletic** suffer their first defeat in a run of **39 home games** going down **2-0** to **Sheffield United** for whom **Brian Deane** scores both goals.

30 **Sheffield United** chairman **Reg Brealey** announces that he has decided not to sell his **63% share-holding** to **Iraqi-born** businessman **Sam Hashimi** or anyone else at the present time.

31 **Liverpool** return to the top of the table on goal difference over **Aston Villa** following their **3-2** victory over **Southampton** in a real thriller with **Bruce Grobbelaar** making his **500th League and Cup** appearance. **Ian Rush** scores the winner. Second Division leaders **Leeds United** go down **1-0** at **Wolves** with **Andy Mutch** seizing on a bad pass-back by **David Batty** to score the vital goal. Pro-motion contenders **Swindon Town** make things difficult for themselves by missing two penalties at home to **Leicester** before drawing **1-1**. In the top-of-the-table GM Vauxhall Conference clash **Darlington** win **2-0** at **Barnet** to keep their chances of a quick return to the Football League alive.

April

1 **Manchester City** register their first away win in the First Division since **January 1986** and of all places it is at **Villa Park** where they put a spoke in the home side's Championship-winning hopes with a **2-1 victory**. **Peter Reid** scores the winner 10 minutes from time. **Celtic** suffer their biggest

defeat of the season so far going down **3-0** to **Rangers** at Ibrox where their defender **Paul Elliott** is **booked** for the **15th time** this season. It is the first season since **1975-76** that **Celtic** have failed to beat **Rangers** in the Premier Division. **Villa's David Platt** is the **PFA's Player of the Year**.

2   After a goalless draw with **Notts County** in the second leg of the **Leyland Daf Cup** Southern Final **Bristol Rovers** win **1-0** on aggregate but **Notts County** are annoyed with referee **Brian Hill's decision** which denied them a possible equaliser and even worse, County's promotions manager **Les Bradd** alleges that Hill hit him when he wanted to question the referee about his decision.

3   **Ian Rush** scores first to put **Liverpool** on the road to a **2-1** home win over **Wimbledon** and open up a three-point lead over **Aston Villa**. **Sunderland** maintain their promotion bid with a surprise **3-1** victory at **Sheffield United** who have now lost two of their last six home games. **Steve Wilkinson**, who cost **Mansfield £80,000** from **Leicester** last September, **scores all of his side's goals** in a **5-2** beating of **Birmingham City** and is the only player to score as many goals in a Football League game this season. **Italy's players** will each pick up about **£250,000** if they **win the World Cup** this summer. **The FA** throw out **Lou Macari's** appeal against his fine over the **Swindon** betting affair. **Rangers** agree a **£20m.** sponsorship deal. **Hamilton Academical** appoint **Billy McLaren** from **Queen of the South** as manager.

4   **Everton** beat **Nottingham Forest 4-0** and were unlucky not to have doubled this score as Forest slide down the table with only one point from their last six games. **Brian Clough** calls his players "**pansies**" and admits "**we were slaughtered.**"

5   **Chester City** want to share **Widnes Rugby League** ground when they leave **Sealand Road** at the end of this season.

6   The **FA** increase former **Swindon Town** chairman **Brian Hillier's suspension** from **six months to three years** but leave **Macari's fine** at **£1,000**. **Chelsea's** proposal that the First Division reverts to **22 clubs** at the end of the season is viewed with apprehension by the FA who are anxious to protect the England team from fixture congestion. **Crewe** push for promotion from the Third Division by registering their **14th game** without defeat – a **2-2** home draw with promotion rivals **Tranmere Rovers**.

7   Beaten **3-1** at home by **Tottenham Hotspur**, **Nottingham Forest** are suffering their worst run since **Brian Clough** became manager. **Luton** suffer their fifth successive away defeat going down **1-0** at **Chelsea**. **Everton** move up to third place with their fifth win in six games – **a 1-0** home victory over **QPR**. In the Second Division, relegation threatened **Bradford Cty** earn a 1-1 draw at top-of-the-table **Leeds** in an exciting match. **Celtic** give one of their worst displays of the season in losing **3-0** to **St. Mirren** at Parkhead. This is **St. Mirren's** first win at **Parkhead** in a run of **19 League visits**.

8   There have never been two more exciting **FA Cup semi-finals** in any season than those in which **Crystal Palace** shock the football fraternity by beating **Liverpool 4-3** and **Manchester United** fight out a **3-3** draw with **Oldham Athletic**. **Both** games went to **extra times**.

10 **Wolves** are still in with a chance of appearing in the **promotion play-offs** thanks to another **hat-trick** from **Steve Bull** in their **5-0** beating of **Leicester City**. **Bob Taylor** nets his **third League hat-trick** of the season in **Bristol City's 4-1** win over **Crewe**. **Exeter City's 1-0** win at **Colchester** places the East Anglian club in danger of losing their Football League status as they are four points adrift at the bottom of the table.

11 A goal by substitute **Mark Robins** in extra time sees **Manchester United** through to the **FA Cup Final** with a **2-1 win over Oldham** in their replay at Maine Road. **Aston Villa** kill off **Arsenal's** championship hopes by winning **1-0** at Highbury with a late goal by **Chris Price**. **Israeli** international **Ronny Rosenthal** makes a dream debut (other than as a substitute) for **Liverpool**. On loan from **Standard Liège**, he scores a **hat-trick** in his side's **4-0** win over **Charlton** at Selhurst Park. Former England international **Ricky Hill** advertises his availability at the end of the season by sending out hundreds of faxes. He is unhappy with **Le Havre** in the **French Second Division**.

13 Recovering from their **FA Cup semi-final** defeat, **Oldham** show what great fighters they are by coming back to beat Second Division leaders **Leeds United 3-1** at Boundary Park. It was their third victory over Leeds this season.

14 Although out of this season's championship race, **Nottingham Forest** keep it alive by drawing **2-2** at **Anfield**, their first point on this ground in their **last nine visits** and their **first goals there** in **seven League games**. **Aston Villa** just manage a **1-0** home win over **Chelsea** who keep them under pressure for most of the second half. **Millwall** are doomed to relegation following their **2-0** defeat at **Derby**. In the Scottish Cup semi-finals **Aberdeen** have an easy passage to Hampden by beating **Dundee United 4-0** and **Celtic** chase a record **30th Final victory** by beating **Clydebank 2-0** with **Andy Walker** scoring both goals.

16 **Millwall** fall further behind by losing to a single goal by **Tottenham's Gary Lineker** at the Den and shortly after the final whistle they appoint **Bruce Rioch** manager with Bob Pearson reverting to his old role as chief-coach. The day's biggest crowd of **32,697** are at Elland Road to see Second Division **Leeds United** emphatically defeat nearest promotion rivals **Sheffield United 4-0** with an all-out attack while their goalkeeper scarcely has a shot to save. **Newcastle** takeover from **Sheffield United** in second place by beating bottom club **Stoke City 3-0** with **Mick Quinn** getting his **31st League goal** of the season. **Bristol City** are six points clear of **Bristol Rovers** at the top of the Third Division after beating **Fulham 5-1**, while **Exeter City** open up a seven-point lead at the top of Division Four with a **2-0** win over **Aldershot**, City's **27th consecutive home League and Cup game** without defeat.

17 **Manchester United's** newest goalscoring star **Mark Robins** scores both of his side's goals in a **2-0** win over **Villa** which shakes the Midlanders' championship hopes. With three games still to play, **Charlton Athletic** will be in the Second Division next season after losing **2-1** at home **to Wimbledon**. The FA decide that **Crystal Palace's** allocation of Cup Final tickets will be **14,000** with **26,000** for **Manchester United**. **Palace** chairman **Ron Noades** is **furious** and predicts a huge black market in tickets. **Juventus** are in a mood to forgive **Liverpool** for their fans rioting at the Heysel stadium and have asked **UEFA** to cut the club's additional three-year ban.

18   New **UEFA president Lennart Johansson** of **Sweden** wants **Liverpool** back in Europe next season but although this may not be possible because UEFA are asking for the British Government's backing they seem certain to return in **1991-92**. Meanwhile the **ban on other British clubs** in Europe next season will be **lifted providing the fans behave** at the **World Cup** this summer. **John Barnes** virtually clinches the championship for **Liverpool** by scoring a late equaliser in a **1-1** draw at **Highbury**. **Newcastle United's** boardroom battle ends with millionaire businessman **John Hall** being co-opted onto the board.

21   While **Liverpool** are beating **Chelsea 4-1** at Anfield, **Aston Villa** keep **two points behind** with a 1-0 home win over **Millwall**. In the **80th League** clash between **Nottingham Forest** and **Southampton** the Forest suffer their eighth defeat in a run of **11 games** at The Dell going down **2-0**. **Spurs** complete their first League double over **Manchester United** for 16 years with a **2-1** win at White Hart Lane. **Rangers** clinch the **Scottish League** championship for the **40th time** by winning **1-0** at Dundee United. Despite drawing **1-1** at **Celtic Park**, **Dundee** can say goodbye to Premier Division football for a spell. **Darlington's 4-0** win at **Stafford** with **John Borthwick** getting a hat-trick seems certain to be enough to carry them **back into** the **Football League**. **Real Madrid** are interested in **John Barnes** and may be willing to pay £5m. for his transfer.

22   Former **Liverpool** striker **John Aldridge** scores afer only **45 seconds** for **Real Sociedad** in a **2-2** draw with **Valencia**.

23   **Alex McLeish** the **Aberdeen** midfielder is voted **Scotland's Player of the Year** by the **Scottish Football Writers**.

24   In **B Internationals, England** beat **Czechoslovakia 2-0** with **Alan Smith** getting both goals at Roker Park, but **Scotland** are beaten **2-1** by **East Germany** at Perth. **Leeds United** suffer their **first home league defeat** of the season losing **2-1** to **Barnsley** who are struggling to avoid relegation. **Walsall** are **relegated** to the Fourth Division a year after dropping out of the Second following their **3-1** defeat at **Cardiff. Exeter City** gain promotion to the Third Division with a **2-1** home win against **Southend United. Carlisle United's 2-1** home defeat by **Lincoln City** ensures a Third Division place next season for **Grimsby Town**.

25   **Paul Gascoigne** stars in **England's 4-2** beating of **Czechoslovakia** setting up three goals and scoring one. **Republic of Ireland** beat the **USSR 1-0** the goal being scored by **Steve Staunton**. This extends their **unbeaten** home run to **18 games. Scotland** go down **1-0** to **East Germany** in a disappointing game, and **Sweden** (in the same World Cup group as Scotland) emphasise the fact that the Scots will have to do better by beating **Wales 4-2**. The Welsh have now gone 10 games without a win.

28   **Liverpool** clinch the League title for the **18th time** (**10 times** in the last 15 years) with a penalty by "Player of the Year" **John Barnes** in a 2-1 home win over **QPR**, while **Villa** finish runners-up being held to a **3-3** draw in a hectic game with **Norwich** which produces **five goals in one 20-minute** spell. **Bradford City** will go down to the Third Division with **Stoke City** after losing **2-1** at **Hull. Grimsby Town** celebrate their return to the Third Division with a 5-1 beating of **Wrexham, Garry Birtles** getting a **hat-trick. St. Johnstone** win the First Division championship with a **2-0** victory at **Ayr** where the home side have veteran **Alan Rough** making his debut for them at the age of 38. **Albion Rovers** and **Alloa** are relegated to the Second Division to be replaced by **Brechin** and either **Kilmarnock or Stirling Albion** who both win away from home and have one more game each to play.

29   **Nottingham Forest** win the Littlewoods' Cup for the second year in succession with a goal by **Nigel Jemson** against **Oldham Athletic**. This was brave **Athletic's 61st game** of the season. **Colchester United's** anticipated drop out of the Football League is confirmed by their **4-0** defeat at **Cambridge** where **Mike Cheetham** scores a hat-trick.

30   At an **extraordinary meeting** of the **Football League** it is proposed that the management committee should consider a **five per cent levy** on all **transfer fees** to be paid to the **Football Trust** to help meet the safety requirements of the **Taylor Report**. It was also suggested that **50 per cent** of the **League's television** contract wih **ITV** should go the same way. **Aldershot** face their **second winding-up order in 12 months** and **Rushmoor Borough Council** who own their ground, refuse them a lease for next season. **Blackpool** can only draw **2-2** at home to **Swansea** and book themselves a place in next season's Fourth Division

May

1   **Liverpool** beat **Derby County 1-0** at Anfield where **Kenny Dalglish** comes on as substitute for a rare appearance in the last **18 minutes** before the club receive the championship trophy. **Barclays Bank** also present them with a cheque for **£100,000. Lou Macari** and **Brian Hillier**, formerly manager and chairman of **Swindon Town**, together with club captain **Colin Calderwood** and former chief accountant **Vince Farrar** are arrested and questioned at **Bristol Central police station** by **Inland Revenue** officials regarding an alleged tax fraud conspiracy. **Calderwood** is later **released** without charge. A packed meetings of **Aldershot** supporters pledge over £44,000 to keep the club going. **Preston North End** appoint their **caretaker manager Les Chapman** as official successor to **John McGrath. Carl Richards**, striker at relegated **Blackpool**, is sacked for allegedly refusing to play the second half of their match with **Chester** last Tuesday.

2   In view of the arrest of Messrs **Macari, Hillier** and **Farrar** the Football League postpone their inquiry into the club's affairs. A record **all-ticket** crowd of **9,813** pack **Twerton Park, Bath** to see the Third Division championship clash between **Bristol Rovers** and **City** which is won **3-0** by **Rovers** with two of the goals scored by **Devon White**. Home secretary **David Waddington** announces a two-year ban on travelling to future **overseas matches** for anyone **convicted** of a football related offence at the **World Cup Finals**. Sad **Celtic** suffer another home defeat going down **3-1** to **Aberdeen** – this is their eighth consecutive Premier League game without a win.

3   **Lou Macari** and **Brian Hillier** are granted conditional bail and former club accountant **Vincent Farrar** unconditional bail when they appear at **Swindon Magistrates Court** accused of tax offences.

Because of a tax snag, the League management committee shelve the idea of a **levy on transfers** to help modernise grounds. They will go ahead with their investigation into the affairs of Swindon Town.

5   **Leeds United** supporters spoil a season of real progress in getting English clubs back into Europe by rioting, looting and assaults at **Bournemouth** before and after the 1-0 victory which clinches promotion for their club and relegation for **Bournemouth**. There are other outbreaks of soccer hooliganism at **Leicestesr, Sheffield, Millwall, Halifax, Shrewsbury, Swansea, Colchester, Bristol** and **Aldershot. Liverpool** celebrate the end of another championship-winning campaign with a **6-1** victory at **Coventry** where **John Barnes** scores a hat-trick. **Kerry Dixon** scores a hat-trick for **Chelsea** in a comfortable **3-1** win at **Millwall. Sheffield Wednesday** are relegated following their **3-0** home defeat **Nottingham Forest. Middlesbrough** hold on to Second Division status with a **4-1** beating of **Newcastle**. The biggest Third Division crowd of the season, **19,483**, are at **Ashton Gate** to see **Bristol City** overwhelm **Walsall 4-0. Exeter City** celebrate their promotion by destroying **Lincoln's** hopes of reaching the **play-offs** with a 5-1 win at Sincil Bank. **Darlington** regain Football League status with a **1-0** victory at **Welling. Rangers** draw 1-1 at **Hearts** and create a **New Premier Division defensive record** by conceding only **19 goals this season**.

6   The Police, who made **120** arrests at **Bournemouth** and **Weymouth** on Saturday, complain that they warned the Football League about holding this particular fixture on a Bank Holiday week-end but their warnings were ignored. The **Football Lague** had also insisted that the game would start promptly at 3 pm. **League president Bill Fox** admits an "error" in not complying with police requests to change the date.

7   **Dorset's Chief Constable Brian Weight**, who blames the Football League for the week-end trouble on the South coast, says that in future the **fixture lists** should be **vetted** by the **police** before being issued. **UEFA president Lennart Johannson** is now **sceptical** about re-admitting English clubs into Europe and announces that a decision will be made at the **UEFA meeting** in **Vienna on 24 May**. Plans are unveiled for the new **65,000 all-seater stadium** in Strathclyde Park, Lanarkshire to replace Hampden Park.

8   **Football League** attendances in **1989-90** showed an increase on the previous season in all divisions except Division 3. The aggregate was 19,445,442 the highest since 1981-82. **John Duncan** becomes the first **Ipswich Town** manager ever to be sacked. **Sir Jack Hayward** completes his **£2.1m.** takeover of **Wolves** and the club's former England skipper **Billy Wright** joins the board.

9   **Mick Mills resigns** as **Colchester United manager** following their relegation from the Football League.

10 The **Scottish FA** fine **Rangers** manager **Graeme Soulness** a record **£5,000** for a furher breach of his touchline ban which is now extended until the end of season **1991-92**.

11 **Ipswich Town** appoint **John Lyall** as their new **manager. Cardiff City** will charge six players **£20** each to replace shirts they threw into the crowd after their **2-0** defeat at **Bury** which brings relegation to the Fourth Division. **Chester** hope to agree a two-year ground sharing deal with **Wrexham**.

12 **Ian Wright**, who has **twice broken his leg** this season, comes on as substitute in the 69th minute in the FA Cup Final to score an equaliser for **Crystal Palace** against **Manchester United** that takes the game into extra time with the sides level at **2-2**. The same player puts Palace ahead with another goal two minutes arter the re-start but Manchester United play their best football of the afternoon before **Mark Hughes** scores their equaliser and his second goal of the match. **Bryan Robson** misses with a header which should have brought United victory. The **Scottish Cup** is won for the first time in a **penalty shoot out** after **Aberdeen** and **Celtic** fail to score in **120 minutes** of scrappy football. **Aberdeen's Dutch goalkeeper Theo Snelders** saves Anton Rogan's kick and **Aberdeen's Brian Irvine** breaks the deadlock with the **20th kick** of the shoot-out. This means that **Celtic** will be **missing from Europe** for the first time in **12 years**.

13 As the League play-offs commence **six players** are booked and **Sunderland** defender **Paul Hardyman** is sent off in a dour derby battle with **Newcastle** which ends in a **goalless draw**. Indeed, four of the six play-off matches end in draws, the exceptions being **Swindon Town's 2-1** win against **Blackburn Rovers** in the Second Division and **Chesterfield's 4-0** victory over **Stockport County** in the Fourth Division with **Calvin Plummer** scoring a hat-trick.

15 While experimenting with their side, **England** just scrape a **1-0** victory over **Denmark** at Wembley as **Gary Lineker** saves the day with his **31st international goal**, **Walsall** appoint **Kenny Hibbitt as manager**.

16 It is reported that **Bobby Robson** will quit as **England manager** after the **World Cup** to manage **Dutch cup-holders PSV Eindhoven. Liam Brady** says farewell after appearing in **Republic of Ireland's 1-1** draw with **Finland** which added about **£250,000** to his testimonial after **72 international appearances. Scotland's** run-up to the World Cup is going badly and this time they suffer the shock of a humiliating **3-1** defeat by unfancied **Egypt** at **Aberdeen. Arsenal** make **David Seaman** England's most expensive goalkeeper when they sign him from **QPR** for **£1.3m.** The play-off finals will be between **Sunderland** (who beat Newcastle) and **Swindon** (beat Blackburn) for promotion to the First Division; **Notts County** (beat Bolton) and **Tranmere** (beat Bury) for promotion to the Second Division; and **Cambridge** and **Chesterfield** for a place in the Third Division. There is trouble at the end of the **Newcastle-Sunderland** derby as **fans invade the pitch** and a number of spectators and police are injured. **Falkirk** appoint **Jim Jefferies** from **Berwick Rangers** as their **new manager**.

17 **Manchester United** equal the record held jointly by **Aston Villa** and **Tottenham** by winning the **FA Cup** for the **seventh time**, beating **Crystal Palace 1-0** in a replay marred by fouls. The vital goal is scored by **Lee Martin** the only local signing in a **£13m.** line-up. Manager **Alex Ferguson** dropped goalkeeper **Jim Leighton** for this game and played **Les Sealey** on loan from **Luton Town**.

18 **Juventus** create a new **world transfer record** by signing Italian international midfielder **Roberto Baggio** from **Fiorentina** for **£7.7m**.

19 **Scottish** morale receives no boost from international which is a 1-1 draw with **Poland**. The visitors are gifted an equaliser by **Liverpool's Gary Gillespie** who sends the ball into his **own net**. **Barrow** play some attractive football to beat **Leek 3-0** and win the **FA Trophy** at **Wembley** in front of a crowd of **19,011**.

20 **Wales** win at last beating **Costa Rica 1-0** at Ninian Park with **Dean Saunders** the scorer. **Tranmere Rovers** win the **Leyland Daf Cup** at Wembley beating **Bristol Rovers 2-1** before a crowd of **48,402**, but the **Bristol Rovers'** captain is so angry at losing after two referees' decisions go against them that he tosses his medal away. Another player picks it up and returns it to him. **Lincoln City** manager **Colin Murphy** leaves the club.

21 **Bobby Robson** announces his **22** for the **World Cup** and biggest surprise is that he has left out **Arsenal's Tony Adams**.

22 **England's unbeaten run of 17 internationals** is brought to an end at **Wembley** by a skilful **Uruguay** who win **2-1** with **Peter Shilton** below his best in his **117th international**. **Luton Town** are bought out by two London property developers **Peter Nelkin** and **David Kohler**. Mr. Nelkin becomes the club's fourth chairman in a year, **Leeds United** make their first and most expensive signing in preparation for next season's First Division football by agreeing to buy back goalkeeper **John Lukic** from **Arsenal** for **£1m**. **Leeds** originally sold him to **Arsenal** for **£125,000**.

23 **Ruud Gullit** demonstrates that he has completely recovered from his operation by dominating the **European Cup final** in which **AC Milan** retain the trophy by defeating **Benfica 1-0**.

24 **Bobby Robson** confirms that he is joining **PSV Eindhoven** for around **£200,000** a year and at a Press conference he shows his anger at a story that he had resigned because a Suffolk divorcee was about to reveal details of an alleged five-year affair. He says that it is all rubbish and a scurrilous article.

25 Although on the short list, **Manchester City** manager **Howard Kendall** says he doesn't wish to be considered for the **England** job.

26 A solitary goal from **Dion Dublin** gives **Cambridge United** victory over **Chesterfield** at Wembley and promotion to the **Third Division**.

27 **Republic of Ireland** already have injury problems for the **World Cup** and these are aggravated in an uninspiring goalless draw with **Turkey** in the 106-degree furnace of the **Izmir's Ataturk Stadium**. **Notts County** win their way back to the **Second Division with a 2-0** victory over **Tranmere Rovers** at **Wembley** with **Tommy Johnson** scoring one and setting up the second for **Craig Short**.

28 **Swindon Town** win promotion to the First Division at the first attempt by beating **Sunderland 1-0** in the Second Division play-off final at Wembley in front of a crowd of **72,873**. A shot by **Alan McLoughlin** is deflected into his own net by **Gary Bennett** but Swindon thoroughly deserved this victory. **Scotland** are again disappointing as they beat **Malta 2-1** after conceding their fifth own goal of the season. Their **Bayern Munich** striker **Alan McInally** gets both of their goals.

29 **Arsenal's** assistant manager **Theo Foley** is appointed manager of **Northampton Town** the club he helped into the First Division as a full-back 25 years ago.

30 **Aston Villa** say they will want **£250,000** compensation from the FA if **Graham Taylor** is appointed England manager.

June

1 The **Football League AGM fails** to give the necessary two-thirds majority vote in favour of **Chelsea chairman Ken Bates'** proposal that the First Division should revert to **22 clubs**, but there was **only one vote** in it. A proposal that **TV fees** for live games should be more **evenly distributed** amongst the clubs was also **lost**.

2 **Steve Bull** saves England's embarrassment with a goal in the last minute in **Tunisia** to make it a 1-1 draw in this **World Cup** warm-up game. **Frank Stapleton** becomes the **Republic of Ireland's** all-time top scorer with his **20th international goal** as they win comfortably **3-0** in **Malta**.

3 **Hearts** shock the football fraternity by making a **£6.12m.** bid to takeover local rivals **Hibernian**. **Lincoln City** appoint **Allan Clarke** as manager.

5 **FIFA** announce a **scale of fines** for players cautioned twice or sent off in the **World Cup** finals. These range from **£2,115** for a player cautioned twice in the first round to **£12,600** for being sent off in the **semi-finals**, **final** and **third-place play-off**. **Hibernian** supporters launch a "Hands off Hibs" campaign to fight **Hearts'** takeover bid. **Gary McAllister** completes his transfer from **Leicester City** to **Leeds United** for **£1m**.

6 The board of **Hibernian** take a **majority though not unanimous vote** to **reject** the Hearts bid.

7 The **Football League** shock newly promoted **Swindon Town** by relegating them from the **First** to the **Third Division** following an eight-hour hearing after the club admit **36 breaches of League rules**, **35** involving **irregular payments** to players. **Peter Shilton's** hopes of creating a new world record of international appearances by beating Irish goalkeeper **Pat Jennings** total of **119** may be shocked by a **FIFA** announcement that they expect to confirm a figure of **129** by **Choi Soon Ho** a winger in **South Korea's** World Cup team.

8 Unfancied **Cameroon** provide the first shock of the World Cup tournament by beating Cup holders **Argentina 1-0** in Milan despite having two players sent off. The **Swindon** crisis deepens as the Football League announce that **further charges** may be brought against individuals with the club during the promotion season just ended and it is alleged that these could include manager **Ossie Ardiles**.

11 **England draw 1-1** with **Republic of Ireland** in a game in which the poor standard of football enrages soccer purists. Scotland's recent poor form lessens the shock of their **1-0** defeat by outsiders **Costa Rica**. **Blackpool** appoint **Graham Carr** as manager.

13 **Swindon Town** will apply for an **injunction** in the **High Court** to set aside the **Football League's** decision to relegate them to the Third Division. Meanwhile the League decide to **promote Sunderland** to the **First Division** in their place with **Tranmere Rovers** moving up into the **Second Division**.

INDEX OF SOME OF THE MORE INTERESTING DIARY ITEMS

THE FOOTBALL TRUST

During the next ten years facilities at British football grounds will undergo a dramatic transformation. Following the publication of Lord Justice Taylor's Final Report into the Hillsborough Stadium disaster the terrace, the traditional home for soccer spectators, will be replaced by seated accommodation at all League grounds. Major stadia will become all seater by 1994 with the remainder scheduled for conversion before the turn of the century.

The Football Trust has been given a lead role in overseeing the far reaching changes recommended by Taylor. The organisation, with its long and impressive tradition of helping the national game, has been entrusted with the responsibility for allocating funds arising from the Government's decision to reduce Pool Betting Duty in the Spring Budget.

Richard Faulkner, First Deputy Chairman, commented: "There were fears when conversion to all seater stadia was first announced that many clubs would be forced out of business. Whilst the game needs substantially more money, the funds from the football pools tax reduction will provide a major boost to safety at grounds. On present forecasts we expect to spend an extra £20 million each year on measures which are essential if Britain is to mount a serious challenge to stage future international tournaments."

Over the last decade the Football Trust has been funded by voluntary donations from the Spotting-the-Ball competition run by Littlewoods, Vernons and Zetters. Its annual budget, over £10 million, has been spent on a broad range of projects which included safety and improvements, anti-hooligan measures, community programmes and the development of the grass roots game.

This source of funding will continue and is added to the £20 million from the tax reduction. Of this £30 million, around £27.5 million will go to the professional game through a variety of grant-aid schemes – the great majority linked to the Taylor Report.

Immediately following the Chancellor's Budget, the establishment of The Football Trust 1990 was announced bringing together the former Football Trust and its sister body the Football Grounds Improvement Trust.

"The game needs a unified coherent approach when dealing with the new challenges facing it," commented Faulkner. "With the Government deciding to channel tax money through the Football Trust, it seemed sensible to approach the task of improving grounds and tackling hooliganism through a single body."

The Trust retained its uniquely representative make-up drawing together members from all areas of the game. The governing bodies in England and Scotland, the local authority associations, the police, professional players, pools companies and the Government now meet at least twelve times a year to discuss applications for grant-aid ranging from closed circuit television enhancement to kit and crutches for the England Amputee side, the current world champions.

Whilst requests for all kinds of assistance are examined by Trustees, the main priority is to facilitate the conversion to all seater stadia using the £100 million from the pools tax for this purpose over the next five years.

With the Taylor Report digested many clubs are now hard at work redesigning their existing facilities. "It's a very exciting time for British football," added Faulkner. "We now have the opportunity to plan our grounds with the modern needs of the supporter in mind. There will be a great many imaginative proposals to consider."

Early meetings of the new 1990 Trust augur well for the game at all levels. Most encouraging is the continued support for community projects. The much praised Football in the Community scheme run by the PFA, Footballers' Further Education and Vocational Training Society, the Football Association and the Football League is getting a massive £4 million boost from the Trust over two years. "Its value is the way it draws football and local people together," explained Richard Faulkner. "Social services such as OAP dances, artificial pitches for local use, women's football and even classrooms at a First Division ground are a few of the excellent projects undertaken. Community football is something we definitely want to promote and encourage."

The Football Trust's programme of activity for 1990–91 is wide ranging. In addition to community projects and implementing the Taylor Report, there will be more family enclosures, covered accommodation, toilets, areas for fans with disabilities, more grass roots pitches with changing rooms and a continued commitment to controlling and reducing hooligan activity.

Richard Faulkner concluded: "The season ahead will be one of the most important in the history of association football. A great deal of time is being invested researching and planning for the future. It's an opportunity the game will take full advantage of and the practical results of this endeavour will be there to judge over the next few years."

THE FOOTBALL LEAGUE

Featuring full details of each of the 92 clubs in the Football League.

Officials, statistics, 1989–90 team photo, full 1989–90 League record and career details of the players.

THE FOOTBALL LEAGUE OFFICIALS

Chief Executive
A. Sandford

President
W. Fox (*Blackburn Rovers*)

Life Vice-Presidents
L. C. Cearns
H. E. McGee
Sir Arthur South
R. Wragg

Management Committee
K. W. Bates (*Chelsea*)
R. T. Chase JP (*Norwich City*)
H. D. Ellis (*Aston Villa*)
W. G. McKeag BA Cantab. (*Newcastle United*)
M. D. B. Sinclair (*York City*)
Sir J. W. Smith CBE, JP, DL (*Liverpool*)
I. H. Stott (*Oldham Athletic*)

Life Members
Sir Matt Busby CBE, KCSG
E. M. Gliksten
N. J. Thomas
The Rt Hon Lord Westwood JP, FCIS
J. F. Wiseman
F. A. Would
R. Wragg

Secretary
David Dent

LEAGUE REVIEW

Although the championship failed to provide the nail-biting, last-minute excitement of the previous season, there was drama enough at the foot of the First Division and sufficient scrambling for play-off places and frenzy to avoid relegation in other divisions to maintain interest in the competition as a whole. Liverpool won their 18th title to compensate for their late disappointment in 1988–89, revealing at times their most fluent and effective qualities which have become a trade mark at Anfield in modern terms, but they lacked the consistency which had featured in other championship campaigns.

Indeed they might well have lost out in the race to Aston Villa who in mid-February had two matches in hand of Liverpool and were only a point behind them. But on 24 February, Villa entertained Wimbledon at Villa Park and were well beaten 3-0. Even so they had a two points lead over their rivals and both teams had completed 26 games.

Liverpool rarely give their opponents more than one chance of catching them, though they did slip up again when beaten 1-0 at Tottenham on 21 March. But this was their only reverse in 23 matches from early December and though it might seem at variance to accuse a team of lacking consistency when it clearly showed the opposite in results, the 1989–90 vintage Liverpool was not one of its most memorable seasons.

In truth, Liverpool are judged by their own high standards. Unfair as this might seem, it remains a reality. There was one newcomer of note at Anfield in the shape of the greying Glenn Hysen, a Swedish international centre-back from Fiorentina of vast experience and the type of equitable temperament one expects from a Scandinavian. If he had a weakness it was in pace.

However Liverpool made a fine start to the season and on Tuesday 12 September they annihilated Crystal Palace 9-0. Eight players managed to figure on the scoresheet including Hysen and even John Aldridge was called off the substitutes bench to score with his first kick from the penalty spot before he was to bid farewell to Liverpool and join Real Sociedad in Spain. Yet only a month later Liverpool were well beaten 4-1 at Southampton where the Saints flank forwards Matthew Le Tissier and Rodney Wallace ran riot through the Liverpool rearguard. This was Liverpool's heaviest defeat of the season, though they also had a more than uncomfortable time of it in the FA Cup semi-final when Crystal Palace exacted sweet revenge upon them and exposed the vulnerability of the Anfield defence to aerial attack.

But apart from losing 3-2 at Queen's Park Rangers in November, Liverpool did not concede more than two goals in any one other League game and given the traditional eccentricities of goalkeeper Bruce Grobbelaar, it said little for the challengers to this Merseyside domination, that more pressure was not put upon them.

Alan Hansen returned to the back four at the start of the season following absence with injury until late in 1988–89, but was not fully fit though he never seemed in any distress and his training was restricted because of his knee problems. But Steve Nicol was hit by injuries himself and missed a third of the programme. Apart from Grobbelaar only Steve McMahon appeared in all 38 League games.

Peter Beardsley and John Barnes looked unplayable at times but Beardsley lost form towards the latter part of the season and also suffered with a niggling injury. It was then that Manager Kenny Dalglish persuaded the Israeli international Ronny Rosenthal to join them on trial. After an impressive run-out in the reserves he was given a game as substitute against Southampton. Two games later he deputised for Ian Rush at centre-forward and scored a hat-trick against Charlton Athletic in a 4-0 win at Selhurst Park. Quick, elusive and strong on the ball, Rosenthal looked a fine prospect. He had been loaned out by Standard Liege in Belgium and had previously had a trial at Luton. At the end of the season he had made eight appearances, three of them as substitute and scored six times, his most telling contribution coming from his appearance as substitute at Highbury against Arsenal on 18 April when he transformed what appeared to be a lethargic Liverpool side into one which salvaged a valuable point.

Defending champions Arsenal never looked a serious threat even when they headed the table for a month or so from the middle of November. George Graham their manager again relied on the players who had snatched victory from the jaws of defeat the previous season, but had a poor second half to the campaign and had to be content with fourth place. One record broken at Highbury was the appearance record set up by George Armstrong and beaten on the last day of the season when David O'Leary came on as substitute at Norwich for his 501st League appearance. Oddly enough in the home game with Norwich he had beaten Armstrong's League and Cup record on his 622nd outing. This game ended

Ronnie Rosenthal breathed new life into Liverpool at a vital period late in the season. Here he leaps over Brian Law (QPR). (USPA)

in a free-for-all among the players following a last minute penalty which led to Arsenal winning 4-3. Both clubs were heavily fined for this disgraceful incident.

Discipline at times was far short of what was considered acceptable, the toll of sendings-off reaching a frighteningly high total. But the most pleasing aspect again concerned attendances which rose for the fourth successive season; something unprecedented in the post-war era. The final figure of 19.4 million was the best since 1981–82 when the figure had reached 20 million.

Manchester United were the best supported team with an average attendance of 39,077 despite spending much of the season dangerously close to the relegation zone. Liverpool came next with 36,589, Arsenal third with 33,713.

Aston Villa, who had to settle for runners-up spot, took time to settle but enjoyed a fine spell mid-season which included seven consecutive wins. My *Sunday Telegraph* colleague Colin Malam reckoned that a team selected from the best Villa and Southampton players might have provided Liverpool with a testing experience in what was certainly a sub-standard season. The Saints also failed when consistency was required and finished seventh.

The relegation writing was on Millwall quite early, but incredibly they were top of the table at the beginning of September. Yet they managed only one win in the last 31 games and had transferred Tony Cascarino for £1.5 million to Aston Villa before the transfer deadline. Millwall also had three managers during the season. They were accompanied by Charlton Athletic, past-masters of the escape routine, but caught in the trap at last. Not so Luton Town who left it until the last match before they survived.

The situation was that on the last day of the season they had to win at Derby and hope Sheffield Wednesday were beaten at home by Nottingham Forest. Wednesday required only a point for survival. In the end it was easy for Luton who won 3-2 while Forest might have won more easily than the scoreline of 3-0 suggested at Hillsborough. Sheffield's troubles had their roots earlier on when they had scored only two goals in the first 11 games, yet astonishingly had won a record away win in the Littlewoods Cup at Aldershot 8-0, having been held by the Fourth Division club to a goalless draw at Hillsborough in the first leg of their tie!

Aldershot faced a financial crisis late in the season and a succession of winding-up orders in the summer which threatened their existence. At Chester City there were problems of a different nature; having had to sell their ground to survive they found attempts to find a

54

temporary home were badly hit. The police vetoed a move to share with Wrexham and Chester then tried Widnes Rugby League club before finally getting approval to move in with Macclesfield of the GM Vauxhall Conference.

But back to the action and if Sheffield was to lose one club from the First Division, they gained another as Sheffield United accompanied another Yorkshire club Leeds United from the Second Division. Leeds had a successful season marred when some of their followers rioted on the weekend of their last game of the season at Bournemouth. The third promoted club eventually became Sunderland, because Swindon Town were finding themselves having to admit guilt over irregular payments to players and officials.

Swindon did manage to successfully appeal to the FA to retain Second Division membership, but the whole affair cast a shadow over half the season and re-opened the rift between the Football League and FA. The West Country club had offered to forego the play-offs because of the pending inquiry, but had they not won through, they might have found themselves relegated to Division Four!

While there was disappointment in the north-east for Newcastle United fans who saw their side fail to make it back into Division One, Middlesbrough saved themselves by beating United 4-1 on the last day of the season and so it was Bournemouth, Bradford City and Stoke City who became the three teams relegated from Division Two.

Swindon's problems out west did not deter Bristol. Rovers won the championship of Division Three and City finished runners-up. Cardiff City, Northampton Town, Blackpool and Walsall were demoted. Walsall then prepared to move to their new headquarters Bescot Stadium. There was more cause for celebration in the West country as Exeter City ran away with the Fourth Division finishing ten points ahead of Grimsby Town. Southend United went up automatically with them and Maidstone United finished a creditable fifth in their first season as members of the Football League. Colchester United dropped out to be replaced by Darlington from the GM Vauxhall Conference who had only been relegated themselves the previous season.

Individual records continued to be broken. At Tranmere Ian Muir overhauled the pre-war scoring record of Bunny Bell with 105 League goals, Mel Pejic broke the appearance record at Hereford while at Plymouth, Kevin Hodges equalled their appearance record.

David O'Leary (second from right) in aerial action for Arsenal against Charlton's Robert Lee (right). O'Leary broke the Arsenal appearance record, previously held by George Armstrong. (Colorsport)

INTRODUCTION TO THE CLUB SECTION

The full page team photographs which appear on the first of each club's six pages in this section of the yearbook were taken at the beginning of the 1989–90 season, and therefore relate to the season covered by this edition's statistics.

The third and fourth pages of each club's section give a complete record of the League season for the club concerned, including date, venue, opponents, result, half-time score, League position, goalscorers, attendance and complete line-ups, including substitutes where used, for every League game in the 1989–90 season. These two pages also include consolidated lists of goalscorers for the club in League, Littlewoods Cup and FA Cup matches and a summary of results in the two main domestic cups. The full League history of the club, a full list of major honours won and best placings achieved, and a note of the team's first and second choice colours appear on the second page of this section. The colours are checked with the clubs, but please note that second choice colours may vary during the season.

Note also that the League position shown after each League result is re-calculated as at every Saturday night plus full holiday programmes, but the position after mid-week fixtures will not normally be up-dated. Please be advised that the attendance figures quoted for each League game are those which appeared in the Press at the time, whereas the attendance statistics published on pages 634 and 635 are those issued officially by the Football League after the season has been completed. However, the figures for each League game are those used by the Football League in their weekly bulletin, in conjunction with the *Sunday Telegraph* and Jack Rollin's column in that newspaper.

On the fourth page of each club's section, the total League appearances for the season are listed at the foot of each player's column. Substitutes are inserted as numbers 12 and 14 where they actually came on to play. The players taken off are respectively given an asterisk (*) and a dagger (†). But in order to give the chart a uniform appearance, where only one substitute has played the number 12 will have been used. Some clubs, Aston Villa for example, have used 13 as their second substitute number, but again for purposes of uniformity, they appear as 14.

In the totals at the foot of each column, substitute appearances are listed separately below the '+' sign, but have been amalgamated in the totals which feature in the player's historical section on the final page for each club.

The final pages for each club lists all the players included on the Football League's 'Retained' list, which is published at the end of May. Here you will find each player's height and weight, where known plus birthplace, birthdate and source, together with total League appearances and goals for each club he has represented. Full names of all other players retained including trainees, non-contract players and schoolboys are also given. In addition more club information is added on these pages

Any transfers which take place between the publication of the League's Retained list and this book going to press will be included in the transfer section between pages 625 and 633, but the player's details will remain under the club which retained him at the end of the season. An asterisk * by a player's name on the fifth and sixth pages mean that he was given a free transfer at the end of the 1988–89 season, a dagger † against a name means that he is a non-contract player, and a double dagger ‡ indicates that the player's registration was cancelled during the season. An § indicates either a Trainee or an Associated Schoolboy who has made Football League appearances.

The play-offs in the Football League are listed separately on pages 612 and 613. Appearances made by players in these play-offs will *not* be included in their career totals on 'page four'.

Four pages, have been included for Darlington, who have returned to the League.

Editor's note: In the Scottish League, two substitutes have been allowed for several seasons. Substitutes where used are listed as 12 and 14. The second player to be taken off is also picked out with a dagger.

ALDERSHOT 1989–90 *Back row (left to right):* Jimmy Devereux, Paul Coombs, David Coles, Steve Osgood, Charlie Henry, Richard Hunt. *Centre row:* Kevan Brown, Jerry Williams, Steve Claridge, Steven Beeks, Dale Banton, Steve Wignall, Adrian Randall, Darren Anderson. *Front row:* Kahota Dumbuya, Daren Hewitt, David Puckett, Colin Smith, Glen Burvill, Ian Phillips, Ian Stewart.

Division 4   **ALDERSHOT**

Recreation Ground, High St., Aldershot GU11 1TW. Telephone Aldershot (0252) 20211. Club call 0898 12 16 30. Aldershot Promotions (0252) 311992

Record attendance: 19,138 v Carlisle U, FA Cup 4th rd replay, 28 January 1970.

Record receipts: £22,949.66 v Sheffield W, Littlewoods Cup, 2nd rd, 2d leg, 3 October, 1989.

Ground capacity: 12,000 (10,000 under cover).

Pitch measurements: 116yd × 76yd.

President: Arthur English.

Chairman: C. Hancock BDS (Lon).

Directors: K. J. Chapman FCA, M. R. Lee.

Team Manager: Len Walker.

Secretary: Jon Pollard.

Team coach: . *Physio:* Jim Lange, Grad. Phys. Dip. MCSP, SRP.

Youth team coach: Ian McDonald. *Marketing and Commercial Manager:*

Year Formed: 1926. *Turned Professional:* 1927. *Ltd Co.:* 1927.

Club Nickname: 'Shots'.

Record League Victory: 8-1 v Gateshead, Division 4, 13 September 1958 – Marshall; Henry, Jackson; Mundy, Price, Gough; Walters, Stepney (3), Lacey (3), Matthews (2), Tyrer.

Record Cup Victory: 7-0 v Chelmsford, FA Cup, 1st rd, 28 November 1931 – Robb; Twine, McDougall (1); Norman Wilson, Gardiner, Middleton (1); Blackbourne, Stevenson (1), Thorn (3), Hopkins (1), Edgar. 7-0 v Newport (I of W)., FA Cup, 2nd rd, 8 December 1945 – Reynolds; Horton, Sheppard; Ray, White, Summerbee: Sinclair, Hold (1), Brooks (5), Fitzgerald, Hobbs (1).

Record Defeat: 0-9 v Bristol C, Division 3(S), 28 December 1946.

Most League Points (2 for a win): 57, Division 4, 1978–9.

Most League Points (3 for a win): 75, Division 4, 1983–84.

Most League Goals: 83, Division 4, 1963–64.

Highest League Scorer in Season: John Dungworth, 26, Division 4, 1978–79.

Most League Goals in Total Aggregate: Jack Howarth, 171, 1965–71 and 1972–77.

Most Capped Player: Peter Scott, 1 (10), Northern Ireland.

Most League Appearances: Murray Brodie, 461, 1970–83.

Record Transfer Fee Received: £150,000 from Wolverhampton W for Tony Lange, July 1989.

Record Transfer Fee Paid: £54,000 to Portsmouth for Colin Garwood, February 1980.

Football League Record: 1932 Elected to Division 3(S); 1958–73 Division 4; 1973–76 Division 3; 1976–87 Division 4; 1987–89 Division 3; 1989– Division 4.

Honours: Football League: best season: 8th, Division 3, 1973–74. *FA Cup:* best season: 5th rd, 1932–33, 5th rd replay, 1978–79. *Football League Cup:* best season: 3rd rd replay 1984–85.

Colours: Red shirts, Royal blue trim, blue shorts red trim, red stockings with Royal blue trim. **Change colours:** All yellow.

ALDERSHOT 1989–90 LEAGUE RECORD

Match No.	Date	Venue	Opponents	Result		H/T Score	Lg. Pos.	Goalscorers	Atten-dance
1	Aug 19	A	Gillingham	D	0-0	0-0	—		3670
2	26	H	Lincoln C	L	0-1	0-0	19		1786
3	Sept 2	A	Peterborough U	D	1-1	1-1	17	Puckett (pen)	3787
4	9	H	Southend U	L	0-5	0-2	21		2255
5	16	A	Chesterfield	L	0-2	0-1	22		2822
6	23	H	Stockport Co	W	2-1	0-1	21	Randall, Puckett	1879
7	26	A	Doncaster R	W	1-0	1-0	—	Banton	1960
8	30	H	Scunthorpe U	W	4-2	2-0	12	Puckett, Claridge 3	1892
9	Oct 7	H	Colchester U	W	4-0	2-0	10	Puckett 2 (1 pen), Wignall, Burvill	2092
10	14	A	Wrexham	D	2-2	0-1	10	Phillips, Claridge	1416
11	17	A	York C	D	2-2	1-1	—	Claridge, Puckett (pen)	2788
12	21	H	Torquay U	L	1-2	0-0	12	Puckett	2244
13	28	A	Burnley	D	0-0	0-0	13		6451
14	31	H	Carlisle U	W	1-0	0-0	—	Henry	2123
15	Nov 4	A	Cambridge U	D	2-2	0-2	13	Henry, Burvill	2565
16	11	H	Hartlepool U	W	6-1	3-0	12	Brown, Puckett 2 (1 pen), Claridge 3	2132
17	25	A	Grimsby T	L	1-2	1-2	12	Puckett	3716
18	Dec 2	H	Halifax T	W	2-0	1-0	11	Claridge 2	1749
19	26	H	Exeter C	L	0-1	0-1	15		3101
20	30	H	Rochdale	D	1-1	1-0	14	Puckett	2095
21	Jan 1	A	Maidstone U	L	1-5	1-3	16	Henry	2206
22	6	A	Scarborough	L	0-1	0-0	—		1623
23	13	A	Lincoln C	W	1-0	0-0	15	Puckett (pen)	3188
24	20	H	Gillingham	W	1-0	0-0	14	Puckett (pen)	2592
25	27	A	Southend U	L	0-5	0-3	15		2821
26	Feb 3	A	Stockport Co	D	1-1	0-0	15	Burvill	2771
27	10	H	Chesterfield	D	0-0	0-0	16		1992
28	17	A	Halifax T	L	1-4	0-3	16	Coombs	1275
29	24	H	Grimsby T	D	0-0	0-0	17		1858
30	27	H	Peterborough U	L	0-1	0-0	—		1138
31	Mar 3	A	Hereford U	L	1-4	1-2	19	Brown	2368
32	6	A	Scunthorpe U	L	2-3	0-1	—	Phillips, Randall	3202
33	10	H	Doncaster R	D	1-1	1-0	18	Puckett (pen)	1512
34	17	A	Colchester U	L	0-1	0-0	20		2682
35	24	H	York C	D	2-2	0-1	20	Anderson, Henry	1556
36	27	H	Wrexham	W	1-0	0-0	—	Puckett	1776
37	31	A	Torquay U	W	2-1	0-0	18	Puckett 2	2086
38	Apr 6	H	Burnley	D	1-1	1-1	—	Baker	2325
39	10	A	Carlisle U	W	3-1	1-1	—	Henry, Puckett, Williams	4998
40	14	H	Maidstone U	L	0-2	0-0	18		2334
41	16	A	Exeter C	L	0-2	0-1	19		6832
42	21	H	Scarborough	D	1-1	0-0	19	Baker	1482
43	24	A	Rochdale	L	0-2	0-0	—		1419
44	28	A	Hartlepool U	L	0-2	0-1	22		2770
45	May 1	H	Hereford U	L	0-2	0-1	—		1412
46	5	H	Cambridge U	L	0-2	0-1	22		3208

Final League Position: 22

GOALSCORERS

League (49): Puckett 18 (7 pens), Claridge 10, Henry 5, Burvill 3, Baker 2, Brown 2, Phillips 2, Randall 2, Anderson 1, Banton 1, Coombs 1, Wignall 1, Williams 1.
Littlewoods Cup (6): Puckett 3 (1 pen), Coyne 1, Henry 1, own goal 1.
FA Cup (0).

Coles	Brown	Phillips	Burvill	Smith	Wignall	Williams	Puckett	Claridge	Henry	Stewart	Coyne	Banton	Randall	Sheffield	Anderson	Coombs	Hunt	Devereux	Ogley	Powell	Beeney	Baker	Beeks	Match No.
1	2	3	4	5	6	7	8	9	10	11														1
1	2	3		5	6	7*	8	9	10	11	4	12												2
1		3	2	5	6	7	8	12	10	11*	4	9												3
1	2*	3	14	5	6†	7	8	12	10	11	4	9												4
1	2	3	4*	5	6	7	8	12	10	11†		9	14											5
	2	3	4	5	6	7†	8	12	10	11*		9	14	1										6
	2	3	4	5	6		8	7	10			9	11	1										7
	2	3	4	5	6	10	8	7		12		9*	11	1										8
	2	3	4	5	6	10*	8	7		12		9	11	1										9
	2	3	4	5	6		8	7	10			9	11	1										10
	2	3	4	5	6		8	7	10	11		9		1										11
	2	3	4	5	6		8	7*	10	11		9†		1	12	14								12
	2	3	4	5	6		8	7	10	11		9*	12	1										13
	2	3	4	5*	6		8	7	10	14		9†	11	1	12									14
	2	3	4		6*		8	7	10	9			11	1	5	12								15
	2	3·	4		6		8	7	10	9*			11	1	5†	12		14						16
1	2	3			6		8	7	10	9		11					4		5					17
1	2	3	10		6		8	7	4	9		11							5					18
1	2	3	10	12	6*		8	7	4	9		11							5					19
1	2	3	10		6		8	7	4	9		11							5					20
1	2	3	4		6		8*	7†	10	9		12	11			14			5					21
1	2	3			6		8	7	4	9		10	11						5					22
1	2				6	9	8	7	10	4*		12	11						5	3				23
1	2				6	4	8	7	10	9			11						5	3				24
1	2	10	4		6		8*	7		9			11		12				5	3				25
1	2	3	4		6		8			9			11			7			5	10				26
1	2	3			6		8		10	9		12	11			7*			5	4				27
1	2	3	4				8		10	9		12	11*		6	7			5					28
1	2*	3	4	12			8		10	9					6	7			5	11				29
1		2	4		6		8		10	9		11				7			5	3				30
1	2	3	4*	12	5	14	8		10	9					6	7†				11				31
1	2	3		5	6	7	8		10	9		11								4				32
1		3	12	5	6	7	8		10	9		11								2	4*			33
1		3		5	6	7	8		10	9		11								2	4			34
	12	3		5	6	7	8		10	9		11†			14					2*	1	4		35
	2	3		5*	6	7	8		10	9		11							12		1	4		36
	2	3			6	7	8		10	9		11							5		1	4		37
	2	3			6	7	8		10	9		11*			12				5		1	4		38
	2	3			6	7	8		10	9		11							5		1	4		39
1	2	3	12		6	7	8		10	9		11*							5			4		40
	2	3	4		6	7	8		10	9*		11			12				5		1			41
	2	3	12		6	7	8			9		11*			14	10†			5		1	4		42
1	2	3	4	14	6	11	8		10	9*		12				7†			5					43
1	2	3	4	6		11†	8*		10	9		12				7		14	5					44
1	2	3	4	6			8		10			7				9	11*		5				12	45
1	2	3	4	6			8		10	9		11				7			5					46
28	41	44	29	22	37	27	46	21	40	40	3	16	31	11	10	7	1	—	27	11	7	7	—	
+1s			+4s	+3s	+1s	+1s		+4s				+3s	+7s	+3s	+6s	+5s	+1s	+1s	+1s			+1s		

Littlewoods Cup   First Round   Peterborough U (a)   0-2
                                                         (h)   6-2
                    Second Round   Sheffield W (a)   0-0
                                                          (h)   0-8

FA Cup   First Round   Cambridge U (h)   0-1

ALDERSHOT

Player and Position	Ht	Wt	Birth Date	Place	Source	Clubs	League App	Gls
Goalkeepers								
David Coles	5 10	12 00	15 6 64	Wandsworth	Apprentice	Birmingham C	—	—
						Mansfield T	3	—
						Aldershot	120	—
						Newport Co (loan)	14	—
					HJK Helsinki	Crystal Palace	—	—
						Brighton & HA	1	—
						Aldershot	28	—
Steve Osgood†	6 0	12 00	20 1 62	Surrey	Farnborough	Aldershot	1	—
Defenders								
Darren Anderson*	6 1	13 05	6 9 66	Merton	Apprentice	Coventry C	—	—
						Charlton Ath	10	1
						Crewe Alex (loan)	5	—
						Aldershot	98	4
Kevan Brown	5 9	11 08	2 1 66	Andover		Southampton	—	—
						Brighton & HA	53	—
						Aldershot	70	2
Jimmy Devereux*	6 4	13 00	20 2 70	Aldershot	Trainee	Aldershot	2	—
Richard Hunt*	6 0	12 10	5 1 71	Reading	QPR§	Aldershot	2	—
Mark Ogley	5 10	11 02	10 3 67	Barnsley	Apprentice	Barnsley	19	—
						Aldershot (loan)	8	—
						Carlisle U	33	1
						Aldershot	28	—
Ian Phillips*	5 9	11 12	23 4 59	Kilwinning	Apprentice	Ipswich T	—	—
						Mansfield T	23	—
						Peterborough U	97	3
						Northampton T	42	1
						Colchester U	150	10
						Aldershot	106	2
Colin Smith*	6 0	12 10	3 11 58	Ruddington	Local	Nottingham F	—	—
						Norwich C	4	—
					See Bee	Cardiff C	50	3
						Aldershot	190	4
Steve Wignall	5 11	12 01	17 9 54	Liverpool	Amateur	Liverpool	—	—
						Doncaster R	130	1
						Nottingham F (loan)	—	—
						Colchester U	281	22
						Brentford	67	2
						Aldershot	147	4
Midfield								
Steve Beeks	5 10	11 05	10 4 71	Ashford	Trainee	Aldershot	1	—
Glen Burvill	5 9	10 10	26 10 62	Canning Town	Apprentice	West Ham U	—	—
						Aldershot	65	15
						Reading	30	—
						Fulham (loan)	9	2
						Aldershot	154	21
Kahota Dumbuya‡	5 7	10 06	10 7 71	Sierra Leone	Trainee	Aldershot	—	—
Charlie Henry	5 11	12 08	13 2 62	Acton	Apprentice	Swindon T	223	26
						Torquay U (loan)	6	1
						Northampton T (loan)	4	1
						Aldershot	40	5
Daren Hewitt‡	5 8	11 06	1 9 69	Chichester	Trainee	Aldershot	2	—
Ian McDonald†	5 9	11 09	10 5 53	Barrow	Apprentice	Barrow	35	2
						Workington	42	4
						Liverpool	—	—
						Colchester U (loan)	5	2
						Mansfield T	56	4
						York C	175	29
						Aldershot	340	49

Foundation: It was through the initiative of Councillor Jack White, a local newsagent who immediately captured the interest of the Town Clerk D. Llewellyn Griffiths, that Aldershot Town was formed in 1926. Having established a limited liability company under the chairmanship of Norman Clinton, an Aldershot resident and chairman of the Hampshire County FA they rented the Recreation Ground from the Aldershot Borough Council.

First Football League game: 27 August, 1932, Division 3(S), v Southend U (h) L 1-2 – Robb; Wade, McDougall; Lawson, Spence, Middleton; Proud, White, Gamble, Douglas, Fishlock (1).

Managers (and Secretary-managers)
Angus Seed 1927–37, Bill McCracken 1937–49, Gordon Clark 1950–55, Harry Evans 1955–59, Dave Smith 1959–71 (GM from 1967), Tommy McAnearney 1967–68, Jimmy Melia 1968–72, Tommy McAnearney 1972–81, Len Walker 1981–84, Ron Harris (GM) 1984–85, Len Walker 1985–   .

Player and Position	Ht	Wt	Birth Date	Place	Source	Clubs	League App	Gls
Jerry Williams	5 11	11 10	24 3 60	Didcot	Apprentice	Reading	309	17
						Gillingham	13	—
						Aldershot	28	1
Forwards								
Dale Banton	5 8	11 00	15 5 61	Kensington	Apprentice	West Ham U	5	—
						Aldershot	106	47
						York C	138	48
						Walsall	10	—
						Grimsby T (loan)	8	1
						Aldershot	23	1
Billy Beggs‡			27 8 67	Ballymena	QPR	Charlton Ath	—	—
						Aldershot	—	—
Paul Coombs	5 11	12 07	4 9 70	Bristol	QPR§	Aldershot	13	1
Paul Holsgrove	6 1	12 00	26 8 69	Wellington	Trainee	Aldershot	3	—
						Wimbledon (loan)	—	—
						WBA (loan)	—	—
David Puckett	5 7	10 05	29 10 60	Southampton	Apprentice	Southampton	95	14
						Nottingham F (loan)	—	—
						Bournemouth	35	14
						Stoke C (loan)	7	—
						Swansea (loan)	8	3
						Aldershot	67	29
Adrian Randall	5 11	11 00	10 11 68	Amesbury	Apprentice	Bournemouth	3	—
						Aldershot	71	4
Ian Stewart	5 7	11 09	10 9 61	Belfast	Juniors	QPR	67	2
						Millwall (loan)	11	3
						Newcastle U	42	3
						Portsmouth	1	—
						Brentford (loan)	7	—
						Aldershot	65	—

Trainees
Barham, David L, Cable, Gary; Cleeve, David; Fisher, Alex J; Jenkinson, Robert R; Kirby, Mark L; Payne, Simon J; Terry, Peter E; Wright, Craig A.

**Non-Contract
McDonald, Ian C; Osgood, Stephen.

Associated Schoolboys
Birmingham, Michael J; Lucas, Kevin G; Stabb, Matthew J.

**Non-Contract Players who are retained must be re-signed before they are eligible to play in League matches.

ARSENAL 1989–90 *Back row (left to right):* Theo Foley (Assistant Manager), Kevin Richardson, Tony Adams, Steve Bould, Alan Smith, Niall Quinn, David O'Leary, Martin Hayes, Kevin Campbell, Michael Thomas, Gary Lewin (Physiotherapist).

Front row: John Lukic, Perry Groves, Nigel Winterburn, Gus Caesar, Lee Dixon, George Graham (Manager), Paul Merson, Paul Davis, David Rocastle, Brian Marwood, Alan Miller.

Division 1 **ARSENAL**

Arsenal Stadium, Highbury, London N5. Telephone 071-226 0304. Recorded information on 01-359 0131. Club call 0898 12 11 70.

Ground Capacity: 47,193.

Record attendance: 73,295 v Sunderland, Div 1, 9 March, 1935.

Record receipts: £233,595 v Everton, Littlewoods Cup Semi-Final, 24 Feb 1988.

Pitch measurements: 110yd × 71yd.

Chairman: P. D. Hill-Wood. *Vice-Chairman:* D. Dein.

Directors: Sir Robert Bellinger CBE, DSC, R. G. Gibbs, C. E. B. L. Carr, R. C. S. Carr.

Managing Director: K. J. Friar.

Manager: George Graham. *Assistant Manager: Coach:* Stewart Houston.

Physio: Gary Lewin. *Reserve Coach:* George Armstrong. *Youth Coach:* Pat Rice.

Secretary: K. J. Friar. *Assistant Secretary:* David Miles. *Commercial Manager:* John Hazell.

Marketing Manager: Phil Carling.

Formed: 1886. *Turned Professional:* 1891. *Ltd Co.:* 1893.

Former Names: 1886 Dial Square; 1886–91, Royal Arsenal; 1891–1914, Woolwich Arsenal.

Club Nickname: 'Gunners'.

Former Grounds: 1886–87, Plumstead Common; 1887–88, Sportsman Ground; 1888–90, Manor Ground; 1890–93, Invicta Ground; 1893–1913, Manor Ground; 1913– Highbury.

Record League Victory: 12-0 v Loughborough T, Division 2, 12 March 1900 – Orr; McNichol, Jackson; Moir, Dick (2), Anderson (1); Hunt, Cottrell (2), Main (2), Gaudie (3), Tennant (2).

Record Cup Victory: 11-1 v Darwen, FA Cup, 3rd rd, 9 January 1932 – Moss; Parker, Hapgood; Jones, Roberts, John; Hulme (2), Jack (3), Lambert (2), James, Bastin (4).

Record Defeat: 0-8 v Loughborough T, Division 2, 12 December, 1896.

Most League Points (2 for a win): 66, Division 1, 1930–31.

Most League Points (3 for a win): 76, Division 1, 1988–89.

Most League Goals: 127. Division 1, 1930–31.

Highest League Scorer in Season: Ted Drake, 42, 1934–35.

Most League Goals in Total Aggregate: Cliff Bastin, 150, 1930–47.

Most Capped Player: Kenny Sansom, 77 (86), England.

Most League Appearances: David O'Leary, 501, 1975–90.

Record Transfer Fee Received: £1,250,000 from Crystal Palace for Clive Allen, August 1980.

Record Transfer Fee Paid: £1,250,000 to QPR for Clive Allen, June 1980.

Football League Record: 1893 Elected to Division 2; 1904–13 Division 1; 1913–19 Division 2; 1919–Division 1.

Honours: Football League: Division 1 – Champions 1930–31, 1932–33, 1933–34, 1934–35, 1937–38, 1947–48, 1952–53, 1970–71, 1988–89; Runners-up 1925–26, 1931–32, 1972–73; Division 2 – Runners-up 1903–04, *FA Cup:* Winners 1929–30, 1935–36,1949–50, 1970–71, 1978–79; Runners-up 1926–27, 1931–32, 1951–52, 1971–72, 1977–78, 1979–80. *Double Performed:* 1970–71. *League Cup:* Winners 1986–87; Runners-up 1967–68, 1968–69, 1987–88. **European Competitions:** *Fairs Cup:* 1963–64, 1969–70 (winners), 1970–71; *European Cup:* 1971–72; *UEFA Cup:* 1978–79, 1981–82, 1982–83; *European Cup-Winners' Cup:* 1979–80 (runners-up).

Colours: Red shirts with white sleeves, white shorts, red stockings. **Change colours:** Yellow shirts, navy blue shorts, yellow stockings.

ARSENAL 1989–90 LEAGUE RECORD

Match No.	Date	Venue	Opponents	Result	H/T Score	Lg. Pos.	Goalscorers	Attendance
1	Aug 19	A	Manchester U	L 1-4	1-1	—	Rocastle	47,245
2	22	H	Coventry C	W 2-0	0-0	—	Marwood, Thomas	33,886
3	26	H	Wimbledon	D 0-0	0-0	12		32,279
4	Sept 9	H	Sheffield W	W 5-0	1-0	8	Merson, Adams, Marwood, Thomas, Smith	30,058
5	16	A	Nottingham F	W 2-1	1-1	6	Merson, Marwood	22,216
6	23	H	Charlton Ath	W 1-0	0-0	4	Marwood (pen)	34,583
7	30	A	Chelsea	D 0-0	0-0	3		31,833
8	Oct 14	H	Manchester C	W 4-0	1-0	2	Groves 2, Thomas, Merson	14,414
9	18	A	Tottenham H	L 1-2	0-2	—	Thomas	33,944
10	21	A	Everton	L 0-3	0-1	5		32,917
11	28	H	Derby Co	D 1-1	1-0	4	Smith	33,189
12	Nov 4	H	Norwich C	W 4-3	0-2	3	Quinn, Dixon 2 (1 pen), O'Leary	35,338
13	11	A	Millwall	W 2-1	1-1	2	Thomas, Quinn	17,265
14	18	H	QPR	W 3-0	1-0	1	Smith, Dixon (pen), Jonsson	38,236
15	26	A	Liverpool	L 1-2	0-1	—	Smith	35,983
16	Dec 3	H	Manchester U	W 1-0	1-0	—	Groves	34,484
17	9	A	Coventry C	W 1-0	0-0	1	Merson	16,255
18	16	H	Luton T	W 3-2	2-1	1	Smith, Merson, Marwood	28,761
19	26	A	Southampton	L 0-1	0-0	2		20,229
20	30	A	Aston Villa	L 1-2	0-1	3	Adams	40,665
21	Jan 1	H	Crystal Palace	W 4-1	4-1	3	Smith 2, Dixon, Adams	38,711
22	13	A	Wimbledon	L 0-1	0-0	3		13,793
23	20	H	Tottenham H	W 1-0	0-0	3	Adams	46,132
24	Feb 17	A	Sheffield W	L 0-1	0-1	3		20,640
25	27	A	Charlton Ath	D 0-0	0-0	—		17,504
26	Mar 3	A	QPR	L 0-2	0-0	4		18,067
27	7	H	Nottingham F	W 3-0	1-0	—	Groves, Adams, Campbell	31,879
28	10	A	Manchester C	D 1-1	0-1	3	Marwood	29,087
29	17	H	Chelsea	L 0-1	0-0	3		33,805
30	24	A	Derby Co	W 3-1	3-0	3	Hayes 2, Campbell	17,514
31	31	H	Everton	W 1-0	1-0	3	Smith	35,223
32	Apr 11	H	Aston Villa	L 0-1	0-0	—		30,060
33	14	A	Crystal Palace	D 1-1	1-0	4	Hayes	28,094
34	18	H	Liverpool	D 1-1	1-0	—	Merson	33,395
35	21	A	Luton T	L 0-2	0-1	5		11,595
36	28	H	Millwall	W 2-0	2-0	4	Davis, Merson	25,607
37	May 2	H	Southampton	W 2-1	0-0	—	Dixon (pen), Rocastle	23,732
38	5	A	Norwich C	D 2-2	1-2	4	Smith 2	19,256

Final League Position: 4

GOALSCORERS

League (54): Smith 10, Merson 7, Marwood 6 (1 pen), Adams 5, Dixon 5 (3 pens), Thomas 5, Groves 4, Hayes 3, Campbell 2, Quinn 2, Rocastle 2, Davis 1, Jonsson 1, O'Leary 1.
Littlewoods Cup (10): Smith 3, Thomas 3, Groves 1, Quinn 1, own goals 2.
FA Cup (1): Quinn 1.

Lukic	Dixon	Winterburn	Thomas	O'Leary	Adams	Rocastle	Richardson	Smith	Merson	Marwood	Caesar	Groves	Hayes	Jonsson	Quinn	Campbell	Davis	Bould	Pates	Ampadu	Match No.
1	2	3	4	5	6*	7	8	9	10†	11	12	14									1
1	2	3	4	5	6	7*	8	9	10	11		12									2
1	2	3	4	5	6	7	8	9	10*	11		12									3
1	2	3	4	5	6	7	8	9	10	11											4
1	2	3	4	5	6	7	8	9	10*	11		12									5
1	2	3	4	5	6	7*	8	9	10	11		12									6
1	2	3	4	5	6	7*	8	9			12	10	11								7
1	2	3	4	5	6	7	8†	9	12	11*		10		14							8
1	2	3	4	5	6	7	8†	9*	12			10	11	14							9
1	2	3	4	5	6	7	8	12	10			11*			9						10
1	2	3†	4	5	6	7	8	9	11							14	10*	12			11
1	2	3	4	5	6	7	8	9	11*		12						10				12
1	2	3	4	5	6	7	8	9		11	12						10*				13
1	2	3	4	5	6	7*	8	9		11†	12					14	10				14
1	2	3	4	5†	6	7	8	9		11	12					14	10*				15
1	2	3	4	5	6	7	8	9	12	11*		10									16
1	2	3	4	5	6	7	8	9	12	11*		10									17
1	2	3	4	5	6	7	8	9*	12	11		10†				14					18
1	2	3	4	5	6	7	8	9	10*	11†		12				14					19
1	2	3	4	5	6	12	8	9	11			7					10*				20
1	2	3†	4	5	6	12	8	9*	11			7				14	10				21
1	2	3		5†	6	12	8	9*	11		14	7					4	10			22
1	2		4	5	6	7	8	9		11							3	10			23
1	2			5	6	7	8†	9	11		12					14	4	10	3*		24
1	2	3	4		6	7	8	9	10	11*						12		5			25
1	2	3	4*	12	6	7	8	9†	10	11						14		5			26
1	2	3	4	12	6	7	8	9	10†	11*						14		5			27
1	2	3	4		6	7*	8	9	11							12	10	5			28
1	2	3	4	12	6	7†	8	9	11							14	10*	5			29
1	2	3	4	12	6		8	9	11			7					10†	5*		14	30
1	2	3	4	12	6		8*	9	11			7					10†	5		14	31
1	2	3	4	8	6			9	12	11		7*					10	5			32
1	2	3	4	8	6			9	12	11		7				14	10*	5†			33
1	2	3	4	8	6			9	10	11†	14	7*						5		12	34
1	2	3	4	8†	6	12		9	10*	11		7		14				5			35
1	2	3	4*		6	7	12	9	10	11†						14	8	5			36
1	2	3	4		6	12	7*	9	10	11†						14	8	5			37
1	2	3	14	12	6	7		9	11						10	4	8†	5*			38
38	38	36	35	28	38	28	32	37	21	17	—	20	8	—	6	8	8	19	1	—	

```
   +   +       +   +   +   +       +   +   + +       +   +           + +
   1s  6s      5s  1s  1s  8s      3s  10s 4s6s      7s  3s          1s2s
```

Littlewoods Cup	Second Round	Plymouth Arg (h)	2-0
		(a)	6-1
	Third Round	Liverpool (h)	1-0
	fourth Round	Oldham Ath (a)	1-3
FA Cup	Third Round	Stoke C (a)	1-0
	Fourth Round	QPR (h)	0-0
		(a)	0-2

ARSENAL

Player and Position	Ht	Wt	Birth Date	Place	Source	Clubs	League App	Gls
Goalkeepers								
John Lukic	6 4	13 07	11 12 60	Chesterfield	Apprentice	Leeds U	146	—
						Arsenal	223	—
Allan Miller	6 2	13 08	29 3 70	Epping	Trainee	Arsenal	—	—
						Plymouth Arg (loan)	13	—
David Seaman	6 3	13 00	19 9 63	Rotherham	Apprentice	Leeds U	—	—
						Peterborough U	91	—
						Birmingham C	75	—
						QPR	141	—
						Arsenal	—	—
Defenders								
Tony Adams	6 1	13 03	10 10 66	London	Apprentice	Arsenal	184	17
Steve Bould	6 3	12 08	16 11 62	Stoke	Apprentice	Stoke C	183	6
						Torquay U (loan)	9	—
						Arsenal	49	2
Gus Caesar	6 0	12 00	5 3 66	London	Apprentice	Arsenal	44	—
Jim Carstairs	6 0	12 05	29 1 71	Fife	Trainee	Arsenal	—	—
Lee Dixon	5 9	10 12	17 3 64	Manchester	Local	Burnley	4	—
						Chester C	57	1
						Bury	45	5
						Stoke C	71	5
						Arsenal	77	6
Lee Francis*	5 10	10 11	24 10 69	Walthamstow	Trainee	Arsenal	—	—
						Chesterfield (loan)	2	—
Charles Hartfield	6 0	12 00	4 9 71	London	Trainee	Arsenal	—	—
Al Hinnigan*	6 0	12 04	26 1 71	Islington	Trainee	Arsenal	—	—
						Torquay U (loan)	7	—
Craig McKernon	5 9	11 00	23 2 68	Gloucester	Apprentice	Mansfield T	94	—
						Arsenal	—	—
Steve Morrow	6 0	11 03	2 7 70	Belfast	Trainee	Arsenal	—	—
David O'Leary	6 1	13 02	2 5 58	London	Apprentice	Arsenal	501	9
Colin Pates	5 11	11 00	10 8 61	Mitcham	Apprentice	Chelsea	281	10
						Charlton Ath	38	—
						Arsenal	2	—
Patrick Scully	6 1	12 07	23 6 70	Dublin	Trainee	Arsenal	—	—
						Preston NE (loan)	13	1
Michael Thomas	5 10	12 04	24 8 67	Lambeth	Apprentice	Arsenal	122	21
						Portsmouth (loan)	3	—
Nigel Winterburn	5 10	10 07	11 12 63	Coventry	Local	Birmingham C	—	—
						Oxford U	—	—
						Wimbledon	165	8
						Arsenal	91	3
Midfield								
Dino Connelly*	5 9	10 08	6 1 70	Glasgow	Trainee	Arsenal	—	—
Paul Davis	5 10	10 10	9 12 61	London	Apprentice	Arsenal	270	26
David Hillier	5 10	11 06	19 12 69	Blackheath	Trainee	Arsenal	—	—
Siggi Jonsson	5 11	11 11	27 9 66	Akranes, Iceland	Akranes FC	Sheffield W	67	4
						Barnsley (loan)	5	—
						Arsenal	6	—
Raymond Lee*	5 8	11 12	19 9 70	Bristol	Trainee	Arsenal	—	—
Gary McKeown	5 10	11 07	19 10 70	Oxford	Trainee	Arsenal	—	—
Brian Marwood	5 7	11 06	5 2 60	Seaham Harbour	Apprentice	Hull C	158	51
						Sheffield W	128	27
						Arsenal	52	16
Andrew Mockler*	5 11	11 13	18 11 70	Stockton	Trainee	Arsenal	—	—
Kevin Richardson	5 9	11 02	4 12 62	Newcastle	Apprentice	Everton	109	16
						Watford	39	2
						Arsenal	96	5
David Rocastle	5 9	11 12	2 5 67	Lewisham	Apprentice	Arsenal	163	18

ARSENAL

Foundation: Formed by workers at the Royal Arsenal, Woolwich in 1886 they began as Dial Square (name of one of the workshops) and included two former Nottingham Forest players Fred Beardsley and Morris Bates. Beardsley wrote to his old club seeking help and they provided the new club with a full set of red jerseys and a ball. The club became known as the "Woolwich Reds" although their official title soon after formation was Woolwich Arsenal.

First Football League game: 2 September, 1893, Division 2, v Newcastle U (h) D 2-2 – Williams; Powell, Jeffrey; Devine, Buist, Howat; Gemmell, Henderson, Shaw (1), Elliott (1), Booth.

Managers (and Secretary-managers)
Sam Hollis 1894–97, Tom Mitchell 1897–98, George Elcoat 1898–99, Harry Bradshaw 1899–1904, Phil Kelso 1904–08, George Morrell 1908–15, Leslie Knighton 1919–25, Herbert Chapman 1925–34, George Allison 1934–47, Tom Whittaker 1947–56, Jack Crayston 1956–58, George Swindin 1958–62, Billy Wright 1962–66, Bertie Mee 1966–76, Terry Neill 1976–83, Don Howe 1984–86, George Graham 1986–   .

Player and Position	Ht	Wt	Birth Date	Place	Source	Clubs	League App	Gls
Forwards								
Kwame Ampadu	5 10	10 13	20 11 70	Bradford	Trainee	Arsenal	2	—
Kevin Campbell	6 0	13 01	4 2 70	Lambeth	Trainee	Arsenal	16	2
						Leyton Orient (loan)	16	9
						Leicester C (loan)	11	5
Andrew Cole	5 11	11 02	15 10 71	Nottingham	Trainee	Arsenal	—	—
Perry Groves	5 11	11 12	19 4 65	London	Apprentice	Colchester U	156	26
						Arsenal	110	17
Martin Hayes	6 0	11 08	21 3 66	Walthamstow	Apprentice	Arsenal	102	26
Neil Heaney	5 9	11 01	3 11 71	Middlesbrough	Trainee	Arsenal	—	—
Colin Hoyle*	5 11	12 03	15 1 72	Derby	Trainee	Arsenal	—	—
						Chesterfield (loan)	3	—
Paul Merson	5 10	11 09	20 3 68	London	Apprentice	Arsenal	88	25
						Brentford (loan)	7	—
Alan Smith	6 3	12 10	21 11 62	Birmingham	Alvechurch	Leicester C	191	73
						Arsenal	113	44
						Leicester C (loan)	9	3

Trainees
Bacon, John P.G; Clements, Steven; Dickov, Paul; Faulkner, Richard A; Flatts, Mark M; Fowler, Kevin A; Gaunt, Craig J; Gooden, Ty M; Joseph, Matthew N.A; Marshall, Scott; Parlour, Raymond; Warden, Danny; Webster, Kenneth D; Will, James A; Young, Stuart R.

Associated Schoolboys
Brissett, Jason C; Clarke, Adrian J; Rawlins, Matthew; Rose, Matthew; Rust, Nicholas C I; Swain, Joel T; Zumrutel, Sonner.

Associated Schoolboys who have accepted the club's offer of a Traineeship/Contract
Charlton, John L; Lee, Justin, D; Read, Paul C; Selley, Ian; Shaw, Paul.

ASTON VILLA 1989–90 *Back row (left to right):* Derek Mountfield, Gareth Williams, Dean Spink, Ian Olney, Kent Nielsen, Ian Ormondroyd, Steve Sims, Nigel Callaghan.
Centre row: Gordon Cowans, Paul McGrath, Nigel Spink, Bobby Downes (Youth Team Coach), Dennis Booth (First Team Coach), Jim Walker (Physiotherapist),
Lee Butler, Kevin Gage, Mark Lillis.
Front row: Paul Birch, Tony Daley, Bernard Gallacher, John Ward (Assistant Manager), Graham Taylor (Manager), Dave Richardson (Assistant Manager), Stuart Gray, Chris Price, David Platt.

Division 1   **ASTON VILLA**

Villa Park, Trinity Rd, Birmingham B6 6HE. Telephone 021-327 6604. Commercial Dept. 021-327 5399. Clubcall: 0898 121148. Ticketline: 0898 12 18 48

Ground Capacity: 42,039.

Record attendance: 76,588 v Derby Co, FA Cup 6th rd, 2 March, 1946.

Record Receipts: £385,678 Everton v Norwich C, FA Cup semi-final, 15 April, 1989.

Pitch measurements: 115yd × 75yd.

President: H. J. Musgrove. *Chairman:* H. D. Ellis.

Directors: J. A. Alderson, Dr D. H. Targett, P. D. Ellis.

Manager: Dr. Jozef Venglos. *Assistant Managers:* Dave Richardson and John Ward.

Secretary: Steven Stride.*Coaches:* Dennis Booth and Bobby Downes.

Physio: Jim Walker. *Youth Coach:* Richard Money.

Commercial Manager: Abdul Rashid.

Year Formed: 1874. *Turned Professional:* 1885. *Ltd Co.:* 1896.

Previous Grounds: 1874–76, Aston Park; 1876–97, Perry Barr; 1897– Villa Park.

Club Nickname: 'The Villans'.

Record League Victory: 12-2 v Accrington S, Division 1, 12 March 1892 – Warner; Evans. Cox; Harry Devey, Jimmy Cowan, Baird; Athersmith (1), Dickson (2), John Devey (4), Campbell L. (4), Hodgetts (1).

Record Cup Victory: 13-0 v Wednesbury Old Ath, FA Cup 1st rd, 30 October 1886 – Warner; Coulton, Simmonds, Yates, Robertson, Burton (2); R. Davis (1), A. Brown (3), Hunter (3), Loach (2), Hodgetts (2).

Record Defeat: 1-8 v Blackburn R, FA Cup 3rd rd, 16 February, 1889.

Most League Points (2 for a win): 70, Division 3, 1971–72.

Most League Points (3 for a win): 78, Division 2, 1987–88.

Most League Goals: 128, Division 1, 1930–31.

Highest League Scorer in Season: 'Pongo' Waring, 49, Division 1, 1930–31.

Most League Goals in Total Aggregate: Harry Hampton, 215, 1904–15 and Billy Walker, 213, 1919–34.

Most Capped Player: Peter McParland 33 (34), Northern Ireland.

Most League Appearances: Charlie Aitken, 561, 1961–76.

Record Transfer Fee Received: £1,469,000 (£1,175,000 basic fee) from Wolverhampton W for Andy Gray, September 1979.

Record Transfer Fee Paid: £1,500,000 to Milwall for Tony Cascarino, March 1990.

Football League Record: 1888 Founder Member of the League; 1936–38 Division 2; 1938–59 Division 1; 1959–60 Division 2; 1960–67 Division 1; 1967–70 Division 2; 1970–72 Division 3; 1972–75 Division 2; 1975–87 Division 1; 1987–88 Division 2; 1988– Division 1.

Honours: Football League: Division 1 – Champions 1893–94, 1895–96, 1896–97, 1898–99, 1899–1900, 1909–10, 1980–81; Runners-up 1888–89, 1902–03, 1907–08, 1910–11, 1912–13, 1913–14, 1930–31, 1932–33, 1989–90; Division 2 – Champions 1937–38, 1959–60; Runners-up 1974–75, 1987–88; Division 3 – Champions 1971–72. *FA Cup:* Winners 1887, 1895, 1897, 1905, 1913, 1920, 1957 (7 wins stands as the joint record); Runners-up 1892, 1924. *Double Performed:* 1896–97. *Football League Cup:* Winners 1961, 1975, 1977; Runners-up 1963, 1971. **European Competitions:** *European Cup:* 1981–82 (winners). 1982–83; *UEFA Cup:* 1975–76, 1977–78, 1983–84; *World Club Championship:* 1982–83; *European Super Cup:* 1982–83 (winners).

Colours: Claret shirts, blue trim, white shorts, claret and blue trim, blue stockings, claret trim. **Change colours:** White shirts, purple/black trim, black shorts, white stockings.

ASTON VILLA 1989–90 LEAGUE RECORD

Match No.	Date		Venue	Opponents	Result		H/T Score	Lg. Pos.	Goalscorers	Attendance
1	Aug	19	A	Nottingham F	D	1-1	1-0	—	Mountfield	26,766
2		23	H	Liverpool	D	1-1	0-1	—	Platt	35,796
3		26	H	Charlton Ath	D	1-1	1-1	13	Olney	15,236
4		29	H	Southampton	L	1-2	0-0	—	Platt	14,401
5	Sept	9	H	Tottenham H	W	2-0	2-0	11	Olney 2	24,769
6		16	A	Sheffield W	L	0-1	0-1	13		17,509
7		23	H	QPR	L	1-3	1-2	17	Platt	14,170
8		30	H	Derby Co	W	1-0	1-0	13	Platt	16,245
9	Oct	14	A	Luton T	W	1-0	1-0	10	Mountfield	9433
10		22	A	Manchester C	W	2-0	1-0	—	Daley, Olney	23,354
11		28	H	Crystal Palace	W	2-1	0-0	7	Platt 2	15,724
12	Nov	5	H	Everton	W	6-2	3-0	—	Cowans, Olney 2, Platt 2, Nielsen	17,637
13		11	A	Norwich C	L	0-1	0-0	5		18,186
14		18	H	Coventry C	W	4-1	2-1	3	Ormondroyd 2, Peake (og), Platt (pen)	22,803
15		25	A	Wimbledon	W	2-0	1-0	2	Platt, Daley	5888
16	Dec	2	H	Nottingham F	W	2-1	1-1	2	Olney, Platt	25,575
17		9	A	Liverpool	D	1-1	1-0	3	Olney	37,435
18		16	A	Millwall	L	0-2	0-0	3		10,528
19		26	H	Manchester U	W	3-0	0-0	3	Olney, Platt, Gage	41,247
20		30	H	Arsenal	W	2-1	1-0	2	Platt, Mountfield	40,665
21	Jan	1	A	Chelsea	W	3-0	1-0	2	Gage, Daley, Platt	23,990
22		13	A	Charlton Ath	W	2-0	1-0	2	Mountfield, McLaughlin (og)	10,513
23		20	H	Southampton	W	2-1	1-0	2	Daley, Gage	33,118
24	Feb	10	H	Sheffield W	W	1-0	0-0	2	Platt	27,168
25		21	A	Tottenham H	W	2-0	0-0	—	Ormondroyd, Platt	32,472
26		24	H	Wimbledon	L	0-3	0-0	1		29,325
27	Mar	4	A	Coventry C	L	0-2	0-0	—		17,891
28		10	H	Luton T	W	2-0	1-0	1	Daley, Platt	22,505
29		17	A	Derby Co	W	1-0	0-0	1	Ormondroyd	21,062
30		20	A	QPR	D	1-1	0-0	--	Nielsen	15,856
31		24	A	Crystal Palace	L	0-1	0-1	1		18,586
32	Apr	1	H	Manchester C	L	1-2	1-1	—	Cowans	24,797
33		11	A	Arsenal	W	1-0	0-0	—	Price	30,060
34		14	H	Chelsea	W	1-0	1-0	2	Cowans	28,361
35		17	A	Manchester U	L	0-2	0-2	—		44,080
36		21	H	Millwall	W	1-0	0-0	2	Platt	21,028
37		28	H	Norwich C	D	3-3	0-1	2	McGrath, Cascarino, Platt	28,988
38	May	5	A	Everton	D	3-3	0-1	2	Cascarino, Cowans, Daley	29,551

Final League Position: 2

GOALSCORERS

League (57): Platt 19 (1 pen), Olney 9, Daley 6, Cowans 4, Mountfield 4, Ormondroyd 4, Gage 3, Cascarino 2, Nielsen 2, McGrath 1, Price 1, own goals 2.
Littlewoods Cup (3): Gray 1, Mountfield 1, Platt 1.
FA Cup (13): Birch 2, Daley 2, Gray 2, Olney 2, Ormondroyd 2, Mountfield 1, Platt 1, own goal 1.

Spink	Price	Gray	McGrath	Mountfield	Nielsen	Birch	Heath	Platt	Cowans	Daley	Olney	Callaghan	Comyn	Williams	Gallacher	Ormondroyd	Gage	Blake	Cascarino	Yorke	Match No.
1	2	3	4	5	6	7	8	9	10*	11†	12	14									1
1		3	4	5	6	7	8†	9	10		12	11*	2	14							2
1	2	3	4	5	6*	7	8	9	10	11†	12					14					3
1	2	10	4	5	6*	7	8	9			12	11†				3	14				4
1	2	10	6	5			8	7		9	11					3		4			5
1	2	10	6	5	12		8*	7		9†	11					3	14	4			6
1	2	10	6	5	12		8	7		9	11†					3	14	4*			7
1	2	11	6	5			8	10	7	9*						3	12	4			8
1	2	11		5	6	14	8†	4	10	12	9					3*		7			9
1	2	11		5	6	12	8	10	7	9						3		4*			10
1	2	11		5	6	12	8	10	7	9†					14	3		4*			11
1	2		4	5	6	12	8	10	7	9*						11	3†	14			12
1	2		4†	5	6		8	10		9	7	3	12	11*	14						13
1	2	3	4	5	6		8	10	7	9*					12	11					14
1	2	3	4	5	6		8	10	7	9						11					15
1	2	3	4	5	6		8	10	7	9						11					16
1	2	3	4	5	6		8	10	7	9						11					17
1	2	3†	4	5	6*		8	10	7	9					12	11	14				18
1			4	5	6	12	8	10	7*	9					3	11	2				19
1			4	5	6		8	10	7	9					3	11	2				20
1	12		4	5	6*		8	10	7	9					3	11	2				21
1	2		4	5	6		8	10	7	9						11	3				22
1	2		4	5	6		8	10	7	9						11	3				23
1	2		4	5	6		8	10	7	9						11	3				24
1	2		4	5	6		8	10	7	9						11	3				25
1	2	14	4	5	6	12	8	10	7	9*						11†	3				26
1	2	14	4	5†	6	12	8	10	7	9						11*	3				27
1	2	5	4		6		8	10	7	9				11			3				28
1	2	5	4		6		8	10	7					11*		12	3		9		29
1	2*	5	4		6		8	10	7	12				11			3		9		30
1	2	5	4		6		8	10	7†	12				11*			3		9	14	31
1		5	4		6		8	10	7	3				11*			2		9	12	32
1	2	12	4		6	11	8	10	7		5					3*			9		33
1	2	3	4	5*	6	11	8	10	7		12								9		34
1	2	3	4	5*	6		8	10	7	12						11			9		35
1	2	3	4	5*	6		8	10	7	12				14		11†			9		36
1	2	3	4	5	6		8	10	7	9						11					37
1	2*	3	4	5	6			10	7	9				12				8	11		38
38	33	26	35	32	34	6	8	37	34	31	27	7	3	4	6	19	22	6	10	—	

Substitute appearances (+):
1s 3s   2s 6s 1s   1s 8s   1s 1s   6s 1s6s   3s 2s

Littlewoods Cup	Second Round	Wolverhampton W (h)	2-1
		(a)	1-1
	Third Round	West Ham U (h)	0-0
		(a)	0-1
FA Cup	Third Round	Blackburn R (a)	2-2
		(h)	3-1
	Fourth Round	Port Vale (h)	6-0
	Fifth Round	WBA (a)	2-0
	Sixth Round	Oldham Ath (a)	0-3

ASTON VILLA

Player and Position	Ht	Wt	Birth Date	Place	Source	Clubs	League App	Gls
Goalkeepers								
Lee Butler	6 2	14 02	30 5 66	Sheffield	Haworth Coll	Lincoln C Aston Villa	30 4	— —
Nigel Spink	6 1	14 06	8 8 58	Chelmsford	Chelmsford C	Aston Villa	249	—
Defenders								
Andy Comyn	6 1	12 00	2 8 68	Manchester	Alvechurch	Aston Villa	4	—
Darrell Duffy	5 11	11 00	18 1 71	Birmingham	Trainee	Aston Villa	1	—
Kevin Gage	5 9	11 02	21 4 64	Chiswick	Apprentice	Wimbledon Aston Villa	168 94	15 8
Bernard Gallacher	5 8	11 02	22 3 67	Johnstone	Apprentice	Aston Villa	55	—
Paul McGrath	6 0	13 02	4 12 59	Ealing	St Patrick's Ath	Manchester U Aston Villa	163 35	12 1
Derek Mountfield	6 1	12 07	2 11 62	Liverpool	Apprentice	Tranmere R Everton Aston Villa	26 106 56	1 19 5
Kent Nielsen	6 2	14 01	28 12 61	Frederiksberg	Brondby	Aston Villa	36	2
Chris Price	5 7	10 02	30 3 60	Hereford	Apprentice	Hereford U Blackburn R Aston Villa	330 83 70	27 11 1
Steve Sims*	6 1	14 04	2 7 57	Lincoln	Apprentice	Leicester C Watford Notts Co Watford Aston Villa	79 152 85 19 41	3 4 5 1 —
Midfield								
Paul Birch	5 6	10 09	20 11 62	West Bromwich	Apprentice	Aston Villa	165	16
Mark Blake	5 11	12 03	16 12 70	Nottingham	Trainee	Aston Villa	9	—
Gordon Cowans	5 9	10 07	27 10 58	Durham	Apprentice Bari	Aston Villa Aston Villa	286 67	42 6
Stuart Gray	5 10	11 05	19 4 60	Withernsea	Local	Nottingham F Bolton W (loan) Barnsley Aston Villa	49 10 120 84	3 — 23 9
Forwards								
Nigel Callaghan	5 9	10 09	12 9 62	Singapore	Apprentice	Watford Derby Co Aston Villa	222 76 24	41 10 1
Tony Cascarino	6 2	11 10	1 9 62	St Paul's Cray	Crockenhill	Gillingham Millwall Aston Villa	219 105 10	78 42 2
Tony Daley	5 9	10 05	18 10 67	Birmingham	Apprentice	Aston Villa	136	19
David Jones	5 9	11 04	6 5 71	Wrexham	Trainee	Aston Villa	—	—
Alan McInally (To Bayern Munich July 1989)	6 1	13 03	10 2 63	Ayr	Ayr U BC	Ayr U Celtic Aston Villa	93 65 58	32 17 18
Tommy Mooney*	5 10	12 05	11 8 71	Teeside North	Trainee	Aston Villa	—	—
Ian Olney	6 1	11 03	17 12 69	Luton	Trainee	Aston Villa	50	11

ASTON VILLA

Foundation: Cricketing enthusiasts of Villa Cross Wesleyan Chapel, Aston, Birmingham decided to form a football club during the winter of 1873–74. Football clubs were few and far between in the Birmingham area and in their first game against Aston Brook St. Mary's Rugby team they played one half rugby and the other soccer. In 1876 they were joined by a Scottish soccer enthusiast George Ramsay who was immediately appointed captain and went on to lead Aston Villa from obscurity to one of the country's top clubs in a period of less than 10 years.

First Football League game: 8 September, 1888, Football League, v Wolverhampton W, (a) D 1-1 – Warner; Cox, Coulton; Yates, H. Devey, Dawson; A. Brown, Green (1), Allen, Garvey, Hodgetts.

Managers (and Secretary-managers)
George Ramsay 1884–1926*, W. J. Smith 1926–34*, Jimmy McMullan 1934–35, Jimmy Hogan 1936–44, Alex Massie 1945–50, George Martin 1950–53, Eric Houghton 1953–58, Joe Mercer 1958–64, Dick Taylor 1965–67, Tommy Cummings 1967–68, Tommy Docherty 1968–70, Vic Crowe 1970–74, Ron Saunders 1974–82, Tony Barton 1982–84, Graham Turner 1984–86, Billy McNeill 1986–87, Graham Taylor 1987–90.

Player and Position	Ht	Wt	Birth Date	Place	Source	Clubs	League App	Gls
Ian Ormondroyd	6 4	13 07	22 9 64	Bradford	Thackley	Bradford C	87	20
						Oldham Ath (loan)	10	1
						Aston Villa	37	5
Mark Parrott	5 11	11 00	14 3 71	Cheltenham	Trainee	Aston Villa	—	—
David Platt	5 10	11 12	10 6 66	Chadderton	Chadderton	Manchester U	—	—
						Crewe Alex	134	55
						Aston Villa	86	31
Gareth Williams	·5 10	11 08	12 3 67	Isle of Wight	Gosport	Aston Villa	12	—
Dwight Yorke	5 10	11 12	3 12 71	Tobago	St Clairs CS	Aston Villa	2	—

Trainees
Bullivant, Russell P; Carruthers, Martin G; Crisp, Richard I; Elliott, John A; Froggatt, Stephen J; Hoban, Neil A; Liddle, Craig G; Livingstone, Glen; Morgan, Steven; Small, Bryan; Smith, Andrew D; Travis, David L; Tyrell, Ian D; Walker, Stephen L; Williams, Lee

Associated Schoolboys
Accison, Keith R; Boyce, Christopher; Carbon, Matthew P; Carter, Trevor J; Cope, Justin A; Cowe, Steven M; Evans, Darren; Ferry, David L; Finney, Nicki D.J; Green, James S; Hackett, Lee J.B; Harrison, Garry M; Hutson, Otis M.F; James, Stuart; King, Ian J; Pearce, Christopher J; Pearce, Dennis A; Rampton, Adrian P; Rose, Brett J; Walker, Steven; Watt, David S; Williams, Graeme E.

Associated Schoolboys who have accepted the club's offer of a Traineeship/Contract
Boden, Christopher; Fenton, Graham A; Goodwin, Craig; Hedigan, Darren; Hodgson, Shaun D; Ibrahim, Kevin A; McCallum, Matthew; Peachey, Wayne T; Pitcher, Steven.

74

BARNS. 1989–90   *Back row (left to right):* Steve Cooper, Carl Tiler, Malcolm Shotton, Steve Lowndes, Paul McGugan, Paul Futcher, Darren Foreman.
Centre row: Eric Winstanley (First Team Coach), Tony Rees, David Currie, Paul Cross, Ian Wardle, Clive Barker, Ian Banks, Gwyn Thomas, Mark Nile (Physiotherapist),
Kevin Fogg (Youth Team Coach).
Front row: John MacDonald, Mark Robinson, Steve Agnew, Allan Clarke (Manager), Joe Joyce, Julian Broddle, Jim Dobbin, Owen Archdeacon.

Division 2   **BARNSLEY**

Oakwell Ground, Grove St, Barnsley. Telephone Barnsley (0226) 295353; Clubcall: 0898 121152; Commercial Office: 0226 286718. Fax: 0226 201000.

Ground Capacity: 30,099 (15,000 under cover).

Record attendance: 40,255 v Stoke C, 15 Feb, 1936, FA Cup 5th rd.

Pitch measurements: 110yd × 75yd.

President: Arthur Raynor. *Vice-Presidents:* N. W. B. Moody, G. Pallister, J. Steele, C. Williams. *Chairman:* J. A. Dennis.

Directors: C. B. Taylor (Vice-Chairman), R. F. Potter, C. H. Harrison, M. R. Hayselden.

Secretary: Michael Spinks. *Commercial Manager:* G. Whewall.

Team Manager: Mel Machin.

Coach: John Deehan. *Physio:* Mark Nile.

Year Formed: 1887. *Turned Professional:* 1888. *Ltd Co.:* 1899.

Previous Name: Barnsley St Peter's, 1887–89

Club Nickname: 'The Tykes', 'Reds' or 'Colliers'.

Record League Victory: 9-0 v Loughborough T, Division 2, 28 January 1899 – Greaves; McCartney, Nixon; Porteous, Burleigh, Howard; Davis (4), Hepworth (1), Lees (1), McCullough (1), Jones (2). 9-0 v Accrington S, Division 3 (N), 3 February 1934 – Ellis; Cookson, Shotton; Harper, Henderson, Whitworth; Spence (2), Smith (1), Blight (4), Andrews (1), Ashton (1).

Record Cup Victory: 6-0 v Blackpool, FA Cup, 1st rd (replay), 20 January 1910 – Mearns; Downs, Ness; Glendinning, Boyle (1), Utley; Bartrop, Gadsby (1), Lillycrop (2), Tufnell (2), Forman. 6-0 v Peterborough U. League Cup, 1st rd (2nd leg), 15 September 1981 – Horn; Joyce, Chambers, Glavin (2), Banks, McCarthy, Evans, Parker (2), Aylott (1), McHale, Barrowclough (1).

Record Defeat: 0-9 v Notts Co, Division 2, 19 November, 1927.

Most League Points (2 for a win): 67, Division 3 (N), 1938–39.

Most League Points (3 for a win): 74, Division 2, 1988–89.

Most League Goals: 118, Division 3 (N), 1933–34.

Highest League Scorer in Season: Cecil McCormack, 33, Division 2, 1950–51.

Most League Goals in Total Aggregate: Ernest Hine, 123, 1921–26 and 1934–38.

Most Capped Player: Eddie McMorran, 9 (15), Northern Ireland.

Most League Appearances: Barry Murphy, 514, 1962–78.

Record Transfer Fee Received: £700,000 from Nottingham F for David Currie, January 1990.

Record Transfer Fee Paid: £150,000 to Darlington for David Currie, February 1988.

Football League Record: 1898 Elected to Division 2; 1932–34 Division 3 (N); 1934–38 Division 2; 1938–39 Division 3 (N); 1946–53 Division 2; 1953–55 Division 3 (N); 1955–59 Division 2; 1959–65 Division 3; 1965–68 Division 4; 1968–72 Division 3; 1972–79 Division 4; 1979–81 Division 3; 1981– Division 2.

Honours: Football League: best season; 3rd, Division 2, 1914–15, 1921–22; Division 3 (N) – Champions 1933–34, 1938–39, 1954–55; Runners-up 1953–54; Division 3 – Runners-up 1980–81; Division 4 – Runners-up 1967–68; Promoted 1978–79. *FA Cup:* Winners 1912; Runners-up 1910. *Football League Cup:* best season, 5th rd. 1981–82.

Colours: Red shirts white trim, white shorts, red stockings. **Change colours:** All white.

BARNSLEY 1989–90 LEAGUE RECORD

Match No.	Date	Venue	Opponents	Result	H/T Score	Lg. Pos.	Goalscorers	Attendance
1	Aug 19	A	Ipswich T	L	1-3	1-0	—	Lowndes	12,100
2	26	H	Brighton & HA	W	1-0	0-0	14	Currie	5920
3	Sept 2	A	Plymouth Arg	L	1-2	0-0	16	MacDonald	7708
4	5	H	Stoke C	W	3-2	2-1	—	Agnew, Cooper, Lowndes	8584
5	9	H	Middlesbrough	D	1-1	1-0	9	Shotton	10,535
6	16	A	Swindon T	D	0-0	0-0	16		6540
7	23	H	Bradford C	W	2-0	1-0	8	Agnew, Foreman	8992
8	26	H	Wolverhampton W	D	2-2	1-1	—	Currie 2	10,161
9	30	A	Blackburn R	L	0-5	0-2	14		8415
10	Oct 7	A	Oldham Ath	L	0-2	0-2	17		6769
11	14	H	Port Vale	L	0-3	0-2	18		6475
12	17	H	Sheffield U	L	1-2	0-1	18	Agnew	16,629
13	21	A	Oxford U	W	3-2	1-0	17	Banks 2, Foreman	3863
14	28	H	Leicester C	D	2-2	0-2	17	Archdeacon, Currie (pen)	6856
15	31	A	Sunderland	L	2-4	0-2	—	Currie, Tiler	14,234
16	Nov 4	H	Portsmouth	L	0-1	0-0	19		5524
17	11	A	WBA	L	0-7	0-3	20		9317
18	18	H	Newcastle U	D	1-1	0-0	20	Currie	10,475
19	25	A	Hull C	W	2-1	0-1	20	Cooper, Currie	5715
20	Dec 2	H	Ipswich T	L	0-1	0-1	21		6097
21	9	A	Stoke C	W	1-0	0-0	20	Cooper	10,163
22	16	A	Bournemouth	L	1-2	0-1	22	Lowndes	5506
23	26	H	Watford	L	0-1	0-0	22		7357
24	30	H	Leeds U	W	1-0	1-0	21	Foreman	14,841
25	Jan 1	A	West Ham U	L	2-4	0-3	22	Dobbin, Archdeacon	18,391
26	13	A	Brighton & HA	D	1-1	0-0	22	Taggart	6856
27	20	H	Plymouth Arg	D	1-1	0-0	23	Smith	7224
28	Feb 3	A	Bradford C	D	0-0	0-0	23		9923
29	10	H	Swindon T	L	0-1	0-1	23		7179
30	24	H	Hull C	D	1-1	1-0	23	Cooper	8901
31	Mar 3	A	Newcastle U	L	1-4	1-3	23	Agnew	18,998
32	10	A	Wolverhampton W	D	1-1	0-0	23	Agnew (pen)	15,995
33	17	H	Oldham Ath	W	1-0	1-0	22	Milligan (og)	10,598
34	19	A	Port Vale	L	1-2	0-1	—	Banks	7036
35	24	A	Sheffield U	W	2-1	0-1	21	Agnew, Saville	15,951
36	31	H	Oxford U	W	1-0	1-0	20	Smith	7096
37	Apr 3	H	Blackburn R	D	0-0	0-0	—		8713
38	7	A	Leicester C	D	2-2	2-0	20	Cooper, Agnew	8620
39	10	A	Sunderland	W	1-0	0-0	—	McCord	11,141
40	14	H	West Ham U	D	1-1	1-1	18	Taggart	10,344
41	17	A	Watford	D	2-2	1-1	—	Lowndes, Agnew (pen)	7289
42	21	H	Bournemouth	L	0-1	0-0	21		7415
43	25	A	Leeds U	W	2-1	0-1	—	O'Connell, Archdeacon	31,700
44	28	H	WBA	D	2-2	0-1	20	O'Connell, Saville	10,334
45	May 2	A	Middlesbrough	W	1-0	1-0	—	Smith	17,015
46	5	A	Portsmouth	L	1-2	0-2	19	Saville	8415

Final League Position: 19

GOALSCORERS

League (49): Agnew 8 (2 pens), Currie 7 (1 pen), Cooper 5, Lowndes 4, Archdeacon 3, Banks 3, Foreman 3, Saville 3, Smith 3, O'Connell 2, Taggart 2, Dobbin 1, McCord 1, MacDonald 1, Shotton 1, Tiler 1, own goal 1.
Littlewoods Cup (2): Archdeacon 1, own goal 1.
FA Cup (6): Cooper 2, Currie 1, Lowndes 1, Smith 1, Taggart 1.

Baker	Tiler	Broddle	Dobbin	Shotton	Futcher	Lowndes	Agnew	Cooper	Currie	Robinson	MacDonald	Banks	Wardle	Foreman	Archdeacon	Cross	Dunphy	Smith	McCord	Marshall	Taggart	Glover	Gray	Thomas	Saville	Fleming	O'Connell	Match No.
1	2	3	4	5	6	7	8	9	10	11																		1
1	2	3	4	5†	6	7	8	9*	10	11	12		14															2
1		3	4	2	6	7	8	12	10	11	9*	5																3
1	12	3	4	2	6*	7	8	9	10	11		5																4
		3	4	2	6	7	8	9	10	11		5						1										5
		3	4	2	6	7*	8	9	10			5			12	11		1										6
	2		4	5	6		8		10	11				7	9	3		1										7
	2		4	5	6		8	12	10	11				7	9*	3		1										8
	2		4	5	6		8		10	11				7	9	3		1										9
	5	5	4	2	6		8	9	10				12	7	11*	3		1										10
1		3	4	2	6	7	8	9	10	11*		5				12												11
1	2		4		6		8		10			5		7	9	3			11									12
1	2		4		6		8		10			5		7	9	3			11									13
1	2		4		6		8		10			5		7	9	3			11									14
1		3	4	2	6		8†	14	10			5*		7	9	12			11									15
	12		4	2	6*		8	14	10			5		7†	9	3		1	11									16
		5	4	2	6		8	12	10				14	7†	11*	3		1	9									17
1		5	4				8	9	10						11	3	6					7						18
1		5	4				8	9	10						11	3	6					7						19
1		5	4*				8	9	10		12				11	3	6					7						20
1		5	4				8	9	10						11	3	6					7						21
1	11	5	4	2			8	9	10*						3		6					7		12				22
1	7	5	4	2			8	9	10		12		14	11†	3*		6											23
1	11	5	4	2			8	9	10					7	3		6											24
1	14	5	4	2		7†	8	12	10						9	3	6*		11									25
1		5	4	2		7	8	9*	10						11	3	6							12				26
1		5	4	2		7	8*	12					14		11†	3	6					9		10				27
1	2*	5	4					12	10	11						3	6					9		8				28
1		5	4					12	10	11*			14			3	6					9		8†	2			29
1				2	6		4		10	11		5	14	7†	8*	3								12	9			30
1				2†	6		4	10		11*		5	14	7	8	3								12	9			31
1				2	6		4		10	11		5		7*	8	3								12	9			32
1				2	6		4	14	10	11*		5		7†	8	3								12	9			33
				2	6		4		10	11		5		7	8	3	1*							12	9			34
1							4		10	11*		5	14	8†	3						6	7		12	9	2		35
1							4		10	11*		5		8	3						6	7		12	9	2		36
1							4		10	11*		5	14	8	3						6	7		12	9	2†		37
1							4		10	11		5	12	8*	3						6	7			9	2		38
1							4		10	11		5		8*	3						6	7		12	9	2		39
1							4		10	11*		5	14	8	3						6	7†		12	9	2		40
1							4		10	11*		5		8	3						6	7		12	9	2		41
1							4*		10	11		5	14	8†	3						6	7		12	9	2		42
1							4		10	11		5	14	8	3						6†			12	9	2	7*	43
1							4		10	11*		5		8	3						6			12	9	2	7	44
1							4		10	11*		5		8	3						6	7		12	9	2		45
1							4		10	11		5	14*	8†	3						6			12	9	2	7	46
37	18	20	28	29	28	20	46	26	24	18	3	33	9	11	17	35	5	25	16	—	20	8	3	1	12	12	2	
+3s	+1s	+4s	+4s		+6s		+1s4s		+6s	+4s	+1s	+1s			+2s	+1s					+2s	+3s				+9s		

Littlewoods Cup	Second Round	Blackpool (h)	1-1
		(a)	1-1 (lost 4-5 on pens)
FA Cup	Third Round	Leicester C (a)	2-1
	Fourth Round	Ipswich T (h)	2-0
	Fifth Round	Sheffield U (a)	2-2
		(h)	0-0
		(h)	0-1

BARNSLEY

Player and Position	Ht	Wt	Birth Date	Place	Source	Clubs	League App	Gls
Goalkeepers								
Clive Baker	5 9	11 00	14 3 59	N Walsham	Amateur	Norwich C	14	—
						Barnsley	245	—
Ian Wardle	5 9	11 00	27 3 70	Doncaster	Schoolboys	Barnsley	9	—
Phil Whitehead	6 2	13 00	17 12 69	Halifax		Halifax T	42	—
						Barnsley	—	—
Defenders								
Paul Cross	5 7	9 06	31 10 65	Barnsley	Apprentice	Barnsley	113	—
Sean Dunphy	6 3	13 05	5 11 70	Rotherham	Trainee	Barnsley	6	—
Gary Fleming	5 9	11 07	17 2 67	Londonderry	Apprentice	Nottingham F	74	—
						Manchester C	14	—
						Notts Co (loan)	3	—
						Barnsley	12	—
Paul Futcher	6 0	12 03	25 9 56	Chester	Apprentice	Chester	20	—
						Luton T	131	1
						Manchester C	37	—
						Oldham Ath	98	1
						Derby Co	35	—
						Barnsley	230	—
Joe Joyce	5 9	10 05	18 3 61	Consett	Amateur	Barnsley	331	4
Brian McCord	5 10	11 06	24 8 68	Derby	Apprentice	Derby Co	5	—
						Barnsley	16	1
Paul McGugan	6 3	13 07	17 7 64	Glasgow	Eastercraigs	Celtic	47	2
						Barnsley	49	2
Darren Rolph*	5 8	11 04	19 11 68	Romford		Barnsley	2	—
Mark Smith	6 2	13 11	21 3 60	Sheffield	Apprentice	Sheffield W	282	16
						Plymouth Arg	82	6
						Barnsley	25	3
Gerry Taggart	6 1	12 03	18 10 70	Belfast	Trainee	Manchester C	12	1
						Barnsley	21	2
Carl Tiler	6 2	13 00	11 2 70	Sheffield	Trainee	Barnsley	26	1
Midfield								
Steve Agnew	5 9	10 06	9 11 65	Shipley	Apprentice	Barnsley	156	21
Ian Banks	5 11	12 12	9 1 61	Mexborough	Apprentice	Barnsley	164	37
						Leicester C	93	14
						Huddersfield T	88	17
						Bradford C	30	3
						WBA	4	—
						Barnsley	37	3
Jonathan Bond*	5 10	11 00	5 11 69	Sheffield	Trainee	Barnsley	—	—
Jim Dobbin	5 10	10 06	17 9 61	Dunfermline	Whitburn BC	Celtic	2	—
						Motherwell (loan)	2	—
						Doncaster R	64	13
						Barnsley	115	12
Colin Marshall	5 5	9 05	1 11 69	Glasgow	Trainee	Barnsley	3	—
Lee Parker‡	6 1	12 07	7 9 70	Hartlepool	Trainee	Barnsley	—	—
Mark Robinson	5 9	11 08	21 11 68	Manchester	Trainee	WBA	2	—
						Barnsley	45	2
Forwards								
Owen Archdeacon	5 7	11 00	4 3 66	Greenock	Gourock U	Celtic	76	7
						Barnsley	21	3
Steve Cooper	5 11	10 12	22 6 64	Birmingham		Birmingham C	—	—
						Halifax (loan)	7	1
						Mansfield T (loan)	—	—
						Newport Co	38	11
						Plymouth Arg	73	15
						Barnsley	65	11

BARNSLEY

Foundation: Many clubs owe their inception to the church and Barnsley are among them, for they were formed in 1887 by the Rev. T. T. Preedy, curate of Barnsley St. Peter's and went under that name until a year after being admitted to the Second Division of the Football League in 1898.

First Football League game: 1 September, 1898, Division 2, v Lincoln C (a) L 0-1 – Fawcett; McArtney, Nixon; King, Burleigh, Porteous; Davis, Lees, Murray, McCullough, McGee.

Managers (and Secretary-managers)
Arthur Fairclough 1898–1901*, John McCartney 1901–04*, Arthur Fairclough 1904–12, John Hastie 1912–14, Percy Lewis 1914–19, Peter Sant 1919–26, John Commins 1926–29, Arthur Fairclough 1929–30, Brough Fletcher 1930–37, Angus Seed 1937–53, Tim Ward 1953–60, Johnny Steele 1960–71 (continued as GM), John McSeveney 1971–72, Johnny Steele (GM) 1972–73, Jim Iley 1973–78, Allan Clarke 1978–80, Norman Hunter 1980–84, Bobby Collins 1984–85, Allan Clarke 1985–89, Mel Machin 1989–   .

Player and Position	Ht	Wt	Birth Date	Place	Source	Clubs	League App	Gls
John Deehan	5 11	13 00	8 8 57	Solihull	Apprentice	Aston Villa	110	42
						WBA	47	5
						Norwich C	162	62
						Ipswich T	49	11
						Manchester C	—	—
						Barnsley	—	—
Brian Irwin‡			20 5 71	Dublin		Barnsley	—	—
Stephen Kaye‡	5 11	11 04	7 12 70	Penistone	Trainee	Barnsley	—	—
Steve Lowndes	5 10	10 13	17 6 60	Cwmbran	Amateur	Newport Co	208	39
						Millwall	96	16
						Barnsley	116	20
Brendan O'Connell	5 10	10 09	12 11 66	London		Portsmouth	—	—
						Exeter C	81	19
						Burnley	64	17
						Huddersfield T (loan)	11	1
						Barnsley	11	2
David Ross‡	6 1	10 03	21 11 69	Durham		Barnsley	—	—
Andrew Saville	6 0	12 00	12 12 64	Hull	Local	Hull C	100	18
						Walsall	38	5
						Barnsley	15	3

Trainees
Beaumont, Wayne; Burton, Mark A; Holmes, Steven; Jackson, Michael; Jarvis, Mark M; Miller, Keith D; Monaghan, Andrew; Roche, Noel J; Tabor, Alexander P; Townley, Stephen E; Wilkinson, Allan D; Winks, Corrie D.

Associated Schoolboys
Bennett, Troy; Bissett, Andrew G; Bochenski, Simon; Brown, Keith D; Craft, Adrian; Cullen, Michael J; Dale, Stephen C; Dobson, Stephen P; Drinkwater, Lee R; Driver, Christopher; Duke, Adrian M; Eaden, Nicholas J; Gartland, Paul M; Goddard, Richard C; Guest, Ashley C; Hall, Richard I; Linney, Kevin; McNicholas, David A; Newsam, Andrew; Nowell, Martyn; O'Sullivan, David J; Oxley, Lea J; Pettinger, Paul A; Poskitt, Adrian; Pullan, Richard; Skelton, Ian S; Tyler, Dean; Warner, Paul C.

Associated Schoolboys who have accepted the club's offer of a Traineeship/Contract
Degnan, Lee A; Eaton, Barry; Firth, Lee; Mercer, Mark S; Morgan, Gregory D; Watson, David N.

BIRMINGHAM CITY 1989–90 *Back row (left to right):* Brian Roberts, Robert Hopkins, Colin Robinson, Martin Thomas, Roger Hansbury, Ian Atkins, Paul Tait, John Frain.
Centre row: Fred Davies (Youth Team Coach), Dean Peer, Mark Yates, Trevor Matthewson, Paul Masefield, Neil Sproston, Phil Sproson, Colin Gordon, Kevin Langley, Matthew Fox,
Peter Henderson (Physiotherapist).
Front row: Ronnie Morris, Dennis Bailey, Simon Sturridge, Paul Shepstone, Bobby Ferguson (Assistant Manager), Dave Mackay (General Manager),
Andy Harris, Andy Williams, Kevin Ashley, Ian Clarkson.

Division 3   **BIRMINGHAM CITY**

St Andrews, Birmingham B9 4NH. Telephone 021-772 0101/2689. Lottery office/Souvenir shop 021 772 1245. Clubcall: 0898 121188. Fax: 021 766 7866. Club Soccer Shop: 021 766 8274.

Ground capacity: 27,689.

Record Attendance: 66,844 v Everton, FA Cup 5th rd, 11 Feb, 1939.

Record receipts: £116,372.50 v Nottingham Forest, FA Cup 5th rd, 20 February 1988.

Pitch measurements: 115yd × 75yd.

Match tickets: Bookable three weeks in advance.

Directors: S. Kumar BA (Chairman), R. Kumar BSC (Vice-Chairman), B. H. Slater BA (HONS), J. F. Wiseman, T. W. J. Edmonds.

Secretary: H. J. Westmancoat FFA, MBIM.

General Manager: Dave Mackay.

Assistant Manager: *Physio:* Peter Henderson MCSP. *Commercial Manager:* Peter Brannan

Year Formed: 1875. *Turned Professional:* 1885. *Ltd Co.:* 1888.

Previous Grounds: Waste ground near Arthur St, 1875; Muntz St. Small Heath, 1877; St Andrews, 1906.

Previous Names: 1875–88, Small Heath Alliance; 1888, dropped 'Alliance'; became Birmingham 1905; became Birmingham City 1945.

Club Nickname: 'Blues'.

Record League Victory: 12-0 v Walsall T Swifts, Division 2, 17 December 1892 – Charnley; Bayley, Jones; Ollis, Jenkyns, Devey; Hallam (2), Walton (3), Mobley (3), Wheldon (2), Hands (2). 12-0 v Doncaster R, Division 2, 11 April 1903 – Dorrington; Goldie, Wassell; Beer, Dougherty (1), Howard; Athersmith (1), Leonard (3), McRoberts (1), Wilcox (4), Field (1). Aston. (1 og).

Record Cup Victory: 9-2 v Burton W, FA Cup, 1st rd, 31 October 1885 – Hedges; Jones, Evetts (1); James (F), Felton, James (A) (1); Davenport (2), Stanley (4), Simms, Figures, Morris (1).

Record Defeat: 1-9 v Sheffield W, Division 1, 13 December, 1930 and v Blackburn R, Division 1, 5 January, 1895.

Most League Points (2 for a win): 59, Division 2, 1947–48.

Most League Points (3 for a win): 82, Division 2, 1984–85.

Most League Goals: 103, Division 2, 1893–94 (only 28 games).

Highest League Scorer in Season: Walter Abbott, 34, Division 2, 1898–99.

Most League Goals in Total Aggregate: Joe Bradford, 249, 1920–35.

Most Capped Player: Malcolm Page, 28, Wales.

Most League Appearances: Frank Womack, 491, 1908–28.

Record Transfer Fee Received: £975,000 from Nottingham F for Trevor Francis, February 1979.

Record Transfer Fee Paid: £350,000 to Derby Co for David Langan, June 1980.

Football League Record: Division 1: 1894–96; 1901–02, 1903–08; 1921–39; 1948–50; 1955–65; 1972–79; 1980–84; 1985–86. Division 2: 1892–94; 1896–1901; 1902–03; 1908–21; 1946–48; 1950–55; 1965–72; 1979–80, 1984–85; 1986–89; Division 3: 1989–.

Honours: Football League: Division 1 best season: 6th, 1955–56; Division 2 – Champions 1892–93, 1920–21, 1947–48, 1954–55; Runners-up 1893–94, 1900–01, 1902–03, 1971–72, 1984–85. *FA Cup:* Runners-up 1931, 1956.*Football League Cup:* Winners 1963. **European Competitions:** *European Fairs Cup:* 1955–58, 1958–60 (runners-up), 1960–61 (runners-up), 1960–62.

Colours: Royal blue shirts, white shorts, blue stockings with white trim. **Change colours:** All yellow.

BIRMINGHAM CITY 1989–90 LEAGUE RECORD

Match No.	Date	Venue	Opponents	Result	H/T Score	Lg. Pos.	Goalscorers	Atten-dance
1	Aug 19	H	Crewe Alex	W 3-0	2-0	—	Yates, Sturridge, Bailey	10,447
2	26	A	Bristol C	L 0-1	0-0	10		8938
3	Sept 2	H	Swansea C	W 2-0	0-0	5	Bailey, Hopkins	8071
4	9	A	Shrewsbury T	L 0-2	0-1	10		4714
5	16	H	Tranmere R	W 2-1	0-0	9	Gordon, Bailey	8604
6	23	A	Brentford	W 1-0	0-0	4	Sturridge	5386
7	26	H	Walsall	W 2-0	1-0	—	Bailey (pen), Tait	10,834
8	30	A	Blackpool	L 2-3	1-2	3	Sturridge, Gleghorn	5737
9	Oct 7	A	Rotherham U	L 1-5	1-1	8	Sturridge	4450
10	14	H	Northampton T	W 4-0	1-0	5	Gleghorn 2, Bailey 2 (1 pen)	8731
11	17	A	Chester C	L 0-4	0-0	—		1882
12	21	H	Huddersfield T	L 0-1	0-0	10		7951
13	28	A	Bury	D 0-0	0-0	11		3383
14	31	H	Cardiff C	D 1-1	0-1	—	Sturridge	7468
15	Nov 4	A	Reading	W 2-0	1-0	10	Sturridge, Hicks (og)	3527
16	11	H	Leyton Orient	D 0-0	0-0	10		7491
17	25	H	Bolton W	W 1-0	0-0	8	Bailey (pen)	8081
18	Dec 1	A	Wigan Ath	L 0-1	0-0	—		2600
19	16	H	Preston NE	W 3-1	1-0	7	Yates, Bailey, Frain	6391
20	26	A	Bristol R	D 0-0	0-0	9		6573
21	30	A	Notts Co	L 2-3	1-2	9	Atkins (pen), Bailey	7786
22	Jan 1	H	Fulham	D 1-1	0-0	9	Gleghorn	8932
23	13	H	Bristol C	L 0-4	0-1	9		11,277
24	20	A	Crewe Alex	W 2-0	0-0	9	Sturridge, Bailey	4681
25	27	H	Shrewsbury T	L 0-1	0-1	9		7461
26	Feb 9	A	Tranmere R	L 1-5	0-1	—	Bailey (pen)	6033
27	13	A	Swansea C	D 1-1	0-0	—	Madden	3603
28	17	H	Wigan Ath	D 0-0	0-0	10		5473
29	24	A	Bolton W	L 1-3	0-1	12	Gordon	7618
30	Mar 3	H	Mansfield T	W 4-1	2-0	11	Sturridge, Bailey 2, Ashley	5746
31	6	H	Blackpool	W 3-1	2-0	—	Peer, Sturridge, Bailey (pen)	7085
32	10	A	Walsall	W 1-0	1-0	9	Gleghorn	6036
33	13	H	Brentford	L 0-1	0-0	—		8169
34	17	H	Rotherham U	W 4-1	1-0	9	Tait, Atkins, Gordon, Sturridge	6985
35	20	A	Northampton T	D 2-2	1-2	—	Peer, Gleghorn	4346
36	24	H	Chester C	D 0-0	0-0	10		7584
37	31	A	Huddersfield T	W 2-1	0-1	10	Bailey, Gleghorn	5837
38	Apr 3	A	Mansfield T	L 2-5	1-4	—	Gleghorn, Bailey	4163
39	7	H	Bury	D 0-0	0-0	10		6808
40	10	A	Cardiff C	W 1-0	0-0	—	Hopkins	3322
41	14	A	Fulham	W 2-1	1-0	7	Hopkins, Gleghorn	4568
42	16	H	Bristol R	D 2-2	2-0	7	Hopkins, Matthewson	12,438
43	21	A	Preston NE	D 2-2	2-1	7	Bailey 2	7680
44	24	H	Notts Co	L 1-2	0-1	—	Hopkins	10,533
45	28	A	Leyton Orient	W 2-1	0-1	7	Hopkins, Peer	5691
46	May 5	H	Reading	L 0-1	0-0	7		14,278

Final League Position: 7

GOALSCORERS

League (60): Bailey 18 (5 pens), Sturridge 10, Gleghorn 9, Hopkins 6, Gordon 3, Peer 3, Atkins 2 (1 pen), Tait 2, Yates 2, Ashley 1, Frain 1, Madden 1, Matthewson 1, own goal 1.
Littlewoods Cup (5): Atkins 2, Bailey 2, Sproson 1.
FA Cup (4): Gleghorn 3, Sturridge 1.

Thomas	Clarkson	Frain	Atkins	Sproson	Matthewson	Peer	Bailey	Yates	Langley	Sturridge	Ashley	Overson	Gordon	Hopkins	Tait	Gleghorn	Deakin	Hansbury	Roberts	Bell	Harris	Madden	Rutherford	Williams	Match No.
1	2	3	4	5	6	7	8	9	10	11															1
1		10	4	5	3	7	8	12		11*		2	6	9											2
1	12	10	4	5	3	7	8	14				2*	6	9†	11										3
1	12		4	5	3	7*	8	9†				2	6	11	14	10									4
1			4	5	3	7*	8					2	6	9	11	10	12								5
	12		4	5	3	7	8		9*			2	6		11	10		1							6
1			4	5	3	7*	8				9	2	6		11	12	10								7
1			4	5	3	7*	8				9	2	6		11	12	10								8
1	12	4	5	6		8		7			2*		9†	11		10	14		3						9
1		3	4	5	6	12	8		11†		9*					10	14		2	7					10
1		3	4	5	6	12	8				14		9†	10	11		2*		7						11
1		3	4	5*	6	12	8		9	2		11†			10	14		7							12
1	5	3	4		6		8		11	9	2				10				7						13
1	2	3	4		5		9*12	11	8						10		7		6						14
1	5	3	4		6	2	8		11	9					10				7						15
1	3†	4		6		8	12	11		2		9*			10	5			7	14					16
1	5	3	4		6		8		11	9	2				10				7						17
1	5	3	4		6		8*		11	9	2		12	10					7						18
1		3	4		6		8	9	11		5			10				2	7						19
1	2	3	4		6		8*	9	11		5		12	10					7						20
1	2*	3	4		6		12	9	11		5		8	10					7						21
1	2	3	4		6		12	9*11†14			5		8	10					7						22
1	2	3	4		6		8	11	9		5	12		10					7*						23
1	2	3	4		6		8	11	9		5	7		10											24
1	2	3	4*		6		8		9		5	7		10					12	11					25
1	2	3	4		6		8		9		5	7		10						11					26
1	12	3	4		6		8	9	7	2*	5		10							11					27
1	2	3	4		6		8	9†	7	5*14			10					12	11						28
1	5*	3	4		6		8	9	7	12			10					2	11						29
1		4		6	5	8	11	7	2	9*			10					3			12				30
1		4		6	5	8	9*11	7	2				10					3			12				31
1		4		6	5	8	9	11	7	2			10					3							32
1	12	4		6	5	8	9*11†7		2	14			10					3							33
1	3	4†		6	5		12	11	7	2	14	9*		8	10										34
1	3	4		6	5		12	11	7	2		9		8*10											35
1	3	4		6	5	12		11†	7	2	14	9		8*10											36
1	14*	3		6	5	8	12	11	7	2	4	9†		10											37
1	3	4		6	9	8		11	7*	2	5	12		10											38
1	3	4		6	7	8	12	11*		2	5	9		10											39
1	3	4		6	7	8		11		2	5	9*12		10											40
1	3	4		6		8		11	7	2	5	9		10											41
1	3	4		6		8		11	7	2	5	9		10											42
1	3	4		6	12	8		11	7*	2	5	9		10											43
	3	4		6	14	8		11†		2	5	12	9*	7	10									1	44
	3	4		6	7	8†		11		2	5	12	9*14	10										1	45
	3	4		6	7		11†	8*	2	5	9	14	10											1	46
42	15 +5s	36 +2s	45	12	46	22 +5s	40 +3s	12 +8s	33	30 +1s	31	27	14 +3s	16 +7s	7 +2s	43 +7s	3 +4s	1	9 +1s	14 +1s	— +1s	5	— +2s	3	

Littlewoods Cup	First Round	Chesterfield (h)	2-1
		(a)	1-1
	Second Round	West Ham U (h)	1-2
		(a)	1-1
FA Cup	First Round	Leyton Orient (a)	1-0
	Second Round	Colchester U (a)	2-0
	Third Round	Oldham Ath (h)	1-1
		(a)	0-1

BIRMINGHAM CITY

Player and Position	Ht	Wt	Birth Date	Place	Source	Clubs	League App	Gls
Goalkeepers								
Martin Thomas	6 1	13 00	28 11 59	Senghennydd	Apprentice	Bristol R	162	—
						Cardiff C (loan)	15	—
						Tottenham H (loan)	—	—
						Southend U (loan)	6	—
						Newcastle U (loan)	3	—
						Newcastle U	115	—
						Middlesbrough(loan)	4	—
						Birmingham C	78	—
Dean Williams§	6 0	11 07	5 1 72	Lichfield	Trainee	Birmingham C	3	—
Defenders								
Kevin Ashley	5 7	10 04	31 12 68	Birmingham	Apprentice	Birmingham C	54	1
Adrian Bird*	6 1	11 07	8 7 69	Bristol	School	Birmingham C	27	—
Ian Clarkson	5 11	12 00	4 12 70	Birmingham	Trainee	Birmingham C	29	—
Matthew Fox	6 0	13 00	13 7 71	Birmingham	Trainee	Birmingham C	3	—
Paul Masefield	5 11	12 08	21 10 70	Birmingham	Trainee	Birmingham C	—	—
Trevor Matthewson	6 1	12 05	12 2 63	Sheffield	Apprentice	Sheffield W	3	—
						Newport Co	75	—
						Stockport Co	80	—
						Lincoln C	43	2
						Birmingham C	46	1
Vince Overson	6 0	13 00	15 5 62	Kettering	Apprentice	Burnley	211	6
						Birmingham C	142	1
Dean Peer	6 2	12 00	8 8 69	Dudley	Trainee	Birmingham C	46	4
Brian Roberts‡	5 8	11 07	6 11 55	Manchester	Apprentice	Coventry C	215	1
						Hereford U (loan)	5	—
						Birmingham C	187	—
Phil Sproson	6 0	12 00	13 10 59	Trent Vale	Amateur	Port Vale	426	33
						Birmingham C	12	—
Neil Sproston‡	6 2	12 03	20 11 70	Dudley	Trainee	Birmingham C	1	—
Midfield								
Ian Atkins	6 0	12 03	16 1 57	Birmingham	Apprentice	Shrewsbury T	278	58
						Sunderland	77	6
						Everton	7	1
						Ipswich T	77	4
						Birmingham C	93	6
Doug Bell	5 11	12 01	5 9 59	Paisley	Cumbernauld	St Mirren	2	1
						Aberdeen	108	6
						Rangers	35	1
						Hibernian	32	3
						Shrewsbury T	50	6
						Hull C (loan)	4	—
						Birmingham C	15	—
Micky Burton	5 9	11 03	5 11 69	Birmingham	Trainee	Birmingham C	4	—
John Deakin	5 8	10 08	29 6 66	Sheffield	Barnsley Apprentice	Doncaster R	23	—
						Grimsby T	—	—
					Shepshed C	Birmingham C	7	—
John Frain	5 7	11 10	8 10 68	Birmingham	Apprentice	Birmingham C	86	7
Andrew Harris	5 10	12 02	17 11 70	Birmingham	Trainee	Birmingham C	1	—
Robert Hopkins	5 7	10 05	25 10 61	Birmingham	Apprentice	Aston Villa	3	1
						Birmingham C	123	21
						Manchester C	7	1
						WBA	83	11
						Birmingham C	27	6
Kevin Langley	6 1	10 03	24 5 64	St Helens	Apprentice	Wigan Ath	160	6
						Everton	16	2
						Manchester C (loan)	9	—
						Manchester C	—	—
						Chester C (loan)	9	—
						Birmingham C	76	2

BIRMINGHAM CITY

Foundation: In 1875 cricketing enthusiasts who were largely members of Trinity Church, Bordesley, determined to continue their sporting relationships throughout the year by forming a football club which they called Small Heath Alliance. For their earliest games played on waste land in Arthur Street, the team included three Edden brothers and two James brothers.

First Football League game: 3 September, 1892, Division 2, v Burslem Port Vale (h) W 5-1 – Charsley; Bayley, Speller; Ollis, Jenkyns, Devey; Hallam (1), Edwards (1), Short (1), Wheldon (2), Hands.

Managers (and Secretary-managers)
Alfred Jones 1892–1908*, Alec Watson 1908–1910, Bob McRoberts 1910–15, Frank Richards 1915–23, Billy Beer 1923–27, Leslie Knighton 1928–33, George Liddell 1933–39, Harry Storer 1945–48, Bob Brocklebank 1949–54, Arthur Turner 1954–58, Pat Beasley 1959–60, Gil Merrick 1960–64, Joe Mallett 1965, Stan Cullis 1965–70, Fred Goodwin 1970–75, Willie Bell 1975–77, Jim Smith 1978–82, Ron Saunders 1982–86, John Bond 1986–87, Garry Pendrey 1987–89, Dave Mackay 1989–   .

Player and Position	Ht	Wt	Birth Date	Place	Source	Clubs	League App	Gls
Ronnie Morris‡	6 0	11 08	25 9 70	Birmingham	Trainee	Birmingham C	11	—
Andrew Williams‡	5 8	10 00	29 9 70	Marston Green	Trainee	Birmingham C	—	—
Forwards								
Dennis Bailey	6 0	11 01	13 11 65	Lambeth		Fulham	—	—
					Farnborough	Crystal Palace	5	1
						Bristol R (loan)	17	9
						Birmingham C	43	18
Nigel Gleghorn	6 0	12 13	12 8 62	Seaham	Seaham Red Star	Ipswich T	66	11
						Manchester C	34	7
						Birmingham C	43	9
Colin Gordon	6 1	12 12	17 1 63	Stourbridge	Oldbury U	Swindon T	72	33
						Wimbledon	3	—
						Gillingham (loan)	4	2
						Reading	24	9
						Bristol C (loan)	8	4
						Fulham	17	2
						Birmingham C	21	3
Mark Rutherford§	5 11	11 00	25 3 72	Birmingham	Trainee	Birmingham C	2	—
Simon Sturridge	5 8	10 00	9 12 69	Birmingham	Trainee	Birmingham C	52	13
Paul Tait	6 1	10 00	31 7 71	Sutton Coldfield	Trainee	Birmingham C	25	2
Mark Yates	5 11	11 09	24 1 70	Birmingham	Trainee	Birmingham C	43	5

Trainees
Brown, Steven M; Casemore, Craig P; Coogan, Mark A; Cook, Alan A.H; Dale, Andrew J; Devery, Brendan J; Duffy, Paul J; Foy, David L; Francis, Sean R; Gray, Brian S; Kodua, Derrick; Larkins, Nigel K; Machin, Jason A; Manifold, Dean P; Naylor, Richard J; Rhodes, Jason P; Rutherford, Mark R; Thorpe, Nicholas S; Williams, Dean; Williams, Richard J.

**Non-Contract
Harrison, Mark

Associated Schoolboys
Afford, Andrew B; Aston, David E; Baker, Lewis M; Black, Simon A; Cook, David R; Cross, Robert B; Gordon, Andrew N; Griffiths, Terence J; Jones, Paul T; Lewis, Craig S; McKeever, Scott J; Potter, Graham S; Richards, Adrian P; Rodgers, Steven J; Savage, Ian R; Steadman, Richard D; Woodward, George; Wratten, Adam P.

Associated Schoolboys who have accepted the club's offer of a Traineeship/Contract
Adams, Carl A; Bignot, Marcus; Halford, John D; Higgins, Matthew; O'Connor, David W.P; Powell, Mark.

**Non-Contract Players who are retained must be re-signed before they are eligible to play in League matches.

BLACKBURN ROVERS 1989–90 *Back row (left to right):* Frank Stapleton, Howard Gayle, Mark Atkins, Andy Kennedy, Terry Gennoe, Darren Collier, Colin Hendry, Keith Hill, Tony Finnigan, John Millar.
Centre row: Jim Furnell (Reserve/Youth Team Manager), David May, Jason Wilcox, Craig Skinner, Neil Oliver, David Mail, Tony Diamond, Scott Sellars, David Hall (Youth Team Coach).
Front row: Ronnie Hildersley, Don Mackay (Manager), Leonard Johnrose, Nicky Reid, Ally Dawson, Chris Sulley, Tony Parkes (Assistant Manager), Simon Garner.

Division 2   **BLACKBURN ROVERS**

Ewood Park, Blackburn BB2 4JF. Telephone Blackburn (0254) 55432.

Ground capacity: 17,819.

Record attendance: 61,783 v Bolton W, FA Cup 6th rd, 2 Mar, 1929.

Record receipts: £60,612 v Liverpool, FA Cup 3rd rd, 8 Jan, 1983.

Pitch measurements: 116yd 2ft × 72yd 2ft.

Chairman: W. Fox. *Vice Chairman:* R. D. Coar BSC.

Directors: T. W. Ibbotson LLB, K. C. Lee, I. R. Stanners, G. R. Root FCMA

Commercial Manager: Ken Beamish.

Secretary: John W. Howarth FAAI.

Manager: Donald Mackay. *Asst. Manager:* Tony Parkes. *Reserve Team Manager:* Jim Furnell.

Physio: Jack Cunningham.

Year Formed: 1875. *Turned Professional:* 1880. *Ltd Co.:* 1897.

Previous Grounds: 1875, Brookhouse Ground; 1876, Alexandra Meadows; 1881, Leamington Road; 1890, Ewood Park.

Previous Name: Blackburn Grammar School OB.

Club Nickname: 'Blue and Whites'.

Record League Victory: 9-0 v Middlesbrough, Division 2, 6 November 1954 – Elvy; Suart, Eckersley; Clayton, Kelly, Bell; Mooney (3), Crossan (2), Briggs, Quigley (3), Langton (1).

Record Cup Victory: 11-0 v Rossendale, FA Cup 1st rd, 13 October 1884 – Arthur; Hopwood, McIntyre; Forrest, Blenkhorn, Lofthouse; Sowerbutts (2), J. Brown (1), Fecitt (4), Barton (3), Birtwistle (1).

Record Defeat: 0-8 v Arsenal, Division 1, 25 February, 1933.

Most League Points (2 for a win): 60, Division 3, 1974–75.

Most League Points (3 for a win): 77, Division 2, 1987–88, 1988–89.

Most League Goals: 114, Division 2, 1954–55.

Highest League Scorer in Season: Ted Harper, 43 Division 1, 1925–26.

Most League Goals in Total Aggregate: Simon Garner, 162, 1978–90.

Most Capped Player: Bob Crompton, 41, England.

Most League Appearances: Derek Fazackerley, 596, 1970–86.

Record Transfer Fee Received: £600,000 from Manchester C for Colin Hendry, November 1989.

Record Transfer Fee Paid: £150,000 to Birmingham C for Andy Kennedy, June 1988.

Football League Record: 1888 Founder Member of the League; 1936–39 Division 2; 1946–47 Division 1; 1947–57 Division 2; 1957–66 Division 1; 1966–71 Division 2; 1971–75 Division 3; 1975-79 Division 2; 1979–80 Division 3; 1980– Division 2.

Honours: Football League: Division 1 – Champions 1911–12, 1913–14; Division 2 – Champions 1938–39; Runners-up 1957–58; Division 3 – Champions 1974–75; Runners-up 1979–80; *FA Cup:* Winners 1884, 1885, 1886, 1890, 1891, 1928; Runners-up 1882. 1960. *Football League Cup:* Semi-final 1961–62. *Full Members' Cup:* Winners 1986–87.

Colours: Blue and white halved shirts, white shorts, blue stockings with red tops. **Change colours:** Yellow shirts, blue stripe, yellow shorts, blue stripe, yellow stockings.

BLACKBURN ROVERS 1989–90 LEAGUE RECORD

Match No.	Date	Venue	Opponents	Result	H/T Score	Lg. Pos.	Goalscorers	Atten- dance
1	Aug 19	H	Oldham Ath	W 1-0	1-0	—	Garner	9939
2	23	A	Leicester C	W 1-0	0-0	—	Sellars	11,411
3	26	A	Leeds U	D 1-1	1-0	2	Atkins	25,045
4	Sept 2	H	Oxford U	D 2-2	1-1	3	Sellars, Gayle	7578
5	9	A	Port Vale	D 0-0	0-0	4		7601
6	16	H	Sunderland	D 1-1	0-0	7	Millar	10,329
7	23	A	Bournemouth	W 4-2	1-1	2	Kennedy, Stapleton, Reid, Sellars	7409
8	27	A	WBA	D 2-2	1-0	—	Garner, Sellars	9269
9	30	H	Barnsley	W 5-0	2-0	4	Garner 3, Sellars, Kennedy	8415
10	Oct 14	A	Portsmouth	D 1-1	1-1	6	Kennedy (pen)	7004
11	18	A	Newcastle U	L 1-2	0-1	—	Kennedy	20,702
12	21	H	Watford	D 2-2	1-1	8	Kennedy (pen), Garner	7950
13	28	A	Plymouth Arg	D 2-2	1-2	9	Gayle, Sellars	6876
14	31	H	Hull C	D 0-0	0-0	—		7456
15	Nov 4	A	Brighton & HA	W 2-1	1-1	9	Garmer, Sellars	7445
16	11	H	Ipswich T	D 2-2	0-1	9	Johnrose, Atkins (pen)	7913
17	18	A	Wolverhampton W	W 2-1	1-1	9	Garner, Reid	14,695
18	21	H	Middlesbrough	L 2-4	0-3	—	Stapleton, Johnrose	8317
19	25	H	West Ham U	W 5-4	4-1	5	Garner, Sellars 2, Stapleton, Johnrose	10,215
20	Dec 1	A	Oldham Ath	L 0-2	0-0	—		10,635
21	9	H	Leicester C	L 2-4	1-2	8	Garner, Gayle	7538
22	26	A	Swindon T	L 3-4	2-3	9	Garner, Kennedy (pen), Gayle	8426
23	30	A	Sheffield U	W 2-1	1-1	8	Kennedy, Garner	17,279
24	Jan 1	H	Bradford C	D 2-2	0-0	9	Kennedy 2 (1 pen)	9957
25	13	H	Leeds U	L 1-2	1-0	11	Garner	14,485
26	20	A	Oxford U	D 1-1	0-0	11	Atkins	5973
27	27	H	Stoke C	W 3-0	2-0	—	Kennedy, Gayle (pen), Sellars	9132
28	Feb 3	H	Bournemouth	D 1-1	0-0	9	Atkins	7947
29	10	A	Sunderland	W 1-0	0-0	8	Reid	16,043
30	17	H	Port Vale	W 1-0	0-0	5	Garner	9240
31	24	A	West Ham U	D 1-1	0-1	6	Sellars	20,052
32	Mar 3	H	Wolverhampton W	L 2-3	2-2	8	Garner, Kennedy	12,054
33	10	H	WBA	W 2-1	1-0	7	Atkins, Reid	8148
34	17	A	Middlesbrough	W 3-0	2-0	5	Garner, Kennedy, Moran	15,259
35	20	H	Portsmouth	W 2-0	2-0	—	Atkins, Garner	8047
36	24	H	Newcastle U	W 2-0	0-0	4	Moran, Sellars	13,285
37	31	A	Watford	L 1-3	0-2	5	Irvine	9096
38	Apr 3	A	Barnsley	D 0-0	0-0	—		8713
39	7	H	Plymouth Arg	W 2-0	0-0	6	Sellars 2	7492
40	10	A	Hull C	L 0-2	0-0	—		5327
41	14	A	Bradford C	W 1-0	1-0	5	Oliver (og)	9082
42	16	H	Swindon T	W 2-1	1-1	4	Garner, Atkins	10,689
43	21	A	Stoke C	W 1-0	0-0	4	Mail (pen)	9305
44	28	A	Ipswich T	L 1-3	1-2	5	Mail (pen)	11,007
45	May 1	H	Sheffield U	D 0-0	0-0	—		15,633
46	5	H	Brighton & HA	D 1-1	0-0	5	Kennedy	9283

Final League Position: 5

GOALSCORERS

League (74): Garner 18, Sellars 14, Kennedy 13 (4 pens), Atkins 7 (1 pen), Gayle 5 (1 pen), Reid 4, Johnrose 3, Stapleton 3, Mail 2 (2 pens), Moran 2, Irvine 1, Millar 1, own goal 1.
Littlewoods Cup (2): Atkins 2.
FA Cup (3): Kennedy 1, Sellars 1, Stapleton 1.

Gennoe	Atkins	Sulley	Finnigan	Hill	May	Gayle	Millar	Stapleton	Garner	Sellars	Kennedy	Hendry	Dawson	Reid	Hildersley	Collier	Irvine	Oliver	Johnrose	Mail	Marriott	Moran	Wilcox	Match No.
1	2	3	4	5	6	7	8	9*	10	11	12													1
1	2	3	4	5	6	7	8	9	10*	11	12													2
1	2	3	4	5		7	8	9	10*	11	12	6												3
1	2	3†	4	5		7	8	9*	10	11	12	6	14											4
1	2	3		5	6	7*	8	9	10	11	12			4										5
1	2	3	10	5	6	7	8	9		11*				4	12									6
1	2	3	12	5	6		8	9	10*	11	7			4										7
1	2	3	12	5	6		8	9*	10	11	7			4										8
	2	3		5	6		8	9	10	11	7			4		1								9
	2	3		5	6		8	9	10	11	7*			4	12	1								10
	2	3		5	6			9	10	11	7	12		4	8*	1								11
	2	3		5	6	14	8†	9	10	11	7*	12		4		1								12
	2	3	12	5		7		9	10*	11		6		4		1	8							13
	2	3		5		7		9	10	11		6		4		1	8							14
	2			5		12	8	9	10*	11		6		4		1	7	3						15
	2	12		5	6		8†	9	10	11				4*		1	7	3	14					16
	2	3		5	6		8	9	10*	11				4		1	7	12						17
	2	3		5	6		8	9		11				4		1	7	10						18
	2	3		5	6			9	10*	11	12			4		1	7	8						19
	2	3		5	6			9	10*	11	12			4		1	7	8						20
	2	3		5	6	12	14	9	10	11				4		1	7*	8†						21
		3		5		12	8*	9	10	11	7†			4		1	14	2		6				22
		3		5		12	8	9	10	11	7		2	4*						6	1			23
		3		5			8	9	10	11	7		2	4						6	1			24
1		3	4	5			8*	9	10	11	7†		2	12			14			6				25
1	5	3	4				8	9	10*	11	7		2				12			6				26
1	2	3				10	8	9		11	7			4						6		5		27
1	2	3				10*	8	9	12	11	7			4						6		5		28
1	2	3				12	8	9	10	11	7*			4						6		5		29
1	2	3				12	8*	9	10	11	7			4						6		5		30
1	2	3				12	8	9	10*	11	7			4						6		5		31
1	2	3	14			12		9†	10	11	7			4			8*			6		5		32
1	2	3	12					9	10	11	7			4			8*			6		5		33
1		3					8	9	10	11	7*		2	4			12			6		5		34
1	2	3				7*	8	9	10	11				4			12			6		5		35
1	2*	3				7†	8	9	10	11	14			4			12			6		5		36
1	2	3					8	9	10	11	7*	14		4			12			6		5†		37
1	2	3				7	8	9	10*	11†	14			4			12			6		5		38
1	2					7*	8	9	10	11		3		4			12			6		5		39
1	2	14				7†	8	9	10	11		3		4			12			6*		5		40
1	2	14					8		10*	11	7	3		4			9†	12		6		5		41
	2	14					8	9	10		7†	3		4		1	12			6		5	11*	42
1	2					12	8	9*	10	11	7	3		4			12			6		5		43
1	2	9				14	8		10†	11	7*	3		4			12			6		5		44
1	2	14				9	8		10	11*	7	3		4			12			6		5†		45
	2	14		5		9	8	12	10	11	7†	3*		4					1	6				46
28	41	36	8	25	17	19	38	42	42	43	26	5	9	42	2	16	13	3	4	25	2	19	1	

```
        +           +   +   +   +         +   +   +         +           +           +
      11s         11s  1s  1s  1s        8s  2s  3s        3s         12s         4s
```

Littlewoods Cup	Second Round	Exeter C (a) 0-3
		(h) 2-1
FA Cup	Third Round	Aston Villa (h) 2-2
		(a) 1-3

BLACKBURN ROVERS

Player and Position	Ht	Wt	Birth Date	Place	Source	Clubs	League App	Gls
Goalkeepers								
Darren Collier	6 0	12 06	1 12 67	Stockton	Middlesbrough	Blackburn R	17	—
Terry Gennoe	6 2	13 03	16 3 53	Shrewsbury	Bricklayers Sp	Bury	3	—
						Blackburn R (loan)	—	—
						Leeds U (loan)	—	—
						Halifax T	78	—
						Southampton	36	—
						Everton (loan)	—	—
						Crystal Palace (loan)	3	—
						Blackburn R	288	—
Defenders								
Mark Atkins	6 1	12 00	14 8 68	Doncaster	School	Scunthorpe U	48	2
						Blackburn R	87	13
Ally Dawson*	5 10	11 10	25 2 58	Glasgow	School	Rangers	218	6
						Blackburn R	40	—
Tony Finnigan	6 0	12 00	17 10 62	Wimbledon	Fulham	Crystal Palace	105	10
						Blackburn R	36	—
Keith Hill	6 0	11 03	17 5 69	Bolton	Apprentice	Blackburn R	41	1
David Mail	5 11	11 12	12 9 62	Bristol	Apprentice	Aston Villa	—	—
						Blackburn R	206	4
David May	6 0	12 00	24 6 70	Oldham	Trainee	Blackburn R	18	—
John Millar	5 7	10 00	8 12 66	Lanark		Chelsea	11	—
						Northampton T (loan)	1	—
						Hamilton A (loan)	10	—
						Blackburn R	92	1
Kevin Moran	5 11	12 09	29 4 56	Dublin	Pegasus (Eire) Sporting Gijon	Manchester U	231	21
						Blackburn R	19	2
Neil Oliver	5 11	11 10	11 4 67	Berwick	Coldstream	Berwick R	93	—
						Blackburn R	3	—
Chris Sulley	5 8	10 00	3 12 59	Camberwell	Apprentice	Chelsea	—	—
						Bournemouth	206	3
						Dundee U	7	—
						Blackburn R	102	—
Midfield								
Lenny Johnrose	5 11	12 00	29 11 69	Preston	Trainee	Blackburn R	9	3
Nicky Reid	5 10	12 04	30 10 60	Ormston	Apprentice	Manchester C	217	2
						Blackburn R	123	6
Scott Sellars	5 7	9 10	27 11 65	Sheffield	Apprentice	Leeds U	76	12
						Blackburn R	163	27
Paul Shepstone	5 8	10 06	8 11 70	Coventry		Coventry C	—	—
						Birmingham C	—	—
						Blackburn R	—	—
Forwards								
Simon Garner	5 9	11 12	23 11 59	Boston	Apprentice	Blackburn R	447	162
Howard Gayle	5 10	10 09	18 5 58	Liverpool	Local	Liverpool	4	1
						Fulham (loan)	14	—
						Birmingham C (loan)	13	1
						Newcastle U (loan)	8	2
						Birmingham C	33	8
						Sunderland	48	2
						Stoke C	6	2
						Blackburn R	88	25
Ron Hildersley*	5 4	9 02	6 4 65	Fife	Apprentice	Manchester C	1	—
						Chester (loan)	9	—
						Chester C	9	—
						Rochdale	16	—
						Preston NE	58	3
						Cambridge U (loan)	9	3
						Blackburn R	30	4

BLACKBURN ROVERS

Foundation: It was in 1875 that some Public School old boys called a meeting at which the Blackburn Rovers club was formed and the colours blue and white adopted. The leading light was John Lewis, later to become a founder of the Lancashire FA, a famous referee who was in charge of two FA Cup Finals, and a vice-president of both the FA and the Football League.

First Football League game: 15 September, 1888, Football League, v Accrington (h) D 5-5 – Arthur; Beverley, James Southworth; Douglas, Almond, Forrest; Beresford (1), Walton, John Southworth (1), Fecitt (1), Townley (2).

Managers (and Secretary-managers)
Thomas Mitchell 1884–96*, J. Walmsley 1896–1903*, R. B. Middleton 1903–25, Jack Carr 1922–26 (TM under Middleton to 1925), Bob Crompton 1926–30 (Hon. TM), Arthur Barritt 1930–36 (had been Sec. from 1927), Reg Taylor 1936–38, Bob Crompton 1938–41, Eddie Hapgood 1944–47, Will Scott 1947, Jack Bruton 1947–49, Jackie Bestall 1949–53, Johnny Carey 1953–58, Dally Duncan 1958–60, Jack Marshall 1960–67, Eddie Quigley 1967–70, Johnny Carey 1970–71, Ken Furphy 1971–73, Gordon Lee 1974–75, Jim Smith 1975–78, Jim Iley 1978, John Pickering 1978–79, Howard Kendall 1979–81, Bobby Saxton 1981–86, Don Mackay 1987– .

Player and Position	Ht	Wt	Birth Date	Birth Place	Source	Clubs	League App	Gls
Alan Irvine	5 9	11 03	12 7 58	Glasgow	Glasgow BC	Queen's Park	88	9
						Everton	60	4
						Crystal Palace	109	12
						Dundee U	24	3
						Blackburn R	25	1
Andy Kennedy	6 1	12 00	8 10 64	Stirling	Sauchie Ath	Rangers	15	3
						Birmingham C	76	18
						Sheffield U (loan)	9	1
						Blackburn R	59	23
Craig Skinner	5 10	11 00	21 10 70	Bury	Trainee	Blackburn R	—	—
Frank Stapleton	6 0	13 01	10 7 56	Dublin	Apprentice	Arsenal	225	75
						Manchester U	223	60
						Ajax	4	—
						Derby Co	10	1
					Le Havre	Blackburn R	43	3
Jason Wilcox	5 10	11 06	15 7 71	Bolton	Trainee	Blackburn R	1	—

Trainees
Ainsworth, Gareth; Baah, Peter H; Beattie, James L; Butterworth, John; Cunningham, Malcolm; Dewhurst, Robert M; Donnelly, Darren C; Gillespie, Lee; Hodson, Steven F; Holt, Matthew J; Latham, Ian D; Sixsmith, Alan L; Smalley, Dylan T; Thorne, Peter L.

Associated Schoolboys
Ainscough, Paul B; Berry, Ian J; Berry, James S; Burch, Damian P; Cunliffe, Scott; Davies, Gareth J; Gaston, Gary M; Gill, Wayne J; Goodall, Daniel J; Greenlees, Paul T; Grunshaw, Steven J; Hassall, Andrew R; Hitchen, Lee A; Man, Wai M; Metcalf, Joshua H; Morris, Andrew N; Moss, Lee; Paver, Mark J; Peake, Warren C; Robinson, Mark A; Scott, Andrew M; Thornton, Scott L; Yeoman, Stephen A.

Associated Schoolboys who have accepted the club's offer of a Traineeship/Contract
Cullen, Anthony; Lindsay, Scott W; McGarry, Ian J; Pickup, Jonathan J.

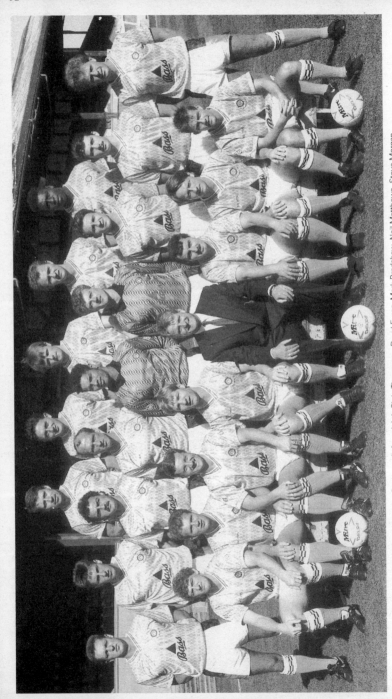

BLACKPOOL 1989-90. *Back row (left to right):* Chris Thompson, David Eyres, Mark Bradshaw, Neil Matthews, Steve Morgan.
Centre row: Simon Rooney, Shaun Dunn, Gary Briggs, Colin Methven, Mark Gayle, Steve McIlhargey, Ian Gore, Steve Burns, Andy Garner.
Front row: Mike Davies, Gordon Owen, David Burgess, Shaun Elliott, Jim Mullen (Manager), Russell Coughlin, Craig Madden, Alan Wright.

Division 4   **BLACKPOOL**

Bloomfield Rd Ground, Blackpool FY1 6JJ. Telephone Blackpool (0253) 404331.

Ground capacity: 12,696.

Record attendance: 38,098 v Wolverhampton W, Division 1, 17 Sept. 1955.

Record receipts: 35,474.18 v Manchester C, FA Cup 3rd rd, 7 February, 1983.

Pitch measurements: 111yd × 73yd.

President: C. A. Sagar BEM.

Chairman: K. Chadwick LLB. ***Vice Chairman:*** G. Bloor.

Managing Director:

Secretary: David Johnson.

Directors: M. H. Melling, T, White, J. Wilde MBE, O. Oyston, J. Allitt, J. Crowther LLB. Mrs. V. Oyston.

Manager: Graham Carr. ***General Manager:*** F. McGrath.

Commercial Manager: Geoffrey Warburton.

Coach: ***Physio:*** Stephen Redmond.

Year Formed: 1887. ***Turned Professional:*** 1887. ***Ltd Co.:*** 1896.

Previous Grounds: 1887, Raikes Hall Gardens; 1897, Athletic Grounds; 1899, Raikes Hall Gardens; 1899, Bloomfield Road.

Previous Name: 'South Shore' combined with Blackpool in 1899, twelve years after the latter had been formed on the breaking up of the old 'Blackpool St John's' club.

Club Nickname: 'The Seasiders'.

Record League Victory: 7-0 v Preston NE (away), Division 1, 1 May 1948 – Robinson; Shimwell, Crosland; Buchan, Hayward, Kelly; Hobson, Munro (1), McIntosh (5), McCall, Rickett (1).

Record Cup Victory: 7-1 v Charlton Ath, League Cup, 2nd rd, 25 September 1963 – Harvey; Armfield, Martin; Crawford, Gratrix, Cranston; Lea, Ball (1), Charnley (4), Durie (1), Oakes (1).

Record Defeat: 1-10 v Small Heath, Division 2, 2 March, 1901 and v Huddersfield T, Division 1, 13 December, 1930.

Most League Points (2 for a win): 58, Division 2, 1929–30.

Most League Points (3 for a win): 86, Division 4, 1984–85.

Most League Goals: 98, Division 2, 1929–30.

Highest League Scorer in Season: Jimmy Hampson, 45, Division 2, 1929–30.

Most League Goals in Total Aggregate: Jimmy Hampson, 247, 1927–38.

Most Capped Player: Jimmy Armfield, 43, England.

Most League Appearances: Jimmy Armfield, 568, 1952–71.

Record Transfer Fee Received: £330,000 from Leeds U for Paul Hart, March 1978.

Record Transfer Fee Paid: £116,666 to Sunderland for Jack Ashurst, October 1979.

Football League Record: 1896 Elected to Division 2; 1899 Failed Re-election; 1900 Re-elected; 1900–30 Division 2; 1930–33 Division 1; 1933–37 Division 2; 1937–67 Division 1; 1967–70 Division 2; 1970–71 Division 1; 1971–78 Division 2; 1978–81 Division 3; 1981–85 Division 4; 1985–90 Division 3; 1990– Division 4.

Honours: *Football League:* Division 1 – Runners-up 1955–56; Division 2 Champions 1929–30; Runners-up 1936–37, 1969–70; Division 4 – Runners-up 1984–85. *FA Cup:* Winners 1953; Runners-up 1948, 1951. *Football League Cup:* Semi-final 1962. *Anglo-Italian Cup:* Winners 1971; Runners-up 1972.

Colours: Tangerine shirts with white trim, tangerine shorts, tangerine stockings with white tops. **Change colours:** All blue.

BLACKPOOL 1989–90 LEAGUE RECORD

Match No.	Date		Venue	Opponents	Result		H/T Score	Lg. Pos.	Goalscorers	Attendance
1	Aug	19	H	Wigan Ath	D	0-0	0-0	—		4561
2		26	A	Notts Co	W	1-0	0-0	9	Burgess	4852
3	Sept	2	H	Shrewsbury T	L	0-1	0-1	13		4109
4		9	A	Bristol C	L	0-2	0-0	19		7172
5		16	H	Crewe Alex	L	1-3	0-2	20	Briggs	4722
6		23	A	Mansfield T	W	3-0	2-0	16	Gabbiadini 2, Diamond	2629
7		26	A	Preston NE	L	1-2	0-0	—	Madden	8920
8		30	H	Birmingham C	W	3-2	2-1	15	Overson (og), Garner (pen), Gabbiadini	5737
9	Oct	6	H	Reading	D	0-0	0-0	—		3321
10		14	A	Leyton Orient	L:	0-2	0-2	16		4126
11		17	A	Northampton T	L	2-4	2-4	—	Briggs, Garner (pen)	3098
12		21	H	Cardiff C	W	1-0	0-0	17	Owen	3502
13		28	A	Rotherham U	D	1-1	0-1	17	Garner	5570
14		31	H	Bury	L	0-1	0-0	—		4184
15	Nov	4	A	Bristol R	D	1-1	0-0	18	Madden	5520
16		11	H	Brentford	W	4-0	1-0	12	Madden 2 (1 pen), Eyres, Morgan	2512
17		25	H	Tranmere R	L	0-3	0-1	15		4106
18	Dec	2	A	Swansea C	D	0-0	0-0	16		4020
19		16	H	Fulham	L	0-1	0-1	19		2648
20		26	A	Bolton W	L	0-2	0-1	22		9944
21		30	A	Chester C	L	0-2	0-1	23		2404
22	Jan	1	H	Huddersfield T	D	2-2	1-1	22	Methven, Garner (pen)	5097
23		13	H	Notts Co	D	0-0	0-0	22		3146
24		20	A	Wigan Ath	D	1-1	0-1	23	Garner	3179
25	Feb	3	H	Mansfield T	W	3-1	3-0	22	Owen, Garner (pen), Richards	4402
26		10	A	Crewe Alex	L	0-2	0-1	23		3978
27		13	A	Shrewsbury T	D	1-1	0-1	—	Eyres	2300
28		23	A	Tranmere R	L	2-4	0-2	—	Garner (pen), Eyres	7873
29	Mar	3	H	Walsall	W	4-3	1-2	23	Bradshaw, Eyres, Methven, Groves	3174
30		6	A	Birmingham C	L	1-3	0-2	—	Richards	7085
31		10	H	Preston NE	D	2-2	2-1	33	Brook, Garner (pen)	8108
32		13	H	Bristol C	L	1-3	0-1	—	Brook	3227
33		17	A	Reading	D	1-1	0-0	23	Owen	3752
34		20	H	Leyton Orient	W	1-0	1-0	—	Richards	2746
35		24	H	Northampton T	W	1-0	0-0	20	Eyres	3296
36		27	A	Walsall	D	1-1	0-0	—	Richards	3134
37		31	A	Cardiff C	D	2-2	1-1	20	Eyres, Brook	2850
38	Apr	7	H	Rotherham U	L	1-2	0-0	21	Brook	3505
39		10	A	Bury	L	0-2	0-1	—		3131
40		14	A	Huddersfield T	D	2-2	1-1	22	Coughlin, Gouck	4845
41		16	H	Bolton W	W	2-1	0-0	21	Brook, Eyres	5435
42		21	H	Fulham	D	0-0	0-0	21		3816
43		24	A	Chester C	L	1-3	0-3	—	Methven	3724
44		28	A	Brentford	L	0-5	0-1	22		4784
45		30	H	Swansea C	D	2-2	0-1	—	Brook, Owen	1842
46	May	5	H	Bristol R	L	0-3	0-2	23		6776

Final League Position: 23

GOALSCORERS

League (49): Garner 8 (6 pens), Eyres 7, Brook 6, Madden 4 (1 pen), Owen 4, Richards 4, Gabbiadini 3, Methven 3, Briggs 2, Bradshaw 1, Burgess 1, Coughlin 1, Diamond 1, Gouck 1, Groves 1, Morgan 1, own goal 1.
Littlewoods Cup (5): Briggs 2, Bradshaw 1, Gabbiadini 1, Garner 1.
FA Cup (9): Eyres 2, Owen 2, Brook 1, Burgess 1, Garner 1, Groves 1, Methven 1.

McIlhargey	Burgess	Morgan	Gore	Briggs	Matthews	Bradshaw	Sinclair	Garner	Coughlin	Wright	Madden	Methven	Owen	Thompson	Elliott	Diamond	Gabbiadini	Eyres	Bartram	Hawkins	Davies	Brook	Groves	Richards	Wood	Gouck	Jones	Match No.
1	2	3	4	5	6	7*	8	9†	10	11	12	14																1
1	2	3	4	5	6			9*	10	11	8	7	12															2
1	2	3	4*	5	12	11		9†	10	7	8	6	14															3
1	2	3	4	5	10	11*		9		7		6			8	12												4
1	2	3	4	5	12				10	14			7		6*	8	9	11†										5
1	2	3	4	11					10			5	7		6	8	9											6
1	2*	3	4	11	6†				10	14	12	8	5	7			9											7
1	2	3	4	11					10			8	5	7	6		9											8
1	2	3	4	11					10	8	12		5	7	6*		9											9
1	2	3	4	11	6*		12		10	8			5	7			9											10
1	2	3	4*	11				9	10	8	6		5	7				12										11
1	2	3	6					9*	10	8	12		5	7	4			11										12
	2			11					10	4	3	8	5	7	6				1	9								13
	2			11					10	4	3	8	5	7*	6			12	1	9								14
	2	3		11	12				10	4		8	5	7	6				1	9*								15
	2	3		11					10*	4		8	5	7†	6	9			1	12		14						16
1	3	2					7†		10	4*		8	5	12	6						11		14	9				17
	7	3	2						10	4		8	5	9	6				1		11							18
	2	3*					7		10	4			5	9	6				1		11	12	8					19
	2†	7							10	4	3	12	5	9*	6				1		11		14	8				20
	14	7						12	10	4	3	5			6				1		11		8†	2*	9			21
	3	7							10	4	2	5	9		6				1		11	8						22
1	3	7							10	4	2	5	9*		6						11	12	8					23
1	3	7	11				8		10	4*	2	5	9†		6						14	12						24
1	3	7						14	10†	4	2	5	9*		6			12				8	11					25
1	3	7						14	10	4*	2	5			6			11†				12	8	9				26
1	3	7						9	10	4	2	5			6*			12				8	11					27
1	3	7						6†	10	4	2	5	14					12			9*	8	11					28
1	3†	7						6	10	4*	2	5						9			12	14	8	11				29
1	3	7						6†	10		2	5						9			14	12	8*	4	11			30
1	3*	7						12	10		2	5						9			6	8	4	11				31
	3	7							10	2*		5			6			9			12	8	4	11	1			32
	2						3		10	7*		5	14		6			9†				8	4	11	1	12		33
	3								10	7		5			6			9			2	8	4	11	1			34
	3								10			5			6			9			7	8	4	11	1		2	35
	3								10			5			6			9			7	8	4	11	1		2	36
	3								10			5	12		6			9*			7	8	4	11	1		2	37
	14		6				3	12	10	11†		5						9			7	8*	4		1		2	38
	3		6						10	11		5						9			7	8	4		1		2	39
	3		6						10	7		5						9				8	12	11	1	4*	2	40
	3		6						10	7		5						9			2	8	4	11*	1	12		41
	3		6						10	11		5						9			7	8			1	4		42
	3		6				12		10	7†		5	14					9			2	8	11*		1	4		43
	3		6				12		10	11		5	7					9			2	8*			1	4		44
	3		6				11*	7	10†			5	14					9			2	12	8		1	4		45
	3		6				14	7	12	11†		5						9			2	8	10*		1	4		46
22	19	36	34	17	8	17	5	45	34	20	9	44	21	2	25	2	5	30	9	4	14	23	18	16	15	6	6	Apps

```
      +        + +  + +  +    + +  +    +       + +  + +            +
     2s      4s4s 4s1s 1s 4s 2s1s 7s  1s1s 1s     5s  3s9s 2s 1s          2s
```

Littlewoods Cup

Littlewoods Cup	First Round	Burnley (h)	2-2
		(a)	1-0
	Second Round	Barnsley (a)	1-1
		(h)	1-1 (won 5-4 on pens)
	Third Round	Exeter C (a)	0-3
FA Cup	First Round	Bolton W (h)	2-1
	Second Round	Chester C (h)	3-0
	Third Round	Burnley (h)	1-0
	Fourth Round	Torquay U (h)	1-0
	Fifth Round	QPR (h)	2-2
		(a)	0-0
		(a)	0-3

BLACKPOOL

Player and Position	Ht	Wt	Birth Date	Place	Source	Clubs	League App	Gls
Goalkeepers								
Mark Gayle*	6 0	12 00	21 10 69	Bromsgrove	Trainee	Leicester C	—	—
						Blackpool	—	—
Steve McIlhargey	6 0	11 07	28 8 63	Ferryhill	Blantyre Celtic	Walsall	—	—
						Rotherham U (loan)	—	—
						Blackpool	22	—
Defenders								
Gary Briggs	6 3	12 10	8 5 58	Leeds	Apprentice	Middlesbrough	—	—
						Oxford U	420	18
						Blackpool	17	2
Dave Burgess	5 10	11 02	20 1 60	Liverpool	Local	Tranmere R	218	1
						Grimsby T	69	
						Blackpool	65	1
Steve Burns	5 11	12 00	28 10 68	Salford	Local	Blackpool	—	—
Shaun Elliott	6 0	11 10	26 1 58	Haltwhistle	Apprentice	Sunderland	321	12
						Norwich C	31	2
						Blackpool	67	
Neil Matthews	6 0	11 07	3 12 67	Manchester	Apprentice	Blackpool	76	1
Colin Methven	6 2	12 07	10 12 55	Kirkcaldy	Leven Royals	East Fife	144	14
						Wigan Ath	296	21
						Blackpool	173	11
Steve Morgan	5 11	13 00	19 9 68	Oldham	Apprentice	Blackpool	144	10
Midfield								
Anthony Abrahams*	5 10	10 11	8 12 69	Liverpool	Trainee	Nottingham F	—	—
						Blackpool	—	—
Mark Bradshaw	5 10	11 05	7 6 69	Ashton	Trainee	Blackpool	41	1
Russell Coughlin	5 8	11 08	15 2 60	Swansea	Apprentice	Manchester C	—	—
						Blackburn R	24	—
						Carlisle U	130	13
						Plymouth Arg	131	18
						Blackpool	102	8
Michael Davies	5 8	10 00	19 1 66	Stretford	Apprentice	Blackpool	189	13
Ian Gore	5 11	12 04	10 1 68	Liverpool		Birmingham C	—	—
					Southport	Blackpool	55	—
Andy Gouck§			8 6 72	Blackpool	Trainee	Blackpool	8	1
Paul Groves	5 11	11 05	28 2 66	Derby	Burton Alb	Leicester C	16	1
						Lincoln C (loan)	8	1
						Blackpool	19	1
Simon Rooney‡	5 11	11 08	10 7 70	Manchester	Trainee	Blackpool	9	—
Trevor Sinclair§			2 3 73	Dulwich	Trainee	Blackpool	9	—
Alan Wright	5 4	9 04	28 9 71	Ashton Under Lyne		Blackpool	41	—
Forwards								
Gary Brook	5 10	12 04	9 5 64	Dewsbury	Frickley Ath	Newport Co	14	2
						Scarborough	64	15
						Blackpool	25	6
George Costa			5 8 66	Finsbury		Blackpool	—	—
Tony Diamond	5 10	10 04	23 8 68	Rochdale	Apprentice	Blackburn R	26	3
						Wigan Ath (loan)	6	2
						Blackpool	3	1
David Eyres	5 10	11 00	26 2 64	Liverpool	Rhyl	Blackpool	35	7
Andy Garner	6 0	12 01	8 3 66	Chesterfield	Apprentice	Derby Co	71	17
						Blackpool	88	19
Nigel Hawkins	5 9	10 07	7 9 68	Bristol	Apprentice	Bristol C	18	2
						Blackpool	7	—

BLACKPOOL

Foundation: Old boys of St. John's School who had formed themselves into a football club decided to establish a club bearing the name of their town and Blackpool FC came into being at a meeting at the Stanley Arms Hotel in the summer of 1887. In their first season playing at Raikes Hall Gardens, the club won both the Lancashire Junior Cup and the Fylde Cup.

First Football League game: 5 September, 1896, Division 2, v Lincoln C (a) L 1-3 – Douglas; Parr, Bowman; Stuart, Stirzaker, Norris; Clarkin, Donnelly, R. Parkinson, Mount (1), J. Parkinson.

Managers (and Secretary-managers)
Tom Barcroft 1903–33* (Hon. Sec.), John Cox 1909–11, Bill Norman 1919–23, Maj. Frank Buckley 1923–27, Sid Beaumont 1927–28, Harry Evans 1928–33 (Hon. TM), Alex "Sandy" Macfarlane 1933–35, Joe Smith 1935–58, Ronnie Suart 1958–67, Stan Mortensen 1967–69, Les Shannon 1969–70, Bob Stokoe 1970–72, Harry Potts 1972–76, Allan Brown 1976–78, Bob Stokoe 1978–79, Stan Ternent 1979–80, Alan Ball 1980–81, Allan Brown 1981–82, Sam Ellis 1982–89, Jimmy Mullen 1989–90, Graham Carr 1990– .

Player and Position	Ht	Wt	Birth Date	Place	Source	Clubs	League App	Gls
Gordon Owen	5 8	10 09	14 6 59	Barnsley	Amateur	Sheffield W	48	5
						Rotherham U (loan)	9	—
						Doncaster R (loan)	9	—
						Chesterfield (loan)	6	2
						Cardiff C	39	14
						Barnsley	68	25
						Bristol C	53	11
						Hull C (loan)	3	—
						Mansfield T	58	8
						Blackpool	28	4
Carl Richards	6 0	13 00	12 1 60	Jamaica	Enfield	Bournemouth	71	15
						Birmingham C	19	2
						Peterborough U	20	5
						Blackpool	16	4
Mark Taylor	5 7	10 00	20 11 64	Hartlepool	Local	Hartlepool U	47	4
						Crewe Alex (loan)	3	—
						Blackpool	90	38

Trainees
Gouck, Andrew S; Sinclair, Trevor L.

**Non-Contract
James, Ryan.

Associated Schoolboys
Alderson, Michael T; Baldwin, Thomas M; Barnes, Terry; Bonner, Mark; Horsfield, Damien J; Leitch, Grant J: Marsh, Simon J; Mitchell, Neil; Murphy, James A; Murphy, Steven A; Murray, Mark; Potter, Ian L; Saddler, Ian D. Stoddard, John A; Thompson, Paul D; Woodhall, Alan C.

**Non-Contract Players who are retained must be re-signed before they are eligible to play in League matches.

BOLTON WANDERERS 1989–90 *Back row (left to right):* Dean Crombie, Mark Came, Dave Felgate, Kevin Rose, Gareth Gray, Mark Winstanley, Barry Cowdrill.
Centre row: Steve Carroll (Youth Coach), Gary Brown, Phil Brown, Julian Darby, David Reeves, Tony Philliskirk, Steve Thompson, Stuart Storer.
Gary Henshaw, Mike Jeffrey, Ewan Simpson (Physiotherapist).
Front row: Ian Stevens, Neil Fisher, Paul Hughes, Nicky Brookman, Mick Brown (First Team Coach), Phil Neal (Manager), Dave Roberts, Jeff Chandler, Robbie Savage, Nicky Spooner.

Division 3   **BOLTON WANDERERS**

Burnden Park, Bolton BL3 2QR. Telephone Bolton (0204) 389200. Information Service: Bolton 21101. Commercial Dept. (0204) 24518.

Ground capacity: 25,000.

Record attendance: 69,912 v Manchester C, FA Cup 5th rd, 18 Feb, 1933.

Record receipts: £53,931 v Everton, League Cup semi-final, 2nd leg, 15 Feb, 1977.

Pitch measurements: 113yd × 76yd.

President: Nat Lofthouse.

Chairman: S. Jones.

Directors: P. A. Gartside, G. Ball, G. Hargreaves, G. Seymour, G. Warburton, W. B. Warburton.

Team Manager: Phil Neal. *Coach:* Mick Brown.

Secretary: Des McBain. *Commercial Manager:*

Physio: E. Simpson.

Year Formed: 1874. *Turned Professional:* 1880. *Ltd Co.:* 1895.

Previous Grounds: Park Recreation Ground and Cockle's Field before moving to Pike's Lane ground 1881; Burnden Park 1895.

Previous Name: 1874–77, Christ Church FC; 1877 became Bolton Wanderers.

Club Nickname: 'The Trotters'.

Record League Victory: 8-0 v Barnsley, Division 2, 6 October 1934 – Jones; Smith, Finney; Goslin, Atkinson, George Taylor; George T. Taylor (2), Eastham, Milsom (1), Westwood (4), Cook. (1 og).

Record Cup Victory: 13-0 v Sheffield U, FA Cup 2nd rd, 1 February 1890 – Parkinson; Robinson (1), Jones; Bullough, Davenport, Roberts; Rushton, Brogan (3), Cassidy (5), McNee, Weir (4).

Record Defeat: 0-7 v Manchester C.., Division 1, 21 March, 1936.

Most League Points (2 for a win): 61, Division 3, 1972–73.

Most League Points (3 for a win): 78, Division 4, 1987–88.

Most League Goals: 96, Division 2, 1934–35.

Highest League Scorer in Season: Joe Smith, 38, Division 1, 1920-21.

Most League Goals in Total Aggregate: Nat Lofthouse, 255, 1946–61.

Most Capped Player: Nat Lofthouse, 33, England.

Most League Appearances: Eddie Hopkinson, 519, 1956–70.

Record Transfer Fee Received: £340,000 from Birmingham C for Neil Whatmore, August 1981.

Record Transfer Fee Paid: £350,000 to WBA for Len Cantello, May 1979.

Football League Record: 1888 Founder Member of the League; 1899–1900 Division 2; 1900–03 Division 1; 1903–05 Division 2; 1905–08 Division 1; 1908–09 Division 2; 1909–10 Division 1; 1910–11 Division 2; 1911–33 Division 1; 1933–35 Division 2; 1935–64 Division 1; 1964–71 Division 2; 1971–73 Division 3; 1973–78 Division 2; 1978–80 Division 1; 1980–83 Division 2; 1983–87 Division 3; 1987–88 Division 4; 1988– Division 3.

Honours: Football League: Division 1 best season: 3rd, 1891–92, 1920–21, 1924–25. Division 2 – Champions 1908–09, 1977–78; Runners-up 1899–1900, 1904–05, 1910–11, 1934–35, Division 3 – Champions 1972–73. *FA Cup:* Winners 1923, 1926, 1929, 1958; Runners-up 1894, 1904, 1953. *Football League Cup:* Semi-final 1976–77. *Freight Rover Trophy:* Runners-up 1986. *Sherpa Van Trophy:* Winners 1989.

Colours: White shirts, navy blue shorts, white stockings. **Change colours:** Red shirts, white shorts, red stockings.

BOLTON WANDERERS 1989–90 LEAGUE RECORD

Match No.	Date	Venue	Opponents	Result	H/T Score	Lg. Pos.	Goalscorers	Atten- dance
1	Aug 19	A	Cardiff C	W 2-0	2-0	—	Philliskirk, Darby	4376
2	26	H	Fulham	D 0-0	0-0	6		5524
3	Sept 2	A	Huddersfield T	D 1-1	1-1	7	Crombie	7872
4	9	H	Bristol R	W 1-0	0-0	4	Reeves	5913
5	16	A	Rotherham U	L 0-1	0-0	12		6846
6	23	H	Leyton Orient	W 2-1	1-0	8	Cowdrill, Philliskirk	5951
7	26	A	Notts Co	L 1-2	0-2	—	Philliskirk	5392
8	30	H	Mansfield T	D 1-1	1-0	11	Winstanley	5797
9	Oct 7	H	Wigan Ath	W 3-2	1-2	6	Philliskirk (pen), Darby 2	6462
10	14	A	Crewe Alex	D 2-2	0-2	7	Reeves 2	4284
11	17	A	Brentford	W 2-1	1-1	—	Reeves 2	4537
12	21	H	Chester C	W 1-0	1-0	5	Philliskirk	6496
13	28	A	Preston NE	W 4-1	2-0	2	Phillskirk, Thompson, Darby, Kelly (og)	9135
14	31	H	Walsall	D 1-1	1-0	–	Darby	7363
15	Nov 4	H	Swansea C	D 0-0	0-0	3		6618
16	11	A	Bristol C	D 1-1	1-1	6	Brown	11,994
17	25	A	Birmingham C	L 0-1	0-0	7		8081
18	Dec 2	H	Northampton T	L 0-3	0-2	8		5501
19	16	A	Shrewsbury T	D 3-3	2-0	9	Thompson 2, Philliskirk	3443
20	26	H	Blackpool	W 2-0	1-0	7	Darby, Cowdrill	9944
21	30	H	Bury	W 3-1	2-1	4	Reeves 2, Storer	10,628
22	Jan 6	A	Tranmere R	W 3-1	0-1	—	Darby, Cowdrill, Storer	8273
23	13	A	Fulham	D 2-2	2-2	5	Pike, Storer	4523
24	20	H	Cardiff C	W 3-1	2-0	4	Philliskirk 2 (1 pen), Comstive	7017
25	28	A	Bristol R	D 1-1	0-1	—	Philliskirk	7772
26	Feb 10	H	Rotherham U	L 0-2	0-1	6		7728
27	17	A	Northampton T	W 2-0	0-0	7	Darby, Thompson	3432
28	24	H	Birmingham C	W 3-1	1-0	5	Reeves 2, Thompson	7618
29	Mar 3	A	Reading	L 0-2	0-1	6		4461
30	6	A	Mansfield T	W 1-0	0-0	—	Darby	3334
31	10	H	Notts Co	W 3-0	1-0	5	Darby, Philliskirk, Reeves	8420
32	16	A	Wigan Ath	L 0-2	0-2	—		6850
33	20	H	Crewe Alex	D 0-0	0-0	—		7241
34	24	H	Brentford	L 0-1	0-1	5		6156
35	27	A	Leyton Orient	D 0-0	0-0	—		3296
36	31	H	Chester C	L 0-2	0-2	5		2738
37	Apr 3	H	Reading	W 3-0	1-0	—	Phillskirk 2, Thompson	4679
38	7	H	Preston NE	W 2-1	0-0	5	Phillskirk 2	8266
39	10	A	Walsall	L 1-2	0-1	—	Philliskirk (pen)	3376
40	14	H	Tranmere R	D 1-1	1-0	5	Storer	9070
41	16	A	Blackpool	L 1-2	0-0	6	Philliskirk	5435
42	21	H	Shrewsbury T	L 0-1	0-1	6		5665
43	24	A	Bury	L 0-2	0-1	—		6551
44	28	H	Bristol C	W 1-0	1-0	6	Green	11,098
45	May 1	H	Huddersfield T	D 2-2	1-1	—	Green, Phillskirk (pen)	8550
46	5	A	Swansea C	D 0-0	0-0	6		5623

Final League Position: 6

GOALSCORERS

League (59): Philliskirk 18 (4 pens), Darby 10, Reeves 10, Thompson 6, Storer 4, Cowdrill 3, Green 2, Brown 1, Comstive 1, Crombie 1, Pike 1, Winstanley 1, own goal 1.
Littlewoods Cup (15): Philliskirk 5 (1 pen), Came 2, Brown 1, Comstive 1, Cowdrill 1, Darby 1, Henshaw 1, Reeves 1, Savage 1, Thompson 1 (pen).
FA Cup (1): Crombie 1.

Rose	Brown	Cowdrill	Savage	Crombie	Winstanley	Storer	Thompson	Reeves	Philliskirk	Darby	Felgate	Henshaw	Jeffrey	Comstive	Chandler	Stevens	Hughes	Came	Brookman	Pike	Gregory	Green	Match No.
1	2	3	4	5	6	7	8	9	10	11													1
	2	3	4	5	6	7	8	9	10	11	1												2
	2	3	4	5	6	7*	8	9	10	11	1	12											3
1	2	3	4	5	6	7	8	9*	10	11			12										4
1	2	3	4*	5	6	7†	8	9	10	11		14	12										5
1	2	3		5	6	7*	8	9	10	11		12		4									6
1	2	3		5	6		8	9	10	11		7		4									7
1	2	3		5	6		8	9	10	11		7		4									8
	2	3		5	6	7*	8	9	10	11	1			4	12								9
	2	3		5	6	7	8	9	10	11	1			4									10
	2	3		5	6	7	8	9	10	11	1			4									11
	2	3		5	6	7*	8	9	10	11	1	12		4									12
	2	3		5	6		8		10	11	1	7		4		9							13
	2	3		5	6		8		10	11	1	7		4		9							14
	2	3		5	6		8		10	11	1	7	12	4		9*							15
	2	3		5	6		8	9	10	11	1	7		4									16
	2	3		5	6		8			11	1	7	10*	4†			14	9	12				17
	2	3		5	6		8		10	11	1	7		4*			9	12					18
	2			5	6	7	8	9	10	11	1			4						3			19
	2	12		5†	6	7	8	9	10	11	1			4*			14			3			20
	2		4	5	6	7	8	9	10	11	1									3			21
	2		4	5	6	7	8	9	10	11	1									3			22
	2			5	6	7	8	9	10*	11	1	12		4			14			3†			23
	2	3		5		7	8	9	10	11	1			4				6					24
	2	3		5		7	8	9	10	11	1			4				6					25
	2	3		5		7	8	9	10	11	1			4				6					26
	2	3		5	6	7	8	9	10	11	1			4									27
	2	3	12	5	6	7	8	9	10	11	1			4*									28
	2	3	12	5†	6	7*	8	9	10	11	1			4			14						29
	2	3			6	7	8	9	10	11	1			4				5					30
	2	3			6	7	8	9	10	11	1			4				5					31
	2	3	12		6	7	8	9	10	11	1			4*				5					32
	2	3			6	7	8	9	10	11*	1			4				5	12				33
	2	3	12		6	7	8†	9	10	11	1			4*				5	14				34
	2	3		5	6	7	8	9	10	11	1			4									35
	2	3		5	6	7		9	10	11	1			4*			12	8					36
	2	3	4	5	6	7	8	9	10	11	1												37
	2	3	4*	5	6	7	8	9	10	11	1								12				38
	2	3		5	6	7†	8	9	10	11	1			12	14				4*				39
	2	3			6	7	8	9	10	11	1			4				5*	12				40
	2	3		5	6	7	8	9	10	11	1			4									41
	2	3		5	6	7	8	9	10	11	1			4*							12		42
	2	3			6	7	8	9	10	11	1							5				4	43
	2	3			6	7*	8	9	10	11	1							5			12	4	44
	2	3	12		6	7*	8	9	10	11	1							5				4	45
	2	3			6	7	8	9	10	11	1							5				4	46
6	46	43	7	36	43	38	45	41	45	46	40	9	1	30	—	3	1	15	—	5	2	4	

```
        +          + +                          + + + +        + + + +        + +
        1s        3s2s                          5s 3s1s 1s    1s 1s4s 2s       5s 1s
```

Littlewoods Cup
First Round — Rochdale (a) 1-2
(h) 5-1
Second Round — Watford (h) 2-1
(a) 1-1
Third Round — Swindon T (a) 3-3
(h) 1-1
(h) 1-1
(a) 1-2

FA Cup
First Round — Blackpool (a) 1-2

BOLTON WANDERERS

Player and Position	Ht	Wt	Birth Date	Birth Place	Source	Clubs	League App	Gls
Goalkeepers								
David Felgate	6 2	13 10	4 3 60	Bl Ffestiniog	Blaenau	Bolton W	—	—
						Rochdale (loan)	35	—
						Bradford C (loan)	—	—
						Crewe Alex (loan)	14	—
						Rochdale (loan)	12	—
						Lincoln C	198	—
						Cardiff C (loan)	4	—
						Grimsby T (loan)	12	—
						Grimsby T	12	—
						Rotherham U (loan)	—	—
						Bolton W	167	—
Gareth Gray	6 0	11 02	24 2 70	Longridge	Darwen	Bolton W	—	—
Kevin Rose	6 1	13 06	23 11 60	Evesham	Ledbury T	Lincoln C	—	—
					Ledbury T	Hereford U	268	—
						Bolton W	6	—
						Halifax T (loan)	—	—
						Carlisle U (loan)	11	—
Defenders								
Phil Brown	5 11	11 06	30 5 59	South Shields	Local	Hartlepool U	217	8
						Halifax T	135	19
						Bolton W	92	5
Mark Came	6 0	12 13	14 9 61	Exeter	Winsford U	Bolton W	165	7
Barry Cowdrill	5 11	11 04	3 1 57	Birmingham	Sutton Coldfield	WBA	131	—
						Rotherham U (loan)	2	—
						Bolton W	82	3
Dean Crombie	6 0	11 12	9 8 57	Lincoln	Ruston Sp	Lincoln C	33	—
						Grimsby T	320	3
						Reading (loan)	4	—
						Bolton W	93	1
Julian Darby	6 0	11 04	3 10 68	Bolton		Bolton W	155	17
Paul Hughes	5 9	11 06	19 12 68	Denton	Trainee	Bolton W	13	—
Phil Neal	5 11	12 02	20 2 51	Irchester	Apprentice	Northampton T	186	29
						Liverpool	455	41
						Bolton W	64	3
Darren Oliver			1 11 71	Liverpool		Bolton W	—	—
Dave Roberts*	5 8	10 00	18 7 71	Ormskirk	Trainee	Bolton W	—	—
Nicky Spooner	5 8	11 00	5 6 71	Manchester	Trainee	Bolton W	—	—
Mark Winstanley	6 1	12 04	22 1 68	St Helens	Trainee	Bolton W	111	2
Midfield								
Gary Brown	5 10	11 02	3 1 69	Beverley	Blackburn R	Bolton W	—	—
Paul Comstive	6 1	12 07	25 11 61	Southport	Amateur	Blackburn R	6	—
						Rochdale (loan)	9	2
						Wigan Ath	35	2
						Wrexham	99	8
						Burnley	82	17
						Bolton W	31	1
Neil Fisher	5 8	11 00	7 11 70	St Helens	Trainee	Bolton W	—	—
John Gregory	6 1	11 00	11 5 54	Scunthorpe	Apprentice	Northampton T	187	8
						Aston Villa	65	10
						Brighton & HA	72	7
						QPR	161	36
						Derby Co	103	22
						Portsmouth	—	—
						Plymouth Arg	3	—
						Bolton W	7	—
Gary Henshaw	5 9	11 08	18 2 65	Leeds	Apprentice	Grimsby T	50	9
						Bolton W	66	4
						Rochdale (loan)	9	1

BOLTON WANDERERS

Foundation: In 1874 boys of Christ Church Sunday School, Blackburn Street, led by their master Thomas Ogden, established a football club which went under the name of the school and whose president was Vicar of Christ Church. Membership was 6d (2½p). When their president began to lay down too many rules about the use of church premises, the club broke away and formed Bolton Wanderers in 1877, holding their earliest meetings at the Gladstone Hotel.

First Football League game: 8 September, 1888, Football League, v Derby C (h), L 3-6 – Harrison; Robinson, Mitchell; Roberts, Weir, Bullough, Davenport (2), Milne, Coupar, Barbour, Brogan (1).

Managers (and Secretary-managers)
Tom Rawthorne 1874–85*, J. J. Bentley 1885–86*, W. G. Struthers 1886–87*, Fitzroy Norris 1887*, J. J. Bentley 1887–95*, Harry Downs 1895–96*, Frank Brettell 1896–98*, John Somerville 1898–1910, Will Settle 1910–15, Tom Mather 1915–19, Charles Foweraker 1919–44, Walter Rowley 1944–50, Bill Ridding 1951–68, Nat Lofthouse 1968–70, Jimmy McIlroy 1970, Jimmy Meadows 1971, Nat Lofthouse 1971 (then admin. man. to 1972), Jimmy Armfield 1971–74, Ian Greaves 1974–80, Stan Anderson 1980–81, George Mulhall 1981–82, John McGovern 1982–85, Charlie Wright 1985, Phil Neal 1985–   .

Player and Position	Ht	Wt	Birth Date	Place	Source	Clubs	League App	Gls
Bob Savage	5 7	11 01	8 1 60	Liverpool	Apprentice	Liverpool	—	—
						Wrexham (loan)	27	10
						Stoke C	7	—
						Bournemouth	82	18
						Bradford C	11	—
						Bolton W	87	11
Steve Thompson	5 11	11 10	2 11 64	Oldham	Apprentice	Bolton W	288	44
Forwards								
Scott Green	6 0	11 12	15 1 70	Walsall	Trainee	Derby Co	—	—
						Bolton W	5	2
Mike Jeffrey	5 9	10 06	11 8 71	Liverpool	Trainee	Bolton W	13	—
Tony Philliskirk	6 1	11 03	10 2 65	Sunderland	Amateur	Sheffield U	80	20
						Rotherham U (loan)	6	1
						Oldham Ath	10	1
						Preston NE	14	6
						Bolton W	45	18
David Reeves	6 0	11 05	19 11 67	Birkenhead	Heswell	Sheffield W	17	2
						Scunthorpe U (loan)	4	2
						Scunthorpe U (loan)	6	4
						Burnley (loan)	16	8
						Bolton W	41	10
Ian Stevens	5 9	12 00	21 10 66	Malta		Preston NE	11	2
						Stockport Co	2	—
					Lancaster C	Bolton W	42	7
Stuart Storer	5 11	11 08	16 1 67	Harborough		Mansfield T	1	—
						Birmingham C	8	—
						Everton	—	—
						Wigan Ath (loan)	12	—
						Bolton W	76	7

Trainees
Bentham, Nicholas J; Birks, Stephen J; Coffey, Steven; Edge, Dean J; Hart, Neil J; Hughes, Kieran M; Mason, Darren J; Sharrock, Simon J; Stubbs, Alan; Vain, Stephen J; Williams, Shane.

Associated Schoolboys
Agnew, Neil; Antrobus, Wayne A; Bancks, Carl; Bebe, Robert E; Farlow, Darren K; Grant, Richard; Harrison, Craig A; Holden, Christian J; Hulme, Ian; McKay, Andrew S; Mason, Andrew; Randles, Martin; Smith, Marcus; Strange, Anthony M; Wildish, Daniel; Woodland, Ian A.

AFC BOURNEMOUTH 1989-90 *Back row (left to right):* John Kirk (Trainer), Luther Blissett, Matthew Holmes, Peter Shearer, Shaun Teale, Kevin Bond, Phil Kite, Gerry Peyton, Trevor Aylott, John Williams, Paul Morrell, Shaun Brooks, George Lawrence, John Dickens (Physiotherapist).
Front row: David Coleman, Sean O'Driscoll, Paul Miller, Denny Mundee, Harry Redknapp (Manager), Mark Newson (Captain), Jimmy Gabriel (Assistant Manager), Gavin Peacock, Shaun Close, Mark O'Connor, Paul Moulden.

Division 3   AFC BOURNEMOUTH

Dean Court Ground, Bournemouth. Telephone Bournemouth (0202) 395381. Fax No: 0202 309797.

Ground capacity: 11,375.

Record attendance: 28,799 v Manchester U, FA Cup 6th rd. 2nd March, 1957.

Record receipts: £33,723 v Manchester U, FA Cup 3rd. 7th Jan, 1984.

Pitch measurements: 112yd × 75yd.

Chairman: J. P. Nolan. *Vice-Chairman:* P. W. Hayward JP.

Managing Director: . *Directors:* E. G. Keep, G. M. C. Hayward, B. E. Willis, C. W. Legg.

Secretary:

Manager: Harry Redknapp.

Coach: Terry Shanahan. *Trainer:* J. Kirk. *Physio:* John Dickens.

Asst. Manager: Jimmy Gabriel.

Commercial Manager:

Club Nickname: 'Cherries'.

Year Formed: 1899. *Turned Professional:* 1912. *Ltd Co.:* 1914.

Previous Names: Boscombe St Johns, 1890–99; Boscombe FC, 1899–1923; Bournemouth & Boscombe Ath FC, 1923–71.

Previous Grounds: 1899–1910. Castlemain Road, Pokesdown; 1910, Dean Court.

Record League Victory: 7-0 v Swindon T, Division 3 (S), 22 September 1956 – Godwin; Cunningham, Keetley; Clayton, Crosland, Rushworth; Siddall (1), Norris (2), Arnott (1), Newsham (2), Cutler (1). 10-0 win v Northampton T at start of 1939–40 expunged from the records on outbreak of war.

Record Cup Victory: 11-0 v Margate, FA Cup, 1st rd, 20 November 1971 – Davies; Machin (1), Kitchener, Benson, Jones, Powell, Cave (1), Boyer, MacDougall (9 incl. 1p), Miller, Scott (De Garis).

Record Defeat: 0-9 v Lincoln C. Division 3, 18 December, 1982.

Most League Points (2 for a win): 62, Division 3, 1971–72.

Most League Points (3 for a win): 97, Division 3, 1986–87.

Most League Goals: 88, Division 3 (S), 1956–57.

Highest League Scorer in Season: Ted MacDougall, 42, 1970–71.

Most League Goals in Total Aggregate: Ron Eyre, 202, 1924–33.

Most Capped Player: Colin Clarke, 6 (24), Northern Ireland.

Most League Appearances: Ray Bumstead, 412, 1958–70.

Record Transfer Fee Received: £465,000 from Manchester C for Ian Bishop, August 1989.

Record Transfer Fee Paid: £210,000 to Gillingham for Gavin Peacock, August 1989.

Football League Record: Elected to Division 3 (S), 1923. Remained a Third Division Club for record number of years until 1970; 1970–71 Division 4; 1971–75 Division 3; 1975–82 Division 4; 1982–87 Division 3; 1987–90 Division 2; 1990– Division 3.

Honours: Football League: Division 3 – Champions 1986–87; Division 3(S) – Runners-up 1947–48. Promotion from Division 4 1970–71 (2nd), 1981–82 (4th). *FA Cup:* best season: 6th rd, 1956–57. *Football League Cup:* best season: 4th rd, 1962, 1964. *Associate Members' Cup:* Winners 1984.

Colours: All red. **Change colours:** All white.

BOURNEMOUTH 1989–90 LEAGUE RECORD

Match No.	Date	Venue	Opponents	Result	H/T Score	Lg. Pos.	Goalscorers	Atten- dance
1	Aug 19	A	Brighton & HA	L 1-2	0-0	—	Newson	9685
2	22	H	WBA	D 1-1	1-0	—	Moulden	8226
3	26	H	Hull C	W 5-4	4-1	8	Swan (og), Moulden 3, Blissett	6454
4	Sept 2	A	Ipswich T	D 1-1	0-0	10	Shearer	11,425
5	9	H	Newcastle U	W 2-1	1-1	6	Moulden 2	9882
6	16	A	Middlesbrough	L 1-2	1-1	11	Blissett	16,077
7	23	H	Blackburn R	L 2-4	1-1	15	Peacock, Blissett (pen)	7409
8	26	H	Port Vale	W 1-0	1-0	—	Blissett	6511
9	30	A	Oxford U	W 2-1	1-0	9	Lawrence, Moulden	5325
10	Oct 7	A	Sunderland	L 2-3	1-1	11	MacPhail (og), Blissett	15,933
11	14	H	Oldham Ath	W 2-0	1-0	9	Moulden, Peacock	6796
12	17	A	Watford	D 2-2	2-1		Brooks, Blissett	9013
13	21	H	Portsmouth	L 0-1	0-1	12		9353
14	Nov 1	H	West Ham U	D 1-1	1-1	—	Blissett	9979
15	4	A	Leeds U	L 0-3	0-2	14		26,484
16	11	H	Sheffield U	L 0-1	0-1	15		8481
17	18	H	Stoke C	W 2-1	1-0	13	Brooks, Moulden	6412
18	25	A	Bradford C	L 0-1	0-1	15		7436
19	Dec 2	H	Brighton & HA	L 0-2	0-2	17		6890
20	5	A	Swindon T	W 3-2	1-1	—	Lawrence, Blissett 2	7326
21	9	A	WBA	D 2-2	0-2	16	Blissett 2	8568
22	16	H	Barnsley	W 2-1	1-0	12	Moulden, Blissett	5506
23	26	A	Leicester C	L 1-2	0-1	12	Williams	14,128
24	30	A	Wolverhampton W	L 1-3	0-2	14	Shearer	15,421
25	Jan 1	H	Plymouth Arg	D 2-2	1-0	15	Holmes, Williams	6939
26	13	A	Hull C	W 4-1	2-0	14	Holmes, Lawrence, Shearer, Blissett	4673
27	20	H	Ipswich T	W 3-1	1-0	12	Blissett 3 (1 pen)	7464
28	Feb 3	A	Blackburn R	D 1-1	0-0	12	Moulden	7947
29	10	A	Middlesbrough	D 2-2	1-0	12	Moulden, Peacock	7630
30	24	H	Bradford C	W 1-0	1-0	12	Moulden	6206
31	28	A	Newcastle U	L 0-3	0-0	—		15,119
32	Mar 3	A	Stoke C	D 0-0	0-0	13		10,988
33	6	H	Oxford U	L 0-1	0-1	—		6319
34	10	A	Port Vale	D 1-1	0-0	14	Brooks	7131
35	17	H	Sunderland	L 0-1	0-0	15		6328
36	20	A	Oldham Ath	L 0-4	0-1	—		10,109
37	24	H	Watford	D 0-0	0-0	15		6737
38	31	A	Portsmouth	L 1-2	1-0	16	Brooks	8835
39	Apr 3	H	Wolverhampton W	D 1-1	0-0	—	Shearer	7448
40	7	H	Swindon T	L 1-2	1-1	18	Blissett	7772
41	11	A	West Ham U	L 1-4	1-2	—	Coleman	20,202
42	14	A	Plymouth Arg	L 0-1	0-0	20		7520
43	17	H	Leicester C	L 2-3	1-3	—	Peacock, Aylott	6781
44	21	A	Bransley	W 1-0	0-0	20	Aylott	7415
45	28	A	Sheffield U	L 2-4	1-2	21	Cadette, Blissett (pen)	20,994
46	May 5	H	Leeds U	L 0-1	0-0	22		9918

Final League Position: 22

GOALSCORERS

League (57): Blissett 18 (3 pens), Moulden 13, Brooks 4, Peacock 4, Shearer 4, Lawrence 3, Aylott 2, Holmes 2, Williams 2, Cadette 1, Coleman 1, Newson 1, own goals 2.
Littlewoods Cup (2): Moulden 1, Shearer 1.
FA Cup (0).

Kite	Newson	Morrell	Teale	Miller	Peacock	Lawrence	Moulden	O'Driscoll	Holmes	Bissett	Barnes	Peyton	O'Connor	Shearer	Brooks	Bond	Coleman	Mundee	Williams	Redknapp	Aylott	Slatter	Cadette	Match No.
1	2	3	4	5	6	7	8	9	10*	11	12													1
	2	3	6	5	4	7	8	9	10	11		1												2
	2	3	4	5	6	7*	8	9	12	11		1	10											3
	2	3*	4	5	6	7	8	9		11		1	10	12										4
		3	4	5	6	7	8	9		11		1		2	10									5
		3	4	5	6	7	8	9		11	12	1		2	10*									6
1		3	4	5	6	7*	8	9		11	12			2	10									7
	2	3	4†	5	6	7	8*	9		11		1		12	10	14								8
	2	3	4	5	6	7†	8	9		11		1		12	10*	14								9
	2	3†	4	5	6*		8	9		11	7	1		12	10	14								10
	2*	3	4	5	6		8	9	7	11		1			10	12								11
		3	4	5	6		8	9	7*	11		1			10	2	12							12
		3†	4	5	6		8	9		11		1	7*	12	10	2	14							13
			4	5			8	9		11		1	7	6	10	2	3							14
1			4		6		8	9		11			7*	5	10	2†	3	14	12					15
			4	5		7	8*	9		11		1		6	10	2	3		12					16
			4	12	6	7†	8	9		11		1	14		10	2	3		5*					17
	7*		4		6	12	8	9		11		1			10	2	3		5					18
			4		6	7	8	9		11		1			10	2	3		5					19
	12		4		6	7	8	9*		11		1			10	2	3		5					20
			4		6	7	8	9		11		1			10	2	3		5					21
	12		4		6	7	8	9*		11		1			10	2	3		5					22
	9		4		6	7	8			11		1			10	2	3		5					23
	9		4	14	6	7	8			11		1		12	10	2	3*		5†					24
	12	3	4		6	7			9	11		1		8	10*	2			5					25
		3	4		6	7	8		10	11		1		9*		2			5	12				26
	12	3	4		6	7	8*		10	11		1		9		2†			5	14				27
	12	3	4		6	7	8†		10	11		1		9		2			5*	14				28
1		3	4		6	7*	8		10	11		1		9		2			5	12				29
		3	4		6	7	8	12	10†	11		1		9		2			5*	14				30
		3	4	5	6	7*	8	10		11		1		9		2				12				31
		3	4	5	6	7*	8†	10		11		1		9	12	2				14				32
			4	5	6†		8	12	10	11		1		9	7	2*	3			14				33
			4	5		12		6	10*	11		1		8	7		3	2		9				34
				5		12		6	10*	11		1		8	7	4	3	2		9				35
				5	6	9		2	10*	11		1		8	7	4	3		12					36
				5		12		6	10*	11		1		8	7†	4	3			9	2	14		37
1				5		7		6	10†	11				12	8	4*	3		14	2	9			38
1					6			7	10	11				5	8		3	4		9	2			39
			5	6*				7	12	11		1		10	8		3	4		9	2			40
			5	6				7	10*	11		1		4			3	12	8	9†	2*	14		41
			5	6				7	10	11		1		4	8		3	2*		9	12			42
1			5	6				7	10*	11		1		4	8		3	2		12	9			43
			5	6				7		11		1		4	8		3	2		9	12	10*		44
			5	6*	12			7		11		1		4	8		3	2		9		10		45
			5	6*	10			7		11		1		4	8	2	3			9		12		46
7	11	21	34	29	41	28	32	37	20	46	1	39	5	27	34	27	25	8	14	1	10	5	4	
+5s		+2s		+5s		+2s	+2s		+3s			+1s 7s	+1s	+4s	+2s		+2s 2s	+3s 8s		+1s	+4s			

Littlewoods Cup	Second Round	Crewe Alex (a)	1-0
		(h)	0-0
	Third Round	Sunderland (a)	1-1
		(h)	0-1
FA Cup	Third Round	Sheffield U (a)	0-2

BOURNEMOUTH

Player and Position	Ht	Wt	Birth Date	Place	Source	Clubs	League App	Gls
Goalkeepers								
Phil Kite	6 1	14 07	26 10 62	Bristol	Apprentice	Bristol R	96	—
						Tottenham H (loan)	—	—
						Southampton	4	—
						Middlesbrough (loan)	2	—
						Gillingham	70	—
						Bournemouth	7	—
Gerry Peyton	6 2	13 09	20 5 56	Birmingham	Atherstone T	Burnley	30	—
						Fulham	345	—
						Southend U (loan)	10	—
						Bournemouth	166	—
Defenders								
Kevin Bond	6 0	13 07	22 6 57	London	Apprentice	Bournemouth	—	—
						Norwich C	142	12
					Seattle S	Manchester C	110	11
						Southampton	140	6
						Bournemouth	58	1
Paul Miller	6 1	12 02	11 10 59	London	Apprentice	Tottenham H	208	7
						Charlton Ath	42	2
						Watford	20	1
						Bournemouth	31	—
						Brentford (loan)	3	—
Paul Morrell	5 11	13 05	23 3 61	Poole	Weymouth	Bournemouth	256	6
Shaun Teale	6 0	13 07	10 3 64	Southport	Weymouth	Bournemouth	54	—
John Williams	6 1	13 12	3 10 60	Liverpool	Amateur	Tranmere R	173	13
						Port Vale	50	2
						Bournemouth	117	9
Midfield								
Shaun Brooks	5 7	11 00	9 10 62	London	Apprentice	Crystal Palace	54	1
						Orient	148	26
						Bournemouth	108	13
David Coleman	5 7	10 08	8 4 67	Salisbury		Bournemouth	43	2
						Colchester U (loan)	6	1
Paul Mitchell			20 10 71	Bournemouth	Trainee	Bournemouth	—	—
Sean O'Driscoll	5 8	11 03	1 7 57	Wolverhampton	Alvechurch	Fulham	148	13
						Bournemouth (loan)	19	1
						Bournemouth	255	15
Gavin Peacock	5 7	11 00	18 11 67	Kent		QPR	17	—
						Gillingham	70	11
						Bournemouth	41	4
Jamie Redknapp§	5 11	11 08	25 6 73	Barton-on-Sea	Trainee	Bournemouth	4	—
Keith Rowland			1 9 71	Portadown	Trainee	Bournemouth	—	—
Forwards								
Trevor Aylott	6 1	14 00	26 11 57	London	Apprentice	Chelsea	29	2
						QPR (loan)	—	–
						Barnsley	96	26
						Millwall	32	5
						Luton T	32	10
						Crystal Palace	53	12
						Barnsley (loan)	9	—
						Bournemouth	138	27
Luther Blissett	5 11	12 00	1 2 58	Jamaica		Watford	246	95
						AC Milan	30	5
						Watford	127	44
						Bournemouth	76	37
Efan Ekoku			8 6 67	Manchester	Sutton U	Bournemouth	—	—
Matt Holmes	5 7	10 07	1 8 69	Luton		Bournemouth	26	3
						Cardiff C (loan)	1	—

AFC BOURNEMOUTH

Foundation: There was a Bournemouth FC as early as 1875, but the present club arose out of the remnants of the Boscombe St John's club (formed 1890). The meeting at which Boscombe FC came into being was held at a house in Gladstone Road in 1899. They began by playing in the Boscombe and District Junior League.

First Football League game: 25 August, 1923, Division 3(S), v Swindon T (a), L 1-3 – Heron; Wingham, Lamb; Butt, C. Smith, Voisey; Miller, Lister (1), Davey, Simpson, Robinson.

Managers (and Secretary-managers)
Vincent Kitcher 1914–23*, Harry Kinghorn 1923–25, Leslie Knighton 1925–28, Frank Richards 1928–30, Billy Birrell 1930–35, Bob Crompton 1935–36, Charlie Bell 1936–39, Harry Kinghorn 1939–47, Harry Lowe 1947–50, Jack Bruton 1950–56, Fred Cox 1956–58, Don Welsh 1958–61, Bill McGarry 1961–63, Reg Flewin 1963–65, Fred Cox 1965–70, John Bond 1970–73, Trevor Hartley 1974–78, John Benson 1975–78, Alec Stock 1979–80, David Webb 1980–82, Don Megson 1983, Harry Redknapp 1983–   .

Player and Position	Ht	Wt	Birth Date	Place	Source	Clubs	League App	Gls
George Lawrence	5 10	12 02	14 9 62	London	Apprentice	Southampton	10	1
						Oxford U (loan)	15	4
						Oxford U	63	21
						Southampton	68	11
						Millwall	28	4
						Bournemouth	33	3
Denny Mundee	5 10	11 00	10 10 68	Swindon	Apprentice	QPR	—	—
						Swindon T	—	—
						Bournemouth	12	—
						Torquay U (loan)	9	—
Peter Shearer	6 0	11 06	4 2 67	Birmingham	Apprentice	Birmingham C	4	—
						Rochdale	1	—
					Cheltenham T	Bournemouth	38	5

Trainees
Bradford, Lee T; Case, Andrew J; Ferris, Eamon R; Giddings, Dean; Lovell, Matthew, W; McCarthy, David; Macauley, Philip P; Masters, Neil B; Morris, David K; Philips, Brett, S; Redknapp, Jamie F; Worsfold, Paul S; Zumrutel, Ender.

Associated Schoolboys
Arnell, Brian; Barfoot, Stuart J; Corbridge, Darren L; Dipper, Guy; Fox, Robert D; Kerr, Stuart P; Maunder, Darren P; Smih, Paul; Wake, Nathan.

BRADFORD CITY 1989–90 *Back row (left to right)*: Norman Hunter (Coach), Brian Mitchell, Dave Evans, Peter Jackson, Gavin Oliver, Paul Tomlinson, Lee Sinnott, Leigh Palin, Mark Leonard, Paul Jewell, Brian Tinnion, Brian Edwards (Physiotherapist).
Front row: Gary Chapman, Alan Davies, Lee Duxbury, Greg Abbott, Terry Yorath (Manager), Jimmy Quinn, Karl Goddard, Mark Ellis, David Campbell.

Division 3   **BRADFORD CITY**

Valley Parade Ground, Bradford BD8 7DY. Telephone Bradford (0274) 306062 (Office); (0274) 307050 (Ticket Office).

Ground capacity: 14,814.

Record attendance: 39,146 v Burnley, FA Cup 4th rd, 11 March, 1911.

Record receipts: £59,250 v Tottenham H, FA Cup 3rd rd, 7 January, 1989.

Pitch measurements: 110yd × 76yd.

Chairman: D. Simpson. *Vice-Chairman:* D. Thompson, FCA.

Directors: P. Wilkowski, D. Taylor, FCA, M. WOODHEAD. *Associate Directors:* M. Smith, G. Lee, H. Williams. M. Scott, P. Brearley.

Manager: John Docherty.

Youth Coach: Leighton James. *Physiotherapist:* Brian Edwards. *Coach:* Arthur Graham.

Secretary: Terry Newman. *Lottery Manager:* Tony Thornton.

Club Nickname: 'The Bantams'.

Year Formed: 1903. *Turned Professional:* 1903. *Ltd Co.:* 1908.

Record League Victory: 11-1 v Rotherham U, Division 3 (N), 25 August 1928 – Sherlaw; Russell, Watson; Burkinshaw (1), Summers, Bauld; Harvey (2), Edmunds (3), White (3), Cairns, Scriven (2).

Record Cup Victory: 11-3 v Walker Celtic, FA Cup, 1st rd (replay) 1 December 1937 – Parker; Rookes, McDermott; Murphy, Mackie, Moore; Bagley (1), Whittingham (1), Deakin (4 incl. 1p), Cooke (1), Bartholomew (4).

Record Defeat: 1-9 v Colchester U, Division 4, 30 December, 1961.

Most League Points (2 for a win): 63, Division 3 (N), 1928–29.

Most League Points (3 for a win): 94, Division 3, 1984–85.

Most League Goals: 128, Division 3 (N), 1928–29.

Highest League Scorer in Season: David Layne, 34, Division 4, 1961–62.

Most League Goals in Total Aggregate: Bobbby Campbell, 121, 1981–84, 1984–86.

Most Capped Player: Harry Hampton, 9, Northern Ireland.

Most League Appearances: Cec Podd, 502, 1970–84.

Record Transfer Fee Received: £850,000 from Everton for Stuart McCall, June 1988.

Record Transfer Fee Paid: £290,000 to Newcastle U for Peter Jackson, October 1988.

Football League Record: 1903 Elected to Division 2; 1908–22 Division 1; 1922–27 Division 2; 1927–29 Division 3 (N); 1929–37 Division 2; 1937–61 Division 3; 1961–69 Division 4; 1969–72 Division 3; 1972–77 Division 4; 1977–78 Division 3; 1978–82 Division 4; 1982–85 Division 3; 1985–90 Division 2; 1990– Division 3.

Honours: Football League: Division 1 best season: 5th, 1910–11; Division 2 – Champions 1907–08; Division 3 – Champions 1984–85; Division 3 (N) – Champions 1928–29; Division 4 – Runners- up 1981–82. *FA Cup:* Winners 1911 (first holders of the present trophy). *Football League Cup* best season: 5th rd, 1965, 1989.

Colours: Yellow shirts with thin claret stripe, claret shorts, amber stockings. **Change colours:** White shirts, black shorts, white stockings.

BRADFORD CITY 1989–90 LEAGUE RECORD

Match No.	Date	Venue	Opponents	Result	H/T Score	Lg. Pos.	Goalscorers	Atten- dance
	Aug 19	H	Port Vale	D	2-2	1-0	—	Jewell, Tinnion	10,242
2	23	A	West Ham U	L	0-2	0-2	—		19,914
3	26	A	Wolverhampton W	D	1-1	1-0	18	Sinnott	13,784
4	Sept 2	H	Portsmouth	D	1-1	0-1	15	Quinn	8425
5	9	A	Oxford U	L	1-2	0-1	22	Davies	4027
6	16	H	Leicester C	W	2-0	1-0	17	Leonard, Quinn	8732
7	23	A	Barnsley	L	0-2	0-1	19		8992
8	26	A	Stoke C	D	1-1	1-0	—	Tinnion	9346
9	30	H	Swindon T	D	1-1	0-0	19	Aizlewood	8334
10	Oct 7	H	Brighton & HA	W	2-0	1-0	19	Adcock, Jewell	7933
11	14	A	Newcastle U	L	0-1	0-0	19		18,898
12	18	H	Ipswich T	W	1-0	0-0	—	Adcock	7350
13	21	A	Sunderland	L	0-1	0-1	18		14,849
14	28	H	Leeds U	L	0-1	0-0	18		12,527
15	31	A	Oldham Ath	D	2-2	1-0	—	Quinn 2	7772
16	Nov 4	A	Plymouth Arg	D	1-1	0-0	18	Campbell	7152
17	11	H	Hull C	L	2-3	0-0	19	Campbell, Jackson	8540
18	18	A	Sheffield U	D	1-1	0-0	18	Jewell	15,419
19	25	H	Bournemouth	W	1-0	1-0	17	Mitchell	7436
20	Dec 2	A	Port Vale	L	2-3	1-2	20	Leonard, Abbott	6762
21	9	H	West Ham U	W	2-1	1-1	19	Leonard, Quinn	9257
22	16	A	Watford	L	2-7	0-5	21	Campbell, Quinn	8554
23	26	H	Middlesbrough	L	0-1	0-1	21		10,008
24	30	H	WBA	W	2-0	1-0	20	Sinnott, Tinnion	8560
25	Jan 1	A	Blackburn R	D	2-2	0-0	19	Jewell, Tinnion (pen)	9957
26	13	H	Wolverhampton W	D	1-1	1-0	20	Leonard	10,680
27	20	A	Portsmouth	L	0-3	0-2	22		8801
28	Feb 3	H	Barnsley	D	0-0	0-0	22		9923
29	10	A	Leicester C	D	1-1	1-1	21	Adcock	10,281
30	17	A	Oxford U	l	1-2	0-1	22	Leonard	7389
31	24	A	Bournemouth	L	0-1	0-1	22		6206
32	Mar 3	H	Sheffield U	L	1-4	0-1	22	Adcock	10,348
33	6	A	Swindon T	L	1-3	1-3	—	Jackson	8483
34	10	H	Stoke C	W	1-0	0-0	22	Woods	9269
35	14	A	WBA	L	0-2	0-1	—		8017
36	17	A	Brighton & HA	L	1-2	0-0	23	McCall	6831
37	21	H	Newcastle U	W	3-2	1-1	—	Abbott, Mitchell, Woods	10,264
38	24	A	Ipswich T	L	0-1	0-1	23		11,074
39	31	H	Sunderland	L	0-1	0-0	23		9826
40	Apr 7	A	Leeds U	D	1-1	0-0	23	Tinnion (pen)	32,316
41	14	H	Blackburn R	L	0-1	0-1	23		9082
42	16	A	Middlesbrough	L	0-2	0-2	23		16,376
43	21	H	Watford	W	2-1	1-0	23	Holdsworth (og), Abbott	5964
44	28	A	Hull C	L	1-2	1-0	23	Duxbury	6514
45	May 5	H	Plymouth Arg	L	0-1	0-1	23		4903
46	7	H	Oldham Ath	D	1-1	0-0	—	Adcock	6798

Final League Position: 23

GOALSCORERS

League (44): Quinn 6, Adcock 5, Leonard 5, Tinnion 5 (2 pens), Jewell 4, Abbott 3, Campbell 3, Jackson 2, Mitchell 2, Sinnott 2, Woods 2, Aizlewood 1, Davies 1, Duxbury 1, McCall 1, own goal 1.
Littlewoods Cup (6): Leonard 2, Abbott 1, Jewell 1, Megson 1, Quinn 1.
FA Cup (1): Tinnion 1 (pen).

Tomlinson	Mitchell	Tinnion	Aizlewood	Sinnott	Evans D	Campbell	Abbott	Jewell	Quinn	Ellis	Chapman	Davies	Duxbury	Wharton	Leonard	Megson	Jackson	Goddard	Oliver	Adcock	Evans M	McCall	Costello	Woods	Morgan	Graham	Lawford	Match No.
1	2	3	4	5	6	7†	8	9*	10	11	12	14																1
1		3	4	5	6		2	9	10	11*	12	8	7															2
1		3	4	5	6	7	2	9	10	12	11*	8																3
1		3	4*	5	6	7	2	9	10	12		8		11														4
1	12	3	4	5	6	7	2*	9	10			8	11†	14														5
1		3	4	5	6	7	2		10			8*	11	9	12													6
1		3	4	5	6	8*	2	12	10				11	9	7													7
1		3	4	5	6†		2		10	12		8	11*	9	7	14												8
1		3	4	5			2†	12	10	11*		8		9	7	6	14											9
1		3		5		8	2	11	10						7	6			4	9								10
1		3		5		12	2	11	10			8			14	7*	6		4	9†								11
1		3	8	5		12	2	11	10							7*	6		4	9								12
1		3	8	5			2	11	10		12				14	7*	6		4	9†								13
1	4	3	8	5			7	2*	11	10			12				6			9								14
1	2	3	4*	5	8	7		11	10								6		12	9								15
	2	3	4	5	8	7		11	10								6			9	1							16
	2	3	4	5	8*	7		11	10					12			6			9	1							17
	2		4	5	8*	12	7	11	10					14			6		3	9†	1							18
	2	3	4*	5	8	12	7	11	10								6			9	1							19
	2	3	4	5	8	12	7	11†	10					9			6			14	1*							20
1	2	3*	4		8		11	6		10		12		9		7			5									21
1	2		4	5	6†	11		12	10			8				7*			3	14	9							22
1	2	3	4	5		11*		12	10			8				7	6			9								23
1	2	3	4	5	6				10			8			7	11				9								24
1	2	3	4	5	6	12			10			8			14	7†	11*			9								25
1	2		4	5	6							8		9		11			3	7		10						26
1	2	3	4	5	14	6	12					8†		9					11	7*		10						27
1	2			5	6	12	4					8		9		7			3	11*		10						28
1	2			5	6		4					8		9		7*			3	11		10	12					29
1	2			5	6		4	12				8		9		7			3	11*		10						30
1	2		7	5	6		4	12				8		9					3	11*		10						31
1	2		7	5	6		4*					8		9					3	12		10		11				32
1	2	3	7	5†			4					8		9		6			14	12		10*		11				33
1	2	3	7	5			4					8		9		6				10				11				34
1	2	3	7	5		11*	4	12				8				6				10			9					35
1	2	3	7	5			4					8				6				9*		10	12	11				36
1	2	3	7	5			4					8				6						10	9	11				37
1	2	3	7	5								8				6						10	9	11	4			38
1	2	3		5	7							8	14	9		6						12	10*	11	4†			39
1	2	3	7	5			4					8		9	11	6						10						40
1	2†	3	7	6			4					14		9	8				5			10*	12		11			41
1	12	11	8	6			2					4		7*					5			10	9		3			42
1	12	11	8	6			2	14				4		7*					5			10†	9		3			43
1	8	11		6			2	12				4		7					5			10*	9		3			44
1	2	11	8	6			10					4							5	7		12	9*		3			45
1	2		8	6			10					4				7†			5	11		12	9*		3		14	46
41	32	37	39	45	24	15	35	20	23	3	1	24	9	5	18	21	25	—	19	25	5	11	8	13	2	6	—	
			+3s			+8s	+10s						+3s	+2s	+2s	+3s	+6s	+2s	+1s	+1s	+3s	+3s		+1s	+4s1s		+1s	

Littlewoods Cup Second Round WBA (a) 3-1
                                    (h) 3-5
FA Cup Third Round Charlton Ath (a) 1-1
                          (h) 0-3

BRADFORD CITY

Player and Position	Ht	Wt	Birth Date	Place	Source	Clubs	League App	Gls
Goalkeepers								
Mark Evans	6 0	11 08	24 8 70	Leeds	Trainee	Bradford C	8	—
Paul Tomlinson	6 2	12 10	22 2 64	Brierley Hill	Amateur	Sheffield U	37	—
						Birmingham C (loan)	11	—
						Bradford C	121	—
Defenders								
David Evans	5 11	12 05	20 5 58	West Bromwich	Apprentice	Aston Villa	2	—
						Halifax T	218	9
						Bradford C	223	3
Karl Goddard	5 9	10 10	29 12 67	Leeds	Apprentice	Manchester U	—	—
						Bradford C	73	—
						Exeter C (loan)	1	—
						Colchester U (loan)	16	1
Peter Jackson	6 1	12 06	6 4 61	Bradford	Apprentice	Bradford C	278	24
						Newcastle U	60	3
						Bradford C	58	5
Brian Mitchell	6 2	13 00	30 7 63	Stonehaven	King Street	Aberdeen	65	1
						Bradford C	138	9
Gavin Oliver	6 0	12 10	6 9 62	Felling	Apprentice	Sheffield W	20	—
						Tranmere R (loan)	17	1
						Brighton & HA (loan)	16	—
						Bradford C	171	2
Martin Pattison	6 0	11 07	21 7 71	Bradford	Trainee	Bradford C	—	—
Lee Sinnott	6 1	12 07	12 7 65	Aldridge	Apprentice	Walsall	40	2
						Watford	78	2
						Bradford C	129	5
Craig Taylor	5 11	11 00	10 12 70	Leeds	Trainee	Bradford C	—	—
Brian Tinnion	6 0	11 05	23 2 68	Newcastle	Apprentice	Newcastle U	32	2
						Bradford C	51	6
Derek Wroe			19 9 70	Stockport	Trainee	Bradford C	—	—
Midfield								
Greg Abbott	5 9	10 07	14 12 63	Coventry	Apprentice	Coventry C	—	—
						Bradford C	255	38
Mark Aizlewood	6 0	12 08	1 10 59	Newport	Apprentice	Newport Co	38	1
						Luton T	98	3
						Charlton Ath	152	9
						Leeds U	70	3
						Bradford C	39	1
David Campbell	5 9	10 09	2 6 65	Eglington	Oxford BC (NI)	Nottingham F	41	3
						Notts Co (loan)	18	2
						Charlton Ath	30	1
						Plymouth Arg (loan)	1	—
						Bradford C	35	4
Alan Davies	5 8	11 04	5 12 61	Manchester	Apprentice	Manchester U	7	—
						Newcastle U	21	1
						Charlton Ath (loan)	1	—
						Carlisle U (loan)	4	1
						Swansea C	84	8
						Bradford C	26	1
Lee Duxbury	5 10	11 07	7 10 69	Skipton	Trainee	Bradford C	13	1
						Rochdale (loan)	10	—
Jimmy Graham	5 11	11 00	15 11 68	Glasgow	Trainee	Bradford C	7	—
						Rochdale (loan)	11	—
Craig Lawford§			25 11 72	Dewsbury	Trainee	Bradford C	1	—
Chris Lee	5 10	11 07	18 6 71	Halifax	Trainee	Bradford C	—	—
Ian Marsh*	5 8	11 00	27 10 69	Swansea	Trainee	Swansea C	1	—
						Bradford C	—	—

BRADFORD CITY

Foundation: Bradford was a rugby stronghold around the turn of the century but after Manningham RFC held an archery contest to help them out of financial difficulties in 1903, they were persuaded to give up the handling code and turn to soccer. So they formed Bradford City and continued at Valley Parade. Recognising this as an opportunity of spreading the dribbling code in this part of Yorkshire, the Football League immediately accepted the new club's first application for membership of the Second Division.

First Football League game: 1 September, 1903, Division 2, v Grimsby T (a), L 0-2 – Seymour; Wilson, Halliday; Robinson, Millar, Farnall; Guy, Beckram, Forrest, McMillan, Graham.

Managers (and Secretary-managers)
Robert Campbell 1903–05, Peter O'Rourke 1905–21, David Menzies 1921–26, Colin Veitch 1926–28, Peter O'Rourke 1928–30, Jack Peart 1930–35, Dick Ray 1935–37, Fred Westgarth 1938–43, Bob Sharp 1943–46, Jack Barker 1946–47, John Milburn 1947–48, David Steele 1948–52, Albert Harris 1952, Ivor Powell 1952–55, Peter Jackson 1955–61, Bob Brocklebank 1961–64, Bill Harris 1965–66, Willie Watson 1966–69, Grenville Hair 1967–68, Jimmy Wheeler 1968–71, Bryan Edwards 1971–75, Bobby Kennedy 1975–78, John Napier 1978, George Mulhall 1978–81, Roy McFarland 1981–82, Trevor Cherry 1982–87, Terry Dolan 1987–89, Terry Yorath 1989–90, John Docherty 1990– .

Player and Position	Ht	Wt	Birth Date	Place	Source	Clubs	League App	Gls
Forwards								
Tony Adcock	5 10	12 04	27 2 63	Bethnal Green	Apprentice	Colchester U	210	98
						Manchester C	15	5
						Northampton T	72	30
						Bradford C	28	5
Peter Costello	6 0	11 07	31 10 69	Halifax	Trainee	Bradford C	20	2
Mark Ellis	5 9	10 09	6 1 62	Bradford	Trinity Ath	Bradford C	218	30
Paul Jewell	5 8	10 08	28 9 64	Liverpool	Apprentice	Liverpool	—	—
						Wigan Ath	137	35
						Bradford C	69	8
Mark Leonard	5 11	11 10	27 9 62	St Helens	Witton A	Everton	—	—
						Tranmere R (loan)	7	—
						Crewe Alex	54	15
						Stockport Co	73	24
						Bradford C	120	25
Ian McCall	5 10	11 07	13 9 64	Dumfries	Motherwell Tech	Queen's Park	66	9
						Dunfermline Ath	47	8
						Rangers	21	2
						Bradford C	12	1
Michael McHugh	5 11	11 00	3 4 71	Donegal		Bradford C	—	—
Kevin Megson	5 11	11 00	1 7 71	Halifax	Trainee	Bradford C	23	—
Neil Woods	6 1	12 12	30 7 66	York	Apprentice	Doncaster R	65	16
						Rangers	3	—
						Ipswich T	27	5
						Bradford C	14	2

Trainees
Bairstow, Scott; Butler, Paul J; Clarkson, Andrew P; Dickinson, Stephen T; Gibson, Christopher M; Inch, Simon M; Jules, Mark A; Lawford, Craig B; McGinley, Martin G; Maloney, Kyle; Quigley, Adrian K; Ryan, Jason; Stergiopoulos, Marcus; Sykes, Matthew J; White, Jonathan G.

Associated Schoolboys
Boardman, Stephen; Bosworth, Harwin; Cawthorne, Paul J; Dover, Paul N; Graystone, Neil J; Higgins, Kevin T; Hutton, Emmott J; Hutton, Samuel P; Mangan, Mark A; Megson, James A; Neil, Jamie W; Nutt, Christopher D; Owen, Gary J; Partridge, Scott M; Renton, Craig D; Stuttard, Andrew J; Sunderland, Andrew D; Sutcliffe, Adrian; Trees, James A; Wilson, Richard J.

Associated Schoolboys who have accepted the club's offer of a Traineeship/Contract
Coy, Paul T; Crabtree, Anthony M; Cressy, Matthew A; Delahaye, Scott; Howe, Jeremy R; Richards, Dean; Smith, Darren P; Tomkinson, Alan P.

116

BRENTFORD 1989–90 *Back row (left to right):* Keith Millen, Robert Larkin, Simon Ratcliffe, John Buttigieg, Terry Evans, Gary Blissett, Kelly Haag, Jamie Bates.
Centre row: Tony Gourvish (Coach), Paul Buckle, Roger Stanislaus, Matthew Howard, Marcus Gayle, Tony Parks, Colin Jones, Kevin Godfrey, Jason Cousins, Mark Fleming, Roy Clare (Physiotherapist).
Front row: Eddie May, Allan Cockram, Andy Ansah, Steve Perryman (Manager), Keith Jones, Phil Holder (Assistant Manager), Richard Cadette, Neil Smillie, Rob Peters.

Division 3　　　　　　　　　　　　**BRENTFORD**

Brentford FC

Griffin Park, Braemar Rd, Brentford, Middlesex TW8 0NT. Telephone 081-847 2511. Commercial Dept: 081-560 6062, Press Office 081-574 3047, Clubcall 0898 12 11 08.

Ground capacity: 10,850.

Record attendance: 39,626 v Preston NE, FA Cup 6th rd, 5 March, 1938.

Record receipts: £55,002 v Liverpool, Milk Cup 2nd rd, 5 Oct, 1983.

Pitch measurements: 111yd × 74yd.

President: W. Wheatley. *Life Vice-President:* F. Edwards.

Chairman: M. M. Lange. *Vice-Chairman:* E. J. Radley-Smith.

Directors: R. J. J. Blindell LLB, D. Tana, G. V. Potter.

Chief Executive: K. A. Loring.

Manager: Steve Perryman. *Asst. Manager:* Phil Holder.

Physiotherapist: Roy Clare.

Youth Team Manager: Joe Gadston.

Community Liaison Officer: Martyn Spong.

Secretary: Polly Kates.

Press Officer/Programme Editor: Eric White (081-574 3047)

Year Formed: 1889. *Turned Professional:* 1899. *Ltd Co.:* 1901.

Club Nickname: 'The Bees'.

Previous Grounds: Clifden Road 1889–91; Benns Fields, Little Ealing 1891–95; Shotters Field 1895–98; Cross Road, S. Ealing 1898–1900; Boston Park 1900–04; Griffin Park 1904.

Record League Victory: 9-0 v Wrexham, Division 3, 15 October 1963 – Cakebread; Coote, Jones; Slater, Scott, Higginson; Summers (1), Brooks (2), McAdams (2), Ward (2), Hales (1). (1 og).

Record Cup Victory: 7-0 v Windsor & Eton (away), FA Cup, 1st rd, 20 November 1982 – Roche; Rowe, Harris (Booker), McNichol (1), Whitehead, Hurlock (2), Kamara, Bowles, Joseph (1), Mahoney (3), Roberts.

Record Defeat: 0-7 v Swansea T, Division 3 (S), 8 November, 1924 and v Walsall, Division 3 (S), 19 January, 1957.

Most League Points (2 for a win): 62, Division 3 (S), 1932–33 and Division 4, 1962–63.

Most League Points (3 for a win): 68, Division 3, 1981–82, 1988–89.

Most League Goals: 98, Division 4, 1962–63.

Highest League Scorer in Season: Jack Holliday, 38, Division 3 (S), 1932–33.

Most League Goals in Total Aggregate: Jim Towers, 153, 1954–61.

Most Capped Player: Dai Hopkins, 12, Wales.

Most League Appearances: Ken Coote, 514, 1949–64.

Record Transfer Fee Received: £350,000 from QPR for Andy Sinton, March 1989.

Record Transfer Fee Paid: £167,000 to Hibernian for Eddie May, July 1989.

Football League Record: 1920 Original Member of Division 3; 1921–33 Division 3 (S); 1933–35 Division 2; 1935–47 Division 1; 1947–54 Division 2; 1954–62 Division 3(S); 1962–63 Division 4; 1963–66 Division 3; 1966–72 Division 4; 1972–73 Division 3; 1973–78 Division 4; 1978– Division 3.

Honours: Football League: Division 1 best season: 5th, 1935–36; Division 2 – Champions 1934–35; Division 3 (S) – Champions 1932–33; Runners-up 1929–30. 1957–58; Division 4 – Champions 1962–63. *FA Cup* best season: 6th rd, 1938, 1946, 1949, 1989. *Football League Cup* best season: 4th rd, 1982–83. *Freight Rover Trophy –* Runners-up 1985.

Colours: Red and white striped shirts, black shorts, red stockings with white tops. **Change colours:** All blue.

BRENTFORD 1989–90 LEAGUE RECORD

Match No.	Date	Venue	Opponents	Result	H/T Score	Lg. Pos.	Goalscorers	Attendance
1	Aug 19	A	Bristol R	L 0-1	0-1	—		5835
2	26	H	Chester C	D 1-1	1-1	15	Evans	5153
3	Sept 2	A	Cardiff C	D 2-2	0-1	19	May 2	3499
4	9	H	Bury	L 0-1	0-1	21		5010
5	16	A	Huddersfield T	L 0-1	0-0	22		5578
6	23	H	Birmingham C	L 0-1	0-0	23		5386
7	26	A	Crewe Alex	W 3-2	1-1	—	Smillie, Jones, Godfrey	3496
8	30	H	Wigan Ath	W 3-1	1-0	17	Blissett, Holdsworth, May	4647
9	Oct 7	H	Bristol C	L 0-2	0-1	19		7421
10	14	A	Preston NE	L 2-4	2-0	21	May, Holdsworth	5956
11	17	H	Bolton W	L 1-2	1-1	—	Holdsworth	4537
12	21	A	Shrewsbury T	L 0-1	0-0	22		3073
13	28	H	Fulham	W 2-0	2-0	21	Evans, Smillie	7962
14	31	A	Notts Co	L 1-3	0-2	—	Moncur	5488
15	Nov 4	A	Tranmere R	L 2-4	1-2	24	May, Ratcliffe	5720
16	11	A	Blackpool	L 0-4	0-1	24		2512
17	25	A	Northampton T	W 2-0	1-0	24	May, Holdsworth	3165
18	Dec 3	H	Leyton Orient	W 4-3	2-0	—	Smillie, May, Holdsworth (pen), Blissett	6434
19	17	H	Mansfield T	W 2-1	2-0	—	Holdsworth 2	5022
20	26	A	Reading	L 0-1	0-1	23		5586
21	30	A	Swansea C	L 1-2	1-2	24	Blissett	4537
22	Jan 1	H	Walsall	W 4-0	2-0	19	Blissett, Smillie, Holdsworth, Jones	5259
23	6	A	Rotherham U	W 4-2	3-0	—	Holdsworth 3, Stanislaus	5624
24	12	A	Chester C	D 1-1	0-0	—	Cockram	2294
25	20	H	Bristol R	W 2-1	0-0	13	Ratcliffe, Cadette	7414
26	27	A	Bury	W 2-0	1-0	11	May, Holdsworth	2963
27	Feb 10	H	Huddersfield T	W 2-1	0-0	9	Holdsworth 2	6774
28	18	A	Leyton Orient	W 1-0	0-0	—	Holdsworth	6572
29	21	H	Cardiff C	L 0-1	0-1	—		5174
30	25	H	Northampton T	W 3-2	1-2	—	Blissett 2, Holdsworth	6391
31	Mar 3	A	Rotherham U	L 1-2	0-1	9	Blissett	5640
32	6	A	Wigan Ath	L 1-2	0-1	—	Blissett	2052
33	10	H	Crewe Alex	L 0-2	0-1	12		5815
34	13	A	Birmingham C	W 1-0	0-0	—	Holdsworth	8169
35	17	A	Bristol C	L 0-2	0-1	11		10,813
36	20	H	Preston NE	D 2-2	2-1	—	Holdsworth, Blissett	4673
37	24	A	Bolton W	W 1-0	1-0	11	Holdsworth	6156
38	31	H	Shrewsbury T	D 1-1	0-0	11	Smillie	5387
39	Apr 7	H	Notts Co	L 0-1	0-0	12		5105
40	10	A	Fulham	L 0-1	0-1	—		6729
41	14	A	Walsall	L 1-2	1-2	13	Sparham	2903
42	16	H	Reading	D 1-1	0-0	15	Driscoll	5594
43	21	A	Mansfield T	W 3-2	0-1	13	Holdsworth 2 (1 pen), Blissett	2346
44	28	H	Blackpool	W 5-0	1-0	13	Evans, Cockram, Holdsworth, Driscoll, Blissett	4784
45	May 2	H	Swansea C	W 2-1	1-0	—	Holdsworth 2	4950
46	5	A	Tranmere R	D 2-2	1-1	13	Godfrey, Steel (og)	5379

Final League Position: 13

GOALSCORERS

League (66): Holdsworth 24 (2 pens), Blissett 11, May 8, Smillie 5, Evans 3, Cockram 2, Driscoll 2, Godfrey 2, Jones 2, Ratcliffe 2, Cadette 1, Moncur 1, Sparham 1, Stanislaus 1, own goal 1.
Littlewoods Cup (7): Blissett 2, May 2, Evans 1, Godfrey 1, Millen 1.
FA Cup (0).

Parks	Buttigieg	Stanislaus	Millen	Evans	Ratcliffe	Jones	May	Godfrey	Blissett	Smillie	Haag	Bates	Ansah	Cadette	Cockram	Fleming	Holdsworth	Perryman	Moncur	Branagan	Cousins	Peters	Gayle	Buckle	Driscoll	Bayes	Scott	Sparham	Miller	Match No.
1	2	3	4	5	6	7	8	9*	10	11	12																			1
1	2*	3	4	5	6	7	8	9†	10	11		12	14																	2
1	2	3	4	5	6	7	8	9*	10	11	12																			3
1	2	3	4	5	6	7	8	12	10	11				9*																4
1	2*	3	4	5	6†	7	8	11	10			9	12			14														5
1	2	3	4	5†	6	7	8		10*	11	12		14	9																6
1	2	3	4	5	6	7	8		10	11	12			9*																7
1	2		4	5	6	7	8		10†	11		12		14		3*	9													8
1			4	5	6	7	8	11	10*			2†		12	14	3	9													9
1			4		6	7	8†	5	10	11	12			14		3	9	2*												10
1			4	5	6	7	8		10	11				14		3	9	2†												11
1			4	5	2	7	8		10	11				12		3	9*		6											12
1	12		4	5	2*	7	8		10	11						3	9		6											13
1	12		4*	5	2	7	8†	14	10	11						3	9		6											14
1	12			5	7		8	14		11		4		10		3	9†	2*	6											15
1			4	5	2	7	8	12		11				10*		3	9		6											16
	12			5	6	7*	8†	14	10	11				2		3	9				1								4	17
	7			5	2		8		10	11				6		3	9				1								4	18
1	3			5		7	8	12	10	11				6*	2		9												4	19
1	3			5		7	8	12	10	11				4	6	2	9*													20
1	3			5	2	7	8		10	11				4	12	6	9*													21
1	3†			5	2	7	8		10*	11				4	12	6	14	9												22
1	3			5	2	7	8		10*	11				4	6*	12	9													23
1	3			5	2	7	8	12	10*	11				4	6		9													24
1	3			5	2	7	8			11		4		10	6		9													25
1	14	3			2	7	8*	12		11†		4		10	6		9				5									26
1	3			5	2	7	8*		10	11				12	6		9				4									27
1	3	4	5	2	7		8*	10	11					12	6		9													28
1	3	4	5	2	7	8		10*	11					12	6		9													29
1	3	4	5	2	7	8		10	11						6		9													30
1	3†	4	5	2	7	8*	12	10	11						6		9				14									31
1	3	4	5	2	7		8*	10	11						6†		9				14	12								32
1	3	4	5	2	7		8*	10	11						9						6†	12	14							33
1	14	3*	4	5		7		8	10	11					9						2	12†	6							34
1	4			5			8†	10	11					12			9				2	3	7*	6	14					35
	14		4†	5	2	7			10	11					3		9*					12	6	8		1				36
	6		4	5	2	7			10						3		9				11	12		8*		1				37
	14		4	5	6†				10	11					3		9*				2	12	7	8		1				38
	2		4	5		7			10*	11							9					12	6	8		1			3	39
10*	3	4	5	6	7					11							9					12		8		1			2	40
	14	3	4*	5		7		12		11							9				2		6	8†		1			10	41
	3	4	5		7				10	11					6		9					12	8*			1			2	42
1	12	3		5		7			8	10	11*				6†		9				4			14					2	43
1		3	4	5		7		14	10	11	12				6†		9				2*			8						44
1		3	4	5		7			10	11					6*		9				2			12	8					45
1		3	4	5		7			10	11					6*		9				2			12	8					46
37	12 +10s	31	32	44	35	42	30	16 +11s	36 +1s	43	1 +4s	10 +5s	— +1s	7 +9s	21 +5s	15 +2s	39	3	5	2	12 +1s	1	1 +1s	6 +8s	10 +4s2s	1	6	5	3	

Littlewoods Cup	First Round	Brighton & HA (a)	3-0
		(h)	1-1
	Second Round	Manchester C (h)	2-1
		(a)	1-4
FA Cup	First Round	Colchester U (h)	0-1

BRENTFORD

Player and Position	Ht	Wt	Birth Date	Place	Source	Clubs	League App	Gls
Goalkeepers								
Ashley Bayes§			19 4 72	Lincoln	Trainee	Brentford	1	—
Tony Parks	5 11	10 08	26 1 63	Hackney	Apprentice	Tottenham H	37	—
						Oxford U (loan)	5	—
						Gillingham (loan)	2	—
						Brentford	70	—
Defenders								
Jamie Bates	6 1	12 12	24 2 68	London	Trainee	Brentford	98	3
John Buttigieg	6 0	11 13	5 10 63	Sliema	Sliema W	Brentford	40	—
Jason Cousins	6 0	11 06	4 10 70	Hillingdon	Trainee	Brentford	13	—
Terry Evans	6 5	15 01	12 4 65	London	Hillingdon B	Brentford	138	13
Mark Fleming	5 9	10 11	11 8 69	Hammersmith	Trainee	QPR	3	—
						Brentford	17	—
Marcus Gayle	6 2	12 13	27 9 70	Hammersmith	Trainee	Brentford	12	—
Robert Larkin‡	5 9	10 09	24 9 70	Aylesbury	Trainee	Brentford	—	—
Keith Millen	6 2	12 04	26 9 66	Croydon	Juniors	Brentford	196	10
Steve Perryman†	5 8	10 10	21 12 51	Ealing	Apprentice	Tottenham H	655	31
						Oxford U	17	—
						Brentford	53	—
Rob Peters	5 8	11 02	18 5 71	Kensington	Trainee	Brentford	2	—
Simon Ratcliffe	5 11	11 09	8 2 67	Davyhulme	Apprentice	Manchester U	—	—
						Norwich C	9	—
						Brentford	44	3
Roger Stanislaus	5 9	12 11	2 11 68	Hammersmith	Trainee	Arsenal	—	—
						Brentford	111	4
Midfield								
Paul Buckle	5 8	10 08	16 12 70	Hatfield	Trainee	Brentford	11	—
Allan Cockram	5 8	10 08	8 10 63	Kensington	Local	Tottenham H	2	—
						Bristol R	1	—
					St Albans	Brentford	70	11
Andy Driscoll			21 10 71	Staines	Trainee	Brentford	13	2
Matthew Howard‡	5 9	11 06	5 12 70	Watford	Trainee	Brentford	1	—
Keith Jones	5 9	10 11	14 10 65	Dulwich	Apprentice	Chelsea	52	7
						Brentford	118	6
Neil Smillie	5 6	10 07	19 7 58	Barnsley	Apprentice	Crystal Palace	83	7
						Brentford (loan)	3	—
						Brighton & HA	75	2
						Watford	16	3
						Reading	39	—
						Brentford	71	7
Forwards								
Paul Birch	6 0	12 05	3 12 68	Reading	Trainee	Arsenal	—	—
						Portsmouth	—	—
						Brentford	18	2
Gary Blissett	6 1	11 13	29 6 64	Manchester	Altrincham	Crewe Alex	122	39
						Brentford	124	31
Richard Cadette	5 8	11 07	21 3 65	Hammersmith	Wembley	Orient	21	4
						Southend U	90	48
						Sheffield U	28	7
						Brentford	48	13
						Bournemouth (loan)	8	1
Kevin Godfrey	5 10	10 11	24 2 60	Kennington	Apprentice	Leyton Orient	285	65
						Plymouth Arg (loan)	7	1
						Brentford	56	10

BRENTFORD

Foundation: Formed as a small amateur concern in 1889 they were very successful in local circles. They won the championship of the West London Alliance in 1893 and a year later the West Middlesex Junior Cup before carrying off the Senior Cup in 1895. After winning both the London Senior Amateur Cup and the Middlesex Senior Cup in 1898 they were admitted to the Second Division of the Southern League.

First Football League game: 28 August, 1920, Division 3, v Exeter C (a), L 0-3 – Young; Rosier, Hodson; Amos, Levitt, Elliott; Henery, Morley, Spredbury, Thompson, Smith.

Managers (and Secretary-managers)
Will Lewis 1900–03*, Dick Molyneux 1903–06, W. G. Brown 1906–08, Fred Halliday 1908–26 (only secretary to 1922), Ephraim Rhodes 1912–15, Archie Mitchell 1921–22, Harry Curtis 1926–49, Jackie Gibbons 1949–52, Jimmy Blain 1952–53, Tommy Lawton 1953, Bill Dodgin Snr 1953–57, Malcolm Macdonald 1957–65, Tommy Cavanagh 1965–66, Billy Gray 1966–67, Jimmy Sirrel 1967–69, Frank Blunstone 1969–73, Mike Everitt 1973–75, John Docherty 1975–76, Bill Dodgin Jnr 1976–80, Fred Callaghan 1980–84, Frank McLintock 1984–87, Steve Perryman 1987–   .

Player and Position	Ht	Wt	Birth Date	Place	Source	Clubs	League App	Gls
Kelly Haag*	6 0	12 03	6 10 70	Enfield	Trainee	Brentford	5	—
Dean Holdsworth	5 11	11 04	8 11 68	London	Trainee	Watford	16	3
						Carlisle U (loan)	4	1
						Port Vale (loan)	6	2
						Swansea C (loan)	5	1
						Brentford (loan)	7	1
						Brentford	39	24
Eddie May	5 9	12 00	30 8 67	Edinburgh	Hutchison Vale	Dundee U	—	—
						Hibernian	109	10
						Brentford	30	8
Colin Scott on loan from Rangers							6	—

Trainees
Bayes, Ashley J; Brand, Nicholas; Ivers, Mark A; Jagroop, Mark A; Moabi, Abrahams K; Moore, Fergus; Ryder, Nicholas J; Thomas, Lee; Tuckerman, Spencer J; Turner, Mark; Webb, Paul A.

**Non-Contract
Perryman, Stephen J.

Associated Schoolboys
Aouf, Tamer; Bradshaw, Ian; Cole, George; Hills, Jamie J; Hutchings, Carl E; Ravenscroft, Craig A; Swaile, Daniel B.

Associated Schoolboys who have accepted the club's offer of a Traineeship/Contract
Brady, Christopher J; Burton, Jamie R; Clubb, Matthew C; Dunkley, Kerry; Grace, Darren M; Hynes, Michael C;Sparks, Christopher.

**Non-Contract Players who are retained must be re-signed before they are eligible to play in League matches.

BRIGHTON AND HOVE ALBION 1989–90 *Back row (left to right)*: Nicky Bissett, Larry May, John Keeley, Mike Trusson, Perry Digweed, Robert Codner.
Centre row: Barry Lloyd (Manager), Gary Chivers, Ted Streeter (Youth Development Officer), Paul McCarthy, Steve Penney, John Robinson, Garry Nelson, Martin Lambert, Dean Wilkins.
Jack Dineen, Ian Chapman, Malcolm Stuart (Physiotherapist), Martin Hinshelwood (Coach), Robert Isaac, Keith Dublin.
Front row: Brian McKenna, John Crumplin, Alan Curbishley, Wayne Stemp, Steve Gatting (Captain), Paul Wood, Kevin Bremner, Adrian Owers, Jimmy Jones.

Division 2   **BRIGHTON & HOVE ALBION**

Goldstone Ground, Old Shoreham Rd, Hove, Sussex BN3 7DE.
Telephone Brighton (0273) 739535. Commercial Dept: 0273-778230. Recorded information (team & ticket news etc): Seagull Line 0898 800 609.

Ground capacity: 18,493.

Record attendance: 36,747 v Fulham, Division 2, 27 December, 1958.

Pitch measurements: 112yd × 75yd.

Chairman: D. C. Sizen. *Vice-Chairman:* J. L. Campbell.

Directors: P. F. Kent, R. A. Bloom, G. A. Stanley, T. H. Appleby, B. E. Clarke.

Manager: Barry Lloyd.

Secretary: Steve Rooke. *Chief Executive:* Ron Pavey.

Coach: Martin Hinshelwood. *Physiotherapist:* Malcolm Stuart.

Marketing Manager: Terry Gill. *Lottery Manager:* Dave Treagus.

Year Formed: 1900. *Turned Professional:* 1900. *Ltd Co.:* 1904.
Previous Name: Brighton & Hove Rangers. *Previous Grounds:* 1900, Withdean; 1901, County Ground; 1902, Goldstone Ground.

Club Nickname: 'The Seagulls'.

Record League Victory: 9-1 v Newport C, Division 3 (S), 18 April 1951 – Ball; Tennant (1p), Mansell (1p); Willard, McCoy, Wilson; Reed, McNichol (4), Garbutt, Bennett (2), Keene (1). 9-1 v Southend U, Division 3, 27 November 1965 – Powney; Magill, Baxter; Leck, Gall, Turner; Gould (1), Collins (1), Livesey (2), Smith (3), Goodchild (2).

Record Cup Victory: 10-1 v Wisbech, FA Cup, 1st rd, 13 November 1965 – Powney; Magill, Baxter; Collins (1), Gall, Turner; Gould, Smith (2), Livesey (3), Cassidy (2), Goodchild (1). (1 og).

Record Defeat: 0-9 v Middlesbrough, Division 2, 23 August, 1958.

Most League Points (2 for a win): 65, Division 3 (S), 1955–56 and Division 3, 1971–72.

Most League Points (3 for a win): 84, Division 3, 1987–88.

Most League Goals: 112, Division 3 (S), 1955–56.

Highest League Scorer in Season: Peter Ward, 32, Division 3, 1976–77.

Most League Goals in Total Aggregate: Tommy Cook, 113, 1922-29.

Most Capped Player: Steve Penney, 17, Northern Ireland.

Most League Appearances: 'Tug' Wilson, 509, 1922–36.

Record Transfer Fee Received: £900,000 from Liverpool for Mark Lawrenson, August 1981.

Record Transfer Fee Paid: £500,000 to Manchester U for Andy Ritchie, October 1980.

Football League Record: 1920 Original Member of Division 3; 1921–58 Division 3 (S); 1958–62 Division 2; 1962–63 Division 3; 1963–65 Division 4; 1965–72 Division 3; 1972–73 Division 2; 1973–77 Division 3; 1977-79 Division 2; 1979–83 Division 1; 1983–87 Division 2; 1987–88 Division 3; 1988– Division 2.

Honours: Football League: Division 1 best season: 16th 1979–80; Division 2 – Runners-up 1978–79; Division 3 (S) – Champions 1957–58; Runners-up 1953–54, 1955–56; Division 3 – Runners-up 1971–72, 1976–77, 1987–88; Division 4 – Champions 1964–65. *FA Cup:* Runners-up 1982–83. *Football League Cup* best season: 5th rd, 1978–79.

Colours: Blue and white striped shirts, blue shorts, blue stockings. **Change colours:** White shirts with red patterned check, red shorts, red stockings with blue and white trim.

BRIGHTON & HOVE ALBION 1989–90 LEAGUE RECORD

Match No.	Date	Venue	Opponents	Result	H/T Score	Lg. Pos.	Goalscorers	Atten-dance
1	Aug 19	H	Bournemouth	W 2-1	0-0	—	Bissett, Codner	9685
2	26	A	Barnsley	L 0-1	0-0	13		5920
3	Sept 2	H	Port Vale	W 2-0	0-0	9	Nelson, Codner (pen)	7218
4	9	A	Sheffield U	L 4-5	1-3	10	Wood 2, Bremner 2	12,653
5	12	A	Wolverhampton W	W 4-2	4-1	—	Nelson, Bremner 2, Codner	12,338
6	16	H	West Ham U	W 3-0	3-0	2	Bremner, Codner, Nelson	12,689
7	23	A	Leicester C	L 0-1	0-0	3		8926
8	27	H	Ipswich T	W 1-0	0-0	—	Wilkins	9770
9	30	A	Plymouth Arg	L 1-2	0-1	6	Wood	7610
10	Oct 7	A	Bradford C	L 0-2	0-1	8		7933
11	14	H	Watford	W 1-0	1-0	7	Bissett	9260
12	18	A	Middlesbrough	D 2-2	0-0	—	Curbishley, Bremner	13,551
13	21	H	Newcastle U	L 0-3	0-1	10		10,756
14	28	A	Hull C	W 2-0	1-0	7	Bissett, Codner	4756
15	Nov 1	H	Swindon T	L 1-2	0-1	—	Wilkins	8070
16	4	H	Blackburn R	L 1-2	1-1	12	Bremner	7445
17	11	A	Stoke C	L 2-3	1-3	12	Codner, Bremner	10,346
18	18	A	Oldham Ath	D 1-1	0-1	12	Codner	7066
19	25	H	Sunderland	L 1-2	1-1	13	Bissett	8681
20	Dec 2	A	Bournemouth	W 2-0	2-0	12	Nelson, Bremner	6890
21	9	H	Wolverhampton W	D 1-1	0-0	11	Wilkins	9817
22	16	A	Leeds U	L 0-3	0-3	15		24,070
23	26	A	Portsmouth	D 0-0	0-0	14		10,800
24	30	H	Oxford U	L 0-1	0-1	17		7738
25	Jan 1	A	WBA	L 0-3	0-2	18		9407
26	13	H	Barnsley	D 1-1	0-0	18	Barham	6856
27	20	A	Port Vale	L 1-2	0-0	20	Codner	8666
28	Feb 10	A	West Ham U	L 1-3	1-0	22	Nelson	19,101
29	17	H	Leicester C	W 1-0	1-0	19	Bremner	7498
30	24	A	Sunderland	L 1-2	0-2	19	Chivers	14,528
31	28	H	Middlesbrough	W 1-0	0-0	—	Barham	5504
32	Mar 3	H	Oldham Ath	D 1-1	0-0	18	Gotsmanov	8229
33	7	H	Plymouth Arg	W 2-1	1-0	—	Morrison (og), Gotsmanov	7418
34	10	A	Ipswich T	L 1-2	1-1	16	Wilkins	10,886
35	14	A	Sheffield U	D 2-2	2-1	—	Whitehurst (og), Chivers	8703
36	17	H	Bradford C	W 2-1	0-0	16	Wilkins 2	6831
37	20	A	Watford	L 2-4	0-3	—	Crumplin, Bissett	8487
38	31	A	Newcastle U	L 0-2	0-0	18		18,746
39	Apr 6	H	Hull C	W 2-0	0-0	—	Bamber (og), Gotsmanov	6789
40	10	A	Swindon T	W 2-1	2-0	—	Bremner, Chivers	8444
41	14	H	WBA	L 0-3	0-2	17		8371
42	16	A	Portsmouth	L 0-3	0-0	17		10,924
43	21	A	Leeds U	D 2-2	0-1	19	Gotsmanov, Crumplin	11,359
44	25	A	Oxford U	W 1-0	0-0	—	Codner	3864
45	28	H	Stoke C	L 1-4	0-0	17	Bremner	9614
46	May 5	A	Blackburn R	D 1-1	0-0	18	Bremner	9283

Final League Position: 18

GOALSCORERS

League (56): Bremner 13, Codner 9 (1 pen), Wilkins 6, Bissett 5, Nelson 5, Gotsmanov 4, Chivers 3, Wood 3, Barham 2, Crumplin 2, Curbishley 1, own goals 3.
Littlewoods Cup (1): Wilkins 1.
FA Cup (5): Barham 1, Codner 1, Curbishley 1, Dublin 1, Nelson 1.

Keeley	Chivers	Chapman	Curbishley	Bissett	Dublin	Wood	Crumplin	Bremner	Codner	Wilkins	Nelson	Lambert	Gatting	Owers	Stemp	Edwards	Barham	Gotsmanov	Digweed	McCarthy	Robinson	Gabbiadini	McGrath	Match No.
1	2	3	4	5	6	7	8	9	10	11														1
1	2	3	4	5	6		8	9	10	11	7													2
1	2	3	4	5	6		8	9	10	11	7													3
1	2	3	4*	5		8	12	9	10	11	7		6											4
1	2	3	4	5		8		9	10	11	7		6											5
1	2	3*	4	5		8		9	10	11	7		6	12										6
1	2		4	4	3		8*	9	10	11	7		6	12										7
1	2		4	5	3		8*	9	10	11	7		6	12										8
1	2		4	5	3	8	12	9	10	11*	7		6											9
1	2	12	4	5	3		8*	9	10	11	7		6											10
1	2	6	4	5	3		8	9	10	11	7													11
1	2	6	4	5	3		8	9	10	11	7													12
1	2	3	4	5	6		8	9*	10	11	7		12											13
1		3	4	5	6		8	9	10	11	7				2									14
1		3	4	5	6		8	9	10	11	7				2									15
1	2	3	4	5	6		8*12	9	10	11	7													16
1	2	3	4	5	6		8 12	9*	10	11	7													17
1	2	3	4	5	6		8	9	10	11	7													18
1	2	3	4	5	6		8 12	9*	10	11	7													19
1	2	3	4	5*	6		8 12	9	10	11	7													20
1	2	3	4		6	8	5	9*	10	11	7		12											21
1	2	3	4		6	8	5		10	11	7		9											22
1	2	3	4	5	6		8*12	9	10	11	7													23
1	2	3	4	5	6		8	9*	10	11	7		12											24
1	2	3	4		6	12	5*	9	10	11	7		8											25
1	2	3	4		6	12		9*	10	11	7	5	8											26
1	2	3	4		6			9	10	11	7	5	8											27
1	2	3	4	9	6				10	11	7	5	8											28
1	2	3	4		6		12	9	10	11	7	5	8*											29
1	2	3*	4		6			9	10	11	7	5	8	12										30
1	2	3	4		6			9	10	11	7*	5	8	12										31
1	2	3	4		6		12	9	10	11		5	8*	7										32
	2	3	4		6		10	9		11		5	8	7	1									33
	3	4*14			6	2	9	10	11	12	5†		8	7	1									34
1	2		4	5	6	3		10	11	9		8	7											35
1	2	3	4	5		12	10	11	9*			8	7†	14										36
1	2	3	4	5	6	12	9	10	11	7		8*												37
	2	3	4	5	6	8	9	10	11			7	1											38
	2	3	4	5	6		9	10	11			7	1											39
	2	3	4	5*	6	12	9	10	11			7	1											40
	2	3	4		6		9	10	11		5	8	7	1										41
	2	3	4*		6	7	9†10	11			5		8	1		12 14								42
	2	3	4		6	5	9	10	11		7	1	8											43
	2	3			6	5	9	10	11		7	1	8	4										44
		3	4		6	2	9	10	11		7	1	5	8										45
		3	4		6	2	9	10	11		7	1	5	8										46

```
35 41 41 45 28 43 24 14 42 45 46 32 — 19 — 2 1 16 14 11 2  4 — 1
      +        +        +  +  +                   +  +       + + +
     1s       1s       2s 11s1s               1s 1s 4s        1s 1s1s
```

Littlewoods Cup	First Round	Brentford (h)	0-3
		(a)	1-1
FA Cup	Third Round	Luton T (h)	4-1
	Fourth Round	Oldham Ath (a)	1-2

BRIGHTON & HOVE ALBION

Player and Position	Ht	Wt	Birth Date	Place	Source	Clubs	League App	Gls
Goalkeepers								
Perry Digweed	6 0	11 04	26 10 59	London	Apprentice	Fulham	15	—
						Brighton & HA	113	—
						WBA (loan)	—	—
						Charlton Ath (loan)	—	—
						Newcastle U (loan)	—	—
						Chelsea (loan)	3	—
John Keeley	6 1	14 02	27 7 61	Plaistow	Apprentice Chelmsford	Southend U	54	—
						Brighton & HA	138	—
Brian McKenna	6 0	13 12	30 1 72	Dublin	Home Farm	Brighton & HA	—	—
Defenders								
Nicky Bissett	6 2	12 10	5 4 64	Fulham	Barnet	Brighton & HA	45	6
Ian Chapman	5 8	11 05	31 5 70	Brighton		Brighton & HA	66	—
Gary Chivers	5 11	11 05	15 5 60	Stockwell	Apprentice	Chelsea	133	4
						Swansea C	10	—
						QPR	60	—
						Watford	14	—
						Brighton & HA	97	9
Keith Dublin	5 11	11 09	29 1 66	Wycombe	Apprentice	Chelsea	51	—
						Brighton & HA	132	5
Steve Gatting	5 11	11 11	29 5 59	Park Royal	Apprentice	Arsenal	58	5
						Brighton & HA	273	18
Robert Isaac	5 11	12 07	30 11 65	Hackney	Apprentice	Chelsea	9	—
						Brighton & HA	30	—
Paul McCarthy	6 0	13 06	4 8 71	Cork	Trainee	Brighton & HA	3	—
Larry May‡	6 1	12 00	26 12 58	Sutton Coldfield	Apprentice	Leicester C	187	12
						Barnsley	122	3
						Sheffield W	31	1
						Brighton & HA	24	3
Wayne Stemp	5 11	11 02	9 9 70	Epsom	Trainee	Brighton & HA	2	—
Midfield								
Mark Barham	5 7	11 00	12 7 62	Folkestone	Apprentice	Norwich C	177	24
						Huddersfield T	27	1
						Middlesbrough	4	—
						WBA	4	—
						Brighton & HA	17	2
John Crumplin	5 8	11 10	26 5 67	Bath	Bognor	Brighton & HA	68	4
Alan Curbishley	5 11	11 10	8 11 57	Forest Gate	Apprentice	West Ham U	85	5
						Birmingham C	130	11
						Aston Villa	36	1
						Charlton Ath	63	6
						Brighton & HA	116	13
Jack Dineen*	5 7	10 10	23 9 70	Brighton	Trainee	Brighton & HA	—	—
Sergei Gotsmanov‡			17 3 59	USSR	Dynamo Minsk	Brighton & HA	16	4
Darren Hinton*			19 2 71	Crawley	Chelsea§	Brighton & HA	—	—
Derek McGrath	5 5	10 01	21 1 72	Dublin	Trainee	Brighton & HA	1	—
Adrian Owers	5 8	10 02	26 2 65	Banbury	Apprentice Chelmsford C	Southend U	27	—
						Brighton & HA	37	4
Steve Penney	5 9	10 04	16 1 64	Ballymena	Ballymena U	Brighton & HA	138	15
John Robinson	5 10	11 05	29 8 71	Rhodesia	Trainee	Brighton & HA	5	—
Dean Wilkins	5 8	11 08	12 7 62	Hillingdon	Apprentice	QPR	6	—
						Brighton & HA	2	—
						Orient (loan)	10	—
					Zwolle	Brighton & HA	133	10

BRIGHTON & HOVE ALBION

Foundation: After barely two seasons in existence, a professional club named Brighton United, consisting mostly of Scotsmen, was forced to disband in 1900. The club's manager John Jackson determined to keep the professional game alive in the town and initiated the movement which led to the formation of Brighton & Hove Rangers that same year.

First Football League game: 28 August, 1920, Division 3, v Southend U (a), L 0-2 – Hayes; Woodhouse, Little; Hall, Comber, Bentley; Longstaff, Ritchie, Doran, Rodgerson, March.

Managers (and Secretary-managers)
John Jackson 1901–05, Frank Scott-Walford 1905–08, John Robson 1908–14, Charles Webb 1919–47, Tommy Cook 1947, Don Welsh 1947–51, Billy Lane 1951–61, George Curtis 1961–63, Archie Macaulay 1963–68, Fred Goodwin 1968–70, Pat Saward 1970–73, Brian Clough 1973–74, Peter Taylor 1974–76, Alan Mullery 1976–81, Mike Bailey 1981–82, Jimmy Melia 1982–83, Chris Cattlin 1983–86, Alan Mullery 1986–87, Barry Lloyd 1987–   .

Player and Position	Ht	Wt	Birth Date	Place	Source	Clubs	League App	Gls
Forwards								
Kevin Bremner	5 9	12 05	7 10 57	Banff	Keith	Colchester U	95	31
						Birmingham C (loan)	4	1
						Wrexham (loan)	4	1
						Plymouth Arg (loan)	5	1
						Millwall	96	33
						Reading	64	22
						Brighton & HA	128	36
Robert Codner	5 11	11 05	23 1 65	Walthamstow	Dagenham Barnet	Leicester C	—	—
						Brighton & HA	73	10
Ally Dick*	5 9	10 07	25 4 65	Stirling	Apprentice Ajax	Tottenham H	17	2
						Brighton & HA	—	—
Alistair Edwards‡			21 6 68	Whyalla	Sydney Olympic	Brighton & HA	1	—
Martin Lambert‡	5 10	11 05	24 9 65	Southampton	Apprentice	Brighton & HA	3	—
						Torquay U	6	2
					Le Havre Sedan			
						Brighton & HA	1	—
Garry Nelson	5 10	11 04	16 1 61	Southend	Amateur	Southend U	129	17
						Swindon T	79	7
						Plymouth Arg	74	20
						Brighton & HA	121	42

Trainees
Barrett, Michael; Brown, Matthew R.N; Coldwell, David J; Danbury, Stuart J; Gumpright, Mark; Jones, James H; Lyons, Christian W; Mummery, Jason; Munday, Stuart C; Nimmo, Andrew K; O'Dowd, Gregory H; Rush, Spencer; Smith, Timothy.

**Non-Contract
Cormack, Lee D.

Associated Schoolboys
Astell, Richard C; Baker, Darren R; Cable, Marc B; Clark, Robertson F; Dale, Stephen P; Hammond, Colin L; Isaac, Stephen; Long, Gareth C; Manuel, Wayne P; Micklethwaite, Marc; Miller, Jan J; Myall, Stuart T; Oliva, Umberto; Pryce-Jones, Liam; Simmonds, Daniel; Tuck, Stuart G.

Associated Schoolboys who have accepted the club's offer of a Traineeship/Contract
Sheriff, Mark.

**Non-Contract Players who are retained must be re-signed before they are eligible to play in League matches.

BRISTOL CITY 1989–90 *Back row (left to right):* David Smith, Paul Mardon, Matt Bryant, Robbie Turner, Ronnie McQuilter, Rob Newman, Paul France.
Centre row: Jimmy Lumsden (Assistant Manager), Alan Theobald, Steve McClaren, Russel Bromage, Andy Leaning, John Pender, Bob Taylor, David Rennie, Glenn Humphries, Buster Footman (Physiotherapist).
Front row: Andy Llewellyn, John Bailey, Paul Wimbleton, Joe Jordan (Manager), Mark Gavin, Jason Eaton, Christ Honor.

Division 2   **BRISTOL CITY**

Ashton Gate, Bristol BS3 2EJ. Telephone Bristol (0272) 632812 (5 lines). Clubcall 0898 12 11 76.

Ground capacity: 25,271.

Record attendance: 43,335 v Preston NE, FA Cup 5th rd, 16 Feb, 1935.

Record receipts: £97,777.50 v Chelsea, FA Cup, 4th round, 27 January, 1990.

Pitch measurements: 115yd × 75yd.

Chairman: D. T. Williams. *Vice-Chairman:* L. J. Kew.

Directors: O. W. Newland, W. I. Williams, P. Manning, M. Fricker, K. Sage. *Commercial Manager:* D. Easton.

Manager: Joe Jordan. *Assistant Manager/Coach:* Jimmy Lumsden.

Physio: Buster Footman. *Football Secretary:* Jean Harris. *Commercial Manager:* John Cox.

Year Formed: 1894. *Turned Professional:* 1897. *Ltd Co.:* 1897. BCFC (1982) PLC.

Previous Grounds: 1894, St John's Lane; 1904, Ashton Gate.

Previous Name: 1894–97, Bristol South End. *Club Nickname:* 'Robins'.

Record League Victory: 9-0 v Aldershot, Division 3(S), 28 December 1946 – Eddols; Morgan, Fox; Peacock, Roberts, Jones (1); Chilcott, Thomas, Clark (4 incl 1p), Cyril Williams (1), Hargreaves (3).

Record Cup Victory: 11-0 v Chichester C, FA Cup, 1st rd, 5 November 1960 – Cook; Collinson, Thresher; Connor, Alan Williams, Etheridge; Tait (1), Bobby Williams (1), Atyeo (5), Adrian Williams (3), Derrick. (1 og).

Record Defeat: 0-9 v Coventry C, Division 3(S), 28 April, 1934.

Most League Points (2 for a win): 70, Division 3 (S), 1954–55.

Most League Points (3 for a win): 91, Division 3, 1989–90.

Most League Goals: 104, Division 3(S), 1926–27.

Highest League Scorer in Season: Don Clark, 36, Division 3(S), 1946–47.

Most League Goals in Total Aggregate: John Atyeo, 314, 1951–66.

Most Capped Player: Billy Wedlock, 26, England.

Most League Appearances: John Atyeo, 597, 1951–66.

Record Transfer Fee Received: £325,000 from Coventry C for Gary Collier, July 1979.

Record Transfer Fee Paid: £235,000 to St Mirren for Tony Fitzpatrick, July 1979.

Football League Record: 1901 Elected to Division 2; 1906–11 Division 1; 1911–22 Division 2; 1922–23 Division 3 (S); 1923-24 Division 2; 1924–27 Division 3(S); 1927–32 Division 2; 1932–55 Division 3(S); 1955–60 Division 2; 1960–65 Division 3; 1965–76 Division 2; 1976–80 Division 1; 1980–81 Division 2; 1981–82 Division 3; 1982–84 Division 4; 1984–90 Division 3; 1990– Division 2.

Honours: Football League: Division 1 – Runners-up 1906–07; Division 2 – Champions 1905–06; Runners-up 1975–76; Division 3(S) – Champions 1922–23, 1926–27, 1954–55; Runners-up 1937–38; Division 3 – Runners-up 1964–65, 1989–90. *FA Cup:* Runners-up 1909. *Football League Cup:* Semi-final 1970–71, 1988–89. *Welsh Cup:* Winners 1934. *Anglo-Scottish Cup:* Winners 1977–78. *Freight Rover Trophy:* Winners 1985–86; Runners-up 1986–87.

Colours: Red shirts, white shorts, red stockings. **Change colours:** Yellow shirts, green shorts, yellow stockings.

BRISTOL CITY 1989–90 LEAGUE RECORD

Match No.	Date	Venue	Opponents	Result	H/T Score	Lg. Pos.	Goalscorers	Attendance
1	Aug 19	A	Bury	D 1-1	0-0	—	Taylor	3399
2	26	H	Birmingham C	W 1-0	0-0	8	Taylor	8938
3	Sept 2	A	Northampton T	L 0-2	0-0	15		4088
4	9	H	Blackpool	W 2-0	0-0	9	Wimbleton (pen), Newman	7172
5	16	A	Cardiff C	W 3-0	1-0	6	Shelton, Taylor, Turner	5970
6	23	H	Bristol R	D 0-0	0-0	5		17,432
7	26	H	Shrewsbury T	W 2-1	1-0	—	Taylor 2	9188
8	29	A	Tranmere R	L 0-6	0-2	—		8974
9	Oct 7	A	Brentford	W 2-0	1-0	5	Wimbleton (pen), Turner	7421
10	14	H	Swansea C	L 1-3	1-1	6	Taylor	8794
11	17	H	Notts Co	W 2-0	1-0	—	Eaton, Short (og)	8331
12	21	A	Mansfield T	L 0-1	0-1	8		2957
13	28	H	Wigan Ath	W 3-0	2-0	6	Shelton, Rennie, Turner	6365
14	31	A	Crewe Alex	W 1-0	1-0	—	Bailey	3554
15	Nov 4	A	Walsall	W 2-0	1-0	1	Taylor, Turner	5286
16	11	H	Bolton W	D 1-1	1-1	3	Newman	11,994
17	25	A	Reading	D 1-1	1-0	4	Rennie	5353
18	Dec 2	H	Rotherham U	D 0-0	0-0	6		9509
19	16	H	Leyton Orient	W 2-1	2-0	3	Taylor 2	7486
20	26	A	Fulham	W 1-0	1-0	3	Taylor	6089
21	30	A	Huddersfield T	L 1-2	0-1	3	Jones	7681
22	Jan 1	H	Preston NE	W 2-1	1-0	3	Swann (og), Newman	11,803
23	13	A	Birmingham C	W 4-0	1-0	1	Taylor 2, Turner, Newman	11,277
24	20	H	Bury	W 1-0	1-0	1	Smith	10,992
25	30	H	Chester C	W 1-0	0-0	—	Newman	8769
26	Feb 10	H	Cardiff C	W 1-0	1-0	1	Shelton	11,982
27	24	H	Reading	L 0-1	0-0	1		10,616
28	Mar 3	A	Chester C	W 3-0	2-0	1	Taylor 3	2496
29	6	H	Tranmere R	L 1-3	0-1	—	Shelton	14,376
30	10	A	Shrewsbury T	W 1-0	0-0	2	Smith	4785
31	13	A	Blackpool	W 3-1	1-0	—	Taylor 2, Shelton	3227
32	17	H	Brentford	W 2-0	1-0	1	Gavin, Rennie	10,813
33	20	A	Swansea C	W 5-0	2-0	—	Taylor 3, Newman, Honor	6867
34	24	A	Notts Co	D 0-0	0-0	1		9598
35	27	H	Northampton T	W 3-1	2-1	—	Turner, Taylor, Shelton	11,965
36	31	H	Mansfield T	D 1-1	0-0	1	Taylor	11,773
37	Apr 3	A	Rotherham U	W 2-1	0-1	—	Johnson (og), Taylor	5274
38	7	A	Wigan Ath	W 3-2	1-1	—	Smith (pen), Taylor, Ferguson	3281
39	10	H	Crewe Alex	W 4-1	3-0	—	Gavin (pen), Taylor 3	13,800
40	14	A	Preston NE	D 2-2	1-1	1	Morgan, Shelton	7599
41	16	H	Fulham	W 5-1	2-1	1	Morgan, Smith, Newman, Ferguson, Shelton	16,139
42	21	A	Leyton Orient	D 1-1	0-1	1	Newman	7273
43	24	H	Huddersfield T	D 1-1	0-1	—	Morgan	17,791
44	28	A	Bolton W	L 0-1	0-1	1		11,098
45	May 2	A	Bristol R	L 0-3	0-1	—		9831
46	5	H	Walsall	W 4-0	2-0	2	Shelton, Gavin (pen), Rennie, Morgan	17,859

Final League Position: 2

GOALSCORERS

League (76): Taylor 27, Shelton 9, Newman 8, Turner 6, Morgan 4, Rennie 4, Smith 4 (1 pen), Gavin 3 (2 pens), Ferguson 2, Wimbleton 2 (2 pens), Bailey 1, Eaton 1, Honor 1, Jones 1, own goals 3.
Littlewoods Cup (4): Taylor 2, Smith 1, Wimbleton 1 (pen).
FA Cup (11): Taylor 5, Turner 3, Gavin 1, Newman 1, Wimbleton 1 (pen).

Leaning	Llewellyn	Bailey	Wimbleton	Pender	Newman	Gavin	Rennie	Taylor	Turner	Smith	Mardon	Eaton	Shelton	Honor	Bromage	Humphries	Mellon	Jones	Sinclair	Miller	Horrix	Jordan	Ferguson	Morgan	Bent	Match No.
1	2	3	4	5	6	7*	8	9	10†	11	12	14														1
1	2	3	4	5	6	7	8	9	10				11													2
1	2		4†	5	8	7*	6	9	12	10		14	11		3											3
1	2		4	5	8	12	6	9	11	10				7*	3											4
1	2		4	5	8		6	9	11	10	12			7*	3											5
1	2		4	5	8	12	6	9	11	10*		14		7	3†											6
1	2		4	5	8	12	6	9	11	10			3	7*												7
1	2		4	5†	8	12	6	9	11	10*			3	7		14										8
1	2	3	4	5	8	7	6	9	11	10																9
1	2	3	4	5	6	7	8	9		11			10													10
1	2	3	12		8	7	6	9	10*	11			4			5										11
1	2†	3	12		8	7	6	9	10	14		11*	4			5										12
1	2	3			8	7	6		11	10*		9	4			5	12									13
1	2	3			8	7	6	9	11	10*		12	4			5										14
1	2	3			8	7	6	9	11	10			4			5										15
1	2	3			8	7	6	9	11	10			4			5										16
1	2	3	12		8	7	6		11	10		9*	4			5										17
1	2	3			8	7	6		11	10			4			5	9									18
	2	3	12		8	7	6	9	14	10*			4			5	11†		1							19
	2	3	12		8	7	6	9	11†	10*			4			5	14		1							20
	2	3			8	7	6	9	11*	10			4			5	12		1							21
	2	3	12		8	7	6	9	11*	10			4			5			1							22
	2	3			8	7	6	9	11	10			4			5			1							23
	2	3			8	7	6	9*	11	10			4			5			1	12						24
	2	3			8	7	6	9*	11	10			4			5			1	12						25
	2	3			8	7	6	9*	11				4	14		5	10†		1	12						26
1	2†	3			8		6	9	11*	10		12	4	14		5	7									27
	2	3			8		6	9*		10		12	4	14		5	7†		1		11					28
	2	3			8			9		10			4	6*		5	7		1	12	11					29
	2	3			8		6	9		10			4	12		5	7*		1		11					30
	2	3			8		6	9		10		11	4			5	7		1							31
	2	3			8	7	6	9	12	10*			4			5	11		1							32
	2	3			8	7	6	9*	11	10		12	4	14		5†			1							33
	2	3			8	7	6	9	11	10			4	12		5*			1							34
	2	3			8	7	6	9*	11	10			4			5			1				12			35
	2	3			8	7	6	9	11*	10			4			5			1				12			36
	2	3			8	7	6	9		10*			4	12		5			1				11			37
	2	3*			8	7	6	9		10			4	12		5			1				11			38
	2				8	7	6	9*	12	10			4†	3		5	14		1				11			39
	2				8	7	6			10			4	3		5			1				11	9		40
	2	3			8	7	6			10			4			5			1				11	9		41
	2	3			8	7	6		12	10			4			5			1				11*	9		42
	2	3			8	7	6		12	10			4			5			1				11*	9		43
	2	3			8	7	6	9*	12	10			4			5			1				11			44
	2	3†			8	7	6		11*	10			4	14		5			1				12	9		45
	2	3†			8	7*	6			10			4	12		5			1				11	9	14	46
19	46	38	10	10	46	36	45	37	26	45	2	6	43	4	3	36	7	2	27	—	3	—	8	7	—	
			+6s			+4s			+7s			+5s	+5s			+10s	+1s	+2s	+2s	+3s	+1s		+3s	+1s		

Littlewoods Cup First Round Reading (h) 2-3
  (a) 2-2

FA Cup First Round Barnet (h) 2-0
  Second Round Fulham (h) 2-1
  Third Round Swindon T (h) 2-1
  Fourth Round Chelsea (h) 3-1
  Fifth Round Cambridge U (h) 0-0
  (a) 1-1
  (a) 1-5

BRISTOL CITY

Player and Position	Ht	Wt	Birth Date	Birth Place	Source	Clubs	League App	Gls
Goalkeepers								
Andy Leaning	6 1	13 07	18 5 62	York	Rowntree M	York C	69	—
						Sheffield U	21	—
						Bristol C	25	—
Ron Sinclair	5 10	11 09	19 11 64	Stirling	Apprentice	Nottingham F		
						Wrexham (loan)	11	—
						Sheffield U (loan)	—	—
						Leeds U (loan)	—	—
						Derby Co (loan)	—	—
						Leeds U	8	—
						Halifax T (loan)	14	—
						Bristol C	27	—
Defenders								
John Bailey	5 8	11 03	1 4 57	Liverpool	Apprentice	Blackburn R	120	1
						Everton	171	3
						Newcastle U	40	—
						Bristol C	73	1
Russel Bromage	5 11	11 05	9 11 59	Stoke	Apprentice	Port Vale	347	13
						Oldham Ath (loan)	2	—
						Bristol C	46	1
Matthew Bryant	6 1	12 11	21 9 70	Bristol	Trainee	Bristol C	—	—
Paul France*	6 1	11 08	10 9 68	Huddersfield	Trainee	Huddersfield T	11	—
						Cobh Ramblers (loan)	—	—
						Bristol C	—	—
Chris Honor	5 9	10 09	5 6 68	Bristol	Apprentice	Bristol C	60	1
						Torquay U (loan)	3	—
						Hereford U (loan)	3	—
Glenn Humphries	6 0	12 00	11 8 64	Hull	Apprentice	Doncaster R	180	8
						Lincoln C (loan)	9	—
						Bristol C	83	—
Andy Llowellyn	5 7	11 12	26 2 66	Bristol	Apprentice	Bristol C	195	3
Ron McQuilter	6 2	12 01	24 12 70	Glasgow		Bristol C	—	—
Paul Mardon	6 0	11 10	14 9 69	Bristol	Trainee	Bristol C	35	—
Rob Newman	6 2	12 00	13 12 63	London	Apprentice	Bristol C	348	44
John Pender	6 0	12 07	19 11 63	Luton	Apprentice	Wolverhampton W	117	3
						Charlton Ath	41	—
						Bristol C	83	3
Midfield								
Michael Melon	5 8	11 03	18 3 72	Paisley	Trainee	Bristol C	9	—
David Rennie	6 0	12 00	29 8 64	Edinburgh	Apprentice	Leicester C	21	1
						Leeds U	101	5
						Bristol C	45	4
Gary Shelton	5 7	11 03	21 3 58	Nottingham	Apprentice	Walsall	24	—
						Aston Villa	24	7
						Notts Co (loan)	8	—
						Sheffield W	198	18
						Oxford U	65	1
						Bristol C	43	9
Forwards								
Junior Bent	5 5	10 06	1 3 70	Huddersfield	Trainee	Huddersfield T	36	6
						Burnley (loan)	9	3
						Bristol C	1	—
Nick Dent‡	6 1	12 04	30 12 67	Bristol		Bristol C	—	—
Jason Eaton	5 10	11 00	29 1 69	Bristol	Trowbridge	Bristol R	3	—
						Bristol C	13	1
Mark Gavin	5 8	10 07	10 12 63	Bailleston	Apprentice	Leeds U	30	3
						Hartlepool U (loan)	7	—
						Carlisle U	13	1
						Bolton W	49	3
						Rochdale	23	6
						Hearts	9	—
						Bristol C	69	6

BRISTOL CITY

Foundation: The name Bristol City came into being in 1897 when the Bristol South End club, formed three years earlier, decided to adopt professionalism and apply for admission to the Southern League after competing in the Western League. The historic meeting was held at The Albert Hall, Bedminster. Bristol City employed Sam Hollis from Woolwich Arsenal as manager and gave him £40 to buy players. In 1901 they merged with Bedminster, another leading Bristol club.

First Football League game: 7 September, 1901, Division 2, v Blackpool (a) W 2-0 – Moles; Tuft, Davies; Jones, McLean, Chambers; Bradbury, Connor, Boucher, O'Brien (2), Flynn.

Managers (and Secretary-managers)
Sam Hollis 1897–99, Bob Campbell 1899–1901, Sam Hollis 1901–05, Harry Thickett 1905–10, Sam Hollis 1911–13, George Hedley 1913–15, Jack Hamilton 1915–19, Joe Palmer 1919–21, Alex Raisbeck 1921–29, Joe Bradshaw 1929–32, Bob Hewison 1932–49 (under suspension 1938–39), Bob Wright 1949–50, Pat Beasley 1950–58, Peter Doherty 1958–60, Fred Ford 1960–67, Alan Dicks 1967–80, Bobby Houghton 1980–82, Roy Hodgson 1982, Terry Cooper 1982–88 (Director from 1983), Joe Jordan 1988– .

Player and Position	Ht	Wt	Birth Date	Birth Place	Source	Clubs	League App	Gls
Dean Horrix (Deceased)	5 11	10 10	21 11 61	Taplow	Apprentice	Millwall	72	19
						Gillingham	14	—
						Reading	158	35
						Cardiff C (loan)	9	3
						Millwall	11	1
						Bristol C	3	—
Joe Jordan†	6 1	12 01	15 12 51	Carluke		Morton	10	1
						Leeds U	169	35
						Manchester U	109	37
						AC Milan	52	12
						Verona	12	1
						Southampton	48	12
						Bristol C	57	8
Nicky Morgan	5 10	12 08	30 10 59	East Ham	Apprentice	West Ham U	21	2
						Portsmouth	95	32
						Stoke C	88	21
						Bristol C	7	4
David Smith	6 0	11 00	25 6 61	Sidcup	Welling U	Gillingham	104	10
						Bristol C	45	4
Bob Taylor	5 10	11 02	3 2 67	Horden	Horden CW	Leeds U	42	9
						Bristol C	49	35
Alan Theobald*	5 6	9 08	28 10 70	Bristol	Trainee	Bristol C	—	—
Cameron Toshack	6 2	12 00	7 3 70	Cardiff	Trainee	Swansea C	—	—
						Bristol C	—	—
Rob Turner	6 3	14 01	18 9 66	Easington	Apprentice	Huddersfield T	1	—
						Cardiff C	39	8
						Hartlepool U (loan)	7	1
						Bristol R	26	2
						Wimbledon	10	—
						Bristol C	52	12
Alan Walsh‡	6 0	11 00	9 12 56	Darlington	Horden CW	Middlesbrough	3	—
						Darlington	251	90
						Bristol C	218	77

Iain Ferguson on loan from Hearts 11 2

Trainees
Campbell, Gary; Clifford, Steven A; Cook, Anthony C; Cutler, Mark A; Fox, Andrew D; Giles, Christopher P.J; Griffiths, Martin S; Keeling, Darren K; Madge, Mark A; Mitchell, Gerard; Smith, Graham J; Smith, Jason M; Torbett, Daniel; Vernon, Deion A; Watkins, Jason; Weaver, Steven A.

Non-Contract
Jordan, Joseph

Associated Schoolboys
Bessell, Wayne; Britten, Anthony P; Cameron, Scott A; Clark, Lee; Davis, Gary; Davis, Michael V; Donaldson, Michael I; Durbin, Gary; Edwards, Duncan; Freeman, Lewis G.E; Harris, Darren; Henson, Steven; Impey, Scott; Kew, Darren; Lucas, Richard; Martin, Simon; Metcalf, Gary; Milson, Paul J; Palmer, Stuart; Perkins, Darron J; Radford, Michael J; Sheridan, Nathan P; Skidmore, Robert; Smith, Stuart; Webb, Lee J; Wilson, Justin; Winter, Steven, D.

Associated Schoolboys who have accepted the club's offer of a Traineeship/Contract
Benton, Stephen; Griffiths, Craig; Mark, Jonathan; Mitchell, Craig A; O'Brien, Paul; Proudfoot, Jamie; Terry, Paul.

**Non-Contract Players who are retained must be re-signed before they are eligible to play in League matches.

BRISTOL ROVERS 1989–90 *Back row (left to right):* Andy Reece, Paul Nixon, Ian Willmott, Steve Yates, Vaughan Jones, Ian Alexander, Phil Purnell.
Centre row: Geoff Twentyman, Chris McClean, Pete Cawley, Nigel Martyn, Devon White, Billy Clark, Ian Hazel, Marcus Browning.
Front row: Roy Dolling (Physiotherapist), Gary Penrice, David Mehew, Des Bulpin (Coach), Gerry Francis (Manager), Kenny Hibbitt (Assistant Manager), Tony Sealy, Ian Holloway.
Ray Kendall (Kit Manager).

Division 2   **BRISTOL ROVERS**

1883

Twerton Park, Twerton, Bath. Telephone: 0272 352508. Training ground: 0272 861743. Match day ticket office: 0025 312327. Offices: 199 Two Mile Road, Kingswood, Bristol BS15 1AZ.
Ground capacity: 9813.
Record attendance: 38,472 v Preston NE, FA Cup 4th rd, 30 Jan, 1960.
Record receipts: £23,275 v Southampton, FA Cup 4th rd, 28 Jan, 1978.
Pitch measurements: 112yd × 75yd.
President: Marquis of Worcester.
Vice-Presidents: Dr W. T. Cussen, A. I. Seager, H. E. L. Brown.
Chairman: D. H. A. Dunford. *Vice-Chairman:* R. D. Redman.
Directors: R. Craig, G. M. H. Dunford, V. Stokes, R. Andrews.
Manager: Gerry Francis. *Assistant Manager:* Ken Hibbitt.
Coach: Des Bulpin. *Physio:* Roy Dolling.
Commercial Manager: A. Wood.
Secretary: R. C. Twyford. *Office Manager:* Mrs Angela Mann.
Year Formed: 1883. *Turned Professional:* 1897.
Ltd Co.: 1896.
Club Nickname: 'Pirates'.
Previous Names: 1883, Black Arabs; 1884, Eastville Rovers; 1897, Bristol Eastville Rovers; 1898, Bristol Rovers.
Previous Grounds: Purdown, Three Acres, Ashley Hill, Rudgeway, Eastville.
Record League Victory: 7-0 v Brighton & HA, Division 3(S), 29 November 1952 – Hoyle; Bamford, Geoff Fox; Pitt, Warren, Sampson; McIlvenny, Roost (2), Lambden (1), Bradford (1), Peterbridge (2). (1 og). 7-0 v Swansea T, Division 2, 2 October 1954 – Radford; Bamford, Watkins; Pitt, Muir, Anderson; Petherbridge, Bradford (2), Meyer, Roost (1), Hooper (2). (2 og). 7-0 v Shrewsbury T, Division 3, 21 March 1964 – Hall, Hillard, Gwyn Jones; Oldfield, Stone (1), Mabbutt; Jarman (2), Brown (1), Biggs (1p), Hamilton, Bobby Jones (2).
Record Cup Victory: 6-0 v Merthyr Tydfil, FA Cup, 1st rd, 14 November 1987 – Martyn; Alexander (Dryden); Tanner, Hibbitt, Twentyman, Jones, Holloway, Meacham (1), White (2), Penrice (3) (Reece). Purnell.
Record Defeat: 0-12 v Luton T, Division 3(S), 13 April, 1936.
Most League Points (2 for a win): 64, Division 3(S), 1952–53.
Most League Points (3 for a win): 93, Division 3, 1989–90.
Most League Goals: 92, Division 3(S), 1952–53.
Highest League Scorer in Season: Geoff Bradford, 33, Division 3(S), 1952–53.
Most League Goals in Total Aggregate: Geoff Bradford, 245, 1949–64.
Most Capped Player: Neil Slatter, 10 (22), Wales.
Most League Appearances: Stuart Taylor, 545, 1966–80.
Record Transfer Fee Received: £1,000,000 from Crystal Palace for Nigel Martyn, November 1989.
Record Transfer Fee Paid: £100,000 to Birmingham C for Stewart Barrowclough, July 1979.
Football League Record: 1920 Original Member of Division 3; 1921–53 Division 3(S); 1953–62 Division 2; 1962–74 Division 3; 1974–81 Division 2; 1981–90 Division 3; 1990–Division 2.
Honours: Football League: Division 2 best season: 6th, 1955–56, 1958–59; Division 3(S) – Champions 1952–53; Division 3 – Champions 1989–90; Runners-up 1973–74. *FA Cup* Best season: 6th rd, 1950–51, 1957–58. *Football League Cup* best season: 5th rd, 1970–71, 1971–72.
Colours: Blue and white quartered shirts, white shorts, blue stockings with two white rings on top. **Change colours:** White shirts, black shorts, white stockings.

BRISTOL ROVERS 1989–90 LEAGUE RECORD

Match No.	Date	Venue	Opponents	Result	H/T Score	Lg. Pos.	Goalscorers	Attendance
1	Aug 19	H	Brentford	W 1-0	1-0	—	Mehew	5835
2	26	A	Mansfield T	W 1-0	0-0	4	Mehew	3050
3	Sept 2	H	Notts Co	W 3-2	3-1	1	Penrice, White, Jones	4753
4	9	A	Bolton W	L 0-1	0-0	3		5913
5	16	H	Preston NE	W 3-0	3-0	1	Twentyman, Penrice, White	4350
6	23	A	Bristol C	D 0-0	0-0	2		17,432
7	26	A	Leyton Orient	W 1-0	1-0	—	Mehew	4675
8	30	H	Reading	D 0-0	0-0	2		6120
9	Oct 7	H	Fulham	W 2-0	0-0	2	Mehew, Penrice	5811
10	14	A	Bury	D 0-0	0-0	2		3969
11	17	A	Cardiff C	D 1-1	0-0	—	Mehew	6372
12	21	H	Northampton T	W 4-2	0-1	1	White, Nixon, Holloway (pen), Quow (og)	4920
13	28	A	Chester C	D 0-0	0-0	1		2618
14	Nov 1	H	Huddersfield T	D 2-2	1-0	—	Nixon, Mehew	6467
15	4	H	Blackpool	D 1-1	0-0	2	Sealy	5520
16	11	A	Shrewsbury T	W 3-2	1-1	1	Sealy 2, Holloway	4746
17	25	A	Swansea C	W 2-0	1-0	1	Mehew, White	5623
18	Dec 2	A	Walsall	W 2-1	1-1	1	White, Mehew	4038
19	15	A	Crewe Alex	L 0-1	0-0	—		3473
20	26	H	Birmingham C	D 0-0	0-0	2		6573
21	30	H	Tranmere R	W 2-0	0-0	2	Nixon, Vickers (og)	6821
22	Jan 1	A	Rotherham U	L 2-3	1-1	2	Mehew, Holloway (pen)	7750
23	13	H	Mansfield T	D 1-1	1-0	3	Twentyman	5339
24	20	A	Brentford	L 1-2	0-0	3	McClean	7414
25	28	H	Bolton W	D 1-1	1-0	—	Reece	7772
26	Feb 10	A	Preston NE	W 1-0	0-0	3	Mehew	5956
27	18	A	Walsall	W 2-0	1-0	—	Saunders 2	6223
28	24	A	Swansea C	D 0-0	0-0	4		5664
29	Mar 3	H	Wigan Ath	W 6-1	2-0	3	Mehew, Saunders 3, Alexander, Holloway	5169
30	6	A	Reading	W 1-0	1-0	—	Mehew	6147
31	11	H	Leyton Orient	D 0-0	0-0	—		7018
32	17	A	Fulham	W 2-1	0-0	3	White 2	5656
33	21	H	Bury	W 2-1	0-1	—	White, Purnell	5552
34	24	A	Cardiff C	W 2-1	0-1	3	Nixon, Mehew	4631
35	31	A	Northampton T	W 2-1	0-0	3	McClean, Holloway	3774
36	Apr 4	A	Wigan Ath	W 2-1	0-1	—	Mehew, McClean	2352
37	7	H	Chester C	W 2-1	2-1	2	Mehew, McClean	6589
38	10	A	Huddersfield T	D 1-1	1-1	—	Reece	4359
39	14	H	Rotherham U	W 2-0	0-0	2	Mehew, Jones	6794
40	16	A	Birmingham C	D 2-2	0-2	2	White, Thomas (og)	12,438
41	21	H	Crewe Alex	D 1-1	0-0	2	White	7250
42	23	A	Tranmere R	W 2-1	0-1	—	Twentyman, Holloway (pen)	12,723
43	26	A	Notts Co	L 1-3	0-1	—	Mehew	10,142
44	28	H	Shrewsbury T	W 1-0	1-0	2	Holloway (pen)	7903
45	May 2	H	Bristol C	W 3-0	1-0	—	White 2, Holloway (pen)	9831
46	5	A	Blackpool	W 3-0	2-0	1	Mehew, Purnell, Nixon	6776

Final League Position: 1

GOALSCORERS

League (71): Mehew 18, White 12, Holloway 8 (5 pens), Nixon 5, Saunders 5, McClean 4, Penrice 3, Sealy 3, Twentyman 3, Jones 2, Purnell 2, Reece 2, Alexander 1, own goals 3.
Littlewoods Cup (1): Penrice 1.
FA Cup (2): Mehew 1, Reece 1.

Martyn	Alexander	Twentyman	Yates	Mehew	Jones	Holloway	Reece	White	Penrice	Willmott	Cawley	Nixon	Sealy	McClean	Parkin	Hazel	Purnell	Browning	Saunders	Byrne	Match No.
1	2	3	4	5	6	7	8	9	10	11											1
1	2	3	4	5	6	7	8	9	10	11*			12								2
1	2	3	4	5	6	7	8	9	10*	11	12										3
1	2	3	4	5	6	7	8	9	10*	11	12										4
1	2	3	4	5	6	7	8*	9	10	11		12									5
1	2	3	4	5	6	7	8	9	10	11											6
1	2	3	4	5	6	7	8	9	10	11											7
1	2	3	4	5	6	7	8	9	10	11											8
1		3	4	5	6	7	8	9	10	11	2*			12							9
1	2	3		5	6	7	8	9	10	11	4*12										10
1	2	3		5	6	7	8	9	10	11	4*12										11
1	2	3		5	6	7	8	9	10*	11	4	12									12
1	2	3	4	5	6	7	8	9				11	10								13
1	2	3	4	5	6	7	8	9				11	10								14
1	2	3	4	5	6	7*	8	9		12		11	10								15
1	2	3	4	5	6	7	8					11	10	9							16
	2	3	4	5	6	7	8	9				11		12	1	10*					17
	2	3		5	6	7	8	9		4*12		11	10		1						18
		3	4	5	6	7	8	9		2		11*10			1	12					19
	2*	3	4	5	6	7	8	9		12		11	10		1						20
	2	3	4	5	6	7	8	9				11*10		12	1						21
	2	3	4	5	6	7	8	9					10	12	1		11*				22
	2	3	4	5	6	7	8	9				11	10*		1		12				23
	2	3	4	5	6	7	8					11*10	9		1		12				24
	2	3	4	5	6	7	8	9				10*			1		11	12			25
	2	3	4	5	6	7	8	9							1		11*	10	12		26
	2	3	4	5*	6	7	8	9							1		11	10	12		27
	2	3	4	5	6	7	8	9							1		11	10			28
	2	3	4	5	6	7	8	9		14		12			1		11†	10*			29
	2	3	4	5	6	7	8	9							1		11	10			30
	2	3	4	5	6	7	8	9							1		11	10			31
	2	3	4	5*	6	7	8	9				12			1		11	10			32
	2	3	4	5	6	7	8	9				12			1		11	10*			33
	2	3	4	5	6	7	8	9				12	10*		1		11				34
	2†	3	4	5	6	7	8			14		10*		9	1		11	12			35
	2	3	4	5	6	7	8*12							9	1		11	10			36
	2	3	4	5	6	7	8*12							9	1		11	10			37
	2	3	4	5	6	7	8 12							9	1		11*	10			38
	2	3	4	5	6	7		9					11*	8	1		12	10			39
		3	4	5	6	7		9		2†			11*	8	1	14	12	10			40
	2	3	4	5	6	7		9					11*	8†	1	14	12	10			41
	2	3	4	5	6	7	8	9					11*	12	1	14		10†			42
	2	3	4	5	6	7	8*	9				12	11		1			10			43
	2	3	4	5	6	7	8	9*				14	12		1		11†	10			44
	2	3	4	5	6	7	8	9							1		11	10			45
	2	3	4	5	6	7	8	9				12			1		11*	10			46
16	43	46	42	46	46	46	43	40	12	14	1	21	12	10	30	2	17	—	19	—	
									+			+	+	+	+		+	+	+	+	
									3s			3s	2s6s	7s	5s		6s5s	1s	1s	2s	

Littlewoods Cup   First Round   Portsmouth (h)   1-0
                                            (a)   0-2
FA Cup   First Round   Reading (h)   1-1
                                       (a)   1-1
                                       (h)   0-1

BRISTOL ROVERS

Player and Position	Ht	Wt	Birth Date	Place	Source	Clubs	League App	Gls
Goalkeepers								
Brian Parkin	6 3	13 00	12 10 65	Birkenhead	Local	Oldham Ath	6	—
						Crewe Alex (loan)	12	—
						Crewe Alex	86	—
						Crystal Palace (loan)	—	—
						Crystal Palace	20	—
						Bristol R	30	—
Defenders								
Bob Bloomer	5 10	11 06	21 6 66	Sheffield		Chesterfield	141	15
						Bristol R	—	—
Peter Cawley*	6 4	13 00	15 9 65	London	Chertsey	Wimbledon	1	—
						Bristol R (loan)	10	—
						Fulham (loan)	5	—
						Bristol R	3	—
Billy Clark	6 0	12 03	19 5 67	Christchurch	Local	Bournemouth	4	1
						Bristol R	42	1
Vaughan Jones	5 8	11 11	2 9 59	Tonyrefail	Apprentice	Bristol R	101	3
						Newport Co	68	4
						Cardiff C	11	—
						Bristol R	223	8
Geoff Twentyman	6 1	13 02	10 3 59	Liverpool	Chorley	Preston NE	98	4
						Bristol R	173	5
Ian Willmott	5 10	12 06	10 7 68	Bristol	Weston Super Mare	Bristol R	17	—
Steven Yates	5 11	12 06	29 1 70	Bristol	Trainee	Bristol R	79	—
Midfield								
Ian Alexander	5 8	10 07	26 1 63	Glasgow	Leicester Juv Pezoporikos	Rotherham U	11	—
						Motherwell	24	2
						Morton	7	1
						Bristol R	152	3
Ian Hazel	5 10	10 04	1 12 67	London	Apprentice	Wimbledon	7	—
						Bristol R (loan)	3	—
						Bristol R	8	—
Ian Holloway	5 7	9 12	12 3 63	Kingswood	Apprentice	Bristol R	111	14
						Wimbledon	19	2
						Brentford (loan)	13	2
						Brentford	17	—
						Torquay U (loan)	5	—
						Bristol R	133	19
Andy Reece	5 11	12 04	5 9 62	Shrewsbury	Willenhall	Bristol R	125	10
Simon Stapleton‡	6 0	12 00	10 12 68	Oxford	Trainee	Portsmouth	—	—
						Bristol R	5	—
Forwards								
Marcus Browning	5 11	12 00	22 4 71	Bristol	Trainee	Bristol R	1	—
Christian McClean	6 4	14 00	17 10 63	Colchester	Clacton	Bristol R	49	6
David Mehew	5 11	11 07	29 10 67	Camberley		Leeds U	—	—
						Bristol R	120	43
Paul Nixon	5 10	11 03	23 09 63	Seaham	New Zealand	Bristol R	28	5
Philip Purnell	5 8	10 02	16 9 64	Bristol	Mangotsfield	Bristol R	132	22

BRISTOL ROVERS

Foundation: Bristol Rovers were formed at a meeting in Stapleton Road, Eastville, in 1883. However, they first went under the name of the Black Arabs (wearing black shirts). Changing their name to Eastville Rovers in their second season, they won the Gloucestershire Senior Cup in 1888–89. Original members of the Bristol & District League in 1892, this eventually became the Western League and Eastville Rovers adopted professionalism in 1897.

First Football League game: 28 August, 1920, Division 3, v Millwall (a) L 0-2 – Stansfield; Bethune, Panes; Boxley, Kenny, Steele; Chance, Bird, Sims, Bell, Palmer.

Managers (and Secretary-managers)
Alfred Homer 1899–1920 (continued as secretary to 1928), Ben Hall 1920–21, Andy Wilson 1921–26, Joe Palmer 1926–29, Dave McLean 1929–30, Albert Prince-Cox 1930–36, Percy Smith 1936–37, Brough Fletcher 1938–49, Bert Tann 1950–68 (continued as GM to 1972), Fred Ford 1968–69, Bill Dodgin Snr 1969–72, Don Megson 1972–77, Bobby Campbell 1978–79, Harold Jarman 1979–80, Terry Cooper 1980–81, Bobby Gould 1981–83, David Williams 1983–85, Bobby Gould 1985–87, Gerry Francis 1987– .

Player and Position	Ht	Wt	Birth Date	Place	Source	Clubs	League App	Gls
Carl Saunders	5 8	10 12	25 11 64	Marston Green	Local	Stoke C	164	23
						Bristol R	20	5
Tony Sealy	5 8	11 08	7 5 59	London	Apprentice	Southampton	7	—
						Crystal Palace	24	5
						Port Vale (loan)	17	6
						QPR	63	18
						Port Vale (loan)	6	4
						Fulham (loan)	5	1
						Fulham	20	9
						Leicester C	39	7
						Bournemouth (loan)	13	2
					Braga	Brentford	12	4
						Swindon T	—	—
						Bristol R	19	3
Devon White	6 3	14 00	2 3 64	Nottingham	Arnold T	Lincoln C	29	4
					Boston U	Bristol R	122	32

Trainees
Archer, Lee; Bourne, Richard M; Chenoweth, Paul; Hervin, Mark P; James, Neil; Jones, Lee W; Maddison, Lee R; Owen, Craig, P; Reeves, Neil R; Stewart, William M.P; Upshall, Jason F.

**Non-Contract
Francis, Gerald C.J; Stevens, Mark A; Thomas, Glenn.

Associated Schoolboys
Charity, Simon N; Crossey, Scott; Dampier, Steven M; Ead, Stephen F; Kempster, Paul G; Marsh, Andrew J; Matthews, Jason L; Paul, Martin L; Robottom, Karl D; Rogers, Stewart; Senior, Nigel A; Smith, Ian S; Stewart, Andrew W; Warke, Derek A; Wills, Andrew K.

**Non-Contract Players who are retained must be resigned before they are eligible to play in League matches.

BURNLEY 1989-90 *Back row (left to right):* Ray Deakin, Steve Gardner, **Paul Comstive**, Dave Williams, Chris Pearce, Roger Eli, Winston White, Joe Jakub.

Centre row: John Deary, Jason Hardy, Paul Atkinson, Tony Hancock, Brendan O'Connell, Mark Monington, Steve Davis, Ian Measham, Jimmy Holland (Physiotherapist).

Front row: Arthur Bellamy (Youth Team Manager), Nigel Smith, Peter Mumby, Andy Farrell, Frank Casper (Manager), Gary Rowell, Neil Grewcock, Mick Docherty (Assistant Manager).

Division 4 **BURNLEY**

Turf Moor, Burnley BB10 4BX. Telephone: Burnley (0282) 27777; Clubcall 0898 121153.
Ground capacity: 25,000.
Record attendance: 54,775 v Huddersfield T, FA Cup 3rd rd, 23 Feb, 1924.
Record Receipts; £63,988 v Sheffield W, FA Cup 6th rd, 12 March, 1983.
Pitch measurements: 115yd × 73yd.
Chairman: F. J. Teasdale.
Vice-Chairman: Dr R. D. Iven MRCS (Eng), LRCP (Lond), MRCGP.
Directors: B. Dearing Llb, B. Rothwell JP, C. Holt, R. Blakeborough.
Manager: Frank Casper. *Assistant Manager:* Mick Docherty.
Secretary: Albert Maddox. *Youth Team Coach:* Leighton James.
Marketing Manager: Mrs. Joyce Pickles. *Physio:* Jimmy Holland.
Year Formed: 1882. *Turned Professional:* 1883.
Ltd. Co.: 1897.
Club Nickname: 'The Clarets'. *Previous Name:* 1881–82, Burnley Rovers.
Previous Grounds: 1881, Calder Vale; 1882, Turf Moor.
Record League Victory: 9-0 v Darwen, Division 1, 9th January 1892 – Hillman; Walker, Lang; McFettridge, Matthews, Keene; Nicol (3), Bowes, Espie (1), McLardie (3), Hill (2).
Record Cup Victory: 9-0 v Crystal Palace, FA Cup, 2nd rd, replay, 10 February 1909 – Dawson; Barron, McLean; Cretney (2), Leake, Moffat (1); Morley, Ogden, Smith (3), Abbott (2), Smethams (1). 9-0 v New Brighton, FA Cup, 4th rd, 26 January 1957 – Black-law; Angus, Winton; Seith, Adamson, Miller; Newlands (1), McIlroy (3), Lawson (3), Cheesebrough (1), Pilkington (1). 9-0 v Penrith (tie drawn away but played at Burnley) FA Cup, 1st rd, 17 November 1984 – Hansbury; Miller, Hampton, Phelan, Overson (Ken-nedy), Hird (3 incl 1p), Grewcock (1), Powell (2), Taylor (3), Biggins, Hutchison.
Record Defeat: 0-10 v Aston Villa, Division 1, 29 August, 1925 and v Sheffield U, Division 1, 19 January, 1929.
Most League Points (2 for a win): 62, Division 2, 1972–73.
Most League Points (3 for a win): 80, Division 3, 1981–82.
Most League Goals: 102, Division 1, 1960–61.
Highest League Scorer in Season: George Beel, 35, Division 1, 1927–28.
Most League Goals in Total Aggregate: George Beel, 178, 1923–32.
Most Capped Player: Jimmy McIlroy, 52 (55), Northern Ireland.
Most League Appearances: Jerry Dawson, 530, 1906–29.
Record Transfer Fee Received: £300,000 from Everton for Martin Dobson, August 1974, and from Derby Co for Leighton James, November 1975.
Record Transfer Fee Paid: £165,000 to QPR for Leighton James, September 1978.
Football League Record: 1888 Original Member of the Football League; 1897–98 Division 2; 1898–1900 Division 1; 1900–13 Division 2; 1913–30 Division 1; 1930–47 Division 2; 1947–71 Division 1; 1971–73 Division 2; 1973–76 Division 1; 1976–80 Division 2; 1980–82 Division 3; 1982–83 Division 2; 1983–85 Division 3; 1985– Division 4.
Honours: Football League: Division 1 – Champions 1920–21, 1959–60; Runners-up 1919–20, 1961–62; Division 2 – Champions 1897–98, 1972–73; Runners-up 1912–13, 1946–47; Division 3 – Champions 1981–82. Record 30 consecutive Division 1 games without defeat 1920–21. *FA Cup:* Winners 1913–14; Runners-up 1946–47, 1961–62. *Football League Cup:* semi-final 1960–61, 1968–69, 1982–83. *Anglo Scottish Cup:* Winners 1978–79. *Sherpa Van Trophy:* Runners-up 1988. **European Competitions;** *European Cup:* 1960–61. *Euro-pean Fairs Cup:* 1966–67.
Colours: Claret shirts with light blue sleeves, white shorts and stockings. **Change colours:** All white with claret facings.

BURNLEY 1989–90 LEAGUE RECORD

Match No.	Date	Venue	Opponents	Result		H/T Score	Lg. Pos.	Goalscorers	Atten- dance
1	Aug 19	A	Rochdale	L	1-2	1-1	—	White (pen)	5420
2	26	H	Stockport Co	D	0-0	0-0	18		6537
3	Sept 2	A	Chesterfield	W	1-0	0-0	10	Mumby	4061
4	9	H	Exeter C	W	1-0	1-0	10	White (pen)	5443
5	16	A	Gillingham	D	0-0	0-0	10		3853
6	23	H	Hereford U	W	3-1	2-1	5	Mumby, O'Connell 2	5827
7	26	H	York C	D	1-1	1-0	—	Mumby	7890
8	30	A	Torquay U	W	1-0	0-0	7	Grewcock	2214
9	Oct 7	A	Maidstone U	W	2-1	1-1	5	O'Connell, Deary	3762
10	14	H	Hartlepool U	D	0-0	0-0	6		7450
11	17	H	Peterborough U	L	1-2	0-1	—	Grewcock	7187
12	21	A	Doncaster R	W	3-2	3-1	7	White (pen), Jakub, Davis	2900
13	28	H	Aldershot	D	0-0	0-0	7		6451
14	Nov 4	H	Southend U	L	2-3	2-2	—	Farrell, O'Connell	3765
15		H	Colchester U	D	0-0	0-0	8		6145
16	11	A	Scunthorpe U	L	0-3	0-3	13		4745
17	25	A	Lincoln C	L	0-1	0-1	13		4079
18	Dec 2	H	Grimsby T	D	1-1	1-0	14	Jakub	5615
19	26	H	Carlisle U	W	2-1	1-1	14	Futcher, Jakub	12,276
20	30	H	Halifax T	W	1-0	1-0	12	Futcher	9105
21	Jan 1	A	Cambridge U	W	1-0	0-0	10	Bent	3738
22	9	H	Scarborough	W	3-0	1-0	—	Futcher, Bent 2	7329
23	13	A	Stockport Co	L	1-3	1-0	8	White	5210
24	20	H	Rochdale	L	0-1	0-1	9		8174
25	Feb 10	H	Gillingham	L	1-2	1-2	13	Walker (og)	7274
26	17	A	Grimsby T	L	2-4	1-1	15	Francis 2	5973
27	24	H	Lincoln C	D	0-0	0-0	15		5897
28	Mar 3	A	Scarborough	L	2-4	0-3	17	Futcher 2	2961
29	6	H	Torquay U	W	1-0	1-0	—	Farrell	4533
30	10	A	York C	W	3-1	2-0	15	White 2 (1 pen), Deary	3216
31	13	A	Wrexham	L	0-1	0-1	—		4362
32	17	A	Maidstone U	D	1-1	1-0	15	Golley (og)	5059
33	20	A	Hartlepool U	L	0-3	0-2	—		3187
34	24	A	Peterborough U	L	1-4	0-2	15	Futcher (pen)	3841
35	28	H	Hereford U	W	1-0	0-0	—	Francis	2389
36	31	H	Doncaster R	L	0-1	0-1	14		5066
37	Apr 3	H	Chesterfield	D	0-0	0-0	—		3959
38	6	A	Aldershot	D	1-1	1-1	—	Jakub	2325
39	10	H	Southend U	D	0-0	0-0	—		3967
40	14	H	Cambridge U	L	1-3	0-2	16	Futcher (pen)	3975
41	16	A	Carlisle U	D	1-1	0-0	16	Saddington (og)	6738
42	21	H	Wrexham	L	2-3	0-2	17	Jakub, Mumby	4512
43	24	A	Halifax T	D	0-0	0-0	—		2556
44	28	H	Scunthorpe U	L	0-1	0-1	17		3902
45	May 1	A	Exeter C	L	1-2	1-0	—	Francis	7544
46	5	A	Colchester U	W	2-1	1-1	16	Taylor (og), White (pen)	2788

Final League Position: 16

GOALSCORERS

League (45): Futcher 7 (2 pens), White 7 (5 pens), Jakub 5, Francis 4, Mumby 4, O'Connell 4, Bent 3, Deary 2, Farrell 2, Grewcock 2, Davis S 1, own goals 4.
Littlewoods Cup (2): Mumby 1, White 1.
FA Cup (11): Eli 3, Futcher 3, Deary 1, Hardy 1, Mumby 1, O'Connell 1, White 1 (pen).

Pearce	Measham	Deakin	Eli	Monington	Harris	White	Mumby	O'Connell	Farrell	Jakub	Deary	Hancock	Grewcock	Davis S	Hardy	McGrory	Atkinson	Futcher	Davis S M	Bent	McKay	Francis	Gardner	Smith	Rowell	Buckley	Williams	Howarth	Match No.
1	2	3	4*	5	6	7	8†	9	10	11	12		14																1
1	2	3*	4	5	6	7	8†	9	11	10	12		14																2
1	2	3		5	6	7	8		10	4	9	11																	3
1	2	3		5	6	7	8		10	4	9	11																	4
1	2	3		5		7	8	12	10	4	9*			6	11														5
1	2	3		5		7	8	11	10	4	9			6															6
1	2	3	12	5		7	8	11	10	4	9*			6															7
1	2	3		5		7	8	11	10	4	9*	12		6															8
1	2	3	14	5		7	8*	11	10	4	9†	12		6															9
1	2	3	4			7	8	11	10	5	9*	12		6															10
1	2	3		5		7	8*	9	10	4	12	11		6															11
1	2	3	12	5		7	8†	9	10	4		11*		6		14													12
1	2	3		5		7	8*	9	11†	10	4	12		6		14													13
1	2		14	5*		7	8	9	11	10	4	12		6	3†														14
1	2			5		7*	8	9	11	10	4	12		6	3														15
1	2			5		7	8*	9	4	10	12			6	3	11													16
1	2						7	12	9	4	10			6*	3	5	11†	8	14										17
1	2						7		9	4	10			5	3*	12	8	6	11										18
1	2	8					7			5	10	4		6	3	11*	9	12											19
1	2	8†					7			5	10	4		6	3*	9	11	14	12										20
1	2						7*			5	10	4		6	3†	14	9	11	8	12									21
1	2*		12				7			5	10	4		6	3		9	11	8										22
1	2						7*			5	10	4	12	6	3†	14	9	11	8										23
1	2						7			5	10	4		6	3*	12	9	11	8										24
1	2						7			5	10			6	3*	9	4	8	12	11									25
1		3	2				7			5	10			6	8*	9	12	4†11		14									26
1		3	2							5	10	4			9	8	7	11	6										27
1		3	8*	12			7			5	10	4			9		2	11	6										28
1		3	12				7			5	10	4			8*	9	2	11	6										29
1		3	9				7			5	10	4			8		2*11	6	12										30
1		3	9	14			7			5	10	4			8†		2*11	6	12										31
1		3	8*	9			7			5	10	4			14		2†11	6	12										32
1		3	2	9			7			5	10*	4			8			11	6	12									33
1	2	3	8							5	10	4		7		9				11						6			34
	2	3	8				7			5	10	4		6		9				11							1		35
	2	3					7†12			5	10	4		8	11*	9						14				6	1		36
	2	3*	8				7			5	10	4		6		9			12			11					1		37
	2		11				7			5	10	4		6	3	9		8									1		38
	2	6	11				7			5	10	4			3*	9		8	12								1		39
	2	12	8				7*			5	10	4			3	9			11			6†14					1		40
1	2	6	8	14						5	10	4			3*12	9†			11			7							41
1	2	3	8	12						5	10	4		6	14	11†		9	7*										42
1	2	3	8				7*			5	10	4		6	11			12	9										43
1	2	3					7			5	10	4		6	11*	14		8†9				12							44
1	2	3	12	8						5	10	4		6	11			9	7*										45
	2	3					7			5	10	4		6	12	11*		9	8†								1	14	46
39	35 +1s	32 +5s	24	13	4	37 +3s	20 +5s	20 +1s	36	46	39 +2s	9	4 +8s	31 +3s	20	6 +2s	5	22 +5s	7 +3s1s	7	8 +2s	18 +2s	8 +4s1s	4 +1s	— +7s1s	5	7	— +1s	

BURNLEY

Player and Position	Ht	Wt	Birth Date	Place	Source	Clubs	League App	Gls
Goalkeepers								
Chris Pearce	6 0	11 04	7 8 61	Newport	Apprentice	Wolverhampton W	—	—
						Blackburn R	—	—
						Rochdale (loan)	5	—
						Barnsley (loan)	—	—
						Rochdale	36	—
						Port Vale	48	—
						Wrexham	25	—
						Burnley	124	—
David Williams	6 0	12 00	18 9 68	Liverpool	Trainee	Oldham Ath	—	—
						Burnley	14	—
Defenders								
Steve Davis	6 0	12 07	26 7 65	Birmingham	Apprentice	Stoke C	—	—
						Crewe Alex	145	1
						Burnley	101	6
Ray Deakin	5 8	11 01	19 6 59	Liverpool	Apprentice	Everton	—	—
						Port Vale	23	6
						Bolton W	105	2
						Burnley	176	6
Roger Eli	5 10	12 00	11 9 65	Bradford	Apprentice	Leeds U	2	
						Wolverhampton W	18	—
						Cambridge U	—	—
						Crewe Alex	27	1
						York C	4	1
						Bury	2	—
						Burnley	29	—
Steve Gardner*	5 9	12 08	3 7 68	Teeside	Apprentice	Manchester U	—	—
						Burnley	95	—
Jim Heggarty‡	6 2	13 08	4 8 65	Larne		Brighton & HA	—	—
						Burnley	36	1
Graham Lawrie	5 8	10 12	4 9 71	Aberdeen	Keith	Burnley	—	—
Shaun McGrory*	5 10	12 00	29 2 68	Coventry		Coventry C	—	—
						Burnley	46	2
Paul McKay	5 8	10 05	28 1 71	Banbury	Trainee	Burnley	12	—
Ian Measham	5 11	11 08	14 12 64	Barnsley	Apprentice	Huddersfield T	17	—
						Lincoln C (loan)	6	—
						Rochdale (loan)	12	—
						Cambridge U	46	—
						Burnley	65	1
Midfield								
Paul Atkinson*	5 10	11 05	14 8 61	Otley	Apprentice	Oldham Ath	143	11
						Watford	11	—
						Oldham Ath	59	2
						Swansea C (loan)	18	3
						Bolton W (loan)	3	—
						Burnley	22	1
John Deary	5 10	11 11	18 10 62	Ormskirk	Apprentice	Blackpool	303	43
						Burnley	41	2
Andy Farrell	5 11	11 00	7 10 65	Colchester	School	Colchester U	105	5
						Burnley	117	9
Jason Hardy	5 8	10 00	14 12 69		Trainee	Burnley	40	1
Neil Howarth§			15 11 71	Farnworth	Trainee	Burnley	1	—
Joe Jakub	5 6	9 06	7 12 56	Falkirk	Apprentice	Burnley	42	—
						Bury	265	27
					AZ 67	Chester C	42	1
						Burnley	46	5
Mark Monington	5 8	11 00	21 10 70	Bilsthorpe	School	Burnley	21	1
Nigel Smith	5 7	10 04	21 12 69	Leeds	Leeds U	Burnley	11	—

BURNLEY

Foundation: The majority of those responsible for the formation of the Burnley club in 1881 were from the defunct rugby club Burnley Rovers. Indeed, they continued to play rugby for a year before changing to soccer and dropping "Rovers" from their name. The changes were decided at a meeting held in May 1882 at the Bull Hotel.

First Football League game: 8 September, 1888, Football League, v PNE (a), L 2-5 – Kay; Bury, Lang; Abrahams, Friel, Keenan; Hibbert, Brady, Poland (1), Gallocher (1), Yates.

Managers (and Secretary-managers)
Arthur F. Sutcliffe 1893–96*, Harry Bradshaw 1896–99*, Ernest Magnall 1899–1903*, Spen Whittaker 1903–10, R. H. Wadge 1910–11*, John Haworth 1911–25, Albert Pickles 1925–32, Tom Bromilow 1932–35, Alf Boland 1935–39*, Cliff Britton 1945–48, Frank Hill 1948–54, Alan Brown 1954–57, Billy Dougall 1957–58, Harry Potts 1958–70 (GM to 1972), Jimmy Adamson 1970–76, Joe Brown 1976–77, Harry Potts 1977–79, Brian Miller 1979–83, John Bond 1983–84, John Benson 1984–85, Martin Buchan 1985, Tommy Cavanagh 1985–86, Brian Miller 1986–89, Frank Casper 1989–

Player and Position	Ht	Wt	Birth Date	Place	Source	Clubs	League App	Gls
Forwards								
John Francis	5 8	11 02	21 11 63	Dewsbury	Emley	Sheffield U	42	6
						Burnley	19	4
Ron Futcher	6 0	12 10	25 9 56	Chester	Apprentice	Chester	4	—
						Luton T	120	40
						Manchester C	17	7
					Minnesota	Barnsley	19	6
					Portland	Oldham Ath	65	30
					NAC Breda	Bradford C	42	18
					Tulsa	Port Vale	52	20
						Burnley	23	7
Neil Grewcock	5 6	11 03	26 4 62	Leicester	Shepshed C	Leicester C	8	1
						Gillingham (loan)	13	1
						Gillingham	21	3
						Burnley	172	25
Peter Mumby	5 9	11 05	22 2 69	Bradford	Trainee	Leeds U	6	—
						Shamrock R (loan)	—	—
						Burnley	25	4
Gary Rowell*	5 10	11 03	6 6 57	Seaham	Apprentice	Sunderland	254	88
						Norwich C	6	1
						Middlesbrough	27	10
						Brighton & HA	12	—
						Dundee	1	—
						Carlisle U	7	—
						Burnley	19	1
Winston White	5 10	10 12	26 10 58	Leicester	Apprentice	Leicester C	12	1
						Hereford U	175	21
						Chesterfield	1	—
						Port Vale	1	—
						Stockport Co	4	—
						Bury	125	11
						Rochdale (loan)	4	—
						Colchester U	65	8
						Burnley	75	12

Trainees
Douglas, Paul A; Eyre, Steven F; Frankum, Noel K; Hill, Dennis J; Hilton, Matthew R; Howarth, Neil; Isherwood, Alvin L; Lancashire, Graham; Pemberton, Paul M; Seals, Taras; Whipp, Kurt M; Whorlow, Sean

**Non-Contract
Kay, Richard H; Mercer, Stephen T.

Associated Schoolboys
Backhouse, Steven J; Carrington, David J; Cox, Simon P; King, Andrew R; Lawson, Andrew P; Livesey, David; McCaffery, Stephen P; Mullin, John; Parry, Christopher M; Ryder, Damian M; Wallace, Simon P.

**Non-Contract Players who are retained must be re-signed before they are eligible to play in League matches.

BURY 1989-90 *Back row (left to right):* Gareth Price, Chris Withe, Jamie Hoyland, Tony Cunningham, Steve Elliott, Andy Feeley, Kevin Hulme.
Centre row: Jack Chapman (Assistant Manager), Ray Pointer (Reserve Coach), Terry Pashley, Charlie Bishop, Kenny Clements, Simon Farnworth, Peter Valentine, Phil Parkinson, Paul Atkin, Alan Knill, Wilf McGuinness (Physiotherapist).
Front row: David Lee, Nigel Greenwood, Andy Hill, Sam Ellis (Manager), Mike Walsh (Player-coach), Sammy McIlroy, Liam Robinson.

Division 3 **BURY**

Gigg Lane, Bury BL9 9HR. Telephone 061-764 4881/2. Commercial Dept. 061-764 7475/705 2144. Clubcall: 0898 121197. Community Programme: 061-797 5423. Social Club: 061-764 6771.

Ground capacity: 8,000.

Record attendance: 35,000 v Bolton, FA Cup 3rd rd, 9 Jan, 1960.

Record receipts: £22,200 v Nottingham F, League Cup quarterfinal, 17 Jan, 1978.

Pitch measurements: 112yd × 72yd.

President:

Chairman: T. Robinson. *Vice-Chairman:* Canon J. R. Smith MA.

Directors: C. H. Eaves, I. Pickup, J. Smith, A. Noonan, F. Mason.

Manager: Sam Ellis. *Assistant Manager:*

Reserve Coach: Ray Pointer. *Physio:* Wilf McGuinness.

Secretary: John Heap. *Commercial Manager:* Neville Neville.

Year Formed: 1885. *Turned professional:* 1885.

Ltd Co.: 1897. **Club Nickname:** 'Shakers'.

Club Sponsors: MacPherson Paints.

Record League Victory: 8-0 v Tranmere R, Division 3, 10 January 1970 – Forrest: Tinney, Saile; Anderson, Turner, McDermott; Hince (1), Arrowsmith (1), Jones (4), Kerr (1), Grundy. (1 og).

Record Cup Victory: 12-1 v Stockton, FA Cup, 1st rd (replay), 2 February 1897 – Montgomery; Darroch, Barbour; Hendry (1), Clegg, Ross (1); Wylie (3), Pangbourn, Millar (4), Henderson (2), Plant. (1 og).

Record Defeat: 0-10 v Blackburn R, FA Cup, preliminary round, 1st October, 1887 and v West Ham U, Milk Cup, 2nd rd, 2nd leg, 25 October, 1983.

Most League Points (2 for a win): 68, Division 3, 1960–61.

Most League Points (3 for a win): 84, Division 4, 1984–85.

Most League Goals: 108, Division 3, 1960–61.

Highest League Scorer in Season: Craig Madden, 35, Division 4, 1981–82.

Most League Goals in Total Aggregate: Craig Madden, 129, 1978–86.

Most Capped Player: Bill Gorman, 11 (13), Eire and (4), Northern Ireland.

Most League Appearances: Norman Bullock, 506, 1920–35.

Record Transfer Fee Received: £150,000 from Chesterfield for Danny Wilson, July 1980 and from Everton for Neville Southall, July 1981.

Record Transfer Fee Paid: £95,000 to Swansea C for Alan Knill, August 1989.

Football League Record: 1894 Elected to Division 2; 1895–1912 Division 1; 1912–24 Division 2; 1924–29 Division 1; 1929–57 Division 2; 1957–61 Division 3; 1961–67 Division 2; 1967–68 Division 3; 1968–69 Division 2; 1969–71 Division 3; 1971–74 Division 4; 1974–80 Division 3; 1980–85 Division 4; 1985– Division 3.

Honours: Football League: Division 1 best season: 4th, 1925–26; Division 2 – Champions 1894–95; Runners-up 1923–24; Division 3 – Champions 1960–61; Runners-up 1967–68. *FA Cup:* Winners 1900, 1903. *Football League Cup:* Semi-final 1963.

Colours: White shirts, navy blue shorts, navy stockings. **Change colours:** Red shirts, white shorts, red stockings.

BURY 1989–90 LEAGUE RECORD

Match No.	Date	Venue	Opponents	Result		H/T Score	Lg. Pos.	Goalscorers	Attendance
1	Aug 19	H	Bristol C	D	1-1	0-0	—	Greenwood	3399
2	26	A	Preston NE	W	3-2	1-0	7	Hoyland, Greenwood, Cunningham	5622
3	Sept 2	H	Wigan Ath	D	2-2	2-2	8	Hoyland 2	3122
4	9	A	Brentford	W	1-0	1-0	6	Cunningham	5010
5	16	H	Mansfield T	W	3-0	3-0	2	Robinson 2 (1 pen), Greenwood	2821
6	23	A	Shrewsbury T	L	1-3	1-2	6	Cunningham	3525
7	26	H	Rotherham U	D	1-1	0-0	—	Robinson	3276
8	30	A	Northampton T	W	1-0	1-0	5	Greenwood	3486
9	Oct 7	A	Chester C	W	4-1	2-0	3	Hoyland, Lee, Cunningham (pen), Withe	2168
10	14	H	Bristol R	D	0-0	0-0	3		3969
11	17	H	Swansea C	W	3-2	3-0	—	Robinson	3336
12	21	A	Fulham	D	2-2	0-0	2	Greenwood, Robinson	3520
13	28	H	Birmingham C	D	0-0	0-0	3		3383
14	31	A	Blackpool	W	1-0	0-0	—	Robinson (pen)	4184
15	Nov 3	A	Cardiff C	L	1-3	1-2	—	Robinson	3437
16	11	H	Reading	W	4-0	1-0	2	Hoyland 2, Lee, Robinson (pen)	3183
17	25	H	Crewe Alex	L	0-3	0-0	5		3637
18	Dec 2	A	Tranmere R	W	4-2	1-2	8	Robinson 3 (2 pens), Bishop	6207
19	16	H	Walsall	L	0-2	0-1	6		2797
20	26	A	Huddersfield T	L	1-2	1-1	6	Robinson	8483
21	30	A	Bolton W	L	1-3	1-2	8	Robinson	10,628
22	Jan 1	H	Leyton Orient	W	2-0	2-0	5	Cunningham, Robinson	2551
23	6	A	Notts Co	W	4-0	3-0	—	Feeley, Cunningham 2, Hoyland	6059
24	13	H	Preston NE	L	1-2	1-2	4	Hill	4715
25	20	A	Bristol C	L	0-1	0-1	6		10,992
26	27	A	Brentford	L	0-2	0-1	8		2963
27	Feb 3	H	Shrewsbury T	D	0-0	0-0	7		2677
28	10	A	Mansfield T	L	0-1	0-1	8		2424
29	13	A	Wigan Ath	D	0-0	0-0	—		2104
30	17	A	Tranmere R	L	1-2	1-0	8	Hoyland	3801
31	24	A	Crewe Alex	L	1-2	0-1	8	Hoyland	3998
32	Mar 3	H	Notts Co	W	3-2	3-1	8	Patterson, Hoyland, Spink	3007
33	6	H	Northampton T	W	1-0	0-0	—	Hulme	2327
34	10	A	Rotherham U	W	3-1	1-1	7	Patterson (pen), Robinson 2	5425
35	17	H	Chester C	W	1-0	0-0	6	Robinson	2851
36	21	A	Bristol R	L	1-2	1-0	—	Hoyland	5552
37	23	A	Swansea C	W	1-0	1-0	—	Lee	3042
38	31	H	Fulham	D	0-0	0-0	6		3000
39	Apr 7	H	Birmingham C	D	0-0	0-0	7		6808
40	10	H	Blackpool	W	2-0	1-0	—	Lee, Patterson	3131
41	14	A	Leyton Orient	W	3-2	0-1	6	Knill, Hoyland (pen), Lee	3535
42	16	H	Huddersfield T	W	6-0	3-0	5	Robinson, Patterson, Lee, Parkinson, Hoyland, Atkin	4621
43	21	A	Walsall	D	2-2	0-0	5	Lee, Hoyland (pen)	3621
44	24	H	Bolton W	W	2-0	1-0	—	Hill, Hoyland	6551
45	28	H	Reading	L	0-1	0-0	5		3259
46	May 5	H	Cardiff C	W	2-0	1-0	5	Hoyland, Parkinson	4224

Final League Position: 5

GOALSCORERS

League (70): Robinson 17 (5 pens), Hoyland 16 (2 pens), Cunningham 8 (1 pen), Lee 8, Greenwood 5, Patterson 4 (1 pen), Feeley 2, Hill 2, Parkinson 2, Atkin 1, Bishop 1, Hulme 1, Knill 1, Spink 1, Withe 1.
Littlewoods Cup (1): Robinson 1.
FA Cup (1): Bishop 1.

Farnworth	Hill	Withe	Hoyland	Knill	Valentine	Lee	Robinson	Cunningham	Parkinson	Feeley	Greenwood	McIlroy	Beresford	Clements	Bishop	Kelly	Hulme	Greenall	Spink	Patterson	Atkin	Price	Match No.
1	2	3	4	5	6	7	8	9	10*	11†	12	14											1
	2	3	4		5	7	12	9	14*	8	10	11†	1	6									2
1	2	3*	4	6	5	7	8	9	14		12	10†		11									3
1	2	3	4	6	5	7	8	9			12	10*		14	11†								4
1	2	3	4	6	5	7†	8	9			12	11	10*	14									5
1	2	3	4	6*	5	7	8	9	10	11†	12	14											6
1	2	3	4	6	5	7	8	9	10*	11†	12	14											7
1	2	3	4	6	5		8	9	12	10*	11	7†	14										8
	2	3*	4	6	5	7	8	9	10	11				12		1							9
	2	3	4	6	5	7	8	9	10	11*				12		1							10
	2	3*	4	6	5	7	8	9	10					12	11	1							11
	2	3*	4	6	5	7	8	9	10	11				12		1							12
	2	3	4	6*	5	7	8†	9	10	11	12			14		1							13
	2	3*	4	6	5	7	8	9	10	12	11†			14		1							14
	2	3	4	6	5	7	8	9	10†	11*	12			14		1							15
	2*		4	6	5	7	8	9	10	11				12	3	1							16
	2	12	4	6	5	7	8		10	11		3*		9		1							17
	2		4	6	5	7	8	9	10					3	11	1							18
	2	3	4	6		7	8	9	10	12				5	11*	1							19
	2	3	4	6		7	8	9	10					5	11	1							20
	2	3*	4	6		7	8	9	10					5	11	1	12						21
	2	3*	4	6		7	8	9	10	12				5	11	1							22
	2		4	6		7	8	9	10					3	11	1			5				23
	2	14	4	6†		7	8	9*	10	12				3	11	1			5				24
	2	11*	4	6		7	8		10	12				3	14	1		9	5†				25
	2		4	6		7	8	9	10*		11			5	3	1	12						26
	2	10	4		5	7	8*							6	3	1	12			9	11		27
	2	14	4	6†	5	7*	8		10					3		1	12			9	11		28
	2		4	6	5	7	8		10					3		1	12			9*11			29
	2		4	6	5	7	8		10					3*		1	12			9	11		30
	2	14	4	6	5	7*	8		10					3†		1	12			9	11		31
	2		4	6	5	7			10					3		1	8			9	11		32
	2		4	6	5	7	8*		10	12				3		1	9				11		33
	2		4	6	5	7	8		10					3		1	9				11		34
	2		4		5	7	8		10					3		1	9				11	6	35
	2		4	6	5	7	8		10					3		1	9				11		36
	2		4	6	5	7	8		10	12				3		1	9*				11		37
	2	12	4	6	5*	7	8		10					3		1	9				11		38
	2	12	4	6	5	7	8†		10*					3		1	9				11	12	39
	2		4	6	5	7	8*		10	9				3		1					11	12	40
	2	14	4	6	5	7	8*		10†	9				3		1					11	12	41
2†12		4	6	5	7	8			10*					3		1				11	9	14	42
	2		4	6	5	7	8*		10					3		1	12			11	9		43
	2		4	6	5	7	8*		10					3		1	12			11	9		44
	2	14	4	6	5	7	8†		10					3*		1	12			11	9		45
	2	3	4	6†	5	7	12	9	10*					14		1				11	8		46
7	46	22	46	43	38	45	43	25	19	26	13	7	1	14	29	38	9	3	6	20	6	—	
		+					+		+	+	+			+	+		+				+	+	
		9s					2s		3s	4s	7s			5s	14s1s		10s				3s	1s	

Littlewoods Cup First Round Stockport Co (a) 0-1
  (h) 1-1
FA Cup First Round Rotherham U (a) 0-0
  (h) 1-2

BURY

Player and Position	Ht	Wt	Birth Date	Place	Source	Clubs	League App	Gls
Goalkeepers								
Aidan Davison	6 1	13 02	11 5 68	Sedgefield	Billingham Syn	Notts Co	1	—
						Leyton Orient (loan)	—	—
						Bury	—	—
						Chester C (loan)	—	—
Simon Farnworth*	6 0	11 10	28 10 63	Chorley	Apprentice	Bolton W	113	—
						Stockport Co (loan)	10	—
						Tranmere R (loan)	7	—
						Bury	105	—
Gary Kelly	5 10	12 03	3 8 66	Fulwood	Apprentice	Newcastle U	53	—
						Blackpool (loan)	5	—
						Bury	38	—
Defenders								
Paul Atkin	6 0	12 04	3 9 69	Nottingham	Trainee	Notts Co	—	—
						Bury	10	1
Charlie Bishop	6 0	12 01	16 2 68	Nottingham	Apprentice	Stoke C	—	—
						Watford	—	—
						Bury	85	4
Kenny Clements	6 1	12 06	9 4 55	Manchester	Amateur	Manchester C	119	—
						Oldham Ath	206	2
						Manchester C (loan)	12	1
						Manchester C	94	—
						Bury	81	1
Shaun Dunn	6 2	11 10	19 1 71	North Shields		Blackpool	—	—
						Bury	—	—
Andy Hill	5 11	12 00	20 1 65	Maltby	Apprentice	Manchester U	—	—
						Bury	252	10
Alan Knill	6 2	10 09	8 10 64	Slough	Apprentice	Southampton	—	—
						Halifax T	118	6
						Swansea C	89	3
						Bury	43	1
Terry Pashley*	5 8	12 00	11 10 56	Chesterfield	Apprentice	Burnley	18	—
						Blackpool	201	7
						Bury	217	5
Gareth Price	5 10	11 00	21 2 70	Swindon	Trainee	Mansfield T	—	—
						Bury	1	—
Mark Simms			17 10 70	Southport	Blackburn R§ Preston NE§	Bury	—	—
Peter Valentine	5 10	12 00	16 4 63	Huddersfield	Apprentice	Huddersfield T	19	1
						Bolton W	68	1
						Bury	202	8
Mick Walsh	6 0	12 00	20 6 56	Manchester		Bolton W	177	4
						Everton	20	—
						Norwich C (loan)	5	—
						Burnley (loan)	3	—
					Ft Lauderdale	Manchester C	4	—
						Blackpool	153	5
						Bury	—	—
Chris Withe	5 10	11 03	25 9 62	Liverpool	Apprentice	Newcastle U	2	—
						Bradford C	143	2
						Notts Co	80	3
						Bury	31	1
Midfield								
Noel Brotherston*	5 7	11 04	18 11 56	Belfast	Apprentice	Tottenham H	1	—
						Blackburn R	317	40
						Bury	38	4
						Scarborough (loan)	5	—

BURY

Foundation: A meeting at the Waggon & Horses Hotel, attended largely by members of Bury Wesleyans and Bury Unitarians football clubs, decided to form a new Bury club. This was officially formed at a subsequent gathering at the Old White Horse Hotel, Fleet Street, Bury on April 24, 1885.

First Football League game: 1 September, 1894, Division 2, v Manchester C (h) W 4-2 – Lowe; Gillespie, Davies; White, Clegg, Ross; Wylie, Barbour (2), Millar (1), Ostler (1), Plant.

Managers (and Secretary-managers)
T. Hargreaves 1887*, H. S. Hamer 1887–1907*, Archie Montgomery 1907–15, William Cameron 1919–23, James Hunter Thompson 1923–27, Percy Smith 1927–30, Arthur Paine 1930–34, Norman Bullock 1934–38, Jim Porter 1944–45, Norman Bullock 1945–49, John McNeil 1950–53, Dave Russell 1953–61, Bob Stokoe 1961–65, Bert Head 1965–66, Les Shannon 1966–69, Jack Marshall 1969, Les Hart 1970, Tommy McAnearney 1970–72, Alan Brown 1972–73, Bobby Smith 1973–77, Bob Stokoe 1977–78, David Hatton 1978–79, Dave Connor 1979–80, Jim Iley 1980–84, Martin Dobson 1984–89, Sam Ellis 1989– .

Player and Position	Ht	Wt	Birth Date	Place	Source	Clubs	League App	Gls
Andy Feeley	5 10	12 07	30 9 61	Hereford	Apprentice	Hereford U	51	3
						Chelsea (loan)	—	—
					Trowbridge T	Leicester C	76	—
						Brentford	67	—
						Bury	30	2
Jamie Hoyland	6 0	12 08	23 1 66	Sheffield	Apprentice	Manchester C	2	—
						Bury	172	35
Dave Lee	5 8	10 02	5 11 67	Manchester	Schools	Bury	161	19
Philip Parkinson	5 10	10 11	1 12 67	Chorley	Apprentice	Southampton	—	—
						Bury	69	3
Mark Patterson	5 6	10 10	24 5 65	Darwen	Apprentice	Blackburn R	101	20
						Preston NE	55	19
						Bury	20	4
Forwards								
Tony Cunningham	6 2	13 10	12 11 57	Jamaica	Stourbridge	Lincoln C	123	32
						Barnsley	42	11
						Sheffield W	28	5
						Manchester C	18	1
						Newcastle U	47	4
						Blackpool	71	17
						Bury	25	8
Kevin Hulme	5 10	11 09	2 12 67	Farnworth	Radcliffe Bor	Bury	24	1
						Chester C (loan)	4	—
Liam Robinson	5 6	11 04	29 12 65	Bradford	School	Nottingham F	—	—
						Huddersfield T	21	2
						Tranmere R (loan)	4	3
						Bury	164	69

Trainees
Ashworth, Adam; Bennett, Ian H; Bradley, Patrick; Bridge, Jason; Dean, John; DeAth, Antony; Denny, Steven; Faulkner, Anthony H; Kent, Daniel; McIlory, Samuel; Newberry, Adrian; Wagstaff, Andrew P.

Associated Schoolboys
Beaumont, Stuart; Brown, Stuart I; Calderbank, Darren P; Chadwick, Craig; Cookson, John; Hartley, Johnathan D; Higgins, Saul J; Motby, Lee A; Phillips, Daniel P; Unsworth, Lee P; Wilkinson, Lee.

Associated Schoolboys who have accepted the club's offer of a Traineeship/Contract
Anderson, Lee C.

CAMBRIDGE UNITED 1989–90 *Back row (left to right):* Paul Bastock, Gary Clayton, Dany O'Shea, Dion Dublin, Phil Chapple, Liam Daish, John Taylor, Colin Bailie, Martin Robinson, Tony Dennis, John Vaughan.
Front row: Michael Cheetham, Steven Claridge, Laurie Ryan, Lee Philpott, John Beck (Team Manager), Gary Johnson (Coach), Chris Leadbitter, Alan Kimble, Andy Fensome, Michael Cook.

Division 3   **CAMBRIDGE UNITED**

Abbey Stadium, Newmarket Rd, Cambridge. Telephone Teversham (0223) 241237. Clubcall: 0898 12 11 41.

Ground capacity: 10,218.

Record attendance; 14,000 v Chelsea, Friendly, 1 May, 1970.

Record receipts: £60,065 v Crystal Palace, FA Cup 6th Rd, 10 March 1990.

Pitch measurements: 110yd × 74yd.

Chairman: D. A. Ruston. *Vice-Chairman:* R. H. Smart.

Directors: R. J. Smith, C. Howlett, J. Howard.

Team Manager: John Beck.

Physio: Roy Johnson.

Secretary: Nigel Pleasants. *Sales Manager:* Gary Johnson.

Year Formed: 1919. *Turned Professional:* 1946. *Ltd Co.:* 1948.

Club Nickname: 'United'.

Previous Name: Abbey United until 1949.

Record League Victory: 6-0 v Darlington, Division 4, 18 September 1971 – Roberts; Thompson, Akers, Guild, Eades, Foote, Collins (1p), Horrey, Hollett, Greenhalgh (4), Phillips. (1 og). 6-0 v Hartlepool, Division 4, 11 February 1989 – Vaughan; Beck, Kimble, Turner, Chapple (1), Daish, Clayton, Holmes, Taylor (3 incl 1p), Bull (1), Leadbitter (1).

Record Cup Victory: 5-1 v Bristol C, FA Cup, 5th rd, second replay, 27 February 1990 – Vaughan; Fensome, Kimble, Bailie (O'Shea), Chapple, Daish, Cheetham, (Robinson), Leadbitter (1), Dublin (2), Taylor (1), Philpott (1).

Record Defeat: 0-6 v Aldershot, Division 3, 13 April, 1974 and v Darlington, Division 4, 28 September, 1974 and v Chelsea, Division 2, 15 January 1983.

Most League Points (2 for a win): 65, Division 4, 1976–77.

Most League Points (3 for a win): 73, Division 4, 1989–90.

Most League Goals: 87, Division 4, 1976–77.

Highest League Scorer in Season: David Crown, 24, Division 4, 1985–86.

Most League Goals in Total Aggregate: Alan Biley, 74, 1975–80.

Most Capped Player: Tom Finney, 7 (15), Northern Ireland.

Most League Appearances: Steve Spriggs, 416, 1975–87.

Record Transfer Fee Received: £350,000 from Derby Co for Alan Biley, January 1980.

Record Transfer Fee Paid: £140,000 to Northampton T for George Reilly, November 1979.

Football League Record: 1970 Elected to Division 4; 1973–74 Division 3; 1974–77 Division 4; 1977–78 Division 3; 1978–84 Division 2; 1984–85 Division 3; 1985–90 Division 4; 1990–Division 3.

Honours: Football League: Division 2 best season: 8th, 1979–80 Division 3 – Runners-up 1977–78; Division 4 – Champions 1976–77; *FA Cup* best season: 6th rd. 1989–90. *Football League Cup:* 4th rd. 1980–81.

Colours: Yellow and black shirts, yellow and black shorts, yellow stockings. **Change colours:** All sky blue with amber and black trim.

CAMBRIDGE UNITED 1989–90 LEAGUE RECORD

Match No.	Date	Venue	Opponents	Result	H/T Score	Lg. Pos.	Goalscorers	Attendance
1	Aug 19	A	Grimsby T	D 0-0	0-0	—		4822
2	26	H	Hereford U	L 0-1	0-0	20		1990
3	Sept 2	A	Scarborough	D 1-1	1-1	18	Taylor	2522
4	9	H	Chesterfield	L 0-1	0-0	20		2215
5	16	A	Exeter C	L 2-3	2-1	21	Chapple, Kimble (pen)	2754
6	22	H	Halifax T	W 1-0	0-0		Philpott	2220
7	26	H	Carlisle U	L 1-2	0-0	—	Leadbitter	2607
8	30	A	Maidstone U	D 2-2	1-1	22	Leadbitter, Pamphlett (og)	1706
9	Oct 7	A	York C	L 2-4	1-2	23	Taylor, Dennis	2061
10	13	H	Torquay U	W 5-2	3-1		Philpott, Taylor 2, Ryan, Kimble (pen)	2085
11	17	H	Doncaster R	W 1-0	1-0	—	Taylor	2483
12	21	A	Wrexham	W 3-2	1-0	15	O'Keefe (og), Philpott, Robinson	1541
13	28	H	Scunthorpe U	W 5-3	4-1	11	Clayton, Taylor, Leadbitter, Dublin 2	2395
14	31	A	Hartlepool U	W 2-1	1-0		Dublin, Cheetham	1726
15	Nov 4	H	Aldershot	D 2-2	2-0	11	Taylor, Dublin	2565
16	10	A	Colchester U	W 2-1	1-1	—	Dennis, Dublin	3771
17	24	A	Southend U	D 0-0	0-0	—		4068
18	Dec 2	H	Rochdale	L 0-3	0-1	12		2289
19	17	H	Peterborough U	W 3-2	2-0	—	Taylor 3	4811
20	26	A	Lincoln C	L 3-4	1-1	12	Chapple, Kimble (pen), Carmichael (og)	4111
21	29	A	Stockport Co	L 1-3	1-1	—	Philpott	3915
22	Jan 1	H	Burnley	L 0-1	0-0	14		3738
23	13	A	Hereford U	W 2-0	2-0	14	Dublin, Cheetham	7302
24	20	H	Grimsby T	W 2-0	0-0	11	Taylor, Dublin	2623
25	Feb 2	A	Halifax T	D 0-0	0-0	—		1526
26	10	H	Exeter C	W 3-2	0-2	11	Cheetham 2, Philpott	3508
27	25	H	Southend U	W 2-1	1-0	—	Taylor, Kimble (pen)	4573
28	Mar 3	A	Gillingham	L 0-1	0-0	14		4215
29	6	H	Maidstone U	W 2-0	2-0	—	Dublin 2	4464
30	16	H	York C	D 2-2	1-1	—	Taylor, Leadbitter	4621
31	20	A	Torquay U	L 0-3	0-2	—		1744
32	25	A	Doncaster R	L 1-2	0-1	—	Dublin	2147
33	27	A	Rochdale	L 0-2	0-1	—		1669
34	30	H	Wrexham	D 1-1	0-0	—	Dublin	3294
35	Apr 2	A	Scarborough	W 5-2	3-0	—	Chapple, Kimble 2 (2 pens), Taylor, Cheetham	3001
36	4	A	Carlisle U	L 1-3	0-2	—	Kimble (pen)	4890
37	7	A	Scunthorpe U	D 1-1	1-0	15	Taylor	2486
38	10	H	Hartlepool U	W 2-1	2-0	—	Claridge, Dublin	3254
39	14	A	Burnley	W 3-1	2-0	11	Dublin, Chapple, Daish	3975
40	17	H	Lincoln C	W 2-1	1-1	—	Claridge, Kimble	4121
41	21	A	Peterborough U	W 2-1	1-0	10	Cheetham, Dublin	9257
42	23	H	Stockport Co	L 0-2	0-1	—		4850
43	25	A	Chesterfield	D 1-1	1-1	—	Claridge	3870
44	29	H	Colchester U	W 4-0	2-0	—	Cheetham 3 (2 pens), Claridge	4558
45	May 1	H	Gillingham	W 2-1	1-0	—	Dublin, Chapple	4963
46	5	A	Aldershot	W 2-0	1-0	6	Cook, Cheetham (pen)	3208

Final League Position: 6

GOALSCORERS

League (76): Dublin 15, Taylor 15, Cheetham 10 (3 pens), Kimble 8 (7 pens), Chapple 5, Philpott 5, Claridge 4, Leadbitter 4, Dennis 2, Clayton 1, Cook 1, Daish 1, Robinson 1, Ryan 1, own goals 3.
Littlewoods Cup (6): Dublin 2, Chapple 1, Leadbitter 1, Robinson 1, Taylor 1.
FA Cup (15): Taylor 5, Dublin 4, Leadbitter 2, Philpott 2, Cheetham 1, own goal 1.

Littlewoods Cup	First Round	Maidstone U (h)	3-1
		(a)	1-0
	Second Round	Derby Co (h)	2-1
		(a)	0-5

Vaughan	Bailie	Kimble	Leadbitter	Chapple	Daish	Dennis	Beck	Dublin	Taylor	Robinson	O'Shea	Ryan	Philpott	Smith	Clayton	Polston	Cheetham	Fensome	Cook	Claridge	Match No.
1	2	3	4	5	6	7	8	9†	10	11*	12	14									1
1	2	3	4	5	6	7	8	9	10†	11*	12	14									2
1	2	3	8	5	6	7		9*	10		4	12	11								3
1	2	3	8	5		7*		9	10	12	4	14	11†	6							4
1	14	3	8	5		7†		12	10		9*	4	11	6	2						5
1	2	3	8	5	6	7		12	10*		9	4	11								6
1	2*	3	8	5	6	7†		12	10		9	14	11	4							7
1		3	8	5	6	7		12	10		9*	4	11		2						8
1		3	8	5	6	7		12	10		9*	4	11		2						9
1		3	8	5	6			12	10	14	4	9*	11†		2		7				10
1		3	8	5	6	7		9	10		12		11*		2		4				11
1		3	8	5	6	7		9*	10		12	14	11		2†		4				12
1		3	8	5	6	7		9	10				11		2		4				13
1		3	8†	5	6	7		9	10*		12	14	11		2		4				14
1		3	8	5	6	7†		9	10		12	14	11*		2		4				15
1		3	8	5	6	7		9	10				11		2		4				16
1	2	3	8*	5	6	7		9	10				11				4				17
1	2	3	8	5	6	7†		9	10*		12	14	11				4				18
1	2	3	8	5	6			9	10		4		11				7				19
1	2	3	8	5	6			9*	10		4	12	11				7				20
1	2	3	8	5	6			9*	10		4	12	11				7				21
1	2	3	8	5	6			12	10		4	9*	11				7				22
1	14	3*	8	5	6			9	10		12		11		4†		7	2			23
1	12	3	8	5	6			9	10				11		4*		7	2			24
1	6	3	8	5				9	10*		12		11		4		7	2			25
1	4	3	8	5	6			9	10				11				7	2			26
1	4	3	14	5	6			12	10*		8		11				7†	2	9		27
1	4	3	8	5	6			9*	10				11				7	2		12	28
1	4*	3	8	5	6			9	10		14		11†				7	2		12	29
1	4	3	8	5	6			9	10*				11				7	2		12	30
1	4†	3	8	5	6			9*	10		14		11				7	2		12	31
1	4†	3	14	5	6			12	10*				11				7	2	8	9	32
1	4	3	7*	5				8	14		6		10†				11	2	12	9	33
1	4	3	8†	5				9	10		6		11*				7	2	14	12	34
1	4	3		5	6			9	10								7	2	8	11	35
1	4	3		5	6			9	10								7	2	8	11	36
1	4	3		5	6			9*	10		12	14	11					2	8†	7	37
1	4	3	14	5	6			9	10*		12						7	2	8	11	38
1	4†	3	14	5	6			9	10		12						7	2	8	11*	39
1		3	4	5	6			9	10*		12						7	2	8	11	40
1	14	3	4	5	6			9	10*		12						7	2	8†	11	41
1	14	3	4	5	6			9	10*		12						7	2	8†	11	42
1	8	3	4	5	6			9			12		11				7*	2†	14	10	43
1	8	3†	4	5	6			9*			12		11				7	2	14	10	44
1	4†	3		5	6			9			12	14	11				7	2	8*	10	45
1	8	3		5	6			9			12	14	11*		4		7	2		10†	46
46	31	44	39	45	42	17	2	37	41	7	14	3	37	4	8	3	36	24	11	15	
+	+					+	+	+	+				+	+					+	+	
5s	4s					9s	4s	9s	12s				7s	5s		2s			4s	5s	

FA Cup

First Round	Aldershot (a)		1-0
Second Round	Woking (h)		3-1
Third Round	Darlington (h)		0-0
		(a)	3-1
Fourth Round	Millwall (a)		1-1
		(h)	1-0
Fifth Round	Bristol C (a)		0-0
		(h)	1-1
		(h)	5-1
Sixth Round	Crystal Palace (h)		0-1

CAMBRIDGE UNITED

Player and Position	Ht	Wt	Birth Date	Place	Source	Clubs	League App	Gls
Goalkeepers								
Paul Bastock†	5 8	10 00	19 5 70	Leamington	Trainee	Coventry C	—	—
						Cambridge U	12	—
John Vaughan	5 10	13 01	26 6 64	Isleworth	Apprentice	West Ham U	—	—
						Charlton Ath (loan)	6	—
						West Ham U	—	—
						Bristol R (loan)	6	—
						Wrexham (loan)	4	—
						Bristol C (loan)	2	—
						Fulham	44	—
						Bristol C (loan)	3	—
						Cambridge U	75	—
Defenders								
Colin Bailie	5 11	10 11	31 3 64	Belfast	Apprentice	Swindon T	107	4
						Reading	84	1
						Cambridge U	59	1
Phil Chapple	6 2	12 07	26 11 66	Norwich	Apprentice	Norwich C	—	—
						Cambridge U	97	9
Liam Daish	6 2	13 05	23 9 68	Portsmouth	Apprentice	Portsmouth	1	—
						Cambridge U	70	1
Andy Fensome	5 8	11 02	18 2 69	Northampton	Trainee	Norwich C	—	—
						Newcastle U (loan)	—	—
						Cambridge U	24	—
Alan Kimble	5 8	11 00	6 8 66	Poole		Charlton Ath	6	—
						Exeter C (loan)	1	—
						Cambridge U	165	16
Danny O'Shea	6 0	12 08	26 3 63	Kennington	Apprentice	Arsenal	6	—
						Charlton Ath (loan)	9	—
						Exeter C	45	2
						Southend U	118	12
						Cambridge U	26	—
Steve Welsh			19 4 68	Glasgow	Army	Cambridge U	—	—
Midfield								
John Beck‡	5 11	11 09	25 5 54	Edmonton	Apprentice	QPR	40	1
						Coventry C	69	6
						Fulham	114	13
						Bournemouth (loan)	4	1
						Bournemouth	133	12
						Cambridge U	112	11
Michael Cheetham	5 11	11 05	30 6 67	Amsterdam	Army	Ipswich T	4	—
						Cambridge U	36	10
Gary Clayton	5 11	12 08	2 2 63	Sheffield	Apprentice Burton Alb	Rotherham U	—	—
						Doncaster R	35	5
						Cambridge U	101	7
Mike Cook	5 9	10 12	18 10 68	Coventry	Trainee	Coventry C	—	—
						York C (loan)	6	1
						Cambridge U	15	1
Lee Philpott	5 9	10 06	21 2 70	Barnet	Trainee	Peterborough U	4	—
						Cambridge U	42	5
Forwards								
Steve Claridge	5 11	11 08	10 4 66	Portsmouth	Fareham Weymouth	Bournemouth	7	1
						Crystal Palace	—	—
						Aldershot	62	19
						Cambridge U	20	4

CAMBRIDGE UNITED

Foundation: The football revival in Cambridge began soon after World War II when the Abbey United club (formed 1919) decided to turn professional and in 1949 changed their name to Cambridge United. They were competing in the United Counties League before graduating to the Eastern Counties League in 1951 and the Southern League in 1958.

First Football League game: 15 August, 1970, Division 4, v Lincoln C (h) D 1-1 – Roberts; Thompson, Meldrum (1), Slack, Eades, Hardy, Leggett, Cassidy, Lindsey, McKinven, Harris.

Managers (and Secretary-managers)
Bill Whittaker 1949–55, Gerald Williams 1955, Bert Johnson 1955–59, Bill Craig 1959–60, Alan Moore 1960–63, Roy Kirk 1964–66, Bill Leivers 1967–74, Ron Atkinson 1974–78, John Docherty 1978–83, John Ryan 1984–85, Ken Shellito 1985, Chris Turner 1985–90, John Beck 1990–

Player and Position	Ht	Wt	Birth Date	Birth Place	Source	Clubs	League App	League Gls
Tony Dennis	5 7	10 02	1 12 63	Eton	Slough	Cambridge U	35	5
Dion Dublin	6 0	12 04	22 4 69	Leicester		Norwich C	—	—
						Cambridge U	67	21
Chris Leadbitter	5 9	10 07	17 10 67	Middlesbrough	Apprentice	Grimsby T	—	—
						Hereford U	36	1
						Cambridge U	74	10
Martin Robinson*	5 8	11 02	17 7 57	Ilford	Apprentice	Tottenham H	6	2
						Charlton Ath	228	58
						Reading (loan)	6	2
						Gillingham	96	24
						Southend U	56	14
						Cambridge U	16	1
Laurie Ryan	5 9	10 12	15 10 63	Watford	Dunstable	Cambridge U	51	13
John Taylor	6 2	11 12	24 10 64	Norwich	Local Sudbury	Colchester U	—	—
						Cambridge U	85	27

Trainees
Banthorpe, Alec N.A; Batch, David J; Giles, Steven P; Harrington, Shaun M; Heard, Stephen J; Kearns, Jamie A; Kelly, John N; Lewis, Stephen R; Merrick, Simon; Parnwell, Giles T; Pincher, Andrew; Pope, Neil L; Proctor, Matthew T; Robinson, David J; Sinclair, Colin N; Vowden, Colin D; Woolf, Gary J.

**Non-Contract
Welsh, Stephen.

Associated Schoolboy
Kennedy, Richard C.

Associated Schoolboys who have accepted the club's offer of a Traineeship/Contract
Ellis, Stephen M.

**Non-Contract Players who are retained must be re-signed before they are eligible to play in League matches.

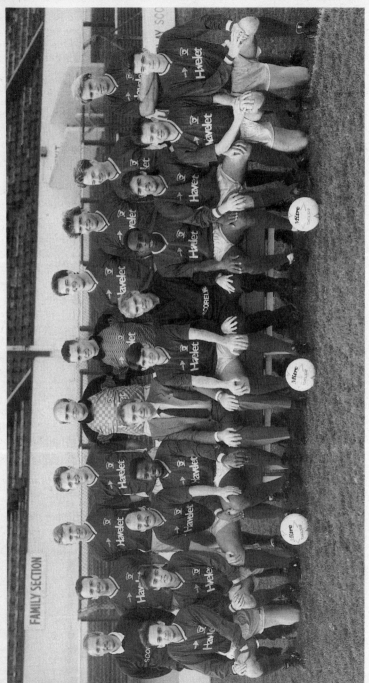

CARDIFF CITY 1989–90 *Back row (left to right):* Jimmy Goodfellow (Physiotherapist), Richard Haig, Gareth Abraham, Morrys Scott, George Wood, Pat O'Hagan, Chris Pike, Roger Gibbins, Jeff Chandler, Leigh Barnard.

Front row: Jonathan Morgan (Captain), Chris Fry, Steve Lynex, Ray Daniel, Tony Clemo (Chairman), Ian Rodgerson, Len Ashurst (Manager), Cohen Griffith, Mark Kelly, Jeff Doman, Jason Perry.

Division 4   **CARDIFF CITY**

Ninian Park, Cardiff CF1 8SX. Telephone Cardiff (0222) 398636. Commercial Office: 0222 220516.
Ground Capacity: 19,300.
Record attendance: 61,566, Wales v England, 14 Oct, 1961.
Club record: 57,893 v Arsenal, Division 1, 22 April, 1953.
Record receipts: £50,517.75 v QPR, FA Cup, 3rd rd, 6 January, 1990.
Pitch Measurements: 114yd × 78yd.
President: Lord Brooks of Tremorfa.
Chairman: J. A. Clemo.
Directors: L. Clemo, R. P. Maughan.
Secretary: Eddie Harrison.
Manager: Len Ashurst. *Commercial Manager:*
Physio: Jimmy Goodfellow. *Coach:* Bobby Smith.
Year Formed: 1899. *Turned Professional:* 1910. *Ltd Co.:* 1910.
Club Nickname: 'Bluebirds'.
Previous Grounds: Riverside, Sophia Gardens, Old Park and Fir Gardens. Moved to Ninian Park, 1910.
Previous Names: 1899–1902 Riverside; 1902–08, Riverside Albion; 1908, Cardiff City.
Record League Victory: 9-2 v Thames, Division 3(S), 6 February 1932 – Farquharson; E. L. Morris, Roberts; Galbraith, Harris, Ronan; Emmerson (1), Keating (1), Jones (1), McCambridge (1), Robbins (5).
Record Cup Victory: 8-0 v Enfield, FA Cup, 1st rd, 28 November 1931 – Farquharson; Smith, Roberts; Harris (1), Galbraith, Ronan; Emmerson (2), Keating (3); O'Neill (2), Robbins, McCambridge.
Record Defeat: 2-11 v Sheffield U, Division 1, 1 January, 1926.
Most League Points (2 for a win): 66, Division 3(S), 1946–47.
Most League Points (3 for a win): 86, Division 3, 1982–83.
Most League Goals: 93, Division 3(S), 1946–47.
Highest League Scorer in Season: Stan Richards, 30, Division 3(S), 1946–47.
Most League Goals in Total Aggregate: Len Davies, 128, 1920–31.
Most Capped Player: Alf Sherwood, 39(41), Wales.
Most League Appearances: Phil Dwyer, 471, 1972–85.
Record Transfer Fee Received: £215,000 from Portsmouth for Jimmy Gilligan, October 1989.
Record Transfer Fee Paid: £180,000 to San Jose Earthquakes for Godfrey Ingram, September 1982.
Football League Record: 1920 Elected to Division 2; 1921–29 Division 1; 1929–31 Division 2; 1931–47 Division 3(S); 1947–52 Division 2; 1952–57 Division 1; 1957–60 Division 2; 1960–62 Division 1; 1962–75 Division 2; 1975–76 Division 3; 1976–82 Division 2; 1982–83 Division 3; 1983–85 Division 2; 1985–86 Division 3; 1986–88 Division 4; 1988–90 Division 3; 1990– Division 4.
Honours: Football League: Division 1 – Runners-up 1923–24; Division 2 – Runners-up 1920–21, 1951–52, 1959–60; Division 3(S) – Champions 1946–47; Division 3 – Runners-up 1975–76, 1982–83; Division 4 – Runners-up 1987–88. *FA Cup:* Winners 1926–27 (only occasion the Cup has been won by a club outside England); Runners-up 1925. *Football League Cup:* Semi-final 1965–66. *Welsh Cup:* Winners 20 times. *Charity Shield:* 1927. European Competitions: *European Cup-Winners' Cup:* 1964–65, 1965–66, 1967–68, 1968–69, 1969–70, 1970–71, 1971–72, 1973–74, 1974–75, 1976–77, 1977–78. 1988–89.
Colours: Blue shirts, white shorts, blue stockings. **Change colours:** All yellow.

CARDIFF CITY 1989–90 LEAGUE RECORD

Match No.	Date	Venue	Opponents	Result	H/T Score	Lg. Pos.	Goalscorers	Attendance
1	Aug 19	H	Bolton W	L 0-2	0-2	—		4376
2	26	A	Tranmere R	L 0-3	0-1	24		5268
3	Sept 2	H	Brentford	D 2-2	1-0	23	Gilligan, Fry	3499
4	9	A	Mansfield T	L 0-1	0-0	24		2766
5	16	H	Bristol C	L 0-3	0-1	24		5970
6	23	A	Wigan Ath	D 1-1	1-0	24	Lynex	2345
7	26	H	Northampton T	L 2-3	1-1	—	Pike, Lynex	2688
8	30	A	Rotherham U	L 0-4	0-2	24		4998
9	Oct 7	A	Huddersfield T	W 3-2	2-1	23	Griffith, Pike 2 (1 pen)	5835
10	13	H	Chester C	D 1-1	0-0	—	Barnard	3675
11	17	H	Bristol R	D 1-1	0-0	—	Kelly	6372
12	21	A	Blackpool	L 0-1	0-0	24		3502
13	28	H	Leyton Orient	D 1-1	1-0	24	Griffith	2370
14	31	A	Birmingham C	D 1-1	1-0	—	Morgan	7468
15	Nov 3	H	Bury	W 3-1	2-1	—	Pike 2, Barnard	3437
16	11	A	Fulham	W 5-2	3-1	23	Pike 2, Griffith, Marshall (og), Morgan	4030
17	25	H	Preston NE	W 3-0	2-0	17	Rodgerson, Pike, Griffith	3270
18	Dec 2	A	Crewe Alex	D 1-1	1-0	19	Morgan	3393
19	16	H	Notts Co	L 1-3	1-1	21	Pike	3610
20	26	A	Swansea C	W 1-0	1-0	17	Barnard	12,244
21	30	A	Walsall	W 2-0	0-0	16	Griffith, Pike	4256
22	Jan 13	H	Tranmere R	D 0-0	0-0	21		4300
23	20	A	Bolton W	L 1-3	0-2	21	Griffith	7017
24	Feb 3	H	Wigan Ath	D 1-1	0-1	21	Rodgerson	3218
25	10	A	Bristol C	L 0-1	0-1	22		11,982
26	17	H	Crewe Alex	D 0-0	0-0	22		2086
27	21	A	Brentford	W 1-0	1-0	—	Abraham	5174
28	24	A	Preston NE	L 0-4	0-1	22		5716
29	Mar 2	H	Shrewsbury T	L 0-1	0-0	—		2751
30	6	H	Rotherham U	W 2-0	1-0	—	Pike, Barnard	2888
31	10	A	Northampton T	D 1-1	1-0	20	Pike	2574
32	13	A	Shrewsbury T	D 0-0	0-0	—		2318
33	17	H	Huddersfield T	L 1-5	0-1	21	Pike	2628
34	20	A	Chester C	L 0-1	0-0	—		1866
35	24	A	Bristol R	L 1-2	1-0	23	Rodgerson	4631
36	27	H	Mansfield T	W 1-0	1-0	—	Barnard	2280
37	31	H	Blackpool	D 2-2	1-1	21	Gibbins, Pike	2850
38	Apr 7	A	Leyton Orient	L 1-3	0-0	22	Pike	3411
39	10	H	Birmingham C	L 0-1	0-0	—		3322
40	14	A	Reading	W 1-0	0-0	21	Griffith	3198
41	16	H	Swansea C	L 0-2	0-1	22		8350
42	21	A	Notts Co	L 1-2	0-2	22	Pike (pen)	5533
43	24	H	Walsall	W 3-1	1-1	—	Barnard, Pike, Griffith	2509
44	28	H	Fulham	D 3-3	1-1	21	Daniel, Barnard, Rodgerson	3932
45	May 1	H	Reading	W 3-2	3-1	—	Barnard, Pike (pen), Griffith	3375
46	5	A	Bury	L 0-2	0-1	21		4224

Final League Position: 21

GOALSCORERS

League (51): Pike 18 (3 pens), Griffith 9, Barnard 8, Rodgerson 4, Morgan 3, Lynex 2, Abraham 1, Daniel 1, Fry 1, Gibbins 1, Gilligan 1, Kelly 1, own goal 1.
Littlewoods Cup (2): Morgan 1, Pike 1.
FA Cup (4): Scott 3, Pike 1.

Wood	Rodgerson	Lynex	Gibbins	Abraham	Perry	Curtis	Morgan	Gilligan	Kelly	Pike	Fry	Gummer	Daniel	Love	Sendall	Kevan	Ward	Barnard	Griffith	Hansbury	Lewis	Tupling	Scott	Powell	Chandler	Haig	Youds	Thompson	Blake	Match No.
1	2	3	4	5	6	7	8	9	10	11*	12																			1
1	2	3	4*	5	6	7	8	9	10	11†	12	14																		2
1	2	4		5	6	7	8	9	10	11*	12		3																	3
1	2	4		5	6	7	8*	9	10		12		3	11†	14															4
1	2	4*		5	6	7	8	9	10		12		3		11															5
1	2	4*		5	6	7	8	9	10		12		3	14	11†															6
1	2	4		5	6	7	8	9	10*	11	12		3																	7
1	2	4	6	5		7			10	11	12		3		9*	8														8
	2	14		5	6	7			10	11	12		3		9*	1		4	8†											9
		9		5	6	7			10	11*			3	12		1		4	8				2							10
	2	7		5	6		12		10	11*			3		9	1		4	8											11
	2	7*	6	5			11		10†				3		9	1		4	8		12				14					12
	2		6	5			7*		10	11			3		9	1		4	8		12									13
	2		6	5			7		10	11			3		9	1		4	8											14
	2		6	5			7*		10	9			3					4	8	1	12				11					15
	2		6	5			7		10	9†			3		12			4	8*	1					14	11				16
	2		6	5			7		10	9†			3		12			4	8	1					14	11*				17
	2	14	6	5			7		10	9*			3		12			4	8	1					11†					18
1	2	7†	6	5*			12		10	9			3					4	8						14	11				19
	2	11	6	5			7†		10	9*			3					4	8	1	12				14					20
	2	11	6	5			7		10	9			3					4	8	1										21
	2		6	5			7*		10	11			3		9			4	8	1	12									22
	2		6	5†			7		10*	11			3		9			4	8	1	12				14					23
	2		6	5			7		10	11*			3	12	9			4	8†	1					14					24
	2	14	6	5			7*		10†	11			3		9			4	8	1	12									25
	2	7	6	5					10	11			3		9			4	8	1										26
	2	11	6	5			7		10	9			3					4	8	1										27
	2	11†	6*	5			7		10	9			3		12			4	8	1					14					28
	2	14	6	5†			7		10	9			3		12			4	8	1					11*					29
	2	12	6	5			7		10*	9			3					4	8	1					11					30
	2		6	5			7		10	9			3		12†			4	8	1					14	11*				31
	2		6	5			7*		10	9			3					4	8	1	12				11†	14				32
	2		6	5			7*		10	11			3	12	9				8	1	12								4*	33
	2		6	5			7		10	9			3*					4	8	1	12				11					34
	2		6	5			7		10	9			3					4	8	1	12				11*			3		35
	2	7*	6	5			12		10	9			3					4	8	1					11					36
	2	7	6	5					10	9			3					4	8	1					11					37
	2		6	5			7		10	9			3					4	8	1					11*			12		38
	2		6	5			7*		10	9			3					4	8	1					11			12		39
	2	14	6	5†			7		10	9			3		12		4		8	1					11*					40
	2		6	5			7		10	9			3		11†		4*		8	1					14			12		41
	2	11*	6	5			7		10	9			3		12			4	8	1										42
	2	11*	6				7		10	9			3		12			4	8	1									5	43
	2	11†	6				7		10	9			3					4	8	1					14			12	5*	44
	2	11	6				7*		10	9			3					4	8	1	12								5	45
	2*	14	6				7		10	9			3					4	8	1	12				11†				5	46
9	45	22	38	34	36	8	29	7	41	41	3	—	43	1	3	6	2	35	38	35	3	—	1	—	21	1	—	1	3	

```
            +        +              +                      +   +   +                       +   +          +          +   +
            4s       3s             3s           20s1s     1s  1s  1s                     8s1s 8s1s       3s        3s1s 1s  3s
```

Littlewoods Cup	First Round	Plymouth Arg (h)	0-3
		(a)	2-0
FA Cup	First Round	Halesowen (h)	1-0
	Second Round	Gloucester C (h)	2-2
		(a)	1-0
	Third Round	QPR (h)	0-0
		(a)	0-2

CARDIFF CITY

Player and Position	Ht	Wt	Birth Date	Place	Source	Clubs	League App	Gls
Goalkeepers								
Roger Hansbury	5 11	12 00	26 1 55	Barnsley	Apprentice	Norwich C	78	—
						Bolton W (loan)	—	—
						Cambridge U (loan)	11	—
						Orient (loan)	—	—
					Eastern Ath	Burnley	83	—
						Cambridge U	37	—
						Birmingham C	57	—
						Sheffield U (loan)	5	—
						Wolverhampton W (loan)	3	—
						Colchester U (loan)	4	—
						Cardiff C	35	—
Pat O'Hagan*	6 0	11 04	15 3 71	Llanbadoc	Trainee	Newport Co	3	—
						Cardiff C	—	—
Jonathan Roberts‡	6 0	12 05	30 12 68	Llwynpia	Trainee	Cardiff C	9	—
Gavin Ward	6 2	12 12	30 6 70	Sutton Coldfield		Shrewsbury T	—	—
						WBA	—	—
						Cardiff C	2	—
George Wood	6 3	14 00	26 9 52	Douglas	East Stirling	East Stirling	44	1
						Blackpool	117	—
						Everton	103	—
						Arsenal	60	—
						Crystal Palace	192	—
						Cardiff C	67	—
						Blackpool (loan)	15	—
Defenders								
Gareth Abraham	6 4	12 11	13 2 69	Merthyr Tydfil	Trainee	Cardiff C	70	4
Phil Bater‡	5 11	12 12	24 10 53	Cardiff	Apprentice	Bristol R	212	2
						Wrexham	73	1
						Bristol R	98	1
						Brentford	19	2
						Cardiff C	76	—
Nathan Blake§	5 10		27 1 72	Newport	Trainee	Cardiff C	6	—
Allan Lewis	6 2	12 10	31 5 71	Pontypridd	Trainee	Cardiff C	11	—
Jason Perry	5 11	10 04	2 4 70	Newport		Cardiff C	40	—
Ian Rodgerson	5 8	11 05	9 4 66	Hereford	Local	Hereford U	100	6
						Cardiff C	85	4
Midfield								
Leigh Barnard	5 8	11 07	29 10 58	Worsley	Apprentice	Portsmouth	79	8
						Peterborough U (loan)	4	—
						Swindon T	217	21
						Exeter C (loan)	6	2
						Cardiff C	35	8
Ray Daniel	5 10	11 00	10 12 64	Luton	Apprentice	Luton T	22	4
						Gillingham (loan)	5	—
						Hull C	58	3
						Cardiff C	43	1
Jeffrey Doman*	5 10	11 00	30 11 70	Llwynypia		Cardiff C	—	—
Roger Gibbins	5 10	11 09	6 9 55	Enfield	Apprentice	Tottenham H	—	—
						Oxford U	19	2
						Norwich C	48	12
					N England	Cambridge U	100	12
						CardiffC	139	17
						Swansea C	35	6
						Newport Co	79	9
						Torquay U	33	5
					Newport Co	Cardiff C	50	1
Jason Gummer*	5 9	11 00	27 10 67	Tredegar	Apprentice	Cardiff C	34	5
						Torquay U (loan)	7	1
Richard Haig*	5 8	11 00	29 12 70	Pontypridd	Trainee	Cardiff C	5	—
Mark Kelly	5 8	10 06	7 10 66	Blackpool		Shrewsbury T	—	—
						Cardiff C	105	2

CARDIFF CITY

Foundation: Credit for the establishment of a first class professional football club in such a rugby stronghold as Cardiff, is due to members of the Riverside club formed in 1899 out of a cricket club of that name. Cardiff became a city in 1905 and in 1908 the local FA granted Riverside permission to call themselves Cardiff City.

First Football League game: 28 August, 1920, Division 2, v Stockport C (a) W 5-2 – Kneeshaw; Brittain, Leyton; Keenor (1), Smith, Hardy; Grimshaw (1), Gill (2), Cashmore, West, Evans (1).

Managers (and Secretary-managers)
Davy McDougall 1910–11, Fred Stewart 1911–33, Bartley Wilson 1933–34, B. Watts-Jones 1934–37, Bill Jennings 1937–39, Cyril Spiers 1939–46, Billy McCandless 1946–48, Cyril Spiers 1948–54, Trevor Morris 1954–58, Bill Jones 1958–62, George Swindin 1962–64, Jimmy Scoular 1964–73, Frank O'Farrell 1973–74, Jimmy Andrews 1974–78, Richie Morgan 1978–82, Len Ashurst 1982–84, Jimmy Goodfellow 1984, Alan Durban 1984–86, Frank Burrows 1986–89, Len Ashurst 1990–

Player and Position	Ht	Wt	Birth Date	Place	Source	Clubs	League App	Gls
Jon Morgan	5 8	10 01	10 7 70	Cardiff	Trainee	Cardiff C	51	3
Forwards								
Jeff Chandler	5 7	10 01	19 6 59	Hammersmith	Apprentice	Blackpool	37	7
						Leeds U	26	2
						Bolton W	157	36
						Derby Co	46	10
						Mansfield T (loan)	6	—
						Bolton W	24	4
						Cardiff C	24	—
Chris Fry	5 9	9 06	23 10 69	Cardiff	Trainee	Cardiff C	32	1
Cohen Griffith	5 10		26 12 62	Georgetown	Kettering T	Cardiff C	38	9
Ian Love*	5 11	11 04	1 3 58	Cardiff	Eastern	Swansea C	41	9
						Torquay U	9	—
						Cardiff C	2	—
Steve Lynex	5 7	11 10	23 1 58	West Bromwich	Apprentice Shamrock R	WBA	—	—
						Birmingham C	46	10
						Leicester C	213	57
						Birmingham C (loan)	10	2
						WBA	29	3
						Cardiff C	62	2
Chris Pike	6 2	12 07	19 10 61	Cardiff	Barry T	Fulham	42	4
						Cardiff C (loan)	6	2
						Cardiff C	41	18
Morrys Scott*	6 3	12 06	17 12 70	Swansea	Trainee	Cardiff C	9	—
Chris Thompson*	5 11	12 02	24 1 60	Walsall	Apprentice	Bolton W	73	18
						Lincoln C (loan)	6	—
						Blackburn R	85	24
						Wigan Ath	74	14
						Blackpool	39	8
						Cardiff C	2	—
Ian Walsh‡	5 9	11 06	4 9 58	St Davids	Apprentice	Crystal Palace	117	23
						Swansea C	37	11
						Barnsley	49	15
						Grimsby T	41	14
						Cardiff C	17	4

Trainees
Blake, Nathan A; Gameson, Leigh J; Gee, Andrew N; Hookings, Stephen P; Jewell, Steven L; Jones, Nathan J; Lasisi, Lee V.B; Morris, Jonathan L; Roberts, Jason L; Searle, Damon P; Semark, Robin H; Stephens, Lee M; Summers, Christopher; Unsworth, Jamie J.

Associated Schoolboys
Bellamy, Nicholas M; Bird, Anthony; Callaway, Nilsson, A.D; Crocker, Matthew; Davies, Russell P; Gorman, Andrew; Hainsworth, Darren J; Heavens, Finbar; Metcalfe, Mark; Sime, Leighton R; Street, Daniel C; Walters, Carl M.P; Williams, Morgan D; Young, Scott.

Associated Schoolboys who have accepted the club's offer of a Traineeship/Contract
Baddeley, Lee M; Popham, Philip H.

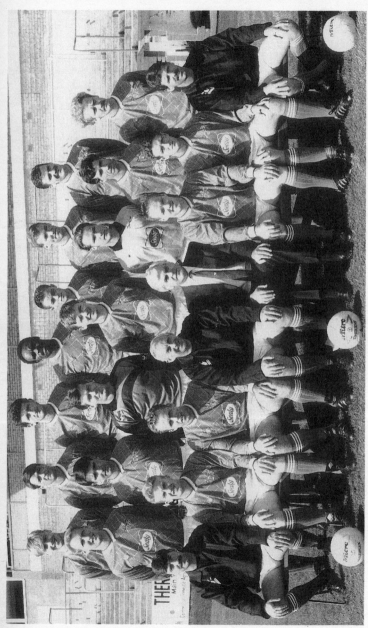

CARLISLE UNITED 1989–90 *Back row (left to right):* Paul Proudlock, Mike Graham, Tony Fyfe, Keith Walwyn, Jim Robertson, Richard Sendall, Brent Hetherington. *Centre row:* Simon Jeffels, Paul Gorman, Dave McKellar, Paul Fitzpatrick, Jason Priestley, Mark Ogley, Nigel Saddington. *Front row:* Peter Hampton (Physiotherapist), Tony Shepherd, Ian Dalziel, Clive Middlemas (Manager), Andrew Jenkins (Chairman), John Halpin, Derek Walsh, Aidan McCaffery (Coach).

Division 4 **CARLISLE UNITED**

Brunton Park, Carlisle CA1 1LL. Telephone Carlisle (0228) 26237. Commercial Dept: (0228) 24014.

Record attendance: 27,500 v Birmingham C, FA Cup 3rd rd, 5 Jan, 1957 and v Middlesbrough, RA Cup 5th rd, 7 Feb, 1970.

Record receipts: £75,988.50 v Liverpool, FA Cup 3rd, 7 January, 1989.

Ground capacity: 18,506.

Pitch measurements: 117yd × 78yd.

President: J. C. Monkhouse. *Vice-Presidents:* J. Johnstone JP, T. L. Sibson, Dr. T. Gardner B, CHB.

Chairman: H. A. Jenkins. *Vice-Chairman:* J. R. Sheffield.

Directors: R. S. Liddell, T. A. Bingley, C. J. Vasey, J. B. Lloyd, A. Liddell, A. Hodgkinson.

Team Manager: Clive Middlemass. *Assistant Manager:* Peter Hampton.

Coach: Aidan McCaffery. *Physio:* Peter Hampton.

Match Secretary: N. Irving. *Commercial Manager:* Frank Layton.

Club Secretary: Miss Alison Moore.

Club Nickname: 'Cumbrians' or 'The Blues'.

Year Formed: 1903. *Ltd Co:* 1921.

Previous Grounds: 1903–5, Milholme Bank; 1905–9, Devonshire Park; 1909– Brunton Park.

Previous name: Shaddowgate United.

Record League Victory: 8-0 v Hartlepools U, Division 3(N), 1 September 1928 – Prout; Smiles, Cook; Robinson (1) Ross. Pigg; Agar (1), Hutchison (1), McConnell (4), Ward (1), Watson, 8-0 v Scunthorpe United, Division 3(N), 25 December 1952 – MacLaren; Hill, Scott; Stokoe, Twentyman, Waters; Harrison (1), Whitehouse (5), Ashman (2), Duffett, Bond.

Record Cup Victory: 6-1 v Billingham Synthonia, FA Cup, 1st rd, 17 November 1956 – Fairley; Hill, Kenny; Johnston, Waters, Thompson; Mooney, Broadis (1), Ackerman (2), Garvie (3), Bond.

Record Defeat: 1-11 v Hull C, Division 3(N), 14 January, 1939.

Most League Points (2 for a win): 62, Division 3(N), 1950–51.

Most League Points (3 for a win): 80, Division 3, 1981–82.

Most League Goals: 113, Division 4, 1963–64.

Highest League Scorer in Season: Jimmy McConnell, 42, Division 3(N), 1928–29.

Most League Goals in Total Aggregate: Jimmy McConnell, 126, 1928–32.

Most Capped Player: Eric Welsh, 4, Northern Ireland.

Most League Appearances: Alan Ross, 466, 1963–79.

Record Transfer Fee Received: £275,000 from Vancouver Whitecaps for Peter Beardsley, April 1981.

Record Transfer Fee Paid: £120,000 to York C for Gordon Staniforth, October 1979.

Football League Record: 1928 Elected to Division 3(N); 1958–62 Division 4; 1962–63 Division 3; 1963–64 Division 4; 1964–65 Division 3; 1965–74 Division 2; 1974–75 Division 1; 1975–77 Division 2; 1977–82 Division 3; 1982–86 Division 2; 1986–87 Division 3; 1987– Division 4.

Honours: Football League: Division 1 best season: 22nd, 1974–75; Promoted from Division 2 (3rd) 1973–74; Division 3 – Champions 1964–65; Runners-up 1981–82; Division 4 – Runners-up 1963–64. *FA Cup:* 6th rd 1974–75. *Football League Cup:* Semi-final 1969–70.

Colours: Blue shirts, white shorts, blue stockings. **Change colours:** Red shirts, white shorts, red stockings.

CARLISLE UNITED 1989–90 LEAGUE RECORD

Match No.	Date	Venue	Opponents	Result	H/T Score	Lg. Pos.	Goalscorers	Attendance
1	Aug 19	A	Hereford U	D 2-2	1-1	—	Ogley, Walsh	2285
2	26	H	Chesterfield	W 4-3	1-2	7	Walwyn, Fyfe 2, Proudlock	3059
3	Sept 2	A	Exeter C	D 0-0	0-0	8		3338
4	9	H	Grimsby T	D 1-1	0-0	13	Fyfe	3360
5	15	A	Halifax T	D 1-1	0-0	—	Walwyn	2121
6	23	H	Gillingham	W 3-0	1-0	6	Proudlock, Miller, Fitzpatrick	3185
7	26	A	Cambridge U	W 2-1	0-0	—	Dalziel, Walwyn	2607
8	30	H	Colchester U	W 1-0	1-0	3	Fyfe	3979
9	Oct 7	H	Wrexham	W 1-0	0-0	3	Hetherington	4235
10	14	A	Doncaster R	D 1-1	0-1	4	Proudlock	2419
11	17	H	Scunthorpe U	L 0-1	0-0	—		4793
12	21	A	Scarborough	L 1-2	1-1	8	Walwyn	2592
13	28	H	Hartlepool U	W 1-0	0-0	6	Hetherington	3699
14	31	A	Aldershot	L 0-1	0-0	—		2123
15	Nov 4	H	Maidstone U	W 3-2	1-0	6	Proudlock, Sendall, Barton (og)	3395
16	11	A	Torquay U	W 2-1	0-0	4	Sendall 2	2266
17	25	A	Rochdale	W 2-1	1-0	4	Saddington, Miller	1920
18	Dec 2	H	Peterborough U	D 0-0	0-0	2		4608
19	17	H	Stockport Co	W 3-1	1-1	—	Proudlock, Miller, Cullen	4971
20	26	A	Burnley	L 1-2	1-1	2	Proudlock	12,276
21	30	A	Lincoln C	W 3-1	1-1	2	Saddington 2, Shepherd	4793
22	Jan 1	H	York C	W 2-1	0-1	2	Jones, Saddington (pen)	6510
23	6	A	Southend U	W 3-0	1-0	—	Walwyn 2, Norris	6196
24	13	A	Chesterfield	L 0-3	0-3	2		4801
25	20	H	Hereford U	W 2-1	0-0	1	Fitzpatrick, Walwyn	4726
26	27	A	Grimsby T	L 0-1	0-0	1		4657
27	Feb 10	H	Halifax T	D 1-1	1-0	1	Fitzpatrick	4844
28	13	H	Exeter C	W 1-0	0-0	—	Shepherd	8461
29	17	A	Peterborough U	L 0-3	0-1	1		4088
30	24	H	Rochdale	L 0-1	0-0	1		4904
31	27	A	Gillingham	L 1-2	1-2	—	Sendall	3177
32	Mar 3	A	Southend U	L 0-2	0-0	3		3465
33	6	A	Colchester U	L 0-4	0-2	—		3752
34	17	A	Wrexham	L 0-1	0-0	8		3409
35	20	H	Doncaster R	W 1-0	0-0	—	Jones	3970
36	24	A	Scunthorpe U	W 3-2	0-1	5	Jones, Saddington (pen), Norris	3406
37	31	H	Scarborough	W 3-1	0-0	4	Saddington 2 (1 pen), Goldsmith	4304
38	Apr 4	H	Cambridge U	W 3-1	2-0	—	Walwyn 2, Walsh	4890
39	7	A	Hartlepool U	L 0-1	0-0	4		3768
40	10	H	Aldershot	L 1-3	1-1	—	Saddington (pen)	4998
41	14	A	York C	W 1-0	1-0	3	Jones	2805
42	16	H	Burnley	D 1-1	0-0	4	Fitzpatrick	6738
43	20	A	Stockport Co	L 1-3	1-2	—	Walwyn	3819
44	24	H	Lincoln C	L 1-2	0-2	—	Saddington (pen)	5064
45	28	H	Torquay U	W 2-0	0-0	5	Norris, Walsh	3997
46	May 5	A	Maidstone U	L 2-5	1-3	8	Walwyn, Saddington	5006

Final League Position: 8

GOALSCORERS

League (61): Walwyn 11, Saddington 10 (5 pens), Proudlock 6, Fitzpatrick 4, Fyfe 4, Jones 4, Sendall 4, Miller 3, Norris 3, Walsh 3, Hetherington 2, Shepherd 2, Cullen 1, Dalziel 1, Goldsmith 1, Ogley 1, own goal 1.
Littlewoods Cup (2): Shepherd 1, Walwyn 1.
FA Cup (3): Proudlock 2, Sendall 1.

McKellar	Graham	Wharton	Saddington	Ogley	Gorman	Shepherd	Walsh	Walwyn	Proudlock	Halpin	Dalziel	Fyfe	Fitzpatrick	Hetherington	Jones	Miller	Sendall	Cullen	Goldsmith	Norris	McCall	Edwards	Robertson	Rose	Match No.
1	2	3	4	5	6	7	8	9	10	11															1
1	2		4	5*		7	8	9	10	11	3	12	6												2
1	2		4	5		7		9	10	11	3	8	6												3
1	2		4	5†	8	7		9*	10	11	3	12	6	14											4
1	2		4			7		9	10	11	3		6		5	8									5
1	2		4				8*	9	10	11	3		6	12	5	7									6
1	2		4				8	9	10	11	3		6		5	7									7
1	2		4			12	8*	9	10	11	3		6		5	7									8
1	2		4		8			9	10*	11	3		6	12	5	7									9
1	2		4		8†			9*	10	11	3	12	6	14	5	7									10
1	2		4		8†			9*	10	11	3	12	6	14	5	7									11
1	2†		4		8			9*	10	11	3	12	6	14	5	7									12
1	2†		4		8			9*	10	11	3		6	14	5	7	12								13
1	2		4		8			9*	10	11	3†		6	14	5	7	12								14
1	2		4			7	8†		10	11		9*	6	14	5	3	12								15
1	2		4			7	12		10†	11	3*		6	14	5	8	9								16
1	2		4			7	12		10	11*	3		6		5	8	9								17
1	2		4			7	14	9			3	12	6	11†	5	8	10*								18
1	2		4			7		9*	10		3	12	6		5	8		11							19
1	2†		4		8			9*	10		3		6		5	7	12	11	14						20
1	2		4		8			9			3		6		5	7			11	10					21
1	2		4		8*	12		9			3		6		5	7			11	10					22
1	2		4		8	12		9			3		6		5*	7			11	10					23
1	2		4		8		5	9	12		3		6*			7			11	10					24
1	5		4		8		2	9	12		3		6			7*			11	10					25
1	5		4		8		2	9	12		3*		6			7			11	10					26
1	4					7	2	9*	12				6		5	8	14		11	10*	3				27
1	4					7	2	9	10				6		5	8			11			3			28
1	2		4			7		9	10*				6		5	8			11	12		3			29
1	2		4			7	14	9	10*				6		5	8†			11	12		3			30
1	2		4			7			10				6		5	8	9		12	11	3*				31
1	5		4			7	2	9†	11				6			8	10		12	14	3*				32
1	5		4			7	2		10				6			8	9		11*12			3			33
1	5		4				7						6	12		8	9		11	10*		3	2		34
1	2		4			12	7						6		5	8	9		11	10*		3			35
	2		4			9	7						6		5	8			11	10		3		1	36
	2		4			12	9†	7*					6		5	8	14		11	10		3		1	37
	2		4			7		9					6		5	8			11	10		3		1	38
	2		4			7		9	12				6		5	8			11*10			3		1	39
	2		4			7		9	12				6		5	8			11	10*		3		1	40
	2		4			7		9	11				6		5	8	10					3		1	41
	2		4		3	7		9	10*				6		5	8	14		11†12					1	42
	2		4		3†	7		9	10				6		5	8	14		12	11*				1	43
			4			7		9*	10				6		5	2	12		11	8		3		1	44
			4			7		9	10				6		5	2			11	8		3		1	45
			4			7		9	10				6		5	2	11		12	8*		3		1	46
35	43	1	44	4	2	30	21	39	34	17	24	6	45	1	36	42	10	2	21	19	6	12	1	11	
						+1s	+7s	+1s	+6s			+7s		+11s			+9s			+5s	+5s				

Littlewoods Cup	First Round	Halifax T (a)	1-3
		(h)	1-0
FA Cup	First Round	Wrexham (h)	3-0
	Second Round	Wigan Ath (a)	0-2

CARLISLE UNITED

Player and Position	Ht	Wt	Birth Date	Place	Source	Clubs	League App	Gls
Goalkeepers								
David McKellar	6 1	13 06	22 5 56	Irvine	Apprentice	Ipswich T	—	—
						Colchester U (loan)	—	—
						Peterborough U (loan)	—	—
					Ardrossan	Derby Co	41	—
						Brentford	84	—
						Carlisle U	82	—
						Hibernian	—	—
						Manchester C (loan)	—	—
						Newcastle U (loan)	10	—
						Hamilton A	52	—
						Dunfermline Ath	6	—
						Hartlepool U (loan)	5	—
						Carlisle U	69	—
						(To Kilmarnock March 1990)		
Jason Priestley	5 11	12 02	25 10 70	Leeds	Trainee	Carlisle U	—	—
						Hartlepool U (loan)	16	—
Defenders								
Ian Dalziel	5 8	11 10	24 10 62	South Shields	Apprentice	Derby Co	22	4
						Hereford U	150	8
						Carlisle U	66	2
Robert Edwards			1 7 73	Kendal		Carlisle U	12	
Mike Graham	5 9	11 07	24 2 59	Lancaster	Apprentice	Bolton W	46	—
						Swindon T	141	1
						Mansfield T	133	1
						Carlisle U	87	2
Peter Hampton‡	5 7	11 02	12 9 54	Oldham	Apprentice	Leeds U	68	2
						Stoke C	138	4
						Burnley	118	2
						Rochdale	19	1
						Carlisle U	12	
John Holliday	6 4	11 00	13 3 70	Penrith		Carlisle U	—	—
Simon Jeffels	6 1	11 08	18 1 66	Barnsley	Apprentice	Barnsley	42	—
						Preston NE (loan)	1	—
						Carlisle U	29	—
Alex Jones	6 2	12 08	27 11 64	Blackburn	Apprentice	Oldham Ath	9	—
						Stockport Co (loan)	3	—
						Preston NE	101	3
						Carlisle U	36	4
David Miller	5 11	11 02	8 1 64	Burnley	Apprentice	Burnley	32	3
						Crewe Alex (loan)	3	—
					Colne Dyn	Tranmere R	29	1
						Preston NE	58	2
						Burnley (loan)	4	—
						Carlisle U	42	3
Jimmy Robertson*	5 9	11 00	24 11 69	Gateshead	Trainee	Carlisle U	13	—
Nigel Saddington	6 1	12 06	9 12 65	Sunderland		Doncaster R	6	—
						Sunderland	3	—
						Carlisle U	97	16
Midfield								
Paul Fitzpatrick	6 4	11 10	5 10 65	Liverpool	Local	Tranmere R	—	—
						Liverpool	—	—
						Preston NE	—	—
						Bolton W	14	—
						Bristol C	44	7
						Carlisle U	77	4
						Preston NE (loan)	2	—
John Halpin	5 10	11 07	15 11 61	Broxburn	Celtic BC	Celtic	7	—
						Sunderland (loan)	—	—
						Carlisle U	132	16
Aiden McCaffery‡	5 11	11 05	30 8 57	Newcastle	Apprentice	Newcastle U	59	4
						Derby Co	37	4
						Bristol R	184	11

CARLISLE UNITED

Foundation: Carlisle United came into being in 1903 through the amalgamation of Shaddongate United and Carlisle Red Rose. The new club was admitted to the Second Division of the Lancashire Combination in 1905–06, winning promotion the following season.

First Football League game: 25 August, 1928, Division 3(N), v Accrington S (a) W 3-2 – Prout; Coulthard, Cook; Harrison, Ross, Pigg; Agar, Hutchison, McConnell (1), Ward (1), Watson. 1 o.g.

Managers (and Secretary-managers)
H. Kirkbride 1904–05*, McCumiskey 1905–06*, J. Houston 1906–08*, Bert Stansfield 1908–10, J. Houston 1910–12, D. Graham 1912–13, George Bristow 1913–30, Billy Hampson 1930–33, Bill Clarke 1933–35, Robert Kelly 1935–36, Fred Westgarth 1936–38, David Taylor 1938–40, Howard Harkness 1940–45, Bill Clark 1945–46*, Ivor Broadis 1946–49, Bill Shankly 1949–51, Fred Emery 1951–58, Andy Beattie 1958–60, Ivor Powell 1960–63, Alan Ashman 1963–67, Tim Ward 1967–68, Bob Stokoe 1968–70, Ian MacFarlane 1970–72, Alan Ashman 1972–75, Dick Young 1975–76, Bobby Moncur 1976–80, Martin Harvey 1980, Bob Stokoe 1980–85, Bryan "Pop" Robson 1985, Bob Stokoe 1985–86, Harry Gregg 1986–87, Cliff Middlemass 1987– .

Player and Position	Ht	Wt	Birth Date	Place	Source	Clubs	League App	Gls
						Bristol C (loan)	6	1
						Torquay U (loan)	6	—
						Exeter C	58	—
						Hartlepool U	6	1
						Carlisle U	14	—
Tony Shepherd	5 9	10 07	16 11 66	Glasgow	Celtic BC	Celtic	28	3
						Bristol C (loan)	3	—
						Carlisle U	31	2
Derek Walsh	5 7	11 05	24 10 67	Hamilton	Apprentice	Everton	1	—
						Hamilton A	2	—
						Carlisle U	63	6
Forwards								
Craig Goldsmith	5 7	11 03	27 8 63	Peterborough	Blackstones	Peterborough U	46	6
						Carlisle U	26	1
Brent Hetherington*	5 7	11 10	6 12 61	Carlisle	Penrith, Workington	Carlisle U	88	23
Steve Norris	5 9	10 08	22 9 61	Coventry	Telford	Scarborough	45	13
						Notts Co (loan)	1	—
						Carlisle U	24	3
Paul Proudlock	5 10	11 00	25 10 65			Hartlepool U	15	—
						Middlesbrough	5	1
						Carlisle U	50	9
Richard Sendell	5 10	11 06	10 7 67	Stamford	Apprentice	Watford	—	—
						Blackpool	11	—
						Carlisle U	48	10
						Cardiff C (loan)	4	—
Keith Walwyn‡	6 1	13 02	17 2 56	Jamaica	Winterton	Chesterfield	3	2
						York C	245	119
						Blackpool	69	16
						Carlisle U	40	11

Trainees
Armstrong, Lee W; Bell, Robert J; Cranston, Nicholas G; Eagling, Mark; Edmondson, Darren S; Elliot, Eamonn G; Graham, Calum I; Heaney, Martin W; Thomson, Marcus E; Thorpe, Jeffrey R; Townley, Derek J.

Associated Schoolboys
Brown, Paul B; Gray, Alan M. Greenhalgh, Andrew M; Little, Simon W; McVitie, Steven G; Otway, Paul; Prins, Jason; Slee, Simon J.

Associated Schoolboys who have accepted the club's offer of a Traineeship/Contract
Caig, Antony; Nugent, Richard; Potts, Craig; Todd, Simon.

CHARLTON ATHLETIC 1989–90   *Back row (left to right):* Kenny Achampong, John Humphrey, Michael Bennett, Colin Walsh.
Centre row: Andy Jones, Steve MacKenzie, Mike Salmon, Joe McLaughlin, Bob Bolder, Carl Leaburn, Tommy Caton.
Front row: Garth Crooks, Mark Reid, Robert Lee, Colin Pates, Paul Mortimer, Paul Williams, Andy Peake.

Division 2   **CHARLTON ATHLETIC**

Selhurst Park, London SE25 6PH. Telephone 01-771 6321.

Ground capacity: 31,000.

Record attendance: 75,031 v Aston Villa, FA Cup 5th rd, 12 Feb, 1938 (at The Valley).

Record receipts: £114,618.70 v Liverpool (at Selhurst Park), Division 1, 23 Jan. 1988.

Pitch measurements: 110yd × 74yd.

Presidents: R. D. Collins, J. A. E. Fryer, J. B. Sunley.

Chairman: R. N. Alwen. *Vice-chairman:* M. J. Norris.

Directors: R. D. Collins, D. G. Ufton, J. B. Sunley.

General Manager: Arnie Warren.

Commercial Manager: Steve Sutherland.

Manager: Lennie Lawrence.

Coach: Mike Flanagan. *Physio:* Jimmy Hendry.

Secretary: Miss Anne Payne.

Year Formed: 1905. *Turned professional:* 1920. *Ltd Co.:* 1919.

Club Nickname: 'Haddicks', 'Robins' or 'Valiants'.

Previous Grounds: 1906, Siemen's Meadow; 1907, Woolwich Common; 1909, Pound Park; 1913, Horn Lane; 1920, The Valley; 1923, Catford (The Mount); 1924, The Valley; 1985 Selhurst Park.

Record League Victory: 8-1 v Middlesbrough, Division 1, 12 September 1953 – Bartram; Campbell, Ellis; Fenton, Ufton, Hammond; Hurst (2), O'Linn (2), Leary (1), Firmani (3), Kiernan.

Record Cup Victory: 7-0 v Burton A, FA Cup 3rd rd, 7 January 1956 – Bartram; Campbell, Townsend; Hewie, Ufton, Hammond; Hurst (1), Gauld (1), Leary (3), White, Kiernan (2).

Record Defeat: 1-11 v Aston Villa, Division 2, 14 November, 1959.

Most League Points (2 for a win): 61, Division 3(S), 1934–35.

Most League Points (3 for a win): 77, Division 2, 1985–86.

Most League Goals: 107, Division 2, 1957–58.

Highest League Scorer in Season: Ralph Allen, 32, Division 3(S), 1934–35.

Most League Goals in Total Aggregate: Stuart Leary, 153, 1953–62.

Most Capped Player: John Hewie, 19, Scotland.

Most League Appearances: Sam Bartram, 583, 1934–56.

Record Transfer Fee Received: £650,000 from Crystal Palace for Mike Flanagan, August 1979.

Record Transfer Fee Paid: £600,000 to Chelsea for Joe McLaughlin, August 1989.

Football League Record: 1921 Elected to Division 3(S); 1929–33 Division 2; 1933–35 Division 3(S); 1935–36 Division 2; 1936–57 Division 1; 1957–72 Division 2; 1972–75 Division 3; 1975–80 Division 2; 1980–81 Division 3; 1981–86; Division 2; 1986–90 Division 1; 1990– Division 2.

Honours: Football League: Division 1 – Runners-up 1936–37; Division 2 – Runners-up 1935–36, 1985–86; Division 3(S) – Champions 1928–29, 1934–35; Promoted from Division 3 (3rd) 1974–75, 1980–81. *FA Cup:* Winners 1947; Runners-up 1946. *Football League Cup* best season: 4th rd. 1962–63, 1965–66, 1978–79. *Full Members Cup:* Runners-up 1987.

Colours: Red shirts, white shorts, white stockings. **Change colours:** All blue.

CHARLTON ATHLETIC 1989–90 LEAGUE RECORD

Match No.	Date	Venue	Opponents	Result	H/T Score	Lg. Pos.	Goalscorers	Attendance
1	Aug 19	H	Derby Co	D 0-0	0-0	—		8543
2	22	A	Millwall	D 2-2	1-0	—	Mortimer, Williams	14,806
3	26	A	Aston Villa	D 1-1	1-1	14	Jones	15,236
4	29	A	Chelsea	W 3-0	2-0	—	Williams 2, Mortimer	17,221
5	Sept 9	A	Luton T	L 0-1	0-0	10		8859
6	16	H	Everton	L 0-1	0-0	12		11,491
7	23	A	Arsenal	L 0-1	0-0	16		34,583
8	30	A	Nottingham F	L 0-2	0-1	19		18,189
9	Oct 14	H	Tottenham H	L 1-3	0-0	19	Williams	17,692
10	21	A	QPR	W 1-0	0-0	18	Mortimer	10,608
11	28	H	Coventry C	D 1-1	1-0	19	Mortimer	6149
12	Nov 4	H	Manchester U	W 2-0	0-0	16	Williams 2	16,065
13	11	A	Sheffield W	L 0-3	0-1	19		16,740
14	18	A	Norwich C	D 0-0	0-0	17		16,084
15	25	H	Manchester C	D 1-1	1-1	17	Williams	8857
16	Dec 2	A	Derby Co	L 0-2	0-2	19		14,590
17	9	H	Millwall	D 1-1	0-0	19	Minto	11,017
18	16	H	Crystal Palace	L 1-2	0-2	19	Walsh	15,763
19	26	A	Wimbledon	L 1-3	0-2	20	Bennett	5988
20	30	A	Liverpool	L 0-1	0-1	20		36,678
21	Jan 1	H	Southampton	L 2-4	1-3	20	Lee, MacKenzie	7614
22	13	H	Aston Villa	L 0-2	0-1	20		10,513
12	20	A	Chelsea	L 1-3	1-2	20	Williams	15,667
24	Feb 10	A	Everton	L 1-2	1-1	20	Williams	21,442
25	19	H	Luton T	W 2-0	1-0		Jones, Walsh	6008
26	24	A	Manchester C	W 2-1	0-0	20	Jones, Mortimer	24,030
27	27	H	Arsenal	D 0-0	0-0	—		17,504
28	Mar 3	H	Norwich C	L 0-1	0-1	20		7918
29	10	A	Tottenham H	L 0-3	0-1	20		21,104
30	17	A	Nottingham F	D 1-1	1-0	20	Williams	6690
31	24	A	Coventry C	W 2-1	0-1	19	Minto, Drinkell (og)	9997
32	31	H	QPR	W 1-0	0-0	19	Maddix (og)	8768
33	Apr 11	A	Liverpool	L 0-4	0-1	—		13,982
34	14	A	Southampton	L 2-3	0-3	19	Jones, Caton	15,275
35	17	H	Wimbledon	L 1-2	0-2	—	Young (og)	5679
36	21	A	Crystal Palace	L 0-2	0-0	19		15,276
37	28	H	Sheffield W	L 1-2	0-1	19	Jones	7029
38	May 5	A	Manchester U	L 0-1	0-1	19		35,389

Final League Position: 19

GOALSCORERS

League (31): Williams 10, Jones 5, Mortimer 5, Minto 2, Walsh 2, Bennett 1, Caton 1, Lee 1, MacKenzie 1, own goals 3.
Littlewoods Cup (4): Jones 2, Walsh 1, Williams 1.
FA Cup (4): Jones 2, Lee 1, Williams 1.

Bolder	Humphrey	Reid	Peake	McLaughlin	Pates	Lee, R	Williams	MacKenzie	Mortimer	Jones	Walsh	Watson	Minto	Leaburn	Achampong	Caton	Bennett	Ferguson	Lee, J	Gritt	Match No.
1	2	3	4	5	6	7	8	9	10*	11†	12	14									1
1	2	3	4	5	6	7	8			11	9*	10	12								2
1	2	3	4	5	6	7	8*			11	9	10†	12	14							3
1	2	3	4	5	6	7	8	12	11		9†	10*	14								4
1	2	3	4	5	6	7	8	12	11		9*	10									5
1	2	3	4*	5	6	7	8	12	11		9†	10	14								6
1	2	3	4	5	6	7	8	12	11		9†	10*	14								7
1	2	3		5	6	7	8	4	11†		9*	10	14	12							8
1	2	3	11	5	6	7	8	4		10		9									9
1	2	3	4	5	6	7	8		10		11	9									10
1	2	3	4*	5	6	7	8	12	10		11	9†14									11
1	2	3	4		6	7	8		11	10				9		5					12
1	2	3	4		6	7	8		10*	11			9†14			5				12	13
1	2	3	4			7	8		10	11		6	9			5					14
1	2	3	4		6	7	8		10	11	14		9†12			5*					15
1	2	3	4		6	7	8		5†	10*	11		12	14	9						16
1	2	3	4			7	8		6	10	11		9*	5		12					17
1	2	3	4			7	8		6	10			11 12	9*	5†14						18
1	2	3		6		11	8	7	5*	4	10†	9		12 14							19
1	2	3	4	5	6	7	8	9	12		10*					11					20
1	2		4	5	6	7	8	9	3		10		12			11*					21
1	2		4	5			7	8	9	3 11	10					6					22
1	2		4	5				8	9	3 11	10	7				6					23
1	2		4	5			7	8	11	9	10		3			6					24
1	2		4	5			7	8 12	11	9	10*		3			6					25
1	2		4	5			7	8 10	11	9*	12		3			6					26
1	2		4	5			7	8 10	11	9			3			6					27
1	2	14	4	5			7*	8	10†11	9	12		3			6					28
1	2	3	4	5			7	8	11	9*	12 10					6					29
1	2	3	4	5			7	9	11	12	8*10					6					30
1	2	3	4	5			7	9	11	12	8*10					6					31
1	2	3	4	5			7	8	11	9	10					6					32
1	2	3	4	5			7	8	11	9*	10		12			6					33
1	2	3	4	5			7	8	11	9	10*		12			6					34
1	2	3	4	5			7	8	11	9	10					6					35
1	2	3	4	5			7	8	11	9	10					6					36
1	2	3	4	5			7	8*	11	9	14					6				10†	37
1	2	3	4	5			7	8	9	14	11†		12			6				10*	38
38	38	30	36	31	17	37	38	11	35	23	24	2	20	8	2	23	2	1	—	2	

+ (Peake) 1s

6s (Lee R) 1s (Williams) 2s (MacKenzie) 3s (Mortimer) 7s 3s (Jones / Walsh) 5s (Minto) 8s 1s (Leaburn / Achampong) 4s (Ferguson) 1s (Lee J)

Littlewoods Cup	Second Round	Hereford U (h)		3-1
		(a)		1-0
	Third Round	Southampton (a)		0-1
FA Cup	Third Round	Bradford C (h)		1-1
		(a)		3-0
	Fourth Round	WBA (a)		0-1

CHARLTON ATHLETIC

Player and Position	Ht	Wt	Birth Date	Place	Source	Clubs	League App	Gls
Goalkeepers								
Bob Bolder	6 3	14 06	2 10 58	Dover	Dover	Sheffield W	196	—
						Liverpool	—	—
						Sunderland	22	—
						Luton T (loan)	—	—
						Charlton Ath	137	—
Mick Salmon	6 2	13 00	14 7 64	Leyland	Local	Blackburn R	1	—
						Chester C (loan)	16	—
						Stockport Co	118	—
						Bolton W	26	—
						Wrexham (loan)	17	—
						Wrexham	83	—
						Charlton Ath	—	—
Matthew Watts			7 10 72	Kettering	Rothwell T	Charlton Ath	—	—
Defenders								
Steve Gritt	5 9	10 10	31 10 57	Bournemouth	Apprentice	Bournemouth	6	3
						Charlton Ath	347	24
						Walsall	20	1
						Charlton Ath	2	—
Paul Bacon	5 9	10 04	20 12 70	London	Trainee	Charlton Ath	—	—
Tommy Caton	6 2	13 00	6 10 62	Liverpool	Apprentice	Manchester C	165	8
						Arsenal	81	2
						Oxford U	53	3
						Charlton Ath	37	2
Miguel De Souza*	5 10	11 00	11 2 70	Newham		Charlton Ath	—	—
John Humphrey	5 10	11 01	31 1 61	Paddington	Apprentice	Wolverhampton W	149	3
						Charlton Ath	194	3
Joe McLaughlin	6 1	12 00	2 6 60	Greenock	School	Morton	134	3
						Chelsea	220	5
						Charlton Ath	31	—
Scott Minto	5 10	10 00	6 8 71	Cheshire	Trainee	Charlton Ath	26	2
Darren Pitcher	5 9	12 02	12 10 69	London	Trainee	Charlton Ath	—	—
						Galway U (loan)	—	—
Mark Reid	5 8	11 05	15 9 61	Kilwinning	Celtic BC	Celtic	124	5
						Charlton Ath	187	13
Marcus Smart*	6 2	12 12	14 3 71	Bromley	Trainee	Charlton Ath	—	—
Midfield								
Steve MacKenzie	5 11	12 05	23 11 61	Romford	Apprentice	Crystal Palace	—	—
						Manchester C	58	8
						WBA	148	23
						Charlton Ath	85	6
Paul Mortimer	5 11	11 03	8 5 68	London	Fulham	Charlton Ath	81	10
Andy Peake	5 10	12 00	1 11 61	Market Harborough	Apprentice	Leicester C	147	13
						Grimsby T	39	4
						Charlton Ath	112	1
Colin Walsh	5 9	10 11	22 7 62	Hamilton	Apprentice	Nottingham F	139	32
						Charlton Ath	76	11
						Peterborough U (loan)	5	1
Forwards								
Kenny Achampong	5 9	10 10	26 6 66	London	Apprentice	Fulham	81	15
						West Ham U (loan)	—	—
						Charlton Ath	10	—
Garth Crooks	5 8	12 01	10 3 58	Stoke	Apprentice	Stoke C	147	48
						Tottenham H	125	48
						Manchester U (loan)	7	2
						WBA	40	16
						Charlton Ath	49	14

CHARLTON ATHLETIC

Foundation: Although formed in 1905 by members of such clubs as East Street Mission, Blundell Mission, and Charlton Reds, Charlton Athletic did not really make their presence felt until adopting professionalism and joining the Southern League in 1920. Before that, they had played in such competitions as the Lewisham, Southern Suburban and London Leagues.

First Football League game: 27 August, 1921, Division 3(S), v Exeter C (h) W 1-0 – Hughes; Mitchell, Goodman; Dowling (1), Hampson, Dunn; Castle, Bailey, Halse, Green, Wilson.

Managers (and Secretary-managers)
Bill Rayner 1920–25, Alex McFarlane 1925–27, Albert Lindon 1928, Alex McFarlane 1928–32, Jimmy Seed 1933–56, Jimmy Trotter 1956–61, Frank Hill 1961–65, Bob Stokoe 1965–67, Eddie Firmani 1967–70, Theo Foley 1970–74, Andy Nelson 1974–79, Mike Bailey 1979–81, Alan Mullery 1981–82, Ken Craggs 1982, Lennie Lawrence 1982–   .

Player and Position	Ht	Wt	Birth Date	Place	Source	Clubs	League App	Gls
Andy Jones	5 11	13 06	9 1 63	Wrexham	Rhyl	Port Vale	90	49
						Charlton Ath	59	15
						Port Vale (loan)	17	3
						Bristol C (loan)	4	1
Carl Leaburn	6 3	12 12	30 3 69	Lewisham	Apprentice	Charlton Ath	60	3
						Northampton T (loan)	9	—
Jason Lee	6 3	13 08	9 5 71	London	Trainee	Charlton Ath	1	—
Robert Lee	5 8	10 12	1 2 66	West Ham	ABTA	Charlton Ath	209	33
Mark Tivey	5 9	10 00	10 2 71	London	Trainee	Charlton Ath	—	—
Gordon Watson	6 0	12 00	20 3 71	Kent	Trainee	Charlton Ath	9	—
Ken Wegner‡			3 3 66	Denmark	Malmo	Charlton Ath	—	—
Paul Williams	5 7	10 03	16 8 65	London	Woodford T	Charlton Ath	82	23
						Brentford (loan)	7	3

Iain Ferguson on loan from Hearts | | | | | | | 1 | — |

Trainees
Barham, Spencer J; Barness, Anthony; Brown, Steven B; Bulgen, Christopher; Crane, Steven J; Franco, Rosario; Grant, Kim T; Harrison, Lee D; Julian, Martin J; Salako, Andrew O; Secker, John R; Wareham, Daniel.

Associated Schoolboys
Appiak, Sam K; Bakes, Sean; Budd, Daniel; Daly, Sean; Forbes, Steven D; Gell, Roger A; Granville, Daniel P; Gray, Andrew J; Jordine, Aundrae; Mills, Daniel R; Newton, Shaun; O'Brien, Paul J; Penn, Tanika; Short, Marlon; Smeeth, Jamie F.

Associated Schoolboys who have accepted the club's offer of a Traineeship/Contract
Donker, Richmond; Nguyen, Vinh; Primus, Linvoy S.

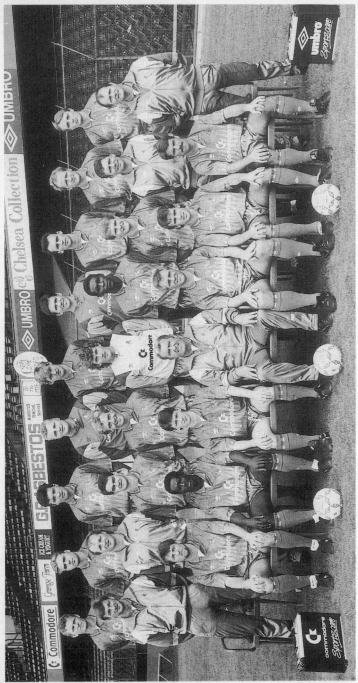

CHELSEA 1989–90 *Back row (left to right):* Mick Hazard, Gareth Hall, Joe McLaughlin, Roger Freestone, David Lee, Kevin Hitchcock, Alan Dickens,
Peter Nicholas, John Bumstead.
Centre row: Eddie Niedzwiecki; Bob Ward (Physiotherapist); Steve Clarke, Kerry Dixon, Dave Beasant, Kenneth Monkou, Gordon Durie, Ian Porterfield (Coach);
Gwyn Williams (Assistant Manager).
Front row: David Mitchell, Clive Wilson, Kevin McAllister, Bobby Campbell (Manager), Graham Roberts, Tony Dorigo, Kevin Wilson.

Division 1 **CHELSEA**

Stamford Bridge, London SW6. Telephone 071-385 5545. Information Service: 071-381 6221. Club call 0898-121159. Ticket News 0898 121859. Lottery office: 071-385-3255.

Ground capacity: 43,900 (21,500 covered).

Record attendance: 82,905 v Arsenal, Division 1, 12 Oct, 1935.

Record receipts: £212,894 v Arsenal, Division 1, 30 September, 1989.

Pitch measurements: 114yd × 71yd.

President: G. M. Thomson.

Chairman: K. W. Bates. *Vice-Chairman:* R. M. Bates.

Directors: C. Hutchinson, Y. S. Todd, S. S. Tollman.

Manager: Bobby Campbell. *Asst. Manager:* Gwyn Williams.

Physio: Bob Ward. *Chief Executive:* C. Hutchinson.

Secretary: Janet Wayth. *Commercial Manager:* John Shaw.

Year formed: 1905. *Turned Professional:* 1905. *Ltd Co.:* 1905.

Club Nickname: 'The Blues'.

Record League Victory: 9-2 v Glossop N E, Division 2, 1 September 1906 – Byrne; Walton, Miller; Key (1), McRoberts, Henderson; Moran, McDermott (1), Hilsdon (5), Copeland (1), Kirwan (1).

Record Cup Victory: 13-0 v Jeunesse Hautcharage, ECWC, 1st rd (2nd leg), 29 September 1971 – Bonetti; Boyle, Harris (1), Hollins (1p), Webb (1), Hinton, Cooke, Baldwin (3), Osgood (5), Hudson (1), Houseman (1).

Record Defeat: 1-8 v Wolverhampton W, Division 1, 26 September, 1953.

Most League Points (2 for a win): 57, Division 2, 1906–07.

Most League Points (3 for a win): 99, Division 2, 1988-89.

Most League Goals: 98, Division 1, 1960–61.

Highest League Scorer in Season: Jimmy Greaves, 41, 1960–61.

Most League Goals in Total Aggregate: Bobby Tambling, 164, 1958–70.

Most Capped Player: Ray Wilkins, 24 (84), England.

Most League Appearances: Ron Harris, 655, 1962–80.

Record Transfer Fee Received: £925,000 from Everton for Pat Nevin, July 1988.

Record Transfer Fee Paid: £725,000 to Newcastle U for Dave Beasant, January 1989.

Football League Record: 1905 Elected to Division 2; 1907–10 Division 1, 1910–12 Division 2; 1912–24 Division 1; 1924–30 Division 2; 1930–62 Division 1; 1962–63 Division 2; 1963–75 Division 1; 1975–77 Division 2; 1977–79 Division 1; 1979–84 Division 2; 1984–88 Division 1; 1988–89 Division 2; 1989– Division 1.

Honours: Football League: Division 1 – Champions 1954–55; Division 2 – Champions 1983–84, 1988–89; Runners-up 1906–7, 1911–12, 1929–30, 1962–63, 1976–77. *FA Cup:* Winners 1970; Runners-up 1914–15, 1966–67. *Football League Cup:* Winners 1964–65, Runners-up 1971–72. *Full Members' Cup:* Winners 1985–86. *Zenith Data Systems Cup:* Winners 1989-90.

European Competitions: *European Fairs Cup:* 1958–60, 1965–66, 1968–69; *European Cup-Winners' Cup:* 1970–71 (winners), 1971–72.

Colours: All royal blue. **Change colours:** Red and white shirts, white shorts, red trim, white stockings.

CHELSEA 1989–90 LEAGUE RECORD

Match No.	Date		Venue	Opponents	Result		H/T Score	Lg. Pos.	Goalscorers	Attendance
1	Aug	19	A	Wimbledon	W	1-0	0-0	—	Wilson K	14,625
2		22	H	QPR	D	1-1	1-1	—	Dorigo	24,354
3		26	H	Sheffield W	W	4-0	3-0	1	Roberts (pen), Harper (og), Dixon, McAllister	16,265
4		29	A	Charlton Ath	L	0-3	0-2	—		17,221
5	Sept	9	H	Nottingham F	D	2-2	1-1	6	Durie, Dixon	21,523
6		16	A	Tottenham H	W	4-1	2-0	4	Dixon, Wilson K 2, Clarke	16,260
7		23	H	Coventry C	W	1-0	1-0	2	Wilson K	18,247
8		30	H	Arsenal	D	0-0	0-0	2		31,833
9	Oct	14	A	Norwich C	L	0-2	0-1	5		19,042
10		21	A	Derby Co	W	1-0	0-0	4	Dixon	17,279
11		28	H	Manchester C	D	1-1	0-0	2	Dixon	21,917
12	Nov	4	H	Millwall	W	4-0	3-0	1	Wilson K 2, Dixon 2	24,969
13		11	A	Everton	W	1-0	0-0	1	Clarke	33,737
14		18	H	Southampton	D	2-2	0-1	2	Monkou, Wilson K	23,093
15		25	A	Manchester U	D	0-0	0-0	3		47,106
16	Dec	2	H	Wimbledon	L	2-5	2-3	4	Dixon, Roberts (pen)	19,975
17		9	A	QPR	L	2-4	1-2	6	Dickens, Clarke	17,935
18		16	H	Liverpool	L	2-5	1-3	7	Durie, Dixon	31,005
19		26	A	Crystal Palace	D	2-2	1-1	7	Dixon, Le Saux	24,680
20		30	A	Luton T	W	3-0	1-0	5	Wilson K 2, Dixon	10,068
21	Jan	1	H	Aston Villa	L	0-3	0-1	7		23,990
22		14	A	Sheffield W	D	1-1	1-0	—	Lee	18,042
23		20	H	Charlton Ath	W	3-1	2-1	6	Wilson K 2, Dixon	15,667
24	Feb	3	A	Coventry C	L	2-3	1-2	6	Dorigo, Dixon	15,243
25		10	H	Tottenham H	L	1-2	0-1	9	Bumstead	28,130
26		17	A	Nottingham F	D	1-1	0-0	8	Roberts	22,500
27		24	H	Manchester U	W	1-0	1-0	6	Hall	29,979
28	Mar	3	A	Southampton	W	3-2	1-2	5	Wilson K, Dorigo, Durie	16,526
29		10	H	Norwich C	D	0-0	0-0	5		18,796
30		17	A	Arsenal	W	1-0	0-0	4	Bumstead	33,805
31		21	A	Manchester C	D	1-1	1-1	—	Durie	24,670
32		31	H	Derby Co	D	1-1	0-0	6	Wilson K	14,265
33	Apr	7	H	Luton T	W	1-0	0-0	6	Durie	15,221
34		14	A	Aston Villa	L	0-1	0-1	6		28,361
35		16	H	Crystal Palace	W	3-0	1-0	6	Dixon, Wilson K, Stuart	16,132
36		21	A	Liverpool	L	1-4	0-2	6	Dixon	38,431
37		28	H	Everton	W	2-1	0-0	6	Dixon 2	18,879
38	May	5	A	Millwall	W	3-1	1-0	5	Dixon 3	12,230

Final League Position: 5

GOALSCORERS

League (58): Dixon 20, Wilson K 14, Durie 5, Clarke 3, Dorigo 3, Roberts 3 (2 pens), Bumstead 2, Dickens 1, Hall 1, Lee 1, Le Saux 1, McAllister 1, Monkou 1, Stuart 1, own goal 1.
Littlewoods Cup (3): Clarke 1, Roberts 1, Wilson K 1.
FA Cup (4): Dixon 2, Clarke 1, Wilson K 1.

Beasant	Clarke	Dorigo	Roberts	Lee	Monkou	Dickens	Nicholas	Dixon	Durie	McAllister	Wilson K	Bumstead	Wilson C	Hazard	Johnsen	Le Saux	Hall	Stuart	Matthew	Match No.
1	2	3	4	5	6	7	8	9	10†	11*	12	14								1
1	2	3	4	5	6	7	8	9	10		11									2
1	2	3	4	5	6	7	8	9		11	10									3
1	2	3	4	5	6	7	8	9	10†	11*	12	14								4
1	2		4	5	6	7†	8	9*	10		12	14	3	11						5
1	2		4	5	6	7*	8	9	10		12		3	11						6
1	2*	3	4	5	6	7	8	9	10		12			11						7
1	2	3	4*	5	6	7	8	9	10		12			11						8
1	2	3		5	6	7*	8	9	12	10	4	14		11†						9
1	2*	3	4	5	6	7	8	9	10		12			11						10
1	2*	3	4	5	6	7	8	9	10		12			11						11
1	2	3	4	5	6	7	8	9	10					11						12
1	2	3	4	5	6	7	8	9	10					11						13
1	2	3	4	5	6	7	8	9	10					11						14
1	2	3	4	5	6	7	8	9	10					11						15
1		3	4	5	6†	7	8*	9	12	10	2	14		11						16
1	2	3	4	5		7		9	12	10	8	14		11†	6*					17
1	2	3	4	5	6	7		9			10	8	11							18
1	2	3	4	5	6			9		7	10	8*11†	12							19
1	2	3	4	5	6			9		7	10	8	11							20
1	2	3	4	5	6	14		9		7	10	8*11†			12					21
1	2		4	8	6			9		11	10	7			5	3				22
1	2	3	4*		6	8		9		7	10				12	5	11			23
1	2	3	4	12		8*		9		7	10	6		11	5					24
1	2	3	4				8	9		7	10	6		11	5					25
1		3	4				8	9		7	10	6		11*	5		12	2		26
1		3	12		6		8	9		7	10	4		11	5		2*			27
1		3	12		6		8	9	14	7	10	4		11†	5		2*			28
1		3			6		8	9		10	7	11	4		5		2			29
1		3			6		8	9		10	7	11	4		5		2			30
1		3			6		8	9		10	7	11	4		5		2			31
1		3			6		8	9		10	7	11	4		5		2			32
1		3	12		6		8	9		10	7	11†	4*14		5		2			33
1		3			6		8	9		10	7	11	4		5		2			34
1		3	12		6		8	9		10†	14				5	11	2	4*	7	35
1		3	12		6		8	9		10	7	11†	4*14		5		2			36
1		3			6			9		10	7	8	4	11	5		2			37
1		3	12		6	14	8†	9		10					5	11	2*	7	4	38
38	24	35	24	23	34	20	29	38	14	21	33	21	12	13	18	4	13	2	2	
				+7s		+2s				+1s	+3s	+4s		+8s	+6s	+3s				

Littlewoods Cup — Second Round — Scarborough (h) 1-1 / (a) 2-3

FA Cup — Third Round — Crewe Alex (h) 1-1 / (a) 2-0 — Fourth Round — Bristol C (a) 1-3

CHELSEA

Player and Position	Ht	Wt	Birth Date	Place	Source	Clubs	League App	Gls
Goalkeepers								
Dave Beasant	6 4	13 00	20 3 59	Willesden	Edgware T	Wimbledon	340	—
						Newcastle U	20	—
						Chelsea	60	—
Roger Freestone	6 2	12 03	19 8 68	Newport		Newport Co	13	—
						Chelsea	42	—
						Swansea C (loan)	14	—
						Hereford U (loan)	8	—
Kevin Hitchcock	6 1	12 02	5 10 62	Custom House	Barking	Nottingham F	—	—
						Mansfield T (loan)	14	—
						Mansfield T	168	—
						Chelsea	11	—
Jason Winters			15 9 71	Oatham	Trainee	Chelsea	—	—
Defenders								
Steve Beattie‡	6 0	12 10	1 9 69	Larne	Trainee	Chelsea	—	—
Steve Clarke	5 9	11 02	29 8 63	Saltcoats	Beith Jnrs	St Mirren	151	6
						Chelsea	114	4
Jason Cundy	6 1	13 10	12 11 69	Wimbledon	Trainee	Chelsea	—	—
Roy Davies	5 6	9 06	19 8 71	Cardiff	Trainee	Chelsea	—	—
Tony Dorigo	5 10	10 00	31 12 65	Melbourne	Apprentice	Aston Villa	111	1
						Chelsea	115	9
Gareth Hall	5 8	10 07	20 3 69	Croydon		Chelsea	49	1
Erland Johnsen	6 0	12 10	5 4 67	Fredrikstad	Bayern Munich	Chelsea	18	—
David Lee	6 3	14 00	26 11 69	Kingswood	Trainee	Chelsea	50	5
Graeme Le Saux	6 0	12 00	17 10 68	Jersey		Chelsea	8	1
Kenneth Monkou	6 0	12 09	29 11 64	Surinam	Feyenoord	Chelsea	36	1
Graham Roberts	5 11	13 10	3 7 59	Southampton	School	Southampton	—	—
						Bournemouth	—	—
					Sholing S	Portsmouth	—	—
					Dorchester T			
					Weymouth	Tottenham H	209	23
						Rangers	55	3
						Chelsea	70	18
Frank Sinclair			3 12 71	Lambeth	Trainee	Chelsea	—	—
Midfield								
John Bumstead	5 7	10 05	27 11 58	Rotherhithe	Apprentice	Chelsea	326	37
Craig Burley	6 1	11 07	24 9 71	Ayr	Trainee	Chelsea	—	—
Alan Dickens	5 11	12 01	3 9 64	Plaistow	Apprentice	West Ham U	192	23
						Chelsea	22	1
Damien Matthew	5 11	10 10	23 9 70	Islington	Trainee	Chelsea	2	—
Edward Newton			13 12 71	Hammersmith	Trainee	Chelsea	—	—
Peter Nicholas	5 8	11 08	10 11 59	Newport	Apprentice	Crystal Palace	127	7
						Arsenal	60	1
						Crystal Palace	47	7
						Luton T	102	1
						Aberdeen	39	3
						Chelsea	68	1
Clive Wilson	5 7	10 00	13 11 61	Manchester	Local	Manchester C	98	9
						Chester C (loan)	21	2
						Manchester C (loan)	11	—
						Chelsea	81	5
Forwards								
Kerry Dixon	6 0	13 00	24 7 61	Luton	Apprentice	Tottenham H	—	—
					Dunstable	Reading	116	51
						Chelsea	267	132

CHELSEA

Foundation: Chelsea may never have existed but for the fact that Fulham rejected an offer to rent the Stamford Bridge ground from Mr. H. A. Mears who had owned it since 1904. Fortunately he was determined to develop it as a football stadium rather than sell it to the Great Western Railway and got together with Frederick Parker, who persuaded Mears of the financial advantages of developing a major sporting venue. Chelsea FC was formed in 1905, and when admission to the Southern League was denied, they immediately gained admission to the Second Division of the Football League.

First Football League game: 2 September, 1905, Division 2, v Stockport C (a) L 0-1 – Foulke; Mackie, McEwan; Key, Harris, Miller; Moran, J.T. Robertson, Copeland, Windridge, Kirwan.

Managers (and Secretary-managers)
John Tait Robertson 1905–07, David Calderhead 1907–33, A. Leslie Knighton 1933–39, Billy Birrell 1939–52, Ted Drake 1952–61, Tommy Docherty 1962–67, Dave Sexton 1967–74, Ron Suart 1974–75, Eddie McCreadie 1975–77, Ken Shellito 1977–78, Danny Blanchflower 1978–79, Geoff Hurst 1979–81, John Neal 1981–85 (Director to 1986), John Hollins 1985–88, Bobby Campbell 1988–   .

Player and Position	Ht	Wt	Birth Date	Place	Source	Clubs	League App	Gls
Billy Dodds (To Dundee Aug 1989)	5 7	10 00	5 2 69	New Cummock	Apprentice	Chelsea	3	—
						Partick T (loan)	30	9
Gordon Durie	6 0	12 00	6 12 65	Paisley	Hill O'Beath	East Fife	81	26
						Hibernian	47	14
						Chelsea	99	39
Kevin McAllister	5 5	11 00	8 11 62	Falkirk		Falkirk	64	18
						Chelsea	93	7
						Falkirk (loan)	6	3
David Mitchell	6 1	11 08	13 6 62	Scotland		Rangers	26	6
					Feyenoord	Chelsea	6	—
Graham Stuart	5 8	11 06	24 10 70	Tooting	Trainee	Chelsea	2	1
Colin West	5 7	11 00	19 9 67	Middlesbrough	Apprentice	Chelsea	16	4
						Partick T (loan)	24	10
						Swansea C (loan)	14	3
Kevin Wilson	5 7	10 10	18 4 61	Banbury	Banbury U	Derby Co	122	30
						Ipswich T	98	34
						Chelsea	108	32

Trainees
Bradley, James J; Chatfield, Ian R; Faulkner, Lee; Forrester, Romon C; Jacobs, Giles; James, Andrew; Kilpatrick, Ian; Vertannes, Desmond M.S.

Associated Schoolboys
Agius, Steven M.F; Bigwood, Jay; Carbon, Vincent; Christie, Terry W; Duberry, Michael W; Goddard, Ryan N.J; Godfrey, Christopher P; Grant, Andrew; Hayfield, Matthew A; Ho, Wai K; Izzet, Mustafa; Luckett, Colin A; McKimm, Stephen J; McLennan, Jason D; Marskell, Ben; Metcalfe, Christian W; Mitchell, Justin A.P; Mitchell, Paul D; Norman, Craig T; Parsons, John; Pearce, Ian A; Skiverton, Terence J; Sullivan, Marc J; Udaw, Emem B; Williams, Andrew D.

Associated Schoolboys who have accepted the club's offer of a Traineeship/Contract
Rowe, Ezekiel; Sell, Richard G.

182

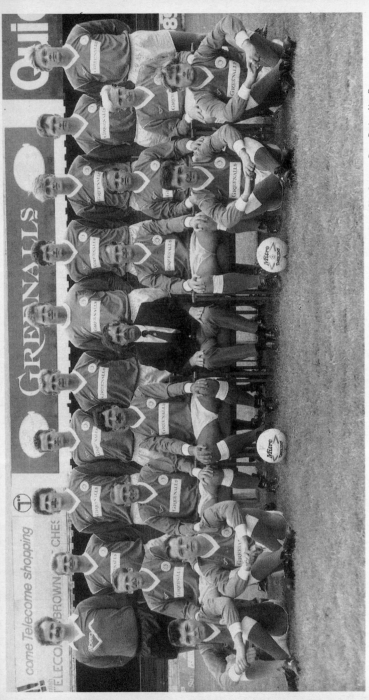

CHESTER CITY 1989–90 *Back row (left to right):* Stuart Walker, Martin Lane, Graham Abel, Chris Lightfoot, David Pugh, Billy Stewart, Barry Butler, Alan Reeves, Colin Woodthorpe, Aiden Newhouse.
Centre row: Carl Dale, David Hamilton, Graham Barrow, Harry McNally (Manager), Joe Hinnigan, Eamonn O'Keefe, Brian Croft.
Front row: Darren Wynne, Robert Painter, Sean Lundon, Michael Carroll.

Division 3 **CHESTER CITY**

The Stadium, Sealand Rd, Chester CH1 4LW. Telephone Chester (0244) 371376. Commercial Dept. (0244) 378162.

Ground: Moss Rose Ground, London Road, Macclesfield.

Ground capacity: 10,000.

Record attendance: 20,500 v Chelsea, FA Cup 3rd rd replay, 16 Jan, 1952.

Record receipts: £30,609 v Sheffield W, FA Cup 4th rd, 31 January, 1987.

Pitch measurements:

Club Patron: Duke of Westminster.

President: Reg Rowlands.

Chairman: R. H. Crofts. Vice-Chairman:

Directors: P. Russell, W. D. MacDonald, N. A. MacLennon, H. McNally.

Team Manager: Harry McNally. *Assistant Manager:* Graham Barrow.

Secretary: R. A. Allan. *Physio:* Joe Hinnigan.

Year Formed: 1884. *Turned Professional:* 1902. *Ltd Co.:* 1909.

Previous name: Chester until 1983.

Club Nicknames: 'Blues'.

Previous Grounds: Faulkner Street; Old Showground; 1904, Whipcord Lane; 1906–90 Sealand Road.

Record League Victory: 12-0 v York C, Division 3(N), 1 February 1936 – Middleton; Common, Hall; Wharton, Wilson, Howarth; Horsman (2), Hughes, Wrightson (4), Cresswell (2), Sargeant (4).

Record Cup Victory: 6-1 v Darlington, FA Cup, 1st rd, 25 November 1933 – Burke; Bennett, Little; Pitcairn, Skitt, Duckworth; Armes (3), Whittam, Mantle (2), Cresswell (1), McLachlan.

Record Defeat: 2-11 v Oldham Ath, Division 3(N), 19 January, 1952.

Most League Points (2 for a win): 56, Division 3(N), 1946–47 and Division 4, 1964–65.

Most League Points (3 for a win): 84, Division 4, 1985–86.

Most League Goals: 119, Division 4, 1964–65.

Highest League Scorer in Season: Dick Yates, 36, Division 3(N), 1946–47.

Most League Goals in Total Aggregate: Gary Talbot, 83, 1963–67 and 1968–70.

Most Capped Player: Bill Lewis, 7 (30), Wales.

Most League Appearances: Ray Gill, 408, 1951–62.

Record Transfer Fee Received: £300,000 from Liverpool for Ian Rush, May 1980.

Record Transfer Fee Paid: £45,000 to Carlisle U for Steve Ludlam, May 1980.

Football League Record: 1931 Elected Division 3(N); 1958–75 Division 4; 1975–82 Division 3; 1982–86 Division 4; 1986– Division 3.

Honours: Football League: Division 3 best season; 5th, 1977–78; Division 3(N) – Runners-up 1935–36; Division 4 – Runners-up 1985–86. *FA Cup* best season: 5th rd, 1976–77, 1979–80. *Football League Cup:* Semi-final 1974–75, *Welsh Cup:* Winners 1908, 1933, 1947. *Debenhams Cup:* Winners 1977.

Colours: Royal blue shirts, white shorts, blue stockings white trim. **Change colours:** Gold shirts and stockings, black shorts.

CHESTER CITY 1989–90 LEAGUE RECORD

Match No.	Date		Venue	Opponents	Result		H/T Score	Lg. Pos.	Goalscorers	Attendance
1	Aug	19	H	Mansfield T	L	0-2	0-1	—		2293
2		26	A	Brentford	D	1-1	1-1	19	Dale	5153
3	Sept	2	H	Crewe Alex	W	2-1	0-1	14	Newhouse, Abel	2170
4		9	A	Swansea C	L	1-2	0-2	17	Newhouse	2738
5		15	H	Notts Co	D	3-3	1-2	—	Newhouse (pen), Lightfoot, Croft	2383
6		23	A	Preston NE	L	0-5	0-1	19		5230
7		26	A	Reading	D	1-1	1-0	—	Lundon	4296
8		30	H	Fulhaam	L	0-2	0-1	21		2135
9	Oct	7	H	Bury	L	1-4	0-2	22	Lundon	2168
10		13	A	Cardiff C	D	1-1	0-0	—	Newhouse	3675
11		17	H	Birmingham C	W	4-0	0-0	—	Croft, Pugh, Painter, Butler	1882
12		21	A	Bolton W	L	0-1	0-1	21		6496
13		28	H	Bristol R	D	0-0	0-0	22		2618
14		31	A	Leyton Orient	W	3-0	2-0	—	Painter, Abel (pen), Butler	3979
15	Nov	4	H	Huddersfield T	W	2-1	1-0	16	Painter, Reeves	2660
16		11	A	Rotherham U	L	0-5	0-2	19		5216
17		24	H	Walsall	D	1-1	1-1	—	Abel (pen)	2507
18	Dec	2	A	Shrewsbury T	L	0-2	0-2	22		2905
19		15	A	Tranmere R	D	0-0	0-0	—		5594
20		26	H	Wigan Ath	D	0-0	0-0	24		3165
21		30	H	Blackpool	W	2-0	1-0	20	Barrow, Abel	2404
22	Jan	1	A	Northampton T	L	0-1	0-0	21		3823
23		6	H	Leyton Orient	W	1-0	1-0	—	Painter	1722
24		12	H	Brentford	D	1-1	0-0	—	Pugh	2294
25		20	A	Mansfield T	L	0-1	0-0	20		2257
26		26	H	Swansea C	W	1-0	0-0	—	Dale	2150
27		30	A	Bristol C	L	0-1	0-0	—		8769
28	Feb	3	H	Preston NE	W	3-1	1-0	12	Woodthorpe, Butler, Croft	2499
29		10	A	Notts Co	D	0-0	0-0	12		5077
30		13	A	Crewe Alex	D	0-0	0-0	—		4260
31		17	H	Shrewsbury T	W	1-0	1-0	9	Abel	2500
32		24	A	Walsall	D	1-1	1-0	10	Butler	3315
33	Mar	3	H	Bristol C	L	0-3	0-2	15		2496
34		6	A	Fulham	L	0-1	0-0	—		3824
35		9	H	Reading	D	1-1	1-0	—	Dale	1978
36		17	A	Bury	L	0-1	0-0	17		2851
37		20	H	Cardiff C	W	1-0	0-0	—	Dale	1866
38		24	A	Birmingham C	D	0-0	0-0	15		7584
39		31	H	Bolton W	W	2-0	2-0	4	Cowdrill (og), Dale	2738
40	Apr	7	A	Bristol R	L	1-2	1-2	16	Reeves	6589
41		14	H	Northampton T	L	0-1	0-1	18		2234
42		16	A	Wigan Ath	L	0-1	0-0	19		2277
43		20	H	Tranmere R	D	2-2	2-0	—	Dale, Pugh	4210
44		24	A	Blackpool	W	3-1	3-0	—	Dale 3	3724
45		28	H	Rotherham U	W	2-0	2-0	16	Bennett, Abel	3827
46	May	5	A	Huddersfield T	L	1-4	0-2	16	Abel	3514

Final League Position: 16

GOALSCORERS

League (43): Dale 9, Abel 7 (2 pens), Butler 4, Newhouse 4 (1 pen), Painter 4, Croft 3, Pugh 3, Lundon 2, Reeves 2, Barrow 1, Bennett 1, Lightfoot 1, Woodthorpe 1, own goal 1.
Littlewoods Cup (0).
FA Cup (4): Abel 1 (pen), Butler 1, Croft 1, Painter 1.

Stewart	Reeves	Woodthorpe	Lane	Able	Hinnigan	Hamilton	Pugh	Newhouse	Dale	Croft	O'Keefe	Hayde	Butler	Painter	Lightfoot	Lundon	Wynne	Hulme	Barrow	Greer	Parsley	Senior	Danzey	Nassari	Bennett	Match No.
1	2	3	4	5	6†	7	8	9	10	11*	12	14														1
1	2	3	4	5	6		8	9	10				7	11												2
1	2	3	6	4			8	9	10	12			7	11*	5											3
1	2	3	6	4	12		8	9	10	11			7		5*											4
1	2	3	6	4			8	9	10	11			7		5											5
1	2	3	6	4			8	9	10	11			7†		5*	12	14									6
1	2	3	6	5	4		8	9	10*	12			7		11											7
1	12	3	6	5*	4		8	9	10†	7			2		14	11										8
1	2†	3		5	4*		8	9	11	12			7		6	10	14									9
1	2	3		5	4		8	9	11	10*			7	12	6											10
1	2	3		5	4		8	9	11				7	10	6											11
1	2	3		5	4*		8	9†	11				7	10	6	12	14									12
1	2*	3		5	4		8		11				7	10	6	12		9								13
1	2	3		5	4		8		11				7	10	6			9								14
1	2	3	5		4		8		12	11			7	10	6			9*								15
1	2*	3	5†	6	4		8		12	11			7	10	14			9								16
1	2†	3	6	5	4				12	11			7	10*	14				8	9						17
1		3	2	5	4*			10	11				7		6	12	14		8	9†						18
1		3	6	5	4		11	9*	12				7	10					8		2					19
1		3	6	9	4	7	11		10	5	12			10					8*		2					20
1		3	6	9	4		11		7	10	5								8		2					21
1		3	6	9	4	12	11		7	10*	5								8		2					22
1		3	6	9	4*	12	11		7	10	5								8		2					23
1		3	6	9	7	12	11	4	10*	5									8		2					24
1	2	3	6	4			9†	7	10*	5	11	14							8		12					25
1	2	3	6	9	4			10	11	7				5					8							26
1	2	3	6	9	4	14	12	10*	11	7†	5								8							27
1	2	3	6	9	4	12	10*	11	7		5								8							28
1	2	3	6	9	4	12	10†	11	7*	14	5								8							29
1	2	3	6	9	4		10	11	7	5									8							30
1	2*	3	6	9	4	12	10	11	7	14	5								8							31
1	2	3	6	4		10	12	11	7	9*	5								8							32
1	2	3	6	4*	10†	9	11	7	12	5									8		14					33
1	2	6	9	4	3	10†	11*	7	12	5									8		14					34
1	2	6	9	4	3	10*	11	7	12	5									8							35
1	2	3	6	5	4*	8	11	7	10	9†	12												14			36
1	2	3	6	5*	12	10	9	11	7	4									8							37
1	2		6	5	3	10	9	11	7	4									8							38
1		3	6	5		10	9	11	2	12	4								8					7*		39
1	2	3	6	5		9	11	7	12	4									8						10*	40
1		3	2	5	4	9	11	7	8	6															10	41
1		3	2	5	4	9	11	7	12	6									8						10*	42
1		3	5	4	7	9	11	2	12	6									8						10*	43
1		3	5	4	7	9	11	2	12	6									8						10*	44
1		3	5	4	7	9	11	2	12	6									8						10*	45
1	14	3	5	4	7	9	11	2*	12	6									8						10†	46
46	28	46	36	41	14	26	31	15	27	41	1	—	44	19	38	5	—	4	28	2	6	—	—	—	8	
	+2s				+1s	+2s	+4s	+3s	+4s	+3s	+2s1s				+2s1s	+2s1s		+13s2s	+6s6s		+1s	+2s	+1s			

Competition	Round	Opponent	Score
Littlewoods Cup	First Round	Crewe Alex (a)	0-4
		(h)	0-2
FA Cup	First Round	Macclesfield (a)	1-1
		(h)	3-2
	Second Round	Blackpool (a)	0-3

CHESTER CITY

Player and Position	Ht	Wt	Birth Date	Birth Place	Source	Clubs	League App	Gls
Goalkeepers								
Steve Farrelly‡	6 3				Knowsley U	Chester C	—	—
Billy Stewart	5 11	11 07	1 1 65	Liverpool	Apprentice	Liverpool	—	—
						Wigan Ath	14	—
						Chester C	148	—
Defenders								
Graham Abel	6 2	13 00	17 9 60	Runcorn	Runcorn	Chester C	190	15
Barry Butler	6 2	13 00	4 6 62	Farnworth	Atherton T	Chester C	153	4
Joe Hinnigan	6 0	12 00	3 12 55	Liverpool	S Liverpool	Wigan Ath	66	10
						Sunderland	63	4
						Preston NE	52	8
						Gillingham	103	7
						Wrexham	29	1
						Chester C	54	2
Martin Lane	5 9	11 04	12 4 61	Altrincham	Amateur	Manchester U		
						Chester C	175	3
						Coventry C	3	—
						Wrexham (loan)	6	—
						Chester C	59	—
Alan Reeves	6 0	12 00	19 11 67	Birkenhead		Norwich C	—	—
						Gillingham (loan)	18	—
						Chester C	30	2
Colin Woodthorpe	5 11	11 08	13 1 69	Ellesmere Pt	Apprentice	Chester C	155	6
Midfield								
David Hamilton*	5 6	10 00	7 11 60	South Shields	Apprentice	Sunderland	—	—
						Blackburn R	114	7
						Cardiff C (loan)	10	—
						Wigan Ath	103	7
						Chester C	28	—
Michael Hayde*			20 6 71	St Helens	Liverpool§	Chester C	1	—
						Linfield (loan)	—	—
Sean Lundon*	5 10	10 10	7 3 69	Liverpool	Apprentice	Chester C	51	4
Derek Nassari§			20 10 71	Pendleton	Trainee	Chester C	1	—
Robert Painter	5 11	11 00	26 1 71	Ince	Trainee	Chester C	42	5
David Pugh	5 10	11 02	19 9 64	Liverpool	Runcorn	Chester C	35	3
Karl Senior§			3 9 72	Northwich	School	Chester C	1	—
Graham Barrow	6 2	13 07	13 6 54	Chorley	Altrincham	Wigan Ath	179	36
						Chester C	142	13
Chris Lightfoot	5 11	11 00	1 4 70	Wimwick	Trainee	Chester C	92	9
Darren Wynne*	5 9	11 05	12 10 70	St Asaph	Trainee	Chester C	12	—
Forwards								
Gary Bennett	6 1	12 06	20 9 63	Liverpool		Wigan Ath	20	3
						Chester C	126	36
						Southend U	42	6
						Chester C	8	1

CHESTER CITY

Foundation: All students of soccer history have read about the medieval games of football in Chester, but the present club was not formed until 1884 through the amalgamation of King's School Old Boys with Chester Rovers. For many years Chester were overshadowed in Cheshire by Northwich Victoria and Crewe Alexandra who had both won the Senior Cup several times before Chester's first success in 1894–95.

First Football League game: 2 September, 1931, Division 3(N), v Wrexham (a) D 1-1 – Johnson; Herod, Jones; Keeley, Skitt, Reilly; Thompson, Ranson, Jennings (1), Cresswell, Hedley.

Managers (and Secretary-managers)
Charlie Hewitt 1930–36, Alex Raisbeck 1936–38, Frank Brown 1938–53, Louis Page 1953–56, John Harris 1956–59, Stan Pearson 1959–61, Bill Lambton 1962–63, Peter Hauser 1963–68, Ken Roberts 1968–76, Alan Oakes 1976–82, Cliff Sear 1982, John Sainty 1982–83, John McGrath 1984, Harry McNally 1985–   .

Player and Position	Ht	Wt	Birth Date	Place	Source	Clubs	League App	Gls
Brian Croft	5 9	10 10	27 9 67	Chester		Chester C	59	3
						Cambridge U	17	2
						Chester C	44	3
Carl Dale	6 0	12 00	29 4 66	Colwyn Bay	Bangor C	Chester C	72	31
Ross Greer‡			23 9 57	Perth, Australia		Chester C	2	—
Eamon O'Keefe‡	5 7	11 05	13 10 53	Manchester	Stalybridge C	Plymouth Arg	—	—
						Hyde U	—	—
						Saudi Arabia	—	—
						Mossley	—	—
						Everton	40	6
						Wigan Ath	58	25
						Port Vale	59	17
						Blackpool	36	23
					Cork C	Chester C	17	4

Trainees
Carroll, Lee J; Cranmer, Martin L.A; Evans, Gary N; Fletcher, Gary G; Griffin, Jamie; McQuillan, Mathew M; Nassari, Derek J; Pickthall, Stuart; Richards, Francis M; Senior, Karl R.

**Non-Contract
Jones, Adrian; Whelan, Spencer R.

Associated Schoolboys
Evans Thomas P; Hillman, Mark; Ingman, David J; Jeanrenaud, Paul; Roberts, Joel H; White, David J; Wilson, Nicholas K.

Associated Schoolboys who have accepted the club's offer of a Traineeship/Contract

**Non-Contract Players who are retained must be re-signed before they are eligible to play in League matches.

CHESTERFIELD 1989–90 *Back row (left to right):* Robert Bloomer, Nigel Thompson, Andy Morris, Trevor Slack, Tony Brien, Jamie Hewitt.
Centre row: Christ McMenemy (Assistant Manager), Reece Simpson, Calvin Plummer, Michael Allison, Michael Leonard, John Ryan, Lee Rogers, Rave Rushbury (Physiotherapist).
Front row: Bryn Gunn, Adrian Shaw, Kevin Arnott, Paul Hart (Manager), Dave Waller, David Hoole, Andrew Rolph.

Division 4   **CHESTERFIELD**

Recreation Ground, Chesterfield S40 4SX. Telephone Chesterfield (0246) 209765. Commercial Dept: (0246) 231535.

Ground capacity: 11,638.

Record attendance: 30,968 v Newcastle U, Division 2, 7 April, 1939.

Record receipts: £32,410 v Sheffield U, Division 3, 25 March, 1989.

Pitch measurements: 112yd × 72yd.

President: His Grace the Duke of Devonshire MC, DL, JP.

Vice-Presidents: P. C. J. T. Kirkman.

Chairman: B. W. Hubbard. *Vice-Chairman:* J. N. Lea.

Associate Directors: B. Watson, J. Croot, J. A. Plant.

Team Manager: Paul Hart.

Physio: Dave Rushbury. *Assistant Manager:* Chris McMenemy.

Secretary: Bob Pepper. *Commercial Manager:* Jim Brown.

Year Formed: 1866. *Turned Professional:* 1891. *Ltd Co:* 1871.

Club Nickname: 'Blues' or 'Spireites'.

Record League Victory: 10-0 v Glossop, Division 2, 17 January 1903 – Clutterbuck; Thorpe, Lerper; Haig, Banner, Thacker; Tomlinson (2), Newton (1), Milward (3), Munday (2), Steel (2).

Record Cup Victory: 5-0 v Wath Ath (away), FA Cup, 1st rd, 28 November 1925 – Birch; Saxby, Dennis; Wass, Abbott, Thompson; Fisher (1), Roseboom (1), Cookson (2), Whitfield (1), Hopkinson.

Record Defeat: 0-10 v Gillingham, Division 3, 5 September, 1987.

Most League Points (2 for a win): 64, Division 4, 1969–70.

Most League Points (3 for a win): 91, Division 4, 1984–85.

Most League Goals: 102, Division 3(N), 1930–31.

Highest League Scorer in Season: Jimmy Cookson, 44, Division 3(N), 1925–26.

Most League Goals in Total Aggregate: Ernie Moss, 161, 1969–76, 1979–81 and 1984–86.

Most Capped Player: Walter McMillen, 4 (7), Northern Ireland.

Most League Appearances: Dave Blakey, 613, 1948–67.

Record Transfer Fee Received: £200,000 from Wolverhampton W for Alan Birch, August 1981.

Record Transfer Fee Paid: £150,000 to Carlisle U for Phil Bonnyman, March 1980.

Football League Record: 1899 Elected to Division 2; 1909 failed re-election; 1921–31 Division 3(N); 1931–33 Division 2; 1933–36 Division 3(N); 1936–51 Division 2; 1951–58 Division 3(N); 1958–61 Division 3; 1961–70 Division 3(N); 1970–83 Division 3; 1983–85 Division 4; 1985–89 Division 3; 1989– Division 4.

Honours: Football League: Division 2 best season: 4th, 1946–47; Division 3(N) – Champions 1930–31, 1935–36; Runners-up 1933–34; Division 4 – Champions 1969–70, 1984–85. *FA Cup* best season: 5th rd. 1932–33, 1937–38, 1949–50. *Football League Cup* best season: 4th rd, 1964–65. *Anglo-Scottish Cup:* Winners 1980–81.

Colours: Blue shirts, white shorts, white stockings. **Change colours:** Yellow shirts, green shorts, yellow stockings.

CHESTERFIELD 1989–90 LEAGUE RECORD

Match No.	Date	Venue	Opponents	Result	H/T Score	Lg. Pos.	Goalscorers	Attendance
1	Aug 19	H	Colchester U	D 1-1	1-1	—	Thompson	3000
2	26	A	Carlisle U	L 3-4	2-1	16	Gunn (pen), Morris, Waller	3059
3	Sept 2	H	Burnley	L 0-1	0-0	21		4061
4	9	A	Cambridge U	W 1-0	0-0	16	Leadbitter (og)	2215
5	16	H	Aldershot	W 2-0	1-0	13	Hewitt, Hart	2822
6	23	A	Maidstone U	W 1-0	1-0	8	Pearce (og)	2147
7	27	A	Hereford U	L 2-3	1-1	—	Waller 2	2620
8	30	H	Rochdale	W 2-1	1-1	8	Waller, Gunn (pen)	3047
9	Oct 7	H	Lincoln C	D 0-0	0-0	9		4723
10	14	A	Exeter C	L 1-2	1-2	11	Waller	3773
11	17	H	Halifax T	W 4-3	1-3	—	Arnott, Gunn (pen), Waller 2	2998
12	21	A	Gillingham	L 0-3	0-2	11		2878
13	28	H	Southend U	D 1-1	1-0	12	Waller	3096
14	Nov 1	A	Scarborough	W 3-2	1-0	—	Arnott, Gunn (pen), Plummer	2341
15	4	A	Grimsby T	W 1-0	0-0	9	Arnott	4513
16	11	H	Stockport Co	D 1-1	0-0	11	Brien	4585
17	25	H	Hartlepool U	W 3-1	3-0	9	Morris, Williams, Gunn (pen)	3488
18	Dec 2	A	Wrexham	W 2-0	0-0	6	Shaw, Gunn	1619
19	16	H	York C	D 0-0	0-0	6		3383
20	26	A	Peterborough U	D 1-1	0-0	7	Hewitt	5422
21	30	A	Scunthorpe U	W 1-0	0-0	4	Plummer	5006
22	Jan 1	H	Doncaster R	L 0-1	0-0	5		5620
23	13	H	Carlisle U	W 3-0	3-0	5	Waller, Plummer 2	4801
24	20	A	Colchester U	L 0-1	0-1	6		3016
25	Feb 3	H	Maidstone U	W 3-1	2-0	5	Gunn (pen), Brien 2	4068
26	10	A	Aldershot	D 0-0	0-0	6		1992
27	17	H	Wrexham	W 3-0	2-0	6	Plummer 2, Dyche	3799
28	24	A	Hartlepool U	L 1-3	1-0	6	Waller	2920
29	Mar 3	H	Torquay U	W 5-1	2-1	7	Plummer, Waller 2, Hewitt, Ryan	3602
30	6	A	Rochdale	L 0-1	0-1	—		2810
31	10	H	Hereford U	W 2-1	2-0	5	Hewitt, Waller	4021
32	13	A	Torquay U	L 0-1	0-1	—		1808
33	17	A	Lincoln C	D 1-1	0-1	7	Plummer	5251
34	20	H	Exeter C	W 2-1	1-1	—	Waller, Bloomer	5319
35	24	A	Halifax T	D 1-1	0-1	7	Waller	2363
36	31	H	Gillingham	W 2-0	1-0	5	Morris, Dyche	4282
37	Apr 3	A	Burnley	D 0-0	0-0	—		3959
38	7	A	Southend U	W 2-0	1-0	3	Morris, Shaw	2892
39	10	H	Scarborough	D 2-2	2-2	—	Waller, Ryan	4916
40	14	A	Doncaster R	L 0-1	0-0	6		3738
41	16	H	Peterborough U	D 1-1	1-0	5	Hart	5696
42	21	A	York C	L 0-4	0-1	5		2374
43	25	A	Cambridge U	D 1-1	1-1	—	Hewitt	3870
44	28	A	Stockport Co	L 1-3	1-1	9	Hewitt	5203
45	May 1	H	Scunthorpe U	D 1-1	0-1	—	Gunn (pen)	3469
46	5	H	Grimsby T	W 2-0	1-0	7	Ryan 2	7501

Final League Position: 7

GOALSCORERS

League (63): Waller 16, Gunn 8 (7 pens), Plummer 8, Hewitt 6, Morris 4, Ryan 4, Arnott 3, Brien 3, Dyche 2, Hart 2, Shaw 2, Bloomer 1, Thompson 1, Williams 1, own goals 2.
Littlewoods Cup (2): Hewitt 1, Waller 1.
FA Cup (3): Gunn 1 (pen), Plummer 1, Waller 1.

Leonard	Gunn	Ryan	Arnott	Brien	Slack	Plummer	Shaw	Waller	Thompson	Morris	Hoole	Hewitt	Hart	Bloomer	Eley	Rolph	Williams	Rogers	Dyche	Hoyle	Chiedozie	Francis	Match No.
1	2	3	4	5	6	7*	8	9	10	11	12												1
1	2	3	4	5	6	7		9	10	11		8											2
1	2	3	4	5		7*		9	10	11		8	6	12									3
1	2	3	4	5		7*		9	10	11		8	6	12									4
1	2	3	4	5		7		9	10*			8	6	12	11								5
1	2	3	4	5		7	12	9	10*			8	6	11									6
1	2	3	4	5		7		9	10			8*	6	11		12							7
1	2	3	4*	5		7	12	9	10†		14	8	6	11									8
1	2	3		5		7	12	9	10*	11		8	6	4									9
1	2	3	10	5		7*		9		11		8	6	4	12								10
1	2	3	10	5				9		11		8	6	4			7						11
1	2	3	10				12	9		11†		8	6	4*		7	14	5					12
1	2	3	10			6	4	9		11		8		12			7*	5					13
1	2	3	10			6	4	9		11		8					7	5					14
1	2	3	10	8		6	4	9		11							7	5					15
1	2	3	10	8		6	4	9		11						12	7*	5					16
1	2	3		8		6	4	9		11						10	7	5					17
1	2		7*	8		6	4	9	12	11		3		14		10†		5					18
1	2	7		8		6†	4	9		11		3		12	14	10*		5					19
1	2	7		8		6*	4	9		11		3			10	12		5					20
1	2	7		8		6	4	9		11		3			10			5					21
1	2	7		8		6	4	9		11		3			10*	12		5					22
1	6	10		5		7	4	9		11		8	3					2					23
1	6	10		5		7	4	9		11		8	3					2					24
1	6	10		5		7†	4	9*		11		8	3	12			14	2					25
1	6	10		5		7	14			11*		8	3	12				2	4	9†			26
1	6	10		5		7				11		8	3					2	4	9			27
1	6	10		5		7		9		12		8	3				11*	2	4				28
1	6	10		5		7		9		11		8	3					2	4				29
1	6	10		5		7		9		11		8	3					2	4				30
1	6	10		5		7		9		11		8	3					2	4				31
1	6	10		5		7		9*		11		8	3	12				2	4				32
1	6	10*		5		7	12	9		11		8	3					2	4				33
1	6			5*		7	12	9		11		8	3	10				2	4				34
1	6		5			7		9		11		8	3					2	4		10		35
1	6	3	5			7		9		11		8						2	4		10		36
1	6	3	5			7		9		11*		8					12	2	4		10		37
1	6	3	5			7	12	9		11		8						2	4		10*		38
1	6	3	5			7	10	9		11		8						2	4				39
1	6	3	5			7	10*	9		11		8						2	4		12		40
1	6	10		5		7		9		11		8	3					2	4				41
1	6	10*		5		7		9		11†		8	3				14	2	4		12		42
1	6	10		5		7		9		11		8	3					2	4				43
1	6	10		5		7		9		11*		8	3				12	2	4				44
1	6	3	5			7				11		8		12			14		4	9†	10*	2	45
1	6	9	5				10*			11		8	3				12		4			2	46
46	46	43	16	43	2	44 +8s	16	43	9 +1s	41 +2s	— +1s	42	27	15 +7s	4 +1s	3 +6s	4 +7s	31 +1s	21 +1s	3	5 +2s	2	

Littlewoods Cup	First Round	Birmingham C (a)	1-2
		(h)	1-1
FA Cup	First Round	Shrewsbury T (a)	3-2
	Second Round	Huddersfield T (h)	0-2

CHESTERFIELD

Player and Position	Ht	Wt	Birth Date	Place	Source	Clubs	League App	Gls
Goalkeepers								
Michael Allison	5 11	11 08	17 3 66	Elderslie	Horwich RMI	Chesterfield	—	—
Mike Astbury	5 10	13 08	22 1 64	Leeds	Apprentice	York C	48	—
						Peterborough U (loan)	4	—
						Darlington	38	—
						Chester C	5	—
						Chesterfield	8	—
Mick Leonard	6 1	12 04	9 5 59	Carshalton	Epsom & Ewell	Halifax T	69	—
						Notts Co	204	—
						Chesterfield	62	—
Defenders								
Tony Brien	6 0	12 00	10 2 69	Dublin	Apprentice	Leicester C	16	1
						Chesterfield	72	4
Bryn Gunn	6 2	13 07	21 8 58	Kettering	Apprentice	Nottingham F	131	1
						Shrewsbury T (loan)	9	—
						Walsall (loan)	6	—
						Mansfield T (loan)	5	—
						Peterborough U	131	14
						Chesterfield	46	8
Nigel Hart	6 0	12 03	1 10 58	Golborne	Local	Wigan Ath	1	—
						Leicester C	—	—
						Blackpool	37	—
						Crewe Alex	142	10
						Bury	45	2
						Stockport Co	39	2
						Chesterfield	27	2
Jamie Hewitt	5 10	10 08	17 5 68	Chesterfield	School	Chesterfield	169	11
Lee Rogers	5 10	12 00	21 10 66	Doncaster	Doncaster R	Chesterfield	135	—
John Ryan	5 10	11 07	18 2 62	Oldham	Apprentice	Oldham Ath	77	8
						Newcastle U	28	1
						Sheffield W	8	1
						Oldham Ath	23	—
						Mansfield T	62	1
						Chesterfield	43	4
Trevor Slack*	6 1	13 02	26 9 62	Peterborough	Apprentice	Peterborough U	202	18
						Rotherham U	15	1
						Grimsby T	21	—
						Northampton T	13	1
						Chesterfield	23	—
Midfield								
Kevin Arnott‡	5 10	11 12	28 9 58	Bensham	Apprentice	Sunderland	133	16
						Blackburn R (loan)	17	2
						Sheffield U	121	11
						Blackburn R (loan)	12	1
						Rotherham U (loan)	9	2
						Chesterfield	71	4
Sean Dyche	6 0	12 04	28 6 71	Kettering	Trainee	Nottingham F		
						Chesterfield	22	2
Mick Henderson‡	5 10	11 04	31 3 56	Gosforth	Apprentice	Sunderland	84	2
						Watford	51	—
						Cardiff C	11	—
						Sheffield U	67	—
						Chesterfield	136	10
David Hoole‡	5 6	10 00	16 10 70	Chesterfield	Trainee	Chesterfield	14	—
Gavin McDonald‡	5 7	10 06	6 10 70	Salford	Trainee	Chesterfield	12	1
Adrian Shaw	5 10	11 07	13 4 66	Easington	Apprentice	Nottingham F	—	1
						Halifax T	100	1
						York C	5	—
						Chesterfield	49	3
Reece Simpson‡	5 8	10 00	5 1 71	Nottingham	Trainee	Chesterfield	—	—
Nigel Thompson‡	5 7	10 07	1 3 67	Leeds	Apprentice	Leeds U	7	—
						Rochdale (loan)	5	—
						Chesterfield	20	1

CHESTERFIELD

Foundation: Chesterfield are fourth only to Stoke, Notts County and Nottingham Forest in age for they can trace their existence as far back as 1866, although it is fair to say that they were somewhat casual in the first few years of their history playing only a few friendlies a year. However, their rules of 1871 are still in existence showing an annual membership of 2s (10p), but it was not until 1891 that they won a trophy (the Barnes Cup) and followed this a year later by winning the Sheffield Cup, Barnes Cup and the Derbyshire Junior Cup.

First Football League game: 2 September, 1899, Division 2, v Sheffield W (a) L 1-5 – Hancock; Pilgrim, Fletcher; Ballantyne, Bell, Downie; Morley, Thacker, Gooing, Munday (1), Geary.

Managers (and Secretary-managers)
E. Russell Timmeus 1891–95*, Gilbert Gillies 1895–1901, E. F. Hind 1901–1902, Jack Hoskin 1902–1906, W. Furness 1906–07, George Swift 1907–10, G. H. Jones 1911–13, R. L. Weston 1913–17, T. Callaghan 1919, J. J. Caffrey 1920–22, Harry Hadley 1922, Harry Parkes 1922–27, Alec Campbell 1927, Ted Davison 1927–32, Bill Harvey 1932–38, Norman Bullock 1938–45, Bob Brocklebank 1945–48, Bobby Marshall 1948–52, Ted Davison 1952–58, Duggie Livingstone 1958–62, Tony McShane 1962–67, Jimmy McGuigan 1967–73, Joe Shaw 1973–76, Arthur Cox 1976–80, Frank Barlow 1980–83, John Duncan 1983–87, Kevin Randall 1987–88, Paul Hart 1988–   .

Player and Position	Ht	Wt	Birth Date	Birth Place	Source	Clubs	League App	Gls
Steven Williams	5 11	11 06	18 7 70	Mansfield		Mansfield T	11	—
						Chesterfield	11	1
Forwards								
Robert Alleyne‡	5 9	11 03	27 9 68	Dudley	Apprentice	Leicester C	3	—
						Wrexham (loan)	10	2
						Chesterfield	40	5
John Chiedozie†	5 7	10 10	18 4 60	Nigeria	Apprentice	Orient	145	20
						Notts Co	111	15
						Tottenham H	53	12
						Derby Co	2	—
						Notts Co	1	—
						Chesterfield	7	—
Kevin Eley‡	5 6	9 07	4 3 68	Mexborough	School	Rotherham U	13	—
						Chesterfield	81	2
Andy Morris	6 5	15 07	17 11 67	Sheffield		Rotherham U	7	—
						Chesterfield	95	13
Calvin Plummer	5 8	10 07	14 2 63	Nottingham	Apprentice	Nottingham F	12	2
						Chesterfield	28	7
						Derby Co	27	3
						Barnsley	54	6
						Nottingham F	8	2
						Derry C (loan)	—	—
						Plymouth Arg	23	1
						Chesterfield	44	8
Andy Rolph	5 6	10 00	28 10 69	Birmingham	Trainee	Birmingham C	—	—
						Chesterfield	21	1
Dave Waller	5 10	10 00	20 12 63	Urmston	Local	Crewe Alex	168	55
						Shrewsbury T	11	3
						Chesterfield	119	53

Trainees
Benjamin, Christopher; Chambers, Scott; Clark, Philip; Cordner, Scott; Godfrey, Paul; Goldring, Mark; Payne, Karl; Pell, Steven M; Preston, Jamie; Sheppard, Craig; Wilkinson, Gareth.

**Non-Contract
Chiedozie, John O; Higginbottom, Andrew J; Rushbury, David G; Wright, Dean B.

Associated Schoolboys
Bennett, Wayne S; Blakemore, Paul D; Campbell, Stephen M; Evans, Lee J; Fitzpatrick, Martin P; Goodwin, Robert; Gregory, Paul Z; Hall, Mark J; Hewitt, Paul S; Hickton, Grant C; Houghton, Darren C; Jones, Alastair D; Pearson, Michael R; Pick, Ashley C; Taylor, Steven; Tomlinson, Ronald J; Vernon, Lee C; Walton, Martin S; Wilcockson, Andrew.

**Non-Contract Players who are retained must be re-signed before they are eligible to play in League matches.

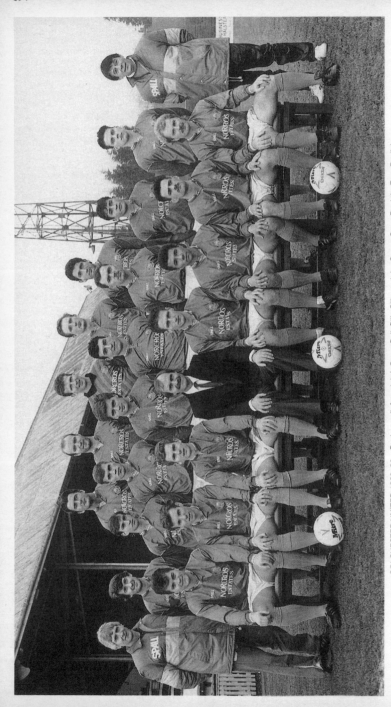

COLCHESTER UNITED 1989–90   *Back row (left to right):* Steve Ball, Billy Gilbert, John Grace, Scott Daniels, Tom English.
Centre row: Brian Owen, Eamonn Collins, Gary Bennett, Clive Stafford, Mark Radford, Trevor Morgan, Stuart Hicks, Richard Wilkins, John Pollard, Sammy Chung (Coach).
Front row: Martin Grainger, Robert Devereaux, Mark Kinsella, Mick Mills (Manager), Tony English, Marcel Bruce, Robert Scott, Les Taylor.

GM Vauxhall Conference   **COLCHESTER UNITED**

Layer Rd Ground, Colchester.

Telephone (0206) 574042. *Commercial Dept:* (0206) 47754.

Ground capacity: 6480.

Record attendance: 19,072 v Reading, FA Cup 1st rd, 27 Nov, 1948.

Record receipts: £22,754 v Manchester U, Milk Cup 3rd rd, 8 Nov, 1983.

Pitch measurements: 110yd × 71yd.

President: M. J. Cadman.

Patron: A. Buck QC, MP.

Chairman: J. T. Crisp. *Deputy-Chairman:* J. H. Schultz.

Chief Executive:

Directors: H. Carson, D. A. Johnson, G. H. Parker, R. Pleydell, J. Wallace, C. Simpson.

Player Manager: Ian Atkins. *Assistant Manager/Coach:* Sammy Chung.

Physio: Brian Owen. *Consultant Physio:* C. Simpson.

Secretary: Mrs Dee Elwood.

Commercial Director: J. T. Carter. *Lottery Manager:* Cyril Harvey. *Programme Editor:* Hal Mason.

Year Formed: 1937. *Turned Professional:* 1937. *Ltd Co.:* 1937.

Club Nickname: 'The U's'.

Record League Victory: 9-1 v Bradford C, Division 4, 30 December 1961 – Ames; Millar, Fowler; Harris, Abrey, Ron Hunt; Foster, Bobby Hunt (4), King (4), Hill (1), Wright.

Record Cup Victory: 7-1 v Yeovil T (away), FA Cup, 2nd rd (replay), 11 December 1958 – Ames; Fisher, Fowler; Parker, Milligan, Hammond; Williams (1), McLeod (2), Langman (4), Evans, Wright.

Record Defeat: 0-8 v Leyton Orient, Division 4, 15 October 1989.

Most League Points (2 for a win): 60, Division 4, 1973–74.

Most League Points (3 for a win): 81, Division 4, 1982–83.

Most League Goals: 104, Division 4, 1961–62.

Highest League Scorer in Season: Bobby Hunt, 37, Division 4, 1961–62.

Most League Goals in Total Aggregate: Martyn King, 131, 1959–65.

Most Capped Player: None.

Most League Appearances: Micky Cook, 613, 1969–84.

Record Transfer Fee Received: £90,000 from Gillingham for Trevor Lee, January 1981.

Record Transfer Fee Paid: £40,000 to Lokeren for Dale Tempest, August 1987.

Football League Record: 1950 Elected to Division 3(S); 1958–61 Division 3; 1961–62 Division 4; 1962–65 Division 3; 1965–66 Division 4; 1966–68 Division 3; 1968–74 Division 4; 1974–76 Division 3, 1976–77 Division 4; 1977–81 Division 3; 1981–90 Division 4.

Honours: Football League: Division 3(S) best season: 3rd , 1956–57; Division 4 – Runners-up 1961–62. *FA Cup* best season: 1970–71, 6th rd (record for a Fourth Division club shared with Oxford United and Bradford City). *Football League Cup:* best season 5th rd 1974–75.

Colours: Blue shirts, white shorts, white stockings. **Change colours:** White shirts, blue shorts, blue stockings.

COLCHESTER UNITED 1989–90 LEAGUE RECORD

Match No.	Date		Venue	Opponents	Result		H/T Score	Lg. Pos.	Goalscorers	Atten- dance
1	Aug	19	A	Chesterfield	D	1-1	1-1	—	Radford	3000
2		26	H	Halifax T	D	2-2	0-0	13	Bennett, Radford (pen)	2404
3	Sept	2	A	Grimsby T	L	1-4	0-2	19	Allinson	4678
4		8	H	Hereford U	D	1-1	1-0	—	Allinson (pen)	3269
5		16	A	Rochdale	D	2-2	1-1	19	Collins, Blake	1466
6		23	A	Scarborough	D	0-0	0-0	20		2420
7		26	H	Maidstone U	W	4-1	1-0	—	Radford, Allinson (pen), Taylor, Bennett (pen)	2946
8		30	A	Carlisle U	L	0-1	0-1	16		3979
9	Oct	7	A	Aldershot	L	0-4	0-2	18		2092
10		13	H	York C	L	0-2	0-2	—		3274
11		17	H	Wrexham	L	1-3	1-1	—	Scott	2564
12		21	A	Scunthorpe U	L	0-4	0-2	23		3254
13		28	H	Peterborough U	L	0-1	0-0	23		3460
14	Nov	1	A	Exeter C	L	1-2	1-1	—	English A	3905
15		4	A	Burnley	D	0-0	0-0	23		6145
16		10	H	Cambridge U	L	1-2	1-1	—	English T (pen)	3771
17		24	A	Gillingham	D	3-3	0-2	—	English T (pen), Bennett, Morgan	3816
18	Dec	2	A	Lincoln C	L	0-1	0-1	23		2517
19		16	H	Torquay U	L	0-3	0-1	23		1720
20		26	A	Southend U	W	2-0	0-0	23	Grainger, English T	5563
21		30	A	Doncaster R	L	0-2	0-1	24		2942
22	Jan	1	H	Hartlepool U	W	3-1	0-1	23	Morgan, Grainger, Radford	3826
23		5	A	Stockport Co	L	0-1	0-0	—		3609
24		12	A	Halifax T	D	1-1	0-1	—	Scott	1397
25		20	H	Chesterfield	W	1-0	1-0	22	Wilkins	3016
26		27	A	York C	L	1-3	1-2	22	Wilkins	2311
27	Feb	3	A	Scarborough	D	2-2	0-0	22	English A, Morgan	1786
28		10	H	Rochdale	L	1-2	12	23	Morgan	2744
29		17	A	Lincoln C	L	1-2	0-2	24	Wilkins	3284
30		20	H	Grimsby T	W	1-0	1-0	—	Bruce	3026
31		23	H	Gillingham	W	2-0	1-0	—	Morgan (pen), Scott	4456
32	Mar	2	A	Stockport Co	D	1-1	0-0	—	Goddard	3452
33		6	H	Carlisle U	W	4-0	2-0	—	Wilkins, Marmon, Morgan 2 (2 pens)	3752
34		10	A	Maidstone U	L	1-4	0-3	23	Morgan (pen)	2856
35		14	A	Hereford U	L	0-2	0-0	—		2253
36		17	H	Aldershot	W	1-0	0-0	24	Morgan	2682
37		24	A	Wrexham	L	2-3	1-0	24	Marmon, Beaumont (og)	4653
38		31	H	Scunthorpe U	W	1-0	1-0	24	Morgan	2920
39	Apr	7	A	Peterborough U	L	0-1	0-1	24		4025
40		10	H	Exeter C	L	0-1	0-0	—		3369
41		14	A	Hartlepool U	W	2-0	0-0	24	Bennett, Collins	3397
42		16	H	Southend U	L	0-2	0-1	24		5283
43		21	A	Torquay U	L	1-4	0-3	24	Morgan (pen)	1521
44		24	H	Doncaster R	W	2-0	2-0	—	Marmon 2	2641
45		29	A	Cambridge U	L	0-4	0-2	—		4558
46	May	5	H	Burnley	L	1-2	1-1	24	Morgan (pen)	2788

Final League Position: 24

GOALSCORERS

League (48): Morgan 12 (6 pens), Bennett 4 (1 pen), Marmon 4, Radford 4 (1 pen), Wilkins 4, Allinson 3 (2 pens), English T 3 (2 pens), Scott 3, Collins 2, English A 2, Grainger 2, Blake 1, Bruce 1, Goddard 1, Taylor 1, own goal 1.
Littlewoods Cup (4): Scott 2, Bennett 1, Collins 1.
FA Cup (1): Bennett 1.

Grace	Hicks	Rooke	English A	Daniels	Radford	Bennett	Collins	Wilkins	Scott	Allinson	Hansbury	Taylor	Kinsella	Pollard	Stafford	Blake	Devereux	Gilbert	English T	Morgan	Bruce	Hagan	Grainger	Warner	Ball	Barrett	Marmon	Goddard	Marriott	Match No.
1	2	3	4	5	6	7	8	9	10	11																				1
	2	3*	4	5	6	7	8	9	10	11†	1	12	14																	2
	2	3	4	5	6*	7	8	9	10†	11	1	12		14																3
	2		4	5		7	8	9		11	1	10				3	6													4
	2		4	5	12	7*	8	9		11	1	10				3	6													5
1	2		3	5	4*	7	8	9		11		10				12	6													6
1	2		3	5	10	7*	8	9	12	11						4	6													7
1	2		6	5	10*	7	8	9	12	11						4	3													8
1	2	3	6	5	11†	14	8	9	10	7*	4	12																		9
1	2		6	5	3	7*	8	9	10	11		4			12															10
1	2		6	5	3	7†	8	9	10*	11		4		14	12															11
1	9		6	5	11*	8†	12	4	2	14		7			10	3														12
1	2		7	5	12		8			11		4				3		6*	10	9										13
1	2		7	5	12		8			11		4				3		6	10	9*										14
1	2		7	5			8			11		4	14	12		3		6	10†	9*										15
1			7	5			8†			11		4	14	12		3		6*	10	9	2									16
1			4	5		7	8			11						3		6	10	9	2									17
1			4	5		7	8			11†	12		14			3		6	10	9*	2									18
1			4	5		7		9	11*			10						6	12		2	8	3							19
1			4	5		7	8		11†			9				3		6*	10		2	12	14							20
1			4	5	6†	7	8*	9					14			3			10	11	2	12								21
1			4	5	6	7	8†		12							3			10*	9	2		11	14						22
1			4	5	6	7	8									3				9	2	11	10							23
			6	5		11*	10†	7	9	14						3		4	12		2		8			1				24
			3	5		11		7	10						12			4		9	2		8*			1	6			25
	14		3	5		11*	12	7	10									4		9	2		8†			1	6			26
			8	5		11*	12	7	10									4		9	2					1	6	3		27
			8	5		11*	12	7	10								14	4†		9	2					1	6	3		28
			8	5		11*		7	10						12			4		9	2					1	6	3		29
			8	5		11*		7	10						12			4		9	2					1	6	3		30
			8	5		11*	12	7	10									4		9	2					1	6	3		31
			8	5		11		7	10									4		9	2					1	6	3		32
			8	5		11		7	10*						12			4		9	2					1	6	3		33
	12		8	5		11*		7	10									4		9	2					1	6	3		34
	12		8	5				7	10						3*			4	11	9	2					1	6			35
	14		3	5		11†	12	7*	10						8			4		9	2					1	6			36
			8	5		11		7	10									4		9	2						6	3	1	37
			8	5		11		7	10									4		9	2						6	3	1	38
			8	5		11		7	10*									4		9	2						6	3	1	39
			8	5		11	12	7*	10									4		9	2						6	3	1	40
	2			5		11*	12	7	10						8			4		9							6	3	1	41
	2			5		11	12	7*	10						8			4†	14	9							6	3	1	42
			8	5*			12	7	10				14					4		9	2	11†					6	3	1	43
			8	5		11		7	10									4		9	2						6	3	1	44
			8	5	3	11*	12	7	10				14					4†		9	2						6		1	45
			4*	5	3	11	8†	7	10				14							9	2		12				6		1	46
19	16	4	44	46	19	26	39	43	14	12	4	30	1	1	15	4	1	26	12	31	28	2	4	1	3	13	22	16	10	
	+4s				+1s	+10s			+11s1s	+1s			+6s	+5s	+6s2s			+1s1s	+1s	+1s	+1s				+3s	+1s	+1s			

Restarick — Match No. 39(12)

Littlewoods Cup	First Round	Southend U (h)	3-4
		(a)	1-2
FA Cup	First Round	Brentford (a)	1-0
	Second Round	Birmingham C (h)	0-2

COLCHESTER UNITED

Player and Position	Ht	Wt	Birth Date	Place	Source	Clubs	League App	Gls
Goalkeepers								
John Grace	6 2	12 07	16 2 64	Dublin	Tolka R	Colchester U	19	—
Defenders								
Marcel Bruce	5 10	11 07	18 3 71	Detroit	Trainee	Colchester U	29	1
Billy Gilbert	5 11	12 00	10 11 59	Lewisham	Apprentice	Crystal Palace	237	3
						Portsmouth	140	—
						Colchester U	27	—
Jim Hagan‡	5 10	10 09	10 8 56	Monkstown	Larne	Coventry C	13	—
						Torquay U (loan)	7	—
						Detroit Express	—	—
						Selko, HK	—	—
						Coventry C	3	—
						Birmingham C	137	—
						Colchester U	2	—
Steve Hetzke‡	6 2	13 04	3 6 55	Marlborough	Apprentice	Reading	261	23
						Blackpool	140	18
						Sunderland	31	—
						Chester C	14	—
						Colchester U	29	2
Stuart Hicks	6 1	12 06	30 5 67	Peterborough	Apprentice	Peterborough U	—	—
					Wisbech	Colchester U	64	—
Lee Hunter‡	5 10	10 08	5 10 69	Oldham	Trainee	Colchester U	9	—
Neale Marmon	6 2	14 00	21 4 61	Bournemouth		Torquay U	4	—
					Hannover 96	Colchester U	22	4
Rodney Rooke‡	5 5	10 03	7 4 70	Orsett	Trainee	Colchester U	4	—
Clive Stafford	6 1	12 02	4 4 63	Ipswich	Diss T	Colchester U	33	—
						Exeter C (loan)	2	—
Midfield								
Ian Allinson‡	5 10	11 00	1 10 57	Hitchin	Apprentice	Colchester U	308	69
						Arsenal	83	16
						Stoke C	9	—
						Luton T	32	3
						Colchester U	38	10
Steve Ball‡	6 0	12 01	2 9 69	Colchester	Trainee	Arsenal	—	—
						Colchester U	4	—
Gary Bennett	5 7	9 13	13 11 70	Enfield	Trainee	Colchester U	45	5
Eamonn Collins	5 6	8 13	22 10 65	Dublin	Apprentice	Blackpool	—	—
						Southampton	3	—
						Portsmouth	5	—
						Exeter C (loan)	9	—
						Gillingham (loan)	—	—
						Colchester U	39	2
Scott Daniels	6 1	11 09	22 11 69	Benfleet	Trainee	Colchester U	73	—
Robert Devereux*	5 8	10 09	31 1 71	Ipswich	Ipswich T§	Colchester U	2	—
Tony English	6 0	11 00	10 10 66	Luton		Colchester U	222	35
Brian Kennedy‡			12 10 68	Co Antrim	Chelsea§	Colchester U	—	—
Mark Kinsella	5 9	11 00	12 8 72	Dublin	Home Farm	Colchester U	6	—
Mark Radford	6 1	11 08	20 12 68	Leicester	Trainee	Colchester U	64	5
Les Taylor	5 8	11 07	4 12 56	North Shields	Apprentice	Oxford U	219	15
						Watford	172	13
						Reading	75	3
						Colchester U	52	1
Richard Wilkins	6 0	12 00	28 5 65	London	Haverhill R	Colchester U	152	22

COLCHESTER UNITED

Foundation: Colchester United was formed in 1937 when a number of enthusiasts of the much older Colchester Town club decided to establish a professional concern as a limited liability company. The new club continued at Layer Road which had been the amateur club's home since 1909.

First Football League game: 19 August, 1950, Division 3(S), v Gillingham (a) D 0-0 – Wright; Kettle, Allen; Bearryman, Stewart, Elder; Jones, Curry, Turner, McKim, Church.

Managers (and Secretary-managers)
Ted Fenton 1946–48, Jimmy Allen 1948–53, Jack Butler 1953–55, Benny Fenton 1955–63, Neil Franklin 1963–68, Dick Graham 1968–72, Jim Smith 1972–75, Bobby Roberts 1975–82, Allan Hunter 1982–83, Cyril Lea 1983–86, Mike Walker 1986–87, Roger Brown 1987–88, Jock Wallace 1989, Mick Mills 1990.

Player and Position	Ht	Wt	Birth Date	Place	Source	Clubs	League App	Gls
Forwards								
Tom English*	5 9	11 06	18 10 61	Cirencester	Colchester U	Coventry C	66	17
						Leicester C	44	3
						Rochdale	3	1
						Plymouth Arg	4	1
						Colchester U	47	17
					Bishop's Stortford	Colchester U	13	3
Martin Grainger§	5 11	11 13	23 8 72	Enfield	Trainee	Colchester U	7	2
Trevor Morgan	6 1	13 01	30 9 56	Forest Gate	Leytonstone	Bournemouth	53	13
						Mansfield T	12	6
						Bournemouth	88	33
						Bristol C	32	8
						Exeter C	30	9
						Bristol R	55	24
						Bristol C	19	8
						Bolton W	77	17
						Colchester U	32	12
John Pollard§	5 11	11 06	17 11 71	Chelmsford	Trainee	Colchester U	9	1
Chris Roll‡			4 11 70	North Walsham	Trainee	Colchester U	—	—
Robert Scott*	5 10	11 07	13 1 64	Broxburn	Whitburn J	Colchester U	37	8
John Warner‡	5 10	12 03	20 11 61	Paddington	Burnham	Colchester U	17	3

Trainees
Baker, Karl J; Cabey, Michael J; Cooper, Simon; Cummins, Desmond N; Grainger, Martin R; Hannigan, Wayne; Leech, Gary R; McCloskey, Gerald J; Patten, George; Pollard, Kelly J; Restarick, Stephen L; Smale-Saunders, Nicholas J; Swan, Matthew; Tuohy, Karl G; Whitley, Simon A.

Associated Schoolboys
Gardiner, Mark A; Townes, Shane.

Associated Schoolboys who have accepted the club's offer of a Traineeship/Contract
Goodwin, James R.A; Leslie, Graham W.

COVENTRY CITY 1989–90 *Back row (left to right)*: Keith Thompson, Gary Bannister, Brian Borrows, Trevor Peake, Cyrille Regis, Tony Dobson, Chris Greenman, Peter Billing.
Centre row: Mick Kearns (Chief Scout), Neil Sillett (Assistant Physiotherapist), Kevin MacDonald, Steve Livingstone, Steve Ogrizovic, Brian Kilcline, Dean Kiely, Howard Clark, Dean Emerson, John Peacock (Football Development Officer), Terry Paine (Youth Team Coach).
Front row: David Smith, Greg Downs, David Speedie, Mick Coop (Reserve Team Coach), John Sillett (Team Manager), George Dalton (Physiotherapist), Michael Gynn, Lloyd McGrath, Dougie McGuire.

Division 1   **COVENTRY CITY**

Highfield Road Stadium, King Richard Street, Coventry CV2 4FW. Telephone Coventry (0203) 257171.

Telex: 312132, answer back code COV AFC. Fax No. 0203 630318.

Ground capacity; 26,218.

Record attendance: 51,455 v Wolverhampton W, Division 2, 29 April, 1967.

Record receipts: £177,271.55 v Nottingham F, Littlewoods Cup, Semi final, 2nd leg, 25 February, 1990.

Pitch measurements: 112yd × 76yd.

Life President: Derrick H. Robbins.

Chairman: J. Poynton. *Vice-chairman:* E. J. Stocker OBE.

Directors: M. F. French FCA, J. F. W. Reason, D. W. Richardson.

Managing Director: G. W. Curtis.

Secretary: G. P. Hover.

Team Manager: John Sillett. *Coach:* Dixie McNeil. *Physio:* G. Dalton.

Year Formed: 1883. *Turned Professional:* 1893. *Ltd Co:* 1907.

Former Names: 1883–98 Singers FC; 1898 Coventry City FC.

Club Nickname: 'Sky Blues'.

Previous Grounds: Binley Rd 1883–87, Stoke Rd 1887–99, Highfield Rd 1899–.

Record League Victory: 9-0 v Bristol C, Division 3(S), 28 April 1934 – Pearson; Brown, Bisby; Perry, Davidson, Frith; White (2), Lauderdale. Bourton (5), Jones (2), Lake.

Record Cup Victory: 7-0 v Scunthorpe U, FA Cup, 1st rd, 24 November 1934 – Pearson; Brown, Bisby; Mason, Davidson, Boileau; Birtley (2), Lauderdale (2), Bourton (1), Jones (1), Liddle (1).

Record Defeat: 2-10 v Norwich C, Division 3(S), 15 March, 1930.

Most League Points (2 for a win): 60, Division 4, 1958–59 and Division 3, 1963–64.

Most League Points (3 for a win): 63, Division 1, 1986–87.

Most League Goals: 108, Division 3(S), 1931–32.

Highest League Scorer in Season: Clarrie Bourton, 49, Division 3(S), 1931–32.

Most League Goals in Total Aggregate: Clarrie Bourton, 171, 1931–37.

Most Capped Player: Dave Clements, 21 (48), Northern Ireland.

Most League Appearances: George Curtis, 486, 1956–70.

Record Transfer Fee Received: £1,250,000 from Nottingham F for Ian Wallace, July 1980.

Record Transfer Fee Paid: £900,000 to Dundee U for Kevin Gallacher, January 1990.

Football League Record: 1919 Elected to Division 2; 1925–26 Division 3(N); 1926–36 Division 3(S); 1936–52 Division 2; 1952–58 Division 3(S); 1958–59 Division 4; 1959–64 Division 3; 1964–67 Division 2; 1967– Division 1.

Honours: Football League: Division 1 best season: 6th, 1969–70; Division 2 – Champions 1966–67; Division 3 – Champions 1963–64; Division 3(S) – Champions 1935–36; Runners-up 1933–34. Division 4 – Runners-up 1958–59. *FA Cup:* Winners 1986–87. *Football League Cup* best season: Semi-final 1980–81; 1989–90. **European Competitions:** *European Fairs Cup:* 1970–71.

Colours: Sky blue and white striped shirts, navy blue shorts, sky blue stockings. **Change colours:** All yellow.

COVENTRY CITY 1989–90 LEAGUE RECORD

Match No.	Date		Venue	Opponents	Result		H/T Score	Lg. Pos.	Goalscorers	Atten- dance
1	Aug	19	H	Everton	W	2-0	0-0	—	Bannister, Speedie	17,981
2		22	A	Arsenal	L	0-2	0-0	—		33,886
3		26	A	Crystal Palace	W	1-0	1-0	4	Kilcline	11,122
4		30	H	Manchester C	W	2-1	0-1	—	Gynn, Smith	16,111
5	Sept	9	A	Millwall	L	1-4	0-3	4	Smith	12,062
6		16	A	Luton T	W	1-0	1-0	3	Bannister	11,152
7		23	A	Chelsea	L	0-1	0-1	6		18,247
8		30	A	Sheffield W	D	0-0	0-0	7		15,054
9	Oct	14	H	Nottingham F	L	0-2	0-1	8		15,722
10		21	H	Manchester U	L	1-4	0-2	11	Drinkell	19,605
11		28	A	Charlton Ath	D	1-1	0-1	12	Speedie	6149
12	Nov	4	A	Liverpool	W	1-0	0-0	9	Regis	36,433
13		11	H	Southampton	W	1-0	0-0	7	Drinkell	12,151
14		18	A	Aston Villa	L	1-4	1-2	10	Gynn	22,803
15		25	H	Norwich C	W	1-0	0-0	6	Regis	11,999
16	Dec	2	A	Everton	L	0-2	0-1	9		21,171
17		9	H	Arsenal	L	0-1	0-0	10		16,255
18		16	H	Wimbledon	W	2-1	1-1	8	Borrows (pen), Curle (og)	8308
19		26	A	QPR	D	1-1	0-1	9	Speedie	9889
20		30	A	Derby Co	L	1-4	0-2	11	Speedie	17,011
21	Jan	1	H	Tottenham H	D	0-0	0-0	11		19,559
22		13	H	Crystal Palace	W	1-0	0-0	11	Speedie	10,858
23		20	A	Manchester C	L	0-1	0-0	12		24,345
24	Feb	3	H	Chelsea	W	3-2	2-1	9	Livingstone, McAllister (og), Regis	15,243
25		17	H	Millwall	W	3-1	2-1	7	Smith, Livingstone 2	10,981
26	Mar	4	H	Aston Villa	W	2-0	0-0	—	Drinkell, Smith	17,891
27		7	A	Luton T	L	2-3	0-1	—	Drinkell, Regis	8244
28		10	A	Nottingham F	W	4-2	2-0	6	Gallacher, Speedie 2, Drinkell	18,750
29		14	A	Norwich C	D	0-0	0-0	—		13,673
30		17	H	Sheffield W	L	1-4	1-1	6	Gynn	13,339
31		24	H	Charlton Ath	L	1-2	1-0	8	Gallacher	9997
32		31	A	Manchester U	L	0-3	0-2	9		39,172
33	Apr	7	H	Derby Co	W	1-0	0-0	8	Wright (og)	11,157
34		14	A	Tottenham H	L	2-3	2-1	9	Smith, Speedie	23,917
35		16	H	QPR	D	1-1	1-1	10	Smith	10,039
36		21	A	Wimbledon	D	0-0	0-0	10		4086
37		28	A	Southampton	L	0-3	0-2	11		16,359
38	May	5	H	Liverpool	L	1-6	1-3	12	Gallacher	23,204

Final League Position: 12

GOALSCORERS

League (39): Speedie 8, Smith 6, Drinkell 5, Regis 4, Gallacher 3, Gynn 3, Livingstone 3, Bannister 2, Borrows 1 (pen), Kilcline 1, own goals 3.
Littlewoods Cup (12): Livingstone 5, Drinkell 2, Downs 1, Kilcline 1 (pen), MacDonald 1, Regis 1, Speedie 1.
FA Cup (0).

Ogrizovic	Borrows	Dobson	Emerson	Kilcline	Peake	Gynn	Speedie	Regis	Bannister	Smith	McGuire	MacDonald	Waugh	Livingstone	Clark	Middleton L	Downs	Thompson	McGrath	Drinkell	Billing	Gallacher	Edwards	Middleton C	Titterton	Match No.
1	2	3	4	5	6	7	8	9	10	11																1
1	2	3	4	5	6	7	8	9	10*	11	12															2
1	2	3	4	5	6	7	8	9	10	11																3
1	2	3	4	5	6	7	8	9	10	11																4
1†	2	3	4	5	6	7*	8	9	10	11	12	14														5
	2	3	4	5	6	7	8	9†	10	11*	12		1	14												6
1	2	3	4*		6	7	8		10	11		9			5	12										7
1	2	3			6	7†	8*		10	11		4		9	12	5	14									8
1	2	3†		5	6	12	8	9	10*	11		4			14		7									9
1	2			5	6	12	8	9		11†		4*			14	3		7	10							10
1	2				6	12	8	9		11		4*			3		7	10	5							11
1	2				6		8	9		11		4			3		7	10	5							12
1	2				6	7	8	9		11		4*			12	3		10	5							13
1	2	3			6	7	8	9*12		11†		4		14				10	5							14
1	2				6	7	8	9		11		4			3			10	5							15
1	2	8	6		7		9			11†		4*		14	3	12		10	5							16
1	2	6	8				9			11		4			3		7	10	5							17
1	2	6	8		5		9			11		4			3		7	10								18
1	2	6	8		5	9				11		4			3		7	10								19
1	2	6	10*		5		8	12		11	14	4†			3			9	7							20
1	2				6	10	8	12		11		3			9		7*	5								21
1	2				6	7	8	9	10*	11		12			3		4	5								22
1	2	3			6	7	8	9		11		10		12	4*			5								23
1	2	12			6		8	9		11		4*		10	3			5	7							24
1	2	4		5	6		8	9		11		10			3			7								25
1	2	3		5	6	4	8	9		11		10*			12			7								26
1	2	5*			6	4	8	9		11		3			10	12	7									27
1	2	3			6	4	8	9		11		10			5		7									28
1	2	3			6	4	8	9		11		10			5		7									29
1	2	3*			6	4	8	9†		11	14	10			5		7	12								30
1	2	3*			6	4	8	9		11†	14	10			5		7	12								31
1	2	12			6	4	8	9		11	14	10†	5*		7		3									32
1	2	5			6	4	8	9		11		10					7	3								33
1	2	5			6	4*	8	9		11		10					7	3	12							34
1	2	5			6		8	9*		11	4	12	10				7	3								35
1	2	5			6			9		11	4	8			10		7	3								36
1	2	5			6	4	8		11	9					10	12	7	3*								37
1		3†			6	4	8	9		11	12		2		5	10*	7						14			38
37	37	28	12	11	33	31	32	32	10	37	1	19	1	6	5	—	16	—	12	21	16	15	6	—	—	

+2s (Dobson) · +3s (Peake) · +2s (Gynn) · +1s (Speedie) · +3s3s (MacDonald/Waugh) · +7s (Clark) · +4s2s · +1s +1s +1s +1s +2s · +2s1s +1s

COVENTRY CITY

Player and Position	Ht	Wt	Birth Date	Place	Source	Clubs	League App	Gls
Goalkeepers								
Steve Ogrizovic	6 5	15 00	12 9 57	Mansfield	ONRYC	Chesterfield	16	—
						Liverpool	4	—
						Shrewsbury T	84	—
						Coventry C	241	1
Keith Waugh	6 1	13 00	27 10 56	Sunderland	Apprentice	Sunderland	—	—
						Peterborough U	195	—
						Sheffield U	99	—
						Cambridge U (loan)	4	—
						Bristol C (loan)	3	—
						Bristol C	167	—
						Coventry C	1	—
Defenders								
Peter Billing	6 2	12 07	24 10 64	Liverpool	S Liverpool	Everton	1	—
						Crewe Alex	88	1
						Coventry C	18	—
Martyn Booty	5 8	12 01	30 5 71	Kirby Muxloe	Trainee	Coventry C	—	—
Brian Borrows	5 10	10 12	20 12 60	Liverpool	Amateur	Everton	27	—
						Bolton W	95	—
						Coventry C	190	3
Howard Clark	5 11	11 01	19 9 68	Coventry	Apprentice	Coventry C	18	1
Tony Dobson	6 1	12 10	5 2 69	Coventry	Apprentice	Coventry C	48	—
Greg Downs*	5 9	10 07	13 12 58	Carlton	Apprentice	Norwich C	169	7
						Torquay U (loan)	1	1
						Coventry C	146	4
Paul Edwards	5 11	11 00	25 12 63	Birkenhead	Altrincham	Crewe Alex	86	6
						Coventry C	8	—
Chris Greenman	5 10	11 06	22 12 68	Bristol	School	Coventry C	—	—
Tony Harwood	5 11	13 11	20 12 70	Chatham	Trainee	Coventry C	—	—
Brian Kilcline	6 2	12 00	7 5 62	Nottingham	Apprentice	Notts Co	158	9
						Coventry C	159	25
Lee Middleton	5 9	11 09	10 9 70	Nuneaton	Trainee	Coventry C	2	—
Trevor Peake	6 0	12 09	6 7 57	Nuneaton	Nuneaton Bor	Lincoln C	171	7
						Coventry C	240	5
Andrew Pearce			20 4 66	Bradford	Halesowen	Coventry C	—	—
David Titterton§			25 9 71	Hatton	Trainee	Coventry C	1	—
Midfield								
Dean Emerson	5 10	11 07	27 12 62	Salford	Local	Stockport Co	156	7
						Rotherham U	55	8
						Coventry C	69	—
Mick Gynn	5 5	10 10	19 8 61	Peterborough	Apprentice	Peterborough U	156	33
						Coventry C	163	19
Lee Hurst	6 0	11 09	21 9 70	Nuneaton	Trainee	Coventry C	—	—
Kevin MacDonald	6 1	12 06	22 12 60	Inverness	Inverness Caley	Leicester C	138	8
						Liverpool	40	1
						Leicester C (loan)	3	—
						Rangers (loan)	3	—
						Coventry C	22	—
Lloyd McGrath	5 9	10 06	24 2 65	Birmingham	Apprentice	Coventry C	124	3
David Smith	5 8	10 02	29 3 68	Gloucester		Coventry C	88	13
Forwards								
Kevin Drinkell	5 11	12 06	18 8 60	Grimsby	Apprentice	Grimsby T	270	89
						Norwich C	121	50
						Rangers	36	12
						Coventry C	22	5
Kevin Gallacher	5 7	9 11	23 11 66	Clydebank	Duntocher BC	Dundee U	131	27
						Coventry C	15	3

COVENTRY CITY

Foundation: Workers at Singer's cycle factory formed a club in 1883. The first success of Singers' FC was to win the Birmingham Junior Cup in 1891 and this led in 1894 to their election to the Birmingham and District League. Four years later they changed their name to Coventry City and joined the Southern League in 1908 at which time they were playing in blue and white quarters.

First Football League game: 28 August, 1920, Division 2, v Rotherham C (a) W 3-2 – Mitchell; Chaplin, Laurence; Fenwick, Hanney, Hadley (1); Dougall, Mercer (1), Parker, Nash, Gibson (1).

Managers (and Secretary-managers)
H. R. Buckle 1909–10, Robert Wallace 1910–13*, Frank Scott-Walford 1913–15, William Clayton 1917–19, H. Pollitt 1919–20, Albert Evans 1920–24, Jimmy Kerr 1924–28, James McIntyre 1928–31, Harry Storer 1931–45, Dick Bayliss 1945–47, Billy Frith 1947–48, Harry Storer 1948–53, Jack Fairbrother 1953–54, Charlie Elliott 1954–55, Jesse Carver 1955–56, Harry Warren 1956–57, Billy Frith 1957–61, Jimmy Hill 1961–67, Noel Cantwell 1967–72, Bob Dennison 1972–81 (became GM), Dave Sexton 1981–83, Bobby Gould 1983–84, Don Mackay 1985–86, George Curtis 1986–87 (became MD), John Sillett 1987–   .

Player and Position	Ht	Wt	Birth Date	Place	Source	Clubs	League App	Gls
Steve Livingstone	6 1	12 07	8 9 69	Middlesbrough	Trainee	Coventry C	21	3
Doug McGuire	5 8	11 00	6 9 67	Bathgate	Celtic BC	Celtic	2	—
						Sunderland (loan)	1	—
						Coventry C	4	—
Craig Middleton	5 9	11 00	10 9 70	Nuneaton	Trainee	Coventry C	1	—
Cyrille Regis	6 0	13 06	9 2 58	Mariapousoula	Hayes	WBA	237	82
						Coventry C	204	43
David Speedie	5 7	11 00	20 2 60	Glenrothes	Amateur	Barnsley	23	—
						Darlington	88	21
						Chelsea	162	47
						Coventry C	104	28
Keith Thompson	5 9	11 02	24 4 65	Birmingham	Apprentice	Coventry C	12	—
						Wimbledon (loan)	3	—
						Northampton T (loan)	10	1
				Oviedo		Coventry C	10	1

Trainees
Barefield, Trevor P; Bickley, Jason L; Bufton, Warren R; Dickson, Darren M; Flemings, Terence M; French, Alun K; Jenkins, Matthew; Kirk, Nicholas T; Knight, Steven J; Moore, Lee; Shepherd, Matthew J; Storer, Darran; Titterton, David S.J; Upton, Richard M; Young, Boyd.

Associated Schoolboys
Carmichael, David; Chadwick, Luke D; O'Brien, Paul W; Smith, Darren W.

Associated Schoolboys who have accepted the club's offer of a Traineeship/Contract
Carr, Gerald J; Davies, Martin L; Procter, David A.O; Smith, Ricky; Stephenson, Michael J.

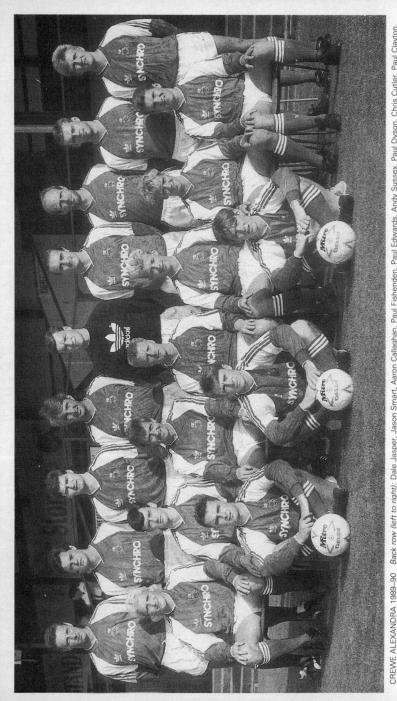

CREWE ALEXANDRA 1989–90 *Back row (left to right):* Dale Jasper, Jason Smart, Aaron Callaghan, Paul Fishenden, Paul Edwards, Andy Sussex, Paul Dyson, Chris Cutler, Paul Clayton. *Centre row:* Mark Gardiner, Aidan Murphy, Kenny Swain, Paul R. Edwards, Steve Walters, Rob Jones, Graham Easter. *Front row:* Rob Edwards, Craig Hignett, Colin Rose.

Division 3　　　　　**CREWE ALEXANDRA**

Football Ground, Gresty Rd, Crewe. Telephone Crewe (0270) 213014.

Ground capacity: 7200.

Record attendance: 20,000 v Tottenham H, FA Cup 4th rd, 30 Jan, 1960.

Record receipts: £24,556 v Chelsea, FA Cup 3rd rd replay, 10 January, 1990.

Pitch measurements: 112yd × 74yd.

President: N. Rowlinson.

Chairman: J. Bowler. *Vice-Chairman:*

Directors: K. Potts, H. Smith, D. Rowlinson, R. Clayton, J. McMillan, J. McMillan.

Manager: Dario Gradi. *Coach/Assistant Manager:* Kenny Swain.

Secretary: Mrs Gill Palin.

Physio: Craig Simmons.

Year Formed: 1877. *Turned Professional:* 1893. *Ltd Co.:* 1892.

Club Nickname: 'Railwaymen'.

Record League Victory: 8-0 v Rotherham U, Division 3 (N), 1st October 1932 – Foster; Pringle, Dawson; Ward, Keenor (1), Turner (1); Gillespie, Swindells (1), McConnell (2), Deacon (2), Weale (1).

Record Cup Victory: 5-0 v Druids, FA Cup, 1st rd, 15 October 1887 – Hicton; Conde, Cope; Bayman, Halfpenny, Osborne (1); Pearson, Payne (1), Price (1), Tinsley, Ellis. (2 scorers unknown.)

Record Defeat: 2-13 v Tottenham H, FA Cup 4th rd replay, 3 February, 1960.

Most League Points (2 for a win): 59, Division 4, 1962–63.

Most League Points (3 for a win): 78, Division 4, 1988–89.

Most League Goals: 95, Division 3 (N), 1931–32.

Highest League Scorer in Season: Terry Harkin, 35, Division 4, 1964–65.

Most League Goals in Total Aggregate: Bert Swindells. 126, 1928–37.

Most Capped Player: Bill Lewis. 12 (30), Wales.

Most League Appearances: Tommy Lowry, 436, 1966–78.

Record Transfer Fee Received: £300,000 from Coventry C for Paul Edwards, March 1990.

Record Transfer Fee Paid: £80,000 to Barnsley for Darren Foreman, March 1990.

Football League Record: 1892 Original Member of Division 2; 1896 Failed re-election; 1921 Re-entered Division 3 (N); 1958–63 Division 4; 1963–64 Division 3; 1964–68 Division 4; 1968–69 Division 3; 1969–89 Division 4; 1989– Division 3.

Honours: Football League: Division 2 best season; 10th, 1892–93. *FA Cup* best season: semi-final 1888. *Football League Cup* best season: 3rd rd. 1974–75, 1975–76, 1978–79.

Colours: Red shirts, white shorts, red stockings. **Change colours:** Blue shirts, white or blue shorts, white stockings.

CREWE ALEXANDRA 1989–90 LEAGUE RECORD

Match No.	Date	Venue	Opponents	Result		H/T Score	Lg. Pos.	Goalscorers	Atten-dance
1	Aug 19	A	Birmingham C	L	0-3	0-2	—		10,447
2	25	H	Reading	D	1-1	1-0	—	Sussex (pen)	3,311
3	Sept 2	A	Chester C	L	1-2	1-0	22	Clayton	2170
4	9	H	Fulham	L	2-3	0-0	23	Sussex, Clayton	3301
5	16	A	Blackpool	W	3-1	2-0	18	Sussex, Edwards P R, Gardiner	4722
6	23	H	Northampton T	W	2-1	1-1	17	Dyson 2	3165
7	26	H	Brentford	L	2-3	1-1	—	Gardiner, Sussex	3496
8	30	H	Shrewsbury T	D	0-0	0-0	18		5118
9	Oct 7	A	Swansea C	L	2-3	2-1	20	Hignett, Fishenden	3847
10	14	H	Bolton W	D	2-2	2-0	20	Clayton, Callaghan	4284
11	17	A	Preston NE	D	0-0	0-0	—		7485
12	21	H	Rotherham U	D	0-0	0-0	20		3647
13	27	A	Tranmere R	D	1-1	0-0	—	Murphy	9020
14	31	H	Bristol C	L	0-1	0-1	—		3554
15	Nov 4	A	Wigan Ath	L	0-1	0-1	22		2727
16	10	H	Mansfield T	W	2-1	1-1	—	Fishenden, Cutler	3333
17	25	A	Bury	W	3-0	0-0	16	Cutler 2, Walters	3637
18	Dec 2	H	Cardiff C	D	1-1	0-1	18	Fishenden	3393
19	15	H	Bristol R	W	1-0	0-0	—	Swain	3473
20	26	A	Walsall	D	1-1	0-1	14	Fishenden	5693
21	30	A	Leyton Orient	L	1-2	0-2	17	Fishenden	3773
22	Jan 1	H	Notts Co	W	1-0	0-0	14	Clayton	4786
23	13	A	Reading	D	1-1	0-1	17	Hignett	4645
24	20	H	Birmingham C	L	0-2	0-0	19		4681
25	27	A	Fulham	D	1-1	0-0	19	Smart	3915
26	Feb 10	H	Blackpool	W	2-0	1-0	15	Hignett, Fishenden	3978
27	13	H	Chester C	D	0-0	0-0	—		4260
28	17	A	Cardiff C	D	0-0	0-0	16		2086
29	24	H	Bury	W	2-1	1-0	14	Sussex 2	3998
30	Mar 3	A	Huddersfield T	W	1-0	0-0	13	Gardiner	5933
31	6	H	Shrewsbury T	D	1-1	1-1	—	Sussex	4318
32	10	A	Brentford	W	2-0	1-0	10	Callaghan, Hignett	5815
33	13	H	Huddersfield T	W	3-0	1-0	—	Sussex, Hignett, Gardiner	4384
34	17	H	Swansea C	D	1-1	1-0	10	Murphy	3898
35	20	A	Bolton W	D	0-0	0-0	—		7241
36	24	H	Preston NE	W	1-0	0-0	9	Joseph	4531
37	31	A	Rotherham U	W	3-1	1-1	8	Hignett, Smart, Joseph	5613
38	Apr 6	H	Tranmere R	D	2-2	0-1	—	Cutler, Hignett	6900
39	10	A	Bristol C	L	1-4	0-3	—	Murphy	13,800
40	14	A	Notts Co	L	0-2	0-1	10		6403
41	16	H	Walsall	W	3-1	1-0	9	Foreman 3	4289
42	21	H	Bristol R	D	1-1	0-0	10	Cutler	7250
43	24	H	Leyton Orient	L	0-1	0-1	—		3808
44	28	A	Mansfield T	L	1-2	0-1	12	McKearney	3071
45	30	A	Northampton T	L	1-3	1-2	—	Hignett	2622
46	May 5	H	Wigan Ath	W	3-2	1-1	12	Gardiner 2, Sussex	3389

Final League Position: 12

GOALSCORERS

League (56): Sussex 9 (1 pen), Hignett 8, Fishenden 6, Gardiner 6, Cutler 5, Clayton 4, Foreman 3, Murphy 3, Callaghan 2, Dyson 2, Joseph 2, Smart 2, Edwards P R 1, McKearney 1, Swain 1, Walters 1.
Littlewoods Cup (6): Gardiner 2, Clayton 1, Dyson 1, Murphy 1, Sussex 1.
FA Cup (6): Sussex 3, Cutler 1, Murphy 1 (pen), Walters 1.

Edwards, P	Swain	Edwards, P R	Callaghan	Dyson	Clayton	Jasper	Murphy	Sussex	Gardiner	Fishenden	Rees	Walters	Cutler	Smart	Hignett	Edwards, R	Disley	McKearney	Greygoose	Rennie	Joseph	Easter	Foreman	Gayle	Jones	Naylor	Curran	Gunn	Match No.
1	2	3	4	5	6*	7	8	9	10	11				12															1
	2	3	4	5	6	7	8	9	10	11*	1	12																	2
	2	3	4	5	6	7	8	9*	10	12	1	11																	3
	2	3	4	5	6	7	8*	9	10		1	11	12																4
	2	3	4	5	6	7	8†	9	10*		1	11	12	14															5
	2	3		5	6	7	8	9	10		1	11*	12	4															6
	2	3		5	6	7	8	9	10		1	11*	12	4															7
1	2	3	14	5	12	7	8	9	10†			11	6*	4															8
1	2	3	12	5	8	7		9		10†		11		4	6*	14													9
1		3	2	5	10	7	8	12		11*			6	4	9														10
1		3	6*	5		7	2	9		11†		10	4	8	14			12											11
1		3	6	5		7	2	9		11†		10*	4	8	14			12											12
1	3		6	5	10	7	2	9*				11†	12	4	8			14											13
1	3		6†	5	10*	7	2	9		14		11	12	4	8														14
	3			5	10*	7	2	9		11†		6	12	4	8				1	14									15
	3		6		14	7*	2	9†		11		10	12	4	8				1	5									16
	3	12	6	5		7	2	9				11	10	4	8*				1										17
	2		6	5	14	7*	8	9†		11		12	10	4				3	1										18
	2	3	6	5			8	9		11		10		4					1		7*12								19
2*	3	6	5		14	8	9		11†			10	12	4					1		7								20
	2	3	6	5†		10*	8	9		11			12	4	14				1		7								21
	2	3	6	5	11		8					10	9	4					1		7								22
	2	3	6	5	9	11	8	12					10†	4	14				1		7*								23
	2	3	6	5		9	8					11	10	4	12				1		7*								24
	2	3	6*	5		7†	8			10	11	9	12	4	14				1										25
	2	3	6	5		7	8			10	11	12		4	9*				1										26
	2	3	6	5*		7		12	10	11		8		4	9†				1				14						27
	2	3	6	5		7		12	10	11		8		4	9*				1										28
	2	3	5			6		9	10†	11		7	12	4	8*14				1										29
	2	3	6			7			5	10	11*	8	12	4	9				1										30
	2	3	6			7			5	10		8	11	4	9				1										31
	2	3	6			7			5	10		8	11*	4	9†				1				14	12					32
	2	3	6			7	14		5	10		8	11*	4	9†				1					12					33
	2		6			7		5				8	11	4	9*		3		1				10†12	14					34
	2		5			7	8					10	11	4	6		3*		1				9	12					35
	2		5			7	8					10	11	4	6		3		1		12		9*						36
	2		5			7	8					10	11	4	6		3		1		12		9*						37
	2		5			7	8	10†				11*		4	6		3		1		12		9	14					38
	2		5			7	8	10				11†		4	6		3		1		12		9*	14					39
	2	5				7	8	10†				11*		4	6		3		1		12		9	14					40
	2	11	5				8	12						4	6*		3		1		10†14		9	7					41
	2		5				7	8	10*14			12		4	6		3		1				9	11†					42
	2		5				7	12	10			11†		4	6		3		1			14	9*	8					43
	2		5*12				7		10†			11		4	6		3		1		7		9	8	14				44
	2		5*				12	10				11†		4	6		3		1		7		9	8	14				45
	2		14				12	10				11		4	6		3†		1		7*			8		5	9		46
8	43	27	38	30	15	39	34	26	24	18	6	27	24	40	30	1	—	14	32	1	9	—	12	—	6	—	1	1	
	+	+	+	+	+	+	+	+	+	+		+	+	+	+	+	+	+		+	+	+	+		+		+	+	
1s	3s	1s	3s	1s	1s	7s	2s	2s				3s	14s	1s	5s		3s	1s		3s		1s	7s	3s	2s	1s	5s	2s	

Littlewoods Cup	First Round	Chester C (h)	4-0
		(a)	2-0
	Second Round	Bournemouth (h)	0-1
		(a)	0-0
FA Cup	First Round	Congleton (h)	2-0
	Second Round	Bishop Auckland (h)	1-1
		(a)	2-0
	Third Round	Chelsea (a)	1-1
		(h)	0-2

CREWE ALEXANDRA

Player and Position	Ht	Wt	Birth Date	Place	Source	Clubs	League App	Gls
Goalkeepers								
Paul Edwards†	5 11	11 08	22 2 65	Liverpool	St Helens T	Crewe Alex	18	—
Dean Greygoose	5 11	11 05	18 12 64	Thetford	Apprentice	Cambridge U	26	—
						Orient (loan)	—	—
						Lincoln C (loan)	6	—
						Orient	1	—
						Crystal Palace	—	—
						Crewe Alex	111	—
Defenders								
Aaron Callaghan	5 11	11 02	8 10 66	Dublin	Apprentice	Stoke C	7	—
						Crewe Alex (loan)	8	—
						Oldham Ath	16	2
						Crewe Alex	82	6
Chris Curran			6 1 71	Manchester	Trainee	Crewe Alex	1	—
Paul Dyson‡	6 2	13 06	27 12 59	Birmingham	Apprentice	Coventry C	140	5
						Stoke C	106	5
						WBA	64	5
						Darlington	12	3
						Crewe Alex	31	2
Wakeley Gage‡	6 4	13 07	5 5 58	Northampton	Desborough T	Northampton T	218	17
						Chester C	17	1
						Peterborough U	73	1
						Crewe Alex	54	1
Rob Jones	5 11	11 00	5 11 71	Wrexham	Trainee	Crewe Alex	35	1
David McKearney	5 10	11 02	20 6 68	Crosby		Bolton W	—	—
						Crewe Alex	17	1
Paul Rennie§			26 10 71	Nantwich	Trainee	Crewe Alex	2	—
Jason Smart	6 0	12 00	15 2 69	Rochdale	Trainee	Rochdale	117	4
						Crewe Alex	41	2
Kenny Swain	5 9	11 07	28 1 52	Birkenhead	Wycombe W	Chelsea C	119	26
						Aston Villa	148	2
						Nottingham F	112	2
						Portsmouth	113	
						WBA (loan)	7	1
						Crewe Alex	84	1
Midfield								
Martin Disley			24 6 71	Ormskirk		Crewe Alex	1	—
Graham Easter†	5 7	10 07	26 9 69	Epsom	Trainee	WBA	—	—
						Huddersfield T	—	—
						Crewe Alex	3	—
Craig Hignett	5 10	10 08	12 1 70	Whiston		Crewe Alex	36	8
Dale Jasper	6 0	11 07	14 1 64	Croydon	Apprentice	Chelsea	10	—
						Brighton & HA	49	6
						Crewe Alex	79	1
Terry Milligan‡	5 10	9 05	10 1 66	Manchester	Apprentice New Zealand	Manchester C	—	—
						Oldham Ath	—	—
						Crewe Alex	77	5
Aidan Murphy	5 10	10 10	17 9 67	Manchester	Apprentice	Manchester U	—	—
						Lincoln C (loan)	2	—
						Oldham Ath (loan)	—	—
						Crewe Alex	90	10
Colin Rose	5 8	10 09	22 1 72	Winsford	Trainee	Crewe Alex	—	—
Warren Thompson‡			24 11 70	Manchester	York C§	Crewe Alex	—	—
Steve Walters	5 10	11 08	9 1 72	Plymouth	Trainee	Crewe Alex	53	2
Forwards								
Paul Clayton	5 11	11 03	4 1 65	Dunstable	Apprentice	Norwich C	13	—
						Darlington	22	3
						Crewe Alex	38	10
Chris Cutler	5 11	11 00	7 4 64	Manchester	Amateur	Bury	23	3
						Crewe Alex	140	24
Robert Edwards†	5 8	11 07	23 2 70	Manchester	Trainee	Crewe Alex	14	1

CREWE ALEXANDRA

Foundation: Crewe Alexandra played cricket and probably rugby before they decided to form a football club in 1877. Whether they took the name "Alexandra" from a pub where they held their meetings, or whether it was after Princess Alexandra, is a matter of conjecture. Crewe's first trophy was the Crewe and District Cup in 1887 and it is worth noting that they reached the semi-finals of the FA Cup the following year.

First Football League game: 3 September, 1892, Division 2, v Burton Swifts (a) L 1-7 – Hickton; Moore, Cope; Linnell, Johnson, Osborne; Bennett, Pearson (1), Bailey, Barnett, Roberts.

Managers (and Secretary-managers)
W. C. McNeill 1892–94*, J. G. Hall 1895–96*, 1897 R. Roberts* (1st team sec.), J. B. Bromerley 1898–1911* (continued as Hon. Sec. to 1925), Tom Bailey 1925–38, George Lillicrop 1938–44, Frank Hill 1944–48, Arthur Turner 1948–51, Harry Catterick 1951–53, Ralph Ward 1953–55, Maurice Lindley 1955–58, Harry Ware 1958–60, Jimmy McGuigan 1960–64, Ernie Tagg 1964–71 (continued as secretary to 1972), Dennis Viollet 1971, Jimmy Melia 1972–73, Ernie Tagg 1974, Harry Gregg 1975–78, Warwick Rimmer 1978–79, Tony Waddington 1979–81, Arfon Griffiths 1981–82, Peter Morris 1982–83, Dario Gradi 1983– .

Player and Position	Ht	Wt	Birth Date	Place	Source	Clubs	League App	Gls
Paul Fishenden	6 0	10 12	2 8 63	Hillingdon	Local	Wimbledon	75	25
						Fulham (loan)	3	—
						Millwall (loan)	3	—
						Orient (loan)	4	—
						Crewe Alex	81	25
Darren Foreman	5 10	10 08	12 2 68	Southampton		Barnsley	47	8
						Crewe Alex	14	3
Mark Gardiner	5 10	10 07	25 12 66	Cirencester	Apprentice	Swindon T	10	1
						Torquay U	49	4
						Crewe Alex	64	16
Andy Gayle*	5 8	11 02	17 9 70	Manchester	Trainee	Oldham Ath	1	—
						Crewe Alex	1	—
Andrew Gunn	6 0	12 01	2 2 71	Barking	Trainee	Watford	—	—
						Crewe Alex	1	—
Francis Joseph‡	5 10	12 00	6 3 60	Kilburn	Hillingdon B	Wimbledon	51	14
						Brentford	110	44
						Wimbledon (loan)	5	1
						Reading	11	2
						Bristol R (loan)	3	—
						Aldershot (loan)	10	2
						Sheffield U	13	3
						Gillingham	18	1
						Crewe Alex	16	2
Tony Naylor	5 8	10 08	29 3 67	Manchester	Droylsden	Crewe Alex	2	—
Tony Rigby			10 8 72	Ormskirk	Trainee	Crewe Alex	—	—
Andy Sussex	6 0	11 06	23 11 64	Enfield	Apprentice	Leyton Orient	144	17
						Crewe Alex	58	13

Trainees
Congerton, Lee D; Cullan, Mark; Evans, Simon J; Fallon, Marcus; Howard, Shane; Johansen, Benjamin R; Jones, Wayne; Reenie, Paul; Sorvel, Neil S; Stewart, Gareth P.N; Wall, Justin W; Watson, Nicholas; Williams, Philip P.

**Non-Contract
Easter, Graham P; Edwards, Paul; Edwards, Robert; Kelsey, Andrew.

Associated Schoolboys
Adebola, Dele; Byrne, Christopher; Ceradlo, Mark; Chapman, Iain A; Cox, Paul J; Dawson, Douglas A; Fairclough, Andrew; Frazer, Stewart A; Heron, Derek J; Lewis, John E; Meeson, Christopher A; Millward, Thomas P; Nichols, Matthew; Ouslem, Joseph A; Paul, Lee S; Rivers, Mark A; Tierney, Francis; Williams, Carwyn.

Associated Schoolboys who have accepted the club's offer of a Traineeship/Contract
Duffy, Christopher J; Garvey, Stephen H; Hughes, Anthony B; Jackson, Michael J; Keen, Ryan H; Maloney, Michael P; Rushton, Paul; Stevenson, Ashlyn R; Whalley, Gareth; Woodward, Andrew S.

**Non-Contract Players who are retained must be re-signed before they are eligible to play in League matches.

212

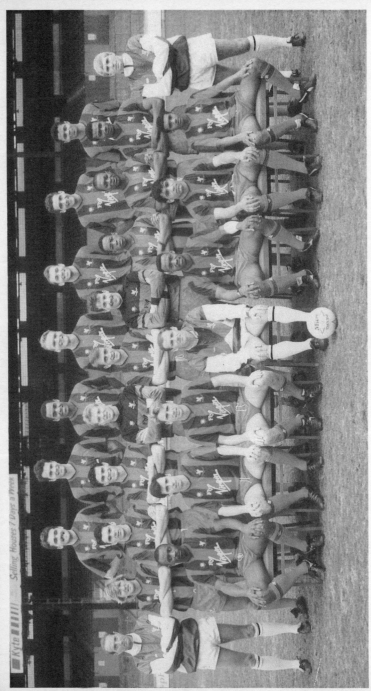

CRYSTAL PALACE 1989–90 *Back row (left to right):* Eddie McGoldrick, Dave Madden, Mark Bright, Geoff Thomas, Phil Barber, John Pemberton, John Salako.
Centre row: Alan Smith (Assistant Manager), Mark Dennis, Jeff Hopkins, Gary O'Reilly, Perry Suckling, Andy Thorn, Nigel Martyn, Ian Wright, Alex Dyer, Rudi Hedman.
Ian Branfoot (First Team Coach).
Front row: Garry Thompson, David Burke, Alan Pardew, Steve Coppell (Manager), Andy Gray, Richard Shaw, David Whyte.

Division 1   **CRYSTAL PALACE**

Selhurst Park, London SE25 6PU. Telephone 01-653 4462. Lottery Office: 01-771 9502. Souvenir Shop: 01-653 5584. Recorded Information: 01-771 5311. Clubcall: 0898 121145. Palace Ticket Line: 0898 121845. Palace Publications: 01-771 8299. Fax No: 01-771 5311.

Ground capacity: 31,439.

Record attendance: 51,482 v Burnley, Division 2, 11 May, 1979.

Record receipts: £179,511 v Liverpool, Division 1, 20 January, 1990.

Pitch measurements: 110yd × 74yd.

President: S. Stephenson.

Chairman: R. G. Noades.

Directors: R. Anderson, B. Coleman, A. S. C. Souza, G. Geraghty, S. Hume-Kendall, M. E. Lee, G. Lucking, P. H. N. Norman, K. A. Sinclair, B. O. Umunna.

Team Manager: Steve Coppell. *Assistant Manager:* Alan Smith. *Coach:* Ian Branfoot. *Physio:* David West.

Company Secretary: Alan Leather. *Club Secretary:* Mike Hurst. *Assistant Secretary:* Terry Byfield. *Club Accountant:* Douglas Miller.

Year Formed: 1905. *Turned Professional:* 1905. *Ltd Co.:* 1905.

Club Nickname: 'The Eagles'.

Club Sponsor: Virgin Atlantic.

Commercial Manager: Graham Drew.

Previous Grounds: 1905, Crystal Palace; 1915, Herne Hill; 1918, The Nest; 1924, Selhurst Park.

Record League Victory: 9-0 v Barrow, Division 4, 10 October 1959 – Rouse; Long, Noakes; Truett, Evans, McNichol; Gavin (1), Summersby (4 incl. 1p), Sexton, Byrne (2), Colfar (2).

Record Cup Victory: 7-0 v Luton T, FA Cup, 3rd rd (replay) 16 January 1929 – Callendar; Weatherby, Charlton; Hamilton (1), Wilde (1), Greener; Harry, Havelock (3), Griffiths (1), Butler (1), Clarke. 7-0 v Stockport C, League Cup, 2nd rd (1st leg), 4 September 1979 – Burridge; Hinshelwood, Sansom, Nicholas, Cannon, Gilbert, Murphy (1), Francis (1) (Walsh (2)), Swindlehurst, Flanagan (2), Hilaire (1).

Record Defeat: 0-9 v Liverpool, Division 1, 12 September, 1989.

Most League Points (2 for a win): 64, Division 4, 1960–61.

Most League Points (3 for a win): 81, Division 2, 1988–89.

Most League Goals: 110, Division 4, 1960–61.

Highest League Scorer in Season: Peter Simpson, 46, Division 3 (S), 1930-31.

Most League Goals in Total Aggregate: Peter Simpson, 154, 1930–36.

Most Capped Player: Paddy Mulligan, 14 (50), Eire; Ian Walsh, 14 (18), Wales; Peter Nicholas, 14 (65) Wales.

Most League Appearances: Jim Cannon, 571, 1973–88.

Record Transfer Fee Received: £800,000 (nett) from Arsenal for Kenny Sansom, August 1980.

Record Transfer Fee Paid: £1,000,000 to Bristol Rovers for Nigel Martyn, November 1989.

Football League Record: 1920 Original Members of Division 3; 1921–25 Division 2; 1925–58 Division 3 (S); 1958–61 Division 4; 1961–64 Division 3; 1964–69 Division 2; 1969–73 Division 1; 1973–74 Division 2; 1974–77 Division 3; 1977–79 Division 2; 1979–81 Division 1; 1981–89 Division 2; 1989– Division 1.

Honours: Football League: Division 1 best season; 13th 1979–80; Division 2 – Champions 1978–79; Runners-up 1968–69; Division 3 – Runners-up 1963–64; Division 3(S) – Champions 1920–21; Runners-up 1928–29, 1930–31, 1938–39; Division 4 – Runners-up 1960–61. *FA Cup* best season: Runners-up 1989–90. *Football League Cup* best season; 5th rd, 1968–69, 1970–71.

Colours: Red and blue shirts, red shorts, red stockings. **Change colours:** White shirts with red and blue diagonal stripe from left shoulder, white shorts with red and blue trimmings, white stockings with red and blue trimmings.

CRYSTAL PALACE 1989–90 LEAGUE RECORD

Match No.	Date	Venue	Opponents	Result		H/T Score	Lg. Pos.	Goalscorers	Attendance
1	Aug 19	A	QPR	L	0-2	0-0	—		16,161
2	22	H	Manchester U	D	1-1	0-1	—	Wright	22,423
3	26	H	Coventry C	L	0-1	0-1	19		11,122
4	Sept 9	A	Wimbledon	W	2-0	1-0	15	Thomas, Wright	12,116
5	12	A	Liverpool	L	0-9	0-3	—		35,779
6	16	A	Southampton	D	1-1	0-1	17	Hopkins	15,368
7	23	H	Nottingham F	W	1-0	0-0	12	Wright	12,899
8	30	H	Everton	W	2-1	2-0	9	Wright, Pardew	15,943
9	Oct 14	A	Derby Co	L	1-3	1-2	13	Pardew	14,585
10	21	H	Millwall	W	4-3	3-1	10	Wright 2, Bright 2	18,920
11	28	A	Aston Villa	L	1-2	0-0	13	Pardew	15,724
12	Nov 4	A	Manchester C	L	0-3	0-2	15		23,768
13	11	H	Luton T	D	1-1	1-0	15	Bright	11,346
14	18	H	Tottenham H	L	2-3	1-2	16	Bright 2	26,266
15	25	A	Sheffield W	D	2-2	1-0	16	Gray, Hopkins	17,227
16	Dec 2	H	QPR	L	0-3	0-2	18		12,784
17	9	A	Manchester U	W	2-1	1-1	16	Bright 2	33,514
18	16	A	Charlton Ath	W	2-1	2-0	12	Thorn, Bright	15,763
19	26	H	Chelsea	D	2-2	1-1	13	Wright, Pemberton	24,680
20	30	H	Norwich C	W	1-0	0-0	12	Wright	14,250
21	Jan 1	A	Arsenal	L	1-4	1-4	14	Pardew	38,711
22	13	A	Coventry C	L	0-1	0-0	14		10,858
23	20	H	Liverpool	L	0-2	0-1	15		29,807
24	Feb 3	A	Nottingham F	L	1-3	0-1	16	Salako	19,739
25	10	H	Southampton	W	3-1	1-0	14	Salako, Gray, Barber	13,363
26	24	H	Sheffield W	D	1-1	0-1	15	Bright	11,857
27	Mar 3	A	Tottenham H	W	1-0	0-0	15	Pardew	26,181
28	17	A	Everton	L	0-4	0-2	15		19,274
29	20	A	Derby Co	D	1-1	0-0	—	Gray	10,051
30	24	H	Aston Villa	W	1-0	1-0	15	Thompson	18,586
31	31	A	Millwall	W	2-1	1-0	15	Bright, Gray	13,332
32	Apr 4	A	Norwich C	L	0-2	0-2	—		12,640
33	14	H	Arsenal	D	1-1	0-1	16	Gray	28,094
34	16	A	Chelsea	L	0-3	0-1	16		16,132
35	21	H	Charlton Ath	W	2-0	0-0	15	Thompson, Bright	15,276
36	28	A	Luton T	L	0-1	0-0	16		10,369
37	May 2	A	Wimbledon	W	1-0	0-0	—	Bright	8209
38	5	H	Manchester C	D	2-2	2-0	15	Pardew, Gray	20,056

Final League Position: 15

GOALSCORERS

League (42): Bright 12, Wright 8, Gray 6, Pardew 6, Hopkins 2, Salako 2, Thompson 2, Barber 1, Pemberton 1, Thomas 1, Thorn 1.
Littlewoods Cup (4): Bright 1, Hopkins 1, Thomas 1, Wright 1.
FA Cup (15): Bright 2, Gray 2 (1 pen), O'Reilly 2, Thomas 2, Wright 2, Barber 1, Hopkins 1, Pardew 1, Salako 1, own goal 1.

Suckling	Pemberton	Burke	Gray	Hopkins	O'Reilly	McGoldrick	Thomas	Bright	Wright	Barber	Pardew	Dyer	Shaw	Madden	Hedman	Parkin	Dennis	Martyn	Salako	Thorn	Thompson	Match No.
1	2	3	4	5	6	7	8	9	10	11*	12											1
1	2	3	4	5	6	7	8	9	10	11												2
1	2	3	4	5	6	7	8	9	10	11												3
1	2	3	4	5	6	7	8	9	10		11											4
1	2	3	4	5	6	7	8	9	10		11											5
1	2	3	4	5	6	7	8	9	10		11											6
1		3	4	5		7	8	9	10		11		6	2								7
1		3	4	5		7	8	9	10	12	11		6*	2								8
1	2		4†	5		7	8	9	10	12	11		6*	3	14							9
1	2		4	5		7	8	9	10	12	11		6*	3								10
1	2		4	5			8	9	10	7	11		6	3								11
1	2		4	5		7	8	9	10	12	11		6*	3†	14							12
	2		4	5		7	8	9	10		11		6			1	3					13
	2		4	5	6	7		9	10		11		8*				3	1	12			14
	2		4	5	12	7	8	9	10*	6	11						3	1				15
2*			4	5	12	7†	8	9	10	6	11						3	1	14			16
	2		4*	5	6		8	9	10	12	11						3	1		7		17
	2		4	5	3	7		9	10	8	11							1		6		18
	2		4	5		7	12	9	10	8	11						3*	1		6		19
	2		4	5		7		9	10	8	11						3	1		6		20
	2		4	5		7	12	9	10	8	11*						3	1		6		21
	2	3		5	4*	12	8	9	10	7	11							1		6		22
	2	3		5		7	8	9	10*	4	11†	14						1	12	6		23
	2	3	4	5			8	9		10	11	7*						1	12	6		24
	2		4	5			8	9		7	11		3					1	10	6		25
	2		4	5			8	9		7	11		3					1	10	6		26
	2		4	5			8	9	12	7	11		3					1	10*	6		27
2*			4		5		8		10	7	11		3	12	14			1	9†	6		28
			4		5		8		10*	7	11		3	12	2			1	9	6		29
			4	5			8	9		7	11		3		2			1		6	10	30
	2		4	5			8	9*		7	11		3		6			1	12		10	31
	2		4	5			8	9		7	11		3		6*			1	12		10	32
	2		4	5			8	9		7	11		3		14			1	12†	6*	10	33
	2		4	5			8	9		7*	11		3	12	6†			1	14		10	34
	2		4	5			8	9		7*	11†		3	14	6			1	12		10	35
	2		4	5			8†	9		7	11*		3	14	6			1	12		10	36
	2						8	9		7	12		3	4	5			1	11*	6	10	37
	2†		4*	5	12			9		3	11		8	14				1	7	6	10	38
12	34	11	35	27	19+2s	20+2s	33+2s	36	25	25+1s	34+5s	10+2s	20	2+1s	8+6s	1+4s	8	25	7+10s	17	9	

Littlewoods Cup	Second Round	Leicester C (h)	1-2
		(a)	3-2
	Third Round	Nottingham F (h)	0-0
		(a)	0-5
FA Cup	Third Round	Portsmouth (h)	2-1
	Fourth Round	Huddersfield T (h)	4-0
	Fifth Round	Rochdale (h)	1-0
	Sixth Round	Cambridge U (a)	1-0
	Semi-final	Liverpool (at Villa Park)	4-3
	Final	Manchester U (at Wembley)	3-3
	Replay	(at Wembley)	0-1

CRYSTAL PALACE

Player and Position	Ht	Wt	Birth Date	Place	Source	Clubs	League App	Gls
Goalkeepers								
Nigel Martyn	6 2	14 00	11 8 66	St Austell	St Blazey	Bristol R	101	—
						Crystal Palace	25	—
Perry Suckling	6 1	11 02	12 10 55	Leyton	Apprentice	Coventry C	27	—
						Manchester C	39	—
						Crystal Palace	56	—
						West Ham U (loan)	6	—
Andrew Woodman	6 1	12 04	11 8 71	Denmark Hill	Trainee	Crystal Palace	—	—
Defenders								
David Burke	5 10	10 13	6 8 60	Liverpool	Apprentice	Bolton W	69	1
						Huddersfield T	189	3
						Crystal Palace	81	—
Mark Dennis	5 9	10 08	2 5 61	Streatham	Apprentice	Birmingham C	130	1
						Southampton	95	2
						QPR	28	—
						Crystal Palace	8	—
Rudi Hedman	6 3	12 00	16 11 64	London	Local	Colchester U	176	10
						Crystal Palace	17	—
						Leyton Orient (loan)	5	—
Jeff Hopkins	6 1	11 11	14 4 64	Swansea	Apprentice	Fulham	219	4
						Crystal Palace	70	2
Gary O'Reilly	5 11	12 00	21 3 61	Isleworth	Amateur	Tottenham H	45	—
						Brighton & HA	79	3
						Crystal Palace	70	2
John Pemberton	5 11	12 03	11 11 64	Oldham	Chadderton	Rochdale	1	—
						Crewe Alex	121	1
						Crystal Palace	78	2
Chris Powell	5 8	11 00	8 9 69	Lambeth	Trainee	Crystal Palace	3	—
						Aldershot (loan)	11	—
Richard Shaw	5 9	11 08	11 9 68	Brentford	Apprentice	Crystal Palace	38	—
						Hull C (loan)	4	—
Gareth Southgate	5 10	11 12	3 9 70	Watford	Trainee	Crystal Palace	—	—
Andy Thorn	6 0	11 05	12 11 66	Carshalton	Apprentice	Wimbledon	107	2
						Newcastle U	36	2
						Crystal Palace	17	1
Midfield								
Phil Barber	5 11	12 06	10 6 65	Tring	Aylesbury U	Crystal Palace	215	34
Darren Carr	5 7	10 04	4 11 69	Birmingham	Burton Alb	Crystal Palace	—	—
Andy Gray	5 11	13 03	22 2 64	Lambeth	Dulwich H	Crystal Palace	98	27
						Aston Villa	37	4
						QPR	11	2
						Crystal Palace	35	6
Mark Hone‡	6 1	12 00	31 3 68	Croydon		Crystal Palace	4	—
Adam Locke*	5 10	11 10	20 8 70	Croydon	Trainee	Crystal Palace	—	—
Eddie McGoldrick	5 10	12 00	30 4 65	London	Nuneaton	Northampton T	107	9
						Crystal Palace	43	—
David Madden*	6 0	11 03	6 1 63	London	Apprentice	Southampton	—	—
						Bournemouth (loan)	5	—
						Arsenal	2	—
						Charlton Ath	20	1
						Reading	9	1
						Crystal Palace	27	5
						Birmingham C (loan)	5	1
Ricky Newman	5 10	11 00	5 8 70	Guildford		Crystal Palace	—	—
Simon Osborn	5 10	11 04	19 1 72	New Addington	Trainee	Crystal Palace	—	—
Alan Pardew	5 10	11 00	18 7 61	Wimbledon	Yeovil	Crystal Palace	101	7
David Stevens	5 11	11 00	19 10 70	Plumstead	Trainee	Crystal Palace	—	—

CRYSTAL PALACE

Foundation: There was a Crystal Palace club as early as 1861 but the present organisation was born in 1905 after the formation of a club by the company that controlled the Crystal Palace (the building that is), had been rejected by the FA who did not like the idea of the Cup Final hosts running their own club. A separate company had to be formed and they had their home on the old Cup Final ground until 1915.

First Football League game: 28 August, 1920, Division 3, v Merthyr T (a) L 1-2 – Alderson; Little, Rhodes; McCracken, Jones, Feebury; Bateman, Conner, Smith, Milligan (1), Whibley.

Managers (and Secretary-managers)
John T. Robson 1905–07, Edmund Goodman 1907–25 (had been secretary since 1905 and afterwards continued in this position to 1933). Alec Maley 1925–27, Fred Maven 1927–30, Jack Tresadern 1930–35, Tom Bromilow 1935–36, R. S. Moyes 1936, Tom Bromilow 1936–39, George Irwin 1939–47, Jack Butler 1947–49, Ronnie Rooke 1949–50, Charlie Slade and Fred Dawes (joint managers) 1950–51, Laurie Scott 1951–54, Cyril Spiers 1954–58, George Smith 1958–60, Arthur Rowe 1960–63, Dick Graham 1963–66, Bert Head 1966–72 (continued as GM to 1973), Malcolm Allison 1973–76, Terry Venables 1976–80, Ernie Walley 1980, Malcolm Allison 1980–81, Dario Gradi 1981, Steve Kember 1981–82, Alan Mullery 1982–84, Dave Bassett 1984, Steve Coppell 1984– .

Player and Position	Ht	Wt	Birth Date	Place	Source	Clubs	League App	Gls
Geoff Thomas	5 10	10 07	5 8 64	Manchester	Local	Rochdale	11	1
						Crewe Alex	125	20
						Crystal Palace	98	12
Forwards								
Mark Bright	6 0	11 00	6 2 62	Stoke	Leek T	Port Vale	29	10
						Leicester C	42	6
						Crystal Palace	148	65
Alex Dyer	5 11	11 12	14 11 65	West Ham	Apprentice	Watford	—	—
						Blackpool	108	19
						Hull C	60	14
						Crystal Palace	17	2
Murray Jones	6 4	14 00	7 10 64	Bexley	Carshalton	Crystal Palace	—	—
John Salako	5 9	11 00	11 2 69	Nigeria	Trainee	Crystal Palace	80	2
						Swansea C (loan)	13	3
Garry Thompson	6 1	14 00	7 10 59	Birmingham	Apprentice	Coventry C	134	38
						WBA	91	39
						Sheffield W	36	7
						Aston Villa	55	17
						Watford	34	8
						Crystal Palace	9	2
David Whyte	5 9	10 06	20 4 71	Greenwich		Crystal Palace	—	—
Ian Wright	5 11	11 11	3 11 63	Woolwich	Greenwich B	Crystal Palace	179	69

Trainees
Brazier, Paul D; Corlett, Stuart A; Doe, Lawrence R; Glass, James R; Gordon, Dean D; Harding, Benjamin; Line, Simon J; Moralee, Jamie D; Myatt, John; Pepper, Mark J; Roberts, Carl; Rodger, Simon L; Thomas, Scott P.

Associated Schoolboys
Bevers, Gary D; Clark, Timothy C; Cripps, Paul; Edwards, Russell J; Finnan, Sean P; Fitzgerald, David; Hilderly, Clifford; Little, Glen; McLynn, Paul; Wade, Tom.

Associated Schoolboys who have accepted the club's offer of a Traineeship/Contract
Cutler, Scott S; Finman, Tony; Holman, Mark B; Oliva, Umberto; Rollison, Simon A; Watts, Grant.

218

DARLINGTON 1989–90 *Back row (left to right):* Mark Hine, David Corner, Keith Granger, Nigel Batch, Mark Prudhoe, Kevan Smith, Gary Coatsworth.
Centre row: Archie Stephens, Paul Emson, Paul Willis, Drew Coverdale, Jim Willis, John Borthwick, Gary Hyde.
Front row: Neil Robinson, Andy Toman, Frank Gray (Coach), Brian Little (Manager), Tony McAndrew (Youth Coach), David Cork, Les McJannet.

Division 4   **DARLINGTON**

Feethams Ground, Darlington. Telephone Darlington (0325) 465097, 467712. Commercial Dept. (0325) 481212.

Ground capacity: 10,932.

Record attendance: 21,023 v Bolton W, League Cup 3rd rd, 14 Nov, 1960.

Record receipts: £25,016 v Middlesbrough, Division 3, 8 November, 1986

Pitch measurements: 110yd × 74yd.

President: J. L. T. Moore.

Chairman: R. Corden. *Vice-Chairman:* A. Noble.

Directors: B. Hadley, D. Mason, A. Moore, B. Sommerville, P. Boddy.

Manager: Brian Little. *Assistant Manager:* Phil Bonnyman.

Secretary: Brian Anderson. *Commercial Manager:* Derek Mason.

Coach/Assistant Manager: Frank Gray. *Physio:* Drew Coverdale.

Year Formed: 1883. *Turned Professional:* 1908. *Ltd Co.:* 1891.

Club Nickname: 'The Quakers'.

Record League Victory: 9-2 v Lincoln C, Division 3 (N), 7 January 1928 – Archibald; Brooks, Mellen; Kelly, Waugh, McKinnell; Cochrane (1), Gregg (1), Ruddy (3), Lees (3), McGiffen (1).

Record Cup Victory: 7-2 v Evenwood T, FA Cup, 1st rd, 17 November 1956 – Ward; Devlin, Henderson; Bell (1p), Greener, Furphy; Forster (1), Morton (3), Tulip (2), Davis, Moran.

Record Defeat: 0-10 v Doncaster R, Division 4, 25 January, 1964.

Most League Points (2 for a win): 59, Division 4, 1965–66.

Most League Points (3 for a win): 85, Division 4, 1984–85.

Most League Goals: 108, Division 3 (N), 1929–30.

Highest League Scorer in Season: David Brown, 39, Division 3 (N), 1924–25.

Most League Goals in Total Aggregate: Alan Walsh, 90, 1978–84.

Most Capped Player: None.

Most League Appearances: Ron Greener, 442, 1955–68.

Record Transfer Fee Received: £150,000 from Barnsley for David Currie, February 1988.

Record Transfer Fee Paid: £40,000 to Hartlepool U for Andy Toman, July 1989.

Football League Record: 1921 Original Member Division 3 (N); 1925–27 Division 2; 1927–58 Division 3 (N); 1958–66 Division 4; 1966–67 Division 3; 1967–85 Division 4; 1985–87 Division 3; 1987–89 Division 4; 1989–90 GM Vauxhall Conference; 1990– Division 4.

Honours: Football League: Division 2 best season: 15th, 1925–26; Division 3 (N) Champions 1924–25; Runners-up 1921–22; Division 4 – Runners-up 1965–66. *FA Cup* best season: 3rd rd, 1910–11, 5th rd. 1957–58. *Football League Cup* best season: 5th rd, 1967–68.

Colours: All white. **Change colours:** All yellow.

DARLINGTON

Player and Position	Ht	Wt	Birth Date	Place	Source	Clubs	League App	Gls
Goalkeepers								
Nigel Batch	5 10	12 07	9 11 57	Huddersfield	Apprentice	Derby Co	—	—
						Grimsby T	348	—
						Lincoln C	—	—
						Darlington	30	—
						Stockport Co (loan)	12	—
Mark Prudhoe	6 0	12 12	8 11 63	Washington	Apprentice	Sunderland	7	—
						Hartlepool U (loan)	3	—
						Birmingham C	1	—
						Walsall	26	—
						Doncaster R (loan)	5	—
						Sheffield W (loan)	—	—
						Grimsby T (loan)	8	—
						Hartlepool U (loan)	13	—
						Bristol C (loan)	3	—
						Carlisle U	34	—
						Darlington	12	—
Defenders								
Gary Coatsworth	6 1	11 06	7 10 68	Sunderland		Barnsley	6	—
						Darlington		
David Corner	6 2	12 13	15 5 66	Sunderland	Apprentice	Sunderland	33	1
						Cardiff C (loan)	6	—
						Peterborough U (loan)	9	—
						Leyton Orient	4	—
						Darlington		
Drew Coverdale	5 11	10 06	20 9 69	Teeside	Trainee	Middlesbrough	—	—
						Darlington	—	—
Frankie Gray	5 10	11 10	27 10 54	Glasgow	Apprentice	Leeds U	193	17
						Nottingham F	81	5
						Leeds U	142	10
						Sunderland	146	8
						Darlington	—	—
Les McJannet	5 8	10 04	2 8 61	Cumnock		Mansfield T	74	—
					Matlock T	Scarborough	34	—
						Darlington	26	1
Kevan Smith	6 3	12 02	13 12 59	Yarm	Stockton	Darlington	245	11
						Rotherham U	59	4
						Coventry C	6	—
						York C	31	5
						Darlington	—	—
Jimmy Willis	6 2	12 04	12 7 68	Liverpool	Blackburn R	Halifax T	—	—
						Stockport Co	10	—
						Darlington	50	2
Midfield								
Paul Emson	5 10	11 00	22 10 58	Lincoln	Brigg T	Derby C	127	13
						Grimsby T	97	15
						Wrexham	49	5
						Darlington	34	5
Gary Gill	5 10	11 09	28 11 64	Middlesbrough	Apprentice	Middlesbrough	77	2
						Hull C (loan)	1	—
						Darlington	—	—
Steve Marden-borough	5 8	11 00	11 9 64	Birmingham	Apprentice	Coventry C	—	—
						Wolverhampton W	9	1
						Cambridge U (loan)	6	—
						Swansea C	36	7
						Newport Co	64	11
						Cardiff C	32	1
						Hereford U	27	—
						Darlington	—	—

DARLINGTON

Foundation: A football club was formed in Darlington as early as 1861 but the present club began in 1883 and reached the final of the Durham Senior Cup in their first season, losing to Sunderland in a replay after complaining that they had suffered from intimidation in the first. The following season Darlington won this trophy and for many years were one of the leading amateur clubs in their area.

First Football League game: 27 August, 1921, Division 3(N), v Halifax T (h) W 2-0 – Ward; Greaves, Barbour; Dickson (1), Sutcliffe, Malcolm; Dolphin, Hooper (1), Edmunds, Wolstenholme, Winship.

Managers (and Secretary-managers)
Tom McIntosh 1902–11, W. L. Lane 1911–12*, Dick Jackson 1912–19, Jack English 1919–28, Jack Fairless 1928–33, George Collins 1933–36, George Brown 1936–38, Jackie Carr 1938–42, Jack Surtees 1942, Jack English 1945–46, Bill Forrest 1946–50, George Irwin 1950–52, Bob Gurney 1952–57, Dick Duckworth 1957–60, Eddie Carr 1960–64, Lol Morgan 1964–66, Jimmy Greenhalgh 1966–68, Ray Yeoman 1968–70, Len Richley 1970–71, Frank Brennan 1971, Ken Hale 1971–72, Allan Jones 1972, Ralph Brand 1972–73, Dick Conner 1973–74, Billy Horner 1974–76, Peter Madden 1976–78, Len Walker 1978–79, Billy Elliott 1979–83, Cyril Knowles 1983–87, Dave Booth 1987–89, Brian Little 1989– .

Player and Position	Ht	Wt	Birth Date	Place	Source	Clubs	League App	Gls
Neil Robinson	5 8	10 06	20 4 57	Liverpool	Apprentice	Everton	16	1
						Swansea C	123	7
						Grimsby T	109	6
						Darlington	38	1
Andy Toman	5 10	11 09	7 3 62	Northallerton	Bishop Auckland	Lincoln C	24	4
						Hartlepool U	112	28
						Darlington	—	—
Paul Willis	5 11	11 07	24 1 70	Liverpool	Trainee	Halifax T	5	—
						Darlington	2	1
Forwards								
Dale Anderson	6 0	10 07	23 8 70	Darlington	Trainee	Darlington	15	—
John Borthwick	6 0	10 12	24 3 64	Hartlepool		Hartlepool U	117	15
						Darlington	—	—
David Cork	5 9	11 08	28 10 62	Doncaster	Apprentice	Arsenal	7	1
						Huddersfield T	110	25
						WBA (loan)	4	—
						Scunthorpe U	15	—
						Darlington	—	—
David Geddist†	6 0	11 08	12 3 58	Carlisle	Apprentice	Ipswich T	43	5
						Luton T (loan)	13	4
						Aston Villa	47	12
						Luton T (loan	4	—
						Barnsley	45	24
						Birmingham C	46	18
						Brentford (loan)	4	—
						Shrewsbury T	39	11
						Swindon T	10	3
						Darlington	—	—
Phil Linacre	6 0	11 00	17 5 62	Middlesbrough	Apprentice	Coventry C	—	—
						Hartlepool U	82	17
					Newcastle Blue Star	Darlington	—	—
Archie Stephens	5 11	12 08	19 5 54	Liverpool	Melksham	Bristol R	127	40
						Middlesbrough	92	24
						Carlisle U	24	3
						Darlington	10	4

DERBY COUNTY 1989–90   *Back row (left to right):* Roy McFarland (Assistant Manager), Phil Gee, Nick Pickering, Michael Forsyth, Peter Shilton, Mark Wright, Martin Taylor, Rob Hindmarch, Ted McMinn, Trevor Hebbard, Gordon Guthrie (Physiotherapist).
Front row: Brian McCord, John Chiedozie, Mel Sage, Paul Blades, Dean Saunders, Arthur Cox (Manager), Paul Goddard, Gary Micklewhite, Geraint Williams, Steve Cross, Mark Patterson.

Division 1　　　　　　　　　**DERBY COUNTY**

Baseball Ground, Shaftesbury Crescent, Derby DE3 8NB. Telephone Derby (0332) 40105. Ramtique Sports Shop: 0332 292081. Clubcall 0898 12 11 87.

Ground capacity: 24,000 (16,000 seats).

Record attendance: 41,826 v Tottenham H, Division 1, 20 Sept, 1969.

Record receipts: £135,789 v West Ham U, Littlewoods Cup, 5th rd replay, 24 January 1990.

Pitch measurements: 110yd × 75yd.

President:

Chairman: I. R. Maxwell, MC. *Vice-Chairman:* I. R. C. Maxwell.

Managing Director: A. S. Webb.

Directors: F. W. Fern, J. N. Kirkland, W. Hart, G. Glossop, C. R. Charlton, C. M. McKerrow, B. E. Fearn, M. McGarry.

Manager: Arthur Cox. *Assistant Manager:* Roy McFarland.

Physio: Gordon Guthrie.

Secretary: Michael Dunford. *Marketing Manager:* C. Tunnicliffe. (Tel. 0332 40105).

Year Formed: 1884. *Turned Professional:* 1884. *Ltd Co.:* 1896.

Club Nickname: 'The Rams'.

Former Grounds: 1884–95, Racecourse Ground; 1895, Baseball Ground.

Record League Victory: 9-0 v Wolverhampton W, Division 1, 10 January 1891 – Bunyan; Archie Goodall, Roberts; Walker, Chalmers, Roulston (1); Bakewell, McLachlan, Johnny Goodall (1), Holmes (2), McMillan (5). 9-0 v Sheffield W, Division 1, 21 January 1899 – Fryer; Methven, Staley; Cox, Archie Goodall, May; Oakden (1), Bloomer (6), Boag, McDonald (1), Allen. (1 og).

Record Cup Victory: 12-0 v Finns Harps, UEFA Cup, 1st rd (1st leg), 15 September 1976 – Moseley; Thomas, Nish, Rioch (1), McFarland, Todd (King), Macken, Gemmill, Hector (5), George (3), James (3).

Record Defeat: 2-11 v Everton, FA Cup 1st rd, 1889–90.

Most League Points (2 for a win): 63, Division 2, 1968–69 and Division 3 (N). 1955–56 and 1956–57.

Most League Points (3 for a win): 84, Division 3, 1985–86 and Division 3, 1986–87.

Most League Goals: 111, Division 3 (N), 1956–57.

Highest League Scorer in Season: Jack Bowers, 37,Division 1, 1930–31 and Ray Straw, 37 Division 3 (N). 1956–57.

Most League Goals in Total Aggregate: Steve Bloomer, 292, 1892–1906 and 1910–14.

Most Capped Player: Peter Shilton, 34 (125), England.

Most League Appearances: Kevin Hector, 486, 1966–78 and 1980–82.

Record Transfer Fee Received: £800,000 from Millwall for Paul Goddard, December 1989.

Record Transfer Fee Paid: £1,000,000 to Oxford U for Dean Saunders, October 1988.

Football League Record: 1888 Founder Member of the Football League: 1907–12 Division 2; 1912–14 Division 1; 1914–15 Division 2; 1915–21 Division 1; 1921–26 Division 2; 1926–53 Division 1; 1953–55 Division 2; 1955–57 Division 3 (N); 1957–69 Division 2; 1969–80 Division 1; 1980–84 Division 2; 1984–86 Division 3; 1986–87 Division 2; 1987– Division 1.

Honours: Football League: Division 1 – Champions 1971–72, 1974–75; Runners-up 1895–96, 1929–30, 1935–36; Division 2 – Champions 1911–12, 1914–15, 1968–69, 1986–87; Runners-up 1925–26; Division 3 (N) Champions 1956–57; Runners-up 1955–56. *FA Cup:* Winners 1945–46; Runners-up 1897–98, 1898–99, 1902–03. *Footbal League Cup:* Semi-final 1967–68. *Texaco Cup:* 1971–72. **European Competitions:** *European Cup:* 1972–73, 1975–76; *UEFA Cup:* 1974–75. 1976–77.

Colours: White shirts, black shorts, black stockings. **Change colours:** Red and black striped shirts, red shorts, red and black stockings.

DERBY COUNTY 1989–90 LEAGUE RECORD

Match No.	Date	Venue	Opponents	Result	H/T Score	Lg. Pos.	Goalscorers	Attendance
1	Aug 19	A	Charlton Ath	D	0-0	0-0	—		8543
2	23	H	Wimbledon	D	1-1	0-1	—	Hebberd	13,874
3	26	H	Manchester U	W	2-0	1-0	6	Goddard, Saunders (pen)	22,175
4	30	A	Nottingham F	L	1-2	1-0	—	Hodge (og)	24,060
5	Sept 9	H	Liverpool	L	0-3	0-0	14		20,034
6	16	A	QPR	W	1-0	0-0	9	Saunders	10,697
7	23	H	Southampton	L	0-1	0-0	11		13,694
8	30	A	Aston Villa	L	0-1	0-1	16		16,245
9	Oct 14	H	Crystal Palace	W	3-1	2-1	11	Goddard 2, Saunders (pen)	14,535
10	21	H	Chelsea	L	0-1	0-0	15		17,279
11	28	A	Arsenal	D	1-1	0-1	15	Goddard	33,189
12	Nov 4	A	Luton T	L	0-1	0-0	17		8919
13	11	H	Manchester C	W	6-0	2-0	12	Wright, Hebberd, Saunders 2 (2 pens), Goddard, Micklewhite	19,239
14	18	H	Sheffield W	W	2-0	1-0	12	Goddard, Saunders	18,085
15	25	A	Tottenham H	W	2-1	0-1	9	Saunders, Goddard	28,075
16	Dec 2	H	Charlton Ath	W	2-0	2-0	6	Saunders, Micklewhite	14,590
17	9	A	Wimbledon	D	1-1	1-0	7	Goddard	5024
18	16	A	Norwich C	L	0-1	0-1	9		16,184
19	26	H	Everton	L	0-1	0-1	11		21,314
20	30	H	Coventry C	W	4-1	2-0	9	Pickering, Hebberd 2, Ramage	17,011
21	Jan 1	A	Millwall	D	1-1	1-0	10	Pickering	12,790
22	13	A	Manchester U	W	2-1	1-0	7	Wright, Pickering	38,985
23	20	A	Nottingham F	L	0-2	0-2	9		24,176
24	Feb 10	H	QPR	W	2-0	1-0	7	Gee, Saunders	14,445
25	24	H	Tottenham H	W	2-1	1-0	7	Saunders, Harford	19,676
26	Mar 3	A	Sheffield W	L	0-1	0-1	8		21,811
27	10	A	Southampton	L	1-2	0-0	10	Saunders	16,430
28	17	H	Aston Villa	L	0-1	0-0	13		21,062
29	20	A	Crystal Palace	D	1-1	0-0	—	Wright	10,051
30	24	H	Arsenal	L	1-3	0-3	14	Briscoe	17,514
31	31	A	Chelsea	D	1-1	0-0	13	Harford	14,265
32	Apr 7	A	Coventry C	L	0-1	0-0	13		11,157
33	14	H	Millwall	W	2-0	0-0	13	Harford 2	13,718
34	16	A	Everton	L	1-2	0-0	14	Wright	23,933
35	21	H	Norwich C	L	0-2	0-1	16		13,758
36	28	A	Manchester C	W	1-0	0-0	14	Wright	29,542
37	May 1	A	Liverpool	L	0-1	0-0	—		38,038
38	5	H	Luton T	L	2-3	2-2	16	Wright, Williams P	17,044

Final League Position: 16

GOALSCORERS

League (43): Saunders 11 (4 pens), Goddard 8, Wright 6, Harford 4, Hebberd 4, Pickering 3, Micklewhite 2, Briscoe 1, Gee 1, Ramage 1, Williams P 1, own goal 1.
Littlewoods Cup (12): Saunders 7 (1 pen), McMinn 3, Goddard 2.
FA Cup (3): Francis 1, Hebberd 1, Ramage 1.

Shilton	Sage	Forsyth	Williams G	Wright	Hindmarch	McMinn	Saunders	Goddard	Pickering	Micklewhite	Cross	Hebberd	Gee	Blades	Ramage	McCord	Harford	Patterson	Francis	Davidson	Briscoe	Williams P	Hayward	Taylor	Match No.
1	2	3	4	5	6	7*	8	9	10	11	12														1
1	2	3	4	5	6	7	8	9†	10*	11		12	14												2
1		3	4	5	6	7*	8	9		11	12	10		2											3
1		3	4	5	6	7*	8	9†		11	12	10	14	2											4
1		3	4	5	6	7*	8	9	12	11		10		2											5
1		3	4	5	6	7	8	9		11		10		2											6
1	12	3	4	5	6	7	8	9	10	11†			14	2*											7
1	2	3	4	5		7	8	9*		11		10	12	6											8
1	2	3	4	5		7	8	9	12	11		10		6*											9
1	2	3	4	5		7	8	9	12	11		10*		6											10
1	2	3	4	5		7	8	9	12	11		10		6*											11
1	2	3	4	5		7	8	9		11		10		6											12
1	2	3	4	5		7	8	9		11		10		6											13
1	2	3	4	5		7	8	9		11		10		6											14
1	2	3	4	5	6	7*	8	9	12	11		10													15
1	2	3	4	5	6		8		7	11		10			9										16
1	2	3	4	5	6		8	9	7	11		10													17
1	2	3	4	5	6†		8	9	7	11	12	10*	14												18
1	2	3	4	5			8	9*	7	11†		10		6	12		14								19
1	2	3	4	5*			8		7		12	10		6	9	11									20
1	2	3	4	5			8		7		12	10		6	9	11*									21
1	2	3	4	5	6		8		7	11		10			9										22
1	2	3	4	5	6		8		7†			10			14		9	11*		12					23
1	2	3	4	5			8		7			10		6			9	11							24
1	2	3	4	5	6		8		11			10					9	7*		12					25
1	2	3	4	5	6		8		11			10	14				9*	7†		12					26
1	2	3	4		5		8		11*			10	14	6			9	7†		12					27
1	2	3	4	5			8		11*			10†	14	6			9	7		12					28
1	2	3	4	5			8		11			10		6			9	7*		12					29
1	2	3	4	5	6		8		10*								9			12	11	7			30
	2	3	4	5	6		8		10*				14				9			12	11	7†		1	31
	2	3	4	5	6		8					10*	14				9			12	11	7†		1	32
1	2	3	4	5	6		8					10					9	7			11				33
	2	3	4	5	6		8					10					9	7*		12	11			1	34
1	2	3	4	5†	6		8					10	14				9	7*		12	11				35
1	2	3	4	5	6		8					10					9	7			11				36
1	2	3	4	5	6		8					10					9	7		12	11*				37
1	2	3	4	5	6		8					10					9	7			11*	12			38
35	33	38	38	36	26	15	38	18	18	18	2	21	4	18	8	2	16	9	—	4	8	9	1	3	
+1s								+5s	+6s2s	+4s1s	+4s	+2s						+8s		+2s	+2s	+1s	+2s		

DERBY COUNTY

Player and Position	Ht	Wt	Birth Date	Place	Source	Clubs	League App	Gls
Goalkeepers								
Peter Shilton	6 0	14 00	18 9 49	Leicester	Apprentice	Leicester C	286	1
						Stoke C	110	—
						Nottingham F	202	—
						Southampton	188	—
						Derby Co	113	—
Martin Taylor	5 11	12 04	9 12 66	Tamworth	Mile Oak R	Derby Co	3	—
						Carlisle U (loan)	10	—
						Scunthorpe U (loan)	8	—
Defenders								
Paul Blades	6 0	10 12	5 1 65	Peterborough	Apprentice	Derby Co	166	1
Robert Briscoe	5 8	10 13	4 9 69	Derby	Trainee	Derby Co	10	1
Jonathan Davidson	5 8	11 11	1 3 70	Cheadle	Trainee	Derby Co	6	—
Mike Forsyth	5 11	12 02	20 3 66	Liverpool	Apprentice	WBA	29	—
						Derby Co	156	4
Rob Hindmarch	6 1	13 4	27 4 61	Stannington	Apprentice	Sunderland	115	2
						Portsmouth (loan)	2	—
						Derby Co	164	9
Mark Patterson	5 10	11 05	13 9 68	Leeds	Trainee	Carlisle U	22	—
						Derby Co	10	—
Steve Round	5 10	11 00	9 11 70	Buxton	Trainee	Derby Co	—	—
Mel Sage	5 8	10 04	24 3 64	Gillingham	Apprentice	Gillingham	132	5
						Derby Co	89	3
Mark Wright	6 3	12 01	1 8 63	Dorchester	Amateur	Oxford U	10	—
						Southampton	170	7
						Derby Co	107	10
Midfield								
Steve Cross	5 10	11 05	22 12 59	Wolverhampton	Apprentice	Shrewsbury T	262	34
						Derby Co	48	3
Steve Hayward	5 10	11 07	8 9 71	Walsall	Trainee	Derby Co	3	—
Trevor Hebberd	6 0	11 04	19 6 58	Winchester	Apprentice	Southampton	97	7
						Bolton W (loan)	6	—
						Leicester C (loan)	4	1
						Oxford U	260	37
						Derby Co	60	9
Jason Kavanagh	5 9	11 00	23 11 71	Birmingham	Birmingham C Schoolboys	Derby Co	—	—
Ted McMinn	6 0	12 11	28 9 62	Castle Douglas	Glenafton Ath	Queen of South	62	5
						Rangers	63	4
					Seville	Derby Co	54	5
Gary Micklewhite	5 7	10 04	21 3 61	Southwark	Apprentice	Manchester U	—	—
						QPR	106	11
						Derby Co	167	27
Nick Pickering	6 0	12 02	4 8 63	Newcastle	Apprentice	Sunderland	179	18
						Coventry C	78	9
						Derby Co	31	3
Steve Taylor	5 8	10 04	10 1 70	Holbrook	Trainee	Derby Co	—	—
Geraint Williams	5 7	10 06	5 1 62	Treorchy	Apprentice	Bristol R	141	8
						Derby Co	207	7
Paul Williams	5 11	12 00	26 3 71	Burton	Trainee	Derby Co	10	1
						Lincoln C (loan)	3	—
Forwards								
Martyn Chalk	5 6	10 00	30 8 69	Louth	Louth U	Derby Co	—	—
Kevin Francis	6 7	15 08	6 12 67	Moseley	Mile Oak Rovers	Derby Co	8	—
Phil Gee	5 9	10 04	19 12 64	Pelsall	Gresley R	Derby Co	103	25

DERBY COUNTY

Foundation: Derby County was formed by members of the Derbyshire County Cricket Club in 1884, when football was booming in the area and the cricketers thought that a football club would help boost finances for the summer game. To begin with, they sported the cricket club's colours of amber, chocolate and pale blue, and went into the game at the top immediately entering the FA Cup.

First Football League game: 8 September, 1888, Football League, v Bolton W (a) W 6-3 – Marshall; Latham, Ferguson, Williamson; Monks, W. Roulstone; Bakewell (2), Cooper (2), Higgins, H. Plackett, L. Plackett (2).

Managers (and Secretary-managers)
Harry Newbould 1896–1906, Jimmy Methven 1906–22, Cecil Potter 1922–25, George Jobey 1925–41, Ted Magner 1944–46, Stuart McMillan 1946–53, Jack Barker 1953–55, Harry Storer 1955–62, Tim Ward 1962–67, Brian Clough 1967–73, Dave Mackay 1973–76, Colin Murphy 1977, Tommy Docherty 1977–79, Colin Addison 1979–82, Johnny Newman 1982, Peter Taylor 1982–84, Roy McFarland 1984, Arthur Cox 1984–

Player and Position	Ht	Wt	Birth Date	Place	Source	Clubs	League App	Gls
Mick Harford	6 2	12 09	12 2 59	Sunderland	Lambton St BC	Lincoln C	115	41
						Newcastle U	19	4
						Bristol C	30	11
						Birmingham C	92	25
						Luton T	139	57
						Derby Co	16	4
Craig Ramage	5 9	11 08	30 3 70	Derby	Trainee	Derby Co	12	1
						Wigan Ath (loan)	10	2
Dean Saunders	5 8	10 06	21 6 64	Swansea	Apprentice	Swansea C	49	12
						Cardiff C (loan)	4	—
						Brighton & HA	72	21
						Oxford U	59	22
						Derby Co	68	25
Kris Sleeuwenhoek	5 7	10 00	2 10 71	Oldham	Wolves Schoolboys	Derby Co	—	—
Robert Straw	5 9	11 08	4 11 70	Derby	Trainee	Derby Co	—	—
John Symonds	5 11	11 07	3 9 70	Coventry	Trainee	Derby Co	—	—

Trainees
Clarke, Mark A; Cooksey, Scott A; Ellerton, Ricky; Grant, Paul S; Hillyer, Jamie A; Holness, Corin J; Phillips, Justin L; Read, Paul M; Smith, Matthew J; Sturridge, Dean C; White, Jason G; Wilkinson, Robert N; Wilson, Kevin P.

Associated Schoolboys
Anderson, Wayne S; Bowers, Kevin; Burton, Michael; Butler, Martin; Canfield, Russell; Curtis, Thomas; Filik, Robert; Flindall, Andrew M; Franklin, Nicholas; Geddis, Stewart R; Gilby, David A; McDermott, Thomas; Matthews, Martin; Mosley, Shaun; Richards, Michael L; Rutter, James; Stallard, Mark; Tunstall, Jamie A; Valerio, Jeremy; Weston, Paul; White, Alan; Wood, Mark; Wood, Mark; Wright, Nicholas, J.

Associated Schoolboys who have accepted the club's offer of a Traineeship/Contract
Allen, Craig; Batey, Darren; Blount, Mark; Carsley, Lee K; Darkes, Craig J; Weston, Kingsby P.

DONCASTER ROVERS 1989–90 *Back row (left to right)*: John Stiles, Lee Turnbull, Gary Jones, Mark Hall, Jack Ashurst (Captain), Steve Gaughan.
Centre row: Steve Beaglehole (Assistant Manager), Eric Brailsford (Physiotherapist), Justin Sumner, Gery Daly, Mark Samways, Dave Cusack, Lee Lamont, John McGinley, Steve Raffell, Dave Blakey (General Manager), Jim Golze (Youth Team Coach).
Front row: Mark Rankine, Grant Morrow, Rufus Brevett, Billy Bremner (Manager), Les Robinson, Colin Douglas, Vince Brockie.

Division 4   **DONCASTER ROVERS**

Doncaster Rovers Football Club Ltd.
(Founded 1879)

Belle Vue Ground, Doncaster. Telephone Doncaster (0302) 539441.

Ground capacity: 4859.

Record attendance: 37,149 v Hull C, Division 3 (N), 2 Oct, 1948.

Record receipts: £22,000 v QPR, FA Cup 3rd rd, 5 Jan, 1985.

Pitch measurements: 111yd × 74½yd.

Vice-Presidents: K. Jackson, R. Jones.

Chairman: B. E. Boldry. *Vice-Chairman:* M. J. H. Collett.

Directors: P. Wetzel, J. J. Burke, T. C. Hamilton, K. Chappell, M. O'Horan, W. Turner.

Manager: Billy Bremner. *Assistant Manager:*

Physio: Gary Delahunt. *Youth Team Manager:* Dave Bentley.

Secretary: Mrs. K. J. Oldale.

Year Formed: 1879. *Turned Professional:* 1885. *Ltd Co.:* 1905 and 1920.

Club Nickname: 'Rovers'.

Previous Grounds: 1880–1916, Intake Ground; 1920–22, Benetthorpe Ground; 1922, Low Pasture, Belle Vue.

Record League Victory: 10-0 v Darlington, Division 4, 25 January 1964 – Potter; Raine, Meadows; Windross (1), White, Ripley (2); Robinson, Book (2), Hale (4), Jeffrey, Broadbent (1).

Record Cup Victory: 7-0 v Blyth Spartans, FA Cup, 1st rd, 27 November 1937 – Imrie; Shaw, Rodgers; McFarlane, Bycroft, Cyril Smith; Burton (1), Kilourhy (4), Morgan (2), Malam, Dutton.

Record Defeat: 0-12 v Small Heath, Division 2, 11 April, 1903.

Most League Points (2 for a win): 72, Division 3(N), 1946-47.

Most League Points (3 for a win): 85, Division 4, 1983-84.

Most League Goals: 123, Division 3 (N), 1946-47.

Highest League Scorer in Season: Clarrie Jordan, 42, Division 3 (N), 1946–47.

Most League Goals in Total Aggregate: Tom Keetley, 180, 1923-29.

Most Capped Player: Len Graham, 14, Northern Ireland.

Most League Appearances: Fred Emery, 406, 1925–36.

Record Transfer Fee Received: £200,000 from Leeds U for Ian Snodin, May 1985.

Record Transfer Fee Paid: £60,000 to Stirling Albion for John Philliben, March 1984.

Football League Record: 1901 Elected to Division 2; 1903 Failed re-election; 1904 Re-elected; 1905 Failed re-election; 1923 Re-elected to Division 3(N); 1935–37 Division 2; 1937–47 Division 3 (N); 1947–48 Division 2; 1948–50 Division 3 (N); 1950-58 Division 2; 1958-59 Division 3; 1959–66 Division 4; 1966–67 Division 3; 1967–69 Division 4; 1969–71 Division 3; 1971–81 Division 4; 1981–83 Division 3; 1983–84 Division 4; 1984–88 Division 3; 1988– Division 4.

Honours: Football League: Division 2 best season: 7th, 1901–02; Division 3 (N) Champions 1934–35, 1946–47, 1949–50; Runners-up 1937–38, 1938–39; Division 4 – Champions 1965–66, 1968–69; Runners-up 1983–84. Promoted 1980–81 (3rd). *FA Cup* best season: 5th rd, 1951–52, 1953–54, 1954–55, 1955–56. *Football League Cup* best season: 5th rd, 1975–76.

Colours: White shirts, red collar and cuffs, red shorts, white stockings. **Change colours:** All green.

DONCASTER ROVERS 1989–90 LEAGUE RECORD

Match No.	Date		Venue	Opponents	Result		H/T Score	Lg. Pos.	Goalscorers	Atten- dance
1	Aug 19	A		Exeter C	L	0-1	0-1	—		3033
2	26	H		Gillingham	D	0-0	0-0	21		1887
3	Sept 2	A		Lincoln C	L	1-2	1-2	22	Turnbull	3906
4	9	H		Peterborough U	L	0-3	0-1	22		2327
5	16	A		Scarborough	W	2-1	0-0	20	Brockie (pen), Turnbull	2750
6	22	H		Southend U	L	0-1	0-1	—		2386
7	26	H		Aldershot	L	0-1	0-1	—		1960
8	30	A		Hartlepool U	W	6-0	3-0	20	Gaughan, Turnbull 3, Robinson 2	1723
9	Oct 7	A		Torquay U	L	0-2	0-2	20		2059
10	14	H		Carlisle U	D	1-1	1-0	20	Brockie	2419
11	17	A		Cambridge U	L	0-1	0-1	—		2483
12	21	H		Burnley	L	2-3	1-3	22	Robinson (pen), Eli (og)	2900
13	28	A		York C	L	1-2	0-1	22	Stiles	2978
14	31	H		Maidstone U	D	1-1	0-1	—	Douglas	1806
15	Nov 4	H		Scunthorpe U	L	1-2	0-1	22	Rankine	3374
16	11	A		Rochdale	W	3-1	2-0	22	Jones D 3	1716
17	25	A		Hereford U	W	1-0	1-0	20	Jones D	2167
18	Dec 2	H		Stockport Co	W	2-1	0-0	20	Jones D, Robinson (pen)	3023
19	15	A		Halifax T	W	2-0	0-0	—	Noteman, Adams	1233
20	26	H		Wrexham	D	2-2	1-1	19	Noteman, Jones D	3668
21	30	H		Colchester U	W	2-0	1-0	19	Robinson (pen), Turnbull	2942
22	Jan 1	A		Chesterfield	W	1-0	0-0	15	Robinson (pen)	5620
23	13	A		Gillingham	L	1-3	1-2	17	Douglas	3820
24	16	H		Grimsby T	D	0-0	0-0	—		4338
25	20	H		Exeter C	W	2-1	2-0	17	Rankine, Robinson (pen)	3492
26	27	A		Peterborough U	L	1-2	0-1	17	Noteman	4080
27	Feb 2	A		Southend U	L	0-2	0-1	—		3174
28	10	H		Scarborough	D	1-1	1-0	18	Turnbull	2899
29	13	H		Lincoln C	L	0-1	0-1	—		3079
30	16	A		Stockport Co	L	1-3	1-1	--	Morrow	3609
31	25	H		Hereford U	L	0-1	0-1	—		2958
32	Mar 3	A		Grimsby T	L	1-2	0-1	21	Jones D	5536
33	6	H		Hartlepool U	D	2-2	1-1	—	Turnbull, Robinson (pen)	2518
34	10	A		Aldershot	D	1-1	0-1	21	Jones D	1512
35	17	H		Torquay U	W	2-1	1-0	19	Stiles, Brockie (pen)	1887
36	20	A		Carlisle U	L	0-1	0-0	—		3970
37	25	H		Cambridge U	W	2-1	1-0	—	Daish (og), Turnbull	2147
38	31	A		Burnley	W	1-0	1-0	19	Jones D	5066
39	Apr 7	H		York C	L	1-2	1-0	21	Muir	2185
40	11	A		Maidstone U	L	0-1	0-1	—		1375
41	14	H		Chesterfield	W	1-0	0-0	20	Jones D	3738
42	16	A		Wrexham	D	0-0	0-0	20		4210
43	21	H		Halifax T	L	3-4	3-0	21	Turnbull, Muir, Grayson	2212
44	24	A		Colchester U	L	0-2	0-2	—		2641
45	28	H		Rochdale	W	4-0	2-0	20	Muir 2, Jones D 2	2189
46	May 5	A		Scunthorpe U	L	1-4	0-4	20	Morrow	3020

Final League Position: 20

GOALSCORERS

League (53): Jones D 12, Turnbull 10, Robinson 8 (6 pens), Muir 4, Brockie 3 (2 pens), Noteman 3, Douglas 2, Morrow 2, Rankine 2, Stiles 2, Adams 1, Gaughan 1, Grayson 1, own goals 2.
Littlewoods Cup (2): Turnbull 2.
FA Cup (1): Noteman 1.

Samways	Robinson	Brevett	Douglas	Ashurst	Raffell	McGinley	Stiles	Turnbull	Rankine	Jones G	Gaughan	Brockie	Sumner	Cusack	Adams	Nicholson	Cygan	Jones D	Noteman	Morrow	Gallagher	Muir	Harle	McKay	Grayson	Reddish	Match No.
1	2	3	4	5	6	7*	8	9	10	11	12																1
1	7	3	4	5	6	12	8	9	10		2	11*															2
1	7	3	4	5	6		8	9	10		2	11															3
1	7	3	4	5	6		8	9	10		12	11*			2												4
1	7	3	4	5	6		8	9	10			11			2												5
1	7	3	4	5	6		8	9	10			11			2												6
1	7	3	4	5	6	12	8	9	10			11			2*												7
1	7	3	4	5	6		8	9	10			11			2												8
1	7	3	4	5	6	12	8	9	10		14	11†			2*												9
1	7	3	4†	5	6	12	8	9	10		14	11			2*												10
1	7	3	4	5	6	12	8	9	10		2*	11															11
1	7	3	2	5	6	4†	8*	9	10		12	14		11													12
1	7	3	2	5	6	12	8		10		4	11			9*												13
1	7	3	2	6	5		8	9	10		4	11															14
1	7	3	2	6†	5		8	9	10		4*	11	12	14													15
1	2	3	6	5			8	9			4				7			10	11								16
1	2	3	6	5			8	9			4				7			10	11								17
1	2	3	6	5	4		8	9							7			10	11								18
1	2	3	6	5			8	9			4				7			10	11								19
1	2	3	6	5			8	12			4	10*			7			9	11								20
1	2	3	6	5			8	9			4	12			7			10	11*								21
1	2	3	6	5			8	9			4	12			7			10	11*								22
1	2	3	6	5	12		8	10*			4				7			9	11								23
1	2	3	6	5			8	9			4				7			10	11								24
1	2	3	6	5			8				4	11			7*			10	9	12							25
1	2	3†	6	5	12		8				4	11			7*			10	9	14							26
1	2	3	6	5	12		8				4	11			7*			10	9								27
1	2	3	6	5			8	9			4				7			10	11*								28
1		3	6	5	2†		8	9			4				7	14	12	10	11*								29
1		3	6	5	2		8				4	11	10		7*			9	12								30
1	2	3		5	6		8*	9			4	14			7†		12	11	10								31
1	2	3	6	5			8	12			4*	14			7†			10	11	9							32
1	2	3	6	5			8†	7			4	14					12	10	11	9*							33
1	2†	3	6	5	7*		8	9			4	14						10	11	12							34
1		3	12				8		10		4	14			2			5	7	9†		11*					35
1		3	6	5			8	9			4				2			10	11			7					36
1		3	6	5			8	9							2			10	11			7	4				37
1			6	5			8	9							2			10	11	3		7	4*		12		38
1	12		6	5			8†	9*							2			10	11	3	14	7	4				39
1		3	6	5			8	9							2			10*	11		14	7†	4				40
1		3	6	5			8	9			12							10	11			7	4		2*		41
1		3	6	5			8	9			12							10	11	14		7†	4		2*		42
1		3†	6	5				9				14			2		12	10	11			7	4			8*	43
1			6	5	3		8	9			12				2*			10	11			7†	4		14		44
1			6	5	3		8	9							2*			10	11			7	4		12		45
1			6	5			8†	9							2			10	11		14	7	4		3†	14	46
46	32	41	45	43	23	4	42	40	36	1	20	19	2	1	23	1	—	27	30	1	—	15	10	—	4	—	

Substitute appearances (+): Brevett 1s — Raffell 4s — McGinley 6s — Turnbull 2s — Brockie 2s 9s — Sumner 5s — Adams 7s — Jones D 1s 1s — Muir 6s 1s — McKay 1s — Grayson 1s — Reddish 2s 1s

Littlewoods Cup	First Round	Huddersfield T (a) 1-1
		(h) 1-2
FA Cup	First Round	Notts Co (h) 1-0
	Second Round	Grimsby T (a) 0-1

DONCASTER ROVERS

Player and Position	Ht	Wt	Birth Date	Birth Place	Source	Clubs	League App	League Gls
Goalkeepers								
Peter Cole*			15 9 70	Manchester		Bury	—	—
						Doncaster R	—	—
Paul Malcolm‡	6 4	13 10	11 12 64	Heworth	Apprentice	Newcastle U	—	—
					Durham C	Rochdale	24	—
						Shrewsbury T		
						Barnsley	3	—
						Doncaster R	34	—
Mark Samways	6 0	11 12	11 11 68	Doncaster	Trainee	Doncaster R	69	—
						Leeds U (loan)	—	—
Defenders								
Jack Ashurst*	6 0	12 04	12 10 54	Renton	Apprentice	Sunderland	140	4
						Blackpool	53	3
						Carlisle U	194	2
						Leeds U	89	1
						Doncaster R	73	1
Rufus Brevett	5 8	11 00	24 9 69	Derby	Trainee	Derby Co	—	—
						Doncaster R	82	—
Vincent Brockie	5 8	10 10	2 2 69	Greenock	Trainee	Leeds U	2	—
						Doncaster R	47	5
Dave Cusack‡	6 1	14 04	6 6 56	Thurcroft	Apprentice	Sheffield W	95	1
						Southend U	186	17
						Millwall	98	9
						Doncaster R	100	4
						Rotherham U	18	—
					Boston U	Doncaster R	1	—
Colin Douglas	6 1	11 00	9 9 62	Hurtford	Celtic BC	Celtic	—	—
						Doncaster R	212	48
						Rotherham U	83	4
						Doncaster R	91	4
Neil Grayson†			1 1 64	York	Rowntree M	Doncaster R	6	1
Mark Hall‡	5 11	11 00	11 5 70	Doncaster	Trainee	Doncaster R	2	—
Jonathan Owen*			18 12 70	Bridgend		Doncaster R	—	—
Steve Raffell*	5 11	11 02	27 4 70	Blyth	Trainee	Doncaster R	54	—
Shane Reddish†	5 10	11 10	5 5 71	Bolsover	Mansfield T§	Doncaster R	1	—
Midfield								
Paul Cygan§			4 3 72	Doncaster		Doncaster R	1	—
Gerry Daly‡	5 8	11 04	30 4 54	Dublin	Bohemians	Manchester U	111	23
						Derby Co	112	31
						Coventry C	84	19
						Leicester C (loan)	17	1
						Burmingham C	32	1
						Shrewsbury T	55	8
						Stoke C	22	1
						Doncaster R	39	4
Steven Gaughan*	5 11	11 02	14 4 70	Doncaster	Trainee	Doncaster R	67	3
David Harle	5 9	10 07	15 8 63	Denaby	Apprentice	Doncaster R	61	3
						Exeter C	43	6
						Doncaster R	83	17
						Leeds U	3	—
						Bristol C (loan)	8	—
						Bristol C	15	2
						Scunthorpe U	89	10
						Peterborough U	22	2
						Doncaster R	10	—
Mark Rankine	5 10	11 01	30 9 69	Doncaster	Trainee	Doncaster R	100	15
John Stiles	5 9	10 12	6 5 64	Manchester	Vancouver W	Leeds U	65	2
						Doncaster R	42	2
Justin Sumner*	5 0	11 00	19 10 70	Harrogate	Leeds U§	Doncaster R	2	—

DONCASTER ROVERS

Foundation: In 1879 Mr. Albert Jenkins got together a team to play a game against the Yorkshire Institution for the Deaf. The players stuck together as Doncaster Rovers joining the Midland Alliance in 1889 and the Midland Counties League in 1891.

First Football League game: 7 September, 1901, Division 2, v Burslem Port Vale (h) D 3-3 – Eggett; Simpson, Layton; Longden, Jones, Wright; Langham, Murphy, Price, Goodson (2), Bailey (1).

Managers (and Secretary-managers)
Arthur Porter 1920–21*, Harry Tufnell 1921–22, Arthur Porter 1922–23, Dick Ray 1923–27, David Menzies 1928–36, Fred Emery 1936–40, Bill Marsden 1944–46, Jackie Bestall 1946–49, Peter Doherty 1949–58, Jack Hodgson and Sid Bycroft (joint managers) 1958, Jack Crayston 1958–59 (continued as Sec-Man to 1961), Jackie Bestall (TM) 1959–60, Norman Curtis 1960–61, Danny Malloy 1961–62, Oscar Hold 1962–64, Bill Leivers 1964–66, Keith Kettleborough 1966–67, George Raynor 1967–68, Lawrie McMenemy 1968–71, Maurice Setters 1971–74, Stan Anderson 1975–78, Billy Bremner 1978–85, Dave Cusack 1985–87, Dave Mackay 1987–89, Billy Bremner 1989–   .

Player and Position	Ht	Wt	Birth Date	Place	Source	Clubs	League App	Gls
Forwards								
Steve Adams	5 8	10 12	7 5 59	Sheffield	Worksop T	Scarborough	48	5
						Doncaster R	30	1
Nicholas Gallagher			28 1 71	Boston		Doncaster R	1	—
David Jones	6 3	14 04	3 7 64	Harrow		Chelsea	—	—
						Bury	1	—
						Leyton Orient	2	—
						Burnley	4	—
						Ipswich T	—	—
						Doncaster R	27	12
Gary Jones‡	5 11	11 06	6 4 69	Huddersfield	Rossington Main	Doncaster R	20	2
John McGinley‡	6 2	13 08	11 6 59	Rowlands Gill	Gateshead Charleroi	Sunderland	3	—
						Lincoln C	71	11
						Rotherham U	3	—
						Lincoln C	21	5
						Hartlepool U (loan)	2	—
						Lincoln C	20	2
						Doncaster R	10	—
Mark McKay			12 11 67	Edinburgh		Doncaster R	1	—
John Muir	6 2	14 06	26 4 63	Sedgley	Dudley T	Doncaster R	16	4
Grant Morrow	5 10	11 07	4 10 70	Glasgow	Rowntree M	Doncaster R	7	2
Max Nicholson§			3 10 71	Leeds	Trainee	Doncaster R	2	—
Kevin Noteman	5 10	10 09	15 10 69	Preston	Trainee	Leeds U	1	—
						Doncaster R	30	3
Robbie Stewart‡			14 6 71	West Lothian	Trainee	Doncaster R	1	—
Lee Turnbull	6 0	11 09	27 9 67	Teeside	Local	Middlesbrough	16	4
						Aston Villa	—	—
						Doncaster R	104	15

Trainees
Almunshi, Haidar M; Bennett, Craig; Clarke, Johnathan P; Cygan, Paul; Driscoll, Michael E; Illman, Mark A; McKenzie, Roger M; Millward, Richard B; Nicholson, Maximilian; Redhead, Christopher A; Rowe, Brian; Veitch, Steven W; Warren, Jason; White, Stuart.

**Non-Contract
Grayson, Neil; Reddish, Shane.

Associated Schoolboys
Bell, Lynden; Beswick, David; Credland, Gary W; Fletcher, Martin L; Nixon, Russell S; Otter, Stephen P; Thompson, Andrew R.

Associated Schoolboys who have accepted the club's offer of a Traineeship/Contract
Limber, Nicholas; Roberts, Jamie S.

**Non-Contract Players who are retained must be re-signed before they are eligible to play in League matches.

EVERTON 1989-90 *Back row (left to right):* Martin Keown, Neville Southall, Dave Watson, Mike Stowell, Mike Newell.

Centre row: Graham Smith (Youth Manager), Terry Darracott (Assistant Manager), Stuart McCall, Neil McDonald, Graeme Sharp, Neil Pointon, Paul Power (Youth Coach), Mike Lyons (Reserve Coach), Chris Goodson (Physiotherapist).

Front row: Tony Cottee, Pat Nevin, Norman Whiteside, John Ebbrell, Kevin Ratcliffe, Colin Harvey (Manager), Raymond Atteveld, Ian Snodin, Kevin Sheedy, Stefan Rehn.

Division 1 **EVERTON**

Goodison Park, Liverpool L4 4EL. Telephone 051-521 2020. Match ticket information: 051-523 6642. Match information: 0898 121 599 Clubcall 0898 12 11 99. Dial-a-seat service: 051-525-1231.

Ground capacity: 41,366 (29,500 seats).

Record attendance: 78,299 v Liverpool, Division 1, 18 Sept, 1948.

Record receipts: £207,780 v Liverpool, FA Cup, 5th rd, 21 February 1988.

Pitch measurements: 112yd × 78yd.

Chairman: P. D. Carter CBE.

Directors: A. W. Waterworth, D. H. Pitcher, K. M. Tamlin, D. A. B. Newton, Dr. D. M. Marsh, W. Kenright.

Manager: Colin Harvey. **Assistant Manager:** Terry Darracott.

Physio: Chris Goodson. **Coach:** Paul Power.

Chief Executive & Secretary: Jim Greenwood.

Marketing Manager: Derek Johnston. **Sales Promotion Manager:** Nigel Coates.

Year Formed: 1878. **Turned Professional:** 1885. **Ltd Co.:** 1892.

Previous name: St Domingo FC, 1878–79.

Club Nickname: 'The Toffees'.

Former Grounds: 1878, Stanley Park; 1882, Priory Road; 1884, Anfield Road; 1892, Goodison Park.

Record League Victory: 9-1 v Manchester C, Division 1, 3 September 1906 – Scott; Balmer, Crelley; Booth, Taylor (1), Abbott (1); Sharp, Bolton (1), Young (4), Settle (2), George Wilson. 9-1 v Plymouth Arg, Division 2, 27 December 1930 – Coggins; Williams, Cresswell; McPherson, Griffiths, Thomson; Critchley, Dunn, Dean (4), Johnson (1), Stein (4).

Record Cup Victory: 11-2 v Derby Co, FA Cup, 1st rd, 18 January 1890 – Smalley; Hannah, Doyle; Kirkwood (3), Holt, Parry; Latta, Brady (3), Geary (2), Chadwick, Millward (3).

Record Defeat: 4-10 v Tottenham H, Division 1, 11, October, 1958.

Most League Points (2 for a win): 66, Division 1, 1969–70.

Most League Points (3 for a win): 90, Division 1, 1984–85.

Most League Goals: 121, Division 2, 1930–31.

Highest League Scorer in Season: William Ralph 'Dixie' Dean, 60, Division 1, 1927–28 (All-time League record).

Most League Goals in Total Aggregate: William Ralph 'Dixie' Dean, 349, 1925–37.

Most Capped Player: Kevin Ratcliffe, 48, Wales.

Most League Appearances: Ted Sagar, 465, 1929–53.

Record Transfer Fee Received: £2,750,000 from Barcelona for Gary Lineker. July 1986.

Record Transfer Fee Paid: £2,000,000 to West Ham U for Tony Cottee, July 1988.

Football League Record: 1888 Founder Member of the Football League; 1930–31 Division 2; 1931–51 Division 1; 1951–54 Division 2; 1954– Division 1.

Honours: *Football League:* Division 1 – Champions 1890–91, 1914–15, 1927–28, 1931–32, 1938–39, 1962–63, 1969–70, 1984–85, 1986–87; Runners-up 1889–90, 1894–95, 1901–02, 1904–05, 1908–09, 1911–12, 1985–86; Division 2 Champions 1930–31; Runners-up 1953–54. *FA Cup:* Winners 1906, 1933, 1966, 1984; Runners-up 1893, 1897, 1907, 1968, 1985, 1986, 1989. *Football League Cup:* Runners-up 1976–77, 1983–84. *League Super Cup:* Runners-up 1986. *Simod Cup:* Runners-up 1989. **European Competitions:** *European Cup:* 1963–64, 1970–71; *European Cup-Winners' Cup:* 1966–67, 1984–85 (winners). *European Fairs Cup:* 1962-63. 1964–65, 1965–66. *UEFA Cup:* 1975–76, 1978–79, 1979–80.

Colours: Royal blue shirts, white shorts, blue stockings with white turnovers. **Change colours:** All yellow.

EVERTON 1989–90 LEAGUE RECORD

Match No.	Date		Venue	Opponents	Result		H/T Score	Lg. Pos.	Goalscorers	Atten- dance
1	Aug	19	A	Coventry C	L	0-2	0-0	—		17,981
2		22	H	Tottenham H	W	2-1	1-1	—	Newell, Sheedy	34,402
3		26	H	Southampton	W	3-0	2-0	3	Whiteside, Newell, McCall	27,807
4		30	A	Sheffield W	D	1-1	1-0	—	Sheedy	19,657
5	Sept	9	H	Manchester U	W	3-2	1-0	2	Newell, Nevin, Sharp	37,916
6		16	A	Charlton Ath	W	1-0	0-0	1	Newell	11,491
7		23	H	Liverpool	L	1-3	1-1	5	Newell	42,453
8		30	A	Crystal Palace	L	1-2	0-2	6	Newell	15,943
9	Oct	14	H	Millwall	W	2-1	0-1	4	Sheedy (pen), Whiteside	26,125
10		21	H	Arsenal	W	3-0	1-0	1	Nevin 2, McDonald	32,917
11		28	A	Norwich C	D	1-1	0-1	1	Cottee	18,627
12	Nov	5	A	Aston Villa	L	2-6	0-3	—	Cottee, McGrath (og)	17,637
13		11	H	Chelsea	L	0-1	0-0	6		33,737
14		18	H	Wimbledon	D	1-1	0-0	7	Sheedy (pen)	21,561
15		25	A	Nottingham F	L	0-1	0-0	12		20,709
16	Dec	2	H	Coventry C	W	2-0	1-0	8	McCall, Watson	21,171
17		9	A	Tottenham H	L	1-2	1-1	9	Cottee	29,374
18		17	H	Manchester C	D	0-0	0-0	—		21,737
19		26	A	Derby Co	W	1-0	1-0	8	McCall	21,314
20		30	A	QPR	L	0-1	0-1	10		11,683
21	Jan	1	H	Luton T	W	2-1	2-0	8	Whiteside, Sharp	21,743
22		13	A	Southampton	D	2-2	1-1	8	Whiteside 2	19,381
23		20	H	Sheffield W	W	2-0	0-0	7	Sheedy 2	25,545
24	Feb	3	A	Liverpool	L	1-2	1-2	7	Sharp	38,730
25		10	H	Charlton Ath	W	2-1	1-1	6	Cottee, Whiteside	21,442
26	Mar	3	A	Wimbledon	L	1-3	1-1	10	Sheedy	6512
27		14	A	Manchester U	D	0-0	0-0	—		37,398
28		17	H	Crystal Palace	W	4-0	2-0	8	Sharp, Cottee 2, Whiteside	19,274
29		21	A	Millwall	W	2-1	1-1	—	Pointon, Cottee	11,495
30		24	H	Norwich C	W	3-1	0-1	4	Cottee 2, Sharp	21,707
31		31	A	Arsenal	L	0-1	0-1	5		35,223
32	Apr	4	H	Nottingham F	W	4-0	3-0	—	Cottee 2, Whiteside 2	17,795
33		7	H	QPR	W	1-0	0-0	3	Cottee (pen)	19,887
34		14	A	Luton T	D	2-2	0-2	3	Cottee, Sharp	9538
35		16	H	Derby Co	W	2-1	0-0	3	Atteveld, Sheedy	23,933
36		21	A	Manchester C	L	0-1	0-0	4		32,144
37		28	A	Chelsea	L	1-2	0-0	5	Nevin	18,879
38	May	5	H	Aston Villa	D	3-3	1-0	6	Cascarino (og), Newell, Sheedy (pen)	29,551

Final League Position: 6

GOALSCORERS

League (57): Cottee 13 (1 pen), Sheedy 9 (3 pens), Whiteside 9, Newell 7, Sharp 6, Nevin 4, McCall 3, Atteveld 1, McDonald 1, Pointon 1, Watson 1, own goals 2.
Littlewoods Cup (7): Newell 3, Sheedy 2, Nevin 1, Whiteside 1.
FA Cup (8): Whiteside 3, Cottee 2, Sheedy 2 (1 pen), Sharp 1.

Southall	Snodin	Pointon	Ratcliffe	Watson	Whiteside	Nevin	McCall	Sharp	Newell	Sheedy	Cottee	Ebbrell	Keown	McDonald	Rehn	Beagrie	Atteveld	Wright	Match No.
1	2	3	4	5	6	7	8	9	10*	11	12								1
1	2	3	4	5	6	7	8	9	10	11									2
1	2	3	4	5	6	7	8	9*	10	11		12							3
1	2	3	4	5*	6	7	8	9		11	10†	12	14						4
1	2	3	4	5	6*	7	8	9	10	11		12							5
1	2	3	4	5		7*	8	9	10	11		12	6						6
1	2	3*	4	5	6†	7	8	9	10	11		12	14						7
1	2		4	5	6*	7	8	9	10	11				3	12				8
1	2†			5	6	7	12	9	11	10	8	4	3	14*					9
1				5	6	7	8		9	11	10	2	4	3					10
1				5	6	7	8		9	11	10	2	4	3					11
1				5†	6*	7	8	12	9	11	10	2	4	3	14				12
1		3				7	8	12	9	11	10*	2	4	5		6			13
1	7	3					8	9	10	11		2	4	5		6			14
1	6	3†		5			8	9	10	11	12	14	4	2		7*			15
1			4	5			8	9		11	10	6	3			7	2		16
1			4	5			8	9	12	11	10	6*	3			7	2		17
1			4	5			8	9	12	11	10	6*	3			7	2		18
1	2		4	5		14	8	9	12	11	10*		3			7	6†		19
1	2		4	5		14	8	9	12	11	10*		3			7	6†		20
1	2		4	5	6	7	8	9	10				3			11*	12		21
1	2		4		6	12	8	9	10	11		5	3			7*			22
1	2		4		6	7	8	9	10	11		5	3						23
1	2		4	5	6	7*	8	9	12	11	10		3						24
1	2		4	12	6	7	8	9		11	10	5	3*						25
1	2		4	5	12		8	9	14	11	10†	7	3*			6			26
1	2	3	4		6		8	9	11*	10		5		12		7*			27
1	2	3	4		6	12	8	9	11	10		5					7*		28
1	2	3	4		6		8	9	11	10		5				12	7*		29
1	2	3	4†		6	14	8	9	11*	10		5				12	7		30
1	2	3		5	6	7	8	9	11*	10		4†	14	12					31
1	2†	3*		5	6	14	8	9	12	10			4	11		7			32
1					6	7*	8	9	12	10	3		4	11			2	5	33
1				5		7	8	9	6	10	3		4	11			2		34
1				5	6	7	8	9	12	10	3		4	11*			2		35
1	3			5	6	7	8	9*	11	10	12		4				2		36
1	3			5	6†	14	8	9	11	10	12		4			7*	2		37
1	3	4		5†		7	8	9	12	10	11*	2	6				14		38
38	25	19	24	28	26	23	37	30	20	33	25	13	19	26	1	14	16	1	

+ + +   + + + + + +
1s 1s 7s   3s 6s 4s 2s 4s 1s 5s   3s5s 2s

Littlewoods Cup	Second Round	Leyton Orient (a)	2-0
		(h)	2-2
	Third Round	Luton T (h)	3-0
	Fourth Round	Nottingham F (a)	0-1
FA Cup	Third Round	Middlesbrough (a)	0-0
		(h)	1-1
		(a)	1-0
	Fourth Round	Sheffield W (a)	2-1
	Fifth Round	Oldham Ath (a)	2-2
		(h)	1-1
		(h)	1-2

EVERTON

Player and Position	Ht	Wt	Birth Date	Place	Source	Clubs	League App	Gls
Goalkeepers								
Jason Kearton	6 1	11 10	9 7 69	Ipswich (Australia)	Brisbane Lions	Everton	—	—
Neville Southall	6 1	12 01	16 9 58	Llandudno	Winsford	Bury	39	—
						Everton	291	—
						Port Vale (loan)	9	—
Mike Stowell	6 2	11 10	19 4 65	Preston	Leyland Motors	Preston NE	—	—
						Everton	—	—
						Chester C (loan)	14	—
						York C (loan)	6	—
						Manchester C (loan)	14	—
						Port Vale (loan)	7	—
						Wolverhampton W (loan)	7	—
						Preston NE (loan)	2	—
Defenders								
Martin Keown	6 1	12 04	24 7 66	Oxford	Apprentice	Arsenal	22	—
						Brighton & HA (loan)	23	1
						Aston Villa	112	3
						Everton	20	—
Neil McDonald	5 11	11 04	2 11 65	Newcastle	Wallsend BC	Newcastle U	180	24
						Everton	56	2
Neil Pointon	5 10	11 00	28 11 64	Warsop Vale	Apprentice	Scunthorpe U	159	2
						Everton	102	5
Kevin Ratcliffe	5 11	12 07	12 11 60	Mancot	Apprentice	Everton	314	2
Dave Watson	6 0	11 12	20 11 61	Liverpool	Amateur	Liverpool	—	—
						Norwich C	212	11
						Everton	133	12
Mark Wright	5 9	10 08	29 1 70	Manchester	Trainee	Everton	1	—
Edward Youds	6 0	11 00	3 5 70	Liverpool	Trainee	Everton	—	—
						Cardiff (loan)	1	—
						Wrexham (loan)	20	2
Midfield								
Ray Atteveld	5 10	12 00	8 9 66	Amsterdam	Haarlem	Everton	18	1
John Ebbrell	5 7	9 12	1 10 69	Bromborough	FA School	Everton	21	—
Marcus Ebdon	5 9	11 00	17 10 70	Pontypool	Trainee	Everton	—	—
Philip Jones	5 8	10 09	1 12 69	Liverpool	Trainee	Everton	1	—
						Blackpool (loan)	6	—
Stuart McCall	5 6	10 01	10 6 64	Leeds	Apprentice	Bradford C	238	37
						Everton	70	3
Stefan Rehn (To Gothenburg Jan 1990)	5 10	10 10	22 9 66	Stockholm	Djurgaarden	Everton	4	—
Kevin Sheedy	5 9	10 11	21 10 59	Builth Wells	Apprentice	Hereford U	51	4
						Liverpool	3	—
						Everton	236	62
Ian Snodin	5 7	8 12	15 8 63	Rotherham	Apprentice	Doncaster R	188	25
						Leeds U	51	6
						Everton	95	2
Trevor Steven (To Rangers July 1989)	5 8	10 09	21 9 63	Berwick	Apprentice	Burnley	76	11
						Everton	214	48
Norman Whiteside	6 0	12 08	7 5 65	Belfast	Apprentice	Manchester U	206	47
						Everton	27	9
Ian Wilson (To Kocaelispor Aug 1989)	5 7	10 10	27 3 58	Aberdeen	Elgin C	Leicester C	285	17
						Everton	34	1

EVERTON

Foundation: St. Domingo Church Sunday School formed a football club in 1878 which played at Stanley Park. Enthusiasm was so great that in November 1879 they decided to expand membership and changed the name to Everton playing in black shirts with a white sash and nicknamed the "Black Watch". After wearing several other colours, royal blue was adopted in 1901.

First Football League game: 8 September, 1888, Football League, v Accrington (h) W 2-1 – Smalley; Dick, Ross; Holt, Jones, Dobson; Fleming (2), Waugh, Lewis, E. Chadwick, Farmer.

Managers (and Secretary-managers)
W. E. Barclay 1888–89*, Dick Molyneux 1889–1901*, William C. Cuff 1901–18*, W. J. Sawyer 1918–19*, Thomas H. McIntosh 1919–35*, Theo Kelly 1936–48, Cliff Britton 1948–56, Ian Buchan 1956–58, Johnny Carey 1958–61, Harry Catterick 1961–73, Billy Bingham 1973–77, Gordon Lee 1977–81, Howard Kendall 1981–87, Colin Harvey 1987– .

Player and Position	Ht	Wt	Birth Date	Place	Source	Clubs	League App	Gls
Forwards								
Peter Beagrie	5 8	9 10	28 11 65	Middlesbrough	Local	Middlesbrough	33	2
						Sheffield U	84	11
						Stoke C	54	7
						Everton	19	—
Tony Cottee	5 8	11 04	11 7 65	West Ham	Apprentice	West Ham U	212	92
						Everton	63	26
Pat Nevin	5 6	10 00	6 9 63	Glasgow	Gartcosh U	Clyde	73	17
						Chelsea	193	36
						Everton	55	6
Mike Newell	6 0	11 00	27 1 65	Liverpool	Amateur	Liverpool	—	—
						Crewe Alex	3	—
						Wigan Ath	72	25
						Luton T	63	18
						Leicester C	81	21
						Everton	26	7
Gary Powell	5 10	10 02	2 4 69	Holylake	Trainee	Everton	—	—
Paul Quinlan			17 4 71	Madrid	Trainee	Everton	—	—
Graeme Sharp	6 1	11 08	16 10 60	Glasgow	Eastercraigs	Dumbarton	40	17
						Everton	295	108

Trainees
Christian, Darren; Clifton, Joseph M; Coy, Chilton S; Darkes, Jason V; Dulson, Craig T; Feeney, David S; Gouldstone, David A; Jenkins, Iain; McDonough, Michael; Monk, Alasdair C; Moore, Neil; O'Neil, John A.J; Reilly, Stephen J; Sang, Neil; Smith, Paul A; Turner, Brendan J; Walsh, Ian J; Whalley, David C; Wilson, David J.

Associated Schoolboys
Ball, Stephen M; Brennan, Jonathan W; Brown, Paul R; Carpenter, James R; Carridge, John J; Dowe, Julian L; Emery, Richard; Gifford, Kenneth J; Grant, Anthony J; Holcroft, Peter I; Jones, Terence P; Lane, Steven; Loupe, Kevin A; McCullagh, Edward J; McGarry, Kevin L; McMahon, Alan D; Malkeson, Alan G; Owen, Phillip G; Powell, Mark A; Price, Christopher; Renforth, Glenn L; Ruffer, Carl J; Ryan, Terence J; Scotton, Alan; Smith, Alex P; Smith, David L; Smith, Dean A; Tait, Paul; Williams, Neil W; Woodhouse, Lee J.

Associated Schoolboys who have accepted the club's offer of a Traineeship/Contract
Bayley, Andrew; Kenny, William A; Langton, Edward P; Norris, Barry; Sharrock, Mark; Unsworth, David G.

EXETER CITY 1989–90 *Back row (left to right):* Richard Young, Dave Walter, Kevin Miller, Lee Rogers.
Centre row: Steve Neville, Herbie Heath, Richard Dryden, Ian Benjamin, Shaun Taylor, Jim McNichol, Phil Lock, Clive Whitehead.
Front row: Paul Batty, Danny Bailey, Scott Hiley, Darran Rowbotham, Chris Vinnicombe, Brian McDermott.

Division 3   **EXETER CITY**

St James Park, Exeter EX4 6PX. Telephone Exeter (0392) 54073. Commercial Dept: (0392) 59466.

Ground capacity: 17, 086.

Record attendance: 20, 984 v Sunderland, FA Cup 6th rd replay, 4 March, 1931.

Record receipts: £32,007 v Newcastle U, FA Cup 5th rd replay, 18 Feb, 1981.

Pitch measurements: 114yd × 73yd.

President: W. C. Hill.

Chairman: A. I. Doble.

Directors: I. M. Couch, A. Gooch JP. M. Holladay, G. Vece, P. Carter, B. J. Snell.

Manager: Terry Cooper. *Coach/Assistant Manager:* Steve Neville.

Secretary M. Holladay.

Commercial Manager: Tony Kellow.

Year Formed: 1904. *Turned Professional:* 1908. *Ltd Co.:* 1908.

Club Nickname: 'The Grecians'.

Record League Victory: 8-1 v Coventry C, Division 3 (S), 4 December 1926 – Bailey; Pollard, Charlton; Pullen, Pool, Garrett; Purcell (2), McDevitt, Blackmore (2), Dent (2), Compton (2). 8-1 v Aldershot, Division 3 (S), 4 May 1935 – Chesters; Gray, Miller; Risdon, Webb, Angus; Jack Scott (1), Wrightson (1), Poulter (3), McArthur (1), Dryden (1). (1 og)

Record Cup Victory: 9-1 v Aberdare, FA Cup 1st rd, 26 November 1927 – Holland; Pollard, Charlton; Phoenix, Pool, Gee; Purcell (2), McDevitt, Dent (4), Vaughan (2), Compton (1).

Record Defeat: 0-9 v Notts Co, Division 3 (S), 16 October, 1948 and v Northampton T, Division 3 (S), 12 April 1958.

Most League Points (2 for a win): 62, Division 4, 1976–77.

Most League Points (3 for a win): 89, Division 4, 1989–90.

Most League Goals: 88, Division 3 (S), 1932–33.

Highest League Scorer in Season: Fred Whitlow, 33, Division 3 (S), 1932–33.

Most League Goals in Total Aggregate: Tony Kellow, 129, 1976–78, 1980–83, 1985–88.

Most Capped Player: Dermot Curtis, 1 (17) Eire.

Most League Appearances: Arnold Mitchell, 495, 1952–66.

Record Transfer Fee Received: £105,000 from Blackpool for Tony Kellow, November 1978.

Record Transfer Fee Paid: £65,000 to Blackpool for Tony Kellow, March 1980.

Football League Record: 1920 Elected Division 3; 1921–1958 Division 3 (S); 1958–64 Division 4; 1964–66 Division 3; 1966–77 Division 4; 1977–84 Division 3; 1984–90 Division 4; 1990– Division 3.

Honours: Football League: Division 3 best season: 8th. 1979–80; Division 3 (S) – Runners-up 1932–33; Division 4 – Champions 1989–90; Runners-up 1976–77. *FA Cup* best season: 6th rd replay. 1931. *Football League Cup:* never beyond 4th rd. Division 3(S) *Cup:* Winners 1934.

Colours: Red and white striped shirts, black shorts, red stockings white stripes. **Change colours:** Blue and white.

EXETER CITY 1989–90 LEAGUE RECORD

Match No.	Date	Venue	Opponents	Result	H/T Score	Lg. Pos.	Goalscorers	Atten- dance
1	Aug 19	H	Doncaster R	W 1-0	1-0	—	Neville	3033
2	26	A	Hartlepool U	W 3-0	2-0	1	Dryden, Taylor, Rowbotham	1726
3	Sept 2	H	Carlisle U	D 0-0	0-0	6		3338
4	9	A	Burnley	L 0-1	0-1	8		5443
5	16	H	Cambridge U	W 3-2	1-2	4	Rowbotham 2, Dryden	2754
6	23	A	Scunthorpe U	L 4-5	2-1	7	Vinnicombe, Neville 2, Dryden	2935
7	27	H	Grimsby T	W 2-1	1-1	—	Rowbotham 2 (1 pen)	3702
8	30	A	Halifax T	W 2-1	0-0	4	Neville, Dryden	1720
9	Oct 7	A	Peterborough U	L 3-4	1-2	6	Robinson (og), Bailey, Rowbotham	3831
10	14	H	Chesterfield	W 2-1	2-1	5	Rowbotham, Whitehead	3773
11	17	A	Rochdale	L 0-1	0-0	—		1337
12	21	H	Hereford U	W 2-0	0-0	5	Dryden, McDermott	3269
13	28	A	Stockport Co	L 1-2	0-1	8	Young	3767
14	Nov 1	H	Colchester U	W 2-1	1-1	—	Neville 2	3905
15	4	H	Lincoln C	W 3-0	2-0	3	McNichol, Rowbotham, Neville	3674
16	11	A	Scarborough	W 2-1	0-1	2	Rowbotham, Batty	2124
17	25	H	Wrexham	D 1-1	1-0	3	Rowbotham	3522
18	Dec 2	A	Maidstone U	L 0-1	0-1	4		1650
19	16	H	Gillingham	W 3-1	1-1	2	Rowbotham 2 (2 pens), Neville	3818
20	26	A	Aldershot	W 1-0	1-0	1	Benjamin	3101
21	30	A	Southend U	W 2-1	1-1	1	Rowbotham 2 (1 pen)	3761
22	Jan 1	H	Torquay U	W 3-0	2-0	1	McNichol, Rowbotham, Whitehead	8154
23	13	A	Hartlepool U	W 3-1	1-0	1	Bennyworth (og) Rowbotham 2	4959
24	20	A	Doncaster R	L 1-2	0-2	2	Neville	3492
25	Feb 10	A	Cambridge U	L 2-3	2-0	2	Whitehead, Rowbotham (pen)	3508
26	13	A	Carlisle U	L 0-1	0-0	—		8461
27	17	H	Maidstone U	W 2-0	0-0	3	Rowbotham, Berry (og)	4181
28	24	A	Wrexham	D 1-1	0-0	2	McNichol	2128
29	Mar 3	H	York C	W 3-1	2-0	1	Neville, Rowbotham 2 (1 pen)	4632
30	7	A	Halifax T	W 2-0	1-0	—	Taylor 2	5528
31	10	A	Grimsby T	L 0-1	0-0	1		6629
32	17	H	Peterborough U	W 2-0	1-0	1	Dryden, Batty (pen)	4676
33	20	A	Chesterfield	L 1-2	1-1	—	Rowe	5319
34	24	H	Rochdale	W 5-0	2-0	1	McNichol 3 (1 pen), Neville 2	4701
35	28	H	Scunthorpe U	W 1-0	0-0	1	Taylor	5805
36	31	A	Hereford U	L 1-2	0-0	1	Dryden	4243
37	Apr 2	A	York C	L 0-3	0-0	—		2091
38	7	H	Stockport Co	D 1-1	1-1	1	McNichol (pen)	4817
39	10	A	Colchester U	W 1-0	0-0	—	McNichol	3369
40	14	A	Torquay U	W 2-0	0-0	1	Taylor, McPherson	3389
41	16	H	Aldershot	W 2-0	1-0	1	Neville, Young	6832
42	21	A	Gillingham	D 1-1	0-0	1	Young	3374
43	25	H	Southend U	W 2-1	1-0	1	Neville, McDermott	8271
44	28	H	Scarborough	W 3-2	1-1	1	Kelly 2 (2 pens), Young	6850
45	May 1	H	Burnley	W 2-1	0-1	—	Whitehead, Young	7544
46	5	A	Lincoln C	W 5-1	2-1	1	Young, Smith (og), Whitehead, McDermott, Rowe	4772

Final League Position: 1

GOALSCORERS

League (83): Rowbotham 21 (6 pens), Neville 14, McNichol 8 (2 pens), Dryden 7, Young 6, Taylor 5, Whitehead 5, McDermott 3, Batty 2 (1 pen), Kelly 2 (2 pens), Rowe 2, Bailey 1, Benjamin 1, McPherson 1, Vinnicombe 1, own goals 4.

Littlewoods Cup (15): Rowbotham 6, McNichol 2, Neville 2, Benjamin 1, Dryden 1, McDermott 1, Vinnicombe 1, Young 1.

FA Cup (10): Rowbotham 4, Bailey 1, Batty 1, Cooper 1, Harrower 1, McDermott 1, Neville 1.

Walter	McNichol	Vinnicombe	Rogers	Taylor	Whitehead	Rowbotham	Bailey	McDermott	Neville	Dryden	Young	Hiley	Benjamin	Rowe	Batty	Cooper	Harrower	Coyle	Frankland	Miller	Elkins	Goddard	Stafford	Eshelby	McPherson	Kelly	Summerfield	Match No.
1	2	3	4	5	6	7	8	9†	10	11*	12		14															1
1		3	4	5	6*	7	8	9	10	11		2	12															2
1		3	4*	5	6	7	8	9	10	11	12	2																3
1		3	4	5	6	7*	8	9	10	11	12	2																4
1		3	4	5	6	7	8	9		11	10*	2	12															5
1		3	4	5	6	7	8	9*	10	11	12	2																6
1		3	4	5	6	7	8	9*	10	11	12	2																7
1		3	4	5	6	7	8	9	10*	11	12	2																8
1	4	3		5	6	7	8		10		9	2	11*	12														9
1	4	3		5	6	7	8	9	10	11		2																10
1	4	3		5	6	7	8	9*	10	11	12	2																11
1	4	3		5	6	7*	8	9	10	11	12	2																12
1	4	3		5	6	7	8	9	10*	11	12	2																13
1	4	3		5		7	8*	9	10	11	12	2			6													14
1	4			5		7	8	9	10*	11	3	2	12		6													15
1	4			5		7	8	9	10	11	3*	2			6	12												16
1	4			5	6	7	8		10			2			9	12	3*	11										17
1	4			5	6	7	8		10			2		11*	9	12	3											18
	4			5	6	7	8	9	10			2		3		12	11*			1								19
				5	6	7	8	9	10			2		3					4	1	11							20
	4			5	6	7	8	9	10			2		3						1	11							21
	4			5	6	7*	8	9	10			2		3†		12				1	11	14						22
	4*			5	6	7	8	9	10			2		3		12				1	11							23
	4	12		5	6	7	8	9*	10			2		3						1	11							24
	4			5	6	7*	8	9	10			2		3		12				1	11							25
	4	12		5	6	7	8	9	10			2		3	14					1		11†						26
	4			5	6*	7	8	9	10			2		3		12	11			1								27
	4			5	6	12	8		10†	11		2		14	9	3*				1			7					28
	4			5	6	7	8	9	10	3		2		11						1								29
	4			5	6	7	8	9	10	3		2		11						1								30
	4			5		7†	8		10	3		2		14	11*		6			1				9				31
	4			5		7*	8	9†	10	3	12	2		11				14		1				6				32
	4			5			8		10	3	9	2		7	11					1				6				33
	4			5*			8	7	10†	11	9	2		14						1					3	12	6	34
	4			5		12	8	7	10*	11	9		3							1					2		6	35
	4			5		9†	8	12	10	11		2		14						1					3	7	6*	36
	4			5	6		8	12		11	9*	2			10					1					3	7		37
	4			5	6		8	9	10		12	2								1					3	7	11*	38
	4			5	6		8	9	10	11		2								1					3	7		39
	4			5			8	9	10	6	11	2								1					3	7		40
	4			5		12	8	9	10	6	11	2								1					3*	7		41
	4*	12		5		3	8	9		6	11	2			10					1						7		42
				5		3	8	9		6	11	2				4				1						7		43
	4			5		3	8	9*	10	6†	11	2		14	12					1						7		44
	4			5		3	8				11	2			6	12				1						7*		45
	4			5		3	8	9			11*	2			10	6	12			1						7		46
18	33	14	13	45	36	31	46	38	42	30	16	45	10	4	15	1	3	1	3	28	5	—	2	1	11	11	4	

+3s   +2s +1s   +3s   +12s +1s   +2s   +6s +5s   +4s +4s   +1s   +1s   +1s

Littlewoods Cup

First Round	Swansea C (h)	3-0
	(a)	1-1
Second Round	Blackburn R (h)	3-0
	(a)	1-2
Third Round	Blackpool (h)	3-0
Fourth Round	Sunderland (h)	2-2
	(a)	2-5

FA Cup

First Round	Dartford (a)	1-1
	(h)	4-1
Second Round	Maidstone U (a)	1-1
	(h)	3-2
Third Round	Norwich C (h)	1-1
	(a)	0-2

EXETER CITY

Player and Position	Ht	Wt	Birth Date	Birth Place	Source	Clubs	League App	Gls
Goalkeepers								
Kevin Miller	6 1	12 10	15 3 69	Falmouth	Newquay	Exeter C	31	—
David Walter	6 3	13 03	3 9 64	Barnstable	Bideford T	Exeter C	44	—
						Plymouth Arg (loan)	—	—
Defenders								
Richard Dryden	6 0	11 02	14 6 69	Stroud		Bristol R	13	—
						Exeter C	51	7
Tony Frankland§	6 1	10 07	11 10 72	Greenwich		Exeter C	4	—
Herbert Heath*	6 0	12 08	29 3 70	Wolverhampton	Darlaston	Exeter C	5	—
Tom Kelly	5 10	11 10	28 3 64	Bellshill	Hibernian	Hartlepool U	15	—
						Torquay U	120	—
						York C	35	2
						Exeter C	12	2
Jim McNichol	6 0	12 10	9 6 58	Glasgow	Apprentice	Ipswich T	—	—
						Luton T	15	—
						Brentford	155	22
						Exeter C	87	10
						Torquay U	124	13
						Exeter C	33	8
Lee Rogers	5 11	12 07	8 4 67	Bristol	Apprentice	Bristol C	30	—
						Hereford U (loan)	13	—
						York C (loan)	7	—
						Exeter C	61	—
Shaun Taylor	6 1	13 00	26 3 63	Plymouth	Bideford	Exeter C	155	12
Clive Whitehead	5 11	11 06	24 11 55	Birmingham	Northfield J	Bristol C	229	10
						WBA	168	6
						Wolverhampton W (loan)	2	—
						Portsmouth	65	2
						Exeter C	38	5
Midfield								
Danny Bailey	5 7	12 07	21 5 64	London	Wealdstone	Exeter C	46	1
Paul Batty	5 7	10 07	9 1 64	E Dington	Apprentice	Swindon T	108	7
						Chesterfield	26	—
						Exeter C	100	11
						Cambridge U (loan)	—	—
Mark Cooper	5 8	11 04	18 12 68	Wakefield	Trainee	Bristol C	—	—
						Exeter C	5	—
						Southend U (loan)	5	—
Tony Coyle‡	5 10	11 12	17 1 60	Glasgow	Avoco Amats	Albion R	46	5
						Stockport Co	219	28
						Chesterfield	76	4
						Stockport Co	23	3
						Exeter C	1	—
Steven Harrower	5 8	11 01	9 10 61	Exeter	Local	Exeter C	187	10
Scott Hiley	5 9	10 07	27 9 68	Plymouth	Trainee	Exeter C	98	6
Steve Neville	5 9	11 00	18 9 57	Walthamstow	Apprentice	Southampton	5	1
						Exeter C	93	22
						Sheffield U	49	6
						Exeter C (loan)	33	17
						Exeter C	59	10
						Bristol C	134	40
						Exeter C	80	28
Darren Rowbotham	5 10	11 05	22 10 66	Cardiff	Trainee	Plymouth Arg	46	2
						Exeter C	100	43
Ben Rowe	5 7	10 00	1 10 70	Hull	Bristol C	Exeter C	10	2
Chris Vinnicombe (To Rangers Nov 1989)	5 9	10 04	20 10 70	Exeter	Trainee	Exeter C	39	1

EXETER CITY

Foundation: Exeter City was formed in 1904 by the amalgamation of St. Sidwell's United and Exeter United. The club first played in the East Devon League and then the Plymouth & District League. After an exhibition match between West Bromwich Albion and Woolwich Arsenal was held to test interest as Exeter was then a rugby stronghold, Exeter City decided at a meeting at the Red Lion Hotel to turn professional in 1908.

First Football League game: 28 August, 1920, Division 3, v Brentford (h) W 3-0 – Pym; Coleburne, Feebury (1p); Crawshaw, Carrick, Mitton; Appleton, Makin, Wright (1), Vowles (1), Dockray.

Managers (and Secretary-managers)
Arthur Chadwick 1910–22, Fred Mavin 1923–27, Dave Wilson 1928–29, Billy McDevitt 1929–35, Jack English 1935–39, George Roughton 1945–52, Norman Kirkham 1952–53, Norman Dodgin 1953–57, Bill Thompson 1957–58, Frank Broome 1958–60, Glen Wilson 1960–62, Cyril Spiers 1962–63, Jack Edwards 1963–65, Ellis Stuttard 1965–66, Jock Basford 1966–67, Frank Broome 1967–69, Johnny Newman 1969–76, Bobby Saxton 1977–79, Brian Godfrey 1979–83, Gerry Francis 1983–84, Jim Iley 1984–85, Colin Appleton 1985–87, Terry Cooper 1988–   .

Player and Position	Ht	Wt	Birth Date	Birth Place	Source	Clubs	League App	Gls
Forwards								
Symon Burgher						Exeter C	14	—
Paul Eshelby			29 5 70	Sheffield		Exeter C	1	—
Brian McDermott	5 8	9 12	8 4 61	Slough	Apprentice	Arsenal	61	12
						Fulham (loan)	3	—
						Oxford U	24	2
						Huddersfield T (loan)	4	1
						Cardiff C	51	8
						Exeter C	60	4
Martin Parker‡	6 0	11 06	3 1 70	Exeter	Trainee	Exeter C	1	—
Richard Young	6 3	13 07	31 12 68	Nottingham	Apprentice	Notts Co	35	5
						Southend U	9	—
						Exeter C	42	10
Angus McPherson on loan from Rangers							11	1

Trainees
Annunziata, Lee J; Day, James A; Frankland, Tony; Hawkins, Jonathan D; Smith, Stuart J.

Associated Schoolboys
Cullen, Marc R; Fairchild, Neil; Hines, Christopher J; Locke, Zak W; Malcolm, Duncan J; Murch, Steven; Phillips, Martin J; Pitts, Kevin J; Powell, Shane M; Reed, Dean; Sercombe, Kevin J; Turvey, Mark A.

Associated Schoolboys who have accepted the club's offer of a Traineeship/Contract
Redwood, Tony R.B; Wright, Andrew J.

FULHAM 1989–90 *Back row (left to right):* Glen Hunter (Physiotherapist), Terry Bullivant (Club Coach), Paul German, Ronnie Mauge, Glen Thomas, Jim Stannard, Shaun Gore, Jeff Eckhardt, Laurence Batty, Andy Sayer, Leo Donnellan, Justin Skinner, Jack Burkett (Assistant Manager), Peter Westacott (Physiotherapist). *Front row:* Steven Greaves, Peter Scott, John Marshall, Jason Howes, Ray Lewington (Manager), Clive Walker, Gordon Davies, Gary Elkins, Gary Barnett.

Division 3 **FULHAM**

Craven Cottage, Stevenage Rd, Fulham, London SW6. Telephone 071-736 6561. Pools Office: 071-736 4634. Clubcall 0898 12 11 98.
Ground capacity: 18,304.
Record attendance: 49,335 v Millwall, Division 2, 8 Oct, 1938.
Record receipts: £80,247 v Chelsea, Division 2, 8 Oct, 1983.
Pitch measurements: 110yd × 75yd.
Chairman: Jimmy Hill.
Directors: Bill Muddyman (Vice-chairman), D. J. Gardner, C. A. Swain, A. Muddyman.
Manager: Alan Dicks. *Assistant Manager:*
Coach: Terry Bullivant. *Physio:* Peter Westacott.
Club Secretary: Mrs Yvonne Haines.
Commercial Manager: Dominic Ostrowski.
Year Formed: 1879. *Turned Professional:* 1898. *Ltd Co.:* 1903. *Reformed:* 1987.
Club Nickname: 'Cottagers'.
Previous Name: 1879–98, Fulham St Andrew's.
Previous Grounds: Lillie Road, Fulham Cross; Barn Elms, Barnes; Ranelagh House; Stansfield's Field, Fulham Road; Half-Moon Cricket Ground, Putney: 1896. Craven Cottage.
Record League Victory: 10-1 v Ipswich T, Division 1, 26th December 1963 – Macedo; Cohen, Langley; Mullery (1), Keetch, Robson (1); Key, Cook (1), Leggat (4), Haynes, Howfield (3).
Record Cup Victory: 6-0 v Wimbledon (away), FA Cup, 1st rd (replay), 3 December 1930 – Iceton; Gibbon, Lilley; Oliver, Dudley, Barrett; Temple, Hammond (1), Watkins (1), Gibbons (2), Penn (2). 6-0 v Bury, FA Cup, 3rd rd, 7 January 1938 – Turner; Bacuzzi, Keeping; Evans, Dennison, Tompkins; Higgins, Worsley, Rooke (6), O'Callaghan. Arnold.
Record Defeat: 0-10 v Liverpool, League Cup 2nd Rd, 1st leg. 23 September 1986.
Most League Points (2 for a win): 60, Division 2, 1958–59 and Division 3, 1970–71.
Most League Points (3 for a win): 78, Division 3, 1981–82.
Most League Goals: 111, Division 3 (S), 1931-32.
Highest League Scorer in Season: Frank Newton, 43, Division 3 (S), 1931–32.
Most League Goals in Total Aggregate: Bedford Jezzard, 154, 1948–56.
Most Capped Player: Johnny Haynes, 56, England.
Most League Appearances: Johnny Haynes, 594, 1952–70.
Record Transfer Fee Received: £333,333 from Liverpool for Richard Money, May 1980.
Record Transfer Fee Paid: £150,000 to Orient for Peter Kitchen, February 1979, and to Brighton & HA for Teddy Maybank, December 1979.
Football League Record: 1907 Elected to Division 2: 1928–32 Division 3 (S); 1932–49 Division 2; 1949–52 Division 1; 1952–59 Division 2; 1959–68 Division 1; 1968–69 Division 2; 1969–71 Division 3; 1971–80 Division 2; 1980–82 Division 3; 1982–86 Division 2; 1986– Division 3.
Honours: Football League: Division 1 best season: 10th. 1959–60; Division 2 – Champions 1948–49; Runners-up 1958–59; Division 3 (S) – Champions 1931–32; Division 3 – Runners-up 1970–71. *FA Cup:* Runners-up 1974–75. *Football League Cup* best season: 5th rd, 1967–68, 1970–71.
Colours: White shirts black trim, black shorts, white stockings black trim. **Change colours:** All red.

FULHAM 1989–90 LEAGUE RECORD

Match No.	Date	Venue	Opponents	Result	H/T Score	Lg. Pos.	Goalscorers	Attendance
1	Aug 19	H	Tranmere R	L 1-2	0-1	—	Eckhardt	4811
2	26	A	Bolton W	D 0-0	0-0	16		5524
3	Sept 2	H	Mansfield T	W 1-0	0-0	12	Skinner	4551
4	9	A	Crewe Alex	W 3-2	0-0	8	Walker, Sayer, Stannard	3301
5	16	H	Swansea C	W 2-0	0-0	7	Thomas, Sayer	4520
6	23	A	Walsall	D 0-0	0-0	7		3969
7	26	H	Huddersfield T	D 0-0	0-0	—		4445
8	30	A	Chester C	W 2-0	1-0	4	Dowie, Marshall	2135
9	Oct 7	A	Bristol R	L 0-2	0-0	7		5811
10	14	H	Rotherham U	D 1-1	0-0	9	Marshall	4375
11	17	A	Reading	L 2-3	0-1	—	Skinner (pen), Sayer	4743
12	21	H	Bury	D 2-2	0-0	11	Walker, Marshall	3520
13	28	A	Brentford	L 0-2	0-2	12		7962
14	31	H	Northampton T	D 1-1	1-1	—	Mauge	3518
15	Nov 5	A	Leyton Orient	D 1-1	1-0	—	Sayer	5817
16	11	H	Cardiff C	L 2-5	1-3	13	Milton, Skinner (pen)	4030
17	25	H	Wigan Ath	W 4-0	1-0	12	Scott, Walker 2, Sayer	3156
18	Dec 2	A	Notts Co	L 0-2	0-1	12		5132
19	16	A	Blackpool	W 1-0	1-0	11	Walker	2648
20	26	H	Bristol C	L 0-1	0-1	11		6089
21	30	H	Shrewsbury T	W 2-1	1-1	11	Walker 2 (1 pen)	3622
22	Jan 1	A	Birmingham C	D 1-1	0-0	12	Scott	8932
23	6	A	Preston NE	L 0-1	0-1	—		5055
24	13	H	Bolton W	D 2-2	2-2	12	Milton, Skinner	4523
25	19	A	Tranmere R	L 1-2	0-0	—	Walker	6154
26	27	H	Crewe Alex	D 1-1	0-0	13	Marshall	3915
27	Feb 10	A	Swansea C	L 2-4	1-3	17	Walker (pen), Milton	3433
28	13	A	Mansfield T	L 0-3	0-0	—		2255
29	17	H	Notts Co	W 5-2	1-1	14	Milton 2, Mauge, Scott, Davies	4625
30	24	A	Wigan Ath	L 1-2	0-0	18	Davies	2163
31	Mar 3	H	Preston NE	W 3-1	1-0	16	Pike, Davies, Walker (pen)	4207
32	6	H	Chester C	W 1-0	0-0	—	Walker	3824
33	10	A	Huddersfield T	W 1-0	0-0	11	Walker	4780
34	17	H	Bristol R	L 1-2	0-0	12	Walker	5656
35	20	A	Rotherham U	L 1-2	1-0	—	Barnett	4511
36	24	H	Reading	L 1-2	0-0	16	Davies	4835
37	31	A	Bury	D 0-0	0-0	16		3000
38	Apr 4	H	Walsall	D 0-0	0-0	—		2652
39	7	A	Northampton T	D 2-2	1-0	17	Davies, Elkins	2822
40	10	H	Brentford	W 1-0	1-0	—	Milton	6729
41	14	H	Birmingham C	L 1-2	0-1	14	Milton	4568
42	16	A	Bristol C	L 1-5	1-2	16	Eckhardt	16,139
43	21	H	Blackpool	D 0-0	0-0	17		3816
44	24	A	Shrewsbury T	L 0-2	0-2	—		2831
45	28	A	Cardiff C	D 3-3	1-1	20	Milton 2, Davies	3932
46	May 5	H	Leyton Orient	L 1-2	1-0	20	Pike	7141

Final League Position: 20

GOALSCORERS

League (55): Walker 13 (3 pens), Milton 9, Davies 6, Sayer 5, Marshall 4, Skinner 4 (2 pens), Scott 3, Eckhardt 2, Mauge 2, Pike 2, Barnett 1, Dowie 1, Elkins 1, Stannard 1, Thomas 1.
Littlewoods Cup (6): Scott 2, Skinner 2 (1 pen), Walker 1, Watson 1.
FA Cup (5): Marshall 1, Peters 1, Scott 1, Walker 1, Watson 1.

Stannard	Mauge	Kimble	Skinner	Eckhardt	Thomas	Marshall	Bremner	Watson	Davies	Sayer	Walker	Lewington	Barnett	Nebbeling	Scott	Dowie	Langley	Donnellan	Elkins	Milton	Vertannes	Burns	Peters	Dowson	Pike	Newson	Batty	Cole	Match No.
1	2	3	4	5	6	7	8†	9	10	11*	12	14																	1
1	2		14	4	6	7	12	9†	10	11			3*	5	8														2
1	2		14	4	6	7	12	9	10	11*			3†	5	8														3
1	2†		14	4	6	7	12	9*	10	11			3	5	8														4
1	2			4	6	7	12		10	11*			3	5	8	9													5
1	2			4	6	7			10	11			3	5	8	9													6
1	2			4	6	7*	12		10	11†		14	3	5	8	9													7
1	2			4	6	7			10	11			3	5	8	9													8
1	2			4*	6	7	12		10	11			3	5	8	9													9
1	2			4	6	7		9†	10	11			3*	5	8			12	14										10
1	2			4	6	7	12		10	11*				5	8			3			9								11
1	2			4	6	7			10	11				5	8			3			9								12
1				4†	6	7		9	10*	11				5	8		12	14	3	2									13
1	10			4	6	7*		9†		11			14	5	8		12		3	2									14
1				4	6	7		9		11				5	8		10	12	3*	2									15
1	8			4	6	7		9†		11		14		5			10	12	3*	2									16
1				4	6	7		9		11				5	8		10		3	2									17
1	3			4†	6	7		9	10	11		14		5	8		12			2*									18
1				4	6	7		9†	10	11				5	8		12	14		2		3*12							19
1	12			4*	6	7		9†	10	11				5	8			14		2		3							20
1				4	6	7		9*	10	11				5	8		12			2		3							21
1				4*	6	7		9	10†	11	12			5	8		14			2		3							22
1				4†	6	7	12	9	10	11		14		5	8*		10			2		3							23
1				4*	6	7	12		10†	11		14		5	8					9		2			3				24
1				4	6	7		2	10†	11*		14		5	8		12			9					3				25
1				4	6	7		2	10*	9	11			5	8		12								3				26
1				4	6	7	12	9*	10	11		14		5	8†					2					3				27
1				4*	6	7	12	2	10	11				5	8					9					3				28
1				4	6	7		2	10	11				5	8					9					3				29
1				4	6	7		2	10	11				5	8					9					3				30
1			12	4	6	7			10	11				5*	8					9					3	2			31
1				4	6	7	5		10	11					8					9					3	2			32
			12	4	6	7	5		10	11					8					9*					3	2		1	33
			12	4	6	7			10*	11					8					9					3	2		1	34
1				4	6	7	5		10	11					8					9					3	2			35
1			12	4	6	7	5		10	11*					8					9					3	2			36
1			12	4	6	7*	5		10	11					8					9				14	3†	2			37
1				4	6	7		2*	10	11					8		12	14		9					3	5			38
1				4	6	7*	12	2	10	11		14			8†					9					3	5			39
1				4	6	7		2	10	11					8					9					3	5			40
1				4†	6	7	12	2	10	11*		14			8					9					3	5			41
1				4†	6		12	2	10	11		14			8					9					3	5		7*	42
1			12	4*	6	7		2	10	11					8					9					3	5			43
1			12	4	6	7*		2	10	11					8					9					3	5			44
1			12	4*	6	7†		2	10	11		14			8					9					3	5			45
1			12	4	6	7		2	10	11†		14			8*					9					3	5			46
44	35	1	24	39	16	34	7	12	19	25	41	2	24	36	41	5	8	8	9	27	—	6	—	4	20	16	2	1	
	+	+	+	+	+	+	+	+		+			+									+		+					
	2s		2s6s	1s	1s	2s	9s2s	4s		4s			2s8s				3s	3s	1s7s	2s		2s							

Littlewoods Cup

	First Round	Oxford U (h)	0-1
		(a)	5-3
	Second Round	Sunderland (a)	1-1
		(h)	0-3

FA Cup

	First Round	Bath C (a)	2-2
		(h)	2-1
	Second Round	Bristol C (a)	1-2

FULHAM

Player and Position	Ht	Wt	Birth Date	Place	Source	Clubs	League App	Gls
Goalkeepers								
Laurence Batty	6 0	13 07	15 2 64	London	Farense	Fulham	7	—
						Crystal Palace (loan)	—	—
Jim Stannard	6 0	13 06	6 10 62	London	Local	Fulham	41	—
						Charlton Ath (loan)	1	—
						Southend U (loan)	17	—
						Southend U	92	—
						Fulham	135	1
Defenders								
Jeff Eckhardt	5 11	11 06	7 10 65	Sheffield		Sheffield U	74	2
						Fulham	112	5
Gary Elkins	5 8	10 10	4 5 66	Wallingford	Apprentice	Fulham	104	2
						Exeter C (loan)	5	—
Paul German*			18 4 71	Chertsey	Trainee	Fulham	—	—
Shaun Gore	6 4	13 01	21 9 68	London		Fulham	26	—
Richard Langley	5 7	11 05	20 3 65	London	Cor Cas	Fulham	46	—
Gavin Nebbeling	6 0	12 04	15 5 63	Johannesburg	Arcadia S	Crystal Palace	151	8
						Northampton T (loan)	11	—
						Fulham	36	—
Mark Newson	5 10	12 06	7 12 60	Stepney	Apprentice Maidstone U	Charlton Ath	—	—
						Bournemouth	177	23
						Fulham	16	—
Gary Peters‡	5 11	11 12	3 8 54	Carshalton	Apprentice Guildford C	Aldershot	—	—
						Reading	156	7
						Fulham	64	2
						Wimbledon	83	7
						Aldershot	17	1
						Reading	100	4
						Fulham	11	2
Martin Pike	5 9	11 04	21 10 64	South Shields	Apprentice	WBA	—	—
						Peterborough U	129	8
						Sheffield U	129	5
						Tranmere R (loan)	2	—
						Bolton W (loan)	5	1
						Fulham	20	2
Doug Rougvie (To Dunfermline Ath Aug 1989)	6 2	13 08	24 5 56	Ballingry		Aberdeen	178	19
						Chelsea	74	3
						Brighton & HA	35	2
						Shrewsbury T	21	3
						Fulham	18	1
Glen Thomas	6 0	11 06	6 10 67	London	Apprentice	Fulham	85	2
Des Vertannes‡			25 4 72	Hounslow	Trainee	Fulham	2	—
Midfield								
Leo Donnellan*	5 10	11 05	19 1 65	Brent	Apprentice	Chelsea	—	—
						Orient (loan)	6	—
						Fulham	79	4
Steve Greaves*	5 9	11 03	17 1 70	London	Trainee	Fulham	1	—
						Waterford (loan)	—	—
						Brighton & HA (loan)	—	—
Ray Lewington	5 6	11 08	7 9 56	Lambeth	Apprentice Vancouver W	Chelsea	85	4
						Wimbledon (loan)	23	—
						Fulham	174	20
						Sheffield U	36	—
						Fulham	60	1
John Marshall	5 10	11 04	18 8 64	Surrey	Apprentice	Fulham	230	21
Peter Scott	5 8	10 10	1 10 63	London	Apprentice	Fulham	215	24
Justin Skinner	6 0	11 03	30 1 69	London	Apprentice	Fulham	103	18

FULHAM

Foundation: Churchgoers were responsible for the foundation of Fulham, which first saw the light of day as Fulham St. Andrew's Church Sunday School FC in 1879. They won the West London Amateur Cup in 1887 and the championship of the West London League in its initial season of 1892–93. The name Fulham had been adopted in 1888.

First Football League game: 3 September, 1907, Division 2, v Hull C (h) L 0-1 – Skene; Ross, Lindsay; Collins, Morrison, Goldie; Dalrymple, Freeman, Bevan, Hubbard, Threlfall.

Managers (and Secretary-managers)
Harry Bradshaw 1904–09, Phil Kelso 1909–24, Andy Ducat 1924–26, Joe Bradshaw 1926–29, Ned Liddell 1929–31, Jim MacIntyre 1931–34, Jim Hogan 1934–35, Jack Peart 1935–48, Frank Osborne 1948–64 (was secretary-manager or GM for most of this period), Bill Dodgin Snr 1949–53, Duggie Livingstone 1956–58, Bedford Jezzard 1958–64 (GM for last two months), Vic Buckingham 1965–68, Bobby Robson 1968, Bill Dodgin Jnr 1969–72, Alec Stock 1972–76, Bobby Campbell 1976–80, Malcolm Macdonald 1980–84, Ray Harford 1984–86, Ray Lewington 1986–90, Alan Dicks 1990– .

Player and Position	Ht	Wt	Birth Date	Birth Place	Source	Clubs	League App	Gls
Forwards								
Gary Barnett	5 5	9 04	11 3 63	Stratford	Apprentice	Coventry C	—	—
						Oxford U	45	9
						Wimbledon (loan)	5	1
						Fulham (loan)	2	1
						Fulham	180	30
Michael Cole	5 11	11 04	3 9 66	Stepney	Amateur	Ipswich T	38	3
						Port Vale (loan)	4	1
						Fulham	46	4
Gordon Davies	5 7	10 12	3 8 55	Merthyr	Merthyr T	Fulham	247	113
						Chelsea	13	6
						Manchester C	31	9
						Fulham	117	39
Jason Howes*	5 8	11 02	24 9 70	London		Fulham	—	—
Ron Mauge	5 10	11 00	10 3 69	Islington	Trainee	Charlton Ath	—	—
						Fulham	50	2
Steve Milton	6 0	12 07	13 4 63	London	Apprentice Whyteleafe	West Ham U	—	—
						Fulham	34	9
Clive Walker	5 8	11 04	26 5 57	Oxford	Apprentice	Chelsea	198	60
						Sunderland	50	10
						QPR	21	1
						Fulham	109	29
John Watson (To Airdrie Feb 1990)	6 0	12 06	13 2 59	Edinburgh	Hong Kong R	Dunfermline Ath	195	72
						Fulham	14	—
Hugh Burns on loan from Dunfermline Ath							6	—

Trainees
Baranowski, Frank M; Budd, Lee P; Ferney, Martin J; Humphreys, Gavin D; Johnson, Ian A; Kemp, Finlay C; McMillan, Jamie; Morgan, Michael I; O'Connor, Daniel T; Onwere, Udo A; Swan, Michael J; Tucker, Mark J.

Associated Schoolboys
Armitage, James A; Bryant, James P; Jupp, Duncan A; Murphy, Gary J; Whitaker, Andrew T; Wright, Stuart J.

Associated Schoolboys who have accepted the club's offer of a Traineeship/Contract
Brodrick, Darren; Gayle, Anthony; Lewis, Leon J

252

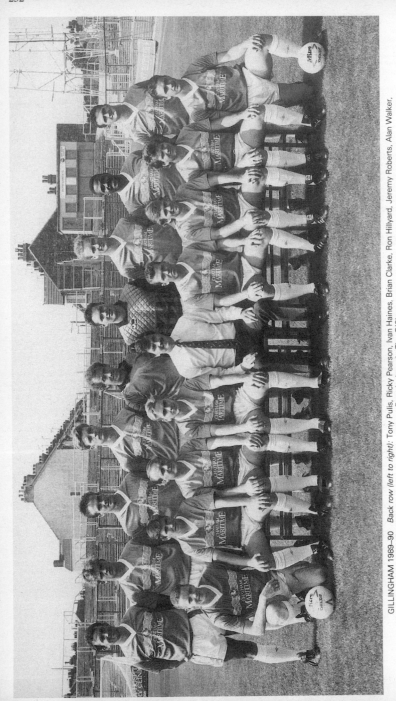

GILLINGHAM 1989–90 *Back row (left to right)*: Tony Pulis, Ricky Pearson, Ivan Haines, Brian Clarke, Ron Hillyard, Jeremy Roberts, Alan Walker, Francis Joseph, Tim O'Shea.
Front row: Gary Smith, Tony Eeles, Paul Haylock, Billy Mannel, Damien Richardson (Manager), Russell Norris, Peter Johnson, Steve Lovell, Lee Palmer.

Division 4 — **GILLINGHAM**

Priestfield Stadium, Gillingham. Telephone Medway (0634) 51854/576828. Commercial Office: 51462.

Ground capacity: 19,581.

Record attendance: 23,002 v QPR, FA Cup 3rd rd. 10 Jan, 1948.

Record receipts: £35,070 v Everton, FA Cup 4th rd, 2nd replay, 4 Feb, 1984.

Pitch measurements: 114yd × 75yd.

President: J. W. Leech. *Vice-Presidents:* G. B. Goodere, G. V. W. Lukehurst, B. B. Moore.

Chairman: M. G. Lukehurst. *Vice-Chairman:* Rt. Hon. Earl Henry Sondes.

Directors: P. H. Giles FCA, G. Trevor Carney. *Managing Director:* A. Smith.

Manager: Damien Richardson. *Assistant Manager:* Ron Hillyard.

Player Coach: Ron Hillyard. *Physio:* Javed Mughal.

Club Secretary: Barry Bright. *Commercial Manager:* John Letley.

Year Formed: 1893. *Turned Professional:* 1894. *Ltd Co.:* 1893.

Club Nickname: 'The Gills'.

Previous Name: New Brompton, 1893–1913.

Record League Victory: 10-0 v Chesterfield, Division 3, 5 September 1987 – Kite; Haylock, Pearce, Shipley (2) (Lillis), West, Greenall (1), Pritchard (2), Shearer (2), Lovell, Elsey (2), David Smith (1).

Record Cup Victory: 10-1 v Gorleston, FA Cup, 1st rd, 16 November 1957 – Brodie; Parry, Hannaway; Riggs, Boswell, Laing; Payne, Fletcher (2), Saunders (5), Morgan (1), Clark (2).

Record Defeat: 2-9 v Nottingham F, Division 3 (S), 18 November, 1950.

Most League Points (2 for a win): 62, Division 4, 1973–74.

Most League Points (3 for a win): 83, Division 3, 1984–85.

Most League Goals: 90, Division 4, 1973–74.

Highest League Scorer in Season: Ernie Morgan, 31, Division 3 (S), 1954–55 and Brian Yeo, 31, Division 4, 1973–74.

Most League Goals in Total Aggregate: Brian Yeo. 135, 1963–75.

Most Capped Player: Tony Cascarino, 3 (26), Republic of Ireland.

Most League Appearances: John Simpson, 571, 1957–72.

Record Transfer Fee Received: £250,000 from Bournemouth for Gavin Peacock, August 1989.

Record Transfer Fee Paid: £102,500 to Tottenham H for Mark Cooper, October 1987.

Football League Record: 1920 Original Member of Division 3; 1921 Division 3 (S); 1938 Failed re-election; Southern League 1938–44; Kent League 1944–46; Southern League 1946–50; 1950 Re-elected to Division 3 (S); 1958–64 Division 4; 1964–71 Division 3; 1971–74 Division 4; 1974–89 Division 3;1989– Division 4.

Honours: Football League: Division 3 best season: 4th, 1978–79, 1984–85; Division 4 – Champions 1963–64; Runners-up 1973–74. *FA Cup* best season: 5th rd. 1969–70. *Football League Cup* best season; 4th rd. 1964.

Colours: Royal blue shirts white trim, white shorts blue trim, white stockings. **Change colours:** Red shirts, white shorts, white stockings.

GILLINGHAM 1989–90 LEAGUE RECORD

Match No.	Date	Venue	Opponents	Result	H/T Score	Lg. Pos.	Goalscorers	Attendance
1	Aug 19	H	Aldershot	D 0-0	0-0	—		3670
2	26	A	Doncaster R	D 0-0	0-0	15		1887
3	Sept 2	H	Scunthorpe U	L 0-3	0-0	20		3467
4	9	A	Hartlepool U	W 2-1	0-1	15	Palmer, Heritage	1691
5	16	H	Burnley	D 0-0	0-0	17		3853
6	23	A	Carlisle U	L 0-3	0-1	18		3185
7	26	H	Southend U	W 5-0	1-0	—	Trusson, Lovell 2 (1 pen), Eeles, Manuel	3842
8	30	A	Peterborough U	D 1-1	0-0	15	Lovell	4199
9	Oct 6	A	Halifax T	W 1-0	0-0	—	Lovell	1776
10	14	H	Stockport Co	L 0-3	0-1	13		3887
11	17	A	Grimsby T	L 0-2	0-1	—		3447
12	21	H	Chesterfield	W 3-0	2-0	13	Palmer, Lovell 2 (2 pens)	2878
13	31	H	Rochdale	W 1-0	0-0	—	Lovell (pen)	3187
14	Nov 4	H	Scarborough	W 2-0	1-0	12	Manuel 2	3436
15	11	A	Lincoln C	W 3-1	3-1	10	Trusson, Heritage, Lovell	3612
16	14	A	Torquay U	W 2-0	1-0	—	Heritage, Palmer	2318
17	24	H	Colchester U	D 3-3	2-0	—	Heritage, Lovell (pen), O'Shea	3816
18	Dec 9	A	York C	L 0-1	0-0	—		2134
19	16	A	Exeter C	L 1-3	1-1	10	Lovell (pen)	3818
20	26	H	Maidstone U	L 1-2	0-0	11	Walker	10,412
21	30	H	Wrexham	W 1-0	1-0	8	Johnson	3733
22	Jan 1	A	Hereford U	W 2-1	1-0	7	Heritage, Johnson	2759
23	13	H	Doncaster R	W 3-1	2-1	7	Heritage, Brevett (og), O'Connor	3820
24	20	A	Aldershot	L 0-1	0-0	7		2592
25	27	H	Hartlepool U	D 0-0	0-0	8		3676
26	Feb 10	A	Burnley	W 2-1	2-1	8	Eeles, Lovell (pen)	7274
27	13	A	Scunthorpe U	D 0-0	0-0	—		2226
28	17	H	York C	D 0-0	0-0	9		3653
29	23	A	Colchester U	L 0-2	0-1	—		4456
30	27	H	Carlisle U	W 2-1	2-1	—	Manuel, Heritage	3177
31	Mar 3	H	Cambridge U	W 1-0	0-0	6	Gavin	4215
32	6	H	Peterborough U	D 0-0	0-0	—		4301
33	9	A	Southend U	L 0-2	0-1	—		4460
34	16	H	Halifax T	W 3-1	2-0	—	Lovell (pen), O'Shea, Heritage	3825
35	19	A	Stockport Co	L 0-1	0-0	—		3378
36	24	H	Grimsby T	L 1-2	0-1	9	Lovell	4150
37	31	A	Chesterfield	L 0-2	0-1	10		4282
38	Apr 7	H	Torquay U	L 0-2	0-1	11		2869
39	10	A	Rochdale	L 0-1	0-0	—		1334
40	14	H	Hereford U	L 0-1	0-0	14		2365
41	16	A	Maidstone U	W 1-0	1-0	12	Heritage	5003
42	21	H	Exeter C	D 1-1	0-0	14	Beadle	3374
43	24	A	Wrexham	L 1-2	0-1	—	Beadle	3498
44	28	H	Lincoln C	D 1-1	0-0	14	Lovell (pen)	2654
45	May 1	A	Cambridge U	L 1-2	0-1	—	Lovell	4963
46	5	A	Scarborough	W 1-0	0-0	14	Lovell	1807

Final League Position: 14

GOALSCORERS

League (46): Lovell 16 (9 pens), Heritage 9, Manuel 4, Palmer 3, Beadle 2, Eeles 2, Johnson 2, O'Shea 2, Trusson 2, Gavin 1, O'Connor 1, Walker 1, own goal 1.
Littlewoods Cup (1): Lovell 1.
FA Cup (0).

	Hillyard	Norris	Johnson	Haines	Pearson	Thompson	Haylock	Eeles	Beadle	Lovell	Manuel	Joseph	Palmer	Smith	Trusson	Gavin	Heritage	Walker	Docker	O'Shea	Place	O'Connor	Pulis	Kimble	Clarke	Lim	Match No.
	1	2	3	4	5	6	7	8	9*10		11	12															1
	1	2	3	4	5	12	7	8	9*10		11†	6	14														2
	1	14	3	4	5		2	8	10		11†	6			7	9*12											3
	1		3	4			2	8	10	11		6			7	9*12	5										4
	1		3	4			2	8	10	11		6			7	9*12	5										5
	1		3	4	14		2	8	10	11		6			7	12	9*	5†									6
	1		3	4			2	8	10	11		6			7	12	9*	5†14									7
	1		3	4			2	8*	9	11		6			7	12	10	5									8
	1		3	4			2	8*	9	11		6			7	12	10	5									9
	1	14	3	4	5		2	8*	9	11		6				12	10		7†								10
	1		3	4	5		2	8	9	11		6				12	10		7*								11
	1		3	4†			2	8	9	11		6			10*12			5	7	14							12
	1		3	4			2	8	9	11		6			7	10*12	5										13
	1		3	4†			2	8*	9	11		6			7	10	12	5	14								14
	1		3				2	8*	9	11		6			7	12	10	5†	14	4							15
	1		3	14			2	8†	9	11		6			7	12	10*	4	5								16
	1		3				2	9	11*			6			7†12	10	4	14	8	5							17
	1		3	4			2	9	11*			6			7	12	10	5	8								18
	1		3	4			2	9	14			6			7	12	10*	5	8†	11							19
	1		3	4†			2	9	10			6			7	12	8*	5	14	11							20
	1		3				2					6			7	9	10	5	8	11	4						21
	1		3				2					6			7	9	10	5	8	11	4						22
	1		3				2	12	7			6				9*10	5	8	11	4							23
	1	2†14		12	3							6			9	10*	5	7	8	11	4						24
	1		3	2	14		9	4				6			12	10*	5	7	8†	11							25
	1		3	6			2	14	9*						12	10	5	7	8	11	4†						26
	1		3	4			2	6	9		12				10	5	7	8	11*								27
	1		3	6			2		9	4					10	5	7	8*	11	12							28
	1		3	6			2	14		4					12	9*10	5	7	8	11†							29
	1		3				2	12	4		6				11*	9	10	5	7	8							30
	1		3				2	12	4		6				11	9	10	5*	8	7							31
	1		3	14			2	12	4		6				11	9	10*	7	8					5†			32
	1		3	14			2	12	7	4	6				11	9	10	8*						5†			33
	1		3				2	7	14		6				11†12	10*	5	8	9	4							34
			3	10			2	12	7	4	6*				9		5	14	8†			11			1		35
	1		3				2	7			6				11	12	10*	5	8	9†	4	14					36
	1		3				14	7*			6				11	9†	5	2	8	12	4	10					37
	1		3				2	14	12	7					10*	5	8	9†	4	11							38
	1		3				2†	7	12	9					10*	5	14	8			4	11	6				39
	1		3				2	7	12	9			6		10*	5	14	8		4†11							40
	1		3				2	7*	9	6					8	5	10	12		4	11						41
	1		3				2	7	12	9*			6		8	5	10	14		4†11							42
	1		3				2	7	12	9			6		8*	5	10	14		4†11							43
			3				2	7	12	9			6		8*	5	10	14		4	11†					1	44
			3				2	14	8	9			6		12	5	10	7†		4*11						1	45
	14		3	4			7†	8*	9		6				12	5	10	2		11					1		46
	42	2	45	23	5	1	44	24	4	36	30	2	38	—	24	18	34	38	15	29	3	14	16	12	3	4	
		+	+	+			+	+		+	+		+		+	+	+	+	+	+		+	+		+		
	3s	3s	1s	1s			9s	6s5s		2s	1s1s		1s		1s	16s8s	5s	7s	1s1s	2s							

GILLINGHAM

Player and Position	Ht	Wt	Birth Date	Place	Source	Clubs	League App	Gls
Goalkeepers								
Ron Hillyard	5 11	11 04	31 3 53	Rotherham	Amateur	York C	61	—
						Hartlepool U (loan)	23	—
						Bury (loan)	—	—
						Brighton & HA (loan)	—	—
						Gillingham	559	—
Harvey Lim	6 0	13 07	30 8 67	Halesworth	Apprentice	Norwich C	—	—
						Plymouth Arg (loan)	—	—
						Gillingham	4	—
Defenders								
Brian Clarke	6 3	13 08	10 10 68	Eastbourne	School	Gillingham	13	—
Ian Docker	5 8	11 02	12 9 69	Gravesend	Trainee	Gillingham	56	—
Ivan Haines	5 9	10 12	14 9 68	Chatham		Gillingham	39	—
Paul Haylock	5 8	11 00	24 3 63	Lowestoft	Apprentice	Norwich C	155	3
						Gillingham	152	—
Peter Johnson	5 9	11 00	5 10 58	Harrogate	Apprentice	Middlesbrough	43	—
						Newcastle U	16	—
						Bristol C (loan)	20	—
						Doncaster R	12	—
						Darlington	89	2
						Crewe Alex	8	—
						Exeter C	5	—
						Southend U	126	3
						Gillingham	45	2
Billy Manuel	5 5	10 00	28 6 69	Hackney	Apprentice	Tottenham H	—	—
						Gillingham	49	5
Russell Norris*	5 9	10 12	1 2 71	Chatham	Trainee	Gillingham	5	—
Tim O'Shea	5 11	11 04	12 11 66	London	School	Tottenham H	3	—
						Newport Co (loan)	10	—
						Leyton Orient	9	1
						Gillingham	53	2
Lee Palmer	6 0	12 04	19 9 70	Gillingham	Trainee	Gillingham	40	3
Ricky Pearson*	5 11	10 09	18 10 70	Maidstone	Trainee	Gillingham	9	—
Brendan Place			13 12 65	Dublin	Athlone T	Gillingham	4	—
Gary Smith‡	5 11	11 08	30 12 68	Chasetown	Apprentice	Walsall	—	—
						Gillingham	1	—
Alan Walker	6 1	12 07	17 12 59	Mossley	Telford U	Lincoln C	75	4
						Millwall	92	8
						Gillingham	67	2
Midfield								
Tony Eeles	5 7	9 12	15 11 70	Chatham	Trainee	Gillingham	36	2
Tony Pulis	5 10	11 08	16 1 58	Newport	Apprentice	Bristol R	85	3
					Happy Valley, HK	Bristol R	45	2
						Newport Co	77	—
						Bournemouth	74	3
						Gillingham	16	—
Steve Thompson§			17 2 72	Manchester	Trainee	Gillingham	2	—
Mike Trusson	5 10	12 04	26 5 59	Northolt	Apprentice	Plymouth Arg	73	15
						Stoke C (loan)	—	—
						Sheffield U	126	31
						Rotherham U	124	19
						Brighton & HA	37	2
						Gillingham	25	2
Forwards								
Peter Beadle	6 0	11 12	13 5 72	London	Trainee	Gillingham	12	2
Lindon Guscott			29 3 72	London	Trainee	Gillingham	2	—
Peter Heritage			8 11 60	Bexhill	Hythe T	Gillingham	42	9

GILLINGHAM

Foundation: The success of the pioneering Royal Engineers of Chatham excited the interest of the residents of the Medway Towns and led to the formation of many clubs including Excelsior. After winning the Kent Junior Cup and the Chatham District League in 1893, Excelsior decided to go for bigger things and it was at a meeting in the Napier Arms, Brompton, in 1893 that New Brompton FC came into being as a professional concern, securing the use of a ground in Priestfield Road.

First Football League game: 28 August, 1920, Division 3, v Southampton (h) D 1-1 – Branfield; Robertson, Sissons; Battiste, Baxter, Wigmore; Holt, Hall, Gilbey (1), Roe, Gore.

Managers (and Secretary-managers)
W. Ironside Groombridge 1896–1906* (previously financial secretary), Steve Smith 1906–08, W. I. Groombridge 1908–19*, George Collins 1919–20, John McMillan 1920–23, Harry Curtis 1923–26, Albert Hoskins 1926–29, Dick Hendrie 1929–31, Fred Maven 1932–37, Alan Ure 1937–38, Bill Harvey 1938–39, Archie Clark 1939–58, Harry Barratt 1958–62, Freddie Cox 1962–65, Basil Hayward 1966–71, Andy Nelson 1971–74, Len Ashurst 1974–75, Gerry Summers 1975–81, Keith Peacock 1981–87, Paul Taylor 1988, Keith Burkinshaw 1988–89, Damien Richardson 1989– .

Player and Position	Ht	Wt	Birth Date	Place	Source	Clubs	League App	Gls
Garry Kimble	5 8	11 00	6 8 66	Poole		Charlton Ath	9	1
						Exeter C (loan)	1	—
						Cambridge U	41	2
						Doncaster R	65	1
						Fulham	3	—
						Maidstone U	—	—
						Gillingham	14	—
Steve Lovell	5 9	12 03	16 7 60	Swansea	Apprentice	Crystal Palace	74	3
						Stockport Co (loan)	12	—
						Millwall	146	44
						Swansea C (loan)	2	1
						Gillingham	132	56
Mark O'Connor	5 7	10 02	10 3 63	Rochdale	Apprentice	QPR	3	—
						Exeter C (loan)	38	1
						Bristol R	80	10
						Bournemouth	128	12
						Gillingham	15	1
Andy Perry‡	5 8	10 03	28 12 62	Dulwich		Portsmouth	4	—
						Gillingham	13	—

Trainees
Berkley, Austin J; Burke, Paul G; Butler, Philip A; Carpenter, Richard; Dempsey, Mark A.P; Dunne, Joseph; Gethin, Barry; Hague, Paul; Harle, Michael J.L; Hume, Lloyd; Jones, Mark; Jordan, David C; Martin, Eliot J; Thompson, Steven; Wood, Simon.

Associated Schoolboys
Allan, Paul S; Bernini, Scott; Chaplin, Matthew J; Christou, Christopher B; Eede, Jason; Foote, Justin P; Hunt, Kevin; Newman, Terry R; Pinch, Spencer J; Russell, Steven J; Symes, Benjamin E; Trott, Robin F; Verrall, Damon F.

Associated Schoolboys who have accepted the club's offer of a Traineeship/Contract
Arnott, Andrew; Cropper, Nicholas M; Harrison, Stuart J; Wren, Nicholas.

258

GRIMSBY TOWN 1989-90 *Back row (left to right):* Paul Agnew, Stephen Stoutt, Steve Sherwood, Paul Reece, Roger Willis, Shaun Cunnington.
Centre row: Peter Jellett (Physiotherapist), Richard O'Kelly, David Gilbert, Gary Childs, Geoff Stephenson, Paul Smaller, Tom Watson, Kevin Jobling, John McDermott, Arthur Mann (Youth Team Coach).
Front row: Tommy Williams, John Cockerill, Keith Alexander, Alan Buckley (Manager), Andy Tillson, Garry Birtles, Mark Lever.

Division 3 **GRIMSBY TOWN**

Blundell Park, Cleethorpes, South Humberside DN35 7PY. Telephone Cleethorpes (0472) 697111. Clubcall 0898 12 15 76.
Ground capacity: 18,496.
Record attendance: 31,651 v Wolverhampton W, FA Cup 5th rd. 20 Feb, 1937.
Record receipts: £44,137 v Norwich C, Milk Cup 5th rd. 16 Jan, 1985.
Pitch measurements: 111yd × 74yd.
Presidents: T. J. Lindley, T. Wilkinson.
Chairman: P. W. Furneaux. *Vice-Chairman:*
Directors: P. W. Furneaux (Chairman), T. Aspinall (Vice-Chairman), W. H. Carr, G. W. Duffield, A. E. Spalding.
Manager: Alan Buckley. *Assistant Manager:* Arthur Mann.
Coach:
Company Secretary: I. Fleming. *Lottery Director:* T. E. Harvey.
Physio: Peter Jellett.
Year Formed. 1878. *Turned Professional:* 1890. *Ltd Co.:* 1890.
Club Nickname: The Mariners'.
Previous Name: Grimsby Pelham.
Previous Grounds: Clee Park; Abbey Park.
Record League Victory: 9-2 v Darwen, Division 2, 15 April 1899 – Bagshaw; Lockie, Nidd; Griffiths, Bell (1), Nelmes; Jenkinson (3), Richards (1), Cockshutt (3), Robinson, Chadburn (1).
Record Cup Victory: 8-0 v Darlington, FA Cup, 2nd rd, 21 November 1885 – G. Atkinson; J. H. Taylor, H. Taylor; Hall, Kimpson, Hopewell; H. Atkinson (1), Garnham, Seal (3), Sharman, Monument (4).
Record Defeat: 1-9 v Arsenal, Division 1, 28 January, 1931.
Most League Points (2 for a win): 68, Division 3 (N), 1955–56.
Most League Points (3 for a win): 79, Division 4, 1989–90.
Most League Goals: 103, Division 2, 1933–34.
Highest League Scorer in Season: Pat Glover, 42, Division 2, 1933–34.
Most League Goals in Total Aggregate: Pat Glover, 182. 1930–39.
Most Capped Player: Pat Glover, 7, Wales.
Most League Appearances: Keith Jobling, 448, 1953–69.
Record Transfer Fee Received: £300,000 from Everton for Paul Wilkinson, March 1985.
Record Transfer Fee Paid: £110,000 to Watford for James Gilligan, July 1985.
Football League Record: 1892 Original Member Division 2; 1901–03 Division 1; 1903 Division 2; 1910 Failed Re-election; 1911 Re-elected Division 2; 1920–21 Division 3; 1921–26 Division 3 (N); 1926–29 Division 2; 1929–32 Division 1; 1932–34 Division 2; 1934–48 Division 1; 1948–51 Division 2; 1951–56 Division 3 (N); 1956–59 Division 2; 1959–62 Division 3; 1962–64 Division 2; 1964–68 Division 3; 1968–72 Division 4; 1972–77 Division 3; 1977–79 Division 3; 1979–80 Division 3; 1980–87 Division 2; 1987–88 Division 3; 1988–90 Division 4; 1990– Division 3.
Honours: Football League: Division 1 best season: 5th, 1934–35; Division 2 – Champions 1900–01, 1933–34; Runners-up 1928–29; Division 3 (N) – Champions 1925–26, 1955–56. Runners-up 1951–52; Division 3 – Champions 1979–80; Runners-up 1961–62, Division 4 – Champions 1971–72; Runners-up 1978–79; 1989–90. *FA Cup:* Semi-finals, 1936, 1939. *Football League Cup:* best season: 5th rd. 1979–80, 1984–85. *League Group Cup:* Winners 1981–82.
Colours: Black and white vertical striped shirts, black shorts with red triangular panel on side, white stockings with red band on turnover. **Change colours:** All blue.

GRIMSBY TOWN 1989–90 LEAGUE RECORD

Match No.	Date	Venue	Opponents	Result	H/T Score	Lg. Pos.	Goalscorers	Attendance
1	Aug 19	H	Cambridge U	D 0-0	0-0	—		4822
2	26	A	Torquay U	W 3-0	0-0	5	Childs, Cunnington, Rees	2525
3	Sept 2	H	Colchester U	W 4-1	2-0	3	Rees 2, Watson, Daniels (og)	4678
4	9	A	Carlisle U	D 1-1	0-0	4	Childs	3360
5	16	H	Maidstone U	L 2-3	2-2	7	Gilbert 2 (1 pen)	5198
6	23	A	York C	W 1-0	0-0	4	Rees	3366
7	27	A	Exeter C	L 1-2	1-1	—	Lever	3702
8	30	H	Hereford U	L 0-2	0-1	11		4832
9	Oct 7	H	Rochdale	L 1-2	0-1	14	Tillson	3996
10	14	A	Scarborough	L 1-3	0-1	15	Gilbert (pen)	2828
11	17	H	Gillingham	W 2-0	1-0	—	Jobling, Hargreaves	3447
12	21	A	Lincoln C	D 1-1	0-0	14	Alexander	6251
13	28	H	Halifax T	D 1-1	0-0	15	Cunnington	4021
14	Nov 1	A	Peterborough U	D 1-1	1-0	—	Gabbiadini	6827
15	4	H	Chesterfield	L 0-1	0-0	17		4513
16	11	A	Wrexham	W 1-0	1-0	15	Birtles	1658
17	25	H	Aldershot	W 2-1	2-1	14	Agnew, Birtles	3716
18	Dec 2	A	Burnley	D 1-1	0-1	15	Cockerill	5615
19	19	H	Southend U	W 2-0	0-0	—	Cockerill 2 (2 pens)	4001
20	26	A	Scunthorpe U	D 2-2	0-2	13	Alexander, Agnew	8384
21	30	A	Hartlepool U	L 2-4	0-2	15	Rees, Alexander	3398
22	Jan 1	H	Stockport Co	W 4-2	1-1	13	Alexander, Rees, Gilbert (pen), Birtles	5717
23	13	H	Torquay U	D 0-0	0-0	13		4586
24	16	A	Doncaster R	D 0-0	0-0	—		4338
25	20	A	Cambridge U	L 0-2	0-0	15		2623
26	27	H	Carlisle U	W 1-0	0-0	12	Alexander	4657
27	Feb 3	H	York C	W 3-0	1-0	9	Tillson, Rees, Alexander	5049
28	10	A	Maidstone U	D 2-2	0-1	10	Childs, Alexander	2365
29	17	H	Burnley	W 4-2	1-1	10	Knight, Cunnington, Childs, Birtles	5973
30	20	A	Colchester U	L 0-1	0-1	—		3026
31	24	A	Aldershot	D 0-0	0-0	9		1858
32	Mar 3	H	Doncaster R	W 2-1	1-0	8	Rees, Gilbert	5536
33	7	A	Hereford U	W 1-0	0-0	—	Childs	3013
34	10	H	Exeter C	W 1-0	0-0	4	Gilbert	6629
35	17	A	Rochdale	W 1-0	0-0	2	Gilbert	3058
36	20	H	Scarborough	W 3-0	3-0	—	Rees 2, Lever	7690
37	24	A	Gillingham	W 2-1	1-0	2	Alexander, Rees	4150
38	31	H	Lincoln C	W 1-0	1-0	2	Gilbert (pen)	11,427
39	Apr 7	A	Halifax T	D 2-2	1-0	2	Rees, Alexander	3620
40	10	H	Peterborough U	L 1-2	0-2	—	Alexander	8123
41	14	A	Stockport Co	W 4-2	2-1	2	Gilbert 2, Birtles, Hargreaves	4065
42	17	H	Scunthorpe U	W 2-1	0-0	—	Tillson, Cockerill	11,894
43	20	A	Southend U	W 2-0	1-0	—	Alexander 2	4945
44	24	H	Hartlepool U	D 0-0	0-0	—		8687
45	28	H	Wrexham	W 5-1	3-1	2	Birtles 3, Cockerill, Rees	8431
46	May 5	A	Chesterfield	L 0-2	0-1	2		7501

Final League Position: 2

GOALSCORERS

League (70): Rees 13, Alexander 12, Gilbert 10 (4 pens), Birtles 8, Childs 5, Cockerill 5 (2 pens), Cunnington 3, Tillson 3, Agnew 2, Hargreaves 2, Lever 2, Gabbiadini 1, Jobling 1, Knight 1, Watson 1, own goal 1.
Littlewoods Cup (5): Alexander 1, Birtles 1, Childs 1, Gilbert 1, Watson 1.
FA Cup (4): Hargreaves 2, Cockerill 1, Gilbert 1.

Sherwood	McDermott	Agnew	Tillson	Lever	Cunnington	Childs	Gilbert	Rees	Cockerill	Alexander	Watson	Hargreaves	Williams	Reece	Birtles	Stephenson	Willis	Jobling	Smaller	Stoutt	Gabbiadini	Knight	Match No.
1	2	3	4	5	6	7	8	9†	10*	11	12	14											1
1	2*	3	4	5	6	7	8	9	10	11			12										2
	2	3	4	5	6	7	8	9		12	10			1	11*								3
	2	3	4	5	6	7	8	9	10	12				1	11*								4
	2		4	5*	6	7	8		10	11	12			1	9			3†	14				5
1	2		4	5	6	7	8	9		12	10				11*			3					6
1	2		4	5	6	7	8	9	10						11			3					7
1	2		4	5	6	7	8	9	10†	12					11			3*	14				8
1			4	5	6	7		9	10	11	2	12			8*			3					9
	2		4	5	6	7*	8	9	10†	11		14	12	1				3					10
			4	5	6	7	8	9		11	2			1		10			3				11
		3	4	5	6	7	8			11	2			1	9	10							12
	2		4	5	6	7	8		10	11*			12	1	9	14		3†					13
	2	3	4	5	6	7	8		10					1	9	11							14
	2	3		5	6	7	8	9†	10				12	1	4*	14		11					15
1	2	3	4	5	6	7	8		10						9	12		11*					16
	2	3	4	5	6	7	8		10	11*	12			1	9								17
	2	3	4	5	6	7	8		10	11*	12			1	9								18
	2	3	4	5	6	7	8	9	10	11				1									19
	2	3	4†	5	6	7	8*	9	10	11			12	1		14							20
	2		4	5	6	7	8*	9		11			14	1	12			3†	10				21
	2		4*	5	6	7	8	9		11			12	1		10		3					22
1	2		4		6	7	8	9	10	11*			12					3				5	23
1			4		6	7	8	9	10	11								3			2	5	24
1			4		6	8*		9	10	14			12		11			3†			2	5	25
1	2		4		6	7†	8	9	10				12		11	14		3*				5	26
1	2		4*		6	7	8	9	10				12		11			3				5	27
1	2*	14	4		6	7	8	9	10				12		11†			3				5	28
1	2		4		6	7	8	9	10				12		11*			3				5	29
1	2	14	4		6	7	8	9	10†				12		11			3				5*	30
1	2		4	5	6	7	8		10	11					9			3					31
1	2†	14	4	5*	6	7	8	9	10				12		11			3					32
1	2	12	4		6	7	8	9	10*			5			11			3					33
1	2	12	4	5	6	7	8	9	10*						11			3					34
1	2	3	4*	5	6	7	8	9					12†		11	14		10					35
1	2	3	4	5	6	7	8	9					12		11*			10					36
1		3	4	12	6*	7	8	9				5		2	11			10					37
1	2	3	4*	5	6	7	8		10	11			12										38
1	2	3	4	5		7	8*	9	10	11			12		4			6					39
1	2	3†	14		6	7	8	9*	10	11			12		5			4					40
1	2*		4	5	6	7	8	9†	10	11			12			14		3					41
1	2		4†	5	6	7*	8	9	10	14			12		11			3					42
1	2		4	5	6	7	8		10	11					9*	12		3					43
1	2		4	5	6	7†	8		10	11*			12		9	14		3					44
1	2	12	4	5	6	7	8	9	10				14		11†			3*					45
1		3†	4	5	6	7	8			11*	2		12		9	14		10					46
31	39	19	42	35	44	44	45	35	33	22	10	5	—	15	36	7	1	30	1	1	3	8	
		+5s		+3s					+16s	+6s				+14s	+1s	+2s		+8s	+3s		+1s		

GRIMSBY TOWN

Player and Position	Ht	Wt	Birth Date	Place	Source	Clubs	League App	Gls
Goalkeepers								
Paul Reece	5 11	12 07	16 7 68	Nottingham	Kettering	Grimsby T	29	—
Steve Sherwood	6 4	14 07	10 12 53	Selby	Apprentice	Chelsea	16	—
						Brighton & HA (loan)—		—
						Millwall (loan)	1	—
						Brentford (loan)	62	—
						Watford	211	1
						Grimsby T	109	—
Defenders								
Paul Agnew	5 9	10 04	15 8 65	Lisburn	Cliftonville	Grimsby T	154	3
John Cockerill	6 0	12 07	12 7 61	Cleethorpes	Stafford R	Grimsby T	62	11
Ian Knight	6 2	12 04	26 10 66	Hartlepool	Apprentice	Barnsley	—	—
						Sheffield W	21	—
						Scunthorpe U (loan)	2	—
						Grimsby T	9	1
Mark Lever	6 3	12 05	29 3 70	Beverley	Trainee	Grimsby T	76	4
John McDermott	5 7	10 07	3 2 69	Middlesbrough		Grimsby T	118	1
Geoff Stephenson*	5 7	11 00	28 4 70	Tynemouth	Trainee	Grimsby T	21	—
Andy Tillson	6 2	12 07	30 6 66	Huntingdon	Kettering	Grimsby T	87	5
Tom Williams*	5 9	11 06	18 12 57	West Lothian	Apprentice	Leicester C	241	10
						Birmingham C	62	1
						Grimsby T	20	—
Midfield								
Gary Childs	5 7	10 08	19 4 64	Birmingham	Apprentice	WBA	3	—
						Walsall	131	17
						Birmingham C	55	2
						Grimsby T	44	5
Shaun Cunnington	5 8	10 04	4 1 66	Bourne	Amateur	Wrexham	199	12
						Grimsby T	103	6
Kevin Jobling	5 9	10 13	1 1 68	Sunderland	Apprentice	Leicester C	9	—
						Grimsby T	80	6
Paul Smaller*	5 9	11 05	18 9 70	Scunthorpe	Trainee	Grimsby T	2	—
Tommy Watson	5 8	10 10	29 9 69	Liverpool	Trainee	Grimsby T	56	5
Forwards								
Keith Alexander	6 4	13 06	14 11 58	Nottingham	Barnet	Grimsby T	82	26
Garry Birtles	6 0	12 00	27 7 56	Nottingham	Long Eaton U	Nottingham F	87	32
						Manchester U	58	11
						Nottingham F	125	38
						Notts Co	63	9
						Grimsby T	38	8
David Gilbert	5 4	10 04	22 6 63	Lincoln	Apprentice	Lincoln C	30	1
						Boston U	Scunthorpe U	1	—
						Northampton T	120	21
						Grimsby T	56	13

GRIMSBY TOWN

Foundation: Grimsby Pelham FC as they were first known, came into being at a meeting held at the Wellington Arms in September 1878. Pelham is the family name of big land-owners in the area, the Earls of Yarborough. The receipts for their first game amounted to 6s. 9d. (approx. 39p). After a year, the club name was changed to Grimsby Town.

First Football League game: 3 September, 1892, Division 2, v Northwich Victoria (h) W 2-1 – Whitehouse; Lundie, T. Frith; C. Frith, Walker, Murrell; Higgins, Henderson, Brayshaw, Riddoch (2), Ackroyd.

Managers (and Secretary-managers)
H. M. Hickson 1903–20*, Haydn Price 1920, George Fraser 1921–24, Wilf Gillow 1924–32, Frank Womack 1932–36, Charles Spencer 1937–51, Bill Shankly 1951–53, Billy Walsh 1954–55, Allenby Chilton 1955–59, Tim Ward 1960–62, Tom Johnston 1962–64, Jimmy McGuigan 1964–67, Don McEvoy 1967–68, Bill Harvey 1968–69, Bobby Kennedy 1969–71, Lawrie McMenemy 1971–73, Ron Ashman 1973–75, Tom Casey 1975–76, Johnny Newman 1976–79, George Kerr 1979–82, David Booth 1982–85, Mike Lyons 1985–87, Bobby Roberts 1987–88, Alan Buckley 1988– .

Player and Position	Ht	Wt	Birth Date	Place	Source	Clubs	League App	Gls
Chris Hargreaves	5 10	10 13	12 5 72	Cleethorpes	Trainee	Grimsby T	19	2
Richard O'Kelly*	5 10	11 08	8 1 57	West Bromwich	Alvechurch	Walsåll	204	56
						Port Vale	28	4
						Walsall	12	1
						Grimsby T	39	10
Tony Rees	5 9	11 13	1 8 64	Merthyr Tydfil	Apprentice	Aston Villa	—	—
						Birmingham C	95	12
						Peterborough U (loan)	5	2
						Shrewsbury T (loan)	2	—
						Barnsley	31	3
						Grimsby T	35	13
Roger Willis	6 1	11 06	17 6 67	Sheffield		Grimsby T	9	—

Trainees
Blake, Robert; Blewitt, Adrian L; Clarke, Mark A; Drury, Robert J; Edwards, Trevor; Ford, Matthew; Liversidge, Scott; Penny, Christian; Stacey, Christopher L; Waiton, Steven M.

Associated Schoolboys
Axcell, Stuart; Dunlop, Simon A; Ellis, Justin; Scrupps, Martyn J; Thomas, Jason W.S.

HALIFAX TOWN 1989–90 *Back row (left to right)*: Terry McPhillips, Phil Horner, Billy Barr, Dean Martin, Shaun Smith, Neil Matthews, Andy Watson. *Centre row*: Graham Broadbent, Ian Juryeff, Chris Hedworth, David Brown, Phil Whitehead, Nick Richardson, Mitch Cook, John Bramhall. *Front row*: Derek Hall, Paul Fleming, Gerry Brook, Bill Ayre, Frank Harrison, Toby Paterson, Brian Butler.

Division 4   **HALIFAX TOWN**

Shay Ground, Halifax HX1 2YS. Offices: 7 Clare Road, Halifax HX1 2HX. Telephone Halifax (0422) 53423/43381. Ground: 0422 361582 (Match day only).

Ground capacity: 5656.

Record attendance: 36,885 v Tottenham H, FA Cup 5th rd, 15 Feb, 1953.

Record receipts: £14,000 v Manchester C, FA Cup 3rd rd, 5 Jan, 1980.

Pitch measurements: 110yd × 70yd.

President: John S. Crowther. *Vice-President:* F. Hinchliffe.

Chairman: S. J. Brown. *Vice-Chairman:* J. Haymer.

Directors: Mrs. P. Burton, I. Stewart, G. Gannon, K. Smyth.

Manager: Jim McCalliog. *Assistant Manager:* Brian Taylor. *Physio:* Mrs. Jane Appleyard. *Youth team coach:* Frank Harrison.

Secretary: Mrs A. Pettifor. *Assistant Secretary:* Miss J. Magee.

Commercial Manager: Paul Kendall.

Year Formed: 1911. *Turned Professional:* 1911. *Ltd Co.:* 1911.

Club Nickname: 'The Shaymen'.

Previous Grounds: Sandhall and Exley.

Record League Victory: 6-0 v Bradford PA, Division 3 (N), 3 December 1955 – Johnson; Griffiths, Ferguson; Watson, Harris, Bell; Hampson (2), Baker (3), Watkinson (1), Capel, Lonsdale. 6-0 v Doncaster R, Division 4, 2 November 1976 – Gennoe; Trainer, Loska (Bradley), McGill, Dunleavy (1), Phelan, Hoy (2), Carroll (1), Bullock (1), Lawson (1), Johnston.

Record Cup Victory: 7-0 v Bishop Auckland, FA Cup 2 rd (replay), 10 January 1967 – White; Russell, Bodell; Smith, Holt, Jeff Lee; Taylor (2), Hutchison (2), Parks (2), Atkins (1), McCarthy.

Record Defeat: 0-13 v Stockport Co, Division 3 (N). 6 January, 1934.

Most League Points (2 for a win): 57, Division 4, 1968–69.

Most League Points (3 for a win): 60, Division 4, 1982–83.

Most League Goals: 83, Division 3 (N), 1957–58.

Highest League Scorer in Season: Albert Valentine. 34, Division 3 (N), 1934–35.

Most League Goals in Total Aggregate: Ernest Dixon, 129, 1922–30.

Most Capped Player: None.

Most League Appearances: John Pickering, 367, 1965–74.

Record Transfer Fee Received: £250,000 from Watford for Wayne Allison, July 1989.

Record Transfer Fee Paid: £40,000 to Leyton Orient for Ian Juryeff, August 1989.

Football League Record: 1921 Original Member of Division 3 (N); 1958–63 Division 3; 1963–69 Division 4; 1969–76 Division 3; 1976– Division 4.

Honours: Football League: Division 3 best season; 3rd. 1970–71; Division 3(N) – Runners-up 1934–35; Division 4 – Runners-up 1968–69. *FA Cup* best season; 5th rd, 1932–33, 1952–53. *Football League Cup* best season: 4th rd, 1964.

Colours: Blue and white shirts, blue shorts, blue stockings. **Change colours:** Blue and yellow shirts, blue and yellow shorts, yellow stockings.

HALIFAX TOWN 1989–90 LEAGUE RECORD

Match No.	Date		Venue	Opponents	Result		H/T Score	Lg. Pos.	Goalscorers	Atten- dance
1	Aug	19	H	Hartlepool U	W	4-0	1-0	—	Watson 2, Hall, Juryeff	1524
2		26	A	Colchester U	D	2-2	2-1	4	Hicks (og), Watson	2404
3	Sept	2	H	Torquay U	W	3-1	0-0	2	Watson, Matthews 2	1893
4		9	A	Wrexham	L	1-2	0-1	6	Hall	1700
5		15	H	Carlisle U	D	1-1	0-0	—	Juryeff	2121
6		22	A	Cambridge U	L	0-1	0-0	—		2220
7		27	A	Scarborough	W	3-2	1-0	—	Watson 2, Juryeff	3147
8		30	H	Exeter C	L	1-2	0-0	10	Matthews	1720
9	Oct	6	H	Gillingham	L	0-1	0-0	—		1776
10		14	A	Lincoln C	L	1-2	1-0	14	Juryeff	4071
11		17	A	Chesterfield	L	3-4	3-1	—	Bramhall, Matthews, Hall	2998
12		21	H	Rochdale	W	1-0	0-0	16	Juryeff	1864
13		28	A	Grimsby T	D	1-1	0-0	18	Bramhall	4021
14		31	H	Hereford U	D	1-1	0-1	—	Matthews	1235
15	Nov	3	A	Stockport Co	W	1-0	0-0	—	Horner	5490
16		10	H	Southend U	L	1-2	0-1	—	Juryeff	1908
17		25	H	Maidstone U	L	1-2	1-0	18	Juryeff	1353
18	Dec	2	A	Aldershot	L	0-2	0-1	18		1749
19		15	H	Doncaster R	L	0-2	0-0	—		1233
20		26	A	York C	W	2-0	1-0	20	Richardson 2	3665
21		30	A	Burnley	L	0-1	0-1	20		9105
22	Jan	1	H	Peterborough U	D	2-2	0-1	20	Naylor, McPhillips	1578
23		6	A	Scunthorpe U	D	1-1	1-1	—	Cowling (og)	3051
24		12	H	Colchester U	D	1-1	1-0	—	Hall	1397
25		20	A	Hartlepool U	L	0-2	0-2	21		2444
26		26	H	Wrexham	W	4-2	3-2	—	Matthews 2, Watson, Richardson	1436
27	Feb	2	H	Cambridge U	D	0-0	0-0	—		1526
28		10	A	Carlisle U	D	1-1	0-1	20	Matthews	4844
29		17	H	Aldershot	W	4-1	3-0	18	Cook, Graham, Matthews, Richardson	1275
30		24	A	Maidstone U	W	2-1	2-0	18	McPhillips, Richardson	2182
31	Mar	3	H	Scunthorpe U	L	0-1	0-0	20		1793
32		7	A	Exeter C	L	0-2	0-1	—		5528
33		10	A	Scarborough	L	1-2	1-2	20	Matthews	1490
34		16	A	Gillingham	L	1-3	0-2	—	Matthews	3825
35		20	H	Lincoln C	L	0-1	0-0	—		1423
36		24	H	Chesterfield	D	1-1	0-1	22	Watson	2363
37		27	A	Torquay U	L	0-1	0-1	—		1911
38		31	A	Rochdale	W	2-0	0-0	22	McPhillips, Watson	2494
39	Apr	7	H	Grimsby T	D	2-2	0-1	22	Watson, Butler	3620
40		11	A	Hereford U	W	1-0	0-0	—	Barr	1817
41		14	A	Peterborough U	L	0-3	0-2	22		4570
42		16	H	York C	D	2-2	2-2	21	Butler, Fleming P (pen)	1605
43		21	A	Doncaster R	W	4-3	0-3	20	Cook, Barr, Richardson, Butler	2212
44		24	H	Burnley	D	0-0	0-0	—		2556
45		27	A	Southend U	L	0-2	0-1	—		3656
46	May	5	H	Stockport Co	L	1-2	1-0	23	Matthews	4744

Final League Position: 23

GOALSCORERS

League (57): Matthews 12, Watson 10, Juryeff 7, Richardson 6, Hall 4, Butler 3, McPhillips 3, Barr 2, Bramhall 2, Cook 2, Fleming P 1 (pen), Graham 1, Horner 1, Naylor 1, own goals 2.
Littlewoods Cup (3): Cook 1, Hall 1, Watson 1.
FA Cup (3): Horner 2, Fleming P 1.

Whitehead	Barr	Cook	Hedworth	Bramhall	Horner	Martin	Watson	Matthews	Butler	Hall	Juryeff	McPhillips	Richardson	Brown	Fleming P	Smith	Broadbent	Harrison	Naylor	Graham	Fleming C	Donnelly	Match No.
1	2	3	4	5	6	7	8	9*10	11	12													1
1	2	3	4	5	6	7	8		10	11	9												2
1	2	3	4†	5	6	7	8*	9	10	11		12	14										3
1	2	3		5	6	7	8	9	4	11	10												4
	2	3	4	5	6	7	8*	9	10	11†14		12		1									5
		3	4	5	6	7	8*	9		11	10	12		1	2								6
12	3	4	5	6	7	8*	9		11	10				1	2								7
14	3	4	5†	6*	7	8	9		11	10	12			1	2								8
		3	4†	5	6	7	8		9	11*10		12	14	1	2								9
1		3		5	6	7	8	9	4	11	10				2								10
1		3		5	6	7		9	4	11	10				2	8							11
1		3	4	5	6	7		9	8*11	10					2	12							12
1		3	4	5	6	7	8	9		11	10				2								13
1		3	4	5	6	7	8*	9		11	10	12			2								14
1		3	4	5	6	7	8	9		11	10				2								15
1			4	5	6	7	8		14	11†10	12				2	3*	9						16
1	14		4	5*	6	7	8	9	3	11†10					2	12							17
1	4				6	7	8	9	3	11	10				2	5							18
	14			5	6	7	8†	4		11				9	1	2	3	12	10*				19
1	8			4	5	6	7							9	2	3	10		11				20
1	8			4	5	6	7		14					9	2	3	10*12	11†					21
1				4	5*	6	7	8†		10			14	9	2	3		12	11				22
1	14			4	5	6		12		10	7			8*	9	2		3	11†				23
	14			4	5	6		11	10	7		12		9	1	2		8*	3†				24
1	8†	3	4		6		12	11	10	7				9		2		14	5*				25
1		3	4		6		8*11		7					9		2		12		5	10		26
		3	4		6	8		11		7				9	1	2				5	10		27
		3	4		6			11		7				8	9	1	2			5	10		28
		3	4		6*		12	11	14	7				8	9	1	2†			5	10		29
		3			6			11	12	7				8*	9	1	2			5	10	4	30
		3			6	12	11			7				8*	9	1	2			5	10	4	31
		3	4		6	8†11			7*					9	1	2		12	14	5	10		32
		3	4		6	8	11						12	9	1	2		7	14	5†10*			33
12	3	4			6	8	11		10					9	1	2*	7†			5	14		34
3*					6	4	8	11	12	10				9	1	2	7†			5	14		35
		3			6	4	10	7	8	11					1	2				5	9		36
7*	3				4	10	12	8					11†	1	2	14		6	9		5		37
	3				4	10*	7	8	11			9	12	1	2			6			5		38
	3				4	10	7	8	11			9		1	2			6			5		39
2	3		4		10	7	8	11				9		1				6			5		40
14	3		4		10	7	8	11*				9†12		1	2			6			5		41
	3		4		10	7	8	11				9*12		1	2			6			5		42
7*	3				4	10	9	8	11†			12		1	2	14		6			5		43
14	3				4	10*	7	8	11†			12	9	1	2			6			5		44
7	3				4	12	10*	8	11			9		1	2			6			5		45
3	11				4	10*	7		14			12	9	1	2			6			5	8†	46

19 15 36 27 23 34 37 33 38 25 40 15 10 21 27 40 6 8 3 5 21 10 2 10 1
\+ +   + + + + + +   + + + +
8s 1s   5s 1s 5s 1s 2s 12s6s   5s 6s 1s 2s

Littlewoods Cup	First Round	Carlisle U (h)	3-1
		(a)	0-1
	Second Round	Middlesbrough (a)	0-4
		(h)	0-1
FA Cup	First Round	Stafford R (a)	3-2
	Second Round	Darlington (a)	0-3

HALIFAX TOWN

Player and Position	Ht	Wt	Birth Date	Birth Place	Source	Clubs	League App	Gls
Goalkeepers								
David Brown	6 1	12 08	28 1 57	Hartlepool	Horden CW	Middlesbrough	10	—
						Plymouth Arg (loan)	5	—
						Oxford U	21	—
						Bury	146	—
						Preston NE	74	—
						Scunthorpe U (loan)	5	—
						Halifax T	27	—
Paddy Roche†	6 1	11 04	4 1 51	Dublin	Shelbourne	Manchester U	46	—
						Brentford	71	—
						Halifax T	184	—
						Chester C	—	—
						Halifax T	—	—
Defenders								
Billy Barr	5 11	11 07	21 1 69	Halifax	Trainee	Halifax T	96	6
Brian Butler	5 6	10 08	4 7 66	Salford	Apprentice	Blackpool	74	5
						Stockport Co	32	2
						Halifax T	30	3
Paul Fleming	5 7	10 00	6 9 67	Halifax		Halifax T	100	1
Frankie Harrison‡	6 1	12 06	19 9 63	Middlesbrough		Middlesbrough	—	—
						Lincoln C	1	—
						Halifax T	54	—
Chris Hedworth	6 1	10 11	5 1 64	Newcastle	Apprentice	Newcastle U	9	—
						Barnsley	25	—
						Halifax T	38	—
Philip Horner	6 1	12 07	10 11 66	Leeds	School	Leicester C	10	—
						Rotherham U (loan)	4	—
						Halifax T	72	4
Toby Paterson‡	6 0	12 00	15 5 71	Scotland	Trainee	Halifax T	1	—
Shaun Smith	5 10	11 00	9 4 71	Leeds	Trainee	Halifax T	7	—
Midfield								
Mitch Cook	5 10	12 00	15 10 61	Scarborough	Scarborough	Darlington	34	4
						Middlesbrough	6	—
						Scarborough	81	10
						Halifax T	37	2
Paul Donnelly	5 8	10 00	23 12 71	Liverpool	Trainee	Halifax T	2	—
Craig Fleming	6 0	11 07	6 10 71	Calder	Trainee	Halifax T	11	—
Tommy Graham	5 9	11 09	31 3 58	Glasgow	Arthurlie	Aston Villa	—	—
						Barnsley	38	13
						Halifax T	71	17
						Doncaster R	11	2
						Scunthorpe U	109	21
						Scarborough	111	11
						Halifax T	21	1
Derek Hall	5 8	11 02	5 1 65	Manchester	Apprentice	Coventry C	1	—
						Torquay U (loan)	10	2
						Torquay U	45	4
						Swindon T	10	—
						Southend U	123	15
						Halifax T	41	4
Dean Martin	5 10	10 02	9 9 67	Halifax	Local	Halifax T	125	6
Dominic Naylor	5 9	11 07	12 8 62	Watford	Trainee	Watford	—	—
						Halifax T	6	1
Nick Richardson	6 0	12 07	11 4 67	Halifax	Local	Halifax T	34	6

HALIFAX TOWN

Foundation: The idea of a soccer club in a Rugby League stronghold was first mooted by a Mr. A. E. Muir who soon interested Joe McClelland (who became secretary-manager of the new club) and Dr. A. H. Muir their first chairman. Following correspondence in *The Halifax Evening Courier* the club was formed at a meeting at the Saddle Hotel in May 1911.

First Football League game: 27 August, 1921, Division 3(N), v Darlington (a) L 0-2 – Haldane; Hawley, Mackrill; Hall, Wellock, Challinor; Pinkey, Hetherington, Woods, Dent, Phipps.

Managers (and Secretary-managers)
A. M. Ricketts 1911–12*, Joe McClelland 1912–30, Alec Raisbeck 1930–36, Jimmy Thomson 1936–47, Jack Breedon 1947–50, William Wootton 1951–52, Gerald Henry 1952–54, Willie Watson 1954–56, Billy Burnikell 1956, Harry Hooper 1957–62, Willie Watson 1964–66, Vic Metcalfe 1966–67, Alan Ball Snr 1967–70, George Kirby 1970–71, Ray Henderson 1971–72, George Mulhall 1972–74, Johnny Quinn 1974–76, Alan Ball Snr 1976–77, Jimmy Lawson 1977–78, George Kirby 1978–81, Mick Bullock 1981–84, Mick Jones 1984–86, Bill Ayre 1986–90, Jim McCalliog 1990– .

Player and Position	Ht	Wt	Birth Date	Birth Place	Source	Clubs	League App	Gls
Forwards								
Graham Broadbent	6 0	12 07	20 12 58	Halifax	Emley	Halifax T	25	2
Tony Fyfe	6 2	12 00	23 2 62	Carlisle		Carlisle U	48	12
						Scarborough (loan)	6	1
						Halifax T	12	—
Terry McPhillips	5 10	11 00	1 10 68	Manchester	Trainee	Liverpool	—	—
						Halifax T	88	28
						Northampton T (loan)	1	—
Neil Matthews	5 11	12 00	19 9 66	Grimsby	Apprentice	Grimsby T	11	1
						Scunthorpe U (loan)	1	—
						Halifax T (loan)	9	2
						Bolton W (loan)	1	—
						Halifax T	105	29
Andy Watson	5 9	11 12	1 4 67	Leeds	Harrogate T	Halifax T	83	15

Trainees
Abbishaw, David S; Ash, Graham M; Brown, Richard A; Cotterill, Darren M; Dixon, Andrew; Fisher, Warren J; Fitzgibbon, Martin J; Gibson, Wayne E; Gilfillan, Daniel; Gourley, Bryan; Griffiths, Neil; Hutchinson, Ian N; Millward, Paul T; Paterson, Jamie R; Pye, Matthew J; Richardson, Joseph C; Smoczyk, Marc R; Stoney, Jarrod P; Tindall, Jonathan D.

**Non-Contract
Roche, Patrick J.

Associated Schoolboys
Higgins, David K; Hook, Steven J; Lister, Howard G; McInall, Stuart; O'Dwyer, Christopher; Orlic, Peter; Radio, Leano; Rancatouri, Ricardo P; Smith, Richard J; Wood, Sean.

Associated Schoolboy who has accepted the club's offer of a Traineeship/Contract
Armstrong, Leighton J.

**Non-Contract Players who are retained must be re-signed before they are eligible to play in League matches.

HARTLEPOOL UNITED 1989–90 *Back row (left to right):* Brian Honour, Simon Grayson, Wayne Stokes, Rob Moverley, Rob McKinnon, Tony Barrass, Paul Dalton.
Centre row: Keith Nobbs, Paul Baker (Captain), Gary Henderson (Physiotherapist), Bryan Robson (Assistant Manager), John Craggs (Coach), Joe Allon, David Stokle.
Front row: Mark Robson, Kenneth Davies, Paul Ogden, Patrick Atkinson, John Tinkler, Russell Doig, Stephen Plaskett.

Division 4 **HARTLEPOOL UNITED**

The Victoria Ground, Clarence Road, Hartlepool. Telephone Hartlepool (0429) 272584. Commercial Dept: (0429) 222077. Fax: 0429 863007.

Ground capacity: 9675.

Record attendance: 17,426 v Manchester U, FA Cup 3rd rd, 5 Jan, 1957.

Record receipts: £17,000 v Leeds U, FA Cup 3rd rd, 18 Jan, 1979.

Pitch measurements: 110yd × 75yd.

President: E. Leadbitter. *Executive Vice-Presidents:* R. Boyes MP, J. C. Thomas, E. Ord.

Chairman: G. Gibson. *Vice-Chairman:* A. Bamford.

Director: D. Dukes.

Manager: Cyril Knowles. *Assistant Manager:* Bryan Robson.

Secretary: M. Kirby. *Sponsorship Manager:*

Coach: John Craggs. *Physio:* Gary Henderson.

Year Formed: 1908. *Turned Professional:* 1908. *Ltd Co.:* 1908.

Club Nickname: 'The Pool'.

Previous Names: Hartlepools United until 1968; Hartlepool until 1977.

Record League Victory: 10-1 v Barrow, Division 4, 4 April 1959 – Oakley; Cameron, Waugh; Johnson, Moore, Anderson; Scott (1), Langland (1), Smith (3), Clark (2), Luke (2). (1 og).

Record Cup Victory: 6-0 v North Shields, FA Cup, 1st rd, 30 November 1946 – Heywood; Brown, Gregory; Spelman, Lambert, Jones; Price, Scott (2), Sloan (4), Moses, McMahon.

Record Defeat: 1-10 v Wrexham, Division 4, 3 March, 1962.

Most League Points (2 for a win): 60, Division 4, 1967–68.

Most League Points (3 for a win): 70, Division 4, 1985–86.

Most League Goals: 90, Division 3 (N), 1956–57.

Highest League Scorer in Season: William Robinson, 28, Division 3 (N), 1927–28.

Most League Goals in Total Aggregate: Ken Johnson, 98, 1949–64.

Most Capped Player: Ambrose Fogarty, 1 (11), Eire.

Most League Appearances: Wattie Moore, 447, 1948–64.

Record Transfer Fee Received: £60,000 from Brighton & HA for Malcolm Poskett, February 1978.

Record Transfer Fee Paid: £17,500 to Chesterfield for Bob Newton, July 1985.

Football League Record: 1921 Original Member of Division 3 (N); 1958–68 Division 4; 1968–69 Division 3; 1969– Division 4.

Honours: Football League: Division 3 best season: 22nd, 1968–69; Division 3 (N) – Runners-up 1956–57. *FA Cup* best season: 4th rd. 1954–55, 1977–78, 1988–89. *Football League Cup best season :* 4th rd. 1974–75.

Colours: All blue. **Change colours:** All yellow.

HARTLEPOOL UNITED 1989–90 LEAGUE RECORD

Match No.	Date	Venue	Opponents	Result		H/T Score	Lg. Pos.	Goalscorers	Atten-dance
1	Aug 19	A	Halifax T	L	0-4	0-1	—		1524
2	26	H	Exeter C	L	0-3	0-2	24		1726
3	Sept 1	A	Southend U	L	0-3	0-3	—		3236
4	9	H	Gillingham	L	1-2	1-0	24	Dalton	1691
5	15	A	Stockport Co	L	0-6	0-3	—		3926
6	23	H	Peterborough U	D	2-2	1-0	24	Allon, Baker	1703
7	26	A	Rochdale	D	0-0	0-0	—		1501
8	30	H	Doncaster R	L	0-6	0-3	24		1723
9	Oct 7	H	Scunthorpe U	W	3-2	2-2	24	Baker, McEwan (pen), Tinkler	1823
10	14	A	Burnley	D	0-0	0-0	24		7450
11	17	A	Torquay U	L	3-4	2-2	—	Allon 2, Hutchison	2108
12	21	H	York C	L	1-2	1-2	24	Dalton	2325
13	28	A	Carlisle U	L	0-1	0-0	24		3699
14	31	H	Cambridge U	L	1-2	0-1	—	Hutchison	1726
15	Nov 4	H	Wrexham	W	3-0	1-0	24	McEwan (pen), Allon, Dalton	1736
16	11	A	Aldershot	L	1-6	0-3	24	Smith	'2137
17	25	A	Chesterfield	L	1-3	0-3	24	Baker	3488
18	Dec 2	H	Hereford U	L	1-2	1-0	24	Dalton	1493
19	16	A	Maidstone U	L	2-4	0-0	24	Baker, Allon	1520
20	26	H	Scarborough	W	4-1	2-1	24	Smith, Baker, Bennyworth, Kamara (og)	3698
21	30	H	Grimsby T	W	4-2	2-0	23	Dalton 2, Bennyworth, Allon	3398
22	Jan 1	A	Colchester U	L	1-3	1-0	24	Dalton	3826
23	6	H	Lincoln C	D	1-1	0-1	—	McKinnon	2499
24	13	A	Exeter C	L	1-3	0-1	24	Allon	4959
25	20	H	Halifax T	W	2-0	2-0	24	Allon, Smith	2444
26	27	A	Gillingham	D	0-0	0-0	23		3676
27	Feb 7	A	Peterborough U	W	2-0	1-0	—	Allon, Tinkler	2813
28	10	H	Stockport Co	W	5-0	3-0	22	Baker 4, MacDonald	3004
29	13	A	Southend U	D	1-1	0-1	—	Allon	3628
30	17	A	Hereford U	L	1-4	0-4	22	Baker	2049
31	24	H	Chesterfield	W	3-1	0-1	22	Baker, Dalton, Allon	2920
32	Mar 3	A	Lincoln C	L	1-4	1-2	22	Allon	3503
33	6	A	Doncaster R	D	2-2	1-1	—	Smith, Allon	2518
34	10	H	Rochdale	W	2-1	0-1	22	Baker, Tupling	2751
35	17	A	Scunthorpe U	W	1-0	0-0	21	Dalton	3868
36	20	H	Burnley	W	3-0	2-0	—	Baker, Olsson, Dalton	3187
37	24	H	Torquay U	D	1-1	0-0	19	Allon	2725
38	31	A	York C	D	1-1	0-0	21	Atkinson Paul	2891
39	Apr 7	H	Carlisle U	W	1-0	0-0	20	Allon	3768
40	10	A	Cambridge U	L	1-2	0-2	—	Smith	3254
41	14	H	Colchester U	L	0-2	0-0	21		3397
42	16	A	Scarborough	L	1-4	0-2	23	Baker	2762
43	21	H	Maidstone U	W	4-2	0-1	23	Berry (og), Allon 2, Baker	2290
44	24	A	Grimsby T	D	0-0	0-0	—		8687
45	28	H	Aldershot	W	2-0	1-0	19	Dalton, Baker	2770
46	May 5	A	Wrexham	W	2-1	0-1	19	Allon, Olsson	2745

Final League Position: 19

GOALSCORERS

League (66): Allon 18, Baker 16, Dalton 11, Smith 5, Bennyworth 2, Hutchison 2, McEwan 2 (2 pens), Olsson 2, Tinkler 2, Atkinson Paul 1, MacDonald 1, McKinnon 1, Tupling 1, own goals 2.
Littlewoods Cup (4): Grayson 2, Baker 1, Dalton 1.
FA Cup (0).

Littlewoods Cup	First Round	York C (h)	3-3
		(a)	1-4
FA Cup	First Round	Huddersfield T (h)	0-2

Bowling	Barrass	McKinnon	Tinkler	Stokes	Stokle	Dalton	Ogen	Baker	Grayson	Atkinson Pat	Curry	Carr	Nobbs	Doig	Davies	Allon	Speirs	Dearden	McEwan	Dunbar	Plaskett	Entwistle	Lamb	Smith M	Trewick	Hutchison	Williams	Moverley	Sinclair	Match No.
1	2	3	4	5	6	7	8	9	10	11*	12																			1
	6	3	4			11	5		10†	12		1	2			7*		8	9	14										2
	6	3	4			11		9					2		8	7		1	5							10				3
	6	3	4			11		9	12						8	7		1	5		2					10*				4
	6	3	4			11	8	9								7		1	5		2					10				5
	6	3	4			11*		9	12						5	7		1	8		2					10				6
	6	3	4			11		9							5	7		1	8		2					10				7
	6	3	4			11		9							5	7		1	8		2					10				8
		3	4			11		9					2			7		1	6					5	8	10				9
		3	4			11		9		12						7		1	2					5	8	10*		6		10
		3	4			11		9		12						7		1	2					5	8	10*		6		11
		3	4			11		9								7		1	2					5	8	10		6		12
		3	4			11										7			2		9		12	5	8	10*		6	1	13
		3	4			11		9*								7			5		2		12		8	10		6	1	14
		3	4			11							2			7			6				12	5	8	10		9*	1	15
14		3				11							2			7			6	9			12	5	8	10†		1	4*	16
		3	4			11		9								7								5		10	8	6	1	17
		3	4			11		9							6	7								5		10*	12	8	1	18
		3	4			11		9						6	8*	7							12	5					10	19
		3	4			11†		9*					10			7			14					5		12				20
		3	4			11		9*					10			7								5						21
		3	4			11		9					10			7								5*						22
		3	4			11		9					10			7								5						23
		3	4			11		9					10			7							12	5						24
		3	4			11		9					10			7								5						25
		3	4			12		9*					10			7								5						26
		3	4			12		9					10			7								5						27
		3	4			11		9*					10			7								5						28
		3	4			11		9					10			7								5						29
		3	4*			12		9					10			7								5						30
		3	4			10		9					2			7								5						31
		3	4			10		9							12	7								5						32
		3	4			10		9					2			7								5						33
		3	4			10		9					2		12	7								5						34
		3	4			10		9					2			7								5						35
		3	4			10		9					2			7							12	5*						36
		3	4			10		9					2			7								5*						37
		3*	4			10		9					2			7								5						38
		3	4			10		9					2			7								5						39
		3	4			14		9					2			7								5		10†				40
		3	4			10		9								7								5						41
		3	4			10†		9							5	7												11		42
		3	4			12		9					2			7								5						43
		3	4					9					2			7								5						44
		3	4			11		9					2			7†								5						45
		3	4			11		9†					2			7								5						46
1	8	46	45	1	1	40	2	43	2	3	—	1	32	2	3	45	—	10	14	1	7	2	4	35	8	12	7	6	4	
		+1s				+5s		5s1s					+3s			+1s			+1s					+6s		+1s		+1s		

McStay — Match No. 17(2) 18(2) 19(2); MacDonald — Match No. 21(12) 22(12) 23(12) 25(2*) 26(2) 27(2*) 28(2) 29(2*) 30(2†) 34(11*) 40(2*) 41(5) 42(14) 43(14) 45(14) 46(14); Tupling — Match No. 20(8) 21(8) 22(8) 23(8) 24(8) 25(8) 26(8) 27(8) 28(8†) 30(8) 31(8) 32(8) 33(8) 34(8) 35(8) 36(8) 37(8) 38(8) 39(8) 40(8) 41(8) 42(8) 43(8) 44(8) 45(8) 46(8); Priestley — Match No. 19(1) 20(1) 21(1) 22(1) 23(1) 24(1) 25(1) 26(1) 27(1) 28(1) 29(1) 30(1) 31(1) 32(1) 33(1) 34(1); Olsson — Match No. 20(2) 21(2) 22(2) 23(2*) 24(2†) 26(11†) 27(14) 28(14) 29(8) 30(14) 32(2) 33(11) 35(11) 36(11) 37(11) 38(11) 40(11) 41(2) 42(2*) 43(10†) 44(10) 45(10*) 46(12); Bennyworth — Match No. 20(6) 21(6) 22(6) 23(6) 24(6*) 25(6) 26(6) 27(6) 28(6) 29(6) 30(6) 31(6) 32(6) 33(6) 34(6) 35(6) 36(6) 37(6) 38(6) 39(6) 40(6) 41(6) 42(6) 43(6) 44(6) 45(6) 46(6); Berryman — Match No. 40(1); Honour — Match No. 24(14) 25(12) 26(14) 27(11†) 28(12) 29(12) 30(11) 31(11) 32(11*); Wilson — Match No. 41(12); Siddall — Match No. 35(1) 36(1) 37(1) 38(1) 39(1) 41(1) 42(1) 43(1) 44(1) 45(1) 46(1); Atkinson Paul — Match No. 36(14) 37(12) 38(12) 39(11) 40(12) 41(11*) 42(12) 43(11*) 44(11) 45(12) 46(10*).

HARTLEPOOL UNITED

Player and Position	Ht	Wt	Birth Date	Birth Place	Source	Clubs	League App	Gls
Goalkeepers								
Steve Berryman†			26 12 66	Blackburn		Hartlepool U	1	—
Graham Carr‡	5 11	11 04	8 12 70	Darlington	Trainee	Hartlepool U	1	—
Rob Moverley	6 3	12 00	16 1 69	Batley	Trainee	Bradford C	—	—
						Hartlepool U	29	—
Barry Siddall*	6 1	14 02	12 9 54	Ellesmere Port	Apprentice	Bolton W	137	—
						Sunderland	167	—
						Darlington (loan)	8	—
						Port Vale	81	—
						Blackpool (loan)	7	—
						Stoke City	20	—
						Tranmere R (loan)	12	—
						Manchester C (loan)	6	—
						Blackpool	110	—
						Stockport Co	21	—
						Hartlepool U	11	—
Defenders								
Tony Barrass*	6 0	12 03	29 3 71	Teesside	Trainee	Hartlepool U	12	—
Ian Bennyworth	6 0	12 07	15 1 62	Hull	Apprentice	Hull C	1	—
					Gainsborough Tr	Scarborough	89	3
					Nuneaton Bor	Hartlepool U	27	2
Stan McEwan‡	6 0	12 07	8 6 57	Cambusrethan	Apprentice	Blackpool	214	24
						Exeter C	65	15
						Hull C	113	25
						Wigan Ath	29	4
						Hartlepool U	14	2
Rob McKinnon	5 11	11 01	31 7 66	Glasgow	Rutherglen G	Newcastle U	1	—
						Hartlepool U	179	5
Keith Nobbs	5 10	11 10	19 9 61	Bishop Auckland	Apprentice	Middlesbrough	1	—
						Halifax T	87	1
					Bishop Auckland	Hartlepool U	172	1
Steve Plaskett*	5 9	10 10	24 4 71	Newcastle	Trainee	Hartlepool U	20	—
Mick Smith	6 1	11 09	28 10 58	Sunderland	Lambton St BC	Lincoln C	25	—
						Wimbledon	205	14
						Aldershot (loan)	7	—
					Seaham Red Star	Hartlepool U	35	5
Tony Smith‡	5 10	12 01	20 2 57	Sunderland	Amateur	Newcastle U	2	—
						Peterborough U	68	5
						Halifax T	83	3
						Hartlepool U	200	8
David Stokle*	6 3	13 00	1 12 69	Hartlepool		Hartlepool U	9	—
Wayne Stokes‡	6 1	13 00	16 2 65	Birmingham	Apprentice	Coventry C	—	—
						Gillingham	3	—
						Stockport Co	18	1
						Hartlepool U	62	1
Paul Williams*	6 2	12 09	8 9 63	Sheffield	Nuneaton	Preston NE	1	—
						Newport Co	26	3
						Sheffield U	8	—
						Hartlepool U	8	—
Midfield								
Patrick Atkinson*	5 9	11 00	22 5 70	Singapore	Trainee	Sheffield U	—	—
						Hartlepool U	21	3
Paul Dalton	5 11	11 07	25 4 67	Middlesbrough	Brandon U	Manchester U	—	—
						Hartlepool U	62	13
Kenneth Davies	6 0	11 00	22 12 70	Stockton	Trainee	Hartlepool U	3	—
Brian Honour	5 7	12 05	16 2 64	Horden	Apprentice	Darlington	74	4
					Peterlee	Hartlepool U	182	11
Steve Locker‡			5 11 70	Ashington	Trainee	Hartlepool U	1	—
Paul Ogden*	5 10	11 02	19 10 69	Salford	Trainee	Oldham Ath	—	—
						Hartlepool U	12	—
Paul Olsson	5 8	10 11	24 12 65	Hull	Apprentice	Hull C	—	—
						Exeter C (loan)	8	—
						Exeter C	35	2
						Scarborough	48	5
						Hartlepool U	23	2

HARTLEPOOL UNITED

Foundation: The inspiration for the launching of Hartlepool United was the West Hartlepool club which won the FA Amateur Cup in 1904–05. They had been in existence since 1881 and their Cup success led in 1908 to the formation of the new professional concern which first joined the North-Eastern League. In those days they were Hartlepools United and won the Durham Senior Cup in their first two seasons.

First Football League game: 27 August, 1921, Division 3(N), v Wrexham (a) W 2-0 – Gill; Thomas, Crilly; Dougherty, Hopkins, Short; Kessler, Mulholland (1), Lister (1), Robertson, Donald.

Managers (and Secretary-managers)
Alfred Priest 1908–12, Percy Humphreys 1912–13, Jack Manners 1913–20, Cecil Potter 1920–22, David Gordon 1922–24, Jack Manners 1924–27, Bill Norman 1927–31, Jack Carr 1932–35 (had been player-coach since 1931), Jimmy Hamilton 1935–43, Fred Westgarth 1943–57, Ray Middleton 1957–59, Bill Robinson 1959–62, Allenby Chilton 1962–63, Bob Gurney 1963–64, Alvan Williams 1964–65, Geoff Twentyman 1965, Brian Clough 1965–67, Angus McLean 1967–70, John Simpson 1970–71, Len Ashurst 1971–74, Ken Hale 1974–76, Billy Horner 1976–83, Johnny Duncan 1983, Mike Docherty 1983, Billy Horner 1984–86, John Bird 1986–88, Bobby Moncur 1988–89, Cyril Knowles 1989– .

Player and Position	Ht	Wt	Birth Date	Place	Source	Clubs	League App	Gls
Mark Robson*	5 10	11 00	25 4 71	Newcastle	Trainee	Hartlepool U	—	—
Jade Sinclair§			6 11 71	Saltburn	Trainee	Hartlepool U	4	—
John Tinkler	5 8	11 07	24 8 68	Trimdon		Hartlepool U	105	5
John Trewick‡	5 10	10 13	3 6 57	Bedlington	Apprentice	WBA	96	11
						Newcastle U	78	8
						Oxford U (loan)	3	—
						Oxford U	111	4
						Birmingham C	37	—
						Hartlepool U	8	—
Steve Tupling	6 0	12 08	11 7 64	Wensleydale	Apprentice	Middlesbrough	—	—
						Carlisle U (loan)	1	—
						Darlington	111	8
						Newport Co	33	2
						Cardiff C	5	—
						Torquay U (loan)	3	—
						Exeter C (loan)	9	1
						Hartlepool U	26	1
Phil Wilson§			5 2 72	Teesside	Trainee	Hartlepool U	1	—
Forwards								
Joe Allon	5 11	11 02	12 11 66	Gateshead		Newcastle U	9	2
						Swansea C	34	11
						Hartlepool U	66	22
Paul Baker	6 1	12 10	5 1 63	Newcastle	Bishop Auckland	Southampton	—	—
						Carlisle U	71	11
						Hartlepool U	122	42
Russell Doig*	5 8	10 09	17 1 64	Millport	St Mirren	E Stirling	109	9
						Leeds U	6	—
						Peterborough U (loan)	7	—
						Hartlepool U	33	1
Ian Dunbar§			6 6 71	Newcastle		Hartlepool U	1	—

(Continued on page 910)

Trainees
Brewis, Stephen L; Brown, Stephen; Clark, Paul J; Fletcher, Stephen M; McGuckin, Thomas I; Oliver, Scott; Percival, Paul; Sinclair, Jade; Todd, Lee; Wilson, Philip M.

**Non-Contract
Berryman, Stephen.

Associated Schoolboy who has accepted the club's offer of a Traineeship/Contract
Dunbar, Ian.

**Non-Contract Players who are retained must be re-signed before they are eligible to play in League matches.

276

HEREFORD UNITED 1989–90 *Back row (left to right):* John Layton, Chris Hemming, Paul Tester, Richard Jones, Tony Elliott, Darren Peacock, Mark Pridav, Russell Bradley, Gary Stevens, Darren Lush, Steve Devine.

Centre row: Ian Bowyer (Manager), Mark Jones, Jon Narbett, Ian Benbow, Mel Pejic, Lee Thomas, Adam Moore, Sean Walton, Mark Jones, Peter Isaac (Physiotherapist).

Front row: Mark Sutton, Shaun Jones, Paul Burton.

Division 4   **HEREFORD UNITED**

*Edgar Street, Hereford.*Telephone Hereford (0432) 276666. Commercial Dept: (0432) 273155.

Ground capacity: 13,777.

Record attendance: 18,114 v Sheffield W, FA Cup 3rd rd, 4 Jan, 1958.

Record receipts: £72,840 v Manchester U, FA Cup 4th rd, 28 January 1990.

Pitch measurements: 111yd × 74yd.

Chairman: P. S. Hill FRICS. *Vice-Chairman:* M. B. Roberts.

Directors: D. H. Vaughan, A. J. Phillips, G. C. E. Hales, H. A. R. Cotterell, J. W. T. Duggan.

Manager: Colin Addison. *Assistant Manager:* Bobby Smith.

Physio: Peter Isaac.

Secretary: David Vaughan. *Commercial Manager:* Paul Roberts.

Year Formed: 1924. *Turned Professional:* 1924. *Ltd Co.:* 1939.

Club Nickname: 'United'.

Record League Victory: 6-0 v Burnley (away), Division 4, 24 January 1987 – Rose; Rodgerson, Devine, Halliday, Pejic, Dalziel, Harvey (1p), Wells, Phillips (3), Kearns (2), Spooner.

Record Cup Victory: 6-1 v QPR, FA Cup, 2nd rd, 7 December 1957 – Sewell; Tomkins, Wade; Masters, Niblett, Horton (2p); Reg Bowen (1), Clayton (1), Fidler, Williams (1), Cyril Beech (1).

Record Defeat: 0-6 v Rotherham U, Division 4, 29 April, 1989.

Most League Points (2 for a win): 63, Division 3, 1975–76.

Most League Points (3 for a win): 77, Division 4, 1984–85.

Most League Goals: 86. Division 3, 1975–76.

Highest League Scorer in Season: Dixie McNeil, 35, 1975–76.

Most League Goals in Total Aggregate: Dixie McNeil, 88, 1974–77, 1982.

Most Capped Player: Brian Evans, 1 (7), Wales.

Most League Appearances: Mel Pejic, 351, 1980–90.

Record Transfer Fee Received: £175,000 from Notts Co for Phil Stant, July 1989.

Record Transfer Fee Paid: £50,000 to Halifax T for Ian Juryeff, December 1989.

Football League Record: 1972 Elected to Division 4; 1973–76 Division 3; 1976–77 Division 2; 1977–78 Division 3; 1978– Division 4.

Honours: Football League: Division 2 best season: 22nd, 1976–77; Division 3 – Champions 1975–76; Division 4 – Runners-up 1972–73. *FA Cup* best season: 4th rd, 1971–72, 1976–77, 1981–82, 1989–90. *Football League Cup* best season: 3rd rd. 1974–75. *Welsh Cup:* Winners: 1990.

Colours: White shirts, black shorts, white stockings. **Change colours:** All red.

HEREFORD UNITED 1989–90 LEAGUE RECORD

Match No.	Date		Venue	Opponents	Result	H/T Score	Lg. Pos.	Goalscorers	Atten- dance
1	Aug	19	H	Carlisle U	D 2-2	1-1	—	Peacock, Gorman (og)	2285
2		26	A	Cambridge U	W 1-0	0-0	8	Devine	1990
3	Sept	2	H	Maidstone U	W 3-0	1-0	5	Benbow, Robinson 2	2627
4		8	A	Colchester U	D 1-1	0-1	—	Pejic	3269
5		16	H	Wrexham	D 0-0	0-0	5		3173
6		23	A	Burnley	L 1-3	1-2	10	Narbett	5827
7		27	H	Chesterfield	W 3-2	1-1	—	Peacock 2, Jones R (pen)	2620
8		30	A	Grimsby T	W 2-0	1-0	6	Jones R, Jones M	4832
9	Oct	7	A	Stockport Co	L 1-2	0-2	7	Jones R (pen)	3428
10		14	H	Southend U	L 0-3	0-2	9		2975
11		18	H	Scarborough	W 3-1	0-0	—	Narbett, Tester 2	2222
12		21	A	Exeter C	L 0-2	0-0	10		3269
13		28	H	Lincoln C	D 2-2	0-2	10	Pejic, Bradley	2392
14		31	A	Halifax T	D 1-1	1-0	—	Oghani	1235
15	Nov	4	H	Rochdale	L 1-3	1-2	14	Jones M A	2235
16		11	A	Peterborough U	D 1-1	0-0	14	Oghani	4983
17		25	H	Doncaster R	L 0-1	0-1	16		2167
18	Dec	2	A	Hartlepool U	W 2-1	0-1	16	Robinson, Jones M	1493
19		16	H	Scunthorpe U	L 1-2	0-2	17	Jones M	1924
20		26	A	Torquay U	D 1-1	0-0	17	Pejic	3005
21		30	A	York C	W 2-1	1-0	16	Narbett, Juryeff	2405
22	Jan	1	H	Gillingham	L 1-2	0-1	17	Hemming	2759
23		13	H	Cambridge U	L 0-2	0-2	18		7302
24		20	A	Carlisle U	L 1-2	0-0	20	Tester	4726
25	Feb	10	A	Wrexham	D 0-0	0-0	21		2171
26		14	A	Maidstone U	L 0-2	0-0	—		1516
27		17	H	Hartlepool U	W 4-1	4-0	21	Jones M (pen), Tester, Juryeff, Pejic	2049
28		25	A	Doncaster R	W 1-0	1-0	—	Wheeler	2958
29	Mar	3	H	Aldershot	W 4-1	2-1	16	Wheeler, Narbett, Tester, Juryeff	2368
30		7	H	Grimsby T	L 0-1	0-0	—		3013
31		10	A	Chesterfield	L 1-2	0-2	17	Wheeler	4021
32		14	H	Colchester U	W 2-0	0-0	—	Wheeler 2	2253
33		17	H	Stockport Co	L 1-2	1-2	17	Pejic	2458
34		20	A	Southend U	L 0-2	0-1	—		2669
35		24	A	Scarborough	W 1-0	1-0	17	Narbett	1873
36		28	H	Burnley	L 0-1	0-0	—		2389
37		31	H	Exeter C	W 2-1	0-0	17	Hemming, Wheeler	4243
38	Apr	7	A	Lincoln C	L 0-1	0-1	17		2501
39		11	H	Halifax T	l 0-1	0-0	—		1817
40		14	A	Gillingham	W 1-0	0-0	17	Jones M	2365
41		16	H	Torquay U	D 0-0	0-0	17		2422
42		21	A	Scunthorpe U	D 3-3	1-2	16	Jones M 2 (1 pen), Bowyer G	2247
43		25	A	York C	L 1-2	0-0	—	Jones M	2007
44		28	H	Peterborough U	L 1-2	0-1	18	Wheeler	2273
45	May	1	A	Aldershot	W 2-0	1-0	—	Wheeler, Robinson	1412
46		5	A	Rochdale	L 2-5	0-2	17	Bowyer G, Burton	1429

Final League Position: 17

GOALSCORERS

League (56): Wheeler 8, Jones M 8 (2 pens), Narbett 5, Pejic 5, Tester 5, Robinson 4, Jones R 3 (2 pens), Juryeff 3, Peacock 3, Bowyer G 2, Hemming 2, Oghani 2, Benbow 1, Bradley 1, Burton 1, Devine 1, Jones M A 1, own goal 1.
Littlewoods Cup (5): Jones R 3 (2 pens), Pejic 1, Robinson 1.
FA Cup (6): Jones M 1 (pen), Jones M A 1, Peacock 1, Pejic 1, Robinson 1, Tester 1.

Elliott	Jones M A	Devine	Hemming	Bradley	Jones R	Pejic	Narbett	Benbow	Peacock	Tester	Robinson	Jones M	Phillips	Stevens	Williams	Thomas	Oghani	Juryeff	Honor	Wheeler	Jones S	Starbuck	Bowyer G	Freestone	Bowyer I	Priday	Burton	Match No.
1	2	3	4†	5	6	7	8	9*	10	11	12	14																1
1	2	3			6	7	4	8	9	5	11	10																2
	2	3			6	7	4	8	9*	5	11	10	1	12														3
	2				6	7	4	8	9	5	11	10	1		3													4
	2	6				7	4	8	9*	5	11	10	1	12	3													5
	2	6				7	4	8*	9	11†	10	5	1	12	3		14											6
	2			6	5	4	8		9	11	10	7	1		3													7
	2	3	12	6	7	4	8		5	11	9	10*	1															8
1	2		4	6	5		8		9	11	10	7			3													9
1	2	4*	6	5†	14	8		9	11	10	7				3		12											10
1	2		4	6		5	8		11	9	7				3		10											11
1	2	12	4	6		5	8		11*	9	7				3		10											12
1	2		4	6		5	8	12	11	9	7				3		10*											13
1	2		4	6		5	8		12	11	9	7			3		10*											14
1	2†	6	4		5		8	14	9	11		7		12	3		10*											15
1	2	12	4	6*			8		5	11	9	7			3		10											16
1	2	6	4		14		8		5	11*	9	7		12	3†		10											17
1	2		4		6		8	10*	5	11	9	7		12	3													18
1	2		4	3	6	12	8	11*	5		9	7						10										19
1	2	3	4		6*	11	8	12	5		9	7						10										20
1	2	3	4	6	14	11*	8	12	5†		9	7						10										21
1		3	4	6		7	8	11*	5		9	12						10			2							22
1	3	12	4		6*	11	8		5		9	7						10			2							23
1	2†	3	4*	6		11	8		5	12	9	7						10			14							24
1	2	3	4		6	8		5	11	9	7							10										25
1	2	3	4		6	8	12	5	11		7							9		10*								26
1	2	3	4	14	6†	8	12	5	11		7*							10		9								27
1		3		4	6		8		5	11*	12	2						9		7	10							28
1	2		4			8		5	11		7						12	9		6*	10	3						29
1	2	3		4	14	8		5	11		6†						12	9		7*	10							30
1	2	3		4	6	8	11*	5		7								9		12	10							31
1	2	3	4	6	8		5		7		11							9		10								32
1	2	3	4	6	8		5	12	7†		11							9		14	10*							33
1	2	3†	4	6		11	5	10	8		12							9		7*	14							34
		3*	4	6	12	8	7	5		2								10		9	14	11†		1				35
			4	6	2	8	7*	5		11								10		9	12	3		1				36
	2*		4	6	7	8		5		11								10		9	12	3		1				37
	2	3	4	6	7	11	5		8*									10		9	12	1						38
	3	4	6	2	11	5	12†	8										10		9	14	7*		1				39
	2	3	4	5	6	8		7										10		9	11			1				40
	2	3	4	5	6	8		7										10		9	11			1				41
	2	3	4*	5	6	8		7										9		10†	12	11		1	14			42
1	2	3	4	5	6*	8		7										9		10	12	11						43
	2	3	4	5	6*	8		7†										9		10	12	11			1	14		44
	2	3	5	4	8†	12	6		9									10*		7	11		14		1			45
	2	3*	5	4	8	9	6		10									7		11			1		12			46
29	41	31	34	33	16	34	36	21	35	24	25	40	6	—	14	—	7	22	2	21	6	6	12	8	—	3	—	
			+3s	+1s		+3s	+4s	+6s	+1s	+2s	+4s	+2s			+6s		+1s	+1s	+3s	+1s		+9s	+2s	+2s	+2s			

Littlewoods Cup

First Round		Torquay U (a)	1-0
		(h)	3-0
Second Round		Charlton Ath (a)	1-3
		(h)	0-1

FA Cup

First Round		Farnborough (a)	1-0
Second Round		Merthyr (h)	3-2
Third Round		Walsall (h)	2-1
Fourth Round		Manchester U (h)	0-1

HEREFORD UNITED

Player and Position	Ht	Wt	Birth Date	Place	Source	Clubs	League App	Gls
Goalkeepers								
Tony Elliott	6 0	12 12	30 11 69	Nuneaton		Birmingham C	—	—
						Hereford U	52	—
Mark Priday§	6 0	11 12	16 10 71	Knighton	Trainee	Hereford U	3	—
Defenders								
Gary Bowyer†			22 6 71	Manchester		Hereford U	14	2
Russell Bradley	6 0	12 05	28 3 66	Birmingham		Nottingham F	—	—
						Hereford U (loan)	12	1
						Hereford	33	1
Steve Devine	5 9	10 07	11 12 64	Strabane	Apprentice	Wolverhampton W	—	—
						Derby Co	11	—
						Stockport Co	2	—
						Hereford U	170	3
Chris Hemming	5 11	11 02	13 4 66	Newcastle	School	Stoke C	93	2
						Wigan Ath (loan)	4	—
						Hereford U	35	2
Mark A. Jones	5 8	10 12	22 10 61	Warley	Apprentice	Aston Villa	24	—
						Brighton & HA	9	—
						Birmingham C	—	—
						Shrewsbury T	34	—
						Hereford U	110	1
Darren Lush‡	5 10	11 00	10 10 69	Salisbury	Bournemouth§	Hereford U	—	—
Darren Peacock	6 2	12 06	3 2 68	Bristol	Apprentice	Newport Co	28	—
						Hereford U	44	3
Mel Pejic*	5 9	10 08	27 4 59	Chesterton	Local	Stoke C	1	—
						Hereford U	351	12
Gary Stevens*	6 1	12 03	30 8 54	Birmingham	Evesham	Cardiff C	150	44
						Shrewsbury T	150	29
						Brentford	32	10
						Hereford U	94	10
Midfield								
Ian Benbow	5 10	11 00	9 1 69	Hereford	Trainee	Hereford U	82	4
Ian Bowyer†	5 10	11 11	6 6 51	Ellesmere Port	Apprentice	Manchester C	50	13
						Orient	78	18
						Nottingham F	239	49
						Sunderland	15	1
						Nottingham F	206	19
						Hereford U	40	1
Darren Goodall‡			9 12 70	Birmingham	WBA§	Hereford U	—	—
Mark Jones	5 8	10 01	4 1 68	Brownhills	Apprentice	Walsall	8	—
						Exeter C (loan)	5	—
						Hereford U	42	8
Richard Jones	5 11	11 01	26 4 69	Pontypool		Newport Co	41	1
						Hereford U	57	4
Shane Jones§	5 9	10 02	8 11 72	Tredegar	Trainee	Hereford U	15	—
Adam Moore‡	5 10	11 04	11 12 70	Cardiff	Newport Co§	Hereford U	—	—
Jon Narbett	5 10	10 08	21 11 68	Birmingham	Apprentice	Shrewsbury T	26	3
						Hereford U	72	12
Lee Thomas*	5 7	11 02	1 11 70	Tredegar	Trainee	Hereford U	1	—
Forwards								
Paul Burton§	5 9	10 01	6 8 73	Hereford		Hereford U	2	1
Ian Juryeff	5 11	12 00	24 11 62	Gosport	Apprentice	Southampton	2	—
						Mansfield T (loan)	12	5
						Reading (loan)	7	1
						Leyton Orient	111	44
						Ipswich T (loan)	2	—
						Halifax T	17	7
						Hereford U	25	3

HEREFORD UNITED

Foundation: A number of local teams amalgamated in 1924 under the chairmanship of Dr. E. W. Maples to form Hereford United and joined the Birmingham Combination. They graduated to the Birmingham League four years later.

First Football League game: 12 August, 1972, Division 4, v Colchester U (a) L 0-1 – Potter; Mallender, Naylor; Jones, McLaughlin, Tucker; Slattery, Hollett, Owen, Radford, Wallace.

Managers (and Secretary-managers)
Eric Keen 1939, George Tranter 1948–49, Alex Massie 1952, George Tranter 1953–55, Joe Wade 1956–62, Ray Daniels 1962–63, Bob Dennison 1963–67, John Charles 1967–71, Colin Addison 1971–74, John Sillett 1974–78, Mike Bailey 1978–79, Frank Lord 1979–82, Tommy Hughes 1982–83, Johnny Newman 1983–87, Ian Bowyer 1987–90, Colin Addison 1990– .

Player and Position	Ht	Wt	Birth Date	Place	Source	Clubs	League App	Gls
Colin Robinson	5 10	10 12	15 5 60	Birmingham	Mile Oak R	Shrewsbury T	194	41
						Birmingham C	37	6
						Hereford U	29	4
Paul Tester	5 8	10 12	10 3 59	Stroud	Cheltenham T	Shrewsbury T	89	12
						Hereford U (loan)	4	—
						Hereford U	70	11
Paul Wheeler	5 11	11 03	3 1 65	Caerphilly	Apprentice Aberaman	Bristol R	—	—
						Cardiff C	101	10
						Hull C	5	—
						Hereford U	21	8

Trainees
Burton, Paul S; Jones, Shane G; McElroy, Stephen L; Priday, Marcus A; Sutton, Mark J.

**Non-Contract
Bowyer, Ian; Bowyer, Gary D; Foley, William; O'Donnell, James A.

Associated Schoolboys
Cocum, Neil; Roberts, Simon P; Sykes, Alex; Watkins, Andrew.

**Non-Contract Players who are retained must be re-signed before they are eligible to play in League matches.

HUDDERSFIELD TOWN 1989–90 *Back row (left to right):* George Mulhall (Coach), Richard Shelton, Simon Trevitt, Ken O'Doherty, Michael Cecere, Steve Hardwick, Iffy Onuora, Gary Leake, Graham Mitchell, Andy Duggan, Mick Byrne, Ian Bray (Youth Development Officer), Gary Williams (Physiotherapist). *Front row:* Chris Marsden, Craig Maskell, Keiron O'Regan, Chris Hutchings, Eoin Hand (Manager), Peter Withe (Assistant Manager), Mark Smith, Junior Bent, Robert Wilson, Dudley Lewis.

Division 3   HUDDERSFIELD TOWN

© 1973

Leeds Rd, Huddersfield HD1 6PE. Telephone (0484) 420335/6. Commercial Dept: (0484) 534867. Recorded Information: (0898) 121635.

Ground capacity: 32,000.

Record attendance: 67,037 v Arsenal, FA Cup 6th rd, 27 Feb, 1932.

Record receipts: £52,607 v Newcastle U, Division 2,7 May, 1984.

Pitch measurements: 115yd × 75yd.

Chairman: K. S. Longbottom. *Vice-Chairman:* D. G. Headey.

Directors: C. Senior, C. Hodgkinson, J. B. Buckley, F. L. Thewlis.

Manager: Eoin Hand. *Assistant Manager:* Peter Withe.

Coach: George Mulhall.

Secretary: G. S. Binns. *Commercial Manager:* Tony Flynn. *Commercial Executive:* Keith Hanvey.

Physio: Gary Williams.

Year Formed: 1908. *Turned Professional:* 1908. *Ltd Co.:* 1908.

Club Nickname: 'The Terriers'.

Record League Victory: 10-1 v Blackpool, Division 1, 13 December 1930 – Turner; Goodall, Spencer; Redfern, Wilson, Campbell; Bob Kelly (1), McLean (4), Robson (3), Davies (1), Smailes (1).

Record Cup Victory: 7-1 v Chesterfield (away), FA Cup, 3rd rd, 12 January 1929: Turvey; Goodall, Wadsworth; Evans, Wilson, Naylor: Jackson (1), Kelly, Brown (3), Cumming (2), Smith. (1 o.g)

Record Defeat: 1-10 v Manchester C, Division 2, 7 November, 1987.

Most League Points (2 for a win): 66, Division 4, 1979–80.

Most League Points (3 for a win): 82, Division 3, 1982–83.

Most League Goals: 101, Division 4, 1979–80.

Highest League Scorer in Season: Sam Taylor, 35, Division 2, 1919–20; George Brown, 35, Division 1, 1925–26.

Most League Goals in Total Aggregate: George Brown, 142, 1921–29 and Jimmy Glazzard, 142, 1946–56.

Most Capped Player: Jimmy Nicholson, 31 (41), Northern Ireland.

Most League Appearances: Billy Smith, 520, 1914–34.

Record Transfer Fee Received: £230,000 from Swindon T for Duncan Shearer, June 1988.

Record Transfer Fee Paid: £110,000 to Mansfield T for Terry Austin, December 1980.

Football League Record: 1910 Elected to Division 2; 1920–52 Division 1; 1952–53 Division 2; 1953–56 Division 1; 1956–70 Division 2; 1970–72 Division 1; 1972–73 Division 2; 1973–75 Division 3; 1975–80 Division 4; 1980–83 Division 3; 1983–88 Division 2; 1988– Division 3.

Honours: Football League: Division 1 – Champions 1923–24, 1924–25, 1925–26; Runners-up 1926–27, 1927–28, 1933–34; Division 2 – Champions 1969–70; Runners-up 1919–20, 1952–53; Division 4 – Champions 1979–80. *FA Cup:* Winners 1922; Runners-up 1920, 1928, 1930, 1938. *Football League Cup:* Semi-final. 1967–68.

Colours: Blue and white striped shirts, white shorts, white stockings. **Change colours:** Red/black striped shirts, black shorts, black stockings.

HUDDERSFIELD TOWN 1989–90 LEAGUE RECORD

Match No.	Date	Venue	Opponents	Result	H/T Score	Lg. Pos.	Goalscorers	Attendance
1	Aug 19	H	Swansea C	W 1-0	0-0	—	Cecere	5775
2	26	A	Walsall	W 3-2	1-1	3	Wilson, Smith, Onuora	4173
3	Sept 2	H	Bolton W	D 1-1	1-1	4	O'Regan	7872
4	9	A	Preston NE	D 3-3	0-1	5	Smith, Hutchings, Wilson	5822
5	16	H	Brentford	W 1-0	0-0	3	Smith	5578
6	22	A	Tranmere R	L 0-4	0-1	—		7375
7	26	A	Fulham	D 0-0	0-0	—		4445
8	30	H	Leyton Orient	W 2-0	2-0	6	Cecere 2 (1 pen)	5258
9	Oct 7	A	Cardiff C	L 2-3	1-2	9	Marsden, O'Regan	5835
10	14	A	Reading	D 0-0	0-0	10		3950
11	17	H	Wigan Ath	W 2-0	0-0	—	Maskell, Smith	5119
12	21	A	Birmingham C	W 1-0	0-0	6	Smith	7951
13	28	H	Shrewsbury T	D 1-1	1-1	7	Bent	6001
14	Nov 1	A	Bristol R	D 2-2	0-1	—	Cecere, Maskell	6467
15	4	A	Chester C	L 1-2	0-1	9	Wilson	2660
16	11	H	Northampton T	D 2-2	1-0	9	Smith, Mitchell	4973
17	25	H	Notts Co	L 1-2	1-2	10	Short (og)	5416
18	Dec 2	A	Mansfield T	W 2-1	1-1	9	Wilson, Hutchings	2966
19	16	A	Rotherham U	D 0-0	0-0	10		6673
20	26	H	Bury	W 2-1	1-1	8	Maskell, O'Connell	8483
21	30	H	Bristol C	W 2-1	1-0	5	Smith, Maskell	7681
22	Jan 1	A	Blackpool	D 2-2	1-1	6	Hutchings, Onuora	5097
23	13	H	Walsall	W 1-0	0-0	6	Marsden	5856
24	21	A	Swansea C	W 3-1	3-0	—	Wilson, Hutchings 2	4488
25	Feb 3	H	Tranmere R	W 1-0	0-0	3	Onuora	7005
26	10	A	Brentford	L 1-2	0-0	4	Wilson	6774
27	17	H	Mansfield T	W 1-0	0-0	4	Maskell	5441
28	24	A	Notts Co	L 0-1	0-0	7		7633
29	Mar 3	A	Crewe Alex	L 0-1	0-0	7		5933
30	6	A	Leyton Orient	L 0-1	0-1	—		3040
31	10	H	Fulham	L 0-1	0-0	8		4780
32	13	A	Crewe Alex	L 0-3	0-1	—		4384
33	17	A	Cardiff C	W 5-1	1-0	8	Maskell 4, O'Regan	2628
34	20	H	Reading	L 0-1	0-1	—		4588
35	24	A	Wigan Ath	W 2-1	1-0	8	Byrne, Maskell	3167
36	31	H	Birmingham C	L 1-2	1-0	9	Withe	5837
37	Apr 3	H	Preston NE	L 0-2	0-2	—		4381
38	7	A	Shrewsbury T	D 3-3	1-1	9	Byrne, Maskell 2 (1 pen)	2867
39	10	A	Bristol R	D 1-1	1-1	—	Kelly	4359
40	14	H	Blackpool	D 2-2	1-1	9	Byrne, Maskell (pen)	4845
41	16	A	Bury	L 0-6	0-3	10		4621
42	21	H	Rotherham U	W 2-1	0-1	8	Edwards 2	4963
43	24	A	Bristol C	D 1-1	1-0	—	Duggan	17,791
44	28	A	Northampton T	L 0-1	0-1	8		2388
45	May 1	A	Bolton W	D 2-2	1-1	—	Edwards, Maskell	8550
46	5	H	Chester C	W 4-1	2-0	8	Byrne, Maskell, Edwards, Reeves (og)	3514

Final League Position: 8

GOALSCORERS
League (61): Maskell 15 (2 pens), Smith 7, Wilson 6, Hutchings 5, Byrne 4, Cecere 4 (1 pen), Edwards 4, Onuora 3, O'Regan 3, Marsden 2, Bent 1, Duggan 1, Kelly 1, Mitchell 1, O'Connell 1, Withe 1, own goals 2.
Littlewoods Cup (7): Maskell 2, Wilson 2, Cecere 1, O'Doherty 1, Onuora 1.
FA Cup (7): Cecere 3 (3 pens), Maskell 2, Smith 1, own goal 1.

Hardwick	Trevitt	Hutchings	May	O'Doherty	Lewis	Mitchell	Wilson	Cecere	Maskell	Smith	Marsden	Onuora	O'Regan	Martin	Byrne	Withe	Bent	Maguire	O'Connell	Bray	Charlton	Duggan	Donovan	Boothroyd	Kelly	Edwards	Match No.
1	2	3	4	5	6	7†	8	9	10	11*12	14																1
1	2	3		5	6		8	9	10	11*			4	12	7												2
1	2	3	4	5	6		8	9	10*11				12	7													3
1	2	3	4	5	6	12	8	9	10†11				14	7*													4
	2	3	4	5	6	7*	8	9	12	11			10		1												5
1	2	3	4	5	6	7*	8	9	10†11	12	14																6
1		3	4	5	6	7	8	9		11	2	12		10*													7
1		3	4	5	6	7	8	9*		11	2	14	12	10†													8
1		3	4	5	6*12		8	9	10	11	2			7†	14												9
1		3	4	5	6		8	9		11	2	12		10*	7												10
1		3	4	5	6		8	9	10	11*	2					7	12										11
1		3	4	5	6		8	9	10	11	2					7											12
1		3	4	5	6		8	9	10	11*	2					7	12										13
1		3	4	5	6		8	9	10	11*	2					12	7										14
1		3	4	5	6		8	9	10	11	2					12	7*										15
1		3	4		6*	5	8	9	10	11	2			14	7†	12											16
1		3	4	5		6	8*	9†10	11	2	7	12	14														17
		3	4		6	8	9	10	11	2	5	1			7												18
		3	4		6	5	8	10*11	2	12	7	1			9												19
		3	4		6	5	8	10	11*	2	12	7	1			9											20
		3	4*	6	5		10	11	2	12	7	1			9	8											21
		3	4	6	5		10	11*	2	12	7	1			9	8											22
		3	4	6	5	7	10	11	2		1				9	8											23
		3	4	6	5	7	10	11	2*	12	1				9	8											24
		3	4	6	5	7	10*11†	2	14	12	1				9	8											25
		3	4	6	5	7	10	11*	12	2	1				9	8											26
		3	4	6	5	7	10	11*	12	2	1				9	8											27
		3	4	6	5	7	10†11	2	14	12	1				9	8											28
		3		6	5	7	9	11	2*10†	4	1			12		8	14										29
		3		6† 5		9	11*	2	12	4	1		10	7		8	14										30
		3	4* 6†	5		9	10	12	2	7	1	11			14	8											31
		3	4*	5		9	10	11	2	1		12	8		6	7											32
		3		5			10	11	7	1	9	4		8			6		2								33
		3		5		12	10	11*	7	1	9	4	14	8†			6		2								34
		3	12	5			10	11	7	1	9	4					6		2			8*					35
		3	8	5	12		10	11	7	1	9†	4*					6		2				14				36
		3	8	5			10	12	7	1	9	4†					6		2		14		11*				37
		3	8	5			10	11	7	1	9	4					6		2								38
		3	8	5			10	11	7	1	9*						6		2		4	12					39
		3*	8	5			10	11	14	7	1	9					6		2		4†12						40
		3	8	5			10	11* 5	7	1	9						6		2		4	12					41
1		3	2	5			10	12	8	7		9*					6				4	11					42
1		3	2	5			10	12	8	7		9*					6				4	11					43
1		3	2	5			10	12	8	7		9†					6		14		4*11						44
1		3	2	5			10		8	7		9					6				4	11					45
1	2*	3	8	12	5		10		7		9						6				4	11					46

21 7 46 40 17 28 35 27 22 40 39 29 3 31 25 17 8 6 — 11 13 1 15 1 9 9 6
+ + + + + + + + + + + + + + + + +
1s 1s 2s 1s 1s 1s 5s 3s 17s6s 2s 4s 1s3s 1s 2s 1s 1s 4s

Littlewoods Cup	First Round	Doncaster R (h)	1-1	
		(a)	2-1	
	Second Round	Nottingham F (a)	1-1	
		(h)	3-3	
FA Cup	First Round	Hartlepool U (a)	2-0	
	Second Round	Chesterfield (a)	2-0	
	Third Round	Grimsby T (h)	3-1	
	Fourth Round	Crystal Palace (a)	0-4	

HUDDERSFIELD TOWN

Player and Position	Ht	Wt	Birth Date	Place	Source	Clubs	League App	Gls
Goalkeepers								
Steve Hardwick	5 11	13 00	6 9 56	Mansfield	Amateur	Chesterfield	38	—
						Newcastle U	92	—
						Oxford U	156	—
						Crystal Palace (loan)	3	—
						Sunderland (loan)	6	—
						Huddersfield T	67	—
Gary Leake‡			30 1 70	Hucknall	Trainee	WBA	—	—
						Chester C (loan)	—	—
						Huddersfield T	—	—
Lee Martin	5 11	11 08	9 9 68	Huddersfield	Trainee	Huddersfield T	43	—
Defenders								
Adrian Boothroyd	5 8	10 12	8 2 77	Bradford	Trainee	Huddersfield T	10	—
Ian Bray*	5 8	11 05	6 12 62	Neath	Apprentice	Hereford U	108	4
						Huddersfield T	89	1
Simon Charlton	7 7	10 11	25 10 71	Huddersfield	Trainee	Huddersfield T	3	—
Andrew Duggan	6 3	13 00	19 9 67	Bradford	Apprentice	Barnsley	2	1
						Rochdale (loan)	3	—
						Huddersfield T	29	3
Dudley Lewis	5 10	10 09	17 11 62	Swansea	Apprentice	Swansea C	230	2
						Huddersfield T	28	—
Graham Mitchell	6 0	11 05	16 2 68	Shipley	Apprentice	Huddersfield T	117	2
Ken O'Doherty	6 0	12 00	30 3 63	Dublin	UCD	Crystal Palace	42	—
						Huddersfield T	55	1
Simon Trevitt	5 11	11 02	20 12 67	Dewsbury	Apprentice	Huddersfield T	94	1
Shaun Weatherhead*	5 11	12 03	3 9 70	Halifax	Trainee	Huddersfield T	—	—
Midfield								
Steven Donald*	5 10	11 02	24 6 70	Paisley	Trainee	Huddersfield T	—	—
Chris Hutchings*	5 10	11 00	5 7 57	Winchester	Harrow Bor	Chelsea	87	3
						Brighton & HA	153	4
						Huddersfield T	110	10
Chris Marsden	5 1J	10 12	3 1 69	Sheffield	Trainee	Sheffield U	16	1
						Huddersfield T	46	3
Andy May	5 8	11 00	26 2 64	Bury	Apprentice	Manchester C	150	8
						Huddersfield T	114	5
						Bolton W (loan)	10	2
Kieran O'Regan	5 9	10 08	9 11 63	Cork	Tranmore Ath	Brighton & HA	86	2
						Swindon T	26	1
						Huddersfield T	73	5
Richard Shelton‡	5 8	10 11	8 6 68	Sheffield	Trainee	Huddersfield T	—	—
Robert Wilson	5 10	11 11	5 6 61	Kensington	Apprentice	Fulham	175	34
						Millwall	28	12
						Luton T	24	1
						Fulham	47	4
						Huddersfield T	28	6
Forwards								
Mick Byrne	5 11	12 03	14 1 60	Dublin	Shamrock R	Huddersfield T	56	11
						Shelbourne (loan)	—	—
Michele Cecere	6 0	11 04	4 1 68	Chester	Apprentice	Oldham Ath	52	8
						Huddersfield T	54	8
						Stockport Co (loan)	1	—
Kevin Donovan	5 7	10 10	17 12 71	Halifax	Trainee	Huddersfield T	1	—
Gary Haycock	6 0	11 12	31 12 70	Bradford	Trainee	Huddersfield T	—	—
						Shelbourne (loan)	—	—
Mark Hurst	5 10	11 02	18 8 70	Derby	Trainee	Nottingham F	—	—
						Huddersfield T	—	—

HUDDERSFIELD TOWN

Foundation: A meeting, attended largely by members of the Huddersfield & District FA, was held at the Imperial Hotel in 1906 to discuss the feasibility of establishing a football club in this rugby stronghold. However, it was not until a man with both the enthusiasm and the money to back the scheme came on the scene, that real progress was made. This benefactor was Mr. Hilton Crowther and it was at a meeting at the Albert Hotel in 1908, that the club formally came into existence with a capital of £2,000 and joined the North-Eastern League.

First Football League game: 3 September, 1910, Division 2, v Bradford PA (a) W 1-0 – Mutch; Taylor, Morris; Beaton, Hall, Bartlett; Blackburn, Wood, Hamilton (1), McCubbin, Jee.

Managers (and Secretary-managers)
Frank Walker 1908–10, Richard Pudan 1910–12, Arthur Fairclough 1912–19, Ambrose Langley 1919–21, Herbert Chapman 1921–25, Cecil Potter 1925–26, Jack Chaplin 1926–29, Clem Stephenson 1929–42, David Steele 1943–47, George Stephenson 1947–52, Andy Beattie 1952–56, Bill Shankly 1956–59, Eddie Boot 1960–64, Tom Johnston 1964–68, Ian Greaves 1968–74, Bobby Collins 1974, Tom Johnston 1975–78 (had been GM since 1975), Mike Buxton 1978–86, Steve Smith 1986–87, Malcolm Macdonald 1987–88, Eoin Hand 1988– .

Player and Position	Ht	Wt	Birth Date	Place	Source	Clubs	League App	Gls
Paul Kirkham‡	5 11	11 05	5 7 69	Manchester	Manchester U	Huddersfield T	1	—
						Waterford (loan)	—	—
Peter Maguire	5 8	9 10	11 9 69	Holmfirth	Trainee	Leeds U	2	—
						Huddersfield T	3	—
Craig Maskell	5 10	11 04	10 4 68	Aldershot	Apprentice	Southampton	6	1
						Swindon T (loan)	—	—
						Huddersfield T	87	43
Iffy Onuora	5 10	11 10	28 7 67	Glasgow		Huddersfield T	20	3
Mark Smith	5 11	11 05	19 12 61	Sheffield		Sheffield U	—	—
					Gainsborough Tr	Scunthorpe U	1	—
					Kettering	Rochdale	27	7
						Huddersfield T	64	9
Peter Withe†	6 1	12 00	30 8 51	Liverpool	Skelmersdale	Southport	3	—
						Barrow	1	—
					Pt Elizabeth/	Wolverhampton W	17	3
					Arcadia S	Birmingham C	35	9
					Portland T	Nottingham F	75	28
						Newcastle U	76	25
						Aston Villa	182	74
						Sheffield U	74	18
						Birmingham C (loan)	8	2
						Huddersfield T	38	1

Trainees
Billy, Christopher A; Byrne, Brian J; Byrne, Jason; Hilditch, John; Johnson, Matthew L; Kelly, Kevin; McKee, Christopher J; Rainton, Karl; Stochero, Daniel M; Thomas, Robert S; Wallace, David A.

**Non-Contract
Gledhill, Richard; Withe, Peter

Associated Schoolboys
Aspinall, Brendan J; Barrett, Anthony M; Cramp, Richard J; Dearnley, Robert; Dyson, Jonathan P; Graley, Marc; Hansgate, Paul M; Hart, Andrew C; Johnson, Dean C; Laycock, Christopher; Payne, Stephen J; Rayne, Dean E; Rowe, Rodney C; Symmonds, Richard A; Tinkler, Jonathan.

Associated Schoolboys who have accepted the club's offer of a Traineeship/Contract
Booth, Andrew D; Collins, Simon; Dysart, John; Ireland, Simon P.

**Non-Contract Players who are retained must be re-signed before they are eligible to play in League matches.

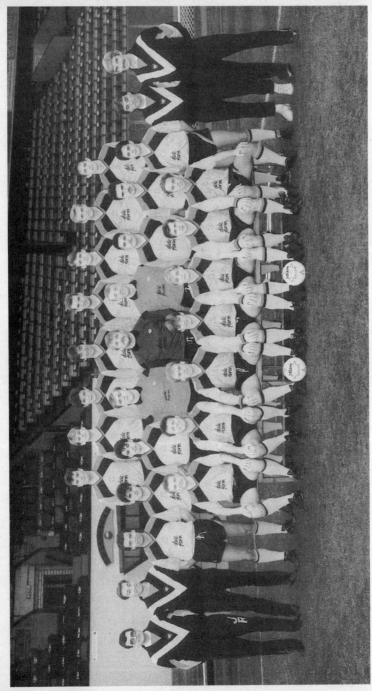

HULL CITY 1989–90 *Back row (left to right):* Steve Terry, Richard Jobson, Neil Buckley, Billy Whitehurst, Peter Swan, Leigh Jenkinson, Lee Warren, Paul Mudd.
Centre row: Jeff Radcliffe (Physiotherapist), Dale Roberts (Youth Team Coach), Ken De Mange, Andy Payton, Malcolm Murray, Gavin Kelly, Iain Hesford, Dave Cleminshaw, Paul Waites, Nicky Brown, Mike Smith, Stan Ternent (Manager), Tom Wilson (Reserve Team Coach).
Front row: Wayne Jacobs, Steve Doyle, Billy Askew, Garreth Roberts, Les Thompson, Ian McParland, Mark Calvert.

Division 2   **HULL CITY**

Boothferry Park, Hull HU4 6EU. Telephone Hull (0482) 51119.
Commercial Manager: (0482) 566050.
Ground capacity: 17,932.
Record attendance: 55,019 v Manchester U, FA Cup 6th rd, 26 Feb, 1949.
Record receipts: £79,604 v Liverpool FA Cup, 5th rd, 18 February, 1989.
Pitch measurements: 112yd × 72yd.
President: T. C. Waite MIRTE.
Vice-Presidents: The Rt. Hon. H. Zammit, Toni Dalli, Max Payne MICM.
Chairman: R. M. Cheetham. *Vice-Chairman:* M. W. Fish FCA.
Directors: D. Robinson, J. Johnson BA, DPA, G. H. C. Needler MA, ACA, C. M. Thorpe LL.B., E. Hughes.
Manager: Stan Ternent. *Assistant Manager/Coach:* Tom Wilson.
Reserve Team Coach: Tom Wilson. *Physio:* Jeff Radcliffe.
Secretary: Frank Boughton. *Commercial Manager:* Simon Cawkill. *Development Manager:* Graham Blakey.
Year Formed: 1904. *Turned Professional:* 1905. *Ltd Co.:* 1905.
Club Nickname: 'The Tigers'.
Previous Grounds: 1904, Boulevard Ground (Hull RFC); 1905, Anlaby Road (Hull CC); 1944/5 Boulevard Grounds; 1946, Boothferry Park.
Record League Victory: 11-1 v Carlisle U, Division 3 (N), 14 January 1939 – Ellis; Woodhead, Dowen; Robinson (1), Blyth, Hardy; Hubbard (2), Richardson (2), Dickinson (2), Davies (2), Cunliffe (2).
Record Cup Victory: 8-2 v Stalybridge Celtic (away), FA Cup, 1st rd, 26 November 1932 – Maddison; Goldsmith, Woodhead; Gardner, Hill (1), Denby; Forward (1), Duncan, McNaughton (1), Wainscoat (4), Sargeant (1).
Record Defeat: 0-8 v Wolverhampton W, Division 2, 4, November, 1911.
Most League Points (2 for a win): 69, Division 3, 1965–66.
Most League Points (3 for a win): 90, Division 4, 1982–83.
Most League Goals: 109, Division 3, 1965–66.
Highest League Scorer in Season: Bill McNaughton, 39, Division 3 (N), 1932–33.
Most League Goals in Total Aggregate: Chris Chilton, 195, 1960–71.
Most Capped Player: Terry Neill, 15 (59), Northern Ireland.
Most League Appearances: Andy Davidson, 520, 1952–67.
Record Transfer Fee Received: £400,000 from Sunderland for Tony Norman, December 1988.
Record Transfer Fee Paid: £200,000 to Leeds U for Peter Swan, March 1989.
Football League Record: 1905 Elected to Division 2; 1930–33 Division 3 (N); 1933–36 Division 2; 1936–49 Division 3 (N); 1949–56 Division 2; 1956–58 Division 3 (N); 1958–59 Division 3; 1959–60 Division 2; 1960–66 Division 3; 1966–78 Division 2; 1978–81 Division 3; 1981–83 Division 4; 1983–85 Division 3; 1985– Division 2.
Honours: Football League: Division 2 best season: 3rd, 1909–10; Division 3 (N) – Champions 1932–33, 1948–49; Division 3 – Champions 1965–66; Runners-up 1958–59; Division 4 – Runners-up 1982–83. *FA Cup* best season: Semi-final, 1930. *Football League Cup* best season: 4th, 1973–74, 1975–76, 1977–78. *Associate Members' Cup:* Runners-up 1984.
Colours: Black and amber vertical stripes, amber sleeve shirts, black shorts, black/amber stockings. **Change colours:** Green and white shirts, white shorts, green trim, green stockings.

290

HULL CITY 1989–90 LEAGUE RECORD

Match No.	Date	Venue	Opponents	Result		H/T Score	Lg. Pos.	Goalscorers	Attendance
1	Aug 19	H	Leicester C	D	1-1	1-1	—	Payton	8158
2	26	A	Bournemouth	L	4-5	1-4	—	Payton 3, McParland	6454
3	Sept 2	H	West Ham U	D	1-1	0-1	17	Swan	9235
4	9	A	Portsmouth	D	2-2	0-0	20	Swan 2	6491
5	12	A	Port Vale	D	1-1	0-0	—	McParland	6168
6	16	H	Leeds U	L	0-1	0-1	21		11,620
7	23	A	Sheffield U	D	0-0	0-0	22		14,969
8	27	A	Middlesbrough	L	0-1	0-1	—		16,382
9	30	H	Newcastle U	L	1-3	1-1	23	McParland	9629
10	Oct 7	H	Swindon T	L	2-3	2-1	23	Swan 2	5366
11	14	A	Stoke C	D	1-1	0-1	23	McParland (pen)	9955
12	17	H	Oldham Ath	D	0-0	0-0	—		5109
13	21	A	WBA	D	1-1	0-1	24	Brown	9228
14	28	H	Brighton & HA	L	0-2	0-1	24		4756
15	31	A	Blackburn R	D	0-0	0-0	—		7456
16	Nov 4	H	Watford	D	0-0	0-0	24		4718
17	11	A	Bradford C	W	3-2	0-0	24	Jobson, Payton, McParland	8540
18	18	A	Oxford U	D	0-0	0-0	23		4029
19	25	H	Barnsley	L	1-2	1-0	23	Payton (pen)	5715
20	Dec 2	A	Leicester C	L	1-2	0-1	24	Jacobs	8616
21	9	H	Port Vale	W	2-1	2-1	23	Payton, Doyle	4207
22	26	A	Wolverhampton W	W	2-1	2-1	23	Brown, Terry	19,524
23	29	A	Plymouth Arg	W	2-1	1-0	—	Swan, Terry	8588
24	Jan 1	H	Sunderland	W	3-2	2-0	21	Payton, Jacobs, Swan	9346
25	13	H	Bournemouth	L	1-4	0-2	23	Payton (pen)	4673
26	20	A	West Ham U	W	2-1	1-1	21	Buckley, Payton	16,847
27	Feb 3	H	Sheffield U	D	0-0	0-0	20		9606
28	10	A	Leeds U	L	3-4	1-2	20	Payton 2 (2 pens). Doyle	29,977
29	17	H	Portsmouth	L	1-2	0-0	21	Terry	4883
30	24	A	Barnsley	D	1-1	0-1	21	Jacobs	8901
31	Mar 3	H	Oxford U	W	1-0	0-0	20	Payton	4503
32	7	A	Newcastle U	L	0-2	0-1	—		20,499
33	10	H	Middlesbrough	D	0-0	0-0	19		6602
34	17	A	Swindon T	W	3-1	2-1	19	Askew, Payton, Bamber	8123
35	20	A	Stoke C	D	0-0	0-0	—		6456
36	24	A	Oldham Ath	L	2-3	0-2	19	Hunter, Jobson	11,472
37	31	H	WBA	L	0-2	0-1	22		5418
38	Apr 6	A	Brighton & HA	L	0-2	0-0	—		6789
39	10	H	Blackburn R	W	2-0	0-0	—	Payton, Bamber	5327
40	14	A	Sunderland	W	1-0	1-0	19	Swan	17,437
41	16	H	Wolverhampton W	W	2-0	1-0	18	Palin, Bamber	7851
42	21	H	Ipswich T	W	1-0	0-0	16	Gayle (og)	9380
43	24	A	Plymouth Arg	D	3-3	1-0	—	Swan, Shotton, Hunter	5256
44	28	H	Bradford C	W	2-1	0-1	14	Swan, Payton	6514
45	May 1	H	Ipswich T	W	4-3	1-0	—	Swan, Shotton, Atkinson, Payton	5306
46	5	A	Watford	L	1-3	0-1	14	Hunter	9827

Final League Position: 14

GOALSCORERS

League (58): Payton 17 (4 pens), Swan 11, McParland 5 (1 pen), Bamber 3, Hunter 3, Jacobs 3, Terry 3, Brown 2, Doyle 2, Jobson 2, Shotton 2, Askew 1, Atkinson 1, Buckley 1, Palin 1, own goal 1.
Littlewoods Cup (1): Payton 1.
FA Cup (0).

290

Hesford	Murray	Jacobs	Swan	Terry	Jobson	Askew	Roberts	Payton	Edwards	Doyle	McParland	Buckley	Thompson	Brown	Jenkinson	Kelly	De Mange	Whitehurst	Warren	Smith	Wheeler	Atkinson	Shaw	Ngata	Bamber	Shotton	Hunter	Palin	Thomas	Match No.
1	2	3	4	5	6	7	8	9*	10†	11	12		14																	1
1*	2	3	4	5	6	7	8			11	9			10†	12	14														2
	2*	3	4	5	6†	7	8			11	10			9	14	1	12													3
		3	4	5	6	7	8			10*	11			9	12	2	1													4
		3	4	5	6	7	8			11	9				2*	1	12	10												5
		3	4	5	6	7	8	14			9				12	2	1	11†	10*											6
		3	4	5	6	7	8			11	9*				2	12	1	10												7
		3	4	5	6	7	8			10†	9*		14		2	11	1	12												8
		3	4	5	6	7	8			10	11			9†	2*	14	1	12												9
		3	4	5	6	7	8			12	10			9*	2	11	1													10
1		3	4	5	6	7	8					11*	9				12	10	2											11
1		3	4	5	6	7	8			12		11	9†		14			10*	2											12
1		3	4	5	6	7						8	11*	2			12	9	10											13
1		3	4	5	6	7						8	11	2			12	9		10*										14
1		3	4	5	6	7				12	10			2			11*	9	8											15
1		3	4	5	6	7				10				2			11*	9	8			12								16
1		3	4†	5	6	7		14		10	12			2			11*	9	8											17
1		3		5	4	7	8			11	10*			2				9	6			12								18
1		3	14	5	4	7	8			11	10			2				9†	6*			12								19
1		3	9	5	4					8†	11		14	2		10*	7		6			12								20
1		3	9	5	4	7*		10†		11				2			8		6			12	14							21
1		3*12	5	4	7	10	8			11				2	14		9†								6					22
1		3	9	5	4	7	10*	8		11				2	12										6					23
1		3	9	5	4	7	10	8		11				2											6					24
1		3	5†	4	7	10	8			11*				2	14		12	9							6					25
1		3	4		10	7	8*			11			5	2			6	9							12					26
1		3	5	4	10	7	8			11				2			6								9					27
1		3	5	4	10	7	8			11				2			6								9					28
1		3	5	4	10†	7	8			11				2*	14		6								12	9				29
1		3	4		10†	7	8			11*			5	2			6					14			12	9				30
1		3	4			7	8*			11	12			2			6					10			9	5				31
1		3	6†	4		7	8			11*12				2		10						14			9	5				32
1		3	4		10	7	8*				12			2			6					11			9	5				33
1		3	4		10	7	8†				12			2			6					11*			9	5		14		34
1		3	4		10†	7	8*				12			2			6					11			9	5		14		35
1		3	4			7	8†							2*			6					12	14		9	5		10	11	36
1		3	12	4							2			6*								11	14		9	5	8†	10	7	37
1		3	4			7	11							2	12		6*								9	5		10	8	38
1		3	12	4		7	8	6*						2											9	5		10	11	39
1		3	4			7	8*	6						2											9	5	12	10	11	40
1		3	4			7	8*	6						2											9	5	12	10	11	41
1		3	8	4		7		6						2											9	5		10	11	42
1		3	9	4		7	8	6						2†								14			5	12	10*	11		43
1		3	10	4		7	8	6						2†								14			9*	5	12		11	44
1		3	10	4		7	8							2											9	5			11	45
1		3	2	4		7	8							6†								14			9*	5	12	10	11	46
38	3	46	27	29	45	32	36	34	2	36	13	7	1	31	9	8	16	15	10	1	—	6	4	—	19	16	1	9	11	

Substitute appearances (+): Swan 4s, Payton 5s, Buckley 7s, Thompson 3s, Brown 3s, Jenkinson 13s, De Mange 5s, Atkinson 5s, Shaw 7s, Ngata 4s, Palin 8s

Waites – Match No. 45(6)

Littlewoods Cup	First Round	Grimsby T (h)	1-0
		(a)	0-2
FA Cup	Third Round	Newcastle U (h)	0-1

HULL CITY

Player and Position	Ht	Wt	Birth Date	Place	Source	Clubs	League App	Gls
Goalkeepers								
David Cleminshaw	6 1	12 09	1 11 70	South Cave	Trainee	Hull C	—	—
Iain Hesford	6 2	13 12	4 3 60	Zambia	Apprentice	Blackpool	202	—
						Sheffield W	—	—
						Fulham (loan)	3	—
						Notts Co (loan)	10	—
						Sunderland	97	—
						Hull C	60	—
Gavin Kelly*	6 0	12 13	29 9 68	Beverley		Hull C	11	—
						Bristol R (loan)	—	—
Defenders								
Nicky Brown	6 0	12 03	16 10 66	Hull	Local	Hull C	58	2
Neil Buckley	6 2	13 06	25 9 68	Hull	Trainee	Hull C	24	1
						Burnley (loan)	5	—
Wayne Jacobs	5 9	10 02	3 2 69	Sheffield	Apprentice	Sheffield W	6	—
						Hull C	85	3
Richard Jobson	6 1	12 02	9 5 63	Hull	Burton A	Watford	28	4
						Hull C	219	17
Paul Mudd	5 8	11 02	13 11 70	Hull	Trainee	Hull C	1	—
Malcolm Shotton	6 3	13 12	16 2 57	Newcastle	Apprentice	Leicester C	—	—
						Nuneaton Bor	—	—
						Oxford U	263	12
						Portsmouth	10	—
						Huddersfield T	16	1
						Barnsley	66	6
						Hull C	16	2
Paul Waites	5 10	12 08	24 1 71	Hull	Trainee	Hull C	1	—
Midfield								
Graeme Atkinson	5 10	10 02	11 11 71	Hull	Trainee	Hull C	13	1
Mark Calvert	5 9	11 05	11 9 70	Newcastle	Trainee	Hull C	5	—
Mark Cooper			12 10 71	Hull	Trainee	Hull C	—	—
Ken De Mange	5 9	11 10	3 9 64	Dublin	Home Farm	Liverpool	—	—
						Scunthorpe U (loan)	3	2
						Leeds U	15	1
						Hull C	62	1
Steve Doyle	5 9	11 09	2 6 58	Port Talbot	Apprentice	Preston NE	197	8
						Huddersfield T	161	6
						Sunderland	100	2
						Hull C	36	2
Gerry Flynn	5 10	11 00	28 3 72	Belfast	Bangor	Hull C	—	—
Herry Ngata‡			24 8 71	New Zealand		Hull C	4	—
Leigh Palin	5 9	10 03	12 9 65	Worcester	Apprentice	Aston Villa	—	—
						Shrewsbury T (loan)	2	—
						Nottingham F	—	—
						Bradford C	71	10
						Stoke C	19	3
						Hull C	9	1
Andy Payton	5 9	10 06	23 10 66	Burnley		Hull C	91	23
Garreth Roberts	5 5	10 08	15 11 60	Hull	Apprentice	Hull C	406	47
Peter Swan	6 0	11 12	28 9 66	Leeds	Local	Leeds U	49	11
						Hull C	42	12
Gwyn Thomas	5 7	11 05	26 9 57	Swansea	Apprentice	Leeds U	89	3
						Barnsley	201	17
						Hull C	11	—
Lee Warren	6 0	11 13	28 2 69	Manchester	Trainee	Leeds U	—	—
						Rochdale	31	1
						Hull C	38	—

HULL CITY

Foundation: The enthusiasts who formed Hull City in 1904 were brave men indeed. More than that they were audacious for they immediately put the club on the map in this Rugby League fortress by obtaining a three-year agreement with the Hull Rugby League club to rent their ground! They had obtained quite a number of conversions to the dribbling code, before the Rugby League forbade the use of any of their club grounds by Association Football clubs. By that time, Hull City were well away having entered the FA Cup in their initial season and the Football League, Second Division after only a year.

First Football League game: 2 September, 1905, Division 2, v Barnsley (h) W 4-1 – Spendiff; Langley, Jones; Martin, Robinson, Gordon (2); Rushton, Spence (1), Wilson (1), Howe, Raisbeck.

Managers (and Secretary-managers)
James Ramster 1904–05*, Ambrose Langley 1905–13, Harry Chapman 1913–14, Fred Stringer 1914–16, David Menzies 1916–21, Percy Lewis 1921–23, Bill McCracken 1923–31, Haydn Green 1931–34, John Hill 1934–36, David Menzies 1936, Ernest Blackburn 1936–46, Major Frank Buckley 1946–48, Raich Carter 1948–51, Bob Jackson 1952–55, Bob Brocklebank 1955–61, Cliff Britton 1961–70 (continued as GM to 1971), Terry Neill 1970–74, John Kaye 1974–77, Bobby Collins 1977–78, Ken Houghton 1978–79, Mike Smith 1979–82, Bobby Brown 1982, Colin Appleton 1982–84, Brian Horton 1984–88, Eddie Gray 1988–89, Colin Appleton 1989, Stan Ternent 1989– .

Player and Position	Ht	Wt	Birth Date	Birth Place	Source	Clubs	League App	Gls
Forwards								
Dave Bamber	6 3	13 10	1 2 59	St Helens	Manchester Univ	Blackpool	86	29
						Coventry C	19	3
						Walsall	20	7
						Portsmouth	4	1
						Swindon T	106	31
						Watford	18	3
						Stoke C	43	8
						Hull C	19	3
Paul Hunter	6 0	12 09	30 8 68	Kirkcaldy	Leven Royal Colts	East Fife	164	56
						Hull C	9	3
Leigh Jenkinson	6 0	12 02	9 7 69	Thorne	Trainee	Hull C	36	1
Ian McParland	5 8	10 08	4 10 61	Edinburgh	Ormiston Pr	Notts Co	221	69
						Hull C	31	6
John Moore‡	6 0	11 11	1 10 66	Consett	Apprentice	Sunderland	16	1
						St Patricks Ath (loan)	—	—
						Newport Co (loan)	2	—
						Darlington (loan)	2	1
						Mansfield T (loan)	5	1
						Rochdale (loan)	10	2
						Hull C	14	1
						Sheffield U (loan)	5	—
Michael Smith	5 8	10 09	19 12 68	Hull		Hull C	13	1
Les Thompson	5 10	11 00	23 9 68	Cleethorpes		Hull C	15	2
						Scarborough (loan)	3	1

Trainees
Atkinson, Steven F; Booth, Grant A; Britt, Peter J; Davison, Lee D; Garbutt, Allan C; Gawthorpe, Robert N; Greenwood, Roger D.M; Hobson, Gary; Holleron, Kevin; Horsley, Richard C; Hutchinson, Mark J; Ledingham, Marc L; Proctor, David N; Robinson, Darren P; Vincent, Steven B; Walmsley, David G; Webster, Wayne A; Whincup, Kirk R; Whitehead, Peter E.

Associated Schoolboys
Bennett, Darren P; Brown, Neil; Fisher, Stephen L; Hopkin, Matthew C; Houghton, Nicholas N; Johnson, Paul A; Jones, Alan; Lowthorpe, Adam; McEvoy, Martin A; McGowan, Timothy A; Malton, David C; Manton, Neil R; Salter, Alan; Shirtliff, Mark A; Smith, Car A; Stowe, Dean; White, Richard C.

Associated Schoolboys who have accepted the club's offer of a Traineeship/Contract
Allison, Neil J; Gallagher, Mark; Morrow, Keith; Noonan, Lee; Welburn, Paul A; Wilson, Stephen L.

IPSWICH TOWN 1989–90 *Back row (left to right):* Simon Milton, Michael Cheetham, Gavin Johnson, Neil Thompson, David Linighan, David Hill, Neil Woods, Ian Redford, David Gregory.
Centre row: Peter Trevivian (First Team Coach), David Lowe, Frank Yallop, Ron Fearon, Craig Forrest, Tony Humes, Chris Kiwomya, John Duncan (Manager).
Front row: Mick Stockwell, Sergei Baltacha, John Wark, Romeo Zondervan, Jason Dozzell, Mich D'Avray, Graham Harbey.

Division 2 **IPSWICH TOWN**

Portman Road, Ipswich, Suffolk IP1 2DA. Telephone Ipswich (0473) 219211 (4 lines). Sales & Marketing Dept: (0473) 212202.

Ground capacity: 31,000.

Record attendance: 38,010 v Leeds U, FA Cup 6th rd, 8 March, 1975.

Record receipts: £105,950 v AZ 67 Alkmaar, UEFA Cup final 1st leg, 6 May, 1981.

Pitch measurements: 112yd × 70yd.

Chairman: P. M. Cobbold.

Directors: J. Kerr MBE, H. R. Smith, J. M. Sangster, K. H. Brightwell, J. Kerridge, D. Sheepshanks.

Manager: John Lyall. *Assistant Manager:* Charlie Woods.

First Team Coach: Peter Trevivian. *Reserve Coach:*

Physio: D. Bingham. *Youth Team Coach:* Bryan Klug.

Secretary: David C. Rose.

Sales & Promotions Manager: M. Noye.

Year Formed: 1878. *Turned Professional:* 1936. *Ltd Co.:* 1936.

Club Nickname: 'Blues' or 'Town'.

Record League Victory: 7-0 v Portsmouth, Division 2, 7 November 1964 – Thorburn; Smith, McNeil; Baxter, Bolton, Thompson; Broadfoot (1), Hegan (2), Baker (1), Leadbetter, Brogan (3). 7-0 v Southampton Division 1, 2 February 1974 – Sivell; Burley, Mills (1), Morris, Hunter, Beattie (1), Hamilton (2), Viljoen, Johnson, Whymark (2), Lambert (1) (Woods). 7-0 v WBA, Division 1, 6 November 1976 – Sivell; Burley, Mills, Talbot, Hunter, Beattie (1), Osborne, Wark (1), Mariner (1) (Bertschin), Whymark (4), Woods.

Record Cup Victory: 10-0 v Floriana, European Cup, Prel. rd, 25 September 1962 – Bailey; Malcolm, Compton; Baxter, Laurel, Elsworthy (1); Stephenson, Moran (2), Crawford (5), Phillips (2), Blackwood.

Record Defeat: 1-10 v Fulham, Division 1, 26 December, 1963.

Most League Points (2 for a win): 64, Division 3 (S), 1953–54 and 1955–56.

Most League Points (3 for a win): 83, Division 1, 1981–82.

Most League Goals: 106, Division 3 (S), 1955–56.

Highest League Scorer in Season: Ted Phillips, 41, Division 3 (S), 1956–57.

Most League Goals in Total Aggregate: Ray Crawford, 203, 1958–63 and 1966–69.

Most Capped Player: Allan Hunter, 47 (53), Northern Ireland.

Most League Appearances: Mick Mills, 591, 1966–82.

Record Transfer Fee Received: £725,000 from Glasgow Rangers for Terry Butcher, August 1986.

Record Transfer Fee Paid: £330,000 to Manchester C for Brian Gayle, January 1990.

Football League Record: 1938 Elected to Division 3 (S); 1954–55 Division 2; 1955–57 Division 3 (S); 1957–61 Division 2; 1961–64 Division 1; 1964–68 Division 2; 1968–86 Division 1; 1986– Division 2.

Honours: Football League: Division 1 – Champions 1961–62; Runners-up 1980–81, 1981–82; Division 2 – Champions 1960–61, 1967–68; Division 3 (S) – Champions 1953–54, 1956–57. *FA Cup:* Winners 1977–78. *Football League Cup* best season: Semi-final 1981–82, 1984–85, *Texaco Cup:* 1972–73. **European Competitions:** *European Cup:* 1962–63; *European Cup-Winners' Cup:* 1978–79; *UEFA Cup:* 1973–74, 1974–75, 1975–76, 1977–78, 1979–80, 1980–81 (winners), 1981–82, 1982–83.

Colours: Blue shirts, white shorts, blue stockings. **Change colours:** All Orange.

IPSWICH TOWN 1989-90 LEAGUE RECORD

Match No.	Date		Venue	Opponents	Result	H/T Score	Lg. Pos.	Goalscorers	Attendance
1	Aug	19	H	Barnsley	W 3-1	0-1	—	Woods, Humes, Lowe	12,100
2		22	H	Sunderland	W 4-2	3-0	—	Lowe 2, Milton, Dozzell	15,965
3		26	A	Sheffield U	L 0-2	0-0	4		13,600
4	Sept	2	H	Bournemouth	D 1-1	0-0	6	Dozzell	11,425
5		9	A	Leeds U	D 1-1	0-1	5	Fairclough (og)	22,972
6		16	H	Wolverhampton W	L 1-3	0-1	12	Westley (og)	14,506
7		23	A	Oxford U	D 2-2	0-1	12	Redford, Penney (og)	5131
8		27	A	Brighton & HA	L 0-1	0-0	—		9770
9		30	H	Stoke C	D 2-2	2-0	16	D'Avray, Dozzell	10,389
10	Oct	7	H	Newcastle U	W 2-1	2-0	13	Wark (pen), Lowe	13,679
11		14	A	Swindon T	L 0-3	0-2	16		8039
12		18	A	Bradford C	L 0-1	0-0	—		7350
13		21	H	Plymouth Arg	W 3-0	2-0	14	Kiwomya 2, Milton	10,362
14		28	A	Portsmouth	W 3-2	1-0	12	Milton 2, Dozzell	7914
15		31	H	Watford	W 1-0	0-0	—	Thompson (pen)	12,557
16	Nov	4	H	WBA	W 3-1	2-1	8	Kiwomya, Lowe, Milton	12,028
17		11	A	Blackburn R	D 2-2	1-0	9	May (og), Wark (pen)	7913
18		18	A	Leicester C	W 1-0	1-0	7	Stockwell	11,664
19		25	H	Oldham Ath	D 1-1	0-0	8	Kiwomya	12,304
20	Dec	2	A	Barnsley	W 1-0	1-0	6	Humes	6097
21		9	H	Sunderland	D 1-1	0-1	5	Wark	13,833
22		26	H	West Ham U	W 1-0	1-0	5	Stockwell	24,365
23		30	H	Middlesbrough	W 3-0	2-0	5	Stockwell, Humes, Donowa	14,290
24	Jan	1	A	Port Vale	L 0-5	0-3	6		8617
25		13	H	Sheffield U	D 1-1	0-1	6	Lowe	16,787
26		20	A	Bournemouth	L 1-3	0-1	7	Thompson (pen)	7464
27	Feb	10	A	Wolverhampton W	L 1-2	1-1	10	Dozzell	18,781
28		17	H	Leeds U	D 2-2	1-2	9	Kiwomya, Wark	17,102
29		24	A	Oldham Ath	L 1-4	0-2	11	Wark	10,193
30	Mar	3	H	Leicester C	D 2-2	2-1	12	Wark, Lowe	12,237
31		6	A	Stoke C	D 0-0	0-0	—		10,815
32		10	H	Brighton & HA	W 2-1	1-1	9	Wark, Milton	10,886
33		13	H	Oxford U	W 1-0	0-0	—	Pennyfather	10,380
34		17	A	Newcastle U	L 1-2	1-0	9	Milton	19,521
35		20	H	Swindon T	W 1-0	0-0	—	Dozzell	11,856
36		24	H	Bradford C	W 1-0	1-0	8	Wark	11,074
37		31	A	Plymouth Arg	L 0-1	0-0	9		6793
38	Apr	7	A	Watford	D 3-3	2-0	10	Stuart 2, Wark	11,158
39		10	H	Portsmouth	L 0-1	0-1	—		11,062
40		14	H	Port Vale	W 3-2	1-1	10	Wark, Dozzell, Thompson (pen)	10,509
41		17	A	West Ham U	L 0-2	0-2	—		25,178
42		21	H	Hull C	L 0-1	0-0	10		9380
43		25	A	Middlesbrough	W 2-1	0-0	—	Lowe, Milton	15,232
44		28	H	Blackburn R	W 3-1	2-1	9	Milton, Lowe 2	11,007
45	May	1	A	Hull C	L 3-4	0-1	—	Lowe 2, Redford	5306
46		5	A	WBA	W 3-1	3-0	9	Lowe, Milton, Dozzell	11,567

Final League Position: 9

GOALSCORERS

League (67): Lowe 13, Milton 10, Wark 10 (2 pens), Dozzell 8, Kiwomya 5, Humes 3, Stockwell 3, Thompson 3 (3 pens), Redford 2, Stuart 2, D'Avray 1, Donowa 1, Pennyfather 1, Woods 1, own goals 4.
Littlewoods Cup (0).
FA Cup (1): Dozzell 1.

Forrest	Yallop	Thompson	Zondervan	Redford	Linighan	Lowe	Dozzell	Wark	Humes	Milton	Woods	Donowa	Johnson	Cheetham	Baltacha	Palmer	Hill	D'Avray	Stockwell	Harbey	Kiwomya	Pennyfather	Gregory	Gayle	Meade	Stuart	Neville	Match No.
1	2	3	4	5*	6	7	8	9	10	11	12																	1
1	2	3	4	5	6	7	8	9	10	11																		2
1	2	3	4	5*	6	7	8	9	10	11	12																	3
1	2	3	4*	5	6	7	8	9	10	11†12	14																	4
1	2	3			6*	7	8	9	10	11	5			4	12													5
1	2	3	4			7	8	9	10	11	5*14	6†			12													6
1	2	3†	4	5	6	7	8	9		11	12							14	10*									7
1†			4	5	6	7	8	9	2	11	10							12	3*14									8
1	14	4	5*	6	7	8	9†	2		12								3	10	11								9
1	3	2			6	7	8	9	5	11								10	4									10
1	5*	3	11		6	7	8		10			4†						9	2	14	12							11
1	5	3	2	12	6	7	8			11*								9	4	10								12
1	5	3	4		6	7	8		11									9	2	10								13
1	2	3	4*		6	7	8		11									5	10	9	12							14
1	5	3			6	7	8	9		11								10	2	4								15
1	5	3	4		6	7*	8	9		11		14						12†	2	10								16
1	5	3	4		6		8	9		11		7							2	10								17
1	5	3	4		6		8	9		11		7*							2	10	12							18
1	5	3	4		6		8	9		11		7*							2	10	12							19
1	5	3	4	12	6		8		9	11		7							2*	10								20
1	5	3	4		6		8	9	2	11		7								10								21
1	5	3	4*		6		8	9	12	11		7						14	2	10†								22
1	5	3			6		8	9	4	11		7							2	10								23
1	5	3			6		8*	9	4	11		7†12	14						2	10								24
1	2	3			6	12	8	9	5	11		7							4	10*								25
1	2	3			6	12	8	9	5	11		7*						4†	10	14								26
1		3			6		8	9	11	12								2	10	7	4*	5						27
1	2	3			6		8	9	11									4	10	7		5						28
1	2	3			6	12	8	9	11			14						4†	10*	7		5						29
1	3	2			6	7	8	9	11*	12								4	10			5						30
1	3	4			6	7	8	9	11									2	10			5						31
1	3	8†	6	7*10		9	11		12									2	14	4		5						32
1	3	8	6	7†10		9	11*		12									2	14	4		5						33
1	3	8	6	7*10		9	11		4									2	12			5						34
1	3	8	6	7 10		9	11		4*									2				5						35
1	3	8	6	7 10		9	11		4*	12								2				5						36
1	3	8†	6	7 10		9	11		4*12									2				5	14					37
1	3	4*	6	7†10		9	12	11										2	14		5		8					38
1	3	4	6	7†10		9	12	11										2*	14		5		8					39
1	2	3	4	11*	6	7†10	9	14											12		5		8					40
1	2	3	4	6	10	9	14	11†											12	7*	5		8					41
1	2	3	4	6†	10	9	14	11	7										12		5		8*					42
1	2	3	4	7	10	9	11	8											6		5							43
1	2	3	4*	7	10	9	12	11	8										6		5							44
1	2	3	14	7	10	9	4	11†	8*										6	12	5							45
	3	4	14	7	10	9†	2	11	8*										6	12	5			1				46
45	31	44	30	14	41	31	46	41	17	41	3	17	3	—	3	3	1	8	34	—	19	7	1	20	—	5	1	

+1s · +4s · +3s · +7s · +4s6s · +3s1s · +5s · +2s · +1s · +4s · +1s · +10s · +1s · +3s · +1s

Littlewoods Cup	Second Round	Tranmere R (h)	0-1
		(a)	0-1
FA Cup	Third Round	Leeds U (a)	1-0
	Fourth Round	Barnsley (a)	0-2

IPSWICH TOWN

Player and Position	Ht	Wt	Birth Date	Place	Source	Clubs	League App	Gls
Goalkeepers								
Ron Fearon	6 0	11 12	19 11 60	Romford	Apprentice	QPR	—	—
						Reading	61	—
					Sutton	Ipswich T	28	—
						Brighton & HA (loan)	7	—
Craig Forrest	6 4	12 03	20 9 67	Vancouver	Apprentice	Ipswich T	73	—
						Colchester U (loan)	11	—
Chris Neville*	6 0	11 10	20 10 70	Cambridge	Trainee	Ipswich T	1	—
Defenders								
Sergei Baltacha‡	6 0	12 00	17 2 58	Ukraine	Dynamo Kiev	Ipswich T	28	1
Jason Dozzell	6 2	12 04	9 12 67	Ipswich	School	Ipswich T	216	28
Brian Gayle	6 1	12 07	6 3 65	London		Wimbledon	83	3
						Manchester C	55	3
						Ipswich T	20	—
Lee Honeywood	5 8	10 10	3 8 71	Chelmsford	Trainee	Ipswich T	—	—
Anthony Humes	5 11	10 10	19 3 66	Blyth	Apprentice	Ipswich T	99	8
Gavin Johnson	6 0	11 01	10 10 70	Ipswich	Trainee	Ipswich T	10	—
David Linighan	6 2	10 12	9 1 65	Hartlepool	Local	Hartlepool U	91	5
						Leeds U (loan)	—	—
						Derby Co	—	—
						Shrewsbury T	65	1
						Ipswich T	82	2
Chris Swailes	6 1	12 11	19 10 70	Gateshead	Trainee	Ipswich T	—	—
Neil Thompson	6 0	13 07	2 10 63	Beverley	Apprentice	Nottingham F	—	—
						Hull C	—	—
						Scarborough	87	15
						Ipswich T	45	3
Frank Yallop	5 11	11 03	4 4 64	Watford	Apprentice	Ipswich T	193	4
Midfield								
Andy Bernal	5 10	12 05	16 7 66	Canberra		Ipswich T	9	
David Gregory	5 10	11 03	23 1 70	Sudbury	Trainee	Ipswich T	6	—
David Hill	5 9	10 03	6 6 66	Nottingham	Local	Scunthorpe U	140	10
						Ipswich T	38	—
Simon Milton	5 9	11 09	23 8 63	London	Bury St	Ipswich T	84	21
					Edmunds	Exeter C (loan)	2	3
						Torquay U (loan)	4	1
Steve Palmer	6 1	12 07	31 3 68	Brighton	Cambridge Univ	Ipswich T	5	—
Glenn Pennyfather	5 8	10 10	11 2 63	Billericay	Apprentice	Southend U	238	36
						Crystal Palace	34	1
						Ipswich T	8	1
Ian Redford	5 10	11 08	5 4 60	Dundee	Errol R	Dundee	85	34
						Rangers	172	23
						Dundee U	101	20
						Ipswich T	42	4
Mike Stockwell	5 6	10 02	14 2 65	Chelmsford	Apprentice	Ipswich T	129	7
John Wark	5 10	11 07	4 8 57	Glasgow	Apprentice	Ipswich T	296	94
						Liverpool	70	28
						Ipswich T	89	23
Romeo Zondervan	5 9	10 02	4 3 59	Surinam	Den Haag	Twente Enschede	—	—
						WBA	84	5
						Ipswich T	212	13
Forwards								
Mich D'Avray*	6 1	13 02	19 2 62	Johannesburg	Apprentice	Ipswich T	211	37
						Leicester C (loan)	3	—

IPSWICH TOWN

Foundation: Considering that Ipswich Town only reached the Football League in 1938, many people outside of East Anglia may be surprised to learn that this club was formed at a meeting held in the Town Hall as far back as 1878 when Mr. T. C. Cobbold, MP, was voted president. Originally it was the Ipswich Association FC to distinguish it from the older Ipswich Football Club which played rugby. These two amalgamated in 1888 and the handling game was dropped in 1893.

First Football League game: 27 August, 1938, Division 3(S), v Southend U (h) W 4-2 – Burns; Dale, Parry; Perrett, Fillingham, McLuckie; Williams, Davies (1), Jones (2), Alsop (1), Little.

Managers (and Secretary-managers)
Mick O'Brien 1936–37, Scott Duncan 1937–55 (continued as secretary), Alf Ramsey 1955–63, Jackie Milburn 1963–64, Bill McGarry 1964–68, Bobby Robson 1969–82, Bobby Ferguson 1982–87, Johnny Duncan 1987–90, John Lyall 1990– .

Player and Position	Ht	Wt	Birth Date	Place	Source	Clubs	League App	Gls
Louie Donowa	5 9	11 00	24 9 64	Ipswich	Apprentice	Norwich C	62	11
						Stoke C (loan)	4	1
					Coruna			
					Willem II	Ipswich T	23	1
Neil Grice*	5 9	10 07	18 4 71	Walthamstow	Trainee	Ipswich T	—	—
Chris Kiwomya	5 10	10 05	2 12 69	Huddersfield		Ipswich T	55	7
David Lowe	5 11	11 00	30 8 65	Liverpool	Apprentice	Wigan Ath	188	40
						Ipswich T	107	36
Raphael Meade‡	5 10	11 09	22 11 62	Islington	Apprentice	Arsenal	41	14
					Sporting Lisbon	Dundee U	11	4
						Luton T	4	—
						Ipswich T	1	—

Trainees
Banks, Andrew C; Betts, Simon R; Boyle, Lee; Doyle, Graeme M; Durrant, Gary J; Gray, David B; Gray, Simon R; Gregory, Neil R; Hooper, Glynn D; Horne, Ian M; Hunter, David M; Hyde, Stephen; McHugh, Shaun; Nicholls, Darren; Pick, Neil J.

Associated Schoolboys
Cotterell, Leo S; Dalrymple, Craig I; Eason, Jeremy J; Gibbs, Paul J; Hewitson, Mark W.G; Jenkins, Stuart I; Lowery, Paul A; Moore, Ian D; Morgan, Philip J; Morley, Jamie D; Powley, Darren L; Snowcroft, James B; Stubbs, Steven; Vaughan, Antony J; Weston, Matthew; Wosahlo, Bradley E.

Associated Schoolboys who have accepted the club's offer of a Traineeship/Contract
Bringloe, Paul D; Cook, Adam; Devine, Declan P; Durrant, Lee R; Harrison, Gary D; Pearn, Steven; Shaw, Marcus; Smedley, Martin.

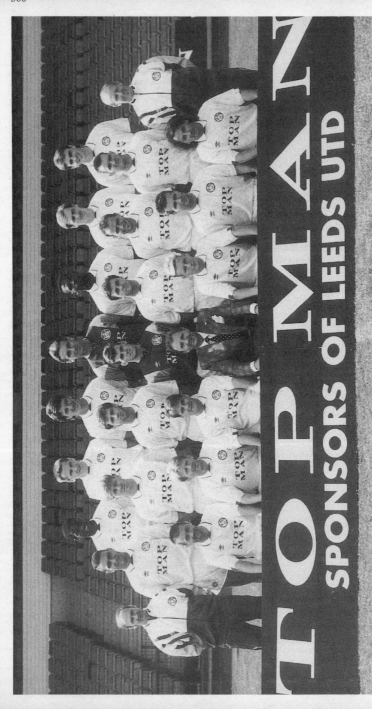

LEEDS UNITED 1989–90 *Back row (left to right):* Chris Fairclough, John McClelland, John Pearson, Mervyn Day, Noel Blake, Peter Haddock, Andy Williams. *Centre row:* Alan Sutton (Physiotherapist), Vinny Jones, Ian Baird, Jim Beglin, Neil Edwards, Bobby Davison, Mel Sterland, Mike Whitlow, Michel Hennigan (Coach). *Front row:* Glynn Snodin, Gordon Strachan, John Hendrie, Howard Wilkinson (Manager), David Batty, Carl Shutt, Mickey Thomas.

Division 1 — LEEDS UNITED

Elland Road, Leeds LS11 0ES. Telephone Leeds (0532) 716037 (4 lines). Ticket Office: 710710. Fax: 706560.

Ground capacity: 40,176.

Record attendance: 57,892 v Sunderland, FA Cup 5th rd replay, 15 March, 1967.

Record receipts: £146,483, FA Cup semi-final replay, Everton v West Ham U, 16 April, 1980.

Pitch measurements: 117yd × 76yd.

President: The Right Hon The Earl of Harewood LLD.

Chairman: L. Silver OBE. *Vice-Chairman:* P. J. Gilman. *Deputy Chairman:* J. W. G. Marjason. *Managing Director:* W. J. Fotherby.

Directors: R. Barker MCIT, MBIM, Coun. M. J. Bedford, E. Carlile, Coun. R. D. Feldman, G. M. Holmes BSC (ECON), Coun. A. Hudson, R. P. Ridsdale.

Manager: Howard Wilkinson. *Assistant Manager:* Mike Hennigan.

Secretary: D. J. Dowse.

Coaches: Mike Hennigan, Peter Gunby, Dick Bate. *Physio:* Alan Sutton.

Commercial Manager: Bob Baldwin.

Year Formed: 1919, as Leeds United after disbandment (by FA order) of Leeds City (formed in 1904). *Turned Professional:* 1920. *Ltd Co.:* 1920.

Club Nickname: United.

Record League Victory: 8-0 v Leicester C, Division 1, 7 April 1934 – Moore; George Milburn, Jack Milburn; Edwards, Hart, Copping; Mahon (2), Firth (2), Duggan (2), Furness (2), Cochrane.

Record Cup Victory: 10-0 v Lyn (Oslo), European Cup, 1st rd (1st leg), 17 September 1969 – Sprake; Reaney, Cooper, Bremner (2), Charlton, Hunter, Madeley, Clarke (2), Jones (3), Giles (2) (Bates), O'Grady (1).

Record Defeat: 1-8 v Stoke C, Division 1, 27 August, 1934.

Most League Points (2 for a win): 67, Division 1, 1968–69.

Most League Points (3 for a win): 85, Division 2, 1989–90.

Most League Goals: 98, Division 2, 1927–28.

Highest League Scorer in Season: John Charles, 42, Division 2, 1953–54.

Most League Goals in Total Aggregate: Peter Lorimer, 168, 1965–79 and 1983–86.

Most Capped Player: Billy Bremner, 54, Scotland.

Most League Appearances: Jack Charlton, 629, 1953–73.

Record Transfer Fee Received: £825,000 from Everton for Ian Snodin, January 1987.

Record Transfer Fee Paid: £930,000 to WBA for Peter Barnes, August 1981.

Football League Record: 1920 Elected to Division 2; 1924–27 Division 1; 1927–28 Division 2; 1928–31 Division 1; 1931–32 Division 2; 1932–47 Division 1; 1947–56 Division 2; 1956–60 Division 1; 1960–64 Division 2; 1964–82 Division 1; 1982–90 Division 2; 1990– Division 1.

Honours: Football League: Division 1 – Champions 1968–69, 1973–74; Runners-up 1964–65, 1965–66, 1969–70, 1970–71, 1971–72; Division 2 – Champions 1923–24, 1963–64, 1989–90; Runners-up 1927–28, 1931–32, 1955–56. *FA Cup:* Winners 1972, Runners-up 1965, 1970, 1973. *Football League Cup:* Winners 1967-68. **European Competitions:** *European Cup:* 1969–70, 1974–75 (runners-up). *European Cup-Winners' Cup:* 1972–73 (runners-up). *European Fairs Cup:* 1965–66, 1966–67 (runners-up), 1967–68 (winners), 1968–69, 1970–71 (winners). *UEFA Cup:* 1971–72, 1973–74, 1979–80.

Colours: All white. **Change colours:** All yellow.

LEEDS UNITED 1989–90 LEAGUE RECORD

Match No.	Date	Venue	Opponents	Result	H/T Score	Lg. Pos.	Goalscorers	Attendance
1	Aug 19	A	Newcastle U	L 2-5	2-1	—	Davison, Baird	24,482
2	23	H	Middlesbrough	W 2-1	1-0	—	Davison, Parkinson (og)	25,004
3	26	H	Blackburn R	D 1-1	0-1	9	Fairclough	25,045
4	Sept 2	A	Stoke C	D 1-1	0-1	11	Strachan	14,570
5	9	H	Ipswich T	D 1-1	1-0	12	Jones	22,972
6	16	A	Hull C	W 1-0	1-0	9	Davison	11,620
7	23	H	Swindon T	W 4-0	2-0	4	Strachan 3 (1 pen), Davison	21,694
8	27	H	Oxford U	W 2-1	2-0	1	Davison, Sterland	24,097
9	30	A	Port Vale	D 0-0	0-0	5		11,156
10	Oct 7	A	West Ham U	W 1-0	1-0	3	Jones	23,539
11	14	H	Sunderland	W 2-0	2-0	2	Davison, Fairclough	27,815
12	17	A	Portsmouth	D 3-3	0-0	—	Davison, Whitlow, Sterland	10,260
13	21	H	Wolverhampton W	W 1-0	1-0	3	Davison	28,204
14	28	A	Bradford C	W 1-0	0-0	2	Davison	12,527
15	Nov 1	H	Plymouth Arg	W 2-1	1-1	—	Strachan (pen), Davison	26,791
16	4	H	Bournemouth	W 3-0	2-0	2	Baird, Strachan (pen), Fairclough	26,484
17	11	A	Leicester C	L 3-4	2-0	2	Baird, Williams, Strachan (pen)	18,032
18	18	H	Watford	W 2-1	0-1	2	Fairclough, Williams	26,921
19	25	A	WBA	L 1-2	0-2	2	Fairclough	15,116
20	Dec 2	H	Newcastle U	W 1-0	0-0	2	Baird	31,715
21	9	A	Middlesbrough	W 2-0	2-0	1	Shutt, Fairclough	19,686
22	16	H	Brighton & HA	W 3-0	3-0	1	Strachan, Hendrie, Jones	24,070
23	26	A	Sheffield U	D 2-2	1-2	1	Sterland, Shutt	31,602
24	30	A	Barnsley	L 0-1	0-1	1		14,841
25	Jan 1	H	Oldham Ath	D 1-1	0-1	1	Hendrie	30,217
26	13	A	Blackburn R	W 2-1	0-1	1	Chapman, Strachan	14,485
27	20	A	Stoke C	W 2-0	0-0	1	Strachan (pen), Hendrie	29,318
28	Feb 4	A	Swindon T	L 2-3	1-1	—	Strachan (pen), Hendrie	16,208
29	10	A	Hull C	W 4-3	2-1	1	Hendrie, Jones, Varadi, Strachan	29,977
30	17	A	Ipswich T	D 2-2	2-1	1	Chapman 2	17,102
31	24	H	WBA	D 2-2	1-0	1	Kamara, Chapman	30,004
32	Mar 3	A	Watford	L 0-1	0-1	1		13,468
33	7	H	Port Vale	D 0-0	0-0	—		28,756
34	10	A	Oxford U	W 4-2	0-2	1	Chapman 2, Varadi, Fairclough	8397
35	17	A	West Ham U	W 3-2	2-0	1	Chapman 2, Strachan	32,536
36	20	A	Sunderland	W 1-0	1-0	1	Sterland	17,851
37	24	H	Portsmouth	W 2-0	1-0	1	Jones, Chapman	27,600
38	31	A	Wolverhampton W	L 0-1	0-1	1		22,419
39	Apr 7	H	Bradford C	D 1-1	0-0	1	Speed	32,316
40	10	A	Plymouth Arg	D 1-1	1-1	—	Chapman	11,382
41	13	A	Oldham Ath	L 1-3	0-1	1	Davison	16,292
42	16	H	Sheffield U	W 4-0	1-0	1	Strachan 2 (1 pen), Chapman, Speed	32,727
43	21	A	Brighton & HA	D 2-2	1-0	1	Speed, Chapman (og)	11,359
44	25	H	Barnsley	L 1-2	1-0	—	Fairclough	31,700
45	28	H	Leicester C	W 2-1	1-0	1	Sterland, Strachan	32,597
46	May 5	A	Bournemouth	W 1-0	0-0	1	Chapman	9918

Final League Position: 1

GOALSCORERS

League (79): Strachan 16 (7 pens), Chapman 12, Davison 11, Fairclough 8, Hendrie 5, Jones 5, Sterland 5, Baird 4, Speed 3, Shutt 2, Varadi 2, Williams 2, Kamara 1, Whitlow 1, own goals 2.
Littlewoods Cup (2): Fairclough 1, Strachan 1.
FA Cup (0).

Day	Sterland	Beglin	Thomas	McClelland	Haddock	Strachan	Batty	Baird	Davison	Hendrie	Shutt	Whitlow	Fairclough	Jones	Speed	Blake	Williams A	Turner	Pearson	Kerr	Snodin	Chapman	Kamara	O'Donnell	Hilaire	Varadi	Match No.
1	2	3	4†	5	6	7	8	9	10*	11	12	14															1
1	2		4*		6	7	8	9†	10	11	12		3	5			14										2
1	2		4†		6	7	8	9	10*	11	12		3	5			14										3
1	2				6	7	8	9	10*	11			3	5	4											12	4
1	2				6	7	8	9	10	11*			3	5	4											12	5
1	2					7	8	9	10	11*			3	6	4	5										12	6
1	2				6	7	8	9	10	11*			3	4		5										12	7
1	2				6	7	8	9	10	11			3	4*		5										12	8
1	2				6	7	8	9	10*	12			3	4†	14	5	11										9
1	2				6	7	8	9	10*	12			3	5	4		11										10
1	2				6	7	8	9	10				3	5	4		11										11
1	2				6	7	8	9	10				3	5	4		11										12
1	2				6	7†	8	9	10	12			3	5	4	14	11*										13
1	2				6	7	8	9	10				3	5	4	12	11*										14
1	2				6	7	8	9	10				3	5	4*	12	11										15
1	2				6	7	8	9	10				3	5	4	12	11*										16
1*	2				6	7	8	9	10	12			3	5	4		11										17
	2				6	7	8	9	10*	12			3	5	4		11	1									18
	2				6	7	8	9	10	12			3	5	4*	14	11†	1									19
1	2					7	8	9	10	12			3	6	4	5	11*										20
1	2					7	8		10				3	6	4	5	11		9								21
1	2				6	7	8		10*	11†	12		3	5	4	14			9								22
1	2					7	8	9	10	11			3	6	4		5										23
1	2				6	7	8	9	10	11*			3†	5	4							12	14				24
1	2				6	7	8	9*	10†	11				5	4						3	12	14				25
1	2*	12			6	7	8		10	11			3	5	4							9					26
1	2				6	7	8		10*	11			3	5	4							9				12	27
1	2				6	7	8			11			3*	5	4	14						9	10†			12	28
1		3†			6	7	8			11				5	4							9*	2	14	12	10	29
1		3			6	7	8			11*				5	4							9	2		12	10	30
1	12	3			6	7	8			11				5	4							9	2			10*	31
1	2	3			6	7	8			12				5	4	14						9	11†			10*	32
1	2	3			6	7	8			11*				5	4	12						9				10	33
1	2	3*			6	7	8†			12				5	4	14	11					9				10	34
1	2				6	7	8			11†	12		3	5	4	14						9				10*	35
1	2				6	7	8			14	12		3*	5	4		11					9				10†	36
1	2	3			6	7*	8			12				5	4	14	11					9				10†	37
1	2				6	7	8			12			3	5	4		11*					9	14			10†	38
1	2	3			6	7	8		10*	12				5	4		11					9					39
1	2	3			6	7	8		10*	12				5	4		11					9					40
1	2	3			6*	7	8			14				5	4	12						9	11			10†	41
1	2	3			6	7			10*		12			5	4		11					9	8				42
1	2	3			6	7				14	12			5	4		11					9	8†			10*	43
1	2	3			6	7			10*					5	4	12	11					9	8				44
1	2	3			6	7			10*	14				5	4†	11						9	8			12	45
1	2	3			6	7			10*	14	12†			5	4	11						9	8				46
44	41	18	3	3	40	46	39	23	25	22	6	27	42	43	12	7	13	2	2	2	3	21	10	—	—	12	

+ + ... + + + + + + ... + + ... + ... + + + ... + + + +

1s 1s ... 3s 1s 4s 5s 14s 2s ... 2s 13s ... 3s ... 5s 3s 1s ... 1s 1s 2s 1s

Littlewoods Cup	Second Round	Oldham Ath (a)	1-2
		(h)	1-2
FA Cup	Third Round	Ipswich T (h)	0-1

LEEDS UNITED

Player and Position	Ht	Wt	Birth Date	Birth Place	Source	Clubs	League App	Gls
Goalkeepers								
Mervyn Day	6 2	15 01	26 6 55	Chelmsford	Apprentice	West Ham U	194	—
						Orient	170	—
						Aston Villa	30	—
						Leeds U	225	—
Neil Edwards	5 8	11 02	5 12 70	Aberdare	Trainee	Leeds U	—	—
Defenders								
Jim Beglin	5 11	11 00	29 7 63	Dublin	Shamrock R	Liverpool	64	2
						Leeds U	19	—
						Plymouth Arg (loan)	5	—
Chris Fairclough	5 11	11 02	12 4 64	Nottingham	Apprentice	Nottingham F	107	1
						Tottenham H	60	5
						Leeds U	53	8
Peter Haddock	5 11	11 05	9 12 61	Newcastle	Apprentice	Newcastle U	57	—
						Burnley (loan)	7	—
						Leeds U	103	1
Dylan Kerr	5 11	12 05	14 1 67	Valetta	Arcadia Shepherds	Leeds U	8	—
Jason Longstaff	5 10	12 03	8 2 71	Leeds	Trainee	Leeds U	—	—
John McClelland	6 2	13 05	7 12 55	Belfast	Portadown Bangor	Cardiff C	4	1
						Mansfield	125	8
						Rangers	96	4
						Watford	184	3
						Leeds U	3	—
						Watford (loan)	1	—
Chris O'Donnell	5 9	12 00	26 5 68	Newcastle	Apprentice	Ipswich T	14	—
						Northampton T (loan)	1	—
						Leeds U	1	—
Brendan Ormsby*	5 11	11 09	1 10 60	Birmingham	Apprentice	Aston Villa	117	4
						Leeds U	46	5
						Shrewsbury T (loan)	1	—
Neil Parsley*	5 10	10 11	25 4 66	Liverpool	Witton Alb	Leeds U	—	—
						Chester C (loan)	6	—
Grenville Shorte	6 1	12 08	14 10 70	Leeds	Trainee	Leeds U	—	—
Mel Sterland	5 10	12 10	1 10 61	Sheffield	Apprentice	Sheffield W	279	37
						Rangers	9	3
						Leeds U	42	5
Midfield								
David Batty	5 7	10 07	2 12 68	Leeds	Trainee	Leeds U	95	1
Darren Edmonds	5 9	11 06	12 4 71	Watford	Trainee	Leeds U	—	—
Simon Grayson	5 11	10 11	16 12 69	Ripon	Trainee	Leeds U	2	—
Vinny Jones	5 11	11 10	5 1 65	Watford	Wealdstone	Wimbledon	77	9
						Leeds U	45	5
Chris Kamara	6 1	12 00	25 12 57	Middlesbrough	Apprentice	Portsmouth	63	7
						Swindon T	147	21
						Portsmouth	11	—
						Brentford	152	28
						Swindon T	87	6
						Stoke C	60	5
						Leeds U	11	1
Glynn Snodin	5 6	9 05	14 2 60	Rotherham	Apprentice	Doncaster R	309	61
						Sheffield W	59	1
						Leeds U	74	10
Gary Speed	5 9	10 06	8 9 69	Hawarden	Trainee	Leeds U	26	3
Gordon Strachan	5 6	10 03	9 2 57	Edinburgh		Dundee	60	13
						Aberdeen	183	55
						Manchester U	160	33
						Leeds U	57	19

LEEDS UNITED

Foundation: Immediately the Leeds City club (founded in 1904) was wound up by the FA in October 1919, following allegations of illegal payments to players, a meeting was called by a Leeds solicitor, Mr. Alf Masser, at which Leeds United was formed. They joined the Midland League playing their first game in that competition in November 1919. It was in this same month that the new club had discussions with the directors of a virtually bankrupt Huddersfield Town who wanted to move to Leeds in an amalgamation. But Huddersfield survived even that crisis.

First Football League game: 28 August, 1920, Division 2, v Port Vale (a) L 0-2 – Down; Duffield, Tillotson; Musgrove, Baker, Walton; Mason, Goldthorpe, Thompson, Lyon, Best.

Managers (and Secretary-managers)
Dick Ray 1919–20, Arthur Fairclough 1920–27, Dick Ray 1927–35, Bill Hampson 1935–47, Willis Edwards 1947–48, Major Frank Buckley 1948–53, Raich Carter 1953–58, Bill Lambton 1958–59, Jack Taylor 1959–61, Don Revie 1961–74, Brian Clough 1974, Jimmy Armfield 1974–78, Jock Stein 1978, Jimmy Adamson 1978–80, Allan Clarke 1980–82, Eddie Gray 1982–85, Billy Bremner 1985–88, Howard Wilkinson 1988– .

Player and Position	Ht	Wt	Birth Date	Place	Source	Clubs	League App	Gls
Mickey Thomas*	5 6	10 07	7 7 54	Mochdre	Amateur	Wrexham	230	33
						Manchester U	90	11
						Everton	10	—
						Brighton & HA	20	—
						Stoke C	57	14
						Chelsea	44	9
						WBA	20	—
						Derby Co (loan)	9	—
					Wichita W	Shrewsbury T	40	1
						Leeds U	3	—
						Stoke C (loan)	5	—
Mick Whitlow	5 11	12 01	13 1 68	Northwich	Witton Alb	Leeds U	49	2
Andy Williams	6 0	11 09	29 7 62	Birmingham	Solihull	Coventry C	9	—
						Rotherham U	87	13
						Leeds U	34	3
Forwards								
Lee Chapman	6 3	13 00	5 12 59	Lincoln	Amateur	Stoke C	99	34
						Plymouth Arg (loan)	4	—
						Arsenal	23	4
						Sunderland	15	3
						Sheffield W	149	63
					Niort	Nottingham F	48	15
						Leeds U	21	12
Bob Davison	5 8	11 08	17 7 59	South Shields	Seaham CW	Huddersfield T	2	—
						Halifax T	63	29
						Derby Co	206	83
						Leeds U	84	30
Darryl Franklin	5 5	10 06	1 3 71	Caerphilly	Trainee	Leeds U	—	—
John Hendrie	5 7	11 04	24 10 63	Lennoxtown	Apprentice	Coventry C	21	2
						Hereford U (loan)	6	—
						Bradford C	173	46
						Newcastle U	34	4
						Leeds U	27	5

(Continued on page 910)

Trainees
Blunt, Scott R; Crosby, Andrew K; Hayward, Darren F; Henderson, Damian M; Jackson, Wayne M; Knop, Michael P; Little, Patrick; Mulrain, Steven; Nicholson, Steven P; Preston, Mark R; Scott, Rogan; Sloanes, Michael D; Smart, Tony G; Stoker, Gareth; Wigley, Russell D.C.G.

Associated Schoolboys
Barker, Philip G; Bowman, Robert A; Byrne, Alexander M; Couzens, Andrew J; Cox, Paul W; Daly, Kevin T; Fitch, Scott; Flanagan, Matthew J; Gilmore, Damian L; Grimston, Andrew; Holmes, Damian L; Hoyle, Michael S; McMichael, Stuart D; Nelson, Dominic; Oliver, Simon J; Owen, Alun H; Robinson, James S; Smith, Stephen P; Sullivan, Christopher J; Tobin, Steven R; Watson, Paul J; Whelan, Noel D; White, Jonathon D; Williams, Scott J.

Associated Schoolboys who have accepted the club's offer of a Traineeship/Contract
Ball, Stephen J; Billy, Marlon K; Curtis, Leonard P; Hepworth, Richard J; Philpott, Marcus.

LEICESTER CITY 1989–90 *Back row (left to right):* Bobby Roberts (Coach), Simon Morgan, Alan Paris, Wayne Clarke, Carl Muggleton, Martin Hodge, Allan Evans, Steve Walsh, Tony James, Gordon Lee (Coach).
Front row: Rob Johnson, Steve Wilkinson, Gary McAllister, Paul Ramsey, Tommy Wright, Ali Mauchlen, David Pleat (Manager), David Puttnam, Tony Spearing, Gary Mills, Marc North, Paul Reid, Darren Williams.

Division 2 **LEICESTER CITY**

City Stadium, Filbert St, Leicester LE2 7FL. Telephone Leicester (0533) 555000. Clubcall: 0898 121185.

Ground capacity: 31,000.

Record attendance: 47,298 v Tottenham H, FA Cup 5th rd, 18 Feb, 1928.

Record receipts: £123,695 v Nottingham F, Littlewoods Cup, 4th rd, 30 November 1988.

Pitch measurements: 112yd × 75yd.

President: T. L. Bennett. *Vice-President:* K. G. Brigstock.

Chairman: T. W. Shipman. *Vice-Chairman:* M. F. George.

Directors: W. G. Page, W. K. Shooter FCA, T. Smeaton, J. M. Elsom FCA.

Manager: David Pleat.*Coach/Assistant Manager:* Gordon Lee.

Secretary: A. K. Bennet.

Physio: Mark Geeson. *PRO:* Alan Birchenall. *Commercial Manager:* P. Hill.

Year Formed: 1884.

Club Nickname: 'Fiberts' or 'Foxes'.

Previous Grounds: 1884, Victoria Park; 1887, Belgrave Road; 1888, Victoria Park; 1891, Filbert Street.

Previous Name: 1884–1919, Leicester Fosse.

Record League Victory: 10-0 v Portsmouth, Division 1, 20 October 1928 – McLaren; Black, Brown; Findlay, Carr, Watson; Adcock, Hine (3), Chandler (6), Lochhead, Barry (1).

Record Cup Victory: 8-1 v Coventry C (away), League Cup, 5th rd, 1 December 1964 – Banks; Sjoberg, Norman (2); Roberts, King, McDerment; Hodgson (2), Cross, Goodfellow, Gibson (1), Stringfellow (2). (1 og).

Record Defeat: 0-12 (as Leicester Fosse) v Nottingham F, Division 1, 21 April, 1909.

Most League Points (2 for a win): 61, Division 2, 1956–57.

Most League Points (3 for a win): 70, Division 2, 1982–83.

Most League Goals: 109, Division 2, 1956–57.

Highest League Scorer in Season: Arthur Rowley, 44, Division 2, 1956–57.

Most League Goals in Total Aggregate: Arthur Chandler, 259, 1923–35.

Most Capped Player: Gordon Banks, 37 (73), England.

Most League Appearances: Adam Black, 528, 1920–35.

Record Transfer Fee Received: £1,050,000 from Everton for Gary Lineker, July 1985.

Record Transfer Fee Paid: £500,000 to Everton for Wayne Clarke, July 1989.

Football League Record: 1894 Elected to Division 2; 1908–09 Division 1; 1909–25 Division 2; 1925–35 Division 1; 1935–37 Division 2; 1937–39 Division 1; 1946–54 Division 2; 1954–55 Division 1; 1955–57 Division 2; 1957–69 Division 1; 1969–71 Division 2; 1971–78 Division 1: 1978–80 Division 2; 1980-81 Division 1; 1981–83 Division 2; 1983–87 Division 1; 1987– Division 2.

Honours: Football League: Division 1 – Runners-up 1928–29; Division 2 – Champions 1924–25, 1936–37, 1953–54, 1956–57, 1970–71, 1979–80; Runners-up 1907–08. *FA Cup:* Runners-up 1949, 1961, 1963, 1969. *Football League Cup:* Winners 1964; Runners-up 1965. **European Competitions:** *European Cup-Winners' Cup:* 1961–62.

Colours: Blue shirts, white shorts, white stockings. **Change colours:** Red shirts, black shorts, black stockings.

LEICESTER CITY 1989–90 LEAGUE RECORD

Match No.	Date		Venue	Opponents	Result		H/T Score	Lg. Pos.	Goalscorers	Attendance
1	Aug	19	A	Hull C	D	1-1	1-1	—	Clarke	8158
2		23	H	Blackburn R	L	0-1	0-0	—		11,411
3		26	H	Newcastle U	D	2-2	1-1	16	McAllister, Spearing	13,384
4	Sept	2	A	Watford	L	1-3	0-2	21	McAllister	10,252
5		9	H	WBA	L	1-3	1-2	24	Reid	10,700
6		16	A	Bradford C	L	0-2	0-1	24		8732
7		23	H	Brighton & HA	W	1-0	0-0	24	Glover	8926
8		27	H	Sunderland	L	2-3	1-1	—	Williams, Paris	10,843
9		30	A	Oldham Ath	L	0-1	0-0	24		6407
10	Oct	7	A	Port Vale	L	1-2	1-0	24	Reid	7268
11		14	H	Oxford U	D	0-0	0-0	24		8199
12		17	A	Plymouth Arg	L	1-3	0-3	—	Reid	10,037
13		21	H	Swindon T	W	2-1	0-0	23	Reid 2	8547
14		28	A	Barnsley	D	2-2	2-0	23	North, Wright	6856
15	Nov	1	H	Wolverhampton W	D	0-0	0-0	—		16,551
16		4	A	Sheffield U	D	1-1	0-1	22	North	15,971
17		11	H	Leeds U	W	4-3	0-2	22	Ramsey 2, Morgan, McAllister	18,032
18		18	H	Ipswich T	L	0-1	0-1	22		11,664
19		25	A	Stoke C	W	1-0	0-0	22	Mills	12,264
20	Dec	2	H	Hull C	W	2-1	1-0	19	Paris, McAllister (pen)	8616
21		9	A	Blackburn R	W	4-2	2-1	18	McAllister (pen), Morgan, Campbell, Wright	7538
22		16	A	Middlesbrough	L	1-4	0-1	19	McAllister (pen)	11,428
23		26	H	Bournemouth	W	2-1	1-0	18	Campbell, Mills	14,128
24		30	H	West Ham U	W	1-0	0-0	13	Mauchlen	16,925
25	Jan	1	A	Portsmouth	W	3-2	1-2	13	Moran, Campbell 2	9387
26		13	A	Newcastle U	L	4-5	2-2	15	Wright, Walsh, McAllister, Campbell	20,847
27		20	H	Watford	D	1-1	1-1	15	Mills	11,466
28	Feb	10	H	Bradford C	D	1-1	1-1	14	Oldfield	10,281
29		17	A	Brighton & HA	L	0-1	0-1	16		7498
30		21	A	WBA	W	1-0	0-0	—	Oldfield	10,902
31		24	H	Stoke C	W	2-1	0-1	13	Oldfield Reid	12,245
32	Mar	3	A	Ipswich T	D	2-2	1-2	14	Walsh, Oldfield	12,237
33		10	A	Sunderland	D	2-2	1-0	15	Agboola (og), James	13,017
34		17	H	Port Vale	W	2-0	2-0	13	North, Walsh	10,076
35		21	A	Oxford U	L	2-4	0-2	—	Reid, McAllister	5,744
36		24	H	Plymouth Arg	D	1-1	1-0	14	McAllister (pen)	9395
37		31	A	Swindon T	D	1-1	1-1	14	Kelly	8561
38	Apr	3	H	Oldham Ath	W	3-0	1-0	—	North, Kelly 2	10,368
39		7	H	Barnsley	D	2-2	0-2	12	Kelly 2	8620
40		10	A	Wolverhampton W	L	0-5	0-2	—		18,175
41		14	H	Portsmouth	D	1-1	0-0	13	James	8407
42		17	A	Bournemouth	W	3-2	3-1	—	North, Oldfield, Reid	6781
43		21	H	Middlesbrough	W	2-1	1-1	12	Kelly 2	9203
44		28	A	Leeds U	L	1-2	0-1	12	McAllister	32,597
45	May	2	A	West Ham U	L	1-3	0-2	—	Ramsey	17,939
46		5	H	Sheffield U	L	2-5	2-4	13	Mills, North	21,134

Final League Position: 13

GOALSCORERS

League (67): McAllister 10 (4 pens), Reid 8, Kelly 7, North 6, Campbell 5, Oldfield 5, Mills 4, Ramsey 3, Walsh 3, Wright 3, James 2, Morgan 2, Paris 2, Clarke 1, Glover 1, Mauchlen 1, Moran 1, Spearing 1, Williams 1, own goal 1.
Littlewoods Cup (4): Clarke 1, Kitson 1, Paris 1, Reid 1.
FA Cup (1): Paris 1.

Hodge	Johnson	Spearing	Mauchlen	Paris	Evans	Russell	Clarke	Wright	McAllister	Mills	Reid	Ramsey	Puttnam	Walsh	James	Wilkinson	Morgan	Kitson	Glover	Williams	North	Oakes	Moran	Campbell	Oldfield	Kelly	Smith	Linton	Fitzpatrick	Match No.
1	2†	3	4	5	6	7	8	9*	10	11	12	14																		1
1	2*	3	4	5	6	7†	8	9	10	11	12				14															2
1		3	2	5	6	12	8	9	10	11*	7	4																		3
1	14	3	2	6*			8	9	10		7	4†		5	12	11														4
1		3	2					9	10		7	4	11	5	8*	6	12													5
1		3	4	2	6					11	10	7*		5		12	9†	8	14											6
1	2	4	12		6						10	7		5*			3	14	9	8†	11									7
1	2	4	5	6*	12						10	7	14				3		9	8†	11									8
1	2*	4	5	6			8				10	7	11	9†			3	14	12											9
1		2	5	6			8			11	10	7	4				3		9*	12										10
1	3	2		6			8			11†	10	7*	4		5		14	9	12											11
1	3*	2	11	6			8				10	7	4		5†		14	9					12							12
1	3	2	12	6			8			11*	10	7	4		5			9												13
1	3	2	12	6	14		8†			11	10	7*	4		5					9										14
1	2*	12								11	10	7	4	14	5	6	3			8†	9									15
1	2	4		6						11	10	7			5		3				8		9							16
1	2	4		6*						11	10	7	12		5		3				8		9							17
1	14	2		6						11	10	12	7*	4†	5		3				8		9							18
1	2*			6						11	10	7	4	5	12		3				8		9							19
1	2									11	10	4	7	5	6		3				8		9							20
1	2		12							11*	10	4	7	5	6		3				8		9							21
1	12	2								11†	10	4	7	5	6		3*	14			8		9							22
1	2		6							11	10	4	7	5			3				8		9							23
1	3*	2	6							11	10	4	7†	5	12			14			8		9							24
1	2	3					12			11	10	4	7	5	6						8*		9							25
1	3	2	6							11	10	4		7	5						9			8						26
1	3	2	6							11	10	4		7	5						9			8						27
1	3	2	6		9†					11	10	4		7	5	12							14		8*					28
1	3	2	6*							11	10	4	14	7	5	12		9†							8					29
1	3	2		12						11	10	4	7	5	6	9*									8					30
1	3	2								11†	10	4	7	12	5	6	9*						14		8					31
1	2†	3		12						11	10	4	7	8*	5	6							14			9				32
1	3	2	9*							11	10	4	7	5	6			12							8					33
1	3	2								11	10	4	7	5	6	12		9*							8					34
1	3*	2	12							11†	10	4	9	7	5	6							14		8					35
1	2	3								12	10	4	11	7*	5	6							14		8†	9				36
1	3	2								10	4	11	7	5	6			12							8*	9				37
1	3	2								11	10	4	7	5	6*										8	9	12			38
1	3†	2								11*	10	4	14	7	5	6									8	12	9			39
1	3*	2								11	4†	10	7	5	6										8	12	9	14		40
1	3	2								11		7	4	5	6			8							10†	9*	12	14		41
1	2	3								11	10	7	4	5	6			8								9				42
1	2	3								11*	10	7	4	5	6			8							12	9				43
1	2	3								11†	10	14	7	4	5	6		8*							12	9				44
1										11	10	2	7	4	6	8	12								5†	9	14	3*		45
1*		2†	3							11	10	7	12	4	6	5		8							9			14		46
46	11	19	38	33	14	4	10	40	43	27	35	31	2	34	26	2	14	8	3	3	15	—	10	11	16	10	—	1	—	

Substitute appearances (below totals):
+2s, +1s, +5s (Hodge, Johnson, Mauchlen); +6s1s, +1s (McAllister, Mills); +2s, +5s, +4s (Ramsey, Puttnam, Walsh); +2s (James); +5s (Morgan); +3s (Glover); +5s, +2s, +1s9s, +2s (North, Moran, Campbell, Oldfield); +4s (Smith); +4s, +1s1s (Linton, Fitzpatrick)

Littlewoods Cup Second Round — Crystal Palace (a) 2-1, (h) 2-3
FA Cup Third Round — Barnsley (h) 1-2

LEICESTER CITY

Player and Position	Ht	Wt	Birth Date	Place	Source	Clubs	League App	Gls
Goalkeepers								
Martin Hodge	6 2	13 07	4 2 59	Southport	Apprentice	Plymouth Arg	43	—
						Everton	25	—
						Preston NE (loan)	44	—
						Oldham Ath (loan)	4	—
						Gillingham (loan)	4	—
						Sheffield W	197	—
						Leicester C	65	—
Carl Muggleton	6 1	11 13	13 9 68	Leicester	Apprentice	Leicester C	3	—
						Chesterfield (loan)	17	—
						Blackpool (loan)	2	—
						Hartlepool U (loan)	8	—
						Stockport Co (loan)	4	—
Paul O'Connor	5 11	12 10	17 8 71	Easington	Trainee	Leicester C	—	—
Defenders								
Allan Evans‡	6 1	12 13	12 10 56	Dunfermline	Dunfermline U	Dunfermline Ath	98	14
						Aston Villa	380	51
						Leicester C	14	—
Tony James	6 3	14 00	27 6 67	Sheffield	Gainsborough T	Lincoln C	29	—
						Leicester C	31	2
Andy Jeffrey	5 10	11 00	15 1 72	Bellshill	Trainee	Leicester C	—	—
Des Linton	6 1	11 13	5 9 71	Birmingham	Trainee	Leicester C	2	—
Simon Morgan	5 11	12 07	5 9 66	Birmingham		Leicester C	160	3
Alan Paris	5 11	10 12	15 8 64	Slough	Slough T	Watford	—	—
						Peterborough U	137	2
						Leicester C	75	3
Richard Smith	6 0	12 00	3 10 70	Leicester	Trainee	Leicester C	4	—
						Cambridge U (loan)	4	—
Tony Spearing	5 9	10 12	7 10 64	Romford	Apprentice	Norwich C	69	—
						Stoke C (loan)	9	—
						Oxford U (loan)	5	—
						Leicester C	56	1
Steve Walsh	6 3	14 00	3 11 64	Fulwood	Local	Wigan Ath	126	4
						Leicester C	117	12
Midfield								
Gary Fitzpatrick	5 10	10 06	5 8 71	Birmingham	Trainee	Leicester C	1	—
Gary Hyde	6 0	9 07	28 12 69	Wolverhampton	Trainee	Darlington	38	3
						Leicester C	—	—
Jamie Ireland‡			4 4 71	Boston	Trainee	Leicester C	—	—
Rob Johnson	5 6	9 12	22 2 62	Bedford	Apprentice	Luton T	97	1
						Lincoln C (loan)	4	—
						Leicester C	13	—
Des Lyttle	5 9	12 00	24 9 71	Wolv'hampton	Trainee	Leicester C	—	—
Gary McAllister	5 10	9 06	25 12 64	Motherwell	Fir Park BC	Motherwell	59	6
						Leicester C	201	47
Ally Mauchlen	5 7	10 05	29 6 60	Kilwinning	Irvine Meadow	Kilmarnock	120	10
						Motherwell	76	4
						Leicester C	179	9
Gary Mills	5 8	11 05	11 11 61	Northampton	Apprentice	Nottingham F	58	8
					Seattle S	Derby Co	18	1
					Seattle S	Nottingham F	79	4
						Notts Co	75	8
						Leicester C	42	4
Scott Oakes	5 10	9 12	5 8 72	Leicester	Trainee	Leicester C	2	—
Patrick O'Toole	5 7	11 00	2 1 65	Dublin	Shelbourne	Leicester C	—	—
Jason Peake	5 9	11 05	29 9 71	Leicester	Trainee	Leicester C	—	—
Paul Ramsey	5 11	13 00	3 9 62	Derry	Apprentice	Leicester C	266	13
Darren Williams	5 10	10 05	15 12 68	Birmingham	YTS	Leicester C	10	2
						Lincoln C (loan)	9	—

LEICESTER CITY

Foundation: In 1884 a number of young footballers who were mostly old boys of Wyggeston School, held a meeting at a house on the Roman Fosse Way and formed Leicester Fosse FC. They collected 9d (less than 4p) towards the cost of a ball, plus the same amount for membership. Their first professional, Harry Webb from Stafford Rangers, was signed in 1888 for 2s 6d (12½p) per week, plus travelling expenses.

First Football League game: 1 September, 1894, Division 2, v Grimsby T (a) L 3-4 – Thraves; Smith, Bailey; Seymour, Brown, Henrys; Hill, Hughes, McArthur (1), Skea (2), Priestman.

Managers (and Secretary-managers)
William Clark 1896–97, George Johnson 1898–1907*, James Blessington 1907–09, Andy Aitken 1909–11, J. W. Bartlett 1912–14, Peter Hodge 1919–26, William Orr 1926–32, Peter Hodge 1932–34, Andy Lochhead 1934–36, Frank Womack 1936–39, Tom Bromilow 1939–45, Tom Mather 1945–46, Johnny Duncan 1946–49, Norman Bullock 1949–55, David Halliday 1955–58, Matt Gillies 1959–68, Frank O'Farrell 1968–71, Jimmy Bloomfield 1971–77, Frank McLintock 1977–78, Jock Wallace 1978–82, Gordon Milne 1982–86, Bryan Hamilton 1986–87, David Pleat 1987–   .

Player and Position	Ht	Wt	Birth Date	Place	Source	Clubs	League App	Gls
Forwards								
Ian Baraclough	6 1	11 02	4 12 70	Leicester	Trainee	Leicester C	—	—
						Wigan Ath (loan)	9	2
Pat Gavin	6 0	12 00	5 6 67	Hammersmith	Hanwell T	Gillingham	13	7
						Leicester C	—	—
						Gillingham (loan)	34	1
David Kelly	5 11	10 10	25 11 65	Birmingham	Alvechurch	Walsall	147	63
						West Ham U	41	7
						Leicester C	10	7
Paul Kitson			9 1 71	Co Durham	Trainee	Leicester C	13	—
Marc North	5 10	11 00	25 9 66	Ware	Apprentice	Luton T	18	3
						Lincoln C (loan)	4	—
						Scunthorpe U (loan)	5	2
						Birmingham C (loan)	5	1
						Grimsby T	67	17
						Leicester C	32	7
David Oldfield	6 0	12 02	30 5 68	Perth, Aust	Apprentice	Luton T	29	4
						Manchester C	26	6
						Leicester C	20	5
Jari Rantanen‡	6 3	15 02	31 12 61	Finland	Gothenburg	Leicester C	13	3
Paul Reid	5 5	10 02	19 1 68	Warley	Apprentice	Leicester C	117	19
Kevin Russell	5 8	10 10	6 12 66	Portsmouth	Apprentice	Brighton & HA	—	—
						Portsmouth	4	1
						Wrexham	84	43
						Leicester C	10	—
Alan Weldrick‡	5 11	11 04	8 10 71	Dublin	Trainee	Leicester C	—	—
Tommy Wright	5 7	9 10	10 1 66	Fife	Apprentice	Leeds U	81	24
						Oldham Ath	112	23
						Leicester C	41	3

Trainees
Duncan, Iain; Holden, Steven A.D; Hoult, Russell; Lannin, Jason N; Moore, Christian; Vassell, Robert A; Williams, Martin K.

Associated Schoolboys
Bedder, Matthew J; Bunting, Nathan J; Carby, Lee; Clines, James; Crane, Adrian P; Eustace, Scott D; Hewitt, Steven J; Joachim, Julian K; Kerr, Christopher J; Macmillan, Paul J; Madigan, Terrance G; Mallett, Carl; Murphy, Benjamin; Nimblette, Wayne C; Orvis, Richard J; Rughoobeer, Danny M; Talbott, Cory R; Thompson, Ian T.

Associated Schoolboys who have accepted the club's offer of a Traineeship/Contract
Foley, Dean; Gallacher, Gordon; Grace, Gary I; Haughton, Warren; Kane, Liam B.D; Mogg, Lewis; Newcombe, Simon; Thorpe, Anthony.

LEYTON ORIENT 1989–90 *Back row (left to right):* Brian Eastwick (Assistant Manager), Greg Berry, Michael Marks, John Sitton, Paul Ward, Terry Howard, Paul Heald, Lee Harvey, Mark Smalley, Mark Cooper, Carl Hoddle, Kevin Nugent, Bill Songhurst (Physiotherapist).
Front row: Jeremy Gill, Alan Hull, Steve Castle, Keith Day, Frank Clark (Manager), Steve Baker, Kevin Dickenson, Kevin Hales, Danny Carter.

Division 3   **LEYTON ORIENT**

*Leyton Stadium, Brisbane Road, Leyton, London E10 5NE.*Telephone 081-539 2223/4. Club Call: 0898 121150.

Ground capacity: 18,869 (7,171 seats).

Record attendance: 34,345 v West Ham U, FA Cup 4th rd, 25 Jan, 1964.

Record receipts: £87,867.92 v West Ham U, FA Cup 3rd rd, 10 January 1987.

Pitch measurements: 110yd × 80yd.

Chairman: T. Wood OBE. *Vice-Chairman:*

Managing Director: Frank Clark.

Directors: A. Pincus, D. L. Weinrabe, H. Linney, M. Pears.

Manager: Frank Clark. *Coach/Assistant Manager:* Brian Eastick. *Physio:* Bill Songhurst.

Secretary: Miss Carol Stokes. *Asst. Sec.:* Mrs Sue Tilling. *Commercial Manager:* Frank Woolf.

Year Formed: 1881. *Turned Professional:* 1903. *Ltd Co.:* 1906.

Club Nickname: 'The O's'.

Previous Names: 1881–86, Glyn Cricket and Football Club; 1886-88, Eagle Football Club; 1888–98, Orient Football Club; 1898–1946, Clapton Orient; 1946–66, Leyton Orient; 1966–87, Orient.

Previous Grounds: Glyn Rd (1884–96), Whittles Athletic Ground (1896–1900). Millfields Rd (1900–30), and Lea Bridge Rd (1930–37).

Record League Victory: 8-0 v Crystal Palace, Division 3 (S), 12 November 1955 – Welton; Lee, Earl; Blizzard, Aldous, McKnight; White (1), Facey (3), Burgess (2), Heckman, Hartburn (2). 8-0 v Colchester U, Division 4, 15 October 1988 – Wells, Howard, Dickenson, Hales (1p), Day (1). Sitton (1), Baker (1), Ward, Hull (3). Juryeff, Comfort (1). 8-0 v Rochdale, Division 4, 20 October 1987 – Wells; Howard, Dickenson, Smalley, Day, Hull, Hales, Castle (Sussex), Shinners, Godfrey (Harvey), Comfort.

Record Cup Victory: 9-2 v Chester, League Cup, 3rd rd, 15 October 1962 – Robertson; Charlton, Taylor; Gibbs, Bishop, Lea; Deeley (1), Waites (3), Dunmore (2), Graham (3), Wedge.

Record Defeat: 0-8 v Aston Villa, FA Cup 4th rd, 30 January, 1929.

Most League Points (2 for a win): 66, Division 3 (S). 1955–56.

Most League Points (3 for a win): 75, Division 4, 1988–89.

Most League Goals: 106, Division 3 (S), 1955–56.

Highest League Scorer in Season: Tom Johnston, 35, Division 2, 1957–58.

Most League Goals in Total Aggregate: Tom Johnston, 121, 1956–58, 1959–61.

Most Capped Player: John Chiedozie, 8 (10), Nigeria.

Most League Appearances: Peter Allen, 432, 1965–78.

Record Transfer Fee Received: £600,000 from Notts Co for John Chiedozie, August 1981.

Record Transfer Fee Paid: £175,000 to Wigan Ath for Paul Beesley, October 1989.

Football League Record: 1905 Elected to Division 2; 1929–56 Division 3 (S); 1956–62 Division 2; 1962–63 Division 1; 1963–66 Division 2; 1966–70 Division 3; 1970–82 Division 2; 1982–85 Division 3; 1985–89 Division 4; 1989– Division 3.

Honours: Football League: Division 1 best season: 22nd, 1962–63; Division 2 – Runners-up 1961–62; Division 3 – Champions 1969–70; Division 3 (S) – Champions 1955–56; Runners-up 1954–55. *FA Cup:* Semi-final 1977–78. *Football League Cup* best season: 5th rd, 1963.

Colours: Red shirts, white shorts, red stockings. **Change colours:** Yellow shirts, blue shorts, yellow stockings.

314

LEYTON ORIENT 1989–90 LEAGUE RECORD

Match No.	Date		Venue	Opponents	Result		H/T Score	Lg. Pos.	Goalscorers	Attendance
1	Aug	19	H	Notts Co	L	0-1	0-1	—		5364
2		26	A	Shrewsbury T	L	2-4	1-1	23	Cooper 2	3299
3	Sept	2	H	Preston NE	W	3-1	1-1	17	Castle, Sitton, Hull	4871
4		9	A	Walsall	W	3-1	1-1	11	Castle 2, Harvey	3894
5		16	H	Wigan Ath	W	1-0	0-0	10	Cooper	4280
6		23	A	Bolton W	L	1-2	0-1	12	Carter	5951
7		26	H	Bristol R	L	0-1	0-1	—		4675
8		30	A	Huddersfield T	L	0-2	0-2	16		5258
9	Oct	6	A	Tranmere R	L	0-3	0-1	—		8223
10		14	H	Blackpool	W	2-0	2-0	15	Howard 2	4126
11		17	A	Rotherham U	L	2-5	1-2	—	Harvey, Cooper	5728
12		21	H	Reading	W	4-1	3-1	13	Castle, Hoddle, Berry, Cooper	4280
13		28	A	Cardiff C	D	1-1	0-1	15	Harvey	2370
14		31	H	Chester C	L	0-3	0-2	—		3979
15	Nov	5	H	Fulham	D	1-1	1-0	—	Cooper	5817
16		11	A	Birmingham C	D	0-0	0-0	17		7491
17		25	H	Mansfield T	W	3-1	1-0	13	Cooper, Howard, Harvey	3317
18	Dec	3	A	Brentford	L	3-4	0-2	—	Howard, Castle 2 (1 pen)	6434
19		16	A	Bristol C	L	1-2	0-2	14	Castle	7486
20		26	H	Northampton T	D	1-1	0-0	16	Cooper	4784
21		30	H	Crewe Alex	W	2-1	2-0	15	Hull, Cooper	3773
22	Jan	1	A	Bury	L	0-2	0-2	18		2551
23		6	A	Chester C	L	0-1	0-1	—		1722
24		13	H	Shrewsbury T	W	1-0	1-0	16	Hales (pen)	3715
25		20	A	Notts Co	L	0-1	0-0	18		5346
26		27	H	Walsall	D	1-1	1-1	18	Hull	3565
27	Feb	10	H	Wigan Ath	W	2-0	1-0	14	Hull 2	2396
28		13	A	Preston NE	W	3-0	2-0	—	Cooper, Hull, Day	4480
29		18	H	Brentford	L	0-1	0-0	—		6572
30		24	A	Mansfield T	L	0-1	0-0	17		2542
31	Mar	3	A	Swansea C	L	0-2	0-0	18		3628
32		6	H	Huddersfield T	W	1-0	1-0	—	Sayer	3040
33		11	A	Bristol R	D	0-0	0-0	—		7018
34		17	H	Tranmere R	L	0-1	0-1	18		4046
35		20	A	Blackpool	L	0-1	0-1	—		2746
36		24	A	Rotherham U	D	1-1	1-1	18	Carter	3359
37		27	H	Bolton W	D	0-0	0-0	—		3296
38		31	A	Reading	D	1-1	0-1	18	Sitton	4130
39	Apr	3	A	Swansea C	W	1-0	1-0	—	Carter	2582
40		7	A	Cardiff C	W	3-1	0-0	15	Hales (pen), Beesley, Harvey	3411
41		14	H	Bury	L	2-3	1-0	16	Howard, Cooper	3535
42		16	A	Northampton T	W	1-0	1-0	14	Carter	3215
43		21	H	Bristol C	D	1-1	1-0	14	Howard	7273
44		24	A	Crewe Alex	W	1-0	1-0	14	Hoddle	3808
45		28	H	Birmingham C	L	1-2	1-0	14	Harvey	5691
46	May	5	A	Fulham	W	2-1	0-1	14	Howard, Carter	7141

Final League Position: 14

GOALSCORERS

League (52): Cooper 11, Castle 7 (1 pen), Howard 7, Harvey 6, Hull 6, Carter 5, Hales 2 (2 pens), Hoddle 2, Sitton 2, Beesley 1, Berry 1, Day 1, Sayer 1.
Littlewoods Cup (9): Carter 2, Castle 2, Cooper 1, Day 1, Harvey 1, Howard 1, Pike 1.
FA Cup (0).

Heald	Baker	Dickenson	Hales	Day	Sitton	Howard	Castle	Harvey	Cooper	Ward	Carter	Hull	Pike	Smalley	Hoddle	Berry	Beesley	Whitbread	Nugent	Hedman	Rees	Campbell	Sayer	Fashanu	Burnett	Match No.
1	2	3	4	5	6	7	8	9	10	11*	12															1
1	2	3	4*	5	6	7	8	9	10		11	12														2
1	2	3	4	5	6	7	8	9	10		11*	12														3
1	2	3	4	5	6	7	8†	9	10*		11	12	14													4
1	2	3	4	5	6	7	8	9	10		11*	12														5
1	2	3	4*	5†	6	7	8	9	10		11	12	14													6
1	2	3	4*		6	7	8	9	10		11	12		5												7
1	2	3		5	6	7	8	9	10	11	12				4*											8
1		3		5	6	7	8		10	12	11	9			4	2*										9
1	12	3		5	6	7	8		10		11	9†			4*	2	14									10
1	12	3		5	6	7		9	10	8	11*				4	2										11
1	4	3	12	5*		7	8	9	10						2	11	6									12
1	4	3			6	7	8	9	10						2	11	5									13
1	4	3	12	5	14	7	8†	9	10						2*	11	6									14
1	4	3	8	5	2	7		9*	10									14	12	11	6†					15
1	3	2		5	6	7	8		10		9				12	11*	4									16
1	6	3	2	5†		7	8	11	10		9*				14	12	4									17
1	6	3	2*			7	8	11	10	9	12					4	5									18
1		3		5	2	7	8		10	9	11*				6	4	12									19
1		3		5		7	8	9	10	6					11	4		2								20
1	12	3†	6	5		7	8	11	10*	9					14	4		2								21
1	6	2†		5		7	8	11*	10			9			12 14	4	3									22
	6		2	5	3		8	11	9	10*12		7				4					1					23
		2	5	3	7	8*11	10	9†				12				4				14	6	1				24
9*		2	5	3	7		11	10		8						4				12	6	1				25
		2	5	3	7	8	11*10	9								4				12	6	1				26
	3	2	5	6	7	8		10	11* 9						12	4					1					27
	3	2	5	6	7	8		10	11* 9						12	4					1					28
	3	2	5	6	7	8		10	11 9						12	4*					1					29
	3	2	5	6	7	8		10*	11 9						4†					14	1	12				30
14	3	2	5	6	7		11	10*							4						1	8†	9	12		31
1	8	3	2	5	6	7		11	10						4							9				32
1	11	3	2	5	6	7		10							8	4						9*12				33
1	6	3	2*	5		7		11	10						8	4					12	9				34
1	6		2	5		7		11	10	12					8	4					3*	9				35
1		2	5	6	7		12		11						8	4					3	9	10*			36
1	14	2	5	6	7		11 12		10						8	4					3†	9*				37
1	3	2	5	6	7		9	10	11						8*	4						12				38
1	3	2		6*	7		9	10	11		12				4	5						8				39
1	3	2	5	6	7		9*10		11	14	12				4							8†				40
1	3	2	5	6	7		9	10	11	8*					4	12										41
1	3	2†		6	7		9	10*	11		12	14			4	5	8									42
1	3	2		6	7		9		11	10*					4	5	8			12						43
1		2	5*	6	7		9		11					10	4	6†	8			12			14			44
1	3	2	5		7		9		11						4	6	8					10*	12			45
1	3	12	5		7		9		11						4	6	8*					10	2			46
37	27 +5s	31	36 +3s	39	36 +1s	45	27	36	38	2	29 +1s	15 +1s	6	1 +1s2s	19 +9s	6	32	8 +8s	5	5 +2s7s	9 +3s	4 +6s	9 +4s	3 +1s	1 +2s +2s	

Littlewoods Cup First Round Gillingham (a) 4-1
                                   (h) 3-0
               Second Round Everton (h) 0-2
                                   (a) 2-2
FA Cup   First Round Birmingham C (h) 0-1

LEYTON ORIENT

Player and Position	Ht	Wt	Birth Date	Place	Source	Clubs	League App	Gls
Goalkeepers								
Paul Heald	6 2	12 05	20 8 68	Wath on Dearne	Trainee	Sheffield U	—	—
						Leyton Orient	65	—
Peter Wells‡	6 1	13 00	13 8 56	Nottingham	Apprentice	Nottingham F	27	—
						Southampton	141	—
						Millwall (loan)	18	—
						Millwall	15	—
						Leyton Orient	148	—
Defenders								
Paul Beesley	6 1	11 05	21 7 65	Wigan		Wigan Ath	155	3
						Leyton Orient	32	1
Gary Campbell‡			4 4 66	Belfast		Arsenal	—	—
						WBA	—	—
						Leyton Orient	8	—
Keith Day	6 1	11 00	29 11 62	Grays	Aveley	Colchester U	113	12
						Leyton Orient	125	6
Kevin Dickenson	5 6	10 06	24 2 62	London	Apprentice	Tottenham H	—	—
						Charlton Ath	75	1
						Leyton Orient	177	3
Jeremy Gill*	5 8	10 10	8 9 70	Bristol	Trowbridge	Leyton Orient	—	—
Kevin Hales	5 7	10 04	13 1 61	Dartford	Apprentice	Chelsea	20	2
						Leyton Orient	256	22
Lee Harvey	5 11	11 07	21 12 66	Harlow	Local	Leyton Orient	124	16
Terry Howard	6 1	11 07	26 2 66	Stepney	Amateur	Chelsea	6	—
						Crystal Palace (loan)	4	—
						Chester C (loan)	2	—
						Leyton Orient	144	16
John Sitton	6 0	12 02	21 10 59	Hackney	Apprentice	Chelsea	13	—
						Millwall	45	1
						Gillingham	107	5
						Leyton Orient	146	7
Adrian Whitbread			22 10 71	Epping	Trainee	Leyton Orient	8	—
Midfield								
Steve Baker	5 5	10 05	2 12 61	Newcastle	Apprentice	Southampton	73	—
						Burnley (loan)	10	—
						Leyton Orient	87	6
Wayne Burnett			4 9 71	Lambeth	Trainee	Leyton Orient	3	—
Steve Castle	5 11	12 05	17 5 56	Ilford	Apprentice	Leyton Orient	161	33
Carl Hoddle	6 0	11 00	8 3 67	Harlow	Bishop's Stortford	Leyton Orient	26	2
Steve Ketteridge‡	5 9	10 07	7 11 59	Stevenage	Apprentice	Derby Co	–	—
						Wimbledon	237	32
						Crystal Palace	59	6
						Leyton Orient	31	—
						Cardiff C (loan)	6	2
Geoff Pike	5 6	11 00	28 9 56	Clapton	Apprentice	West Ham U	291	32
						Notts Co	82	17
						Leyton Orient	14	—
Chris Zoricich			3 5 69	New Zealand		Leyton Orient	—	—
Forwards								
Greg Berry	5 11	12 00	5 3 71	Essex	East Thurrock	Leyton Orient	9	1
Danny Carter	5 11	11 12	29 6 69	Hackney	Billericay	Leyton Orient	32	5
Mark Cooper	6 1	13 00	5 4 67	Watford	Apprentice	Cambridge U	71	17
						Tottenham H	—	—
						Shrewsbury T (loan)	6	2
						Gillingham	49	11
						Leyton Orient	53	15

LEYTON ORIENT

Foundation: There is some doubt about the foundation of Leyton Orient, and, indeed, some confusion with clubs like Leyton and Clapton over their early history. As regards the foundation, the most favoured version is that Leyton Orient was formed originally by members of Homerton Theological College who established Glyn Cricket Club in 1881 and then carried on through the following winter playing football. Eventually many employees of the Orient Shipping Line became involved and so the name Orient was chosen in 1888.

First Football League game: 2 September, 1905, Division 2, v Leicester Fosse (a) L 1-2 – Butler; Holmes, Codling; Lamberton, Boden, Boyle; Kingaby (1), Wootten, Leigh, Evenson, Bourne.

Managers (and Secretary-managers)
Sam Omerod 1905–06, Ike Ivenson 1906, Billy Holmes 1907–22, Peter Proudfoot 1922–29, Arthur Grimsdell 1929–30, Peter Proudfoot 1930–31, Jimmy Seed 1931–33, David Pratt 1933–34, Peter Proudfoot 1935–39, Tom Halsey 1939–40, Billy Wright 1940–45, Billy Hall 1945, Billy Wright 1945–46, Charlie Hewitt 1946–48, Neil McBain 1948–49, Alec Stock 1949–56, 1956–57, 1957–59, Johnny Carey 1961–63, Benny Fenton 1963–64, Dave Sexton 1965, Dick Graham 1966–68, Jimmy Bloomfield 1968–71, George Petchey 1971–77, Jimmy Bloomfield 1977–81, Paul Went 1981, Ken Knighton 1981, Frank Clark 1982– .

Player and Position	Ht	Wt	Birth Date	Place	Source	Clubs	League App	Gls
Justin Fashanu‡	6 1	12 07	18 8 62	Kensington	Apprentice	Norwich C	90	35
						Nottingham F	32	3
						Southampton (loan)	9	3
						Notts Co	64	20
						Brighton & HA	16	2
					Edmonton	Manchester C	2	—
						West Ham U	2	—
						Leyton Orient	5	—
Alan Hull	5 9	11 00	4 9 62	Rochford	Barking	Leyton Orient	77	16
Michael Marks‡	6 0	12 06	23 3 68	Lambeth		Millwall	36	10
						Mansfield T (loan)	1	—
						Leyton Orient	3	—
Kevin Nugent	6 1	12 04	10 4 69	Edmonton	Trainee	Leyton Orient	25	3
						Cork C (loan)	—	—
Andy Sayer	5 9	10 12	6 6 66	Brent	Apprentice	Wimbledon	58	15
						Cambridge U (loan)	5	—
						Fulham	53	15
						Leyton Orient	10	1

Trainees
Baker, Adam; Jordan, Dean B; Moncur, Lloyd; Murphy, James; O'Hanlon, George T; O'Neill, Mark A; Sharman, Keith E; Tomlinson, Michael L; Warne, Colin.

**Non-Contract
Welsh, Alexander.

Associated Schoolboys
Beckett, Nathan J; Bird, Robert J; Collinson, David J; Denny, Neil R; Fowler, Lee P; Howard, Anthony; McDermott, Dean P; Ramage, Andrew; Rayment, Stuart; Rolls, George E; Ross, Anthony; Singh, Wayne; Smith, Murray H; Sweetman, Nicholas E; Warren, Mark W; Wedlock, Grant.

Associated Schoolboys who have accepted the club's offer of a Traineeship/Contract
Bart-Williams, Christopher; Elliott, Colin E; McCarthy, John; Okai, Stephen P; Patience, Brett J; Sheikh, Azzaz; Stephenson, Andrew; Thompson, David; Walker, Scott P.

**Non-Contract Players who are retained must be re-signed before they are eligible to play in League matches.

318

LINCOLN CITY 1989–90 *Back row (left to right):* John Schofield, Tony Lormor, Matt Carmichael, Keith Scott, Andrew Gorton, Mark Wallington, Ian Bowling, Grant Brown, Darren Davis, Graham Bressington, Neil Smith.

Front row: Philip Brown, Paul Casey, David Puttnam, Stephen Stoutt, Colin Murphy (Manager), John Pickering (Assistant Manager), Steve Thompson, John Pickering (Assistant Manager), Gordon Hobson, Paul Smith, Shane Nicholson, David Clarke.

Division 4   **LINCOLN CITY**

Sincil Bank, Lincoln LN5 8LD. Telephone Lincoln (0522) 522224 and 510263.Fax No. 0522 520564. Social Club 0522 20960.

Ground capacity: 10,369.

Record attendance: 23,196 v Derby Co, League Cup 4th rd, 15 November, 1967.

Record receipts: £34,843.30 v Tottenham H, Milk Cup 2nd rd, 26 October 1983.

Pitch measurements: 110yd × 75yd.

Hon. Life Presidents: V. C. Withers, D. W. L. Bocock.

President: H. Dove.

Chairman: K. J. Reames. *Vice-Chairman:* M. B. Pryor.

Directors: G. D. Overton, G. R. Davey (Managing), R. Staples, D. Barron.

Hon. Consultant Surgeon: Mr. Brian Smith. *Hon. Club Doctor:* Nick Huntley.

Secretary: G. R. Davey. *Club Doctor:* Malcolm Locker.

Manager: Allan Clarke. *Assistant Manager:* John Pickering.

Physio: Adrian Davies. *Commercial Manager:* Wayne Jenner.

Year Formed: 1883. *Turned Professional:* 1892. *Ltd Co.:* 1892.

Club Nickname: 'The Red Imps'.

Previous Grounds: 1883, John O'Gaunt's; 1894, Sincil Bank.

Record League Victory: 11-1 v Crewe Alex, Division 3(N), 29 September 1951 – Jones; Green (1p), Varney; Wright, Emery, Grummett (1); Troops (1), Garvey, Graver (6), Whittle (1), Johnson (1).

Record Cup Victory: 8-1 v Bromley, FA Cup, 2nd rd, 10 December 1938 – McPhail; Hartshorne, Corbett; Bean, Leach, Whyte (1); Hancock, Wilson (1), Ponting (3), Deacon (1), Clare (2).

Record Defeat: 3-11 v Manchester C, Division 2, 23 March, 1895.

Most League Points (2 for a win): 74, Division 4, 1975–76.

Most League Points (3 for a win): 77, Division 3, 1981–82.

Most League Goals: 121, Division 3(N), 1951–52.

Highest League Scorer in Season: Allan Hall, 42, Division 3(N), 1931–32.

Most League Goals in Total Aggregate: Andy Graver, 144, 1950–55 and 1958–61.

Most Capped Player: David Pugh, 3 (7), Wales and George Moulson, 3, Eire.

Most League Appearances: Tony Emery, 402, 1946–59.

Record Transfer Fee Received: £180,000 from Newcastle U for Mick Harford, December 1980.

Record Transfer Fee Paid: £60,000 to Southampton for Gordon Hobson, September 1988, £60,000 to Sheffield U for Alan Roberts, October 1989, and £60,000 to Leicester C for Grant Brown, January 1990.

Football League Record: 1892 founder member of Division 2. Remained in Division 2 until 1920 when they failed re-election but also missed seasons 1908–09 and 1911–12 when not re-elected. 1921–32 Division 3(N); 1932–34 Division 2; 1934–48 Division 3(N); 1948–49 Division 2; 1949–52 Division 3(N); 1952–61 Division 2; 1961–62 Division 3; 1962–76 Division 4; 1976–79 Division 3; 1979–81 Division 4; 1981–86 Division 3; 1986–87 Division 4; 1987–88 GM Vauxhall Conference; 1988– Division 4.

Honours: Football League: Divison 2 best season: 5th, 1901–02; Division 3(N) – Champions 1931–32, 1947–48, 1951–52; Runners-up 1927–28. 1930–31, 1936–37; Division 4 – Champions 1975–76; Runners-up 1980–81. *FA Cup:* best season: 1st rd of Second Series (5th rd equivalent), 1886–87, 2nd rd (5th rd equivalent), 1889–90, 1901–02. *Football League Cup:* best season: 4th rd, 1967–68.

Colours: Red and white striped shirts, black shorts, red stockings with white trim. **Change colours:** Green and white check shirts, green (or white) shorts, green stockings.

LINCOLN CITY 1989–90 LEAGUE RECORD

Match No.	Date	Venue	Opponents	Result	H/T Score	Lg. Pos.	Goalscorers	Attendance
1	Aug 19	H	Scunthorpe U	W 1-0	0-0	—	Carmichael	4504
2	26	A	Aldershot	W 1-0	0-0	3	Carmichael	1786
3	Sept 2	H	Doncaster R	W 2-1	2-1	1	Bressington, Groves	3906
4	9	A	Torquay U	W 3-0	3-0	1	Brown, Sertori 2	2081
5	16	H	York C	D 0-0	0-0	2		4149
6	23	A	Wrexham	W 2-0	0-0	2	Sertori 2	2002
7	27	H	Peterborough U	W 1-0	0-0	—	Clarke (pen)	6106
8	30	A	Southend U	L 0-2	0-1	2		4833
9	Oct 7	A	Chesterfield	D 0-0	0-0	2		4723
10	14	H	Halifax T	W 2-1	0-1	2	Sertori, Waitt	4071
11	18	A	Maidstone U	L 0-2	0-2	—		2199
12	21	H	Grimsby T	D 1-1	0-0	3	Smith	6251
13	28	A	Hereford U	D 2-2	2-0	5	Carmichael, Smith	2392
14	Nov 1	H	Stockport Co	D 0-0	0-0	—		5003
15	4	A	Exeter C	L 0-3	0-2	7		3674
16	11	H	Gillingham	L 1-3	1-3	8	Bressington	3612
17	25	H	Burnley	W 1-0	1-0	8	Schofield	4079
18	Dec 2	A	Colchester U	W 1-0	1-0	5	Nicholson	2517
19	16	A	Rochdale	L 0-1	0-0	7		1216
20	26	H	Cambridge U	W 4-3	1-1	5	Bailie (og), Hobson (pen), Carmichael, Smith	4111
21	30	H	Carlisle U	L 1-3	1-1	6	Hobson (pen)	4793
22	Jan 1	A	Scarborough	L 0-2	0-2	8		2441
23	6	A	Hartlepool U	D 1-1	1-0	—	Hobson	2499
24	13	H	Aldershot	L 0-1	0-0	9		3188
25	20	A	Scunthorpe U	D 1-1	0-0	10	Puttnam	3830
26	Feb 3	H	Wrexham	W 1-0	0-0	8	Lormor	3030
27	10	A	York C	D 0-0	0-0	9		2687
28	13	A	Doncaster R	W 1-0	1-0	—	Hobson	3079
29	17	H	Colchester U	W 2-1	2-0	5	Lormor, Smith	3284
30	24	A	Burnley	D 0-0	0-0	5		5897
31	Mar 3	H	Hartlepool U	W 4-1	2-1	5	Cornforth, Lormor 2, Clarke (pen)	3503
32	7	H	Southend U	W 2-0	1-0	—	Smith (og), Schofield	4860
33	13	A	Peterborough U	L 0-1	0-0	—		6204
34	17	H	Chesterfield	D 1-1	1-0	4	Lormor	5251
35	20	A	Halifax T	W 1-0	0-0	—	Smith P	1423
36	25	H	Maidstone U	L 1-2	0-1	—	Brown	4302
37	31	A	Grimsby T	L 0-1	0-1	7		11,427
38	Apr 4	H	Torquay U	D 2-2	2-1	—	Hobson, Scott	2573
39	7	H	Hereford U	W 1-0	1-0	6	Lormor	2501
40	9	A	Stockport Co	D 1-1	0-1	—	Hobson	3394
41	14	H	Scarborough	D 0-0	0-0	8		3310
42	17	A	Cambridge U	L 1-2	1-1	—	Lormor	4121
43	21	H	Rochdale	L 1-2	0-2	9	Lormor	2470
44	24	A	Carlisle U	W 2-1	2-0	—	Hobson, Carmichael	5064
45	28	A	Gillingham	D 1-1	0-0	8	Scott	2654
46	May 5	H	Exeter C	L 1-5	1-2	10	Hobson	4772

Final League Position: 10

GOALSCORERS

League (48): Hobson 8 (2 pens), Lormor 8, Carmichael 5, Sertori 5, Smith P 5, Bressington 2, Brown 2, Clarke 2 (2 pens), Schofield 2, Scott 2, Cornforth 1, Groves 1, Nicholson 1, Puttnam 1, Waitt 1, own goals 2.
Littlewoods Cup (0).
FA Cup (1): Nicholson 1.

Gorton	Casey	Clarke	Cook	James	Davis	Anderson	Bressington	Carmichael	Sertori	Nicholson	Thompson	Brown G	Groves	Cumming	Schofield	Waitt	Roberts	Smith P	Williams P	Wallington	Williams D	Hobson	Stoutt	Cornforth	Brown P	Puttnam	Lormor	Smith N	Scott	Match No.
1	2	3	4	5	6	7	8	9	10	11																				1
1	2	3	4				8	10	9	12	5	6	7	11*																2
1	2	3		12			8	10	9		5*	6	7	11	4															3
1	2	3					8	10	9		5	6	7	11	4															4
1	2	3		12			8	10	9		5	6*	7†	11	4	14														5
1	2	3					8		9		5	6	7	11	4	10														6
1	2	3					8	12	9		5	6	7	11	4	10*														7
1	2	3					8		9		5	6	7	11	4	10														8
1	2	3					8		9		5	6	7	11	4	10														9
1	2	3					8		9		5	6		11	4	10	7													10
1	2	3					8		9		5	6		11	4*	10	7	12												11
1	2	3					8	11	9		5	6			4		7	10												12
1		3		12			8	11	9	4	5*	6			2		7	10												13
1		3	4	5			8	11	9			6			2	10	7													14
1		3	4	5			8	12	9			6		11*	2		7	10												15
1		3*			6		8	11	9		5			12	4		7	10	2											16
		3			6		8	10	9	4	5				7				2	1	11									17
		3			6		8	10	9	4	5				7				2	1	11									18
		3			6		8		9	4	5				2		10			1	7	11								19
1		3*	4		6		8	11			5				2		7	10				9				12				20
1					6		8	11†	14	3	5				4*		7	10				9	2			12				21
1		3			6*		8	12	14		5				4		7	10†				9	2			11				22
1					6		8	11		3	5				4		7	10				9	2							23
							5	12	10*	3		6			8†		7			1		9	2	4		14	11			24
							8	12	14	3*	5†	6			7			10		1		9	2	4		11				25
		3			6		8				5							7		1		9	2	4		11	10			26
		3*			6		8	12			5							7		1		9	2	4		11	10			27
		3			6		8				5							7		1		9	2	4		11	10			28
		3			6		8	12			5							7		1		9	2	4		11*	10			29
					6		8			3	5							7		1		9	2	4		11	10			30
		3			6						5				8			7		1		9	2	4		11	10			31
					6					3	5				8			7		1		9	2	4		11	10			32
					6		4*	12		3	5				8†			7		1		9	2	14		11	10			33
		3			6					4	5				8			7		1		9	2			11	10			34
		3			6		8				5							7		1		9	2			11	10	4		35
		3			6		8				5							7		1		9	2*			11	10	4	12	36
		3†			6		8				5		14					7		1		9	2			11	10	4*	12	37
		3*			6		8				5				2					1	12	7		4		11	10		9*	38
							8	12		3	5	6			2					1		7		4		11	10		9*	39
					6		8	12		3	5				2					1		7		4		11	10		9*	40
		3					8				5	6			2					1	12	7		4*		11	10		9	41
					6		8	12		3	5*				2					1		7		4		11	10		9	42
		3					5	12				6	14	7†	2					1		8		4		11	10		9*	43
					6		8	9		3	5				2					1		7		4		11	10			44
					6		8	9*		3	5				2					1		7		4		11	10		12	45
							8*	9		3	5			14	2					1		7		4		11	10	6†	12	46
20	12	30	6	1	31+	1	43+	16+	21+	18	27	34	8	11	28+	7+	10	32+	3	26	7	29+	21	9	1+	23	21	4	6+	

Substitute appearances: Davis +3s; Carmichael +10s; Sertori +3s; Nicholson +5s; Schofield +1s; Waitt +1s; Roberts +1s; Smith P +1s; Wallington +2s; Brown P +4s; Smith N +4s

Littlewoods Cup	First Round	Wolverhampton W (a)	0-1
		(h)	0-2
FA Cup	First Round	Billingham Syn (h)	1-0
	Second Round	Rochdale (a)	0-3

LINCOLN CITY

Player and Position	Ht	Wt	Birth Date	Place	Source	Clubs	League App	Gls
Goalkeepers								
Ian Bowling	6 3	14 08	27 7 65	Sheffield	Gainsborough T	Lincoln C	8	–
						Hartlepool U (loan)	1	—
Andy Gorton	5 11	11 04	23 9 66	Salford		Oldham Ath	26	—
						Stockport Co (loan)	14	—
						Tranmere R (loan)	1	—
						Stockport Co	34	—
						Lincoln C	20	—
Mark Wallington	6 1	14 11	17 9 52	Grantham	Amateur	Walsall	11	—
						Leicester C	412	—
						Derby Co	67	—
						Lincoln C	64	—
Defenders								
Grant Brown	6 0	11 12	19 11 69	Sunderland	Trainee	Leicester C	14	—
						Lincoln C	34	2
Paul Casey*	5 8	10 06	6 10 61	Rinteln	Apprentice	Sheffield U	25	1
					Boston U	Lincoln C	20	—
Darren Davis	6 0	11 00	5 2 67	Sutton Ashfield	Apprentice	Notts Co	92	1
						Lincoln C	72	2
Shane Nicholson	5 10	11 06	3 6 70	Newark	Trainee	Lincoln C	64	1
Stephen Stoutt	5 8	11 06	5 4 64	Halifax	Local	Huddersfield T	6	—
						Wolverhampton W	94	5
						Grimsby T	3	1
						Lincoln C	21	—
Steve Thompson	6 1	14 04	28 7 55	Sheffield	Boston U	Lincoln C	154	8
						Charlton Ath	95	—
						Leicester C	—	—
						Sheffield U	20	1
						Lincoln C	27	—
Midfield								
Nicky Anderson‡	5 10	10 10	29 3 69	Lincoln	Trainee	Mansfield T	20	—
						Lincoln C	1	—
Graham Bressington	6 0	12 06	8 7 66	Eton	Wycombe W	Lincoln C	73	3
Phil Brown*	5 8	9 07	16 1 66	Sheffield	Apprentice	Chesterfield	87	19
						Stockport Co	23	1
						Lincoln C	43	3
David Clarke	5 10	11 00	3 12 64	Nottingham	Apprentice	Notts Co	123	7
						Lincoln C	66	6
Mark Cook‡	6 0	11 11	7 8 70	Boston	Trainee	Lincoln C	7	—
Bob Cumming‡	5 8	10 05	7 12 55	Aidrie	Bailleston Jrs	Grimsby T	365	57
						Lincoln C	41	5
Alan Roberts	5 9	10 00	8 12 64	Newcastle	Apprentice	Middlesbrough	38	2
						Darlington	119	19
						Sheffield U	36	2
						Lincoln C	10	—
Jon Schofield	5 11	11 03	16 5 65	Barnsley	Gainsborough T	Lincoln C	58	4
George Shipley‡	5 8	10 08	7 3 59	Newcastle	Apprentice	Southampton	3	—
						Reading (loan)	12	1
						Blackpool (loan)	—	—
						Lincoln C	223	39
						Charlton Ath	61	6
						Gillingham	29	3
						Lincoln C	—	—
Neil Smith	5 10	10 12	10 2 70	Warley	Trainee	Shrewsbury T	1	—
					Redditch	Lincoln C	4	—

LINCOLN CITY

Foundation: Although there was a Lincoln club as far back as 1861, the present organisation was formed in 1883 winning the Lincolnshire Senior Cup in only their fourth season. They were Founder members of the Midland League in 1889 and that competition's first champions.

First Football League game: 3 September, 1892, Division 2, v Sheffield U (a) L 2-4 – W. Gresham; Coulton, Neill; Shaw, Mettam, Moore; Smallman, Irving (1), Cameron (1), Kelly, J. Gresham.

Managers (and Secretary-managers)
David Calderhead 1900–07, John Henry Strawson 1907–14 (had been secretary), George Fraser 1919–21, David Calderhead Jnr. 1921–24, Horace Henshall 1924–27, Harry Parkes 1927–36, Joe McClelland 1936–46, Bill Anderson 1946–65 (GM to 1966), Roy Chapman 1965–66, Ron Gray 1966–70, Bert Loxley 1970–71, David Herd 1971–72, Graham Taylor 1972–77, George Kerr 1977–78, Willie Bell 1977–78, Colin Murphy 1978–85, John Pickering 1985, George Kerr 1985–87, Peter Daniel 1987, Colin Murphy 1987–90, Allan Clarke 1990– .

Player and Position	Ht	Wt	Birth Date	Place	Source	Clubs	League App	Gls
Forwards								
Matt Carmichael*	6 2	11 07	13 5 64	Singapore	Army	Lincoln C	26	5
Malcolm Dunkley*	6 5	14 00	12 7 61	Wolverhampton	Bromsgrove R	Lincoln C	11	4
Gordon Hobson	5 9	10 07	27 11 57	Sheffield	Sheffield RGRS	Lincoln C	272	73
						Grimsby T	52	18
						Southampton	33	8
						Lincoln C	61	22
Anth Lormor	6 1	12 03	29 10 70	Ashington	Trainee	Newcastle U	8	3
						Norwich C (loan)	—	—
						Lincoln C	21	8
David Puttnam	5 10	11 09	3 2 67	Leicester	Leicester U	Leicester C	7	—
						Lincoln C	23	1
Keith Scott	6 3	12 00	10 6 67	London	Leicester U	Lincoln C	10	2
Paul Smith	5 11	10 09	9 11 64	Rotherham	Apprentice	Sheffield U	36	1
						Stockport Co (loan)	7	5
						Port Vale	44	7
						Lincoln C	61	15
Mick Waitt‡	6 4	12 00	25 6 60	Hexham	Keyworth U	Notts Co	82	27
						Lincoln C	8	1

Trainees
Briggs, Steven; Davis, Jason M; Hardwick, James; Harrison, Richard C; Hurford, Lee R; McCormick, Craig L; Mulhall, Stuart; West, Dean.

**Non-Contract
Davidson, Michael; Humphreys, John; Langford, Timothy; Statham, Thomas; Topliss, Kevin.

Associated Schoolboys
Barker, Adrian; Brown, Michael A.

**Non-Contract Players who are retained must be re-signed before they are eligible to play in League matches.

324

LIVERPOOL 1989-90 *Back row (left to right):* Jan Molby, Gary Gillespie, Mike Hooper, Gary Ablett, Bruce Grobbelaar, Steve Staunton, Glenn Hysen.
Centre row: Roy Evans (First Team Coach), Ray Houghton, Ian Rush, Alec Watson, John Aldridge, Barry Venison, David Burrows, Ronnie Moran (Chief Coach).
Front row: John Barnes, Steve Nicol, Alan Hansen (Captain), Kenny Dalglish (Player Manager), Ronnie Whelan, Steve McMahon, Peter Beardsley.

Division 1 **LIVERPOOL**

Anfield Road, Liverpool 4. Telephone 051-263 2361. Clubcall: 0898-121184. Ticket and Match Information: 051-260-9999 (24-hour service) or 051-260-8680 (office hours) or 0898 12 1584 for Ticket Call.

Ground Capacity: 39,772.

Record attendance: 61,905 v Wolverhampton W, FA Cup 4th rd, 2 Feb, 1952.

Record receipts: £227,351 v QPR, FA Cup, 6th rd replay, 14 March, 1990.

Pitch measurements: 110yd × 75yd.

Directors: Sir J. W. Smith CBE, DL, JP, Coun. S. T. Moss JP, S. C. Reakes JP, J. T. Cross, R. Paisley OBE, MSC (HON), G. A. Ensor LLB, N. White, D. Moores.

Vice-Presidents: C. J. Hill, H. E. Roberts.

Team Manager: Kenny Dalglish. *Coach:* Ron Moran.

Chief Executive/General Secretary: Peter Robinson.

Commercial Manager: K. Addison.

Year Formed: 1892. *Turned Professional:* 1892. *Ltd Co.:* 1892.

Club Nickname: 'Reds' or 'Pool'.

Record League Victory: 10-1 v Rotherham T, Division 2, 18 February 1896 – Storer; Goldie, Wilkie; McCarthy, McQueen, Holmes; McVean (3), Ross (2), Allan (4), Becton (1), Bradshaw.

Record Cup Victory: 11-0 v Stomsgodset Drammen, ECWC 1st rd (1st leg), 17 September 1974 – Clemence; Smith (1), Lindsay (1p), Thompson (2), Cormack (1), Hughes (1), Boersma (2), Hall, Heighway (1), Kennedy (1), Callaghan (1).

Record Defeat: 1-9 v Birmingham C, Division 2, 11 December, 1954.

Most League Points (2 for a win): 68, Division 1, 1978–79.

Most League Points (3 for a win): 90, Division 1, 1987–88.

Most League Goals: 106, Division 2, 1895–96.

Highest League Scorer in Season: Roger Hunt, 41, Division 2, 1961–62.

Most League Goals in Total Aggregate: Roger Hunt, 245, 1959–69.

Most Capped Player: Emlyn Hughes, 59 (62), England.

Most League Appearances: Ian Callaghan, 640, 1960–78.

Record Transfer Fee Received: £3,200,000 from Juventus for Ian Rush, June 1986.

Record Transfer Fee Paid: £2,800,000 to Juventus for Ian Rush, August 1988.

Football League Record: 1893 Elected to Division 2; 1894–95 Division 1; 1895–96 Division 2; 1896–1904 Division 1; 1904–05 Division 2; 1905–54 Division 1; 1954–62 Division 2; 1962– Division 1.

Honours: Football League: Division 1 – Champions 1900–01, 1905–06, 1921–22, 1922–23, 1946–47, 1963–64, 1965–66, 1972–73, 1975–76, 1976–77, 1978–79, 1979–80, 1981–82, 1982–83, 1983–84, 1985–86, 1987–88, 1989–90 (Liverpool have a record number of 18 League Championship wins); Runners-up 1898–99, 1909–10, 1968–69, 1973–74, 1974–75, 1977–78, 1984–85, 1986–87, 1988–89; Division 2 – Champions 1893–94, 1895–96, 1904–05, 1961–62; *FA Cup:* Winners 1965, 1974, 1986, 1989; Runners-up 1914, 1950, 1971, 1977, 1988; *Football League Cup:* Winners 1981, 1982, 1983, 1984. Runners-up 1977–78, 1986–87. League Super Cup-Winners: 1985–86. **European Competitions;** *European Cup:* 1964–65, 1966–67, 1973–74, 1976–77 (winners), 1977–78 (winners), 1978–79, 1979–80, 1980–81 (winners), 1981–82, 1982–83, 1983–84 (winners), 1984–85 (runners-up); *European Cup-Winners' Cup:* 1965–66 (runners-up), 1971–72, 1974–75; **European Fairs Cup:** 1967–68, 1968–69, 1969–70, 1970–71; *UEFA Cup:* 1972–73 (winners), 1975–76 (winners); *Super Cup:* 1977 (winners), 1978; *World Club Championship;* 1981 (runners-up).

Colours: All red. **Change colours:** All silver grey.

LIVERPOOL 1989–90 LEAGUE RECORD

Match No.	Date	Venue	Opponents	Result	H/T Score	Lg. Pos.	Goalscorers	Attendance
1	Aug 19	H	Manchester C	W 3-1	1-1	—	Barnes (pen), Beardsley, Nicol	37,628
2	23	A	Aston Villa	D 1-1	1-0	—	Barnes	35,796
3	26	A	Luton T	D 0-0	0-0	5		11,124
4	Sept 9	A	Derby Co	W 3-0	0-0	5	Rush, Barnes (pen), Beardsley	20,034
5	12	H	Crystal Palace	W 9-0	3-0	—	Nicol 2, McMahon, Rush, Gillespie, Beardsley, Aldridge (pen), Barnes, Hysen	35,779
6	16	H	Norwich C	D 0-0	0-0	2		36,885
7	23	A	Everton	W 3-1	1-1	1	Barnes, Rush 2	42,453
8	Oct 14	A	Wimbledon	W 2-1	1-0	1	Beardsley, Whelan	13,510
9	21	A	Southampton	L 1-4	0-2	2	Beardsley (pen)	20,501
10	29	H	Tottenham H	W 1-0	1-0	—	Barnes	36,550
11	Nov 4	H	Coventry C	L 0-1	0-0	2		36,433
12	11	A	QPR	L 2-3	1-2	3	Barnes 2 (1 pen)	18,804
13	19	A	Millwall	W 2-1	1-1	—	Barnes, Rush	13,547
14	26	H	Arsenal	W 2-1	1-0	—	McMahon, Barnes	35,983
15	29	A	Sheffield W	L 0-2	0-0	—		32,732
16	Dec 2	A	Manchester C	W 4-1	1-0	1	Rush 2, Beardsley, McMahon	31,641
17	9	H	Aston Villa	D 1-1	0-1	2	Beardsley	37,435
18	16	H	Chelsea	W 5-2	3-1	2	Beardsley, Rush 2, Houghton, McMahon	31,005
19	23	H	Manchester U	D 0-0	0-0	—		37,426
20	26	H	Sheffield W	W 2-1	1-0	1	Molby, Rush	37,488
21	30	H	Charlton Ath	W 1-0	1-0	—	Barnes	36,678
22	Jan 1	A	Nottingham F	D 2-2	2-0	1	Rush 2	24,518
23	13	H	Luton T	D 2-2	1-0	1	Barnes, Nicol	35,312
24	20	A	Crystal Palace	W 2-0	1-0	1	Rush, Beardsley	29,807
25	Feb 3	H	Everton	W 2-1	2-1	1	Barnes, Beardsley (pen)	38,730
26	10	A	Norwich C	D 0-0	0-0	1		20,210
27	Mar 3	H	Millwall	W 1-0	0-0	1	Gillespie	36,427
28	18	A	Manchester U	W 2-1	1-0	—	Barnes 2 (1 pen)	46,629
29	21	H	Tottenham H	L 0-1	0-0	—		25,656
30	31	H	Southampton	W 3-2	1-1	1	Barnes, Osman (og), Rush	37,027
31	Apr 3	H	Wimbledon	W 2-1	2-0	—	Rush, Gillespie	33,319
32	11	A	Charlton Ath	W 4-0	1-0	—	Rosenthal 3, Barnes	13,982
33	14	H	Nottingham F	D 2-2	2-0	1	Rosenthal, McMahon	37,265
34	18	A	Arsenal	D 1-1	0-1	—	Barnes	33,395
35	21	H	Chelsea	W 4-1	2-0	1	Rosenthal, Nicol 2, Rush	38,431
36	28	H	QPR	W 2-1	1-1	1	Rush, Barnes (pen)	37,758
37	May 1	H	Derby Co	W 1-0	0-0	—	Gillespie	38,038
38	5	A	Coventry C	W 6-1	3-1	1	Rush, Barnes 3, Rosenthal 2	23,204

Final League Position: 1

GOALSCORERS

League (78): Barnes 22 (5 pens), Rush 18, Beardsley 10 (2 pens), Rosenthal 7, Nicol 6, McMahon 5, Gillespie 4, Aldridge 1 (pen), Houghton 1, Hysen 1, Molby 1, Whelan 1, own goal 1.
Littlewoods Cup (8): Staunton 3, Rush 2, Barnes 1, Beardsley 1, Hysen 1.
FA Cup (20): Rush 6, Barnes 5 (1 pen), Beardsley 4 (1 pen), Nicol 3, McMahon 1, Whelan 1.

Grobbelaar	Hysen	Burrows	Nicol	Whelan	Hansen	Beardsley	Venison	Rush	Barnes	McMahon	Aldridge	Gillespie	Molby	Staunton	Houghton	Ablett	Marsh	Tanner	Rosenthal	Dalglish	Match No.
1	2	3	4	5	6	7	8	9	10	11											1
1	2	3	4	5	6	7	8	9	10	11											2
1	2	3	4	5	6	7*		9	10	11	12	8									3
1	2	3	4	5	6	7		9	10	11		8									4
1	2	3	4	5	6	7*		9	10	11†	12	8	14								5
1	2	3	4	5	6	7		9	10	11		8									6
1	2	3	4	5	6	7	8	9	10	11											7
1	2	3	4	5	6	7	8		10	11			9								8
1	2	3	4	5	6	7	8*	9	10	11				12							9
1	2	3		5		7	4*	9	10	11			12	8	6						10
1	2	3		5	6	7		9	10	11*			12	8	4						11
1	2	3	4*	5	6	7		9	10	11			12	8							12
1	2			5	6	7		9	10	11			4	3	8						13
1	2		4	5	6	12	7*	9	10	11				3	8						14
1		12		5		7		9	10*	11	2	6	3	8	4						15
1	2			5		7		9		11	6†	10	3*	8	4	12	14				16
1	2			5		7		9	10*	11	6	3	8	4	12						17
1	2	12		5	6	7	3	9		11			10*	8	4						18
1	2	12		5	6*	7	3	9		11			10	8	4						19
1	2	12	4	5		7	3*	9		11†			10	14	8	6					20
1	2		4	5	6	12	3	9	10	14			11†	8		7*					21
1	2	8	4	5	6	7	3	9	10	11											22
1	2	12	4	5	6	7	3	9	10	11			8*								23
1	2		4	5	6	7	3	9	10	11			8								24
1	2	8	4	5	6	7	3	9	19	11											25
1	2	8	4	5	6	7	3	9	10	11											26
1		8*	4	5	6	7	3	9	10	11	2		12								27
1	2			5	6	7	3	9	10	11			4	8							28
1	2			5	6	7	3	9	10	11			4	8							29
1	2			5	6	7	3*	9	10	11†	12		4	8			14				30
1	2	3		5	6			9	10	11			4	7	8						31
1		3		5	6	2*			10	11†			12	7	4	14		8	9		32
1	2	3		5	6			9	10	11			4	12				7*	8		33
1	2	3	4	5*	6			9	10	11			12	8†	7			14			34
1	2	3	4		6			9	10	11			5*	7	12				8		35
1	2	3*	4		6†		5	9	10	11			14	7	12	8					36
1	2	3						9	10	11			5	7†	6*	8		4	12	14	37
1	2	3						9	10	11			5	7	6	4		8			38
38	35	23 +3s	21 +2s	34	31	27 +2s	25	36	34	37	— +1s	11 +2s	12 +2s	18 +5s	16 +2s	13 +3s	— +2s	2 +2s	5 +3s	— +1s	

Littlewoods Cup	Second Round	Wigan Ath (h)	5-2
		(a)	3-0
		(played at Anfield)	
	Third Round	Arsenal (a)	0-1
FA Cup	Third Round	Swansea C (a)	0-0
		(h)	8-0
	Fourth Round	Norwich C (a)	0-0
		(h)	3-1
	Fifth Round	Southampton (h)	3-0
	Sixth Round	QPR (a)	2-2
		(h)	1-0
	Semi-final	Crystal Palace (at Villa Park)	3-4

LIVERPOOL

Player and Position	Ht	Wt	Birth Date	Place	Source	Clubs	League App	Gls
Goalkeepers								
Mark Brack*	6 0	12 02	18 9 70	Liverpool	Trainee	Liverpool	—	—
Bruce Grobbelaar	6 1	13 00	6 10 57	Durban	Vancouver W	Crewe Alex	24	1
						Vancouver W	—	—
						Liverpool	338	—
Michael Hooper	6 2	13 05	10 2 64	Bristol	Local	Bristol C	1	—
						Wrexham (loan)	20	—
						Wrexham	14	—
						Liverpool	30	—
Defenders								
Gary Ablett	6 0	11 04	19 11 65	Liverpool	Apprentice	Liverpool	72	1
						Derby Co (loan)	6	—
						Hull C (loan)	5	—
David Burrows	5 8	11 00	25 10 68	Dudley	Apprentice	WBA	46	1
						Liverpool	47	—
John Carroll	6 1	11 08	13 10 71	Dublin	Home Farm	Liverpool	—	—
David Collins	6 1	12 10	30 10 71	Dublin	Trainee	Liverpool	—	—
Gary Gillespie	6 2	12 07	5 7 60	Stirling	School	Falkirk	22	—
						Coventry C	172	6
						Liverpool	126	13
Alan Hansen	6 1	13 00	13 6 55	Alloa	Sauchie BC	Partick T	86	6
						Liverpool	434	8
Glenn Hysen	6 1	12 08	30 10 59	Gothenburg	Fiorentina	Liverpool	35	1
Barry Jones	6 0	12 00	30 6 70	Liverpool	Prescot T	Liverpool	—	—
Steve Nicol	5 10	12 00	11 12 61	Irvine	Ayr U BC	Ayr U	70	7
						Liverpool	207	31
John Smyth*	5 10	11 00	28 4 70	Dundalk	Dundalk	Liverpool	—	—
Steve Staunton	5 11	11 02	19 1 69	Drogheda	Dundalk	Liverpool	41	—
						Bradford C (loan)	8	—
Barry Venison	5 10	11 09	16 8 64	Consett	Apprentice	Sunderland	173	2
						Liverpool	91	—
Alex Watson	6 0	10 12	6 4 68	Liverpool	Apprentice	Liverpool	4	—
Midfield								
Steve Harkness	5 9	10 11	27 8 71	Carlisle	Trainee	Carlisle U	13	—
						Liverpool	—	—
Ray Houghton	5 8	11 04	9 1 62	Glasgow	Amateur	West Ham U	1	—
						Fulham	129	16
						Oxford U	83	10
						Liverpool	85	13
Craig Johnston	5 8	10 13	8 12 60	Johannesburg	Sydney C	Middlesbrough	64	16
						Liverpool	190	30
Steve McMahon	5 9	11 08	20 8 61	Liverpool	Apprentice	Everton	100	11
						Aston Villa	75	7
						Liverpool	167	28
Jim Magilton	5 10	12 07	6 5 69	Belfast	Apprentice	Liverpool	—	—
Jan Molby	6 1	14 07	4 7 63	Denmark	Ajax	Liverpool	132	25
Peter Sermanni*	5 9	11 02	9 9 71	Glasgow	Celtic BC	Liverpool	—	—
Nick Tanner	6 1	13 10	24 5 65	Bristol	Mangotsfield	Bristol R	107	3
						Liverpool	4	—
						Norwich C (loan)	6	—
Ronnie Whelan	5 9	10 13	25 9 61	Dublin	Home Farm	Liverpool	298	43
Forwards								
John Aldridge (To Real Sociedad Sept 1989)	5 11	10 04	18 9 58	Liverpool	South Liverpool	Newport Co	170	69
						Oxford U	114	72
						Liverpool	83	50

LIVERPOOL

Foundation: But for a dispute between Everton FC and their landlord at Anfield in 1892, there may never have been a Liverpool club. This dispute persuaded the majority of Evertonians to quit Anfield for Goodison Park, leaving the landlord, Mr. John Houlding, to form a new club. He originally tried to retain the name "Everton" but when this failed, he founded Liverpool Association FC on 15 March, 1892.

First Football League game: 2 September, 1893, Division 2, v Middlesbrough (a) W 2-0 – McOwen; Hannah, McLean; Henderson, McQue (1), McBride; Gordon, McVean (1), M. McQueen, Stott, H. McQueen.

Managers (and Secretary-managers)
W. E. Barclay 1892–96, Tom Watson 1896–1915, David Ashworth 1920–22, Matt McQueen 1923–28, George Patterson 1928–36 (continued as secretary), George Kay 1936–51, Don Welsh 1951–56, Phil Taylor 1956–59, Bill Shankly 1959–74, Bob Paisley 1974–83, Joe Fagan 1983–85, Kenny Dalglish 1985–   .

Player and Position	Ht	Wt	Birth Date	Place	Source	Clubs	League App	Gls
John Barnes	5 11	12 00	7 11 63	Jamaica	Sudbury Court	Watford	233	65
						Liverpool	105	45
Peter Beardsley	5 8	11 07	18 1 61	Newcastle	Wallsend BC	Carlisle U	102	22
					Vancouver W	Manchester U	—	—
					Vancouver W	Newcastle U	147	61
						Liverpool	104	35
Charlie Boyd*	5 6	9 04	20 9 69	Liverpool	Trainee	Liverpool	—	—
Kenny Dalglish†	5 8	11 13	4 3 51	Glasgow	Cumb'n'ld U	Celtic	204	112
						Liverpool	355	118
Wayne Harrison	5 8	10 07	15 11 67	Stockport	Apprentice	Oldham Ath	5	1
						Liverpool	—	—
						Oldham Ath (loan)	1	—
						Crewe Alex (loan)	3	1
Steve McManaman	5 11	10 02	11 2 72	Liverpool	School	Liverpool	—	—
Mike Marsh	5 8	10 14	21 7 69	Liverpool	Kirkby T	Liverpool	3	—
Russell Payne	5 10	11 08	8 7 70	Wigan	Skelmersdale	Liverpool	—	—
Ronny Rosenthal†	5 10	11 12	11 10 63	Haifa	Standard Liege	Luton T	—	—
						Liverpool	8	7
Ian Rush	6 0	12 06	20 10 61	St Asaph	Apprentice	Chester	34	14
						Liverpool	224	139
						Juventus	29	7
						Liverpool	60	25

Trainees
Brownbill, Barry K; Gandy, Ian; Godfrey, Warren; Hagan, Kevin K; Hollis, Stephen J; Howard, Andrew P; Kelly, Johnathan J; Lampkin, Kevin; Levene, Kevin; Meskell, Vincent W; Murray, Joseph E; Robinson, Jamie; Roscoe, Andrew R; Rubbery, Howard A; Russell, Alexander J; Taylor, Andrew J.

Associated Schoolboys
Brough, Steven L; Collom, Delme G; Coogan, Neil M; Deegan, Mark; Fitzpatrick, Kevin; Frodsham, Ian T; Grindley, David E; Jones, Stuart J; Li, Christian; Meekin, Tony; Prescott, Mark; Stalker, Mark E; Whittaker, Stuart.

Associated Schoolboys who have accepted the club's offer of a Traineeship/Contract
Dennis, Wayne A; Fox, Michael J; Matteo, Dominic; Matthews, Anthony; Walsh, Stephen J.

330

LUTON TOWN 1989–90 *Back row (left to right):* Jason Rees, Mick O'Brien, Alec Chamberlain, Graham Rodger, Les Sealey, Iain Dowie, John Dreyer, Richard Cooke.
Centre row: Les Shannon (Coach), John Faulkner (First Team Coach), Julian James, Marvin Johnson, Tim Allpress, Kurt Nogan, Sean Farrell, Darron McDonough, Richard Harvey.
Paul Gray, Dave Galley (Physiotherapist), George Ley (Coach).
Front row: David Preece, Mick Kennedy, Danny Wilson (Captain), Jim Ryan (Manager), Tim Breacker, Kingsley Black, Lars Elstrup.

Division 1   **LUTON TOWN**

Kenilworth Road Stadium, 1 Maple Rd, Luton, Beds., LU4 8AW.
Telephone, Offices: Luton (0582) 411622; Credit Hotline (0582) 30748 (24 hrs); Banquetting: (0582) 411526.

Ground capacity: 13,023.

Record attendance: 30,069 v Blackpool, FA Cup 6th rd replay, 4 March, 1959.

Record receipts: £77,000 v Oxford U, Littlewoods Cup Semifinal, 28 Feb, 1988.

Pitch measurements: 110yd × 72yd. (Artificial surface).

President: Bert Ward.

Chairman: R. Smith.

General Manager/Secretary: Bill J. Tomlins.

Directors: David Evans MP, T. W. Bailey, S. Pearson, M. Watson Challis, C. J. Hudson, H. Richardson.

Commercial Manager: Wendy Grzybowska.

Manager: Jim Ryan.

Coaches: John Faulkner, Les Shannon and George Ley.

Physio: Dave Galley.

Year Formed: 1885. *Turned Professional:* 1890. *Ltd Co.:* 1897.

Club Nickname: 'The Hatters'.

Previous Grounds: 1885, Excelsior, Dallow Lane; 1897, Dunstable Road; 1905, Kenilworth Road.

Record League Victory: 12-0 v Bristol R, Division 3(S), 13 April 1936 – Dolman; Mackey, Smith; Finlayson, Nelson, Godfrey; Rich, Martin (1), Payne (10), Roberts (1), Stephenson.

Record Cup Victory: 9-0 v Clapton, FA Cup, 1st rd (replay after abandoned game), 30 November 1927 – Abbott; Kingham, Graham; Black, Rennie, Fraser; Pointon, Yardley (4), Reid (2), Woods (1), Dennis (2).

Record Defeat: 0-9 v Small Heath, Division 2, 12 November, 1898.

Most League Points (2 for a win): 66, Division 4, 1967–68.

Most League Points (3 for a win): 88, Division 2, 1981–82.

Most League Goals: 103, Division 3(S), 1936–37.

Highest League Scorer in Season: Joe Payne, 55, Division 3(S), 1936–37.

Most League Goals in Total Aggregate: Gordon Turner, 243, 1949–64.

Most Capped Player: Mal Donaghy, 58 (64), Northern Ireland.

Most League Appearances: Bob Morton, 494, 1948–64.

Record Transfer Fee Received: £1,000,000 from QPR for Roy Wegerle, December 1989.

Record Transfer Fee Paid: £850,000 to Odense for Lars Elstrup, August 1989.

Football League Record: 1897 Elected to Division 2; 1900 failed re-election; 1920 Division 3; 1921 Division 3(S); 1937–55 Division 2; 1955–60 Division 1; 1960–63 Division 2; 1963–65 Division 3; 1965–68 Division 4; 1968–70 Division 3; 1970–74 Division 2; 1974–75 Division 1; 1975–82 Division 2; 1982– Division 1.

Honours: Football League: Division 1 best season : 7th, 1986–87; Division 2 – Champions 1981–82; Runners-up 1954–55, 1973–74; Division 3 – Runners-up 1969–70; Division 4 – Champions 1967–68; Division 3(S) – Champions 1936–37; Runners-up 1935–36. *FA Cup:* Runners-up 1959. *Football League Cup:* Winners 1987–88; Runners-up 1988–89. *Simod Cup:* Runners-up 1988.

Colours: White shirts with navy and orange trim, navy shorts, white stockings. **Change colours:** All royal blue.

Special Loupe system for deaf and blind in our handicapped area. New Health Line Club – featuring multi gym, sauna, spa pool, situated beneath our executive boxes. Tel: 41622. SoccerLine, 0898 700 273 for latest news and views about Luton Town.

LUTON TOWN 1989–90 LEAGUE RECORD

Match No.	Date		Venue	Opponents	Result		H/T Score	Lg. Pos.	Goalscorers	Atten-dance
1	Aug	19	A	Tottenham H	L	1-2	0-1	—	Wegerle	17,668
2		22	H	Sheffield W	W	2-0	1-0	—	Wilson (pen), Black	9503
3		26	H	Liverpool	D	0-0	0-0	10		11,124
4		30	A	QPR	D	0-0	0-0	—		10,565
5	Sept	9	H	Charlton Ath	W	1-0	0-0	7	Wilson (pen)	8859
6		16	A	Coventry C	L	0-1	0-1	8		11,152
7		23	H	Wimbledon	D	1-1	1-1	10	Wegerle (pen)	8449
8		30	A	Manchester C	L	1-3	1-2	14	Black	23,863
9	Oct	14	H	Aston Villa	L	0-1	0-1	16		9433
10		21	H	Norwich C	W	4-1	1-0	12	Black, Dreyer, Wilson, Williams	9038
11		28	A	Millwall	D	1-1	1-1	14	Elstrup	11,140
12	Nov	4	H	Derby Co	W	1-0	0-0	11	Dowie	8919
13		11	A	Crystal Palace	D	1-1	0-1	10	Wilson	11,346
14		18	H	Manchester U	L	1-3	0-2	13	Wilson	11,141
15		25	A	Southampton	L	3-6	1-2	13	Dreyer, Black, Elstrup	14,014
16	Dec	2	H	Tottenham	D	0-0	0-0	15		12,620
17		9	A	Sheffield W	D	1-1	0-1	15	James	16,339
18		16	A	Arsenal	L	2-3	1-2	18	Elstrup 2 (1 pen)	28,761
19		26	H	Nottingham F	D	1-1	0-1	17	Cooke	10,754
20		30	H	Chelsea	L	0-3	0-1	19		10,068
21	Jan	1	A	Everton	L	1-2	0-2	19	Wilson (pen)	21,743
22		13	A	Liverpool	D	2-2	0-1	19	Black, Nogan	35,312
23		20	H	QPR	D	1-1	1-1	19	Preece	9703
24	Feb	14	A	Wimbledon	W	2-1	0-0	—	Nogan, Dowie	3496
25		19	A	Charlton Ath	L	0-2	0-1	—		6008
26		24	H	Southampton	D	1-1	1-1	18	Dowie	9417
27	Mar	3	A	Manchester U	L	1-4	0-3	18	Black	35,327
28		7	H	Coventry C	W	3-2	1-0	—	Black, Gray, Dowie	8244
29		10	A	Aston Villa	L	0-2	0-1	17		22,505
30		17	H	Manchester C	D	1-1	0-0	17	Wilson (pen)	9765
31		24	H	Millwall	W	2-1	1-0	17	McCarthy (og), Black	9027
32		31	A	Norwich C	L	0-2	0-1	17		14,451
33	Apr	7	A	Chelsea	L	0-1	0-0	18		15,221
34		14	H	Everton	D	2-2	2-0	18	Dowie 2	9538
35		16	A	Nottingham F	L	0-3	0-0	18		17,001
36		21	H	Arsenal	W	2-0	1-0	18	Dowie, Black	11,595
37		28	H	Crystal Palace	W	1-0	0-0	18	Dowie	10,369
38	May	5	A	Derby Co	W	3-2	2-2	17	Breacker, Black 2	17,044

Final League Position: 17

GOALSCORERS

League (43): Black 11, Dowie 8, Wilson 7 (4 pens), Elstrup 4 (1 pen), Dreyer 2, Nogan 2, Wegerle 2 (1 pen), Breacker 1, Cooke 1, Gray 1, James 1, Preece 1, Williams 1, own goal 1.
Littlewoods Cup (11): Elstrup 5, Wegerle 4, Dreyer 1, Preece 1.
FA Cup (1): Wilson 1.

Chamberlain	Breacker	Dreyer	Williams	McDonough	Beaumont	Kennedy	Wegerle	Wilson	Preece	Black	Dowie	Harvey	Farrell	Elstrup	Cooke	Johnson	Rodger	James	Gray	Donaghy	Harford	Rees	Nogan	Allpress	Hughes	Poutch	Match No.
1	2	3	4†	5	6	7	8	9	10*	11	12	14															1
1	2	3	4	5	6	7	8	9	10	11*				12													2
1	2	3	4*	5	6	7†	8	9	10	11		14		12													3
1	2	3	4	5	6	7	8	9	10	11*				12													4
1	2	3		5	6	7	8	4	10	11				9													5
1	2	3		5†	6	7	8	4	10*	11		14		9			12										6
1	2	3		5†	6	7	8	4	10	11		14		9*			12										7
1	2	3			6	7†	8	4	10	11		5		9*		12		14									8
1	2	3	7		6		8*	4	10	11		14		9			12		5†								9
1	2	3	7		6		8	4	10	11*	12	14		9					5†								10
1	2	3	7	5†	6	10	8*	4		11	12	14		9													11
1	2	3	7		6	10		4		12	11*	8		9			5										12
1	2	3	7		6†	10	12	4		11		8	14	9*			5										13
1	2	6	7*			10	8	4		11	9	3				12	5										14
1	2	6				10	12	4	7*	11	9	3				8	5†	14									15
1	2	6	7			10	8	4†	14	11*	9	3				12	5										16
1	2	6	7					4		11	9	3				10	12		5*	8							17
1	2	6	7			4†				11*	9	3				10	12			8	14	5					18
1	2	3	7			4				11	9		14			10*	8	6†	5	12							19
1	2	6				4*	8		10	11	9	3				7		5		12							20
1	2	6				4			7	10	9	3						8		11†	5*	12	14				21
1	2	6				4			7	10	11	3						5		9			8				22
1	2	6				4			7	10*	11	3		9				5				12	8				23
1	2	6				4			7	10	11*	3		9		12		5					8				24
1	2	6				4			7	10	11†	3		9*		12	14	5					8				25
1	2	6				4*			7	10	11	3		9				5				12	8				26
1	2	6							7	10*	11	3†		9		12	14	5				4	8				27
1	2	6							7	10*	11	3†		9		14		5		12		4	8				28
1	2	6				4				11		9						5		12		7†	8	3	10*	14	29
1	2	6				4			7	10†	11	3		9				5		12			14	8*			30
1	2	6				4			7	10	11	3		9				5		8*		12					31
1	2	6	3			4			7	10	11	9						5				12		8*			32
1	2	6	3	14		4†			7	10	11	9			8*			5				12					33
1	2	6	3	14		4†			7	10	11	9				12		5					8*				34
1	2	6	3	14		4†			7	10	11	9				12		5					8*				35
1	2	6	3			4			7	10	11*	9				12	14	5†					8				36
1	2	6	3†			4	14		7	10	11*	9				12		5					8				37
1	2	6	3			4	14		7	10	11	9				12		5†					8*				38
38	38	38	14	15	16	30	13	35	30	36	26	17	—	13	3	7	2	19	2	5	1	8	10	1	1	—	
					+3s	+2s	+2s		+2s		+3s	+9s	+1s		+10s	+8s	+5s			+1s	+5s		+3s	+6s		+1s	

Littlewoods Cup	Second Round	Mansfield T (a)	4-3
		(h)	7-2
	Third Round	Everton (a)	0-3
FA Cup	Third Round	Brighton & HA (a)	1-4

LUTON TOWN

Player and Position	Ht	Wt	Birth Date	Birth Place	Source	Clubs	League App	Gls
Goalkeepers								
Alec Chamberlain	6 2	13 00	20 6 64	March	Ramsey T	Ipswich T	—	—
						Colchester U	184	—
						Everton	—	—
						Tranmere R (loan)	15	—
						Luton T	44	—
Les Sealey	6 1	12 08	29 9 57	Bethnal Green	Apprentice	Coventry C	158	—
						Luton T	207	—
						Plymouth Arg (loan)	6	—
						Manchester U (loan)	2	—
Andy Petterson	6 1	14 04	26 9 69	Freemantle		Luton T	—	—
						Swindon T (loan)	—	—
Defenders								
Tim Allpress	6 0	12 00	27 1 71	Hitchin	Trainee	Luton T	1	—
Dave Beaumont	5 10	11 05	10 12 63	Edinburgh	'S' Form	Dundee U	89	3
						Luton T	34	
Tim Breacker	6 0	12 06	2 7 65	Bicester		Luton T	202	3
John Dreyer	6 0	11 10	11 6 63	Alnwick	Wallingford T	Oxford U	60	2
						Torquay U (loan)	5	—
						Fulham (loan)	12	2
						Luton T	56	3
Ken Gillard	5 9	11 08	30 4 72	Dublin	Trainee	Luton T	—	—
Richard Harvey	5 9	11 10	17 4 69	Letchworth	Apprentice	Luton T	43	—
Marvin Johnson	5 11	11 06	29 10 68	Wembley	Apprentice	Luton T	37	—
Mark Pembridge	5 7	11 01	29 11 70	Merthyr	Trainee	Luton T	—	—
Neil Poutch*	5 8	11 09	27 11 69	Dublin	Trainee	Luton T	1	—
						Leicester C (loan)	—	—
Graham Rodger	6 2	11 11	1 4 67	Glasgow	Apprentice	Wolverhampton W	1	—
						Coventry C	36	2
						Luton T	2	—
Darren Salton	6 1	12 01	16 3 72	Edinburgh	Trainee	Luton T	—	—
Kevin Shanley	5 11	11 11	8 9 70	Ireland	Trainee	Luton T	—	—
Midfield								
Kingsley Black	5 8	10 11	22 6 68	Luton	School	Luton T	86	19
Gary Cobb*	5 8	11 05	6 8 68	Luton	Apprentice	Luton T	9	—
						Northampton T (loan)	1	—
						Swansea C (loan)	5	—
Sean Farrell	6 1	12 08	28 2 69	Watford	Apprentice	Luton T	—	—
						Colchester U (loan)	9	1
Ricky Hill (To Le Havre June 1989)	5 11	13 00	5 3 59	London	Apprentice	Luton T	436	54
Ceri Hughes	5 9	11 06	26 2 71	Pontypridd	Trainee	Luton T	1	—
Julian James	5 10	11 11	22 3 70	Tring	Trainee	Luton T	24	1
Mick Kennedy	5 10	10 06	9 4 61	Salford	Apprentice	Halifax T	76	4
						Huddersfield T	81	9
						Middlesbrough	68	5
						Portsmouth	129	4
						Bradford C	45	2
						Leicester C	9	—
						Luton T	32	—
Darron McDonough	5 11	12 06	7 11 62	Antwerp	Apprentice	Oldham Ath	183	14
						Luton T	70	5
Michael O'Brien	5 10	11 04	28 11 70	Dublin	Trainee	Luton T	—	—
Alan O'Sullivan*	5 5	10 01	26 8 71	Cork	Trainee	Luton T	—	—
David Preece	5 5	10 00	28 5 63	Bridgnorth	Apprentice	Walsall	111	5
						Luton T	147	5

LUTON TOWN

Foundation: Formed by an amalgamation of two leading local clubs, Wanderers and Excelsior a works team, at a meeting in Luton Town Hall in April 1885. The Wanderers had three months earlier changed their name to Luton Town Wanderers and did not take too kindly to the formation of another Town club but were talked around at this meeting. Wanderers had already appeared in the FA Cup and the new club entered in its inaugural season.

First Football League game: 4 September, 1897, Division 2, v Leicester Fosse (a) D 1-1 – Williams; McCartney, McEwen; Davies, Stewart, Docherty; Gallacher, Coupar, Birch, McInnes, Ekins (1).

Managers (and Secretary-managers)
Charlie Green 1901–28*, George Thomson 1925, John McCartney 1927–29, George Kay 1929–31, Harold Wightman 1931–35, Ted Liddell 1936–38, Neil McBain 1938–39, George Martin 1939–47, Dally Duncan 1947–58, Syd Owen 1959–60, Sam Bartram 1960–62, Bill Harvey 1962–64, George Martin 1965–66, Allan Brown 1966–68, Alec Stock 1968–72, Harry Haslam 1972–78, David Pleat 1978–86, John Moore 1986–87, Ray Harford 1987–89, Jim Ryan 1990– .

Player and Position	Ht	Wt	Birth Date	Place	Source	Clubs	League App	Gls
Jason Rees	5 5	9 08	22 12 69	Pontpridd	Trainee	Luton T	14	—
Ian Scott	5 10	11 05	25 11 68	Luton	Apprentice	Luton T	—	—
Paul Telfer	5 9	10 02	21 10 71	Edinburgh	Trainee	Luton T	—	—
Aaron Tighe	5 9	10 09	11 7 69	Banbury	Apprentice	Luton T	—	—
						Leicester C (loan)	— .	—
Steve Williams	5 11	10 11	12 7 58	London	Apprentice	Southampton	278	18
						Arsenal	95	4
						Luton T	24	1
Danny Wilson	5 6	11 04	1 1 60	Wigan	Wigan Ath	Bury	90	8
						Chesterfield	100	13
						Nottingham F	10	1
						Scunthorpe U (loan)	6	3
						Brighton & HA	135	33
						Luton T	110	24
Forwards								
Richard Cooke	5 6	9 00	4 9 65	Islington	Apprentice	Tottenham H	11	2
						Birmingham C (loan)	5	—
						Bournemouth	57	13
						Luton T	17	1
Gary Crawshaw	5 8	10 08	4 2 71	Reading	Trainee	Luton T	—	—
Iain Dowie	6 0	13 03	9 1 65		Hendon	Luton T	37	9
						Fulham (loan)	5	1
Lars Elstrup	5 11	11 11	24 3 63	Roby, Denmark	OB Odense	Luton T	23	4
Paul Gray	5 9	11 08	28 1 70	Portsmouth	Trainee	Luton T	7	1
Kurt Nogan	5 10	11 01	9 9 70	Cardiff	Trainee	Luton T	10	2

Trainees
Brown, Stuart, W; Campbell, Jamie; Cooper, David B.E; Gormley, David P; Lawford, John S; McGonagle, Mark B; Rutherford, Ian S; Thompson, Darren J; Watkiss, Richard K.

Associated Schoolboys
Benton, James; Brittain, Vincent J; Carey, Andrew R; Dickeson, Mark J; Fleet, Matthew J; Goodfellow, Scott; Green, Mark; Hartson, John; Jackson, Matthew A; Jukes, Andrew; Mann, David J; Pack, Nathan R; Smith, Wayne J; Watkins, Neil S.

Associated Schoolboys who have accepted the club's offer of a Traineeship/Contract
Hancock, Paul J; Holtham, Matthew D; Newman, Paul S; Rogers, Lee.

336

MAIDSTONE UNITED 1989–90 *Back row (left to right)*: Graham Pearce, Tony Sorrell, Warren Barton, Karl Elsey, Mark Gall, Paul Rumble.
Centre row: Ken Steggles (Physiotherapist), Jason Lillis, Jesse Roast, Steve Butler, Tony Pamphlett, Mark Beeney, Stuart Weaver, Darren Oxbrow, Les Berry, Mark Golley, Ken Charlery.
Tommy Taylor (Assistant Manager).
Front row: Mark Brewer, Gary Stebbing, Dennis Berry (Director), Geoff Pearson (Director), Keith Peacock (Team Manager), Jim Thompson (Chairman), Bill Williams (General Manager),
Jim Dawkins (Vice-Chairman), Michael Frank (Club Physician), Steve Galliers, Gary Cooper.

Division 4   **MAIDSTONE UNITED**

Watling Street, Dartford, Kent DA2 6EN. Telephone (0622) 754403.

Ground capacity: 5250.

Record Attendance: (at The Stadium, London Road, Maidstone): 10,591 v Charlton Ath., FA Cup 3rd rd replay, 15 Jan 1979.

Pitch Measurement: 110yd × 75yd.

Manager: Keith Peacock. *Coach:* Tommy Taylor.

Directors: J. C. Thompson (Chairman), J. G. Dawkins, G. Pearson, D. Berry.

Secretary: W. T. Williams. *Physio:* Ken Steggles.

Year formed: 1897.

Club Nickname: 'Stones'.

Previous Leagues: East Kent, Thames & Medway Combination, Kent, Corinthian, Athenian, Isthmian, Southern, GM Vauxhall Conference.

Record League Victory: 5-1 v Aldershot, Division 4, 1 January 1990 – Beeney; Barton, Cooper (1), Berry, Oxbrow, Golley, Gall (1), Elsey (1), Pritchard (2), Butler, Sorrell.

Record Defeat: 1-4 v Colchester U, Division 4, 26 September 1989.

Most League Points (3 for a win): 73, Division 4, 1989–90.

Most League Goals: 77, Division 4, 1989–90.

Highest League Scorer in Season: Steve Butler, 21, Division 4, 1989–90.

Most League Goals in Total Aggregate: Steve Butler, 21, Division 4, 1989–90.

Most Capped Player: None.

Most League Appearances: Mark Golley, 45, 1989–90.

Football League Record: 1989 Promoted to Division 4.

Honours: Football League: best season: 5th, Division 4, 1989–90. *FA Cup:* Never past 3rd rd. *Football League Cup:* Never past 1st rd.

Record Transfer Fee paid: £35,000 to Fisher Athletic for Ken Charlery, March 1989.

Colours: Amber shirts, black shorts, black stockings with gold trim.

MAIDSTONE UNITED 1989–90 LEAGUE RECORD

Match No.	Date	Venue	Opponents	Result	H/T Score	Lg. Pos.	Goalscorers	Atten-dance
1	Aug 19	A	Peterborough U	L	0-1	0-0	—		6522
2	26	H	Scarborough	W	4-1	3-0	9	Butler 3 (1 pen), Lillis	3372
3	Sept 2	A	Hereford U	L	0-3	0-1	16		2627
4	9	H	Stockport Co	L	0-1	0-1	18		2020
5	16	A	Grimsby T	W	3-2	2-2	16	Gall 2, Butler	5198
6	23	H	Chesterfield	L	0-1	0-1	17		2147
7	26	A	Colchester U	L	1-4	0-1	—	Cooper (pen)	2946
8	30	H	Cambridge U	D	2-2	1-1	21	Smith (og), Lillis	1706
9	Oct 7	H	Burnley	L	1-2	1-1	21	Cooper (pen)	3762
10	14	A	Scunthorpe U	L	0-1	0-0	22		3165
11	18	H	Lincoln C	W	2-0	2-0	—	Elsey, Lillis (pen)	2199
12	21	A	Southend U	W	1-0	1-0	19	Butler	4016
13	28	H	Wrexham	W	2-0	2-0	17	Butler, Elsey	1768
14	31	A	Doncaster R	D	1-1	1-0	—	Golley	1806
15	Nov 4	A	Carlisle U	L	2-3	0-1	18	Gall 2	3395
16	11	H	York C	W	1-0	0-0	16	Butler	2043
17	25	A	Halifax T	W	2-1	0-1	15	Gall, Golley	1353
18	Dec 2	H	Exeter C	W	1-0	1-0	13	Gall	1650
19	16	H	Hartlepool U	W	4-2	0-0	11	Rumble, Cooper, Gall 2	1520
20	26	A	Gillingham	W	2-1	0-0	8	Butler, Gall	10,412
21	30	A	Torquay U	L	1-2	0-1	9	Gall	2344
22	Jan 1	H	Aldershot	W	5-1	3-1	6	Elsey, Gall, Cooper, Pritchard 2	2206
23	13	A	Scarborough	W	1-0	1-0	6	Butler	1961
24	20	H	Peterborough U	D	1-1	0-1	5	Butler	2707
25	27	A	Stockport Co	W	2-1	0-0	5	Butler 2	4161
26	Feb 3	A	Chesterfield	L	1-3	0-2	6	Butler	4068
27	10	H	Grimsby T	D	2-2	1-0	7	Gall, Elsey	2365
28	14	H	Hereford U	W	2-0	0-0	—	Butler, Gall	1516
29	17	A	Exeter C	L	0-2	0-0	7		4181
30	24	H	Halifax T	L	1-2	0-2	7	Golley	2182
31	Mar 3	A	Rochdale	L	2-3	0-2	10	Sorrell, Charlery	2085
32	6	A	Cambridge U	L	0-2	0-2	—		4464
33	10	H	Colchester U	W	4-1	3-0	10	Lillis 3, Butler	2856
34	17	A	Burnley	D	1-1	0-1	11	Gall	5059
35	21	H	Scunthorpe U	D	1-1	1-0	—	Gall	1299
36	25	A	Lincoln C	W	2-1	1-0	—	Lillis 2	4302
37	31	H	Southend U	W	3-0	1-0	8	Brush (og), Butler, Lillis	3550
38	Apr 4	H	Rochdale	W	2-0	0-0	—	Rumble, Lillis	1501
39	7	A	Wrexham	L	2-4	1-2	8	Butler 2	2806
40	11	H	Doncaster R	W	1-0	1-0	—	Butler	1375
41	14	A	Aldershot	W	2-0	0-0	4	Lillis, Sorrell	2334
42	16	H	Gillingham	L	0-1	0-1	6		5003
43	21	A	Hartlepool U	L	2-4	1-0	6	Gall, Butler	2290
44	25	H	Torquay U	W	5-1	4-0	—	Lillis 2, Pritchard 2, Butler	2223
45	28	A	York C	D	0-0	0-0	6		2362
46	May 5	H	Carlisle U	W	5-2	3-1	5	Gall 2, Charlery, Lillis, Sorrell	5006

Final League Position: 5

GOALSCORERS

League (77): Butler 21 (1 pen), Gall 18, Lillis 14 (1 pen), Cooper 4 (2 pens), Elsey 4, Pritchard 4, Golley 3, Sorrell 3, Charlery 2, Rumble 2, own goals 2.
Littlewoods Cup (1): Butler 1.
FA Cup (5): Gall 2, Barton 1, Butler 1, Elsey 1.

Beeney	Barton	Cooper	Berry	Golley	Lillis	Elsey	Sorrell	Butler	Gall	Charlery	Pamphlett	Galliers	Pearce	Rumble	Stebbing	Roast	Oxbrow	Johns	Pritchard	Match No.
1	2†	3	4	5		7*	8	9	10	11	12		6		14					1
1		3	6	5	7	2	9	10	11*	12	4	8								2
1		3	6	5	7†	2	9	10	12	11	4	8*	14							3
1	12	3		5		2	9	10	11	7*	4	8	6							4
1	2	7		5			8	9	10	11*	12	4	6	3						5
1	2	7		5			8	9†	10	11	12	4	6	3*	14					6
1	2	7		5			12	8	9	10	11	4	6	3*						7
1	2	3		5		7	8	9	10*12	11†	4	6			14					8
1	2	3†		5		7	8	12		11*	9		6		14	10	4			9
11		4*	9	7	8			10	12				6	3		2	5	1		10
	2		4	9	7	8		10					6	3			5	1	11	11
1	2		4	9	7*	8		10	12				6	3			5		11	12
1	2		4	9	7	8		10					6	3			5		11	13
1	2		4	9	7*	8		10	12				6	3			5		11	14
1	2	14	4†	9	7*	8		10	12				6	3			5		11	15
1	2		4	9		8		10	7				6	3			5		11	16
1	11	3	4	9				10	7*12			8	6			2	5			17
1	2	3	4	5			8		10	7	11		9	6						18
1	2	3	4	6			8	11	10	7	12	14					5*		9†	19
1	2	3	4	5			8	11	10	7	6								9	20
1	2	3	4	5			8	11†10		7	12	6*14							9	21
1	2	3	4	6			8	11	10	7							5		9	22
1	2	3	4	6			8		10	7		11					5		9	23
1	2	3	4	6			8	11	10	7	12						5*		9	24
1	2	3	4	6	14		8	11	10	7†	12						5*		9	25
1	2	3	4	5	12		8	11	10	7	6*								9	26
1	2	3	4	6	12		8	11	10	7*							5		9	27
1	2	3	4	6	12		8	11†10*		7	14						5		9	28
1	2	3*	4	6			8	14	10	7	12	11					5		9†	29
1		3	4	6	8		9	10		7	12	11				2	5*			30
1		3*	4	6	14		8	11	10	7	12	9				2	5†			31
1	2	14	4*	6	12		8	9	10	7†11		5	3							32
1	2	3	4	6	7		8	11	10		9		5							33
	2	3		6	11		8		7	9	4		10				5	1		34
	2	3		6	11		8	10	7	9	4*	12					5	1		35
	2	3	12	6	11		8	10*	7	9	4						5	1		36
	2		4	5	11		8	10	7*	9		3	6				1		12	37
	2		4	5	11		8	10	7*	9		3	6				1		12	38
	2		4	5	11*	8		10	12	9		3	6				1		7	39
	2		4	5	11		8	10	7	9*		3	6				1		12	40
	2		4		11		8	12	10	7†	9*	14	3			6	5	1		41
	2		4	5	11		8	14	10	12	9*	3				6†	1		7	42
	2		4	5	11		8	12	10	7	9	3*	6				1			43
1	2	3	4	5	11*	8		10		9	12		6						7	44
1	2†	3	4	5	11	8	14	10		12		6					9		7*	45
	2	3	4	5	11	8	12	10	7*	9		6					1			46
33	41	31	37	45	26	44	21	44	33	19	7	7	24	19	2	15	24	13	21	

+ + +   +   + +   + + +   + +   +

1s 2s 1s   7s   7s   8s 11s   1s3s 4s   4s1s   3s

Littlewoods Cup	First Round	Cambridge U (a)	1-3	
			0-1	
FA Cup	First Round	Yeovil (h)	2-1	
	Second Round	Exeter C (h)	1-1	
		(a)	2-3	

MAIDSTONE UNITED

Player and Position	Ht	Wt	Birth Date	Place	Source	Clubs	League App	Gls
Goalkeepers								
Mark Beeney	6 4	13 00	30 12 67	Pembury		Gillingham	2	—
						Maidstone U	33	—
						Aldershot (loan)	7	—
Nicky Johns	6 2	11 05	8 6 57	Bristol	Minehead	Millwall	50	—
						Tampa Bay R	—	—
						Sheffield U (loan)	1	—
						Charlton Ath	288	—
						QPR	10	—
						Maidstone U	13	—
Defenders								
Warren Barton	6 0	11 00	19 3 69	London	Leytonstone/ Ilford	Maidstone U	42	—
Les Berry	6 2	11 13	4 5 56	Plumstead	Apprentice	Charlton Ath	358	11
						Brighton & HA	23	—
						Gillingham (loan)	11	—
						Gillingham	20	—
						Maidstone U	38	—
Darren Oxbrow	6 1	12 06	1 9 69	Ipswich	Trainee	Ipswich T	—	—
						Maidstone U	24	—
Tony Pamphlett*	6 3	13 07	13 4 60	Westminster	Dartford	Maidstone U	7	—
Graham Pearce*	5 9	11 00	8 7 59	Hammersmith	Barnet	Brighton & HA	88	2
						Gillingham	65	—
						Brentford	18	—
						Maidstone U	27	—
Jesse Roast	6 1	12 07	16 3 64	Barking	Barking	Maidstone U	16	—
Paul Rumble	5 11	11 05	14 3 69	Hemel Hempstead	Trainee	Watford	—	1
						Scunthorpe U (loan)	8	1
						Maidstone U	23	2
Gary Stebbing	5 9	11 00	11 8 65	Croydon	Apprentice	Crystal Palace	102	3
						Southend U (loan)	5	—
					KV Ostend	Maidstone U	6	—
Midfield								
Gary Cooper	5 8	11 03	20 11 65	Edgware	Fisher Ath	Maidstone U	33	4
Karl Elsey	5 10	12 00	20 11 58	Swansea	Pembroke B	QPR	7	—
						Newport Co	123	15
						Cardiff C	59	5
						Gillingham	128	13
						Reading	44	3
						Maidstone U	44	4
Steve Galliers	5 6	9 07	21 8 57	Fulwood	Chorley	Wimbledon	155	10
						Crystal Palace	13	—
						Wimbledon	146	5
						Bristol C (loan)	9	—
						Bristol C	68	6
						Maidstone U	8	—
Mark Golley	6 1	13 00	28 10 62	Beckenham	Sutton U	Maidstone U	45	3
Tony Sorrell	5 10	12 04	17 10 66	Bromchurch	Bishops Stortford	Maidstone U	28	3

MAIDSTONE UNITED

Foundation: First appeared as Maidstone Invicta in December 1891 playing in the Maidstone & District League and the Kent League before changing name to Maidstone United in 1897. Then employed part-time professionals until reverting to amateur status in 1927, Re-adopted professionalism when joining the Southern League in 1971.

First Football League game: 19 August, 1989, Division 4, v Peterborough U (a) L 0-1 – Beeney; Barton (Stebbing), Cooper, Berry, Golley, Pearce, Lillis (Charlery), Elsey, Sorrell, Butler, Gall.

Managers (and Secretary-managers)
Ken Spurgeon 1971, Roy Houghton 1971–72, Ernie Morgan 1972–73, Robin Stepney 1973–75, Terry Adlington 1975–77, Barry Watling 1977–80, Bill Williams 1980–85, Barry Fry 1985–86, Bill Williams 1980–85, Barry Fry 1985–86, Bill Williams 1986–87 (Continued as General Manager), John Still 1987–89, Keith Peacock 1989–   .

Player and Position	Ht	Wt	Birth Date	Birth Place	Source	Clubs	League App	Gls
Forwards								
Steve Butler	6 2	11 01	27 1 62	Birmingham	Army	Brentford	21	3
						Maidstone U	44	21
Ken Charlery	6 1	12 07	28 11 64	Stepney	Fisher Ath	Maidstone U	30	2
Mark Gall	5 10	12 00	14 5 63	Brixton	Greenwich Bor	Maidstone U	41	18
Jason Lillis	5 11	11 10	1 10 69	Chatham	Trainee	Gillingham	29	3
						Maidstone U	33	14
Howard Pritchard	5 10	12 07	18 10 58	Cardiff	Apprentice	Bristol C	38	2
						Swindon T	65	11
						Bristol C	119	22
						Gillingham	88	20
						Walsall	45	7
						Maidstone U	24	4

Trainees
Brewer, Mark A; King, Richard C; Paris, Spencer P.C; Reilly, James L; Toms, Matthew; Weaver, Stuart N.

MANCHESTER CITY 1989–90 *Back row (left to right):* Colin Hendry, Andy Hinchcliffe, Mark Seagraves, David White, Gary Megson, Paul Lake.
Centre row: Roy Bailey (Medical Trainer), Tony Book (Reserve/Youth Team Coach), Jason Beckford, Ashley Ward, Andy Dibble, Paul Cooper, Gary Fleming, Wayne Clarke.
Mick Heaton (Assistant Manager).
Front row: Alan Harper, Peter Reid, Steve Redmond (Captain). Howard Kendall (Manager), Mark Ward, Ian Brightwell, Clive Allen.

Division 1 **MANCHESTER CITY**

Maine road, Moss Side, Manchester M14 7WN. Telephone 061-226 1191/2. Ticket Office: 061-226 2224. Development Office: 061-226 3143. Clubcall: 0898 12 11 91. Ticket call: 0898 12 15 91.
Ground capacity: 48,500.
Record attendance: 84,569 v Stoke C, FA Cup 6th rd, 3 March, 1934 (British record for any game outside London or Glasgow).
Record receipts: £239,476. Everton v Liverpool, Milk Cup Final replay, 28 March, 1984.
Pitch measurements: 118yd × 76yd.
Chairman: P. J. Swales. *Vice-Charman:* F. Pye.
Directors: I. L. G. Niven, C. B. Muir OBE, M. T. Horwich, W. C. Adams, A. Thomas, G. Doyle, W. A. Miles, B. Turnbull, J. Greibach.
Secretary: Bernard Halford.
Commercial Manager: P. Critchley.
General Manager: Jimmy Frizzell. *Manager:* Howard Kendall.
Player-Coach: Peter Reid. *Assistant Manager:* Mick Heaton.
Medical Trainer: Roy Bailey.
Year formed: 1887 as Ardwick FC; 1894 as Manchester City.
Turned Professional: 1887 as Ardwick FC. *Ltd Co.:* 1894.
Nickname: Blues.
Previous Names: 1887–94, Ardwick FC (formed through the amalgamation of West Gorton and Gorton Athletic, the latter having been formed in 1880).
Previous Grounds: 1880–81, Clowes Street; 1881–82, Kirkmanshulme Cricket Ground; 1882–84, Queens Road; 1884–87, Pink Bank Lane; 1887–1923, Hyde Road (1894–1923, as City); 1923, Maine Road.
Record League Victory: 10-1 Huddersfield T, Division 2, 7 November 1987 – Nixon; Gidman, Hinchcliffe, Clements, Lake, Redmond, White (3), Stewart (3), Adcock (3), McNab (1) Simpson.
Record Cup Victory: 10-1 v Swindon T, FA Cup, 4th rd, 29 January 1930 – Barber; Felton, McCloy; Barrass, Cowan, Heinemann; Toseland, Marshall (5), Tait (3), Johnson (1), Brook (1).
Record Defeat: 1-9 v Everton, Division 1, 3 September, 1906.
Most League Points (2 for a win): 62, Division 2, 1946–47.
Most League Points (3 for a win): 82, Division 2, 1988–89.
Most League Goals: 108, Division 2, 1926–27.
Highest League Scorer in Season: Tommy Johnson, 38, Division 1, 1928–29.
Most League Goals in Total Aggregate: Tommy Johnson, 158, 1919–30.
Most Capped Player: Colin Bell, 48, England.
Most League Appearances: Alan Oakes, 565, 1959–76.
Record Transfer Fee Received: £1,700,000 from Tottenham H for Paul Stewart, June 1988.
Record Transfer Fee Paid: £1,437,500 to Wolverhampton W for Steve Daley, September 1979 (£1,150,000 basic fee).
Football League Record: 1892 Ardwick elected founder member of Division 2, 1894 Newly-formed Manchester C elected to Division 2; Division 1 1899–1902, 1903–09, 1910–26, 1928–38, 1947–50, 1951–63, 1966–83, 1985–87, 1989–; Division 2 1902–03, 1909–10, 1926–28, 1938–47, 1950–51, 1963–66, 1983–85, 1987–89.
Honours: Football League: Division 1 – Champions 1936–37, 1967–68; Runners-up 1903–04, 1920–21, 1976–77; Division 2 – Champions 1898–99, 1902–03, 1909–10, 1927–28, 1946–47, 1965–66; Runners-up 1895–96, 1950–51. *FA Cup:* Winners 1904, 1934, 1956, 1969; Runners-up 1926, 1933, 1955, 1981. *Football League Cup:* Winners 1970, 1976; Runners-up 1973–74.
European Competitions: *European Cup:* 1968–69. *European Cup-Winners' Cup:* 1969–70 (winners), 1970–71. *UEFA Cup:* 1972–73, 1976–77, 1977–78, 1978–79.
Colours: Sky blue shirts, dark blue collar, white shorts, navy blue stockings. **Change colours:** Alternate maroon and white striped shirts with fine blue stripe between, England neckline with button down neck, integral shadow diamond weave, maroon shorts with 1½″ blue stripe and white stripe, maroon stockings with sky blue diamond on turnover.

MANCHESTER CITY 1989–90 LEAGUE RECORD

Match No.	Date	Venue	Opponents	Result	H/T Score	Lg. Pos.	Goalscorers	Atten- dance
1	Aug 19	A	Liverpool	L 1-3	1-1	—	Hinchliffe	37,628
2	23	H	Southampton	L 1-2	0-1	—	Gleghorn	25,416
3	26	H	Tottenham H	D 1-1	1-1	18	White	32,004
4	30	A	Coventry C	L 1-2	1-0	—	White	16,111
5	Sept 9	H	QPR	W 1-0	1-0	18	Allen	23,420
6	16	A	Wimbledon	L 0-1	0-1	18		6815
7	23	H	Manchester U	W 5-1	3-0	13	Oldfield 2, Morley, Bishop, Hinchliffe	43,246
8	30	H	Luton T	W 3-1	2-1	10	Oldfield, Bishop, Brightwell	23,863
9	Oct 14	A	Arsenal	L 0-4	0-1	14		40,414
10	22	H	Aston Villa	L 0-2	0-1	—		23,354
11	28	A	Chelsea	D 1-1	0-0	16	Allen	21,917
12	Nov 4	H	Crystal Palace	W 3-0	2-0	14	White, Morley, Allen	23,768
13	11	A	Derby Co	L 0-6	0-2	18		19,239
14	18	H	Nottingham F	L 0-3	0-2	19		26,238
15	25	A	Charlton Ath	D 1-1	1-1	19	Allen	8857
16	Dec 2	H	Liverpool	L 1-4	0-1	20	Allen (pen)	31,641
17	9	A	Southampton	L 1-2	1-0	20	Allen	15,832
18	17	A	Everton	D 0-0	0-0	—		21,737
19	26	H	Norwich C	W 1-0	0-0	19	Allen	29,534
20	30	H	Millwall	W 2-0	1-0	16	White 2	28,084
21	Jan 1	A	Sheffield W	L 0-2	0-1	18		28,756
22	13	A	Tottenham H	D 1-1	0-1	17	Hendry	26,384
23	20	H	Coventry C	W 1-0	0-0	14	White	24,345
24	Feb 3	A	Manchester U	D 1-1	0-0	14	Brightwell	40,274
25	10	H	Wimbledon	D 1-1	0-0	16	Hendry	24,126
26	24	H	Charlton Ath	L 1-2	0-0	17	White	24,030
27	Mar 3	A	Nottingham F	L 0-1	0-0	17		22,644
28	10	H	Arsenal	D 1-1	1-0	18	White	29,087
29	17	A	Luton T	D 1-1	0-0	18	Allen (pen)	9765
30	21	H	Chelsea	D 1-1	1-1	—	Quinn	24,670
31	Apr 1	A	Aston Villa	W 2-1	1-1	—	Ward, Reid	24,797
32	7	A	Millwall	D 1-1	0-1	17	Ward	10,265
33	11	A	QPR	W 3-1	1-1	—	Allen, Hendry, Ward	8437
34	14	H	Sheffield W	W 2-1	1-0	15	Quinn, Heath	33,022
35	16	A	Norwich C	W 1-0	1-0	13	Heath	18,914
36	21	H	Everton	W 1-0	0-0	13	Quinn	32,144
37	28	H	Derby Co	L 0-1	0-0	13		29,542
38	May 5	A	Crystal Palace	D 2-2	0-2	14	Allen (pen), Quinn	20,056

Final League Position: 14

GOALSCORERS

League (43): Allen 10 (3 pens), White 8, Quinn 4, Hendry 3, Oldfield 3, Ward 3, Bishop 2, Brightwell 2, Heath 2, Hinchliffe 2, Morley 2, Gleghorn 1, Reid 1.
Littlewoods Cup (8): Morley 2, Oldfield 2, White 2, Allen 1, Bishop 1.
FA Cup (2): Hendry 1, Lake 1.

Dibble	Lake	Hinchcliffe	Bishop	Gayle	Redmond	Oldfield	Allen	Morley	McNab	Gleghorn	White	Fleming	Cooper	Brightwell	Beckford	Fashanu	Hendry	Seagraves	Taggart	Ward M	Harper	Reid	Megson	Clarke	Heath	Quinn	Ward A	Match No.
1	2	3	4	5	6	7*	8	9	10	11	12																	1
1	2	3	4†	5	6	7	8	9*	10	11	12	14																2
	11	3	4	5	6		8	9	10		7	2	1															3
		3	4	5	6		8	9	10		7	2	1	11														4
	11*	3	4	5	6		8	9	10		7	2	1	12														5
	11	3	4	5	6		8	9	10*		7	2	1	12														6
	11*	3	4	5	6		8	9			7	2	1	10	12													7
	11*	3	4	5	6		8	9		12	7	2	1	10														8
	11	3	4	5	6		8	9		12	7	2*	1	10														9
1	11	3	4†	5	6		8	9		12	7	2		10*	14													10
1	11	3*	4	5	6		8	9	10	12	7	2																11
1	11	3	4	5	6		8	9	10		7	2																12
1		3	4	5	6		8	9	10		7	2*		11†	12	14												13
1		3	4		6		8	9	10		7	2		11			5											14
1		3	4	8	6			9*	10	12	7	2		11			5											15
1	11		4		6		8	9		12	7			10			5	2	3*									16
1	11	3	4		6		10*	9		8	7						5	2									12	17
1		3	14		6		8*	9†		12	7						11		5				2	4	10			18
1	11	3	8		6			9*		12	7			14					5				2	4	10†			19
1	11	3			6			9			7			12					5			8	2	4*	10			20
1	11	3			6			9*		12	7			14					5			8	2	4	10†			21
1	11	3			6			9*			7			14					5			8	2	4†	10	12		22
1	11	3			6						7			14	12				5			8	2*	4	10†	9		23
1	11	3			6						7			4	12				5			8	2		10	9*		24
1	11*	3			6					12	7			4					5			8	2		10	9		25
1	11	3			6*						7			14					5			8	2	4†	10	9	12	26
1	11	3			6						7			14					5			8	2	4†	10*	12	9	27
1	11	3			6					12	7								5			8*	2	4	10	9		28
1	4*	3			6			9			7			14					5			8	2		10†	12	11	29
1		3			6			9			7								5			8	2	4	11	10		30
1	2				6			9†			7			14					5			8	3	4	11	12	10*	31
1	2				6			9†			7			14					5			8	3	4	11*	12	10	32
1	2				6			9*			7			14					5			8	3	4	11	12	10†	33
1	2†				6			9*			7			14					5			8	3	4	11	12	10	34
1	14				6			9†			7	2							5			8	3	4	11	12	10*	35
1	14				6						7*	2			12				5			8	3	4	11†	9	10	36
1	11				6					12	7	2							5*			8	3	4		9	10	37
1	11	14			6					12	7*	2†							5			8	3	4		9	10	38

Appearances:
31 31 28 18 14 38 10 23 17 11 2 35 13 7 14 1 — 10 — 25 2 1 19 21 18 19 4 7 9 —
+ + + + + + + + +
3s 1s 5s 7s 1s 2s 1s 14s 4s2s 5s 5s 1s

Littlewoods Cup	Second Round	Brentford (a)	1-2
		(h)	4-1
	Third Round	Norwich C (h)	3-1
	Fourth Round	Coventry C (h)	0-1
FA Cup	Third Round	Millwall (h)	0-0
		(a)	1-1
		(a)	1-3

MANCHESTER CITY

Player and Position	Ht	Wt	Birth Date	Place	Source	Clubs	League App	Gls
Goalkeepers								
Paul Cooper	5 11	13 10	21 12 53	Brierley Hill	Apprentice	Birmingham C	17	—
						Ipswich T	447	—
						Leicester C	56	—
						Manchester C	15	—
Andy Dibble	6 2	13 07	8 5 65	Cwmbran	Apprentice	Cardiff C	62	—
						Luton T	30	—
						Sunderland (loan)	12	—
						Huddersfield T (loan)	5	—
						Manchester C	69	—
Defenders								
Colin Hendry	6 1	12 02	7 12 65	Keith	Islavale	Dundee	41	2
						Blackburn R	102	22
						Manchester C	25	3
Andy Hinchcliffe	5 10	12 10	5 2 69	Manchester	Apprentice	Manchester C	112	8
Neil Lennon*	5 9	11 06	25 6 71	Lurgan	Trainee	Manchester C	1	—
Steve Redmond	5 11	12 13	2 11 67	Liverpool	Apprentice	Manchester C	167	3
Mark Seagraves	6 1	12 10	22 10 66	Bootle	Local	Liverpool	—	—
						Norwich C (loan)	3	—
						Manchester C	42	—
Midfield								
David Brightwell	6 1	13 05	7 1 71	Lutterworth		Manchester C	—	—
Ian Brightwell	5 10	11 07	9 4 68	Lutterworth	Trainee	Manchester C	103	14
Alan Harper	5 8	10 09	1 11 60	Liverpool	Apprentice	Liverpool	—	—
						Everton	127	4
						Sheffield W	35	—
						Manchester C	21	—
Michael Hughes	5 6	10 08	2 8 71	Larne	Carrick R	Manchester C	1	—
Paul Kelly			6 3 71	Urmston	Trainee	Manchester C	—	—
Paul Lake	6 0	12 02	28 10 68	Manchester	Trainee	Manchester C	105	7
Gary Megson	5 10	11 06	2 5 59	Manchester	Apprentice	Plymouth Arg	78	10
						Everton	22	2
						Sheffield W	123	13
						Nottingham F	—	—
						Newcastle U	24	1
						Sheffield W	110	12
						Manchester C	41	1
Mike Quigley	5 6	9 04	2 10 70	Manchester	Trainee	Manchester C	—	—
Peter Reid	5 8	10 07	20 6 56	Huyton	Apprentice	Bolton W	225	23
						Everton	159	8
						QPR	29	1
						Manchester C	18	1
Ian Thompstone	6 0	11 03	17 1 71		Trainee	Manchester C	1	1
Michael Wallace	5 8	10 02	5 10 70	Farnworth	Trainee	Manchester C	—	—
Mark Ward	5 6	9 12	10 10 62	Prescot	Apprentice Northwich V	Everton	—	—
						Oldham Ath	84	12
						West Ham U	165	12
						Manchester C	19	3
Forwards								
Clive Allen	5 10	12 03	20 5 61	London	Apprentice	QPR	49	32
						Arsenal	—	—
						Crystal Palace	25	9
						QPR	87	40
						Tottenham H	105	60
					Bordeaux	Manchester C	30	10
Jason Beckford	5 9	12 04	14 2 70	Manchester	Trainee	Manchester C	18	1

MANCHESTER CITY

Foundation: Manchester City was formed as a Limited Company in 1894 after their predecessors Ardwick had been forced into bankruptcy. However, many historians like to trace the club's lineage as far back as 1880 when St. Mark's Church, West Gorton added a football section to their cricket club. They amalgamated with Gorton Athletic in 1884 as Gorton FC. Because of a change of ground they became Ardwick in 1887.

First Football League game: 3 September, 1892, Division 2, v Bootle (h) W 7-0 – Douglas; McVickers, Robson; Middleton, Russell, Hopkins; Davies (3), Morris (2), Angus (1), Weir (1), Milarvie.

Managers (and Secretary-managers)
Joshua Parlby 1894–95*, Sam Omerod 1895–1902, Tom Maley 1902–06, Harry Newbould 1906–12, Ernest Magnall 1912–24, David Ashworth 1924–25, Peter Hodge 1926–32, Wilf Wild 1932–46 (continued as secretary to 1950), Sam Cowan 1946–47, John "Jock" Thomson 1947–50, Leslie McDowall 1950–63, George Poyser 1963–65, Joe Mercer 1965–71 (continued as GM to 1972), Malcolm Allison 1972–73, Johnny Hart 1973, Ron Saunders 1973–74, Tony Book 1974–79, Malcolm Allison 1979–80, John Bond 1980–83, John Benson 1983, Billy McNeill 1983–86, Jimmy Frizzell 1986–87 (continued as GM), Mel Machin 1987–89, Howard Kendall 1990–   .

Player and Position	Ht	Wt	Birth Date	Place	Source	Clubs	League App	Gls
Wayne Clarke	6 0	11 08	28 2 61	Wolverhampton	Apprentice	Wolverhampton W	148	30
						Birmingham C	92	38
						Everton	57	18
						Leicester C	11	1
						Manchester C	9	—
Adrian Heath	5 6	10 01	11 1 61	Stoke	Apprentice	Stoke C	95	16
						Everton	226	71
					Espanol	Aston Villa	9	—
						Manchester C	12	2
Niall Quinn	6 4	12 04	6 10 66	Dublin	Eire Youth	Arsenal	67	14
						Manchester C	9	4
Ashley Ward	6 1	11 07	24 11 70	Middleton	Trainee	Manchester C	1	—
David White	6 1	12 09	30 10 67	Manchester		Manchester C	150	28
Darren Wilson‡			30 9 71	Manchester		Manchester C	—	—

Trainees
Agius, Mark S; Davies, Allan; Dyer, Simon R; Flitcroft, Gary W; Graham, Andrew G; Jackson, Robert G; Locke, Stuart J; McCullough, Ronald K; Margetson, Martyn W; Mulvey, Eamon M; Peters, Mark; Sheron, Michael N; Williams, Paul J; Wills, John; Wilson, Darren A.

Associated Schoolboys
Beech, Christopher; Bell, Stephen J; Callaghan, Matthew; Downer, Lee J; Edghill, Richard; Hughes, Robert M; Ingram, Rae; Lydiate, Joseph L; McDowell, Stephen A; McHugh, Darren R; Murray, William A; Roe, David; Smith, Daniel S; Thomas, Scott L; Turner, David E.

Associated Schoolboys who have accepted the club's offer of a Traineeship/Contract
Bibby, Richard; Foster, John C; Foster, Matthew R; Harkin, Sean C; Lewis, Ian R; Lomas, Steven; Mike, Adrian.

MANCHESTER UNITED 1989–90 *Back row (left to right):* Viv Anderson, Neil Webb, Mike Duxbury, Billy Garton, Lee Sharpe, Mike Phelan, Lee Martin, Mal Donaghy, Steve Bruce.
Centre row: Jim McGregor (Physiotherapist), Archie Knox (Assistant Manager), Guiliano Maiorana, Gary Walsh, Jim Leighton, David Wilson, Russell Beardsmore, Norman Davies (Kit Manager).
Front row: Mark Robins, Tony Gill, Colin Gibson, Bryan Robson, Alex Ferguson (Manager), Brian McClair, Mark Hughes, Clayton Blackmore, Ralph Milne.

Division 1   **MANCHESTER UNITED**

Old Trafford, Manchester M16 0RA. Telephone 061-872 1661. Ticket and Match Information: 061-872 0199. Membership enquiries: 061-872 5208. Souvenir shop: 061-872 3398.
Ground capacity: 50,726.
Record attendance: 76,962 Wolverhampton W v Grimsby T, FA Cup semi-final. 25 March, 1939.
Club record: 70,504 v Aston Villa, Division 1, 27 December, 1920.
Record receipts: £232,173.70 v Nottingham F, FA Cup 6th rd, 18 March, 1989.
Pitch measurements: 116yd × 76yd.
President: Sir Matt Busby CBE, KCSG.
Vice-Presidents: J. A. Gibson, W. A. Young, J. G. Gulliver, R. L. Edwards.
Chairman/Chief Executive: C. M. Edwards.
Directors: J. M. Edelson, R. Charlton CBE, E. M. Watkins LL.M., A. M. Midani, N. Burrows, R. L. Olive, M. Knighton.
Manager: Alex Ferguson. *Assistant Manager/Coach:* Archie Knox.
Secretary: Kenneth Merrett.
Commercial Manager: D. A. McGregor.
Physio: Jim McGregor.
Year Formed: 1878 as Newton Heath LYR; 1902, Manchester United.
Turned Professional: 1885. *Ltd Co.:* 1907.
Previous Name: Newton Heath, 1880–1902. *Nickname:* 'Red Devils'.
Previous Grounds: 1880–93, North Road, Monsall Road; 1893, Bank Street; 1910, Old Trafford (played at Maine Rd 1941–49).
Record League Victory: 10-1 v Wolverhampton W, Division 2, 15 October 1892 – Warner; Mitchell, Clements; Perrins, Stewart (3), Erentz; Farman (1), Hood (1), Donaldson (3), Carson (1), Hendry (1).
Record Cup Victory: 10-0 v RSC Anderlecht, European Cup, Prel. rd (2nd leg), 26 September 1956 – Wood; Foulkes; Byrne; Colman, Jones, Edwards; Berry (1), Whelan (2), Taylor (3), Viollet (4), Pegg.
Record Defeat: 0-7 v Blackburn R, Division 1, 10 April, 1926 and v Aston Villa, Division 1, 27 December, 1930 and v Wolverhampton W. Division 2, 26 December, 1931.
Most League Points (2 for a win): 64, Division 1, 1956–57.
Most League Points (3 for a win): 81, Division 1, 1987–88.
Most League Goals: 103, Division 1, 1956–57 and 1958–59.
Highest League Scorer in Season: Dennis Viollet, 32, 1959–60.
Most League Goals in Total Aggregate: Bobby Charlton, 199, 1956–73.
Most Capped Player: Bobby Charlton, 106, England.
Most League Appearances: Bobby Charlton, 606, 1956–73.
Record Transfer Fee Received: £1,800,000 from Barcelona for Mark Hughes, August 1986.
Record Transfer Fee Paid: £2,300,000 to Middlesbrough for Gary Pallister, August 1989.
Football League Record: 1892 Newton Heath elected to Division 1; 1894–1906 Division 2; 1906–22 Division 1; 1922–25 Division 2; 1925–31 Division 1; 1931–36 Division 2; 1936–37 Division 1; 1937–38 Division 2; 1938–74 Division 1; 1974–75 Division 2; 1975– Division 1.
Honours: Football League: Division 1 – Champions 1907–8, 1910–11, 1951–52, 1955–56, 1956–57, 1964–65, 1966–67; Runners-up 1946–47, 1947–48, 1948–49, 1950–51, 1958–59, 1963–64, 1967–68, 1979–80, 1987–88. Division 2 – Champions 1935–36, 1974–75; Runners-up 1896–97, 1905–06, 1924–25, 1937–38. *FA Cup:* Winners 1909, 1948, 1963, 1977, 1983, 1985, 1990 (7 wins stands as the joint record); Runners-up 1957, 1958, 1976, 1979, *League Cup:* 1982–83 (Runners-up). European Competitions: *European Cup:* 1956–57 (s-f), 1957-58 (s-f), 1965–66 (s-f), 1967–68 (winners), 1968–69 (s-f). *European Cup-Winners' Cup:* 1963–64, 1977–78, 1983–84. *European Fairs Cup:* 1964–65. *UEFA Cup:* 1976–77, 1980–81, 1982–83, 1984–85.
Colours: Red shirts, white shorts, black stockings. **Change colours:** Royal blue on white shirts, navy/royal blue shorts, navy stockings.

MANCHESTER UNITED 1989–90 LEAGUE RECORD

Match No.	Date		Venue	Opponents	Result	H/T Score	Lg. Pos.	Goalscorers	Atten- dance
1	Aug	19	H	Arsenal	W 4-1	1-1	—	Bruce, Hughes, Webb, McClair	47,245
2		22	A	Crystal Palace	D 1-1	1-0	—	Robson	22,423
3		26	A	Derby Co	L 0-2	0-1	9		22,175
4		30	H	Norwich C	L 0-2	0-1	—		39,610
5	Sept	9	A	Everton	L 2-3	0-1	16	McClair, Beardsmore	37,916
6		16	H	Millwall	W 5-1	2-1	11	Hughes 3, Robson, Sharpe	42,746
7		23	A	Manchester C	L 1-5	0-3	14	Hughes	43,246
8	Oct	14	H	Sheffield W	D 0-0	0-0	17		41,492
9		21	A	Coventry C	W 4-1	2-0	14	Bruce, Hughes 2, Phelan	19,605
10		28	H	Southampton	W 2-1	1-1	11	McClair 2	37,122
11	Nov	4	A	Charlton Ath	L 0-2	0-0	13		16,065
12		12	H	Nottingham F	W 1-0	1-0	—	Pallister	34,182
13		18	A	Luton T	W 3-1	2-0	9	Wallace, Blackmore, Hughes	11,141
14		25	H	Chelsea	D 0-0	0-0	10		47,106
15	Dec	3	A	Arsenal	L 0-1	0-1	—		34,484
16		9	H	Crystal Palace	L 1-2	1-1	12	Beardsmore	33,514
17		16	H	Tottenham H	L 0-1	0-0	13		36,230
18		23	A	Liverpool	D 0-0	0-0	—		37,426
19		26	A	Aston Villa	L 0-3	0-0	15		41,247
20		30	A	Wimbledon	D 2-2	0-1	15	Hughes, Robins	9622
21	Jan	1	H	QPR	D 0-0	0-0	15		34,824
22		13	H	Derby Co	L 1-2	0-1	15	Pallister	38,985
23		21	A	Norwich C	L 0-2	0-0	—		17,370
24	Feb	3	H	Manchester C	D 1-1	0-0	17	Blackmore	40,274
25		10	A	Millwall	W 2-1	0-1	15	Wallace, Hughes	15,491
26		24	A	Chelsea	L 0-1	0-1	16		29,979
27	Mar	3	H	Luton T	W 4-1	3-0	16	McClair, Hughes, Wallace, Robins	35,327
28		14	H	Everton	D 0-0	0-0	—		37,398
29		18	H	Liverpool	L 1-2	0-1	—	Whelan (og)	46,629
30		21	A	Sheffield W	L 0-1	0-1	—		33,260
31		24	A	Southampton	W 2-0	0-0	16	Gibson, Robins	20,510
32		31	H	Coventry C	W 3-0	2-0	16	Hughes 2, Robins	39,172
33	Apr	14	A	QPR	W 2-1	0-1	14	Robins, Webb	18,997
34		17	H	Aston Villa	W 2-0	2-0	—	Robins 2	44,080
35		21	A	Tottenham H	L 1-2	0-2	14	Bruce (pen)	33,317
36		30	H	Wimbledon	D 0-0	0-0	—		29,281
37	May	2	A	Nottingham F	L 0-4	0-4	—		21,186
38		5	H	Charlton Ath	W 1-0	1-0	13	Pallister	35,389

Final League Position: 13

GOALSCORERS

League (46): Hughes 13, Robins 7, McClair 5, Bruce 3 (1 pen), Pallister 3, Wallace 3, Beardsmore 2, Blackmore 2, Robson 2, Webb 2, Gibson 1, Phelan 1, Sharpe 1, own goal 1.
Littlewoods Cup (3): Ince 2, Wallace 1.
FA Cup (15): McClair 3, Robins 3, Hughes 2, Robson 2, Wallace 2, Blackmore 1, Martin 1, Webb 1.

Leighton	Duxbury	Blackmore	Bruce	Phelan	Donaghy	Robson	Webb	McClair	Hughes	Sharpe	Martin	Graham	Pallister	Robins	Anderson	Beardsmore	Ince	Wallace	Maiorana	Milne	Brazil	Gibson	Sealey	Bosnich	Match No.
1	2	3	4	5	6	7	8	9	10	11*	12														1
1	2	3	4	5	6	7	8	9	10	11															2
1	2	6	4	5		7	8	9	10	11	3*	12													3
1	2	3†	4	5		7*	8	9	10	11	12		6	14											4
1	2*	8	4	5	7			9	10	11	3†		6		12	14									5
1	12		4†	5	3	7		9	10	11			6		2	14	8*								6
1			4	5	3			9	10	12			6		2	7*	8	11							7
1	2*		4	5	3	7		9	10	14	12		6				8	11†							8
1	12		4	5	2	7		9	10	11†	3		6				8*		14						9
1		12	4	5	2	7		9	10	11	3		6				8*								10
1		12	4	5	2†	7		9	10	11*	3		6				8	14							11
1		2	4	5		7		9	10	12	3		6				8	11*							12
1		2	4	5		7		9	10		3		6				8	11							13
1	12	2	4	5		7		9	10		3*		6		14		8	11†							14
1		2*	4	5		7		9	10		3		6		12		8	11							15
1		14	4	5†	7			9	10*	12	3		6		2		8	11							16
1		14	4*	5	7			9	10		3		6	12	2†		8	11							17
1		2	4	5		7		9	10	12	3		6				8	11*							18
1	12	7†	4	5				9	10	11	3*		6	14	2		8								19
1		7	4	5				9	10	12	3		6	11	2		8*								20
1	12	8†	4	5				9	10	7*	3		6	11	2	14									21
1	12	8*	4	5				9	10		3		6	11	2	7†			14						22
1		14	4	5†				9	10		3		6	7	2	12	8*	11							23
1	8	7		5	4*			9	10		3		6	14	2	12		11†							24
1	8	7†		5				9	10		3		6	14	2*	4		11		12					25
1		7*	4	5	14			9	10		3		6		2†	12	8	11							26
1			4	5				9	10		3		6	7	2	12	8	11*							27
1	2	14	4	5				9	10*		3		6	7†		12	8	11							28
1	12	7	4	5				9	10		3		6		2*	14	8	11†							29
1	11*		4	5	2			9	10		3		6	7†	12	14						8			30
1			4	5	2	12		9	10†		3		6			14	8	11				7*			31
1			4	5	2*	7		9	10	12	3		6			14	8	11†				3			32
			4*	5		7	8	9	10†		3		6	14	2			11		12			1		33
		14		5		7	8	9	10				6	4	2*	12		11				3†	1		34
1		14	4	5		7	8†	9	10		3		6		2	12		11*							35
		14	4	5					10		3		6	9*	2	7	8	11†		12				1	36
1	2	3	4	5			8	9	10				6			7		11							37
1			4	5		7	8	9	10		3		6		2			11							38
35	12	19	34	38	13	20	10	37	36	13	28	—	35	10	14	8	25	23	—	—	—	5	2	1	
	+	+						+		+		+		+	+	+	+	+		+	+	+			
	7s	9s			1s			1s		1s		1s		5s	4s	1s	7s	2s	13s	1s	3s	1s	1s	1s	

Littlewoods Cup	Second Round	Portsmouth (a)	3-2
		(h)	0-0
	Third Round	Tottenham H (h)	0-3
FA Cup	Third Round	Nottingham F (a)	1-0
	Fourth Round	Hereford U (a)	1-0
	Fifth Round	Newcastle U (a)	3-2
	Sixth Round	Sheffield U (a)	1-0
	Semi-final	Oldham Ath	3-3
		(at Maine Road)	
	Replay	(at Maine Road)	2-1
	Final	Crystal Palace	
		(at Wembley)	3-3
	Replay	(at Wembley)	1-0

MANCHESTER UNITED

Player and Position	Ht	Wt	Birth Date	Birth Place	Source	Clubs	League App	Gls
Goalkeepers								
Mark Bosnich†			13 1 72	Sydney, Australia		Manchester U	1	—
Jim Leighton	6 1	12 08	24 7 58	Johnstone	Dalry T	Aberdeen	300	—
						Manchester U	73	—
Gary Walsh	6 1	12 12	21 3 68	Wigan		Manchester U	30	—
						Airdrie (loan)	3	—
Defenders								
Viv Anderson	6 0	11 01	29 8 56	Nottingham	Apprentice	Nottingham F	328	15
						Arsenal	120	9
						Manchester U	53	2
Derek Brazil	6 0	12 00	14 12 68	Dublin	Rivermount BC	Manchester U	2	—
Steve Bruce	6 0	12 06	31 12 60	Newcastle	Apprentice	Gillingham	205	29
						Norwich C	141	14
						Manchester U	93	7
Brian Carey			31 5 68		Cork C	Manchester U	—	—
Mal Donaghy	5 10	12 07	13 9 57	Belfast	Larne	Luton T	410	16
						Manchester U	44	—
						Luton T (loan)	5	—
Mike Duxbury*	5 9	11 02	1 9 59	Accrington	Apprentice	Manchester U	299	6
Billy Garton (Retired)	5 11	11 08	15 3 65	Salford	Apprentice	Manchester U	41	—
						Birmingham C (loan)	5	—
Colin Gibson	5 8	10 08	6 4 60	Bridport	Apprentice	Aston Villa	185	10
						Manchester U	79	9
Tony Gill	5 9	10 00	6 3 68	Bradford	Apprentice	Manchester U	10	1
Lee Martin	5 11	11 05	5 2 68	Hyde		Manchester U	57	1
Gary Pallister	6 4	13 00	30 6 65	Ramsgate	Billingham	Middlesbrough	156	5
						Darlington (loan)	7	—
						Manchester U	35	3
Midfield								
Russell Beardsmore	5 6	8 10	28 9 68	Wigan	Apprentice	Manchester U	44	4
Clayton Blackmore	5 9	11 03	23 9 64	Neath	Apprentice	Manchester U	104	12
Wayne Bullimore	5 9	10 06	12 9 70	Sutton-in-Ashfield	Trainee	Manchester U	—	—
Paul Ince	5 11	11 06	21 10 67	Ilford	Trainee	West Ham U	72	7
						Manchester U	26	—
Paul McGuinness	5 7	11 05	2 3 66	Manchester	Local	Manchester U	—	—
						Crewe Alex	13	—
						Manchester U	—	—
Ralph Milne	5 9	12 00	13 5 61	Dundee	School	Dundee U	179	44
						Charlton Ath	22	—
						Bristol C	30	6
						Manchester U	23	3
						West Ham U (loan)	—	—
Mike Phelan	5 11	12 03	24 9 62	Nelson	Apprentice	Burnley	168	9
						Norwich C	156	9
						Manchester U	38	1
Bryan Robson	5 11	11 12	11 1 57	Chester-Le-Street	Apprentice	WBA	197	39
						Manchester U	272	67
Lee Sharpe	5 11	11 04	27 5 71	Birmingham	Trainee	Torquay U	14	3
						Manchester U	40	1
John Shotton*	5 8	10 06	17 8 71	Hartlepool	Trainee	Manchester U	—	—
Neil Webb	6 1	13 02	30 7 63	Reading	Apprentice	Reading	72	22
						Portsmouth	123	34
						Nottingham F	146	47
						Manchester U	11	2
David Wilson	5 9	10 10	20 3 69	Burnley	Apprentice	Manchester U	4	—
Paul Wratten	5 7	9 13	29 11 70	Middlesbrough	Trainee	Manchester U	—	—

MANCHESTER UNITED

Foundation: Manchester United was formed as comparatively recently as 1902 after their predecessors, Newton Heath, went bankrupt. However, it is usual to give the date of the club's foundation as 1878 when employees of the Lancashire and Yorkshire Railway Company formed Newton Heath L and YR. Cricket and Football Club. They won the Manchester Cup in 1886 and as Newton Heath FC were admitted to the Second Division in 1892.

First Football League game: 3 September, 1892, Division 1, v Blackburn R (a) L 3–4 – Warner; Clements, Brown; Perrins, Stewart, Erentz; Farman (1), Coupar (1), Donaldson (1), Carson, Mathieson.

Managers (and Secretary-managers)
Ernest Magnall 1900–12, John Robson 1914–21, John Chapman 1921–26, Clarence Hildrith 1926–27, Herbert Bamlett 1927–31, Walter Crickmer 1931–32, Scott Duncan 1932–37, Jimmy Porter 1938–44, Walter Crickmer 1944–45*, Matt Busby 1945–69 (continued as GM then Director), Wilf McGuinness 1969–70, Frank O'Farrell 1971–72, Tommy Docherty 1972–77, Dave Sexton 1977–81, Ron Atkinson 1981–86, Alex Ferguson 1986– .

Player and Position	Ht	Wt	Birth Date	Place	Source	Clubs	League App	Gls
Forwards								
Deiniol Graham	5 10	10 05	4 10 69	Cannock	Trainee	Manchester U	2	—
Mark Hughes	5 8	12 05	1 11 63	Wrexham	Apprentice	Manchester U	89	37
					Barcelona	Manchester U	75	27
Brian McClair	5 9	12 02	8 12 63	Airdrie	Apprentice	Aston Villa	—	—
						Motherwell	39	15
						Celtic	145	99
						Manchester U	115	39
Giuliano Maiorana	5 9	11 08	18 4 69	Cambridge	Histon	Manchester U	7	—
Andy Rammell	5 10	11 07	10 2 67	Nuneaton	Atherstone U	Manchester U	—	—
Mark Robins	5 7	10 01	22 12 69	Ashton-under-Lyme	Apprentice	Manchester U	27	7
Danny Wallace	5 4	10 06	21 1 64	London	Apprentice	Southampton	155	64
						Manchester U	26	3

Trainees
Baggaley, Phillip J; Brameld, Marcus J; Carter, Stephen G; Costa, Lee A; Ferguson, Darren; Gordon, Mark; Lawton, Craig T; Lydiate, Jason L; McAuley, Sean; McKee, Colin; McReavie, Alan S; Pollitt, Michael F; Potts, Leslie A; Sallis, Roger J; Sharples, John B; Shields, James J; Sixsmith, Paul; Smyth, Peter W; Stanger, Jonathan N; Taylor, Christopher; Toal, Kieran M; Tonge, Alan J; Wilkinson, Ian M.

**Non-Contract
Bosnich, Mark J.

Associated Schoolboys
Appleton, Michael A; Barnes, Lee M; Bates, Simon; Beckham, David R.J; Brown, Karl D; Butt, Nicholas; Devine, Paul V; Edwards, Marc; Gillespie, Keith R; Hemmings, Marvin; Kirby, Dean J; Lacey, Nicholas; McShane, Patrick; Mitton, Paul J; Monaghan, Matthew S; Murdoch, Colin J; Neville, Gary A; O'Kane, John A; O'Keefe, Paul; Parkin, Daniel J; Rawlinson, Mark D; Roberts, Joseph; Ryan, Mark; Savage, Robert W; Scholes, Paul; Thornley, Benjamin L; Twynam, Gary S.

Associated Schoolboys who have accepted the club's offer of a Traineeship/Contract
Burke, Raphael E; Davies, Simon I; Giggs, Ryan J; Gough, Paul; Noone, Andrew C; Switzer, George; Taylor, Leonard A; Telford, Colin L.

**Non-Contract Players who are retained must be re-signed before they are eligible to play in League matches.

354

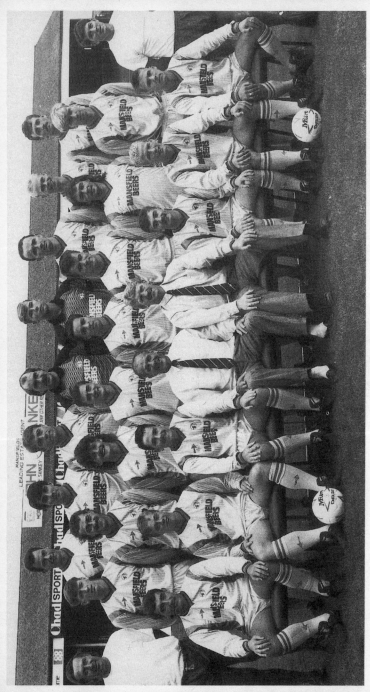

MANSFIELD TOWN 1989–90 *Back row (left to right):* Steve Charles, Tony Lowery, David Hunt, Brian Cox, Jason Pearcey, Trevor Christie, Steve Williams, Mark Kearney (Captain). *Centre row:* Kevin Randall (Youth Team Coach), Steve Chambers, Kevin Kent, Craig McKernon, Shane Reddish, Ian Stringfellow, David Hodges, Tony Kenworthy, Simon Coleman, Dennis Pettit (Physiotherapist). *Front row:* Steve Prindiville, Graham Leishman, Gary McDonald, Bill Dearden (Assistant Manager), George Foster (Manager/Player), Ian Hathaway, Mark Place, Tony Clarke.

Division 3 **MANSFIELD TOWN**

Field Mill Ground, Quarry Lane, Mansield. Telepone Mansfield (0623) 23567. Commercial Office: 0623 658070. Fax: 0623-25014

Ground capacity: 10,468.

Record attendance: 24,467 v Nottingham F, FA Cup 3rd rd, 10 Jan, 1953.

Record receipts: £33,321 v Wimbledon, FA Cup 4th rd, 30 Jan, 1988.

Pitch measurements: 115yd × 72yd.

Chairman: J. W. Pratt. *Vice-Chairman:* J. B. Almond JP

Directors: G. Hall, J. A. Brown.

Player-Manager: George Foster. *Assistant Manager/Coach:* Bill Dearden.

Coach: Bill Dearden. *Physio:* Dennis Pettitt.

Secretary: J. D. Eaton. *Commercial Manager:* J.Slater.

Year Formed: 1910. *Turned Professional:* 1910. *Ltd Co.:* 1910.

Previous name: Mansfield Wesleyans 1891–1910.

Club Nickname: 'The Stags'.

Record League Victory: 9-2 v Rotherham U, Division 3(N), 27 December 1932 – Wilson; Anthony, England; Davies, Robinson (S), Slack; Prior, Broom, Readman (3), Hoyland (3), Bowater (3).

Record Cup Victory: 8-0 v Scarborough (away), FA Cup, 1st rd, 22 November 1952 – Bramley; Chessell, Bradley; Field, Plummer, Lewis; Scott, Fox (3), Marron (2), Sid Watson (1), Adam (2).

Record Defeat: 1-8 v Walsall, Division 3(N), 19 January, 1933.

Most League Points (2 for a win): 68, Division 4, 1974–75.

Most League Points (3 for a win): 81, Division 4, 1985–86.

Most League Goals: 108, Division 4, 1962–63.

Highest League Scorer in Season: Ted Harston, 55, Division 3(N), 1936–37.

Most League Goals in Total Aggregate: Harry Johnson, 104, 1931–36.

Most Capped Player: John McClelland, 6 (53), Northern Ireland.

Most League Appearances: Rod Arnold, 440, 1970–83.

Record Transfer Fee Received: £500,000 from Middlesbrough for Simon Coleman, September 1989.

Record Transfer Fee Paid: £80,000 to Leicester C for Steve Wilkinson, September 1989.

Football League Record: 1931 Elected to Division 3(S); 1932–37 Division 3(N); 1937–47 Division 3(S); 1947–58 Division 3(N); 1958–60 Division 3; 1960–63 Division 4; 1963–72 Division 3; 1972–75 Division 4; 1975–77 Division 3; 1977–78 Division 2; 1978–80 Division 3, 1980–86 Division 4; 1986– Division 3.

Honours: Football League: Division 2 best season: 21st 1977–78; Division 3 – Champions 1976–77; Division 4 – Champions 1974–75; Division 3(N) – Runners-up 1950–51. *FA Cup* best season: 6th rd, 1968–69. *Football League Cup* Best season: 5th rd, 1975–76. *Freight Rover Trophy* – Winners 1986–87.

Colours: Amber shirts, blue shorts, amber stockings. **Change colours:** Green shirt, white shorts, white stockings.

356

MANSFIELD TOWN 1989–90 LEAGUE RECORD

Match No.	Date	Venue	Opponents	Result	H/T Score	Lg. Pos.	Goalscorers	Attendance
1	Aug 19	A	Chester C	W 2-0	1-0	—	Charles, Christie	2293
2	26	H	Bristol R	L 0-1	0-0	11		3050
3	Sept 2	A	Fulham	L 0-1	0-0	16		4551
4	9	H	Cardiff C	W 1-0	0-0	13	Charles	2766
5	16	A	Bury	L 0-3	0-3	15		2821
6	23	H	Blackpool	L 0-3	0-2	18		2629
7	30	A	Bolton W	D 1-1	0-1	20	Charles	5797
8	Oct 7	A	Shrewsbury T	W 1-0	0-0	17	Kent	3148
9	14	H	Walsall	L 0-2	0-0			3229
10	16	A	Tranmere R	D 1-1	0-0	—	Charles (pen)	6909
11	21	H	Bristol C	W 1-0	1-0	18	Christie	2957
12	24	H	Swansea C	W 4-0	0-0	—	Kent, Stringfellow 2, Christie	2643
13	28	A	Reading	L 0-1	0-0	13		3242
14	31	A	Preston NE	D 2-2	0-2	—	Wilkinson 2	3129
15	Nov 4	H	Notts Co	L 1-3	1-0	15	Wilkinson	6016
16	10	A	Crewe Alex	L 1-2	1-1	—	Christie	3333
17	25	A	Leyton Orient	L 1-3	0-1	19	Wilkinson	3317
18	Dec 2	H	Huddersfield T	L 1-2	1-1	20	Kearney	2966
19	17	A	Brentford	L 1-2	0-2	—	Wilkinson	5022
20	26	H	Rotherham U	W 3-1	2-0	20	Smalley, Stringfellow, Christie	6348
21	30	H	Northampton T	L 1-2	1-0	21	Christie	3200
22	Jan 1	A	Wigan Ath	L 0-4	0-1	23		2477
23	13	A	Bristol R	D 1-1	0-1	23	Leishman	5339
24	20	H	Chester C	W 1-0	0-0	22	Wilkinson	2257
25	Feb 3	A	Blackpool	L 1-3	0-3	23	Wilkinson	4402
26	10	H	Bury	W 1-0	1-0	21	Wilkinson	2424
27	13	H	Fulham	W 3-0	0-0	—	Charles, Hathaway, Christie	2255
28	17	A	Huddersfield T	L 0-1	0-0	20		5441
29	24	H	Leyton Orient	W 1-0	0-0	19	Wilkinson	2542
30	Mar 3	A	Birmingham C	L 1-4	-02	19	Christie	5746
31	6	H	Bolton W	L 0-1	0-0	—		3334
32	10	A	Swansea C	L 0-1	0-0	21		3304
33	17	H	Shrewsbury T	W 2-1	1-1	19	Charles, Christie	2230
34	20	A	Walsall	L 0-1	0-1	—		3017
35	24	H	Tranmere R	W 1-0	0-0	19	Wilkinson	3362
36	27	A	Cardiff C	L 0-1	0-1	—		2280
37	31	A	Bristol C	D 1-1	0-0	19	Kearney	11,773
38	Apr 3	H	Birmingham C	W 5-2	4-1	—	Wilkinson 5	4163
39	7	H	Reading	D 1-1	1-1	19	Christie (pen)	2563
40	10	A	Preston NE	L 0-4	0-3	—		5035
41	14	H	Wigan Ath	W 1-0	1-0	17	Charles	2421
42	16	A	Rotherham U	D 0-0	0-0	17		5096
43	21	H	Brentford	L 2-3	1-0	18	Clark, Christie	2346
44	24	A	Northampton T	W 2-1	2-0	—	Kearney, Christie	2119
45	28	H	Crewe Alex	W 2-1	1-0	15	Swain (og), Hodges	3071
46	May 5	A	Notts Co	L 2-4	0-3	15	Kent, Christie (pen)	6943

Final League Position: 15

GOALSCORERS

League (50): Wilkinson 15, Christie 13 (2 pens), Charles 7 (1 pen), Kearney 3, Kent 3, Stringfellow 3, Clark 1, Hathaway 1, Hodges 1, Leishman 1, Smalley 1, own goal 1.
Littlewoods Cup (8): Christie 3, Stringfellow 3, Kearney 1, Wilkinson 1.
FA Cup (0).

Beasley	McKernon	Prindiville	Hunt	Foster	Coleman	Lowery	Stringfellow	Christie	Charles	Kearney	Cox	Chambers	Leishman	Hathaway	McDonald	Kenworthy	Place	Hodges	O'Riordan	Kent	Wilkinson	Gray	Smalley	Murray	Fairclough	Clark	Pearcey	Match No.
1	2	3	4	5	6	7	8	9	10	11																		1
	2	3*	4	5	6	7	8			11	1	12		9	10													2
	2	3	4	5	6	7	8	9	10	11	1																	3
	2	3	4	5	6		8	9	10	11	1			7														4
	2	3*	4	5	6	7	8†	9	10	11	1		12	14														5
		3	4			7†	8	9	10	11	1		12	2		5			6*14									6
1		3	4	5*		7	8	9	10	11			12					2	6									7
1		3	2*	5			8	4	10	14	11		12						6†	7	9							8
1	2			5			8	4*	10		11		12				3		6	7	9							9
	2			5			8	4	10	11	1		12						6	7	9*	3						10
	2			5			8	4	10	11	1								6	7	9	3						11
	2			5			8	4	10	11	1								6	7	9	3						12
	2	3		5			8	4	10	11	1									7	9		6					13
	2	3*		5		11	8	4	10		1		12							7	9		6					14
	2			5			8*	4	10	3	1		12	11						7	9		6					15
	2			5		11	8	4	10	3	1									7	9		6					16
	2	11	10	5			8	4		3	1		14	12						7*	9		6†					17
	2	3		5		7		4	10	6	1		12	11							9*	8						18
		3		5		11		4	10	8	1									7	9		6	2				19
1		3		5			8	4	10	11										7	9		6	2				20
1		3		5				4	10	11				8						7	9		6	2				21
1		12		5				4	10	3				11			14			7	9†	8	6*	2				22
1		3		5			8	4	10†	11			14	12						7	9		6*	2				23
1		3		5			8†	4	10	11			12	14						7	9		6	2*				24
1		3		5				4	10	11*			12	8						7	9		6					25
1		3		5				4	10	11										7	9	8	6	2				26
1		3		5			8	4	10	11										7	9		6	2				27
1		3		5			8	4	10											7	9	11	6	2				28
1		3		5			8	4	10	11										7	9		6	2				29
1		3					8	4	10	11*			12							7	9	5	6	2				30
1		3					8	4*	10†				14	12						7	9	5	6	2	11			31
1							8	4	11	3										7	9	5	6	2	10			32
1				5				4	11	3										7	9		6	2	10	8		33
1				5				4	11*	3			12							7	9		6	2	10	8		34
1				5				4	11	3										7	9		6	2	10	8		35
1				5				4*	11	3			14	12						7	9		6	2	10†	8		36
1				5				4	11	3		14		12						7*	9		6	2	10	8†		37
				5				4	11	3				12						7	9		6	2	10	8*	1	38
		3		5				4	11									10		7	9		6	2		8	1	39
				5				4	11	3†		14		14						7	9	10†	6	2		8	1	40
				5				4	11	3								10		7	9		6	2		8	1	41
				5				4	11	3										7	9		6	2	10	8	1	42
1				5				4	11	3				12						7	9*		6	2	10	8		43
1				5				4	11	3									9	7			6	2	10	8		44
1				5				4	11	3									9	7	12		6	2	10*	8		45
1				5				4	11*	3				12					9	7			6	2	10	8		46
26	7	22	21	42	5	14	17	43	42	41	15	4	1	11	1	1	1	8	6	38	36	16	28	28	13	14	5	

Substitutes: Lowery +1s; Christie +2s, Charles +2s, Kearney +1s; Chambers +3s, Leishman +3s, Hathaway +11s, McDonald +1s; Hodges +11s; Gray +1s

Littlewoods Cup	First Round	Northampton T (h)	1-1
		(a)	2-0
	Second Round	Luton T (h)	3-4
		(a)	2-7
FA Cup	First Round	Wigan Ath (a)	0-2

MANSFIELD TOWN

Player and Position	Ht	Wt	Birth Date	Place	Source	Clubs	League App	Gls
Goalkeepers								
Andy Beasley	6 2	12 01	5 2 64	Sedgley	Apprentice	Luton T	—	—
						Mansfield T	43	—
						Gillingham (loan)	—	—
						Peterborough U (loan)	7	—
						Scarborough (loan)	4	—
Brian Cox*	6 1	13 10	7 5 61	Sheffield	Apprentice	Sheffield W	22	—
						Huddersfield T	213	—
						Mansfield T	54	—
Jason Pearcey	6 1	13 05	23 7 71	Leamington Spa	Trainee	Mansfield T	6	—
Defenders								
Tony Clarke‡	5 10	11 02	21 9 70	Leamington Spa		Mansfield T	—	—
Wayne Fairclough	5 10	9 12	27 4 68	Nottingham	Apprentice	Notts Co	71	—
						Mansfield T	13	—
George Foster	5 10	11 02	26 9 56	Plymouth	Apprentice	Plymouth Arg	212	6
						Torquay U (loan)	6	3
						Exeter C (loan)	28	—
						Derby Co	30	—
						Mansfield T	305	—
Mark Kearney	5 10	11 00	12 6 62	Ormskirk	Marine	Everton	—	—
						Mansfield T	230	29
Tony Kenworthy*	5 10	10 07	31 10 58	Leeds	Apprentice	Sheffield U	286	34
						Mansfield T (loan)	13	—
						Mansfield T	87	—
Malcolm Murray	5 11	11 02	26 7 64	Buckie	Buckie T	Hearts	27	—
						Hull C	11	—
						Mansfield T	28	—
Mark Place*	5 11	10 08	16 11 69		Trainee	Mansfield T	15	—
Steve Prindiville	5 9	11 04	26 12 68	Harlow	Apprentice	Leicester C	1	—
						Chesterfield	43	1
						Mansfield T	22	—
Mark Smalley	5 11	11 06	2 1 65	Newark	Apprentice	Nottingham F	3	—
						Birmingham C (loan)	7	—
						Bristol R (loan)	10	—
						Leyton Orient	64	4
						Mansfield T	28	1
Midfield								
Steve Chambers‡	5 10	10 10	20 7 68	Worksop	Apprentice	Sheffield W	—	—
						Mansfield T	25	—
Steve Charles	5 9	10 07	10 5 60	Sheffield	Sheffield Univ	Sheffield U	123	10
						Wrexham	113	37
						Mansfield T	135	26
Kevin Gray§	6 0	13 00	7 1 72	Sheffield	Trainee	Mansfield T	17	—
David Hodges	5 9	10 02	17 1 70	Hereford		Mansfield T	83	7
David Hunt	5 11	13 09	17 4 59	Leicester	Apprentice	Derby Co	5	—
						Notts Co	336	28
						Aston Villa	13	—
						Mansfield T	22	—
Tony Lowery	5 9	11 01	6 7 61	Wallsend	Ashington	WBA	1	—
						Walsall (loan)	6	1
						Mansfield T	245	19
Forwards								
Keith Cassells	5 10	11 12	10 7 57	London	Wembley T	Watford	12	—
						Peterborough U (loan)	8	—
						Oxford U	45	13
						Southampton	10	4
						Brentford	86	28
						Mansfield T	163	52

MANSFIELD TOWN

Foundation: Many records give the date of Mansfield Town's formation as 1905. But the present club did not come into being until 1910 when the Mansfield Wesleyans (formed 1891) and playing in the Notts and District League, decided to spread their wings and changed their name to Mansfield Town, joining the new Central Alliance in 1911.

First Football League game: 29 August, 1931, Division 3(S), v Swindon T (h) W 3-2 – Wilson; Clifford, England; Wake, Davis, Blackburn; Gilhespy, Readman (1), Johnson, Broom (2), Baxter.

Managers (and Secretary-managers)
John Baynes 1922–25, Ted Davison 1926–28, J. Hickling 1928–33, Henry Martin 1933–35, Charlie Bell 1935, Harold Wightman 1936, Harold Parkes 1936–38, Jack Poole 1938–39, Lloyd Barke 1939–45, Roy Goodall 1945–49, Freddie Steele 1949–51, George Jobey 1952–53, Stan Mercer 1953–55, Charlie Mitten 1956–58, Sam Weaver 1958–60, Raich Carter 1960–63, Tommy Cummings 1963–67, Tommy Eggleston 1967–70, Jock Basford 1970–71, Danny Williams 1971–74, Dave Smith 1974–76, Peter Morris 1976–78, Billy Bingham 1978–79, Mick Jones 1979–81, Stuart Boam 1981–83, Ian Greaves 1983–89, George Foster 1989– .

Player and Position	Ht	Wt	Birth Date	Birth Place	Source	Clubs	League App	Gls
Trevor Christie	6 2	12 00	28 2 59	Newcastle	Apprentice	Leicester C	31	8
						Notts Co	187	64
						Nottingham F	14	5
						Derby Co	65	22
						Manchester C	9	3
						Walsall	99	22
						Mansfield T	57	14
Wayne Davidson	5 9	11 00	7 12 68	Wallsend		Mansfield T	—	—
Ian Hathaway	5 8	10 06	22 8 68	Worsley	Bedworth U	Mansfield T	34	2
Kevin Kent	5 11	11 00	19 3 65	Stoke	Apprentice	WBA	2	—
						Newport Co	33	1
						Mansfield T	202	32
Graham Leishman	5 9	10 07	6 4 68	Manchester	Irlam T	Mansfield T	16	2
Gary McDonald*	5 9	11 12	20 11 69	Sunderland	Ipswich T§	Mansfield T	2	—
Ian Stringfellow	5 9	10 02	8 5 69	Nottingham	Apprentice	Mansfield T	82	16
Steve Wilkinson	6 0	10 12	1 9 68	Lincoln	Apprentice	Leicester C	7	1
						Rochdale (loan)	—	—
						Crewe Alex (loan)	5	2
						Mansfield T	37	15

Trainees
Bircumshaw, Gary; Elkington, Justin C; Gray, Kevin J; Hall, Geoffrey; Hodges, Christopher; Jones, Adam; Milner, Jason; Morgan, Peter C; O'Brien, Damian; Shaw, Paul.

Associated Schoolboys
Cann, Scott A; Doughty, Stephen J; Foster, Stephen; Holland, Paul; Kerrigan, Jonathan R; Kingston, Christopher L; Martin, Stephen A; Mowbray, Scott G; Richardson, Paul S.; Smith, Dean R; Smith, Kevin; Timmons, Christopher B; Travis, Steven; Wain, Lee J; Ward, Darren.

MIDDLESBROUGH 1989–90 *Back row (left to right):* Mark Proctor, Kevin Poole, Steve Pears, Matthew Coddington, Alan Comfort. *Centre row:* Peter Davenport, Stuart Ripley, Bernie Slaven, Ian Baird, Nicky Mohan, Simon Coleman, Gary Parkinson, Michael Trotter. *Front row:* Gary Hamilton, Colin Cooper, Mark Burke, Paul Kerr, Tony Mowbray, Mark Brennan, Alan Kernaghan, Owen McGee.

Division 2   **MIDDLESBROUGH**

Ayresome Park, Middlesbrough, Cleveland TS1 4PB. Telephone Middlesbrough (0642) 819659/815996. Commercial Dept. 0642 826664. Clubcall, 0898 121181. Special Answering Service available on (0642) 825383.

Ground capacity; 30,000.

Record attendance: 53,596 v Newcastle U, Division 1, 27 Dec, 1979.

Record receipts: £82,835.95 v Everton. FA Cup, 4th rd replay, 3 Feb, 1988.

Pitch measurements: 115yd × 75yd.

Chairman: M. C. Henderson.

Directors: G. Fordy, S. Gibson, R. Corbidge.

Chief Executive: Keith Lamb.

Manager: Colin Todd. *Coach:*

Physiotherapist: Tommy Johnson.

Secretary: Tom Hughes.

Commercial Manager: Alan Murray.

Year Formed: 1876. *Turned Professional:* 1889; became amateur 1892, and professional again, 1899. *Ltd Co:* 1892.

Club Nickname: 'The Boro'.

Previous Grounds: 1877, Old Archery Ground, Linhorpe Rd; 1903, Ayresome Park.

Record League Victory: 9-0 v Brighton & HA, Division 2, 23 August 1958 – Taylor; Bilcliff, Robinson; Harris (2 pens), Phillips, Walley; Day, McLean, Clough (5), Peacock (2), Holliday.

Record Cup Victory: 9-3 v Goole T, FA Cup, 1st rd, 9 January 1915 – Williamson; Haworth, Weir; Davidson, Cook, Malcolm; Wilson, Carr (3), Elliott (3), Tinsley (3), Davies.

Record Defeat: 0-9 v Blackburn R, Division 2, 6 Novmber, 1954.

Most League Points (2 for a win): 65, Division 2, 1973–74.

Most League Points (3 for a win): 94, Division 3, 1986–87.

Most League Goals: 122, Division 2, 1926–27.

Highest League Scorer in Season: George Camsell, 59, Division 2, 1926–27 (Second Division record).

Most League Goals in Total Aggregate: George Camsell, 326, 1925–39.

Most Capped Player: Wilf Mannion, 26, England.

Most League Appearances: Tim Williamson, 563, 1902–23.

Record Transfer Fee Received: £2,300,000 from Manchester United for Gary Pallister, August 1989.

Record Transfer Fee Paid: £700,000 to Manchester U for Peter Davenport, November 1988.

Football League Record: 1899 Elected to Division 2; 1902–24 Division 1; 1924–27 Division 2; 1927–28 Division 1; 1928–29 Division 2; 1929–54 Division 1; 1954–66 Division 2; 1966–67 Division 3; 1967–74 Division 2; 1974–82 Division 1; 1982–86 Division 2; 1986–87 Division 3; 1987–88 Division 2; 1988–89 Division 1; 1989– Division 2.

Honours: Football League: Division 1 best season : 3rd, 1913–14. Division 2 – Champions 1926–27, 1928–29, 1973–74; Runners-up 1901–02. Division 3 – Runners-up 1966–67, 1986–87. *FA Cup* best season; 6th rd, 1935–36, 1946–47, 1969–70, 1974–75, 1976–77, 1977–78; old last eight 1900–01, 1903–04. *Football League Cup:* Semi-final 1975–76. *Amateur Cup:* Winners 1895, 1898, *Anglo-Scottish Cup:* Winners 1975–76.

Colours: Red shirts, white shorts, red stockings. **Change colours:** All sky blue.

MIDDLESBROUGH 1989–90 LEAGUE RECORD

Match No.	Date	Venue	Opponents	Result	H/T Score	Lg. Pos.	Goalscorers	Attendance
1	Aug 19	H	Wolverhampton W	W 4-2	2-0	—	Slaven 2, Proctor, Davenport	21,727
2	23	A	Leeds U	L 1-2	0-1	—	Comfort	25,004
3	27	A	Sunderland	L 1-2	1-0	—	Slaven	21,569
4	Sept 2	H	Sheffield U	D 3-3	1-1	12	Slaven 2, Comfort	17,897
5	9	A	Barnsley	D 1-1	0-1	13	Burke	10,535
6	16	H	Bournemouth	W 2-1	1-1	10	Slaven, Proctor	16,077
7	23	A	Portsmouth	L 1-3	0-3	14	Slaven	7305
8	27	H	Hull C	W 1-0	1-0	—	Proctor	16,382
9	30	A	Watford	L 0-1	0-1	15		10,102
10	Oct 14	H	Plymouth Arg	L 0-2	0-0	20		15,003
11	18	H	Brighton & HA	D 2-2	0-0	—	Mowbray, Parkinson (pen)	13,551
12	21	A	Oldham Ath	L 0-2	0-1	20		6835
13	28	H	WBA	D 0-0	0-0	19		14,076
14	30	A	Port Vale	D 1-1	1-1	—	Kernaghan	7708
15	Nov 4	A	Newcastle U	D 2-2	1-1	20	Proctor, Brennan	23,349
16	11	H	Swindon T	L 0-2	0-0	21		13,720
17	18	A	West Ham U	L 0-2	0-1	21		18,720
18	21	A	Blackburn R	W 4-2	3-0	—	Kernaghan 3, Slaven	8317
19	25	H	Oxford U	W 1-0	1-0	16	Slaven	13,756
20	Dec 2	A	Wolverhampton W	L 0-2	0-0	18		12,357
21	9	H	Leeds U	L 0-2	0-2	21		19,686
22	16	H	Leicester C	W 4-1	1-0	18	Cooper 2, Slaven, Ripley	11,428
23	26	A	Bradford C	W 1-0	1-0	17	Slaven	10,008
24	30	A	Ipswich T	L 0-3	0-2	18		14,290
25	Jan 1	H	Stoke C	L 0-1	0-0	20		16,238
26	14	H	Sunderland	W 3-0	2-0	—	Davenport, Slaven, Parkinson	17,698
27	20	A	Sheffield U	L 0-1	0-1	19		15,950
28	Feb 3	H	Portsmouth	W 2-0	1-0	16	Kerr, Slaven	15,295
29	10	A	Bournemouth	D 2-2	0-1	17	Mowbray, Slaven	7630
30	24	A	Oxford U	L 1-3	0-1	18	Brennan	5949
31	28	A	Brighton & HA	L 0-1	0-0	—		5504
32	Mar 3	H	West Ham U	L 0-1	0-0	21		23,617
33	7	H	Watford	L 1-2	0-0	—	Coleman	14,008
34	10	A	Hull C	D 0-0	0-0	20		6602
35	17	H	Blackburn R	L 0-3	0-2	21		15,259
36	20	A	Plymouth Arg	W 2-1	1-0	—	Baird, Brennan	7,185
37	31	H	Oldham Ath	W 1-0	1-0	19	Slaven	17,238
38	Apr 7	A	WBA	D 0-0	0-0	19		9458
39	11	H	Port Vale	L 2-3	1-0	—	Slaven, Davenport	14,973
40	14	A	Stoke C	D 0-0	0-0	22		8636
41	16	H	Bradford C	W 2-0	2-0	20	Slaven, Baird	16,376
42	21	A	Leicester C	L 1-2	1-1	22	Slaven	9203
43	25	H	Ipswich T	L 1-2	1-0	—	Baird	15,232
44	28	A	Swindon T	D 1-1	1-0	22	Slaven	9,532
45	May 2	H	Barnsley	L 0-1	0-1	—		17,015
46	5	H	Newcastle U	W 4-1	0-0	21	Slaven 2, Baird 2	18,484

Final League Position: 21

GOALSCORERS

League (52): Slaven 21, Baird 5, Kernaghan 4, Proctor 4, Brennan 3, Davenport 3, Comfort 2, Cooper 2, Mowbray 2, Parkinson 2 (1 pen), Burke 1, Coleman 1, Kerr 1, Ripley 1.
Littlewoods Cup (6): Slaven 4, Comfort 1, Kernaghan 1.
FA Cup (1): Parkinson 1.

Poole	Parkinson	Mohan	Mowbray	Putney	Pallister	Slaven	Proctor	Davenport	Kerr	Comfort	Ripley	Kernaghan	Brennan	Burke	Coleman	Gill	Cooper	Pears	McGee	Baird	Phillips	Match No.
1	2	3	4	5	6	7	8	9	10*	11	12											1
1	2	3	4	5	6	7	8	9		11	10											2
1	2	3	4	5	6	7	8	9		11	10*	12										3
1	2	3	4	6		7	8	9*		11	12	5	10									4
1	2	3	4	6†		7	8	12		11		9*	5	10	14							5
1	2	3	4	6		7	8	12		11		9*	5	10†	14							6
1	2	3	4	6		7	8	12		11		9*	5	10†	14							7
1	2	3	4	6		7	8			11		9	5	10								8
1	2	3	4	6		7	8			11		9†	5	10*	12	14						9
1		3	4	6		7	8	9*		11	12	5	2	10†	14							10
1	2		4	6		7*	8			11		9	12	10	5		3					11
1	2		4	6		7	8			11		9	10		5		3					12
1	2		4	6		7	8			11		9	5	10*	12		3					13
1	2		4	6		7	8			11		9	5	10			3					14
1	2		4	6		7	8			11*		9†	5	10	12	14	3					15
1	2	12	4	6		7	8			11		5	10	9†	14		3*					16
1	2	3	4	6		7	8			11	12	10	9*		5							17
1	2	3	4	6		7	8			11		9	10		5							18
1	2	3	4	6		7	8			11		9	10		5							19
1	14	2†	4			7	8			11		9*	6	10	12	5	3					20
1	2		4	10		7	8			11		9	6*	12	5		3					21
	2		4	6		7	8			11	12†	9*	10	14	5		3	1				22
	2		4	6		7	8			11	12	9*	10		5		3	1				23
	2		4	6*		7	8			11	12	9	10		5		3	1				24
	2		4			7	8			11	6	9*	10	12	5		3	1				25
	2		4	9*		7	8			11	12	6	10		5		3	1				26
	2		4			7	8			11	6	9	10*		5		3	1	12			27
	2		4	10		7	8	12		11		6*			5		3	1		9		28
	2	3	4			7	8			11*	12	10			5			1	6	9		29
	2	3	4			7	8			11*	12	10			5			1	6	9		30
	2	3	4			7	8*			11	12	10			5			1	6	9		31
	2		4			7	8*			11	12	10			5			1	6	9	3	32
	2		4			7	8			11		10			5			1	6	9	3	33
	2		4			7	8			11		10			5			1	6	9	3	34
			4†			7	8			11	10*	6	14	12	5		2	1		9	3	35
	2		4			7*	8			11	12	10			5			1	6	9	3	36
	2		4			7	8			11	12	10			5	14		1	6†	9*	3	37
	2		4			7	8			11		10			5		12	1	6*	9	3	38
	2		4			7	8			11	12	10			5			1	6	9*	3	39
	2		4			7	8			11	12	10			5			1	6*	9	3	40
	2		4			7	8			11	12	10*			5			1	6	9	3	41
	2		4			7	8			11	12	10*			5			1	6	9	3	42
	2		4			7*	8			11	12	10			5			1	6	9	3	43
			4			7	8			11	10				5		2	1	6	9	3	44
			4			7	8			11	10	12			5*		2	1	6	9	3	45
			4			7	8			11	10				5		2	1	6	9	3	46
21	40	21	28	25	3	46	45	30	13	15	26	34	36	3	33	1	18	25	12	19	12	
	+	+						+	+			+	+	+	+	+	+	+				
	1s	1s						5s	4s			13s	3s	4s	9s	3s	3s	1s				

Littlewoods Cup	Second Round	Halifax T (h)		4-0
		(a)		1-0
	Third Round	Wimbledon (h)		1-1
		(a)		0-1
FA Cup	Third Round	Everton (h)		0-0
		(a)		1-1
		(a)		0-1

MIDDLESBROUGH

Player and Position	Ht	Wt	Birth Date	Place	Source	Clubs	League App	Gls
Goalkeepers								
Matt Coddington*	6 1	11 05	17 9 69	Lytham St Annes	Trainee	Middlesbrough	—	—
						Bury (loan)	—	—
						Halifax T (loan)	—	—
Stephen Pears	6 0	12 11	22 1 62	Brandon	Apprentice	Manchester U	4	—
						Middlesbrough (loan)	12	—
						Middlesbrough	178	—
Kevin Poole	5 10	11 10	21 7 63	Bromsgrove	Apprentice	Aston Villa	28	—
						Northampton T (loan)	3	—
						Middlesbrough	34	—
Defenders								
Simon Coleman	6 0	10 08	13 3 68	Worksop		Mansfield T	96	7
						Middlesbrough	36	1
Colin Cooper	5 10	10 00	28 2 67	Durham		Middlesbrough	156	6
Lee Crosby			23 1 72	Hartlepool	Trainee	Middlesbrough	—	—
Owen McGee	5 7	10 07	20 4 70	Teeside	Trainee	Middlesbrough	13	—
Nicky Mohan	6 2	12 00	6 10 70	Middlesbrough	Trainee	Middlesbrough	28	—
Tony Mowbray	6 1	12 02	22 11 63	Saltburn	Apprentice	Middlesbrough	291	22
Gary Parkinson	5 10	11 11	10 1 68	Middlesbrough	Amateur	Everton	—	—
						Middlesbrough	161	4
Jim Phillips	6 0	12 07	8 2 66	Bolton	Apprentice	Bolton W	108	2
						Rangers	25	—
						Oxford U	79	8
						Middlesbrough	12	—
Mark Sunley			13 10 71	Stockton		Middlesbrough	—	—
Michael Trotter	6 3	12 02	27 10 69	Hartlepool	Trainee	Middlesbrough	—	—
						Doncaster R (loan)	3	—
Midfield								
Gary Agnew*	5 11	12 03	27 1 71	Dumfries	Trainee	Middlesbrough	—	—
Mark Brennan	5 10	10 13	4 10 65	Rossendale	Apprentice	Ipswich T	168	19
						Middlesbrough	65	6
Gary Hamilton	5 8	11 02	27 12 65	Glasgow	Apprentice	Middlesbrough	229	25
Dan Holmes			13 6 72	Clophill	Trainee	Middlesbrough	—	—
Paul Kerr	5 8	11 04	9 6 64	Portsmouth	Apprentice	Aston Villa	24	3
						Middlesbrough	101	7
Robert Lake			13 10 71	Stockton	Trainee	Middlesbrough	—	—
Mark Nesbitt			11 1 72	Doncaster R	Trainee	Middlesbrough	—	—
Mark Proctor	5 10	12 08	30 1 61	Middlesbrough	Apprentice	Middlesbrough	109	12
						Nottingham F	64	5
						Sunderland (loan)	5	—
						Sunderland	112	19
						Sheffield W	59	4
						Middlesbrough	55	4
Trevor Putney	5 7	10 11	11 2 61	Harold Hill	Brentwood W	Ipswich T	103	8
						Norwich C	82	9
						Middlesbrough	25	—
Martin Russell	5 9	10 05	27 4 67	Dublin	Apprentice	Manchester U	—	—
						Birmingham C (loan)	5	—
						Leicester C	20	—
						Norwich C (loan)	—	—
						Scarborough	51	9
						Middlesbrough	—	—

MIDDLESBROUGH

Foundation: The story of how the idea of a Middlesbrough football club was first mooted at a tripe supper at the Corporation Hotel in 1876 is well known locally. But the club was formally established at a meeting in the Talbot Hotel the following year and is one of the oldest clubs in the North East.

First Football League game: 2 September, 1899, Division 2, v Lincoln C (a) L 0-3 – Smith; Shaw, Ramsey; Allport, McNally, McCracken; Wanless, Longstaffe, Gettins, Page, Pugh.

Managers (and Secretary-managers)
John Robson 1899–1905, Alex Massie 1905–06, Andy Aitken 1906–09, J. Gunter 1908–10, Andy Walker 1910–11, Tom McIntosh 1911–19, James Howie 1920–23, Herbert Bamlett 1923–26, Peter McWilliam 1927–34, Wilf Gillow 1934–44, David Jack 1944–52, Walter Rowley 1952–54, Bob Dennison 1954–63, Raich Carter 1963–66, Stan Anderson 1966–73, Jack Charlton 1973–77, John Neal 1977–81, Bobby Murdoch 1981–82, Malcolm Allison 1982–84, Willie Maddren 1984–86, Bruce Rioch 1986–90, Colin Todd 1990– .

Player and Position	Ht	Wt	Birth Date	Place	Source	Clubs	League App	Gls
Forwards								
Ian Arnold			4 7 72	Durham City	Trainee	Middlesbrough	—	—
Ian Baird	6 0	12 09	1 4 64	Southampton	Apprentice	Southampton	17	3
						Cardiff C (loan)	12	6
						Southampton	5	2
						Newcastle U (loan)	5	1
						Leeds U	85	33
						Portsmouth	20	1
						Leeds U	77	17
						Middlesbrough	19	5
Mark Burke	5 10	11 08	12 2 69	Solihull	Apprentice	Aston Villa	7	—
						Middlesbrough	57	6
Alan Comfort	5 7	11 02	8 12 64	Aldershot	Apprentice	QPR	—	—
						Cambridge U	63	5
						Leyton Orient	150	47
						Middlesbrough	15	2
Peter Davenport	5 11	11 03	24 3 61	Birkenhead	Amateur Cammel Laird	Everton	—	—
						Nottingham F	118	54
						Manchester U	92	22
						Middlesbrough	59	7
Andy Fletcher			12 8 71	Cleveland	Trainee	Middlesbrough	—	—
Paul Hanford			4 1 72	Middlesbrough	Trainee	Middlesbrough	—	—
Alan Kernaghan	6 2	12 12	25 4 67	Otley	Apprentice	Middlesbrough	122	11
Stuart Ripley	5 11	12 06	20 11 67	Middlesbrough	Apprentice	Middlesbrough	171	17
						Bolton W (loan)	5	1
Lee Roxby			18 10 71	Stockton	Trainee	Middlesbrough	—	—
Bernie Slaven	5 11	10 10	13 11 60	Paisley		Morton	22	1
						Airdrie	2	—
						Q of the S	2	—
						Albion R	42	27
						Middlesbrough	205	82
Lee Tucker			14 9 71	Middlesbrough	Trainee	Middlesbrough	—	—

Trainees
Devine, Michael; Green, Scott; Keavney, David G; McDonagh, Dermot; Martin, Stephen; Melling, Paul; Napier, Stephen; Peverell, Nicholas J; Templeman, Richard J; Waller, Michael A; White, Karl A; White, Neil.

Associated Schoolboys
Barron, Michael J; Cullen, Levi; Gate, Paul; Holman, Anthony R; Illman, Neil D; Jenkins, Paul; Johnson, Ian; Law, Andrew J; Lee, Anthony S; McGargle, Stephen; McNeil, Damien; Maddick, Kevin A; Maughan, Lee J; Maughan, Neil G; Norton, Paul; Ripley, Andrew I; Taylor, Mark S.

Associated Schoolboys who have accepted the club's offer of a Traineeship/Contract
Collett, Andrew A; Pollock, Jamie.

MILLWALL 1989–90 *Back row (left to right):* Darren Treacy, Phil Babb, Teddy Sheringham, Stephen Torpey, David Thompson, Tony Cascarino, Steve Anthrobus, Manus Magill, Steve Wood.
Centre row: Peter Melville (Physiotherapist), George Lawrence, Paul Stephenson, Alan McLeary, Brian Horne, Dean Horrix, Kevin Branagan, Keith Stevens, Terry Hurlock.
Wesley Reid, Frank Sibley (Coach).
Front row: Danis Salman, Jimmy Carter, Sean Sparham, Ian Dawes, John Docherty (Manager), Les Briley, Frank McLintock (Assistant Manager), Darren Morgan, Kevin O'Callaghan,
Alan Dowson, Nicky Coleman.

Division 2 **MILLWALL**

The Den, Cold Blow Lane, London, SE14 5RH. Telephone 071-639 3143, Commercial Dept. 071-639 4590, 071-277 6877 Credit Card Bookings.
Ground capacity: 26,000.
Record Attendance: 48,672 v Derby Co, FA Cup 5th rd, 20 Feb, 1937.
Record Receipts: £52,637 v Leicester C, FA Cup 5th rd, 19 Feb, 1985.
Pitch measurements: 112yd × 74yd.
President: Lord Mellish.
Chairman: R. I. Burr. *Vice-Chairman:* P. W. Mead. *Directors:* J. D. Burnige, B. E. Mitchell, P. M. Mead, D. Sullivan.
Chief Executive Secretary: G. I. S. Hortop.
Manager: Bruce Rioch. *Assistant Manager:* Frank Sibley.
Coach: Wally Downes.
Commercial Manager: W. W. Neil.
Chief Scout: *Physio:* Peter Melville.
Year Formed: 1885. *Turned Professional:* 1893. *Ltd Co.:* 1894.
Club Nickname: 'The Lions'.
Previous Grounds: 1885, Glengall Road, Millwall; 1886, Back of 'Lord Nelson'; 1890, East Ferry Road; 1901, North Greenwich; 1910, The Den.
Previous Names: 1885, Millwall Rovers; 1889, Millwall Athletic.
Record League Victory: 9-1 v Torquay U, Division 3(S), 29 August 1927 – Lansdale; Tilling, Hill; Amos, Bryant (3), Graham; Chance, Hawkins (3), Landells (1), Phillips (2), Black. 9-1 v Coventry C, Division 3(S), 19 November 1927 – Lansdale; Fort, Hill; Amos, Collins (1), Graham; Chance, Landells (4), Cock (2), Phillips (2), Black.
Record Cup Victory: 7-0 v Gateshead, FA Cup, 2nd rd, 12 December 1936 – Yuill; Ted Smith, Inns; Brolly, Hancock, Forsyth; Thomas (1), Mangnall (1), Ken Burditt (2), McCartney (2), Thorogood (1).
Record Defeat: 1-9 v Aston Villa, FA Cup 4th rd, 28 January, 1946.
Most League Points (2 for a win): 65, Division 3(S), 1927–28 and Division 3, 1965–66.
Most League Points (3 for a win): 90, Division 3, 1984–85.
Most League Goals: 127, Division 3(S), 1927–28.
Highest League Scorer in Season: Richard Parker, 37, Division 3(S), 1926–27.
Most League Goals in Total Aggregate: Derek Possee, 79, 1967–73.
Most Capped Player: Eamonn Dunphy, 22 (23), Eire.
Most League Appearances: Barry Kitchener, 523, 1967–82.
Record Transfer Fee Received: £1,500,000 from Aston Villa for Tony Cascarino, March 1990.
Record Transfer Fee Paid: £800,000 to Derby Co for Paul Goddard, December 1989.
Football League Record: 1920 Original Members of Division 3; 1921 Division 3(S); 1928–34 Division 2; 1934–38 Division 3(S); 1938–48 Division 2; 1948–58 Division 3(S); 1958–62 Division 4; 1962–64 Division 3; 1964–65 Division 4; 1965–66 Division 3; 1966–75 Division 2; 1975–76 Division 3; 1976–79 Division 2; 1979–85 Division 3; 1985–88 Division 2; 1988–90 Division 1; 1990– Division 2.
Honours: Football League: Division 2 – Champions 1987–88; Division 3(S) – Champions 1927–28, 1937–38; Runners-up 1952–53; Division 3 – Runners–up 1965–66, 1984–85; Division 4 – Champions 1961–62; Runners-up 1964–65. *FA Cup:* Semi-final 1900, 1903, 1937 (first Division 3 side to reach semi-final). *Football League Cup* best season: 5th rd, 1973–74, 1976–77. *Football League Trophy* – Winners 1982–83.
Colours: Blue shirts, white shorts, blue stockings. **Change colours:** Yellow shirts, black shorts, black stockings.

MILLWALL 1989–90 LEAGUE RECORD

Match No.	Date	Venue	Opponents	Result		H/T Score	Lg. Pos.	Goalscorers	Atten- dance
1	Aug 19	A	Southampton	W	2-1	1-0	—	Briley, Cascarino	14,201
2	22	H	Charlton Ath	D	2-2	0-1	—	Sheringham, Dawes	14,806
3	26	H	Nottingham F	W	1-0	0-0	2	Carter	12,140
4	29	A	Wimbledon	D	2-2	1-1	—	Anthrobus, Cascarino	8865
5	Sept 9	H	Coventry C	W	4-1	3-0	1	Sheringham 2, Anthrobus, Dawes	12,062
6	16	A	Manchester U	L	1-5	1-2	5	Sheringham	42,746
7	23	H	Sheffield W	W	2-0	0-0	3	Carter, Cascarino	11,287
8	30	H	Norwich C	L	0-1	0-0	5		13,925
9	Oct 14	A	Everton	L	1-2	1-0	7	Sheringham	26,125
10	21	A	Crystal Palace	L	3-4	1-3	9	Hopkins (og), Cascarino, Anthrobus	18,920
11	28	H	Luton T	D	1-1	1-1	10	Dawes	11,140
12	Nov 4	A	Chelsea	L	0-4	0-3	12		24,969
13	11	A	Arsenal	L	1-2	1-1	14	Sheringham	17,265
14	19	H	Liverpool	L	1-2	1-1	—	Thompson	13,547
15	25	A	QPR	D	0-0	0-0	15		9141
16	Dec 2	H	Southampton	D	2-2	1-1	16	Cascarino, Stephenson	10,470
17	9	A	Charlton Ath	D	1-1	0-0	17	Anthrobus	11,017
18	16	H	Aston Villa	W	2-0	0-0	15	Cascarino, Stephenson	10,528
19	26	A	Tottenham H	L	1-3	0-3	16	Cascarino	26,874
20	30	A	Manchester C	L	0-2	0-1	17		28,084
21	Jan 1	H	Derby Co	D	1-1	0-1	17	Dawes	12,790
22	13	A	Nottingham F	L	1-3	0-1	18	Sheringham	18,065
23	20	H	Wimbledon	D	0-0	0-0	18		11,780
24	Feb 3	A	Sheffield W	D	1-1	1-1	18	Sheringham	17,737
25	10	H	Manchester U	L	1-2	1-0	18	Morgan	15,491
26	17	A	Coventry C	L	1-3	1-2	19	Cascarino	10,981
27	24	H	QPR	L	1-2	0-1	19	Cascarino	11,505
28	Mar 3	A	Liverpool	L	0-1	0-0	19		36,427
29	17	A	Norwich C	D	1-1	0-0	19	Sheringham	14,699
30	21	H	Everton	L	1-2	1-1	—	Goddard	11,495
31	24	A	Luton T	L	1-2	0-1	20	Briley	9027
32	31	H	Crystal Palace	L	1-2	0-1	20	Allen	13,332
33	Apr 7	H	Manchester C	D	1-1	1-0	20	Thompson	10,265
34	14	A	Derby Co	L	0-2	0-0	20		13,718
35	16	H	Tottenham H	L	0-1	0-0	20		10,574
36	21	A	Aston Villa	L	0-1	0-0	20		21,028
37	28	A	Arsenal	L	0-2	0-2	20		25,607
38	May 5	H	Chelsea	L	1-3	0-1	20	Allen	12,230

Final League Position: 20

GOALSCORERS

League (39): Cascarino 9, Sheringham 9, Anthrobus 4, Dawes 4, Allen 2, Briley 2, Carter 2, Stephenson 2, Thompson 2, Goddard 1, Morgan 1, own goal 1.
Littlewoods Cup (4): Burlock 2, Cascarino 1, Sheringham 1.
FA Cup (5): Sheringham 2, Carter 1, Cascarino 1, Goddard 1.

Horne	Salman	Dawes	Hurlock	Wood	McLeary	Stevens	Briley	Sheringham	Cascarino	Anthrobus	Carter	Thompson	Torpey	Sparham	Waddock	Stephenson	Coleman	Goddard	Branagan	Treacy	Morgan	Horrix	Reid	Cunningham	Allen	McCarthy	Match No.
1	2	3	4	5	6	7	8	9	10	11																	1
1	2	3	4	5	6	7	8	9	10	11*	12																2
1		3	4		6	2	8	9	10	11	7	5															3
1		3	4		6	2	8	9	10	11*	7	5	12														4
1		3	4		6	2	8	9	10	11	7	5															5
1		3	4	12	6	2	8	9	10	11	7†	5*	14														6
1		3	4	5	6	2	8*	9	10	11	7		12														7
1		3	4		6	2		9	10	11*	7†	5	12	14	8												8
1		3	4		6	2	8*	9	10	11	7	5	12														9
1		3	4		6			9	10	11	7	5	2	8													10
1		3	4	5	6	2		9	10	11*	7	12	8														11
1		3	4	5*	6	2		9	10		7	12	11	8													12
1		3	4		6	2		9	10		7	5	11*	8	12												13
1		3	4		6	2		9	10		7	5	11	8													14
1		3			6	2		9*	10		7	5	11	8	12	4											15
1		3			6	2	4	10	9		7	5	8	11													16
1		3			6	2	4	10	9		7	5	8	11													17
1		3	8		6	2	4	10			7	5	9	11													18
1		3	8		6	2	4	10	14	7*	5	9†	12	11													19
1		3	8	5	6	2	4	10	12	7	9*		11														20
1		3	8	5	6	2	4	10		7	11	9															21
	2	3	8	5	6	4*	12	10	14	11					7†	9			1								22
	2	3	8	5	6		7	10	12	4	11				9*				1								23
	2	3			6	8	7	10	5	11	9				1	4											24
	2	3			6	10	7	5	11	9*	1	4	8	12													25
	2	8			6	9*	10	12	5	11	3	7	1	4													26
		3	8		6	2*	4	9†	10	7	5	14	11	12	1												27
7		3			6	2	8	9	10	5	11	1	4														28
		3	4		6	8	9	5	11*	10	1	12	7	2													29
		3	4		6	2	8*	9	5	11	10	1	7	12													30
		3	8		6	2	14	12	5	11*	10	1	7†	9	4												31
		3	8		6†	2	7	12	5	11	10*	1	14	9	4												32
		3	8		6	4	7	10	11	5	1	2	9														33
		3	8		6	4	7	10	5	11	1	2	9														34
		3	8		6	4	10	12	7	11*	1	2	9	5													35
		3	4	2	6†	8	10	11*	14	7	12	9	1	5													36
		3			6	2	8	10	7	4	11	9*	1	12	5												37
1		3			6	8	10†	7	14	4*	12	11	2	9	5												38
22	7	38	29	21	30 +1s	28	25 +1s	28 +3s	28	13	25 +2s	25 +3s	3 +2s	5	14 +4s	19 +4s	3 +4s	13 +4s	16	4 +1s	1	—	4 +1s	5 +1s	6 +1s	6 +2s	

Littlewoods Cup	Second Round	Stoke C (a)	0-1
		(h)	2-0
	Third Round	Tranmere R (a)	2-3
FA Cup	Third Round	Manchester C (a)	0-0
		(h)	1-1
		(h)	3-1
	Fourth Round	Cambridge U (h)	1-1
		(a)	0-1

MILLWALL

Player and Position	Ht	Wt	Birth Date	Place	Source	Clubs	League App	Gls
Goalkeepers								
Keith Branagan	6 1	13 02	10 7 66	Fulham		Cambridge U	110	—
						Millwall	16	—
						Brentford (loan)	2	—
Brian Horne	5 11	13 13	5 10 67	Billericay	Apprentice	Millwall	135	—
Peter Hucker	6 2	12 12	28 10 59	London	Apprentice	QPR	160	—
						Cambridge U (loan)	—	—
						Oxford U	66	—
						WBA (loan)	7	—
						Manchester U (loan)	—	—
						Millwall	—	—
Defenders								
Philip Babb	6 0	12 03	30 11 70		Lambeth	Millwall	—	—
Nicky Coleman	5 10	11 12	6 5 66	Crayford	Apprentice	Millwall	88	—
						Swindon T (loan)	13	4
Ken Cunningham	5 11	11 02	28 6 71	Dublin		Millwall	5	—
Ian Dawes	5 7	11 11	22 2 63	Croyden	Apprentice	QPR	229	3
						Millwall	68	5
Alan Dowson	5 8	10 06	17 6 70	Gateshead	Trainee	Millwall	—	—
						Fulham (loan)	4	—
Mick McCarthy	6 2	12 12	7 2 59	Barnsley	Apprentice	Barnsley	272	7
						Manchester C	140	2
						Celtic	48	—
					Lyon	Millwall	6	—
Alan McLeary	5 11	10 08	6 10 64	London	Apprentice	Millwall	231	5
Sean Sparham	5 7	10 10	4 12 68	Bexley		Millwall	28	—
						Brentford (loan)	5	—
David Thompson	6 3	12 07	20 11 68	N'humberland	Trainee	Millwall	47	3
Steve Wood	6 0	11 09	2 2 63	Bracknell	Apprentice	Reading	219	9
						Millwall	78	—
Midfield								
Les Briley	5 6	11 00	2 10 56	Lambeth	Apprentice	Chelsea	—	—
						Hereford U	61	2
						Wimbledon	61	2
						Aldershot	157	3
						Millwall	206	12
Terry Hurlock	5 9	13 02	22 9 58	Hackney	Leytonstone	Brentford	220	18
						Reading	29	—
						Millwall	104	8
Darren Morgan	5 6	9 05	5 11 67	Camberwell	Apprentice	Millwall	35	2
						Bradford C (loan)	2	—
Wesley Reid	5 8	11 03	10 9 68	Lewisham	Trainee	Arsenal	—	—
						Millwall	6	—
Keith Stevens	6 0	12 05	21 6 64	Merton	Apprentice	Millwall	246	3
Gary Waddock	5 9	12 07	17 3 62	Kingsbury	Apprentice	QPR	203	8
					Charleroi	Millwall	18	—
Forwards								
Malcolm Allen	5 8	10 06	21 3 67	Deiniolen	Apprentice	Watford	39	5
						Aston Villa (loan)	4	—
						Norwich C	35	8
						Millwall	8	2
Jimmy Carter	5 10	10 04	9 11 65	London	Apprentice	Crystal Palace	—	—
						QPR	—	—
						Millwall	86	8

Foundation: Formed in 1885 as Millwall Rovers by employees of Morton & Co, a jam and marmalade factory in West Ferry Road. The founders were predominantly Scotsmen. Their first headquarters was the The Islanders pub in Tooke Street, Millwall. Their first trophy was the East End Cup in 1887.

First Football League game: 28 August, 1920, Division 3, v Bristol R (h) W 2-0 – Lansdale; Fort, Hodge; Voisey (1), Riddell, McAlpine; Waterall, Travers, Broad (1), Sutherland, Dempsey.

Managers (and Secretary-managers)
Willie Henderson 1894–95*, John Beveridge 1895–1907* (continued as secretary until 1915), Fred Kidd 1907–08, George Saunders 1908–09, Herbert Lipsham 1913–19, Robert Hunter 1919–33, Bill McCracken 1933–36, Charlie Hewitt 1936–40, Bill Voisey 1940–44, Jack Cock 1944–48, Charlie Hewitt 1948–56, Ron Gray 1956–57, Jimmy Seed 1958–59, Reg Smith 1959–61, Ron Gray 1961–63, Billy Gray 1963–66, Benny Fenton 1966–74, Gordon Jago 1974–77, George Petchey 1978–80, Peter Anderson 1980–82, George Graham 1982–86, John Docherty 1986–90, Bob Pearson 1990, Bruce Rioch 1990– .

Player and Position	Ht	Wt	Birth Date	Place	Source	Clubs	League App	Gls
Paul Goddard	5 8	12 00	12 10 59	Harlington	Apprentice	QPR	70	23
						West Ham U	170	54
						Newcastle U	61	19
						Derby Co	49	15
						Millwall	14	1
Manus Magill	6 0	11 07	2 8 71	Ballymena		Millwall	—	—
Kevin O'Callaghan	5 8	11 04	19 10 61	London	Apprentice	Millwall	20	3
						Ipswich T	115	3
						Portsmouth	87	16
						Millwall	56	12
Teddy Sheringham	5 8	12 04	2 4 66	Highams Park	Apprentice	Millwall	174	60
						Aldershot (loan)	5	—
Paul Stephenson	5 10	10 09	2 1 68	Newcastle	Apprentice	Newcastle U	61	1
						Millwall	35	3
Stephen Torpey	6 2	12 11	8 12 70	Islington	Trainee	Millwall	7	—
Darren Treacy	5 10	12 09	6 9 70	Lambeth	Trainee	Millwall	7	—

Trainees
Emberson, Carl W; Henry, Ansell A; Kerry, Nicholas C; Pope, Barry D; Rogerson, Colin C; Thompson, Darren; Walker, Lee M.D.

Associated Schoolboys
Beard, Mark; Chapman, Daniel G; French, Jermaine; Gordon, Neville; Gratwick; Elliott, P; Hart, Aiden, M; Irving, Paul R; McArthur, Frank P; McIntyre, Ian S; Middleton, Mathew J; Munoz, Mark; Nixon, Andrew W; Okyere-Darkoh, Joseph; Omogbehin, Colin; Ritrovato, Anthony; Smith, Brett R; Spaine, Vidal E; Thatcher, Ben D; Whymark, Chay A.E.

Associated Schoolboys who have accepted the club's offer of a Traineeship/Contract
Bedford, Roy D; Dickson, Hugh J; Dolby, Tony C; Foran, Mark J; Franklin, Jeffrey; Holloway, Jamie D; Lee, Brian R; Manning, Paul J; Owen, Daniel; Roberts, Andrew J.

NEWCASTLE UNITED 1989–90 *Back row (left to right):* Bobby Saxton (First Team Coach), Wayne Fereday, Tommy Wright, John Anderson, Liam O'Brien, Andy Thorn, Rob McDonald, Kevin Scott, Bjorn Kristensen, Mick Quinn, Gary Kelly, Michael O'Neill, Derek Wright (Physiotherapist), *Front row:* Gary Brazil, John Gallacher, Paul Sweeney, Mark McGhee, Jim Smith (Manager), Kevin Dillon, Kevin Brock, Ray Ranson, Mark Stimson.

Division 2   **NEWCASTLE UNITED**

St James' Park, Newcastle-upon-Tyne NE1 4ST. Telephone Tyne-side (091) 232 8361. Commercial Managers: (091) 232 2285. Club Shop: (091) 261 6357. Recorded information: (091) 261 1571. Fax: 091-232 9875. Clubcall 0898-121190. Harveys (Restaurant) 2221860.

Ground capacity: 37,637.

Record attendance: 68,386 v Chelsea, Division 1, 3 Sept, 1930.

Record receipts: £135,000 v Watford, FA Cup 3rd rd 2nd replay, 16 January, 1989.

Pitch measurements: 115yd × 75yd.

Chairman: W.G. McKeag. **Vice-Chairman:** G. R. Forbes.

Directors: Stan Seymour, J. Rush AFC, Sir George Bowman JP, E. Dunn, G. R. Dickson, P. Mallinger.

Manager: Jim Smith. *Asst. Manager:* Bobby Saxton.

Coach: Colin Suggett. *Physio:* Derek Wright.

General Manager/Secretary: R. Cushing.

Assistant Secretary: K. Slater. *Commercial Manager:* G. McDonnell.

Year Formed: 1881. *Turned Professional:* 1889. *Ltd Co.:* 1890.

Club Nickname: 'Magpies'.

Previous Names: Stanley 1881; Newcastle East End 1882–1892.

Previous Ground: South Byker 1881; Chillingham Road, Heaton, 1886 to 1892.

Record League Victory: 13-0 v Newport Co, Division 2, 5 October 1946 – Garbutt; Cowell, Graham; Harvey, Brennan, Wright; Milburn (2), Bentley (1), Wayman (4), Shackleton (6), Pearson.

Record Cup Victory: 9-0 v Southport (at Hillsborough) FA Cup, 4th rd, 1 February 1932 – McInroy; Nelson, Fairhurst; McKenzie, Davidson, Weaver (1); Boyd (1), Jimmy Richardson (3), Cape (2), McMenemy (1), Lang (1).

Record Defeat: 0-9 v Burton Wanderers, Division 2, 15 April, 1895.

Most League Points (2 for a win): 57, Division 2, 1964–65.

Most League Points (3 for a win): 80, Division 2, 1983–84 and Division 2, 1989–90.

Most League Goals: 98, Division 1, 1951–52.

Highest League Scorer in Season: Hughie Gallacher, 36, Division 1, 1926–27.

Most League Goals in Total Aggregate: Jackie Milburn, 178, 1946–57.

Most Capped Player: Alf McMichael, 40, Northern Ireland.

Most League Appearances: Jim Lawrence. 432, 1904–22.

Record Transfer Fee Received: £2,000,000 from Tottenham H for Paul Gascoigne, July 1988.

Record Transfer Fee Paid: £850,000 to Wimbledon for Dave Beasant, June 1988 and £850,000 to Wimbledon for Andy Thorn, August 1988.

Football League Record: 1893 Elected to Division 2; 1898–1934 Division 1; 1934–48 Division 2; 1948–61 Division 1; 1961–65 Division 2; 1965–78 Division 1; 1978–84 Division 2; 1984–89 Division 1; 1989– Division 2.

Honours: Football League; Division 1 – Champions 1904–05, 1906–07, 1908–09, 1926–27; Division 2 – Champions 1964–65; Runners-up 1897–98, 1947–48. *FA Cup:* Winners 1910, 1924, 1932, 1951, 1952, 1955; Runners-up 1905, 1906, 1908, 1911, 1974. *Football League Cup:* Runners-up 1975–76. *Texaco Cup:* Winners 1973–74, 1974–75. **European Competitions;** *European Fairs Cup:* 1968–69 (winners), 1969–70, 1970–71, *UEFA Cup:* 1977–78. *Anglo-Italian Cup:* Winners 1973.

Colours: Black and white striped shirts, black shorts, black stockings. **Change colours:** Yellow and green striped shirts, green shorts, yellow stockings.

NEWCASTLE UNITED 1989–90 LEAGUE RECORD

Match No.	Date	Venue	Opponents	Result	H/T Score	Lg. Pos.	Goalscorers	Atten- dance
1	Aug 19	H	Leeds U	W 5-2	1-2	—	Quinn 4 (1 pen), Gallacher	24,482
2	26	A	Leicester C	D 2-2	1-1	6	Quinn, Gallacher	13,384
3	Sept 2	H	Oldham Ath	W 2-1	1-0	5	Quinn 2 (1 pen)	20,804
4	9	A	Bournemouth	L 1-2	1-1	8	Quinn	9882
5	13	A	Oxford U	L 1-2	1-1	—	Quinn	7313
6	16	H	Portsmouth	W 1-0	0-0	6	Thorn	19,589
7	24	A	Sunderland	D 0-0	0-0	—		29,499
8	27	H	Watford	W 2-1	2-1	—	Gallacher, Quinn	17,040
9	30	A	Hull C	W 3-1	1-1	3	Anderson, Brazil, McGhee	9629
10	Oct 7	A	Ipswich T	L 1-2	0-2	5	McGhee	13,679
11	14	H	Bradford C	W 1-0	0-0	3	McGhee	18,898
12	18	H	Blackburn R	W 2-1	1-0	—	McGhee, Quinn	20,702
13	21	A	Brighton & HA	W 3-0	1-0	2	Quinn 3	10,756
14	28	H	Port Vale	D 2-2	1-0	3	McGhee, Quinn	17,809
15	Nov 1	A	WBA	W 5-1	2-1	—	Robson (og), Brazil, Brock. McGhee, O'Brien	12,339
16	4	H	Middlesbrough	D 2-2	1-1	3	McGhee. O'Brien	23,349
17	11	A	West Ham U	D 0-0	0-0	3		25,892
18	18	A	Barnsley	D 1-1	0-0	3	Quinn	10,475
19	25	H	Sheffield U	W 2-0	2-0	3	Gallacher, Quinn	28,092
20	Dec 2	A	Leeds U	L 0-1	0-0	3		31,715
21	9	H	Oxford U	L 2-3	1-1	4	Stimson, Quinn (pen)	16,685
22	26	A	Stoke C	L 1-2	1-0	6	Scott	14,878
24	30	A	Swindon T	D 1-1	1-0	6	Quinn	11,657
25	Jan 1	H	Wolverhampton W	L 1-4	0-0	7	Brock	22,054
25	13	H	Leicester C	W 5-4	2-2	7	McGhee 2, Quinn 2, Gallacher	20,847
26	20	A	Oldham Ath	D 1-1	0-0	6	McGhee	11,194
27	Feb 4	H	Sunderland	D 1-1	0-0	—	McGhee	31,572
28	10	A	Portsmouth	D 1-1	0-0	7	Quinn	14,204
29	24	A	Sheffield U	D 1-1	1-0	8	Morris (og)	21,035
30	28	H	Bournemouth	W 3-0	0-0	—	Anderson, Quinn 2	15,119
31	Mar 3	H	Barnsley	W 4-1	3-1	5	Anderson, Scott, Aitken, McGhee (pen)	18,998
32	7	A	Hull C	W 2-0	1-0	—	McGhee 2 (1 pen)	20,499
33	10	A	Watford	D 0-0	0-0	4		12,069
34	17	H	Ipswich T	W 2-1	0-1	4	Quinn 2	19,521
35	21	A	Bradford C	L 2-3	1-1	—	McGhee (pen), Aizlewood (og)	10,264
36	24	A	Blackburn R	L 0-2	0-0	5		13,285
37	31	H	Brighton & HA	W 2-0	0-0	4	Gallacher, Quinn	18,746
38	Apr 3	H	Plymouth Arg	W 3-1	1-1	—	Quinn, McGhee 2 (1 pen)	16,558
39	7	A	Port Vale	W 2-1	2-0	3	Quinn, McGhee	10,290
40	11	H	WBA	W 2-1	1-0	—	Anderson, Quinn	19,460
41	14	A	Wolverhampton W	W 1-0	1-0	3	Scott	19,507
42	16	H	Stoke C	W 3-0	2-0	2	Kristensen 2, Quinn	26,190
43	21	A	Plymouth Arg	D 1-1	1-1	3	McGhee	11,702
44	25	H	Swindon T	D 0-0	0-0	—		26,568
45	28	H	West Ham U	W 2-1	0-1	3	Kristensen, Quinn	31,496
46	May 5	A	Middlesbrough	L 1-4	0-0	3	McGee (og)	18,484

Final League Position: 3

GOALSCORERS

League (80): Quinn 32 (3 pens), McGhee 19 (4 pens), Gallacher 6, Anderson 4, Kristensen 3, Scott 3, Brazil 2, Brock 2, O'Brien 2, Aitken 1, Stimson 1, Thorn 1, own goals 4.
Littlewoods Cup (5): Brazil 1 (pen), Brock 1, Gallacher 1, McGhee 1, Thorn 1.
FA Cup (10): McGhee 5 (1 pen), Quinn 2, O'Brien 1, Robinson 1, Scott 1.

Wright	Ranson	Sweeney	Dillon	Scott	Thorn	Gallacher	Brock	Quinn	McGhee	Fereday	Brazil	Stimson	Kristensen	Anderson	Kelly	Burridge	O'Brien	Bradshaw	Aitken	Robinson	Askew	Match No.
1	2	3*	4	5	6	7	8	9	10	11	12											1
1	2		4	5	6	7	8*	9	10	11		3	12									2
1	2†		4	5	6	7*	8	9	10	11	12	3	14									3
1	2	8*	4	5	6	7†		9	10	11		3	14	12								4
1	2		4*	5	6		8	9	10	11	7	3	12									5
	2			5	6	7	8	9	10	11		3	4*	12	1							6
			4	5	6	7*	8	9	10		12	3	11	2	1							7
			4	5	6	7	8	9	10	11		3		2	1							8
			4	5	6	7*	8	9†	10	11	12	3	14	2	1							9
			4	5	6†	7*	8	9	10	11	12	3	14	2	1							10
			4	5		7	8	9	10			3	6	2		1	11					11
			4	5		7*	8†	9	10	14	12	3	6	2		1	11					12
			4	5		7*	8	9	10	14	12	3	6	2†		1	11					13
	2		4	5			8	9	10		7	3	6			1	11					14
	2	14	4*	5			8	9	10		7	3	6	11†		1	12					15
	2†	14	4	5			8	9	10		7	3	6	11*		1	12					16
	2	14	4	5			8*	9	10		7†	3	6	12		1	11					17
	2*		4	5			8	9	10	14	7†	3	6	12		1	11					18
	2		4	5		7*	8	9	10		12	3	6			1	11					19
	2		4	5		7†	8	9	10	14		3*	6	12		1	11					20
	2	14	4*	5			8	9	10†	7		3	6	12		1	11					21
	2	3	4	5		7*	8	9	10	14	12†		6			1	11					22
			12	5		7*	8	9	10			3	6	2		1	11		4			23
			12	5		7	8	9	10			3	6	2		1	11		4*			24
		14	12	5	6†	7*	8	9	10			3		2		1	11		4			25
			3	5	6	7	8	9	10					2		1	11		4			26
	11†		2	5		7	8	9	10	14		3	6*	12		1			4			27
1	11		2	5		7	8	9	10			3	6*	12					4			28
1	6		2	5		7	8	9	10	11		3							4			29
1	6		2	5		7	8	9	10	11		3							4			30
1	6		2	5		7	8	9	10	11*	12	3							4			31
1	6		2	5		7	8	9	10	11	12	3*							4			32
1	6	3	2	5		7	8	9	10	11									4			33
1	6	3	2	5		7	8*	9	10	11†	12			14					4			34
1	6	3	2	5		7	8†	9	10	11*	12			14					4			35
1	6	3†	2	5		7	8	9	10		12							14*	4		11	36
	6	3	2	5		7*	8	9	10							1			4		11	37
	6	3	2	5†		7*	8	9	10		12			14		1			4		11	38
	6	3	2	5		7	8	9	10							1			4		11	39
	6	3	2	5		7	8	9	10	11*	12					1			4			40
	6		2	5		7	8	9	10	11		3				1			4			41
	6†		2	5		7	8*	9	10	11	12	3		14		1			4			42
	6		2	5		7	8	9	10	11		3				1			4			43
	6		2	5		7	8	9	10	11		3				1			4			44
	6		2	5		7	8*	9	10	11	12	3				1			4			45
	6		2†	5		7	8	9*	10	11	12	3		14		1			4			46
14	33	14	43	42	10	21	43	45	46	21	4	35	25	29	4	28	14	9	22	—	4	
		+5s				+7s	+1s				+4s	+12s	+2s	+8s	+8s		+5s		+3s		+1s	

Littlewoods Cup	Second Round	Reading (a)		1-3	
		(h)		4-0	
FA Cup	Third Round	WBA (h)		0-1	
	Third Round	Hull C (a)		1-0	
	Fourth Round	Reading (a)		3-3	
		(h)		4-1	
	Fifth Round	Manchester U (h)		2-3	

NEWCASTLE UNITED

Player and Position	Ht	Wt	Birth Date	Place	Source	Clubs	League App	Gls
Goalkeepers								
John Burridge	5 11	12 11	3 12 51	Workington	Apprentice	Workington	27	—
						Blackpool	134	—
						Aston Villa	65	—
						Southend U (loan)	6	—
						Crystal Palace	88	—
						QPR	39	—
						Wolverhampton W	74	—
						Derby Co (loan)	6	—
						Sheffield U	109	—
						Southampton	62	—
						Newcastle U	28	—
Tommy Wright	6 1	13 05	29 8 63	Belfast	Linfield	Newcastle U	23	—
Defenders								
John Anderson	5 11	11 06	7 11 59	Dublin	Apprentice	WBA	—	—
						Preston NE	51	—
						Newcastle U	272	13
Matthew Appleby	5 10	11 02	16 4 72	Middlesbrough	Trainee	Newcastle U	—	—
Darren Bradshaw	5 10	11 03	19 3 67	Sheffield	Matlock T	Chesterfield	18	—
						York C	59	3
						Newcastle U	12	—
Graeme Carter*	6 0	12 00	18 11 69	Castle Eden	Trainee	Newcastle U	—	—
Craig Chapman*	5 7	10 05	9 12 70	Middlesbrough	Trainee	Newcastle U	—	—
Bjorn Kristensen	6 1	12 05	10 10 63	Malling	Aarhus	Newcastle U	38	3
Philip Mason	5 6	10 07	3 12 71	Consett	Trainee	Newcastle U	—	—
Michael Parkinson	5 7	11 04	8 6 71	Sunderland	Trainee	Newcastle U	—	—
Ray Ranson	5 9	11 12	12 6 60	St Helens	Apprentice	Manchester C	183	1
						Birmingham C	137	—
						Newcastle U	47	1
David Roche	5 11	12 01	13 12 70	Newcastle	Trainee	Newcastle U	2	—
Kevin Scott	6 2	11 06	17 12 66	Easington		Newcastle U	78	5
Mark Stimson	5 11	11 00	27 12 67	Plaistow		Tottenham H	2	—
						Leyton Orient (loan)	10	—
						Gillingham (loan)	18	—
						Newcastle U	37	1
Midfield								
Roy Aitken	6 0	12 00	24 11 58	Irvine	Celtic BC	Celtic	483	40
						Newcastle U	22	1
Billy Askew	5 5	10 10	2 10 59	Lumley	Apprentice	Middlesbrough	12	—
						Blackburn R (loan)		—
						Hull C	253	19
						Newcastle U	4	—
Kevin Brock	5 9	10 12	9 9 62	Middleton Stoney	Apprentice	Oxford U	246	26
						QPR	40	2
						Newcastle U	65	4
Lee Clark	5 7	11 07	27 10 72	Wallsend	Trainee	Newcastle U	—	—
Kevin Dillon	6 0	12 07	18 12 59	Sunderland	Apprentice	Birmingham C	186	15
						Portsmouth	215	45
						Newcastle U	43	—
Wayne Fereday	5 9	11 00	16 6 63	Warley	Apprentice	QPR	197	21
						Newcastle U	25	—
Archie Gourlay	5 8	10 00	29 6 69	Greenock		Morton	2	—
						Newcastle U	1	—
						Morton (loan)	4	—
Liam O'Brien	6 1	13 03	5 9 64	Dublin	Shamrock R	Manchester U	31	2
						Newcastle U	39	6
Paul Sweeney	5 7	10 00	10 1 65	Glasgow	St Kentigerns Acad	Raith R	205	8
						Newcastle U	27	—
Paul Tinmouth*	5 8	10 08	7 11 70	South Shields	Trainee	Newcastle U	—	—

NEWCASTLE UNITED

Foundation: It stemmed from a newly formed club called Stanley in 1881. In October 1882 they changed their name to Newcastle East End to avoid confusion with Stanley in Co. Durham. Shortly afterwards another club Rosewood merged with them. Newcastle West End had been formed in August 1882 and they played on a ground which is now St. James' Park. In 1889, West End went out of existence after a bad run and the remaining committee men invited East End to move to St. James' Park. They accepted and at a meeting in Bath Lane Hall in 1892, changed their name to Newcastle United.

First Football League game: 2 September, 1893, Division 2, v Royal Arsenal (a) D 2–2 – Ramsay; Jeffery, Miller; Crielly, Graham, McKane; Bowman, Crate (1), Thompson, Sorley (1), Wallace. Graham and not Crate scored according to some reports.

Managers (and Secretary-managers)
Frank Watt 1895–32 (continued as secretary to 1932), Andy Cunningham 1930–35, Tom Mather 1935–39, Stan Seymour 1939–47 (Hon-manager), George Martin 1947–50, Stan Seymour 1950–54 (Hon-manager), Duggie Livingstone 1954–56, Stan Seymour (Hon-manager 1956–58), Charlie Mitten 1958–61, Norman Smith 1961–62, Joe Harvey 1962–75, Gordon Lee 1975–77, Richard Dinnis 1977, Bill McGarry 1977–80, Arthur Cox 1980–84, Jack Charlton 1984, Willie McFaul 1985–88, Jim Smith 1988– .

Player and Position	Ht	Wt	Birth Date	Birth Place	Source	Clubs	League App	League Gls
Forwards								
Gary Brazil	5 11	9 13	19 9 62	Tunbridge Wells	Apprentice	Crystal Palace	—	—
						Sheffield U	62	9
						Port Vale (loan)	6	3
						Preston NE	166	58
						Mansfield T (loan)	—	—
						Newcastle U	23	2
John Gallacher	5 10	10 08	26 1 69	Glasgow		Falkirk	18	5
						Newcastle U	28	6
Mark Gill*	5 9	11 01	6 6 66	Dublin	Home Farm	Newcastle U	—	—
Steve Howey	6 1	10 09	26 10 71	Sunderland	Trainee	Newcastle U	1	—
Rob McDonald‡	6 2	13 00	22 1 59	Hull	Apprentice	Hull C	25	2
					PSV Eindhoven	Newcastle U	10	1
Mark McGhee	5 10	12 00	25 5 57	Glasgow	Apprentice	Bristol C	—	—
						Morton	64	37
						Newcastle U	28	5
						Aberdeen	164	63
						Hamburg	30	7
						Celtic	88	27
						Newcastle U	46	19
Mirandinha‡	5 8	11 00	2 7 59	Sao Paulo	Fluminense	Newcastle U	54	20
Michael O'Neill (To Dundee U Aug 1989)	5 11	10 10	5 7 69	Portadown	Coleraine	Newcastle U	48	15
Frank Pingel‡	6 1	13 08	9 5 64	Resskov	Aarhus	Newcastle U	14	1
Mick Quinn	5 9	13 00	2 5 62	Liverpool	Apprentice	Derby Co	—	—
						Wigan Ath	69	19
						Stockport Co	63	39
						Oldham Ath	80	34
						Portsmouth	121	54
						Newcastle U	45	32
David Robinson	6 0	13 02	27 11 69	Newcastle	Trainee	Newcastle U	2	—

Trainees
Cleary, David J; Cole, Anthony R; English, Michael; Heron, Thomas; Makel, Lee R; Neilson, Alan B; Reay, Simon; Young, Michael.

**Non-Contract
Bennett, Ian M.

Associated Schoolboys
Alderson, Richard; Appleby, Richard D; Dinning, Tony; Foster, Gary H; Geddes, Paul A; Gower, Mark S; Morton, Graeme F; Murray, Nathan A; Ternent, Neill S.

Associated Schoolboys who have accepted the club's offer of a Traineeship/Contract
Cornish, Darren; Elliott, Robert J; Lewis, Stephen; Milner, John F; Thompson, Alan; Watson, John I; Watson, Stephen C.

**Non-Contract Players who are retained must be re-signed before they are eligible to play in League matches.

NORTHAMPTON TOWN 1989–90   *Back row (left to right)*: Bradley Sandeman, Matt Terry, Wayne Williams, Steve Berry, Dean Thomas, Paul Wilson, Irvin Gernon. *Centre row*: Dennis Casey (Physiotherapist), Phil Chard, Bobby Barnes, Keith McPherson, Peter Gleasure, Dave Johnson, Steve Brown, Darren Collins, Clive Walker (Coach). *Front row*: Trevor Quow, David Scope, Martin Singleton, Graham Carr (Manager), Russell Wilcox, Warren Donald.

Division 4   **NORTHAMPTON TOWN**

County Ground, Abington Avenue, Northampton NN1 4PS. Telephone Northampton (0604) 234100. Commercial Dept. (0604) 234100. Information Line, 0898 700 275.

Ground capacity: 11,907.

Record attendance: 24,523 v Fulham, Division 1, 23 April, 1966.

Record receipts: £47,292.40 v Coventry C, FA Cup 3rd rd, 6 January, 1990.

Pitch measurements: 112yd × 75yd.

Chairman: R. J. Underwood. *Vice-Chairman:* B. Stonhill.

Directors: D. Kerr, M. Church, R. Church, M. Deane, B. Hancock.

Secretary: Philip Mark Hough.

Manager: Theo Foley.

Coach: Clive Walker.

Physio: Dennis Casey.   *Commercial Manager:* Mark Underwood.

Year Formed: 1897. *Turned Professional:* 1901. *Ltd Co.:* 1901.

Club Nickname: 'The Cobblers'.

Record League Victory: 10-0 v Walsall, Division 3 (S), 5 November 1927 – Hammond; Watson, Jeffs; Allen, Brett, Odell, Daley, Smith (3), Loasby (3), Hoten (1), Wells (3).

Record Cup Victory: 9-1 v Metropolitan Police, FA Cup, 1st rd, 28 November 1931 – Hammond; English, Fred Dawes; Dowsey, O'Dell, Davies; Scott, Riches (1), Bowen (2), Albert Dawes (3), Wells (2). (1 og).

Record Defeat: 0-11 v Southampton, Southern League, 28 December, 1901.

Most League Points (2 for a win): 68, Division 4, 1975–76.

Most League Points (3 for a win): 99, Division 4, 1986–87.

Most League Goals: 109. Division 3, 1962–63 and Division 3 (S), 1952–53.

Highest League Scorer in Season: Cliff Holton, 36, Division 3, 1961–62.

Most League Goals in Total Aggregate: Jack English, 135, 1947–60.

Most Capped Player: E. Lloyd Davies, 12 (16), Wales.

Most League Appearances: Tommy Fowler, 521, 1946–61.

Record Transfer Fee Received: £265,000 from Watford for Richard Hill, July 1987.

Record Transfer Fee Paid: £85,000 to Manchester C for Tony Adcock, January 1988.

Football League Record: 1920 Original Member of Division 3; 1921 Division 3 (S); 1958–61 Division 4; 1961–63 Division 3; 1963–65 Division 2; 1965–66 Division 1; 1966–67 Division 2; 1967–69 Division 3; 1969–76 Division 4; 1976–77 Division 3; 1977–87 Division 4; 1987–90 Division 3; 1990– Division 4.

Honours: Football League: Division 1 best season: 21st. 1965–66; Division 2 – Runners-up 1964–65; Division 3 – Champions 1962–63; Division 3 (S) – Runners-up 1927–28, 1949–50; Division 4 – Champions 1986–87; Runners-up 1975–76. *FA Cup* best season: 5th rd, 1933–34, 1949–50, 1969–70. *Football League Cup* best season: 5th rd, 1964–65, 1966–67.

Colours: Yellow shirts, solid claret strip on right hand side, yellow shorts, claret trim, yellow stockings, with claret hoops. **Change colours:** Dark blue shirts blue trim, dark blue shorts white triangle, dark blue stockings white tops.

NORTHAMPTON TOWN 1989–90 LEAGUE RECORD

Match No.	Date	Venue	Opponents	Result		H/T Score	Lg. Pos.	Goalscorers	Atten- dance
1	Aug 19	A	Walsall	L	0-1	0-0	—		5020
2	26	A	Swansea C	D	1-1	0-1	17	Collins	3495
3	Sept 2	H	Bristol C	W	2-0	0-0	10	Thomas, Adcock (pen)	4088
4	9	A	Wigan Ath	D	0-0	0-0	14		2459
5	16	H	Shrewsbury T	W	2-1	1-1	11	Collins, Adcock (pen)	3131
6	23	A	Crewe Alex	L	1-2	1-1	14	Collins	3165
7	26	A	Cardiff C	W	3-2	1-1	—	Quow, Adcock, Abraham (og)	2688
8	30	H	Bury	L	0-1	0-1	13		3486
9	Oct 7	H	Preston NE	L	1-2	0-1	14	Collins	3039
10	14	A	Birmingham C	L	0-4	0-1	17		8731
11	17	H	Blackpool	W	4-2	4-2	—	Donald, Wilcox, Barnes, Collins	3098
12	21	A	Bristol R	L	2-4	1-0	16	Brown, Barnes (pen)	4920
13	28	H	Notts Co	D	0-0	0-0	16		3734
14	31	A	Fulham	D	1-1	1-1	—	Barnes (pen)	3518
15	Nov 4	H	Rotherham U	L	1-2	0-0	17	Barnes (pen)	3598
16	11	A	Huddersfield T	D	2-2	0-1	18	Gernon, Barnes	4973
17	25	H	Brentford	L	0-2	0-1	21		3165
18	Dec 2	A	Bolton W	W	3-0	2-0	15	Barnes 2, Donald	5501
19	17	H	Reading	W	2-1	2-1	—	Barnes, Collins	3025
20	26	A	Leyton Orient	D	1-1	0-0	13	Barnes	4784
21	30	A	Mansfield T	W	2-1	0-1	13	Berry, Barnes	3200
22	Jan 1	H	Chester C	W	1-0	0-0	11	Berry	3823
23	13	H	Swansea C	D	1-1	0-1	10	Barnes	3799
24	Feb 17	H	Bolton W	L	0-2	0-1	19		3432
25	20	H	Walsall	D	1-1	1-0	—	Collins	2617
26	25	A	Brentford	L	2-3	2-1	—	Thomas, Collins	6391
27	Mar 3	H	Tranmere R	L	0-4	0-1	20		3147
28	6	A	Bury	L	0-1	0-0	—		2327
29	10	A	Cardiff C	D	1-1	0-1	22	Barnes (pen)	2574
30	13	H	Wigan Ath	D	1-1	0-0	—	Chard	2172
31	17	A	Preston NE	D	0-0	0-0	22		5681
32	20	H	Birmingham C	D	2-2	2-1	—	Terry, Wilcox	4346
33	24	A	Blackpool	L	0-1	0-0	22		3296
34	27	A	Bristol C	L	1-3	1-2	—	Barnes	11,965
35	31	H	Bristol R	L	1-2	0-0	23	Thorpe	3774
36	Apr 3	A	Shrewsbury T	L	0-2	0-1	—		2314
37	7	H	Fulham	D	2-2	0-1	23	Sandeman, Thorpe	2822
38	10	A	Notts Co	L	2-3	0-1	23	Terry, Barnes	5396
39	14	A	Chester C	W	1-0	1-0	23	Barnes (pen)	2234
40	16	H	Leyton Orient	L	0-1	0-1	23		3215
41	21	A	Reading	L	2-3	1-1	23	Barnes (pen), McPherson	3140
42	24	A	Mansfield T	L	1-2	0-2	—	Wilcox	2119
43	28	H	Huddersfield T	W	1-0	1-0	23	Barnes	2388
44	30	H	Crewe Alex	W	3-1	2-1	—	Barnes (pen), Chard, Thorpe	2622
45	May 2	A	Tranmere R	D	0-0	0-0	—		5363
46	5	A	Rotherham U	L	0-2	0-0	22		3420

Final League Position: 22

GOALSCORERS

League (51): Barnes 18 (7 pens), Collins 8, Adcock 3 (2 pens), Thorpe 3, Wilcox 3, Berry 2, Chard 2, Donald 2, Terry 2, Thomas 2, Brown 1, Gernon 1, McPherson 1, Quow 1, Sandeman 1, own goal 1.
Littlewoods Cup (1): Adcock 1.
FA Cup (3): Barnes 1, Berry 1 Thomas 1.

Gleasure	Williams	Wilson	Thomas	Wilcox	McPherson	Quow	Culpin	Donald	Adcock	Berry	Sandeman	Collins	Scope	Donegal	Brown	Barnes	Gernon	Chard	Singleton	McPhillips	Terry	Leaburn	Thorpe	Johnson	Bell	Match No.
1	2	3	4	5	6	7*	8†	9	10	11	12	14														1
1		3	4	5	6	7		9	10	11	2	8														2
1		3	4	5	6	7		9	10	11	2	8														3
1		3	4	5	6	7	12	9	10	11	2	8*														4
1	12	3	4	5	6	7		9*	10	11	2	8														5
1		3	4	5	6	7	12		10	11	2	8	9*													6
1	9	3	4	5	6	7			10	11	2*	8	12													7
1	2	3	4	5	6	7	12	14	10	11		8*	9†													8
1	2*	3	4	5	6	7		9		11		8		10	12											9
1		3	4	5	6	2		9*		7		8	12		11	10										10
1		3	4	5*	6	2		9		7	12	8			11	10										11
1			4	5	6	2		9		7	12	8			11*	10	3									12
1			4	5	6			9		7		8			11	10	3	2								13
1			4	5	6			9*		7	12	8	14		11†	10	3	2								14
1			4	5	6			9†		7	12	8*			11	10	3	2	14							15
1			4	5	6			9		7†	12	8			11*	10	3	2	14							16
1			4	5	6			9		7		8*	14		11†	10	3	2	12							17
1		3	4	5	6			9		7		8			11*	10		2	12							18
1			4	5	6			9		7	12	8*			11	10	3	2								19
1			4	5	6			9		7	12	8			11*	10	3	2								20
1			4	5	6			9		7	12	8*			11	10	3	2								21
1			4	5	6			9		7		8			11	10	3	2								22
1			4	5	6			9		7		8†	14		11	10	3	2*	12							23
1		3	4	5	6	2		9		7		8			11*	10			12							24
1		3	4	5	6	2		9		7		8			11	10										25
1		3	4	5	6	2		9		7		8			11	10										26
1		3	4	5	6	2		9		7		8*	14		11†	10			12							27
1	12		4	5	6			9		7		8			11	10	3*	2								28
1		3	4	5	6			9*		7	12	8			11	10		2								29
1		3	9	5	6					7		8			11	10		2			4					30
1		3	9	5	6					7		8			11	10		2			4					31
1		3*	9	5	6					7	12	8			11	10		2			4					32
1				5	6					7	12	8				10		2	3		4	9	11*			33
1		3		5	6*					7	12	8				10		2			4	9	11			34
1		3		5	6					7	12	8				10		2*			4	9	11			35
1	2	3		5	6†					7	12	8				10			14		4	9	11*			36
1	2	3		5	6					7		8				10					4	9	11			37
1	2			5	6					7	12	8				10		3			4	9*	11			38
1	2	3		5	6					7		8				10					4	9	11			39
1	2	3		5	6					7†	12	8*	14			10					4	9	11			40
1				5	6					7	12	8			11*	10		2	14		4	9		3†		41
1	2			5	6							8				10					4	9	11	3	7	42
1	2			5	6							8				10					4	9	11	3	7	43
1	2			5	6							8				10					4	9	11	3	7	44
1	2			5	6						12	8	14			10					4	9*	11	3	7†	45
1	2†			5	6						12	8	14			10					4	9	11	3*	7	46
46	14	26	31	46	43	25	1	20	8	41	20	33	2	1	15	37	12	29	6	—	17	9	13	6	5	

Substitute appearances:
+1s +1s ... +5s +3s 7s ... +9s 2s 5s 6s ... +4s 1s ... +1s 1s

Littlewoods Cup First Round Mansfield T (a) 1-1
  (h) 0-2

FA Cup First Round Kettering (a) 1-0
  Second Round Aylesbury (h) 0-0
  (a) 1-0
  Third Round Coventry C (h) 1-0
  Fourth Round Rochdale (a) 0-3

NORTHAMPTON TOWN

Player and Position	Ht	Wt	Birth Date	Place	Source	Clubs	League App	Gls
Goalkeepers								
Peter Gleasure	5 11	12 13	8 10 60	Luton	Apprentice	Millwall	55	—
						Northampton T (loan)	11	—
						Northampton T	317	—
Defenders								
Mickey Bodley‡	5 11	12 00	14 9 67	Hayes	Apprentice	Chelsea	6	1
						Northampton T	20	
Irving Gernon	6 2	12 01	30 12 62	Birmingham	Apprentice	Ipswich T	76	—
						Northampton T (loan)	9	—
						Gillingham	35	1
						Reading	25	—
						Northampton T	12	1
David Johnson†	5 10	11 02	10 3 67	Northampton	Irthlingborough D	Northampton T	7	
Keith McPherson	5 11	10 11	11 9 63	Greenwich	Apprentice	West Ham U	1	—
						Cambridge U (loan)	11	1
						Northampton T	182	8
Matthew Tarry*	5 9	11 00	14 10 70	Northampton	Trainee	Northampton T	—	—
Steve Terry	6 1	13 03	14 6 62	Clapton	Apprentice	Watford	160	14
						Hull C	62	4
						Northampton T	17	2
Russell Wilcox	6 0	11 10	25 3 64	Hemsworth	Apprentice	Doncaster R	1	—
						Cambridge U	—	—
					Frickley	Northampton T	138	9
Wayne Williams	5 11	11 09	17 11 63	Telford	Apprentice	Shrewsbury T	221	7
						Northampton T	41	1
Paul Wilson	5 10	10 12	2 8 68	Bradford	Trainee	Huddersfield T	15	—
						Norwich C	—	—
						Northampton T	81	2
Midfield								
Michael Bell§			15 11 71	Newcastle	Trainee	Northampton T	6	—
Steve Berry	5 7	11 06	4 4 63	Gosport	Apprentice	Portsmouth	28	2
						Aldershot (loan)	7	—
						Sunderland	35	2
						Newport Co	60	6
						Swindon T	4	—
						Aldershot	48	6
						Northampton T	75	5
Philip Chard	5 8	11 03	16 10 60	Corby	Nottingham F	Peterborough U	172	18
						Northampton T	115	27
						Wolverhampton W	34	5
						Northampton T	29	2
Warren Donald*	5 7	10 01	7 10 64	Uxbridge	Apprentice	West Ham U	2	—
						Northampton T (loan)	11	2
						Northampton T	177	11
Trevor Quow	5 7	10 12	28 9 60	Peterborough	Apprentice	Peterborough U	203	17
						Gillingham	79	3
						Northampton T	48	2
Bradley Sandeman	5 10	10 08	24 2 70	Northampton	Trainee	Northampton T	53	3
Martin Singleton*	5 10	11 00	2 8 63	Banbury	Apprentice	Coventry C	23	1
						Bradford C	71	3
						WBA	19	1
						Northampton T	50	4

NORTHAMPTON TOWN

Foundation: Formed in 1897 by school teachers connected with the Northampton and District Elementary Schools' Association, they survived a financial crisis at the end of their first year when they were £675 in the red and became members of the Midland League – a fast move indeed for a new club. They achieved Southern League membership in 1901.

First Football League game: 28 August, 1920, Division 3, v Grimsby T (a) L 0-2 – Thorpe; Sproston, Hewison; Jobey, Tomkins, Pease; Whitworth, Lockett, Thomas, Freeman, MacKechnie.

Managers (and Secretary-managers)
Arthur Jones 1897–1907*, Herbert Chapman 1907–12, Walter Bull 1912–13, Fred Lessons 1913–19, Bob Hewison 1920–25, Jack Tresadern 1925–30, Jack English 1931–35, Syd Puddefoot 1935–37, Warney Cresswell 1937–39, Tom Smith 1939–49, Bob Dennison 1949–54, Dave Smith 1954–59, David Bowen 1959–67, Tony Marchi 1967–68, Ron Flowers 1968–69, Dave Bowen 1969–72 (continued as GM and secretary to 1985 when joined the board), Billy Baxter 1972–73, Bill Dodgin Jnr 1973–76, Pat Crerand 1976–77, Bill Dodgin Jnr 1977, John Petts 1977–78, Mike Keen 1978–79, Clive Walker 1979–80, Bill Dodgin Jnr 1980–82, Clive Walker 1982–84, Tony Barton 1984–85, Graham Carr 1985–90, Theo Foley 1990–   .

Player and Position	Ht	Wt	Birth Date	Place	Source	Clubs	League App	Gls
Forwards								
Bobby Barnes	5 7	10 05	17 12 62	Kingston	Apprentice	West Ham U	43	5
						Scunthorpe U (loan)	6	—
						Aldershot	49	26
						Swindon T	45	13
						Bournemouth	14	—
						Northampton T	37	18
Steve Brown	5 9	10 12	6 7 66	Northampton	Irthlingborough D	Northampton T	21	1
Darren Collins	5 11	12 00	24 5 67	Winchester	Petersfield U	Northampton T	43	8
Glenville Donegal‡	6 2	12 08	20 6 69		Trainee	Northampton T	20	3
David Scope	5 8	10 12	10 5 67	Newcastle	Blyth Sp	Northampton T	7	—
Adrian Thorpe	5 6	11 00	20 11 63	Chesterfield	Heanor T	Bradford C	17	1
						Tranmere R (loan)	5	3
						Notts Co	59	9
						Walsall	27	1
						Northampton T	13	3

Trainees
Ashdjian, John A; Barrett, James D.A; Bell, Michael; Burnham, Jason J; Capone, Julian; Carlin, Scott; Carr, Matthew J; Douglas, Michael J; Hall, Stephen J; Hallcro, Darren; Hallcro, Wayne; Kitching, Lee; Magill, Andrew C; Parker, Sean; Proud, Andrew, J; Shaw Jon T; Shearman, Robert M; Taylor, Martin P; Waldock, Casey K.C; Watts, Darren J.

**Non-Contract
Johnson, David D.

Associated Schoolboys
Bingham, Matthew J; Knight, Stuart A; Lamb, Paul D; Underwood, Simon S; Willis, Ian.

Associated Schoolboys who have accepted the club's offer of a Traineeship/Contract
Harrald, Russell M; Kiernan, Daniel J; Waring, James M.

**Non-Contract Players who are retained must be re-signed before they are eligible to play in League matches.

NORWICH CITY 1989–90. *Back row (left to right)*: Mike Flynn, Andy Townsend, Tim Sherwood, Andy Linighan, Paul Cook, Adrian Pennock, Dean Coney.
Centre row: Tim Sheppard (Physiotherapist), Jeremy Goss, Andy Theodosiou, Jonathan Sheffield, Ian Butterworth, Bryan Gunn, Robert Rosario, Mark Walton, Ian Culverhouse, Ian Crook, David Williams (Assistant Manager).
Front row: David Smith, Malcolm Allen, David Phillips, Robert Fleck, David Stringer (Manager), Dale Gordon, Mark Bowen, Ruel Fox, Jason Minett.

Division 1   **NORWICH CITY**

Carrow Road, Norwich NR1 1JE. Telephone Norwich (0603) 612131. Commercial Dept. (0603) 615011. Box Office (0603) 761661. Clubcall: 0898 12 11 44. Match Information Line: 0898 121514.

NORWICH CITY FC

Ground capacity: 24,284.

Record attendance: 43,984 v Leicester C, FA Cup 6th rd, 30 March, 1963.

Record receipts: £126,395 v West Ham U, FA Cup 6th rd replay, 22 March, 1989.

Pitch measurements: 114yd × 74yd.

President: G. C. Watling.

Chairman: Robert T. Chase JP. *Vice-Chairman:* J. A. Jones.

Directors: F. J. Kennedy, B. W. Lockwood, G. A. Paterson, A. Scholes DMS, IPFA.

Manager: Dave Stringer. *Assistant Manager/Coach:* Dave Williams.

Commercial Manager: Ray Cossey.

Physio: Tim Sheppard MCSP, SRP.

Secretary: A. R. W. Neville.

Year Formed: 1902. *Turned Professional:* 1905. *Ltd Co.:* 1905.

Club Nickname: 'The Canaries'.

Previous Grounds: 1902, Newmarket Road; 1908–35. The Nest, Rosary Road.

Record League Victory: 10-2 v Coventry C, Division 3 (S), 15 March 1930 – Jarvie; Hannah, Graham; Brown, O'Brien, Lochhead (1); Porter (1), Anderson, Hunt (5), Scott (2), Slicer (1).

Record Cup Victory: 8-0 v Sutton U, FA Cup, 4th rd, 28 January 1989 – Gunn; Culverhouse, Bowen, Butterworth, Linighan, Townsend (Crook), Gordon, Fleck (3), Allen (4), Phelan, Putney (1).

Record Defeat: 2-10 v Swindon T, Southern League, 5, September, 1908.

Most League Points (2 for a win): 64, Division 3 (S), 1950–51.

Most League Points (3 for a win): 84, Division 2, 1985–86.

Most League Goals: 99, Division 3(S), 1952–53.

Highest League Scorer in Season: Ralph Hunt, 31. Division 3 (S), 1955–56.

Most League Goals in Total Aggregate: Johnny Gavin, 122, 1945–54, 1955–58.

Most Capped Player: Martin O'Neill, 18 (64), Northern Ireland.

Most League Appearances: Ron Ashman, 592, 1947–64.

Record Transfer Fee Received: £1,000,000 from Manchester C.for Kevin Reeves, March 1980 and from Nottingham F for Justin Fashanu, August 1981, and from Everton for Dave Watson, August 1986.

Record Transfer Fee Paid: £550,000 to Coventry C for David Phillips, July 1989.

Football League Record: 1920 Original Member of Division 3; 1921 Division 3 (S): 1934–39 Division 2; 1946–58 Division 3 (S); 1958–60 Division 3; 1960–72 Division 2; 1972–74 Division 1; 1974–75 Division 2; 1975–81 Division 1; 1981–82 Division 2; 1982–85 Division 1; 1985–86 Division 2; 1986– Division 1.

Honours: Football League: Division 1 best season: 4th, 1988–89; Division 2 – Champions 1971–72, 1985–86. Division 3 (S) – Champions 1933–34; Division 3 – Runners-up 1959–60. *FA Cup:* Semi-finals 1959, 1989. *Football League Cup:* Winners 1962, 1985; Runners-up 1973, 1975.

Colours: Yellow shirts green trim, green shorts yellow trim, yellow stockings. **Change colours:** White shirts green trim, white shorts green trim, white stockings.

NORWICH CITY 1989–90 LEAGUE RECORD

Match No.	Date	Venue	Opponents	Result	H/T Score	Lg. Pos.	Goalscorers	Attendance
1	Aug 19	A	Sheffield W	W 2-0	1-0	—	Phillips, Fleck	19,142
2	23	H	Nottingham F	D 1-1	1-0	—	Gordon	18,267
3	26	H	QPR	D 0-0	0-0	7		14,021
4	30	A	Manchester U	W 2-0	1-0	—	Gordon, Fleck (pen)	39,610
5	Sept 9	A	Southampton	D 4-4	1-2	3	Rosario 2, Sherwood, Fleck	14,259
6	16	A	Liverpool	D 0-0	0-0	7		36,885
7	23	H	Tottenham H	D 2-2	0-2	7	Phillips, Bowen	20,095
8	30	A	Millwall	W 1-0	0-0	4	Bowen	13,925
9	Oct 14	A	Chelsea	W 2-0	1-0	3	Bowen, Fleck (pen)	19,042
10	21	A	Luton T	L 1-4	0-1	6	Allen (pen)	9038
11	28	H	Everton	D 1-1	1-0	6	Linighan	18,627
12	Nov 4	A	Arsenal	L 3-4	2-0	6	Allen, Phillips, Sherwood	35,338
13	11	A	Aston Villa	W 2-0	0-0	4	Mountfield (og), Linighan	18,186
14	18	H	Charlton Ath	D 0-0	0-0	4		16,084
15	25	A	Coventry C	L 0-1	0-0	8		11,999
16	Dec 2	H	Sheffield W	W 2-1	2-1	5	Townsend (pen), King (og)	15,341
17	9	A	Nottingham F	W 1-0	1-0	4	Bowen	18,939
18	16	H	Derby Co	W 1-0	1-0	4	Rosario	16,184
19	26	A	Manchester C	L 0-1	0-0	4		29,534
20	30	A	Crystal Palace	L 0-1	0-0	6		14,250
21	Jan 1	H	Wimbledon	L 0-1	0-0	6		16,680
22	13	A	QPR	L 1-2	0-0	9	Gordon	11,439
23	21	H	Manchester U	W 2-0	0-0	—	Fleck 2	17,370
24	Feb 4	A	Tottenham H	L 0-4	0-2	—		19,599
25	10	H	Liverpool	D 0-0	0-0	10		20,210
26	27	A	Southampton	L 1-4	1-0	—	Allen	13,668
27	Mar 3	A	Charlton Ath	W 1-0	1-0	11	Fleck	7918
28	10	A	Chelsea	D 0-0	0-0	9		18,796
29	14	H	Coventry C	D 0-0	0-0	—		13,673
30	17	H	Millwall	D 1-1	0-0	10	Townsend	14,699
31	24	A	Everton	L 1-3	1-0	11	Phillips	21,707
32	31	H	Luton T	W 2-0	1-0	8	Townsend (pen), Bowen	14,451
33	Apr 4	H	Crystal Palace	W 2-0	2-0	—	Sherwood, O'Reilly (og)	12,640
34	14	A	Wimbledon	D 1-1	1-0	8	Bowen	4638
35	16	H	Manchester C	L 0-1	0-1	9		18,914
36	21	A	Derby Co	W 2-0	1-0	8	Rosario, Fox	13,758
37	28	A	Aston Villa	D 3-3	1-0	8	Fox, Mountfield (og), Rosario	28,988
38	May 5	H	Arsenal	D 2-2	2-1	10	Bowen, Fox	19,256

Final League Position: 10

GOALSCORERS

League (44): Bowen 7, Fleck 7 (2 pens), Rosario 5, Phillips 4, Allen 3 (1 pen), Fox 3, Gordon 3, Sherwood 3, Townsend 3 (2 pens), Linighan 2, own goals 4.
Littlewoods Cup (4): Fleck 3, Gordon 1.
FA Cup (4): Fleck 2, Gordon 1, Rosario 1.

Gunn	Culverhouse	Bowen	Butterworth	Linighan	Townsend	Gordon	Fleck	Coney	Crook	Phillips	Cook	Sherwood	Rosario	Fox	Allen	Goss	Mortensen	Pennock	Tanner	Smith	Walton	Power	Match No.
1	2	3	4	5	6	7	8	9	10	11													1
1	2	3	4*	5	6	7	8	9	10	11	12												2
1	2	3		5	6	7	8	9	10	11			4										3
1	2*	3	4	5	6	7	8		10	11		12	9										4
1		3	4	5	6	7	8		10	11	12	2*	9										5
1		3	4	5	6	7	8		10	11		2	9										6
1		3	4	5	6	7	8		10	11		2	9										7
1		3	4	5	6	7	8		10	11		2	9										8
1		3	4	5	6	7	8		10	11		2	9										9
1		3	4	5		7	8*		10	11		2	9	6†	12	14							10
1	2	3	4	5	6*	7	8		10†	11		14	9	12									11
1	2	3	4	5		7				11		6	9	8	10								12
1	2	3	4	5	10	7		9		11		6		8									13
1	2	3	4	5	6*	7		9†12		11		10	14	8									14
1	2	3	4	5	6	7				11		10	9	8									15
1	14	3	4	5	6	7		12	10	11		2†	9*				8						16
1	2	3	4	5	6	7			10	11			9				8						17
1	2	3	4	5	6	7			10	11			9				8						18
1	2	3	4	5	6	7			10	11		12	9				8*						19
1	2	3	4	5	6	7	12		10†	11		14	9				8*						20
1	2	3	4	5	6	7	8		10	11			9										21
1	2	3*	4	5	6	7	8		10	11		12	9										22
1	2	3	4	5	6	7	8		10	11†			9										23
1	2	3		5	6	7	8	12	10	11†		4	9*		14								24
1	2	3		5	6	7	8	9*	10	11		4			12								25
1	2	3	5*	6	7†	8			10	11			9	14	12		4						26
1	2	3		5	6		8		10	11			5	9	7				4				27
1	2	3		5	6		8		10	11			12	9	7*				4				28
1	2	3		5	6		8		10	11			9*	7	12				4				29
1	2	3		5	6		8		10	11			7	9					4				30
1	2	3		5	6		8		10	11		7	9						4				31
1	2	3		5	6		12		10	11		7	9*14		8†				4				32
1	2	3		5	6				10	11		4	9	7			8						33
1	2	3		5	6				10	11		4	9	7*		12	8						34
1	2	3		5	6		12		10	11		4	9			7	8*						35
1	2	3		5	6		8*		10	11		4	9†	7		12			14				36
	2	3		5	6		8*		10	11		4	9	7							1	12	37
1	2	3		5			8		10	11		4	9	7	6								38
37	31	38	22	37	35	26	25	6	34	38	—	22	29	6	9	3	12	1	6	—	1	—	
							+	+ +				+	+	+	+	+	+ +		+		+		
							1s	2s	3s1s			2s	5s	2s	1s	3s	4s3s		1s		1s		

Littlewoods Cup	Second Round	Rotherham U (h)	1-1
		(a)	2-0
	Third Round	Manchester C (a)	1-3
FA Cup	Third Round	Exeter C (a)	1-1
		(h)	2-0
	Fourth Round	Liverpool (h)	0-0
		(a)	1-3

NORWICH CITY

Player and Position	Ht	Wt	Birth Date	Place	Source	Clubs	League App	Gls
Goalkeepers								
Bryan Gunn	6 2	13 13	22 12 63	Thurso	Invergordon BC	Aberdeen	15	—
						Norwich C	141	—
Jon Sheffield	5 11	11 07	1 2 69	Bedworth		Norwich C	1	—
						Aldershot (loan)	11	—
						Ipswich T (loan)	—	—
Mark Walton	6 2	13 13	1 6 69	Merthyr	Swansea C	Luton T	—	—
						Colchester U	40	—
						Norwich C	1	—
Defenders								
Mark Bowen	5 8	11 13	7 12 63	Neath	Apprentice	Tottenham H	17	2
						Norwich C	97	10
Ian Butterworth	6 1	12 10	25 1 64	Nantwich	Apprentice	Coventry C	90	—
						Nottingham F	27	—
						Norwich C	122	2
Ian Culverhouse	5 10	11 02	22 9 64	B Stortford	Apprentice	Tottenham H	2	—
						Norwich C	158	—
Andy Linighan	6 3	12 06	18 8 62	Hartlepool	Smiths BC	Hartlepool U	110	4
						Leeds U	66	3
						Oldham Ath	87	6
						Norwich C	86	8
Adrian Pennock	6 0	12 04	27 3 71	Ipswich	Trainee	Norwich C	1	—
Andy Theodosiou	6 0	12 10	30 10 70	Stoke Newington	Tottenham H	Norwich C	—	—
Midfield								
Ian Crook	5 8	10 06	18 1 63	Romford	Apprentice	Tottenham H	20	1
						Norwich C	117	7
Dale Gordon	5 10	11 08	9 1 67	Gt Yarmouth	Apprentice	Norwich C	155	20
Jeremy Goss	5 9	10 09	11 5 65	Cyprus	Amateur	Norwich C	36	2
Jason Minett	5 10	10 02	2 8 71	Peterborough	Trainee	Norwich C	—	—
David Phillips	5 10	11 02	29 7 63	Wegberg	Apprentice	Plymouth Arg	73	15
						Manchester C	81	13
						Coventry C	100	8
						Norwich C	38	4
Tim Sherwood	6 1	11 04	6 2 69	St Albans	Trainee	Watford	32	2
						Norwich C	27	3
David Smith	5 9	11 12	26 12 70	Liverpool	Trainee	Norwich C	1	—
Andy Townsend	5 11	12 07	23 7 63	Maidstone	Weymouth	Southampton	83	5
						Norwich C	71	8
David Williams†	5 10	11 08	11 3 55	Cardiff	Clifton Ath	Bristol R	352	66
						Norwich C	60	11
Forwards								
Dean Coney	6 0	13 04	18 9 63	Dagenham	Apprentice	Fulham	211	56
						QPR	48	7
						Norwich C	17	1
Robert Fleck	5 8	11 08	11 8 65	Glasgow	Possil Y M	Partick Th	2	1
						Rangers	85	29
						Norwich C	78	24
Ruel Fox	5 6	10 00	14 1 68	Ipswich	Apprentice	Norwich C	48	5
Henrik Mortensen	5 10	11 07	12 2 68	Odder, Denmark	Aarhus	Norwich C	15	—
Lee Power§	5 11	11 02	30 6 72	Lewisham	Trainee	Norwich C	1	—
Robert Rosario	6 3	12 01	4 3 66	Hammersmith	Hillingdon Bor	Norwich C	117	18
						Wolverhampton W (loan)	2	1

NORWICH CITY

Foundation: Formed in 1902, largely through the initiative of two local schoolmasters who called a meeting at the Criterion Cafe, they were shocked by an FA Commission which in 1904 declared the club professional and ejected them from the FA Amateur Cup. However, this only served to strengthen their determination. New officials were appointed and a professional club established at a meeting in the Agricultural Hall in March 1905.

First Football League game: 28 August, 1920, Division 3, v Plymouth A (a) D 1-1 – Skermer; Gray, Gadsden; Wilkinson, Addy, Martin; Laxton, Kidger, Parker, Whitham (1), Dobson.

Managers (and Secretary-managers)
John Bowman 1905–07, James McEwen 1907–08, Arthur Turner 1909–10, Bert Stansfield 1910–15, Major Frank Buckley 1919–20, Charles O'Hagan 1920–21, Albert Gosnell 1921–26, Bert Stansfield 1926, Cecil Potter 1926–29, James Kerr 1929–33, Tom Parker 1933–37, Bob Young 1937–39, Jimmy Jewell 1939, Bob Young 1939–45, Cyril Spiers 1946–47, Duggie Lochhead 1945–50, Norman Low 1950–55, Tom Parker 1955–57, Archie Macaulay 1957–61, Willie Reid 1961–62, George Swindin 1962, Ron Ashman 1962–66, Lol Morgan 1966–69, Ron Saunders 1969–73, John Bond 1973–80, Ken Brown 1980–87, Dave Stringer 1987– .

Player and Position	Ht	Wt	Birth Date	Place	Source	Clubs	League App	Gls
Alan Taylor‡	5 9	10 06	14 11 53	Hinckley	Morecambe	Rochdale	55	7
						West Ham U	98	25
						Norwich C	24	5
					Vancouver W	Cambridge U	8	2
					Vancouver W	Hull C	14	3
						Burnley	64	23
						Bury	62	10
						Norwich C	4	1
Robert Taylor	6 0	11 07	30 4 71	Norwich	Trainee	Norwich C	—	—

Trainees
Brown, Nicholas J; Church, Philip R; De Melo, Armando; Ewens, David T; Hamilton, John T; Ling, Marcus R; Loss, Colin P; Pauling, Gavin J; Power, Lee M; Roberts, Mark G; Rocastle, Stephen O; Sutch, Daryl; Sutton, Christopher R; Ullathorne, Robert; Wooding, Timothy D.

**Non-Contract
Williams, David M.

Associated Schoolboys
Akinbiyi, Adelola; Cleveland, Darren L; Cousin, Scott; Cubitt, Samuel W; Cureton, Jamie; Eadie, Darren M; Ewins, Scott R; Hall, Darren D; Harrington, Justin D; Heald, Gregory J; Herd, Stuart A.L; Jackson, Daniel A; Marshall, Andrew J; Martin, Richard B.T; Prior, Adam G; Roberts, Glyn S; Rule, Keith C; Ruse, Barry J; Snowling, Scott; Southon, Jamie P; Wright, Jonathan.

Associated Schoolboys who have accepted the club's offer of a Traineeship/Contract
Collins, Sean C; Johnson, Andrew; Mortimer, Philip D.

**Non-Contract Players who are retained must be re-signed before they are eligible to play in League matches.

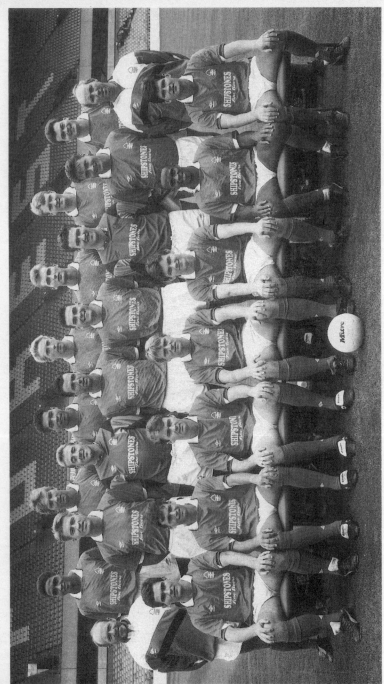

NOTTINGHAM FOREST 1989–90 *Back row (left to right):* Gary Charles, Garry Parker, Des Walker, Terry Wilson, Darren Wassall, Brian Rice, Steve Hodge. *Centre row:* Archie Gemmill (Coach), Lee Chapman, Steve Sutton, Colin Foster, Steve Chettle, Mark Crossley, Tommy Gaynor, Liam O'Kane (Coach). *Front row:* Nigel Clough, Gary Crosby, John Sheridan, Stuart Pearce (Captain), Lee Glover, Franz Carr, Brian Laws.

Division 1   **NOTTINGHAM FOREST**

City Ground, Nottingham NG2 5FJ. Telephone Nottingham (0602) 822202. Information Desk: 821122.
Commercial Manager: 820444.
Ground capacity: 31,920 (15,114 seats).
*Record attendance:*49,945 v Manchester U, Division 1, 28 Oct. 1967.
Record receipts: £186,000 v Tottenham H, Littlewoods Cup, 5th rd, 17 January, 1990.
Pitch measurements: 115 × 78yd.
Chairman: M. Roworth. *Vice Chairman:* F. T. C. Pell FCA.
Directors: G. E. Macpherson JP, F. Reacher, J. F. Hickling, I. I. Korn, J. M. Smith, C. Wootton.
Manager: Brian Clough. *Assistant Manager:* Ron Fenton.
Secretary: P. White. *Commercial Manager:* Dave Pullan.
Coach: Liam O'Kane. *Physio:* G. Lyas.
Year Formed: 1865. *Turned Professional:* 1889. *Ltd Co.:* 1982.
Club Nickname: 'Reds'.
Previous Grounds: 1865, Forest Racecourse: 1879. The Meadows; 1880, Trent Bridge Cricket Ground; 1882, Parkside, Lenton; 1885, Gregory, Lenton; 1890. Town Ground; 1898, City Ground.
Record League Victory: 12-0 v Leicester Fosse, Division 1, 12 April 1909 – Iremonger; Dudley, Maltby; Hughes (1), Needham, Armstrong; Hooper (3), Marrison, West (3), Morris (2), Spouncer (3 incl. 1p).
Record Cup Victory: 14-0 v Clapton (away), FA Cup, 1st rd, 17 January 1891 – Brown: Earp, Scott; Smith (A), Russell, Jeacock; McCallum (2), 'Tich' Smith (1), Higgins (5), Lindley (4), Shaw (2).
Record Defeat: 1-9 v Blackburn R, Division 2, 10 April, 1937.
Most League Points (2 for a win): 70, Division 3 (S), 1950–51.
Most League Points (3 for a win): 74, Division 1, 1983–84.
Most League Goals: 110, Division 3 (S), 1950–51.
Highest League Scorer in Season: Wally Ardron. 36, Division 3(S), 1950–51.
Most League Goals in Total Aggregate: Grenville Morris, 199, 1898–1913.
Most Capped Player: Martin O'Neill, 36 (64), Northern Ireland.
Most League Appearances: Bob McKinlay, 614, 1951–70.
Record Transfer Fee Received: £1,500,000 from Manchester U for Neil Webb, August 1989.
Record Transfer Fee Paid: £1,250,000 to Coventry C for Ian Wallace, July 1980.
Football League Record: 1892 Elected to Division 1; 1906–07 Division 2; 1907–11 Division 1; 1911–22 Division 2; 1922–25 Division 1; 1925–49 Division 2; 1949–51 Division 3 (S); 1951–57 Division 2; 1957–72 Division 1; 1972–77 Division 2; 1977– Division 1.
Honours: Football League: Division 1 – Champions 1977–78; Runners-up 1966–67, 1978–79, Division 2 – Champions 1906–07, 1921–22. Runners-up 1956–57; Division 3 (S) – Champions 1950–51. *FA Cup:* Winners 1898, 1959. *Anglo-Scottish Cup:* Winners 1976–77, *Football League Cup:* Winners 1977–78, 1978–79, 1988–89, 1989–90; Runners-up 1979–80. *Simod Cup:* Winners 1989. **European Competitions:** *Fairs Cup:* 1961–62, 1967–68. *European Cup:* 1978–79 (winners), 1979–80 (winners), 1980–81. *Super Cup:* 1979–80 (winners), 1980–81 (runners-up). *World Club Championship:* 1980–81 (runners-up). *UEFA Cup:* 1983–84, 1984–85.
Colours: Red shirts, white shorts, red stockings. **Change colours:** White shirts, black shorts, white stockings.

NOTTINGHAM FOREST 1989–90 LEAGUE RECORD

Match No.	Date	Venue	Opponents	Result	H/T Score	Lg. Pos.	Goalscorers	Atten- dance
1	Aug 19	H	Aston Villa	D 1-1	0-1	—	Parker	26,766
2	23	A	Norwich C	D 1-1	0-1	—	Chapman	18,267
3	26	A	Millwall	L 0-1	0-0	16		12,140
4	30	H	Derby Co	W 2-1	0-1		Crosby, Pearce	24,060
5	Sept 9	A	Chelsea	D 2-2	1-1	13	Chapman 2	21.523
6	16	H	Arsenal	L 1-2	1-1	15	Parker	22,216
7	23	A	Crystal Palace	L 0-1	0-0	18		12,899
8	30	H	Charlton Ath	W 2-0	1-0	12	Laws, Chapman	18,189
9	Oct 14	A	Coventry C	W 2-0	1-0	9	Crosby, Rice	15,722
10	21	A	Wimbledon	W 3-1	2-1	8	Hodge, Parker, Pearce (pen)	5184
11	28	H	QPR	D 2-2	1-0	9	Crosby, Chapman	19,442
12	Nov 4	H	Sheffield W	L 0-1	0-0	10		21,864
13	12	A	Manchester U	L 0-1	0-1	—		34,182
14	18	A	Manchester C	W 3-0	2-0	11	Clough 2 (1 pen), Rice	26,238
15	25	H	Everton	W 1-0	0-0	7	Clough (pen)	20,709
16	Dec 2	A	Aston Villa	L 1-2	1-1	10	Chapman	25,575
17	9	H	Norwich C	L 0-1	0-1	11		18,939
18	17	H	Southampton	W 2-0	1-0	—	Hodge, Chapman	16,437
19	26	A	Luton T	D 1-1	1-0	10	Hodge	10.754
20	30	A	Tottenham H	W 3-2	2-1	8	Clough, Crosby, Parker	33,401
21	Jan 1	A	Liverpool	D 2-2	0-2	9	Hodge, Clough (pen)	24,518
22	13	A	Millwall	W 3-1	1-0	5	Clough, Laws, Hodge	18,065
23	20	A	Derby Co	W 2-0	2-0	4	Hodge, Jemson	24,176
24	Feb 3	H	Crystal Palace	W 3-1	1-0	4	Clough, Hodge, Jemson	19,739
25	17	H	Chelsea	D 1-1	0-0	4	Orlygsson	22,500
26	Mar 3	H	Manchester C	W 1-0	0-0	3	Crosby	22,644
27	7	A	Arsenal	L 0-3	0-1	—		31,879
28	10	H	Coventry C	L 2-4	0-2	4	Currie, Laws	18,750
29	17	A	Charlton Ath	D 1-1	0-1	5	Hodge	6690
30	24	A	QPR	L 0-2	0-1	7		14,653
31	31	H	Wimbledon	L 0-1	0-1	7		16,821
32	Apr 4	A	Everton	L 0-4	0-3	—		17,795
33	7	H	Tottenham H	L 1-3	0-2	11	Hodge	21,669
34	14	A	Liverpool	D 2-2	0-2	11	Hodge, Jemson	37,265
35	16	H	Luton T	W 3-0	0-0	8	Carr, Parker, Clough	17,001
36	21	A	Southampton	L 0-2	0-1	12		17,006
37	May 2	H	Manchester U	W 4-0	4-0	—	Parker, Pearce, Clough, Chettle	21,186
38	5	A	Sheffield W	W 3-0	1-0	9	Pearce 2, Jemson	29,762

Final League Position: 9

GOALSCORERS

League (55): Hodge 10, Clough 9 (3 pens), Chapman 7, Parker 6, Crosby 5, Pearce 5 (1 pen), Jemson 4, Laws 3, Rice 2, Carr 1, Chettle 1, Currie 1, Orlygsson 1.
Littlewoods Cup (18): Hodge 4, Clough 3 (1 pen), Crosby 3, Jemson 2, Pearce 2, Chapman 1, Gaynor 1, Parker 1, own goal 1.
FA Cup (0).

Sutton	Laws	Pearce	Walker	Foster	Hodge	Carr	Parker	Clough	Chapman	Crosby	Rice	Wilson	Gaynor	Starbuck	Chettle	Wassall	Crossley	Orlygsson	Jemson	Charles	Currie	Williams	Match No.
1	2	3	4	5	6	7	8	9	10	11													1
1	2	3	4	5	6	7	8	9	10	11													2
1	2	3	4	5	6	7*	8	9	10	11	12												3
1	2	3	4	5	6		8	9	10	7	11												4
1	2	3	4	5	6*		8	9	10	7	11	12											5
1	2	3	4	5	6		11	9	10*	7			8†12	14									6
1	2		4		6		8	9	10	7	11*	5	12		3								7
1	2		4		6	7	8	9	10	11*			12		3	5							8
1	2	3	4		6		8	9	10	7	11	5											9
1	2	3	4		6		8	9*	10	7		5	12	11									10
1	2	3	4		6*		8	9	10	7	12	5		11									11
1	2	3	4		6	12	8	9	10	7		5		11*									12
	2	3	4		6		8	9	10	7	11	5*	12				1						13
	2	3	4		6		8	9	10	7	11	5					1						14
	2	3	4		6		8	9	10	7	11	5					1						15
	2	3	4		6		8	9	10	7	11	5					1						16
1	2	3	4		6		8	9	10	7	11	5											17
1	2	3	4		6			9	10	7	11	5					8						18
1	2	3	4		6		8	9		7					5			11	10				19
1	2	3	4		6		8	9		7*					5			11	10	12			20
1	2	3	4		6		8	9		7					5			11	10				21
1	2	3	4		6*		8	9		7	12				5			11	10				22
1	2	3	4		6		8	9		7					5			11	10*	12			23
1	2	3	4		6		8	9		7					5			11*	10	12			24
1	2	3	4		6		8	9		7					5			11	10				25
1	2	3	4		6		8	9		7		12			5*			11	10				26
1	2	3	4				8	9		7	6				5			11	10				27
1	2	3	4				8†	9		7	6	5		14				11*	12		10		28
1	2	3	4		6		8*	9		7	12	5		14				11	10†				29
1	2†	3	4			7	8*	9		6	11	5		14					10	12			30
1	2	3	4			11	8	9		7	6	5							10				31
1	2		4		6	12	14	9		7	11	8†			5				10*	3			32
1	2		4		6	11	8	9		7		5			3				10				33
	2	3	4		6	7	11	9		8					5		1		10				34
	2	3	4		6	7	11	9		8					5		1		10				35
	2	3	4		6*	7	11	9		8†14					5		1		10	12			36
	2	3	4		6	12	8	9		7	11				5†14		1				10*		37
1	2	3	4		6	12	8	9		7	11*				5				10				38
30	38	34	38	6	34	10	36	38	18	34	15	18	5	—	21	2	8	11	17	—	4	1	
						+	+				+	+	+	+	+			+	+	+	+		
						4s	1s				3s	3s	6s	2s	1s			1s	1s	1s	4s		

Littlewoods Cup	Second Round	Huddersfield T (h)	1-1
		(a)	3-3
	Third Round	Crystal Palace (a)	0-0
		(h)	5-0
	Fourth Round	Everton (h)	1-0
	Fifth Round	Tottenham H (h)	2-2
		(a)	3-2
	Semi-final	Coventry C (h)	2-1
		(a)	0-0
	Final	Oldham Ath (at Wembley)	1-0
FA Cup	Third Round	Manchester U (h)	0-1

NOTTINGHAM FOREST

Player and Position	Ht	Wt	Birth Date	Place	Source	Clubs	League App	Gls
Goalkeepers								
Mark Crossley	6 0	13 09	16 6 69	Barnsley		Nottingham F	10	—
						Manchester U (loan)		—
Andrew Marriott	6 0	12 07	11 10 70	Nottingham	Trainee	Arsenal	—	—
						Nottingham F	—	—
						WBA (loan)	3	—
						Blackburn R (loan)	2	—
						Colchester U (loan)	10	—
Steve Sutton	6 1	13 07	16 4 61	Hartington	Apprentice	Nottingham F	199	—
						Mansfield T (loan)	8	—
						Derby Co (loan)	14	—
Defenders								
Craig Boardman	6 0	11 08	30 11 70	Barnsley	Trainee	Nottingham F	—	—
Stuart Cash	5 11	11 10	5 9 65	Tipton	Halesowen	Nottingham F	—	—
						Rotherham U (loan)	8	1
Gary Charles	5 9	10 13	13 4 70	London		Nottingham F	2	—
						Leicester C (loan)	8	—
Steve Chettle	6 1	12 00	27 9 68	Nottingham	Apprentice	Nottingham F	80	3
Jason Fletcher	5 11	11 10	29 9 69	Nottingham	Trainee	Nottingham F	—	—
Brian Laws	5 10	11 05	14 10 61	Wallsend	Apprentice	Burnley	125	12
						Huddersfield T	56	1
						Middlesbrough	107	12
						Nottingham F	60	4
Stuart Pearce	5 10	12 09	24 4 62	Shepherds Bush	Wealdstone	Coventry C	51	4
						Nottingham F	173	23
Kevin Sharp*	5 10	11 00	1 11 70	Stapleford	Trainee	Nottingham F	—	—
Des Walker	5 11	11 03	26 11 65	Hackney	Apprentice	Nottingham F	194	—
Darren Wassall	5 11	11 09	27 6 68	Edgbaston		Nottingham F	6	—
						Hereford U (loan)	5	—
						Bury (loan)	7	1
Brett Williams	5 10	11 11	19 3 68	Dudley	Apprentice	Nottingham F	21	—
						Stockport Co (loan)	2	—
						Northampton T (loan)	4	—
						Hereford U (loan)	14	—
Midfield								
Martin Clark	5 9	10 11	13 10 68	Uddington	Hamilton A	Clyde	51	2
						Nottingham F	—	—
						Falkirk (loan)	3	1
						Mansfield T (loan)	14	1
Gary Crosby	5 7	9 11	8 5 64	Sleaford	Lincoln U Grantham	Lincoln C	7	—
						Nottingham F	61	6
Scot Gemmill	5 10	10 01	2 1 71	Paisley	School	Nottingham F	—	—
Steve Hodge	5 7	9 12	25 10 62	Nottingham	Apprentice	Nottingham F	123	30
						Aston Villa	53	12
						Tottenham H	45	7
						Nottingham F	68	17
Anthony Loughlan	6 0	12 03	19 1 70	Surrey	Leicester U	Nottingham F	—	—
Thorvaldur Orlygsson	5 11	10 08	2 8 66	Odense	Akureyri	Nottingham F	12	1
Garry Parker	5 10	11 00	7 9 65	Oxford	Apprentice	Luton T	42	3
						Hull C	84	8
						Nottingham F	61	13
Brian Rice	6 0	11 10	11 10 63	Glasgow	Whitburn Central	Hibernian	84	11
						Nottingham F	90	9
						Grimsby T (loan)	4	—
						WBA (loan)	3	—
Mark Smith	5 9	10 04	16 12 64	Bellshill	St Mirren BC	Queen's Park	82	7
						Celtic	6	1
						Dunfermline Ath	53	6
						Stoke C (loan)	2	—
						Nottingham F	—	—

NOTTINGHAM FOREST

Foundation: One of the oldest football clubs in the world, Nottingham Forest was formed at a meeting in the Clinton Arms in 1865. Known originally as the Forest Football Club, the game which first drew the founders together was "shinney" a form of hockey. When they determined to change to football in 1865, one of their first moves was to buy a set of red caps to wear on the field.

First Football League game: 3 September, 1892, Division 2, v Everton (a) D 2-2 – Brown; Earp, Scott; Hamilton, A. Smith, McCracken; McCallum, W. Smith, Higgins (2), Pike, McInnes.

Managers (and Secretary-managers)
Harry Radford 1889–97*, Harry Haslam 1897–1909*, Fred Earp 1909–12, Bob Masters 1912–25, John Baynes 1925–29, Stan Hardy 1930–31, Noel Watson 1931–36, Harold Wightman 1936–39, Billy Walker 1939–60, Andy Beattie 1960–63, John Carey 1963–68, Matt Gillies 1969–72, Dave Mackay 1972, Allan Brown 1973–75, Brian Clough 1975–   .

Player and Position	Ht	Wt	Birth Date	Birth Place	Source	Clubs	League App	Gls
Steven Stone	5 9	11 03	20 8 71	Gateshead	Trainee	Nottingham F	—	—
Terry Wilson	6 0	10 10	8 2 69	Broxburn	Apprentice	Nottingham F	84	6
Ian Woan	5 10	11 09	14 12 67	Wirral	Runcorn	Nottingham F	—	—
Forwards								
Franz Carr	5 7	10 12	24 9 66	Preston	Apprentice	Blackburn R	—	—
						Nottingham F	118	15
						Sheffield W (loan)	12	—
Nigel Clough	5 9	11 04	19 3 66	Sunderland	AC Hunters	Nottingham F	198	72
David Currie	5 11	12 09	27 11 62	Stockton	Local	Middlesbrough	113	31
						Darlington	76	33
						Barnsley	80	30
						Nottingham F	8	1
Michael Danzey*	6 1	12 12	8 2 71	Widnes	Trainee	Nottingham F	—	—
						Chester C (loan)	2	—
Tommy Gaynor	6 1	13 02	29 1 63	Limerick	Limerick	Doncaster R	33	7
						Nottingham F	42	7
Lee Glover	5 10	12 01	24 4 70	Kettering	Trainee	Nottingham F	20	3
						Leicester C (loan)	5	1
						Barnsley (loan)	8	—
Nigel Jemson	5 10	11 10	10 8 69	Preston	Trainee	Preston NE	32	8
						Nottingham F	18	4
						Bolton W (loan)	5	—
						Preston NE (loan)	9	2
Neil Lyne	6 1	12 04	4 4 70	Leicester	Leicester U	Nottingham F	—	—
						Walsall (loan)	7	—
Stephen McLoughlin	5 10	10 09	21 11 69	Nottingham	Trainee	Nottingham F	—	—
Philip Starbuck	5 10	10 13	24 11 68	Nottingham	Apprentice	Nottingham F	24	2
						Birmingham C (loan)	3	—
						Hereford U (loan)	6	—

Trainees
Allum, Peter J; Brown, Warren J; Browne, Shaun M; Dobson, Richard J; Dunn, Colin F; Edwards, Alex D; Gilchrist, Phillip; Hodder, Steven J; Hope, Stephen F; Jarrett, Justin M; Mallabar, Gavin W; Nevitt, Gary J; Roddis, Nicholas P; Smith, Mark A; Stobbart, Loy.

Associated Schoolboys
Armstrong, Steven C; Brooks, Mark L; Connelly, Martin J; Fowkes, Graham L; Glasser, Neil; Helliwell, Craig; Jackson, Grant S; Johnson, Dean M; Keay, Christopher J; McGregor, Paul A; McMahon, Sam K; Marshall, Lee; Mitchell, Andrew; Ring, Gerrard; Rookyard, Carl; Shaw, Darren R; Storer, Richard; Walker, Justin; Ward, Andrew D; Warner, Vance J; Wright, Dale C.

Associated Schoolboys who have accepted the club's offer of a Traineeship/Contract
Bell, Stephen; Fancutt, Martin S; Forrest, Sean F; Hogg, Andrew K; Howe, Stephen; Kilford, Ian A; Noble, Barrett; Pearce, Dale; Yates, Luke.

NOTTS COUNTY 1989-90 *Back row (left to right):* Geoff Pike, David Norton, Willie McStay, Wayne Fairclough, Scott Machin, Paul Cox, David Kevan.
Centre row: Philip Robinson, Charles Palmer, Nicky Law, Dean Yates, Steve Cherry, Aidan Davison, Craig Short, Don O'Riordan, Philip Stant, John Newman (Assistant Manager).
Front row: Gary Lund, Paul Barnes, Tommy Johnson, Neil Warnock (Manager), Philip Turner, Mark Draper, Nicky Platnauer.

Division 2   **NOTTS COUNTY**

County Ground, Meadow Lane, Nottingham NG2 3HJ. Telephone Nottingham (0602) 861155. Clubcall: 0898 121101. Football in the Community 863656. County '75 864718. Supporters Club 866802.

Ground capacity: 21,097.

Record attendance: 47,310 v York C, FA Cup 6th rd, 12 March, 1955.

Record receipts: £63,505 v Everton, FA Cup 6th rd, 10 March, 1984.

Pitch measurements: 114yd × 74yd.

Chairman: D. C. Pavis. *Vice Chairman:* J. Mounteney.

Directors: W. A. Hopcroft, M. Pavis.

Team Manager: Neil Warnock. *Commerical Manager:* Fiona Green.

Coach: Mick Jones.

Chief Executive: N. E. Hook, M.INST.M.

Physio: David Wilson BA, MCSP, DIPTP, GRAD DIP PHYS SRP.

Year Formed: 1862 *(see Foundation).*

Turned Professional: 1885. *Ltd Co.:* 1888.

Previous Grounds: 1862, The Park; 1864, The Meadows; 1877, Beeston Cricket Ground; 1880, Castle Ground; 1883, Trent Bridge; 1910, Meadow Lane.

Club Nickname: 'Magpies'.

Record League Victory: 11-1 v Newport C, Division 3 (S), 15 January 1949 – Smith; Southwell, Purvis; Gannon, Baxter, Adamson; Houghton (1), Sewell (4), Lawton (4), Pimbley, Johnston (2).

Record Cup Victory: 15-0 v Rotherham T (at Trent Bridge), FA Cup, 1st rd, 24 October 1885 – Sherwin; Snook, H. T. Moore; Dobson (1), Emmett (1), Chapman; Gunn (1), Albert Moore (2), Jackson (3), Daft (2), Cursham (4). (1 og).

Record Defeat: 1-9 v Blackburn R, Division 1, 16 November, 1889 and v Aston Villa, Division 1, 29 September, 1888 and v Portsmouth, Division 2, 9 April, 1927.

Most League Points (2 for a win): 69, Division 4, 1970–71.

Most League Points (3 for a win): 87, Division 3, 1989–90.

Most League Goals: 107, Division 4, 1959–60.

Highest League Scorer in Season: Tom Keetley, 39, Division 3 (S), 1930–31.

Most League Goals in Total Aggregate: Les Bradd, 124, 1967–78.

Most Capped Player: Harry Cursham, 8, England; Martin O'Neill, 8, Northern Ireland.

Most League Appearances: Albert Iremonger, 564, 1904–26.

Record Transfer Fee Received: £350,000 from Tottenham H for John Chiedozie, August 1984.

Record Transfer Fee Paid: £600,000 to Orient for John Chiedozie, August 1981.

Football League Record: 1888 Founder Member of the Football League; 1893–97 Division 2; 1897–1913 Division 1; 1913–14 Division 2; 1914–20 Division 1; 1920–23 Division 2; 1923–26 Division 1; 1926–30 Division 2; 1930–31 Division 3 (S); 1931–35 Division 2; 1935–50 Division 3 (S); 1950–58 Division 2; 1958–59 Division 3; 1959–60 Division 4; 1960–64 Division 3; 1964–71 Division 4; 1971–73 Division 3; 1973–81 Division 2; 1981–84 Division 1; 1984–85 Division 2; 1985–90 Division 3; 1990– Division 2.

Honours: Football League: Division 1 best season: 3rd, 1890–91, 1900–01; Division 2 – Champions 1896–97, 1913–14, 1922–23; Runners-up 1894–95, 1980–81; Division 3(S) – Champions 1930–31, 1949–50; Runners-up 1936–37; Division 3 – Runners-up 1972-73; Division 4 – Champions 1970–71; Runners-up 1959–60. *FA Cup:* Winners 1893–94; Runners-up 1890–91. *Football League Cup* best season: 5th rd, 1963–64, 1972–73, 1975–76.

Colours: Black and white broad striped shirts, amber sleeve and neck trim, black shorts, with white side flash, white stockings. **Change colours:** All sky blue.

NOTTS COUNTY 1989–90 LEAGUE RECORD

Match No.	Date		Venue	Opponents	Result		H/T Score	Lg. Pos.	Goalscorers	Atten- dance
1	Aug	19	A	Leyton Orient	W	1-0	1-0	—	Stant	5364
2		26	H	Blackpool	L	0-1	0-0	13		4852
3	Sept	2	A	Bristol R	L	2-3	1-3	18	Yates, Johnson	4753
4		9	H	Reading	D	0-0	0-0	15		4697
5		15	A	Chester C	D	3-3	2-1	—	Chapman, Short, Draper	2383
6		23	H	Rotherham U	W	2-0	1-0	13	Chapman 2	5891
7		26	H	Bolton W	W	2-1	2-0	—	Johnson, Lund	5392
8		30	A	Swansea C	D	0-0	0-0	10		3075
9	Oct	7	A	Walsall	D	2-2	2-1	11	Johnson, Draper	4592
10		14	H	Tranmere R	W	1-0	1-0	8	Chapman	6332
11		17	A	Bristol C	L	0-2	0-1	—		8331
12		21	H	Preston NE	W	2-1	0-1	9	Palmer, Johnson	5284
13		28	A	Northampton T	D	0-0	0-0	9		3734
14		31	H	Brentford	W	3-1	2-0	—	Turner, Lund 2	5488
15	Nov	4	A	Mansfield T	W	3-1	0-1	7	Robinson, Johnson 2	6016
16		11	H	Wigan Ath	D	1-1	0-1	7	Lund	5449
17		25	A	Huddersfield T	W	2-1	2-1	6	Turner, Yates	5416
18	Dec	2	H	Fulham	W	2-0	1-0	4	Johnson, Robinson	5132
19		16	A	Cardiff C	W	3-1	1-1	2	Stant 2, Turner	3610
20		26	H	Shrewsbury T	W	4-0	1-0	1	Stant 2, Yates, Turner	7819
21		30	H	Birmingham C	W	3-2	2-1	1	Palmer, Johnson, Lund	7786
22	Jan	1	A	Crewe Alex	L	0-1	0-0	1		4786
23		6	H	Bury	L	0-4	0-3	—		6059
24		13	A	Blackpool	D	0-0	0-0	2		3146
25		20	H	Leyton Orient	W	1-0	0-0	2	Palmer	5346
26	Feb	3	A	Rotherham U	W	2-1	1-0	2	Barnes, Yates	7251
27		10	H	Chester C	D	0-0	0-0	2		5077
28		17	A	Fulham	L	2-5	1-1	2	Yates, Johnson	4625
29		24	H	Huddersfield T	W	1-0	0-0	2	Lund	7633
30	Mar	3	A	Bury	L	2-3	1-3	4	Johnson, Draper (pen)	3007
31		6	H	Swansea C	W	2-1	2-0	—	Lund, Palmer	4862
32		10	A	Bolton W	L	0-3	0-0	4		8420
33		17	H	Walsall	W	2-0	1-0	4	Bartlett, Johnson	5207
34		19	A	Tranmere R	L	0-2	0-2	—		9718
35		24	H	Bristol C	D	0-0	0-0	4		9598
36		31	A	Preston NE	W	4-2	2-2	4	Norton, Yates, Bartlett 2	5810
37	Apr	7	A	Brentford	W	1-0	0-0	4	Bartlett	5105
38		10	H	Northampton T	W	3-2	1-0	—	Johnson (pen), Thomas, Stant	5396
39		14	H	Crewe Alex	W	2-0	1-0	4	Johnson, Bartlett	6403
40		17	A	Shrewsbury T	D	2-2	0-1	—	Johnson, Bartlett	3536
41		21	H	Cardiff C	W	2-1	2-0	4	Short, Bartlett	5533
42		24	A	Birmingham C	W	2-1	1-0	—	Lund, Palmer	10,533
43		26	H	Bristol R	W	3-1	1-0	—	Turner, Johnson 2 (1 pen)	10,142
44		28	A	Wigan Ath	D	1-1	1-0	3	Johnson (og)	2433
45	May	3	A	Reading	D	1-1	0-0	—	Bartlett	3132
46		5	H	Mansfield T	W	4-2	3-0	3	Lund, Turner, Johnson 2 (1 pen)	6943

Final League Position: 3

GOALSCORERS

League (73): Johnson 18 (3 pens), Lund 9, Bartlett 8, Stant 6, Turner 6, Yates 6, Palmer 5, Chapman 4, Draper 3 (1 pen), Robinson 2, Short 2, Barnes 1, Norton 1, Thomas 1, own goal 1.
Littlewoods Cup (3): Robinson 1, Short 1, Stant 1.
FA Cup (0).

Cherry	Palmer	Platnauer	Fairclough	Yates	Robinson	Draper	O'Riordan	Lund	Stant	Turner	Short	Johnson	Barnes	McStay	Kevan	Chapman	Norris	Norton	Law	Chiedozie	Fleming	Bartlett	Thomas	Match No.
1	2	3	4	5	6	7	8	9	10	11														1
1	2	3		5	6	7	8*	9†10		11	4	12	14											2
1	2	3	7	5	6	12	8*	9	10		4	11†		14										3
1	2	3		5	6	7			10		8	4	11		9									4
1	2†	3		5	6	7		9	10*		8	4	12	14		11								5
1	2	3		5	6	7		9			8	4	10			11								6
1	2	3		5	6	7		9			8	4	10			11								7
1	2	3		5	6	7		9	12		8	4	10*			11								8
1	2	3		5	6	7		9			8	4	10			11								9
1	2	3		5	6	7		9			8	4	10*12			11								10
1	2	3		5	6	7†		9	12		8	4	10	14		11*								11
1	2	3		5	6	7		9			8	4	10			11								12
1	2	3		5	6	7	10	9	12		8	4				11*								13
1	2	3		5	6	7	14	9	12		8	4	10†			11*								14
1	2	3		5	6	7		9	12		8	4	10			11*								15
1	2	3		5	6	7		9	12		8	4	10			11*								16
1	2	3		5	6	7		9	10	11	8	4												17
1	2	3		5	6	12		9	10†	11	8	4				7*	14							18
1	2	3		5	6*	7		9	10	11	8	4				12								19
1	2	3	12	5	6	7*		9	10		8	4				11								20
1	2	3	12	5	6*	7		9	10		8	4				11								21
1	2	3	8	5	6	7	11*	9	10†			4		14		12								22
1	2	3	12	5	6*	7		9	10†		8	4		14		11								23
1	2	3		5	6	7		9			8	4	10			11								24
1	2	3		5	6	7		9			8	4	10			11								25
1	2	3		5	6	7		9		11	8	4	10											26
1	3*	2†		5	6	12		9		11	8	4				7		10	14					27
1		3		5	6	7		9†		11	8	4	12					10	2*	14				28
1	2	3		5	6	7		9			8	4	10*			11		12						29
1	2	3		5	6†12			9		11	8	4				7		10*		14				30
1	2			5	6	7†		9			8	4				11*	14	10			3	12		31
1		3		5	6†	7	14	9			8	4				11	12	10*	2					32
1		3		5	6	7		9			8	4				11†	12	14	2				10*	33
1	2*			5	6			9		11	8	4	12			7					3		10	34
1		3		5	6					11	8	4				7		2				9	10	35
1		3		5	6†	7	14				8	4				11*	12	2				9	10	36
1		3		5	6	12					8	4				11	7*	2				9	10	37
1		3		5	6	7					8	4				11		2				9	10	38
1		3		5	6	7					8	4				11		2				9	10	39
1	12	3		5	6	7					8	4				11		2				9	10*	40
1	2	3		5	6				10		8	4				11*	12	7				9		41
1	2	3		5	6	12			10		8	4				11*		7				9		42
1	2	3		5	6				10		8	4				11						9	7	43
1	2	3		5	6				10		8	4				11†	12	14				9	7*	44
1	2	3		5	6				10		8	4				11						9	7	45
1	2	3		5	6				10		8	4				11						9	7	46
46	36	44	5	45	46	29	15	40	14	44	44	34	10	—	1	13	—	11	2	—	3	14	10	
	+1s		+3s			+5s	+2s		+8s			+6s	+3s	+3s		+2s	+6s	+1s	+4s		+1s	+1s		

Littlewoods Cup First Round Shrewsbury T (a) 0-3
                                               (h) 3-1
FA Cup First Round Doncaster R (a) 0-1

NOTTS COUNTY

Player and Position	Ht	Wt	Birth Date	Place	Source	Clubs	League App	Gls
Goalkeepers								
Kevin Blackwell	5 11	12 10	21 12 58	Luton	Boston U	Barnet	—	—
						Scarborough	44	—
						Notts Co	—	—
Steve Cherry	5 11	11 00	5 8 60	Nottingham	Apprentice	Derby Co	77	—
						Port Vale (loan)	4	—
						Walsall	71	—
						Plymouth Arg	73	—
						Chesterfield (loan)	10	—
						Notts Co	64	—
Paul Dolan	6 4	13 05	16 4 66	Ottawa	Vancouver W	Notts Co	—	—
Defenders								
Paul Cox	5 11	11 12	1 1 72	Nottingham	Trainee	Notts Co	—	—
Nicky Law	6 0	13 05	8 9 61	Greenwich	Apprentice	Arsenal	—	—
						Barnsley	114	1
						Blackpool	66	1
						Plymouth Arg	38	5
						Notts Co	47	4
						Scarborough (loan)	12	—
David Norton	5 7	11 03	3 3 65	Cannock	Apprentice	Aston Villa	44	2
						Notts Co	23	1
Charlie Palmer	5 11	12 03	10 7 63	Aylesbury	Apprentice	Watford	10	1
						Derby Co	51	2
						Hull C	70	1
						Notts Co	48	5
Nicky Platnauer	5 10	12 12	10 6 61	Leicester	Bedford T	Bristol R	24	7
						Coventry C	44	6
						Birmingham C	28	2
						Reading (loan)	7	—
						Cardiff C	115	6
						Notts Co	44	—
Craig Short	6 0	11 04	25 6 68	Bridlington	Pickering T	Scarborough	63	7
						Notts Co	44	2
Dean Thomas	5 9	11 08	19 12 61	Bedworth	Nuneaton Bor Dusseldorf	Wimbledon	57	8
						Northampton T	74	11
						Notts Co	10	1
Dean Yates	6 1	10 04	26 10 67	Leicester	Apprentice	Notts Co	226	27
Midfield								
Gary Chapman	5 10	12 00	1 5 64	Leeds		Bradford C	5	—
						Notts Co	19	4
Mark Draper	5 10	10 00	11 11 70	Derbyshire	Trainee	Notts Co	54	6
Willie McStay*	5 10	11 0	26 11 61	Hamilton	Celtic BC	Celtic	68	2
						Huddersfield T	9	—
						Notts Co	45	1
						Hartlepool U (loan)	3	—
						Partick T (loan)	5	—
Don O'Riordan	6 0	11 12	14 5 57	Dublin	Apprentice	Derby Co	6	1
						Doncaster R (loan)	2	—
					Tulsa	Preston NE	158	8
						Carlisle U	84	18
						Middlesbrough	41	2
						Grimsby T	86	14
						Notts Co	60	3
						Mansfield T (loan)	6	—
Philip Robinson	5 9	10 10	6 1 67	Stafford	Apprentice	Aston Villa	3	1
						Wolverhampton W	71	8
						Notts Co	46	2
Eddie Snook	5 7	10 01	18 10 68	Washington	Apprentice	Notts Co	—	—
Mark Telford			17 12 71	South Shields	Trainee	Notts Co	—	—

NOTTS COUNTY

Foundation: For many years the foundation date of the Football League's oldest club was given as 1862 and the club celebrated its centenary in 1962. However, the researches of Keith Warsop have since shown that the club was on a very haphazard basis at that time, playing little more than practice matches. The meeting which put it on a firm footing was held at the George IV Hotel in December 1864, when they became known as the Notts Football Club.

First Football League game: 15 September, 1888, Football League, v Everton (a) L 1-2 – Holland; Guttridge, McLean; Brown, Warburton, Shelton; Hodder, Harker, Jardine, Moore (1), Wardle.

Managers (and Secretary-managers)
Edwin Browne 1883–93*, Tom Featherstone 1893*, Tom Harris 1893–13*, Albert Fisher 1913–27, Horace Henshall 1927–34, Charlie Jones 1934–35, David Pratt 1935, Percy Smith 1935–36, Jimmy McMullan 1936–37, Harry Parkes 1938–39, Tony Towers 1939–42, Frank Womack 1942–43, Major Frank Buckley 1944–46, Arthur Stollery 1946–49, Eric Houghton 1949–53, George Poyser 1953–57, Tommy Lawton 1957–58, Frank Hill 1958–61, Tim Coleman 1961–63, Eddie Lowe 1963–65, Tim Coleman 1965–66, Jack Burkitt 1966–67, Andy Beattie (GM 1967), Billy Gray 1967–68, Jimmy Sirrel 1969–75, Ron Fenton 1975–77, Jimmy Sirrel 1978–82 (continues as GM to 1984), Howard Wilkinson 1982–83, Larry Lloyd 1983–84, Richie Barker 1984–85, Jimmy Sirrel 1985–87, John Barnwell 1987–88, Neil Warnock 1989– .

Player and Position	Ht	Wt	Birth Date	Birth Place	Source	Clubs	League App	Gls
Phil Turner	5 8	10 13	12 2 62	Sheffield	Apprentice	Lincoln C	241	19
						Grimsby T	62	8
						Leicester C	24	2
						Notts Co	60	8
Forwards								
Kevin Bartlett	5 9	10 12	12 10 62	Portsmouth	Apprentice	Portsmouth	3	—
					Fareham	Cardiff C	82	25
						WBA	37	10
						Notts Co	14	8
Tommy Johnson	5 10	10 00	15 1 71	Newcastle	Trainee	Notts Co	50	22
Gary Lund	5 11	11 00	13 9 64	Grimsby	School	Grimsby T	60	24
						Lincoln C	44	13
						Notts Co	122	37
Scott Machin	6 0	12 00	29 9 70	Leicester	Trainee	Notts Co	—	—
Phil Stant	6 1	12 07	13 10 62	Bolton	Camberley Army	Reading	4	2
						Hereford U	89	38
						Notts Co	22	6

Trainees
Aldridge, Stephen P; Barrow, Lee A; Brough, John R; Crossland, Daniel; Finch, Craig B; Harmon, Darren J; Hearne, Darren J; Johnson, Michael O; Moore, James W; Patterson, Gary; Powell, Darren L; Slawson, Stephen M; Thompson, John A; Walker, James B; Walker, Richard N; Wells, Mark A.

**Non-Contract
Whitehead, Matthew J.

Associated Schoolboys
Armeni, Christopher; Dodson, Matthew J; Gallagher, Thomas D; Galloway, Michael A; Lawley, Edward W.H; McDermott, Stephen R; Marshall, Daniel J; Ridgeway, Ian D; Smith, Paul A; Wells, Iain D; Whitehurst, Nicolas.

Associated Schoolboys who have accepted the club's offer of a Traineeship/Contract
Blatherwick, Steven S; Lister, Ian; Rogers, Kevin A; Saunders, Darren D; Sherlock, Paul G; Simpson, Michael.

**Non-Contract Players who are retained must be re-signed before they are eligible to play in League matches.

OLDHAM ATHLETIC 1989–90 *Back row (left to right):* Tony Barlow, Frank Bunn, Paul Warhurst, Mark Stewart, Andy Holden (Club Captain), Jason Allen, Andrew Woodcock, Andy Ritchie, John Kelly.

Centre row: Bill Urmson (Coach), Ronnie Evans (Kit Manager), Steve Bramwell, Simon Mooney, Andy Rhodes, Steve Morgan, Jon Hallworth, Clark Wood, Andy Gayle, Norman Kelly, Neil Adams, Willie Donachie (Player/Coach), Ian Liversidge (Physiotherapist).

Front row: Mike Milligan, Nick Henry, Earl Barrett, Dennis Irwin, Ian Marshall, Joe Royle (Manager), Andy Barlow, Tommy Wright, Roger Palmer, Garry Williams, Scott McGarvey.

Division 2   **OLDHAM ATHLETIC**

Boundary Park, Oldham. Telephone 061-624-4972. Commercial Dept. 061-652-0966. Clubcall, 0898 121142.

Ground capacity: 19,432.

Record attendance: 47,671 v Sheffield W, FA Cup 4th rd. 25 Jan, 1930.

Record receipts: £82,320 v West Ham U, Littlewoods Cup semi-final, first leg, 14 February 1990.

Pitch measurements: 110yd × 74yd. (Artificial surface).

President: R. Schofield.

Chairman & Chief Executive: I. H. Stott, *Vice-Chairman:* D. A. Brierley.

Directors: G. T. Butterworth, R. Adams, D. R. Taylor, P. Chadwick, J. Slevin, N. Holden.

Manager: Joe Royle.

Secretary: Terry Cale. *Commercial Manager:* Alan Hardy.

Player-Coach: Willie Donachie. *Coach:* Billy Urmson.

Physio: Ian Liversedge.

Year Formed: 1895. *Turned Professional:* 1899. *Ltd Co.:* 1906.

Club Nickname: 'The Latics'.

Previous Names: 1895, Pine Villa; 1899, Oldham Athletic.

Previous Ground: Sheepfoot Lane; 1905, Boundary Park.

Record League Victory: 11-0 v Southport, Division 4, 26 December 1962 – Hollands; Branagan, Marshall; McCall, Williams, Scott; Ledger (1), Johnstone, Lister (6), Colquhoun (1), Whitaker (3).

Record Cup Victory: 10-1 v Lytham, FA Cup, 1st rd, 28 November 1925 – Gray; Wynne, Grundy; Adlam, Heaton, Naylor (1), Douglas, Pynegar (2), Ormston (2), Barnes (3), Watson (2).

Record Defeat: 4-13 v Tranmere R, Division 3 (N), 26 December, 1935.

Most League Points (2 for a win): 62, Division 3, 1973–74.

Most League Points (3 for a win): 75, Division 2, 1986–87.

Most League Goals: 95, Division 4, 1962–63.

Highest League Scorer in Season: Tom Davis, 33, Division 3 (N), 1936–37.

Most League Goals in Total Aggregate: Roger Palmer, 129, 1980–90.

Most Capped Player: Albert Gray, 9 (24), Wales.

Most League Appearances: Ian Wood, 525, 1966–80.

Record Transfer Fee Received: £350,000 from Norwich City for Andy Linighan, March 1988, and £350,000 from Hibernian for Andy Goram, November 1987.

Record Transfer Fee Paid: £225,000 to Bournemouth for Paul Moulden, March 1990.

Football League Record: 1907 Elected to Division 2; 1910–23 Division 1; 1923–35 Division 2; 1935–53 Division 3 (N); 1953–54 Division 2; 1954–58 Division 3 (N); 1958–63 Division 4; 1963–69 Division 3; 1969–71 Division 4; 1971–74 Division 3; 1974– Division 2.

Honours: Football League: Division 1 – Runners-up 1914–15; Division 2 – Runners-up 1909–10; Division 3 (N) – Champions 1952–53; Division 3 – Champions 1973–74; Division 4 – Runners-up 1962–63. *FA Cup:* Semi-final 1913, 1989–90. *Football League Cup:* Runners-up 1990.

Colours: All blue with red piping. **Change colours:** All red with blue piping.

404

OLDHAM ATHLETIC 1989–90 LEAGUE RECORD

Match No.	Date	Venue	Opponents	Result	H/T Score	Lg. Pos.	Goalscorers	Attendance
1	Aug 19	A	Blackburn R	L 0-1	0-1	—		9939
2	22	H	Watford	D 1-1	1-0	—	Holden R	6230
3	26	H	Swindon T	D 2-2	0-1	17	Palmer 2	5531
4	Sept 2	A	Newcastle U	L 1-2	0-1	19	Holden R	20,804
5	9	H	Plymouth Arg	W 3-2	1-0	15	Palmer, Holden R, Ritchie	4940
6	16	A	Stoke C	W 2-1	2-0	13	Palmer, Ritchie	10,673
7	23	H	WBA	W 2-1	0-0	7	Ritchie 2 (1 pen)	6907
8	26	A	Sheffield U	L 1-2	0-0	—	Bunn	14,314
9	30	H	Leicester C	W 1-0	0-0	8	Morgan (og)	6407
10	Oct 7	H	Barnsley	W 2-0	2-0	6	Bunn, Milligan	6769
11	14	A	Bournemouth	L 0-2	0-1	10		6796
12	17	A	Hull C	D 0-0	0-0	—		5109
13	21	H	Middlesbrough	W 2-0	1-0	7	Ritchie 2	6835
14	28	A	Wolverhampton W	D 1-1	0-0	8	Milligan	15,278
15	31	H	Bradford C	D 2-2	0-1	—	Barlow, Ritchie (pen)	7772
16	Nov 4	H	Sunderland	W 2-1	1-0	6	Ritchie, Warhurst	8829
17	11	A	Oxford U	W 1-0	1-0	4	Ritchie	4480
18	18	H	Brighton & HA	D 1-1	1-0	6	Milligan	7066
19	25	A	Ipswich T	D 1-1	0-0	6	Yallop (og)	12,304
20	Dec 1	H	Blackburn R	W 2-0	0-0	—	Holden R, Ritchie	10,635
21	9	A	Watford	L 0-3	0-3	6		9399
22	16	A	West Ham U	W 2-0	2-0	4	Milligan, Foster (og)	14,960
23	26	H	Port Vale	W 2-1	1-0	4	Adams, Barrett	11,274
24	30	H	Portsmouth	D 3-3	2-3	4	Milligan 2, Palmer	8815
25	Jan 1	A	Leeds U	D 1-1	1-0	4	Palmer	30,217
26	13	A	Swindon T	L 2-3	0-1	5	McGarvey, Adams	7785
27	20	H	Newcastle U	D 1-1	1-0	4	Ritchie	11,194
28	Feb 3	A	WBA	D 2-2	1-1	3	Ritchie (pen), Palmer	12,237
29	10	H	Stoke C	W 2-0	0-0	4	Palmer, Ritchie	10,028
30	24	H	Ipswich T	W 4-1	2-0	4	Marshall 2, Palmer, Irwin	10,193
31	Mar 3	A	Brighton & HA	D 1-1	1-0	4	Adams	8229
32	17	A	Barnsley	L 0-1	0-1	8		10,598
33	20	H	Bournemouth	W 4-0	1-0	—	Redfearn, Milligan, Palmer 2	10,109
34	24	H	Hull C	W 3-2	2-0	6	Palmer 2, Marshall	11,472
35	28	H	Sheffield U	L 0-2	0-1	—		14,160
36	31	A	Middlesbrough	L 0-1	0-1	8		17,238
37	Apr 3	A	Leicester C	L 0-3	0-1	—		10,368
38	13	H	Leeds U	W 3-1	1-0	—	Holden R 2 (1 pen), Bunn	16,292
39	16	A	Port Vale	L 0-2	0-1	9		11,451
40	18	A	Plymouth Arg	L 0-2	0-2	—		8146
41	21	H	West Ham U	W 3-0	0-0	9	Ritchie (pen), Bunn 2	12,190
42	24	A	Portsmouth	L 1-2	1-2	—	Barrett	9601
43	May 1	H	Oxford U	W 4-1	1-0	—	Holden R 3, Palmer	12,616
44	3	H	Wolverhampton W	D 1-1	1-0	—	Palmer	17,468
45	5	A	Sunderland	W 3-2	1-1	8	Adams, Ritchie, Palmer	22,243
46	7	A	Bradford C	D 1-1	0-0	—	Redfearn	6798

Final League Position: 17

GOALSCORERS

League (70): Palmer 16, Ritchie 15 (4 pens), Holden R 9 (1 pen), Milligan 7, Bunn 5, Adams 4, Marshall 3, Barrett 2, Redfearn 2, Barlow 1, Irwin 1, McGarvey 1, Warhurst 1, own goals 3.
Littlewoods Cup (24): Ritchie 10, Bunn 7, Holden R 2, Adams 1, Barrett 1, Henry 1, Milligan 1, Palmer 1.
FA Cup (16): Marshall 3 (1 pen), Palmer 3, Ritchie 3 (1 pen), Holden R 2, Barrett 1, Bunn 1, McGarvey 1, Redfearn 1, own goal 1.

Littlewoods Cup	Second Round	Leeds U (h)	2-1
		(a)	2-1
	Third Round	Scarborough (h)	7-0
	Fourth Round	Arsenal (h)	3-1
	Fifth Round	Southampton (a)	2-2
		(h)	2-0
	Semi-final	West Ham U (h)	6-0
		(a)	0-3
	Final	Nottingham F (at Wembley)	0-1

Rhodes	Irwin	Barlow	Henry	Barrett	Holden A	Adams	Ritchie	Bunn	Milligan	Holden R	Palmer	Marshall	Warhurst	Williams	Hallworth	Donachie	Heseltine	Redfearn	McGarvey	Moulden	Match No.
1	2	3	4	5	6	7*	8	9†	10	11	12	14									1
1	2		3		6	7	8	9	10	11	4	5									2
1	2	14	12	3	6	7*	8	9	10	11	4	5†									3
1	2	3	4	5			8	9*	10	11	7		6	12							4
1	2	3	4	5			8	9	10	11	7		6								5
1	2	3	4	6			8	9	10	11	7	5									6
1	2	3	4	6			8	9	10	11	7		5								7
1	2	3	4	6			8	9	10	11	7		5								8
	2	3	4	6			8	9	10	11	7	5			1						9
1	2	3	4	6			8	9	10	11	7				5						10
1	2	3*	4	6	12		8	9	10	11	7				5						11
1	2	3	4	6			8	9	10	11	7				5						12
1	2	3	4	6			8	9	10	11	7		5								13
1	2	3	4	6		7	8	9	10	11			5								14
1	2	3	4	5		7	8		10	11	9		6								15
1	2	3	4	5			8		10	11	7	9	6								16
1	2	3	4	5			8	9	10	11	7	12	6*								17
1	2	3	4	5			8	9	10	11	7*	12	6								18
1	2	3	4	5			8		10	11	7	9	6								19
1	2	3	4	5		7	8			11	10	9	6								20
1	2	3*	4	5			8	9	10	11	12	7	6								21
1	2	3	4	5			8	9	10	11	12	7	6*								22
1	2	3	4	5		7	8	9	10	11			6								23
1	2	3	4	5		7	8*	9	10	11	12		6								24
	2	3	4	5		7		9	10	11	8	6			1						25
	2		4	6		7			10	11	8	5			1		3*	9	12		26
	2*	3	4	6	12		8		10	11	9		5		1			7			27
	2	3	4	6		7	8		10	11	12	5			1				9*		28
	2	3	4	6		7	8		10	11	12	5			1				9*		29
	2	3	4	5		7			10	11	8	9*	6		1				12		30
	2	3	4	5	12		8		10	11	7	9	6*		1						31
	2	3	4	5	12				10	11	8	9	6*		1			7			32
	2	3	4*	5	12				10	11	8	9	6		1			7			33
	2	3	4	5	12				10*	11	8	9	6		1			7			34
	2	3*	4	5	12				10	11	8	9	6		1			7†	14		35
1	2	3	4	5	6			9	10	11†	8	12						7*	14		36
1	2	3	4*	5	6		8		10		12	9						7	11		37
	2	3	4	5	12	7†	9		10	11			6		1			14	8*		38
	2	3	4	5	14		8	9		11	12		6*		1			7	10†		39
	2	3	4	5	12		8	9		11	10		6*		1			7			40
1	2	3	4	5			8	9	10	11			6					7			41
1	2	3	4†	5*	6		8	9	10	11	12	14						7			42
1		3		5		7	8*	9†	10	11	4		6			2		12	14		43
1		3		5		7	8	12	10*	11		9	6			2		4			44
1		3		5		7	8			11		9	6*	12		2		4		10	45
1		3		5		7	8			11		9	6			2		4		10	46
31	42	43	40	46	6	18	37	28	41	45	33	22	28	1	15	7	1	15	2	5	
		+	+		+	+	+				+	+	+	+				+	+	+	
		1s	1s		9s	1s	1s				9s	3s	2s	2s				2s	2s	3s	

FA Cup

Third Round	Birmingham C (a)	1-1
	(h)	1-0
Fourth Round	Brighton & HA (h)	2-1
Fifth Round	Everton (h)	2-2
	(a)	1-1
	(h)	2-1
Sixth Round	Aston Villa (h)	3-0
Semi-final	Manchester U	
	(at Maine Road)	3-3
Replay	(at Maine Road)	1-2

OLDHAM ATHLETIC

Player and Position	Ht	Wt	Birth Date	Place	Source	Clubs	League App	Gls
Goalkeepers								
Jon Hallworth	6 2	12 10	26 10 65	Stockport	School	Ipswich T	45	—
						Swindon T (loan)	—	—
						Bristol R (loan)	2	—
						Fulham (loan)	—	—
						Oldham Ath	31	—
Andy Rhodes	6 0	12 00	23 8 64	Doncaster	Apprentice	Barnsley	36	—
						Doncaster R	106	—
						Oldham Ath	69	—
Defenders								
Jason Allen*	6 0	11 02	8 6 70	Belfast	Trainee	Oldham Ath	—	—
Andrew Barlow	5 9	11 01	24 11 65	Oldham		Oldham Ath	173	3
Anthony Barlow*	5 8	10 08	11 9 70	Manchester	Trainee	Oldham Ath	—	—
Earl Barrett	5 10	11 00	28 4 67	Rochdale	Apprentice	Manchester C	3	—
						Chester C (loan)	12	—
						Oldham Ath	108	2
Chris Blundell	5 10	10 09	7 12 69	Billlinge	Trainee	Oldham Ath	3	—
Willie Donachie	5 9	11 03	5 10 51	Glasgow	Juniors	Manchester C	351	2
					Portland T	Norwich C	11	—
					Portland T	Burnley	60	3
						Oldham Ath	152	3
Wayne Heseltine	5 9	11 06	3 12 69	Bradford	Trainee	Manchester U	—	—
						Oldham Ath	1	—
Andy Holden	6 1	13 00	14 9 62	Flint	Rhyl	Chester C	100	17
						Wigan Ath	49	4
						Oldham Ath	19	4
Dennis Irwin	5 7	9 07	31 10 65	Cork	Apprentice	Leeds U	72	1
						Oldham Ath	167	4
Ian Marshall	6 1	12 12	20 3 66	Liverpool	Apprentice	Everton	15	1
						Oldham Ath	76	7
Simon Mooney*	5 9	10 04	23 9 70	Rochdale	Trainee	Oldham Ath	—	—
Paul Warhurst	6 1	14 00	26 9 69	Stockport	Trainee	Manchester C	—	—
						Oldham Ath	34	1
Midfield								
Nick Henry	5 6	9 08	21 2 69	Liverpool	Trainee	Oldham Ath	64	—
Norman Kelly	5 8	11 00	10 10 70	Belfast	Trainee	Oldham Ath	2	—
						Wigan Ath (loan)	4	—
Mike Milligan	5 8	11 00	20 2 67	Manchester	Apprentice	Oldham Ath	162	17
Steve Morgan	5 9	11 05	28 12 70	Wrexham	Trainee	Oldham Ath	2	—
						Wrexham (loan)	7	1
Neil Redfearn	5 10	12 04	20 6 65	Dewsbury	Apprentice	Nottingham F	—	—
						Bolton W	35	1
						Lincoln C (loan)	10	1
						Lincoln C	90	12
						Doncaster R	46	14
						Crystal Palace	57	10
						Watford	24	3
						Oldham Ath	17	2
Clark Wood*	5 8	10 00	25 9 70	Bury	Trainee	Oldham Ath	—	—
Andrew Woodcock*	5 8	10 12	8 2 71	Stretford	Trainee	Oldham Ath	—	—
Forwards								
Neil Adams	5 8	10 08	23 11 65	Stoke	Local	Stoke C	32	4
						Everton	20	—
						Oldham Ath (loan)	9	—
						Oldham Ath	27	4
Steve Bramwell*	5 7	10 00	9 10 70	Stockport	Trainee	Oldham Ath	1	—
						Wigan Ath (loan)	—	—

OLDHAM ATHLETIC

Foundation: It was in 1895 that John Garland, the landlord of the Featherstall and Junction Hotel, decided to form a football club. As Pine Villa they played in the Oldham Junior League. In 1899 the local professional club Oldham County, went out of existence and one of the liquidators persuaded Pine Villa to take over their ground at Sheepfoot Lane and change their name to Oldham Athletic.

First Football League game: 9 September, 1907, Division 2, v Stoke (a) W 3-1 – Hewitson; Hodson, Hamilton; Fay, Walders, Wilson; Ward, W. Dodds (1), Newton (1), Hancock, Swarbrick (1).

Managers (and Secretary-managers)
David Ashworth 1906–14, Herbert Bamlett 1914–21, Charlie Roberts 1921–22, David Ashworth 1923–24, Bob Mellor 1924–27, Andy Wilson 1927–32, Jimmy McMullan 1933–34, Bob Mellor 1934–45 (continued as secretary to 1953), Frank Womack 1945–47, Billy Wootton 1947–50, George Hardwick 1950–56, Ted Goodier 1956–58, Norman Dodgin 1958–60, Jack Rowley 1960–63, Les McDowall 1963–65, Gordon Hurst 1965–66, Jimmy McIlroy 1966–68, Jack Rowley 1968–69, Jimmy Frizzell 1970–82, Joe Royle 1982–   .

Player and Position	Ht	Wt	Birth Date	Place	Source	Clubs	League App	Gls
Frankie Bunn	5 11	10 06	6 11 62	Birmingham	Apprentice	Luton T	59	9
						Hull C	95	23
						Oldham Ath	78	26
Rick Holden	5 11	12 07	9 9 64	Skipton		Burnley	1	—
						Halifax T	67	12
						Watford	42	8
						Oldham Ath	45	9
Scott McGarvey	6 0	11 05	22 4 63	Glasgow	Apprentice	Manchester U (loan)	25	3
						Wolverhampton W	13	2
						Portsmouth	23	6
						Carlisle U (loan)	10	3
						Carlisle U	25	8
						Grimsby T	50	7
						Bristol C	26	9
						Oldham Ath	4	1
						Wigan Ath (loan)	3	—
Paul Moulden	5 10	11 00	6 9 67	Farnworth	Apprentice	Manchester C	64	18
						Bournemouth	32	13
						Oldham Ath	8	—
Roger Palmer	5 10	11 00	30 1 59	Manchester	Apprentice	Manchester C	31	9
						Oldham Ath	391	129
Andy Ritchie	5 9	11 11	28 11 60	Manchester	Apprentice	Manchester U	33	13
						Brighton & HA	89	23
						Leeds U	136	40
						Oldham Ath	105	48
Mark Stewart*	6 0	12 00	26 7 67	Bury		Oldham Ath	—	—
Gary Williams	5 8	10 11	8 6 63	Bristol	Apprentice	Bristol C	100	1
						Portsmouth	—	—
						Swansea C	6	—
						Bristol R	—	—
						Oldham Ath	59	12

Trainees
Bamber, Neil S;Bennett, Ian M; Bernard, Paul R.J;Bradshaw, Gary; Challender, Gregory L; Fisk, Jason T; Gerrard, Paul W; Halstead, Christopher; Huyton, Darren J; Kenton, Andrew M; Leeming, Daniel J; Makin, Christopher; Miller, Robert J; Raynor, Steven; Vigon, Adam M.S; Wall, David M; Wilson, Greg J.

Associated Schoolboys
Adams, Christian; Berry, Matthew; Boden, Liam T; Everingham, Nicholas P; Eyre, John R; Frost, John A; Hall, David; Haworth, Steven J.A; Hilton, Robert C; Hoolickin, Anthony P; Johnson, Bradley R; Jones, Michael C; Knapman, Stephen C; Lockley, Richard J; Mayo, Jonathan P; Miller, Peter D; Morton, Christopher P; Owen, Jonathon K; Petts, Samuel; Price, Robert J; Shard, Anthony; Speak, Matthew I; Stevenson, Martyn J; Walker, Ian S; Woods, Andrew N.

OXFORD UNITED 1989-90 *Back row (left to right)*: Phillip Heath, Neil Slater, Peter Hucker, Ceri Evans, Paul Kee, Jimmy Phillips, Alan Judge, Colin Greenall, Garry Smart.
Centre row: Matthew McDonnell, Robbie Mustoe, Richard Hill, John Clinkard (Physiotherapist), Michael Ford, David Fogg (Coach), John Durnin, David Moss (Coach), Paul Simpson, Maurice Evans (General Manager), Lee Nogan, Joey Beauchamp, Mark Hewitson.
Front row: Gary Shelton, David Penney, Martin Foyle, Steve Foster, Brian Horton (Manager), Mickey Lewis, David Bardsley, Peter Rhoades-Brown, Les Phillips.

Division 2 **OXFORD UNITED**

OXFORD UNITED
F.C.

Manor Ground, Headington, Oxford. Telephone Oxford (0865) 61503. Supporters Club: 0865 63063. Clubcall: 0898 121172. Fax No. 0865 741820.

Ground capacity: 11,117.

Record attendance: 22,750 v Preston NE, FA Cup 6th rd, 29 Feb, 1964.

Record receipts: £71,304 v Aston Villa, Milk Cup semi-final, 12 March, 1986.

Pitch measurements: 110yd × 75yd.

President: The Duke of Marlborough.

Managing Director: P. D. McGeough.

Directors: G. E. Coppock, J. A. Hunt, Miss G. N. A. Maxwell, P. Reeves.

Manager: Brian Horton. *Coach:* David Fogg.

Physio: John Clinkard.

Secretary: Mick Brown *Commercial Manager:* Nick Johnson.

Year Formed: 1893. *Turned Professional:* 1949. *Ltd Co.:* 1949.

Club Nickname: 'The U's'.

Previous Names: 1893, Headington; 1894, Headington United; 1960, Oxford United.

Previous Grounds: 1893–94 Headington Quarry; 1894–98 Wooton's Field; 1898–1902 Sandy Lane Ground; 1902–09 Britannia Field; 1909–10 Sandy Lane; 1910–14 Quarry Recreation Ground; 1914–22 Sandy Lane; 1922–25 The Paddock Manor Road; 1925– Manor Ground.

Record League Victory: 7-0 v Barrow, Division 4, 19 December 1964 – Fearnley; Beavon, Quartermann; Ron Atkinson (1), Kyle, Jones; Morris, Booth (3), Willey (1), Graham Atkinson (1), Harrington (1).

Record Cup Victory: 6-0 v Gillingham, League Cup, 2nd rd (1st leg), 24 September 1986 – Judge; Langan, Trewick, Phillips (Brock), Briggs, Shotton, Houghton (1), Aldridge (4) (incl. 1p), Charles (Leworthy), Hebberd, Slatter. (1 og).

Record Defeat: 0-6 v Liverpool, Division 1, 22 March 1986.

Most League Points (2 for a win): 61, Division 4, 1964–65.

Most League Points (3 for a win): 95, Division 3, 1983–84.

Most League Goals: 91, Division 3, 1983–84.

Highest League Scorer in Season: John Aldridge, 30, Division 2, 1984–85.

Most League Goals in Total Aggregate: Graham Atkinson, 73, 1962–73.

Most Capped Player: Ray Houghton, 12 (34), Eire and Neil Slatter, 12 (22), Wales.

Most League Appearances: John Shuker, 478, 1962–77.

Record Transfer Fee Received: £1,000,000 from Derby Co for Dean Saunders, October 1988.

Record Transfer Fee Paid: £265,000 to Watford for David Bardsley, September 1987.

Football League Record: 1962 Elected to Division 4; 1965–68 Division 3; 1968–76 Division 2; 1976–84 Division 3; 1984–85 Division 2; 1985–88 Division 1; 1988– Division 2.

Honours: Football League: Division 1 best season: 18th, 1985–86, 1986–87; Division 2 – Champions 1984–85; Division 3 – Champions 1967–68, 1983–84; Division 4 – Promoted 1964–65 (4th). *FA Cup* best season: 6th rd, 1963-64 (record for 4th Division club). *Football League Cup:* Winners 1985–86.

Colours: Gold, navy blue sleeves, navy blue shorts, gold stockings. **Change colours:** All red.

OXFORD UNITED 1989–90 LEAGUE RECORD

Match No.	Date	Venue	Opponents	Result		H/T Score	Lg. Pos.	Goalscorers	Attendance
1	Aug 19	A	Plymouth Arg	L	0-2	0-0	—		8509
2	26	H	Watford	D	1-1	0-1	23	Durnin	5664
3	Sept 2	A	Blackburn R	D	2-2	1-1	20	Hendry (og), Foyle	7578
4	9	H	Bradford C	W	2-1	1-0	16	Simpson, Mustoe	4027
5	13	H	Newcastle U	W	2-1	1-1	—	Ranson (og), Mustoe	7313
6	16	A	WBA	L	2-3	0-0	14	Durnin, Foyle	9628
7	23	H	Ipswich T	D	2-2	1-0	13	Penney, Durnin	5131
8	27	A	Leeds U	L	1-2	0-2	—	Stein	24,097
9	30	H	Bournemouth	L	1-2	0-1	18	Stein	5325
10	Oct 7	H	Portsmouth	W	2-1	2-0	16	Phillips J (pen), Durnin	5192
11	14	A	Leicester C	D	0-0	0-0	15		8199
12	17	A	Swindon T	L	0-3	0-2	—		10,741
13	21	H	Barnsley	L	2-3	0-1	19	Durnin, Stein	3863
14	28	A	West Ham U	L	2-3	1-1	20	Stein, Mustoe	19,177
15	Nov 1	H	Stoke C	W	3-0	1-0	—	Durnin, Foster, Mustoe	4375
16	4	A	Port Vale	W	2-1	1-0	13	Ford, Durnin	6994
17	11	H	Oldham Ath	L	0-1	0-1	14		4480
18	18	H	Hull C	D	0-0	0-0	16		4029
19	25	A	Middlesbrough	L	0-1	0-1	18		13,756
20	Dec 2	H	Plymouth Arg	W	3-2	1-1	15	Evans, Simpson, Phillips J	4403
21	9	A	Newcastle U	W	3-2	1-1	14	Evans, Phillips J (pen), Simpson	16,685
22	16	H	Wolverhampton W	D	2-2	1-1	16	Mustoe, Stein	7825
23	26	A	Sunderland	L	0-1	0-0	16		24,075
24	30	H	Brighton & HA	W	1-0	1-0	12	Stein	7738
25	Jan 1	H	Sheffield U	W	3-0	1-0	12	Simpson 2, Stein	7883
26	13	A	Watford	W	1-0	0-0	9	Lewis	10,040
27	20	H	Blackburn R	D	1-1	0-0	10	Penney	5973
28	Feb 10	H	WBA	L	0-1	0-1	13		6749
29	17	A	Bradford C	W	2-1	1-0	11	Mustoe, Stein	7389
30	24	H	Middlesbrough	W	3-1	1-0	10	Simpson, Durnin 2	5949
31	Mar 3	A	Hull C	L	0-1	0-0	11		4503
32	6	A	Bournemouth	W	1-0	1-0	—	Durnin	6319
33	10	H	Leeds U	L	2-4	2-0	12	Durnin, Simpson	8397
34	13	A	Ipswich T	L	0-1	0-0	—		10,380
35	17	A	Portsmouth	L	1-2	0-2	12	Foster	6749
36	21	H	Leicester C	W	4-2	2-0	—	Mustoe, Durnin, James (og), Stein	21,629
37	24	H	Swindon T	D	2-2	2-1	12	Foster 2	8382
38	31	A	Barnsley	L	0-1	0-1	13		7096
39	Apr 7	H	West Ham U	L	0-2	0-0	14		8371
40	10	A	Stoke C	W	2-1	0-1	—	Simpson 2 (1 pen)	8139
41	14	A	Sheffield U	L	1-2	0-0	12	Durnin	16,752
42	16	H	Sunderland	L	0-1	0-0	12		6053
43	21	A	Wolverhampton W	L	0-2	0-1	14		13,556
44	25	H	Brighton & HA	L	0-1	0-0	—		3864
45	May 1	A	Oldham Ath	L	1-4	0-1	—	Ford	12,616
46	5	H	Port Vale	D	0-0	0-0	17		4728

Final League Position: 17

GOALSCORERS

League (57): Durnin 13, Simpson 9 (1 pen), Stein 9, Mustoe 7, Foster 4, Phillips J 3 (2 pens), Evans 2, Ford 2, Foyle 2, Penney 2, Lewis 1, own goals 3.
Littlewoods Cup (4): Simpson 2, Durnin 1, Foyle 1.
FA Cup (1): Simpson 1.

Hucker	Bardsley	Phillips J	Phillips L	Foster	Greenall	Penney	Mustoe	Foyle	Durnin	Simpson	Ford	Smart	Lewis	McClaren	Slatter	Judge	Stein	Evans	Heath	Byrne	Nogan	Beauchamp	Kee	Muttock	Robinson	Jackson	Match No.
1	2	3	4	5	6	7†	8*	9	10	11	12	14															1
1	2	3		5	6	7		9	10	11				4	8												2
1	2	3	8	5		7		9	10	11				4	6												3
		3		5		7	12	9	10	11			2	4	8*	6	1										4
		3		5		7	8	9	10	11			2	4		6	1										5
		3		5		7	8†	9	10	11*	12		2	4		6	1	14									6
		3		5		7	8*	9	10†	11	12		2	4		6	1	14									7
		3		5		7*	8	9	10	11				4	2	6	1	12									8
1		3		5		14	8	9	10†	11	12			4	2*	6	7										9
1		3				7	8	9*	12	11			2	4		6	10	5									10
1		3			9	7	8			11			2	4		6	10	5									11
1		3			6	7*	8	9		11				4	2		10	5	12								12
1		3					8	9		11				4	6*		10	5	7	12							13
		3		5	6	7			9	12		8	2	4		1	10	11*									14
		3*		5	6	7†			9	14		8	2	4	12	1	10	11									15
		3		5	6	7			9	8			2	4		1	10	11									16
		3		5	6	12	7		9	14		8*	2	4		1	10	11†									17
		3		5		12	7			14			2	4*	8	1†	10	6	9	11							18
		3		5			7		9				2	4	8		10	6		11*	12		1				19
		3		5			9	7*	12	14			2	4	8		10	6	11†				1				20
		3		5					9	11			2	4	8		10	6	7				1				21
		3		5			8		9	11	6		2	4			10		7				1				22
		3*		5			8*		9†	11	14		2	4	12		10	6	7				1				23
		3		5					9	11			2	4	8		10	6	7				1				24
		3		5					9	11			2	4	8		10	6	7				1				25
		3		5					9	11			2	4	8		10	6	7				1				26
		3		5			12		9*	11			2	4	8		10	6	7				1				27
		3		5			9†	12		11		6	2	4	8*		10		7			14	1				28
		3		5			7		9	11	6		2	4	8		10						1				29
		3		5			7		9	11	6		2	4	8		10						1				30
		3		5			14	7	9	11†	6		2	4	8*		10	12					1				31
		3		5			8	7	9	11	6		2	4			10						1				32
		3		5			8*	7	9	11	6		2	4			10	12					1				33
		3		5			8	7	9	11	6		2	4			10						1				34
				5			8*	7	9	11	6		2	4			10	3	12				1				35
				5			12	8*	9	11	3		2	4			10	6	7				1				36
				5			8		9	11	3		2	4			10	6	7				1				37
				5			14	8	9†	11	3		2	4			10	6	12		7*		1				38
				5			8	12	9	11	3		2	4			10	6	7*				1				39
				5			7	8	9	11	3		2	4		1	10	6									40
			12	5			7*	8	9	11†	3		2	4		1	10	6				14					41
			12	5			7*	8	9	11	3		2	4		1	10	6									42
			7	5			8*	14		11	3		2	4	12	1	10	6						9†			43
			8	5			14	7	9†	11	3		2	4*	12	1	10	6									44
			8	5			7*	12	9	11	3		2	4		1	10	6									45
			8†	5			14		9	11	3			4*	12	1	10		7						2	6	46
8	3	34	6 +2s	35	15	20 +9s	36 +2s	11 +2s	39 +3s	38 +4s	25 +6s	39 +1s	45	17 +5s	10	17	38 +3s	24	16 +5s	2 +1s	2 +2s	2 +1s	21	1	1	1	

Littlewoods Cup	First Round	Fulham (a)	1-0
		(h)	3-5
FA Cup	Third Round	Plymouth Arg (a)	1-0
	Fourth Round	Southampton (a)	0-1

OXFORD UNITED

Player and Position	Ht	Wt	Birth Date	Place	Source	Clubs	League App	Gls
Goalkeepers								
Alan Judge	5 11	11 06	15 5 60	Kingsbury	Amateur	Luton T	11	—
						Reading (loan)	33	—
						Reading	44	—
						Oxford U	74	—
						Lincoln C (loan)	2	—
						Cardiff C (loan)	8	—
Paul Kee	6 3	12 12	8 11 69	Belfast	Ards	Oxford U	21	—
Defenders								
Ceri Evans	6 1	14 02	2 10 63	Christchurch	Otaga Univ. Worcester Coll (Oxford)	Oxford U	28	2
Paul Evans	5 7	11 01	16 3 72	Shrewsbury	Trainee	Oxford U	—	—
Mike Ford	5 11	12 05	9 2 66	Bristol		Leicester C	—	—
					Devizes	Cardiff C	145	13
						Oxford U	41	3
Steve Foster	6 0	14 00	24 9 57	Portsmouth	Apprentice	Portsmouth	109	6
						Brighton HA	172	6
						Aston Villa	15	3
						Luton T	163	11
						Oxford U	35	4
Colin Greenall	5 10	11 06	30 12 63	Billinge	Apprentice	Blackpool	183	9
						Gillingham	62	4
						Oxford U	67	2
						Bury (loan)	3	—
Darren Jackson	6 1	12 08	24 9 71	Bristol	Trainee	Oxford U	1	—
Jon Muttock	6 2	13 00	23 12 71	Oxford	Trainee	Oxford U	1	—
Neil Slatter*	5 11	10 09	30 5 64	Cardiff	Apprentice	Bristol R	148	4
						Oxford U	91	6
						Bournemouth (loan)	6	—
Gary Smart	5 9	11 03	29 4 64	Totnes	Wokingham	Oxford U	57	—
Midfield								
Paul Byrne	5 9	11 06	30 6 72	Dublin	Trainee	Oxford U	3	—
Mark Hewitson*	5 8	10 10	27 2 71	Oxford	Trainee	Oxford U	—	—
Richard Hill	6 0	12 04	20 9 63	Hinckley		Leicester C	—	—
					Nuneaton	Northampton T	86	46
						Watford	4	—
						Oxford U	63	13
Mickey Lewis	5 8	12 07	15 2 65	Birmingham	School	WBA	24	—
						Derby Co	43	1
						Oxford U	81	1
Steve McClaren	5 7	9 08	3 5 61	Fulford	Apprentice	Hull C	178	16
						Derby Co	25	—
						Lincoln C (loan)	8	—
						Bristol C	61	2
						Oxford U	22	—
Robbie Mustoe	5 10	10 08	28 8 68	Oxford		Oxford U	91	10
Les Phillips	5 8	10 06	7 1 63	London	Apprentice	Birmingham C	44	3
						Oxford U	136	8
Leslie Robinson	5 8	11 05	1 3 67	Mansfield		Mansfield T	15	—
						Stockport Co	67	3
						Doncaster R	82	12
						Oxford U	1	—
Graham Waters	5 8	11 02	5 11 71	St Austell	Trainee	Oxford U	—	—
Forwards								
Joey Beauchamp	5 11	11 03	13 3 71	Oxford	Trainee	Oxford U	4	—

OXFORD UNITED

Foundation: There had been an Oxford United club around the time of World War I but only in the Oxfordshire Thursday League and there is no connection with the modern club which began as Headington in 1893, adding "United" a later. Playing first on Quarry Fields and subsequently Wooton's Fields, they owe much to a Dr. Hitchings for their early development.

First Football League game: 18 August, 1962, Division 4, v Barrow (a) L 2-3 – Medlock; Beavon, Quartermain; R. Atkinson, Kyle, Jones; Knight, G. Atkinson (1), Houghton (1), Cornwell, Colfar.

Managers (and Secretary-managers)
Harry Thompson 1949–58 (Player Manager 1949-51), Arthur Turner 1959–69 (continued as GM to 1972), Ron Saunders 1969, George Summers 1969–75, Mike Brown 1975–79, Bill Asprey 1979–80, Ian Greaves 1980–82, Jim Smith 1982–85, Maurice Evans 1985–88, Mark Lawrenson 1988, Brian Horton 1988–   .

Player and Position	Ht	Wt	Birth Date	Place	Source	Clubs	League App	Gls
John Durnin	5 10	11 10	18 8 65	Liverpool	Waterloo Dock	Liverpool	—	—
						WBA (loan)	5	2
						Oxford U	61	16
Martin Foyle	5 10	11 02	2 5 63	Salisbury	Amateur	Southampton	12	1
						Blackburn R (loan)	—	—
						Aldershot	98	35
						Oxford U	90	26
Philip Heath	5 9	12 02	24 11 64	Stoke	Apprentice	Stoke C	156	17
						Oxford U	37	1
Matt McDonnell	5 10	10 10	10 4 71	Reading	Trainee	Oxford U	—	—
Lee Nogan	5 10	11 00	21 5 69	Cardiff	Apprentice	Oxford U	10	—
						Brentford (loan)	11	2
						Southend U (loan)	6	1
David Penney	5 8	10 07	17 8 64	Wakefield	Pontefract	Derby Co	19	—
						Oxford U	29	2
Peter Rhoades-Brown*	5 9	11 04	2 1 62	Hampton	Apprentice	Chelsea	96	4
						Oxford U	112	13
Paul Simpson	5 6	11 11	26 7 66	Carlisle	Apprentice	Manchester C	118	18
						Oxford U	67	17
Mark Stein	5 3	9 02	28 1 66	Capetown, SA		Luton T	54	19
						Aldershot (loan)	2	1
						QPR	33	4
						Oxford U	41	9

Trainees
Allen, Christopher A; Aris, Shane A; Fisher, Stuart M; Harwood, Paul D.A; Keeble, Matthew E; McLean, Richard G; Maciak, Michael.

Associated Schoolboys
Bayliss, Gary J; Conneely, Michael; Ford, Robert J; Fowler, Jason K. G. Girolami, Adriano; Goodall, Grant S; Greig, Neil J; Howard, Carl W; Jefferd, Kenneth M; Judge, Kevin A; Kennett, Wilson; Lawton, Daniel P; McGregor, Christian N; Maisey, Darren; Morrisey, Terry; Purnell, Rhydian M; Stevens, Greg R; Wright, Andrew L.

Associated Schoolboys who have accepted the club's offer of a Traineeship/Contract
Cane, Michael F; Didcock, Tristan; Druce, Mark A; Kelly, Leighton; Mutchell, Robert D; Tavinor, Stephen J; Wallbridge, Andrew J; Wanless, Paul S; Wild, Robert P.

414

PETERBOROUGH UNITED 1989–90

Back row (left to right):
Phil Crosby,
Steve Osborne,
Gary Andrews,
Noel Luke,
Robert Atkin.

Middle row:
Milton Graham,
Gerry McElhinney,
David Robinson,
Tony Godden,
Paul Crichton,
Carl Richards,
Adrian Speed,
Sean Willis.

Front row:
Worrell Sterling,
Robert Sullivan,
David Longhurst,
Mick Halsall,
Garry Butterworth,
Craig Goldsmith.

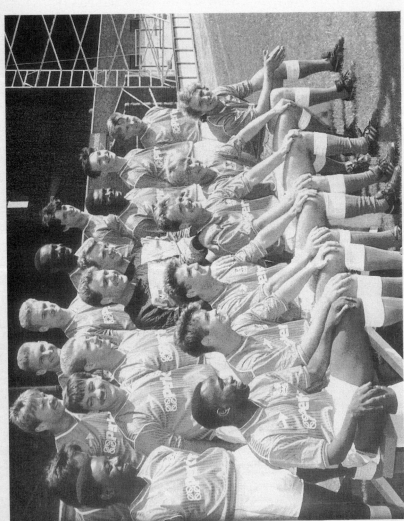

Division 4 **PETERBOROUGH UNITED**

London Road Ground, Peterborough PE2 8AL. Telephone Peterborough (0733) 63947.

Ground capacity: 28,000.

Record attendance: 30,096 v Swansea T, FA Cup 5th rd, 20 Feb, 1965.

Record receipts: £51,315 v Brighton & HA, 5th rd, 15 Feb, 1986.

Pitch measurements: 112yd × 76yd.

President: C. W. Swift OBE.

Chairman: J. F. Devaney. *Vice-Chairman:* M. C. Lewis.

Directors: R. D. Bowerman, M. G. Cook, FCA, M. B. Devaney (Mrs), A. Devaney (Miss), J. T. Dykes, A. Palkovich.

General Manager:

Manager: Mark Lawrenson. *Assistant Manager:* David Booth.

Secretary: Arnold V. Blades.

Physio: Bill Harvey.

Commercial Manager: J. Hill.

Year Formed: 1934. *Turned Professional:* 1934. *Ltd Co.:* 1934.

Club Nickname: 'The Posh'.

Record League Victory: 8-1 v Oldham Ath, Division 4, 26 November 1969 – Drewery; Potts, Noble; Conmy, Wile, Wright; Moss (1), Price (3), Hall (4), Halliday, Robson.

Record Cup Victory: 6–0 v Redditch, FA Cup, 1st rd (replay), 22 November 1971 – Drewery; Carmichael, Brookes; Oakes, Turner, Wright; Conmy, Price (1), Hall (2), Barker (2), Robson (1).

Record Defeat: 1-8 v Northampton T, FA Cup 2nd rd 2nd replay, 18 December, 1946.

Most League Points (2 for a win): 66, Division 4, 1960–61.

Most League Points (3 for a win): 82, Division 4, 1981–82.

Most League Goals: 134, Division 4, 1960–61.

Highest League Scorer in Season: Terry Bly, 52, Division 4, 1960–61.

Most League Goals in Total Aggregate: Jim Hall, 122, 1967–75.

Most Capped Player: Tony Millington, 8 (21), Wales.

Most League Appearances: Tommy Robson, 482, 1968–81.

Record Transfer Fee Received: £110,000 from Blackpool for Bob Doyle, July 1979.

Record Transfer Fee Paid: £100,000 to Halifax T for David Robinson, July 1989.

Football League Record: 1960 Elected to Division 4; 1961–68 Division 3, when they were demoted for financial irregularities; 1968–74 Division 4; 1974–79 Division 3; 1979– Division 4.

Honours: Football League: Division 3 best season: 4th, 1977–78. Division 4 – Champions 1960–61, 1973–74, *FA Cup* best season: 6th rd, 1965. *Football League Cup:* Semi-final 1966.

Colours: Royal blue shirts, white shorts, white stockings, two royal blue bars. **Change colours:** White shirts, royal blue trim, white shorts, royal blue trim, royal blue stockings, two white bars.

PETERBOROUGH UNITED 1989–90 LEAGUE RECORD

Match No.	Date	Venue	Opponents	Result	H/T Score	Lg. Pos.	Goalscorers	Attendance
1	Aug 19	H	Maidstone U	W 1-0	0-0	—	Halsall	6522
2	26	A	York C	L 0-1	0-0	10		2569
3	Sept 2	H	Aldershot	D 1-1	1-1	11	Robinson	3787
4	9	A	Doncaster R	W 3-0	1-0	7	Luke, Richards, Halsall	2327
5	16	H	Scunthorpe U	D 1-1	0-1	8	Richards	4350
6	23	A	Hartlepool U	D 2-2	0-1	9	Halsall, Butterworth	1703
7	27	A	Lincoln C	L 0-1	0-0	—		6106
8	30	H	Gillingham	D 1-1	0-0	13	Graham (pen)	4199
9	Oct 7	H	Exeter C	W 4-3	2-1	9	Harle (pen), McNichol (og), Sterling, Graham	3831
10	14	H	Rochdale	W 2-1	0-0	8	Luke, Culpin	1767
11	17	A	Burnley	W 2-1	1-0	—	Luke 2	7187
12	21	H	Stockport Co	W 2-0	1-0	4	Halsall 2	4804
13	28	A	Colchester U	W 1-0	0-0	3	Osborne	3460
14	Nov 1	H	Grimsby T	D 1-1	0-1	—	Robinson	6827
15	4	A	Southend U	D 0-0	0-0	4		4895
16	11	H	Hereford U	D 1-1	0-0	5	Osborne	4983
17	25	H	Torquay U	D 1-1	0-0	6	Richards	4175
18	Dec 2	A	Carlisle U	D 0-0	0-0	7		4608
19	17	A	Cambridge U	L 2-3	0-2	—	Osborne, Halsall	4811
20	26	H	Chesterfield	D 1-1	0-0	10	Osborne	5422
21	30	H	Scarborough	L 1-2	0-2	11	Richards	4153
22	Jan 1	A	Halifax T	D 2-2	1-0	12	Harle (pen), Butterworth	1578
23	6	A	Wrexham	L 1-2	0-0	—	Osborne	1937
24	13	H	York C	D 1-1	0-1	11	Richards	3678
25	20	A	Maidstone U	D 1-1	1-0	12	Hine	2707
26	27	H	Doncaster R	W 2-1	1-0	9	Oakes, Sterling	4080
27	Feb 7	H	Hartlepool U	L 0-2	0-1	—		2813
28	10	A	Scunthorpe U	D 0-0	0-0	12		3188
29	17	H	Carlisle U	W 3-0	1-0	11	Butterworth, Jepson, Hine	4088
30	24	A	Torquay U	L 1-2	0-1	12	Robinson	2467
31	27	A	Aldershot	W 1-0	0-0	—	Hine	1138
32	Mar 3	H	Wrexham	W 3-1	2-1	9	Jepson, Riley, Culpin	3990
33	6	A	Gillingham	D 0-0	0-0	—		4301
34	13	H	Lincoln C	W 1-0	0-0	—	Jepson	6204
35	17	A	Exeter C	L 0-2	0-1	9		4676
36	21	H	Rochdale	L 0-1	0-1	—		3485
37	24	H	Burnley	W 4-1	2-0	8	Halsall, Riley, Robinson (pen), Jepson	3841
38	30	A	Stockport Co	D 0-0	0-0	—		3651
39	Apr 7	H	Colchester U	W 1-0	1-0	9	Sterling	4025
40	10	A	Grimsby T	W 2-1	2-0	—	Sterling, Riley	8123
41	14	H	Halifax T	W 3-0	2-0	7	Halsall, Riley, Jepson	4570
42	16	A	Chesterfield	D 1-1	0-1	7	Riley	5696
43	21	H	Cambridge U	L 1-2	0-1	7	Luke	9257
44	25	A	Scarborough	L 1-2	0-1	—	Sterling	1838
45	28	A	Hereford U	W 2-1	1-0	7	Halsall, Hine	2273
46	May 5	H	Southend U	L 1-2	0-2	9	Halsall	7958

Final League Position: 9

GOALSCORERS

League (59): Halsall 10, Jepson 5, Luke 5, Osborne 5, Richards 5, Riley 5, Sterling 5, Hine 4, Robinson 4 (1 pen), Butterworth 3, Culpin 2, Graham 2 (1 pen), Harle 2 (2 pens), Oakes 1, own goal 1.
Littlewoods Cup (4): Richards 2, Halsall 1, Sterling 1.
FA Cup (3): Andrews 1, Robinson 1, Sterling 1.

Godden	Luke	Crosby	Halsall	Robinson	Oakes	Sterling	Graham	Richards	Longhurst	Goldsmith	Andrews	Osborne	Crichton	Butterworth	McElhinney	Culpin	Harle	Barber	Hine	Jepson	Moore	Riley	Watkins	Match No.
1	2	3	4	5	6	7	8	9	10	11														1
1	2*	3	4	5	6	7	8	9	10†	11	12	14												2
	2		4	5	6	7	8	9	12	11			10*	1	3									3
	2	3	4	5	6	7	8	9	10	11*				1	12									4
1	2*	3	4	5	6	7	8	9	10	11†			14	1	12									5
		3	4	5	6	7	8	9	10*			2	12	1	11									6
		3	4	5	6	7	8	9	12			2		1	11*	10								7
		3	4	5	6	7	8	9†	12			2	14	1	11	10*								8
	2	3	4	5	6	7	14	9*	12					1	11		8		10†					9
	2	3	4	5	6	7	12	9						1	11*		8		10					10
	2	3	4	5		7	14	12	9*					11†	6		8		10	1				11
	2*	3	4	5		7	12		9					11	6		8		10	1				12
	2	3	4	5		7		9				12		11	6		8*		10	1				13
	2	3	4	5		7		9					14	11†	6*		8		10	1				14
	2	3	4	5		7	12	9					14	11†	6		8		10*	1				15
	2	3	4	5		7		9	8†				14	11	6		12		10*	1				16
1	2	3	4	5		7	10	9				12	14	11	6*		8†							17
1	2	3	4	5		7	10	9*				12		11	6		8							18
1	2	3	4	5		7		9	14			6	10	11†	12		8*							19
1	2		4	5		7		9	12			3	10*	11	6				8					20
1	2	3†	4	5		7		9	12			11*	10	14	6				8					21
1	2	3	4	5	12	7		9					10*	11	6				8					22
1	2	3	4	5		7		12	9			10		11*	6				8					23
1	2	3	4		5	7		12	9†			10		11	6*		14		8					24
10		3	4	5	11	7						2	9*	1	12	6			8					25
10		3	4	5	11	7						2		1	12	6			8*	9				26
10		3†	4	5	6	7						2*	14	1	12				8	9	11			27
	2		4	5	10	7							1	3	6				8	9	11			28
	2		4	5	10	7							1	3	6				8	9	11			29
	2	12	4	5	10	7							1	3	6*				8	9	11			30
1	2	12	4	5		7							10	3	6				8	9	11*			31
1	2	3	4	5		7							14*	11	6	12			8	9†		10		32
1	2	3	4	5		7		9						11	6				8			10		33
1	2	3	4	5		7								11	6	8				9		10		34
1	2	3	4	5	14	7†								11*	6	8				9		10		35
1	2	3	4	5		7*									12	14			8	9	11†	10		36
1	2	3	4	5	11	7									12	6			8	9		10*		37
1	2	3	4	5	11	7									12	6			8	9		10*		38
1	2	3	4	5	11	7									12	6			8	9*		10		39
1	2	3	4	5	11	7										6			8	9		10		40
1	2	3†	4	5	11	7							14		12	6			8	9		10*		41
1	2	3	4	5	11	7										6			8	9		10		42
1	2	3†	4	5	11	7							14		12	6*			8	9		10		43
1	2	3	4	5	11*	7							14		12	6†			8	9		10		44
	2	3	4	5	6	7							9	1	11				8			10		45
	2	3*	4	5	6	7							9	1	11				8†		12	10	14	46
24	43	40	46	45	27	46	10	16	14	5	9	12	16	29	34	9	14	6	22	18	6	15	—	

Subs (+): Oakes +2s · Graham +2s · Richards +5s · Longhurst +4s · Goldsmith +7s · Andrews +1s · Osborne +1s · Crichton +20s · Culpin +10s · Harle +3s · Barber +1s · Jepson +1s · Riley +1s · Watkins +1s

Littlewoods Cup First Round	Aldershot (h)	2-0
	(a)	2-6
FA Cup First Round	Hayes (h)	1-1
	(a)	1-0
Second Round	Swansea C (a)	1-3

PETERBOROUGH UNITED

Player and Position	Ht	Wt	Birth Date	Place	Source	Clubs	League App	Gls
Goalkeepers								
Paul Crichton*	6 1	12 05	3 10 68	Pontefract	Apprentice	Nottingham F	—	—
						Notts Co (loan)	5	—
						Darlington (loan)	5	—
						Peterborough U (loan)	4	—
						Darlington (loan)	3	—
						Swindon T (loan)	4	—
						Rotherham U (loan)	6	—
						Torquay U (loan)	13	—
						Peterborough U	47	—
Tony Godden*	6 0	13 00	2 8 55	Gillingham	Ashford T	WBA	267	—
						Preston NE (loan)	—	—
						Luton T (loan)	12	—
						Walsall (loan)	19	—
						Chelsea (loan)	8	—
						Chelsea	26	—
						Birmingham C	29	—
						Bury (loan)	1	—
						Sheffield W (loan)	—	—
						Peterborough U	24	—
Defenders								
Gary Andrews*	5 11	12 01	12 5 68	Nottingham		Nottingham F	—	—
						Peterborough U	43	—
Steve Collins‡	5 8	12 04	21 3 62	Stamford	Apprentice	Peterborough U	94	1
						Southend U	51	—
						Lincoln C (loan)	13	—
						Lincoln C	11	—
						Peterborough U	122	2
Phil Crosby	5 9	10 08	9 11 62	Leeds	Apprentice	Grimsby T	39	1
						Rotherham U	183	2
						Peterborough U	42	—
Gerry McElhinney	6 1	13 10	19 9 56	Londonderry	Distillery	Bolton W	109	2
						Rochdale (loan)	20	1
						Plymouth Arg	91	2
						Peterborough U	67	1
Keith Oakes	5 10	12 02	3 7 56	Bedworth	Apprentice	Peterborough U	62	2
						Newport Co	232	27
						Gillingham	86	7
						Fulham	76	3
						Peterborough U	70	6
David Robinson	6 0	12 03	14 1 65	Cleveland	Billingham	Hartlepool U	66	1
						Halifax T	72	1
						Peterborough U	45	4
Midfield								
Garry Butterworth	5 8	10 11	8 9 69	Peterborough	Trainee	Peterborough U	59	3
Milton Graham	5 10	12 04	2 11 62	Tottenham	Local	Bournemouth	73	12
						Chester C	129	11
						Peterborough U	15	2
Mick Halsall	5 10	11 04	21 7 61	Bootle	Apprentice	Liverpool	—	—
						Birmingham C	36	3
						Carlisle U	92	11
						Grimsby T	12	—
						Peterborough U	133	15
Mark Hine	5 8	9 11	18 5 64	Middlesbrough	Local	Grimsby T	22	1
						Darlington	128	8
						Peterborough U	22	4
Noel Luke	5 11	10 11	28 12 64	Birmingham	School	WBA	9	1
						Mansfield T	50	9
						Peterborough U	161	25
Martin Moore*			10 1 66	Middlesbrough	Stockton	Peterborough U	7	—

PETERBOROUGH UNITED

Foundation: The old Peterborough & Fletton club, founded in 1923, was suspended by the FA during season 1932–33 and disbanded. Local enthusiasts determined to carry on and in 1934 a new professional club Peterborough United was formed and entered the Midland League the following year.

First Football League game: 20 August, 1960, Division 4, v Wrexham (h) W 3-0 – Walls; Stafford, Walker; Rayner, Rigby, Norris; Halls, Emery (1), Bly (1), Smith, McNamee (1).

Managers (and Secretary-managers)
Jock Porter 1934–36, Fred Taylor 1936–37, Vic Poulter 1937–38, Sam Madden 1938–48, Jack Blood 1948–50, Bob Gurney 1950–52, Jack Fairbrother 1952–54, George Swindin 1954–58, Jimmy Hagan 1958–62, Jack Fairbrother 1962–64, Gordon Clark 1964–67, Norman Rigby 1967–69, Jim Iley 1969–72, Noel Cantwell 1972–77, John Barnwell 1977–78, Billy Hails 1978–79, Peter Morris 1979–82, Martin Wilkinson 1982–83, John Wile 1983–86, Noel Cantwell 1986–88 (continued as GM), Mick Jones 1988–89, Mark Lawrenson 1990– .

Player and Position	Ht	Wt	Birth Date	Birth Place	Source	Clubs	League App	Gls
Forwards								
Paul Culpin	5 10	11 10	8 2 62	Kirby Muxloe		Leicester C	—	—
					Nuneaton	Coventry C	9	2
						Northampton T	63	23
						Peterborough U	12	2
Nicky Cusack (To Motherwell Aug 1989)	6 0	11 13	24 12 65	Rotherham	Alvechurch	Leicester C	16	1
						Peterborough U	44	10
Mike Nuttell‡	6 1	12 00	22 11 68	Boston	Trainee	Peterborough U	21	—
						Crewe Alex (loan)	3	1
						Carlisle U (loan)	3	—
Steve Osborne	5 10	11 11	3 3 69	Middlesbrough	South Bank	Peterborough U	41	6
David Riley	5 7	10 10	8 12 60	Northampton	Keyworth U	Nottingham F	12	2
						Darlington (loan)	6	2
						Peterborough U (loan)	12	2
						Port Vale	76	11
						Peterborough U	15	5
Worrell Sterling	5 8	10 08	8 6 65	Bethnal Green	Apprentice	Watford	94	14
						Peterborough U	58	8
Dale Watkins§			4 11 71	Peterborough	Trainee	Peterborough U	1	—

Trainees
Bradley, Martin P; Clark, Darrin W; Cooper, Darren; Curtis, Hamish; Herrick, Mark J; Hill, Paul J; Islam, Russell; Jones, Timothy P; Phillips, Michael P; Roberts, Shaun; Smith, Robert L; Tuffs, Andrew G; Watkins, Dale A.
Associated Schoolboy
Stanhope, Andrew P.

420

PLYMOUTH ARGYLE 1989-90 *Back row (left to right):* Martin Barlow, Lee Cooper, David Byrne, Darren Garner, Owen Pickard, Jason Rowbotham, Lee Cansfield, Kenny Brown, Kevin Hodges, Stuart Casey.
Centre row: Martin Harvey (Coach), Paul Rowe, Ian Angus, Greg Campbell, Rhys Wilmot, Gary Penhaligon, Tommy Tynan, John Brimacombe, Mark Stuart, Malcolm Musgrove.
Front row: Andrew Morrison, Andrew Thomas, Peter Whiston, Adrian Burrows, Ken Brown, Kevin Summerfield, Sean McCarthy, Nicky Marker, Mark Smith.

Division 2   **PLYMOUTH ARGYLE**

Home Park, Plymouth, Devon PL2 3DQ. Telephone Plymouth (0752) 562561-2-3. Lottery Shop: 561041.

Ground capacity: 26,000.

Record attendance: 43,596 v Aston Villa, Division 2, 10 Oct, 1936.

Record receipts: £96,989.57 v Derby Co, FA Cup 6th rd, 10 March, 1984.

Pitch measurements: 112yd × 75yd.

President: S. Rendell.

Chairman: P. D. Bloom.

Directors: B. L. Hooper, R. Burroughs ARICS. G. E. Jasper, J. E. C. Kent, D. Forshaw, C. Hartley.

Manager: David Kemp. *Coach:* Alan Gillett.

Secretary: Graham Little. *Commercial Manager:* D. Potham.

Physio: Malcolm Musgrove.

Year Formed: 1886. *Turned Professional:* 1903. *Ltd Co.:* 1903.

Club Nickname: 'The Pilgrims'.

Previous Name: 1886–1903. Argyle Athletic Club.

Record League Victory: 8-1 v Millwall, Division 2, 16 January 1932 – Harper; Roberts, Titmuss; Mackay, Pullan, Reed; Grozier, Bowden (2), Vidler (3), Leslie (1), Black (1). (1 og).

Record Cup Victory: 6-0 v Corby T, FA Cup, 3rd rd, 22 January 1966 – Leiper; Book, Baird; Williams, Nelson, Newman; Jones (1), Jackson (1), Bickle (3), Piper (1), Jennings.

Record Defeat: 0-9 v Stoke C, Division 2, 17 December, 1960.

Most League Points (2 for a win): 68, Division 3 (S), 1929–30.

Most League Points (3 for a win): 87, Division 3, 1985–86.

Most League Goals: 107, Division 3 (S), 1925–26 and 1951–52.

Highest League Scorer in Season: Jack Cock, 32, Division 3 (S), 1925–26.

Most League Goals in Total Aggregate: Sammy Black, 180, 1924–38.

Most Capped Player: Moses Russell, 20 (23), Wales.

Most League Appearances: Sammy Black, 470, 1924–38. Kevin Hodges, 470, 1978–90.

Record Transfer Fee Received: £250,000 from Everton for Gary Megson, February 1980.

Record Transfer Fee Paid: £170,000 to Sheffield W for Mark Smith, January 1987.

Football League Record: 1920 Original Member of Division 3; 1921–30 Division 3 (S); 1930–50 Division 2; 1950–52 Division 3 (S); 1952–56 Division 2; 1956–58 Division 3 (S); 1958–59 Division 3; 1959–68 Division 2; 1968–75 Division 3; 1975–77 Division 2; 1977–86 Division 3; 1986– Division 2.

Honours: Football League: Division 2 best season: 4th, 1931–32, 1952–53; Division 3 (S) – Champions 1929–30, 1951–52; Runners-up 1921–22, 1922–23, 1923–24, 1924–25, 1925–26, 1926–27 (record of six consecutive years); Division 3 – Champions 1958–59; Runners-up 1974–75, 1985–86. *FA Cup* best season: semi-final 1983–84. *Football League Cup:* Semi-final, 1965, 1974.

Colours: Green shirts, black shorts, white stockings green tops. **Change colours:** White shirts, white shorts, white stockings green tops.

PLYMOUTH ARGYLE 1989–90 LEAGUE RECORD

Match No.	Date	Venue	Opponents	Result	H/T Score	Lg. Pos.	Goalscorers	Attendance
1	Aug 19	H	Oxford U	W 2-0	0-0	—	Stuart 2	8509
2	26	A	West Ham U	L 2-3	0-1	11	Stuart 2	20,231
3	Sept 2	H	Barnsley	W 2-1	0-0	8	Campbell, McCarthy	7708
4	9	A	Oldham Ath	L 2-3	0-1	11	McCarthy, Thomas	4940
5	12	A	Portsmouth	W 3-0	1-0	—	Tynan 2 (1 pen), Thomas	6865
6	16	H	Sheffield U	D 0-0	0-0	5		10,884
7	23	A	Wolverhampton W	L 0-1	0-0	11		13,762
8	26	A	Swindon T	L 0-3	0-1	—		6862
9	30	A	Brighton & HA	W 2-1	1-0	11	Hodges, Tynan	7610
10	Oct 7	H	Stoke C	W 3-0	1-0	7	Hodges, Tynan (pen), Thomas	6940
11	14	A	Middlesbrough	W 2-0	0-0	—	Stuart, Thomas	15,003
12	17	H	Leicester C	W 3-1	3-0	—	Hodges, Thomas, Evans (og)	10,037
13	21	A	Ipswich T	L 0-3	0-2	5		10,362
14	28	H	Blackburn R	D 2-2	2-1	6	McCarthy 2	6876
15	Nov 1	A	Leeds U	L 1-2	1-1	—	Thomas	26,791
16	4	H	Bradford C	D 1-1	0-0	10	Tynan	7152
17	11	A	Watford	W 2-1	0-0	8	Tynan, Thomas	9401
18	18	A	Sunderland	L 1-3	1-2	10	Campbell	15,033
19	25	H	Port Vale	L 1-2	1-2	10	Tynan	7034
20	Dec 2	A	Oxford U	L 2-3	1-1	11	Thomas, Tynan (pen)	4403
21	10	H	Portsmouth	L 0-2	0-1	—		9988
22	26	H	WBA	D 2-2	0-2	13	Thomas, Summerfield	9782
23	29	H	Hull C	L 1-2	0-1	—	Campbell	8588
24	Jan 1	A	Bournemouth	D 2-2	0-1	17	Tynan (pen), Thomas	6939
25	13	H	West Ham U	D 1-1	1-0	16	Tynan	11,671
26	20	A	Barnsley	D 1-1	0-0	16	Thomas	7224
27	Feb 3	H	Wolverhampton W	L 0-1	0-1	18		10,873
28	10	A	Sheffield U	L 0-1	0-1	19		13,530
29	24	A	Port Vale	L 0-3	0-1	20		7254
30	Mar 3	H	Sunderland	W 3-0	2-0	19	Tynan 2, McCarthy	7299
31	7	A	Brighton & HA	L 1-2	0-1	—	Stuart	7418
32	10	H	Swindon T	L 0-3	0-2	21		8364
33	17	A	Stoke C	D 0-0	0-0	20		9452
34	20	H	Middlesbrough	L 1-2	0-1	—	Byrne	7185
35	24	A	Leicester C	D 1-1	0-1	22	Marker	9395
36	31	H	Ipswich C	W 1-0	0-0	21	Morrison	6793
37	Apr 3	A	Newcastle U	L 1-3	1-1	—	Hodges	16,558
38	7	A	Blackburn R	L 0-2	0-0	21		7492
39	10	H	Leeds U	D 1-1	1-1	—	Tynan (pen)	11,382
40	14	H	Bournemouth	W 1-0	0-0	21	Tynan (pen)	7520
41	16	A	WBA	W 3-0	1-0	19	McCarthy 3	9728
42	18	A	Oldham Ath	W 2-0	2-0	—	McCarthy 2	8146
43	21	A	Newcastle U	D 1-1	1-1	18	Tynan	11,702
44	24	A	Hull C	D 3-3	0-1	—	Fiore, Burrows, Thomas	5256
45	28	H	Watford	D 0-0	0-0	18		8564
46	May 5	A	Bradford C	W 1-0	1-0	16	McCarthy	4903

Final League Position: 16

GOALSCORERS

League (58): Tynan 15 (6 pens), Thomas 12, McCarthy 11, Stuart 6, Hodges 4, Campbell 3, Burrows 1, Byrne 1, Fiore 1, Marker 1, Morrison 1, Summerfield 1, own goal 1.
Littlewoods Cup (4): Tynan 3, McCarthy 1.
FA Cup (0).

Wilmot	Brown	Brimacombe	Marker	Burrows	Smith	Byrne	McCarthy	Tynan	Thomas	Stuart	Hodges	Campbell	Morrison	Barlow	Whiston	Beglin	Pickard	Damerell	Summerfield	Robson	Garner	Broddle	Cooper	Gregory	Fiore	Salman	Blackwell	King	Match No.
1	2	3	4	5	6	7	8	9	10	11																			1
1	2	3	4	5	6	7	8	9	10	11																			2
1	2	3	4	5	6	7*	8	9†	10	11	12	14																	3
1	2	3	4	5	6		8	9	10	11	7																		4
1	2	3	4	5	6		8	9	10	11	7																		5
1	2	3	4	5	6	12	8	9	10*	11	7																		6
1	2	3	4	5		6	8	9	10	11	7																		7
1	2	3	4	5		6	8	9	10	11	7																		8
1	2	3	4	5*		10		9	12	11	7	8	6																9
1	2	3	4	5		7		9	12	11	8*	10	6																10
1	2	3	4	5				9	8	11	7	10	6																11
1	2	3	4	5		12	9*	8	11	7†	10	6	14																12
1	2	3	4	5		12	9*	8	11	7	10	6†	14																13
1	2	3	4	5		14	8	9*	10	11	7	12	6†																14
1	2	3	4	5		7	8	9	10	11	6																		15
1	2	3	4	5		7	8*	9	10	11	6	12																	16
1	2	3	4	5		7		9	10	11	6	8																	17
1	2	3*	4	5		7		9	10	11	6	8	12																18
1	2		4	5				9	10	11	7	8	6		3														19
1	2		4	5		7		9	10		6	8			3				11										20
1	2		4	5		7		9	10		6	8*			3				11†	12		14							21
1	2		4	5		7		9*	10		6	8				3			11			12							22
1	2		4	5		7			10		6	8				3			11			9							23
1	2		4	5				9	10		6	8*				3			11	7		12							24
1	2		4	5		8*	9	10			6	12				3			11	7									25
1	2		4	5		8	9	10			6	12				3*			11	7									26
1	2		4	5		8*	9†	10	14		6	12							11	7		3							27
1	2		4	5				9	10	12	6	8*							11	7		3							28
1	2		4	5				9	10	8	6	12							11	7		3*							29
1	2	14	4	5		8*	9		11		6†								12	7		3		10					30
1	2	12	4	5		8	9		11		6									7		3		10*					31
1	2			5		14	8	9	11†		6	12							4*	7		3		10					32
1	2			5		10	8	9			6									7		3			11		4		33
1	2		4	5		14	8*	9			6	12								7†					11	3	10		34
1	2		4	5		7	9	8	10		6														11*	3		12	35
1	2		4	5		7	8	9*	10		6								12						11	3			36
1	2		4	5		7	8	9*	10		6								12						11	3†	14		37
1	2			5		7	8	9	10	12	6								3						11*		4		38
1			4	5		7	8	9	11	10	6*															3	2	12	39
1			4	5		7*	8	9	10	6									12						11	3	2		40
1	2		4	5		7	8	9	10	6									12						11	3*			41
1	2		4	5		7	8	9	10	6															11	3			42
1	2		4	5		7	8	9	10*	6															11	3		12	43
1	2		4	5		7	8	9	12	6															11	3	10*		44
1	2		4	5		7	8	9	10†	6	14														11*	3		12	45
1	2		4	5		7	8		6	10	9														11*	3		12	46
46	44	18	43	46	6	28	30	44	33	23	43	15	18	—	3	5	1	—	8	7	—	9	2	3	11	10	5	5	
		+				+	+	+	+	+	+	+	+		+				+	+		+			+	+	+	+	
		2s				4s	2s	3s	2s	1s	7s	1s	1s		5s				4s1s	2s		1s			1s	1s	2s	3s	

Littlewoods Cup	First Round	Cardiff C (a)	3-0
		(h)	0-2
	Second Round	Arsenal (a)	0-2
		(h)	1-6
FA Cup	Third Round	Oxford U (h)	0-1

PLYMOUTH ARGYLE

Player and Position	Ht	Wt	Birth Date	Place	Source	Clubs	League App	Gls
Goalkeepers								
Garry Penhaligon‡	6 0	12 01	13 5 70	St Austell	Trainee	Plymouth Arg	1	—
Rhys Wilmot	6 1	12 00	21 2 62	Newport	Apprentice	Arsenal	8	—
						Hereford U (loan)	9	—
						Orient (loan)	46	—
						Swansea C (loan)	16	—
						Plymouth Arg (loan)	17	—
						Plymouth Arg	46	—
Defenders								
John Brimacombe	5 11	11 10	25 11 58	Plymouth	Liskeard/Saltash	Plymouth Arg	98	3
Julian Broddle	5 9	11 03	1 11 64	Laughton	Apprentice	Sheffield U	1	—
						Scunthorpe U	144	32
						Barnsley	77	4
						Plymouth Arg	9	—
Kenny Brown	5 8	11 06	11 7 67	Barking	Apprentice	Norwich C	25	—
						Plymouth Arg	83	1
Adrian Burrows	5 11	11 12	16 1 59	Sutton	Local	Mansfield T	78	5
						Northampton T	88	4
						Plymouth Arg	175	6
						Southend U (loan)	6	—
Leigh Cooper*	5 8	10 09	7 5 61	Reading	Apprentice	Plymouth Arg	323	15
Nick Marker	6 1	13 00	3 5 65	Exeter	Apprentice	Exeter C	202	3
						Plymouth Arg	112	8
Andy Morrison	5 11	12 00	30 7 70	Inverness	Trainee	Plymouth Arg	22	1
Jason Rowbotham	5 9	11 00	3 1 69	Cardiff	Trainee	Plymouth Arg	9	—
Danis Salman	5 10	11 08	12 3 60	Cyprus	Apprentice	Brentford	325	8
						Millwall	93	4
						Plymouth Arg	11	—
Midfield								
Dougie Anderson‡	6 0	10 05	29 8 63	Hong Kong	Port Glasgow	Oldham Ath	9	—
						Tranmere R	126	15
						Plymouth Arg	19	1
						Cambridge U (loan)	8	2
						Northampton T (loan)	5	—
Stuart Casey*	5 7	10 07	5 9 69	Plymouth	Trainee	Plymouth Arg	—	—
Mark Fiore	5 10	11 10	18 11 69	Southwark	Trainee	Wimbledon	1	—
						Plymouth Arg	12	1
Darren Garner	5 6	11 01	10 12 71	Plymouth	Trainee	Plymouth Arg	2	—
Kevin Hodges	5 8	10 00	12 6 60	Bridport	Apprentice	Plymouth Arg	470	78
Adam King	5 11	11 12	4 10 69	Hillingdon	Trainee	West Ham U	—	—
						Plymouth Arg	8	—
Kevin Summerfield	5 11	11 00	7 1 59	Walsall	Apprentice	WBA	9	4
						Birmingham C	5	1
						Walsall	54	17
						Cardiff C	10	1
						Plymouth Arg	138	26
						Exeter C (loan)	4	—
Andy Thomas	6 0	10 10	16 12 62	Oxford	Apprentice	Oxford U	116	32
						Fulham (loan)	4	2
						Derby Co (loan)	1	—
						Newcastle U	31	6
						Bradford C	23	5
						Plymouth Arg	36	12
Peter Whiston	6 0	11 06	4 1 68	Widnes		Plymouth Arg	10	—
						Torquay U (loan)	8	1

PLYMOUTH ARGYLE

Foundation: The Plymouth Argyle Association Football Club developed out of the Argyle Athletic club which was formed in 1886 at a meeting in Argyle Terrace, Mutley. Plymouth was a rugby stronghold, but servicemen brought soccer to the town and it spread quickly. At first Argyle Athletic Club played both soccer and rugby in colours of green and black. The rugby section was eventually disbanded, and after a number of exhibition games had satisfied the locals of the feasibility of running a professional club, Plymouth Argyle was formed in 1903.

First Football League game: 28 August, 1920, Division 3, v Norwich C (h) D 1-1 – Craig; Russell, Atterbury; Logan, Dickinson, Forbes; Kirkpatrick, Jack, Bowler, Heeps (1), Dixon.

Managers (and Secretary-managers)
Frank Brettell 1903–05, Bob Jack 1905–06, Bill Fullerton 1906–07, Bob Jack 1910–38, Jack Tresadern 1938–47, Jimmy Rae 1948–55, Jack Rowley 1955–60, Neil Dougall 1961, Ellis Stuttard 1961–63, Andy Beattie 1963–64, Malcolm Allison 1964–65, Derek Ufton 1965–68, Billy Bingham 1968–70, Ellis Stuttard 1970–72, Tony Waiters 1972–77, Mike Kelly 1977–78, Malcolm Allison 1978–79, Bobby Saxton 1979–81, Bobby Moncur 1981–83, Johnny Hore 1983–84, Dave Smith 1984–88, Ken Brown 1988–90, David Kemp 1990– .

Player and Position	Ht	Wt	Birth Date	Place	Source	Clubs	League App	Gls
Forwards								
Martin Barlow	5 7	10 03	25 6 71	Barnstable	Trainee	Plymouth Arg	2	—
David Byrne	5 8	11 00	5 3 61	London	Kingstonian	Gillingham	23	3
						Millwall	63	6
						Cambridge U (loan)	4	—
						Blackburn R (loan)	4	—
						Plymouth Arg	45	2
						Bristol R (loan)	2	—
Greg Campbell*	5 11	11 05	13 7 65	Portsmouth	Apprentice	West Ham U	5	—
						Brighton & HA (loan)	2	—
						Plymouth Arg	35	6
Lee Cansfield‡	5 8	11 00	4 8 71	Plymouth	Trainee	Plymouth Arg	—	—
Mark Damerell	5 9	11 00	31 7 65	Plymouth	St Blazey	Plymouth Arg	1	—
Sean McCarthy	6 0	12 02	12 9 67	Bridgend	Bridgend	Swansea C	91	25
						Plymouth Arg	70	19
Owen Pickard	5 10	11 03	18 11 69	Barnstaple	Trainee	Plymouth Arg	7	—
Paul Robinson	6 4	14 07	21 2 71	Nottingham	Notts Co§ Bury§	Scarborough	20	3
						Plymouth Arg	—	—
Paul Rowe	5 10	10 12	1 8 71	Wadebridge	Trainee	Plymouth Arg	—	—
Mark Stuart	5 8	11 02	15 12 66	Hammersmith	QPR schoolboy	Charlton Ath	107	28
						Plymouth Arg	57	11
						Ipswich T (loan)	5	2
Tommy Tynan*	5 10	12 09	17 11 55	Liverpool	Apprentice	Liverpool	—	—
						Swansea C (loan)	6	2
						Sheffield W	91	31
						Lincoln C	9	1
						Newport Co	183	66
						Plymouth Arg	80	43
						Rotherham U	32	13
						Plymouth Arg (loan)	9	9
						Plymouth Arg	173	73

Trainees
Adcock, Paul M; Balsdon, Mark A; Browne, Martyn A; Casey, Robert N; Clode, Mark J; Cross, Ryan; Davies, Lee K; Edworthy, Marc; Evans, Michael J; Goddard, Scott; Jones, Jason S; Maxwell, Paul J; Smith, Paul A; Tallon, Darren J.B.

Associated Schoolboys
Anbany, Simon J; Balfour, Dax; Crocker, Marcus; Hayward, Shaun; Hicks, Nathan J; Jones, Gerard; Morgan, James A; Morris, Mark G; Plumb, Gareth L; Salt, Neil B; Smith, Damian B; Sullivan, Martyn G; Underhay, Leigh A; Williams, Keith R.

PORTSMOUTH 1989-90 *Back row (left to right):* Terry Connor, Warren Neill, Micky Fillery, Warren Aspinall, Mark Chamberlain.
Centre row: Gordon Neave (Kitman), Lee Sandford, Alan Knight, Graeme Hogg, Andy Gosney, Guy Whittingham, Neil Sillett (Physiotherapist).
Front row: Steve Wigley, Shaun Murray, Gavin Maguire, Kenny Black, John Gregory (Manager), Kevin Ball, Martin Kuhl, John Beresford, Mark Kelly.

Division 2   **PORTSMOUTH**

Fratton Park, Frogmore Rd, Portsmouth PO4 8RA. Telephone Portsmouth (0705) 731204. Commercial Dept: 0705-827111. Ticket Office: 0705-750825. Lottery Office: 0705 825016. Club-call: 0898 121182.

Ground capacity: 28,000.

Record attendance: 51,385 v Derby Co, FA Cup 6th rd, 26 Feb, 1949.

Record receipts: £122,000 v Southampton, FA Cup 4th rd, 28 Jan, 1984.

Pitch measurements: 116yd × 73yd.

President: B. J. Deacon CBE. *Vice-Presidents:* Sir A. L. Blake MC, LLB, KCVO, Mrs J. Deacon.

Chairman: J. A. Gregory. *Vice-Chairman:* D. K. Deacon.

Directors: M. H. Gregory, R. Stainton, J. W. Slaon, J. P. R. Prevost FCA., M. Murphy, R. Jones, D. Deacon, B. Henson, J. Dunnett.

Team Manager: Frank Burrows. *Coach:* Steve Wicks.

Chief Executive/Company Secretary: P. Weld. *Commercial Manager:* Ray Stainton.

Physio: John Dickens. *Youth Team Coach:* Graham Paddon.

Year Formed: 1898. *Turned Professional:* 1898. *Ltd Co.:* 1898.

Club Nickname: 'Pompey'.

Record League Victory: 9-1 v Notts Co, Division 2, 9 April 1927 – McPhail; Clifford, Ted Smith; Reg Davies (1), Foxall, Moffat; Forward (1), Mackie (2), Haines (3), Watson, Cook (2).

Record Cup Victory: 7-0 v Stockport Co, FA Cup, 3rd rd, 8 January 1949 – Butler; Rookes, Ferrier; Scoular, Flewin, Dickinson; Harris (3), Barlow, Clarke (2), Phillips (2), Froggatt.

Record Defeat: 0-10 v Leicester C, Division 1, 20 October, 1928.

Most League Points (2 for a win): 65, Division 3, 1961–62.

Most League Points (3 for a win): 91, Division 3, 1982–83.

Most League Goals: 91, Division 4, 1979–80.

Highest League Scorer in Season: Billy Haines, 40. Division 2, 1926–27.

Most League Goals in Total Aggregate: Peter Harris, 194, 1946–60.

Most Capped Player: Jimmy Dickinson, 48, England.

Most League Appearances: Jimmy Dickinson, 764, 1946–65.

Record Transfer Fee Received: £915,000 from AC Milan for Mark Hateley, June 1984.

Record Transfer Fee Paid: £315,000 to Aston Villa for Warren Aspinall, August 1988.

Football League Record: 1920 Original Member of Division 3; 1921 Division 3 (S); 1924–27 Division 2; 1927–59 Division 1; 1959–61 Division 2; 1961–62 Division 3; 1962–76 Division 2; 1976–78 Division 3; 1978–80 Division 4; 1980–83 Division 3; 1983–87 Division 2; 1987–88 Division 1; 1988– Division 2.

Honours: Football League: Division 1 – Champions 1948–49, 1949–50; Division 2 – Runners-up 1926–27, 1986–87; Division 3 (S) – Champions 1923–24; Division 3 – Champions 1961–62, 1982–83. *FA Cup:* Winners 1939; Runners-up 1929, 1934. *Football League Cup* best season: 5th rd, 1960–61, 1985–86.

Colours: Blue shirts, white shorts, red stockings. **Change colours:** Yellow shirts, blue shorts, black stockings.

PORTSMOUTH 1989–90 LEAGUE RECORD

Match No.	Date		Venue	Opponents	Result		H/T Score	Lg. Pos.	Goalscorers	Atten- dance
1	Aug	19	A	Watford	L	0-1	0-1	—		10,164
2		26	H	Stoke C	D	0-0	0-0	20		7433
3	Sept	2	A	Bradford C	D	1-1	1-0	18	Fillery	8425
4		9	H	Hull C	D	2-2	0-0	21	Whittingham, Ball	6491
5		12	H	Plymouth Arg	L	0-3	0-1	—		6865
6		16	A	Newcastle U	L	0-1	0-1	23		19,589
7		23	H	Middlesbrough	W	3-1	3-0	20	Chamberlain, Kuhl, Whittingham	7305
8		26	H	West Ham U	L	0-1	0-0	—		12,632
9		30	A	Wolverhampton W	L	0-5	0-0	22		13,677
10	Oct	7	A	Oxford U	L	1-2	0-2	22	Whittingham	5192
11		14	H	Blackburn R	D	1-1	1-1	22	Whittingham	7004
12		17	H	Leeds U	D	3-3	0-0	—	Kuhl (pen), Whittingham 2	10,260
13		21	A	Bournemouth	W	1-0	1-0	22	Whittingham	9353
14		28	H	Ipswich T	L	2-3	0-1	22	Neill, Kuhl	7914
15		31	A	Sheffield U	L	1-2	0-0	—	Gilligan	14,718
16	Nov	4	A	Barnsley	W	1-0	0-0	21	Gilligan	5524
17		11	H	Port Vale	W	2-0	1-0	17	Black, Whittingham	7708
18		18	H	WBA	D	1-1	1-0	17	Kuhl (pen)	9069
19		26	A	Swindon T	D	2-2	0-1	19	Kuhl (pen), Whittingham	10,438
20	Dec	2	H	Watford	L	1-2	0-1	22	Whittingham	7933
21		10	A	Plymouth Arg	W	2-0	1-0	—	Chamberlain, Whittingham	9988
22		16	H	Sunderland	D	3-3	1-2	20	Kuhl (pen), Wigley, Ball	7127
23		26	A	Brighton & HA	D	0-0	0-0	20		10,800
24		30	A	Oldham Ath	D	3-3	3-2	22	Whittingham 3	8815
25	Jan	1	H	Leicester C	L	2-3	2-1	23	Fillery, Wigley	9387
26		13	A	Stoke C	W	2-1	2-0	19	Whittingham, Hazard	12,051
27		20	H	Bradford C	W	3-0	2-0	17	Fillery, Chamberlain, Stevens	8801
28	Feb	3	A	Middlesbrough	L	0-2	0-1	19		15,295
29		10	H	Newcastle U	D	1-1	0-1	18	Gilligan	14,204
30		17	A	Hull C	W	2-1	0-0	15	Chamberlain, Whittingham	4883
31		24	H	Swindon T	D	1-1	1-0	16	Black	10,300
32	Mar	3	A	WBA	D	0-0	0-0	16		10,502
33		6	H	Wolverhampton W	L	1-3	0-1	—	Whittingham	12,284
34		10	A	West Ham U	L	1-2	0-1	17	Kuhl	20,961
35		17	H	Oxford U	W	2-1	2-0	18	Gilligan, Whittingham	6749
36		20	A	Blackburn R	L	0-2	0-2	—		8047
37		24	A	Leeds U	L	0-2	0-1	18		27,600
38		31	H	Bournemouth	W	2-1	0-1	—	Whittingham 2	8835
39	Apr	7	A	Sheffield U	W	3-2	0-0	16	Fillery, Chamberlain, Whittingham	9004
40		10	A	Ipswich T	W	1-0	1-0	—	Whittingham	11,062
41		14	A	Leicester C	D	1-1	0-0	16	Connor	8407
42		16	H	Brighton & HA	W	3-0	0-0	13	Whittingham, Hogg, Gilligan	10,924
43		21	A	Sunderland	D	2-2	0-1	13	Connor, Wigley	14,379
44		24	H	Oldham Ath	W	2-1	2-1	—	Wigley, Chamberlain	9601
45		28	A	Port Vale	D	1-1	1-1	13	Kuhl (pen)	7942
46	May	5	H	Barnsley	W	2-1	2-0	12	Connor, Kuhl	8415

Final League Position: 12

GOALSCORERS

League (62): Whittingham 23, Kuhl 9 (5 pens), Chamberlain 6, Gilligan 5, Fillery 4, Wigley 4, Connor 3, Ball 2, Black 2, Hazard 1, Hogg 1, Neill 1, Stevens 1.
Littlewoods Cup (4): Black 2, Fillery 1, Kuhl 1.
FA Cup (1): Whittingham 1.

Knight	Neill	Beresford	Fillery	Sandford	Ball	Wigley	Aspinall	Kelly	Connor	Black	Hogg	Chamberlain	Maguire	Whittingham	Kuhl	Russell	Gilligan	Symons	Stevens	Hazard	Match No.
1	2	3	4†	5	6	7	8*	9	10	11	12	14									1
1	2		4	5	6	7		9*	10	11		8	3	12							2
1	2*		4	5	6	7		9	10	11†	12	8	3	14							3
1			4	5	6	7		9*	10	11	2	8†	3	12	14						4
1			4	5	6	7			10	11*	2	9	3	12	8						5
1		3	4	5	6	7			14	11†	12	10*	2	9	8						6
1		3	4	5	6	7			12	11		9	2	10*	8						7
1	12	3	4	5	6	7*				11		10	2	9	8						8
1	12	3	4	5	6	7			14	11		10†	2	9	8*						9
1	2		11		6	7				3		4	9	8	5	10					10
1	2	3	11	5	6	7						4	9	8		10					11
1	2	3	11*	5†	6	7			12	14		4	9	8			10				12
1	2	3	4		6	7				11	5		9	8			10				13
1	2	3	4*		6	7				11	5	12	9	8			10				14
1	2	3			6	7*			12	11	5	14	4	9†	8		10				15
1	2	3			6	7				11	5		4	9	8		10				16
1	2	3			6	7				11	5		4	9	8		10				17
1	2†	3				7*			14	11	5	12	4	9	8		10	6			18
1		3			6	7				11	5	2	4	9	8		10				19
1		3			6	7†12		14		11*	5	2	4	9	8		10				20
1	3*				6	7				11	5	2	4	9	8	12	10				21
1	2				6	7		12		11	5		4	9	8	3	10*				22
1	2	3	12		6	7		10		11	5		4	9	8*						23
1		3	4		6	7				11	5	2	9	8			10				24
1		3	4		6	7		12		11*	5	2	9	8			10				25
1	2	12	4		6	7†				8	5*11	9		14					3	10	26
1	2	3	4		6	7				12	5 11	9					10			8*	27
1	2		4		6	7			10*	5	11	9†12		14					3	8	28
1	2		4		6	7			10*	5	11	9	12	14					3	8†	29
1	2		4		6	7			10	5	11	9	12						3	8*	30
1	2		4†		6	7*			10	5	11	9	12	14					3	8	31
1	2		4		6	7			10	5*11	9	12						3	8		32
1	2		4		6	7			10	5	11	9	12	14					3*	8†	33
1	2		4*		6	7			10	5	11	9	8	12					3		34
1	2		4		6	7			10	5	11*	9	12	8					3		35
1	2		4		6			14	12	10	5	11*	9	8	7				3†		36
1	2		4*			7		14	10	5	11	6	9†12	8					3		37
1	2		4			7			10	5	11	6	9	8					3		38
1	2	10	4			7				5	11	6	9	8					3		39
1	2	10				7				5	11	6	9	4	8				3		40
1	2	10				7	12	8*	9	5	11	6		4					3		41
1	2	10				7				5	11	6	9	4	8				3		42
1	2	10				7		12	14	5	11†6	9	4		8*				3		43
1	2				6	7			8*10	5	11		9	4	12				3		44
1	2	10				7			8	14	5	11	6	9*	4†		12		3		45
1	2	10				7*			8	12	5	11	6		4		9		3		46
46	35	27	28	13	36	45	1	6	9	36	36	34	29	39	30	2	24	1	21	8	

Substitutes (+): Beresford 2s, Fillery 1s, Sandford 1s, Aspinall 2s, Kelly 7s, Connor 6s, Black 5s, Hogg 3s, Chamberlain 4s, Kuhl 3s, Gilligan 10s, Symons 1s, Stevens 8s

Littlewoods Cup	First Round	Bristol R (a)	0-1
		(h)	2-0
	Second Round	Manchester U (h)	2-3
		(a)	0-0
FA Cup	Third Round	Crystal Palace (a)	1-2

PORTSMOUTH

Player and Position	Ht	Wt	Birth Date	Place	Source	Clubs	League App	Gls
Goalkeepers								
Andy Gosney	6 4	13 05	8 11 63	Southampton	Apprentice	Portsmouth	23	—
Alan Gough	5 10	12 01	10 3 71	Watford	Shelbourne	Portsmouth	—	—
Alan Knight	6 1	13 02	3 7 61	Ballham	Apprentice	Portsmouth	379	—
Defenders								
Andy Awford	5 9	11 09	14 7 72	Worcester	Trainee	Portsmouth	4	—
Kevin Ball	5 9	11 06	12 11 64	Hastings	Amateur	Coventry C	—	—
						Portsmouth	105	4
Shaun Gale	6 0	11 06	8 10 69	Reading	Trainee	Portsmouth	—	—
Jason Hall	5 6	10 04	28 10 70	Epping	Trainee	Portsmouth	—	—
Graeme Hogg	6 1	12 12	17 6 64	Aberdeen	Apprentice	Manchester U	83	1
						WBA (loan)	7	—
						Portsmouth	80	2
Gavin Maguire	5 10	11 08	24 11 67	Hammersmith	Apprentice	QPR	40	—
						Portsmouth	47	—
Warren Neill	5 8	11 10	21 11 62	Acton	Apprentice	QPR	181	3
						Portsmouth	80	—
Gary Stevens	6 0	12 00	30 3 62	Hillingdon	Apprentice	Brighton & HA	133	2
						Tottenham H	147	6
						Portsmouth	21	1
Kit Symons	6 1	11 09	5 3 71	Basingstoke	Trainee	Portsmouth	3	—
Chris White	5 11	11 10	11 12 70	Chatham	Trainee	Portsmouth	—	—
Midfield								
John Beresford	5 5	10 04	4 9 66	Sheffield	Apprentice	Manchester C	—	—
						Barnsley	88	5
						Portsmouth	30	—
Kenny Black	5 9	12 01	29 11 63	Stenhousemuir	Linlithgow Rose	Rangers	22	1
						Motherwell	17	—
						Hearts	178	15
						Portsmouth	41	2
Mark Chamberlain	5 8	10 07	19 11 61	Stoke	Apprentice	Port Vale	96	17
						Stoke C	112	17
						Sheffield W	66	8
						Portsmouth	66	12
Lee Darby	6 0	11 06	20 9 69	Salford		Portsmouth	1	—
Mike Fillery	5 11	13 00	17 9 60	Mitcham	Apprentice	Chelsea	161	32
						QPR	97	9
						Portsmouth	64	6
Lee Gosling	5 10	11 07	5 3 70	Basingstoke	Trainee	Portsmouth	—	—
Micky Hazard	5 7	10 05	5 2 60	Sunderland	Apprentice	Tottenham H	91	13
						Chelsea	81	9
						Portsmouth	8	1
Martin Kuhl	5 11	11 13	10 1 65	Frimley	Apprentice	Birmingham C	111	5
						Sheffield U	38	4
						Watford	4	—
						Portsmouth	72	10
Lee Russell	5 11	11 04	3 9 69	Southampton	Trainee	Portsmouth	5	—
Micky Turner	5 10	12 07	15 10 71	Cuckfield	Trainee	Portsmouth	—	—
Forwards								
Darren Anderton	6 0	11 07	3 3 72	Southampton	Trainee	Portsmouth	—	—
Warren Aspinall	5 9	12 05	13 9 67	Wigan	Apprentice	Wigan Ath	51	22
						Everton	7	—
						Aston Villa	44	14
						Portsmouth	43	11
Terry Connor	5 9	11 08	9 11 62	Leeds	Apprentice	Leeds U	98	19
						Brighton & HA	156	51
						Portsmouth	48	12

PORTSMOUTH

Foundation: At a meeting held in his High Street, Portsmouth offices in 1898, solicitor Alderman J. E. Pink and five other business and professional men agreed to buy some ground close to Goldsmith Avenue for £4,950 which they developed into Fratton Park in record breaking time. A team of professionals was signed up by manager Frank Brettell and entry to the Southern League obtained for the new club's September 1899 kick-off.

First Football League game: 28 August, 1920, Division 3, v Swansea T (h) W 3-0 – Robson; Probert, Potts; Abbott, Harwood, Turner; Thompson, Stringfellow (1), Reid (1), James (1), Beedie.

Managers (and Secretary-managers)
Frank Brettell 1898–1901, Bob Blyth 1901–04, Richard Bonney 1905–08, Bob Brown 1911–20, John McCartney 1920–27, Jack Tinn 1927–47, Bob Jackson 1947–52, Eddie Lever 1952–58, Freddie Cox 1958–61, George Smith 1961–70, Ron Tindall 1970–73 (GM to 1974), John Mortimore 1973–74, Ian St. John 1974–77, Jimmy Dickinson 1977–79, Frank Burrows 1979–82, Bobby Campbell 1982–84, Alan Ball 1984–89, John Gregory 1989–90, Frank Burrows 1990– .

Player and Position	Ht	Wt	Birth Date	Place	Source	Clubs	League App	Gls
Jimmy Gilligan	6 2	11 07	24 1 64	Hammersmith	Apprentice	Watford	27	6
						Lincoln C (loan)	3	—
						Grimsby T	25	4
						Swindon T	17	5
						Lincoln C	11	1
						Newport Co (loan)	5	1
						Cardiff C	97	35
						Portsmouth	32	5
Mark Kelly	5 8	9 10	27 11 69	Sutton		Portsmouth	44	1
Shaun Murray	5 8	11 02	7 2 70	Newcastle	Trainee	Tottenham H	—	—
						Portsmouth	—	—
Darryl Powell	6 0	12 03	15 11 71	London	Trainee	Portsmouth	3	—
Mike Ross	5 6	9 13	2 9 71	Southampton	Trainee	Portsmouth	1	—
Guy Whittingham	5 10	11 12	10 11 64	Evesham	Yeovil, Army	Portsmouth	42	23
Steve Wigley	5 9	10 05	15 10 61	Ashton	Curzon Ashton	Nottingham F	82	2
						Sheffield U	28	1
						Birmingham C	87	4
						Portsmouth	56	4

Trainees
Cheverton, Darren L; Daughtry, Paul W; Davies, Shaun; Doling, Stuart J; Knott, Alan; Male, Christopher; Perrett, Russell; Pettican, David J; Robbins, Ian; Smith, Lee A; Tierling, Lee A.

Associated Schoolboys
Bromige, Glyn J; Burton, Nicholas J; Cornwall, Martin I; Cunningham, Aaron M; Elliott, Simon J; Fazakerley, Jacob K; Gardner, Christopher D; Green, Bjay; Igoe, Samuel G; Loveridge, Jon S; Martin, Adam D.A; Miles, Graeme D; Mosedale, Anthony J; Ogburn, Mark; Ollrenshaw, Scott, R; O'Mahony, Sean S; Pattison, Marc D; Pinhorne, Lee A; Pinhorne, Stephen M; Rowe, David J; Scaddan, Richard J; Stewart, Paul T; Sutton, Graham W.

Associated Schoolboys who have accepted the club's offer of a Traineeship/Contract
Askham, Paul N; Bluck, Lee; Merry, Kai; O'Brien, Simon; Owen, Christian P; Price, Benjamin; Watts, Christian J; Wiseman, Simon L; Young, Roy E.

PORT VALE 1989–90 *Back row (left to right):* Simon Mills, Ron Futcher, Robbie Earle, Paul Millar, Ron Jepson, Gary West, Kevin Finney, Neil Aspin, Dean Glover.
Centre row: Mike Pejic (Coach), Martin Copeland (Physiotherapist), Nicky Cross, Alan Webb, Mark Grew, Trevor Wood, Matt Booth, Darren Hughes,
Steve Hunt (Youth Coach), John Rudge (Manager).
Front row: David Riley, Ian Miller, Andy Porter, Ray Walker (Captain), Gary Ford, John Jeffers, Paul Atkinson, Glen Shepherd.

Division 2 **PORT VALE**

Vale Park, Burslem, Stoke-on-Trent. Telephone Stoke-on-Trent (0782) 814134. Commercial Dept. 0782-835524. Clubcall 0898 12 16 36. Fax: 834981.
Ground capacity: 20,950.
Record attendance: 50,000 v Aston Villa, FA Cup 5th rd, 20 Feb, 1960.
Record receipts: £92,658 v Derby Co, FA Cup 3rd rd, 7 January, 1990.
Pitch measurements: 116yd × 76yd.
President: J. Burgess.
Chairman: W. T. Bell Tech. Eng. MIMI.
Executive Director: J. Cooper.
Directors: D. P. McGrath, N. C. Tizley, I. McPherson, A. Belfield.
Manager: John Rudge.
Secretary: A. R. Waterhouse. *Commercial Manager:* M. Brooks.
Coach: Mike Pejic. *Physio:* R. Gray.
Year Formed: 1876. *Turned Professional:* 1885. *Ltd Co.:* 1911.
Club Nickname: 'Valiants'.
Previous Name: Burslem Port Vale; became Port Vale, 1913.
Previous Grounds: 1876, Limekin Lane, Longport; 1881, Westport; 1884, Moorland Road, Burslem; 1886, Athletic Ground, Cobridge; 1913, Recreation Ground, Hanley; 1950, Vale Park.
Record League Victory: 9-1 v Chesterfield, Division 2, 24 September 1932 – Leckie; Shenton, Poyser; Sherlock, Round, Jones; McGrath, Mills, Littlewood (6), Kirkham (2), Morton (1).
Record Cup Victory: 7-1 v Irthlingborough (away), FA Cup, 1st rd, 12 January 1907 – Matthews; Dunn, Hamilton; Eardley, Baddeley, Holyhead; Carter, Dodds (2), Beats, Mountford (2), Coxon (3).
Record Defeat: 0-10 v Sheffield U, Division 2, 10 December, 1892 and v Notts Co, Division 2, 26 February, 1895.
Most League Points (2 for a win): 69, Division 3 (N), 1953–54.
Most League Points (3 for a win): 88, Division 4, 1982–83.
Most League Goals: 110, Division 4, 1958–59.
Highest League Scorer in Season: Wilf Kirkham 38, Division 2, 1926–27.
Most League Goals in Total Aggregate: Wilf Kirkham, 154, 1923–29, 1931–33.
Most Capped Player: Sammy Morgan, 7 (18), Northern Ireland.
Most League Appearances: Roy Sproson, 761, 1950–72.
Record Transfer Fee Received: £300,000 from Charlton Ath for Andy Jones, September 1987.
Record Transfer Fee Paid: £200,000 to Middlesbrough for Dean Glover, February 1989, and £200,000 to Leeds U for Neil Aspin, July 1989.
Football League Record: Original Member of Division 2, 1892–96; Failed re-election in 1896; Re-elected 1898; Resigned 1907; Returned in Oct, 1919, when they took over the fixtures of Leeds City; 1929–30 Division 3 (N); 1930–36 Division 2; 1936–38 Division 3 (N); 1938–52 Division 3 (S); 1952–54 Division 3 (N); 1954–57 Division 2; 1957–58 Division 3(S); 1958–59 Division 4; 1959–65 Division 3; 1965–70 Division 4; 1970–78 Division 3; 1978–83 Division 4; 1983–84 Division 3; 1984–86 Division 4; 1986–89 Division 3; 1989– Division 2.
Honours: Football League: Division 2 best season: 5th, 1930–31; Division 3 (N) – Champions 1929–30, 1953–54; Runners-up 1952–53; Division 4 – Champions 1958–59; Promoted 1969–70 (4th). *FA Cup:* Semi-final 1954, when in Division 3. *Football League Cup:* never past 2nd rd.
Colours: White shirts with black trim, black shorts, white stockings black rings. **Change colours:** All yellow.

PORT VALE 1989–90 LEAGUE RECORD

Match No.	Date	Venue	Opponents	Result	H/T Score	Lg. Pos.	Goalscorers	Atten- dance
1	Aug 19	A	Bradford C	D 2-2	0-1	—	Glover, Beckford	10,242
2	26	H	WBA	W 2-1	0-1	7	Glover (pen), Futcher	7695
3	Sept 2	A	Brighton & HA	L 0-2	0-0	13		7218
4	9	H	Blackburn R	D 0-0	0-0	17		7601
5	12	H	Hull C	D 1-1	0-0	—	Earle	6168
6	16	A	Watford	L 0-1	0-0	19		8445
7	23	A	Stoke C	D 1-1	0-0	18	Earle	27,032
8	26	A	Bournemouth	L 0-1	0-1	—		6511
9	30	H	Leeds U	D 0-0	0-0	20		11,156
10	Oct 7	H	Leicester C	W 2-1	0-1	20	Beckford, Cross	7268
11	14	A	Barnsley	W 3-0	2-0	13	Earle, Cross 2	6475
12	17	A	Wolverhampton W	L 0-2	0-2	—		18,123
13	21	H	West Ham U	D 2-2	0-1	16	Martin (og), Futcher	8899
14	28	A	Newcastle U	D 2-2	0-1	15	Earle, Futcher	17,809
15	30	H	Middlesbrough	D 1-1	1-1	—	Glover (pen)	7708
16	Nov 4	H	Oxford U	L 1-2	0-1	15	Jeffers	6994
17	11	A	Portsmouth	L 0-2	0-1	16		7708
18	18	H	Swindon T	W 2-0	2-0	15	Beckford, Cross	7393
19	25	A	Plymouth Arg	W 2-1	2-1	14	Cross 2	7034
20	Dec 2	H	Bradford C	W 3-2	2-1	13	Beckford, Earle 2	6762
21	9	A	Hull C	L 1-2	1-2	13	Earle	4207
22	16	H	Sheffield U	D 1-1	1-0	14	Cross	9813
23	26	A	Oldham Ath	L 1-2	0-1	15	Parkin	11,274
24	30	A	Sunderland	D 2-2	1-0	16	Kay (og), Millar	21,354
25	Jan 1	H	Ipswich T	W 5-0	3-0	14	Beckford 2, Earle, Cross, Miller	8617
26	13	A	WBA	W 3-2	2-0	12	Cross, Beckford, Porter	13,575
27	20	H	Brighton & HA	W 2-1	0-0	9	Cross 2	8666
28	Feb 3	H	Stoke C	D 0-0	0-0	10		22,075
29	10	H	Watford	W 1-0	0-0	9	Earle	7063
30	17	A	Blackburn R	L 0-1	0-0	10		9240
31	24	H	Plymouth Arg	W 3-0	0-0	9	Hughes, Beckford, Mills	7254
32	Mar 3	A	Swindon T	L 0-3	0-3	9		8314
33	7	A	Leeds U	D 0-0	0-0	—		28,756
34	10	H	Bournemouth	D 1-1	0-0	11	Millar	7131
35	17	A	Leicester C	L 0-2	0-2	11		10,076
36	19	H	Barnsley	W 2-1	1-0	—	Saville (og), Beckford	7036
37	24	H	Wolverhampton W	W 3-1	3-0	11	Millar, Beckford, Earle	12,509
38	31	A	West Ham U	D 2-2	0-0	11	Beckford, Cross	20,507
39	Apr 7	H	Newcastle U	L 1-2	0-2	11	Earle	10,290
40	11	A	Middlesbrough	W 3-2	0-1	—	Glover (pen), Beckford 2	14,973
41	14	A	Ipswich T	L 2-3	1-1	11	Earle, Cross (pen)	10,509
42	16	H	Oldham Ath	W 2-0	1-0	11	Beckford 2	11,451
43	21	A	Sheffield U	L 1-2	0-0	11	Beckford	16,809
44	28	H	Portsmouth	D 1-1	1-1	11	Beckford	7942
45	May 1	H	Sunderland	L 1-2	1-2	—	Millar	9447
46	5	A	Oxford U	D 0-0	0-0	11		4728

Final League Position: 11

GOALSCORERS

League (62): Beckford 17, Cross 13 (1 pen), Earle 12, Glover 4 (3 pens), Millar 4, Futcher 3, Hughes 1, Jeffers 1, Miller 1, Mills 1, Parkin 1, Porter 1, own goals 3.
Littlewoods Cup (4): Beckford 3, Futcher 1.
FA Cup (4): Beckford 1, Cross 1, Walker 1, own goal 1.

Grew	Webb	Hughes	Mills	Aspin	Glover	Porter	Earle	Futcher	Cross	Jeffers	Beckford	Miller	Jepson	Walker	Finney	West	Millar	Wood	Parkin	Riley	Match No.
1	2	3	4	5	6	7	8	9*10		11	12										1
1	2	3	4	5	6	7	8	9		11	10										2
1	2	3	4	5	6	7*	8	9	12	11	10										3
1	2	3	4	5	6	7	8	9*10		11	12										4
1	2	3	4	5	6	7†	8	12	9*11		10	14									5
1	2	3	4	5	6	7†	8		9	11*10		14		12							6
1	2	3	4	5	6	7	8*	9		11	10†	14		12							7
1	2	3	4	5	6	7		9	10		12					8	11*				8
1	2	3	4	5	6	7		9		11*10		14				8	12†				9
1	2	3	11	5	6*	8	9		10			7		4	12						10
1	2	3	11	5	6	8	9		10			7		4							11
1	2	3	11†	5	6	8	12	9*	10			7		4	14						12
1	2	3	11	5	6	8	12	9	14	10		7*		4†							13
1	2*	3†11		5	6	8	12	9	14	10		7		4							14
1		11		5	6	8	9*	3	10			7		4		2	12				15
1		11		5	6	8	9	3	10*			7		4		2	12				16
1		11		5	12	8	9	3	10			7		4		2	6*				17
1		3	2	5	6		8		9	11	10	7		4							18
1		3	2	5	6	7	8		9	11	10			4							19
		3	2	5	6		8		9	11	10	7		4				1			20
1		3	2	5	6		8		9	11	10*	7		4	12						21
1		3	2		6	12	8		9	11*	10†	7	14	4					5		22
1		3	2		6	14	8		9*11		10	7†		4	12				5		23
1		3	2	5	6	7	8	9*			10			4	12		11				24
1		3	2	5	6	7†	8	9*			10	14		4	12		11				25
1		3	4	5	6	7	8		9	11	10			4							26
1		3	2	5	6	7	8†		9	11*10		14		4	12						27
1		3	2	5	6	7	8		9*11		10			4	12						28
1		3	2	5	6	7	8		9	11				4	10						29
1		3	2	5	6*	7	8		9	11	10			4			12				30
1		3	2	5	6	7	8		9	11	10			4							31
1		3	2	5†	6	7	8		9	11	10*			4	12		14				32
1		3	2	5	6	7	8		9	11	10			4							33
1		3	2	5	6	7*	8		9	11	10			4	12						34
1		3	2	5	6	7	8		9*11		10			4	12						35
1		3	2	5	6		8		12	11	10	7*		4			9				36
1		3	2		6	7	8		12	11	10			4			9*		5		37
1		3	2		6	7	8		12	11	10			4			9*		5		38
1		3	2	14	6	7†	8		12	11	10			4			9*		5		39
1		3	2	5	6	7	8		9	11	10			4							40
1		3		5	6	7†	8		9*11		10	14		4	12				2		41
1	8			5	6	7		9	3	10				4	11				2		42
1	2			5	6	12	8	9	3		10			4	11*				7		43
1	2			5	6	7	8	3	9	11	10†12	14		4					3*		44
	2			5	6	7*	8	9	3	14		4	11†	10				1		12	45
	2			5	6	7	8	9	3	12		4	11	10*				1			46
43	14	38	45	41	44	32	43	7	37	38	40	14	—	38	4	3	11	3	9	2	
				+		+			++	+	+	+		+	+	+	+		+		
				1s		4s			4s 5s	2s	2s	7s		5s	2s	4s	12s		3s		

Littlewoods Cup

	First Round	Walsall (a)	2-1
		(h)	1-0
	Second Round	Wimbledon (h)	1-2
		(a)	0-3
FA Cup	Third Round	Derby Co (h)	1-1
		(a)	3-2
	Fourth Round	Aston Villa (a)	0-6

PORT VALE

Player and Position	Ht	Wt	Birth Date	Place	Source	Clubs	League App	Gls
Goalkeepers								
Mark Grew	5 11	12 08	15 2 58	Bilston	Amateur	WBA	33	—
						Wigan Ath (loan)	4	—
						Notts Co (loan)	—	—
						Leicester C	5	—
						Oldham Ath (loan)	5	—
						Ipswich T	6	—
						Fulham (loan)	4	—
						WBA (loan)	1	—
						Derby Co (loan)	—	—
						Port Vale	124	—
Trevor Wood	6 0	12 06	3 11 68	Jersey	Apprentice	Brighton & HA	—	—
						Port Vale	5	—
Defenders								
Neil Aspin	6 0	12 03	12 4 65	Gateshead	Apprentice	Leeds U	207	5
						Port Vale	42	—
Matt Booth	6 0	11 09	10 12 70	Stoke	Trainee	Port Vale	—	—
Dean Glover	5 10	11 11	29 12 63	Birmingham	Apprentice	Aston Villa	28	—
						Sheffield U (loan)	5	—
						Middlesbrough	50	5
						Port Vale	66	4
Darren Hughes	5 11	10 11	6 10 65	Prescot	Apprentice	Everton	3	—
						Shrewsbury T	37	1
						Brighton & HA	26	2
						Port Vale	125	2
Tim Parkin	6 2	13 03	31 12 57	Penrith	Apprentice Malmo Almondsbury G	Blackburn R	13	—
						Bristol R	206	12
						Swindon T	110	6
						Port Vale	12	1
Wayne Simpson‡	5 9	11 00	19 9 68	Stoke	Trainee	Port Vale	—	—
Alan Webb	5 10	12 00	1 1 63	Wellington	Apprentice	WBA	24	—
						Lincoln C (loan)	11	—
						Port Vale	183	2
Gary West	6 2	12 07	25 8 64	Scunthorpe	Apprentice	Sheffield U	75	1
						Lincoln C	83	4
						Gillingham	52	3
						Port Vale	17	1
Midfield								
Robbie Earle	5 9	10 10	27 1 65	Newcastle, Staffs	Amateur	Stoke C	—	—
						Port Vale	259	66
Kevin Finney	6 0	12 00	19 10 69	Newcastle-U-Lyme	Apprentice	Port Vale	37	1
Gary Ford	5 8	11 10	8 2 61	York	Apprentice	York C	366	52
						Leicester C	16	2
						Port Vale	45	10
						Walsall (loan)	13	2
Simon Mills	5 8	11 04	16 8 64	Sheffield	Apprentice	Sheffield W	5	—
						York C	99	5
						Port Vale	107	6
Andy Porter	5 9	11 02	17 9 68	Manchester	Trainee	Port Vale	57	2
Glen Shepherd‡	5 9	10 00	4 1 71	Dudley	Trainee	Port Vale	—	—
Ray Walker	5 10	12 00	6 7 81	North Shields	Apprentice	Aston Villa	23	—
						Port Vale (loan)	15	1
						Port Vale	170	15
Forwards								
Paul Atkinson	5 9	10 02	19 1 66	Chester-Le-Street	Apprentice	Sunderland	60	5
						Port Vale	4	3
						Hartlepool U (loan)	11	1

Foundation: Formed in 1876 as Port Vale, adopting the prefix 'Burslem' in 1884 upon moving to that part of the city. It was dropped in 1911.

First Football League game: 3 September, 1892, Division 2, v Small Heath (a) L 1-5 – Frail; Clutton, Elson; Farrington, McCrindle, Delves; Walker, Scarratt, Bliss (1), Jones. (Only 10 men).

Managers (and Secretary-managers)
Sam Gleaves 1896–1905*, Tom Clare 1905–11, A. S. Walker 1911–12, H. Myatt 1912–14, Tom Holford 1919–24 (continued as trainer), Joe Schofield 1924–30, Tom Morgan 1930–32, Tom Holford 1932–35, Warney Cresswell 1936–37, Tom Morgan 1937–38, Billy Frith 1945–46, Gordon Hodgson 1946–51, Ivor Powell 1951, Freddie Steele 1951–57, Norman Low 1957–62, Freddie Steele 1962–65, Jackie Mudie 1965–67, Sir Stanley Matthews (GM) 1965–68, Gordon Lee 1968–74, Roy Sproson 1974–77, Colin Harper 1977, Bobby Smith 1977–78, Dennis Butler 1978–79, Alan Bloor 1979, John McGrath 1980–83, John Rudge 1983– .

Player and Position	Ht	Wt	Birth Date	Place	Source	Clubs	League App	Gls
Darren Beckford	6 1	11 01	12 5 67	Manchester	Apprentice	Manchester C	11	—
						Bury (loan)	12	5
						Port Vale (loan)	11	4
						Port Vale	124	46
Nicky Cross	5 9	11 04	7 2 61	Birmingham	Apprentice	WBA	105	15
						Walsall	109	45
						Leicester C	58	15
						Port Vale	42	13
Steve Davies‡	6 0	11 09	16 7 60	Liverpool	Congleton	Port Vale	6	—
John Jeffers	5 10	11 10	5 10 68	Liverpool	Trainee	Liverpool	—	—
						Port Vale	55	1
Ronnie Jepson	6 1	13 02	12 5 63	Stoke	Nantwich	Port Vale	7	—
						Peterborough U (loan)	18	5
Gary McKinstry	5 9	10 08	7 1 72	Banbridge	Portadown	Port Vale	—	—
Paul Millar	6 2	12 07	16 1 66	Belfast	Portadown	Port Vale	23	4
Ian Miller	5 8	11 12	13 5 55	Perth		Bury	15	—
						Nottingham F	—	—
						Doncaster R	124	14
						Swindon T	127	9
						Blackburn R	268	16
						Port Vale	21	1
Brian Mills	5 9	10 10	26 12 71	Stone	Trainee	Port Vale	—	—

Trainees
Banks, Ian G; Bedson, Nicholas S; Beeby, Matthew; Bennett, Tony; Boswell, Christopher W; Brown, Saxton; Craig, Nickolas; Harrison, Michael; Johnson, John; Kidd, Ryan A; Llewellyn, Paul; Lowe, David E; Moore, Paul C; Myatt, Robert J; Rushton, David.

Associated Schoolboys
Brown, Christopher E; Byrne, Paul T; McCarthy, Anthony M; Mountford, Wayne; Palmer, Shane M; Rushton, Marc A; Stirk, Mark A; Tweats, Timothy A.

Associated Schoolboys who have accepted the club's offer of a Traineeship/Contract
Blake, Martin G; Dyass, Mark W; Gillard, Christopher; Lovatt, Gregory; Mitchell, Richard D; Royall, Adam; Shea, Gareth D.

438

PRESTON NORTH END 1989-90 *Back row (left to right):* Bob Atkins, Gary Walker, Andy Gill, Alan Kelly, Roy Tunks, Chris Hollis, Adrian Hughes, Alex Jones.
Centre row: Mark Patterson, Warren Joyce, Gary Swann, Martin James, Graham Shaw, Steven Harper, Mick Bennett, Steven Anderton, Paul Maloney.
Front row: David Miller, Neil Williams, Brian Mooney, Tony Ellis, Simon Snow, Jeff Wrightson, Mick Rathbone, Andy McAteer.

Division 3 **PRESTON NORTH END**

Deepdale, Preston PR1 6RU. Telephone Preston (0772) 795919. Answerphone (0772) 709170. Commercial Dept. (0772) 795465/795156. Pitch Hire: (0772) 705468. Community Office: (0772) 704275.

Ground capacity: 17,000.

Record attendance: 42,684 v Arsenal, Division 1, 23 Apr, 1938.

Record receipts: £54,000 v Burnley, Sherpa Van Trophy, Northern Final, second leg, 19 April, 1988.

Pitch measurements: 110yd × 72yd. (artificial surface.)

President: Tom Finney, OBE, JP.

Vice President: T. C. Nicholson JP, FCIOB.

Chairman: Keith W. Leeming.

Vice-Chairmen: J. T. Garratt, M. J. Woodhouse.

Directors: B. J. Campbell, J. Francis, E. Griffith BVSC, MRCVS (Company Secretary), J. E. Wignall, J. W. Wilding, J. T. Worden.

Manager: Les Chapman. *Asst. Manager:*

Physio: Andy Jones.

Secretary: D. J. Allan. *Promotions Manager:* Wayne Dore.

Year Formed: 1881. *Turned Professional:* 1885. *Ltd Co.:* 1893.

Club Nickname: 'The Lilywhites' or 'North End'.

Record League Victory: 10-0 v Stoke, Division 1, 14 September 1889 – Trainer; Howarth, Holmes; Kelso, Russell (1), Graham; Gordon, Jimmy Ross (2), Nick Ross (3), Thomson (2), Drummond (2).

Record Cup Victory: 26-0 v Hyde, FA Cup, 1st rd, 15 October 1887 – Addison; Howarth, Nick Ross; Russell (1), Thomson (5), Graham (1); Gordon (5), Jimmy Ross (8), John Goodall (1), Dewhurst (3), Drummond (2).

Record Defeat: 0-7 v Blackool, Division 1, 1 May, 1948.

Most League Points (2 for a win): 61, Division 3, 1970–71.

Most League Points (3 for a win): 90, Division 4, 1986–87.

Most League Goals: 100, Division 2, 1927–28 and Division 1, 1957–58.

Highest League Scorer in Season: Ted Harper, 37, Division 2, 1932–33.

Most League Goals in Total Aggregate: Tom Finney, 187, 1946–60.

Most Capped Player: Tom Finney, 76, England.

Most League Appearances: Alan Kelly, 447, 1961–75.

Record Transfer Fee Received: £765,000 from Manchester C for Michael Robinson, June 1979.

Record Transfer Fee Paid: £125,000 to Norwich C for Mike Flynn, December 1989.

Football League Record: 1888 Founder Member of League; 1901–04 Division 2; 1904–12 Division 1; 1912–13 Division 2; 1913–14 Division 1; 1914–15 Division 2; 1919–25 Division 1; 1925–34 Division 2; 1934–49 Division 1; 1949–51 Division 2; 1951–61 Division 1; 1961–70 Division 2; 1970–71 Division 3; 1971–74 Division 2; 1974–78 Division 3; 1978–81 Division 2, 1981–85 Division 3; 1985–87 Division 4; 1987– Division 3.

Honours: Football League; Division 1 – Champions 1888–89 (first champions, 1889–90; Runners-up 1890–91, 1891–92, 1892–93, 1905–06, 1952–53, 1957–58; Division 2 – Champions 1903–04, 1912–13, 1950–51; Runners-up 1914–15, 1933–34; Division 3 – Champions 1970–71; Division 4 Runners-up 1986–87. *FA Cup:* Winners 1889, 1938; Runners-up 1888, 1922, 1937, 1954, 1964. *Double Performed:* 1888–89. *Football League Cup* best season: 4th rd, 1963, 1966, 1972, 1981.

Colours: All white. **Change colours:** All yellow.

PRESTON NORTH END 1989–90 LEAGUE RECORD

Match No.	Date	Venue	Opponents	Result	H/T Score	Lg. Pos.	Goalscorers	Attendance
1	Aug 19	A	Rotherham U	L 1-3	0-2	—	Shaw	5951
2	26	H	Bury	L 2-3	0-1	22	Shaw, Harper	5622
3	Sept 2	A	Leyton Orient	L 1-3	1-1	24	Ellis	4871
4	9	H	Huddersfield T	D 3-3	1-0	22	Bogie, Swann, Mooney	5822
5	16	A	Bristol R	L 0-3	0-3	23		4350
6	23	H	Chester C	W 5-0	1-0	20	Mooney 3, Harper 2 (1 pen)	5230
7	26	H	Blackpool	W 2-1	0-0	—	Bradshaw (og), Atkins	8920
8	30	A	Walsall	L 0-1	0-0	19		4045
9	Oct 7	A	Northampton T	W 2-1	1-0	16	Harper, Ellis	3039
10	14	H	Brentford	W 4-2	0-2	14	Ellis, Joyce, Harper, Swann	5956
11	17	H	Crewe Alex	D 0-0	0-0	—		7485
12	21	A	Notts Co	L 1-2	1-0	15	Williams	5284
13	28	H	Bolton W	L 1-4	0-2	19	Scully	9135
14	31	A	Mansfield T	D 2-2	2-0	—	Mooney, Joyce	3129
15	Nov 4	H	Shrewsbury T	W 2-1	1-0	14	Swann, Patterson	5418
16	11	A	Swansea C	L 1-2	0-1	15	Patterson	3843
17	25	A	Cardiff C	L 0-3	0-2	18		3270
18	Dec 2	H	Reading	W 1-0	1-0	14	Swann	5067
19	16	H	Birmingham C	L 1-3	0-1	15	Patterson (pen)	6391
20	26	H	Tranmere R	D 2-2	1-2	18	Swann 2	8300
21	30	H	Wigan Ath	D 1-1	1-1	18	Patterson	7220
22	Jan 1	A	Bristol C	L 1-2	0-1	20	Mooney	11,803
23	6	H	Fulham	W 1-0	1-0	—	Shaw	5055
24	13	A	Bury	W 2-1	2-1	15	Joyce, Mooney	4715
25	20	H	Rotherham U	L 0-1	0-0	16		6088
26	Feb 3	A	Chester C	L 1-3	0-1	18	Harper	2499
27	10	H	Bristol R	L 0-1	0-0	20		5956
28	13	H	Leyton Orient	L 0-3	0-2	—		4480
29	17	A	Reading	L 0-6	0-4	21		3998
30	24	H	Cardiff C	W 4-0	1-0	21	Harper 3, Joyce	5716
31	Mar 3	A	Fulham	L 1-3	0-1	21	Shaw	4207
32	6	H	Walsall	W 2-0	1-0	—	Swann, Thomas	5210
33	10	A	Blackpool	D 2-2	1-2	19	Shaw, Mooney	8108
34	17	H	Northampton T	D 0-0	0-0	20		5681
35	20	A	Brentford	D 2-2	1-2	—	Joyce, Williams	4673
36	24	A	Crewe Alex	L 0-1	0-0	21		4531
37	31	H	Notts Co	L 2-4	2-2	22	Joyce 2	5810
38	Apr 3	A	Huddersfield T	W 2-0	2-0	—	Joyce, Bogie	4381
39	7	A	Bolton W	L 1-2	0-0	20	Bogie	8266
40	10	A	Mansfield T	W 4-0	3-0	—	Joyce 2, Foster (og), Hughes	5035
41	14	H	Bristol C	D 2-2	1-1	20	Flynn, Harper	7599
42	16	A	Tranmere R	L 1-2	0-0	20	Joyce	10,187
43	21	H	Birmingham C	D 2-2	1-2	20	Thomas, Mooney	7680
44	24	A	Wigan Ath	W 1-0	1-0	—	Thomas	4454
45	28	H	Swansea C	W 2-0	0-0	18	Swann, Williams	6695
46	May 5	A	Shrewsbury T	L 0-2	0-0	19		5319

Final League Position: 19

GOALSCORERS

League (65): Joyce 11, Harper 10 (1 pen), Mooney 9, Swann 8, Shaw 5, Patterson 4 (1 pen), Bogie 3, Ellis 3, Thomas 3, Williams 3, Atkins 1, Flynn 1, Hughes 1, Scully 1, own goals 2.
Littlewoods Cup (4): Shaw 4 (1 pen).
FA Cup (1): Joyce 1.

Tunks	Miller	Swann	Atkins	Jones	Hughes	Mooney	Ellis	Joyce	Shaw	Patterson	Rathbone	Wrightson	Snow	Harper	Kelly	Bogie	Williams	Scully	Bennett	Flynn	Greenwood	Stowell	McIlroy	Thomas	Anderton	Match No.
1	2	3	4	5	6	7	8	9	10	11																1
1	11	3	4	5		7		9	10			2	6	8*	12											2
	2*	11	4	5		7	8	9	10			3	6		1	12										3
		3			6	7	8*	9	10	12				4	1	11	2	5								4
		3*	14		6	7	8	9	10	12				4†	1	11	2	5								5
		3	4		6	7	8	9						10	1	11	2	5								6
		3	4		6	7	8	9						10	1	11	2	5								7
		3	4		6	7*	8	9	12					10	1	11	2	5								8
		3	4		6	7	8	9	12					10	1	11*	2	5								9
		3	4			7	8	9				6		10	1	11	2	5								10
		3	4		6	7	8	9						10	1	11	2	5								11
		3	4		6	7	8	9	12					10*	1	11	2	5								12
		3	4		6*	7	8	9	12					10	1	11	2	5								13
		3	4		6	7	8*	5	10	9	12				1	11	2									14
		3	4			7*		5	10	9	12			8	1	11	2	6								15
		3	4		14		8	5	10*	11	12			7†	1	9	2	6								16
		3	4		14	7	8	5	10*	11				12	1	9	2	6†								17
		3	4		6	7	8	5	10	11					1	9	2									18
		9†	4		6*	12	8	10	14	7				11	1		2		3	5						19
		8			6	7		9	10					11	1	4	2		3	5						20
		8			6	7		9	10					11	1	4	2		3	5						21
		8			6	7		9	10					11	1	4	2		3	5						22
		8			6	7		9	11	10					1	4	2		3	5						23
		4				7		9	10	8				6	11	1	2		3	5						24
		4			6	7		9*	10	8				11	1	12	2		3	5						25
		4			6*	7		9	10					8	12	1	2		3	5	11					26
		3				7		9	10					6	11		2		5	8	1		4			27
		2				7		9	10*					6	11	12			3	5	8	1	4			28
		2			6	7		9						4	1	11			3	5	8		10			29
		3				7		9	8					6	11	1	2			5			4	10		30
		3			6	7	8	5						11	1	9	2			5			4	10		31
		3			6	7		10	8					5	11	1	2						4	9		32
		3			6	7		5	8					4	1		2				10		11	9		33
		3				7		10	8					6	11	1	2			5			4	9		34
		3	11*			8	7	10	14					6	12	1	2			5			4	9†		35
		3	11*			8†	7	10	9					6	12	1	14			2			5	4		36
		3	12			7		9*	10†					6	11	1	14			2			5	8	4	37
		3	10			8	7	9						6	1	11	2			5			4			38
		3	10			8	7	9						6	1	11	2			5			4			39
		3	10			8	7	9*						6	12	1	11	2		5			4†	14		40
		3	10*			8	7	9						6	12	1	11	2		5			4			41
		3	10			12	7†	8		14				6	1	11	2			5*			4	9		42
		3	12			7	8	14						6	11†	1	10	2		5*			4	9		43
		3	5			7	8							6	11	1	10	2					4	9		44
		3	5			7	8							6	11	1	10	2					4	9		45
		3	5			12	7	8	14					6	11†	1	10	2					4*	9		46
2	3	46	27	3	29	44	17	44	24	12	3	26	1	28	42	30	41	13	10	23	5	2	20	11	—	
				+	+6s	+1s		+7s		+1s		+5s			+8s	+5s								+1s		
				1s																						

PRESTON NORTH END

Player and Position	Ht	Wt	Birth Date	Place	Source	Clubs	League App	Gls
Goalkeepers								
Andy Gill*	6 0	13 00	28 9 70	Manchester	Trainee	Preston NE	—	—
Chris Hollis*	6 1	12 12	8 11 70	St Helens	Trainee	Preston NE	—	—
Alan Kelly	6 2	12 05	11 8 68	Preston		Preston NE	96	—
Roy Tunks	6 1	13 11	21 1 51	Wuppertal	Apprentice	Rotherham U	138	—
						York C (loan)	4	—
						Ipswich T (loan)	—	—
						Newcastle U (loan)	—	—
						Preston NE	277	—
						Wigan Ath	245	—
						Hartlepool U	5	—
						Preston NE	25	—
Defenders								
Bob Atkins	6 0	12 02	16 10 62	Leicester	Local	Sheffield U	40	3
						Preston NE	200	5
Michael Bennett*	5 7	10 00	24 12 62	Bolton	Apprentice	Bolton W	65	1
						Wolverhampton W	6	—
						Cambridge U	76	—
						Bradford C	—	—
						Preston NE	86	1
Les Chapman†	5 7	10 04	27 9 48	Oldham	High Barn	Oldham Ath	76	9
						Huddersfield T	133	8
						Oldham Ath	187	11
						Stockport Co	32	1
						Bradford C	139	3
						Rochdale	88	—
						Stockport Co	38	3
						Preston NE	53	1
Mike Flynn	6 0	11 00	23 2 69	Oldham	Trainee	Oldham Ath	40	1
						Norwich C	—	—
						Preston NE	23	1
Adrian Hughes	6 2	12 12	19 12 70	Billinge	Trainee	Preston NE	59	2
Andy McAteer*	5 10	11 10	24 4 61	Preston	Apprentice	Preston NE	238	8
						Blackpool	41	—
						Preston NE	13	1
Mike Rathbone	5 10	11 12	6 11 58	Birmingham	Apprentice	Birmingham C	20	—
						Blackburn R	273	2
						Preston NE	78	3
Gary Walker‡	6 1	12 05	12 9 69	Billinge	Trainee	Preston NE	—	—
Jeff Wrightson	5 11	11 00	18 5 68	Newcastle	Apprentice	Newcastle U	4	—
						Preston NE	89	—
Midfield								
Steven Anderton	5 8	11 05	2 10 69	Lancaster	Trainee	Preston NE	1	—
Ian Bogie	5 7	10 02	6 12 67	Newcastle	Apprentice	Newcastle U	14	—
						Preston NE	48	4
Martin James	5 10	11 07	18 5 71	Formby	Trainee	Preston NE	—	—
Warren Joyce	5 9	11 11	20 1 65	Oldham	Local	Bolton W	184	17
						Preston NE	106	20
Sammy McIlroy	5 10	11 08	2 8 54	Belfast	Apprentice	Manchester U	342	57
						Stoke C	133	14
						Manchester C	13	1
						Bury	43	6
					Modling	Bury	57	2
						Preston NE	20	—
Paul Maloney*	5 6	9 10	10 11 69	St Helens	Trainee	Preston NE	—	—
Brian Mooney	5 11	11 02	2 2 66	Dublin	Home Farm	Liverpool	—	—
						Wrexham (loan)	9	2
						Preston NE	119	18
Gary Swann	5 9	11 02	11 4 62	York	Apprentice	Hull C	186	9
						Preston NE	140	27
Neil Williams	5 11	11 04	23 10 64	Waltham Abbey	Apprentice	Watford	—	—
						Hull C	91	10
						Preston NE	82	5

PRESTON NORTH END

Foundation: North End Cricket and Rugby Club which was formed in 1863, indulged in most sports before taking up soccer in about 1879. In 1881 they decided to stick to football to the exclusion of other sports and even a 16–0 drubbing by Blackburn Rovers in an invitation game at Deepdale, a few weeks after taking this decision, did not deter them for they immediately became affiliated to the Lancashire FA.

First Football League game: 8 September, 1888, Football League, v Burnley (h) W 5-2 – Trainer; Haworth, Holmes; Robertson, W. Graham, J. Graham; Gordon (1), Ross (2), Goodall, Dewhurst (2), Drummond.

Managers (and Secretary-managers)
Charlie Parker 1906–15, Vincent Hayes 1919–23, Jim Lawrence 1923–25, Frank Richards 1925–27, Alex Gibson 1927–31, Lincoln Hayes 1931–1932 (run by committee 1932–36), Tommy Muirhead 1936–37, (run by committee 1937–49), Will Scott 1949–53, Scot Symon 1953–54, Frank Hill 1954–56, Cliff Britton 1956–61, Jimmy Milne 1961–68, Bobby Seith 1968–70, Alan Ball Sr 1970–73, Bobby Charlton 1973–75, Harry Catterick 1975–77, Nobby Stiles 1977–81, Tommy Docherty 1981, Gordon Lee 1981–83, Alan Kelly 1983–85, Tommy Booth 1985–86, Brian Kidd 1986, John McGrath 1986–90, Les Chapman 1990– .

Player and Position	Ht	Wt	Birth Date	Birth Place	Source	Clubs	League App	League Gls
Forwards								
Sean Curry‡	5 8	10 11	13 11 66	Liverpool	Apprentice	Liverpool	—	—
						Blackburn R	38	6
						Hartlepool U	1	—
						Preston NE	—	—
Nigel Greenwood	5 11	12 00	27 11 66	Preston	Apprentice	Preston NE	45	14
						Bury	110	25
						Preston NE	5	—
Tony Hancock	6 1	12 12	31 1 67	Manchester	Stockport Georgians	Stockport Co	22	5
						Burnley	17	—
						Preston NE	—	—
Steve Harper	5 10	11 05	3 2 69	Stoke	Trainee	Port Vale	28	2
						Preston NE	41	10
Graham Shaw	5 8	10 01	7 6 67	Newcastle	Apprentice	Stoke C	99	18
						Preston NE	31	5
Simon Snow‡	5 10	13 00	3 4 66	Sheffield	Sutton U	Preston NE	1	—
John Thomas	5 8	11 03	5 8 58	Wednesbury		Everton	—	—
						Tranmere R (loan)	11	2
						Halifax T (loan)	5	—
						Bolton W	22	6
						Chester	44	20
						Lincoln C	67	20
						Preston NE	78	38
						Bolton W	73	31
						WBA	18	1
						Preston NE	11	3

Trainees
Ashcroft, Lee; Burrow, David R; Cartwright, Lee; Christie, David; Cunningham, Richard A; Dalgarno, Alan W; Eaves, David M.C; Gallagher, Lee; Kerfoot, Jason J; Lambert, Matthew R; McCullough, Gary; Middlemass, Scott L; Peel, Nathan J; Rapsey, Jason A; Raynor, Kevin B.C; Siddall, Adam M; Simpson, Mark A.

**Non-Contract
Chapman, Leslie; Johnson, Steven E; Keighley, John P; Nixon, Craig G.

Associated Schoolboys
Alder, Joseph; Allardyce, Craig S; Baker, Alistair M; Brandes, Christopher M; Duffell, Paul; England, Kieran J; Fowler, John A; Hall, Andrew B; Heavey, Paul A; Holland, Christopher J: Iles, Thomas W.S; Kellett, Ian; Linford, Paul R; Molyneux, Steven B; Morris, Darren A; Morris, Paul I; Moylon, Craig; Myhan, Jeremy; O'Neill, John P; Parkinson, Christopher; Parkinson, Stuart G; Pearson, Scott; Raywood, Matthew J; Sheridan, Brian J; Squires; James A; Sumner, Craig R; Sutcliffe, Keith C.

Associated Schoolboys who have accepted the club's offer of a Traineeship/Contract
Bagnall, John A; Burton, Simon P; Close, Jamie T; Critchley, Adam D; Finney, Stephen K; Flitcroft, David J; Hindle, Paul J; O'Connor, Kerry J; Rimmer, David J; Schofield, Christopher; Williams, Christopher.

**Non-Contract Players who are retained must be re-signed before they are eligible to play in League matches.

444

QUEEN'S PARK RANGERS 1989–90   *Back row (left to right):* Roy Wegerle, Colin Clarke, Brian Law, Nicky Johns, Tony Roberts, David Seaman, Alan McDonald, Mark Falco, David Bardsley.

Centre row: Justin Channing, Les Boyle (Youth Team Trainer), George Smith (Youth Team Coach), Cliff Speight (Physiotherapist), Don Howe (First Team Coach), Roger Cross (Reserve Team Coach), Ron Berry (Kit Manager), Mike Varney (Physiotherapist), Simon Barker.

Front row: Leslie Ferdinand, Kenny Sansom, Andy Sinton, Paul Parker, Ray Wilkins, Paul Wright, Danny Maddix.

Division 1 **QUEEN'S PARK RANGERS**

South Africa Road, W12 7PA. Telephone 081-743 0262. Box Office 081-749 5744. Supporters Club: 081-749 6771. Club Shop: 081-749 6862. Marketing: 081-740 8737.
Ground capacity: 23,480 (23,000 covered).
Record attendance: 35,353 v Leeds U, Division 1, 27 April, 1974.
Record receipts: £114,743 v Tottenham H, Division 1, 12 January, 1985.
Pitch measurements: 112yd × 72yd.
Chairman: R. C. Thompson. *Vice-Chairman:* R. P. B. Noonan.
Directors: C. B. Berlin (Managing), (Corporate): R. B. Copus, A. Ingham, A Chandler, B. Evans, B. Rowe, G. Bierers.
Chief Coach: Don Howe.
Secretary: Miss S. F. Marson. *Commercial Manager:* B. Rowe.
Reserve Team Coach: Roger Cross.
Physio: Brian Morris.
Year Formed: 1885 *(see Foundation).* *Turned Professional;* 1898. *Ltd Co.:* 1899.
Club Nickname: 'Rangers' or 'Rs'. *Previous Name:* 1885–87, St Jude's.
Previous Grounds: 1885 *(see Foundation),* Welford's Fields; 1888–89: London Scottish Ground, Brondesbury, Home Farm, Kensal Rise Green, Gun Club Wormwood Scrubs, Kilburn Cricket Ground; 1899, Kensal Rise Athletic Ground; 1901, Latimer Road, Notting Hill; 1904, Agricultural Society, Park Royal; 1907, Park Royal Ground; 1917, Loftus Road; 1931, White City; 1933, Loftus Road; 1962, White City; 1963, Loftus Road.
Record League Victory: 9-2 v Tranmere R, Division 3, 3 December 1960 – Drinkwater; Woods, Ingham; Keen, Rutter, Angell; Lazarus (2), Bedford (2), Evans (2), Andrews (1), Clark (2).
Record Cup Victory: 8-1 (away) v Bristol R (away), FA Cup, 1st rd, 27 November 1937 – Gilfillan; Smith, Jefferson; Lowe, James, March; Cape, Mallett, Cheetham (3), Fitzgerald (3) Bott (2). 8-1 v Crewe Alex, Milk Cup, 1st rd, 3 October 1983 – Hucker; Neill, Dawes, Waddock (1), McDonald (1), Fenwick, Micklewhite (1), Stewart (1), Allen (1), Stainrod (3), Gregory.
Record Defeat: 1-8 v Mansfield T, Division 3, 15 March, 1965 and v Manchester U, Division 1, 19 March, 1969.
Most League Points (2 for a win): 67, Division 3, 1966–67.
Most League Points (3 for a win): 85, Division 2, 1982–83.
Most League Goals: 111, Division 3, 1961–62.
Highest League Scorer in Season: George Goddard, 37, Division 3(S), 1929–30.
Most League Goals in Total Aggregate: George Goddard, 172, 1926–34.
Most Capped Player: Don Givens, 26 (56), Eire.
Most League Appearances: Tony Ingham, 519, 1950–63.
Record Transfer Fee Received: £1,250,000 from Arsenal for Clive Allen, June 1980.
Record Transfer Fee Paid: £1,000,000 to Luton T for Roy Wegerle, December 1989.
Football League Record: 1920 Original Members of Division 3; 1921 Division 3(S); 1948–52 Division 2; 1952–58 Division 3(S); 1958–67 Division 3; 1967–68 Division 2; 1968–69 Division 1; 1969–73 Division 2; 1973–79 Division 1; 1979–83 Division 2; 1983– Division 1.
Honours: Football League: Division 1 – Runners-up 1975–76; Division 2 – Champions 1982–83; Runners-up 1967–68, 1972–73; Division 3(S) – Champions 1947–48; Runners-up 1946–47; Division 3 – Champions 1966–67. *FA Cup:* Runners-up 1982. *Football League Cup:* Winners 1966–67. Runners-up 1985–86. (In 1966–67 won Division 3 and Football League Cup.) **European Competition:** *UEFA Cup:* 1976–77, 1984–85.
Colours: Blue and white hooped shirts, white shorts, white stockings with 3 blue bands at top. **Change colours:** Red and black hooped shirts, black shorts, black stockings with 4 red bands at top.

QUEEN'S PARK RANGERS 1989–90 LEAGUE RECORD

Match No.	Date		Venue	Opponents	Result		H/T Score	Lg. Pos.	Goalscorers	Atten- dance
1	Aug 19	H		Crystal Palace	W	2-0	0-0	—	Wright 2 (1 pen)	16,161
2	22	A		Chelsea	D	1-1	1-1	—	Clarke	24,345
3	26	A		Norwich C	D	0-0	0-0	8		14,021
4	30	H		Luton T	D	0-0	0-0	—		10,565
5	Sept 9	A		Manchester C	L	0-1	0-1	12		23,420
6	16	H		Derby Co	L	0-1	0-0	14		10,697
7	23	A		Aston Villa	W	3-1	2-1	9	Francis 3	14,170
8	30	A		Tottenham H	L	2-3	0-2	11	Bardsley, Francis	23,781
9	Oct 14	H		Southampton	L	1-4	0-1	15	Francis	10,022
10	21	H		Charlton Ath	L	0-1	0-0	17		10,608
11	28	A		Nottingham F	D	2-2	0-1	18	Sinton, Wright	19,442
12	Nov 4	A		Wimbledon	D	0-0	0-0	19		5912
13	11	H		Liverpool	W	3-2	2-1	17	Wright 2 (1 pen), Falco	18,804
14	18	A		Arsenal	L	0-3	0-1	18		38,236
15	25	H		Millwall	D	0-0	0-0	18		9141
16	Dec 2	A		Crystal Palace	W	3-0	2-0	14	Maddix, Sinton 2	12,784
17	9	H		Chelsea	W	4-2	2-1	13	Ferdinand 2, Falco, Clarke	17,935
18	16	A		Sheffield W	L	0-2	0-2	14		14,569
19	26	H		Coventry C	D	1-1	1-0	14	Falco	9889
20	30	H		Everton	W	1-0	1-0	13	Sinton	11,683
21	Jan 1	A		Manchester U	D	0-0	0-0	13		34,824
22	13	H		Norwich C	W	2-1	0-0	13	Falco, Clarke	11,439
23	20	A		Luton T	D	1-1	1-1	13	Falco	9703
24	Feb 10	A		Derby Co	L	0-2	0-1	13		14,445
25	24	A		Millwall	W	2-1	1-0	13	Barker, Wegerle	11,505
26	Mar 3	H		Arsenal	W	2-0	0-0	13	Wilkins, Wegerle	18,067
27	17	H		Tottenham H	W	3-1	1-0	12	Clarke, Sinton, Barker	16,691
28	20	H		Aston Villa	D	1-1	0-0	—	Clarke	15,856
29	24	H		Nottingham F	W	2-0	1-0	10	Sinton, Barker	14,653
30	31	A		Charlton Ath	L	0-1	0-0	12		8768
31	Apr 3	A		Southampton	W	2-0	0-0	—	Maddix, Wegerle	14,757
32	7	A		Everton	L	0-1	0-0	9		19,887
33	11	A		Manchester C	L	1-3	1-1	—	Wegerle	8437
34	14	H		Manchester U	L	1-2	1-0	10	Channing	18,997
35	16	A		Coventry C	D	1-1	1-1	11	Maddix	10,039
36	21	H		Sheffield W	W	1-0	1-0	9	Clarke	10,488
37	28	A		Liverpool	L	1-2	1-1	10	Wegerle	37,758
38	May 5	H		Wimbledon	L	2-3	1-1	11	Wegerle (pen), Channing	9676

Final League Position: 11

GOALSCORERS

League (45): Clarke 6, Sinton 6, Wegerle 6 (1 pen), Falco 5, Francis 5, Wright 5 (2 pens), Barker 3, Maddix 3, Channing 2, Ferdinand 2, Bardsley 1, Wilkins 1.
Littlewoods Cup (3): Clarke 1, Spackman 1, Wright 1 (pen).
FA Cup (11): Barker 2 (1 pen), Clarke 2, Sansom 2, Sinton 2, Wilkins 2, Wegerle 1.

Seaman	Channing	Sansom	Parker	McDonald	Spackman	Allen	Reid	Clarke	Wright	Sinton	Falco	Maddix	Barker	Kerslake	Stein	Bardsley	Francis	Rutherford	Ferdinand	Roberts	Law	Wilkins	Wegerle	Herrera	Iorfa	Match No.
1	2	3	4	5	6	7	8†	9*	10	11	12	14														1
1	2	3	4	5	6	7	8	9	10*	11†	12	14														2
1	2	3	4	5	6		8	9†	10*	11	12					7	14									3
1	2	3	4	5	6		8†	9	10	11	12	14				7*	·									4
1	2	3	4	5	6		8	9	10†	11		14				7*	12									5
1	2	3	4	5	6		8†	9	10*	11		14				7	12									6
1	2	3	4	5	6		8†	9	12	11		14				7	10*									7
1	2	3	4	5	6			9		11	12		8			7	10*									8
1	2		4*	5	6		8†	9	12	11			3	14		7	10									9
1	2	3		5	6*			9	10	11		4	8			7	12									10
1	2	3	4	5			8	9	12	11		6				7	10*									11
1	2	3	4	5	6		8	9		11*	10					7	12									12
1	2	3	4	5			8	12	10*	11		9	6			7										13
	2†	3	4	5	14		8	12	10	11	9*					7				1	6					14
		3	4	5	14		8†	9	12	11		6	7			2				1	10*					15
		3	4	5			8		12	11		9	6			2				1	10*	7				16
		3	4	5			8†		12	11		9	6	14		2				1	10*	7				17
14		3	4	5				9		11		6	8			2†			10*	1		7	12			18
1		3	4	5				9		11		6	8			2						7	10			19
1		3		5				9		11		6	8			2					4	7	10			20
1		3		5				9	12	11		6	8			2					4	7	10*			21
1		3	4	5				9*	12	11		6	8			2						7	10			22
1		3	4	5				9*	12	11		6	8			2						7	10			23
1	14	3	4	5				9	12	11		6†	8			2						7	10*			24
1		3		5				9		11		6	8			2					4	7	10			25
1		3	4	5				9		11		6	8			2						7	10			26
1		3	4	5				9*		11	12	6	8			2						7	10			27
1		3	4	5				9*		11	12	6	8			2						7	10			28
1		3	4	5				9*		11	12	6	8			2						7	10			29
1		3	4					9		11	12	6	8			2			5			7	10*			30
1		3	4					9		11		6	8			2			5			7	10			31
1	12	3	4					9		11		6	8			2			5*			7	10			32
1	12	3	4					9		11		6	8*			2			5			7	10			33
1	8	3	4	5				9*		11	12	6				2			10			7				34
1	8	3*	4	5				9		11	12	6				2			10			7				35
1	8	3	4	5				9		11		6				2						7	10			36
1	8			5				9		11		6*				2			12		4	7	10	3		37
1	8	3		5				9*		11		6				2			12		4	7	10†		14	38
33	19	36	32	34	11	2	15	27	9	38	11	28	24	—	1	31	3	1	6	5	10	23	18	1	—	
				+4s		+2s		+7s	+6s		+10s	+4s	+4s	+1s				+1s	+1s	+3s			+1s		+1s	

QUEEN'S PARK RANGERS

Player and Position	Ht	Wt	Birth Date	Place	Source	Clubs	League App	Gls
Goalkeepers								
Peter Caldwell			5 6 72	Dorchester	Trainee	QPR	—	—
Tony Roberts	6 0	12 00	4 8 69	Bangor	Trainee	QPR	6	—
Defenders								
David Bardsley	5 10	10 06	11 9 64	Manchester	Apprentice	Blackpool	45	—
						Watford	100	3
						Oxford U	74	7
						QPR	31	1
Justin Channing	5 10	11 03	19 11 68	Reading	Apprentice	QPR	48	4
Roberto Herrera	5 7	10 06	12 6 70	Torbay	Trainee	QPR	3	—
Anthony Joyce			24 9 71	Wembley	Trainee	QPR	—	—
Brian Law	6 2	11 10	1 1 70	Merthyr	Apprentice	QPR	17	—
Alan McCarthy			11 1 72	London	Trainee	QPR	—	—
Alan McDonald	6 2	12 07	12 10 63	Belfast	Apprentice	QPR	202	8
						Charlton Ath (loan)	9	—
Danny Maddix	5 11	11 00	11 10 67	Ashford	Apprentice	Tottenham H	—	—
						Southend U (loan)	2	—
						QPR	74	5
David Pizanti‡	5 10	11 00	27 5 62	Israel	Cologne	QPR	22	—
Kenny Sansom	5 6	11 08	26 9 58	Camberwell	Apprentice	Crystal Palace	172	3
						Arsenal	314	6
						Newcastle U	20	—
						QPR	36	—
Paul Vowels			26 8 71	Neath	Trainee	QPR	—	—
Midfield								
Simon Barker	5 9	11 00	4 11 64	Farnworth	Apprentice	Blackburn R	182	35
						QPR	53	4
Greg Costello‡	5 11	10 06	5 4 70	Dublin	Apprentice	QPR	—	—
Steven Crocker			23 3 72	London	Trainee	QPR	—	—
David Macciochi			14 9 72	Harlow	Trainee	QPR	—	—
Michael Meaker			18 8 71	Greenford	Trainee	QPR	—	—
Paul Parker	5 7	10 09	4 4 64	Essex	Apprentice	Fulham	153	2
						QPR	108	—
Michael Rutherford			6 6 72	Sidcup	Trainee	QPR	2	—
Andy Sinton	5 7	10 07	19 3 66	Newcastle	Apprentice	Cambridge U	93	13
						Brentford	149	28
						QPR	48	9
Nigel Spackman (To Rangers Nov 1989)	6 1	12 04	2 12 60	Romsey	Andover	Bournemouth	119	10
						Chelsea	141	12
						Liverpool	51	—
						QPR	29	1
Ray Wilkins	5 8	11 02	14 9 56	Hillingdon	Apprentice	Chelsea	179	27
						Manchester U	160	7
						AC Milan	73	2
					Paris St Germain	Rangers	70	2
						QPR	23	1
Forwards								
Bradley Allen	5 7	10 00	13 9 71	Harold Wood	Schoolboys	QPR	1	—
Colin Clarke	5 11	12 10	30 10 62	Newry	Apprentice	Ipswich T	—	—
						Peterborough U	82	18
						Gillingham (loan)	8	1
						Tranmere R	45	22
						Bournemouth	46	26
						Southampton	82	36
						Bournemouth (loan)	4	2
						QPR	46	11

QUEEN'S PARK RANGERS

Foundation: There is an element of doubt about the date of the foundation of this club, but it is believed that in either 1885 or 1886 it was formed through the amalgamation of Christchurch Rangers and St. Jude's Institute FC. The leading light was George Wodehouse, whose family maintained a connection with the club until comparatively recent times. Most of the players came from the Queen's Park district so this name was adopted after a year as St. Jude's Institute.

First Football League game: 28 August, 1920, Division 3, v Watford (h) L 1-2 – Price; Blackman, Wingrove; McGovern, Grant, O'Brien; Faulkner, Birch (1), Smith, Gregory, Middlemiss.

Managers (and Secretary-managers)
James Cowan 1906–13, James Howie 1913–20, Ted Liddell 1920–24, Will Wood 1924–25 (had been secretary since 1903), Bob Hewison 1925–30, John Bowman 1930–31, Archie Mitchell 1931–33, Mick O'Brien 1933–35, Billy Birrell 1935–39, Ted Vizard 1939–44, Dave Mangnall 1944–52, Jack Taylor 1952–59, Alec Stock 1959–65 (GM to 1968), Jimmy Andrews 1965, Bill Dodgin Jnr 1968, Tommy Docherty 1968, Les Allen 1969–70, Gordon Jago 1971–74, Dave Sexton 1974–77, Frank Sibley 1977–78, Steve Burtenshaw 1978–79, Tommy Docherty 1979–80, Terry Venables 1980–84, Gordon Jago 1984, Alan Mullery 1984, Frank Sibley 1984–85, Jim Smith 1985–88, Trevor Francis 1988–90, Don Howe 1990– .

Player and Position	Ht	Wt	Birth Date	Place	Source	Clubs	League App	Gls
Maurice Doyle	5 8	10 07	17 10 69	Ellesmere Port	Trainee	Crewe Alex	8	2
						QPR	—	—
Mark Falco	6 0	12 00	22 10 60	Hackney	Apprentice	Tottenham H	174	67
						Chelsea (loan)	3	—
						Watford	33	14
						Rangers	14	5
						QPR	67	22
Les Ferdinand	5 11	13 05	18 12 66	London	Hayes	QPR	12	2
						Brentford (loan)	3	—
						Besiktas (loan)	—	—
Dominic Iorfa			1 10 68	Lagos	Antwerp	QPR	1	—
Kevin Kingsmore‡	5 7	11 02	14 10 70	Belfast	Trainee	QPR	—	—
Steve Lynch‡	5 9	10 08	25 9 69	Belfast	Trainee	QPR	—	—
Roy Wegerle	5 8	10 02	19 3 64	South Africa	Tampa Bay R	Chelsea	23	3
						Swindon T (loan)	7	1
						Luton T	45	10
						QPR	19	6
Paul Wright (To Hibs March 1990)	5 8	10 08	17 8 67	East Kilbride	'S' Form	Aberdeen	68	16
						QPR	15	5

Trainees
Allsop, Justin P; Bixby, Michael E; Bromage, Raymond P; McEnroe, David J; Parker, Thomas G.P; Patterson, Herbert A; Ready, Karl.

Associated Schoolboys
Barrett, Sean M; Boswell, Peter K.A; Bowder, Stanley R; Bryan, Marvin L; Challis, Trevor M; Davey, Joe L; Dichio, Daniele; Dickinson, Steven D; Gallen, Kevin A; Graham, Mark R; Hart, David P; Jackson, Stephen; Mark, Robert J; Millard, Martyn L.

Associated Schoolboys who have accepted the club's offer of a Traineeship/Contract
Duong, Vinh-Tam; Finlay, Darren J; Wilkinson, Gary R.

READING 1989–90 *Back row (left to right)*: Mick Tait, Dave Leworthy, Mark Whitlock, Phil Burns, Steve Francis, Lee Payne, Michael Gilkes, Nashim Bashir. *Centre row*: Lew Chatterley (Assistant Manager), Adrian Williams, Mick Conroy, Domenyk Newman, Martin Hicks, Trevor Senior, Irvin Gernon, Darren Wood, John Haselden (Physiotherapist), Stewart Henderson (Coach).

Front row: George Friel, Stuart Beavon, Steve Moran, Richard Cox, Ian Branfoot (Manager), Scott Taylor, Keith Knight, Steve Richardson, Linden Jones.

Division 3   **READING**

Elm Park, Norfolk Road, Reading. Telephone Reading (0734) 507878.

Ground capacity: 12,500.

Record attendance: 33,042 v Brentford, FA Cup 5th rd, 19 Feb, 1927.

Record receipts: £70,693.79 v Arsenal, FA Cup 3 rd, 10 January 1987.

Pitch measurements: 112yd × 77yd.

Life President: J. H. Brooks.

Chairman: Roger Smee. *Vice-Chairman:*

Directors: J. Campbell, C. M. Brooks, M. J. King.

Manager: Ian Porterfield. *Assistant Manager:* Eddie Niedzwiecki. *Coach:* Stewart Henderson.

Physio: John Hasleden.

Commercial Manager: Tony Mundell.

Secretary:

Year Formed: 1871. *Turned Professional:* 1895 *Ltd Co.:* 1895.

Club Nickname: 'The Royals'.

Previous Grounds: 1871, Reading Recreation; Reading Cricket Ground; 1882, Coley Park; 1889, Caversham Cricket Ground; 1896, Elm Park.

Record League Victory: 10-2 v Crystal Palace, Division 3(S), 4 September 1946 – Groves; Glidden, Gulliver; McKenna, Ratcliffe, Young; Chitty, Maurice Edelston (3), McPhee (4), Barney (1), Deverell (2).

Record Cup Victory: 6-0 v Leyton, FA Cup, 2nd rd, 12 December 1925 – Duckworth; Eggo, McConnell; Wilson, Messer, Evans; Smith (2), Braithwaite (1), Davey (1), Tinsley, Robson (2).

Record Defeat: 0-18 v Preston NE, FA Cup 1st rd, 1893–94.

Most League Points (2 for a win): 65, Division 4, 1978–79.

Most League Points (3 for a win): 94, Division 3, 1985–86.

Most League Goals: 112, Division 3(S), 1951–52.

Highest League Scorer in Season: Ronnie Blackman, 39, Division 3(S), 1951–52.

Most League Goals in Total Aggregate: Ronnie Blackman, 156, 1947–54.

Most Capped Player: Billy McConnell, 8, Northern Ireland.

Most League Appearances: Steve Death, 471, 1969–82.

Record Transfer Fee Received: £325,000 from Watford for Trevor Senior, July 1987.

Record Transfer Fee Paid: £250,000 to Leicester C for Steve Moran, November 1987.

Football League Record: 1920 Original Member of Division 3; 1921–26 Division 3(S); 1926–31 Division 2; 1931–58 Division 3(S); 1958–71 Division 3; 1971–76 Division 4; 1976–77 Division 3; 1977–79 Division 4; 1979–83 Division 3; 1983–84 Division 4; 1984–86 Division 3; 1986–88 Division 2; 1988– Division 3.

Honours: Football League: Division 2 best season: 13th 1986–87; Division 3 – Champions 1985–86. Division 3(S) – Champions 1925–26; Runners-up 1931–32, 1934–35, 1948–49, 1951–52; Division 4 – Champions 1978–79. *FA Cup;* Semi-final 1927. *Football League Cup* best season: 4th rd, 1965, 1966, 1978. *Simod Cup:* Winners 1987–88.

Colours: Sky blue shirts, navy blue shorts, sky blue stockings. **Change colours:** All gold.

READING 1989–90 LEAGUE RECORD

Match No.	Date	Venue	Opponents	Result		H/T Score	Lg. Pos.	Goalscorers	Attendance
1	Aug 19	H	Shrewsbury T	D	3-3	1-2	—	Taylor, Hicks, Gilkes	3909
2	25	A	Crewe Alex	D	1-1	0-1	—	Williams	3311
3	Sept 2	H	Tranmere R	W	1-0	0-0	9	Conroy	4548
4	9	A	Notts Co	D	0-0	0-0	12		4697
5	16	H	Walsall	L	0-1	0-0	14		3819
6	23	A	Swansea C	W	6-1	3-1	11	Senior 3, Hicks, Knight, Wood	3511
7	26	H	Chester C	D	1-1	0-0	—	Bashir	4296
8	30	A	Bristol R	D	0-0	0-0	12		6120
9	Oct 6	A	Blackpool	D	0-0	0-0	—		3321
10	14	H	Huddersfield T	D	0-0	0-0	13		3950
11	17	H	Fulham	W	3-2	1-0	—	Senior, Beavon (pen), Mauge (og)	4743
12	21	A	Leyton Orient	L	1-4	1-3	12	Leworthy	4280
13	28	H	Mansfield T	W	1-0	0-0	10	Leworthy	3242
14	31	A	Wigan Ath	L	1-3	1-1	—	Senior	2029
15	Nov 4	H	Birmingham C	L	0-2	0-1	12		3527
16	11	A	Bury	L	0-4	0-1	14		3183
17	25	H	Bristol C	D	1-1	0-1	14	Senior	5353
18	Dec 2	A	Preston NE	L	0-1	0-1	17		5067
19	17	A	Northampton T	L	1-2	1-2	—	Beavon	3025
20	26	H	Brentford	W	1-0	1-0	15	Senior	5586
21	30	H	Rotherham U	W	3-2	0-1	14	Senior, Moran 2 (1 pen)	3924
22	Jan 13	H	Crewe Alex	D	1-1	1-0	18	Gooding	4645
23	20	A	Shrewsbury T	D	1-1	0-1	17	Moran	3504
24	Feb 11	A	Walsall	D	1-1	1-1	19	Senior	3506
25	12	A	Tranmere R	L	1-3	0-0	—	Moran	5264
26	17	H	Preston NE	W	6-0	4-0	18	Moran, Senior 2, Bennett (og), Leworthy 2	3998
27	20	H	Swansea T	D	1-1	1-0	—	Moran (pen)	4064
28	24	A	Bristol C	W	1-0	0-0	13	Leworthy	10,616
29	Mar 3	H	Bolton W	W	2-0	1-0	12	Tait, Gooding	4461
30	6	H	Bristol R	L	0-1	0-1	—		6147
31	9	A	Chester C	D	1-1	0-1	—	Leworthy	1978
32	17	H	Blackpool	D	1-1	0-0	16	Moran (pen)	3752
33	20	A	Huddersfield T	W	1-0	1-0	—	Tait	4588
34	24	A	Fulham	W	2-1	0-0	12	Beavon, Conroy	4835
35	31	H	Leyton Orient	D	1-1	1-0	13	Leworthy	4130
36	Apr 3	A	Bolton W	L	0-3	0-1	—		4679
37	7	A	Mansfield T	D	1-1	1-1	13	Tait	2563
38	10	H	Wigan Ath	W	2-0	1-0	—	Moran, Williams	3099
39	14	H	Cardiff C	L	0-1	0-0	12		3198
40	16	A	Brentford	D	1-1	0-0	11	Gooding	5594
41	21	H	Northampton T	W	3-2	1-1	12	Moran 2, Senior	3140
42	24	A	Rotherham U	D	1-1	0-1	—	Senior	3719
43	28	H	Bury	W	1-0	0-0	10	Wood	3259
44	May 1	A	Cardiff C	L	2-3	1-3	—	Moran, Senior	3375
45	3	H	Notts Co	D	1-1	0-0	—	Taylor	3132
46	5	A	Birmingham C	W	1-0	0-0	10	Gilkes	14,278

Final League Position: 10

GOALSCORERS

League (57): Senior 14, Moran 11 (3 pens), Leworthy 7, Beavon 3 (1 pen), Gooding 3, Tait 3, Conroy 2, Gilkes 2, Hicks 2, Taylor 2, Williams 2, Wood 2, Bashir 1, Knight 1, own goals 2.
Littlewoods Cup (8): Gilkes 4, Senior 3, Taylor 1.
FA Cup (12): Senior 4, Jones 3, Moran 2, Beavon 1 (pen), Conroy 1, Gilkes 1.

Francis	Richardson	Gernon	Beavon	Hicks	Wood	Jones	Taylor	Senior	Gilkes	Payne	Williams	Conroy	Leworthy	Bashir	Knight	Tait	Friel	Whitlock	Moran	Lemon	Gooding	Match No.
1	2	3	4	5	6	7	8	9	10·11													1
1	3		4	5	6	7	8	9	10	11	2											2
1	3		4	5	6	7	8	9	10		2	11										3
1	3		4	5	6	7	8	9	10		2	11*12										4
1	3		4	5	6	7	8†	9	10	11*	2	12		14								5
1	3		4	5	6	2	8*	9	10	11		12				7						6
1	3		4	5	6	2		9	10	11		12			8	7*						7
1	3	8	4	5	6	2		9	10	11*		12				7						8
1	3	11	4	5	6	2	8	9	10							7						9
1	3		4	5	6	2	8	9*10				12 11				7						10
1	3		4	5	6	2	8	9	10			11				7						11
1	3		4	5	6	2	8*	9	10			12 11				7†14						12
1	3		4	5	6	2	12	9	10			11				7	8*					13
1	3		4	5	6	2	8	9				12 11				7*	10					14
1			4	5	6	2	8*	9	10	14		12 11				7†		3				15
1			4	5	6	2	8	9		10	7	12 11*						3				16
1	3		4	5		2	12	9		11		10†				7	8*		6		14	17
1	3		4	5		2	12	9		11†		10				7*	8		6		14	18
1	3		4	5		2		9	12	11					8			6	10*	7		19
1	3	12		5		2		9	10						8			6	11	7	4*	20
1	3			5		2		9	10						8			6	11	7	4	21
1	3		7	5		2		9	10						8			6	11		4	22
1	3		7	5		2		9	10			8*12						6	11		4	23
1	3	6		2		7		9	10			12			8			5	11*		4	24
1	3			5		2	7	9	10						6	12		8	11*		4	25
1	3			5	4	2		9	10						6	12		8	11*		7	26
1	3			5	4	2		9*10							6	12		8	11		7	27
1	3			5	4	2		9*10							6	12		8	11		7	28
1	3	12		5	4	2			10						6	9		8	11*		7	29
1	3	12		5	4				10	14					6	9†	2	8	11*		7	30
1	3			5	4				10		2				6	9		8	11		7	31
1	3			5	4	2			10						6	9		8	11		7	32
1	3	11		5	4	2*12			10						6	9†		8	14		7	33
1		11		5	4	2	8		10		3				6	9					7	34
1	3	11		5	4	2			10*						6	9		8	12		7	35
1	3	11		5	4*	2	12		10						6	9†		8	14		7	36
1	3	11		5	4	2			10						6			8	9		7	37
1	3	11		5		2			10		4	6			8				9		7	38
1	3	11†		5		2	14		10		4	6 12			8				9*		7	39
1	3			5		2*10		9	12		4	6			8				11		7	40
1	3			5		2		9	10		4	6			8				11		7	41
1	3			5	12	2		9*10			4	6			8				11		7	42
1	3			5	2		14	9*10			4	6 12			8†				11		7	43
1	3			5	2†14	8		9	10		4*	6 12							11		7	44
1	3			5		2		9	10		4	6 12			8†14				11*		7	45
1	3			5		2		9	10		4	6			8				11		7	46

Francis	Richardson	Gernon	Beavon	Hicks	Wood	Jones	Taylor	Senior	Gilkes	Payne	Williams	Conroy	Leworthy	Bashir	Knight	Tait	Friel	Whitlock	Moran	Lemon	Gooding
46	43	3	29	44	31	38	22	35	40	10	16	27	16	1	13	27	2	10	23	3	27
	+3s		+1s	+1s	+7s		+2s	+2s				+7s	+12s	+2s		+1s	+1s		+5s		

Littlewoods Cup	First Round	Bristol C (a)		3-2	
		(h)		2-2	
	Second Round	Newcastle U (h)		3-1	
		(a)		0-4	
FA Cup	First Round	Bristol R (a)		1-1	
		(h)		1-1	
		(a)		1-0	
	Second Round	Welling (h)		0-0	
		(a)		1-1	
		(h)		0-0	
		(a)		2-1	
	Third Round	Sunderland (h)		2-1	
	Fourth Round	Newcastle U (h)		3-3	
		(a)		1-4	

READING

Player and Position	Ht	Wt	Birth Date	Place	Source	Clubs	League App	Gls
Goalkeepers								
Phil Burns	6 0	12 00	18 12 66	Stockport	Army	Reading	—	—
Gary Phillips‡	6 0	14 00	20 9 61	St Albans	Barnet	WBA	—	—
						Brentford	143	—
						Reading	24	—
						Hereford U (loan)	6	—
Steve Francis	5 11	11 05	29 5 64	Billericay	Apprentice	Chelsea	71	—
						Reading	116	—
Defenders								
Adrian Chatterley‡	6 1	12 09	29 6 70	Walsall		Reading	—	—
Martin Hicks	6 3	13 06	27 2 57	Stratford on Avon	Stratford T	Charlton Ath	—	—
						Reading	456	23
Linden Jones	5 6	10 08	5 3 61	Tredegar	Apprentice	Cardiff C	145	2
						Newport Co	142	5
						Reading	96	6
Domenyk Newman‡	6 0	12 03				Reading	—	—
Steve Richardson	5 5	10 03	11 2 62	Slough	Apprentice	Southampton	—	—
						Reading	295	2
Mark Whitlock	6 0	12 02	14 3 61	Portsmouth	Apprentice	Southampton	61	1
						Grimsby T (loan)	8	—
						Aldershot (loan)	14	—
						Bournemouth	99	1
						Reading	27	—
Adrian Williams	5 10	11 00	16 8 71	Reading	Trainee	Reading	24	2
Darren Wood	6 1	12 08	22 10 68	Derby	Trainee	Chesterfield	67	3
						Reading	32	2
Midfield								
Naseem Bashir*	5 6	10 06	12 9 69	Amersham		Reading	3	1
Stuart Beavon	5 6	10 04	30 11 58	Wolverhampton	Apprentice	Tottenham H	4	—
						Notts Co (loan)	6	—
						Reading	396	44
Mick Gooding	5 7	10 08	12 4 59	Newcastle	B Auckland	Rotherham U	102	10
						Chesterfield	12	—
						Rotherham U	156	33
						Peterborough U	47	21
						Wolverhampton W	44	4
						Reading	27	3
Colin Mitchell‡	5 6	9 03	24 3 71			Reading	—	—
Mick Tait*	5 11	12 05	30 9 56	Wallsend	Apprentice	Oxford U	64	23
						Carlisle U	106	20
						Hull C	33	3
						Portsmouth	240	30
						Reading	99	9
Scott Taylor	5 9	11 00	28 11 70	Portsmouth	Trainee	Reading	32	2
Forwards								
Mike Conroy	6 0	11 00	31 12 65	Glasgow	Apprentice	Coventry C	—	—
						Clyde Bank	114	38
						St Mirren	10	1
						Reading	47	6
George Friel	5 8	10 11	11 10 70	Reading	Trainee	Reading	3	—
Michael Gilkes	5 8	10 02	20 7 65	Hackney		Reading	159	19
Andy King‡	6 0	11 07	30 3 70	Newbury		Reading	1	—
Keith Knight	5 8	11 00	16 2 69	Cheltenham	Cheltenham T	Reading	42	8
David Leworthy	5 9	12 00	22 10 62	Portsmouth	Apprentice Fareham T	Portsmouth	1	—
						Tottenham H	11	3
						Oxford U	37	8
						Shrewsbury T (loan)	6	3
						Reading	28	7

READING

Foundation: Reading was formed as far back as 1871 at a public meeting held at the Bridge Street Rooms. They first entered the FA Cup as early as 1877 when they amalgamated with the Reading Hornets. The club was further strengthened in 1889 when Earley FC joined them. They were the first winners of the Berks and Bucks Cup in 1878–79.

First Football League game: 28 August, 1920, Division 3, v Newport C (a) W 1-0 – Crawford; Smith, Horler; Christie, Mavin, Getgood; Spence, Weston, Yarnell, Bailey (1), Andrews.

Managers (and Secretary-managers)
Thomas Sefton 1897–1901*, James Sharp 1901–02, Harry Matthews 1902–20, Harry Marshall 1920–22, Arthur Chadwick 1923–25, H. S. Bray 1925–26 (secretary only since 1922 and 26–35), Andrew Wylie 1926–31, Joe Smith 1931–35, Billy Butler 1935–39, John Cochrane 1939, Joe Edelston 1939–47, Ted Drake 1947–52, Jack Smith 1952–55, Harry Johnston 1955–63, Roy Bentley 1963–69, Jack Mansell 1969–71, Charlie Hurley 1972–77, Maurice Evans 1977–84, Ian Branfoot 1984–89, Ian Porterfield 1990– .

Player and Position	Ht	Wt	Birth Date	Place	Source	Clubs	League App	Gls
Steve Moran	5 8	11 00	10 1 61	Croydon	Amateur	Southampton	180	78
						Leicester C	43	14
						Reading	90	22
Lee Payne	5 10	11 05	12 12 66	Luton	Barnet	Newcastle U	7	—
						Reading	27	3
Trevor Senior	6 1	12 08	28 11 61	Dorchester	Dorchester T	Portsmouth	11	2
						Aldershot (loan)	10	7
						Reading	164	102
						Watford	24	1
						Middlesbrough	10	2
						Reading	72	30

Trainees
Beel, Mark A; Brown, Iain C; Butler, Steven J; Fealey, Nathan J; Henderson, Daniel J; Hodgson, David N; Holzman, Mark R; Honey, Daniel W; Lovell, Stuart A; Malins, Martin J; Rodgers, Brendan J.K; Saunders, Paul B; Schonberger, David P; Seymour, Christopher D; Stevens, Gary.

Associated Schoolboys
Barkus, Lee P; Bass, David; Beech, Matthew P; Bullock, Ian S; Champion, Marc G; Clift, David R; Ferguson, Gary; Gregory, Paul; Harvey, Michael; Horner, Duncan R; Lockey, Richard A; Maskell, Gary P; Mukabaa, Antony G; Pugh, Gareth D; Rose, Andrew R; Thorpe, Michael S; Timothy, David.

Associated Schoolboys who have accepted the club's offer of a Traineeship/Contract
Emery, Barry; Gardner, Dudley J; Giamattei, Aaron P; Liney, Paul; McCance, Darren; McGuigan, Gareth J.; Silvey, Paul S.

ROCHDALE 1989–90   *Back row (left to right):* Dave Sutton (Physiotherapist), Jonathon Hill, Neil Edmonds, Dean Walling, Steve O'Shaughnessy, Tony Brown, Keith Welch, Stuart Cramer, David Cole, Zac Hughes, Kevin Stonehouse, Steve Taylor, Willie Burns, Bernard Ellison (Youth Development Officer).

Centre row: Colin Small, Jason Hasford, Michael Holmes, Wayne Goodison, Terry Dolan (Manager), Alan Ainscow, Jeff Lee (Assistant Manager), Robbie Whellans, Jason Dawson, Peter Ward, Vinny Chapman.

Front row: Neil Jones, Chris Lucketti, Jamie Hedderman, Paul Buckley, Andy Smith, Phil Lockett, Spencer Barrow, Steve Milligan, Paul Herring, Carl Alford.

Division 4   **ROCHDALE**

Spotland, Willbutts Lane, Rochdale OL11 5DA. Telephone Rochdale (0706) 44648-9. Fax: 0706 48466

Ground capacity: 10,250.

Record attendance: 24,231 v Notts Co, FA Cup 2nd rd, 10 Dec, 1949.

Record receipts: £28,371.20 v Northampton T, FA Cup 4th rd, 27 January 1990.

Pitch measurements: 113yd × 75yd.

President: Mrs L. Stoney.

Chairman: D. F. Kilpatrick. *Vice-Chairman:* G. Morris.

Directors: W. A. C. Dromsfield, E. Lord, L. Hilton, G. R. Brierley, J. Marsh, C. D. Walkden.

Manager: Terry Dolan.

Secretary: Bill Kenyon JP. *Asst. Manager:*

Commercial Manager: Mrs Sheila Hodgkinson. *Lottery Manager:* B. Johnson.

Physio: Dave Sutton. *Coach:* J. Lee.

Year Formed: 1907. *Turned Professional:* 1907. *Ltd Co.:* 1910.

Club Nickname: 'The Dale'.

Record League Victory: 8-1 v Chesterfield, Division 3(N), 18 December 1926 – Hill; Brown, Ward; Hillhouse, Parkes, Braidwood; Hughes, Bertram, Whitehurst (5), Schofield (2), Martin (1).

Record Cup Victory: 8-2 v Crook T, FA Cup, 1st rd, 26 November 1927 – Moody; Hopkins, Ward; Braidwood, Parkes, Barker; Tompkinson, Clennell (3) Whitehurst (4), Hall, Martin (1).

Record Defeat: 0-8 v Wrexham, Division 3(N), 28 December, 1929, 0-8 v Leyton Orient, Division 4, 20 October, 1987, and 1-9 v Tranmere R, Division 3(N), 25 December, 1931.

Most League Points (2 for a win): 65, Division 4, 1978–79.

Most League Points (3 for a win): 66, Division 4, 1989–90.

Most League Goals: 105, Division 3(N), 1926–27.

Highest League Scorer in Season: Albert Whitehurst, 44, Division 3(N), 1926–27.

Most League Goals in Total Aggregate: Reg Jenkins, 119, 1964–73.

Most Capped Player: None.

Most League Appearances: Graham Smith, 317, 1966–74.

Record Transfer Fee Received: £50,000 from Huddersfield T for Mark Smith, January 1989, and £50,000 from Stockport Co for David Frain, July 1989.

Record Transfer Fee Paid: £25,000 to Bolton W for Mark Gavin, October 1987.

Football League Record: 1921 Elected to Division 3(N); 1958–59 Division 3; 1959–69 Division 4; 1969–74 Division 3; 1974– Division 4.

Honours: Football League: Division 3 best season: 9th, 1969–70; Division 3(N) – Runners-up 1923–24, 1926–27. *FA Cup:* best season: 5th rd, 1989–90. *Football League Cup:* Runners-up 1962 (record for 4th Division club).

Colours: All Royal blue. **Change colours:** All yellow.

ROCHDALE 1989–90 LEAGUE RECORD

Match No.	Date	Venue	Opponents	Result	H/T Score	Lg. Pos.	Goalscorers	Attendance
1	Aug 19	H	Burnley	W 2-1	1-1	—	Walling, Harris (og)	5420
2	26	A	Scunthorpe U	W 1-0	1-0	2	Cole	2808
3	Sept 2	H	Wrexham	L 0-3	0-2	7		2331
4	9	A	York C	L 0-1	0-1	14		2250
5	16	H	Colchester U	D 2-2	1-1	15	Whellans, Walling	1466
6	23	A	Torquay U	L 0-1	0-0	16		1809
7	26	H	Hartlepool U	D 0-0	0-0	—		1501
8	30	A	Chesterfield	L 1-2	1-1	19	Stonehouse (pen)	3047
9	Oct 7	A	Grimsby T	W 2-1	1-0	15	Elliott, Jobling (og)	3996
10	14	H	Peterborough U	L 1-2	0-0	17	Elliott	1767
11	17	H	Exeter C	W 1-0	0-0	—	Holmes	1337
12	21	A	Halifax T	L 0-1	0-0	18		1864
13	28	H	Scarborough	W 1-0	0-0	14	Johnson	1402
14	31	A	Gillingham	L 0-1	0-0	—		3187
15	Nov 4	A	Hereford U	W 3-1	2-1	15	Johnson, Elliott 2	2235
16	11	H	Doncaster R	L 1-3	0-2	17	Goodison (pen)	1716
17	25	H	Carlisle U	L 1-2	0-1	17	O'Shaughnessy	1920
18	Dec 2	A	Cambridge U	W 3-0	1-0	17	O'Shaughnessy, Elliott, Dawson	2289
19	16	H	Lincoln C	W 1-0	0-0	14	Stonehouse (pen)	1216
20	26	A	Stockport Co	L 1-2	0-2	16	Goodison (pen)	4215
21	30	A	Aldershot	D 1-1	0-1	17	Ward	2095
22	Jan 1	H	Southend U	L 0-1	0-1	18		1521
23	13	H	Scunthorpe U	W 3-0	0-0	16	Burns (pen), O'Shaughnessy 2	1781
24	20	A	Burnley	W 1-0	1-0	16	Ward	8174
25	Feb 3	H	Torquay U	D 0-0	0-0	16		1909
26	6	H	York C	L 0-1	0-0	—		1821
27	10	A	Colchester U	W 2-1	2-1	14	Cole, Johnson	2744
28	13	A	Wrexham	D 1-1	0-0	—	Cole	1552
29	24	A	Carlisle U	W 1-0	0-0	13	Walling	4904
30	Mar 3	H	Maidstone U	W 3-2	2-0	13	Cole, Holmes, Johnson	2085
31	6	H	Chesterfield	W 1-0	1-0	—	Ward	2810
32	10	A	Hartlepool U	L 1-2	1-0	12	O'Shaughnessy	2751
33	17	H	Grimsby T	L 0-1	0-0	12		3058
34	21	A	Peterborough U	W 1-0	1-0	—	Ward	3485
35	24	A	Exeter C	L 0-5	0-2	12		4701
36	27	H	Cambridge U	W 2-0	1-0	—	Milner, O'Shaughnessy	1669
37	31	H	Halifax T	L 0-2	0-0	11		2494
38	Apr 4	A	Maidstone U	L 0-2	0-0	—		1501
39	7	A	Scarborough	L 1-2	1-0	12	Cole	1799
40	10	H	Gillingham	W 1-0	0-0	—	Ward	1334
41	14	A	Southend U	L 2-3	0-1	12	Small, Goodison (pen)	2464
42	16	H	Stockport Co	D 1-1	0-0	13	Goodison (pen)	3194
43	21	A	Lincoln C	W 2-1	2-0	11	Milligan, Elliott	2470
44	24	H	Aldershot	W 2-0	0-0	—	Henshaw, Dawson	1419
45	28	A	Doncaster R	L 0-4	0-2	12		2189
46	May 5	H	Hereford U	W 5-2	2-0	12	O'Shaughnessy 2 (1 pen), Milner 3	1429

Final League Position: 12

GOALSCORERS

League (52): O'Shaughnessy 8 (1 pen), Elliott 6, Cole 5, Ward 5, Goodison 4 (4 pens), Johnson 4, Milner 4, Walling 3, Dawson 2, Holmes 2, Stonehouse 2 (2 pens), Burns 1 (pen), Henshaw 1, Milligan 1, Small 1, Whellans 1, own goals 2.
Littlewoods Cup (3): Burns 1, Goodison 1, Holmes 1.
FA Cup (8): Johnson 2, O'Shaughnessy 2, Dawson 1, Goodison 1 (pen), Stonehouse 1, Ward 1.

Welch	Goodison	Chapman	Brown	Cole	Ward	Aincsow	Holmes	Walling	Burns	Stonehouse	Hill	Edmonds	Whellans	O'Shaughnessy	Small	Hasford	Elliott	Johnson	Graham	Dawson	Milner	Duxbury	Henshaw	Milligan	Lockett	Match No.
1	2	3	4	5	6	7	8	9	10	11																1
1	2		4	5	6	7	8	9	10	11	3															2
1	2		4	5	6*	7	8	9†10		11	3	12	14													3
1	2	3*	4	5	6	7	8		10	11				9	12											4
1	2		4	5		7	8	10	12	11*	3			9	6											5
1	2		4	5		7	8	10	12	11	3			9*	6†14											6
1	2	3†	4	5			8	10	6		11	7		9*			14	12								7
1	2		4	5	6	14	8*10	7	11		3			12		9†										8
1	2		4	5	6*	7	8	12	10	11	3							9								9
1	2		4	5	12	7	8	10	6	11*	3							9								10
1	2		4	5	6	7	8	12	10		3	11*						9								11
1	2		4	5	6	7*	8	14	10†		3	12					9	11								12
1	2			5	6	7	12		10	11*	3			4			9	8								13
1	2			5	6	7*12	14	10	11†		3			4			9	8								14
1	2	5		6		7		10			3			4			9	8	11							15
1	2	5	14	6		7*12	10†				3			4			9	8	11							16
1	2		4	5	6			9	3*	7				10			12	8	11							17
1	2*		4	5	6		7		3					10			9	8	11	12						18
1	2		4	5			7		3	6				10				8	11	9						19
1	2		4	5	6		7		3		14		12	10*			8†11		9							20
1	2		4	5	6		7		3					10			12	8	11	9*						21
1	2			5	6		7		3	12		4					10	8*11	9							22
1	2		4	5	6		7		3					10			8	11	9							23
1	2		4	5	6		7		3			12	10				11	9*	8							24
1	2		4	5	6*		7			3				12	11		9	8	10							25
1	2		4	5	6		7*		3†	11				10			12	9	8	14						26
1	2		4	5	6				3	11				10			8	9		7						27
1	2	11*	4	5	6				3					10			8	9	12	7						28
1	2		4	5	6		7	12	3					10			8	9*		11						29
1	2		4	5	6		7	12	3					10			8	9*		11						30
1	2		4	5	6		7	12	3					10			8	9*		11						31
1	2		4	5	6*		7	9	3		14		12	10†			8			11						32
1	2		4	5	6		7		3		14		12	10†			8	9*		11						33
1	2		4	5	6		7		3	10							9*12	11	8							34
1	2		4	5*			7	12	3	6							8	9	11	10						35
1	2		4	5			7		3	6				10			12	9*11		8						36
1	2		4	5	9		7†		3	6				10			14	12		11	8*					37
1	2		4	5*	6	7		12	3					11	8	10		9								38
1	2†		4	5	6	7	14		3					10	8	9		12	11*							39
1			4	5	6	2			3						8	9		10	7			11				40
1	11		4	5	6	2			3						10	9		8*	7	12						41
1	2		4	5	6	11			3						9			10	7	8						42
1	2		4		6	11			3						9			10	7		8	5				43
1	2		4		6	11*14			3					12				9	10	7		8	5†			44
1	2		4	5†6		14			3					12				9	10*	7		8	11			45
1	2	4	12	6		11			5*					10				9	8	7			3†14			46
46	45	4	43	41	39	19	33	9	42	13	22	2	5	27	5	—	19	20	11	25	14	9	8	5	—	

+ 2s + 1s + 1s + 5s + 10s2s + 1s + 3s + 2s + 6s3s + 2s1s + 3s + 4s + 2s + 2s + 1s + 1s + 1s

Littlewoods Cup	First Round	Bolton W (h)	2-1
		(a)	1-5
FA Cup	First Round	Marine (a) (at Anfield)	1-0
	Second Round	Lincoln C (h)	3-0
	Third Round	Whitley Bay (h)	1-0
	Fourth Round	Northampton T (h)	3-0
	Fifth Round	Crystal Palace (a)	0-1

ROCHDALE

Player and Position	Ht	Wt	Birth Date	Place	Source	Clubs	League App	Gls
Goalkeepers								
Lee Lamont*	5 11	11 10	16 5 71	Leeds	Trainee	Doncaster R	—	—
						Rochdale	—	—
Keith Welch	6 0	12 00	3 10 68	Bolton	Trainee	Bolton W	—	—
						Rochdale	162	—
Defenders								
Tony Brown	6 2	12 07	17 9 58	Bradford	Thackley	Leeds U	24	1
						Doncaster (loan)	14	—
						Doncaster R	73	2
						Scunthorpe U	54	2
						Rochdale	43	—
Willie Burns	5 11	10 10	10 12 69	Motherwell	Trainee	Manchester C	—	—
						Rochdale	44	1
Vincent Chapman	5 9	11 00	5 12 67	Newcastle	Tow Law T	Huddersfield T	6	—
						York C (loan)	—	—
						Rochdale	4	—
David Cole	6 0	11 10	28 9 62	Barnsley		Sunderland	—	—
						Swansea C	8	—
						Swindon T	69	3
						Torquay U	110	6
						Rochdale	43	5
Neil Edmonds‡	5 8	10 08	18 10 68	Accrington	Trainee	Oldham Ath	5	—
						Rochdale	43	8
Wayne Goodison	5 8	11 07	23 9 64	Wakefield	Apprentice	Barnsley	36	—
						Crewe Alex	94	1
						Rochdale	45	4
Jonathan Hill	5 10	11 10	20 8 70	Wigan	Trainee	Rochdale	25	—
Zac Hughes	5 11	11 12	6 6 71	Bentley, Australia	Trainee	Rochdale	2	—
Chris Lucketti§			28 9 71	Littleborough	Trainee	Rochdale	1	—
Steve O'Shaughnessy	6 2	13 00	13 10 67		Wrexham	Leeds U	—	—
						Bradford C	1	—
						Rochdale	71	14
Midfield								
Alan Ainscow*	5 8	11 05	15 7 53	Bolton	Apprentice	Blackpool	192	28
						Birmingham C	108	16
						Everton	28	3
						Barnsley (loan)	2	—
					Eastern	Wolverhampton W	58	5
						Blackburn R	65	5
						Rochdale	20	—
Carl Alford‡			11 2 72	Manchester	Trainee	Rochdale	4	—
Phil Lockett§	5 9	11 02	6 9 72	Stockton	Trainee	Rochdale	1	—
Joe McIntyre‡			19 6 71	Manchester	Port Vale§	Rochdale	4	—
Steve Milligan§	5 9	11 00	13 6 73	Hyde	Trainee	Rochdale	5	1
Colin Small*	5 8	11 00	9 11 70	Stockport	Manchester C§	Rochdale	7	1
Jason Dawson	5 7	11 05	9 2 71	Burslem	Port Vale§	Rochdale	27	2
Steve Elliott	6 0	11 10	15 9 58	Haltwistle	Apprentice	Nottingham F	4	—
						Preston NE	208	70
						Luton T	12	3
						Walsall	69	21
						Bolton W	60	11
						Bury	31	11
						Rochdale	22	6
Jason Hasford*	5 8	10 12	1 4 71	Manchester	Manchester C§	Rochdale	1	—
Micky Holmes	5 8	10 12	9 9 65	Blackpool		Bradford C	5	—
						Burnley	—	—
						Wolverhampton W	83	13
						Huddersfield T	7	—
						Cambridge U	11	—
						Rochdale	38	2

ROCHDALE

Foundation: Considering the love of rugby in their area, it is not surprising that Rochdale had difficulty in establishing an Association Football club. The earlier Rochdale Town club formed in 1900 went out of existence in 1907 when the present club was immediately established and joined the Manchester League, before graduating to the Lancashire Combination in 1908.

First Football League game: 27 August, 1921, Division 3(N), v Accrington Stanley (h) W 6-3 – Crabtree; Nuttall, Sheehan; Hill, Farrer, Yarwood; Hoad, Sandiford, Dennison (2), Owens (3), Carney (1).

Managers (and Secretary-managers)
Billy Bradshaw 1920, (run by committee 1920–22), Tom Wilson 1922–23, Jack Peart 1923–30, Will Cameron 1930–31, Herbert Hopkinson 1932–34, Billy Smith 1934–35, Ernest Nixon 1935–37, Sam Jennings 1937–38, Ted Goodier 1938–52, Jack Warner 1952–53, Harry Catterick 1953–58, Jack Marshall 1958–60, Tony Collins 1960–68, Bob Stokoe 1967–68,

Len Richley 1968–70, Dick Conner 1970–73, Walter Joyce 1973–76, Brian Green 1976–77, Mike Ferguson 1977–78, Doug Collins 1979, Bob Stokoe 1979–80, Peter Madden 1980–83, Jimmy Greenhoff 1983–84, Vic Halom 1984–86, Eddie Gray 1986–88, Danny Bergara 1988–89, Terry Dolan 1989– .

Player and Position	Ht	Wt	Birth Date	Place	Source	Clubs	League App	Gls
Steve Johnson	6 0	12 09	23 6 57	Liverpool	Altrincham	Bury	154	52
						Rochdale	19	7
						Wigan Ath	51	18
						Bristol C	21	3
						Rochdale (loan)	6	1
						Chester C (loan)	10	6
						Scunthorpe U	72	20
						Chester C	38	10
					Huskvarna	Rochdale	24	4
Andy Milner	5 11	11 07	10 2 67	Kendal	Netherfield	Manchester C	—	—
						Rochdale	16	4
Kevin Stonehouse	5 11	11 01	20 9 59	Bishop Auckland	Shildon	Blackburn R	85	27
						Huddersfield T	22	4
						Blackpool	55	19
						Darlington	72	20
						Carlisle U (loan)	3	—
						Rochdale	14	2
Steve Taylor‡	5 10	10 09	18 10 55	Royton	Apprentice	Bolton W	40	16
						Port Vale (loan)	4	2
						Oldham Ath	47	25
						Luton T	20	1
						Mansfield T	37	7
						Burnley	86	37
						Wigan Ath	30	7
						Stockport Co	26	8
						Rochdale	84	42
						Preston NE	5	2
						Burnley	45	6
						Rochdale	17	4
Dean Walling*	6 0	10 08	17 4 69	Leeds		Leeds U	—	—
						Rochdale	65	8
Peter Ward	6 0	11 10	15 10 64	Co Durham	Chester-le-Street	Huddersfield T	37	2
						Rochdale	40	5
Robbie Whellans*	5 8	10 09	10 12 69	Harrogate	Trainee	Bradford C	—	—
						Hartlepool U (loan)	11	1
						Rochdale	11	1

Trainees
Barrow, Spencer J; Griffin, Steven W; Hedderman, Jamie T; Herring, Paul J; Lockett, Philip B; Lucketti, Christopher J; Milligan, Stephen J.F; Smith, Andrew J.

Associated Schoolboys
Clayton, Michael; Dockray, Martin; Eyres, Kenneth L; Hirst, Richard T; Hoyle, Dominic W; Knaggs, Martin T; Legg, Stuart A; Lennigan, Neil R; Taylor, Wayne A; Weston, Daniel B; Yale, Lee D.

Associated Schoolboys who have accepted the club's offer of a Traineeship/Contract
Anders, Jason S; Grimbaldeston, David A.

ROTHERHAM UNITED 1989–90 *Back row (left to right):* Phil Henson (Assistant Manager), Ian Bailey (Physiotherapist), Billy Russell, Pat Heard, Ronnie Robinson, Nigel Johnson, Billy Mercer, Stewart Evans, Kelham O'Hanlon, Paul Haycock, Andy Barnsley, Neil Richardson, Nigel Pepper, John Breckin (Youth Team Coach).
Front row: Simon Thompson, John Buckley, Shaun Goodwin, Martin Scott, Tony Grealish, Billy McEwan (Manager), Bobby Williamson, Clive Mendonca, Des Hazel, Mark Dempsey, Andy Ainscow.

Division 3   **ROTHERHAM UNITED**

Millmoor Ground, Rotherham. Telephone Rotherham (0709) 562434.

Ground Capacity: 15,736.

Record attendance: 25,000 v Sheffield U, Division 2, 13 Dec, 1952 and v Sheffield W, Division 2, 26 Jan, 1952.

Record receipts: £44,091 v Manchester U, Littlewoods Cup, 2nd rd, 1st leg, 28 September, 1989.

Pitch measurements. 115yd × 75yd.

President: Sir J. Layden.

Chairman: K. F. Booth.

Directors: R. Hull (Vice-Chairman), B. J. Peacock, C. A. Luckock, J. A. Webb.

Manager: Billy McEwan. *Asst. Manager:* Phil Henson. *Physio:* Ian Bailey.

*Secretary:*N. Darnill.

Commercial Manager: D. Nicholls.

Year Formed: 1884. *Turned Professional:* 1905. *Ltd Co.:* 1920.

Club Nickname: 'The Merry Millers'.

Previous Names: 1884, Thornhill United; 1905, Rotherham County; 1925, amalgamated with Rotherham Town under Rotherham United.

Previous Grounds: Red House Ground; 1907, Millmoor.

Record League Victory: 8-0 v Oldham Ath, Division 3(N), 26 May 1947 – Warnes; Selkirk, Ibbotson; Edwards, Horace Williams, Danny Williams; Wilson (2), Shaw (1), Ardron (3), Guest (1), Hainsworth (1).

Record Cup Victory: 6-0 v Spennymoor U, FA Cup 2nd rd, 17 December 1977 – McAlister; Forrest, Breckin, Womble, Stancliffe, Green, Finney, Phillips (3), Gwyther (2) (Smith), Goodfellow, Crawford (1). 6-0 v Wolverhampton W. FA Cup, 1st rd, 16 November 1985 – O'Hanlon, Forrest, Dungworth, Gooding (1), Smith (1), Pickering, Birch (2), Emerson, Tynan (1), Simmons (1), Pugh.

Record Defeat: 1-11 v Bradford C, Division 3(N), 25 August, 1928.

Most League Points (2 for a win): 71, Division 3(N), 1950–1.

Most League Points (3 for a win): 82, Division 4, 1988–89.

Most League Goals: 114, Division 3(N), 1946–47.

Highest League Scorer in Season: Wally Ardron, 38, Division 3(N), 1946–47.

Most League Goals in Total Aggregate: Gladstone Guest, 130, 1946–56.

Most Capped Player: Harold Millership, 6, Wales.

Most League Appearances: Danny Williams, 459, 1946–62.

Record Transfer Fee Received: £180,000 from Everton for Bobby Mimms, May 1985.

Record Transfer Fee Paid: £100,000 to Cardiff C for Ronnie Moore, August 1980.

Football League Record: 1893 Rotherham Town elected to Division 2; 1896 failed re-election; 1919 Rotherham County elected to Division 2; 1923–51 Division 3(N); 1951–68 Division 2; 1968–73 Division 3; 1973–75 Division 4; 1975–81 Division 3; 1981–83 Division 2; 1983–88 Division 3; 1988–89 Division 4; 1989– Division 3.

Honours: Football League: Division 2 best season: 3rd, 1954–55 (equal points with champions and runners-up); Division 3 – Champions 1980–81; Division 3(N) – Champions 1950–51; Runners-up 1946–47, 1947–48, 1948–49; Division 4 – Champions 1988–89. *FA Cup* best season: 5th rd, 1953, 1968. *Football League Cup:* Runners-up 1961.

Colours: Red shirts, white shorts, red stockings. **Change colours:** Yellow shirts, blue shorts, yellow stockings.

ROTHERHAM UNITED 1989–90 LEAGUE RECORD

Match No.	Date		Venue	Opponents	Result	H/T Score	Lg. Pos.	Goalscorers	Attendance
1	Aug	19	H	Preston NE	W 3-1	2-0	—	Dempsey, Williamson, Mendonca	5951
2		26	A	Wigan Ath	W 3-0	0-0	1	Williamson, Buckley, Mendonca	2659
3	Sept	2	H	Walsall	D 2-2	0-0	2	Buckley, Williamson	5926
4		9	A	Tranmere R	L 1-2	1-1	7	Barnsley	4912
5		16	H	Bolton W	W 1-0	0-0	4	Heard	6846
6		23	A	Notts Co	L 0-2	0-1	10		5891
7		26	A	Bury	D 1-1	0-0	—	Williamson	3276
8		30	H	Cardiff C	W 4-0	2-0	7	Williamson 3 (1 pen), Mendonca	4998
9	Oct	7	H	Birmingham C	W 5-1	1-1	4	Scott, Williamson 3, Buckley	4450
10		14	A	Fulham	D 1-1	0-0	4	Barnsley	4375
11		17	H	Leyton Orient	W 5-2	2-1	—	Williamson, Mendonca 2, Robinson, Buckley	5728
12		21	A	Crewe Alex	D 0-0	0-0	4		3647
13		28	H	Blackpool	D 1-1	1-0	5	Johnson	5570
14		31	A	Swansea C	L 0-1	0-0	—		4077
15	Nov	4	A	Northampton T	W 2-1	0-0	6	Buckley, Goodwin	3598
16		11	H	Chester C	W 5-0	2-0	4	Goodwin, Williamson 2, Buckley, Hazel	5216
17		25	H	Shrewsbury T	W 4-2	2-2	2	Williamson (pen), Evans, Pepper, Johnson	5694
18	Dec	2	A	Bristol C	D 0-0	0-0	2		9509
19		16	H	Huddersfield T	D 0-0	0-0	4		6673
20		26	A	Mansfield T	L 1-3	0-2	4	Goodwin	6348
21		30	A	Reading	L 2-3	1-0	6	Barnsley, Williamson (pen)	3924
22	Jan	1	H	Bristol R	W 3-2	1-1	4	Evans, Hazel, Williamson (pen)	7750
23		6	A	Brentford	L 2-4	0-3	—	Goater, Fleming (og)	5624
24		13	H	Wigan Ath	L 1-2	1-1	7	Goodwin	6055
25		20	A	Preston NE	W 1-0	0-0	5	Evans	6088
26		27	H	Tranmere R	D 0-0	0-0	6		6386
27	Feb	3	H	Notts Co	L 1-2	0-1	6	Yates (og)	7251
28		10	A	Bolton W	W 2-0	1-0	5	Mendonca 2	7728
29		17	H	Swansea C	W 3-2	1-1	5	Williamson (pen), Mendonca, Heard	5062
30		24	A	Shrewsbury T	D 1-1	1-0	6	Goodwin	3282
31	Mar	3	H	Brentford	W 2-1	1-0	5	Williamson, Goater	5640
32		6	A	Cardiff C	L 0-2	0-1	—		2888
33		10	H	Bury	L 1-3	1-1	6	Goodwin	5425
34		17	A	Birmingham C	L 1-4	0-1	7	Mendonca	6985
35		20	H	Fulham	W 2-1	0-1	—	Mendonca 2	4511
36		24	A	Leyton Orient	D 1-1	1-1	7	Heard	3359
37		31	H	Crewe Alex	L 1-3	1-1	7	Williamson (pen)	5613
38	Apr	3	H	Bristol C	L 1-2	1-0	—	Buckley	5274
39		7	A	Blackpool	W 2-1	0-0	6	Cash, Mendonca	3505
40		14	A	Bristol R	L 0-2	0-0	8		6794
41		16	H	Mansfield T	D 0-0	0-0	8		5096
42		21	H	Huddersfield T	L 1-2	1-0	9	Dempsey	4963
43		24	H	Reading	D 1-1	1-0	—	Mendonca	3719
44		28	A	Chester C	L 0-2	0-2	9		3827
45	May	1	A	Walsall	D 1-1	0-1	—	Dempsey	5697
46		5	H	Northampton T	W 2-0	0-0	9	Evans, Mendonca	3420

Final League Position: 9

GOALSCORERS

League (71): Williamson 19 (6 pens), Mendonca 14, Buckley 7, Goodwin 6, Evans 4, Barnsley 3, Dempsey 3, Heard 3, Goater 2, Hazel 2, Johnson 2, Cash 1, Pepper 1, Robinson 1, Scott 1, own goals 2.
Littlewoods Cup (3): Williamson 2 (1 pen), Mendonca 1.
FA Cup (2): Evans 1, Hazel 1.

O'Hanlon	Russell	Robinson	Grealish	Barnsley	Scott	Buckley	Dempsey	Williamson	Haycock	Hazel	Mendonca	Goodwin	Johnson	Heard	Thompson	Pepper	Ainscow	Evans	Goater	Mercer	Pickering	Cash	Ford	Richardson	Match No.
1	2	3	4	5	6	7	8	9	10*	11	12														1
1	2	3	4*	5	6†	7	8	9		11	10	12	14												2
1	2	3	4*	5	6	7†	8	9		11	10	12	14												3
1	2	6	3			7	8	9	12	11	10*	4	5												4
1	2	12	6			7*	8	9	10†	11		4	5	3	14										5
1	2	3	4*	6	10	7†	8	9					5		11	12	14								6
1	2	3	4	6	11	7	8	9			12	10*	5												7
1	2	3	4*	6	8	7		9			11†	10	12	5	14										8
1	2	3	4	6	11	7		9			10	8	5												9
1	2	3	4	6	11			9				8	5	10	7										10
1	2	3	4	6	11	7*		9			10	8	5	12											11
1	2	3	4	6	11	7		9			10*	8	5	12											12
1	2	3	4*	6	11	7		9			14	10†	8	5	12										13
1	2	3†	4	6	11			9			14	10*	8	5	7	12									14
1			4	2	3	7		9			11	10*	8	5	6	12									15
1			4	2	3	7		9			11		8	5	6	10*	12								16
1		3	4†	2	6	7		9			11	8	5	14		10*	12								17
1		3	4	2	6	7		9			11		5			8	10								18
1		3	4	2*	6	7		9			11†	10	8	5	14	12									19
1	2	3	4†	14	6	7		9				10*	8	5	11	12									20
1		3	4*	2	6	7		9			11	10	8	5		12									21
	5	3	4	2	6	7*		9			11	8				12					10	1			22
	5	3	4	2†	6			9			11	8	14			7*					10	12	1		23
1		3	14	2	6			9			11	12	8	5	7†	4					10*				24
1	2	3	4	14	6	7		9*			12	8	5	11†							10				25
1	2	3			6	7		9			12	8	5	11*		4					10				26
1	2	3	4†	14	6	7		9			11*	8	5								10	12			27
1	2	3	4		6	7*		9			12	10	8	5		11									28
1	2	3	4*			7		9			12	10	8	5		11									29
1	2	3	4		6	7		9			10*	8	5			11		12							30
1	2	3	4	12	6*	7		9			11	8	5					10							31
1		3	4		6	7		9			11*	8	5	12				10	2						32
1	14	3	4		6	7		9				8	5	11†		12	10*		2						33
1	2	3			6	7†	8	9			11*	10		5				4				12	14		34
1	2	3				7	8	9			10	11	5	6				4							35
1	2	3				7	8	9			10		5	6				4			11				36
1	2	3				7	8	9			14	10*	4	5	6			12			11†				37
1		3		2		7	8	9			12	10†	4	5	6*	14					11				38
1					6	7	8					10	4	5		11		9			2	3			39
		3			6	7	8*					10	4	5		11	12	9			2		1		40
1					6	8					7	12		11	9*	4	5	10			2	3			41
1		6	4	12		11	8	9				10	7*	5							2	3			42
1		6	4*12			11	8†	9			14	10		5	7						2	3			43
1		6		2		11	8	9*			14	10	4	5	7†	12						3			44
1		6		2		8					11	10	4	5		12		9				7*	3		45
1		6		2		8					11	10	5	4		12		9				7*	3		46
43	28	43	31 +1s	31 +2s	28 +6s	40	22	41	2	22 +1s	30 +1s	35 +1s	40 +11s	13 +2s	3 +3s	15 +3s	— +1s	12 +8s	5 +4s	2 +1s	9 +8s	8 +7s	1	2 +1s	

Littlewoods Cup First Round Sheffield U (a) 1-1
                              (h) 1-0
                 Second Round Norwich C (a) 1-1
                              (h) 0-2
FA Cup First Round Bury (h) 0-0
                    (a) 2-1
        Second Round Walsall (a) 0-1

ROTHERHAM UNITED

Player and Position	Ht	Wt	Birth Date	Place	Source	Clubs	League App	Gls
Goalkeepers								
Stuart Ford	5 11	11 13	20 7 71	Sheffield	Trainee	Rotherham U	1	—
Billy Mercer	6 1	11 00	22 5 69	Liverpool	Trainee	Liverpool	—	—
						Rotherham U	2	—
Kelham O'Hanlon	6 1	13 03	16 5 62	Saltburn	Apprentice	Middlesbrough	87	—
						Rotherham U	215	—
Defenders								
Andy Barnsley	6 0	11 11	9 6 62	Sheffield	Denaby U	Rotherham U	28	—
						Sheffield U	77	1
						Rotherham U	64	3
Pat Heard*	5 9	11 05	17 3 60	Hull	Apprentice	Everton	11	—
						Aston Villa	24	2
						Sheffield W	25	3
						Newcastle U	34	2
						Middlesbrough	25	2
						Hull C	80	5
						Rotherham U	44	7
Nigel Johnson	6 2	12 08	23 6 64	Rotherham	Apprentice	Rotherham U	54	1
						Nottingham F (loan)	—	—
						Rotherham U	35	—
						Manchester C	4	—
						Rotherham U	92	4
Ally Pickering	5 9	10 08	22 6 67	Manchester	Buxton	Rotherham U	10	—
Neil Richardson	5 10	10 08	3 6 68	Sunderland		Rotherham U	2	—
Ronnie Robinson	5 9	11 00	22 10 66	Sunderland	Vaux Breweries	Ipswich T	—	—
						Leeds U	27	—
						Doncaster R	78	5
						WBA	1	—
						Rotherham U	43	1
Billy Russell	5 10	11 04	14 9 59	Glasgow	Apprentice	Everton	—	—
						Celtic	—	—
						Doncaster R	244	15
						Scunthorpe U	117	7
						Rotherham U	73	2
Martin Scott	5 8	9 10	7 1 68	Sheffield	Apprentice	Rotherham U	81	2
						Nottingham F (loan)	—	—
Midfield								
Mark Dempsey	5 8	10 04	14 1 64	Manchester	Apprentice	Manchester U	1	—
						Swindon T (loan)	5	—
						Sheffield U	63	9
						Chesterfield (loan)	3	—
						Rotherham U	49	4
Shaun Goodwin	5 7	8 10	14 6 69	Rotherham	Trainee	Rotherham U	82	10
Tony Grealish*	5 7	11 08	21 9 56	Paddington	Apprentice	Orient	171	10
						Luton T	78	2
						Brighton & HA	100	6
						WBA	65	5
						Manchester C	11	—
						Rotherham U	110	6
Nigel Pepper	5 10	10 03	25 4 68	Rotherham	Apprentice	Rotherham U	45	1
Simon Thompson	5 8	10 08	27 2 70	Sheffield	Trainee	Rotherham U	12	—
Forwards								
Andy Ainscow‡	5 10	10 11	1 10 68	Orrell	Trainee	Wigan Ath	22	4
						Rotherham U	1	—
John Buckley	5 9	10 07	10 5 62	Glasgow	Queen's Park	Partick Th	45	5
						Doncaster R	84	11
						Leeds U	10	1
						Leicester C (loan)	5	—
						Doncaster R (loan)	6	—
						Rotherham U	102	12

ROTHERHAM UNITED

Foundation: This club traces its history back to the formation of Thornhill United in 1878 (reformed 1884). They changed their name to Rotherham County in 1905. Confusion exists because of the existence of the Rotherham Town club (founded c. 1885) and in the Football League as early as 1893 but this club was not the one previously mentioned. The Town amalgamated with Rotherham County to form Rotherham United in 1925.

First Football League game: 2 September, 1893, Division 2, Rotherham T v Lincoln C (a) D 1-1 – McKay; Thickett, Watson; Barr, Brown, Broadhead; Longden, Cutts, Leatherbarrow, McCormick, Pickering. 1 o.g. 30 August, 1919, Division 2, Rotherham C v Nottingham F (h) W 2-0 – Branston; Alton, Baines; Bailey, Coe, Stanton; Lee (1), Cawley (1), Glennon, Lees, Lamb.

Managers (and Secretary-managers)
Billy Heald 1925–29 (secretary only for long spell), Stanley Davies 1929–30, Billy Heald 1930–33, Reg Freeman 1934–52, Andy Smailes 1952–58, Tom Johnston 1958–62, Danny Williams 1962–65, Jack Mansell 1965–67, Tommy Docherty 1967–68, Jimmy McAnearney 1968–73, Jimmy McGuigan 1973–79, Ian Porterfield 1979–81, Emlyn Hughes 1981–83, George Kerr 1983–85, Norman Hunter 1985–87, Dave Cusack 1987–88, Billy McEwan 1988– .

Player and Position	Ht	Wt	Birth Date	Place	Source	Clubs	League App	Gls
Stewart Evans	6 4	11 05	15 11 60	Maltby	Apprentice	Rotherham U	—	—
					Gainsborough T	Sheffield U	—	—
						Wimbledon	175	50
						WBA	14	1
						Plymouth Arg	45	10
						Rotherham U	45	10
Shaun Goater	6 2	12 10	25 2 70	Bermuda		Manchester U	—	—
						Rotherham U	12	2
Paul Haycock	6 1	12 00	8 7 62	Sheffield	Burton Alb	Rotherham U	97	22
Desmond Hazel	5 10	10 04	15 7 67	Bradford	Apprentice	Sheffield W	6	—
						Grimsby T (loan)	9	2
						Rotherham U	75	8
Clive Mendonca	5 10	11 07	9 9 68	Tullington	Apprentice	Sheffield U	13	4
						Doncaster R (loan)	2	—
						Rotherham U	50	17
Bobby Williamson	5 10	11 00	13 8 61	Glasgow	Auchengill	Clydebank	70	28
						Rangers	41	12
						WBA	53	11
						Rotherham U	84	46

Trainees
Brooks, Christopher; Cox, Darren J; Foster, Fraser P; Hodges, Mark; Howard, Jonathan; Jarvis, Craig E; Kinnair, Michael R; Melville, Philip T; Saunders, Anthony; Saunders, Paul; Seddons, Darren M; Smith, Lee; Staniforth, Andrew J; Taylor, Andrew; Tompkins, David A; Wilson, Mark; Wood, Lee.

Associated Schoolboys
Batty, Neil R; Bennett, Paul S; Breckin, Ian; Bridgewater, Nicholas J; Bunting, James R.S; Chappell, Christopher A; Charlton, Thomas J; Day, Paul E; Dolby, Christopher J; Glossop, Alistair J; Gray, Andrew R; Hardwick, Matthew; Hinshelwood, Shane; Hurst, Paul; Jarvis, Steven M: Kirk; Darren; McCormick, Andrew J; Marples, Simon J; Parkes, Nicholas S; Partington, Dean J; Pinder, Scott K; Williams, Matthew; Wroe, David A.

Associated Schoolboys who have accepted the club's offer of a Traineeship/Contract
Anson, Simon D; Clark, Matthew; Lawler, Shane; Tesh, John A.

SCAREOROUGH 1989–90 *Back row (left to right):* Roy McHale (Manager), Barry Richardson, Michael Clarke, Paul Robson, Adrian Meyer, Steve Richards, Lee Hirst, Paul Robinson, George Oghani, Chris Short, Ian Ironside, Phil Chambers (Youth Team Coach).

Front row: Steve Saunders, Martin Butler, Martin Russell, Alan Kamara, John Macdonald, Mick Matthews, Phil Wilson, Mark Ash, Lee Slingsby.

Division 4 **SCARBOROUGH**

The Athletic Ground, Seamer Road, Scarborough YO12 4HF.
Telephone 0723-375094.

Ground capacity: 7600.

Record Attendance: 11,130 v Luton T, FA Cup 3rd rd, 8 January 1938. Football League: 7314 v Wolverhampton W, Division 4, 15 August, 1987.

Record receipts: £19,754 v Wolverhampton W, Division 4, 15 August, 1987.

Pitch measurements: 120yd × 75yd.

President: John Birley.

Chairman: G. Richmond.

Directors: M. L. Jones FCA, J. W. Fawcett, A. D. Mollon, M. Bramham, J. Lawrence, A. Jenkinson, J. R. Birley (President and Chief Executive).

Manager: Ray McHale. *Assistant Manager:*

Secretary: E. V. Hall.

Assistant Secretary: Miss S. B. Wright.

Commercial Manager: *Physio:* K. Warner.

Year Formed: 1879. *Turned Professional:* 1926. *Ltd Co.:* 1933.

Club Nickname: 'The Boro'.

Previous Grounds: 1879–87, Scarborough Cricket Ground; 1887–98, Recreation Ground; 1898– Athletic Ground.

Record League Victory: 4-0 v Bolton W, Division 4, 29 August 1987 – Blackwell; McJannet, Thompson, Bennyworth (Walker), Richards (1) (Cook), Kendall, Hamill (1), Moss, McHale, Mell (1), Graham. (log). 4-0 v Newport C, Division 4, 12 April 1988 – Ironside; McJannet, Thompson, Kamara, Richards (1), Short (1), Adams (Cook 1), Brook, Outhart (1), Russell, Graham.

Record Cup Victory: 6-0 v Rhyl Ath, FA Cup, 1st rd, 29 November 1930 – Turner; Severn, Belton; Maskell, Robinson, Wallis; Small (1), Rand (2), Palfreman (2), Hill A. D. (1), Mickman.

Record Defeat: 1-16 v Southbank, Northern League, 15 November, 1919.

Most League Points (3 for a win): 77, Division 4, 1988–89.

Most League Goals: 67, Division 4, 1988–89

Highest League Scorer in Season: Gary Brook, 12, Division 4, 1988–89.

Most League Goals in Total Aggregate: Paul Dobson, 20, 1989–90.

Most Capped Player: None.

Most League Appearances: Steve Richards, 119, 1987–90.

Record Transfer Fee Received: £175,000 from Middlesbrough for Martin Russell, March 1990.

Record Transfer Fee Paid: £102,000 to Leicester C for Martin Russell, March 1989.

Football League Record: Promoted to Division 4 1987.

Honours: Football League: Division 4 best season: 5th, 1988–89. *FA Cup:* best seasons: 3rd rd, 1931, 1938, 1976, 1978. *Football League Cup:* best season: 3rd rd 1989.

Colours: All red. **Change colours:** All white.

SCARBOROUGH 1989–90 LEAGUE RECORD

Match No.	Date		Venue	Opponents	Result		H/T Score	Lg. Pos.	Goalscorers	Atten-dance
1	Aug	19	H	Wrexham	W	2-1	1-1	—	Dobson, Richards	2700
2		26	A	Maidstone U	L	1-4	0-3	12	Dobson	3372
3	Sept	2	H	Cambridge U	D	1-1	1-1	13	Russell	2522
4		9	A	Scunthorpe U	W	1-0	1-0	12	Russell (pen)	3330
5		16	H	Doncaster R	L	1-2	0-0	14	Norris	2750
6		23	A	Colchester U	D	0-0	0-0	14		2420
7		27	H	Halifax T	L	2-3	0-1	—	Norris, Short	3147
8		30	A	Stockport Co	L	2-3	1-3	18	Russell, Olsson	3086
9	Oct	7	A	Southend U	L	0-1	0-0	19		3432
10		14	H	Grimsby T	W	3-1	1-0	16	Kamara, Norris 2	2828
11		18	A	Hereford U	L	1-3	0-0	—	Brook	2222
12		21	H	Carlisle U	W	2-1	1-1	17	Brook, Robinson	2592
13		28	A	Rochdale	L	0-1	0-0	19		1402
14	Nov	1	H	Chesterfield	L	2-3	0-1	—	Rogers (og), Brook	2341
15		4	A	Gillingham	L	0-2	0-1	20		3436
16		11	H	Exeter C	L	1-2	1-0	20	Dobson	2124
17		24	H	York C	L	1-3	1-2	—	Dobson	3602
18	Dec	2	A	Torquay U	L	2-3	2-0	22	Russell, Spink	1858
19		9	H	Stockport Co	W	2-0	1-0	—	Spink, Dobson	1780
20		26	A	Hartlepool U	L	1-4	1-2	21	MacDonald	3698
21		30	A	Peterborough U	W	2-1	2-0	21	Wilson, Clarke	4153
22	Jan	1	H	Lincoln C	W	2-0	2-0	21	Fyfe, Dobson	2441
23		6	H	Aldershot	W	1-0	0-0	—	Russell	1623
24		9	A	Burnley	L	0-3	0-1	—		7329
25		13	H	Maidstone U	L	0-1	0-1	20		1961
26		20	A	Wrexham	W	2-0	0-0	19	Richards, Russell	1756
27		27	H	Scunthorpe U	D	0-0	0-0	19		2329
28	Feb	3	H	Colchester U	D	2-2	0-0	19	Dobson, Russell (pen)	1786
29		10	A	Doncaster R	D	1-1	0-1	19	Matthews	2899
30		17	H	Torquay U	D	0-0	0-0	20		1725
31		24	H	York C	W	2-1	0-1	19	Dobson 2	3551
32	Mar	3	H	Burnley	W	4-2	3-0	15	Meyer, MacDonald, Dobson, Oghani	2961
33		10	A	Halifax T	W	2-1	2-1	16	Saunders, Richards	1490
34		17	H	Southend U	D	1-1	0-0	16	Richards	2179
35		20	A	Grimsby T	L	0-3	0-3	—		7690
36		24	H	Hereford U	L	0-1	0-1	18		1873
37		31	A	Carlisle U	L	1-3	0-0	20	Matthews	4304
38	Apr	2	A	Cambridge U	L	2-5	0-3	—	Dobson, Oghani (pen)	3001
39		7	H	Rochdale	W	2-1	0-1	19	MacDonald, Matthews	1799
40		10	A	Chesterfield	D	2-2	2-2	—	MacDonald, Robinson	4916
41		14	A	Lincoln C	D	0-0	0-0	19		3310
42		16	H	Hartlepool U	W	4-1	2-0	18	MacDonald, Oghani (pen), Dobson, Meyer	2762
43		21	A	Aldershot	D	1-1	0-0	18	Dobson	1482
44		25	H	Peterborough U	W	2-1	1-0	—	Oghani, Robinson	1838
45		28	A	Exeter C	L	2-3	1-1	16	Dobson 2	6850
46	May	5	H	Gillingham	L	0-1	0-0	18		1807

Final League Position: 18

GOALSCORERS

League (60): Dobson 15, Russell 7 (2 pens), MacDonald 5, Norris 4, Oghani 4 (2 pens), Richards 4, Brook 3, Matthews 3, Robinson 3, Meyer 2, Spink 2, Clarke 1, Fyfe 1, Kamara 1, Olsson 1, Saunders 1, Short 1, Wilson 1, own goal 1.
Littlewoods Cup (7): Brook 1, Dobson 1, Graham 1, Richards 1, Robinson 1, Russell 1 (pen), own goal 1.
FA Cup (0).

Blackwell	Kamara	Clarke	Short	Richards	Bennyworth	Saunders	Graham	Dobson	Brook	Russell	Norris	Olsson	Robinson	Ironside	Law	MacDonald	Spink	Butler	Ash	Matthews	Richardson	Wilson	Fyfe	Meyer	Dixon	Oghani	Slingsby	Hirst	Holmes	Match No.
1	2	3	4	5	6	7	8	9	10	11																				1
1	2	3	4	5	6†	7*	8	9	10	11	12		14																	2
1	2	3	4†	5	6	7*	8	9	10	11	12		14																	3
1	2	3	4	5	6	7†	8	9*	10	11	12		14																	4
1	2	3	4	5	6	7	8	9*	10†	11	12		14																	5
1	2	3	4	5	6	12	8		14	11	9	7*	10†																	6
1	2	3	4	5†	6*	7	8	12	11	9	14		10																	7
1	2	3†	4	5	6	7	8*	12	11	9	14		10																	8
	2	14	4	5	6	7	8	12	11	9*	3†		10	1																9
	2	12	4*	5	6	7	8		11	9	3		10	1																10
	2	14	4	5	6	7	8†	12	11	9	3		10*	1																11
	2	3	4	5	6	8	12	7	11	9*	14		10†	1																12
	2	3		5	6	7	8	9	10	11	4*		12	1																13
	2	3		5	6	7*	8	9	10	12	4		11	1																14
	2	3	4	5		7	8	9	10	11*	6			1																15
	3	12	2	5	6	7*	8	9†	10	11	14			1	4															16
	2	3		5			8	9		11					4	1	6	7	10											17
	2	3†	4	5			8*	9		11	14					1	6	7	10	12										18
		3		5			8*	9		11	12					1	6	7	10	2	4									19
		3	14	5			8	9		11	10*					1	6	7	12	2†	4									20
		3	11†	2	5		12	14		10						1				6	8	4		7*		9				21
		3		2	5		14	12	8	10						1				6	11	4		7†		9*				22
		3		2	5		12	8†		10						1				6	11	14	4	7*		9				23
		3		2†	5		12	8*		10						1				6	11	14	4	7		9				24
		3	5	2			12		8	10						1				6	11		4	7*		9				25
		3	10	2	5					8						1				6	11		4	7		9				26
		10		2	5		14		12	8						1				6	11	9*	3	4		7†				27
		3	9	2	5			10		8						1					11	4		6		7				28
		3	9	2	5			10		8						1					11	4		6		7				29
		3		2	5		14	10		9						1				11†	4	8		6		7*12				30
		3		2	5		12	10		9						1				11	4	8*		6		7				31
		3		2	5		8*	10†		9						1				11	14	4	12	6		7				32
		3		2	5		7	10		8						1				11		4		6		9				33
		3	7	2	5		8*	10		9						1				11	12	4		6						34
		3	7	2	5		12	10		9						1				11	8	4		6*						35
		3		2	5†		7	10		9						1				11	12	8	4	6					14*	36
	3	14	2*				9	10			1					1				11	12	8	4	6		7		5†		37
	3*14		2				7†	10			1					1				11	12	8	4	6		9		5		38
6		3					9*	10		12						1				11		2	4	1	8	7		5		39
6		3	2					9								1				11	4	1	8	10		7		5		40
		3	10	2				12		9						1				11	4*	1	8	6		7		5		41
		3	9	2				4	10	11						1					8		6			7		5		42
		3	9	2				4	10	11										1	8		6			7		5		43
		3	9	2					10*	12						11†				4	1	8		6		7		5	14	44
		3	9	2				12†	10	14						11				4*	1	8		6		7		5		45
		3	9	2					10	12						11				1	8		6			7		5	4*	46
8	45	30	40	35	15	23	20	34	10	31	8	9	13	14	12	29	3	1	7	21	24	23	6	18	3	13	—	10	1	
					+	+		+	+	+	+		+	+			+	+			+	+				+		+	+	
					6s	1s		9s	4s	3s	5s		6s	7s7s			5s	4s			1s					1s	1s		1s	

Morris — Match No. 15(12).

Littlewoods Cup	First Round	Scunthorpe U (h)	2-0
		(a)	1-1
	Second Round	Chelsea (a)	1-1
		(h)	3-2
	Third Round	Oldham Ath (a)	0-7
FA Cup	First Round	Whitley Bay (h)	0-1

SCARBOROUGH

Player and Position	Ht	Wt	Birth Date	Birth Place	Source	Clubs	League App	Gls
Goalkeepers								
Ian Ironside	6 2	13 00	8 3 64	Sheffield	Apprentice	Barnsley	—	—
					N Ferriby U	Scarborough	48	—
Barry Richardson	6 0	12 00	5 8 69	Willington Key	Trainee	Sunderland	—	—
						Scunthorpe U	—	—
						Scarborough	24	—
Defenders								
Mark Ash	5 9	11 04	22 1 68	Sheffield	Apprentice	Rotherham U	20	—
						Scarborough	11	—
Lee Hirst	6 2	12 07	26 1 69	Sheffield		Scarborough	10	—
David Holmes§			22 11 72	Derby	Trainee	Scarborough	2	—
Alan Kamara	5 9	10 12	15 7 58	Sheffield	Kiveton Park	York C	10	—
						Darlington	134	1
					Burton Alb	Scarborough	118	2
Adrian Meyer	6 0	14 00	22 9 70	Bristol	Trainee	Scarborough	18	2
Darren Mountain†	5 9	10 09	16 8 70	Sheffield	Trainee	Scunthorpe U	—	—
						Scarborough	—	—
Steve Richards	6 0	12 00	24 10 61	Dundee	Apprentice	Hull C	58	2
					Gainsborough T	York C	7	—
						Lincoln C	21	—
						Cambridge U	4	2
						Scarborough	119	10
Chris Short	5 10	12 02	9 5 70	Munster		Scarborough	43	1
Midfield								
John MacDonald	5 9	10 08	15 4 61	Glasgow	Clydebank	Rangers	160	44
						Charlton Ath	2	—
						Barnsley	94	20
						Scarborough	29	5
Mike Matthews	5 8	11 03	25 9 60	Hull	Apprentice	Wolverhampton W	76	7
						Scunthorpe U	58	5
						Halifax T	99	8
						Scarborough	7	1
						Stockport Co	35	3
						Scarborough	21	3
Steve Saunders	5 7	10 06	21 9 64	Warrington	Apprentice	Bolton W	3	—
						Crewe Alex	22	1
						Preston NE	—	—
						Grimsby T	76	13
						Scarborough	32	1
Lee Slingsby	5 7	11 04	27 11 70	Doncaster	Doncaster R§	Scarborough	1	—
Phil Wilson‡	5 6	11 13	16 10 60	Hemsworth	Apprentice	Bolton W	39	4
						Huddersfield T	233	16
						York C	46	2
					Macclesfield	Scarborough	24	1
Forwards								
Martin Butler‡	5 8	10 09	3 3 66	Hull		York C	65	9
						Aldershot (loan)	2	1
						Exeter C (loan)	4	1
						Carlisle U (loan)	1	—
						Scunthorpe U	2	—
						Scarborough	6	—
`Michael Clarke	5 11	11 05	22 12 67	Birmingham		Barnsley	40	3
						Scarborough	36	1
Paul Dobson	5 9	10 06	17 12 62	Hartlepool	Amateur	Newcastle U	—	—
						Hartlepool U	31	8
					Horden	Hartlepool U	80	24
						Torquay U	77	38
						Doncaster R	24	10
						Scarborough	55	20

SCARBOROUGH

Foundation: Scarborough came into being as early as 1879 when they were formed by members of the town's cricket club and went under the name of Scarborough Cricketers' FC with home games played on the North Marine Road Cricket Ground.

First Football League game: 15 August, 1987, Division 4, v Wolverhampton W (h) D 2-2 – Blackwell; McJannet, Thompson, Bennyworth, Richards, Kendall, Hamill, Moss, McHale (1), Mell (1), Graham.

Managers (and Secretary-managers)
B. Chapman 1945–47*, George Hall 1946–47, Harold Taylor 1947–48, Frank Taylor 1948–50, A. C. Bell (Director & Hon. TM) 1950–53, Reg Halton 1953–54, Charles Robson (Hon. TM) 1954–57, George Higgins 1957–58, Andy Smailes 1959–61, Eddie Brown 1961–64, Albert Franks 1964–65, Stuart Myers 1965–66, Graham Shaw 1968–69, Colin Appleton 1969–73, Ken Houghton 1974–75, Colin Appleton 1975–81, Jimmy McAnearney 1981–82, John Cottam 1982–84, Harry Dunn 1984–86, Neil Warnock 1986–88, Colin Morris 1989, Ray McHale 1989– .

Player and Position	Ht	Wt	Birth Date	Place	Source	Clubs	League App	Gls
Colin Morris‡	5 7	10 06	22 8 53	Blyth	Apprentice	Burnley	10	—
						Southend U	133	25
						Blackpool	87	26
						Sheffield U	240	68
						Scarborough	24	3
Mike Norbury‡			22 1 69	Kemsworth	Ossett	Scarborough	—	—
George Oghani	5 11	12 03	2 9 60	Manchester	Hyde U	Bolton W	99	27
						Wrexham (loan)	7	—
						Burnley	74	21
						Stockport Co	8	2
						Hereford U	8	2
						Scarborough	14	4

Trainees
Breden, Gary; Gee, Michael P; Glenister, Andrew A; Heblich, Kieron; Hewitt, Stephen; Hird, Paul R; Holmes, David J; McCrorie, Craig D; Pollington, Miguel C; Rocca, Jon C; Silk, Matthew; Slade, Paul A; Suddes, Lee; Taylor, Stephen P; Williams, David J.

**Non-Contract
Mountain, Darren.

Associated Schoolboys
Brooks, Duncan S; Hill, Philip; Shipton, Jason; Ward, Richard; Williamson, David M.

Associated Schoolboys who have accepted the club's offer of a Traineeship/Contract
Pratt, Jeremy; Swales, Stephen C; Tomlinson, Sean; Wignall, Adrian.

**Non-Contract Players who are retained must be re-signed before they are eligible to play in League matches.

SCUNTHORPE UNITED 1989–90 *Back row (left to right):* William Green (Assistant Manager), Peter Brooks, Wayne Sykes, Matthew Barbrook, Paul Smalley, Andy Stevenson, Peter Litchfield, Paul Musselwhite, Steve Thatcher, Paul Nicol, Richard Hall, Perry Cotton, Andy Flounders, Richard Money, Phil McLoughlin (Physiotherapist).
Centre row: Paul Longden, David Cowling, Gordon Tucker, Steve Lister, Michael Buxton (Manager), Gary Marshall, Kevin Taylor, Andrew Hodkinson, Tony Daws.
Front row: Lee McGlinchey, Graham Alexander, Steve McCormick, Andrew Godfrey, Allan Evans, Paul Gibbs, Darren Lelliott, Darren Spooner, Sean Creaton, Neil Cox.

Division 4 **SCUNTHORPE UNITED**

Glanford Park, Scunthorpe, South Humberside. Telephone Scunthorpe (0724) 848077.

Ground capacity: 10,300.

Record attendance: Old Showground: 23,935 v Portsmouth, FA Cup 4th rd, 30 Jan, 1954. Glanford Park: 8775 v Rotherham U, Division 4, 1 May 1989.

Record receipts: £30,857 v Grimsby T, Division 4, 26 December, 1989.

Pitch measurements: 111yd × 73yd.

President: Sir Reginald Sheffield, Bt.

Vice-Presidents: I. T. Botham, G. Johnson.

Chairman: G. Pearson. *Vice-Chairman:* *Deputy Chairman:* T. E. Belton.

Directors: R. Garton, G. Pearson, D. M. Fletton, J. B. Borrill.

Manager: Mick Buxton. *Asst. Manager:* W. Green. *Youth Development Officer:* D. Moore.

Physio: Phil McLoughlin.

Secretary: A. D. Rowing. *Commercial Manager:* A. D. Rowing.

*Year Formed:*1899. *Turned Professional:* 1912. *Ltd Co.:* 1912.

Club Nickname: 'The Iron'.

Previous Names: Amalgamated with Brumby Hall: North Lindsey United to become Scunthorpe & Lindsey United, 1910; dropped '& Lindsey' in 1958.

Record League Victory: 8-1 v Luton T, Division 3, 24 April 1965 – Sidebottom; Horstead, Hemstead; Smith, Neale, Lindsey; Bramley (1), Scott, Thomas (5), Mahy (1), Wilson (1).

Record Cup Victory: 9-0 v Boston U, FA Cup, 1st rd, 21 November 1953 – Malan; Hubbard, Brownsword; Sharpe, White, Bushby; Mosby (1), Haigh (3), Whitfield (2), Gregory (1), Mervyn Jones (2).

Record Defeat: 0-8 v Carlisle U, Division 3(N), 25 December, 1952.

Most League Points (2 for a win): 66, Division 3(N), 1957, 1957–58.

Most League Points (3 for a win): 83, Division 4, 1982–83.

Most League Goals: 88, Division 3(N), 1957–58.

Highest League Scorer in Season: Barrie Thomas, 31, Division 2, 1961–62.

Most League Goals in Total Aggregate: Steve Cammack, 110, 1979–81, 1981–86.

Most Capped Player: None.

Most League Appearances: Jack Brownsword, 595, 1950–65.

Record Transfer Fee Received: £90,000 from Ipswich T for Dave Hill, July 1988.

Record Transfer Fee Paid: £50,000 to Carlisle U for Gary Marshall, July 1989.

Football League Record: 1950 Elected to Division 3(N); 1958–64 Division 2; 1964–68 Division 3; 1968–72 Division 4; 1972–73 Division 3; 1973–83 Division 3; 1983–84 Division 3; 1984– Division 4.

Honours: Football League: Division 2 best season: 4th, 1961–62; Division 3(N) – Champions 1957–58. *FA Cup:* best season; 5th rd. 1957–58, 1969–70. *Football League Cup:* never past 3rd rd.

Colours: Claret and blue striped shirts, blue shorts claret band, blue stockings claret band.
Change colours: White shirts, claret and blue trim, claret shorts blue band, white stockings claret band.

SCUNTHORPE UNITED 1989–90 LEAGUE RECORD

Match No.	Date		Venue	Opponents	Result		H/T Score	Lg. Pos.	Goalscorers	Atten-dance
1	Aug	19	A	Lincoln C	L	0-1	0-0	—		4504
2		26	H	Rochdale	L	0-1	0-1	23		2808
3	Sept	2	A	Gillingham	W	3-0	0-0	14	Taylor (pen), Flounders 2	3467
4		9	H	Scarborough U	L	0-1	0-1	17		3330
5		16	A	Peterborough U	D	1-1	1-0	18	Taylor	4350
6		23	H	Exeter C	W	5-4	1-2	15	Lillis 2, Hamilton 2, Taylor	2935
7		26	H	Torquay U	W	2-0	2-0	—	Flounders, Lillis (pen)	3242
8		30	A	Aldershot	L	2-4	0-2	14	Lillis, Tucker	1892
9	Oct	7	A	Hartlepool U	L	2-3	2-2	16	Lillis, Daws	1823
10		14	H	Maidstone U	W	1-0	0-0	12	Lister (pen)	3165
11		17	A	Carlisle U	W	1-0	0-0	—	Lillis	4793
12		21	H	Colchester U	W	4-0	2-0	9	Stevenson, Daws, Hamilton, Taylor	3254
13		28	A	Cambridge U	L	3-5	1-4	9	Marshall, Daws, Hamilton	2395
14		31	H	York C	D	1-1	1-1	—	Flounders	3800
15	Nov	4	A	Doncaster R	W	2-1	1-0	10	Daws, Flounders	3374
16		11	H	Burnley	W	3-0	3-0	7	Marshall, Ward (pen), Hamilton	4745
17		25	A	Stockport Co	L	2-4	1-1	10	Ward, Flounders	3259
18	Dec	2	H	Southend U	D	1-1	0-1	10	Ward	3714
19		16	A	Hereford U	W	2-1	2-0	9	Lillis, Nicol	1924
20		26	H	Grimsby T	D	2-2	2-0	9	Daws, Marshall	8384
21		30	H	Chesterfield	L	0-1	0-0	10		5006
22	Jan	1	A	Wrexham	D	0-0	0-0	11		1887
23		6	H	Halifax T	D	1-1	1-1	—	Taylor	3051
24		13	A	Rochdale	L	0-3	0-0	12		1781
25		20	H	Lincoln C	D	1-1	0-0	13	Lillis	3830
26		27	A	Scarborough	D	0-0	0-0	13		2329
27	Feb	10	H	Peterborough U	D	0-0	0-0	15		3188
28		· 13	H	Gillingham	D	0-0	0-0	—		2226
29		16	A	Southend U	D	0-0	0-0	—		3154
30		24	H	Stockport Co	W	5-0	3-0	11	Lillis 2, Daws 2, Ward	3280
31	Mar	3	A	Halifax T	W	1-0	0-0	12	Daws	1793
32		6	H	Aldershot	W	3-2	1-0	—	Lillis, Hamilton, Flounders	3202
33		10	A	Torquay U	W	3-0	0-0	9	Daws, Flounders, Lillis	1935
34		17	A	Hartlepool U	L	0-1	0-0	10		3868
35		21	A	Maidstone U	D	1-1	0-1	—	Flounders	1299
36		24	H	Carlisle U	L	2-3	1-0	10	Flounders, Lillis (pen)	3406
37		28	A	Exeter C	L	0-1	0-0	—		5805
38		31	H	Colchester U	L	0-1	0-1	12		2920
39	Apr	7	H	Cambridge U	D	1-1	0-1	13	Taylor	2486
40		10	A	York C	W	1-0	0-0	—	Taylor	2232
41		14	H	Wrexham	W	3-1	0-1	10	Flounders 2 (1 pen), Taylor	2820
42		17	A	Grimsby T	L	1-2	0-0	—	Flounders	11,894
43		21	H	Hereford U	D	3-3	2-1	12	Flounders 2 (1 pen), Pejic (og)	2247
44		28	A	Burnley	W	1-0	1-0	13	Cotton	3902
45	May	1	A	Chesterfield	D	1-1	1-0	—	Daws	3469
46		5	H	Doncaster R	W	4-1	4-0	11	Flounders 3, Daws	3020

Final League Position: 11

GOALSCORERS

League (69): Flounders 18 (2 pens), Lillis 13 (2 pens), Daws 11, Taylor 8 (1 pen), Hamilton 6, Ward 4 (1 pen), Marshall 3, Cotton 1, Lister 1 (pen), Nicol 1, Stevenson 1, Tucker 1, own goal 1.
Littlewoods Cup (1): Flounders 1.
FA Cup (7): Lillis 3, Taylor 2, Daws 1, Hodkinson 1.

Litchfield	Smalley	Longden	Taylor	Knight	Tucker	Hodkinson	Cowling	Cotton	Flounders	Marshall	Nicol	Money	Butler	Musselwhite	Daws	Hamilton	Stevenson	Lillis	Lister	Ward	Hall	Bramhall	Match No.
1	2	3	4	5	6	7	8*	9	10	11	12												1
1	2	12	4	3	6*		8		10	11	5	7	9										2
	2	3	4		6	7	8		10	11	5			1	9*	12							3
	2	3	4		6	7			10	11	5			1	9	8							4
	2	3	4		6	7			10	11	5		9*	1	8	12							5
	2	3	4		6	7*12			10	11	5			1	8		9						6
	2	3	4		6	7			10	11	5			1	8		9						7
	2*	3	4		6	7†12			10	11	5			1	14	8	9						8
1	2	3	4		6†	7*12		14		11	5				10	8	9						9
1	2	3	4*			7			12	11					10	8	6	9	5				10
1	2	3	4	14		7†			12	11					10*	8	6	9	5				11
1	2	3	4			7				11					10	8	6	9	5				12
1	2	3	4*			7		14		11					10	8	6†	9	5	12			13
1	2	3		5		7			10	11					9	8	6			4			14
1		3			2				10	11	5				9	8	6	7		4			15
1		3			2		9		10	11	5					8	6	7		4			16
1	12	3			2		9		10	11*	5					8	6	7		4			17
1	2	3				8	9*	14	10	11	5				6	7	12			4			18
1	2	3	4			8†		14	12	11	6				9*	10		7		5			19
1	2	3	4				8		12	11	6				9*	10		7			5		20
	2	3	4				8	9		11*	6			1	12	10	5	7					21
	2	3	4			7			10	11	6			1	9	8	5						22
	2	3	4*			7			10	11	6			1	12	8	5	9					23
	2	3	4			7			10	11	6			1	9	8	5						24
	2	3			6*	7	8	14	10†					1	9	11	12			4		5	25
	2	3			6	7	8							1	9	11	10			4		5	26
	2	3			6*	7	8		12					1	9	11	10			4		5	27
	2	3			6	7*	8	9						1	12	11	10			4		5	28
	2	3			6		8*		10					1	9	11	12	7		4		5	29
	2	3			6		8*		10					1	9	11	12	7		4		5	30
	2	3				7	8		10					1	9	11	6			4		5	31
	2	3					8		10		12			1	9*	11	6	7		4		5	32
	2	3			6		8*		10					1	9	11	12	7		4		5	33
	2	3			6		8	14	10	12	5†			1	9	11		7*		4			34
	2	3			6	7	8		10					1	9	11				4		5	35
	2	3			6	7	8	9	10					1		11	12			4*		5	36
	2	3			6		8	9	10					1		11		7		4		5	37
	2	3			6	14	8*	9†	10					1	12	11				4		5	38
	2	3			6			10	12					1	9	11	8	7*		4		5	39
	2	3			6	7		9	10					1		11	8			4		5	40
	2	3	4		6	7		9	10					1		11	8					5	41
	2	3	4		6	7		9	10					1		11	8					5	42
	2	3	4*		6	7		9	10					1	8	11	12					5	43
1	2	3			6	7		9	10						8	11				4		5	44
1	2	3			6	7		9	10						8	11				4		5	45
1	2	3			6	7		9	10						8	11				4		5	46
17	43	45	37	2	14	21	29	14	37	31	17	1	2	29	28	42	19	27	5	24	1	21	
	+	+	+		+		+	+	+	+					+	+	+	+		+		+	
	1s	1s	2s		1s		3s	3s	7s	3s					5s	1s	5s	2s		1s		1s	

Littlewoods Cup — First Round — Scarborough (a) — 0-2
(h) — 1-1

FA Cup — First Round — Matlock (h) — 4-1
Second Round — Burnley (h) — 2-2
(a) — 1-1
(a) — 0-5

SCUNTHORPE UNITED

Player and Position	Ht	Wt	Birth Date	Place	Source	Clubs	League App	Gls
Goalkeepers								
Peter Litchfield	6 1	12 12	27 7 56	Manchester	Droylsden	Preston NE	107	—
						Bradford C	88	—
						Oldham Ath (loan)	3	—
						Scunthorpe U	17	—
Paul Musselwhite	6 2	12 07	22 12 68	Portsmouth	Portsmouth†	Scunthorpe U	70	—
Defenders								
Graham Alexander	5 10	11 00	10 10 71	Coventry	Trainee	Scunthorpe U	—	—
John Bramhall	6 2	13 06	20 11 56	Warrington	Amateur	Tranmere R	170	7
						Bury	167	17
						Chester C (loan)	4	—
						Rochdale	86	13
						Halifax T	62	5
						Scunthorpe U	21	—
Richard Hall	6 1	13 00	14 3 72	Ipswich	Trainee	Scunthorpe U	1	—
Steve Lister	6 1	11 00	18 11 61	Doncaster	Apprentice	Doncaster R	237	30
						Scunthorpe U	156	29
Paul Longden	5 9	11 00	28 9 62	Wakefield	Apprentice	Barnsley	5	—
						Scunthorpe U	261	—
Richard Money‡	5 11	11 07	13 10 55	Lowestoft	Lowestoft T	Scunthorpe U	173	4
						Fulham	106	3
						Liverpool	14	—
						Derby Co (loan)	5	—
						Luton T	44	1
						Portsmouth	17	—
						Scunthorpe U	106	—
Paul Nicol*	6 1	12 00	31 10 67	Scunthorpe		Scunthorpe U	75	2
Paul Smalley	5 11	11 00	17 11 66	Nottingham	Apprentice	Notts Co	118	—
						Scunthorpe U	83	1
Gordon Tucker	5 11	11 12	5 1 68	Manchester	Derby Co	Huddersfield T	35	—
						Scunthorpe U	15	1
Midfield								
David Cowling	5 7	11 04	27 11 58	Doncaster	Apprentice	Mansfield T	—	—
						Huddersfield T	340	43
						Scunthorpe U (loan)	1	—
						Reading	10	1
						Scunthorpe U	71	2
Perry Cotton	5 11	11 12	11 11 65	Chislehurst		Scunthorpe U	18	1
Neil Cox	5 11	12 10	8 10 71	Scunthorpe	Trainee	Scunthorpe U	—	—
Ian Hamilton	5 9	11 03	14 12 67	Stevenage	Apprentice	Southampton	—	—
						Cambridge U	24	1
						Scunthorpe U	70	7
Mark Lillis	6 0	13 06	17 1 60	Manchester	Local	Huddersfield T	206	56
						Manchester C	39	11
						Derby Co	15	1
						Aston Villa	31	4
						Scunthorpe U	29	13
Andy Stevenson	6 0	12 03	29 9 67	Scunthorpe	School	Scunthorpe U	67	1
Kevin Taylor	5 10	11 00	22 1 61	Sheffield	Apprentice	Sheffield W	125	21
						Derby Co	22	2
						Crystal Palace	87	14
						Scunthorpe U	115	21
Paul Ward	5 11	1205	15 9 63	Bedlington	Apprentice	Chelsea	—	—
						Middlesbrough	76	1
						Darlington	124	9
						Leyton Orient	31	1
						Scunthorpe U	25	4

SCUNTHORPE UNITED

Foundation: The year of foundation for Scunthorpe United has often been quoted as 1910, but the club can trace its history back to 1899 when Brumby Hall FC, who played on the Old Showground, consolidated their position by amalgamating with some other clubs and changing their name to Scunthorpe United. The year 1910 was when that club amalgamated with North Lindsey United as Scunthorpe and Lindsey United. The link is Mr. W. T. Lockwood whose chairmanship covers both years.

First Football League game: 19 August, 1950, Division 3(N), v Shrewsbury T (h) D 0-0 – Thompson; Barker, Brownsword; Allen, Taylor, McCormick; Mosby, Payne, Gorin, Rees, Boyes.

Managers (and Secretary-managers)
Harry Allcock 1915–53*, Tom Crilly 1936–37, Bernard Harper 1946–48, Leslie Jones 1950–51, Bill Corkhill 1952–56, Ron Suart 1956–58, Tony McShane 1959, Bill Lambton 1959, Frank Soo 1959–60, Dick Duckworth 1960–64, Fred Goodwin 1964–66, Ron Ashman 1967–73, Ron Bradley 1973–74, Dick Rooks 1974–76, Ron Ashman 1976–81, John Duncan 1981–83, Allan Clarke 1983–84, Frank Barlow 1984–87, Mick Buxton 1987– .

Player and Position	Ht	Wt	Birth Date	Place	Source	Clubs	League App	Gls
Forwards								
Tony Daws	5 9	10 02	10 9 66	Sheffield		Notts Co	8	1
						Sheffield U	11	3
						Scunthorpe U	89	38
Andy Flounders	5 11	11 06	13 12 63	Hull	Apprentice	Hull C	159	54
						Scunthorpe U	150	64
Andrew Hodkinson*	5 6	10 10	4 11 65	Ashton	Apprentice	Bolton W	—	—
						Oldham Ath	5	1
						Stockport Co	118	18
						Scunthorpe U	62	8
Gary Marshall	5 11	10 10	20 4 64	Bristol	Shepton Mallet	Bristol C	68	7
						Torquay U (loan)	7	1
						Carlisle U	21	2
						Scunthorpe U	34	3

Trainees
Barbrook, Matthew A; Clayton, Paul; Creaton, Sean T; Evans, Allan; Gibbs, Paul D; Godfrey, Andrew P; Lelliott, Darren F; McCormick, Steven A; McGlinchey, Lee J; Spooner, Darren; Sykes, Wayne; Thatcher, Stephen.

**Non-Contract
Moore, David.

Associated Schoolboy
Hall, James M.

Associated Schoolboys who have accepted the club's offer of a Traineeship/Contract
McCullagh, Paul A.

**Non-Contract Players who are retained must be re-signed before they are eligible to play in League matches.

SHEFFIELD UNITED 1989–90 *Back row (left to right):* Geoff Taylor (Coach), Ian Bryson, Tony Agana, Paul Stancliffe, Simon Webster, Graham Benstead, Matthew Dickins, Brian Deane. *Centre row:* John Dungworth (Youth Development Officer), Martin Pike, Julian Winter, Mark Morris, Simon Tracey, Darren Carr, James Gannon, Colin Hill, Cliff Powell, Bob Booker, Chris Wilder, Brian Smith, Keith Mincher (Youth Coach). *Front row:* Peter Duffield, John Francis, John Gannon, Dave Bassett (Team Manager), David Danes, Alan Roberts, Mark Todd. Derek French (Physiotherapist).

Division 1   **SHEFFIELD UNITED**

Bramall Lane Ground, Sheffield, S2 4SU. Telephone Sheffield (0742) 738955/6/7. Bladesline (recorded message), 0898 888 650.

Ground capacity: 35,618 (13,600 seats).

Record attendance: 68,287 v Leeds U, FA Cup 5th rd, 15 Feb, 1936.

Record receipts: £171,000 v Manchester U, FA Cup 6th rd, 11 March, 1990.

Pitch measurements: 113yd × 72yd.

President: R. Wragg M. INST. BM.

Chairman: R. J. Brealey.

Directors: R. Wragg, P. G. Woolhouse, A. H. Laver, M. Wragg, D. Dooley.

Manager: Dave Bassett. *Coach:* Geoff Taylor.

Assistant Manager: *Physio:* Derek French.

Secretary: D. Capper. *Commercial Manager:* Andy R. Daykin.

Year Formed: 1889. *Turned Professional:* 1889. *Ltd Co.:* 1899.

Club Nickname: 'The Blades'.

Record League Victory: 10-0 v Burslem Port Vale, Division 2, 10 December 1892 – Howlett; Witham, Lilley; Howell, Hendry, Needham; Drummond (1), Wallace (1), Hammond (4), Davies (2), Watson (2).

Record Cup Victory: 5-0 v Newcastle U (away), FA Cup, 1st rd, 10 January 1914 – Gough; Cook, English; Brelsford, Howley, Sturgess; Simmons (2), Gillespie (1), Kitchen (1), Fazackerley, Revill (1). 5-0 v Corinthians, FA Cup, 1st rd, 10 January 1925 – Sutcliffe; Cook, Milton; Longworth, King, Green; Partridge, Boyle (1), Johnson 4), Gillespie, Tunstall. 5-0 v Barrow, FA Cup, 3rd rd, 7 January 1956 – Burgin; Coldwell, Mason; Fountain, Johnson, Iley; Hawksworth (1), Hoyland (2), Howitt, Wragg (1), Grainger (1).

Record Defeat: 0-13 v Bolton W, FA Cup 2nd rd, 1 February, 1890.

Most League Points (2 for a win): 60, Division 2, 1952–53.

Most League Points (3 for a win): 96, Division 4, 1981–82.

Most League Goals: 102, Division 1, 1925–26.

Highest League Scorer in Season: Jimmy Dunne, 41, Division 1, 1930–31.

Most League Goals in Total Aggregate: Harry Johnson, 205, 1919–30.

Most Capped Player: Billy Gillespie, 25, Northern Ireland.

Most League Appearances: Joe Shaw, 629, 1948–66.

Record Transfer Fee Received: £400,000 from Leeds U for Alex Sabella, May 1980.

Record Transfer Fee Paid: £300,000 to Leyton Orient for Paul Beesley, July 1990 and £300,000 to Crystal Palace for John Pemberton, July 1990.

Football League Record: 1892 Elected to Division 2; 1893–1934 Division 1; 1934–39 Division 2; 1946–49 Division 1; 1949–53 Division 2; 1953–56 Division 1; 1956–61 Division 2; 1961–68 Division 1; 1968–71 Division 2; 1971–76 Division 1; 1976–79 Division 2; 1979–81 Division 3; 1981–82 Division 4; 1982–84 Division 3; 1984–88 Division 2; 1988–89 Division 3; 1989–90 Division 2; 1990– Division 1.

Honours: Football League: Division 1 – Champions 1897–98; Runners-up 1896–97, 1899–1900; Division 2 – Champions 1952–53; Runners-up 1892–93, 1938–39, 1960–61, 1970–71, 1989–90; Division 4 – Champions 1981–82. *FA Cup:* Winners 1899, 1902, 1915, 1925; Runners-up 1901, 1936. *Football League Cup* best season: 5th rd, 1961–62, 1966–67, 1971–72.

Colours: Red (thin) and white striped shirts, red and white trim, black shorts, black stockings red trim. **Change colours:** Lime green shirts, red shorts, red stockings, black trim.

SHEFFIELD UNITED 1989–90 LEAGUE RECORD

Match No.	Date	Venue	Opponents	Result	H/T Score	Lg. Pos.	Goalscorers	Atten- dance
1	Aug 19	A	WBA	W 3-0	1-0	—	Agana 2, Deane	14,907
2	26	H	Ipswich T	W 2-0	0-0	3	Deane, Morris	13,600
3	Sept 2	A	Middlesbrough	D 3-3	1-1	4	Francis, Bryson 2	17,897
4	9	H	Brighton & HA	W 5-4	3-1	1	Booker, Deane, Francis 2, Bryson (pen)	12,653
5	12	H	Swindon T	W 2-0	0-0	1	Booker, Deane	13,920
6	16	A	Plymouth Arg	D 0-0	0-0	1		10,884
7	23	H	Hull C	D 0-0	0-0	1		14,969
8	26	H	Oldham Ath	W 2-1	0-0	—	Deane, Agana	14,314
9	30	A	Sunderland	D 1-1	1-1	1	Bryson	22,760
10	Oct 7	A	Wolverhampton W	W 2-1	1-1	1	Rostron, Gannon	19,328
11	14	H	West Ham U	L 0-2	0-1	1		20,822
12	17	A	Barnsley	W 2-1	1-0	1	Bradshaw, Bryson (pen)	16,629
13	21	H	Stoke C	W 2-1	2-0	1	Bradshaw, Booker	16,873
14	28	A	Watford	W 3-1	1-0	1	Deane, Francis 2	11,623
15	31	H	Portsmouth	W 2-1	0-0	—	Duffield 2 (2 pens)	14,718
16	Nov 4	H	Leicester C	D 1-1	1-0	1	Evans (og)	15,971
17	11	A	Bournemouth	W 1-0	1-0	1	Bradshaw	8481
18	18	H	Bradford C	D 1-1	0-0	1	Gannon	15,419
19	25	A	Newcastle U	L 0-2	0-2	1		28,092
20	Dec 2	H	WBA	W 3-1	1-0	1	Booker 2, Deane	14,094
21	10	A	Swindon T	W 2-0	1-0	—	Gittens (og). Morris	10,282
22	16	A	Port Vale	D 1-1	0-1	2	Bryson	9813
23	26	H	Leeds U	D 2-2	2-1	2	Rostron, Agana	31,602
24	30	H	Blackburn R	L 1-2	1-1	2	Deane	17,279
25	Jan 1	A	Oxford U	L 0-3	0-1	2		7883
26	13	A	Ipswich T	D 1-1	1-0	2	Deane	16,787
27	20	H	Middlesbrough	W 1-0	1-0	2	Agana	15,950
28	Feb 3	A	Hull C	D 0-0	0-0	2		9606
29	10	H	Plymouth Arg	W 1-0	1-0	2	Deane	13,530
30	24	H	Newcastle U	D 1-1	0-1	2	Deane	21,035
31	Mar 3	A	Bradford C	W 4-1	1-0	2	Whitehouse, Deane, Stancliffe, Agana	10,348
32	14	A	Brighton & HA	D 2-2	1-2	—	Wood, Booker	8703
33	17	H	Wolverhampton W	W 3-0	1-0	2	Deane, Gannon (pen), Whitehurst	18,735
34	21	A	West Ham U	L 0-5	0-1	—		21,629
35	24	H	Barnsley	L 1-2	1-0	2	Wood	15,951
36	28	A	Oldham Ath	W 2-0	1-0	—	Deane 2	14,160
37	31	A	Stoke C	W 1-0	0-0	2	Deane	14,898
38	Apr 3	H	Sunderland	L 1-3	1-0	2	Deane	20,588
39	7	A	Portsmouth	L 2-3	0-0	2	Todd, Morris	9004
40	10	H	Watford	W 4-1	1-1	—	Agana, Booker, Deane, Whitehurst	14,653
41	14	H	Oxford U	W 2-1	0-0	2	Booker, Ford (og)	16,752
42	16	A	Leeds U	L 0-4	0-1	3		32,727
43	21	H	Port Vale	W 2-1	0-0	2	Bryson, Deane	16,809
44	28	H	Bournemouth	W 4-2	2-1	2	Bryson 2, Agana, Deane	20,994
45	May 1	A	Blackburn R	D 0-0	0-0	—		15,633
46	5	A	Leicester C	W 5-2	4-2	2	Wood, Deane, Agana 2, Rostron	21,134

Final League Position: 2

GOALSCORERS

League (78): Deane 21, Agana 10, Bryson 9 (2 pens), Booker 8, Francis 5, Bradshaw 3, Gannon 3 (1 pen), Morris 3, Rostron 3, Wood 3, Duffield 2 (2 pens), Whitehurst 2, Stancliffe 1, Todd 1, Whitehouse 1, own goals 3.
Littlewoods Cup (1): Deane 1.
FA Cup (8): Agana 2 (1 pen), Bryson 2, Bradshaw 1, Deane 1, Stancliffe 1, own goal 1.

Tracey	Hill	Barnes	Booker	Stancliffe	Morris	Roberts	Gannon	Agana	Deane	Bryson	Francis	Whitehouse	Pike	Bradshaw	Todd	Rostron	Duffield	Webster	Lake	Wilder	Wood	Whitehurst	Match No.
1	2	3	4	5	6	7	8	9	10	11													1
1	2	3	4	5	6	7	8	9	10	11													2
1	2	3	4	5	6	7	8†		10	11	9*	12	14										3
1	2	3	4	5	6	7*	8		10	11	9	12											4
1	2	3	4	5	6	7*	8		10	11	9	12											5
1	2		4	5	6		8		10	11	9*	7		3	12								6
1	2		4	5	6		12		10	11	9†	7*		3	14	8							7
1	2		4	5	6	7*	8	9	10	11		12		3									8
1	2		4	5	6	12	8	9*	10	11		7		3									9
1	2		4	5	6		8	9	10	11	12			7*		3							10
1	2†		4	5	6		8	9	10	11*	12			7	14	3							11
1	2		4	5	6		8	9	10	11	12			7*		3							12
1	2		4	5	6		8	9	10	11*	12			7		3							13
1	2		4	5	6		8	9*	10		12	11		7		3							14
1	2		4†	5	6		8		10		9	11*		7	14	3	12						15
1	2		4	5	6		8		10		9†	11*		7	14	3	12						16
1	2		4	5	6		8		10		9	11*		7		3	12						17
1	2		4	5	6		8	9*	10	11	12			7		3							18
1	2		4	5	6		8		10	11	9*				3	12	14	7†					19
1	2		4	5	6		8		10	11		7*		3		9		12					20
1	2		4†	5	6		8		10	11	12	7		3	9*		14						21
1	2		4	5	6		12		10	11	9	7*		3		8							22
1	2		4	5	6*		8	9	10	11		7		3		12							23
1	2		4*	5			8†	9	10	11	12	7		14	3	6							24
1	2		4†	5	6			9	10	11	12	7*	8	3	14								25
1	2	3			6			9	10	11	7*		12		14	8			4†	5			26
1	2	3		5		4		9	10	11	12	7*				8				6			27
1	2	3	12	5	6		8*	9	10		11	7				4							28
1	2	3	12	5	6		8*	9†	10	11		7				4					14		29
1	2	3	4	5	6		8	9	10			14		12							7†	11*	30
1	2	3	4	5	6*		8	9	10		11	7†		12							14		31
1		3	4	5			8*		10	11†	14	6		12		2					7	9	32
1			4	5*			8		10	11		6	3	12		2					7	9	33
1	12		4	5			8		10	11		14	6*	3		2					7†	9	34
1	2	3	4	5			8*		10	11†	14	6		12							7	9	35
1	2	3		5	6		8		10	11		9		4							7		36
1	2	3	14	5	6		8	12	10	11		4									7†	9*	37
1	2	3		5	14		8	12	10	11*		4		6							7	9†	38
1		3	14	5	6		8	9		11		4	2†		12						7*	10	39
1	2	3	4	5	6		8	9	10	11											7*	12	40
1	2	3	4	5	6		8	9	10	11†		14									7*	12	41
1	2	3	4	5	6		8†	12	10	11		7									14	9*	42
1	2	3	4	5*	6		8†	9	10	11	12			14							7		43
1	2	3	4†		6			9*	10	11		12		8		14			5	7			44
1	2	3	4		6			9	10	11				8					5	7*	12		45
1	2	3	4		6			9	10*	11			14	8					5	7†	12		46
46	42	24	38	40	41	6	39	26	45	39	11	8	2	20	10	24	2	9	2	8	15	9	
	+1s	+4s	+1s	+1s	+5s		+9s	+4s	+1s	+10s	+6s	+2s		+3s	+11s	+2s		+2s		+2s	+5s		

Littlewoods Cup	First Round	Rotherham U (h)	1-1
		(a)	0-1
FA Cup	Third Round	Bournemouth (h)	2-0
	Fourth Round	Watford (h)	1-1
		(a)	2-1
	Fifth Round	Barnsley (h)	2-2
		(a)	0-0
		(a)	1-0
	Sixth Round	Manchester U (h)	0-1

SHEFFIELD UNITED

Player and Position	Ht	Wt	Birth Date	Place	Source	Clubs	League App	Gls
Goalkeepers								
Graham Benstead	6 1	13 07	20 8 63	Aldershot	Apprentice	QPR	—	—
						Norwich C (loan)	1	—
						Norwich C	15	—
						Colchester U (loan)	18	—
						Sheffield U (loan)	8	—
						Sheffield U	39	—
Matthew Dickins‡	6 4	14 00	3 9 70	Sheffield	Trainee	Sheffield U	—	—
						Leyton Orient (loan)	—	—
Simon Tracey	6 0	13 00	9 12 67	Woolwich	Apprentice	Wimbledon	1	—
						Sheffield U	53	—
Defenders								
David Barnes	5 10	11 01	16 11 61	London	Apprentice	Coventry C	9	—
						Ipswich T	17	—
						Wolverhampton W	88	4
						Aldershot	69	1
						Sheffield U	24	—
Darren Carr	6 0	12 07	4 9 68	Bristol		Bristol R	30	—
						Newport Co	9	—
						Sheffield U	13	1
Martin Dickinson‡	5 10	12 03	14 3 63	Leeds	Apprentice	Leeds U	103	2
						WBA	50	2
						Sheffield U	1	—
John Flower	6 4	15 04	9 12 64	Northampton	Corby T	Sheffield U	—	—
Colin Hill	5 11	12 02	12 11 63	Hillingdon	Apprentice	Arsenal	46	1
						Brighton & HA (loan)	—	—
					Maritimo	Colchester U	69	—
						Sheffield U	43	—
Mark Morris	6 0	11 10	26 9 62	Morden	Apprentice	Wimbledon	168	9
						Aldershot (loan)	14	—
						Watford	41	1
						Sheffield U	42	3
Cliff Powell	6 0	12 00	21 2 68	Watford	Apprentice	Watford	—	—
						Hereford U (loan)	7	—
						Sheffield U	10	—
						Doncaster R (loan)	4	—
						Cardiff C (loan)	1	—
Wilf Rostron*	5 7	11 11	29 9 56	Sunderland	Apprentice	Arsenal	17	2
						Sunderland	76	17
						Watford	317	22
						Sheffield W	7	—
						Sheffield U	26	3
Brian Smith	5 9	11 02	27 10 66	Sheffield	Local	Sheffield U	84	—
						Scunthorpe U (loan)	6	1
Paul Stancliffe	6 2	12 13	5 5 58	Sheffield	Apprentice	Rotherham U	285	8
						Sheffield U	275	12
Mitchum Ward	5 8	10 07	18 6 71	Sheffield	Trainee	Sheffield U	—	—
Simon Webster	6 0	11 07	20 1 64	Earl Shilton	Apprentice	Tottenham H	3	—
						Exeter C (loan)	26	—
						Norwich C (loan)	—	—
						Huddersfield T	118	4
						Sheffield U	37	3
Chris Wilder	5 10	10 08	23 9 67	Wortley	Apprentice	Southampton	—	—
						Sheffield U	73	1
						Walsall (loan)	4	—
Midfield								
Bob Booker	6 2	12 04	25 1 58	Watford	Bedmond Sp	Brentford	251	41
						Sheffield U	68	10
Ian Bryson	5 11	11 11	26 11 62	Kilmarnock		Kilmarnock	215	40
						Sheffield U	76	17

SHEFFIELD UNITED

Foundation: In March 1889, Yorkshire County Cricket Club formed Sheffield United six days after an FA Cup semi-final between Preston North End and West Bromwich Albion had finally convinced Charles Stokes, a member of the cricket club, that the formation of a professional football club would prove successful at Bramall Lane. The United's first secretary, Mr. J. B. Wostinholm was also secretary of the cricket club.

First Football League game: 3 September, 1892, Division 2, v Lincoln C (h) W 4-2 – Lilley; Witham, Cain; Howell, Hendry, Needham (1); Wallace, Dobson, Hammond (3), Davies, Drummond.

Managers (and Secretary-managers)
J. B. Wostinholm 1889–1899*, John Nicholson 1899–1932, Ted Davison 1932–52, Reg Freeman 1952–55, Joe Mercer 1955–58, Johnny Harris 1959–68 (continued as GM to 1970), Arthur Rowley 1968–69, Johnny Harris (GM resumed TM duties) 1969–73, Ken Furphy 1973–75, Jimmy Sirrel 1975–77, Harry Haslam 1978–81, Martin Peters 1981, Ian Porterfield 1981–86, Billy McEwan 1986–88, Dave Bassett 1988–   .

Player and Position	Ht	Wt	Birth Date	Place	Source	Clubs	League App	Gls
John Gannon	5 8	10 10	18 12 66	Wimbledon	Apprentice	Wimbledon	16	2
						Crewe Alex (loan)	15	—
						Sheffield U (loan)	16	1
						Sheffield U	39	3
Michael Lake	6 1	13 07	16 11 66	Manchester	Macclesfield T	Sheffield U	4	—
Richard Lucas	5 10	11 04	22 9 70	Sheffield	Trainee	Sheffield U	—	—
Mark Todd	5 7	10 00	4 12 67	Belfast	Trainee	Manchester U	—	—
						Sheffield U	67	5
Dane Whitehouse	5 8	10 12	14 10 70	Sheffield	Trainee	Sheffield U	17	1
Julian Winter	6 0	11 02	6 9 65	Huddersfield	Local	Huddersfield T	93	5
						Scunthorpe U (loan)	4	—
						Sheffield U	—	—
Forwards								
Tony Agana	5 11	12 02	2 10 63	London	Weymouth	Watford	15	1
						Sheffield U	89	36
Carl Bradshaw	6 0	11 00	2 10 68	Sheffield	Apprentice	Sheffield W	32	4
						Barnsley (loan)	6	1
						Manchester C	5	—
						Sheffield U	30	3
Brian Deane	6 3	12 07	7 2 68	Leeds	Apprentice	Doncaster R	66	12
						Sheffield U	88	43
Peter Duffield	5 6	10 07	4 2 69	Middlesbrough		Middlesbrough	—	—
						Sheffield U	54	14
						Halifax T (loan)	12	6
Billy Whitehurst	6 0	13 00	10 6 59	Thurnscoe	Mexborough	Hull C	193	47
						Newcastle U	28	7
						Oxford U	40	4
						Reading	17	8
						Sunderland	17	3
						Hull C	36	5
						Sheffield U	14	2
Paul Wood	5 9	10 01	1 11 64	Middlesbrough	Apprentice	Portsmouth	47	6
						Brighton & HA	92	8
						Sheffield U	17	3

Trainees
Atkinson, Timothy; Circuit, Steven; Fenwick, Ashley J.C; Ford, Reece; Harrison, Richard; Heywood, Colin L.J; Ingram, Stephen; Jaques, John W; Morris, Lee; Reed, John P; Wagstaff, Russell J.

Associated Schoolboys
Archbold, John D; Batten, Ian G; Battersby, Anthony; Beal, Nicholas P; Butterfield, Timothy; Camacho, Luiz M.C; Clarke, Simon J; Cope, Steven G; Dickerson, Ian; Fickling, Ashley D.S; Foreman, Matthew, B; Johnson, Andrew P; Letts, Simon C; Lumsden, Jamie; Myhill, Craig S; Risdale, Scott; Stevens, Paul J; Tee, Jason K; Thompson, Martin R; Wainwright, Daniel J; Wainwright, Lee; Ward, Timothy M.J; Watts, Gregory; Whitehouse, Ryan.

Associated Schoolboys who have accepted the club's offer of a Traineeship/Contract
Brocklehurst, David; Cherrill, Matthew G; Evans, James D; Godwin, Jon B; Reaney, Andrew.

SHEFFIELD WEDNESDAY 1989–90 *Back row (left to right):* Carlton Palmer, Chris Turner, Dalian Atkinson, Kevin Pressman, Peter Shirtliff.
Centre row: Richie Barker (Assistant Manager), Lawrie Madden, Craig Shakespeare, Steve Whitton, Greg Fee, Nigel Worthington, David Hirst, Alan Smith (Physiotherapist).
Front row: Alan Harper, Darren Wood, Mark Taylor, Ron Atkinson (Manager), Nigel Pearson, David Bennett, Dean Barrick.

Division 2   **SHEFFIELD WEDNESDAY**

Hillsborough, Sheffield, S6 1SW. Telephone (Sheffield (0742) 343122. Box Office: Sheffield 337233. Clubcall: 0898-121186.

Ground capacity: 38,780.

Record attendance: 72,841 v Manchester C, FA Cup 5th rd, 17 Feb, 1934.

Record receipts: £398,134, Liverpool v Nottingham F, FA Cup semi-final, 9 April, 1988.

Pitch measurements: 115yd × 75yd.

Chairman: D. G. Richards. *Vice-Chairman:* K. T. Addy.

Directors: C. Woodward, E. Barron, G. K. Hulley, R. M. Grierson FCA, J. Ashton MP.

Manager: Ron Atkinson. *Assistant Manager:* Richie Barker.

Physio: A. Smith.

Secretary: G. H. Mackrell FCCA. *Commercial Manager:* R. Gorrill (Tel. 0742-337235).

Club Nickname: 'The Owls'.

Year Formed: 1867 (fifth oldest League Club).

Turned Profesional: 1887. *Ltd Co.:* 1899.

Previous Grounds: 1867, Highfield; 1869, Myrtle Road; 1877, Sheaf House; 1887, Olive Grove; 1899, Owlerton (since 1912 known as Hillsborough). Some games were played at Endcliffe in the 1880s. Until 1895 Bramall Lane was used for some games.

Record League Victory: 9-1 v Birmingham, Division 1, 13 December 1930 – Brown; Walker, Blenkinsop; Strange, Leach, Wilson; Hooper (3), Seed (2), Ball (2), Burgess (1), Rimmer (1).

Record Cup Victory: 12-0 v Halliwell, FA Cup, 1st rd, 17 January 1891 – Smith; Thompson, Brayshaw; Harry Brandon (1), Betts, Cawley (2); Winterbottom, Mumford (2), Bob Brandon (1), Woolhouse (5), Ingram (1).

Record Defeat: 0-10 v Aston Villa, Division 1, 5 October, 1912.

Most League Points (2 for a win): 62, Division 2, 1958–59.

Most League Points (3 for a win): 88, Division 2, 1983–84.

Most League Goals: 106, Division 2, 1958–59.

Highest League Scorer in Season: Derek Dooley, 46, Division 2, 1951–52.

Most League Goals in Total Aggregate: Andy Wilson, 199, 1900–20.

Most Capped Player: Ron Springett, 33, England.

Most League Appearances: Andy Wilson, 502, 1900–20.

Record Transfer Fee Received: £800,000 from Rangers for Mel Sterland, March 1989.

Record Transfer Fee Paid: £750,000 to WBA for Carlton Palmer, February 1989.

Football League Record: 1892 Elected to Division 1; 1899–1900 Division 2; 1900–20 Division 1; 1920–26 Division 2; 1926–37 Division 1; 1937–50 Division 2; 1950–51 Division 1; 1951–52 Division 2; 1952–55 Division 1; 1955–56 Division 2; 1956–58 Division 1; 1958–59 Division 2; 1959–70 Division 1; 1970–75 Division 2; 1975–80 Division 3; 1980–84 Division 2; 1984–90; 1990– Division 2.

Honours: Football League: Division 1 – Champions 1902–03, 1903–04, 1928–29, 1929–30; Runners-up 1960–61; Division 2 – Champions 1899–1900, 1925–26, 1951–52, 1955–56, 1958–59; Runners-up 1949–50, 1983–84. *FA Cup:* Winners 1896, 1907, 1935; Runners-up 1890, 1966. *Football League Cup* best season: 5th rd, 1982–83, 1983–84, 1984–85. **European Competitions:** *Fairs Cup:* 1961–62, 1963–64.

Colours: Blue and white striped shirts, black shorts, blue stockings. **Change colours:** Yellow shirts, sky blue shorts, yellow stockings.

SHEFFIELD WEDNESDAY 1989–90 LEAGUE RECORD

Match No.	Date	Venue	Opponents	Result	H/T Score	Lg. Pos.	Goalscorers	Atten-dance
1	Aug 19	H	Norwich C	L 0-2	0-1	—		19,142
1	22	A	Luton T	L 0-2	0-1	—		9503
3	26	A	Chelsea	L 0-4	0-3	20		16,265
4	30	H	Everton	D 1-1	0-1	—	Atkinson	19,657
5	Sept 9	A	Arsenal	L 0-5	0-1	20		30,058
6	16	H	Aston Villa	W 1-0	1-0	13	Atkinson	17,509
7	23	A	Millwall	L 0-2	0-0	20		11,287
8	30	H	Coventry C	D 0-0	0-0	20		15,054
9	Oct 14	A	Manchester U	D 0-0	0-0	20		41,492
10	21	A	Tottenham H	L 0-3	0-2	20		26,909
11	28	H	Wimbledon	L 0-1	0-0	20		13,728
12	Nov 4	A	Nottingham F	W 1-0	0-0	20	Wilson (og)	21,864
13	11	H	Charlton Ath	W 3-0	1-0	20	Atkinson, Hirst 2	16,740
14	18	A	Derby Co	L 0-2	0-1	20		18,085
15	25	H	Crystal Palace	D 2-2	0-1	20	Whitton, Hirst (pen)	17,227
16	29	H	Liverpool	W 2-0	0-0	—	Hirst, Atkinson	32,732
17	Dec 2	A	Norwich C	L 1-2	1-2	17	Hirst	15,341
18	9	H	Luton T	D 1-1	1-0	18	Dreyer (og)	16,339
19	16	H	QPR	W 2-0	2-0	17	Atkinson, Hirst	14,569
20	26	A	Liverpool	L 1-2	0-1	18	Atkinson	37,488
21	30	A	Southampton	D 2-2	1-1	18	Atkinson, Shirtliff	16,417
22	Jan 1	H	Manchester C	W 2-0	1-0	16	Hirst, Pearson	28,756
23	14	A	Chelsea	D 1-1	0-1	—	Atkinson	18,042
24	20	A	Everton	L 0-2	0-0	16		25,545
25	Feb 3	H	Millwall	D 1-1	1-1	15	Hirst	17,737
26	10	A	Aston Villa	L 0-1	0-0	17		27,168
27	17	H	Arsenal	W 1-0	1-0	14	Bould (og)	20,640
28	24	A	Crystal Palace	D 1-1	1-0	14	Worthington	11,857
29	Mar 3	H	Derby Co	W 1-0	1-0	14	Sheridan	21,811
30	17	A	Coventry C	W 4-1	1-1	14	Hirst, Worthington, Sheridan, Atkinson	13,339
31	21	H	Manchester U	W 1-0	1-0	—	Hirst	33,260
32	24	A	Wimbledon	D 1-1	0-0	13	Shirtliff	5034
33	31	H	Tottenham H	L 2-4	1-1	14	Hirst, Atkinson	26,582
34	Apr 7	H	Southampton	L 0-1	0-0	14		18,329
35	14	A	Manchester C	L 1-2	0-1	17	Hirst	33,022
36	21	A	QPR	L 0-1	0-1	17		10,448
37	28	A	Charlton Ath	W 2-1	1-0	17	Hirst 2	7029
38	May 5	H	Nottingham F	L 0-3	0-1	18		29,762

Final League Position: 18

GOALSCORERS

League (35): Hirst 14 (1 pen), Atkinson 10, Sheridan 2, Shirtliff 2, Worthington 2, Pearson 1, Whitton 1, own goals 3.
Littlewoods Cup (9): Whitton 4, Atkinson 3, Hirst 1 (pen), Shakespeare 1.
FA Cup (3): Atkinson 1, Hirst 1, Shirtliff 1.

Turner	Harper	Worthington	Palmer	Pearson	Madden	Bennett	Barrick	Whitton	Atkinson	Shakespeare	Hirst	Fee	Taylor	Wood	Shirtliff	Newsome	Pressman	Varadi	King	Sheridan	Nilsson	Carr	Francis	McCall	Match No.
1	2	3	4	5	6	7	8	9*	10	11	12														1
1	8*	3	4	5	6	12		9		11	10	2	7												2
1	2	3		5	6		4	9		11	10		7	8											3
1	8	3		5	6	12	4	9		11	10		7			2*									4
1	8†	3		5	6	12	4	9		11	10*		7	14		2									5
		3	4		6		8	9		11	10		7		5	2	1								6
12		3	4		6		8†	9		11	10		7*	14	5	2	1								7
12		3	4		6		8	9		11	10		7		5	2*	1								8
		3	4		6	7	8	9*	10	11	12				5	2	1								9
1		3	4		6	7	8	9†	10	11*	12			14	5	2									10
1		3	4		6	7*	8	9	10	11†	12			14	5	2									11
	2		4		6	7		9	10	11	12				5		1		3*	8					12
	2		4		6	7		9	10	11					5		1		3	8					13
	2	11	4		6	7*		9	10		12				5		1		3	8					14
		11	4	2*	6	7		9	10		12				5		1		3	8					15
	2		4		6	7		9	10	11					5		1		3	8					16
	2		4		6	7		9	10	11*	12				5		1		3	8					17
		11	4		6	7*		9	10		12				5		1		3	8	2				18
		11	4		6	7*		9	10		12				5		1		3	8	2				19
		11	4		6			9	10						5		1		3	8	2	7			20
		11	4		6			9	10						5		1		3	8	2	7			21
		11	4		6			9	10		12				5		1*		3	8	2	7			22
1		11	4		6			9	10		12				5				3	8	2*	7			23
1		3	4		6			9	10	11*	12				5				2	8		7			24
1		11	4		6			9	10						5				3	8	2	7*	12		25
1		11*	4		6			9	10						5				3	8	2	7	12		26
1		11	4		6			9	10		12				5*				3	8	2	14	7†		27
1		11	4	5	6			9	10										3	8	2	12	7*		28
1		11	4		6			9†	10		12				5				3	8	2	14	7*		29
1		11	4		6			9†	10		12			14	5				3*	8	2	7			30
1		11	4		6			9	10						5				3	8	2	7			31
1		11*	4		6			9	10		12			14	5				3	8	2		7†		32
1			4		6			9	10	11	12			14	5				3*	8	2		7†		33
1		3	4		6			9	10	11*	12				5					8	2		7		34
1		3	4		6			9	10	11	12				5					8	2		7*		35
1		11†	4		6			9	10		12				5				3	8*	2	7	14		36
1		11	4		6			9	10		12				5				3†	8	2	7*	14		37
1		11	4		6			9	10		12				5				3	8	2		7*		38
23	9 +2s	32	34	33	18 +7s	10 +8s	3	10 +9s	38	15 +2s	36 +2s	1	8 +1s	3 +1s	33	5	15 +1s	— +2s	25	27	20	9 +3s2s	10 +2s	1	

Littlewoods Cup	Second Round	Aldershot (h) 0-0
		(a) 8-0
	Third Round	Derby Co (a) 1-2
FA Cup	Third Round	Wolverhampton W (a) 2-1
	Fourth Round	Everton (h) 1-2

SHEFFIELD WEDNESDAY

Player and Position	Ht	Wt	Birth Date	Birth Place	Source	Clubs	League App	Gls
Goalkeepers								
Marlon Beresford	6 1	10 11	2 9 69	Lincoln	Trainee	Sheffield W	—	—
						Bury (loan)	1	—
						Ipswich T (loan)	—	—
Lance Key			13 5 68	Kettering	Histon	Sheffield W	—	—
Kevin Pressman	6 1	13 00	6 11 67	Fareham	Apprentice	Sheffield W	35	—
Chris Turner	6 0	12 04	15 9 58	Sheffield	Apprentice	Sheffield W	91	—
						Lincoln C (loan)	5	—
						Sunderland	195	—
						Manchester U	64	—
						Sheffield W	52	—
						Leeds U (loan)	2	—
Defenders								
Scott Cam	5 9	10 00	3 5 70	Sheffield	Trainee	Sheffield W	—	—
Kevin Elshaw*	6 1	13 11	11 9 70	Sheffield	Trainee	Sheffield W	—	—
Greg Fee	6 1	12 00	24 6 64	Halifax		Bradford C	7	—
					Boston U	Sheffield W	26	—
Phillip King	5 10	12 00	28 12 67	Bristol		Exeter C	27	—
						Torquay U	24	3
						Swindon T	116	4
						Sheffield W	25	—
Steve McCall	5 11	11 03	15 10 60	Carlisle	Apprentice	Ipswich T	257	7
						Sheffield W	10	—
						Carlisle U (loan)	6	—
Lawrie Madden	5 11	13 01	28 9 55	London	Amateur Manchester Univ	Arsenal	—	—
						Mansfield T	10	—
						Charlton Ath	113	7
						Millwall	47	2
						Sheffield W	207	2
Jon Newsome	6 2	13 11	6 9 70	Sheffield	Trainee	Sheffield W	6	—
Roland Nilsson	6 0	11 06	27 11 63	Helsingborg	Gothenburg	Sheffield W	20	—
Carlton Palmer	5 10	11 00	5 12 65	West Bromwich	Trainee	WBA	121	4
						Sheffield W	47	1
Nigel Pearson	6 1	13 07	21 8 63	Nottingham	Heanor T	Shrewsbury T	153	5
						Sheffield W	89	5
Peter Shirtliff	6 2	13 04	6 4 61	Barnsley	Apprentice	Sheffield W	188	4
						Charlton Ath	103	7
						Sheffield W	33	2
Shaun Sowden			25 3 68	Blackburn	Histon	Sheffield W	—	—
Mark Taylor	5 10	11 00	22 2 66	Walsall	Local	Walsall	113	4
						Sheffield W	9	—
David Wetherall	6 3	12 00	14 3 71	Sheffield	School	Sheffield W	—	—
Darren Wood	5 10	11 08	9 6 64	Scarborough	Apprentice	Middlesbrough	101	6
						Chelsea	144	3
						Sheffield W	11	—
Nigel Worthington	5 10	12 06	4 11 61	Ballymena	Ballymena U	Notts Co	67	4
						Sheffield W	200	4
Midfield								
Dean Barrick	5 9	11 04	30 9 69	Hemsworth	Trainee	Sheffield W	11	2
Tony Gregory	5 8	10 10	21 3 68	Doncaster	Apprentice	Sheffield W	18	1
Graham Hyde	5 7	11 07	10 11 70	Doncaster	Trainee	Sheffield W	—	—
John Sheridan	5 9	10 08	1 10 64	Stretford	Local	Leeds U	230	47
						Nottingham F	—	—
						Sheffield W	27	2
Forwards								
Dalian Atkinson	6 1	12 10	21 3 68	Shrewsbury		Ipswich T	60	18
						Sheffield W	38	10

SHEFFIELD WEDNESDAY

Foundation: Sheffield, being one of the principal centres of early Association Football, this club was formed as long ago as 1867 by the Sheffield Wednesday Cricket Club (formed 1825) and their colours from the start were blue and white. The inaugural meeting was held at the Adelphi Hotel and the original committee included Charles Stokes who was subsequently a founder member of Sheffield United.

First Football League game: 3 September, 1892, Division 1, v Notts C (a) W 1-0 – Allan; T. Brandon (1), Mumford; Hall, Betts, H. Brandon; Spiksley, Brady, Davis, R.N. Brown, Dunlop.

Managers (and Secretary-managers)
Arthur Dickinson 1891–1920*, Robert Brown 1920–33, Billy Walker 1933–37, Jimmy McMullan 1937–42, Eric Taylor 1942–58 (continued as GM to 1974), Harry Catterick 1958–61, Vic Buckingham 1961–64, Alan Brown 1964–68, Jack Marshall 1968–69, Danny Williams 1969–71, Derek Dooley 1971–73, Steve Burtenshaw 1974–75, Len Ashurst 1975–77, Jackie Charlton 1977–83, Howard Wilkinson 1983–88, Peter Eustace 1988–89, Ron Atkinson 1989–   .

Player and Position	Ht	Wt	Birth Date	Place	Source	Clubs	League App	Gls
Dave Bennett	5 9	10 07	11 7 59	Manchester	Amateur	Manchester C	52	9
						Cardiff C	77	18
						Coventry C	172	25
						Sheffield W	28	—
Trevor Francis	5 10	11 07	19 4 54	Plymouth	Apprentice	Birmingham C	280	118
						Nottingham F	70	28
						Manchester C	26	12
						Sampdoria	68	17
						Atalanta	21	1
						Rangers	18	—
						QPR	32	12
						Sheffield W	12	—
Sam Goodacre	5 10	11 00	1 12 70	Sheffield	School	Sheffield W	—	—
Kevin Haigh*	5 6	10 00	16 7 70	Sheffield	Local	Sheffield W	—	—
David Hirst	5 11	12 05	7 12 67	Barnsley	Apprentice	Barnsley	28	9
						Sheffield W	115	30
David Hodgson‡	5 9	12 02	1 11 60	Gateshead	Amateur	Middlesbrough	125	16
						Liverpool	28	4
						Sunderland	40	5
						Norwich C	6	1
						Middlesbrough (loan)	2	—
					Jerez	Sheffield W	11	1
David Johnson	6 2	13 08	29 10 70	Rother Valley	Trainee	Sheffield W	—	—
David Lycett	5 11	13 08	9 9 70	Sheffield	Trainee	Sheffield W	—	—
Jason Swann*	5 10	11 04	27 1 71	Sheffield	Trainee	Sheffield W	—	—
Steve Whitton	6 0	12 07	4 12 60	East Ham	Apprentice	Coventry C	74	21
						West Ham U	39	6
						Birmingham C (loan)	8	2
						Birmingham C	95	28
						Sheffield W	31	4

Trainees
Burton, Paul; Chambers, Leroy D; Curry, Ian; Dickinson, Mark A; Downing, Nigel; Dunn, Gareth T; Holmshaw, Richard J; Jones, Ryan A; Robinson, Nicholas; Roden, Andrew P; Smith, Mark A.

Associated Schoolboys
Barker, Richard I; Bekisz, Paul D; Brookfield, Nicholas; Brown, Steven M; Burrows, Marc L; Faulkner, David P; Flint, Jonathan A; Frank, Ian D; Harrison, James; Holmes, Darren P; Linighan, Brian; Linighan, John; McCarthy, Lawrence J; McManus, Steven; McVeigh, Michael B; Nankivell, Lee M; Newton, Paul; Parker, Scott; Robinson, Paul; Rowntree, Michael C; Simpson, Ronald J; Wright, Jeremy H.

492

SHREWSBURY TOWN 1989–90 *Back row (left to right):* Alan Finley, Steve Perks, Richard Pratley, Ken Hughes, Wayne McLean.
Centre row: Asa Hartford (Player Coach), Victor Kasule, Richard Green, Steve Pittman, Michael Brown, Tony Kelly, David Moyes, Les Helm (Physiotherapist).
Front row: Phil Priest, Carl Griffiths, Ian McNeill (Manager), Jim Melrose, Dougie Bell, Brian Williams (Youth Team Coach).
Sitting: Mark Roberts, Graeme Worsley, Jon Purdie, John McGinlay.

Division 3   SHREWSBURY TOWN

Gay Meadow, Shrewsbury. Telephone Shrewsbury (0743) 60111. Commercial Dept. 56316. Club call: 0898 121194.

Match information: 8040.

*Ground capacity:*15,000.

Record attendance: 18,917 v Walsall, Division 3, 26 Apr, 1961.

Record receipts: £36,240 v Ipswich T, FA Cup 5th rd, 13 Feb, 1982.

Pitch measurements: 116yd × 76yd.

President: *Vice-President:* Dr. J. Millard Bryson.

Chairman: K. R. Woodhouse.

Directors: A. C. Williams, F. C. G. Fry, R. Bailey, M. J. Starkey, G. W. Nelson, W. H. Richards.

Manager: Asa Hartford. *Commercial Manager:* M. Thomas.

Physio: L. Helm. *Coach:*

Secretary: M. J. Starkey.

Club Nickname: 'Town' or 'Shrews'.

Year Formed: 1886. *Turned Professional:* 1905 (approx). *Ltd Co.:* 1936.

Previous Ground: Old Shrewsbury Racecourse.

Record League Victory: 7-0, v Swindon T, Division 3(S), 6 May 1955 – McBride; Bannister, Keech; Wallace, Maloney, Candlin; Price, O'Donnell (1), Weigh (4), Russell, McCue (2).

Record Cup Victory: 7-1 v Banbury Spencer, FA Cup, 1st rd, 4 November 1961 – Gibson; Walters, Skeech; Wallace, Pountney, Harley; Kenning (2), Pragg, Starkey (1), Rowley (2), McLaughlin (2).

Record Defeat: 1-8 v Norwich C, Division 3(S), 1952–53 and v Coventry C, Division 3, 22 October, 1963.

Most League Points (2 for a win): 62, Division 4, 1974–75.

Most League Points (3 for a win): 65, Division 2, 1984–85.

Most League Goals: 101, Division 4, 1958–59.

Highest League Scorer in Season: Arthur Rowley, 38, Division 4, 1958–59.

Most League Goals in Total Aggregate: Arthur Rowley, 152, 1958–65 (thus completing his League record of 434 goals).

Most Capped Player: Jimmy McLaughlin, 5 (12), Northern Ireland and Bernard McNally, 5, Northern Ireland.

Most League Appearances: Colin Griffin, 406, 1975–89.

Record Transfer Fee Received: £385,000 from WBA for Bernard McNally, July 1989.

Record Transfer Fee Paid: £100,000 to Aldershot for John Dungworth, November 1979.

Football League Record: 1950 Elected to Division 3(N); 1951–58 Division 3(S); 1958–59 Division 4; 1959–74 Division 3; 1974–75 Division 4; 1975–79 Division 3; 1979–89 Division 2; 1989– Division 3.

Honours: Football League: Division 2 best season: 8th, 1983–84, 1984–85; Division 3 – Champions 1978–79; Division 4 – Runners-up 1974–5. *FA Cup* best season: 6th rd, 1978–79, 1981–82. *Football League Cup:* Semi-final 1961. *Welsh Cup:* Winners 1891, 1938, 1977, 1979, 1984, 1985; Runners-up 1931, 1948, 1980.

Colours: White shirts, blue trim, blue shorts, white stockings, blue and gold trim. **Change colours:** Red Shirts, white shorts, red stockings.

SHREWSBURY TOWN 1989–90 LEAGUE RECORD

Match No.	Date	Venue	Opponents	Result		H/T Score	Lg. Pos.	Goalscorers	Atten- dance
1	Aug 19	A	Reading	D	3-3	2-1	—	Bell, Griffiths, Kelly	3909
2	26	H	Leyton Orient	W	4-2	1-1	5	Moyes, McGinlay 2, Pratley	3299
3	Sept 2	A	Blackpool	W	1-0	1-0	3	Bell	4109
4	9	H	Birmingham C	W	2-0	1-0	1	Naughton (pen), McGinlay	4714
5	16	A	Northampton T	L	1-2	1-1	5	Pittman	3131
6	23	H	Bury	W	3-1	2-1	1	Bell, McGinlay, Griffiths	3525
7	26	A	Bristol C	L	1-2	0-1	—	Purdie	9188
8	30	H	Crewe Alex	D	0-0	0-0	8		5118
9	Oct 7	H	Mansfield T	L	0-1	0-0	10		3148
10	14	A	Wigan Ath	D	0-0	0-0	11		2279
11	17	A	Walsall	W	2-0	0-0	—	Moyes, Pittman	4266
12	21	H	Brentford	W	1-0	0-0	7	Moyes	3073
13	28	A	Huddersfield T	D	1-1	1-1	8	Moyes	6001
14	31	H	Tranmere R	W	3-1	1-1	—	McGinlay 2, Finley	4927
15	Nov 4	A	Preston NE	L	1-2	0-1	8	Naughton	5418
16	11	H	Bristol R	L	2-3	1-1	8	McGinlay, Griffiths	4746
17	25	A	Rotherham U	L	2-4	2-2	9	Brown, Griffiths	5694
18	Dec 2	H	Chester C	W	2-0	2-0	7	McGinlay, Greer (og)	2905
19	16	H	Bolton W	D	3-3	0-2	8	Gorman, McGinlay, Moyes	3443
20	26	A	Notts Co	L	0-4	0-1	10		7819
21	30	A	Fulham	L	1-2	1-1	10	McGinlay	3622
22	Jan 1	H	Swansea C	D	1-1	1-0	10	McGinlay	3515
23	13	A	Leyton Orient	L	0-1	0-1	11		3715
24	20	H	Reading	D	1-1	1-0	10	McGinlay	3504
25	27	A	Birmingham C	W	1-0	1-0	10	McGinlay	7461
26	Feb 3	A	Bury	D	0-0	0-0	9		2677
27	13	H	Blackpool	D	1-1	1-0	—	Kelly	2300
28	17	A	Chester C	L	0-1	0-1	11		2500
29	24	H	Rotherham U	D	1-1	0-1	11	Naughton	3282
30	Mar 2	A	Cardiff C	W	1-0	0-0	—	Perry (og)	2751
31	6	A	Crewe Alex	D	1-1	1-1	—	McGinlay	4318
32	10	H	Bristol C	L	0-1	0-0	14		4785
33	13	H	Cardiff C	D	0-0	0-0	—		2318
34	17	A	Mansfield T	L	1-2	1-1	15	Spink	2230
35	20	H	Wigan Ath	L	1-3	0-2	—	Kelly	2297
36	24	H	Walsall	W	2-0	2-0	14	Moyes, Kelly	3225
37	31	A	Brentford	D	1-1	0-0	15	Kelly	5387
38	Apr 3	H	Northampton T	W	2-0	1-0	—	McGinlay, Moyes	2314
39	7	H	Huddersfield T	D	3-3	1-1	—	McGinlay 3 (1 pen)	2867
40	9	A	Tranmere R	L	1-3	1-2	—	Moyes	7812
41	14	A	Swansea C	W	1-0	0-0	11	McGinlay	3386
42	17	H	Notts Co	D	2-2	1-0	—	Spink 2	3536
43	21	A	Bolton W	W	1-0	1-0	11	McGinlay	5665
44	24	H	Fulham	W	2-0	2-0	—	Spink, McGinlay	2831
45	28	A	Bristol R	L	0-1	0-1	11		7903
46	May 5	H	Preston NE	W	2-0	0-0	11	McGinlay, Spink	5319

Final League Position: 11

GOALSCORERS

League (59): McGinlay 22 (1 pen), Moyes 8, Kelly 5, Spink 5, Griffiths 4, Bell 3, Naughton 3 (1 pen), Pittman 2, Brown 1, Finley 1, Gorman 1, Pratley 1, Purdie 1, own goals 2.
Littlewoods Cup (5): Naughton 2 (1 pen), Green 1, Melrose 1, Pratley 1.
FA Cup (2): McGinlay 2 (2 pens).

Perks	Green	Pittman	Kelly	Pratley	Moyes	Brown	Bell	Melrose	Griffiths	Naughton	Kasule	Hartford	McGinlay	Purdie	Priest	Finley	Worsley	Gorman	Wassell	Cornforth	Lynch	Wimbleton	Ormsby	Weir	Spink	Blake	Parrish	Match No.
1	2	3	4	5	6	7	8	9†	10*	11	12	14																1
1	2	3	4	5	6	7	8	9*		11	12		10															2
1	2	3	4	5	6	7	8			11		9	10															3
1	2	3	4	5	6	7	8			11		9	10															4
1	2	3	4	5	6	7	8			11		9*	10	12														5
1	2	3	4	5	6	7	8		12	11			10*	9														6
1	2		4	5	6	7	8		12	11			10*	9	3													7
1	2	3†	4		6	7	8		12	11			10*	9	14	5												8
1	2	3	4		6	7	8	9*		11			10	12		5												9
1	2	3	4		6	7			12	11		14	10*	9	8†	5												10
1	2	3	4		6	7				11		8	10	9		5												11
1	2†	3*	4		6	7			12	11		8	10	9		5	14											12
1	2	3†	4		6	7*			12	11		8	10	9		5	14											13
1	2	3	4		6	7				11		8	10	9		5												14
1	2	3*	4		6	7				11		8	10	9		5	12											15
1	2	3	4		6	7*			12	11†		8	10		14	5	9											16
1	2	3	4		6	7				11			10			5	12	8*		9								17
1	2	3	4		6	7			12	11†		14	10*			5		8		9								18
1	2	3†	4		6	7				11*		14	10	12		5		8		9								19
1	2		4*		6	7			12	11			10	9†	3	5	14	8										20
1	2	3	4		6	7			12	11		14	10†	9*		5		8										21
1	2	3	4		6	7			12	11		9*	10			5		8										22
1	2	3			6	7			12	11		9*	10	4		5		8										23
1	2				6	7		9		11			10	12				8			3		4*			5		24
1	2		4		6	7			12	11		9*	10			5	14	8			3†							25
1	2		4		6	7			12	11		9*	10			5		8			3							26
1	2		4		6	7			12	11		9*	10			5	14	8†			3							27
1	2		4		6	7			12	11*		9	10			5		8			3							28
1	2		4		6	7				11		9	10			5		8			3							29
1	2		4		6	7†				11		9*	10	12		5	14	8			3							30
1	2		4		6	7†				11		9*	10	12		5	14	8			3							31
1	2		4		6	7			12	11		9*	10			5	14				3	8†						32
1	2		4		6	7			12	11*			10			5					3	8			9			33
1	2		4		6	7*				11			10			5					3	8		12	9			34
1	2		4		6	7*				11			10			5					3	8		12	9			35
1	2		4		6	7*			12	11			10								3	8			9	5		36
1	2		4		6	7			12	11			10*								3	8			9	5		37
1	2		4		6	7				11			10								3	8			9	5		38
1	2		4		6	7			12	11			10				14				3	8			9*	5†		39
1	2*		4		6	7				11			10			5					3	8		12	9			40
1			4		6	7				11*			10	2							3	8		12	9	5		41
1			4		6	7				11			10	2							3	8			9	5		42
1			4		6	7				11*			10	2							3	8		12	9	5		43
1			4		6	7			12	11			10*	2							3†	8		14	9	5		44
1			4		6	7				11*			10	2							3	8†		12	9	5	14	45
1			4		6	7			12	11*			10	2							3	8†			9	5	14	46
46	40	20	43	7	46	42	9	5	10	40	3	14	44	9	7	28	7	17	—	3	22	16	1	4	13	10	—	
							+1s				+14s	+8s		+3s	+2s	+3s	+3s	+4s	+1s	+8s	+2s	+2s			+5s		+2s	

Littlewoods Cup — First Round — Notts Co (h) — 3-0
(a) — 1-3
Second Round — Swindon T (h) — 0-3
(a) — 1-3
FA Cup — First Round — Chesterfield (h) — 2-3

SHREWSBURY TOWN

Player and Position	Ht	Wt	Birth Date	Place	Source	Clubs	League App	Gls
Goalkeepers								
Ken Hughes	6 0	11 08	9 1 66	Barmouth		Crystal Palace	—	—
						Shrewsbury T	15	—
Steve Perks	6 0	12 02	19 4 63	Shrewsbury	Apprentice	Shrewsbury T	211	—
Defenders								
Paul Bywater‡	5 11	13 05	10 8 71	Bridgnorth	Trainee	Shrewsbury T	—	—
Alan Finley	6 3	14 03	10 12 67	Liverpool	Marine	Shrewsbury T	63	2
Richard Green	6 0	11 08	22 11 67	Wolverhampton		Shrewsbury T	125	5
Wayne McLean‡	6 1	12 03	8 1 71	Wordsley	Trainee	Shrewsbury T	—	—
David Moyes	6 1	11 05	25 4 63	Blythswood	Drumchapel A	Celtic	24	—
						Cambridge U	79	1
						Bristol C	83	6
						Shrewsbury T	96	11
Sean Parrish§			14 3 72	Wrexham	Trainee	Shrewsbury T	2	—
Steve Pittman‡	5 9	12 05	18 7 67	Livingstone		East Fife	68	10
						Shrewsbury T	32	2
						Dunfermline Ath (loan)	—	—
Richard Pratley*	6 2	14 02	12 1 63	Banbury	Banbury U	Derby Co	31	1
						Scunthorpe U (loan)	10	—
						Shrewsbury T	46	—
Brian Williams*	5 9	12 1	5 11 55	Salford	Apprentice	Bury	159	19
						QPR	19	—
						Swindon T	99	8
						Bristol R	172	20
						Bristol C	77	3
						Shrewsbury T	65	1
Graeme Worsley	5 10	11 02	4 1 69	Liverpool	Bootle	Shrewsbury T	21	—
Midfield								
Paul Gorman	5 10	11 08	6 8 63	Dublin	Apprentice	Arsenal	6	—
						Birmingham C	6	—
						Carlisle U	148	7
						Shelbourne (loan)	—	—
						Shrewsbury T	19	1
Asa Hartford	5 7	11 04	24 10 50	Clydebank	Amateur	WBA	213	18
						Manchester C	185	22
						Nottingham F	3	—
						Everton	81	6
						Manchester C	75	7
						Norwich C	28	2
						Bolton W	81	8
						Stockport Co	45	—
						Oldham Ath	7	—
						Shrewsbury T	17	—
Tony Kelly	5 10	11 09	1 10 64	Liverpool	Apprentice	Liverpool	—	—
						Derby Co	—	—
						Wigan Ath	101	15
						Stoke C	36	4
						WBA	26	1
						Chester C (loan)	5	—
						Colchester U (loan)	13	2
						Shrewsbury T	63	10
Tommy Lynch	6 0	12 06	10 10 64	Limerick	Limerick	Sunderland	4	—
						Shrewsbury T	22	—
Philip Priest*	5 7	10 06	9 9 66	Warley	School	Chelsea	—	—
						Blackpool (loan)	1	—
						Brentford (loan)	5	1
						Shrewsbury T	60	3
Mark Roberts‡	5 8	10 10	20 7 71	Shrewsbury	Trainee	Shrewsbury T	—	—
Paul Wimbleton	5 8	10 06	13 11 64	Havant	Apprentice	Portsmouth	10	—
						Cardiff C	119	17
						Bristol C	16	2
						Shrewsbury T	16	—

SHREWSBURY TOWN

Foundation: Shrewsbury School having provided a number of the early England and Wales internationals it is not surprising that there was a Town club as early as 1876 which won the Birmingham Senior Cup in 1879. However, the present Shrewsbury Town club was formed in 1886 and won the Welsh FA Cup as early as 1891.

First Football League game: 19 August, 1950, Division 3(N), v Scunthorpe U (a) D 0-0 – Eggleston; Fisher, Lewis; Wheatley, Depear, Robinson; Griffin, Hope, Jackson, Brown, Barker.

Managers (and Secretary-managers)
W. Adams 1905–12*, A. Weston 1912–34*, Jack Roscamp 1934–35, Sam Ramsey 1935–36, Ted Bousted 1936–40, Leslie Knighton 1945–49, Harry Chapman 1949–50, Sammy Crooks 1950–54, Walter Rowley 1955–57, Harry Potts 1957–58, Johnny Spuhler 1958, Arthur Rowley 1958–68, Harry Gregg 1968–72, Maurice Evans 1972–73, Alan Durban 1974–78, Richie Barker 1978, Graham Turner 1978–84, Chic Bates 1984–87, Ian McNeill 1987–90, Asa Hartford 1990– .

Player and Position	Ht	Wt	Birth Date	Place	Source	Clubs	League App	Gls
Forwards								
Mike Brown	5 9	10 12	8 2 68	Birmingham		Shrewsbury T	147	8
Carl Griffiths	5 9	10 06	15 7 71	Oswestry	Trainee	Shrewsbury T	46	10
Alan Irvine‡	6 2	11 06	29 11 62	Broxburn		Hibernian	—	—
						Falkirk	110	17
						Liverpool	2	—
						Dundee U	7	—
						Shrewsbury T	37	6
Vic Kasule (To Hamilton A Oct 1989)	5 10	10 03	28 5 65	Glasgow	Motherwell M	Albion R	132	18
						Meadowbank Th	35	7
						Shrewsbury T	40	4
John McGinlay	5 9	11 06	8 4 64	Inverness	Elgin C	Shrewsbury T	60	27
Jim Melrose*	5 9	10 01	7 10 58	Glasgow	Eastercraigs	Partick Th	122	31
						Leicester C	72	21
						Coventry C	24	8
						Celtic	29	7
						Wolverhampton W (loan)	7	2
						Manchester C	34	8
						Charlton Ath	48	19
						Leeds U	4	—
						Shrewsbury T	49	3
Willie Naughton	6 0	12 08	20 3 62	Catrine	Apprentice	Preston NE	162	10
						Walsall	151	16
						Shrewsbury T	43	3
Jon Purdie‡	5 9	11 12	22 2 67	Corby	Apprentice	Arsenal	—	—
						Wolverhampton W	89	12
						Cambridge U (loan)	7	2
						Oxford U	11	—
						Brentford	6	—
						Shrewsbury T	12	1
Dean Spink	5 11	13 08	22 1 67	Birmingham	Halesowen T	Aston Villa	—	—
						Scarborough (loan)	3	2
						Bury (loan)	6	1
						Shrewsbury T	13	5
Kim Wassell‡	5 8	11 08	9 6 57	Wolverhampton	Apprentice	Northampton T	20	—
					Finland	Aldershot	—	—
					Finland	Hull C	1	—
						Swansea C	2	—
						Wolverhampton W	2	—
					Finland	Shrewsbury T	2	—
Billy Weir	5 5	9 12	11 4 68	Baillieston	Baillieston J	Shrewsbury T	9	—

Trainees
Ball, Ian S; Copeland, Stephen; Evans, Andrew N; Jones, Dale; Parrish, Sean; Ryan, Darren T; Silletto, John B; Thomson, Scott M.

Associated Schoolboys
Bailey, Steven P; Davies, Ashley; Evans, Paul S; Hodgin, Christopher; Humphries, Lee M; Jenkins, Sam B; Malpass, Jody; Rhodes, John; Williams, David J; Williams, Mark; Yates, Jason.

Associated Schoolboys who have accepted the club's offer of a Traineeship/Contract
Barton, Michael; Doster, David; Evans, Jason S; Hanmer, Gareth C; Seabury, Kevin.

498

SOUTHAMPTON 1989–90 *Back row (left to right):* Micky Adams, Barry Horne, Neil Maddison, Jeff Kenna, Dean Radford, Steve Davis, Lee Luscombe, Paul Rideout, Jamie Webb.
Francis Benali, Andy Cook, Nicky Banger.
Centre row: Don Taylor (Physiotherapist), Dave Merrington (Youth Team Coach), Paul Masters, Gerry Forrest, Matthew Le Tissier, Mark Blake, Tim Flowers, Neil Ruddock, John Burridge.
Alan Shearer, Graham Baker, Jason Dodd, Raymond Wallace, Ray Graydon (Reserve Teamn Coach).
Front row: John Mortimore (Assistant Manager, Russell Osman, Danny Wallace, Kevin Moore, Chris Nicholl (Manager), Jimmy Case, Rodney Wallace, Glenn Cockerill,
Dennis Rofe (First Team Trainer).

The Dell, Milton Road, Southampton SO9 4XX. Telephone Southampton (0703) 220505. Ticket enquiries 0703-228575.

Ground capacity: 21,900.

Record attendance: 31,044 v Manchester U, Division 1, 8 Oct, 1969.

Record receipts: £128,730 v Oldham Ath, Littlewoods Cup 5th rd, 24 January 1990.

Pitch measurements: 110yd × 72yd.

Chairman: F. G. L. Askham FCA.

Vice-Chairman: K. St. J. Wiseman.

Directors: J. Corbett, E. T. Bates, I. L. Gordon, B. H. D. Hunt, M. R. Richards FCA.

Manager: Chris Nicholl. *Assistant Manager:* John Mortimore.

Coach: Dennis Rofe. *Physio:* Don Taylor.

Secretary: Brian Truscott. *Commercial Manager:* Bob Russell.

Club Nickname: 'The Saints'.

Year Formed: 1885. *Turned Professional:* 1894. *Ltd Co.:* 1897.

Previous Name: Southampton St Mary's until 1885.

Previous Grounds: 1885, Antelope Ground; 1897, County Cricket Ground: 1898, The Dell.

Record League Victory: 9-3 v Wolverhampton W, Division 2, 18 September 1965 – Godfrey; Jones, Williams; Walker, Knapp, Huxford; Paine (2), O'Brien (1), Melia, Chivers (4), Sydenham (2).

Record Cup Victory: 7-1 v Ipswich T, FA Cup, 3rd rd, 7 January 1961 – Reynolds; Davies, Traynor; Conner, Page, Huxford; Paine (1), O'Brien (3 incl. 1p), Reeves, Mulgrew (2), Penk (1).

Record Defeat: 0-8 v Tottenham H, Division 2, 28 March, 1936 and v Everton, Division 1, 20 November, 1971.

Most League Points (2 for a win): 61, Division 3 (S), 1921–22 and Division 3, 1959–60.

Most League Points (3 for a win): 77, Division 1, 1983–84.

Most League Goals: 112, Division 3 (S), 1957–58.

Highest League Scorer in Season: Derek Reeves, 39, Division 3, 1959–60.

Most League Goals in Total Aggregate: Mike Channon, 185, 1966–77, 1979–82.

Most Capped Player: Peter Shilton 49 (125), England.

Most League Appearances: Terry Paine, 713, 1956–74.

Record Transfer Fee Received: £1,200,000 from Manchester U for Danny Wallace, September 1989.

Record Transfer Fee Paid: £700,000 to Portsmouth for Barry Horne, March 1989.

Football League Record: 1920 Original Member of Division 3; 1921 Division 3 (S); 1922–53 Division 2; 1953–58 Division 3(S); 1958–60 Division 3; 1960–66 Division 2; 1966–74 Division 1; 1974–78 Division 2; 1978– Division 1.

Honours: Football League: Division 1 – Runners-up 1983–84; Division 2 – Runners-up 1965–66, 1977–78; Division 3 (S) – Champions 1921–22; Runners-up 1920–21; Division 3 – Champions 1959–60. *FA Cup:* Winners 1975–76; Runners-up 1900, 1902. *Football League Cup:* Runners-up 1978–79. **European Competitions:** *European Fairs Cup:* 1969–70, *UEFA Cup:* 1971–72, 1981–82, 1982–83, 1984–85; *European Cup-Winners' Cup:* 1976–77.

Colours: Red and white striped shirts, black shorts, white stockings, red trim. **Change colours:** White shirts, Solent green trim, white shorts, white stockings, Solent green trim.

SOUTHAMPTON 1989–90 LEAGUE RECORD

Match No.	Date	Venue	Opponents	Result	H/T Score	Lg. Pos.	Goalscorers	Atten-dance
1	Aug 19	H	Millwall	L 1-2	0-1	—	Ruddock	14,201
2	23	A	Manchester C	W 2-1	1-0	—	Wallace D 2	25,416
3	26	A	Everton	L 0-3	0-2	15		27,807
4	29	H	Aston Villa	W 2-1	0-0	—	Cockerill, Case	14,401
5	Sept 9	A	Norwich C	D 4-4	2-1	9	Rideout 2, Wallace Rod 2	14,259
6	16	H	Crystal Palace	D 1-1	1-0	10	Horne	15,368
7	23	A	Derby Co	W 1-0	0-0	8	Wallace Rod	13,694
8	30	H	Wimbledon	D 2-2	0-1	8	Le Tissier 2 (1 pen)	12,904
9	Oct 14	A	QPR	W 4-1	1-0	6	Wallace Rod 2, Le Tissier (pen), Shearer	10,022
10	21	H	Liverpool	W 4-1	2-0	3	Rideout, Wallace Rod 2, Le Tissier	20,501
11	28	A	Manchester U	L 1-2	1-1	5	Le Tissier	37,122
12	Nov 4	H	Tottenham H	D 1-1	0-1	8	Cockerill	19,601
13	11	A	Coventry C	L 0-1	0-0	8		12,151
14	18	A	Chelsea	D 2-2	1-0	8	Le Tissier 2 (1 pen)	23,093
15	25	H	Luton T	W 6-3	2-1	5	Rideout 2, Le Tissier, Wallace Rod 2, Shearer	14,014
16	Dec 2	A	Millwall	D 2-2	1-1	7	Rideout, Le Tissier (pen)	10,470
17	9	H	Manchester C	W 2-1	0-1	5	Wallace Rod, Horne	15,832
18	17	A	Nottingham F	L 0-2	0-1	—		16,437
19	26	H	Arsenal	W 1-0	0-0	6	Wallace Rod	20,229
20	30	H	Sheffield W	D 2-2	1-1	4	Le Tissier 2 (1 pen)	16,417
21	Jan 1	A	Charlton Ath	W 4-2	3-1	4	Le Tissier, Osman, Wallace Rod 2	7614
22	13	H	Everton	D 2-2	1-1	4	Osman 2	19,381
23	20	A	Aston Villa	L 1-2	0-1	5	Cockerill	33,118
24	Feb 10	A	Crystal Palace	L 1-3	0-1	8	Osman	13,363
25	24	A	Luton T	D 1-1	1-1	10	Shearer	9417
26	27	H	Norwich C	W 4-1	0-1	—	Le Tissier 3, Moore	13,668
27	Mar 3	H	Chelsea	L 2-3	2-1	6	Wallace Rod 2	16,526
28	10	H	Derby Co	W 2-1	0-0	7	Wallace Rod, Le Tissier	16,430
29	17	A	Wimbledon	D 3-3	1-2	7	Le Tissier 3 (1 pen)	5382
30	24	H	Manchester U	L 0-2	0-0	9		20,510
31	31	A	Liverpool	L 2-3	1-1	11	Rideout, Case	37,027
32	Apr 3	H	QPR	L 0-2	0-0	—		14,757
33	7	A	Sheffield W	W 1-0	0-0	10	Cockerill	18,329
34	14	H	Charlton Ath	W 3-2	3-0	7	Ruddock 2, Case	15,275
35	21	H	Nottingham F	W 2-0	1-0	7	Wallace Rod 2	17,006
36	28	H	Coventry C	W 3-0	2-0	7	Le Tissier (pen), Horne, Osman	16,359
37	May 2	A	Arsenal	L 1-2	0-0	—	Horne	23,732
38	5	A	Tottenham H	L 1-2	0-2	7	Cook	31,038

Final League Position: 7

GOALSCORERS

League (71): Le Tissier 20 (7 pens), Wallace Rod 18, Rideout 7, Osman 5, Cockerill 4, Horne 4, Case 3, Ruddock 3, Shearer 3, Wallace D 2, Cook 1, Moore 1.
Littlewoods Cup (8): Le Tissier 3 (1 pen), Wallace Rod 2, Cockerill 1, Horne 1, Rideout 1.
FA Cup (4): Horne 1, Le Tissier 1, Ruddock 1, Wallace Rod 1.

Flowers	Wallace Ray	Adams	Case	Ruddock	Osman	Le Tissier	Horne	Rideout	Baker	Wallace D	Moore	Wallace Rod	Cockerill	Benali	Shearer	Forrest	Dodd	Maddison	Davis	Lee	Andrews	Cook	Cherednik	Match No.
1	2	3	4	5	6*	7	8	9	10†	11	12		14											1
1	2	3	4	5		7	10	9		11*		6	12	8										2
1	2	3	4	5		7†	10	9		11*		6	12	8	14									3
1	2	3	4	5			10	9		11		6	7	8										4
1	2	3	4	5	12		10	9		11		6*	7	8										5
1	2	3	4	5	6	11*	10	9			12	7	8											6
1	2	3*	4	5	6	11	10	9			12	7	8											7
1	2	3†	4	5	6	7	10	12		11		8	14		9*									8
1			4	5	6	7	10					11	8	3	9		2							9
1			4	5	6	7	10	12				11	8	3	9*		2							10
1			4	5	6	7	10					11	8	3	9		2							11
1			4	5	6	7		10				11	8	3	9		2							12
1			4	5	6	7	10					11	8	3	9		2							13
1			4	5	6	7	10					11	8	3	9		2							14
1			4	5	6	7	10					11	8	3	9		2							15
1			4	5	6	7	10					11	8	3	9		2							16
1			4	5	6	7	12	10*	14			11	8	3	9†		2							17
1	14		4		6	7	10	9			12	5	11	8*	3		2†							18
1			4		6	7	10	9				5	11	8	3		2							19
1			4	14	6	7	10†	9*			12	5	11	8	3		2							20
1			4		6	7	10	9				5	11	8	3		2							21
1			4		6	7	10	9				5	11	8	3		2							22
1		2	4		6	7	10	9				5	11	8	3									23
1			4	5	6	7	2	9			12	11*	8	3	10									24
1			4		6	11	10	9			12	5	7*	8	3		2							25
1			4		6	11	10	9				5	7	8	3		2							26
1			4†		6	11*	10	9			12	5	7	8	3		2		14					27
			4		6*	11	10	9			12	5	7	8	3		2				1			28
			4		6	11	10	9				5	7	8	3		2				1			29
			4		6	11	10	9			12	5	7	8	3		2*				1			30
1			4	8*	6	11	10	9			12	5	7	3†			2						14	31
1			4	8	6	11	10	9			12	5*	7	3					14				2†	32
1		3	4	5	6	11*	10	9				7†	12	8			2					14		33
1		3	4	5	6	11*	10	9				7	12	8									2	34
1		3	4	5	6	11	10	9				7		8									2	35
1		3	4	5	6	11*	10	9				7	12	8					14				2†	36
1		3†	4	5	6	11	10	9*			12	7	14	8									2	37
1			4	5	6	11	10	9				7*	3	8						12			2	38
35	8	15	33	25	34	35	28	30	2	5	18	35	35	23	19	1	21	—	4	—	3	2	7	
+1s				+4s	+1s		+1s	+1s	+1s		+3s	+3s	+1s	+4s	+7s		+1s	+2s		+2s		+2s	+1s	

SOUTHAMPTON

Player and Position	Ht	Wt	Birth Date	Birth Place	Source	Clubs	League App	Gls
Goalkeepers								
Ian Andrews	6 2	12 02	1 12 64	Nottingham	Apprentice	Leicester C	126	—
						Swindon T (loan)	1	—
						Celtic	5	—
						Leeds U (loan)	1	—
						Southampton	3	—
Tim Flowers	6 2	13 04	3 2 67	Kenilworth	Apprentice	Wolverhampton W	63	—
						Southampton (loan)	—	—
						Southampton	60	—
						Swindon T (loan)	2	—
						Swindon T (loan)	5	—
Gary French	5 11	11 10	21 11 71	Ilminster	Trainee	Southampton	—	—
Defenders								
Mick Adams	5 7	10 10	8 11 61	Sheffield	Apprentice	Gillingham	92	5
						Coventry C	90	9
						Leeds U	73	2
						Southampton	23	—
Francis Benali	5 9	11 01	30 12 68	Southampton	Apprentice	Southampton	34	—
Mark Blake	6 0	12 04	19 12 67	Portsmouth	Apprentice	Southampton	18	2
						Colchester U (loan)	4	1
						Shrewsbury T (loan)	10	—
Aleksey Cherednik	5 9	11 07	12 12 60	USSR	Dnepr	Southampton	8	—
Andy Cook	5 9	10 12	10 8 69	Romsey	Apprentice	Southampton	9	1
Steve Davis	6 2	12 08	30 10 68	Hexham	Trainee	Southampton	4	—
						Burnley (loan)	9	—
Jason Dodd	5 10	11 10	2 11 70	Bath		Southampton	22	—
Gerry Forrest*	5 10	10 11	21 1 57	Stockton	South Bank	Rotherham U	357	7
						Southampton	115	—
Jeff Kenna	5 11	11 09	27 8 70	Dublin	Trainee	Southampton	—	—
Kevin Moore	5 11	12 02	29 4 58	Grimsby	Local	Grimsby T	400	27
						Oldham Ath	13	1
						Southampton	81	7
Russell Osman	6 0	11 10	14 2 59	Repton	Apprentice	Ipswich T	294	17
						Leicester C	108	8
						Southampton	71	5
Dean Radford	5 11	11 05	14 11 70	London	Trainee	Southampton	—	—
Neil Ruddock	6 2	12 06	9 5 68	London	Apprentice	Millwall	—	—
						Tottenham H	9	—
						Millwall	2	1
						Southampton	42	6
Ray Wallace	5 6	10 02	2 10 69	Lewisham	Trainee	Southampton	35	—
Midfield								
Graham Baker*	5 9	10 08	3 12 58	Southampton	Apprentice	Southampton	113	22
						Manchester C	117	19
						Southampton	60	9
						Aldershot (loan)	7	2
Jimmy Case	5 9	12 07	18 5 54	Liverpool	S Liverpool	Liverpool	186	23
						Brighton & HA	127	10
						Southampton	190	9
Glenn Cockerill	6 0	12 04	26 8 50	Grimsby	Louth U	Lincoln C	71	10
						Swindon T	26	1
						Lincoln C	115	25
						Sheffield U	62	10
						Southampton	181	26
Barry Horne	5 10	11 06	18 5 62	St Asaph	Rhyl	Wrexham	136	16
						Portsmouth	70	7
						Southampton	40	4
Sammy Lee	5 7	10 01	7 2 59	Liverpool	Apprentice	Liverpool	197	13
						QPR	30	—
					Osasuna	Southampton	2	—

SOUTHAMPTON

Foundation: Formed largely by players from the Deanery FC, which had been established by school teachers in 1880. Most of the founders were connected with the young men's association of St. Mary's Church. At the inaugural meeting held in November 1885 the club was named Southampton St. Mary's and the church's curate was elected president.

First Football League game: 28 August, 1920, Division 3, v Gillingham (a) D 1-1 – Allen; Parker, Titmuss; Shelley, Campbell, Turner; Barratt, Dominy (1), Rawlings, Moore, Foxall.

Managers (and Secretary-managers)
Cecil Knight 1894–95*, Charles Robson 1895–97, E. Arnfield 1897–1911* (continued as secretary), George Swift 1911–12, E. Arnfield 1912–19, Jimmy McIntyre 1919–24, Arthur Chadwick 1925–31, George Kay 1931–36, George Gross 1936–37, Tom Parker 1937–43, J. R. Sarjantson stepped down from the board to act as secretary-manager 1943–47 with the next two listed being team managers during this period), Arthur Dominy 1943–46, Bill Dodgin Snr 1946–49, Sid Cann 1949–51, George Roughton 1952–55, Ted Bates 1955–73, Lawrie McMenemy 1973–85, Chris Nicholl 1985– .

Player and Position	Ht	Wt	Birth Date	Place	Source	Clubs	League App	Gls
Neil Maddison	5 9	11 08	2 10 69	Darlington	Trainee	Southampton	7	2
Paul Masters*	5 6	10 07	16 1 71	Southampton	Trainee	Southampton	—	—
Jamie Webb‡	5 8	10 06	7 12 69	Portsmouth	Trainee	Southampton	—	—
Tommy Widdrington	5 8	11 01	21 11 71	Newcastle	Trainee	Southampton	—	—
Forwards								
Nicky Banger	5 8	10 06	25 2 71	Southampton	Trainee	Southampton	—	—
Matthew Le Tissier	6 0	11 06	14 10 68	Guernsey	Vale Recreation	Southampton	106	35
Lee Luscombe	6 0	12 04	16 7 71	Guernsey	Trainee	Southampton	—	—
Paul Rideout	5 11	12 01	14 8 64	Bournemouth	Apprentice	Swindon T	95	38
						Aston Villa	54	19
						Bari	99	23
						Southampton	55	13
Andy Rowland	6 2	13 10	1 10 65	Taunton		Southampton	—	—
Alan Shearer	5 11	11 03	13 8 70	Newcastle	Trainee	Southampton	41	6
Rodney Wallace	5 7	10 01	2 10 69	Lewisham	Trainee	Southampton	91	31

Trainees
Allsopp, Daniel; Bound, Matthew, T; Burnett, Darren D; Good, Nicholas R.J; Hopkins, Colin J; Lamport, David M; Owen, Dean M; Peters, Jason G; Phillips, Kevin; Powell, Lee; Roast, Stephen; Taylor, Gareth K; White, Christian J.

Associated Schoolboys
Baker, Jonathan; Chesney, Adrian M; Cleeve, Anthony G; Davies, Andrew, I; Davies, Neil; Elliott, Jamie; Fleming, Sean; Hopper, Neil; Jones, Stephen; Kamara, Abdul S; McNally, Aron A; Murphy, Kevin; Pitman, Jamie R; Puckrin, Glenn; Reed, Adam M; Robinson, Matthew R; Rowe, Damion; Shakespeare, Jason P; Shiers, Benjamin D; Skedd, Antony S; Smith, Justin M.F; Tekell, Lee; Tisdale, Paul R; Walker, Matthew; Waters, Jamie S; Watson, Paul D; White, Nicholas.

Associated Schoolboys who have accepted the club's offer of a Traineeship/Contract
Crowley, Thomas; Frost, Neil; Savage, Ian; Selby, Neil S; Thomas, Martin; Thorne, Kevin M; Whitman, Nathan; Wright, Scott.

SOUTHEND UNITED 1989–90 *Back row (left to right)*: Steve Tilson, Martin Lawrence, Gary Bennett, Mario Walsh, David Crown, Matt Jones, Justin Edinburgh. *Centre row*: Paul Clark (Assistant Manager), David Martin, Roy McDonough, Paul Sansome, Paul Newell, Spencer Prior, Ian O'Connell, Kevin Lock (Coach). *Front row*: Nicky Smith, Peter Butler, Paul Roberts, David Webb (General Manager), Paul Brush, Martin Ling, Jason Cook.

Division 3 **SOUTHEND UNITED**

Roots Hall Football Ground, Victoria Avenue, Southend-on-Sea SS2 6NQ. Telephone Southend (0702) 340707. Commercial Dept: (0702) 332113. Soccerline: 0898 700 279.

Ground capacity: 11,863.

Record attendance: 31,090 v Liverpool FA Cup 3rd rd, 10 Jan, 1979.

Record receipts: £36,599 v Liverpool, FA Cup 3rd rd, 10 Jan, 1979.

Pitch measurements: 110yd × 74yd.

President: N. J. Woodcock.

Chairman: V. T. Jobson. *Vice-Chairman:* J. W. Adams.

Secretary: J. W. Adams.

Directors: R. F. Moore OBE, M. Markscheffel, J. Foster, W. E. Parsons, R. J. Osborne.

Manager: David Webb *Assistant Manager:* Kevin Lock. *Youth Team Manager:* Danny Greaves.

Commercial Manager: Harry Stobart. *Physio:*

Club Nickname: 'The Shrimpers'.

Year Formed: 1906. *Turned Professional:* 1906. *Ltd Co.:* 1919.

Previous Grounds: 1906, Roots Hall, Prittlewell; 1920, Kursaal; 1934, Southend Stadium; 1955, Roots Hall Football Ground.

Record League Victory: 9-2 v Newport Co, Division 3 (S), 5 September 1936 – McKenzie; Nelson, Everest (1); Deacon, Turner, Carr; Bolan, Lane (1), Goddard (4), Dickinson (2), Oswald (1).

Record Cup Victory: 10-1 v Golders Green, FA Cup, 1st rd, 24 November 1934 – Moore; Morfitt, Kelly; Mackay, Joe Wilson, Carr (1); Lane (1), Johnson (5), Cheesmuir (2), Deacon (1), Oswald. 10-1 v Brentwood, FA Cup, 2nd rd, 7 December 1968 – Roberts; Bentley, Birks; McMillan (1) Beesley, Kurila; Clayton, Chisnall, Moore (4), Best (5), Hamilton.

Record Defeat: 1-9 v Brighton & HA, Division 3, 27 November, 1965.

Most League Points (2 for a win): 67, Division 4, 1980–81.

Most League Points (3 for a win): 80, Division 4, 1986–87.

Most League Goals: 92, Division 3 (S), 1950–51.

Highest League Scorer in Season: Jim Shankly, 31, 1928–29 and Sammy McCrory, 1957–58, both in Division 3 (S).

Most League Goals in Total Aggregate: Roy Hollis, 122, 1953–60.

Most Capped Player: George Mackenzie, 9, Eire.

Most League Appearances: Sandy Anderson, 451, 1950–63.

Record Transfer Fee Received: £150,000 from Crystal Palace for Glenn Pennyfather, November 1987, and £150,000 from Wolverhampton W for Shane Westley, June 1989.

Record Transfer Fee Paid: £111,111 to Blackpool for Derek Spence, December 1979.

Football League Record: 1920 Original Member of Division 3; 1921 Division 3 (S); 1958–66 Division 3; 1966–72 Division 4; 1972–76 Division 3; 1976–78 Division 4; 1978–80 Division 3; 1980–81 Division 4; 1981–84 Division 3; 1984–87 Division 4; 1987–89 Division 3; 1989–90 Division 4; 1990– Division 3.

Honours: Football League: Division 3 (S) best season; 3rd, 1931–32, 1949–50; Division 4 – Champions 1980–81; Runners-up 1971–72, 1977–78. *FA Cup* best season: old 3rd rd, 1920–21, 5th rd, 1925-26, 1951-52, 1975-76. *Football League Cup:* never past 3rd rd.

Colours: Blue shirts yellow trim, yellow shorts blue trim, blue stockings. **Change colours:** All yellow.

506

SOUTHEND UNITED 1989–90 LEAGUE RECORD

Match No.	Date	Venue	Opponents	Result	H/T Score	Lg. Pos.	Goalscorers	Attendance
1	Aug 19	H	York C	W 2-0	1-0	—	Walsh, Crown	2725
2	26	A	Wrexham	D 3-3	1-1	6	Prior, Crown, Bennett	2011
3	Sept 1	H	Hartlepool U	W 3-0	3-0	—	Ling 2, Walsh	3236
4	9	A	Aldershot	W 5-0	2-0	2	Bennett, Brown (og), Crown 2, Smith (og)	2255
5	15	H	Torquay U	W 1-0	1-0	—	Bennett	7070
6	22	A	Doncaster R	W 1-0	1-0	—	Crown (pen)	2386
7	26	A	Gillingham	L 0-5	0-1	—		3842
8	30	H	Lincoln C	W 2-0	1-0	1	Butler, McDonough	4833
9	Oct 7	H	Scarborough	W 1-0	0-0	1	Crown	3432
10	14	A	Hereford U	W 3-0	2-0	1	Crown 2, McDonough	2975
11	16	A	Stockport Co	L 0-1	0-0	—		6593
12	21	H	Maidstone U	L 0-1	0-1	1		4016
13	28	A	Chesterfield	D 1-1	0-1	2	Crown	3096
14	31	H	Burnley	W 3-2	2-2	—	McDonough, Crown (pen), Bennett	3765
15	Nov 4	H	Peterborough U	D 0-0	0-0	1		4895
16	10	A	Halifax T	W 2-1	1-0	—	Ling, Martin	1908
17	24	H	Cambridge U	D 0-0	0-0	—		4068
18	Dec 2	A	Scunthorpe U	D 1-1	1-0	1	Ling	3714
19	19	A	Grimsby T	L 0-2	0-0	—		4001
20	26	H	Colchester U	L 0-2	0-0	4		5563
21	30	H	Exeter C	L 1-2	1-1	5	McDonough	3761
22	Jan 1	A	Rochdale	W 1-0	1-0	4	Ling	1521
23	6	A	Carlisle U	L 0-3	0-1	—		6196
24	12	A	Wrexham	W 2-1	1-0	—	Crown, Cook	3005
25	20	A	York C	L 1-2	0-0	4	Crown (pen)	2397
26	27	H	Aldershot	W 5-0	3-0	3	Ling 2, Crown 3	2821
27	Feb 2	H	Doncaster R	W 2-0	1-0	—	McDonough, Ling	3174
28	6	A	Torquay U	L 0-3	0-1	—		2077
29	13	A	Hartlepool U	D 1-1	1-0	—	Ling	3628
30	16	H	Scunthorpe U	D 0-0	0-0	—		3154
31	25	A	Cambridge U	L 1-2	0-1	—	Crown	4573
32	Mar 3	H	Carlisle U	W 2-0	0-0	2	Butters 2	3465
33	7	A	Lincoln C	L 0-2	0-1	—		4860
34	9	H	Gillingham	W 2-0	1-0	—	Benjamin, Butters	4460
35	17	A	Scarborough	D 1-1	0-0	3	Smith N	2179
36	20	H	Hereford U	W 2-0	1-0	—	Benjamin, Martin	2669
37	23	H	Stockport Co	W 2-0	2-0	—	Butler, Benjamin	3917
38	31	A	Maidstone U	L 0-3	0-1	3		3550
39	Apr 7	H	Chesterfield	L 0-2	0-1	5		2892
40	10	A	Burnley	D 0-0	0-0	—		3967
41	14	A	Rochdale	W 3-2	1-0	5	Brown (og), Ansah, Martin	2464
42	16	A	Colchester U	W 2-0	1-0	3	Benjamin, Daley	5283
43	20	H	Grimsby T	L 0-2	0-1	—		4945
44	25	A	Exeter C	L 1-2	0-1	—	Crown	8271
45	27	H	Halifax T	W 2-0	1-0	—	Ling, Smith P	3656
46	May 5	A	Peterborough U	W 2-1	2-0	3	Crown 2	7958

Final League Position: 3

GOALSCORERS

League (61): Crown 19 (3 pens), Ling 10, McDonough 5, Benjamin 4, Bennett 4, Butters 3, Martin 3, Butler 2, Walsh 2, Ansah 1, Cook 1, Daley 1, Prior 1, Smith N 1, Smith P 1, own goals 3.
Littlewoods Cup (9): Bennett 4, Crown 3 (1 pen), Martin 2.
FA Cup (0).

Sansome	Dixon	Roberts	Martin	Prior	Brush	Cook	Butler	Crown	Walsh	Bennett	McDonough	Ling	Tilson	Edinburgh	Daley	Jones	Smith N	Clark	Edwards	Butters	Benjamin	O'Connell	Smith P	Ansah	Austin	Cooper	Match No.
1	2	3	4	5	6	7	8	9	10*	11	12																1
1	2	3	4	5	6	7	8	9	10	11																	2
1	2	3	4	5		7	8	9	10	11		6															3
1	2	3	4	5		7	8	9	10	11		6															4
1	2	3	4	5		7	8	9	10	11		6															5
1	2	3	4	5	12	7	8	9	10†	11	14	6*															6
1	2	3	4	5	12	7	8	9	10†	11	14		6*														7
1	2	3	4	5	6	7	8	9		11	10																8
1	2		4	5	6	7*	8	9		11	10	12	3														9
1	2			5	6	7	8	9*		11†	10	4	3	12		14											10
1	2			5	6	7	8	9			10	4	3	11*		12											11
1	2			5	6	7*	8	9	10†	11		4	3	12		14											12
1	2		4	5	6	7	8	9		11	10		3														13
1	2		4	5	6	7	8	9		11	10		3														14
1	2		4	5*	6	7	8	9		10	11	12	3														15
1	2		4		6	7	8	9		10	11	5*	3			12											16
1	2		4		6	7	8	9		10	11	5	3														17
1	2		4		6	5	8	9		10	11		3				7										18
1	2		4		6	5†	8*	9		10	11	12	3	14			7										19
1	2		4		6	7		9*	12	10	11		3					8	5								20
1	2					7	8	9	4	10	11		3					6	5								21
1	2					7	8	9	4	10	11		3					6	5								22
1	2†	14				7	8	9*	12	10	11	4	3					6	5								23
1	2	3	4		6	7	8	9		11	10							5									24
1	2	3	4		6	7*	8	9		11	10	12						5									25
1	2	3	4		6		8	9		10	11						7	5									26
1	2	3	4		6		8	9	12	10	11						7*	5									27
1	2	3	4				8	9	12	10	11						7*	5	6								28
1	2	3	4			7	8	9	12	10	11*							6	5								29
1	2	3†	4	14		7	8	9	12	10	11*							6	5								30
1	2		4	3			8	9		10							11*	7	6	5	12						31
1	2		4*	3			8	9				11					7	6	5	10	12						32
1	2		4	3			8		9	11*							7	6	5	10	12						33
1	2		4	3			8	9	11								7	6	5	10							34
1	2			3	4			9	11†	12							7	6	5	10	14*		8				35
1	2		4	3	7*	8	9			11								6	5	10	12						36
1	2		4	3		8	9*		12	7							11	6	5	10							37
1	2		4	3		8	9			7*							11	6	5	10	12						38
1	2		4	3†		8			12	7							11	6	5	10	14		9*				39
1			4		12			6					3				11	5	10	8	9			2	7*		40
1			4					9					3	11*		6		5	10	8	7			2	12		41
1			4					9	5			3	12				6	10	8*	7			2	11			42
1	14		4					9	5	12		3					6	10	8†	7*			2	11			43
1	4†						5	9	7	12		3				6	14	10	8				2	11*			44
1						5	9		7			3	12			6	4	10	8*	11			2				45
1			4			11	9		7			3	12			6	5	10	8*				2				46
46	24	30	38	15	28	29	40	41	10	20	27	24	11	22	—	2	12	24	7	16	15	—	8	6	7	4	
	+	+			+	+			+	+	+	+	+			+	+	+	+	+			+	+	+	+	
	1s	1s			3s	1s			1s	5s	6s	1s	5s			5s	2s	2s	1s	1s			4s	2s	1s	1s	

Littlewoods Cup	First Round	Colchester U (a)	4-3
		(h)	2-1
	Second Round	Tottenham H (a)	0-1
		(h)	3-2
FA Cup	First Round	Aylesbury (a)	0-1

SOUTHEND UNITED

Player and Position	Ht	Wt	Birth Date	Birth Place	Source	Clubs	League App	Gls
Goalkeepers								
Paul Newell	6 1	11 05	23 2 69	Greenwich	Trainee	Southend U	15	—
Paul Sansome	6 0	12 00	6 10 61	N Addington	Apprentice	Crystal Palace	—	—
						Milwall	156	—
						Southend U	96	—
Defenders								
Dean Austin	6 0	12 04	26 4 70	Hemel Hempstead	St Albans	Southend U	7	—
Paul Brush*	5 11	12 02	22 2 58	Plaistow	Apprentice	West Ham U	151	1
						Crystal Palace	50	3
						Southend U	73	1
Andy Dixon*	6 1	10 11	19 4 68	Louth	Apprentice	Grimsby T	38	—
						Southend U	24	—
Justin Edinburgh	5 9	11 06	18 12 69	Brentwood	Trainee	Southend U	37	—
						Tottenham H (loan)	—	—
Chris Hyslop			14 6 72	Watford	Trainee	Southend U	—	—
David Martin	6 1	11 08	25 4 63	East Ham	Apprentice	Millwall	140	6
						Wimbledon	35	3
						Southend U	149	6
Spencer Prior	6 3	12 10	22 4 71	Rochford	Trainee	Southend U	29	2
Paul Roberts*	5 9	11 13	27 4 62	London	Apprentice	Millwall	146	—
						Brentford	62	—
						Swindon T	27	—
						Southend U	38	—
						Aldershot	39	—
						Exeter C	3	—
						Southend U	54	—
Midfield								
Peter Butler	5 9	11 01	27 8 66	Halifax	Apprentice	Huddersfield T	5	—
						Cambridge U (loan)	14	1
						Bury	11	—
						Cambridge U	55	9
						Southend U	91	7
Paul Clark	5 10	12 12	14 9 58	Benfleet	Apprentice	Southend U	33	1
						Brighton & HA	79	9
						Reading (loan)	2	—
						Southend U	236	3
Jason Cook	5 7	10 06	29 12 69	Edmonton	Trainee	Tottenham H	—	—
						Southend U	29	1
Peter Daley	5 10	11 00	14 2 70	Liverpool	Liverpool§	Southend U	5	1
Andy Edwards	6 2	12 06	17 9 71	Epping	Trainee	Southend U	9	—
Matthew Jones*	5 11	12 00	9 10 70	Chiswick	Trainee	Southend U	5	—
Martin Ling	5 7	9 12	15 7 66	West Ham	Apprentice	Exeter C	116	14
						Swindon T	2	—
						Southend U	135	31
Iain O'Connell*	6 0	11 07	9 10 70	Rochford	Trainee	Southend U	4	—
Nick Smith*	5 8	10 00	28 1 69	Berkley	Trainee	Southend U	60	6
Paul Smith	5 11	12 00	18 9 71	London	Trainee	Southend U	10	1
Forwards								
Andy Ansah	5 10	11 01	19 3 69	Lewisham		Crystal Palace	—	—
						Brentford	8	2
						Southend U	7	1

SOUTHEND UNITED

Foundation: The leading club in Southend around the turn of the century was Southend Athletic, but they were an amateur concern. Southend United was a more ambitious professional club when they were founded in 1906, employing Bob Jack as secretary-manager and immediately joining the Second Division of the Southern League.

First Football League game: 28 August, 1920, Division 3, v Brighton & HA (a) W 2-0 – Capper; Reid, Newton; Wileman, Henderson, Martin; Nicholls, Nuttall, Fairclough (2), Myers, Dorsett.

Managers (and Secretary-managers)
Bob Jack 1906–10, George Molyneux 1910–11, O. M. Howard 1911–12, Joe Bradshaw 1912–19, Ned Liddell 1919–20, Tom Mather 1920–21, Ted Birnie 1921–34, David Jack 1934–40, Harry Warren 1946–56, Eddie Perry 1956–60, Frank Broome 1960, Ted Fenton 1961–65, Alvan Williams 1965–67, Ernie Shepherd 1967–69, Geoff Hudson 1969–70, Arthur Rowley 1970–76, Dave Smith 1976–83, Peter Morris 1983–84, Bobby Moore 1984–86, Dave Webb 1986–87, Dick Bate 1987, Paul Clark 1987–88, Dave Webb (GM) 1988– .

Player and Position	Ht	Wt	Birth Date	Place	Source	Clubs	League App	Gls
Ian Benjamin	5 11	12 00	11 12 61	Nottingham	Apprentice	Sheffield U	5	3
						WBA	2	—
						Notts Co	—	—
						Peterborough U	80	14
						Northampton T	150	59
						Cambridge U	25	2
						Chester C	22	2
						Exeter C	32	4
						Southend U	15	4
David Crown	5 10	11 04	16 2 58	Enfield	Walthamstow A	Brentford	46	8
						Portsmouth	28	2
						Exeter C (loan)	7	3
						Reading	88	15
						Cambridge U	106	45
						Southend U	113	61
Martyn Lawrence‡	5 11	11 10	3 9 70	Rochford	Trainee	Southend U	—	—
Roy McDonough	6 1	11 11	16 10 58	Solihull	Apprentice	Birmingham C	2	1
						Walsall	82	15
						Chelsea	—	—
						Colchester U	93	24
						Southend U	22	4
						Exeter C	20	1
						Cambridge U	32	5
						Southend U	186	30
Steve Tilson	5 11	11 10	27 7 66	Essex	Burnham	Southend U	32	2
Mario Walsh	6 1	11 12	19 1 66	Paddington	Apprentice	Portsmouth	—	—
						Torquay U	100	18
						Colchester U	38	12
						Southend U	11	2
Adrian West			6 12 71	Bedford	Trainee	Southend U	—	—

Trainees
Afror, Louis K.J; Furzur, Lee T; Grayburn, Marlon S; Hayden, Jason R; Matthews, Lee D; Schneider, Matthew J; Sugrue, Simon; Travi, Lee C.

Associated Schoolboy
Watson, Mark.

STOCKPORT COUNTY 1989–90 *Back row (left to right):* Alan Dean, Ian McInerney, Brett Angell, Barry Siddall, David Redfern, Andy Thorpe, Gary Leonard, Gary Dooner. *Centre row:* Rodger Wylde (Physiotherapist), Chris Downes, George Oghani, Malcolm Brown, Gary McDonald, Chris Beaumont, John Cooke, Mark Payne, Tony Caldwell, Paul Jones (Youth Manager). *Front row:* Steve Bullock, David Logan, Mick Matthews, Bill Williams, Danny Bergara (Manager), Nigel Hart, David Frain, Mark Howard, Paul Williams.

Division 4   **STOCKPORT COUNTY**

Edgeley Park, Hardcastle Road, Stockport, Cheshire SK3 9DD.
Telephone 061–480 8888. Clubcall: 0898 12 16 38. Promotions
Office: 061-480 1247.
Ground capacity: 8520.
Record attendance: 27,833 v Liverpool, FA Cup 5th rd, 11 Feb, 1950.
Record receipts: £23,515 v Liverpool, Milk Cup 2nd rd, 1st leg, 24 Sept, 1984.
Pitch measurements: 110yd × 71yd.
Hon. Vice-Presidents: Mike Yarwood OBE, Freddie Pye, Andrew Barlow.
Chairman: B. Elwood. *Vice-Chairman:* G. White.
Directors: M. Baker, B. Taylor, M. H. Rains, H. T. Stephenson.
Chief Executive/Secretary: J. D. Simpson.
Manager: Danny Bergara. *Asst. Manager:* John Sainty.
Coach: *Physio:* Rodger Wylde.
Assistant Secretary/Commercial Manager:
General Manager: John Higgins. *Programme Editors:* Steve Bellis and Todd White.
Year Formed: 1883. *Turned Professional:* 1891. *Ltd Co.:* 1908.
Club Nickname: 'County' or 'Hatters'.
Previous Names: Heaton Norris Rovers 1883–88, Heaton Norris 1888–90.
Previous Grounds: 1883 Heaton Norris Recreation Ground; 1884 Heaton Norris Wanderers Cricket Ground; 1885 Chorlton's Farm, Chorlton's Lane; 1886 Heaton Norris Cricket Ground; 1887 Wilkes' Field, Belmont Street; 1889 Nursery Inn, Green Lane; 1902 Edgeley Park.
Record League Victory: 13-0 v Halifax T, Division 3 (N), 6 January 1934 – McGann; Vincent (1p), Jenkinson; Robinson, Stevens, Len Jones; Foulkes (1), Hill (3), Lythgoe (2), Stevenson (2), Downes (4).
Record Cup Victory: 6-2 v West Auckland T (away), FA Cup, 1st rd, 14th November 1959 – Lea; Betts (1), Webb; Murray, Hodder, Porteous; Wilson (1), Holland, Guy (2), Ritchie (1), Davock (1).
Record Defeat: 1-8 v Chesterfield, Division 2, 19 April, 1902.
Most League Points (2 for a win): 64, Division 4, 1966–67.
Most League Points (3 for a win): 74, Division 4, 1989–90.
Most League Goals: 115, Division 3 (N), 1933–34.
Highest League Scorer in Season: Alf Lythgoe, 46, Division 3 (N), 1933–34.
Most League Goals in Total Aggregate: Jack Connor, 132, 1951–56.
Most Capped Player: Harry Hardy, 1, England.
Most League Appearances: Bob Murray, 465, 1952–63.
Record Transfer Fee Received: £80,000 from Manchester C for Stuart Lee, September 1979.
Record Transfer Fee Paid: £50,000 to Rochdale for David Frain, July 1989 and £50,000 to Hull C for Keith Edwards, September 1989.
Football League Record: 1900 Elected to Division 2; 1904 failed re-election; 1905–21 Division 2; 1921-22 Division 3 (N); 1922–26 Division 2; 1926–37 Division 3 (N); 1937–38 Division 2; 1938-58 Division 3 (N); 1958–59 Division 3; 1959–67 Division 4; 1967–70 Division 3; 1970– Division 4.
Honours: Football League: Division 2 best season: 10th, 1905–06; Division 3 (N) – Champions 1921–22, 1936–37; Runners-up 1928–29, 1929-30; Division 4 – Champions 1966–67.
FA Cup best season: 5th rd. 1935, 1950. *Football League Cup* best season: 4th rd, 1972–73.
Colours: White shirts, royal blue shorts, white stockings. **Change colours:** All red.

STOCKPORT COUNTY 1989–90 LEAGUE RECORD

Match No.	Date		Venue	Opponents	Result		H/T Score	Lg. Pos.	Goalscorers	Atten- dance
1	Aug	19	H	Torquay U	D	1-1	1-1	—	Beaumont	2356
2		26	A	Burnley	D	0-0	0-0	14		6537
3	Sept	1	H	York C	D	2-2	1-1	—	Oghani, Matthews	2793
4		5	A	Wrexham	W	1-0	0-0	—	Payne	2333
5		9	A	Maidstone U	W	1-0	1-0	3	Logan	2020
6		15	H	Hartlepool U	W	6-0	3-0	—	Angell 4 (1 pen), Cooke, Oghani (pen)	3926
7		23	A	Aldershot	L	1-2	1-0	3	Angell (pen)	1879
8		30	H	Scarborough	W	3-2	3-1	5	Edwards, McInerney, Angell	3086
9	Oct	7	H	Hereford U	W	2-1	2-0	4	Edwards, Angell	3428
10		14	A	Gillingham	W	3-0	1-0	3	Angell 2, Edwards	3887
11		16	H	Southend U	W	1-0	0-0	—	Angell	6593
12		21	A	Peterborough U	L	0-2	0-1	2		4804
13		28	H	Exeter C	W	2-1	1-0	1	McInerney, Edwards	3767
14	Nov	1	A	Lincoln C	D	0-0	0-0	—		5003
15		3	H	Halifax T	L	0-1	0-0	—		5490
16		11	A	Chesterfield	D	1-1	0-0	3	McInerney	4585
17		25	H	Scunthorpe U	W	4-2	1-1	2	Payne, Angell 3 (1 pen)	3259
18	Dec	2	A	Doncaster R	L	1-2	0-0	3	Matthews	3023
19		9	A	Scarborough	L	0-2	0-1	—		1780
20		17	A	Carlisle U	L	1-3	1-1	—	McInerney	4971
21		26	H	Rochdale	W	2-1	2-0	3	Angell, Brown	4215
22		29	H	Cambridge U	W	3-1	1-1	—	Downes, Edwards 2	3915
23	Jan	1	A	Grimsby T	L	2-4	1-1	3	Beaumont, Edwards	5717
24		5	A	Colchester U	W	1-0	0-0	—	Frain	3609
25		13	H	Burnley	W	3-1	0-1	3	Payne 2, Logan	5210
26		20	A	Torquay U	L	0-3	0-0	3		2228
27		27	H	Maidstone U	L	1-2	0-0	4	McInerney	4161
28	Feb	3	H	Aldershot	D	1-1	0-0	4	Payne	2771
29		10	A	Hartlepool U	L	0-5	0-3	5		3004
30		13	A	York C	W	3-0	2-0	—	Angell 2, McInerney	2256
31		16	H	Doncaster R	W	3-1	1-1	—	Edwards 2, Angell	3609
32		24	A	Scunthorpe U	L	0-5	0-3	3		3280
33	Mar	2	H	Colchester U	D	1-1	0-0	—	Angell	3452
34		9	H	Wrexham	L	0-2	0-1	—		4177
35		17	A	Hereford U	W	2-1	2-1	5	Payne, Beaumont	2458
36		19	H	Gillingham	W	1-0	0-0	—	Edwards	3378
37		23	A	Southend U	L	0-2	0-2	—		3917
38		30	H	Peterborough U	D	0-0	0-0	—		3651
39	Apr	7	A	Exeter C	D	1-1	1-1	7	Angell	4817
40		9	H	Lincoln C	D	1-1	1-0	—	Angell	3394
41		14	H	Grimsby T	L	2-4	1-2	9	Logan, McInerney	4065
42		16	A	Rochdale	D	1-1	0-0	9	Frain	3194
43		20	H	Carlisle U	W	3-1	2-1	—	Gannon, Brown, Angell	3819
44		23	A	Cambridge U	W	2-0	1-0	—	Angell 2	4850
45		28	H	Chesterfield	W	3-1	1-1	4	Rogers (og), Beaumont, Logan	5203
46	May	5	A	Halifax T	W	2-1	0-1	4	Beaumont, McInerney	4744

Final League Position: 4

GOALSCORERS

League (68): Angell 23 (3 pens), Edwards 10, McInerney 8, Payne 6, Beaumont 5, Logan 4, Brown 2, Frain 2, Matthews 2, Oghani 2 (1 pen), Cooke 1, Downes 1, Gannon 1, own goal 1.
Littlewoods Cup (3): McDonald 1, McInerney 1, Matthews 1.
FA Cup (2): Angell 1, Edwards 1.

Siddall	Brown	Hart	Payne	Williams B	Thorpe	Beaumont	Frain	Angell	Cooke	Williams P	Oghani	Robertson	Matthews	Bullock	MacDonald	Howard	Logan	McInerney	Caldwell	Edwards	Jones	Leonard	Downes	Redfern	Knowles	Muggleton	Gannon	Hope	Ritchie	Match No.
1	2	3	4	5	6	7	8	9†	10	11*	12		14																	1
1	2		8	5	6				10		12	3	4			7	9		11*											2
1	2		8	5	6		11	10	9			4	7*			3			12											3
1	2		8	5	6		11	10	9*			4				3	7		12											4
1	2		8	5	6		11*	10	9			4				3	7		12											5
1	2		8	5	6		11	10	12	9*		4				3	7													6
1	2		8	5	6		11*	10	12	9		4				3	7													7
1	2		8†	5	6		11	10*	12			3	4	14			7		9											8
1	2		5	8		12	11	10				4	3				7		9*	6										9
1	2		8	5	6		11	10				4	3				7		9											10
1	2		8	5	6		11	10				4	3				7		9											11
1			5	2		8	11					12	4	3			7		9	6		10*								12
1	2		5	8		11	10					4	3				7		9	6										13
1	2		5	8		11	10					4	3				7		9	6										14
1	2		8	5	6		11	10				4	3				7		9											15
1	2		8	5	6		11	10				4	3				7		9											16
1	2		8	5	6	4	11	10				3					7		9											17
1	2		8	5	6	7	11*	12				3	4			10			9											18
1	2		8	5		12	4	11	10			3†					7*		9	6		14								19
1			8	5	6	7	9	11			2	3				10			4											20
	2			5		4	11	10				3	7			9	6					8	1							21
	2			5		4	11	10				3	7			9	6					8	1							22
	2†			5		11	4	10	12		14	3	7*			9	6					8	1							23
	7			5		4	11	10				2	3			9	6					8	1							24
	7			5	12	4†	11	2				3	10*			9	6					8	1	14						25
	7			5	12	4	11	2				3*	10			9	6					8	1							26
1	2		7	5	8*	4	11				12	10				9	6		3											27
	2		4	5	6	12	11	10				3	7†			9*			8	1		14								28
	2		8	5	6	9	11	10*				3	14			12			4	1		7†								29
	2		8	5	4	7	11					3	10			9	6			1										30
	2		8	5	4	7	11					3	10			9	6			1										31
	2		8	5		7	11		4			3	10			9	6			1										32
	2			5	7*	8	11	12				3	10			9	6		4				1							33
	2	12		4	14	8	11		7*			3	10†			9	6						1			5				34
	2		8	5	4*	9	12	11				3	10			1			6				7†	14						35
	2		8	5	4	9†	12	14				3	10			11			1			6*		7						36
	2		8	5	4	9*	11	12				3	10			6									7				37
	2		8	5	4	9	6	11				3	10											7*						38
			8		4	9	10	11				2	3			5			6											39
	8		5	2	9	4	11					3	10			6	7													40
	8	5†	2	9	4	11*						3	10			6	14					7								41
	2	8		5	9	4	11	12				3	10†			6			7*											42
	2			5	9	4	11					3	12			6			7*			8								43
	2			5	9	4	11					3	12			6			7*			8								44
				5	9	4	11		6			3				2						7			8					45
	2			5	9	4	11		6			3	12			14			7*			8								46
21	37	1	33	37	39	19	25	43	23	2	5	6	16	23	1	25	36	—	26	25	4	10	11	7	4	7	4	—		
	+1s		+1s	+3s	+4s	+1s	+1s	+5s	+3s	+3s	+4s						+4s	+2s	+1s		+2s1s	+2s		+1s						

Brookman — Match No. 38(12) 42(14) 43(10) 44(10) 45(10) 46 (10†); Brabin — Match No. 39(7); Cecere — Match No. 41(12); Barrett — Match No. 37(1) 38(1) 39(1) 40(1) 41(1) 42(1) 43(1) 44(1) 45(1) 46(1).

Littlewoods Cup	First Round	Bury (h)	1-0
		(a)	1-1
	Second Round	QPR (a)	1-2
		(h)	0-0
FA Cup	First Round	Burnley (a)	1-1
		(h)	1-2

STOCKPORT COUNTY

Player and Position	Ht	Wt	Birth Date	Birth Place	Source	Clubs	League App	League Gls
Goalkeepers								
David Redfern	6 2	13 08	8 11 62	Sheffield	School	Sheffield W	—	—
						Doncaster R (loan)	—	—
						Rochdale (loan)	19	—
						Rochdale	68	—
					Gainsborough T	Stockport Co	11	—
Defenders								
Malcolm Brown	6 2	12 06	13 12 56	Salford	Apprentice	Bury	11	—
						Huddersfield T	256	16
						Newcastle U	39	—
						Huddersfield T	96	1
						Rochdale	11	—
						Stockport Co	37	2
Steven Bullock	5 8	11 01	5 10 66	Stockport	Apprentice	Oldham Ath	18	—
						Tranmere R	30	1
						Stockport Co	90	—
Chris Downes	5 10	10 08	17' 1 69	Sheffield	Trainee	Sheffield U	2	—
						Scarborough (loan)	2	—
						Stockport Co	11	1
Jim Gannon	6 2	12 06	7 9 68	London	Dundalk	Sheffield U	—	—
						Halifax T (loan)	2	—
						Stockport Co	7	1
Mark Howard*	5 8	11 00	21 10 64	Kings Lynn		Norwich C	—	—
						Stockport Co	19	2
						Cambridge U (loan)	2	—
Paul Jones*	6 1	12 09	13 5 53	Ellesmere Pt.	Apprentice	Bolton W	444	37
						Huddersfield T	73	8
						Oldham Ath	32	1
						Blackpool	37	—
					Galway	Wigan Ath	—	—
						Rochdale	14	2
						Stockport Co	25	—
David Logan	5 9	10 11	5 12 63	Middlesbrough	Whitby	Mansfield T	67	1
						Northampton T	41	1
						Halifax T	3	—
						Stockport Co	60	4
Paul Robertson	5 7	11 06	5 2 72	Stockport	York C§	Stockport Co	9	—
Andy Thorpe	5 11	12 00	15 9 60	Stockport	Amateur	Stockport Co	314	3
						Tranmere R	53	—
						Stockport Co	101	—
Bill Williams	6 1	12 11	7 10 60	Rochdale	Local	Rochdale	95	2
						Stockport Co	104	1
						Manchester C	1	—
						Stockport Co	65	2
Midfield								
Gary Brabin			9 12 70	Liverpool	Trainee	Stockport Co	1	—
Nick Brookman	5 9	10 07	28 10 68	Manchester	Trainee	Bolton W	57	10
						Stockport Co	6	—
Gary Dooner‡	5 7	10 00	14 9 70	St Helens	Trainee	Stockport Co	1	—
David Frain	5 8	10 05	11 10 62	Sheffield	Rowlinson YC	Sheffield U	44	6
						Rochdale	42	12
						Stockport Co	29	2
Darren Knowles	5 6	10 01	8 10 70	Sheffield	Trainee	Sheffield U	—	—
						Stockport Co	9	—
Gary Leonard*	5 9	10 12	28 11 65	Newcastle	Apprentice	WBA	—	—
						Shrewsbury T	67	1
						Hereford U (loan)	11	1
						Bury	9	1
						Stockport Co	17	1
Mark Payne	5 9	11 09	3 8 60	Cheltenham		Stockport Co	56	7

STOCKPORT COUNTY

Foundation: Formed at a meeting held at Wellington Road South by members of Wycliffe Congregational Chapel in 1883, they called themselves Heaton Norris Rovers until changing to Stockport County in 1890, a year before joining the Football Combination.

First Football League game: 1 September, 1900, Division 2, v Leicester Fosse (a) D 2-2 – Moores; Earp, Wainwright; Pickford, Limond, Harvey; Stansfield, Smith (1), Patterson, Foster, Betteley (1).

Managers (and Secretary-managers)
Fred Stewart 1894–1911, Harry Lewis 1911–14, David Ashworth 1914–19, Albert Williams 1919–24, Fred Scotchbrook 1924–26, Lincoln Hyde 1926–31, Andrew Wilson 1932–33, Fred Westgarth 1934–36, Bob Kelly 1936–38, George Hunt 1938–39, Bob Marshall 1939–49, Andy Beattie 1949–52, Dick Duckworth 1952–56, Billy Moir 1956–60, Reg Flewin 1960–63, Trevor Porteous 1963–65, Bert Trautmann (GM) 1965–66, Eddie Quigley (TM) 1965–66, Jimmy Meadows 1966–69, Wally Galbraith 1969–70, Matt Woods 1970–71, Brian Doyle 1972–74, Jimmy Meadows 1974–75, Roy Chapman 1975–76, Eddie Quigley 1976–77, Alan Thompson 1977–78, Mike Summerbee 1978–79, Jimmy McGuigan 1979–82, Eric Webster 1982–85, Colin Murphy 1985, Les Chapman 1985–86, Jimmy Melia 1986, Colin Murphy 1986–87, Asa Hartford 1987–89, Danny Bergara 1989– .

Player and Position	Ht	Wt	Birth Date	Place	Source	Clubs	League App	Gls
Forwards								
Brett Angell	6 1	12 03	20 8 68	Marlborough		Portsmouth	—	—
					Cheltenham T	Derby Co	—	—
						Stockport Co	70	28
Chris Beaumont	5 11	11 07	5 12 65	Sheffield	Denaby	Rochdale	34	7
						Stockport Co	22	5
Tony Caldwell‡	5 9	11 07	21 3 58	Salford	Horwich RMI	Bolton W	139	58
						Bristol C	17	3
						Chester C (loan)	4	—
						Grimsby T	3	—
						Stockport Co	26	5
John Cooke*	5 8	11 00	25 4 62	Salford	Apprentice	Sunderland	55	4
						Carlisle U (loan)	6	2
						Sheffield W	—	—
						Carlisle U	106	11
						Stockport Co	58	7
Alan Dean‡	5 8	10 00	28 11 70	Stockport	York C§	Stockport Co	—	—
Keith Edwards	5 8	10 03	16 7 57	Stockton		Sheffield U	70	29
						Hull C	132	57
						Sheffield U	191	114
						Leeds U	38	6
						Aberdeen	9	2
						Hull C	55	29
						Stockport Co	27	10
						Huddersfield T (loan)	10	4
Darren Hope	5 6	10 05	3 4 71	Stoke	Trainee	Stoke C	—	—
						Stockport Co	4	—
John Mannion			23 7 71	Altrincham	Trainee	Stockport Co	—	—
Ian McInerney	5 10	11 08	26 1 64	Liverpool	Blue Star	Huddersfield T	10	1
						Stockport Co	40	8
David Ritchie	5 11	11 01	20 1 71	Newcastle	Trainee	Stoke C	—	—
						Stockport Co	1	—
Paul Williams	5 6	10 07	11 9 69	Leicester	Trainee	Leicester C	—	—
						Stockport Co	7	—

Trainees
Bancroft, David P; Barrett, Lee S; Burnside, Scott; Fieldsend; Shaun M; Foley, Paul; Hibbert, Andrew; Middleton, Andrew P; Parker, Philip; Shepherd, Wayne D; Spofforth, Ian.

STOKE CITY 1989–90. *Back row (left to right):* Darren Boughey, Paul Ware, Mark Higgins, Dave Bamber, George Berry, Carl Beeston, Wayne Biggins.
Centre row: Tony Lacey (Youth Coach), Keith Rowley (Physiotherapist), Derek Statham, Ian Scott, Peter Fox, Scott Barrett, Nicky Morgan, Carl Saunders, Sammy Chung (Coach), Mick Mills (Manager).
Front row: Cliff Carr, Peter Beagrie, Chris Kamara, Ian Cranson, Gary Hackett.

Division 3   **STOKE CITY**

Victoria Ground, Stoke-on-Trent. Telephone Stoke-on-Trent (0782) 413511. Commercial Dept. 0782 45840. Soccerline Information: 0898 700278.

Ground capacity: 35,812.

Record attendance: 51,380 v Arsenal, Division 1, 29 Mar, 1937.

Record receipts: £97,000 v Liverpool, FA Cup 3rd rd, 9 January 1988.

Pitch measurements: 116yd × 75yd.

Vice-President: J. A. M. Humphries.

Chairman: P. Coates. *Vice-Chairman:* T. E. Weetman.

Directors: G. L. Manning, M. Nield, K. A. Humphreys, J. M. Loftus.

Manager: Alan Ball.

Coach: Sammy Chung. *Physio:* Keith Rowley.

Secretary: M. J. Potts.

Sales & Marketing Manager: M. J. Cullerton.

Year Formed: 1863 *(see Foundation).

Turned Professional: 1885. *Ltd Co.:* 1908.

Club Nickname: 'The Potters'.

Previous Grounds: 1875, Sweeting's Field; 1878, Victoria Ground (previously known as the Athletic Club Ground).

Record League Victory: 10-3 v WBA, Division 1, 4 February 1937 – Doug Westland; Brigham, Harbot; Tutin, Turner (1p), Kirton; Matthews, Antonio (2), Fred Steele (5), Jimmy Westland, Johnson (2).

Record Cup Victory: 7–1 v Burnley, FA Cup, 2nd rd (replay), 20 February 1896 – Clawley; Clare, Eccles; Turner, Grewe, Robertson; Willie Maxwell, Dickson, Maxwell (A) (3), Hyslop (4), Schofield.

Record Defeat: 0–10 v Preston NE, Division 1, 14 September, 1889.

Most League Points (2 for a win): 63, Division 3 (N), 1926–27.

Most League Points (3 for a win): 62, Division 2, 1987–88.

Most League Goals: 92, Division 3 (N), 1926–27.

Highest League Scorer in Season: Freddie Steele, 33, Division 1, 1936–37.

Most League Goals in Total Aggregate: Freddie Steele, 142, 1934–49.

Most Capped Player: Gordon Banks, 36, (73), England.

Most League Appearances: Eric Skeels, 506, 1958–76.

Record Transfer Fee Received: £750,000 from Everton for Peter Beagrie, October 1989.

Record Transfer Fee Paid: £480,000 to Sheffield W for Ian Cranson, July 1989.

Football League Record: 1888 Founder Member of Football League; 1890 Not re-elected; 1891 Re-elected; Relegated in 1907, and after one year in Division 2, resigned for financial reasons; Re-elected to Division 2 in 1919; 1922–23 Division 1; 1923–26 Division 2; 1926–27 Division 3(N); 1927–33 Division 2; 1933–53 Division 1; 1953–63 Division 2; 1963–77 Division 1; 1977–79 Division 2; 1979–85 Division 1; 1985–90 Division 2; 1990– Division 3.

Honours: Football League: Division 1 best season: 4th, 1935–36, 1946–47; Division 2 – Champions 1932–33, 1962–63; Runners-up 1921–22; Promoted 1978–79 (3rd); Division 3 (N) – Champions 1926–27. *FA Cup:* Semi-finals 1899, 1971, 1972. *Football League Cup:* Winners 1971–72. **European Competitions:** *UEFA Cup:* 1972–73, 1974–75.

Colours: Red and white striped shirts, white shorts, red stockings. **Change colours:** Yellow shirts, black shorts, yellow stockings.

518

STOKE CITY 1989–90 LEAGUE RECORD

Match No.	Date	Venue	Opponents	Result	H/T Score	Lg. Pos.	Goalscorers	Attendance
1	Aug 19	H	West Ham U	D 1-1	0-1	—	Biggins	16,058
2	26	A	Portsmouth	D 0-0	0-0	15		7433
3	Sept 2	H	Leeds U	D 1-1	1-0	14	Cranson	14,570
4	5	A	Barnsley	L 2-3	1-2	—	Berry (pen), Morgan	8584
5	9	A	Wolverhampton W	D 0-0	0-0	19		15,659
6	16	H	Oldham Ath	L 1-2	0-2	22	Bamber	10,673
7	23	H	Port Vale	D 1-1	0-0	23	Palin	27,032
8	26	H	Bradford C	D 1-1	0-1	—	Cranson	9346
9	30	A	Ipswich T	D 2-2	0-2	21	Palin (pen), Saunders	10,389
10	Oct 7	A	Plymouth Arg	L 0-3	0-1	21		6940
11	14	H	Hull C	D 1-1	1-0	21	Biggins	9955
12	17	H	WBA	W 2-1	2-0	—	Hackett, Biggins	11,991
13	21	A	Sheffield U	L 1-2	0-2	21	Palin (pen)	16,873
14	28	H	Sunderland	L 0-2	0-0	21		12,480
15	Nov 1	A	Oxford U	L 0-3	0-1	—		4375
16	4	A	Swindon T	L 0-6	0-2	23		7825
17	11	H	Brighton & HA	W 3-2	3-1	23	Beeston, Bamber, Kamara	10,346
18	18	A	Bournemouth	L 1-2	0-1	24	Hilaire	6412
19	25	H	Leicester C	L 0-1	0-0	24		12,264
20	Dec 2	A	West Ham U	D 0-0	0-0	23		17,704
21	9	H	Barnsley	L 0-1	0-0	24		10,163
22	26	H	Newcastle U	W 2-1	0-1	24	Biggins, Beeston	14,878
23	30	H	Watford	D 2-2	2-1	24	Biggins 2 (1 pen)	13,228
24	Jan 1	A	Middlesbrough	W 1-0	0-0	24	Ellis	16,238
25	13	H	Portsmouth	L 1-2	0-2	24	Sandford	12,051
26	20	A	Leeds U	L 0-2	0-0	24		29,318
27	27	A	Blackburn R	L 0-3	0-2	—		9132
28	Feb 3	A	Port Vale	D 0-0	0-0	24		22,075
29	10	A	Oldham Ath	L 0-2	0-0	24		10,028
30	17	H	Wolverhampton W	W 2-0	0-0	24	Biggins, Hackett	17,870
31	24	A	Leicester C	L 1-2	1-0	24	Biggins	12,245
32	Mar 3	H	Bournemouth	D 0-0	0-0	24		10,988
33	6	H	Ipswich T	D 0-0	0-0	—		10,815
34	10	A	Bradford C	L 0-1	0-0	24		9269
35	17	H	Plymouth Arg	D 0-0	0-0	24		9452
36	20	A	Hull C	D 0-0	0-0	—		6456
37	24	A	WBA	D 1-1	0-1	24	Ellis	12,771
38	31	H	Sheffield U	L 0-1	0-0	24		14,898
39	Apr 7	A	Sunderland	L 1-2	0-0	24	Ellis	17,119
40	10	H	Oxford U	L 1-2	1-0	—	Sandford	8139
41	14	H	Middlesbrough	D 0-0	0-0	24		8636
42	16	A	Newcastle U	L 0-3	0-2	24		26,190
43	21	H	Blackburn R	L 0-1	0-0	24		9305
44	24	A	Watford	D 1-1	1-1	—	Biggins	8073
45	28	A	Brighton & HA	W 4-1	0-0	24	Ellis 2, Biggins, Scott	9614
46	May 5	H	Swindon T	D 1-1	1-1	24	Ellis	11,386

Final League Position: 24

GOALSCORERS

League (35): Biggins 10 (1 pen), Ellis 6, Palin 3 (2 pens), Bamber 2, Beeston 2, Cranson 2, Hackett 2, Sandford 2, Berry 1 (pen), Hilaire 1, Kamara 1, Morgan 1, Saunders 1, Scott 1.
Littlewoods Cup (1): Morgan 1.
FA Cup (0).

Fox	Butler	Statham	Kamara	Cranson	Beeston	Hackett	Scott	Bamber	Biggins	Beagrie	Saunders	Morgan	Berry	Ware	Boughey	Palin	Barrett	Higgins	Hilaire	Carr	Fowler	Holmes	Ellis	Sandford	Kelly	Kevan	Blake	Smith	Brooke	Match No.
1	2	3	4	5	6	7	8*	9	10	11	12																			1
1	2	3	4	5	6	7	8	9	10*	11		12																		2
1	2	3	4	5	6	7	8	9		11		10*	12																	3
1	2	3	4	5		7	8	9		11	12	10*	6																	4
1	2	3	4	5	6	7	8*	9	10	11			12																	5
1	2	3	4	5	6	7		9		11		8*	10†	12	14															6
1	2	3	4	5	6		12	9		11			14	10		7*	8†													7
1	2	3	4	5	6	7		9		11	12			10*		8														8
1	2	3	4	5	6	7		9		11			10			8														9
	2	3	4	5	6	7*		9	10	11	12					8	1													10
	2	3	4	5*	6			9	10	11			14	12		8	1		7†											11
	2	3	4	5*	6	7†		9	10	11			14	12		8	1													12
	2	3	4	5	6			9	10	11	12	7*				8	1													13
	2	3	4	5	6		8*	9	10	11	12					7	1													14
	2	3	4	5	6		8*	9	10	11†	12		14			7	1													15
	2	3	4	5		7	14	9	10	11	12					8*	1			6†										16
1	2	3	4	5			8	9	10*	11	12	6	14							7†										17
1	2	3	4	5†			8	9	10		12	6	14*							7	11									18
1	2		4				8	7	9	10*	12			6		5				11	3									19
1	2		4				8	7	9	10				6		5				11	3									20
1	2		4				8	7*	9	10				6		5				11	3									21
1			4	5		7*		10						2		8				3	6	12	9	11						22
1	2		4				8	12	10					7*						3	6	5	9	11						23
1	2		4				8		10	12				7						3	6*	5	9	11						24
1	2		4				8	12		7		10*	14							3	6	5†	9	11						25
1	2						8	12	10	4		7*	14							3†	6	5	9	11						26
1	2	3	4						10	12		7		9						6*	5		8	11						27
1	2		4		6		12	9	10											3	8	5	7*	11						28
1	2		4				12	9	10											3	8	6	11*	7	5					29
1	2		4		6		12		10							11				8	3		9	5	7*					30
1	2		4		6	7			10							11*				8	3	12	9	5						31
1	2		4		6		12									11				8	3	10*	9	5		7				32
1	2		4		6*				10							11	12			8	3		9	5		7				33
1	2		4		6		12		10							11*				8	3		9	5		7				34
1	2		4				12		10							3				8*	6		9	5	7	11				35
1	2		4		6		8		10		12									3	11		9	5		7*				36
1	2						12		10*							3†	11			8	6	14	9	5						37
1	2		4		6*		12		10							8				3	11		5	7†						38
1	2		4													3				8	6	7*11	5	12						39
1	2		4						10							3				8	6	11	5	12						40
1	2		4				12		10*							11	3			8	6	14	7†	5						41
1	2						12		10	6						3				8*	4		11	5						42
1			4						10				2	7		3				8	6	12	11*	5						43
1	2		4						10	7						3				8	6	12	11*	5						44
1	2		4				12	9	10							7†				3	8	6	11*	5						45
	2		4			7		9	10	11						3*				8			5							46
38	44	19	22	17	38	18	14	20	35	13	12	6	15	9	4	17	7	4	5	22	13	5	24	23	5	17	18	2	6	
							+8s	+5s	+10s	+7s	+1s		+7s	+3s	+2s				+2s		+2s	+1s		+4s					+2s	

Thomas — Match No. 37(4) 38(9) 39(10) 40(9) 41(9) 42(9) 43(9*) 44(9†)
Barnes — Match No. 37(7) 38(14) 39(9) 40(7*) 42(7)
Gallimore — Match No. 43(12)
Farrell — Match No. 44(14) 46(12)
Sale — Match No. 45(14) 46(14)
Noble — Match No. 46(1)
Wright — Match No. 46(6†)

Littlewoods Cup	Second Round	Millwall (h)		1-0
		(a)		0-2
FA Cup	Third Round	Arsenal (h)		0-1

STOKE CITY

Player and Position	Ht	Wt	Birth Date	Place	Source	Clubs	League App	Gls
Goalkeepers								
Scott Barrett	6 0	12 11	2 4 63	Ilkeston	Amateur	Wolverhampton W	30	—
						Stoke C	51	—
						Colchester U (loan)	13	—
						Stockport Co (loan)	10	—
Peter Fox	5 11	12 10	5 7 57	Scunthorpe	Apprentice	Sheffield W	49	—
						West Ham U (loan)	—	—
						Barnsley (loan)	1	—
						Stoke City	355	—
Daniel Noble	5 11	12 09	2 9 70	Hull	Trainee	Stoke C	1	—
Defenders								
George Berry*	6 0	13 04	19 11 57	Rostrup, W Germ	Apprentice	Wolverhampton W	124	4
						Stoke C	237	27
						Doncaster R (loan)	1	—
Noel Blake	6 0	13 05	12 1 62	Kingston, Jamaica	Sutton C T	Walsall	—	—
						Aston Villa	4	—
						Shrewsbury T (loan)	6	—
						Birmingham C	76	5
						Portsmouth	144	10
						Leeds U	51	4
						Stoke C	18	—
John Butler	5 11	11 07	7 2 62	Liverpool	Prescot Cables	Wigan Ath	245	15
						Stoke C	69	1
Cliff Carr	5 5	10 04	19 6 64	London	Apprentice	Fulham	145	14
						Stoke C	104	1
Ian Cranson	5 11	12 04	2 7 64	Easington	Apprentice	Ipswich T	131	5
						Sheffield W	30	—
						Stoke C	17	2
Lee Fowler	5 7	11 11	26 1 69	Nottingham	Trainee	Stoke C	16	—
Mark Higgins	6 1	13 05	29 9 58	Buxton	Apprentice	Everton	152	6
						Manchester U	6	—
						Bury	68	—
						Stoke C	39	1
Andrew Holmes*	6 1	12 12	7 1 69	Stoke	Apprentice	Stoke C	8	—
Paul Rennie	5 9	11 02	9 5 70	Sandbach		Stoke C	—	—
Lee Sandford	6 1	12 02	22 4 68	Basingstoke	Apprentice	Portsmouth	72	1
						Stoke C	23	2
Derek Statham	5 5	11 05	24 3 59	Wolverhampton	Apprentice	WBA	299	8
						Southampton	64	2
						Stoke C	19	—
Ian Wright	5 11	12 02	10 3 72	Lichfield	Trainee	Stoke C	1	—
Midfield								
Carl Beeston	5 9	10 03	30 6 67	Stoke	Apprentice	Stoke C	79	4
Darren Boughey	5 9	10 13	30 11 70	Stoke	Trainee	Stoke C	7	—
Stephen Farrell§			8 3 73	Kilmarnock	Trainee	Stoke C	2	—
Tony Gallimore§			21 2 72	Crewe	Trainee	Stoke C	1	—
Tony Henry‡	5 11	12 00	26 11 57	Sunderland	Apprentice	Manchester C	79	6
						Bolton W	70	22
						Oldham Ath	190	25
						Stoke C	62	11
Tony Kelly	5 9	10 12	14 2 66	Meridan	St Albans C	Stoke C	9	—
David Kevan	5 8	9 10	31 8 68	Wigtown	Apprentice	Notts Co	89	3
						Cardiff C (loan)	7	—
						Stoke C	17	—
Kevin Lewis‡			17 10 70	Hull	Trainee	Stoke C	1	—
Ian Scott	5 9	11 04	20 9 67	Radcliffe	Apprentice	Manchester C	24	3
						Stoke C	19	1
Paul Ware	5 8	11 02	7 11 70	Congleton	Trainee	Stoke C	28	1

STOKE CITY

Foundation: The date of the formation of this club has long been in doubt. The year 1863 was claimed, but more recent research by Wade Martin has uncovered nothing earlier than 1868, when a couple of Old Carthusians, who were apprentices at the local works of the old North Staffordshire Railway Company, met with some others from that works, to form Stoke Ramblers. It should also be noted that the old Stoke club went bankrupt in 1908 when a new club was formed.

First Football League game: 8 September, 1888, Football League, v WBA (h) L 0-2 – Rowley; Clare, Underwood; Ramsey, Shutt, Smith; Sayer, McSkimming, Staton, Edge, Tunnicliffe.

Managers (and Secretary-managers)
Tom Slaney 1874–83*, Walter Cox 1883–84*, Harry Lockett 1884–90, Joseph Bradshaw 1890–92, Arthur Reeves 1892–95, William Rowley 1895–97, H. D. Austerberry 1897–1908, A. J. Barker 1908–14, Peter Hodge 1914–15, Joe Schofield 1915–19, Arthur Shallcross 1919–23, John "Jock" Rutherford 1923, Tom Mather 1923–35, Bob McGrory 1935–52, Frank Taylor 1952–60, Tony Waddington 1960–77, George Eastham 1977–78, Alan A'Court 1978, Alan Durban 1978–81, Richie Barker 1981–83, Bill Asprey 1984–85, Mick Mills 1985–89, Alan Ball 1989– .

Player and Position	Ht	Wt	Birth Date	Place	Source	Clubs	League App	Gls
Forwards								
Paul Barnes	5 10	10 02	16 11 67	Leicester	Apprentice	Notts Co	53	14
						Stoke C	5	—
Wayne Biggins	5 11	11 00	20 11 61	Sheffield	Apprentice	Lincoln C	8	1
					Kings Lynn	Burnley	78	29
						Norwich C	79	16
						Manchester C	32	9
						Stoke C	35	10
Tony Ellis	5 11	11 00	20 10 64	Salford	Northwich V	Oldham Ath	8	—
						Preston NE	86	26
						Stoke C	24	6
Mark McGinley (To Hamilton A Aug 1989)	5 6	9 13	30 3 71	Dumbarton	Trainee	Stoke C	—	—
Mark Sale§	6 5	13 08	27 2 72	Burton-on-Trent	Trainee	Stoke C	2	—
Simon Stainrod‡	5 10	12 09	1 2 59	Sheffield	Apprentice	Sheffield U	67	14
						Oldham Ath	69	21
						QPR	145	48
						Sheffield W	15	2
						Aston Villa	63	16
						Stoke C	28	6
						Strasbourg (loan)	—	—
Mark Smith on loan from Dunfermline Ath							2	—

Trainees
Baines, Paul; Berks, John A; Berks, Peter R; Bright, David J; Devlin, Mark A; Farrell, Stephen; Gallimore, Anthony M; Hobbs, David J; Martin, Daniel; Morris, Christopher S; Reaney, Scott; Sale, Mark D; Skilling, Mark J; Wright, Ian M.

Associated Schoolboys
Amesbury, Martin P; Coker, Jonathan P; Davies, Andrew; Henry, Stephen; Lovelock, Owen J; Marsh, Christopher T; Meer, Stuart W; Mosely, Christopher K; Naguthney, Nadeem; Stewart, Jeremy; Winstone, Simon J; Woodier, Garry K.

Associated Schoolboys who have accepted the club's offer of a Traineeship/Contract
Jennings, Gareth J; Lees, Ian W; McLeish, Alexander P; Percival, Jason C; Potts, Adrian H; Robinson, Jason L; Wileman, Matthew L.

SUNDERLAND 1989–90   *Back row (left to right):* Gordon Armstrong, John Cornforth, Gary Bennett, Micky Heathcote, John MacPhail, Richard Ord, Gary Owers.
Centre row (standing): Viv Busby (Chief Coach), Tony Norman, Tim Carter, Denis Smith (Manager).
Centre row (sitting): Paul Lemon, Reuben Agboola, Thomas Hauser, Thomas Lynch, John Kay.
Front row: Marco Gabbiadini, Eric Gates, Anthony Cullen, Colin Pascoe, Paul Hardyman.

Division 1   SUNDERLAND

Roker Park Ground, Sunderland. Telephone Sunderland 091 5140332. Commercial Dept: 091-5672275.
Ground capacity: 31,887.
Record attendance: 75,118 v Derby Co, FA Cup 6th rd replay, 8 Mar, 1933.
Record receipts: £130,000 v Newcastle U, Division 2, 24 September 1989.
Pitch measurements: 113yd × 74yd.
Chairman: R. S. Murray FCCA.
Director: G. Davidson FCA., G. W. Hodgson FCA.
Associate Directors: J. Donnolly, G. S. Wood.
Manager: Denis Smith.
General Manager/Secretary: G. Davidson FCA.
Chief Coach: Viv Busby. *Reserve Coach:* Malcolm Crosby.
Physio: Steve Smelt. *Youth Coach:* Roger Jones.
Commercial Manager: Alec King.
Year Formed: 1879. *Turned Professional:* 1886. *Ltd Co.:* 1906.
Club Nickname: Rokermen.
Previous Grounds: 1879, Blue House Field, Hendon; 1882, Groves Field, Ashbrooke; 1883, Horatio Street; 1884, Abbs Field, Fulwell; 1886, Newcastle Road; 1898, Roker Park.
Previous Name: 1879–80, Sunderland and District Teacher's AFC.
Record League Victory: 9-1 v Newcastle U, Division 1, 5 December 1908 – Roose; Forster, Melton; Daykin, Thomson, Low; Mordue, Hogg (4), Brown, Holley (3), Bridgett (2).
Record Cup Victory: 11-1 v Fairfield, FA Cup, 1st rd, 2 February 1895 – Doig; McNeill, Johnston; Dunlop, McCreadie (1), Wilson; Gillespie (1), Millar (5), Campbell, Hannah (3), Scott (1).
Record Defeat: 0-8 v West Ham U, Division 1, 19 October, 1968 and v Watford, Division 1, 25 September, 1982.
Most League Points (2 for a win): 61, Division 2, 1963–64.
Most League Points (3 for a win): 93, Division 3, 1987–88.
Most League Goals: 109, Division 1, 1935–36.
Highest League Scorer in Season: Dave Halliday, 43, Division 1, 1928–29.
Most League Goals in Total Aggregate: Charlie Buchan, 209, 1911–25.
Most Capped Player: Martin Harvey, 34, Northern Ireland.
Most League Appearances: Jim Montgomery, 537, 1962–77.
Record Transfer Fee Received: £275,000 from Manchester C for Dennis Tueart, March 1974, from Manchester U for Chris Turner, August 1985 and from Sheffield W for Mark Proctor, September 1987.
Record Transfer Fee Paid: £450,000 to Hull C for Tony Norman, December 1988.
Football League Record: 1890 Elected to Division 1; 1958–64 Division 2; 1964–70 Division 1; 1970–76 Division 2; 1976–77 Division 1; 1977–80 Division 2; 1980–85 Division 1; 1985–87 Division 2; 1987–88 Division 3; 1988–90 Division 2; 1990– Division 1.
Honours: Football League: Division 1 – Champions 1891–92, 1892–93, 1894–95, 1901–02, 1912–13, 1935–36; Runners-up 1893–94; 1897–98, 1900–01, 1922–23, 1934–35; Division 2 – Champions 1975–76; Runners-up 1963–64, 1979–80; Division 3 – Champions 1987–88. *FA Cup:* Winners 1937, 1973; Runners-up 1913. *Football League Cup:* Runners-up 1984–85.
European Competitions: *Cup-Winners' Cup:* 1973–74.
Colours: Red and white striped shirts, black shorts, red stockings white turnover. **Change colours:** Blue shirts, white shorts, blue stockings white turnover.
Largest non-season ticket membership scheme in Football League over 42,000 members.

SUNDERLAND 1989–90 LEAGUE RECORD

Match No.	Date		Venue	Opponents	Result		H/T Score	Lg. Pos.	Goalscorers	Atten- dance
1	Aug	19	A	Swindon T	W	2-0	1-0	—	Gates, Hawke	10,199
2		22	H	Ipswich T	L	2-4	0-3	—	Gates, Gabbiadini	15,965
3		27	H	Middlesbrough	W	2-1	0-1	—	Bennett, Pascoe	21,569
4	Sept	2	A	WBA	D	1-1	0-0	7	Gabbiadini	10,885
5		9	H	Watford	W	4-0	3-0	2	Armstrong, Gabbiadini 3	15,042
6		16	A	Blackburn R	D	1-1	0-0	3	MacPhail	10,329
7		24	H	Newcastle U	D	0-0	0-0	—		29,499
8		27	A	Leicester C	W	3-2	1-1	—	Armstrong, Hardyman (pen), Owers	10,843
9		30	H	Sheffield U	D	1-1	1-1	4	Deane (og)	22,760
10	Oct	7	H	Bournemouth	W	3-2	1-1	2	Gates 2, Gabbiadini	15,933
11		14	A	Leeds U	L	0-2	0-2	5		27,815
12		18	A	West Ham U	L	0-5	0-3	—		20,901
13		21	H	Bradford C	W	1-0	1-0	6	MacPhail	14,849
14		28	A	Stoke C	W	2-0	0-0	5	Bracewell, Gabbiadini	12,480
15		31	H	Barnsley	W	4-2	2-0	—	Gates 2, Hardyman (pen), Bennett	14,234
16	Nov	4	A	Oldham Ath	L	1-2	0-1	4	Owers	8829
17		11	H	Wolverhampton W	D	1-1	0-0	5	Hardyman (pen)	20,660
18		18	H	Plymouth Arg	W	3-1	2-1	4	Gabbiadini, Owers, Ord	15,033
19		25	A	Brighton & HA	W	2-1	1-1	4	Gabbiadini, Owers	8681
20	Dec	2	H	Swindon T	D	2-2	0-1	4	Armstrong, Hauser	15,849
21		9	A	Ipswich T	D	1-1	1-0	3	Owers	13,833
22		16	A	Portsmouth	D	3-3	2-1	3	Bennett, Hardyman, Gabbiadini	7127
23		26	H	Oxford U	W	1-0	0-0	3	Gabbiadini	24,075
24		30	H	Port Vale	D	2-2	0-1	3	Gabbiadini, Hauser	21,354
25	Jan	1	A	Hull C	L	2-3	0-2	3	Hauser, Owers	9346
26		14	A	Middlesbrough	L	0-3	0-2	—		17,698
27		20	H	WBA	D	1-1	1-0	5	Gabbiadini	15,583
28	Feb	4	A	Newcastle U	D	1-1	0-0	—	Gabbiadini	31,572
29		10	H	Blackburn R	L	0-1	0-0	6		16,043
30		17	A	Watford	D	1-1	1-1	7	Hauser	9093
31		24	H	Brighton & HA	W	2-1	2-0	5	Hauser 2	14,528
32	Mar	3	A	Plymouth Arg	L	0-3	0-2	7		7299
33		10	H	Leicester C	D	2-2	0-1	8	Gabbiadini, Armstrong	13,017
34		17	A	Bournemouth	W	1-0	0-0	7	Gabbiadini	6328
35		20	H	Leeds U	L	0-1	0-1	—		17,851
36		24	H	West Ham U	W	4-3	1-1	9	Brady, Hardyman (pen), Owers, Gabbiadini	13,896
37		31	A	Bradford C	W	1-0	0-0	7	Brady	9826
38	Apr	3	A	Sheffield U	W	3-1	0-1	—	Bracewell, Gabbiadini 2	20,588
39		7	H	Stoke C	W	2-1	0-0	5	Gabbiadini, Armstrong	17,119
40		10	A	Barnsley	L	0-1	0-0	—		11,141
41		14	H	Hull C	L	0-1	0-1	6		17,437
42		16	A	Oxford U	W	1-0	0-0	6	Gabbiadini	6053
43		21	H	Portsmouth	D	2-2	1-0	6	Armstrong 2	14,379
44		28	A	Wolverhampton W	W	1-0	0-0	6	Hardyman	19,463
45	May	1	A	Port Vale	W	2-1	2-1	—	Owers, Hardyman	9447
46		5	H	Oldham Ath	L	2-3	1-1	6	Owers, Armstrong	22,243

Final League Position: 6

GOALSCORERS

League (70): Gabbiadini 21, Owers 9, Armstrong 8, Hardyman 7 (4 pens), Gates 6, Hauser 6, Bennett 3, Bracewell 2, Brady 2, MacPhail 2, Hawke 1, Ord 1, Pascoe 1, own goal 1.
Littlewoods Cup (13): Gabbiadini 4, Armstrong 3, Gates 3, Hardyman 2 (1 pen), Pascoe 1.
FA Cup (1): Armstrong 1.

Norman	Agboola	Hardyman	Bennett	MacPhail	Owers	Cullen	Armstrong	Gates	Gabbiadini M	Pascoe	Cornforth	Hawke	Ord	Bracewell	Carter	Hauser	Kay	Gabbiadini R	Atkinson	Heathcote	Brady	Williams	Match No.
1	2	3	4*	5	6	7†	8	9	10	11	12	14											1
1	2	3		5	6	7	8	9	10	11			4										2
1	2	3	4	5	6		8	9	10	11				7									3
1	2	3	4	5	6		8	9*	10	11		12		7									4
	2	3	4	5	6	12	8	9'	10	11*				7	1								5
	2	3	4	5	6*	12	8	9†	10	11				7	1	14							6
	2	3	4	5	6		8	9	10	11				7	1								7
	2	3	4	5	6		8	9	10	11				7	1								8
	2*	3	4	5	6	12	8	9†	10	11				7	1	14							9
		3	4	5	6		8	9	10	11				7	1		2						10
	2	3	4	5	6	12	8	9*	10†	11				7	1				14				11
		3	4	5	6	12	8	9†	10	11*				7	1	14	2						12
		3	4	5	6		8	9	10	11				7	1		2						13
		3*	4	5	6	12	8	9	10	11				7	1		2						14
		3	4	5†	6	12	8	9	10	11			14	7*	1		2						15
	2	3†	4		6	12	8	9*	10	11				5	1				7	14			16
		3	4		6		8	9	10	11				5	1	7	2						17
	2	3*	4		6		8	9	10	11				5	1				7	12			18
		3	4		6		8	9	10	11				5	7*	1			12		2		19
	2	3	4		6		8	9	10	11†				5*	1	14	12		7				20
	2	3	4		6		8	9	10	11					1		5		7				21
1	2	3	4	7	6		8	9*	10	11							12		5				22
1	2	3	4		6		8	9*	10	11	7						12		5				23
1	2	3	4		6		8	9*	10	11			14				12		5		7†		24
1	14	3†	4	5	6		8	9*	10	11				7			12		2				25
1	3*	9	4	5	6		8		10	11				7			12		2				26
12	3	4	5*	6	11†		8		10				14	7	1	9	2						27
1		4	3	5	6	12	8*	9	10					7			2		11				28
1		4	3	5			8	9*	10	11				7		12	2		6				29
1		4	3	5	11*		8		10					7		9	2		6				30
1		3	4	5	11		8		10					7		9	2		6				31
1	12	3*	4	5	11		8		10				14	7		9†	2		6				32
1	3		4	5	6		8		10	12				7		9	2				11*		33
1	3		4	5	6		8		10	12				7		9†	2		14		11*		34
1	3		4	5	6		8	9*	10	11				7		12	2						35
1	12	3*		5	6		8		10	11				7			2			4	9		36
1	12	3	4*	5	6		8	9	10					7			2				11		37
1	3			5	6		8		10	11				7			2			4	9		38
1	3			5	6		8	12	10	9				7			2			4	11*		39
1	3			5	6		8	12	10	9				7			2			4	11*		40
1	12	3	4	5	6	14	8	9	10					7†			2				11*		41
1	11	3	4†	5	6	14	8	9	10							12	2		7*				42
1	11	3		5	6		8	9	10					7			2			4			43
1	11	3	4	5	6		8	9	10					7			2						44
1	11	3	4*	5	6		8	9	10					7			2			12			45
1	11†	3		5	6		8	9*	10					7		12	2			4		14	46
28	30	42	36	38	43	5	46	34	46	32	1	1	6	36	18	6	31	—	11	6	9	1	
						+6s		+11s	+2s	+1s				+1s	+7s	+1s	+1s		+12s	+1s	+2s	+2s	

Littlewoods Cup	Second Round	Fulham (h)	1-1
		(a)	3-0
	Third Round	Bournemouth (h)	1-1
		(a)	1-0
	Fourth Round	Exeter C (a)	2-2
		(h)	5-2
	Fifth Round	Coventry C (h)	0-0
		(a)	0-5
FA Cup	Third Round	Reading (a)	1-2

SUNDERLAND

Player and Position	Ht	Wt	Birth Date	Place	Source	Clubs	League App	Gls
Goalkeepers								
Tim Carter	6 1	12 00	5 10 67	Bristol	Apprentice	Bristol R	47	—
						Newport Co (loan)	1	—
						Sunderland	21	—
						Carlisle U (loan)	4	—
						Bristol C (loan)	3	—
Tony Norman	6 2	12 08	24 2 58	Mancot	Amateur	Burnley	—	—
						Hull C	372	—
						Sunderland	52	—
Andy Sams	6 0	13 01	18 12 70	Bishop Auckland	Trainee	Sunderland	—	—
Defenders								
Reuben Agboola	5 9	11 02	30 5 62	London	Apprentice	Southampton	90	—
						Sunderland	134	—
						Charlton Ath (loan)	1	—
Gary Bennett	6 1	12 01	4 12 61	Manchester	Amateur	Manchester C	—	—
						Cardiff C	87	11
						Sunderland	220	18
Andy Fox‡			1 1 70	Hartlepool	Trainee	Sunderland	—	—
Paul Hardyman	5 8	11 04	11 3 64	Portsmouth	Fareham	Portsmouth	117	3
						Sunderland	42	7
Mike Heathcote	6 2	12 05	10 9 65	Durham		Middlesbrough	—	—
					Spennymoor U	Sunderland	9	—
						Halifax T (loan)	7	1
						York C (loan)	3	—
John Kay	5 10	11 06	29 1 64	Sunderland	Apprentice	Arsenal	14	—
						Wimbledon	63	2
						Middlesbrough (loan)	8	—
						Sunderland	89	—
John MacPhail	6 0	12 03	7 12 55	Dundee	St Columba's	Dundee	68	7
						Sheffield U	135	7
						York C	142	24
						Bristol C	26	1
						Sunderland	129	22
Richard Ord	6 2	12 08	3 3 70	Easington	Trainee	Sunderland	49	2
						York C (loan)	3	—
Jonathan Trigg	5 8	10 06	8 5 71	Jersey	Trainee	Sunderland	—	—
Paul Williams	6 0	12 02	25 9 70	Liverpool	Trainee	Sunderland	2	—
Midfield								
Gordon Armstrong	6 0	11 02	15 7 67	Newcastle	Apprentice	Sunderland	187	28
Paul Bracewell	5 8	10 09	19 7 62	Stoke	Apprentice	Stoke C	129	5
						Sunderland	38	4
						Everton	95	7
						Sunderland	37	2
Tony Callender			15 11 70	Hexham		Sunderland	—	—
John Cornforth	6 1	11 05	7 10 67	Whitley Bay	Apprentice	Sunderland	30	2
						Doncaster R (loan)	7	3
						Shrewsbury T (loan)	3	—
						Lincoln C (loan)	9	1
Martin Gray	5 9	10 11	17 8 71	Stockton	Trainee	Sunderland	—	—
Gary Owers	5 10	11 10	3 10 68	Newcastle	Apprentice	Sunderland	118	16
Forwards								
Brian Atkinson	5 10	12 00	19 1 71	Darlington	Trainee	Sunderland	16	—
Kieron Brady	5 9	11 13	17 9 71	Glasgow	Trainee	Sunderland	11	2
Tony Cullen	5 6	11 07	30 9 69	Newcastle		Sunderland	23	—
						Carlisle U (loan)	2	1

SUNDERLAND

Foundation: A Scottish schoolmaster named James Allan, working at Hendon Boarding School, took the initiative in the foundation of Sunderland in 1879 when they were formed as The Sunderland and District Teachers' Association FC at a meeting in the Adults School, Norfolk Street. Because of financial difficulties, they quickly allowed members from outside the teaching profession and so became Sunderland AFC in October 1880.

First Football League game: 13 September, 1890, Football League, v Burnley (h) L 2-3 – Kirtley; Porteous, Oliver; Wilson, Auld, Gibson; Spence (1), Miller, Campbell (1), Scott, D. Hannah.

Managers (and Secretary-managers)
Tom Watson 1888–96, Bob Campbell 1896–99, Alex Mackie 1899–1905, Bob Kyle 1905–28, Johnny Cochrane 1928–39, Bill Murray 1939–57, Alan Brown 1957–64, George Hardwick 1964–65, Ian McColl 1965–68, Alan Brown 1968–72, Bob Stokoe 1972–76, Jimmy Adamson 1976–78, Ken Knighton 1979–81, Alan Durban 1981–84, Len Ashurst 1984–85, Lawrie McMenemy 1985–87, Denis Smith 1987–   .

Player and Position	Ht	Wt	Birth Date	Place	Source	Clubs	League App	Gls
Marco Gabbiadini	5 10	11 02	20 1 68	Nottingham	Apprentice	York C	60	14
						Sunderland	117	60
Ricardo Gabbiadini	6 0	13 05	11 3 70	Newport	Trainee	York C	1	—
						Sunderland	1	—
						Blackpool (loan)	5	3
						Brighton & HA (loan)	1	—
						Grimsby T (loan)	3	1
Eric Gates*	5 6	10 08	28 6 55	Ferryhill	Apprentice	Ipswich T	296	73
						Sunderland	181	43
Thomas Hauser	6 3	12 06	10 4 65	West Germany	Berne OB	Sunderland	31	8
Warren Hawke	5 10	10 11	20 9 70	Durham	Trainee	Sunderland	12	1
Paul Lemon	5 10	11 07	3 6 66	Middlesbrough	Apprentice	Sunderland	107	15
						Carlisle U (loan)	2	—
						Walsall (loan)	2	—
						Reading (loan)	3	—
Colin Pascoe	5 9	10 00	9 4 65	Bridgend	Apprentice	Swansea C	174	39
						Sunderland	81	15
David Rush	5 11	10 10	15 5 71	Sunderland	Trainee	Sunderland	—	—

Trainees
Armstrong, Andrew; Atkinson, Jonathan; Bone, William; Brodie, Stephen E; Egen, Jonathan D; Gooding, Robert; Guthrie, Simon; Maskell, Stuart; Moore, Paul; Morson, David; Patterson, Ian D; Smith, Anthony; Snowball, David; Walls, Wayne M.

Associated Schoolboys
Barrass, Keith D; Hails, Stuart A; Lawson, Ian D; Musgrave, Sean; Redman, Stephen; Scothern, Andrew; Smith, Martin.

Associated Schoolboys who have accepted the club's offer of a Traineeship/Contract
Carr, David; Harwood, Paul; Robinson, Anthony; Russell, Craig S; Wales, David J.

SWANSEA CITY 1989–90 *Back row (left to right):* Jason Prew, Terry Boyle, David Hough, Peter Lloyd.
Centre row: Ron Walton (Youth Team Coach), Stewart Phillips, Cameron Toshack, James Heeps, Lee Bracey, Chris Coleman, Des Trick, Ken Davey (Physiotherapist).
Front row: David D'Auria, Bryan Wade, Paul Raynor, Tommy Hutchison (Player Coach), Andrew Melville, Ian Evans (Manager), Steve Thornber, Andrew Legg, Robbie James.
Sitting: Simon Davey, Philip Evans.

Division 3 **SWANSEA CITY**

Vetch Field, Swansea SA1 3SU. Telephone Swansea (0792) 474114. Fax: 0792 646120.

Ground capacity: 16,098.

Record attendance: 32,796 v Arsenal, FA Cup 4th rd, 17 Feb, 1968.

Record receipts: £36,477.42 v Liverpool, Division 1, 18 Sept, 1982.

Pitch measurements: 112yd × 74yd.

President: I. C. Pursey MBE.

Chairman: D. J. Sharpe.

Directors: D. G. Hammond FCA, MBIM (Vice-Chairman), M. Griffiths.

Team Manager: Terry Yorath. *Assistant Manager:* Tommy Hutchinson.

Youth Team Manager: Ron Walton. *Physio:* Ken Davey.

Commercial and Marketing Manager: Steve Sanders.

Year Formed: 1912. *Turned Professional:* 1912. *Ltd Co.:* 1912.

Club Nickname: 'The Swans'.

Secretary: George Taylor.

Previous Name: Swansea Town until Feb 1970.

Record League Victory: 8-0 v Hartlepool U, Division 4, 1 April 1978 – Barber; Evans, Bartley, Lally (1) (Morris), May, Bruton, Kevin Moore, Robbie James (3 incl. 1p), Curtis (3), Toshack (1), Chappell.

Record Cup Victory: 12-0 v Sliema W (Malta), ECWC 1st rd (1st leg). 15 September 1982 – Davies; Marustik, Hadziabdic (1), Irwin (1), Kennedy, Rajkovic (1), Loveridge (2) (Leighton James), Robbie James, Charles (2), Stevenson (1), Latchford (1) (Walsh (3)).

Record Defeat: 0-8 v Liverpool, FA Cup 3rd rd replay, 9 January, 1990.

Most League Points (2 for a win): 62, Division 3 (S), 1948–49.

Most League Points (3 for a win): 70, Division 4, 1987–88.

Most League Goals: 90, Division 2, 1956–57.

Highest League Scorer in Season: Cyril Pearce, 35, Division 2, 1931–32.

Most League Goals in Total Aggregate: Ivor Allchurch, 166, 1949–58, 1965–68.

Most Capped Player: Ivor Allchurch, 42 (68), Wales.

Most League Appearances: Wilfred Milne, 585, 1919–37.

Record Transfer Fee Received: £370,000 from Leeds U for Alan Curtis, May 1979.

Record Transfer Fee Paid: £340,000 to Liverpool for Colin Irwin, August 1981.

Football League Record: 1920 Original Member of Division 3; 1921–25 Division 3 (S); 1925–47 Division 2; 1947–49 Division 3 (S); 1949–65 Division 2; 1965–67 Division 3; 1967–70 Division 4; 1970–73 Division 3; 1973–78 Division 4; 1978–79 Division 3; 1979–81 Division 2; 1981–83 Division 1; 1983–84 Division 2; 1984–86 Division 3; 1986–88 Division 4; 1988– Division 3.

Honours: Football League: Division 1 best season: 6th 1981–82; Division 2 – Promoted 1980–81 (3rd); Division 3 (S) – Champions 1924–25, 1948–49; Division 3 – Promoted 1978–79 (3rd); Division 4 – Promoted 1969–70 (3rd), 1977–78 (3rd). *FA Cup:* Semi-finals 1926, 1964. *Football League Cup* best season; 4th rd, 1964–65, 1976–77. *Welsh Cup:* Winners 8 times: Runners-up 8 times. **European Competitions:** *European Cup-Winners' Cup:* 1961–62, 1966–67, 1981–82, 1982–83, 1983–84.

Colours: White shirts, white shorts, black stockings. **Change colours:** All red.

SWANSEA CITY 1989–90 LEAGUE RECORD

Match No.	Date	Venue	Opponents	Result		H/T Score	Lg. Pos.	Goalscorers	Attendance
1	Aug 19	A	Huddersfield T	L	0-1	0-0	—		5775
2	26	H	Northampton T	D	1-1	1-0	18	Melville	3495
3	Sept 2	A	Birmingham C	L	0-2	0-0	21		8071
4	9	H	Chester C	W	2-1	2-0	18	Raynor 2	2738
5	16	A	Fulham	L	0-2	0-0	19		4520
6	23	H	Reading	L	1-6	1-3	22	Phillips	3511
7	30	H	Notts Co	D	0-0	0-0	22		3075
8	Oct 7	H	Crewe Alex	W	3-2	1-2	21	Melville 2, Hutchison	3847
9	14	A	Bristol C	W	3-1	1-1	18	Raynor, Salako 2	8794
10	17	A	Bury	L	2-3	0-3	—	Salako, Curtis	3336
11	20	H	Tranmere R	W	1-0	0-0	—	Curtis	3669
12	24	A	Mansfield T	L	0-4	0-0	—		2643
13	28	A	Walsall	W	1-0	0-0	14	James	3469
14	31	H	Rotherham U	W	1-0	0-0	—	Curtis	4077
15	Nov 4	A	Bolton W	D	0-0	0-0	11		6618
16	11	H	Preston NE	W	2-1	1-0	11	Boyle, Melville	3843
16	25	A	Bristol R	L	0-2	0-1	11		5623
18	Dec 2	H	Blackpool	D	0-0	0-0	11		4020
19	16	A	Wigan Ath	L	0-2	0-1	12		2034
20	26	H	Cardiff C	L	0-1	0-1	12		12,244
21	30	H	Brentford	W	2-1	2-1	12	Coleman, Hughes	4537
22	Jan 1	A	Shrewsbury T	D	1-1	0-1	13	Chalmers	3515
23	13	A	Northampton T	D	1-1	1-0	13	Melville	3799
24	21	H	Huddersfield T	L	1-3	0-3	—	James (pen)	4488
25	26	A	Chester C	L	0-1	0-0	—		2150
26	Feb 10	H	Fulham	W	4-2	3-1	13	Hutchison, Chalmers 3	3433
27	13	H	Birmingham C	D	1-1	0-0	—	Harris	3603
28	17	A	Rotherham U	L	2-3	1-1	15	Davey, Raynor	5062
29	20	A	Reading	D	1-1	0-1	—	Coleman	4064
30	24	H	Bristol R	D	0-0	0-0	16		5664
31	Mar 3	A	Leyton Orient	W	2-0	0-0	14	Hough, Davey	3628
32	6	A	Notts Co	L	1-2	0-2	—	Hughes	4862
33	10	H	Mansfield T	W	1-0	0-0	13	Legg	3304
34	17	A	Crewe Alex	D	1-1	0-1	14	Harris	3898
35	20	H	Bristol C	L	0-5	0-2	—		6867
36	23	H	Bury	L	0-1	0-1	—		3042
37	30	A	Tranmere R	L	0-3	0-1	—		8111
38	Apr 3	H	Leyton Orient	L	0-1	0-1	—		2582
39	7	H	Walsall	W	2-0	1-0	18	Hughes, Raynor	2474
40	14	H	Shrewsbury T	L	0-1	0-0	19		3386
41	16	A	Cardiff C	W	2-0	1-0	18	Hughes, Wade	8350
42	21	H	Wigan Ath	W	3-0	1-0	16	Legg, James 2 (1 pen)	3141
43	28	A	Preston NE	L	0-2	0-0	19		6695
44	30	A	Blackpool	D	2-2	1-0	—	Legg, Raynor	1842
45	May 2	A	Brentford	L	1-2	0-1	—	Thornber	4950
46	5	H	Bolton W	D	0-0	0-0	17		5623

Final League Position: 17

GOALSCORERS

League (45): Raynor 6, Melville 5, Chalmers 4, Hughes 4, James 4 (2 pens), Curtis 3, Legg 3, Salako 3, Coleman 2, Davey 2, Harris 2, Hutchison 2, Boyle 1, Hough 1, Phillips 1, Thornber 1, Wade 1.
Littlewoods Cup (1): Raynor 1.
FA Cup (6): Chalmers 2, Melville 2, Davies 1, Raynor 1 (pen).

Bracey	Hough	Coleman	Melville	Boyle	James	Cobb	D'Auria	Raynor	Salako	Hutchison	Phillips	Legg	Harris	Trick	Freestone	Davey	Wade	Curtis	Thornber	Hughes	Chalmers	Walker	Heeps	Match No.
1	2	3	4	5	6	7	8	9*	10	11	12													1
1	2	3	4	5	6	7		12	10	11*	9	8												2
1	2	3	4	5	6	7	11	12	10		9	8*												3
1	2	3	4	5	6	7*	8	11	10	9	12													4
1	2	3	4	5		7	6	11	10	9	8													5
1		3	4*	5	6			11	10	7	9	8	2	12										6
	2	3*	4	5	6			11†	10	9		8	7		1	12	14							7
	2	3	4	5	6			11*	10	9			7		1	12		8						8
	2	3	4	5	6			11	10	9			7		1			8						9
	2	3	4	5	6			11*	10	9	12		7		1			8						10
	2	3	4	5	6			11	10	9*	12		7		1			8						11
	2	3	4	5	6			11*	10	9	12		7		1			8						12
	2	3	4	5	6*				10	9			7		1	12		8	11					13
	2	3	4	5						9			7		1	11	10	8	6					14
	2†	3	4	5						9	12		7	14	1	11	10*	8	6					15
	2	3	4	5						9		10	7		1	11*	12	8	6					16
	2	3	4	5						9*		10	11	12	1	7		8†	6	14				17
	2	3	4							7		10	11*	12	1			8	6	9		5		18
		3	4	5*			7					10	11	12	1	2		8	6	9†	14			19
		3	4					7				10	11†	14	1	2	12	8*	6	9		5		20
1		3	4					10*					11	7		2		8	6	9	12	5		21
1		3	4										11	7		2		8	6	9	10	5		22
1		3	4					12					11	7		2		8*	6	9	10	5		23
1		3†	4	8				7				10	11	14		2		12	6	9		5*		24
	2	3	4	5				7				10†	11					8	6	12	9*	14	1	25
1	2*	3	4	5	12			7				10	11†					8	6	14	9			26
1	2	3	4	5*	12			7				10	11					8†	6	14	9			27
1	2	3	4	5	12			7				10	11					8*	6		9			28
1	2	3	4	5				7				10	11					8	6		9			29
1	2	3	4	5*				7				10	11					8	6	12	9			30
1	2	3	4	5				7				10†	11	14				8	6	12	9*			31
1	2	3	4	5				7				10*	11	14				8	6	12	9†			32
1	2*	3	4	5				7				10	11	12				8	6	9				33
1		3	5		2			7				10	11	14	4*			8	6	9†	12			34
1		3	4	5				7				10*	11	14		2	12	8†	6	9				35
1		3	4	5				7		9		10	11			2		8*	6		12			36
1		3	4	12				7		9		10	11†			2		8	6	14		5*		37
1		3	4	7								11	9	14		2		8*	6	12		5	10†	38
1		3	4	8			2	7				11	5						6	9	10			39
1		3	2	6		7*	8					11	5			14	12	10		9†		4		40
1	2	3	4	8				7			12	11	5	14				10*	6	9†				41
1	2	3	4	8				7				11	5				12	10*	6	9				42
1	2	3	4	8				7				11†	5				12	10*	6	9		14		43
1	2	3	4	8				7				11†	5				14	12	6	9		10*		44
1	2	3	4	8				7			12	11*	5			12	14		6	9		10†		45
1	2	3	4	8				7				11	5					10	6	9				46
31	32	46	46	27	25	5	6	38	13	31	6	20	41	11	14	16	2	21	34	16	13	11	1	
				+5s		+1s2s			+5s			+8s6s		+3s		+2s			+9s5s		+8s	+3s	+2s	

Littlewoods Cup	First Round	Exeter C (a)	0-3
		(h)	1-1
FA Cup	First Round	Kidderminster H (a)	3-2
	Second Round	Peterborough U (h)	3-1
	Third Round	Liverpool (h)	0-0
		(a)	0-8

SWANSEA CITY

Player and Position	Ht	Wt	Birth Date	Place	Source	Clubs	League App	Gls
Goalkeepers								
Lee Bracey	6 1	12 08	11 9 68	Ashford	Trainee	West Ham U	—	—
						Swansea C	61	—
Philip Heeps			16 5 71	Luton	Trainee	Swansea C	1	—
Lee Jones‡	6 2	12 10	9 8 70	Pontyprid	Trainee	Swansea C	—	—
Defenders								
Terry Boyle	5 10	12 04	29 10 58	Ammanford	Apprentice	Tottenham H	—	—
						Crystal Palace	26	1
						Wimbledon (loan)	5	1
						Bristol C	37	—
						Newport Co	166	11
						Cardiff C	128	7
						Swansea C	27	1
Chris Coleman	6 2	12 10	10 6 70	Swansea	Apprentice	Swansea C	119	2
Philip Evans	5 10	11 00	1 3 71	Swansea	Trainee	Swansea C	—	—
Mark Harris	6 1	13 00	15 7 63	Reading	Wokingham	Crystal Palace	2	—
						Burnley (loan)	4	—
						Swansea C	41	2
Andy Melville	6 1	12 06	29 11 68	Swansea	School	Swansea C	175	22
Jason Prew*	5 11	11 10	15 12 70	Cwmbran	Trainee	Swansea C	—	—
Des Trick	6 0	12 00	7 11 69	Swansea	Trainee	Swansea C	14	—
Midfield								
David D'Auria	5 8	11 00	26 3 70	Swansea	Trainee	Swansea C	25	2
David Hough	5 11	11 02	20 2 66	Crewe	Apprentice	Swansea C	181	9
Tommy Hutchison†	5 11	11 02	22 9 47	Cardenden	Dundonald B	Alloa	68	4
						Blackpool	165	10
						Coventry C	314	24
					Bulova	Manchester C	46	4
						Burnley	92	4
						Swansea C	169	9
Andy Legg	5 8	10 07	28 7 66	Neath	Briton Ferry	Swansea	32	3
Peter Lloyd*	5 9	10 11	28 5 71	Swansea	Trainee	Swansea C	—	—
Steve Thornber	5 10	11 02	11 10 65	Dewsbury	Local	Halifax T	104	4
						Swansea C	65	1
Keith Walker	6 0	11 09	17 4 66	Edinburgh	ICI Juveniles	Stirling Alb	91	17
						St Mirren	43	6
						Swansea C	13	—
Forwards								
Paul Chalmers	5 10	10 03	31 10 63	Glasgow	Eastercraigs	Celtic	4	1
						Bradford C (loan)	2	—
						St Mirren	101	23
						Swansea C	16	4
Alan Curtis*	5 11	12 05	16 4 54	Rhondda	Amateur	Swansea C	248	72
						Leeds U	28	5
						Swansea C	90	21
						Southampton	50	5
						Stoke C (loan)	3	—
						Cardiff C	125	10
						Swansea C	26	3
Simon Davey	5 10	11 02	1 10 70	Swansea	Trainee	Swansea C	26	2
John Hughes	6 0	13 07	9 9 64	Edinburgh	Newtongrange S	Berwick R	41	14
						Swansea C	24	4
Robbie James	5 11	13 00	23 3 57	Swansea	Apprentice	Swansea C	394	99
						Stoke C	48	6
						QPR	87	4
						Leicester C	23	—
						Swansea C	90	16

SWANSEA CITY

Foundation: The earliest Association Football in Wales was played in the Northern part of the country and no international took place in the South until 1894, when a local paper still thought it necessary to publish an outline of the rules and an illustration of the pitch markings. There had been an earlier Swansea club, but this has no connection with Swansea Town (now City) formed at a public meeting in June 1912.

First Football League game: 28 August, 1920, Division 3, v Portsmouth (a) L 0-3 – Crumley; Robson, Evans; Smith, Holdsworth, Williams; Hole, I. Jones, Edmundson, Rigsby, Spottiswood.

Managers (and Secretary-managers)
Walter Whittaker 1912–14, William Bartlett 1914–15, Joe Bradshaw 1919–26, Jimmy Thomson 1927–31, Neil Harris 1934–39, Haydn Green 1939–47, Bill McCandless 1947–55, Ron Burgess 1955–58, Trevor Morris 1958–65, Glyn Davies 1965–66, Billy Lucas 1967–69, Roy Bentley 1969–72, Harry Gregg 1972–75, Harry Griffiths 1975–77, John Toshack 1978–83 (resigned October re-appointed in December) 1983–84, Colin Appleton 1984, John Bond 1984–85, Tommy Hutchison 1985–86, Terry Yorath 1986–89, Ian Evans 1989–90, Terry Yorath 1990– .

Player and Position	Ht	Wt	Birth Date	Place	Source	Clubs	League App	Gls
Stewart Phillips	6 0	11 07	30 12 61	Halifax	Amateur	Hereford U	293	83
						WBA	15	4
						Swansea C	20	1
Paul Raynor	6 0	11 04	29 4 66	Nottingham	Apprentice	Nottingham F	3	—
						Bristol R (loan)	8	—
						Huddersfield T	50	9
						Swansea C	122	20
						Wrexham (loan)	6	—
Bryan Wade*	5 8	11 05	25 6 63	Bath	Trowbridge T	Swindon T	60	19
						Swansea C	36	5

Trainees
Baldwin, Nicholas; Bowen, Jason; Corcoran, Glen; Jenkins, Stephen; Johnson, Alec; Thomas, Christopher.

**Non-Contract
Hutchison, Thomas

Associated Schoolboys
Brown, Lee J; Palser, Christopher R; Thomas, David J; Thomas, Richard M.

Associated Schoolboys who have accepted the club's offer of a Traineeship/Contract
Bishop, Matthew; West, Martyn S.

**Non-Contract Players who are retained must be re-signed before they are eligible to play in League matches.

534

SWINDON TOWN 1989–90 *Back row (left to right):* Dave Hockaday, Duncan Shearer, Nick Hammond, Adrian Viveash, Tony Galvin, Phil King, John Cornwell, Fraser Digby, Tim Parkin, Steve White.

Centre row: Chic Bates (Coach), John Trollope (Coach), Tom Jones, Ross MacLaren (Coach), Jon Gittens, Neil Tomlinson, Leigh Barnard, Andy Rowland (Coach), Kevin Morris (Physiotherapist). *Front row:* Paul Hunt, Steve Foley, Mark Jones, Colin Calderwood, Ossie Ardiles (Player-Manager), Alan McLoughlin, Paul Bodin, Fitzroy Simpson, Nick Summerbee.

Division 2   **SWINDON TOWN**

County Ground, Swindon, Wiltshire. Telephone Swindon (0793) 642984. Fax: 536170 (after 5pm). Clubcall: 0898 121640.

Ground capacity: 16,153.

Record attendance: 32,000 v Arsenal, FA Cup 3rd rd, 15 Jan, 1972.

Record receipts: £56,024 v Tottenham H, FA Cup 4th rd, 26 Jan, 1980.

Pitch measurements: 114yd × 72yd.

President: C. J. Green.

Chairman: G. Herbert. *Vice-Chairman:* C. Howard.

Directors:

Company Secretary: R. M. Mattick.

Manager: Ossie Ardiles. *Asst. Manager:* Chic Bates.

Coach: Andy Rowland. *Physio:* Kevin Morris.

Secretary: Lisa Maberly. *Youth Team Manager:* John Trollope.

Commercial Manager: Doug Buswell.

Club Nickname: 'Robins'.

Year Formed: 1881 *(see Foundation).* *Turned Professional:* 1894. *Ltd Co.:* 1894.

Previous Ground: 1881–96, The Croft.

Record League Victory: 9-1 v Luton T, Division 3 (S), 28 August 1920 – Nash; Kay, Macconachie; Langford, Hawley, Wareing; Jefferson (1), Fleming (4), Rogers, Batty (2), Davies (1), (1og).

Record Cup Victory: 10-1 v Farnham U Breweries (away), FA Cup, 1st rd (replay), 28 November 1925 – Nash; Dickenson, Weston: Archer, Bew, Adey; Denyer (2), Wall (1), Richardson (4), Johnson (3), Davies.

Record Defeat: 1-10 v Manchester C, FA Cup 4th rd replay, 25 January, 1930.

Most League Points (2 for a win): 64, Division 3, 1968–69.

Most League Points (3 for a win): 102, Division 4, 1985–86 (League record).

Most League Goals: 100, Division 3 (S), 1926–27.

Highest League Scorer in Season: Harry Morris, 47, Division 3 (S), 1926–27.

Most League Goals in Total Aggregate: Harry Morris, 216, 1926–33.

Most Capped Player: Rod Thomas, 30 (50), Wales.

Most League Appearances: John Trollope, 770, 1960–80.

Record Transfer Fee Received: £400,000 from Sheffield W for Phil King, November 1989.

Record Transfer Fee Paid: £250,000 to Huddersfield T for Duncan Shearer, June 1988.

Football League Record: 1920 Original Member of Division 3; 1921–58 Division 3 (S); 1958–63 Division 3; 1963–65 Division 2; 1965–69 Division 3; 1969–74 Division 2; 1974–82 Division 3; 1982–86 Division 4; 1986–87 Division 3; 1987– Division 2.

Honours: Football League: Division 2 best season; 4th, 1989–90; Division 3 – Runners-up 1962–63, 1968–69; Division 4 – Champions 1985–86 (with record 102 points). *FA Cup:* Semi-finals 1910, 1912. *Football League Cup:* Winners 1968–69. *Anglo-Italian Cup:* Winners 1970.

Colours: Red and white. **Change colours:** White and black.

SWINDON TOWN 1989–90 LEAGUE RECORD

Match No.	Date		Venue	Opponents	Result		H/T Score	Lg. Pos.	Goalscorers	Attendance
1	Aug	19	H	Sunderland	L	0-2	0-1	—		10,199
2		26	A	Oldham Ath	D	2-2	1-0	22	McLoughlin, Shearer	5531
3	Sept	3	H	Wolverhampton W	W	3-1	2-0	—	Jones, Shearer, McLoughlin	10,312
4		9	A	West Ham U	D	1-1	0-1	14	Gittens	21,469
5		12	A	Sheffield U	L	0-2	0-0	—		13,920
6		16	H	Barnsley	D	0-0	0-0	18		6540
7		23	A	Leeds U	L	0-4	0-2	21		21,694
8		26	H	Plymouth Arg	W	3-0	1-0	—	Jones, King, Bodin	6862
9		30	A	Bradford C	D	1-1	0-0	17	White	8334
10	Oct	7	A	Hull C	W	3-2	1-2	14	Simpson, McLoughlin, Parkin	5366
11		14	H	Ipswich T	W	3-0	2-0	11	Shearer, McLoughlin, Stockwell (og)	8039
12		17	H	Oxford U	W	3-0	2-0	—	Calderwood, White 2	10,741
13		21	A	Leicester C	L	1-2	0-0	9	McLoughlin	8547
14	Nov	1	A	Brighton & HA	W	2-1	1-0	—	MacLaren, Gittens	8070
15		4	H	Stoke C	W	6-0	2-0	7	McLoughlin, Shearer 2, Bamber (og), White 2	7825
16		11	A	Middlesbrough	W	2-0	0-0	6	Shearer, Mohan (og)	13,720
17		18	A	Port Vale	L	0-2	0-2	8		7393
18		26	H	Portsmouth	D	2-2	1-0	—	Shearer 2	10,438
19	Dec	2	A	Sunderland	D	2-2	1-0	9	McLoughlin, Shearer	15,849
20		5	H	Bournemouth	L	2-3	1-1	—	Bodin (pen), White	7326
21		10	H	Sheffield U	L	0-2	0-1	—		10,282
22		17	A	WBA	W	2-1	1-0	—	Shearer, White	9884
23		26	H	Blackburn R	W	4-3	3-2	7	Shearer 2, Bodin, Foley	8426
24		30	H	Newcastle U	D	1-1	0-1	7	Shearer	11,657
25	Jan	1	A	Watford	W	2-0	0-0	5	McLoughlin 2	13,708
26		13	H	Oldham Ath	W	3-2	1-0	3	McLoughlin, White 2	7785
27		20	A	Wolverhampton W	L	1-2	0-0	3	White	17,210
28	Feb	4	H	Leeds U	W	3-2	1-1	—	McLoughlin, Foley, MacLaren	16,208
29		10	A	Barnsley	W	1-0	1-0	3	Calderwood	7179
30		18	H	West Ham U	D	2-2	1-1	—	White, MacLaren	16,105
31		24	A	Portsmouth	D	1-1	0-1	3	McLoughlin	10,300
32	Mar	3	H	Port Vale	W	3-0	3-0	3	Calderwood, White, Shearer	8314
33		6	H	Bradford C	W	3-1	3-1	—	Shearer 2, Foley	8483
34		10	A	Plymouth Arg	W	3-0	2-0	2	White 2, Shearer	8364
35		17	H	Hull C	L	1-3	1-2	3	Shearer	8123
36		20	A	Ipswich T	L	0-1	0-0	—		11,856
37		24	A	Oxford U	D	2-2	1-2	3	White, Bodin (pen)	8382
38		31	H	Leicester C	D	1-1	1-1	3	Spearing (og)	8561
39	Apr	7	A	Bournemouth	W	2-1	1-1	4	Simpson, Gittens	7772
40		10	H	Brighton & HA	L	1-2	0-2	—	White	8444
41		14	H	Watford	W	2-0	0-0	4	Shearer, White	8520
42		16	A	Blackburn R	L	1-2	1-1	5	Gittens	10,689
43		21	H	WBA	W	2-1	0-0	5	Bodin, White	8495
44		25	A	Newcastle U	D	0-0	0-0	—		26,568
45		28	H	Middlesbrough	D	1-1	0-1	4	Foley	9532
46	May	5	A	Stoke C	D	1-1	1-1	4	Shearer	11,386

Final League Position: 4

GOALSCORERS

League (79): Shearer 20, White 18, McLoughlin 12, Bodin 5 (2 pens), Foley 4, Gittens 4, Calderwood 3, MacLaren 3, Jones 2, Simpson 2, King 1, Parkin 1, own goals 4.
Littlewoods Cup (15): White 5, McLoughlin 4, Shearer 4, MacLaren 2.
FA Cup (1): Shearer 1.

Digby	Hockaday	King	McLoughlin	Parkin	Calderwood	Galvin	Shearer	White	MacLaren	Simpson	Cornwell	Ardiles	Barnard	Gittens	Jones	Summerbee	Close	Bodin	Hunt	Foley	Kerslake	Dearden	Match No.
1	2	3	4	5*	6	7†	8	9	10	11	12	14											1
1		3	4	5	6	7	8*	9	10	11	12		2										2
1		3	4		6	11	8†	9	10		12		2*	5	7	14							3
1		3	4	5		11*		9	10		12		2	6	7		8						4
1		3	4	5		11		9	10	14	12		2*	6	7†		8						5
1		3	4		6		8		10†	11			2	5	7*		9	12	14				6
1	2	3	4	5		12	8		10	11*				6	7			9					7
1	2	3	4	5		14	8†		10	11				6	7*			9	12				8
1	2	3	4*	5		11†	8	12	10	14				6	7			9					9
1	2	3*	4		6		8	9	10	11	12			5	7								10
1	2	3	4		6		8	9	10		12			5	7			11*					11
1	2	3	4		6		14	9	10		12			5	7			11*	8†				12
1	2	3	4		6			9	10					5	7			11	8				13
1	2	3*	4	5			8	9	10	11				6	7†			12	14				14
1	2		4	5			8	9	10	11				6	7			3					15
1			4		5		12	8	9	10	11*	2		6	7			3					16
1			4		5		8	9†10		11	2*			6	7		14	3	12				17
1			4		5		8	9	10*11					6	7			3		12	2		18
1			4		5		8	9*10	12	14				6	7			3		11†	2		19
1			4		5		8	9	10	12				6	7			3		11*	2		20
1			4		5		8	9	10	12				6	7			3		11	2*		21
1			4		5	14	8	9*10		12				6	7†			3		11	2		22
1	14		4		5		8	9†10		12				6	7			3		11	2*		23
1	12		4		5		8	9	10					6	7			3		11*	2		24
1			4		5		8	9	10	12				6	7*			3		11	2		25
1			4		5		8	9	10	12				6	7*			3		11	2		26
1	12		4		5		8	9	10					6	7			3		11*	2		27
1			4		5		8	9	10					6	7			3		11	2		28
1			4		5		8	9†10		12				6	7*		14	3		11	2		29
1			4		5		8	9	10					6	7			3		11	2		30
1			4		5		8	9*10	12					6	7			3		11	2		31
1	14		4		5		8	9	10†12					6	7			3		11*	2		32
1	14		4†		5		8	9	10	12				6	7			3		11*	2		33
1			4		5		8	9	10	11				6	7			3			2		34
1			4		5		8	9*10		11				6	7		12	3			2		35
1	14		4		5		8	9*10		11				6	7†		12	3			2		36
1			4		5		8	9	10*11	12				6	7			3			2		37
1	12		4		5		8	9	10	11*				6	7			3			2		38
			4†		5		8	9*10		11		14		6	7		12	3			2	1	39
1	14		4		5		8*	9	10	11†				6	7		12	3			2		40
1			4*		5		8	9	10	11†				6	7		12	3		14	2		41
1			4		5		8	9	10	12		14		6	7			3		11*	2†		42
1	2		4		5		8	9	10	12				6	7			3		11*			43
1			4		5		8	9	10					6	7			3		11	2		44
1	14		4		5		8	9	10	12				6	7			3		11*	2†		45
1			4		5		8†	9	10	12		14		6	7*			3		11	2		46
45	11	14	46	6	46	6	42	42	46	19	2	—	5	40	43	—	4	38	2	20	28	1	
	+9s						+5s	+1s		+11s	+17s	+2s			+1s	+1s		+7s	+3s	+2s	+3s		

Littlewoods Cup Second Round Shrewsbury T (a) 3-0
          (h) 3-1
      Third Round Bolton W (h) 3-3
          (a) 1-1
          (a) 1-1
          (h) 2-1
      Fourth Round Southampton (h) 0-0
          (a) 2-4
FA Cup Third Round Bristol C (a) 1-2

SWINDON TOWN

Player and Position	Ht	Wt	Birth Date	Place	Source	Clubs	League App	Gls
Goalkeepers								
Fraser Digby	6 1	12 12	23 4 67	Sheffield	Apprentice	Manchester U	—	—
						Oldham Ath (loan)	—	—
						Swindon T (loan)	—	—
						Swindon T	161	—
Nicky Hammond	6 0	11 13	7 9 67	Hornchurch	Apprentice	Arsenal	—	—
						Bristol R (loan)	3	—
						Peterborough U (loan)	—	—
						Aberdeen (loan)	—	—
						Swindon T	4	—
Defenders								
David Barnett‡	5 6	9 13	20 11 69	Swindon	Trainee	Swindon T	—	—
Colin Calderwood	6 0	11 09	20 1 65	Stranraer	Amateur	Mansfield T	100	1
						Swindon T	215	11
Dean Casserly‡			9 10 69	Wiltshire	Trainee	Swindon T	—	—
Paul O'Driscoll‡			25 2 71	Swindon	Southampton§	Swindon T	—	—
Curtis Fleming‡	5 8	11 04	8 10 68	Manchester	St Patrick's Ath	Swindon T	—	—
Jon Gittens	5 11	12 06	22 1 64	Moseley	Paget R	Southampton	18	—
						Swindon T	98	5
David Hockaday	5 10	10 09	9 11 57	Billingham	Amateur	Blackpool	147	24
						Swindon T	242	6
Ross MacLaren	5 10	12 12	14 4 62	Edinburgh	Rangers	Shrewsbury T	161	18
						Derby Co	122	4
						Swindon T	83	7
Adrian Viveash	6 1	11 12	30 9 69	Swindon	Trainee	Swindon T	—	—
Midfield								
Ossie Ardiles‡	5 6	9 10	3 8 52	Cordoba	Huracan	Tottenham H	140	13
						Paris St Germain	14	1
						Tottenham H	98	3
						Blackburn R (loan)	5	—
						QPR	8	—
						Swindon T	2	—
Paul Bodin	6 0	12 01	13 9 64	Cardiff	Chelsea	Newport Co	—	—
						Cardiff C	57	3
					Bath C	Newport Co	6	1
						Swindon T	62	7
John Cornwell	6 0	12 00	13 10 64	Bethnal Green	Apprentice	Orient	202	35
						Newcastle U	33	1
						Swindon T	25	—
Peter Coyne	5 9	10 07	13 11 58	Manchester	Apprentice	Manchester U	2	1
					Ashton U	Crewe Alex	134	47
					Hyde U	Swindon T	110	30
						Aldershot (loan)	3	—
Steve Foley	5 7	10 12	4 10 62	Liverpool	Apprentice	Liverpool	—	—
						Fulham (loan)	3	—
						Grimsby T	31	2
						Sheffield U	66	14
						Swindon T	98	16
Mark Jones*	5 8	9 12	26 9 61	Berinsfield	Apprentice	Oxford U	129	7
						Swindon T	40	9
Tommy Jones	5 10	11 07	7 10 64	Aldershot	Weymouth	Aberdeen	28	3
						Swindon T	84	8
David Kerslake	5 8	11 04	19 6 66	London	Apprentice	QPR	58	6
						Swindon T	28	—
Alan McLoughlin	5 8	10 00	20 4 67	Manchester	Local	Manchester U	—	—
						Swindon T	9	—
						Torquay U	24	4
						Swindon T	80	15

SWINDON TOWN

Foundation: It is generally accepted that Swindon Town came into being in 1881, although there is no firm evidence that the club's founder, Rev. William Pitt, captain of the Spartans (an offshoot of a cricket club) changed his club's name to Swindon Town before 1883, when the Spartans amalgamated with St. Mark's Young Men's Friendly Society.

First Football League game: 28 August, 1920, Division 3, v Luton T (h) W 9-1 – Nash; Kay, Macconachie; Langford, Hawley, Wareing; Jefferson (1), Fleming (4), Rogers, Batty (2), Davies (1). 1 o.g.

Managers (and Secretary-managers)
Sam Allen 1902–33, Ted Vizard 1933–39, Neil Harris 1939–41, Louis Page 1945–53, Maurice Lindley 1953–55, Bert Head 1956–65, Danny Williams 1965–69, Fred Ford 1969–71, Dave Mackay 1971–72, Les Allen 1972–74, Danny Williams 1974–78, Bobby Smith 1978–80, John Trollope 1980–83, Ken Beamish 1983–84, Lou Macari 1984–89, Ossie Ardiles 1989– .

Player and Position	Ht	Wt	Birth Date	Place	Source	Clubs	League App	Gls
Jim Reynolds‡	5 9	10 10	27 10 67	Swindon	Apprentice	Swindon T	2	—
Fitzroy Simpson	5 8	10 07	26 2 70	Trowbridge	Trainee	Swindon T	37	2
Paul Trollope	6 0	12 02	3 6 72	Swindon	Trainee	Swindon T	—	—
Forwards								
Shaun Close	5 8	10 01	8 9 66	Islington	Trainee	Tottenham H	9	—
						Bournemouth	39	8
						Swindon T	11	
Tony Galvin	5 9	11 05	12 7 56	Huddersfield	Goole T	Tottenham H	201	20
						Sheffield W	36	1
						Swindon T	11	
Paul Hunt	5 5	10 02	8 10 71	Swindon	Trainee	Swindon T	4	—
Duncan Shearer	5 10	10 09	28 8 62	Fort William	Inverness Clach	Chelsea	2	1
						Huddersfield T	83	38
						Swindon T	78	34
Nick Summerbee	5 11	11 08	26 8 71	Altrincham	Trainee	Swindon T	1	—
Neil Tomlinson	5 11	12 00	14 10 69	Birmingham	Shrewsbury T	Swindon T	—	—
Steve White	5 11	11 04	2 1 59	Chipping Sodbury	Mangotsfield U	Bristol R	50	20
						Luton T	72	25
						Charlton Ath	29	12
						Lincoln C (loan)	3	—
						Luton T (loan)	4	—
						Bristol R	101	24
						Swindon T	146	57

Trainees
Braidwood, Jason P; Dixon, Liam J; Graham, Alex; Hall, Darren M; Lea, Mark J; Lovegrove, Ryan B; Murray, Edwin J; Spalding, Lee A; Spence, Robert J; Thompson, Paul S; Walker, Richard D.

Associated Schoolboys
Bates, Andrew; Chew, Paul; Corry, David J; O'Driscoll, Mark A; Pitman, Andrew R; Skinner, Neil J; Sly, Simon J; Underwood, Jamie; Worrall, Benjamin J.

Associated Schoolboys who have accepted the club's offer of a Traineeship/Contract
O'Sullivan, Wayne S.J; Phillips, Marcus S; Thomson, Andrew J.

TORQUAY UNITED 1989-90 *Back row (left to right):* Robbie Taylor, Paul Hirons, Sean Joyce, Paul Holmes.
Centre row: Carl Airey, John Matthews, Mark Loram, Matt Elliott, Ken Veysey, Mark Coombe, John Uzzell, Phil Lloyd, Alan Hay, Dean Edwards.
Front row: John Morrison, Ian Weston, Norman Medhurst (Physiotherapist), Dave Smith (Manager), Sean Haslegrave (Assistant Manager), Paul Smith, Jim Smith.

Division 4   **TORQUAY UNITED**

Plainmoor Ground, Torquay, Devon TQ1 3PS. Telephone Torquay (0803) 328666/7. Clubcall 0898 12 16 41.

Ground capacity: 5539.

Record attendance: 21,908 v Huddersfield T, FA Cup 4th rd, 29 Jan, 1955.

Record receipts: £21,000 v West Ham U, FA Cup, 3rd rd, 6 January 1990.

Pitch measurements: 112 yd × 74yd.

President: A. J. Boyce.

Chairman: L. W. Pope. *Vice-Chairman:* G. J. Harvey.

Directors: W. W. Rogers, R. Harvey, F. M. Mosley TD, M. Beer, M. Bateson.

Team Manager: Dave Smith. *Assistant Manager:* Sean Haslegrave.

Physio: Norman Medhurst.

Company Secretary: D. F. Turner. *Lottery Administrators:* C. Munslow and A. Sandford.

Nickname: 'The Gulls'.

Year Formed: 1898. *Turned Professional:* 1921. *Ltd Co.:* 1921.

Previous Name: 1910, Torquay Town; 1921, Torquay United,

Previous Grounds: 1898, Teignmouth Road; 1901, Torquay Recreation Ground; 1905, Cricket Field Road; 1907–10, Torquay Cricket Ground.

Record League Victory: 9-0 v Swindon T, Division 3 (S), 8 March 1952 – George Webber; Topping, Ralph Calland; Brown, Eric Webber, Towers; Shaw (1), Marchant (1), Northcott (2), Collins (3), Edds (2).

Record Cup Victory: 7-1 v Northampton T, FA Cup, 1st rd, 14 November 1959 – Gill; Penford, Downs; Bettany, George Northcott, Rawson; Baxter, Cox, Tommy Northcott (1), Bond (3), Pym (3).

Record Defeat: 2-10 v Fulham, Division 3 (S), 7 September, 1931 and v Luton T, Division 3 (S), 2 September, 1933.

Most League Points (2 for a win): 60, Division 4, 1959–60.

Most League Points (3 for a win): 77, Division 4, 1987–88.

Most League Goals: 89, Division 3 (S), 1956–57.

Highest League Scorer in Season: Sammy Collins, 40, Division 3 (S), 1955–56.

Most League Goals in Total Aggregate: Sammy Collins, 204, 1948–58.

Most Capped Player: None.

Most League Appearances: Dennis Lewis, 443, 1947–59.

Record Transfer Fee Received: £125,000 from Manchester U for Lee Sharpe, May 1988.

Record Transfer Fee Paid: £25,000 to Exeter C for Vince O'Keefe, March 1980.

Football League Record: 1927 Elected to Division 3 (S); 1958–60 Division 4; 1960–62 Division 3; 1962–66 Division 4; 1966–72 Division 3; 1972– Division 4.

Honours: Football League: Division 3 best season: 4th, 1967–68, Division 3(S) – Runners-up 1956–57; Division 4 – Promoted 1959–60 (3rd), 1965–66 (3rd). *FA Cup* best season: 4th rd, 1949, 1955, 1971, 1983, 1990. *Football League Cup:* never past 3rd rd. *Sherpa Van Trophy:* Runners-up 1989.

Colours: All yellow. **Change colours:** All white.

TORQUAY UNITED 1989–90 LEAGUE RECORD

Match No.	Date		Venue	Opponents	Result		H/T Score	Lg. Pos.	Goalscorers	Attendance
1	Aug	19	A	Stockport Co	D	1-1	1-1	—	Airey	2356
2		26	H	Grimsby T	L	0-3	0-0	22		2525
3	Sept	2	A	Halifax T	L	1-3	0-0	23	Loram (pen)	1893
4		9	H	Lincoln C	L	0-3	0-3	23		2081
5		15	A	Southend U	L	0-1	0-1	—		7070
6		23	H	Rochdale	W	1-0	0-0	23	Loram	1809
7		26	A	Scunthorpe U	L	0-2	0-2	—		3242
8		30	H	Burnley	L	0-1	0-0	23		2214
9	Oct	7	H	Doncaster R	W	2-0	2-0	22	Airey, Smith P	2059
10		13	A	Cambridge U	L	2-5	1-3	—	Loram, Airey	2085
11		17	H	Hartlepool U	W	4-3	2-2	—	Joyce 2, Airey, Smith P	2108
12		21	A	Aldershot	W	2-1	0-0	20	Airey, Joyce	2244
13		31	A	Wrexham	D	1-1	1-1	—	Airey	1225
14	Nov	4	A	York C	D	1-1	0-0	19	Airey	2496
15		11	H	Carlisle U	L	1-2	0-0	19	Airey	2266
16		14	H	Gillingham	L	0-2	0-1	—		2318
17		25	A	Peterborough U	D	1-1	0-0	19	Smith J	4715
18	Dec	2	H	Scarborough	W	3-2	0-2	19	Smith P 2, Holmes	1858
19		16	A	Colchester U	W	3-0	1-0	18	Loram, Caldwell, Smith P	1720
20		26	H	Hereford U	D	1-1	0-0	18	Loram	3005
21		30	H	Maidstone U	W	2-1	1-0	18	Edwards, Loram	2344
22	Jan	1	A	Exeter C	L	0-3	0-2	19		8154
23		13	A	Grimsby T	D	0-0	0-0	19		4586
24		20	H	Stockport Co	W	3-0	0-0	18	Joyce, Caldwell, Taylor	2228
25	Feb	3	A	Rochdale	D	0-0	0-0	18		1909
26		6	H	Southend U	W	3-0	1-0	—	Elliott, Smith P, Loram	2077
27		17	A	Scarborough	D	0-0	0-0	17		1725
28		24	H	Peterborough U	W	2-1	1-0	16	Loram (pen), Holmes	2467
29	Mar	3	A	Chesterfield	L	1-5	1-2	18	Ryan (og)	3602
30		6	A	Burnley	L	0-1	0-1	—		4533
31		10	H	Scunthorpe U	L	0-3	0-0	19		1935
32		13	H	Chesterfield	W	1-0	1-0	—	Caldwell	1808
33		17	A	Doncaster R	L	1-2	0-1	18	Uzzell	1887
34		20	H	Cambridge U	W	3-0	2-0	—	Lloyd, Edwards, Caldwell	1744
35		24	A	Hartlepool U	D	1-1	0-0	16	Loram (pen)	2725
36		27	H	Halifax T	W	1-0	1-0	—	Whiston	1911
37		31	H	Aldershot	L	1-2	0-0	15	Uzzell	2086
38	Apr	4	A	Lincoln C	D	2-2	1-2	—	Edwards, Loram (pen)	2573
39		7	A	Gillingham	W	2-0	1-0	14	Caldwell 2	2869
40		10	H	Wrexham	L	0-1	0-0	—		1774
41		14	H	Exeter C	L	0-2	0-0	15		3389
42		16	A	Hereford U	D	0-0	0-0	15		2422
43		21	A	Colchester U	W	4-1	3-0	15	Cookson, Gilbert (og), Elliott, Loram	1521
44		25	A	Maidstone U	L	1-5	0-4	—	Loram	2223
45		28	A	Carlisle U	L	0-2	0-0	15		3997
46	May	5	H	York C	D	1-1	0-1	15	Joyce	1564

Final League Position: 15

GOALSCORERS

League (53): Loram 12 (4 pens), Airey 8, Caldwell 6, Smith P. 6, Joyce 5, Edwards 3, Elliott 2, Holmes 2, Uzzell 2, Cookson 1, Lloyd 1, Smith J. 1, Taylor 1, Whiston 1, own goals 2.
Littlewoods Cup (0).
FA Cup (9): Elliott 2, Smith J 2, Hirons 1, Lloyd 1, Loram 1, Uzzell 1, own goal 1.

Veysey	Pugh	Holmes	Matthews	Elliott	Uzzell	Bastow	Lloyd	Edwards	Loram	Morrison	Airey	Joyce	Hirons	Smith P	Miller	Davies	Weston	Hay	Taylor	Mundee	Smith J	Hall	Caldwell	Cookson	Whiston	Hannigan	Curran	Match No.
1	2	3	4	5	6	7*	8	9	10	11†	12	14																1
1	2		4	5	6		8	9	10	11*	3	7	12															2
1	3	2	4		6		8	9	12		10†	14			11	5	7*											3
1		2	4†	5	6		8*			11		14		10	12			3*	7	9								4
1		2	4		6			12	14	8†		11		10		5		3*	7	9								5
1		2	4		6		3	12	10			11		8		5		7*	9									6
1	6			5			3	7†	10	4		11		12		5*		14	9									7
1		2		5			3	9	10	14		6		7	11†			8*	4	12								8
1		2		5			3	9	10					8	6	7	11		4									9
1			5	2			3	9*	10					8	6	7	11		12	4								10
1		2	5	12			3	9	10†					8*	6	14	7		11	4								11
1		2	5	10			3	9	12					8	6	7*	11		4									12
1		2	5	4	10		3	9	12					8	6	7*	11											13
1		2	5	4	10		3	9	7					8	6		11*		12									14
1		2	5*	4	10		3	9	7					8	6		11		12									15
1		2		4	10		3	9†	7					8	6	12	11*			14								16
1		2		4	10		3		7	11				6	9*12	5			8									17
1		2		4*10			3		7†14			6			9	11	5	12		8								18
1		2	5*	4		12	3	8	7	11				6		9							10					19
1		2	12	4			3	8	7	11				6*		9			5				10					20
1		2	4		6		3	8	7	11				9			5					12	10*					21
1		2	4		6		3	8	7*11					9		14	5†		10	12								22
1		2	4*	5	6	12	3	8		11				14	7		9†						10					23
1		2		5	6	9	3					8*4	11	7		12							10					24
1		2		5	6		3		9*			4	12	7		11			8				10					25
1		2		5	6		3	9				4	8	7		11							10					26
1		2		5	6		3	9				4	8	7		11							10					27
1		2	12	5	6		3	9				4	8*	7		11			10									28
1		2	12	5	6		3	9				4	8*	7		11			10									29
1		2		5	6		3	9				4		7		11			10			8						30
1		2		5	6	10	3	9				4	11*	7					8				12					31
1		2		5	6	11	3	9				4		7					12	10		8*						32
1		2		5*	6	11	3	9				4		7	14				12	10†	8							33
1		2	5		6		3	8	9			4		7			11					10*12						34
1			5		6		3	8*	9			4		7			11	12						2	10			35
1		2			6		3		9			4		7			11			12		10*		8	5			36
1	2*				6		3		9					7			11		4	12		10		8	5			37
1		2			6		3	8	9	4	12			7			11					10*			5			38
1		2			6		3	8	9	14	4			7*			11†		12	10					5			39
1		2			6		3	8	9	7	4		11*						12	10				5†14				40
1		2	12		6		3	8	9	7	4								10†14			5		11*				41
1		2	5	8	6*		3		9		4			11								7	10		12			42
1		2	5	8*			3	12	9†			14		11							7	10	4	6				43
1		2	5	8			3	12	9	4	14			6†11							7	10*						44
1		2	5	8			3	6	9	4*				11			14		7	10†				12				45
1		2	5*	6		12	3	8	9	4	14			11						7	10†							46
46	3	44	22	32	35	6	45	26	39	11	11	38	9	31	3	6	25	8	11	9	2	7	17	7	8	5	—	
		+3s	+1s	+1s		+3s1s	+4s	+3s	+3s	+1s	+3s			+7s2s		+1s	+4s		+7s			+8s3s		+3s		+2s1s		

TORQUAY UNITED

Player and Position	Ht	Wt	Birth Date	Place	Source	Clubs	League App	Gls
Goalkeepers								
Mark Coombe*	6 1	12 06	17 9 68	Torquay	Trainee	Bournemouth	—	—
						Bristol C	—	—
						Carlisle U (loan)	—	—
						Colchester U	3	—
						Torquay U	8	—
Ken Veysey	5 11	11 08	8 6 67	Hackney		Torquay U	71	—
Defenders								
Chris Curran§			17 9 71	Birmingham	Trainee	Torquay U	1	—
Andy Davies§	6 0	11 06	6 6 72	Wolverhampton	Trainee	Torquay U	13	—
Matthew Elliott	6 3	13 06	1 11 68	Surrey	Epsom & Ewell	Charlton Ath	—	—
						Torquay U	46	4
Alan Hay	6 0	12 06	28 11 58	Dunfermine	Amateur	Bolton W	—	—
						Bristol C	74	1
						St Mirren (loan)	—	—
						York C	150	3
						Tranmere R	28	—
						York C	1	—
						Sunderland	1	—
						Torquay U	8	—
Paul Holmes	5 10	11 00	18 2 68	Sheffield	Apprentice	Doncaster R	47	1
						Torquay U	69	2
Philip Lloyd	5 11	11 11	26 12 64	Hemsworth	Apprentice	Middlesbrough	—	—
						Barnsley	—	—
						Darlington	127	3
						Torquay U	138	7
John Morrison	5 6	10 04	27 7 70	Kettering	Trainee	Torquay U	32	—
Phil Underhill‡	5 6	9 09	26 10 69	Bristol	Trainee	Southampton	—	—
						Torquay U	—	—
John Uzzell	5 10	11 03	31 3 59	Plymouth	Apprentice	Plymouth Arg	302	6
						Torquay U	36	2
Midfield								
Ian Bastow	5 8	9 02	12 8 71	Torquay	Trainee	Torquay U	11	—
Sean Joyce	5 8	10 05	15 2 67	Doncaster		Doncaster R	41	2
						Exeter C (loan)	1	—
						Torquay U	71	8
John Matthews	6 0	12 06	1 11 55	London	Apprentice	Arsenal	45	2
						Sheffield U	103	14
						Mansfield T	72	6
						Chesterfield	38	1
						Plymouth Arg	135	4
						Torquay U	25	—
Daral Pugh‡	5 8	10 03	5 6 61	Crynant	Apprentice	Doncaster R	154	15
						Huddersfield T	84	7
						Rotherham U	112	6
						Cambridge U (loan)	6	1
						Torquay U	32	—
Jim Smith*	5 9	10 07	22 11 69	Johnstone	Trainee	Torquay U	45	5
Ian Weston*	5 10	11 10	6 5 68			Bristol R	16	—
						Torquay U	62	2
						Shamrock R (loan)	—	—
Forwards								
Carl Airey*	6 0	12 06	6 2 65	Wakefield	Apprentice	Barnsley	38	5
						Bradford C (loan)	5	—
						Darlington	75	28
					Charleroi	Chesterfield	26	4
						Rotherham U	32	11
						Torquay U	29	11
						Shamrock R (loan)	—	—

TORQUAY UNITED

Foundation: The idea of establishing a Torquay club was agreed by old boys of Torquay College and Torbay College, while sitting in Princess Gardens listening to the band. A proper meeting was subsequently held at Tor Abbey Hotel at which officers were elected. This was in 1898 and the club's first competition was the Eastern League (later known as the East Devon League).

First Football League game: 27 August, 1927, Division 3(S), v Exeter C (h) D 1–1 – Millsom; Cook, Smith; Wellock, Wragg, Connor, Mackey, Turner (1), Jones, McGovern, Thomson.

Managers (and Secretary-managers)
Percy Mackrill 1927–29*, A. H. Hoskins 1929*, Frank Womack 1929–32, Frank Brown 1932–38, Alf Steward 1938–40, Billy Butler 1945–46, Jack Butler 1946–47, John McNeil 1947–50, Bob John 1950, Alex Massie 1950–51, Eric Webber 1951–65, Frank O'Farrell 1965–68, Alan Brown 1969–71, Jack Edwards 1971–73, Malcolm Musgrove 1973–76, Mike Green 1977–81, Frank O'Farrell 1981–82 (continued as GM to 1983), Bruch Rioch 1982–84, Dave Webb 1984–85, John Sims 1985, Stuart Morgan 1985–87, Cyril Knowles 1987–89, Dave Smith 1989– .

Player and Position	Ht	Wt	Birth Date	Place	Source	Clubs	League App	Gls
Dave Caldwell*	5 10	10 08	31 7 60	Aberdeen	Inverness Caley	Mansfield T	157	57
						Carlisle U (loan)	4	—
						Swindon T (loan)	5	—
						Chesterfield	68	17
						Torquay U	24	4
					Overpelt	Torquay U	17	6
Steven Cookson§	6 1	10 10	19 2 72	Wolverhampton	Trainee	Torquay U	10	1
Dean Edwards	5 11	11 07	25 2 62	Wolverhampton	Apprentice	Shrewsbury T	13	1
					Telford U	Wolverhampton W	31	9
						Exeter C	54	17
						Torquay U	70	11
Paul Hall§	5 9	10 02	3 7 72	Manchester	Trainee	Torquay U	10	—
Paul Hirons*	5 11	11 00	6 3 71	Bristol	Bristol C§	Torquay U	21	—
Mark Loram	6 0	12 00	13 8 67	Paignton	Brixham	Torquay U	52	8
						QPR (loan)	—	—
						QPR	—	—
						Torquay U (loan)	13	4
						Torquay U	124	24
Alan Miller‡			13 9 70	Preston	Bury§	Torquay U	4	—
Paul Smith	5 8	9 09	5 10 67	London	Apprentice	Arsenal	—	—
						Brentford	17	1
						Bristol R	16	1
						Torquay U	44	7
Robbie Taylor*	5 9	10 10	3 12 67	Plymouth		Portsmouth	—	—
						Newport Co	44	7
						Torquay U	18	1
Richard Thompson‡	6 2	12 01	11 4 69	Bristol	Watford	Newport Co	13	2
						Torquay U	15	4

Trainees
Attwood, Darren R; Convy, Alan L; Cookson, Steven J; Crook, Alexander L; Curran, Christopher; Davies, Andrew J; Davis, Arron; Edwards, Fraser L; Gaisford, Darren W; Gilbert, Asa J; Hall, Paul A; Kidd, Steven R; Nock, Paul A; Ryder, Ciaran H; Taylor, Scott R; Whittaker, Matthew J.

Associated Schoolboys who have accepted the club's offer of a Traineeship/Contract
Poblocki, Dean

546

TOTTENHAM HOTSPUR 1989–90 *Back row (left to right)*: Andy Polston, Paul Stewart, Erik Thorstvedt, Guy Butters, Bobby Mimms, Gary Stevens, Steve Sedgley.. *Centre row*: Gudni Bergsson, Philip Gray, Brian Statham, Paul Gascoigne, Vinny Samways, David Howells, Nayim, Chris Hughton. *Front row*: Paul Walsh, Mark Robson, Terry Fenwick, Gary Mabbutt, Gary Lineker, John Polston, Paul Moran.

Division 1   **TOTTENHAM HOTSPUR**

748 High Rd, Tottenham, London, N17. Telephone 081-808
8080. Commercial Dept: 081-808 0281. Recorded information:
0898 100 515. Dial-a-seat: 01-808 3030. Telex: 24739 and
295261. Spurs Line: 0898 100 500. Fax: 01-885 1951.
Ground Capacity: 29,700.
Record attendance: 75,038 v Sunderland, FA Cup 6th rd, 5
March, 1938.
Record receipts: £245,632.10 v Anderlecht, UEFA Cup Final
2nd leg, 23 May, 1984.
Pitch measurements: 110yd × 73yd.
Chairman: I. A. Scholar. *Vice-Chairman:* D. A. Alexiou.
Directors: F. P. Sinclair, P. A. Bobroff, A. G. Berry.
Financial Director: D. R. Peter.
Manager: Terry Venables.
Assistant Manager: Doug Livermore. *Physios:* John Sheridan and Dave Butler.
Secretary: Peter Barnes. *Commercial Manager:* Mike Rollo. *PRO:* John Fennelly.
Year Formed: 1882. *Turned Professional:* 1895. *Ltd Co.:* 1898.
Club Nickname: 'Spurs'.
Previous Grounds: 1882, Tottenham Marshes; 1885, Northumberland Park; 1898, White
Hart Lane.
Previous Name: 1882–85, Hotspur Football Club.
Record League Victory: 9-0 v Bristol R, Division 2, 22 October 1977 – Davies; Naylor,
Holmes, Hoddle (1), McAllister, Perryman, Pratt, McNab, Morris (3), Lee (4), Taylor
(1).
Record Cup Victory: 13-2 v Crewe Alex, FA Cup, 4th rd (replay), 3 February 1960 – Brown;
Hills, Henry; Blanchflower, Norman, Mackay; White, Harmer (1), Smith (4), Allen (5),
Jones (3 incl. 1p).
Record Defeat: 0-7 v Liverpool, Division 1, 2 September, 1978.
Most League Points (2 for a win): 70, Division 2, 1919–20.
Most League Points (3 for a win): 77, Division 1, 1984–85.
Most League Goals: 115, Division 1, 1960-61.
Highest League Scorer in Season: Jimmy Greaves, 37, Division 1, 1962–63.
Most League Goals in Total Aggregate: Jimmy Greaves, 220, 1961–70.
Most Capped Player: Pat Jennings, 74 (119), Northern Ireland.
Most League Appearances: Steve Perryman, 655, 1969–86.
Record Transfer Fee Received: £4,500,000 from Marseille for Chris Waddle, July 1989.
Record Transfer Fee Paid: £2,000,000 to Newcastle U for Paul Gascoigne, July 1988.
Football League Record: 1908 Elected to Division 2; 1909–15 Division 1; 1919–20 Division
2; 1920–28 Division 1; 1928–33 Division 2; 1933–35 Division 1; 1935–50 Division 2; 1950–77
Division 1; 1977–78 Division 2; 1978– Division 1.
Honours: Football League: Division 1 – Champions 1950–51, 1960–61; Runners-up
1921–22, 1951–52, 1956–57, 1962–63; Division 2 – Champions 1919–20, 1949–50; Runners-
up 1908–09, 1932–33; Promoted 1977–78 (3rd). *FA Cup:* Winners 1901 (as non-League
club). 1921, 1961, 1962, 1967, 1981, 1982 (7 wins stands as the joint record): Runners-up
1986–87. *Football League Cup:* Winners 1970–71, 1972–73; Runners-up 1981–82. **European
Competitions:** *European Cup:* 1961–62; *European Cup-Winners' Cup:* 1962–63 (winners),
1963–64, 1967–68, 1981–82 (runners-up), 1982–83); *UEFA Cup:* 1971–72 (winners),
1973–74 (runners-up), 1983–84 (winners), 1984–85.
Colours: White shirts, navy blue shorts, white stockings. **Change colours:** All yellow.

TOTTENHAM HOTSPUR 1989-90 LEAGUE RECORD

Match No.	Date	Venue	Opponents	Result	H/T Score	Lg. Pos.	Goalscorers	Attendance
1	Aug 19	H	Luton T	W 2-1	1-0	—	Stewart, Allen	17,668
2	22	A	Everton	L 1-2	1-1	—	Allen	34,402
3	26	A	Manchester C	D 1-1	1-1	11	Gascoigne	32,004
4	Sept 9	A	Aston Villa	L 0-2	0-2	17		24,769
5	16	H	Chelsea	L 1-4	0-2	19	Gascoigne	16,260
6	23	A	Norwich C	D 2-2	2-0	19	Gascoigne, Lineker	20,095
7	30	H	QPR	W 3-2	2-0	17	Lineker 3	23,781
8	Oct 14	A	Charlton Ath	W 3-1	0-0	12	Thomas, Lineker, Gascoigne	17,692
9	18	H	Arsenal	W 2-1	2-0	—	Samways, Walsh	33,944
10	21	H	Sheffield W	W 3-0	2-0	7	Lineker 2, Moran	26,909
11	29	A	Liverpool	L 0-1	0-1	—		36,550
12	Nov 4	A	Southampton	D 1-1	1-0	8	Gascoigne	19,601
13	11	H	Wimbledon	L 0-1	0-0	9		26,876
14	18	A	Crystal Palace	W 3-2	2-1	6	Howells, Lineker (pen), Samways	26,266
15	25	H	Derby Co	L 1-2	1-0	11	Stewart	28,075
16	Dec 2	A	Luton T	D 0-0	0-0	11		12,620
17	9	H	Everton	W 2-1	1-1	8	Lineker, Stewart	29,374
18	16	A	Manchester U	W 1-0	0-0	5	Lineker	36,230
19	26	H	Millwall	W 3-1	3-0	5	Samways, Lineker, McLeary (og)	26,874
20	30	H	Nottingham F	L 2-3	1-2	7	Lineker 2	33,401
21	Jan 1	A	Coventry C	D 0-0	0-0	5		19,559
22	13	H	Manchester C	D 1-1	1-0	6	Howells	26,384
23	20	A	Arsenal	L 0-1	0-0	8		46,132
24	Feb 4	H	Norwich C	W 4-0	2-0	—	Lineker 3 (1 pen), Howells	19,599
25	10	A	Chelsea	W 2-1	1-0	5	Howells, Lineker	28,130
26	21	H	Aston Villa	L 0-2	0-0	—		32,472
27	24	A	Derby Co	L 1-2	0-1	5	Moncur	19,676
28	Mar 3	H	Crystal Palace	L 0-1	0-0	7		26,181
29	10	H	Charlton Ath	W 3-0	1-0	8	Polston J, Lineker, Howells	21,104
30	17	A	QPR	L 1-3	0-1	9	Walsh	16,691
31	21	H	Liverpool	W 1-0	0-0	—	Stewart	25,656
32	31	A	Sheffield W	W 4-2	1-1	4	Allen, Lineker 2, Stewart	26,582
33	Apr 7	A	Nottingham F	W 3-1	2-0	5	Stewart, Allen 2	21,669
34	14	H	Coventry C	W 3-2	1-2	5	Lineker 2, Stewart	23,917
35	16	A	Millwall	W 1-0	0-0	4	Lineker	10,574
36	21	H	Manchester U	W 2-1	2-0	3	Gascoigne, Lineker	33,317
37	28	A	Wimbledon	L 0-1	0-1	3		12,800
38	May 5	H	Southampton	W 2-1	2-0	3	Stewart, Allen	31,038

Final League Position: 3

GOALSCORERS

League (59): Lineker 24 (2 pens), Stewart 8, Allen 6, Gascoigne 6, Howells 5, Samways 3, Walsh 2, Moncur 1, Moran 1, Polston J 1, Thomas 1, own goal 1.
Littlewoods Cup (16): Nayim 3, Allen 2, Lineker 2, Fenwick 1, Gascoigne 1, Howells 1, Mabbutt 1, Samways 1, Sedgley 1, Stewart 1, Walsh 1, own goal 1.
FA Cup (1): Howells 1.

Thorstvedt	Butters	Bergsson	Fenwick	Howells	Mabbutt	Samways	Gascoigne	Stewart	Lineker	Allen	Walsh	Sedgley	Stevens	Van Den Hauwe	Thomas	Robson	Nayim	Moran	Polston, J	Mimms	Hughton	Moncur	Polston, A	Match No.
1	2	3	4	5	6	7!	8*	9	10	11	12	14												1
1	2		4	5	6	14	8*	9	10	11	12	7†		3										2
1	2		4	5*	6	14	8	9	10	11†	12	7		3										3
1	2†		4	5	6	7*	8	9	10	11	12		14	3										4
1			4	5†	6		8	9	10	11	7		3*	2	12	14								5
1	2		4		6	7†	8	9	10*	11	12			3	5	14								6
1	2		4		6		8	9	10	12		11		3	5*	7								7
1	2*		4		6	14	8	9	10	5		11		3	12	7†								8
1			4	12	6	9*	8		10	5	7	11		3	2									9
1			4	7	6	9	8*		10	5		11		3	2		12							10
1	4			7	6	9			10	5†	12	11		3	2		8*14							11
1	4			7	6	9*	8		10	5	12	11		3	2									12
1	4			5	6	9†	8	12	10	14	7*	11		3	2									13
1	4			5	6	7	8	9	10*		12			3	2		11							14
1		5*	6	7†	8	9	10	11	12	4				3	2		14							15
1	3		5	6	7	8	9	10*	4	12	11			2										16
1	12		5	6	7*	8	9	10		4		11		3	2									17
		5	6	7	8	9	10		4		11			3	2					1				18
	3		5	6	7	8	9	10		4		11	12		2*					1				19
	2†		5	6	7*	8	9	10		4	12	11	14	3						1				20
	2		5	6	7	8*	9	10		4		11		3					12	1				21
1			5		7		9	10	4		11			3	2				8		6			22
1			5	6	7†		9	10	4	12	11			3*	2		14		8					23
1			5	6		8		10*	7	11				3			9	12	4		2			24
1			5	6		8		10†	7*	11				3			9	12	4		2	14		25
1			5	6		8†		10	7	11				3			9*	12	4		2	14		26
1			5	6				10	12	7	11*			3	14		9		4		2†	8		27
1			5	6		8*		10		7				3			9	12	4		2	11†14		28
1			5	6		8		10	11	7				3			9		4		2			29
1			5	6		8	12	10	11	7				3*			9	4†			2	14		30
1	2		5†	6		8	12	10	11	7*	4			3	14		9							31
1	2		5	6		8	12	10	11	7*	4			3	14		9†							32
1	2		5†	6		8	7*	10	11	12	4			3	14		9							33
1	2			6		8	7	10	11		4			3	5		9							34
1	2		5	6		8*	7	10	11	12	4			3	14		9†							35
1	2		5	6	12	8	7	10	11		4			3			9*							36
1	2*		5		12	8	7	10	11		4			3†14			9	6						37
1	2*		5	6		8	7	10	11		4			3	12		9							38
34	7	17	10	33	36	18	34	24	38	29	12	31	4	31	17	—	18	—	11	4	8	2	—	
	+1s			+1s		+5s		+4s		+3s		+14s1s		+3s			+9s		+3s	+1s	+5s	+2s	+3s1s	

Littlewoods Cup	Second Round	Southend U (h)	1-0
		(a)	2-3
	Third Round	Manchester U (a)	3-0
	Fourth Round	Tranmere R (a)	2-2
		(h)	4-0
	Fifth Round	Nottingham F (a)	2-2
		(h)	2-3
FA Cup	Third Round	Southampton (h)	1-3

TOTTENHAM HOTSPUR

Player and Position	Ht	Wt	Birth Date	Place	Source	Clubs	League App	Gls
Goalkeepers								
Kevin Dearden	5 11	12 08	8 3 70	Luton	Trainee	Tottenham H	—	—
						Cambridge U (loan)	15	—
						Hartlepool U (loan)	10	—
						Oxford U (loan)	—	—
						Swindon T (loan)	1	—
Peter Guthrie‡	6 1	12 13	10 10 61	Newcastle	Weymouth	Tottenham H	—	—
						Swansea C (loan)	14	—
						Charlton Ath (loan)	—	—
Gareth Howells	6 1	12 08	13 6 70	Guildford	Trainee	Tottenham H	—	—
						Swindon T (loan)	—	—
						Leyton Orient (loan)	—	—
Bobby Mimms	6 2	12 13	12 10 63	York	Apprentice	Halifax T	—	—
						Rotherham U	83	—
						Everton	29	—
						Notts Co (loan)	2	—
						Sunderland (loan)	4	—
						Blackburn R (loan)	6	—
						Manchester C (loan)	3	—
						Tottenham H	37	—
						Aberdeen (loan)	6	—
Erik Thorstvedt	6 3	14 04	28 10 62	Stavanger	IFK Gothenburg	Tottenham H	52	—
Ian Walker	6 1	11 09	31 10 71	Watford	Trainee	Tottenham H	—	—
Defenders								
Gudni Bergsson	5 10	10 07	21 7 65	Iceland	Valur	Tottenham H	26	—
Guy Butters	6 3	13 00	30 10 69	Hillingdon	Trainee	Tottenham H	35	1
						Southend U (loan)	16	3
Terry Fenwick	5 11	11 01	17 11 59	Camden, Co. Durham	Apprentice	Crystal Palace	70	—
						QPR	256	33
						Tottenham H	61	8
Ian Hendon	6 0	12 10	5 12 71	Ilford	Trainee	Tottenham H	—	—
Chris Hughton	5 7	11 05	11 12 58	West Ham	Amateur	Tottenham H	297	12
David McDonald	5 10	11 00	2 1 71	Dublin	Trainee	Tottenham H	—	—
Gary Mabbutt	5 9	10 10	23 8 61	Bristol	Apprentice	Bristol R	131	10
						Tottenham H	264	21
John Moncur	5 7	9 10	22 9 66	Stepney	Apprentice	Tottenham H	12	1
						Doncaster R (loan)	4	—
						Cambridge U (loan)	4	—
						Portsmouth (loan)	7	—
						Brentford (loan)	5	1
Andy Polston	5 10	11 00	26 7 70	Walthamstow	Trainee	Tottenham H	1	—
						Cambridge U (loan)	3	—
John Polston	5 11	11 00	10 6 68	London	Apprentice	Tottenham H	24	1
Steve Sedgley	6 1	12 06	26 5 68	Enfield	Apprentice	Coventry C	84	3
						Tottenham H	32	—
Brian Statham	5 11	11 00	21 5 69	Zimbabwe	Apprentice	Tottenham H	24	—
Mitchell Thomas	6 0	12 00	2 10 64	Luton	Apprentice	Luton T	107	1
						Tottenham H	126	6
David Tuttle	6 1	12 10	6 2 72	Reading	Trainee	Tottenham H	—	—
Pat Van Den Hauwe	6 0	10 08	16 12 60	Dendermonde	Apprentice	Birmingham C	123	1
						Everton	135	2
						Tottenham H	31	—
Midfield								
Paul Allen	5 7	10 10	28 8 62	Aveley	Apprentice	West Ham U	152	6
						Tottenham H	178	14
Matthew Edwards	5 10	9 08	15 6 71	Hammersmith	Trainee	Tottenham H	—	—
Peter Garland	5 9	12 00	20 1 71	Croydon	Trainee	Tottenham H	—	—
Paul Gascoigne	5 10	11 07	27 5 67	Gateshead	Apprentice	Newcastle U	92	21
						Tottenham H	66	12

TOTTENHAM HOTSPUR

Foundation: The Hotspur Football Club was formed from an older cricket club in 1882. Most of the founders were old boys St. John's Presbyterian School and Tottenham Grammar School. The Casey brothers were well to the fore as the family provided the club's first goalposts (painted blue and white) and their first ball. They soon adopted the local YMCA as their meeing place, but after a couple of moves settled at the Red House, which is still their headquarters, although now known simply as 748 High Road.

First Football League game: 1 September, 1908, Division 2, v Wolverhampton W (h) W 3-0 – Hewitson; Coquet, Burton; Morris (1), Steel (D), Darnell; Walton, Woodward (2), Macfarlane, R. Steel, Middlemiss.

Managers (and Secretary-managers)
Frank Brettell 1897–98, John Cameron 1901–12, Peter McWilliam 1913–27, Billy Minter 1927–30, Percy Smith 1935, Jack Tresadern 1935–38, Peter McWilliam 1938–42, Joe Hulme 1945–49, Arthur Rowe 1949–55, Jimmy Anderson 1955–58, Bill Nicholson 1958–74, Terry Neill 1974–76, Keith Burkinshaw 1976–84, Peter Shreeves 1984–86, David Pleat 1986–87, Terry Venables 1987–   .

Player and Position	Ht	Wt	Birth Date	Place	Source	Clubs	League App	Gls
Eddie Gormley*	5 7	10 07	23 10 68	Dublin	Bray W	Tottenham H	—	—
						Chesterfield (loan)	4	—
						Motherwell (loan)	—	—
						Shrewsbury T (loan)	—	—
Nayim	5 8	11 04	5 11 66	Ceuta	Barcelona	Tottenham H	30	2
Vinny Samways	5 8	9 00	27 10 68	Bethnal Green	Apprentice	Tottenham H	70	6
Forwards								
Ian Gilzean	6 1	12 08	10 12 69	Enfield	Trainee	Tottenham H	—	—
Philip Gray	5 10	11 07	2 10 68	Belfast	Apprentice	Tottenham H	3	—
						Barnsley (loan)	3	—
David Howells	5 11	11 01	15 12 67	Guildford	Trainee	Tottenham H	74	9
Richard Johnston*	5 9	10 10	15 10 69	Portadown	Trainee	Tottenham H	—	—
Gary Lineker	5 11	12 02	30 11 60	Leicester	Apprentice	Leicester C	194	95
						Everton	41	30
					Barcelona	Tottenham H	38	24
Paul Moran	5 10	11 00	22 5 68	Enfield	Trainee	Tottenham H	27	2
						Portsmouth (loan)	3	—
						Leicester C (loan)	10	1
Mark Robson	5 7	10 05	22 5 69	Newham	Trainee	Exeter C	26	7
						Tottenham H	8	—
						Reading (loan)	7	—
						Watford (loan)	1	—
						Plymouth Arg (loan)	7	—
Paul Stewart	5 11	11 10	7 10 64	Manchester	Apprentice	Blackpool	201	56
						Manchester C	51	26
						Tottenham H	58	20
Chris Waddle (To Marseille July 1989)	6 0	11 05	14 12 60	Hepworth	Tow Law T	Newcastle U	170	46
						Tottenham H	138	33
Paul Walsh	5 7	10 08	1 10 62	Plumstead	Apprentice	Charlton Ath	87	24
						Luton T	80	24
						Liverpool	77	25
						Tottenham H	70	9

Trainees
Bence, Steven M; Cheesewright, John A; Dang, Hung Q; Fulling, Lee; Hackett, Warren J; Hall, Mark A; Hardwicke, Victor; Houghton, Scott A; Howell, Gregory C; Mahorn, Paul G; Morah, Olisa H; Nethercott, Stuart D; Potts, Anthony J; Smith, Kevin; Smith, Neil J; Young, Neil A.

Associated Schoolboys
Binks, Spencer C; Burdett, Christopher R; Campbell, Sulzeer; Clark, Alex J; Day, Christopher; Foot, Daniel F; Hardy, Danny P; Hill, Daniel, R.L; Hoddle, Mark D; Hughton, Leon A; Knott, Gareth R; Landon, Christopher S; McDougald, David; McDougall, Alan J; McGinley, Terrence D; Overton, Graham J; Reynolds, Andrew; Reynolds, Christopher C; Robinson, Stephen; Smith, Daneal; Smith, Jason L; Theodorou, Theodorus S; Winyard, Alfred P.

Associated Schoolboys who have accepted the club's offer of a Traineeship/Contract
Barmby, Nicholas J; Caskey, Darren M; Culverhouse, David P; Deanus, Del; Hodges, Lee L; Kinnear, Colin B.T; Marlowe, Andrew D; Smart, Lee; Thompson-Minton; Jeffrey S; Watson, Kevin E; Wood, Dean B.

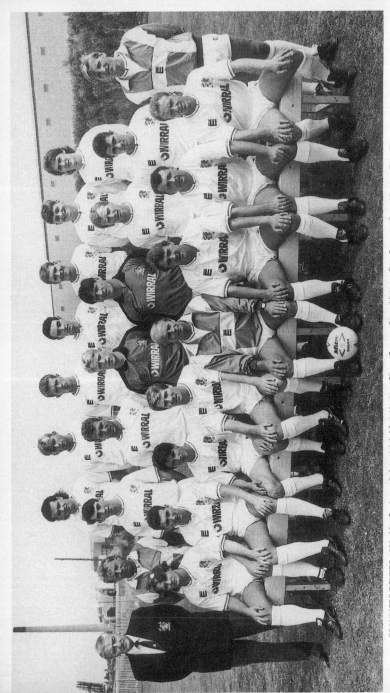

TRANMERE ROVERS 1989–90   *Back row (left to right):* Mark Hughes, Shaun Garnett, Steve Vickers, Gary Bauress, Dave Higgins, Tony Thomas, John Norman.
Centre row: Norman Wilson (Secretary), Kenny Jones (Trainer), Chris Malkin, Jim Steel, Paul Collings, Eric Nixon, Dave Fairclough, Eddie Bishop, Ronnie Moore (Coach).
Front row: John Morrissey, Dave Martindale, John Smith, Steve Mungall, John King (Manager), Ian Muir, Mark McCarrick, Jimmy Harvey.

Division 3 **TRANMERE ROVERS**

Prenton Park, Prenton Road West, Birkenhead. Telephone 051-608 4194. Commercial/Cashline 051-608 0371. Valley Road Training Centre 051-652 2578. Shop 051-608 0438.

Ground capacity: 14,200.

Record attendance: 24,424 v Stoke C, FA Cup 4th rd, 5 Feb, 1972.

Record receipts: £48,597 v Tottenham H, Littlewoods Cup, 4th rd, 22 November, 1989.

Pitch measurements: 112yd × 71yd.

President: H. B. Thomas.

Chairman: P. R. Johnson. *Vice-Chairman and Chief Executive:* F. D. Corfe.

Directors: A. J. Adams BDS, G. E. H. Jones LLB, F. J. Williams, J. J. Holsgrove, FCA, G. A. Higham MSC TECH LRSC, M INST PI.

Secretary: Norman Wilson FAAI. *Commercial Manager:* Nigel Coates.

Development Manager: Nobby Abbott.

Manager: John King. *Trainer:* Kenny Jones.

Youth Development Manager: Warwick Rimmer.

Coach: Ronnie Moore. *Physio:* Alec McLellaw.

Year Formed: 1885. *Turned Professional:* 1912. *Ltd Co.:* 1920.

Previous name: Belmont AFC 1884–85.

Previous grounds: 1884 Steeles Field, 1887 Ravenshaws Field/Old Prenton Park, 1912 Prenton Park.

Club Nickname: 'The Rovers'.

Record League Victory: 13-4 v Oldham Ath, Division 3 (N), 26 December 1935 – Gray; Platt, Fairhurst; McLaren, Newton, Spencer; Eden, MacDonald (1), Bell (9), Woodward (2), Urmson (1).

Record Cup Victory: 9-0 v AP Leamington, FA Cup, 1st rd, 24 November 1979 – Johnson; Mathias, Flood (Mungall), Bramhall, Edwards, Evans (2), O'Neil (2 incl 1p), Parry, Peplow, Lumby (3), Beamish (1). (1 og).

Record Defeat: 1-9 v Tottenham H, FA Cup 3rd rd replay, 14 January, 1953.

Most League Points (2 for a win): 60, Division 4, 1964–65.

Most League Points (3 for a win): 80, Division 4, 1988–89 and Division 3, 1989–90.

Most League Goals: 111, Division 3 (N), 1930–31.

Highest League Scorer in Season: Bunny Bell, 35, Division 3(N), 1933–34.

Most League Goals in Total Aggregate: Ian Muir, 105, 1985–90.

Most Capped Player: Albert Gray, 3 (24), Wales.

Most League Appearances: Harold Bell, 595, 1946–64 (inc. League record 401 consecutive appearances).

Record Transfer Fee Received: £120,000 from Cardiff C for Ronnie Moore, February 1979.

Record Transfer Fee Paid: £125,000 to Manchester C for Neil McNab, January 1990.

Football League Record: 1921 Original Member of Division 3 (N): 1938–39 Division 2; 1946–58 Division 3 (N); 1958–61 Division 3; 1961–67 Division 4; 1967–75 Division 3; 1975–76 Division 4; 1976–79 Division 3; 1979–89 Division 4; 1989– Division 3.

Honours: Football League Division 2 best season: 22nd, 1938–39; Division 3 (N) – Champions 1937–38; Promotion to 3rd Division: 1966–67, 1975–76; Division 4 – Runners-up 1988–89. *FA Cup* best season: 5th rd, 1967–68. *Football League Cup* best season: 4th rd, 1961, 1982, 1989, 1990. *Welsh Cup:* Winners 1935. Runners-up 1934.

Colours: All white. **Change colours:** Claret/sky blue shirts, sky blue shorts and stockings.

TRANMERE ROVERS 1989–90 LEAGUE RECORD

Match No.	Date		Venue	Opponents	Result		H/T Score	Lg. Pos.	Goalscorers	Atten- dance
1	Aug	19	A	Fulham	W	2-1	1-0	—	Bishop, Malkin	4811
2		26	H	Cardiff C	W	3-0	1-0	2	Harvey, McCarrick, Morrissey	5268
3	Sept	2	A	Reading	L	0-1	0-0	6		4548
4		9	H	Rotherham U	W	2-1	1-1	2	Malkin, Fairclough	4912
5		16	A	Birmingham C	L	1-2	0-0	8	Muir	8604
6		22	H	Huddersfield T	W	4-0	1-0	—	Malkin, Muir, Higgins, Morrissey	7375
7		26	A	Wigan Ath	W	3-1	1-0	—	Muir 2, Hughes	3136
8		29	H	Bristol C	W	6-0	2-0	—	Malkin 2, Rennie (og), Muir, Bishop 2	8974
9	Oct	6	H	Leyton Orient	W	3-0	1-0	—	Muir 2, Malkin	8223
10		14	A	Notts Co	L	0-1	0-1	1		6332
11		16	H	Mansfield T	D	1-1	0-0	—	Muir (pen)	6909
12		20	A	Swansea C	L	0-1	0-0	—		3669
13		27	H	Crewe Alex	D	1-1	0-0	—	Muir	9020
14		31	A	Shrewsbury T	L	1-3	1-1	—	Hughes	4927
15	Nov	4	A	Brentford	W	4-2	2-1	5	Harvey 2, Steel, Muir	5720
16		10	H	Walsall	W	2-1	1-0	—	McCarrick, Bishop	6281
17		25	A	Blackpool	W	3-0	1-0	3	Methven (og). Vickers, Martindale	4106
18	Dec	2	H	Bury	L	2-4	2-1	5	Martindale, Malkin	6207
19		15	H	Chester C	D	0-0	0-0	—		5594
20		26	A	Preston NE	D	2-2	2-1	5	Harvey, Steel	8300
21		30	A	Bristol R	L	0-2	0-0	7		6821
22	Jan	6	H	Bolton W	L	1-3	1-0	—	Muir (pen)	8273
23		13	A	Cardiff C	D	0-0	0-0	8		4300
24		19	H	Fulham	W	2-1	0-0	—	Morrissey 2	6154
25		27	A	Rotherham U	D	0-0	0-0	7		6386
26	Feb	3	A	Huddersfield T	L	0-1	0-0	8		7005
27		9	H	Birmingham C	W	5-1	1-0	—	McNab, Steel, Malkin, Hughes, Muir	6033
28		12	H	Reading	W	3-1	0-0	—	Steel, Harvey, Muir	5264
29		17	A	Bury	W	2-1	0-1	3	Muir (pen), Malkin	3801
30		23	H	Blackpool	W	4-2	2-0	—	Malkin 2, Vickers, McCarrick	7873
31	Mar	3	A	Northampton	W	4-0	1-0	2	Muir, Bishop 2, Hughes	3147
32		6	A	Bristol C	W	3-1	1-0	—	McCarrick, Muir, Bishop	14,376
33		9	H	Wigan Ath	W	2-0	1-0	—	Thomas, Muir	9604
34		17	A	Leyton Orient	W	1-0	1-0	2	Malkin	4046
35		19	H	Notts Co	W	2-0	2-0	—	Malkin 2	9718
36		24	A	Mansfield T	L	0-1	0-0	2		3362
37		30	H	Swansea C	W	3-0	1-0	—	Malkin, Harvey, Thomas	8111
38	Apr	6	A	Crewe Alex	D	2-2	1-0	—	Muir, Steel	6900
39		9	H	Shrewsbury T	W	3-1	2-1	—	Harvey, Vickers, Finley (og)	7812
40		14	A	Bolton W	D	1-1	0-1	3	Muir	9070
41		16	H	Preston NE	W	2-1	0-0	3	Mungall, Muir	10,187
42		20	A	Chester C	D	2-2	0-2	—	Malkin, Muir (pen)	4210
43		23	H	Bristol R	L	1-2	1-0	—	Muir	12,723
44		28	A	Walsall	L	1-2	1-0	4	Malkin	3287
45	May	2	H	Northampton T	D	0-0	0-0	—		5363
46		5	H	Brentford	D	2-2	1-1	4	Muir, Malkin	5379

Final League Position: 4

GOALSCORERS

League (86): Muir 23 (4 pens), Malkin 18, Bishop 7, Harvey 7, Steel 5, Hughes 4, McCarrick 4, Morrissey 4, Vickers 3, Martindale 2, Thomas 2, Fairclough 1, Higgins 1, McNab 1, Mungall 1, own goals 3.
Littlewoods Cup (14): Malkin 4, Muir 4 (2 pens), Bishop 2, Steele 2, McCarrick 1, Vickers 1.
FA Cup (0).

Nixon	Higgins	McCarrick	Bishop	Hughes	Vickers	Morrissey	Harvey	Steel	Muir	Thomas	Malkin	Fairclough	Martindale	Garnett	Mungall	Pike	Irons	McNab	Bauress	Match No.
1	2	3	4	5	6	7	8	9*	10	11	12									1
1	2	3	4	5	6	7	8		10	11	9									2
1	2	3	4	5*	6	7	8		10	11	9	12								3
1	2	3	4	5	6	7*	8		10	11	9	12								4
1	2	3	4*	5†	6	7	8		10	11	9	12	14							5
1	2	3	12	5	6	7	8		10	11	9				4*					6
1	2	3	12	5	6	7†	8	14	10	11	9				4*					7
1	2	3	12	5	6	7	8		10	11	9				4*					8
1	2	3		5	6	7	8		10	11	9				4					9
1	2	3*12		5	6	7	8		10	11	9				4					10
1	2	3	12	5	6†	7	8	14	10	11	9				4*					11
1	2	3	12	5		7	8	14	10	11	9†				4* 6					12
1	2	3	4	5	6	7	8		10	11	9									13
1	2	3*	4	5	6	7	8	12	10	11	9									14
1	2	3	4	5		7	8	9	10					6	11					15
1	2	3	4	5	6	7	8*	9	10		12				11					16
1	2			5	6†		8	9	10	11	7	12	14	4*	3					17
1	2	12		5*	6		8	9	10	11	7		14	4† 11	3 14					18
1	2	3		5	6		8	9	10	11	7	12			4*					19
1	2	3	11	5	6		8*	9	10	12	7				4					20
1	2	3	12	5	6		8†	9	10	11	7*		14		4					21
1	2	3		5*	6	7	8	12	10	11	9							4		22
1	2	3		5	6	7	8	12	10	11	9*							4		23
1	2	3	14	5	6	7	8†12		10	11	9*							4		24
1	2	3		5	6	7	8	9	10	11								4		25
1	2	3	12	5†	6	7	8*	9	10	11			14					4		26
1	2	3		5	6	7*	8	9	10	11	12							4		27
1	2	3		5	6		8	9	10	11	7							4		28
1	2	3	12	5*	6		8	9	10	11	7							4		29
1		3		5	6		8	9	10	11*	7	12				2		4		30
1	2	3	4	5	6		8	9	10*11		7	12								31
1	2	3*	4	5	6		8	9	10	11	7	12								32
1	2		4	5	6		8	9	10	11*	7	12			3					33
1	2	12		5		7	8*	9	10	11				6	3			4		34
1	2			5		7	8	9	10	11				6	3			4		35
1	2			5*	6	7	8	9	10	11	12				3			4		36
1	2			5	6	7*	8	9	10	11	12				3			4		37
1	2	12		5	6	7*	8	9	10	11			14		3†			4		38
1	2			5	6	7*12	8	9	10	11					3			4		39
1	2	12		5	6	7	8*	9	10	11					3			4		40
1	2			5	6	7	8	9	10	11					3			4		41
1	2			5	6	7	8	9	10	11	12				3*			4		42
1	2	12		5†	6	7	8*	9	10	11			14		3			4		43
1	2	3		5†	6	7	8	9	10	11	12		14		4*					44
1	2	3		5	6	7†12	8	9	10	11*			14					4		45
1	2	12			6	7	8	9	10*11						3			4	5	46
46	45	32	13	45	42	24	45	29	46	42	36	3	13	4	16	2	—	22	1	
			+15s			+3s	+1s	+7s			+4s		+11s	+6s	+1s			+3s		

Littlewoods Cup First Round   Preston NE (a)   4-3
                                                (h)   3-1
             Second Round   Ipswich T (a)   1-0
                                                (h)   1-0
             Third Round   Millwall (h)   3-2
             Fourth Round   Tottenham H (h) 2-2
                                          (a)   0-4

FA Cup   First Round   Preston NE (a)   0-1

TRANMERE ROVERS

Player and Position	Ht	Wt	Birth Date	Place	Source	Clubs	League App	Gls
Goalkeepers								
Paul Collings	6 2	12 00	30 9 68	Liverpool		Tranmere R	1	—
Eric Nixon	6 2	14 03	4 10 62	Manchester	Curzon Ashton	Manchester C	58	—
						Wolverhampton W (loan)	16	—
						Bradford C (loan)	3	—
						Southampton (loan)	4	—
						Carlisle U (loan)	16	—
						Tranmere R (loan)	8	—
						Tranmere R	91	—
Defenders								
Gary Bauress	6 0	12 00	19 1 71	Liverpool	Trainee	Tranmere R	1	—
Dave Higgins	6 0	11 00	19 8 61	Liverpool	Eagle	Tranmere R	28	—
					Caernarfon	Tranmere R	121	3
Mark Hughes	6 1	12 10	3 2 62	Morriston	Apprentice	Bristol R	74	3
						Torquay U (loan)	9	1
						Swansea C	12	—
						Bristol C	22	—
						Tranmere R	172	6
Mark McCarrick	5 8	10 08	4 2 62	Liverpool	Witton A	Birmingham C	15	—
						Lincoln C	44	—
						Crewe Alex	11	—
					Runcorn	Tranmere R	114	12
Steve Mungall	5 8	11 02	22 5 58	Bellshill		Motherwell	20	—
						Tranmere R	382	8
John Norman*	5 8	11 07	26 6 71	Birkenhead	Trainee	Tranmere R	—	—
Tony Thomas	5 11	12 05	12 7 71	Liverpool	Trainee	Tranmere R	51	4
Stephen Vickers	6 2	12 00	13 10 67	B Auckland	Spennymoor U	Tranmere R	173	9
Midfield								
Eddie Bishop	5 8	11 07	28 11 62	Liverpool	Runcorn	Tranmere R	68	16
Shaun Garnett	6 2	11 00	22 11 69	Wallasey	Trainee	Tranmere R	5	—
Jimmy Harvey	5 9	11 04	2 5 58	Lurgan	Glenavon	Arsenal	3	—
						Hereford U (loan)	11	—
						Hereford U	267	39
						Bristol C	3	—
						Wrexham (loan)	6	—
						Tranmere R	121	14
Neil McNab	5 7	11 00	4 6 57	Greenock		Morton	14	—
						Tottenham H	72	3
						Bolton W	35	4
						Brighton & HA	103	4
						Leeds U (loan)	5	—
						Portsmouth (loan)	—	—
						Manchester C	221	16
						Tranmere R	22	1
Dave Martindale	5 11	11 10	9 4 64	Liverpool	Apprentice	Liverpool	—	—
					Caernarfon	Tranmere R	85	7
John Smith	5 7	10 12	23 7 70	Liverpool		Tranmere R	2	—
Forwards								
David Fairclough*	5 10	11 00	5 1 57	Liverpool	Apprentice	Liverpool	98	34
					Lucerne	Norwich C	2	—
						Oldham Ath	17	1
						Rochdale	—	—
					Beveren	Tranmere R	14	1
Kenny Irons	5 9	11 00	4 11 70	Liverpool	Trainee	Tranmere R	3	—
Ken McKenna‡	5 10	12 00	2 7 60	Birkenhead	Local	Tranmere R	4	—
					Telford U	Tranmere R	15	3
Chris Malkin	6 0	10 12	4 6 67	Bebington	Overpool	Tranmere R	65	22

TRANMERE ROVERS

Foundation: Formed in 1884 as Belmont they adopted their present title the following year and eventually joined their first league, the West Lancashire League in 1889–90, the same year as their first success in the Wirral Challenge Cup. The club almost folded in 1899–1900 when all the players left en bloc to join a rival club, but they survived the crisis and went from strength to strength winning the 'Combination' title in 1907–08 and the Lancashire Combination in 1913–14. They joined the Football League in 1920 from the Central League.

First Football League game: 27 August, 1921, Division 3(N), v Crewe Alex (h) W 4-1 – Bradshaw; Grainger, Stuart (1); Campbell, Milnes (1), Heslop; Moreton, Groves (1), Hyam, Ford (1), Hughes.

Managers (and Secretary-managers)
Bert Cooke 1919–35, Jackie Carr 1935–36, Jim Knowles 1936–39, Bill Ridding 1939–45, Ernie Blackburn 1946–55, Noel Kelly 1955–57, Peter Farrell 1957–60, Walter Galbraith 1961, Dave Russell 1961–69, Jackie Wright 1969–72, Ron Yeats 1972–75, John King 1975–80, Bryan Hamilton 1980–85, Frank Worthington 1985–87, Ronnie Moore 1987, John King 1987– .

Player and Position	Ht	Wt	Birth Date	Place	Source	Clubs	League App	Gls
John Morrissey	5 8	11 04	8 3 65	Liverpool	Apprentice	Everton	1	—
						Wolverhampton W	10	1
						Tranmere R	178	24
Ian Muir	5 7	10 10	5 5 63	Coventry	Apprentice	QPR	2	2
						Burnley (loan)	2	1
						Birmingham C	1	—
						Brighton & HA	4	—
						Swindon T (loan)	2	—
						Tranmere R	213	105
Jim Steel	6 3	14 00	4 12 59	Dumfries	Apprentice	Oldham Ath	108	24
						Wigan Ath (loan)	2	2
						Wrexham (loan)	9	6
						Port Vale	28	6
						Wrexham	164	51
						Tranmere R	109	19

Trainees
Barton, Stewart A; Brannon, Gerard D; Dunne, Jamie C; Hughes, Mark A; James, Scott; Kelly, Kevin J; McGreal, John; Taylor, Scott C; Young, Neil.

Associated Schoolboys
Atkins, Sean; Clayton, John E; Foster, Michael G; Hill, Christopher; Johnson, Philip; Jones, Gary S; Keegan, Kevin T; McGuiness, Lee; Thompson, Paul D.

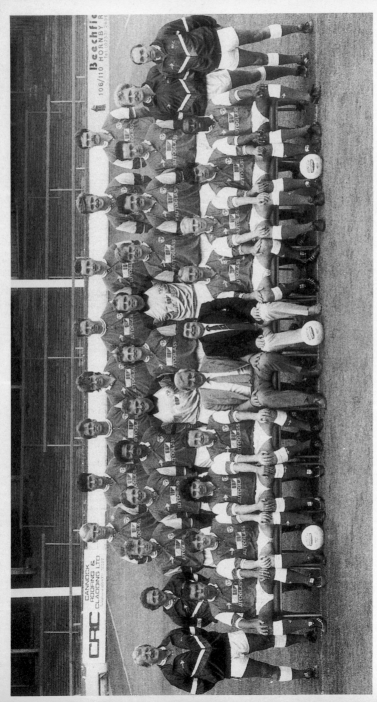

WALSALL 1989–90 *Back row (left to right):* Mark Goodwin, Phil Hawker, Keith Bertschin, Howard Pritchard, Andy Saville, Steve O'Hara, Chris Marsh, Peter Hart.
Centre row: John Barnwell (Manager), Ray Train, Paul Jones, Peter Skipper, Ken Mower, Fred Barber, Graeme Forbes, Ron Green, Dean Smith, Willie Naughton, Martin Goldsmith, Paul Taylor (General Manager), Tom Bradley (Physiotherapist).
Front row: Mark Rees, Alex Taylor, Andy Dornan, John Kelly, R. Clift (Director), B. Blower (Chairman), Steve Gritt, Mark Jones, Stuart Rimmer, Adrian Littlejohn.

Division 4 **WALSALL**

Bescot Stadium, Bescot Crescent, Walsall ES1 4SA. Telephone Walsall (0922) 22791. Commercial Dept. (0922) 22791. Lottery: (0922) 30696. Clubcall: 0898 121104.

Ground capacity: 12,000.

Record attendance: 25,453 v Newcastle U, Division 2, 29 Aug, 1961.

Record receipts: £50,926.50 v Watford, FA Cup 5th rd, 2nd replay, 2 March, 1987.

Pitch measurements: 110yd × 73yd.

President:

Chairman: B. S. Blower.

Managing Director:

Directors: J. Bowser, R. Clift, T. F. Hargreaves, M. Miller, K. R. Whalley.

Team Manager: Kenny Hibbitt. *General Manager:* Paul Taylor.

Physio: Tom Bradley.

Secretary/Commercial Manager: K. R. Whalley.

Year Formed: 1888. *Turned Professional:* 1888. *Ltd Co.:* 1921.

Club Nickname: 'The Saddlers'.

Previous Names: Walsall Swifts (founded 1877) and Walsall Town (founded 1879) amalgamated in 1888 and were known as Walsall Town Swifts until 1895.

Record League Victory: 10-0 v Darwen, Division 2, 4 March 1899 – Tennent; Peers (E) (1), Davies; Hickinbotham, Jenkyns, Taggart; Dean (3), Vail (2), Aston (4), Martin, Griffin.

Record Cup Victory: 6-1 v Leytonstone (away). FA Cup, 1st rd, 30 November 1946 – Lewis, Netley, Skidmore; Crutchley, Foulkes, Newman; Maund (1), Talbot, Darby (1), Wilshaw (2), Davies (2). 6–1 v Margate, FA Cup, 1st rd (replay), 24 November 1955 – Davies; Haddington, Vinall; Dorman, McPherson, Crook; Morris, Walsh (3), RIchards (2), McLaren (1), Moore.

Record Defeat: 0-12 v Small Heath, 17 December, 1892 and v Darwen, 26 December, 1896, both Division 2.

Most League Points (2 for a win): 65, Division 4, 1959–60.

Most League Points (3 for a win): 82, Division 3, 1987–88.

Most League Goals: 102, Division 4, 1959–60.

Highest League Scorer in Season: Gilbert Alsop, 40, Division 3 (N), 1933–34 and 1934–35.

Most League Goals in Total Aggregate: Tony Richards, 184, 1954–63, and Colin Taylor, 184, 1958–63, 1964–68, 1969–73.

Most Capped Player: Mick Kearns, 15 (18), Eire.

Most League Appearances: Colin Harrison, 467, 1964–82.

Record Transfer Fee Received: £600,000 from West Ham U for David Kelly, July 1988.

Record Transfer Fee Paid: £175,000 to Birmingham C for Alan Buckley, June 1979.

Football League Record: 1892 Elected to Division 2; 1895 failed re-election; 1896–1901 Division 2; 1901 failed re-election; 1921 Original Member of Division 3 (N); 1927–31 Division 3 (S); 1931–36 Division 3 (N); 1936–58 Division 3 (S); 1958–60 Division 4; 1960–61 Division 3; 1961–63 Division 2; 1963–79 Division 3; 1979–80 Division 4; 1980–88 Division 3; 1988–89 Division 2; 1989–90 Division 3; 1990– Division 4.

Honours: Football League: Division 2 best season: 6th, 1898–99; Division 3 – Runners-up 1960–61; Division 4 – Champions 1959–60; Runners-up 1979–80. *FA Cup* best season: 5th rd, 1939, 1975, 1978, and last 16 1888–89. *Football League Cup:* Semi-final 1983–84.

Colours: Red shirts, white shorts, red stockings with white hoop. **Change colours:** Blue shirts, white shorts, blue stockings with white hoop.

WALSALL 1989–90 LEAGUE RECORD

Match No.	Date	Venue	Opponents	Result		H/T Score	Lg. Pos.	Goalscorers	Attendance
1	Aug 19	H	Northampton T	W	1-0	0-0	—	Rimmer (pen)	5020
2	26	H	Huddersfield T	L	2-3	1-1	12	Rimmer, Pritchard	4173
3	Sept 2	A	Rotherham U	D	2-2	0-0	11	Hawker, Thorpe	5926
4	9	H	Leyton Orient	L	1-3	1-1	16	Rimmer	3894
5	16	A	Reading	W	1-0	0-0	13	Gritt	3819
6	23	H	Fulham	D	0-0	0-0	15		3969
7	26	A	Birmingham C	L	0-2	0-1	—		10,834
8	30	H	Preston NE	W	1-0	0-0	14	Saville (pen)	4045
9	Oct 7	H	Notts Co	D	2-2	1-2	13	Kelly, Rimmer	4592
10	14	A	Mansfield T	W	2-0	0-0	12	Taylor, Bertschin	3229
11	17	H	Shrewsbury T	L	0-2	0-0	—		4266
12	21	A	Wigan Ath	L	0-3	0-1	14		2229
13	28	H	Swansea C	L	0-1	0-0	18		3469
14	31	A	Bolton W	D	1-1	0-1	—	Bertschin	7363
15	Nov 4	H	Bristol C	L	0-2	0-1	20		5286
16	10	A	Tranmere R	L	1-2	0-1	—	Rimmer (pen)	6281
17	24	A	Chester C	D	1-1	0-1	—	Rimmer	2507
18	Dec 2	H	Bristol R	L	1-2	1-1	23	Bertschin	4038
19	16	A	Bury	W	2-0	1-0	20	Bertschin 2	2797
20	26	H	Crewe Alex	D	1-1	1-0	21	Walters (og)	5693
21	30	H	Cardiff C	L	0-2	0-0	22		4256
22	Jan 1	A	Brentford	L	0-4	0-2	24		5259
23	13	A	Huddersfield T	L	0-1	0-0	24		5856
24	27	A	Leyton Orient	D	1-1	1-1	24	Rimmer	3565
25	Feb 10	H	Reading	D	1-1	1-1	24	Forbes	3506
26	18	A	Bristol C	L	0-2	0-1	—		6223
27	20	A	Northampton T	D	1-1	0-1	—	Taylor	2617
28	24	H	Chester C	D	1-1	0-1	24	Rimmer	3315
29	Mar 3	A	Blackpool	L	3-4	2-1	24	Rimmer 2, Morgan (og)	3174
30	6	A	Preston NE	L	0-2	0-1	—		5210
31	10	H	Birmingham C	L	0-1	0-1	24		6036
32	17	A	Notts Co	L	0-2	0-1	24		5207
33	20	H	Mansfield T	W	1-0	1-0	—	Rees	3017
34	24	A	Shrewsbury T	L	0-2	0-2	24		3225
35	27	H	Blackpool	D	1-1	0-0	—	Skipper	3134
36	31	H	Wigan Ath	L	1-2	1-1	24	Ford	3182
37	Apr 4	A	Fulham	D	0-0	0-0	—		2652
38	7	A	Swansea C	L	0-2	0-1	24		2474
39	10	H	Bolton W	W	2-1	1-0	—	Bertschin 2	3376
40	14	H	Brentford	W	2-1	2-1	24	Bertschin 2	2903
41	16	A	Crewe Alex	L	1-3	0-1	24	Shaw	4289
42	21	H	Bury	D	2-2	0-0	24	Ford, Shaw (pen)	3621
43	24	A	Cardiff C	L	1-3	1-1	—	Shaw	2509
44	28	H	Tranmere R	W	2-1	0-1	24	Forbes, Taylor	3287
45	May 1	H	Rotherham U	D	1-1	1-0	—	Dornan	5697
46	5	A	Bristol C	L	0-4	0-2	24		17,859

Final League Position: 24

GOALSCORERS

League (40): Rimmer 10 (2 pens), Bertschin 9, Shaw 3 (1 pen), Taylor 3, Forbes 2, Ford 2, Dornan 1, Gritt 1, Hawker 1, Kelly 1, Pritchard 1, Rees 1, Saville 1 (pen), Skipper 1, Thorpe 1, own goals 2.
Littlewoods Cup (1): Pritchard 1.
FA Cup (5): Bertschin 2, Rimmer 2, Forbes 1.

Barber	Gritt	Mower	Kelly	Forbes	Skipper	Pritchard	Rimmer	Saville	Goodwin	Thorpe	Hawker	Bertschin	Green	Smith	Rees	Jones	Taylor	O'Hara	Marsh	Wilder	Lemon	Dorman	Littlejohn	Whitehouse	Hart	Ford	Lyne	Bremmer	Shaw	Match No.
1	2	3	4	5*	6	7	8	9	10	11	12																			1
1	2	3	4*	5	6	7	8†	9	10	11	12	14																		2
	2	3*	12	5	6	7†	8	9	4	11	10	14	1																	3
	2	3	10	5	6	7*	8	9	4	11	12		1																	4
	2	3	4		6		8*	9		11	12		1		5	7	10													5
	2	3	4		6		8	9		11	12		1		5	7	10*													6
	2		4	5	6		8*	9		11	3	12	1			7	10													7
	2	3	12	5	6			9		11	10	8	1		7*		4													8
	2	3	7	5	6			12	9	10	11*	8	1				4													9
	2*		7	5	6			9	10	11		8	1				4	12	3											10
	2		7	5	6			12	9	10*	11	8	1				4	3												11
	2†		7	5	6			12	9	10	11	8	1				4*	3	14											12
	2		7	5	6		8	9*		11	10	12	1				4	3												13
	2		7	5	6		8	12	14	11	10†	9	1				3	4*												14
			7	5	6		8	12		10*	11	9	1					3	2	4										15
			7	5	6		8	12			11	9	1					3*	10	2	4									16
	4	3	7	5	6		8	12		11		9	1					10*	2											17
		3	7	5	6		8		4	11		9	1					10	2											18
	2	3	7	5	6		8*	12	4	11		9	1					10												19
	2	3	7†	5	6		8	12	4	11		9	1				14	10*												20
1	2	3		5			8	12	4	11		10	9	6			7*													21
1	2		7*	5			8		4	11		10	9	6			12	3												22
1		3	7	5	6		8	14	10	12		9†					4					2	11*							23
1				5	6		8	7		10		9					4					2	11	3						24
1				5	6		8	7	14	10†		9					4	12				2	11†	3						25
1		10		5	6		8	12		7	11	9*					4					2		3						26
1		12	7	5	6		8			11	14*	9					4					2		3	10†					27
1		7*		5	6		8	12				9					10					2	11	3	4					28
1				5	6		8	12	10	7		9					4					2	11*	3						29
1		3		5	6		8	11	10	7		9					4					2								30
1		3		5	6		8	7	10	12		9					4					2	11*							31
1		3	11	5	6		8	7	10			9					4					2								32
1		3		5	6		8		10	9		7*					4	12				2	11							33
1		3		5	6		8		10*	14		4						11†				2				7	9	12		34
1		3		5	6		8		10*			4						11				2				7†	9	12		35
1		3		5	6		8		10*			4						11†				2				7	9	12	14	36
1		3		5	6		8					4						2	11							7	9	10		37
1		3		5	6*		8	12	10	9		4						2	11*							7	9†	10	14	38
1		3		5			8		10	9		4					11					2								39
1		3		5			8		10	9		4					11	2							6	7				40
1		3		5			8		10	9		4					11	2							6	7*	12			41
1		3		5			8		10	9		4					11*	2							6	7	12			42
1		3		5			8		10			4					11*	2							6	7	12	9		43
		3		5	7								1	6			4	12				2	11			8	10*	9		44
		3		5	6			12					1	4			10	8*				2	11			7		9		45
				5	6	8†		3					1	4*			10	11				2				7	12	9		46
25	20	29	24	44	40	4	38	16	22	24	22	29	21	7	7	3	30	14	8	4	2	18	11	9	10	13	6	2	4	
		+1s	+2s				+3s	+10s 2s	+3s	+8s	+6s						+2s	+4s	+1s								+1s	+4s	+5s	

Goldsmith — Match No. 46(14)

Littlewoods Cup	First Round	Port Vale (h)	1-2
		(a)	0-1
FA Cup	First Round	Telford U (a)	3-0
	Second Round	Rotherham U (h)	1-0
	Third Round	Hereford U (a)	1-2

WALSALL

Player and Position	Ht	Wt	Birth Date	Place	Source	Clubs	League App	Gls
Goalkeepers								
Fred Barber	5 11	11 07	28 8 63	Ferryhill	Apprentice	Darlington	135	—
						Everton	—	—
						Walsall	151	—
						Peterborough (loan)	6	—
Ron Green	6 2	14 00	3 10 56	Birmingham	Alvechurch	Walsall	163	—
						WBA (loan)	—	—
						Shrewsbury T	19	—
						Bristol R (loan)	18	—
						Bristol R	38	—
						Scunthorpe U	78	—
						Wimbledon	4	—
						Shrewsbury T (loan)	17	—
						Manchester C (loan)	—	—
						Walsall	23	—
Defenders								
Andy Dornan*	5 9	11 03	19 8 61	Aberdeen	King St	Aberdeen	2	—
						Motherwell	92	3
						Walsall	118	1
Graeme Forbes	6 0	12 00	29 7 58	Forfar	Lochee U	Motherwell	185	16
						Nottingham F (loan)	—	—
						Walsall	173	9
Peter Hart*	5 11	12 07	14 8 57	Mexborough	Apprentice	Huddersfield T	210	7
						Walsall	390	12
Ken Mower	6 1	12 04	1 12 60	Walsall	Apprentice	Walsall	398	8
Peter Skipper	5 11	12 05	11 4 58	Hull	Local	Hull C	23	2
						Scunthorpe U (loan)	1	—
						Darlington	91	4
						Hull C	265	17
						Oldham Ath	27	1
						Walsall	40	1
Dean Smith	6 0	12 01	19 3 71	West Bromwich	Trainee	Walsall	22	—
Phil Whitehouse	5 6	10 09	23 3 71	Wolverhampton	Trainee	WBA	—	—
						Walsall	9	—
Midfield								
Des Bremner*	5 10	11 08	7 9 52	Aberchirder	Deveronvale	Hibernian	199	18
						Aston Villa	174	9
						Birmingham C	168	5
						Fulham	16	—
						Walsall	6	—
Paul Evason‡			18 9 70	Bridgnorth	Trainee	Walsall	—	—
Mark Goodwin*	5 10	10 09	23 2 60	Sheffield	Apprentice	Leicester C	91	8
						Notts Co	237	24
						Walsall	92	2
Phil Hawker*	6 1	11 07	7 12 62	Solihull	Apprentice	Birmingham C	35	1
						Walsall	177	10
John Kelly	5 10	10 09	20 10 60	Bebbington	Cammellaird	Tranmere R	64	9
						Preston NE	130	27
						Chester C	85	17
						Swindon T	7	1
						Oldham Ath	52	6
						Walsall	26	1
						Huddersfield T (loan)	10	—
Steve O'Hara	6 1	12 02	21 1 71	Bellshill	Trainee	Walsall	18	—
Stuart Sadler*			15 9 70	Birmingham	Trainee	Walsall	—	—
Alex Taylor	5 7	10 11	13 6 62	Bailleston	Blantyre St. J	Dundee U	33	6
						Hamilton A	66	5
						Walsall	45	6

Foundation: Two of the leading clubs around Walsall in the 1880s were Walsall Swifts (formed 1877) and Walsall Town (formed 1879). The Swifts were winners of the Birmingham Senior Cup in 1881, while the Town reached the 4th round (5th round modern equivalent) of the FA Cup in 1883. These clubs amalgamated as Walsall Town Swifts in 1888, becoming simply Walsall in 1895.

First Football League game: 3 September, 1892, Division 2, v Darwen (h) L 1-2 – Hawkins; Withington, Pinches; Robinson, Whitrick, Forsyth; Marshall, Holmes, Turner, Gray (1), Pangbourn.

Managers (and Secretary-managers)
H. Smallwood 1888–91*, A. G. Burton 1891–93, J. H. Robinson 1893–95, C. H. Ailso 1895–96*, A. E. Parsloe 1896–97*, L. Ford 1897–98*, G. Hughes 1898–99*, L. Ford 1899–1901*, J. E. Shutt 1908–13*, Haydn Price 1914–20, Joe Burchell 1920–26, David Ashworth 1926–27, Jack Torrance 1927–28, James Kerr 1928–29, S. Scholey 1929–30, Peter O'Rourke 1930–32, G. W. Slade 1932–34, Andy Wilson 1934–37, Tommy Lowes 1937–44, Harry Hibbs 1944–51, Tony McPhee 1951, Brough Fletcher 1952–53, Major Frank Buckley 1953–55, John Love 1955–57, Billy Moore 1957–64, Alf Wood 1964, Reg Shaw 1964–68, Dick Graham 1968, Ron Lewin 1968–69, Billy Moore 1969–72, John Smith 1972–73, Doug Fraser 1973–77, Dave Mackay 1977–78, Alan Ashman 1978, Frank Sibley 1979, Alan Buckley 1979–86, Neil Martin (joint manager with Buckley) 1981–82, Tommy Coakley 1986–88, John Barnwell 1989–90, Kenny Hibbitt 1990– .

Player and Position	Ht	Wt	Birth Date	Place	Source	Clubs	League App	Gls
Forwards								
Keith Bertschin	6 1	11 08	25 8 56	Enfield	Barnet	Ipswich T	32	8
						Birmingham C	118	29
						Norwich C	114	29
						Stoke City	88	29
						Sunderland	36	7
						Walsall	55	9
Martin Goldsmith	6 0	11 11	4 11 69	Walsall	Trainee	Walsall	3	—
						Larne (loan)	—	—
Adrian Littlejohn	5 10	10 04	26 9 70	Wolverhampton	WBA§	Walsall	11	—
Chris Marsh	5 10	12 11	14 1 70	Dudley	Trainee	Walsall	25	—
Mark Rees*	5 10	11 10	13 10 61	Smethwick	Apprentice	Walsall	237	37
						Rochdale (loan)	3	—
Stuart Rimmer	5 7	9 04	12 10 64	Southport	Apprentice	Everton	3	—
						Chester C	114	67
						Watford	10	1
						Notts Co	4	2
						Walsall	61	18
Gary Shaw*	5 9	12 00	21 1 61	Birmingham	Apprentice	Aston Villa	165	59
						Blackpool (loan)	6	—
					Klagenfurt	Walsall	9	3

Trainees
Ayres, Michael; Baddams, Adrian A; Beckett, Mark D; Cooke, Paul J; Dean, Martin J; Green, Richard S; Knight, Craig; McCall, Gary; Millen, William F; Preece, John B; Riley, Darren S; Sweeney, David; Williams, James A.

Associated Schoolboys
Brown, Stuart J; Cooper, Matthew T; Draper, Terence; Eivors, Gerard; Fieldhouse, Lee S; Fullelove, Christopher H; Harding, Andrew; Hillin, Stephen A; Instone, Wayne A; McFarlane, Anders I; Norman, Karl M; Oldaker, Steven A; Reynolds, Simon D; Simcox, Robert S; Simkins, Ian M; Wilkes, David T.

Associated Schoolboys who have accepted the club's offer of a Traineeship/Contract
Brown, Richard C; Harrison, Seth; Knight, Richard; Read, Paul J; Richardson, Jason P; Tolson, Neil; Turner, Emlyn A; Ward, Anthony.

564

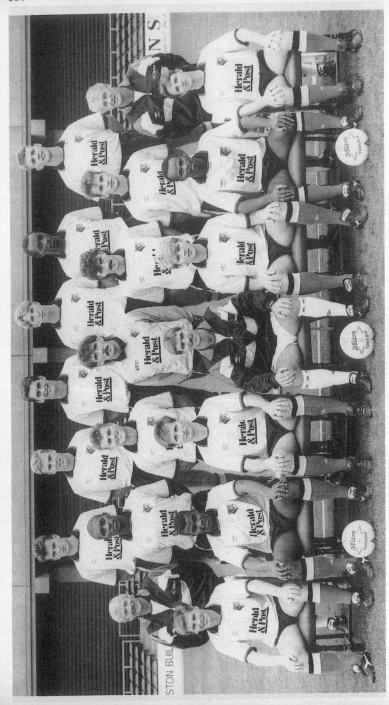

WATFORD 1989-90 *Back row (left to right):* Lee Richardson, Kenny Jackett, Willie Falconer, Iwan Roberts, Garry Thompson, David Holdsworth. *Centre row:* Billy Hails (Physiotherapist), Wayne Allison, Neil Redfearn, Tony Coton, Paul Wilkinson, Dean Holdsworth, Tom Walley (First Team Coach). *Front row:* Nigel Gibbs, Liburd Henry, Glenn Roeder, Steve Harrison (Manager), Glyn Hodges, Rod Thomas, Gary Porter.

Division 2

WATFORD

Vicarage Road Stadium, Watford WD1 8ER. Telephone Watford (0923) 30933. Answerphone Service: Watford 35133 for information. 0898 700 272 – The 'Hornet Hotline' 24-hour club news service. Ticket Office: 220393. Club shop: 220847. Catering: 221457. Junior Hornets Club: 53836. Marketing: 225761.

Ground capacity: 26,996.

Record attendance: 34,099 v Manchester U, FA Cup 4th rd replay, 3 Feb, 1969.

Record receipts: £104,347 v Liverpool, FA Cup 6th rd replay. 17 March, 1986.

Pitch measurements: 115yd × 75yd.

Chairman: Elton John. *Vice-Chairman:* G. A. Smith.

Directors: J. Harrowell, Bertie Mee OBE, J. Reid. H. M. Stratford JP, M. Winwood.

Chief Executive: Eddie Plumley FAAI.

Team Manager: Colin Lee.

Coach: Tom Walley. *Physio:* Billy Hails.

Marketing Manager: Chris Childs. *Public Relations Manager:* Ed Coan.

Year Formed: 1891*(see Foundation). **Turned Professional:** 1897. **Ltd Co.:** 1909.

Club Nickname: 'The Hornets'.

Previous Name: West Herts.

Previous Grounds: 1899, Cassio Road; 1922, Vicarage Road.

Record League Victory: 8-0 v Sunderland, Division 1, 25 September 1982 – Sherwood; Rice, Rostron, Taylor, Terry, Bolton, Callaghan (2), Blissett (4), Jenkins (2), Jackett, Barnes.

Record Cup Victory: 10-1 v Lowestoft T, FA Cup, 1st rd, 27 November 1926 – Yates; Prior, Fletcher (1); Smith (F), 'Bert' Smith, Strain; Stephenson, Warner (3), Edmonds (2), Swan (2), Daniels (1). (1 og)

Record Defeat: 0-10 v Wolverhampton W, FA Cup 1st rd replay, 13 January, 1912.

Most League Points (2 for a win): 71, Division 4, 1977–78.

Most League Points (3 for a win): 80, Division 2, 1981–82.

Most League Goals: 92, Division 4, 1959–60.

Highest League Scorer in Season: Cliff Holton, 42, Division 4, 1959–60.

Most League Goals in Total Aggregate: Tommy Barnett, 144, 1928–39.

Most Capped Player: John Barnes, 31 (58), England and Kenny Jackett, 31, Wales.

Most League Appearances: Duncan Welbourne, 411, 1963–74.

Record Transfer Fee Received: £1,000,000 from AC Milan for Luther Blissett, July 1983.

Record Transfer Fee Paid: £550,000 to AC Milan for Luther Blissett, August 1984.

Football League Record: 1920 Original Member of Division 3; 1921–58 Division 3 (S), 1958–60 Division 4; 1960–69 Division 3; 1969–72 Division 2; 1972–75 Division 3; 1975–78 Division 4; 1978–79 Division 3; 1979–82 Division 2; 1982–88 Division 1; 1988– Division 2.

Honours: Football League: Division 1 – Runners-up 1982–83; Division 2 – Runners-up 1981–82; Division 3 – Champions 1968–69, Runners-up 1978–79; Division 4 – Champions 1977–78; Promoted 1959–60 (4th). *FA Cup:* Runners-up 1984. *Football League Cup:* Semi-final 1978–79. **European Competitions:** *UEFA Cup:* 1983–84.

Colours: Yellow shirts (black/red piping), black shorts, red stockings (yellow/black tops). **Change colours:** White shirts (black/red piping), white shorts, white stockings.

WATFORD 1989–90 LEAGUE RECORD

Match No.	Date	Venue	Opponents	Result		H/T Score	Lg. Pos.	Goalscorers	Attendance
1	Aug 19	H	Portsmouth	W	1-0	1-0	—	Wilkinson	10,164
2	22	A	Oldham Ath	D	1-1	0-1	—	Holdsworth Dean	6230
3	26	A	Oxford U	D	1-1	1-0	5	Thomas	5664
4	Sept 2	H	Leicester C	W	3-1	2-0	2	Wilkinson, Porter (pen), Thompson	10,252
5	9	A	Sunderland	L	0-4	0-3	7		15,042
6	16	H	Port Vale	W	1-0	0-0	4	Wilkinson	8445
7	23	A	West Ham U	L	0-1	0-1	9		20,728
8	27	A	Newcastle U	L	1-2	1-2	—	Wilkinson	17,040
9	30	H	Middlesbrough	W	1-0	1-0	10	Wilkinson	10,102
10	Oct 7	H	WBA	L	0-2	0-1	12		10,444
11	14	A	Brighton & HA	L	0-1	0-1	14		9260
12	17	H	Bournemouth	D	2-2	1-2	—	Porter (pen), Holdsworth David	9013
13	21	A	Blackburn R	D	2-2	1-1	15	Holdsworth David, Wilkinson	7950
14	28	H	Sheffield U	L	1-3	0-1	16	Porter	11,623
15	31	A	Ipswich T	L	0-1	0-0	—		12,557
16	Nov 4	A	Hull C	D	0-0	0-0	17		4718
17	11	H	Plymouth Arg	L	1-2	0-0	18	Redfearn	9401
18	18	A	Leeds U	L	1-2	1-0	19	Penrice	26,921
19	25	H	Wolverhampton W	W	3-1	1-1	19	Penrice, Wilkinson, Falconer	12,736
20	Dec 2	A	Portsmouth	W	2-1	1-0	16	Wilkinson, Penrice	7933
21	9	H	Oldham Ath	W	3-0	3-0	15	Wilkinson, Hodges, Penrice	9399
22	16	H	Bradford C	W	7-2	5-0	11	Wilkinson 2, Penrice, Ashby, Henry, Richardson, Porter	8554
23	26	A	Barnsley	W	1-0	0-0	8	Wilkinson	7357
24	30	A	Stoke C	D	2-2	1-2	9	Hodges, Penrice	13,228
25	Jan 1	H	Swindon T	L	0-2	0-0	11		13,708
26	13	H	Oxford U	L	0-1	0-0	13		10,040
27	20	A	Leicester C	D	1-1	1-1	14	Roeder	11,466
28	Feb 10	A	Port Vale	L	0-1	0-0	16		7063
29	17	H	Sunderland	D	1-1	1-1	14	Thomas	9093
30	24	A	Wolverhampton W	D	1-1	1-1	15	Wilkinson	16,187
31	Mar 3	H	Leeds U	W	1-0	1-0	15	Thomas	13,468
32	7	A	Middlesbrough	W	2-1	0-0	—	Hodges 2 (1 pen)	14,008
33	10	H	Newcastle U	D	0-0	0-0	13		12,069
34	13	H	West Ham U	L	0-1	0-0	—		15,682
35	17	A	WBA	L	0-2	0-1	14		9915
36	20	H	Brighton & HA	W	4-2	3-0	—	Penrice 2, Hodges, Thomas	8487
37	24	A	Bournemouth	D	0-0	0-0	13		6737
38	31	H	Blackburn R	W	3-1	2-0	12	Wilkinson, Holdsworth David, Penrice	9096
39	Apr 7	H	Ipswich T	D	3-3	0-2	13	Hodges 2 (2 pens), Penrice	11,158
40	10	A	Sheffield U	L	1-4	1-1	—	Penrice	14,653
41	14	A	Swindon T	L	0-2	0-0	14		8520
42	17	H	Barnsley	D	2-2	1-1	15	Wilkinson, Thomas	7289
43	21	A	Bradford C	L	1-2	0-1	15	Falconer	5964
44	24	H	Stoke C	D	1-1	1-1	—	Thomas	8073
45	28	A	Plymouth Arg	D	0-0	0-0	15		8564
46	May 5	H	Hull C	W	3-1	1-0	15	Penrice 2, Falconer	9827

Final League Position: 15

GOALSCORERS

League (58): Wilkinson 15, Penrice 13, Hodges 7 (3 pens), Thomas 6, Porter 4 (2 pens), Falconer 3, Holdsworth David 3, Ashby 1, Henry 1, Holdsworth Dean 1, Redfearn 1, Richardson 1, Roeder 1, Thompson 1.
Littlewoods Cup (2): Roberts 2.
FA Cup (4): Hodges 1, Penrice 1, Porter 1 (pen), Roeder 1.

Coton	Gibbs	Jackett	Richardson	Holdsworth David	Roeder	Thomas	Wilkinson	Thompson	Porter	Redfearn	Holdsworth Dean	Falconer	Roberts	Henry	Hodges	Robson	Allison	Drysdale	Pullan	Penrice	Ashby	McClelland	Williams	Harrison	Bazeley	Match No.
1	2	3	4	5	6	7	8	9*	10	11	12															1
1	2	3	4†	5	6	7	8	9*	10	11	12	14														2
1	2	3	4†	5	6	7	8	9*	10	11	12	14														3
1	2	3	4	5	6	7	8	9	10	11																4
1	2	3	4	5	6	7	8	9*	10	11†	12	14														5
1	2	3	4	5	6	7	8		10	11				9												6
1	2	3	4†	5	6	7	8		10			14	9*12	11												7
1	2	3	4*	5	6	7	8		10			12	9	11												8
1	2	3		5	6	7	8*		10			4	9	12	11											9
1	2	3	4	5	6					12	14	10	9*	8	11†											10
1	2	3	4	5	6	7†	8		10	12		9			11*		14									11
1	2	3	4	5	6	7	8		10	12					11*		9									12
1	2	3	4	5	6	7	8		10						11		9									13
1	2	3	4	5	6	7	8		10						11		9									14
1	2	4		5	6		8	12	10			7	9		11*						3					15
1	2	4		5	6		8	12	10			7	9*		11						3					16
1	2			5	6		8	9	10	7		4			11						3					17
1	2			5	6		8	12	10	7†		4			11		3	14		9*						18
1	2	4		5	6		8		10			7			11					9	3					19
1	2	4		5	6		8		10			7*			11			12		9	3					20
1	2	7*	4	5	6		8		10						11			12		9	3					21
																										22
1	2	4		5	6		8		10			7			11					9	3					23
1	2	4		5	6		8		10			7			11					9	3					24
1	2*	4		5	6	12	8		10			7			11					9	3					25
1	2	4			6		8		10			7			11					9	3	5				26
1	2	4			6				10			9	7		11	8					3	5				27
1	2	6	5			14	8	9†	10	12					11*		7				3		4			28
1	2	6	5			7	8		10	12					11					9	3		4*			29
1	2			5	6	7	8		10			4			11			3		9						30
1	2			5	6	7	8		10			4			11					9	3					31
1	2†	12		5	6	7	8		10*			4			11			14		9	3					32
1			4	5	6	7	8		10						11			3		9				2		33
1			4	5	6	7	14	12	8*						11†		3			9	10			2		34
1	2			5	6	7	8		10						11			3		9			4			35
1	2			5	6	7	8	12	10						11			3		9*			4			36
1	2			5	6	7	8		10						11			3		9			4			37
1	12	4*		5	6	7	8		10						11			3		9				2		38
1				5	6	7	8		10						11			3		9	12		2*	4		39
1				5	6	7	8		10						11			3		9			4	2		40
1	2			5	6	7	8		10						11		14			9	12		3†	4*		41
1	2			5	6	7	8		10						11			3		9			4			42
1	2			5	6	12	8*		10						11		7	3		9			4			43
1	2	4†		5	6	11	8		10						7*12					9	3		14			44
1	2	4		5	6	5*	6	7†	8						11					9	7		3			45
1	2	4	5*	6	7†	8			10						11			3		9	12				14	46
46	41	16	31	44	44	30	43	7	31	10	—	23	8	7	35	1	6	18	1	29	14	1	18	2	—	

```
        + +        + +        + + + +        + +              + +          +        + +
        1s 1s      1s 2s      6s1s 2s 4s 7s  1s 2s            1s2s 3s      4s       1s1s
```

Littlewoods Cup	Second Round	Bolton W (a)		1-2
		(h)		1-1
FA Cup	Third Round	Wigan Ath (h)		2-0
	Fourth Round	Sheffield U (a)		1-1
		(h)		1-2

WATFORD

Player and Position	Ht	Wt	Birth Date	Place	Source	Clubs	League App	Gls
Goalkeepers								
Tony Coton	6 1	11 08	19 5 61	Tamworth	Mile Oak	Birmingham C	94	—
						Hereford U (loan)	—	—
						Watford	233	—
David James	6 4	14 07	1 8 70	Welwyn	Trainee	Watford	—	—
Melvyn Rees	6 2	12 12	25 1 67	Cardiff	Trainee	Cardiff C	31	—
						Watford	3	—
						Crewe Alex (loan)	6	—
						Southampton (loan)	—	—
						Leyton Orient (loan)	9	—
Defenders								
Barry Ashby	6 2	12 03	21 11 70	London	Trainee	Watford	18	1
Jason Drysdale	5 10	10 07	17 11 70	Bristol	Trainee	Watford	20	—
David Evans	5 7	10 02	28 8 72	Bangor	Trainee	Watford	—	—
Willie Falconer	6 1	12 10	5 4 66	Aberdeen	Lewis Utd	Aberdeen	77	13
						Watford	63	8
Martin Gardener*	5 11	12 00	29 10 69	Tredegar	School	Watford	—	—
Nigel Gibbs	5 7	10 02	20 11 65	St Albans	Apprentice	Watford	187	2
David Holdsworth	5 11	11 04	8 11 68	London	Trainee	Watford	77	4
Glenn Roeder	6 0	12 13	13 12 55	Woodford	Apprentice	Orient	115	4
						QPR	157	17
						Notts Co (loan)	4	—
						Newcastle U	193	8
						Watford	45	1
Jason Soloman	6 1	11 09	6 10 70	Welwyn	Trainee	Watford	—	—
Paul Towler	5 10	11 10	1 2 72	Bristol	Trainee	Watford	—	—
Gary Williams	5 9	11 01	17 6 60	Wolverhampton	Apprentice	Leeds U	39	3
						Watford	18	—
Midfield								
Gerry Harrison	5 10	12 02	15 4 72	Lambeth	Trainee	Watford	3	—
Kenny Jackett	5 11	11 13	5 1 62	Watford	Apprentice	Watford	335	26
Gary Porter	5 5	9 10	6 3 66	Sunderland	Apprentice	Watford	159	22
Jonathan Price	5 10	11 07	18 9 71	Hemel Hempstead	Trainee	Watford	—	—
Chris Pullan	5 8	10 12	14 12 67	Durham	School	Watford	10	—
						Halifax T (loan)	5	1
Lee Richardson	5 11	11 00	12 3 69	Halifax	School	Halifax T	56	2
						Watford	41	1
Forwards								
Wayne Allison	6 1	12 06	16 10 68	Huddersfield		Halifax T	84	23
						Watford	7	—
Darren Bazeley§			5 10 72	Northampton	Trainee	Watford	1	—

WATFORD

Foundation: Tracing this club's foundation proves difficult. Nowadays it is suggested that Watford was formed as Watford Rovers in 1891. Another version is that Watford Rovers were not forerunners of the present club whose history began in 1898 with the amalgamation of West Herts and Watford St. Mary's.

First Football League game: 28 August, 1920, Division 3, v QPR (a) W 2-1 – Williams; Horseman, F. Gregory; Bacon, Toone, Wilkinson; Bassett, Ronald (1), Hoddinott, White (1), Waterall.

Managers (and Secretary-managers)
John Goodall 1903–10, Harry Kent 1910–26, Fred Pagnam 1926–29, Neil McBain 1929–37, Bill Findlay 1938–47, Jack Bray 1947–48, Eddie Hapgood 1948–50, Ron Gray 1950–51, Haydn Green 1951–52, Len Goulden 1952–55 (GM to 1956), Johnny Paton 1955–56, Neil McBain 1956–59, Ron Burgess 1959–63, Bill McGarry 1963–64, Ken Furphy 1964–71, George Kirby 1971–73, Mike Keen 1973–77, Graham Taylor 1977–87, Dave Bassett 1987–88, Steve Harrison 1988–90, Colin Lee 1990–   .

Player and Position	Ht	Wt	Birth Date	Place	Source	Clubs	League App	Gls
Liburd Henry	5 11	11 00	29 8 67	Dominica	Leytonstone/ Ilford	Watford	10	1
						Halifax T (loan)	5	—
Glyn Hodges	6 0	12 03	30 4 63	Streatham	Apprentice	Wimbledon	232	49
						Newcastle U	7	—
						Watford	86	15
Gary Penrice	5 7	10 00	23 3 64	Bristol	Mangotsfield	Bristol R	188	54
						Watford	29	13
Iwan Roberts	6 3	12 05	26 6 68	Banour		Watford	63	9
Rod Thomas	5 6	10 03	10 10 70	London	Trainee	Watford	54	8
Paul Wilkinson	6 0	11 00	30 10 64	Louth	Apprentice	Grimsby T	71	27
						Everton	31	7
						Nottingham F	34	5
						Watford	88	34

Trainees
Alsford, Julian; Bazeley, Darren S; Fuller, Adrian J; Gallen, Joseph M; Kendall, Stuart J; Meara, James S; Proctor, Neil S.C; Rice, Marc G; Sheppard, Simon; Wild, Matthew J.

Associated Schoolboys
Bennellick, James A; Boachie, Nana; Buoy, Nicholas; Durrant, Kevin J; Edgar, Nicholas; Evans, Paul A; Flowers, Paul A; Georgiou, Jimmy; Hutchins, Neil; McIntosh, Craig; Merritt, Justin; Morrisey, Tobi; North, Tyronne L; Page, Robert J; Porter, Gareth; Riddick, Alexander G; Slinn, Kevin P; Young, Matthew.

Associated Schoolboys who have accepted the club's offer of a Traineeship/Contract
Dalli, Marc J; Lavin, Gerard; Nwaokolo, Daniel; Pugh, Stephen; Snowdon, Trevor.

WEST BROMWICH ALBION 1989–90 *Back row (left to right):* Darren Bradley, Colin West, Chris Whyte, Paul Raven, Stacey North, John Thomas.
Centre row: Tony Ford, Kevin Bartlett, Stuart Naylor, Paul Bradshaw, Colin Anderson, Simeon Hodson.
Front row: Bernard McNally, Don Goodman, Stuart Pearson (First Team Coach), Brian Talbot (Manager), Gary Robson, Steve Parkin.

Division 2   WEST BROMWICH ALBION

The Hawthorns, West Bromwich B71 4LF. Telephone 021-525 8888 (all Depts). Fax: 021 553 6634.

Ground capacity: 36,159 (10,865 seats).

Record attendance: 64,815 v Arsenal, FA Cup 6th rd, 6 March 1937.

Record receipts: £161,632.50 v Aston Villa, FA Cup 5th rd, 17 February, 1990.

Pitch measurements: 115yd × 75yd.

President: F. A. Millichip. *Vice-President:* C. E. Edwards.

Chairman: J. G. Silk. *Vice-Chairman:* D. B. Boundy.

Directors: J. W. Brandrick, J. S. Lucas, M. C. McGinnity, T. J. Summers, A. B. Hale.

Player-Manager: Brian Talbot. *Assistant Manager:*

Coach: Stuart Pearson. *Physio:* John MacGowan MCSP, SRP. *Secretary:* Dr. J. J. Evans.

Club Statistician: Tony Matthews. *Commercial Manager:* Alan Stevenson.

Year Formed: 1879. *Turned Professional:* 1885. *Ltd Co.:* 1892.

Club Nicknames: 'Throstles', 'Baggies', 'Albion'.

Previous Grounds: 1879, Coopers Hill; 1879, Dartmouth Park; 1881, Bunns Field, Walsall Street; 1882, Four Acres (Dartmouth Cricket Club); 1885, Stoney Lane; 1900, The Hawthorns.

Previous Name: 1879–81, West Bromwich Strollers.

Record League Victory: 12-0 v Darwen, Division 1, 4 April 1892 – Reader; Horton, McCulloch; Reynolds (2), Perry, Groves; Bassett (3), McLeod, Nicholls (1), Pearson (4), Geddes (1). (1 og).

Record Cup Victory: 10-1 v Chatham (away), FA Cup, 3rd rd, 2 March 1889 – Roberts; Horton, Green; Timmins (1), Charles Perry, Horton; Bassett (2), Perry (1), Bayliss (2), Pearson, Wilson (3). (1 og).

Record Defeat: 3-10 v Stoke C, Division 1, 4 February, 1937.

Most League Points (2 for a win): 60, Division 1, 1919–20.

Most League Points (3 for a win): 72, Division 2, 1988–89.

Most League Goals: 105, Division 2, 1929–30.

Highest League Scorer in Season: William 'Ginger' Richardson, 39, Division 1, 1935–36.

Most League Goals in Total Aggregate: Tony Brown, 218, 1963–79.

Most Capped Player: Stuart Williams, 33 (43), Wales.

Most League Appearances: Tony Brown, 574, 1963–80.

Record Transfer Fee Received: £1,500,000 from Manchester U for Bryan Robson, October 1981.

Record Transfer Fee Paid: £748,000 to Manchester C for Peter Barnes, July 1979.

Football League Record: 1888 Founder Member of Football League; 1901–02 Division 2; 1902–04 Division 1; 1904–11 Division 2; 1911–27 Division 1; 1927–31 Division 2; 1931–38 Division 1; 1938–49 Division 2; 1949–73 Division 1; 1973–76 Division 2; 1976–86 Division 1; 1986– Division 2.

Honours: Football League: Division 1 – Champions 1919–20; Runners-up 1924–25, 1953–54, Division 2 – Champions 1901–02, 1910–11; Runners-up 1930–31, 1948–49; Promoted to Division 1 1975–76 (3rd). *FA Cup:* Winners 1888, 1892, 1931, 1954, 1968; Runners-up 1886, 1887, 1895, 1912, 1935. *Football League Cup:* Winners 1965–66; Runners-up 1966–67, 1969–70. **European Competitions:** *European Cup-Winners' Cup:* 1968–69; *European Fairs Cup:* 1966–67; *UEFA Cup:* 1978–79, 1979–80, 1981–82.

Colours: Navy blue and white striped shirts, navy blue shorts, white stockings. **Change colours:** Green and yellow striped shirts, green shorts, yellow stockings.

WEST BROMWICH ALBION 1989–90 LEAGUE RECORD

Match No.	Date	Venue	Opponents	Result	H/T Score	Lg. Pos.	Goalscorers	Attendance
1	Aug 19	H	Sheffield U	L 0-3	0-1	—		14,907
2	22	A	Bournemouth	D 1-1	0-1		Goodman	8226
3	26	A	Port Vale	L 1-2	1-0	24	Whyte	7695
4	Sept 2	H	Sunderland	D 1-1	0-0	22	Goodman	10,885
5	9	A	Leicester C	W 3-1	2-1	18	West, Whyte, Goodman	10,700
6	16	A	Oxford U	W 3-2	0-0	15	Robson, Greenall (og), Bradley	9628
7	23	A	Oldham Ath	L 1-2	0-0	16	West	6907
8	27	H	Blackburn R	D 2-2	0-1	—	Goodman, Ford	9269
9	30	A	West Ham U	W 3-2	2-0	13	Ford, McNally 2 (1 pen)	19,739
10	Oct 7	A	Watford	W 2-0	1-0	9	Thomas, Whyte	10,444
11	15	H	Wolverhampton W	L 1-2	1-1	—	Talbot	21,316
12	17	A	Stoke C	L 1-2	0-2	—	Bartlett	11,991
13	21	H	Hull C	D 1-1	1-0	13	Parkin	9228
14	28	A	Middlesbrough	D 0-0	0-0	14		14,076
15	Nov 1	H	Newcastle U	L 1-5	1-2	—	Goodman	12,339
16	4	A	Ipswich T	L 1-3	1-2	16	Goodman	12,028
17	11	H	Barnsley	W 7-0	3-0	13	Goodman 3, Ford, Bartlett 2, McNally (pen)	9317
18	18	A	Portsmouth	D 1-1	0-1	14	McNally (pen)	9069
19	25	H	Leeds U	W 2-1	2-0	11	Goodman, Bartlett	15,116
20	Dec 2	A	Sheffield U	L 1-3	0-1	14	Robson	14,094
21	9	H	Bournemouth	D 2-2	2-0	17	Goodman, Bartlett	8568
22	17	H	Swindon T	L 1-2	0-1	—	Goodman (pen)	9884
23	26	H	Plymouth Arg	D 2-2	2-0	19	Goodman 2	9782
24	30	A	Bradford C	L 0-2	0-1	19		8560
25	Jan 1	H	Brighton & HA	W 3-0	2-0	16	Robson, Bartlett, West	9407
26	13	H	Port Vale	L 2-3	0-2	17	Goodman, Ford	13,575
27	20	A	Sunderland	D 1-1	0-1	18	Robson	15,583
28	Feb 3	H	Oldham Ath	D 2-2	1-1	17	Robson, West	12,237
29	10	A	Oxford U	W 1-0	1-0	15	Shakespeare	6749
30	21	H	Leicester C	L 0-1	0-0	—		10,902
31	24	A	Leeds U	D 2-2	0-1	17	Goodman, Bartlett	30,004
32	Mar 3	H	Portsmouth	D 0-0	0-0	17		10,502
33	10	A	Blackburn R	L 1-2	0-1	18	Ford	8148
34	14	H	Bradford C	W 2-0	1-0	—	Ford, McNally	8017
35	17	H	Watford	W 2-0	1-0	17	Hackett, Whyte	9915
36	20	A	Wolverhampton W	L 1-2	1-1	—	Foster	24,475
37	24	H	Stoke C	D 1-1	1-0	16	Ford	12,771
38	31	A	Hull C	W 2-0	1-0	15	Goodman, Hackett	5418
39	Apr 4	H	West Ham U	L 1-3	1-2	—	Goodman	11,556
40	7	H	Middlesbrough	D 0-0	0-0	15		9458
41	11	A	Newcastle U	L 1-2	0-1	—	Goodman	19,460
42	14	A	Brighton & HA	W 3-0	2-0	15	Goodman, Ford, Bannister	8371
43	16	H	Plymouth Arg	L 0-3	0-1	16		9728
44	21	A	Swindon T	L 1-2	0-0	17	Goodman	8495
45	28	A	Barnsley	D 2-2	1-0	19	Tiler (og), Bradley	10,334
46	May 5	H	Ipswich T	L 1-3	0-3	20	Bannister	11,567

Final League Position: 20

GOALSCORERS

League (67): Goodman 21 (1 pen), Ford 8, Bartlett 7, McNally 5 (3 pens), Robson 5, West 4, Whyte 4, Bannister 2, Bradley 2, Hackett 2, Foster 1, Parkin 1, Shakespeare 1, Talbot 1, Thomas 1, own goals 2.
Littlewoods Cup (7): Thomas 3, Whyte 2, McNally 1, Talbot 1.
FA Cup (3): Bartlett 1, Ford 1, Robson 1.

Bradshaw	Bradley	Parkin	Talbot	Whyte	North	Ford	Goodman	West	McNally	Anderson	Robson	Thomas	Burgess	Marriott	Naylor	Barham	Bartlett	Hodson	Allardyce	Harbey	Bennett	Raven	Andersen	Dobbins	Cartwright	Foster	Shakespeare	Hackett	Bannister	Match No.
1	2	3	4*	5	6	7	8†	9	10	11	12	14																		1
1	2	3		5	6	7	8	9*	10	11			4	12																2
1	6	3	12	5		7	8	9	10*	11†			4	14	2															3
1†	6	3	12	5		7	8*	9	10	11			4	14	2															4
	6	3	12	5		7	8	9	10	11			4*		2	1														5
	6	3		5		12	7	8	9	10	11		4†	14	2*	1														6
	2			5	6	7	8	9	10	11*	4	12		3	1															7
	2		12	5	6	7	8	9*	10	11†	4	14		3	1															8
	2		12	5	6	7	8		10	11	4*	9		3	1															9
	2		4	5	6	11		10		9	3	1				7	8													10
	2*		4	5	6	11	8		10		12	9		3	1	7														11
	2	12	5	6	7	8	10	4*	9	3	1	11†	14																	12
	2	12	5	6	7	8	10	4	9	3	1	11*																		13
	2	4	5	6	7	8	10	11	9	1	3																			14
	2	4	5	6	7	8	10	11*	9†	1	12	3	14																	15
		4	5	6	11	8	10	12	2	1	7*	9	3																	16
	11	4	6	7	8	10	14	12	1	9†	2	3	5*																	17
	11	4	6	7	8	10	1	9	2	3	5																			18
	11	4*	6	7	8	10	12	2	1	9	3	5																		19
	11	4*	6	7	8	10	12	14	2	1	9†	3	5																	20
		6	7	8	12	10	11†	4	2	1	9*	3	5	14																21
		6	12	7	8	9	10	11†	4	2	1	14	3	5*																22
		6	5	7	8	9	10	11†	4*	1	14	3			2	12														23
		6	5	7	8	10*	11†	4	9	1	14	3			2	12														24
		6	5	7	8	9	10	4	1	11	3			2																25
		6	7	8	9	10	4	1	11	3	5	2																		26
	14	6	7	8	9	10†	4	12	1	11	3	5	2*																	27
		6	5	7*	9	10	4	2	1	11	3			12	8															28
		6	5	9	10	4	2	1	11	3			8	7																29
14		4†	6	5	8	9*	10	2	1	3	11	12	7																	30
4		5	8	12	10	6	1	11	2	3	9*	7																		31
4		5	8*	9	10	6	1	11	2	3	7	12																		32
	14	5	7	9*	10	6†	1	2	3	12	4	11	8																	33
12	6	5	7	10*	2	1	3	9	4	11	8																			34
10	6	5	7	2	1	3	9	4	11	8																				35
10†	6	5	7	12	2	1	3	14	9*	4	11	8																		36
10	6	5	7	8	2	1	3	4	11	9																				37
10	6	5	7	8	2*	1	3	12	4	11	9																			38
2	6	5	7	8	1	3	10	12	4	11*	9																			39
2	6	5	7	8	10	1	3	4	11	9																				40
2	6	5	7	8	10	14	1	3	12	4	11†	9*																		41
11	6	5	7	8	10	2	1	3	12	4	9*																			42
11	6	5	7	8	10	2*	1	3	14	4	12	9†																		43
11	6	5	7	8	10	1	2	3	9	4*	12																			44
11	6	7	8	10	5	1	2*	3	4	12	9																			45
2*	4†	6	7	8	10	5	1	3	14	11	12	9																		46
4	25	14	12	43	32	42	39	18	41	13	21	8	31	3	39	4	15	10	—	30	1	7	—	5	2	7	18	9	13	
+2s					+8s	+1s	+2s						+3s				+4s	+10s +3s				+5s	+1s			+1s		+5s +7s	+5s	

Littlewoods Cup	Second Round	Bradford C (h)		1-3
		(a)		5-3
	Third Round	Newcastle U (a)		1-0
	Fourth Round	Derby Co (a)		0-2
FA Cup	Third Round	Wimbledon (h)		2-0
	Fourth Round	Charlton Ath (h)		1-0
	Fifth Round	Aston Villa (h)		0-2

WEST BROMWICH ALBION

Player and Position	Ht	Wt	Birth Date	Place	Source	Clubs	League App	Gls
Goalkeepers								
Paul Bradshaw*	6 3	13 04	28 4 56	Altrincham	Apprentice	Blackburn R	78	—
						Wolverhampton W	200	—
					Vancouver W	WBA	8	—
						Bristol R	5	—
						Newport Co	23	—
						WBA	6	—
Stuart Naylor	6 4	12 10	6 12 62	Wetherby	Yorkshire A	Lincoln C	49	—
						Peterborough U (loan)	8	—
						Crewe Alex (loan)	55	—
						WBA	172	—
Defenders								
Arthur Albiston (To Dundee July 1989)	5 7	11 05	14 7 57	Edinburgh	Apprentice	Manchester U	379	6
						WBA	43	2
Sam Allardyce	6 1	14 00	19 10 54	Dudley	Apprentice	Bolton W	184	21
						Sunderland	25	2
						Millwall	63	2
						Coventry C	28	1
						Huddersfield T	37	—
						Bolton W	14	—
						Preston NE	90	2
						WBA	1	—
Martyn Bennett‡	6 0	12 12	4 8 61	Birmingham	Apprentice	WBA	182	9
Daryl Burgess	5 11	12 03	20 4 71	Birmingham	Trainee	WBA	34	—
Graham Harbey	5 8	10 08	29 8 64	Chesterfield	Apprentice	Derby Co	40	1
						Ipswich T	59	1
						WBA	30	—
Simeon Hodson	5 9	10 02	5 3 66	Lincoln	Apprentice	Notts Co	27	—
						Charlton Ath	5	—
						Lincoln C	56	—
						Newport Co	34	1
						WBA	26	—
Stacey North	6 2	12 06	25 11 64	Luton	Apprentice	Luton T	25	—
						Wolverhampton W (loan)	3	—
						WBA	98	—
Paul Raven	6 0	12 03	28 7 70	Salisbury	Schools	Doncaster R	52	4
						WBA	10	—
Darren Rogers	5 10	11 04	9 4 71	Birmingham	Trainee	WBA	—	—
Chris Whyte	6 1	11 10	2 9 61	London	Amateur	Arsenal	90	8
						Crystal Palace (loan)	13	—
					Los Angeles	WBA	84	7
Steve Parkin	5 6	10 07	7 11 65	Mansfield	Apprentice	Stoke C	113	5
						WBA	14	1
Ken Wharton‡	5 7	8 10	28 11 60	Newcastle	Grainger Park BC	Newcastle U	290	26
						Middlesbrough	—	—
						Carlisle U	1	—
						Bradford C	5	—
						WBA	—	—
Midfield								
Vetle Andersen‡			20 4 64	Kristiansand		WBA	1	—
Colin Anderson	5 9	10 07	26 4 62	Newcastle	Apprentice	Burnley	6	—
						Torquay U	100	11
						QPR (loan)	—	—
						WBA	117	8
Darren Bradley	5 10	11 04	24 11 65	Birmingham	Apprentice	Aston Villa	20	—
						WBA	96	3
Wayne Dobbins	5 7	10 08	30 8 68	Bromsgrove	Apprentice	WBA	37	—
Bernard McNally	5 7	10 11	17 2 63	Shrewsbury	Apprentice	Shrewsbury T	282	23
						WBA	41	5
Gary Robson	5 5	10 10	6 7 65	Co Durham	Apprentice	WBA	133	15

WEST BROMWICH ALBION

Foundation: There is a well known story that when employees of Salter's Spring Works in West Bromwich decided to form a football club in 1879, they had to send someone to the nearby Association Football stronghold of Wednesbury to purchase a football. A weekly subscription of 2d (less than 1p) was imposed and the name of the new club was West Bromwich Strollers.

First Football League game: 8 September, 1888, Football League, v Stoke (a) W 2-0 – Roberts; J. Horton, Green; E. Horton, Perry, Bayliss; Bassett, Woodhall (1), Hendry, Pearson, Wilson (1).

Managers (and Secretary-managers)
Louis Ford 1890–92*, Henry Jackson 1892–94*, Edward Stephenson 1894–95*, Clement Keys 1895–96*, Frank Heaven 1896–1902*, Fred Everiss 1902–48, Jack Smith 1948–52, Jesse Carver 1952, Vic Buckingham 1953–59, Gordon Clark 1959–61, Archie Macaulay 1961–63, Jimmy Hagan 1963–67, Alan Ashman 1967–71, Don Howe 1971–75, Johnny Giles 1975–77, Ronnie Allen 1977, Ron Atkinson 1978–81, Ronnie Allen 1981–82, Ron Wylie 1982–84, Johnny Giles 1984–85, Ron Saunders 1986–87, Ron Atkinson 1987–88, Brian Talbot 1988– .

Player and Position	Ht	Wt	Birth Date	Birth Place	Source	Clubs	League App	Gls
Craig Shakespeare	5 10	11 05	26 10 63	Birmingham	Apprentice	Walsall	284	45
						Sheffield W	17	—
						WBA	18	1
Brian Talbot	5 10	12 00	21 7 53	Ipswich	Apprentice	Ipswich T	177	25
						Arsenal	254	40
						Watford	48	8
						Stoke C	54	5
						WBA	74	5
Forwards								
Gary Bannister	5 8	11 01	22 7 60	Warrington	Apprentice	Coventry C	22	3
						Sheffield W	118	55
						QPR	136	56
						Coventry C	43	11
						WBA	13	2
Neil Cartwright	5 9	10 13	20 2 71	Stourbridge	Trainee	WBA	8	—
Tony Ford	5 9	12 08	14 5 59	Grimsby	Apprentice	Grimsby T	354	54
						Sunderland (loan)	9	1
						Stoke C	112	13
						WBA	53	9
Adrian Foster	5 9	11 00	20 7 71	Kidderminster	Trainee	WBA	14	1
Donald Goodman	5 10	11 00	9 5 66	Leeds		Bradford C	70	14
						WBA	125	45
Gary Hackett	5 8	10 13	11 10 62	Stourbridge	Bromsgrove R	Shrewsbury T	150	17
						Aberdeen	15	—
						Stoke C	73	7
						WBA	14	2
Colin West	6 2	13 11	13 11 62	Wallsend	Apprentice	Sunderland	102	21
						Watford	45	20
						Rangers	10	2
						Sheffield W	45	8
						WBA	38	12
Jason Withe‡			16 8 71	Liverpool	Trainee	WBA	—	—

Trainees
Ashton, Mark A; Birch, Matthew J; Bowen, Stuart A; Colcombe, Scott; Ehiogu, Ugochuku; Hall, Scott M; Hollier, Nigel T; Love, Craig; Mahoney, Timothy M; Morris, Simon R.J; Norman, Justin; Palmer, Leslie J; Patterson, Matthew; Price, Lyndon P; Pritchard, David M; Shepard, Matthew; Sweeney, Paul A; Whalley, David; Wright, Dean T.J.

Associated Schoolboys
Ball, Steven G; Darton, Scott R; Dwyer, James C; Evans, Lee J; Flint, Richard; Harris, Lee P; Harris, Richard J; Hicks, Daniel; Hinett, Gregory J; Hunter, Roy I; Johnson, Jonathan J; Love, Brett A; Mansell, Craig E; Miles, Anthony T; Owen, Darren L; Ward, Jonathan.

Associated Schoolboys who have accepted the club's offer of a Traineeship/Contract
Coldicott, Stacy; Hammond, Kirk; Howse, Justin J; Nelson, Matthew; Nightingale, Jonathan; Sinfield, Marc R; Tymon, Carl L.

WEST HAM UNITED 1989–90   *Back row (left to right):* Paul Hilton (Youth Team Coach), Gary Strodder, Phil Parkes, Tony Gale, Alvin Martin, Allen McKnight, Stewart Robson, Leroy Rosenior. *Centre row:* Kevin Keen, Steve Potts, George Parris, Ray Stewart, Paul Ince, Eamonn Dolan, David Kelly. *Front row:* Mark Ward, Julian Dicks, Frank McAvennie, Liam Brady, Stuart Slater, Tommy McQueen.

Division 2 — WEST HAM UNITED

Boleyn Ground, Green Street, Upton Park, London E13. Telephone 01-472 2740. Commercial Dept. 01-472 5756. Answerphone 01-470 1325. Hammer Line: 01-475 0555. Dial-a-seat: 01-472 3322.

Ground capacity: 35,510.

Record attendance: 42,322 v Tottenham H, Division 1, 17 Oct, 1970.

Record receipts: £146,074 v Tottenham H, League Cup 5th rd, 27 January 1987.

Pitch measurements: 112yd × 72yd.

Chairman: L. C. Cearns. *Vice-Chairman:* W. F. Cearns.

Directors: J. Petchey, M. W. Cearns AIB., C. J. WARNER MA.

Manager: Billy Bonds.

Secretary: T. M. Finn. *Commercial Manager:* Brian Blower.

Year Formed: 1895. *Turned Professional:* 1900. *Ltd Co.:* 1900.

Previous names: Thames Ironworks FC 1895–1900.

Previous Grounds: Memorial Recreation Ground, Canning Town: 1904 Boleyn Ground.

Club Nickname: 'The Hammers'.

Record League Victory: 8-0 v Rotherham U, Division 2, 8 March 1958 – Gregory; Bond, Wright; Malcolm, Brown, Lansdowne, Grice, Smith (2), Keeble (2), Dick (4), Musgrove. 8-0 v Sunderland, Division 1, 19 October 1968 – Ferguson; Bonds, Charles; Peters, Stephenson, Moore (1); Redknapp, Boyce, Brooking (1), Hurst (6), Sissons.

Record Cup Victory: 10-0 v Bury, League Cup, 2nd rd (2nd leg), 25 October 1983 – Parkes; Stewart (1), Walford, Bonds (Orr), Martin (1), Devonshire (2), Allen, Cottee (4), Swindlehurst, Brooking (2), Pike.

Record Defeat: 2-8 v Blackburn R, Division 1, 26 December, 1963.

Most League Points (2 for a win): 66, Division 2, 1980–81.

Most League Points (3 for a win): 84, Division 1, 1985–86.

Most League Goals: 101, Division 2, 1957–58.

Highest League Scorer in Season: Vic Watson, 41 Division 1, 1929–30.

Most League Goals in Total Aggregate: Vic Watson, 306, 1920–35.

Most Capped Player: Bobby Moore, 108, England.

Most League Appearances: Billy Bonds, 663, 1967–88.

Record Transfer Fee Received: £2,000,000 from Everton for Tony Cottee, July 1988.

Record Transfer Fee Paid: £1,250,000 to Celtic for Frank McAvennie, March 1989.

Football League Record: 1919 Elected to Division 2; 1923–32 Division 1; 1932–58 Division 2; 1958–78 Division 1; 1978–81 Division 2; 1981–89 Division 1; 1989– Division 2.

Honours: Football League: Division 1 best season: 3rd, 1985–86, Division 2 – Champions 1957–58, 1980–81; Runners-up 1922–23. *FA Cup:* Winners 1964, 1975, 1980; Runners-up 1922–23. *Football League Cup:* Runners-up 1966, 1981. **European Competitions:** *European Cup-Winner's Cup:* 1964–65 (winners), 1965–66, 1975–76 (runners-up), 1980–81.

Colours: Claret and blue shirts, white shorts, white stockings. **Change colours:** White shirts, blue shorts, blue stockings.

WEST HAM UNITED 1989–90 LEAGUE RECORD

Match No.	Date	Venue	Opponents	Result	H/T Score	Lg. Pos.	Goalscorers	Atten-dance
1	Aug 19	A	Stoke C	D 1-1	1-0	—	Keen	16,058
2	23	H	Bradford C	W 2-0	2-0	—	Slater 2	19,914
3	26	H	Plymouth Arg	W 3-2	1-0	1	Kelly, Allen, Keen	20,231
4	Sept 2	A	Hull C	D 1-1	1-0	1	Ward	9235
5	9	H	Swindon T	D 1-1	1-0	3	Allen	21,469
6	16	A	Brighton & HA	L 0-3	0-3	8		12,689
7	23	H	Watford	W 1-0	1-0	5	Dicks (pen)	20,728
8	26	A	Portsmouth	W 1-0	0-0	—	Rosenior	12,632
9	30	H	WBA	L 2-3	0-2	7	Dolan, Parris	19,739
10	Oct 7	H	Leeds U	L 0-1	0-1	10		23,539
11	14	A	Sheffield U	W 2-0	1-0	8	Ward 2 (1 pen)	20,822
12	18	H	Sunderland	W 5-0	3-0	—	Allen, Slater, Keen, Dolan 2	20,901
13	21	A	Port Vale	D 2-2	1-0	4	Keen, Slater	8899
14	28	H	Oxford U	W 3-2	1-1	4	Parris, Slater, Dicks	19,177
15	Nov 1	A	Bournemouth	D 1-1	1-1	—	Strodder	9979
16	4	A	Wolverhampton W	L 0-1	0-0	5		22,231
17	11	H	Newcastle U	D 0-0	0-0	7		25,842
18	18	H	Middlesbrough	W 2-0	1-0	5	Slater, Dicks (pen)	18,720
19	25	A	Blackburn R	L 4-5	1-4	7	Brady, Dicks (pen), Slater, Ward	10,215
20	Dec 2	H	Stoke C	D 0-0	0-0	7		17,704
21	9	A	Bradford C	L 1-2	1-1	7	Ward	9257
22	16	H	Oldham Ath	L 0-2	0-2	8		14,960
23	26	A	Ipswich T	L 0-1	0-1	10		24,365
24	30	A	Leicester C	L 0-1	0-0	11		16,925
25	Jan 1	H	Barnsley	W 4-2	3-0	10	Allen, Keen 2, Dicks (pen)	18,391
26	13	A	Plymouth Arg	D 1-1	0-1	10	Quinn	11,671
27	20	H	Hull C	L 1-2	1-1	13	Morley	16,847
28	Feb 10	H	Brighton & HA	W 3-1	0-1	11	Gatting (og), Dicks, Quinn	19,101
29	18	A	Swindon T	D 2-2	1-1	—	Quinn 2	16,105
30	24	H	Blackburn R	D 1-1	1-0	14	Quinn	20,052
31	Mar 3	A	Middlesbrough	W 1-0	0-0	10	Allen	23,617
32	10	H	Portsmouth	W 2-1	1-0	10	Allen, Dicks (pen)	20,961
33	13	A	Watford	W 1-0	0-0	—	Morley	15,682
34	17	A	Leeds U	L 2-3	0-2	10	Morley, Foster	32,536
35	21	H	Sheffield U	W 5-0	1-0	—	Morley, Quinn 3 (1 pen), Allen	21,629
36	24	A	Sunderland	L 3-4	1-1	10	Quinn 2, Morley	13,896
37	31	H	Port Vale	D 2-2	0-0	10	Morley, Gale	20,507
38	Apr 4	A	WBA	W 3-1	2-1	—	Quinn, Bishop, Keen	11,556
39	7	A	Oxford U	W 2-0	0-0	8	Morley, Quinn	8,371
40	11	H	Bournemouth	W 4-1	2-1	—	Miller (og), Bishop, Dicks (pen), Allen	20,202
41	14	A	Barnsley	D 1-1	1-1	7	Morley	10,344
42	17	H	Ipswich T	W 2-0	2-0	—	Allen, Keen	25,178
43	21	A	Oldham Ath	L 0-3	0-0	7		12,190
44	28	A	Newcastle U	L 1-2	1-0	7	Dicks (pen)	31,496
45	May 2	H	Leicester C	W 3-1	2-0	—	Rosenior, Keen, Morley	17,939
46	5	H	Wolverhampton W	W 4-0	2-0	7	Keen, Morley, Robson, Brady	22,509

Final League Position: 7

GOALSCORERS

League (80): Quinn 12 (1 pen), Keen 10, Morley 10, Allen 9, Dicks 9 (7 pens), Slater 7, Ward 5 (1 pen), Dolan 3, Bishop 2, Brady 2, Parris 2, Rosenior 2, Foster 1, Gale 1, Kelly 1, Robson 1, Strodder 1, own goals 2.
Littlewoods Cup (11): Dicks 4 (1 pen), Allen 2, Slater 2, Keen 1, Kelly 1, Martin 1.
FA Cup (0).

Parkes	Potts	Parris	Gale	Martin	Keen	Ward	McAvennie	Slater	Brady	Ince	Kelly D	Dicks	Allen	Devonshire	Dolan	Rosenior	Foster	Strodder	Fashanu	McQueen	Suckling	Bishop	Morley	Quinn	Kelly P.	Robson	Miklosko	Match No.
1	2	3	4	5	6	7	8*	9	10	11	12																	1
1	2	11	4	5	6	7		9	10			8	3															2
1	2	11	4	5	6	7			10			8	3	9														3
1	2		4	5	6	7		11	10*			8	3	9	12													4
1	2	11	4	5	6	7			10*			8†	3	9	12	14												5
1	2	11	4	5	6	7		8	10				3	9														6
1	2	11	4	5	6			8					3	7		9*12	10											7
1	2	11	4	5	6			8					3	7		9	10											8
1	2	11	4	5	6			8				9*	3	7		12	10											9
1	2	11	4*	5	6	7		8	12				3	9			10											10
1	2	11		5	6	7		8					3			9	10	4										11
1	2	11		5	6	7		8	12				3*10			9		4										12
1	2	11		5	6	7		8					3	10		9		4										13
1	2	11		5	6			8	7				3	10		9		4										14
1	2	11		5	6*12			8	7				3	10		9		4										15
1	2	11		5	6*12			8†	7				3	10		9		14	4									16
1	2	11		5	6	10		8	7*	14			3		12	9†		4										17
1	2	11		5	6	10		8	7				3	9				4										18
1	2			5		10		8	7				3	9	6			4	11									19
1	2			5	9	10		8	7	12			3		6*		14	4	11†									20
1	2		6	5	9	10		8	7					11				4	3									21
	2		6	5	14	10		8	7				3	11	12	9*	4†				1							22
	2	12	6	5	9	10		8†	7*	14			3	11			4				1							23
	2	11	6	5					10				3	7			4				1	8	9					24
	2	4	6	5	9*							12	3	11							1	8	10	7				25
	2	14	4	5	9†				12				3	7	6*						1	8	10	11				26
	2†		6	5	11				7				12				4*		3		1	8	10	9	14			27
1			4*	6	5	11			10	7			9	3								8		12	2			28
			4	6	5	11†			10*	7		14	3	8								12	9		2	1		29
			4	6	5	11			10	7*		14	3	8								12	9		2†	1		30
			4	6	5	11			10	7*			3	8								12	14	9†	2	1		31
			4	6					10		2	7†	11	3	8	9*	5					12		14	1			32
			4	6					10		2		3	8			5					7	11	9	1			33
			4*	6					10		2	12		8			5			3		7	11	9	1			34
			4	6					10		2			8			5			3		7	11	9	1			35
			4	6					10*		2	12		8			5					7	11	9	1			36
			4	6					10*	14	2	12		3	8		5					7	11	9†	1			37
			4	6					10		2		3	8			5					7	11	9	1			38
			4	6					10*		2		3	8			5		12			7	11	9	1			39
		12	4*	6					10	14	2		3	8			5					7	11†	9	1			40
			4	6		7					2	11	3	8			5					10		9	1			41
		12	4	6					10	14	2	7*	3	8			5					11†		9	1			42
			4	6					10		2	7	3	8			5		12			11*		9	1			43
		4	12	6					10	14	2		3	8			5					11*		9†	1	7		44
		4		6					10*		2	12	3	8		9	5					11			1	7		45
		4		6					10*		2	12	3	8		9	5					11	14		1	7		46
22	30 +2s	35 +3s	36	31	43 +1s	17 +2s	1 +4s	40 +8s	25	1 +8s	8	40	39	3	8 +4s	4 +2s	20 +1s2s	16	2	5 +2s	6	13 +4s	18 +1s	18 +3s	— +1s	7	18	

Littlewoods Cup

Littlewoods Cup	Second Round	Birmingham C (a)	2-1
		(h)	1-1
	Third Round	Aston Villa (a)	0-0
		(h)	1-0
	Fourth Round	Wimbledon (h)	1-0
	Fifth Round	Derby Co (h)	1-1
		(a)	0-0
		(h)	2-1
	Semi-final	Oldham Ath (a)	0-6
		(h)	3-0
FA Cup	Third Round	Torquay U (a)	0-1

WEST HAM UNITED

Player and Position	Ht	Wt	Birth Date	Place	Source	Clubs	League App	Gls
Goalkeepers								
Steven Banks	5 11	11 04	9 2 72	Hillingdon	Trainee	West Ham U	—	—
Allen McKnight	6 1	13 07	27 1 64	Antrim	Distillery	Celtic	12	—
						Albion R (loan)	36	—
						West Ham U	23	—
Ludek Miklosko	6 3	12 08	9 12 61	Ostrava	Banik Ostrava	West Ham U	18	—
Phil Parkes	6 3	15 01	8 8 50	Sedgeley	Amateur	Walsall	52	—
						QPR	344	—
						West Ham U	344	—
Defenders								
Julian Dicks	5 7	10 08	8 8 68	Bristol	Apprentice	Birmingham C	89	1
						West Ham U	82	11
Colin Foster	6 4	13 10	16 7 64	Chislehurst	Apprentice	Orient	174	10
						Nottingham F	72	5
						West Ham U	22	1
Tony Gale	6 1	13 10	19 11 59	London	Apprentice	Fulham	277	19
						West Ham U	196	3
Chris Harwood	5 11	12 00	19 4 70	Hendon	Trainee	West Ham U	—	—
Paul Hilton‡	6 1	11 06	8 10 59	Oldham	Amateur	Bury	148	39
						West Ham U	60	7
Tommy McQueen	5 7	11 01	1 4 63	Bellshill	Gartcosh U	Clyde	112	1
						Aberdeen	53	4
						West Ham U	30	—
Alvin Martin	6 1	13 03	29 7 58	Bootle	Apprentice	West Ham U	374	23
George Parris	5 9	12 00	11 9 64	Ilford	Apprentice	West Ham U	158	7
Andy Pearson*	5 7	10 06	27 11 69	London	Trainee	West Ham U	—	—
Steven Potts	5 7	10 04	7 5 67	Hartford, USA	Apprentice	West Ham U	78	—
Ray Stewart	5 11	11 11	7 9 59	Perth	Errol Rovers	Dundee U	44	5
						West Ham U	340	62
Gary Strodder	6 1	11 04	1 4 65	Leeds	Apprentice	Lincoln C	132	6
						West Ham U	65	2
Midfield								
Martin Allen	5 10	11 00	14 8 65	Reading	School	QPR	136	16
						West Ham U	39	9
Ian Bishop	5 9	10 06	29 5 65	Liverpool	Apprentice	Everton	1	—
						Crewe Alex (loan)	4	—
						Carlisle U	132	14
						Bournemouth	44	2
						Manchester U	19	2
						West Ham U	17	2
Liam Brady*	5 9	11 02	13 2 56	Dublin	Apprentice	Arsenal	235	43
						Juventus	57	13
						Sampdoria	57	6
						Internazionale	58	5
						Ascoli	17	—
						West Ham U	89	9
Alan Devonshire*	5 11	11 00	13 4 56	London	Southall & Ealing	West Ham U	358	29
Kevin Keen	5 6	9 08	25 2 67	Amersham	Apprentice	West Ham U	104	14
Paul Kelly	5 7	10 13	12 10 69	Bexley	Trainee	West Ham U	1	—
Simon Livett	5 10	12 02	8 1 69	Newham	YTS	West Ham U	—	—
Stewart Robson	5 11	11 13	6 11 64	Billericay	Apprentice	Arsenal	151	16
						West Ham U	68	4
Matthew Rush	5 11	12 10	6 8 71	Dalston	Trainee	West Ham U	—	—
Forwards								
Simon Clarke	5 11	11 02	23 9 71	Chelmsford	Trainee	West Ham U	—	—
Eamonn Dolan	5 10	12 03	20 9 67	Essex	Apprentice	West Ham U	15	3
						Bristol C (loan)	3	—

WEST HAM UNITED

Foundation: Thames Ironworks FC was formed by employees of this shipbuilding yard in 1895 and entered the FA Cup in their initial season at Chatham and the London League in their second. Short of funds, the club was wound up in June 1900 and relaunched a month later as West Ham United. Connection with the Ironworks was not finally broken until four years later.

First Football League game: 30 August, 1919, Division 2, v Lincoln City (h) D 1-1 – Hufton; Cope, Lee; Lane, Fenwick, McCrae; D. Smith, Moyes (1), Puddefoot, Morris, Bradshaw.

Managers (and Secretary-managers)
Syd King 1902–32, Charlie Paynter 1932–50, Ted Fenton 1950–61, Ron Greenwood 1961–74 (continued as GM to 1977), John Lyall 1974–89, Lou Macari 1989–90, Billy Bonds 1990– .

Player and Position	Ht	Wt	Birth Date	Birth Place	Source	Clubs	League App	Gls
Frank McAvennie	5 9	11 00	22 11 59	Glasgow	Johnstone B	St Mirren	135	50
						West Ham U	85	33
						Celtic	55	27
						West Ham U	14	—
Paul McMenemy‡	5 10	11 12	5 11 66	Farnborough	Apprentice	West Ham U	—	—
						Aldershot (loan)	10	5
						Northampton T (loan)	4	2
Trevor Morley	5 11	12 01	20 3 62	Nottingham	Nuneaton	Northampton T	107	39
						Manchester C	72	18
						West Ham U	19	10
Jimmy Quinn	6 1	12 00	18 11 59	Belfast	Oswestry T	Swindon T	49	10
						Blackburn R	71	17
						Swindon T	64	30
						Leicester C	31	6
						Bradford C	35	14
						West Ham U	21	12
Leroy Rosenior	6 1	11 10	24 3 64	London	School	Fulham	54	16
						QPR	38	7
						Fulham	34	20
						West Ham U	42	14
Stuart Slater	5 9	10 04	27 3 69	Sudbury	Apprentice	West Ham U	60	8

Trainees
Beard, Simon A; Gibbons, Anthony G; Hancock, Darren J; Heffer, Steven P; Horlock, Kevin; Macari, Michael; Marquis, Paul R; Padington, John P; Purdie, John D; Reed, Peter M.

Associated Schoolboys
Bates, Jonathon P; Canham, Scott; Fleming, Shaun A; Fletcher, Paul A; Geraghty, Jason W; Gore, Kevin E; Holman, Mathias J; Johnson, Roy J; Knight, Jason G; Pallecaros, George K; Pearson, Philip; Perkins, Declan O; Rainbow, James R; Read, Paul; Reeve, Mark E; Reeves, Steven T; Rose, Christopher A; Stone, Damon T; Victory, Jamie C.

Associated Schoolboys who have accepted the club's offer of a Traineeship/Contract
Basham, Michael; Comerford, Anthony M; Harriott, Marvin; Lowe, John; Miller, Simon R; Small, Keith; White, David T; Williamson, Daniel A.

582

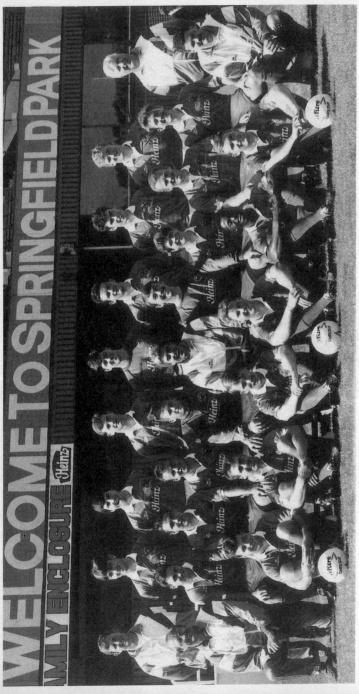

WIGAN ATHLETIC 1989-90 *Back row (left to right):* David Philpotts (Coach). Darren Patterson, Paul Beesley. Joe Parkinson. Phil Hughes. Alan Johnson. Allen Tankard. Peter Atherton.
Tommy Cavanagh (Coach).
Centre row: David Crompton (Coaching). Jonathon Crompton, Andrew Pilling, Steve Senior, Ian Banford. Bryan Hamilton (Manager), Nigel Adkins. Neill Rimmer. David Thompson,
Ray Woods, Alex Cribley (Physiotherapist).
Front row: Shaun Fallon. Tony Ward, Bryan Griffiths, Simon Andrews. Don Page. Jimmy Carberry.

Division 3   **WIGAN ATHLETIC**

Springfield Park, Wigan. Telephone Wigan (0942) 44433. Commercial Dept: (0942) 43067. Latics Line: 0898 888 636.

Ground capacity: 11,434.

Record attendance: 27,500 v Hereford U, 12 Dec, 1953.

Record receipts: £40,577 v Leeds U, FA Cup 6th rd, 15 Mar, 1987.

Pitch measurements: 117yd × 72yd.

President: T. Hitchen.

Chairman: W. Kenyon. *Vice-Chairman:*

Directors: J. A. Bennett, J. D. Fillingham, W. Howard, S. Jackson, W. Pearce.

Chief Executive: Bryan Hamilton. *Vice-President:* J. H. Farrimond.

Secretary: Mark A. Blackbourne. *Commercial Manager:* John Crossley.

Manager: Bryan Hamilton. *Assistant Manager:*

Coaches: Dave Philpotts and Alex Cribley. *Physio:* Alex Cribley.

Year Formed: 1932.

Club Nickname: The Latics'.

Record League Victory: 7-2 v Scunthorpe U (away), Division 4, 12 March 1982 – Tunks; McMahon, Glenn, Wignall, Cribley, Methven (1), O'Keefe, Barrow (1), Bradd (3), Houghton (2), Evans.

Record Cup Victory: 6-0 v Carlisle U (away), FA Cup, 1st rd, 24 November 1934 – Caunce; Robinson, Talbot; Paterson, Watson, Tufnell; Armes (2), Robson (1), Roberts (2), Felton, Scott (1).

Record Defeat: 1-6 v Bristol R, Division 3, 3 March, 1990.

Most League Points (2 for a win): 55, Division 4, 1978–79 and 1979–80.

Most League Points (3 for a win): 91, Division 4, 1981–82.

Most League Goals: 80, Division 4, 1981–82.

Highest League Scorer in Season: Les Bradd, 19, Division 4, 1981–82.

Most League Goals in Total Aggregate: Peter Houghton, 62, 1978–84.

Most Capped Player: None.

Most League Appearances: Colin Methven, 296, 1979–86.

Record Transfer Fee Received: £175,000 from Leyton Orient for Paul Beesley, October 1989.

Record Transfer Fee Paid: £65,000 to Everton for Eamon O'Keefe, January 1982.

Football League Record: 1978 elected to Division 4; 1982 – Division 3.

Honours: Best season in Division 3; 4th, 1985–86, 1986–87; Division 4 – Promoted (3rd) 1981–82. *FA Cup:* 4th rd 1979–80, 1985–86. *Football League Cup* best season: 4th rd, 1981–82. *Freight Rover Trophy:* Winners 1984–85.

Colours: Blue shirts, white shorts, blue stockings. **Change colours:** White shirts, black short, white stockings.

WIGAN ATHLETIC 1989–90 LEAGUE RECORD

Match No.	Date	Venue	Opponents	Result	H/T Score	Lg. Pos.	Goalscorers	Atten- dance
1	Aug 19	A	Blackpool	D	0-0	0-0	—	4561
2	26	H	Rotherham U	L	0-3	0-0	21	2659
3	Sept 2	A	Bury	D	2-2	2-2	20	Hilditch 2	3122
4	9	H	Northampton T	D	0-0	0-0	20		2459
5	16	A	Leyton Orient	L	0-1	0-0	21		4280
6	23	H	Cardiff C	D	1-1	0-1	21	Pilling	2345
7	26	H	Tranmere R	L	1-3	0-1	—	Griffiths (pen)	3136
8	30	A	Brentford	L	1-3	0-1	23	Pilling	4647
9	Oct 7	A	Bolton W	L	2-3	2-1	24	Brown (og), Hilditch	6462
10	14	H	Shrewsbury T	D	0-0	0-0	24		2279
11	17	A	Huddersfield T	L	0-2	0-0	—		5119
12	21	H	Walsall	W	3-0	1-0	23	Taylor (og), Carberry, Daley	2229
13	28	A	Bristol C	L	0-3	0-2	23		6365
14	31	H	Reading	W	3-1	1-1	—	Hilditch, Ward, Tankard (pen)	2029
15	Nov 4	H	Crewe Alex	W	1-0	1-0	21	Daley	2727
16	11	A	Notts Co	D	1-1	1-0	22	Carberry	5449
17	25	A	Fulham	L	0-4	0-1	23		3156
18	Dec 1	H	Birmingham C	W	1-0	0-0	—	Ward	2600
19	16	H	Swansea C	W	2-0	1-0	16	Daley 2	2034
20	26	A	Chester C	D	0-0	0-0	19		3165
21	30	A	Preston NE	D	1-1	1-1	19	Rimmer	7220
22	Jan 1	A	Mansfield T	W	4-0	1-0	16	Thompson, Hilditch 3	2477
23	13	A	Rotherham U	W	2-1	1-1	14	Daley, Pilling	6055
24	20	H	Blackpool	D	1-1	1-0	14	Pilling	3179
25	Feb 3	A	Cardiff C	D	1-1	1-0	15	Pilling	3218
26	10	H	Leyton Orient	L	0-2	0-1	18		2396
27	13	H	Bury	D	0-0	0-0	—		2104
28	17	A	Birmingham C	D	0-0	0-0	17		5473
29	24	H	Fulham	W	2-1	0-0	15	Griffiths 2 (1 pen)	2163
30	Mar 3	A	Bristol R	L	1-6	0-2	17	Carberry	5169
31	6	H	Brentford	W	2-1	1-0	—	Pilling, Thompson	2052
32	9	A	Tranmere R	L	0-2	0-1	—		9604
33	13	A	Northampton T	D	1-1	0-0	—	Daley	2172
34	16	H	Bolton W	W	2-0	2-0	—	Griffiths, Brown (og)	6850
35	20	A	Shrewsbury T	W	3-1	2-0	—	Thompson 3	2297
36	24	H	Huddersfield T	L	1-2	0-1	13	Parkinson	3167
37	31	A	Walsall	W	2-1	1-1	12	Griffiths, Skipper (og)	3182
38	Apr 4	H	Bristol R	L	1-2	1-0	—	Baraclough	2352
39	7	H	Bristol C	L	2-3	1-1	14	Baraclough, Parkinson	3281
40	10	A	Reading	L	0-2	0-1	—		3099
41	14	A	Mansfield T	L	0-1	0-1	15		2421
42	16	H	Chester C	W	1-0	0-0	13	Griffiths (pen)	2277
43	21	A	Swansea C	L	0-3	0-0	15		3141
44	24	H	Preston NE	L	0-1	0-1	—		4454
45	28	H	Notts Co	D	1-1	0-1	17	Patterson	2433
46	May 5	A	Crewe Alex	L	2-3	1-1	18	Griffiths, Johnson	3389

Final League Position: 18

GOALSCORERS

League (48): Griffiths 7 (3 pens), Hilditch 7, Daley 6, Pilling 6, Thompson 5, Carberry 3, Baraclough 2, Parkinson 2, Ward 2, Johnson 1, Patterson 1, Rimmer 1, Tankard 1 (pen), own goals 4.
Littlewoods Cup (7): Thompson 2, Griffiths 1, Hilditch 1, Page 1, Parkinson 1, Senior 1.
FA Cup (4): Griffiths 1, Hilditch 1, Johnson 1, Page 1.

Appearance grid (shirt numbers worn each match; * and † denote substitutions). Player columns left → right: Adkins, Senior, Tankard, Rimmer, Atherton, Beesley, Thompson, Parkinson, Hilditch, Page, Carberry, Patterson, Fallon, Johnson, Griffiths, Pilling, Nugent, McGarvey, Crompton, Ward, Daley, Kelly, Hughes, Rogerson, Taylor, Whitworth, Baraclough.

Adkins	Senior	Tankard	Rimmer	Atherton	Beesley	Thompson	Parkinson	Hilditch	Page	Carberry	Patterson	Fallon	Johnson	Griffiths	Pilling	Nugent	McGarvey	Crompton	Ward	Daley	Kelly	Hughes	Rogerson	Taylor	Whitworth	Baraclough	Match No.
1	2	3	4	5	6	7	8	9	10	11*	12																1
1	2		4	5	6	7	8*	9	10	11†		3	12	14													2
1	2	3	4	5	6	7	8	9	10*14				11†12														3
1	2	3	4	5	6	7	8	9	10*12				11														4
1	2*	3	4	5	6	7	8		10†	9	12		11		14												5
1	2	3	4	5	6	7	8		10†	9*12			11	14													6
1	2	3	4	5	6	7	8		10†14	12			11	9*													7
1	2	3	4*	5	6	7		14		12			11	8	9		10†										8
1		3	4	2	6		10		14	5	12		11†	8	9		7*										9
1	2	3	4	5	6	7	8	10		11	12								9*								10
1	2	3	4	5	6	7		9	10†14	12			11	8*													11
1	2	3	4	5			8	7	6	11				9*					12	10							12
1	2	3	4	5		7*	9		6	12	11								8†10	14							13
	2	3		5		8	10	7	6	11*			4	9	12							1					14
	2	3		5	10	8†	7*	6	12	11			4	9	14							1					15
	2	3		5		8	10	7*	6	12	11		4†	9	14							1					16
	2	3		5	14	8*10†	7	6	12	11		4	9									1					17
	2	3	8	5	14	7*	6	12	11†	9		4	10									1					18
	2	3	8	5		7	4	12	6	11	9*								10			1					19
	2†	3	8	5	7	4	9		6*	12	11	14						10				1					20
	2	3	8	5		7	4	9	12	6	11*							10				1					21
	2	3	8	5		7†	4	9	12	6	11*14						10					1					22
	2	3	8	5		7	4*		6	11	9	12	10									1					23
	2	3		5	7	4	12	6*11	9	8†10												1	14				24
	2†	3	8	5	7		4*11	6	12	9			10									1	14				25
		3	8	5	7	9*12	6	11†	4	10			1	14												2	26
		3	8	5	7	2	9†11*	6	12	4	14	10	1														27
	2	3	8	5	7	4	11	12	6		9		10*									1					28
	2	3	8	5	7	4†	11*14	6	12	9		10											1					29
	2	3		5	7	4	12	14	6	11†	9	10										1	8*				30
	2	3	8	5	7	4	6	11	9	10												1					31
	2	3	8	5	7	4	12	14	6	11†	9*	10										1					32
	2	3	8	5	7	4	12	6	11	9	10*											1					33
	2	3	8	5	7	4	6	11	9	10												1					34
	2	3	8	5	7	4	12	14	6	11*	9	10†										1					35
	2	3	8	5	7	4	6	11	9*	10†												1	14		12		36
	2	3	8	5	4	14	12	6	11*	7†	10											1				9	37
	2	3		5	4	8	14	7*12	6	11	10†											1				9	38
	2	3		5	7	4	10	12	8	6	11*											1				9	39
	2	3	8	12	7	4	10†	5	6	11	14											1				9*	40
	2	3	8	5	7	4	10†12	14	6	11												1				9*	41
	2	3	8	5	7	4	12	6	11	10												1				9*	42
	2	3	8	5	7	4	12	14	6	11	10†											1				9*	43
	2	3	8	5	7	4	10	12†14	6	11												1				9*	44
	2	3	8	5	7	4	10	12	14	6	11*	9†										1					45
	2	3	8	5	7	4	10*12	14	6	11	9†											1					46
13	43	45	38	45	11	38	33	20	18	15	12	1	26	40	21	—	3	1	8	32	—	33	1	—	1	8	Totals

Substitute appearances: + 1s (Atherton) · + 1s (Thompson) · + 1s 7s 17s 17s (Hilditch, Page, Carberry, Patterson) · + 1s 7s (Johnson) · + 5s 5s 1s (Griffiths, Pilling) · + 3s 1s 4s (Daley, Kelly) · + 2s 1s (Hughes, Rogerson) · + 1s 1s (Whitworth, Baraclough)

Littlewoods Cup	First Round	Wrexham (a)	0-0
		(h)	5-0
	Second Round	Liverpool (a)	2-5
		(h)	0-3
		(at Anfield)	
FA Cup	First Round	Mansfield T (a)	2-0
	Second Round	Carlisle U (h)	2-0
	Third Round	Watford (a)	0-2

WIGAN ATHLETIC

Player and Position	Ht	Wt	Birth Date	Place	Source	Clubs	League App	Gls
Goalkeepers								
Nigel Adkins	5 11	12 07	11 3 65	Birkenhead	Apprentice	Tranmere R	86	—
						Wigan Ath	53	—
Ian Banford‡	6 0	12 00	13 5 71	Liverpool	Trainee	Wigan Ath	—	—
Philip Hughes	5 11	12 07	19 11 64	Manchester	Apprentice	Manchester U	—	—
						Leeds U	6	—
						Bury	80	—
						Wigan Ath	80	—
Defenders								
Peter Atherton	5 11	12 03	6 4 70	Orrell	Trainee	Wigan Ath	102	1
Darren Patterson	6 1	12 00	15 10 69	Belfast	Trainee	WBA	—	—
						Wigan Ath	29	1
Steve Senior*	5 8	11 04	15 5 64	Sheffield	Apprentice	York C	168	6
						Darlington (loan)	5	—
						Northampton T	4	—
						Wigan Ath	109	3
Allen Tankard	5 10	11 07	21 5 69	Fleet	Apprentice	Southampton	5	—
						Wigan Ath	78	2
Neil Whitworth§			12 4 72	Ince		Wigan Ath	2	—
Midfield								
James Carberry	5 10	11 02	13 10 60	Liverpool	Trainee	Everton	—	—
						Wigan Ath	32	3
Shaun Fallon*	5 9	10 12	10 9 70	Widnes	Trainee	Wigan Ath	3	—
Alan Johnson	5 11	11 12	19 2 71	Ince	Trainee	Wigan Ath	41	2
Joe Parkinson	5 11	12 02	11 6 71	Eccles	Trainee	Wigan Ath	45	3
Andy Pilling	5 10	11 04				Wigan Ath	85	11
Neill Rimmer	5 6	10 03	13 11 67	Liverpool	Apprentice	Everton	1	—
						Ipswich T	22	3
						Wigan Ath	63	4
Lee Rogerson			21 3 67	Darwen	Clitheroe	Wigan Ath	3	—
David Thompson	5 11	12 04	27 5 62	Manchester	Local	Rochdale	155	13
						Manchester U (loan)	—	—
						Notts Co	55	8
						Wigan Ath	108	14
Tony Ward*	5 6	10 02	4 4 70	Warrington	Trainee	Everton	—	—
						Doncaster R (loan)	4	—
						Wigan Ath	11	2
Forwards								
Simon Andrews	5 10	11 00	26 9 70	Macclesfield	Trainee	Manchester U	—	—
						Wigan Ath	—	—
Jonathan Crompton‡	5 9	10 07	25 1 70	Orrell	Trainee	Wigan Ath	1	—

WIGAN ATHLETIC

Foundation: Following the demise of Wigan Borough and their resignation from the Football League in 1931, a public meeting was called in Wigan at the Queen's Hall in May 1932 at which a new club Wigan Athletic, was founded in the hope of carrying on in the Football League. With this in mind, they bought Springfield Park for £2,250, but failed to gain admission to the Football League until 46 years later.

First Football League game: 19 August, 1978, Division 4, v Hereford U (a) D 0-0 – Brown; Hinnigan, Gore, Gillibrand, Ward, Davids, Corrigan, Purdie, Houghton, Wilkie, Wright.

Managers (and Secretary-managers)
Charlie Spencer 1932–37, Jimmy Milne 1946–47, Bob Pryde 1949–52, Ted Goodier 1952–54, Walter Crook 1954–55, Ron Suart 1955–56, Billy Cooke 1956, Sam Barkas 1957, Trevor Hitchen 1957–58, Malcolm Barrass 1958–59, Jimmy Shirley 1959, Pat Murphy 1959–60, Allenby Chilton 1960, Johnny Ball 1961–63, Allan Brown 1963–66, Alf Craig 1966–67, Harry Leyland 1967–68, Alan Saunders 1968, Ian McNeill 1968–70, Gordon Milne 1970–72, Les Rigby 1972–74, Brian Tiler 1974–76, Ian McNeill 1976–81, Larry Lloyd 1981–83, Harry McNally 1983–85, Bryan Hamilton 1985–86, Ray Mathias 1986–89, Bryan Hamilton 1989–   .

Player and Position	Ht	Wt	Birth Date	Birth Place	Source	Clubs	League App	Gls
Phil Daley			12 4 67	Walton	Newton	Wigan Ath	33	6
Bryan Griffiths	5 9	11 00	26 1 65	Prescot	St Helens T	Wigan Ath	74	15
Mark Hilditch*	6 0	12 01	20 8 60	Royton	Amateur	Rochdale	197	40
						Tranmere R	49	12
						Wigan Ath	103	26
Steve Nugent§			7 5 73	Wigan	Trainee	Wigan Ath	1	—
Don Page	5 10	11 04	18 1 64	Manchester	Runcorn	Wigan Ath	40	2
Robin Taylor*			14 1 71	Rinteln	Leicester C†	Wigan Ath	1	—
Ray Woods	5 11	11 00	7 6 65	Birkenhead	Apprentice	Tranmere R	7	2
					Colne D	Wigan Ath	8	—

Trainees
Appleton, Stephen; Blakemore, Colin; Bourne, George M; Cunliffe, Lee J; Derbyshire, Scott L; Dykes, Steven; Edwardson, Barry J; Hulme, Gary B; Maddox, Daniel W; Mason, Graham; Musker, Paul H; Nugent, Stephen; Phoenix, Stuart G; Sonner, Daniel J; Whitworth, Neil A; Wilson, Adam J; Woodward, Christopher J.

Associated Schoolboys
Brown, David; Brown, Jason; Chamberlain, Stuart; Cunliffe, Lee J; Curd, Collin D; Dixon, Stephen; Gallagher, Andrew N; Gallagher, Simon K; Gwinnett, Martin; Harrison, Anthony; Hunt, Mark; Kenyon, Terence A; Kirwin, Paul; Lewis, Gary; Little, Wayne; O'Brien, Stephen J; Peoples, Martin; Riley, Michael P; Saint, Darren; Strong, Greg; Taylor, Steven; Thomas, Craig; Wallace, Jeffrey R; Williamson, Colin.

Associated Schoolboys who have accepted the club's offer of a Traineeship/Contract
Leyland, Neil T; Roberts, Andrew; Robertson, John.

588

WIMBLEDON 1989–90 *Back row (left to right):* Gerald Dobbs, David Cooper, Garry Brooke, Scott Fitzgerald, Lawrie Sanchez, Steve Allen (Physiotherapist), John Scales, Keith Curle, Detzi Kruszynski, Mark Quamina, Mark Fiore.
Centre row: Dean Blackwell, Alan Cork, Carlton Fairweather, John Fashanu, Eric Young, John Gayle, Paul Miller, Steve Cotterill, Clive Goodyear, Roger Joseph.
Front row: Bobby Gould (Manager), Terry Gibson, Terry Phelan, Hans Segers, Neil Sullivan, Dennis Wise, Vaughan Ryan, David Kemp (Coach).

Division 1 **WIMBLEDON**

Plough Lane Ground, Durnsford Road, Wimbledon, London SW19 (first used in 1912). Telephone 01-946 6311. Commercial Manager: 01-947 0867.

Ground capacity: 13,806.

Record attendance: 18,000 v HMS Victory in FA Amateur Cup 3rd rd, 1934–35.

Record receipts: £80,680 v Chelsea, Division 1, 19 August 1989.

Pitch measurements: 110yd × 73yd.

President: Rt Hon Lord Michael Havers of Bury St Edmunds.

Chairman: S. G. Reed. *Vice-Chairman:* J. Lelliott.

Managing Director: S. Hammam.

Directors: P. Cork, P. R. Cooper, N. N. Namman.

Manager: Bobby Gould.

Coach: Ray Harford. *Physio:* Steve Allen.

Secretary: Adrian Cook. *Commercial Manager:* Reg Davis.

Year Formed: 1889. *Turned Professional:* 1964. *Ltd Co.:* 1964.

Previous Name: Wimbledon Old Centrals 1899–1905.

Club Nickname: 'The Dons'.

Record League Victory: 6-0 v Newport C, Division 3, 3 September 1983 – Beasant; Peters, Winterburn, Galliers, Morris, Hatter, Evans (2), Ketteridge (1), Cork (3 incl. 1p), Downes, Hodges (Driver).

Record Cup Victory: 7-2 v Windsor & Eton, FA Cup, 1st rd, 22 November 1980 – Beasant; Jones, Armstrong, Galliers, Mick Smith (2), Cunningham (1), Ketteridge, Hodges, Leslie, Cork (1), Hubbick (3).

Record Defeat: 0-8 v Everton, League Cup 2nd rd, 29 August, 1978.

Most League Points (2 for a win): 61, Division 4, 1978–79.

Most League Points (3 for a win): 98, Division 4, 1982–83.

Most League Goals: 97, Division 3, 1983–84.

Highest League Scorer in Season: Alan Cork, 29, 1983–84.

Most League Goals in Total Aggregate: Alan Cork, 138, 1977–90.

Most Capped Player: Glyn Hodges 5 (13), Wales.

Most League Appearances: Alan Cork, 386, 1977–90.

Record Transfer Fee Received: £850,000 from Newcastle U for Dave Beasant, June 1988 and £850,000 from Newcastle U for Andy Thorn, August 1988.

Record Transfer Fee Paid: £500,000 to Reading for Keith Curle, October 1988.

Football League Record: 1977 Elected to Division 4; 1979–80 Division 3; 1980–81 Division 4; 1981–82 Division 3; 1982–83 Division 4; 1983–84 Division 3; 1984–86 Division 2; 1986 Division 1.

Honours: Football League: Division 1 best season 6th, 1986–87, Division 3 – Runners-up 1983–84; Division 4 – Champions 1982–83. *FA Cup:* Winners 1987–88. *Football League Cup* best season: 4th rd, 1979–80, 1983–84, 1988–89. *League Group Cup:* runners-up 1981–82.

Colours: Blue shirts yellow trim, blue shorts yellow trim, blue stockings yellow trim. **Change colours:** Red shirts green trim, red shorts green trim, red stockings green trim.

WIMBLEDON 1989–90 LEAGUE RECORD

Match No.	Date		Venue	Opponents	Result		H/T Score	Lg. Pos.	Goalscorers	Attendance
1	Aug	19	H	Chelsea	L	0-1	0-0	—		14,625
2		23	A	Derby Co	D	1-1	1-0	—	Cork	13,874
3		26	A	Arsenal	D	0-0	0-0	17		32,279
4		29	H	Millwall	D	2-2	1-1	16	Fairweather, Cork	8865
5	Sept	9	A	Crystal Palace	L	0-2	0-1	19		12,116
6		16	H	Manchester C	W	1-0	1-0	16	Fashanu	6815
7		23	A	Luton T	D	1-1	1-1	15	Kruszynski	8449
8		30	A	Southampton	D	2-2	1-0	15	Young, Wise	12,904
9	Oct	14	H	Liverpool	L	1-2	0-1	18	Wise	13,510
10		21	H	Nottingham F	L	1-3	1-2	19	Young	5184
11		28	A	Sheffield W	W	1-0	0-0	17	Gibson	13,728
12	Nov	4	H	QPR	D	0-0	0-0	18		5912
13		11	A	Tottenham H	W	1-0	0-0	13	Sanchez	26,876
14		18	A	Everton	D	1-1	0-0	14	Cotterill	21,561
15		25	H	Aston Villa	L	0-2	0-1	14		5888
16	Dec	2	A	Chelsea	W	5-2	3-2	13	Gibson 2, Wise 2, Cork	19,976
17		9	H	Derby Co	D	1-1	0-1	14	Scales	5024
18		16	A	Coventry C	L	1-2	1-1	16	Young	8308
19		26	H	Charlton Ath	W	3-1	2-0	12	Curle (pen), Kruszynski, Gayle	5988
20		30	H	Manchester U	D	2-2	1-0	14	Young, Cork	9622
21	Jan	1	A	Norwich C	W	1-0	0-0	12	Gibson	16,680
22		13	H	Arsenal	W	1-0	0-0	12	Bennett	13,793
23		20	A	Millwall	D	0-0	0-0	11		11,780
24	Feb	10	A	Manchester C	D	1-1	0-0	12	Cork	24,126
25		14	H	Luton T	L	1-2	0-0	—	Wise	3496
26		24	A	Aston Villa	W	3-0	0-0	11	Fashanu 2 (1 pen), Miller	29,325
27	Mar	3	H	Everton	W	3-1	1-1	9	Fashanu 2 (1 pen), Wise	6512
28		17	H	Southampton	D	3-3	2-1	11	Young, Scales, Fashanu	5382
29		24	H	Sheffield W	D	1-1	0-0	12	Fashanu (pen)	5034
30		31	A	Nottingham F	W	1-0	1-0	10	Wise	16,821
31	Apr	3	A	Liverpool	L	1-2	0-2	—	Gibson	33,319
32		14	H	Norwich C	D	1-1	0-1	12	Fashanu	4638
33		17	A	Charlton Ath	W	2-1	2-0	—	Wise, Fashanu (pen)	5679
34		21	H	Coventry C	D	0-0	0-0	11		4086
35		28	H	Tottenham H	W	1-0	1-0	9	Fashanu	12,800
36		30	A	Manchester U	D	0-0	0-0	—		29,281
37	May	2	H	Crystal Palace	L	0-1	0-0	—		8209
38		5	A	QPR	W	3-2	1-1	8	Fashanu, Miller, Curle	9676

Final League Position: 8

GOALSCORERS

League (47): Fashanu 11 (4 pens), Wise 8, Cork 5, Gibson 5, Young 5, Curle 2 (1 pen), Kruszynski 2, Miller 2, Scales 2, Bennett 1, Cotterill 1, Fairweather 1, Gayle 1, Sanchez 1.
Littlewoods Cup (7): Gibson 3, Fashanu 2 (1 pen), Fairweather 1, McGee 1.
FA Cup (0).

Segers	Curle	Phelan	Kruszynski	Young	Scales	Joseph	Cork	Gayle	Sanchez	Wise	Brooke	McGee	Fashanu	Fairweather	Gibson	Ryan	Miller	Blackwell	Cotterill	McAllister	Bennett	Anthrobus	Goodyear	Newhouse	Fitzgerald	Match No.
1	2	3	4	5	6	7*	8	9	10	11	12															1
1	2	3	4	5	6	14	8		10	11†		7*	9	12												2
1	2	3	4	5	6		8		10	11			9	7												3
1	2	3	4	5	6		8		10	11			9*	7	12											4
1	2	3	4	5	6	14	8†		10	11			9	7*12												5
1	5	3	4		6	2†				11			9	7	10*	8	12 14									6
1	2	3	4*	5	6				14	12	11		9†	7	10	8										7
1	2	3	4	5	6		12			10*11			9	7		8										8
1	2	3	4*	5	6		14			12	11		9†	7	10	8										9
1	2	3		5	6		12	14	10	11			9†	7	4	8*										10
1	6	3		5		2			8*10	11			4†	7	9	14	12									11
1	6	3		5		2			8*10	11			4	7	9	12										12
1	6	3		5		2	12			10	11			7	9*	4	8									13
1	6	3		5		2	12			10†11			14	7	4	8*	9									14
1	6	3		5	14	2†12				11			4*	9	7	10	8									15
1	6	3	12	5	4	2	8			11				7*	9	10										16
1	6	3		5	4	2	8			11				7	9*10	12										17
1	6	3		5	4	2	8			11 12				7*	9	10										18
1	6	3	2	5	4	14	8*12			11†				7	9	10										19
1	6	3	2	5	4	12				11*			8	7	9	10										20
1	6	3	2	5	4	12				11*			8	7	9	10										21
1	6		2	5	4	8		9	10	11									3		7					22
1	6	3	8		4	2	12	9	10	11				5							7*					23
1	6	3	4		5	2†12		9	10	7			11				14				8*					24
1	2	3	4	6	5		8	9*10		11			14				12				7†					25
1	6			5	2		12		10*11			3	9		4	8						7				26
1	6			5	2					11		3	9	10	4	8						7				27
1	6			5	2		10			11		3*	9		4	8	12					7				28
1	6	3	8	5	2		12 10*			11			9		4							7				29
1	6	3	8	5	2					11			9	10*	4		14					7†				30
1	6	3	8	5	2		12			11			9	10	4							7*				31
1	6	3	8	5	2		12			11			9	10	4							7*				32
1	6	3	10	5						11			9		4	8					7*		2	12		33
1	6	3	10	5		14 12				11			9*		4	8					7†		2			34
1	6	3	10	5			12			11†			9		4	8					7*		14			35
1	6	3	10	5		2	7*								4	8	14					12 11		9†		36
1	6	3	10	5			12			11			7* 9		4	8							2			37
1	6	3	10	5		2	12			11			9†		4	8	14					7*				38
38	38	34	26	35	27	15	12	8	16	35	—	11	24	20	16	28	11	—	2	1	6	10	4	1	—	
		+		+	+	+	+	+	+			+	+			+	+	+	+			+	+			
		1s		1s	4s	19s	3s2s			2s	2s			1s	2s	3s	4s	3s			2s	1s		1s1s		

Littlewoods Cup

Littlewoods Cup	Second Round	Port Vale (a)	2-1
		(h)	3-0
	Third Round	Middlesbrough (a)	1-1
		(h)	1-0
	Fourth Round	West Ham U (a)	0-1
FA Cup	Third Round	WBA (a)	0-2

WIMBLEDON

Player and Position	Ht	Wt	Birth Date	Place	Source	Clubs	League App	Gls
Goalkeepers								
Hans Segers	5 11	12 07	30 10 61	Eindhoven	PSV Eindhoven	Nottingham F	58	—
						Stoke C (loan)	1	—
						Sheffield U (loan)	10	—
						Dunfermline Ath (loan)	4	—
						Wimbledon	71	—
Neil Sullivan	6 0	12 01	24 2 70	Sutton	Trainee	Wimbledon	—	—
Defenders								
Dean Blackwell	6 1	12 10	5 12 69	London	Trainee	Wimbledon	3	—
						Plymouth Arg (loan)	7	—
Andy Clement*	5 8	11 00	12 11 67	Cardiff	Apprentice	Wimbledon	26	—
						Bristol R (loan)	6	—
						Newport Co (loan)	5	1
Keith Curle	6 0	11 09	14 11 63	Bristol	Bristol	Bristol R	32	4
						Torquay U	16	5
						Bristol C	121	1
						Reading	40	—
						Wimbledon	56	2
Gerald Dobbs	5 8	11 07	24 1 71	London	Trainee	Wimbledon	—	—
Scott Fitzgerald	6 0	12 02	13 8 69	London	Trainee	Wimbledon	1	—
Clive Goodyear	6 0	11 04	15 1 61	Lincoln	Local	Luton T	90	4
						Plymouth Arg	106	5
						Wimbledon	26	—
Roger Joseph	5 11	11 13	24 12 65	Paddington	Juniors	Brentford	104	2
						Wimbledon	50	—
Brian McAllister	5 11	12 05	30 11 70	Glasgow	Trainee	Wimbledon	3	—
Terry Phelan	5 8	10 00	16 3 67	Manchester		Leeds U	14	—
						Swansea C	45	—
						Wimbledon	93	—
John Scales	6 0	12 02	4 7 66	Harrogate		Leeds U	—	—
						Bristol R	72	2
						Wimbledon	91	8
Eric Young	6 2	13 00	25 3 60	Singapore	Slough T	Brighton & HA	126	10
						Wimbledon	99	9
Midfield								
Michael Bennett	5 10	11 11	27 7 69	London	Apprentice	Charlton Ath	35	2
						Wimbledon	7	1
Detsi Kruszynski	6 0	12 12	14 10 61	Divschav	Homburg	Wimbledon	43	2
Paul McGee	5 6	9 10	17 5 68	Dublin	Bohemians	Colchester U	3	—
						Wimbledon	14	1
Aiden Newhouse	6 0	12 00	23 5 72	Wallasey	Trainee	Chester C	44	6
						Wimbledon	2	—
Mark Quamina	5 10	11 07	25 11 69	St Helier	Trainee	Wimbledon	1	—
Vaughan Ryan	5 8	10 12	2 9 68	Westminster		Wimbledon	59	1
						Sheffield U (loan)	3	—
Lawrie Sanchez	5 11	11 07	22 10 59	Lambeth	Amateur	Reading	262	28
						Wimbledon	183	24
Dennis Wise	5 6	9 05	15 12 66	Kensington		Wimbledon	135	27
Forwards								
Steve Anthrobus	6 2	12 13	10 11 68	Lewisham		Millwall	21	4
						Southend U (loan)	—	—
						Wimbledon	10	—
Garry Brooke*	5 7	11 00	24 11 60	Bethnal Green	Apprentice Groningen	Tottenham H	73	15
						Norwich C	14	2
						Wimbledon	12	—
						Stoke C (loan)	8	—

WIMBLEDON

Foundation: Old boys from Central School formed this club as Wimbledon Old Centrals in 1889. Their earliest successes were in the Clapham League before switching to the Southern Suburban League in 1902.

First Football League game: 20 August, 1978, Division 4, v Halifax T (h) D 3-3 – Guy; Bryant (1), Galvin, Donaldson, Aitken, Davies, Galliers, Smith, Connell (1), Holmes, Leslie (1).

Managers (and Secretary-managers)
Les Henley 1955–71, Mike Everitt 1971–73, Dick Graham 1973–74, Allen Batsford 1974–78, Dario Gradi 1978–81, Dave Bassett 1981–87, Bobby Gould 1987–90,   .

Player and Position	Ht	Wt	Birth Date	Place	Source	Clubs	League App	Gls
David Cooper	5 10	11 10	23 6 71	London	Trainee	Wimbledon	—	—
Alan Cork	6 0	12 00	4 3 59	Derby	Amateur	Derby Co	—	—
						Lincoln C (loan)	5	—
						Wimbledon	386	138
Steve Cotterill	6 1	12 05	20 7 64	Cheltenham	Burton Albion	Wimbledon	6	2
Carlton Fairweather	5 11	11 00	22 9 61	London	Tooting	Wimbledon	127	25
John Fashanu	6 1	11 12	18 9 62	Kensington	Amateur	Cambridge U	—	—
						Norwich C	7	1
						C Palace (loan)	1	—
						Lincoln C	36	10
						Millwall	50	12
						Wimbledon	138	52
John Gayle	6 4	13 01	30 7 64	Birmingham	Burton Albion	Wimbledon	13	1
Terry Gibson	5 5	10 00	23 12 62	Walthamstow	Apprentice	Tottenham H	18	4
						Coventry C	98	43
						Manchester U	23	1
						Wimbledon	52	16
Paul Miller	6 0	11 00	31 1 68	Bisley	Trainee	Wimbledon	38	7
						Newport Co (loan)	6	2
						Bristol C	3	—

Trainees
Alexander, Matthew J; Ardley, Neil C; Bond, Wayne; Castledine, Stewart M; Cooper, Keith B; Hudson, David P; McCarthy, Jamie; Pearson, Matthew J; Perry, Christopher J; Skinner, Justin J.

Associated Schoolboys
Andrews, Lee R; Bassey, Simon J; Bevis, Colin; Bowdery, David J; Di Rubbo, Franco; Fairbairn, Neil; Fewings, Neil L; Laker, Barry J; McCormack, David R; Mosley, David; Payne, Gary; Payne, Grant; Swift, Kieron; Thomas, Mark.

Associated Schoolboys who have accepted the club's offer of a Traineeship/Contract
Fear, Peter S; Marchant, Giles R; Orriss, Craig J; Rootes, Michael G; Taylor, Geoffrey J.

WOLVERHAMPTON WANDERERS 1989–90 *Back row (left to right):* Ally Robertson, Gary Bellamy, Nick Clarke, Mark Kendall, Vince Bartram, Tony Lange, Shane Westley, Floyd Streete, Mark Venus. *Centre row:* John Paskin, Robert Kelly, Andy Mutch, Steve Bull, Paul Darby (Physiotherapy), Barry Powell (Coach), Garry Pendrey (Coach), Phil Robinson, Robbie Dennison, Phil Chard, Paul McLoughlin. *Front row:* Tim Steele, Richard Hartigan, Mick Gooding, Nigel Vaughan, J. Harris (Chairman), Graham Turner (Manager), Andy Thompson, Keith Downing, Matt Green, Tom Bennett.

Division 2 WOLVERHAMPTON WANDERERS

Molineux Grounds, Wolverhampton WV1 4QR. Telephone Admin office: Wolverhampton (0902) 712181; lottery shop: 0902-27524. Commercial Office: (0902) 23166.

Ground capacity: 25,000.

Record attendance: 61,315 v Liverpool, FA Cup 5th rd, 11 Feb, 1939.

Record receipts: £110,623 v Sheffield W, FA Cup 3rd rd, 6 Jan, 1990.

Pitch measurements: 115yd × 72yd.

President: Sir Jack Haywood.

Chairman: J. Harris.

Directors: A. C. Gallagher, D. M. Gallagher, H. P. D. Glaister (Company Secretary).

Team Manager: Graham Turner.

Coaches: Garry Pendrey and Barry Powell. *Physio:* Paul Darby.

Chief Executive:

Secretary: Keither Pearson ACIS. *Commercial Manager:* Keith Butler.

Year Formed: 1877*(see Foundation). **Turned Professional:** 1888. **Ltd Co.:** 1982.

Previous Grounds: 1877, Goldthorn Hill; 1884, Dudley Road; 1889, Molineux.

Club Nickname: 'Wolves'.

Previous Name: 1880, St Luke's, Blakenhall combined with The Wanderers to become Wolverhampton Wanderers (1923) Ltd until 1982.

Record League Victory: 10-1 v Leicester C, Division 1, 15 April 1938 – Sidlow; Morris, Dowen; Galley, Cullis, Gardiner; Maguire (1), Horace Wright, Westcott (4), Jones (1), Dorsett (4).

Record Cup Victory: 14-0 v Cresswell's Brewery, FA Cup, 2nd rd, 13 November 1886 – I. Griffiths; Baugh, Mason; Pearson, Allen (1), Lowder; Hunter (4), Knight (2), Brodie (4), B. Griffiths (2), Wood. Plus one goal 'scrambled through'.

Record Defeat: 1-10 v Newton Heath, Division 1, 15 October, 1892.

Most League Points (2 for a win): 64, Division 1, 1957–58.

Most League Points (3 for a win): 92, Division 4, 1988–89.

Most League Goals: 115, Division 2, 1931–32.

Highest League Scorer in Season: Dennis Westcott, 38, Division 1, 1946–47.

Most League Goals in Total Aggregate: Bill Hartill, 164, 1928–35.

Most Capped Player: Billy Wright, 105, England (70 consecutive).

Most League Appearances: Derek Parkin, 501, 1967–82.

Record Transfer Fee Received: £1,150,000 from Manchester C for Steve Daley, September 1979.

Record Transfer Fee Paid: £1,175,000 to Aston Villa for Andy Gray, September 1979.

Football League Record: 1888 Founder Member of Football League: 1906–23 Division 2; 1923–24 Division 3 (N); 1924–32 Division 2; 1932–65 Division 1; 1965–67 Division 2; 1967–76 Division 1; 1976–77 Division 2; 1977–82 Division 1; 1982–83 Division 2; 1983–84 Division 1; 1984–85 Division 2; 1985–86 Division 3; 1986–88 Division 4; 1988–89 Division 3; 1989– Division 2.

Honours: Football League: Division 1 – Champions 1953–54, 1957–58, 1958–59; Runners-up 1937–38, 1938–39, 1949–50, 1954–55, 1959–60; Division 2 – Champions 1931–32, 1976–77; Runners-up 1966–67, 1982–83; Division 3 (N) – Champions 1923–24; Division 3– Champions 1988–89; Division 4 – Champions 1987–88. *FA Cup:* Winners 1893, 1908, 1949, 1960; Runners-up 1889, 1896, 1921, 1939. *Football League Cup:* Winners 1973–74, 1979–80. *Texaco Cup:* 1970–71; *Sherpa Van Trophy:* Winners 1988. **European Competitions:** *European Cup:* 1958–59, 1959–60. *European Cup-Winners' Cup:* 1960–61. *UEFA Cup:* 1971–72 (runners-up), 1973-74, 1974–75, 1980–81.

Colours: Gold shirts, black shorts, gold stockings. **Change colours:** All sky blue.

WOLVERHAMPTON WANDERERS 1989–90 LEAGUE RECORD

Match No.	Date	Venue	Opponents	Result		H/T Score	Lg. Pos.	Goalscorers	Atten- dance
1	Aug 19	A	Middlesbrough	L	2-4	0-2	—	Mutch, Thompson (pen)	21,727
2	26	H	Bradford C	D	1-1	0-1	21	Bull	13,784
3	Sept 3	A	Swindon T	L	1-3	0-2	—	Thompson (pen)	10,312
4	9	H	Stoke C	D	0-0	0-0	23		15,659
5	12	H	Brighton & HA	L	2-4	1-4	—	Bull, Mutch	12,338
6	16	A	Ipswich T	W	3-1	1-0	20	Mutch 2, Bellamy	14,506
7	23	H	Plymouth Arg	W	1-0	0-0	17	Paskin	13,762
8	26	A	Barnsley	D	2-2	1-1	—	Bull 2	10,161
9	30	H	Portsmouth	W	5-0	0-0	12	Dennison 2, Venus, Bull 2	13,677
10	Oct 7	H	Sheffield U	L	1-2	1-1	15	Hill (og)	19,328
11	15	A	WBA	W	2-1	1-1	—	Dennison, Bull	21,316
12	17	H	Port Vale	W	2-0	2-0	—	Mutch, Bull	18,123
13	21	A	Leeds U	L	0-1	0-1	11		28,204
14	28	H	Oldham Ath	D	1-1	0-0	10	Thompson (pen)	15,278
15	Nov 1	A	Leicester C	D	0-0	0-0	—		16,551
16	4	H	West Ham U	W	1-0	0-0	11	Bull	22,231
17	11	A	Sunderland	D	1-1	0-0	11	Mutch	20,660
18	18	H	Blackburn R	L	1-2	1-1	11	Paskin	14,695
19	25	H	Watford	L	1-3	1-1	12	Mutch	12,736
20	Dec 2	H	Middlesbrough	W	2-0	0-0	10	Cook, Thompson (pen)	12,357
21	9	A	Brighton & HA	D	1-1	0-0	10	Dennison	9817
22	16	A	Oxford U	D	2-2	1-1	10	Venus, Dennison	7825
23	26	H	Hull C	L	1-2	1-2	11	Bull	19,524
24	30	H	Bournemouth	W	3-1	2-0	10	Downing, Dennison, Mutch	15,421
25	Jan 1	A	Newcastle U	W	4-1	0-0	8	Bull 4	22,054
26	13	A	Bradford C	D	1-1	0-1	8	Bull	10,680
27	20	H	Swindon T	W	2-1	0-0	8	McLoughlin 2	17,210
28	Feb 3	A	Plymouth Arg	W	1-0	1-0	6	Mutch	10,873
29	10	H	Ipswich T	W	2-1	1-1	5	Bull, Linighan (og)	18,781
30	17	A	Stoke C	L	0-2	0-0	6		17,870
31	24	H	Watford	D	1-1	1-1	7	Bull	16,187
32	Mar 3	A	Blackburn R	W	3-2	2-2	6	McLoughlin 2, Downing	12,054
33	6	A	Portsmouth	W	3-1	1-0	—	Bellamy, Fillery (og), Bull	12,284
34	10	H	Barnsley	D	1-1	0-0	5	Bull	15,995
35	17	A	Sheffield U	L	0-3	0-1	6		18,735
36	20	H	WBA	W	2-1	1-1	—	Cook, Bull	24,475
37	24	A	Port Vale	L	1-3	0-3	7	Mutch	12,509
38	31	H	Leeds U	W	1-0	1-0	6	Mutch	22,419
39	Apr 3	A	Bournemouth	D	1-1	0-0	—	Bellamy	7448
40	10	H	Leicester C	W	5-0	2-0	—	Bull 3, Dennison 2	18,175
41	14	H	Newcastle U	L	0-1	0-1	8		19,507
42	16	A	Hull C	L	0-2	0-1	8		7851
43	21	H	Oxford U	W	2-0	1-0	8	Downing, Bull	13,556
44	28	H	Sunderland	L	0-1	0-0	8		19,463
45	May 3	A	Oldham Ath	D	1-1	0-1	—	Steele	17,468
46	5	A	West Ham U	L	0-4	0-2	10		22,509

Final League Position: 10

GOALSCORERS

League (67): Bull 24, Mutch 11, Dennison 8, McLoughlin 4, Thompson 4 (4 pens), Bellamy 3, Downing 3, Cook 2, Paskin 2, Venus 2, Steele 1, own goals 3.
Littlewoods Cup (5): Bull 2, Dennison 1, Mutch 1, Westley 1.
FA Cup (1): Bull 1.

Lange	Bellamy	Venus	Robertson	Westley	Vaughan	Thompson	Gooding	Bull	Mutch	Dennison	Downing	Chard	Steele	Paskin	McLoughlin	Kendall	Streete	Bennett	Clarke	Cook	Jones	Match No.
1	2*	3	4	5	6	7	8	9	10	11	12											1
1		3	4	5	6	7	8	9	10	11	2*12											2
1		3	4	5	6*	7	8	9	10	11			2	12								3
1		3	4	5	6	7	8	9	10	11			2*		12							4
1	2	3	4	5	6	7	8*	9	10	11†			12	14								5
	2	3		5	6		8		10	11				9		1	4	7				6
	2	3			6		8	9	10†	11*12				14		1	4	7	5			7
	2	3			6		8	9		11			10			1	4	7	5			8
	2	3	4		6		8*	9		11	12	14		10		1		7	5†			9
	2	3	4		6		8	9	10	11				7		1	5					10
	2	3		5	6*	7	8	9	10	11	12					1	4					11
		3		5	6	7		9	10	11		8	4			1		2				12
	4	3		5	14	7*	8†	9	10	11	6				12	1		2				13
	4	3		5		7	8	9	10	11	6					1		2				14
	4	3		5		7		9	10	11	6					1		2		8		15
	4	3		5		7		9	10	11	6					1		2		8		16
	4	3		5	8	7		9	10	11	6					1		2				17
	4	3		5	12	7			10	11	6*		9	14		1		2†		8		18
	4	3	2	5		7			10	11			9	14		1	6†			8*	12	19
	4	3	2	5		7			10*	11			9	12		1	6			8		20
	4	3	2	5		7		9	10	11						1	6			8		21
	4	3	2	5		7		9	10	11						1	6			8		22
	4	3	2*	5		7†		9	10	11	12		14			1	6			8		23
	4	3						9	10	11			5	7		1	6	2		8		24
	4	3						9	10	11†	5*			7	14	1	6	2		8	12	25
	4	3						9	10	11	5				12	1	6	2		8*	7	26
	4	3						9	10*	11	5				12	1	6	2		8	7	27
		3	4		12			9	10	11	5*					1	6	2		8	7	28
		3	4					9	10	11	5					1	6	2		8	7	29
		3	4					9	10	11	5				12	1	6	2		8	7*	30
	6	3	4		2			9		11	5			7		1		10		8		31
	6	3	4		2			9		11	5*			7		1		10		8	12	32
	6	3	4		2			9		11	5			7		1		10		8		33
	6	3	4		2			9	12	11				7*		1		10		8	5	34
	6	3	4		14			9	12	11	5				10†	1		2		8	7*	35
	6	3	4	5				9	10	11	7					1		2		8		36
	6	3	4	5				9	10	11	7					1		2		8		37
	6	3	4					9	10*	11	5			7		1		2		8		38
	6	3	4					9	10	11	5			7		1		2		8		39
	6		4	8	3			9	10	11	5*			7		1		2			12	40
	6	4		8	3			9	10	11				7	14	1		2†		5*12		41
	6	4	5	3				9	10*11					7	12	1		2		8		42
	6		5	3				9		11	8			7	12	10*	1		2				43
	6	4		5	3			9		11	8			7	12	10*	1		2				44
	6	4	5		3			9		11*	8			12	10		1		2		7		45
	6	4	5		3			9		11	8†			10	14	1		2		7*12		46
5	39	44	5	37	23	31	13	42	35	46	26	4	13	10	7	41	17	30	3	28	7	
	+2s	+2s			+2s						+5s	+2s	+2s	+7s	+12s					+6s		

Littlewoods Cup First Round Lincoln C (h) 1-0
  (a) 2-0
  Second Round Aston Villa (a) 1-2
  (h) 1-1
FA Cup Third Round Sheffield W (h) 1-2

WOLVERHAMPTON WANDERERS

Player and Position	Ht	Wt	Birth Date	Place	Source	Clubs	League App	Gls
Goalkeepers								
Vincent Bartram	6 2	13 04	7 8 68	Birmingham	Amateur	Wolverhampton W	1	—
						Blackpool (loan)	9	—
Mark Kendall*	6 0	12 04	20 9 58	Blackwood	Apprentice	Tottenham H	29	—
						Chesterfield (loan)	9	—
						Newport Co	272	—
						Wolverhampton W	147	—
Tony Lange	6 0	12 09	10 12 64	London	Apprentice	Charlton Ath	12	—
						Aldershot (loan)	7	—
						Aldershot	125	—
						Wolverhampton W	5	—
Defenders								
Gary Bellamy	6 2	11 05	4 7 62	Worksop	Apprentice	Chesterfield	184	7
						Wolverhampton W	106	6
Tom Bennett	5 11	11 08	12 12 69	Falkirk	Trainee	Aston Villa		
						Wolverhampton W	32	—
Nicky Clarke	5 11	12 00	20 8 67	Walsall	Apprentice	Wolverhampton W	66	1
Alistair Robertson*	5 9	12 04	9 9 52	Philipstoun	Apprentice	WBA	506	8
						Wolverhampton W	107	—
Floyd Streete*	5 11	14 00	5 5 59	Jamaica	Rivet S Utrecht	Cambridge U	125	19
						Derby Co	35	—
						Wolverhampton W	159	6
Mark Venus	6 0	11 08	6 4 67	Hartlepool		Hartlepool U	4	—
						Leicester C	61	1
						Wolverhampton W	83	2
Shane Westley	6 2	12 10	16 6 65	Canterbury	Apprentice	Charlton Ath	8	—
						Southend U	144	10
						Norwich C (loan)	—	—
						Wolverhampton W	37	—
Midfield								
Paul Cook	5 11	10 10	22 2 67	Liverpool		Wigan Ath	83	14
						Norwich C	6	—
						Wolverhampton W	28	2
Robert Dennison	5 7	11 00	30 4 63	Banbridge	Glenavon	WBA	16	1
						Wolverhampton W	142	22
Keith Downing	5 8	11 00	23 7 65	Oldbury	Mile Oak	Notts Co	23	1
						Wolverhampton W	97	5
Matt Green*	5 11	11 07	6 11 70	Dudley	Trainee	Wolverhampton W	—	—
Paul Jones	5 9	10 04	6 9 65	Walsall	Apprentice	Walsall	143	15
						Wrexham (loan)	5	—
						Wolverhampton W	13	—
Robert Kelly‡	5 9	10 13	21 12 64	Birmingham	Apprentice	Leicester C	24	1
						Tranmere R (loan)	5	2
						Wolverhampton W	16	2
Andy Thompson	5 4	10 06	9 11 67	Carnock	Apprentice	WBA	24	1
						Wolverhampton W	150	20
Nigel Vaughan*	5 5	8 10	20 5 59	Caerleon	Apprentice	Newport Co	224	32
						Cardiff C	149	42
						Reading (loan)	5	1
						Wolverhampton W	93	10
Forwards								
Steve Bull	5 11	11 04	28 3 65	Tipton	Apprentice	WBA	4	2
						Wolverhampton W	161	109
Richard Hartigan*	5 6	9 04	10 9 70	Solihull	Trainee	Wolverhampton W	—	—

WOLVERHAMPTON WANDERERS

Foundation: Another club where precise details of information are confused, due in part to the existence of an earlier Wolverhampton club which played rugby. However, it is now considered likely that it came into being in 1879 when players from St. Luke's (founded 1877) and Goldthorn (founded 1876) broke away to form Wolverhampton Wanderers Association FC.

First Football League game: 8 September, 1888, Football League, v Aston Villa (h) D 1-1 – Baynton; Baugh, Mason; Fletcher, Allen, Lowder; Hunter, Cooper, Anderson, White, Cannon. Scorer – Cox o.g.

Managers (and Secretary-managers)
George Worrall 1877–85*, John Addenbrooke 1885–1922, George Jobey 1922–24, Albert Hoskins 1924–26 (had been secretary since 1922), Fred Scotchbrook 1926–27, Major Frank Buckley 1927–44, Ted Vizard 1944–48, Stan Cullis 1948–64, Andy Beattie 1964–65, Ronnie Allen 1966–68, Bill McGarry 1968–76, Sammy Chung 1976–78, John Barnwell 1978–81, Ian Greaves 1982, Graham Hawkins 1982–84, Tommy Docherty 1984–85, Bill McGarry 1985, Sammy Chapman 1985–86, Brian Little 1986, Graham Turner 1986– .

Player and Position	Ht	Wt	Birth Date	Place	Source	Clubs	League App	Gls
Paul McLoughlin	5 10	10 07	23 12 63	Bristol	Bristol C	Cardiff C	49	4
					Gisborne C	Hereford U	74	14
						Wolverhampton W	19	4
Andy Mutch	5 10	11 00	28 12 63	Liverpool	Southport	Wolverhampton W	184	70
John Paskin	5 10	11 10	1 2 62	Capetown	Seiko	WBA	25	5
						Wolverhampton W	17	2
Tim Steele	5 9	11 00	1 2 67	Coventry	Apprentice	Shrewsbury T	61	5
						Wolverhampton W	26	2
Colin Taylor	6 0	12 07	25 12 71	Liverpool	Trainee	Wolverhampton W	—	—

Trainees
Briggs, Martyn B; Butler, David J; Farrington, Jamie G; Fennel, Neville R; Garner, James; Harnett, Andrew J; Jones, Warren G; Kelly, Andrew; Leeding, Stuart; Morgan, Stephen W; Nicholls, Alan; Read, David L; Tonner, Ian S; Urbicki, Stephen; Wilson, Justin A.

Associated Schoolboys
Allison, Steven; Beardshaw, Richard N; Capewell, Matthew J; Challenor, David; Colley, Nicholas; Crosby, David, W; Ewart, Robert; Fletcher, Mark; Goode, Mark G; Haswell, Gordon; Robbins, Simon; Smith, Jason J; Voice, Scott H; Wagstaff, Andrew T; Wakeman, Lee; Williams, Eifion W; Woodbine, Kevin.

Associated Schoolboys who have accepted the club's offer of a Traineeship/Contract
De Bont, Andrew; Williams, Lee.

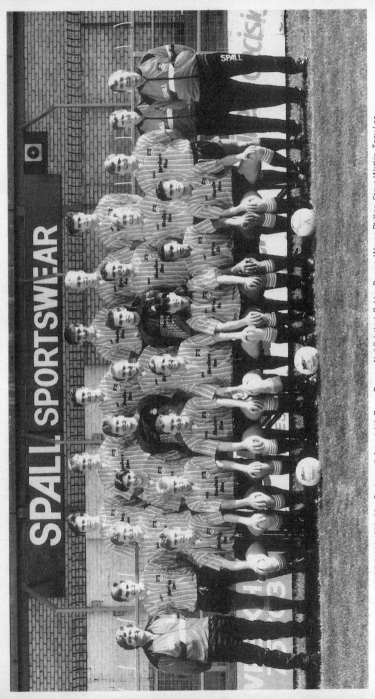

WREXHAM 1989–90 *Back row (left to right):* Roger Preece, Neil Salathiel, Robbie Barnes, Wayne Phillips, Steve Watkin, Tony Lee.
Centre row: Dixie McNeil (Manager), Mike Williams, Ollie Kearns, Gary Worthington, Vince O'Keefe, Jon Bowden, Mark Morris, Martin Filson, Darren Wright, Nigel Beaumont, Cliff Sear (Youth Team Coach), George Showell (Assistant Manager/Physiotherapist).
Front row: Mark Wrench, Geoff Hunter, Sean Reck, Joey Jones (Captain), Graham Cooper, Chris Armstrong, Andy Thackeray.

Division 4   **WREXHAM**

Racecourse Ground, Mold Road, Wrexham. Telephone Wrexham (0978) 262129. Commercial Dept: (0978) 352536. Fax No. 0978 357821. Clubcall 0898 12 16 42.

Ground capacity: 20,000 (18,000 covered).

Record attendance: 34,445 v Manchester U, FA Cup 4th rd, 26 Jan, 1957.

Record receipts: £49,761.70 v AS Roma, European Cup-Winners' Cup, 2nd rd 2nd leg, 7 Nov, 1984.

Pitch measurements: 111yd × 71yd.

President: F. Wellum.

Chairman: W. P. Griffiths.

Vice-Chairman/Managing Director: D. L. Rhodes.

Directors: F. J. Tomlinson, C. Griffiths, S. Mackreth, D. Wood, G. Palletta, B. Williams.

Manager: Brian Flynn. *Assistant Manager:* Kevin Reeves.

Secretary: D. L. Rhodes. *Player-coach:* Joey Jones.

Commercial Manager: P. Stokes. *Physio:* George Showell.

Year Formed: 1873 (oldest Club in Wales).

Turned Professional: 1912. *Ltd Co.:* 1912.

Previous Ground: Acton Park.

Club Nickname: 'Robins'.

Record League Victory: 10-1 v Hartlepools, Division 4, 3 March 1962 – Keelan; Peter Jones, McGavan; Tecwyn Jones, Fox, Ken Barnes; Ron Barnes (3), Bennion (1), Davies (3), Ambler (3), Ron Roberts.

Record Cup Victory: 6-0 v Gateshead, FA Cup, 1st rd, 20 November 1976 – Lloyd; Evans, Whittle, Davis, Roberts, Thomas (Hill), Shinton (3 incl. 1p), Sutton, Ashcroft (2), Lee (1), Griffiths. 6-0 v Charlton Ath, FA Cup, 3rd rd, 5 January 1980 – Davies; Darracott, Kenworthy, Davis, Jones (Hill), Fox, Vinter (3), Sutton, Edwards (1), McNeil (2), Carrodus.

Record Defeat: 0-9 v Brentford, Division 3, 15 October, 1963.

Most League Points (2 for a win): 61, Division 4, 1969–70 and Division 3, 1977–78.

Most League Points (3 for a win): 71, Division 4, 1988–89.

Most League Goals: 106, Division 3 (N), 1932–33.

Highest League Scorer in Season: Tom Bamford, 44, Division 3 (N), 1933–34.

Most League Goals in Total Aggregate: Tom Bamford, 175, 1928–34.

Most Capped Player: Dai Davies, 28 (51), Wales.

Most League Appearances: Arfon Griffiths, 592, 1959–61, 1962–79.

Record Transfer Fee Received: £300,000 from Manchester U for Mickey Thomas, November 1978 and from Manchester C for Bobby Shinton, July 1979.

Record Transfer Fee Paid: £210,000 to Liverpool for Joey Jones, October 1978.

Football League Record: 1921 Original Member of Division 3 (N); 1958–60 Division 3; 1960–62 Division 4; 1962–64 Division 3; 1964–70 Division 4; 1970–78 Division 3; 1978–82 Division 2; 1982–83 Division 3; 1983– Division 4.

Honours: Football League: Division 2 best season: 15th, 1978–79; Division 3 – Champions 1977–78; Division 3 (N) – Runners-up 1932–33; Division 4 – Runners-up 1969–70. *FA Cup* best season: 6th rd, 1973–74, 1977–78. *Football League Cup:* best season: 5th rd, 1961, 1978. *Welsh Cup:* Winners 21 times. Runners-up 19 times. Record number of victories and appearances in finals. **European Competition:** *European Cup-Winners' Cup:* 1972-73, 1975–76, 1978–79, 1979–80, 1984–85.

Colours: Red shirts, white shorts, red stockings. **Change colours:** Green shirts, green shorts, green stockings.

WREXHAM 1989–90 LEAGUE RECORD

Match No.	Date	Venue	Opponents	Result		H/T Score	Lg. Pos.	Goalscorers	Attendance
1	Aug 19	A	Scarborough	L	1-2	1-1	—	Worthington	2700
2	26	H	Southend	D	3-3	1-1	17	Jones, Buxton (pen), Thackeray	2011
3	Sept 2	A	Rochdale	W	3-0	2-0	9	Beaumont, Flynn 2	2331
4	5	H	Stockport C	L	0-1	0-0	—		2333
5	9	H	Halifax T	W	2-1	1-0	9	Worthington 2	1700
6	16	A	Hereford U	D	0-0	0-0	9		3173
7	23	H	Lincoln C	L	0-2	0-0	12		2002
8	30	A	York C	L	0-1	0-0	17		2196
9	Oct 7	A	Carlisle U	L	0-1	0-0	17		4235
10	14	H	Aldershot	D	2-2	1-0	19	Worthington, Kearns	1416
11	17	A	Colchester U	W	3-1	1-1	—	Reck, Worthington 2 (1 pen)	2564
12	21	H	Cambridge U	L	2-3	0-1	21	Cooper, Kearns	1541
13	28	A	Maidstone U	L	0-2	0-2	21		1768
14	31	H	Torquay U	D	1-1	1-1	—	Worthington	1225
15	Nov 4	A	Hartlepool U	L	0-3	0-1	21		1736
16	11	H	Grimsby T	L	0-1	0-1	21		1658
17	25	A	Exeter C	D	1-1	0-1	21	Hunter	3522
18	Dec 2	H	Chesterfield	L	0-2	0-0	21		1619
19	26	A	Doncaster R	D	2-2	1-1	22	Hunter, Buxton (pen)	3668
20	30	A	Gillingham	L	0-1	0-1	22		3733
21	Jan 1	H	Scunthorpe U	D	0-0	0-0	22		1887
22	6	H	Peterborough U	W	2-1	0-0	—	Buxton, Hunter	1937
23	12	A	Southend U	L	1-2	0-1	—	Buxton (pen)	3005
24	20	H	Scarborough	L	0-2	0-0	23		1756
25	26	A	Halifax T	L	2-4	2-3	—	Cooper 2	1436
26	Feb 3	A	Lincoln C	L	0-1	0-0	24		3030
27	10	H	Hereford U	D	0-0	0-0	24		2171
28	13	H	Rochdale	D	1-1	0-0	—	Chapman (og)	1552
29	17	A	Chesterfield	L	0-3	0-2	23		3799
30	24	H	Exeter C	D	1-1	0-0	24	Beaumont	2128
31	Mar 3	A	Peterborough U	L	1-3	1-2	24	Youds	3990
32	6	H	York C	W	2-0	0-0	—	Sertori, Preece R	1780
33	9	A	Stockport Co	W	2-0	1-0	—	Beaumont, Wright	4177
34	13	H	Burnley	W	1-0	1-0	—	Thackeray	4362
35	17	H	Carlisle U	W	1-0	0-0	23	Thackeray	3409
36	24	H	Colchester U	W	3-2	0-1	23	Worthington 2, Thackeray	4653
37	27	A	Aldershot	L	0-1	0-0	—		1776
38	30	A	Cambridge U	D	1-1	0-0	—	Thackeray	3294
39	Apr 7	H	Maidstone U	W	4-2	2-1	23	Youds, Worthington 2, Sertori	2806
40	10	A	Torquay U	W	1-0	0-0	—	Thackeray	1774
41	14	A	Scunthorpe U	L	1-3	1-0	23	Thackeray	2820
42	16	H	Doncaster R	D	0-0	0-0	22		4210
43	21	A	Burnley	W	3-2	2-0	22	Morgan, Armstrong 2	4512
44	24	H	Gillingham	W	2-1	1-0	—	Bowden, Armstrong	3498
45	28	A	Grimsby T	L	1-5	1-3	21	Preece A	8431
46	May 5	H	Hartlepool U	L	1-2	1-0	21	Worthington	2745

Final League Position: 21

GOALSCORERS

League (51): Worthington 12 (1 pen), Thackeray 7, Buxton 4 (3 pens), Armstrong 3, Beaumont 3, Cooper 3, Hunter 3, Flynn 2, Kearns 2, Sertori 2, Youds 2, Bowden 1, Jones 1, Morgan 1, Preece A 1, Preece R 1, Reck 1, Wright 1, own goal 1.
Littlewoods Cup (0).
FA Cup (0).

O'Keefe	Salathiel	Wright	Reck	Beaumont	Jones J	Buxton	Thackeray	Kearns	Worthington	Bowden	Preece R	Flynn	Cooper	Barnes	Wrench	Hunter	Filson	Williams	Armstrong	Morris	Owen	Madden	Jones R	Youds	Phillips	Sertori	Morgan	Kennedy	Preece A	Match No.
1	2	3	4*	5	6	7	8	9	10	11†12	14																			1
1	2	3		5	6		9	8	10	11*12	4	7																		2
1				5	6	9	14	10	7	12	4	11		2*	3	8†														3
1				5	6	9	14	10	11		8†	7*	2	3	4	12														4
1	3			5	6	9*	2	12	10		7	8	11		4															5
1	3			5	6	12	2	9*10	11		7	8			4															6
1	3	14		5	6		2	9*10	11		7	8†12			4															7
1	3	14		5	6		2	9	10	11*	7	8	12		4†															8
1	3†14			5	6	12	2	9	10		7*	5	11		4															9
1	3	14		5	6	7†	2	9	10	12		8*11			4															10
1			4	3	6			9	10	11		12	7	2	8*		5													11
1			4	3	6	8	9	10	7*			12	11	2			5													12
1	2		4	3	6	9	8*	10	11		12	7					5													13
1	2		4	3	6	9		10	11*12	8	7					5														14
1	2†		4	3	6	11	14	12	10		7		8		5	9*														15
	2	3†		6		9	14	10	7		11	4*			5	12	1	8												16
	2		4	3	6	12	9*10	7†11			8	5	1	14																17
	2			3	6	12	9	10	7*11		8	5	1	4																18
1	2*		4	6		9	11	10†	12	7	3	8	5	14																19
1			4	6		9	11	10	12	2	7†	3	8*	5	14															20
1			4	6		9	7	12	11*	2		3	8	5	10															21
1			4	3	6	10	7	12	11*	2		8	5	9†	14															22
1			4	3	6	10	7		11	2		8	5*	9	12															23
1			4	5	6		7*	12	11	2		3	8	9	10															24
1	3			5	6	7		10	4	2	11	8†		12	9*14															25
1	3			5	6	12		10	4	2	7	11	8*	9																26
1	2	3	4	5				10		7	8*									11			6	12	9					27
1	2	3	4	5				10		7	8								12	11*			6		9					28
1	2	3	4	5				10		7	8								12	11*			6		9					29
1	2	3	4	5				10	11	7*									12		8		6		9					30
1	2	3		5	14			12	10	11	7†	4*							8				6		9					31
1	2	3	4	5				10	11	7											8		6		9					32
1	2	3	4	5				10	11	7											8		6		9					33
1	2	3		5		4*		10	11	7											8		6	12	9					34
1	2	3				4		10	11	7											8		6	5	9					35
1	2	3		5		4		10	11	7*								12			8		6		9					36
1	2	3		5		4		10		7								12			8*		6		9	11				37
1	2	3†4	5			8		10	11*	7													6		9			14	12	38
1	2		4	5		8		10	11	7*								12					6		9		3			39
1	2		4	5		8		10	11	7*													6		9		3	12		40
1	2	4†		5		8		10	11										14				6		9	7	3*12			41
1	2	3†4	5			8		10*11										12	14				6		9	7				42
1	2		4	5		8		11										9					6		7	3	10			43
1	2		4	5		8		11										9					6		7	3	10			44
1	2		4	5*		8												7	14				6	12	9	7†3	10			45
1	2†		4					10										12	14				6	5	9	7*		11		46
43	29	24	28	43	23	16	29	10	39	31	27	19	16	8	2	21	—	13	10	3	8	6	—	20	2	18	7	6	4	
			+4s			+1s	+5s	+5s	+2s	+3s	+2s	+5s	+4s	+2s		+1s			+12s		+5s	+2s1s		+3s				+1s	+3s	

Hardy — Match No. 46(3).

Littlewoods Cup	First Round	Wigan Ath (h)	0-0
		(a)	0-5
FA Cup	First Round	Carlisle U (a)	0-3

WREXHAM

Player and Position	Ht	Wt	Birth Date	Place	Source	Clubs	League App	Gls
Goalkeepers								
Mark Morris	5 11	12 00	1 8 68	Chester		Wrexham	15	—
Vince O'Keefe	6 2	13 00	2 4 57	Coleshill	Local	Birmingham C	—	—
						Peterborough U (loan)	—	—
						Walsall	—	—
					AP Leamington	Exeter C	53	—
						Torquay U	108	—
						Blackburn R	68	—
						Bury (loan)	2	—
						Blackpool (loan)	7	—
						Wrexham	43	—
Defenders								
Robert Barnes	5 8	10 08	26 11 69	Stoke	Trainee	Manchester C	—	—
						Wrexham	8	—
Nigel Beaumont	6 1	12 07	11 2 67	Pontefract		Bradford C	2	—
						Wrexham	64	3
Robert Filson‡	5 11	12 00	25 6 68	St Helens	Everton†	Preston†	—	—
						Wrexham	2	—
Phil Hardy§			9 4 73	Chester		Wrexham	1	—
Joey Jones	5 10	11 07	4 3 55	Llandudno	Amateur	Wrexham	98	2
						Liverpool	72	3
						Wrexham	146	6
						Chelsea	78	2
						Huddersfield T	68	3
						Wrexham	100	9
Robert Jones§			12 11 71	Liverpool	Crewe Alex§	Wrexham	1	—
Alan Kennedy†	5 9	10 07	31 8 54	Sunderland	Apprentice	Newcastle U	158	9
						Liverpool	251	15
						Sunderland	54	2
						Hartlepool U	5	—
						Wigan Ath	22	—
					Colne Dyn	Wrexham	7	—
Wayne Phillips	5 10	11 00	15 12 70	Bangor	Trainee	Wrexham	5	—
Neil Salathiel*	5 7	12 00	19 11 62	Wrexham	Amateur	Sheffield W	—	—
						Wrexham	4	—
						Crewe Alex	65	—
					South Africa	Wrexham	240	3
Mike Williams	5 10	10 12	6 2 65	Mancot	Apprentice	Chester C	34	4
						Wrexham	178	3
Mark Wrench*	5 10	11 00	27 9 69	Warrington	Trainee	Wrexham	6	—
Darren Wright	5 10	11 04	14 3 68	West Bromwich	Apprentice	Wolverhampton W	1	—
						Wrexham	110	4
Midfield								
John Bowden	6 0	11 07	21 1 63	Stockport	Local	Oldham Ath	82	5
						Port Vale	70	7
						Wrexham	101	12
Graham Cooper	5 10	10 09	18 11 65	Huddersfield	Local	Huddersfield T	74	13
						Wrexham	54	14
Brian Flynn	5 4	12 00	12 10 55	Pt Talbot	Limerick	Burnley	120	8
						Leeds U	154	11
						Burnley (loan)	2	—
						Burnley	80	11
						Cardiff C	32	—
						Doncaster R	27	—
					Limerick	Bury	19	—
						Doncaster R	24	1
						Wrexham	81	4
Geoff Hunter	5 10	10 12	27 10 59	Hull	Apprentice	Manchester U	—	—
						Crewe Alex	87	8
						Port Vale	221	15
						Wrexham	98	11
Gareth Owens§			21 10 71	Chester	Trainee	Wrexham	13	—
Roger Preece*	5 9	10 12	9 6 69	Much Wenlock	Apprentice	Coventry C	—	—
						Wrexham	110	12

WREXHAM

Foundation: The oldest club still in existence in Wales, Wrexham was founded in 1873 by a group of local businessmen initially to play a 17-a-side game against the Provincial Insurance team. By 1875 their team formation was reduced to 11 men and a year later they were among the founders of the Welsh FA.

First Football League game: 27 August, 1921, Division 3(N), v Hartlepools U (h) L 0-2 – Godding; Ellis, Simpson; Matthias, Foster, Griffiths; Burton, Goode, Cotton, Edwards, Lloyd.

Managers (and Secretary-managers)
Ted Robinson 1912–25* (continued as secretary to 1930), Charlie Hewitt 1925–29, Jack Baynes 1929–31, Ernest Blackburn 1932–36, Jimmy Logan 1937–38, Arthur Cowell 1938, Tom Morgan 1938–40, Tom Williams 1940–49, Les McDowall 1949–50, Peter Jackson 1951–54, Cliff Lloyd 1954–57, John Love 1957–59, Billy Morris 1960–61, Ken Barnes 1961–65, Billy Morris 1965, Jack Rowley 1966–67, Alvan Williams 1967–68, John Neal 1968–77, Arfon Griffiths 1977–81, Mel Sutton 1981–82, Bobby Roberts 1982–85, Dixie McNeil 1985–89, Brian Flynn 1989–   .

Player and Position	Ht	Wt	Birth Date	Place	Source	Clubs	League App	Gls
Sean Reck	5 10	12 07	5 5 67	Oxford	Apprentice	Oxford U	14	—
						Newport Co (loan)	15	—
						Reading (loan)	1	—
						Wrexham	32	1
Andy Thackeray	5 9	11 00	13 2 68	Huddersfield		Manchester C		—
						Huddersfield T	2	—
						Newport Co	54	4
						Wrexham	69	9
Forwards								
Chris Armstrong	6 0	11 00	19 6 71	Newcastle	Local	Wrexham	22	3
Steve Buxton*	5 5	11 02	13 3 60	Birmingham	Amateur	Wrexham	109	21
						Stockport Co	18	1
						Torquay U	—	—
						Wrexham	121	25
Ollie Kearns*	6 0	12 00	12 6 56	Banbury	Banbury U	Reading	86	40
						Oxford U	18	4
						Walsall	38	11
						Hereford U	170	58
						Wrexham	46	14
Tony Lee‡	5 7	10 07	2 3 70	Wirral	Trainee	Wrexham	—	—
Andy Preece†	6 1	12 00	27 3 67	Evesham		Northampton T	1	—
					Worcester C	Wrexham	7	1
Mark Sertori	6 3	12 00	1 9 67	Manchester		Stockport Co	4	—
						Lincoln C	50	9
						Wrexham	18	2
Jason Taylor‡			29 8 70	Wrexham	Aston Villa§	Wrexham	1	—
Gary Worthington	5 10	10 05	10 11 66	Cleethorpes	Apprentice	Manchester U		—
						Huddersfield T	—	—
						Darlington	40	15
						Wrexham	42	12
Steve Watkin	5 10	11 00	16 6 71	Wrexham	School	Wrexham	—	—

Trainees
Barker, Paul; Goss, Alexander J; Hardy, Philip; Jones, Robert S; Kelly, James; O'Gorman, David J; Owen, Gareth; Weaver, Steven; Williams, Jamie L; Young, Steven J.

**Non-Contract
Kennedy, Alan P; Preece, Andrew P;

Associated Schoolboys
Barnes, Richard I; Beamish, Michael; Brammer, David; Burke, Damien P.W; Coulthard, Christopher; Cross, Jonathan; Darracott, Neale; Holman, Matthew J.; Johnson, Stuart M; Jones, Richard N; Jones, Simon; Merrick, David G; Oldfield, Damon M; Sadler, Phillip A; Thomas, David N; Wright, Ian.

Associated Schoolboys who have accepted the club's offer of a Traineeship/Contract
Douglas, Iain S; Durkin, Kieron J; Knight, Craig; Lunt, Robert J; Smith, Mark A.

**Non-Contract Players who are retained must be re-signed before they are eligible to play in League matches.

606

YORK CITY 1989–90   *Back row (left to right):* Alan Little (Coach), Kevin Dixon, Darren Bradshaw, Steve Spooner, Ian Helliwell, Chris Marples, Ricky Greenough, Steven Tutill, Bob Colville, Tom Kelly, Jeff Miller (Physiotherapist).

Front row: Tony Barrett, Tony Canham, Gary Himsworth, Gary Howlett, John Bird (Manager), Shaun Reid, Wayne, Iain Dunn, Andy McMillan.

Division 4   **YORK CITY**

Bootham Crescent, York. Telephone York (0904) 624447.

Ground capacity: 14,109.

Record attendance: 28,123 v Huddersfield T, FA Cup 6th rd, 5 Mar, 1938.

Record receipts: £38,054 v Liverpool, FA Cup 5th rd, 15 Feb, 1986.

Pitch measurements: 115yd × 75yd.

Chairman: M. D. B. Sinclair.

Directors: D. M. Craig OBE, JP, BSC, FICE, FI, MUN E, FCI ARB, M CONS E, B. A. Houghton, C. Webb, E. B. Swallow, J. E. H. Quickfall FCA.

Manager: John Bird. *Assistant Manager:* Alan Little.

Secretary: Keith Usher. *Commercial Manager:* Mrs. Sheila Smith.

Physio: Jeff Miller.

Hon. Orthopaedic Surgeon: Mr Peter De Boer, MA, FRCS. *Medical Officer:* Dr A. I. MacLeod.

Year Formed: 1922. *Turned Professional:* 1922. *Ltd Co.:* 1922.

Club Nickname: 'Minstermen'.

Previous Grounds: 1922, Fulfordgate; 1932, Bootham Crescent.

Record League Victory: 9-1 v Southport, Division 3 (N), 2 February 1957 – Forgan; Phillips, Howe; Brown (1), Cairney, Mollatt; Hill, Bottom (4 incl. 1p), Wilkinson (2), Wragg (1), Fenton (1).

Record Cup Victory: 6-0 v South Shields (away), FA Cup, 1st rd, 16 November 1968 – Widdowson; Baker (1p), Richardson; Carr, Jackson, Burrows; Taylor, Ross (3), MacDougall (2), Hodgson, Boyer.

Record Defeat: 0-12 v Chester, Division 3 (N), 1 February, 1936.

Most League Points (2 for a win): 62, Division 4, 1964–65.

Most League Points (3 for a win): 101, Division 4, 1983–84.

Most League Goals: 96, Division 4, 1983–84.

Highest League Scorer in Season: Bill Fenton, 31, Division 3 (N), 1951-52; Arthur Bottom, 31, Division 3 (N), 1954–55 and 1955–56.

Most League Goals in Total Aggregate: Norman Wilkinson, 125, 1954–66.

Most Capped Player: Peter Scott, 7 (10), Northern Ireland.

Most League Appearances: Barry Jackson, 481, 1958–70.

Record Transfer Fee Received: £100,000 from Carlisle U for Gordon Staniforth, October 1979, and from QPR for John Byrne, October 1985.

Record Transfer Fee Paid: £50,000 to Aldershot for Dale Banton, November 1984.

Football League Record: 1929 Elected to Division 3 (N); 1958–59 Division 4; 1959–60 Division 3; 1960–65 Division 4; 1965–66 Division 3; 1966–71 Division 4; 1971–74 Division 3; 1974–76 Division 2; 1976–77 Division 3; 1977–84 Division 4; 1984–88 Division 3; 1988– Division 4.

Honours: Football League: Division 2 best season: 15th, 1974–75; Division 3 – Promoted 1973–74 (3rd); Division 4 – Champions 1983–84. *FA Cup:* Semi-finals 1955, when in Division 3. *Football League Cup* best season: 5th rd, 1962.

Colours: Red shirts, blue shorts, white stockings. **Change colours:** White shirts, blue shorts, red stockings.

YORK CITY 1989–90 LEAGUE RECORD

Match No.	Date	Venue	Opponents	Result		H/T Score	Lg. Pos.	Goalscorers	Atten- dance
1	Aug 19	A	Southend U	L	0-2	0-1	—		2725
2	26	H	Peterborough U	W	1-0	0-0	11	Hall	2569
3	Sept 1	A	Stockport Co	D	2-2	1-1	—	Howlett, Helliwell	2793
4	9	H	Rochdale	W	1-0	1-0	11	Spooner (pen)	2250
5	16	A	Lincoln C	D	0-0	0-0	11		4149
6	23	H	Grimsby T	L	0-1	0-0	13		3366
7	26	A	Burnley	D	1-1	0-1	—	Warburton	7890
8	30	H	Wrexham	W	1-0	0-0	9	Dunn	2196
9	Oct 7	H	Cambridge U	W	4-2	2-1	8	Barratt, Dixon, Helliwell, Spooner	2061
10	13	A	Colchester U	W	2-0	2-0	—	Himsworth 2	3274
11	17	H	Aldershot	D	2-2	1-1	—	Helliwell, Dixon	2788
12	21	A	Hartlepool U	W	2-1	2-1	6	Himsworth, Howlett	2325
13	28	H	Doncaster R	W	2-1	1-0	4	Dixon, Warburton	2978
14	31	A	Scunthorpe U	D	1-1	1-1	—	Helliwell	3800
15	Nov 4	H	Torquay U	D	1-1	0-0	5	Kelly (pen)	2496
16	11	A	Maidstone U	L	0-1	0-0	6		2043
17	24	A	Scarborough	W	3-1	2-1	—	Helliwell, Howlett, Canham	3602
18	Dec 9	H	Gillingham	W	1-0	0-0	—	Canham	2134
19	16	A	Chesterfield	D	0-0	0-0	3		3383
20	26	H	Halifax T	L	0-2	0-1	6		3665
21	30	H	Hereford U	L	1-2	0-1	7	Dixon	2405
22	Jan 1	A	Carlisle U	L	1-2	1-0	9	Kelly (pen)	6510
23	13	A	Peterborough U	D	1-1	1-0	10	Hall	3678
24	20	H	Southend U	W	2-1	0-0	8	Helliwell 2	2397
25	27	H	Colchester U	W	3-1	2-1	6	Longhurst 2, Reid	2311
26	Feb 3	A	Grimsby T	L	0-3	0-1	7		5049
27	6	A	Rochdale	W	1-0	0-0	—	Helliwell	1821
28	10	H	Lincoln C	D	0-0	0-0	4		2687
29	13	H	Stockport Co	L	0-3	0-2	—		2256
30	17	A	Gillingham	D	0-0	0-0	8		3653
31	24	A	Scarborough	L	1-2	1-0	8	Helliwell	3551
32	Mar 3	A	Exeter C	L	1-3	0-2	11	Reid	4632
33	6	A	Wrexham	L	0-2	0-0	—		1780
34	10	H	Burnley	L	1-3	0-2	13	Reid (pen)	3216
35	16	A	Cambridge U	D	2-2	1-1	—	Howlett, Hail	4621
36	24	A	Aldershot	D	2-2	1-0	13	Spooner, Helliwell	1556
37	31	H	Hartlepool U	D	1-1	0-0	13	Reid	2891
38	Apr 2	H	Exeter C	W	3-0	0-0	—	Barratt, Canham, Helliwell	2091
39	7	A	Doncaster R	W	2-1	0-1	10	Spooner, Himsworth	2185
40	10	H	Scunthorpe U	L	0-1	0-0	—		2232
41	14	H	Carlisle U	L	0-1	0-1	13		2805
42	16	A	Halifax T	D	2-2	2-2	14	Canham, Helliwell	1605
43	21	H	Chesterfield	W	4-0	0-0	13	Barratt, Helliwell, Dunn, Spooner	2374
44	25	A	Hereford U	W	2-1	0-0	—	Helliwell, Barratt	2007
45	28	H	Maidstone U	D	0 0	0-0	11		2362
46	May 5	A	Torquay U	D	1-1	1-0	13	Spooner	1564

Final League Position: 13

GOALSCORERS

League (55): Helliwell 14, Spooner 6 (1 pen), Barratt 4, Canham 4, Dixon 4, Himsworth 4, Howlett 4, Reid 4 (1 pen), Hall 3, Dunn 2, Kelly 2 (2 pens), Longhurst 2, Warburton 2.
Littlewoods Cup (7): Spooner 3, Colville 2, Helliwell 1, Warburton 1.
FA Cup (1): Warburton 1.

Marples	Barratt	Kelly	Reid	Greenough	Warburton	Howlett	Spooner	Helliwell	Colville	Hall	Dunn	Tutill	Dixon	Canham	McMillan	Himsworth	Heathcote	Longhurst	Naylor	Ord	Madden	Crossley	Match No.
1	2	3	4	5	6	7	8	9	10	11*	12												1
1	2	3	4	12	6	7	8	9	10	11		5*											2
1	2	3	4		6	7	8	9	10	11*	12	5											3
1	2	3	4*		6	7	8	9	10	12		5	11										4
1	2	3	4		6	7	8	9	10		11	5											5
1	2	3	4		6	7	8	9	10	12	11*	5											6
1	2	3			6	7	8	9	10	4*	12	5	11†	14									7
1	4	3			6	7	8	9	10*		11	5	12	2									8
1	2	3	4		6	7	8	9				5		10		11							9
1	4	3			6	7	8	9				5		10	12	2	11*						10
1	4	3			6	7	8	9				5		10	12	2	11*						11
1	4	3			6	7	8	9				5		10		2	11						12
1	4	3			6	7	8	9				5		10	12	2	11*						13
1	4	3			6	7	8	9	12	10*		5	2	11									14
1	4	3			6	7	8	9	10*	12		5	14	2	11†								15
1	4*	3			6	7	8	9				5	12	10	2	11							16
1	4	3			6	7	8	9				5	11	10	2								17
1	4	3			6	7	8	9				5	11	10	2								18
1	4	3			6	7	8	9				5	11	10*	2	12							19
1	2	3			6	7*	8	9	12			5	11†	10		2	14						20
1	2†	3			6	7	8	9*	12			5	11	10	14	4							21
1	2	3			6	7	8	12	9			5	11	10		4*							22
1	2	3			7	14	9†	8	12			5		10	11	4*		6					23
1	2	3			6	7		9	12	8†		5	14	11*			4	10					24
1	8	3	4*		6	7		9	12			5		11		2		10					25
1	2	3	4		6	7	8	9				5		11				10					26
1	2	3	4		6	7	8	9	12			5		11	10*								27
1	2	3	4		6	7	8	9	10			5		11									28
1	2	3	4*		6	7	8	9	10†	12	14	5		11									29
1	2	3			6	7	8	9	10*	4		5		11				12					30
1	2	3	4		6	7		9	10	8	11*	5	12										31
1	2	3	4		6	7*	9	8	10	12	11	5											32
1	2	3	4*		12	8	9	11†				5	14			7				6	10		33
1	2	3	4		6	7	8	9				5†	11	14	12			10*					34
1	2	3	4		6	7	8	9	11			5		10									35
1	2				6	7	8	9	3			5	4	11		10*					12		36
1	2		4		6	7†	8	9	3	12		5		11	14	10*							37
1	7		4		6		8	9	3	10		5	11			2							38
1	7		4		6		8	9	3	10*		5	11			2		12					39
1	7		4		6		8	9	3	10*		5	11			2		12					40
1	7		4*		6	12	8	9	14	3			11			2				10†		5	41
1	7		6		4		8	9	10†	3	14	5		11*		2		12					42
1	7	12	6		4		8	9	3	10		5		11*		2							43
1	7		4		6	11	8	9	12	3	10*	5				2							44
1	7		4		6	11*	8	9	14	3	10†	5	12			2							45
1	7		6		4		8	9	10*	3		5	11			2		12					46
46	46	35	24	2	43	41	41	44	17	22	10	42	15	28	21	15	3	4	—	3	3	1	
		+	+			+	+		+	+	+		+	+	+	+				+		+	
		1s	1s			2s	2s		7s	5s	8s		4s	6s	4s	8s				1s		1s	

Littlewoods Cup	First Round	Hartlepool U (a)	3-3	
		(h)	4-1	
	Second Round	Southampton (h)	0-1	
		(a)	0-2	
FA Cup	First Round	Grimsby T (h)	1-2	

YORK CITY

Player and Position	Ht	Wt	Birth Date	Place	Source	Clubs	League App	Gls
Goalkeepers								
Scott Endersby‡	5 10	12 04	24 2 62	Lewisham	Kettering T	Ipswich T	—	—
						Tranmere R	79	—
						Swindon T	85	—
						Carlisle U	52	—
						York C	35	—
						Cardiff C (loan)	4	—
						Rochdale (loan)	—	—
Dean Kiely	5 11	11 08	10 10 70	Manchester	WBA§	Coventry C	—	—
						Ipswich T (loan)	—	—
						York C	—	—
Chris Marples	5 11	11 12	3 8 64	Chesterfield		Chesterfield	84	—
						Stockport Co	57	—
						York C	91	—
Defenders								
Tony Barratt	5 8	10 02	18 10 65	Salford	Billingham T	Grimsby T	22	—
						Hartlepool U	98	4
						York C	58	4
Richard Crossley			5 9 70	Huddersfield	Huddersfield T§	York C	1	—
Ricky Greenough*	6 1	13 06	30 5 61	Mexborough	Alfreton T	Chester C	132	15
						Scarborough	—	—
						York C	29	1
Andy McMillan	5 10	10 13	22 6 68	South Africa		York C	49	—
Steve Tutill	6 0	11 10	1 10 69	Derwent	Trainee	York C	85	1
Ray Warburton	6 0	11 05	7 10 67	Rotherham	Apprentice	Rotherham U	4	—
						York C	43	2
Midfield								
Wayne Hall	5 8	10 04	25 10 68	Rotherham	Darlington†	York C	29	3
Gary Howlett	5 8	10 04	2 4 63	Dublin	Home Farm	Coventry C	—	—
						Brighton HA	32	2
						Bournemouth	60	7
						Aldershot (loan)	1	—
						Chester C (loan)	6	1
						York C	84	10
Shaun Reid	5 8	11 08	13 10 65	Huyton	Local	Rochdale	133	4
						Preston NE (loan)	3	—
						York C	49	6
Steve Spooner	5 10	12 00	25 1 61	Sutton	Apprentice	Derby Co	8	—
						Halifax T	72	13
						Chesterfield	93	14
						Hereford U	84	19
						York C	72	11
Forwards								
Tony Canham	5 8	10 07	8 6 60	Leeds	Harrogate R	York C	175	38
Bob Colville*	5 10	12 00	27 4 63	Nuneaton	Rhos U	Oldham Ath	32	4
						Bury	11	1
						Stockport Co	71	20
						York C	24	—
Kevin Dixon‡	5 10	10 06	27 7 60	Blackhill	Tow Law T	Carlisle U	9	—
						Hartlepool U (loan)	6	3
						Hartlepool U	107	26
						Scunthorpe U (loan)	14	2
						Scunthorpe U	41	4
						Hartlepool U	14	4
						York C	38	8
						Scarborough (loan)	3	—

YORK CITY

Foundation: Although there was a York City club formed in 1903 by a soccer enthusiast from Darlington, this has no connection with the modern club because it went out of existence during World War I. Unlike many others of that period who restarted in 1919, York City did not re-form until 1922 and the tendency now is to ignore the modern club's pre-1922 existence.

First Football League game: 31 August, 1929, Division 3(N), v Wigan Borough (a) W 2-0 – Farmery; Archibald, Johnson; Beck, Davis, Thompson; Evans, Gardner, Cowie (1), Smailes, Stockhill (1).

Managers (and Secretary-managers)
Bill Sherrington 1924–60 (was secretary for most of this time but virtually secretary-manager for a long pre-war spell), John Collier 1929–36, Tom Mitchell 1936–50, Dick Duckworth 1950–52, Charlie Spencer 1952–53, Jimmy McCormick 1953–54, Sam Bartram 1956–60, Tom Lockie 1960–67, Joe Shaw 1967–68, Tom Johnston 1968–75, Wilf McGuinness 1975–77, Charlie Wright 1977–80, Barry Lyons 1980–81, Denis Smith 1982–87, Bobby Saxton 1987–88, John Bird 1988–   .

Player and Position	Ht	Wt	Birth Date	Place	Source	Clubs	League App	Gls
Iain Dunn	5 10	11 07	1 4 70	Derwent	School	York C	44	8
Ian Helliwell	6 3	13 12	7 12 62	Rotherham	Matlock T	York C	119	33
Gary Himsworth	5 7	9 08	19 12 69	Appleton	Trainee	York C	86	8
David Longhurst	5 8	10 12	15 1 65	Northampton	Apprentice	Nottingham F	—	—
						Halifax T	85	24
						Northampton T	37	7
						Peterborough U	58	7
						York C	4	2
Craig Madden‡	5 8	11 08	25 9 58	Manchester	Northern Nomads	Bury	297	129
						WBA	12	3
						Blackpool	91	24
						Wrexham (loan)	8	—
						York C	4	—
Glenn Naylor	5 9		11 8 72	York	Trainee	York C	1	—
Tony Hall on loan from East Fife							—	—

Trainees
Alker, Simon; Bushwell, Stephen P; Cartwright, Mark N; Cunningham, Andrew; Curtis, Andrew; Ede, Stuart; Howard, Michael J; Pybus, Darren J; Thompson, Geoffrey; Vardy, Richard; Wood, Mark; Woodward, Simon C.

**Non-Contract
McCarthy, Jonathan.

Associated Schoolboys
Crowther, Nicky A; Ellis, Robert; Harvey, David E; Henry, Craig L; Higgins, Neil F; Jefferson, Nicholas; Mannell, Nick; Marwick, Brett; Pallant, Shaun; Rigby, Ian W; Smith, Michael J; Vause, Adam; Wood, Paul.

Associated Schoolboys who have accepted the club's offer of a Traineeship/Contract
Hall, Craig; Smith, Andrew.

**Non-Contract Players who are retained must be re-signed before they are eligible to play in League matches.

END OF SEASON PLAY-OFFS 1989–90

Cutting down on the number of play-off games by switching the finals of each division to Wembley produced aggregate attendances of 291,523 for the 15 matches involved. Although the Fourth and Third Division finals attracted only 26,404 and 29,252 crowds respectively, Sunderland and Swindon provided a Second Division sell-out of 72,873.

For the fourth year in succession, the team finishing sixth in the Fourth Division succeeded in gaining promotion through the system. This time it was Cambridge United who prevailed, initially against the League's newest entry Maidstone and then in the final with Chesterfield who missed a number of chances before United's 77th minute winner.

Chesterfield, in sharp contrast, had had little difficulty in disposing of Stockport County, beating them 6-0 on aggregate scores.

Playing at home in the first leg semi-finals did nothing for either Bolton or Bury where they were held respectively by Notts County and Tranmere. Notts and Rovers each won their home legs 2-0. Then in the final Notts again succeeded by two clear goals against Tranmere.

In the north-east derby between Sunderland and Newcastle at Roker Park, Sunderland missed many chances and a penalty from Paul Hardyman which was saved by John Burridge in the United goal. Hardyman followed up and was sent off for a foul on the goalkeeper. The goalless draw set up the return at Newcastle with the tie well balanced.

However, on a heavy pitch, United were unable to make any impression and were struggling from the 13th minute after Eric Gates forced the ball in for Sunderland's opening goal. When Marco Gabbiadini added a second five minutes from time, Newcastle fans invaded the pitch and the referee George Courtney took the teams off the field for 21 minutes.

Swindon did all the damage to Blackburn at Ewood Park in the first leg winning far more easily than the 2-1 scoreline suggested. Rovers did better at Swindon but again lost 2-1.

At Wembley, Swindon completely dominated the exchanges with Sunderland yet had to settle for one goal scored by Alan McLoughlin, whose drive took a wicked deflection off Gary Bennett the Sunderland captain to wrong-foot goalkeeper Tony Norman in the 27th minute.

DIVISION 2, Semi-final, First Leg
13 MAY

Blackburn R (0) 1 *(Kennedy)*
Swindon T (1) 2 *(White, Foley)* 15,636
Blackburn R: Gennoe; Atkins, Dawson, Reid, Moran, Mail, Stapleton (Kennedy), Millar, Gayle, Garner, Sellars.
Swindon T: Digby; Kerslake, Bodin, McLoughlin (Simpson), Calderwood, Gittens, Jones, Shearer, White, MacLaren, Foley.

Sunderland (0) 0
Newcastle U (0) 0 26,641
Sunderland: Norman; Kay, Hardyman, Bennett, MacPhail, Owers, Bracewell, Armstrong, Gates, Gabbiadini, Agboola.
Newcastle U: Burridge; Scott, Stimson, Aitken, Anderson, Ranson, (O'Brien), Brock, Askew, Quinn, McGhee, Kristensen.

DIVISION 3, Semi-final, First Leg

Bolton W (1) 1 *Philliskirk (pen))*
Notts Co (1) 1 *(Lund)* 15,108
Bolton W: Felgate; Brown, Cowdrill, Green, Came, Winstanley, Storer, Thompson, Reeves (Comstive), Philliskirk, Darby.

Notts Co: Cherry; Palmer, Platnauer, Short (Norton), Yates, Robinson, Thomas, Turner, Bartlett, Lund, Johnson.

Bury (0) 0
Tranmere R (0) 0 7019
Bury: Kelly; Hill, Clements (Bishop), Hoyland, Knill, Valentine, Lee, Robinson, Cunningham, Parkinson, Patterson.
Tranmere R: Nixon; Higgins, Mungall, McNab, Hughes, Vickers, Malkin, Harvey, Steel, Muir, Thomas.

DIVISION 4, Semi-final, First Leg

Cambridge U (0) 1 *(Cheetham (pen))*
Maidstone U (0) 1 *(Gall)* 7264
Cambridge U: Vaughan; Fensome, Leadbitter (O'Shea), Bailie, Chapple, Daish, Cheetham, Cook, Dublin, Claridge, Philpott (Taylor).
Maidstone U: Johns; Barton, Cooper, Berry, Golley, Roast, Gall, Elsey, Charlery, Butler, Lillis (Sorrell).

Chesterfield (2) 4 *(Plummer 3, Ryan)*
Stockport Co (0) 0 8277
Chesterfield: Leonard; Francis, Ryan, Dyche, Brien, Gunn, Plummer, Hewitt, Chiedozie, Rogers, Morris.
Stockport Co: Barrett; Leonard, Logan (Knowles), Frain, Thorpe, Bullock, McInerney, Gannon, Beaumont, Brookman (Brabin), Angell.

DIVISION 2, Semi-final, Second Leg
16 MAY

Newcastle U (0) 0
Sunderland (1) 2 *(Gates, Gabbiadini)* 32,216
Newcastle U: Burridge; Bradshaw (Dillon), Stimson, Aitken, Anderson, Scott, Brock, Askew, (O'Brien), Quinn, McGhee, Kristensen.
Sunderland: Norman; Kay, Agboola, Bennett, MacPhail, Owers, Bracewell, Armstrong, Gates, Gabbiadini, Hawke.

Swindon T (2) 2 *(Shearer, White)*
Blackburn R (0) 1 *(Gayle)* 12,416
Swindon T: Digby; Kerslake, Bodin, McLoughlin (Simpson), Calderwood, Gittens, Jones, Shearer, White, MacLaren, Foley.
Blackburn R: Gennoe; Atkins, Sulley (Garner), Reid, Moran (Dawson), Mail, Kennedy, Millar, Stapleton, Gayle, Sellars.

DIVISION 3, Semi-final, Second Leg

Notts Co (1) 2 *(Johnson, Bartlett)*
Bolton W (0) 0 15,197
Notts Co: Cherry; Norton, Platnauer, Palmer, Yates, Robinson, Thomas, Bartlett, Lund, Johnson, Turner.
Bolton W: Felgate; Brown, Cowdrill, Green, Came (Crombie), Winstanley, Storer (Gregory), Thompson, Reeves, Philliskirk, Darby.

Tranmere R (1) 2 *(Malkin, Muir (pen))*

Bury (0) 0   10,343

Tranmere R: Nixon; Higgins, Mungall, McNab, Hughes, Vickers, Malkin, Harvey, Steel, Muir, Thomas.
Bury: Kelly; Hill, Clements (Atkin), Hoyland, Valentime, Knill, Lee, Hulme, Cunningham, Parkinson, Patterson.

DIVISION 4, Semi-final, Second Leg

Maidstone U (0) 0

Cambridge U (0) 2 *(Dublin, Cheetham (pen)) aet*
                                                                  5538

Maidstone U: Johns; Barton (Oxbrow), Cooper, Berry, Golley, Roast, Gall, Elsey, Charley (Lillis), Butler, Sorrell.
Cambridge U: Vaughan; Fensome, Kimble, Bailie, Chapple, Daish, Cheetham, Leadbitter (O'Shea), Dublin, Claridge (Taylor), Philpott.

Stockport Co (0) 0

Chesterfield (1) 2 *(Plummer, Chiedozie)*   7339

Stockport Co: Barrett; Brown (Bullock), Williams P, Frain, Thorpe, Jones, Knowles (Brookman), Brabin, Beaumont, McInerney, Angell.
Chesterfield: Leonard; Francis, Ryan, Dyche, Brien, Gunn, Plummer (Waller), Hewitt, Chiedozie, Rogers, Morris.

DIVISION 4, Final *(at Wembley)*

16 May

Cambridge U (0) 1 *(Dublin)*

Chesterfield (0) 0   26,404

Cambridge U: Vaughan; Fensome, Kimble, Bailie, Chapple, O'Shea, Cheetham, Leadbitter (Cook), Dublin, Taylor (Claridge), Philpott.
Chesterfield: Leonard; Francis, Ryan, Dyche, Brien, Gunn, Plummer, Hewitt, Chiedozie (Waller), Rogers, Morris.

DIVISION 3, Final *(at Wembley)*

27 MAY

Notts Co (1) 2 *(Johnson, Short)*

Tranmere R (0) 0   29,252

Notts Co: Cherry; Palmer, Platnauer, Short, Yates, Robinson, Thomas, Turner, Bartlett, Lund, Johnson.
Tranmere R: Nixon; Garnett, Mungall (Fairclough), McNab, Hughes, Vickers, Malkin, Harvey (Bishop), Steel, Muir, Thomas.

DIVISION 2, Final *(at Wembley)*

28 May

Sunderland (0) 0

Swindon T (1) 1 *(McLoughlin)*   72,873

Sunderland: Norman; Kay, Agboola, Bennett, MacPhail, Owers, Bracewell, Armstrong, Gates (Hauser), Gabbiadini, Pascoe (Atkinson).
Swindon T: Digby; Kerslake, Bodin, McLoughlin, Calderwood, Gittens, Jones, Shearer, White, MacLaren, Foley.

Marco Gabbiadini (left) finds his progress for Sunderland hampered by Swindon's Colin Calderwood in the play-off final at Wembley. Swindon won 1-0 but then the bottom fell out of their world. (Bob Thomas).

BARCLAYS LEAGUE FINAL TABLES 1989–90

DIVISION 1

		P	Home W	D	L	Goals F	A	Away W	D	L	Goals F	A	GD	Pts
1	Liverpool	38	13	5	1	38	15	10	5	4	40	22	+41	79
2	Aston Villa	38	13	3	3	36	20	8	4	7	21	18	+19	70
3	Tottenham Hotspur	38	12	1	6	35	24	7	5	7	24	23	+12	63
4	Arsenal	38	14	3	2	38	11	4	5	10	16	27	+16	62
5	Chelsea	38	8	7	4	31	24	8	5	6	27	26	+8	60
6	Everton	38	14	3	2	40	16	3	5	11	17	30	+11	59
7	Southampton	38	10	5	4	40	27	5	5	9	31	36	+8	55
8	Wimbledon	38	5	8	6	22	23	8	8	3	25	17	+7	55
9	Nottingham F	38	9	4	6	31	21	6	5	8	24	26	+8	54
10	Norwich C	38	7	10	2	24	14	6	4	9	20	28	+2	53
11	QPR	38	9	4	6	27	22	4	7	8	18	22	+1	50
12	Coventry C	38	11	2	6	24	25	3	5	11	15	34	−20	49
13	Manchester U	38	8	6	5	26	14	5	3	11	20	33	−1	48
14	Manchester C	38	9	4	6	26	21	3	8	8	17	31	−9	48
15	Crystal Palace	38	8	7	4	27	23	5	2	12	15	43	−24	48
16	Derby Co	38	9	1	9	29	21	4	6	19	14	19	+3	46
17	Luton T	38	8	8	3	24	18	2	5	12	19	39	−14	43
18	Sheffield W	38	8	6	5	21	17	3	4	12	14	34	−16	43
19	Charlton Ath	38	4	6	9	18	25	3	3	13	13	32	−26	30
20	Millwall	38	4	6	9	23	25	1	5	13	16	40	−26	26

DIVISION 2

		P	Home W	D	L	Goals F	A	Away W	D	L	Goals F	A	GD	Pts
1	Leeds U	46	16	6	1	46	18	8	7	8	33	34	+27	85
2	Sheffield U	46	14	5	4	43	27	10	8	5	35	31	+20	85
3	Newcastle U	46	17	4	2	51	26	5	10	8	29	29	+25	80
4	Swindon T	46	12	6	5	49	29	8	8	7	30	30	+20	74
5	Blackburn R	46	10	9	4	43	30	9	8	6	31	29	+15	74
6	Sunderland	46	10	8	5	41	32	10	6	7	29	32	+6	74
7	West Ham	46	14	5	4	50	22	6	7	10	30	35	+23	72
8	Oldham Ath	46	15	7	1	50	23	4	7	12	20	34	+13	71
9	Ipswich T	46	13	7	3	38	22	6	5	12	29	44	+1	69
10	Wolverhampton W	46	12	5	6	37	20	6	8	9	30	40	+7	67
11	Port Vale	46	11	9	3	37	20	4	7	12	25	37	+5	61
12	Portsmouth	46	9	8	6	40	34	6	8	9	22	31	−3	61
13	Leicester C	46	10	8	5	34	29	5	6	12	33	50	−12	59
14	Hull C	46	7	8	8	27	31	7	8	8	31	34	−7	58
15	Watford	46	11	6	6	41	28	3	9	11	17	32	−2	57
16	Plymouth Arg	46	9	8	6	30	23	5	5	13	28	40	−5	55
17	Oxford U	46	8	7	8	35	31	7	2	14	22	35	−9	54
18	Brighton & HA	46	10	6	7	28	27	5	3	15	28	45	−16	54
19	Barnsley	46	7	9	7	22	23	6	6	11	27	48	−22	54
20	West Bromwich A	46	6	8	9	35	37	6	7	10	32	34	−4	51
21	Middlesbrough	46	10	3	10	33	29	3	8	12	19	34	−11	50
22	AFC Bournemouth	46	8	6	9	30	31	4	6	13	27	45	−19	48
23	Bradford C	46	9	6	8	26	24	0	8	15	18	44	−24	41
24	Stoke C	46	4	11	8	20	24	2	8	13	15	39	−28	37

DIVISION 3

		P	Home W	D	L	Goals F	A	Away W	D	L	Goals F	A	GD	Pts
1	Bristol R	46	15	8	0	43	14	11	7	5	28	21	+36	93
2	Bristol C	46	15	5	3	40	16	12	5	6	36	24	+36	91
3	Notts Co	46	17	4	2	40	18	8	8	7	33	35	+20	87
4	Tranmere R	46	15	5	3	54	22	8	6	9	32	27	+37	80
5	Bury	46	11	7	5	35	19	10	4	9	35	30	+21	74
6	Bolton W	46	12	7	4	32	19	6	8	9	27	29	+11	69
7	Birmingham C	46	19	7	6	33	19	8	5	10	27	40	+1	66
8	Huddersfield T	46	11	5	7	30	23	6	9	8	31	39	−1	65
9	Rotherham U	46	12	6	5	48	28	5	7	11	23	34	+9	64
10	Reading	46	10	9	4	33	21	5	10	8	24	32	+4	64
11	Shrewsbury T	46	10	9	4	38	24	6	6	11	21	30	+5	63
12	Crewe Alex	46	10	8	5	32	24	5	9	9	24	29	+3	62
13	Brentford	46	11	4	8	41	31	7	3	13	25	35	0	61
14	Leyton Orient	46	9	6	8	28	24	7	4	12	24	32	−4	58
15	Mansfield T	46	13	2	8	34	25	3	5	15	16	40	−15	55
16	Chester C	46	11	7	5	30	23	2	8	13	13	32	−12	54
17	Swansea C	46	10	6	7	25	27	4	6	13	20	36	−18	54
18	Wigan Ath	46	10	6	7	29	22	3	8	12	19	42	−16	53
19	Preston NE	46	10	7	6	42	30	4	3	16	23	49	−14	52
20	Fulham	46	8	8	7	33	27	4	7	12	22	39	−11	51
21	Cardiff C	46	6	9	8	30	35	6	5	12	21	35	−19	50
22	Northampton T	46	7	7	9	27	31	4	7	12	24	37	−17	47
23	Blackpool	46	8	6	9	29	33	2	10	11	20	40	−24	46
24	Walsall	46	6	8	9	23	30	3	6	14	17	42	−32	41

DIVISION 4

		P	Home W	D	L	Goals F	A	Away W	D	L	Goals F	A	GD	Pts
1	Exeter C	46	20	3	0	50	14	8	2	13	33	34	+35	89
2	Grimsby T	46	14	4	5	41	20	8	9	6	29	27	+23	79
3	Southend U	46	15	3	5	35	14	7	6	10	26	34	+13	75
4	Stockport C	46	13	6	4	45	27	8	5	10	23	35	+6	74
5	Maidstone U	46	14	4	5	49	21	8	3	12	28	40	+16	73
6	Cambridge U	46	14	3	6	45	30	7	7	9	31	36	+10	73
7	Chesterfield	46	12	9	2	41	19	7	5	11	22	31	+13	71
8	Carlisle U	46	15	4	4	38	20	6	4	13	23	40	+1	71
9	Peterborough U	46	10	8	5	35	23	7	9	7	24	23	+13	68
10	Lincoln C	46	11	6	6	30	27	7	8	8	18	21	0	68
11	Scunthorpe U	46	9	9	5	42	25	8	6	9	27	29	+15	66
12	Rochdale	46	11	4	8	28	23	9	2	12	24	32	−3	66
13	York C	46	10	5	8	29	24	6	11	6	26	29	+2	64
14	Gillingham	46	9	8	6	28	21	8	3	12	18	27	−2	62
15	Torquay U	46	12	2	9	33	29	3	10	10	20	37	−13	57
16	Burnley	46	6	10	7	19	18	8	4	11	26	37	−10	56
17	Hereford U	46	7	4	12	31	32	8	6	9	25	30	−6	55
18	Scarborough	46	10	5	8	35	28	5	5	13	25	45	−13	55
19	Hartlepool U	46	12	4	7	45	33	3	6	14	21	55	−22	55
20	Doncaster R	46	7	7	9	29	29	7	2	14	24	31	−7	51
21	Wrexham	46	8	8	7	28	28	5	4	14	23	39	−16	51
22	Aldershot	46	8	7	8	28	26	4	7	12	21	43	−20	50
23	Halifax T	46	5	9	9	31	29	7	4	12	26	36	−8	49
24	Colchester U	46	9	3	11	26	25	2	7	14	22	50	−27	43

FOOTBALL LEAGUE 1888–89 to 1989–90

FOOTBALL LEAGUE

	First	Pts	Second	Pts	Third	Pts
1888–89a	Preston NE	40	Aston Villa	29	Wolverhampton W	28
1889–90a	Preston NE	33	Everton	31	Blackburn R	27
1890–91a	Everton	29	Preston NE	27	Notts Co	26
1891–92b	Sunderland	42	Preston NE	37	Bolton W	36

FIRST DIVISION

Maximum points: a 44; b 52; c 60; d 68; e 76; f 84; g 126; h 120; k 114

	First	Pts	Second	Pts	Third	Pts
1892–93c	Sunderland	48	Preston NE	37	Everton	36
1893–94c	Aston Villa	44	Sunderland	38	Derby Co	36
1894–95c	Sunderland	47	Everton	42	Aston Villa	39
1895–96c	Aston Villa	45	Derby Co	41	Everton	39
1896–97c	Aston Villa	47	Sheffield U*	36	Derby Co	36
1897–98c	Sheffield U	42	Sunderland	37	Wolverhampton W*	35
1898–99d	Aston Villa	45	Liverpool	43	Burnley	39
1899–1900d	Aston Villa	50	Sheffield U	48	Sunderland	41
1900–01d	Liverpool	45	Sunderland	43	Notts Co	40
1901–02d	Sunderland	44	Everton	41	Newcastle U	37
1902–03d	The Wednesday	42	Aston Villa*	41	Sunderland	41
1903–04d	The Wednesday	47	Manchester C	44	Everton	43
1904–05d	Newcastle U	48	Everton	47	Manchester C	46
1905–06e	Liverpool	51	Preston NE	47	The Wednesday	44
1906–07e	Newcastle U	51	Bristol C	48	Everton*	45
1907–08e	Manchester U	52	Aston Villa*	43	Manchester C	43
1908–09e	Newcastle U	53	Everton	46	Sunderland	44
1909–10e	Aston Villa	53	Liverpool	48	Blackburn R*	45
1910–11e	Manchester U	52	Aston Villa	51	Sunderland*	45
1911–12e	Blackburn R	49	Everton	46	Newcastle U	44
1912–13e	Sunderland	54	Aston Villa	50	Sheffield W	49
1913–14e	Blackburn R	51	Aston Villa	44	Middlesbrough*	43
1914–15e	Everton	46	Oldham Ath	45	Blackburn R*	43
1919–20f	WBA	60	Burnley	51	Chelsea	49
1920–21f	Burnley	59	Manchester C	54	Bolton W	52
1921–22f	Liverpool	57	Tottenham H	51	Burnley	49
1922–23f	Liverpool	60	Sunderland	54	Huddersfield T	53
1923–24f	Huddersfield T*	57	Cardiff C	57	Sunderland	53
1924–25f	Huddersfield T	58	WBA	56	Bolton W	55
1925–26f	Huddersfield T	57	Arsenal	52	Sunderland	48
1926–27f	Newcastle U	56	Huddersfield T	51	Sunderland	49
1927–28f	Everton	53	Huddersfield T	51	Leicester C	48
1928–29f	Sheffield W	52	Leicester C	51	Aston Villa	50
1929–30f	Sheffield W	60	Derby Co	50	Manchester C*	47
1930–31f	Arsenal	66	Aston Villa	59	Sheffield W	52
1931–32f	Everton	56	Arsenal	54	Sheffield W	50
1932–33f	Arsenal	58	Aston Villa	54	Sheffield W	51
1933–34f	Arsenal	59	Huddersfield T	56	Tottenham H	49
1934–35f	Arsenal	58	Sunderland	54	Sheffield W	49
1935–36f	Sunderland	56	Derby Co*	48	Huddersfield T	48
1936–37f	Manchester C	57	Charlton Ath	54	Arsenal	52
1937–38f	Arsenal	52	Wolverhampton W	51	Preston NE	49
1938–39f	Everton	59	Wolverhampton W	55	Charlton Ath	50
1946–47f	Liverpool	57	Manchester U*	56	Wolverhampton W	56
1947–48f	Arsenal	59	Manchester U*	52	Burnley	52
1948–49f	Portsmouth	58	Manchester U*	53	Derby Co	53
1949–50f	Portsmouth*	53	Wolverhampton W	53	Sunderland	52
1950–51f	Tottenham H	60	Manchester U	56	Blackpool	50
1951–52f	Manchester U	57	Tottenham H*	53	Arsenal	53
1952–53f	Arsenal*	54	Preston NE	54	Wolverhampton W	51
1953–54f	Wolverhampton W	57	WBA	53	Huddersfield T	51
1954–55f	Chelsea	52	Wolverhampton W*	48	Portsmouth*	48
1955–56f	Manchester U	60	Blackpool*	49	Wolverhampton W	49
1956–57f	Manchester U	64	Tottenham H*	56	Preston NE	56
1957–58f	Wolverhampton W	64	Preston NE	59	Tottenham H	51
1958–59f	Wolverhampton W	61	Manchester U	55	Arsenal*	50
1959–60f	Burnley	55	Wolverhampton W	54	Tottenham H	53
1960–61f	Tottenham H	66	Sheffield W	58	Wolverhampton W	57

* Won or placed on goal average.

	First	Pts	Second	Pts	Third	Pts
1961–62f	Ipswich T	56	Burnley	53	Tottenham H	52
1962–63f	Everton	61	Tottenham H	55	Burnley	54
1963–64f	Liverpool	57	Manchester U	53	Everton	52
1964–65f	Manchester U*	61	Leeds U	61	Chelsea	56
1965–66f	Liverpool	61	Leeds U*	55	Burnley	55
1966–67f	Manchester U	60	Nottingham F*	56	Tottenham H	56
1967–68f	Manchester C	58	Manchester U	56	Liverpool	55
1968–69f	Leeds U	67	Liverpool	61	Everton	57
1969–70f	Everton	66	Leeds U	57	Chelsea	55
1970–71f	Arsenal	65	Leeds U	64	Tottenham H*	52
1971–72f	Derby Co	58	Leeds U*	57	Liverpool*	57
1972–73f	Liverpool	60	Arsenal	57	Leeds U	53
1973–74f	Leeds U	62	Liverpool	57	Derby Co	48
1974–75f	Derby Co	53	Liverpool*	51	Ipswich T	57
1975–76f	Liverpool	60	QPR	59	Manchester U	56
1976–77f	Liverpool	57	Manchester C	56	Ipswich T	52
1977–78f	Nottingham F	64	Liverpool	57	Everton	55
1978–79f	Liverpool	68	Nottingham F	60	WBA	59
1979–80f	Liverpool	60	Manchester U	58	Ipswich T	53
1980–81f	Aston Villa	60	Ipswich T	56	Arsenal	53
1981–82g	Liverpool	87	Ipswich T	83	Manchester U	78
1982–83g	Liverpool	82	Watford	71	Manchester U	70
1983–84g	Liverpool	80	Southampton	77	Nottingham F*	74
1984–85g	Everton	90	Liverpool*	77	Tottenham H	77
1985–86g	Liverpool	88	Everton	86	West Ham	84
1986–87g	Everton	86	Liverpool	77	Tottenham H	71
1987–88h	Liverpool	90	Manchester U	81	Nottingham F	73
1988–89k	Arsenal*	76	Liverpool	76	Nottingham F	64
1989–90k	Liverpool	79	Aston Villa	70	Tottenham H	63

No official competition during 1915–19 and 1939–46.

SECOND DIVISION

Maximum points: a 44; b 56; c 60; d 68; e 76; f 84; g 126; h 132; k 138.

	First	Pts	Second	Pts	Third	Pts
1892–93a	Small Heath	36	Sheffield U	35	Darwen	30
1893–94b	Liverpool	50	Small Heath	42	Notts Co	39
1894–95c	Bury	48	Notts Co	39	Newton Heath*	38
1895–96c	Liverpool*	46	Manchester C	46	Grimsby T*	42
1896–97c	Notts Co	42	Newton Heath	39	Grimsby T	38
1897–98c	Burnley	48	Newcastle U	45	Manchester C	39
1898–99d	Manchester C	52	Glossop NE	46	Leicester Fosse	45
1899–1900d	The Wednesday	54	Bolton W	52	Small Heath	46
1900–01d	Grimsby T	49	Small Heath	48	Burnley	44
1901–02d	WBA	55	Middlesbrough	51	Preston NE*	42
1902–03d	Manchester C	54	Small Heath	51	Woolwich A	48
1903–04d	Preston NE	50	Woolwich A	49	Manchester U	48
1904–05d	Liverpool	58	Bolton W	56	Manchester U	53
1905–06e	Bristol C	66	Manchester U	62	Chelsea	53
1906–07e	Nottingham F	60	Chelsea	57	Leicester Fosse	48
1907–08e	Bradford C	54	Leicester Fosse	52	Oldham Ath	50
1908–09e	Bolton W	52	Tottenham H*	51	WBA	51
1909–10e	Manchester C	54	Oldham Ath*	53	Hull C*	53
1910–11e	WBA	53	Bolton W	51	Chelsea	49
1911–12e	Derby Co*	54	Chelsea	54	Burnley	52
1912–13e	Preston NE	53	Burnley	50	Birmingham	46
1913–14e	Notts Co	53	Bradford PA*	49	Woolwich A	49
1914–15e	Derby Co	53	Preston NE	50	Barnsley	47
1919–20f	Tottenham H	70	Huddersfield T	64	Birmingham	56
1920–21f	Birmingham*	58	Cardiff C	58	Bristol C	51
1921–22f	Nottingham F	56	Stoke C*	52	Barnsley	52
1922–23f	Notts Co	53	West Ham U*	51	Leicester C	51
1923–24f	Leeds U	54	Bury*	51	Derby Co	51
1924–25f	Leicester C	59	Manchester U	57	Derby Co	55
1925–26f	Sheffield W	60	Derby Co	57	Chelsea	52
1926–27f	Middlesbrough	62	Portsmouth*	54	Manchester C	54
1927–28f	Manchester C	59	Leeds U	57	Chelsea	54
1928–29f	Middlesbrough	55	Grimsby T	53	Bradford*	48
1929–30f	Blackpool	58	Chelsea	55	Oldham Ath	53
1930–31f	Everton	61	WBA	54	Tottenham H	51
1931–32f	Wolverhampton W	56	Leeds U	54	Stoke C	52
1932–33f	Stoke C	56	Tottenham H	55	Fulham	50
1933–34f	Grimsby T	59	Preston NE	52	Bolton W*	51
1934–35f	Brentford	61	Bolton W*	56	West Ham U	56
1935–36f	Manchester U	56	Charlton Ath	55	Sheffield U*	52
1936–37f	Leicester C	56	Blackpool	55	Bury	52

* Won or placed on goal average/goal difference.

	First	Pts	Second	Pts	Third	Pts
1937–38f	Aston Villa	57	Manchester U*	53	Sheffield U	53
1938–39f	Blackburn R	55	Sheffield U	54	Sheffield W	53
1946–47f	Manchester C	62	Burnley	58	Birmingham C	55
1947–48f	Birmingham C	59	Newcastle U	56	Southampton	52
1948–49f	Fulham	57	WBA	56	Southampton	55
1949–50f	Tottenham H	61	Sheffield W*	52	Sheffield U*	52
1950–51f	Preston NE	57	Manchester C	52	Cardiff C	50
1951–52f	Sheffield W	53	Cardiff C*	51	Birmingham C	51
1952–53f	Sheffield U	60	Huddersfield T	58	Luton T	52
1953–54f	Leicester C*	56	Everton	56	Blackburn R	55
1954–55f	Birmingham C*	54	Luton T*	54	Rotherham U	54
1955–56f	Sheffield W	55	Leeds U	52	Liverpool*	48
1956–57f	Leicester C	61	Nottingham F	54	Liverpool	53
1957–58f	West Ham U	57	Blackburn R	56	Charlton Ath	55
1958–59f	Sheffield W	62	Fulham	60	Sheffield U*	53
1959–60f	Aston Villa	59	Cardiff C	58	Liverpool*	50
1960–61f	Ipswich T	59	Sheffield U	58	Liverpool	52
1961–62f	Liverpool	62	Leyton O	54	Sunderland	53
1962–63f	Stoke C	53	Chelsea*	52	Sunderland	52
1963–64f	Leeds U	63	Sunderland	61	Preston NE	56
1964–65f	Newcastle U	57	Northampton T	56	Bolton W	50
1965–66f	Manchester C	59	Southampton	54	Coventry C	53
1966–67f	Coventry C	59	Wolverhampton W	58	Carlisle U	52
1967–68f	Ipswich T	59	QPR*	58	Blackpool	58
1968–69f	Derby Co	63	Crystal Palace	56	Charlton Ath	50
1969–70f	Huddersfield T	60	Blackpool	53	Leicester C	51
1970–71f	Leicester C	59	Sheffield U	56	Cardiff C*	53
1971–72f	Norwich C	57	Birmingham C	56	Millwall	55
1972–73f	Burnley	62	QPR	61	Aston Villa	50
1973–74f	Middlesbrough	65	Luton T	50	Carlisle U	49
1974–75f	Manchester U	61	Aston Villa	58	Norwich C	53
1975–76f	Sunderland	56	Bristol C*	53	WBA	53
1976–77f	Wolverhampton W	57	Chelsea	55	Nottingham F	52
1977–78f	Bolton W	58	Southampton	57	Tottenham H*	56
1978–79f	Crystal Palace	57	Brighton*	56	Stoke C	56
1979–80f	Leicester C	55	Sunderland	54	Birmingham C*	53
1980–81f	West Ham U	66	Notts Co	53	Swansea C*	50
1981–82g	Luton T	88	Watford	80	Norwich C	71
1982–83g	QPR	85	Wolverhampton W	75	Leicester C	70
1983–84g	Chelsea*	88	Sheffield W	88	Newcastle U	80
1984–85g	Oxford U	84	Birmingham C	82	Manchester C	74
1985–86g	Norwich C	84	Charlton Ath	77	Wimbledon	76
1986–87g	Derby Co	84	Portsmouth	78	Oldham Ath††	75
1987–88h	Millwall	82	Aston Villa*	78	Middlesbrough	78
1988–89k	Chelsea	99	Manchester C	82	Crystal Palace	81
1989–90k	Leeds U*	85	Sheffield U	85	Newcastle U††	80

No competition during 1915–19 and 1939–46.
††Not promoted after play-offs

THIRD DIVISION
Maximum points: 92; 138 from 1981–82

	First	Pts	Second	Pts	Third	Pts
1958–59	Plymouth Arg	62	Hull C	61	Brentford*	57
1959–60	Southampton	61	Norwich C	59	Shrewsbury T*	52
1960–61	Bury	68	Walsall	62	QPR	60
1961–62	Portsmouth	65	Grimsby T	62	Bournemouth*	59
1962–63	Northampton T	62	Swindon T	58	Port Vale	54
1963–64	Coventry C*	60	Crystal Palace	60	Watford	58
1964–65	Carlisle U	60	Bristol C*	59	Mansfield T	59
1965–66	Hull C	69	Millwall	65	QPR	57
1966–67	QPR	67	Middlesbrough	55	Watford	54
1967–68	Oxford U	57	Bury	56	Shrewsbury T	55
1968–69	Watford*	64	Swindon T	64	Luton T	61
1969–70	Orient	62	Luton T	60	Bristol R	56
1970–71	Preston NE	61	Fulham	60	Halifax T	56
1971–72	Aston Villa	70	Brighton	65	Bournemouth*	62
1972–73	Bolton W	61	Notts Co	57	Blackburn R	55
1973–74	Oldham Ath	62	Bristol R*	61	York C	61
1974–75	Blackburn R	60	Plymouth Arg	59	Charlton Ath	55
1975–76	Hereford U	63	Cardiff C	57	Millwall	56
1976–77	Mansfield T	64	Brighton & HA	61	Crystal Palace*	59
1977–78	Wrexham	61	Cambridge U	58	Preston NE*	56
1978–79	Shrewsbury T	61	Watford*	60	Swansea C	60
1979–80	Grimsby T	62	Blackburn R	59	Sheffield W	58
1980–81	Rotherham U	61	Barnsley*	59	Charlton Ath	59
1981–82	Burnley*	80	Carlisle U	80	Fulham	78

Won on goal average/goal difference.

	First	Pts	Second	Pts	Third	Pts
1982–83	Portsmouth	91	Cardiff C	86	Huddersfield T	82
1983–84	Oxford U	95	Wimbledon	87	Sheffield U*	83
1984–85	Bradford C	94	Millwall	90	Hull C	87
1985–86	Reading	94	Plymouth Arg	87	Derby Co	84
1986–87	Bournemouth	97	Middlesbrough	94	Swindon T	87
1987–88	Sunderland	93	Brighton & HA	84	Walsall	82
1988–89	Wolverhampton W	92	Sheffield U	84	Port Vale	84
1989–90	Bristol R	93	Bristol C	91	Notts Co	87

FOURTH DIVISION

Maximum points: 92; 138 from 1981–82

1958–59	Port Vale	64	Coventry C*	60	York C	60	Shrewsbury T	58
1959–60	Walsall	65	Notts Co*	60	Torquay U	60	Watford	57
1960–61	Peterborough U	66	Crystal Palace	64	Northampton T*	60	Bradford PA	60
1961–62†	Millwall	56	Colchester U	55	Wrexham	53	Carlisle U	52
1962–63	Brentford	62	Oldham Ath*	59	Crewe Alex	59	Mansfield T*	57
1963–64	Gillingham*	60	Carlisle U	60	Workington T	59	Exeter C	58
1964–65	Brighton	63	Millwall*	62	York C	62	Oxford U	61
1965–66	Doncaster R*	59	Darlington	59	Torquay U	58	Colchester U*	56
1966–67	Stockport Co	64	Southport*	59	Barrow	59	Tranmere R	58
1967–68	Luton T	66	Barnsley	61	Hartlepools U	60	Crewe Alex	58
1968–69	Doncaster R	59	Halifax T	57	Rochdale*	56	Bradford C	56
1969–70	Chesterfield	64	Wrexham	61	Swansea C	60	Port Vale	59
1970–71	Notts Co	69	Bournemouth	60	Oldham Ath	59	York C	56
1971–72	Grimsby T	63	Southend U	60	Brentford	59	Scunthorpe U	57
1972–73	Southport	62	Hereford U	58	Cambridge U	57	Aldershot*	56
1973–74	Peterborough U	65	Gillingham	62	Colchester U	60	Bury	59
1974–75	Mansfield T	68	Shrewsbury T	62	Rotherham U	59	Chester*	57
1975–76	Lincoln C	74	Northampton T	68	Reading	60	Tranmere R	58
1976–77	Cambridge U	65	Exeter C	62	Colchester U*	59	Bradford C	59
1977–78	Watford	71	Southend U	60	Swansea C*	56	Brentford	56
1978–79	Reading	65	Grimsby T*	61	Wimbledon*	61	Barnsley	61
1979–80	Huddersfield T	66	Walsall	64	Newport Co	61	Portsmouth*	60
1980–81	Southend U	67	Lincoln C	65	Doncaster R	56	Wimbledon	55
1981–82	Sheffield U	96	Bradford C*	91	Wigan Ath	91	AFC Bournemouth	88
1982–83	Wimbledon	98	Hull C	90	Port Vale	88	Scunthorpe U	83
1983–84	York C	101	Doncaster R	85	Reading*	82	Bristol C	82
1984–85	Chesterfield	91	Blackpool	86	Darlington	85	Bury	84
1985–86	Swindon T	102	Chester C	84	Mansfield T	81	Port Vale	79
1986–87	Northampton T	99	Preston NE	90	Southend U	80	Wolverhampton W††	79
1987–88	Wolverhampton W	90	Cardiff C	85	Bolton W	78	Scunthorpe U††	77
1988–89	Rotherham U	82	Tranmere R	80	Crewe Alex	78	Scunthorpe U††	77
1989–90	Exeter C	89	Grimsby T	79	Southend U	75	Stockport Co††	74

†*Maximum points:* 88 owing to Accrington Stanley's resignation.   ††*Not promoted after play-offs.*

THIRD DIVISION—SOUTH (1921–1958)

Maximum points: a 84; b 76; c 80; d 92.

1920–21a	Crystal Palace	59	Southampton	54	QPR	53
1921–22a	Southampton*	61	Plymouth Arg	61	Portsmouth	53
1922–23a	Bristol C	59	Plymouth Arg*	53	Swansea T	53
1923–24a	Portsmouth	59	Plymouth Arg	55	Millwall	54
1924–25a	Swansea T	57	Plymouth Arg	56	Bristol C	53
1925–26a	Reading	57	Plymouth Arg	56	Millwall	53
1926–27a	Bristol C	62	Plymouth Arg	60	Millwall	56
1927–28a	Millwall	65	Northampton T	55	Plymouth Arg	53
1928–29a	Charlton Ath*	54	Crystal Palace	54	Northampton T*	52
1929–30a	Plymouth Arg	68	Brentford	61	QPR	51
1930–31a	Notts Co	59	Crystal Palace	51	Brentford	50
1931–32a	Fulham	57	Reading	55	Southend U	53
1932–33a	Brentford	62	Exeter C	58	Norwich C	57
1933–34a	Norwich C	61	Coventry C*	54	Reading*	54
1934–35a	Charlton Ath	61	Reading	53	Coventry C	51
1935–36a	Coventry C	57	Luton T	56	Reading	54
1936–37a	Luton T	58	Notts Co	56	Brighton	53
1937–38a	Millwall	56	Bristol C	55	QPR*	53
1938–39a	Newport Co	55	Crystal Palace	52	Brighton	49
1939–46	Competition cancelled owing to war.					
1946–47a	Cardiff C	66	QPR	57	Bristol C	51
1947–48a	QPR	61	Bournemouth	57	Walsall	51
1948–49a	Swansea T	62	Reading	55	Bournemouth	52
1949–50a	Notts Co	58	Northampton T*	51	Southend U	51

* *Won on goal average.*

	First	Pts	Second	Pts	Third	Pts
1950–51d	Nottingham F	70	Norwich C	64	Reading*	57
1951–52d	Plymouth Arg	66	Reading*	61	Norwich C	61
1952–53d	Bristol R	64	Millwall*	62	Northampton T	62
1953–54d	Ipswich T	64	Brighton	61	Bristol C	56
1954–55d	Bristol C	70	Leyton O	61	Southampton	59
1955–56d	Leyton O	66	Brighton	65	Ipswich T	64
1956–57d	Ipswich T*	59	Torquay U	59	Colchester U	58
1957–58d	Brighton	60	Brentford*	58	Plymouth Arg	58

THIRD DIVISION—NORTH (1921–1958)

Maximum points: a 84; b 76; c 80; d 92.

	First	Pts	Second	Pts	Third	Pts
1921–22b	Stockport Co	56	Darlington*	50	Grimsby T	50
1922–23b	Nelson	51	Bradford PA	47	Walsall	46
1923–24a	Wolverhampton W	63	Rochdale	62	Chesterfield	54
1924–25a	Darlington	58	Nelson*	53	New Brighton	53
1925–26a	Grimsby T	61	Bradford PA	60	Rochdale	59
1926–27a	Stoke C	63	Rochdale	58	Bradford PA	55
1927–28a	Bradford PA	63	Lincoln C	55	Stockport Co	54
1928–29a	Bradford C	63	Stockport Co	62	Wrexham	52
1929–30a	Port Vale	67	Stockport Co	63	Darlington*	50
1930–31a	Chesterfield	58	Lincoln C	57	Wrexham*	54
1931–32c	Lincoln C*	57	Gateshead	57	Chester	50
1932–33a	Hull C	59	Wrexham	57	Stockport Co	54
1933–34a	Barnsley	62	Chesterfield	61	Stockport Co	59
1934–35a	Doncaster R	57	Halifax T	55	Chester	54
1935–36a	Chesterfield	60	Chester*	55	Tranmere R	55
1936–37a	Stockport Co	60	Lincoln C	57	Chester	53
1937–38a	Tranmere R	56	Doncaster R	54	Hull C	53
1938–39a	Barnsley	67	Doncaster R	56	Bradford C	52
1939–46	Competition cancelled owing to war.					
1946–47a	Doncaster R	72	Rotherham U	64	Chester	56
1947–48a	Lincoln C	60	Rotherham U	59	Wrexham	50
1948–49a	Hull C	65	Rotherham U	62	Doncaster R	50
1949–50a	Doncaster R	55	Gateshead	53	Rochdale*	51
1950–51d	Rotherham U	71	Mansfield T	64	Carlisle U	62
1951–52d	Lincoln C	69	Grimsby T	66	Stockport Co	59
1952–53d	Oldham Ath	59	Port Vale	58	Wrexham	56
1953–54d	Port Vale	69	Barnsley	58	Scunthorpe U	57
1954–55d	Barnsley	65	Accrington S	61	Scunthorpe U*	58
1955–56d	Grimsby T	68	Derby Co	63	Accrington S	59
1956–57d	Derby Co	63	Hartlepools U	59	Accrington S[2]	58
1957–58d	Scunthorpe U	66	Accrington S	59	Bradford C	57

* Won or placed on goal average/goal difference.

PROMOTED AFTER PLAY-OFFS
(Not accounted for in previous section)

1986–87	Aldershot to Division 3.
1987–88	Swansea C to Divison 3.
1988–89	Leyton Orient to Division 3.
1989–90	Cambridge U to Division 3; Sunderland to Division 1.

LEAGUE TITLE WINS

LEAGUE DIVISION 1 – Liverpool 18, Arsenal 9, Everton 9, Manchester U 7, Aston Villa 7, Sunderland 6, Newcastle U 4, Sheffield W 4, Huddersfield T 3, Wolverhampton W 3, Blackburn R 2, Portsmouth 2, Preston NE 2, Burnley 2, Manchester C 2, Tottenham H 2, Leeds U 2, Derby Co 2, Chelsea 1, Sheffield U 1, WBA 1, Ipswich T 1, Nottingham F 1 each.

LEAGUE DIVISION 2 – Leicester C 6, Manchester C 6, Sheffield W 5, Birmingham C (one as Small Heath) 4, Derby Co 4, Liverpool 4, Leeds U 3, Preston NE 3, Middlesbrough 3, Grimsby T 2, Norwich C 2, Nottingham F 2, Tottenham H 2, WBA 2, Aston Villa 2, Stoke C 2, Ipswich T 2, Burnley 2, Chelsea 2, Manchester U 2, West Ham U 2, Wolverhampton W 2, Bolton W 2, Huddersfield 1, Bristol C, Brentford, Bury, Bradford C, Everton, Fulham, Sheffield U, Newcastle U, Coventry C, Blackpool, Blackburn R, Sunderland, Crystal Palace, Luton T, QPR, Oxford U, Millwall 1 each.

LEAGUE DIVISION 3 – Portsmouth 2, Oxford U 2, Plymouth Arg, Southampton, Bury, Northampton T, Coventry C, Carlisle U, Hull C, QPR, Watford, Leyton O, Preston NE, Aston Villa, Bolton W, Oldham Ath, Blackburn R, Hereford U, Mansfield T, Wrexham, Shrewsbury T, Grimsby T, Rotherham U, Burnley, Bradford C, Bournemouth, Reading, Sunderland, Wolverhampton W, Bristol R, 1 each.

LEAGUE DIVISION 4 – Chesterfield 2, Doncaster R 2, Peterborough U 2, Port Vale, Walsall, Millwall, Brentford, Gillingham, Brighton, Stockport Co, Luton T, Notts Co, Grimsby T, Southport, Mansfield T, Lincoln C, Cambridge U, Watford, Reading, Huddersfield T, Southend U, Sheffield U, Wimbledon, York C, Swindon T, Northampton T, Rotherham U, Wolverhampton W, Exeter C, 1 each.

To 1957–58

DIVISION 3 (South) – Bristol C 3; Charlton Ath, Ipswich T, Millwall, Notts Co, Plymouth Arg, Swansea T 2 each; Brentford, Bristol R, Cardiff C, Crystal Palace, Coventry C, Fulham, Leyton O, Luton T, Newport Co, Nottingham F, Norwich C, Portsmouth, QPR, Reading, Southampton, Brighton 1 each.

DIVISION 3 (North) – Barnsley, Doncaster R, Lincoln C 3 each; Chesterfield, Grimsby T, Hull C, Port Vale, Stockport Co 2 each; Bradford PA, Bradford C, Darlington, Derby Co, Nelson, Oldham Ath, Rotherham U, Stoke C, Tranmere R, Wolverhampton W, Scunthorpe U 1 each.

RELEGATED CLUBS

1891–92 League extended. Newton Heath, Sheffield W and Nottingham F admitted. *Second Division formed* including Darwen.
1892–93 In Test matches, Sheffield U and Darwen won promotion in place of Notts Co and Accrington S.
1893–94 In Tests, Liverpool and Small Heath won promotion. Newton Heath and Darwen relegated.
1894–95 After Tests, Bury promoted, Liverpool

1895–96 After Tests, Liverpool promoted, Small Heath relegated.
1896–97 After Tests, Notts Co promoted, Burnley relegated.
1897–98 Test system abolished after success of Stoke C and Burnley. League extended. Blackburn R and Newcastle U elected to First Division. *Automatic promotion and relegation introduced.*

DIVISION 1 TO DIVISION 2

1898–99 Bolton W and Sheffield W
1899–1900 Burnley and Glossop
1900–01 Preston NE and WBA
1901–02 Small Heath and Manchester C
1902–03 Grimsby T and Bolton W
1903–04 Liverpool and WBA
1904–05 League extended. Bury and Notts Co, two bottom clubs in First Division, re-elected.
1905–06 Nottingham F and Wolverhampton W
1906–07 Derby Co and Stoke C
1907–08 Bolton W and Birmingham C
1908–09 Manchester C and Leicester Fosse
1909–10 Bolton W and Chelsea
1910–11 Bristol C and Nottingham F
1911–12 Preston NE and Bury
1912–13 Notts Co and Woolwich Arsenal
1913–14 Preston NE and Derby Co
1914–15 Tottenham H and Chelsea*
1919–20 Notts Co and Sheffield W
1920–21 Derby Co and Bradford
1921–22 Bradford C and Manchester U
1922–23 Stoke C and Oldham Ath
1923–24 Chelsea and Middlesbrough
1924–25 Preston NE and Nottingham F
1925–26 Manchester C and Notts Co
1926–27 Leeds U and WBA
1927–28 Tottenham H and Middlesbrough
1928–29 Bury and Cardiff C
1929–30 Burnley and Everton
1930–31 Leeds U and Manchester U
1931–32 Grimsby T and West Ham U
1932–33 Bolton W and Blackpool
1933–34 Newcastle U and Sheffield U
1934–35 Leicester C and Tottenham H
1935–36 Aston Villa and Blackburn R
1936–37 Manchester U and Sheffield W
1937–38 Manchester C and WBA
1938–39 Birmingham C and Leicester C
1946–47 Brentford and Leeds U
1947–48 Blackburn R and Grimsby T
1948–49 Preston NE and Sheffield U

1949–50 Manchester C and Birmingham C
1950–51 Sheffield W and Everton
1951–52 Huddersfield and Fulham
1952–53 Stoke C and Derby Co
1953–54 Middlesbrough and Liverpool
1954–55 Leicester C and Sheffield W
1955–56 Huddersfield and Sheffield U
1956–57 Charlton Ath and Cardiff C
1957–58 Sheffield W and Sunderland
1958–59 Portsmouth and Aston Villa
1959–60 Luton T and Leeds U
1960–61 Preston NE and Newcastle U
1961–62 Chelsea and Cardiff C
1962–63 Manchester C and Leyton O
1963–64 Bolton W and Ipswich T
1964–65 Wolverhampton W and Birmingham C
1965–66 Northampton T and Blackburn R
1966–67 Aston Villa and Blackpool
1967–68 Fulham and Sheffield U
1968–69 Leicester C and QPR
1969–70 Sunderland and Sheffield W
1970–71 Burnley and Blackpool
1971–72 Huddersfield T and Nottingham F
1972–73 Crystal Palace and WBA
1973–74 Southampton, Manchester U, Norwich C
1974–75 Luton T, Chelsea, Carlisle U
1975–76 Wolverhampton W, Burnley, Sheffield U
1976–77 Sunderland, Stoke C, Tottenham H
1977–78 West Ham U, Newcastle U, Leicester C
1978–79 QPR, Birmingham C, Chelsea
1979–80 Bristol C, Derby Co, Bolton W
1980–81 Norwich C, Leicester C, Crystal Palace
1981–82 Leeds U, Wolverhampton W, Middlesbrough
1982–83 Manchester C, Swansea C, Brighton & HA
1983–84 Birmingham C, Notts Co, Wolverhampton W
1984–85 Norwich C, Sunderland, Stoke C
1985–86 Ipswich T, Birmingham C, WBA
1986–87 Leicester C, Manchester C, Aston Villa
1987–88 Chelsea,** Portsmouth, Watford, Oxford U
1988–89 Middlesbrough, West Ham U, Newcastle U
1989–90 Sheffield W, Charlton Ath, Millwall

*Subsequently re-elected to Division 1 when League was extended after the War.

DIVISION 2 TO DIVISION 3

1920–21 Stockport Co
1921–22 Bradford and Bristol C
1922–23 Rotherham C and Wolverhampton W
1923–24 Nelson and Bristol C
1924–25 Crystal Palace and Coventry C
1925–26 Stoke C and Stockport Co
1926–27 Darlington and Bradford C
1927–28 Fulham and South Shields
1928–29 Port Vale and Clapton O
1929–30 Hull C and Notts Co
1930–31 Reading and Cardiff C
1931–32 Barnsley and Bristol C
1932–33 Chesterfield and Charlton Ath
1933–34 Millwall and Lincoln C
1934–35 Oldham Ath and Notts Co

1935–36 Port Vale and Hull C
1936–37 Doncaster R and Bradford C
1937–38 Barnsley and Stockport Co
1938–39 Norwich C and Tranmere R
1946–47 Swansea T and Newport Co
1947–48 Doncaster R and Millwall
1948–49 Nottingham F and Lincoln C
1949–50 Plymouth Arg and Bradford
1950–51 Grimsby T and Chesterfield
1951–52 Coventry C and QPR
1952–53 Southampton and Barnsley
1953–54 Brentford and Oldham Ath
1954–55 Ipswich T and Derby Co
1955–56 Plymouth Arg and Hull C
1956–57 Port Vale and Bury

1957–58 Doncaster R and Notts Co	1974–75 Millwall, Cardiff C, Sheffield W
1958–59 Barnsley and Grimsby T	1975–76 Oxford U, York C, Portsmouth
1959–60 Bristol C and Hull C	1976–77 Carlisle U, Plymouth Arg, Hereford U
1960–61 Lincoln C and Portsmouth	1977–78 Blackpool, Mansfield T, Hull C
1961–62 Brighton and Bristol R	1978–79 Sheffield U, Millwall, Blackburn R
1962–63 Walsall and Luton T	1979–80 Fulham, Burnley, Charlton Ath
1963–64 Grimsby T and Scunthorpe U	1980–81 Preston NE, Bristol C, Bristol R
1964–65 Swindon T and Swansea T	1981–82 Cardiff C, Wrexham, Orient
1965–66 Middlesbrough and Leyton O	1982–83 Rotherham U, Burnley, Bolton W
1966–67 Northampton T and Bury	1983–84 Derby Co, Swansea C, Cambridge U
1967–68 Plymouth Arg and Rotherham U	1984–85 Notts Co, Cardiff C, Wolverhampton W
1968–69 Fulham and Bury	1985–86 Carlisle U, Middlesbrough, Fulham
1969–70 Preston NE and Aston Villa	1986–87 Sunderland**, Grimsby T, Brighton & HA
1970–71 Blackburn R and Bolton W	1987–88 Huddersfield T, Reading, Sheffield U**
1971–72 Charlton Ath and Watford	1988–89 Shrewsbury T, Birmingham C, Walsall
1972–73 Huddersfield T and Brighton	1989–90 Bournemouth, Bradford, Stoke C
1973–74 Crystal Palace, Preston NE, Swindon T	

DIVISION 3 TO DIVISION 4

1958–59 Rochdale, Notts Co, Doncaster R and Stockport Co	1972–73 Rotherham U, Brentford, Swansea C, Scunthorpe U
1959–60 Accrington S, Wrexham, Mansfield T and York C	1973–74 Cambridge U, Shrewsbury T, Southport, Rochdale
1960–61 Chesterfield, Colchester U, Bradford C and Tranmere R	1974–75 AFC Bournemouth, Tranmere R, Watford, Huddersfield T
1961–62 Newport Co, Brentford, Lincoln C and Torquay U	1975–76 Aldershot, Colchester U, Southend U, Halifax T
1962–63 Bradford, Brighton, Carlisle U and Halifax T	1976–77 Reading, Northampton T, Grimsby T, York C
1963–64 Millwall, Crewe Alex, Wrexham and Notts Co	1977–78 Port Vale, Bradford C, Hereford U, Portsmouth
1964–65 Luton T, Port Vale, Colchester U and Barnsley	1978–79 Peterborough U, Walsall, Tranmere R, Lincoln C
1965–66 Southend U, Exeter C, Brentford and York C	1979–80 Bury, Southend U, Mansfield T, Wimbledon
1966–67 Doncaster R, Workington T, Darlington and Swansea T	1980–81 Sheffield U, Colchester U, Blackpool, Hull C
1967–68 Scunthorpe U, Colchester U, Grimsby T and Peterborough U (demoted)	1981–82 Wimbledon, Swindon T, Bristol C, Chester
	1982–83 Reading, Wrexham, Doncaster R, Chesterfield
1968–69 Oldham Ath, Crewe Alex, Hartlepool and Northampton T	1983–84 Scunthorpe U, Southend U, Port Vale, Exeter C
	1984–85 Burnley, Orient, Preston NE, Cambridge U
1969–70 Bournemouth, Southport, Barrow, Stockport Co	1985–86 Lincoln C, Cardiff C, Wolverhampton W, Swansea C
1970–71 Reading, Bury, Doncaster R, Gillingham	1986–87 Bolton W**, Carlisle U, Darlington, Newport Co
1971–72 Mansfield T, Barnsley, Torquay U, Bradford C	1987–88 Doncaster R, York C, Grimsby T, Rotherham U**
**Relegated after play-offs	1988–89 Southend U, Chesterfield, Gillingham, Aldershot
	1989–90 Cardiff C, Northampton T, Blackpool, Walsall

APPLICATIONS FOR RE-ELECTION
FOURTH DIVISION
Eleven: Hartlepool U.
Seven: Crewe Alex
Six: Barrow (lost League place to Hereford U 1972), Halifax T, Rochdale, Southport (lost League place to Wigan Ath 1978), York C
Five: Chester C, Darlington, Lincoln C, Stockport Co, Workington (lost League place to Wimbledon 1977)
Four: Bradford PA (lost League place to Cambridge U 1970), Newport Co, Northampton T
Three: Doncaster R, Hereford U
Two: Bradford C, Exeter C, Oldham Ath, Scunthorpe U, Torquay U
One: Aldershot, Colchester U, Gateshead (lost League place to Peterborough U 1960), Grimsby T, Swansea C, Tranmere R, Wrexham, Blackpool, Cambridge U, Preston NE
Accrington S resigned and Oxford U were elected 1962.
Port Vale were forced to re-apply following expulsion in 1968.

THIRD DIVISIONS NORTH & SOUTH
Seven: Walsall.
Six: Exeter C, Halifax T, Newport Co.
Five: Accrington S, Barrow, Gillingham, New Brighton, Southport.
Four: Rochdale, Norwich C.
Three: Crystal Palace, Crewe Alex, Darlington, Hartlepool, Merthyr T, Swindon T.
Two: Aberdare Ath, Aldershot, Ashington, Bournemouth, Brentford, Chester, Colchester U, Durham C, Millwall, Nelson, QPR, Rotherham U, Southend U, Tranmere R, Watford, Workington
One: Bradford C, Bradford PA, Brighton, Bristol R, Cardiff C, Carlisle U, Charlton Ath, Gateshead, Grimsby T, Mansfield T, Shrewsbury T, Torquay U, York C.

LEAGUE STATUS FROM 1986–87
RELEGATED FROM LEAGUE	**PROMOTED TO LEAGUE**
1986–87 Lincoln C	Scarborough
1987–88 Newport Co	Lincoln C
1988–89 Darlington	Maidstone U
1989–90 Colchester U	Darlington

LEADING SCORERS 1989–90

DIVISION 1	League	FA Cup	Littlewoods Cup	Other Cups	Total
John Barnes (Liverpool)	22	5	1	0	28
Gary Lineker (Tottenham H)	24	0	2	0	26
Ian Rush (Liverpool)	18	6	2	0	26
Kerry Dixon (Chelsea)	20	2	0	3	25
Matthew Le Tissier (Southampton)	20	1	3	0	24
David Platt (Aston Villa)	19	1	1	3	24
Dean Saunders (Derby Co)	11	0	7	3	21
Rodney Wallace (Southampton)	18	1	2	0	21
Kevin Wilson (Chelsea)	14	1	1	4	20
Mark Bright (Crystal Palace)	12	2	1	2	17
David Hirst (Sheffield W)	14	1	1	0	16
Dalian Atkinson (Sheffield W)	10	1	3	1	15
Peter Beardsley (Liverpool)	10	4	1	0	15
Tony Cottee (Everton)	13	2	0	0	15
Mark Hughes (Manchester U)	13	2	0	0	15
John Fashanu (Wimbledon)	11	0	2	1	14
Steve Hodge (Nottingham F)	10	0	4	0	14

DIVISION 2	League	FA Cup	Littlewoods Cup	Other Cups	Total
Mick Quinn (Newcastle U)	32	2	0	2	36
Bernie Slaven (Middlesbrough)	21	0	4	7	32
Andy Ritchie (Oldham Ath)	15	3	10	0	28
Steve Bull (Wolverhampton W)	24	1	2	0	27
Duncan Shearer (Swindon T)	20	1	4	1	26
Marco Gabbiadini (Sunderland)	21	0	4	0	25
Mark McGhee (Newcastle U)	19	5	1	0	25
Steve White (Swindon T)	18	0	5	2	25
Brian Deane (Sheffield U)	21	1	1	1	24
Guy Whittingham (Portsmouth)	23	1	0	0	24
Paul Hunter (Hull C)	16	4	2	0	22
Including all but 3 League for East Fife)					
Darren Beckford (Port Vale)	17	1	3	0	21
Don Goodman (WBA)	21	0	0	0	21
Lee Chapman (Leeds U)	19	0	1	0	20
(Including 7 League, 1 Littlewoods for Nottingham F)					
Roger Palmer (Oldham Ath)	16	3	1	0	20
Luther Blissett (Bournemouth)	18	0	0	1	19
Gary Penrice (Watford)	16	1	1	1	19
(Including 3 League, 1 Littlewoods for Bristol R)					
Jimmy Quinn (West Ham U)	18	0	1	0	19
(Including 6 League, 1 Littlewoods for Bradford C)					

DIVISION 3	League	FA Cup	Littlewoods Cup	Other Cups	Total
Bob Taylor (Bristol C)	27	5	2	0	34
Ian Muir (Tranmere R)	23	0	4	6	33
Dean Holdsworth (Brentford)	25	0	0	4	29
(Including 1 League for Watford)					
John McGinlay (Shrewsbury T)	22	2	0	2	26
Tony Philliskirk (Bolton W)	18	0	5	1	24
Chris Malkin (Tranmere R)	17	0	4	2	23
Bobby Williamson (Rotherham U)	19	0	2	1	22
Craig Maskell (Huddersfield T)	15	2	2	2	21
David Mehew (Bristol R)	18	1	0	2	21
Trevor Senior (Reading)	14	3	3	1	21
Dennis Bailey (Birmingham C)	18	0	2	0	20
Bobby Barnes (Northampton T)	18	1	0	1	20
Chris Pike (Cardiff)	18	1	1	0	20
Tommy Johnson (Notts Co)	18	0	0	0	18
Stuart Rimmer (Walsall)	10	2	0	6	18
Liam Robinson (Bury)	17	0	1	0	18
Trevor Christie (Mansfield T)	13	0	3	1	17

DIVISION 4	League	FA Cup	Littlewoods Cup	Other Cups	Total
Darren Rowbotham (Exeter C)	20	4	6	0	30
Brett Angell (Stockport Co)	23	1	0	4	28
Steve Butler (Maidstone U)	21	1	1	3	26
Mark Gall (Maidstone U)	18	2	0	6	26
David Crown (Southend U)	19	0	3	1	23
David Puckett (Aldershot)	18	0	3	1	22
Dion Dublin (Cambridge U)	15	4	2	0	21
John Taylor (Cambridge U)	15	5	1	0	21
Andy Flounders (Scunthorpe U)	18	0	1	1	20
Mike Helliwell (York C)	14	0	1	4	19
Joe Allon (Hartlepool U)	18	0	0	0	18
Paul Baker (Hartlepool U)	16	0	1	1	18
Steve Lovell (Gillingham)	16	0	1	1	18
Steve Neville (Exeter C)	14	1	2	1	18
Dave Waller (Chesterfield)	16	1	1	0	18

FA CHARITY SHIELD WINNERS 1908–89

1908	Manchester U v QPR	4-0 after 1-1 draw	1956	Manchester U v Manchester C		1-0
1909	Newcastle U v Northampton T	2-0	1957	Manchester U v Aston Villa		4-0
1910	Brighton v Aston Villa	1-0	1958	Bolton W v Wolverhampton W		4-1
1911	Manchester U v Swindon T	8-4	1959	Wolverhampton W v Nottingham F		3-1
1912	Blackburn R v QPR	2-1	1960	Burnley v Wolverhampton W		2-2*
1913	Professionals v Amateurs	7-2	1961	Tottenham H v FA XI		3-2
1919	WBA v Tottenham H	2-0	1962	Tottenham H v Ipswich T		5-1
1920	Tottenham H v Burnley	2-0	1963	Everton v Manchester U		4-0
1921	Huddersfield v Liverpool	1-0	1964	Liverpool v West Ham U		2-2*
1922	Not played		1965	Manchester U v Liverpool		2-2*
1923	Professionals v Amateurs	2-0	1966	Liverpool v Everton		1-0
1924	Professionals v Amateurs	3-1	1967	Manchester U v Tottenham H		3-3*
1925	Amateurs v Professionals	6-1	1968	Manchester C v WBA		6-1
1926	Amateurs v Professionals	6-3	1969	Leeds U v Manchester C		2-1
1927	Cardiff C v Corinthians	2-1	1970	Everton v Chelsea		2-1
1928	Everton v Blackburn R	2-1	1971	Leicester C v Liverpool		1-0
1929	Professionals v Amateurs	3-0	1972	Manchester C v Aston Villa		1-0
1930	Arsenal v Sheffield W	2-1	1973	Burnley v Manchester C		1-0
1931	Arsenal v WBA	1-0	1974	Liverpool† v Leeds		1-1
1932	Everton v Newcastle U	5-3	1975	Derby Co v West Ham U		2-0
1933	Arsenal v Everton	3-0	1976	Liverpool v Southampton		1-0
1934	Arsenal v Manchester C	4-0	1977	Liverpool v Manchester U		0-0*
1935	Sheffield W v Arsenal	1-0	1978	Nottingham F v Ipswich T		5-0
1936	Sunderland v Arsenal	2-1	1979	Liverpool v Arsenal		3-1
1937	Manchester C v Sunderland	2-0	1980	Liverpool v West Ham U		1-0
1938	Arsenal v Preston NE	2-1	1981	Aston Villa v Tottenham H		2-2*
1948	Arsenal v Manchester U	4-3	1982	Liverpool v Tottenham H		1-0
1949	Portsmouth v Wolverhampton W	1-1*	1983	Manchester U v Liverpool		2-0
1950	World Cup Team v Canadian Touring Team	4-2	1984	Everton v Liverpool		1-0
1951	Tottenham H v Newcastle U	2-1	1985	Everton v Manchester U		2-0
1952	Manchester U v Newcastle U	4-2	1986	Everton v Liverpool		1-1*
1953	Arsenal v Blackpool	3-1	1987	Everton v Coventry		1-0
1954	Wolverhampton W v WBA	4-4*	1988	Liverpool v Wimbledon		2-1
1955	Chelsea v Newcastle U	3-0				

Each club retained shield for six months. † Won on penalties

FA CHARITY SHIELD 1989

Liverpool (1) 1, Arsenal (0) 0
At Wembley, 12 August, 1989, attendance 63,000

Liverpool: Grobbelaar; Hysen, Burrows, Nicol, Whelan, Hansen, Beardsley, Venison, Rush, Barnes, McMahon.

Scorer: Beardsley.

Arsenal: Lukic; Dixon, Winterburn, Thomas, O'Leary, Adams, Rocastle, Richardson, Smith (Quinn), Caesar (Marwood), Merson.

Referee: A. Gunn (Sussex).

Peter Beardsley (left) seems unconcerned by the attempted tackle from Arsenal's Michael Thomas. Beardsley's goal won the Charity Shield for Liverpool. (Bob Thomas)

TRANSFERS 1989–90

		From	To
July 1989			
26	Allison, Wayne	Halifax Town	Watford
7	Archdeacon, Owen D.	Glasgow Celtic	Barnsley
28	Aspin, Neil	Leeds United	Port Vale
11	Barnes, David	Aldershot	Sheffield United
21	Beaumont, Christopher P.	Rochdale	Stockport County
28	Beglin, James M.	Liverpool	Leeds United
21	Black, Kenneth G.	Heart of Midlothian	Portsmouth
26	Bradley, Russell	Nottingham Forest	Hereford United
6	Brown, Malcolm	Rochdale	Stockport County
27	Clarke, Wayne	Everton	Leicester City
20	Comfort, Alan	Leyton Orient	Middlesbrough
25	Cranson, Ian	Sheffield Wednesday	Stoke City
18	Deary, John S.	Blackpool	Burnley
26	Elsey, Karl W.	Reading	Maidstone United
13	Foster, Stephen B.	Luton Town	Oxford United
21	Frain, David	Rochdale	Stockport County
24	Gunn, Brynley C.	Peterborough United	Chesterfield
25	Hardyman, Paul G.	Portsmouth	Sunderland
17	Harkness, Steven	Carlisle United	Liverpool
25	Jakub, Janek	Chester City	Burnley
13	Lange, Anthony S.	Aldershot	Wolverhampton Wanderers
11	Lewis, Dudley K.	Swansea City	Huddersfield Town
13	McLoughlin, Paul B.	Hereford United	Wolverhampton Wanderers
27	McNally, Bernard A.	Shrewsbury Town	West Bromwich Albion
20	Marshall, Gary	Carlisle United	Scunthorpe United
26	May, Edward	Hibernian	Brentford
11	Morris, Mark J.	Watford	Sheffield United
31	Nebbeling, Gavin M.	Crystal Palace	Fulham
27	Newell, Michael C.	Leicester City	Everton
1	Phelan, Michael C.	Norwich City	Manchester United
31	Phillips, David O.	Coventry City	Norwich City
27	Plummer, Calvin A.	Plymouth Argyle	Chesterfield
18	Reck, Sean M.	Oxford United	Wrexham
31	Rennie, David	Leeds United	Bristol City
14	Richards, Carroll L.	Birmingham City	Peterborough United
28	Robinson, David A.	Halifax Town	Peterborough United
7	Rose, Kevin P.	Hereford United	Bolton Wanderers
6	Salman, Michael B.	Wrexham	Charlton Athletic
10	Scott, Ian	Manchester City	Stoke City
28	Sedgley, Stephen P.	Coventry City	Tottenham Hotspur
24	Shaw, Graham P.	Stoke City	Preston North End
19	Shepherd, Anthony	Glasgow Celtic	Carlisle United
18	Sherwood, Timothy A.	Watford	Norwich City
26	Shirtliff, Peter A.	Charlton Athletic	Sheffield Wednesday
27	Short, Jonathan C.	Scarborough	Notts. County
10	Skipper, Peter D.	Oldham Athletic	Walsall
10	Smart, Jason	Rochdale	Crewe Alexandra
18	Stant, Philip R.	Hereford United	Notts. County
28	Sterland, Melvyn	Glasgow Rangers	Leeds United
21	Thomas, Andrew M.	Bradford City	Plymouth Argyle
27	Thomas, John W.	Bolton Wanderers	West Bromwich Albion
20	Tucker, Gordon	Huddersfield Town	Scunthorpe United
18	Walsh, Mario M.	Colchester United	Southend United
24	Webb, Neil J.	Nottingham Forest	Manchester United
20	Wilmot, Rhys J.	Arsenal	Plymouth Argyle
24	Wilson, Robert J.	Fulham	Huddersfield Town
11	Winter, Julian	Huddersfield Town	Sheffield United
31	Withe, Christopher	Notts. County	Bury
28	Wood, Darren	Chesterfield	Reading
August 1989			
16	Adams, Neil J.	Everton	Oldham Athletic
23	Ainscow, Andrew P.	Wigan Athletic	Rotherham United
16	Aizlewood, Mark	Leeds United	Bradford City
24	Allen, Martin J.	Queens Park Rangers	West Ham United
3	Bailey, Dennis L.	Crystal Palace	Birmingham City
18	Banton, Dale C.	Walsall	Aldershot
2	Banks, Ian F.	West Bromwich Albion	Barnsley
10	Biggins, Wayne	Manchester City	Stoke City
2	Bishop, Ian W.	A.F.C. Bournemouth	Manchester City
18	Boyle, Terrence D. J.	Cardiff City	Swansea City
2	Butler, Brian F.	Stockport County	Halifax Town
18	Clarke, Michael D.	Barnsley	Scarborough
2	Cook, Mitchell	Scarborough	Halifax Town
17	Croft, Brian G. A.	Cambridge United	Chester City
17	Crosby, Philip A.	Rotherham United	Peterborough United
2	Cunningham, Anthony E.	Blackpool	Bury
2	Cusack, Nicholas J.	Peterborough United	Motherwell
22	Daniel, Raymond C.	Hull City	Cardiff City

		From	*To*
18	Dennis, Mark E.	Queens Park Rangers	Crystal Palace
25	Diamond, Anthony J.	Blackburn Rovers	Blackpool
18	Dickens, Alan W.	West Ham United	Chelsea
4	Dodds, William	Chelsea	Dundee
3	Downes, Christopher B.	Sheffield United	Stockport County
14	Doyle, Stephen C.	Sunderland	Hull City
1	Feeley, Andrew J.	Brentford	Bury
17	Fleming, Gary J.	Nottingham Forest	Manchester City
8	Galliers, Steven	Bristol City	Maidstone United
18	Galvin, Anthony	Sheffield Wednesday	Swindon Town
3	Graham, Milton M.	Chestesr City	Peterborough United
18	Gray, Andrew A.	Queens Park Rangers	Crystal Palace
29	Gregory, John C.	Derby County	Portsmouth
31	Hart, Nigel	Stockport County	Chesterfield
17	Hemming, Christopher A. J.	Stoke City	Hereford United
4	Henry, Charles A.	Swindon Town	Aldershot
1	Hill, Colin F.	Colchester United	Sheffield United
18	Holden, Richard W.	Watford	Oldham Athletic
23	James, Anthony C.	Lincoln City	Leicester City
18	Johnson, Robert S.	Luton Town	Leicester City
17	Jones, Mark	Walsall	Hereford United
10	Juryeff, Ian M.	Leyton Orient	Halifax Town
9	Kelly, John	Oldham Athletic	Walsall
18	Kennedy, Michael F.	Leicester City	Luton Town
7	Keown, Martin R.	Aston Villa	Everton
16	Kite, Philip D.	Gillingham	A.F.C. Bournemouth
18	Knill, Alan R.	Swansea City	Bury
18	Lawrence, George R.	Millwall	A.F.C. Bournemouth
25	McClaren, Stephen	Bristol City	Oxford United
4	McGhee, Mark	Glasgow Celtic	Newcastle United
3	McGrath, Paul	Manchester United	Aston Villa
3	McIlhargey, Stephen	Walsall	Blackpool
17	McLaughlin, Joseph	Chelsea	Charlton Athletic
3	Matthewson, Trevor	Lincoln City	Birmingham City
18	Miller, Paul R.	Watford	A.F.C. Bournemouth
2	Moulden, Paul A.	Manchester City	A.F.C. Bournemouth
16	Naughton, William B. S.	Walsall	Shrewsbury Town
17	Oliver, Neil	Berwick Rangers	Blackburn Rovers
15	O'Neill, Michael A.	Newcastle United	Dundee United
2	Owen, Gordon	Mansfield Town	Blackpool
29	Palliser, Garry A.	Middlesbrough	Manchester United
16	Peacock, Gavin K.	Gillingham	A.F.C Bournemouth
1	Platnauer, Nicholas R.	Cardiff City	Notts. County
22	Pulis, Anthony R.	A.F.C. Bournemouth	Gillingham
14	Putney, Trevor A.	Norwich City	Middlesbrough
18	Quinn, Michael	Portsmouth	Newcastle United
17	Rees, Anthony A.	Barnsley	Grimsby Town
18	Reeves, Alan	Norwich City	Chester City
17	Reeves, David	Sheffield Wednesday	Bolton Wanderers
18	Robinson, Colin R.	Birmingham City	Hereford United
18	Robinson, Philip J.	Wolverhampton Wanderers	Notts County
18	Robinson, Ronald	West Bromwich Albion	Rotherham United
1	Rodger, Graham	Coventry City	Luton Town
4	Rougvie, Douglas	Fulham	Dunfermline Athletic
15	Saunders, Steven J.	Grimsby Town	Scarborough
24	Shelton, Gary	Oxford United	Bristol City
3	Sheridan, John J.	Leeds United	Nottingham Forest
3	Smith, David A.	Gillingham	Bristol City
18	Sproson, Philip J.	Port Vale	Birmingham City
18	Statham, Derek J.	Southampton	Stoke City
7	Stiles, John C.	Leeds United	Doncaster Rovers
17	Thompson, Steven P.	Sheffield United	Lincoln City
15	Thorpe, Adrian	Notts. County	Walsall
11	Uzzell, John E.	Plymouth Argyle	Torquay United
25	Van Den Hauwe, Patrick W. R.	Everton	Tottenham Hotspur
15	Walton, Mark A.	Colchester United	Norwich City
19	Watson, John M.	Dunfermline Athletic	Fulham
18	Waugh, Keith	Bristol City	Coventry City
1	Whiteside, Norman	Manchester United	Everton
14	Wright, Thomas E.	Oldham Athletic	Leicester City

Temporary Transfers

25	Beresford, Marlon	Sheffield Wednesday	Bury
23	Bracewell, Paul W.	Everton	Sunderland
16	Bradshaw, Darren S.	York City	Newcastle United
17	Bowling, Ian	Lincoln City	Hartlepool United
20	Brown, Grant A.	Leicester City	Lincoln City
14	Cobb, Gary E.	Luton Town	Swansea City
16	Coddington, Matthew J.	Middlesbrough	Bury
17	Coyne, Peter D.	Swindon Town	Aldershot
31	Dearden, Kevin C.	Tottehham Hotspur	Hartlepool United
20	Groves, Paul	Leicester City	Lincoln City
24	Hansbury, Roger	Birmingham City	Colchester United
7	Harris, Mark A.	Crystal Palace	Burnley

		From	To
1	Holsgrove, Paul	Aldershot	West Bromwich Albion
17	Knight, Ian J.	Sheffield Wednesday	Scunthorpe United
24	Rees, Melvyn J.	Watford	Crewe Alexandra
14	Salako, John A.	Crystal Palace	Swansea City

September 1989

15	Bardsley, David J.	Oxford United	Queens Park Rangers
29	Bracewell, Paul W.	Everton	Sunderland
14	Bradshaw, Darren S.	York City	Newcastle United
2	Carey, Brian P.	Cork City	Manchester United
8	Close, Shaun C.	A.F.C. Bournemouth	Swindon Town
26	Coleman, Simon	Mansfield Town	Middlesbrough
20	Comstive, Paul T.	Burnley	Bolton Wanderers
29	Edwards, Keith	Hull City	Stockport County
22	Foster, Colin J.	Nottingham Forest	West Ham United
9	Gleghorn, Nigel W.	Manchester City	Birmingham City
22	Harris, Mark A.	Crystal Palace	Swansea City
29	Holdsworth, Dean C.	Watford	Brentford
14	Ince, Paul E. C.	West Ham United	Manchester United
22	Jones, Alexander	Preston North End	Carlisle United
8	Jonsson, Sigurdur	Sheffield Wednesday	Arsenal
14	Knowles, Darren T.	Sheffield United	Stockport County
21	Lillis, Mark A.	Aston Villa	Scunthorpe United
14	Miller, David B.	Preston North End	Carlisle United
1	Pike, Geoffrey A.	Notts. County	Leyton Orient
1	Sinclair, Ronald M.	Leeds United	Bristol City
15	Stein, Earl M. S.	Queens Park Rangers	Oxford United
1	Trusson, Michael S.	Brighton & Hove Albion	Gillingham
18	Wallace, David L.	Southampton	Manchester United

Temporary Transfers

29	Airey, Carl	Torquay United	Shamrock Rovers
29	Beresford, Marlon	Sheffield Wednesday	Ipswich Road
5	Blake, Mark C.	Southampton	Colchestesr United
7	Bradshaw, Carl	Manchester City	Sheffield United
13	Chapman, Gary A.	Bradford City	Notts. County
15	Clark, Martin J.	Nottingham Forest	Falkirk
29	Cobb, Gary E.	Swansea City	Luton Town (Tr. Back)
25	Coddington, Matthew J.	Middlesbrough	Halifax Town
7	Davison, Aidan J.	Notts. County	Leyton Orient
13	Dowie, Iain	Luton Town	Fulham
29	Freestone, Roger	Chelsea	Swansea City
14	Gabbiadini, Ricardo	Sunderland	Blackpool
1	Gavin, Patrick J.	Leicester City	Gillingham
14	Glover, Edward L.	Nottingham Forest	Leicester City
2	Gormley, Edward J.	Tottenham Hotspur	Shrewsbury Town
23	Hansbury, Roger	Colchester United	Birmingham City (Tr. Back)
13	Jones, Alexander	Preston North End	Carlisle United
28	Kevan, David J.	Notts. County	Cardiff City
21	Lamb, Alan	Nottingham Forest	Hartlepool United
28	Lamont, Lee S.	Doncaster Rovers	Rochdale
28	McGarvey, Scott T.	Oldham Athletic	Wigan Athletic
6	Maguire, Peter J.	Leeds United	Huddersfield Town
6	Marriott, Andrew	Nottingham Forest	West Bromwich Albion
7	Mundee, Denny W. J.	A.F.C. Bournemouth	Torquay United
28	O'Riordan, Donald J.	Notts. County	Mansfield Town
15	Palin, Leigh G.	Bradford City	Stoke City
1	Phillips, Gary C.	Reading	Hereford United
19	Rostron, John W.	Sheffield Wednesday	Sheffield United
7	Scully, Patrick J.	Arsenal	Preston North End
7	Sendall, Richard A.	Carlisle United	Cardiff City
22	Sheffield, Jonathon	Norwich City	Aldershot
6	Smith, Richard G.	Leicester City	Cambridge United
29	Weston, Jan P.	Torquay United	Shamrock Rovers
6	Williams, Brett	Nottingham Forest	Hereford United

October 1989

6	Adcock, Anthony C.	Northamnpton Town	Bradford City
7	Barnard, Leigh K.	Swindon Town	Cardiff City
13	Barnes, David O.	A.F.C. Bournemouth	Northampton Town
20	Beesley, Paul	Wigan Athletic	Leyton Orient
13	Bell, Douglas K.	Shrewsbury Town	Birmingham City
5	Bradshaw, Carl	Manchestesr City	Sheffield United
3	Burridge, John	Southampton	Newcastle United
26	Chard, Phillip J.	Wolverhampton W.	Northampton Town
6	Culpin, Paul	Northampton Town	Peterborough United
6	Curtis, Alan T.	Cardiff City	Swansea City
3	Drinkell, Kevin	Glasgow Rangers	Coventry City
20	Gernon, Fredeick A. J.	Reading	Northampton Town
3	Gilligan, James M.	Cardiff City	Portsmouth
24	Hawkins, Nigel	Bristol City	Blackpool
13	Lamb, Alan	Nottingham Forest	Hartlepool United
2	Maguire, Peter J.	Leeds United	Huddersfield Town
27	Morgan, Trevor J.	Bolton Wanderers	Colchester United

		From	*To*
25	Pennyfather, Howard K.	Crystal Palace	Ipswich Town
18	Pritchard, Howard K.	Walsall	Maidstone United
13	Roberts, Alan	Sheffield United	Lincoln City
20	Ward, Paul T.	Leyton Orient	Scunthorpe United
2	Wilkinson, Stephen J.	Leicester City	Mansfield Town

Temporary Transfers

12	Adams, Stephen	Scarborough	Doncaster Rovers
6	Airey, Carl	Shamrock Rovers	Torquay United (Tr. Back)
16	Barber, Frederick	Walsall	Peterborough United
27	Bartram, Vincent L.	Wolverhampton Wanderers	Blackpool
18	Beresford, Marlon	Ipswich Town	Sheffield Wednesday (Tr. Back)
11	Cheetham, Michael M.	Ipswich Town	Cambridge United
7	Davison, Aidan J.	Notts. County	Bury
5	Elliott, Stephen B.	Bury	Rochdale
30	Gabbiadini, Ricardo	Sunderland	Grimsby Town
25	Goater, Leonard S.	Manchester United	Rotherham United
13	Gorman, Paul A.	Carlisle United	Shelbourne
10	Hansbury, Roger	Birmingham City	Cardiff City
26	Hulme, Kevin	Bury	Chester City
25	Irvine, James A.	Dundee United	Blackburn Rovers
12	Johns, Nicholas P.	Queens Park Rangers	Maidstone United
5	Kelly, Gary A.	Newcastle United	Bury
19	Kelly, Norman	Oldham Athletic	Wigan Athletic
30	Kiely, Dean L.	Coventry City	Ipswich Town
19	Moncur, John F.	Tottenham Hotspur	Brentford

November 1989

2	Beagrie, Peter S.	Stoke City	Everton
15	Brook, Gary	Scarborough	Blackpool
23	Chalmers, Paul	St. Mirren	Swansea City
3	Chandler, Jeffrey G.	Bolton Wanderers	Cardiff City
1	Cook, Paul A.	Norwich City	Wolverhampton Wanderers
17	Davison, Aidan J.	Notts. County	Bury
10	Elliott, Stephen B.	Bury	Rochdale
20	Fashanu, Justinus S.	Manchester City	West Ham United
13	Futcher, Ronald	Port Vale	Burnley
16	Hendry, Edward C. J.	Blackburn Rovers	Manchestesr City
16	Hucker, Peter I.	Oxford United	Millwall
24	Hughes, John	Berwick Rangers	Swansea City
22	Irvine, James A.	Dundee United	Blackburn Rovers
9	Jones, Paul A.	Walsall	Wolverhampton Wanderers
24	Kerslake, David	Queens Park Rangers	Swindon Town
30	King, Philip G.	Swindon Town	Sheffield Wednesday
3	Lamont, Lee S.	Doncaster Rovers	Rochdale
23	MacDonald, John	Barnsley	Scarborough
21	Martyn, Antony N.	Bristol Rovers	Crystal Palace
10	Noteman, Kevin S.	Leeds United	Doncaster Rovers
14	Penrice, Gary K.	Bristol Rovers	Watford
3	Sheridan, John J.	Nottingham Forest	Sheffield Wednesday
30	Spackman, Nigel J.	Queens Park Rangers	Glasgow Rangers
3	Vinnicombe, Christopher	Exeter City	Glasgow Rangers
23	Walker, Keith C.	St. Mirren	Swansea City

Temporary Transfers

30	Beglin, James	Leeds United	Plymouth Argyle
30	Bent, Junior A.	Huddersfield Town	Burnley
8	Blackwell, Kevin P.	Scarborough	Notts. County
24	Branagan, Keith G.	Millwall	Brentford
8	Campbell, Kevin J.	Arsenal	Leicester City
8	Chapman, Gary	Notts. County	Bradford City (Tr. Back)
23	Cornforth, John M.	Sunderland	Shrewsbury Town
21	Davis, Stephen M.	Southampton	Burnley
2	Dickens, Matthew J.	Sheffield United	Leyton Orient
29	Ferguson, Iain J. H.	Heart of Midlothian	Charlton Athletic
17	Gorman, Paul A.	Carlisle United	Shrewsbury Town
3	Graham, James	Bradford City	Rochdale
14	Hamilton, Lindsay	Glasgow Rangers	Leeds United
9	Harbey, Graham K.	Ipswich Town	West Bromwich Albion
9	Hilaire, Vincent M.	Leeds United	Stoke City
30	Jones, Andrew M.	Charlton Athletic	Bristol City
1	Kevan, David J.	Cardiff City	Notts. County (Tr. Back)
2	King, Philip G.	Swindon Town	Sheffield Wednesday
10	Law, Nicholas	Notts. County	Scarborough
2	Lemon, Paul A.	Sunderland	Walsall
30	Lemon, Paul A.	Walsall	Sunderland (Tr. Back)
16	McCord, Brian J.	Derby County	Barnsley
23	McPhillips, Terence	Halifax Town	Northampton Town
22	McStay, William	Notts. County	Hartlepool United
17	Martyn, Antony N.	Bristol Rovers	Crystal Palace
22	Miller, Paul R.	A.F.C. Bournemouth	Brentford
2	Moran, Paul	Tottenham Hotspur	Leicester City
1	Mundee, Denny W. J.	Torquay United	A.F.C. Bournemouth (Tr. Back)
8	Norris, Stephen M.	Scarborough	Notts County

		From	To
10	O'Connell, Brendan	Burnley	Huddersfield Town
10	Ogley, Mark A.	Carlisle United	Aldershot
11	Parkin, Brian	Crystal Palace	Bristol Rovers
10	Pike, Martin R.	Sheffield United	Tranmere Rovers
1	Powell, Clifford G.	Sheffield United	Cardiff City
22	Rees, Melvyn J.	Watford	Southampton
29	Smalley, Mark A.	Leyton Orient	Mansfield Town
16	Smith, Mark C.	Plymouth Argyle	Barnsley
20	Spink, Dean P.	Ason Villa	Scarborough
15	Turner, Christopher R.	Sheffield Wednesday	Leeds United
2	Wilder, Christopher J.	Sheffield United	Walsall
23	Williams, Darren	Leicester City	Lincoln City
9	Williams, Paul D.	Derby County	Lincoln City

December 1989

		From	To
14	Adams, Stephen	Scarborough	Doncaster Rovers
26	Bennyworth, Ian R.	Scarborough	Hartlepool
28	Bishop, Ian W.	Manchester City	West Ham United
14	Blackwell, Kevin P.	Scarborough	Notts. County
20	Ellis, Anthony J.	Preston North End	Stoke City
4	Flynn, Michael A.	Norwich City	Preston North End
29	Goddard, Paul	Derby County	Millwall
23	Goldsmith, Craig S. W.	Peterborough United	Carlisle United
26	Gooding, Michael C.	Wolverhampton Wanderers	Reading
14	Gorman, Paul A.	Carlisle United	Shrewsbury
23	Hansbury, Roger	Birmingham City	Cardiff City
6	Harbey, Graham K.	Ipswich town	West Bromwich Albion
15	Harper, Alan	Sheffield Wednesday	Manchester City
22	Heseltine, Wayne A.	Manchestesr United	Oldham Athletic
14	Juryeff, Ian M.	Halifax Town	Hereford United
1	Kasule, Victor	Shrewsbury Town	Hamilton Academical
1	Kelly, Gary A.	Newcastle United	Bury
26	MacDonald, Garry	Stockport County	Hartlepool United
22	McKernon, Craig A.	Mansfield Town	Arsenal
7	Matthews, Michael	Stockport County	Scarborough
28	Morley, Trevor W.	Manchester City	West Ham United
14	Murray, Malcom	Hull City	Mansfield Town
15	O'Connor, Mark A.	A.F.C. Bournemouth	Gillingham
26	Olsson, Paul	Scarborough	Hartlepool United
8	Parkin, Timothy J.	Swindon Town	Port Vale
15	Reid, Peter	Queens Park Rangers	Manchester City
22	Sandford, Lee R.	Portsmouth	Stoke City
18	Smith, Mark C.	Plymouth Argyle	Barnsley
29	Stoutt, Stephen P.	Grimsby Town	Lincoln City
5	Thorn, Andrew	Newcastle United	Crystal Palace
22	Tupling, Stephen	Cardiff City	Hartlepool United
29	Ward, Mark W.	West Ham United	Manchester City
14	Wegerle, Roy C.	Luton Town	Queen's Park Rangers

Temporary Transfers

		From	To
7	Adams, Stephen	Doncaster Rovers	Scarborough (Tr. Back)
22	Andrews, Ian E.	Celtic	Southampton
13	Branagan, Keith G.	Brentford	Millwall (Tr. Back)
13	Burns, Hugh	Dunfermline Athletic	Fulham
6	Byrne, Michael	Huddersfield Town	Shelbourne
22	Carr, Franz A.	Nottingham Forest	Sheffield Wednesday
13	Cullen, Anthony	Sunderland	Carlisle United
14	Dearden, Kevin C.	Tottentham Hotspur	Oxford United
14	Donaghy, Malachy	Manchester United	Luton Town
23	Elkins, Gary	Fulham	Exeter City
28	Fyfe, Tony	Carlisle United	Scarborough
28	Goddard, Karl E.	Bradford City	Exeter City
15	Hedman, Rudolph G.	Crystal Palace	Leyton Orient
29	Honor, Christian R.	Bristol City	Hereford United
10	Joseph, Francis	Gillingham	Crewe Alexandra
15	Lemon, Paul A.	Sunderland	Reading
29	Marriott, Andrew	Nottingham Forest	Blackburn Rovers
6	Naylor, Dominic J.	Watford	Halifax Town
28	Norris, Stephen M.	Scarborough	Carlisle United
13	Parsley, Neil	Leeds United	Chester City
14	Pike, Martin R.	Sheffield United	Bolton Wanderers
15	Priestley, Jason A.	Carlisle United	Hartlepool United
30	Quinn, James M.	Bradford City	West Ham United
22	Robson, Mark A.	Tottehham Hotspur	Plymouth Argyle
6	Rostron, John W.	Sheffield United	Sheffield Wednesday (Tr. Back)
14	Sealey, Leslie J.	Luton Town	Manchester United
14	Shaw, Richard E.	Crystal Palace	Hull City
15	Suckling, Perry J.	Crystal Palace	West Ham United
29	Youds, Edward P.	Everton	Cardiff City

January 1990

		From	To
11	Aitken, Robert S.	Celtic	Newcastle United
29	Baird, Ian J.	Leeds United	Middlesbrough
9	Bennett, Michael R.	Charlton Athletic	Wimbledon

		From	*To*
18	Bramhall, John	Halifax Town	Scunthorpe United
10	Broddle, Julian R.	Barnsley	Plymouth Argyle
4	Brown, Grant A.	Leicester City	Lincoln City
11	Chapman, Lee R.	Nottingham Forest	Leeds United
11	Cheetham, Michael M.	Ipswich Town	Cambridge United
12	Clarke, Wayne	Leicester City	Manchestesr City
19	Currie, David N.	Barnsley	Nottingham Forest
24	Francis, John A.	Sheffield United	Burnley
24	Fyfe, Tony	Carlisle United	Halifax Town
29	Gallacher, Kevin W.	Dundee United	Coventry City
19	Gayle, Brian W.	Manchester City	Ipswich Town
19	Goater, Leonard S.	Manchester United	Rotherham United
26	Graham, Thomas	Scarborough	Halifax Town
25	Groves, Paul	Leicester City	Blackpool
26	Hancock, Anthony E.	Burnley	Preston North End
18	Harford, Michael G.	Luton Town	Derby County
11	Hazard, Michael	Chelsea	Portsmouth
9	Joseph, Francis	Gillingham	Crewe Alexandra
29	Kamara, Christopher	Stoke City	Leeds United
18	Longhurst, David J.	Peterborough United	York City
29	Lormor, Anthony	Newcastle United	Lincoln City
11	McCall, Ian H.	Rangers	Bradford City
5	McNab, Neil	Manchester City	Tranmere Rovers
18	Milner, Andrew J.	Manchester City	Rochdale
8	Naylor, Dominic J.	Watford	Halifax Town
19	Norris, Stephen M.	Scarborough	Carlisle United
12	Ogley, Mark A.	Carlisle United	Aldershot
12	Oldfield, David C.	Manchester City	Leicestesr City
11	Parkin, Brian	Crystal Palace	Bristol Rovers
22	Pates, Colin G.	Charlton Athletic	Arsenal
8	Quinn, James M.	Bradford City	West Ham United
12	Redfearn, Neil D.	Watford	Oldham Athletic
25	Richards, Carroll L.	Peterborough United	Blackpool
22	Smalley, Mark A.	Leyton Orient	Mansfield Town
10	Taggart, Gerald P.	Manchester City	Barnsley
18	Williams, Gary	Leeds United	Watford
18	Wimbleton, Paul P.	Bristol City	Shrewsbury Town

Temporary Transfers

10	Barrett, Scott	Stoke City	Colchester United
13	Butters, Guy	Tottenham Hotspur	Southend United
11	Cornforth, John M.	Sunderland	Lincoln City
15	Crossley, Mark G.	Nottingham Forest	Manchester United
5	Dickins, Matthew J.	Leyton Orient	Sheffield United (Tr. Back)
11	Dowson, Alan P.	Millwall	Fulham
18	Duxbury, Lee E.	Bradford City	Rochdale
11	Edinburgh, Justin C.	Southend United	Tottenham Hotspur
24	Fyfe, Tony	Scarborough	Carlisle United (Tr. Back)
18	Glover, Edward L.	Nottingham Forest	Barnsley
31	Goddard, Karl E.	Bradford City	Colchester United
5	Gourlay, Archibald M.	Newcastle United	Greenock Norton
17	Gray, Philip	Tottenham Hotspur	Barnsley
1	Greenall, Colin A.	Oxford United	Bury
12	Haylock, Garry A.	Huddersfield Town	Shelbourne
4	Heathcote, Michael	Sunderland	York City
16	Howells, Gareth J.	Tottenham Hotspur	Swindon Town
25	Jepson, Ronald F.	Port Vale	Peterborough United
25	Kevan, David J.	Notts. County	Stoke City
11	Knight, Ian J.	Sheffield Wednesday	Grimsby Town
16	Lynch, Thomas	Sunderland	Shrewsbury Town
10	McClelland, John	Leeds United	Watford
12	McStay, William	Notts. County	Partick Thistle
3	Madden, Craig A.	Blackpool	Wrexham
25	Madden, David J.	Crystal Palace	Birmingham City
11	Miller, Paul A.	Wimbledon	Bristol City
22	Milne, Ralph	Manchester United	West Ham United
18	Ormsby, Brendon T. C.	Leeds United	Shrewsbury Town
11	Powell, Christopher G. R.	Crystal Palace	Aldershot
11	Puttnam, David P.	Leicester City	Lincoln City
5	Rees, Melvyn J.	Watford	Leyton Orient
19	Shaw, Richard E.	Hull City	Crystal Palace (Tr. Back)
11	Stevens, Gary A.	Tottenham Hotspur	Portsmouth
22	Suckling, Perry J.	West Ham United	Crystal Palace (Tr. Back)

February 1990

15	Andrews, Ian E.	Celtic	Southampton
16	Anthrobus, Stephen A.	Millwall	Wimbledon
1	Bamber, John D.	Stoke City	Hull City
9	Blake, Noel L. G.	Leeds United	Stoke City
23	Chapman, Gary A.	Bradford City	Notts. County
8	Claridge, Stephen E.	Aldershot	Cambridge United
15	Gayle, Andrew K.	Oldham Athletic	Crewe Alexandra
2	Greenwood, Nigel P.	Bury	Preston North End
20	Gritt, Stephen J.	Walsall	Charlton Athletic

		From	*To*
26	Gunn, Andrew C.	Watford	Crewe Alexandra
23	Heath, Adrian P.	Aston Villa	Manchester City
15	Kevan, David J.	Notts. County	Stoke City
26	Knight, Ian J.	Sheffield Wednesday	Grimsby Town
22	Lynch, Thomas	Sunderland	Shrewsbury Town
9	McIlroy, Samuel B.	Bury	Preston North End
22	Newhouse, Aidan	Chester City	Wimbledon
28	Newson, Mark	A.F.C. Bournemouth	Fulham
7	O'Toole, Christopher P.	Shelbourne	Leicester City
1	Patterson, Mark A.	Preston North End	Bury
8	Pike, Martin R.	Sheffield United	Fulham
2	Saunders, Carl S.	Stoke City	Bristol Rovers
28	Sayer, Andrew	Fulham	Leyton Orient
9	Sertori, Mark A.	Lincoln City	Wrexham
28	Shotton, Malcolm	Barnsley	Hull City
23	Thomas, John W.	West Bromwich Albion	Preston North End
16	Varadi, Imre	Sheffield Wednesday	Leeds United
9	Watson, John M.	Fulham	Airdrieonians
7	Whitehurst, William	Hull City	Sheffield United
9	Wood, Paul A.	Brighton & Hove Albion	Sheffield Utd.

Temporary Transfers

9	Anthrobus, Stephen A.	Millwall	Southend United
13	Anthrobus, Stephen A.	Southend United	Millwall (Tr. Back)
1	Byrne, David S.	Plymouth Argyle	Bristol Rovers
27	Danzey, Michael	Nottingham Forest	Chester City
16	Davis, Stephen M.	Burnley	Southampton (Tr. Back)
1	Dixon, Kevin L.	York City	Scarborough
1	Dyche, Sean M.	Nottingham Forest	Chesterfield
11	Gannon, James P.	Sheffield United	Halifax Town
2	Goldsmith, Martin	Walsall	Larne
8	Hedman, Rudolph G.	Leyton Orient	Crystal Palace (Tr. Back)
8	Hoyle, Colin R.	Arsenal	Chesterfield
10	Hurst, Mark D.	Nottingham Forest	Huddersfield Town
8	McCall, Stephen H.	Sheffield Wednesday	Carlisle United
16	Mimms, Robert A.	Tottenham Hotspur	Aberdeen
22	Ord, Richard J.	Sunderland	York City
9	Pittman, Stephen	Shrewsbury Town	Dunfermline Athletic
22	Powell, Christopher G. R.	Crystal Palace	Aldershot
17	Robson, Mark A.	Plymouth Argyle	Tottenham Hotspur (Tr. Back)
1	Rose, Kevin P.	Bolton Wanderers	Halifax Town
8	Shakespeare, Craig R.	Sheffield Wednesday	West Bromwich A.
15	Smith, Mark	Dunfermline Athletic	Stoke City
1	Spink, Dean P.	Aston Villa	Bury
8	Stafford, Clive A.	Colchester United	Exeter City
19	Starbuck, Philip M.	Nottingham Forest	Hereford United
8	Stowell, Michael	Everton	Preston North End
20	Stowell, Michael	Preston North End	Everton (Tr. Back)
8	Veradi, Imre	Sheffield Wednesday	Leeds United
8	Youds, Edward P.	Everton	Wrexham

March 1990

20	Allen, Malcolm	Norwich City	Millwall
29	Ansah, Andrew	Brentford	Southend United
23	Askew, William	Hull City	Newcastle United
9	Bannister, Gary	Coventry City	West Bromwich Albion
23	Barnes, Paul L.	Notts. County	Stoke City
13	Bartlett, Kevin	West Bromwich Albion	Notts. County
2	Benjamin, Ian	Exeter City	Southend United
22	Bent, Junior A.	Huddersfield	Bristol Rovers
22	Bloomer, Robert	Chesterfield	Bristol Rovers
26	Brookman, Nicholas A.	Bolton Wanderers	Stockport County
16	Cascarino, Anthony G.	Millwall	Aston Villa
1	Dyche, Sean	Nottingham Forest	Chesterfield
16	Edwards, Paul R.	Crewe Alexandra	Coventry City
5	Fairclough, Wayne R.	Notts. County	Mansfield Town
16	Fiore, Mark J.	Wimbledon	Plymouth Argyle
23	Fleming, Gary J.	Manchester City	Barnsley
8	Foreman, Darren	Barnsley	Crewe Alexandra
7	Gannon, James P.	Sheffield United	Stockport County
17	Green, Scott P.	Derby County	Bolton Wanderers
1	Hackett, Gary S.	Stoke City	West Bromwich Albion
22	Harle, David	Peterborough United	Doncaster Rovers
14	Hope, Darren	Stoke City	Stockport County
2	Horrix, Dean V.	Millwall	Bristol City
15	Hunter, Paul	East Fife	Hull City
12	Johns, Nicholas	Queens Park Rangers	Maidstone United
22	Kelly, David	West Ham United	Leicester City
22	Kelly, Thomas J.	York City	Exeter City
16	King, Adam	West Ham United	Plymouth Argyle
9	McCord, Brian	Derby County	Barnsley
22	McKellar, David	Carlisle United	Kilmarnock
23	Morgan, Nicholas	Stoke City	Bristol City
23	Moulden, Paul	A.F.C. Bournemouth	Oldham Athletic

		From	To
23	O'Connell, Brendan J.	Burnley	Barnsley
22	Palin, Leigh	Stoke City	Hull City
15	Philips, James N.	Oxford United	Middlesbrough
21	Puttnam, David	Leicester City	Lincoln City
21	Quinn, Niall	Arsenal	Manchester City
15	Ritchie, David M.	Stoke City	Stockport County
19	Robinson, Leslie	Doncaster Rovers	Oxford United
15	Russell, Martin	Scarborough	Middlesbrough
20	Salman, Danis M. M.	Millwall	Plymouth Argyle
9	Saville, Andrew V.	Walsall	Barnsley
6	Shakespeare, Craig R.	Sheffield Wednesday	West Bromwich Albion
27	Smith, Mark	Dunfermline	Nottingham Forest
15	Spink, Dean P.	Aston Villa	Shrewsbury Town
22	Stevens, Gary A.	Tottenham Hotspur	Portsmouth
12	Terry, Steve G.	Hull City	Northampton Town
22	Thomas, David G.	Barnsley	Hull City
21	Thomas, Dean R.	Northampton Town	Notts. County
24	Thompson, Garry	Watford	Crystal Palace
23	Thorpe, Adrian	Walsall	Northampton Town
9	Whitehead, Philip M.	Halifax Town	Barnsley
1	Woods, Neil	Ipswich Town	Bradford City
2	Wright, Paul H.	Queens Park Rangers	Hibernian

Temporary Transfers

16	Atkinson, Paul	Port Vale	Hartlepool United
22	Baker, Graham	Southampton	Aldershot
22	Baraclough, Ian R.	Leicester City	Wigan Athletic
22	Barrett, Scott	Stoke City	Stockport County
22	Batty, Paul W.	Exeter City	Cambridge U
22	Beeney, Mark R.	Maidstone United	Aldershot
15	Blackwell, Dean R.	Wimbledon	Plymouth Argyle
22	Blake, Mark C.	Southampton	Shrewsbury Town
1	Brooke, Garry J.	Wimbledon	Stoke City
22	Buckley, Neil A.	Hull City	Burnley
22	Cadette, Richard	Brentford	A.F.C. Bournemouth
22	Cecere, Michele J.	Huddersfield Town	Stockport County
22	Cash, Stuart P.	Nottingham Forest	Rotherham United
15	Clarke, Martin J.	Nottingham Forest	Mansfield Town
22	Cooper, Mark N.	Exeter City	Southend United
21	Davison, Aidan	Bury	Chester City
20	Dearden, Kevin C.	Tottenham Hotspur	Swindon Town
22	Duxbury, Lee	Rochdale	Bradford City (Tr. Back)
22	Edwards, Keith	Stockport County	Huddersfield Town
21	Ferguson, Iain J. H.	Heart of Midlothian	Bristol City
8	Fleming, Gary J.	Manchestesr City	Notts. County
22	Fleming, Gary J.	Notts. County	Manchester City (Tr. Back)
22	Ford, Gary	Port Vale	Walsall
17	Francis, Lee C.	Arsenal	Chesterfield
22	Freestone, Roger	Chelsea	Hereford United
22	Gabbiadini, Ricardo	Sunderland	Brighton & Hove Albion
7	Gannon, James P.	Halifax Town	Sheffield United (Tr. Back)
22	Hall, Anthony D.	East Fife	York City
21	Hannigan, Al J.	Arsenal	Torquay United
23	Hayde, Michael	Chester City	Lichfield
19	Henshaw, Gary	Bolton Wanderers	Rochdale
16	Hilaire, Vincent M.	Leeds United	Charlton Athletic
21	Howells, Gareth	Tottenham Hotspur	Leyton Orient
22	Hurst, Mark	Huddersfield Town	Nottingham Forest (Tr. Back)
22	Jones, Philip A.	Everton	Blackpool
22	Kelly, Gavin J.	Hull City	Bristol Rovers
22	Kelly, John	Walsall	Huddersfield Town
9	Kiely, Dean	Coventry City	York City
22	Leaburn, Carl W.	Charlton Athletic	Northampton Town
22	Lyne, Neil	Nottingham Forest	Walsall
9	McPherson, Angus	Glasgow Rangers	Exeter City
3	Madden, Craig	Wrexham	Blackpool (Tr. Back)
21	Marriott, Andrew	Nottingham Forest	Colchester United
22	Morgan, Darren	Millwall	Bradford City
22	Morgan, Steven	Oldham Athletic	Wrexham
1	Muggleton, Carl D.	Leicester City	Stockport County
22	Muggleton, Carl D.	Stockport County	Leicester City (Tr. Back)
22	Ord, Richard J.	York City	Sunderland (Tr. Back)
22	Poutch, Neil	Luton Town	Leicester City
1	Riley, David	Port Vale	Peterborough United
8	Robertson, Stuart	Clyde	Stockport County
22	Rose, Kevin P.	Bolton Wanderers	Carlisle United
22	Scott, Colin	Rangers	Brentford
21	Sealey, Leslie J.	Luton Town	Manchester United
21	Sheffield, Jon	Norwich City	Ipswich Town
22	Slatter, Neil	Oxford United	A.F.C. Bournemouth
22	Sparham, Sean	Millwall	Brentford
22	Stuart, Mark R. N.	Plymouth Argyle	Ipswich Town
22	Summerfield, Kevin	Plymouth Argyle	Exeter City
1	Tanner, Nicholas	Liverpool	Norwich City

		From	To
20	Thomas, Michael R.	Leeds United	Stoke City
8	Walter, David W.	Exeter City	Plymouth Argyle
21	Whiston, Peter M.	Plymouth Argyle	Torquay United
23	Williams, Darren	Leicester City	Lincoln City
12	Wood, George	Cardiff City	Blackpool

April 1990

11	McKinstry, Gary	Portadown	Port Vale
3	Riley, David S.	Port Vale	Peterborough United

Temporary Transfers

30	Baraclough, Ian R.	Wigan Athletic	Leicester City (Tr. Back)
30	Blackwell, Dean R.	Plymouth Argyle	Wimbledon (Tr. Back)
27	Bramwell, Steven	Oldham Athletic	Wigan Athletic
26	Brooke, Garry J.	Stoke City	Wimbledon (Tr. Back)
25	Freestone, Roger	Hereford United	Chelsea (Tr. Back)
30	Greaves, Steven R.	Fulham	Brighton & Hove Albion
20	Johnston, Richard W.	Tottenham Hotspur	Dunfermline Athletic
13	Mimms, Robert A.	Aberdeen	Tottenham Hotspur (Tr. Back)
23	Morgan, Darren J.	Bradford City	Millwall (Tr. Back)
20	Scott, Colin	Brentford	Rangers (Tr. Back)

May 1990

18	Kiely, David L.	Coventry City	York City
18	Seaman, David A.	Queens Park Rangers	Arsenal

Summer moves . . .

Warren Barton, Maidstone U – Wimbledon; Adrian Boothroyd, Huddersfield T – Bristol R; Colin Clarke, QPR – Portsmouth; Lee Francis, Arsenal – Chesterfield; Rob Hindmarch, Derby Co – Wolverhampton W; John Humphrey, Charlton Ath – Crystal Palace; Denis Irwin, Oldham Ath – Manchester U; Chris Lee, Bradford C – Rochdale; John Lukic, Arsenal – Leeds U; Ian McCall, Bradford C – Dunfermline Ath; Mike Stowell, Everton – Wolverhampton W; Peter Whiston, Plymouth Arg – Torquay U; Ian Thompstone, Manchester C – Oldham Ath; Mark Kelly, Cardiff C – Fulham; Liburd Henry, Watford – Maidstone U; Neil Matthews, Halifax T – Stockport Co; Dennis Wise, Wimbledon – Chelsea; John Hendrie, Leeds U – Middlesbrough; Andy Linighan, Norwich – Arsenal; Sean McCarthy, Plymouth Arg – Bradford C; Robbie Mustoe, Oxford U – Middlesbrough; Andy Townsend, Norwich C – Chelsea; Clive Wilson, Chelsea – QPR; Kevin Ball, Portsmouth – Sunderland; Peter Costello, Bradford C – Rochdale; Peter Davenport, Middlesbrough – Sunderland; Jimmy Graham, Bradford C – Rochdale; Colin Greenall, Oxford U – Bury; Mike Heathcote, Sunderland – Shrewsbury T; Andy Hinchcliffe, Manchester C – Everton; Glyn Hodges, Watford – Crystal Palace; Jamie Hoyland, Bury – Sheffield U; John McGinlay, Shrewsbury T – Bury; Nigel Pepper, Rotherham U – York C; Neil Pointon, Everton – Manchester C; Steve Spooner, York C – Rotherham U; Colin Woodthorpe, Chester C – Norwich C; Tony Coton, Watford – Manchester C; Mark Brennan, Middlesbrough – Manchester City; Keith Dublin, Brighton & HA – Watford; David Walter, Exeter C – Plymouth Arg; John Pemberton, Crystal Palace – Sheffield U; Paul Beesley, Leyton Orient – Sheffield U; Kevin Richardson, Arsenal – Real Sociedad; Martin Hayes, Arsenal – Celtic; Mark Hateley, Monaco – Rangers; Anders Limpar, Cremonese – Arsenal.

Continued from page 15

THE WORLD CUP 1930–1990

Year	Winners		Runners-up		Venue	Attendance	Referee
1930	Uruguay	4	Argentina	2	Montevideo	90,000	Langenus (B)
1934	Italy	2	Czechoslovakia	1	Rome	50,000	Eklind (Se)
	(after extra time)						
1938	Italy	4	Hungary	2	Paris	45,000	Capdeville (F)
1950	Uruguay	2	Brazil	1	Rio de Janeiro	199,854	Reader (E)
1954	West Germany	3	Hungary	2	Berne	60,000	Ling (E)
1958	Brazil	5	Sweden	2	Stockholm	49,737	Guigue (F)
1962	Brazil	3	Czechoslovakia	1	Santiago	68,679	Latychev (USSR)
1966	England	4	West Germany	2	Wembley	93,802	Dienst (Sw)
	(after extra time)						
1970	Brazil	4	Italy	1	Mexico City	107,412	Glockner (EG)
1974	West Germany	2	Holland	1	Munich	77,833	Taylor (E)
1978	Argentina	3	Holland	1	Buenos Aires	77,000	Gonella (I)
	(after extra time)						
1982	Italy	3	West Germany	1	Madrid	90,080	Coelho (Br)
1986	Argentina	3	West Germany	2	Mexico City	114,580	Filho (Br)
1990	West Germany	1	Argentina	0	Rome	73,603	Codesal (Mex)

GOALSCORING AND ATTENDANCES IN WORLD CUP FINAL ROUNDS

	Matches	Goals (avge)	Attendance (avge)
1930, Uruguay	18	70 (3.8)	434,500 (24,138)
1934, Italy	17	70 (4.1)	395,000 (23,235)
1938, France	18	84 (4.6)	483,000 (26,833)
1950, Brazil	22	88 (4.0)	1,337,000 (60,772)
1954, Switzerland	26	140 (5.3)	943,000 (36,270)
1958, Sweden	35	126 (3.6)	868,000 (24,800)
1962, Chile	32	89 (2.7)	776,000 (24,250)
1966, England	32	89 (2.7)	1,614,677 (50,458)
1970, Mexico	32	95 (2.9)	1,673,975 (52,311)
1974, West Germany	38	97 (2.5)	1,774,022 (46,684)
1978, Argentina	38	102 (2.6)	1,610,215 (42,374)
1982, Spain	52	146 (2.8)	1,766,277 (33,967)
1986, Mexico	52	132 (2.5)	2,199,941 (42,307)
1990, West Germany	52	115 (2.21)	2,510,686* (48,282)

BARCLAYS LEAGUE ATTENDANCES 1989–90

	TOTAL ATTENDANCES	AVERAGE ATTENDANCES
TOTAL	19,445,442	9550
DIVISION 1	7,883,039	20,744
DIVISION 2	6,867,674	12,441
DIVISION 3	2,803,551	5078
DIVISION 4	1,891,178	3426

DIVISION ONE STATISTICS

	Average gate			Season 1989/90	
	1988/89	1989/90	+/−%	Highest	Lowest
Arsenal	35,595	33,713	−5.3	46,133	23,732
Aston Villa	23,310	25,544	+9.6	41,247	14,170
Charlton Athletic	9398	10,748	+14.4	17,806	5679
Chelsea	15,731	21,531	+36.9	31,285	13,114
Coventry City	16,040	14,312	−10.8	23,204	8294
Crystal Palace	10,655	17,105	+60.5	29,870	10,051
Derby County	17,536	17,426	−0.6	24,190	13,694
Everton	27,765	26,280	−5.3	41,443	17,591
Liverpool	38,574	36,589	−5.1	38,730	33,319
Luton Town	9504	9886	+4.0	12,620	8244
Manchester City	23,500	27,975	+19.0	43,246	23,354
Manchester United	36,488	39,077	+7.1	47,245	29,281
Millwall	15,416	12,413	−19.5	17,265	10,267
Norwich City	16,785	16,737	−0.3	20,210	12,640
Nottingham Forest	20,785	20,606	−0.9	26,766	16,437
Queens Park Rangers	12,281	13,218	+7.6	18,997	8437
Sheffield Wednesday	20,037	20,930	+4.5	33,260	13,728
Southampton	15,590	16,463	+5.6	20,510	12,904
Tottenham Hotspur	24,467	26,588	+8.7	33,944	17,668
Wimbledon	7824	7756	−0.9	14,738	3 618

DIVISION TWO STATISTICS

	Average gate			Season 1989/90	
	1988/89	1989/90	+/−%	Highest	Lowest
AFC Bournemouth	8087	7454	−7.8	9970	5506
Barnsley	7215	9033	+25.2	16,629	5524
Blackburn Rovers	8891	9624	+8.2	15,633	7494
Bradford City	10,524	8777	−16.6	12,527	4903
Brighton & Hove Albion	9048	8679	−4.1	12,689	5504
Hull City	6666	6518	−2.2	11,620	4207
Ipswich Town	12,650	12,913	+2.1	25,326	9430
Leeds United	21,811	28,210	+29.3	32,697	21,884
Leicester City	10,694	11,716	+9.6	21,134	8199
Middlesbrough	19,999	16,269	−18.7	23,617	11,428
Newcastle United	22,921	21,590	−5.8	31,665	15,163
Oldham Athletic	7204	9727	+35.0	17,451	4940
Oxford United	6352	5820	8.4	8397	3863
Plymouth Argyle	8628	8749	+1.4	11,702	6793
Portsmouth	10,201	8959	−12.2	14,204	6496
Port Vale	6943	8978	+29.3	22,075	6168
Sheffield United	12,222	16,989	+39.0	31,602	12,653
Stoke City	9817	12,449	+26.8	27,004	8139
Sunderland	14,878	17,728	+19.2	28,499	13,014
Swindon Town	8687	9394	+8.1	16,208	6540
Watford	12,292	10,353	−15.8	15,682	7289
West Bromwich Albion	12,757	11,308	−11.4	21,316	8017
West Ham United	20,738	20,311	−2.1	25,892	14,960
Wolverhampton W.	14,392	17,045	+18.4	24,475	12,338

DIVISION THREE STATISTICS

	Average gate			Season 1989/90	
	1988/89	1989/90	+/-%	Highest	Lowest
Birmingham City	6265	8558	+36.6	14,278	5473
Blackpool	4276	4075	-4.7	8108	1842
Bolton Wanderers	5705	7286	+27.7	11,098	4679
Brentford	5681	5662	-0.3	7962	4537
Bristol C	8120	11,544	+42.2	19,483	6365
Bristol Rovers	5259	6202	+17.9	9813	4350
Bury	3367	3450	+2.5	6551	2327
Cardiff City	4384	3642	-16.9	8356	2086
Chester City	3055	2506	-18.0	4218	1730
Crewe Alexandra	3296	4008	+21.6	6900	3165
Fulham	4938	4484	-9.2	7141	2652
Huddersfield Town	5821	5630	-3.3	8483	3514
Leyton Orient	3793	4365	+15.1	7273	3040
Mansfield Town	4005	3129	-21.9	6384	2231
Northampton Town	3918	3187	-18.7	4346	2119
Notts County	5675	6151	+8.4	10,151	4586
Preston North End	7737	6313	-18.4	9105	4480
Reading	5105	4060	-20.5	6147	3009
Rotherham United	5063	5612	+10.8	7724	3420
Shrewsbury Town	4706	3521	-25.2	5319	2297
Swansea City	5088	4223	-17.0	12,244	2474
Tranmere Rovers	5331	7449	+39.7	12,723	4912
Walsall	6108	4077	-33.3	6036	2903
Wigan Athletic	3151	2758	-12.5	6850	1934

DIVISION FOUR STATISTICS

	Average gate			Season 1989/90	
	1988/89	1989/90	+/-%	Highest	Lowest
Aldershot	2609	2022	-22.5	3208	1139
Burnley	7062	6222	-11.9	12,277	3959
Cambridge United	2653	3359	+26.6	4963	1990
Carlisle United	3176	4740	+49.2	8462	3059
Chesterfield	3717	4181	+12.5	7501	2822
Colchester United	2893	3150	+8.9	5283	1720
Doncaster Rovers	2158	2706	+25.4	4336	1806
Exeter City	2679	4859	+81.4	8271	2754
Gillingham	3675	3887	+5.8	11,605	2382
Grimsby Town	4302	5984	+39.1	11,894	3447
Halifax Town	1946	1895	-2.6	4744	1233
Hartlepool United	2048	2503	+22.2	3724	1379
Hereford United	2132	2676	+25.5	7302	1567
Lincoln City	3887	4071	+4.7	6251	2470
Maidstone United	1037	2427	+134.0	5006	1299
Peterborough United	3264	4804	+47.3	9257	2813
Rochdale	1968	2027	+3.0	5420	1216
Scarborough	2961	2325	-21.5	3602	1623
Scunthorpe United	4547	3524	-22.5	8384	2226
Southend United	3699	3836	+3.7	7070	2584
Stockport County	2792	3899	+39.6	6593	2356
Torquay United	2349	2147	-8.6	3389	1521
Wrexham	2636	2368	-10.2	4653	1225
York City	2613	2615	+0.1	3665	2061

LEAGUE ATTENDANCES SINCE 1946–47

Season	Matches	Total	Div. 1	Div. 2	Div. 3 (S)	Div. 3 (N)
1946–47	1848	35,604,606	15,005,316	11,071,572	5,664,004	3,863,714
1947–48	1848	40,259,130	16,732,341	12,286,350	6,653,610	4,586,829
1948–49	1848	41,271,414	17,914,667	11,353,237	6,998,429	5,005,081
1949–50	1848	40,517,865	17,278,625	11,694,158	7,104,155	4,440,927
1950–51	2028	39,584,967	16,679,454	10,780,580	7,367,884	4,757,109
1951–52	2028	39,015,866	16,110,322	11,066,189	6,958,927	4,880,428
1952–53	2028	37,149,966	16,050,278	9,686,654	6,704,299	4,708,735
1953–54	2028	36,174,590	16,154,915	9,510,053	6,311,508	4,198,114
1954–55	2028	34,133,103	15,087,221	8,988,794	5,996,017	4,051,071
1955–56	2028	33,150,809	14,108,961	9,080,002	5,692,479	4,269,367
1956–57	2028	32,744,405	13,803,037	8,718,162	5,622,189	4,601,017
1957–58	2028	33,562,208	14,468,652	8,663,712	6,097,183	4,332,661

Season	Matches	Total	Div. 1	Div. 2	Div. 3	Div. 4
1958–59	2028	33,610,985	14,727,691	8,641,997	5,946,600	4,276,697
1959–60	2028	32,538,611	14,391,227	8,399,627	5,739,707	4,008,050
1960–61	2028	28,619,754	12,926,948	7,033,936	4,784,256	3,874,614
1961–62	2015	27,979,902	12,061,194	7,453,089	5,199,106	3,266,513
1962–63	2028	28,885,852	12,490,239	7,792,770	5,341,362	3,261,481
1963–64	2028	28,535,022	12,486,626	7,594,158	5,419,157	3,035,081
1964–65	2028	27,641,168	12,708,752	6,984,104	4,436,245	3,512,067
1965–66	2028	27,206,980	12,480,644	6,914,757	4,779,150	3,032,429
1966–67	2028	28,902,596	14,242,957	7,253,819	4,421,172	2,984,648
1967–68	2028	30,107,298	15,289,410	7,450,410	4,013,087	3,354,391
1968–69	2028	29,382,172	14,584,851	7,382,390	4,339,656	3,075,275
1969–70	2028	29,600,972	14,868,754	7,581,728	4,223,761	2,926,729
1970–71	2028	28,194,146	13,954,337	7,098,265	4,377,213	2,764,331
1971–72	2028	28,700,729	14,484,603	6,769,308	4,697,392	2,749,426
1972–73	2028	25,448,642	13,998,154	5,631,730	3,737,252	2,081,506
1973–74	2027	24,982,203	13,070,991	6,326,108	3,421,624	2,163,480
1974–75	2028	25,577,977	12,613,178	6,955,970	4,086,145	1,992,684
1975–76	2028	24,896,053	13,089,861	5,798,405	3,948,449	2,059,338
1976–77	2028	26,182,800	13,647,585	6,250,597	4,152,218	2,132,400
1977–78	2028	25,392,872	13,255,677	6,474,763	3,332,042	2,330,390
1978–79	2028	24,540,627	12,704,549	6,153,223	3,374,558	2,308,297
1979–80	2028	24,623,975	12,163,002	6,112,025	3,999,328	2,349,620
1980–81	2028	21,907,569	11,392,894	5,175,442	3,637,854	1,701,379
1981–82	2028	20,006,961	10,420,793	4,750,463	2,836,915	1,998,790
1982–83	2028	18,766,158	9,295,613	4,974,937	2,943,568	1,552,040
1983–84	2028	18,358,631	8,711,448	5,359,757	2,729,942	1,557,484
1984–85	2028	17,849,835	9,761,404	4,030,823	2,667,008	1,390,600
1985–86	2028	16,488,577	9,037,854	3,551,968	2,490,481	1,408,274
1986–87	2028	17,379,218	9,144,676	4,168,131	2,350,970	1,715,441
1987–88	2030	17,959,732	8,094,571	5,341,599	2,751,275	1,772,287
1988–89	2036	18,464,192	7,809,993	5,887,805	3,035,327	1,791,067
1989–90	2036	19,445,442	7,883,039	6,867,674	2,803,551	1,891,178

This is the first time since the war that attendances have risen for four consecutive seasons.

THE LITTLEWOODS/MILK LEAGUE CUP
and
OTHER FOOTBALL LEAGUE COMPETITIONS:

ZENITH DATA SYSTEMS CUP

LEYLAND DAF CUP

LEAGUE CUP FINALISTS 1961–90

Played as a two-leg final until 1966. All subsequent finals at Wembley.

Year	Winners	Runners-up	Score
1961	Aston Villa	Rotherham U	0-2, 3-0 (aet)
1962	Norwich C	Rochdale	3-0, 1-0
1963	Birmingham C	Aston Villa	3-1, 0-0
1964	Leicester C	Stoke C	1-1, 3-2
1965	Chelsea	Leicester C	3-2, 0-0
1966	WBA	West Ham U	1-2, 4-1
1967	QPR	WBA	3-2
1968	Leeds U	Arsenal	1-0
1969	Swindon T	Arsenal	3-1 (aet)
1970	Manchester C	WBA	2-1 (aet)
1971	Tottenham H	Aston Villa	2-0
1972	Stoke C	Chelsea	2-1
1973	Tottenham H	Norwich C	1-0
1974	Wolverhampton W	Manchester C	2-1
1975	Aston Villa	Norwich C	1-0
1976	Manchester C	Newcastle U	2-1
1977	Aston Villa	Everton	0-0, 1-1 (aet), 3-2 (aet)
1978	Nottingham F	Liverpool	0-0 (aet), 1-0
1979	Nottingham F	Southampton	3-2
1980	Wolverhampton W	Nottingham F	1-0
1981	Liverpool	West Ham U	1-1 (aet), 2-1
MILK CUP			
1982	Liverpool	Tottenham H	3-1 (aet)
1983	Liverpool	Manchester U	2-1 (aet)
1984	Liverpool	Everton	0-0 (aet), 1-0
1985	Norwich C	Sunderland	1-0
1986	Oxford U	QPR	3-0
LITTLEWOODS CUP			
1987	Arsenal	Liverpool	2-1
1988	Luton T	Arsenal	3-2
1989	Nottingham F	Luton T	3-1
1990	Nottingham F	Oldham Ath	1-0

LEAGUE CUP WINS
Liverpool 4, Nottingham F 4, Aston Villa 3, Manchester C 2, Norwich C 2, Tottenham H 2, Wolverhampton W 2, Arsenal 1, Birmingham C 1, Chelsea 1, Leeds U 1, Leicester C 1, Luton T 1, Oxford U 1, QPR 1, Stoke C 1, Swindon T 1, WBA 1.

APPEARANCES IN FINALS
Liverpool 6, Aston Villa 5, Nottingham F 5, Arsenal 4, Norwich C 4, Manchester C 3, Tottenham H 3, WBA 3, Chelsea 2, Everton 2, Leicester C 2, Luton T 2, QPR 2, Stoke C 2, West Ham U 2, Wolverhampton W 2, Birmingham C 1, Leeds U 1, Manchester U 1, Newcastle U 1, Oldham Ath 1, Oxford U 1, Rochdale 1, Rotherham U 1, Southampton 1, Sunderland 1, Swindon T 1.

APPEARANCES IN SEMI-FINALS
Aston Villa 8, Liverpool 8, Tottenham H 7, West Ham U 7, Arsenal 6, Manchester C 5, Norwich C 5, Nottingham F 5, Chelsea 4, Manchester U 4, WBA 4, Burnley 3, Everton 3, Leeds U 3, QPR 3, Wolverhampton W 3, Birmingham C 2, Bristol C 2, Coventry C 2, Ipswich T 2, Leicester C 2, Luton T 2, Oxford U 2, Plymouth Arg 2, Southampton 2, Stoke C 2, Sunderland 2, Swindon T 2, Blackburn R 1, Blackpool 1, Bolton W 1, Bury 1, Cardiff C 1, Carlisle U 1, Chester C 1, Derby Co 1, Huddersfield T 1, Middlesbrough 1, Newcastle U 1, Oldham Ath 1, Peterborough U 1, Rochdale 1, Rotherham U 1, Shrewsbury T 1, Walsall 1, Watford 1.

LITTLEWOODS CUP 1989-90

FIRST ROUND FIRST LEG

21 AUG

Stockport Co (0) 1 *(MacDonald)*
Bury (0) 0   2851
Stockport Co: Siddall; Brown, Robertson, Payne, Williams, Thorpe, Beaumont (Oghani), Matthews, MacDonald, Cooke, Frain (Howard).
Bury: Farnworth; Hill, Withe, Hoyland, Valentine, Clements, Lee, Feeley, Cunningham, Robinson (Greenwood), Parkinson (McIlroy).

22 AUG

Birmingham C (1) 2 *(Atkins, Bailey)*
Chesterfield (0) 1 *(Waller)*   6722
Birmingham C: Thomas; Clarkson, Frain, Atkins, Sproson, Matthewson, Peer, Bailey, Yates (Overson), Langley (Gordon), Sturridge.
Chesterfield: Leonard; Gunn, Ryan, Arnott, Brien, Slack, Plummer, Hewitt, Waller, Thompson, Morris.

Blackpool (1) 2 *(Briggs, Garner)*
Burnley (1) 2 *(Mumby, White)*   4540
Blackpool: McIlhargey; Burgess, Morgan, Gore, Briggs, Eyres (Thompson), Methven, Madden, Garner, Coughlin, Wright.
Burnley: Pearce; Measham, Deakin, Eli, Monington (Deary), Harris, White, Mumby, O'Connell, Jakub, Farrell.

Bristol C (1) 2 *(Wimbleton (pen), Smith)*
Reading (2) 3 *(Gilkes 3)*   6318
Bristol C: Leaning; Llewellyn, Bailey, Wimbleton, Pender, Rennie, Gavin, Newman, Taylor, Smith, Eaton.
Reading: Francis; Williams, Richardson, Beavon, Hicks, Wood, Jones, Taylor, Senior, Gilkes, Payne.

Cambridge U (2) 3 *(Dublin 2, Leadbitter)*
Maidstone U (1) 1 *(Butler)*   2405
Cambridge U: Vaughan; Bailie, Kimble, Leadbitter, Chapple, Daish, Dennis, Beck, Dublin, Taylor, Robinson (O'Shea).
Maidstone U: Beeney; Elsey, Cooper, Pamphlett, Golley, Berry, Lillis, Galliers (Barton), Sorrell, Butler, Gall (Charlery).

Cardiff C (0) 0
Plymouth Arg (0) 3 *(Tynan 2 (1pen), McCarthy)*2620
Cardiff C: Wood; Rodgerson, Gibbins, Abraham, Perry, Lynex, Curtis, Morgan, Kelly, Gilligan, Pike (Fry).
Plymouth Arg: Wilmot; Brown, Marker, Burrows, Brimacombe, Smith, Byrne, McCarthy, Tynan, Thomas, Stuart.

Colchester U (2) 2 *(Scott 2, Bennett)*
Southend U (1) 4 *(Bennett, Crown 2, Martin)* 3537
Colchester U: Grace; Hicks, Rooke, English A, Daniels, Radford (Taylor), Bennett, Collins, Wilkins, Scott, Allinson.
Southend U: Sansome; Dixon, Roberts, Martin, Prior, Brush, Cook, Butler, Crown, Walsh, Bennett.

Crewe Alex (2) 4 *(Sussex, Clayton, Murphy, Gardiner)*
Chester C (0) 0   3200
Crewe Alex: Edwards P; Swain, Edwards PR (Walters), Callaghan, Dyson, Clayton, Jasper, Murphy, Sussex, Gardiner, Fishenden (Cutler).
Chester C: Stewart; Hamilton, Woodthorpe, Hinnigan, Lane, Butler, Abel, Pugh, Newhouse (Painter), Dale, Croft.

Gillingham (0) 1 *(Lovell)*
Leyton Orient (2) 4 *(Howard, Harvey, Cooper, Castle)* 3258
Gillingham: Hillyard; Norris, Johnson, Haines, Pearson (Joseph), Thompson, Haylock, Eeles, Beadle, Lovell, Manuel (Palmer).
Leyton Orient: Heald; Baker, Dickenson, Hales, Day, Sitton, Howard, Castle, Harvey, Cooper, Carter.

Halifax T (1) 3 *(Cook, Hall, Watson)*
Carlisle U (1) 1 *(Shepherd)*   1604
Halifax T: Whitehead; Barr, Cook, Hedworth, Bramhall, Horner, Martin, Watson (McPhillips), Juryeff, Butler (Richardson), Hall.
Carlisle U: McKellar; Robertson, Wharton, Saddington, Ogley, Graham, Shepherd, Walsh, Walwyn, Proudlock (Hetherington), Halpin.

Huddersfield T (0) 1 *(Onuora)*
Doncaster R (1) 1 *(Turnbull)*   3983
Huddersfield T: Hardwick; Trevitt, Hutchings, Marsden, O'Doherty, Lewis, O'Regan, Wilson, Cecere, Maskell, Smith (Onuora).
Doncaster R: Samways; Douglas, Brevett, Raffell, Ashurst, Cusack (Brockie), Robinson, Stiles, Turnbull, Rankine, Gaughan.

Hull C (1) 1 *(Payton)*
Grimsby T (0) 0   5045
Hull C: Hesford; Murray (Brown), Jacobs, Swan, Terry, Jobson, Askew, Payton, McParland, Edwards (Jenkinson), Doyle.
Grimsby T: Sherwood; Williams, Agnew, Tillson, Lever, Cunnington, Childs, Gilbert, Rees, Watson, Alexander (Birtles).

Mansfield T (0) 1 *(Stringfellow)*
Northampton T (0) 1 *(Adcock)*   3095
Mansfield T: Beasley; McKernon, Prindiville, Hunt, Foster, Coleman, Lowery, Stringfellow, Charles (Chambers), Christie (Leishman), Kearney.
Northampton T: Gleasure; Williams (Sandeman), Wilson, Thomas, Wilcox, McPherson, Quow, Culpin (Collins), Donald, Adcock, Berry.

Preston NE (2) 3 *(Shaw 3 (1 pen))*

Tranmere R (2) 4 *(Malkin 2, Muir, Bishop)*   4632

Preston NE: Gill; Miller, Swann, Atkins, Jones, Hughes (Patterson), Mooney, Bogie (Rathbone), Joyce, Shaw, Harper.
Tranmere R: Nixon; Higgins, McCarrick, Bishop, Hughes, Vickers, Morrissey, Harvey, Malkin, Muir, Thomas.

Rochdale (1) 2 *(Holmes, Goodison)*

Bolton W (1) 1 *(Thompson)*   3464

Rochdale: Welch; Goodison, Hill, Brown, Cole, Ward, Ainscow, Holmes, Walling, Burns, Stonehouse.
Bolton W: Rose; Brown, Cowdrill, Savage, Crombie, Winstanley, Storer (Henshaw), Thompson, Reeves, Philliskirk, Darby.

Sheffield U (1) 1 *(Deane)*

Rotherham U (0) 1 *(Mendonca)*   11,136

Sheffield U: Tracey; Hill, Barnes, Booker, Stancliffe, Morris, Roberts, Gannon, Agana (Francis), Deane, Bryson.
Rotherham U: O'Hanlon; Russell, Robinson, Grealish, Barnsley, Scott, Buckley, Dempsey, Williamson, Mendonca, Hazel.

Shrewsbury T (1) 3 *(Melrose, Green, Pratley)*

Notts Co (0) 0   2848

Shrewsbury T: Perks; Green, Pittman (Kasule), Kelly, Pratley, Moyes, Brown, Bell, Melrose (Purdie), McGinlay, Naughton.
Notts Co: Cherry; Palmer, Platnauer, Fairclough, Yates, Robinson, Draper (McStay), O'Riordan, Lund (Johnson), Stant, Turner.

Torquay U (0) 0

Hereford U (1) 1 *(Jones R)*   2340

Torquay U: Veysey; Pugh (Airey), Holmes, Matthews, Elliott, Uzzell, Smith P, Lloyd, Edwards, Loram, Joyce.
Hereford U: Elliott; Jones MA, Devine, Pejic, Peacock, Bradley, Jones R, Narbett, Benbow, Robinson, Tester.

Walsall (1) 1 *(Pritchard)*

Port Vale (1) 2 *(Beckford 2)*   4774

Walsall: Barber; Gritt, Mower, Kelly, Forbes, Skipper, Pritchard, Rimmer, Saville, Hawker, Thorpe.
Port Vale: Grew; Webb, Hughes, Mills, Aspin, Glover, Porter, Earle, Futcher (Cross), Beckford, Jeffers.

Wolverhampton W (1) 1 *(Westley)*

Lincoln C (0) 0   11,071

Wolverhampton W: Lange; Downing, Venus, Robertson, Westley, Vaughan, Thompson, Gooding, Bull, Mutch, Dennison.
Lincoln C: Gorton; Casey, Clarke, Cook, Brown, Davies, Groves, Bressington, Sertori, Carmichael, Nicholson.

Wrexham (0) 0

Wigan Ath (0) 0   2042

Wrexham: O'Keefe; Salathiel, Wright, Reck (Flynn),

Beaumont, Jones, Buxton, Thackeray, Kearns (Cooper), Worthington, Bowden.
Wigan Ath: Adkins; Senior, Tankard, Rimmer, Atherton, Beesley, Thompson, Parkinson, Hilditch, Page, Carberry (Griffiths).

23 AUG

Brighton & HA (0) 0

Brentford (2) 3 *(Millen, Godfrey, May)*   6045

Brighton & HA: Keeley; Chivers, Chapman, Curbishley, Bissett, Dublin, Nelson, Crumplin (Lambert), Wood, Codner, Wilkins.
Brentford: Parks; Buttigieg, Ratcliffe (Ansah), Stanislaus, Millen, Evans, Jones, May, Godfrey (Bates), Blissett, Smillie.

Bristol R (1) 1 *(Penrice)*

Portsmouth (0) 0   4727

Bristol R: Martyn; Alexander, Twentyman, Yates, Mehew, Jones, Holloway, Reece, White, Penrice, Wilmott.
Portsmouth: Knight; Neill, Beresford, Fillery, Sandford, Ball, Wigley, Chamberlain, Kelly, Connor, Black.

Exeter C (0) 3 *(Rowbotham 2, McDermott)*

Swansea C (0) 0   2777

Exeter C: Walter; Hiley, Vinnicombe, Rogers, Taylor, Whitehead, Rowbotham, Bailey, McDermott, Neville, Dryden.
Swansea C: Bracey; Hough (Legg), Coleman, Melville, Boyle, James, Cobb, D'Auria, Phillips, Raynor (Trick), Hutchison.

Fulham (0) 0

Oxford U (1) 1 *(Foyle)*   3376

Fulham: Stannard; Mauge, Kimble, Skinner, Eckhardt (Walker), Thomas, Marshall, Scott, Watson, Davies, Barnett.
Oxford U: Hucker; Barnsley, Phillips, Lewis, Foster, Greenall, Penney, Ford, Foyle, Durnin, Simpson.

Hartlepool U (1) 3 *(Grayson 2, Baker)*

York C (1) 3 *(Colville 2, Helliwell)*   1507

Hartlepool U: Carr; Nobbs, McKinnon, Tinkler, Barrass, Stokle, Doig, Davies, Baker, Grayson, Dalton.
York C: Marples; Barratt, Kelly, Reid, Greenough, Warburton, Howlett, Spooner, Helliwell, Colville, Dunn.

Peterborough U (2) 2 *(Sterling, Richards)*

Aldershot (0) 0   3397

Peterborough U: Godden; Luke, Crosby, Halsall, Robinson, Oakes, Sterling, Graham, Richards (Osborne), Longhurst, Goldsmith.
Aldershot: Coles, Brown, Phillips, Coyne, Smith, Wignall, Williams, Puckett, Claridge, Henry, Stewart.

Scarborough (2) 2 *(Brook, Richards)*

Scunthorpe U (0) 0   2259

Scarborough: Blackwell; Kamara, Clarke, Short, Richards, Bennyworth, Saunders, Graham, Dobson, Brook, Russell.
Scunthorpe U: Litchfield; Smalley, Longden, Taylor,

Nicol, Tucker, Money, Cowling, Cotton (Stevenson), Flounders, Marshall.

Stockport Co: Siddall; Brown, Robertson (Howard), Matthews, Thorpe, Williams, Payne, Bullock, Cooke, MacDonald (McInerney), Angell.
Stockport Co won 2-1 on aggregate

FIRST ROUND SECOND LEG

28 AUG

Port Vale (0) 1 *(Beckford)*

Walsall (0) 0   4441

Port Vale: Grew; Webb, Hughes, Mills, Aspin, Glover, Porter, Earle, Futcher (Cross), Beckford, Jeffers.
Walsall: Green; Gritt, Mower, Goodwin, Forbes, Skipper, Pritchard (Bertschin), Rimmer, Saville, Hawker, Thorpe (Kelly).
Port Vale won 3-1 on aggregate

29 AUG

Aldershot (1) 6 *(Puckett 3 (1 pen), Coyne, Henry, Oakes (og))*

Peterborough U (0) 2 *(Richards, Halsall) aet*   1587

Aldershot: Coles; Brown, Phillips, Coyne, Smith, Wignall, Williams (Burvill), Puckett, Banton, Henry, Stewart (Claridge).
Peterborough U: Godden; Andrews, Crosby, Halsall, Robinson, Oakes, Sterling, Graham, Richards, Longhurst, Goldsmith.
Aldershot won 6-4 on aggregate

Bolton W (2) 5 *(Philliskirk, Reeves, Savage, Cowdrill, Darby)*

Rochdale (0) 1 *(Burns)*   4637

Bolton W: Felgate; Brown, Cowdrill, Savage, Crombie, Winstanley, Storer, Thompson, Reeves, Philliskirk, Darby.
Rochdale: Welch; Goodison, Hill, Brown, Cole, Ward, Ainscow, Holmes, Walling (Whellans), Burns, Stonehouse.
Bolton W won 6-3 on aggregate

Brentford (1) 1 *(Blissett)*

Brighton & HA (1) 1 *(Wilkins)*   4306

Brentford: Parks; Buttigieg (Bates), Stanislaus, Millen, Evens, Ratcliffe (Cockram), Jones, May, Godfrey, Blissett, Smillie.
Brighton & HA: Keeley; Chivers, Chapman, Curbishley, Bissett, Dublin, Nelson, Wood, Bremner, Codner, Wilkins.
Brentford won 4-1 on aggregate

Burnley (0) 0

Blackpool (0) 1 *(Bradshaw)*   6085

Burnley: Pearce; Eli, Deakin, Farrell (Grewcock), Monington, Harris, White, Mumby (Hancock), O'Connell, Jakub, Deary.
Blackpool: McIlhargey; Burgess, Morgan, Gore, Briggs, Methven, Wright, Coughlin, Madden, Garner, Bradshaw.
Blackpool won 3-2 on aggregate

Bury (0) 1 *(Robinson)*

Stockport Co (1) 1 *(Matthews)*   2590

Bury: Farnworth; Hill, Withe, Hoyland, Valentine, Clements, Lee, Feeley, Cunningham, Greenwood (Robinson), Barnes (McIlroy).

Carlisle U (0) 1 *(Walwyn)*

Halifax T (0) 0   3045

Carlisle U: McKellar; Graham, Dalziel, Saddington, Ogley (Fyfe), Fitzpatrick, Shepherd (Wharton), Walsh, Walwyn, Proudlock, Halpin.
Halifax T: Whitehead; Barr, Cook, Hedworth, Bramhall, Horner, Martin, Watson (Richardson), Broadbent (McPhillips), Butler, Hall.
Halifax T won 3-2 on aggregate

Chester C (0) 0

Crewe Alex (0) 2 *(Dyson, Gardiner)*   1758

Chester C: Stewart; Reeves, Woodthorpe, Abel, Lightfoot, Lane, Butler, Pugh, Newhouse, Dale, Painter.
Crewe Alex: Edwards P; Swain, Edwards PR, Callaghan, Dyson (Smart), Clayton, Jasper, Murphy, Sussex, Gardiner, Walters.
Crewe Alex won 6-0 on aggregate

Chesterfield (0) 1 *(Hewitt)*

Birmingham C (0) 1 *(Bailey)*   3313

Chesterfield: Leonard; Gunn, Ryan, Arnott, Brien, Slack, Plummer, Hewitt, Waller, Thompson, Morris.
Birmingham C: Thomas; Ashley, Matthewson, Atkins, Sproson, Overson, Peer, Bailey, Gordon, Frain, Yates (Hopkins).
Birmingham C won 3-2 on aggregate

Doncaster R (0) 1 *(Turnbull)*

Huddersfield T (2) 2 *(Wilson 2)*   3583

Doncaster R: Samways; Brockie, Brevett, Douglas, Ashurst, Raffell, Robinson, Stiles (Gaughan), Turnbull, Rankine, Jones G (McGinley).
Huddersfield T: Hardwick; Trevitt, Hutchings, Marsden (Mitchell), O'Doherty, Lewis, O'Regan, Wilson, Cecere, Maskell, Bent (Onuora).
Huddersfield T won 3-2 on aggregate

Grimsby T (1) 2 *(Alexander, Childs)*

Hull C (0) 0 *aet*   6758

Grimsby T: Reece; Williams (Watson), Agnew, Tillson, Lever, Cunnington, Gilbert, Cockerill, Childs, Rees (Birtles), Alexander.
Hull C: Kelly; Murray (Edwards), Brown, Terry, Jacobs, Jobson, Askew, Payton (Swan), McParland, Doyle, Jenkinson.
Grimsby T won 2-1 on aggregate

Leyton Orient (0) 3 *(Day, Castle, Carter)*

Gillingham (0) 0   2818

Leyton Orient: Heald; Baker, Dickenson, Hales, Day, Sitton, Howard, Castle, Cooper, Harvey (Hull), Carter.
Gillingham: Hillyard; Norris (Smith), Johnson, Haines, Pearson, Palmer, Haylock, Eeles (Thompson), Beadle, Lovell, Joseph.
Leyton Orient won 7-1 on aggregate

642

Notts Co (1) 3 *(Robinson, Short, Stant)*
Shrewsbury T (0) 1 *(Naughton)*   2559

Notts Co: Cherry; Palmer, Platnauer, Short, Yates, Robinson, Draper, Johnson, Lund, Stant, Turner (Fairclough).
Shrewsbury T: Perks; Green, Pittman, Kelly, Pratley, Moyes, Brown, Bell, Melrose (Kasule), McGinlay, Naughton.
Shrewsbury T won 4-3 on aggregate

Plymouth Arg (0) 0
Cardiff C (1) 2 *(Pike, Morgan)*   5728

Plymouth Arg: Wilmot; Brown, Brimacombe, Marker, Burrows, Smith, Byrne (Hodges), McCarthy, Tynan, Thomas, Stuart.
Cardiff C: Wood; Rodgerson, Daniel, Lynex, Abraham, Perry, Curtis (Gummer), Morgan, Gilligan, Kelly, Pike (Fry).
Plymouth Arg won 3-2 on aggregate

Portsmouth (0) 2 *(Fillery, Black)*
Bristol R (0) 0   5287

Portsmouth: Knight; Neill, Maguire, Fillery, Sandford, Ball, Wigley, Chamberlain, Kelly, Connor, Black.
Bristol R: Martyn; Alexander, Twentyman, Yates, Mehew, Jones, Holloway, Reece, White, Penrice (McClean), Willmott.
Portsmouth won 2-1 on aggregate

Reading (0) 2 *(Senior, Gilkes)*
Bristol C (2) 2 *(Taylor 2)*   4457

Reading: Francis; Williams, Richardson, Beavon, Hicks, Wood, Jones, Taylor S, Senior, Gilkes, Payne (Conroy).
Bristol C: Leaning; Llewellyn, Honor, Wimbleton (Mardon), Pender, Rennie, Gavin (Eaton), Newman, Taylor, Smith, Shelton.
Reading won 5-4 on aggregate

Rotherham U (0) 1 *(Williamson (pen))*
Sheffield U (0) 0   11,833

Rotherham U: O'Hanlon; Russell, Robinson, Grealish (Goodwin), Barnsley, Scott, Buckley, Dempsey, Williamson, Mendonca, Hazel.
Sheffield U: Tracey; Hill, Barnes, Booker (Todd), Stancliffe, Morris, Roberts (Francis), Gannon, Agana, Deane, Bryson.
Rotherham U won 2-1 on aggregate

Scunthorpe U (0) 1 *(Flounders)*
Scarborough (0) 1 *(Dobson)*   2853

Scunthorpe U: Musselwhite; Smalley, Longden, Taylor, Nicol, Tucker, Hodkinson, Cowling, Butler, Flounders, Marshall.
Scarborough: Blackwell; Kamara, Clarke, Short, Richards, Bennyworth, Saunders, Graham, Dobson, Brook, Russell.
Scarborough won 3-1 on aggregate

Southend U (1) 2 *(Crown (pen), Bennett)*
Colchester U (0) 1 *(Collins)*   3763

Southend U: Sansome; Dixon, Roberts, Martin, Prior, Brush (Smith), Cook, Butler, Crown, Walsh, Bennett.
Colchester U: Grace; Hicks, Rooke, English A, Daniels, Radford (Taylor), Bennett, Collins, Wilkins, Scott (Kinsella), Allinson.
Southend U won 6-4 on aggregate

Swansea C (0) 1 *(Raynor)*
Exeter C (1) 1 *(Rowbotham)*   1987

Swansea C: Bracey; Hough, Coleman, Melville, Boyle, James, Cobb, D'Auria, Phillips, Raynor, Legg.
Exeter C: Walter; Hiley, Vinnicombe, McNichol, Taylor, Whitehead, Rowbotham, Bailey, McDermott, Neville, Dryden.
Exeter C Won 4-1 on aggregate

Tranmere R (0) 3 *(Muir 2 (2 pens), Malkin)*
Preston NE (0) 1 *(Shaw)*   5275

Tranmere R: Nixon; Higgins (Martindale), McCarrick, Bishop, Hughes, Vickers, Morrissey (Fairclough), Harvey, Malkin, Muir, Thomas.
Preston NE: Tunks; Miller, Rathbone, Atkins, Jones, Wrightson, Mooney, Joyce (Bogie), Snow, Shaw, Swann.
Tranmere R won 7-4 on aggregate

Wigan Ath (4) 5 *(Hilditch, Senior, Parkinson, Thompson, Page)*
Wrexham (0) 0   1871

Wigan Ath: Adkins; Senior, Tankard, Rimmer, Atherton, Beesley, Thompson, Parkinson, Hilditch, Page (Pilling), Griffiths.
Wrexham: O'Keefe; Salathiel, Wright, Flynn, Beaumont, Jones, Cooper (Preece), Thackeray, Buxton, Worthington (Armstrong), Bowden.
Wigan Ath won 5-0 on aggregate

York C (1) 4 *(Warburton, Spooner 3)*
Hartlepool U (0) 1 *(Dalton)*   2236

York C: Marples; Barratt, Kelly, Reid, Tutill, Warburton, Howlett, Spooner, Helliwell, Colville, Hall.
Hartlepool U: Carr; Nobbs, McKinnon, Tinkler, McEwan, Barrass, Allon, Davies (Doig), Baker, Speirs, Dalton.
York C won 7-4 on aggregate

30 AUG

Hereford U (2) 3 *(Jones R (pen), Pejic, Robinson)*
Torquay U (0) 0   2444

Hereford U: Elliott; Jones MA, Devine, Pejic, Peacock, Bradley, Jones R, Narbett, Benbow (Hemming), Robinson, Tester.
Torquay U: Veysey; Holmes, Pugh, Matthews, Davies, Uzzell, Weston, Lloyd, Edwards (Smith P), Airey (Morrison), Loram.
Hereford U won 4-0 on aggregate

Lincoln C (0) 0
Wolverhampton W (1) 2 *(Bull, Dennison)*   6733

Lincoln C: Gorton; Casey, Clarke, Davis, Thompson, Brown G, Groves, Bressington, Sertori, Carmichael, Brown P (Waitt).
Wolverhampton W: Lange; Thompson, Venus, Robertson, Westley, Vaughan, Chard, Gooding, Bull, Mutch, Dennison.
Wolverhampton W won 3-0 on aggregate

Maidstone U (0) 0
Cambridge U (0) 1 *(Taylor)* 2700
Maidstone U: Beeney; Elsey, Cooper, Pamphlett (Charlery), Golley, Berry, Lillis, Galliers (Barton), Sorrell, Butler, Poole.
Cambridge U: Vaughan; Bailie, Kimble, O'Shea, Chapple, Daish, Dennis, Leadbitter, Dublin, Taylor, Philpott (Robinson).
Cambridge U won 4-1 on aggregate

Oxford U (2) 3 *(Simpson 2, Durnin)*
Fulham (2) 5 *(Scott 2, Skinner 2 (1 pen), Walker)* 3896
Oxford U: Hucker; Bardsley, Phillips J, Lewis, Foster (Ford), Greenall, Penney, McClaren, Foyle, Durnin, Simpson.
Fulham: Stannard; Mauge, Barnett (Bremner), Skinner, Nebbeling, Thomas, Marshall, Scott, Watson (Kimble), Sayer, Walker.
Fulham Won 5-4 on aggregate

5 SEPT

Northampton T (0) 0
Mansfield T (2) 2 *(Christie, Stringfellow)* 3963
Northampton T: Gleasure; Sandeman (Williams), Wilson, Donald, Wilcox, McPherson, Quow (Culpin), Collins, Thomas, Adcock, Berry.
Mansfield T: Cox; McKernon, Prindiville, Hunt, Foster, Coleman, Lowery, Stringfellow, Christie, Charles, Kearney.
Mansfield T won 3-1 on aggregate

SECOND ROUND FIRST LEG

18 SEPT

Port Vale (1) 1 *(Futcher)*
Wimbledon (1) 2 *(Fairweather, Fashanu)* 5827
Port Vale: Grew; Webb, Hughes, Walker, Aspin, Glover, Cross, Earle, Futcher, Beckford, Mills (Miller).
Wimbledon: Segers; Curle, Phelan, Kruszynski, Young, Scales, Fairweather, Ryan, Fashanu, Gibson, Wise.

19 SEPT

Arsenal (1) 2 *(Smith, Brimacombe (og))*
Plymouth Arg (0) 0 26,865
Arsenal: Lukic; Dixon, Winterburn, Thomas, O'Leary, Adams, Rocastle, Richardson, Smith, Merson (Groves), Marwood.
Plymouth Arg: Wilmot; Brown, Brimacombe, Marker, Burrows, Smith, Hodges, McCarthy, Tynan, Thomas, Stuart.

Barnsley (1) 1 *(Archdeacon)*
Blackpool (1) 1 *(Gabbiadini)* 7515
Barnsley: Wardle; Shotton, Broddle, Dobbin, Banks, Futcher, Lowndes, Agnew, Cooper, MacDonald (Foreman), Archdeacon.
Blackpool: McIlhargey; Burgess, Morgan (Wright), Gore, Methven, Elliott, Owen, Diamond (Madden), Gabbiadini, Garner, Briggs.

Birmingham C (0) 1 *(Sproson)*
West Ham U (1) 2 *(Allen, Slater)* 10,987
Birmingham C: Thomas; Ashley, Matthewson, Atkins, Sproson, Overson, Peer, Bailey, Gordon (Sturridge), Gleghorn, Hopkins.
West Ham U: Parkes; Potts, Dicks, Gale, Martin, Keen, Ward (Brady), Slater, Allen, Dolan, Parris.

Bolton W (1) 2 *(Philliskirk 2)*
Watford (0) 1 *(Roberts)* 6856
Bolton W: Rose; Brown, Cowdrill, Henshaw, Crombie, Winstanley, Storer, Thompson, Reeves, Philliskirk, Darby.
Watford: Coton; Gibbs, Jackett, Richardson, Holdsworth, Roeder, Thomas, Wilkinson, Roberts, Porter, Redfearn.

Brentford (1) 2 *(Evans, Blissett)*
Manchester C (0) 1 *(Oldfield)* 6065
Brentford; Parks; Buttigieg, Stanislaus, Millen, Evans, Ratcliffe (Cockram), Jones, May, Cadette (Haag), Blissett, Smillie.
Manchester C: Cooper; Fleming, Hinchcliffe, Bishop, Gayle, Redmond, White, Morley, Oldfield, McNab, Lake.

Cambridge U (1) 2 *(Chapple, Robinson)*
Derby Co (0) 1 *(Goddard)* 5333
Cambridge U: Vaughan; Bailie, Kimble, O'Shea, Chapple, Smith, Dennis, Leadbitter, Robinson, Taylor, Philpott (Dublin).
Derby Co: Shilton; Blades, Forsyth, Williams, Wright, Hindmarch, McMinn, Saunders, Goddard, Hebberd (Pickering), Micklewhite.

Chelsea (1) 1 *(Roberts)*
Scarborough (1) 1 *(Monkou (og))* 10,349
Chelsea: Beasant; Clarke, Dorigo, Roberts, Lee, Monkou, Dickens (Wilson C), Nicholas, Dixon, Wilson K, Hazard.
Scarborough: Blackwell; Kamara, Clarke, Short, Richards, Bennyworth, Olsson, Graham, Norris, Brook (Dobson), Russell.

Crewe Alex (0) 0
Bournemouth (1) 1 *(Moulden)* 3504
Crewe Alex: Edwards P; Swain, Edwards PR, Callaghan (Smart), Dyson, Clayton, Jasper, Cutler (Murphy), Sussex, Gardiner, Walters.
Bournemouth: Peyton; Shearer, Morrell, Teale, Miller, Peacock, Lawrence, Moulden, O'Driscoll, Brooks, Blissett.

Crystal Palace (0) 1 *(Wright)*
Leicester C (1) 2 *(Kitson, Reid)* 7382
Crystal Palace: Suckling; Pemberton (Dyer), Burke, Gray, Hopkins, O'Reilly (Shaw), McGoldrick, Thomas, Bright, Wright, Pardew.
Leicester C: Hodge; Johnson, Morgan, Mauchlen, Walsh, Evans, Reid, Williams, Kitson (North), McAllister, Wright (Paris).

Grimsby T (1) 3 *(Gilbert, Watson, Birtles)*
Coventry C (0) 1 *(Kilcline (pen))* 10,150
Grimsby T: Sherwood; McDermott, Stephenson, Till-

son, Lever, Cunnington, Childs, Gilbert, Rees, Watson, Birtles.
Coventry C: Waugh; Borrows, Dobson, Emerson (Livingstone), Kilcline, Peake, Gynn (Thompson), Speedie, MacDonald, Bannister, Smith.

Ipswich T (0) 0
Tranmere R (1) 1 *(Muir)*   7757
Ipswich T: Forrest; Baltacha, Thompson, Zondervan, Redford, Palmer (Donowa), Lowe, Dozzell, Wark, Humes (Yallop), Milton.
Tranmere R: Nixon; Higgins, McCarrick, Martindale, Hughes, Garnett (Bishop), Morrissey (Steel), Harvey, Malkin, Muir, Thomas.

Leyton Orient (0) 0
Everton (1) 2 *(Newell, Sheedy)*   8214
Leyton Orient: Heald; Baker, Dickenson, Hales, Day, Sitton, Howard, Castle, Cooper, Harvey (Hull), Carter.
Everton: Southall; Snodin, Pointon, Ratcliffe, Watson, Rehn, Nevin, McCall, Sharp, Newell, Sheedy.

Liverpool (1) 5 *(Hysen, Rush 2, Beardsley, Barnes)*
Wigan Ath (1) 2 *(Griffiths, Thompson)*   19,231
Liverpool: Grobbelaar; Hysen, Burrows, Nicol, Whelan, Hansen, Beardsley (Staunton), Gillespie (Venison), Rush, Barnes, Molby.
Wigan Ath: Adkins; Atherton, Tankard, Rimmer, Patterson, Beesley, Thompson, Parkinson, Carberry (Nugent), Page (Johnson), Griffiths.

Mansfield T (3) 3 *(Stringfellow, Christie 2)*
Luton T (2) 4 *(Wegerle 2, Elstrup 2)*   5361
Mansfield T: Cox; McKernon, Hathaway, Hunt, Foster, Coleman, Lowery (Prindiville), Stringfellow, Christie, Charles, Kearney.
Luton T: Chamberlain; Breacker, Dreyer, Wilson, McDonough, Beaumont, Kennedy, Wegerle, Elstrup, Preece, Williams (Black).

Oldham Ath (2) 2 *(Ritchie, Holden R)*
Leeds U (1) *(Strachan)*   8415
Oldham Ath: Rhodes; Irwin, Barlow, Henry, Marshall, Barrett, Palmer, Ritchie, Bunn, Milligan, Holden R.
Leeds U: Day; Sterland, Whitlow, Jones, Fairclough (Blake), Haddock, Strachan, Batty, Baird, Davison (Williams A), Hendrie.

Reading (1) 3 *(Senior 2, Taylor)*
Newcastle U (0) 1 *(Gallacher)*   7960
Reading: Francis; Jones, Richardson, Beavon, Hicks, Wood, Knight (Bashir), Taylor, Senior, Gilkes, Payne.
Newcastle U: Kelly; Ranson, Stimson, Dillon, Scott, Thorn, Gallacher, Brock, Quinn, McGhee, Fereday.

Shrewsbury T (0) 0
Swindon T (3) 3 *(Shearer, McLoughlin 2)*   3518
Shrewsbury T: Perks; Green, Pittman, Kelly (Griffiths), Pratley, Moyes, Brown, Bell, Purdie (Priest), McGinlay, Naughton.
Swindon T: Digby; Hockaday, King, McLoughlin, Calderwood, Gittens, Jones, Shearer (Galvin), Bodin, MacLaren, Simpson.

Stoke C (1) 1 *(Morgan)*
Millwall (0) 0   8030
Stoke C: Fox; Butler, Statham, Kamara, Cranson, Higgins, Palin (Hackett), Ware, Bamber, Morgan, Beagrie.
Millwall: Horne; Stevens, Dawes, Hurlock, Wood, McLeary, Carter, Briley, Sheringham, Cascarino, Anthrobus (Waddock).

Sunderland (1) 1 *(Hardyman (pen))*
Fulham (1) 1 *(Watson)*   11,416
Sunderland: Carter; Agboola (Cullen), Hardyman, Bennett, MacPhail, Owers, Cornforth (Rush), Armstrong, Gates, Hauser, Pascoe.
Fulham: Stannard; Mauge, Thomas (Bremner), Skinner, Nebbeling, Eckhardt, Marshall, Scott, Watson, Sayer, Walker.

20 SEPT

Aston Villa (1) 2 *(Platt, Gray)*
Wolverhampton W (0) 1 *(Mutch)*   27,400
Aston Villa: Spink; Price, Gallagher, Gage, Mountfield, McGrath, Platt, Heath (Nielsen), Olney, Gray, Callaghan.
Wolverhampton W: Kendall; Bellamy, Venus, Streete, Clarke, Vaughan (Downing), Bennett, Gooding, Bull (Paskin), Mutch, Dennison.

Charlton Ath (2) 3 *(Jones 2, Walsh)*
Hereford U (1) *(Jones R (pen))*   3618
Charlton Ath: Bolder; Humphrey, Reid, Peake, McLaughlin, Pates, Lee, Williams, Jones, Walsh, MacKenzie.
Hereford U: Priday; Jones MA, Williams, Pejic, Peacock, Bradley (Devine), Jones R, Narbett, Benbow (Jones M), Robinson, Tester.

Exeter C (0) 3 *(Vinnicombe, Dryden, Young)*
Blackburn R (0) 0   4808
Exeter C: Walter; Hiley, Vinnicombe, Rogers, Taylor, Whitehead, Rowbotham, Bailey (Young), McDermott, Neville, Dryden.
Blackburn R: Gennoe (Gayle); Atkins, Sulley, Reid, Hill, May, Kennedy, Millar, Stapleton, Finnigan (Hildersley), Sellars.

Middlesbrough (2) 4 *(Comfort, Slaven 2, Kernaghan)*
Halifax T (0) 0   10,613
Middlesbrough: Poole; Parkinson, Mohan, Mowbray, Kernaghan, Putney, Slaven, Proctor, Ripley, Brennan, Comfort.
Halifax T: Brown; Barr (Fleming), Cook, Butler, Bramhall, Horner, Martin, Watson, Matthews, Juryeff, Hall (Richardson).

Norwich C (1) 1 *(Fleck)*
Rotherham U (1) *(Williamson)*   9531
Norwich C: Gunn; Sherwood, Bowen, Butterworth, Linighan, Townsend, Gordon, Fleck, Rosario, Crook, Phillips.
Rotherham U: O'Hanlon; Russell, Barnsley, Grealish, Johnson, Robinson, Buckley, Dempsey, Williamson, Haycock, Thompson.

Nottingham F (1) 1 *(Crosby)*

Huddersfield T (1) *(O'Doherty)*   18,976

Nottingham F: Sutton; Laws, Pearce, Walker, Foster, Hodge, Crosby, Sheridan, Clough, Chapman, Parker.
Huddersfield T: Hardwick; Trevitt, Hutchings, May, O'Doherty, Lewis, Mitchell, Wilson, Cecere, Maskell (Marsden), Smith.

Portsmouth (0) 2 *(Black, Kuhl)*

Manchester U (3) 3 *(Ince 2, Wallace)*   18,072

Portsmouth: Knight; Maguire, Beresford, Fillery, Sandford, Ball, Wigley, Kuhl, Whittingham, Chamberlain, Black.
Manchester U: Leighton; Anderson, Donaghy, Beardsmore, Phelan, Pallister, Robson (Duxbury), Ince, McClair (Sharpe), Hughes, Wallace.

QPR (2) 2 *(Spackman, Clarke)*

Stockport Co (0) 1 *(McInerney)*   6745

QPR: Seaman; Channing, Sansom, Parker, McDonald, Spackman, Francis (Reid), Barker, Clarke (Falco), Wright, Sinton.
Stockport Co: Siddall; Brown, Logan, Matthews, Williams, Thorpe, McInerney, Payne, Oghani, Cooke, Angell (Knowles).

Sheffield W (0) 0

Aldershot (0) 0   9237

Sheffield W: Pressman; Newsome, Worthington, Palmer, Shirtliff, Madden, Taylor, Whitton (Harper), Atkinson, Hirst, Shakespeare.
Aldershot: Coles; Brown, Phillips, Burvill, Smith, Wignall, Williams, Puckett, Banton, Henry, Stewart.

Tottenham H (0) 1 *(Fenwick)*

Southend U (0) 0   15,734

Tottenham H: Thorstvedt; Butters, Van den Hauwe, Fenwick, Thomas (Samways), Mabbutt, Walsh, Gascoigne, Stewart, Sedgley, Robson.
Southend U: Sansome; Dixon, Roberts, Martin, Prior, Ling, Cook, Butler, Crown, Walsh, Bennett.

WBA (0) 1 *(McNally)*

Bradford C (2) 3 *(Leonard 2, Megson)*   7771

WBA: Ward; Bradley, Parkin, Robson, Whyte, North, Ford, Goodman, West, McNally, Anderson.
Bradford C: Tomlinson; Abbott, Tinnion, Aizlewood, Sinnott, Evans, Megson, Campbell, Leonard, Quinn, Jewell.

York C (0) 0

Southampton (0) 1 *(Wallace Rod)*   4526

York C: Marples; Barratt, Kelly, Reid, Tutill, Warburton, Howlett, Spooner, Helliwell, Colville (Dixon), Dunn.
Southampton: Flowers; Wallace Ray, Adams, Case, Ruddock, Osman, Wallace Rod, Cockerill, Rideout (Le Tissier), Horne, Shearer.

SECOND ROUND SECOND LEG

2 OCT

Stockport Co (0) 0

QPR (0) 0   5997

Stockport Co: Siddall; Brown, Bullock, Matthews, Williams, Jones, McInerney, Thorpe, MacDonald (Howard), Cooke, Angell.
QPR: Seaman; Channing, Sansom, Parker, McDonald, Spackman, Barker, Reid, Clarke, Francis, Sinton.
QPR won 2-1 on aggregate

3 OCT

Aldershot (0) 0

Sheffield W (4) 8 *(Whitton 4, Atkinson 3, Shakespeare)*   4011

Aldershot: Coles; Brown, Phillips, Burvill, Smith, Wignall, Claridge, Puckett, Stewart (Anderson), Williams (Coombs), Randall.
Sheffield W: Pressman; Newsome, Worthington, Palmer (Hirst), Shirtliff, Madden, Bennett, Harper, Whitton (Varadi), Atkinson, Shakespeare.
Sheffield W won 8-0 on aggregate.

Blackburn R (1) 2 *(Atkins 2)*

Exeter C (0) 1 *(Rowbotham)*   6608

Blackburn R: Collier; Atkins, Finnigan (Skinner), Reid, Hill, May, Kennedy, Millar, Stapleton, Garner, Sellars.
Exeter C: Walter; Hiley, Vinnicombe, Rogers, Taylor, Whitehead, Rowbotham, Bailey, Young, Neville, Dryden (Harrower).
Exeter C won 4-2 on aggregate

Blackpool (1) 1 *(Briggs)*

Barnsley (0) 1 *(Briggs og)*   aet 5251

Blackpool: McIlhargey; Burgess (Wright), Morgan, Gore (Eyres), Methven, Elliott, Owen, Coughlin, Gabbiadini, Garner, Briggs.
Barnsley: Wardle; Shotton, Cross, Dobbin, (Archdeacon), Broddle, Futcher, Banks, Agnew, Cooper, Currie, Robinson.
Aggregate 2-2; Blackpool won 5-4 on penalties

Bournemouth (0) 0

Crewe Alex (0) 0   5343

Bournemouth: Peyton; Newson, Morrell, Teale, Miller, Peacock, Barnes, Moulden, O'Driscoll, Shearer, Blissett.
Crewe Alex: Edwards P; Swain, Edwards PR, Smart, Dyson, Cutler (Clayton), Jasper, Murphy, Sussex, Fishenden, Walters.
Bournemouth won 1-0 on aggregate

Everton (0) 2 *(Whiteside, Sheedy)*

Leyton Orient (1) 2 *(Carter, Pike)*   10,128

Everton: Southall; Snodin, McDonald, Ratcliffe (Rehn), Watson, Whiteside, Nevin, McCall, Sharp (Cottee), Newell, Sheedy.
Leyton Orient: Heald; Hoddle, Dickenson, Pike, Day (Baker); Sitton, Howard, Castle, Cooper, Harvey, Carter.
Everton won 4-2 on aggregate

Fulham (0) 0

Sunderland (2) 3 *(Gabbiadini 2, Armstrong)* 6314

Fulham: Stannard; Mauge, Thomas, Skinner, Marshall, Eckhardt, Barnett (Donnellan), Scott, Watson, Sayer, Walker.
Sunderland: Carter; Kay, Hardyman, Bennett, MacPhail, Owers, Bracewell, Armstrong, Gates, Gabbiadini, Pascoe.
Sunderland won 4-1 on aggregate

Halifax T (0) 0

Middlesbrough (0) 1 *(Slaven)* 1641

Halifax T: Brown; Fleming, Cook, Hedworth, Bramhall, Horner, Martin (Butler), Watson, McPhillips, Juryeff, Hall (Richardson).
Middlesbrough: Poole; Parkinson, Mohan, Gill, Kernaghan, Putney (McGee), Slaven, Davenport, Burke, Brennan, Comfort.
Middlesbrough won 5-0 on aggregate

Huddersfield T (1) 3 *(Maskell 2, Cecere)*

Nottingham F (1) 3 *(Gaynor, Crosby, Clough)*
aet 13,262

Huddersfield T: Hardwick; O'Doherty, Lewis, Mitchell (O'Regan), Wilson, Cecere, Maskell, Smith (Onuora), Marsden, Hutchings, May.
Nottingham F: Sutton; Laws, Pearce, Walker, Wassall, Hodge, Crosby, Parker (Wilson), Clough, Chapman, Gaynor.
Nottingham F won on away goals after 4-4 on aggregate

Leeds U (0) 1 *(Fairclough)*

Oldham Ath (2) 2 *(Bunn, Ritchie)* 18,092

Leeds U: Day; Sterland, Whitlow, Jones (Speed), Blake (Fairclough), Haddock, Strachan, Batty, Baird, Davison, Williams.
Oldham Ath: Hallworth; Irwin, Barlow, Henry, Warhurst, Barrett, Palmer, Ritchie, Bunn, Milligan, Holden R.
Oldham Ath won 4-2 on aggregate

Luton T (3) 7 *(Wegerle 2, Preece, Elstrup 3, Dreyer)*

Mansfield T (1) 2 *(Kearney, Wilkinson)* 6519

Luton T: Chamberlain; Breacker, Dreyer, Wilson, Rodger, Beaumont, Kennedy, Wegerle, Elstrup, Preece, Black.
Mansfield T: Beasley; Hodges (Hathaway), Prindiville, Hunt, Gray, Wilkinson, Lowery, Stringfellow, Christie, Charles, Kearney.
Luton T won 11-5 on aggregate

Manchester U (0) 0

Portsmouth (0) 0 26,698

Mancheser U: Leighton; Duxbury, Donaghy, Bruce, Phelan, Pallister, Robson, Ince, McClair, Hughes, Wallace.
Portsmouth: Knight; Neill, Beresford, Maguire, Russell, Ball, Wigley, Kuhl, Whittingham, Fillery, Connor.
Manchester U won 3-2 on aggregate

Millwall (1) 2 *(Sheringham, Cascarino)*

Stoke C (0) 0 aet 8637

Millwall: Horne; Stevens, Dawes, Hurlock, Sparham, Thompson, Carter, Waddock, Sheringham, Cascarino, Anthrobus.
Stoke C: Fox; Butler, Statham, Kamara, Cranson,
Higgins (Saunders), Hackett, Beeston, Bamber, Palin, Beagrie.
Millwall won 2-1 on aggregate

Plymouth Arg (1) 1 *(Tynan)*

Arsenal (1) 6 *(Byrne (og), Thomas 3, Groves, Smith)*
17,360

Plymouth Arg: Wilmot; Brown, Brimacombe, Marker, Burrows, Morrison, Hodges (Thomas), Byrne, Tynan (Pickard), Campbell, Stuart.
Arsenal: Lukic; Dixon (Caesar), Winterburn, Thomas, O'Leary, Adams, Rocastle, Richardson, Smith, Groves (Merson), Hayes.
Arsenal won 8-1 on aggregate

Rotherham U (0) 0

Norwich C (2) 2 *(Gordon, Fleck)* 9064

Rotherham U: O'Hanlon; Russell, Robinson, Grealish, Johnson, Barnsley, Buckley, Scott (Goodwin), Williamson, Mendonca (Thompson), Hazel.
Norwich C: Gunn; Sherwood, Bowen, Butterworth, Linighan, Townsend, Gordon, Fleck, Rosario, Crook, Phillips.
Norwich C won 3-1 on aggregate

Southampton (1) 2 *(Shearer 2)*

York C (0) 0 8096

Southampton: Flowers; Wallace Ray (Dodd), Benali, Case, Ruddock, Osman, Le Tissier, Cockerill, Shearer, Rideout (Moore), Wallace Ray.
York C: Marples; McMillan, Kelly, Barratt, Tutill, Warburton, Howlett, Spooner, Helliwell (Colville), Dixon, Dunn.
Southampton won 3-0 on aggregate

Swindon T (0) 3 *(White 2, Shearer)*

Shrewsbury T (0) 1 *(Naughton (pen))* 5544

Swindon T: Digby; Hockaday, King (Close), Bodin, Calderwood, Gittens, Jones (McLoughlin), Shearer, White, MacLaren, Simpson.
Shrewsbury T: Perks; Green, Hartford, Kelly, Finley, Moyes, Brown, Bell, Purdie (Griffiths), McGinlay, Naughton.
Swindon T won 6-1 on aggregate

Tranmere R (1) 1 *(Malkin)*

Ipswich T (0) 0 10,050

Tranmere R: Nixon; Higgins, McCarrick, Martindale (Bishop), Hughes, Vickers, Morrissey (Steel), Harvey, Malkin, Muir, Thomas.
Ipswich T: Forrest; Zondervan, Thompson, Stockwell, Humes, Linighan, Lowe, Dozzell, D'Avray, Palmer (Donowa), Hill (Johnson).
Tranmere R won 2-0 on aggregate

Watford (0) 1 *(Roberts)*

Bolton W (0) 1 *(Comstive)* 8452

Watford: Coton; Gibbs, Jackett, Falconer, Holdsworth, Roeder, Thomas, Henry (Thompson), Roberts, Porter, Hodges (Richardson).
Bolton W: Felgate; Brown, Cowdrill, Comstive, Crombie, Winstanley, Storer, Thompson, Reeves, Philliskirk, Darby.
Bolton W won 3-2 on aggregate

4 OCT

Bradford C (2) 3 *(Abbott, Jewell, Quinn)*
WBA (3) 5 *(Thomas 3, Talbot, Whyte) aet* 5731
Bradford C: Tomlinson; Abbot, Tinnion, Oliver, Sinnott, Jackson, Megson, Campbell, Leonard (Costello), Quinn, Jewell.
WBA: Naylor; Bradley, Burgess, Talbot, Whyte, North, Barham, Goodman (Foster), Thomas, McNally, Bartlett.
WBA won on away goals after 6-6 on aggregate

Coventry C (2) 3 *(Drinkell, Speedie, MacDonald)*
Grimsby T (0) 0 15,327
Coventry C: Ogrizovic; Borrows, Dobson, MacDonald, Downs, Peake, Drinkell, Speedie, Regis, Bannister, Smith.
Grimsby T: Sherwood; McDermott, Jobling (Willis), Tillson, Lever, Cunnington, Childs, Gilbert, Rees, Cockerill, Alexander.
Coventry C won 4-3 on aggregate

Derby Co (1) 5 *(Saunders 3, Goddard, McMinn)*
Cambridge U (0) 0 12,525
Derby Co: Shilton; Sage, Forsyth, Williams, Wright, Blades, McMinn, Saunders, Goddard, Hebberd, Micklewhite.
Cambridge U: Vaughan; Clayton, Kimble, O'Shea, Chapple, Daish, Dennis, Leadbitter, Robinson (Ryan), Taylor (Dublin), Philpott.
Derby Co won 6-2 on aggregate

Hereford U (0) 0
Charlton Ath (1) 1 *(Williams)* 4777
Hereford U: Elliott; Jones MA, Devine, Pejic, Jones R, Bradley, Jones M, Narbett (Hemming), Peacock, Robinson, Tester.
Charlton Ath: Bolder; Humphrey, Reid, MacKenzie, McLaughlin, Pates, Lee, Williams, Jones, Walsh, Mortimer.
Charlton Ath won 4-1 on aggregate

Leicester C (0) 2 *(Clarke, Paris)*
Crystal Palace (0) 3 *(Hopkins, Thomas, Bright)*
  aet 10,283
Leicester C: Hodge; Mauchlen, Morgan, Ramsey, Paris, Evans, (Spearing), Reid, Clarke, Kitson (Puttnam), McAllister, Wright.
Crystal Palace: Suckling; Shaw (Pemberton), Burke, Gray, Hopkins, Dyer (Barber), McGoldrick, Thomas, Bright, Wright, Pardew.
Crystal Palace won on away goals after 4-4 on aggregate

Manchester C (1) 4 *(White, Morley 2, Oldfield)*
Brentford (1) 1 *(May)* 17,874
Manchester C: Cooper; Fleming, Hinchcliffe, Bishop, Gayle, Redmond, White, Morley, Oldfield, Brightwell, Lake.
Brentford: Parks; Bates, Stanislaus (Buttigieg), Millen, Evans, Ratcliffe, Jones, May (Cadette), Holdsworth, Blissett, Smillie.
Manchester C won 5-3 on aggregate

Newcastle U (1) 4 *(Brazil (pen), Brock, Thorn, McGhee)*
Reading (0) 0 15,220
Newcastle U: Burridge; Anderson (Sweeney), Stimson, Dillon, Scott, Thorn, Gallacher, Brock, Brazil, McGhee, Kristensen.
Reading: Francis; Jones, Richardson, Beavon, Hicks, Wood, Knight, Taylor, Senior, Gilkes, Conroy (Leworthy).
Newcastle U won 5-3 on aggregate

Scarborough (0) 3 *(Graham, Robinson, Russell (pen))*
Chelsea (0) 2 *(Clarke, Wilson K)* 5086
Scarborough: Blackwell; Short, Richards, Bennyworth, Olsson, Graham, Russell, Kamara, Saunders, Norris (Brook), Robinson.
Chelsea: Beasant; Lee, Clarke, Dorigo, Bumstead, Monkou, Hazard (McAllister), Dickens (Wilson C), Nicholas, Dixon, Wilson K.
Scarborough won 4-3 on aggregate

Southend U (2) 3 *(Martin, Bennett 2)*
Tottenham H (1) 2 *(Allen, Nayim) aet* 10,400
Southend U: Sansome; Dixon (Edinburgh), Roberts, Martin, Prior, Brush, Cook (Walsh), Butler, Crown, McDonough, Bennett.
Tottenham H: Thorstvedt; Thomas (Howells), Van Den Hauwe, Fenwick, Allen, (Walsh), Mabbutt, Nayim, Gascoigne, Stewart, Lineker, Sedgley.
Tottenham H won on away goals after 3-3 on aggregate

West Ham U (0) 1 *(Dicks)*
Birmingham C (0) 1 *(Atkins)* 12,187
West Ham U: Parkes; Potts, Dicks, Gale, Martin, Keen, Allen, Slater, Dolan (Kelly), Ward (Brady), Parris.
Birmingham C: Thomas; Ashley, Matthewson, Atkins, Sproson, Overson, Tait (Peer), Bailey, Sturridge (Roberts), Gleghorn, Hopkins.
West Ham U won 3-2 on aggregate

Wigan Ath (0) 0
Liverpool (0) 3 *(Staunton 3) At Anfield* 17,954
Wigan Ath: Adkins; Senior, Tankard, Rimmer, Atherton, Beesley, Thompson (Carberry), Pilling, Hilditch (Patterson), Page, Griffiths.
Liverpool: Grobbelaar; Hysen, Burrows, Nicol, Whelan, Hansen, Beardsley (Molby), Venison (Staunton), Houghton, McMahon.
Liverpool won 8-2 on aggregate

Wimbledon (0) 3 *(Fashanu (pen), Gibson 2)*
Port Vale (0) 0 2757
Wimbledon: Segers; Curle, Phelan, Kruszynski, Young, Scales, Fairweather, Ryan, Fashanu, Gibson, Wise.
Port Vale; Grew; Webb, Hughes, Walker, Aspin, Glover (Earle), Porter (Finney), Mills, Futcher, Beckford, Miller.
Wimbledon won 5-1 on aggregate

Wolverhampton W (0) 1 *(Bull)*
Aston Villa (1) 1 *(Mountfield)* 22,754
Wolverhampton W: Kendall; Bellamy, Venus, Streete (Downing), Westley, Vaughan, Bennett (Chard), Gooding, Bull, Paskin, Dennison.
Aston Villa: Spink; Price, Gallacher, Gage (Heath), Mountfield, McGrath, Daley, Platt, Olney, Cowans, Gray.
Aston Villa won 3-2 on aggregate

THIRD ROUND

23 OCT

Tranmere R (1) 3 *(McCarrick, Steel, Bishop)*

Millwall (1) 2 *(Hurlock 2)*   11,626

Tranmere R: Nixon; Higgins (Martindale), McCarrick, Bishop, Hughes, Steel, Morrissey (Fairclough), Harvey, Malkin, Muir, Thomas.
Millwall: Horne; Stevens, Dawes, Hurlock, Thompson, Wood, Carter, Waddock (Torpey), Sheringham, Cascarino, Anthrobus (Sparham).

24 OCT

Crystal Palace (0) 0

Nottingham F (0) 0   14,250

Crystal Palace: Suckling; Pemberton, Shaw, Gray, Hopkins, Dyer, McGoldrick (Barber), Thomas, Bright, Wright, Pardew.
Nottingham F: Sutton; Laws, Pearce, Walker, Wilson, Hodge, Crosby, Parker, Clough, Chapman, Chettle.

Everton (0) 3 *(Newell 2, Nevin)*

Luton T (0) 0   18,428

Everton: Southall; Ebbrell, McDonald, Keown, Watson, Whiteside, Nevin, McCall, Newell, Cottee (Sharp), Sheedy.
Luton T: Chamberlain; Breacker, Dreyer (Dowie), Wilson, McDonough, Beaumont, Harvey, Wegerle, Elstrup, Preece (Johnson), Black.

Southampton (0) 1 *(Cockerill)*

Charlton Ath (0) 0   13,590

Southampton: Flowers; Dodd, Benali, Case, Ruddock, Osman, Le Tissier, Cockerill, Shearer, Rideout, Wallace Rod.
Charlton Ath: Bolder; Humphrey, Reid, Peake, McLaughlin, Pates, Lee, Williams, Leaburn (Jones), Walsh, Mortimer (Achampong).

Sunderland (1) 1 *(Gabbiadini)*

Bournemouth (1) 1 *(Shearer)*   12,595

Sunderland: Carter; Kay, Hardyman, Bennett, MacPhail, Owers, Bracewell, Armstrong, Gates, Gabbiadini, Pascoe (Cullen).
Bournemouth: Peyton; Bond, Coleman, Teale, Miller, Shearer, O'Connor, Moulden, O'Driscoll, Brooks, Blissett.

Swindon T (1) 3 *(McLoughlin, Shearer, MacLaren)*

Bolton W (1) 3 *(Henshaw, Philliskirk, Came)*   8318

Swindon T: Digby; Hockaday (Jones), King, McLoughlin, Calderwood, Gittens, Bodin (Hunt), Shearer, White, MacLaren, Simpson.
Bolton W: Felgate; Brown, Cowdrill, Comstive, Crombie, Winstanley, Henshaw (Came), Thompson, Reeves (Chandler), Philliskirk, Darby.

25 OCT

Arsenal (0) 1 *(Smith)*

Liverpool (0) 0   40,814

Arsenal: Lukic; Dixon, Winterburn, Thomas, O'Leary, Adams, Rocastle, Richardson, Quinn, Merson, Hayes (Smith).

Liverpool: Grobbelaar; Watson, Burrows, Ablett, Whelan, Molby, Houghton, Venison, Rush, Barnes, McMahon (Beardsley).

Aston Villa (0) 0

West Ham U (0) 0   20,898

Aston Villa: Spink; Price, Gage, Birch (Ormondroyd), Mountfield, Nielsen, Daley (Blake), Platt, Olney, Cowans, Gray.
West Ham U: Parkes; Potts, Dicks, Strodder, Martin, Keen, Brady (Kelly), Slater, Dolan, Allen, Parris.

Derby Co (0) 2 *(Saunders 2 (1 pen))*

Sheffield W (0) 1 *(Hirst (Pen))*   18,042

Derby Co: Shilton; Sage, Forsyth, Williams, Wright, Blades, McMinn, Saunders, Goddard, Hebberd, Micklewhite.
Sheffield W: Turner; Newsome, Worthington, Palmer, Shirtliff, Madden, Taylor, Pearson, Whitton (Hirst), Atkinson, Shakespeare.

Exeter C (2) 3 *(McNichol, Neville, Rowbotham)*

Blackpool (0) 0   6508

Exeter C: Walter; Hiley, Vinnicombe, McNichol, Taylor, Whitehead, Rowbotham, Bailey, McDermott, Neville, Dryden.
Blackpool: Gayle; Burgess, Morgan, Thompson (Madden), Methven, Wright, Owen, Coughlin, Hawkins, Garner, Briggs.

Manchester C (1) 3 *(White, Bishop, Allen)*

Norwich C (0) 1 *(Fleck)*   20,126

Manchester C: Dibble; Fleming, Hinchcliffe, Bishop, Gale, Redmond, White, Morley, Allen, McNab, Lake.
Norwich C: Gunn; Sherwood (Allen), Bowen, Butterworth, Linighan, Townsend, Gordon, Fleck, Rosario, Crook, Phillips.

Manchester U (0) 0

Tottenham H (1) 3 *(Lineker, Samways, Nayim)*   45,759

Manchester U: Leighton; Donaghy, Martin (Maiorana), Bruce, Phelan, Pallister, Robson, Ince, McClair, Hughes, Sharpe.
Tottenham H: Thorstvedt; Thomas, Van Den Hauwe, Fenwick (Moran), Allen, Howells, Mabbutt, Nayim, Samways, Lineker, Sedgley.

Middlesbrough (0) 1 *(Slaven)*

Wimbledon (1) 1 *(Gibson)*   12,933

Middlesbrough: Poole; Parkinson, Cooper, Mowbray, Kernaghan, Putney, Slaven, Proctor, Ripley, Brennan, Comfort.
Wimbledon: Segers; Joseph, Phelan, McGee (Fiore), Young, Curle, Fairweather, Gayle (Miller), Gibson, Sanchez, Wise.

Newcastle U (0) 0

WBA (1) 1 *(Whyte)*   22,639

Newcastle U: Burridge; Ranson, Stimson, Dillon, Scott, Kristensen, Gallacher (Fereday), Brock (Brazil), Quinn, McGhee, O'Brien.
WBA: Naylor; Parkin, Hodson, Talbot, Whyte, North, Ford, Goodman, Thomas, McNally, Robson (Anderson).

Oldham Ath (5) 7 *(Bunn 6, Ritchie)*
Scarborough (0) 0   7712
Oldham Ath: Rhodes; Irwin, Barlow, Henry, War-
hurst, Barrett, Adams, Ritchie, Bunn, Milligan,
Holden R
Scarborough: Ironside; Kamara, Clarke, Short (Ols-
son), Richards, Bennyworth, Brook, Graham, Norris
(Saunders), Robinson, Russell.

QPR (0) 1 *(Wright (pen))*
Coventry C (1) 2 *(Downs, Drinkell)*   9277
QPR: Seaman; Channing, Sansom, Maddix, McDon-
ald, Barker, Reid, Wright, Clarke, Francis (Ruther-
ford), Sinton.
Coventry C: Ogrizovic; Burrows, Downs, McDonald,
Kilcline (Billing), Peake, McGrath, Speedie, Regis,
Drinkell, Smith.

THIRD ROUND REPLAYS
1 NOV

Nottingham F (4) 5 *(Hodge 2, Clough, Pearce, Hop-
kins (og))*
Crystal Palace (0) 0   18,625
Nottingham F: Sutton; Laws, Pearce, Walker, Wilson
(Chettle), Hodge, Crosby (Rice), Parker, Clough,
Chapman, Gaynor.
Crystal Palace: Suckling; Pemberton (Hedman),
Shaw, Gray, Hopkins, Dyer, Barber (Salako),
Thomas, Bright, Wright, Pardew.

7 NOV

Bolton W (0) 1 *(Brown)*
Swindon T (0) 1 *(Shearer) aet*   11,533
Bolton W: Felgate; Brown, Cowdrill, Comstive,
Crombie, Winstanley, Henshaw (Came), Thompson,
Reeves (Jeffrey), Philliskirk, Darby.
Swindon T: Digby; Hockaday (Cornwell), Bodin,
McLoughlin, Calderwood, Gittens, Jones, Shearer,
White (Hunt), MacLaren, Simpson.

Bournemouth (0) 0
Sunderland (1) 1 *(Gabbiadini)*   7349
Bournemouth: Kite; Bond, Coleman, Teale, Shearer,
Peacock, O'Connor (Williams), Moulden, O'Dri-
scoll, Brooks, Blissett.
Sunderland: Carter; Williams, Agboola, Bennett,
Ord, Owers, Atkinson, Armstrong, Gates (Hauser),
Gabbiadini, Pascoe.

8 NOV

West Ham U (1) 1 *(Dicks)*
Aston Villa (0) 0   23,833
West Ham U: Parkes; Potts, Dicks, Strodder, Martin,
Keen, Brady, Slater, Dolan, Ward, Parris.
Aston Villa: Spink; Price, Gage (Comyn), McGrath,
Mountfield, Nielsen, Daley (Callaghan), Platt,
Olney, Cowans, Ormondroyd.

Wimbledon (1) 1 *(McGee)*
Middlesbrough (0) 0   3554
Wimbledon: Segers; Joseph, Phelan, McGee, Young,
Curle, Fairweather, Miller, Gibson, Sanchez, Wise.
Middlesbrough: Poole; Parkinson, Cooper, Mow-
bray, Kernaghan, Putney, Proctor, Burke, Brennan,
Davenport, Slaven.

THIRD ROUND SECOND REPLAY
14 NOV

Bolton W (1) 1 *(Philliskirk (pen))*
Swindon T (1) 1 *(White) aet*   14,129
Bolton W: Felgate; Brown, Cowdrill, Comstive,
Crombie, Winstanley, Henshaw, Thompson, Reeves,
Philliskirk, Darby.
Swindon T: Digby; Cornwell, Bodin, McLoughlin
(Galvin), Calderwood, Gittens, Jones, Shearer,
White (Close), MacLaren, Simpson.

THIRD ROUND THIRD REPLAY
21 NOV

Swindon T (0) 2 *(White, MacLaren)*
Bolton W (0) 1 *(Came) aet*   11,238
Swindon T: Digby; Cornwell (Galvin), Bodin,
McLoughlin, Calderwood, Gittens, Foley, Shearer,
White (Close), MacLaren, Simpson.
Bolton W: Felgate; Brown, Cowdrill, Comstive,
Crombie, Winstanley, Hughes (Neal), Thompson,
Came (Stevens), Jeffrey, Darby.

FOURTH ROUND
22 NOV

Derby Co (1) 2 *(McMinn 2)*
WBA (0) 0   21,313
Derby Co: Shilton; Sage, Forsyth, Williams, Wright,
Blades (Cross), McMinn, Saunders, Goddard, Heb-
berd, Micklewhite.
WBA: Naylor; Hodson (Burgess), Harbey, Talbot,
Raven, Whyte, Ford, Goodman, Bartlett, McNally,
Parkin.

Manchester C (0) 0
Coventry C (1) 1 *(Regis)*   23,355
Manchester C: Dibble; Fleming (Brightwell), Hinch-
cliffe, Bishop, Hendry, Redmond, White, Gayle,
Allen, McNab, Lake (Oldfield).
Coventry C: Ogrizovic; Burrows, Dobson, Clark,
Billing, Peake, Gynn, Speedie (MacDonald), Regis,
Drinkell, Smith.

Nottingham F (0) 1 *(Chapman)*
Everton (0) 0   21,324
Nottingham F: Crossley; Laws, Pearce, Walker, Chet-
tle, Hodge, Crosby, Parker, Clough, Chapman, Rice.
Everton: Southall; McDonald, Pointon, Keown, Sno-
din, Ebbrell, Nevin (Cottee), McCall, Sharp, Newell,
Sheedy.

Oldham Ath (1) 3 *(Ritchie 2, Henry)*
Arsenal (0) 1 *(Quinn)*   14,924
Oldham Ath: Rhodes; Irwin, Barlow, Henry, Barrett,
Warhurst, Marshall, Ritchie, Bunn, Milligan, Holden
R.
Arsenal: Lukic; Dixon, Winterburn, Thomas, O'Le-
ary, Adams, Rocastle, Richardson, Smith, Quinn,
Jonsson (Groves).

Tranmere R (0) 2 *(Vickers, Steel)*
Tottenham H (1) 2 *(Gascoigne, Higgins (og))* 13,789
Tranmere R: Nixon; Higgins, Pike, Bishop (Martin-
dale), Hughes, Vickers, Morrissey (Malkin), Harvey,
Steel, Muir, Mungall.

Tottenham H: Thorstvedt; Thomas, Polston J, Bergsson (Stevens), Howells, Mabbutt, Samways, Gascoigne, Stewart (Walsh), Lineker, Allen.

West Ham U (0) 1 *(Allen)*

Wimbledon (0) 0   24,746

West Ham U: Parkes; Potts, Dicks, Strodder, Martin, Keen (Fashanu), Brady, Slater, Allen, Ward, Parris (Devonshire).
Wimbledon: Segers; Joseph, Phelan, Ryan, Young, Curle, Fairweather, Miller (Cork), Cotterill, Sanchez (Scales), Wise.

29 NOV

Exeter C (1) 2 *(Rowbotham, Neville)*

Sunderland (0) 2 *(Armstrong, Gates)*   8643

Exeter C: Walter; Hiley, Harrower, McNichol, Taylor, Whitehead, Rowbotham, Bailey, Batty, Neville, Benjamin.
Sunderland: Carter; Agboola, Hardyman, Bennett, Ord, Owers (Hauser), Atkinson, Armstrong, Gates, Gabbiadini, Pascoe.

Swindon T (0) 0

Southampton (0) 0   15,085

Swindon T: Digby; Kerslake (Cornwell), Bodin, McLoughlin, Calderwood, Gittens, Jones, Shearer, White (Simpson), MacLaren, Foley.
Southampton: Flowers; Dodd, Benali, Case, Ruddock, Osman, Le Tissier, Cockerill, Shearer (Horne), Rideout, Wallace Rod.

FOURTH ROUND REPLAYS

Tottenham H (1) 4 *(Howells, Stewart, Mabbutt, Allen)*

Tranmere R (0) 0   23,724

Tottenham H: Thorstvedt; Thomas, Van Den Hauwe, Allen, Howells, Mabbutt, Samways, Gascoigne, Stewart, Lineker, Sedgley.
Tranmere R: Nixon; Higgins, Pike, Martindale (Fairclough), Hughes, Vickers, Malkin (Bishop), Harvey, Steel, Muir, Mungall.

5 DEC

Sunderland (2) 5 *(Pascoe, Armstrong, Gates 2, Hardyman (pen))*

Exeter C (1) 2 *(Benjamin, McNichol)*   18,130

Sunderland: Carter; Agboola, Hardyman, Bennett, Owers, Atkinson, Kay, Armstrong (Brady), Gates, Gabbiadini (Hauser), Pascoe.
Exeter C: Walter; Hiley, Harrower (Cooper), McNichol, Taylor, Whitehead, Rowbotham, Bailey, Batty, Neville, Benjamin (Coyle).

16 JAN

Southampton (0) 4 *(Horne, Rideout, Le Tissier, Wallace Rod)*

Swindon T (2) 2 *(McLoughlin, White) aet*   19,018

Southampton: Flowers; Dodd (Shearer), Benali, Case, Moore (Ruddock), Osman, Le Tissier, Cockerill, Rideout, Horne, Wallace Rod.
Swindon T: Digby; Kerslake, Bodin, McLoughlin, Calderwood, Gittens, Jones (Cornwall), Shearer, White, MacLaren, Foley.

FIFTH ROUND
17 JAN

Nottingham F (1) 2 *(Crosby, Parker)*

Tottenham H (0) 2 *(Lineker, Sedgley)*   30,044

Nottingham F: Sutton; Laws, Pearce, Walker, Chettle, Hodge, Crosby, Parker, Clough, Jemson, Orlygsson (Rice).
Tottenham H: Thorstvedt; Thomas, Van Den Hauwe, Allen, Howells, Mabbutt, Samways, Polston J (Nayim), Stewart, Lineker, Sedgley.

Sunderland (0) 0

Coventry C (0) 0   27,218

Sunderland: Carter; Kay, Hardyman, Bennett, MacPhail, Owers, Bracewell, Armstrong, Gates (Agboola), Gabbiadini (Hauser), Pascoe.
Coventry C: Ogrizovic; Borrows, Dobson, McGrath, Billing, Peake, Gynn, Speedie, Regis, Livingstone, Smith.

West Ham U (1) 1 *(Dicks)*

Derby Co (0) 1 *(Saunders)*   25,035

West Ham U: Parkes; Potts, Dicks, Parris, Martin, Gale, Brady, Kelly, Rosenior (Slater), Allen, Keen.
Derby Co: Shilton; Sage, Forsyth, Williams, Wright, Hindmarch, Pickering, Saunders, Ramage (Francis), Hebberd, Cross (Patterson).

24 JAN

Southampton (1) 2 *(Le Tissier (1 pen))*

Oldham Ath (0) 2 *(Ritchie 2)*   21,026

Southampton: Flowers; Dodd, Benali, Case, Moore, Osman, Le Tissier, Cockerill, Rideout, Horne, Wallace Rod.
Oldham Ath: Hallworth; Barrett, Barlow, Henry, Marshall, Warhurst (Donachie), Adams (McGarvey), Ritchie, Palmer, Milligan, Holden R.

FIFTH ROUND REPLAYS

Coventry C (2) 5 *(Livingstone 4, Gynn)*

Sunderland (0) 0   21,219

Coventry C: Ogrizovic; Borrows, Downs, Gynn, Billing (Dobson), Peake, MacDonald, Speedie, Regis, Livingstone, Smith.
Sunderland: Carter; Kay, Hardyman, Bennett (Agboola), Ord, Owers, Bracewell, Armstrong, Gates (Hauser), Gabbiadini, Lemon.

Derby Co (0) 0

West Ham U (0) 0 *aet*   22,510

Derby Co: Taylor; Sage, Forsyth, Williams, Wright, Hindmarch, Patterson, Saunders, Harford (Francis), Hebberd, McCord (Briscoe).
West Ham U: Parkes; Strodder, McQueen, Parris, Martin, Gale, Brady (Milne), Kelly, Slater, Robson (Devonshire), Keen.

Tottenham H (1) 2 *(Nayim, Walsh)*

Nottingham F (2) 3 *(Hodge 2, Jemson)*   32,357

Tottenham H: Thorstvedt; Thomas, Polston J, Van Den Hauwe (Hughton), Allen, Howells, Mabbutt, Nayim, Stewart (Walsh), Lineker, Sedgley.
Nottingham F: Sutton; Laws, Pearce, Walker, Chettle, Hodge, Crosby, Parker, Clough, Jemson, Orlygsson.

31 JAN
FIFTH ROUND REPLAY

Oldham Ath (1) 2 *(Ritchie, Milligan)*

Southampton (0) 0   18,862

Oldham Ath: Hallworth; Irwin, Barlow, Henry, Marshall, Barrett, Adams, Ritchie, McGarvey, Milligan, Holden R.
Southampton: Flowers; Dodd (Maddison), Benali, Case, Ruddock, Osman, Le Tissier, Cockerill, Rideout, Horne, Wallace Rod (Shearer).

FIFTH ROUND SECOND REPLAY

West Ham U (1) 2 *(Slater, Keen)*

Derby Co (0) 1 *(Saunders)*   25,166

West Ham U: Parkes; Potts (McQueen), Dicks, Parris, Martin, Gale, Brady, Kelly, Slater, Robson, Keen.
Derby Co: Taylor; Sage, Forsyth, Williams G, Patterson, Davidson, Francis (Ramage), Saunders, Harford, Hebberd, Briscoe.

SEMI-FINAL FIRST LEG
11 FEB

Nottingham F (1) 2 *(Clough (pen), Pearce)*

Coventry C (0) 1 *(Livingstone)*   26,153

Nottingham F: Sutton; Laws, Pearce, Walker, Chettle, Hodge, Crosby, Parker, Clough, Jemson, Orlygsson (Starbuck).
Coventry C: Ogrizovic; Borrows, Downs, Dobson, Kilcline, Peake, Gallacher, Gynn, Regis, Livingstone, Smith.

14 FEB

Oldham Ath (3) 6 *(Adams, Ritchie 2, Barrett, Holden R, Palmer)*

West Ham U (0) 0   19,263

Oldham Ath: Hallworth; Irwin, Barlow, Henry, Marshall, Barrett, Adams, Ritchie, Palmer, Milligan, Holden R.

West Ham U: Parkes; Robson, Dicks, Parris, Martin, Gale, Brady, Slater, Strodder (Devonshire), Kelly, Keen.

SEMI-FINAL SECOND LEG

25 FEB

Coventry C (0) 0

Nottingham F (0) 0   25,900

Coventry C: Ogrizovic; Borrows, Downs, Speedie, Kilcline (Dobson), Peake, Gallacher (Drinkell), Gynn, Regis, Livingstone, Smith.
Nottingham F: Sutton; Laws, Pearce, Walker, Chettle, Hodge, Crosby, Parker, Clough, Jemson, Wilson.
Nottingham F won 2-1 on aggregate

7 MAR

West Ham U (1) 3 *(Martin, Dicks (pen), Kelly)*

Oldham Ath (0) 0   15,431

West Ham U: Miklosko; Slater, Dicks, Parris, Martin, Gale, Brady (McQueen), Allen, Rosenior, Kelly, Keen.
Oldham Ath: Hallworth; Irwin, Barlow, Henry, Barrett, Warhurst, Adams, Palmer, Marshall, Milligan, Holden R.
Oldham Ath won 6-3 on aggregate

FINAL at Wembley

29 APR

Nottingham F (0) 1 *(Jemson)*

Oldham Ath (0) 0   74,343

Nottingham F: Sutton; Laws, Pearce, Walker, Chettle, Hodge, Crosby, Parker, Clough, Jemson, Carr.
Oldham Ath: Rhodes; Irwin, Barlow, Henry, Barrett, Warhurst, Adams, Ritchie, Bunn (Palmer), Milligan, Holden R.
Referee: J. Martin (Alton)

Nottingham Forest winger Franz Carr (left) links arms with Oldham full-back Dennis Irwin during the Littlewoods Cup Final at Wembley. Forest won 1-0 with a Nigel Jemson goal. (Colorsport)

ZENITH DATA SYSTEMS CUP 1989-90

FIRST ROUND

7 NOV

Leeds U (1) 1 *(Davison)*

Blackburn R (0) 0   5070

Leeds U: Day; Sterland (Speed), Whitlow, Jones, Fairclough, Haddock, Strachan, Batty, Baird, Davison, Williams.
Blackburn R: Collier; Atkins (Finnigan), Oliver, Reid, Hill, Hendry, Skinner (Gayle), Millar, Stapleton, Garner, Sellars.

Sheffield U (1) 1 *(Francis)*

Wolverhampton W (0) 0   4926

Sheffield U: Tracey; Webster, Barnes, Booker, Stancliffe, Morris, Todd, Gannon, Francis, Duffield, Whitehouse (Wood).
Wolverhampton W: Kendall; Bennett (Paskin), Venus, Bellamy, Westley, Downing (Vaughan), Thompson, Cooke, Bull, Mutch, Dennison.

8 NOV

Oxford U (1) 2 *(Durnin, Phillips J)*

Luton T (1) 3 *(Dowie 2, Gray) aet*   1754

Oxford U: Judge; Smart, Phillips J, Lewis, Foster, Greenall, Mustoe, Ford (McClaren), Durnin, Stein, Heath.
Luton T: Chamberlain; Breacker, Harvey, Wilson, Johnson, Beaumont, Cooke (Gray), Wegerle, Dowie, Kennedy (Tighe), Preece.

14 NOV

Sunderland (1) 1 *(Armstrong (pen))*

Port Vale (1) 2 *(Walker, Cross)*   7035

Sunderland: Norman; Agboola, Williams, Bennett, Ord, Owers, Bracewell, Armstrong, Hauser, Gabbiadini, Cullen (Atkinson).
Port Vale: Grew; Mills, Jeffers, Walker, Aspin, Porter, Miller, Earle, Cross, Beckford, Riley.

SECOND ROUND

Charlton Ath (0) 2 *(Minto, Humphrey)*

Leicester C (1) 1 *(Campbell)*   1565

Charlton Ath: Bolder; Humphrey, Reid, Peake, Caton, Smart (Mortimer), Bennett, Achampong, Crooks, Walsh (Leaburn), Minto.
Leicester C: Hodge; Mauchlen (Baraclough), Johnson, Ramsey, Walsh, Paris, Reid, Williams, Campbell, Peake (James), Wright.

21 NOV

Ipswich T (3) 4 *(Gregory 3, Redford)*

Watford (0) 1 *(Penrice)*   5078

Ipswich T: Forrest; Gregory, Thompson, Redford, Yallop, Linighan, Donowa, Dozzell, Wark (Stockwell), Woods, Milton.
Watford: Coton; Gibbs, Drysdale, Falconer, Solomon, Roeder, Pullen (Thomas), Wilkinson (Ashby), Penrice, Porter, Henry.

Sheffield W (1) 3 *(Atkinson, Palmer, Sheridan)*

Sheffield U (1) 2 *(Deane, Booker) aet*   30,464

Sheffield W: Pressman; Pearson, King, Palmer, Shirtliff, Madden, Bennett (Shakespeare), Sheridan, Hirst, Atkinson, Worthington.

Sheffield U: Tracey; Hill, Barnes, Booker, Stancliffe, Morris, Bradshaw (Francis), Gannon, Agana (Webster), Deane, Bryson.

27 NOV

Crystal Palace (0) 4 *(Wright, Pardew, Bright 2)*

Luton T (1) 1 *(Dowie)*   3747

Crystal Palace: Martyn; Pemberton, Dennis, Gray (O'Reilly), Hopkins, Barber, McGoldrick, Thomas, Bright, Wright (Salako), Pardew.
Luton T: Chamberlain; Breacker, Harvey, Wilson, Allpress (Cooke), Dreyer, Preece, Dowie, James, Wegerle, Tighe (Gray).

28 NOV

Barnsley (1) 1 *(Dobbin)*

Leeds U (2) 2 *(Strachan (pen), Williams)*   6136

Barnsley: Baker; Dobbin, Cross, Banks (Tiler), Shotton, Futcher, Broddle, Agnew, Cooper, Currie, Archdeacon (Lowndes).
Leeds U: Edwards; Sterland, Whitlow, Jones, Fairclough, Haddock (Kerr), Strachan, Batty, Baird, Davison (Shutt), Williams.

Bournemouth (0) 2 *(Blissett, Shearer)*

Chelsea (0) 3 *(Dickens 3) aet*   6214

Bournemouth: Peyton; Bond, Coleman, Teale, Williams, Peacock, Lawrence (Shearer), Moulden, O'Driscoll, Brooks, Blissett (O'Connor).
Chelsea: Beasant; Clarke, Dorigo, Roberts, Lee, Monkou, Dickens, Bumstead (Wilson C), Dixon, Wilson K, Hazard (McAllister).

Hull C (0) 1 *(Jenkinson)*

Aston Villa (0) 2 *(Mountfield, Platt)*   2888

Hull C: Hesford; Brown, Jacobs, Jobson, Terry, Buckley (McParland), Askew (De Mange), Payton, Swan, Jenkinson, Doyle.
Aston Villa: Butler; Price, Gray, McGrath, Mountfield, Nielsen, Daley, Platt, Olney, Cowans, Ormondroyd.

Newcastle U (1) 2 *(Quinn 2)*

Oldham Ath (0) 0   6167

Newcastle U: Burridge; Ranson, Stimson (Fereday), Dillon, Bradshaw, Kristensen, Gallacher, Brock, Quinn, McGhee (Brazil), O'Brien.
Oldham Ath: Rhodes; Irwin, Blundell, Donachie, Barrett, Williams, Adams, Ritchie, McGarvey, Milligan (Palmer), Holden R (Kelly).

Stoke C (2) 2 *(Berry (pen), Bamber)*

Bradford C (0) 1 *(Mitchell)*   4616

Stoke C: Fox; Butler, Carr, Kamara, Higgins, Berry, Hackett, Beeston, Bamber, Higgins, Palin.
Bradford C: Evans M; Mitchell, Tinnion, Oliver (Leonard), Sinnott, Jackson, Abbott, Evans D, Adcock (Campbell), Quinn, Jewell.

29 NOV

FIRST ROUND

Coventry C (1) 1 *(Gynn)*

Wimbledon (0) 3 *(Scales, Cork, Gibson) aet*   3781

Coventry C: Ogrizovic; Borrows, Downs, Kilcline (Dobson), Billing, Peake, Gynn, Emerson (Clark), Regis, Drinkell, Smith.

Wimbledon: Segers; Scales, Phelan, Ryan, Young, Curle, Miller (Fairweather), Cotterill (Cork), Gibson, Kruszynski, Fiore.

SECOND ROUND

Middlesbrough (0) 3 *(Slaven 2, Coleman)*
Port Vale (1) 1 *(Jeffers)*   6691

Middlesbrough: Poole; Mohan, Cooper, Mowbray, Coleman, Putney (Burke), Slaven, Proctor, Ripley, Brennan, Davenport.
Port Vale: Wood; Mills, Hughes, Walker, Aspin, Glover, Porter (Riley), Earle, Cross, Beckford (Millar), Jeffers.

Norwich C (2) 5 *(Mortensen, Crook, Sherwood, Gordon, Rosario)*
Brighton & HA (0) 0   5704

Norwich C: Gunn; Sherwood, Bowen, Butterworth, Linighan, Townsend, Gordon, Mortensen, Rosario, Crook, Phillips.
Brighton & HA: Keeley; Chivers, Chapman, Curbishley, Bissett, Dublin, Nelson, Wood, Crumplin, Codner, Wilkins.

Nottingham F (1) 3 *(Pearce (pen), Carr, Crosby)*
Manchester C (1) 2 *(White, Oldfield)*   9729

Nottingham F: Crossley; Laws, Pearce, Walker, Chettle, Hodge, Carr, Parker, Gaynor (Rice), Chapman (Clough), Crosby.
Manchester C: Dibble; Fleming, Taggart, Bishop, Gayle, Redmond, White, Morley, Hinchcliffe (Brightwell), McNab (Oldfield), Lake.

WBA (0) 0
Derby Co (1) 5 *(Saunders 3, Goddard, Micklewhite)*   4880

WBA: Naylor; Burgess (Robson), Harbey, Talbot, Raven, Whyte, Ford, Goodman, Bartlett (Thomas), McNally, Parkin.
Derby Co: Shilton; Sage, Forsyth, Williams, Wright, Hindmarch, Pickering, Saunders (Francis), Goddard, Hebberd, Micklewhite.

West Ham U (1) 5 *(Keen, Dolan, Dicks, Martin, Slater)*
Plymouth Arg (0) 2 *(Thomas 2) aet*   5409

West Ham U: Parkes; Potts, Dicks, Strodder, Martin, Keen, Devonshire, Slater, Allen, Ward (Dolan), Kelly (Foster).
Plymouth Arg: Wilmot; Brown, Whiston, Marker, Burrows, Hodges, Byrne (Morrison), Campbell, Tynan, Thomas, Stuart (Pickard).

5 DEC

Portsmouth (0) 0
Wimbledon (0) 1 *(Curle (pen))*   2499

Portsmouth: Knight; Chamberlain, Beresford, Maguire, Hogg, Ball, Wigley, Kuhl, Whittingham, Gilligan (Connor), Black (Kelly).
Wimbledon: Segers; Joseph, McAllister, Scales, Young, Curle, Fairweather, Cork, Gibson (Cotterill), Ryan (Kruszynski), Sanchez.

13 DEC

Swindon T (1) 2 *(White, Thompson (og))*
Millwall (0) 1 *(Waddock)*   3223

Swindon T: Digby; Kerslake, Bodin, McLoughlin, Calderwood, Gittens, Jones, Shearer, White, MacLaren, Foley (Cornwell).

Millwall: Branagan; Stevens, Coleman, Hurlock, Thompson, McLeary, Carter, Waddock, Anthrobus, Cascarino, Briley (Dawes).

THIRD ROUND

19 DEC

Crystal Palace (1) 2 *(Gray, Wright)*
Charlton Ath (0) 0   6621

Crystal Palace: Martyn; Pemberton, O'Reilly, Gray, Hopkins, Thorn, McGoldrick, Barber (Salako), Bright, Wright, Pardew (Thomas).
Charlton Ath: Bolder; Bacon (Lee J), Reid, Peake (Watson), Humphrey, Mortimer, Lee R, Bennett, Leaburn, Achampong, Minto.

Stoke C (1) 2 *(Kamara, Biggins)*
Leeds U (0) 2 *(Shutt 2) aet*   5792

Stoke C: Fox; Butler, Carr, Kamara, Holmes, Fowler (Morgan), Hackett, Ware (Scott), Biggins, Saunders, Palin.
Leeds U: Day; Sterland, Whitlow (Kerr), Jones, Blake, Haddock, Strachan, Batty, Pearson (Shutt), Baird, Hendrie.
Leeds U won 5-4 on penalties.

20 DEC

Middlesbrough (2) 4 *(Slaven 3, Kernaghan)*
Sheffield W (1) 1 *(Bennett)*   8716

Middlesbrough: Pears; Parkinson, Cooper, Mowbray, Coleman, Putney, Slaven, Proctor, Kernaghan, Brennan (Kerr), Davenport.
Sheffield W: Pressman; Nilsson, King, Palmer, Shirtliff, Pearson, Bennett (Whitton), Sheridan, Hirst, Atkinson, Worthington.

Newcastle U: (1) 3 *(O'Brien, Gallacher, Cross (og))*
Derby Co (1) 2 *(Cross 2) aet*   6800

Newcastle U: Burridge; Ranson, Sweeney (Anderson), Dillon, Scott, Kristensen, Gallacher, Brock (Fereday), Quinn, McGhee, O'Brien.
Derby Co: Shilton; Sage, Forsyth, Williams, Wright, Hindmarch (Blades), Gee (Ramage), Saunders, Goddard, Hebberd, Cross.

21 DEC

Ipswich T (0) 3 *(Thompson (pen), Milton, Johnson)*
Wimbledon (0) 1 *(Fashanu (pen))*   7918

Ipswich T: Forrest; Stockwell (Johnson), Thompson, Zondervan, Yallop, Linighan, Woods (Donowa), Dozzell, Wark, Kiwomya, Milton.
Wimbledon: Segers; Joseph (Kruszynski), Phelan, Sanchez, Young, Curle, Fairweather, Fashanu, Gibson, Ryan, Wise.

22 DEC

Aston Villa (0) 2 *(Platt (pen), Mountfield)*
Nottingham F (1) 1 *(Pearce)*   6530

Aston Villa: Spink; Price, Gage, McGrath, Mountfield, Nielsen, Daley, Platt, Olney, Cowans, Ormondroyd (Williams).
Nottingham F: Sutton; Laws (Charles), Pearce, Walker, Chettle, Hodge, Crosby, Parker, Clough, Chapman, Rice (Orlygsson).

THIRD ROUND

Chelsea (1) 4 *(Dixon, Roberts (pen), Lee, Wilson K)*
West Ham U (0) 3 *(Keen, Slater, Kelly)*   8418
Chelsea: Beasant; Clarke, Le Saux, Roberts, Lee, Monkou, McAllister, Bumstead, Dixon, Durie (Wilson K), Wilson C.
West Ham U: Parkes; Potts, Dicks, Strodder, Keen, Gale, Brady (Kelly), Slater, Foster, Ward, Allen.

SEMI-FINALS (Northern Area)

17 JAN

Aston Villa (0) 2 *(Gray, Platt (pen))*
Leeds U (0) 0   17,543
Aston Villa: Spink; Price, Gage, Gray, Mountfield, Nielsen, Daley (Birch), Platt, Olney, Cowans, Ormondroyd.
Leeds U: Day; Blake, Whitlow, Jones, Fairclough, Haddock, Strachan, Batty, Baird, Hendrie (Pearson), Beglin (Kerr).

23 JAN

Middlesbrough (0) 1 *(Cooper)*
Newcastle U (0) 0   16,948
Middlesbrough: Pears; Parkinson, Cooper, Mowbray, Coleman, Ripley, Slaven, Proctor, Kerr, Brennan, Davenport (McGhee).
Newcastle U: Burridge; Fereday, Sweeney, Aitken, Scott, Ranson, Dillon, Kristensen, Gallacher, McGhee, O'Brien.

SEMI-FINALS (Southern Area)

Ipswich T (1) 2 *(Donowa, Gregory)*
Chelsea (1) 3 *(Thompson (og), Wilson K 2)*   13,365
Ipswich T: Forrest; Yallop, Thompson, Stockwell (Pennyfather), Gregory, Linighan, Lowe, Dozzell, Wark, Donowa, Milton.
Chelsea: Beasant; Clarke, Dorigo, Bumstead, Johnsen, Monkou, McAllister, Dickens, Dixon, Wilson K, Le Saux.

THIRD ROUND

24 JAN

Swindon T (2) 4 *(Shearer, Foley, Bodin, White)*
Norwich C (1) 1 *(Phillips)*   5314
Swindon T: Digby; Kerslake, Bodin, McLoughlin, Calderwood, Gittens, Jones, Shearer, White, McLaren, Foley.
Norwich C: Gunn; Culverhouse, Bowen, Butterworth, Linighan, Townsend, Gordon, Fleck, Rosario (Allen), Crook, Phillips (Sherwood).

NORTHERN FINAL First Leg

30 JAN

Aston Villa (1) 1 *(Birch)*
Middlesbrough (1) 2 *(Slaven, Brennan)*   16,547
Aston Villa: Spink;; Gage, Mountfield, McGrath (Price), Neilsen, Gray, Birch (Daley), Platt, Olney, Cowans, Ormondroyd.
Middlesbrough: Pears; Parkinson, Mohan, Coleman, McGee, Kirk, Proctor, Brennan, Slaven, Ripley, Kernaghan.

NORTHERN FINAL Second Leg

6 FEB

Middlesbrough (0) 2 *(Slaven, Kerr)*
Aston Villa (0) 1 *(Gray) aet*   20,806
Middlesbrough: Pears; Parkinson, Mohan, Mowbray, Coleman, Ripley (Davenport), Slaven, Proctor, Kernaghan, Putney (McGhee), Kerr.
Aston Villa: Spink; Price, Gage, McGrath, Mountfield, Nielsen, Daley, Platt, Olney, Cowans, Ormondroyd (Gray).
Middlesbrough won 4-2 on aggregate.

SEMI-FINAL (Southern Area)

13 FEB

Crystal Palace (1) 1 *(Gray)*
Swindon T (0) 0   6027
Crystal Palace: Martyn; Pemberton, Shaw, Gray, Hopkins, Thorn, Barber, Thomas, Bright, Salako, Pardew.
Swindon T: Digby; Kerslake, Bodin, McLoughlin, Calderwood, Gittens, Jones, Shearer, White, MacLaren, Foley.

SOUTHERN FINAL First Leg   21 FEB

Crystal Palace (0) 0
Chelsea (2) 2 *(Dixon, Wilson K)*   14,839
Crystal Palace: Martyn; Pemberton, Shaw, Gray, Hopkins, Thorn, Barber (Dyer), Thomas, Bright, Salako, Pardew.
Chelsea: Beasant; Hall, Dorigo, Roberts, Johnsen, Bumstead, McAllister, Nicholas, Dixon, Wilson K, Wilson C.

SOUTHERN FINAL Second Leg   12 MAR

Chelsea (0) 2 *(Bumstead, Hall)*
Crystal Palace (0) 0   15,061
Chelsea: Beasant; Hall, Dorigo, Bumstead, Johnsen, Monkou, McAllister, Nicholas, Dixon, Durie, Wilson K.
Crystal Palace: Martyn; Hedman, Shaw, Gray, Dyer (O'Reilly), Thorn, Barber, Thomas, Salako, Wright (Whyte), Pardew.
Chelsea won 4-0 on aggregate.

FINAL (at Wembley)

25 MAR

Chelsea (1) 1 *(Dorigo)*
Middlesbrough (0) 0   76,369
Chelsea: Beasant; Hall, Dorigo, Bumstead, Johnsen, Monkou, McAllister, Nicholas, Dixon, Durie, Wilson K.
Middlesbrough: Pears; Parkinson, Cooper, Kernaghan, Coleman, McGee, Slaven, Proctor, Ripley, Brennan, Davenport.
Referee: R. Milford) Bristol.

ZENITH DATA SYSTEMS CHALLENGE CUP

19 DEC

Rangers (0) 1 *(Johnston)*
Arsenal (1) 2 *(Davis, Quinn)*   31,118
Rangers: Woods (Ginzburg); Stevens, Gough (Cowan), Butcher, Brown (Dodds), Ferguson I, Spackman, Steven, Munro, Johnston, Walters.
Arsenal: Lukic; Dixon, Winterburn, Davis, O'Leary (Caesar), Adams, Rocastle, Richardson, Quinn, Merson (Hayes), Marwood (Groves).
Referee: D. Syme (Rutherglen).

LEYLAND DAF CUP 1989–90

PRELIMINARY ROUND

Southern Area

7 NOV

Brentford (0) 3 *(Holdsworth 2, May)*
Leyton Orient (0) 0   2544
Brentford: Parks; Ratcliffe, Perryman (Buttigieg), Bates, Evans, Moncur, Jones, May, Holdsworth (Godfrey), Cadette, Smillie.
Leyton Orient: Heald; Hoddle, Dickenson, Baker, Day, Sitton, Howard, Pike (Nugent), Smalley, Cooper, Berry.

Cardiff C (0) 3 *(Powell, Barnard, Abraham)*
Walsall (1) 5 *(Skipper, Bertschin 2, Rimmer, Kelly)*
                                                          1487
Cardiff C: Ward; Rodgerson, Daniel, Barnard, Abraham, Gibbins, Morgan (Fry), Griffith, Pike (Powell), Kelly, Chandler.
Walsall: Green; Wilder, O'Hara, Lemon, Forbes, Skipper, Kelly, Rimmer, Bertschin, Marshall, Thorpe.

Colchester U (0) 0
Northampton T (1) 3 *(Barnes, Chard, Collins)* 1780
Colchester U: Grace; Hicks (Pollard), Stafford, Kinsella, Daniels, Gilbert, Bennett, Collins, Morgan, English T (Scott), Wilkins.
Northampton T: Gleasure; Chard, Gernon, Thomas, Wilcox, McPherson, Berry, Singleton, Sandeman (Collins), Barnes, Scope.

Southend U (0) 1 *(Tilson)*
Gillingham (0) 0   1650
Southend U: Sansome; Roberts, Edinburgh, Martin, Tilson, Brush, Cook, Butler, Crown, McDonough (Walsh), O'Connell (Ling).
Gillingham: Hillyard; Haylock, Johnson, O'Shea, Place, Palmer, Trusson, Eeles, Lovell, Heritage (Gavin), Manuel.

Torquay U (0) 1 *(Loram)*
Bristol R (0) 0   2218
Torquay U: Veysey; Holmes, Lloyd, Elliott, Matthews, Joyce, Loram, Airey, Edwards, Uzzell, Weston.
Bristol R: Martyn; Alexander, Twentyman, Yates, Mehew, Jones, Holloway, Reece, White, Sealy, Nixon.

Northern Area

Halifax T (2) 3 *(Cook, Juryeff, Martin)*
Lincoln C (0) 0   824
Halifax T: Whitehead; Fleming, Cook (Butler), Hedworth, Bramhall, Horner, Martin, Watson, Broadbent, Juryeff, Hall.
Lincoln C: Gorton; Schofield, Clarke, Cumming, Davis (Nicholson), Brown G, Roberts, Bressington, Sertori, Smith, Carmichael.

Huddersfield T (0) 2 *(Smith, Maskell)*
Doncaster R (1) 2 *(Rankine, Adams)*   1714
Huddersfield T: Hardwick; Marsden, Hutchings, May, O'Doherty, Lewis, Bent, Wilson (O'Regan), Cecere, Maskell, Smith.
Doncaster R: Samways; Douglas, Brevett, Gaughan (Nicholson), Ashurst, McGinley, Robinson, Stiles, Turnbull, Rankine, Adams.

Preston NE (1) 3 *(Ellis 2, Joyce)*
Burnley (0) 0   5241
Preston NE: Kelly; Williams, Swann, Scully, Joyce, Hughes, Harper, Ellis, Bogie, Shaw, Patterson.
Burnley: Pearce; Measham, Hardy (McGrory), Deary, Eli, Davis, White, Mumby, O'Connell, Jakub, Farrell.

Scunthorpe U (0) 1 *(Flounders)*
Scarborough (0) 0   1496
Scunthorpe U: Litchfield; Cowling, Longden, Ward, Nicol, Stevenson, Lillis, Hamilton, Hodkinson, Flounders, Marshall.
Scarborough: Ironside; Kamara, Clarke, Short, Richards, Olsson, Saunders, Graham, Dobson (Robinson), Brook, Bennyworth.

Tranmere R (1) 1 *(Muir)*
Chester C (0) 0   10,559
Tranmere R: Nixon; Higgins, McCarrick (Fairclough), Bishop, Hughes, Garnett, Morrissey (Malkin), Martindale, Steel, Muir, Mungall.
Chester C: Stewart; Reeves, Woodthorpe, Hamilton, Abel, Lane, Butler, Pugh, Dale (Newhouse), Painter, Croft.

Wrexham (1) 1 *(Cooper)*
Blackpool (0) 0   1092
Wrexham: O'Keefe; Salathiel, Wright, Hunter, Williams, Beaumont, Preece R (Thackeray), Owen, Kearns (Buxton), Cooper, Worthington.
Blackpool: Bartram; Burgess, Morgan, Coughlin, Methven, Elliott, Owen, Madden, Hawkins (Eyres), Garner (Wright), Briggs.

York C (4) 7 *(Helliwell 3, Spooner, Tutill, Canham 2)*
Hartlepool U (1) 1 *(McEwan (pen))*   1444
York C: Marples; McMillan, Kelly, Barratt (Colville), Tutill, Warburton, Howlett, Spooner, Helliwell, Canham, Himsworth (Dunn).
Hartlepool U: Moverley; Plaskett, McKinnon, Tinkler, McEwan, Baker, Allon, Trewick, Lamb (Atkinson), Hutchison, Dalton.

8 NOV

Southern Area

Hereford U (1) 3 *(Hemming, Robinson, Stevens)*
Aldershot (1) 2 *(Claridge, Randall)*   1194
Hereford U: Elliott; Jones M A, Williams, Hemming, Peacock, Bradley, Jones M, Narbett, Robinson, Benbow (Stevens), Tester.
Aldershot: Sheffield; Brown, Phillips, Burvill, Anderson, Randall, Claridge, Puckett, Williams, Henry, Stewart.

Peterborough U (0) 1 *(Andrews)*
Fulham (0) 0   1939
Peterborough U: Crichton; Luke, Crosby (Speed), Graham, Robinson, Andrews, Sterling, Culpin (Osborne), Richards, Harle, Butterworth.
Fulham: Stannard; Langley, Elkins, Skinner, Nebbeling, Marshall, Barnett, Scott, Watson, Milton, Walker.

28 NOV

Aldershot (1) 3 *(Ogley, Puckett, Claridge)*

Birmingham C (0) 0   1148

Aldershot: Coles; Brown, Phillips, Henry, Ogley, Williams, Claridge, Puckett, Stewart (Beeks), Burvill, Randall (Hunt).
Birmingham C: Thomas; Ashley, Frain, Atkins, Clarkson (Tait), Matthewson, Bell, Bailey, Sturridge, Gleghorn, Langley.

Fulham (0) 0

Notts Co (1) 1 *(Palmer)*   1317

Fulham: Stannard; Langley (Barnett), Elkins, Donnellan, Nebbeling, Eckhardt, Marshall, Scott (Ferney), Sayer, Milton, Walker.
Notts Co: Cherry; Palmer, Platnauer, Short, Yates, Robinson, Draper (Johnson), Turner, Lund, Stant (Fairclough), O'Riordan.

Gillingham (0) 2 *(Lovell, Walker)*

Cambridge U (0) 0   1044

Gillingham: Lim; Haylock, Johnson, Walker, Place (Haines), Palmer, Gavin, O'Shea, Lovell (Docker), Heritage, Manuel.
Cambridge U: Vaughan; Bailie, Kimble, Cheetham, Chapple, Daish, Dennis, Leadbitter, Dublin, Taylor (Robinson), Philpott.

Leyton Orient (1) 2 *(Beesley, Christie (og))*

Mansfield T (0) 0   1133

Leyton Orient: Heald; Hales, Dickenson, Beesley, Whitbread, Baker, Howard, Castle, Carter, Cooper (Berry), Harvey.
Mansfield T: Cox; McKernon, Kearney, Christie, Foster, Prindiville, Hunt, Lowery, Wilkinson (Stringfellow), Charles (Kent), Hathaway.

Northampton T (2) 2 *(Wilcox, Gernon)*

Maidstone U (3) 4 *(Gall 3, Golley)*   1165

Northampton T: Gleasure; Williams (McPhillips), Gernon, Thomas, Wilcox, McPherson, Sandeman (Collins), Chard, Berry, Barnes, Wilson.
Maidstone U: Beeney; Roast, Cooper, Berry, Golley, Pearce, Gall (Charlery), Elsey, Galliers, Butler, Barton.

Walsall (0) 0

Shrewsbury T (0) 1 *(Melrose)*   2120

Walsall: Green; Wilder, Mower, Gritt, Forbes, Skipper, Kelly (Taylor), Rimmer, Bertschin, Saville, Thorpe.
Shrewsbury T: Perks; Green, Pittman, Kelly (Hartford), Finley, Moyes, Brown, Gorman, Cornforth, McGinlay (Melrose), Griffiths.

Northern Area
Blackpool (0) 4 *(Garner, Owen 2, Knill (og))*

Bury (0) 0   1408

Blackpool: McIlhargey; Gore, Morgan, Coughlin, Methven, Elliott, Davies, Madden, Owen, Garner, Eyres.
Bury: Kelly; Hill (Withe), Bishop, Parkinson, Valentine, Knill, Lee, Robinson, Cunningham, Feeley, Greenwood (Hulme).

Bolton W (1) 2 *(Darby, Brookman)*

Crewe Alex (0) 0   3868

Bolton W: Felgate; Brown, Cowdrill, Hughes, Crombie, Winstanley, Henshaw, Thompson, Came, Brookman, Darby.
Crewe Alex: Greygoose; Swain (McKearney), Edwards P R, Smart, Dyson, Callaghan, Jasper, Murphy, Sussex, Cutler (Fishenden), Walters.

Burnley (0) 0

Stockport Co (1) 2 *(Beaumont, Angell)*   3352

Burnley: Pearce; Measham, Hardy, Farrell, Davis, Hancock, White, Futcher, O'Connell, Jakub, McGrory.
Stockport Co: Siddall; Bullock, Robertson, Frain, Jones, Thorpe, Beaumont, Payne, Edwards (McInerney), Cooke (Downs), Angell.

Chester C (0) 0

Rochdale (0) 0   1222

Chester C: Stewart; Lundon, Woodthorpe, Hamilton, Abel, Lane, Butler, Barrow, Greer, Newhouse (Lightfoot), Croft.
Rochdale: Welch; Goodison, Hill, Brown, Cole, Ward, Holmes, Johnson, Elliott, O'Shaughnessy, Graham.

Doncaster R (0) 1 *(Robinson (pen))*

Grimsby T (0) 0   1551

Doncaster R: Samways; Robinson, Brevett, Rankine (Gaughan), Ashurst, Douglas, Adams, Stiles, Turnbull, Jones D, Noteman.
Grimsby T: Reece; McDermott, Agnew, Tilson, Lever, Cunnington, Childs (Alexander), Gilbert, Birtles, Cockerill, Hargreaves (Jobling).

Hartlepool U (1) 1 *(Baker)*

Rotherham U (2) 4 *(Plaskett (og), Robinson, Williams (og), Grealish)*   818

Hartlepool U: Moverley; Plaskett, McKinnon, Tinkler, Smith, Williams, Allon, Davies, Baker, Brown (Atkinson), Dalton.
Rotherham U: O'Hanlon; Barnsley, Robinson, Grealish, Johnson, Scott (Pepper), Buckley, Goodwin, Williamson, Evans, Hazel (Goater).

Northern Area
29 NOV

Lincoln C (0) 3 *(Sertori 2, Carmichael)*

Chesterfield (0) 0   1178

Lincoln C: Wallington; Williams P, Clarke, Nicholson, Cook, Davis, Schofield, Bressington, Sertori, Carmichael, Williams D.
Chesterfield: Allison; Gunn, Ryan, Shaw, Rogers, Plummer, Bloomer (Hewitt), Brien, Waller, Williams, Morris.

Scarborough (0) 0

Carlisle U (1) *(Dalziel)*   826

Scarborough: Ironside; Kamara, Clarke, Olsson, Richards, Bennyworth, McDonald, Dobson, Graham, Spink, Saunders (Short).
Carlisle U: McKeller; Graham, Dalziel, Saddington, Jones, Fitzpatrick, Shepherd, Miller, Sendall, Proudlock (Walwyn), Hetherington.

Southern Area
5 DEC

Bristol C (2) 2 *(Jones, Shelton)*

Swansea C (1) 1 *(Raynor (pen))*   3488

Bristol C: Leaning; Llewellyn, Pender, Shelton (Wimbleton), Humphries, Rennie, Gavin, Newman, Jones, Smith, Turner.
Swansea C: Freestone; Hough, Coleman, Melville, Trick, Thornber (Legg), Harris, Chalmers, Hughes, Raynor (Curtis), Hutchison.

Northern Area

Wigan Ath (1) 1 *(Daley)*

Bolton W (0) 0   2306

Wigan Ath: Hughes; Senior, Tankard, Taylor (Johnson), Atherton, Patterson, Carberry, Rimmer, Pilling (Griffiths), Daley, Thompson.
Bolton W: Felgate; Brown, Cowdrill, Brookman, Crombie, Winstanley, Henshaw (Storer), Thompson, Came, Philliskirk, Darby.

9 DEC

Bury (3) 4 *(Cunningham 2, Lee, Barnes (og))*

Wrexham (1) 1 *(Worthington (pen))*   1371

Bury: Kelly; Hill, Clements (Withe), Hoyland, Valentine, Knill, Lee, Robinson (Hulme), Cunningham, Feeley, Bishop.
Wrexham: O'Keefe; Salathiel, Barnes, Jones, Reck, Beaumont, Preece R (Lee), Thackeray, Kearns (Buxton), Cooper, Worthington.

Southern Area

Mansfield T (1) 2 *(Charles 2)*

Brentford (1) 1 *(Holdsworth)*   1445

Mansfield T: Cox; Hunt (Gray), Prindiville, Christie, Foster, Stringfellow, Kent, Kearney, Wilkinson, Charles, Hathaway.
Brentford: Branagan; Ratcliffe (Cousins), Fleming, Millen, Evans, Cockram, Stanislaus, May, Holdsworth (Godfrey), Blissett, Smillie.

12 DEC

Birmingham C (1) 1 *(Atkins)*

Hereford U (0) 0   3168

Birmingham C: Thomas; Clarkson (Roberts), Frain, Atkins, Overson, Matthewson, Bell, Bailey, Yates (Deakin), Gleghorn, Langley.
Hereford U: Elliott; Jones M A, Devine (Bradley), Pejic, Peacock, Hemming, Jones M, Narbett, Robinson, Jones R, Tester (Oghani).

Cambridge U (1) 3 *(Leadbitter, Cheetham, Daish)*

Southend U (2) 3 *(Walsh, Edinburgh, Ling)* 1304

Cambridge U: Vaughan; Bailie, Kimble, Cheetham, Chapple, Daish, O'Shea, Leadbitter, Dublin, Taylor (Ryan), Philpott (Robinson).
Southend U: Sansome; Roberts, Edinburgh, Martin, Cook (Smith), Brush, Clark, Butler, Walsh, McDonough (Tilson), Ling.

Notts Co (1) 2 *(Draper, Lund)*

Peterborough U (1) 2 *(Luke, Harle)*   1616

Notts Co: Cherry; Harle, Platnauer, Short, Yates (O'Riordan), Fairclough, Draper, Turner, Lund, Stant (Barnes), Johnson.
Peterborough U: Godden; Luke, Crosby, Halsall, Robinson, Andrews, Sterling, Harle, Richards, Longhurst (Osborne), Butterworth (Goldsmith).

Northern Area

Chesterfield (0) 2 *(Williams, Shaw)*

Halifax T (0) 1 *(Richardson)*   1275

Chesterfield: Leonard; Gunn, Hewitt, Shaw, Rogers, Plummer (Eley), Thompson, Brien, Waller, Williams, Morris.
Halifax T: Brown; Fleming, Smith, Barr (Matthews), Bramhall, Horner, Martin, Watson (Broadbent), Richardson, Harrison, Hall.

Grimsby T (1) 3 *(Cockerill, Alexander, Rees)*

Huddersfield T (2) 3 *(Onuora, Maskell (pen), Duggan)*   995

Grimsby T: Reece; Jobling, Agnew, Birtles (Watson), Lever (Hargreaves), Cunnington, Childs, Gilbert, Rees, Cockerill, Alexander.
Huddersfield T: Martin; Marsden, Hutchings, May, Mitchell, Duggan, O'Regan, Wilson, Onuora, Maskell (Withe), Smith.

Rochdale (0) 0

Tranmere R (0) 1 *(Muir)*   1078

Rochdale: Welch; Goodison, Burns, Brown, Elliott (Stonehouse), Ward, Holmes, Johnson, Dawson, O'Shaughnessy, Graham.
Tranmere R: Nixon; Higgins (Garnett), McCarrick, Martindale, Hughes, Vickers, Malkin, Harvey, Steel, Muir, Thomas.

Rotherham U (2) 3 *(Barnsley, Williamson, Grealish)*

York C (0) 1 *(Kelly (pen))*   1996

Rotherham U: O'Hanlon; Barnsley, Robinson, Grealish, Johnson, Scott, Buckley (Pepper), Goodwin, Williamson, Evans (Mendonca), Hazel.
York C: Marples; McMillan (Himsworth), Kelly, Barratt, Tutill, Warburton, Howlett, Spooner, Helliwell (Colville), Canham, Dixon.

13 DEC

Stockport Co (1) 2 *(Angell (pen), Thorpe)*

Preston NE (3) 4 *(Ellis, Shaw 2, Hughes)* 1545

Stockport Co: Shepherd; Leonard, Logan (Bullock), Frain, Williams B, Thorpe, McInerney, Payne, Edwards (Williams P), Beaumont, Angell.
Preston NE: Kelly; Williams, Bennett, Atkins, Flynn, Hughes, Bogie (Rathbone), Ellis, Swann, Shaw, Harper.

19 DEC

Crewe Alex (1) 1 *(Joseph)*

Wigan Ath (0) 0   1984

Crewe Alex: Greygoose; Swain, Edwards P R, Smart, Dyson, Callaghan, Joseph, Murphy, Sussex (McKearney), Walters, Fishenden (Easter).
Wigan Ath: Hughes; Senior, Tankard, Parkinson, Atherton, Patterson, Thompson, Rimmer, Pilling (Page), Daley, Griffiths.

Southern Area

Shrewsbury T (3) 4 *(McGinlay 2, Naughton (pen), Priest)*

Cardiff C (0) 0   1058

Shrewsbury T: Perks; Green, Priest, Kelly, Finley, Moyes, Brown, Gorman, Cornforth (Griffiths), McGinlay, Naughton (Purdie).
Cardiff C: Ward; Rodgerson, Searle, Barnard (Roberts), Perry, Lewis, Morgan, Miethig, Scott, Haig (Blake), Lynex.

20 DEC

Rochdale (1) 1 *(Holmes)*

Chester C (2) 2 *(Lightfoot 2)*   787

Rochdale: Welch; Goodison, Burns, Hughes, Cole, Stonehouse, Holmes, Walling (Hill), Dawson, O'Shaughnessy (Ainscow), Graham.
Chester C: Stewart; Parsley, Woodthorpe (Lundon), Hamilton, Lane, Lightfoot, Butler, Barrow, Abel, Painter, Pugh (Croft).
Chester C won play-off match to reach First Round.

658

22 DEC

Carlisle U (1) 1 *(Proudlock)*

Scunthorpe U (0) 1 *(Taylor)* 1942

Carlisle U: McKellar; Graham, Dalziel (Hetherington), Saddington, Jones, Fitzpatrick, Miller, Shepherd, Walwyn (Fyfe), Proudlock, Cullen.
Scunthorpe U: Musselwhite; Smalley, Longden, Alexander, Hall, Stevenson, Cotton, Taylor (Cox), Daws, Flounders, Hamilton.

Southern Area

9 JAN

Mansfield T (1) 2 *(Kearney, Gray)*

Leyton Orient (0) 1 *(Sitton)* 1938

Mansfield T: Beasley; Murray, Prindiville, Christie, Foster, Gray, Kent, Hunt, Wilkinson, Charles, Kearney.
Leyton Orient: Rees; Hales (Berry), Sitton, Beesley, Day, Baker, Hoddle, Castle, Carter, Nugent, Harvey.
Mansfield T won play-off match to reach First Round.

FIRST ROUND

Aldershot (1) 1 *(Forbes (og))*

Walsall (2) 4 *(Rimmer 2, Forbes, Kelly)* 1214

Aldershot: Coles; Brown, Williams, Banton, Ogley, Wignall, Claridge, Puckett, Stewart (Hunt), Henry, Randall.
Walsall: Barber; Dornan, Gritt, Taylor, Forbes, Skipper, Kelly, Rimmer, Bertschin (Saville), Goodwin, Littlejohn.

Northern Area
Bolton W (1) 2 *(Reeves 2)*

Lincoln C (0) 1 *(Hobson)* 4420

Bolton W: Felgate; Brown, Pike, Comstive, Crombie, Winstanley, Storer, Thompson, Reeves (Henshaw), Philliskirk, Darby.
Lincoln C: Gorton; Stoutt, Nicholson, Brown G, Thompson, Davies, Schofield, Brown P, Hobson, Smith, Sertori.

Carlisle U (0) 1 *(Saddington (pen))*

Stockport Co (0) 2 *(Angell, Edwards) aet* 2814

Carlisle U: McKellar; Robertson, Walsh, Saddington, Graham, Fitzpatrick, Miller, Shepherd (Edwards), Walwyn (Sendall), Hetherington, Cullen.
Stockport Co: Redfern; Bullock, Logan, Frain, Williams, Jones, Beaumont (Cooke), Downes, Edwards, McInerney, Angell.

Doncaster R (1) 2 *(Stiles, Jones D)*

Bury (0) 0 2847

Doncaster R: Samways; Robinson, Brevett, Rankine, Ashurst, Douglas, Adams, Stiles, Gaughan, Jones D, Noteman.
Bury: Kelly; Hill, Clements (Hulme), Hoyland, Greenall, Knill, Lee, Robinson, Cunningham, Parkinson (Greenwood), Bishop.

Halifax T (0) 1 *(Horner)*

York C (0) 1 *(Helliwell) aet* 1063

Halifax T: Whitehead; Fleming P, Harrison, Hedworth, Bramhall, Horner, Hall (Barr), Broadbent, Richardson, Butler (Fleming C), Matthews.
York C: Marples; Barratt, Kelly, Himsworth (Dunn), Tutill, Heathcote, Howlett, Hall, Colville, Dixon (Helliwell), Canham.
Halifax T won 7-6 on penalties.

Preston NE (0) 1 *(Mooney)*

Wigan Ath (0) 2 *(Daley, Rimmer)* 4539

Preston NE: Kelly; Williams, Bennett (Rathbone), Bogie, Flynn, Hughes (Wrightson), Mooney, Swann, Joyce, Patterson, Shaw.
Wigan Ath: Hughes; Senior, Tankard, Parkinson, Atherton, Johnson, Thompson, Rimmer, Pilling, Daley, Griffiths.

Rotherham U (1) 3 *(Mendonca, Hazel, Scott)*

Huddersfield T (0) 0 3519

Rotherham U: O'Hanlon; Barnsley, Robinson, Pepper, Johnson, Scott, Heard (Goater), Goodwin, Evans, Mendonca, Hazel.
Huddersfield T: Martin; Marsden, Hutchings, May, Duggan, Lewis, O'Regan (Onuora), Bray, Wilson, Maskell, Smith.

Tranmere R (1) 2 *(McCarrick, Malkin)*

Scunthorpe U (1) 1 *(Cotton)* 2766

Tranmere R: Nixon; Higgins, McCarrick, McNab, Hughes, Vickers, Morrissey, Harvey, Malkin, Muir, Thomas.
Scunthorpe U: Musselwhite; Smalley, Longden, Taylor, Stevenson (Nicol), Cotton, Marshall, Hamilton, Daws, Flounders, Cowling (Hodkinson).

Southern Area

10 JAN

PRELIMINARY ROUND

Maidstone U (2) 2 *(Gall, Butler)*

Colchester U (0) 1 *(Ball)* 1176

Maidstone U: Beeney; Barton, Cooper, Berry, Oxbrow, Golley, Gall, Elsey (Rumble), Pritchard, Butler (Charley), Sorrell.
Colchester U: Grace; Taylor, Radford, Collins, Daniels, English A, Bennett, Ball, Morgan (Kinsella), Scott, Grainger (Wilkins).

FIRST ROUND

Peterborough U (0) 0

Hereford U (0) 1 *(Jones M)* 1824

Peterborough U: Godden; Luke, Oakes (Crosby), Halsall, Robinson, McElhinney, Sterling, Hine, Longhurst, Osborne (Harle), Butterworth.
Hereford U: Elliott; Jones M A, Devine, Hemming, Peacock, Bradley (Jones R), Jones M (Jones S), Narbett, Robinson, Benbow, Pejic.

PRELIMINARY ROUND

15 JAN

Exeter C (0) 2 *(Benjamin, Neville)*

Torquay U (0) 0 4737

Exeter C: Miller; Hiley, Benjamin, Rogers, Taylor, Whitehead, Rowbotham, Bailey, McDermott, Neville, Goddard.
Torquay U: Veysey; Holmes, Lloyd, Joyce, Elliott, Uzzell, Smith P, Airey, Bastow, Caldwell, Hirons.

Reading (1) 1 *(Moran)*

Bristol C (0) 1 *(Gavin)* 1784

Reading: Burns; Williams, Richardson, Gooding, Hicks, Whitlock, Payne, Tait, Conroy (Leworthy), Gilkes, Moran.
Bristol C: Sinclair; Llewellyn, Bailey, Shelton, Humphries, Rennie (Melon), Gavin, Newman, Miller, Smith, Turner.

Northern Area

16 JAN

FIRST ROUND

Blackpool (0) 0

Chester C (1) 1 *(Newhouse)*   1433

Blackpool: Bartram; Wright, Morgan, Coughlin, Briggs, Elliott, Gore, Hawkins, Owen, Garner, Diamond (Bradshaw).
Chester C: Stewart; Woodthorpe, Lundon, Hinnigan, Lightfoot, Lane, Butler, Barrow, Newhouse, Pugh (Pointer), Croft.

PRELIMINARY ROUND

Southern Area

17 JAN

Bristol R (1) 3 *(Holloway (pen), Sealy, Mehew)*

Exeter C (0) 0   3136

Bristol R: Parkin; Alexander, Twentyman, Yates, Mehew, Jones, Holloway, Reece, McClean, Sealy, Nixon (Browning).
Exeter C: Walter; Hiley, Frankland, Rogers, Heath, Cooper, Eshelby, Batty, Locke (Bailey), McDermott, Benjamin.

Swansea C (1) 1 *(Trick)*

Reading (1) 2 *(Tait, Senior)*   1829

Swansea C: Bracey; Trick, Coleman, Melville, Walker, Thornber, Harris, James, Hughes, Chalmers (Hutchinson), Legg.
Reading: Francis; Jones, Richardson, Gooding, Hicks, Whitlock, Beavon, Tait (Taylor), Senior, Gilkes, Moran.

FIRST ROUND

Maidstone U (0) 2 *(Butler, Gall)*

Mansfield T (0) 1 *(Christie)*   1020

Maidstone U: Beeney; Barton, Cooper, Berry, Oxbrow, Golley, Gall (Lillis), Elsey, Pritchard, Butler, Stebbing (Charley).
Mansfield T: Beasley; Murray, Prindiville (McDonald), Christie, Foster, Gray, Kent, Hunt, Wilkinson, Leishman (Chambers), Kearney.

Southend U (2) 2 *(Cook, Crown)*

Northampton T (0) 1 *(Collins)*   1346

Southend U: Sansome; Dixon, Roberts, Martin, Butters, Brush, Cook, Butler, Crown, McDonough, Bennett.
Northampton T: Gleasure; Sandeman, Gernon, Thomas, Wilcox, McPherson, Berry, Singleton (Wilson), Collins, Barnes, Donald.

23 JAN

Brentford (2) 2 *(May, Cadette)*

Reading (1) 1 *(Moran (pen))*   3928

Brentford: Parks; Ratcliffe, Stanislaus, Bates, Evans, Cockram, Jones, May (Godfrey), Holdsworth, Cadette, Smillie.
Reading: Francis; Jones, Richardson, Gooding, Hicks, Whitlock, Beavon, Conroy (Taylor), Senior (Leworthy), Gilkes, Moran.

Bristol C (0) 0

Notts Co (0) 1 *(Barnes)*   4902

Bristol C: Sinclair; Llewellyn, Bailey, Madge (Smith), Pender, Newman, Rennie, Gavin, Taylor, Miller, Melon.
Notts Co: Cherry; Palmer, Platnauer, Short, Yates, Robinson, Draper, Turner, Lund, Barnes, O'Riordan.

Shrewsbury T (0) 0

Exeter C (0) 1 *(McDermott)*   1462

Shrewsbury T: Perks; Green, Lynch, Kelly, Finley, Moyes, Brown, Gorman, Melrose, McGinlay, Naughton.
Exeter C: Miller; Hiley, Benjamin, McNichol, Taylor, Whitehead, Rowbotham, Bailey, McDermott, Neville, Goddard.

24 JAN

Bristol R (1) 1 *(Nixon)*

Gillingham (0) 0   2724

Bristol R: Parkin; Alexander, Twentyman, Yates, Mehew, Jones, Holloway, Reece, White, Sealy (Nixon), Purnell.
Gillingham: Lim; Haylock, Manuel, Pulis (Eeles), Walker, Palmer, Docker, O'Shea, Gavin (Lovell), Heritage, O'Connor.

QUARTER-FINALS

30 JAN

Walsall (2) 4 *(Rimmer 3, Bertschin)*

Southend U (0) 1 *(Butler)*   2255

Walsall: Barber; Dornan, Whitehouse, Taylor, Forbes, Skipper, Goodwin, Rimmer, Bertschin, Hawker, Littlejohn.
Southend U: Sansome; Dixon, Roberts, Martin, Butters, Brush (Clark), Tilson, Butler, Crown, McDonough (Bennett), Ling.

Northern Area

Halifax T (1) 3 *(Matthews 2, Hall)*

Stockport Co (1) 1 *(Angell)* aet   1779

Halifax T: Brown; Fleming P, Cook, Hedworth, Harrison, Horner, Hall, Martin, Richardson, Butler (Naylor), Matthews.
Stockport Co: Siddall; Brown, Robertson (Williams P), Downes, Williams B, Thorpe, Payne, Knowles, Beaumont, Frain, Angell.

Wigan Ath (0) 0 *(Carberry)*

Doncaster R (0) 2 *(Turnbull, Jones D)* aet   2742

Wigan Ath: Hughes; Senior, Tankard, Parkinson (Rogerson), Atherton, Johnson, Thompson, Ward, Pilling (Carberry), Daley, Griffiths.
Doncaster R: Samways; Robinson, Brevett, Turnbull, Ashurst, Douglas, Adams, Stiles, Noteman, Jones D, Gaughan.

31 JAN

Bolton W (0) 1 *(Storer)*

Rotherham U (0) 0   6838

Bolton W: Felgate; Brown, Cowdrill, Comstive, Crombie, Came, Storer, Thompson, Reeves, Philliskirk, Darby.
Rotherham U: O'Hanlon; Russell (Barnsley), Robinson, Pepper, Johnson, Scott, Buckley, Goodwin, Williamson, Evans (Goater), Hazel.

6 FEB

Tranmere R (0) 3 *(McNab, Muir, Morrissey)*

Chester C (0) 0   4183

Tranmere R: Nixon; Higgins, McCarrick, McNab, Hughes, Vickers, Morrissey, Harvey (Bishop), Steel, Muir, Thomas.
Chester C: Stewart; Reeves, Woodthorpe, Hamilton, Lightfoot, Lane, Butler (Painter), Barrow, Abel (Newhouse), Dale, Croft.

Southern Area

Brentford (1) 2 *(Smillie, Holdsworth)*

Bristol R (1) 2 *(Holloway (pen), Saunders)* aet   4409

Brentford: Parks; Ratcliffe, Stanislaus, Cousins (Buttigieg), Bates, Cockram, Jones, May, Holdsworth, Cadette (Blissett), Smillie.
Bristol R: Parkin; Alexander, Twentyman, Yates, Mehew (Byrne), Jones, Holloway, Reece, White, Saunders, Purnell.
Bristol R won 4-3 on penalties.

Northern Area

20 FEB

SEMI-FINALS

Doncaster R (2) 3 *(Brockie, Turnbull, Noteman)*
Halifax T (0) 0   5754

Doncaster R: Samways; Robinson, Brevett, Rankine, Ashurst, Douglas (Raffell), Brockie, Stiles (Adams), Turnbull, Muir, Noteman.
Halifax T: Brown; Fleming P, Cook, Hedworth, Naylor, Martin, Hall, Watson, Richardson, Butler (Fleming C). Matthews.

Tranmere R (0) 2 *(Muir, Steel)*
Bolton W (1) 1 *(Philliskirk)*   9315

Tranmere R: Nixon; Mungall, McCarrick, McNab, Hughes, Vickers, Malkin, Harvey, Steel, Muir, Thomas.
Bolton W: Felgate; Brown, Cowdrill, Comstive, Crombie, Winstanley, Storer, Thompson, Reeves, Philliskirk, Darby.

Southern Area

QUARTER-FINALS

21 FEB

Hereford U (0) 1 *(Hemming)*
Notts Co (0) 1 *(Barnes) aet*   3409

Hereford U: Elliott; Jones M A, Devine, Hemming (Robinson), Peacock, Pejic (Jones R), Jones M, Narbett, Wheeler, Starbuck, Tester.
Notts Co: Cherry; Palmer, Platnauer (O'Riordan), Short, Yates, Robinson, Fairclough, Turner, Stant (Lund), Barnes, Johnson.
Notts Co won 4-3 on penalties.

Maidstone U (1) 2 *(Butler, Gall)*
Exeter C (0) 0   1685

Maidstone U: Beeney; Barton, Cooper, Berry, Oxbrow, Golley, Gall, Elsey, Roast, Butler, Lillis (Charlery).
Exeter C: Miller; Batty, Benjamin, McNichol, Taylor, Whitehead, Rowbotham (Rogers), Bailey, McDermott, Neville, Frankland.

Northern Area Final

FIRST LEG

12 MAR

Tranmere R (1) 2 *(Muir, Malkin)*
Doncaster R (0) 0   10,004

Tranmere R: Nixon, Higgins, Mungall, McNab, Hughes, Vickers (Bishop), Malkin, Harvey (Morrissey), Steel, Muir, Thomas.
Doncaster R: Samways; Brockie, Brevett, Rankine, Ashurst, Douglas, Muir, Stiles (Adams), Turnbull, Jones D, Noteman.

Southern Area

SEMI-FINALS

14 MAR

Bristol R (0) 0
Walsall (0) 0 *aet*   4740

Bristol R: Parkin; Alexander, Twentyman, Yates, Mehew (Sealy), Jones, Holloway, Reece, White, Saunders, Purnell.

Walsall: Barber; Rees, Mower, Taylor, Forbes, Skipper, Goodwin, Rimmer, Bertschin (Hart), Hawker, Littlejohn.
Bristol R won 3-2 on penalties.

Maidstone U (0) 0
Notts Co (0) 1 *(Turner) aet*   2114

Maidstone U: Johns; Barton (Gall), Cooper, Berry, Rumble, Golley, Lillis, Elsey, Charlery, Butler, Sorrell.
Notts Co: Cherry; Fleming, Platnauer, Law, Yates, Robinson, Norton, Turner, Lund, Bartlett, O'Riordan.

FINAL

First Leg

28 MAR

Bristol R (0) 1 *(Mehew)*
Notts Co (0) 0   6480

Bristol R: Parkin; Alexander, Twentyman, Yates, Mehew, Jones, Holloway, Reece (McClean), White, Nixon, Purnell.
Notts Co: Cherry; Norton, Platnauer, Short, Yates, Robinson, O'Riordan, Turner, Bartlett (Stant), Chapman, Johnson.

FINAL

Second Leg

2 APR

Notts Co (0) 0
Bristol R (0) 0   10,857

Notts Co: Cherry; Norton, Platnauer, Short, Yates, Robinson, O'Riordan (Lund), Turner, Bartlett, Chapman (Stant), Johnson.
Bristol R: Parkin; Alexander, Twentyman, Yates, Mehew, Jones, Holloway, Reece, McClean, Saunders, Purnell (Nixon).
Bristol R won 1-0 on aggregate.

Northern Area Final

Second Leg

3 APR

Doncaster R (0) 1 *(Jones D)*
Tranmere R (0) 1 *(Muir)*   6670

Doncaster R: Samways; Brockie, Brevett, Rankine, Ashurst, Douglas, Muir, Stiles, Turnbull, Jones D, Noteman.
Tranmere R: Nixon; Higgins, Mungall, McNab, Hughes, Vickers, Morrissey, Harvey, Steel, Muir, Thomas.

FINAL (at Wembley)

20 MAY

Bristol R (0) 1 *(White)*
Tranmere R (1) 2 *(Muir, Steel)*   48,402

Bristol R: Parkin; Alexander (Nixon), Twentyman, Yates, Mehew, Jones, Holloway, Reece, White, Saunders, Purnell (McClean).
Tranmere R: Nixon; Garnett, Mungall, McNab, Hughes, Vickers, Malkin, Harvey, Steel, Muir, Thomas.
Referee: V. Callow (Solihull).

THE FA CUP

THE FOOTBALL ASSOCIATION OFFICIALS

Patron: HER MAJESTY THE QUEEN

President: HRH THE DUKE OF KENT

Honorary Vice-Presidents
His Grace the Duke of Marlborough; The Rt Hon
The Earl of Derby MC; Air Marshall Michael
Simmons KCB, AFC, RAF; General Sir John
Stibbon KCB, OBE; Admiral of the Fleet Sir John
Fieldhouse GCB, GBE, ADC; Right Hon Earl of
Harewood KBE, LLD; Sir Walter Winterbottom CBE;
Rt Hon Lord Westwood FCIS, JP; E. A. Croker CBE

Chairman of the Council
F. A. Millichip (West Bromwich Albion FC)

Vice-Chairman of the Council
C. H. Wilcox (Gloucestershire FA)

Life Vice-Presidents
A. D. McMullen MBE (Bedfordshire FA);
E. D. Smith MBE JP (Cumberland FA);
L. G. Webb (Somerset and Avon South FA);
R. Wragg F.Inst.B.M. (Sheffield United FC);
R. H. Speake (Kent Co FA);
B. W. Mulrenan (Universities Athletic Union);
Sq/Ldr G. A. Hadley (Royal Air Force);
L. T. Shipman (Leicester City FC);
Dr J. O'Hara MB, ChB, AMRCGP (Sussex Co. FA);
S. A. Rudd (Liverpool Co FA);
E. A. Brown (Suffolk FA)

Vice-Presidents
F. A. Millichip (West Bromwich Albion FC);
E. G. Powell FIBA (Herefordshire FA);
Sir Leonard Smith CBE (Commonwealth
  Caribbean);
W. T. Annable (Nottinghamshire FA);
L. Smart (Swindon Town FC)

Secretary
R. H. G. Kelly, FCIS, 16 Lancaster Gate, London
W2 3LW

FA Challenge Cup Committee
E. A. Brown (Chairman),
W. T. Annable, W. Fox, W. G. Halsey,
W. G. McKeag, Dr. J. O'Hara, P. Rushton,
I. A. Scholar, S. Seymour, T. W. Shipman,
L. Smart, A. L. Smith, J. W. Smith

FA CUP FINALS 1872–1990

1872 and 1874–92	Kennington Oval	1911	Replay at Old Trafford
1873	Lillie Bridge	1912	Replay at Bramall Lane
1886	Replay at Derby		
1893	Fallowfield, Manchester	1915	Old Trafford, Manchester
1894	Everton	1920–22	Stamford Bridge
1895–1914	Crystal Palace	1923 to date	Wembley
1901	Replay at Bolton	1970	Replay at Old Trafford
1910	Replay at Everton	1981	Replay at Wembley

Year	Winners	Runners-up	Score
1872	Wanderers	Royal Engineers	1-0
1873	Wanderers	Oxford University	2-0
1874	Oxford University	Royal Engineers	2-0
1875	Royal Engineers	Old Etonians	2-0 (after 1-1 draw aet)
1876	Wanderers	Old Etonians	3-0 (after 1-1 draw aet)
1877	Wanderers	Oxford University	2-1 (aet)
1878	Wanderers*	Royal Engineers	3-1
1879	Old Etonians	Clapham R	1-0
1880	Clapham R	Oxford University	1-0
1881	Old Carthusians	Old Etonians	3-0
1882	Old Etonians	Blackburn R	1-0
1883	Blackburn Olympic	Old Etonians	2-1 (aet)
1884	Blackburn R	Queen's Park, Glasgow	2-1
1885	Blackburn R	Queen's Park, Glasgow	2-0
1886	Blackburn R†	WBA	2-0 (after 0-0 draw)
1887	Aston Villa	WBA	2-0
1888	WBA	Preston NE	2-1
1889	Preston NE	Wolverhampton W	3-0
1890	Blackburn R	Sheffield W	6-1
1891	Blackburn R	Notts Co	3-1
1892	WBA	Aston Villa	3-0
1893	Wolverhampton W	Everton	1-0
1894	Notts Co	Bolton W	4-1
1895	Aston Villa	WBA	1-0
1896	Sheffield W	Wolverhampton W	2-1
1897	Aston Villa	Everton	3-2
1898	Nottingham F	Derby Co	3-1
1899	Sheffield U	Derby Co	4-1
1900	Bury	Southampton	4-0
1901	Tottenham H	Sheffield U	3-1 (after 2-2 draw)
1902	Sheffield U	Southampton	2-1 (after 1-1 draw)
1903	Bury	Derby Co	6-0
1904	Manchester C	Bolton W	1-0
1905	Aston Villa	Newcastle U	2-0
1906	Everton	Newcastle U	1-0
1907	Sheffield W	Everton	2-1
1908	Wolverhampton W	Newcastle U	3-1
1909	Manchester U	Bristol C	1-0
1910	Newcastle U	Barnsley	2-0 (after 1-1 draw)
1911	Bradford C	Newcastle U	1-0 (after 0-0 draw)
1912	Barnsley	WBA	1-0 (aet, after 0-0 draw)
1913	Aston Villa	Sunderland	1-0
1914	Burnley	Liverpool	1-0
1915	Sheffield U	Chelsea	3-0
1920	Aston Villa	Huddersfield T	1-0 (aet)
1921	Tottenham H	Wolverhampton W	1-0
1922	Huddersfield T	Preston NE	1-0
1923	Bolton W	West Ham U	2-0
1924	Newcastle U	Aston Villa	2-0
1925	Sheffield U	Cardiff C	1-0
1926	Bolton W	Manchester C	1-0
1927	Cardiff C	Arsenal	1-0
1928	Blackburn R	Huddersfield T	3-1
1929	Bolton W	Portsmouth	2-0
1930	Arsenal	Huddersfield T	2-0
1931	WBA	Birmingham	2-1
1932	Newcastle U	Arsenal	2-1
1933	Everton	Manchester C	3-0
1934	Manchester C	Portsmouth	2-1
1935	Sheffield W	WBA	4-2
1936	Arsenal	Sheffield U	1-0
1937	Sunderland	Preston NE	3-1
1938	Preston NE	Huddersfield T	1-0 (aet)
1939	Portsmouth	Wolverhampton W	4-1
1946	Derby Co	Charlton Ath	4-1 (aet)
1947	Charlton Ath	Burnley	1-0 (aet)
1948	Manchester U	Blackpool	4-2
1949	Wolverhampton W	Leicester C	3-1
1950	Arsenal	Liverpool	2-0
1951	Newcastle U	Blackpool	2-0
1952	Newcastle U	Arsenal	1-0

Year	Winners	Runners-up	Score
1953	Blackpool	Bolton W	4-3
1954	WBA	Preston NE	3-2
1955	Newcastle U	Manchester C	3-1
1956	Manchester C	Birmingham C	3-1
1957	Aston Villa	Manchester U	2-1
1958	Bolton W	Manchester U	2-0
1959	Nottingham F	Luton T	2-1
1960	Wolverhampton W	Blackburn R	3-0
1961	Tottenham H	Leicester C	2-0
1962	Tottenham H	Burnley	3-1
1963	Manchester U	Leicester C	3-1
1964	West Ham U	Preston NE	3-2
1965	Liverpool	Leeds U	2-1 (aet)
1966	Everton	Sheffield W	3-2
1967	Tottenham H	Chelsea	2-1
1968	WBA	Everton	1-0 (aet)
1969	Manchester C	Leicester C	1-0
1970	Chelsea	Leeds U	2-1 (aet)
	(after 2-2 draw, after extra time, at Wembley)		
1971	Arsenal	Liverpool	2-1 (aet)
1972	Leeds U	Arsenal	1-0
1973	Sunderland	Leeds U	1-0
1974	Liverpool	Newcastle U	3-0
1975	West Ham U	Fulham	2-0
1976	Southampton	Manchester U	1-0
1977	Manchester U	Liverpool	2-1
1978	Ipswich T	Arsenal	1-0
1979	Arsenal	Manchester U	3-2
1980	West Ham U	Arsenal	1-0
1981	Tottenham H	Manchester C	3-2
	(after 1-1 draw, after extra time, at Wembley)		
1982	Tottenham H	QPR	1-0
	(after 1-1 draw, after extra time, at Wembley)		
1983	Manchester U	Brighton &'HA	4-0
	(after 2-2 draw, after extra time, at Wembley)		
1984	Everton	Watford	2-0
1985	Manchester U	Everton	1-0 (aet)
1986	Liverpool	Everton	3-1
1987	Coventry C	Tottenham H	3-2 (aet)
1988	Wimbledon	Liverpool	1-0
1989	Liverpool	Everton	3-2 (aet)
1990	Manchester U	Crystal Palace	1-0
	(after 3-3 draw, after extra time, at Wembley)		

* *Won outright, but restored to the Football Association.*

† *A special trophy was awarded for third consecutive win.*

FA CUP WINS

Aston Villa 7, Manchester U 7, Tottenham H 7, Blackburn R 6, Newcastle U 6, Arsenal 5, The Wanderers 5, WBA 5, Sheffield U 4, Bolton W 4, Everton 4, Liverpool 4, Wolverhampton W 4, Manchester C 4, Sheffield W 3, West Ham U 3, Bury 2, Old Etonians 2, Preston NE 2, Nottingham F 2, Sunderland 2, Barnsley 1, Blackburn Olympic 1, Blackpool 1, Bradford C 1, Burnley 1, Cardiff C 1, Charlton Ath 1, Chelsea 1, Clapham R 1, Coventry C 1, Derby Co 1, Huddersfield T 1, Notts Co 1, Old Carthusians 1, Oxford University 1, Portsmouth 1, Royal Engineers 1, Leeds U 1, Southampton 1, Ipswich T 1, Wimbledon 1.

APPEARANCES IN FINALS

Arsenal 11, Everton 11, Manchester U 11, Newcastle U 11, WBA 10, Aston Villa 9, Liverpool 9, Blackburn R 8, Manchester C 8, Tottenham H 8, Wolverhampton W 8, Bolton W 7, Preston NE 7, Old Etonians 6, Sheffield U 6, Huddersfield T 5, *The Wanderers 5, Sheffield W 5, Derby Co 4, Oxford University 4, Royal Engineers 4, Leeds U 4, Leicester C 4, West Ham U 4, Blackpool 3, Burnley 3, Chelsea 3, Portsmouth 3, Sunderland 3, Southampton 3, Barnsley 2, Birmingham C 2, *Bury 2, Cardiff C 2, Charlton Ath 2, Clapham R 2, Notts Co 2, Queen's Park (Glasgow) 2, *Nottingham F 2, *Blackburn Olympic 1, *Bradford C 1, Bristol C 1, Coventry C 1, Crystal Palace 1, *Old Carthusians 1, Luton T 1, Fulham 1, *Ipswich T 1, QPR 1, Brighton & HA 1, Watford 1, *Wimbledon 1.

* *Denotes undefeated.*

APPEARANCES IN SEMI-FINALS

Everton 22, WBA 19, Liverpool 18, Manchester U 18, Aston Villa 17, Blackburn R 16, Arsenal 16, Sheffield W 15, Derby Co 13, Newcastle U 13, Wolverhampton W 13, Bolton W 12, Tottenham H 12, Nottingham F 11, Southampton 10, Sunderland 10, Preston NE 10, Manchester C 10, Sheffield U 10, Chelsea 10, Birmingham C 9, Southampton 9, Burnley 8, Leeds U 8, Huddersfield T 7, Leicester C 7, Old Etonians 6, Oxford University 6, The Wanderers 5, Notts Co 5, Fulham 5, West Ham U 5, Portsmouth 4, Queen's Park (Glasgow) 4, Royal Engineers 4, Blackpool 3, Cardiff C 3, Clapham R 3, Millwall 3, Old Carthusians 3, The Swifts 3, Stoke C 3, Ipswich T 3, Luton T 3, Watford 3, Barnsley 2, Blackburn Olympic 2, Bristol C 2, Bury 2, Charlton Ath 2, Crystal Palace (professional club) 2, Grimsby T 2, Norwich C 2, Oldham Ath 2, Swansea T 2, Swindon T 2, Bradford C 1, Cambridge University 1, Coventry C 1, Crewe Alex 1, Crystal Palace (amateur club) 1, Darwen 1, Derby Junction 1, Glasgow R 1, Hull C 1, Marlow 1, Old Harrovians 1, Port Vale 1, Reading 1, Shropshire W 1, York C 1, Orient 1, QPR 1, Brighton & HA 1, Plymouth Arg 1, Wimbledon 1.

FA CUP 1989–90

PRELIMINARY AND QUALIFYING ROUNDS

There was an original entry of 541 clubs for the 1989–90 competition. Clubs in the First and Second Divisions of the Football League are exempt to the Third Round Proper, while clubs in the Third and Fourth Divisions are exempt to the First Round Proper. In addition, last season's FA Trophy finalists (Macclesfield Town and Telford United) and two other clubs at the discretion of the FA (Kettering Town and Sutton United) are exempt to the First Round Proper. The following 20 clubs are exempt to the Fourth Round Qualifying: Altrincham, Aylesbury United, Bath City, Bognor Regis Town, Burton Albion, Chelmsford City, Chorley, Dagenham, Darlington, Enfield, Farnborough Town, Halesowen Town, Hayes, Kidderminster Harriers, Merthyr Tydfil, Northwich Victoria, Runcorn, VS Rugby, Welling United, Yeovil Town.

Preliminary Round

Alnwick Town v Peterlee Newtown	1-1, 2-1
Horden CW v Whitley Bay	0-3
Cleator Moor Celtic v Thackley	1-1, 3-1
Harworth CI v Ashington	0-3
Consett v Ferryhill Athletic	1-3
Northallerton Town v Netherfield	3-3, 1-2
Bridlington Trinity v Darlington CB	
(match awarded to Darlington CB)	
Clitheroe v Bedlington Terriers	4-0
Washington v Chester-le-Street Town	0-0, 1-2
Norton & Stockton Ancients v South Bank	1-7
Langley Park Welfare v Guiseley	5-4
Seaham Red Star v Easington Colliery	1-0
Crook Town v Workington	0-0, 1-0
Annfield Plain v Shotton Comrades	2-3
Prudhoe East End v Harrogate Town	1-0
Evenwood Town v Durham City	0-1
Esh Winning v North Shields	2-6
Penrith v Murton	2-3
Darwin v Lancaster City	0-3
Prescot Cables v Ossett Albion	2-1
Atherton LR v Accrington Stanley	1-1, 5-2
Droylsden v Blackpool Wren Rovers	3-2
Skelmersdale United v Curzon Ashton	1-1, 0-2
Glossop v Maine Road	0-4
Congleton Town v Irlam Town	1-1, 2-0
Colwyn Bay v Ilkeston Town *(at Rhyl FC)*	5-1
Burscough v Bootle	2-0
Heanor Town v Formby	2-0
Leyland Motors v Rossendale United	0-1
Sheffield v Armthorpe Welfare	1-0
Oakham United v Worksop Town	4-2
Belper Town v Ashton United	1-0
Radcliffe Borough v Bridgnorth Town	2-2, 2-0
Walsall Wood v Winsford United	2-0
North Ferriby United v Long Eaton United	1-0
Brigg Town v St Helens Town	0-2
Chadderton v Gresley Rovers	1-2
Mile Oak Rovers v Warrington Town	1-2
Friar Lane Old Boys v Farsley Celtic	1-2
Eastwood Town v Grantham Town	1-2
Hinckley Athletic v Highgate United	2-0
Chasetown v Spalding United	2-2, 0-3
Princes End United v Alfreton Town	0-2
Sutton Town v Rushall Olympic	1-1, 0-3
Nuneaton Borough v Willenhall Town	1-1, 0-1
Sutton Coldfield Town v Harrisons	7-0
Stratford Town v Wellingborough Town	0-0, 4-3
Brackley Town v Coventry Sporting	
(walkover for Brackley Town FC)	
Tividale v Stourbridge	1-3
MK Wolverton Town v Irthlingborough Diamonds	2-1
Bilston Town v Desborough Town	1-1, 1-2
Hednesford Town v Lye Town	0-2
March Town United v Chatteris Town	5-0

Halesowen Harriers v Rushden Town	2-5
Oldbury United v Kings Lynn	1-1, 1-3
Soham Town Rangers v Rothwell Town	0-1
Wisbech Town v Eynesbury Rovers	5-0
Northampton Spencer v Paget Rangers	3-3, 0-2
Racing Club Warwick v Haverhill Rovers	1-1, 0-1
Hitchin v Leicester United	3-1
Purfleet v Stamford	1-1, 2-1
Braintree Town v Newmarket Town	1-1, 0-1
Great Yarmouth Town v Stevenage Borough	0-2
Langford v Canvey Island	0-3
Saffron Walden Town v Burnham Ramblers	2-1
Lowestoft Town v Gorleston	2-1
Bury Town v Clapton	0-5
Basildon United v Stowmarket	0-1
Barkingside v Harlow Town	2-5
Witham Town v Clacton Town	2-1
Heybridge Swifts v Ford United	1-1, 2-0
Welwyn Garden City v Halstead Town	1-1, 2-4
Wootton Blue Cross v Cheshunt	0-2
Wivenhoe Town v Harwich & Parkeston	2-0
Felixstowe Town v Tring Town	0-2
Ware v Tiptree United	2-1
Boreham Wood v Harefield United	1-0
Hoddesdon Town v Berkhamsted Town	2-3
(at Hertford Town)	
Baldock Town v Cray Wanderers	3-0
Aveley v Chesham United	0-0, 1-0
Beckenham Town v Walthamstow Pennant	0-5
Yeading v Buckingham Town	4-0
Burgess Hill Town v Wandsworth & Norwood	1-2
Edgware Town v Burnham	1-3
Billericay Town v Dunstable	0-1
Barton Rovers v Chipstead	0-0, 3-2
Darenth Heathside v Hertford Town	3-3, 1-4
Hounslow v Horsham YMCA	2-2, 1-0
Letchworth Garden City v Royston Town	1-3
Northwood v Hampton	1-3
Rayners Lane v Wembley	1-0
Epsom & Ewell v Metropolitan Police	0-0, 2-0
Hailsham Town v Eton Manor	2-2, 1-0
Collier Row v Corinthian	3-1
Lewes v Hanwell Town	2-1
Erith & Belvedere v Chatham Town	5-1
Southwick v Rainham Town	3-0
Ruislip Manor v Portfield	0-0, 2-0
Merstham v Hornchurch *(at Hornchurch FC)*	
Tooting & Mitcham United v Worthing	2-2, 1-0
Herne Bay v Horsham	3-1
Lancing v Canterbury City	0-1
Ringmer v Molesey *(at Molesey FC)*	0-1
Tunbridge Wells v Deal Town	1-1, 1-2
Three Bridges v Banstead Athletic	1-0
Peacehaven & Telscombe v Corinthian Casuals	0-0, 2-1
(Replay at Leatherhead FC)	
Margate v Wick	2-1
Steyning Town v Eastbourne United *(at Eastbourne U)*	2-5
Croydon v Havant Town *(at Metropolitan Police FC)*	3-2
Egham Town v Sheppey United	4-1
Abingdon United v Newport IOW	1-4
Andover v Camberley Town	2-2, 5-1
Haywards Heath v AFC Totton	1-2
Flackwell Heath v Horndean	3-0
Bournemouth v Bracknell Town	2-0
Chertsey Town v Arundel	3-1
Littlehampton Town v Calne Town	1-1, 1-0
Witney Town v Chichester City	4-1
Petersfield United v Poole Town	0-4
Wimborne Town v Swanage Town & Herston	0-2

Romsey Town v Westbury United	5-1
Salisbury v Sholing Sports	6-0
Cwmbran Town v Bridgend Town	1-0
(at Bridgend Town FC)	
Welton Rovers v Thatcham Town	0-5
Thame United v Frome Town	7-0
Newbury Town v Bristol Manor Farm	2-2, 1-3
Tiverton Town v Trowbridge Town	1-1, 1-3
Sharpness v Chippenham Town	1-1, 0-1
Chard Town v Yate Town	2-1
Glastonbury v Maesteg Park	0-1
Ton Pentre v Mangotsfield United 2-2, 0-1*, 1-1, 3-3, 1-3	
Paulton Rovers v Radstock Town	4-2
Evesham United v Malvern Town	0-1
Clevedon Town v Ilfracombe Town	0-1
Torrington v Falmouth Town	1-1, 2-4
Taunton Town v Minehead	9-1
*Abandoned 41 min, floodlight failure.	

First Qualifying Round

Whitley Bay v Willington	6-0
Billingham Town v Spennymoor United	1-1, 1-2
Cleator Moor Celtic v Barrow	1-4
Ashington v Alnwick Town	0-5
Netherfield v Ryhope CA	3-1
Billingham Synthonia v Guisborough Town	2-0
Darlington CB v Gateshead	0-1
Clitheroe v Ferryhill Athletic	2-2, 1-1, 3-4
South Bank v Shildon	2-0
Whitby Town v Hebburn	1-3
Langley Park Welfare v Brandon United	3-1
Bishop Auckland v Chester-le-Street Town	3-2
Crook Town v West Auckland Town	5-1
Gretna v Tow Law Town	3-5
Shotton Comrades v Bridlington Town	0-5
Prudhoe East End v Seaham Red Star	0-0, 2-3
North Shields v Whickham	1-0
Newcastle Blue Star v Stockton	1-1, 3-1
Murton v Blyth Spartans	0-3
Lancaster City v Durham City	0-1
Accrington Stanley v Borrowash Victoria	4-0
Mossley v South Liverpool	0-0, 3-0
Droylsden v Fleetwood Town	0-0, 1-1, 1-0
Curzon Ashton v Prescot Cables	2-0
Congleton Town v Denaby United	2-1
Caernarfon Town v Horwich RMI	3-1
Colwyn Bay v Morecambe (at Rhyl FC)	4-1
Burscough v Maine Road	1-2
Rossendale United v Vauxhall GM	2-1
Marine v Eastwood Hanley	1-1, 2-1
Sheffield v Hyde United	0-1
Bangor City v Heanor Town	3-1
Belper Town v Arnold Town	2-2, 1-3
Southport v Stalybridge Celtic	3-2
Radcliffe Borough v Rhyl	1-2
Walsall Wood v Oakham United	0-1
St Helens Town v Sandwell Borough	0-1
Buxton v Emley	3-1
Gresley Rovers v Witton Albion	2-2, 0-1
Warrington Town v North Ferriby United	1-0
Grantham Town v Louth United	2-1
Dudley Town v Boston	0-1
Hinckley Athletic v Frickley Athletic	1-3
Goole Town v Farsley Celtic	1-0
Alfreton Town v Rocester	1-0
Boston United v Leek Town	3-3, 3-0
Rushall Olympic v Matlock Town	0-1
Willenhall Town v Spalding United	1-1, 2-0
Stratford Town v Histon	2-0
Alvechurch v Bedworth United	0-1
Brackley Town v Shepshed Charterhouse	2-1
Gainsborough Trinity v Sutton Coldfield Town	1-2
MK Wolverton Town v Baker Perkins	2-1
Stafford Rangers v Hinckley Town	1-0
Desborough Town v Atherstone United	1-0
Lye Town v Stourbridge	2-0

Rushden Town v Holbeach United	4-5
Boldmere St Michaels v Tamworth	2-3
Kings Lynn v Bromsgrove Rovers	0-3
Rothwell Town v March Town United	0-2
Paget Rangers v Ely City	2-1
Moor Green v Redditch United	0-1
Haverhill Rovers v Corby Town	1-1, 3-2
Hitchin Town v Wisbech Town	3-2
Newmarket Town v Leighton Town	1-0
Bishops Stortford v Barnet	0-1
Stevenage Borough v Cambridge City	3-5
Canvey Island v Purfleet	3-0
Lowestoft Town v Arlesey Town	1-1, 4-0
Barking v Hendon	1-1, 2-2, 1-2
Clapton v Sudbury Town	1-2
Stowmarket Town v Saffron Walden Town	5-3
Witham Town v Finchley	3-1
Redbridge Forest v Dartford	2-4
Heybridge Swifts v Grays Athletic	2-1
Halstead Town v Harlow Town	3-2
Wivenhoe Town v Potton United	3-0
St Albans City v Wealdstone	1-2
Tring Town v Leyton-Wingate	0-4
Ware v Cheshunt	2-0
Berkhamsted Town v East Thurrock United	1-0
Harrow Borough v Gravesend & Northfleet	1-2
Baldock Town v Wycombe Wanderers	0-2
Aveley v Boreham Wood	0-1
Yeading v Chalfont St Peter	0-0, 5-0
Uxbridge v Hemel Hempstead	1-0
Wandsworth & Norwood v Carshalton Athletic	1-1, 1-3
Slough Town v Walthamstow Pennant	5-1
Dunstable v Vauxhall Motors	3-0
Crawley Town v Staines Town	0-1
Barton Rovers v Windsor & Eton	2-0
Hertford Town v Burnham	0-1
Royston Town v Feltham	2-1
Bromley v Kingsbury Town	1-1, 2-2, 2-0
Hampton v Fisher Athletic	3-1
Rayners Lane v Hounslow	1-2
Hailsham Town v Tonbridge AFC	2-0
Dorking v Tilbury	1-2
Collier Row v Dulwich Hamlet	1-2
Lewes v Epsom & Ewell	2-0
Southwick v Shoreham	5-0
Kingstonian v Woking	1-5
Ruislip Manor v Ashford Town	1-3
Hornchurch v Erith & Belvedere	1-2
Redhill v Ramsgate	1-0
Folkestone v Leatherhead	2-1
Herne Bay v Dover Athletic	0-6
Canterbury City v Tooting & Mitcham United	2-0
Deal Town v Whitstable Town	1-3
Hastings Town v Walton & Hersham	0-3
Three Bridges v Hythe Town	0-2
Peacehaven & Telscombe v Molesey	0-1
Eastbourne United v Malden Vale	1-2
Whyteleafe v Sittingbourne	1-0
Croydon v Wokingham Town (at Sutton United FC)	0-3
Egham Town v Margate	0-1
Andover v Devizes Town	2-0
Pagham v Marlow	0-1
AFC Totton v Whitehawk	4-2
Flackwell Heath v Newport IOW	0-2
Chertsey Town v Eastleigh	4-0
Basingstoke Town v Bashley	1-1, 3-2
Littlehampton Town v Waterlooville	3-1
Witney Town v Bournemouth	1-0
Swanage Town & Herston v Melksham Town	4-0
Gosport Borough v Hungerford Town	2-0
Romsey Town v Fareham Town	1-1, 2-1
Salisbury v Poole Town	1-1, 1-3
Thatcham Town v Stroud	2-2, 1-2
Banbury United v Maidenhead United	1-3
Thame United v Abingdon Town	0-3

666

Bristol Manor Farm v Cwmbran Town	0-1
Chippenham Town v Weston-Super-Mare	1-2
Cheltenham Town v Saltash United	1-0
Chard Town v Dorchester Town	0-2
Maesteg Park v Trowbridge Town	1-2
Paulton Rovers v Shortwood United	2-3
Worcester City v Clandown	3-0
Malvern Town v Barry Town	1-5
Gloucester City v Mangotsfield United	4-0
Falmouth Town v St Blazey	1-1, 0-1
Weymouth v Barnstable Town	6-2
Taunton Town v Bideford	3-0
Exmouth Town v Ilfracombe Town	2-0

Second Qualifying Round

Spennymoor United v Whitley Bay	2-4
Barrow v Alnwick Town	3-1
Billingham Synthonia v Netherfield	0-0, 2-1
Gateshead v Ferryhill Athletic	3-0
Hebburn v South Bank	0-0, 0-3
Langley Park Welfare v Bishop Auckland	2-5
Tow Law Town v Crook Town	4-2
Bridlington Town v Seaham Red Star	2-1
North Shields v Newcastle Blue Star	1-1, 4-2
Blyth Spartans v Durham City	4-1
Mossley v Accrington Stanley	3-1
Droylsden v Curzon Ashton	0-1
Caernarfon Town v Congleton Town	1-2
Colwyn Bay v Maine Road (at Rhyl FC)	2-1
Marine v Rossendale United	2-0
Hyde United v Bangor City	2-1
Southport v Arnold Town	2-1
Rhyl v Oakham United	2-0
Buxton v Sandwell Borough	1-1, 1-1, 3-2
Witton Albion v Warrington Town	2-0
Boston v Grantham Town	1-2
Frickley Athletic v Goole Town	1-1, 0-1
Boston United v Alfreton Town	1-0
Matlock Town v Willenhall Town	5-0
Bedworth United v Stratford Town	3-0
Brackley Town v Sutton Coldfield Town	1-2
Stafford Rangers v MK Wolverton Town	2-0
Desborough Town v Lye Town	1-1, 2-5
Tamworth v Holbeach United	1-0
Bromsgrove Rovers v March Town United	4-0
Redditch United v Paget Rangers	5-0
Haverhill Rovers v Hitchin Town	2-3
Barnet v Newmarket Town	4-2
Cambridge City v Canvey Island	3-0
Hendon v Lowestoft Town	7-0
Sudbury Town v Stowmarket Town	3-2
Dartford v Witham Town	3-1
Heybridge Swifts v Halstead Town	1-0
Wealdstone v Wivenhoe Town	0-1
Leyton Wingate v Ware	2-1
Gravesend & Northfleet v Berkhamsted Town	1-0
Wycombe Wanderers v Boreham Wood	3-1
Uxbridge v Yeading	1-0
Carshalton Athletic v Slough Town	0-2
Staines Town v Dunstable	

(1-0 abandoned 38 mins tie awarded to Staines Town)

Barton Rovers v Burnham	1-1, 2-3
Bromley v Royston Town	3-0
Hampton v Hounslow	2-0
Tilbury v Hailsham Town	2-2, 1-2*, 2-3
Dulwich Hamlet v Lewes	4-1
Woking v Southwick	4-1
Ashford Town v Erith & Belvedere	0-1
Folkestone v Redhill	1-1, 1-0
Dover Athletic v Canterbury City	0-0, 2-0
Walton & Hersham v Whitstable Town	0-1
Hythe Town v Molesey	2-1
Whyteleafe v Malden Vale	2-0
Wokingham Town v Margate	1-0
Marlow v Andover	3-2
AFC Totton v Newport IOW	1-3
Basingstoke Town v Chertsey Town	3-1
Littlehampton Town v Witney Town	0-4

Gosport Borough v Swanage Town & Herston	1-1, 2-0
Romsey Town v Poole Town	1-2
Maidenhead United v Stroud	2-0
Abingdon Town v Cwmbran Town	0-0, 4-3
Cheltenham Town v Weston-Super-Mare	7-0
Trowbridge Town v Dorchester Town	0-0, 0-2
Worcester City v Shortwood United	3-0
Barry Town v Gloucester City	2-2, 0-2
Weymouth v St Blazey	2-0
Taunton Town v Exmouth Town	0-0, 2-2, 0-0, 0-1

*Abandoned in extra time

Third Round Qualifying

Barrow v Whitley Bay	2-2, 1-3
Gateshead v Billingham Synthonia	0-2
Bishop Auckland v South Bank	1-1, 3-1
Bridlington Town v Tow Law Town	0-0, 0-0, 2-3
Blythe Spartans v North Shields	0-3
Curzon Ashton v Mossley	1-1, 1-3
Colwyn Bay v Congleton Town (at Rhyl FC)	1-1, 0-4
Hyde United v Marine	0-1
Rhyl v Southport	0-3
Witton Albion v Buxton	1-1, 6-4
Goole Town v Grantham Town	2-1
Matlock Town v Boston United	1-1, 1-0
Sutton Coldfield Town v Bedworth United	1-2
Lye Town v Stafford Rangers	1-2
Bromsgrove Rovers v Tamworth	2-0
Hitchin Town v Redditch United	0-2
Cambridge City v Barnet	3-4
Sudbury Town v Hendon	1-2
Heybridge Swifts v Dartford	0-1
Leyton Wingate v Wivenhoe Town	0-0, 0-2
Wycombe Wanderers v Gravesend & Northfleet	1-1, 1-1, 3-0
Slough Town v Uxbridge	0-0, 2-1
Burnham v Staines Town	0-1
Hampton v Bromley	0-1
Dulwich Hamlet v Hailsham Town	1-1, 4-3
Erith & Belvedere v Woking	1-1, 0-5
Dover Athletic v Folkestone	0-1
Hythe Town v Whitstable Town	2-0
Wokingham Town v Whyteleafe	1-1, 2-1
Newport IOW v Marlow	0-1
Witney Town v Basingstoke Town	0-2
Poole Town v Gosport Borough	1-0
Abingdon Town v Maidenhead United	3-1
Dorchester Town v Cheltenham Town	2-1
Gloucester City v Worcester City	4-2
Exmouth Town v Weymouth	2-0

Fourth Round Qualifying

Northwich Victoria v Goole Town	2-0
Billingham Synthonia v North Shields	2-1
Southport v Whitley Bay	1-3
Chorley v Marine	1-1, 0-0, 0-3
Tow Law Town v Altrincham	2-0
Darlington v Runcorn	4-2
Congleton Town v Witton Albion	1-0
Mossley v Bishop Auckland	1-1, 0-3
Stafford Rangers v Wycombe Wanderers	4-1
Redditch United v Bedworth United	1-1, 2-0
Wivenhoe Town v Halesowen Town	0-0, 2-3
Welling United v Bromley	5-2
Kidderminster Harriers v Chelmsford City	2-2, 3-1
Matlock Town v Enfield	3-1
Dartford v Dagenham	3-1
Burton Albion v Barnet	2-2, 0-1
Bromsgrove Rovers v VS Rugby	1-0
Aylesbury United v Hendon	4-1
Bognor Regis Town v Dorchester Town	1-1, 1-5
Dulwich Hamlet v Merthyr Tydfil	1-1, 2-4
Basingstoke Town v Marlow	1-1, 2-1
Folkestone v Gloucester City	0-1
Hythe Town v Hayes	0-0, 0-3
Wokingham Town v Woking	1-3
Staines Town v Yeovil Town	0-3
Poole Town v Bath City	2-2, 0-3
Abingdon Town v Slough Town	0-3
Exmouth Town v Farnborough Town	1-4

FA CUP 1989–90

FIRST ROUND
17 NOV

Aldershot (0) 0
Cambridge U (0) 1 *(Taylor)*   3408
Aldershot: Coles; Brown, Phillips, Burvill, Ogley, Williams (Devereux), Claridge, Puckett, Stewart, Henry, Randall.
Cambridge U: Vaughan; Clayton, Kimble, Cheetham, Chapple, Daish, Dennis, Leadbitter, Dublin, Taylor, Philpott (Robinson).

Marine (0) 0
Rochdale (0) 1 *(Stonehouse)*   *at Anfield* 3525
Marine: O'Brien; Draper, Gautrey, Smith, Johnson K, McDonough (Rowlands), Roche, Grant, Bennett, Meachin, King.
Rochdale: Welch; Goodison, Hill, Brown, Cole, Ward (Ainscow), Edmonds, Johnson, Stonehouse, O'Shaughnessy, Graham.

18 NOV

Aylesbury (0) 1 *(Donegal)*
Southend U (0) 0   4043
Aylesbury: Garner; Reed, Mason, Day, Hutter, Pluckrose, Smith, Donegal, Hercules (Wright), Ketteridge, Wilson.
Southend U: Sansome; Roberts, Edinburgh, Martin, Tilson, Brush, Cook, Butler, Crown, McDonough, Ling (Walsh).

Basingstoke (2) 3 *(Clarkson 2, Webb)*
Bromsgrove (0) 0   2361
Basingstoke: Simpkins; Baird (Lawrence), Davies, Wiltshire, Ingman, Webb, Greenwood (Robinson), Whale, Clarkson, Mottashed, Coombs.
Bromsgrove: Taylor; Trusswell, Brighton, O'Connell, Richardson, Cunningham, Webb, Stott, Hanks, Parmenter, Ford (Booth).

Bishop Auckland (0) 2 *(Grant, Healey)*
Tow Law T (0) 0   1521
Bishop Auckland: Owers; Liddle, Morgan, Farquhar, Magee, Lormor, Fothergill, Grant, Grady, Healey, Deacey.
Tow Law T: Young; Haley, Clasper, Gardiner, Gibson, Knox, Thompson (Davison), Carr, Barker, White, Deverdics.

Blackpool (0) 2 *(Eyres, Garner)*
Bolton W (0) 1 *(Crombie)*   7309
Blackpool: McIlhargey; Gore, Morgan, Coughlin, Methven, Elliott, Matthews (Davies), Madden, Brook, Garner, Eyres.
Bolton W: Felgate; Brown, Cowdrill, Comstive, Crombie, Winstanley, Henshaw (Storer), Thompson, Reeves (Came), Philliskirk, Darby.

Brentford (0) 0
Colchester U (0) 1 *(Bennett)*   4171
Brentford: Parks; Perryman (Godfrey), Peters, Millen, Evans, Ratcliffe, Jones, May, Holdsworth (Haag), Blissett, Smillie.
Colchester U: Grace; Bruce, Stafford, English A, Daniels, Gilbert, Bennett, Collins, Morgan, English T (Taylor), Wilkins.

Bristol C (2) 2 *(Taylor, Turner)*
Barnet (0) 0   7538
Bristol C: Leaning; Llewellyn, Bailey, Shelton, Humphries, Newman, Rennie, Gavin, Taylor, Smith (Eaton), Turner.
Barnet: Guthrie; Wilson, Stacey, Poole, Reilly, Payne (Clarke), Stein (Gridelet), Murphy, Bull, Cooper, Bodley.

Bristol R (1) 1 *(Reece)*
Reading (1) 1 *(Conroy)*   6115
Bristol C: Parkin; Alexander, Twentyman, Yates, Mehew, Jones, Holloway, Reece, McClean, Willmott (Hazel), Nixon.
Reading: Francis; Jones, Gilkes (Whitlock), Beavon, Hicks, Wood, Knight, Tait, Senior, Conroy, Payne.

Burnley (0) 1 *(White (pen))*
Stockport Co (0) 1 *(Angell)*   8030
Burnley: Pearce; Measham, Hardy, Farrell, Eli (Hancock), Davis, White, Futcher, O'Connell, Jakub, Atkinson.
Stockport Co: Siddall; Brown, Bullo~k, Matthews, Williams (Jones), Thorpe, McInerney, Payne, Edwards (Frain), Cooke, Angell.

Cardiff C (1) 1 *(Pike)*
Halesowen (0) 0   3972
Cardiff C: Wood; Rogerson, Daniel, Barnard, Abraham, Gibbins, Morgan, Griffith, Pike, Kelly, Chandler (Fry).
Halesowen: Clarke; Penn, Price, Smith, Pearce, Hemans, Hazelwood, Flynn, Joinson L, Joinson P, Hunter (Field).

Carlisle U (1) 3 *(Sendall, Proudlock 2)*
Wrexham (0) 0   4588
Carlisle U: McKellar; Graham, Walsh, Saddington, Jones, Fitzpatrick, Shepherd, Miller, Sendall, Proudlock, Halpin.
Wrexham: Morris; Salathiel, Beaumont, Hunter, Williams, Jones, Preece (Barnes), Flynn (Owen), Buxton, Worthington, Cooper.

Crewe Alex (0) 2 *(Cutler, Sussex)*
Congleton (0) 0   5867
Crewe Alex: Greygoose; Murphy, Swain, Smart, Dyson, Callaghan, Jasper, Hignett, Sussex, Walters (Clayton), Cutler.
Congleton: Searle; Young, Woolley, Clack, Peel, Ridgeway, Thornhill, Reeves-Jones, Biddle, Piggott, Dutton (Owen).

Darlington (3) 6 *(Cork, McJannet, Corner 2, Toman, Anderson)*
Northwich (2) 2 *(Hanchard, Callaghan)*   3334
Darlington: Prudhoe; McJannet, Gray, Willis, Smith, Corner, Hine (Anderson) Toman, Borthwick, Cork, Emson.
Northwich: Ryan; Young, Jones, Maguire, McAughtrie, Macowat (O'Connor), Coyle (Parker), Callaghan, Hanchard, Morton, Wintersgale.

668

Dartford (0) 1 *(Hessenthaler)*

Exeter C (1) 1 *(Rowbotham)*   3129

Dartford: Harrold; Myers, Johnson, Mossley, Brown, Sowerby, Hessenthaler, Garvey, Keen, Leslie, Taylor.
Exeter C: Walter; Hiley, Harrower, McNichol, Taylor, Whitehead, Rowbotham, Bailey, Batty, Neville, Dryden (Young).

Doncaster R (0) 1 *(Noteman)*

Notts Co (0) 0   3817

Doncaster R: Samways; Robinson, Brevett, Rankine, Ashurst, Douglas, Gaughan, Stiles, Turnbull, Jones, Noteman.
Notts Co: Cherry; Palmer, Platnauer, Short, Yates, Robinson, Draper, Turner, Lund, Johnson, Norris (Stant).

Farnborough (0) 0

Hereford U (0) 1 *(Peacock)*   1921

Farnborough: Gray; Turkington, Mason, Fielder, Bye, Wigmore, McDonald (Horton), Holsgrove, Brathwaite, Read, Rogers.
Hereford U: Elliott; Jones M A, Williams, Peacock, Hemming, Devine, Jones M, Narbett, Stevens, Oghani (Jones R), Tester.

Gillingham (0) 0

Welling (0) 0   5598

Gillingham: Hillyard; Haylock, Johnson, Haines, Place, Palmer, Trusson, Eeles (Gavin), Lovell, Heritage, Manuel.
Welling: Barron; Hone, Horton, Glover, Ransom, Clemmence, White, Burgess, Booker, Robbins, Reynolds.

Gloucester (1) 1 *(Talboys)*

Dorchester (0) 0   1754

Gloucester: Shaw; Hedges, Williams, Lander, Green, Steel, Talboys, Hughes, Morrison, Payne, Noble.
Dorchester: Jones; Coates, White, Morrell, Loveridge, Joyce, Borthwick, Greeno, Diaz, Morrison, Hampson (Flint).

Hartlepool U (0) 0

Huddersfield T (2) 2 *(Cecere 2 (2 pens))*   3160

Hartlepool U: Moverley; McEwan, McKinnon, Tinkler, Williams, Barrass, Allon, Sinclair (Atkinson), Baker, Hutchison (Lamb), Dalton.
Huddersfield T: Hardwick; Marsden, Hutchings, O'Regan, O'Doherty, Mitchell, Onuora (Withe), Wilson, Cecere, Maskell, Smith.

Kettering (0) 0

Northampton T (0) 1 *(Thomas)*   6100

Kettering: Shoemake; Nightingale, Slack, Brown (Moss), Collins, Keast, Richardson, Wright, Genovese (Edwards), Horwood, Cooke.
Northampton T: Gleasure; Chard, McPherson, Wilcox, Gernon, Quow, Thomas, Sandeman, Collins, Barnes, Berry.

Kidderminster H (0) 2 *(Forsyth, Bancroft)*

Swansea C (2) 3 *(Melville 2, Davies)*   3248

Kidderminster H: Jones; Barton, Bancroft, Weir, Boxall, Forsyth, Dearlove, Casey, Whitehouse, Blair (Howell), Sugrue.
Swansea C: Bracey; Hough, Coleman, Melville, Boyle, Thornber, Harris, Curtis, Legg, Raynor, Davey.

Leyton Orient (0) 0

Birmingham C (0) 1 *(Sturridge)*   4063

Leyton Orient: Heald; Hales, Dickenson, Beesley, Day, Sitton (Baker), Howard, Castle, Carter, Cooper, Berry.
Birmingham C: Thomas; Ashley, Frain, Atkins, Clarkson, Matthewson, Bell, Bailey, Sturridge (Tait), Gleghorn, Langley.

Lincoln C (0) 1 *(Nicholson)*

Billingham Syn (0) 0   2903

Lincoln C: Wallington; Williams, Clarke, Nicholson, Thompson, Davis, Roberts (Hobson), Bressington, Sertori, Carmichael, Cumming (Schofield).
Billingham Syn: Mullen; Steer, Parry, Granycome, Lynch, Coleby, McMullen, Mallone, Butler, Singh (Cochrane), Allen.

Macclesfield (0) 1 *(Burr)*

Chester C (1) 1 *(Painter)*   4200

Macclesfield: Zelem; Farrelly, Johnson, Edwards, Tobin, Hanlon, Askey, Timmons, Ellis, Burr, Wilson (Imrie).
Chester C: Stewart; Reeves, Woodthorpe, Hamilton, Abel, Lane, Butler, Pugh, Dale, Painter, Croft.

Peterborough U (1) 1 *(Sterling)*

Hayes (0) 1 *(Barrowcliffe)*   5172

Peterborough U: Crichton; Luke, Crosby, Halsall, Robinson, McElhinney, Sterling, Culpin (Graham), Osborne (Richards), Longhurst, Butterworth.
Hayes: Hyde; Court, Taylor, Arden, Leather, Dixon (Whiskey), Barrowcliffe, Marshall, Seabrook, Fraser, Walton.

Preston NE (0) 0 *(Joyce)*

Tranmere R (0) 0   7521

Preston NE: Kelly; Williams, Swann, Atkins, Joyce, Hughes, Mooney, Ellis, Bogie, Shaw (Harper), Patterson.
Tranmere R: Nixon; Higgins, Pike, Bishop, Hughes, Vickers, Morrissey (Malkin), Harvey, Steel, Muir, Mungall.

Redditch (0) 1 *(Campbell)*

Merthyr (1) 3 *(Thompson 2, Rodgers)*   1975

Redditch: Burke; Smith, Kemp, Judd, George, Hooman, O'Hare, Campbell, Andrews (Brown), Buchanan (Dale), Whittington.
Merthyr: Wager; Tong, Evans, Stevenson, Williams S, Beattie, Rodgers, Giles, Green, Webley, Thompson.

Rotherham U (0) 0

Bury (0) 0   6305

Rotherham U: O'Hanlon; Barnsley, Robinson, Grealish, Johnson, Scott, Buckley, Goodwin, Williamson, Evans, Hazel.
Bury: Kelly; Clements, Bishop, Hoyland, Valentine, Knill, Lee, Robinson, Pashley (McIlroy), Feeley, Greenwood.

Scarborough (0) 0

Whitley Bay (0) 1 *(Scott)*   2085

Scarborough: Ironside; Short, Kamara (Clarke), Law, Richards, Bennyworth, Saunders, Olsson, Dobson, Robinson (Graham), Russell.

Whitley Bay: Dickson; Liddle, Teasdale, Robinson, Gowans, Scott, Walker (Gamble), Dawson, Chandler (Pearson), Todd, Johnson.

Scunthorpe U (2) 4 *(Lillis 3, Hodkinson)*
Matlock (0) 1 *(Walker)*   4307

Scunthorpe U: Litchfield; Cowling, Longden, Ward, Nicol (Smalley), Stevenson, Lillis, Hamilton, Hodkinson, Flounders, Marshall.
Matlock: Wilson; Franklin, Mitchell, Marsh, Hunter, Wragg, Mullins, Sheppard, Walker (Jones), Gee (Thompson), Greaves.

Shrewsbury T (1) 2 *(McGinlay 2 (2 pens))*
Chesterfield (2) 3 *(Gunn (pen), Waller, Plummer)*   3842

Shrewsbury T: Perks; Green, Pittman (Wassell), Kelly, Finley, Moyes, Brown, Hartford, Worsley, McGinlay, Griffiths (Melrose).
Chesterfield: Leonard; Gunn, Ryan, Shaw, Rogers, Plummer, Bloomer, Brien, Waller, Williams, Morris.

Slough (1) 1 *(Langley)*
Woking (1) 2 *(Buzaglo, Mulvaney)*   2182

Slough: Bunting; How, Mallinson (Johnson), Knight, Bateman, Dell B, Dell A, Stanley, Langley, Thompson, Adams.
Woking: Caulfield; Mitchell, Cowler, Russell, Baron, Wye S, Parr, Biggins, Mulvaney, Buzaglo, Franks.

Stafford R (1) 2 *(Camden 2 (2 pens))*
Halifax T (1) 3 *(Fleming, Horner 2)*   2508

Stafford R: Price; Simpson, Upton, Curilo, Essex, Wood (Campbell), Wharton, Gill, Camden, Cavell, Turley.
Halifax T: Whitehead; Fleming, Hedworth, Bramhall, Horner, Martin, Watson, Juryeff, Hall, Butler, Matthews.

Sutton U (1) 1 *(McKinnon)*
Torquay U (0) 1 *(Uzzell)*   2987

Sutton U: Sullivan; Gates, Dawson, Rains, Hemsley, Rogers, Hanlan, Massey, Seagrove (Dennis), McKinnon, Hawkins.
Torquay U: Veysey; Holmes, Lloyd, Elliott, Davies, Joyce, Loram, Airey (Hirons), Edwards, Uzzell, Morrison.

Telford U (0) 0
Walsall (1) 3 *(Rimmer, Bertschin, Forbes)*   2832

Telford U: Charlton; McGinty, Hancock, Wiggins, Nelson, Brindley, Griffiths, Sankey (Lloyd), Stringer, McKenna, Eves.
Walsall: Green; Wilder, Kelly, Forbes, Skipper, Marsh, Rimmer, Bertschin, Thorpe, Gritt, Mower.

York C (0) 0 *(Warburton)*
Grimsby T (0) 2 *(Hargreaves 2)*   4128

York C: Marples; McMillan, Kelly, Barratt, Tutill, Warburton, Howlett, Spooner (Hall), Helliwell, Canham, Dixon.
Grimsby T: Sherwood; McDermott, Agnew, Tillson, Lever, Cunnington, Childs, Gilbert, Birtles, Cockerill, Hargreaves.

19 NOV
Bath C (0) 2 *(Freegard, Randall)*
Fulham (0) 2 *(Peters, Walker)*   4283

Bath C: Preston; Stevens, Palmer, Ricketts, Banks, Brown, Smith, Cousins (Singleton), Freegard, Randall, Smart.

Fulham: Stannard; Peters, Elkins, Skinner, Nebbeling, Marshall, Barnett (Donnellan), Lewington, Sayer, Eckhardt, Walker.

Maidstone U (1) 2 *(Gall, Barton)*
Yeovil (0) 1 *(Spencer)*   2625

Maidstone U: Beeney; Barton, Rumble, Berry, Oxbrow, Pearce, Gall, Elsey, Golley, Butler, Pritchard (Cooper).
Yeovil: Fry; Sherwood, Lowe, Shail, Dawkins, Conning (Cordice), Quinn, Wallace, Blackman (Thompson), Spencer, Donnellan.

Wigan Ath (2) 2 *(Page, Hilditch)*
Mansfield T (0) 0   3087

Wigan Ath: Hughes; Senior, Tankard, Ward, Atherton, Patterson, Carberry, Hilditch, Daley (Thompson), Page, Griffiths.
Mansfield T: Cox; Hunt, Prindiville, Christie, Foster, Kearney, Kent, Lowery, Wilkinson (Stringfellow), Charles, Hodges (Gray).

First Round Replays
21 NOV

Bury (1) 1 *(Bishop)*
Rotherham U (1) 2 *(Hazel, Evans)*   5009

Bury: Kelly; Clements, Bishop, Hoyland, Valentine, Knill, Lee, Robinson, Hill, Feeley (McIlroy), Greenwood.
Rotherham U: O'Hanlon; Barnsley, Robinson, Grealish, Johnson, Scott, Buckley, Goodwin (Russell), Williamson, Evans, Hazel.

Chester C (2) 3 *(Abel (pen), Butler, Croft)*
Macclesfield (1) 2 *(Burr 2)*   4202

Chester C: Stewart; Lane, Woodthorpe, Hamilton, Abel, Lightfoot, Butler, Pugh (Barrow), Dale (Newhouse), Painter, Croft.
Macclesfield: Zelem; Farrelly, Johnson, Edwards, Tobin, Hanlon, Askey, Timmons, Ellis (Connor), Burr, Imrie.

Hayes (0) 0
Peterborough U (1) 1 *(Robinson)*   4000

Hayes: Hyde; Court, Taylor, Arden, Leather, Dixon (Whiskey), Barrowcliffe, Marshall, Seabrook, Fraser, Walton.
Peterborough U: Godden; Luke, Crosby, Halsall, Robinson, McElhinney, Sterling, Culpin (Osborne), Richards, Graham, Butterworth.

Reading (0) 1 *(Senior)*
Bristol R (0) 1 *(Mehew)*   *aet* 6015

Reading: Francis; Jones, Richardson, Beavon, Hicks, Wood (Whitlock), Knight (Moran), Tait, Senior, Conroy, Payne.
Bristol R: Parkin; Alexander, Twentyman, Yates, Mehew, Jones, Holloway, Reece, McClean, Nixon, Willmott.

22 NOV
Exeter C (1) 4 *(Bailey, Batty, Harrower, Neville)*
Dartford (0) 1 *(Johnson)*   4900

Exeter C: Walter; Hiley, Harrower (Rowe), McNichol, Taylor, Whitehead, Rowbotham, Bailey, Batty, Neville (Benjamin), Frankland.

Dartford: Harold; Myers (Sowerby), Johnson, Mossley (Leslie), Brown, Connor, Hassenthaler, Garvey, Keen, Robinson, Taylor.

Fulham (1) 2 *(Marshall, Watson)*

Bath C (1) 1 *(Smart)* 3506

Fulham: Stannard; Peters, Elkins, Skinner, Nebbeling, Eckhardt, Marshall, Lewington (Donnellan), Sayer, Watson, Walker.
Bath C: Preston; Stevens, Palmer, Ricketts, Banks, Brown, Smith, Cousins (Singleton), Freegard, Randall, Smart.

Stockport Co (0) 1 *(Edwards)*

Burnley (0) 2 *(Futcher, O'Connell)* 6257

Stockport Co: Siddall; Brown, Bullock (Jones), Matthews, Williams, Thorpe, McInerney, Payne, Edwards, Cooke (Frain), Angell.
Burnley: Pearce; Measham, Hardy, Farrell, McGrory, Hancock (Mumby), White, Futcher, O'Connell, Jakub, Atkinson.

Torquay U (2) 4 *(Lloyd, Smith 2, Elliott)*

Sutton U (0) 0 2736

Torquay U: Veysey; Holmes, Lloyd, Elliott, Davies, Joyce, Loram, Smith J, Hirons, Uzzell, Morrison.
Sutton U: Sullivan; Gates, Robinson, Rains, Hemsley, Rogers, Hanlan, Massey (Rondeau), Ekoku, McKinnon, Hawkins (Seagrove).

Welling (1) 1 *(Hone)*

Gillingham (0) 0 4020

Welling: Barron; Hone, Horton, Glover, Ransom, Clemmence, White, Burgess, Booker, Robbins, Reynolds.
Gillingham: Hillyard; Haylock, Johnson, Haines, Place, Palmer, Trusson, O'Shea (Docker), Lovell, Heritage, Manuel (Gavin).

FIRST ROUND, SECOND REPLAY
27 NOV

Bristol R (0) 0

Reading (0) 1 *(Senior)* 6782

Bristol R: Parkin; Alexander, Twentyman, Yates, Mehew, Jones, Holloway, Reece (McClean), White, Sealy, Nixon.
Reading: Francis; Jones, Richardson, Beavon, Hicks, Whitlock, Knight, Tait, Senior, Conroy, Payne (Taylor).

SECOND ROUND
9 DEC

Basingstoke (1) 2 *(Blankley, Clarkson)*

Torquay U (1) 3 *(Elliott, Mottashed og, Loram)* 4091

Basingstoke: Simpkins; Blankley, Davies, Wiltshire, Ingman, Webb, Greenwood, Whale, Clarkson, Mottashed, O'Donnell (Cameron).
Torquay U: Veysey; Holmes, Lloyd, Elliott, Taylor, Joyce, Loram, Smith, Edwards, Uzzell, Weston (Davies).

Blackpool (2) 3 *(Brook, Burgess, Owen)*

Chester (0) 0 4099

Blackpool: McIlhargey; Burgess, Morgan, Coughlin, Methven, Elliott (Davies), Gore, Brook, Owen, Garner, Eyres.

Chester C: Stewart; Butler, Woodthorpe, Hamilton, Lightfoot (Pugh) (Newhouse), Lane, Greer, Barrow, Abel, Painter, Croft.

Bristol C (0) 2 *(Taylor, Wimbleton (pen))*

Fulham (1) 1 *(Scott)* 7662

Bristol C: Sinclair; Llewellyn, Bailey, Wimbleton, Humphries, Rennie, Gavin, Newman, Taylor, Smith, Turner.
Fulham: Stannard; Donnellan, Mauge (Skinner), Lewington (Barnett), Nebbeling, Peters, Marshall, Scott, Sayer, Watson, Langley.

Cambridge U (2) 3 *(Cheetham, Leadbitter, Taylor)*

Woking (1) 1 *(Mulvainy)* 3477

Cambridge U: Vaughan; Bailie, Kimble, Cheetham, Chapple, Daish, O'Shea, Leadbitter, Dublin, Taylor, Philpott.
Woking: Caulfield; Mitchell, Moss (Davies), Russell, Barron, Wye S (Biggins), Parr, Hall, Mulvainy, Buzaglo, Wye L.

Cardiff C (0) 2 *(Scott 2)*

Gloucester (1) 2 *(Talboys, Townsend)* 4531

Cardiff C: Wood; Rodgerson, Daniel, Barnard, Abraham, Gibbins, Morgan (Haig), Griffith (Lynex), Scott, Kelly, Chandler.
Gloucester: Shaw; Hedges, Williams, Lander (Chandler), Green, Steel, Talboys, Payne, Morrison, Townsend, Noble.

Chesterfield (0) 0

Huddersfield T (0) 2 *(Cecere (pen), Maskell)* 6687

Chesterfield: Leonard; Gunn, Hewitt, Shaw, Rogers, Plummer, Thompson, Bien, Waller, Williams, Morris.
Huddersfield T: Martin; Marsden, Hutchings, May, Mitchell, Lewis, O'Regan, Wilson, Cecere, Maskell, Smith.

Colchester U (0) 0

Birmingham C (1) 2 *(Gleghorn 2)* 3858

Colchester U: Grace; Bruce, Hagan, English A, Daniels, Gilbert, Bennett, Collins (Taylor), Morgan (Collins, English T, Wilkins.
Birmingham C: Thomas; Ashley, Frain, Atkins, Overson, Matthewson, Bell, Bailey, Sturridge (Hopkins), Gleghorn, Langley.

Crewe Alex (0) 1 *(Murphy (pen))*

Bishop Auckland (0) 1 *(Healey)* 3907

Crewe Alex: Greygoose; Swain, Callaghan, Dyson, Smart (Clayton), Edwards, Murphy, Jasper, Sussex (Walters), Fishenden, Cutler.
Bishop Auckland: Owers; Liddle, MacGee, Lormor, Morgan, Fothergill (Shaw), Deacy, Healey, Farquhar, Grady, Grant (Blackburn).

Darlington (1) 3 *(Coverdale, McJannet, Borthwick)*

Halifax T (0) 0 4041

Darlington: Prudhoe; McJannet, Coverdale, Willis, Smith, Corner, Hine, Toman, Borthwick, Cork, Emson.
Halifax T: Whitehead; Fleming, Butler, Broadbent (Harrison), Bramhall, Horner, Martin, Watson, Matthews (Barr), Juryeff, Hall.

Grimsby T (0) 1 *(Cockerill)*

Doncaster R (0) 0   6623

Grimsby T: Reece; McDermott, Agnew, Tillson, Lever, Cunnington, Childs, Gilbert, Birtles, Cockerill, Alexander (Rees).
Doncaster R: Samways; Robinson, Brevett, Raffell, Ashurst, Douglas, Gaughan, McGinley, Turnbull, Jones, Noteman.

Hereford U (2) 3 *(Robinson, Jones M A, Tester)*

Merthyr (0) 2 *(Webley 2)*   4539

Hereford U: Elliott; Jones M A, Devine, Hemming, Peacock, Jones R, Jones M, Narbett, Robinson, Benbow, Tester.
Merthyr: Wager; Tong, Jones, Stevenson, Evans, Tupling, Giles (Williams), Webley (Hamer), Thompson, Beattie, Green.

Maidstone U (0) 1 *(Elsey)*

Exeter C (0) 1 *(Cooper)*   2385

Maidstone U: Beeney; Barton, Cooper, Berry, Oxbrow (Sorrell), Pearce, Gall (Charlery), Elsey, Galliers, Butler, Golley.
Exeter C: Miller; Hiley, Benjamin, McNichol, Taylor, Whitehead, Rowbotham, Bailey, McDermott, Neville, Cooper.

Northampton T (0) 0

Aylesbury (0) 0   6098

Northampton T: Gleasure; Chard, Wilson, Thomas, Wilcox, McPherson, Berry, Donald, Collins, Barnes, Brown.
Aylesbury: Garner; Reed (Welsh), Mason, Day, Hutter, Pluckrose, Smith, Donegal, Hercules, Ketteridge, Wilson.

Reading (0) 0

Welling (0) 0   4998

Reading: Burns; Jones, Richardson, Beavon, Hicks, Whitlock, Knight (Moran), Tait (Taylor), Senior, Conroy, Payne.
Welling: Barron; Hone, Horton, Glover, Ransom, Clemmence, White, Handford, Booker, Robbins, Reynolds.

Rochdale (2) 3 *(Ward, Johnson, O'Shaughnessy)*

Lincoln C (0) 0   2369

Rochdale: Welch; Goodison, Burns, Brown, Cole, Ward, Holmes, Dawson, Johnson, O'Shaughnessy, Graham.
Lincoln C: Wallington; Williams, Clarke, Nicholson, Thompson, Davis, Schofield (Smith), Bressington, Sertori, Carmichael (Darrin), Hobson.

Scunthorpe U (1) 2 *(Taylor 2)*

Burnley (1) 2 *(Mumby, Deary)*   5698

Scunthorpe U: Litchfield; Cowling (Smalley), Longden, Ward, Lister, Stevenson, Lillis, Taylor, Hodkinson, Flounders, Marshall.
Burnley: Pearce; Measham, Mumby, Farrell, McGrory, Davis, White, Deary, Futcher, Jakub, Atkinson.

Swansea C (1) 3 *(Raynor (pen), Chalmers 2)*

Peterborough U (0) 1 *(Andrews)*   4175

Swansea C: Bracey; Trick, Coleman, Melville, Boyle, Thornber, Harris, Curtis, Chalmers, Raynor, Legg.

Peterborough U: Godden; Luke, Crosby, Halsall, Robinson, McElhinney (Culpin), Sterling, Andrews, Richards, Graham (Longhurst), Butterworth.

Walsall (1) 1 *(Rimmer)*

Rotherham U (0) 0   4240

Walsall: Green; Gritt, Mower, Goodwin, Skipper, Kelly, Rimmer, Bertschin, Marsh, Thorpe, Smith.
Rotherham U: O'Hanlon; Barnsley, Robinson, Grealish (Goodwin), Johnson, Scott, Buckley, Pepper, Williamson, Evans (Goater), Hazel.

Whitley Bay (1) 1 *(Robinson, Todd)*

Preston NE (0) 0   4500

Whitley Bay: Dickson; Liddle, Teasdale, Robinson, Gowans, Johnson, Walker (Haire), Dawson, Chandler (Gamble), Todd, Pearson.
Preston NE: Kelly; Williams, Swann, Atkins, Joyce, Hughes, Mooney (Flynn), Ellis, Bogie, Patterson, Harper.

Wigan Ath (0) 2 *(Johnson, Griffiths)*

Carlisle U (0) 0   4151

Wigan Ath: Hughes; Senior, Tankard, Parkinson, Atherton, Patterson, Carberry (Johnson), Rimmer, Pilling (Griffiths), Daley, Thompson.
Carlisle U: McKellar; Graham, Dalziel, Saddington, Jones, Walsh, Shepherd, Miller (Hetherington), Walwyn, Proudlock, Sendall (Fyfe).

SECOND ROUND REPLAYS

12 DEC

Burnley (1) 1 *(Eli)*

Scunthorpe U (0) 1 *(Daws)*   aet 7682

Burnley: Pearce; Measham, McGrory, Deary, Farrell, Davis, White, Mumby (Eli), Futcher, Jakub, Atkinson (Hardy).
Scunthorpe U: Litchfield; Smalley, Longden, Ward (Hodkinson), Lister, Stevenson, Lillis, Taylor, Daws (Flounders), Hamilton, Marshall.

Gloucester (0) 0

Cardiff C (1) 1 *(Scott)*   3877

Gloucester: Shaw; Hedges, Williams, Payne, Green, Steel, Talboys, Hughes (Lander), Morrison, Townsend, Noble (Hyde).
Cardiff C: Wood; Rodgerson, Daniel, Barnard, Abraham, Gibbins, Morgan (Lynex), Scott, Pike, Kelly, Chandler.

13 DEC

Aylesbury (0) 0

Northampton T (0) 1 *(Barnes)*   aet 4895

Aylesbury: Garner; Welsh (Mason), Cox, Day, Hutter, Pluckrose, Smith, Donegal, Hercules, Ketteridge, Wilson.
Northampton T: Gleasure; Chard, Gernon, Thomas, Wilcox, McPherson, Berry, Donald (Singleton), Collins, Barnes, Brown (McPhillips).

Bishop Auckland (0) 0

Crewe Alex (1) 2 *(Sussex 2)*   2740

Bishop Auckland: Owers; Liddle, Morgan, Farquhar, Magee, Lormor, Fothergill, Grady, Grant (Shaw), Healey, Deacey.

672

Crewe Alex: Greygoose; Swain, Edwards P, Smart, Dyson, Callaghan, Easter (Edwards R) (Clayton), Murphy, Sussex, Walters, Fishenden.

Exeter C (2) 3 *(Rowbotham 2, McDermott)*
Maidstone U (1) 2 *(Butler, Gall)* 4125

Exeter C: Miller; Hiley, Benjamin, McNichol, Taylor, Whitehead, Rowbotham, Bailey, McDermott, Neville, Cooper (Batty).
Maidstone U: Beeney; Barton, Cooper, Berry (Charlery), Golley, Pearce, Gall, Elsey, Galliers (Rumble), Butler, Sorrell.

Welling (0) 1 *(Glover)*
Reading (0) 1 *(Beavon (pen))* aet 3444

Welling: Barron; Hone, Horton, Glover, Ransom, Clemmence, White, Handford, Booker, Robbins, Reynolds.
Reading: Francis; Jones, Richardson, Beavon, Hicks, Whitlock, Wood, Tait, Senior, Moran, Payne.

SECOND ROUND SECOND REPLAYS

18 DEC

Burnley (2) 5 *(Eli 2, Futcher 2, Hardy)*
Scunthorpe U (0) 0 7429

Burnley: Pearce; Measham, McGrory (Hardy), Deary, Farrell, Davis, White, Eli (McKay), Futcher, Jakub, Atkinson.
Scunthorpe U: Litchfield; Smalley, Longden, Hodkinson (Cotton), Lister, Nicol, Lillis, Taylor, Daws, Hamilton, Marshall (Flounders).

19 DEC

Reading (0) 0
Welling (0) 0 aet 4138

Reading: Burns; Jones, Richardson, Beavon, Hicks, Whitlock, Wood, Tait (Leworthy), Senior, Gilkes, Payne.
Welling: Barron; Hone, Horton, Glover, Ransom, Clemmence, White (Burgess), Handford, Booker, Robbins, Reynolds.

SECOND ROUND THIRD REPLAY

22 DEC

Welling (1) 1 *(Robbins)*
Reading (0) 2 *(Moran 2)* 2737

Welling: Barron; Hone, Horton, Glover, Ransom, Clemmence, White, Handford, Booker, Robbins, Reynolds.
Reading: Francis; Jones, Richardson, Beavon, Hicks, Whitlock, Wood, Tait, Senior, Gilkes, Moran.

THIRD ROUND

6 JAN

Birmingham C (0) 1 *(Gleghorn)*
Oldham Ath (0) 1 *(Bunn)* 13,131

Birmingham C: Thomas; Clarkson, Frain, Atkins, Overson, Matthewson, Bell (Hopkins), Bailey, Sturridge, Gleghorn, Langley.
Oldham Athletic: Hallworth; Irwin, Barlow, Henry, Marshall, Barrett, Adams, Palmer, Bunn, Milligan, Holden R.

Blackburn R (1) 2 *(Stapleton, Sellars)*
Aston Villa (1) 2 *(Olney, Ormondroyd)* 14,456

Blackburn R: Gennoe; Reid, Sulley, Finnigan, Hill, Mail, Kennedy, Millar, Stapleton (Gayle), Garner, Sellars.
Aston Villa: Spink; Gage, Williams, McGrath, Mountfield, Nielsen, Daley, Platt, Olney, Cowans, Ormondroyd.

Blackpool (0) 1 *(Methven)*
Burnley (0) 0 7790

Blackpool: McIlhargey; Wright, Morgan, Coughlin, Methven, Elliott, Gore, Brook, Owen, Garner, Eyres.
Burnley: Pearce; Measham, Hardy, Deary, Farrell, Davis, White, Eli, Futcher, Jakub, McKay (Hancock).

Brighton & HA (0) 4 *(Dublin, Nelson, Codner, Curbishley)*
Luton T (0) 1 *(Wilson)* 10,361

Brighton & HA: Keeley; Chivers, Chapman, Curbishley, Gatting, Dublin, Nelson, Barham, Bremmer, Codner, Wilkins.
Luton T: Chamberlain; Breacker, Harvey, James (Dowie), Johnson, Dreyer, Wilson, Kennedy, Harford, Preece, Black.

Bristol C (2) 2 *(Taylor, Newman)*
Swindon T (1) 1 *(Shearer)* 17,422

Bristol C: Sinclair; Llewellyn, Bailey, Shelton, Humphries, Rennie, Gavin, Newman, Taylor, Smith, Turner.
Swindon T: Digby; Kerslake, Bodin, McLoughlin, Calderwood, Gittens, Jones (Hockaday), Shearer, White, MacLaren, Foley.

Cambridge U (0) 0
Darlington (0) 0 4281

Cambridge U: Vaughan; Bailie, Kimble, Clayton (Fensome), Chapple, Daish, Cheetham, Leadbitter, Dublin, Taylor, Philpott.
Darlington: Prudhoe; Gray, Coverdale, Willis, Smith, Corner, Borthwick, Toman, Stephens, Cork (Hyde), Emson.

Cardiff C (0) 0
QPR (0) 0 13,834

Cardiff C: Hansbury; Rodgerson, Daniel, Barnard, Abraham, Gibbins, Morgan, Griffith, Pike, Perry, Lynex (Kelly).
QPR: Seaman; Bardsley, Sansom, Parker, McDonald, Maddix, Wilkins, Barker, Falco, Wegerle, Sinton.

Chelsea (0) 1 *(Clarke)*
Crewe Alex (0) 0 18,066

Chelsea: Beasant; Clarke, Wilson C (McAllister), Roberts, Johnsen, Monkou, Lee, Bumstead, Dixon, Wilson K, Le Saux.
Crewe Alex: Greygoose; Swain, Edwards P, Smart, Dyson, Callaghan, Joseph, Murphy, Clayton (Sussex), Cutler, Walters.

Crystal Palace (0) 2 *(Thomas, Gray (pen))*
Portsmouth (1) 1 *(Whittingham)* 12,644

Crystal Palace: Martyn; Pemberton, O'Reilly, Gray, Hopkins (Thomas), Thorn, Salako, Barber, Bright, Wright, Pardew.

Portsmouth: Knight; Neill, Beresford, Maguire, Hogg, Ball, Wigley, Kuhl, Whittingham (Gilligan), Fillery, Chamberlain.

Exeter C (0) 1 *(Rowbotham)*

Norwich C (0) 1 *(Fleck)* 9061

Exeter C: Miller; Hiley, Benjamin, McNichol, Taylor, Whitehead, Rowbotham, Bailey, McDermott, Neville, Frankland.
Norwich C: Gunn; Culverhouse, Bowen, Butterworth, Linighan, Townsend, Gordon, Fleck, Rosario, Crook, Phillips.

Hereford U (0) 2 *Jones M (pen), Pejic)*

Walsall (1) 1 *(Bertschin)* 5569

Hereford U: Elliott; Jones M A, Devine, Hemming, Peacock, Pejic, Jones M, Narbett, Robinson, Jones R, Benbow.
Walsall: Barber; Gritt (Marsh), Mower, Taylor, Forbes, Skipper, Goodwin, Rimmer, Bertschin, Hawker, Littlejohn.

Huddersfield T (1) 3 *(Smith, Maskell, Lever (og))*

Grimsby T (1) 1 *(Gilbert)* 9901

Huddersfield T: Martin; Marsden, Hutchings, May, Mitchell, Lewis, O'Regan, Bray, Onuora (Cecere), Maskell, Smith.
Grimsby T: Reece; McDermott, Cockerill, Tillson, Lever (Hargreaves), Cunnington, Childs, Gilbert, Rees, Birtles (Jobling), Alexander.

Hull C (0) 0

Newcastle U (0) 1 *(O'Brien)* 10,743

Hull C: Hesford; Brown, Jacobs, Jobson, Terry, De Mange, Roberts (Jenkinson), Payton, Swan (Whitehurst), Askew, Doyle.
Newcastle U: Burridge; Anderson, Stimson, Dillon, Scott, Kristensen, Fereday, Brock, Quinn, McGhee, O'Brien.

Leeds U (0) 0

Ipswich T (0) 1 *(Dozzell)* 26,766

Leeds U: Day; Sterland, Kerr, Jones, Fairclough, Haddock, Strachan, Batty, Baird (Pearson), Shutt, (Snodin), Hendrie.
Ipswich T: Forrest; Stockwell, Thompson, Yallop, Humes, Linighan, Donowa, Dozzell, Wark, Kiwomya, Milton.

Leicester C (1) 1 *(Paris)*

Barnsley (0) 2 *(Currie, Lowndes)* 16,278

Leicester C: Hodge; Mauchlen, Paris, Mills, Walsh (Morgan), James, Reid, Russell, Baraclough (Ramsey), McAllister, Wright.
Barnsley: Baker; Dobbin, Cross, Futcher, Shotton, Smith, Lowndes, Agnew (Banks), Cooper (Foreman), Currie, Archdeacon.

Manchester C (0) 0

Millwall (0) 0 25,038

Manchester C: Dibble; Harper, Hinchcliffe, Reid, Hendry, Redmond, White, Ward M, Allen (Ward A), Megson, Lake.
Millwall: Branagan; Stevens, Dawes, Briley, Wood, McLeary, Carter, Hurlock, Goddard, Cascarino, Stephenson.

Middlesbrough (0) 0

Everton (0) 0 20,075

Middlesbrough: Pears; Parkinson, Cooper, Mowbray, Coleman, Ripley, Slaven, Proctor (Kerr), Kernaghan, Brennan, Davenport.
Everton: Southall; Snodin, McDonald, Ratcliffe, Watson, Whiteside, Atteveld, McCall, Sharp, Newell, Beagrie.

Northampton T (1) 1 *(Berry)*

Coventry C (0) 0 11,648

Northampton T: Gleasure; Chard, Gernon, Thomas, Wilcox, McPherson, Berry, Quow, Collins, Barnes, Brown.
Coventry C: Ogrizovic; Borrows, Downs, MacDonald, Billing, Peake, Drinkell, Speedie, McGrath, Gynn (Regis), Smith.

Plymouth Arg (0) 0

Oxford U (0) 1 *(Simpson)* 7384

Plymouth Arg: Wilmot; Brown, Whiston, Marker, Burrows, Hodges, Byrne, Morrison, Tynan, Thomas, Summerfield.
Oxford U: Kee; Smart, Phillips L, Lewis, Foster, Evans, Heath, McClaren, Durnin, Stein, Simpson.

Reading (0) 2 *(Jones 2)*

Sunderland (1) 1 *(Armstrong)* 9344

Reading: Francis; Jones, Richardson, Gooding, Hicks, Whitlock, Beavon, Tait, Senior, Gilkes, Moran.
Sunderland: Norman; Kay, Lynch, Agboola, MacPhail, Owers, Bracewell, Armstrong, Gates (Hauser), Gabbiadini, Pascoe.

Rochdale (0) 1 *(Johnson)*

Whitley Bay (0) 0 5781

Rochdale: Welch; Goodison, Burns, Brown, Cole, Ward, Holmes (Hill), Johnson, Dawson, O'Shaughnessy, Graham.
Whitley Bay: Harrison; Liddle (Scott), Teasdale, Robinson, Gowens, Wharton, Walker (Haire), Dawson, Pearson, Todd, Johnson.

Sheffield U (2) 2 *(Bryson, Agana)*

Bournemouth (0) 0 11,944

Sheffield U: Tracey; Hill, Barnes, Booker (Rostron), Stancliffe, Morris, Bradshaw (Francis), Webster, Agana, Lake, Bryson.
Bournemouth: Peyton; Bond, Morrell, Teale (Moulden), Williams, Peacock, Lawrence, Shearer, Holmes, Miller, Blissett.

Stoke C (0) 0

Arsenal (0) 1 *(Quinn)* 23,827

Stoke C: Fox; Butler, Carr, Kamara, Holmes, Fowler, Ware (Hackett), Beeston, Saunders, Biggins, Sandford.
Arsenal: Lukic; Dixon, Davis, Thomas (Jonsson), O'Leary, Adams, Quinn, Richardson, Groves, Bould, Merson (Rocastle).

Swansea C (0) 0

Liverpool (0) 0 16,098

Swansea C: Bracey; Trick, Coleman, Melville, Walker, Thornber, Harris, Curtis, Hughes, Chalmers, Legg.

Liverpool: Grobbelaar; Hysen, Venison, Nicol, Whelan, Hansen, Beardsley, Staunton, Rush, Barnes, McMahon.

Torquay U (0) 1 *(Hirons)*

West Ham U (0) 0 5342

Torquay U: Veysey; Holmes, Lloyd, Matthews, Elliott, Uzzell, Smith P, Edwards, Taylor, Caldwell (Hirons), Weston.
West Ham U: Parkes; Potts, Dicks, Parris (Rosenior), Martin, Gale, Quinn, Bishop, Keen, Morley, Allen.

Tottenham H (0) 1 *(Howells)*

Southampton (2) 3 *(Le Tissier, Horne, Wallace Rod)* 33,134

Tottenham H: Mimms; Thomas, Hughton, Bergsson, Howells, Mabbutt, Samways (Walsh), Allen, Stewart, Lineker, Sedgley.
Southampton: Flowers; Dodd, Benali, Case, Moore, Osman, Le Tissier, Horne, Rideout (Shearer) Cockerill, Wallace Rod.

Watford (0) 2 *(Roeder, Hodges)*

Wigan Ath (0) 0 10,069

Watford: Coton; Gibbs, Ashby, Richardson, Holdsworth, Roeder, Henry, Wilkinson, Penrice, Porter, Hodges.
Wigan Ath: Hughes; Senior, Tankard, Parkinson, Atherton, Johnson, Thompson, Hilditch, Rimmer (Pilling), Daley, Carberry (Griffiths).

WBA (1) 2 *(Robson, Bartlett)*

Wimbledon (0) 0 12,986

WBA: Naylor; Dobbins, Harvey, Robson, North, Whyte, Ford, Goodman, West, McNally, Bartlett.
Wimbledon: Segers; Kruszynski, Phelan, Scales, Young, Curle, Fairweather, Fashanu (Cork), Gibson, Ryan (Joseph), Wise.

Wolverhampton W (0) 1 *(Bull)*

Sheffield W (0) 2 *(Shirtliff, Atkinson)* 23,800

Wolverhampton W: Kendall; Bennett, Venus, Streete, Paskin (Jones), Bellamy, Downing, Dennison, Bull, Mutch, Cook.
Sheffield W: Turner; Nilsson, King, Palmer, Shirtliff, Pearson, Carr, Sheridan, Hirst, Atkinson, Worthington.

7 JAN

Charlton Ath (0) 1 *(Jones)*

Bradford C (1) 1 *(Tinnion (pen))* 5357

Charlton Ath: Bolder; Humphrey, Mortimer, Peake, McLaughlin, Caton, Lee, Williams, McKenzie, Walsh, Jones.
Bradford C: Tomlinson; Mitchell, Tinnion, Aizlewood, Sinnott, Evans, Abbott, Davies, Leonard, Jewell, Jackson.

Nottingham F (0) 0

Manchester U (0) 1 *(Robins)* 23,072

Nottingham F: Sutton; Laws (Charles), Pearce, Walker, Chettle, Hodge, Crosby, Parker, Clough, Jemson, Orlygsson (Wilson).
Manchester U: Leighton; Anderson, Martin, Bruce, Phelan, Pallister, Beardsmore, Blackmore (Duxbury), McClair, Hughes, Robins.

Port Vale (0) 1 *(Beckford)*

Derby Co (1) 1 *(Hebberd)* 17,478

Port Vale: Grew; Mills, Hughes, Walker, Aspin, Glover, Porter, Earle, Cross, Beckford, Riley (Millar).
Derby Co: Shilton; Sage, Forsyth, Williams, Hindmarch, Blades (Cross), Pickering, Saunders, Ramage (Francis), Hebberd, McCord.

THIRD ROUND REPLAYS

9 JAN

Darlington (1) 1 *(McJannet)*

Cambridge U (0) 3 *(Taylor, Philpott, Dublin)* 9003

Darlington: Prudhoe; McJannet, Gray, Willis, Smith, Corner, Borthwick, Toman, Stephens, Cork, Emson.
Cambridge U: Vaughan; Bailie (Fensome), Kimble, Clayton (O'Shea), Chapple, Daish, Cheetham, Leadbitter, Dublin, Taylor, Philpott.

Liverpool (3) 8 *(Barnes 2, Whelan, Beardsley, Nicol, Rush 3)*

Swansea C (0) 0 29,149

Liverpool: Grobbelaar; Hysen, Venison, Nicol, Whelan, Hansen, Beardsley, Staunton, Rush, Barnes, McMahon.
Swansea C: Bracey; Trick (Hutchison), Coleman, Melville, Walker, Thornber, Harris, Curtis (James), Hughes, Chalmers, Legg.

Millwall (1) 1 *(Carter)*

Manchester C (0) 1 *(Hendry)* aet 17,696

Millwall: Branagan; Stevens, Dawes, Briley, Wood, McLeary, Carter (Coleman), Hurlock, Goddard, Cascarino, Stephenson.
Manchester C: Dibble; Harper, Hinchcliffe, Reid, Hendry, Redmond, White, Ward M, Allen, Megson, Lake.

10 JAN

Aston Villa (2) 3 *(Ormondroyd, Daley, May (og))*

Blackburn R (1) 1 *(Kennedy)* 31,169

Aston Villa: Spink; Gage, Williams (Birch), McGrath, Mountfield, Price, Daley, Platt, Olney, Cowans, Ormondroyd.
Blackburn R: Gennoe; Reid (Johnrose), Sulley (Gayle), Finnigan, May, Mail, Kennedy, Millar, Stapleton, Garner, Sellars.

Bradford C (0) 0

Charlton Ath (2) 3 *(Lee, Williams, Jones)* 8424

Bradford C: Tomlinson; Mitchell, Tinnion, Aizlewood, Sinnott, Evans, Jackson, Abbott (Campbell), Davies, Leonard, Jewell.
Charlton Ath: Bolder; Humphrey, Mortimer, Peake, McLaughlin, Caton, Lee, Williams, MacKenzie, Walsh, Jones.

Crewe Alex (0) 0

Chelsea (1) 2 *(Dixon 2)* 7200

Crewe Alex: Greygoose; Swain, Edwards P, Callaghan, Dyson (Jasper), Smart, Joseph, Murphy, Cutler, Clayton (Hignett), Walters.
Chelsea: Beasant; Clarke, Le Saux, Roberts, Monkou, Johnsen, Bumstead, Nicholas, Dixon, Durie (Lee), Wilson K.

Derby Co (0) 2 *(Ramage, Francis)*
Port Vale (0) 3 *(Hindmarch (og), Walker, Cross)*
                                                    21,389
Derby Co: Shilton; Sage, Forsyth, Williams, Wright, Hindmarch, Pickering, Saunders, Ramage (Francis), Hebberd, McCord.
Port Vale: Grew; Mills, Hughes, Walker, Aspin, Glover, Porter, Earle, Cross, Beckford, Jeffers.

Everton (1) 1 *(Sheedy)*
Middlesbrough (0) 1 *(Parkinson)*   aet 24,352
Everton: Southall; Snodin, McDonald, Ratcliffe, Keown, Whiteside (Cottee), Beagrie (Nevin), McCall, Sharp, Newell, Sheedy.
Middlesbrough: Pears; Parkinson, Cooper, Mowbray, Coleman, Ripley, Slaven, Proctor, Kernaghan (Kerr), Brennan, Davenport.

Norwich C (1) 2 *(Rosario, Gordon)*
Exeter C (0) 0   18,202
Norwich C: Gunn; Culverhouse, Bowen, Butterworth, Linighan, Townsend, Gordon, Fleck, Rosario, Crook, Phillips.
Exeter C: Miller; Hiley, Benjamin, McNichol, Taylor, Whitehead, Rowbotham, Bailey, McDermott (Cooper), Neville (Batty), Frankland.

Oldham Ath (0) 1 *(Holden R)*
Birmingham C (0) 0   9982
Oldham Ath: Hallworth; Irwin, Barlow (Heseltine), Henry, Barrett, Marshall, Adams, Palmer, McGarvey, Milligan, Holden R.
Birmingham C: Thomas; Clarkson, Frain, Atkins, Overson, Matthewson, Bell (Yates), Bailey, Sturridge, Gleghorn, Langley.

QPR (0) 2 *(Wilkins, Wegerle)*
Cardiff C (0) 0   12,226
QPR: Seaman; Bardsley, Sansom, Parker, McDonald, Maddix, Wilkins, Barker, Falco, Wegerle, Sinton.
Cardiff C: Hansbury; Rodgerson, Daniel, Barnard (Youds), Abraham, Gibbins, Morgan, Griffith, Pike, Perry, Kelly.

THIRD ROUND SECOND REPLAYS

15 JAN

Millwall (2) 3 *(Goddard, Sheringham 2)*
Manchester C (0) 1 *(Lake)*   17,771
Millwall: Branagan; Salman, Dawes, Waddock, Wood, McLeary, Sheringham, Hurlock (Briley), Goddard, Cascarino, Stephenson.
Manchester C: Dibble; Harper, Hinchcliffe, Reid, Hendry, Redmond, White, Ward M, Allen (Brightwell) (Ward A), Megson, Lake.

17 JAN

Everton (0) 1 *(Whiteside)*
Middlesbrough (0) 0   23,866
Everton: Southall; Snodin, McDonald, Ratcliffe, Keown, Whiteside, Nevin, McCall, Sharp, Newell (Cottee), Sheedy (Atteveld).
Middlesbrough: Pears; Parkinson, Cooper, Mowbray, Coleman, Ripley, Slaven, Proctor, Kerr, Brennan, Davenport (Kernaghan).

FOURTH ROUND

27 JAN

Arsenal (0) 0
QPR (0) 0   43,483
Arsenal: Lukic; Dixon, Winterburn, Davis (Thomas), O'Leary, Adams, Rocastle, Richardson, Smith, Bould (Merson), Groves.
QPR: Seaman; Bardsley, Sansom, Parker, McDonald, Maddix, Wilkins, Barker, Clarke, Wegerle (Wright), Sinton.

Aston Villa (2) 6 *(Platt, Birch, Olney, Gray 2)*
Port Vale (0) 0   36,532
Aston Villa: Spink; Price, Gage, McGrath, Mountfield (Gray), Nielsen, Birch, Platt, Olney (Heath), Cowans, Ormondroyd.
Port Vale: Grew; Mills, Hughes, Walker, Aspin, Glover, Porter (Millar), Earle, Cross, Beckford, Jeffers.

Barnsley (2) 2 *(Taggart, Cooper)*
Ipswich T (0) 0   14,440
Barnsley: Baker; Dobbin, Taggart, Futcher, Shotton, Smith, Lowndes, Agnew, Glover, Gray (Tiler), Cooper.
Ipswich T: Forrest; Humes, Thompson, Stockwell (Gayle), Gregory (Yallop), Linighan, Lowe, Dozzell, Wark, Donowa, Milton.

Blackpool (0) 1 *(Owen)*
Torquay U (0) 0   6781
Blackpool: McIlhargey; Wright, Morgan, Coughlin (Bradshaw), Methven, Elliott, Gore, Groves, Owen (Davies), Garner, Eyres.
Torquay U: Veysey; Holmes, Lloyd, Joyce (Matthews), Elliott, Uzzell, Smith P, Taylor (Airey), Bastow, Caldwell, Hirons.

Bristol C (1) 3 *(Turner 2, Gavin)*
Chelsea (0) 1 *(Wilson K)*   24,535
Bristol C: Sinclair; Llewellyn, Bailey, Shelton, Humphries, Rennie, Gavin, Newman, Taylor, Smith, Turner.
Chelsea: Beasant; Clarke, Dorigo, Roberts, Johansen, Monkou (Lee), McAllister, Bumstead, Dixon, Wilson K, Le Saux.

Crystal Palace (2) 4 *(Hopkins, Lewis (og), Bright, Salako)*
Huddersfield T (0) 0   12,920
Crystal Palace: Martyn; Pemberton, Burke, Gray, Hopkins, Thorn, Dyer, Thomas, Bright, Salako, Barber.
Huddersfield T: Martin; Marsden (O'Regan), Hutchings, May, Mitchell, Lewis, Wilson, Bray, Cecere (Onuora), Maskell, Smith.

Millwall (1) 1 *(Cascarino)*
Cambridge U (0) 1 *(Taylor)*   14,573
Millwall: Branagan; Salman, Dawes, Waddock (Briley), Wood, McLeary, Sheringham, Hurlock, Goddard (Carter), Cascarino, Stephenson.
Cambridge U: Vaughan; Fensome, Kimble, Bailie, Chapple, Daish, Cheetham, Leadbitter, Dublin, Taylor, Philpott.

Oldham Ath (0) 2 *(McGarvey, Ritchie)*
Brighton & HA (0) 1 *(Barham)*   11,034
Oldham Ath: Hallworth; Irwin, Barlow, Henry, Barrett, Marshall, Redfearn (Adams), Ritchie (Palmer), McGarvey, Milligan, Holden R.

Brighton & HA: Keeley; Chivers, Chapman, Curbishley, Gatting, Dublin, Nelson, Barham, Bremner (Wood), Codner, Wilkins.

Reading (2) 3 *(Jones, Senior, Gilkes)*

Newcastle U (2) 3 *(Quinn, McGhee 2)*   11,989

Reading: Francis; Jones, Richardson, Gooding (Leworthy), Hicks, Whitlock, Beavon, Tait (Conroy), Senior, Moran, Gilkes.
Newcastle U: Burridge; Stimson, Ranson, Aitken, Scott, Kristensen, Gallacher, Sweeney, Quinn, McGhee, O'Brien (Dillon).

Rochdale (0) 3 *(O'Shaughnessy, Dawson, Goodison (og))*

Northampton T (0) 0   9048

Rochdale: Welch; Goodison, Burns, Brown, Cole, Ward, Holmes, Milner, Dawson, O'Shaughnessy, Graham.
Northampton T: Gleasure; Chard, Wilson, Thomas, Wilcox, McPherson, Berry (Singleton), Quow (Donald), Collins, Barnes, Brown.

Sheffield U (1) 1 *(Ashby (og))*

Watford (0) 1 *(Penrice)*   19,435

Sheffield U: Benstead; Hill, Barnes, Webster, Stancliffe, Morris, Bradshaw, Gannon, Agana, Deane, Bryson.
Watford: Coton; Gibbs, Ashby, Williams, Holdsworth, Roeder, Henry, Penrice, Roberts (Thompson), Porter, Hodges.

Southampton (0) 1 *(Ruddock)*

Oxford U (0) 0   19,802

Southampton: Flowers; Dodd, Benali, Case, Ruddock, Osman, Le Tissier, Cockerill, Rideout (Shearer), Horne, Wallace Rod.
Oxford U: Kee; Smart, Phillips, Lewis, Foster, Evans, Heath (Nogan), McClaren, Penney, Stein, Simpson.

WBA (0) 1 *(Ford)*

Charlton Ath (0) 0   18,172

WBA: Naylor; Burgess, Harbey, Robson (Talbot), North, Whyte (Foster), Ford, Goodman, West, McNally, Bartlett.
Charlton Ath: Salmon; Humphrey, Minto, Peake, McLaughlin, Caton, Lee (MacKenzie), Williams, Jones (Leaburn), Walsh, Mortimer.

28 JAN

Hereford U (0) 0

Manchester U (0) 1 *(Blackmore)*   13,777

Hereford U: Elliott; Jones M A, Devine, Hemming, Peacock, Pejic, Jones M, Narbett, Robinson, Benbow, Tester.
Manchester U: Leighton; Anderson, Martin, Donaghy, Duxbury, Pallister, Blackmore, Ince (Beardsmore), McClair, Hughes, Wallace.

Norwich C (0) 0

Liverpool (0) 0   23,162

Norwich C: Gunn; Culverhouse, Bowen, Butterworth, Linighan, Townsend, Gordon, Fleck, Rosario, Crook, Phillips.
Liverpool: Grobbelaar; Hysen, Venison, Nicol, Whelan, Hansen, Beardsley, Stanton, Rush, Barnes, McMahon.

Sheffield W (1) 1 *(Hirst)*

Everton (2) 2 *(Whiteside 2)*   31,754

Sheffield W: Turner; Nilsson, King, Palmer, Shirtliff, Pearson, Carr (Whitton), Sheridan, Hirst, Atkinson, Worthington.

Everton: Southall; Snodin, McDonald, Ratcliffe, Watson, Whiteside, Keown, McCall, Sharp, Newell (Nevin), Sheedy.

FOURTH ROUND REPLAYS

30 JAN

Cambridge U (0) 1 *(Thompson (og))*

Millwall (0) 0   *aet* 9591

Cambridge U: Vaughan; Fensome, Kimble, Bailie, Chapple, Daish, Cheetham, Leadbitter, Dublin, Taylor, Philpott.
Millwall: Branagan; Thompson, Dawes, Treacy, Wood, McLeary, Carter (Goddard), Briley, Sheringham, Cascarino, Stephenson.

Watford (1) 1 *(Porter (pen))*

Sheffield U (1) 2 *(Deane, Stancliffe)*   13,922

Watford: Coton; Gibbs, Ashby, Williams, Holdsworth, Roeder, Henry, Penrice, Thompson, Porter, Hodges (Wilkinson).
Sheffield U: Treacy; Hill (Booker), Barnes, Webster, Stancliffe, Morris, Bradshaw, Gannon, Agana, Deane, Bryson (Whitehouse).

31 JAN

Liverpool (1) 3 *(Nicol, Barnes, Beardsley (pen))*

Norwich C (1) 1 *(Fleck)*   29,339

Liverpool: Grobbelaar; Hysen, Venison, Nicol, Whelan, Hansen, Beardsley, Staunton (Burrows), Rush, Barnes, McMahon.
Norwich C: Gunn; Culverhouse, Bowen, Butterworth, Linighan, Townsend, Gordon, Fleck, Rosario, Crook, Phillips.

Newcastle U (2) 4 *(McGhee 2, Quinn, Robinson)*

Reading (0) 1 *(Senior)*   26,233

Newcastle U: Burridge; Ranson (Robinson), Stimson, Aitken (Bradshaw), Scott, Kristensen, Gallacher, Dillon, Quinn, McGhee, Sweeney.
Reading: Francis; Jones, Richardson, Gooding, Hicks, Whitlock (Wood), Beavon, Tait, Senior, Gilkes, Moran (Conroy).

QPR (0) 2 *(Sansom, Sinton)*

Arsenal (0) 0   21,547

QPR: Seaman; Bardsley, Sansom, Parker, McDonald, Maddix, Wilkins, Barker, Clarke, Wegerle, Sinton.
Arsenal: Lukic; Dixon, Winterburn, Thomas, O'Leary, Adams, Rocastle, Richardson, Smith, Bould, Groves (Merson).

FIFTH ROUND

17 FEB

Bristol C (0) 0

Cambridge U (0) 0   20,676

Bristol C: Sinclair; Llewellyn, Bailey, Shelton, Humphries, Rennie, Gavin, Newman, Taylor, Smith, Turner.
Cambridge U: Vaughan; Fensome, Bailie (O'Shea), Leadbitter, Chapple, Daish, Cheetham, Kimble, Dublin, Taylor, Philpott.

Crystal Palace (0) 1 *(Barber)*

Rochdale (0) 0   17,044

Crystal Palace: Martyn; Pemberton, Shaw, Gray (Dyer), Hopkins, Thorn, Barber, Thomas, Bright, Salako, Pardew.
Rochdale: Welch; Goodison, Burns, Brown, Cole, Ward, Holmes, Duxbury, Dawson (Johnson), O'Shaughnessy (Hill), Milner.

Liverpool (1) 3 *(Rush, Beardsley, Nicol)*
Southampton (0) 0   35,961
Liverpool: Grobbelaar; Hysen, Venison, Nicol, Whelan, Hansen, Beardsley, Burrows, Rush, Barnes (Houghton), McMahon.
Southampton: Flowers; Horne, Benali, Case, Moore, Osman, Wallace Ray (Lee), Cockerill, Rideout, Shearer (Maddison), Wallace Rod.

Oldham Ath (0) 2 *(Ritchie (pen), Palmer)*
Everton (2) 2 *(Sharp, Cottee)*   19,320
Oldham Ath: Hallworth; Irwin, Barlow, Henry, Marshall, Barrett, Adams (Warhurst), Ritchie, Palmer, Milligan, Holden R.
Everton: Southall; Snodin, McDonald, Ratcliffe, Watson, Whiteside, Ebbrell, McCall, Sharp, Cottee, Sheedy.

WBA (0) 0
Aston Villa (1) 2 *(Mountfield, Daley)*   26,585
WBA: Naylor; Burgess, Harbey, Robson (Talbot), North, Whyte, Shakespeare, Goodman, West (Foster), McNally, Bartlett.
Aston Villa: Spink; Price, Gage, McGrath, Mountfield, Nielsen, Daley, Platt, Olney, Cowans, Ormondroyd.

18 FEB

Blackpool (1) 2 *(Groves, Eyres)*
QPR (1) 2 *(Clarke 2)*   9641
Blackpool: McIlhargey; Wright, Morgan, Coughlin, Methven, Bradshaw, Gore, Groves, Brook (Owen), Garner, Eyres.
QPR: Seaman; Bardsley, Sansom, Parker, McDonald, Maddix, Wilkins, Barker, Clarke, Wegerle, Sinton.

Newcastle U (0) 2 *(McGhee (pen), Scott)*
Manchester U (1) 3 *(Robins, Wallace, McClair)*
                                                31,748
Newcastle U: Burridge; Ranson, Stimson, Aitken, Scott, Bradshaw, Brock, Dillon, Quinn, McGhee, Sweeney (Brazil).
Manchester U: Leighton; Anderson, Martin, Bruce, Phelan, Pallister, Robins (Beardsmore), Duxbury (Ince), McClair, Hughes, Wallace.

Sheffield U (1) 2 *(Bradshaw, Bryson)*
Barnsley (2) 2 *(Smith, Cooper)*   33,113
Sheffield U: Tracey; Hill, Barnes, Webster (Booker), Stancliffe, Morris, Bradshaw (Whitehouse), Gannon, Agana, Deane, Bryson.
Barnsley: Baker; Lowndes, Taggart, Futcher, Shotton, Smith (Cross), Robinson (Foreman), Banks, Glover, Agnew, Cooper.

FIFTH ROUND REPLAYS

21 FEB

Barnsley (0) 0
Sheffield U (0) 0   *aet* 27,672
Barnsley: Baker; Lowndes, Taggart, Futcher, Cross, Tiler, Robinson, Banks, Glover, Agnew, Cooper.
Sheffield U: Tracey; Hill (Webster), Barnes, Booker, Stancliffe, Morris, Bradshaw (Todd), Gannon, Agana, Deane, Whitehouse.

Cambridge U (0) 0 *(Dublin)*
Bristol C (0) 1 *(Taylor)*   *aet* 9796
Cambridge U: Vaughan; Fensome, Kimble, Bailie, Chapple, Daish, Cheetham, Leadbitter, Dublin, Taylor, Philpott.

Bristol C: Sinclair; Llewellyn, Bailey, Shelton, Humphries, Rennie, Gavin, Newman, Taylor, Smith, Turner.

Everton (0) 1 *(Sheedy (pen))*
Oldham Ath (0) 1 *(Marshall)*   *aet* 36,663
Everton: Southall; Snodin, McDonald (Nevin), Ratcliffe, Watson, Whiteside, Atteveld (Newell), McCall, Sharp, Cottee, Sheedy.
Oldham Ath: Hallworth; Irwin, Barlow, Henry (Redfearn), Warhurst, Barrett, Adams, Palmer, Marshall, Milligan, Holden R.

QPR (0) 0
Blackpool (0) 0   *aet* 15,323
QPR: Seaman; Bardsley, Sansom, Parker, McDonald, Maddix, Wilkins, Barker, Clarke, Wegerle (Wright), Sinton.
Blackpool: McIlhargey; Wright, Morgan (Davies), Owen (Diamond), Methven, Bradshaw, Gore, Groves, Brook, Garner, Eyres.

FIFTH ROUND SECOND REPLAYS

26 FEB

QPR (0) 3 *(Sinton, Sansom, Barker (pen))*
Blackpool (0) 0   12,775
QPR: Seaman; Bardsley, Sansom, Parker, McDonald, Maddix, Wilkins, Barker, Clarke, Wegerle, Sinton.
Blackpool: McIlhargey; Wright, Morgan (Owen), Coughlin (Davies), Methven, Bradshaw, Gore, Groves, Brook, Garner, Eyres.

27 FEB

Cambridge U (1) 5 *(Leadbitter, Philpott, Dublin 2, Taylor)*
Bristol C (0) 1 *(Taylor)*   9047
Cambridge U: Vaughan; Fensome, Kimble, Bailie (O'Shea), Chapple, Daish, Cheetham (Robinson), Leadbitter, Dublin, Taylor, Philpott.
Bristol C: Leaning; Llewellyn, Bailey, Shelton, Humphries, Rennie, Gavin (Mellon), Newman, Taylor, Smith, Turner.

5 MAR

Barnsley (0) 0
Sheffield U (0) 1 *(Agana (pen))*   *aet* 26,560
Barnsley: Baker; Lowndes (Deehan), Taggart, Futcher, Cross, Tiler, Robinson (Archdeacon), Banks, Glover, Agnew, Cooper.
Sheffield U: Tracey; Hill, Barnes, Booker, Stancliffe, Todd, Bradshaw (Bryson), Gannon, Agana (Carr), Deane, Whitehouse.

10 MAR

Oldham Ath (1) 2 *(Palmer, Marshall (pen))*
Everton (1) 1 *(Cottee)*   *aet* 19,346
Oldham Ath: Hallworth; Irwin, Barlow, Henry, Barrett, Redfearn, Adams (Warhurst), Palmer, Marshall, Milligan, Holden R.
Everton: Southall; Snodin, McDonald (Newell), Ratcliffe, Keown, Ebbrell, Attveld (Beagrie), McCall, Sharp, Cottee, Sheedy.

SIXTH ROUND

Cambridge U (0) 0
Crystal Palace (0) 1 *(Thomas)*   10,084
Cambridge U: Vaughan; Fensome, Kimble, Bailie, Chapple, Daish, Cheetham, Leadbitter, Dublin, Taylor, Philpott.

*Crystal Palace:*Martyn; Pemberton, Shaw, Gray, O'Reilly, Thorn, Barber, Thomas, Salako, Wright, Pardew.

11 MAR

QPR (1) 2 *(Wilkins, Barker)*

Liverpool (0) 2 *(Barnes, Rush)*   21,057

QPR: Seaman; Bardsley, Sansom, Parker, McDonald, Maddix, Wilkins, Barker, Clarke, Wegerle (Falco), Sinton.
Liverpool: Grobbelaar; Hysen, Venison (Gillespie), Nicol, Whelan, Hansen, Beardsley (Staunton), Houghton, Rush, Barnes, McMahon.

Sheffield U (0) 0

Manchester U (1) 1 *(McClair)*   34,344

Sheffield U: Tracey; Hill, Barnes, Booker, Stancliffe, Todd, Bradshaw (Bryson), Gannon, Agana, Deane, Whitehouse (Rostron).
Manchester U: Leighton; Anderson (Duxbury), Martin, Bruce, Phelan, Pallister, Robins, Ince, McClair, Hughes, Wallace.

14 MAR

Oldham Ath (1) 3 *(Holden R, Price (og), Redfearn)*

Aston Villa (0) 0   19,490

Oldham Ath: Hallworth; Irwin, Barlow, Henry, Warhurst, Barrett, Redfearn, Palmer, Marshall, Milligan, Holden R.
Aston Villa: Spink; Price, Gage, McGrath, Gray, Nielsen, Daley (Birch), Platt, Olney, Cowans, Gallacher.

SIXTH ROUND REPLAY

Liverpool (1) 1 *(Beardsley)*

QPR (0) 0   38,090

Liverpool: Grobbelaar; Hysen, Venison, Nicol, Whelan, Hansen, Beardsley, Houghton, Rush, Barnes, McMahon.
QPR: Seaman; Bardsley, Sansom, Parker, McDonald, Maddix, Wilkins, Barker, Clarke, Wegerle (Falco), Sinton.

SEMI-FINALS

8 APR

Crystal Palace (0) 4 *(Bright, O'Reilly, Gray, Pardew)*

Liverpool (1) 3 *(Rush, McMahon, Barnes (pen))*
    at Villa Park aet 38,389

Crystal Palace: Martyn; Pemberton, Shaw, Gray, O'Reilly, Thorn, Barber, Thomas, Bright, Salako, Pardew.

Liverpool: Grobbelaar; Hysen, Burrows, Gillespie (Venison), Whelan, Hansen, Beardsley, Houghton, Rush (Staunton), Barnes, McMahon.

Manchester U (1) 3 *(Robson, Webb, Wallace)*

Oldham Ath (1) 3 *(Barrett, Marshall, Palmer)*
    at Maine Road aet 44,026

Manchester U: Leighton; Martin (Robins), Gibson, Bruce, Phelan, Pallister, Robson (Wallace), Ince, McClair, Hughes, Webb.
Oldham Ath: Hallworth; Irwin, Barlow, Henry (Warhurst), Barrett, Holden A, Redfearn, Ritchie (Palmer), Marshall, Milligan, Holden R.

SEMI-FINAL REPLAY

11 APR

Manchester U (0) 2 *(McClair, Robins)*

Oldham Ath (0) 1 *(Ritchie) at Maine Road aet* 35,005

Manchester U: Leighton; Ince, Martin (Robins), Bruce, Phelan, Pallister, Robson, Webb, McClair, Hughes, Wallace.
Oldham Ath: Hallworth; Irwin, Barlow (Palmer), Henry, Barrett, Holden A, Redfearn, Ritchie, Marshall (Warhurst), Milligan, Holden R.

FINAL AT WEMBLEY

12 MAY

Crystal Palace (1) 3 *(O'Reilly, Wright 2)*

Manchester U (1) 3 *(Robson, Hughes 2)*   80,000

Crystal Palace: Martyn; Pemberton, Shaw, Gray (Madden), O'Reilly, Thorn, Barber (Wright), Thomas, Bright, Salako, Pardew.
Manchester U: Leighton; Ince, Martin (Blackmore), Bruce, Phelan, Pallister (Robins), Robson, Webb, McClair, Hughes, Wallace.
Referee: A. Gunn (South Chailey).

REPLAY AT WEMBLEY

17 MAY

Crystal Palace (0) 0

Manchester U (0) 1 *(Martin)*   80,000

Crystal Palace: Martyn; Pemberton, Shaw, Gray, O'Reilly, Thorn, Barber (Wright), Thomas, Bright, Salako (Madden), Pardew.
Manchester U: Sealey; Ince, Martin, Bruce, Phelan, Pallister, Robson, Webb, McClair, Hughes, Wallace.
Referee: A. Gunn (South Chailey).

Lee Martin (3) shoots high into the Crystal Palace net in some style for Manchester United's winner in the FA Cup Final replay at Wembley. (Colorsport)

SCOTTISH FOOTBALL

Secretary
P. Donald

The Scottish Season, 1989–90

Foul weather on a Saturday in mid-December; only five league matches played, and those probably should not have been on. There is the expected call for a winter break. All right: when? The end of December and the whole of January is a suggested period (six weeks). That would mean a start again at the beginning of February. Brrrh! If you look at recent statistics, you will find that many of the worst cancellations have been in February. A longer break perhaps? That leaves us with a start in March which, although better and lighter, is by no means blameless. And how about all the good open weather which might be missed in December and January?

No, those who say that we are the only countries in Europe not to have a winter break forget that geographically we have a maritime climate and do not have a big freeze on a regular basis. My vote is for maintaining the status quo, and the odd shiver or two at times unspecified in the period November to March. Also, perhaps a readiness by the League authorities to postpone games on the previous day if the weather forecast suggests that that would be sensible.

What of the season itself? In the League, there was an appalling start by Rangers, who did look to be the strongest team. They pulled gradually up the table, and by Christmas were pulling ahead. By February they had a lead of seven points, and, whatever might be said and written, there was no way they were going to forego that – and they did not. At the lower end of the table, Dundee were seven points in arrears. There did not seem much chance of their pulling that back. And they did not, though for a moment it did just look as if they might have a chance if others faltered considerably.

Aberdeen and Hearts never looked like heading Rangers, but there was a good tussle between them for second place, which the former won. Celtic had, for them, a bad season; three spells of three games in a row without a goal, and another spell of four games in a row without a goal spelt out a depressing fact, and, although interest was there till the end, it was no real surprise when they failed to qualify for Europe, and Dundee United eased into fourth place, and maintained their proud record of appearances in European competition.

United had a season of reconstruction, with many young players blooded and, though they too suffered from a lack of goals, they could be well pleased with their overall results. Motherwell, clearly helped by a rejuvenated Davie Cooper, and Hibs both had periods of success, and both finished well up in the points, and well clear of any foot-of-the-table trouble. That was left to St Mirren and Dunfermline, but they both kept well clear of Dundee, and it was particularly pleasing to find Dunfermline establishing themselves in this company; indeed, on 8 November they stood at the top of the Premier Division for the first time in their history. It is not easy for a promoted side to find time to adjust to the demands of the Premier Division.

In the First Division the outstanding fight between St Johnstone and Airdrieonians was for the one ticket to the Premier Division; but it was a long struggle, only resolved when, at the end of March, in front of a full house at the magnificent new McDiarmid Park, Saints won a superb game to deny their opponents the title. The Perth team look equipped to enter the top ranks, and they now have a ground with facilities which must be the envy of many another club: when the opportunity arose, they showed imagination and enterprise in leading the way into the '90s.

The fact of two teams away ahead of the others, and with only one place to play for, did not altogether help the First Division. There were too many games which meant not all that much, for there was not much left to play for. But it did raise yet again the question of league reorganisation. Various proposals were made, but none got very far. The real problem is that for the top clubs, there are already sufficient fixtures, and a return to the forty-four league games of a couple of seasons ago is unthinkable, whilst the ideas of three fixtures between the teams is not at all satisfactory.

Some favour a larger Premier Division, with teams playing each other only twice: but that does look like a return to 1974, and there were distinct disadvantages then as the big teams drew further and further away from the others. In the end, I suppose, it does mean a new league for the big teams, and reconstruction for the others. At the other end, it does seem a pity that some arrangement cannot be found to introduce new blood at the foot of the league: there are teams which would flourish, and would provide good weekly crowds. But to some of the lowly league teams it would mean extinction, and the entrenched establishment of many years supports the continuation of the present system.

The lower end of the First Division was interesting, but gradually one team after another drew away from the relegation zone, and the last weeks were a battle amongst Forfar (who had not helped their cause by losing two points for playing an unregistered player), Alloa and Albion Rovers. Forfar just won the encounter, so the two who had been promoted last season returned to the Second Division, adjustment to the higher ranks had again proved too difficult.

Then to the Second Division. It took a couple of months to sort out which teams were going to be in the running for promotion, and which were destined to fill the lower places. Later on, Brechin City established a good lead, but the group below were all in with a shout. Kilmarnock should have been comfortably placed, for they looked the best team in the Division, but though they had several good runs, they also had some poor perform- ances, and lost games which they should have won. Dumbarton looked to be making a challenge, but trouble with the state of their ground meant that they were many games behind the others, and that is never the recipe for garnering the points; in the end they could not last the pace. Stirling Albion had their customary late thrust, and Stenhousemuir were well in the race, but in the end it was Kilmarnock who deservedly took the second promotion place, Brechin having already taken the first, and, though without much confi- dence in the final stages, the championship of the Division.

The Skol Cup once again proved an interesting start to the season, with plenty of the games going to extra time, and not a few to penalties to settle the issue. There were few upsets: St Johnstone lost to Queen of the South in the second round, and Clydebank nearly won against the Hibs, losing the penalty shootout in the end; otherwise, the senior teams were successful, and it was thus perhaps proper that the final should once again be contested by the teams who finished at the top of the table. It was the third in a row between Aberdeen and Rangers, and this time the Dons took the cup home – after extra time.

The Scottish Cup had its fair share of drama. Elgin City and Inverness Caley both had their successes against league clubs, the latter disposing, after a replay and penalties, of Airdrieonians, who were then in the middle of a good run in the league. Caley went on to face Stirling Albion, with a quarter-final place for the winner. This time the league side proved too strong after a well-contested match. Stirling now met Clydebank, fresh from their win over St Mirren, a last minute goal in the first game having given them a reprieve and a replay at home, which they just won.

Now it was a First v Second Division draw to see which would oppose Celtic in a semi- final at Hampden: it would be a first for either club. Celtic had meantime moved uneasily forward against Forfar in the third round, and had disposed of Rangers by an odd goal in the fourth: it was the first time that these two clubs had been drawn together before the semi-finals for many years. Celtic faced Clydebank, and they won comfortably, though the Bankies enjoyed every minute of their prominence and certainly did not disgrace themselves.

Aberdeen, having conceded first minute goals against both Partick and Morton in earlier rounds, had come back to win on both occasions, and had then removed Hearts in a workmanlike manner; they played Dundee U in the other semi-final, and were too good for them. And so to the final. It was by no means a bad game, but it lacked goals, and went to extra time. Still no goals, so – for the first time – a penalty shoot-out and no replay. It took twenty kicks to settle the issue. Aberdeen and Celtic each missed once, but neither goalkeeper touched the ball till the nineteenth kick which was moving into the net when Theo Snelders, with an acrobatic leap, managed to deflect it.

So Aberdeen won, and the arguments started. Was this the way to finish a cup final? Of course it is not the ideal way, but it does produce an immediate result, and the crowd coming from far and wide for this, the climax of the season, are entitled to a winner; not to the thought of a mid-week replay to which many cannot come. There was the additional thought that, for the players in the imminent World Cup, enough was enough. So it was, but the general argument in favour of the penalty shoot-out is, I think, good. I hope that it will continue to be available as the last line, but hope that it will not be used too frequently.

Our clubs did not have a distinguished season in Europe, and were all eliminated in the early stages, though not without giving a good account of themselves. Rangers went out to Bayern Munich in the first round, and Aberdeen and Celtic joined them, though the latter had a hectic scramble against Partizan Belgrade in which the newly-joined Polish player, Dariusz Dziekanowski, scored four times, but his side still managed to lose. Dundee United and Hibernian both reached the next stage, but were then eliminated – Hibs by only the narrowest of margins.

ALAN ELLIOTT

ABERDEEN

Premier Division

Year Formed: 1903. *Ground & Address:* Pittodrie Stadium, Pittodrie St, Aberdeen AB2 1QH. *Telephone:* 0224 632328.
Ground Capacity: total: 22,568 seated: All. *Size of Pitch:* 110yd×72yd.
Chairman: Richard M. Donald. *Secretary:* Ian J. Taggart. *Commercial Executive:* Dave Johnston.
Managers: Alex Smith and Jocky Scott. *Assist. Manager:* Drew Jarvie. *Physio:* David Wylie. *Coach:* Teddy Scott.
Managers since 1975: Ally MacLeod; Billy McNeill; Alex Ferguson; Ian Porterfield; Alex Smith and Jocky Scott.
Club Nickname(s): The Dons. *Previous Grounds:* None.
Record Attendance: 45,061 v Hearts, Scottish Cup 4th rd; 13 Mar, 1954.
Record Transfer Fee received: £800,000 for Steve Archibald to Tottenham Hotspur (1980).
Record Transfer Fee paid: £650,000 for Hans Gillhaus from PSV Eindhoven November 1989.
Record Victory: 13-0 v Peterhead, Scottish Cup; 9 Feb, 1923.
Record Defeat: 0-8 v Celtic, Division I; 30 Jan, 1965.

1989–90 LEAGUE RECORD

Match No.	Date	Venue	Opponents	Result	H/T Score	Lg. Pos.	Goalscorers	Atten- dance
1	Aug 12	H	Hibernian	W 1-0	0-0	—	Mason	16,000
2	19	A	Motherwell	D 0-0	0-0	2		6491
3	26	H	Dundee	W 1-0	0-0	2	Jess	12,500
4	Sept 9	A	Rangers	L 0-1	0-0	3		40,283
5	16	H	Dunfermline Ath	W 2-1	1-0	2	Mason, Robertson C	13,000
6	23	A	St Mirren	W 2-0	1-0	1	Mason, Grant	5872
7	30	H	Celtic	D 1-1	0-0	1	McLeish	21,374
8	Oct 4	A	Dundee U	L 0-2	0-1	—		11,879
9	14	H	Hearts	L 1-3	0-1	5	Van der Ark	15,000
10	25	A	Hibernian	W 3-0	1-0	—	Robertson C, Mason, Van der Ark	12,000
11	28	H	Motherwell	W 1-0	1-0	2	Bett (pen)	13,500
12	Nov 4	A	Dundee	D 1-1	1-0	2	Connor	7041
13	18	A	Dunfermline Ath	W 3-0	2-0	2	Gillhaus 2, Robertson D	11,882
14	22	H	Rangers	W 1-0	1-0	—	Gillhaus	23,000
15	25	H	St Mirren	W 5-0	3-0	1	Nicholas 3, McLeish, Mason	13,500
16	Dec 2	A	Celtic	L 0-1	0-0	1		38,300
17	9	H	Dundee U	W 2-0	0-0	1	Nicholas, Mason	15,500
18	20	A	Hearts	D 1-1	0-1	—	Grant	11,370
19	26	H	Hibernian	L 1-2	0-1	—	Grant	16,500
20	30	A	Motherwell	D 2-2	1-0	2	Van der Ark 2	7267
21	Jan 2	H	Dundee	W 5-2	4-2	2	Grant, Van der Ark 2, Bett, Nicholas	16,054
22	6	A	Rangers	L 0-2	0-0	2		41,351
23	13	H	Dunfermline Ath	W 4-1	4-1	2	Grant, Mason, Nicholas, Bett	14,000
24	27	A	St Mirren	L 0-1	0-1	3		7855
25	Feb 3	H	Hearts	D 2-2	2-1	3	Nicholas 2 (1 pen)	15,000
26	10	A	Dundee U	D 1-1	1-0	2	Mason	10,533
27	17	H	Celtic	D 1-1	1-0	2	Nicholas	22,100
28	Mar 3	A	Dunfermline Ath	W 4-2	1-0	2	Mason, Nicholas, Gillhaus 2	8228
29	10	A	Hibernian	L 2-3	0-1	2	Van der Ark, Hunter (og)	9500
30	24	H	Motherwell	W 2-0	1-0	2	Gillhaus 2	10,000
31	31	A	Dundee	D 1-1	1-1	2	Gillhaus	8071
32	Apr 8	H	Rangers	D 0-0	0-0	—		23,000
33	18	A	Dundee U	W 1-0	0-0	—	Grant	10,000
34	21	A	Hearts	L 0-1	0-0	3		11,616
35	28	H	St Mirren	W 2-0	0-0	3	Irvine, Nicholas	7977
36	May 2	A	Celtic	W 3-1	0-1	—	Jess 2, Graham Watson	20,154

Final League Position: 2

GOALSCORERS

League: (56): Nicholas 11 (1 pen), Mason 9, Gillhaus 8, Van der Ark 7, Grant 6, Bett 3 (1 pen), Jess 3, McLeish 2, Robertson C 2, Connor 1, Irvine 1, Robertson D 1, Graham Watson 1, own goal 1
Scottish Cup: (16): Gillhaus 3, Van der Ark 3, Irvine 2, Nicholas 2, Bett 1, Grant 1, Mason 1, own goals 3.
Skol Cup: (12): Mason 5, Bett 2, Cameron 2, Robertson D 1, Van der Ark 1, own goal 1.

Most Capped Players: Alex McLeish, 72, Scotland.
Most League Appearances: 556: Willie Miller, 1973–90.
Most League Goals in Season (Individual): 38: Benny Yorston, Division I; 1929–30.
Most Goals Overall (Individual): 199: Joe Harper.

Honours
League Champions: Division I 1954–55. Premier Division 1979–80, 1983–84, 1984–85; *Runners-up:* Division I 1910–11, 1936–37, 1955–56, 1970–71, 1971–72. Premier Division 1977–78, 1980–81, 1981–82, 1988–89, 1989–90.
Scottish Cup Winners: 1947, 1970, 1982, 1983, 1984, 1986, 1990; *Runners-up:* 1937, 1953, 1954, 1959, 1967, 1978.
League Cup Winners: 1955–56, 1976–77, 1985–86, 1989–90; *Runners-up:* 1946–47, 1978–79, 1979–80, 1987–88, 1988–89.
Drybrough Cup Winners: 1971, 1980.
European: *European Cup* 12 matches (1980–81, 1984–85, 1985–86); *Cup Winners Cup Winners:* 1982–83. Semi-finals 1983–84. 31 matches (1967–68, 1970–71, 1978–79, 1982–83, 1983–84, 1986–87); *UEFA Cup* 30 matches (1968–69 *Fairs Cup;* 1971–72, 1972–73, 1973–74, 1977–78, 1979–80, 1981–82, 1987–88, 1988–89).
Club colours: Shirt, Shorts, Stockings: Red with white trim.

Snelders, T	McKinnie, S	Robertson, D	Grant, B	Irvine, B	Miller, W	Nicholas, C	Bett, J	Van der Ark, W	Connor, R	Mason, P	Dodds, D	Robertson, C	Simpson, N	Cameron, I	McLeish, A	Jess, E	Robertson, I	Harvie, S	Gillhaus, H	Watt, M	Watson, Gregg	Minns, R	Watson,Graham	Wright, S	Booth, S	Match No.
1	2	3	4	5	6	7	8	9*10		11	12															1
1	2	3		5	6	7	8	9*10		12			4	11												2
1	2	3	4†		6	7	8	10	9			14	12		5	11*										3
1	2	3	4		6	7	8	11*10	9				12		5											4
1	2	3			6	7	8	12	10	9		4			5	11*										5
1	2	3	4		6	7	8	12	10	9				11*	5											6
1	2		4*12		6	7	8	14	10	9		3		11†	5											7
1	2		4 12		6	7	8	11	10	9†		3*		14	5											8
1	2	3 12			6	7*8		14	10	9		4		11†	5											9
1	2	3		6		14	8*		7	9		4			5	11†10	12									10
1	2	3*	12		6	7	8	11	10	9		4			5											11
1	2		12 3		6		8	7	10	9		4*			5	11										12
1	2	3	4	6		7	8*14		10	9		12			5				11†							13
1	2	3	4	6		7*8		12	10	9					5				11							14
1	2	3* 4		6		7	8	14	10	9†		12			5				11							15
1	2	3	4* 6			7†8		14	10	9		12			5				11							16
1	2	3	4	6		7	8	12	10*9						5				11							17
1	2	3	4	6		7	8		10	9					5				11							18
	2	3	4* 6			7	8	14	10	9		12			5				11†	1						19
	2		4 6			7		11*10	9			12	8	3	5					1						20
	2		4 6			7	8	11	10†9*			12		5	14					1	3					21
	2		4 6			7†8		11	10	9		14	12	5						1	3*					22
	2	3	4* 6			7	8	11†10	9			12		5	14					1						23
	2		4 6			7†		11	10	9		12	8	5		3*		14		1						24
1	2		4 6			7		11	10					5		3		9	8							25
	2		4 6			7		8	10	9		12		5	3			11*		1						26
	2		4 6			7	8†	10	9			12	14	5	3*11							1				27
	2		4 3	6	7	8		10	9					5				11				1				28
	2		4*3†6		7	8	14	10	9			12		5				11				1				29
	2	12	6		7	8*10†		9			4			5	14	3	11				1					30
	2		4 6			7	8	10*3	9			12		5				11				1				31
	2		4 6			7	8	3	9			10*12		5				11				1				32
1		3	4 6			7	8	10	9†				5	14		11	2*	12								33
1		3	4 6				8*	10	9			12		5	7		11					2				34
1			4 5	6	7*		10	9		2				8			11				3†12	14				35
1	2	3		5	6			7	8	11				10					12	4*	9					36
23	33	20	28	28	15	32	30	15	34	33	—	10	5	6	32	7	5	1	19	7	3	6	3	—	1	
		+	+	+		+	+	+	+	+	+	+	+	+		+	+		+		+	+	+	+	+	
		3s	3s	1s		11s	1s	1s	12s	4s	5s	4s	1s1s	1s		1s1s	1s		1s1s		1s					

AIRDRIEONIANS   First Division

Year Formed: 1878.   *Ground & Address:* Broomfield Park, Gartlea Rd, Airdrie ML6 9JL.   *Telephone:* 0236 62067.
Ground Capacity: total: 11,830   seated: 1350.   *Size of Pitch:* 112yd×67yd.
Chairman: Robert H. Davidson.   *Secretary:* George W. Peat CA.   *Commercial Manager:* Elma Nelson.
Manager: Jim Bone.   *Assistant Manager:* Ian Bird.   *Physio:* Gerry McElhill.   *Coach:* Joe Craig.
Managers since 1975: I. McMillan; J. Stewart; R. Watson; W. Munro; A. MacLeod; D. Whiteford; G. McQueen; J. Bone.
Club Nickname(s): The Diamonds or The Waysiders.   *Previous Grounds:* Mavisbank.
Record Attendance: 24,000 v Hearts, Scottish Cup; 8 Mar, 1952.
Record Transfer Fee received: £200,000 for Sandy Clark to West Ham U, May 1982.
Record Transfer Fee paid: £175,000 for Owen Coyle from Clydebank, February 1990.

1989–90 LEAGUE RECORD

Match No.	Date	Venue	Opponents	Result	H/T Score	Lg. Pos.	Goalscorers	Attendance
1	Aug 12	A	Clyde	L	0-1	0-0	—		1200
2	19	H	Hamilton A	W	1-0	1-0	7	Lawrence	2304
3	26	H	Albion R	W	1-0	0-0	6	McDonald (og)	2200
4	Sept 2	A	Morton	W	1-0	0-0	6	Lawrence	1850
5	5	H	Falkirk	D	1-1	0-0	—	Macdonald K	4319
6	9	A	Raith R	W	4-0	1-0	3	Gray, Macdonald K 2, Butler	1817
7	16	H	St Johnstone	D	2-2	1-1	3	Macdonald K, Irvine	3000
8	23	A	Partick T	L	1-2	0-1	3	Irvine	5301
9	30	H	Alloa	W	2-1	1-0	3	Boyle, Macdonald K	1250
10	Oct 7	A	Ayr U	W	3-1	1-1	3	MacDonald I, Auld, Lawrence	3371
11	14	H	Meadowbank T	W	3-1	2-0	3	Conn, Irvine (pen), Stewart	1400
12	21	A	Clydebank	W	3-0	1-0	3	Harvey, Balfour 2	1239
13	28	H	Forfar Ath	W	4-1	3-1	2	Conn, Morris (og), Irvine 2 (1 pen)	1300
14	Nov 4	A	Falkirk	L	1-3	0-3	3	Lawrence	3500
15	11	H	Raith R	W	3-2	1-1	3	Balfour, McPhee, Harvey	1800
16	18	A	St Johnstone	W	2-1	1-0	3	MacDonald I, McAdam	7123
17	25	H	Partick T	D	1-1	0-0	3	Harvey	4381
18	Dec 2	A	Alloa	W	2-0	1-0	2	Irvine, Stewart	1366
19	9	H	Ayr U	D	1-1	1-0	2	Harvey	2200
20	20	A	Meadowbank T	W	1-0	0-0	—	Lawrence	600
21	26	H	Clyde	W	1-0	1-0	—	Lawrence	2500
22	Jan 2	A	Albion R	W	2-0	2-0	—	Balfour, Gray	2682
23	6	H	Morton	W	4-1	2-1	1	MacDonald I, Lawrence, Speirs (pen), Irvine	2491
24	13	A	Forfar Ath	D	1-1	0-0	2	Lawrence	1156
25	30	H	Clydebank	D	2-2	0-2	—	Rowe (og), Grant	2200
26	Feb 3	A	Clyde	W	1-0	0-0	2	Jack	1300
27	7	A	Hamilton A	L	2-3	2-0	—	Harris (og), Gray	2699
28	10	H	Ayr U	W	6-0	1-0	1	Gray (pen), Coyle 3, MacDonald I, Harvey	2800
29	17	H	Partick T	W	3-2	1-2	1	Gray (pen), Coyle, Lawrence	3000
30	Mar 3	A	Albion R	W	2-1	1-0	1	Jack, Gray (pen)	2270
31	10	A	Forfar Ath	W	3-2	0-1	1	Balfour, Butler, Harvey	1341
32	24	H	Alloa	W	3-1	0-0	1	Coyle 2 (1 pen), Grant	1700
33	31	A	St Johnstone	L	1-3	0-0	2	Gray	9644
34	Apr 3	H	Clydebank	L	3-4	3-3	—	Coyle 2, Harvey	2600
35	7	A	Falkirk	L	1-3	1-1	2	Gray (pen)	4200
36	14	H	Meadowbank T	D	1-1	1-0	2	Watson	1750
37	21	H	Raith R	L	0-1	0-0	2		1700
38	28	A	Morton	D	1-1	1-0	2	Stewart	1235
39	May 5	H	Hamilton A	W	3-1	2-0	2	Coyle 2, Harvey	1000

Final League Position: 2

GOALSCORERS

League: (77): Coyle 10 (1 pen), Lawrence 9, Gray 8 (4 pens), Harvey 8, Irvine 7 (2 pens), Balfour 5, Macdonald K 5, MacDonald I 4, Stewart 3, Butler 2, Conn 2, Grant 2, Jack 2, Auld 1, Boyle 1, McAdam 1, McPhee 1, Speirs 1 (pen), Watson 1, own goals 4.
Scottish Cup: (3): Gray 1, Harvey 1, Lawrence 1.
Skol Cup: (4): Lawrence 2 (1 pen), Balfour 1, Butler 1.

Record Victory: 15-1 v Dundee Wanderers, Division II; 1 Dec, 1894.
Record Defeat: 1-11 v Hibernian, Division I; 24 Oct, 1959.
Most Capped Player: Jimmy Crapnell, 9, Scotland.
Most League Appearances: 523: Paul Jonquin, 1962–79.
Most League Goals in Season (Individual): 52, Hugh Baird, Division II, 1954–55.
Most Goals Overall (Individual): —.

Honours

League Champions: Division II 1902–03, 1954–55, 1973–74; *Runners-up:* Division I 1922–23, 1923–24, 1924–25, 1925–26. First Division 1979–80, 1989–90. Division II 1900–01, 1946–47, 1949–50, 1965–66.
Scottish Cup Winners: 1924; *Runners-up:* 1975.   *Scottish Spring Cup Winners:* 1976.
League Cup:—.
Club colours: Shirt: White with Red diamond. Shorts: White. Stockings: Red with white diamond tops.

Martin, J	Boyle, J	Jack, P	McKeown, B	Grant, D	McPhee, I	Lawrence, A	Balfour, E	Butler, J	Conn, S	MacDonald, I	Lawrie, D	Stewart, A	Macdonald, K	Gray, S	Walsh, R	Irvine, W	Auld, S	Harvey, G	McAdam, T	Speirs, G	Coyle, O	Watson, J	Hendry, A	Kelly, J	Match No.
1	2	3	4	5	6	7	8*	9	10	11†	12	14													1
1	2	3	4	5	6	7	8	9*	10	11			12												2
1	2	3	4	5	6	7	8	9	10	12			11*												3
1	2	3	4	5	6	11	8	9†	10*	12			14	7											4
1	2	3	4	5	6	11	8		10				9	7											5
1	2	3	4	5	6	11	8†	14	10				9	7*	12										6
1	2	3*	4	5	6	11	8		10				9	7	12										7
1	2	3	4	5*	6	11	8			12	10†		9	7	14										8
1	2	3†	4		6		10	8		11	14	12	7*	9	5										9
1	2		4			3	10	8	7	6	11		9	5											10
1	2		4	12		3	10†	8	7*	6	11		14	9	5										11
1	2		4			3		8	7	6	11		12	9	5	10*									12
1	2		4	12		3		8	7	6*	11		14	9	5	10†									13
1	2		4			3	11	8	7*	6	14		12	9†	5	10									14
1	2		4			3	10	8		6	11			7		5	9								15
1		2	12			3	10	8*		6	11			7		5	9†	4	14						16
1		2				3	10†	8*	12	6	11			7		14	5	9	4						17
1		2				3		12	8*	11	14			7		10	5	9	4	6†					18
1		2				3*	10	8		6	11			7		12	5	9	4						19
1	3	2					10†	8		12	11			7		14	5	9	4	6*					20
1	2	12					10†	8		3	11			7		14	5	9	4	6*					21
1	2						10†	8	6	3	11*			7		14	5	9	4	12					22
1	2						10		6	3	11			7		12	5	9*	4						23
1	2	12	4				10	14	6†	3	11			7			5*	9		8					24
1	2	6	12				10	8		3†	11			7		9	5*	14	4						25
1	2	6	5		10*	8				3	14			7		9		12	4	11†					26
1	2	6	5			10	8			3†	11			7		9*		12	4	14					27
1	2	6	5			12	9			3	11*			7†		14	4				8	10			28
1	2	6	5			12	9			3	11*			7			4				8	10			29
1		6	2	5		11	9			3				7		12	4				8	10*			30
1	2		4	5		11*	9	6		12				7		3	14				8	10†			31
1	12		4	5			7	6		11†				2		9	5*			10	8	14			32
1	2		4	5	12	9	6	3*	11†				7		14					10	8				33
1	2		4	5	12	6*	9		11†				7		3	8				10	14				34
1	2		4	5	14	6		11					7		12	3	9			10†	8*				35
1	2	6	5		10			3†	14				7		12	4	9			11*	8				36
1		6†	12		10			3	11				7	2		5	9			8	14	4*			37
1	2				8	10		3	11	12			7†	4	6*	5	9			14					38
1	2				6			3	14	12			7†	4		5	9			10	8*	11			39
39	30	24	21	20	19	29	34	17	29	30	—	—	5	30	3	11	25	20	15	6	10	10	1	1	
+1s	+2s		+5s			+5s	+2s	+2s	+2s	+7s	+1s	+8s	+3s1s	+1s10s		+7s		+3s		+1s	+3s				

ALBION ROVERS   Second Division

Year Formed: 1882. *Ground & Address:* Cliftonhill Stadium, Main St, Coatbridge ML5 9XX. *Telephone:* 0236 32350.
Ground Capacity: total: 8780 seated: 474. *Size of Pitch:* 110yd×70yd.
Chairman: David Forrester C.A.. *Secretary:* D. Forrester C.A.. *Commercial Manager:* Robin W. Marwick J.P.,
R.I.B.A..
Manager: David Provan. *Assistant Manager:* Joe Baker. *Physio:* Jim Maitland. *Coach:* —.
Managers since 1975: G. Caldwell; S. Goodwin; D. Whiteford; W. Wilson; T. Gemmell; D. Provan.
Club Nickname(s): The Wee Rovers. *Previous Grounds:* Meadow Park, Whifflet.
Record Attendance: 27,381 v Rangers, Scottish Cup 2nd rd; 8 Feb, 1936.
Record Transfer Fee received: £40,000 from Motherwell for Bruce Cleland.

1989–90 LEAGUE RECORD

Match No.	Date	Venue	Opponents	Result	H/T Score	Lg. Pos.	Goalscorers	Attendance
1	Aug 12	H	Ayr U	W 3-1	2-0	—	Chapman, McAnenay, Graham	1380
2	19	A	Partick T	L 0-4	0-2	9		3003
3	26	A	Airdrieonians	L 0-1	0-0	10		2200
4	Sept 2	H	Clydebank	L 3-4	0-0	11	Watson, Graham, McAnenay	861
5	5	A	Alloa	L 1-4	0-1	—	McKenzie	998
6	9	A	St Johnstone	L 1-2	0-2	13	McAnenay	4470
7	16	A	Raith R	L 1-2	1-2	14	McAnenay	1224
8	23	H	Clyde	W 2-0	1-0	13	McAnenay 2	1001
9	30	A	Falkirk	L 0-6	0-1	14		2724
10	Oct 7	H	Forfar Ath	L 0-2	0-1	14		655
11	14	A	Hamilton A	D 0-0	0-0	14		1420
12	21	H	Meadowbank T	D 0-0	0-0	14		437
13	28	A	Morton	D 0-0	0-0	14		1400
14	Nov 4	H	Alloa	D 1-1	1-0	14	Clark G	538
15	11	H	St Johnstone	L 1-3	0-1	14	McAnenay	1793
16	18	H	Raith R	D 2-2	1-0	13	McTeague, Watson	621
17	29	A	Clyde	D 0-0	0-0	—		1100
18	Dec 2	H	Falkirk	W 2-1	0-1	13	Clark G, Graham	1614
19	9	A	Forfar Ath	L 0-3	0-1	13		448
20	26	A	Ayr U	L 0-2	0-0	—		3151
21	30	H	Partick T	W 5-4	2-3	13	Cougan 3, Watson, Haddow	2212
22	Jan 2	H	Airdrieonians	L 0-2	0-2	—		2682
23	6	A	Clydebank	W 3-1	0-1	13	McKeown, Maher (og), Cowan	838
24	9	H	Hamilton A	D 0-0	0-0	—		1006
25	13	H	Morton	D 1-1	0-0	12	Cowan	902
26	27	A	Meadowbank T	L 2-3	1-2	12	Graham, Chapman (pen)	400
27	Feb 3	H	Falkirk	D 2-2	0-0	12	Chapman (pen), Clark G	1777
28	10	A	Raith R	L 2-3	0-1	12	Clark G 2	1035
29	Mar 3	H	Airdrieonians	L 1-2	0-1	14	Chapman (pen)	2270
30	10	A	St Johnstone	L 2-5	1-0	14	Chapman (pen), Irvine	1321
31	17	A	Morton	L 0-3	0-0	14		755
32	27	A	Alloa	W 4-3	2-1	—	McAnenay, Graham 2, Irvine	630
33	31	H	Meadowbank T	L 1-2	1-2	14	Clark G	400
34	Apr 4	A	Clyde	L 1-2	1-1	—	Graham	550
35	7	H	Forfar Ath	D 2-2	1-1	14	Oliver, Edgar	526
36	14	A	Ayr U	W 2-0	1-0	13	Chapman (pen), McAnenay	1477
37	21	A	Hamilton A	W 2-1	1-0	13	Harris (og), McAnenay	1229
38	28	H	Partick T	D 2-2	0-2	13	Clark G, Lauchlan	1345
39	May 5	H	Clydebank	L 1-2	1-1	13	Clark G	471

Final League Position: 13

GOALSCORERS

League: (50): McAnenay 10, Clark G 8, Graham 7, Chapman 6 (5 pens), Cougan 3, Watson 3, Cowan 2, Irvine 2, Edgar 1, Haddow 1, Lauchlan 1, McKenzie 1, McKeown 1, McTeague 1, Oliver 1, own goals 2.
Scottish Cup: (0).
Skol Cup: (0).

Record transfer fee paid: £150,000 for Gerry McTeague to Stirling Albion.
Record Victory: 12-0 v Airdriehill, Scottish Cup; 3 Sept, 1887.
Record Defeat: 1-9 v Motherwell, Division I; 2 Jan, 1937.
Most Capped Player: Jock White, 1 (2), Scotland.
Most League Appearances: 399, Monty Walls, 1921–36.
Most League Goals in Season (Individual): 41: Jim Renwick, Division II; 1932–33.
Most Goals Overall (Individual): 105: Bunty Weir, 1928–31.

Honours

League Champions: Division II 1933–34, Second Division 1988–89; *Runners-up:* Division II 1913–14, 1937–38, 1947–48.
Scottish Cup Runners-up: 1920.
League Cup:—.
Club colours: Shirt: Yellow with red & white trim. Shorts: Red with yellow stripes. Stockings: Yellow with red band.

McCulloch, R	McDonald, D	McGowan, M	McKenzie, P	Oliver, M	Clark, R	Watson, S	Cadden, S	Graham, A	Chapman, J	McAnenay, M	Teevan, P	Bishop, J	Granger, C	Diver, D	McTeague, G	Cormack, D	Millar, G	Haddow, L	Cougan, C	Clark, G	Edgar, D	Lauchlan, G	Cowan, S	McKeown, D	Irvine, W	Match No.
1	2	3	4	5	6	7	8	9	10	11*12																1
1	2	3	7	5	6	4*	8	9†10	11	12			14													2
1	2	3	7	5	6	4		9†10	11	12			8*14													3
1	2	3	4	5	6	7*	8	9†10	11				12	14												4
1	2†	3	4	5	6	12	8	9	10*11	7			14													5
1		3	4	6	7	2*	8	9	10	11	12				5											6
1	2†	3*	4	6	7	12	10	9	8	11			14		5											7
1	2		8	6	3	12	4*	9†10	7	14			11		5											8
1	3		8†	6		2	4	9	10	7	12		14	11*	5											9
			6†	3	12	4		8	11	7			10*	9	5	1	2	14								10
1			6	2	4	9	8	11*		10					5		3			12	7					11
1		4†	6	2	8	9	11	7		10*					5		3			12	14					12
1		4	6	2	8		7			10	9				5		3			11*12						13
1	3	4		6	8*10		7			9					5		2	12		11						14
1	3	4		6	8	10	7			9†					5		2*14	12		11						15
1	3	4		6	8	10	12	7*		14					5		2	9		11†						16
1	3	4	6		2	8	9	10	7*12						5					11						17
1	3	4	6		2	8	9	10	7*						5		12			11						18
1	3		6	4		8	9	10	7†	12					5		2*14			11						19
1	2	3*	6	4		9	10		12						5		11†			7	8		14			20
1	2	3	6	4		9	10		12						5		11	7			8*					21
1	2	3	6	12	4	9	10								5*		14	7		11†	8					22
1	2	3	6	4*	7		8	14							5		12	11†					9	10		23
1	2		6	4	8	9*10	12								5			7		11	3					24
1			6	4	8		10*14								5	2	12	7†11		9	3					25
1	3		6	7*		9	4								5	14	2†	8	12	11	10					26
1	2*	3	6	4		14	8	7							5		11	12			9†10					27
1	2*	3	6	4†			8	7					14		5		11	12		9	10					28
1			6	8	2	4†	9	10	7*				14		5		12	11			3					29
1	3*		6		2	4		8	12				14		5		7	11			10†	9				30
1	2		6	4		12	8	14					3	10†	5	7*11					9					31
1	2		6	4		9	8*	7†					14		5		12	11		3	10					32
1	2		6	4†		9	8	7*					14		5		12	10		3	11					33
1	2†		6	4*12		9	8	14							5		11	10		3	7					34
1	2	5	6	4	12	9	8	14					3				11†	7*		10						35
1	2	5	6	4		7	9	10	12								11*	8		3						36
1	2	5	6	4		8	9	10	12								11†	7*14		3						37
1	2	5	6	4*10		9	8	12									11	7†14		3						38
1	14		6	4		9	8	7*					5	3			10	2†12		11						39
38	24	20	16	22	31	32	29	28	35	23	4	—	5	6	30	1	12	5	7	25	9	—	6	16	5	

+ 1s   + + + +   1s 4s 2s 3s   + + + +   10s 7s1s 6s 4s   + + +   4s 10s 8s   + +   3s4s

ALLOA   Second Division

Year Formed: 1883.   *Ground & Address:* Recreation Park, Clackmannan Rd, Alloa FK10 1RR.   *Telephone:* 0259 722695.
Ground Capacity: total: 3100   seated: 180.   *Size of Pitch:* 110yd×75yd.
Chairman: George Ormiston.   *Secretary:* E. G. Cameron.   *Commercial Manager:* William McKie.
Manager: Hugh McCann.   *Assistant Manager:* —.   *Physio:* —.   *Coach:* —.
Managers since 1975: H. Wilson; A Totten; W. Garner; J. Thomson; D. Sullivan; G. Abel; B. Little.
Club Nickname(s): The Wasps.   *Previous Grounds:* None.
Record Attendance: 13,000 v Dunfermline Athletic, Scottish Cup 3rd rd replay; 26 Feb, 1939.
Record Transfer Fee received: £30,000 for Martin Nelson to Hamilton A (1988).
Record Transfer Fee paid: —.

1989–90 LEAGUE RECORD

Match No.	Date		Venue	Opponents	Result	H/T Score	Lg. Pos.	Goalscorers	Attendance
1	Aug	12	H	St Johnstone	L 0-1	0-1	—		1744
2		19	A	Meadowbank T	W 3-1	1-0	5	McCallum 3	500
3		26	H	Falkirk	D 1-1	1-1	7	Lytwyn	2831
4	Sept	2	A	Hamilton A	L 0-1	0-0	9		1751
5		5	H	Albion R	W 4-1	1-0	—	Lamont, McCallum 2, Irvine	998
6		9	A	Clyde	W 4-2	1-1	4	Irvine 2, McCallum, Gibson	800
7		16	A	Morton	L 2-3	0-2	5	Lamont, McCallum	1500
8		23	H	Ayr U	D 1-1	0-0	5	Ramsay	1295
9		30	A	Airdrieonians	L 1-2	0-1	6	Lamont	1250
10	Oct	7	H	Raith R	W 2-0	1-0	5	Lee I, Lamont	1675
11		14	A	Forfar Ath	D 3-3	2-1	5	Lamont, Gibson, Irvine	758
12		21	A	Partick T	D 3-3	1-3	6	Irvine 2, Lamont	3781
13		28	H	Clydebank	L 1-4	0-3	6	Millen	850
14	Nov	4	A	Albion R	D 1-1	0-1	8	Irvine	538
15		11	H	Clyde	D 1-1	0-0	7	Lee I	1181
16		18	H	Morton	D 1-1	1-0	6	Lee I	834
17		25	A	Ayr U	L 0-3	0-0	9		2056
18	Dec	2	H	Airdrieonians	L 0-2	0-1	11		1366
19		9	A	Raith R	D 1-1	0-0	11	Irvine	1118
20		23	H	Forfar Ath	L 0-2	0-2	12		610
21		26	A	St Johnstone	L 0-3	0-1	—		6033
22		30	H	Meadowbank T	L 0-1	0-0	12		755
23	Jan	2	A	Falkirk	L 0-1	0-1	—		3231
24		6	H	Hamilton A	L 0-2	0-2	12		879
25		13	A	Clydebank	L 1-3	0-1	13	Gibson	797
26	Feb	3	A	Morton	L 0-2	0-1	13		1262
27		10	H	Clyde	W 1-0	0-0	13	Ramsay	641
28		28	H	Partick T	W 1-0	0-0	—	McCallum (pen)	959
29	Mar	3	A	Forfar Ath	L 2-3	0-3	12	Gibson, Millen	564
30		17	A	St Johnstone	L 0-6	0-2	13		3100
31		20	H	Falkirk	D 0-0	0-0	—		1149
32		24	A	Airdrieonians	L 1-3	0-0	13	Hayton	1700
33		27	H	Albion R	L 3-4	1-2	—	Sorbie, Lee I, Lamont	630
34		31	H	Hamilton A	D 1-1	0-0	13	Sorbie	692
35	Apr	7	A	Meadowbank T	D 1-1	0-1	13	Lamont	400
36		14	H	Raith R	L 0-4	0-0	14		760
37		21	A	Partick T	L 0-1	0-0	14		1763
38		28	H	Clydebank	D 1-1	0-0	14	Lamont	765
39	May	5	H	Ayr U	D 0-0	0-0	14		528

Final League Position: 14

GOALSCORERS

League: (41): Lamont 9, Irvine 8, McCallum 8 (1 pen), Gibson 4, Lee I 4, Millen 2, Ramsay 2, Sorbie 2, Hayton 1, Lytwyn 1.
Scottish Cup: (2): Irvine 2.
Skol Cup: (0).

Record Victory: 9-2 v Forfar Ath, Division II; 18 Mar, 1933.
Record Defeat: 0-10 v Dundee, Division II; 8 Mar, 1947: v Third Lanark, League Cup, 8 Aug, 1953.
Most Capped Player: Jock Hepburn, 1, Scotland.
Most League Appearances: —.
Most League Goals in Season (Individual): 49: William 'Wee' Crilley, Division II; 1921–22.
Most Goals Overall (Individual): —.

Honours

League Champions: Division II 1921–22; *Runners-up:* Division II 1938–39. Second Division 1976–77, 1981–82, 1984–85, 1988–89.
Scottish Cup:—.
League Cup:—.
Club colours: Shirt: Gold with black trim. Shorts: Black. Stockings: Gold.

Lowrie, R	Robertson, R	Haggart, L	Lee, R	McCulloch, K	Gibson, J	Blackie, W	Ramsay, S	McCallum, M	Erwin, H	Lytwyn, C	Paxton, W	Hayton, G	Lee, I	Lamont, P	Millen, A	Irvine, J	Currie, M	Lee, D	Shanks, D	Miller, S	McGuinness, S	Ormond, J	Sorbie, S	Holmes, J	Match No.
1	2	3	4	5	6	7	8*	9	10	11	12														1
1	4	2	3		6	7	12	9	5	11†	8*		10	14											2
1	12	2	3		6*	14		9†	5	11	8		10	7	4										3
1	12	2	3		6	7		9†	5		8	14	10*	11	4										4
1	2		3*		6		12	9	5		8		10	7	4	11									5
1	12	2	3		6		8	9	5*			14	10	7	4	11†									6
1	2		3		6		8	9	5		12		10*	7	4	11									7
1	2		3		6		8	9	5		12		10	7	4	11*									8
1	6	2†	3	5				9*				7	10	8	4	11	14	12							9
1	2		3	5				9*			12		10	7	4	11	6†	14	8						10
1	2		3		6†		5	9*			12		10	7	4	11	14	8							11
1	12	2	3	5	6			9*				14	10	7	4	11	8†								12
1	2		3	5	6		8†	9			12	14	10	7	4	11*									13
1	2		3	5	6		8	9*		11	12		10	7	4										14
1	2*		3		6		8				12	7	10	9	4	11		5							15
1	2*		3		6		8			11†	14	7	10	9	4	12		5							16
1	2		3		6		8†				12	7*	10	9	4	11	14	5							17
1	2		3		6			9*					10	7	4	11	8	5	12						18
	2		3		6	14	8*						10†	9	4	11	7	5	12		1				19
1	2		3		6	14	12	8†					10	9	4	11		5	7*						20
1	2		3		6*		8	9			12		10	7	4	11		5							21
1	2		3		6		8*	9		14	12		10	7	4	11†		5							22
1	2		3	14	11†			9*				6	10	7	4	12	8	5							23
1	2		3		6			9		11			10†	7	4	12	8*	5	14						24
1	2†		3	14	6		8	9			12		10	7*	4	5	11								25
1		3	2		6		5	9	8			10		12	4	11		7*							26
1	2		3	5	6†	7	8	9		14			10*		4	11	12								27
1		3		5	6	7	12	9*		11			10		4			2					8		28
1	12	3*		5	6	7	14	4†		11			10					2					8		29
1	2					7	5	9*	10	8			4	11†	14	3		12	6						30
1		3		5	7		6	9	10	11*		2	12		4								8		31
1	2*			5	12		6	9	10	11†		4	14		8								7	3	32
1	12			5	7		4†	11	10	9		2	14		6*								8	3	33
1	12	3*		5	7		6	11	10	9†		4	14		8								2		34
1		3		5	7			11†	10	9		4	12		6*	14							8	2	35
1		3		5	7			11	10	9		4	12		6*		8							2	36
1		3		5	6		8			12		11	4	10*	7		9							2	37
1		3		5	7			10	11			4	9		6*	12		8						2	38
1		3		5	6			12	10	7		4	11		8*		9							2	39
38	13	18	35	17	30	3	20	13	26	14	8	13	35	33	37	23	6	19	3	5	1	2	9	8	

+ + + + + + + + + + + + + + + + + +
4s 3s 1s 2s 1s4s 2s 4s 5s 1s11s1s 2s 7s 6s2s 3s 4s

ARBROATH Second Division

Year Formed: 1878.   *Ground & Address:* Gayfield Park, Arbroath DD11 1QB.   *Telephone:* 0241 72157.
Ground Capacity: total: 10,000   seated: 896.   *Size of Pitch:* 115yd×71yd.
Chairman: H. B. Crockatt (President).   *Secretary:* Ronald McLeish.   *Commercial Manager:* David Kean.
Manager: Ian Gibson.   *Assistant Manager:* George Mackie.   *Physio:* William Shearer.   *Coach:* James Cant.
Managers since 1975: A. Henderson; I. J. Stewart; G. Fleming; J. Bone; J Young.
Club Nickname(s): The Red Lichties.   *Previous Grounds:* None.
Record Attendance: 13,510 v Rangers, Scottish Cup 3rd rd; 23 Feb, 1952.
Record Transfer Fee received: £50,000 for Mark McWalter to St Mirren (June 1987).

1989–90 LEAGUE RECORD

Match No.	Date	Venue	Opponents	Result		H/T Score	Lg. Pos.	Goalscorers	Atten- dance
1	Aug 12	A	Stirling Albion	W	3-2	1-1	—	Brand 3	500
2	19	H	Kilmarnock	D	1-1	0-1	3	Brand	1070
3	26	H	Stenhousemuir	W	2-1	0-1	3	Bennett M, Fotheringham	380
4	Sept 2	A	Brechin C	D	2-2	1-0	3	Bennett M, Richardson	900
5	9	A	Queen of the S	D	2-2	0-0	3	Kerr, Stewart	750
6	16	H	Montrose	D	2-2	1-1	3	Fotheringham, Brand	730
7	23	A	East Stirling	D	1-1	1-0	4	Carlin	200
8	30	H	Queen's Park	D	2-2	1-2	4	Brand 2 (2 pens)	661
9	Oct 7	H	Dumbarton	W	2-1	1-0	2	Brand 2	611
10	14	A	Stranraer	L	1-2	0-1	3	Carlin	670
11	21	A	Cowdenbeath	D	1-1	1-1	5	Marshall	230
12	28	H	Berwick R	W	1-0	0-0	3	Gibson	418
13	Nov 4	A	East Fife	L	0-3	0-1	5		604
14	11	A	Brechin C	L	0-1	0-1	7		829
15	18	A	Queen's Park	W	2-1	1-1	6	Marshall, Fotheringham	531
16	25	H	East Stirling	W	2-0	0-0	4	Marshall 2	402
17	Dec 2	A	Dumbarton	D	0-0	0-0	3		450
18	20	H	Stranraer	W	2-0	1-0	—	Smith 2	329
19	23	A	Kilmarnock	L	0-3	0-0	3		3336
20	26	H	Stirling Albion	L	1-2	0-1	—	Fotheringham	720
21	Jan 2	A	Stenhousemuir	L	0-3	0-2	—		300
22	13	A	Queen of the S	L	1-0	1-0	5	Carlin	380
23	20	A	Montrose	L	2-4	2-2	6	Richardson, Marshall	450
24	27	H	Cowdenbeath	D	0-0	0-0	6		348
25	31	H	East Fife	W	3-0	0-0	—	Fotheringham, Bennett M, Smith	480
26	Feb 3	A	Berwick R	L	1-3	0-1	4	Marshall	387
27	10	A	East Stirling	L	0-1	0-0	5		300
28	17	H	Kilmarnock	L	2-4	1-1	8	Smith, Marshall	891
29	27	H	Brechin C	L	0-2	0-0	—		452
30	Mar 3	A	East Fife	W	3-2	2-2	6	Marshall 2, Fotheringham	546
31	17	H	Montrose	W	3-0	2-0	7	Marshall 3	365
32	24	H	Queen's Park	D	1-1	0-1	7	Richardson	376
33	31	A	Stenhousemuir	L	0-1	0-1	8		500
34	Apr 7	H	Queen of the S	W	1-0	0-0	8	Richardson	310
35	14	A	Stirling Albion	L	2-3	2-1	8	McKillop, Hamilton	720
36	21	H	Cowdenbeath	L	0-1	0-1	9		237
37	24	A	Dumbarton	L	0-2	0-2	—		450
38	28	A	Stranraer	L	1-2	1-0	11	Hamilton	500
39	May 5	A	Berwick R	L	0-5	0-1	12		413

Final League Position: 12

GOALSCORERS

League: (47): Marshall 12, Brand 9 (2 pens), Fotheringham 6, Richardson 4, Smith 4, Bennett M 3, Carlin 3, Hamilton 2, Gibson 1, Kerr 1, McKillop 1, Stewart 1.
Scottish Cup: (1): Fotheringham 1.
Skol Cup: (1) Fotheringham 1.

Record Transfer Fee paid: £20,000 for Douglas Robb from Montrose (1981).
Record Victory: 36-0 v Bon Accord, Scottish Cup 1st rd; 12 Sept, 1885.
Record Defeat: 0-8 v Kilmarnock, Division II; 3 Jan, 1949.
Most Capped Player: Ned Doig, 2 (5), Scotland.
Most League Appearances: 445: Tom Cargill, 1966–81.
Most League Goals in Season (Individual): 45: Dave Easson, Division II; 1958–59.
Most Goals Overall (Individual): 120: Jimmy Jack; 1966–71.

Honours
League Champions Runners-up: Division II 1934–35, 1958–59, 1967–68, 1971–72.
Scottish Cup:—.
League Cup:—.
Club colours: Shirt: Maroon with white neck & cuffs. Shorts: White. Stockings: Maroon with white hoop tops.

Jackson, D	Hamilton, J	Gallagher, J	Mitchell, B	Carlin, G	Fleming, J	Stewart, I	Richardson, A	Brand, R	Fotheringham, J	Dewar, G	Smith, R	Tindal, K	Bennett, M	Gibson, I	McNab, S	Kerr, B	Farnan, C	Marshall, J	Bennett, W	Balfour, D	Florence, S	McKillop, A	Match No.
1	2	3	4	5	6	7	8	9	10*	11	12												1
1	2	3	4	5	6	7*	8	9	10†	11	14	12											2
1	2	3	7	5	4			10	12	11			6	8	9*								3
1	2	3*	7	5	4	12	11	9	10				6	8									4
1	2	3	4	5	6	7	8	9*	12	11								10					5
1	2		4		3	12	7*	9†	10	11			6	8		14	5						6
1	2	3	7	5	4			9	10	11			6	8									7
1	2		4	5	3	12		9		11			6	8		7		10*					8
1	2		4	5	3			9		11			6	8		7*		10	12				9
1	2		4	5	3			9	12	11*			6	8				10	7				10
1	2		4	5	6			9*	11				7	8		12		10	3				11
1	2		4	5	3	6	9	11						8		12		10	7*				12
1	2		4	5	3	7	9	11					6	8				10					13
1	2		7	5	3	8	9	11					6					10	4				14
1	12	11*	4	5	3	6		9			7			8				10	2				15
1		11	4	5	3	6		9			7			8				10	2				16
1		14	4	5	3		11	12	10*		7†	6	8					9	2				17
1	12		4	5	3		10		9	11	7	6	8*					2					18
1	2	12	4	5	3		10			11	9	7	6*	8				9					19
1	2		4	5	3		7		10	11			6	8				9					20
	2		4		3	7	8	10	11*	12	14	6				5†	9		1				21
	2	6†	7	5			11	10*	14	12	8						9	3	1	4			22
	2	6†	7	5		14	11	10*	12		8						9	4	1				23
	2	3	7	5			8	10	11	6							9	4	1				24
	2		8		3	7	11	10		9	12	6	5*					4	1				25
	2		8	5†	3	7	11	10*		9		6	14					12	4	1			26
	6†		8		3	14	7	10		9*	2			11				12	4	1		5	27
	7	2		3		11		12	10†		6*	8	14					9	4	1		5	28
	7	4		3		11	12	10*			6	8†	14					9	2	1		5	29
		3	7		6	11		10			8							9	2	1	4	5	30
	7	3		6		11	12	10*			8							9	2	1	4	5	31
	7	3		6		11		10			8							9	2	1	4	5	32
	7	3	12		6	11		10		14		8*						9†	2	1	4	5	33
1	7	3	8		6			11		12	10							9*	2		4	5	34
1	7	3	8		6				11		10							9	2		4	5	35
1	4		2		11			7†	14		10	8					12	9	3		6*	5	36
1	8	12	4		3			7*	14	10	11†			6				9	2			5	37
1	8	6	2	5						11	10					7		9	3		4		38
1	8	12	2	5	6				11*	10						7		9	3		4		39
26	34	18	36	25	35	6	28	15	25	19	12	9	20	23	1	7	2	27	26	13	9	13	

```
 +  +  +           +  +  +  +  +  +        +           +  +  +
2s 4s 1s          5s 3s 6s 3s 5s 3s       1s          6s 2s 1s
```

AYR UNITED

First Division

Year Formed: 1910.   *Ground & Address:* Somerset Park, Tryfield Place, Ayr KA8 9NB.   *Telephone:* 0292 263435.
Ground Capacity: total: 18,500   seated: 1200.   *Size of Pitch:* 111yd×72yd.
Chairman: Robert A. Loudon.   *Secretary:* David Quayle.   *Commercial Manager:* Mike James.
Manager: Alistair R. MacLeod.   *Assistant Manager:* David Wells.   *Physio:* Robert Pender.   *Coach:* David Wells.
Managers since 1975: Alex Stuart; Ally MacLeod; Wllie McLean; George Caldwell; Ally MacLeod.
Club Nickname(s): The Honest Men.   *Previous Grounds:* None.
Record Attendance: 25,225 v Rangers, Division I; 13 Sept, 1969.
Record Transfer Fee received: £300,000 for Steven Nicol to Liverpool (Oct 1981).
Record Transfer Fee paid: £50,000 for Peter Weir from St Mirren, June 1990.
Record Victory: 11-1 v Dumbarton, League Cup; 13 Aug, 1952.

1989–90 LEAGUE RECORD

Match No.	Date		Venue	Opponents	Result	H/T Score	Lg. Pos.	Goalscorers	Attendance
1	Aug	12	A	Albion R	L 1-3	0-2	—	McIntyre (pen)	1380
2		19	H	Forfar Ath	D 1-1	0-1	11	McAllister	2031
3		26	H	Hamilton A	L 0-1	0-0	12		2652
4	Sept	2	A	Clyde	D 2-2	1-2	10	Templeton, Walker	1400
5		5	H	Morton	L 2-3	1-3	—	Templeton, Walker	2492
6		9	A	Falkirk	W 1-0	1-0	10	Kennedy	3000
7		16	H	Clydebank	W 3-2	2-0	9	Bryce, Walker, McCann	2440
8		23	A	Alloa	D 1-1	0-0	8	Walker	1295
9		30	H	Partick T	D 0-0	0-0	9		4524
10	Oct	7	H	Airdrieonians	L 1-3	1-1	9	Willock	3371
11		14	A	Raith R	L 0-2	0-2	11		1571
12		21	H	St Johnstone	D 2-2	1-0	11	Bryce, Conlan	3115
13		28	A	Meadowbank T	W 2-1	1-0	10	Sludden, Walker	400
14	Nov	4	A	Morton	D 1-1	1-1	9	Scott	1900
15		11	H	Falkirk	D 3-3	1-1	10	Templeton, Bryce, Scott	3716
16		18	A	Clydebank	L 1-4	0-2	11	Bryce	1301
17		25	H	Alloa	W 3-0	0-0	10	Kennedy, Templeton, Walker	2056
18	Dec	2	A	Partick T	W 2-1	0-1	7	Templeton 2	3592
19		9	A	Airdrieonians	D 1-1	0-1	7	Bryce	2200
20		16	A	Raith R	W 1-0	0-0	5	Templeton	1745
21		26	H	Albion R	W 2-0	0-0	—	Walker, McCracken	3151
22		30	H	Forfar Ath	L 0-1	0-1	5		816
23	Jan	2	A	Hamilton A	L 0-4	0-1	—		1533
24		6	H	Clyde	W 1-0	0-0	6	Bryce	2410
25		13	H	Meadowbank T	D 0-0	0-0	7		2195
26		27	A	St Johnstone	L 0-4	0-3	7		5057
27	Feb	3	H	Partick T	W 2-1	1-1	7	McIntyre, Bryce	3247
28		10	A	Airdrieonians	L 0-6	0-1	9		2800
29		28	A	Forfar Ath	D 1-1	0-0	—	Bryce (pen)	1311
30	Mar	3	A	Clydebank	W 1-0	1-0	6	Walker	1152
31		14	H	Clyde	D 1-1	0-1	—	Templeton	1617
32		17	A	Hamilton A	L 1-2	1-1	8	Bryce	1119
33		24	H	Falkirk	D 1-1	1-0	8	McAllister	2190
34		31	A	Raith R	L 2-5	1-4	9	Bryce, McCracken	1117
35	Apr	7	A	Morton	W 1-0	1-0	8	McCracken	1175
36		14	H	Albion R	L 0-2	0-1	9		1477
37		21	A	Meadowbank T	L 0-1	0-1	9		400
38		28	H	St Johnstone	L 0-2	0-1	10		5114
39	May	5	A	Alloa	D 0-0	0-0	10		528

Final League Position: 10

GOALSCORERS

League: (41): Bryce 10 (1 pen), Templeton 8, Walker 8, McCracken 3, Kennedy 2, McAllister 2, McIntyre 2 (1 pen), Scott 2, Conlan 1, McCann 1, Sludden 1, Willock 1.
Scottish Cup: (1): McCracken 1.
Skol Cup: (0).

Record Defeat: 0-9 in Division I v Rangers (1929); v Hearts (1931); v Third Lanark (1954).
Most Capped Player: Jim Nisbet, 3, Scotland.
Most League Appearances: 371: Ian McAllister, 1977–90.
Most League Goals in Season (Individual): 66: Jimmy Smith, 1927–28.
Most Goals Overall (Individual): —.

Honours

League Champions: Division II 1911–12, 1912–13, 1927–78, 1936–37, 1958–59, 1965–66. Second Division 1987–88; *Runners-up:* Division II 1910–11, 1955–56, 1968–69.
Scottish Cup:—.
League Cup:—.
Club colours: Shirt: White with broad black chest panel and pinstripe. Shorts: Black. Stockings: White with black diamond tops.

Watson, G	McIntyre, S	Kennedy, D	Henderson, J	McAllister, I	Brown, R	Willock, A	Scott, R	Walker, T	Sludden, J	Cowell, J	Fraser, A	Shaw, G	Hughes, J	Furphy, W	Evans, S	Templeton, H	Bryce, T	Wilson, K	McCann, J	Love, J	Ross, B	Conlan, P	McCracken, D	Purdie, D	Lewis, D	Gillespie, A	Gilmour, G	Smyth, D	Rough, A	Match No.
1	2	3	4	5	6*	7	8	9	10	11	12																			1
1	2	11		5			8	9†			12		14	3*	4	6	7		10											2
1	2*	8		5				9		11	12			3	4	6	7		10											3
1	2†	8		5			12	9		11*				3	4	6	7		10	14										4
1	14	2		5		11†		9	10					3	4	6	7*		8	12										5
1	2	11		5		7*	8	9			12			3	4	6			10†	14										6
1	2	11		5		7*		9		12				3	4	6			10	14	8†									7
1	2	11		5		7*		9						3	4	6†12	10				8	14								8
1		11		5		7*	8	9						3	4	6	12	10		12										9
1		11		5		7		9						3*	4	6	8	10			2	12								10
1		11		5		7	8*	9	14					3	4	6		10†			2		12							11
1		3		5			8	9	12						4	6	7*10				2		11							12
1		3		5		12	8	9	10						4	6	7				2		11*							13
1		3		5		14	8*	9	10						4	6	7	12			2		11†							14
1		3					8	9	10						4	6	7	11			2		5							15
1		3		5		12	8†	9	10*						4	6	7	11			2		14							16
	2	8		5	4		12	9						3			11	7*10						1	6					17
	2	8		5			12	9						3	4	6	7	10						1	11*					18
	2	8		5		11		9						3	4	6	7	10						1						19
	2	11		5		8*		9						3	4	6	7	10	12					1						20
	2	11*				8		9						3	4	6	7	10	12				5	1						21
	2	11		5		8*		9						3	4	6†	7	10	12				14	1						22
	2	11		5		8*		9						3		6	7	10	12				4	1						23
		11		5		8*	2	9							4	6	7	10	12	3				1						24
		11		5		8*	2	9							4	6	7	10	12	3				1						25
		11		5	2†	8		9							4	6	7*10	14		3			12	1						26
	2	11						9							4	6	7	10		3	8		5	1						27
		11						9		12				2	4	6	7*10			3	8		5	1						28
	2	11		5		8		9							4	6	7	10		3				1						29
	2	11		5		8*		9							4	6	7	10	12	3				1						30
	2	11		5				9							4	6	7	10		3	8*		12	1						31
	2	11*						8						4		7	10	12	3	9			6	1		5				32
	2			5	11			8						4		10	7	3		9			9	1		6				33
	2			5			12	8†						4	14	11*10	7	3		9			9	1		6				34
	7			5			8	6						3	4	11		10		2			9	1						35
	8			5†	12		6*							3	4	11	7	10		2			9	1		14				36
					4	7*		10						8	11			12	2	9			9	1		5	3	6		37
	8			4				11		9	10	7						2		12			5		3*	6	1			38
	8						10*	3	4					11			7		2				12	1		5				39
16	21	36	1	31	5	20	12	32	6	3	5	2	21	34	34	31	34	4	19	4	7	3	11	22	2	6	2	3	1	
	+1s				+7s		+1s	+3s		+2s	+3s	+1s				+1s	+2s	+1s	+13s				+3s			+1s6s		+1s		

Also played: Ellis, C — Match 39 (9).

BERWICK RANGERS Second Division

Year Formed: 1881.   *Ground & Address:* Shielfield Park, Tweedmouth, Berwick-upon-Tweed TD15 2EF.   *Telephone:* 0289 307424.
Ground Capacity: total: 10,673   seated: 1473.   *Size of Pitch:* 112yd×76yd.
Chairman: George Deans.   *Secretary:* Dennis McCleary.   *Commercial Manager:* —.
Manager: Ralph Callachan.   *Assistant Manager:* —. *Physio:* Gordon Roberts.   *Coach:* R. Johnson, I. Oliver.
Managers since 1975: H. Melrose; G. Haig; D. Smith; F. Connor; J. McSherry; E Tait; J. Thomson; J. Jefferies.
Club Nickname(s): The Borderers.   *Previous Grounds:* Bull Stot Close, Pier Field, Meadow Field, Union Park, Old Shielfield.
Record Attendance: 13,365 v Rangers, Scottish Cup 1st rd; 28 Jan, 1967.

1989–90 LEAGUE RECORD

Match No.	Date		Venue	Opponents	Result	H/T Score	Lg. Pos.	Goalscorers	Attendance
1	Aug	12	H	Cowdenbeathh	W 2-0	1-0	—	Cass, Kerr (og)	647
2		19	A	Queen of the S	L 2-4	1-2	8	Thorpe, McLaren	704
3		26	H	Stirling Albion	D 1-1	0-0	8	Sloan	516
4	Sept	2	A	Dumbarton	W 5-1	5-1	5	Porteous 2, Thorpe 3	550
5		9	H	East Fife	D 1-1	0-1	5	Thorpe	620
6		16	A	Queen's Park	L 1-3	0-1	7	Hughes	529
7		23	A	Kilmarnock	L 0-2	0-1	10		1975
8		30	H	Montrose	W 2-0	1-0	8	Hughes, Sloan	447
9	Oct	7	A	East Stirling	L 1-3	1-1	10	Sloan	200
10		14	H	Stenhousemuir	L 0-2	0-0	10		473
11		21	H	Brechin C	D 1-1	0-0	11	Graham	433
12		28	A	Arbroath	L 0-1	0-0	11		418
13	Nov	4	A	Stranraer	W 3-1	2-0	10	Sloan, Porteous, Hughes	500
14		11	H	Dumbarton	L 1-2	1-1	11	Hughes	487
15		18	A	Montrose	L 1-2	1-2	11	Paterson (og)	200
16		25	H	Kilmarnock	W 3-2	3-0	11	Wharton, Sloan, Fraser (pen)	784
17	Dec	2	A	East Stirling	L 1-2	1-0	11	Graham	150
18		23	A	Queen of the S	L 2-3	1-1	13	Sloan, Locke	461
19		26	H	Cowdenbeath	L 1-2	1-1	—	Locke	201
20	Jan	2	A	Stirling Albion	L 2-3	0-0	—	Tait, Sokoluk	500
21		6	H	Queen's Park	W 2-0	2-0	13	Bickmore, Sokoluk	363
22		9	A	Stenhousemuir	W 3-1	2-0	—	Bickmore 2, Fraser	400
23		13	A	East Fife	D 2-2	0-2	12	Sokoluk, Davidson (pen)	707
24		16	A	Stranraer	W 3-1	1-0	—	Bickmore, Tait, Sloan	421
25		27	A	Brechin C	L 0-1	0-0	12		400
26	Feb	3	H	Arbroath	W 3-1	1-0	10	Tait, Sloan 2	387
27		10	H	Stenhousemuir	W 1-0	1-0	9	Fraser	458
28		24	H	Kilmarnock	L 1-4	1-1	11	Sokoluk	992
29		28	A	Montrose	W 2-0	1-0	—	Frizell 2	155
30	Mar	3	H	Queen of the S	D 1-1	0-0	8	Sloan	348
31		10	H	East Fife	W 2-0	0-0	5	Sokoluk, Bickmore	382
32		27	A	Cowdenbeath	L 1-3	1-2	9	Bickmore	250
33		31	H	Dumbarton	W 3-2	2-1	9	Sloan, Bickmore, Tait	436
34	Apr	4	A	Stirling Albion	L 0-4	0-2	—		300
35		7	H	Stranraer	W 2-1	0-1	9	Sloan, Graham	335
36		14	H	East Stirling	W 1-0	0-0	6	Sokoluk	404
37		21	A	Queen's Park	W 3-0	2-0	7	Sloan 2, Neil	478
38		28	H	Brechin C	W 1-0	0-0	7	Callachan	554
39	May	5	H	Arbroath	W 5-0	1-0	5	Cass 2, Sloan 2, Sokoluk	413

Final League Position: 5

GOALSCORERS

League: (66): Sloan 16, Bickmore 7, Sokoluk 7, Thorpe 5, Hughes 4, Tait 4, Cass 3, Fraser 3 (1 pen), Graham 3, Porteous 3, Frizell 2, Locke 2, Callachan 1, Davidson 1 (pen), McLaren 1, Neil 1, Wharton 1, own goals 2.
Scottish Cup: (1): Neil 1.
Skol Cup: (3): Sloan 2, Thorpe 1.

Record Transfer Fee received: —.
Record Transfer Fee paid: —.
Record Victory: 8-1 v Forfar Ath, Division II; 25 Dec, 1965: v Vale of Leithen, Scottish Cup; Dec, 1966.
Record Defeat: 1-9 v Hamilton A, First Division; 9 Aug, 1980.
Most Capped Player: —.
Most League Appearances: 435: Eric Tait, 1970–87.
Most League Goals in Season (Individual): 38: Ken Bowron, Division II; 1963–64.
Most Goals Overall (Individual): 115: Eric Tait, 1970–87.

Honours
League Champions: Second Division 1978–79.
Scottish Cup:—.
League Cup: Semi-final 1963–64.
Club colours: Shirt: Black and gold shadow pinstripe. Shorts: Black. Stockings: Black.

Neilson, D	Fraser, S	O'Donnell, J	Muir, L	Cass, M	Locke, S	Graham, T	Thorpe, B	Sloan, S	Hughes, J	Callachan, R	Porteous, S	McLaren, P	Davidson, G	Tait, G	Bickmore, S	Sokoluk, J	Maxwell, D	Leitch, G	Telford, M	Neil, M	Ainslie, G	Wharton, K	Marshall, B	Leetion, P	Scally, D	Frizell, I	Watson, S	Match No.
1	2	3	4	5	6	7	8*	9	10	11†12	14																	1
1		3	4	5	6		8	7	11	9	10*	2	12															2
1	2	3	4	5	6	7*	8	9	10	11	12																	3
1	2	3	4	5	6	12	8†	7*	10	11	9		14															4
1	2	3	4	5*	6	12	8†	7	10	11	9																	5
1	2	3	4	5*	6	12	8†	7	10	11	9		14															6
1	2	3	4	5	6	7	8	14	10	11†	12			9*														7
1	2	3	4		6	7*	8	12	10	11		5		9														8
1	2	3	4	14	6		8	7	10	11		5*		9†12														9
1	2	3		5	6				10			8*	4	14	9†	7	11	12										10
1	2	3		5	6	11			10			4		7	9	8												11
1	2	3		5	6	11*	12		10			4		7	9	8†14												12
1	2	3	8	5	6		7	10		11		4		9														13
1	2	3	8*	5	6		7	10		11†		4		14	9	12												14
1	2	3		5	6		10	7†		8*	4			9	14	12	11											15
1	3*				6	10	7		10*		4	9		14	5†	8	11											16
1				5	8	7		10	11†	4	9		3*	12		6												18
1	2	3			5		7	11†14	8	6	9	12				10*	4											19
1	2	3			5	7*		10		6	9	11	8				4	12										20
1	2	3			5	7		10		6	9	11*	8				4	12										21
1	2	3			5	7		10†		6	9	11	8*	12			4	14										22
1	2*	3			5	7			12	6	9	11	8	10†			4	14										23
1	2*	3			5	4	7	10		6	9	11	8†	12				14										24
1	2	3			5	7		10		6	9	11†12	8*				4	14										25
1	2	3			5	7		10		6	9	11†	8*	12			4	14										26
1	2	3			5	7		10		6	9	11†	8				4											27
1	2	3			5	7		10		6	9	11†	8	12			4*	14										28
1	2	3	8		5			10		6	9	11		12				7*	4									29
1	2	3	4*		5	7		10	12	6	8		9					14	11†									30
1	2	3			5	7		10		6	9	11	8				4											31
1	2	3	12		5	7		10		6	9	11*	8†				4	14										32
1	2	3	12		5	7		10†14		6	9	11	8*				4											33
1	2	3	12		5	7		10		6	9	11*	8	14			4†											34
	2	3		5	9	11*	7	10		6	8		12				4									1		35
	2	3		5	9*12	7	10†		6	8		11	14				4									1		36
	2	3	5*		12	7		14	6	8	11†10		9				4									1		37
	2	3	5	12	7	14		6	8	11	10*		9†				4									1		38
	2	3	5*	12	7	10		6	4†11	8		9		14												1		39
34	37	38	11	21	24	9	21	32	14	30	7	6	31	25	19	18	3	11	—	8	1	2	19	—	2	1	5	
		+	+	+	+	+	+	+	+	+	+	+	+	+	+	+		+		+		+	+		+	+	+	
		1s		5s		3s	4s	3s		1s	5s	6s		1s	3s	4s		3s 7s		1s		2s	1s		1s	2s	9s	

BRECHIN CITY
First Division

Year Formed: 1906. *Ground & Address:* Glebe Park, Trinity Rd, Brechin, Angus DD9 6BJ. *Telephone:* 03562 2856.
Ground Capacity: total: 3491 seated: 291. *Size of Pitch:* 110yd×67yd.
Chairman: David H. Will. *Secretary:* George C. Johnston. *Commercial Manager:* —.
Manager: John Ritchie. *Assistant Manager:* Dick Campbell. *Physio:* Jack Sunter. *Coach:* Brian Reid; Eric Martin.
Managers since 1975: Charlie Dunn; Ian Stewart; Doug Houston; Ian Fleming; John Ritchie.
Club Nickname(s): The City. *Previous Grounds:* Nursery Park.
Record Attendance: 8122 v Aberdeen, Scottish Cup 3rd rd; 3 Feb, 1973.
Record Transfer Fee received: £46,000 for Ken Eadie to Falkirk (1986).
Record Transfer Fee paid: £15,000 for Gerry Lesslie from Dundee U.

1989–90 LEAGUE RECORD

Match No.	Date	Venue	Opponents	Result	H/T Score	Lg. Pos.	Goalscorers	Attendance
1	Aug 12	A	Kilmarnock	W 2-0	0-0	—	Pryde, Brown	2402
2	19	H	Dumbarton	W 4-0	1-0	1	Brash, Sexton, Hill, Pryde	500
3	26	A	Montrose	W 1-0	1-0	1	Wardell	600
4	Sept 2	H	Arbroath	D 2-02	0-1	1	Brash, Ritchie	900
5	9	A	Stirling Albion	L 0-2	0-0	2		760
6	16	H	Queen of the S	W 3-1	1-1	1	Buckley, Lees, Wardell	400
7	23	A	East Fife	L 1-3	0-1	2	Hutt	949
8	30	H	Stenhousemuir	L 1-2	1-0	6	Hutt	300
9	Oct 7	A	Cowdenbeath	D 1-1	1-0	5	Lees	250
10	14	H	East Stirling	W 2-1	1-1	2	Hill, Brown	308
11	21	A	Berwick R	D ¾ 1-1	0-0	4	Candlish (pen)	433
12	028	H	Stranraer	W 1-0	0-0	2	Brash	300
13	Nov 4	H	Queen's Park	W 1-0	0-0	2	Lees	450
14	11	A	Arbroath	W 1-0	1-0	1	Paterson I A	829
15	18	A	Stenhousemuir	L 0-2	0-0	1		300
16	25	H	East Fife	W 2-1	0-1	1	Lees, Ritchie	602
17	Dec 2	H	Cowdenbeath	W 1-0	0-0	1	Scott	500
18	23	A	Dumbarton	D 1-1	0-1	1	Sexton	700
19	26	H	Kilmarnock	W 3-1	1-1	—	Lees, Pryde, Ritchie	1050
20	Jan 1	H	Montrose	D 1-1	1-0	—	Ritchie	600
21	10	A	East Stirling	L 0-2	0-1	—		400
22	13	H	Stirling Albion	W 3-1	2-0	1	Ritchie 3	800
23	17	A	Queen's Park	W 3-0	1-0	—	Sexton, Mirner (og), Lees	350
24	27	H	Berwick R	W 1-0	0-0	1	Ritchie	400
25	Feb 3	A	Stranraer	W 4-2	3-1	1	Lees 2, Candlish (pen), Paterson I A	700
26	7	A	Queen of the S	L 1-3	0-1	—	Brown	750
27	10	H	Cowdenbeath	L 1-3	0-0	1	Conway	400
28	20	A	Stenhousemuir	D 1-1	0-0	—	Pryde	707
29	27	A	Arbroath	W 2-0	0-0	1	Ritchie, Pryde	452
30	Mar 3	H	Queen's Park	W 1-0	1-0	1	Lees	550
31	10	A	Queen of the S	D 2-2	1-0	1	Hutt, Paterson I A	802
32	17	H	Dumbarton	W 3-0	2-0	1	Lees, Paterson I A 2	600
33	24	H	Montrose	D 2-2	1-1	1	Sexton, Candlish (pen)	800
34	31	A	Kilmarnock	D 2-2	1-0	1	Lees, Brash	4887
35	Apr 7	H	Stirling Albion	L 1-5	1-3	1	Candlish (pen)	900
36	14	A	East Fife	W 3-1	1-0	1	Pryde, Sexton, Lees	649
37	21	H	Stranraer	D 0-0	0-0	1		750
38	28	A	Berwick R	L 0-1	0-0	1		554
39	May 5	H	East Stirling	D 0-0	0-0	1		1150

Final League Position: 1

GOALSCORERS

League: (59): Lees 12, Ritchie 9, Pryde 6, Paterson I A 5, Sexton 5, Brash 4, Candlish 4 (4 pens), Brown 3, Hutt 3, Hill 2, Wardell 2, Buckley 1, Conway 1, Scott 1, own goal 1.
Scottish Cup: (13): Lees 5, Hutt 3, Ritchie 3, Brown 1, Paterson I A 1.
Skol Cup: (4): Hill 1, Paterson I G 1, Ritchie 1, Sexton 1.

Record Victory: 12-1 v Thornhill, Scottish Cup 1st rd; 28 Jan, 1926.
Record Defeat: 0-10 v Airdrieonians, Albion R and Cowdenbeath, all in Division II, 1937–38.
Most Capped Player: —.
Most League Appearances: 459: David Watt, 1975–89.
Most League Goals in Season (Individual): 26: W. McIntosh, Division II; 1959–60.
Most Goals Overall (Individual): —.

Honours
League Champions: Second Division 1982–83. C Division 1953–54. Second Division Champions 1989–90. *Runners-up:*—.
Scottish Cup:—.
League Cup:—.
Club colours: Shirt, Shorts, Stockings: Red with white trimmings.

Lawrie, D	Paterson, I G	Scott, D	Brown, R	Stevens, G	Hamilton, R	Wardell, S	Hill, H	Ritchie, P	Sexton, P	Buckley, G	Pryde, I	Hutt, G	Brash, A	Lees, G	Watt, D	Paterson, I A	Yule, R	Candlish, C	Wilkie, S	Baillie, R	Conway, F	Moffatt, J	Grant, B	Match No.
1	2	3	4	5	6	7	8†	9	10	11*	12	14												1
1	2	3	4		6	7*	8	9	10	11	12			5										2
1	2	3	4		6*	7	8	9	10	11†	14	12		5										3
1	2	3	4		6†	7	8	9	10	12	11*	14		5										4
1	2	3	4		6	7	8	9	10	11*		14		5†	12									5
1	6	3	4			14	12	10	11				8	5	7†	9*					2			6
1	6†	3	4			12	14	9	10	11			8	5	7*						2			7
1	2	3		14	7	6		9†	10	11			8	5		12					4*			8
1	2	3	4		14	6		11†	10	12			8	5	7	9*								9
1	2	3	4		6	7	12		10	11			8	5		9*								10
1	2†	10	4		6	7*	8		12	11		14		5		9		3						11
1	2	6	4			7	8		10	11	12			5		9*		3						12
1	2	10	4		6	7	8			11*	12			5		9		3						13
1	2†	6	4			7	8		10*	11	12	14		5		9		3						14
1		3	4		6†	7	8		10*	11	12	14		5		9					2			15
1		3	4		6	7†	8		10	11	12			5		9*				14	2			16
1			4		6	7	8	9	10	11				5				3			2			17
		3	4		6	7	8		10	11	12			5		9*					2		1	18
1		3	4		6	7	8	9	10	11				5							2			19
1		3	4		6	7	8	9	10	11*	12			5							2			20
1			4		6	7		9	10	11†	12	14	8*	5				3			2			21
1			4		6	7	8	9	10	11*	12			5				3			2			22
1	14		4		6†	7*	8	9	10	11	12			5				3			2			23
1	12		4		6	7	8*	9	10	11†		14		5				3			2			24
1	12		4		6	7	8	9	10	11†		14		5				3			2*			25
1	14	3	4		6	7	8	9*	10†	11	12			5							2			26
1		3	4		6	7	8	9	10	11*	12			5							2			27
1	14	3	4		6	7	8	9*	10†	11	12			5							2			28
1	10*	3	4		6	7	8	9		11	12			5							2			29
1	10	3	4		6	7	8	9*		11	12			5							2			30
1	10	3			6	7*	8	9		11	12			5						4	2			31
1	6*		4			7†	8	9	10	11	12	14		5				3			2			32
1	12				6	7	8	9	10	11*				5				3		4	2		7	33
1	2		4		6	7*	8	9†	10	11	12			5				3				14		34
1	2		4		6	7*	8	9	10	11†	12	14		5				3			2			35
1	12		4		6	7	8	9	10	11†		14		5				3*			2			36
1	12		4		6	7	8	9†	10	11		14		5				3*			2			37
1	10		4		6	7	8	9*		11	12	14		5				3			2†			38
1	10		4		6†	7	8	9		11*	12	14		5				3			2			39
38	20	28	28	7	6	14	36	25	28	5	22	27	36	32	5	23	1	20	—	4	22	1	1	

```
38  20  28  28   7   6  14  36  25  28   5  22  27  36  32   5  23   1  20   —   4  22   1   1
 +   +               +   +   +   +   +   +       +   +           +       +       +   +
2s  5s             2s 12s 1s  13s 1s      1s 6s      4s          1s      6s      3s  5s
```

CELTIC

Premier Division

Year Formed: 1888. *Ground & Address:* Celtic Park, 95 Kerrydale St, Glasgow G40 3RE. *Telephone:* 041 554 2611
Ground Capacity: total: 60,800 seated: 9000. *Size of pitch:* 114×75yd.
Chairman: John C. McGinn. *Secretary:* Chris D. White, CA. *Commercial Manager:* John C. McGinn.
Manager: Billy McNeill. *Assistant Manager:* Tommy Craig. *Physio:* Brian Scott. *Coach:* Bobby Lennox.
Managers since 1975: Jock Stein; Billy McNeill; David Hay; Billy McNeill.
Club Nickname(s): The Bhoys. *Previous Grounds:* None.
Record Attendance: 92,000 v Rangers, Division I; 1 Jan, 1938.
Record Transfer Fee received: £850,000 for Brian McClair to Manchester United (1987).
Record Transfer Fee paid: £725,000 for Frank McAvennie from West Ham United (1987).
Record Victory: 11-0 v Dundee, Division I; 26 Oct, 1895.
Record Defeat: 0-8 v Motherwell, Division I; 30 Apr, 1937.
Most Capped Player: Danny McGrain, 62, Scotland.
Most League Appearances: 486: Billy McNeill, 1957–75.

1989–90 LEAGUE RECORD

Match No.	Date	Venue	Opponents	Result	H/T Score	Lg. Pos.	Goalscorers	Atten- dance
1	Aug 12	A	Hearts	W 3-1	2-0	—	Coyne 3 (1 pen)	25,932
2	19	H	Dunfermline Ath	W 1-0	0-0	1	Galloway	34,000
3	26	H	Rangers	D 1-1	1-1	1	Dziekanowski	54,000
4	Sept 9	A	St Mirren	L 0-1	0-1	1		19,813
5	16	A	Dundee U	D 2-2	1-0	4	Morris, Coyne	16,624
6	23	H	Motherwell	D 1-1	1-1	4	McStay	29,000
7	30	A	Aberdeen	D 1-1	0-0	4	Miller	21,374
8	Oct 4	H	Hibernian	W 3-1	0-1	—	Walker 2, Dziekanowski	36,000
9	14	A	Dundee	W 3-1	2-0	1	Dziekanowski, Aitken, Coyne	16,215
10	21	H	Hearts	W 2-1	0-1	1	Aitken, Coyne	38,105
11	28	A	Dunfermline Ath	L 0-2	0-2	1		19,588
12	Nov 4	A	Rangers	L 0-1	0-0	4		41,598
13	18	H	Dundee U	L 0-1	0-0	5		32,350
14	22	H	St Mirren	D 1-1	1-1	—	Miller	23,100
15	25	A	Motherwell	D 0-0	0-0	4		16,029
16	Dec 2	H	Aberdeen	W 1-0	0-0	3	Walker (pen)	38,300
17	9	A	Hibernian	W 3-0	2-0	3	Dziekanowski, Wdowczyk, Walker	18,000
18	16	H	Dundee	W 4-1	1-1	3	Walker, McStay, Dziekanowski, Miller	17,860
19	26	A	Hearts	D 0-0	0-0	—		23,259
20	30	H	Dunfermline Ath	L 0-2	0-1	3		30,548
21	Jan 2	H	Rangers	L 0-1	0-1	—		54,000
22	6	A	St Mirren	W 2-0	2-0	4	Miller, Dziekanowski	14,813
23	13	A	Dundee U	L 0-2	0-0	4		16,635
24	27	H	Motherwell	L 0-1	0-0	4		23,000
25	Feb 3	A	Dundee	D 0-0	0-0	4		14,100
26	10	H	Hibernian	D 1-1	1-1	4	Dziekanowski	25,000
27	17	A	Aberdeen	D 1-1	0-1	4	McStay	22,100
28	Mar 3	H	Dundee U	W 3-0	1-0	4	Galloway, Miller, Whyte	23,541
29	10	H	Hearts	D 1-1	1-1	4	Coyne	34,792
30	24	A	Dumfermline Ath	D 0-0	0-0	4		14,044
31	Apr 1	A	Rangers	L 0-3	0-2	—		41,926
32	7	H	St Mirren	L 0-3	0-2	5		18,481
33	17	A	Hibernian	L 0-1	0-0	—		11,000
34	21	H	Dundee	D 1-1	0-0	4	Creaney	15,115
35	28	A	Motherwell	D 1-1	1-1	4	Dziekanowski	10,322
36	May 2	H	Aberdeen	L 1-3	1-0	—	Walker	20,154

Final League Position: 5

GOALSCORERS

League: (37): Dziekanowski 8, Coyne 7 (1 pen), Walker 6 (1 pen), Miller 5, McStay 3, Aitken 2, Galloway 2, Creaney 1, Morris 1, Wdowczyk 1, Whyte 1.
Scottish Cup: (8): Coyne 2, Walker 2, Dziekanowski 1, McStay 1, Miller 1, Morris 1 (pen).
Skol Cup: (7): Dziekanowski 3, Burns 1, Grant 1, McStay 1, Walker 1.

Most League Goals in Season (Individual): 50: James McGrory, Division I; 1935–36.
Most Goals Overall (Individual): 397: James McGrory; 1922–39.

Honours

League Champions: (35 times) Division I 1892–93, 1893–94, 1895–96, 1897–98, 1904–05, 1905–06, 1906–07, 1907–08, 1908–09, 1909–10, 1913–14, 1914–15, 1915–16, 1916–17, 1918–19, 1921–22, 1925–26, 1935–36, 1937–38, 1953–54, 1965–66, 1966–67, 1967–68, 1968–69, 1969–70, 1970–71, 1971–72, 1972–73, 1973–74. Premier Division 1976–77, 1978–79, 1980–81, 1981–82, 1985–86, 1987–88; *Runners-up:* 21 times.
Scottish Cup Winners: (27 times) 1892, 1899, 1900, 1904, 1907, 1908, 1911, 1912, 1914, 1923, 1925, 1927, 1931, 1933, 1937, 1951, 1954, 1965, 1967, 1969, 1971, 1972, 1974, 1975, 1977, 1980, 1985, 1988, 1989; *Runners-up:* 16 times.
League Cup Winners: (9 times) 1956–57, 1957–58, 1965–66, 1966–67, 1967–68, 1968–69, 1969–70, 1974–75, 1982–83; *Runners-up:* 8 times.
European: *European Cup Winners:* 1966–67. 74 matches (1966–67 winners, 1967–68, 1968–69, 1969–70 runners-up, 1970–71, 1971–72 semi-finals, 1972–73, 1973–74 semi-finals, 1974–75, 1977–78, 1979–80, 1981–82, 1982–83, 1986–87); *Cup Winners Cup:* 33 matches (1963–64 semi-finals, 1965–66 semi-finals, 1975–76, 1980–81, 1984–85, 1985–86); *UEFA Cup:* 16 matches (1962–63, 1964–65 *Fairs Cup;* 1976–77, 1983–84, 1987–88).
Club colours: Shirt: Green and white hoops. Shorts: White. Stockings: White

Bonner, P	Morris, C	Burns, T	Aitken, R	Whyte, D	Grant, P	Galloway, M	McStay, P	Dziekanowski, D	Coyne, T	Fulton, S	Walker, A	Rogan, A	Hewitt, J	McCahill, S	Miller, J	Elliott, P	Mathie, A	Wdowczyk, D	Creaney, G	Stark, W	Match No.
1	2	3	4	5	6	7	8	9*	10	11	12										1
1	2	3	4	5	6	7	8	9	10						11						2
1	2	3	4	5	6	7	8	9	10						11						3
1	2	3*	4	5	6	7	8	9	10			14	12		11†						4
1	2		4	5		7	8	9*	10	11	12	3				6					5
1	2		4	6		7	8	9	10*	11	12	3				5					6
1	2		4	6		7	8	9	12		10*	3			11	5					7
1	2		4	6		7	8	9	10			3			11	5					8
1	2	12	4	6		7	8*	9	14		10†	3		5	11						9
1	2	3	4	6		7	8	9	14	10†	12			5	11*						10
1	2	3	4	6		7	8	9	10		12				11*	5					11
1	2	3	4	6		7	8	9*	10		12				11	5					12
1	2	3		12	6†	7	8	9	10*		4	14			11	5					13
1	2			6		7	12	8	9		10	3	14		11†	5	4*				14
1	2			6		7	12	8	9		10	3†14			11*	5	4				15
1	2		4	6	7	12	8	9			10*				11	5		3			16
1	2		4	6	8	7	9				10				11	5		3			17
1	2		4	6	7	12	8	9			10				5*11†	14		3			18
1	2		4	6	12	7*	8	9†14	10						11	5		3			19
1	2		4	6	7†	8	9	14	10*			11	12			5		3			20
1	2		4	6	7	10†	8	12	9	14					11*	5		3			21
1			4	6	2	8	9†	10	12	14					11	5	7*	3			22
1	2		6	4	8	9	10	12							11	5	7*	3			23
1	2		6	4	8	9	14	11	10†						7*12	5		3			24
1	2		6	7*	4	8	9	10†12	14						11	5		3			25
1	2		6	7	4*	8	9	10†11	14	12						5		3			26
1	2		6	7	4	8	9	10	11*	12						5		3			27
1	2		6	7	4	8	9	10	11							5		3			28
1	2		6	7	4	8	9*10	12							11	5		3			29
1	2		6	7		8	10*12	9	4†							5	14	3	11		30
1	2		6	2	7	8	9†10	12	14		4*				11	5		3			31
1	2		6	7	4	8	10	9*							5	11†12		3	14		32
1	2		6	7†	4*	8	14	11	10						5	12		3	9		33
1	2		6	4	8		11*10	12	9†						5	7		3	14		34
1			6	4	2	8	9*	11	10†						5	12		3	14	7	35
1			6	4	2	8	9	11*10							5	12		3	14	7†	36
36	32	8	18	35	24	29	35	31	17	13	19	16	8	2	16	25	5	23	2	2	
		+		+	+	+	+	+	+	+	+				+	+		+	+		
		1s		2s	4s	2s	6s	3s	13s	2s	4s				8s	2s		1s	4s		

CLYDE

First Division

Year Formed: 1878.   *Ground & Address:* Firhill Park, 90 Firhill Rd, Glasgow G20 7AL.   *Telephone:* 041 946 9000.
Ground Capacity: total: 20,600   seated: 3264.   *Size of Pitch:* 106yd×72yd.
Chairman: John F. McBeth F.R.I.C.S..   *Secretary:* John D. Taylor.   *Commercial Manager:* John Donnelly.
Manager: John Clark.   *Assistant Manager:* John Cushley.   *Physio:* J. Watson.   *Coach:* —.
Managers since 1975: S. Anderson; C. Brown; J. Clark.
Club Nickname(s): The Bully Wee.   *Previous Grounds:* None.
Record Attendance: 52,000 v Rangers, Division I; 21 Nov, 1908.
Record Transfer Fee received: £95,000 for Pat Nevin to Chelsea (July 1983).
Record Transfer Fee paid: £14,000 for Harry Hood from Sunderland (1966).

1989–90 LEAGUE RECORD

Match No.	Date		Venue	Opponents	Result	H/T Score	Lg. Pos.	Goalscorers	Attendance
1	Aug	12	H	Airdrieonians	W 1-0	0-0	—	McGlashan	1200
2		19	A	Morton	W 1-0	1-0	4	Clarke	1400
3		26	A	Partick T	D 2-2	2-2	4	Callaghan, McGlashan (pen)	4037
4	Sept	2	H	Ayr U	D 2-2	2-1	5	McCabe 2	1400
5		5	A	Clydebank	L 1-2	0-1	—	McGlashan	1009
6		9	H	Alloa	L 2-4	1-1	6	Callaghan, McCabe	800
7		16	H	Forfar Ath	D 0-0	0-0	7		600
8		23	A	Albion R	L 0-2	0-1	9		1001
9		30	H	Hamilton A	D 1-1	1-1	10	Rooney	600
10	Oct	7	A	Meadowbank T	L 1-2	0-0	10	McGlashan	500
11		14	H	St Johnstone	L 0-2	0-2	13		1435
12		21	A	Raith R	W 2-0	1-0	8	Clarke, McGlashan	1543
13		28	H	Falkirk	W 2-0	1-0	8	Fairlie, McGlashan	1650
14	Nov	4	H	Clydebank	W 2-0	0-0	6	Clarke, Fairlie	850
15		11	A	Alloa	D 1-1	0-0	6	Speirs	1181
16		18	A	Forfar Ath	D 1-1	1-0	5	McCabe	567
17		29	H	Albion R	D 0-0	0-0	—		1100
18	Dec	2	A	Hamilton A	W 1-0	0-0	4	McCabe	1254
19		9	H	Meadowbank T	L 0-3	0-0	5		700
20		16	A	St Johnstone	L 0-2	0-2	6		2465
21		26	A	Airdrieonians	L 0-1	0-1	—		2500
22		30	A	Morton	D 1-1	1-0	9	Knox	900
23	Jan	2	H	Partick T	D 3-3	2-0	—	McGlashan 2, Nolan	3450
24		6	A	Ayr U	L 0-1	0-0	10		2410
25		13	A	Falkirk	L 0-3	0-0	11		2200
26	Feb	3	H	Airdrieonians	L 0-1	0-0	11		1300
27		10	A	Alloa	L 0-1	0-0	11		641
28	Mar	3	A	Partick T	W 3-0	2-0	11	Shanks, Clarke, Thompson	2419
29		14	A	Ayr U	D 1-1	1-0	—	Clarke	1617
30		17	H	Raith R	W 1-0	0-0	11	Speirs	500
31		21	H	Raith R	D 0-0	0-0	—		500
32		27	H	Hamilton A	L 0-1	0-0	—		480
33		31	A	Forfar Ath	D 2-2	1-0	11	McGlashan, Clarke	804
34	Apr	4	H	Albion R	W 2-1	1-1	—	McGlashan, Thompson	550
35		7	A	Clydebank	L 1-2	0-2	11	Thompson	800
36		14	H	Falkirk	D 0-0	0-0	10		1200
37		21	A	St Johnstone	D 1-1	1-1	11	Knox	5323
38		28	H	Meadowbank T	D 1-1	0-1	11	Speirs	733
39	May	5	A	Morton	W 3-2	3-0	9	Thompson, Clarke, McGlashan (pen)	809

Final League Position: 9

GOALSCORERS

League: (39): McGlashan 11 (2 pens), Clarke 7, McCabe 5, Thompson 4, Speirs 3, Callaghan 2, Fairlie 2, Knox 2, Nolan 1, Rooney 1, Shanks 1.
Scottish Cup: (0).
Skol Cup: (1): McCabe 1.

Record Victory: 11-1 v Cowdenbeath, Division II; 6 Oct, 1951.
Record Defeat: 0-11 v Dumbarton, Scottish Cup 4th rd, 22 Nov, 1879; v Rangers, Scottish Cup 4th rd, 13 Nov, 1880.
Most Capped Player: Tommy Ring, 12, Scotland.
Most League Appearances: 428: Brian Ahern.
Most League Goals in Season (Individual): 32: Bill Boyd, 1932–33.
Most Goals Overall (Individual): —.

Honours
League Champions: Division II 1904–05, 1951–52, 1956–57, 1961–62, 1972–73. Second Division 1977–78, 1981–82; *Runners-up:* Division II 1903–04, 1905–06, 1925–26, 1963–64.
Scottish Cup Winners: 1939, 1955, 1958; *Runners-up:* 1910, 1912, 1949.
League Cup:—.
Club colours: Shirt: White with red and black trim. Shorts: Black. Stockings: White.

Robertson, S	McFarlane, R	Spence, T	Reid, W	Speirs, C	Nolan, M	Fairlie, J	Knox, K	McGlashan, C	Rooney, J	McCabe, G	McGuiness, B	Nugent, S	Callaghan, W	Clarke, S	Atkins, D	Quinn, S	McVie, Gary	Cowell, J	McVie, Graeme	Tracey, P	Shanks, P	Scott, M	Thompson, D	Ross, S	Mallan, S	Match No.
1	2	3	4	5	6	7	8	9	10	11																1
1		3	4	5	6	12	14	9	10	11†	2		7*	8												2
1	10	3	4	5	6	12	8	9		7	2		11*													3
1	10	3	4	5	6		12	9		7	2		11	8*											·	4
1	2†	3	4	5	6	12	14	9	10	7			11*	8												5
1		3	4	5	6	14	12	9	10	11	2		7†	8*												6
	2	3	4	5	6	7†12		9	8*10		14				1	11										7
		3	4	5	6		8	9	10	7*	2	12			1	11†14										8
	4	3		5	6	7	8	9	10*12	2			1			11										9
	6		4	5	2		8	9	10	7			1			11	3									10
	2	3	4	5	6		8	9	10	7†			1		14	11*12										11
	8		4	5	6	7	2	9		10			11	1			3									12
	8		4	5	6	7	2	9		10			11	1			3							·		13
	8		4	5	6	7	2	9		10			11	1			3									14
	8		4	5	6	7	2	9	12	10			11*	1			3									15
	8	4†		5	6	7*	2	9	14	10			11	1			12	3								16
	8			5	6	10*	2	9	4	7	14		11†	1			12	3								17
	8			5	6	10	2	9	4	7			11*	1			12	3								18
	8			6		7	2	9	4*10	5				1	12		11	3								19
	8	3		5	6	7*	2	9		10	4		11†	1			12		14							20
	8			5	6	7	2	9	4*10				11	1			12	3								21
	8			5	6	7	2	9	4	10			11	1				3								22
	8			5	6	7*	2	9	4	10			11	1			12	3								23
	8			5	6	7	2	9	4	10			11*	1				3	12							24
	8			5	6		2	9	12	10†			11	1		14		3	4*	7						25
	2			5	6	11*	4	9					10	1				3		8	12	7				26
	4			5	6	12	2	9		10			11	1				3*		8		7				27
				5*	6		2	9	4	11	12		8					3		10		7	1			28
		12	5	6	14		2	9	4	11†	3		10							8*		7	1			29
		4	5	6	8		2	9		11	3									10*		7	1	12		30
	6		4	5		7	2	9	8		3									10			1	11		31
	8		4	5	6†		2	9	10	11*	3									14		7	1	12		32
	6		4	5	12		2	9	10		3		8									7*	1	11		33
	6		4	5	14		2	9	10†12		3		8									7	1*11			34
	6		4	5	12		2	9		10	3*		8									7	1	11		35
	6		4	5	8		2	9			3		10*								12	7	1	11		36
	6		4	5	12		2	9	10	11*			8					3				1		7		37
	6†		4	5			2	9	10*12	14			8					3				7	1	11		38
	6*		4	5	12		2	9		14			10					3			8†	7	1	11		39
6	33	12	24	38	32	19	34	39	24	31	16	—	5	28	21	2	—	4	20	—	8	1	12	12	8	
			+	+	+	+			+	+	+						+	+	+	+	+	+			+	
			1s	5s	6s	5s			3s	4s	3s	2s					2s2s		6s1s	1s	3s	1s			2s	

CLYDEBANK

First Division

Year Formed: 1965.   *Ground & Address:* Kilbowie Park, Arran Place, Clydebank G81 2PB.   *Telephone:* 041 952 2887.
Ground Capacity: total: 9900 seated: All.   *Size of Pitch:* 110yd×68yd.
Chairman: C. A. Steedman.   *Secretary:* I. C. Steedman.   *Commercial Manager:* David Curwood.
Manager: J. S. Steedman.   *Managing Director:* J. S. Steedman.   *Assistant Manager:* —.   *Physio:* John Jolly.   *Coach:*
Jim Fallon.
Managers since 1975: William Munro; J. S. Steedman.
Club Nickname(s): The Bankies.   *Previous Grounds:* None.
Record Attendance: 14,900 v Hibernian, Scottish Cup 1st rd; 10 Feb, 1965.
Record Transfer Fee received: £175,000 for Owen Coyle from Airdrieonians, February 1990.

1989–90 LEAGUE RECORD

Match No.	Date		Venue	Opponents	Result		H/T Score	Lg. Pos.	Goalscorers	Atten-dance
1	Aug	12	H	Partick T	L	1-2	1-2	—	Eadie (pen)	2915
2		19	A	St Johnstone	L	1-2	1-1	12	Hughes	7267
3		26	H	Morton	W	3-1	1-1	9	Coyle O 2, Collins (og)	1152
4	Sept	2	A	Albion R	W	4-3	0-0	7	Davies, Hughes, Coyle O, Eadie	861
5		5	H	Cyde	W	2-1	1-0	—	Hughes, Eadie	1009
6		9	A	Forfar Ath	D	2-2	2-1	5	Coyle O, Auld	584
7		16	A	Ayr U	L	2-3	0-2	6	Davies, Eadie (pen)	2440
8		23	H	Meadowbank T	D	1-1	1-0	6	Coyle O	735
9		30	A	Raith R	L	0-1	0-0	8		1300
10	Oct	7	H	Hamilton A	D	2-2	0-1	7	Eadie, Kelly	1192
11		14	A	Falkirk	L	1-2	0-1	8	Kelly	2574
12		21	A	Airdrieonians	L	0-3	0-1	9		1239
13		28	A	Alloa	W	4-1	3-0	9	Eadie 2 (1 pen), Coyle O 2	850
14	Nov	4	A	Clyde	L	0-2	0-0	10		850
15		11	H	Forfar Ath	W	3-2	2-1	9	Harvey, Coyle O 2	738
16		18	H	Ayr U	W	4-1	2-0	8	Coyle T, Sweeney, Dickson, Coyle O	1301
17		25	A	Meadowbank T	D	1-1	1-1	7	Coyle O	500
18	Dec	2	H	Raith R	W	3-1	2-1	6	Coyle O, Coyle T, Eadie	988
19		9	A	Hamilton A	L	1-2	0-0	6	Kelly	1148
20		23	H	Falkirk	D	3-3	1-0	6	Eadie 2, Davies	1464
21		26	A	Partick T	D	1-1	0-0	—	Coyle T	3934
22		30	H	St Johnstone	W	4-0	3-0	4	Coyle T, Coyle O, Eadie 2	2105
23	Jan	3	A	Morton	D	2-2	0-0	—	Davies, Rowe	1300
24		6	H	Albion R	L	1-3	1-0	7	Coyle O	838
25		13	A	Alloa	W	3-1	1-0	6	Coyle O, Eadie 2	797
26		30	A	Airdrieonians	D	2-2	2-0	—	Gray (og), Coyle O	2200
27	Feb	3	A	Hamilton A	W	3-1	0-0	5	Coyle O, Harris (og), Eadie	1407
28		10	H	Forfar Ath	W	3-2	1-1	5	Eadie, Davies, Coyle T	655
29		21	A	Falkirk	W	1-0	0-0	—	Harvey	2800
30	Mar	3	H	Ayr U	L	0-1	0-1	4		1152
31		24	H	Raith R	D	2-2	1-2	5	Harvey, Kelly	738
32		27	H	Meadowbank T	W	2-1	2-1	—	Eadie, Coyle T	350
33		31	A	Partick T	L	0-4	0-2	5		3002
34	Apr	3	A	Airdrieonians	W	4-3	3-3	—	Coyle T, Eadie, Kelly, Crawford	2600
35		7	H	Clyde	W	2-1	2-0	4	Kelly 2	800
36		17	A	St Johnstone	W	3-1	2-1	—	Eadie, Rowe, Caffrey	7328
37		21	H	Morton	L	0-1	0-0	4		1061
38		28	A	Alloa	D	1-1	0-0	4	Eadie	765
39	May	5	A	Albion R	W	2-1	1-1	3	Rowe, Eadie	471

Final League Position: 3

GOALSCORERS

League: (74): Eadie 21 (3 pens), Coyle O 17, Coyle T 7, Kelly 7, Davies 5, Harvey 3, Hughes 3, Rowe 3, Auld 1, Caffrey 1, Crawford 1, Dickson 1, Sweeney 1, own goals 3.
Scottish Cup: (8): Davies 4, Eadie 2, Kelly 1, own goal 1.
Skol Cup: (3): Eadie 2, McGurn 1.

Record Transfer Fee paid: £50,000 for Gerry McCabe from Clyde.
Record Victory: 8-1 v Arbroath, First Division; 3 Jan, 1977.
Record Defeat: 1-9 v Gala Fairydean, Scottish Cup qual. rd; 15 Sept, 1965.
Most Capped Player: —.
Most League Appearances: 620: Jim Fallon, 1968–86.
Most League Goals in Season (Individual): 28: Blair Millar, First Division; 1978–79.
Most Goals Overall (Individual): 84, Blair Millar, 1977–83.

Honours
League Champions: Second Division 1975–76; *Runners-up:* First Division 1976–77, 1984–85.
Scottish Cup: Semi-finalists 1990.
League Cup: —.
Club colours: Shirt: White with red zig-zag band. Shorts: White. Stockings: White with red hooped tops.

Stevenson, H	Traynor, J	Rodger, J	Maher, J	Sweeney, S	Auld, S	Davies, J	Harvey, P	Eadie, K	Bryce, T	Coyle, O	McGurn, G	Caffrey, H	Gallacher, J	Dickson, J	Hughes, J	Robertson, J	Campbell, K	Crawford, J	Lansdown, A	Coyle, T	Duncanson, J	Rowe, G	Smith, B	Kelly, P	Dick, I	Ferguson, W	Hamilton, L	Arrol, A	O'Brien, J	Match No.
1	2*	3	4	5	6	7	8	9	10†	11	12	14																		1
		3	4	5	6	7	8	9		11	12	14	1	2*	10†															2
		3*	4	5	6	7	8†	9		11	12	14	1	2	10															3
		3	4	5	6	7	8*	9		11	12		1	2	10															4
		3	4	5	6	7	8*	9†		11	12	14	1	2	10															5
		3	4	5	6	7	8†	9		11	12	14	1	2	10*															6
		3	4	5	6	7	8*	9		11	12	14	1	2	10†															7
		3	4	5		7	8	9*		11	12	14	1	2	10					6†										8
		3*	4	5		7	8	9		11†	12	14	1	2	10					6										9
		3	4*	5		7	8	9		11	12	14	1	2	10					6†										10
		3	4	5		7	8	9		11	12		1	2*	10					6										11
		3	4	5		7†	8*	9		11	12	14	1	2	10					6										12
		3	4	5		7	8	9		11			1	2	10					6										13
		3	4	5		7	8	9		11			1	2	10			12		6*										14
		3	4	5		7	8	9		11			1	2	10*			14		6†				12						15
		3	4*	5		7	8	9		11			1	2	10			12		6										16
		3	4	5		7	8	9		11			1	2	10*			12		6										17
		3	4	5		7	8	9		11			1	2				12		6		10*								18
		3*	4	5		7	8	9		11			1	2				12		6†		10		14						19
		3	4	5		7	8	9		11				2						6		10					1			20
			4	5		7	8	9		11			1	2					3	6		10								21
		3	4	5		7	8	9		11			1	2						6		10								22
		3*	4	5		7	8	9		11			1	2				12		6		10								23
			4	5		7	8	9		11			1	2				12	3	6		10*								24
			4	5		7	8	9		11			1	2					3	6		10								25
			4	5		7		9†		11			1	2				12	3	6	8*	10		14						26
			4	5		7	8	9		11			1	2					3	6		10								27
			4	5		7	8	9					1	2					3	6		10	11*	12						28
		3	4	5		7*	8	9		11†			1	2				12		6		10		14						29
		3	4	5		7	8	9*						2				12	14	6		10†	11	5					1	30
		3	4	5		7	8	9					1	2*				12		6		10	11							31
			4	5		7		9					1	2*				14	3	6	8†	10	11	12						32
		3	4	5		7		9					1	2				12		6*	8†	10	11	14						33
		3	4	5		7	8	9						2				12		6*		10	11							34
		3†	4*	5		7	8	9						2				14		6		10	11	12						35
			4	5		7	8	9*		11			1	2				12	3	6		10								36
			4	5		7	8	9		11			1	2					3	6		10								37
			4	5		7		9		11†			1	2*				12	3	6	8	10		14						38
			4	5		7	8	9					1	2				12	3	6		10	11*							39
1	1	28	28	33	7	31	34	37	1	27	4	12	34	30	10	1	2	14	5	26	5	25	11	13	2	2	1	1	1	

+1s +1s · · 1s6s · 1s · 7s 2s9s · 3s1s 1s4s 5s 4s · 1s 4s

Also played: Thomson W – Match 34 (1), 35 (1).

COWDENBEATH Second Division

Year Formed: 1881. *Ground & Address:* Central Park, Cowdenbeath KY4 9EY. *Telephone:* 0383 511205.
Ground Capacity: total: 7250 seated: 2750. *Size of Pitch:* 110yd×70yd.
Chairman: Thomas Currie. *Secretary:* J. Ronald Fairbairn. *Commercial Manager:* James Colvin.
Manager: John Brownlie. *Assistant Manager:* —. *Physio:* James Reekie. *Coach:* John Brownlie.
Managers since 1975: D. McLindon; F. Connor; P. Wilson; A Rolland; H. Wilson; W. McCulloch; J. Clark; J. Craig;
R. Campbell; J. Blackley; J. Brownlie.
Club Nickname(s): Cowden. *Previous Grounds:* North End Park, Cowdenbeath.
Record Attendance: 25,586 v Rangers, League Cup quarter final; 21 Sept, 1949.
Record Transfer Fee received: —.
Record Transfer Fee paid: —.

1989–90 LEAGUE RECORD

Match No.	Date		Venue	Opponents	Result		H/T Score	Lg. Pos.	Goalscorers	Atten- dance
1	Aug	12	A	Berwick R	L	0-2	0-1	—		647
2		19	H	Montrose	L	0-1	0-0	14		250
3		26	H	East Fife	L	0-1	0-0	14		350
4	Sept	2	A	Stranraer	L	1-3	1-0	14	Spence	750
5		9	A	Kilmarnock	D	0-0	0-0	13		1804
6		16	H	Stirling Albion	W	4-0	2-0	13	Spence 2, Mailer 2	350
7		23	A	Queen's Park	D	0-0	0-0	13		591
8		30	H	Dumbarton	L	1-5	0-1	13	MacKenzie	250
9	Oct	7	H	Brechin C	D	1-1	0-1	13	MacKenzie	250
10		14	A	Queen of the S	W	4-2	1-2	12	Malone 2, Hamill, Herd	500
11		21	H	Arbroath	D	1-1	1-1	13	Ross	230
12		28	A	East Stirling	D	1-1	1-0	12	Ross	150
13	Nov	4	A	Stenhousemuir	L	1-3	0-1	13	Ross	200
14		11	H	Stranraer	L	3-4	0-2	12	Scott 2, Malone (pen)	250
15		18	A	Dumbarton	D	2-2	1-0	13	MacKenzie, Spence	500
16		25	H	Queen's Park	D	0-0	0-0	12		200
17	Dec	2	A	Brechin C	L	0-1	0-0	14		500
18		20	H	Queen of the S	W	4-2	3-1	—	Scott 2, Ross, Malone	150
19		23	A	Montrose	L	0-2	0-1	14		250
20		26	H	Berwick R	W	2-1	1-1	—	Mailer, Ross	201
21	Jan	2	A	East Fife	D	0-0	0-0	—		962
22		6	H	Stenhousemuir	L	0-1	0-1	12		200
23		13	H	Kilmarnock	W	2-1	1-0	13	Scott, Hamill	781
24		27	A	Arbroath	D	0-0	0-0	13		348
25	Feb	3	H	East Stirling	W	4-0	1-0	13	Spence 3, Ross	200
26		7	A	Stirling Albion	D	1-1	1-1	—	Ross	700
27		10	A	Brechin C	W	3-1	0-0	10	Buckley, Ross 2	400
28		17	H	East Fife	D	2-2	0-0	9	Wright, Scott	543
29	Mar	3	A	Stenhousemuir	L	1-2	1-0	11	Wright	400
30		7	H	Queen of the S	W	2-1	2-0	—	Malone, Buckley (pen)	360
31		13	H	Stirling Albion	D	1-1	0-1	—	Buckley	290
32		17	A	Queen's Park	W	2-0	0-0	8	Wright 2	264
33		27	A	Berwick R	W	3-1	2-1	—	Buckley 2 (1 pen), Duffy	250
34		31	A	Stranraer	W	2-1	2-0	5	Ross 2	400
35	Apr	7	H	Montrose	L	2-4	2-1	6	Ross, Buckley (pen)	200
36		14	A	Dumbarton	W	3-1	1-0	5	Ross 2, Buckley	400
37		21	A	Arbroath	W	1-0	1-0	5	Malone	237
38		28	H	East Stirling	D	3-3	2-0	6	Ross 2, Archibald	200
39	May	5	A	Kilmarnock	L	1-2	0-1	7	Malone	8419

Final League Position: 7

GOALSCORERS

League: (58): Ross 16, Buckley 7 (3 pens), Malone 7 (1 pen), Spence 7, Scott 6, Wright 4, MacKenzie 3, Mailer 3, Hamill 2, Archibald 1, Duffy 1, Herd 1.
Scottish Cup: (6): Ross 4, Wright 1, own goal 1.
Skol Cup: (0).

Record Victory: 12-0 v St Johnstone, Scottish Cup 1st rd; 21 Jan, 1928.
Record Defeat: 1-11 v Clyde, Division II; 6 Oct, 1951.
Most Capped Player: Jim Paterson, 3, Scotland.
Most League Appearances: —.
Most League Goals in Season (Individual): 40: Willie Devlin, Division II; 1925–26.
Most Goals Overall (Individual): —.

Honours

League Champions: Division II 1913–14, 1914–15, 1938–39; *Runners-up:* Division II 1921–22, 1923–24, 1969–70.
Scottish Cup:—.
League Cup:—.
Club colours: Shirt: Royal blue shadow vertical stripe with white chest band. Shorts: White with blue side stripe. Stockings: Royal blue.

Allan, R	Watt, D	Rae, J	Malone, D	McGovern, D	Kerr, G	Spence, W	Frith, J	Mailer, J	Ross, A	Scott, C	MacKenzie, A	Wright, J	Herd, W	Douglas, H	McConville, J	Baillie, R	Lamont, W	Cullen, D	Hamill, K	Archibald, E	Callaghan, W	Duffy, D	Smith, M	Buckley, G	Match No.
1	2*	3	4	5†	6	7	8	9	10	11	12	14													1
1	2	3	4*		6	7	10†	9	11	14	12	8	5												2
1	2		4		6	7	12	9	11	8*	10	5	3												3
1	2	3	8		6	7*	12	9	11	10	4	5													4
	2		4		6	7	9*	12	11	10	8†	5	3				1		14						5
	2		4		6	7	9	12	11	10*	8	5	3				1								6
	2		4		6	7*	9	12	11†	10	8	5	14	3			1								7
	2		8		6	7	9*	10	11†	12	14	4	5	3			1								8
	2		4		6	7*	12	11	9	10	8	5	3				1								9
	2		8*		6	7	12	9	10	4	5	3					1		11†	14					10
	2		4†		6	7*	12	10	9	14	8	5					1		11	3					11
	2				6	12	14	7	11	9*	10†	4	5				1		8	3					12
	2		8		6	7	10	4	5	12							1		11*	3	9				13
	2		8		6	12	7*	11	10	4	3						1		14	5	9†				14
	2		8		6	7	12	11	10*	4	3						1			5	9				15
			8		6	7	10	11	12	4						2	1		3	5	9*				16
	2		8	4	6	7	10*	11†	9	14							1		3	5	12				17
	2		8	4*	6	9	10	11	12								1		3	5	7				18
	2		8	4*	6	9	10	11	12								1		3	5	7				19
	2		8	4*	6	9	10	11	12								1		3	5	7				20
			8	4	6*	9†	10	11	14	7						2	1		12	5	3				21
			8	4	6	9	10	11								2	1		12	5	3			7*	22
	2		8		6	7	9	10	4								1		11*	5			3	12	23
	2		8	5	6	7	9	10	4								1		11	3					24
	2		8	5	6	7	9	10*	4								1		11	14			12	3†	25
	2		8	5†	6	7	9*	10	4	3							1		11	14			12		26
	2		8		6	7†	9	10	4								1		11*	5	14		3	12	27
	2		8		6	7*	9	10	4								1		11	5			3	12	28
	2		12	8	6	9	10*	4	14								1		11	5			3	7†	29
	2		8	10	6	9	4										1		11	5		12	3	7*	30
	2		8	10†	6	12	9	4	14								1		11*	5			3	7	31
	2		8	10	6	9*	11†	14	4								1			5		12	3	7	32
	2†		8		6	12	11	4*	14	3							1		10	5		9		7	33
	2		4†	8	6	9	11	14	3								1		10	5		12		7*	34
	2		4	8	6	9	11	14	3								1		10†	5		12		7*	35
	2*		4	8	6	7†	9	11	14	3	12						1			5				10	36
	2		4	8	6	7*	14	9†	11	12							1		3	5				10	37
	2		4	8	6	7	9	11†	14								1		3	5			10*	12	38
	2		8		6	7*	9	11	14	3							1		4	5		12		10†	39
4	36	3	34	22	39	26	2	14	30	33	11	17	12	14	12	4	35	—	24	26	4	6	11	10	Total
	+1s		+4s	+5s	+2s	+4s		+9s	+7s			+7s	+2s	+1s		+1s	+3s	+3s					+8s	+5s	Subs

DUMBARTON   Second Division

Year Formed: 1872.   *Ground & Address:* Boghead Park, Miller St, Dumbarton G82 2JA.   *Telephone:* 0389 62569/67864.
Ground Capacity: total: 10,700   seated: 700.   *Size of Pitch:* 110yd×75yd.
Chairman: R. Campbell Ward.   *Secretary:* C. Cleary & Co..   *Commercial Manager:* John Holden.
Manager: Billy Lamont.   *Assistant Manager:* Billy Simpson.   *Physio:* Robert McCallum.   *Coach:* —.
Managers since 1975: A. Wright; D. Wilson; S. Fallon; W. Lamont; D. Wilson; D. Whiteford; A. Totten; M. Clougherty;
R. Auld.
Club Nickname(s): The Sons.   *Previous Grounds:* None.
Record Attendance: 18,000 v Raith Rovers, Scottish Cup; 2 Mar, 1957.
Record Transfer Fee received: £125,000 for Graeme Sharp to Everton (March 1982).
Record Transfer Fee paid: £40,000 for Charlie Gibson from Stirling Albion 1989.

1989–90 LEAGUE RECORD

Match No.	Date	Venue	Opponents	Result	H/T Score	Lg. Pos.	Goalscorers	Atten-dance
1	Aug 12	H	Queen of the S	W 2-1	0-0	—	MacIver, Cairney	650
2	19	A	Brechin C	L 0-4	0-1	10		500
3	26	A	East Stirling	W 2-1	2-1	5	McQuade J (pen), MacIver	200
4	Sept 2	H	Berwick R	L 1-5	1-5	9	Spence	550
5	9	H	Stranraer	W 5-2	4-0	8	Gibson, Cairney, MacIver 2, Doyle	500
6	16	A	East Fife	D 2-2	0-0	6	McQuade A, Gibson	624
7	23	H	Stirling Albion	D 2-2	0-1	7	Gibson, Reid	800
8	30	A	Cowdenbeath	W 5-1	1-0	5	Gibson 3, MacIver, Spence	250
9	Oct 7	A	Arbroath	L 1-2	0-1	7	Gibson	611
10	14	H	Queen's Park	W 2-1	0-0	5	Gibson, Spence	700
11	21	H	Stenhousemuir	W 1-0	0-0	3	Gibson	348
12	28	A	Kilmarnock	L 0-3	0-0	5		2867
13	Nov 4	H	Montrose	W 3-2	1-2	3	Gibson 2, McQuade A	400
14	11	A	Berwick R	W 2-1	1-1	3	Quinn, Gibson	487
15	18	A	Cowdenbeath	D 2-2	0-1	2	MacIver 2	500
16	25	A	Stirling Albion	L 1-4	1-0	5	Hughes	570
17	Dec 2	H	Arbroath	D 0-0	0-0	4		450
18	16	A	Queen's Park	D 2-2	1-1	2	Gibson, MacIver	587
19	23	H	Brechin C	D 1-1	1-0	4	Spence	700
20	Jan 6	A	Montrose	D 2-2	0-0	5	Hughes, MacIver	300
21	10	A	Queen of the S	W 4-1	1-0	—	Andrews (og), MacIver 2, Gibson	923
22	13	A	Stranraer	D 4-4	1-1	4	Hughes (pen), MacIver, McQuade J, Spence	400
23	27	A	Stenhousemuir	L 3-4	2-2	4	Milligan (og), Hughes (pen), MacIver	500
24	Feb 10	H	Queen of the S	D 1-1	0-0	4	MacIver	822
25	Mar 14	A	East Fife	L 1-3	0-1	—	MacIver	609
26	17	A	Brechin C	L 0-3	0-2	10		600
27	20	H	East Stirling	W 3-0	1-0	—	Quinn, Hughes 2	500
28	24	H	Kilmarnock	L 0-2	0-0	10		1881
29	27	A	Montrose	W 2-1	1-0	—	Morrison, McQuade J	350
30	31	A	Berwick R	L 2-3	1-2	10	Gibson, Boyd	436
31	Apr 3	H	Kilmarnock	L 1-3	1-2	—	Gibson	1000
32	7	A	Stenhousemuir	W 3-1	1-1	10	Hughes, Gibson, MacIver	600
33	10	A	Stranraer	D 1-1	0-1	—	Morrison (pen)	300
34	14	H	Cowdenbeath	L 1-3	0-1	9	Gibson	400
35	17	H	East Stirling	W 2-1	2-0	—	Gibson 2	300
36	21	H	East Fife	W 3-1	2-0	6	MacIver, Morrison (2 pens)	500
37	24	H	Arbroath	W 2-0	2-0	—	Boyd, MacIver	450
38	28	H	Stirling Albion	L 1-2	0-1	5	MacIver	600
39	May 5	A	Queen's Park	L 0-1	0-0	6		586

Final League Position: 6

GOALSCORERS

League: (70): Gibson 20, MacIver 19, Hughes 7 (2 pens), Spence 5, Morrison 4 (3 pens), McQuade J 3 (1 pen),
Boyd 2, Cairney 2, McQuade A 2, Quinn 2, Doyle 1, Reid 1, own goals 2.
Scottish Cup: (2): McQuade J 1, Quinn 1.
Skol Cup: (3): MacIver 2, Gibson 1.

Record Victory: 13-1 v Kirkintilloch Cl. 1st Rd 1 September 1888.
Record Defeat: 1-11 v Albion Rovers, Division II; 30 Jan, 1926: v Ayr United, League Cup; 13 Aug, 1952.
Most Capped Player: John Lindsay, 8, Scotland; James McAulay, 8, Scotland.
Most League Appearances: —.
Most League Goals in Season (Individual): 38: Kenny Wilson, Division II; 1971–72.
Most Goals Overall (Individual): —.

Honours

League Champions: Division I 1890–91 (shared with Rangers), 1891–92. Division II 1910–11, 1971–72; *Runners-up:* First Division 1983–84. Division II 1907–08.
Scottish Cup Winners: 1883; *Runners-up:* 1881, 1882, 1887, 1891, 1897.
League Cup:—.
Club colours: Shirt: Gold with white chest band. Shorts: Black. Stockings: Gold and black.

Strachan, B	McQuade, A	Wharton, P	Dickie, G	Cairney, P	Spence, C	McQuade, J	Reid, W	Gibson, C	MacIver, S	Meechan, J	Gow, S	McGrogan, P	Quinn, P	Grant, B	Doyle, J	Dempsey, J	Stevens, G	Hughes, J	Stevenson, H	Morrison, S	Boyd, J	Wilson, D	McGinley, J	Match No.
1	2	3	4	5	6	7*	8	9	10	11	12													1
1	2	3	4	5	6	12		9*10	11			7	8											2
1	2		4	5	6	7	8		10	3			9	11										3
1	2	14	4	5	6	7	8			3		11†	9	10*12										4
1	7	3		5	6		12	9†10*		2			14	11	8	4								5
1	7	3			5	12	6	9	10		2			11*	8	4								6
1	7	3			5		6	9	10		2		12	11*	8	4								7
1	7	3	12		5		6	9	10†11	2	14			8*	4									8
1	7	3	12	5			6	9	10	11	2			8*	4									9
1	7	3		5	6		8	9	10	11*	2		12		4									10
1	2	3		5	8		6	9	10	12			7	11*	4									11
1	2		8	5	11		6	9	10*	3		7	12		4									12
1	2	3†	4*	5	6		7	9	12	11		10		14		8								13
1	2			5	6		7	9		3		11		10	4		8							14
1	2	14		5	6		7*	9	12	3		11		10†	4		8							15
1	2			12	5		6	9	11	3		10		8*	4	7								16
	2	3		5	8	12		9	10*			11			4	6	7	1						17
	2	3		5	8†	7*14		9	10			12			4	6	11	1						18
	2	3		5	8			9	10			7			4	6	11	1						19
	2	3		5	8		4*	9	10			12	7		6	11	1							20
	2	14	5	6			7*	9†10				12		8	3	4	11	1						21
		3	6			8	12	2	9	10*		7			4	5	11	1						22
	2				3		12	9	10			11		6*	4	5	8	1	7					23
	2	14			5	12	4	9	10			11*	6	7				1†	8	3				24
	4			5	8		2	9	10			12	7*		11	1	6	3						25
	2				5		8	9	10				6	4		11	1	7	3					26
1	2	12		5	14	8	9					10†		6*	4		11		7	3				27
1	2	12		5		8†	9	10				14		6*	4		11		7	3				28
1	2	6		5	7		9*10					12		4		11		8	3					29
1	2	6		5	7*		9	10				12		4		11		8	3					30
1	2	6		5	12		9	10				7		4		11*		8	3					31
1	7	6		5			9*10			2		12		4		11		8	3					32
1	7	6		5	10*12					2	9			4		11		8	3					33
1	7	14	6*	5		12	9			2	10			4		11		8†	3					34
1	4	3		5		12	9	10		2			8			11*		7	6					35
1	4	3		6			9	10		2			7*	5		12		8	11					36
1	2	5		4		8	9	10			12			6	7		11	3*						37
1	2	5	8		4	12	9	10						6			11	3	7*					38
	2	12			5	7		9*10			14			6		8	1	11	3			4†		39
28	38	19	14	18	38	8	23	36	32	12	11	3	17	7	18	29	8	24	11	17	16	1	1	
		+	+	+		+	+		+			+	+	+	+ +		+							
		5s	5s	1s		8s6s			2s	1s	1s	3s11s			3s		1s							

DUNDEE

First Division

Year Formed: 1893.   *Ground & Address:* Dens Park, Sandeman St, Dundee DD3 7JY.   *Telephone:* 0382 826104.
Ground Capacity: total: 22,381   seated: 12,130.   *Size of Pitch:* 113yd×73yd.
Chairman: Angus Cook.   *Secretary:* John Campbell.   *Commercial Manager:* —.
Manager: Gordon Wallace.   *Assistant Manager:* John Blackley.   *Physio:* Eric Ferguson.   *Coach:* Bert Slater.
Managers since 1975: David Whyte; Tommy Gemmell; Donald Mackay; Archie Knox; Jocky Scott; Dave Smith; Gordon Wallace.
Club Nickname(s): The Dark Blues or The Dee.   *Previous Grounds:* Carolina Port 1893–98.
Record Attendance: 43,024 v Rangers, Scottish Cup; 1953.
Record Transfer Fee received: £500,000 for Tommy Coyne to Celtic, March 1989.
Record Transfer Fee paid: £110,000 for Willie Jamieson from Hamilton A, January 1990.
Record Victory: 10–0 Division II v Alloa; 9 Mar, 1947 and v Dunfermline Ath; 22 Mar, 1947.

1989–90 LEAGUE RECORD

Match No.	Date	Venue	Opponents	Result	H/T Score	Lg. Pos.	Goalscorers	Attendance
1	Aug 12	A	Dunfermline Ath	L	1-2	1-1	—	Beedie	8987
2	19	H	Dundee U	W	4-3	2-2	4	Wright 3, McBride	13,616
3	26	A	Aberdeen	L	0-1	0-0	7		12,500
4	Sept 9	H	Hearts	D	2-2	1-2	7	Wright, Harvey	8440
5	16	A	Rangers	D	2-2	0-1	6	Craig, Wright	35,836
6	23	H	Hibernian	D	0-0	0-0	6		6842
7	30	A	Motherwell	L	0-3	0-2	9		4463
8	Oct 4	A	St Mirren	L	2-3	2-1	—	Wright, Dodds	3612
9	14	H	Celtic	L	1-3	0-2	10	Craib	16,215
10	21	H	Dunfermline Ath	L	1-2	1-1	10	Dodds (pen)	7058
11	28	A	Dundee U	D	0-0	0-0	10		11,529
12	Nov 4	H	Aberdeen	D	1-1	0-1	10	Dodds	7041
13	11	A	Hearts	L	3-6	1-3	10	Dodds 2, Saunders	11,869
14	18	A	Rangers	L	0-2	0-0	10		14,536
15	25	A	Hibernian	L	2-3	0-2	10	Beedie, Dodds	6000
16	Dec 2	H	Motherwell	W	2-1	1-0	10	Dodds (pen), Craig	4099
17	9	H	St Mirren	D	3-3	0-1	10	Dodds (pen), Chisholm, Forsyth	4043
18	16	A	Celtic	L	1-4	1-1	10	Beedie	17,860
19	26	A	Dunfermline Ath	L	0-1	0-0	—		9282
20	30	H	Dundee U	D	1-1	0-0	10	Chisholm	12,803
21	Jan 2	A	Aberdeen	L	2-5	2-4	—	Campbell D, Wright	16,054
22	6	H	Hearts	L	0-1	0-0	10		8300
23	13	A	Rangers	L	0-3	0-1	10		36,993
24	27	H	Hibernian	W	2-0	1-0	10	Wright, Chisholm	5720
25	Feb 3	H	Celtic	D	0-0	0-0	10		14,100
26	10	A	St Mirren	D	0-0	0-0	10		5010
27	17	A	Motherwell	L	1-3	0-2	10	Dodds	5508
28	Mar 3	H	Rangers	D	2-2	1-1	10	Campbell A, Dodds	12,743
29	10	A	Dunfermline Ath	W	1-0	1-0	10	Dodds	7247
30	24	A	Dundee U	W	2-1	2-1	10	Wright, Shannon	11,918
31	31	H	Aberdeen	D	1-1	1-1	10	Wright	8071
32	Apr 4	A	Hearts	D	0-0	0-0	—		10,761
33	14	H	St Mirren	L	1-2	1-1	10	Campbell A	7415
34	21	A	Celtic	D	1-1	0-0	10	Dodds (pen)	15,115
35	28	A	Hibernian	D	1-1	1-0	10	Dodds	4665
36	May 5	H	Motherwell	L	1-2	0-1	10	Wright	2846

Final League Position: 10

GOALSCORERS

League: (41): Dodds 13 (4 pens), Wright 11, Beedie 3, Chisholm 3, Campbell A 2, Craig 2, Campbell D 1, Craib 1, Forsyth 1, Harvey 1, McBride 1, Saunders 1, Shannon 1
Scottish Cup: (0).
Skol Cup: (5): Harvey 2, McBride 2, Wright 1.

Record Defeat: 0-11 v Celtic, Division I; 26 Oct, 1895.
Most Capped Player: Alex Hamilton, 24, Scotland.
Most League Appearances: 341: Doug Cowie 1945–61.
Most League Goals in Season (Individual): 38: Dave Halliday, Division I; 1923–24.
Most Goals Overall (Individual): 113: Alan Gilzean.

Honours
League Champions: Division I 1961–62. First Division 1978–79. Division II 1946–47; *Runners-up:* Division I 1902–03, 1906–07, 1908–09, 1948–49, 1980–81.
Scottish Cup Winners: 1910; *Runners-up:* 1925, 1952, 1964.
League Cup Winners: 1951–52, 1952–53, 1973–74; *Runners-up:* 1967–68, 1980–81.
European: *European Cup:* 1962–63 (semi-final). *Cup Winners Cup:* 1964–65.
UEFA Cup: (Fairs Cup 1967–68 semi-final), 1971–72, 1973–74, 1974–75.
Club colours: Shirt: Dark blue with red and white trim. Shorts: White. Stockings: Blue and White.

Geddes, R	Forsyth, S	Albiston, A	McGeachie, G	Chisholm, G	Craib, M	Craig, A	Shannon, R	Wright, K	Campbell, D	Beedie, S	McBride, J	Dodds, W	Harvey, G	McLeod, G	Campbell, A	Saunders, W	Frail, S	Angus, I	Smith, J	Carson, T	Dinnie, A	Holt, J	McSkimming, S	Campbell, S	Jamieson, W	McMartin, G	Ferguson, D	Duffy, J	Mathers, P	Match No.
1	2	3	4*	5	6	7	8	9	10†	11	14	12																		1
1	6	3		5	4	7	2	9	8*	11		10	12																	2
1	6	3	7	5	4*		2	9	8	11	14	12	10†																	3
1	6	3		5	4	7	2	9	10*	8	11	12																		4
1	6*	3		5	4	7	2	9	8	11	12	10																		5
1	6	3		5	4	7	2	9	8*	11	12	10																		6
1	6	3*		5	4	7	2	9	8	11	12	10†	14																	7
1	6	3		5	4*	7	2	9	8	11	12	10†	14																	8
1	6	3*		5	4	7†	2	9	8	11	12	10	14																	9
1	12	3		5	6	7†	2	9	8	11	14	10		4*																10
	6	3		5*	12	7†	2	9	8	11	14	10		4						1										11
	12	3		5	6	7*	2	9	8†	11	14	10		4						1										12
	12	3*		5	6	7	2	9	8	11†	14	10		4						1										13
	12	3		5†	6	7*	2	9	8	11	14	10		4						1										14
	12	3		5	6	7*	2	9	8	11		10		4						1										15
1	12	3		5	6*	7	2	9	8	11		10		4																16
1	12	3		5	6	7	2	9	8	11*	14	10		4†																17
	12	3		5	6	7	2	9	8	11*		10	14	4†						1										18
	12	3		5	6	7	2	9	8	11†		10	14	4*						1										19
		3*		5	6	7†	2	9	8	11	12	10	14	4						1										20
		3		5	6	7	2	9	8*	11	12	10		4						1										21
		3		5	6	7	2†	9	8*	11	12	10	14	4						1										22
		3			6	7	2*	9	8†	11	12	10	14	4						1				5					23
		3			6	7	2	9	8	11	12	10*		4						1				5					24
		3			6	7	2	9	8	11	12	10		4*						1				5					25
		3			6	7	2	9†	8	11	12	10*	14	4						1				5					26
		3			6	7	2†	9*	8	11	12	10	14	4						1				5					27
	2	3				7*	8	9	12	11		10		4						1				5			6		28
	2	3				7	8	9		11		10		4										5			6	1	29
	2	3				7	8	9		11		10		4										5			6	1	30
	2	3				7*	8	9	12	11		10		4										5			6	1	31
	2	3				7	8	9	12	11		10		4										5			6*	1	32
	2	3			6	7	8*	9	12	11†	14	10		4										5			6	1	33
	2	3			6	7*	8	9		11		10		4										5			6	1	34
	2	3				7†	8	9		11*		10		4										5			6	1	35
	2	3					8*	9		11†		10		4										5			6	1	36
12	33	9	2	34	20	12	36	34	6	19	10	29	4	24	8	7	6	4	4	16	21	2	6	—	14	3	4	8	8	

Appearances (substitute): +1s +1s +2s +8s +9s2s +8s +1s +2s3s +7s +2s +1s +1s2s +1s

Also played: Bain K – Match 36 (12); McQuillan J – Match 35 (12), 36 (7); Kerr M – Match 35 (14), 36 (14).

DUNDEE UNITED

Premier Division

Year Formed: 1909 (1923).   *Ground & Address:* Tannadice Park, Tannadice St, Dundee DD3 7JW.   *Telephone:* 0382
833166.
Ground Capacity: total: 22,310   seated: 2252.   *Size of Pitch:* 110×74yd.
Chairman: James Y. McLean.   *Secretary:* —.   *Commercial Manager:* James Connor.
Manager: James Y. McLean.   *Assistant Manager:* —.   *Physio:* Graham Doig.   *Coach:* Paul Sturrock.
Managers since 1975: J. McLean.
Club Nickname(s): The Terrors.   *Previous Grounds:* None.
Record Attendance: 28,000 v Barcelona, Fairs Cup; 16 Nov, 1966.
Record Transfer Fee received: £750,000 for Richard Gough to Tottenham Hotspur (Aug 1986).
Record Transfer Fee paid: £350,000 for Michael O'Neill from Newcastle U, August 1989.
Record Victory: 14-0 v Nithsdale Wanderers, Scottish Cup 1st rd; 17 Jan, 1931.
Record Defeat: 1-12 v Motherwell, Division II; 23 Jan, 1954.

1989–90 LEAGUE RECORD

Match No.	Date	Venue	Opponents	Result	H/T Score	Lg. Pos.	Goalscorers	Attendance
1	Aug 12	H	Motherwell	D 1-1	1-1	—	French	8596
2	19	A	Dundee	L 3-4	2-2	9	Malpas, O'Neill M, Paatelainan	13,616
3	26	H	Dunfermline Ath	W 2-1	2-1	5	Van der Hoorn, O'Neill M	9158
4	Sept 9	A	Hibernian	L 0-2	0-1	9		7000
5	16	H	Celtic	D 2-2	0-1	7	Van der Hoorn, French	16,624
6	23	A	Hearts	D 1-1	0-0	7	McInally	14,008
7	30	H	St Mirren	D 0-0	0-0	7		6643
8	Oct 4	H	Aberdeen	W 2-0	1-0	—	McInally, Malpas	11,879
9	14	A	Rangers	L 1-2	0-0	8	O'Neill M (pen)	36,062
10	21	A	Motherwell	L 2-3	1-1	8	O'Neill M 2	8184
11	28	H	Dundee	D 0-0	0-0	8		11,529
12	Nov 4	A	Dunfermline Ath	D 1-1	1-1	8	Paatelainan (pen)	10,804
13	8	H	Hibernian	W 1-0	1-0	—	Jackson	8247
14	18	A	Celtic	W 1-0	0-0	7	Gallacher	32,350
15	25	H	Hearts	W 2-1	0-1	5	Bowman, Paatelainan	12,201
16	Dec 9	A	Aberdeen	L 0-2	0-0	5		15,500
17	13	A	St Mirren	L 0-1	0-1	—		2800
18	16	H	Rangers	D 1-1	1-1	5	Paatelainan	15,947
19	23	A	Motherwell	D 1-1	1-1	5	Paatelainan (pen)	6169
20	30	A	Dundee	D 1-1	0-0	6	Jackson	12,803
21	Jan 3	H	Dunfermline Ath	W 1-0	1-0	—	Jackson	11,148
22	6	A	Hibernian	D 0-0	0-0	5		6500
23	13	H	Celtic	W 2-0	2-0	5	Connolly 2	16,635
24	27	A	Hearts	L 2-3	0-2	5	Connolly, Paatelainan (pen)	13,083
25	Feb 3	A	Rangers	L 1-3	1-3	6	Clark	39,058
26	10	H	Aberdeen	D 1-1	0-1	6	McInally	10,533
27	17	H	St Mirren	W 2-0	0-0	6	Jackson, Connolly	5957
28	Mar 3	A	Celtic	L 0-3	0-1	6		23,541
29	10	A	Motherwell	W 1-0	1-0	5	Jackson	4697
30	24	H	Dundee	L 1-2	1-2	6	Connolly	11,918
31	31	A	Dunfermline Ath	W 1-0	0-0	5	Jackson	6945
32	Apr 7	H	Hibernian	W 1-0	0-0	4	Paatelainan (pen)	6633
33	18	A	Aberdeen	L 0-1	0-0	—		10,000
34	21	H	Rangers	L 0-1	0-0	5		15,995
35	28	H	Hearts	D 1-1	0-0	5	Jackson	7679
36	May 5	A	St Mirren	D 0-0	0-0	4		4312

Final League Position: 4

GOALSCORERS

League: (36): Jackson 7, Paatelainan 7 (4 pens), Connolly 5, O'Neill M 5 (1 pen), McInally 3, French 2, Malpas 2,
Van der Hoorn 2, Bowman 1, Clark 1, Gallacher 1.
Scottish Cup: (4): Clark 1, Connolly 1, Jackson 1, Paatelainan 1.
Skol Cup: (2): Hinds 1, O'Neill M 1.

Most Capped Player: Maurice Malpas, 37, Scotland.
Most League Appearances: 625: Hamish McAlpine; 1969–85.
Most League Goals in Season (Individual): 41: John Coyle, Division II; 1955–56.
Most Goals Overall (Individual): 158: Peter McKay.

Honours
League Champions: Premier Division 1982–83. Division II 1924–25, 1928–29; *Runners-up:* Division II 1930–31, 1959–60.
Scottish Cup Runners-up: 1974, 1981, 1985, 1987, 1988.
League Cup Winners: 1979–80, 1980–81; *Runners-up:* 1981–82, 1984–85.
Summer Cup Runners-up: 1964–65.
Scottish War Cup Runners-up: 1939–40.
European: *European Cup:* 8 matches 1983–84 (semi-finals), 1988–89; *Cup Winners Cup:* 4 matches 1974–75; *UEFA Cup Runners-up:* 1986–87. 74 matches (1966–67, 1969–70, 1970–71 *Fairs Cup;* 1971–72, 1975–76, 1977–78, 1978–79, 1979–80, 1980–81, 1981–82, 1982–83, 1984–85, 1985–86, 1986–87, 1987–88, 1989–90).
Club colours: Tangerine jersey, black shorts. Change colours: all white.

Thomson, S	Vander Hoorn F	Malpas, M	McInally, J	Hegarty, P	Narey, D	Irvine, J A	Jackson, D	Connolly, P	French, H	Paatelainen, M	Clark, J	Bowman, D	Gallacher, K	O'Neill, M	McKinlay, W	Krivokapic, M	Hinds, P	Thomson, W	Cleland, A	McGinnis, G	Preston, A	McLeod, J	Main, A	McKinnon, R	O'Neil, J	Welsh, B	Match No.
1	2	3	4	5	6	7*	8†	9	10	11	14	12															1
1	3	4	8	5	6		14	12	11	2			7	9†	10*												2
	2	3	4		6		10	12	5	8	9*		7	11				1									3
	4	3	2	5	6		10	12		8	11	9*	7					1									4
	4	3	10	5	6		14	11†		12	8	7	9					1	2*								5
	4	3	10	5	6		14	11†		12	8	7	9					1	2*								6
	4*	3	10		6				5	8	7	14	12	9				1	2	11†							7
		3	4		6		7*			5	8	9	10†	11				1	2	12	14						8
		3	4		6		7		14	5	8	9	10†	11				1	2*12								9
	4	3			6		7*		10	5	8	9	2	11†14				1	12								10
	2	3	4		6				10	8	7	9*11				5			12				1				11
	2	3	4		6				10	8	11*	9	7			5			12				1				12
	2	3	4*		6		11†		10	12	8	9	7			5	14						1				13
	2*	3	4		6				10	5	8	11†	9	7		14			12				1				14
	2*	3	4		6				10	12	8	11	9	7	5								1				15
	2	3	4		6				10†	8	11	9	7*	14	12	5							1				16
	2	3	4		6				10	12	8*	9	7	5	11								1				17
	2	3	4		6					8	11	7	9	10	5								1				18
	2	3	4		6					8	11	7	9	10*	5				12				1				19
	2	3	4		6					9	11	8	6	10	5						7		1				20
	2*	3	4		6					9	10†	11	8	12	14	5					7		1				21
		3	4		6		2			9	10*	11	7	8	5				12				1				22
	2	3	4		6					9	10*	11	7	12	8	5							1				23
	2	3	4		6					12	10	11	7*	5	8	9							1				24
	2	3	4		6					9	10†	11	5*	14	12	7					8		1				25
	2	3	4		6					9	10*	11	12	5	7						8		1				26
	2	3	4		6					9	14	11	12	5	3	10*					8		1	7†			27
	2	3	4		6					9	7	11	5	8	10*				12				1				28
	2	3	4		6					9*10†	14	11	7	5	8				12				1				29
	2	3*	4		6					9	10	14	11	8	12	5							1		7†		30
	2		4		6					9	10*	11	8	5	12	7							1			3	31
	2		4		6					9	10*	14	12	8	5	11†			7				1			3	32
	4		6							9†	8	14	2	5	12	11					1	10*	7		3	33
	4		6				7			8	9		10	5	2	11*			1			12				3	34
	2		4		6†					9	14	10	12	5*	8				1		11	7				3	35
	2	3	4		6*					9	11	10	5	7	8				1		12						36
2	31	30	35	5	31	1	24	12	7	27	18	20	17	15	13	25	7	7	12	4	8	—	27	7	6	5	

+ + + + + + + + + + + + + +
1s 3s 5s4s 11s4s 3s 1s 6s 3s 3s 2s 3s 4s

DUNFERMLINE ATHLETIC Premier Division

Year Formed: 1885. *Ground & Address:* East End Park, Halbeath Rd, Dunfermline KY12 7RB. *Telephone:* 0383 724295.
Ground Capacity: total: 19,904 seated: 4000. *Size of Pitch:* 114yd×72yd.
Chairman: William M. Rennie. *Secretary:* James McConville J.P.. *General Manager:* Jack E. Kyle. *Commercial Manager:* Audrey Kelly.
Co-Managers: Jim Leishman/Iain Munro. *Assistant Manager:* —. *Physio:* Philip Yeates, M.C.S.P.. *Coach:* Iain Munro.
Managers since 1975: G. Miller; H. Melrose; P. Stanton; T. Forsyth; J. Leishman.
Club Nickname(s): The Pars. *Previous Grounds:* None.
Record Attendance: 27,816 v Celtic, Division I; 30 April 1968.
Record Transfer Fee received: £200,000 for Ian McCall to Rangers (Aug 1987).
Record Transfer Fee paid: £540,000 for Istvan Kozma from Bordeaux, September 1989.

1989–90 LEAGUE RECORD

Match No.	Date	Venue	Opponents	Result	H/T Score	Lg. Pos.	Goalscorers	Attendance
1	Aug 12	H	Dundee	W 2-1	1-1	—	Smith P, Irons	8987
2	19	A	Celtic	L 0-1	0-0	5		34,000
3	26	A	Dundee U	L 1-2	1-2	8	Jack	9158
4	Sept 9	H	Motherwell	D 1-1	0-0	8	Jack	8715
5	16	A	Aberdeen	L 1-2	0-1	10	Jack (pen)	13,000
6	23	H	Rangers	D 1-1	1-1	9	Jack	17,765
7	30	A	Hibernian	D 2-2	1-1	8	Robertson 2	13,000
8	Oct 4	A	Hearts	W 2-1	0-0	—	Jack, Smith P	14,165
9	14	H	St Mirren	W 5-1	2-1	6	Jack 2 (1 pen), Kozma 3	7656
10	21	A	Dundee	W 2-1	1-1	3	Jack, Smith P	7058
11	28	H	Celtic	W 2-0	2-0	3	Jack, Kozma	19,588
12	Nov 4	H	Dundee U	D 1-1	1-1	3	Kozma	10,804
13	8	A	Motherwell	D 1-1	0-1	—	Jack	9138
14	18	H	Aberdeen	L 0-3	0-2	4		11,882
15	25	A	Rangers	L 0-3	0-2	6		39,121
16	Dec 2	H	Hibernian	D 0-0	0-0	6		9303
17	9	H	Hearts	L 0-2	0-1	6		11,295
18	26	H	Dundee	W 1-0	0-0	—	Kozma	9282
19	30	A	Celtic	W 2-0	1-0	5	Rafferty, Jack	30,548
20	Jan 3	A	Dundee U	L 0-1	0-1	—		11,148
21	6	H	Motherwell	L 0-5	0-3	7		8525
22	10	A	St Mirren	L 0-2	0-2	—		4501
23	13	A	Aberdeen	L 1-4	1-4	8	Irons	14,000
24	27	H	Rangers	L 0-1	0-1	9		17,350
25	Feb 3	H	St Mirren	W 1-0	0-0	7	O'Boyle	7068
26	10	A	Hearts	W 2-0	1-0	7	Jack, O'Boyle	14,204
27	17	A	Hibernian	L 1-2	0-1	8	Tierney	7000
28	Mar 3	H	Aberdeen	L 2-4	0-1	8	Tierney, Gallagher	8228
29	10	A	Dundee	L 0-1	0-1	8		7247
30	24	H	Celtic	D 0-0	0-0	8		14,044
31	31	H	Dundee U	L 0-1	0-0	8		6945
32	Apr 7	A	Motherwell	W 3-1	1-1	8	Smith P, Jack 2 (2 pens)	6351
33	14	H	Hearts	L 0-1	0-0	9		10,829
34	21	A	St Mirren	W 2-1	1-0	8	O'Boyle (pen), Jack	5830
35	28	A	Rangers	L 0-2	0-0	8		40,769
36	May 5	H	Hibernian	D 1-1	1-0	8	Jack	9681

Final League Position: 8

GOALSCORERS

League: (37): Jack 16 (4 pens), Kozma 6, Smith P 4, O'Boyle 3 (1 pen), Irons 2, Robertson 2, Tierney 2, Gallagher 1, Rafferty 1.
Scottish Cup: (3): Jack 2 (1 pen), O'Boyle 1.
Skol Cup: (7): Jack 3, Rougvie 2, Abercromby 1, Smith P 1.

Record Victory: 11-2 v Stenhousemuir, Division II; 27 Sept, 1930.
Record Defeat: 0-10 v Dundee, Division II; 22 Mar, 1947.
Most Capped Player: Andy Wilson, 6 (12), Scotland.
Most League Appearances: 360: Bobby Robertson; 1977–88.
Most League Goals in Season (Individual): 55: Bobby Skinner, Division II; 1925–26.
Most Goals Overall (Individual): 154: Charles Dickson.

Honours

League Champions: First Division 1988–89. Division II 1925–26. Second Division 1985–86; *Runners-up:* First Division 1986–87. Division II 1912–13, 1933–34, 1954–55, 1957–58, 1972–73. Second Division 1978–79.
Scottish Cup Winners: 1961, 1968; *Runners-up:* 1965.
League Cup Runners-up: 1949–50.
European: *European Cup:*—. *Cup Winners Cup:* 1961–62, 1968–69 (semi-finals). *UEFA Cup:* 1962–63, 1964–65, 1965–66, 1966–67, 1969–70 (*Fairs Cup*).
Club colours: Shirt: Broad black and white vertical stripes. Shorts: Black. Stockings: Black with red diamond tops.

Westwater, I	Nicholl, J	Rougvie, D	McCathie, N	Tierney, G	Abercromby, W	Smith, P	Farningham, R	Jack, R	O'Boyle, G	Irons, D	Sharp, R	Gallagher, E	Rafferty, S	Kozma, I	Robertson, G	Wilson, T	Bonnyman, P	Clark, A	Williamson, A	Sinclair, C	Match No.
1	2	3	4	5	6	7	8	9	10*	11	12										1
1	2	3	4	5	6	7	8	9*	10†	11	12	14									2
1	2*	3	4	5	6	7		9	10†	11	12	14	8								3
1	2	3	4	5	12	7		9	10	11			8*	6							4
1		3	4	5	6	7		9	10	11			8		2						5
1		3	4	5		7*	12	9	10		6		8	11	2						6
1		3	4	5		7		9	10	12	6		8	11*	2						7
1		3	4	5		7	12	9	10*		6		8	11	2						8
1		3	4	5		7		9	10	12	6		8	11*	2						9
1		3	4	5		7	12	9	10		6		8	11*	2						10
1		3	4	5		7		9	10	12	6*		8	11	2						11
1		3	4	5		7		9	10		6		8	11	2						12
1		3	4	5*		7		9	10		6		8	11	2	12					13
1		3	4	5*		7	14	9	10		6		8	11†	2	12					14
1		3	4	5*		7	14	9	10†	12	6		8	11	2						15
1		3	4	5		7		9	10		6		8	11	2						16
1		3†	4	5		7	14	9	10*		6	12	8	11	2						17
1		3	4	5			8	9*	10		6	12	7	11	2						18
1		3	4	5		7		9	10		6		8	11*	12	2					19
1		3	4	5		7		9	10		6*	12	8	11	14	2†					20
1		3	4	5	14	7		9*	10		6	12	8	11†	2						21
1	2		4	5	14	7	6*	9	10	3†	11		8	12							22
1	2*	3	4		6	12	14	9	10	11†	7		8			5					23
1	2†	5	4			7		9	10*	11		14	8	6	3	12					24
1	2*	6	4	5	12	7		9†	10			14	8	11	3						25
1		3	4	5		7		9	10		6		8	11	2						26
1		3†	4	5		7		9*	10	14	6	12	8	11	2						27
1	2		4	5		7		9	10	6			8	11	3						28
1	6*	3	4	5		7		9	10		12		8	11	2						29
1	2		4	5		7		9	10		6	3	8	11							30
1	2		4	5		7	6	9	10			3	8	11							31
1	6	3	4	5		7	8	9	12			14		11†	2			10*			32
1		3	4	5*	6	7	8	9	10†		12	14		11	2						33
1		3	4	5	6	7	8	9†	10*		12	14		11	2						34
1		3*	4	5	6	7		9	10		12		8	11	2						35
1		3	4			7*	6	9	10			14	8	12	2				5	11†	36
36	17	28	36	33	5	32	11	34	28	13	22	4	31	32	15	13	1	3	1	1	

Substitute appearances: + + + + (4s1s 6s 2s) + + + + + + (10s5s 10s1s 1s 2s 2s) + (1s)

EAST FIFE   Second Division

Year Formed: 1903. *Ground & Address:* Bayview Park, Methil Fife KY8 3AG. *Telephone:* 0333 26323. *Fax:* 26376.
Ground Capacity: total: 5150 seated: 600. *Size of Pitch:* 110yd×71yd.
Chairman: James Baxter. *Secretary:* Mrs I. McCammon. *Commercial Manager:* James Bonthrone.
Manager: Gavin Murray. *Assistant Manager:* —. *Physio:* Bud Porteous. *Coach:* David Gorman.
Managers since 1975: Frank Christie; Roy Barry; David Clarke; Gavin Murray.
Club Nickname(s): The Fifers. *Previous Grounds:* None.
Record Attendance: 22,515 v Raith Rovers, Division I; 2 Jan, 1950.
Record Transfer Fee received: £100,000 for Paul Hunter from Hull C, March 1990.
Record Transfer Fee paid: £29,000 for Ray Charles from Montrose (1987).

1989–90 LEAGUE RECORD

Match No.	Date		Venue	Opponents	Result	H/T Score	Lg. Pos.	Goalscorers	Atten- dance
1	Aug	12	A	East Stirling	W 2-0	0-0	—	Mitchell, Hunter	180
2		19	H	Stenhousemuir	L 2-3	1-2	6	Cairney (og), Mitchell	667
3		26	A	Cowdenbeath	W 1-0	0-0	4	Hope	350
4	Sept	2	H	Queen's Park	D 1-1	0-0	6	Hunter	801
5		9	A	Berwick R	D 1-1	1-0	7	McGonigal	620
6		16	H	Dumbarton	D 2-2	0-0	5	Lennox, Brown W	624
7		23	H	Brechin C	W 3-1	1-0	3	Hunter, McGonigal, Mitchell	949
8		30	A	Stranraer	D 1-1	0-1	3	Taylor P (pen)	700
9	Oct	7	H	Queen of the S	D 2-2	1-0	3	Hunter, Rogerson	796
10		14	A	Kilmarnock	L 0-1	0-0	7		2456
11		21	A	Stirling Albion	L 1-3	1-2	8	Mitchell	636
12		28	H	Montrose	W 4-1	2-1	6	Sheran (og), Taylor P (pen), Brown W 2	578
13	Nov	4	H	Arbroath	W 3-0	1-0	4	Mitchell, Brown W, Taylor P (pen)	604
14		11	A	Queen's Park	L 1-2	1-1	6	Lennox	687
15		18	H	Stranraer	L 1-2	1-1	8	Mitchell	420
16		25	A	Brechin C	L 1-2	1-0	9	Hamilton (og)	602
17	Dec	2	A	Queen of the S	L 1-5	0-3	10	Brown I	531
18		23	A	Stenhousemuir	D 2-2	2-1	10	Taylor P (pen), Hunter	430
19		26	H	East Stirling	D 1-1	1-1	—	Mitchell	772
20	Jan	2	H	Cowdenbeath	D 0-0	0-0	—		962
21		10	H	Kilmarnock	W 4-2	1-1	—	Mitchell, Brown W 2, Hunter	1109
22		13	A	Berwick R	D 2-2	2-0	8	Brown W, Hunter	707
23		27	H	Stirling Albion	W 1-0	1-0	7	Hunter	976
24		31	A	Arbroath	L 0-3	0-0	—		480
25	Feb	3	A	Montrose	D 2-2	0-1	7	Mitchell, Hunter	450
26		10	A	Queen's Park	W 3-1	1-2	6	Hunter 2, Taylor P (pen)	624
27		17	A	Cowdenbeath	D 2-2	0-0	5	Hunter, Mitchell	543
28		28	A	Stranraer	W 2-0	0-0	—	Hunter, Charles	500
29	Mar	3	H	Arbroath	L 2-3	2-2	5	Mitchell, Hunter	546
30		10	A	Berwick R	L 0-2	0-0	6		382
31		14	H	Dumbarton	W 3-1	1-0	—	Wilson 2, Crolla	609
32		17	H	East Stirling	D 1-1	0-1	5	Lennox	321
33		24	H	Queen of the S	L 1-2	1-2	6	Brown I	510
34		31	A	Montrose	W 2-0	0-0	6	Brown W, Paterson (og)	350
35	Apr	7	A	Kilmarnock	L 1-2	0-0	5	Mitchell	3266
36		14	H	Brechin C	L 1-3	0-1	7	Brown W	649
37		21	A	Dumbarton	L 1-3	0-2	8	Bell	500
38		28	H	Stenhousemuir	W 2-1	1-0	8	Wilson, Hope	914
39	May	5	A	Stirling Albion	L 0-2	0-1	9		1020

Final League Position: 9

GOALSCORERS

League: (60): Hunter 14, Mitchell 12, Brown W 9, Taylor P 5 (5 pens), Lennox 3, Wilson 3, Brown I 2, Hope 2, McGonigal 2, Bell 1, Charles 1, Crolla 1, Rogerson 1, own goals 4.
Scottish Cup: (8): Hunter 4, Brown I 1, Brown W 1, Crolla 1, Mitchell 1.
Skol Cup: (2): Hunter 2.

Record Victory: 13-2 v Edinburgh City, Division II; 11 Dec, 1937.
Record Defeat: 0-9 v Hearts, Division I; 5 Oct, 1957.
Most Capped Player: George Aitken, 5 (8), Scotland.
Most League Appearances: 517: David Clarke, 1968–86.
Most League Goals in Season (Individual): 41: Jock Wood, Division II; 1926–27 and Henry Morris, Division II; 1947–48.
Most Goals Overall (Individual): 196: George Dewar (149 in League).

Honours
League Champions: Division II 1947–48; *Runners-up:* Division II 1929–30, 1970–71. Second Division 1983–84.
Scottish Cup Winners: 1938; *Runners-up:* 1927, 1950.
League Cup Winners: 1947–48, 1949–50, 1953–54.
Club colours: Shirt: Black and gold stripes. Shorts: Black with gold flashes. Stockings: Black with gold and white tops.

Charles, R	Harrow, A	Taylor, P	Lennox, S	Reid, G	Crolla, C	Mitchell, A	Brown, W	Hunter, P	McGonigal, A	Hope, D	Brown, I	Bell, G	Hall, A	Halliday, D	Collins, N	Gallacher, W	Rogerson, S	Banner, A	Taylor, P H	Bryce, G	McPhee, W	Hogarth, G	Wilson, S	Prior, S	Moffat, J	Atkins, D	Match No.
1	2	3	4*	5	6	7	8†	9	10	11	12	14															1
1	2	3	4	5	6	7	8†	9	10	11*	12	14															2
1	2	3	4	5	8	7	10	9*	12	11				6													3
1	2	3	4	5	8	7	12	9	10	11*				6													4
1	2	3	4	5	8	7	12	9	10*	11				6													5
1	2†	3	4	5	8*	7	12	9	10	11			14	6													6
1	2*	3	4	5		7	8	9	10	11				6		12											7
1	2	3	4	5			8	9	10	7				6		12	11*										8
1		3	4	10			8	9	7	11				6*		2	12		5								9
1		3	4			7	8	9	10	11				6		2			5								10
		3	4	14	7	8		9	10†	11*				6		2	12		5	1							11
		3	4	10	7†	8			9*	12	14			6		2	11		5	1							12
1		3	4		8	7		9	14	10†	12			6		2*	11		5								13
1		3	4		8	7	10*	9	12	14				6		2	11†		5								14
1		3	4*	5	8	7		9†	10	12	14			6		2	11										15
1		3	4		8	7		9	10	12				6		2	11*		5								16
1		3	4		8	7		9	10	11	14			6		2†	12		5*								17
1		3	4			7*		9	8	12	11	2				10	5		6								18
1		3	8			7		9	4	12	11	2		14		10†	5		6*								19
1		3	4	14		7	8	9†		10		2			12	11*	5		6								20
1		3	4	12		7	8	9†	14	10		2*				11	5		6								21
1		3	4*	12		7	8	9	14	10		2				11†	5		6								22
1		3	4		8	7*		9		12	10†	2				11	5		6	14							23
1		3	4	12		7	8	9	14	10*		2				11†	5		6								24
1		3			6	7	8	9	4	10*		2				11	5		12								25
1		3		4		7	8*	9	12	10†		2				11	5		6	14							26
1		3	4			7	8	9		10		2				11	5		6								27
1		3	4		8		10*	9		11		2				7	5		6	12							28
1		3	4		8	7		9		11*		2				10	5		6	12							29
1						8	7	9		12	4	2			3		5		6	11*	10						30
1		3	8	11		7		9*	4†			2		14		5			6	12			10				31
1		3	8	11		7		9*	4			2							6	12			10	5			32
1†		3			8*	7		4	9			2		11		6			12	14			10	5			33
		3				7	9		11	10*		2			4				6	12			8	5		1	34
		3				7	9	4		10*		2				11			6	12			8	5		1	35
		3	8*			7	9		11			2			4†	14	6		12				10	5		1	36
		3	8			7	10*	11	12			2			4		6						9	5		1	37
1		3	4	14			9	7*	12			2				11	8	6†					10	5			38
1		3	4	12		7		11†	10			2				8*		6	14				9	5			39
33	8	38	33	9	22	35	24	28	17	20	18	22	15	12	1	23	25	2	21	1	1	—	9	8	2	2	
		+			+	+	+	+	+	+	+	+				+	+		+				+	+			
		7s			3s	1s	2s	12s	8s	3s	2s	2s				4s	1s		11s	1s	1s						

EAST STIRLINGSHIRE   Second Division

Year Formed: 1881. *Ground & Address:* Firs Park, Firs St, Falkirk FK2 7AY. *Telephone:* 0324 23583.
Ground Capacity: total: 6000   seated: 2000.   *Size of Pitch:* 112yd×72yd.
Chairman: John P. Turnbull.   *Secretary:* Peter I. McKay.   *Commercial Manager:* —.
Manager: Alan Mackin.   *Assistant Manager:* Bobby McCulley.   *Physio:* Angus Williamson.   *Coach:* —.
Managers since 1975: I. Ure; D. McLinden; W. P. Lamont; M. Ferguson; W. Little; D. Whiteford; D. Lawson; J. D.
Connell, A. Mackin.
Club Nickname(s): The Shire.   *Previous Grounds:* Burnhouse, Randyford Park, Merchiston Park, New Kilbowie
Park.
Record Attendance: 11,500 v Hibernian, Scottish Cup; 10 Feb, 1969.
Record Transfer Fee received: £35,000 for Jim Docherty to Chelsea (1978).

1989–90 LEAGUE RECORD

Match No.	Date	Venue	Opponents	Result	H/T Score	Lg. Pos.	Goalscorers	Attendance
1	Aug 12	H	East Fife	L 0-2	0-0	—		180
2	19	A	Queen's Park	L 2-3	0-2	13	O'Brien, Wilcox	400
3	26	H	Dumbarton	L 1-2	1-2	13	Arthur Grant	200
4	Sept 2	A	Kilmarnock	L 0-2	0-1	13		1749
5	9	H	Stenhousemuir	L 0-3	0-1	14		200
6	16	A	Stranraer	D 1-1	1-1	14	Wilcox (pen)	350
7	23	H	Arbroath	D 1-1	0-1	14	Dewar (og)	200
8	30	A	Queen of the S	D 2-2	0-1	14	Durie, Lex Grant	350
9	Oct 7	H	Berwick R	W 3-1	1-1	14	O'Brien, McNeill, Wilcox	200
10	14	A	Brechin C	L 1-2	1-1	14	Lex Grant	308
11	21	H	Montrose	L 0-2	0-1	14		150
12	28	H	Cowdenbeath	D 1-1	0-1	14	Bateman	150
13	Nov 4	A	Stirling Albion	L 0-4	0-1	14		530
14	11	H	Kilmarnock	W 2-1	0-0	14	McNeill, Wilson	1375
15	18	H	Queen of the S	W 1-0	0-0	14	Wilson	220
16	25	A	Arbroath	L 0-2	0-0	14		402
17	Dec 2	H	Berwick R	W 2-1	0-1	13	Wilson, Diver	150
18	23	H	Queen's Park	W 1-0	1-0	12	Feeney	300
19	26	A	East Fife	D 1-1	1-1	—	Durie	772
20	Jan 6	H	Stirling Albion	L 0-2	0-1	14		600
21	10	H	Brechin C	W 2-0	1-0	—	Workman, McNeill	400
22	13	A	Stenhousemuir	L 0-2	0-1	14		400
23	Feb 3	A	Cowdenbeath	L 0-4	0-1	14		200
24	10	H	Arbroath	W 1-0	0-0	14	O'Brien	300
25	Mar 3	A	Kilmarnock	L 0-2	0-1	14		2747
26	14	H	Montrose	D 1-1	0-0	—	Henderson	200
27	17	A	East Fife	D 1-1	1-0	14	Byrne	321
28	20	A	Dumbarton	L 0-3	0-1	—		500
29	27	H	Stirling Albion	L 0-2	0-2	—		450
30	31	A	Queen of the S	D 1-1	0-0	14	Durie	663
31	Apr 4	H	Stranraer	L 0-3	0-2	—		119
32	7	A	Queen's Park	L 1-2	1-2	14	Brannigan	425
33	11	H	Stenhousemuir	W 4-2	1-1	—	McNeill, Diver, Workman (pen), Wilcox	300
34	14	A	Berwick R	L 0-1	0-0	14		404
35	17	A	Dumbarton	L 1-2	0-2	—	Byrne	300
36	21	A	Montrose	L 0-3	0-0	14		163
37	24	H	Stranraer	L 0-1	0-0	—		300
38	28	A	Cowdenbeath	D 3-3	0-2	14	Wilson, Bateman (pen), Diver	200
39	May 5	A	Brechin C	D 0-0	0-0	14		1150

Final League Position: 14

GOALSCORERS

League: (34): McNeill 4, Wilcox 4 (1 pen), Wilson 4, Diver 3, Durie 3, O'Brien 3, Bateman 2 (1 pen), Byrne 2, Lex Grant
2, Workman 2 (1 pen), Brannigan 1, Feeney 1, Arthur Grant 1, Henderson 1, own goal 1.
Scottish Cup: (3): Armstrong 1, Arthur Grant 1, Wilson 1.
Skol Cup: (0).

Record Transfer Fee paid: —.
Record Victory: 10–1 v Stenhousemuir, Scottish Cup 1st rd; 1 Sept, 1888.
Record Defeat: 1-12 v Dundee United, Division II; 13 Apr, 1936.
Most Capped Player: Humphrey Jones, 5 (14), Wales.
Most League Appearances: Gordon Simpson, 1967–79.
Most League Goals in Season (Individual): 36: Malcolm Morrison, Division II; 1938–39.
Most Goals Overall (Individual): —.

Honours

League Champions: Division II 1931–32; *Runners-up:* Division II 1962–63. Second Division 1979–80.
Scottish Cup:—.
League Cup:—.
Club colours: Shirt: White. Shorts: White. Stockings: Black.

Kelly, C	Peters, A	Russell, G	Wilcox, D	Gilchrist, A	Purdie, B	Grant, Arthur	Drew, D	Durie, C	Scott, R	Feeney, P	Wood, D	McEntegart, T	McIntosh, S	O'Brien, P	Wilson, C	McNeill, W	Bateman, A	Grant, Lex	Brown, G	Cairns, M	Workman, J	Lauchlan, G	Mackin, A	Brannigan, K	Love, D	Diver, D	McLaren, P	Watson, G	Granger, C	Match No.
1	2	3	4	5	6	7	8	9*	10	11	12																			1
1	2		4	5		7*	6	9	10		12	8	3	11																2
1	2		4	11	6	7*	10	8	14		12	5†	3		9															3
1	2	14	4	5		7	11	10*	12			6	3		8†	9														4
1	2		4	5		7	8	10†12	14			6*	3		11	9														5
1		5	4		7	2*	8	12	11			6	3		10	9														6
1		5	4	2		6	14		12			3	7†10	11*	8	9														7
1	2		4	5	6	7		12				3	14	10†11*	8	9														8
1	2		4	5	6	8		12				3	7	11*10	9															9
1		5	4		6	8		12				3	7	11	10	9*	2													10
		2	4	5		14	3†11		6				9	7*12	8	10		1												11
		2	4	5	6		12		7				8	9	10			1			3			11*						12
		2	4	5	10	7		11				12	3	6*	9	8		1												13
		2		6	9	10						4	7	11*	8			1			3	12	5							14
		2		6	11	10		12				4	7	9	8			1			3*		5							15
		2		6	11	7	12	14				4	10	9†	8*			1			3		5							16
		2		6	7							4	8	9	10			3					5	1	11					17
		2	6		5	10		12				7	8	9*	4			3						1	11					18
		2	6		10	11*		12				4	7		8			3					5	1	9					19
		2	8		6*10	11		12				4	7					3					5	1	9					20
1		2	6			4		7				9	8					3					5		11	10				21
1		2	6			10†		14				4	7*	9	8			3					5		11	12				22
		2		4	12	11*						3	8	7	9			10					5		6			1		23
		2		12								7	14		10			3			4	5		9†11*		1	6			24
		2		12								10*	7		11			3			4	5		9		1				25
		2				7		4				12	11*					3					5	9		1	10			26
		2				14		11*				7	4	12				3					5	9		1	10†			27
		2				14		11*				7	4		12			3					5	9		1	10†			28
		4	6			7	12	14				3	11†		10								5	9		1				29
		2	6			7	8†12	14				11*	4					3					5	9		1				30
		4	2			7	8†					12	11*14					3					5	9		1				31
		4*	2			7		12				11	14	10†				3					5	9		1	6			32
		2				7		8				11						3			4	5		9		1				33
		6				7		8				9		10				3			4	5				1				34
		2				7*		8				14	11	12				3			4	5		9		1				35
		4				12		10*				7	11	8†				3					5	9	14	1				36
		2				14						4	10					3					5	9	12	1	6			37
		4				12						6	10					5					9			1	3		38
		2	4			12						6						3					5	9		10	1			39
12	4	30	29	6	14	27	12	18	3	4	—	8	18	16	25	23	26	5	1	6	24	1	6	24	4	21	4	17	7	

Substitute appearances: 1s (Russell); + 9s 3s 4s 4s12s3s (Grant Arthur, Drew, Durie, Scott); 1s; + 1s 4s 4s 3s (Wilson, McNeill, Bateman); + 1s (Brannigan); + 3s (Granger).

FALKIRK

First Division

Year Formed: 1876. *Ground & Address:* Brockville Park, Hope St, Falkirk FK1 5AX. *Telephone:* 0324 24121.
Ground Capacity: total: 18,000 seated: 2661. *Size of Pitch:* 110yd×70yd.
Chairman: David Holmes. *Secretary:* W. Barrie Scott, C.A.. *Commercial Manager:* Alastair McKenzie.
Manager: Jim Jefferies. *Assistant Manager:* W. Brown. *Physio:* B. Cairney. *Coach:* —.
Managers since 1975: J. Prentice; G. Miller; W. Little; J. Hagart; A. Totten; G. Abel; W. Lamont; D. Clarke; J. Duffy.
Club Nickname(s): The Bairns. *Previous Grounds:* Randyford; Blinkbonny Grounds; Hope Street.
Record Attendance: 23,100 v Celtic, Scottish Cup 3rd rd; 21 Feb, 1953.
Record Transfer Fee received: £150,000 for Roddie Manley from St Mirren, 1989.
Record Transfer Fee paid: £70,000 for Gordon Marshall from East Fife, 1987.
Record Victory: 21-1 v Laurieston, Scottish Cup 2nd rd; 23 Mar, 1893.

1989–90 LEAGUE RECORD

Match No.	Date	Venue	Opponents	Result	H/T Score	Lg. Pos.	Goalscorers	Attendance
1	Aug 12	A	Forfar Ath	W 2-1	1-0	—	Robertson, Baptie	2081
2	19	H	Raith R	L 0-2	0-0	8		3000
3	26	A	Alloa	D 1-1	1-1	8	McGivern	2831
4	Sept 2	H	Meadowbank T	D 1-1	1-1	8	Burgess	3119
5	5	A	Airdrieonians	D 1-1	0-0	—	Baptie	4319
6	9	H	Ayr U	L 0-1	0-1	9		3000
7	16	H	Hamilton A	D 3-3	2-1	10	McWilliams, Clark, Rae	3000
8	23	A	St Johnstone	L 0-2	0-1	12		7011
9	30	H	Albion R	W 6-0	1-0	7	Rae 4, McWilliams, Callaghan	2724
10	Oct 7	A	Partick T	L 0-1	0-1	8		8369
11	14	H	Clydebank	W 2-1	1-0	7	McWilliams (pen), Baptie	2574
12	21	H	Morton	W 1-0	0-0	7	McWilliams (pen)	3000
13	28	A	Clyde	L 0-2	0-1	7		1650
14	Nov 4	H	Airdrieonians	W 3-1	3-0	5	McCoy, McWilliams, Baptie	3500
15	11	A	Ayr U	D 3-3	1-1	5	McWilliams, Baptie, McCoy	3716
16	18	A	Hamilton A	L 0-1	0-1	7		2640
17	25	H	St Johnstone	D 3-3	1-3	6	McWilliams (pen), Rutherford 2	3400
18	Dec 2	A	Albion R	L 1-2	1-0	9	Hetherston	1614
19	9	H	Partick T	D 1-1	0-0	9	McGivern	4000
20	23	A	Clydebank	D 3-3	0-1	9	Hetherston, McWilliams, McCoy	1464
21	26	H	Forfar Ath	W 4-0	1-0	—	Baptie, McWilliams 2, McCoy	2500
22	30	A	Raith R	L 0-4	0-1	8		2765
23	Jan 2	H	Alloa	W 1-0	1-0	—	McWilliams	3231
24	6	A	Meadowbank T	W 2-1	0-0	5	Rae, McWilliams (pen)	1200
25	13	H	Clyde	W 3-0	0-0	5	McWilliams 2, Baptie	2200
26	27	A	Morton	W 2-0	1-0	4	Rutherford, McWilliams (pen)	2158
27	Feb 3	A	Albion R	D 2-2	0-0	4	McWilliams (pen), Beaton	1777
28	10	H	St Johnstone	W 1-0	1-0	3	Rae	4738
29	21	H	Clydebank	L 0-1	0-0	—		2800
30	Mar 3	A	Hamilton A	D 2-2	0-0	5	Beaton, McWilliams (pen)	1891
31	17	H	Partick T	W 2-0	1-0	4	Hay, Rutherford	3200
32	20	A	Alloa	D 0-0	0-0	—		1149
33	24	A	Ayr U	D 1-1	0-1	3	Rutherford	2190
34	31	H	Morton	W 2-0	0-0	3	Mooney 2	1700
35	Apr 7	A	Airdrieonians	W 3-1	1-1	3	Logan, Rutherford, Rae	4200
36	14	A	Clyde	D 0-0	0-0	3		1200
37	21	H	Forfar Ath	D 2-2	0-2	3	McKinnon, Burgess	2300
38	28	A	Raith R	D 1-1	0-0	3	Baptie	1733
39	May 5	A	Meadowbank T	L 0-1	0-1	4		886

Final League Position: 4

GOALSCORERS

League: (59): McWilliams 17 (7 pens), Baptie 8, Rae 8, Rutherford 6, McCoy 4, Beaton 2, Burgess 2, Hetherston 2, McGivern 2, Mooney 2, Callaghan 1, Clark 1, Hay 1, Logan 1, McKinnon 1, Robertson 1.
Scottish Cup: (0).
Skol Cup: (4): Burgess 2 (1 pen), Beaton 1, McGivern 1.

Record Defeat: 1-11 v Airdrieonians, Division I; 28 Apr, 1951.
Most Capped Player: Alex Parker, 14 (15), Scotland.
Most League Appearances: —.
Most League Goals in Season (Individual): 43: Evelyn Morrison, Division I; 1928–29.
Most Goals Overall (Individual): —.

Honours

League Champions: Division II 1935–36, 1969–70, 1974–75. Second Division 1979–80; *Runners-up:* Division I 1907–08, 1909–10. First Division 1985–86. Division II 1904–05, 1951–52, 1960–61.
Scottish Cup Winners: 1913, 1957.
League Cup Runners-up: 1947–48.
Club colours: Shirt: Dark blue with white flashings. Shorts: White. Stockings: Red.

Marshall, G	Holmes, J	Hay, G	Brannigan, K	Burgess, G	Hetherston, P	Callaghan, T	Rae, A	Robertson, D	Baptie, C	McWilliams, D	Rutherford, P	McGivern, S	Beaton, D	Houston, P	Smith, G	McNair, C	Mooney, M	McKinnon, C	Clark, M	Melvin, M	Logan, S	McCoy, G	McKenzie, P	Cowell, J	Hamilton, G	Match No.
1	2	3	4†	5	6	7	8	9	10*	11	14	12														1
1	2	3		5	4†	7	9	8*	14	11	12	10	6													2
1	2			5	12		8*		9	7†	11	6	3	4	10	14										3
1	2	3	6	5		7	10	9*	14	11†	12			8	4											4
1		3	2	5	9†	7*	8		10			12	4	6	11	14										5
1		3	2	5		7	8†	9	11			12	4	6*	10	14										6
1	2	3		5			10	12	9	11*			4	8†	7	14	6									7
1		3	2	5			7		8	11		12	4	14	9*	10	6†									8
1		3	6		12		7		8	11		5	4	10*	9		2									9
1		5		3			7		8	11		6	4	10*	9†	12	2	14								10
1		3*		5	14	10	7		8	9		12	4		6†		2	11								11
1		3		5	14	8	6		9	11		12	4						2*			7†	10			12
1		3		5	12	8	6		7*	11		9†	4		14		2	10								13
1	12	5†		6			7		11	9*			3	2	4					14		8	10			14
1	12	5		6			7		11	9*			3	2	4							8	10			15
1				5	6		9*		7	11	14		3	2	4					12		8†	10			16
1				5	11		8†		3	12	9	6	2	4						14		7	10*			17
1				11			8*		6	3	7	9	5	2	4					12		14	10†			18
1		5					8		9	11*		12	3	6	2						4	10	7			19
1		5	6				8		9	7			3	4	2						12	11*	10			20
1		3		5			8		4	7*	12	11	9	6	2								10			21
1		3		5			7		8*	11	14	9	2†	6	4							10	12			22
1			6	5			7*			11	12	9		2	4					3		10	8			23
1			6	5			7			11	10*	9†	3	2	4							12	8	14		24
1		5					7		8	11		9	3	2	6					12		4	10*			25
1		5							8	11		9*	3	2	6					14	12	10	4	7†		26
1		5					7		8	11*	12	9	3	2		6				14		10		4†		27
1		5					7		8	11*		9†	3	4	2	6					14	10	12			28
1		5					7		4	11*		9	3	2	10	6				8†	14	12				29
1		5					7†		11		12	9	3	2		6				14	4	10*	8			30
1		5†	4				8		10	11		9	3	2		6					14	7*		12		31
1		5	4				8*		10	11		9	3	2		6	14					7†		12		32
1		5	4				14		8	11		9	3	2		6						12	10*	7†		33
1		5	4				8*		7	11		9	3†	2		6						12	10		14	34
1		5					7		8	11		9	3*	2		6					4	10	12			35
1		4					8		5	11†		9	14	2	6	7					3	10*			12	36
1		3		5					9	8	11*		2	4		12	14					10		6†	7	37
1		3		5			12		9	11			2	4		6						7	10		8*	38
1		4		5			10		9	11			2				8*	6†			3	7		12	14	39
39	7	25	10	28	14	9	34	4	32	33	18	12	21	28	36	6	8	3	2	14	15	18	10	3	—	
	+		+	+			+ +		+ +	+ +			+ +		+ +	+ +	+ +			+ +	+ +	+ +	+ +			
	2s		9s	1s			1s 2s		10s 3s	2s 3s			1s 7s		8s	1s 1s	6s	1s			4s		6s 1s			

FORFAR ATHLETIC First Division

Year Formed: 1885.   *Ground & Address:* Station Park, Carseview Road, Forfar.   *Telephone:* 0307 63576.
Ground Capacity: total: —   seated: —.   *Size of Pitch:* 115yd×69yd.
Chairman: Gordon Webster.   *Secretary:* David McGregor.   *Commercial Manager:* —.
Manager: Bobby Glennie.   *Assistant Manager:* Ian Fleming.   *Physio:* Andy Dickson.   *Coach:* Billy McGann.
Managers since 1975: Jerry Kerr; Archie Knox; Alex Rae; Doug Houston; Henry Hall.
Club Nickname(s): Sky Blues.   *Previous Grounds:* None.
Record Attendance: 10,780 v Rangers, Scottish Cup 2nd rd, 2 Feb, 1970.
Record Transfer Fee received: £44,000 for Kenny Macdonald from Airdrieonians, 1988.
Record Transfer Fee paid: £30,000 for Tom McCafferty from East Fife, 1989.

1989–90 LEAGUE RECORD

Match No.	Date	Venue	Opponents	Result	H/T Score	Lg. Pos.	Goalscorers	Atten- dance
1	Aug 12	H	Falkirk	L	1-2	0-1	—	Grant	2081
2	19	A	Ayr U	D	1-1	1-0	10	Brewster	2031
3	26	A	St Johnstone	L	1-3	1-2	11	Whyte	4310
4	Sept 2	H	Partick T	L	0-3	0-1	13		1416
5	5	A	Meadowbank T	L	1-3	1-3	—	Morton	750
6	9	H	Clydebank	D	2-2	1-2	14	Morton, Grant	584
7	16	A	Clyde	D	0-0	0-0	13		600
8	23	H	Raith R	D	2-2	2-0	14	Morton, Brewster	757
9	30	A	Morton	D	1-1	0-1	13	Clinging	1300
10	Oct 7	A	Albion R	W	2-0	1-0	13	Glennie, Morton (pen)	655
11	14	H	Alloa	D	3-3	1-2	10	Brazil, Clinging, Clark	758
12	21	A	Hamilton A	L	0-1	0-1	13		722
13	28	A	Airdrieonians	L	1-4	1-3	13	Mennie	1300
14	Nov 4	H	Meadowbank T	L	1-3	0-0	13	Whyte	545
15	11	A	Clydebank	L	2-3	1-2	13	McCafferty, Brewster	738
16	18	H	Clyde	D	1-1	0-1	14	Brewster (pen)	567
17	25	A	Raith R	L	0-1	0-0	14		1249
18	Dec 2	H	Morton	L	0-1	0-0	14		552
19	9	H	Albion R	W	3-0	2-0	14	Clark 2, Adam	448
20	23	A	Alloa	W	2-0	2-0	14	Whyte, Clark	610
21	26	A	Falkirk	L	0-4	0-1	—		2500
22	30	H	Ayr U	W	1-0	1-0	14	Clinging	816
23	Jan 2	H	St Johnstone	L	1-5	0-4	—	Clinging	3619
24	6	A	Partick T	D	0-0	0-0	14		2795
25	13	H	Airdrieonians	D	1-1	0-0	14	Brewster (pen)	1156
26	Feb 3	H	Raith R	D	2-2	1-1	14	Clark, Clinging	717
27	10	A	Clydebank	L	2-3	1-1	14	Whyte, McCafferty	655
28	14	A	Hamilton A	D	1-1	0-1	—	Brewster (pen)	902
29	28	A	Ayr U	D	1-1	0-0	—	Brewster	1311
30	Mar 3	H	Alloa	W	3-2	3-0	13	Hendry, Morris, Winter (pen)	564
31	10	H	Airdrieonians	L	2-3	1-0	13	Winter (pen), Hendry	1341
32	17	A	Meadowbank T	W	3-0	1-0	12	Adam, Leslie 2	400
33	27	A	Morton	L	0-2	0-1	—		600
34	31	H	Clyde	D	2-2	0-1	12	Hendry, Whyte	804
35	Apr 7	A	Albion R	D	2-2	1-1	12	Hendry, Leslie	526
36	14	H	Partick T	W	2-0	0-0	12	Hendry, Clinging	940
37	21	A	Falkirk	D	2-2	2-0	12	Brewster, Whyte	2300
38	28	H	Hamilton A	W	2-0	1-0	12	Lorimer, Hendry	778
39	May 5	A	St Johnstone	L	0-1	0-0	12		7966

Final League Position: 12

GOALSCORERS

League: (51): Brewster 8 (3 pens), Clinging 6, Hendry 6, Whyte 6, Clark 5, Morton 4 (1 pen), Leslie 3, Adam 2, Grant 2, McCafferty 2, Winter 2 (2 pens), Brazil 1, Glennie 1, Lorimer 1, Mennie 1, Morris 1.
Scottish Cup: (1): Brewster 1.
Skol Cup: (0).

Record Victory: 14-1 v Lindertis, Scottish Cup 1st rd; 1 Sept 1988.
Record Defeat: 2-12 v King's Park, Division II; 2 Jan, 1930.
Most Capped Player: —.
Most League Appearances: 376: Alex Brash, 1974–86.
Most League Goals in Season (Individual): 45: Dave Kilgour, Division II; 1929–30.
Most Goals Overall (Individual): 124, John Clark.

Honours
League Champions: Second Division 1983–84. C Division 1948–49.
Scottish Cup: Semi-finals 1982.
League Cup: Semi-finals 1977–78.
Club colours: Shirt: Sky blue. Shorts: Navy. Stockings: Sky blue.

Kennedy, S	Lorimer, R	Hamill, A	Morris, R	Smith, P	Morton, J	Ormond, J	McCafferty, T	Whyte, G	Brewster, C	Grant, B	Clark, J	Bennett, W	Brazil, A	Hutton, G	Ward, K	Moffat, J	Winter, G	McNaughton, B	Allan, R	Morland, D	Glennie, R	Peacock, B	Clinging, I	Leslie, A	Mennie, V	Robertson, D	Thompson, G	Adam, C	Hendry, J	Match No.
1	2	3	4	5	6	7	8*	9	10	11	12																			1
1	12	3	4		6		8	9	10	7	11	2	5*																	2
1*		3	4		6	14	7	9	10		11	2	5†	8	12															3
		3	4		6		8	9	10			2	5	7*	1	11	12													4
	2	6	4		3		8	9*10		14	7		5†		1	11	12													5
	12	6	4		3†		8	9	10	11			5	2*	1	7	14													6
	7†	4	6	5	3	14	8	9	10		12	2			1		11*													7
		5	6		2		3*14	8	7 10	9			4				11†		1		12									8
		5	6		3		8*14	10					2				7		12	1	4		9†11							9
		5	6		3		8	9	10	12			2				7*		1	4	11									10
		5	6		3		8	7*10		9			4				12		1	2	11									11
		5	6		3		7	9†10					2				11*		1	14	4		8 12							12
		3	6	5			8		10*12	14							11†		1	4	2		9	7						13
		3	6		12		8	11	10			2*							1	4	5		7		9					14
		5	6	14			3*12	8	7 10								11†		1	2	9					4				15
		5	6				3*12	8	7 10								11		1	2	9					4				16
		5	4	3			8	7	10	12							11*		1	2	9					6				17
		3		12			8	14	10	9†		2	5*				1		6	11						4	7			18
	10	2	12				7	9				5	3		1	6	11*			4	8									19
12	3	2			8*	7 14	9			4	5	6		1			11			10†										20
	3	6		4*		7 12	9			2	5	11		1			8			10										21
	8	2		12		7	9	6	10*			5	3		1		4		11											22
	6	2		12		7	9	14	10			5	3		1		4†		11				8*							23
	6	4		3†		8	9	10*			12	5		11	1		2		7				14							24
	6	4†14	3			8	7*10		12			2	5		1		11		9											25
12	8	4*	2			7	10	9				6	5		3	1			11											26
12	6	2			8	7	10	9			4	5		3	1		11*													27
7	6	2			8	9	10			4	5		3	1					11											28
7	6	2			8	11*10				4	5		3	1					12										9	29
7	6	2			11	14				4	5		3	1					12						8*10†				9	30
7	6	2			11*14					4	5		3†	1					12						8 10				9	31
7*	6	2			11	14				4	5		3	1					12						8†10				9	32
7	6				8					4	5		3	1	2*				11†12				14	10					9	33
2*	6				7	11	8			4	5†		3	1					12				14	10					9	34
7	6	2†			11	8				4			3	1			5		14	12				10*					9	35
7	2				6	11*10				4			3	1			5		12	14				8†					9	36
7	6	2			10	11†	8			4			3	1			5*		14	12									9	37
7	6	2			10	11	8			4			3	1			5		12										9	38
7	6	4	2		10	11†	8						3*	1			5		12	9										39
3	15	38	36	6	17	1	32	35	32	4	11	2	29	21	1	4	32	—	32	3	20	1	20	2	1	1	11	9	10	
+				+	+		+	+	+		+		+	+		+	+		+		+		+				+			
5s			2s4s		6s		2s	6s			2s6s		1s			1s	1s		4s		2s		4s		10s		3s			

Also played: Dolan S – Match 39 (14).

HAMILTON ACADEMICAL   First Division

Year Formed: 1875.   *Ground & Address:* Douglas Park, Douglas Park Lane, Hamilton ML3 0DF.   *Telephone:* 0698 286103.
Ground Capacity: total: 14,505   seated: 1505.   *Size of Pitch:* 110yd×70yd.
Chairman: Robert D. Gibb.   *Secretary:* David S. Morrison.   *Commercial Manager:* George Miller.
Manager: Billy McLaren.   *Assistant Manager:* —.   *Physio:* Frank Ness.   *Coach:* Colin Miller.
Managers since 1975: J. Eric Smith; Dave McParland; John Blackley; Bertie Auld; John Lambie; Jim Dempsey.
Club Nickname(s): The Accies.   *Previous Grounds:* Bent Farm, South Avenue, South Haugh.
Record Attendance: 28,690 v Hearts, Scottish Cup 3rd rd, 3 Mar, 1937.
Record Transfer Fee received: £110,000 for Willie Jamieson to Dundee, January 1990.

1989–90 LEAGUE RECORD

Match No.	Date	Venue	Opponents	Result	H/T Score	Lg. Pos.	Goalscorers	Atten- dance
1	Aug 12	H	Meadowbank T	W 2-0	1-0	—	Archer, Weir	1404
2	19	A	Airdrieonians	L 0-1	0-1	6		2304
3	26	A	Ayr U	W 1-0	0-0	5	Morrison	2652
4	Sept 2	H	Alloa	W 1-0	0-0	4	Morrison (pen)	1751
5	5	A	St Johnstone	L 0-3	0-1	—		6203
6	9	H	Partick T	L 1-4	0-3	8	Morrison	3774
7	16	A	Falkirk	D 3-3	1-2	8	Harris, Morrison, McCluskey	3000
8	23	H	Morton	D 2-2	1-0	7	Harris (pen), Morrison	1569
9	30	A	Clyde	D 1-1	1-1	5	Morrison	600
10	Oct 7	A	Clydebank	D 2-2	1-0	6	Napier, Smith	1192
11	14	H	Albion R	D 0-0	0-0	6		1420
12	21	A	Forfar Ath	W 1-0	1-0	4	McCluskey	722
13	28	H	Raith R	W 3-2	2-1	4	Harris, Miller, Morrison	1447
14	Nov 4	H	St Johnstone	D 3-3	1-2	4	McCluskey, Gordon, Donaghy	2582
15	11	A	Partick T	L 1-3	1-1	4	Harris	6021
16	18	H	Falkirk	W 1-0	1-0	4	Burgess (og)	2640
17	25	A	Morton	D 0-0	0-0	4		1600
18	Dec 2	H	Clyde	L 0-1	0-0	5		1254
19	9	H	Clydebank	W 2-1	0-0	4	McDonald, McGachie	1148
20	23	A	Meadowbank T	L 0-1	0-0	4		435
21	Jan 2	H	Ayr U	W 4-0	1-0	—	McCluskey, McDonald, McGachie, Napier	1533
22	6	A	Alloa	W 2-0	2-0	4	Napier, McDonald	879
23	9	A	Albion R	D 0-0	0-0	—		1006
24	13	A	Raith R	W 3-1	2-0	4	McLeod (og), McGachie 2	1595
25	Feb 3	H	Clydebank	L 1-3	0-0	6	Napier	1407
26	7	H	Airdrieonians	W 3-2	0-2	—	McCluskey, McAdam (og), Smith	2699
27	10	A	Meadowbank T	D 1-1	1-1	4	McKee	500
28	14	H	Forfar Ath	D 1-1	1-0	4	Smith	902
29	Mar 3	H	Falkirk	D 2-2	0-0	3	Harris, Napier	1891
30	14	A	Partick T	L 1-4	1-2	—	Harris	2779
31	17	H	Ayr U	W 2-1	1-1	3	Harris (pen), McGachie	1119
32	24	H	St Johnstone	L 2-3	1-0	4	Harris, McCluskey	2196
33	27	A	Clyde	W 1-0	0-0	—	Napier	480
34	31	A	Alloa	D 1-1	0-0	4	McCluskey	692
35	Apr 7	A	Raith R	D 0-0	0-0	5		1191
36	14	H	Morton	W 2-0	0-0	4	Martin, Harris	1077
37	21	H	Albion R	L 1-2	0-1	5	McGinlay	1229
38	28	A	Forfar Ath	L 0-2	0-1	6		778
39	May 5	A	Airdrieonians	L 1-3	0-2	6	McCluskey	1000

Final League Position: 6

GOALSCORERS

League: (52): Harris 9 (2 pens), McCluskey 8, Morrison 7 (1 pen), Napier 6, McGachie 5, McDonald 3. Smith 3, Archer 1, Donaghy 1, Gordon 1, McGinlay 1, McKee 1, Martin 1, Miller 1, Weir 1, own goals 3.
Scottish Cup: (0).
Skol Cup: (3): Carr 1, McDonald 1, McKee 1.

Record Transfer Fee paid: £60,000 for Paul Martin from Kilmarnock, 1988.
Record Victory: 10-2 v Cowdenbeath, Division I, 15 Oct, 1932.
Record Defeat: 1-11 v Hibernian, Division I, 6 Nov, 1965.
Most Capped Players: Colin Miller, 5, Canada.
Most League Appearances: 447: Rikki Ferguson, 1974–8.
Most League Goals in Season (Individual): 34: David Wilson, Division I; 1936–37.
Most Goals Overall (Individual): 246: David Wilson, 1928–39.

Honours
League Champions: First Division 1985–86, 1987–88. Division II 1903–04; *Runners-up:* Division II 1952–53, 1964–65.
Scottish Cup Runners-up: 1911, 1935.
League Cup:—.
Club colours: Shirt: Red and white hoops. Shorts: White. Stockings: White.

Ferguson, A	McKee, K	Napier, C	Weir, J	Jamieson, W	Miller, C	Harris, C	Morrison, S	Gordon, S	Archer, S	McDonald, P	McGuigan, R	Carr, S	Prentice, A	Donaghy, P	Martin, P	McCluskey, G	Smith, M	McGachie, J	Murdoch, A	Moore, S	Hillcoat	McFarlane, I	Kasule, V	Smith, T	McLean, S	McGinlay, M	Match No.
1	2	3	4	5	6	7	8	9	10*	11	12																1
1	2	3	4	5	6	7	9	11	10	12	8*																2
1	2	3	4	5	6	7	14	8†	11	9*10	12																3
1	2	3	4	5	6		9	11	7	8	10*	12															4
1	2	3	4	5	6	9	8	11	12	7†10*	14																5
1	2	3	4	5	6*	7	12	8	10							9	11										6
1	2	3	4	5	6	7	8		10*12							9	11										7
1	2	3	4	5	6	7	8	12		11						9	10*										8
1	2	3		5	6	4	8		10†	12		14	7			9*11											9
1	2	4	12	5	6		8	3	11	10*						9	7										10
1	2	4	12	5	6	8†		3	11	14					7*	9	10										11
1	2	3		5	6	10		14	11	12					7*	9†	8	4									12
1†	2	3		5	6	7	8	14		11	12					9*	10	4									13
	2	3	14	5		7	8*	6†		11	12					9	10	1					4				14
	2	3	8†	5	6	7*10				11	12					9		1	14				4				15
	2	3	12	5	6	7	8			11*		14				9	10†				4	1					16
	2	3	12		6	7	8			11*		10		5		9†		1	14		4						17
	2	3	14		6	9	8			11		10		5		12†	1			4		7*					18
1	2	3			6	7				11			10			5		9			4		8				19
1	2	3	14		6	7				11			10			5 12		9†			4		8*				20
1	2	3		5	6	7	8			11						9*	10				4		12				21
1	2	3	14	5	6	7*	8†			11						9	10				4		12				22
1	2	3			5	8	7			11*					6	9	10				4		12				23
1	2	3				6	7	12		11†10*					5	9	8				4		14				24
1	2	3	10			6	7			11	14				5	9	8*		12	4†							25
1	2	3	4†			6	8			14	11				5	9		12					10* 7				26
1	2	3				6	7			4	11				5	9							8 10				27
1	2	3	14			6	7			4	11*				5	9		12					10† 8				28
1	2	3	4			6	7			8	11				12 5	9*		10†					14				29
1	2	3	8†			6	7			4	11				12	14* 5		9					10				30
1	2	3				6	7			4†11	10*				5	9	8	12								14	31
1	2	3	10*			6	7			4	11				12	5	9	8									32
1	2	3	10†			6	7			4	11		14		5	9*	8	12									33
1	2	3	10			6	7			4*11	14				5	9	8†	12									34
1	2	3	10			6	7			4	11				5	9*	12	8									35
1	2	3	10			6	7			4	11				5	9	12							8*			36
1	2	6† 8		4		7	3			11	14				5	9*	12							10			37
1	2	3†10				6	7			4	11		14		5	9	8*	12									38
1	2	3†10				7	4			11	6				5* 9		12						14 8				39
34	39	39	21	19	37	35	17	4	19	37	6	3	4	7	21	27	5	21	4	2	14	1	7	3	—	3	
+						+		+	+	+	+	+	+	+	+	+		+			+		+	+	+	+	
9s						2s		3s2s	1s	10s	3s	1s	7s2s	1s		5s		8s			5s		2s	1s			

HEART OF MIDLOTHIAN Premier Division

Year Formed: 1874. *Ground & Address:* Tynecastle Park, Gorgie Rd, Edinburgh EH11 2NL. *Telephone:* 031 337 6132.
Ground Capacity: total: 29,000 seated: 9000. *Size of Pitch:* 110yd×76yd.
Chairman: A. Wallace Mercer. *Secretary:* L. W. Porteous. *Commercial Manager:* Charles Burnett.
Manager: Alex MacDonald. *Assistant Manager:* —. *Physio:* Alan Rae. *Coach:* (1) Walter Borthwick, (2) John Binnie.
Managers since 1975: J. Hagart; W. Ormond; R. Moncur; A. MacDonald; A. MacDonald & W. Jardine; A. MacDonald.
Club Nickname(s): Jam Tarts. *Previous Grounds:* The Meadows 1873, Powderhall 1878, Tyneside 1881, (Tynecastle Park, 1886).
Record Attendance: 53,496 v Rangers, Scottish Cup 3rd rd; 13 Feb, 1932.
Record Transfer Fee received: £700,000 for John Robertson to Newcastle U (April 1988).
Record Transfer Fee paid: £350,000 for Dave McPherson from Rangers (July 1987).
Record Victory: 18-0 v Vale of Lothian, Edinburgh Shield; 17 Sept, 1887.

1989–90 LEAGUE RECORD

Match No.	Date		Venue	Opponents	Result		H/T Score	Lg. Pos.	Goalscorers	Attendance
1	Aug	12	H	Celtic	L	1-3	0-2	—	McPherson	25,932
2		19	A	St Mirren	W	2-1	2-0	8	Berry, Musemic	7064
3		26	H	Hibernian	W	1-0	1-0	4	Musemic	22,728
4	Sept	9	A	Dundee	D	2-2	2-1	4	McPherson, Crabbe	8440
5		16	A	Motherwell	W	3-1	1-0	1	Crabbe 2, Robertson	8948
6		23	H	Dundee U	D	1-1	0-0	2	McPherson	14,008
7		30	A	Rangers	L	0-1	0-1	5		39,554
8	Oct	4	H	Dunfermline Ath	L	1-2	0-0	—	Musemic	14,165
9		14	A	Aberdeen	W	3-1	1-0	4	McKinlay, Crabbe 2	15,000
10		21	A	Celtic	L	1-2	1-0	5	Crabbe	38,105
11		28	H	St Mirren	W	4-0	1-0	5	Crabbe, Robertson 2, Colquhoun	9911
12	Nov	4	A	Hibernian	D	1-1	1-1	5	Bannon	18,501
13		11	H	Dundee	W	6-3	3-1	1	Foster, Robertson, Colquhoun 3, Crabbe	11,869
14		18	H	Motherwell	W	3-0	0-0	1	Colquhoun, Sandison, Crabbe	12,035
15		25	A	Dundee U	L	1-2	1-0	3	Crabbe	12,201
16	Dec	2	H	Rangers	L	1-2	1-0	4	Bannon	24,771
17		9	A	Dunfermline Ath	W	2-0	1-0	4	Robertson 2	11,295
18		20	A	Aberdeen	D	1-1	1-0	—	Robertson	11,370
19		26	H	Celtic	D	0-0	0-0	—		23,259
20		30	A	St Mirren	L	0-2	0-0	4		7287
21	Jan	1	H	Hibernian	W	2-0	1-0	—	Robertson 2	25,224
22		6	A	Dundee	W	1-0	0-0	3	Craib (og)	8300
23		13	A	Motherwell	W	3-0	1-0	3	Robertson 2 (1 pen), Colquhoun	8822
24		27	H	Dundee U	W	3-2	2-0	2	Kidd, Crabbe, Robertson	13,083
25	Feb	3	A	Aberdeen	D	2-2	1-2	2	Sandison, Ferguson	15,000
26		10	H	Dunfermline Ath	L	0-2	0-1	3		14,204
27		17	A	Rangers	D	0-0	0-0	3		41,884
28	Mar	3	H	Motherwell	W	2-0	0-0	3	Crabbe, Robertson	9205
29		10	A	Celtic	D	1-1	1-1	3	Robertson	34,792
30		24	H	St Mirren	D	0-0	0-0	3		8066
31		31	A	Hibernian	W	2-1	1-1	3	Robertson 2	17,500
32	Apr	4	H	Dundee	D	0-0	0-0	—		10,761
33		14	A	Dunfermline Ath	W	1-0	0-0	2	McPherson	10,829
34		21	A	Aberdeen	W	1-0	0-0	2	Mackay	11,616
35		28	A	Dundee U	D	1-1	0-0	2	McLaren	7679
36	May	5	H	Rangers	D	1-1	1-1	3	Robertson (pen)	20,283

Final League Position: 3

GOALSCORERS

League: (54): Robertson 17 (2 pens), Crabbe 12, Colquhoun 6, McPherson 4, Musemic 3, Bannon 2, Sandison 2, Berry 1, Ferguson 1, Foster 1, Kidd 1, McKinlay 1, McLaren 1, own goal 1.
Scottish Cup: (7): Robertson 4, Colquhoun 2, Crabbe 1.
Skol Cup: (9): Crabbe 4, Bannon 1, Kidd 1, Kirkwood 1, Musemic 1, Robertson 1.

Record Defeat: 0-7 v Hibernian, Division I; 1 Jan, 1973.
Most Capped Player: Bobby Walker, 29, Scotland.
Most League Appearances: —.
Most League Goals in Season (Individual): 44: Barney Battles.
Most Goals Overall (Individual): 206: Jimmy Wardhaugh, 1946–59.

Honours

League Champions: Division I 1894–85, 1896–97, 1957–58, 1959–60. First Division 1979–80; *Runners-up:* Division I 1893–94, 1898–99, 1903–04, 1905–06, 1914–15, 1937–38, 1953–54, 1956–57, 1958–59, 1964–65. Premier Division 1985–86. First Division 1977–78, 1982–83.
Scottish Cup Winners: 1891, 1896, 1901, 1906, 1956; *Runners-up:* 1903, 1907, 1968, 1976, 1986.
League Cup Winners: 1954–55, 1958–59, 1959–60, 1962–63; *Runners-up:* 1961–62.
European: *European Cup* 4 matches (1958–59, 1960–61). *Cup Winners Cup* 4 matches (1976–77). *UEFA Cup:* 15 matches (1961–62, 1963–64, 1965–66 *Fairs Cup*; 1984–85, 1986-87).
Club colours: Shirt: Maroon. Shorts: White. Stockings: Maroon with white tops.

Smith, H	McLaren, A	Kirkwood, D	Levein, C	Berry, N	McPherson, D	Colquhoun, J	Mackay, G	Musemic, H	Ferguson, I	Bannon, E	Crabbe, S	Kidd, W	Whittaker, B	McKinlay, T	Robertson, J	McCreery, D	Foster, W	Sandison, J	Wright, G	Match No.
1	2	3	4	5	6	7	8	9	10	11*	12									1
1	3	10		5	6	7	8*	9†14	12	11	2	4								2
1	2		4	5	6	7	8	9†12		11	10*14			3						3
1	2		4	5	6	7	8	9†		11	10*			3	12	14				4
1	12	5	4		6	7	8			10*	2			3	9	11				5
1	2	5	4		6	7	8	12		10*				3	9	11				6
1	2	5	4		6	7	8			12	10*			3	9	11				7
1	2	12	4		6	9	8†14		7	10				3	11*	5				8
1	2		4		6	7	8			11	10			3	12	5	9*			9
1	2	14	4		6	7	8			11	10†			3	12	5	9*			10
1	2	14	4		6	7	8			11	10*			3	12	5	9†			11
1	2	14	4		6	7	8			11*	10†			3	12	5	9			12
1	2	5	4*		6	7	8†			11	12	14		3	10		9			13
1	2	5	4			7	8			12	11	10*		3		9	6			14
1	2	5	4		6	7	8			12	11	10		3	9*					15
1	2		4		6	7	8			11	10*14			3	12	5†	9			16
1	2	14	4		6	7				11	12	8†		3	10*	5	9			17
1	2		4		6	7	8			11	10*12			3	9	5†	14			18
1	2*		4		6	7	8			11	10	14		3	9	5†	12			19
1			4		6	7	8			12	11	10	2*	3	9	5				20
1	14		4		6	7†	8			11	12		2	3	10		9*	5		21
1			4		6	7	8			12	11	9*	2	3	10			5		22
1			4		6	7	8			12	11	10†	2	3	9*14			5		23
1			4		6	7*14				12	11	10	2	3	9	5†	8			24
1			4		6	7	12			14	11	10	2	3†	9	5*	8			25
1	2*		4		6	7	8			12	11	10		3	9			5		26
1			4		6	7	8*			11	10		2	3	9	5	12			27
1			4	8	6	7				11	10*		2†	3	9	5	12	14		28
1			4	8	6	7*				11	10		2	3	9	5	12			29
1	2		4		6	7	8			11*10				3	9	5	12			30
1	2	14	4	5	6	7	8			11	12			3	9*	10†				31
1	2		4	5	6	7	8			11				3	9	10				32
1	2	14	4	5	6	7†	8			11	12			3	9*	10				33
1	2	14	4	5	6	7†	8			11*	12			3	9	10				34
1	2		4	5	6	7	8			11	9*			3	12	10				35
1	2		4	5	6	7*	8†				12			3	9	10	11	14		36

```
36 26 10 35 10 35 36 31  4  1 31 27 12  6 29 25 20 14  8  —
 +  +                 +  +  +  +  +           +  +  +  +
1s 9s               2s 2s10s2s 8s 5s        7s 2s 3s 4s1s
```

HIBERNIAN   Premier Division

Year Formed: 1875.   *Ground & Address:* Easter Road Stadium, Albion Rd, Edinburgh EH7 5QG.   *Telephone:* 031 661 2159.
Ground Capacity: total: 23,353   seated: 5853.   *Size of Pitch:* 112yd×74yd.
Chairman: David F. Duff.   *Secretary:* Cecil F. Graham, F.A.A.I., M.Inst. C.M..   *Commercial Manager:* Raymond Sparkes.
Manager: Alex Miller.   *Assistant Manager:* Peter Cormack.   *Physio:* Stewart Collie.   *Coach:* —.
Managers since 1975: Eddie Turnbull; Willie Ormond; Bertie Auld; Pat Stanton; John Blackley; Alex Miller.
Club Nickname(s): Hibees.   *Previous Grounds:* Meadows 1875–78, Powderhall 1878–79, Mayfield 1875–80, First Easter Road 1880–92, Second Easter Road 1892–.
Record Attendance: 65,860 v Hearts, Division I; 2 Jan, 1950.
Record Transfer Fee received: £382,000 for Gordon Durie to Chelsea (May 1986).
Record Transfer Fee paid: £325,000 for Andy Goram from Oldham Ath.
Record Victory: 22-1 v 42nd Highlanders; 3 Sept, 1881.

1989–90 LEAGUE RECORD

Match No.	Date		Venue	Opponents	Result		H/T Score	Lg. Pos.	Goalscorers	Atten- dance
1	Aug	12	A	Aberdeen	L	0-1	0-0	—		16,000
2		19	H	Rangers	W	2-1	1-0	3	Houchen, Weir	21,500
3		26	A	Hearts	L	0-1	0-1	6		22,728
4	Sept	9	A	Dundee U	W	2-0	1-0	5	Evans, Fellenger	7000
5		16	H	St Mirren	W	3-1	2-1	3	Houchen 2, Collins	6000
6		23	A	Dundee	D	0-0	0-0	3		6842
7		30	H	Dunfermline Ath	D	2-2	1-1	2	Houchen, Collins	13,000
8	Oct	4	A	Celtic	L	1-3	1-0	—	Evans	36,000
9		14	H	Motherwell	W	3-2	2-0	2	Houchen, Weir, Collins	8000
10		25	H	Aberdeen	L	0-3	0-1	—		12,000
11		28	A	Rangers	L	0-3	0-0	7		35,260
12	Nov	4	H	Hearts	D	1-1	1-1	7	Archibald	18,501
13		8	A	Dundee U	L	0-1	0-1	—		8247
14		18	A	St Mirren	D	0-0	0-0	8		4500
15		25	H	Dundee	W	3-2	2-0	8	Collins, McGinlay, Evans	6000
16	Dec	2	A	Dunfermline Ath	D	0-0	0-0	8		9303
17		9	H	Celtic	L	0-3	0-2	8		18,000
18		26	A	Aberdeen	W	2-1	1-0	—	Archibald, Kane	16,500
19		30	H	Rangers	D	0-0	0-0	7		17,000
20	Jan	1	A	Hearts	L	0-2	0-1	—		25,224
21		6	H	Dundee U	D	0-0	0-0	8		6500
22		9	A	Motherwell	W	2-0	1-0	—	McGinlay, Sneddon	6447
23		13	H	St Mirren	L	0-1	0-1	7		6000
24		27	A	Dundee	L	0-2	0-1	7		5720
25	Feb	3	H	Motherwell	L	1-2	0-1	8	Collins	5524
26		10	A	Celtic	D	1-1	1-1	8	Collins	25,000
27		17	H	Dunfermline Ath	W	2-1	1-0	7	Hamilton, Sneddon	7000
28	Mar	3	A	St Mirren	W	1-0	1-0	7	Houchen	4073
29		10	H	Aberdeen	W	3-2	1-0	7	Orr, McGinlay, Wright	9500
30		24	A	Rangers	W	1-0	0-0	5	Houchen	37,542
31		31	H	Hearts	L	1-2	1-1	6	Weir	17,500
32	Apr	7	A	Dundee U	L	0-1	0-0	6		6633
33		17	H	Celtic	W	1-0	0-0	—	Kane (pen)	11,000
34		21	A	Motherwell	L	0-1	0-1	6		4435
35		28	H	Dundee	D	1-1	0-1	6	Houchen	4665
36	May	5	A	Dunfermline Ath	D	1-1	0-1	7	Kane	9681

Final League Position: 7

GOALSCORERS

League: (34): Houchen 8, Collins 6, Evans 3, Kane 3 (1 pen), McGinlay 3, Weir 3, Archibald 2, Sneddon 2, Fellenger 1, Hamilton 1, Orr 1, Wright 1.
Scottish Cup: (7): Houchen 3, McGinlay 2, Collins 1, Orr 1.
Skol Cup: (3): Sneddon 2, Collins 1.

Record Defeat: 0-10 v Rangers; 24 Dec, 1898.
Most Capped Player: Lawrie Reilly, 38, Scotland.
Most League Appearances: 446: Arthur Duncan.
Most League Goals in Season (Individual): 42: Joe Baker.
Most Goals Overall (Individual): 364: Gordon Smith.

Honours
League Champions: Division I 1902–03, 1947–48, 1950–51, 1951–52. First Division 1980–81. Division II 1893–94, 1894–95, 1932–33; *Runners-up:* Division I 1896–97, 1946–47, 1949–50, 1952–53, 1973–74.
Scottish Cup Winners: 1887, 1902; *Runners-up:* 1896, 1914, 1923, 1924, 1947, 1958, 1972, 1979.
League Cup Winners: 1972–73; *Runners-up:* 1950–51, 1968–69, 1974–75.
European: *European Cup* 6 matches (1955–56 semi-finals). *Cup Winners Cup* 6 matches (1972–73). *UEFA Cup* 54 matches (1960–61 semi-finals, 1961–62, 1962–63, 1965–66, 1967–68, 1968–69, 1970–71 *Fairs Cup*; 1973–74, 1974–75, 1975–76, 1976–77, 1978–79).
Club colours: Shirt: Green with white sleeves. Shorts: White. Stockings: Green with white trim.

Goram, A	Kane, P	Sneddon, A	Cooper, N	Mitchell, G	Hunter, G	Weir, M	Orr, N	Evans, G	Hamilton, B	Findlay, W	Tortolano, J	Houchen, K	Collins, J	Fellenger, D	Milne, C	McGinlay, P	Archibald, S	Reid, C	Rae, G	Miller, W	Wright, P	Match No.
1	2	3	4	5	6	7*	8	9	10	11	12											1
1	2	3	4	5	6	7	8		11			9	10									2
1	2	3	4	5	6	7	8*14		12	11†		9	10									3
1	2†	3	4	5	6	7	8		11*14			9	10	12								4
1			4	3	6		5	11	7			9	10	8	2							5
1			4	3*	6		5	11	7			9	10	8†	2	12	14					6
1	2	3	4		6	7*	8†11		5			9	10	12	14							7
1	2	3	4		6		11	8	7			9	10	5								8
1	2	3	4	5*	6	7†	11	8				9	10	12	14							9
1	2		4	5*	6	7	8	11	3			9†10		12	14							10
1	2	3	4	5	6	12	11	8*				9	10	7								11
1	2†	3	4	5	6	7	11*	9					10	14	12	8						12
1	2	3	4	5*	6	12	11	9					10	7	8							13
1	2	3	4		6	5	7*					9	10	12	11	8						14
1	2	3	4†		6	14	11	8				9*10		7	5	12						15
		3	4		6	12	11	8				9	10	7*	2	5			1			16
		3	4	5*	6	14	12	11	7				10	9†	2	8			1			17
1	2	3	4	5	6	7	9	11				12	10			8*						18
1	2	3	4	5		7	9	11				10				8		6				19
1	2	3	4	5		7	9†11*					12	10			14	8	6				20
1	2	3	4	12	6	7*11†	5					9	10	14		8						21
1	2	3	4†	5	6	7*14		12				9	10	11		8						22
1	2	3	4	5†	6	7	14		12			9	10	11*		8						23
1	2	3	4	12	6	8*	9†	5	14	11		10		7								24
1	2	3	4	12	6	14	8		7†			9	10	11*		5						25
1	2	3		5	6	7	8					9	10			11				4		26
1	2	3		5	6	7	12	8				9*10				11				4		27
1	2	3		5	6	7	8					9	10			11				4		28
1	2	3		5	6	7*	8					9	10			11				4	12	29
1	2	3		5	11	6	8*					9	10			12				4	7	30
1		3	5	11	6	7	4	14				9	10	12						2†	8*	31
1	2		5	6	7	8*12	11	3				10	9							4		32
1	2		5	6	7*12	11	3					9	10			8				4		33
1	2		5	6	12	7*11	3					9	10			8				4		34
1	2†		5	6	7*14	11	12	3				9	10			8				4		35
1	2	14	5	6	12	7†11	3					9*10				8				4		36
34	31	28	27	28	34	12	24	23	26	5	6	27	35	8	3	20	8	2	2	11	2	
	+1s		+3s			+6s	+5s	+5s	+2s		+5s		+1s2s			+4s	+8s	+5s			+1s	

KILMARNOCK

First Division

Year Formed: 1869.   *Ground & Address:* Rugby Park, Kilmarnock KA1 2DP.   *Telephone:* 0563 25184.
Ground Capacity: total: 17,528   seated: 4011.   *Size of Pitch:* 115yd×75yd.
Chairman: Robert Fleeting.   *Secretary and General Manager:* Walter W. McCrae.   *Commercial Manager:* —.
Manager: Jim Fleeting.   *Assistant Manager:* Jim McSherry.   *Physio:* Hugh Allan.   *Coach:* Frank Coulston.
Managers since 1975: W. Fernie; D. Sneddon; J. Clunie; E. Morrison; J. Fleeting.
Club Nickname(s): Killie.   *Previous Grounds:* None.
Record Attendance: 34,246 v Rangers, League Cup, Aug, 1963.
Record Transfer Fee received: £120,000 for Davie Provan from Celtic, 1978.
Record Transfer Fee paid: £80,000 for Bobby Geddes to Dundee, May 1990.
Record Victory: 13-2 v Saltcoats Victoria, Scottish Cup 2nd rd; 12 Sept, 1896.

1989–90 LEAGUE RECORD

Match No.	Date		Venue	Opponents	Result		H/T Score	Lg. Pos.	Goalscorers	Atten- dance
1	Aug	12	H	Brechin C	L	0-2	0-0	—		2402
2		19	A	Arbroath	D	1-1	1-0	12	Curran	1070
3		26	A	Queen's Park	L	0-1	0-0	12		1846
4	Sept	2	H	East Stirling	W	2-0	1-0	10	Watters, Montgomerie	1749
5		9	H	Cowdenbeath	D	0-0	0-0	10		1804
6		16	A	Stenhousemuir	W	3-0	0-0	9	Thompson H 2, Thompson D	1753
7		23	H	Berwick R	W	2-0	1-0	6	Curran, Thompson H	1975
8		30	A	Stirling Albion	W	1-0	1-0	2	Curran	1920
9	Oct	7	A	Montrose	W	1-0	0-0	1	Watters	800
10		14	H	East Fife	W	1-0	0-0	1	Reilly	2456
11		21	A	Stranraer	L	0-1	0-0	1		2500
12		28	H	Dumbarton	W	3-0	0-0	1	Watters 2, Tait	2867
13	Nov	4	A	Queen of the S	W	2-0	1-0	1	Reilly, Thompson D	2896
14		11	A	East Stirling	L	1-2	0-0	2	MacCabe	1375
15		18	H	Stirling Albion	L	1-2	0-2	3	Tait	2473
16		25	A	Berwick R	L	2-3	0-3	7	Curran, Marshall	784
17	Dec	2	H	Montrose	D	1-1	0-0	6	MacFarlane	2095
18		23	H	Arbroath	W	3-0	0-0	5	Watters 3	3336
19		26	A	Brechin C	L	1-3	1-1	—	Burns	1050
20	Jan	2	H	Queen's Park	W	2-0	1-0	—	Watters, Callaghan	4843
21		10	A	East Fife	L	2-4	1-1	—	Watters, Burns	1109
22		13	A	Cowdenbeath	L	1-2	0-1	6	Reilly	781
23		20	H	Stenhousemuir	W	2-0	1-0	5	Watters, Montgomerie	2777
24		27	H	Stranraer	L	0-1	0-1	5		3550
25	Feb	17	A	Arbroath	W	4-2	1-1	4	Callaghan, Tait, Sludden, Watters	891
26		24	H	Berwick R	W	4-1	1-1	4	Watters 3, Sludden	992
27	Mar	3	A	East Stirling	W	2-0	1-0	4	Burns, Reilly	2747
28		6	H	Stirling Albion	W	1-0	1-0	—	Watters	3369
29		10	H	Queen's Park	W	3-0	2-0	3	Watters 2, Montgomerie	3767
30		13	A	Queen of the S	L	1-2	0-2	—	Flexney	1500
31		17	A	Stenhousemir	L	1-2	0-0	3	Sludden	1717
32		24	A	Dumbarton	W	2-0	0-0	3	Sludden, Tait	1881
33		31	H	Brechin C	D	2-2	0-1	3	Tait, Watters	4887
34	Apr	3	A	Dumbarton	W	3-1	2-1	—	Sludden, Watters 2	1000
35		7	H	East Fife	W	2-1	0-0	2	Porteous, Tait	3266
36		14	A	Stranraer	L	1-2	0-0	3	Watters	2556
37		21	H	Queen of the S	W	4-1	2-0	2	Watters, Sludden, McArthur, MacKinnon	3262
38		28	A	Montrose	W	3-1	1-0	2	Sludden, Watters, Mackay (og)	1650
39	May	5	H	Cowdenbeath	W	2-1	1-0	2	Flexney, MacKinnon (pen)	8419

Final League Position: 2

GOALSCORERS

League: (67): Watters 23, Sludden 7, Tait 6, Curran 4, Reilly 4, Burns 3, Montgomerie 3, Thompson H 3, Callaghan 2, Flexney 2, MacKinnon 2 (1 pen), Thompson D 2, McArthur 1, MacCabe 1, MacFarlane 1, Marshall 1, Porteous 1, own goal 1.
Scottish Cup: (1): Watters 1.
Skol Cup: (1): Thompson D 1.

Record Defeat: 0-8 v Hibernian, Division I; 22 Aug, 1925: v Rangers, Division I; 27 Feb, 1937.
Most Capped Player: Joe Nibloe, 11, Scotland.
Most League Appearances: 478: Alan Robertson, 1972–89.
Most League Goals in Season (Individual): 35: Peerie Cunningham, Division I; 1927–28.
Most Goals Overall (Individual): 148: W. Culley; 1912–23.

Honours
League Champions: Division I 1964–65. Division II 1897–98, 1898–99; *Runners-up:* Division I 1959–60, 1960–61, 1962–63, 1963–64. First Division 1975–76, 1978–79, 1981–82. Division II 1953–54, 1973–74, Second Division 1989–90.
Scottish Cup Winners: 1920, 1929; *Runners-up:* 1898, 1932, 1938, 1957, 1960.
League Cup Runners-up: 1952–53, 1960–61, 1962–63.
European: *European Cup* 1965–66. *Cup Winners Cup* —. *UEFA Cup Fairs Cup:* 1966–67 (semi-finals), 1969–70.
Club colours: Shirt: Blue and white hoops. Shorts: Blue. Stockings: Blue.

McCulloch, A	Wilson, K	Davidson, F	Jenkins, E	Cody, S	Flexney, P	Thompson, D	Tait, T	Thompson, M	Reilly, R	Watters, W	Curran, P	Montgomerie, R	McLean, S	MacFarlane, D	Walker, David	MacKinnon, D	MacCabe, D	Geraghty, M	Callaghan, T	Marshall, S	Sludden, J	Burns, T	Spence, T	Wylde, G	McArthur, M	Quinn, S	Geddes, R	Porteous, I	McKellar, D	Match No.
1	2	3	4	5	6	7	8†	9*	10	11	12		14																	1
1	2		4	7	6		8		10	11	9		3	5																2
1	2	3*		6	5	7†	8		10	11	9		14	12	4															3
1	2	3*	14		5†	7	8		10	11	9		12	6	4															4
1	2		14		5	7*	8†	12	10	11	9		3	6	4															5
1	12			10*	5	14	8	9	11		7†	2				6			3	4										6
1				10*	5	14	8	9	11	12	7†	2				6			3	4										7
1				12	5	7†	8	9	10*	14	11	2				6			3	4										8
1	10*				5	14	8	12	9	11	7†	2				6			3	4										9
1	10†				5	12	8	14	9	11	7*	2				6			3	4										10
1	10				5	7	8	9		11		2				6			3	4										11
1	12				5	7*	8	10		11		2				6			3	4	9†	14								12
1	10*				5	12	8	9		11		2				6			3	4			7							13
1	14				5	12	8	9		11*		2				6			3	4	7	10†								14
1					5	10†	8	9	12	11						6	3	2			7*	14	4							15
1	14			12			8	9		11	7	2				6	3†		4		10*		5							16
1	12			7*	5			10		11	9				6†	8	3	2	14	4										17
1					5		8			11	14	2				6	12		3		7†	4*		9	10					18
1			4*		5		8		7	11	12	2				6†	14		3					9	10					19
1	12		4*		5		8			11	14	2				6					7		3	9†	10					20
1					5	4*	8		7†	11		2	12		14	6			3					9	10					21
1					5		8	12		11		2			3*		7	6	14	4				9†	10					22
1	14				5					11*		2				6			8		9	10	3	4	7†	12				23
1					5			12		11		2				6			8		9	10	3	4*	7†	14				24
				12	5		8			9		2				4					7	10	6	3	11*		1			25
				11*	5		8			9		2				4					7	10	6	3		12	1			26
					5		8			11	9	2				4					7	10	6	3			1			27
					5		8			11*	9	2				4					7	10	6	3		12	1			28
					5		8			11†	9	2				4					7	10	6*	3		12	1	14		29
					5		8				9	2				4			12		7*	10	6	3			1	11		30
					5		8				9	2				4			12		6†	10	11	3	14		1	7*		31
	14				5		8			11†	9	2				4			12			10	6	3	7*		1			32
	4†				5		8			11	9	2				4			14	12		10	6	3	7*		1			33
	12				5		8			11	9	2				4			14		7*	10†	6	3			1			34
	14*				5		8			11	9	2				4					7	10	6	3†				12	1	35
					5		8			11	9	2				4					7*	10	6	3				12	1	36
					5		8			11*	9	2				4						10	6	3	12			7	1	37
					5		8			11*	9	2				4						10	6	3	12			7	1	38
	14				5		8			11*	9	2				4						10†	6	3	12			7	1	39
24	6	3	7	12	34	8	37	4	30	35	12	32	19	5	13	33	4	2	20	1	22	22	17	5	2	—	10	5	5	

+1s; 6s8s; 7s1s 3s1s 3s 4s 3s 2s; 2s1s; 9s1s; 6s 1s3s; 2s

MEADOWBANK THISTLE   First Division

Year Formed: 1974.   *Ground & Address:* Meadowbank Stadium, London Rd, Edinburgh EH7 6AE.   *Telephone:* 031 661 5351.
Ground Capacity: total: 16,500   seated: 16,500.   *Size of Pitch:* 105yd×72yd.
Chairman: John P. Blacklaw.   *Secretary:* William L. Mill.   *Commercial Manager:* Sean Pinkman.
Manager: Terence Christie.   *Assistant Manager:* Lawrie Glasson.   *Physio:* Arthur Duncan.   *Coach:* Tam McLaren.
Managers since 1975: John Bain; Alec Ness; Willie MacFarlane; Terry Christie.
Club Nickname(s): Thistle; Wee Jags.   *Previous Grounds:* None.
Record Attendance: 4000 v Albion Rovers, League Cup 1st rd; 9 Sept, 1974.
Record Transfer Fee received: £70,000 for Darren Jackson to Newcastle U (1986).

1989–90 LEAGUE RECORD

Match No.	Date		Venue	Opponents	Result		H/T Score	Lg. Pos.	Goalscorers	Atten- dance
1	Aug	12	A	Hamilton A	L	0-2	0-1	—		1404
2		19	H	Alloa	L	1-3	0-1	14	McGachie	500
3		26	H	Raith R	L	1-2	0-0	13	Inglis	650
4	Sept	2	A	Falkirk	D	1-1	1-1	12	Roseburgh	3119
5		5	H	Forfar Ath	W	3-1	3-1	—	Park 2, Forrest	750
6		9	A	Morton	D	0-0	0-0	11		1200
7		16	H	Partick T	D	1-1	1-0	11	Forrest	2000
8		23	A	Clydebank	D	1-1	0-1	10	Boyd	735
9		30	H	St Johnstone	L	1-3	0-1	12	Park	1500
10	Oct	7	H	Clyde	W	2-1	0-0	11	Roseburgh, Armstrong (pen)	500
11		14	A	Airdrieonians	L	1-3	0-2	12	McNaughton	1400
12		21	A	Albion R	D	0-0	0-0	12		437
13		28	H	Ayr U	L	1-2	0-1	12	Roseburgh (pen)	400
14	Nov	4	*A	Forfar Ath	W	3-1	0-0	11	Williamson, Sprott, Forrest	545
15		11	H	Morton	D	0-0	0-0	11		500
16		18	A	Partick T	L	0-2	0-1	12		3338
17		25	H	Clydebank	D	1-1	1-1	12	Williamson	500
18	Dec	2	A	St Johnstone	L	0-1	0-1	12		3888
19		9	A	Clyde	W	3-0	0-0	12	Scott, McNaughton, Boyd	700
20		20	H	Airdrieonians	L	0-1	0-0	—		600
21		23	H	Hamilton A	W	1-0	0-0	11	McNaughton	435
22		30	A	Alloa	W	1-0	0-0	10	McNaughton	755
23	Jan	2	A	Raith R	W	2-1	2-1	—	Roseburgh, Inglis	1897
24		6	H	Falkirk	L	1-2	0-0	9	Park	1200
25		13	A	Ayr U	D	0-0	0-0	10		2195
26		27	H	Albion R	W	3-2	2-1	8	Irvine, McTeague (og), McNaughton	400
27	Feb	3	A	St Johnstone	W	2-1	0-1	8	Boyd, McNaughton	4162
28		10	H	Hamilton A	D	1-1	1-1	7	Forrest	500
29		28	A	Raith R	L	0-3	0-1	—		708
30	Mar	3	H	Morton	W	1-0	0-0	9	Forrest	300
31		17	H	Forfar Ath	L	0-3	0-1	10		400
32		24	H	Partick T	D	1-1	1-1	9	Inglis	1000
33		27	A	Clydebank	L	1-2	1-2	—	Roseburgh	350
34		31	A	Albion R	W	2-1	2-1	8	Roseburgh, Boyd	400
35	Apr	7	H	Alloa	D	1-1	1-0	9	Roseburgh	400
36		14	A	Airdrieonians	D	1-1	0-1	8	Conn (og)	1750
37		21	A	Ayr U	W	1-0	1-0	8	McNaughton	400
38		28	A	Clyde	D	1-1	1-0	8	McNaughton	733
39	May	5	H	Falkirk	W	1-0	1-0	7	Forrest	886

Final League Position: 7

GOALSCORERS

League: (41): McNaughton 8, Roseburgh 7 (1 pen), Forrest 6, Boyd 4, Park 4, Inglis 3, Williamson 2, Armstrong 1 (pen), Irvine 1, McGachie 1, Scott 1, Sprott 1, own goals 2.
Scottish Cup: (1): Armstrong 1.
Skol Cup: (1): Roseburgh 1.

Record Transfer Fee paid: £28,000 for Victor Kasule from Albion Rovers (1987).
Record Victory: 6-0 v Raith R, Second Division; 9 Nov, 1985.
Record Defeat: 0-8 v Hamilton A, Division II; 14 Dec, 1974.
Most Capped Player: —.
Most League Appearances: 446: Walter Boyd, 1979–89.
Most League Goals in Season (Individual): 21: John McGachie, 1986–87. *(Team):* 69; Second Division, 1986–87.
Most Goals Overall (Individual): 63: Adrian Sprott, 1980–85.

Honours
League Champions: Second Division 1986-87; *Runners-up:* Second Division 1982–83. First Division 1987–88.
Scottish Cup: —.
League Cup: Semi-finals 1984–85.
Club colours: Shirt: Amber with black trim. Shorts: Black. Stockings: Amber.

McQueen, J	McCormack, J	Armstrong, G	Boyd, W	Williamson, S	Roseburgh, D	Logan, S	Irvine, N	Forrest, R	Sprott, A	McGachie, J	Banks, A	Inglis, J	Carswell, A	Perry, J	Park, D	Scott, G	Prentice, A	McNaughton, B	Bullen, L	Christie, M	Match No.
1	2	3	4	5	6	7	8	9†	10	11*14	12										1
2*	3	4	5	6	7	8	9	10†	11			1		12	14						2
1	2	3		5	6	7	8	14	10	11*		4		9†	12						3
1	2	3	6	5	9	7	8	12	10	11*		4									4
1	2	3		5	9	7	8	11	10			4		6							5
1		3	2	5		7	8	11	10			4		9	6						6
1	2	3	5			7	8	11*10	12	14		4		9†	6						7
1	2	3	12	5	9†	7	8	14	10	11*		4		6							8
1	2	3	8*	5	9	7		11	10			4		6	12						9
1	2	3	12	5	11		8		10	14		4		7		6*		9†			10
1	2	3		5	10		8		11			4		7	12	6*14		9†			11
1	2	3	14	5	10*		8	7	11			4†			12	6		9			12
1	2	3		5	10		8	7	11			4			12	6*		9			13
1		3	14	5	10		6	12	11			4		7†			2	9*	8		14
1		3		5	10		6	12†	11			4		7	14		2	9*	8		15
1	8	3	12	5			6*	11				4		7	14		2†	9		10	16
1	2	3	14	5	10		6†	11				4		7	12			9*	8		17
1	8	3	6*	5	10			11	12	14		4		7			2	9			18
1	8	3	6	5	10			11				4		7*	12		2	9			19
1	8	3	6	5	10*			11				4		7	12		2†14	9			20
1		3	12	5	10		6		11			4		7			2	9*	8		21
1		3	12	5	10		6		11			4		7			2	9*	8		22
1		3	12	5	10		6*		11			4		7			2	9	8		23
1		3	12	5	10		6*		11			4		7	14		2	9†	8		24
1	6	3		5	10			8*11				4		7	12		2	9			25
1	4	3				6	7	11				5					2	9	8	10	26
1	4	12		3		6*	7	11				5		14			2	9	8	10†	27
1	4	12		3		6*	7	11				5		14			2	9	8†	10	28
1		3	14	5	6			8*11				4†		7			2	9	12	10	29
1	2	3		5	6*		8	7	11			4			12			9		10	30
1		3	2	5	6		8	10	11*			4		7†14				9	12		31
1		3		5	6		8	7*11				4					2	9	12	10	32
1		3	12	5	6		8	7	11			4					2†	9*14		10	33
1	7	3	2	5	6		8		12			4						9	11*10		34
1	7	3	2	5	6		8*14	12				4						9†11		10	35
1	7	3	2	5	6		8*12	11				4		14				9†		10	36
1	2	3	12	5	6			14	11		8*	4		7†				9		10	37
1	2	3	12	5	6				11		8*	4		7				9		10	38
1	2†	3	12	5			14	6	11		8*	4		7				9		10	39
38	25	39	13 +17s	35	35	9 +1s	29 +8s	19 +2s	37	5	3 +1s	37 +4s1s	1	21 +5s	9	12	20	24 +11s1s	5 +4s	13 +4s	

MONTROSE

Second Division

Year Formed: 1879. *Ground & Address:* Links Park, Wellington St, Montrose DD10 8QD. *Telephone:* 0674 73200.
Ground Capacity: total: 6500 seated: 324. *Size of Pitch:* 113yd×70yd.
Chairman: Brian Keith. *Secretary:* Malcolm J. Watters. *Commercial Manager:* John Archbold.
Manager: Ian Stewart. *Assistant Manager:* John Smith. *Physio:* Andy Bell. *Coach:* Chic McLelland.
Managers since 1975: A. Stuart; K. Cameron; R. Livingstone; S. Murray; D. D'Arcy; I. Stewart.
Club Nickname(s): The Gable Endies. *Previous Grounds:* None.
Record Attendance: 8983 v Dundee, Scottish Cup 3rd rd; 17 Mar, 1973.
Record Transfer Fee received: £50,000 for Gary Murray to Hibernian (Dec, 1980).
Record Transfer Fee paid: —.

1989–90 LEAGUE RECORD

Match No.	Date		Venue	Opponents	Result	H/T Score	Lg. Pos.	Goalscorers	Atten-dance
1	Aug	12	H	Stranraer	D 2-2	2-2	—	Ewing (og), Murray	350
2		19	A	Cowdenbeath	W 1-0	0-0	4	McGlashan	250
3		26	H	Brechin C	L 0-1	0-1	9		600
4	Sept	2	A	Stenhousemuir	L 0-1	0-0	11		240
5		9	H	Queen's Park	W 4-1	4-1	9	Dolan, Murray 2, Maver	370
6		16	A	Arbroath	D 2-2	1-1	8	Maver, Powell	730
7		23	H	Queen of the S	D 0-0	0-0	8		354
8		30	H	Berwick R	L 0-2	0-1	11		447
9	Oct	7	H	Kilmarnock	L 0-1	0-0	11		800
10		14	A	Stirling Albion	L 0-2	0-1	11		570
11		21	A	East Stirling	W 2-0	1-0	10	Murray 2	150
12		28	A	East Fife	L 1-4	1-2	13	Murray	578
13	Nov	4	A	Dumbarton	L 2-3	2-1	12	Paterson, McGlashan	400
14		11	H	Stenhousemuir	L 0-2	0-0	13		250
15		18	H	Berwick R	W 2-1	2-1	12	Powell, Brown (pen)	200
16		25	A	Queen of the S	L 2-3	1-2	13	Powell, McGlashan	650
17	Dec	2	A	Kilmarnock	D 1-1	0-0	12	Allan	2095
18		20	H	Stirling Albion	D 3-3	2-0	—	Brown 2, Murray	300
19		23	H	Cowdenbeath	W 2-0	1-0	11	Powell 2	250
20		26	A	Stranraer	W 2-1	0-0	—	Maver 2	850
21	Jan	1	A	Brechin C	D 1-1	0-1	—	Allan	600
22		6	H	Dumbarton	D 2-2	0-0	9	Powell, McGlashan	300
23		13	A	Queen's Park	L 1-2	1-1	11	McGlashan	472
24		20	H	Arbroath	W 4-2	2-2	10	Powell 2, Sheran, McGlashan	450
25	Feb	3	A	East Fife	D 2-2	1-0	11	King, McGlashan	450
26		10	A	Stranraer	L 0-2	0-2	13		300
27		28	H	Berwick R	L 0-2	0-1	—		155
28	Mar	3	A	Stirling Albion	W 3-2	1-1	12	Maver, Powell 2	450
29		10	H	Stenhousemuir	D 1-1	1-1	12	Allan	200
30		14	A	East Stirling	D 1-1	0-0	—	McGlashan	200
31		17	A	Arbroath	L 0-3	0-2	12		365
32		24	A	Brechin C	D 2-2	1-1	11	Allan, Murray	800
33		27	H	Dumbarton	L 1-2	0-1	—	McGlashan	350
34		31	H	East Fife	L 0-2	0-0	12		350
35	Apr	7	A	Cowdenbeath	W 4-2	1-2	12	Maver, Brown, Murray 2	200
36		14	H	Queen's Park	L 0-1	0-0	13		200
37		21	H	East Stirling	W 3-0	0-0	13	Brown (pen), Powell, Maver	163
38		28	H	Kilmarnock	L 1-3	0-1	13	Allan	1650
39	May	5	H	Queen of the S	D 1-1	1-1	13	Allan	250

Final League Position: 13

GOALSCORERS

League: (53): Powell 11, Murray 10, McGlashan 9, Maver 7, Allan 6, Brown 5 (2 pens), Dolan 1, King 1, Paterson 1, Sheran 1, own goal 1.
Scottish Cup: (1): Allan 1.
Skol Cup: (4): Murray 4.

Record Victory: 12-0 v Vale of Leithen, Scottish Cup 2nd rd; 4 Jan, 1975.
Record Defeat: 0-13 v Aberdeen; 17 Mar, 1951.
Most Capped Player: Alexander Keillor, 2 (6), Scotland.
Most League Appearances: —.
Most League Goals in Season (Individual): 28: Brian Third, Division II; 1972–73.
Most Goals Overall (Individual): —.

Honours
League Champions: Second Division 1984–85.
Scottish Cup: Quarter-finals 1973, 1976.
League Cup: Semi-finals 1975–76.
Club colours: Shirt: Blue with white pin stripe. Shorts: White. Stockings: Red.

Larter, D	Morrison, B	King, S	Paterson, D	Halley, K	Selbie, A	Allan, H	Lyons, A	Maver, C	McGlashan, J	Murray, G	Mackay, H	Wright, A	Greig, I	Powell, D	Brown, K	Dolan, A	Duffy, A	Sheran, J	Young, J	Walker, A	McLelland, C	Price, R	Match No.
1	2	3	4	5	6†	7*	8	9	10	11	12	14											1
1	2	3	4	5	6*	7	8	9	10	11			12							.			2
1	2	3	4	5	6*	7	8	9	10	11				12									3
1	2	3	4	5†	6*	7	8	9	10	11	12				14								4
1	2	3	5		12	7†	8*	9	10	11	14			4	6								5
1	2	3	5			7	8	9†10	11				14	4	6*12								6
1	2	3	5		14	7	8†	9	10	11			12	4	6*								7
1	2	3	4		14		8	7	10	11	9*		12		6†	5							8
1	2	3	6		7*14			8	11	9†		12	4	10	5								9
1	2	3	6			7	8*	9	10	11†12		14	4		5								10
1	2	3	4			7	8	9	10†11	12				6*14	5								11
1	2	3	4			7	8	9	10	11				6*12	5								12
1	2		6	3		12	7	10	11†	9			14	4	8*	5							13
1	2	3	6			12	14	7	10	11	9*			4	8†	5							14
1	2	3	6			7	12	9	10		14		11†	4	8*	5							15
1	2	3	6†			7	8*	9	10		12		11	4	14	5							16
1		3†	2		14	7	8	9	10	12			11	4	6*	5							17
1		3	2			6*	8	10	11				7	4	12	14			5	9†			18
1		3*	2		14		8	9	10	11	12		7	4	6†	5							19
1		3	2			6	12	8†	7	10		9	14	11*	4	5							20
1	2	6			3	7	8	9	5	11†14			12		10*	4							21
1	2	3			6	7*	8	9	10	12	14		11†	4		5							22
1	2	3			6†	7	8	9	10	12	14		11*	4		5							23
1	2	3			6	7*	8†	9	10		12		11	4		5				14			24
1	2†	3	5*		6	7		9	10		8		12	11	4			14					25
1		3†	4		6*	7		9	10	12	8		14	11	2			5					26
1		3†	6*			7	8	9	10	12	2		14	11	4			5					27
1		3	2			7	8	9		5			10	11	4					6			28
1	2	3	5			7	8	9	10		6		11	4									29
1	2	3	14			7	8†	9	10	12	5		11	4*							6		30
1	2	3	4			7	8	9	10	12	5*		6†11		14								31
1	2	3	5			7	8	9	10	12	6†		11*	4	14								32
1	2	3	5		14	7	8	9†10	12				11	4	6*								33
1	2	3	5			6	7	8	9	10*12			11	4									34
1	2	3	5			6	7	8	9	10			11	4									35
1	2	3	4			7	8	9	10	12			6†11*							14			36
1	2	3				7	8	9	10†12				14	11	4*			5			6		37
1	2	3				7	8	9	10	4			11*		12			5			6		38
1	2	3	6			7	8		11*14				10†12	4	9			5					39
39	32	38	32	4	15	32	33	37	33	22	14 —		4	23	28	11		5	21	1	1	3	1
	+		+	+	+					+	+		+	+	+	+		+	+			+	
	1s		6s	3s	3s					10s	15s1s		6s9s	1s	5s			4s1s				2s	

MORTON

First Division

Year Formed: 1874.   *Ground & Address:* Cappielow Park, Sinclair St, Greenock.   *Telephone:* 0475 23511.
Ground Capacity: total: 16,000   seated: 5500.   *Size of Pitch:* 110yd×71yd.
Chairman: John Wilson.   *Secretary:* Mrs Jane Rankin.   *Commercial Manager:* Iain Baxter.
Manager: Allan McGraw.   *Assistant Manager:* John McMaster.   *Physio:* John Tierney.   *Coach:* Billy Osborne.
Managers since 1975: Joe Gilroy; Benny Rooney; Alex Miller; Tommy McLean; Willie McLean; Allan McGraw.
Club Nickname(s): The Ton.   *Previous Grounds:* Grant Street 1874, Garvel Park 1875, Cappielow Park 1879, Lady-
burn Park 1882, (Cappielow Park 1883).
Record Attendance: 23,000 v Celtic; 1922.
Record Transfer Fee received: £350,000 for Neil Orr to West Ham U.
Record Transfer Fee paid: £35,000 for Roddy MacDonald from Hearts.
Record Victory: 11-0 v Carfin Shamrock, Scottish Cup 1st rd; 13 Nov, 1886.

1989–90 LEAGUE RECORD

Match No.	Date	Venue	Opponents	Result	H/T Score	Lg. Pos.	Goalscorers	Attendance
1	Aug 12	A	Raith R	L 0-2	0-1	—		1529
2	19	H	Clyde	L 0-1	0-1	13		1400
3	26	A	Clydebank	L 1-3	1-1	14	Alexander	1152
4	Sept 2	H	Airdrieonians	L 0-1	0-0	14		1850
5	5	A	Ayr U	W 3-2	3-1	—	Reid, Jim Boag, Alexander	2492
6	9	H	Meadowbank T	D 0-0	0-0	12		1200
7	16	H	Alloa	W 3-2	2-0	12	Pickering, Deeney, Alexander	1500
8	23	A	Hamilton A	D 2-2	0-1	11	Deeney, O'Hara	1569
9	30	H	Forfar Ath	D 1-1	1-0	11	McDonald	1300
10	Oct 7	A	St Johnstone	D 1-1	0-1	12	Alexander	6730
11	14	H	Partick T	D 2-2	1-2	9	Alexander 2	3790
12	21	A	Falkirk	L 0-1	0-0	10		3000
13	28	H	Albion R	D 0-0	0-0	11		1400
14	Nov 4	H	Ayr U	D 1-1	1-1	12	Ronald	1900
15	11	A	Meadowbank T	D 0-0	0-0	12		500
16	18	A	Alloa	D 1-1	0-1	10	Robertson	834
17	25	H	Hamilton A	D 0-0	0-0	11		1600
18	Dec 2	A	Forfar Ath	W 1-0	0-0	10	Turner	552
19	9	H	St Johnstone	D 0-0	0-0	10		2970
20	23	H	Raith R	D 1-1	1-1	10	Alexander	1310
21	30	A	Clyde	D 1-1	0-1	11	Turner	900
22	Jan 3	H	Clydebank	D 2-2	0-0	—	McGraw, Alexander	1300
23	6	A	Airdrieonians	L 1-4	1-2	11	Turner	2491
24	9	A	Partick T	W 2-1	1-1	—	McGraw, Alexander	2446
25	13	A	Albion R	D 1-1	0-0	9	McGraw	902
26	27	H	Falkirk	L 0-2	0-1	10		2158
27	Feb 3	H	Alloa	W 2-0	1-0	9	O'Hara, McNeil	1262
28	10	A	Partick T	W 1-0	0-0	8	Alexander	2559
29	27	H	St Johnstone	L 1-2	0-0	—	McInnes	1920
30	Mar 3	A	Meadowbank T	L 0-1	0-0	10		300
31	10	A	Raith R	L 1-2	0-1	10	Roberts	1182
32	17	H	Albion R	W 3-0	0-0	9	Pickering 2, Turner	755
33	27	H	Forfar Ath	W 2-0	1-0	—	Turner, Fowler (pen)	600
34	31	A	Falkirk	L 0-2	0-0	10		1700
35	Apr 7	H	Ayr U	L 0-1	0-1	10		1175
36	14	A	Hamilton A	L 0-2	0-0	11		1077
37	21	A	Clydebank	W 1-0	0-0	10	O'Hara	1061
38	28	H	Airdrieonians	D 1-1	1-0	9	Turner	1235
39	5	H	Clyde	L 2-3	0-3	11	Fowler, Alexander	809

Final League Position: 11

GOALSCORERS

League: (38): Alexander 11, Turner 6, McGraw 3, O'Hara 3, Pickering 3, Deeney 2, Fowler 2 (1 pen), Jim Boag 1,
McDonald 1, McInnes 1, McNeil 1, Reid 1, Roberts 1, Robertson 1, Ronald 1.
Scottish Cup: (6): Alexander 3, Fowler 1, O'Hara 1, Turner 1.
Skol Cup: (2): Alexander 1, Turner 1.

Record Defeat: 1-10 v Port Glasgow Ath, Division II; 5 May, 1894: v St Bernards, Division II; 14 Oct, 1933.
Most Capped Player: Jimmy Cowan, 25, Scotland.
Most League Appearances: 358: David Hayes, 1969-84.
Most League Goals in Season (Individual): 58: Allan McGraw, Division II; 1963-64.
Most Goals Overall (Individual): —.

Honours

League Champions: First Division 1977-78, 1983-84, 1986-87. Division II 1949-50, 1963-64, 1966-67.
Scottish Cup Winners: 1922; Runners-up: 1948.
League Cup Runners-up: 1963-64.
European: European Cup —. Cup Winners Cup —. UEFA Cup (Fairs): 1968-69.
Club colours: Shirt: Blue and white hoops. Shorts: White. Stockings: Blue.

Wylie, D	Collins, D	Pickering, M	Reid, B	Boag, John	Hunter, J	Ronald, G	Turner, T	Alexander, R	O'Hara, A	Deeney, M	Roberts, P	McCrystal, R	Boag, Jim	McDonald, I	McGoldrick, K	Goodwin, J	McInnes, D	Fowler, J	McGraw, M	Robertson, D	Gourlay, A	Strain, B	Kelly, G	McNeil, J	Hopkin, D	Cowie, G	Match No.
1	2	3	4	5	6	7	8	9	10	11																	1
1	2	3	4	5	6*	7	8	9	10	11	12																2
1	2		4	5	6	7†	8	9	10	11	14	3*		12													3
1	2	3	4	5	6		10	9	12	11†	14			7			8*										4
1	2	3	4	5	6		10	9	12	11†				7*			8	14									5
1	2	3	4	5	6		10	9		11*				7			8	12									6
1		3	4	5	6		10	9	2	11				7*			8†	12	14								7
1	12	3*	4	5	6	14	10	9	2	11				7†			8										8
1	12	3*	4	5	6	7†	10	9	2	11				14			8										9
1	2	3	4	5	6	7	10	9	14	11*				12			8†										10
1	2	3	4	5	6	7*10		9	14	11†				12			8										11
1	2	3	4	5	6	7	10	9		11*				12			8										12
1	2	3	4	5	6			9		11†				7			8	14	12	10*							13
1	2	3	4	5	6	7*		9		11				12			8	10									14
1	2	3	4	5	6	7		9						12			8†	14	10	11*							15
1	2	3	4	5	6	11		9						8			10	7									16
1	2†	3	4	5	6	11		9	12					8			10*14		7								17
1	2*	3		5	6	11		9	4	12				8			10†14		7								18
1	2	3		5	6	11		9	4	12				8*10†14					7								19
1	2	3	4	5*	6	11		9	12					8†10			14		7								20
1	2	3	4	5	6	11†10		9	12	14				8*					7								21
1	2	3	4	5	6			9	12	11				8†			10	14	7*								22
1	2	3	4	5	6	11		9	12	7*				8†			14	10									23
1	2	3	4		6	11		9	5					8			14	6	10*12	7†							24
1	2	3	4		6			9	5					8*			12	11	10	7							25
1	2		4					9	7†14					8	5	10	11*	3	6	12							26
1	2	3	4		6			9	5					8*			12	11	10					7			27
1	2	3	4	12	6		10	9	5					8			11							7*			28
1	2	3	4	14	6	7		9	5					8			12	10*						11†			29
1	2	3	4*12		6	7		9	5	14				8			10†11										30
1	2		3	6	14	7		9	5	10				8*			12				4		11†				31
1	2	3†	4	8	6	7		9*	12	5				10			11							14			32
1	2		4	5	6	7		9	12	11*				10			8			3†				14			33
1	2		4	5	6	7		9	11*	12				10			8†							14	3		34
1	2		4	5	6	7		9	12	14				10			8†							11*	3		35
1	2		4	5	6	7		9	14	10				12			11*							8†	3		36
1	2		4		6	7		9		5				10†			8*		14	11	12				3		37
1	2		4		6	7		9	14	5				10					3	12				11†	8*		38
1	2	3†	4			7*	11	9	10	5				8					14	12				6			39
39	36	30	36	29	36	13	30	38	19	17	4	1	6	22	—	—	15	24	5	7	4	2	1	7	3	5	
	+2s			+3s			+2s		+10s	+5s	+4s			+7s	+3s	+2s	+4s	+8s	+1s	+6s	+1s			+3s	+1s	+5s	

735

MOTHERWELL Premier Division

Year Formed: 1886.   *Ground & Address:* Fir Park, Motherwell ML1 2QN.   *Telephone:* 0698 61437/8.
Ground Capacity: total: 18,000   seated: 3500.   *Size of Pitch:* 110yd×75yd.
Chairman: John C. Chapman.   *Secretary:* Alan C. Dick.   *Commercial Manager:* John Swinburne.
Manager: Tommy McLean.   *Assistant Manager:* Tom Forsyth.   *Physio:* Jim Maitland.   *Coach:* Cameron Murray.
Managers since 1975: Ian St John; Willie McLean; Rodger Hynd; Ally MacLeod; David Hay; Jock Wallace; Bobby Watson; Tommy McLean.
Club Nickname(s): The 'Well.   *Previous Grounds:* Roman Road (1886–95), Dalziel Park.
Record Attendance: 35,632 v Rangers, Scottish Cup 4th rd replay; 12 Mar, 1952.
Record Transfer Fee received: £375,000 for Andy Walker to Celtic (1987).
Record Transfer Fee paid: £100,000 for Mike Larnach from Newcastle U and £100,000 for Nick Cusack from Peterborough U, July 1989.

1989–90 LEAGUE RECORD

Match No.	Date	Venue	Opponents	Result	H/T Score	Lg. Pos.	Goalscorers	Attendance
1	Aug 12	A	Dundee U	D 1-1	1-1	—	Cusack	8596
2	19	H	Aberdeen	D 0-0	0-0	7		6491
3	26	H	St Mirren	W 3-1	2-0	3	Kirk, Cusack 2	4703
4	Sept 9	A	Dunfermline Ath	D 1-1	0-0	1	Paterson	8715
5	16	H	Hearts	L 1-3	0-1	5	McCart	8948
6	23	A	Celtic	D 1-1	1-1	5	Paterson	29,000
7	30	H	Dundee	W 3-0	2-0	3	Kirk, O'Neill (pen), Cooper	4463
8	Oct 3	H	Rangers	W 1-0	1-0	—	Russell	17,667
9	14	A	Hibernian	L 2-3	0-2	3	Cusack 2	8000
10	21	H	Dundee U	W 3-2	1-1	2	Boyd, Cooper (pen), Arnott	8184
11	28	A	Aberdeen	L 0-1	0-1	6		13,500
12	Nov 4	A	St Mirren	D 2-2	1-0	6	Cusack, Cooper	4585
13	8	H	Dunfermline Ath	D 1-1	1-0	—	Cusack	9138
14	18	A	Hearts	L 0-3	0-0	6		12,035
15	25	H	Celtic	D 0-0	0-0	7		16,029
16	Dec 2	A	Dundee	L 1-2	0-1	7	Kirk	4099
17	9	A	Rangers	L 0-3	0-1	7		33,549
18	23	A	Dundee U	D 1-1	1-1	7	Russell	6169
19	30	H	Aberdeen	D 2-2	0-1	8	Cooper 2 (1 pen)	7267
20	Jan 2	H	St Mirren	W 2-0	0-0	—	Arnott, Kirk	8253
21	6	A	Dunfermline Ath	W 5-0	3-0	6	Cusack 2, Gahagan 2, Kirk	8525
22	9	H	Hibernian	L 0-2	0-1	—		6447
23	13	H	Hearts	L 0-3	0-1	6		8822
24	27	A	Celtic	W 1-0	0-0	6	Cusack	23,000
25	Feb 3	A	Hibernian	W 2-1	1-0	5	Arnott, Paterson	5524
26	10	H	Rangers	D 1-1	1-0	5	Arnott	17,647
27	17	H	Dundee	W 3-1	2-0	5	Kirk 2, Gahagan	5508
28	Mar 3	A	Hearts	L 0-2	0-0	5		9205
29	10	H	Dundee U	L 0-1	0-1	6		4697
30	24	A	Aberdeen	L 0-2	0-1	7		10,000
31	31	A	St Mirren	D 0-0	0-0	7		5448
32	Apr 7	H	Dunfermline Ath	L 1-3	1-1	7	McCathie (og)	6351
33	14	A	Rangers	L 1-2	0-0	7	Cusack	39,305
34	21	H	Hibernian	W 1-0	1-0	7	Arnott	4435
35	28	H	Celtic	D 1-1	1-1	7	Cooper (pen)	10,322
36	May 5	A	Dundee	W 2-1	1-0	6	Russell, Kirk	2846

Final League Position: 6

GOALSCORERS

League: (43): Cusack 11, Kirk 8, Cooper 6 (3 pens), Arnott 5, Gahagan 3, Paterson 3, Russell 3, Boyd 1, McCart 1, O'Neill 1 (pen), own goal 1.
Scottish Cup: (7): Arnott 1, Bryce 1, Cooper 1 (pen), Gahagan 1, Kirk 1, McCart 1, Russell 1.
Skol Cup: (4): Cusack 2, Dolan 1, Kirk 1.

Record Victory: 12-1 v Dundee U, Division II; 23 Jan, 1954.
Record Defeat: 0-8 v Aberdeen, Premier Division; 26 Mar, 1979.
Most Capped Player: George Stevenson, 12, Scotland.
Most League Appearances: 626: Bobby Ferrier, 1918–37.
Most League Goals in Season (Individual): 52: Willie McFadyen, Division I; 1931–32.
Most Goals Overall (Individual): 283: Hugh Ferguson, 1916–25.

Honours

League Champions: Division I 1931–32. First Division 1981–82, 1984–85. Division II 1953–54, 1968–69; *Runners-up:* Division I 1926–27, 1929–30, 1932–33, 1933–34. Division II 1894–95, 1902–03.
Scottish Cup: 1952; *Runners-up:* 1931, 1933, 1939, 1951.
League Cup: 1950–51; *Runners-up:* 1954–55.
Club colours: Shirt: Amber with claret band. Shorts: Claret. Stockings: Amber.

Maxwell, A	Burley, G	Boyd, T	Dolan, J	Philliben, J	McCart, C	Russell, R	O'Neill, C	Cusack, N	Kirk, S	Mair, G	Arnott, D	McLean, P	Paterson, C	McBride, M	Cooper, D	Gahagan, J	McAdam, T	Reilly, M	Griffin, J	Bryce, S	MacCabe, D	McNair, C	Gardner, J	Match No.
1	2	3	4†	5	6	7	8	9	10*	11	12	14												1
1	2	3	4	5	6	7	8	9*	10†	11	12	14												2
1	2	3	12	5	8*	4	9	10					6	7†	11	14								3
1	2	3		5	7	4	9	10					8*	6	11	12								4
1	2	3	14	5	7	4*	9	10†					8	6	11	12								5
1	2	3	14	6	7	8	10†	9*					4		11	12	5							6
1	2	3	6	7†	8	9*	10	12					4		11	14	5							7
1	2	3	6	7	8	9*	10	12					4		11†	14	5							8
1	2	6*	7	8†	9	10	12						4		11		5	3	14					9
1	2	3	14	5	6	10	9*						4		11	7†	8	12						10
1	2	3	14	6	7	12	10	9*					4		11		5	8†						11
1	2	3	12	6*	7†	8	9	10					4		11	14	5							12
1	2	3	14	6	7†	4	9*	10	8				5		11	12								13
1		3		5	6	7	8	9	10				4		11	12	2*							14
1	3	2		5	6	10*	8	9					4		11	7	12							15
1	2	3	8	5	6	7	9*	10	12				4		11									16
1	2	3		5	6	8	9	10	12				4		11	7*								17
1	2	3		5	6	8	12	10	7	9			4†		11*	14								18
1	2	3	5*	6	12	8	9	10	7				4		11†	14								19
1	2	3		6	8	4	10	12	9				5		11	7*								20
1	2	3	12	6	8	4	9	10					5		11*	7†	14							21
1	2	3	8	6	4*	9	10						5		11	7†	12	14						22
1	2	3		6	8	4	10	7*	9				5		11	12								23
1	2	3	14	6	8	4	9	10	7*				5		11†	12								24
1	2	3	14	6	8	4	9	10	7†				5		11*	12								25
1	2	3	14	6	8	4	9†	10	7				5		11*	12								26
1	2	3		6	8†	4	9	10	7				5		11*	12	14							27
1	2	3		5	6	7	8	9	10	11			4											28
1	2	3		6	8	4†	10	11*	9				5			7	12	14						29
1	2		4	6	8	9	10	11*	7				12						5	3				30
1	2	14	5	6	8†	9	10	7*					4		11	12							3	31
1	2*	3	5	6†	8	9	10	7*					4		11	12	14							32
1	2	3	5	6†	8	9	14	7*					4		11	12	10							33
1	2	3	5	6	9	8	7						4		11		10							34
1	2	3	5	6	8*	9	12	7					4		11		10							35
1	2*	3	5	12	8	9	10	14	7†				4		11		6							36
36	34	33	5	19	33	32	24	29	32	7	23	—	33	1	31	7	6	3	6	—	—	1	1	
		+	+	+	+			+	+		+	+	+	+					+		+	+	+	
		7s	5s	1s	1s			2s	2s		2s	7s	2s						19s		1s	5s3s	1s 1s	

PARTICK THISTLE

First Division

Year Formed: 1876.   *Ground & Address:* Firhill Park, 90 Firhill Rd, Glasgow G20 7AL.   *Telephone:* 041 946 2673.
Ground Capacity: total: 20,600   seated: 3264.   *Size of Pitch:* 106yd×72yd.
Chairman: Jim Donald.   *Secretary:* Campbell Gillan.   *Commercial Manager:* Dorothy Martin.
Manager: John Lambie.   *Assistant Manager:* Gerry Collins.   *Physio:* Jim Martin.   *Coach:* Ian Jardine.
Managers since 1975: R. Auld; P. Cormack; B. Rooney; R. Auld; D. Johnstone; W. Lamont, S. Clark, J. Lambie.
Club Nickname(s): The Jags.   *Previous Grounds:* Jordanvale Park; Muirpark; Inchview; Meadowside Park.
Record Attendance: 49,838 v Rangers, Division I; 18 Feb, 1922.
Record Transfer Fee received: £100,000 for Mo Johnston from Watford.
Record Transfer Fee paid: £60,000 for Cammy Duncan from Motherwell, October 1989.
Record Victory: 16-0 v Royal Albert, Scottish Cup 1st rd; 17 Jan, 1931.

1989–90 LEAGUE RECORD

Match No.	Date	Venue	Opponents	Result	H/T Score	Lg. Pos.	Goalscorers	Attendance
1	Aug 12	A	Clydebank	W 2-1	2-1	—	Campbell, Charnley	2915
2	19	H	Albion R	W 4-0	2-0	1	McCoy 3, Campbell	3003
3	26	H	Clyde	D 2-2	2-2	3	Kerr, Wright	4037
4	Sept 2	A	Forfar Ath	W 3-0	1-0	2	Charnley 3 (2 pens)	1416
5	5	H	Raith R	W 3-1	1-0	—	Wright, Campbell, Charnley (pen)	3390
6	9	A	Hamilton A	W 4-1	3-0	2	Campbell 2, Dinnie, Peebles	3774
7	16	A	Meadowbank T	D 1-1	0-1	2	Flood	2000
8	23	H	Airdrieonians	W 2-1	1-0	2	Flood, Kennedy	5301
9	30	A	Ayr U	D 0-0	0-0	2		4524
10	Oct 7	H	Falkirk	W 1-0	1-0	2	Dinnie	8369
11	14	A	Morton	D 2-2	2-1	2	Adam, Campbell	3790
12	21	H	Alloa	D 3-3	3-1	2	Campbell 2, Adam	3781
13	28	A	St Johnstone	L 1-2	0-0	3	Charnley (pen)	10,091
14	Nov 4	A	Raith R	D 1-1	0-0	2	Campbell	2433
15	11	H	Hamilton A	W 3-1	1-1	2	Law, Campbell, Charnley (pen)	6021
16	18	H	Meadowbank T	W 2-0	1-0	2	Perry (og), Campbell	3338
17	25	A	Airdrieonians	D 1-1	0-0	2	Charnley (pen)	4381
18	Dec 2	H	Ayr U	L 1-2	1-0	3	Craig	3592
19	9	A	Falkirk	D 1-1	0-0	3	Charnley	4000
20	26	H	Clydebank	D 1-1	0-0	—	Campbell	3934
21	30	A	Albion R	L 4-5	3-2	3	Flood 3, Campbell	2212
22	Jan 2	A	Clyde	D 3-3	0-2	—	Flood, Campbell 2	3450
23	6	H	Forfar Ath	D 0-0	0-0	3		2795
24	9	H	Morton	L 1-2	1-1	—	Charnley (pen)	2446
25	13	H	St Johnstone	L 0-1	0-0	3		5484
26	Feb 3	A	Ayr U	L 1-2	1-1	3	Campbell	3247
27	10	H	Morton	L 0-1	0-0	6		2559
28	17	A	Airdrieonians	L 2-3	2-1	6	Flood 2	3000
29	28	A	Alloa	L 0-1	0-0	—		959
30	Mar 3	H	Clyde	L 0-3	0-2	7		2419
31	14	H	Hamilton A	W 4-1	2-1	—	Martin (og), Mitchell, McFarlane, English	2779
32	17	A	Falkirk	L 0-2	0-1	6		3200
33	24	A	Meadowbank T	D 1-1	1-1	7	Wright	1000
34	31	H	Clydebank	W 4-0	2-0	7	Wright 2, Campbell, Smith	3002
35	Apr 7	H	St Johnstone	L 0-2	0-1	7		5300
36	14	A	Forfar Ath	L 0-2	0-0	7		940
37	21	H	Alloa	W 1-0	0-0	7	Campbell	1763
38	28	A	Albion R	D 2-2	2-0	7	Flood, Charnley	1345
39	May 5	H	Raith R	D 1-1	1-0	8	English	2252

Final League Position: 8

GOALSCORERS

League: (62): Campbell 18, Charnley 11 (7 pens), Flood 9, Wright 5, McCoy 3, Adam 2, Dinnie 2, English 2, Craig 1, Kennedy 1, Kerr 1, Law 1, MacFarlane 1, Mitchell 1, Peebles 1, Smith 1, own goals 2.
Scottish Cup: (2): Campbell 1, Charnley 1 (pen).
Skol Cup: (0).

Record Defeat: 0-10 v Queen's Park, Scottish Cup; 3 Dec, 1881.
Most Capped Player: Alan Rough, 51 (53), Scotland.
Most League Appearances: 410: Alan Rough, 1969–82.
Most League Goals in Season (Individual): 41: Alec Hair, Division I; 1926–27.
Most Goals Overall (Individual): —.

Honours
League Champions: First Division 1975–76. Division II 1896–97, 1899–1900, 1970–71; *Runners-up:* Division II 1901–02.
Scottish Cup Winners: 1921; *Runners-up:* 1930.
League Cup Winners: 1971–72; *Runners-up:* 1953–54, 1956–57, 1958–59.
European: *European Cup* —. *Cup Winners Cup* —. *UEFA Cup* 6 matches (1963–64 *Fairs Cup*; 1972–73).
Club colours: Shirts: Amber with red shoulders and sleeves. Shorts: Red with amber stripe. Stockings: Red.

Murdoch, A	Dinnie, A	Smith, R	Kerr, J	MacDonald, R	Kennedy, A	Flood, J	Wright, B	Campbell, C	McCoy, G	Charnley, J	Gallagher, B	Peebles, G	Mitchell, J	McGuire, W	Law, R	Adam, C	Dempsey, J	Duncan, C	Craig, D	Clarke, S	Collins, G	Jardine, I	Corrie, T	McStay, W	MacFarlane, D	Grant, A	Rae, G	English, I	Wylie, R	Match No.
1	2	3	4	5	6	7	8	9	10	11																				1
1	2	3	4	5†	6		7	9	10	11	14	8*12																		2
1	2	3	4	5	6	12	8	9	10	11		7*																		3
1	2	3	4	5	6		7	9	10	11		8																		4
1	2	3	4	5	6	12	7	9	10*11			8†	14																	5
1	2	3	4	5	6	10	7	9		11		8																		6
1	2	3†	4	5	6	10	7	9		11	12	8*		14																7
1	2		4	5	6	10*	8	9	12	11			14		3	7†														8
1	2		4	5	6	10†	8	9	12	11			14		3	7*														9
1	2	3	4	5	6		7	9	10	11		8																		10
1	2		4	5	6	12	8	9		11	7*14				3	10†														11
1	2	3	4		5	12	10	9		11	7*				6	8														12
1	2		4		6	10	8	9		11		12			3	7*	5													13
	2		4	5*	6	10†	8	9		11	14	7			3	12		1												14
		6	4*				8	9		11	10†	2	7		3			1	12	14	5									15
		6	4				8	9		11	10†	2	7*		3	14		1	12		5									16
		6	4*				8	9†		11	10	2		12	3			1	7	14	5									17
		6			5	14	8	9		11	10		12	7†	3			1	2*		4									18
		3				10	8	9		11	12			7*	2			1	6		5	4								19
	2				5	14	8	9			12		10	7*				1	3	11†	6	4								20
3	2				5	7	8	9		11								1	10		6	4								21
3	2				5	7	8	9		11		6						1	10*			4	12							22
3	4	5				7	8	9		11	7	12						1				10	2*							23
3	4	5				7		9		11	12		10		6			1				8	2*							24
	4				12			9		11	10	6			3			1			5	8	7*	2						25
	14	5				10	4	9		11		6		12	3			1				8*	7†	2						26
12	3					10	8	9		11	6			5				1				7*		2	4					27
	3	5				10	8	9			7	4			11			1					2	6						28
3	4	5				10	8	9			7*	6				2†		1				12	11	14						29
3†	4				6	10	8				5	7			2*			1	14			12	11	9						30
3	4				5	10	8				9	11			2			1				7*		12†		6	14			31
3	4				6*	9	10			8	11	7†			2			1					12		5	14				32
	6	3				10	8	9		11	7*	4	12		2			1								5				33
	6	3				10	8	9*		11		4	7		2			1						12	5					34
	6	3				10	8			11	12	4	7†	9*	2			1								5	14			35
	3	2			6	10	8			11			7	12	4			1								5	9*			36
	3					10	6	9		11		7*		2			1					12		5	8	4				37
	3					10	8	9		11		7		2								4*		12	5	9	6			38
	3	12				10		8*		11		14	7		2			1				4		6†	5					39
13	14	29	33	17	22	26	36	34	6	29	15	22	14	4	27	6	1	25	6	1	8	12	4	4	5	1	9	3	2	
		+	+			+					+	+	+	+	+								+	+	+		+			
		1s	2s			7s					2s	7s	2s	7s	4s1s	2s							3s	2s		2s	1s	4s	2s		3s	

Also played: Graham P – Match 38 (1).

QUEEN OF THE SOUTH   Second Division

Year Formed: 1919.   *Ground & Address:* Palmerston Park, Terregles St, Dumfries DG2 9BA.   *Telephone:* 0387 54853.
Ground Capacity: total: 13,000   seated: 1300.   *Size of Pitch:* 112yd×72yd.
Chairman: W. J. Harkness C.B.E..   *Secretary:* Mrs Doreen Alcorn.   *Commercial Manager:* J. Anderson.
Manager: Frank McGarvey.   *Assistant Manager:* —.   *Physio:* —.   *Coach:* I. McChesney.
Managers since 1975: M. Jackson; G. Herd; A. Busby; R. Clark; M. Jackson; D. Wilson; W. McLaren.
Club Nickname(s): The Doonhamers.   *Previous Grounds:* None.
Record Attendance: 24,500 v Hearts, Scottish Cup 3rd rd; 23 Feb, 1952.
Record Transfer Fee received: £100,000 for Ted McMinn from Rangers, 1985.
Record Transfer Fee paid: —.
Record Victory: 11-1 v Stranraer, Scottish Cup 1st rd; 16 Jan, 1932.

1989–90 LEAGUE RECORD

Match No.	Date	Venue	Opponents	Result	H/T Score	Lg. Pos.	Goalscorers	Attendance
1	Aug 12	A	Dumbarton	L 1-2	0-0	—	Andrews	650
2	19	H	Berwick R	W 4-2	2-1	5	Moore 2, Fraser (pen), McGuire	704
3	26	H	Stranraer	D 2-2	0-1	6	Andrews, Moore	1250
4	Sept 2	A	Stirling Albion	L 0-5	0-2	12		700
5	9	H	Arbroath	D 2-2	0-0	12	Andrews, Sim	750
6	16	A	Brechin C	L 1-3	1-1	12	Thomson I	400
7	23	A	Montrose	D 0-0	0-0	12		354
8	30	H	East Stirling	D 2-2	1-0	12	McGhie, Thomson A	350
9	Oct 7	A	East Fife	D 2-2	0-1	12	Mills, Possee	796
10	14	H	Cowdenbeath	L 2-4	2-1	13	McGuire, Johnston	500
11	21	H	Queen's Park	W 3-1	3-0	12	McGhie, McGuire 2	560
12	28	A	Stenhousemuir	W 3-1	0-0	10	Andrews, Sim, Sloan	250
13	Nov 4	A	Kilmarnock	L 0-2	0-1	11		2896
14	11	H	Stirling Albion	W 3-1	0-1	10	Andrews, Gordon, Sim	720
15	18	A	East Stirling	L 0-1	0-0	10		220
16	25	H	Montrose	W 3-2	2-1	10	Sloan, Fraser, Johnston	650
17	Dec 2	H	East Fife	W 5-1	3-0	9	Fraser 2 (1 pen), Sloan, Gordon 2	531
18	20	A	Cowdenbeath	L 2-4	1-3	—	Robertson, Fraser (pen)	150
19	23	H	Berwick R	W 3-2	1-1	7	Gordon, Andrews, McGhie	461
20	Jan 2	A	Stranraer	W 2-0	2-0	—	Gordon, Sloan	650
21	10	H	Dumbarton	L 1-4	1-1	—	Gordon	923
22	13	A	Arbroath	L 0-1	0-1	9		380
23	27	A	Queen's Park	D 0-0	0-0	9		754
24	Feb 3	H	Stenhousemuir	D 1-1	1-1	8	Robertson (pen)	940
25	7	H	Brechin C	W 3-1	1-0	—	Robertson 2 (1 pen), Thomson I	750
26	10	H	Dumbarton	D 1-1	0-0	7	Sloan	822
27	17	A	Stirling Albion	D 1-1	0-0	7	Possee	750
28	Mar 3	A	Berwick R	D 1-1	0-0	7	McGhie	348
29	7	A	Cowdenbeath	L 1-2	0-2	—	Sloan	360
30	10	H	Brechin C	D 2-2	0-1	7	Gordon, Thomson A	802
31	13	H	Kilmarnock	W 2-1	2-0	—	Thomson A 2	1500
32	17	A	Stranraer	L 0-3	0-1	6		950
33	24	H	East Fife	W 2-1	2-1	5	Robertson (pen), Thomson A	510
34	31	H	East Stirling	D 1-1	0-0	7	Gordon	663
35	Apr 7	A	Arbroath	L 0-1	0-0	7		310
36	14	H	Stenhousemuir	L 0-4	0-2	10		758
37	21	A	Kilmarnock	L 1-4	0-2	10	Thomson A	3262
38	28	H	Queen's Park	D 0-0	0-0	10		374
39	May 5	A	Montrose	D 1-1	1-1	10	Sloan	250

Final League Position: 10

GOALSCORERS
League: (58): Gordon 8, Sloan 7, Andrews 6, Thomson A 6, Fraser 5 (3 pens), Robertson 5 (3 pens), McGhie 4, McGuire 4, Moore 3, Sim 3, Johnston 2, Possee 2, Thomson I 2, Mills 1.
Scottish Cup: (7): Gordon 3, Fraser 1, McGhie 1, Sloan 1, Thomson A 1.
Skol Cup: (1): Fraser 1 (pen).

Record Defeat: 2-10 v Dundee, Division I; 1 Dec, 1962.
Most Capped Player: Billy Houliston, 3, Scotland.
Most League Appearances: 619: Allan Ball; 1962–83.
Most League Goals in Season (Individual): 33: Jimmy Gray, Division II; 1927–28.
Most Goals Overall (Individual): —.

Honours
League Champions: Division II 1950–51; *Runners-up:* Division II 1932–33, 1961–62, 1974–75. Second Division 1980–81, 1985–86.
Scottish Cup:—.
League Cup:—.
Club colours: Shirt: Royal blue. Shorts: White. Stockings: Royal blue with white tops.

McLean, A	McGhie, W	Gray, W	Sim, W	Mills, D	McGuire, J	Andrews, G	Fraser, G	Moore, S	Johnston, G	Sloan, T	Telfer, G	Stewart, R	Shanks, M	Hetherington, K	Thomson, I	McCafferty, T	Thomson, A	Holland, B	Possee, M	Gordon, S	Davidson, A	Robertson, J	Archer, S	Donaldson, S	Bain, A	Dawson, L	Match No.
1	2	3	4	5	6*	7†	8	9	10	11	12	14															1
1	2	3	4	5	11*12	6	9	8	7				10														2
1	2†	3	4	5	11	12	10	9	8	7			6*14														3
1	2	3	4			12	10	9*	6	7			8	5	11†14												4
1	2		14	5	11*	9	10		8	7		12	6†	4	3												5
1	2		3	5		9	10*		7	11		12	8†	4	6		14										6
1	2		4	5	11	9*	6		8	7		12		10	3												7
1	2		4	5	11*	9†	6		8		7	12	10	3		14											8
	2		6†	5	11*12			7	9			4	8	3		10	1	14									9
	2		6*	5†11	12			7	9			4	8	3		10	1	14									10
	2		6		11†14	8*		7	9			12	5	3	4	10	1										11
	2		6		11	12	10	7*	9				5	3	4	8	1										12
	2		6		11	12	10	7*	9			14	5†	3	4	8	1										13
	2		10			7	8		6			3	5		4	12	1	11*	9								14
	2	12	6		11	7		10				5	3	4	8*			9	1								15
	2				11	8		7	6			5	3	4	10	1		9									16
	2				7	6		8	10			5	3	4				9	1	11							17
	2		14	12		7	6		8†10*			3	5	4				9	1	11							18
	2					7	6*		8	10		3	5	4			12	9	1	11							19
	2*		10	12		11			7	6		8	5	4				9	1		3						20
			3	2		7*			10	6		8	5		4	14	12	9	1		11†						21
	2	6						7*	9			8	5	3	4			12	11	1		10					22
	2		3					7	11			8	5	6	4			9	1	12	10*						23
	2	10†12						8	7*				5	3	4	14		9	1	11	6						24
	2	6	3					8	7				5	10	4			9	1	11							25
	2	6	3					8*	7				5	10	4	12		9	1	11							26
	5	4	2					8	10				3		9		7	6	1	11							27
	5	6	2	12					7			3	4	9		11	8	1				10*					28
	5	6†	2	10*					7	14		3	4	9		12	8	1	11								29
	2*	14	3					7	12			5	6	4	10		9†	8	1	11							30
	2	8	3					7				5	6	4	10			9	1	11							31
	2	6*	3					8				5	10	4	7		12	9	1	11							32
		6	2					8	10			5	3	4	7			9	1	11							33
	2	6						8	10			5	3	4	7			9	1	11*				12			34
		6						8	10			5	3	4	7			9	1	11					2		35
		6		14				8	10			2	5		4	7		12	9	1	11*					3†	36
	2	3						8	10			6	5		4	7			9	1	11						37
	2	3	5		7			8*10				6	4		12	9		11		1							38
	2		5		12			8*10				3	4		6	7			9	1	11						39
8	35	4+	30+	23+	12+	14	17	4	31	39	—	1	18	33	27	27+	20+	7	5	25	24+	17	5	1	1	1	
		4s	3s	1s	10s							1s		6s3s	1s	2s	6s				8s		1s		1s		

QUEEN'S PARK
Second Division

Year Formed: 1867. *Ground & Address:* Hampden Park, Mount Florida, Glasgow G42 9BA. *Telephone:* 041 632 1275.
Ground Capacity: total: 74,730 seated: 10,000. *Size of Pitch:* 115yd×75yd.
President: Austin Reilly. *Chairman:* —. *Secretary:* James C. Rutherford. *Commercial Manager:* —.
Physio: A. P. McEwan. *Coach:* Edward Hunter.
Coaches since 1975: D. McParland, J. Gilroy, E. Hunter.
Club Nickname(s): The Spiders. *Previous Grounds:* 1st Hampden (Titwood Park), 2nd Hampden, 3rd Hampden.
Record Attendance: 95,772 v Rangers, Scottish Cup; 18 Jan, 1930.
Record for ground: 149,547, Scotland v England, 1937.
Record Transfer Fee received: —.

1989–90 LEAGUE RECORD

Match No.	Date	Venue	Opponents	Result	H/T Score	Lg. Pos.	Goalscorers	Atten- dance
1	Aug 12	A	Stenhousemuir	W 3-1	2-1	—	Caven, O'Brien P, Hendry	260
2	19	H	East Stirling	W 3-2	2-0	2	Hendry, O'Brien P, Ogg	400
3	26	H	Kilmarnock	W 1-0	0-0	2	McEntegart	1846
4	Sept 2	A	East Fife	D 1-1	0-0	2	Caven	801
5	9	A	Montrose	L 1-4	1-4	4	O'Brien P	370
6	16	H	Berwick R	W 3-1	1-0	2	Hendry 2, Ogg	529
7	23	H	Cowdenbeath	D 0-0	0-0	1		591
8	30	A	Arbroath	D 2-2	2-1	1	Hendry, McKenzie	661
9	Oct 7	H	Stranraer	L 0-2	0-1	4		771
10	14	A	Dumbarton	L 1-2	0-0	8	Caven	700
11	21	A	Queen of the S	L 1-3	0-3	9	Caven	560
12	28	H	Stirling Albion	W 2-1	1-0	7	Hendry 2	725
13	Nov 4	A	Brechin C	L 0-1	0-0	9		450
14	11	H	East Fife	W 2-1	1-1	8	Hendry, McEntegart	687
15	18	H	Arbroath	L 1-2	1-1	9	Hendry	531
16	25	A	Cowdenbeath	D 0-0	0-0	8		200
17	Dec 2	A	Stranraer	W 1-0	0-0	8	McKenzie	550
18	16	H	Dumbarton	D 2-2	1-1	8	O'Brien P, Rodden	587
19	23	A	East Stirling	L 0-1	0-1	9		300
20	26	H	Stenhousemuir	D 0-0	0-0	—		526
21	Jan 2	A	Kilmarnock	L 0-2	0-1	—		4843
22	6	A	Berwick R	L 0-2	0-2	8		363
23	13	H	Montrose	W 2-1	1-1	7	Armstrong, O'Brien P	472
24	17	H	Brechin C	L 0-3	0-1	—		350
25	27	H	Queen of the S	D 0-0	0-0	8		754
26	Feb 3	A	Stirling Albion	L 0-1	0-1	9		770
27	10	A	East Fife	L 2-3	2-1	12	Elder, Elliot	624
28	20	H	Stranraer	W 3-0	2-0	—	O'Brien P 2, Ogg	455
29	27	H	Stenhousemuir	D 1-1	0-1	—	McFadyen	228
30	Mar 3	A	Brechin C	L 0-1	0-1	10		550
31	10	A	Kilmarnock	L 0-3	0-2	11		3767
32	17	H	Cowdenbeath	L 0-2	0-0	13		264
33	24	A	Arbroath	D 1-1	1-0	12	McNamee	376
34	31	H	Stirling Albion	W 3-1	0-1	11	Elliott, Ogg, Hendry	607
35	Apr 7	H	East Stirling	W 2-1	2-1	11	McKenzie, O'Brien P	425
36	14	A	Montrose	W 1-0	0-0	11	O'Brien P (pen)	200
37	21	H	Berwick R	L 0-3	0-2	11		478
38	28	A	Queen of the S	D 0-0	0-0	12		374
39	May 5	H	Dumbarton	W 1-0	0-0	11	McKenzie	586

Final League Position: 11

GOALSCORERS

League: (40): Hendry 10, O'Brien P 9 (1 pen), Caven 4, McKenzie 4, Ogg 4, Elliot 2, McEntegart 2, Armstrong 1, Elder 1, McFadyen 1, McNamee 1, Rodden 1.
Scottish Cup: (1): Rodden 1.
Skol Cup: (2): McKenzie 1, O'Brien P 1.

Record Transfer Fee paid: —.
Record Victory: 16-0 v St Peters, Scottish Cup 1st rd; 29 Aug, 1885.
Record Defeat: 0-9 v Motherwell, Division I; 26 Apr, 1930.
Most Capped Player: Walter Arnott, 14, Scotland.
Most League Appearances: 473: J. B. McAlpine.
Most League Goals in Season (Individual): 30: William Martin, Division 1; 1937–38.
Most Goals Overall (Individual): 163: J. B. McAlpine.

Honours
League Champions: Division II 1922–23. B Division 1955–56. Second Division 1980–81.
Scottish Cup Winners: 1874, 1875, 1876, 1880, 1881, 1882, 1884, 1886, 1890, 1893; *Runners-up:* 1892, 1900.
League Cup:—.
FA Cup runners-up: 1884, 1885
Club colours: Shirt: White and black hoops. Shorts: White. Stockings: White with black hoops.

Monaghan, M.	McLean, S.	Armstrong, P.	Elder, G.	McNamee, P.	Hendry, M	Caven, R	O'Brien, J	Rodden, J	McKenzie, K	O'Brien, P	Ogg, J	McEntegart, S	Morton, C	Jack, S	Elliot, D	Kinnie, R	Mirner, E	Flannigan, M	McFadyen, J	Greig, D	Match No.
1	2	3	4	5	6	7	8†	9*	10	11	12	14									1
1	2		4	5	10†	7	8*	14	11	9	3	6		12							2
1			4	5	9†	7	8*	10	11	3	6	12		2	14						3
1		3	4	5*	9†	7	8	10	11	6	12	2		14							4
1		8	4	5*	9	7	10	11	3	6	2	12									5
1	2	8	4*	7	9	14	10†	11	3	6	5	12									6
1	2	8	4	9†	7	12	10	11	3	6*	5	14									7
1	2	8	4	7	9	10	11	3	5	6											8
1	2	8	4	9*	7	12	10	11	3	5	6										9
1	2	8*	4	5	9	7	12	10	11	3	6										10
1	2		4	5	9	7	12	10*	11	3	6	8									11
1	2	8†	4	5	10	7	14	12	11	3	6	9*									12
1	2		4	7	10	8	12	11*	3	6	5	9									13
1	2		4	5	9	7	8*	14	10†	11	3	6		12							14
1	2*		4	5	10	7	8	11†	12	9	3	6		14							15
1		3	4	5	10	7*	8	14	12	11†	6	2		9							16
1		3	4	5	11*	7	8	12	10	6	9	2									17
1		3	4	11	7	8*	12	10	6	5	9	2									18
1	2	8	4	7	11	10	6	3	5	9											19
1	2	3	4	10	7	11*	14	6†	8	5	9	12									20
1	2	8	4	10*	7	12	9†	3	6	5	11	14									21
1	2	8	4	6*	7	10	9	3	12	5	11†	14									22
1	2	8†	4	5	11*	7	12	10	6	3	14	9									23
1	2		4	5	11†	7	14	10	6	3*	8	12		9							24
1	2	8	4	7	10*	11	12	6	3	5	9										25
1	2	8	4	5	7	11*	10	6	3	9	12										26
1	2		4	7	10	8	6*	3	12	5	9	11									27
1	2	5	7*	8	10†	9	3	6	4	11	12	14									28
1	2		4	7	8	10*	11	3	6	5	9	12									29
1	7	5	4	8	10	11	3	6	2	9*	12										30
1	2	3	4	7	12	8	10†	11	6*	5	9	14									31
1	2	3	4	7	12	10	8†	6	14	5	9	11*									32
1	2	8	4	7	10	11*	6	3	5	9	12										33
1	2	8	4	7	11	10	9	3	5*	6	12										34
1	2	8	4	5	11*	7	10	6	3	9	12										35
1	2	8	4	5	10	7	11*	6	3	9	12										36
1	2	8	4	11	7	10*	6	3	5	9	12										37
1	2	8*	4	10	7	12	6	3	5	9	11										38
1	2	7	4	11	8*	10	6	3	12	5	9†	14									39
39	32	29	39	29	30	31	18	5	27	39	31	19	—	26	28	1	1	3	1	1	
		+1s	+1s	+1s	+14s	+6s			+1s	+6s	+3s				+7s		+1s	+5s	+4s	+6s	

RAITH ROVERS   First Division

Year Formed: 1883. *Ground & Address:* Stark's Park, Pratt St, Kirkcaldy KY1 1SA. *Telephone:* 0592 263514.
Ground Capacity: total: 9500   seated: 3075.   *Size of Pitch:* 113yd×67yd.
Chairman: John Urquhart.   *Secretary:* P. J. Campsie.   *Commercial Manager:* Alex Kilgour.
Manager: Frank Connor. *Assistant Manager:* Murray Cheyne. *Physio:* David Campbell. *Coach:* Alex Kinninmouth. *Reserve Coach:* Andy Harrow.
Managers since 1975: R. Paton; A. Matthews; W. McLean; G. Wallace; R. Wilson; F. Connor.
Club Nickname(s): Rovers.   *Previous Grounds:* Robbie's Park.
Record Attendance: 31,306 v Hearts, Scottish Cup 2nd rd; 7 Feb, 1953.
Record Transfer Fee received: £85,000 for Andy Harrow to Luton T (Oct 1980).
Record Transfer Fee paid: £35,000 for Willie Gibson from Partick Th (Oct 1981).

1989–90 LEAGUE RECORD

Match No.	Date	Venue	Opponents	Result	H/T Score	Lg. Pos.	Goalscorers	Attendance
1	Aug 12	H	Morton	W 2-0	1-0	—	Fraser (pen), Coyle	1529
2	19	A	Falkirk	W 2-0	0-0	2	Ferguson, Dalziel	3000
3	26	A	Meadowbank T	W 2-1	0-0	1	Ferguson 2	650
4	Sept 2	H	St Johnstone	L 0-2	0-2	3		4979
5	5	A	Partick T	L 1-3	0-1	—	Dalziel	3390
6	9	H	Airdrieonians	L 0-4	0-1	7		1817
7	16	H	Albion R	W 2-1	2-1	4	Dalziel, Logan	1224
8	23	A	Forfar Ath	D 2-2	0-2	4	Dalziel 2	757
9	30	H	Clydebank	W 1-0	0-0	4	Nelson	1300
10	Oct 7	A	Alloa	L 0-2	0-1	4		1675
11	14	H	Ayr U	W 2-0	2-0	4	Dalziel, Ferguson	1571
12	21	H	Clyde	L 0-2	0-1	5		1543
13	28	A	Hamilton A	L 2-3	1-2	5	Dalziel 2	1447
14	Nov 4	H	Partick T	D 1-1	0-0	7	Sorbie	2433
15	11	A	Airdrieonians	L 2-3	1-1	8	Dalziel, Romaines	1800
16	18	A	Albion R	D 2-2	0-1	9	Dalziel, Macdonald	621
17	25	H	Forfar Ath	W 1-0	0-0	5	McStay	1249
18	Dec 2	A	Clydebank	L 1-3	1-2	8	Macdonald (pen)	988
19	9	H	Alloa	D 1-1	0-0	8	Logan	1118
20	16	A	Ayr U	L 0-1	0-0	8		1745
21	23	A	Morton	D 1-1	1-1	8	Logan	1310
22	30	H	Falkirk	W 4-0	1-0	6	Logan, Dalziel, Macdonald (pen), McStay	2765
23	Jan 2	H	Meadowbank T	L 1-2	1-2	—	Dalziel	1897
24	6	A	St Johnstone	W 2-1	1-0	8	Dalziel 2	5293
25	13	H	Hamilton A	L 1-3	0-2	8	Dalziel	1595
26	Feb 3	A	Forfar Ath	D 2-2	1-1	10	Macdonald, Fraser	717
27	10	H	Albion R	W 3-2	1-0	10	Macdonald 2, Nelson	1035
28	28	A	Meadowbank T	W 3-0	1-0	—	Macdonald, Dalziel, Coyle	708
29	Mar 3	A	St Johnstone	D 0-0	0-0	8		3852
30	10	H	Morton	W 2-1	1-0	6	McStay, Macdonald	1182
31	17	A	Clyde	L 0-1	0-0	7		500
32	21	A	Clyde	D 0-0	0-0	—		500
33	24	A	Clydebank	D 2-2	2-1	6	Logan, Macdonald (pen)	738
34	31	H	Ayr U	W 5-2	4-1	6	Dalziel 2, Nelson, Simpson, Ferguson	1117
35	Apr 7	H	Hamilton A	D 0-0	0-0	6		1191
36	14	A	Alloa	W 4-0	0-0	6	Logan, Nelson, Burn, Ferguson	760
37	21	A	Airdrieonians	W 1-0	0-0	6	Macdonald	1700
38	28	H	Falkirk	D 1-1	0-0	5	Dalziel	1733
39	May 5	A	Partick T	D 1-1	0-1	5	Dalziel	2252

Final League Position: 5

GOALSCORERS

League: (57): Dalziel 20, Macdonald 10 (3 pens), Ferguson 6, Logan 6, Nelson 4, McStay 3, Coyle 2, Fraser 2 (1 pen), Burn 1, Romaines 1, Simpson 1, Sorbie 1.
Scottish Cup: (3): Dalziel 1, Logan 1, own goal 1.
Skol Cup: (0).

Record Victory: 10-1 v Coldstream, Scottish Cup 2nd rd; 13 Feb, 1954.
Record Defeat: 2-11 v Morton, Division II; 18 Mar, 1936.
Most Capped Player: Dave Morris, 6, Scotland.
Most League Appearances: 430: Willie McNaught.
Most League Goals in Season (Individual): 38: Norman Haywood, Division II; 1937–38.
Most Goals Overall (Individual): 105: Ernie Copland *(League).*

Honours
League Champions: Division II 1907–08, 1909–10 (shared), 1937–38, 1948–49; *Runners-up:* Division II 1908–09, 1926–27, 1966–67. Second Division 1975–76, 1977–78, 1986–87.
Scottish Runners-up: 1913.
League Cup Runners-up: 1948–49.
Club colours: Shirt: Royal blue. Shorts: White. Stockings: Royal blue; all with red-white trimmings.

Arthur, G	McStay, J	Murray, D	Fraser, C	Glennie, R	MacLeod, I	Simpson, S	Dalziel, G	Ferguson, I	Coyle, R	Nelson, M	Romaines, S	Burn, P	Dennis, S	Logan, A	Sorbie, S	McGeachie, G	Macdonald, K	Buchanan, N	Match No.
1	2	3	4	5	6	7	8	9	10*	11†	12		14						1
1	2	3	4	5	10	7*	8	9	12	11		6							2
1	2	3	4	5	10	7*	8	9	12	11		6							3
1*	2	3	4	5	10	7	8	9	12	11†	14	6							4
1	2	3	4	5	10	7*	8†	9	12	11		6	14						5
1	2	3	4	5	10	7*	8	9†	12	11		6	14						6
1	2	3		5	6	8	14	4	11*	7	10					9†	12		7
1	2	3	4		10	8†	14	5	11	7	6					9*	12		8
1	2	3	4		6	8	12		11	7	10			5		9*			9
1	2	3	4		6	14	8	12	10	11	7†			5		9*			10
1	2	3	4		6	7*	8	9	11†	10	14		12	5					11
1	2	3			6	7*	8	12	4	10	11			5		9			12
1		3		2	12	8	7*	6		10	11			5		9	4		13
1	2	3			6	7†	8	14	4	10	11		12	5*		9			14
1	2	3	4*		6	7	8†	5	10	14	11		9	12					15
1	5	3				7*	10	4	6	8	12	11	9					2	16
1	2	3			6	12	8	7*	4	11†	10		14	5		9			17
1	2	3			6	12	8	4	11*	7	10		14	5†		9			18
1	2	3			6	8	4	11	7	10	12			5		9*			19
1	5	3	2		8	12	11	10	6	7*					4		9		20
1	5	3	2		8	12	11	10	6	7*					4		9		21
1	5	3	2		8	12	6	11	10	14	7*				4†		9		22
1	5	3	2		8	12	4	11	10	6†	7*	14					9		23
1	5	3	4	2		7*	8	12	6	11	10					14	9†		24
1	5	3*	4	2		7	8	12	6	11						10	9†	14	25
1	5	3	4	2		7†	8*	14	6	11	10					12	9		26
1	2	3	4			7*	8†	14	6	11	10			5		12	9		27
1	2		4			7*	8	10†	6	11	12	14		5		3	9		28
1	2	4	3			7	8*	12	6	11	10			5			9		29
1	2	4*	3			7	8	14	10	11	12	6†		5			9		30
1	2	4	3			7*	8	6	11	10	12			5			9		31
1	2	4	3			8	12	6	11	10				5		7	9*		32
1	2	14	4	3		8	12	6	11	10†				5		7	9*		33
1	2	4	3			14	8†	7	6	11	12	10*		5			9		34
1	2	4*	3			7	8†	14	6	11	12	10		5			9		35
1	2	3				8*	12	4	11	6	10			5		7	9		36
1	2	3				8	4	11	6	10				5		7	9		37
1	2	3	4	12	8	11	6	10	5							7*	9		38
1	2	3	4	12	8	9	11	6	10	5						7*			39
39	38	28	23	7	37	20	39	12	28	27	26	25	18	16	5	14	25	2	
		+1s				+7s	+20s		+5s	+3s	+4s		+10s	+9s		+1s	+1s		

RANGERS

Premier Division

Year Formed: 1873. *Ground & Address:* Ibrox Stadium, Edminston Drive, Glasgow G51 2XD. *Telephone:* 041 427 5232/041 427 1117 (Information Service).
Ground Capacity: total: 44,500 seated: 36,500. *Size of Pitch:* 115yd×75yd.
Chairman: David Murray. *Secretary:* R. C. Ogilvie. *Commercial Manager:* —.
Manager: Graeme Souness. *Assistant Manager:* Walter Smith. *Physio:* Phil Boersma. *Coach:* Phil Boersma, Peter McCloy.
Managers since 1975: Jock Wallace; John Greig; Jock Wallace; Graeme Souness.
Club Nickname(s): The Gers. *Previous Grounds:* None.
Record Attendance: 118,567 v Celtic, Division I; 2 Jan, 1939.
Record Transfer Fee received: £580,000 for Robert Fleck to Norwich C (Dec. 1987).
Record Transfer Fee paid: £1,500,000 for Trevor Steven from Everton, 1989.
Record Victory: 14-2 v Blairgowrie, Scottish Cup 1st rd; 20 Jan, 1934.
Record Defeat: 2-10 v Airdrieonians, 1886.
Most Capped Player: George Young, 53, Scotland.
Most League Appearances: 496: John Greig, 1962–78.

1989–90 LEAGUE RECORD

Match No.	Date		Venue	Opponents	Result	H/T Score	Lg. Pos.	Goalscorers	Attendance
1	Aug	12	H	St Mirren	L 0-1	0-1	—		39,951
2		19	A	Hibernian	L 0-2	0-1	10		21,500
3		26	A	Celtic	D 1-1	1-1	10	Butcher	50,000
4	Sept	9	H	Aberdeen	W 1-0	0-0	10	Johnston	40,283
5		16	H	Dundee	D 2-2	1-0	8	McCoist 2	35,836
6		23	A	Dunfermline Ath	D 1-1	1-1	8	McCoist	17,765
7		30	H	Hearts	W 1-0	1-0	6	Johnston	39,554
8	Oct	3	A	Motherwell	L 0-1	0-1	—		17,667
9		14	H	Dundee U	W 2-1	0-0	7	Johnston, McCoist	36,062
10		25	A	St Mirren	W 2-0	1-0	—	McCoist, Johnston	15,130
11		28	A	Hibernian	W 3-0	0-0	4	McCoist 2, Johnston (pen)	35,260
12	Nov	4	H	Celtic	W 1-0	0-0	1	Johnston	41,598
13		18	A	Dundee	W 2-0	0-0	2	Walters, Johnston	14,536
14		22	A	Aberdeen	L 0-1	0-1	—		23,000
15		25	H	Dunfermline Ath	W 3-0	2-0	2	Johnston, Butcher, McCoist	39,121
16	Dec	2	H	Hearts	W 2-1	0-1	2	Walters, Steven	24,771
17		9	H	Motherwell	W 3-0	1-0	2	Butcher, McCoist, Brown	33,549
18		16	A	Dundee U	D 1-1	1-1	1	Johnston	15,947
19		23	H	St Mirren	W 1-0	1-0	1	Dodds	31,797
20		30	A	Hibernian	D 0-0	0-0	1		17,000
21	Jan	2	A	Celtic	W 1-0	1-0	—	Spackman	54,000
22		6	H	Aberdeen	W 2-0	0-0	1	Walters, McCoist	41,351
23		13	H	Dundee	W 3-0	1-0	1	McCoist, Dodds, Johnston	36,993
24		27	A	Dunfermline Ath	W 1-0	1-0	1	Stevens	17,350
25	Feb	3	H	Dundee U	W 3-1	3-1	1	Walters, McCoist, Johnston	39,058
26		10	A	Motherwell	D 1-1	0-1	1	Johnston	17,647
27		17	H	Hearts	D 0-0	0-0	1		41,884
28	Mar	3	A	Dundee	D 2-2	1-1	1	Johnston, Dodds	12,743
29		17	A	St Mirren	D 0-0	0-0	1		15,122
30		24	H	Hibernian	L 0-1	0-0	1		37,542
31	Apr	1	H	Celtic	W 3-0	2-0	—	Walters (pen), Johnston, McCoist (pen)	41,926
32		8	A	Aberdeen	D 0-0	0-0	—		23,000
33		14	H	Motherwell	W 2-1	0-0	1	Steven, Johnston	39,305
34		21	A	Dundee U	W 1-0	0-0	1	Steven	15,995
35		28	H	Dunfermline Ath	W 2-0	0-0	1	McCoist, Dodds	40,769
36	May	5	A	Hearts	D 1-1	1-1	1	Munro	20,283

Final League Position: 1

GOALSCORERS

League: (48): Johnston 15 (1 pen), McCoist 14 (1 pen), Walters 5 (1 pen), Dodds 4, Butcher 3, Steven T 3, Brown 1, Munro 1, Spackman 1, Stevens G 1.
Scottish Cup: (3): Brown 1, Johnston 1, Walters 1.
Skol Cup: (15): McCoist 5, Walters 4 (2 pens), Ferguson I 2, Steven 2, Johnston 1, own goal 1.

Most League Goals in Season (Individual): 44: Sam English, Division I; 1931–32.
Most Goals Overall (Individual): 233: Bob McPhail; 1927–39.

Honours

League Champions: (39 times) Division I 1890–91 (shared), 1898–99, 1899–1900, 1900–01, 1901–02, 1910–11, 1911–12, 1912–13, 1917–18, 1919–20, 1920–21, 1922–23, 1923–24, 1924–25, 1926–27, 1927–28, 1928–29, 1929–30, 1930–31, 1932–33, 1933–34, 1934–35, 1936–37, 1938–39, 1946–47, 1948–49, 1949–50, 1952–53, 1955–56, 1956–57, 1958–59, 1960–61, 1962–63, 1963–64, 1974–75. Premier Division 1975–76, 1977–78, 1986–87, 1988–89, 1989–90; *Runners-up:* 23 times.
Scottish Cup Winners: (24 times) 1894, 1897, 1898, 1903, 1928, 1930, 1932, 1934, 1935, 1936, 1948, 1949, 1950, 1953, 1960, 1962, 1963, 1964, 1966, 1973, 1976, 1978, 1979, 1981; *Runners-up:* 15 times.
League Cup Winners: (15 times) 1946–47, 1948–49, 1960–61, 1961–62, 1963–64, 1964–65, 1970–71, 1975–76, 1977–78, 1978–79, 1981–82, 1983–84, 1984–85, 1986–87, 1987–88, 1988–89; *Runners-up:* 7 times.
European: *European Cup:* 51 matches (1956–57, 1957–58, 1959–60 semi-finals, 1961–62, 1963–64, 1964–65, 1975–76, 1976–77, 1978–79, 1987–88).
Cup Winners Cup Winners: 1971–72. 50 matches (1960–61 runners-up, 1962–63, 1966–67 runners-up, 1969–70, 1971–72 winners, 1973–74, 1977–78, 1979–80, 1981–82, 1983–84). *UEFA Cup:* 34 matches (1967–68, 1968–69 semi-finals, 1970–71 Fairs Cup; 1982–83, 1984–85, 1985–86, 1986–87).
Club colours: Shirt: Royal blue with red and white trim. Shorts: White. Stockings: Red.

Woods, C	Stevens, G	Munro, S	Gough, R	Wilkins, R	Butcher, T	Steven, T	Ferguson, I	McCoist, A	Johnston, M	Walters, M	Drinkell, K	Ferguson, D	Ginzburg, B	Nisbet, S	Brown, J	Cowan, T	Dodds, D	Cooper, N	McCall, I	Spackman, N	Vinnicombe, C	Robertson, A	Souness, G	Match No.
1*	2	3	4	5	6	7	8	9†	10	11	14	12												1
	2	3	4	5	6	7	8	9	10	11*	12		1											2
	2	3	4	5	6	7	8	12	10	9*			1		11									3
1	2	3		5	6	7	8	14	10†	11	9	12			4*									4
1	2	3		5*	6	7	12	9	10	11			8		4									5
1	2	3	4	5	6	7	12	9	10	11					8*									6
	2	3	4	5	6	7	8†	9	10	11*			1			12	14							7
	2	3	4	5	6	7		9	10				1			8	11*	12						8
1	2	3	4	5	6	7		9	10	11*						12	8†	14						9
1	2	3	4	5	6	7	8	9	10										11					10
1	2	3	4*	5	6	7	8	9	10								14	12	11†					11
1	2	3		5	6	7	8	9	10	11					4									12
1	2†	3		5	6	7	8	9	10	11*			14		4	12								13
1	2	3		5	6	7	8	9	10	11					4									14
1	2	3		5	6	7	8	9	10	11					4									15
1	2	3			6	7	8	9	10	11					4					5				16
1	2	3*	4		6	7	8	9	10						11					5	12			17
1	2	3	4		6	7	8	9	10						11					5				18
1	2	3†	4		6	7*	8	9	10						11			12		5	14			19
1	2	3	4			7		9	10	11					11	8				5				20
1	2	3*	4		6	7		9	10	8					11					5	12			21
1	2	3	4		6	7		9	10	8*					11					5	12			22
1	2	3	4		6	7		9*	10	8					11			12		5				23
1	2	3	4		6	7	8	9	10						11					5				24
1	2	3	4			7	8*	9	10						11					5	6	12		25
1	2	3	4*		6	7	8	9	10						11			12		5				26
1	2	3	4		6	7	8	9	10						11					5				27
1	2	3			6	7	8		10				4*	11	9					5	12			28
1	2	3	4		6	7	8	9	10						11*			12		5				29
1	2	3	4		6	7	12	9	10	8					11*					5				30
1	2	3	4		6	7*	8	9	10						11			12		5				31
1	2†	3	4		6	7	8*	9	10						11		14	12		5				32
1	2*	3	4		6	7	8†	9	10				14		11	12				5				33
1	2	3	4		6	7		9	10						11		8*	12		5				34
1	2	3†	4		6	7		9*	10						11		8	12		5			14	35
1	2	3	4		6	7		9*	10						11		8†		14	5	12			36
32	35	36	26	15	34	34	21	32	36	27	2	3	4	4	24	1	4	2	2	21	1	—	—	

+ + 3s 2s   + + 2s 2s   + + 3s3s 2s10s 1s 2s   + + 6s1s 1s

ST JOHNSTONE Premier Division

Year Formed: 1884. *Ground & Address:* McDiarmid Park, Crieff Road, Perth PH1 2SJ. *Telephone:* 0738 26961.
Ground Capacity: total: 10,169 seated: all. *Size of Pitch:* 115yd×75yd.
Chairman: G. S. Brown. *Secretary:* S. Duff. *General Manager:* John Litster. *Commercial Manager:* —.
Manager: Alex Totten. *Assistant Manager:* Bert Paton. *Physio:* J. Peacock. *Coach:* T. Campbell.
Managers since 1975: J. Stewart, J. Storrie; A. Stuart; A. Rennie; I. Gibson; A. Totten.
Club Nickname(s): Saints. *Previous Grounds:* Recreation Grounds, Muirton Park.
Record Attendance: 29,972 v Dundee, Scottish Cup 2nd rd; 10 Feb, 1952.
Record Transfer Fee received: £400,000 for Ally McCoist to Sunderland (1982).
Record Transfer Fee paid: £90,000 for Gary McGinnis from Dundee U, February 1990..
Record Victory: 8-1 v Partick Th, League Cup; 16 Aug, 1969.

1989–90 LEAGUE RECORD

Match No.	Date	Venue	Opponents	Result	H/T Score	Lg. Pos.	Goalscorers	Attendance
1	Aug 12	A	Alloa	W 1-0	1-0	—	Johnston	1744
2	19	H	Clydebank	W 2-1	1-1	3	Curran, McVicar (pen)	7267
3	26	H	Forfar Ath	W 3-1	2-1	2	Moore 3	4310
4	Sept 2	A	Raith R	W 2-0	2-0	1	Moore, Grant	4979
5	5	H	Hamilton A	W 3-0	1-0	—	Moore, Grant 2	6203
6	9	H	Albion R	W 2-1	2-0	1	Heddle 2	4470
7	16	A	Airdrionians	D 2-2	1-1	1	Jenkins 2	3000
8	23	H	Falkirk	W 2-0	1-0	1	Burgess (og), Grant	7011
9	30	A	Meadowbank T	W 3-1	1-0	1	Grant, Cherry, Maskrey	1500
10	Oct 7	H	Morton	D 1-1	1-0	1	Jenkins	6730
11	14	A	Clyde	W 2-0	2-0	1	McVicar, Moore	1435
12	21	A	Ayr U	D 2-2	0-1	1	Ward, McVicar (pen)	3115
13	28	H	Partick T	W 2-1	0-0	1	Moore, Maskrey	10,091
14	Nov 4	A	Hamilton A	D 3-3	2-1	1	Maskrey 2, Moore	2582
15	11	A	Albion R	W 3-1	1-0	1	Maskrey, Cherry, Grant	1793
16	18	H	Airdrieonians	L 1-2	0-1	1	Heddle	7123
17	25	A	Falkirk	D 3-3	3-1	1	Maskrey, Ward, Curran	3400
18	Dec 2	H	Meadowbank T	W 1-0	1-0	1	Heddle	3888
19	9	A	Morton	D 0-0	0-0	1		2970
20	16	H	Clyde	W 2-0	2-0	1	Treanor, Moore	2465
21	26	H	Alloa	W 3-0	1-0	—	Heddle, Maskrey, Grant	6033
22	30	A	Clydebank	L 0-4	0-3	1		2105
23	Jan 2	A	Forfar Ath	W 5-1	4-0	—	Johnston, Curran, Grant, Hutton (og), Hamill (og)	3619
24	6	H	Raith R	L 1-2	0-1	2	Grant	5293
25	13	A	Partick T	W 1-0	0-0	1	Treanor (pen)	5484
26	27	H	Ayr U	W 4-0	3-0	1	Maskrey, Grant 3	5057
27	Feb 3	H	Meadowbank T	L 1-2	1-0	1	Grant	4162
28	10	A	Falkirk	L 0-1	0-1	2		4738
29	27	A	Morton	W 2-1	0-0	—	Johnston, Moore	1920
30	Mar 3	H	Raith R	D 0-0	0-0	2		3852
31	10	A	Albion R	W 5-2	0-1	2	Cherry, Grant 2, Johnston 2	1321
32	17	H	Alloa	W 6-0	2-0	2	Ward, Moore, Treanor, Johnston 2, Hegarty	3100
33	24	A	Hamilton A	W 3-2	0-1	2	Grant, Moore, Maskrey	2196
34	31	H	Airdrieonians	W 3-1	0-0	1	Treanor (pen), Grant, Ward	9644
35	Apr 7	A	Partick T	W 2-0	1-0	1	Maskrey 2	5300
36	17	H	Clydebank	L 1-3	1-2	1	Grant	7328
37	21	H	Clyde	D 1-1	1-1	1	Moore	5323
38	28	A	Ayr U	W 2-0	1-0	1	Cherry, Maskrey	5114
39	5	H	Forfar Ath	W 1-0	0-0	1	Grant	7966

Final League Position: 1

GOALSCORERS

League: (81): Grant 19, Moore 13, Maskrey 12, Johnston 7, Heddle 5, Cherry 4, Treanor 4 (2 pens), Ward 4, Curran 3, Jenkins 3, McVicar 3 (2 pens), Hegarty 1, own goals 3.
Scottish Cup: (0).
Skol Cup: (0)

Record Defeat: 0-12 v Cowdenbeath, Scottish Cup, 21 January 1928.
Most Capped Player: Sandy McLaren, 5, Scotland.
Most League Appearances: 298: Drew Rutherford.
Most League Goals in Season (Individual): 36: Jimmy Benson, Division II; 1931–32.
Most Goals Overall (Individual): 114: John Brogan, 1977–83.

Honours
League Champions: First Division 1982–83, 1989–90. Division II 1923–24, 1959–60, 1962–63; *Runners-up:* Division II 1931–32. Second Division 1987–88.
Scottish Cup: Semi-finals 1934, 1968, 1989.
League Cup Runners-up: 1969.
European: *European Cup*—. *Cup Winners Cup*—. *UEFA Cup:* 1971–72.
Club colours: Shirt: Royal blue with white semi-circular chest panel. Shorts: Royal blue. Stockings: Royal blue.

Balavage, J	Thomson, K	McVicar, D	Newbigging, W	Cherry, P	Thompson, G	Curran, H	Johnston, S	Moore, A	Jenkins, G	Heddle, I	Sorbie, S	Grant, R	Nicolson, K	Treanor, M	Maher, G	Smith, M	Blackie, W	Maskrey, S	Ward, K	McKillop, A	Barron, D	Hegarty, P	McGinnis, G	Butter, J	Bingham, D	Match No.
1	2	3	4	5	6†	7	8	9	10*11	14	12															1
1	4	3	2	12	8	6	7	10	11*14	9†	5															2
1	4	3		5	8	6†	7	10	11	12	9*			2	14											3
1	4	3*		5	12	8	6	7	10	11		9†			14											4
1	4	3		5	12	8	6†	7	10	11*		9		2			14									5
1	4	3		5	12	8*	6	7	10	11		9		2		14	9†									6
1	4	3		5	12	8*6	7	10	11			9†		2			14									7
1	4	3		5	8	6	7	10†11				9*		2		12	14									8
1	4	3		5	8	6	7	10†11				9*		2		12	14									9
1	4	3		5	8	6	7	10	11†			9*		2		14	12									10
1	4	3		5	14	8†	6	7	10	11		9*		2		12										11
1	4	3		5	8	6	7	10†11				9*		2		12	14									12
1	4	3	2		8†	6	7	10*11	12									9	14	5						13
1	4	3	2		8†	6	7	10*11										9	12	5	14					14
1	4	3	8	12	6	7	10†11*	14			2							9	5							15
1	4	3	8	12	6*		10†11	14			2							9	7	5						16
1	4	3†	6		8	14	12	11	10		2							9	7*	5						17
1	4	3	5		8	6*	12	11	10		2					14		9	7†							18
1	2	3	5		8	6	12	11	10									9	7*	4						19
1	4	3	5		8	6	7	12	11	10	2							9*								20
1	4	3	5		8		7	6	11	10	2							9								21
1	4	3	5		8	12	7	6	11	10*	2							9								22
1	4	3	5		8†	6	7	12	11	10*	2					14		9								23
1	4	3	5		8*	6	7	11	10		2					12		9								24
1		3	5		8	6	12	11	10*		2					7		9		4						25
1		3	2		8	6	7	11	10									9		4	5					26
1		3	2		8*	6	7	12	11†	10								9	14	4	5					27
1		3	8		6*	7		11	10									9	12	4	5				2	28
		3	2		6	7	9	11	10											4	5	8		1		29
1		3	12	14	6	7	9*11†	10		2										4	5	8				30
1		3	8		9	7	11*	10	2							12				4	5	6				31
1		3	8		6	7	14	11†	10*	2						12	9			4	5					32
1		3	8		6†	7	11	10	2							12	9*			4	5	14				33
1		3	8		6*	7	12	10	2							9	14			4	5	11†				34
1		3	8			7	11	10*	2							9	12			4	5	6				35
1			8		6	7	11*	10	2							9	12			4	5	3				36
1		8*	12	6	7	11	10	2								9†14				4	5	3				37
1		8	12	6*	7	11	10	2								9†14				4	5	3				38
1		7		8†12	3	10	2									9	14			4	5	6			11*	39
38	24	35	1	38	1	26	34	33	20	38	—	33	1	30	—	—	2	22	6	5	16	14	10	1	1	
	+						+	+	+		+	+	+			+	+		+	+	+	+	+			
	1s		6s5s		3s		8s	1s	3s		4s			1s	2s			8s7s	12s		1s		1s			

ST MIRREN   Premier Division

Year Formed: 1877.   *Ground & Address:* St Mirren Park, Love St, Paisley PA3 2EJ.   *Telephone:* 041 889 2558/041 840 1337.
Ground Capacity: total: 25,344   seated: 1344.   *Size of Pitch:* 112yd×73yd.
Chairman: Lewis Kane.   *Secretary:* George N. Pratt.   *Commercial Manager:* Jack Copland.
Manager: Tony Fitzpatrick.   *Assistant Manager:* —.   *Physio:* Bobby Holmes.   *Coach:* Gordon McQueen.
Managers since 1975: Alex Ferguson; Jim Clunie; Rikki MacFarlane; Alex Miller; Alex Smith; Tony Fitzpatrick.
Club Nickname(s): The Buddies.   *Previous Grounds:* Short Roods 1877–79, Thistle Park Greenhill 1879–83, Westmarch 1883–94.
Record Attendance: 47,428 v Celtic, Scottish Cup 4th rd; 7 Mar, 1925.
Record Transfer Fee received: £850,000 for Ian Ferguson to Rangers (1988).
Record Transfer Fee paid: £285,000 for Fraser Wishart from Motherwell, August 1989.
Record Victory: 15-0 v Glasgow University, Scottish Cup 1st rd; 30 Jan, 1960.

1989–90 LEAGUE RECORD

Match No.	Date	Venue	Opponents	Result	H/T Score	Lg. Pos.	Goalscorers	Atten-dance
1	Aug 12	A	Rangers	W 1-0	1-0	—	McDowall	39,951
2	19	H	Hearts	L 1-2	0-2	5	Godfrey	7064
3	26	A	Motherwell	L 1-3	0-2	9	Torfason	4703
4	Sept 9	H	Celtic	W 1-0	1-0	6	Walker	19,813
5	16	A	Hibernian	L 1-3	1-2	9	Black	6000
6	23	H	Aberdeen	L 0-2	0-1	10		5872
7	30	A	Dundee U	D 0-0	0-0	10		6643
8	Oct 4	H	Dundee	W 3-2	1-2	—	Torfason 2, Walker	3612
9	14	A	Dunfermline Ath	L 1-5	1-2	9	Torfason	7656
10	25	H	Rangers	L 0-2	0-1	—		15,130
11	28	A	Hearts	L 0-4	0-1	9		9911
12	Nov 4	H	Motherwell	D 2-2	0-1	9	Torfason, Lambert	4585
13	18	H	Hibernian	D 0-0	0-0	9		4500
14	22	A	Celtic	D 1-1	1-1	—	Torfason	21,000
15	25	A	Aberdeen	L 0-5	0-3	9		13,500
16	Dec 9	A	Dundee	D 3-3	1-0	9	Lambert, Torfason (pen), Godfrey	4043
17	13	H	Dundee U	W 1-0	1-0	—	Torfason	2800
18	23	A	Rangers	L 0-1	0-1	9		31,797
19	30	H	Hearts	W 2-0	0-0	9	Davies, Torfason	7287
20	Jan 2	A	Motherwell	L 0-2	0-0	—		8253
21	6	H	Celtic	L 0-2	0-2	9		14,813
22	10	H	Dunfermline Ath	W 2-0	2-0	—	Torfason, McDowall	4501
23	13	A	Hibernian	W 1-0	1-0	9	Torfason	6000
24	27	H	Aberdeen	W 1-0	1-0	8	McDowall	7855
25	Feb 3	A	Dunfermline Ath	L 0-1	0-0	9		7068
26	10	H	Dundee	D 0-0	0-0	9		5010
27	17	A	Dundee U	L 0-2	0-0	9		5957
28	Mar 3	H	Hibernian	L 0-1	0-1	9		4073
29	17	H	Rangers	D 0-0	0-0	9		15,122
30	24	A	Hearts	D 0-0	0-0	9		8066
31	31	H	Motherwell	D 0-0	0-0	9		5448
32	Apr 7	A	Celtic	W 3-0	2-0	9	Torfason, Shaw, Lambert	18,481
33	14	A	Dundee	W 2-1	1-1	8	Shaw, Martin	7415
34	21	H	Dunfermline Ath	L 1-2	0-1	9	Martin	5830
35	28	A	Aberdeen	L 0-2	0-0	9		7977
36	May 5	H	Dundee U	D 0-0	0-0	9		4312

Final League Position: 9

GOALSCORERS

League: (28): Torfason 12 (1 pen), Lambert 3, McDowall 3, Godfrey 2. Martin 2, Shaw 2, Walker 2, Black 1, Davies 1.
Scottish Cup: (5): Davies 2, McDowall 1, McWalter 1, Shaw 1.
Skol Cup: (4): Kinnaird 1, McDowall 1, Shaw 1, Torfason 1.

Record Defeat: 0-9 v Rangers, Division I; 4 Dec, 1897.
Most Capped Player: Iain Munro & Billy Thomson, 7, Scotland.
Most League Appearances: 287: Billy Abercromby, 1976–87.
Most League Goals in Season (Individual): 45: Dunky Walker, Division I; 1921–22.
Most Goals Overall (Individual): —.

Honours
League Champions: First Division 1976–77. Division II 1967–68; Runners-up 1935–36.
Scottish Cup Winners: 1926, 1959, 1987; Runners-up: 1908, 1934, 1962.
League Cup Runners-up: 1955–56.
Victory Cup: 1919–20.
Summer Cup: 1943–44.
Anglo-Scottish Cup: 1979–80.
European: European Cup—. Cup Winners Cup: 1987–88. UEFA Cup: 1980–81, 1983–84, 1985–86.
Club colours: Shirt: Narrow black and white striped with white chest panel. Shorts: Black. Stockings: Black. Change colours: All red.

Money, C	Dawson, R	Wilson, T	Walker, K	Godfrey, P	Winnie, D	McDowall, K	Martin, B	Torfason, G	Davies, W	Weir, P	Chalmers, P	Lambert, P	Wishart, F	Kinnaird, P	McIntosh, M	McGarvey, F	Shaw, G	Hutchinson, T	Black, T	Manley, R	McWhirter, N	Fridge, L	McWalter, M	McEwan, A	McGowne, K	Stickroth, T	McGill, D	Match No.
1	2	3	4	5	6	7	8	9†	10*	11	12	14																1
1		3	4	5	6		8	9	10*	11†	7	12		2	14													2
1		2	4	5			8	7	10	11†		6				3	9*12	14										3
1		2	4		6		8	9*10				7		12			7†14		3	5	11							4
1		2	4		6		8	9	10*12				7†14						3	5	11							5
	2	4†	6			8	9*14	12		11		7			3	5			1	10								6
	2	4				8	9	6	11	12				7		3	5		1	10*								7
	2	4	6†			8	9*11		12				7		3	5	14	1	10									8
1	2	4*	6			8	9	7	11	12			14		3	5			10†									9
1		4†	6			8	9*	7	11	12		2	14		3	5			10									10
1		5	7*	8			10	4	2	14		12		3	6	11	9†											11
1		5	6	10†	8	9	12		14	4*	2	7		3	11													12
1		5	10†	8	9	12		4	2	7*			3	6	11	14												13
1		5	10	8	9			4	2	7			3	6	11													14
1		5*	10†	8	9	12		4	2	7			3	6	11	14												15
	5	3	10	2	9	12		4*		11		7		8	6	1												16
	5*	10†	2	9	12		4	11		7		3	8	6	1	14												17
	5	10†	2	9	12		4*	11		7		3	8	6	1	14												18
	5	10	2	9	4		12	11		7*		3		6	1	8												19
	5	10	2	9	4	12		11*		7		3		6	1	8												20
1		5	10*	9	4	14		2	11		7†		3	8	6	12												21
1		5	10	7	9*	4		2	11				3	8	6	12												22
1		5	12	10†	7	9	4		2	11			3	8	6*	14												23
1		5	10	7	4		8	2	11			3	6	9														24
1*		5	10	7	9	4	8			11		3	6	12	2													25
1		5	10*	7		4	11	8	12			3	6	9	2†14													26
1		5	7	9	4	11	8	2*		12		3	6	10														27
1		5	12	7	9	4	11†	14	2*			3	8	6	10													28
1		5	10	2	4*		12	11		7		3	8	6	9†	14												29
1		5	10	2	4		12	11*		7		3	8	6	9													30
1	5	10	9	8			4	2		7		3	6	12	11*													31
1		5	12	8	9*	4	2	11		7		3	6	10														32
1		5	8	10	4	2	11		7			3	6	9														33
1		5	12	8	10	9*	4	2	11		7		3	6														34
1			8*10	4	2†11	14	7		3	6	5			9	12													35
1			8	4	2	11	7			6	5			3	9	10												36
28	1	9	10	22	16	20	35	29	22	9	2	19	19	22	1	2	18	—	31	30	20	8	13	2	1	6	1	
		+1s	+3s				+7s		+3s	+7s6s	+1s	+3s		+1s	+1s5s	+1s			+1s		+9s		+1s	+1s	+1s			

STENHOUSEMUIR Second Division

Year Formed: 1884.   *Ground & Address:* Ochilview Park, Gladstone Rd, Stenhousemuir FK5 5QL.   *Telephone:* 0324 562992.
Ground Capacity: total: 4000   seated: 350.   *Size of Pitch:* 113yd×78yd.
Chairman: John Cook.   *Secretary:* A. T. Bulloch.   *Commercial Manager:* John Young.
Manager: James Meakin.   *Assistant Manager:* —.   *Physio:* B. Porteous.   *Coach:* H. Nicol.
Managers since 1975: H. Glasgow; J. Black; A. Rose; W. Henderson; A. Rennie; J. Meakin.
Club Nickname(s): The Warriors.   *Previous Grounds:* Tryst Ground 1884–86, Goschen Park 1886–90.
Record Attendance: 12,500 v East Fife, Scottish Cup 4th rd; 11 Mar, 1950.
Record Transfer Fee received: £25,000 for Lindsay Hamilton to Rangers.
Record Transfer Fee paid: —.

1989–90 LEAGUE RECORD

Match No.	Date		Venue	Opponents	Result	H/T Score	Lg. Pos.	Goalscorers	Atten-dance
1	Aug	12	H	Queen's Park	L 1-3	1-2	—	Bell	260
2		19	A	East Fife	W 3-2	2-1	9	Walker 2, Yardley	667
3		26	A	Arbroath	L 1-2	1-0	10	McGurn	380
4	Sept	2	H	Montrose	W 1-0	0-0	8	McGurn	240
5		9	A	East Stirling	W 3-0	1-0	6	McGurn, Walker, Clouston	200
6		16	H	Kilmarnock	L 0-3	0-0	10		1753
7		23	H	Stranraer	L 0-2	0-1	11		200
8		30	A	Brechin C	W 2-1	0-1	10	McCormick 2 (1 pen)	300
9	Oct	7	H	Stirling Albion	W 2-1	1-0	8	Walker, McGurn	500
10		14	A	Berwick R	W 2-0	0-0	6	Milligan, McCormick	473
11		21	A	Dumbarton	L 0-1	0-0	7		348
12		28	H	Queen of the S	L 1-3	0-0	9	McCormick	250
13	Nov	4	A	Cowdenbeath	W 3-1	1-0	7	Walker, Speirs, McCormick	200
14		11	A	Montrose	W 2-0	0-0	4	Walker, Bell	250
15		18	H	Brechin C	W 2-0	0-0	4	Kemp, McCormick (pen)	300
16		25	A	Stranraer	D 2-2	2-2	2	McCormick (pen), Speirs	450
17	Dec	2	A	Stirling Albion	D 1-1	0-1	2	Aitchison	600
18		23	H	East Fife	D 2-2	1-2	6	Kemp, Walker	430
19		26	A	Queen's Park	D 0-0	0-0	—		526
20	Jan	2	H	Arbroath	W 3-0	2-0	—	McCormick 3 (2 pens)	300
21		6	A	Cowdenbeath	W 1-0	1-0	3	Tracey	200
22		9	H	Berwick R	L 1-3	0-2	—	Kemp	400
23		13	H	East Stirling	W 2-0	1-0	3	Nelson, Quinton	400
24		20	A	Kilmarnock	L 0-2	0-1	3		2777
25		27	H	Dumbarton	W 4-3	2-2	2	Nelson, McCormick, Speirs, Kemp	500
26	Feb	3	A	Queen of the S	D 1-1	1-1	2	Cairney	940
27		10	A	Berwick R	L 0-1	0-1	3		458
28		20	H	Brechin C	D 1-1	0-0	—	Anderson	707
29		27	A	Queen's Park	D 1-1	1-0	—	McCormick	228
30	Mar	3	H	Cowdenbeath	W 2-1	0-1	2	McCormick, Speirs	400
31		10	A	Montrose	D 1-1	1-1	2	Speirs	200
32		17	H	Kilmarnock	W 2-1	0-0	2	Nelson, Bell	1717
33		31	A	Arbroath	W 1-0	1-0	2	McCormick	500
34	Apr	7	H	Dumbarton	L 1-3	1-1	4	Nelson	600
35		11	A	East Stirling	L 2-4	1-1	—	Speirs, Clouston	300
36		14	A	Queen of the S	W 4-0	2-0	4	Speirs 2, Anderson, Aitchison	758
37		21	A	Stirling Albion	W 3-1	2-0	3	McCormick, Cairney, Speirs	1260
38		28	H	East Fife	L 1-2	0-1	4	Nelson	914
39	May	5	A	Stranraer	L 1-4	1-3	4	Speirs	600

Final League Position: 4

GOALSCORERS

League: (60): McCormick 15 (5 pens), Speirs 10, Walker 7, Nelson 5, Kemp 4, McGurn 4, Bell 3, Aitchison 2, Anderson 2, Cairney 2, Clouston 2, Milligan 1, Quinton 1, Tracey 1, Yardley 1.
Scottish Cup: (2): McCormick 1, Speirs 1.
Skol Cup: (0).

Record Victory: 9-2 v Dundee U, Division II; 19 Apr, 1937.
Record Defeat: 2-11 v Dunfermline Ath, Division II; 27 Sept, 1930.
Most Capped Player: —.
Most League Appearances: 189: T. Mullen.
Most League Goals in Season (Individual): 31: Evelyn Morrison, Division II; 1927–28; Robert Murray, Division II; 1936–37.
Most Goals Overall (Individual): —.

Honours
League Champions:—.
Scottish Cup: Semi-finals 1902–03.
League Cup:—.
Club colours: Shirt: Maroon with white pinstripe. Shorts: White. Stockings: Maroon with three white hoops.

McKeown, K	Milligan, J	Elliott, T	Cairney, H	Aitchison, T	Kemp, B	Bell, A	McGurn, J	Yardley, K	Clouston, B	Walker, C	Quinton, I	Gavin, S	Tracey, K	McCormick, S	Condie, T	Speirs, A	McNab, J	Paterno, J	Hoggan, K	Clark, R	Nelson, M	Anderson, P	Aitken, N	Kelly, C	McKinlay, J	Match No.
1	2	3	4	5	6	7	8	9	10	11*	12															1
1	8	3	4	5*	6	7	10	11†	2	9	14	12														2
1	8†	3	4		6	7	10	11*	2	9	14	12	5													3
1		3	4		10	7†	8	11*	2	9	6	12	5	14												4
1		3	4		6	7	8		2	10	11	12	5	9*												5
1		3	4		6	7*	8	14	2	10	11†	12	5	9												6
1	12	3†	4		10	14	8	11	2	9		5	6	7*												7
1	2	3	4		6	10*	8	7		11†		5	9	12	14											8
1	2		4		6	3	12	8		7	11*	5	9			10										9
1	2	3	4		6	10	12	8†		7		14	5	9	11*											10
1†	2	3	4	10	6	8		7		14		5*	9	12	11											11
	2	3	4	6	10	14	7	8†		5	9	12	11*							1						12
	6	10	4	2	3		8	12		5	9		11							1	7*					13
	6		4	2	3	12	8	10		5	9		11							1	7*					14
	6		4		3	7	8	10	12	5	9		11*							1	2					15
	6		4	2	3	7*	8	10	12	5†	9		11							1	14					16
	6†		4	2	3	8	10	14		5	9	11*	12							1	7					17
	3*	4	14	11	7†	6	10	12		5	9									1		2	8			18
	12	4	3	6	7	8	10	11		9										1		2*	5			19
	3	4	12	10	2		11		5	9	8*									1		7	6			20
	3	4		10	2		11		5	9	7									1		8	6			21
14	3	4	12	10	2		11		5†	9	7*									1		8	6			22
	3	4		10	12	2	11		5	9*										1		7	8	6		23
	3*	4		10	2	11			5	9	12									1		8	7	6		24
3†	4		10	7			5	9	12	11*					1			2	8		6		14			25
		4	10	7	3	12	11*		5	9					1			8	6		2					26
		4	2	10	7	11	14		5	9†	12							8*	6	3	1					27
		4	14	3	7*	2	10	12	5	9	11†								6	8	1					28
		4	12	3	8	10	14		5	9	11†		7*						6	2	1					29
		4	7†	3	14	8	10	12	5	9	11*								6	2	1					30
		4	8	3	12	7	10*	14	5†	9	11								6	2	1					31
	3	4		10	7		12		5	9	11*							8	6	2	1					32
	3	4		10	7*	14	12		5	9	11							8†	6	2	1					33
	3	4	14	10	7	2	11*		5	9†								8	6	12	1					34
3†	4		10	12	8	14		5	9	11		7*						6	2	1						35
		4	14	10	11	3	12		5	9†			8*					7	6	2	1					36
		4	10	7*	3	12			5	9	11							8	6	2	1					37
	3	4		10	7*	8	12		5	9	11							5	6	2	1					38
		4	10	7†	8		3*		5	9	11	14							6	2	1				12	39
11	10	27	39	15	39	21	9	5	31	24	15	2	34	33	5	20	1	15	2	7	19	19	13	13	—	
		+	+	+	+		+		+	+	+	+	+	+		+		+	+		+		+	+		
2s	1s		7s		9s				1s1s	1s	19s	7s		1s	3s5s						2s		2s	1s		

STIRLING ALBION   Second Division

Year Formed: 1945.   *Ground & Address:* Annfield Park, St Ninians Rd, Stirling FK8 2HE.   *Telephone:* 0786 50399.
Ground Capacity: total: 12,0000   seated: 643.   *Size of Pitch:* 110yd×74yd.
Chairman: Peter McKenzie.   *Secretary:* Duncan McCallum.   *Commercial Manager:* —.
Manager: John Brogan.   *Assistant Managers:* Tom O'Neill, Jimmy Sinclair.   *Physio:* Fred Rae.   *Coach:* Jim McSherry.
Managers since 1975: A. Smith; G. Peebles; J. Fleeting; J. Brogan.
Club Nickname: The Binos.   *Previous Grounds:* None.
Record Attendance: 26,400 v Celtic, Scottish Cup 4th rd; 14 Mar, 1959.
Record Transfer Fee received: £70,000 for John Philliben to Doncaster R (Mar 1984).
Record Transfer Fee paid: £17,000 for Douglas Lawrie from Airdrieonians, December 1989.

1989–90 LEAGUE RECORD

Match No.	Date	Venue	Opponents	Result	H/T Score	Lg. Pos.	Goalscorers	Atten- dance
1	Aug 12	H	Arbroath	L 2-3	1-1	—	George, Docherty	500
2	19	A	Stranraer	W 2-0	0-0	6	Reid, Robertson	895
3	26	A	Berwick R	D 1-1	0-0	7	Moore (pen)	516
4	Sept 2	A	Queen of the S	W 5-0	2-0	4	Moore 2 (1 pen), Mitchell, Lloyd, Docherty	700
5	9	H	Brechin C	W 2-0	0-0	1	Lloyd, Reid	760
6	16	A	Cowdenbeath	L 0-4	0-2	4		350
7	23	A	Dumbarton	D 2-2	1-0	5	Reid, Conway	800
8	30	H	Kilmarnock	L 0-1	0-1	7		1920
9	Oct 7	A	Stenhousemuir	L 1-2	0-1	9	Robertson	500
10	14	H	Montrose	W 2-0	1-0	9	George 2	570
11	21	H	East Fife	W 3-1	2-1	6	Lloyd 3	636
12	28	A	Queen's Park	L 1-2	0-1	8	Lloyd	725
13	Nov 4	H	East Stirling	W 4-0	1-0	6	Moore 2, Tennant, Derek Walker	530
14	11	A	Queen of the S	L 1-3	1-0	9	George	720
15	18	A	Kilmarnock	W 2-1	2-0	7	Reid, Lloyd	2473
16	25	H	Dumbarton	W 4-1	0-1	6	Reid, Lloyd, Lawrie, Derek Walker	570
17	Dec 2	H	Stenhousemuir	D 1-1	1-0	5	Moore	600
18	20	A	Montrose	D 3-3	0-2	—	Reid 2, Derek Walker	300
19	23	H	Stranraer	W 1-0	1-0	2	Robertson	400
20	26	A	Arbroath	W 2-1	1-0	—	Lawrie, Lloyd	720
21	Jan 2	H	Berwick R	W 3-2	0-0	—	Moore, Docherty, Reid	500
22	6	A	East Stirling	W 2-0	1-0	1	Moore (pen), Derek Walker	600
23	13	A	Brechin C	L 1-3	0-2	2	Reid	800
24	27	A	East Fife	L 0-1	0-1	3		976
25	Feb 3	H	Queen's Park	W 1-0	1-0	3	Lloyd	770
26	7	H	Cowdenbeath	D 1-1	1-1	—	Lloyd	700
27	17	H	Queen of the S	D 1-1	0-0	2	Gilmour	750
28	Mar 3	H	Montrose	L 2-3	1-1	3	Gilmour, Moore (pen)	450
29	6	A	Kilmarnock	L 0-0	0-1	—		3369
30	13	A	Cowdenbeath	D 1-1	1-0	—	Lloyd	290
31	24	H	Stranraer	W 2-1	1-1	4	Reid 2	510
32	27	A	East Stirling	W 2-0	2-0	—	Lawrie, Reid	450
33	31	A	Queen's Park	L 1-3	1-0	4	Reid	607
34	Apr 4	H	Berwick R	W 4-0	2-0	—	Moore 2, Lloyd, Docherty	300
35	7	A	Brechin C	W 5-1	3-1	3	Moore, Reid 2, Brash (og), George	900
36	14	H	Arbroath	W 3-2	1-2	2	Reid, Docherty, Mitchell	720
37	21	H	Stenhousemuir	L 1-3	0-2	4	Lloyd	1260
38	28	A	Dumbarton	W 2-1	1-0	3	Moore, George	600
39	May 5	H	EastFife	W 2-0	1-0	3	Lloyd, Moore	1020

Final League Position: 3

GOALSCORERS

League: (73): Reid 16, Lloyd 15, Moore 14 (4 pens), George 6, Docherty 5, Derek Walker 4, Lawrie 3, Robertson 3, Gilmour 2, Mitchell 2, Conway 1, Tennant 1, own goal 1.
Scottish Cup: (15): Lloyd 7, Docherty 2, Gilmour 2, Moore 2 (1 pen), George 1, Reid 1.
Skol Cup: (0).

Record Victory: 20-0 v Selkirk, Scottish Cup, 1st rd; 8 Dec, 1984.
Record Defeat: 0-9 v Dundee U, Division I; 30 Dec, 1967.
Most Capped Player: —.
Most League Appearances: 504: Matt McPhee, 1967–81.
Most League Goals in Season (Individual): 29: Joe Hughes, Division II; 1969–70.
Most Goals Overall (Individual): 129: Billy Steele, 1971–83.

Honours
League Champions: Division II 1952–53, 1957–58, 1960–61, 1964–65. Second Division 1976–77; *Runners-up:* Division II 1948–49, 1950–51.
Scottish Cup—.
League Cup—.
Club colours: Shirt: Red with white sleeves. Shorts: White. Stockings: White.

Graham, A	Michell, C	Given, J	Hughes, M	Moore, V	Woods, J	George, D	McConville, R	Reid, J	Robertson, S	Docherty, R	Gilmour, J	Conway, M	Tennant, S	Lloyd, D	Hamilton, L	McGeown, M	Blackwood, I	Lawrie, D	Walker, Derek	Brown, M	Walker, David	Mooney, M	Hannigan, P	Match No.
1	2	3	4*	5	6	7	8	9	10	11	12													1
1	2	6		8	5	7*	4†	9	10	11	12	14	3											2
1	2	6	12	8	5	7	4†	9*	10	11		14	3											3
1*	2	6		8	5	7†	4	9	10	11		14	3	12										4
	2	6		8	5	7*	12		10	11		4	3	9		1								5
	2	6	14	8	5	7	12		10	11		4†	3	9*		1								6
	2	6	14		5	7	8†	9*	10	11		4	3	12		1								7
	2	6		8	5	7	10†	9*		11		14	4	3	12	1								8
	2	6		8*	5	12		9	10	11		14	4	3	7†	1								9
	2	6	14	8	5	7	12		10	11		4†		9*		1	3							10
	2	6		8	5	7*	12		10	11		4	3	9		1								11
	2	6		8	5†	7*	12	14	10	11		4	3	9		1								12
	2	6		8		7*	12		10†	11		4	3	9		1		5	14					13
	2			8*	14	7	12		10	11		4	3	9		1		5	6†					14
	2			8		7*	12		10	11		4	3	9†		1		5	14	6				15
	2†			8	14	7*	12		10	11		4	3	9		1		5	6					16
	2			8	14	7*	12		10	11		4	3	9		1		5	6†					17
	2	12		8		7			10	11		4*	3	9		1		5	14	6†				18
	2	6		8		7†	4*		10	11		14	3	9		1		5	12					19
	2	6		8		7†	4		10*	11		14	3	9		1		5	12					20
	2*	3		8	6	7	12		10	11		4		9		1		5						21
	2	3		8	6	7†	4*		10	11		14		9		1		5	12					22
	2	3		8		7	4		10*	11		12	9			1		5			6			23
	2	6		8		7	4*		10	11		14	3	9		1		5	12					24
	2	6		8		7	12		10	11		14	3	9*		1		5	4					25
	2	6		8		7	12		10	11			3†	9*		1		5	4	14				26
	2	6		8			12		10†	11*		14		9		1		5	4		3	7		27
	2	6		8			12			11		4†		9		1		5	10	14	3	7*		28
	2	6		8		7*	12		10	11†		4	3	9		1		5	14					29
	2	6		8		7†			10	11		4	3	9*		1		5	12		14			30
	2	6		8		7			10	11		4		9		1		5			3			31
	2	3		8	6	7	12		10	11		4		9*		1		5						32
	2	3*		8	6	7†	12		10	11		4		9		1		5			14			33
	2	3		8	6	7†	12		10*	11		4		9		1		5				14		34
	2	3		8*	6	7	12		10	11		4		9†		1		5				14		35
	2	3		8	6	7	9*		10	11		4				1		5				12		36
	2	3*		8	6†	7	12		10	11		4		9		1		5				14		37
1	2	3†		8	6	7*	12		10	11		4		9				5			14			38
	2	3		8	6*	7	12		10	11†		4		9		1		5				14		39
5	39	31	1	36	18	15	22	28	33	39	7	23	23	31	5	29	1	27	9	2	3	2	—	

Substitute appearances (+): Given +1s; Moore +4s; George +15s, McConville +4s; Reid +7s; Conway +12s, Tennant +4s; Lloyd +3s; Walker, Derek +9s; Brown +1s; Walker, David +4s; Mooney +5s.

STRANRAER

Second Division

Year Formed: 1870. *Ground & Address:* Stair Park, London Rd, Stranraer DG9 8BS. *Telephone:* 0776 3271.
Ground Capacity: total: 4000 seated: 250. *Size of Pitch:* 110×70yd.
Chairman: T. Rice. *Secretary:* Graham Rodgers. *Commercial Manager:* —.
Manager: Alex McAnespie. *Assistant Manager:* —. *Physio:* —. *Coach:* John McNiven.
Managers since 1975: J. Hughes; N. Hood; G. Hamilton; D. Sneddon; J. Clark; R. Clark; A. McAnespie.
Club Nickname(s): The Blues. *Previous Grounds:* None.
Record Attendance: 6500 v Rangers, Scottish Cup 1st rd; 24 Jan, 1948.
Record Transfer Fee received: —.
Record Transfer Fee paid: £15,000 for Colin Harkness from Kilmarnock, August 1989.

1989–90 LEAGUE RECORD

Match No.	Date		Venue	Opponents	Result	H/T Score	Lg. Pos.	Goalscorers	Attendance
1	Aug	12	A	Montrose	D 2-2	2-2	—	Henderson, Harkness	350
2		19	H	Stirling Albion	L 0-2	0-0	11		895
3		26	A	Queen of the S	D 2-2	1-0	11		1250
4	Sept	2	H	Cowdenbeath	W 3-1	0-1	7	McCutcheon (pen), Harkness, Henderson	750
5		9	A	Dumbarton	L 2-5	0-4	11	Duncan, Harkness	500
6		16	H	East Stirling	D 1-1	1-1	11	Duncan	350
7		23	A	Stenhousemuir	W 2-0	1-0	9	Henderson, Cook	200
8		30	H	East Fife	D 1-1	1-0	9	Henderson	700
9	Oct	7	A	Queen's Park	W 2-0	1-0	6	Cook, McNiven	771
10		14	H	Arbroath	W 2-1	1-0	4	Cook, Ewing	670
11		21	H	Kilmarnock	W 1-0	0-0	2	Cook	2500
12		28	A	Brechin C	L 0-1	0-0	4		300
13	Nov	4	H	Berwick R	L 1-3	0-2	8	Lindsay	500
14		11	A	Cowdenbeath	W 4-3	2-0	5	McCutcheon, Harkness, Henderson, McNiven	250
15		18	A	East Fife	W 2-1	1-1	5	McCutcheon, Duncan	420
16		25	H	Stenhousemuir	D 2-2	2-2	3	McNiven, Cook	450
17	Dec	2	H	Queen's Park	L 0-1	0-0	7		550
18		20	A	Arbroath	L 0-2	0-1	—		329
19		23	A	Stirling Albion	L 0-1	0-1	8		400
20		26	H	Montrose	L 1-2	0-0	—	Duncan	850
21	Jan	2	A	Queen of the S	L 0-2	0-2	—		650
22		13	H	Dumbarton	D 4-4	1-1	10	Henderson 2, McNiven, Ewing	400
23		16	A	Berwick R	L 1-3	0-1	—	Cook	421
24		27	A	Kilmarnock	W 1-0	1-0	10	Henderson	3550
25	Feb	3	A	Brechin C	L 2-4	1-3	12	McCutcheon 2	700
26		10	H	Montrose	W 2-0	2-0	11	Harkness 2	300
27		20	A	Queen's Park	L 0-3	0-2	—		455
28		28	H	East Fife	L 0-2	0-0	—		500
29	Mar	17	H	Queen of the S	W 3-0	1-0	11	Harkness 3	950
30		24	A	Stirling Albion	L 1-2	1-1	13	Cook	510
31		31	H	Cowdenbeath	L 1-2	0-2	13	Harkness	400
32	Apr	4	A	East Stirling	W 3-0	2-0	—	McNiven, Cook 2	119
33		7	A	Berwick R	L 1-2	1-0	13	Harkness	335
34		10	A	Dumbarton	D 1-1	1-0	—	Harkness	300
35		14	H	Kilmarnock	W 2-1	0-0	12	Henderson 2	2556
36		21	A	Brechin C	D 0-0	0-0	12		750
37		24	A	East Stirling	W 1-0	0-0	—	McNiven	300
38		28	H	Arbroath	W 2-1	0-1	9	Duncan, Cook	500
39	May	5	H	Stenhousemuir	W 4-1	3-1	8	McMillan, McNiven, Cook, Duncan	600

Final League Position: 8

GOALSCORERS

League: (57): Harkness 13, Cook 11, Henderson 10, McNiven 7, Duncan 6, McCutcheon 5 (1 pen), Ewing 2, Lindsay 2, McMillan 1.
Scottish Cup: (2): Harkness 2.
Skol Cup: (3): Harkness 2, Cuthbertson 1.

757

Record Victory: 7-0 v Brechin C, Division II; 6 Feb, 1965.
Record Defeat: 1-11 v Queen of the South, Scottish Cup 1st rd; 16 Jan, 1932.
Most Capped Player: —.
Most League Appearances: 256: Dan McDonald.
Most League Goals in Season (Individual): —. 27: Derek Frye, Second Division; 1977–78.
Most Goals Overall (Individual): —.

Honours
League Champions:—.
Scottish Cup:—.
League Cup:—.
Club colours: Shirt: Royal blue with amber chest band. Shorts: Royal blue. Stockings: Royal blue.

Duffy, B	Lowe, L	Workman, J	McNiven, J	Gallagher, A	McCutcheon, D	Ewing, A	Harkness, C	Cook, D	Henderson, D	Lindsay, C	Duncan, G	McInnes, I	Barr, R	Spittal, I	McMillan, G	Cuthbertson, S	Martin, P	Millar, D	Shirkie, S	Teevan, P	Doherty, J	Hamilton, D	Corrie, T	Muir, W	Dougan, M	Match No.
1	2	3	4	5	6	7	8†	9*	10	11	12	14														1
1	2	3†	4	5	6	7	8	9*	10	11	12		14													2
1			4	5		6	8	12	10	11	9	7*	2	3												3
1	2†		4	5	6	14	8	12	10	3	9	7	11*													4
1	2		4	5*	6	11	8	9	10†	3	12	7		14												5
1	2	3			6	8	14	12	11	9	7*		5	4	10†											6
1	2	3	4		6	8	12	11†	9	14		10		7*	5											7
1	2*	3	4	6	10	14		8	11	7†	9	12		5												8
1	2		4	5	6	7	8†	9	11*	3	12	14	10													9
1	2		4	5	6	7	8*	9†	11	3	12	14	10													10
1	2†		4	5	6	7	8*	9	11	3	12	14	10													11
1	2†		4	5	6	7*	8	9	11	3	12	14	10													12
1	2		4*	5	6	8	9	11	3	7	12	10†	14													13
1	2		4	5	6	7†	9	8	10*	3	12	11	14													14
1	2		4	5	6	7	9†	8*	11	3	12	10	14													15
1	2		4	5	6	7	9†	8*	3	11	10	12	14													16
1	2*		4	5	6	7	9	8	11†	3	12	10	14													17
1	2		4	5	6	11	9		3	8	10*	7		12												18
1	2†		4	5	6	10*	9	8	3	7	14	11	12													19
1	2	6		5		11	8	9	3*	10	7		4†	12	14											20
1	2		4	5*	6	7		8	10	3	9		11				12									21
1			4			7		8	10	3	6	12		5	9	2				11*						22
1		2		5		7		9	10	3	6†	12		4	8		14	11*								23
1	2		4	5	6	7		8	10	3	12	14		9*	11†											24
1	2		5	6		9†	8	10	3	11	12		14	4						7*						25
1			5	6	4	9	8	11	3	14	7*		2†	12	10											26
1			4	5	6	11	9	8*	10	3	12	7		14	2†											27
1	2		4	5	6	7		8	10*	12		11†	9			3	14									28
1			4	5	6	3*	9	12	11	2	7		8			10†	14									29
1			4	5	6		9	8	11	2	7		10		3*	12										30
1			4	5	6		9	12	11	3	7		8*		10†	2	14									31
1			4	5	6		9	8	10*	11	12	3	7		2											32
1			4*	5	6		8	7	11	10	12	3	9		2											33
1	12		4	5	6		9†	8	11	3	7	14	10		2	4*										34
1	2*		4	5	6	10		11	3	7	12	9		8												35
1	12		4	5	6		9†	3	7		8		10	2	11*	14										36
1			4	5	6	8	3	9	7*	11		2	12		10*											37
1			4	5		10	3	9	7*	11	8		6		2	12										38
1	2†		4	5	6	12	9	3	10	14	8*			11	7											39
39	25	5	35	36	34	23	28	32	30	30	24	15	2	24	18	6	1	—	8	3	—	—	8	3	—	

Substitute appearances: 2s (Duffy) … 2s (Ewing) 1s (Harkness) 6s (Cook) 1s (Henderson) … 14s (Duncan) 15s (McInnes) 1s (Barr) 4s (Spittal) 10s (McMillan) 2s (Cuthbertson) … 2s (Shirkie) 1s (Teevan) … 1s (Corrie) 1s (Muir) … 2s (Muir) 2s1s (Dougan)

B & Q SCOTTISH LEAGUE FINAL TABLES
1989–90

PREMIER DIVISION

			Home		Goals			Away			Goals			
		P	W	D	L	F	A	W	D	L	F	A	GD	Pts
1	Rangers	36	14	2	2	32	7	6	9	3	16	12	+29	51
2	Aberdeen	36	12	4	2	33	13	5	6	7	23	20	+23	44
3	Hearts	36	8	6	4	28	17	8	6	4	26	18	+19	44
4	Dundee U	36	8	8	2	21	12	3	5	10	15	27	−3	35
5	Celtic	36	6	6	6	21	20	4	8	6	16	17	0	34
6	Motherwell	36	7	6	5	23	21	4	6	8	20	26	−4	34
7	Hibernian	36	8	5	5	25	23	4	5	9	9	18	−7	34
8	Dunfermline Ath	36	5	6	7	17	23	6	2	10	20	27	−13	30
9	St Mirren	36	6	6	6	14	15	4	4	10	14	33	−20	30
10	Dundee	36	4	8	6	23	26	1	6	11	18	39	−24	24

DIVISION 1

			Home		Goals			Away			Goals			
		P	W	D	L	F	A	W	D	L	F	A	GD	Pts
1	St Johnstone	39	13	3	4	40	16	12	5	2	41	23	+42	58
2	Airdrieonians	39	12	6	2	45	23	11	2	6	32	22	+32	54
3	Clydebank	39	10	4	5	39	29	7	6	7	35	35	+10	44
4	Falkirk	39	11	5	3	38	17	3	10	7	21	29	+13	43
5	Raith Rovers	39	10	4	5	30	22	5	8	7	27	28	+7	42
6	Hamilton A	39	9	5	5	33	27	5	8	7	19	26	−1	41
7	Meadowbank Th	39	7	6	7	22	25	6	7	6	19	21	−5	39
8	Partick Th	39	9	5	6	33	22	3	9	7	29	31	+9	38
9	Clyde	39	5	9	5	18	20	5	6	9	21	26	−7	35
10	Ayr U	39	6	8	5	24	23	5	5	10	17	39	−21	35
11	Morton	39	4	10	6	21	20	5	6	8	17	26	−8	34
12	Forfar Ath*	39	5	7	7	29	33	3	8	9	22	32	−14	29
13	Albion R	39	4	8	8	31	38	4	3	12	19	40	−28	27
14	Alloa	39	4	8	8	18	27	2	5	12	23	43	−29	25

DIVISION 2

			Home		Goals			Away			Goals			
		P	W	D	L	F	A	W	D	L	F	A	GD	Pts
1	Brechin C	39	12	5	3	33	20	7	6	6	26	24	+15	49
2	Kilmarnock	39	14	3	3	35	11	8	1	10	32	28	+28	48
3	Stirling A	39	13	3	4	44	20	7	4	8	29	30	+23	47
4	Stenhousemuir	39	10	2	7	30	29	8	6	6	30	24	+7	44
5	Berwick R	39	13	4	3	36	19	5	1	13	30	38	+9	41
6	Dumbarton	39	9	5	5	33	29	6	5	9	37	44	−3	40
7	Cowdenbeath	39	7	6	6	35	30	6	7	7	23	24	+4	39
8	Stranraer	39	8	4	8	32	31	7	4	8	25	28	−2	38
9	East Fife	39	7	7	5	37	29	5	5	10	23	34	−3	36
10	Queen of the S	39	8	8	3	40	34	3	6	11	18	35	−11	36
11	Queen's Park	39	10	5	5	26	23	3	5	11	14	28	−11	36
12	Arbroath	39	9	5	5	26	18	3	5	12	21	43	−14	34
13	Montrose	39	5	7	8	28	29	5	5	9	25	34	−10	32
14	East Stirling	39	8	3	8	20	25	0	7	13	14	41	−32	26

* 2 points deducted for breach of rules.

SCOTTISH LEAGUE 1890–91 to 1989–90

*On goal average/difference.   †Held jointly after indecisive play-off.   ‡Won on deciding match.
††Held jointly.   ¶Two points deducted for fielding ineligible player.
Competition suspended 1940–45 during war.   ‡‡Two points deducted for registration irregularities.

PREMIER DIVISION

Maximum points: 72

	First	Pts	Second	Pts	Third	Pts
1975–76	Rangers	54	Celtic	48	Hibernian	43
1976–77	Celtic	55	Rangers	46	Aberdeen	43
1977–78	Rangers	55	Aberdeen	53	Dundee U	40
1978–79	Celtic	48	Rangers	45	Dundee U	44
1979–80	Aberdeen	48	Celtic	47	St Mirren	42
1980–81	Celtic	56	Aberdeen	49	Rangers*	44
1981–82	Celtic	55	Aberdeen	53	Rangers	43
1982–83	Dundee U	56	Celtic*	55	Aberdeen	55
1983–84	Aberdeen	57	Celtic	50	Dundee U	47
1984–85	Aberdeen	59	Celtic	52	Dundee U	47
1985–86	Celtic*	50	Hearts	50	Dundee U	47

Maximum points: 88

1986–87	Rangers	69	Celtic	63	Dundee U	60
1987–88	Celtic	72	Hearts	62	Rangers	60

Maximum points: 72

1988–89	Rangers	56	Aberdeen	50	Celtic	46
1989–90	Rangers	51	Aberdeen*	44	Hearts	44

FIRST DIVISION

Maximum points: 52

1975–76	Partick Th	41	Kilmarnock	35	Montrose	30

Maximum points: 78

1976–77	St Mirren	62	Clydebank	58	Dundee	51
1977–78	Morton*	58	Hearts	58	Dundee	57
1978–79	Dundee	55	Kilmarnock*	54	Clydebank	54
1979–80	Hearts	53	Airdrieonians	51	Ayr U	44
1980–81	Hibernian	57	Dundee	52	St Johnstone	51
1981–82	Motherwell	61	Kilmarnock	51	Hearts	50
1982–83	St Johnstone	55	Hearts	54	Clydebank	50
1983–84	Morton	54	Dumbarton	51	Partick Th	46
1984–85	Motherwell	50	Clydebank	48	Falkirk	45
1985–86	Hamilton A	56	Falkirk	45	Kilmarnock	44

Maximum points: 88

1986–87	Morton	57	Dunfermline Ath	56	Dumbarton	53
1987–88	Hamilton A	56	Meadowbank Th	52	Clydebank	49

Maximum points: 78

1988–89	Dunfermline Ath	54	Falkirk	52	Clydebank	48
1989–90	St Johnstone	58	Airdrieonians	54	Clydebank	44

SECOND DIVISION

Maximum points: 52

1975–76	Clydebank*	40	Raith R	40	Alloa	35

Maximum points: 78

1976–77	Stirling A	55	Alloa	51	Dunfermline Ath	50
1977–78	Clyde*	53	Raith R	53	Dunfermline Ath	48
1978–79	Berwick R	54	Dunfermline Ath	52	Falkirk	50
1979–80	Falkirk	50	East Stirling	49	Forfar Ath	46
1980–81	Queen's Park	50	Queen of the S	46	Cowdenbeath	45
1981–82	Clyde	59	Alloa*	50	Arbroath	50
1982–83	Brechin C	55	Meadowbank Th	54	Arbroath	49
1983–84	Forfar Ath	63	East Fife	47	Berwick R	43
1984–85	Montrose	53	Alloa	50	Dunfermline Ath	49
1985–86	Dunfermline Ath	57	Queen of the South	55	Meadowbank Th	49
1986–87	Meadowbank Th	55	Raith R*	52	Stirling A	52
1987–88	Ayr U	61	St Johnstone	59	Queen's Park	51
1988–89	Albion R	50	Alloa	45	Brechin C	43
1989–90	Brechin C	49	Kilmarnock	48	Stirling A	47

FIRST DIVISION to 1974–75

Maximum points: a 36; b 44; c 40; d 52; e 60; f 68; g 76; h 84.

	First	Pts	Second	Pts	Third	Pts
1890–91a††	Dumbarton	29	Rangers	29	Celtic	24
1891–92b	Dumbarton	37	Celtic	35	Hearts	30
1892–93a	Celtic	29	Rangers	28	St Mirren	23
1893–94a	Celtic	29	Hearts	26	St Bernard's	22
1894–95a	Hearts	31	Celtic	26	Rangers	21
1895–96a	Celtic	30	Rangers	26	Hibernian	24
1896–97a	Hearts	28	Hibernian	26	Rangers	25
1897–98a	Celtic	33	Rangers	29	Hibernian	22
1898–99a	Rangers	36	Hearts	26	Celtic	24
1899–1900a	Rangers	32	Celtic	25	Hibernian	24
1900–01c	Rangers	35	Celtic	29	Hibernian	25
1901–02a	Rangers	28	Celtic	26	Hearts	22
1902–03b	Hibernian	37	Dundee	31	Rangers	29
1903–04d	Third Lanark	43	Hearts	39	Rangers*	38
1904–05d	Celtic‡	41	Rangers	41	Third Lanark	35
1905–06e	Celtic	49	Hearts	43	Airdrieonians	38
1906–07f	Celtic	55	Dundee	48	Rangers	45
1907–08f	Celtic	55	Falkirk	51	Rangers	50
1908–09f	Celtic	51	Dundee	50	Clyde	48
1909–10f	Celtic	54	Falkirk	52	Rangers	46
1910–11f	Rangers	52	Aberdeen	48	Falkirk	44
1911–12f	Rangers	51	Celtic	45	Clyde	42
1912–13f	Rangers	53	Celtic	49	Hearts*	41
1913–14g	Celtic	65	Rangers	59	Hearts*	54
1914–15g	Celtic	65	Hearts	61	Rangers	50
1915–16g	Celtic	67	Rangers	56	Morton	51
1916–17g	Celtic	64	Morton	54	Rangers	53
1917–18f	Rangers	56	Celtic	55	Kilmarnock	43
1918–19f	Celtic	58	Rangers	57	Morton	47
1919–20h	Rangers	71	Celtic	68	Motherwell	57
1920–21h	Rangers	76	Celtic	66	Hearts	56
1921–22h	Celtic	67	Rangers	66	Raith R	56
1922–23g	Rangers	55	Airdrieonians	50	Celtic	46
1923–24g	Rangers	59	Airdrieonians	50	Celtic	41
1924–25g	Rangers	60	Airdrieonians	57	Hibernian	52
1925–26g	Celtic	58	Airdrieonians*	50	Hearts	50
1926–27g	Rangers	56	Motherwell	51	Celtic	49
1927–28g	Rangers	60	Celtic*	55	Motherwell	55
1928–29g	Rangers	67	Celtic	51	Motherwell	50
1929–30g	Rangers	60	Motherwell	55	Aberdeen	53
1930–31g	Rangers	60	Celtic	58	Motherwell	56
1931–32g	Motherwell	66	Rangers	61	Celtic	48
1932–33g	Rangers	62	Motherwell	59	Hearts	50
1933–34g	Rangers	66	Motherwell	62	Celtic	47
1934–35g	Rangers	55	Celtic	52	Hearts	50
1935–36g	Celtic	66	Rangers*	61	Aberdeen	61
1936–37g	Rangers	61	Aberdeen	54	Celtic	52
1937–38g	Celtic	61	Hearts	58	Rangers	49
1938–39g	Rangers	59	Celtic	48	Aberdeen	46
1946–47e	Rangers	46	Hibernian	44	Aberdeen	39
1947–48e	Hibernian	48	Rangers	46	Partick Th	36
1948–49e	Rangers	46	Dundee	45	Hibernian	39
1949–50e	Rangers	50	Hibernian	49	Hearts	43
1950–51e	Hibernian	48	Rangers*	38	Dundee	38
1951–52e	Hibernian	45	Rangers	41	East Fife	37
1952–53e	Rangers*	43	Hibernian	43	East Fife	39
1953–54e	Celtic	43	Hearts	38	Partick Th	35
1954–55e	Aberdeen	49	Celtic	46	Rangers	41
1955–56f	Rangers	52	Aberdeen	46	Hearts*	45
1956–57f	Rangers	55	Hearts	53	Kilmarnock	42
1957–58f	Hearts	62	Rangers	49	Celtic	46
1958–59f	Rangers	50	Hearts	48	Motherwell	44
1959–60f	Hearts	54	Kilmarnock	50	Rangers*	42
1960–61f	Rangers	51	Kilmarnock	50	Third Lanark	42
1961–62f	Dundee	54	Rangers	51	Celtic	46
1962–63f	Rangers	57	Kilmarnock	48	Partick Th	46
1963–64f	Rangers	55	Kilmarnock	49	Celtic*	47
1964–65f	Kilmarnock*	50	Hearts	50	Dunfermline Ath	49
1965–66f	Celtic	57	Rangers	55	Kilmarnock	45
1966–67f	Celtic	58	Rangers	55	Clyde	46

	First	Pts	Second	Pts	Third	Pts
1967–68f	Celtic	63	Rangers	61	Hibernian	45
1968–69f	Celtic	54	Rangers	49	Dunfermline Ath	45
1969–70f	Celtic	57	Rangers	45	Hibernian	44
1970–71f	Celtic	56	Aberdeen	54	St Johnstone	44
1971–72f	Celtic	60	Aberdeen	50	Rangers	44
1972–73f	Celtic	57	Rangers	56	Hibernian	45
1973–74f	Celtic	53	Hibernian	49	Rangers	48
1974–75f	Rangers	56	Hibernian	49	Celtic	45

SECOND DIVISION to 1974–75
Maximum points: a 76; b 72; c 68; d 52; e 60; f 36; g 44; h 52.

	First	Pts	Second	Pts	Third	Pts
1893–94f	Hibernian	29	Cowlairs	27	Clyde	24
1894–95f	Hibernian	30	Motherwell	22	Port Glasgow	20
1895–96f	Abercorn	27	Leith Ath	23	Renton	21
1896–97f	Partick Th	31	Leith Ath	27	Kilmarnock	21
1897–98f	Kilmarnock	29	Port Glasgow	25	Morton	22
1898–99f	Kilmarnock	32	Leith Ath	27	Port Glasgow	25
1899–1900f	Partick Th	29	Morton	26	Port Glasgow	20
1900–01f	St Bernard's	26	Airdrieonians	23	Abercorn	21
1901–02g	Port Glasgow	32	Partick Th	31	Motherwell	26
1902–03g	Airdrieonians	35	Motherwell	28	Ayr U	27
1903–04g	Hamilton A	37	Clyde	29	Ayr U	28
1904–05g	Clyde	32	Falkirk	28	Hamilton A	27
1905–06g	Leith Ath	34	Clyde	31	Albion R	27
1906–07g	St Bernard's	32	Vale of Leven*	27	Arthurlie	27
1907–08g	Raith R	30	Dumbarton	‡‡27	Ayr U	27
1908–09g	Abercorn	31	Raith R*	28	Vale of Leven	28
1909–10g‡	Leith Ath	33	Raith R	33	St Bernard's	27
1910–11g	Dumbarton	31	Ayr U	27	Albion R	25
1911–12g	Ayr U	35	Abercorn	30	Dumbarton	27
1912–13h	Ayr U	34	Dunfermline Ath	33	East Stirling	32
1913–14g	Cowdenbeath	31	Albion R	27	Dunfermline Ath	26
1914–15h	Cowdenbeath*	37	St Bernard's*	37	Leith Ath	37
1921–22a	Alloa	60	Cowdenbeath	47	Armadale	45
1922–23a	Queen's Park	57	Clydebank	¶50	St Johnstone	¶45
1923–24a	St Johnstone	56	Cowdenbeath	55	Bathgate	44
1924–25a	Dundee U	50	Clydebank	48	Clyde	47
1925–26a	Dunfermline Ath	59	Clyde	53	Ayr U	52
1926–27a	Bo'ness	56	Raith R	49	Clydebank	45
1927–28a	Ayr U	54	Third Lanark	45	King's Park	44
1928–29b	Dundee U	51	Morton	50	Arbroath	47
1929–30a	Leith Ath*	57	East Fife	57	Albion R	54
1930–31a	Third Lanark	61	Dundee U	50	Dunfermline Ath	47
1931–32a	East Stirling*	55	St Johnstone	55	Raith Rovers*	46
1932–33c	Hibernian	54	Queen of the S	49	Dunfermline Ath	47
1933–34c	Albion R	45	Dunfermline Ath*	44	Arbroath	44
1934–35c	Third Lanark	52	Arbroath	50	St Bernard's	47
1935–36c	Falkirk	59	St Mirren	52	Morton	48
1936–37c	Ayr U	54	Morton	51	St Bernard's	48
1937–38c	Raith R	59	Albion R	48	Airdrieonians	47
1938–39c	Cowdenbeath	60	Alloa*	48	East Fife	48
1946–47d	Dundee	45	Airdrieonians	42	East Fife	31
1947–48e	East Fife	53	Albion R	42	Hamilton A	40
1948–49e	Raith R*	42	Stirling Albion	42	Airdrieonians*	41
1949–50e	Morton	47	Airdrieonians	44	St Johnstone*	36
1950–51e	Queen of the S*	45	Stirling Albion	45	Ayr U*	36
1951–52e	Clyde	44	Falkirk	43	Ayr U	39
1952–53e	Stirling Albion	44	Hamilton A	43	Queen's Park	37
1953–54e	Motherwell	45	Kilmarnock	42	Third Lanark*	36
1954–55e	Airdrieonians	46	Dunfermline Ath	42	Hamilton A	39
1955–56b	Queen's Park	54	Ayr U	51	St Johnstone	49
1956–57b	Clyde	64	Third Lanark	51	Cowdenbeath	45
1957–58b	Stirling Albion	55	Dunfermline Ath	53	Arbroath	47
1958–59b	Ayr U	60	Arbroath	51	Stenhousemuir	40
1959–60b	St Johnstone	53	Dundee U	50	Queen of the S	49
1960–61b	Stirling Albion	55	Falkirk	54	Stenhousemuir	50
1961–62b	Clyde	54	Queen of the S	53	Morton	44
1962–63b	St Johnstone	55	East Stirling	49	Morton	48
1963–64b	Morton	67	Clyde	53	Arbroath	46
1964–65b	Stirling Albion	59	Hamilton A	50	Queen of the S	45
1965–66b	Ayr U	53	Airdrieonians	50	Queen of the S	49
1966–67b	Morton	69	Raith R	58	Arbroath	57

1967–68b	St Mirren	62	Arbroath	53	East Fife	40
1968–69b	Motherwell	64	Ayr U	53	East Fife*	47
1969–70b	Falkirk	56	Cowdenbeath	55	Queen of the S	50
1970–71b	Partick Th	56	East Fife	51	Arbroath	46
1971–72b	Dumbarton*	52	Arbroath	52	Stirling Albion	50
1972–73b	Clyde	56	Dunfermline Ath	52	Raith R*	47
1973–74b	Airdrieonians	60	Kilmarnock	59	Hamilton A	55
1974–75a	Falkirk	54	Queen of the S	53	Montrose	53

Elected to First Division: 1894 Clyde; 1897 Partick Th; 1899 Kilmarnock; 1900 Partick Th; 1902 Partick Th; 1903 Airdrieonians; 1905 Falkirk, Aberdeen and Hamilton A; 1906 Clyde; 1910 Raith R; 1913 Ayr U.

RELEGATED FROM PREMIER DIVISION

1975–76 Dundee, St Johnstone
1976–77 Hearts, Kilmarnock
1977–78 Ayr U, Clydebank
1978–79 Hearts, Motherwell
1979–80 Dundee, Hibernian
1980–81 Kilmarnock, Hearts
1981–82 Partick Th, Airdrieonians
1982–83 Morton, Kilmarnock
1983–84 St Johnstone, Motherwell
1984–85 Dumbarton, Morton
1985–86 No relegation due to League reorganisation
1986–87 Clydebank, Hamilton A
1987–88 Falkirk, Dunfermline Ath, Morton
1988–89 Hamilton A
1989–90 Dundee

RELEGATED FROM DIVISION 1

1975–76 Dunfermline Ath, Clyde
1976–77 Raith R, Falkirk
1977–78 Alloa Ath, East Fife
1978–79 Montrose, Queen of the S
1979–80 Arbroath, Clyde
1980–81 Stirling A, Berwick R
1981–82 East Stirling, Queen of the S
1982–83 Dunfermline Ath, Queen's Park
1983–84 Raith R, Alloa
1984–85 Meadowbank Th, St Johnstone
1985–86 Ayr U, Alloa
1986–87 Brechin C, Montrose
1987–88 East Fife, Dumbarton
1988–89 Kilmarnock, Queen of the S
1989–90 Albion R, Alloa

RELEGATED FROM DIVISION 1 (to 1973–74)

1921–22 *Queen's Park, Dumbarton, Clydebank
1922–23 Albion R, Alloa Ath
1923–24 Clyde, Clydebank
1924–25 Third Lanark, Ayr U
1925–26 Raith R, Clydebank
1926–27 Morton, Dundee U
1927–28 Dunfermline Ath, Bo'ness
1928–29 Third Lanark, Raith R
1929–30 St Johnstone, Dundee U
1930–31 Hibernian, East Fife
1931–32 Dundee U, Leith Ath
1932–33 Morton, East Stirling
1933–34 Third Lanark, Cowdenbeath
1934–35 St Mirren, Falkirk
1935–36 Aidrieonians, Ayr U
1936–37 Dunfermline Ath, Albion R
1937–38 Dundee, Morton
1938–39 Queen's Park, Raith R
1946–47 Kilmarnock, Hamilton A
1947–48 Airdrieonians, Queen's Park
1948–49 Morton, Albion R
1949–50 Queen of the S, Stirling Albion
1950–51 Clyde, Falkirk

1951–52 Morton, Stirling Albion
1952–53 Motherwell, Third Lanark
1953–54 Airdrieonians, Hamilton A
1954–55 No clubs relegated
1955–56 Stirling Albion, Clyde
1956–57 Dunfermline Ath, Ayr U
1957–58 East Fife, Queen's Park
1958–59 Queen of the S, Falkirk
1959–60 Arbroath, Stirling Albion
1960–61 Ayr U, Clyde
1961–62 St Johnstone, Stirling Albion
1962–63 Clyde, Raith R
1963–64 Queen of the S, East Stirling
1964–65 Airdrieonians, Third Lanark
1965–66 Morton, Hamilton A
1966–67 St Mirren, Ayr U
1967–68 Motherwell, Stirling Albion
1968–69 Falkirk, Arbroath
1969–70 Raith R, Partick Th
1970–71 St Mirren, Cowdenbeath
1971–72 Clyde, Dunfermline Ath
1972–73 Kilmarnock, Airdrieonians
1973–74 East Fife, Falkirk

*Season 1921–22 – only 1 club promoted, 3 clubs relegated.

The Scottish Football League was reconstructed into three divisions at the end of the 1974–75 season, so the usual relegation statistics do not apply. Further reorganisation took place at the end of the 1985–86 season. From 1986–87, the Premier and First Division had 12 teams each. The Second Division remains at 14. From 1988–89, the Premier Division reverted to 10 teams, and the First Division to 14 teams.

SCOTTISH LEAGUE SKOL CUP FINALS 1946–90

Season	Winners	Runners-up	Score
1946–47	Rangers	Aberdeen	4-0
1947–48	East Fife	Falkirk	4-1 after 0-0 draw
1948–49	Rangers	Raith R	2-0
1949–50	East Fife	Dunfermline Ath	3-0
1950–51	Motherwell	Hibernian	3-0
1951–52	Dundee	Rangers	3-2
1952–53	Dundee	Kilmarnock	2-0
1953–54	East Fife	Partick T	3-2
1954–55	Hearts	Motherwell	4-2
1955–56	Aberdeen	St Mirren	2-1
1956–57	Celtic	Partick T	3-0 after 0-0 draw
1957–58	Celtic	Rangers	7-1
1958–59	Hearts	Partick T	5-1
1959–60	Hearts	Third Lanark	2-1
1960–61	Rangers	Kilmarnock	2-0
1961–62	Rangers	Hearts	3-1 after 1-1 draw
1962–63	Hearts	Kilmarnock	1-0
1963–64	Rangers	Morton	5-0
1964–65	Rangers	Celtic	2-1
1965–66	Celtic	Rangers	2-1
1966–67	Celtic	Rangers	1-0
1967–68	Celtic	Dundee	5-3
1968–69	Celtic	Hibernian	6-2
1969–70	Celtic	St Johnstone	1-0
1970–71	Rangers	Celtic	1-0
1971–72	Partick T	Celtic	4-1
1972–73	Hibernian	Celtic	2-1
1973–74	Dundee	Celtic	1-0
1974–75	Celtic	Hibernian	6-3
1975–76	Rangers	Celtic	1-0
1976–77	Aberdeen	Celtic	2-1
1977–78	Rangers	Celtic	2-1
1978–79	Rangers	Aberdeen	2-1
1979–80	Dundee U	Aberdeen	3-0 after 0-0 draw
1980–81	Dundee U	Dundee	3-0
1981–82	Rangers	Dundee U	2-1
1982–83	Celtic	**Rangers**	2-1
1983–84	Rangers	Celtic	3-2
1984–85	Rangers	Dundee U	1-0
1985–86	Aberdeen	Hibernian	3-0
1986–87	Rangers	Celtic	2-1
1987–88	Rangers	Aberdeen	3-3
		(Rangers won 5-3 on penalties)	
1988–89	Rangers	Aberdeen	3-2
1989–90	Aberdeen	Rangers	2-1

SCOTTISH LEAGUE CUP WINS

Rangers 16, Celtic 9, Hearts 4, Aberdeen 4, Dundee 3, East Fife 3, Dundee U 2, Hibernian 1, Motherwell 1, Partick Th 1.

APPEARANCES IN FINALS

Rangers 22, Celtic 19, Aberdeen 9, Dundee 5, Hearts 5, Hibernian 5, Dundee U 4, Partick Th 4, East Fife 3, Kilmarnock 3, Motherwell 2, Dunfermline Ath 1, Falkirk 1, Morton 1, Raith R 1, St Johnstone 1, St Mirren 1, Third Lanark 1.

Rangers missed out on the Skol Cup, but no other club can match their record in it. They had the consolation of the Premier Championship and here John Brown (Rangers) watches Trevor Smith (Dunfermline Athletic) fail in his bid to tackle him. (Action Images)

SKOL CUP 1989–90

FIRST ROUND

8 AUG

Dumbarton (1) 3 *(MacIver 2, Gibson)*
Stenhousemuir (0) 0   569
Dumbarton: Strachan; McQuade A, Wharton, Dickie, Cairney, Meechan, McQuade J, Spence, Gibson, MacIver, Grant.
Stenhousemuir: Paterno; Milligan, Elliott, Cairney, Aitchison, Kemp, Bell (Quinton), Clouston (Gavin), Walker, McGurn, Condie.

9 AUG

Arbroath (0) 1 *(Fotheringham)*
East Stirling (0) 0   655
Arbroath: Jackson; Hamilton, Gallacher, Fleming, Carlin, Bennett, Mitchell, Richardson, Brand (Smith), Fotheringham, Dewar.
East Stirling: Kelly; Russell, McIntosh, Wilcox D, McEntegart, Gilchrist, Grant, Drew, McNeill (Feeney), O'Brien, Durie.

Cowdenbeath (0) 0
Montrose (0) 4 *(Murray 4 [2 pens])*   391
after extra time
Cowdenbeath: Allan; Baillie (McKenzie), Rae, Malone (Frith), McGovern, Kerr, Spence, Herd, Mailer, Ross, Scott.
Montrose: Larter; Morrison, King (Wright), Paterson, Halley, McGlashan, Allan (McLelland), Lyons, Maver, Selbie, Murray.

East Fife (2) 2 *(Hunter 2)*
Queen's Park (0) 2 *(McKenzie, O'Brien P)*   858
East Fife: Charles; Halliday (Harrow), Taylor, Lennox, Reid, Crolla, Mitchell, Brown W, Hunter, McGonigal (Brown I), Hope.
Queen's Park: Monaghan; McLean, Armstrong, Elder, McNamee, Hendry, Caven, O'Brien J (Ogg), Rodden (McEntegart), McKenzie, O'Brien P.
(Queen's Park won 7-6 on penalties after extra time.)

Stirling Albion (0) 0
Berwick R (0) 3 *(Thorpe, Sloan 2)*   *at Ochilview* 492
Stirling Albion: Graham; Mitchell, Tennant (Conway), Hughes (Moore), Woods, Given, George, McConville, Reid, Robertson, Docherty.
Berwick R: Neilson; Fraser, O'Donnell, Muir, Cass, Locke, Graham, Thorpe, Porteous (Ainslie), Sloan, Callachan (McLaren).

Stranraer (1) 3 *(Harkness 2, Cuthbertson)*
Brechin C (3) 4 *(Sexton, Paterson I G, Hill, Ritchie)* 735
after extra time
Stranraer: Duffy; Lowe, Workman, McNiven, Gallagher, McCutcheon, McInnes (Ewing), Harkness, Cook (Duncan), Henderson, Cuthbertson.
Brechin C: Lawrie; Watt, Scott, Brown, Stevens, Paterson I G, Wardell (Pryde), Hill, Ritchie (Hamilton), Sexton, Buckley.

SECOND ROUND

15 AUG

Airdrieonians (3) 4 *(Lawrence 2 [1 pen], Butler, Balfour)*
Forfar Ath (0) 0   1320
Airdrieonians: Martin; Boyle, Jack, McKeown, Grant, McPhee, Lawrence, Balfour (Stewart), Butler, Conn, MacDonald I (Macdonald K).
Forfar Ath: Kennedy; Lorimer, Hamill, Morris, Smith, Morton, Ormond, McCafferty (Grant), Whyte, Brewster, Clark (Brazil).

Ayr U (0) 0
Hamilton A (0) 1 *(McDonald)*   2616
Ayr U: Watson; McIntyre, Hughes, Kennedy, McAllister, Evans, Templeton, Scott, Walker, Sludden (Fraser), Willock (Cowell).
Hamilton A: Ferguson; McKee, Napier, Weir, Jamieson, Miller, Harris, Morrison (McGuigan), Gordon, Archer (Carr), McDonald.

Berwick R (0) 0
St Mirren (1) 2 *(McDowall, Torfason)*   1643
Berwick R: Neilson; Fraser, O'Donnell, Muir, Cass, Locke, Leitch (McLaren), Thorpe (Porteous), Sloan, Hughes, Callachan.
St Mirren: Money; Dawson, Wishart, Walker, Martin, Winnie, Shaw, McDowall, Torfason, Davies, Kinnaird.

Dumbarton (0) 0
Celtic (2) 3 *(McStay, Dziekanowski, Burns)* 8500
Dumbarton: Strachan; McQuade A, Wharton, Dickie, Cairney, Spence, McQuade J (Quinn), Reid, Gibson, MacIver (McGrogan), Meechan.
Celtic: Bonner; Morris, Burns, Aitken, Whyte, Grant, Galloway, McStay (Rogan), Dziekanowski, Coyne (Walker), Hewitt.

Dundee (1) 5 *(McBride 2, Harvey 2, Wright)*
Clyde (1) 1 *(McCabe)*   3021
Dundee: Geddes; Shannon, Albiston, Frail (Craib), Chisholm, Forsyth, Craig, Beedie, Wright (Campbell A), Harvey, McBride.
Clyde: Robertson; McFarlane, Spence, Reid, Speirs, Nolan, Knox, Clarke (Fairlie), McGlashan, Rooney, McCabe.

Dunfermline Ath (0) 3 *(Rougvie, Abercromby, Jack)*
Raith R (0) 0   6381
Dunfermline Ath: Westwater; Robertson, Rougvie, McCathie, Tierney, Abercromby, Smith P, Farningham, Jack, O'Boyle, Irons.
Raith R: Arthur; McStay, Murray, Fraser, Glennie, Dennis, Simpson, Dalziel, Ferguson, MacLeod (Burn), Romaines (Nelson).

Hibernian (1) 2 *(Sneddon 2)*

Alloa (0) 0   6600

Hibernian: Goram; Kane, Sneddon, Cooper, Mitchell, Hunter, Weir, Orr (Tortolano), Houchen, Hamilton, Findlay (McCluskey).
Alloa: Lowrie; Robertson, Lee R, Erwin, McCulloch (Ramsay), Gibson, Blackie, Paxton, McCallum, Lee I, Lytwyn (Lamont).

Kilmarnock (0) 1 *(Thompson D)*

Motherwell (2) 4 *(Kirk, Cusack 2, Dolan)*   3903

Kilmarnock: McCulloch; Wilson, Davidson (Montgomerie), Jenkins, Cody, Flexney, Thompson D, McLean, Thompson M (Curran), Reilly, Watters.
Motherwell: Maxwell; Burley, Boyd, O'Neill, Philliben, McCart, Russell (Mair), Arnott (Dolan), Cusack, Kirk, Cooper.

Queen's Park (0) 0

Morton (1) 1 *(Turner)*   997

Queen's Park: Monaghan; McLean, Ogg, Elder, McNamee, McEntegart, Caven, Armstrong, O'Brien P, Hendry (Rodden), McKenzie.
Morton: Wylie; Collins, Pickering, Reid, John Boag, Hunter, Ronald, Turner, Alexander, O'Hara, Deeney.

Rangers (2) 4 *(McCoist 3, Ferguson)*

Arbroath (0) 0   31,762

Rangers: Ginzburg; Stevens G (Ferguson D), Munro, Gough, Wilkins, Butcher, Steven T, Ferguson I, McCoist, Johnston, Walters (Drinkell).
Arbroath: Jackson; Hamilton, Gallagher, Fleming, Carlin (Kerr), Bennett M, Stewart, Richardson, Brand, Mitchell, Fotheringham.

Albion R (0) 0 *at Fir Park*

Aberdeen (1) 2 *(Robertson, Van der Ark)*   2384

Albion R: McCulloch; McDonald, McGowan, McKenzie, Oliver, Clark, Watson (Teevan), Cadden, Graham, Chapman, Granger (McAnenay).
Aberdeen: Snelders; McKimmie, Robertson D, Grant, Irvine, Miller, Nicholas, Bett, Dodds (Cameron), Connor, Mason (Van der Ark).

Brechin C (0) 0

Falkirk (1) 3 *(McGivern, Burgess [pen], Beaton)*   1179

Brechin C: Lawrie; Paterson I G, Scott, Brown, Brash, Hamilton (Hutt), Wardell, Hill, Ritchie, Sexton, Buckley (Pryde).
Falkirk: Marshall; Holmes, Hay, Hetherston, Beaton, Burgess, Callaghan (McNair), Robertson (Rutherford), Baptie, Rae, McGivern.

Clydebank (1) 3 *(Eadie 2, McGurn)*

Meadowbank T (1) 1 *(Roseburgh)*   765

Clydebank: Gallacher; Dickson, Rodger, Maher, Sweeney, Hughes (Bryce), Davies, Harvey, Eadie, Robertson (McGurn), Coyle O.
Meadowbank T: McQueen; McCormack, Armstrong, Boyd, Williamson, Roseburgh, Logan, Irvine, Perry (Banks), Sprott, McGachie (Inglis).

Dundee U (0) 1 *(O'Neill)*

Partick T (0) 0   7041

Dundee U: Thomson S; McInally, Van der Hoorn (Hegarty), Malpas, Clark, Narey, Gallacher, Jackson, O'Neill, McKinlay, Paatelainan.
Partick T: Murdoch; Dinnie, Smith, Kerr, MacDonald, Kennedy, Wright, Peebles (McCoy), Flood (Mitchell), Campbell, Charnley.

Hearts (3) 3 *(Crabbe 2, Musemic)*

Montrose (0) 0   7027

Hearts: Smith; McLaren, Kirkwood, Levein (Whittaker), Berry, McPherson, Colquhoun, MacKay, Musemic, Crabbe, Bannon.
Montrose: Larter; Morrison, King, Paterson, Halley, Wright (Selbie), Allan (Mackay), Lyons, Maver, McGlashan, Murray.

Queen of the S (1) 1 *(Fraser [pen])*

St Johnstone (0) 0   1046

Queen of the S: McLean; McGhie, Gray, Sim, Mills, Fraser, Sloan, Johnston, Moore, Shanks, McGuire (Telfer).
St Johnstone: Balavage; Thomson K, McVicar, Newbigging (Smith), Cherry, Thompson G (Grant), Curran, Johnston, Moore, Jenkins, Heddle.

THIRD ROUND

22 AUG

Celtic (1) 2 *(Grant, Dziekanowski)*

Queen of the S (0) 0   20,074

Celtic: Bonner; Morris, Rogan, Aitken, Whyte, Grant (Fulton), Galloway, McStay, Dziekanowski, Walker, Hewitt.
Queen of the S: McLean; McGhie, Gray, Sim, Mills, Johnston, Sloan (Andrews), Shanks, Moore, Fraser, McGuire (Telfer).

Hibernian (0) 0

Clydebank (0) 0   6669

Hibernian: Goram; Kane, Sneddon, Cooper, Mitchell (Findlay), Hunter, Weir, Orr, Houchen, Collins, Hamilton (Evans).
Clydebank: Gallacher; Dickson, Rodger, Maher (McGurn), Auld, Sweeney, Davies, Harvey, Eadie, Hughes (Robertson J), Coyle O.
(Hibernian won 5-3 on penalties after extra time)

23 AUG

Aberdeen (2) 4 *(Mason 2, Cameron, Bett)*

Airdrieonians (0) 0   10,000

Aberdeen: Snelders; McKimmie, Robertson D, Irvine (Grant), McLeish, Miller, Nicholas, Bett, Mason, Connor, Cameron (Jess).
Airdrieonians: Martin; Boyle, Jack, McKeown, Grant, McPhee, Lawrence, Balfour, Butler, Conn, MacDonald I (Macdonald K).

Dunfermline Ath(1) 1 *(Jack)*

Dundee (0) 0   8026

Dunfermline Ath: Westwater; Nicholl, Rougvie (Smith M), McCathie, Tierney, Abercromby, Smith P, Rafferty (Sharp), Jack, O'Boyle, Irons.
Dundee: Geddes; Shannon, Albiston, Craib, Chisholm, Forsyth, Craig, Beedie, Wright, Harvey (Campbell A), McBride.

Falkirk (1) 1 *(Burgess)*
Hearts (2) 4 *(Bannon, Crabbe, Kirkwood, Kidd)*
9046
Falkirk: Marshall; Holmes, McWilliams, Callaghan, Beaton, Burgess, Robertson (Rutherford), McNair, Baptie, Rae, McGivern (Houston).
Hearts: Smith; Levein, Kidd, Whittaker, Berry (McLaren), McPherson, Colquhoun, Kirkwood, Musemic, Crabbe (Ferguson), Bannon.

Hamilton A (1) 2 *(Carr, McKee)*
Dundee U (0) 1 *(Hinds)*
2675
Hamilton A: Ferguson; McKee (Donaghy), Napier, Weir, Jamieson, Miller, Harris, Gordon, Carr (Morrison), Prentice, McDonald.
Dundee U: Thomson W; Van der Hoorn, Malpas, McInally, Clark, Narey, Krivikapic, Adam (Bowman), O'Neill M, Gallacher, Paatelainan (Hinds).

Morton (1) 1 *(Alexander)*
Rangers (1) 2 *(Walters, Pickering (og))*
11,821
Morton: Wylie; Collins, Pickering, Reid, John Boag, Hunter, Ronald (Roberts), Turner, Alexander, O'Hara (McCrystal), Deeney.
Rangers: Ginzburg; Stevens G, Munro, Nisbet, Wilkins, Butcher, Steven T, Ferguson I, Drinkell, Johnston, Walters.

St Mirren (1) 1 *(Kinnaird)*
Motherwell (0) 0
4754
St Mirren: Money; Wishart (Lambert), Wilson, Walker, Godfrey, Winnie, Kinnaird, Martin, McGarvey, Davies, Weir.
Motherwell: Maxwell; Burley, Boyd, Paterson, Philliben (Dolan), McCart, Russell, O'Neill, Arnott, Kirk, Mair (McBride).

QUARTER-FINALS

29 AUG

Hibernian (0) 1 *(Collins)*
Dunfermline Ath (1) 3 *(Rougvie, Smith P, Jack)* 13,454
after extra time
Hibernian: Goram; Kane, Sneddon, Cooper, Mitchell (Findlay), Hunter, Weir, Orr (Hamilton), Houchen, Collins, Evans.
Dunfermline Ath: Westwater; Nicholl, Rougvie, McCathie, Tierney, Abercromby (Sharp), Smith P, Rafferty, Jack, O'Boyle (Gallagher), Irons.

30 AUG

Aberdeen (1) 3 *(Mason, Bett, Winnie (og))*
St Mirren (0) 1 *(Shaw)*
11,500
Aberdeen: Snelders; McKimmie, Robertson D, Grant (Simpson), McLeish, Miller, Nicholas, Bett, Mason, Connor, Jess (Cameron).
St Mirren: Money; Wilson, Black (Godfrey), Walker, Martin, Winnie, Shaw, Kinnaird, Torfason, Davies (Lambert), Weir.

Hamilton A (0) 0
Rangers (1) 3 *(Walters 2 [1 pen], Steven T)* 9162
Hamilton A: Ferguson; McKee, Napier, Weir, Jamieson, Miller, Harris, Gordon (Donaghy), Morrison, Prentice (Carr), McDonald.
Rangers: Ginzburg; Stevens G, Munro, Brown, Wilkins, Butcher, Steven T, Ferguson I, McCoist, Johnston, Walters.

Hearts (1) 2 *(Crabbe, Robertson)*
Celtic (0) 2 *(Dziekanowski, Walker)*
25,218
Hearts: Smith; McLaren, Whittaker (Kidd), Kirkwood, Levein, McPherson, Colquhoun, MacKay, Musemic, Crabbe (Robertson), Bannon.
Celtic: Bonner; Morris, Burns, Aitken, Whyte, Grant, Galloway, McStay, Dziekanowski, Coyne, Hewitt (Walker).
(Celtic won 3-1 on penalties after extra time)

SEMI-FINALS

19 SEPT *at Hampden Park*

Rangers (3) 5 *(Steven T, Johnston, McCoist 2, Ferguson I)*
Dunfermline Ath (0) 0
41,643
Rangers: Woods; Stevens G, Munro, Gough, Wilkins (Ferguson I), Butcher, Steven T, Ferguson D, McCoist, Johnston, Walters.
Dunfermline Ath: Westwater; Robertson, Rougvie (Smith P), McCathie, Tierney, Abercromby, Farningham (Rafferty), Kozma, Jack, O'Boyle, Irons.

20 SEPT

Aberdeen (0) 1 *(Cameron)*
Celtic (0) 0
45,367
Aberdeen: Snelders; McKimmie, Robertson D, Robertson C (Grant), McLeish, Miller, Nicholas, Bett, Mason, Connor, Cameron (Van der Ark).
Celtic: Bonner; Morris, Rogan, Aitken, McCahill, Burns, Galloway, McStay, Dziekanowski, Coyne, Fulton (Miller) (Walker).

FINAL

22 OCT *at Hampden Park*

Aberdeen (1) 2 *(Mason 2)*
Rangers (1) 1 *(Walters [pen])*
61,190
after extra time
Aberdeen: Snelders; McKimmie, Robertson D, Grant (Van der Ark), McLeish, Miller, Nicholas, Bett, Mason, Connor, Jess (Irvine).
Rangers: Woods; Stevens G, Munro, Gough, Wilkins, Butcher, Steven T, Ferguson I, McCoist, Johnston, Walters (McCall).

Referee: G B Smith (Edinburgh).

SCOTTISH CUP FINALS 1874–1990

Year	Winners	Runners-up	Score
1874	Queen's Park	Clydesdale	2-0
1875	Queen's Park	Renton	3-0
1876	Queen's Park	Third Lanark	2-0 after 1-1 draw
1877	Vale of Leven	Rangers	3-2 after 0-0 and 1-1 draws
1878	Vale of Leven	Third Lanark	1-0
1879	Vale of Leven*	Rangers	
1880	Queen's Park	Thornlibank	3-0
1881	Queen's Park†	Dumbarton	3-1
1882	Queen's Park	Dumbarton	4-1 after 2-2 draw
1883	Dumbarton	Vale of Leven	2-1 after 2-2 draw
1884	Queen's Park‡	Vale of Leven	
1885	Renton	Vale of Leven	3-1 after 0-0 draw
1886	Queen's Park	Renton	3-1
1887	Hibernian	Dumbarton	2-1
1888	Renton	Cambuslang	6-1
1889	Third Lanark§	Celtic	2-1
1890	Queen's Park	Vale of Leven	2-1 after 1-1 draw
1891	Hearts	Dumbarton	1-0
1892	Celtic¶	Queen's Park	5-1
1893	Queen's Park	Celtic	2-1
1894	Rangers	Celtic	3-1
1895	St Bernard's	Renton	2-1
1896	Hearts	Hibernian	3-1
1897	Rangers	Dumbarton	5-1
1898	Rangers	Kilmarnock	2-0
1899	Celtic	Rangers	2-0
1900	Celtic	Queen's Park	4-3
1901	Hearts	Celtic	4-3
1902	Hibernian	Celtic	1-0
1903	Rangers	Hearts	2-0 after 1-1 and 0-0 draws
1904	Celtic	Rangers	3-2
1905	Third Lanark	Rangers	3-1 after 0-0 draw
1906	Hearts	Third Lanark	1-0
1907	Celtic	Hearts	3-0
1908	Celtic	St Mirren	5-1
1909	••		
1910	Dundee	Clyde	2-1 after 2-2 and 0-0 draws
1911	Celtic	Hamilton A	2-0 after 0-0 draw
1912	Celtic	Clyde	2-0
1913	Falkirk	Raith R	2-0
1914	Celtic	Hibernian	4-1 after 0-0 draw
1920	Kilmarnock	Albion R	3-2
1921	Partick T	Rangers	1-0
1922	Morton	Rangers	1-0
1923	Celtic	Hibernian	1-0
1924	Airdrieonians	Hibernian	2-0
1925	Celtic	Dundee	2-1
1926	St Mirren	Celtic	2-0
1927	Celtic	East Fife	3-1
1928	Rangers	Celtic	4-0
1929	Kilmarnock	Rangers	2-0
1930	Rangers	Partick T	2-1 after 0-0 draw
1931	Celtic	Motherwell	4-2 after 2-2 draw
1932	Rangers	Kilmarnock	3-0 after 1-1 draw
1933	Celtic	Motherwell	1-0
1934	Rangers	St Mirren	5-0
1935	Rangers	Hamilton A	2-1
1936	Rangers	Third Lanark	1-0
1937	Celtic	Aberdeen	2-1
1938	East Fife	Kilmarnock	4-2 after 1-1 draw
1939	Clyde	Motherwell	4-0
1947	Aberdeen	Hibernian	2-1
1948	Rangers	Morton	1-0 after 1-1 draw
1949	Rangers	Clyde	4-1
1950	Rangers	East Fife	3-0
1951	Celtic	Motherwell	1-0
1952	Motherwell	Dundee	4-0

Year	Winners	Runners-up	Score
1953	Rangers	Aberdeen	1-0 after 1-1 draw
1954	Celtic	Aberdeen	2-1
1955	Clyde	Celtic	1-0 after 1-1 draw
1956	Hearts	Celtic	3-1
1957	Falkirk	Kilmarnock	2-1 after 1-1 draw
1958	Clyde	Hibernian	1-0
1959	St Mirren	Aberdeen	3-1
1960	Rangers	Kilmarnock	2-0
1961	Dunfermline Ath	Celtic	2-0 after 0-0 draw
1962	Rangers	St Mirren	2-0
1963	Rangers	Celtic	3-0 after 1-1 draw
1964	Rangers	Dundee	3-1
1965	Celtic	Dunfermline Ath	3-2
1966	Rangers	Celtic	1-0 after 0-0 draw
1967	Celtic	Aberdeen	2-0
1968	Dunfermline Ath	Hearts	3-1
1969	Celtic	Rangers	4-0
1970	Aberdeen	Celtic	3-1
1971	Celtic	Rangers	2-1 after 1-1 draw
1972	Celtic	Hibernian	6-1
1973	Rangers	Celtic	3-2
1974	Celtic	Dundee U	3-0
1975	Celtic	Airdrieonians	3-1
1976	Rangers	Hearts	3-1
1977	Celtic	Rangers	1-0
1978	Rangers	Aberdeen	2-1
1979	Rangers	Hibernian	3-2 after 0-0 and 0-0 draws
1980	Celtic	Rangers	1-0
1981	Rangers	Dundee U	4-1 after 0-0 draw
1982	Aberdeen	Rangers	4-1 (aet)
1983	Aberdeen	Rangers	1-0 (aet)
1984	Aberdeen	Celtic	2-1 (aet)
1985	Celtic	Dundee U	2-1
1986	Aberdeen	Hearts	3-0
1987	St Mirren	Dundee U	1-0 (aet)
1988	Celtic	Dundee U	2-1
1989	Celtic	Rangers	1-0
1990	Aberdeen	Celtic	0-0 (aet)

(Aberdeen won 9-8 on penalties)

*Vale of Leven awarded cup, Rangers failed to appear for replay after 1-1 draw.

†After Dumbarton protested the first game, which Queen's Park won 2-1.

‡Queen's Park awarded cup, Vale of Leven failing to appear.

§Replay by order of Scottish FA because of playing conditions in first match, won 3-0 by Third Lanark.

¶After mutual protested game which Celtic won 1-0.

•• Owing to riot, the cup was withheld after two drawn games – Celtic 2-1, Rangers 2-1.

SCOTTISH CUP WINS

Celtic 29, Rangers 24, Queen's Park 10, Aberdeen 7, Hearts 5, Clyde 3, St Mirren 3, Vale of Leven 3, Dunfermline Ath 2, Falkirk 2, Hibernian 2, Kilmarnock 2, Renton 2, Third Lanark 2, Airdrieonians 1, Dumbarton 1, Dundee 1, East Fife 1, Morton 1, Motherwell 1, Partick Th 1, St Bernard's 1.

APPEARANCES IN FINAL

Celtic 46, Rangers 40, Aberdeen 13, Queen's Park 12, Hearts 10, Hibernian 10, Kilmarnock 7, Vale of Leven 7, Clyde 6, Dumbarton 6, St Mirren 6, Third Lanark 6, Dundee U 5, Motherwell 5, Renton 5, Dundee 4, Dunfermline Ath 3, East Fife 3, Airdrieonians 2, Falkirk 2, Hamilton A 2, Morton 2, Partick Th 2, Albion R 1, Cambuslang 1, Clydesdale 1, Raith R 1, St Bernard's 1, Thornibank 1.

SCOTTISH CUP 1990

FIRST ROUND

9 DEC *at Ochilview Park*

Berwick R (1) 1 *(Neil)*

Stenhousemuir (1) 1 *(McCormick)*   300

Berwick R: Neilson; Fraser, O'Donnell, Marshall, Cass, Davidson, Sloan, Neil, Tait, Callachan, Leitch.
Stenhousemuir: Paterno; Clouston, Kemp, Cairney, Tracey, Aitchison, Bell, Clark, McCormick, Walker (Quinton), Speirs (Elliott).

Brechin C (0) 3 *(Lees, Hutt, Paterson)*

Montrose (0) 1 *(Allan)*   630

Brechin C: Lawrie; Watt, Scott, Brown, Conway, Hutt, Lees, Hill, Ritchie, Sexton (Candlish), Pryde (Paterson I A).
Montrose: Larter; Brown, King, Paterson, Sheran, McGlashan, Allan, Lyons, Powell, Maver, Murray (Dolan).

Elgin City (1) 2 *(Teasdale J, McKay (pen))*

Arbroath (1) 1 *(Fotheringham)*   1542

Elgin C: Ure; McArthur, Maclennan, Mone, Cran, Mackay, Ferris, Teasdale M, Jappy, Teasdale J (Slavin), McGinlay (Bennett).
Arbroath: Jackson; Bennett W, Fleming, Mitchell, Carlin, Bennett M, Richardson, Gibson, Marshall (Dewar), Fotheringham, Gallacher (Tindal).

Queen of the S (0) 2 *(Sloan, Fraser)*

Cove Rangers (0) 1 *(Cormack)*   870

Queen of the S: Davidson; Bain (Mills), Thomson I, McCafferty, Hetherington, Sim, Andrews (Thomson A), Johnston, Gordon, Fraser, Sloan.
Cove Rangers: Beckett; Thompson (Smith), Whyte, Dobbins, Paterson A, Taylor, Cormack, Megginson, Yule, Paterson S, Duncan.

Queen's Park (0) 1 *(Rodden)*

Dumbarton (1) 2 *(McQuade J, Quinn)*   784

Queen's Park: Monaghan; Kinnie, Armstrong, Elder, McNamee, O'Brien P, Caven, O'Brien J, Elliott, McKenzie (McEntegart), Rodden (Hendry).
Dumbarton: Stevenson; McQuade A, Wharton, Dempsey, Cairney, Stevens, Hughes, Spence, Gibson, MacIver, McQuade J (Quinn).

Stirling Albion (0) 4 *(Lloyd 3, George)*

Coldstream (0) 0   500

Stirling Albion: McGeown; Mitchell, Tennant, Conway, Brown, Walker, Reid, Moore, Lloyd, McConville (George), Docherty (Gilmour).
Coldstream: Kerr; Herbert, Gilmour, Middlemiss, Mitchell, Hunter, Ritchie, Hume, Williamson, Lawson, Byrne.

FIRST ROUND REPLAY

12 DEC

Stenhousemuir (0) 1 *(Speirs)*

Berwick R (0) 0   500

Stenhousemuir: Paterno; Aitchison, Elliott, Cairney, Tracey, Kemp, Quinton, Clouston, McCormick, Walker (Bell), Speirs (Clark).

Berwick R: Neilson; Fraser, O'Donnell, Marshall, Cass, Davidson, Sloan, Neil, Tait, Callachan, Leitch.

SECOND ROUND

30 DEC

Dumbarton (0) 0

Cowdenbeath (1) 2 *(Ross 2)*   700

Dumbarton: Stevenson; McQuade A, Wharton, Dempsey, Cairney, Stevens, Quinn, Spence, Gibson, MacIver, Hughes.
Cowdenbeath: Lamont; Watt, Hamill, Malone, Archibald, Kerr, Wright, McGovern, Mailer, Ross, Scott.

Elgin City (0) 2 *(McHardy, Bennett)*

Brechin C (1) 2 *(Lees, Hutt)*   3370

Elgin City: Clark; Cran (McGinlay), Maclennan, Mone, McHardy, Mackay, Ferris, Teasdale M, Jappy, Teasdale J (Bennett), McArthur.
Brechin C: Lawrie; Conway, Scott, Brown, Brash, Hutt, Lees, Hill, Ritchie, Sexton, Pryde (Paterson I A).

Gala Fairydean (1) 2 *(Thorburn, Smith)*

Inverness Caledonian (1) 2 *(MacDonald, Polworth)*650

Gala Fairydean: Ramage; Henry, Nichol, Smith, Frizzel I, Thomson (McCormack), Collins, Frizzel R, Lochrie, Loughran, Thorburn.
Inverness Caledonian: Morrison; Davidson, McAllister, Hill (Murphy), Mann, Docherty, MacDonald (Polworth), Lisle, Urquhart, Christie, Robertson.

Stenhousemuir (0) 0

Queen of the S (0) 1 *(Gordon)*   750

Stenhousemuir: Paterno; Nelson (Aitchison), Elliott, Cairney, Tracey, Anderson, Milligan (Bell), Clouston, McCormick, Kemp, Quinton.
Queen of the S: Davidson; McGhie, Shanks, McCafferty, Hetherington, Sloan, Andrews, Johnston, Possee, Gordon, Robertson (Sim).

Stirling Albion (1) 3 *(Lloyd 2, Gilmour)*

Whitehill Welfare (0) 0   583

at Firs Park

Stirling Albion: McGeown; Mitchell, Tennant, McConville, Lawrie, Given, Reid, Moore, Lloyd, Robertson (Derek Walker), Docherty (Gilmour).
Whitehill Welfare: Frazer; Lansborough, Robertson, Mealyou, Anderson, Johnston, McCartney, Rushford, McKenna, Connachan (McGill), Livingston (Armstrong).

Stranraer (1) 1 *(Harkness)*

Kilmarnock (0) 1 *(Watter)*   3600

Stranraer: Duffy; Lowe, Lindsay, McNiven, Gallagher, McCutcheon, Ewing, Cook, Harkness, Henderson (Duncan), Spittal (McMillan).
Kilmarnock: McCulloch; Montgomerie, McLean, Cody, Flexney, MacKinnon, Callaghan, Tait, Thompson H, Burns, Watters (Jenkins).

Vale of Leithen (1) 1 *(Cross)*
East Stirling (1) 3 *(Wilson, Armstrong, Grant)* 350
Vale of Leithen: McDermott; Ross G, Graham, Bird, Armstrong, Woodburn, Ross C, Williams, Hogarth, Spence (Gaffney), McKinlay (Cormack).
East Stirling: Love; Russell, Workman, McIntosh, Branninган, Wilcox, Arthur Grant, Bateman, Durie, Wilson (Drew), Diver (Feeney).

7 JAN

Ross County (1) 1 *(Williamson)*
East Fife (1) 4 *(Brown W, Hunter, Brown I, Crolla)* 1750
Ross County: Cathcart; Somerville, Campbell, Williamson, Bellshaw, Lemmon, O'Brien (McKay), Robertson, Grant, Connelly, Stewart (Wilson).
East Fife: Charles; Bell, Taylor P, Lennox, Rogerson, Taylor P H, Mitchell (Crolla), Brown W, Hunter, Brown I, Gallacher (Hope).

SECOND ROUND REPLAYS

6 JAN

Brechin C (2) 8 *(Ritchie 3, Brown, Lees 3, Hutt)*
Elgin City (0) 0 1500
Brechin C: Lawrie; Watt, Candlish, Brown, Brash, Hutt, Lees, Hill, Ritchie, Sexton, Paterson I A.
Elgin City: Clark; Slavin, McLennan, Mone, McHardy, Mackay, Ferries, Teasdale M, Jappy, McArthur, McGinlay.

Inverness Caledonian (1) 4 *(Polwoth 3, Robertson)*
Gala Fairydean (1) 1 *(Lochrie)* 1595
Inverness Caledonian: Morrison; Davidson, Polson, Docherty, Mann, McAllister, Hill (Mackay), Lisle, Urquhart, Polworth, Robertson.
Gala Fairydean: Ramage; Henry, Nichol (Collins), Smith, Frizzel I, Thomson, Notman, Frizzel R, Lochrie, Loughran, Thorburn (McCormack).

Kilmarnock (0) 0
Stranraer (0) 0 5033
after extra time. Stranraer won 4-3 on penalties.
Kilmarnock: McCulloch; Montgomerie, Callaghan, Jenkins, Flexney, MacKinnon, Geraghty, Tait, Reilly, Burns (Curran), Watters (Thompson D).
Stranraer: Duffy; Lowe, Lindsay, McNiven, Shirkie, McCutcheon, Ewing, Cook, McMillan, Henderson (Duncan), Spittal (McInnes).

THIRD ROUND

20 JAN

Airdrieonians (1) 2 *(Harvey, Lawrence)*
Inverness Caledonian (0) 2 *(Andrew, Polwoith)* 2516
Airdrieonians: Martin; Boyle, Conn, McAdam, Auld, Speirs, Gray, Butler (Irvine), Harvey, Lawrence, MacDonald.
Inverness Caledonian: Morrison; Davidson, Mann, Docherty, Andrew, Christie, MacDonald, Lisle, Urquhart, Polworth, Robertson.

Albion R (0) 0
Clydebank (0) 2 *(Davies 2)* 984
Albion R: McCulloch; Watson, McKeown, Cadden, McTeague, Clark R, Edgar, Chapman (Lauchlan), Graham, Haddow (Cougan), Clark G.
Clydebank: Gallacher; Dickson, Rodger (Crawford), Maher, Sweeney, Coyle T, Davies, Harvey, Kelly (Caffrey), Row, Coyle O.

Ayr U (0) 0
St Mirren (0) 0 7869
Ayr U: Purdie; Scott, McCann, Furphy, McAllister, Evans, Templeton, Willock, Walker, Bryce (Wilson), Kennedy.
St Mirren: Money; Wishart, Black, Davies, Godfrey, Winnie, Lambert, Manley, Torfason, McDowall (McWalter), Kinnaird (Shaw).

Brechin C (0) 0
Hibernian (0) 2 *(Houchen, Orr)* 3007
Brechin C: Lawrie; Conway, Candlish, Brown, Brash, Scott, Lees, Hill, Ritchie, Sexton, Paterson I A.
Hibernian: Goram; Kane, Sneddon, Cooper, Hamilton (McGinlay), Hunter, Evans, Orr, Houchen, Collins, Tortolano.

Cowdenbeath (1) 3 *(Ross 2, McCutcheon (og))*
Stranraer (0) 1 *(Harkness)* 587
Cowdenbeath: Lamont; Watt, Smith, Wright (McGovern), Archibald, Kerr, Spence, Malone, Ross, Scott, Hamill.
Stranraer: Duffy; Lowe (McInnes), Lindsay (Harkness), McNiven, Gallagher, McCutcheon, McMillan, Cuthbertson, Cook, Ewing, Spittal.

Dundee (0) 0
Dundee U (0) 0 14,276
Dundee: Carson; Dinnie; Shannon, Chisholm, Forsyth, Craib, Craig, McLeod, Wright, Dodds, McSkimming.
Dundee U: Main; Bowman, Malpas, McInally, Krivokapic, Narey, Clark, Jackson, Gallacher (Hinds), Connolly (Van Der Hoorn), Paatelainan.

Dunfermline Ath (0) 0
Hamilton A (0) 0 6439
Dunfermline Ath: Westwater; Nicholl, Rougvie, McCathie, Bonnyman, Sharp, Smith P, Kozma, Jack (Smith M), Rafferty (O'Boyle), Irons.
Hamilton A: Ferguson; McKee, Napier, Hillcoat, Martin, Harris, McCluskey, McGachie, Weir, McDonald.

East Fife (1) 3 *(Hunter 3)*
Meadowbank T (1) 1 *(Armstrong)* 1100
East Fife: Charles; Bell, Taylor P, Lennox, Rogerson, Taylor P H, Mitchell (Hope), Brown W, Hunter, Brown I (Crolla), Gallacher.
Meadowbank T: McQueen; Prentice, Armstrong, Inglis, Williamson (Irvine), McCormack, Forrest (Perry), Boyd, McNaughton, Roseburgh, Sprott.

Forfar Ath (1) 1 *(Brewster)*
Celtic (1) 2 *(Morris (pen), Dziekanowski)* 8388
Forfar Ath: Allan; Brazil, Smith, Hutton, Winter, McCafferty, Hamill, Clark, Brewster, Clinging, Whyte (Leslie).

Celtic: Bonner; Morris, McCahill, Whyte, Wdowczyk, Mathie (Walker), Galloway, McStay, Fulton, Dziekanowski, Miller.

Hearts (0) 2 *(Robertson 2)*
Falkirk (0) 0 14,259
Hearts: Smith; Kidd, Whittaker, Levein, McCreery, McPherson, Colquhoun, Kirkwood, Robertson, Crabbe (Ferguson), Bannon.
Falkirk: Marshall; Melvin, Beaton, McKenzie, Burgess, Smith, Rae (Logan), Baptie, Rutherford, McCoy, McWilliams.

Morton (0) 2 *(Alexander, O'Hara)*
Raith R (2) 2 *(McDonald (og), Dalziel)* 3100
Morton: Wyllie; Collins, Pickering, Reid, O'Hara, Fowler, Ronald (Deeney), McDonald (McInnes), Alexander, McGraw, Gourlay.
Raith R: Arthur; MacLeod, Murray, Fraser, McStay, Coyle, Simpson (Ferguson), Dalziel, Logan (Macdonald), Sorbie, Nelson.

Motherwell (2) 7 *(McCart, Cooper (pen), Arnott, Russell, Bryce, Kirk, Gahagan)*
Clyde (0) 0 4077
Motherwell: Maxwell; Burley, Boyd, O'Neill (Philliben), Paterson, McCart, Gahagan, Russell, Arnott (Bryce), Kirk, Cooper.
Clyde: Ross; Knox, McVie, Rooney, Speirs, Nolan, Fairlie, McFarlane, McGlashan, McCabe, Clarke.

Partick T (2) 2 *(Campbell, Charnley (pen))*
Aberdeen (2) 6 *(Van Der Ark 3, Grant, Kerr (og), Mason)* 11,875
Partick T: Duncan; Kennedy (Mitchell), Law, Kerr, Collins, Flood, Corrie, Jardine (Craig), Campbell, Gallagher, Charnley.
Aberdeen: Watt; McKimmie, Robertson I, Grant, McLeish, Irvine, Nicholas (Jess), Simpson, Mason, Connor, Van Der Ark (Robertson C).

Queen of the S (0) 0
Alloa (0) 0 1100
Queen of the S: Davidson; McGhie, McCafferty, Mills, Hetherington, Shanks, Sloan, Sim, Gordon, Thomson I, Possee.
Alloa: Lowrie; McCulloch, Lee R, Millen, Lee D, Gibson, Hayton, Ramsay, McCallum, Lee I, Lamont (Miller).

Rangers (1) 3 *(Johnston, Brown, Walters)*
St Johnstone (0) 0 39,003
Rangers: Woods; Stevens G, Munro, Gough (Vinnicombe), Spackman, Butcher, Steven T, Walters, McCoist, Johnston, Brown.
St Johnstone: Balavage; Thomson K, McVicar, Barron, Cherry, Johnston, Moore, Curran, Maskrey, Blackie (Grant), Heddle.

29 JAN

East Stirling (0) 0
Stirling Albion (1) 1 *(Docherty)* 527
East Stirling: Watson; Russell, Workman, McIntosh, Brannigan, Purdie, Arthur Grant, Drew, McNeill, Durie, Diver (Bateman).
Stirling Albion: McGeown; Mitchell, Tennant, Walker, Lawrie, Given, Reid, Moore, Lloyd, Robertson, Docherty (George).

THIRD ROUND REPLAYS

23 JAN

Dundee U (0) 1 *(Clark)*
Dundee (0) 0 15,503
Dundee U: Main; Van Der Hoorn, Malpas, McInally, Krivokapic, Narey, Clark, O'Neill M (Bowman), Jackson, Preston, Paatelainen.
Dundee: Carson; Dinnie, Shannon, Chisholm, Forsyth, Craib (Frail), Craig, McLeod, Wright, Dodds, McSkimming (McBride).

24 JAN

Inverness Caledonian (1) 1 *(Robertson)*
Airdrieonians (1) 1 *(Gray)* 3200
after extra time; Inverness Caledonian won 5-4 on penalties
Inverness Caledonian: Morrison; Davidson, Mann, Docherty, Andrew, Christie, MacDonald, Lisle, Urquhart, Polworth, Robertson.
Airdrieonians: Martin; Boyle, Conn, McAdam, Auld, Butler, Gray, Balfour, Harvey, Lawrence, Macdonald.

St Mirren (2) 2 *(Davies, McDowall)*
Ayr U (0) 1 *(McCracken)*
St Mirren: Money; Wishart, Black, Davies, Godfrey, Manley, McGowne (Shaw), Lambert, Torfason, McDowall, Kinnaird (McWalter).
Ayr U: Purdie; Scott, McCann, Furphy, McAllister, Evans, Templeton, Willock, Shaw (McCracken), Bryce, Kennedy.

29 JAN

Alloa (2) 2 *(Irvine 2)*
Queen of the S (1) 3 *(Gordon, McGhie, Thomson A)* 1073
after extra time
Alloa: Lowrie; McCulloch, Lee R, Millen, Lee D, Gibson, Lytwyn, Ramsay, McCallum (Lamont), Lee I, Irvine (Erwin).
Queen of the S: Davidson; McGhie, Mills, McCafferty, Hetherington, Gordon, Shanks (Robertson), Thomson I, Sloan, Archer, Possee (Thomson A).

Raith R (1) 1 *(Logan)*
Morton (1) 3 *(Fowler, Alexander 2)* 2740
Raith R: Arthur; MacLeod, Murray, Fraser, McStay, Coyle (Ferguson), Simpson, Dalziel, Logan, Sorbie, Nelson.
Morton: Wyllie; Collins, Pickering, Reid, O'Hara, Hunter, McNeil (Kelly), McDonald, Alexander, McGraw, Fowler (McInness).

31 JAN

Hamilton A (0) 0
Dunfermline Ath (1) 1 *(O'Boyle)* 4200
Hamilton A: Ferguson; McKee, Napier, Hillcoat, Martin, Miller, Harris, McCluskey, Mcgachie, Weir, McDonald (Moore).
Dunfermline Ath: Westwater; Nicholl, Robertson, McCathie, Tierney, Rougvie, Smith P, Rafferty, Jack, O'Boyle, Irons (Abercromby).

FOURTH ROUND

24 FEB

Aberdeen (0) 2 *(Gillhaus, Nicholas)*
Morton (1) 1 *(Turner)* 14,500

Aberdeen: Mimms; McKimmie, Robertson I, Grant, McLeish, Irvine, Nicholas, Bett, Mason, Connor, Gillhaus.
Morton: Wyllie; Collins, Pickering, Reid, O'Hara, Hunter, Turner, McDonald (McInnes), Alexander, Fowler, McNeil (John Boag).

Hearts (3) 4 *(Robertson 2, Colquhoun, Crabbe)*
Motherwell (0) 0 19,161

Hearts: Smith; Kidd, McKinlay, Levein, McCreery (Berry), McPherson, Colquhoun, Mackay, Robertson, Crabbe (Foster), Bannon.
Motherwell: Maxwell; Burley, Boyd, O'Neill, Paterson, Philliben, MacCabe (Mair), Russell, Cusack, Kirk, Gahagan (Dolan).

Hibernian (3) 5 *(McGinlay 2, Houchen 2, Collins*
East Fife (0) 1 *(Mitchell)* 7232

Hibernian: Goram; Kane, Sneddon, Orr (Findlay), Mitchell, Hunter, McGinlay, Hamilton, Houchen, Collins, Tortolano.
East Fife: Charles; Bell (Brown I), Taylor P, Lennox, Rogerson, Taylor P H, Mitchell, Crolla, Hunter, Brown W, Gallacher (Bryce).

25 FEB

Celtic (1) 1 *(Coyne)*
Rangers (0) 0 53,000

Celtic: Bonner; Morris, Wdowczyk, Grant, Elliott, Whyte, Galloway, McStay, Dziekanowski, Coyne (Walker), Miller.
Rangers: Woods; Stevens G, Munro, Ferguson I, Spackman, Butcher, Steven T, Walters (Vinnicombe) (Dodds), McCoist, Johnston, Brown.

26 FEB

Dundee U (1) 2 *(Connolly, Paatelainan)*
Queen of the S (1) 1 *(Gordon)* 5948

Dundee U: Main; Van Der Hoorn, Malpas, McInally, Krivokapic, Narey, Connolly, McKinnon, Jackson, Preston (Bowman), Paatelainan.
Queen of the S: Davidson; Mills, McCafferty, McGhie, Thomson I, Johnston (Possee), Sim, Sloan, Thomson A, Gordon, Robertson (McGuire).

27 FEB *at Starks Park*

Cowdenbeath (0) 1 *(Wright)*
Dunfermline Ath (1) 2 *(Jack 2 (1 pen))*

Cowdenbeath: Lamont; Watt, Smith, Wright, Archibald (Malone), Kerr, Spence (Buckley), McGovern, Ross, Hamill, Scott.
Dunfermline Ath: Westwater; Nicholl, Sharp, McCathie, Tierney, Irons, Smith P, Rafferty, Jack, O'Boyle (Gallagher), Kozma.

28 FEB

St Mirren (0) 1 *(McWalter)*
Clydebank (0) 1 *(Manley (og))* 5800

St Mirren: Money; Wishart, Black, Davies, Godfrey, Manley, Martin, Lambert, Torfaso, McDowall (McWalter), Kinnaird.

Clydebank: Gallacher; Dickson, Rodger, Maher, Sweeney, Coyle, Harvey, Davies, Eadie, Rowe, Caffrey (Kelly).

Stirling Albion (3) 6 *(Lloyd 2, Reid, Docherty, Moore, Gilmour)*
Inverness Caledonian (2) 2 *(Robertson, Christie)* 3495

Stirling Albion: McGeown; Mitchell, Walker, Conway, Lawrie, Given (McConville), Reid, Moore, Lloyd (Gilmour), Robertson, Docherty.
Inverness Caledonian: Morrison; Davidson, Mann, Docherty (Hill), Andrew, Murphy, MacDonald (Mackay), Lisle, Urquhart, Christie, Robertson.

FOURTH ROUND REPLAY

12 MAR

Clydebank (2) 3 *(Eadie 2, Davies)*
St Mirren (2) 2 *(Shaw, Davies)* 6333

Clydebank: Gallacher; Dickson, Rodger, Smith, Sweeney, Coyle, Harvey, Davies, Eadie, Rowe, Kelly.
St Mirren: Money; Martin, Black, Davies, Manley, McWhirter, Shaw, Lambert, Torfason, McWalter (Kinnaird), McDowall.

QUARTER-FINALS

17 MAR

Aberdeen (1) 4 *(Bett, Gillhaus, Irvine, Nicholas)*
Hearts (1) 1 *(Colquhoun)* 22,500

Aberdeen: Mimms; McKimmie, Connor, Grant (Robertson C), McLeish, Irvine, Nicholas, Bett, Mason, Van Der Ark (Cameron), Gillhaus.
Hearts: Smith; Kidd, McKinlay, Levein, McCreery, McPherson, Colquhoun, Berry, Robertson, Crabbe (Foster), Bannon (MacKay).

Clydebank (1) 1 *(Davies)*
Stirling Albion (0) 1 *(Moore (pen))* 2595

Clydebank: Gallacher; Rowe, Rodger, Smith, Sweeney, Coyle, Harvey, Davies, Eadie, Duncanson (Caffrey), Kelly.
Stirling Albion: McGeown; Mitchell, Tennant, McConville (George), Lawrie, Woods, Gilmour, Moore, Lloyd (Conway), Robertson, Docherty.

Dundee U (1) 1 *(Jackson)*
Hibernian (0) 0 13,847

Dundee U: Main; Van Der Hoorn, Malpas, McInally, Krivokapic, Narey, McKinlay (Bowman), Clark, Jackson, Connolly, Paatelainan.
Hibernian: Goram; Kane, Sneddon, Mitchell, Hunter, Orr (Wright), Hamilton, Houchen, Collins, McGinlay (Tortolano).

Dunfermline Ath (0) 0
Celtic (0) 0 19,568

Dunfermline Ath: Westwater; Robertson, McCathie, Tierney, Rougvie, Smith, Rafferty, Jack, Irons, Kozma.
Celtic: Bonner; Morris, Wdowczyk, Rogan, Elliott, Whyte, Grant, McStay, Dziekanowski, Coyne, Miller.

QUARTER-FINALS REPLAYS

21 MAR

Celtic (2) 3 *(McStay, Coyne, Miller)*
Dunfermline Ath (0) 0   40,798
Celtic: Bonner; Morris, Wdowczyk, Rogan, Elliott, Whyte, Grant, McStay, Dziekanowski, Coyne, Miller (Walker).
Dunfermline Ath: Westwater; Robertson (Smith T), Sharp (Gallagher), McCathie, Tierney, Rougvie, Smith P, Rafferty, Jack, Irons, Kozma.

Stirling Albion (0) 0
Clydebank (0) 1 *(Kelly)*   3738
at Brockville Park
Stirling Albion: McGeown; Mitchell, Tennant, Conway (George), Lawrie, Woods, Gilmour (Reid), Walker, Lloyd, Robertson, Docherty.
Clydebank: Gallacher; McGurn, Rodger, Smith, Sweeney, Coyle, Harvey, Davies, Kelly, Rowe, Caffrey.

SEMI-FINALS

14 APR *at Hampden Park*

Celtic (1) 2 *(Walker 2)*
Clydebank (0) 0   34,768
Celtic: Bonner; Morris, Wdowczyk, Fulton, Galloway, Whyte, Grant, McStay, Dziekanowski, Walker, Miller.

Clydebank: Gallacher; Dickson, Rodger (Smith), Maher, Sweeney, Crawford (Caffrey), Harvey, Davies, Eadie, Rowe, Kelly.

at Tynecastle Park

Aberdeen (2) 4 *(Irvine, Paatelainen (og), Van Der Hoorn (og), Gillhaus)*
Dundee U (0) 0   16,581
Aberdeen: Snelders; McKimmie; Robertson D, Grant (Graham Watson), McLeish, Irvine, Nicholas (Van Der Ark), Bett, Mason, Connor, Gillhaus.
Dundee U: Main; Van Der Hoorn, Clark, McInally, Krivokapic, Narey, McKinlay, Bowman, Jackson, Connolly (French), Paatelainen.

FINAL

12 MAY *at Hampden Park*

Aberdeen (0) 0
Celtic (0) 0   60,493
after extra time; Aberdeen won 9-8 on penalties.
Aberdeen: Snelders; McKimmie, Robertson D, Grant, McLeish, Irvine, Nicholas, Bett, Mason (Graham Watson), Connor, Gillhaus.
Celtic: Bonner; Wdowczyk, Rogan, Grant, Elliott, Whyte, Stark (Galloway), McStay, Dziekanowski, Walker (Coyne), Miller.
Referee: G. B. Smith (Edinburgh).

Theo Snelders the Aberdeen goalkeeper dives to save the deciding spot kick from Anton Rogan of Celtic and the first Scottish Cup Final determined by penalty kicks is won by the Dons. (Action Images)

SPORT AND THE LAW

The Law could hardly avoid Sport during season 1989–90.

The Government called in the Home Secretary and the judiciary after Hillsborough. Takeover tussles for more than one club caused them to call in their lawyers. The Inland Revenue caused the Football League to take legal advice before pursuing its own investigation into Swindon town's off-field affairs; and a court decided that £12,000 could be the appropriate damages awarded for a foul tackle resulting in a broken leg.

This is the civil compensation remedy for which the criminal courts have now graded 18 months imprisonment for deliberate, violent, foul play at both rugby as well as soccer. The on-field hooligans cannot say that they have not been warned.

The Government also passed its Football Spectators Act 1989 during November sandwiched between Lord Justuce Taylor's Interim and Final Reports on the Hillsborough disaster. It did not come into force under 24 April 1990 by a Home Office Order.

It is not the fault of successive Government Ministers with responsibility for Sport that they are locked in the Department of the Environment, either as a Minister of State with access to Cabinet papers, or as an Under-Secretary with no such access; but in any event, never as part of the Home Office which carries the can for Law and Order.

After all the fears about the proposed Government National Football Membership Scheme, Lord Justice Taylor's Final Report exposed its impracticability for any realistic action. This was separate and apart from the basic legal flaw that it belonged to neither the company law shareholding membership or the equally well known unincorporated club members' concept.

More significantly, the Act gives courts powers to impose restriction orders on football crowd offenders convicted abroad; but it can only take effect in the United Kingdom if someone presses the button to initiate a crossover process which will bring the U.K. courts into the picture, by a technical process of laying on information or issuing a warrant for arrest. Even then, the courts have a discretion whether to restrict or not. The Act does not go as far as the drink-driven hooligan legislation which provides for *mandatory* disqualifications for convicted motorists. Why this discretion has been maintained can never be properly or rationally explained.

More positively, however, the little known or little publicised Local Government Finance Act of 1988 *for sport* was followed up in November 1989 by a Government Practice Note which re-affirms a long standing practice of Discretionary Rate Relief if sports clubs for all games do the schools' work of physically educating young people who cannot obtain adequate sports facilities because of lack of staff or equipment in the schools.

In the long term this aspect of the Law in Sport may have the most beneficial effect for sport and football's future beyond any other help which the Law alone can provide for Sport if Sport does not keep its own house in order – on the field as well as off it.

EDWARD GRAYSON

Football hooliganism erupted on the final day of the full programme of League matches; the worst incidents being recorded at Bournemouth where Leeds United followers were Involved. (Action Images)

WELSH
and
NORTHERN IRISH
FOOTBALL

LEAGUE TABLES, CUP WINNERS
AND HONOURS PAST AND PRESENT

WELSH FOOTBALL 1989–90

THE ABACUS WELSH FOOTBALL LEAGUE

National Division

	P	W	D	L	F	A	Pts
Haverfordwest County	30	19	5	6	70	25	62
Aberystwyth Town	30	18	7	5	69	31	61
Abergavenny Thur.	30	18	7	5	66	34	61
Cwmbran Town	30	19	3	8	55	33	60
Llanelli	30	16	6	8	61	38	54
Briton Ferry Athletic	30	16	6	8	58	43	54
AFC Cardiff	30	14	6	10	44	40	48
Pembroke Borough	30	13	7	10	46	38	46
Ton Pentre	30	11	6	13	44	54	39
Bridgend Town	30	9	8	13	38	49	35
Port Talbot Athletic	30	7	11	12	41	46	32
Brecon Corinthians	30	8	7	15	37	50	31
Maesteg Park Athletic	30	6	9	15	31	36	27
Ammanford Town	30	7	6	17	32	54	27
Pontllanfraith	30	3	7	20	33	73	16
Ebbw Vale	30	4	3	23	26	104	15

Premier Division

	P	W	D	L	F	A	Pts
Sully	34	24	6	4	120	38	78
Ferndale	34	22	7	5	73	34	73
Afan Lido	34	20	6	8	78	43	66
Milford United	34	19	6	9	73	38	63
Ynysybwl	34	18	5	11	67	56	59
Llanwern	34	17	5	12	62	51	56
Clydach United	34	15	8	11	63	60	53
Blaenrhondda	34	14	10	10	63	55	52
Seven Sisters	34	12	8	14	62	74	44
BP Llandarcy	34	12	7	15	48	59	43
Panteg	34	12	5	17	60	76	41
Garw	34	10	7	17	49	66	37
Morriston Town	34	10	7	17	56	81	37
Cardiff Corinthians	34	10	7	17	47	72	37
Newport YMCA	34	9	9	16	42	66	36
Caerleon	34	9	6	19	46	63	33
Tonyrefail Welfare	34	6	9	19	40	75	27
Trelewis	34	4	8	22	43	85	20

Division One

	P	W	D	L	F	A	Pts
Caldicot Town	32	20	5	7	66	32	65
Methyr Tydfil	32	21	1	10	118	50	64
Aberaman	32	18	9	5	87	43	63
Blaenavon Blues	32	20	2	10	83	49	62
Taffs Well	32	18	5	9	63	45	59
Carmarthen Town	32	16	3	13	69	56	51
South Wales Police	32	12	13	7	48	32	49
Treharris Athletic	32	15	4	13	65	41	49
Skewen Athletic	32	12	9	11	48	47	45
Pontlottyn	32	12	6	14	54	62	42
Caerau	32	11	5	16	39	74	38
Pontardawe	32	9	9	14	47	67	36
Pontyclun	32	8	10	14	57	65	34
SGIHE	32	9	6	17	40	63	33
Tondu Robins	32	9	5	18	57	68	32
Abercynon Athletic	32	7	8	17	48	90	29
Blaine West Side	32	3	4	25	28	122	13

Clydach United have withdrawn from the league for the season 1990–91. Blaina West Side failed to gain re-election. They will be replaced by Risca United and Cardiff Civil Service. AFC Cardiff and Sully have merged to form a new club – Inter Cardiff – which will play in the top division in season 1990–91. The three divisions will be retitled divisons 1, 2 and 3 in season 1990–91.

MANWEB LEAGUE

	P	W	D	L	F	A	Pts
Caersws	28	25	1	2	81	20	76
Welshpool	28	18	3	7	74	33	57
Penrhyncoch	28	17	3	8	67	37	54
Morda	28	16	3	9	58	33	51
Tywyn & Bryncrug	28	16	2	10	61	36	50
Llandrindod Wells	28	13	6	9	48	39	45
Carno	28	13	5	10	52	50	44
Knighton Town	28	13	3	12	50	59	42
Llanidloes Town	28	11	4	13	50	50	37
Talgarth	28	8	10	10	51	51	34
Newtown	28	10	4	14	36	61	34
Builth Wells	28	8	6	14	31	52	26
Aberystwyth Town***	28	7	5	16	30	63	23
Rhayader Town	28	4	3	21	23	76	15
UCW Aberystwyth	28	2	2	24	23	75	8

3 points deducted.

Caersws, Welshpool, Penrhyncoch, Carno and Llanidloes Town will join the newly-formed Cymru Alliance League in 1990–91.

League Challenge Cup – Winners: Caersws; Runners-up: Tywyn/Bryncrug.
Youth Challenge Cup – Winners: Tywyn/Bryncrug; Runners-up: Newtown.
Summer Cup – Winners: Caersws; Runners-up: Knighton.
CWFA Challenge Cup – Winners: Welshpool; Runners-up: Tywyn/Bryncrug.
J. Emrys Morgan Cup – Winners: Llangedwyn; Runners-up: Crickhowell.
CWFA Youth Cup – Winners: Newtown Yth; Runners-up: Penrhyncoch Yth.

Gwent Senior Cup
Pill A.F.C. 2, Rogerstone A.F.C. 1

Gwent Amateur Cup
Albion Rovers A.F.C. 1, Civil Service Newport A.F.C. 0

WARWICK INTERNATIONAL WELSH ALLIANCE LEAGUE

	P	W	D	L	F	A	Pts
Porthmadog	34	26	4	4	98	26	82
Bangor City	34	23	10	1	90	30	79
Connah's Quay N.	34	23	4	7	89	39	73
Nantlle Vale	34	20	7	7	81	47	67
Bethesda Athletic	34	18	6	10	89	53	60
Locomotive Llanberis	34	17	8	9	89	72	59
Flint Town United	34	16	5	13	61	54	53
Llanfairpwll	34	16	3	15	70	66	51
Conwy United	34	14	6	14	70	61	48
Llandudno	34	13	6	15	76	74	45
Y Felinheli	34	12	8	14	56	68	44
Rhyl***	34	12	6	16	45	61	39
Mochdre	34	9	7	18	49	82	34
Holywell Town***	34	8	8	18	44	68	29
Pilkingtons	34	7	7	20	53	78	28
Llanrwst United	34	6	9	19	46	85	27
Colwyn Bay	34	5	5	24	43	108	20
Caernarfon Town	34	4	5	25	38	115	17

***3 pts deducted.
Holywell Town, Porthmadog, Connah's Quay Nomads and Conwy United will join the newly-formed Cymru Alliance League in season 1990–91.

WELSH INTERMEDIATE CUP 1989–90

First Round
Locomotive Llanberis v Harlech Town	5-0
Cemaes Bay v Llangefni Town	1-2
C.P.D. Llanerchymedd v Nefyn United	4-1
Tie awarded to Nefyn United – ineligible player)	
Blaenau Amateurs v Holyhead Town	3-3, 0-5
(Tie awarded to Blaenau Amateurs – ineligible player)	
Rhydymwyn v Denbigh Town	4-1
Rhos United v Mochdre	2-5
Shotton Westminster v British Aerospace	1-0
Morda United v Penley	2-1, 1-0
Bradley Sports Club v Druids United	1-0
Bala Town v Ruthin Town	2-1
Overton Athletic v Hawkesbury Villa	5-1
Barmouth & Duffryn v Tywyn Bryncrug	1-3
Abermule v Penparcau	0-3
Welshpool Rangers v Montgomery	w/o
(Tie awarded to Montgomery – Welshpool failed to appear)	

Second Round
Llangefni Town v Landudno	2-1
Bethesda Athletic v Y Felinheli	0-2
Conwy United v Locomotive Llanberis	3-1
Nantlle Vale v Llanrug United	2-2, (aet) 3-2
Llanrwst United v Llanfairpwll PG	4-2
Connah's Quay Nomads v Buckley	1-1, 5-2
Rhydymwyn v Shotton Westminster	0-1
Mochdrew v Holywell Town	1-1, 0-2
Mostyn v Pilkington (St. Asaph)	1-1, 7-0
Morda United v Rhos Aelwyd	(aet, pens) 2-2, 8-7
Gresford Athletic v Corwen Amateurs	2-0
Overton Athletic v Llay Welfare	1-2
Brymbo Steelworks v Llay Royal B Legion	1-2
Welshpool Town v Rhostyllen M.V.	1-1, 5-0
Bradley Sports Club v Chirk A.A.A.	1-3
Cefn Albion v Penycae	1-1, 3-0
Bala Town v Lex XI	3-3, 2-3
Penparcau v Llanidloes Town	3-3, 4-0
Penrhyncoch v Montgomery	0-2
Rhayader Town v Tywyn v Tywyn & Bryncrug	2-2, 3-4
Llandrindod Wells v Knighton Town	1-2
Carno v Builth Wells	0-1
(Tie awarded to Carno – ineligible player)	
Llwydcoed Welfare v Llangeinor	0-1
A.F.C. Porth v Albion Rovers	4-1
Treorchy v Croesyceiliog	0-2

Third Round
Y Felinheli v Flint Town United	3-1
Blaenau Amateurs v Porthmadog	1-5
Connah's Quay Nomads v Holywell Town	2-0
Nantlle Vale v Conwy United	5-0
Shotton Westminster v Llanrwst United	1-2
Llangefni Town v Mostyn	2-1
Llay Royal B Legion v Lex XI	1-1, 4-5
Chirk A.A.A. v Llay Welfare	1-0
Cefn Albion v Gresford Athletic	4-7
Knighton Town v Penparcau	(aet, pens) 1-1, 6-7

Montgomery v Machynlleth	5-1
Morda United v Tywyn & Bryncrug	4-2
Carno v Welshpool Town	0-2
S. Glam Inst Higher Education v Risca United	1-1, 2-4
Taffs Well v Llantwit Fardre	4-2
A.F.C. Porth v Carmarthen Town	2-0
B.S.C. (Port Talbot) v Trelewis	4-1
Tondu Robins v Llantwit Major	2-1
Morriston Town v Bryntirion Athletic	3-3, 2-0
Newport Corinthians v Llangeninor	3-2
Afan Lido v Kenfig Hill	0-0, 1-3
Cardiff Corinthians v Caldicot Town	1-1, 4-2
Fields Park Athletic v Brecon Corinthians	0-1
Pontyclun v Treharris Athletic	3-1
A.F.C. Cardiff v Croesyceiliog	5-0
Abertillery Town v Hirwaun Welfare	2-4
Cardiff Civil Service v Porthcawl	0-4
Clydach United v Ragged School	1-3

Fourth Round
Y Felinheli v Nantlle Vale	1-2
Connah's Quay Nomads v Welshpool	1-1
Montgomery v Llangefni Town	1-1
Morda United v Llanrwst United	4-2
Penparcau v Caersws	1-5
Aberystwyth Town v Gresford Athletic	3-0
Porthmadog v Chirk A.A.A.	4-2
Lex XI v Mold Alexandra	2-3
Ragged School v Tondu Robins	3-2
Risca United v Porthcawl	2-4
Morriston Town v Abergavenny Thursdays	0-2
Pontyclun v Hirwaun Welfare	3-2
B.S.C. (Port Talbot) v Cardiff Corinthians	0-1
A.F.C. Cardiff v A.F.C. Porth	7-2
Newport Corinthians v Taffs Well	0-3
Kenfig Hill v Brecon Corinthians	3-2

Fifth Round
Llangefni Town v Cardiff Cor.	1-0
Porthcawl Town v Caersws	2-1
Aberystwyth Town v Pontyclun	5-0
Mold Alexandra v Connah's Quay	2-2, 6-2
Abergavenny Thursdays v A.F.C. Cardiff	2-3
Kenfig Hill v Nantlle Vale	1-1, 1-2
Taffs Well v Ragged School	1-4
Porthmadog v Morda United	0-0, 2-0

Quarter-Finals
Llangefni Town v Porthcawl Town	1-3
Aberystwyth Town v Mold Alexandra	0-0, 0-2
A.F.C. Cardiff v Nantlle Vale	5-1
Ragged School v Porthmadog	2-1

Semi-finals
Porthcawl Town v Mold Alexandra	2-0
A.F.C. Cardiff v Ragged School	1-2

Final
Porthcawl Town v Ragged School	0-2
(at Vetch Field, Swansea)	

ALLBRIGHT BITTER WELSH CUP 1989–90

First Round
Conwy United v Felinheli	3-3, 1-0
Porthmadog v CPD Llanerchymedd	3-0
Llanrwst United v Nantlle Vale	1-3
Llanfair PG v Bethesda Athletic	1-2
Shotton Westminster v Connah's Quay Nomads	1-7
Mostyn v Llandudno	5-2
Flint Town United v Holywell Town	4-0
Pilkington's (St. Asaph) v Rhydymwyn	3-1
Tywyn & Bryncrug v Knighton Town	3-2
Druids United v Bradley Sports Club	2-1
Brymbo Steelworks v Buckley	4-2
Mold Alexandra v Gresford Athletic	2-4
Llay Royal B Legion v British Aerospace	1-0
Bala Town v Penycae	1-2

Corwen Amateurs v Morda United	1-4
Rhos Aelwyd v Cefn Albion	(aet, pens) 1-1, 3-5
Chirk A.A.A. v Ruthin Town	2-1
Lex XI v Llay Welfare	10-0
Llanidloes Town v Rhayader Town	1-1, 2-3
Builth Wells v Llandrindod Wells	5-1
Penrhyncoch v Machynlleth	8-0
Bridgend Town v Cwmbran Town	2-2, 3-2
A.F.C. Cardiff v Tonyrefail Welfare	3-1
Pontyclun v Risca Town	2-1
Trelewis v Skewen Athletic	1-2
S. Glam. Inst Higher Educn. v Brecon Corinthians	0-3
Ferndale Athletic v Newport Y.M.C.A.	10-0
Caerau v Taffs Well	2-3
Port Talbot Athletic v Caldicot Town	1-0

Caerleon v Briton Ferry Athletic	1-4
Pontllanfraith v Abergavenny Thursdays	2-2, 2-1
(Tie awarded to Pontllanfraith – ineligible player)	
B.P. Llandarcy v Ammanford Town	0-2
Afan Lido v Abercynon Athletic	4-0
Seven Sisters v Cardiff Corinthians	3-4
Carmarthen Town v Llanwern	2-1
Haverfordwest v Sully	1-1, 2-3
Pembroke Borough v Pontardawe	0-0, 2-1
Llanelli v Milford United	2-0
Bath City v Cheltenham Town	1-1, 2-1
Stourbridge v Worcester City	0-2
A.F.C. Newport v Stroud (at Moreton)	3-1

Second Round

Pilkington's (St. Asaph) v Rhyl	1-3
Bethesda Athletic v Porthmadog	0-3
Nantlle Vale v Colwyn Bay	0-3
Conwy United v Bangor City	1-1, 0-8
Flint town United v Caernarfon Town	1-0
Penycae v Cefn Albion	2-0
Lex XI v Gresford Athletic	2-1
Connah's Quay Nomads v Llay Royal B Legion	2-1
Druids United v Chirk A.A.A.	0-1
Mostyn v Brymbo Steelworks	2-2, 1-4
Builth Wells v Caersws	0-3
Rhayader Town v Morda United	0-5
Aberystwyth Town v Penrhyncoch	3-0
Tywyn & Bryncrug v Newtown	2-0
Port Talbot Athletic v Briton Ferry Athletic	1-0
Worcester City v Ebbw Vale	4-0
Pontllanfraith v Llanelli	0-3
Bridgend Town v A.F.C. Cardiff	2-3
Sully v Maesteg Park	1-1, 1-2
Taffs Well v Ton Pentre	0-2
Skewen Athletic v Cardiff Corinthians	0-0, 1-5
Carmarthen Town v Ammanford	1-2
Pontyclun v Bath City (at Bath)	0-9
Ferndale Athletic v Pembroke Borough	0-4
A.F.C. Newport v Brecon Corinthians (at Glos.)	1-0
Afan Lido v Merthyr Tydfil (at Merthyr)	2-3

Third Round

Maesteg Park Athletic v Worcester City	1-1, 0-1
Ton Pentre v Port Talbot Athletic	0-2
Ammanford Town v Llanelli	1-3
Aberystwyth Town v Cardiff Corinthians	2-1
Swansea City v Merthyr Tydfil	0-3
Pembroke Borough v A.F.C. Cardiff	1-7
Cardiff City v A.F.C. Newport	1-0
Barry Town v Bath City	3-2
Hereford United v Connah's Quay Nomads	9-0
Porthmadog v Wrexham	1-4
Penycae v Caersws	0-2
Bangor City v Flint Town United	7-1
Brymbo Steelworks v Colwyn Bay	1-8
Morda United v Kidderminster Harriers	1-2
Tywyn & Bryncrug v Lex XI	2-1
Chirk A.A.A. v Rhyl	1-6

Fourth Round

Rhyl v Llanelli	3-1
Caersws v Tywyn & Bryncrug	3-0
Port Talbot v Cardiff City (at Cardiff)	1-4
A.F.C. Cardiff v Aberystwyth Town	2-2, 0-1
Colwyn Bay v Barry Town	0-1
Merthyr Tydfil v Bangor City	0-3
Kidderminster Harriers v Hereford United	1-3
Worcester City v Wrexham	0-1

Quarter-Finals

Caersws v Barry Town	1-2
Wrexham v Rhyl	1-1, 2-0
Cardiff City v Aberystwyth Town	2-0
Bangor City v Hereford United	1-1, 0-4

Semi-finals

Barry Town v Wrexham	0-1, 0-0
Cardiff City v Hereford United	0-3, 3-1

Final: Wrexham 1, Hereford United 2

(at the National Stadium, Cardiff, 13 May 1990). Att.: 4182.

Wrexham: O'Keefe; Salathiel, Kennedy, Reck, Beaumont, Phillips, Morgan, Thackeray, Sertori (Armstrong), Worthington, Bowden.

Scorer: Worthington.

Hereford United: Elliott; Jones M. A., Devine, Pejic, Peacock, Bradley, Jones S. (Tester), Jones M., Benbow, Robinson, Bowyer G.

Scorers: Robinson, Benbow.

Referee: John Deakin.

WELSH YOUTH CUP 1989–90

First Round

West End v Afan Lido	w/o
Mynydd Ida v Machynlleth	12-1
Wrexham Schools v Bala Town	6-1
Rhyl Vic. Club v Prestatyn Town	0-0, 2-0
Aberaman v Cogan Coronation	0-7
Caldicot Town v Treorchy Athletic	9-0
Y Felinheli v Trearddur Bay	4-0

Second Round

Caersws v Tregarron Turfs	3-3, 2-4
Cwmbran Town v West End	2-1
Caerau v Trelewis	2-2, 2-1
Hawarden Rangers v Rhyl	3-2
Mynydd Isa v Colwyn Bay	1-1, 2-0
Wrexham Schools v Rhyl Victory Club	4-1
Cogan Coronation v Caldicot Town	2-5
Llantwit Fadre v Caerleon	2-4
Briton Ferry Ath. v Abergavenny	5-3
Llanrwst United v Felinheli	4-3
Caernarfon Town v Porthmadog	2-2, 0-1

Third Round

Tregarron Turfs v Cardiff City	0-15
(at Cardiff)	

Cwmbran Town v Caerau	1-4
Hawarden Rangers v Mynydd Isa	4-1
Hereford United v Wrexham Schools	1-2
Swansea City v Caldicot Town	8-0
Caerleon v Briton Ferry Ath.	0-2
Llanrwst United v Porthmadog	3-1
Newtown v Wrexham	0-8

Quarter-Finals

Cardiff City v Caerau	7-2
Hawarden Rangers v Wrexham Schools	3-1
Swansea City v Briton Ferry Ath.	4-1
Llanrwst United v Wrexham	0-1

Semi-finals

Cardiff City v Hawarden Rangers	7-0
(at Recreation Ground, Carno)	
Swansea City v Wrexham	4-1
(at Vetch Field, Swansea)	

Final

Cardiff City v Swansea City	5-0
(at Penydarren Park, Merthyr Tydfil)	

TIB WELSH NATIONAL LEAGUE (WREXHAM AREA)

Premier Division

	P	W	D	L	F	A	Pts
Mold Alexandra	30	25	3	2	110	39	78
Wrexham	30	23	1	6	92	30	70
Llay RBL	30	18	8	4	81	39	62
Brymbo Steelworks	30	17	4	9	68	37	55
Lex XI	30	14	6	10	61	45	48
Gresford Athletic	30	14	4	12	61	49	46
Ruthin Town***	30	13	5	12	53	45	41
Corwen Amateurs	30	11	4	15	38	49	37
Chirk AAA***	30	11	7	12	42	56	37
Penycae	30	10	7	13	56	71	37
Rhos Aelwyd	30	9	5	16	47	60	32
Cefn Albion	30	8	8	14	44	69	32
Bradley Sports Club	30	9	4	17	39	60	31
Rhostyllen M. Villa	30	8	2	20	49	76	26
Buckley	30	7	3	20	41	94	24
Smithfield Athletic	30	5	5	20	43	106	20

Division 1

	P	W	D	L	F	A	Pts
Bala Town	26	18	5	3	66	30	59
Marchwiel Villa	26	18	1	7	72	42	55
Penley	26	15	6	5	70	38	51
Ruthin Town	26	12	9	5	63	36	45
Druids United	26	13	6	7	64	49	45
Llay Welfare	26	13	6	7	56	50	45
Cefn Albion	26	10	3	13	65	69	33
Brymbo Steelworks	26	10	2	14	56	62	32
Mynydd Isa	26	9	4	13	65	69	31
Overton Athletic	26	9	2	15	55	65	29
Johnstown Athletic	26	9	2	15	47	55	29
Rubery Owen R.	26	8	4	14	51	69	28
Lex XI***	26	8	6	12	52	51	27
Hawkesbury Villa	26	2	0	24	20	102	6

Division 2

	P	W	D	L	F	A	Pts
New Broughton	24	19	3	2	75	18	60
Castell Alun Colts	24	15	5	4	74	28	50
Rhos Aelwyd	24	13	5	6	68	45	44
Treuddyn Villa	24	13	4	7	77	45	43
Flint Town United	24	13	3	8	48	28	42
New Brighton Villa	24	13	2	9	71	39	41
Minera	24	13	0	11	69	54	39
Kelloggs	24	11	4	9	55	50	37
Corwen	24	9	3	12	43	61	30
Penycae***	24	6	2	16	33	67	17
Llay RBL	24	5	1	17	22	75	16
Druids United*	24	7	1	16	37	98	16
Bala Town Res	24	2	1	21	13	83	7

Division 3

	P	W	D	L	F	A	Pts
Kelloggs	18	14	3	1	58	19	45
Ruthin	18	11	6	1	46	15	39
New Broughton	18	11	2	5	48	28	35
New Broughton	18	11	2	5	48	28	35
Llangollen	18	9	4	5	48	35	31
Penley Res	18	9	0	9	38	42	27
Glynceiriog	18	7	4	7	42	43	25
Gresford Athletic	18	7	3	8	41	41	24
JCB Transmissions	18	6	2	10	37	56	20
Overton Athletic	18	2	2	14	32	63	8
Llay Welfare	18	0	2	16	19	67	2

***3 pts deducted.
*6 pts deducted.

OCS CLWYD LEAGUE

Premier Division

	P	W	D	L	F	A	Pts
Connah's Quay N.	20	15	3	2	56	17	48
Mostyn	20	15	2	3	56	23	47
Mold Alexandra 2000	20	11	1	8	39	31	34
Deeside	20	11	1	8	46	48	34
Abergele RBL	20	9	6	5	56	39	33
Saltney Town*	20	9	4	7	40	45	28
Shotton Westminster	20	7	5	8	36	46	25
Rhyl Victory Club	20	4	6	10	44	49	17
Point of Ayr	20	3	7	10	33	54	16
Pilkingtons	20	4	1	15	24	53	13
Rhydymwyn	20	2	4	14	25	47	10

Division 1

	P	W	D	L	F	A	Pts
Holywell Town	20	16	3	1	53	19	51
Connah's Quay A.	20	16	2	2	59	23	50
Meliden	20	13	0	7	56	34	39
Rhuddlan Town	20	10	5	5	59	35	35
Abbey Life	20	8	5	7	47	41	29
Llandyrnog United	20	6	5	9	43	36	23
Trefnant Village	20	6	3	11	41	50	21
Halkyn United	20	5	2	13	27	61	17
Caerwys	20	4	4	12	32	65	16
Denbigh Town‡	20	6	6	8	44	35	15
Brynford†	20	2	3	15	15	71	3

Division 2

	P	W	D	L	F	A	Pts
Nove	24	21	1	2	88	26	64
Bagillt Hotspurs	24	18	2	4	70	36	56
Abergele RBL	24	14	5	5	63	34	47
Denbigh YC	24	13	5	6	80	36	44
Kwik Save	24	13	2	9	74	48	41
Albion Social	24	12	2	10	77	32	37
Llandyrnog United	24	11	5	8	63	59	37
Denbigh Town	24	10	4	10	63	59	34
Trefnant Village	24	7	4	13	66	72	25
Rhuddlan Town*	24	8	3	13	41	55	24
Quay Aztecs	24	3	4	17	36	94	13
Prestatyn Victoria	24	3	1	20	42	122	10
Mostyn Albion	24	2	2	20	23	113	8

*3 pts deducted.
†6 pts deducted.
‡9 pts deducted.

Mostyn will join the newly-formed Cymru Alliance League in 1990–91.

SOUTH WALES AMATEUR LEAGUE

First Division

	P	W	D	L	F	A	Pts
Porthcawl Town	30	19	6	5	85	31	63
Hirwaun Welfare	30	18	7	5	80	48	61
Hoover Sports	30	18	7	5	57	35	61
AFC Cardiff	30	15	6	9	58	48	51
Cilfynydd	30	14	6	10	63	43	48
British Steel	30	13	9	8	55	40	48
Sully	30	14	6	10	69	56	48
Barry Athletic	30	13	5	12	53	55	44
Cardiff Civil Service	30	10	11	9	58	53	41
Kenfig Hill	30	12	4	14	56	64	40
Llantwit Major	30	8	11	11	34	42	35
Ynyshir & W. BC	30	9	5	16	55	82	32
Ynysddu Welfare	30	8	6	16	39	60	30
Llantwit Fadre	30	7	6	17	43	76	27
Bryntirion Athletic	30	5	4	21	30	74	19
Ton Pentre & Gelli BC	30	3	9	18	40	68	18

Continued on Page 877

NORTHERN IRISH FOOTBALL 1989–90

History was made in Northern Ireland football last season when Portadown won the Smirnoff Irish League Championship for the first time in their 66 year history – a magnificent achievement after heading the Championship table from mid-November. Their manager Ronnie McFall was nominated Manager of the Year.

McFall's professionalism and expertise earned him justifiable all-round praise. His team was dogged by injury and a lengthy suspension of striker Marty Magee, but he went shrewdly into the transfer market and obtained a number of players on loan, including Dougie Bell (Motherwell), Vic Kasule (Hamilton) and Sandy Fraser (Motherwell).

Glentoran were the chief rivals with manager Tommy Jackson winning four trophies – the Irish Cup, Budweiser Cup, Lombard and Ulster Cup and the Country Antrim Shield. Glenavon, celebrating their centenary, won the Roadferry Cup, but for Linfield it was a disastrous season. Their only triumph was in the TNT Gold Cup; they lost seven matches to arch-rivals Glentoran and failed for the first time in a decade to qualify for any of the UEFA competitions.

The depressing run culminated with the dramatic resignation of manager Roy Coyle after 14½ years of incredible success during which the team won more than 30 senior trophies. He had been subject to severe verbal criticism by fans.

And there were other managerial departures as well – Peter Dornan at Ards and Jim Platt, the former Middlesbrough goalkeeper, at Coleraine, where he has been succeeded by Willie McFaul, the former Newcastle United manager. Eric Bowyer, Cliftonville coach and distinguished ex-Linfield captain, took over at Windsor Park.

For the Irish League it was a season which brought increased sponsorship, further grants from the Football Trusts and the announcement that Manchester Utd will meet them in a match at Windsor Park as part of their centenary celebrations. An Official History of the League is also being published.

Northern Ireland's international performances can only be described as indifferent. They were eliminated from the World Cup after the 3-0 defeat by the Republic in Dublin, lost 1-0 in Belfast to Norway, but there was a glimmer of light at the end of the tunnel when the Under 21 and Under 23 matches against Israel and the Republic proved a success, producing a number of young hopefuls, and then came the refreshing 1-0 victory over World Cup finalists Uruguay. "At last I feel I am getting a settled side and I look forward now with a lot more confidence," said manager Billy Bingham, who was appointed as a FIFA Technical Officer at the World Cup.

Northern Ireland oppose Yugoslavia, Austria, Denmark and the Faroe Islands in the European Championship; an uphill task and the odds are that they will not make it to the finals in Sweden 1992.

Linfield may not have had an outstanding season, but they hit the jackpot when they accepted an invitation to play against Argentina at Windsor Park – part of the world champions' build-up to Italia 90. They did not let themselves down and fought determinedly before losing 1-0 to the South Americans.

The Irish FA also introduced a six-a-side competition sponsored by Guinness. Now this is to be enlarged, with invitations sent to English, Scottish and Republic of Ireland clubs. It will be a definite date in their calendar.

MALCOLM BRODIE

SMIRNOFF IRISH LEAGUE CHAMPIONSHIP FINAL TABLE

	P	W	D	L	F	A	Pts
Portadown	26	18	7	3	42	17	55
Glenavon	26	16	6	4	52	26	54
Glentoran	26	12	8	6	43	24	44
Linfield	26	14	2	10	54	40	44
Ballymena United	26	12	7	7	37	25	43
Bangor	26	11	5	10	26	22	28
Newry Town	26	11	4	11	42	37	37
Cliftonville	26	9	8	9	36	39	35
Larne	26	8	7	11	29	38	31
Carrick Rangers	26	8	6	12	33	36	30
Coleraine	26	8	6	12	36	44	30
Ards	26	5	6	15	25	43	21
Crusaders	26	4	8	14	27	55	20
Distillery	26	4	8	14	27	53	20

BUDWEISER CUP

Final

(Windsor Park, March 7, 1990)

Glentoran 4 *(Macartney 2, Campbell, Caskey)*

Linfield 2 *(McGaughey, Bailie)*

Glentoran: Smyth; Morrison, Heath, Devine, Moore, Bowers, Campbell, Caskey, Macartney, Douglas, Craig (Jameson).
Linfield: Dunlop; Dornan, Bailie, Doherty, Spiers, Coyle, Grattan (Baxter), McKeown, McGaughey, Kerr, Burrows.
Referee: G. Hyndes (Portadown).
Attendance: 6,000.
Previous winners: 1988: Glentoran; 1989: Glenavon.
Semi-finals Glenavon 1, Linfield 2 *(at the Oval)*

Glentoran 4, Newry Town 0 *(at Ballyskeagh)*

IRISH LEAGUE CHAMPIONSHIP WINNERS

1891	Linfield	1914	Linfield	1936	Belfast Celtic	1956	Linfield
1892	Linfield	1915	Belfast Celtic	1937	Belfast Celtic	1957	Glentoran
1893	Linfield	1920	Belfast Celtic	1938	Belfast Celtic	1958	Ards
1894	Glentoran	1921	Glentoran	1939	Belfast Celtic	1959	Linfield
1895	Linfield	1922	Linfield	1940	Belfast Celtic	1960	Glenavon
1901	Distillery	1923	Linfield	1948	Belfast Celtic	1961	Linfield
1902	Linfield	1924	Queen's Island	1949	Linfield	1962	Linfield
1903	Distillery	1925	Glentoran	1950	Linfield	1963	Distillery
1904	Linfield	1926	Belfast Celtic	1896	Distillery	1964	Glentoran
1905	Glentoran	1927	Belfast Celtic	1897	Glentoran	1965	Derry City
1906	Cliftonville/Dist	1928	Belfast Celtic	1898	Linfield	1966	Linfield
1907	Linfield	1929	Belfast Celtic	1899	Distillery	1967	Glentoran
1908	Linfield	1930	Linfield	1900	Belfast Celtic	1968	Glentoran
1909	Linfield	1931	Glentoran	1951	Glentoran	1969	Linfield
1910	Cliftonville	1932	Linfield	1952	Glenavon	1970	Glentoran
1911	Linfield	1933	Belfast Celtic	1953	Glentoran	1971	Linfield
1912	Glentoran	1934	Linfield	1954	Linfield	1972	Glentoran
1913	Glentoran	1935	Linfield	1955	Linfield	1973	Crusaders
						1974	Coleraine
						1975	Linfield
						1976	Crusaders
						1977	Glentoran
						1978	Linfield
						1979	Linfield
						1980	Linfield
						1981	Glentoran
						1982	Linfield
						1983	Linfield
						1984	Linfield
						1985	Linfield
						1986	Linfield
						1987	Linfield
						1988	Glentoran
						1989	Linfield
						1990	Portadown

LOMBARD ULSTER CUP

SECTIONAL TABLES

Section A	P	W	D	L	F	A	Pts
Glenavon	3	3	0	0	7	2	9
Linfield	3	1	1	0	3	2	4
Ards	3	1	1	1	5	7	4
Ballymena	3	0	0	3	3	7	0

Section B	P	W	D	L	F	A	Pts
Glentoran	3	3	0	0	8	1	9
Larne	3	1	1	0	4	8	4
Distillery	3	1	0	2	4	5	3
Portadown	3	0	1	2	1	3	1

Section C	P	W	D	L	F	A	Pts
Cliftonville	3	2	1	0	7	3	7
Ballyclare	3	1	0	2	2	4	5
Coleraine	3	1	1	0	8	6	4
Newry Town	3	0	1	2	3	9	1

Section D	P	W	D	L	F	A	Pts
Carrick Rangers	3	2	1	0	9	5	7
Bangor	3	1	2	0	7	4	5
Crusaders	3	1	1	1	4	5	4
Omagh Town	3	0	0	3	2	8	0

Quarter-finals

Carrick Rangers 0, Coleraine 2; Glenavon 2, Larne 0; Glentoran 3, Linfield 1; Cliftonville 3, Bangor 0.

Semi-finals

Coleraine 0, Glentoran 2; *(Windsor Park, Belfast)*
Larne 2, Portadown 1 *(The Oval, Belfast)*

Final

(at Windsor Park, Belfast, October 3, 1989)
Attendance 8,000

Glentoran 3 *(Macartney 2, Caskey)*

Glenavon 1 *(Blackledge)*

Glentoran: Smyth; McGreevy, McCaffrey, Campbell, Moore, Devine, Totten, Caskey, Macartney, Craig (Cleeland), Douglas (Mathieson).
Glenavon: Beck; McKeown, Scappaticci, McCann, Byrne, Lowry, McConville, Ferris, Blackledge, McBridge, Conville.
Referee: R. Stewart (Dunmurry).

Winners

1949	Linfield	1960	Linfield	1971	Linfield	1982	Glentoran
1950	Larne	1961	Ballymena U	1972	Coleraine	1983	Glentoran
1951	Glentoran	1962	Linfield	1973	Ards	1984	Linfield
1952		1963	Crusaders	1974	Linfield	1985	Coleraine
1953	Glentoran	1964	Linfield	1975	Coleraine	1986	Coleraine
1954	Crusaders	1965	Coleraine	1976	Glentoran	1987	Larne
1955	Glenavon	1966	Glentoran	1977	Linfield	1988	Glentoran
1956	Linfield	1967	Linfield	1978	Linfield	1989	Glentoran
1957	Linfield	1968	Coleraine	1979	Linfield		
1958	Distillery	1969	Coleraine	1980	Ballymena U		
1959	Glenavon	1970	Linfield	1981	Glentoran		

TNT GOLD CUP

FINAL SECTIONAL TABLES

Section A	P	W	D	L	F	A	Pts
Linfield	3	2	1	0	6	4	7
Bangor	3	0	3	0	2	2	3
Ballymena United	3	0	2	1	2	3	2
Cliftonville	3	0	2	1	2	3	2

Section B	P	W	D	L	F	A	Pts
Glentoran	3	2	1	0	5	2	7
Ards	3	1	1	0	4	4	4
Newry Town	3	1	0	2	5	4	3
Carrick Rangers	3	0	2	1	1	6	2

Section C	P	W	D	L	F	A	Pts
Portadown	5	4	1	0	10	2	13
Glenavon	5	4	1	0	12	3	13
Larne	5	2	1	2	8	10	7
Coleraine	5	2	0	3	6	7	6
Distillery	5	1	1	3	7	8	4
Crusaders	5	0	0	5	2	15	0

Semi-finals

Portadown 5, Glentoran 2 *(at Windsor Park)*
Linfield 1 Glenavon 0 *(at Windsor Park)*

Final

(The Oval, Belfast, November 7, 1988). Attendance 6,000

Linfield 0

Portadown 0

Linfield: Dunlop; Dornan, Easton, (Dehnoun), Doherty, Jeffrey, Coyle, Mitchell, Mooney, McGaughey, Baxter, Bailie.
Portadown: Keenan; Major, Curliss, McKeever, McCullough, Stewart, Mills, Williamson, Cunningham, Magee, Fraser, McCreadie.
Referee: F. McKnight (Newtownards).

Replay

(The Oval, November 22, 1989). Attendance 4,500

Linfield 2 *(McCallan, 23; McKeown, 63)*

Portadown 0

Linfield: Dunlop; Dornan, Mooney, Doherty, McKeown, Coyle, Bailie, Knell, Baxter, McCallan (McGaughey), Burrows.
Portadown: Keenan; Major, Curliss, McKeever, McCullough, Stewart, Davidson (Robinson), Cunningham (Williamson), Magee, Fraser, McCreadie.
Referee: F. McKnight (Newtownards).

Winners (from 1946)

1946	Celtic	1958	Coleraine	1970	Linfield	1982	Linfield
1947	Celtic	1959	Linfield	1971	Linfield	1983	Glentoran
1948	Linfield	1960	Glentoran	1972	Portadown	1984	Linfield
1949	Linfield	1961	Linfield	1973	Linfield	1985	Linfield
1950	Linfield	1962	Glentoran	1974	Ards	1986	Crusaders
1951	Glentoran	1963	Linfield	1975	Ballymena U	1987	Glentoran
1952	Portadown	1964	Derry City	1976	Coleraine	1988	Linfield
1953	Ards	1965	Linfield	1977	Glentoran	1989	Linfield
1954	Glenavon	1966	Glentoran	1978	Glentoran	1990	Linfield
1955	Linfield	1967	Linfield	1979	Portadown		
1956	Glenavon	1968	Linfield	1980	Linfield		
1957	Linfield	1969	Coleraine	1981	Cliftonville		

BASS IRISH CUP 1989–90

First Round
F.C. Enkalon v GEC (Larne)	1-1, 0-1
Armoy Utd v Dundela	0-3
Annagh Utd v Loughgall	1-5
Drumaness Mills v Crewe Utd	1-0
Star of the Sea v H and W Welders	1-8
Hanover v Crumlin	0-1
Ballyclare Comrades v Tandragee Rovers	3-0
H and W Sports v Armagh Thistle	4-0
Islandmagee v Fisher Body	3-2
Rathfriland Rangers v Institute	2-5
Dromore Amateurs v Ballynahinch Utd	0-2
Killyleagh v Annalong Swifts	3-1
UU Jordanstown v Cromac Albion	1-3
Civil Service v UU Coleraine	3-2
1st Bangor v Killymoon Rangers	2-0
Orangefield OB v Ards Rangers	1-1, 1-5
Larne Tech OB v Newtownabbey Town	2-2, 0-2
Queens University v 1st Liverpool	1-0
Armagh City v Bangor Amateur	6-3
Roe Valley v Connor	3-1
Dromara Village v Downshire	1-2
Kilmore Rec v Ballymoney Utd	3-1
Comber Rec v RUC	0-1

Second Round
1st Bangor v Downshire	2-0
Islandmagee v H and W Sports & Rec	2-4
Dundela v Newtownabbey Town	6-0
Cromac Albion v Roe Valley	3-3, 0-1
Armagh City v Barn Utd	3-3, 2-2
(5-6 pens)	
Ards Rangers v Ballynahinch Utd	3-1
Killyleagh v Ballyclare Comrades	3-3
Blue Circle v Drumaness Mills	0-6
Moyola Park v Shorts	1-1, 1-4
Loughgall v Kilmore Rec	2-1
H. & W Welders v Portstewart	1-0
GEC (Larne) v Queens University	2-0
Oxford Utd Stars v AFC	4-1
Limavady Utd v Macosquin	1-0
RUC v Saintfield Utd	4-0
Institute v Crumlin Utd	0-2
Standard Telephones v Sirocco Works	0-0, 4-1

Third Round
Oxford Utd Stars v Dundela	2-2, 3-4
Ards Rangers v H and W Sports & Rec	1-2

Fourth Round
Barn Utd v Roe Valley	4-1
Standard Telephones v H & Sports & Rec	2-0
H and W Welders v Limavady Utd	2-0
Crumlin Utd v Drumaness Mills	1-3
Ballyclare Comrades v RUC	1-1
GEC (Larne) v 1st Bangor	1-2
Shorts v Dundela	0-1

Fifth Round
Bangor v RUC	1-1, 3-0
(Replay at Clandeboye)	
Ballymena v Dungannon Swifts	1-1, 1-1
(2-4 on pens)	
Brantwood v Banbridge Town	1-2
Carrick Rangers v Coagh Utd	2-0
Chimney Corner v STC	1-0
Coleraine v Dunmurry R	2-0
Cookstown v Donegal	0-5
Crusaders v Drumaness Mills	3-1
Distillery v 1st Bangor	3-0
Glentoran v Cliftonville	1-1, 1-0
Linfield v Glenavon	1-1, 1-0
Larne v H and W Welders	1-0
Loughgall v Barn Utd	0-1
Omagh Town v Ards	0-3
Portadown v Dundela	1-0
Tobermore Utd v Newry	0-2

Sixth Round
Ards v Larne	0-2
Banbridge Town v Chimney Corner	2-1
Bangor v RUC	3-0
Carrick Rangers v Portadown	0-2
Coleraine v Crusaders	2-0
Donegal C v Linfield	1-2
Glentoran v Barn Utd	2-1
Newry Town v Dungannon Swifts	4-1

Note: rioting occurred at the Donegal Celtic v Linfield game with 48 policemen and 15 civilians injured.

Linfield and Donegal Celtic were later each fined £1,000 for spectators throwing missiles and Linfield £750 for a spectator encroaching on to the pitch.

Quarter-finals
Banbridge Town v Coleraine	0-1
Larne v Linfield	1-2
Newry Town v Glentoran	2-3
Portadown v Bangor	2-1

Semi-finals
Portadown v Coleraine	3-0
(Oval, Friday 26 April)	
Glentoran v Linfield	2-0
(Windsor Park, Saturday 7 April)	

Final

(Windsor Park, Belfast, May 5, 1990, attendance 12,000)

Glentoran 3 *(Neill (59), Douglas (83), Morrison (86))*
Portadown 0

Glentoran: Smyth; Neill, McCaffrey, Devine, Moore, Bowers, Campbell, Caskey, Macartney (Totten), Douglas, Jameson.

Portadown: Keenan; Major, Curliss, McKeever (Bell), Strain, Stewart, Mills (Cunningham), McCreadie, Cowan, Fraser, Davidson.

Referee: A. Snoddy (Carryduff).

IRISH CUP FINALS (from 1946–47)

1946–47	Belfast Celtic 1, Glentoran 0	1969–70	Linfield 2, Ballymena U 1
1947–48	Linfield 3, Coleraine 0	1970–71	Distillery 3, Derry City 0
1948–49	Derry City 3, Glentoran 1	1971–72	Coleraine 2, Portadown 1
1949–50	Linfield 2, Distillery 1	1972–73	Glentoran 3, Linfield 2
1950–51	Glentoran 3, Ballymena U 1	1973–74	Ards 2, Ballymena U 1
1951–52	Ards 1, Glentoran 0	1974–75	Coleraine 1:0:1, Linfield 1:0:0
1952–53	Linfield 5, Coleraine 0	1975–76	Carrick Rangers 2, Linfield 1
1953–54	Derry City 1, Glentoran 0	1976–77	Coleraine 4, Linfield 1
1954–55	Dundela 3, Glenavon 0	1977–78	Linfield 3, Ballymena U 1
1955–56	Distillery 1, Glentoran 0	1978–79	Cliftonville 3, Portadown 2
1956–57	Glenavon 2, Derry City 0	1979–80	Linfield 2, Crusaders 0
1957–58	Ballymena U 2, Linfield 0	1980–81	Ballymena U 1, Glenavon 0
1958–59	Glenavon 2, Ballymena U 0	1981–82	Linfield 2, Coleraine 1
1959–60	Linfield 5, Ards 1	1982–83	Glentoran 1:2, Linfield 1:1
1960–61	Glenavon 5, Linfield 1	1983–84	Ballymena U 4, Carrick Rangers 1
1961–62	Linfield 4, Portadown 0	1984–85	Glentoran 2, Coleraine 1
1962–63	Linfield 2, Distillery 1	1984–85	Glentoran 1,1, Linfield 1, 0
1963–64	Derry City 2, Glentoran 0	1985–86	Glentoran 2, Coleraine 1
1964–65	Coleraine 2, Glenavon 1	1986–87	Glentoran 1, Larne 0
1965–66	Glentoran 2, Linfield 0	1987–88	Glenavon 0, Glentoran 1
1966–67	Crusaders 3, Glentoran 1	1988–89	Ballymena U 1, Larne 0
1967–68	Crusaders 2, Linfield 0	1989–90	Glentoran 3, Portadown 0
1968–69	Ards 4, Distillery 2		

INTERNATIONAL FOOTBALL

INTERNATIONAL DIRECTORY

EUROPEAN CHAMPIONSHIP

EUROPEAN CLUB RESULTS

BRITISH AND IRISH INTERNATIONAL RESULTS
AND APPEARANCES

UNDER-21, UNDER-18 AND UNDER-16

SCHOOLS AND YOUTH FOOTBALL

SOUTH AMERICA AND OTHER
INTERNATIONAL FOOTBALL

OLYMPICS

INTERNATIONAL DIRECTORY

The latest available information has been given regarding numbers of clubs and players registered with FIFA, the world governing body. Where known, official colours are listed. With European countries, League tables show a number of signs. * indicates relegated teams, + play-offs, *+ relegated after play-offs. In Yugoslavia, drawn matches result in penalty shoot-outs, the winners receiving more points than losers.

There are 166 FIFA members. These include the four home countries, England, Scotland, Northern Ireland and Wales, dealt with elsewhere in the Yearbook; but basic details appear in this directory.

EUROPE

ALBANIA

Founded: 1932.
Number of Clubs: 49.
Number of Players: 3757.
National Colours: Red shirts, black shorts, red stockings.

International matches 1989

1 Jan, Tirana: v Greece (h) drew 1-1 *(Minga)*
8 Mar, Tirana: v England (h) lost 0-2
26 Apr, Wembley: v England (a) lost 0-5
8 Oct, Stockholm: v Sweden (a) lost 1-3 *(Kushta)*
15 Nov, Tirana: v Poland (h) lost 1-2 *(Kushta)*

League Championship wins (1945–90)

Dinamo Tirana 15; Partizan Tirana 14; 17 Nentori 8; Vlaznia 6; Labinoti 1.

Cup wins (1948–90)

Dinamo Tirana 12; Partizan Tirana 11; 17 Nentori 6; Vlaznia 5; Flamurtari 2; Labinoti 1.

Final League Table 1989–90

	P	W	D	L	F	A	Pts
Dinamo	33	19	9	5	45	22	50
Partizani	33	20	8	5	56	25	49
Flamurtari	33	15	7	11	39	27	39
17 Nentori	33	13	8	12	40	34	36
Vllaznia	33	12	9	12	45	46	33
Apolonia	33	13	7	13	42	46	30
Luftetari	33	13	5	15	31	39	30
Besa	33	7	14	12	31	47	26
Tomori	33	6	15	12	26	36	25
Lokomotiva	33	8	9	16	33	45	25
Labinoti	33	11	5	17	27	41	24
Beselidhja*	33	7	12	14	31	38	23

Beselidhja 3 points deducted, Partizani 2 and Apolonia 1.
Cup Final: Dinamo 1, Flamurtari 1 aet. Dinamo won 4-2 on penalties.
Top scorer: Majaci (Apolonia) 19.

AUSTRIA

Founded: 1904.
Number of Clubs: 1992.
Number of Players: 253,576.
National Colours: White shirts, black shorts, black stockings.

International matches 1989

24 Mar, Vienna: v Italy (H) lost 0-1
12 Apr, Graz: v Czechoslovakia (h) lost 1-2 *(Herzog)*
20 May, Leipzig: v East Germany (a) drew 1-1 *(Polster)*
31 May, Oslo: v Norway (a) lost 1-4 *(Ogris)*
14 June, Reykjavik: v Iceland (a) drew 0-0
24 Aug, Salzburg: v Iceland (h) won 2-1 *(Pfeifenberger, Zsak)*

6 Sept, Vienna: v USSR (h) drew 0-0
8 Oct, Valetta: v Malta (a) won 2-1 *(Glatzmeyer, Rodax)*
25 Oct, Istanbul: v Turkey (a) lost 0-3
15 Nov, Vienna: v East Germany (h) won 3-0 *(Polster 3 (1 pen))*

League Championship wins (1912–90)

Rapid Vienna 29; Austria/Vienna (prev. Austria/WAC, FK Austria and WAC) 19; Admira-Energie-Wacker (prev. Sportklub Admira & Admira-Energie); First Vienna 6; Tirol-Svarowski-Innsbruck (prev. Wacker Innsbruck) 7; Wiener Sportklub 3; FAC 1; Hakoah 1; Linz ASK 1; Wacker Vienna 1; WAF 1; Voest Linz 1.

Cup wins (1919–90)

Austria/WAC 23; Rapid Vienna 13; TS Innsbruck (prev. Wacker Innsbruck) 6; Admira-Energie-Wacker (prev. Sportklub Admira & Admira-Energie) 5; First Vienna 3; Linz ASK 1; Wacker Vienna 1; WAF 1; Wiener Sportklub 1, Graz 1.

Final League Table 1989–90

	P	W	D	L	F	A	Pts
Tirol	22	13	8	1	44	21	34
FK Austria	22	14	3	5	50	30	31
Admira Wacker	22	13	3	6	58	38	29
Rapid	22	11	6	5	44	30	28
Sturm Graz	22	6	11	5	23	17	23
Vienna	22	7	7	8	38	40	21
Salzburg	22	5	11	6	29	31	21
St Polten	22	7	7	8	25	31	21
Kremser	22	7	6	9	32	33	20
Vorwaerts Steyr	22	3	8	11	22	40	14
Graz	22	4	3	15	21	43	11
Wiener SC	22	4	3	15	19	46	11

Final Round

	P	W	D	L	F	A	Pts
Tirol	36	24	9	4	72	37	38
FK Austria	36	21	5	10	76	42	30
Rapid	36	17	10	9	69	52	30
Admira Wacker	36	17	8	11	79	55	28
Sturm Graz	36	10	15	11	34	30	25
Salzburg	36	10	11	11	49	52	25
St Polten	36	9	16	11	43	54	24
Vienna	36	10	9	17	51	78	19

Cup Final: FK Austria 3, Rapid 1 aet
Top scorer: Rodax (Admira Wacker) 35

BELGIUM

Founded: 1895.
Number of Clubs: 3362.
Number of Players: 289,770.
National Colours: Red shirts with tri-coloured trim, red shorts, red stockings with trim.

International matches 1989

16 Feb, Lisbon: v Portugal (a) drew 1-1 *(Gerets)*
29 Apr, Brussels: v Czechoslovakia (h) won 2-1 *(De Gryse 2)*
27 May, Brussels: v Yugoslavia: (h) won 1-0 *(Van der Linden)*
1 June, Lille: v Luxembourg (a) won 5-0 *(Van der Linden 4, Vervoort)*
8 June, Ottawa: v Canada (a) won 2-0 *(Ceulemans, De Gryse)*
24 Aug, Brugge: v Denmark (h) won 3-0 *(De Gryse, Ceulemans 2 (1 pen))*
6 Sept, Brussels: v Portugal (h) won 3-0 *(Ceulemans, Van der Linden 2)*
11 Oct, Basle: v Switzerland (a) drew 2-2 *(De Gryse, Geiger (og))*
25 Oct, Brussels: v Luxembourg (h) drew 1-1 *(Versavel)*

League Championship wins (1925–90)

CFKA Sredets (prev. CSKA Sofia, CDNA) 26; Levski Spartak (prev. Levski Sofia) 16; Slavia Sofia 6; Vladislav Varna 3; Lokomotiv Sofia 3; Trakia Plovdiv 2; AS 23 Sofia 1; Botev Plovdiv 1; SC Sofia 1; Sokol Varna 1; Saprtak Plovdiv 1, Tichka Varna 1; ZSK Sofia 1; Beroe Stara Zagora 1.

Cup wins (1946–90)

Levski Spartak (prev. Levski Sofia) 15; CFKA Sredets (prev. CSKA Sofia, CDNA) 13; Slavia Sofia 6; Lokomotive Sofia 3; Botev Plovdiv 1; Spartak Plovdiv 1; Spartak Sofia 1; Marek Stanke 1; Trakia Plovdiv 1; Spartak Varna 1; Sliven 1.

League Championship wins (1896–1990)

Anderlecht 20; Union St Gilloise 11; Standard Liège 8; Beerschot 7; FC Brugge 8; RC Brussels 6; FC Liège 5; Daring Brussels 5; Antwerp 4; Mechelen 4; Lierse SK 3; SV Brugge 3; Beveren 2; RWD Molenbeek 1.

Cup wins (1954–90)

Anderlecht 7; Standard Liège 4; FC Brugge 4; Beerschot 2; Waterschei 2; Beveren 2; Gent 2; Antwerp 1; Lierse SK 1; Racing Doornik 1; Waregem 1; SV Brugge 1; Mechelen 1; FC Liège 1.

Final League Table 1989–90

	P	W	D	L	F	A	Pts
FC Brugge	34	25	7	2	76	19	57
Anderlecht	34	24	5	5	76	21	53
Mechelen	23	19	12	3	65	14	50
Antwerp	34	15	13	6	63	32	43
Standard	34	16	10	8	54	33	42
Gent	34	12	12	10	45	39	36
Kortrijk	34	13	7	14	39	46	33
Beerschot	34	11	10	13	34	47	32
SV Brugge	34	12	7	15	46	47	31
FC Liege	34	8	12	14	35	45	28
Lierse	34	11	6	17	42	66	28
Lokeren	34	9	10	15	34	66	28
Ekeren	34	10	7	17	38	52	27
Charleroi	34	9	9	16	41	56	27
Saint-Trond	34	8	11	15	25	45	27
Waregem	34	8	9	17	35	63	25
Beveren*	34	8	8	18	32	57	24
Racing*	34	5	11	18	29	61	21

Cup Final: FC Liege 2, Ekeren 1
Top scorer: Farina (FC Brugge) 24

BULGARIA

Founded: 1923.
Number of Clubs: 4328.
Number of Players: 442,829.
National Colours: White shirts, green shorts, red stockings.

International matches 1989

21 Feb, Sofia: v USSR (h) lost 1-2 *(Kostadinov)*
22 Mar, Sofia: v West Germany (h) lost 1-2 *(Iliev)*
26 Apr, Sofia: v Denmark (h) lost 0-2
17 May, Bucharest: v Rumania (a) lost 0-1
24 Aug, Erfurt: v East Germany (a) drew 1-1 *(Jordanov)*
20 Sept, Cesena: v Italy (a) lost 0-4
11 Oct, Varna: v Greece (h) won 4-0 *(Ivanov, Bankov, Iskrenov, Stoichkov)*
15 Nov, Athens: v Greece (a) lost 0-1

Final League Table 1989–90

	P	W	D	L	F	A	Pts
CSKA Sofia	30	19	9	2	86	29	47
Levski	30	12	12	6	57	38	36
Slavia Sofia	30	13	10	7	37	29	36
Etur	30	14	7	9	51	32	35
Pirin	30	13	8	9	46	32	34
Lokomotiv Sofia	30	14	5	11	52	41	33
Botev Plovdiv	30	14	4	12	42	39	32
Gorna	30	11	8	11	28	32	30
Sliven	30	12	5	13	41	44	29
Beroe	30	10	9	11	43	48	29
Chernomoretz	30	11	7	12	36	41	29
Dounav	30	9	9	12	30	38	27
Lokomotiv Plovdiv	30	9	9	12	36	47	27
Hebar*	30	10	5	15	29	43	25
Chernomore*	30	6	4	20	28	63	16
Vratza*	30	5	5	20	25	65	15

Cup Final: Sliven 2, CSKA Sofia 0
Top scorer: Stoichkov (CSKA Sofia) 38

CYPRUS

Founded: 1934.
Number of Clubs: 87.
Number of Players: 23,000.
National Colours: Sky blue shirts, white shorts, blue and white stockings.

International matches 1989

8 Feb, Limassol: v Scotland (h) los· 23 *(Koliandris, Ioannou)*
26 Apr, Hampden Park: v Scotland (a) lost 1-2 *(Nicolaou)*
21 May, Oslo: v Norway (a) lost 1-3 *(Koliandris)*
15 Oct, Nicosia: v Malta (h) drew 0-0
28 Oct, Athens: v Yugoslavia (a) lost 1-2 *(Pittas (pen))*
18 Nov, Toulouse: v France (a) lost 0-2

League Championship wins (1935–90)

Omonia 16; Apoel 14; Anorthosis 6; AEL 5; EPA 3; Olympiakos 3; Pezoporikos 2; Chetin Kayal 1; Trast 1.

Cup wins (1935–90)

Apoel 12; Omonia 8; AEL 6; EPA 5; Anorthosis 4; Apollon 3; Trast 3; Chetin Kayal 2; Olympiakos 1; Pezoporikos 1; Salamina 1.

Final League Table 1989–90

	P	W	D	L	F	A	Pts
Apoel	26	18	5	3	46	19	41
Omonia	25	15	5	5	52	20	35
Pezoporikos	26	10	11	5	37	27	31
Aris	26	11	8	7	43	31	30
Apollon	26	11	7	8	43	28	29
AEL	26	8	11	7	31	30	27
Anortosi	26	10	7	9	20	28	27
Paralimni	26	7	12	7	39	40	26
Olympiakos	26	6	11	9	32	35	23
Apop	26	6	10	10	30	46	22
Salamina	25	6	9	10	25	31	21
Alki	26	6	9	11	27	35	21
Evagoras*	26	5	9	12	23	41	19
Ethnikos*	26	3	4	19	15	52	10

Cup Final: Salamina 3, Omonia 2
Top scorer: Gogic (Apoel) 19

CZECHOSLOVAKIA

Founded: 1906.
Number of Clubs: 5972.
Number of Players: 374,421.
National Colours: Red shirts, white shorts, blue stockings.

International matches 1989

12 Apr Graz: v Austria (a) won 2-1 *(Griga 2)*
29 Apr, Brussels: Belgium (a) lost 1-2 *(Luhovy)*
9 May, Prague: v Luxembourg (h) won 4-0 *(Griga, Skuhravy 2, Bilek)*
7 June, Berne: v Switzerland (a) won 1-0 *(Skuhravy)*
5 Sept, Nitra: v Rumania (h) won 2-0 *(Vik, Bilek)*
5 Oct, Prague: v Portugal (h) won 2-1 *(Bilek 2 (1 pen))*
25 Oct, Prague: v Switzerland (h) won 3-0 *(Skuhravy, Bilek, Moravcik)*
15 Nov. Lisbon: v Portugal (a) drew 0-0

League Championship wins (1926–90)

Sparta Prague 19; Slavia Prague 12; Dukla Prague (prev. UDA) 11; Slovan Bratislava 6; Spartak Trnava 5; Banik Ostrava 3; Inter-Bratislava 1; Spartak Hradec Kralove 1; Viktoria Zizkov 1; Zbrojovka Brno 1; Bohemians 1; Vitkovice 1.

Cup wins (1961–90)

Dukla Prague 8; Sparta Prague 7; Slovan Bratislava 5; Spartak Trnava 4; Banik Ostrava 2; Lokomotiv Kosice 2; TJ Gottwaldov 1; Dunajska Streda 1.

Final League Table 1989–90

	P	W	D	L	F	A	Pts
Sparta Prague	30	21	4	5	77	27	46
Banik Ostrava	30	16	9	5	50	24	41
Inter	30	15	6	9	55	30	36
Bohemians	30	14	7	9	43	31	35
Slovan	30	10	15	5	29	25	35
Nitra	30	15	4	11	50	37	34
Dukla Prague	30	13	7	10	42	31	33
Olomouc	30	13	6	11	40	42	32
Vitkovice	30	13	4	13	41	52	30
Slavia Prague	30	9	12	9	37	40	27
Cheb	30	11	5	14	28	34	27
Zbrojovka	30	9	8	13	38	50	26
Banska Bystrica	30	9	6	15	35	43	24
Dunajska	30	9	6	15	30	43	24
Trnava*	30	4	8	18	24	66	16
Povaszka*	30	6	2	22	25	69	14

Cup Final: Dukla Prague 1, Inter Bratislava 1
(Dukla won 5-4 on penalties aet)
Top scorer: Luhovy (Inter) 20

DENMARK

Founded: 1889.
Number of Clubs: 1510.
Number of Players: 323,605.
National Colours: Red shirts, white shorts, red stockings.

International matches 1989

8 Feb, Valetta: v Malta (a) won 2-0 *(Elstrup, Larsen H)*
10 Feb, Valetta: v Finland (n) drew 0-0
12 Feb, Valetta: v Algeria (n) drew 0-0
22 Feb, Pisa: v Italy (a) lost 0-1
12 Apr, Aalborg: v Canada (h) won 2-0 *(Elstrup, Vilfort)*
26 Apr, Sofia: v Bulgaria (a) won 2-0 *(Povlsen, Laudrup B)*
17 May, Copenhagen: v Greece (h) won 7-1 *(Laudrup B, Bartram, Nielsen K, Povlsen, Vilfort, Andersen H, Laudrup M (pen))*
7 June, Copenhagen: v England (h) drew 1-1 *(Elstrup)*
14 June, Copenhagen: v Sweden (h) won 6-0 *(Povlsen, Elstrup 2, Andersen H, Bartram, Laudrup M)*
18 June, Copenhagen: v Brazil (h) won 4-0 *(Olsen M (pen), Laudrup M 2, Olsen L)*
24 Aug, Brugge: v Belgium (a) lost 0-3
6 Sept, Amsterdam: v Holland (a) drew 2-2 *(Bartram, Heintze)*
11 Oct, Copenhagen: v Rumania (h) won 3-0 *(Nielsen K, Laudrup B, Povlsen)*
15 Nov, Bucharest: v Rumania (a) lost 1-3 *(Povlsen)*

League Championship wins (1913–89)

KB Copenhagen 15; B 93 Copenhagen 9; AB (Akademisk) 9; B 1903 Copenhagen 7; Frem 6; Esbjergs BK 5; Vejle BK 5; AGF Aarhus 5; Hvidovre 3; Brondby 3; Odense BK 3; B 1909 Odense 2; Koge BK 2; Lyngby 1.

Cup wins (1955–89)

Aarhus GF 7; Vejle BK 6; Randers Freja 3; BK 09 Odense 2; Aalborg BK 2; Esbjerg BK 2; Frem 2; B 1903 Copenhagen 2; Lyngby 2; B93 Copenhagen 1; KB Copenhagen 1; Vanlose 1; Hvidovre 1; Odense Bk 1; Brondby 1.

Final League Table 1989

	P	W	D	L	F	A	Pts
Odense	26	17	7	2	4	19	41
Brondby	26	17	4	5	52	26	38
Lyngby	26	15	8	3	48	24	38
Vejle	26	14	6	6	45	27	34
Aarhus	26	10	13	3	39	22	33
B 1903	26	8	11	7	33	28	27
Silkeborg	26	7	11	8	31	29	25
Frem	26	9	5	12	34	38	23
Naestved	26	8	7	11	35	40	23
Ikast	26	6	9	11	28	43	21
Aalborg	26	5	9	12	30	39	19
Herfolge	26	5	6	15	17	45	16
B 1913*	26	4	5	17	25	52	13
Bronshoj*	26	4	5	11	26	56	13

Cup Final: Brondby beat Ikast 6-3 on penalties after 0-0 draw.
Top scorer: Miklos Molnar (Frem) 14
Lars Jakobsen 14

ENGLAND

Founded: 1863.
Number of Clubs: 41,750.
Number of Players: 1,005,000.
National Colours: White shirts, navy blue shorts, white stockings.

FAEROE ISLANDS

Founded: 1979.
Number of Clubs: 22.
Number of Players: 3500.

Final League Table 1989

	P	W	D	L	F	A	Pts
B71	18	13	5	0	37	13	31
HB	18	8	6	4	43	30	22
B68	18	7	8	3	25	20	22
VB	18	8	5	5	33	21	21
KI	18	8	5	5	36	32	21
H36	18	8	3	7	27	26	19
GI	18	7	2	9	28	33	16
SIF	18	5	5	8	24	29	15
IF*	18	2	6	10	11	30	10
LIF*	18	0	3	15	8	38	3

Cup Final: HB 2, B71 0 *(after 1-1 draw aet)*
Top scorer: Steinthorsson (VB) 15

FINLAND

Founded: 1907.
Number of Clubs: 1140.
Number of Players: 57,732.
National Colours: White shirts, blue shorts, white stockings.

International matches 1989

11 Jan, El Mahalla: v Egypt (a) lost 12 *(Paatelainen)*
13 Jan, Cairo: v Egypt (a) lost 1-2 *(Tarkkio)*
8 Feb, Valetta: v Algeria (a) lost 0-2
10 Feb, Valetta: v Denmark (n) drew 0-0
12 Feb, Valetta: v Malta (a) drew 0-0
22 Mar, Dresden: v East Germany (a) 1-1 *(Lipponen)*
31 May, Helsinki: Holland (h) lost 0-1
24 Aug, Helsinki: Yugoslavia (h) drew 2-2 (Tarkkio, Ukkonen)
6 Sept, Helsinki: v Wales (h) won 1-0 *(Lipponen)*
4 Oct, Dortmund: v West Germany (a) lost 1-6 *(Lipponen)*
22 Oct, Port of Spain: v Trinidad & Tobago (a) won 1-0 *(Lius)*
25 Oct, Port of Spain: v Trinidad & Tobago (a) lost 0-2
15 Nov, Rotterdam: v Holland (a) lost 0-3

League Championship wins (1949–89)

Helsinki JK 7; Turun Palloseura 5; Kupion Palloseura 5; Valkeakosken Haka 4; Lahden Reipas 3; Kuusysi 3; Ilves-Kissat 2; IF Kamraterna 2; Kotkan TP 2; ÖPS Oulu 2; Torun Pyrkivä 1; IF Kronohagens 1; Helsinki PS 1; Kokkolan PV 1; IF Kamraterna 1; Vasa 1.

Cup wins (1955–89)

Valkeakosken Haka 9; Lahden Reipas 7; Kotkan TP 4; Helsinki JK 3; Mikkelin 2; Kuusysi 2; Kuopion Palloseura 2; IFK Abo 1; Drott 1; Helsinki PS 1; Pallo-Peikot 1; Ilves Tampere 1; Rovaniemi PS 1.

Final League Table 1989

	P	W	D	L	F	A	Pts
Kuusysi	27	17	7	3	51	23	41
TPS Turku	27	15	9	3	46	21	39
Rovaniemi	27	12	10	5	45	27	34
Haka	27	12	6	9	38	30	30
HJK	27	11	7	9	36	28	29
Ilves	27	10	6	11	45	43	26
Kups	27	12	5	10	39	37	29
Reipas Lahti	27	11	5	11	56	48	27
Oulu	27	7	8	12	31	43	22
Mikkeli	27	7	8	12	34	50	22
KePS*	27	2	10	15	27	66	14
Jaro*	27	3	5	19	27	39	11

Cup Final: Kups 3, Haka 2
Top scorer: Lius (Kuusysi) 15

FRANCE

Founded: 1919.
Number of Clubs: 22,829.
Number of Players: 1,608,470.
National Colours: Blue shirts, white shorts, red stockings.

International matches 1989

7 Feb, Dublin: v Rep of Ireland (a) drew 0-0
8 Mar, Hampden Park: v Scotland (a) lost 0-2
29 Apr, Paris: v Yugoslavia (h) drew 0-0
16 Aug, Stockholm: v Sweden (a) won 4-2 *(Cantona 2, Papin 2)*
5 Sept, Oslo: v Norway (a) drew 1-1 *(Papin (pen))*
11 Oct, Paris: v Scotland (h) won 3-0 *(Deschamps, Cantona, Nicol (og))*
18 Nov, Toulouse: v Cyprus (h) won 2-0 *(Deschamps, Blanc)*

League Championship wins (1933–90)

Saint Etienne 10; Olympique Marseille 6; Stade de Reims 6; Nantes 6; AS Monaco 5; OGC Nice 4; Girondins Bordeaux 4; Lille OSC 3; FC Sete 2; Sochaux 2; Racing Club Paris 1; Roubaix-Tourcoing 1; Strasbourg 1; Paris St Germain 1.

Cup wins (1918–90)

Olympique Marseille 10; Saint Etienne 6; Lille OSC 5; Racing Club Paris 5; Red Star 5; AS Monaco 4; Olympique Lyon 3; Girondins Bordeaux 3; CAS Genereaux 2; Nancy 2; OGC Nice 2; Racing Club Strasbourg 2; Sedan 2; FC Sete 2; Stade de Reims 2; SO Montpellier 2; Stade Rennes 2; Paris St Germain 2; AS Cannes 1; Club Français 1; Excelsior Roubaix 1; Le Havre 1; Olympique de Pantin 1; CA Paris 1; Sochaux 1; Toulouse 1; Bastia 1; Nantes 1; Metz 1.

Final League Table 1989–90

	P	W	D	L	F	A	Pts
Marseille	38	22	9	7	75	34	53
Bordeaux	38	22	7	9	51	25	51
Monaco	38	15	16	7	38	24	46
Sochaux	38	17	9	12	46	39	43
Paris-SG	38	18	6	14	50	48	42
Auxerre	38	14	13	11	49	40	41
Nantes	38	13	14	1	42	34	40
Lyon	38	14	11	13	43	41	39
Toulouse	38	13	12	13	39	39	38
Brest	38	15	8	15	39	44	38
Cannes	38	12	12	14	44	50	36
Toulon	38	12	11	15	35	50	35
Montpellier	38	12	10	16	49	48	34
Metz	38	8	18	12	33	36	34
St. Etienne	38	11	12	15	38	46	34
Caen	38	12	10	16	34	48	34
Lille	38	12	9	17	43	52	33
Nice	38	9	13	16	34	48	31
Paris Racing*	38	10	10	18	39	59	30
Mulhouse*	39	9	10	19	42	58	28

Cup Final: Montpellier 2, Paris Racing 1 (aet)
Top scorer: Papin (Marseille) 30

EAST GERMANY

Founded: 1948.
Number of Clubs: 5771.
Number of Players: 577,700.
National Colours: White shirts, blue shorts, white stockings.

International matches 1989

13 Feb, Cairo: v Egypt (a) won 4-0 (Kirsten 2, Thom 2)
8 Mar, Athens: v Greece (a) lost 2-3 *(Halata, Thom)*
22 Mar, Dresden: v Finland (h) drew 1-1 *(Trautmann)*
12 Apr, Magdeburg: v Turkey (h) lost 0-2
26 Apr, Kiev: v USSR (a) lost 0-3
20 May, Leipzig: v Austria (h) drew 1-1 *(Kirsten)*
24 Aug, Erfurt: v Bulgaria (h) drew 1-1 *(Kirsten)*
6 Sept, Reykjavik: v Iceland (a) won 3-0 *(Sammer, Ernst, Doll)*
8 Oct, Karl-Marx-Stadt: v USSR (h) won 2-1 *(Thom, Sammer)*
25 Oct, Maletta: v Malta (a) won 4-0 *(Doll 2, Steinmann 2 (1 pen))*
15 Nov, Vienna: v Austria (a) lost 0-3

League Championship wins (1950–90)

Dynamo Berlin 10; Dynamo Dresden 7; ASK Vorwaerts 6; Wismut Krl-Marx-Stadt 4; FC Magdeburg 4; Carl Jena (prev. Motor Jena) 3; Chemie Leipzig 2; Turbine Erfurt 2; Turbine Halle 1; Zwickau Horch 1; Empor Rostock 1; ZSG Halle 1; Planitz 1.

Cup wins (1949–90)

Dynamo Dresden 7; Carl Zeiss Jena (prev. Motor Jena) 5; Lokomotive Leipzig 5; FC Magdeburg 4; Dynamo Berlin 3; Chemie Leipzig 2; Magdeburg Aufbau 2; Motor Zwickau 2; ASK Vorwaerts 2; Dresden Einheit SC 1; Dresden VP 1; Halle Chemie SC 1; North Dessau Waggonworks 1; Thale EHW 1; Union East Berlin 1; Wismut Karl-Marx Stadt 1; Sachsenring Zwickau 1.

Final League Table 1989–90

	P	W	D	L	F	A	Pts
Dynamo Dresden	26	12	12	2	47	26	36
Magdeburg	26	14	7	5	42	21	35
Karl-Marx-Stadt	26	13	9	4	34	23	35
FC Berlin	26	9	12	5	38	35	30
Carl Zeiss Jena	26	11	8	7	29	27	30
Hansa Rostock	26	9	9	8	38	33	27
Cottbus	26	10	7	9	36	37	27
Lokomotiv Leipzig	26	9	7	10	34	33	25
Chemie Halle	26	8	8	10	38	38	24
Brandenburg	26	6	12	8	35	37	24
Rot-Weiss Erfurt	26	5	9	12	27	40	19
Eisenhuttenstadt	26	2	14	10	22	31	18
Wismut Aue*	26	5	8	13	25	36	18
Bischofswerda*	26	7	2	17	22	50	16

Cup Final: Dynamo Dresden 2, Schwerin 1
Top scorer: Gutschow (Dynamo Dresden) 18

WEST GERMANY

Founded: 1900.
Number of Clubs: 21,510.
Number of Players: 4,765,146.
National Colours: White shirts, black shorts, white stockings.

International matches 1989

22 Mar, Sofia: v Bulgaria (a) won 2-1 *(Voller, Littbarski)*
26 Apr, Rotterdam: v Holland (a) drew 1-1 *(Riedle)*
31 May, Ninian Park: v Wales (a) drew 0-0
6 Sept, Dublin: v Rep Ireland (a) drew 1-1 *(Dorfner)*
4 Oct, Dortmund: v Finland (h) won 6-1 *(Moller 2, Littbarski, Klinsmann, Voller, Matthaus (pen))*
15 Nov, Cologne: v Wales (h) won 2-1 *(Voller, Hassler)*

League Championship wins (1903–90)

Bayern Munich 12; IFC Nuremberg 9; Schalke 04 7; SV Hamburg 6; Borussia Moenchengladbach 5; VfB Leipzig 3; VfB Stuttgart 3; Sp Vgg Furth 3; Borussia Dortmund 3; IFC Cologne 3; Viktoria Berlin 2; Hertha Berlin 2; Hanover 96 2; Dresden SC 2; IFC Kaiserslautern 2; SV Werder Bremen 2; Munich 1860 1; Union Berlin 1; FC Freibourg 1; Phoenix Karlsruhe 1; Karlsruhe FV 1; Holstein Kiel 1; Fortuna Dusseldorf 1; Rapid Vienna 1; VfB Mannheim 1; Rot-Weiss Essen 1; Eintracht Frankfurt 1; Eintracht Brunswick.

Cup wins (1935–90)

Bayern Munich 8; IFC Cologne 4; Eintracht Frankfurt 4; IFC Nuremberg 3; SV Hamburg 3; Dresden SC 2; Fortuna Dusseldorf 2; Karlsruhe SC 2; Munich 1860 2; Schalke 04 2; VfB Stuttgart 2; Borussia Moenchengladbach 2; Borussis Dortmund 2; First Vienna 1; VfB Leipzig 1; Kickers Offenbach 1; Rapid Vienna 1; Rot-Weiss Essen 1; SW Essen 1; Werder Bremen 1; Bayer Uerdingen 1; IFC Kaiserslautern 1.

West Germany 1990 World Cup winners: Back row left to right: Thomas Berthold, Bodo Illgner, Jurgen Kohler, Guido Buchwald, Rudi Voller, Klaus Augenthaler; Front: Pierre Littbarski, Andreas Brehme, Thomas Hassler, Jurgen Klinsmann, Lothar Matthaus. (ASP)

Final League Table 1989–90

	P	W	D	L	F	A	Pts
Bayern Munich	34	19	11	4	64	28	49
Cologne	34	17	9	8	54	43	43
E. Frankfurt	34	15	11	8	61	40	43
Dortmund	34	15	11	8	51	35	41
Leverkusen	34	12	15	7	40	32	39
Stuttgart	34	15	6	13	53	47	36
Werder Bremen	34	10	14	10	49	41	34
Nuremberg	34	11	11	12	42	46	33
F. Dusseldorf	34	10	12	12	41	41	32
Karlsruhe	34	10	12	12	32	39	32
Hamburg	34	13	5	16	39	46	31
Kaiserslautern	34	10	11	13	41	55	31
St. Pauli	34	9	13	12	31	46	31
Uerdingen	34	10	10	14	41	48	30
Moenchengladbach	34	11	8	15	37	45	30
Bochum	34	11	7	16	44	53	29
Mannheim*	34	10	6	18	36	53	26
Homburg*	34	8	8	18	33	51	24

Cup Final: Kaiserslautern 3, Werder Bremen 2
Top scorer: Andersen (Eintracht Frankfurt) 18

GREECE

Founded: 1926.
Number of Clubs: 3678.
Number of Players: 282,550.
National Colours: White shirts, blue shorts, white stockings.

International matches 1989

18 Jan, Tirana: v Albania (a) drew 1-1 *(Tsiantakis)*
25 Jan, Athens: v Portugal (h) lost 1-2 *(Bormpokis)*
8 Feb, Athens: v England (h) lost 1-2 *(Saravakos (pen))*
22 Feb, Athens: v Norway (h) won 4-2 *(Samaras, Vakalopoulos, Tsalouhidis, Saravakas)*
8 Mar, Athens: v East Germany (h) won 3-2 *(Saravakos 2, Wahl (og))*
29 Mar, Athens: v Turkey (h) lost 0-1
5 Apr, Athens: v Yugoslavia (h) lost 1-4 *(Mitropoulos)*
26 Apr, Athens: v Rumania (h) drew 0-0
17 May, Copenhagen: Denmark (a) lost 1-7 *(Samaras)*
24 Aug, Oslo: v Norway (a) drew 0-0
5 Sept, Warsaw: v Poland (a) lost 0-3
20 Sept, Novi Sad: v Yugoslavia (a) lost 0-3
11 Oct, Varna: v Bulgaria (a) lost 0-4
25 Oct, Budapest: v Hungary (a) drew 1-1 *(Borbokis)*
15 Nov, Athens: v Bulgaria (h) won 1-0 *(Noblias)*

League Championship wins (1928–90)

Olympiakos 25; Panathinaikos 15; AEK Athens 8; Aris Salonika 3; PAOK Salonika 2; Larissa 1.

Cup wins (1932–90)

Olympiakos 19; Panathinaikos 11; AEK Athens 9; PAOK Salonika 2; Aris Salonika 1; Ethnikos 1; Iraklis 1; Panionios 1; Kastoria 1; Larissa 1; Ofi Crete 1.

Final League Table 1989–90

	P	W	D	L	F	A	Pts
Panathinaikos	34	21	11	2	75	35	53
AEK Athens	34	20	10	4	64	18	50
PAOK	34	19	8	7	51	31	46
Olympiakos	34	18	9	7	60	37	45
Iraklis	34	14	11	9	43	35	39
Ofi Crete	34	16	4	14	52	41	36
Aris Salonika	34	11	13	10	37	40	35
Larissa	34	12	10	12	35	38	34
Levadiakos	34	12	8	14	34	45	32
Panionios	34	8	14	12	43	52	30
Doxa	34	9	11	14	35	39	29
Panserraikos	34	9	11	14	30	42	29
Xanthi	34	12	5	17	33	51	29
Apollon	34	8	12	14	39	36	28
Ionikos	34	8	12	14	27	47	28
Kalamaria*	34	7	13	14	30	38	27
Volos*	34	10	2	22	32	63	22
Ethnikos*	34	7	6	21	20	52	20

Cup Final: Olympiakos 4, Ofi Crete 2
Top scorer: Mavros (Panionios) 22

HOLLAND

Founded: 1889.
Number of Clubs: 7912.
Number of Players: 978,324.
National Colours: Orange shirts, white shorts, orange stockings.

International matches 1989

4 Jan, Tel Aviv: v Israel (a) won 2-0 *(Wouters, Van Loen)*
22 Mar, Eindhoven: v USSR (h) won 2-0 *(Van Basten, Koeman R (pen))*
26 Apr, Rotterdam: v West Germany (h) drew 1-1 *(Van Basten)*
31 May, Helsinki: v Finland (a) won 1-0 *(Kieft)*
6 Sept, Amsterdam: v Denmark (h) drew 2-2 *(Koeman R, Wouters)*
11 Oct, Wrexham: v Wales (a) won 2-1 *(Rutjes, Bosman)*
15 Nov, Rotterdam: v Finland (h) won 3-0 *(Bosman, Koeman E, Koeman R (pen))*
20 Dec, Rotterdam: v Brazil (h) lost 0-1

League Championship wins (1898–1990)

Ajax Amsterdam 23; Feyenoord 13; PSV Eindhoven 11; HVV The Hague 8; Sparta Rotterdam 6; Go Ahead Deventer 4; HBS The Hague 3; Willem II Tilburg 3; RCH Haarlem 2; RAP 2; Heracles 2; ADO The Hague 2; Quick The Hague 1; BVV Scheidam 1; NAC Breda 1; Eindhoven 1; Enschede 1; Volewijckers Amsterdam 1; Limburgia 1; Rapid JC Haarlem 1; DOS Utrecht 1; DWS Amsterdam 1; Haarlem 1; Be Quick Groningen 1; SVV Scheidam 1; AZ 67 Alkmaar 1.

Cup wins (1899–1990)

Ajax Amsterdam 11; PSV Eindhoven 7; Feyenoord 6; Quick The Hague 4; AZ 67 Alkmaar 3; HEC 3; Sparta Rotterdam 3; DFC 2; Fortuna Geleen 2; Haarlem 2; HBS The Hague 2; RCH 2; VOC 2; Wageningen 2; Willem II Tilburg 2; FC Den Haag 2; Concordia Rotterdam 1; CVV 1; Eindhoven 1; HVV The Hague 1; Longa 1; Quick Njimegen 1; RAP 1; Roermond 1; Schoten 1; Velocitas Breda 1; Velocitas Groningen 1; VSV 1; VUC 1; VVV Groningen 1; ZFC 1; NAC Breda 1; Twente Enschede 1; Utrecht 1.

Final League Table 1989–90

	P	W	D	L	F	A	Pts
Ajax	34	19	11	4	67	23	49
PSV Eindhoven	34	20	8	6	94	36	48
Twente	34	16	10	8	48	34	42
Vitesse	34	15	11	8	49	31	41
Roda	34	14	13	7	53	39	41
Volendam	34	15	9	10	43	38	39
Fortuna Sittard	34	12	14	8	42	35	38
RKC	34	13	11	10	45	47	37
Groningen	34	10	15	9	50	46	35
Den Haag	34	13	7	14	58	63	33
Feyenoord	34	9	13	12	51	45	31
Sparta	34	12	7	15	51	61	31
Willem II	34	7	13	14	42	49	27
Utrecht	34	8	11	15	27	45	27
MVV	34	7	13	14	38	61	27
NEC*	34	5	16	13	32	55	26
Den Bosch*	34	6	13	15	30	51	25
Haarlem*	34	4	7	23	22	74	15

Cup Final: PSV Eindhoven 1, Vitesse 0
Top scorer: Romario (PSV Eindhoven) 23

HUNGARY

Founded: 1901.
Number of Clubs: 2503.
Number of Players: 129,087.
National Colours: Red shirts, white shorts, green stockings.

International matches 1989

8 Mar, Budapest: v Rep of Ireland (h) drew 0-0
12 Apr, Budapest: v Malta (h) drew 1-1 *(Boda (pen))*
26 Apr, Tarente: v Italy (a) lost 0-4
3 June, Dublin: v Rep of Ireland (a) lost 0-2
6 Sept, Belfast: v N. Ireland (a) won 2-1 *(Kovacs K, Bognar G)*
11 Oct, Budapest: v Spain (h) drew 2-2 *(Pinter 2)*
25 Oct, Budapest: v Greece (h) drew 1-1 *(Szekeres)*
15 Nov, Seville: v Spain (a) lost 0-4

League Championship wins (1901–90)

Ferencvaros (prev. FRC) 23; MTK-VM Budapest (prev. Hungaria, Bastay and Vörös Lobogo) 19; Ujpest Dozsa 19; Honved 11; Vasas Budapest 6; Csepel 3; Raba Györ (prev. Vasas Györ) 3; BTC 2; Nagyvarad 1.

Cup wins (1910–90)

Ferencvaros (prev. FRC) 14; MTK-VM Budapest (prev. Hungaria, Bastay and Vörös Lobogo) 9; Ujpest Dozsa 7; Raba Györ (prev. Vasas Györ) 4; Vasas Budapest 3; Honved 3; Diösgyör 2; Bocskai 1; III Ker 1; Kispesti AC 1; Soroksar 1; Szolnoki MAV 1; Siofok Banyasz 1; Bekescsaba 1; Pecs 1.

* *Cup not held regularly until 1964*

Final League Table 1989–90

	P	W	D	L	F	A	Pts
Ujpest Dozsa	30	18	4	8	43	20	58
MTK VM	30	18	4	8	48	26	58
Ferencvaros	30	13	9	8	48	34	48
Pecs	30	13	9	8	37	23	48
Tatabanya	30	13	4	13	24	28	43
Veszprem	30	10	11	9	27	24	41
Siofok	30	10	9	11	31	34	39
Vasas	30	10	9	11	35	42	39
Videoton	30	9	11	10	26	30	38
Bekescsaba	29	10	7	12	25	33	37
Raba Eto	30	7	14	9	34	30	35
Vac	29	8	11	10	29	30	35
Honved	30	9	8	13	31	39	35
Debrecen	30	7	14	9	20	30	35
Haladas*	30	9	6	15	33	46	33
Csepel*	30	5	10	15	27	49	25

Cup Final: Pecs 2, Honved 0
Top scorer: Dzurjak (Ferencvaros) 18

ICELAND

Founded: 1929.
Number of Clubs: 82.
Number of Players: 19,400.
National Colours: Blue shirts, white shorts, blue stockings.

International matches 1989

31 May, Moscow: v USSR (a) drew 1-1 *(Askelsson)*
14 June, Reykjavik: v Austria (h) drew 0-0.
24 Aug, Salzburg: v Austria (a) lost 1-2 *(Margeirsson)*
6 Sept, Reykjavik: v East Germany (h) lost 0-3
20 Sept, Reyjavik: v Turkey (h) won 2-1 *(Petursson 2)*

League Championship wins (1912–89)

KR 20; Valur 19; Fram 17; IA Akranes 12; Vikingur 4; IBK Keflavik 3; IBV Vestmann 2; KA Akureyri 1.

Cup wins (1960–89)

KR 7; Fram 7; IA Akranes 5; Valur 5; IBV Vestmann 3; IBA Akureyri 1; Vikingur 1; IBK Keflavik 1.

Final League Table 1989

	P	W	D	L	F	A	Pts
KA Akureyri	18	9	7	2	29	15	34
FH	18	9	5	4	26	16	32
Fram	18	10	2	6	22	16	32
KR Reykjavik	18	8	5	5	28	22	29
Valur	18	8	4	6	21	15	28
IA Akranes	18	8	2	8	19	20	26
Thor	18	4	6	8	20	30	18
Vikingur	18	4	5	9	24	31	17
Filkyr*	18	5	2	11	18	31	17
IB Keflavik*	18	3	6	9	18	29	15

Cup Final: Fram 3, KR Reykjavik 1
Top scorer: Magnusson (FH) 12

REPUBLIC OF IRELAND

Founded: 1921.
Number of Clubs: 3503.
Number of Players: 33,028.
National Colours: Green shirts, white shorts, green stockings.

International matches 1989

8 Mar, Budapest: v Hungary (a) drew 0-0
26 Apr, Dublin: v Spain (h) won 1-0 *(Michel (og))*
27 May, Dublin: v Malta (h) won 2-0 *(Houghton, Moran)*
3 June, Dublin: v Hungary (h) won 2-0 *(McGrath, Cascarino)*
6 Sept, Dublin: v West Germany (h) drew 1-1 *(Stapleton)*
11 Oct, Dublin: v N. Ireland (h) won 3-0 *(Whelan, Cascarino, Houghton)*
15 Nov, Valetta: v Malta (a) won 2-0 *(Aldridge 2 (1 pen))*

League Championship wins (1922–90)

Shamrock Rovers 24; Shelbourne 7, Bohemians 7; Dundalk 7; Waterford 6; Cork United 5; Drumcondra 5; St Patrick's Athletic 4; Cork United 3; Cork Athletic 2; Sligo Rovers 2; Limerick 2; Athlone Town 2; Dolphin 1; Cork Hibernians 1; Cork Celtic 1; Derry City 1.

Cup wins (1922–90)

Shamrock Rovers 23; Dundalk 8, Drumcondra 5; Bohemians 4; Shelbourne 3; Cork Athletic 2; Cork United 2; St James's Gate 2; St Patrick's Athletic 2; Cork Hibernians 2; Limerick 2; Waterford 2; Alton United 1; Athlone Town 1; Cork 1; Fordsons 1; Transport 1; Finn Harps 1; Home Farm 1; Sligo 1; UCD 1; Derry City 1; Bray Wanderers 1.

Final League Table 1989–90

	P	W	D	L	F	A	Pts
St. Patrick's	33	22	8	3	51	22	52
Derry City	33	20	9	4	72	18	49
Dundalk	33	17	8	8	50	26	42
Shamrock R	33	16	8	9	45	37	40
Cork City	33	14	7	12	35	24	35
Bohemians	33	14	7	12	35	32	35
Shelbourne	33	10	13	10	39	39	33
Galway Utd	33	10	9	14	39	61	29
Limerick City	33	7	8	18	28	50	22
Athlone Town	33	5	12	16	28	53	22
Drogheda Utd*	33	5	8	20	20	44	18
UCD*	33	6	5	22	25	61	17

Cup Final: Bray Wanderers 3, St Francis 0
Top scorer: Ennis (St. Patrick's) 19

ITALY

Founded: 1898.
Number of Clubs: 20,117.
Number of Players: 1,129,667.
National Colours: Blue shirts, white shorts, blue stockings, white trim.

International matches 1989

22 Feb, Pisa: v Denmark (h) won 1-0 *(Bergomi)*
24 Mar, Vienna: v Austria (a) won 1-0 *(Berti)*
29 Mar, Sibiu: v Rumania (a) lost 0-1
22 Apr, Verona: v Uruguay (h) drew 1-1 *(Baggio)*
26 Apr, Tarente: v Hungary (h) won 4-0 *(Vialli, Ferri, Berti, Carnevale)*
20 Sept, Cesena: v Bulgaria (h) won 4-0 *(Baggio 2, (1 pen) Carnevale, Iliev og)*
14 Oct, Bologna: v Brazil (h) lost 0-1
11 Nov, Vicenza: v Algeria (h) won 1-0 *(Serena)*
15 Nov, Wembley: v England (a) drew 0-0
21 Dec, Cagliari: v Argentina (h) drew 0-0

League Championship wins (1898–1990)

Juventus 22; Inter-Milan 13; AC Milan 11; Genoa 9; Torino 8; Pro Vercelli 7; Bologna 7; Fiorentina 2; Napoli 2; AS Roma 2; Casale 1; Novese 1; Cagliari 1; Lazio 1; Verona 1.

Cup wins (1922–90)

Juventus 8; AS Roma 6; Torino 4; Fiorentina 4; AC Milan 4; Inter-Milan 3; Napoli 3; Sampdoria 3; Bologna 2; Atalanta 1; Genoa 1; Lazio 1; Vado 1; Venezia 1.

Final League Table 1988–89

	P	W	D	L	F	A	Pts
Internazionale	34	26	6	2	67	19	58
Napoli	34	18	11	5	57	28	47
AC Milan	34	16	14	4	61	25	46
Juventus	34	15	13	6	51	36	43
Sampdoria	34	14	11	9	43	25	39
Atalanta	34	11	14	9	37	32	36
Fiorentina	34	12	10	12	44	43	34
Roma	34	11	12	11	33	40	34
Lecce	34	8	15	11	25	35	31
Lazio	34	5	19	10	23	32	29
Verona	34	5	19	10	18	27	29
Ascoli	34	9	11	14	30	41	29
Cesena	34	8	13	13	24	39	29
Bologna	34	8	13	13	26	43	29
Torino*	34	8	11	15	37	49	27
Pescara*	34	5	17	12	28	43	27
Pisa*	34	6	11	17	17	39	23
Como*	34	6	10	18	24	49	22

N.B. Play-off for UEFA Cup place, in Perugia: Fiorentina 1 Roma 0

Cup Final: Napoli – Sampdoria 1-0, 0-4
Top Scorer: Serena (Internazionale) 22

Final League Table 1989–90

	P	W	D	L	F	A	Pts
Napoli	34	21	9	4	57	31	51
Milan	34	22	5	7	56	27	49
Internazionale	34	17	10	7	55	21	44
Juventus	34	15	14	5	56	36	44
Sampdoria	34	16	11	7	46	26	43
Roma	34	14	13	7	45	40	41
Atalanta	34	12	11	11	36	43	35
Bologna	34	9	16	9	29	36	34
Lazio	34	8	15	11	34	33	31
Bari	34	6	19	9	34	37	31
Genoa	34	6	17	11	27	31	29
Fiorentina	34	7	14	13	41	42	28
Cesena	34	6	16	12	26	36	28
Lecce	34	10	8	16	29	46	28
Udinese*	34	6	15	13	37	51	27
Verona*	34	6	13	15	27	44	25
Cremonese*	34	5	13	16	29	50	23
Ascoli*	34	4	13	17	29	43	21

Cup Final: Juventus – AC Milan 0-0, 1-0
Top scorer: Van Basten (AC Milan) 19

LIECHTENSTEIN

Founded: 1933.
Number of Clubs: 7.
Number of Players: 1300.
National Colours: Blue & red shirts, red shorts, blue stockings.

No international matches 1989

Liechtenstein has no national league. Teams compete in Swiss regional leagues.

LUXEMBOURG

Founded: 1908.
Number of Clubs: 199.
Number of Players: 23,252.
National Colours: Red shirts, white shorts, blue stockings.

International matches 1989

9 May, Prague: v Czechoslovakia (a) lost 0-4
1 June, Lille: v Belgium (n) lost 0-5
11 Oct, Sarrebrucken: v Portugal (n) lost 0-3
25 Oct, Brussels: v Belgium (a) drew 1-1 *(Hellers)*
15 Nov, St Gallen: v Switzerland (a) lost 1-2 *(Malget)*

League Championship wins (1910–90)

Jeunesse Esch 21; Spora Luxembourg 11; Stade Dudelange 10; Red Boys Differdange 6; US Hollerich-Bonnevoie 5; Fola Esch 5; Avenir Beggen 4; US Luxembourg 4; Aris Bonnevoie 3; Progres Niedercorn 3.

Cup wins (1922–90)

Red Boys Differdange 16; Jeunnesse Esch 9; Spora Luxembourg 8; US Luxembourg 8; Stade Dudelange 4; Progres Niedercorn 4; Fola Esch 3; Avenir Beggen 3; Alliance Dudelange 2; US Rumelange 2; Aris Bonnevoie 1; US Dudelange 1; Jeunesse Hautcharage 1; National Schiffige 1; Racing Luxembourg 1; SC Tetange 1; Hesperange 1.

Final League Table 1989–90

Qualifying	P	W	D	L	F	A	Pts
Avenir Beggen	18	14	3	1	57	12	31
Union	18	12	3	3	38	17	27
Fola Esch	18	7	8	3	23	14	22
Spora	18	9	4	5	28	23	22
Jeunnesse Esch	18	6	9	3	23	20	21
Grevenmacher	18	6	5	7	21	22	17
Red Boys	18	4	8	6	25	18	16
Aris	18	4	6	8	11	27	14
Hesperange	18	1	4	13	14	44	6
Alliance*	18	0	4	14	12	55	4

Play-offs	P	W	D	L	F	A	Pts
Union	10	7	2	1	37	6	29.5
Avenir Beggen	10	5	2	3	26	16	27.5
Jeunesse Esch	10	7	2	1	19	12	26.5
Spora	10	3	3	4	14	15	20
Fola Esch	10	2	1	7	12	33	16
Grevenmacher	10	0	2	8	8	41	10.5

Cup Final: Hesperange 7, Differdange 1 (after 3-3 draw)
Top scorer: Krähen (Avenir Beggen) 30

MALTA

Founded: 1900.
Number of Clubs: 242.
Number of Players: 4024.
National Colours: Red shirts, white shorts, red stockings.

International matches 1989

11 Jan, Valetta: v Israel (h) lost 1-2 *(Carabott)*
22 Jan, Valetta: v Spain (h) lost 0-2
8 Feb, Valetta: v Denmark (h) lost 0-2
10 Feb, Valetta: v Algeria (h) lost 0-1
12 Feb, Valetta: v Finland (h) drew 0-0
23 Mar, Seville: v Spain (a) lost 0-4
12 Apr, Budapest: v Hungary (a) drew 1-1 *(Busuttil)*
26 Apr, Valetta: v Northern Ireland (h) lost 0-2
27 May, Dublin: v Rep of Ireland (a) lost 0-2
8 Oct, Valetta: v Austria (h) lost 1-2 *(Zarb)*
15 Oct, Nicosia: v Cyprus (a) drew 0-0
25 Oct, Valetta: v East Germany (h) lost 0-4
15 Nov, Valetta: v Rep of Ireland (h) lost 0-2

League Championship wins (1910–90)

Floriana 24; Sliema Wanderers 22; Valletta 13; Hibernians 6; Hamrun Spartans 5; Rabat Ajax 2; St George's 1; KOMR 1.

Cup wins (1935–90)

Sliema Wanderers 17; Floriana 16; Valletta 5; Hibernians 5; Hamrun Spartans 5; Gzira United 1; Melita 1; Zurrieq 1; Rabat Ajax 1.

Final League Table 1989–90

	P	W	D	L	F	A	Pts
Valetta	16	13	2	1	28	6	28
Sliema Wanderers	16	11	2	3	35	11	24
Hamrun	16	10	3	3	37	13	23
Hibernians	16	10	3	3	30	12	23
Floriana	16	8	1	7	24	17	17
Naxxar Lions	16	2	7	7	17	27	11
Zurrieq	16	2	5	9	13	30	9
Zebbug	16	2	1	13	7	45	5
Tarxien	16	1	2	13	8	38	4

Cup Final: Sliema Wanderers 1, Birkirkara 0
Top scorer: Zarb (Valetta)

NORTHERN IRELAND

Founded: 1880.
Number of Clubs: 1,555.
Number of Players: 24,558.
National Colours: Green shirts, white shorts, green stockings.

NORWAY

Founded: 1902.
Number of Clubs: 3449.
Number of Players: 298,400.
National Colours: Red shirts, white shorts, blue & white stockings.

International matches 1989

22 Feb, Athens: v Greece (a) lost 2-4 *(Bratseth, Sorloth)*
2 May, Oslo: v Poland (h) lost 0-3
21 May, Oslo: v Cyprus (h) won 3-1 *(Osvold, Sorloth, Bratseth)*
31 May, Oslo: v Austria (h) won 4-1 *(Halle, Fjortoft, Loken, Kojedal)*
14 June, Oslo: v Yugoslavia (h) lost 1-2 *(Fjortoft)*
24 Aug, Oslo: v Greece (h) drew 0-0
5 Sept, Oslo: v France (h) drew 1-1 *(Bratseth)*
11 Oct, Sarajevo: v Yugoslavia (a) lost 0-1
25 Oct, Kuwait: v Kuwait (a) drew 2-2 *(Sorloth, Fjortoft)*
15 Nov, Hampden Park: v Scotland (a) drew 1-1 *(Johnsen)*

League Championship wins (1938–89)

Fredrikstad 9; Viking Stavanger 7; Lillestroem 6; Rosenborg Trondheim 5; Valerengen 4; Larvik Turn 3; Brann Bergen 2; Lyn Oslo 2; IK Start 2; Friedig 1; Fram 1; Skeid Odo 1; Strömgodset Drammen 1; Moss 1.

Cup wins (1902–89)

Odds Bk, Skien 11; Fredrikstad 10; Lyn Oslo 8; Skeid Oslo 8; Sarpsborg FK 6; Brann Bergen 5; Orn F Horten 4; Lillestroem 4; Rosenborg Trondheim 4, Viking Stavanger 4; Frigg 3; Stromgodset Drammen 3; Mjondalens F 3; Mercantile 2, Grane Nordstrand 1; Kvik Halden; Sparta 1; Gjovik 1; Bodo-Glimt 1; Valerengen 1; Moss 1; Tromso 1; Byrne 1.
(Until 1937 the cup-winners were regarded as champions.)

Final League Table 1989

	P	W	D	L	F	A	Pts
Lillestrom	22	16	4	2	31	13	52
Rosenborg	22	13	5	4	56	29	44
Tromso	22	11	4	7	36	25	37
Molde	22	11	4	7	40	32	37
Kongsvinger	22	10	4	8	34	25	34
Viking Stavanger	22	9	4	9	36	33	31
Brann	22	9	3	10	28	32	30
Moss	22	7	5	10	35	36	26
Start	22	5	8	9	26	34	23
Valerengen	22	7	2	13	29	52	23
Sogndal*	22	4	6	12	31	45	18
Mjondalen*	22	4	3	15	23	50	15

Cup Final: Viking 2, Molde 2 aet. Viking 2, Molde 1
Top scorer: Jakobsen (Rosenborg) 18

POLAND

Founded: 1923.
Number of Clubs: 5881.
Number of Players: 317,442.
National Colours: White shirts, red shorts, white & red stockings.

International matches 1989

8 Feb, San Jose: v Costa Rica (a) won 4-2 *(Warzycha K 2, Kosecki, Urban)*
13 Feb, Guatemala: v Guatemala (a) won 1-0 *(Warzycha K)*
14 Feb, Puebla: v Mexico (a) lost 1-3 *(Kosecki)*
12 Apr, Warsaw: v Rumania (h) won 2-1 *(Urban, Tarasiewicz)*
2 May, Oslo: v Norway (a) won 3-0 *(Furtok 2, Wdowczyk)*
7 May, Stockholm: v Sweden (a) lost 1-2 *(Tarasiewicz)*
3 June, Wembley: v England (a) lost 0-3
24 Aug, Lublin: v USSR (h) drew 1-1 *(Wodowczyk)*
5 Sept, Warsaw: v Greece (h) 3-0 *(Warzycha K, Dziekanowski, Ziober)*
20 Sept, Coruna: v Spain (a) lost 0-1
11 Oct, Chorzow: v England (h) drew 0-0
25 Oct, Chorzow: v Sweden (h) lost 0-2
15 Nov, Tirana: Albania (a) won 2-1 *(Tarasiewicz, Ziober)*

League Championship wins (1921–90)

Gornik Zabrze 14; Ruch Chorzow 13; Wisla Krakow 6; Cracovia 5; Pogon Lwow 4; Legia Warsaw 4; Lech Poznan 3; Warta Poznan 2; Polonia Bytom 2; Stal Mielec 2; Widzew Lodz 2; Garbarnia Krakow 1; Polonia Warsaw 1; LKS Lodz 1; Slask Wroclaw 1; Szombierki Bytom 1.

Cup wins (1951–90)

Legia Warsaw 9, Gornik Zabrze 6; Zaglebie Sosnowiec 4; Lech Poznan 3; Ruch Chorzow 2, Slask Wroclaw 2; Gwardia Warsaw 1; LKS Lodz 1; Polonia Warsaw 1; Wisla Krakow 1; Stal Rzeszow 1; Arka Gdynia 1; Lechia Gdansk 1; Widzew Lodz 1; GKS Katowice 1.

Final League Table 1989–90

	P	W	D	L	F	A	Pts
Lech Poznan	30	13	12	5	46	26	42
Zaglebie Lubin	30	14	10	6	37	23	40
Katowice	30	12	14	4	31	17	40
Bydgoszcz	30	13	7	10	36	25	37
Gornik Zabrze	30	13	10	7	37	27	36
Olimpia	30	12	10	8	35	23	35
Legia Warsaw	30	10	16	4	27	18	35
LKS Lodz	30	12	10	8	34	30	33
Wisla Krakow	30	8	12	10	32	33	31
Slask Wroclaw	30	8	10	12	30	34	26
Ruch Chorzow	30	8	9	13	31	36	25
Stal Mielec	30	8	10	12	27	38	25
Sosnowiec	30	6	12	12	22	36	22
Motor Lublin	30	6	13	11	18	35	22
Widzew Lodz*	30	4	12	14	23	40	17
Bialystok*	30	3	13	14	19	45	14

One extra point for victories over three goals; one deducted for defeats conceding over three goals.
Cup Final: Legia Warsaw 2, Katowice 0
Top scorer: Jusnowiak (Lech Poznan) 18

PORTUGAL

Founded: 1914.
Number of Clubs: 1605.
Number of Players: 55,499.
National Colours: Red shirts, white shorts, red stockings.

International matches 1989

25 Jan, Athens: v Greece (a) won 2-1 *(Nunes, Paneira)*
16 Feb, Lisbon: v Belgium (h) drew 1-1 *(Paneira)*
29 Mar, Lisbon: v Angola (h) won 6-0 *(Oliveira, Frederico 2, Andre, Nunes, Semedo)*
26 Apr, Lisbon: v Switzerland (h) won 3-1 *(Joao Pinto, Frederico, Paneira)*
8 June, Rio de Janeiro: v Brazil (a) lost 0-4
31 Aug, Setubal: v Rumania (h) drew 0-0
6 Sept, Brussels: v Belgium (a) lost 0-3
20 Sept, Neuchatel: v Switzerland (a) won 2-1 *(Futre, Rui Aguas)*
5 Oct, Prague: v Czechoslovakia (a) lost 1-2 *(Rui Aguas)*
11 Oct, Sarrebrucken: v Luxembourg (a) won 3-0 *(Rui Aguas 2, Rui Barros)*
15 Nov, Lisbon: v Czechoslovakia (h) drew 0-0

League Championship wins (1935-90)

Benfica 28; Sporting Lisbon 16; FC Porto 11; Belenenses 1.

Cup wins (1939-90)

Benfica 21; Sporting Lisbon 11; FC Porto 6; Boavista 3; Belenenses 3; Vitoria Setubal 2; Academica Coimbra 1; Leixoes Porto 1; Sporting Braga 1; Amadora 1.

Final League Table 1989-90

	P	W	D	L	F	A	Pts
Porto	34	27	5	2	72	16	59
Benfica	34	23	9	2	76	18	55
Sporting	34	17	12	5	42	24	46
Guimaraes	34	17	11	6	46	28	45
Chaves	34	12	14	8	38	38	38
Belenenses	34	16	4	14	32	33	36
Setubal	34	14	8	12	39	34	36
Boavista	34	13	8	13	49	36	34
Tirsense	34	7	16	11	21	32	30
Maritimo	34	7	15	12	25	38	29
Beira Mar	34	10	9	15	22	39	29
Braga	34	8	12	14	32	42	28
Estrela Amadora	34	10	8	16	35	34	28
Nacional	34	7	14	13	34	46	28
Penafiel	34	9	8	17	24	50	26
Uniao Madeira*	34	5	14	15	24	45	24
Portimonense*	34	7	7	20	30	57	21
Farense*	34	5	10	19	25	57	20

Cup Final: Amadora 2, Farense 0 (after 1-1 draw aet)
Top scorer: Magnusson (Benfica) 33

RUMANIA

Founded: 1908.
Number of Clubs: 5453.
Number of Players: 179,987.
National Colours: Yellow shirts, blue shorts, red stockings.

International matches 1989

29 Mar, Sibiu: v Italy (h) won 1-0 *(Sabau)*
12 Apr, Warsaw: v Poland (a) lost 1-2 *(Sabau)*
26 Apr, Athens: v Greece (a) drew 0-0
17 May, Bucharest: v Bulgaria (h) won 1-0 *(Popescu)*
31 Aug, Setubal: v Portugal (a) drew 0-0
5 Sept, Nitra: v Czechoslovakia (a) lost 0-2
11 Oct, Copenhagen: v Denmark (a) lost 0-3
15 Nov, Bucharest: v Denmark (h) won 3-1 *(Balint 2, Sabau)*

League Championship wins (1910-90)

Steaua Bucharest (prev. CCA) 14; Dinamo Bucharest 13; Venus Bucharest 7; CSC Temesvar 6; UT Arad 6; Ripensia Temesvar 4; Uni Craiova 3; Petrolul Ploesti 3; Rapid Bucharest 2; Olimpia Bucharest 2; CAC Bucharest 2; Arges Pitesti 2; Soc RA Bucharest 1; Prahova Ploesti 1; CSC Brasov 1; Juventus Bucharest 1; SSUD Reita 1; Craiova Bucharest 1; Progresul 1; Ploesti United 1; Unirea Tricolor 1.

Cup wins (1934-90)

Steaua Bucharest (prev. CCA) 17; Rapid Bucharest 9; Dinamo Bucharest 7; Uni Craiova 4; UT Arad 2; Progresul 2; Ripensia 2; ICO Oradeo 1; Metal Ochimia Resita 1; Petrolul Ploesti 1; Stinta Cluj 1; Stinta Timisoara 1; Turnu Severin 1; Chimia Rannicu 1; Jiul Petroseni 1; Poli Timisoara 1.

Final League Table 1989-90

	P	W	D	L	F	A	Pts
Dinamo	34	26	5	3	96	23	57
Steaua	34	26	4	4	89	30	56
Uni. Craiova	34	19	6	9	56	27	44
Petrolul	34	17	7	10	54	40	41
Timisoara	34	17	7	10	65	40	41
Sibiu	34	16	4	14	52	42	36
Brasov	34	13	9	12	42	57	35
Corvinul	34	14	4	16	37	56	32
Farul	34	11	9	14	54	54	31
Bihor	34	13	4	17	61	59	30
Sportul	34	12	6	16	43	57	30
Arges	34	13	3	18	38	45	29
Uni. Cluj	34	10	9	15	40	60	29
Jiul	34	12	5	17	41	54	29
Bacau	34	12	5	17	43	56	29
Flacara	34	10	8	16	37	48	28

Victoria and Olt were withdrawn, there record expunged and opponents awarded points.
Cup Final: Dinamo 6, Steaua 4
Top scorer: Balint (Steaua) 19

SAN MARINO

Founded: 1931.
Number of Clubs: 17.
Number of Players: 920.
Colours: Blue and white.

No International results 1989

SCOTLAND

Founded: 1873.
Number of Clubs: 6,148.
Number of Players: 139,000.
National Colours: Dark blue shirts, white shorts, red stockings.

SPAIN

Founded: 1913.
Number of Clubs: 30,920.
Number of Players: 343,657.
National Colours: Red shirts, dark blue shorts, black stockings, yellow trim.

International matches 1989

22 Jan, Valetta: v Malta (a) won 2-0 *(Michel, Beguiristain)*
8 Feb, Belfast: v Northern Ireland (a) won 2-0 *(Andrinua, Manolo)*
23 Mar, Seville: v Malta (h) won 4-0 *(Michel 2, (1 pen), Manolo 2)*
26 April, Dublin: v Rep of Ireland (a) lost 0-1
20 Sept, Coruna: v Poland (h) won 1-0 *(Michel)*.
11 Oct, Budapest: v Hungary (a) drew 2-2 *(Julio Salinas, Michel)*
15 Nov, Seville: v Hungary (h) won 4-0 *(Manolo, Butragueno, Juanito, Fernando)*
13 Dec, Tenerife: v Switzerland (h) won 2-1 *(Michel (pen), Felice)*

League Championship wins (1945-90)

Real Madrid 25; Barcelona 10; Atletico Madrid 8; Athletic Bilbao 8; Valencia 4; Real Sociedad 2; Real Betis 1; Seville 1.

794

Cup wins (1902–90)
Athletic Bilbao 23; Barcelona 22; Real Madrid 16; Atletico Madrid 6; Valencia 5; Real Union de Irun 3; Seville 3; Real Zaragoza 3; Espanol 2; Arenas 1; Ciclista Sebastian 1; Racing de Irun 1; Vizcaya Bilbao 1; Real Betis 1; Real Sociedad 1.

Final League Table 1989–90

	P	W	D	L	F	A	Pts
Real Madrid	38	26	10	2	107	38	62
Valencia	38	20	13	5	67	42	53
Barcelona	38	23	5	10	83	39	51
Atletico Madrid	38	20	10	8	55	35	50
Real Sociedad	38	15	14	9	43	35	44
Sevilla	38	18	7	13	64	46	43
Logrones	38	18	5	15	47	51	41
Osasuna	38	14	12	12	42	42	40
Zaragoza	38	16	8	14	52	52	40
Mallorca	38	11	17	10	36	34	39
Oviedo	38	12	15	11	41	46	39
Bilbao	38	11	15	12	37	39	37
Gijon	38	12	10	16	37	34	34
Castellon	38	9	14	15	30	48	32
Cadiz	38	12	6	20	28	63	30
Valladolid	38	8	14	16	31	41	30
Malaga†	38	9	10	19	23	50	28
Tenerife†	38	8	10	20	42	60	26
Celta*	38	5	12	21	24	51	22
Rayo Vallecano*	38	6	7	25	32	75	19

Cup Final: Barcelona 2, Real Madrid 0
Top scorer: Sanchez (Real Madrid) 38

SWEDEN

Founded: 1904.
Number of Clubs: 3400.
Number of Players: 437,000.
National Colours: Yellow shirts, blue shorts, yellow and blue stockings.

International matches 1989
26 Apr, Wrexham: v Wales (a) won 2-0 *(Schiller, Ratcliffe (og))*
7 May, Stockholm: v Poland (h) won 2-1 *(Ljung, Larsson N)*
31 May, Orebro: Algeria (h) won 2-0 *(Ingesson 2)*
14 June, Copenhagen: v Denmark (a) lost 0-6
16 June, Copenhagen: v Brazil (n) won 2-1 *(Rehn, Ljung (pen))*
16 Aug, Stockholm: v France (h) lost 2-4 *(Lindqvist, Thern)*
6 Sept, Stockholm: v England (h) drew 0-0
8 Oct, Stockholm: v Albania (h) won 3-1 *(Magnusson, Ingesson, Engqvist)*
25 Oct, Chorzow: v Poland (a) won 2-0 *(Larsson P, Ekstrom)*

League Championship wins (1896–89)
Oergryte IS Gothenburg 14; Malmo FF 13; IFK Norrköping 12; IFK Gothenburg 11; Djurgaarden 8; AIK Stockholm 8; GAIS Gothenburg 6; IF Halsingborg 5; Boras IF Elfsborg 4; Oster Vaxjo 4; Halmstad 2; Atvidaberg 2; IFK Ekilstuue 1; IF Gavic Brynas 1; IF Gothenburg 1; Fassbergs 1; Norrköping IK Sleipner 1.

Cup wins (1941–89)
Malmo FF 13; AIK Stockholm 4; IFK Norrköping 4; IFK Gothenburg 3; Atvidaberg 2; Kalmar 2; GAIS Gothenburg 1; IF Halsinborg 1; Raa 1; Landskroma 1; Oster Vaxjo 1; Djurgaarden 1.

Final League Table 1989–90

	P	W	D	L	F	A	Pts
Malmo	22	12	7	3	35	11	31
Norrkoping	22	12	5	5	45	24	29
GAIS Gothenburg	22	9	8	5	31	20	26
Orebro	22	10	6	6	25	21	26
Halmstad	22	11	3	8	30	31	25
Djurgaarden	22	9	5	8	23	24	23
IFK Gothenburg	22	9	4	9	34	29	22
AIK Stockholm	22	5	11	6	26	29	21
Orgryte	22	6	9	7	19	28	21
Brage	22	6	5	11	22	31	17
Sundsvall*	22	4	5	13	30	40	13
Vastra Frolund*	22	3	4	15	24	56	10

Play-offs: Malmo beat GAIS Gothenburg 3-2 on aggregate; Norrkopoing beat Orebro 4-1 on aggregate; *Final:* Malmo 2, Norrkoing 0; Norrkoping 1, Malmo 0.
Deciding game: Norrkoping 0, Malmo 0 (Norrkoping won 4-3 on penalties).
Cup Final: Djurgaarden 3, Hacken 0
Top scorer: Hellstrom (Norrkoping) 13

SWITZERLAND

Founded: 1895.
Number of Clubs: 1480.
Number of Players: 182,953.
National Colours: Red shirts, white shorts, red stockings.

International matches 1989
26 Apr, Lisbon: v Portugal (a) lost 1-3 *(Zuffi)*
7 June, Berne: v Czechoslovakia (h) lost 0-1
21 June, Basle: v Brazil (h) 1-0 *(Turkyilmaz (pen))*
20 Sept, Neuchatel: v Portugal (h) lost 1-2 *(Turkyilmaz (pen))*
11 Oct, Basle: v Belgium (h) drew 2-2 *(Knup, Turkyilmaz)*
25 Oct, Prague: v Czechoslovakia (a) lost 0-3
15 Nov, Sion: v Luxembourg (h) won 2-1 *(Bonvin, Turkyilmaz)*
13 Dec, Tenerife: v Spain (a) lost 1-2 *(Knup)*

League Championship wins (1898–90)
Grasshoppers 21; Servette 15; Young Boys Berne 11; FC Zurich 9; FC Basle 8; Lausanne 7; La Chaux-de-Fonds 3; FC Lugano 3; Winterthur 3; FX Aarau 2; Neuchatel Xamax 2; FC Anglo-American 1; St Gallen 1; FC Brühl 1; Cantonal-Neuchatel 1; Biel 1; Bellinzona 1; FC Etoile La Chaux-de-Fonds 1; Lucerne 1.

Cup wins (1926–90)
Grasshoppers 17; Lausanne 7; La Chaux-de-Fonds 6; Young Boys Berne 6; Servette 6; FC Basle 5; FC Zurich 5; FC Sion 5; FC Lugano 1; FC Granges 1; Lucerne 1; St Gallen 1; Urania Geneva 1; Young Fellows Zurich 1; Aarau 1.

League Table 1989–90

	P	W	D	L	F	A	Pts
St Gallen	22	9	10	3	40	24	28
Neuchatel	22	11	5	6	38	32	27
Grasshoppers	22	9	7	6	31	24	25
Lucerne	22	9	6	7	39	29	24
Sion	22	9	5	8	29	31	23
Lausanne	22	6	10	6	28	27	22
Lugano	22	8	6	8	36	35	22
Young Boys	22	7	7	8	29	29	21
Servette	22	7	7	8	34	36	21
Wettingen	22	7	5	10	18	27	19
Aarau	22	5	7	10	20	30	17
Bellinzona	22	5	5	12	31	49	15

Final Round

	P	W	D	L	F	A	Q	F	T
Grasshoppers	14	9	0	5	28	15	13	18	31
Neuchatel	14	5	6	3	18	14	14	16	30
Lucerne	14	6	4	4	20	22	12	16	28
St Gallen	14	4	5	5	19	15	14	13	27
Lugano	14	4	4	6	11	23	11	12	23
Young Boys	14	2	6	6	11	20	11	10	21
Sion	14	1	5	8	10	22	12	7	19

Promotion/relegation

Group 1

	P	W	D	L	F	A	Pts
Servette	14	8	4	2	29	13	20
Zurich	14	8	4	2	30	17	20
Basle	14	6	5	3	27	17	17
Bellinzona	14	5	5	4	19	16	15
Yverdon	14	3	7	4	14	16	13
Fribourg	14	4	3	7	17	27	11
Chur	14	3	3	8	9	21	9
Schaffhausen	14	2	3	9	15	33	7

Group 2

	P	W	D	L	F	A	Pts
Aarau	14	10	2	2	35	10	22
Wettingen	14	9	4	1	29	9	22
Bulle	14	6	5	3	24	18	17
Baden	14	6	4	4	31	25	16
Locarno	14	4	5	5	15	17	13
Grenchen	14	2	5	7	18	28	9
Winterthur	14	2	3	9	15	38	7
Chenois	14	3	1	9	12	34	6

Cup Final: Grasshoppers 2, Neuchatel 1
Top scorer: Zamorano (St Gallen) 23

TURKEY

Founded: 1923.
Number of Clubs: 3754.
Number of Players: 87,200.
National Colours: White shirts, white shorts, red and white stockings.

International matches 1989

29 Mar, Athens: v Greece (a) won 1-0 *(Retvan)*
12 Apr, Magdeburg: v East Germany (a) won 2-0 *(Colak, Ridvan)*
10 May, Istanbul: v USSR (h) lost 0-1
20 Sept, Reykjavik: v Iceland (a) lost 1-2 *(Feyyaz)*
25 Oct, Istanbul: v Austria (h) won 3-0 *Ridvan 2, Feyyaz)*
15 Nov, Simferopol: v USSR (a) lost 0-2

League Championship wins (1960–90)

Fenerbahce 12; Galatasaray 8; Besiktas 7; Trabzonspor 6.

Cup wins (1963–90)

Galatasaray 8; Fenerbahce 4; Besiktas 4; Trabzonspor 3; Goztepe Izmir 2; Atay Ismir 2; Ankaragucu 2; Eskisehirspor 1; Bursapor 1; Genclerbirligi 1; Sakaryaspor 1.

Final League Table 1989–90

	P	W	D	L	F	A	Pts
Besiktas	34	24	6	4	83	20	78
Trabzonspor	34	20	8	6	58	28	68
Fenerbahce	34	21	4	9	69	39	67
Galatasaray	34	19	6	9	59	26	63
Sariyer	34	15	11	8	52	44	56
Ankaragucu	34	14	7	13	33	41	49
Bursaspor	34	13	8	13	46	45	47
Konyaspor	34	13	7	14	40	42	46
Karsiyaka	34	14	4	16	47	50	46
Zeytinburnu	34	13	6	15	39	39	45
Genclerbirligi	34	11	12	11	50	51	45
Adana	34	12	9	13	48	53	45
Boluspor	34	11	12	11	32	39	45
Malatya	34	12	8	14	43	46	44
Altay Izmir*	34	9	8	17	38	56	35
Samsunspor*	34	7	6	21	24	50	27
Adanademir*	34	5	8	21	31	83	23
Sakarya*	34	5	6	23	33	73	21

Cup Final: Besiktas 2, Trabzonspor 0
Top scorer: Feyyaz (Besiktas) 28

WALES

Founded: 1876.
Number of Clubs: 1,923.
Number of Players: 51,578.
National Colours: All red.

USSR

Founded: 1912.
Number of Clubs: 50,198.
Number of Players: 4,800,300.
National Colours: Red shirts, white shorts, red stockings.

International matches 1989

21 Feb, Sofia: v Bulgaria (a) won 2-1 *(Rats, Borodyuk)*
22 Mar, Eindhoven: v Holland (a) lost 0-2
26 Apr, Kiev: v East Germany (h) won 3-0 *(Dobrovolski, Litovchenko, Protasov)*
10 May, Istanbul: v Turkey (a) won 1-0 *(Mikhailichenko)*
31 May, Moscow: v Iceland (h) drew 1-1 *(Dobrovolski)*
24 Aug, Lublin: v Poland (a) drew 1-1 *(Kirakov)*
6 Sept, Vienna: v Austria (a) drew 0-0
8 Oct, Karl-Marx-Stadt: v East Germany (a) lost 1-2 *(Litovchenko)*
15 Nov, Simferopol: v Turkey (h) won 2-0 *(Protasov, Gokhan (og))*

League Championship wins (1936–89)

Spartak Moscow 12; Dynamo Kiev 12; Dynamo Moscow 11; CSKA Moscow 6; Torpedo Moscow 3; Dynamo Tbilisi 2; Dnepr Dnepropetrovsk 2; Saria Voroshilovgrad 1; Ararat Erevan 1; Dynamo Minsk 1; Zenit Leningrad 1.

Cup wins (1936–89)

Spartak Moscow 9; Dynamo Kiev 9; Torpedo Moscow 6; Dynamo Moscow 6; CSKA Moscow 4; Donets Shaktyor 4; Lokomotiv Moscow 2; Dynamo Tbilisi 2; Ararat Erevan 2; Karpaty Lvov 1; SKA Rostov 1; Zenit Leningrad 1; Metalist Khartov 1; Dnepr 1.

Final League Table 1989–90

	P	W	D	L	F	A	Pts
Spartak Moscow	30	17	10	3	46	19	44
Dnepr	30	18	6	6	47	28	42
Dynamo Kiev	30	13	12	5	44	27	38
Jalgiris	30	14	8	8	39	26	36
Moscow Torpedo	30	11	13	6	40	26	35
Chernomorets	30	11	9	10	40	41	31
Moscow Dynamo	30	9	12	9	31	26	30
Metallist	30	10	10	10	30	33	30
Dynamo Minsk	30	11	7	12	35	33	29
Volgograd	30	9	9	12	28	35	27
Dynamo Tbilisi	30	6	13	11	27	32	25
Ararat	30	8	8	14	25	41	24
Dushanbe	30	7	10	13	21	38	24
Donetsk	30	9	5	16	24	36	23
Lokomotiv Moscow*	30	7	9	14	20	32	23
Zenit*	30	5	9	16	24	48	19

Cup Final: Dnepr 1, Torpedo Moscow 0
Top scorer: Rodionov (Moscow Spartak) 16

YUGOSLAVIA

Founded: 1919.
Number of Clubs: 7455.
Number of Players: 270,229.
National Colours: Blue shirts, white shorts, red stockings.

International matches 1989

5 Apr, Athens: v Greece (a) won 4-1 *(Zlatko Vujovic 2, Tuce, Jakovljevic)*
29 Apr, Paris: v France (a) drew 0-0
27 May, Brussels: v Belgium (a) lost 0-1
14 June, Oslo: v Norway (a) won 2-1 *(Stojkovic, Zlatko Vujovic)*
24 Aug, Helsinki: v Finland (a) drew 2-2 *(Pancev, Savicevic)*
6 Sept, Zagreb: v Scotland (h) won 3-1 *(Katanec, Nicol (og), Gillespie (og))*
20 Sept, Novi Sad: v Greece (h) won 3-0 *(Brnovic, Prosinecki, Pancev)*
11 Oct, Sarajevo: Norway (h) won 1-0 *(Hadzibegic (og))*
28 Oct, Athens: v Cyprus (h) won 2-1 *(Pancev, Stanojkovic)*
13 Nov, Joao Pessoa: v Brazil (a) drew 0-0
13 Dec, Wembley: v England (a) lost 1-2 *(Skoro)*

League Championship wins (1923–90)

Red Star Belgrade 17; Partizan Belgrade 11; Hajduk Split 9; Gradjanski Zagreb 5; BSK Belgrade 5; Dynamo Zagreb 4; Jugoslavija Belgrade 2; Concordia Zagreb 2; FC Sarajevo 2; Vojvodina Novi Sad 2; HASK Zagreb 1; Zeljeznicar 1.

Cup wins (1947–90)

Red Star Belgrade 12; Dynamo Zagreb 8; Hajduk Split 8; Partizan Belgrade 5; BSK Belgrade 2; OFK Belgrade 2; Rejeka 2; Velez Mostar 2; Vardar Skopje 1; Borac Banjaluka 1.

Final League Table 1989–90

	P	W	D	W	D	L	L	F	A	Pts
Red Star	34	24	3		2	5		79	29	51
Dinamo Zagreb	34	18	8		3	5		56	24	42
Hajduk Split	34	18	2		1	13		50	35	38
Partizan	34	18	1		3	12		51	37	37
Rad	34	16	4		2	12		40	32	36
Rijeka	34	14	5		2	13		28	36	33
Zeljeznicar	34	14	4		2	14		37	40	32
Olimpija	34	14	2		4	14		48	39	30
Sloboda	34	15	0		4	15		43	46	30
Vojvodina	34	13	3		3	15		43	51	29
Buducnost	34	13	3		5	13		30	35	29
Spartak	34	12	4		2	16		28	40	28
Borac	34	12	3		4	15		27	39	27
Radnicki	34	12	2		6	14		42	48	26
Osijek	34	12	2		2	18		28	47	26
Velez	34	11	3		3	17		38	51	25
Sarajevo*	34	12	1		3	18		45	52	25
Vardar*	34	8	1		1	24		33	64	17

Cup Final: Red Star 1, Hajduk Split 0
Top scorer: Pancev (Red Star) 24

SOUTH AMERICA

ARGENTINA

Founded: 1893.
Number of Clubs: 3,035.
Number of Players: 306,365.
National Colours: Blue and white shirts, black shorts, white stockings.

International matches 1989

9 Mar, Barranquilla: v Colombia (a) lost 0-1
13 Apr, Guayaquil: v Ecuador (a) drew 2-2 *(Aviles, Cuvi (pen))*
20 Apr, Santiago: v Chile (a) drew 1-1 *(Airez)*
2 July, Goiania: v Chile (n) won 1-0 *(Caniggia)*
4 July, Goiania: v Ecuador (n) drew 0-0
8 July, Goiania: v Uruguay (n) won 1-0 *(Caniggia)*
10 July, Goiania: v Bolivia (n) drew 0-0
12 July, Rio de Janeiro: v Brazil (a) lost 0-2
14 July, Rio de Janeiro: v Uruguay (n) lost 0-2
16 July, Rio de Janeiro: v Paraguay (n) drew 0-0
21 Dec, Cagliari: v Italy (a) drew 0-0

BOLIVIA

Founded: 1925.
Number of Clubs: 305.
Number of Players: 15,290.
National Colours: Green shirts, white shorts, green stockings.

International matches 1989

25 May, Cochabamba: v Paraguay (h) won 3-2 *(Pena, Garcia 2)*
1 June, Asuncion: v Paraguay (a) lost 0-2
8 June, Santa Cruz: v Uruguay (h) drew 0-0
14 June, Montevideo: v Uruguay (a) lost 0-1
22 June, Santa Cruz: v Chile (h) lost 0-1
27 June, Santiago: v Chile (a) lost 1-2 *(Garcia)*
4 July, Goiania: v Uruguay (n) lost 0-3
6 July, Goiania: v Ecuador (n) drew 0-0
8 July, Goiania: v Chile (n) lost 0-5
10 July, Goiania: v Argentina (n) drew 0-0
20 Aug, La Paz: v Peru (h) won 2-1 *(Melgar (pen), Ramallo)*

3 Sept, La Paz: v Uruguay (h) won 2-1 *(Dominguez (og), Pena)*
10 Sept, Lima: v Peru (a) won 2-1 *(Montano, Sanchez)*
17 Sept, Montevideo: v Uruguay (a) lost 0-2

BRAZIL

Founded: 1914.
Number of Clubs: 12,9877.
Number of Players: 551,358.
National Colours: Yellow shirts, blue shorts, white stockings, green trim.

International matches 1989

15 Mar, Curiatiba: v Ecuador (h) won 1-0 *(Bebeto)*
29 Mar, Jeddah: v Saudi Arabia (a) won 3-1 *(Bebeto 2, Washington)*
12 Apr, Teresina: v Paraguay (h) won 2-0 *(Cristovao, Vivinho)*
10 May, Fortaleza: v Peru (h) won 4-1 *(Ze do Carmo, Bebeto, Charles 2)*
24 May, Lima: v Peru (a) drew 1-1 *(Cristovao)*
8 June, Rio de Janeiro: v Portugal (h) won 4-0 *(Bebeto 2, Ricardo, Charles)*
16 June, Copenhagen: v Sweden (n) lost 1-2 *(Cristovao)*
18 June, Copenhagen: v Denmark (a) lost 0-4
21 June, Basle: v Switzerland (a) lost 0-1
1 July, Salvador: v Venezuela (h) won 3-1 *(Bebeto, Geovani (pen), Baltazar)*
3 July, Salvador: v Peru (h) drew 0-0
7 July, Salvador: v Colombia (h) drew 0-0
9 July, Recife: v Paraguay (h) won 2-0 *(Bebeto 2)*
12 July, Rio de Janeiro: v Argentina (h) won 2-0 *(Bebeto, Romario)*
14 July, Rio de Janeiro: v Paraguay (h) won 3-0 *(Bebeto 2, Romario)*
16 July, Rio de Janeiro: v Uruguay (h) won 1-0 *(Romario)*
30 July, Caracas: v Venezuela (a) won 4-0 *(Branco, Romario, Bebeto 2)*
13 Aug, Santiago: v Chile (a) drew 1-1 *(Gonzalez (og))*
20 Aug, Sao Paulo: v Venezuela (h) won 6-0 *(Careca 4, Silas, Acosta)*
3 Sept, Rio de Janeiro: v Chile (h) *(match abandoned 70 mins, Brazil leading 1-0; awarded to Brazil 2-0)*

14 Oct, Bologna: v Italy (a) won 1-0 (*Andre Cruz*)
13 Nov, Joao Pessoa: v Yugoslavia (h) drew 0-0
20 Dec, Rotterdam: v Holland (a) won 1-0 (*Careca*)

CHILE

Founded: 1895.
Number of Clubs: 4,598.
Number of Players: 609,724
National Colours: Red shirts, blue shorts, white stockings.

International matches 1989

29 Jan, Guayaquil: v Ecuador (a) lost 0-1
1 Feb, Armenia: v Peru (n) drew 0-0
5 Feb, Armenia: v Colombia (a) lost 0-1
20 Apr, Santiago: v Argentina (h) drew 1-1 (*Espinoza*)
6 May, Los Angeles: v Guatemala (n) won 1-0 (*Martinez*)
7 May, Miami: v El Salvador (n) won 1-0 (*Ormeno*)
23 May, Wembley: v England (a) drew 0-0
26 May, Belfast: v N. Ireland (a) won 1-0 (*Astengo*)
30 May, Hampden Park: v Scotland (a) lost 0-2
3 June, Cairo: v Egypt (a) lost 0-2
19 June, Montevideo: v Uruguay (a) drew 2-2 (*Gonzalez, Pizarro*)
22 June, Santa Cruz: v Bolivia (a) won 1-0 (*Covarrubias*)
27 June, Santiago: v Bolivia (h) won 2-1 (*Covarrubias, Pizarro (pen)*)
2 July, Goiania: v Argentina (n) lost 0-1
6 July, Goiania: v Uruguay (n) lost 0-3
8 July, Goiania: v Bolivia (n) won 5-0 (*Olmos, Ramirez, Astengo. Pizarro (pen), Reyes*)
10 July, Goiania: v Ecuador (n) won 2-1 (*Olmos, Letelier*)
6 Aug, Caracas: v Venezuela (a) won 3-1 (*Aravena 2, Zamorano*)
13 Aug, Santiago: v Brazil (h) drew 1-1 (*Basay*)
27 Aug, Mendoza: v Venezuela (n) won 5-0 (*Letelier 3, Yanez, Vera*)
3 Sept, Rio de Janeiro: v Brazil (a) (*match abandoned 70 mins, Brazil leading 1-0; awarded to Brazil 2-0*)

COLOMBIA

Founded: 1925.
Number of Clubs: 3685.
Number of Players: 188,050
National Colours: Red shirts, blue shorts, tricolour stockings.

International matches 1989

3 Feb, Pereira: v Peru (h) won 1-0 (*Higuita (pen)*)
5 Feb, Armenia: v Chile (h) won 1-0 (*Redin*)
9 Mar, Barranquilla: v Argentina (h) won 1-0 (*Iguaran*)
25 June, Miami: v USA (a) won 1-0 (*Valderrama*)
3 July, Salvador: v Venezuela (n) won 4-2 (*Higuita (pen), Iguaran 2, De Avila*)
5 July, Salvador: v Paraguay (n) lost 0-1
7 July, Salvador: v Brazil (a) drew 0-0
9 July, Recife: v Peru (n) drew 1-1 (*Iguaran*)
6 Aug, Montevideo: v Uruguay (a) drew 0-0
20 Aug, Barranquilla: v Ecuador (h) won 2-0 (*Iguaran 2*)
27 Aug, Asuncion: v Paraguay (a) lost 1-2 (*Iguaran*)
3 Sept, Guayaquil: v Ecuador (a) drew 0-0
17 Sept, Barranquilla: v Paraguay (h) won 2-1 (*Iguaran, Hernandez*)
15 Oct, Barranquilla: v Israel (h) won 1-0 (*Usurriaga*)
30 Oct, Tel Aviv: v Israel (a) drew 0-0

ECUADOR

Founded: 1925.
Number of Clubs: 170.
Number of Players: 15,700.
National Colours: Yellow shirts, blue shorts, red stockings.

International matches 1989

29 Jan, Guayaquil: v Chile (h) won 1-0 (*Aviles*)
15 Mar, Guritiba: v Brazil (a) lost 0-1
13 Apr, Guayaquil: v Argentina (h) drew 2-2 (*Aviles, Cuvi (pen)*)
3 May, Montevideo: v Uruguay (a) lost 1-3 (*Aviles*)
23 May, Quito: v Uruguay (h) drew 1-1 (*Aviles*)
18 June, Port of Spain: v N. Ireland Select (n) drew 1-1 (*Izquierdo*)
20 June, Port of Spain: v Peru (n) lost 1-2 (*Guerrero*)
2 July, Goiania: v Uruguay (n) won 1-0 (*Benitez*)
4 July, Goiania: v Argentina (n) drew 0-0
6 July, Goiania: v Bolivia (n) drew 0-0
10 July, Goiania: v Chile (n) lost 1-2 (*Aviles*)
20 Aug, Barranquilla: v Colombia (a) lost 0-2
3 Sept, Guayaquil: v Colombia (h) drew 0-0
10 Sept, Asuncion: v Paraguay (a) lost 1-2 (*Aviles*)
24 Sept, Guayaquil: v Paraguay (h) won 3-1 (*Aguinaga, Marsetti, Aviles*)

PARAGUAY

Founded: 1906.
Number of Clubs: 1500.
Number of Players: 140,000
National Colours: Red and white shirts, blue shorts, blue stockings.

International matches 1989

12 Mar, Kingston: v Jamaica (n) won 3-0 (*Jacquet, Palacios, Gabino Roman*)
19 Mar, Port of Spain: v Trinidad & Tobago (a) drew 2-2 (*Caceres, Palacios*)
23 Mar, Arima: v Trinidad & Tobago (a) drew 1-1 (*Franco*)
26 Mar, Caracas: v Venezuela (a) won 2-1 (*Ferreyra, Franco*)
30 Mar, Maturin: v Venezuela (a) drew 0-0
12 Apr, Teresina: v Brazil (a) lost 0-2
6 May, Los Angeles: v El Salvador (n) won 2-1
7 May, Miami: v Guatemala (n) won 2-1 (*Britez Roman, Ferreyra*)
15 May, Asuncion: v Peru (h) drew 1-1 (*Britez Roman*)
25 May, Cochabamba: v Bolivia (a) lost 2-3 (*Rojas, Franco*)
1 June, Asuncion: v Bolivia (h) won 2-0 (*Ferreyra 2*)
1 July, Salvador: v Peru (n) won 5-2 (*Canete 2, Neffa, Mendoza, Del Solar (og)*)
5 July, Salvador: v Colombia (n) won 1-0 (*Mendoza*)
7 July, Salvador: v Venezuela (n) won 3-0 (*Neffa, Ferreyra 2*)
9 July, Recife: v Brazil (a) lost 0-2
12 July, Rio de Janeiro: v Uruguay (n) lost 0-3
14 July, Rio de Janeiro: v Brazil (a) lost 0-3
16 July, Rio de Janeiro: v Argentina (n) drew 0-0
27 Aug, Asuncion: v Colombia (h) won 2-1 (*J. Ferreira, Chilavert (pen)*)
10 Sept, Asuncion: v Ecuador (h) won 2-1 (*Cabanas, J. Ferreira*)
17 Sept, Barranquilla: v Colombia (a) lost 1-2 (*Mendoza*)
24 Sept, Guayaquil: v Ecuador (a) lost 1-3 (*Neffa*)

PERU

Founded: 1922.
Number of Clubs: 10,000.
Number of Players: 325,650
National Colours: White shirts, red trim, white shorts, white stockings.

International matches 1989

1 Feb, Armenia: v Chile (n) drew 0-0
3 Feb, Pereira: v Colombia (a) lost 0-1
10 May, Fortaleza: v Brazil (a) lost 1-4 (*Torres*)
15 May, Asuncion: v Paraguay (a) drew 1-1 (*Requena (pen)*)
18 May, Lima: v Venezuela (n) won 2-1 (*Zegarra, Rey Munoz*)
24 May, Lima: v Brazil (h) drew 1-1 (*Dall'Orso*)
4 June, New York: v USA (a) lost 0-3
18 June, Port of Spain: v Trinidad & Tobago (a) lost 1-2
20 June, Port of Spain: v Ecuador (n) won 2-1 (*Franco Navarro, Olaechea*)
25 June, San Cristobal: v Venezuela (a) lost 1-3 (*Rodriguez*)
1 July, Salvador: v Paraguay (n) lost 2-5 (*Hirano, Manassero*)

3 July, Salvador: v Brazil (a) drew 0-0
5 July, Salvador: v Venezuela (n) drew 1-1 (*Navarro*)
9 July, Recife: v Colombia (n) drew 1-1 (*Hirano*)
20 Aug, La Paz: v Bolivia (a) lost 1-2 (*Del Solar*)
27 Aug, Lima: v Uruguay (h) lost 0-2
10 Sept, Lima: v Bolivia (h) lost 1-2 (*Gonzalez*)
24 Sept, Montevideo: v Uruguay (a) lost 0-2

URUGUAY

Founded: 1900.
Number of Clubs: 1091.
Number of Players: 134,310.
National Colours: Light blue shirts, black shorts, black stockings.

International matches 1989

22 Apr, Verona: v Italy (a) drew 1-1 (*Aguilera*)
3 May, Montevideo: v Ecuador (h) won 3-1 (*Martinez, Aguilera 2*)
23 May, Quito: v Ecuador (a) drew 1-1 (*Herrera*)
8 June, Santa Cruz: v Bolivia (a) drew 0-0
14 June, Montevideo: v Bolivia (h) won 1-0 (*Herrera*)
19 June, Montevideo: v Chile (h) drew 2-2 (*Correa 2*)
2 July, Goiania: v Ecuador (h) won 1-0 (*Benitez*)
4 July, Goiania: v Bolivia (h) won 3-0 (*Ostolaza 2, Sosa*)
6 July, Goiania: v Chile (n) won 3-0 (*Sosa, Alzamendi, Francescoli*)
8 July, Goiania: v Argentina (n) lost 0-1
12 July, Rio de Janeiro: v Paraguay (n) won 3-0 (*Francescoli, Alzamendi, Paz*)
14 July, Rio de Janeiro: v Argentina (n) won 2-0 (*Sosa 2*)

16 July, Rio de Janeiro: v Brazil (a) lost 0-1
6 Aug, Montevideo: v Colombia (h) drew 0-0
27 Aug, Lima: v Peru (a) won 2-0 (*Sosa, Alzamendi*)
3 Sept, La Paz: v Bolivia (a) lost 1-2 (*Sosa*)
17 Sept, Montevideo: v Bolivia (h) won 2-0 (*Sosa, Francescoli*)
24 Sept, Montevideo: v Peru (h) won 2-0 (*Sosa 2*)

VENEZUELA

Founded: 1926.
Number of Clubs: 1753.
Number of Players: 63,175
National Colours: Magenta shirts, white shorts, white stockings.

International matches 1989

26 Mar, Caracas: v Paraguay (h) lost 1-2 (*Marquez*)
30 Mar, Maturin: v Paraguay (h) drew 0-0
18 May, Lima: v Peru (a) lost 1-2 (*Dominguez*)
25 June, San Cristobal: v Peru (h) won 3-1 (*H. Rivas, Febles, S. Rivas*)
1 July, Salvador: v Brazil (a) lost 1-3 (*Maldonado*)
3 July, Salvador: v Colombia (n) lost 2-4 (*Maldonado 2*)
5 July, Salvador: v Peru (n) drew 1-1 (*Maldonado*)
7 July, Salvador: v Parguay (n) lost 0-3
30 July, Caracas: v Brazil (h) lost 0-4
6 Aug, Caracas: v Chile (h) lost 1-3 (*Fernandez*)
20 Aug, Sao Paulo: v Brazil (a) lost 0-6
27 Aug, Mendoza: v Chile (n) lost 0-5

ASIA

AFGHANISTAN

Founded: 1922.
Number of Clubs: 30.
Number of Players: 3,300.
National Colours: White shirts, white shorts, white stockings.

BAHRAIN

Founded: 1951.
Number of Clubs: 25.
Number of Players: 2,030.
National Colours: White shirts, red shorts, white stockings.

BANGLADESH

Founded: 1972.
Number of Clubs: 1,265.
Number of Players: 30,385.
National Colours: Orange shirts, white shorts, green stockings.

BRUNEI

Founded: 1959.
Number of Clubs: 22.
Number of Players: 830.
National Colours: Gold shirts, black shorts, gold stockings.

BURMA

Founded: 1947.
Number of Clubs: 600.
Number of Players: 21,000.
National Colours: Red shirts, white shorts, red stockings.

CHINA

Founded: 1924.
Number of Clubs: 1,045.
Number of Players: 2,250,200.
National Colours: Red shirts, white shorts, red stockings.

HONG KONG

Founded: 1914.
Number of Clubs: 69.
Number of Players: 3,274.
National Colours: Red shirts, white shorts, red stockings.

INDIA

Founded: 1937.
Number of Clubs: 2,000.
Number of Players: 56,000.
National Colours: Light blue shirts, white shorts, dark blue stockings.

INDONESIA

Founded: 1930.
Number of Clubs: 2,880.
Number of Players: 97,000.
National Colours: Red shirts, white shorts, red stockings.

IRAN

Founded: 1920.
Number of Clubs: 6,326.
Number of Players: 306,000.
National Colours: Green shirts, white shorts, red stockings.

IRAQ

Founded: 1948.
Number of Clubs: 155.
Number of Players: 4,400.
National Colours: White shirts, white shorts, white stockings.

ISRAEL

Founded: 1928.
Number of Clubs: 544.
Number of Players: 30,449.
National Colours: White shirts, blue shorts, white stockings.

JAPAN

Founded: 1921.
Number of Clubs: 13,047.
Number of Players: 358,989.
National Colours: Blue shirts, white shorts, blue stockings.

JORDAN

Founded: 1949.
Number of Clubs: 98.
Number of Players: 4,305.
National Colours: White shirts, white shorts, white stockings.

KAMPUCHEA

Founded: 1933.
Number of Clubs: 30.
Number of Players: 650.
National Colours: Blue shirts, white shorts, red stockings.

KOREA, NORTH

Founded: 1945.
Number of Clubs: 90.
Number of Players: 3,420.
National Colours: Red shirts, white shorts, red stockings.

KOREA, SOUTH

Founded: 1928.
Number of Clubs: 476.
Number of Players: 2,047.
National Colours: Red shirts, red shorts, red stockings.

KUWAIT

Founded: 1952.
Number of Clubs: 14 (senior).
Number of Players: 1,526.
National Colours: Blue shirts, white shorts, blue stockings.

LAOS

Founded: 1951.
Number of Clubs: 76.
Number of Players: 2,060.
National Colours: Red shirts, white shorts, blue stockings.

LEBANON

Founded: 1933.
Number of Clubs: 105.
Number of Players: 8,125.
National Colours: Red shirts, white shorts, red stockings.

MACAO

Founded: 1939.
Number of Clubs: 52.
Number of Players: 800.
National Colours: Green shirts, white shorts, green and white stockings.

MALDIVES

Founded: 1986.
National Colours: Green shirts, white shorts, red stockings.

MALAYSIA

Founded: 1933.
Number of Clubs: 450.
Number of Players: Players 11,250.
National Colours: Black and gold shirts, white shorts, black and gold stockings.

NEPAL

Founded: 1951.
Number of Clubs: 85.
Number of Players: 2,550.
National Colours: Red shirts, blue shorts, blue and white stockings.

OMAN

Founded: 1978.
Number of Clubs: 47.
Number of Players: 2,340.
National Colours: White shirts, red shorts, white stockings.

PAKISTAN

Founded: 1948.
Number of Clubs: 882.
Number of Players: 21,000.
National Colours: Green shirts, white shorts, green stockings.

PHILLIPPINES

Founded: 1907.
Number of Clubs: 650.
Number of Players: 45,000.
National Colours: Blue shirts, white shorts, blue stockings.

QATAR

Founded: 1960.
Number of Clubs: 8 (senior).
Number of Players: 1,380.
National Colours: White shirts, maroon shorts, white stockings.

SAUDI ARABIA

Founded: 1959.
Number of Clubs: 120.
Number of Players: 9,600.
National Colours: White shirts, white shorts, white stockings.

SINGAPORE

Founded: 1892.
Number of Clubs: 250.
Number of Players: 8,000.
National Colours: Sky blue shirts, sky blue shorts, sky blue stockings.

SRI LANKA

Founded: 1939.
Number of Clubs: 600.
Number of Players: 18,825.
National Colours: Maroon shirts, white shorts, white stockings.

SYRIA

Founded: 1936.
Number of Clubs: 102.
Number of Players: 30,600.
National Colours: White shirts, white shorts, white stockings.

THAILAND

Founded: 1916.
Number of Clubs: 168.
Number of Players: 15,000.
National Colours: Crimson shirts, white shorts, crimson stockings.

UNITED ARAB EMIRATES

Founded: 1971.
Number of Clubs: Clubs 23 (senior).
Number of Players: 1,787.
National Colours: White shirts, white shorts, white stockings.

VIETNAM

Founded: 1962.
Number of Clubs: 55 (senior).
Number of Players: 16,000.
National Colours: Red shirts, white shorts, red stockings.

YEMEN, ARAB REPUBLIC

Founded: 1962.
Number of Clubs: 61 (senior).
Number of Players: 22,600.
National Colours: Green shirts, green shorts, green stockings.

YEMEN, PDR

Founded: 1940.
Number of Clubs: 36.
Number of Players: 1,700.
National Colours: Light blue shirts, white shorts, light blue stockings.

CONCACAF

ANTIGUA

Founded: 1928.
Number of Clubs: 60.
Number of Players: 1,008.
National Colours: Gold shirts, black shorts, black stockings.

BAHAMAS

Founded: 1967.
Number of Clubs: 14.
Number of Players: 700.
National Colours: Yellow shirts, black shorts, yellow stockings.

BARBADOS

Founded: 1910.
Number of Clubs: 92.
Number of Players: 1,100.
National Colours: Royal blue shirts, gold shorts, royal blue stockings.

BELIZE

Founded: 1986.
National Colours: Blue shirts, red and white trim, white shorts, blue stockings.

BERMUDA.

Founded: 1928.
Number of Clubs: 30.
Number of Players: 1,947
National Colours: Blue shirts, white shorts, white stockings.

CANADA

Founded: 1912.
Number of Clubs: 1,600.
Number of Players: 224,290.
National Colours: Red shirts, red shorts, red stockings.

COSTA RICA

Founded: 1921.
Number of Clubs: 431.
Number of Players: 12,429.
National Colours: Red shirts, blue shorts, white stockings.

CUBA

Founded: 1924.
Number of Clubs: 70.
Number of Players: 12,900.
National Colours: White shirts, blue shorts, white stockings.

801

DOMINICAN REPUBLIC

Founded: 1953.
Number of Clubs: 128.
Number of Players: 10,706
National Colours: Blue shirts, white shorts, red stockings.

EL SALVADOR

Founded: 1936.
Number of Clubs: 944.
Number of Players: 21,294.
National Colours: Blue shirts, blue shorts, blue stockings.

GRENADA

Founded: 1924.
Number of Clubs: 15.
Number of Players: 200.
National Colours: Green and yellow shirts, red shorts, green and yellow stockings.

GUATEMALA

Founded: 1933.
Number of Clubs: 1,611.
Number of Players: 43,516.
National Colours: Blue shirts, white shorts, blue stockings.

GUYANA

Founded: 1902.
Number of Clubs: 103.
Number of Players: 1,665.
National Colours: Green and yellow shirts, black shorts, white and green stockings.

HAITI

Founded: 1904.
Number of Clubs: 40.
Number of Players: 4,000.
National Colours: Red shirts, black shorts, red stockings.

HONDURAS

Founded: 1951.
Number of Clubs: 1,050.
Number of Players: 15,300.
National Colours: Blue shirts, blue shorts, blue stockings.

JAMAICA

Founded: 1910.
Number of Clubs: 266.
Number of Players: 45,200.
National Colours: Green shirts, black shorts, green and gold stockings.

MEXICO

Founded: 1927.
Number of Clubs: 77 (senior).
Number of Players: 14,022,700.
National Colours: Green shirts, white shorts, green stockings.

NETHERLANDS ANTILLES

Founded: 1921.
Number of Clubs: 85.
Number of Players: 4,500.
National Colours: White shirts, white shorts, red stockings.

NICARAGUA

Founded: 1968.
Number of Clubs: 31.
Number of Players: 160 (senior).
National Colours: Blue shirts, blue shorts, blue stockings.

PANAMA

Founded: 1937.
Number of Clubs: 65.
Number of Players: 4,225.
National Colours: Red and white shirts, blue shorts, red stockings.

PUERTO RICO

Founded: 1940.
Number of Clubs: 175.
Number of Players: 4,200.
National Colours: White and red shirts, blue shorts, white and blue stockings.

SURINAM

Founded: 1920.
Number of Clubs: 168.
Number of Players: 4,430.
National Colours: Red shirts, white shorts, white stockings.

TRINIDAD AND TOBAGO

Founded: 1906.
Number of Clubs: 124.
Number of Players: 5,050.
National Colours: Red shirts, black shorts, red stockings.

USA

Founded: 1913.
Number of Clubs: 7,000.
Number of Players: 1,411,500.
National Colours: White shirts, blue shorts, red stockings.

Recent additions: ARUBA, SANTA LUCIA, ST. VINCENT and the GRENADINES. Aruba is an island in the Caribbean with 1,500 registered players. St. Lucia is another island in the same area with 4,000 players. St Vincent and the Grenadines is similarly situated and has 5,000 players.

OCEANIA

AUSTRALIA

Founded: 1961.
Number of Clubs: 6,816.
Number of Players: 433,957.
National Colours: Gold shirts, green shorts, white stockings.

FIJI

Founded: 1946.
Number of Clubs: 140.
Number of Players: 21,500.
National Colours: White shirts, black shorts, black stockings.

NEW ZEALAND

Founded: 1891.
Number of Clubs: 312.
Number of Players: 52,969.
National Colours: White shirts, black shorts, white stockings.

PAPUA-NEW GUINEA

Founded: 1962.
Number of Clubs: 350.
Number of Players: 8,250.
National Colours: Red shirts, black shorts, red stockings.

Founded: 1936.
Number of Clubs: 53.
Number of Players: 17,350.
National Colours: Blue shirts, white shorts, red stockings.

WESTERN SAMOA

Founded: 1986.
National Colours: Blue shirts, white shorts, blue and white stockings.

Recent additions: SOLOMON ISLANDS, VANUATA. The Solomon Islands are situated in the South Pacific to the south-east of Papua New Guinea. There are 4,000 registered players. Vanuatu was formerly known as the New Hebrides and is a double chain of islands to the south-east of the Solomons.

AFRICA

ALGERIA

Founded: 1962.
Number of Clubs: 780.
Number of Players: 58,567.
National Colours: Green shirts, white shorts, red stockings.

BURKINA FASO

Founded: 1960.
Number of Clubs: 57.
Number of Players: 4,672.
National Colours: Black shirts, white shorts, red stockings.

ANGOLA

Founded: 1977.
Number of Clubs: 276.
Number of Players: 4,269.
National Colours: Red shirts, black shorts, red stockings.

BENIN

Founded: 1968.
Number of Clubs: 117.
Number of Players: 6,700.
National Colours: Green shirts, green shorts, green stockings.

BOTSWANA

Founded: 1976.
National Colours: Sky blue shirts, white shorts, sky blue stockings.

BURUNDI

Founded: 1948.
Number of Clubs: 132.
Number of Players: 3,930.
National Colours: Red shirts, white shorts, green stockings.

CAMEROON

Founded: 1960.
Number of Clubs: 200.
Number of Players: 9,328.
National Colours: Green shirts, red shorts, yellow stockings.

CAPE VERDE ISLANDS

Founded: 1986.
National Colours: Green shirts, green shorts, green stockings.

CENTRAL AFRICA

Founded: 1937.
Number of Clubs: 256.
Number of Players: 7,200.
National Colours: Grey and blue shirts, white shorts, red stockings.

CONGO

Founded: 1962.
Number of Clubs: 250.
Number of Players: 5,940.
National Colours: Red shirts, red shorts, white stockings.

EGYPT

Founded: 1921.
Number of Clubs: 168.
Number of Players: 11,695.
National Colours: Red shirts, white shorts, black stockings.

ETHIOPIA

Founded: 1943.
Number of Clubs: 767.
Number of Players: 20,594.
National Colours: Green shirts, yellow shorts, red stockings.

GABON

Founded: 1962.
Number of Clubs: 320.
Number of Players: 10,000.
National Colours: Blue shirts, white shorts, white stockings.

GAMBIA

Founded: 1952.
Number of Clubs: 30.
Number of Players: 860.
National Colours: White and red shirts, white shorts, white stockings.

GHANA

Founded: 1957.
Number of Clubs: 347.
Number of Players: 11,275.
National Colours: White shirts, white shorts, white stockings.

GUINEA

Founded: 1959.
Number of Clubs: 351.
Number of Players: 10,000
National Colours: Red shirts, yellow shorts, green stockings.

GUINEA-BISSAU

Founded: 1986.
National Colours: Green shirts, green shorts, green stockings.

GUINEA, EQUATORIAL

Founded: 1986.

IVORY COAST

Founded: 1960.
Number of Clubs: 84 (senior).
Number of Players: 3,655.
National Colours: Orange shirts, white shorts, green stockings.

KENYA

Founded: 1960.
Number of Clubs: 351.
Number of Players: 8,800.
National Colours: Red shirts, red shorts, red stockings.

LESOTHO

Founded: 1932.
Number of Clubs: 88.
Number of Players: 2,076.
National Colours: White shirts, blue shorts, white stockings.

LIBERIA

Founded: 1962.
National Colours: Blue and white shirts, white shorts, blue and white stockings.

LIBYA

Founded: 1963.
Number of Clubs: 89.
Number of Players: 2,941.
National Colours: Green shirts, white shorts, green stockings.

MADAGASCAR

Founded: 1961.
Number of Clubs: 775.
Number of Players: 23,536.
National Colours: Red shirts, white shorts, green stockings.

MALAWI

Founded: 1966.
Number of Clubs: 465.
Number of Players: 12,500.
National Colours: Red shirts, red shorts, red stockings.

MALI

Founded: 1960.
Number of Clubs: 128.
Number of Players: 5,480.
National Colours: Green shirts, yellow shorts, red stockings.

MAURITANIA

Founded: 1961.
Number of Clubs: 59.
Number of Players: 1,930.
National Colours: Green and yellow shirts, blue shorts, green stockings.

MAURITIUS

Founded: 1952.
Number of Clubs: 397.
Number of Players: 29,375.
National Colours: Red shirts, white shorts, red stockings.

MOROCCO

Founded: 1955.
Number of Clubs: 350.
Number of Players: 19,768.
National Colours: Red shirts, green shorts, red stockings.
Championship Table 1988

MOZAMBIQUE

Founded: 1978.
Number of Clubs: 144.
National Colours: Red shirts, red shorts, red stockings.

NIGER

Founded: 1967.
Number of Clubs: 64.
Number of Players: 1,525.
National Colours: Orange shirts, white shorts, green stockings.

NIGERIA

Founded: 1945.
Number of Clubs: 326.
Number of Players: 80,190.
National Colours: Green shirts, white shorts, green stockings.

RWANDA

Founded: 1972.
Number of Clubs: 167
National Colours: Red shirts, red shorts, red stockings.

SENEGAL

Founded: 1960.
Number of Clubs: 75 (senior).
Number of Players: 3,977.
National Colours: Green shirts, yellow shorts, red stockings.

SEYCHELLES

Founded: 1986.
National Colours: Green shirts, yellow shorts, red stockings.

ST. THOMAS AND PRINCIPE

Founded: 1986.
National Colours: Green shirts, green shorts, green stockings.

SIERRA LEONE

Founded: 1967.
Number of Clubs: 104.
Number of Players: 8,120.
National Colours: Green shirts, white shorts, blue stockings.

SOMALIA

Founded: 1951.
Number of Clubs: 46 (senior).
Number of Players: 1,150.
National Colours: Sky blue shirts, white shorts, white stockings.

SUDAN

Founded: 1936.
Number of Clubs: 750.
Number of Players: 42,200.
National Colours: White shirts, white shorts, white stockings.

SWAZILAND

Founded: 1976.
Number of Clubs: 136.
National Colours: Blue and gold shirts, white shorts, blue and gold stockings.

TANZANIA

Founded: 1930.
Number of Clubs: 51.
National Colours: Yellow shirts, yellow shorts, yellow stockings.

TOGO

Founded: 1960.
Number of Clubs: 144.
Number of Players: 4,346.
National Colours: Red shirts, white shorts, red stockings.

TUNISIA

Founded: 1957.
Number of Clubs: 215.
Number of Players: 18,300.
National Colours: Red shirts, white shorts, red stockings.

UGANDA

Founded: 1924.
Number of Clubs: 400.
Number of Players: 1,518.
National Colours: Yellow shirts, black shorts, yellow stockings.

ZAIRE

Founded: 1919.
Number of Clubs: 3,800.
Number of Players: 64,627.
National Colours: Green shirts, yellow shorts, yellow stockings.

ZAMBIA

Founded: 1929.
Number of Clubs: 20 (senior).
Number of Players: 4,100.
National Colours: Green shirts, white shorts, black stockings.

ZIMBABWE

Founded: 1965.
National Colours: White shirts, black shorts, black stockings.

Recent addition: CHAD (readmitted). This landlocked country was once a FIFA member up to 1974 and has now been reaffiliated.

EUROPEAN FOOTBALL CHAMPIONSHIP

(formerly EUROPEAN NATIONS' CUP)

Year	Winners	Runners-up	Venue	Attendance	Referee
1960	USSR 2	Yugoslavia 1	Paris	17,966	Ellis (E)
	(after extra time)				
1964	Spain 2	USSR 1	Madrid	120,000	Holland (E)
1968	Italy 2	Yugoslavia 0	Rome	60,000	Dienst (Sw)
	(after extra time; after 1-1 draw)			75,000	
1972	West Germany 3	USSR 0	Brussels	43,437	Marschall (A)
1976	Czechoslovakia 2	West Germany 2	Belgrade	45,000	Gonella (I)
	(Czechoslovakia won 5-3 on penalties)				
1980	West Germany 2	Belgium 1	Rome	47,864	Rainea (R)
1984	France 2	Spain 0	Paris	80,000	Christov (Cz)
1988	Holland 2	USSR 0	Munich	72,308	Vautrot (F)

FINAL SERIES DATA

Year	Venue	Matches	Attendances	Average
1960	France	4	78,958	19,739
1964	Spain	4	156,253	39,063
1968	Italy	5	192,119	38,424
1972	Belgium	4	106,949	26,737
1976	Yugoslavia	4	106,087	26,522
1980	Italy	14	389,838	27,845
1984	France	15	603,977	40,266
1988	West Germany	15	938,541	62,569

EUROPEAN CHAMPIONSHIP 1990–92

GROUP 1

Reykjavik, 31 May, 1990, 6500

Iceland (1) 2 *(Gudjohnsen 42, Edvaldsson 88)*
Albania (0) 0

Iceland: Christensson; Thordarsson, Edvaldsson, Orlogsson (Jonsson C 46), Gretarsson, Jonsson S, Berg, Ormslev, Torvarsson (Orloggson O 67), Petursson, Gudjohnsen.
Albania: Strakosha; Noga (Illiadhe 75), Lekbello, Kovi, Vapa, Jera, Shehu (Arbere 46), Josa, Millo, Abazi, Demollari.

DATES FOR THE QUALIFYING MATCHES IN THE 7TH EUROPEAN FOOTBALL CHAMPIONSHIP 1992 – HENRI DELAUNAY CUP

Group 1
1990
30.5	Iceland – Albania
5.9	Iceland – France
26.9	Czechoslovakia – Iceland
10.10	Spain – Iceland
13.10	France – Czechoslovakia
14.11	Czechoslovakia – Spain
17.11	Albania – France
19.12	Spain – Albania

1991
20.2	France – Spain
30.3	France – Albania
1.5	Albania – Czechoslovakia
26.5	Albania – Iceland
5.6	Iceland – Czechoslovakia
4.9	Czechoslovakia – France
25.9	Iceland – Spain
12.10	Spain – France
16.10	Czechoslovakia – Albania
13.11	Spain – Czechoslovakia
13/20.11	France – Iceland
18.12	Albania – Spain

Group 2
1990
12.9	Switzerland – Bulgaria
12.9	Scotland – Rumania
17.10	Rumania – Bulgaria
17.10	Scotland – Switzerland
14.11	Bulgaria – Scotland
14.11	San Marino – Switzerland
5.12	Rumania – San Marino

1991
27.3	Scotland – Bulgaria
27.3	San Marino – Rumania
3.4	Switzerland – Rumania
1.5	Bulgaria – Switzerland
1.5	San Marino – Scotland
22.5	San Marino – Bulgaria
5.6	Switzerland – San Marino
11.9	Switzerland – Scotland
16.10	Bulgaria – San Marino
16.10	Rumania – Scotand
13.11	Scotland – San Marino
13.11	Rumania – Switzerland
20.11	Bulgaria – Rumania

Group 3
1990
12.9	USSR – Norway
10.10	Norway – Hungary
17.10	Hungary – Italy
31.10	Hungary – Cyprus
3.11	Italy – USSR
14.11	Cyprus – Norway
22.12	Cyprus – Italy

1991
3.4	Cyprus – Hungary
17.4	Hungary – USSR
1.5	Italy – Hungary
1.5	Norway – Cyprus
22/29.5	USSR – Cyprus
5.6	Norway – Italy
28.8	Norway – USSR
25.9	USSR – Hungary
12.10	USSR – Italy
30.10	Hungary – Norway
13.11	Italy – Norway
13.11	Cyprus – USSR
21.12	Italy – Cyprus

Group 4
1990
12.9	Northern Ireland – Yugoslavia
12.9	Faroe Islands – Austria
10.10	Denmark – Faroe Islands
17.10	Northern Ireland – Denmark
31.10	Yugoslavia – Austria
14.11	Denmark – Yugoslavia
14.11	Austria – Northern Ireland

1991
27.3	Yugoslavia – Northern Ireland
1.5	Yugoslavia – Denmark
1.5	Northern Ireland – Faroe Islands
14/15.5	Yugoslavia – Faroe Islands
22.5	Austria – Faroe Islands
5.6	Denmark – Austria
11.9	Faroe Islands – Northern Ireland
25.9	Faroe Islands – Denmark
9.10	Austria – Denmark
16.10	Faroe Islands – Yugoslavia
16.10	Northern Ireland – Austria
13.11	Denmark – Northern Ireland
13.11	Austria – Yugoslavia

Group 5 (*East Germany withdrew*)
1990
17.10	Wales – Belgium
14.11	Luxembourg – Wales

1991
27.2	Belgium – Luxembourg
27.3	Belgium – Wales
1.5	West Germany – Belgium
5.6	Wales – West Germany
11.9	Luxembourg – Belgium
16.10	West Germany – Wales
13.11	Wales – Luxembourg
20.11	Belgium – West Germany
17.12	West Germany – Luxembourg

Group 6
1990
12.9	Finland – Portugal
17.10	Portugal – Holland
31.10	Greece – Malta
21.11	Holland – Greece
25.11	Malta – Finland
19/23.12	Malta – Holland

1991
23.1	Greece – Portugal
9.2	Malta – Portugal
20.2	Portugal – Malta
13.3	Holland – Malta
17.4	Holland – Finland
16.5	Finland – Malta
5.6	Finland – Holland
11.9	Portugal – Finland
9.10	Finland – Greece
16.10	Holland – Portugal
30.10	Greece – Finland
20.11	Portugal – Greece
4.12	Greece – Holland
22.12	Malta – Greece

Group 7
1990
17.10	England – Poland
17.10	Rep. of Ireland – Turkey
14.11	Rep. of Ireland – England
14.11	Turkey – Poland

1991
27.3	England – Rep. of Ireland
17.4	Poland – Turkey
1.5	Turkey – England
1.5	Rep. of Ireland – Poland
16.10	Poland – Rep. of Ireland
16.10	England – Turkey
13.11	Turkey – Rep. of Ireland
13.11	Poland – England

International Records

MOST GOALS IN AN INTERNATIONAL

England	Malcolm Macdonald (Newcastle U) 5 goals v Cyprus, at Wembley	16.4.1975
	Willie Hall (Tottenham H) 5 goals v Ireland, at Old Trafford	16.11.1938
	G. O. Smith (Corinthians) 5 goals v Ireland, at Sunderland	18.2.1899
	Steve Bloomer (Derby Co) 5 goals* v Wales, at Cardiff	16.3.1896
	Oliver Vaughton (Aston Villa) 5 goals v Ireland, at Belfast	18.2.82
Scotland	Charles Heggie (Rangers) 5 goals v Ireland, at Belfast	20.3.1886
Ireland	Joe Bambick (Linfield) 6 goals v Wales, at Belfast	1.2.1930
Wales	James Price (Wrexham) 4 goals v Ireland, at Wrexham	25.2.1882
	Mel Charles (Cardiff C) 4 goals v Ireland, at Cardiff	11.4.1962
	Ian Edwards (Chester) 4 goals v Malta, at Wrexham	25.10.1978

* There are conflicting reports which make it uncertain whether Bloomer scored four or five goals in this game.

MOST GOALS IN AN INTERNATIONAL CAREER

		Goals	Games
England	Bobby Charlton (Manchester U)	49	106
Scotland	Denis Law (Huddersfield T, Manchester C, Torino, Manchester U)	30	55
	Kenny Dalglish (Celtic, Liverpool)	30	102
Ireland	Billy Gillespie (Sheffield U)	12	25
	Joe Bambrick (Linfield, Chelsea)	12	11
	Gerry Armstrong (Tottenham H, Watford, Real Mallorca, WBA, Chesterfield)	12	63
Wales	Trevor Ford (Swansea T, Aston Villa, Sunderland, Cardiff C)	23	38
	Ivor Allchurch (Swansea T, Newcastle U, Cardiff C)	23	68
Republic of Ireland	Frank Stapleton (Arsenal, Manchester U, Ajax, Derby Co, Le Havre, Blackburn R)	20	70

HIGHEST SCORES

World Cup Match	New Zealand	13	Fiji	0	1981
Olympic Games	Denmark	17	France	1	1908
	Germany	16	USSR	0	1912
International Match	Germany	13	Finland	0	1940
	Spain	13	Bulgaria	0	1933
European Cup	Feyenoord	12	Reykjavik	2	1969
European Cup-Winners' Cup	Sporting Lisbon	16	Apoel Nicosia	1	1963
Fairs & UEFA Cups	Ajax	14	Red Boys	0	1984

GOALSCORING RECORDS

World Cup Final	Geoff Hurst (England) 3 goals v West Germany	1966
World Cup Final tournament	Just Fontaine (France) 13 goals	1958
Major European Cup game	Lothar Emmerich (Borussia Dortmund) v Floriana in Cup-Winners' Cup – 6 goals	1965
Career	Arthur Friedenreich (Brazil) 1329 goals	1910–30
	Pele (Brazil) 1281 goals	*1956–78
	Franz 'Bimbo' Binder (Austria, Germany) 1006 goals	1930–50

*Pelé has since scored two goals in Testimonial matches making his total 1283.

MOST CAPPED INTERNATIONALS IN BRITISH ISLES

England	Peter Shilton	125 appearances	1970–90
Northern Ireland	Pat Jennings	119 appearances	1964–86
Scotland	Kenny Dalglish	102 appearances	1971–86
Wales	Joey Jones	72 appearances	1975–87
Republic of Ireland	Liam Brady	72 appearances	1974–90

Milestones in British transfers

£1000 Alf Common, Sunderland to Middlesbrough, 1905
£10,000 David Jack, Bolton Wanderers to Arsenal, 1928

£100,000 Denis Law, Torino to Manchester U, 1962
£200,000 Martin Peters, West Ham U to Tottenham, 1970
£500,000 Kevin Keegan, Liverpool to SV Hamburg, 1977

TRANSFERS

British players £2 million and over

£3,200,000 Ian Rush, Liverpool to Juventus, June 1987
£2,800,000 Ian Rush, Juventus to Liverpool, August 1988
£2,750,000 Gary Lineker, Everton to Barcelona, June 1986
£2,300,000 Mark Hughes, Manchester U to Barcelona, May 1986
£2,300,000 Gary Pallister, Middlesbrough to Manchester U, August 1989
£2,200,000 Tony Cottee, West Ham U to Everton, July 1988
£2,000,000 Paul Gascoigne, Newcastle U to Tottenham H, July 1988

World records

£7,700,000 Roberto Baggio, Fiorentina to Juventus, June 1990
£6,900,000 Diego Maradona, Barcelona to Napoli, June 1984
£5,500,000 Ruud Gullit, PSV Eindhoven to AC Milan, June 1987
£5,500,000 Karl-Heinz Riedle, Werder Bremen to Lazio, June 1990
£5,500,000 Thomas Hassler, Cologne to Juventus, June 1990
£4,800,000 Diego Maradona, Argentinos Juniors to Barcelona, June 1982
£4,800,000 Lajos Detari, Eintracht Frankfurt to Olympiakos, July 1988
£4,800,000 Dragan Stojkovic, Red Star Belgrade to Marseille, June 1990

EUROPEAN CLUB RESULTS 1989–90

BELGIUM — FRANCE — WEST GERMANY — HOLLAND — ITALY — SPAIN

BELGIUM – LEAGUE RESULTS 1989–90

	Anderlecht	Antwerp	Beerschot	Beveren	CS Brugge	FC Brugge	Charleroi	Kortrijk	Ekeren	Gent	Liege	Lierse	Lokeren	Mechelen	Racing Mechelen	St Truiden	Standard	Waregem
Anderlecht	—	0-1	2-0	1-0	4-0	0-0	5-0	3-0	2-0	0-1	4-2	2-1	7-0	0-3	1-0	3-0	1-0	6-0
Antwerp	2-2	—	4-0	0-0	1-1	0-4	3-0	2-0	4-1	2-2	1-1	4-1	5-0	1-1	1-0	2-0	2-1	4-0
Beerschot	1-3	1-1	—	4-1	0-0	0-0	2-0	0-2	1-0	2-0	1-0	0-0	2-3	0-0	2-1	0-0	0-3	2-0
Beveren	1-1	3-1	0-0	—	1-4	0-1	4-0	4-1	0-3	1-0	2-1	0-0	0-2	1-3	3-4	0-0	0-1	1-0
CS Brugge	1-2	2-0	0-2	0-1	—	0-2	3-3	1-2	1-1	1-0	1-0	1-2	3-1	0-0	4-1	2-1	3-1	3-1
FC Brugge	3-0	0-2	3-0	2-0	2-1	—	1-0	1-1	4-0	4-1	2-0	2-0	3-1	3-0	4-0	3-0	2-1	3-0
Charleroi	0-0	3-3	4-0	1-1	2-1	0-1	—	0-0	4-0	2-1	2-0	3-1	3-1	0-3	3-0	0-1	0-2	0-2
Kortrijk	0-2	0-6	3-1	4-0	0-3	0-3	3-2	—	3-1	1-0	1-0	5-0	0-1	0-0	6-2	2-1	0-1	1-2
Ekeren	3-1	1-3	0-1	3-0	2-1	2-2	1-0	2-0	—	0-1	0-0	4-1	2-2	0-1	2-0	1-0	1-4	3-1
Gent	1-2	1-1	2-0	2-1	1-1	2-2	3-1	0-0	2-1	—	3-0	1-1	0-0	0-0	4-1	2-1	5-1	2-2
Liege	0-1	1-1	3-1	3-2	0-0	0-0	0-1	3-1	2-0	2-2	—	4-2	4-0	0-0	0-0	2-0	0-0	2-0
Lierse	0-4	2-1	3-2	4-0	1-3	1-5	2-1	3-0	2-1	0-1	2-1	—	4-3	1-1	0-0	1-3	0-4	2-0
Lokeren	1-3	0-0	0-2	0-3	2-1	0-3	3-1	0-1	2-1	1-1	1-1	1-3	—	0-0	0-0	0-0	0-0	1-1
Mechelen	0-0	0-0	2-2	4-0	3-0	3-1	1-1	1-0	3-0	3-0	7-0	2-0	3-0	—	5-1	4-0	4-0	2-0
Racing Mechelen	0-3	0-0	1-3	1-0	1-2	1-2	1-1	0-0	1-1	2-0	1-1	1-1	3-4	0-4	—	3-0	1-0	0-0
St.Truiden	0-4	1-0	1-1	1-1	1-0	1-4	0-0	1-1	0-0	2-1	1-1	2-0	0-1	1-0	0-0	—	1-1	1-1
Standard	0-2	2-1	1-1	1-1	4-1	1-1	5-1	0-0	2-0	1-1	2-0	2-0	5-0	2-0	2-1	2-1	—	1-1
Waregem	0-5	1-4	4-0	4-0	2-1	1-3	2-2	0-1	1-1	0-2	3-1	2-1	1-1	0-2	2-1	0-3	1-1	—

FRANCE – LEAGUE RESULTS 1989–90

	Auxerre	Bordeaux	Brest	Caen	Cannes	Lille	Lyon	Marseille	Metz	Monaco	Montpellier	Mulhouse	Nantes	Nice	Paris-St Germain	Racing	St-Etienne	Sochaux	Toulon	Toulouse
Auxerre	—	1-1	3-1	3-0	1-0	3-0	0-1	0-2	1-1	0-0	2-1	3-1	0-0	1-0	2-0	2-0	2-1	1-1	2-0	2-2
Bordeaux	0-1	—	3-0	2-1	2-0	3-1	2-0	3-0	1-0	0-0	2-0	1-0	3-0	3-0	4-0	1-0	1-0	2-1	2-1	
Brest	2-1	2-0	—	2-1	2-0	1-0	0-2	2-1	2-0	1-1	1-1	2-0	3-2	3-0	0-1	2-0	0-0	1-0	2-1	0-0
Caen	1-0	1-0	2-1	—	1-0	2-0	1-0	0-2	1-0	1-1	3-2	1-0	2-0	1-1	2-0	1-0	3-2	1-1	2-2	0-1
Cannes	2-2	3-0	1-1	3-1	—	3-0	2-1	2-2	1-0	0-0	1-1	4-1	2-1	1-0	3-1	3-1	0-0	1-1	0-0	2-2
Lille	2-1	0-1	1-2	1-0	2-1	—	0-0	2-1	1-1	1-0	1-1	1-1	1-0	2-0	2-1	2-2	5-0	3-0	3-0	
Lyon	1-1	0-0	4-0	2-1	0-1	2-1	—	1-4	0-0	0-2	3-1	3-1	·	2-0	1-2	1-1	0-0	0-4	3-2	3-0
Marseille	1-1	2-0	1-0	1-0	1-1	4-1	0-1	—	2-1	2-2	2-0	3-1	1-0	3-0	2-1	4-1	2-0	6-1	3-0	6-1
Metz	2-1	0-0	1-1	0-0	2-2	1-1	2-3	3-2	—	1-0	1-0	1-1	1-1	0-0	0-1	0-0	1-0	2-0	0-0	3-0
Monaco	2-4	2-0	2-0	2-1	0-0	1-1	1-0	1-3	1-0	—	1-0	0-0	0-0	2-0	4-0	0-0	2-1	2-1	2-0	
Montpellier	1-0	1-2	1-1	5-1	4-1	5-0	2-0	1-1	1-1	0-0	—	3-3	2-1	1-0	2-0	2-1	3-3	2-0	3-0	1-0
Mulhouse	1-2	0-0	2-0	0-0	1-0	2-1	4-4	1-2	2-2	1-1	2-0	—	0-2	1-0	1-0	4-2	1-2	1-2	4-0	0-1
Nantes	2-1	2-1	1-0	0-0	1-0	1-0	2-1	0-0	0-0	1-1	3-2	—	2-2	0-1	5-1	2-0	0-1	4-0	0-1	
Nice	1-1	1-0	0-1	1-0	2-0	1-1	1-0	1-1	0-0	1-0	3-0	2-0	1-2	—	3-3	2-0	1-3	2-4	1-2	1-1
Paris St. Germain	1-1	1-1	3-1	3-1	5-1	2-1	0-1	2-1	1-0	2-1	2-1	0-0	2-2	2-1	—	1-2	2-0	1-0	1-1	0-0
Racing	3-1	1-3	1-1	0-0	3-2	2-0	0-1	1-1	1-1	0-0	0-0	2-1	5-1	2-2	—	3-0	1-1	0-2	1-0	
St-Etienne	4-1	1-1	2-0	0-0	1-0	2-1	1-0	0-0	4-3	0-2	1-0	3-0	0-0	0-0	1-2	0-1	—	0-2	1-2	0-3
Sochaux	0-0	2-0	1-0	5-0	3-0	1-0	1-0	0-2	0-0	1-0	3-1	0-0	1-3	1-1	1-0	2-0	2-3	—	1-0	1-0
Toulon	1-0	0-2	2-0	0-0	0-1	1-1	1-1	0-4	1-1	2-0	3-0	2-1	0-0	1-1	0-3	1-0	2-0	2-1	—	0-0
Toulouse	1-1	0-1	2-1	2-1	4-0	3-1	0-0	2-1	2-0	0-1	0-0	3-0	1-1	0-1	4-1	1-0	1-1	0-0	0-0	—

WEST GERMANY – LEAGUE RESULTS 1989–90

	Bochum	Werder Bremen	Borussia Dortmund	Fortuna Dusseldorf	Eintracht Frankfurt	Hamburg	Homburg	Kaiserslautern	Karlsruhe	Cologne	Bayer Leverkusen	Waldhof Mannheim	Moenchengladbach	Bayern Munich	Nuremberg	St. Pauli	Stuttgart	Bayer Uerdingen
Bochum	—	0-0	2-3	1-2	2-2	3-1	1-0	2-0	2-0	0-1	0-2	2-0	2-1	0-0	3-3	3-3	2-0	2-1
Werder Bremen	1-1	—	2-0	2-2	1-2	2-1	0-0	4-0	4-0	0-0	0-1	0-0	2-2	4-0	2-1	6-1	0-0	
Borussia Dortmund	0-1	4-1	—	1-0	0-0	1-0	3-0	1-1	2-0	0-0	1-1	2-0	3-2	2-1	3-1	2-0	1-0	
Fortuna Dusseldorf	2-2	2-1	1-1	—	1-0	1-1	1-0	1-1	0-0	1-1	2-0	0-0	0-1	1-2	0-0	7-0	4-2	2-1
Eintracht Frankfurt	4-0	1-0	0-2	2-0	—	2-0	1-1	1-1	1-1	3-1	0-3	3-1	3-0	1-2	5-1	4-1	5-1	2-1
Hamburg	1-4	4-0	1-1	1-0	1-1	—	2-0	3-0	1-0	0-2	1-1	1-0	3-0	0-3	1-0	0-0	1-0	6-0
Homburg	1-0	1-1	3-3	1-0	2-3	0-1	—	2-2	2-0	0-1	2-1	2-1	1-3	1-3	0-1	0-2	4-2	1-2
Kaiserslautern	2-1	2-2	2-2	1-0	2-1	1-3	3-1	—	5-1	1-2	2-0	2-3	2-1	0-0	0-2	1-1	1-2	2-1
Karlsruhe	2-0	2-1	2-1	2-2	1-0	2-0	0-2	0-0	—	0-0	2-1	4-0	0-1	3-3	0-0	0-0	1-0	0-1
Cologne	2-0	4-2	1-1	1-3	3-5	2-0	1-0	4-1	0-5	—	1-1	6-0	3-0	1-1	2-1	1-0	0-0	0-1
Bayer Leverkusen	2-1	1-3	1-0	3-3	2-0	1-0	3-1	1-1	1-1	0-2	—	3-0	0-0	0-0	2-0	1-1	1-1	1-1
Waldhof Mannheim	3-2	0-0	2-1	0-1	1-1	4-1	1-2	4-0	1-0	2-3	1-1	—	4-2	1-0	1-1	0-1	2-1	1-1
Moenchengladbach	1-2	4-0	0-0	3-1	2-1	1-3	0-0	3-1	0-0	0-2	1-1	2-0	—	0-0	3-0	4-1	3-1	0-1
Bayern Munich	5-1	1-1	3-0	0-0	1-0	4-0	1-0	3-0	4-1	5-1	0-1	2-0	2-0	—	3-2	1-3	3-1	3-0
Nuremberg	2-1	1-1	1-3	3-0	1-0	2-0	2-0	0-0	2-0	1-1	2-2	2-0	2-0	4-0	—	0-1	0-2	1-1
St. Pauli	2-0	0-0	2-1	1-0	2-2	0-0	1-1	0-2	1-1	1-1	3-0	2-1	2-1	0-2	0-1	—	0-0	1-1
Stuttgart	1-0	3-1	3-1	4-0	1-1	3-0	2-2	0-1	2-0	3-1	1-0	1-0	4-0	2-1	4-0	4-0	—	1-0
Bayer Uerdingen	3-1	0-1	1-3	0-1	1-1	5-2	3-0	3-2	1-0	2-3	0-2	0-2	0-0	2-2	3-3	1-0	4-1	—

HOLLAND – LEAGUE RESULTS 1989–90

	Ajax	Den Bosch	Feyenoord	Fortuna Sittard	Groningen	Den Haag	Haarlem	Maastricht	Nijmegen	PSV Eindhoven	RKC	Roda	Sparta	Twente	Utrecht	Vitesse	Volendam	Willem II
Ajax	—	6-0	1-1	1-0	3-2	1-0	5-0	5-0	3-0	3-2	0-0	2-2	1-2	4-0	3-0	5-2	0-0	1-0
Den Bosch	0-1	—	1-1	1-1	0-0	0-1	1-0	0-3	1-0	1-1	1-2	1-1	3-0	4-2	2-0	1-2	0-0	1-1
Feyenoord	0-1	2-0	—	0-2	3-3	0-2	5-0	2-0	2-1	4-0	5-0	2-2	6-1	2-3	0-0	0-0	1-1	4-1
Fortuna Sittard	0-0	2-0	1-1	—	0-0	2-1	1-0	1-1	1-1	4-1	1-1	1-1	2-1	2-3	1-0	0-0	4-1	3-0
Groningen	0-1	0-0	3-3	0-0	—	2-1	3-3	5-2	1-1	0-0	1-2	1-1	2-2	5-0	2-0	3-1	3-0	1-1
Den Haag	0-4	3-1	2-0	4-1	2-2	—	6-1	6-1	2-2	1-5	1-1	1-3	1-0	3-1	1-1	2-1	2-1	0-3
Haarlem	0-4	2-0	3-1	0-3	0-1	1-2	—	1-1	1-1	0-2	0-2	0-0	0-4	0-1	1-2	0-2	2-1	0-2
Maastricht	1-0	3-0	1-1	1-1	1-3	3-0	1-1	—	2-0	0-1	3-0	1-1	1-2	0-0	0-0	1-5	0-1	2-1
Nijmegen	1-1	2-2	0-0	1-0	1-1	3-3	3-1	0-0	—	1-4	2-1	0-1	1-2	2-2	0-0	0-4	2-2	2-2
PSV Eindhoven	2-0	1-1	1-1	2-0	2-0	9-2	4-0	8-1	6-0	—	4-0	3-4	9-1	1-1	1-0	0-1	2-2	2-1
RKC	0-3	1-1	3-0	3-1	3-1	3-2	1-0	1-1	3-1	0-3	—	3-1	3-0	0-0	3-3	0-1	1-1	2-2
Roda	1-1	0-3	2-0	0-1	1-1	3-1	5-0	3-2	0-0	3-1	3-0	—	1-1	2-0	1-0	0-1	2-1	4-1
Sparta	1-2	4-2	2-2	4-1	3-0	3-1	0-1	2-2	1-2	0-4	2-1	3-1	—	3-0	0-1	1-1	2-0	1-1
Twente	2-1	4-1	1-0	1-1	4-1	1-0	2-2	3-0	2-1	0-0	0-1	1-1	2-0	—	3-1	1-1	1-0	2-0
Utrecht	0-0	1-1	3-0	0-1	1-0	2-1	0-0	0-0	3-0	1-7	1-1	0-1	2-1	1-2	—	1-2	0-3	2-1
Vitesse	1-1	0-0	2-1	1-1	0-1	1-1	4-0	2-1	0-0	0-2	1-1	2-0	2-1	1-2	5-1	—	0-1	2-0
Volendam	2-2	3-0	2-0	2-2	1-2	0-2	1-0	4-1	1-0	0-0	1-0	2-0	2-0	2-1	1-0	1-0	—	2-1
Willem II	1-1	1-0	0-1	2-0	3-0	1-1	3-2	1-1	0-1	3-4	0-2	2-2	1-1	0-0	0-0	1-1	5-1	—

ITALY – LEAGUE RESULTS 1989–90

	Ascoli	Atalanta	Bari	Bologna	Cesena	Cremonese	Fiorentina	Genoa	Internazionale	Juventus	Lazio	Lecce	AC Milan	Napoli	Roma	Sampdoria	Udinese	Verona
Ascoli	—	1-1	1-1	1-1	0-0	0-1	2-1	0-0	0-1	1-2	0-0	0-2	1-0	0-1	1-1	2-1	1-0	1-1
Atalanta	1-0	—	0-0	1-0	2-0	0-0	1-0	2-1	1-2	4-0	2-1	0-1	0-2	3-0	2-2	1-0	1-0	1-0
Bari	2-2	4-0	—	0-0	2-0	2-0	1-1	0-0	0-0	1-1	0-0	0-1	0-1	1-1	1-2	0-2	3-1	2-1
Bologna	2-1	0-0	3-1	—	1-0	1-1	1-0	2-2	1-1	1-1	2-1	0-0	2-4	1-1	1-0	0-0	1-0	1-0
Cesena	1-0	0-0	2-2	0-0	—	1-1	1-1	1-1	2-3	1-1	0-0	4-0	0-3	0-0	0-0	1-2	1-1	1-0
Cremonese	2-1	1-1	0-2	2-1	1-2	—	1-2	0-1	0-1	2-2	1-1	1-0	1-1	0-1	0-3	2-2	1-1	
Fiorentina	5-1	4-1	2-2	0-1	0-0	0-0	—	0-0	2-2	2-2	1-0	3-0	2-3	0-1	1-2	3-1	1-2	3-1
Genoa	2-0	2-2	0-0	0-0	2-3	1-0	1-1	—	0-0	2-3	2-2	1-0	1-1	1-1	0-2	1-2	0-0	0-1
Internazionale	0-0	7-2	1-1	3-0	1-1	2-1	2-0	1-0	—	2-1	3-0	0-3	3-1	3-0	2-0	2-0	0-0	
Juventus	3-1	0-1	1-0	1-1	1-1	4-0	3-1	1-1	1-0	—	1-0	3-0	3-0	1-1	1-1	1-0	1-1	2-1
Lazio	3-0	1-2	2-2	3-0	4-0	1-1	1-1	0-0	2-1	1-1	—	3-0	1-3	3-0	0-1	0-2	0-0	0-0
Lecce	1-1	2-1	1-1	1-0	2-1	2-1	1-0	2-1	0-0	2-3	0-0	—	1-2	1-1	0-2	0-0	1-0	1-0
AC Milan	2-1	3-1	4-0	1-0	3-0	2-1	1-1	1-0	1-3	3-2	0-1	2-0	—	3-0	1-0	1-0	3-1	0-0
Napoli	1-0	3-1	3-0	2-0	1-0	3-0	3-2	2-1	2-0	3-1	1-0	3-2	3-0	—	3-1	1-1	1-0	2-0
Roma	0-0	4-1	1-0	2-2	1-0	3-2	0-0	0-1	1-1	1-0	1-1	2-1	0-4	1-1	—	1-1	3-1	5-2
Sampdoria	2-0	1-0	0-0	3-0	0-0	1-1	3-0	0-0	2-0	0-0	2-0	1-0	1-1	2-1	4-2	—	3-1	1-0
Udinese	2-0	0-0	2-2	1-1	1-0	1-1	1-1	2-4	4-3	2-2	0-2	3-1	0-2	2-2	1-1	3-3	—	2-1
Verona	0-0	1-1	1-1	3-2	0-2	1-1	1-0	1-1	0-3	1-4	1-1	0-0	2-1	1-2	2-2	1-0	2-0	—

SPAIN – LEAGUE RESULTS 1989–90

	Athletic Bilbao	Atletico Madrid	Barcelona	Cadix	Castellon	Celta Vigo	Logrones	Malaga	Mallorca	Osasuna	Oviedo	Rayo Vallecano	Real Madrid	Real Sociedad	Seville	Sporting Gijon	Tenerife	Valencia	Valladolid	Zaragoza
Athletic Bilbao	—	1-1	1-2	3-1	2-1	2-0	1-0	3-0	0-0	1-1	0-0	3-2	1-1	1-0	1-1	1-0	1-1	1-1	2-2	2-0
Atletico Madrid	2-0	—	1-0	1-0	4-1	2-1	3-1	2-0	1-0	0-1	1-1	2-0	3-3	0-0	1-0	3-1	2-0	1-1	1-0	2-1
Barcelona	4-2	0-2	—	5-0	2-0	6-0	4-2	1-0	1-1	4-0	0-0	7-1	3-1	2-3	3-4	2-0	3-0	2-1	1-0	3-1
Cadix	1-0	0-1	0-4	—	1-0	1-0	0-1	0-2	1-1	0-0	1-0	3-1	0-3	1-0	0-4	2-0	1-0	0-2	1-0	1-1
Castellon	1-0	0-0	1-0	1-1	—	1-0	0-0	1-1	1-2	1-2	1-1	1-0	0-0	0-2	3-1	1-0	0-0	0-1	1-1	2-1
Celta Vigo	0-0	2-0	1-2	5-1	1-0	—	0-1	1-1	2-2	1-1	0-0	0-0	0-0	0-1	0-0	1-0	1-2	0-0	2-2	
Logrones	1-0	0-2	1-2	1-1	1-0	4-1	—	1-0	0-1	1-1	2-0	1-5	1-0	2-1	1-0	4-1	1-0	1-0	2-1	
Malaga	0-1	0-0	0-1	1-0	1-1	1-1	0-2	—	0-2	1-1	1-0	1-0	1-2	0-2	2-1	1-0	2-1	1-1	0-1	0-3
Mallorca	1-0	0-0	1-0	5-1	1-1	2-0	3-1	2-0	—	2-2	2-2	1-0	0-0	0-0	1-1	1-1	0-2	0-1	1-1	0-1
Osasuna	1-1	2-1	0-3	1-0	1-2	1-0	3-0	2-0	1-0	—	4-0	2-1	0-2	1-1	2-1	0-1	3-0	2-2	1-0	2-0
Oviedo	1-0	3-0	2-0	4-3	1-1	1-0	0-4	0-0	0-2	2-0	—	3-2	0-1	5-0	0-3	1-0	2-1	0-0	0-0	2-2
Rayo Vallecano	0-0	4-4	1-4	0-1	0-2	2-0	0-2	1-0	0-0	1-1	1-1	—	1-2	0-3	2-1	1-2	1-0	2-2	2-1	2-2
Real Madrid	4-0	3-1	3-2	4-1	7-0	3-0	3-3	4-0	1-1	4-1	5-2	5-2	—	3-0	5-2	2-0	5-2	6-2	4-0	7-2
Real Sociedad	0-0	0-0	2-2	2-0	2-0	1-0	1-0	1-1	2-0	1-0	1-1	4-1	2-1	—	2-1	1-2	1-0	2-2	1-1	2-1
Seville	3-2	1-1	1-1	3-2	2-1	3-1	3-1	3-0	1-1	1-2	4-0	1-2	0-1	—	1-0	1-0	4-0	0-0	4-0	
Sporting Gijon	0-1	2-1	0-2	4-0	0-0	3-0	5-1	0-1	3-0	0-0	0-0	1-0	1-1	0-0	0-1	—	1-0	1-1	3-0	1-1
Tenerife	1-1	2-3	1-4	0-1	3-0	2-1	3-1	2-2	1-1	2-0	2-1	1-0	2-3	2-2	1-2	1-1	—	1-0	1-0	1-2
Valencia	1-1	1-3	2-1	3-0	2-2	2-0	4-0	3-0	1-0	3-1	3-0	4-1	1-1	3-1	1-1	2-0	2-1	—	4-3	2-1
Valladolid	3-1	2-0	2-0	1-2	0-0	0-1	0-1	0-1	0-0	1-1	1-1	1-0	0-0	1-0	3-0	1-3	1-2	0-2	—	2-1
Zaragoza	1-0	0-2	2-0	1-0	3-1	1-1	1-0	3-0	1-0	1-0	2-0	3-0	0-1	2-1	1-0	2-1	3-3	0-1	2-2	—

BRITISH INTERNATIONAL RESULTS 1872–1990

BRITISH INTERNATIONAL CHAMPIONSHIP 1883–1984

Year	Champions	Pts	Year	Champions	Pts	Year	Champions	Pts
1883–84	Scotland	6	1920–21	Scotland	6	1956–57	England	5
1884–85	Scotland	5	1921–22	Scotland	4	1957–58	{ England	4
1885–86	{ England	5	1922–23	Scotland	5		{ N. Ireland	4
	{ Scotland	5	1923–24	Wales	6	1958–59	{ N. Ireland	4
1886–87	Scotland	6	1924–25	Scotland	6		{ England	4
1887–88	England	6	1925–26	Scotland	6	1959–60	{ England	4
1888–89	Scotland	5	1926–27	{ Scotland	4		{ Scotland	4
1889–90	{ Scotland	5		{ England	4		{ Wales	4
	{ England	5	1927–28	Wales	5	1960–61	England	6
1890–91	England	6	1928–29	Scotland	6	1961–62	Scotland	6
1891–92	England	6	1929–30	England	6	1962–63	Scotland	6
1892–93	England	6	1930–31	{ Scotland	4	1963–64	{ Scotland	4
1893–94	Scotland	5		{ England	4		{ England	4
1894–95	England	5	1931–32	England	6		{ N. Ireland	4
1895–96	Scotland	5	1932–33	Wales	5	1964–65	England	5
1896–97	Scotland	5	1933–34	Wales	5	1965–66	England	5
1897–98	England	6	1934–35	{ England	4	1966–67	Scotland	5
1898–99	England	6		{ Scotland	4	1967–68	England	5
1899–1900	Scotland	6	1935–36	Scotland	4	1968–69	England	6
1900–01	England	5	1936–37	Wales	6	1969–70	{ England	4
1901–02	Scotland	5	1937–38	England	4		{ Scotland	4
1902–03	{ England	4	1938–39	{ England	4		{ Wales	4
	{ Ireland	4		{ Scotland	4	1970–71	England	5
	{ Scotland	4		{ Wales	4	1971–72	{ England	4
1903–04	England	5	1946–47	England	5		{ Scotland	4
1904–05	England	5	1947–48	England	5	1972–73	England	6
1905–06	{ England	4	1948–49	Scotland	6	1973–74	{ England	4
	{ Scotland	4	1949–50	England	6		{ Scotland	4
1906–07	Wales	5	1950–51	Scotland	6	1974–75	England	4
1907–08	{ Scotland	5	1951–52	{ Wales	5	1975–76	Scotland	6
	{ England	5		{ England	5	1976–77	Scotland	5
1908–09	England	6	1952–53	{ England	4	1977–78	England	6
1909–10	Scotland	4		{ Scotland	4	1978–79	England	5
1910–11	England	5	1953–54	England	6	1979–80	N. Ireland	5
1911–12	{ England	5	1954–55	England	6	1980–81	*Not completed*	
	{ Scotland	5	1955–56	{ England	3	1981–82	England	6
1912–13	England	4		{ Scotland	3	1982–83	England	5
1913–14	Ireland	5		{ Wales	3	1983–84	N. Ireland	3
1919–20	Wales	4		{ N. Ireland	3			

Note: In the results that follow, wc = World Cup, ec = European Championship. For Ireland, read Northern Ireland from 1921.

ENGLAND v SCOTLAND

Played: 107; England won 43, Scotland won 40, Drawn 24. *Goals:* England 188, Scotland 168.

	E	S		E	S		E	S
1872 Glasgow	0	0	1887 Blackburn	2	3	1902 Birmingham	2	2
1873 Kennington Oval	4	2	1888 Glasgow	5	0	1903 Sheffield	1	2
1874 Glasgow	1	2	1889 Kennington Oval	2	3	1904 Glasgow	1	0
1875 Kennington Oval	2	2	1890 Glasgow	1	1	1905 Crystal Palace	1	0
1876 Glasgow	0	3	1891 Blackburn	2	1	1906 Glasgow	1	2
1877 Kennington Oval	1	3	1892 Glasgow	4	1	1907 Newcastle	1	1
1878 Glasgow	2	7	1893 Richmond	5	2	1908 Glasgow	1	1
1879 Kennington Oval	5	4	1894 Glasgow	2	2	1909 Crystal Palace	2	0
1880 Glasgow	4	5	1895 Everton	3	0	1910 Glasgow	0	2
1881 Kennington Oval	1	6	1896 Glasgow	1	2	1911 Everton	1	1
1882 Glasgow	1	5	1897 Crystal Palace	1	2	1912 Glasgow	1	1
1883 Sheffield	2	3	1898 Glasgow	3	1	1913 Chelsea	1	0
1884 Glasgow	0	1	1899 Birmingham	2	1	1914 Glasgow	1	3
1885 Kennington Oval	1	1	1900 Glasgow	1	4	1920 Sheffield	5	4
1886 Glasgow	1	1	1901 Crystal Palace	2	2	1921 Glasgow	0	3

Year	Venue			Year	Venue			Year	Venue		
1922	Aston Villa	0	1	wc1950	Glasgow	1	0	1971	Wembley	3	1
1923	Glasgow	2	2	1951	Wembley	2	3	1972	Glasgow	1	0
1924	Wembley	1	1	1952	Glasgow	2	1	1973	Glasgow	5	0
1925	Glasgow	0	2	1953	Wembley	2	2	1973	Wembley	1	0
1926	Manchester	0	1	wc1954	Glasgow	4	2	1974	Glasgow	0	2
1927	Glasgow	2	1	1955	Wembley	7	2	1975	Wembley	5	1
1928	Wembley	1	5	1956	Glasgow	1	1	1976	Glasgow	1	2
1929	Glasgow	0	1	1957	Wembley	2	1	1977	Wembley	1	2
1930	Wembley	5	2	1958	Glasgow	4	0	1978	Glasgow	1	0
1931	Glasgow	0	2	1959	Wembley	1	0	1979	Wembley	3	1
1932	Wembley	3	0	1960	Glasgow	1	1	1980	Glasgow	2	0
1933	Glasgow	1	2	1961	Wembley	9	3	1981	Wembley	0	1
1934	Wembley	3	0	1962	Glasgow	0	2	1982	Glasgow	1	0
1935	Glasgow	0	2	1963	Wembley	1	2	1983	Wembley	2	0
1936	Wembley	1	1	1964	Glasgow	0	1	1984	Glasgow	1	1
1937	Glasgow	1	3	1965	Wembley	2	2	1985	Glasgow	0	1
1938	Wembley	0	1	1966	Glasgow	4	3	1986	Wembley	2	1
1939	Glasgow	2	1	ec1967	Wembley	2	3	1987	Glasgow	0	0
1947	Wembley	1	1	ec1968	Glasgow	1	1	1988	Wembley	1	0
1948	Glasgow	2	0	1969	Wembley	4	1	1989	Glasgow	2	0
1949	Wembley	1	3	1970	Glasgow	0	0				

ENGLAND v WALES

Played: 97; England won 62, Wales won 14, Drawn 21. *Goals:* England 239, Wales 90.

Year	Venue	E	W	Year	Venue	E	W	Year	Venue	E	W
1879	Kennington Oval	2	1	1911	Millwall	3	0	1955	Cardiff	1	2
1880	Wrexham	3	2	1912	Wrexham	2	0	1956	Wembley	3	1
1881	Blackburn	0	1	1913	Bristol	4	3	1957	Cardiff	4	0
1882	Wrexham	3	5	1914	Cardiff	2	0	1958	Aston Villa	2	2
1883	Kennington Oval	5	0	1920	Highbury	1	2	1959	Cardiff	1	1
1884	Wrexham	4	0	1921	Cardiff	0	0	1960	Wembley	5	1
1885	Blackburn	1	1	1922	Liverpool	1	0	1961	Cardiff	1	1
1886	Wrexham	3	1	1923	Cardiff	2	2	1962	Wembley	4	0
1887	Kennington Oval	4	0	1924	Blackburn	1	2	1963	Cardiff	4	0
1888	Crewe	5	1	1925	Swansea	2	1	1964	Wembley	2	1
1889	Stoke	4	1	1926	Crystal Palace	1	3	1965	Cardiff	0	0
1890	Wrexham	3	1	1927	Wrexham	3	3	ec1966	Wembley	5	1
1891	Sunderland	4	1	1927	Burnley	1	2	ec1967	Cardiff	3	0
1892	Wrexham	2	0	1928	Swansea	3	2	1969	Wembley	2	1
1893	Stoke	6	0	1929	Chelsea	6	0	1970	Cardiff	1	1
1894	Wrexham	5	1	1930	Wrexham	4	0	1971	Wembley	0	0
1894	Queen's Club, Kensington	1	1	1931	Liverpool	3	1	1972	Cardiff	3	0
1896	Cardiff	9	1	1932	Wrexham	0	0	wc1972	Cardiff	1	0
1897	Sheffield	4	0	1933	Newcastle	1	2	wc1973	Wembley	1	1
1898	Wrexham	3	0	1934	Cardiff	4	0	1973	Wembley	3	0
1899	Bristol	4	0	1935	Wolverhampton	1	2	1974	Cardiff	2	0
1900	Cardiff	1	1	1936	Cardiff	1	2	1975	Wembley	2	2
1901	Newcastle	6	0	1937	Middlesbrough	2	1	1976	Wrexham	2	1
1902	Wrexham	0	0	1938	Cardiff	2	4	1976	Cardiff	1	0
1903	Portsmouth	2	1	1946	Manchester	3	0	1977	Wembley	0	1
1904	Wrexham	2	2	1947	Cardiff	3	0	1978	Cardiff	3	1
1905	Liverpool	3	1	1948	Aston Villa	1	0	1979	Wembley	0	0
1906	Cardiff	1	0	wc1949	Cardiff	4	1	1980	Wrexham	1	4
1907	Fulham	1	1	1950	Sunderland	4	2	1981	Wembley	0	0
1908	Wrexham	7	1	1951	Cardiff	1	1	1982	Cardiff	1	0
1909	Nottingham	2	0	1952	Wembley	5	2	1983	Wembley	2	1
1910	Cardiff	1	0	wc1953	Cardiff	4	1	1984	Wrexham	0	1
				1954	Wembley	3	2				

ENGLAND v IRELAND

Played: 96; England won 74, Ireland won 6, Drawn 16. *Goals:* England 319, Ireland 80.

	E	I		E	I		E	I
1882 Belfast	13	0	1914 Middlesbrough	0	3	1957 Wembley	2	3
1883 Liverpool	7	0	1919 Belfast	1	1	1958 Belfast	3	3
1884 Belfast	8	1	1920 Sunderland	2	0	1959 Wembley	2	1
1885 Manchester	4	0	1921 Belfast	1	1	1960 Belfast	5	2
1886 Belfast	6	1	1922 West Bromwich	2	0	1961 Wembley	1	1
1887 Sheffield	7	0	1923 Belfast	1	2	1962 Belfast	3	1
1888 Belfast	5	1	1924 Everton	3	1	1963 Wembley	8	3
1889 Everton	6	1	1925 Belfast	0	0	1964 Belfast	4	3
1890 Belfast	9	1	1926 Liverpool	3	3	1965 Wembley	2	1
1891 Wolverhampton	6	1	1927 Belfast	0	2	EC1966 Belfast	2	0
1892 Belfast	2	0	1928 Everton	2	1	EC1967 Wembley	2	0
1893 Birmingham	6	1	1929 Belfast	3	0	1969 Belfast	3	1
1894 Belfast	2	2	1930 Sheffield	5	1	1970 Wembley	3	1
1895 Derby	9	0	1931 Belfast	6	2	1971 Belfast	1	0
1896 Belfast	2	0	1932 Blackpool	1	0	1972 Wembley	0	1
1897 Nottingham	6	0	1933 Belfast	3	0	1973 Everton	2	1
1898 Belfast	3	2	1935 Everton	2	1	1974 Wembley	1	0
1899 Sunderland	13	2	1935 Belfast	3	1	1975 Belfast	0	0
1900 Dublin	2	0	1936 Stoke	3	1	1976 Wembley	4	0
1901 Southampton	3	0	1937 Belfast	5	1	1977 Belfast	2	1
1902 Belfast	1	0	1938 Manchester	7	0	1978 Wembley	1	0
1903 Wolverhampton	4	0	1946 Belfast	7	2	EC1979 Wembley	4	0
1904 Belfast	3	1	1947 Everton	2	2	1979 Belfast	2	0
1905 Middlesbrough	1	1	1948 Belfast	6	2	EC1979 Belfast	5	1
1906 Belfast	5	0	wc1949 Manchester	9	2	1980 Wembley	1	1
1907 Everton	1	0	1950 Belfast	4	1	1982 Wembley	4	0
1908 Belfast	3	1	1951 Aston Villa	2	0	1983 Belfast	0	0
1909 Bradford	4	0	1952 Belfast	2	2	1984 Wembley	1	0
1910 Belfast	1	1	wc1953 Everton	3	1	wc1985 Belfast	1	0
1911 Derby	2	1	1954 Belfast	2	0	wc1985 Wembley	0	0
1912 Dublin	6	1	1955 Wembley	3	0	EC1986 Wembley	3	0
1913 Belfast	1	2	1956 Belfast	1	1	EC1987 Belfast	2	0

SCOTLAND v WALES

Played: 101; Scotland won 60, Wales won 18, Drawn 23. *Goals:* Scotland 238, Wales 111.

	S	W		S	W		S	W
1876 Glasgow	4	0	1910 Kilmarnock	1	0	1955 Glasgow	2	0
1877 Wrexham	2	0	1911 Cardiff	2	2	1956 Cardiff	2	2
1878 Glasgow	9	0	1912 Tynecastle	1	0	1957 Glasgow	1	1
1879 Wrexham	3	0	1913 Wrexham	0	0	1958 Cardiff	3	0
1880 Glasgow	5	1	1914 Glasgow	0	0	1959 Glasgow	1	1
1881 Wrexham	5	1	1920 Cardiff	1	1	1960 Cardiff	0	2
1882 Glasgow	5	0	1921 Aberdeen	2	1	1961 Glasgow	2	0
1883 Wrexham	4	1	1922 Wrexham	1	2	1962 Cardiff	3	2
1884 Glasgow	4	1	1923 Paisley	2	0	1963 Glasgow	2	1
1885 Wrexham	8	1	1924 Cardiff	0	2	1964 Cardiff	2	3
1886 Glasgow	4	1	1925 Tynecastle	3	1	EC1965 Glasgow	4	1
1887 Wrexham	2	0	1926 Cardiff	3	0	EC1966 Cardiff	1	1
1888 Edinburgh	5	1	1927 Glasgow	3	0	1967 Glasgow	3	2
1889 Wrexham	0	0	1928 Wrexham	2	2	1969 Wrexham	5	3
1890 Paisley	5	0	1929 Glasgow	4	2	1970 Glasgow	0	0
1891 Wrexham	4	3	1930 Cardiff	4	2	1971 Cardiff	0	0
1892 Edinburgh	6	1	1931 Glasgow	1	1	1972 Glasgow	1	0
1893 Wrexham	8	0	1932 Wrexham	3	2	1973 Wrexham	2	0
1894 Kilmarnock	5	2	1933 Edinburgh	2	5	1974 Glasgow	2	0
1895 Wrexham	2	2	1934 Cardiff	2	3	1975 Cardiff	2	2
1896 Dundee	4	0	1935 Aberdeen	3	2	1976 Glasgow	3	1
1897 Wrexham	2	2	1936 Cardiff	1	1	wc1977 Glasgow	1	0
1898 Motherwell	5	2	1937 Dundee	1	2	1977 Wrexham	0	0
1899 Wrexham	6	0	1938 Cardiff	1	2	wc1977 Liverpool	2	0
1900 Aberdeen	5	2	1939 Edinburgh	3	2	1978 Glasgow	1	1
1901 Wrexham	1	1	1946 Wrexham	1	3	1979 Cardiff	0	3
1902 Greenock	5	1	1947 Glasgow	1	2	1980 Glasgow	1	0
1903 Cardiff	1	0	wc1948 Cardiff	3	1	1981 Swansea	0	2
1904 Dundee	1	1	1949 Glasgow	2	0	1982 Glasgow	1	0
1905 Wrexham	1	3	1950 Cardiff	3	1	1983 Cardiff	2	0
1906 Edinburgh	0	2	1951 Glasgow	0	1	1984 Glasgow	2	1
1907 Wrexham	0	1	wc1952 Cardiff	2	1	wc1985 Glasgow	0	1
1908 Dundee	2	1	1953 Glasgow	3	3	wc1985 Cardiff	1	1
1909 Wrexham	2	3	1954 Cardiff	1	0			

SCOTLAND v IRELAND

Played: 91; Scotland won 60, Ireland won 15, Drawn 16. *Goals:* Scotland 253, Ireland 81.

Year	Venue	S	I	Year	Venue	S	I	Year	Venue	S	I
1884	Belfast	5	0	1920	Glasgow	3	0	1957	Belfast	1	1
1885	Glasgow	8	2	1921	Belfast	2	0	1958	Glasgow	2	2
1886	Belfast	7	2	1922	Glasgow	2	1	1959	Belfast	4	0
1887	Glasgow	4	1	1923	Belfast	1	0	1960	Glasgow	5	2
1888	Belfast	10	2	1924	Glasgow	2	0	1961	Belfast	6	1
1889	Glasgow	7	0	1925	Belfast	3	0	1962	Glasgow	5	1
1890	Belfast	4	1	1926	Glasgow	4	0	1963	Belfast	1	2
1891	Glasgow	2	1	1927	Belfast	2	0	1964	Glasgow	3	2
1892	Belfast	3	2	1928	Glasgow	0	1	1965	Belfast	2	3
1893	Glasgow	6	1	1929	Belfast	7	3	1966	Glasgow	2	1
1894	Belfast	2	1	1930	Glasgow	3	1	1967	Belfast	0	1
1895	Glasgow	3	1	1931	Belfast	0	0	1969	Glasgow	1	1
1896	Belfast	3	3	1932	Glasgow	3	1	1970	Belfast	1	0
1897	Glasgow	5	1	1933	Belfast	4	0	1971	Glasgow	0	1
1898	Belfast	3	0	1934	Glasgow	1	2	1972	Glasgow	2	0
1899	Glasgow	9	1	1935	Belfast	1	2	1973	Glasgow	1	2
1900	Belfast	3	0	1936	Edinburgh	2	1	1974	Glasgow	0	1
1901	Glasgow	11	0	1937	Belfast	3	1	1975	Glasgow	3	0
1902	Belfast	5	1	1938	Aberdeen	1	1	1976	Glasgow	3	0
1903	Glasgow	0	2	1939	Belfast	2	0	1977	Glasgow	3	0
1904	Dublin	1	1	1946	Glasgow	0	0	1978	Glasgow	1	1
1905	Glasgow	4	0	1947	Belfast	0	2	1979	Glasgow	1	0
1906	Dublin	1	0	1948	Glasgow	3	2	1980	Belfast	0	1
1907	Glasgow	3	0	1949	Belfast	8	2	wc1981	Glasgow	1	1
1908	Dublin	5	0	1950	Glasgow	6	1	1981	Glasgow	2	0
1909	Glasgow	5	0	1951	Belfast	3	0	wc1981	Belfast	0	0
1910	Belfast	0	1	1952	Glasgow	1	1	1982	Belfast	1	1
1911	Glasgow	2	0	1953	Belfast	3	1	1983	Glasgow	0	0
1912	Belfast	4	1	1954	Glasgow	2	2	1984	Belfast	0	2
1913	Dublin	2	1	1955	Belfast	1	2				
1914	Belfast	1	1	1956	Glasgow	1	0				

WALES v IRELAND

Played: 90; Wales won 42, Ireland won 27, Drawn 21. *Goals:* Wales 181, Ireland 126.

Year	Venue	W	I	Year	Venue	W	I	Year	Venue	W	I
1882	Wrexham	7	1	1912	Cardiff	2	3	wc1954	Wrexham	1	2
1883	Belfast	1	1	1913	Belfast	1	0	1955	Belfast	3	2
1884	Wrexham	6	0	1914	Wrexham	1	2	1956	Cardiff	1	1
1885	Belfast	8	2	1920	Belfast	2	2	1957	Belfast	0	0
1886	Wrexham	5	0	1921	Swansea	2	1	1958	Cardiff	1	1
1887	Belfast	1	4	1922	Belfast	1	1	1959	Belfast	1	4
1888	Wrexham	11	0	1923	Wrexham	0	3	1960	Wrexham	3	2
1889	Belfast	3	1	1924	Belfast	1	0	1961	Belfast	5	1
1890	Shrewsbury	5	2	1925	Wrexham	0	0	1962	Cardiff	4	0
1891	Belfast	2	7	1926	Belfast	0	3	1963	Belfast	4	1
1892	Bangor	1	1	1927	Cardiff	2	2	1964	Belfast	2	3
1893	Belfast	3	4	1928	Belfast	2	1	1965	Belfast	5	0
1894	Swansea	4	1	1929	Wrexham	2	2	1966	Cardiff	1	4
1895	Belfast	2	2	1930	Belfast	0	7	EC1967	Belfast	0	0
1896	Wrexham	6	1	1931	Wrexham	3	2	EC1968	Wrexham	2	0
1897	Belfast	3	4	1932	Belfast	0	4	1969	Belfast	0	0
1898	Llandudno	0	1	1933	Wrexham	4	1	1970	Swansea	1	0
1899	Belfast	0	1	1934	Belfast	1	1	1971	Belfast	0	1
1900	Llandudno	2	0	1935	Wrexham	3	1	1972	Wrexham	0	0
1901	Belfast	1	0	1936	Belfast	2	3	1973	Everton	0	1
1902	Cardiff	0	3	1937	Wrexham	4	1	1974	Wrexham	1	0
1903	Belfast	0	2	1938	Belfast	0	1	1975	Belfast	0	1
1904	Bangor	0	1	1939	Wrexham	3	1	1976	Swansea	1	0
1905	Belfast	2	2	1947	Belfast	1	2	1977	Belfast	1	1
1906	Wrexham	4	4	1948	Wrexham	2	0	1978	Wrexham	1	0
1907	Belfast	3	2	1949	Belfast	2	0	1979	Belfast	1	1
1908	Aberdare	0	1	wc1950	Wrexham	0	0	1980	Cardiff	0	1
1909	Belfast	3	2	1951	Belfast	2	1	1982	Wrexham	3	0
1910	Wrexham	4	1	1952	Swansea	3	0	1983	Belfast	1	0
1911	Belfast	2	1	1953	Belfast	3	2	1984	Swansea	1	1

OTHER BRITISH INTERNATIONAL RESULTS 1908–1990
ENGLAND

v ALBANIA			E	A
wc1989	8 Mar	Tirana	2	0
wc1989	26 Apr	Wembley	5	0

v ARGENTINA			E	A
1951	9 May	Wembley	2	1
1953	17 May	Buenos Aires	0	0
(abandoned after 21 mins)				
wc1962	2 June	Rancagua	3	1
1964	6 June	Rio de Janeiro	0	1
wc1966	23 July	Wembley	1	0
1974	22 May	Wembley	2	2
1977	12 June	Buenos Aires	1	1
1980	13 May	Wembley	3	1
wc1986	22 June	Mexico City	1	2

v AUSTRALIA			E	A
1980	31 May	Sydney	2	1
1983	11 June	Sydney	0	0
1983	15 June	Brisbane	1	0
1983	18 June	Melbourne	1	1

v AUSTRIA			E	A
1908	6 June	Vienna	6	1
1908	8 June	Vienna	11	1
1909	1 June	Vienna	8	1
1930	14 May	Vienna	0	0
1932	7 Dec	Chelsea	4	3
1936	6 May	Vienna	1	2
1951	28 Nov	Wembley	2	2
1952	25 May	Vienna	3	2
wc1958	15 June	Boras	2	2
1961	27 May	Vienna	1	3
1962	4 Apr	Wembley	3	1
1965	20 Oct	Wembley	2	3
1967	27 May	Vienna	1	0
1973	26 Sept	Wembley	7	0
1979	13 June	Vienna	3	4

v BELGIUM			E	B
1921	21 May	Brussels	2	0
1923	19 Mar	Highbury	6	1
1923	1 Nov	Antwerp	2	2
1924	8 Dec	West Bromwich	4	0
1926	24 May	Antwerp	5	3
1927	11 May	Brussels	9	1
1928	19 May	Antwerp	3	1
1929	11 May	Brussels	5	1
1931	16 May	Brussels	4	1
1936	9 May	Brussels	2	3
1947	21 Sept	Brussels	5	2
1950	18 May	Brussels	4	1
1952	26 Nov	Wembley	5	0
wc1954	17 June	Basle	4	4*
1964	21 Oct	Wembley	2	2
1970	25 Feb	Brussels	3	1
EC1980	12 June	Turin	1	1
wc1990	27 June	Bologna	1	0

*After extra time

v BOHEMIA			E	B
1908	13 June	Prague	4	0

v BRAZIL			E	B
1956	9 May	Wembley	4	2
wc1958	11 June	Gothenburg	0	0
1959	13 May	Rio de Janeiro	0	2
wc1962	10 June	Vina del Mar	1	3
1963	8 May	Wembley	1	1
1964	30 May	Rio de Janeiro	1	5
1969	12 June	Rio de Janeiro	1	2
wc1970	7 June	Guadalajara	0	1
1976	23 May	Los Angeles	0	1
1977	8 June	Rio de Janeiro	0	0
1978	19 Apr	Wembley	1	1
1981	12 May	Wembley	0	1
1984	10 June	Rio de Janeiro	2	0
1987	19 May	Wembley	1	1
1990	28 Mar	Wembley	1	0

v BULGARIA			E	B
wc1962	7 June	Rancagua	0	0
1968	11 Dec	Wembley	1	1
1974	1 June	Sofia	1	0
EC1979	6 June	Sofia	3	0
EC1979	22 Nov	Wembley	2	0

v CAMEROON			E	C
wc1990	1 July		3	2

v CANADA			E	C
1986	24 May	Burnaby	1	0

v CHILE			E	C
wc1950	25 June	Rio de Janeiro	2	0
1953	24 May	Santiago	2	1
1984	17 June	Santiago	0	0
1989	23 May	Wembley	0	0

v COLOMBIA			E	C
1970	20 May	Bogota	4	0
1988	24 May	Wembley	1	1

v CYPRUS			E	C
EC1975	16 Apr	Wembley	5	0
EC1975	11 May	Limassol	1	0

v CZECHOSLOVAKIA			E	C
1934	16 May	Prague	1	2
1937	1 Dec	Tottenham	5	4
1963	29 May	Bratislava	4	2
1966	2 Nov	Wembley	0	0
wc1970	11 June	Guadalajara	1	0
1973	27 May	Prague	1	1
EC1974	30 Oct	Wembley	3	0
EC1975	30 Oct	Bratislava	1	2
1978	29 Nov	Wembley	1	0
wc1982	20 June	Bilbao	2	0
1990	25 Apr	Wembley	4	2

v DENMARK			E	D
1948	26 Sept	Copenhagen	0	0
1955	2 Oct	Copenhagen	5	1
wc1956	5 Dec	Wolverhampton	5	2
wc1957	15 May	Copenhagen	4	1
1966	3 July	Copenhagen	2	0
EC1978	20 Sept	Copenhagen	4	3
EC1979	12 Sept	Wembley	1	0
EC1982	22 Sept	Copenhagen	2	2
EC1983	21 Sept	Wembley	0	1
1988	14 Sept	Wembley	1	0
1989	7 June	Copenhagen	1	1
1990	15 May	Wembley	1	0

v ECUADOR			E	Ec
1970	24 May	Quito	2	0

v EGYPT			E	Eg
1986	29 Jan	Cairo	4	0
wc1990	21 June	Cagliari	1	0

v FIFA			E	FIFA
1938	26 Oct	Highbury	3	0
1953	21 Oct	Wembley	4	4
1963	23 Oct	Wembley	2	1

v FINLAND			E	F
1937	20 May	Helsinki	8	0
1956	20 May	Helsinki	5	1
1966	26 June	Helsinki	3	0
wc1976	13 June	Helsinki	4	1
wc1976	13 Oct	Wembley	2	1
1982	3 June	Helsinki	4	1
wc1984	17 Oct	Wembley	5	0
wc1985	22 May	Helsinki	1	1

814

v FRANCE

			E	F
1923	10 May	Paris	4	1
1924	17 May	Paris	3	1
1925	21 May	Paris	3	2
1927	26 May	Paris	6	0
1928	17 May	Paris	5	1
1929	9 May	Paris	4	1
1931	14 May	Paris	2	5
1933	6 Dec	Tottenham	4	1
1938	26 May	Paris	4	2
1947	3 May	Highbury	3	0
1949	22 May	Paris	3	1
1951	3 Oct	Highbury	2	2
1955	15 May	Paris	0	1
1957	27 Nov	Wembley	4	0
EC1962	3 Oct	Sheffield	1	1
EC1963	27 Feb	Paris	2	5
wc1966	20 July	Wembley	2	0
1969	12 Mar	Wembley	5	0
wc1982	16 June	Bilbao	3	1
1984	29 Feb	Paris	0	2

v GERMANY

			E	G
1930	10 May	Berlin	3	3
1935	4 Dec	Tottenham	3	0
1938	14 May	Berlin	6	3

v EAST GERMANY

			E	EG
1963	2 June	Leipzig	2	1
1970	25 Nov	Wembley	3	1
1974	29 May	Leipzig	1	1
1984	12 Sept	Wembley	1	0

WEST GERMANY

			E	WG
1954	1 Dec	Wembley	3	1
1956	26 May	Berlin	3	1
1965	12 May	Nuremberg	1	0
1966	23 Feb	Wembley	1	0
wc1966	30 July	Wembley	4	2*
1968	1 June	Hanover	0	1*
wc1970	14 June	Leon	2	3*
EC1972	29 Apr	Wembley	1	3
EC1972	13 May	Berlin	0	0
1975	12 Mar	Wembley	2	0
1978	22 Feb	Munich	1	2
wc1982	29 June	Madrid	0	0
1982	13 Oct	Wembley	1	2
1985	12 June	Mexico City	3	0
1987	9 Sept	Dusseldorf	1	3
wc1990	4 July	Turin	1	1

*After extra time

v GREECE

			E	G
EC1971	21 Apr	Wembley	3	0
EC1971	1 Dec	Athens	2	0
EC1982	17 Nov	Wembley	3	0
EC1983	30 Mar	Wembley	0	0
1989	8 Feb	Athens	2	1

v HOLLAND

			E	N
1935	18 May	Amsterdam	1	0
1946	27 Nov	Huddersfield	8	2
1964	9 Dec	Amsterdam	1	1
1969	5 Nov	Amsterdam	1	0
1970	14 Jan	Wembley	0	0
1977	9 Feb	Wembley	0	2
1982	25 May	Wembley	2	0
1988	23 Mar	Wembley	2	2
EC1988	15 June	Dusseldorf	1	3
wc1990	16 June	Cagliari	0	0

v HUNGARY

			E	H
1908	10 June	Budapest	7	0
1909	29 May	Budapest	4	2
1909	31 May	Budapest	8	2
1934	10 May	Budapest	1	2
1936	2 Dec	Highbury	6	2
1953	25 Nov	Wembley	3	6
1954	23 May	Budapest	1	7
1960	22 May	Budapest	0	2
wc1962	31 May	Rancagua	1	2
1965	5 May	Wembley	1	0
1978	24 May	Wembley	4	1
wc1981	6 June	Budapest	3	1
wc1982	18 Nov	Wembley	1	0
EC1983	27 Apr	Wembley	2	0
EC1983	12 Oct	Budapest	3	0
1988	27 Apr	Budapest	0	0

v ICELAND

			E	I
1982	2 June	Reykjavik	1	1

v REPUBLIC OF IRELAND

			E	RI
1946	30 Sept	Dublin	1	0
1949	21 Sept	Everton	0	2
wc1957	8 May	Wembley	5	1
wc1957	19 May	Dublin	1	1
1964	24 May	Dublin	3	1
1976	8 Sept	Wembley	1	1
EC1978	25 Oct	Dublin	1	1
EC1980	6 Feb	Wembley	2	0
1985	26 Mar	Wembley	2	1
EC1988	12 June	Stuttgart	0	1
wc1990	11 June	Cagliari	1	1

v ISRAEL

			E	Is
1986	26 Feb	Ramat Gan	2	1
1988	17 Feb	Tel Aviv	0	0

v ITALY

			E	I
1933	13 May	Rome	1	1
1934	14 Nov	Highbury	3	2
1939	13 May	Milan	2	2
1948	16 May	Turin	4	0
1949	30 Nov	Tottenham	2	0
1952	18 May	Florence	1	1
1959	6 May	Wembley	2	2
1961	24 May	Rome	3	2
1973	14 June	Turin	0	2
1973	14 Nov	Wembley	0	1
1976	28 May	New York	3	2
wc1976	17 Nov	Rome	0	2
wc1977	16 Nov	Wembley	2	0
EC1980	15 June	Turin	0	1
1985	6 June	Mexico City	1	2
1989	15 Nov	Wembley	0	0
wc1990	7 July	Bari	1	2

v KUWAIT

			E	K
wc1982	25 June	Bilbao	1	0

v LUXEMBOURG

			E	L
1927	21 May	Luxembourg	5	2
wc1960	19 Oct	Luxembourg	9	0
wc1961	28 Sept	Highbury	4	1
wc1977	30 Mar	Wembley	5	0
wc1977	12 Oct	Luxembourg	2	0
EC1982	15 Dec	Wembley	9	0
EC1983	16 Nov	Luxembourg	4	0

v MALTA

			E	M
EC1971	3 Feb	Valletta	1	0
EC1971	12 May	Wembley	5	0

v MEXICO

			E	M
1959	24 May	Mexico City	1	2
1961	10 May	Wembley	8	0
wc1966	16 July	Wembley	2	0
1969	1 June	Mexico City	0	0
1985	9 June	Mexico City	0	1
1986	17 May	Los Angeles	3	0

v MOROCCO

			E	Mo
wc1986	6 June	Monterrey	0	0

v NORWAY

			E	N
1937	14 May	Oslo	6	0
1938	9 Nov	Newcastle	4	0
1949	18 May	Oslo	4	1
1966	29 June	Oslo	6	1
wc1980	10 Sept	Wembley	4	0
wc1981	9 Sept	Oslo	1	2

v PARAGUAY

			E	Pa
wc1986	18 June	Mexico City	3	0

v PERU

			E	P
1959	17 May	Lima	1	4
1962	20 May	Lima	4	0

v POLAND

			E	P
1966	5 Jan	Everton	1	1
1966	5 July	Chorzow	1	0
wc1973	6 June	Chorzow	0	2
wc1973	17 Oct	Wembley	1	1
wc1986	11 June	Monterrey	3	0
wc1989	3 June	Wembley	3	0
wc1989	11 Oct	Katowice	0	0

v PORTUGAL

			E	P
1947	25 May	Lisbon	10	0
1950	14 May	Lisbon	5	3
1951	19 May	Everton	5	2
1955	22 May	Oporto	1	3
1958	7 May	Wembley	2	1
wc1961	21 May	Lisbon	1	1
wc1961	25 Oct	Wembley	2	0
1964	17 May	Lisbon	4	3
1964	4 June	São Paulo	1	1
wc1966	26 July	Wembley	2	1
1969	10 Dec	Wembley	1	0
1974	3 Apr	Lisbon	0	0
EC1974	20 Nov	Wembley	0	0
EC1975	19 Nov	Lisbon	1	1
wc1986	3 June	Monterrey	0	1

v RUMANIA

			E	R
1939	24 May	Bucharest	2	0
1968	6 Nov	Bucharest	0	0
1969	15 Jan	Wembley	1	1
wc1970	2 June	Guadalajara	1	0
wc1980	15 Oct	Bucharest	1	2
wc1981	29 April	Wembley	0	0
wc1985	1 May	Bucharest	0	0
wc1985	11 Sept	Wembley	1	1

v SAUDI ARABIA

			E	SA
1988	16 Nov	Riyadh	1	1

v SPAIN

			E	S
1929	15 May	Madrid	3	4
1931	9 Dec	Highbury	7	1
wc1950	2 July	Rio de Janeiro	0	1
1955	18 May	Madrid	1	1
1955	30 Nov	Wembley	4	1
1960	15 May	Madrid	0	3
1960	26 Oct	Wembley	4	2
1965	8 Dec	Madrid	2	0
1967	24 May	Wembley	2	0
EC1968	3 Apr	Wembley	1	0
EC1968	8 May	Madrid	2	1
1980	26 Mar	Barcelona	2	0
EC1980	18 June	Naples	2	1
1981	25 Mar	Wembley	1	2
wc1982	5 July	Madrid	0	0
1987	18 Feb	Madrid	4	2

v SWEDEN

			E	S
1923	21 May	Stockholm	4	2
1923	24 May	Stockholm	3	1
1937	17 May	Stockholm	4	0
1947	19 Nov	Highbury	4	2
1949	13 May	Stockholm	1	3
1956	16 May	Stockholm	0	0
1959	28 Oct	Wembley	2	3
1965	16 May	Gothenburg	2	1
1968	22 May	Wembley	3	1
1979	10 June	Stockholm	0	0
1986	10 Sept	Stockholm	0	1
wc1988	19 Oct	Wembley	0	0
wc1989	6 Sept	Stockholm	0	0

v TUNISIA

			E	T
1990	2 June	Tunis	1	1

v SWITZERLAND

			E	S
1933	20 May	Berne	4	0
1938	21 May	Zurich	1	2
1947	18 May	Zurich	0	1
1948	2 Dec	Highbury	6	0
1952	28 May	Zurich	3	0
wc1954	20 June	Berne	2	0
1962	9 May	Wembley	3	1
1963	5 June	Basle	8	1
EC1971	13 Oct	Basle	3	2
EC1971	10 Nov	Wembley	1	1
1975	3 Sept	Basle	2	1
1977	7 Sept	Wembley	0	0
wc1980	19 Nov	Wembley	2	1
wc1981	30 May	Basle	1	2
1988	28 May	Lausanne	1	0

v TURKEY

			E	T
wc1984	14 Nov	Istanbul	8	0
wc1985	16 Oct	Wembley	5	0
EC1987	29 Apr	Izmir	0	0
EC1987	14 Oct	Wembley	8	0

v USA

			E	USA
wc1950	29 June	Belo Horizonte	0	1
1953	8 June	New York	6	3
1959	28 May	Los Angeles	8	1
1964	27 May	New York	10	0
1985	16 June	Los Angeles	5	0

v URUGUAY

			E	U
1953	31 May	Montevideo	1	2
wc1954	26 June	Basle	2	4
1964	6 May	Wembley	2	1
wc1966	11 July	Wembley	0	0
1969	8 June	Montevideo	2	1
1977	15 June	Montevideo	0	0
1984	13 June	Montevideo	0	2
1990	22 May	Wembley	1	2

v USSR

			E	USSR
1958	18 May	Moscow	1	1
wc1958	8 June	Gothenburg	2	2
wc1958	17 June	Gothenburg	0	1
1958	22 Oct	Wembley	5	0
1967	6 Dec	Wembley	2	2
EC1968	8 June	Rome	2	0
1973	10 June	Moscow	2	1
1984	2 June	Wembley	0	2
1986	26 Mar	Tbilisi	1	0
EC1988	18 June	Frankfurt	1	3

v YUGOSLAVIA

			E	Y
1939	18 May	Belgrade	1	2
1950	22 Nov	Highbury	2	2
1954	16 May	Belgrade	0	1
1956	28 Nov	Wembley	3	0
1958	11 May	Belgrade	0	5
1960	11 May	Wembley	3	3
1965	9 May	Belgrade	1	1
1966	4 May	Wembley	2	0
EC1968	5 June	Florence	0	1
1972	11 Oct	Wembley	1	1
1974	5 June	Belgrade	2	2
EC1986	12 Nov	Wembley	2	0
EC1988	11 Nov	Belgrade	4	1
1989	13 Dec	Wembley	2	1

SCOTLAND

v ARGENTINA			S	A
1977	18 June	Buenos Aires	1	1
1979	2 June	Glasgow	1	3
1990	28 Mar	Glasgow	1	0

v AUSTRIA			S	A
1931	16 May	Vienna	0	5
1933	29 Nov	Glasgow	2	2
1937	9 May	Vienna	1	1
1950	13 Dec	Glasgow	0	1
1951	27 May	Vienna	0	4
wc1954	16 June	Zurich	0	1
1955	19 May	Vienna	4	1
1956	2 May	Glasgow	1	1
1960	29 May	Vienna	1	4
1963	8 May	Glasgow	4	1
		(abandoned after 79 mins)		
wc1968	6 Nov	Glasgow	2	1
wc1969	5 Nov	Vienna	0	2
EC1978	20 Sept	Vienna	2	3
EC1979	17 Oct	Glasgow	1	1

v AUSTRALIA			S	Au
wc1985	20 Nov	Glasgow	2	0
wc1985	4 Dec	Melbourne	0	0

v BELGIUM			S	B
1947	18 May	Brussels	1	2
1948	28 Apr	Glasgow	2	0
1951	20 May	Brussels	5	0
EC1971	3 Feb	Liège	0	3
EC1971	10 Nov	Aberdeen	1	0
1974	2 June	Brussels	1	2
EC1979	21 Nov	Brussels	0	2
EC1979	19 Dec	Brussels	1	3
EC1982	15 Dec	Brussels	2	3
EC1983	12 Oct	Glasgow	1	1
EC1987	1 Apr	Brussels	1	4
EC1987	14 Oct	Glasgow	2	0

v BRAZIL			S	B
1966	25 June	Glasgow	1	1
1972	5 July	Rio de Janeiro	0	1
1973	30 June	Glasgow	0	1
wc1974	18 June	Frankfurt	0	0
1977	23 June	Rio de Janeiro	0	2
wc1982	18 June	Seville	1	4
1987	26 May	Glasgow	0	2
wc1990	20 June	Turin	0	1

v BULGARIA			S	B
1978	22 Feb	Glasgow	2	1
EC1986	10 Sept	Glasgow	0	0
EC1987	11 Nov	Sofia	1	0

v CANADA			S	C
1983	12 June	Vancouver	2	0
1983	16 June	Edmonton	3	0
1983	20 June	Toronto	2	0

v CHILE			S	C
1977	15 June	Santiago	4	2
1989	30 May	Glasgow	2	0

v COLOMBIA			S	C
1988	17 May	Glasgow	0	0

v COSTA RICA			S	CR
wc1990	11 June	Genoa	0	1

v CYPRUS			S	C
wc1968	17 Dec	Nicosia	5	0
wc1969	11 May	Glasgow	8	0
wc1989	8 Feb	Limassol	3	2
wc1989	26 Apr	Glasgow	2	1

v CZECHOSLOVAKIA			S	C
1937	22 May	Prague	3	1
1937	8 Dec	Glasgow	5	0
wc1961	14 May	Bratislava	0	4
wc1961	26 Sept	Glasgow	3	2
wc1961	29 Nov	Brussels	2	4*
1972	2 July	Porto Alegre	0	0
wc1973	26 Sept	Glasgow	2	1
wc1973	17 Oct	Prague	0	1
wc1976	13 Oct	Prague	0	2
wc1977	21 Sept	Glasgow	3	1

After extra time.

v DENMARK			S	D
1951	12 May	Glasgow	3	1
1952	25 May	Copenhagen	2	1
1968	16 Oct	Copenhagen	1	0
EC1970	11 Nov	Glasgow	1	0
EC1971	9 June	Copenhagen	0	1
wc1972	18 Oct	Copenhagen	4	1
wc1972	15 Nov	Glasgow	2	0
EC1975	3 Sept	Copenhagen	1	0
EC1975	29 Oct	Glasgow	3	1
wc1986	4 June	Nezahualcayotl	0	1

v EGYPT			S	E
1990	16 May	Aberdeen	1	3

v FINLAND			S	F
1954	25 May	Helsinki	2	1
wc1964	21 Oct	Glasgow	3	1
wc1965	27 May	Helsinki	2	1
1976	8 Sept	Glasgow	6	0

v FRANCE			S	F
1930	18 May	Paris	2	0
1932	8 May	Paris	3	1
1948	23 May	Paris	0	3
1949	27 Apr	Glasgow	2	0
1950	27 May	Paris	1	0
1951	16 May	Glasgow	1	0
wc1958	15 June	Orebro	1	2
1984	1 June	Marseilles	0	2
wc1989	8 Mar	Glasgow	2	0
wc1989	11 Oct	Paris	0	3

v GERMANY			S	G
1929	1 June	Berlin	1	1
1936	14 Oct	Glasgow	2	0

v EAST GERMANY			S	EG
1974	30 Oct	Glasgow	3	0
1977	7 Sept	East Berlin	0	1
EC1982	13 Oct	Glasgow	2	0
EC1983	16 Nov	Halle	1	2
1985	16 Oct	Glasgow	0	0
1990	25 Apr	Glasgow	0	1

v WEST GERMANY			S	WG
1957	22 May	Stuttgart	3	1
1959	6 May	Glasgow	3	2
1964	12 May	Hanover	2	2
wc1969	16 Apr	Glasgow	1	1
wc1969	22 Oct	Hamburg	2	3
1973	14 Nov	Glasgow	1	1
1974	27 Mar	Frankfurt	1	2
1986	8 June	Queretaro	1	2

v HOLLAND			S	N
1929	4 June	Amsterdam	2	0
1938	21 May	Amsterdam	3	1
1959	27 May	Amsterdam	2	1
1966	11 May	Glasgow	0	3
1968	30 May	Amsterdam	0	0
1971	1 Dec	Rotterdam	1	2
wc1978	11 June	Mendoza	3	2
1982	23 Mar	Glasgow	2	1
1986	29 Apr	Eindhoven	0	0

v HUNGARY			S	H
1938	7 Dec	Glasgow	3	1
1954	8 Dec	Glasgow	2	4
1955	29 May	Budapest	1	3
1958	7 May	Glasgow	1	1
1960	5 June	Budapest	3	3
1980	31 May	Budapest	1	3
1987	9 Sept	Glasgow	2	0

v ICELAND

			S	I
wc1984	17 Oct	Glasgow	3	0
wc1985	28 May	Reykjavik	1	0

v IRAN

			S	I
wc1978	7 June	Cordoba	1	1

v REPUBLIC OF IRELAND

			S	RI
wc1961	3 May	Glasgow	4	1
wc1961	7 May	Dublin	3	0
1963	9 June	Dublin	0	1
1969	21 Sept	Dublin	1	1
EC1986	15 Oct	Dublin	0	0
EC1987	18 Feb	Glasgow	0	1

v ISRAEL

			S	I
wc1981	25 Feb	Tel Aviv	1	0
wc1981	28 Apr	Glasgow	3	1
1986	28 Jan	Tel Aviv	1	0

v ITALY

			S	I
1931	20 May	Rome	0	3
wc1965	9 Nov	Glasgow	1	0
wc1965	7 Dec	Naples	0	3
1988	22 Dec	Perugia	0	2

v LUXEMBOURG

			S	L
1947	24 May	Luxembourg	6	0
EC1986	12 Nov	Glasgow	3	0
1987	2 Dec	Esch	0	0

v MALTA

			S	M
1988	22 Mar	Valletta	1	1
1990	28 May	Valletta	2	1

v NEW ZEALAND

			S	NZ
wc1982	15 June	Malaga	5	2

v NORWAY

			S	N
1929	28 May	Oslo	7	3
1954	5 May	Glasgow	1	0
1954	19 May	Oslo	1	1
1963	4 June	Bergen	3	4
1963	7 Nov	Glasgow	6	1
1974	6 June	Oslo	2	1
EC1978	25 Oct	Glasgow	3	2
EC1979	7 June	Oslo	4	0
wc1988	14 Sept	Oslo	2	1
wc1989	15 Nov	Glasgow	1	1

v PARAGUAY

			S	P
wc1958	11 June	Norrkoping	2	3

v PERU

			S	P
1972	26 Apr	Glasgow	2	0
wc1978	3 June	Cordoba	1	3
1979	12 Sept	Glasgow	1	1

v POLAND

			S	P
1958	1 June	Warsaw	2	1
1960	4 May	Glasgow	2	3
wc1965	23 May	Chorzow	1	1
wc1965	13 Oct	Glasgow	1	2
1980	28 May	Poznan	0	1
wc1990	19 May	Glasgow	1	1

v PORTUGAL

			S	P
1950	21 May	Lisbon	2	2
1955	4 May	Glasgow	3	0
1959	3 June	Lisbon	0	1
1966	18 June	Glasgow	0	1
EC1971	21 Apr	Lisbon	0	2

EC1971	13 Oct	Glasgow	2	1
1975	13 May	Glasgow	1	0
EC1978	29 Nov	Lisbon	0	1
EC1980	26 Mar	Glasgow	4	1
wc1980	15 Oct	Glasgow	0	0
wc1981	18 Nov	Lisbon	1	2

v RUMANIA

			S	R
EC1975	1 June	Bucharest	1	1
EC1975	17 Dec	Glasgow	1	1
1986	26 Mar	Glasgow	3	0

v SAUDI ARABIA

			S	SA
1988	17 Feb	Riyadh	2	2

v SPAIN

			S	Sp
wc1957	8 May	Glasgow	4	2
wc1957	26 May	Madrid	1	4
1963	13 June	Madrid	6	2
1965	8 May	Glasgow	0	0
EC1974	20 Nov	Glasgow	1	2
EC1975	5 Feb	Valencia	1	1
1982	24 Feb	Valencia	0	3
wc1984	14 Nov	Glasgow	3	1
wc1985	27 Feb	Seville	0	1
1988	27 Apr	Madrid	0	0

v SWEDEN

			S	Sw
1952	30 May	Stockholm	1	3
1953	6 May	Glasgow	1	2
1975	16 Apr	Gothenburg	1	1
1977	27 Apr	Glasgow	3	1
wc1980	10 Sept	Stockholm	1	0
wc1981	9 Sept	Glasgow	2	0
wc1990	16 June	Genoa	2	1

v SWITZERLAND

			S	Sw
1931	24 May	Geneva	3	2
1948	17 May	Berne	1	2
1950	26 Apr	Glasgow	3	1
wc1957	19 May	Basle	2	1
wc1957	6 Nov	Glasgow	3	2
1973	22 June	Berne	0	1
1976	7 Apr	Glasgow	1	0
EC1982	17 Nov	Berne	0	2
EC1983	30 May	Glasgow	2	2

v TURKEY

			S	T
1960	8 June	Ankara	2	4

v URUGUAY

			S	U
wc1954	19 June	Basle	0	7
1962	2 May	Glasgow	2	3
1983	21 Sept	Glasgow	2	0
wc1986	13 June	Nezahualcoyotl	0	0

v USA

			S	USA
1952	30 Apr	Glasgow	6	0

v USSR

			S	USSR
1967	10 May	Glasgow	0	2
1971	14 June	Moscow	0	1
wc1982	22 June	Malaga	2	2

v YUGOSLAVIA

			S	Y
1955	15 May	Belgrade	2	2
1956	21 Nov	Glasgow	2	0
wc1958	8 June	Vasteras	1	1
1972	29 June	Belo Horizonte	2	2
wc1974	22 June	Frankfurt	1	1
1984	12 Sept	Glasgow	6	1
wc1988	19 Oct	Glasgow	1	1
wc1989	6 Sept	Zagreb	1	3

v ZAIRE

			S	Z
wc1974	14 June	Dortmund	2	0

WALES

v AUSTRIA			W	A
1954	9 May	Vienna	0	2
EC1955	23 Nov	Wrexham	1	2
EC1974	4 Sept	Vienna	1	2
1975	19 Nov	Wrexham	1	0

v BELGIUM			W	B
1949	22 May	Liège	1	3
1949	23 Nov	Cardiff	5	1

v BULGARIA			W	B
EC1983	27 Apr	Wrexham	1	0
EC1983	16 Nov	Sofia	0	1

v BRAZIL			W	B
wc1958	19 June	Gothenburg	0	1
1962	12 May	Rio de Janeiro	1	3
1962	16 May	São Paulo	1	3
1966	14 May	Rio de Janeiro	1	3
1966	18 May	Belo Horizonte	0	1
1983	12 June	Cardiff	1	1

v CANADA			W	Ca
1986	10 May	Toronto	0	2
1986	20 May	Vancouver	3	0

v CHILE			W	C
1966	22 May	Santiago	0	2

v COSTA RICA			W	CR
1990	20 May	Cardiff	1	0

v CZECHOSLOVAKIA			W	C
wc1957	1 May	Cardiff	1	0
wc1957	26 May	Prague	0	2
EC1971	21 Apr	Swansea	1	3
EC1971	27 Oct	Prague	0	1
wc1977	30 Mar	Wrexham	3	0
wc1977	16 Nov	Prague	0	1
wc1980	19 Nov	Cardiff	1	0
wc1981	9 Sept	Prague	0	2
EC1987	29 Apr	Wrexham	1	1
EC1987	11 Nov	Prague	0	2

v DENMARK			W	D
wc1964	21 Oct	Copenhagen	0	1
wc1965	1 Dec	Wrexham	4	2
EC1987	9 Sept	Cardiff	1	0
EC1987	14 Oct	Copenhagen	0	1

v FINLAND			W	F
EC1971	26 May	Helsinki	1	0
EC1971	13 Oct	Swansea	3	0
EC1987	10 Sept	Helsinki	1	1
EC1987	1 Apr	Wrexham	4	0
wc1988	19 Oct	Swansea	2	2
wc1989	6 Sept	Helsinki	0	1

v FRANCE			W	F
1933	25 May	Paris	1	1
1939	20 May	Paris	1	2
1953	14 May	Paris	1	6
1982	2 June	Toulouse	1	0

v EAST GERMANY			W	EG
wc1957	19 May	Leipzig	1	2
wc1957	25 Sept	Cardiff	4	1
wc1969	16 Apr	Dresden	1	2
wc1969	22 Oct	Cardiff	1	3

v WEST GERMANY			W	WG
1968	8 May	Cardiff	1	1
1969	26 Mar	Frankfurt	1	1
1976	6 Oct	Cardiff	0	2
1977	14 Dec	Dortmund	1	1
EC1979	2 May	Wrexham	0	2
EC1979	17 Oct	Cologne	1	5
wc1989	31 May	Cardiff	0	0
wc1989	15 Nov	Cologne	1	2

v GREECE			W	G
wc1964	9 Dec	Athens	0	2
wc1965	17 Mar	Cardiff	4	1

v HOLLAND			W	H
wc1988	14 Sept	Amsterdam	0	1
wc1989	11 Oct	Wrexham	1	2

v HUNGARY			W	H
wc1958	8 June	Sanviken	1	1
wc1958	17 June	Stockholm	2	1
1961	28 May	Budapest	2	3
EC1962	7 Nov	Budapest	1	3
EC1963	20 Mar	Cardiff	1	1
EC1974	30 Oct	Cardiff	2	0
EC1975	16 Apr	Budapest	2	1
1985	16 Oct	Cardiff	0	3

v ICELAND			W	I
wc1980	2 June	Reykjavik	4	0
wc1981	14 Oct	Swansea	2	2
wc1984	12 Sept	Reykjavik	0	1
wc1984	14 Nov	Cardiff	2	1

v IRAN			W	I
1978	18 Apr	Teheran	1	0

v REPUBLIC OF IRELAND			W	RI
1960	28 Sept	Dublin	3	2
1979	11 Sept	Swansea	2	1
1981	24 Feb	Dublin	3	1
1986	26 Mar	Dublin	1	0
1990	28 Mar	Dublin	0	1

v ISRAEL			W	I
wc1958	15 Jan	Tel Aviv	2	0
wc1958	5 Feb	Cardiff	2	0
1984	10 June	Tel Aviv	0	0
1989	8 Feb	Tel Aviv	3	3

v ITALY			W	I
1965	1 May	Florence	1	4
wc1968	23 Oct	Cardiff	0	1
wc1969	4 Nov	Rome	1	4
1988	4 June	Brescia	1	0

v KUWAIT			W	K
1977	6 Sept	Wrexham	0	0
1977	20 Sept	Kuwait	0	0

v LUXEMBOURG			W	L
EC1974	20 Nov	Swansea	5	0
EC1975	1 May	Luxembourg	3	1

v MALTA			W	M
EC1978	25 Oct	Wrexham	7	0
EC1979	2 June	Valletta	2	0
1988	1 June	Valletta	3	2

v MEXICO			W	M
wc1958	11 June	Stockholm	1	1
1962	22 May	Mexico City	1	2

NORWAY			W	M
EC1982	22 Sept	Swansea	1	0
EC1983	21 Sept	Oslo	0	0
1984	6 June	Trondheim	0	1
1985	26 Feb	Wrexham	1	1
1985	5 June	Bergen	2	4

v POLAND

			W	P
wc1973	28 Mar	Cardiff	2	0
wc1973	26 Sept	Katowice	0	3

v PORTUGAL

			W	P
1949	15 May	Lisbon	2	3
1951	12 May	Cardiff	2	1

v RUMANIA

			W	R
EC1970	11 Nov	Cardiff	0	0
EC1971	24 Nov	Bucharest	0	2
1983	12 Oct	Wrexham	5	0

v SAUDI ARABIA

			W	SA
1986	25 Feb	Dahran	2	1

v SPAIN

			W	S
wc1961	19 Apr	Cardiff	1	2
wc1961	18 May	Madrid	1	1
1982	24 Mar	Valencia	1	1
wc1984	17 Oct	Seville	0	3
wc1985	30 Apr	Wrexham	3	0

v SWEDEN

			W	S
wc1958	15 June	Stockholm	0	0
1988	27 Apr	Stockholm	1	4
1989	26 Apr	Wrexham	0	2
1990	25 Apr	Stockholm	2	4

v SWITZERLAND

			W	S
1949	26 May	Berne	0	4
1951	16 May	Wrexham	3	2

v TURKEY

			W	T
EC1978	29 Nov	Wrexham	1	0
EC1979	21 Nov	Izmir	0	1
wc1980	15 Oct	Cardiff	4	0
wc1981	25 Mar	Ankara	1	0

v REST OF UNITED KINGDOM

			W	UK
1951	5 Dec	Cardiff	3	2
1969	28 July	Cardiff	0	1

v URUGUAY

			W	U
1986	21 Apr	Wrexham	0	0

v USSR

			W	USSR
wc1965	30 May	Moscow	1	2
wc1965	27 Oct	Cardiff	2	1
wc1981	30 May	Wrexham	0	0
wc1981	18 Nov	Tbilisi	0	3
1987	18 Feb	Swansea	0	0

v YUGOSLAVIA

			W	Y
1953	21 May	Belgrade	2	5
1954	22 Nov	Cardiff	1	3
EC1976	24 Apr	Zagreb	0	2
EC1976	22 May	Cardiff	1	1
EC1982	15 Dec	Titograd	4	4
EC1983	14 Dec	Cardiff	1	1
1988	23 Mar	Swansea	1	2

NORTHERN IRELAND

v ALBANIA

			NI	A
wc1965	7 May	Belfast	4	1
wc1965	24 Nov	Tirana	1	1
EC1982	15 Dec	Tirana	0	0
EC1983	27 Apr	Belfast	1	0

v ALGERIA

			NI	A
wc1986	3 June	Guadalajara	1	1

v ARGENTINA

			NI	A
wc1958	11 June	Halmstad	1	3

v AUSTRIA

			NI	A
wc1982	1 July	Madrid	2	2
EC1982	13 Oct	Vienna	0	2
EC1983	21 Sept	Belfast	3	1

v AUSTRALIA

			NI	A
1980	11 June	Sydney	2	1
1980	15 June	Melbourne	1	1
1980	18 June	Adelaide	2	1

v BELGIUM

			NI	B
wc1976	10 Nov	Liège	0	2
wc1977	16 Nov	Belfast	3	0

v BRAZIL

			NI	B
wc1986	12 June	Guadalajara	0	3

v BULGARIA

			NI	B
wc1972	18 Oct	Sofia	0	3
wc1973	26 Sept	Sheffield	0	0
EC1978	29 Nov	Sofia	2	0
EC1979	2 May	Belfast	2	0

v CHILE

			NI	C
1989	26 May	Belfast	0	1

v CYPRUS

			NI	C
EC1971	3 Feb	Nicosia	3	0
EC1971	21 Apr	Belfast	5	0
wc1973	14 Feb	Nicosia	0	1
wc1973	8 May	London	3	0

v CZECHOSLOVAKIA

			NI	C
wc1958	8 June	Halmstad	1	0
wc1958	17 June	Malmo	2	1*

*After extra time

v DENMARK

			NI	D
EC1978	25 Oct	Belfast	2	1
EC1979	6 June	Copenhagen	0	4
1986	26 Mar	Belfast	1	1

v FINLAND

			NI	F
wc1984	27 May	Pori	0	1
wc1984	14 Nov	Belfast	2	1

v FRANCE

			NI	F
1951	12 May	Belfast	2	2
1952	11 Nov	Paris	1	3
wc1958	19 June	Norrkoping	0	4
1982	24 Mar	Paris	0	4
wc1982	4 July	Madrid	1	4
1986	26 Feb	Paris	0	0
1988	27 Apr	Belfast	0	0

v WEST GERMANY

			NI	WG
wc1958	15 June	Malmo	2	2
wc1960	26 Oct	Belfast	3	4
wc1961	10 May	Hamburg	1	2
1966	7 May	Belfast	0	2
1977	27 Apr	Cologne	0	5
EC1982	17 Nov	Belfast	1	0
EC1983	16 Nov	Hamburg	1	0

Page 820

NORTHERN IRELAND (continued)

v GREECE

			NI	G
wc1961	3 May	Athens	1	2
wc1961	17 Oct	Belfast	2	0
1988	17 Feb	Athens	2	3

v HOLLAND

			NI	N
1962	9 May	Rotterdam	0	4
wc1965	17 Mar	Belfast	2	1
wc1965	7 Apr	Rotterdam	0	0
wc1976	13 Oct	Rotterdam	2	2
wc1977	12 Oct	Belfast	0	1

v HONDURAS

			NI	H
wc1982	21 June	Zaragoza	1	1

v HUNGARY

			NI	H
wc1988	19 Oct	Budapest	0	1
wc1989	6 Sept	Belfast	1	2

v ICELAND

			NI	I
wc1977	11 June	Reykjavik	0	1
wc1977	21 Sept	Belfast	2	0

v REPUBLIC OF IRELAND

			NI	RI
EC1978	20 Sept	Dublin	0	0
EC1979	21 Nov	Belfast	1	0
wc1988	14 Sept	Belfast	0	0
wc1989	11 Oct	Dublin	0	3

v ISRAEL

			NI	I
1968	10 Sept	Jaffa	3	2
1976	3 Mar	Tel Aviv	1	1
wc1980	26 Mar	Tel Aviv	0	0
wc1981	18 Nov	Belfast	1	0
1984	16 Oct	Belfast	3	0
1987	18 Feb	Tel Aviv	1	1

v ITALY

			NI	I
wc1957	25 Apr	Rome	0	1
1957	4 Dec	Belfast	2	2
wc1958	15 Jan	Belfast	2	1
1961	25 Apr	Bologna	2	3

v MALTA

			NI	M
1988	21 May	Belfast	3	0
wc1989	26 Apr	Valetta	2	0

v MEXICO

			NI	M
1966	22 June	Belfast	4	1

v MOROCCO

			NI	Mo
1986	23 Apr	Belfast	2	1

v NORWAY

			NI	N
EC1974	4 Sept	Oslo	1	2
EC1975	29 Oct	Belfast	3	0
1990	27 Mar	Belfast	2	3

v POLAND

			NI	P
EC1962	10 Oct	Katowice	2	0
EC1962	28 Nov	Belfast	2	0
1988	23 Mar	Belfast	1	1

v PORTUGAL

			NI	P
wc1957	16 Jan	Lisbon	1	1
wc1957	1 May	Belfast	3	0
wc1973	28 Mar	Coventry	1	1
wc1973	14 Nov	Lisbon	1	1
wc1980	19 Nov	Lisbon	0	1
wc1981	29 Apr	Belfast	1	0

v RUMANIA

			NI	R
wc1984	12 Sept	Belfast	3	2
wc1985	16 Oct	Bucharest	1	0

v SPAIN

			NI	S
1958	15 Oct	Madrid	2	6
1963	30 May	Bilbao	1	1
1963	30 Oct	Belfast	0	1
EC1970	11 Nov	Seville	0	3
EC1972	16 Feb	Hull	1	1
wc1982	25 June	Valencia	1	0
1985	27 Mar	Palma	0	0
wc1986	7 June	Guadalajara	1	2
wc1988	21 Dec	Seville	0	4
wc1989	8 Feb	Belfast	0	2

v SWEDEN

			NI	S
EC1974	30 Oct	Solna	2	0
EC1975	3 Sept	Belfast	1	2
wc1980	15 Oct	Belfast	3	0
wc1981	3 June	Solna	0	1

v SWITZERLAND

			NI	S
wc1964	14 Oct	Belfast	1	0
wc1964	14 Nov	Lausanne	1	2

v TURKEY

			NI	T
wc1968	23 Oct	Belfast	4	1
wc1968	11 Dec	Istanbul	3	0
EC1983	30 Mar	Belfast	2	1
EC1983	12 Oct	Ankara	0	1
wc1985	1 May	Belfast	2	0
wc1985	11 Sept	Izmir	0	0
EC1986	12 Nov	Izmir	0	0
EC1987	11 Nov	Belfast	1	0

v URUGUAY

			NI	U
1964	29 Apr	Belfast	3	0
1990	18 May	Belfast	1	0

v USSR

			NI	USSR
wc1969	10 Sept	Belfast	0	0
wc1969	22 Oct	Moscow	0	2
EC1971	22 Sept	Moscow	0	1
EC1971	13 Oct	Belfast	1	1

v YUGOSLAVIA

			NI	Y
EC1975	16 Mar	Belfast	1	0
EC1975	19 Nov	Belgrade	0	1
wc1982	17 June	Zaragoza	0	0
EC1987	29 Apr	Belfast	1	2
EC1987	14 Oct	Sarajevo	0	3

REPUBLIC OF IRELAND

v ALGERIA

			RI	A
1982	28 Apr	Algiers	0	2

v ARGENTINA

			RI	A
1951	13 May	Dublin	0	1
1979	29 May	Dublin	0	0*
1980	16 May	Dublin	0	1

v AUSTRIA

			RI	A
1952	7 May	Vienna	0	6
1953	25 Mar	Dublin	4	0
1958	14 Mar	Vienna	1	3
1962	8 Apr	Dublin	2	3
EC1963	25 Sept	Vienna	0	0
EC1963	13 Oct	Dublin	3	2
1966	22 May	Vienna	0	1
1968	10 Nov	Dublin	2	2
EC1971	30 May	Dublin	1	4
EC1971	10 Oct	Linz	0	6

v BELGIUM

			RI	B
1928	12 Feb	Liège	4	2
1929	30 Apr	Dublin	4	0
1930	11 May	Brussels	3	1
wc1934	25 Feb	Dublin	4	4

* Not considered a full international

821

1949	24 Apr	Dublin	0	2
1950	10 May	Brussels	1	5
1965	24 Mar	Dublin	0	2
1966	25 May	Liège	3	2
wc1980	15 Oct	Dublin	1	1
wc1981	25 Mar	Brussels	0	1
EC1986	10 Sept	Brussels	2	2
EC1987	29 Apr	Dublin	0	0

v BRAZIL RI B

1974	5 May	Rio de Janeiro	1	2
1982	27 May	Uberlandia	0	7
1987	23 May	Dublin	1	0

v BULGARIA RI B

wc1977	1 June	Sofia	1	2
wc1977	12 Oct	Dublin	0	0
EC1979	19 May	Sofia	0	1
EC1979	17 Oct	Dublin	3	0
EC1987	1 Apr	Sofia	1	2
EC1987	14 Oct	Dublin	2	0

v CHILE RI C

1960	30 Mar	Dublin	2	0
1972	21 June	Recife	1	2
1974	12 May	Santiago	2	1
1982	22 May	Santiago	0	1

v CYPRUS RI C

wc1980	26 Mar	Nicosia	3	2
wc1980	19 Nov	Dublin	6	0

v CZECHOSLOVAKIA RI C

1938	18 May	Prague	2	2
EC1959	5 Apr	Dublin	2	0
EC1959	10 May	Bratislava	0	4
wc1961	8 Oct	Dublin	1	3
1979	26 Sept	Prague	1	4
wc1961	29 Oct	Prague	1	7
EC1967	21 May	Dublin	0	2
EC1967	22 Nov	Prague	2	1
wc1969	4 May	Dublin	1	2
wc1969	7 Oct	Prague	0	3
1981	29 Apr	Dublin	3	1
1986	27 May	Reykjavik	1	0

v DENMARK RI D

wc1956	3 Oct	Dublin	2	1
wc1957	2 Oct	Copenhagen	2	0
wc1968	4 Dec	Dublin	1	1
(abandoned after 51 mins)				
wc1969	27 May	Copenhagen	0	2
wc1969	15 Oct	Dublin	1	1
EC1978	24 May	Copenhagen	3	3
EC1979	2 May	Dublin	2	0
wc1984	14 Nov	Copenhagen	0	3
wc1985	13 Nov	Dublin	1	4

v ECUADOR RI E

1972	19 June	Natal	3	2

v EGYPT RI E

wc1990	17 June	Palermo	0	0

v ENGLAND RI E

1946	30 Sept	Dublin	0	1
1949	21 Sept	Everton	2	0
wc1957	8 May	Wembley	1	5
wc1957	19 May	Dublin	1	1
1964	24 May	Dublin	1	3
1976	8 Sept	Wembley	1	1
EC1978	25 Oct	Dublin	1	1
EC1980	6 Feb	Wembley	0	2
1985	26 Mar	Wembley	1	2
EC1988	12 June	Stuttgart	1	0
wc1990	11 June	Cagliari	1	1

v FINLAND RI F

wc1949	8 Sept	Dublin	3	0
wc1949	9 Oct	Helsinki	1	1
1990	16 May	Dublin	1	1

v FRANCE RI F

1937	23 May	Paris	2	0
1952	16 Nov	Dublin	1	1
wc1953	4 Oct	Dublin	3	5
wc1953	25 Nov	Paris	0	1
wc1972	15 Nov	Dublin	2	1
wc1973	19 May	Paris	1	1
wc1976	17 Nov	Paris	0	2
wc1977	30 Mar	Dublin	1	0
wc1980	28 Oct	Paris	0	2
wc1981	14 Oct	Dublin	3	2
1989	7 Feb	Dublin	0	0

v GERMANY RI G

1935	8 May	Dortmund	1	3
1936	17 Oct	Dublin	5	2
1939	23 May	Bremen	1	1

v WEST GERMANY RI WC

1951	17 Oct	Dublin	3	2
1952	4 May	Cologne	0	3
1955	28 May	Hamburg	1	2
1956	25 Nov	Dublin	3	0
1960	11 May	Dusseldorf	1	0
1966	4 May	Dublin	0	4
1970	9 May	Berlin	1	2
1975	1 Mar	Dublin	1	0†
1979	22 May	Dublin	1	3
1981	21 May	Bremen	0	3†
1989	6 Sept	Dublin	1	1

†v West Germany 'B'

v HOLLAND RI N

1932	8 May	Amsterdam	2	0
1934	8 Apr	Amsterdam	2	5
1935	8 Dec	Dublin	3	5
1955	1 May	Dublin	1	0
1956	10 May	Rotterdam	4	1
wc1980	10 Sept	Dublin	2	1
wc1981	9 Sept	Rotterdam	2	2
EC1982	22 Sept	Rotterdam	1	2
EC1983	12 Oct	Dublin	2	3
EC1988	18 June	Gelsenkirchen	0	1
wc1990	21 June	Palermo	1	1

v HUNGARY RI H

1934	15 Dec	Dublin	2	4
1936	3 May	Budapest	3	3
1936	6 Dec	Dublin	2	3
1939	19 Mar	Cork	2	2
1939	18 May	Budapest	2	2
wc1969	8 June	Dublin	1	2
wc1969	5 Nov	Budapest	0	4
wc1989	8 Mar	Budapest	0	2
wc1989	4 June	Dublin	2	0

v ICELAND RI I

EC1962	12 Aug	Dublin	4	2
EC1962	2 Sept	Reykjavik	1	1
EC1982	13 Oct	Dublin	2	0
EC1983	21 Sept	Reykjavik	3	0
1986	25 May	Rekjavik	2	1

v IRAN RI I

1972	18 June	Recife	2	1

v N. IRELAND RI NI

EC1978	20 Sept	Dublin	0	0
EC1979	21 Nov	Belfast	0	1
wc1988	14 Sept	Belfast	0	0
wc1989	11 Oct	Dublin	3	0

v ISRAEL RI I

1984	4 Apr	Tel Aviv	0	3
1985	27 May	Tel Aviv	0	0
1987	10 Nov	Dublin	5	0

v ITALY RI I

1926	21 Mar	Turin	0	3
1927	23 Apr	Dublin	1	2
EC1970	8 Dec	Rome	0	3
EC1971	10 May	Dublin	1	2
1985	5 Feb	Dublin	1	2
wc1990	30 June	Rome	0	1

v LUXEMBOURG			RI	L
1936	9 May	Luxembourg	5	1
wc1953	28 Oct	Dublin	4	0
wc1954	7 Mar	Luxembourg	1	0
EC1987	28 May	Luxembourg	2	0
EC1987	9 Sept	Dublin	2	1

v MALTA			RI	M
EC1983	30 Mar	Valletta	1	0
EC1983	16 Nov	Dublin	8	0
wc1989	28 May	Dublin	2	0
wc1989	15 Nov	Valletta	2	0
1990	2 June	Valletta	3	0

v MEXICO			RI	M
1984	8 Aug	Dublin	0	0

v NORWAY			RI	N
wc1937	10 Oct	Oslo	2	3
wc1937	7 Nov	Dublin	3	3
1950	26 Nov	Dublin	2	2
1951	30 May	Oslo	3	2
1954	8 Nov	Dublin	2	1
1955	25 May	Oslo	3	1
1960	6 Nov	Dublin	3	1
1964	13 May	Oslo	4	1
1973	6 June	Oslo	1	1
1976	24 Mar	Dublin	3	0
1978	21 May	Oslo	0	0
wc1984	17 Oct	Oslo	0	1
wc1985	1 May	Dublin	0	0
1988	1 June	Oslo	0	0

v POLAND			RI	P
1938	22 May	Warsaw	0	6
1938	13 Nov	Dublin	3	2
1958	11 May	Katowice	2	2
1958	5 Oct	Dublin	2	2
1964	10 May	Cracow	1	3
1964	25 Oct	Dublin	3	2
1968	15 May	Dublin	2	2
1968	30 Oct	Katowice	0	1
1970	6 May	Dublin	1	2
1970	23 Sept	Dublin	0	2
1973	16 May	Wroclaw	0	2
1973	21 Oct	Dublin	1	0
1976	26 May	Posnan	2	0
1977	24 Apr	Dublin	0	0
1978	12 Apr	Lodz	0	3
1981	23 May	Bydgoszcz	0	3
1984	23 May	Dublin	0	0
1986	12 Nov	Warsaw	0	1
1988	22 May	Dublin	3	1

v PORTUGAL			RI	P
1946	16 June	Lisbon	1	3
1947	4 May	Dublin	0	2
1948	23 May	Lisbon	0	2
1949	22 May	Dublin	1	0
1972	25 June	Recife	1	2

v RUMANIA			RI	R
1988	23 Mar	Dublin	2	0
wc1990	25 June	Genoa	0	0

v SCOTLAND			RI	S
wc1961	3 May	Glasgow	1	4
wc1961	7 May	Dublin	0	3
1963	9 June	Dublin	1	0
1969	21 Sept	Dublin	1	1
EC1986	15 Oct	Dublin	0	0
EC1987	18 Feb	Glasgow	1	0

v SPAIN			RI	S
1931	26 Apr	Barcelona	1	1
1931	13 Dec	Dublin	0	5
1946	23 June	Madrid	1	0
1947	2 Mar	Dublin	3	2
1948	30 May	Barcelona	1	2
1949	12 June	Dublin	1	4
1952	1 June	Madrid	0	6
1955	27 Nov	Dublin	2	2
EC1964	11 Mar	Seville	1	5
EC1964	8 Apr	Dublin	0	2
wc1965	5 May	Dublin	1	0
wc1965	27 Oct	Seville	1	4
wc1965	10 Nov	Paris	0	1
EC1966	23 Oct	Dublin	0	0
EC1966	7 Dec	Valencia	0	2
1977	9 Feb	Dublin	0	1
EC1982	17 Nov	Dublin	3	3
EC1983	27 Apr	Zaragosa	0	2
wc1985	26 May	Cork	0	0
wc1988	16 Nov	Seville	0	2
wc1989	26 Apr	Dublin	1	0

v SWEDEN			RI	S
wc1949	2 June	Stockholm	1	3
wc1949	13 Nov	Dublin	1	3
1959	1 Nov	Dublin	3	2
1960	18 May	Malmo	1	4
EC1970	14 Oct	Dublin	1	1
EC1970	28 Oct	Malmo	0	1

v SWITZERLAND			RI	S
1935	5 May	Basle	0	1
1936	17 Mar	Dublin	1	0
1937	17 May	Berne	1	0
1938	18 Sept	Dublin	4	0
1948	5 Dec	Dublin	0	1
EC1975	11 May	Dublin	2	1
EC1975	21 May	Berne	0	1
1980	30 Apr	Dublin	2	0
wc1985	2 June	Dublin	3	0
wc1985	11 Sept	Berne	0	0

v TRINIDAD & TOBAGO			RI	TT
1982	30 May	Port of Spain	1	2

v TUNISIA			RI	TU
1988	19 Oct	Dublin	4	0

v TURKEY			RI	T
EC1966	16 Nov	Dublin	2	1
EC1967	22 Feb	Ankara	1	2
EC1974	20 Nov	Izmir	1	1
EC1975	29 Oct	Dublin	4	0
1976	13 Oct	Ankara	3	3
1978	5 Apr	Dublin	4	2
1990	26 May	Izmir	0	0

v URUGUAY			RI	U
1974	8 May	Montevideo	0	2
1986	23 Apr	Dublin	1	1

v USA			RI	USA
1979	29 Oct	Dublin	3	2

v USSR			RI	USSR
wc1972	18 Oct	Dublin	1	2
wc1973	13 May	Moscow	0	1
EC1974	30 Oct	Dublin	3	0
EC1975	18 May	Kiev	1	2
wc1984	12 Sept	Dublin	1	0
wc1985	16 Oct	Moscow	0	2
EC1988	15 June	Hanover	1	1
1990	25 Apr	Dublin	1	0

v WALES			RI	W
1960	28 Sept	Dublin	2	3
1979	11 Sept	Swansea	1	2
1981	24 Feb	Dublin	1	3
1986	26 Mar	Dublin	0	1
1990	28 Mar	Dublin	1	0

v YUGOSLAVIA			RI	Y
1955	19 Sept	Dublin	1	4
1988	27 Apr	Dublin	2	0

OTHER BRITISH AND IRISH INTERNATIONAL MATCHES 1989–90

Dublin, 6 September 1989, 48,000

Rep of Ireland (1) 1 *(Stapleton)*

West Germany (1) 1 *(Dorfner)*

Rep of Ireland: Bonner; Morris, Staunton, McCarthy, O'Leary, Brady (Townsend), McGrath, Aldridge (Cascarino), Stapleton (Byrne), Whelan, Galvin.
West Germany: Illgner (Aumann); Reuter, Pflugler, Buchwald (Reinhardt), Augenthaler, Dorfner (Bein), Moller, Thon, Wohlfarth, Littbarski, Hassler.

Wembley, 15 November 1989, 75,000

England (0) 0

Italy (0) 0

England: Shilton (Beasant); Stevens, Pearce (Winterburn), Walker, Butcher, McMahon (Hodge), Robson (Phelan), Beardsley (Platt), Barnes, Lineker, Waddle.
Italy: Zenga; Bergomi, Maldini, Baresi, Ferri, Berti, Donadoni, De Napoli, Vialli (Baggio), Giannini, Carnevale (Serena).

Wembley, 13 December 1989, 34,796

England (1) 2 *(Robson 2)*

Yugoslavia (1) 1 *(Skoro)*

England: Shilton (Beasant); Parker, Pearce (Dorigo), Thomas (Platt), Walker, Butcher, Robson (McMahon), Rocastle (Hodge), Bull, Lineker, Waddle.
Yugoslavia: Ivkovic; Stanojkovic, Spasic (Petric), Brnovic (Panadic), Hadzibegic, Vulic, Skoro, Susic (Prosinecki), Mihajlovic, Stojkovic, Savevski.

Belfast, 27 March 1990, 3500

N. Ireland (1) 2 *(Quinn, Wilson K)*

Norway (0) 3 *(Skammelstrud, Anderson, Hansen)*

N. Ireland: Kee; Hill, Donaghy, McClelland, Taggart, McCreery (Rogan), Wilson D, Quinn, Clarke (Dowie), Wilson K, Black.
Norway: Thorstvedt; Hansen, Johnsen, Halvorsen, Halle, Loken, Ahlsen, Gulbrandsen, Skammelstrud, Andersen, Fjortoft (Jakobsen).

Wembley, 28 March 1990, 80,000

England (1) 1 *(Lineker)*

Brazil (0) 0

England: Shilton (Woods); Stevens, Pearce, McMahon, Walker, Butcher, Platt, Waddle, Beardsley (Gascoigne), Lineker, Barnes.
Brazil: Taffarel; Jorginho, Mozer (Aldair), Mauro Galvao, Branco, Ricardo, Bebeto (Muller), Dunga, Careca, Silas (Alemao), Valdo (Bismarck).

Dublin, 28 March 1990, 41,350

Rep of Ireland (0) 1 *(Slaven)*

Wales (0) 0

Rep of Ireland: Bonner; Morris, Staunton (Hughton), McCarthy, Moran (O'Leary), Whelan (Sheedy), Townsend, Byrne, Slaven, Cascarino, Sheridan.
Wales: Southall; Hall, Phillips, Nicholas, Aizlewood, Melville, Maguire, Horne, Rush, Allen, Davies.

Glasgow, 28 March 1990, 51,537

Scotland (1) 1 *(McKimmie)*

Argentina (0) 0

Scotland: Leighton; Gough, McKimmie, Levein, McLeish, MacLeod, Bett (Aitken), McCall, McInally (McClair), McStay, Fleck.
Argentina: Pumpido; Batista, Bauza, Sensini, Fabbri, Ruggeri (Monzon), Calderon, Basualdo, Burruchaga (Troglio), Valdano, Caniggia.

Wembley, 25 April 1990, 21,342

England (2) 4 *(Bull 2, Pearce, Gascoigne)*

Czechoslovakia (1) 2 *(Skuhravy, Kubik)*

England: Shilton (Seaman); Dixon, Pearce (Dorigo), Steven, Walker (Wright), Butcher, Robson (McMahon), Gascoigne, Bull, Lineker, Hodge.
Czechoslovakia: Miklosko; Bielik, Straka (Kadlec), Hasek, Kocian, Kinier, Bilek, Kubik, Knoflicek, Skuhravy (Weiss), Moravcik.

Glasgow, 25 April 1990, 21,868

Scotland (0) 0

East Germany (0) 1 *(Doll (pen))*

Scotland: Goram; Gillespie (McStay), MacLeod, Levein, McLeish, Gough, McAllister, McCall, Durie (McCoist), Johnston, Collins.
East Germany: Brautigam; Boger, Peschke, Lindner, Schuster, Sammer, Herzog, Steubner (Buttner), Kirsten, Ernst, Doll.

Stockholm, 25 April 1990, 13,981

Sweden (2) 4 *(Brolin 2, Ingesson 2)*

Wales (1) 2 *(Saunders 2)*

Sweden: Ravelli; Nilsson, Hysen, Larsson P, Ljung, Engqvist, Limpar, Ingesson, Schwarz, Brolin, Magnusson (Pettersson).
Wales: Southall; Phillips, Bowen, Melville, Law, Maguire, Nicholas, Horne, Allen, Saunders, Hodges.

Dublin, 25 April 1990, 43,990

Rep of Ireland (0) 1 *(Staunton)*

USSR (0) 0

Rep of Ireland: Peyton; Morris (Hughton), Staunton, McCarthy, O'Leary (Moran), Waddock, McGrath, Townsend, Quinn, Kelly D, Sheedy.
USSR: Uvarov; Fokin, Kuznetsov, Khidiatulin, Gorlukovich, Tishenko, Zigmantovich, Bzoshin, (Cherenkov), Bozodjuk, Ljuty (Savictav), Belanov.

Wembley, 15 May 1990, 27,643

England (0) 1 *(Lineker)*

Denmark (0) 0

England: Shilton (Woods); Stevens, Pearce (Dorigo), McMahon (Platt), Walker, Butcher, Hodge, Gascoigne, Waddle (Rocastle), Lineker (Bull), Barnes.
Denmark: Schmeichel; Sivebaek, Nielsen, Olsen, Andersen, Bartram, Jensen, Vilfort, Povlsen (Brunn), Laudrup M (Jakobsen), Laudrup B

824

Dublin, 16 May 1990, 31,556

Rep of Ireland (0) 1 *(Sheedy)*

Finland (0) 1 *(Tauriainen P)*

Rep of Ireland; Bonner; Hughton, Staunton (Morris), McCarthy, O'Leary, Brady (Townsend), McGrath, Houghton, Slaven (Aldridge), Cascarino, Byrne (Sheedy).
Finland: Huttunen; Vuorela, Sulonen, Heikkinen, Jantti (Turunen), Kanerva, Jorvinen, Tauriainen P, Litmanen (Tauriainen A), Myyry (Aaltonen), Paatelainen.

Aberdeen, 16 May 1990, 23,000

Scotland (0) 1 *(McCoist)*

Egypt (2) 3 *(Abdelhamid, Hassan H, Yousef)*

Scotland: Gunn; McKimmie (McCall), Malpas, Gillespie, McLeish (Levein), Gough, Durie, Bett, McCoist, McStay, Cooper.
Egypt: Shoubeir; Hassan I, Yakan, Yassin, Hassan H, El Kass (El Batel), Ramzy H, Abdelhany, Ramzy A, Youssef, Abdelhamid.

Belfast, 18 May 1990, 4000

N. Ireland (1) 1 *(Wilson K)*

Uruguay (0) 0

N. Ireland: Wright; Hill (Devine), Worthington, Taggart, McDonald, Rogan (Morrow), Dennison (McCreery), Wilson K, Dowie, Black.
Uruguay: Zeoli; Gutierrez, De Leon, Herrera (Saldana), Perdomo, Dominguez, Alzamendi (Aguilera), Ostolaza, Francescoli, Bengoechea (Paz), Sosa.

Glasgow, 19 May 1990, 25,142

Scotland (1) 1 *(Johnston)*

Poland (0) 1 *(Gillespie (og))*

Scotland: Goram; Gillespie, Malpas, Gough, Aitken, Levein, McCall, McAllister (McStay), McCoist, Johnston (McInally), MacLeod (Collins).
Poland: Bako; Kubicki, Lukasik (Soczynski), Wdowczyk, Kaczmarek, Prusik, Czachowski, Nawrocki (Pisz), Dziekanowski, Kosecki, Ziober.

Cardiff, 20 May 1990, 5977

Wales (1) 1 *(Saunders)*

Costa Rica (0) 0

Wales: Southall; Blackmore, Bodin, Aizlewood, Young (Melville), Hopkins, Horne, Nicholas, Saunders, Hughes (Allen), Hodges (Speed).
Costa Rica: Conejo; Flores, Medford (Marin), Chavel, Guimarez (Jaibel), Chavarria, David, Cayasso, Marchena, Montero, Ramirez.

Wembley, 22 May 1990, 38,751

England (0) 1 *(Barnes)*

Uruguay (1) 2 *(Ostolaza, Perdomo)*

England: Shilton; Parker, Pearce, Hodge (Beardsley), Walker, Butcher, Robson, Gascoigne, Waddle, Lineker (Bull), Barnes.
Uruguay: Pereira; Gutierrez, De Leon, Herrera, Perdomo, Dominguez, Alzamendi, Ostolaza, Francescoli, Paz, Sosa (Martinez).

Izmir, 27 May 1990, 5000

Turkey (0) 0

Rep of Ireland (0) 0

Turkey: Engin; Riza, Tugay, Gokhan B, Kemal (Gokhan K), Ogun, Mustafa (Heyrettin) Unal (Mehmet), Feyyaz (Savas), Oguz, Metin.
Rep of ireland: Bonner; Morris, Staunton (Hughton), McGrath, McCarthy, O'Leary (Slaven), Townsend (Sheridan), Waddock (Byrne), Aldridge, Cascarino, Sheedy.

Valetta, 28 May 1990, 3000

Malta (1) 1 *(Degiorgio)*

Scotland (1) 2 *(McInally 2)*

Malta: Cini; Vella S, Carabott, Calea (Camilleri), Laferia, Buttigieg, Zerafa, Vella R, Gregory (Zarb), Degiorgio, Licari (Scerri).
Scotland: Goram (Leighton); Gough, Aitken, McPherson, Gillespie (Levein), Malpas, McStay (Collins), McCall, Bett (McAllister), McInally, Johnston (McCoist).

Valetta, 2 June 1990, 800

Malta (0) 0

Rep of Ireland (1) 3 *(Quinn, Townsend, Stapleton)*

Malta: Cini; Vella S (Delia), Laferia, Galea (Camilleri), Gregory (Zarb), Buttigieg, Zerafa, Vella R, Carabott, Degiorgio, Licari.
Rep of Ireland: Peyton; Hughton, Staunton, O'Leary, Moran, McLoughlin, Sheridan, Byrne, Quinn, Kelly (Stapleton), Slaven (Townsend).

Tunis, 2 June 1990, 25,000

Tunisia (1) *(Hergal)*

England (0) 1 *(Bull)*

Tunisia: Zitouni; Mbadbi, Neji, Hishiri, Yahia, Mahjoubi, Sellimi, Tarak, Hergal (Dermach), Rouissi, Khemiri (Rashid).
England: Shilton; Stevens, Pearce, Hodge (Beardsley), Walker, Butcher (Wright), Robson, Gascoigne, Waddle (Platt), Lineker (Bull), Barnes.

Peter Shilton bowed out of international football at the end of the World Cup in Italy after 125 appearances for his country. He had broken Bobby Moore's record of 108 caps in June 1989. (Bob Thomas)

INTERNATIONAL APPEARANCES

This is a list of full international appearances by Englishmen, Irishmen, Scotsmen and Welshmen in matches against the Home Countries and against foreign nations. It does not include unofficial matches against Commonwealth and Empire countries. The year indicated refers to the season: ie 1990 is the 1989-90 season.

Explanatory code for matches played by all five countries: A represents Austria; Alb, Albania; Alg, Algeria; Arg, Argentina; Aus, Australia; B, Bohemia; Bel, Belgium; Br, Brazil; Bul, Bulgaria; Ca, Canada; Cam, Cameroon; Ch, Chile; Chn, China; Co, Colombia; Cr, Costa Rica; Cy, Cyprus; Cz, Czechoslovakia; D, Denmark; E, England; Ec, Ecuador; Ei, Eire; EG, East Germany; Eg, Egypt; F, France; Fi, Finland; G, Germany (pre-war); Gr, Greece; H, Hungary; Ho, Holland; Hon, Honduras; I, Italy; Ic, Iceland; Ir, Iran; Is, Israel; K, Kuwait; L, Luxembourg; M, Mexico; Ma, Malta; Mor, Morocco; N, Norway; Ni, Northern Ireland; Nz, New Zealand; P, Portugal; Par, Paraguay; Pe, Peru; Pol, Poland; R, Rumania; R of E, Rest of Europe; R of W, Rest of World; S.Ar, Saudi Arabia; S, Scotland; Se, Sweden; Sp, Spain; Sw, Switzerland; T, Turkey; Tr, Trinidad & Tobago; Tun, Tunisia; U, Uruguay; UK, Rest of United Kingdom; US, United States of America; USSR; W, Wales; WG, West Germany; Y, Yugoslavia.
As at 8 July 1990.

ENGLAND

Abbott, W. (Everton), 1902 v W (1)

A'Court, A. (Liverpool), 1958 v Ni, Br, A, USSR; 1959 v W (5)

Adams, T. A. (Arsenal), 1987 v Sp, T, Br; 1988 v WG, T, Y, Ho, H, S, Co, Sw, Ei, Ho, USSR ; 1989 v D, Se, S.Ar. (17)

Adcock, H. (Leicester C), 1929 v F, Bel, Sp; 1930 v Ni, W (5)

Alcock, C. W. (Wanderers), 1875 v S (1)

Alderson, J. T. (C Palace), 1923 v F (1)

Aldridge, A. (WBA), 1888 v Ni; (with Walsall Town Swifts), 1889 v Ni (2)

Allen, A. (Stoke C) 1960 v Se, W, Ni (3)

Allen, A. (Aston Villa), 1888 v Ni (1)

Allen, C. (QPR), 1984 v Br (sub), U, Ch; (with Tottenham H), 1987 v T; 1988 v Is (5)

Allen, H. (Wolverhampton W), 1888 v S, W, Ni; 1889 v S; 1890 v S (5)

Allen, J. P. (Portsmouth), 1934 v Ni, W (2)

Allen, R. (WBA), 1952 v Sw; 1954 v Y, S; 1955 v WG, W (5)

Alsford, W. J. (Tottenham H), 1935 v S (1)

Amos, A. (Old Carthusians), 1885 v S; 1886 v W (2)

Anderson, R. D. (Old Etonians), 1879 v W (1)

Anderson, S. (Sunderland), 1962, v A, S (2)

Anderson, V. (Nottingham F), 1979 v Cz, Se; 1980 v Bul, Sp; 1981 v N, R, W, S; 1982 v Ni, Ic; 1984 v Ni; (with Arsenal), 1985 v T, Ni, Ei, R, Fi, S, M, US; 1986 v USSR, M; 1987 v Se, Ni (2), Y, Sp, T; (with Manchester U), 1988 v WG, H, Co (30)

Angus, J. (Burnley), 1961 v A (1)

Armfield, J. C. (Blackpool), 1959 v Br, Pe, M, US; 1960 v Y, Sp, H, S; 1961 v L, P, Sp, M, I, A, W, Ni, S; 1962 v A, Sw, Pe, W, Ni, S, L, P, H, Arg, Bul, Br; 1963 v F (2), Br, EG, Sw, Ni, W, S; 1964 v R of W, W, Ni, S; 1966 v Y, Fi (43)

Armitage, G. H. (Charlton Ath), 1926 v Ni (1)

Armstrong, D. (Middlesbrough), 1980 v Aus; (with Southampton), 1983 v WG; 1984 v W (3)

Armstrong, K. (Chelsea), 1955 v S (1)

Arnold, J. (Fulham), 1933 v S (1)

Arthur, J. W. H. (Blackburn R), 1885 v S, W, Ni; 1886 v S, W; 1887 v W, Ni (7)

Ashcroft, J. (Woolwich Arsenal), 1906 v Ni, W, S (3)

Ashmore, G. S. (WBA), 1926 v Bel (1)

Ashton, C. T. (Corinthians), 1926 v Ni (1)

Ashurst, W. (Notts Co), 1923 v Se (2); 1925 v S, W, Bel (5)

Astall, G. (Birmingham C), 1956 v Fi, WG (2)

Astle, J. (WBA), 1969 v W; 1970 v S, P, Br (sub), Cz (5)

Aston, J. (Manchester U), 1949 v S, W, D, Sw, Se, N, F; 1950 v S, W, Ni, Ei, I, P, Bel, Ch, US; 1951 v Ni (17)

Athersmith, W. C. (Aston Villa), 1892 v Ni, 1897 v S, W,

Ni; 1898 v S, W, Ni; 1899 v S, W, Ni; 1900 v S, W (12)

Atyeo, P. J. W. (Bristol C), 1956 v Br, Se, Sp; 1957 v D, Ei (2) (6)

Austin, S. W. (Manchester C), 1926 v Ni (1)

Bach, P. (Sunderland), 1899 v Ni (1)

Bache, J. W. (Aston Villa), 1903 v W; 1904 v W, Ni; 1905 v S; 1907 v Ni; 1910 v Ni; 1911 v S (7)

Baddeley, T. (Wolverhampton W), 1903 v S, Ni; 1904 v S, W, Ni (5)

Bagshaw, J. J. (Derby Co), 1920 v Ni (1)

Bailey, G. R. (Manchester U), 1985 v Ei, M (2)

Bailey, H. P. (Leicester Fosse), 1908 v W, A (2), H, B (5)

Bailey, M. A. (Charlton Ath), 1964 v US; 1965 v W (2)

Bailey, N. C. (Clapham Rovers), 1878 v S; 1879 v S, W; 1880 v S; 1881 v S; 1882 v S, W; 1883 v S, W; 1884 v S, W, Ni; 1885 v Ni; 1886 v S, W; 1887 v S, W (19)

Baily, E. F. (Tottenham H), 1950 v Sp; 1951 v Y, Ni, W; 1952 v A (2), Sw, W; 1953 v Ni (9)

Bain, J. (Oxford University), 1887 v S (1)

Baker, A. (Arsenal), 1928 v W (1)

Baker, B. H. (Everton), 1921 v Bel; (with Chelsea), 1926 v Ni (2)

Baker, J. H. (Hibernian), 1960 v Y, Sp, H, Ni, S; (with Arsenal) 1966 v Sp, Pol, Ni (8)

Ball, A. J. (Blackpool), 1965 v Y, WG, Se; 1966 v S, Sp, Fi, D, U, Arg, P, WG (2), Pol (2); (with Everton), 1967 v W, S, Ni, A, Cz, Sp; 1968 v W, S, USSR, Sp (2), Y, WG; 1969 v W, S, R (2), M, Br, U; 1970 v P, Co, Ec, R, Br, Cz (sub), WG, W, S, Bel; 1971 v Ma, EG, Gr, Ma (sub), Ni, S; 1972 v Sw, Gr; (with Arsenal) WG (2), S; 1973 v W (3), Y, S (2), Cz, Ni, Pol; 1974 v P (sub); 1975 v WG, Cy (2), Ni, W, S (72)

Ball, J. (Bury), 1928 v Ni (1)

Balmer, W. (Everton), 1905 v Ni (1)

Bamber, J. (Liverpool), 1921 v W (1)

Bambridge, A. L. (Swifts), 1881 v W; 1883 v W; 1884 v Ni (3)

Bambridge, E. C. (Swifts), 1879 v S; 1880 v S; 1881 v S; 1882 v S, W, Ni; 1883 v W; 1884 v S, W, Ni; 1885 v S, W, Ni; 1886 v S, W; 1887 v S, W, Ni (18)

Bambridge, E. H. (Swifts), 1876 v S (1)

Banks, G. (Leicester C), 1963 v S, Br, Cz, EG; 1964 v W, Ni, S, R of W, U, P (2), US, Arg; 1965 v Ni, S, H, Y, WG, Se; 1966 v Ni, S, Sp, Pol (2), WG (2), Y, Fi, U, M, F, Arg, P; 1967 v Ni, W, S, Cz; (with Stoke C), 1968 v W, Ni, S, USSR (2), Sp, WG, Y; 1969 v Ni, S, R (2), F, U, Br; 1970 v W, Ni, S, Ho, Bel, Co, Ec, R, Br, Cz; 1971 v Gr, Ma (2), Ni, S; 1972 v Sw, Gr, WG (2), W, S (73)

Banks, H. E. (Millwall), 1901 v Ni (1)

Banks, T. (Bolton W), 1958 v USSR (3), Br, A; 1959 v Ni (6)

Bannister, W. (Burnley), 1901 v W; (with Bolton W), 1902 v Ni (2)

Barclay, R. (Sheffield W), 1932 v S; 1933 v Ni; 1936 v S (3)

Barham, M. (Norwich C), 1983 v Aus (2) (2)

Barkas, S. (Manchester C), 1936 v Bel; 1937 v S; 1938 v W, Ni, Cz (5)

Barker, J. (Derby Co), 1935 v I, Ho, S, W, Ni; 1936 v G, A, S, W, Ni; 1937 v W (11)

Barker, R. (Herts Rangers), 1872 v S (1)

Barker, R. R. (Casuals), 1895 v W (1)

Barlow, R. J. (WBA), 1955 v Ni (1)

Barnes, J. (Watford), 1983 v Ni (sub), Aus (sub), Aus (2); 1984 v D, L (sub), F (sub), S, USSR, Br, U, Ch; 1985 v EG, Fi, T, Ni, R, Fi, S, I (sub), M, WG (sub), US (sub); 1986 v R (sub), Is (sub), M (sub), Ca (sub), Arg (sub); 1987 v Se, T (sub), Br; (with Liverpool), 1988 v WG, T, Y, Is, Ho, S, Co, Sw, Ei, Ho, USSR; 1989 v Se, Gr, Alb, Pol, D; 1990 v Se, I, Br, D, U, Tun, Ei, Ho, Eg, Bel, Cam (58)

Barnes, P. S. (Manchester C), 1978 v I, WG, Br, W, S, H; 1979 v D, Ei, Cz, Ni (2), S, Bul, A; (with WBA), 1980 v D, W; 1981 v Sp (sub), Br, W, Sw (sub); (with Leeds U), 1982 v N (sub), Ho (sub) (22)

Barnet, H. H. (Royal Engineers), 1882 v Ni (1)

Barrass, M. W. (Bolton W), 1952 v W, Ni; 1953 v S (3)

Barrett, A. F. (Fulham), 1930 v Ni (1)

Barrett, J. W. (West Ham U), 1929 v Ni (1)

Barry, L. (Leicester C), 1928 v F, Bel; 1929 v F, Bel, Sp (5)

Barson, F. (Aston Villa), 1920 v W (1)

Barton, J. (Blackburn R), 1890 v Ni (1)

Barton, P. H. (Birmingham), 1921 v Bel; 1922 v Ni; 1923 v F; 1924 v Bel, S, W; 1925 v Ni (7)

Bassett, W. I. (WBA), 1888 v Ni, 1889 v S, W; 1890 v S, W; 1891 v S, Ni; 1892 v S; 1893 v S, W; 1894 v S; 1895 v S, Ni; 1896 v S, W, Ni (16)

Bastard, S. R. (Upton Park), 1880 v S (1)

Bastin, C. S. (Arsenal), 1932 v W; 1933 v I, Sw; 1934 v S, Ni, W, H, Cz; 1935 v S, Ni, I; 1936 v S, W, G, A; 1937 v W, Ni; 1938 v S, G, Sw, F (21)

Baugh, R. (Stafford Road), 1886 v Ni; (with Wolverhampton W) 1890 v Ni (2)

Bayliss, A. E. J. M. (WBA), 1891 v Ni (1)

Baynham, R. L. (Luton T), 1956 v Ni, D, Sp (3)

Beardsley, P. A. (Newcastle U), 1986 v Eg (sub), Is, USSR, M, Ca (sub), P (sub), Pol, Para, Arg; 1987 v Ni (2), Y, Sp, Br, S; (with Liverpool), 1988 v WG, T, Is, Ho, H, S, Co, Sw, Ei, Ho; 1989 v D, Se, S.Ar, Gr (sub), Alb (sub), Alb, Pol, D; 1990 v Se, Pol, I, Br, U (sub), Tun (sub), Ei, Eg (sub), Cam (sub), WG, I (45)

Beasant, D. J. (Chelsea), 1990 v I (sub), Y (sub) (2)

Beasley, A. (Huddersfield T), 1939 v S (1)

Beats, W. E. (Wolverhampton W), 1901 v W; 1902 v S (2)

Beattie, T. K. (Ipswich T), 1975 v Cy (2), S; 1976 v Sw, P; 1977 v Fi, I (sub), Ho; 1978 v L (sub) (9)

Becton, F. (Preston NE), 1895 v Ni; (with Liverpool), 1897 v W (2)

Bedford, H. (Blackpool), 1923 v Se; 1925 v Ni (2)

Bell, C. (Manchester C), 1968 v Se, WG; 1969 v W, Bul, F, U, Br; 1970 v Ni (sub), Ho (2), P, Br (sub), Cz, WG (sub); 1972 v Gr, WG (2), W, Ni, S; 1973 v W (3), Y, S (2), Ni, Cz, Pol; 1974 v A, Pol, I, W, Ni, S, Arg, EG, Bul, Y; 1975 v Cz, P, WG, Cy (2), Ni, S; 1976 v Sw, Cy (48)

Bennett, W. (Sheffield U), 1901 v S, W (2)

Benson, R. W. (Sheffield U), 1913 v Ni (1)

Bentley, R. T. F. (Chelsea), 1949 v Se; 1950 v S, P, Bel, Ch, USA; 1953 v W, Bel; 1955 v W, WG, Sp, P (12)

Beresford, J. (Aston Villa), 1934 v Cz (1)

Berry, A. (Oxford University), 1909 v Ni (1)

Berry, J. J. (Manchester U), 1953 v Arg, Ch, U; 1956 v Se (4)

Bestall, J. G. (Grimsby T), 1935 v Ni (1)

Betmead, H. A. (Grimsby T), 1937 v Fi (1)

Betts, M. P. (Old Harrovians), 1877 v S (1)

Betts, W. (Sheffield W), 1889 v W (1)

Beverley, J. (Blackburn R), 1884 v S, W, Ni (3)

Birkett, R. H. (Clapham Rovers), 1879 v S (1)

Birkett, R. J. E. (Middlesbrough), 1936 v Ni (1)

Birley, F. H. (Oxford University), 1874 v S; (with Wanderers), 1875 v S (2)

Birtles, G. (Nottingham F), 1980 v Arg (sub), I; 1981 v R (3)

Bishop, S. M. (Leicester C), 1927 v S, Bel, L, F (4)

Blackburn, F. (Blackburn R), 1901 v S; 1902 v Ni; 1904 v S (3)

Blackburn, G. F. (Aston Villa), 1924 v F (1)

Blenkinsop, E. (Sheffield W), 1928 v F, Bel; 1929 v S, W, Ni, F, Bel, Sp; 1930 v S, W, Ni, G, A; 1931 v S, W, Ni, F, Bel; 1932 v S, W, Ni, Sp; 1933 v S, W, Ni, A (26)

Bliss, H. (Tottenham H), 1921 v S (1)

Blissett, L. (Watford), 1983 v WG (sub), L, W, Gr (sub), H, Ni, S (sub), Aus (1+sub); 1984 v D (sub), H, W (sub), S, USSR (14)

Blockley, J. P. (Arsenal), 1973 v Y (1)

Bloomer, S. (Derby Co), 1895 v S, Ni; 1896 v W, Ni; 1897 v S, W, Ni; 1898 v S; 1899 v S, W, Ni; 1900 v S; 1901 v S, W; 1902 v S, W, Ni; 1904 v S; 1905 v S, W, Ni; (with Middlesbrough), 1907 v S, W (23)

Blunstone, F. (Chelsea), 1955 v W, S, F, P; 1957 v Y (5)

Bond, R. (Preston NE), 1905 v Ni, W; 1906 v S, W, Ni; (with Bradford C), 1910 v S, W, Ni (8)

Bonetti, P. P. (Chelsea), 1966 v D; 1967 v Sp, A; 1968 v Sp; 1970 v Ho, P, WG (7)

Bonsor, A. G. (Wanderers), 1873 v S; 1875 v S (2)

Booth, F. (Manchester C), 1905 v Ni (1)

Booth, T. (Blackburn R.), 1898 v W; (with Everton), 1903 v S (2)

Bowden, E. R. (Arsenal), 1935 v W, I; 1936 v W, Ni, A; 1937 v H (6)

Bower, A. G. (Corinthians), 1924 v Ni, Bel; 1925 v W, Bel; 1927 v W (5)

Bowers, J. W. (Derby Co), 1934 v S, Ni, W (3)

Bowles, S. (QPR), 1974 v P, W, Ni; 1977 v I, Ho (5)

Bowser, S. (WBA), 1920 v Ni (1)

Boyer, P. J. (Norwich C), 1976 v W (1)

Boyes, W. (WBA), 1935 v Ho; (with Everton), 1939 v W, R of E (3)

Boyle, T. W. (Burnley), 1913 v Ni (1)

Brabrook, P. (Chelsea), 1958 v USSR; 1959 v Ni; 1960 v Sp (3)

Bracewell, P. W. (Everton), 1985 v WG (sub), US; 1986 v Ni (3)

Bradford, G. R. W. (Bristol R), 1956 v D (1)

Bradford, J. (Birmingham), 1924 v Ni; 1925 v Bel; 1928 v S; 1929 v Ni, W, F, Sp; 1930 v S, Ni, G, A; 1931 v W (12)

Bradley, W. (Manchester U), 1959 v I, US, M (sub) (3)

Bradshaw, F. (Sheffield W), 1908 v A (1)

Bradshaw, T. H. (Liverpool), 1897 v Ni (1)

Bradshaw, W. (Blackburn R), 1910 v W, Ni; 1912 v Ni; 1913 v W (4)

Brann, G. (Swifts), 1886 v S, W; 1891 v W (3)

Brawn, W. F. (Aston Villa), 1904 v W, Ni (2)

Bray, J. (Manchester C), 1935 v W; 1936 v S, W, Ni, G; 1937 v S (6)

Brayshaw, E. (Sheffield W), 1887 v Ni (1)

Bridges, B. J. (Chelsea), 1965 v S, H, Y; 1966 v A (4)

Bridgett, A. (Sunderland), 1905 v S; 1908 v S, A (2), H, B; 1909 v Ni, W, H (2), A (11)

Brindle, T. (Darwen), 1880 v S, W (2)

Brittleton, J. T. (Sheffield W), 1912 v S, W, Ni; 1913 v S; 1914 v W (5)

Britton, C. S. (Everton), 1935 v S, W, Ni, I; 1937 v S, Ni, H, N, Se (9)

Broadbent, P. F. (Wolverhampton W), 1958 v USSR; 1959 v S, W, Ni, I, Br; 1960 v S (7)

Broadis, I. A. (Manchester C), 1952 v S, A, I; 1953 v S, Arg, Ch, U, US; (with Newcastle U), 1954 v S, H, Y, Bel, Sw, U (14)

Brockbank, J. (Cambridge University), 1872 v S (1)

Brodie, J. B. (Wolverhampton W), 1889 v S, Ni; 1891 v Ni (3)

Bromilow, T. G. (Liverpool), 1921 v W; 1922 v S, W; 1923 v Bel; 1926 v Ni (5)

Bromley-Davenport, W. E. (Oxford University), 1884 v S, W (2)

Brook, E. F. (Manchester C), 1930 v Ni; 1933 v Sw: 1934 v S, W, Ni, F, H, Cz; 1935 v S, W, Ni, I; 1936 v S, W, Ni; 1937 v H; 1938 v W, Ni (18)

Brooking, T. D. (West Ham U), 1974 v P, Arg, EG, Bul, Y; 1975 v Cz (sub), P; 1976 v P, W, Br, I, Fi; 1977 v Ei, Fi, I, Ho, Ni, W; 1978 v I, WG, W, S (sub), H; 1979 v D, Ei, Ni, W (sub), S, Bul, Se (sub), A; 1980 v D, Ni, Arg (sub), W, Ni, S, Bel, Sp; 1981 v Sw, Sp, R, H; 1982 v H, S, Fi, Sp (sub) (47)

Brooks, J. (Tottenham H), 1957 v W, Y, D (3)

Broome, F. H. (Aston Villa), 1938 v G, Sw, F; 1939 v N, I, R, Y (7)

Brown, A. (Aston Villa), 1882 v S, W, Ni (3)

Brown, A. S. (Sheffield U), 1904 v W; 1906 v Ni (2)

Brown, A. (WBA), 1971 v W (1)

Brown, G. (Huddersfield T), 1927 v S, W, Ni, Bel, L, F; 1928 v W; 1929 v S; (with Aston Villa), 1933 v W (9)

Brown, J. (Blackburn R), 1881 v W; 1882 v Ni; 1885 v S, W, Ni (5)

Brown, J. H. (Sheffield W), 1927 v S, W, Bel, L, F; 1930 v Ni (6)

Brown, K. (West Ham U), 1960 v Ni (1)

Brown, W. (West Ham U), 1924 v Bel (1)

Bruton, J. (Burnley), 1928 v F, Bel; 1929 v S (3)

Bryant, W. I. (Clapton), 1925 v F (1)

Buchan, C. M. (Sunderland), 1913 v Ni; 1920 v W; 1921 v W, Bel; 1923 v F; 1924 v S (6)

Buchanan, W. S. (Clapham R), 1876 v S (1)

Buckley, F. C. (Derby Co), 1914 v Ni (1)

Bull, S. G. (Wolverhampton W), 1989 v S (sub), D (sub); 1990 v Y, Cz, D (sub), U (sub), Tun (sub), Ei (sub), Ho (sub), Eg, Bel (sub) (11)

Bullock, F. E. (Huddersfield T), 1921 v Ni (1)

Bullock, N. (Bury), 1923 v Bel; 1926 v W; 1927 v Ni (3)

Burgess, H. (Manchester C), 1904 v S, W, Ni; 1906 v S (4)

Burgess, H. (Sheffield W), 1931 v S, Ni, F, Bel (4)

Burnup, C. J. (Cambridge University), 1896 v S (1)

Burrows, H. (Sheffield W), 1934 v H, Cz; 1935 v Ho (3)

Burton, F. E. (Nottingham F), 1889 v Ni (1)

Bury, L. (Cambridge University), 1877 v S; (with Old Etonians), 1879 v W (2)

Butcher, T. (Ipswich T), 1980 v Aus; 1981 v Sp; 1982 v W, S, F, Cz, WG, Sp; 1983 v D, WG, L, W, Gr, H, Ni, S, Aus (3); 1984 v D, H, L, F, Ni; 1985 v EG, Fi, T, Ni, Ei, R, Fi, S, I, WG, US; 1986 v Is, USSR, S, M, Ca, P, Mor, Pol, Para, Arg; (with Rangers) 1987 v Se, Ni (2), Y, Sp, Br, S; 1988 v T, Y; 1989 v D, Se, Gr, Alb, Alb, Ch, S, Pol, D; 1990 v Se, Pol, I, Y, Br, Cz, D, U, Tun, Ei, Ho, Bel, Cam, WG (77)

Butler, J. D. (Arsenal), 1925 v Bel (1)

Butler, W. (Bolton W), 1924 v S (1)

Byrne, G. (Liverpool), 1963 v S; 1966 v N (2)

Byrne, J. J. (C Palace), 1962 v Ni; (with West Ham U), 1963 v Sw; 1964 v S, U, P (2), Ei, Br, Arg; 1965 v W, S (11)

Byrne, R. W. (Manchester U), 1954 v S, H, Y, Bel, Sw, U; 1955 v S, W, Ni, WG, F, Sp, P; 1956 v S, W, Ni, Br, Se, Fi, WG, D, Sp; 1957 v S, W, Ni, Y, D (2), Ei (2); 1958 v W, Ni, F (33)

Callaghan, I. R. (Liverpool), 1966 v Fi, F; 1978 v Sw, L (4)

Calvey, J. (Nottingham F), 1902 v Ni (1)

Campbell, A. F. (Blackburn R), 1929 v W, Ni; (with Huddersfield T), 1931 v W, S, Ni; 1932 v W, Ni, Sp (8)

Camsell, G. H. (Middlesbrough), 1929 v F, Bel; 1930 v Ni, W; 1934 v F; 1936 v S, G, A, Bel (9)

Capes, A. J. (Stoke C), 1903 v S (1)

Carr, J. (Middlesbrough), 1920 v Ni; 1923 v W (2)

Carr, J. (Newcastle U), 1905 v Ni; 1907 v Ni (2)

Carr, W. H. (Owlerton, Sheffield), 1875 v S (1)

Carter, H. S. (Sunderland), 1934 v S, H; 1936 v G; 1937 v S, Ni, H; (with Derby Co), 1947 v S, W, Ni, Ei, Ho, F, Sw (13)

Carter, J. H. (WBA), 1926 v Bel; 1929 v Bel, Sp (3)

Catlin, A. E. (Sheffield W), 1937 v W, Ni, H, N, Se (5)

Chadwick, A. (Southampton), 1900 v S, W (2)

Chadwick, E. (Everton), 1891 v S, W; 1892 v S; 1893 v S; 1894 v S; 1896 v Ni; 1897 v S (7)

Chamberlain, M (Stoke C), 1983 v L (sub); 1984 v D (sub), S, USSR, Br, U, Ch; 1985 v Fi (sub) (8)

Chambers, H. (Liverpool), 1921 v S, W, Bel; 1923 v S, W, Ni, Bel; 1924 v Ni (8)

Channon, M. R. (Southampton), 1973 v Y, S (2), Ni, W, Cz, USSR, I; 1974 v A, Pol, I, P, W, Ni, S, Arg, EG, Bul, Y; 1975 v Cz, P, WG, Cy (2), Ni (sub), W, S; 1976 v Sw, Cz, P, W, Ni, S, Br, I, Fi; 1977 v Fi, I, L, Ni, W, S, Br (sub), Arg, U; (with Manchester C), 1978 v Sw (46)

Charlton, J. (Leeds U), 1965 v S, H, Y, WG, Se; 1966 v W, Ni, S, A, Sp, Pol (2), WG (2), Y, Fi, D, U, M, F, Arg, P; 1967 v W, S, Ni, Cz; 1968 v W, Sp; 1969 v W, R, F; 1970 v Ho (2), P, Cz (35)

Charlton, R. (Manchester U), 1958 v S, P, Y; 1959 v S, W, Ni, USSR, I, Br, Pe, US; 1960 v W, S, Se, Y, Sp, H; 1961 v Ni, W, S, L, P, Sp, M, I, A; 1962 v W, Ni, S, A, Sw, Pe, L, P, H, Arg, Bul, Br; 1963 v S, F, Br, Cz, EG, Sw; 1964 v S, W, Ni, R of W, U, P, Ei, Br, Arg, US (sub); 1965 v Ni, S, Ho; 1966 v W, Ni, S, A, Sp, WG (2), Y, Fi, N, Pol, U, M, F, Arg, P; 1967 v Ni, W, S, Cz; 1968 v W, Ni, S, USSR (2), Sp (2), Se, Y; 1969 v S, W, Ni, R (2), Bul, M, Br; 1970 v W, Ho (2), P, Co, Ec, Cz, R, Br, WG (106)

Charnley, R. O. (Blackpool), 1963 v F (1)

Charsley, C. C. (Small Heath), 1893 v Ni (1)

Chedgzoy, S. (Everton), 1920 v W; 1921 v W, S, Ni; 1922 v Ni; 1923 v S; 1924 v W; 1925 v Ni (8)

Chenery, C. J. (C Palace), 1872 v S; 1873 v S; 1874 v S (3)

Cherry, T. J. (Leeds U), 1976 v W, S (sub), Br, Fi; 1977 v Ei, I, L, Ni, S (sub), Br, Arg, U; 1978 v Sw, L, I, Br, W; 1979 v Cz, W, Se; 1980 v Ei, Arg (sub), W, Ni, S, Aus, Sp (sub) (27)

Chilton, A. (Manchester U), 1951 v Ni; 1952 v F (2)

Chippendale, H. (Blackburn R), 1894 v Ni (1)

Chivers, M. (Tottenham H), 1971 v Ma (2), Gr, Ni, S; 1972 v Sw (1+1 sub), Gr, WG (2), Ni (sub), S; 1973 v W (3), S (2), Ni, Cz, Pol, USSR, I; 1974 v A, Pol (24)

Christian, E. (Old Etonians), 1879 v S (1)

Clamp, E. (Wolverhampton W), 1958 v USSR (2), Br, A (4)

Clapton, D. R. (Arsenal), 1959 v W (1)

Clare, T. (Stoke C), 1889 v Ni; 1892 v Ni; 1893 v W; 1894 v S (4)

Clarke, A. J. (Leeds U), 1970 v Cz; 1971 v EG, Ma, Ni, W (sub), S (sub); 1972 v S (2), W, Cz, Pol, USSR, I; 1974 v A, Pol, I; 1975 v P; 1976 v Cz, P (sub) (19)

Clarke, H. A. (Tottenham H), 1954 v S (1)

Clay, T. (Tottenham H), 1920 v W; 1922 v W, S, Ni (4)

Clayton, R. (Blackburn R), 1956 v Ni, Br, Se, Fi, WG, Sp; 1957 v S, W, Ni, Y, D (2), Ei (2); 1958 v S, W, Ni, F, P, Y, USSR; 1959 v S, W, Ni, USSR, I, Br, Pe, M, US; 1960 v W, Ni, S, Se, Y (35)

Clegg, J. C. (Sheffield W), 1872 v S (1)

Clegg, W. E. (Sheffield W), 1873 v S; (with Sheffield Albion), 1879 v W (2)

Clemence, R. N. (Liverpool), 1973 v W (2); 1974 v EG, Bul, Y; 1975 v Cz, P, WG, Cy, Ni, W, S; 1976 v Sw, Cz, P, W (2), Ni, S, Br, Fi; 1977 v Ei, Fi, I, Ho, L, S, Br, Arg, U; 1978 v Sw, L, I, WG, Ni, S; 1979 v D, Ei, Ni (2), S, Bul, A (sub); 1980 v D, Bul, Ei, Arg, W, S, Bel, Sp; 1981 v R, Sp, Br, Sw, H; (with Tottenham H), 1982 v N, Ni, Fi; 1983 v L; 1984 v L (61)

Clement, D. T. (QPR), 1976 v W (sub), W, I; 1977 v I, Ho (5)

Clough, B. H. (Middlesbrough), 1960 v W, Se (2)

Clough, N. H. (Nottingham F), 1989 v Ch (1)

Coates, R. (Burnley), 1970 v Ni; 1971 v Gr (sub); (with Tottenham H), Ma, W (4)

Cobbold, W. N. (Cambridge University), 1883 v S, Ni; 1885 v S, Ni; 1886 v S, W; (with Old Carthusians), 1887 v S, W, Ni (9)

Cock, J. G. (Huddersfield T), 1920 v Ni; (with Chelsea), v S (2)

Cockburn, H. (Manchester U), 1947 v W, Ni, Ei; 1948 v S, I; 1949 v S, Ni, D, Sw, Se; 1951 v Arg, P; 1952 v F (13)

Cohen, G. R. (Fulham), 1964 v U, P, Ei, US, Br; 1965 v W, S, Ni, Bel, H, Ho, Y, WG, Se; 1966 v W, S, Ni, A, Sp, Pol (2), WG (2), N, D, U, M, F, Arg, P; 1967 v W, S, Ni, Cz, Sp; 1968 v W, Ni (37)

Coleclough, H. (C Palace), 1914 v W (1)

Coleman, E. H. (Dulwich Hamlet), 1921 v W (1)

Coleman, J. (Woolwich Arsenal), 1907 v Ni (1)

Common, A. (Sheffield U), 1904 v W, Ni; (with Middlesbrough), 1906 v W (3)

Compton, L. H. (Arsenal), 1951 v W, Y (2)

Conlin, J. (Bradford C), 1906 v S (1)

Connelly, J. M. (Burnley), 1960 v W, N, S, Se; 1962 v W, A, Sw, P; 1963 v W, F; (with Manchester U), 1965 v H, Y, Se; 1966 v W, Ni, S, A, N, D, U (20)

Cook, T. E. R. (Brighton), 1925 v W (1)

Cooper, N. C. (Cambridge University), 1893 v Ni (1)

Cooper, T. (Derby Co), 1928 v Ni; 1929 v W, Ni, S, F, Bel, Sp; 1931 v F; 1932 v W, Sp; 1933 v S; 1934 v S, H, Cz; 1935 v W (15)

Cooper, T. (Leeds U), 1969 v W, S, F, M; 1970 v Ho, Bel, Co, Ec, R, Cz, Br, WG; 1971 v EG, Ma, Ni, W, S; 1972 v Sw (2); 1975 v P (20)

Coppell, S. J. (Manchester U), 1978 v I, WG, Br, W, Ni, S, H; 1979 v D, Ei, Cz, Ni (2), W (sub), S, Bul, A; 1980 v D, Ni, Ei (sub), Sp, Arg, W, S, Bel, I; 1981 v R (sub), Sw, R, Br, W, S, Sw, H; 1982 v H, S, Fi, F, Cz, K, WG; 1983 v L, Gr (42)

Copping, W. (Leeds U), 1933 v I, Sw; 1934 v S, Ni, W, F; (with Arsenal), 1935 v Ni, I; 1936 v A, Bel; 1937 v N, Se, Fi; 1938 v S, W, Ni, Cz; 1939 v W, R of E; (with Leeds U), R (20)

Corbett, B. O. (Corinthians), 1901 v W (1)

Corbett, R. (Old Malvernians), 1903 v W (1)

Corbett, W. S. (Birmingham), 1908 v A, H, B (3)

Corrigan, J. T. (Manchester C), 1976 v I (sub), Br; 1979 v W; 1980 v Ni, Aus; 1981 v W, S; 1982 v W, Ic (9)

Cottee, A. R. (West Ham U), 1987 v Se (sub), Ni (sub); 1988 v H (sub); (with Everton) 1989 v D (sub), Se (sub), Ch (sub), S (7)

Cotterill, G. H. (Cambridge University), 1891 v Ni; (with Old Brightonians), 1892 v W; 1893 v S, Ni (4)

Cottle, J. R. (Bristol C), 1909 v Ni (1)

Cowan, S. (Manchester C), 1926 v Bel; 1930 v A; 1931 v Bel (3)

Cowans, G. (Aston Villa), 1983 v W, H, Ni, S, Aus (3); (with Bari), 1986 v Eg, USSR (9)

Cowell, A. (Blackburn R), 1910 v Ni (1)

Cox, J. (Liverpool), 1901 v Ni; 1902 v S; 1903 v S (3)

Cox, J. D. (Derby Co), 1892 v Ni (1)

Crabtree, J. W. (Burnley), 1894 v Ni; 1895 v Ni, S; (with

Aston Villa), 1896 v W, S, Ni; 1899 v S, W, Ni; 1900 v S, W, Ni; 1901 v W; 1902 v W (14)

Crawford, J. F. (Chelsea), 1931 v S (1)

Crawford, R. (Ipswich T), 1962 v Ni, A (2)

Crawshaw, T. H. (Sheffield W), 1895 v Ni; 1896 v S, W, Ni; 1897 v S, W, Ni; 1901 v Ni; 1904 v W, Ni (10)

Crayston, W. J. (Arsenal), 1936 v S, W, G, A, Bel; 1938 v W, Ni, Cz (8)

Creek, F. N. S. (Corinthians), 1923 v F (1)

Cresswell, W. (South Shields), 1921 v W; (with Sunderland), 1923 v F; 1924 v Bel; 1925 v Ni; 1926 v W; 1927 v Ni; (with Everton), 1930 v Ni (7)

Crompton, R. (Blackburn R), 1902 v S, W, Ni; 1903 v S, W; 1904 v S, W, Ni; 1906 v S, W, Ni; 1907 v S, W, Ni; 1908 v S, W, Ni, A (2), H, B; 1909 v S, W, Ni, H (2), A; 1910 v S, W; 1911 v S, W, Ni; 1912 v S, W, Ni; 1913 v S, W, Ni; 1914 v S, W, Ni (41)

Crooks, S. D. (Derby Co), 1930 v S, G, A; 1931 v S, W, Ni, F, Bel; 1932 v S, W, Ni, Sp; 1933 v Ni, W, A; 1934 v S, Ni, W, F, H, Cz; 1935 v Ni; 1936 v S, W; 1937 v W, H (26)

Crowe, C. (Wolverhampton W), 1963 v F (1)

Cuggy, F. (Sunderland), 1913 v Ni; 1914 v Ni (2)

Cullis, S. (Wolverhampton W), 1938 v S, W, Ni, F, Cz; 1939 v S, Ni, R of E, N, I, R, Y (12)

Cunliffe, A. (Blackburn R), 1933 v Ni, W (2)

Cunliffe, D. (Portsmouth), 1900 v Ni (1)

Cunliffe, J. N. (Everton), 1936 v Bel (1)

Cunningham, L. (WBA), 1979 v W, Se, A (sub); (with Real Madrid), 1980 v Ei, Sp (sub); 1981 v R (sub) (6)

Currey, E. S. (Oxford University), 1890 v S, W (2)

Currie, A. W. (Sheffield U), 1972 v Ni; 1973 v USSR, I; 1974 v A, Pol, I; 1976 v Sw; (with Leeds U), 1978 v Br, W (sub), Ni, S, H (sub); 1979 v Cz, Ni (2), W, Se (17)

Cursham, A. W. (Notts Co), 1876 v S; 1877 v S; 1878 v S; 1879 v W; 1883 v S, W (6)

Cursham, H. A. (Notts Co), 1880 v W; 1882 v S, W, Ni; 1883 v S, W, Ni; 1884 v Ni (8)

Daft, H. B. (Notts Co), 1889 v Ni; 1890 v S, W; 1891 v Ni; 1892 v Ni (5)

Danks, T. (Nottingham F), 1885 v S (1)

Davenport, P. (Nottingham F), 1985 v Ei (sub) (1)

Davenport, J. K. (Bolton W), 1885 v W; 1890 v Ni (2)

Davis, G. (Derby Co), 1904 v W, Ni (2)

Davis, H. (Sheffield W), 1903 v S, W, Ni (3)

Davison, J. E. (Sheffield W), 1922 v W (1)

Dawson, J. (Burnley), 1922 v S, Ni (2)

Day, S. H. (Old Malvernians), 1906 v Ni, W, S (3)

Dean, W. R. (Everton), 1927 v S, W, F, Bel, L; 1928 v S, W, Ni, F, Bel; 1929 v S, W, Ni; 1931 v S; 1932 v Sp; 1933 v Ni (16)

Deeley, N. V. (Wolverhampton W), 1959 v Br, Pe (2)

Devey, J. H. G. (Aston Villa), 1892 v Ni; 1894 v Ni (2)

Devonshire, A. (West Ham U), 1980 v Aus (sub), Ni; 1982 v Ho, Ic; 1983 v WG, W, Gr; 1984 v L (8)

Dewhurst, F. (Preston NE), 1886 v W, Ni; 1887 v S, W, Ni; 1888 v S, W, Ni; 1889 v W (9)

Dewhurst, G. P. (Liverpool Ramblers), 1895 v W (1)

Dickinson, J. W. (Portsmouth), 1949 v N, F; 1950 v S, W, Ei, P, Bel, Ch, US, Sp; 1951 v Ni, W, Y; 1952 v W, Ni, S, A (2), I, Sw; 1953 v W, Ni, S, Bel, Arg, Ch, U, US; 1954 v W, Ni, S, R of E, H (2), Y, Bel, Sw, U; 1955 v Sp, P; 1956 v W, Ni, S, D, Sp; 1957 v W, Y, D (48)

Dimmock, J. H. (Tottenham H), 1921 v S; 1926 v W, Bel (3)

Ditchburn, E. G. (Tottenham H), 1949 v Sw, Se; 1953 v US; 1957 v W, Y, D (6)

Dix, R. W. (Derby Co), 1939 v N (1)

Dixon, J. A. (Notts Co), 1885 v W (1)

Dixon, K. M. (Chelsea), 1985 v M (sub), WG, US; 1986 v Ni, Is, M (sub), Pol (sub); 1987 v Se (8)

Dixon, L. M. (Arsenal), 1990 v Cz (1)

Dobson, A. T. C. (Notts Co), 1882 v Ni; 1884 v S, W, Ni (4)

Dobson, C. F. (Notts Co), 1886 v Ni (1)

Dobson, J. M. (Burnley), 1974 v P, EG, Bul, Y; (with Everton), 1975 v Cz (5)

Doggart, A. G. (Corinthians), 1924 v Bel (1)

Dorigo, A. R. (Chelsea), 1990 v Y (sub), Cz (sub), D (sub), I (4)

Dorrell, A. R. (Aston Villa), 1925 v W, Bel, F; 1926 v Ni (4)

Douglas, B. (Blackburn R), 1958 v S, W, Ni, F, P, Y, USSR (2), Br, A; 1959 v S, USSR; 1960 v Y, H; 1961 v Ni, W, S, L, P, Sp, M, I, A; 1962 v W, Ni, S, Pe, L, P, H, Arg, Bul, Br; 1963 v S, Br, Sw (36)

Downs, R. W. (Everton), 1921 v Ni (1)

Doyle, M. (Manchester C), 1976 v W, S (sub), Br, I; 1977 v Ho (5)

Drake, E. J. (Arsenal), 1935 v Ni, I; 1936 v W; 1937 v H; 1938 v F (5)

Ducat, A. (Woolwich Arsenal), 1910 v S, W, Ni; (with Aston Villa), 1920 v S, W; 1921 v Ni (6)

Dunn, A. T. B. (Cambridge University), 1883 v Ni; 1884 v Ni; (with Old Etonians), 1892 v S, W (4)

Duxbury, M. (Manchester U), 1984 v L, F, W, S, USSR, Br, U, Ch; 1985 v EG, Fi (10)

Earle, S. G. J. (Clapton), 1924 v F; (with West Ham U), 1928 v Ni (2)

Eastham, G. (Arsenal), 1963 v Br, Cz, EG; 1964 v W, Ni, S, R of W, U, P, Ei, US, Br, Arg; 1965 v H, WG, Se; 1966 v Sp, Pol, D (19)

Eastham, G. R. (Bolton W), 1935 v Ho (1)

Eckersley, W. (Blackburn R), 1950 v Sp; 1951 v S, Y, Arg, P; 1952 v A (2), Sw; 1953 v Ni, Arg, Ch, U, US; 1954 v W, Ni, R of E, H (17)

Edwards, D. (Manchester U), 1955 v S, F, Sp, P; 1956 v S, Br, Se, Fi, WG; 1957 v S, Ni, Ei (2), D (2); 1958 v W, Ni, F (18)

Edwards, J. H. (Shropshire Wanderers), 1874 v S (1)

Edwards, W. (Leeds U), 1926 v S, W; 1927 v W, Ni, S, F, Bel, L; 1928 v S, F, Bel; 1929 v S, W, Ni; 1930 v W, Ni (16)

Ellerington, W. (Southampton), 1949 v N, F (2)

Elliott, G. W. (Middlesbrough), 1913 v Ni; 1914 v Ni; 1920 v W (3)

Elliott, W. H. (Burnley), 1952 v I, A; 1953 v Ni, W, Bel (5)

Evans, R. E. (Sheffield U), 1911 v S, W, Ni; 1912 v W (4)

Ewer, F. H. (Casuals), 1924 v F; 1925 v Bel (2)

Fairclough, P. (Old Foresters), 1878 v S (1)

Fairhurst, D. (Newcastle U), 1934 v F (1)

Fantham, J. (Sheffield W), 1962 v L (1)

Fashanu, J. (Wimbledon), 1989 v Ch, S (2)

Felton, W. (Sheffield W), 1925 v F (1)

Fenton, M. (Middlesbrough), 1938 v S (1)

Fenwick, T. (QPR), 1984 v W (sub), S, USSR, Br, U, Ch; 1985 v Fi, S, M, US; 1986 v R, T, Ni, Eg, M, P, Mor, Pol, Arg; (with Tottenham H), 1988 v Is (sub) (20)

Field, E. (Clapham Rovers), 1876 v S; 1881 v S (2)

Finney, T. (Preston NE), 1947 v W, Ni, Ei, Ho, F, P; 1948 v S, W, Ni, Bel, Se, I; 1949 v S, W, Ni, Se, N, F; 1950 v S, W, Ni, Ei, I, P, Bel, Ch, US, Sp; 1951 v W, S, Arg, P; 1952 v W, Ni, S, F, I, Sw, A; 1953 v W, Ni, S, Bel, Arg, Ch, U, US; 1954 v W, S, Bel, Sw, U, H, Y; 1955 v WG; 1956 v S, W, Ni, D, Sp; 1957 v S, W, Y, D (2), Ei (2); 1958 v W, S, F, P, Y, USSR (2); 1959 v Ni, USSR (76)

Fleming, H. J. (Swindon T), 1909 v S, H (2); 1910 v W, Ni; 1911 v W, Ni; 1912 v S; 1913 v S, W; 1914 v S (11)

Fletcher, A. (Wolverhampton W), 1889 v W; 1890 v W (2)

Flowers, R. (Wolverhampton W), 1955 v F; 1959 v S, W, I, Br, Pe, US, M (sub); 1960 v W, Ni, S, Se, Y, Sp, H;

1961 v Ni, W, S, L, P, Sp, M, I, A; 1962 v W, Ni, S, A, Sw, Pe, L, P, H, Arg, Bul, Br; 1963 v Ni, W, S, F (2), Sw; 1964 v Ei, US, P; 1965 v W, Ho, WG; 1966 v N (49)

Forman, Frank (Nottingham F), 1898 v S, Ni; 1899 v S, W, Ni; 1901 v S; 1902 v S, Ni; 1903 v W (9)

Forman, F. R. (Nottingham F), 1899 v S, W, Ni (3)

Forrest, J. H. (Blackburn R), 1884 v W; 1885 v S, W, Ni; 1886 v S, W; 1887 v S, W, Ni; 1889 v S; 1890 v Ni (11)

Fort, J. (Millwall), 1921 v Bel (1)

Foster, R. E. (Oxford University), 1900 v W; (with Corinthians), 1901 v W, Ni, S; 1902 v W (5)

Foster, S. (Brighton & HA), 1982 v Ni, Ho, K (3)

Foulke, W. J. (Sheffield U), 1897 v W (1)

Foulkes, W. A. (Manchester U), 1955 v Ni (1)

Fox, F. S. (Gillingham), 1925 v F (1)

Francis, G. C. J. (QPR), 1975 v Cz, P, W, S; 1976 v Sw, Cz, P, W, Ni, S, Br, Fi (12)

Francis, T. (Birmingham C), 1977 v Ho, L, S, Br; 1978 v Sw, L, I (sub), WG (sub), Br, W, S, H; (with Nottingham F), 1979 v Bul (sub), Se, A (sub); 1980 v Ni, Bul, Sp; 1981 v Sp, R, S (sub), Sw; (with Manchester C), 1982 v N, Ni, W, S (sub), Fi (sub), F, Cz, K, WG, Sp; (with Sampdoria), 1983 v D, Gr, H, Ni, S, Aus (3); 1984 v D, Ni, USSR; 1985 v EG (sub), T (sub), Ni (sub), R, Fi, S, I, M; 1986 v S (52)

Franklin, C. F. (Stoke C), 1947 v S, W, Ni, Ei, Ho, F, Sw, P; 1948 v S, W, Ni, Bel, Se, I; 1949 v S, W, Ni, D, Sw, N, F, Se; 1950 v W, S, Ni, Ei, I (27)

Freeman, B. C. (Everton), 1909 v S, W; (with Burnley), 1912 v S, W, Ni (5)

Froggatt, J. (Portsmouth), 1950 v Ni, I; 1951 v S; 1952 v S, A (2), I, Sw; 1953 v Ni, W, S, Bel, US (13)

Froggatt, R. (Sheffield W), 1953 v W, S, Bel, US (4)

Fry, C. B. (Corinthians), 1901 v Ni (1)

Furness, W. I. (Leeds U), 1933 v I (1)

Galley, T. (Wolverhampton W), 1937 v N, Se (2)

Gardner, T. (Aston Villa), 1934 v Cz; 1935 v Ho (2)

Garfield, B. (WBA), 1898 v Ni (1)

Garratty, W. (Aston Villa), 1903 v W (1)

Garrett, T. (Blackpool), 1952 v S, I; 1954 v W (3)

Gascoigne, P. J. (Tottenham H), 1989 v D (sub), S.Ar (sub), Alb (sub), Ch, S (sub); 1990 v Se (sub), Br (sub), Cz, D, U, Tun, Ei, Ho, Eg, Bel, Cam, WG (17)

Gates, E. (Ipswich T), 1981 v N, R (2)

Gay, L. H. (Cambridge University), 1893 v S; (with Old Brightonians), 1894 v S, W (3)

Geary, F. (Everton), 1890 v Ni; 1891 v S (2)

Geaves, R. L. (Clapham Rovers), 1875 v S (1)

Gee, C. W. (Everton), 1932 v W, Sp; 1937 v Ni (3)

Geldard, A. (Everton), 1933 v I, Sw; 1935 v S; 1938 v Ni (4)

George, C. (Derby Co), 1977 v Ei (1)

George, W. (Aston Villa), 1902 v S, W, Ni (3)

Gibbins, W. V. T. (Clapton), 1924 v F; 1925 v F (2)

Gidman, J. (Aston Villa), 1977 v L (1)

Gillard, I. T. (QPR), 1975 v WG, W; 1976 v Cz (3)

Gilliat, W. E. (Old Carthusians), 1893 v Ni (1)

Goddard, P. (West Ham U), 1982 v Ic (sub) (1)

Goodall, F. R. (Huddersfield T), 1926 v S; 1927 v S, F, Bel, L; 1928 v S, W, F, Bel; 1930 v S, G, A; 1931 v S, W, Ni, Bel; 1932 v Ni; 1933 v W, Ni, A, I, Sw; 1934 v W, Ni, F (25)

Goodall, J. (Preston NE), 1888 v S, W; 1889 v S, W; (with Derby Co), 1891 v S, W; 1892 v S; 1893 v W; 1894 v S; 1895 v S, Ni; 1896 v S, W; 1898 v W (14)

Goodhart, H. C. (Old Etonians), 1883 v S, W, Ni (3)

Goodwyn, A. G. (Royal Engineers), 1873 v S (1)

Goodyer, A. C.(Nottingham F), 1879 v S (1)

Gosling, R. C. (Old Etonians), 1892 v W; 1893 v S; 1894 v W; 1895 v W, S (5)

Gosnell, A. A. (Newcastle U), 1906 v Ni (1)

Gough, H. C. (Sheffield U), 1921 v S (1)

Goulden, L. A. (West Ham U), 1937 v Se, N; 1938 v W, Ni, Cz, G, Sw, F; 1939 v S, W, R of E, I, R, Y (14)
Graham, L. (Millwall), 1925 v S, W (2)
Graham, T. (Nottingham F), 1931 v F; 1932 v Ni (2)
Grainger, C. (Sheffield U), 1956 v Br, Se, Fi, WG; 1957 v W, Ni; (with Sunderland), 1957 v S (7)
Greaves, J. (Chelsea), 1959 v Pe, M, US; 1960 v W, Se, Y, Sp; 1961 v Ni, W, S, L, P, Sp, I, A; (with Tottenham H), 1962 v S, Sw, Pe, H, Arg, Bul, Br; 1963 v Ni, W, S, F (2), Br, Cz, Sw; 1964 v W, Ni, R of W, P (2), Ei, Br, U, Arg; 1965 v Ni, S, Bel, Ho, H, Y; 1966 v W, A, Y, N, D, Pol, U, M, F; 1967 v S, Sp, A (57)
Green, F. T. (Wanderers), 1876 v S (1)
Green, G. H. (Sheffield U), 1925 v F; 1926 v S, Bel, W; 1927 v W, Ni; 1928 v F, Bel (8)
Greenhalgh, E. H. (Notts Co), 1872 v S; 1873 v S (2)
Greenhoff, B. (Manchester U), 1976 v W, Ni; 1977 v Ei, Fi, I, Ho, Ni, W, S, Br, Arg, U; 1978 v Br, W, Ni, S (sub), H (sub); (with Leeds U), 1980 v Aus (sub) (18)
Greenwood, D. H. (Blackburn R), 1882 v S, Ni (2)
Gregory, J. (QPR), 1983 v Aus (3); 1984 v D, H, W (6)
Grimsdell, A. (Tottenham H), 1920 v S, W; 1921 v S, Ni; 1923 v W, Ni (6)
Grosvenor, A. T. (Birmingham), 1934 v Ni, W, F (3)
Gunn, W. (Notts Co), 1884 v S, W (2)
Gurney, R. (Sunderland), 1935 v S (1)

Hacking, J. (Oldham Ath), 1929 v S, W, Ni (3)
Hadley, N. (WBA), 1903 v Ni (1)
Hagan, J. (Sheffield U), 1949 v D (1)
Haines, J. T. W. (WBA), 1949 v Sw (1)
Hall, A. E. (Aston Villa), 1910 v Ni (1)
Hall, G. W. (Tottenham H), 1934 v F; 1938 v S, W, Ni, Cz; 1939 v S, Ni, R of E, I, Y (10)
Hall, J. (Birmingham C), 1956 v S, W, Ni, Br, Se, Fi, WG, D, Sp; 1957 v S, W, Ni, Y, D (2), Ei (2) (17)
Halse, H. J. (Manchester U), 1909 v A (1)
Hammond, H. E. D. (Oxford University), 1889 v S (1)
Hampson, J. (Blackpool), 1931 v Ni, W; 1933 v A (3)
Hampton, H. (Aston Villa), 1913 v S, W; 1914 v S, W (4)
Hancocks, J. Wolverhampton W), 1949 v Sw; 1950 v W; 1951 v Y (3)
Hapgood, E. (Arsenal), 1933 v I, Sw; 1934 v S, Ni, W, H, Cz; 1935 v S, Ni, W, I, Ho; 1936 v S, Ni, W, G, A, Bel; 1937 v Fi; 1938 v S, G, Sw, F; 1939 v S, W, Ni, R of E, N, I, Y (30)
Hardinge, H. T. W. (Sheffield U), 1910 v S (1)
Hardman, H. P. (Everton), 1905 v W; 1907 v S, Ni; 1908 v W (4)
Hardwick, G. F. M. (Middlesbrough), 1947 v S, W, Ni, Ei, Ho, F, Sw, P; 1948 v S, W, Ni, Bel, Se (13)
Hardy, H. (Stockport Co), 1925 v Bel (1)
Hardy, S. (Liverpool), 1907 v S, W, Ni; 1908 v S; 1909 v S, W, Ni, H (2), A; 1910 v S, W, Ni; 1912 v Ni; (with Aston Villa), 1913 v S; 1914 v Ni, W, S; 1920 v S, W, Ni (21)
Harford, M. G. (Luton T), 1988 v Is (sub); 1989 v D (2)
Hargreaves, F. W. (Blackburn R), 1880 v W; 1881 v W: 1882 v Ni (3)
Hargreaves, J. (Blackburn R), 1881 v S, W (2)
Harper, E. C. (Blackburn R), 1926 v S (1)
Harris, G. (Burnley), 1966 v Pol (1)
Harris, P. P. (Portsmouth), 1950 v Ei; 1954 v H (2)
Harris, S. S. (Cambridge University), 1904 v S; (with Old Westminsters), 1905 v Ni, W; 1906 v S, W, Ni (6)
Harrison, A. H. (Old Westminsters), 1893 v S, Ni (2)
Harrison, G. (Everton), 1921 v Bel; 1922 v Ni (2)
Harrow, J. H. (Chelsea), 1923 v Ni, Se (2)
Hart, E. (Leeds U), 1929 v W; 1930 v W, Ni; 1933 v S, A; 1934 v S, H, Cz (8)
Hartley, F. (Oxford C), 1923 v F (1)
Harvey, A. (Wednesbury Strollers), 1881 v W (1)
Harvey, J. C. (Everton), 1971 v Ma (1)

Hassall, H. W. (Huddersfield T), 1951 v S, Arg, P; 1952 v F; (with Bolton W), 1954 v Ni (5)
Hateley, M. (Portsmouth), 1984 v USSR (sub), Br, U, Ch; (with AC Milan), 1985 v EG (sub), Fi, Ni, Ei, Fi, S, I, M; 1986 v R, T, Eg, S, M, Ca, P, Mor, Para (sub); 1987 v T (sub), Br (sub), S; (with Monaco), 1988 v WG (sub), Ho (sub), H (sub), Co (sub), Ei (sub), Ho (sub), USSR (sub) (31)
Haworth, G. (Accrington), 1887 v Ni, W, S; 1888 v S; 1890 v S (5)
Hawtrey, J. P. (Old Etonians), 1881 v S, W (2)
Hawkes, R. M. (Luton T), 1907 v Ni; 1908 v A (2), H, B (5)
Haygarth, E. B. (Swifts), 1875 v S (1)
Haynes, J. N. (Fulham), 1955 v Ni; 1956 v S, Ni, Br, Se, Fi, WG, Sp; 1957 v W, Y, D, Ei (2); 1958 v W, Ni, S, F, P, Y, USSR (3), Br, A; 1959 v S, Ni, USSR, I, Br, Pe, M, US; 1960 v Ni, Y, Sp, H; 1961 v Ni, W, S, L, P, Sp, M, I, A; 1962 v W, Ni, S, A, Sw, Pe, P, H, Arg, Bul, Br (56)
Healless, H. (Blackburn R), 1925 v Ni; 1928 v S (2)
Hector, K. J. (Derby Co), 1974 v Pol (sub), I (sub), (2)
Hedley, G. A. (Sheffield U), 1901 v Ni (1)
Hegan, K. E. (Corinthians), 1923 v Bel, F; 1924 v Ni, Bel (4)
Hellawell, M. S. (Birmingham C), 1963 v Ni, F (2)
Henfrey, A. G. (Cambridge University), 1891 v Ni; (with Corinthians), 1892 v W; 1895 v W; 1896 v S, W (5)
Henry, R. P. (Tottenham H), 1963 v F (1)
Heron, F. (Wanderers), 1876 v S (1)
Heron, G. H. H. (Uxbridge), 1873 v S; 1874 v S; (with Wanderers), 1875 v S; 1876 v S; 1878 v S (5)
Hibbert, W. (Bury), 1910 v S (1)
Hibbs, H. E. (Birmingham), 1930 v S, W, A, G; 1931 v S, W, Ni; 1932 v W, Ni, Sp; 1933 v S, W, Ni, A, I, Sw; 1934 v Ni, W, F; 1935 v S, W, Ni, Ho; 1936 v G, W (25)
Hill, F. (Bolton W), 1963 v Ni, W (2)
Hill, J. H. (Burnley), 1925 v W; 1926 v S; 1927 v S, Ni, Bel, F; 1928 v Ni, W; 1929 v F, Bel, Sp (11)
Hill, G. A. (Manchester U), 1976 v I; 1977 v Ei (sub), Fi (sub), L; 1978 v Sw (sub), L (6)
Hill, R. (Luton T), 1983 v D (sub), WG; 1986 v Eg (sub) (3)
Hill, R. H. (Millwall), 1926 v Bel (1)
Hillman, J. (Burnley), 1899 v Ni (1)
Hills, A. F. (Old Harrovians), 1879 v S (1)
Hilsdon, G. R. (Chelsea), 1907 v Ni; 1908 v S, W, Ni, A, H, B; 1909 v Ni (8)
Hine, E. W. (Leicester C), 1929 v W, Ni; 1930 v W, Ni; 1932 v W, Ni (6)
Hinton, A. T. (Wolverhampton W), 1963 v F; (with Nottingham F), 1965 v W, Bel (3)
Hitchens, G. A. (Aston Villa), 1961 v M, I, A; (with Inter-Milan), 1962 v Sw, Pe, H, Br (7)
Hobbis, H. H. F. (Charlton Ath), 1936 v A, Bel (2)
Hoddle, G. (Tottenham H), 1980 v Bul, W, Aus, Sp; 1981 v Sp, W, S; 1982 v N, Ni, W, Ic, Cz (sub), K; 1983 v L (sub), Ni, S; 1984 v H, L, F; 1985 v Ei (sub), S, I (sub), M, WG, US; 1986 v R, T, Ni, Is, USSR, S, M, Ca, P, Mor, Pol, Para, Arg; 1987 v Se Ni, Y, Sp, T, S; (with Monaco), 1988 v WG, T (sub), Y (sub), Ho (sub), H (sub), Co (sub), Ei (sub), Ho, USSR (53)
Hodge, S. B. (Aston Villa), 1986 v USSR (sub), S, Ca, P (sub), Mor (sub), Pol, Para, Arg; 1987 v Se, Ni, Y (with Tottenham H), Sp, Ni, T, S; 1989 (with Nottingham F) v D; 1990 v I (sub), Y (sub), Cz, D, U, Tun (22)
Hodgetts, D. (Aston Villa), 1888 v S, W, Ni; 1892 v S, Ni; 1894 v Ni (6)
Hodgkinson, A. (Sheffield U), 1957 v S, Ei (2), D; 1961 v W (5)
Hodgson, G. (Liverpool), 1931 v S, Ni, W (3)
Hodkinson, J. (Blackburn R), 1913 v W, S; 1920 v Ni (3)
Hogg, W. (Sunderland), 1902 v S, W, Ni (3)

Holdcroft, G. H. (Preston NE), 1937 v W, Ni (2)

Holden, A. D. (Bolton W), 1959 v S, I, Br, Pe, M (5)

Holden, G. H. (Wednesday OA), 1881 v S; 1884 v S, W, Ni (4)

Holden-White, C. (Corinthians), 1888 v W, S (2)

Holford, T. (Stoke), 1903 v Ni (1)

Holley, G. H. (Sunderland), 1909 v S, W, H (2), A; 1910 v W; 1912 v S, W, NI; 1913 v S (10)

Holliday, E. (Middlesbrough), 1960 v W, Ni, Se (3)

Hollins, J. W. (Chelsea), 1967 v Sp (1)

Holmes, R. (Preston NE), 1888 v Ni; 1891 v S; 1892 v S; 1893 v S, W; 1894 v Ni; 1895 v Ni (7)

Holt, J. (Everton), 1890 v W; 1891 v S, W; 1892 v S, Ni; 1893 v S; 1894 v S, Ni; 1895 v S; (with Reading), 1900 v Ni (10)

Hopkinson, E. (Bolton W), 1958 v W, Ni, S, F, P, Y; 1959 v S, I, Br, Pe, M, US; 1960 v W, Se (14)

Hossack, A. H. (Corinthians), 1892 v W; 1894 v W (2)

Houghton, W. E. (Aston Villa), 1931 v Ni, W, F, Bel; 1932 v S, Ni; 1933 v A (7)

Houlker, A. E. (Blackburn R), 1902 v S; (with Portsmouth), 1903 v S, W; (with Southampton), 1906 v W, Ni (5)

Howarth, R. H. (Preston NE), 1887 v Ni; 1888 v S, W; 1891 v S; (with Everton), 1894 v Ni (5)

Howe, D. (WBA), 1958 v S, W, Ni, F, P, Y, USSR (3), Br, A; 1959 v S, W, Ni, USSR, I, Br, Pe, M, US; 1960 v W, Ni, Se (23)

Howe, J. R. (Derby Co), 1948 v I; 1949 v S, Ni (3)

Howell, L. S. (Wanderers), 1873 v S (1)

Howell, R. (Sheffield U), 1895 v Ni; (with Liverpool) 1899 v S (2)

Hudson, A. A. (Stoke C), 1975 v WG, Cy (2)

Hudson, J. (Sheffield), 1883 v Ni (1)

Hudspeth, F. C. (Newcastle U), 1926 v Ni (1)

Hufton, A. E. (West Ham U), 1924 v Bel; 1928 v S, Ni; 1929 v F, Bel, Sp (6)

Hughes, E. W. (Liverpool), 1970 v W, Ni, S, Ho, P, Bel; 1971 v EG, Ma (2), Gr, W; 1972 v Sw, Gr, Wg (2), W, Ni, S; 1973 v W (3), S (2), Pol, USSR, I; 1974 v A, Pol, I, W, Ni, S, Arg, EG, Bul, Y; 1975 v Cz, P, Cy (sub), Ni; 1977 v I, L, W, S, Br, Arg, U; 1978 v Sw, L, I, WG, Ni, S, H; 1979 v D, Ei, Ni, W, Se; (with Wolverhampton W), 1980 v Sp (sub), Ni, S (sub) (62)

Hughes, L. (Liverpool), 1950 v Ch, US, Sp (3)

Hulme, J. H. A. (Arsenal), 1927 v S, Bel, F; 1928 v S, Ni, W; 1929 v Ni, W; 1933 v S (9)

Humphreys, P. (Notts Co), 1903 v S (1)

Hunt, G. S. (Tottenham H), 1933 v I, Sw, S (3)

Hunt, Rev K. R. G. (Leyton), 1911 v S, W (2)

Hunt, R. (Liverpool), 1962 v A; 1963 v EG; 1964 v S, US, P; 1965 v W; 1966 v S, Sp, Pol (2), WG (2), Fi, N, U, M, F, Arg, P; 1967 v Ni, W, Cz, Sp, A; 1968 v W, Ni, USSR (2), Sp (2), Se, Y; 1969 v R (2) (34)

Hunt, S. (WBA), 1984 v S (sub), USSR (sub) (2)

Hunter, J. (Sheffield Heeley), 1878 v S; 1880 v S, W; 1881 v S, W; 1882 v S, W (7)

Hunter, N. (Leeds U), 1966 v WG, Y, Fi, Sp (sub); 1967 v A; 1968 v Sp, Se, Y, WG, USSR; 1969 v R, W; 1970 v Ho, WG (sub); 1971 v Ma; 1972 v WG (2), W, Ni, S; 1973 v W (2) USSR (sub); 1974 v A, Pol, Ni (sub), S; 1975 v Cz (28)

Hurst, G. C. (West Ham U), 1966 v S, WG (2), Y, Fi, D, Arg, P; 1967 v Ni, W, S, Cz, Sp, A; 1968 v W, Ni, S, Se (sub), WG, USSR (2); 1969 v Ni, S, R (2), Bul, F, M, U, Br; 1970 v W, Ni, S, Ho (1+1 sub), Bel, Co, Ec, R, Br, WG; 1971 v EG, Gr, W, S; 1972 v Sw (2), Gr, WG (49)

Iremonger, J. (Nottingham F), 1901 v S; 1902 v Ni (2)

Jack, D. N. B. (Bolton W), 1924 v S, W; 1928 v F, Bel; (with Arsenal), 1930 v S, G, A; 1933 v W, A (9)

Jackson, E. (Oxford University), 1891 v W (1)

Jarrett, B. G. (Cambridge University), 1876 v S; 1877 v S; 1878 v S (3)

Jefferis, F. (Everton), 1912 v S, W (2)

Jezzard, B. A. G. (Fulham), 1954 v H; 1956 v Ni (2)

Johnson, D. E. (Ipswich T), 1975 v W, S; 1976 v Sw; (with Liverpool), 1980 v Ei, Arg, Ni, S, Bel (8)

Johnson, E. (Saltley College), 1880 v W; (with Stoke C), 1884 v Ni (2)

Johnson, J. A. (Stoke C), 1937 v N, Se, Fi, S, Ni (5)

Johnson, T. C. F. (Manchester C), 1926 v Bel; 1930 v W; (with Everton), 1932 v S, Sp; 1933 v Ni (5)

Johnson, W. H. (Sheffield U), 1900 v S, W, Ni; 1903 v S, W, Ni (6)

Johnston, H. (Blackpool), 1947 v S, Ho; 1951 v S; 1953 v Arg, Ch, U, US; 1954 v W, Ni, H (10)

Jones, A. (Walsall Town Swifts), 1882 v S, W; (with Great Lever), 1883 v S (3)

Jones, H. (Blackburn R), 1927 v S, Bel, L, F; 1928 v S, Ni (6)

Jones, H. (Nottingham F), 1923 v F (1)

Jones, M. D. (Sheffield U), 1965 v WG, Se; (with Leeds U), 1970 v Ho (3)

Jones, W. (Bristol C), 1901 v Ni (1)

Jones, W. H. (Liverpool), 1950 v P, Bel (2)

Joy, B. (Casuals), 1936 v Bel (1)

Kail, E. I. L. (Dulwich Hamlet), 1929 v F, Bel, Sp (3)

Kay, A. H. (Everton), 1963 v Sw (1)

Kean, F. W. (Sheffield Wed), 1923 v S, Bel; 1924 v W; 1925 v Ni; 1926 v Ni, Bel; 1927 v L; (with Bolton W), 1929 v F, Sp (9)

Keegan, J. K. (Liverpool), 1973 v W (2); 1974 v W, Ni, Arg, EG, Bul, Y; 1975 v Cz, WG, Cy (2), Ni, S; 1976 v Sw, Cz, P, W (2), Ni, S, Br, Fi; 1977 v Ei, I, Ho, L; (with SV Hamburg), W, Br, Arg, U; 1978 v Sw, I, WG, Br, H; 1979 v D, Ei, Cz, Ni, W, S, Bul, Se, A; 1980 v D, Ni, Ei, Sp (2), Arg, Bel, I; (with Southampton), 1981 v Sp, Sw, H; 1982 v N, H, Ni, S, Fi, Sp (sub) (63)

Keen, E. R. L. (Derby Co), 1933 v A; 1937 v W, Ni, H (4)

Kelly, R. (Burnley), 1920 v S; 1921 v S, W, Ni; 1922 v S, W; 1923 v S; 1924 v Ni; 1925 v W, Ni, S; (with Sunderland), 1926 v W; (with Huddersfield T), 1927 v L; 1928 v S (14)

Kennedy, A. (Liverpool), 1984 v Ni, W (2)

Kennedy, R. (Liverpool), 1976 v W (2), Ni, S; 1977 v L, W, S, Br (sub), Arg (sub); 1978 v Sw, L; 1980 v Bul, Sp, Arg, W, Bel (sub), I (17)

Kenyon-Slaney, W. S. (Wanderers), 1873 v S (1)

Kevan, D. T. (WBA), 1957 v S; 1958 v W, Ni, S, P. Y, USSR (3), Br, A; 1959 v M, US; 1961 v M (14)

Kidd, B. (Manchester U), 1970 v Ni, Ec (sub) (2)

King, R. S. (Oxford University), 1882 v Ni (1)

Kingsford, R. K. (Wanderers), 1874 v S (1)

Kingsley, M. (Newcastle U), 1901 v W (1)

Kinsey, R. (Wolverhampton), 1892 v W; 1893 v S; (with Derby Co), 1896 v W, Ni (4)

Kirchen, A. J. (Arsenal), 1937 v N, Se, Fi (3)

Kirton, W. J. (Aston Villa), 1922 v Ni (1)

Knight, A. E. (Portsmouth), 1920 v Ni (1)

Knowles, C. (Tottenham H), 1968 v USSR, Sp, Se, WG (4)

Labone, B. L. (Everton), 1963 v Ni, W, F; 1967 v Sp, A; 1968 v S, Sp, Se, Y, USSR, Wg; 1969 v Ni, S, R, Bul, M, U, Br; 1970 v S, W, Bel, Co, Ec, R, Br, WG (26)

Lampard, F. R. G. (West Ham U), 1973 v Y; 1980 v Aus (2)

Langley, E. J. (Fulham), 1958 v S, P, Y (3)

Langton, R. (Blackburn R), 1947 v W, Ni, Ei, Ho, F, Sw; 1948 v Se; (with Preston NE), 1949 v D, Se; (with Bolton W), 1950 v S; 1951 v Ni (11)

Latchford, R. D. (Everton), 1978 v I, Br, W; 1979 v D, Ei, Cz (sub), Ni (2), W, S, Bul, A (12)

Latheron, E. G. (Blackburn R), 1913 v W; 1914 v Ni (2)

Lawler, C. (Liverpool), 1971 v Ma, W, S; 1972 v Sw (4)

Lawton, T. (Everton), 1939 v S, W, Ni, R of E, N, I, R, Y; (with Chelsea), 1947 v S, W, Ni, Ei, Ho, F, Sw, P; 1948 v W, Ni, Bel; (with Notts Co), 1948 v S, Se, I; 1949 v D (23)

Leach, T. (Sheffield W), 1931 v W, Ni (2)

Leake, A. (Aston Villa), 1904 v S, Ni; 1905 v S, W, Ni (5)

Lee, E. A. (Southampton), 1904 v W (1)

Lee, F. H. (Manchester C), 1969 v Ni, W, S, Bul, F, M, U; 1970 v W, Ho (2), P, Bel, Co, Ec, R, Br, WG; 1971 v EG, Gr, Ma, Ni, W, S; 1972 v Sw (2), Gr, WG (27)

Lee, J. (Derby Co), 1951 v Ni (1)

Lee, S. (Liverpool), 1983 v Gr, L, W, Gr, H, S, Aus; 1984 v D, H, L, F, Ni, W, Ch (sub) (14)

Leighton, J. E. (Nottingham F), 1886 v Ni (1)

Lilley, H. E. (Sheffield U), 1892 v W (1)

Linacre, H. J. (Nottingham F), 1905 v W, S (2)

Lindley, T. (Cambridge University), 1886 v S, W, Ni, 1887 v S, W, Ni; 1888 v S, W, Ni; (with Nottingham F), 1889 v S; 1890 v S, W; 1891 v Ni (13)

Lindsay, A. (Liverpool), 1974 v Arg, EG, Bul, Y (4)

Lindsay, W. (Wanderers), 1877 v S (1)

Lineker, G. (Leicester C), 1984 v S (sub); 1985 v Ei, R (sub), S (sub), I (sub), WG, US; (with Everton), 1986 v R, T, Ni, Eg, USSR, Ca, P, Mor, Pol, Para, Arg; (with Barcelona), 1987 v Ni (2), Y, Sp, T, Br; 1988 v WG, T, Y, Ho, H, S, Co, Sw, Ei, Ho, USSR; 1989 v Se, S.Ar, Gr, Alb, Alb, Pol, D; (with Tottenham H) 1990 v Se, Pol, I, Y, Br, Cz, D, U, Tun, Ei, Ho, Eg, Bel, Cam, WG, I (58)

Lintott, E. H. (QPR), 1908 v S, W, Ni; (with Bradford C), 1909 v S, Ni, H (2) (7)

Lipsham, H. B. (Sheffield U), 1902 v W (1)

Little, B. (Aston Villa), 1975 v W (sub) (1)

Lloyd, L. V. (Liverpool), 1971 v W; 1972 v Sw, Ni; (with Nottingham F), 1980 v W (4)

Lockett, A. (Stoke C), 1903 v Ni (1)

Lodge, L. V. (Cambridge University), 1894 v W; 1895 v S, W; (with Corinthians), 1896 v S, Ni (5)

Lofthouse, J. M. (Blackburn R), 1885 v S, W, Ni; 1887 v S, W; (with Accrington), 1889 v Ni; (with Blackburn R), 1890 v Ni (7)

Lofthouse, N. (Bolton W), 1951 v Y; 1952 v W, Ni, S, A (2), I, Sw; 1953 v W, Ni, S, Bel, Arg, Ch, U, US; 1954 v W, Ni, R of E, Bel, U; 1955 v Ni, S, F, Sp, P; 1956 v W, S, Sp, D, Fi (sub); 1959 v W, USSR (33)

Longworth, E. (Liverpool), 1920 v S; 1921 v Bel; 1923 v S, W, Bel (5)

Lowder, A. (Wolverhampton W), 1889 v W (1)

Lowe, E. (Aston Villa), 1947 v F, Sw, P (3)

Lucas, T. (Liverpool), 1922 v Ni; 1924 v F; 1926 v Bel (3)

Luntley, E. (Nottingham F), 1880 v S, W (2)

Lyttelton, Hon. A. (Cambridge University), 1877 v S (1)

Lyttelton, Hon. E. (Cambridge University), 1878 v S (1)

McCall, J. (Preston NE), 1913 v S, W; 1914 v S; 1920 v S; 1921 v Ni (5)

McDermott, T. (Liverpool), 1978 v Sw, L; 1979 v Ni, W, Se; 1980 v D, Ni (sub), Ei, Ni, S, Bel (sub), Sp; 1981 v N, R, Sw, R (sub), Br, Sw (sub); H; 1982 v N, H, W (sub), Ho, S (sub), Ic (25)

McDonald, C. A. (Burnley), 1958 v USSR (3), Br, A; 1959 v W, Ni, USSR (8)

McFarland, R. L. (Derby Co), 1971 v Gr, Ma (2), Ni, S; 1972 v Sw, Gr, W, S; 1973 v W (3), Ni, S, Cz, Pol, USSR, I; 1974 v A, Pol, I, W, Ni; 1976 v Cz, S; 1977 v Ei, I (28)

McGarry, W. H. (Huddersfield T), 1954 v Sw, U; 1956 v W, D (4)

McGuinness, W. (Manchester U), 1959 v Ni, M (2)

McInroy, A. (Sunderland), 1927 v Ni (1)

McMahon, S. (Liverpool), 1988 v Is, H, Co, USSR; 1989 v D (sub); 1990 v Se, Pol, I, Y (sub), Br, Cz (sub), D, Ei (sub), Eg, Bel, I (16)

McNab, R. (Arsenal), 1969 v Ni, Bul, R (1+1 sub) (4)

McNeal, R. (WBA), 1914 v S, W (2)

McNeil, M. (Middlesbrough), 1961 v W, Ni, S, L, P, Sp, M, I; 1962 v L (9)

Mabbutt, G. (Tottenham H), 1983 v WG, Gr, L, W, Gr, H, Ni, S (sub); 1984 v H; 1987 v Y, Ni, T; 1988 v WG (13)

Macaulay, R. H. (Cambridge University), 1881 v S (1)

Macdonald, M. (Newcastle U), 1972 v W, Ni, S (sub); 1973 v USSR (sub); 1974 v P, S (sub), Y (sub); 1975 v WG, Cy (2), Ni; 1976 v Sw (sub), Cz, P (14)

Macrae, S. (Notts Co), 1883 v S, W, Ni; 1884 v S, W, Ni (6)

Maddison, F. B. (Oxford University), 1872 v S (1)

Madeley, P. E. (Leeds U), 1971 v Ni; 1972 v Sw (2), Gr, WG (2), W, S; 1973 v S, Cz, Pol, USSR, I; 1974 v A, Pol, I; 1975 v Cz, P, Cy; 1976 v Cz, P, Fi; 1977 v Ei, Ho (24)

Magee, T. P. (WBA), 1923 v W, Se; 1925 v S, Bel, F (5)

Makepeace, H. (Everton), 1906 v S; 1910 v S; 1912 v S, W (4)

Male, C. G. (Arsenal), 1935 v S, Ni, I, Ho; 1936 v S, W, Ni, G, A, Bel; 1937 v S, Ni, H, N, Se, Fi; 1939 v I, R, Y (19)

Mannion, W. J. (Middlesbrough), 1947 v S, W, Ni, Ei, Ho, F, Sw, P; 1948 v W, Ni, Bel, Se, I; 1949 v N, F; 1950 v S, Ei, P, Bel, Ch, US; 1951 v Ni, W, S, Y; 1952 v F (26)

Mariner, P. (Ipswich T), 1977 v L (sub), Ni; 1978 v L, W (sub), S; 1980 v W, Ni (sub), S, Aus, I (sub), Sp (sub); 1981 v N, Sw, Sp, Sw, H; 1982 v N, H, Ho, S, Fi, F, Cz, K, WG, Sp; 1983 v D, WG, Gr, W; 1984 v D, H, L; (with Arsenal), 1985 v EG, R (35)

Marsden, J. T. (Darwen), 1891 v Ni (1)

Marsden, W. (Sheffield W), 1930 v W, S, G (3)

Marsh, R. W. (QPR), 1972 v Sw (sub); (with Manchester C), WG (sub+1), Ni, S; 1973 v W (2), Y (9)

Marshall, T. (Darwen), 1880 v W; 1881 v W (2)

Martin, A. (West Ham U), 1981 v Br, S (sub); 1982 v H, Fi; 1983 v Gr, L, W, Gr, H; 1984 v H, L, W; 1985 v Ni; 1986 v Is, Ca, Para; 1987 v Se (17)

Martin, H. (Sunderland), 1914 v Ni (1)

Marwood, B. (Arsenal), 1989 v S.Ar (sub) (1)

Maskrey, H. M. (Derby Co), 1908 v Ni (1)

Mason, C. (Wolverhampton W), 1887 v Ni; 1888 v W; 1890 v Ni (3)

Matthews, R. D. (Coventry C), 1956 v S, Br, Se, WG; 1957 v Ni (5)

Matthews, S. (Stoke C), 1935 v W, I; 1936 v G; 1937 v S; 1938 v S, W, Cz, G, Sw, F; 1939 v S, W, Ni, R of E, N, I, Y; 1947 v S; (with Blackpool), 1947 v Sw, P; 1948 v S, W, Ni, Bel, I; 1949 v S, W, Ni, D, Sw; 1950 v Sp; 1951 v Ni, S; 1954 v Ni, R of E, H, Bel, U; 1955 v Ni, W, S, F, WG, Sp, P; 1956 v W, Br; 1957 v S, W, Ni, Y, D (2) Ei (54)

Matthews, V. (Sheffield U), 1928 v F, Bel (2)

Maynard, W. J. (1st Surrey Rifles), 1872 v S; 1876 v S (2)

Meadows, J. (Manchester C), 1955 v S (1)

Medley, L. D. (Tottenham H), 1951 v Y, W; 1952 v F, A, W, Ni (6)

Meehan, T. (Chelsea), 1924 v Ni (1)

Melia, J. (Liverpool), 1963 v S, Sw (2)

Mercer, D. W. (Sheffield U), 1923 v Ni, Bel (2)

Mercer, J. (Everton), 1939 v S, Ni, I, R, Y (5)

Merrick, G. H. (Birmingham C), 1952 v Ni, S, A (2), I, Sw; 1953 v Ni, W, S, Bel, Arg, Ch, U; 1954 v W, Ni, S, R of E, H (2), Y, Bel, Sw, U (23)

Metcalfe V. (Huddersfield T), 1951 v Arg, P (2)

Mew, J. W. (Manchester U), 1921 v Ni (1)

Middleditch, B. (Corinthians), 1897 v Ni (1)

Milburn, J. E. T. (Newcastle U), 1949 v S, W, Ni, Sw; 1950 v W, P, Bel, Sp; 1951 v W, Arg, P; 1952 v F; 1956 v D (13)

Miller, B. G. (Burnley), 1961 v A (1)

Miller, H. S. (Charlton Ath), 1923 v Se (1)

Mills, G. R. (Chelsea), 1938 v W, Ni, Cz (3)

Mills, M. D. (Ipswich T), 1973 v Y; 1976 v W (2), Ni, S, Br, I (sub), Fi; 1977 v Fi (sub), I, Ni, W, S; 1978 v WG, Br, W, Ni, S, H; 1979 v D, Ei, Ni (2), S, Bul, A; 1980 v D, Ni, Sp (2); 1981 v Sw (2), H; 1982 v N, H, S, Fi, F, Cz, K, WG, Sp (42)

Milne, G. (Liverpool), 1963 v Br, Cz, EG; 1964 v W, Ni, S, R of W, U, P, Ei, Br, Arg; 1965 v Ni, Bel (14)

Milton, C. A. (Arsenal), 1952 v A (1)

Milward, A. (Everton), 1891 v S, W; 1897 v S, W (4)

Mitchell, C. (Upton Park), 1880 v W; 1881 v S; 1883 v S, W; 1885 v W (5)

Mitchell, J. F. (Manchester C), 1925 v Ni (1)

Moffat, H. (Oldham Ath), 1913 v W (1)

Molyneux, G. (Southampton), 1902 v S; 1903 v S, W, Ni (4)

Moon, W. R. (Old Westminsters), 1888 v S, W; 1889 v S, W; 1890 v S, W; 1891 v S (7)

Moore, H. T. (Notts Co), 1883 v Ni; 1885 v W (2)

Moore, J. (Derby Co), 1923 v Se (1)

Moore, R. F. (West Ham U), 1962 v Pe, H, Arg, Bul, Br; 1963 v W, Ni, S, F (2), Br, Cz, EG, Sw; 1964 v W, Ni, S, R of W, U, P (2), Ei, Br, Arg; 1965 v Ni, S, Bel, H, Y, WG, Se; 1966 v W, Ni, S, A, Sp, Pol (2), WG (2), N, D, U, M, F, Arg, P; 1967 v W, Ni, S, Cz, Sp, A; 1968 v W, Ni, S, USSR (2), Sp (2), Se, Y, WG; 1969 v Ni, W, S, R, Bul, F, M, U, Br; 1970 v W, Ni, S, Ho, P, Bel, Co, Ec, R, Br, Cz, WG; 1971 v EG, Gr, Ma, Ni, S; 1972 v Sw (2), Gr, WG (2), W, S; 1973 v W (3), Y, S (2), Ni, Cz, Pol, USSR, I; 1974 v I (108)

Moore, W. G. B. (West Ham U), 1923 v Se (1)

Mordue, J. (Sunderland), 1912 v Ni; 1913 v Ni (2)

Morice, C. J. (Barnes), 1872 v S (1)

Morley, A. (Aston Villa), 1982 v H (sub), Ni, W, Ic; 1983 v D, Gr (6)

Morley, H. (Notts Co), 1910 v Ni (1)

Morren, T. (Sheffield U), 1898 v Ni (1)

Morris, F. (WBA), 1920 v S; 1921 v Ni (2)

Morris, J. (Derby Co), 1949 v N, F; 1950 v Ei (3)

Morris, W. W. (Wolverhampton W), 1939 v S, Ni, R (3)

Morse, H. (Notts Co), 1879 v S (1)

Mort, T. (Aston Villa), 1924 v W, F; 1926 v S (3)

Morten, A. (C Palace), 1873 v S (1)

Mortensen, S. H. (Blackpool), 1947 v P; 1948 v W, S, Ni, Bel, Se, I; 1949 v S, W, Ni, Se, N; 1950 v S, W, Ni, I, P, Bel, Ch, US, Sp; 1951 v S, Arg; 1954 v R of E, H (25)

Morton, J. R. (West Ham U), 1938 v Cz (1)

Mosforth, W. (Sheffield W), 1877 v S; (with Sheffield Albion), 1878 v S; 1879 v S, W; 1880 v S, W; (with Sheffield W), 1881 v W; 1882 v S, W (9)

Moss, F. (Arsenal), 1934 v S, H, Cz; 1935 v I (4)

Moss, F. (Aston Villa), 1922 v S, Ni; 1923 v Ni; 1924 v S, Bel (5)

Mosscrop, E. (Burnley), 1914 v S, W (2)

Mozley, B. (Derby Co), 1950 v W, Ni, Ei (3)

Mullen, J. (Wolverhampton W), 1947 v S; 1949 v N, F; 1950 v Bel (sub), Ch, US; 1954 v W, Ni, S, R of E, Y, Sw (12)

Mullery, A. P. (Tottenham H), 1965 v Ho; 1967 v Sp, A; 1968 v W, Ni, S, USSR, Sp (2), Se, Y; 1969 v Ni, S, R, Bul, F, M, U, Br; 1970 v W, Ni, S (sub), Ho (sub), Bel, P, Co, Ec, R, Cz, WG, Br; 1971 v Ma, EG, Gr; 1972 v Sw (35)

Neal, P. G. (Liverpool), 1976 v W, I; 1977 v W, S, Br, Arg, U; 1978 v Sw, I, WG, Ni, S, H; 1979 v D, Ei, Ni (2), S, Bul, A; 1980 v D, Ni, Sp, Arg, W, Bel, I; 1981 v R, Sw, Sp, Br, H; 1982 v N, H, W, Ho, Ic, F (sub), K; 1983 v D, G, L, W, Gr, H, Ni, S, Aus (2); 1984 v D (50)

Needham, E. (Sheffield U), 1894 v S; 1895 v S; 1897 v S, W, Ni; 1898 v S, W; 1899 v S, W, Ni; 1900 v S, Ni; 1901 v S, W, Ni; 1902 v W (16)

Newton, K. R. (Blackburn R), 1966 v S, WG; 1967 v Sp, A; 1968 v W, S, Sp, Se, Y, WG; 1969 v Ni, W, S, R, Bul, M, U, Br, F; (with Everton), 1970 v Ni, S, Ho, Co, Ec, R, Cz, WG (27)

Nicholls, J. (WBA), 1954 v S, Y (2)

Nicholson, W. E. (Tottenham H), 1951 v P (1)

Nish, D. J. (Derby Co), 1973 v Ni; 1974 v P, W, Ni, S (5)

Norman, M. (Tottenham H), 1962 v Pe, H, Arg, Bul, Br; 1963 v S, F, Br, Cz, EG; 1964 v W, Ni, S, R of W, U, P (2), US, Br, Arg; 1965 v Ni, Bel, Ho (23)

Nuttall, H. (Bolton W), 1928 v W, Ni; 1929 v S (3)

Oakley, W. J. (Oxford University), 1895 v W; 1896 v S, W, Ni; (with Corinthians), 1897 v S, W, Ni; 1898 v S, W, Ni; 1900 v S, W, Ni; 1901 v S, W, Ni (16)

O'Dowd, J. P. (Chelsea), 1932 v S; 1933 v Ni, Sw (3)

O'Grady, M. (Huddersfield T), 1963 v Ni; (with Leeds U), 1969 v F (2)

Ogilvie, R. A. M. M. (Clapham R), 1874 v S (1)

Oliver, L. F. (Fulham), 1929 v Bel (1)

Olney, B. A. (Aston Villa), 1928 v F, Bel (2)

Osborne, F. R. (Fulham), 1923 v Ni, F; (with Tottenham H), 1925 v Bel; 1926 v Bel (4)

Osborne, R. (Leicester C), 1928 v W (1)

Osgood, P. L. (Chelsea), 1970 v Bel, R (sub), Cz (sub), 1974 v I (4)

Osman, R. (Ipswich T), 1980 v Aus; 1981 v Sp, R, Sw; 1982 v N, Ic; 1983 v D, Aus (3); 1984 v D (11)

Ottaway, C. J. (Oxford University), 1872 v S; 1874 v S (2)

Owen, J. R. B. (Sheffield), 1874 v S (1)

Owen, S. W. (Luton T), 1954 v H, Y, Bel (3)

Page, L. A. (Burnley), 1927 v S, W, Bel, L, F; 1928 v W, Ni (7)

Paine, T. L. (Southampton), 1963 v Cz, EG; 1964 v W, Ni, S, R of W, U, US, P; 1965 v Ni, H, Y, WG, Se; 1966 v W A, Y, N, M (19)

Pallister, G. A. (Middlesbrough), 1988 v H; 1989 v S.Ar (2)

Pantling, H. H. (Sheffield U), 1924 v Ni (1)

Paravacini, P. J. de (Cambridge University), 1883 v S, W, Ni (3)

Parker, P. A. (QPR), 1989 v Alb (sub), Ch, D; 1990 v Y, U, Ho, Eg, Bel, Cam, WG, I (11)

Parker, T. R. (Southampton), 1925 v F (1)

Parkes, P. B. (QPR), 1974 v P (1)

Parkinson, J. (Liverpool), 1910 v S, W (2)

Parr, P. C. (Oxford University), 1882 v W (1)

Parry, E. H. (Old Carthusians), 1879 v W; 1882 v W, S (3)

Parry, R. A. (Bolton W), 1960 v Ni, S (2)

Patchitt, B. C. A. (Corinthians), 1923 v Se (2) (2)

Pawson, F. W. (Cambridge University), 1883 v Ni; (with Swifts), 1885 v Ni (2)

Payne, J. (Luton T), 1937 v Fi (1)

Peacock, A. (Middlesbrough), 1962 v Arg, Bul; 1963 v Ni, W; (with Leeds U), 1966 v W, Ni (6)

Peacock, J. (Middlesbrough), 1929 v F, Bel, Sp (3)

Pearce, S. (Nottingham F), 1987 v Br, S; 1988 v WG (sub), Is, H; 1989 v D, Se, S.Ar., Gr, Alb, Alb, Ch, S, Pol, D; 1990 v Se, Pol, I, Y, Br, Cz, D, U, Tun, Ei, Ho, Eg, Bel, Cam, WG (30)

Pearson, H. F. (WBA), 1932 v S (1)

Pearson, J. H. (Crewe Alex), 1892 v Ni (1)

Pearson, J. S. (Manchester U), 1976 v W, Ni, S, Br, Fi;

1977 v Ei, Ho (sub), W, S, Br, Arg, U; 1978 v I (sub), WG, Ni (15)

Pearson, S. C. (Manchester U), 1948 v S; 1949 v S, Ni; 1950 v Ni, I; 1951 v P; 1952 v S, I (8)

Pease, W. H. (Middlesbrough), 1927 v W (1)

Pegg, D. (Manchester U), 1957 v Ei (1)

Pejic, M. (Stoke C), 1974 v P, W, Ni, S (4)

Pelly, F. R. (Old Foresters), 1893 v Ni; 1894 v S, W (3)

Pennington, J. (WBA), 1907 v S, W; 1908 v S, W, Ni, A; 1909 v S, W, H (2), A; 1910 v S, W; 1911 v S, W, Ni; 1912 v S, W, Ni; 1913 v S, W; 1914 v S, Ni; 1920 v S, W (25)

Pentland, F. B. (Middlesbrough), 1909 v S, W, H (2), A (5)

Perry, C. (WBA), 1890 v Ni; 1891 v Ni; 1893 v W (3)

Perry, T. (WBA), 1898 v W (1)

Perry, W. (Blackpool), 1956 v Ni, S, Sp (3)

Perryman, S. (Tottenham H), 1982 v Ic (sub) (1)

Peters, M. (West Ham U), 1966 v Y, Fi, Pol, M, F, Arg, P, WG; 1967 v Ni, W, S, Cz; 1968 v W, Ni, S, USSR (2), Sp (2), Se, Y; 1969 v Ni, S, R, Bul, F, M, U, Br; 1970 v Ho (2), P (sub), Bel; (with Tottenham H), W, Ni, S, Co, Ec, R, Br, Cz, WG; 1971 v EG, Gr, Ma (2), Ni, W, S; 1972 v Sw, Gr, WG (1+1 sub) Ni (sub) 1973 v S (2), Ni, W, Cz, Pol, USSR, I; 1974 v A, Pol, I, P, S (67)

Phelan, M. C. (Manchester U), 1990 v I (sub) (1)

Phillips, L. H. (Portsmouth), 1952 v Ni; 1955 v W, WG (3)

Pickering, F. (Everton), 1964 v US; 1965 v Ni, Bel (3)

Pickering, N. (Sunderland), 1983 v Aus (1)

Pickering, J. (Sheffield U), 1933 v S (1)

Pike, T. M. (Cambridge University), 1886 v Ni (1)

Pilkington, B. (Burnley), 1955 v Ni (1)

Plant, J. (Bury), 1900 v S (1)

Platt, D. (Aston Villa), 1990 v I (sub), Y (sub), Br, D (sub), Tun (sub), Ho (sub), Eg (sub), Bel (sub), Cam, WG, I (11)

Plum, S. L. (Charlton Ath), 1923 v F (1)

Pointer, R. (Burnley), 1962 v W, L, P (3)

Porteous, T. S. (Sunderland), 1891 v W (1)

Priest, A. E. (Sheffield U), 1900 v Ni (1)

Prinsep, J. F. M. (Clapham Rovers), 1879 v S (1)

Puddefoot, S. C. (Blackburn R), 1926 v S, Ni (2)

Pye, J. (Wolverhampton W), 1950 v Ei (1)

Pym, R. H. (Bolton W), 1925 v S, W; 1926 v W (3)

Quantrill, A. (Derby Co), 1920 v S, W; 1921 v W, Ni (4)

Quixall, A. (Sheffield W), 1954 v W, Ni, R of E; 1955 v Sp, P (sub) (5)

Radford, J. (Arsenal), 1969 v R; 1972 v Sw (sub) (2)

Raikes, G. B. (Oxford University), 1895 v W; 1896 v W, Ni, S (4)

Ramsey, A. E. (Southampton), 1949 v Sw; (with Tottenham H), 1950 v S, I, P, Bel, Ch, US, Sp; 1951 v S, Ni, W, Y, Arg, P; 1952 v S, W, Ni, F, A (2), I, Sw; 1953 v Ni, W, S, Bel, Arg, Ch, U, US; 1954 v R of E, H (32)

Rawlings, A. (Preston NE), 1921 v Bel (1)

Rawlings, W. E. (Southampton), 1922 v S, W (2)

Rawlinson, J. F. P. (Cambridge University), 1882 v Ni (1)

Rawson, H. E. (Royal Engineers), 1875 v S (1)

Rawson, W. S. (Oxford University), 1875 v S; 1877 v S (2)

Read, A. (Tufnell Park), 1921 v Bel (1)

Reader, J. (WBA), 1894 v Ni (1)

Reaney, P. (Leeds U), 1969 v Bul (sub); 1970 v P; 1971 v Ma (3)

Reeves, K. (Norwich C), 1980 v Bul; (with Manchester C), Ni (2)

Regis, C. (WBA), 1982 v Ni (sub), W (sub), Ic; 1983 v WG; (with Coventry C), 1988 v T (sub) (5)

Reid, P. (Everton), 1985 v M (sub), WG, US (sub); 1986

v R, S (sub), Ca (sub), Pol, Para, Arg; 1987 v Br; 1988 v WG, Y (sub), Sw (sub) (13)

Revie, D. G. (Manchester C), 1955 v Ni, S, F; 1956 v W, D; 1957 v Ni (6)

Reynolds, J. (WBA), 1892 v S; 1893 v S, W; (with Aston Villa), 1894 v S, Ni; 1895 v S; 1897 v S, W (8)

Richards, C. H. (Nottingham F), 1898 v Ni (1)

Richards, G. H. (Derby Co), 1909 v A (1)

Richards, J. P. (Wolverhampton W), 1973 v Ni (1)

Richardson, J. R. (Newcastle U), 1933 v I, Sw (2)

Richardson, W. G. (WBA), 1935 v Ho (1)

Rickaby, S, (WBA), 1954 v Ni (1)

Rigby, A. (Blackburn R), 1927 v S, Bel, L, F; 1928 v W (5)

Rimmer, E. J. (Sheffield W), 1930 v S, G, A; 1932 v Sp (4)

Rimmer, J. J. (Arsenal), 1976 v I (1)

Rix, G. (Arsenal), 1981 v N, R, Sw (sub), Br, W, S; 1982 v Ho (sub), Fi (sub), F, Cz, K, WG, Sp; 1983 v D, WG (sub), Gr (sub); 1984 v Ni (17)

Robb, G. (Tottenham H), 1954 v H (1)

Roberts, C. (Manchester U), 1905 v Ni, W, S (3)

Roberts, F. (Manchester C), 1925 v S, W, Bel, F (4)

Roberts, G. (Tottenham H), 1983 v Ni, S; 1984 v F, Ni, S, USSR (6)

Roberts, H. (Arsenal), 1931 v S (1)

Roberts, H. (Millwall), 1931 v Bel (1)

Roberts, R. (WBA), 1887 v S; 1888 v Ni; 1890 v Ni (3)

Roberts, W. T. (Preston NE), 1924 v W, Bel (2)

Robinson, J. (Sheffield W), 1937 v Fi; 1938 v G, Sw; 1939 v W (4)

Robinson, J. W. (Derby Co), 1897 v S, Ni; (with New Brighton Tower), 1898 v S, W, Ni; (with Southampton), 1899 v W, S; 1900 v S, W, Ni; 1901 v Ni (11)

Robson, B. (WBA), 1980 v Ei, Aus; 1981 v N, R, Sw, Sp, R, Br, W, S, Sw, H; 1982 v N (with Manchester U), H, Ni, W, Ho, S, Fi, F, Cz, WG, Sp; 1983 v D, Gr, L, S; 1984 v H, L, F, Ni, S, USSR, Br, U, Ch; 1985 v EG, Fi, T, Ei, R, Fi, S, M, I, WG, US; 1986 v R, T, Is, M, P, Mor; 1987 v, Ni (2), Sp, T, Br, S; 1988 v T, Y, Ho, H, S, Co, Sw, Ei, Ho, USSR; 1989 v S, Se, S.Ar, Gr, Alb, Alb, Ch, S, Pol, D; 1990 v Pol, I, Y, Cz, U, Tun, Ei, Ho (87)

Robson, R. (WBA), 1958 v F, USSR (2), Br, A; 1960 v Sp, H; 1961 v Ni, W, S, L, P, Sp, M, I; 1962 v W, Ni, Sw, L, P (20)

Rocastle, D. (Arsenal), 1989 v D, S.Ar., Gr, Alb, Alb, Pol (sub), D; 1990 v Se (sub), Pol, Y, D (sub) (11)

Rose, W. C. (Wolverhampton W), 1884 v S, W, Ni; (with Preston NE), 1886 v Ni; (with Wolverhampton W), 1891 v Ni (5)

Rostron, T. (Darwen), 1881 v S, W (2)

Rowe, A. (Tottenham H), 1934 v F (1)

Rowley, J. F. (Manchester U), 1949 v Sw, Se, F; 1950 v Ni, I; 1952 v S (6)

Rowley, W. (Stoke C), 1889 v Ni; 1892 v Ni (2)

Royle, J. (Everton), 1971 v Ma; 1973 v Y; (with Manchester C), 1976 v Ni (sub), I; 1977 v Fi, L (6)

Ruddlesdin, H. (Sheffield W), 1904 v W, Ni; 1905 v S (3)

Ruffell, J. W. (West Ham U), 1926 v S; 1927 v Ni; 1929 v S, W, Ni; 1930 v W (6)

Russell, B. B. (Royal Engineers), 1883 v W (1)

Rutherford, J. (Newcastle U), 1904 v S; 1907 v S, Ni, W; 1908 v S, Ni, W, A (2), H, B (11)

Sadler, D. (Manchester U), 1968 v Ni, USSR; 1970 v Ec (sub); 1971 v EG (4)

Sagar, C. (Bury), 1900 v Ni; 1902 v W (2)

Sagar, E. (Everton), 1936 v S, Ni, A, Bel (4)

Sandford, E. A. (WBA), 1933 v W (1)

Sandilands, R. R. (Old Westminsters), 1892 v W; 1893 v Ni; 1894 v W; 1895 v W; 1896 v W (5)

Sands, J. (Nottingham F), 1880 v W (1)

Sansom, K. (C Palace), 1979 v W; 1980 v Bul, Ei, Arg, W (sub), Ni, S, Bel, I; (with Arsenal), 1981 v N, R, Sw, Sp, R, Br, W, S, Sw; 1982 v Ni, W, Ho, S, Fi, F, Cz, WG, Sp; 1983 v D, WG, Gr, L, Gr, H, Ni, S; 1984 v D, H, L, F, S, USSR, Br, U, Ch; 1985 v EG, Fi, T, Ni, Ei, R, Fi, S, I, M, WG, US; 1986 v R, T, Ni, Eg, Is, USSR, S, M, Ca, P, Mor, Pol, Para, Arg; 1987 v Se, Ni (2), Y, Sp, T; 1988 v WG, T, Y, Ho, S, Co, Sw, Ei, Ho, USSR (86)

Saunders, F. E. (Swifts), 1888 v W (1)

Savage, A. H. (C Palace), 1876 v S (1)

Sayer, J. (Stoke C), 1887 v Ni (1)

Scattergood, E. (Derby Co), 1913 v W (1)

Schofield, J. (Stoke C), 1892 v W; 1893 v W; 1895 v Ni (3)

Scott, L. (Arsenal), 1947 v S, W, Ni, Ei, Ho, F, Sw, P; 1948 v S, W, Ni, Bel, Se, I; 1949 v W, Ni, D (17)

Scott, W. R. (Brentford), 1937 v W (1)

Seaman, D. A. (QPR), 1989 v S.Ar., D (sub); 1990 v Cz (sub) (3)

Seddon, J. (Bolton W), 1923 v F, Se (2); 1924 v Bel; 1927 v W; 1929 v S (6)

Seed, J. M. (Tottenham H), 1921 v Bel: 1923 v W, Ni, Bel; 1925 v S (5)

Settle, J. (Bury), 1899 v S, W, Ni; (with Everton), 1902 v S, Ni; 1903 v Ni (6)

Sewell, J. (Sheffield W), 1952 v Ni, A, Sw; 1953 v Ni; 1954 v H (2) (6)

Sewell, W. R. (Blackburn R), 1924 v W (1)

Shackleton, L. F. (Sunderland), 1949 v W, D; 1950 v W; 1955 v W, WG (5)

Sharp, J. (Everton), 1903 v Ni; 1905 v S (2)

Shaw, G. E. (WBA), 1932 v S (1)

Shaw, G. L. (Sheffield U), 1959 v S, W, USSR, I; 1963 v W (5)

Shea, D. (Blackburn R), 1914 v W, Ni (2)

Shellito, K. J. (Chelsea), 1963 v Cz (1)

Shelton A. (Notts Co), 1889 v Ni; 1890 v S, W; 1891 v S, W; 1892 v S (6)

Shelton, C. (Notts Rangers), 1888 v Ni (1)

Shepherd, A. (Bolton W), 1906 v S; (with Newcastle U), 1911 v Ni (2)

Shilton, P. L. (Leicester C), 1971 v EG, W; 1972 v Sw, Ni; 1973 v Y, S (2), Ni, W, Cz, Pol, USSR, I; 1974 v A, Pol, I, W, Ni, S, Arg; (with Stoke C), 1975 v Cy; 1977 v Ni, W; (with Nottingham F), 1978 v W, H; 1979 v Cz, Se, A; 1980 v Ni, Sp, I; 1981 v N, Sw, R; 1982 v H, Ho, S, F, Cz, K, WG, Sp; (with Southampton), 1983 v D, WG, Gr, W, Gr, H, Ni, S, Aus (3); 1984 v D, H, F, Ni, W, S, USSR, Br, U, Ch; 1985 v EG, Fi, T, Ni, R, Fi, S, I, WG; 1986 v R, T, Ni, Eg, Is, USSR, S, M, Ca, P, Mor, Pol, Para, Arg; 1987 v Se, Ni (2), Sp, Br; (with Derby Co), 1988 v WG, T, Y, Ho, S, Co, Sw, Ei, Ho; 1989 v D, Se, Gr, Alb, Alb, Ch, S, Pol, D; 1990 v Se, Pol, I, Y, Br, Cz, D, U, Tun, Ei, Ho, Eg, Bel, Cam, WG, I (125)

Shimwell, E. (Blackpool), 1949 v Se (1)

Shutt, G. (Stoke C), 1886 v Ni (1)

Silcock, J. (Manchester U), 1921 v S, W; 1923 v Se (3)

Sillett, R. P. (Chelsea), 1955 v F, Sp, P (3)

Simms, E. (Luton T), 1922 v Ni (1)

Simpson, J. (Blackburn R), 1911 v S, W, Ni; 1912 v S, W, Ni; 1913 v S; 1914 v W (8)

Slater, W. J. (Wolverhampton W), 1955 v W, WG; 1958 v S, P, Y, USSR (3); 1959 v USSR; 1960 v S (12)

Smalley, T. (Wolverhampton W), 1937 v W (1)

Smart, T. (Aston Villa), 1921 v S; 1924 v S, W; 1926 v Ni; 1930 v W (5)

Smith, A. M. (Arsenal), 1989 v S.Ar., (sub), Gr, Alb (sub), Pol (sub) (4)

Smith, A. (Nottingham F), 1891 v S, W; 1893 v Ni (3)

Smith, A. K. (Oxford University), 1872 v S (1)

Smith, B. (Tottenham H), 1921 v S; 1922 v W (2)

Smith, C. E. (C Palace), 1876 v S (1)

Smith, G. O. (Oxford University), 1893 v Ni; 1894 v W, S; 1895 v W; 1896 v Ni, W, S; (with Old Carthusians), 1897 v Ni, W, S; 1898 v Ni, W, S; (with Corinthians), 1899 v Ni, W, S; 1899 v Ni, W, S; 1901 v S (20)

Smith, H. (Reading), 1905 v W, S; 1906 v W, Ni (4)

Smith, J. (WBA), 1920 v Ni; 1923 v Ni (2)

Smith, Joe (Bolton W), 1913 v Ni; 1914 v S, W; 1920 v W, Ni (5)

Smith, J. C. R. (Millwall), 1939 v Ni, N (2)

Smith, J. W. (Portsmouth), 1932 v Ni, W, Sp (3)

Smith, Leslie (Brentford), 1939 v R (1)

Smith, Lionel (Arsenal), 1951 v W; 1952 v W, Ni; 1953 v W, S, Bel (6)

Smith, R. A. (Tottenham H), 1961 v Ni, W, S, L, P, Sp; 1962 v S; 1963 v S, F, Br, Cz, EG; 1964 v W, Ni, R of W (15)

Smith, S. (Aston Villa), 1895 v S (1)

Smith, S. C. (Leicester C), 1936 v Ni (1)

Smith, T. (Birmingham C), 1960 v W, Se (2)

Smith, T. (Liverpool), 1971 v W (1)

Smith, W. H. (Huddersfield T), 1922 v W, S; 1928 v S (3)

Sorby, T. H. (Thursday Wanderers, Sheffield), 1879 v W (1)

Southworth, J. (Blackburn R), 1889 v W; 1891 v W; 1892 v S (3)

Sparks, F. J. (Herts Rangers), 1879 v S; (with Clapham Rovers), 1880 v S, W (3)

Spence, J. W. (Manchester U), 1926 v Bel; 1927 v Ni (2)

Spence, R. (Chelsea), 1936 v A, Bel (2)

Spencer, C. W. (Newcastle U), 1924 v S; 1925 v W (2)

Spencer, H. (Aston Villa), 1897 v S, W; 1900 v W; 1903 v Ni; 1905 v W, S (6)

Spiksley, F. (Sheffield W), 1893 v S, W; 1894 v S, Ni; 1896 v Ni; 1898 v S, W (7)

Spilsbury, B. W. (Cambridge University), 1885 v Ni; 1886 v Ni, S (3)

Spink, N. (Aston Villa), 1983 v Aus (sub) (1)

Spouncer, W. A. (Nottingham F), 1900 v W (1)

Springett, R. D. G. (Sheffield W), 1960 v Ni, S, Y, Sp, H; 1961 v Ni, S, L, P, Sp, M, I, A; 1962 v W, Ni, S, A, Sw, Pe, L, P, H, Arg, Bul, Br; 1963 v Ni, W, F (2), Sw; 1966 v W, A, N (33)

Sproston, B. (Leeds U), 1937 v W; 1938 v S, W, Ni, Cz, G, Sw, F; (with Tottenham H), 1939 v W, R of E; (with Manchester C), N (11)

Squire, R. T. (Cambridge University), 1886 v S, W, Ni (3)

Stanbrough, M. H. (Old Carthusians), 1895 v W (1)

Staniforth, R. (Huddersfield T), 1954 v S, H, Y, Bel, Sw, U; 1955 v W, WG (8)

Starling, R. W. (Sheffield W), 1933 v S; (with Aston Villa), 1937 v S (2)

Statham, D. (WBA), 1983 v W, Aus (2) (3)

Steele, F. C. (Stoke C), 1937 v S, W, Ni, N, Se, Fi (6)

Stein, B. (Luton T), 1984 v F (1)

Stephenson, C. (Huddersfield T), 1924 v W (1)

Stephenson, G. T. (Derby Co), 1928 v F, Bel; (with Sheffield W), 1931 v F (3)

Stephenson, J. E. (Leeds U), 1938 v S; 1939 v Ni (2)

Stepney, A. C. (Manchester U), 1968 v Se (1)

Sterland, M. (Sheffield W), 1989 v S.Ar., (1)

Steven, T. M. (Everton), 1985 v Ni, Ei, R, Fi, I, US (sub); 1986 v T (sub), Eg, USSR (sub), M (sub), Pol, Para, Arg; 1987 v Se, Y (sub), Sp (sub); 1988 v T, Y, Ho, H, S, Sw, Ho, USSR; 1989 v S; (with Rangers), 1990 v Cz, Cam (sub), WG (sub), I (29)

Stevens, G. A. (Tottenham H), 1985 v Fi (sub), T (sub), Ni; 1986 v S (sub), M (sub), Mor (sub), Para (sub) (7)

Stevens, M. G. (Everton), 1985 v I, WG; 1986 v R, T, Ni, Eg, Is, S, Ca, P, Mor, Pol, Para, Arg; 1987 v Br, S; 1988 v T, Y, Is, Ho, H (sub), S, Sw, Ei, Ho, USSR; (with Rangers), 1989 D, Se, Gr, Alb, Alb, S, Pol; 1990 v Se, Pol, I, Br, D, Tun, Ei, I (41)

Stewart, J. (Sheffield W), 1907 v S, W; (with Newcastle U), 1911 v S (3)

Stiles, N. P. (Manchester U), 1965 v S, H, Y, Se; 1966 v W, Ni, S, A, Sp, Pol (2), WG (2), N, D, U, M, F, Arg, P; 1967 v Ni, W, S, Cz; 1968 v USSR; 1969 v R; 1970 v Ni, S (28)

Stoker, J. (Birmingham), 1933 v W; 1934 v S, H (3)

Storer, H. (Derby Co), 1924 v F; 1928 v Ni (2)

Storey, P. E. (Arsenal), 1971 v Gr, Ni, S; 1972 v Sw, WG, W, Ni, S; 1973 v W (3), Y, S (2), Ni, Cz, Pol, USSR, I (19)

Storey-Moore, I. (Nottingham F), 1970 v Ho (1)

Strange, A. H. (Sheffield W), 1930 v S, A, G; 1931 v S, W, Ni, F, Bel; 1932 v S, W, Ni, Sp; 1933 v S, Ni, A, I, Sw; 1934 v Ni, W, F (20)

Stratford, A. H. (Wanderers), 1874 v S (1)

Streten, B. (Luton T), 1950 v Ni (1)

Sturgess, A. (Sheffield U), 1911 v Ni; 1914 v S (2)

Summerbee, M. G. (Manchester C), 1968 v S, Sp, WG; 1972 v Sw, WG (sub), W, Ni; 1973 v USSR (sub) (8)

Sunderland, A. (Arsenal), 1980 v Aus (1)

Sutcliffe, J. W. (Bolton W), 1893 v W; 1895 v S, Ni; 1901 v S; (with Millwall), 1903 v W (5)

Swan, P. (Sheffield W), 1960 v Y, Sp, H; 1961 v Ni, W, S, L, P, Sp, M, I, A; 1962 v W, Ni, S, A, Sw, L, P (19)

Swepstone, H. A. (Pilgrims), 1880 v S; 1882 v S, W; 1883 v S, W, Ni (6)

Swift, F. V. (Manchester C), 1947, v S, W, Ni, Ei, Ho, F, Sw, P; 1948 v S, W, Ni, Bel, Se, I; 1949 v S, W, Ni, D, N (19)

Tait, G. (Birmingham Excelsior), 1881 v W (1)

Talbot, B. (Ipswich T), 1977 v Ni (sub), S, Br, Arg, U; (with Arsenal), 1980 v Aus (6)

Tambling, R. V. (Chelsea), 1963 v W, F; 1966 v Y (3)

Tate, J. T. (Aston Villa), 1931 v F, Bel; 1933 v W (3)

Taylor, E. (Blackpool), 1954 v H (1)

Taylor, E. H. (Huddersfield T), 1923 v S, W, Ni, Bel; 1924 v S, Ni, F; 1926 v S (8)

Taylor, J. G. (Fulham), 1951 v Arg, P (2)

Taylor, P. J. (C Palace), 1976 v W (sub), W, Ni, S (4)

Taylor, P. H. (Liverpool), 1948 v W, Ni, Se (3)

Taylor, T. (Manchester U), 1953 v Arg, Ch, U; 1954 v Bel, Sw; 1956 v S, Br, Se, Fi, WG; 1957 v Ni, Y (sub), D (2), Ei (2); 1958 v W, Ni, F (19)

Temple, D. W. (Everton), 1965 v WG (1)

Thickett, H. (Sheffield U), 1899 v S, W (2)

Thomas, D. (Coventry C), 1983 v Aus (1+1 sub) (2)

Thomas, D. (QPR), 1975 v Cz (sub), P, Cy (sub+1), W, S (sub); 1976 v Cz (sub), P (sub) (8)

Thomas, M. L. (Arsenal), 1989 v S.Ar; 1990 v Y (2)

Thompson, P. (Liverpool), 1964 v P (2), Ei, US, Br, Arg; 1965 v Ni, W, S, Bel, Ho; 1966 v Ni; 1968 v Ni, WG; 1970 v S, Ho (sub) (16)

Thompson, P. B. (Liverpool), 1976 v W (2), Ni, S, Br, I, Fi; 1977 v Fi; 1979 v Ei (sub), Cz, Ni, S, Bul, Se (sub), A; 1980 v D, Ni, Bul, Ei, Sp (2), Arg, W, S, Bel, I; 1981 v N, R, H; 1982 v N, H, W, Ho, S, Fi, F, Cz, K, WG, Sp; 1983 v WG, Gr (42)

Thompson, T. (Aston Villa), 1952 v W; (with Preston NE), 1957 v S (2)

Thomson, R. A. (Wolverhampton W), 1964 v Ni, US, P, Arg; 1965 v Bel, Ho, Ni, W (8)

Thornewell, G. (Derby Co), 1923 v Se (2); 1924 v F; 1925 v F (4)

Thornley, I. (Manchester C), 1907 v W (1)

Tilson, S. F. (Manchester C), 1934 v H, Cz; 1935 v W; 1936 v Ni (4)

Titmuss, F. (Southampton), 1922 v W; 1923 v W (2)

Todd, C. (Derby Co), 1972 v Ni; 1974 v P, W, Ni, S, Arg, EG, Bul, Y; 1975 v P (sub), WG, Cy (2), Ni, W, S; 1976 v Sw, Cz, P, Ni, S, Br, Fi; 1977 v Ei, Fi, Ho (sub), Ni (27)

Toone, G. (Notts Co), 1892 v S, W (2)

Topham, A. G. (Casuals), 1894 v W (1)

Topham, R. (Wolverhampton W), 1893 v Ni; (with Casuals) 1894 v W (2)

Towers, M. A. (Sunderland), 1976 v W, Ni (sub), I (3)

Townley, W. J. (Blackburn R), 1889 v W; 1890 v Ni (2)

Townrow, J. E. (Clapton Orient), 1925 v S; 1926 v W (2)

Tremelling, D. R. (Birmingham), 1928 v W (1)

Tresadern, J. (West Ham U), 1923 v S, Se (2)

Tueart, D. (Manchester C), 1975 v Cy (sub), Ni; 1977 v Fi, Ni, W (sub), S (sub) (6)

Tunstall, F. E. (Sheffield U), 1923 v S; 1924 v S, W, Ni, F; 1925 v Ni, S (7)

Turnbull, R. J. (Bradford), 1920 v Ni (1)

Turner, A. (Southampton), 1900 v Ni; 1901 v Ni (2)

Turner, H. (Huddersfield T), 1931 v F, Bel (2)

Turner, J. A. (Bolton W), 1893 v W; (with Stoke C) 1895 v Ni; (with Derby Co) 1898 v Ni (3)

Tweedy, G. J. (Grimsby T), 1937 v H (1)

Ufton, D. G. (Charlton Ath), 1954 v R of E (1)

Underwood A. (Stoke C), 1891 v Ni; 1892 v Ni (2)

Urwin, T. (Middlesbrough), 1923 v Se (2); (with Newcastle U) 1924 v Bel; 1926 v W (4)

Utley, G. (Barnsley), 1913 v Ni (1)

Vaughton, O. H. (Aston Villa), 1882 v S, W, Ni; 1884 v S, W (5)

Veitch, C. C. M. (Newcastle U), 1906 v S, W, Ni; 1907 v S, W; 1909 v W (6)

Veitch, J. G. (Old Westminsters), 1894 v W (1)

Venables, T. F. (Chelsea), 1965 v Ho, Bel (2)

Vidal, R. W. S. (Oxford University), 1873 v S (1)

Viljoen, C. (Ipswich T), 1975 v Ni, W (2)

Viollet, D. S. (Manchester U), 1960 v H; 1962 v L (2)

Von Donop (Royal Engineers), 1873 v S; 1875 v S (2)

Wace, H. (Wanderers), 1878 v S; 1879 v S, W (3)

Waddle, C. R. (Newcastle U), 1985 v Ei, R (sub), Fi (sub), S (sub), I, M (sub), WG, US; (with Tottenham H), 1986 v R, T, Ni, Is, USSR, S, M, Ca, P, Mor, Pol (sub), Arg (sub); 1987 v Se (2); 1988 v Y, Sp, T, Br, S; 1988 v WG, Is, H, S (sub), Co, Sw (sub), Ei, Ho (sub); 1989 v Se, S.Ar., Alb, Alb, Ch, S, Pol, D (sub); (with Marseille), 1990 v Se, Pol, I, Y, Br, D, U, Tun, Ei, Ho, Eg, Bel, Cam, WG, I (sub) (59)

Wadsworth, S. J. (Huddersfield T), 1922 v S; 1923 v S, Bel; 1924 v S, Ni; 1925 v S, Ni; 1926 v W; 1927 v Ni (9)

Wainscoat, W. R. (Leeds U), 1929 v S (1)

Waiters, A. K. (Blackpool), 1964 v Ei, Br; 1965 v W, Bel, Ho (5)

Walker, D. S. (Nottingham F), 1989 v D (sub), Se (sub), Gr, Alb, Alb, Ch, S, Pol, D; 1990 v Se, Pol, I, Y, Br, Cz, D, U, Tun, Ei, Ho, Eg, Bel, Cam, WG, I (25)

Walden, F. I. (Tottenham H), 1914 v S; 1922 v W (2)

Walker, W. H. (Aston Villa), 1921 v Ni; 1922 v Ni, W, S; 1923 v Se (2); 1924 v S; 1925 v Ni, W, S, Bel, F; 1926 v Ni, W, S; 1927 v Ni, W; 1933 v A (18)

Wall, G. (Manchester U), 1907 v W; 1908 v Ni; 1909 v S; 1910 v W, S; 1912 v S; 1913 v Ni (7)

Wallace, C. W. (Aston Villa), 1913 v W; 1914 v Ni; 1920 v S (3)

Wallace, D. L. (Southampton), 1986 v Eg (1)

Walsh, P. (Luton T), 1983 v Aus (2+1 sub) (3)

Walters, A. M. (Cambridge University), 1885 v S, N; 1886 v S; 1887 v S, W; (with Old Carthusians) 1889 v S, W; 1890 v S, W (9)

Walters, P. M. (Oxford University), 1885 v S, Ni; (with Old Carthusians), 1886 v S, W, Ni; 1887 v S, W; 1888 v S, Ni; 1889 v S, W; 1890 v S, W (13)

Walton, N. (Blackburn R) 1890 v Ni (1)

Ward, J. T. (Blackburn Olympic), 1885 v W (1)

Ward, P. (Brighton & HA), 1980 v Aus (sub) (1)

Ward, T. V. (Derby Co), 1948 v Bel; 1949 v W (2)

Waring, T. (Aston Villa), 1931 v F, Bel; 1932 v S, W, Ni (5)

Warner, C. (Upton Park), 1878 v S (1)

Warren, B. (Derby Co), 1906 v S, W, Ni; 1907 v S, W, Ni; 1908 v S, W, Ni, A (2), H, B; (with Chelsea), 1909 v S, Ni, W, H (2), A; 1911 v S, Ni, W (22)

Waterfield, G. S. (Burnley), 1927 v W (1)

Watson, D. (Norwich C), 1984 v Br, U, Ch; 1985 v M, US (sub); 1986 v S; (with Everton), 1987 v Ni; 1988 v Is, Ho, S, Sw (sub), USSR (12)

Watson, D. V. (Sunderland), 1974 v P, S (sub), Arg, EG, Bul, Y; 1975 v Cz, P, WG, Cy (2), Ni, W, S; (with Manchester C) 1976 v Sw, Cz (sub), P; 1977 v Ho, L, Ni, W, S, Br, Arg, U; 1978 v Sw, L, I, WG, Br, W, Ni, S, H; 1979 v D, Ei, Cz, Ni (2), W, S, Bul, Se, A; (with Werder Bremen), 1980 v D; (with Southampton) Ni, Bul, Ei, Sp (2), Arg, Ni, S, Bel, I; 1981 v N, R, Sw, R, W, S, Sw, H; (with Stoke C), 1982 v Ni, Ic (65)

Watson, V. M. (West Ham U), 1923 v W, S; 1930 v S, G, A (5)

Watson, W. (Burnley), 1913 v S; 1914 v Ni; 1920 v Ni (3)

Watson, W. (Sunderland), 1950 v Ni, I; 1951 v W, Y (4)

Weaver, S. (Newcastle U), 1932 v S, 1933 v S, Ni (3)

Webb, G. W. (West Ham U), 1911 v S, W (2)

Webb, N. J. (Nottingham F), 1988 v WG (sub), T, Y, Is, Ho, S, Sw, Ei, USSR (sub); 1989 v D, Se, Gr, Alb, Alb, Ch, S, Pol, D; (with Manchester U), 1990 v Se, I (sub) (20)

Webster, M. (Middlesbrough), 1930 v S, A, G (3)

Wedlock, W. J. (Bristol C), 1907 v S, Ni, W; 1908 v S, Ni, W, A (2), H, B; 1909 v S, W, Ni, H (2), A; 1910 v S, W, Ni; 1911 v S, W, Ni; 1912 v S, W, Ni; 1914 v W (26)

Weir, D. (Bolton W), 1889 v S, Ni (2)

Welch, R. de C. (Wanderers), 1872 v S; (with Harrow Chequers) 1874 v S (2)

Weller, K. (Leicester C), 1974 v W, Ni, S, Arg (4)

Welsh, D. (Charlton Ath), 1938 v G, Sw; 1939 v R (3)

West, G. (Everton), 1969 v W, Bul, M (3)

Westwood, R. W. (Bolton W), 1935 v S, W, Ho; 1936 v Ni, G; 1937 v W (6)

Whateley, O. (Aston Villa), 1883 v S, Ni (2)

Wheeler, J. E. (Bolton W), 1955 v Ni (1)

Wheldon, G. F. (Aston Villa), 1897 v Ni; 1898 v S, W, Ni (4)

White, T. A. (Everton), 1933 v I (1)

Whitehead, J. (Accrington), 1893 v W; (with Blackburn R) 1894 v Ni (2)

Whitfeld, H. (Old Etonians), 1879 v W (1)

Whitham, M. (Sheffield U), 1892 v Ni (1)

Whitworth, S. (Leicester C), 1975 v WG, Cy, Ni, W, S; 1976 v Sw, P (7)

Whymark, T. J. (Ipswich T), 1978 v L (sub) (1)

Widdowson, S. W. (Nottingham F), 1880 v S (1)

Wignall, F. (Nottingham F), 1965 v W, Ho (2)

Wilkes, A. (Aston Villa), 1901 v S, W; 1902 v S, W, Ni (5)

Wilkins, R. G. (Chelsea), 1976 v I; 1977 v Ei, Fi, Ni, Br, Arg, U; 1978 v Sw (sub), L, I, WG, W, Ni, S, H; 1979 v D, Ei, Cz, Ni, W, S, Bul, Se (sub), A; (with Manchester U) 1980 v D, Ni, Bul, Sp (2), Arg, W (sub), Ni, S, Bel, I; 1981 v Sp (sub), R, Br, W, S, Sw, H (sub); 1982 v Ni, W, Ho, S, Fi, F, Cz, K, WG, Sp; 1983 v D, WG, 1984 v D, Ni, W, S, USSR, Br, U, Ch; (with AC Milan), 1985 v EG, Fi, T, Ni, Ei, R, Fi, S, I, M; 1986 v T, Ni, Is, Eg, USSR, S, M, Ca, P, Mor; 1987 v Se, Y (sub) (84)

Wilkinson, B. (Sheffield U), 1904 v S (1)

Wilkinson, L. R. (Oxford University), 1891 v W (1)

Williams, B. F. (Wolverhampton W), 1949 v F; 1950 v S, W, Ei, I, P, Bel, Ch, US, Sp; 1951 v Ni, W, S, Y, Arg, P; 1952 v W, F; 1955 v S, WG, F, Sp, P; 1956 v W (24)

Williams, O. (Clapton Orient), 1923 v W, Ni (2)

Williams, S. (Southampton), 1983 v Aus (1+1 sub); 1984 v F; 1985 v EG, Fi, T (6)

Williams, W. (WBA), 1897 v Ni; 1898 v W, Ni, S; 1899 v W, Ni (6)

Williamson, E. C. (Arsenal), 1923 v Se (2) (2)

Williamson, R. G. (Middlesbrough), 1905 v Ni; 1911 v Ni, S, W; 1912 v S, W; 1913 v Ni (7)

Willingham, C. K. (Huddersfield T), 1937 v Fi; 1938 v S, G, Sw, F; 1939 v S, W, Ni, R of E, N, I, Y (12)

Willis, A. (Tottenham H), 1952 v F (1)

Wilshaw, D. J. (Wolverhampton W), 1954 v W, Sw, U; 1955 v S, F, Sp, P; 1956 v W, Ni, Fi, WG; 1957 v Ni (12)

Wilson, C. P. (Hendon), 1884 v S, W (2)

Wilson, C. W. (Oxford University), 1879 v W; 1881 v S (2)

Wilson, G. (Sheffield W), 1921 v S, W, Bel; 1922 v S, Ni; 1923 v S, W, Ni, Bel; 1924 v W, Ni, F (12)

Wilson, G. P. (Corinthians), 1900 v S, W (2)

Wilson, R. (Huddersfield T), 1960 v S, Y, Sp, H; 1962 v W, Ni, S, A, Sw, Pe, P, H, Arg, Bul, Br; 1963 v Ni, F, Br, Cz, EG, Sw; 1964 v W, S, R of W, U, P (2), Ei, Br, Arg; (with Everton), 1965 v S, H, Y, WG, Se; 1966 v WG (sub), W, Ni, A, Sp, Pol (2), Y, Fi, D, U, M, F, Arg, P, WG; 1967 v Ni, W, S, Cz, A; 1968 v Ni, S, USSR (2), Sp (2), Y (63)

Wilson, T. (Huddersfield T), 1928 v S (1)

Winckworth, W. N. (Old Westminsters), 1892 v W; 1893 v Ni (2)

Windridge, J. E. (Chelsea), 1908 v S, W, Ni, A (2), H, B; 1909 v Ni (8)

Wingfield-Stratford, C. V. (Royal Engineers), 1877 v S (1)

Winterburn, N. (Arsenal), 1990 v I (sub) (1)

Withe, P. (Aston Villa), 1981 v Br, W, S; 1982 v N (sub), W, Ic; 1983 v H, Ni, S; 1984 v H (sub); 1985 v T (11)

Wollaston, C. H. R. (Wanderers), 1874 v S; 1875 v S; 1877 v S; 1880 v S (4)

Wolstenholme, S. (Everton), 1904 v S; (with Blackburn R), 1905 v W, Ni (3)

Wood, H. (Wolverhampton W), 1890 v S, W; 1896 v S (3)

Wood, R. E. (Manchester U), 1955 v Ni, W; 1956 v Fi (3)

Woodcock, A. S. (Nottingham F), 1978 v Ni; 1979 v Ei (sub), Cz, Bul (sub), Se; 1980 v Ni; (with Cologne), Bul, Ei, Sp (2), Arg, Bel, I; 1981 v N, R, Sw, R, W (sub), S; 1982 v Ni (sub), Ho, Fi (sub), WG (sub), Sp; (with Arsenal), 1983 v WG (sub), Gr, L, Gr; 1984 v L, F (sub), Ni, W, S, Br, U (sub); 1985 v EG, Fi, T, Ni; 1986 v R (sub), T (sub), Is (sub) (42)

Woodger, G. (Oldham Ath), 1911 v Ni (1)

Woodhall, G. (WBA), 1888 v S, W (2)

Woodley, V. R. (Chelsea), 1937 v S, N, Se, Fi; 1938 v S, W, Ni, Cz, G, Sw, F; 1939 v S, W, Ni, R of E, N, I, R, Y (19)

Woods, C. C. E. (Norwich C), 1985 v US; 1986 v Eg (sub), Is (sub), Ca (sub); (with Rangers), 1987 v Y, Sp (sub), Ni (sub), T, S; 1988 v Is, H, Sw (sub), USSR; 1989 v D (sub); 1990 v Br (sub), D (sub) (16)

Woodward, V. J. (Tottenham H), 1903 v S, W, Ni; 1904 v S, Ni; 1905 v S, W, Ni; 1907 v S; 1908 v S, W, Ni, A (2), H, B; 1909 v W, Ni, H (2), A; (with Chelsea), 1910 v Ni; 1911 v W (23)

Woosnam, M. (Manchester C), 1922 v W (1)

Worrall, F. (Portsmouth), 1935 v Ho; 1937 v Ni (2)

Worthington, F. S. (Leicester C), 1974 v Ni (sub), S, Arg, EG, Bul, Y; 1975 v Cz, P (sub) (8)

Wreford-Brown, C. (Oxford University), 1889 v Ni; (with Old Carthusians), 1894 v W; 1895 v W; 1898 v S (4)

Wright, E, G. D. (Cambridge University), 1906 v W (1)

Wright, J. D. (Newcastle U), 1939 v N (1)

Wright, M. (Southampton), 1984 v W; 1985 v EG, Fi, T, Ei, R, I, WG; 1986 v R, T, Ni, Eg, USSR; 1987 v Y, Ni, S; (with Derby Co), 1988 v Is, Ho (sub), Co, Sw, Ei, Ho; 1990 v Cz (sub), Tun (sub, Ho, Eg, Bel, Cam, WG, I (30)

Wright, T. J. (Everton), 1968 v USSR; 1969 v R (2), M (sub), U, Br; 1970 v W, Ho, Bel, R (sub), Br (11)
Wright, W. A. (Wolverhampton W), 1947 v S, W, Ni, Ei, Ho, F, Sw, P; 1948 v S, W, Ni, Bel, Se, I; 1949 v S, W, Ni, D, Sw, Se, N, F; 1950 v S, W, Ni, Ei, I, P, Bel, Ch, US, Sp; 1951 v Ni, S, Arg; 1952 v W, Ni, S, F, A (2), I, Sw; 1953 v Ni, W, S, Bel, Arg, Ch, U, US; 1954 v W, Ni, S, R of E, H (2), Y, Bel, Sw, U; 1955 v W, Ni, S, WG, F, Sp, P; 1956 v Ni, W, S, Br, Se, Fi, WG, D, Sp; 1957 v S, W, Ni, Y, D (2), Ei (2); 1958 v W, Ni, S, P, Y, USSR (3), Br, A, F; 1959 v W, Ni, S, USSR, I, Br, Pe, M, US (105)

Wylie, J. G. (Wanderers), 1878 v S (1)

Yates, J. (Burnley), 1889 v Ni (1)
York, R. E. (Aston Villa), 1922 v S; 1926 v S (2)
Young, A. (Huddersfield T), 1933 v W; 1937 v S, H, N, Se; 1938 v G, Sw, F; 1939 v W (9)
Young, G. M. (Sheffield W), 1965 v W (1)

R. E. Evans also played for Wales against E, Ni, S; J. Reynolds also played for Ireland against E, W, S.

NORTHERN IRELAND

Aherne, T. (Belfast C), 1947 v E; 1948 v S; 1949 v W; (with Luton T), 1950 v W (4)
Alexander, A. (Cliftonville), 1895 v S (1)
Allen, C. A. (Cliftonville), 1936 v E (1)
Allen, J. (Limavady), 1887 v E (1)
Anderson, T. (Manchester U), 1973 v Cy, E, S, W; 1974 v Bul, P; (with Swindon T), 1975 v S (sub); 1976 v Is; 1977 v Ho, Bel, WG, E, S, W, Ic; 1978 v Ic, Ho, Bel; (with Peterborough U), S, E, W; 1979 v D (22)
Anderson, W. (Linfield), 1898 v W, E, S; 1899 v S (4)
Andrews, W. (Glentoran), 1908 v S; (with Grimsby T), 1913 v E, S (3)
Armstrong, G. (Tottenham H), 1977 v WG, E, W (sub), Ic (sub); 1978 v Bel, S, E, W; 1979 v Ei, D, Bul, E, Bul, E, S, W, D; 1980 v E, Ei, Is, S, E, W, Aus (3); 1981 v Se; (with Watford), P, S, P, S, Se; 1982 v S, Is, E, F, W, Y, Hon, Sp, A, F; 1983 v A, T, Alb, S, E, W; (with Real Mallorca), 1984 v A, WG, E, W, Fi; 1985 v R, Fi, E, Sp; (with WBA), 1986 v T, R (sub), E (sub), F (sub); (with Chesterfield), D (sub), Br (sub) (63)

Baird, G. (Distillery), 1896 v S, E, W (3)
Baird, H. (Huddersfield T), 1939 v E (1)
Balfe, J. (Shelbourne), 1909 v E; 1910 v W (2)
Bambrick, J. (Linfield), 1929 v W, S, E; 1930 v W, S, E; 1932 v W; (with Chelsea), 1935 v W; 1936 v E, S; 1938 v W (11)
Banks, S. J. (Cliftonville), 1937 v W (1)
Barr, H. H. (Linfield), 1962 v E; (with Coventry C), 1963 v E, Pol (3)
Barron, H. (Cliftonville), 1894 v E, W, S; 1895 v S; 1896 v S; 1897 v E, W (7)
Barry, H. (Bohemians), 1900 v S (1)
Baxter, R. A. (Cliftonville), 1887 v S, W (2)
Bennett, L. V. (Dublin University), 1889 v W (1)
Berry, J. (Cliftonville), 1888 v S, W; 1889 v E (3)
Best, G. (Manchester U), 1964 v W, U; 1965 v E, Ho (2), S, Sw (2), Alb; 1966 v S, E, Alb; 1967 v E; 1968 v S; 1969 v E, S, W, T; 1970 v S, E, W, USSR; 1971 v Cy (2), Sp, E, S, W; 1972 v USSR, Sp; 1973 v Bul; 1974 v P; (with Fulham), 1977 v Ho, Bel, WG; 1978 v Ic, Ho (37)
Bingham, W. L. (Sunderland), 1951 v F; 1952 v E, S, W; 1953 v E, S, F, W; 1954 v E, S, W; 1955 v E, S, W; 1956 v E, S, W; 1957 v E, S, W, P (2), I; 1958 v S, E, W, I (2), Arg, Cz (2), WG, F; (with Luton T), 1959 v E, S, W, Sp; 1960 v S, E, W; (with Everton), 1961 v E, S, WG (2), Gr, I; 1962 v E, Gr; 1963 v E, S, Pol (2), Sp; (with Port Vale), 1964 v S, E, Sp (56)
Black, J. (Glentoran), 1901 v E (1)
Black, K. (Luton T), 1988 v Fr (sub), Ma (sub); 1989 v Ei, H, Sp, Sp, Ch (sub); 1990 v H, N, U (10)
Blair, H. (Portadown), 1931 v S; 1932 v S; (with Swansea), 1934 v S (3)
Blair, J. (Cliftonville), 1907 v W, E, S; 1908 v E, S (5)
Blair, R. V. (Oldham Ath), 1975 v Se (sub), S (sub), W; 1976 v Se, Is (5)

Blanchflower, R. D. (Barnsley), 1950 v S, W; 1951 v E, S; (with Aston Villa), F; 1952 v W; 1953 v E, S, W, F; 1954 v E, S, W; (with Tottenham H), 1955 v E, S, W; 1956 v E, S, W; 1957 v E, S, W, I, P (2); 1958 v E, S, W, I (2), Cz (2), Arg, F, WG; 1959 v E, S, W, Sp; 1960 v E, S, W; 1961 v E, S, W, WG (2); 1962 v E, S, W, Gr, Ho; 1963 v E, S, Pol (2) (56)
Blanchflower, J. (Manchester U), 1954 v W; 1955 v E, S; 1956 v S, W; 1957 v S, E, P; 1958 v S, E, I (2) (12)
Bookman, L. O. (Bradford C), 1914 v W; (with Luton T), 1921 v S, W; 1922 v E (4)
Bothwell, A. W. (Ards), 1926 v S, E, W; 1927 v E, W (5)
Bowler, G. C. (Hull C), 1950 v E, S, W (3)
Boyle, P. (Sheffield U), 1901 v E; 1902 v E; 1903 v S, W; 1904 v E (5)
Braithwaite, R. S. (Linfield), 1962 v W; 1963 v P, Sp; (with Middlesbrough), 1964 v W, U; 1965 v E, S, Sw (2), Ho (10)
Breen, T. (Belfast C), 1935 v E, W; 1937 v E, S; (with Manchester U), 1937 v W; 1938 v E, S; 1939 v W, S (9)
Brennan, B. (Bohemians), 1912 v W (1)
Brennan, R. A. (Luton T), 1949 v W; (with Birmingham C), 1950 v E, S, W; (with Fulham), 1951 v E (5)
Briggs, W. R. (Manchester U), 1962 v W; (with Swansea T), 1965 v Ho (2)
Brisby, D. (Distillery), 1891 v S (1)
Brolly, T. (Millwall), 1937 v W; 1938 v W; 1939 v E, W (4)
Brookes, E. A. (Shelbourne), 1920 v S (1)
Brotherston, N. (Blackburn R), 1980 v S, E, W, Aus (3); 1981 v Se, P; 1982 v S, Is, E, F, S, W, Hon (sub), A (sub); 1983 v A (sub), WG, Alb, T, Alb, S (sub), E (sub), W; 1984 v T; 1985 v Is (sub), T (27)
Brown, J. (Glenavon), 1921 v W; (with Tranmere R), 1924 v E, W (3)
Brown, J. (Wolverhampton W), 1935 v E, W; 1936 v E; (with Coventry C), 1937 v E, W; 1938 v S, W; (with Birmingham C), 1939 v E, S, W (10)
Brown, W. G. (Glenavon), 1926 v W (1)
Brown, W. M. (Limavady), 1887 v E (1)
Browne, F. (Cliftonville), 1887 v E, S, W; 1888 v E, S (5)
Browne, R. J. (Leeds U), 1936 v E, W; 1938 v E, W; 1939 v E, S (6)
Bruce, W. (Glentoran), 1961 v S; 1967 v W (2)
Buckle, H. (Cliftonville), 1882 v E (1)
Buckle, H. R. (Sunderland), 1904 v E; (with Bristol R), 1908 v W (2)
Burnett, J. (Distillery), 1894 v E, W, S; (with Glentoran), 1895 v E, W (5)
Burnison, J. (Distillery), 1901 v E, W (2)
Burnison, S. (Distillery), 1908 v E; 1910 v E, S; (with Bradford), 1911 v E, S, W; (with Distillery), 1912 v E; 1913 v W (8)
Burns, J. (Glenavon), 1923 v E (1)
Butler, M. P. (Blackpool), 1939 v W (1)

Campbell, A. C. (Crusaders), 1963 v W; 1965 v Sw (2)

Campbell, D. A. (Nottingham F), 1986 v Mor (sub), Br; 1987 v E (2), T, Y; 1988 v Y (with Charlton Ath), T (sub), Gr (sub), Pol (sub) (10)

Campbell, J. (Cliftonville), 1896 v W; 1897 v E, S, W; (with Distillery), 1898 v E, S, W; (with Cliftonville), 1899 v E; 1900 v E, S; 1901 v S, W; 1902 v S; 1903 v E; 1904 v S (15)

Campbell, J. P. (Fulham), 1951 v E, S (2)

Campbell, R. (Bradford C), 1982 v S, W (sub) (2)

Campbell, W. G. (Dundee), 1968 v S, E; 1969 v T; 1970 v S, W, USSR (6)

Carey, J. J. (Manchester U), 1947 v E, S, W; 1948 v E; 1949 v E, S, W (7)

Carroll, E. (Glenavon), 1925 v S (1)

Casey, T. (Newcastle U), 1955 v W; 1956 v W; 1957 v E, S, W, I, P (2); 1958 v WG, F; (with Portsmouth), 1959 v E, Sp (12)

Cashin, M. (Cliftonville), 1898 v S (1)

Caskey, W. (Derby Co), 1979 v Bul, E, Bul, E, D (sub); 1980 v E (sub); (with Tulsa R), 1982 v F (sub) (7)

Cassidy, T. (Newcastle U), 1971 v E (sub); 1972 v USSR (sub); 1974 v Bul (sub), S, E, W; 1975 v N; 1976 v S, E, W; 1977 v WG (sub); 1980 v E, Ei (sub), Is, S, E, W, Aus (3); (with Burnley), 1981 v Se, P; 1982 v Is, Sp (sub) (24)

Caughey, M. (Linfield), 1986 v F (sub), D (sub) (2)

Chambers, J. (Distillery), 1921 v W; (with Bury), 1928 v E, S, W; 1929 v E, S, W; 1930 v S, W; (with Nottingham F), 1932 v E, S, W (12)

Chatton, H. A. (Partick T), 1925 v E, S; 1926 v E (3)

Christian, J. (Linfield), 1889 v S (1)

Clarke, C. J. (Bournemouth), 1986 v F, D, Mor, Alg (sub), Sp, Br; (with Southampton), 1987, v E, T, Y; 1988 v Y, T, Gr, Pol, F, Ma; 1989 v Ei, H, Sp, Sp (sub) (with QPR) Ma, Ch; 1990 v H, Ei, N (24)

Clarke, R. (Belfast C), 1901 v E, S (2)

Cleary, J. (Glentoran), 1982 v S, W; 1983 v W (sub); 1984 v T (sub); 1985 v Is (5)

Clements, D. (Coventry C), 1965 v W, Ho; 1966 v M; 1967 v S, W; 1968 v S, E; 1969 v T (2), S, W; 1970 v S, E, W, USSR (2); 1971 v Sp, E, S, W, Cy; (with Sheffield W), 1972 v USSR (2), Sp, E, S, W; 1973 v Bul, Cy (2), P, E, S, W; (with Everton), 1974 v Bul, P, S, E, W; 1975 v N, Y, E, S, W; 1976 v Se, Y; (with New York Cosmos), E, W (48)

Clugston, J. (Cliftonville), 1888 v W; 1889 v W, S, E; 1890 v E, S; 1891 v E, W; 1892 v E, S, W; 1893 v E, S, W (14)

Cochrane, D. (Leeds U), 1939 v E, W; 1947 v E, S, W; 1948 v E, S, W; 1949 v S, W; 1950 v S, E (12)

Cochrane, M. (Distillery), 1898 v S, W, E; 1899 v E; 1900 v E, S, W; (with Leicester Fosse), 1901 v S (8)

Cochrane, T. (Coleraine), 1976 v N; (with Burnley), 1978 v S (sub), E (sub), W (sub); 1979 v Ei (sub); (with Middlesbrough), D, Bul, E, Bul, E; 1980 v Is, E (sub), W (sub), Aus (1+2 sub); 1981 v Se (sub), P (sub), S, P, S, Se; 1982 v E (sub), F; (with Gillingham), 1984 v S, Fi (sub) (26)

Collins, F. (Glasgow C), 1922 v S (1)

Condy, J. (Distillery), 1882 v W; 1886 v E, S (3)

Connell, T. (Coleraine), 1978 v W (sub) (1)

Connor, J. (Glentoran), 1901 v S, E; (with Belfast C), 1905 v E, S, W; 1907 v E, S; 1908 v E, S; 1909 v W; 1911 v S, E, W (13)

Connor, M. J. (Brentford), 1903 v S, W; (with Fulham), 1904 v E (3)

Cook, W. (Celtic), 1933 v E, W, S; (with Everton), 1935 v E; 1936 v S, W; 1937 v E, S, W; 1938 v E, S, W; 1939 v E, S, W (15)

Cooke, S. (Belfast YMCA), 1889 v E; (with Cliftonville), 1890 v E, S (3)

Coulter, J. (Belfast C), 1934 v E, S, W; (with Everton),

1935 v E, S, W; 1937 v S, W; (with Grimsby T), 1938 v S, W; (with Chelmsford C), 1939 v S (11)

Cowan, J. (Newcastle U), 1970 v E (sub) (1)

Cowan, T. S. (Queen's Island), 1925 v W (1)

Coyle, F. (Coleraine), 1956 v E, S; 1957 v P (with Nottingham F), 1958 v Arg (4)

Coyle, L. (Derry C), 1989 v Ch (sub) (1)

Coyle, R. I. (Sheffield W), 1973 v P, Cy (sub), W (sub); 1974 v Bul (sub), P (sub) (5)

Craig, A. B. (Rangers), 1908 v E, S, W; 1909 v S; (with Morton), 1912 v S, W; 1914 v E, S, W (9)

Craig, D. J. (Newcastle U), 1967 v W; 1968 v W; 1969 v T (2), E, S, W; 1970 v E, S, W, USSR; 1971 v Cy (2), S, S (sub); 1972 v USSR, S (sub); 1973 v Cy (2), E, S, W; 1974 v Bul, P; 1975 v N (25)

Crawford, S. (Distillery), 1889 v E, W; (with Cliftonville), 1891 v E, S, W; 1893 v E, W (7)

Croft, T. (Queen's Island), 1924 v E (1)

Crone, R. (Distillery), 1889 v S; 1890 v E, S, W (4)

Crone, W. (Distillery), 1882 v W; 1884 v E, S, W; 1886 v E, S, W; 1887 v E; 1888 v E, W; 1889 v S; 1890 v W (12)

Crooks, W. (Manchester U), 1922 v W (1)

Crossan, E. (Blackburn R), 1950 v S; 1951 v E; 1955 v W (3)

Crossan, J. A. (Sparta-Rotterdam), 1960 v E; (with Sunderland), 1963 v W, P, Sp; 1964 v E, S, W, U, Sp; 1965 v E, S, Sw (2); (with Manchester C), W, Ho (2), Alb; 1966 v S, E, Alb, WG; 1967 v E, S; (with Middlesbrough), 1968 v S (24)

Crothers, C. (Distillery), 1907 v W (1)

Cumming, L. (Huddersfield T), 1929 v W, S; (with Oldham Ath), 1930 v E (3)

Cunningham, R. (Ulster), 1892 v S, E, W; 1893 v E (4)

Cunningham, W. E. (St Mirren), 1951 v W; 1953 v E; 1954 v S; 1955 v S; (with Leicester C), 1956 v E, S, W; 1957 v E, S, W, I, P (2); 1958 v S, W, I, Cz (2), Arg, WG, F; 1959 v E, S, W; 1960 v E, S, W; (with Dunfermline Ath), 1961 v W; 1962 v W, Ho (30)

Curran, S. (Belfast C), 1926 v S, W; 1928 v S (3)

Curran, J. J. (Glenavon), 1922 v W; (with Pontypridd), 1923 v E, S; (with Glenavon), 1924 v E (4)

Cush, W. W. (Glenavon), 1951 v E, S; 1954 v S, E; 1957 v W, I, P (2); (with Leeds U), 1958 v I (2), W, Cz (2), Arg, WG, F; 1959 v E, S, W, Sp; 1960 v E, S, W; (with Portadown), 1961 v WG, Gr; 1962 v Gr (26)

Dalton, W. (YMCA), 1888 v S; (with Linfield), 1890 v S, W; 1891 v S, W; 1892 v E, S, W; 1894 v E, S, W (11)

D'Arcy, S. D. (Chelsea), 1952 v W; 1953 v E; (with Brentford), 1953 v S, W, F (5)

Darling, J. (Linfield), 1897 v E, S; 1900 v S; 1902 v E, S, W; 1903 v E, S, W; 1905 v E, S, W; 1906 v E, S, W; 1908 v W; 1909 v E; 1910 v E, S, W; 1912 v S (21)

Davey, H. H. (Reading), 1926 v E; 1927 v E, S; 1928 v E; (with Portsmouth), 1928 v W (5)

Davis, T. L. (Oldham Ath), 1937 v E (1)

Davison, J. R. (Cliftonville), 1882 v E, W; 1883 v E, W; 1884 v E, W, S; 1885 v E (8)

Dennison, R. (Wolverhampton W), 1988 v F, Ma; 1989 v H, Sp, Ch (sub); 1990 v Ei, U (7)

Devine, J. (Glentoran), 1900 v U (sub) (1)

Devine, W. (Limavady), 1886 v E, W; 1887 v W; 1888 v W (4)

Dickson, D. (Coleraine), 1970 v S (sub); 1973 v Cy, P (4)

Dickson, T. A. (Linfield), 1957 v S (1)

Dickson, W. (Chelsea), 1951 v W, F; 1952 v E, S, W; 1953 v E, S, W, F; (with Arsenal), 1954 v E, W; 1955 v E (12)

Diffin, W. (Belfast C), 1931 v W (1)

Dill, A. H. (Knock and Down Ath), 1882 v E, W; (with Cliftonville), 1883 v W; 1884 v E, S, W; 1885 v E, S, W (9)

Doherty, I. (Belfast C), 1901 v E (1)

Doherty, J. (Cliftonville), 1933 v E, W (2)

Doherty, L. (Linfield), 1985 v Is; 1988 v T (sub) (2)

Doherty, M. (Derry C), 1938 v S (1)

Doherty, P. D. (Blackpool), 1935 v E, W; 1936 v E, S; (with Manchester C), 1937 v E, W; 1938 v E, S; 1939 v E, W; (with Derby Co), 1947 v E; (with Huddersfield T), 1947 v W; 1948 v E, W; 1949 v S; (with Doncaster R), 1951 v S (16)

Donaghy, M. (Luton T), 1980 v S, E, W; 1981 v Se, P, S (sub); 1982 v S, Is, E, F, S, W, Y, Hon, Sp, F; 1983 v A, WG, Alb, T, Alb, S, E, W; 1984 v A, T, WG, S, E, W, Fi; 1985 v R, Fi, E, Sp, T; 1986 v T, R, E, F, D, Mor, Alg, Sp, Br; 1987 v E (2), T, Is, Y; 1988 v Y, T, Gr, Pol, F, Ma; 1989 v Ei, H (with Manchester U), Sp, Sp, Ma, Ch; 1990 v Ei, N (64)

Donnelly, L. (Distillery), 1913 v W (1)

Doran, J. F. (Brighton), 1921 v E; 1922 v E, W (3)

Dougan, A. D. (Portsmouth), 1958 v Cz; (with Blackburn R), 1960 v S; 1961 v E, W, I, Gr; (with Aston Villa), 1963 v S, P (2); (with Leicester C), 1966 v S, E, W, M, Alb, WG; 1967 v E, S; (with Wolverhampton W), 1967 v W; 1968 v S, W, Is; 1969 v T (2), E, S, W; 1970 v S, E, USSR (2); 1971 v Cy (2), Sp, E, S, W; 1972 v USSR (2), E, S, W; 1973 v Bul, Cy (43)

Douglas, J. P. (Belfast C), 1947 v E (1)

Dowd, H. O. (Glenavon), 1974 v W; 1975 v N (sub), Se (3)

Dowie, I. (Luton T), 1990 v N (sub), U (2)

Duggan, H. A. (Leeds U), 1930 v E; 1931 v E, W; 1933 v E; 1934 v E; 1935 v S, W; 1936 v S (8)

Dunlop, G. (Linfield), 1985 v Is; 1987 v E, Y; 1990 v Ei (4)

Dunne, J. (Sheffield U), 1928 v W; 1931 v W, E; 1932 v E, S; 1933 v E, W (7)

Eames, W. L. E. (Dublin U), 1885 v E, S, W (3)

Eglington, T. J. (Everton), 1947 v S, W; 1948 v E, S, W; 1949 v E (6)

Elder, A. R. (Burnley), 1960 v W; 1961 v S, E, W, WG (2), Gr; 1962 v E, S, Gr; 1963 v E, S, W, P (2), Sp; 1964 v W, U; 1965 v E, S, W, Sw (2), Ho (2), Alb; 1966 v E, S, W, M, Alb; 1967 v E, S, W; (with Stoke C), 1968 v E, W; 1969 v E (sub), S, W; 1970 v USSR (40)

Elleman, A. R. (Cliftonville), 1889 v W; 1890 v E (2)

Elwood, J. H. (Bradford), 1929 v W; 1930 v E (2)

Emerson, W. (Glenavon), 1920 v E, S, W; 1921 v E; 1922 v E, S; (with Burnley), 1922 v W; 1923 v E, S, W; 1924 v E (11)

English, S. (Glasgow R), 1933 v W, S (2)

Enright, J. (Leeds C), 1912 v S (1)

Falloon, E. (Aberdeen), 1931 v S; 1933 v S (2)

Farquharson, T. G. (Cardiff C), 1923 v S, W; 1924 v E, S, W; 1925 v E, S (7)

Farrell, P. (Distillery), 1901 v S, W (2)

Farrell, P. (Hibernian), 1938 v W (1)

Farrell, P. D. (Everton), 1947 v S, W; 1948 v E, S, W; 1949 v E, W (7)

Feeney, J. M. (Linfield), 1947 v S; (with Swansea T), 1950 v E (2)

Feeney, W. (Glentoran), 1976 v Is (1)

Ferguson, W. (Linfield), 1966 v M; 1967 v E (2)

Ferris, J. (Belfast Celtic), 1920 v E, W; (with Chelsea), 1921 v S, E; (with Belfast C), 1928 v S (5)

Ferris, R. O. (Birmingham), 1950 v S; 1951 v F; 1952 v S (3)

Finney, T. (Sunderland), 1975 v N, E (sub), S, W; 1976 v N, Y, S; (with Cambridge U), 1980 v E, Is, S, E, W, Aus (2) (14)

Fitzpatrick, J. C. (Bohemians), 1896 v E, S (2)

Flack, H. (Burnley), 1929 v S (1)

Fleming, J. G. (Nottingham F), 1987 v E (2), Is, Y; 1988

v T, Gr, Pol; 1989 v Ma, Ch; (with Manchester C), 1990 v H, Ei (11)

Forbes, G. (Limavady), 1888 v W; (with Distillery), 1891 v E, S (3)

Forde, J. T. (Ards), 1959 v Sp; 1961 v E, S, WG (4)

Foreman, T. A. (Cliftonville), 1899 v S (1)

Forsyth, J. (YMCA), 1888 v E, S (2)

Fox, W. (Ulster), 1887 v E, S (2)

Fulton, R. P. (Belfast C), 1930 v W; 1931 v E, S, W; 1932 v W, E; 1933 v E, S; 1934 v E, W, S; 1935 v E, W, S; 1936 v S, W; 1937 v E, S, W; 1938 v W (20)

Gaffikin, J. (Linfield Ath), 1890 v S, W; 1891 v S, W; 1892 v E, S, W; 1893 v E, S, W; 1894 v E, S, W; 1895 v E, W (15)

Galbraith, W. (Distillery), 1890 v W (1)

Gallagher, P. (Celtic), 1920 v E, S; 1922 v S; 1923 v S, W; 1924 v S, W; 1925 v S, W, E; (with Falkirk), 1927 v S (11)

Gallogly, C. (Huddersfield T), 1951 v E, S (2)

Gara, A. (Preston NE), 1902 v E, S, W (3)

Gardiner, A. (Cliftonville), 1930 v S, W; 1931 v S; 1932 v E, S (5)

Garrett, J. (Distillery), 1925 v W (1)

Gaston, R. (Oxford U), 1969 v Is (sub) (1)

Gaukrodger, G. (Linfield), 1895 v W (1)

Gaussen, A. W. (Moyola Park), 1884 v E, S; 1888 v E, W; 1889 v E, W (6)

Geary, J. (Glentoran), 1931 v S; 1932 v S (2)

Gibb, J. T. (Wellington Park) 1884 v S, W; 1885 v S, E, W; 1886 v S; 1887 v S, E, W; 1889 v S (10)

Gibb, T. J. (Cliftonville), 1936 v W (1)

Gibson W. K. (Cliftonville), 1894 v S, W, E; 1895 v S; 1897 v W; 1898 v S, W, E; 1901 v S, W, E; 1902 v S, W (13)

Gillespie, R. (Hertford), 1886 v E, S, W; 1887 v E, S, W (6)

Gillespie, W. (Sheffield U), 1913 v E, S; 1914 v E, W; 1920 v S, W; 1921 v E; 1922 v E, S, W; 1923 v E, S, W; 1924 v E, S, W; 1925 v E, S; 1926 v S, W; 1927 v E, W; 1928 v E; 1929 v E; 1931 v E (25)

Gillespie, W. (West Down), 1889 v W (1)

Goodall, A. L. (Derby Co), 1899 v S, W; 1900 v E, W; 1901 v E; 1902 v S; 1903 v E, W; (with Glossop), 1904 v E, W (10)

Goodbody, M. F. (Dublin University), 1889 v E; 1891 v W (2)

Gordon, H. (Linfield), 1891 v S; 1892 v E, S, W; 1893 v E, S, W; 1895 v E, W; 1896 v E, S (11)

Gordon, T. (Linfield), 1894 v W; 1895 v E (2)

Gorman, W. C. (Brentford), 1947 v E, S, W; 1948 v W (4)

Gowdy, J. (Glentoran), 1920 v E; (with Queen's Island), 1924 v W; (with Falkirk), 1926 v E, S; 1927 v E, S (6)

Gowdy, W. A. (Hull C), 1932 v S; (with Sheffield W), 1933 v S; (with Linfield), 1935 v E, S, W; (with Hibernian), 1936 v W (6)

Graham, W. G. L. (Doncaster R), 1951 v W, F; 1952 v E, S, W; 1953 v S, F; 1954 v E, W; 1955 v S, W; 1956 v E, S; 1959 v E (14)

Greer, W. (QPR), 1909 v E, S, W (3)

Gregg, H. (Doncaster R), 1954 v W; 1957 v E, S, W, I, P (2); 1958 v E, I; (with Manchester U), 1958 v Cz, Arg, WG, F, W; 1959 v E, W; 1960 v S, E, W; 1961 v E, S; 1962 v S, Gr; 1964 v S, E (25)

Hall, G. (Distillery), 1897 v E (1)

Halligan, W. (Derby Co), 1911 v W; (with Wolverhampton W), 1912 v E (2)

Hamill, M. (Manchester U), 1912 v E; 1914 v E, S; (with Belfast C), 1920 v E, S, W; (with Manchester C), 1921 v S (7)

Hamilton, B. (Linfield), 1969 v T; 1971 v Cy (2), E, S, W; (with Ipswich T), 1972 v USSR (1+1 sub), Sp; 1973 v

842

v E, S, W; 1904 v E, S, W; 1905 v E, S, W; (with Chelsea), 1906 v E, S, W; 1907 v W; (with Clyde), 1909 v S (17)

Lacey, W. (Everton), 1909 v E, S, W; 1910 v E, S, W; 1911 v E, S, W; 1912 v E; (with Liverpool), 1913 v W; 1914 v E, S, W; 1920 v E, S, W; 1921 v E, S, W; 1922 v E, S; (with New Brighton), 1925 v E (23)

Lawther, W. I. (Sunderland), 1960 v W; 1961 v I; (with Blackburn R), 1962 v S, Ho (4)

Leatham, J. (Belfast C), 1939 v W (1)

Ledwidge, J. J. (Shelbourne), 1906 v S, W (2)

Lemon, J. (Glentoran), 1886 v W; 1888 v S; (with Belfast YMCA), 1889 v W (3)

Leslie, W. (YMCA), 1887 v E (1)

Lewis, J. (Glentoran), 1899 v S, E, W; (with Distillery), 1900 v S (4)

Little, J. (Glentoran), 1898 v W (1)

Lockhart, H. (Rossall School), 1884 v W (1)

Lockhart, N. (Linfield), 1947 v E; (with Coventry C), 1950 v W; 1951 v W; 1952 v W; (with Aston Villa), 1954 v S, E; 1955 v W; 1956 v W (8)

Lowther, R. (Glentoran), 1888 v E, S (2)

Loyal, J. (Clarence), 1891 v S (1)

Lutton, R. J. (Wolverhampton W), 1970 v S, E; (with West Ham U), 1973 v Cy (sub), S (sub), W (sub); 1974 v P (6)

Lyner, D. (Glentoran), 1920 v E, W; 1922 v S, W; (with Manchester U), 1923 v E; (with Kilmarnock), 1923 v W (6)

McAdams, W. J. (Manchester C), 1954 v W; 1955 v S; 1957 v E; 1958 v S, I; (with Bolton W), 1961 v E, S, W, I, WG (2), Gr; 1962 v E, Gr; (with Leeds U), Ho (15)

McAlery, J. M. (Cliftonville), 1882 v E, W (2)

McAlinden, J. (Belfast C), 1938 v S; 1939 v S; (with Portsmouth), 1947 v E; (with Southend U), 1949 v E (4)

McAllen, J. (Linfield), 1898 v E; 1899 v E, S, W; 1900 v E, S, W; 1901 v W; 1902 v S (9)

McAlpine, W. J. (Cliftonville), 1901 v S (1)

McArthur, A. (Distillery), 1886 v W (1)

McAuley, J. L. (Huddersfield T), 1911 v E, W; 1912 v E, S; 1913 v E, S (6)

McAuley, P. (Belfast C), 1900 v S (1)

McCabe, J. J. (Leeds U), 1949 v S, W; 1950 v E; 1951 v W; 1953 v W; 1954 v S (6)

McCabe, W. (Ulster), 1891 v E (1)

McCambridge, J. (Ballymena), 1930 v S, W; (with Cardiff C), 1931 v W; 1932 v E (4)

McCandless, J. (Bradford), 1912 v W; 1913 v W; 1920 v W, S; 1921 v E (5)

McCandless, W. (Linfield), 1920 v E, W; 1921 v E; (with Rangers), 1921 v W; 1922 v S; 1924 v W, S; 1925 v S; 1929 v W (9)

McCann, P. (Belfast C), 1910 v E, S, W; 1911 v E; (with Glentoran), 1911 v S; 1912 v E; 1913 v W (7)

McCashin, J. (Cliftonville), 1896 v W; 1898 v S, W; 1899 v S (4)

McCavana, W. T. (Coleraine), 1955 v S; 1956 v E, S (3)

McCaw, D. (Distillery), 1882 v E (1)

McCaw, J. H. (Linfield), 1927 v W; 1930 v S; 1931 v E, S, W (5)

McClatchey, J. (Distillery), 1886 v E, S, W (3)

McClatchey, R. (Distillery), 1895 v S (1)

McCleary, J. W. (Cliftonville), 1955 v W (1)

McCleery, W. (Cliftonville), 1922 v N; 1930 v E, W; 1931 v E, S, W; 1932 v S, W; 1933 v E, W (10)

McClelland, J. (Arsenal), 1961 v W, I, WG (2), Gr; (with Fulham), 1967 v M (6)

McClelland, J. (Mansfield T), 1980 v S (sub), Aus (3); 1981 v Se, S, (with Rangers), S, Se; 1982 v S, W, Y, Hon, Sp, A, F; 1983 v A, WG, Alb, T, Alb, S, E, W; 1984 v A, T, WG, S, E, W, Fi; 1985 v R, (with Watford),

Fi, Is, E, Sp, T; 1986 v T, F (sub); 1987 v E (2), T, Is, Y; 1988 v T, Gr, F, Ma; 1989 v Ei, H, Sp, Sp, Ma; (with Leeds U), 1990 v N (53)

McCluggage, A. (Bradford), 1924 v E; (with Burnley), 1927 v S, W; 1928 v S, E, W; 1929 v S, E, W; 1930 v W; 1931 v E, W (12)

McClure, G. (Cliftonville), 1907 v S, W; 1908 v E; (with Distillery), 1909 v E (4)

McConnell, E. (Cliftonville), 1904 v S, W; (with Glentoran), 1905 v S; (with Sunderland), 1906 v E; 1907 v E; 1908 v S, W; (with Sheffield W), 1909 v S, W; 1910 v S, W, E (12)

McConnell, P. (Doncaster R), 1928 v W; (with Southport), 1932 v E (2)

McConnell, W. G. (Bohemians), 1912 v W; 1913 v E, S; 1914 v E, S, W (6)

McConnell, W. H. (Reading), 1925 v E, W; 1926 v E, W; 1927 v E, S, W; 1928 v E, W (8)

McCourt, F. J. (Manchester C), 1952 v E, W; 1953 v E, S, W, F (6)

McCoy, J. (Distillery), 1896 v W (1)

McCoy, R. (Coleraine), 1987 v T (sub) (1)

McCracken, R. (C Palace), 1921 v E; 1922 v E, S, W (4)

McCracken, W. (Distillery), 1902 v E, W; 1903 v E; 1904 v E, S, W; (with Newcastle U), 1905 v E, S, W; 1907 v E; 1920 v E; 1922 v E, S, W; (with Hull C), 1923 v S (15)

McCreery, D. (Manchester U), 1976 v S (sub), E, W; 1977 v Ho, Bel, WG, E, S, W, Ic; 1978 v Ic, Ho, Bel, S, E, W; 1979 v Ei, D, Bul, E, Bul, W, D; (with QPR), 1980 v E, Ei, S (sub), E (sub), W (sub), Aus (1+sub); 1981 v Se (sub), P (sub); (with Tulsa R), S, P, Se; 1982 v S, Is, E (sub), F, Y, Hon, Sp, A; 1984 v T (sub); 1985 v R, Sp (sub); 1986 v T (sub), R, E, F, D, Alg, Sp, Br; 1987 v T, E, Y; 1988 v Y; 1989 v Sp, Ma, Ch; (with Hearts), 1990 v H, Ei, N, U (sub) (67)

McCrory, S. (Southend U), 1958 v E (1)

McCullough, K. (Belfast C), 1935 v W; 1936 v E; (with Manchester C), 1936 v S; 1937 v E, S (5)

McCullough, W. J. (Arsenal), 1961 v I; 1963 v Sp; 1964 v S, E, W, U, Sp; 1965 v E, Sw; (with Millwall), 1967 v E (10)

McCurdy, C. (Linfield), 1980 v Aus (sub) (1)

McDonald, A. (QPR), 1986 v R, E, F, D, Mor, Alg, Sp, Br; 1987 v E (2), T, Is, Y; 1988 v Y, T, Pol, F, Ma; 1989 v Ei, H, Sp, Ch; 1990 v H, Ei, U (25)

McDonald, R. (Glasgow R), 1930 v S; 1932 v E (2)

McDonnell, J. (Bohemians), 1911 v E, S; 1912 v W; 1913 v W (4)

McElhinney, G. (Bolton W), 1984 v WG, S, E, W, Fi; 1985 v R (6)

McFaul, W. S. (Linfield), 1967 v E (sub); (with Newcastle U), 1970 v W; 1971 v Sp; 1972 v USSR; 1973 v Cy; 1974 v Bul (6)

McGarry, J. K. (Cliftonville), 1951 v W, F, S (3)

McGaughey, M. (Linfield), 1985 v Is (sub) (1)

McGee, G. (Wellington Park), 1885 v E, S, W (3)

McGrath, R. C. (Tottenham H), 1974 v S, E, W; 1975 v N; 1976 v Is (sub); 1977 v Ho (with Manchester U), Bel, WG, E, S, W, Ic; 1978 v Ic, Ho, Bel, S, E, W; 1979 v Bul (sub), E (sub), E (sub) (21)

McGregor, S. (Glentoran), 1921 v S (1)

McGrillen, J. (Clyde), 1924 v S; (with Belfast C), 1927 v S (2)

McGuire, E. (Distillery), 1907 v S (1)

McIlroy, H. (Cliftonville), 1906 v E (1)

McIlroy, J. (Burnley), 1952 v E, S, W; 1953 v E, S, W; 1954 v S, W; 1955 v E, S; 1956 v E, S, W; 1957 v E, S, W, I, P (2); 1958 v E, S, W, I (2), Cz (2), Arg, WG, F; 1959 v E, S, W, Sp; 1960 v E, S, W; 1961 v E, W, WG (2), Gr; 1962 v E, S, Gr, Ho; 1963 v E, S, Pol (2); (with Stoke C), 1963 v W; 1966 v S, E, Alb (55)

McIlroy, S. B. (Manchester U), 1972 v Sp, S (sub); 1974

v S, E, W; 1975 v N, Se, Y, E, S, W; 1976 v Se, N, Y, S, E, W; 1977 v Ho, Bel, E, S, W, Ic; 1978 v Ic, Ho, Bel, S, E, W; 1979 v Ei, D, Bul, E, Bul, E, S, W, D; 1980 v E, Ei, Is, S, E, W; 1981 v Se, P, S, P, S, Se; 1982 v S, Is; (with Stoke C), E, F, S, W, Y, Hon, Sp, A, F; 1983 v A, WG, Alb, T, Alb, S, E, W; 1984 v A, T, S, E, W, Fi; 1985 v Fi, E, T; (with Manchester C), 1986 v T, R, E, F, D, Mor, Alg, Sp, Br; 1987 v E (sub) (88)

McIlvenny, J. (Distillery), 1890 v E; 1891 v E (2)

McIlvenny, P. (Distillery), 1924 v W (1)

McKeag, W. (Glentoran), 1968 v S, W (2)

McKee, F. W. (Cliftonville), 1906 v S, W; (with Belfast C), 1914 v E, S, W (5)

McKelvie, H. (Glentoran), 1901 v W (1)

McKenna, J. (Huddersfield), 1950 v E, S, W; 1951 v E, S, F; 1952 v E (7)

McKenzie, H. (Distillery), 1923 v S (1)

McKenzie, R. (Airdrie), 1967 v W (1)

McKeown, H. (Linfield), 1892 v E, S, W; 1893 v S, W; 1894 v S, W (7)

McKie, H. (Cliftonville), 1895 v E, S, W (3)

McKinney, D. (Hull C), 1921 v S; (with Bradford C), 1924 v S (2)

McKinney, V. J. (Falkirk), 1966 v WG (1)

McKnight, A. (Celtic), 1988 v Y, T, Gr, Pol, F, Ma; 1989 (with West Ham U) v Ei, H, Sp, Sp (10)

McKnight, J. (Preston NE), 1912 v S; (with Glentoran), 1913 v S (2)

McLaughlin, J. C. (Shrewsbury T), 1962 v E, S, W, Gr; 1963 v W; (with Swansea T), 1964 v W, U; 1965 v E, W, Sw (2); 1966 v W (12)

McLean, T. (Limavady), 1885 v S (1)

McMahon, J. (Bohemians), 1934 v S (1)

McMaster, G. (Glentoran), 1897 v E, S, W (3)

McMichael, A. (Newcastle U), 1950 v E, S; 1951 v E, S, F; 1952 v E, S, W; 1953 v E, S, W, F; 1954 v E, S, W; 1955 v E, W; 1956 v W; 1957 v E, S, W, I, P (2); 1958 v E, S, W, I (2), Cz (2), Arg, WG, F; 1959 v S, W, Sp; 1960 v E, S, W (40)

McMillan, G. (Distillery), 1903 v E; 1905 v W (2)

McMillan, S. (Manchester U), 1963 v E, S (2)

McMillen, W. S. (Manchester U), 1934 v E; 1935 v S; 1937 v S; (with Chesterfield), 1938 v S, W; 1939 v E, S (7)

McMordie, A. S. (Middlesbrough), 1969 v Is, T (2), E, S, W; 1970 v E, S, W, USSR; 1971 v Cy (2), E, S, W; 1972 v USSR, Sp, E, S, W; 1973 v Bul (21)

McMorran, E. J. (Belfast C), 1947 v E; (with Barnsley), 1951 v E, S, W; 1952 v E, S, W; 1953 v E, S, F; (with Doncaster R), 1953 v W; 1954 v E; 1956 v W; 1957 v I, P (15)

McMullan, D. (Liverpool), 1926 v E, W; 1927 v S (3)

McNally, B. A. (Shrewsbury T), 1986 v Mor; 1987 v T (sub); 1988 v Y, Gr, Ma (sub) (5)

McNinch, J. (Ballymena), 1931 v S; 1932 v S, W (3)

McParland, P. J. (Aston Villa), 1954 v W; 1955 v E, S; 1956 v E, S; 1957 v E, S, W, P; 1958 v E, S, W, I (2), Cz (2), Arg, WG, F; 1959 v E, S, W, Sp; 1960 v E, S, W; 1961 v E, S, W, I, WG (2), Gr; (with Wolverhampton W), 1962 v Ho (34)

McShane, J. (Cliftonville), 1899 v S; 1900 v E, S, W (4)

McVickers, J. (Glentoran), 1888 v E; 1889 v S (2)

McWha, W. B. R. (Knock), 1882 v E, W; (with Cliftonville), 1883 v E, W; 1884 v E; 1885 v E, W (7)

Macartney, A. (Ulster), 1903 v S, W; (with Linfield), 1904 v S, W; (with Everton), 1905 v E, S; (with Belfast C), 1907 v E, S, W; 1908 v E, S, W; (with Glentoran), 1909 v E, S, W (15)

Mackie, J. (Arsenal), 1923 v W; (with Portsmouth), 1935 v S, W (3)

Madden, O. (Norwich C), 1938 v E (1)

Magill, E. J. (Arsenal), 1962 v E, S, Gr; 1963 v E, S, W, Pol (2), Sp; 1964 v E, S, W, U, Sp; 1965 v E, S, Sw (2),

Ho, Alb; 1966 v S, E; (with Brighton), 1966 v Alb, W, WG, M (26)

Maginnis, H. (Linfield), 1900 v E, S, W; 1903 v S, W; 1904 v E, S, W (8)

Maguire, E. (Distillery), 1907 v S (1)

Mahood, J. (Belfast C), 1926 v S; 1928 v E, S, W; 1929 v E, S, W; 1930 v W; (with Ballymena), 1934 v S (9)

Manderson, R. (Glasgow R), 1920 v W, S; 1925 v S, E; 1926 v S (5)

Mansfield, J. (Dublin Freebooters), 1901 v E (1)

Martin, C. J. (Glentoran), 1947 v S; (with Leeds U), 1948 v E, S, W; (with Aston Villa), 1949 v E; 1950 v W (6)

Martin, D. (Bo'ness), 1925 v S (1)

Martin, D. C. (Cliftonville), 1882 v E, W; 1883 v E (3)

Martin, Đ. K. (Belfast C), 1934 v E, S, W; 1935 v S; (with Wolverhampton W), 1935 v E; 1936 v W; (with Nottingham F), 1937 v S; 1938 v E, S; 1939 v S (10)

Mathieson, A. (Luton T), 1921 v W; 1922 v E (2)

Maxwell, J. (Linfield), 1902 v W; 1903 v W, E; (with Glentoran), 1905 v W, S; (with Belfast C), 1906 v W; 1907 v S (7)

Meek, H. L. (Glentoran), 1925 v W (1)

Mehaffy, J. A. C. (Queen's Island), 1922 v W (1)

Meldon, J. (Dublin Freebooters), 1899 v S, W (2)

Mercer, H. V. A. (Linfield), 1908 v E (1)

Mercer, J. T. (Distillery), 1898 v E, S, W; 1899 v E; (with Linfield), 1902 v E, W; (with Distillery), 1903 v S, W; (with Derby Co), 1904 v E, W; 1905 v S (11)

Millar, W. (Barrow), 1932 v W; 1933 v S (2)

Miller, J. (Middlesbrough), 1929 v W, S; 1930 v E (3)

Milligan, D. (Chesterfield), 1939 v W (1)

Milne, R. G. (Linfield), 1894 v E, S, W; 1895 v E, W; 1896 v E, S, W; 1897 v E, S; 1898 v E, S, W; 1899 v E, W; 1901 v W; 1902 v E, S, W; 1903 v E, S; 1904 v E, S, W; 1906 v E, S, W (27)

Mitchell, C. (Glentoran), 1934 v W (1)

Mitchell, E. J. (Cliftonville), 1933 v S (1)

Mitchell, W. (Distillery), 1932 v E, W; 1933 v E, W; (with Chelsea), 1934 v W, S; 1935 v S, E; 1936 v S, E; 1937 v E, S, W; 1938 v E, S (15)

Molyneux, T. B. (Ligoniel), 1883 v E, W; (with Cliftonville), 1884 v E, W; 1885 v E; 1886 v E, W, S; 1888 v S (11)

Montgomery, F. J. (Coleraine), 1955 v E (1)

Moore, C. (Glentoran), 1949 v W (1)

Moore, J. (Linfield Ath), 1891 v E, S, W (3)

Moore, P. (Aberdeen), 1933 v E (1)

Moore, T. (Ulster), 1887 v S, W (2)

Moore, W. (Falkirk), 1923 v S (1)

Moorhead, F. W. (Dublin University), 1885 v E (1)

Moorhead, G. (Linfield), 1923 v S; 1928 v S; 1929 v S (3)

Moran, J. (Leeds C), 1912 v S (1)

Moreland, V. (Derby Co), 1979 v Bul (sub), Bul (sub), E, S; 1980 v E, Ei (6)

Morgan, F. G. (Linfield), 1923 v E; (with Nottingham F), 1924 v S; 1927 v E; 1928 v E, S, W; 1929 v E (7)

Morgan, S. (Port Vale), 1972 v Sp; 1973 v Bul (sub), P, Cy, E, S, W; (with Aston Villa), 1974 v Bul, P, S, E; 1975 v Se; 1976 v Se (sub), N, Y; (with Brighton & HA), S, W (sub); (with Sparta Rotterdam), 1979 v D (18)

Morrison, J. (Linfield Ath), 1891 v E, W (2)

Morrison, T. (Glentoran), 1895 v E, S, W; (with Burnley), 1899 v W; 1900 v W; 1902 v E, S (7)

Morrogh, E. (Bohemians), 1896 v S (1)

Morrow, S. J. (Arsenal), 1990 v U (sub) (1)

Morrow, W. J. (Moyola Park), 1883 v E, W; 1884 v S (3)

Muir, R. (Oldpark), 1885 v S, W (2)

Mullan, G. (Glentoran), 1983 v S, E, W, Alb (sub) (4)

Mulholland, S. (Celtic), 1906 v S, E (2)

Mulligan, J. (Manchester C), 1921 v S (1)

Murphy, J. (Bradford C), 1910 v E, S, W (3)

Murphy, N. (QPR), 1905 v E, S, W (3)

844

Murray, J. M. (Motherwell), 1910 v E, S; (with Sheffield W), 1910 v W (3)

Napier, R. J. (Bolton W), 1966 v WG (1)

Neill, W. J. T. (Arsenal), 1961 v I, Gr, WG; 1962 v E, S, W, Gr; 1963 v E, W, Pol, Sp; 1964 v S, E, W, U, Sp; 1965 v E, S, W, Sw, Ho (2), Alb; 1966 v S, E, W, Alb, WG, M; 1967 v S, W; 1968 v S, E; 1969 v E, S, W, Is, T (2); 1970 v S, E, W, USSR (2); (with Hull C), 1971 v Cy, Sp; 1972 v USSR (2), Sp, S, E, W; 1973 v Bul, Cy (2), P, E, S, W (59)

Nelis, P. (Nottingham F), 1923 v E (1)

Nelson, S. (Arsenal), 1970 v W, E (sub); 1971 v Cy, Sp, E, S, W; 1972 v USSR (2), Sp, E, S, W; 1973 v Bul, Cy, P; 1974 v S, E; 1975 v Se, Y; 1976 v Se, N, Is, E; 1977 v Bel (sub), WG, W, Ic; 1978 v Ic, Ho, Bel; 1979 v Ei, D, Bul, E, Bul, E, S, W, D; 1980 v E, Ei, Is; 1981 v S, P, S, Se; (with Brighton & HA), 1982 v E, S, Sp (sub), A (51)

Nicholl, C. J. (Aston Villa), 1975 v Se, Y, E, S, W; 1976 v Se, N, Y, S, E, W; 1977 v W; (with Southampton), 1978 v Bel (sub), S, E, W; 1979 v Ei, Bul, E, Bul, E, W; 1980 v Ei, Is, S, E, W, Aus (3); 1981 v Se, P, S, P, S, Se; 1982 v S, Is, E, F, W, Y, Hon, Sp, A, F; 1983 v S (sub), E, W; (with Grimsby T), 1984 v A, T (51)

Nicholl, H. (Belfast C), 1902 v E, W; 1905 v E (3)

Nicholl, J. M. (Manchester U), 1976 v Is, W (sub); 1977 v Ho, Bel, E, S, W, Ic; 1978 v Ic, Ho, Bel, S, E, W; 1979 v Ei, D, Bul, E, Bul, E, S, W, D; 1980 v E, Ei, Is, S, E, W, Aus (3); 1981 v Se, P, S, P, S, Se; 1982 v S, Is, E; (with Toronto B), F, W, Y, Hon, Sp, A, F; (with Sunderland), 1983 v A, WG, Alb, T, Alb, (with Toronto B), S, E, W; (with Rangers), 1984 v T, WG, S, E, (with Toronto B), Fi; 1985 v R, (with WBA) Fi, E, Sp, T; 1986 v T, R, E, F, Alg, Sp, Br (73)

Nicholson, J. J. (Manchester U), 1961 v S, W; 1962 v E, W, Gr, Ho; 1963 v E, S, Pol (2); (with Huddersfield T), 1965 v W, Ho (2), Alb; 1966 v S, E, W, Alb, M; 1967 v S, W; 1968 v S, E, W; 1969 v S, E, W, T (2); 1970 v S, E, W, USSR (2); 1971 v Cy (2), E, S, W; 1972 v USSR (2) (41)

Nixon, R. (Linfield), 1914 v S (1)

Nolan-Whelan, J. V. (Dublin Freebooters), 1901 v E, W; 1902 v S, W (4)

O'Brien, M. T. (QPR), 1921 v S; (with Leicester C), 1922 v S, W; 1924 v S, W; (with Hull C), 1925 v S, E, W; 1926 v W; (with Derby Co), 1927 v W (10)

O'Connell, P. (Sheffield W), 1912 v E, S; (with Hull C), 1914 v E, S, W (5)

O'Doherty, A. (Coleraine), 1970 v E, W (sub) (2)

O'Driscoll, J. F. (Swansea T), 1949 v E, S, W (3)

O'Hagan, C. (Tottenham H), 1905 v S, W; 1906 v S, W, E; (with Aberdeen), 1907 v E, S, W; 1908 v S, W; 1909 v E (11)

O'Hagan, W. (St Mirren), 1920 v E, W (2)

O'Hehir, J. C. (Bohemians), 1910 v W (1)

O'Kane, W. J. (Nottingham F), 1970 v E, W, S (sub); 1971 v Sp, E, S, W; 1972 v USSR (2); 1973 v P, Cy; 1974 v Bul, P, S, E, W; 1975 v N, Se, E, S (20)

O'Mahoney, M. T. (Bristol R), 1939 v S (1)

O'Neill, C. (Motherwell), 1989 Ch (sub); 1990 v Ei (sub) (2)

O'Neill, J. (Leicester C), 1980 v Is, S, E, W, Aus (3); 1981 v P, S, P, S, Se; 1982 v S, Is, E, F, S, F (sub); 1983 v A, WG, Alb, T, Alb, S; 1984 v S (sub); 1985 v Is, Fi, E, Sp, T; 1986 v T, R, E, F, D, Mor, Alg, Sp, Br (39)

O'Neill, J. (Sunderland), 1962 v W (1)

O'Neill, M. A. (Newcastle U), 1988 v Gr, Pol, F, Ma; 1989 v Ei, H, Sp (sub), Sp (sub), Ma (sub), Ch; (with Dundee U), 1990 v H (sub), Ei (12)

O'Neill, M. H. (Distillery), 1972 v USSR (sub), (with Nottingham F), Sp (sub), W (sub); 1973 v P, Cy, E, S, W;

1974 v Bul, P, E (sub), W; 1975 v Se, Y, E, S; 1976 v Y; 1977 v E (sub), S; 1978 v Ic, Ho, S, E, W; 1979 v Ei, D, Bul, E, Bul, D; 1980 v Ei, Is, Aus (3); 1981 v Se, P (with Norwich C), P, S, Se; (with Manchester C), 1982 v S (with Norwich C), E, F, S, Y, Hon, Sp, A, F; 1983 v A, WG, Alb, T, Alb, S, E; (with Notts Co), 1984 v A, T, WG, E, W, Fi; 1985 v R, Fi (64)

O'Reilly, H. (Dublin Freebooters), 1901 v S, W; 1904 v S (3)

Parke, J. (Linfield), 1964 v S; (with Hibernian), 1964 v E, Sp; (with Sunderland), 1965 v Sw, S, W, Ho (2), Alb; 1966 v WG; 1967 v E, S; 1968 v S, E (14)

Peacock, R. (Celtic), 1952 v S; 1953 v F; 1954 v W; 1955 v E, S; 1956 v E, S; 1957 v W, I, P; 1958 v S, E, W, I (2), Arg, Cz (2), WG; 1959 v E, S, W; 1960 v S, E; 1961 v E, S, I, WG (2), Gr; (with Coleraine), 1962 v S (31)

Peden, J. (Linfield), 1887 v S, W; 1888 v W, E; 1889 v S, E; 1890 v W, S; 1891 v W, E; 1892 v W, E; 1893 v E, S, W; (with Distillery), 1896 v W, E, S; 1897 v W, S; 1898 v W, E, S; (with Linfield), 1899 v W (24)

Penney, S. (Brighton & HA), 1985 v Is; 1986 v T, R, E, F, D, Mor, Alg, Sp; 1987 v E, T, Is; 1988 v Pol, F, Ma; 1989 v Ei, Sp (17)

Percy, J. C. (Belfast YMCA), 1889 v W (1)

Platt, J. A. (Middlesbrough), 1976 v Is (sub); 1978 v S, E, W; 1980 v S, E, W, Aus (3); 1981 v Se, P; 1982 v F, S, W (sub), A; 1983 v A, WG, Alb, T; (with Ballymena U), 1984 v E, W (sub); (with Coleraine), 1986 v Mor (sub) (23)

Ponsonby, J. (Distillery), 1895 v S; 1896 v E, S, W; 1897 v E, S, W; 1899 v E (8)

Potts, R. M. C. (Cliftonville), 1883 v E, W (2)

Priestley, T. J. (Coleraine), 1933 v S; (with Chelsea), 1934 v E (2)

Pyper, Jas. (Cliftonville), 1897 v S, W; 1898 v S, E, W; 1899 v S; 1900 v E (7)

Pyper, John (Cliftonville), 1897 v E, S, W; 1899 v E, W; 1900 v E, W, S; 1902 v S (9)

Pyper, M. (Linfield), 1932 v W (1)

Quinn, J. M. (Blackburn R), 1985 v Is, Fi, E, Sp, T; 1986 v T, R, E, F, D (sub), Mor (sub); 1987 v E (sub), T; (with Swindon T), 1988 v Y (sub), T, Gr, Pol, F (sub), Ma; 1989 (with Leicester C) v Ei, H (sub), Sp (sub), Sp (with Bradford C), Ma, Ch; 1990 v H (with West Ham U), N (27)

Rafferty, P. (Linfield), 1980 v E (sub) (1)

Ramsey, P. (Leicester C), 1984 v A, WG, S; 1985 v Is, E, Sp, T; 1986 v T, Mor; 1987 v Is, E, Y (sub); 1988 v Y; 1989 v Sp (14)

Rankine, J. (Alexander), 1883 v E, W (2)

Raper, E. O. (Dublin University), 1886 v W (1)

Rattray, D. (Avoniel), 1882 v E; 1883 v E, W (3)

Rea, B. (Glentoran), 1901 v E (1)

Redmond, J. (Cliftonville), 1884 v W (1)

Reid, G. H. (Cardiff C), 1923 v S (1)

Reid, J. (Ulster), 1883 v E; 1884 v W; 1887 v S; 1889 v W; 1890 v S, W (6)

Reid, S. E. (Derby Co), 1934 v E, W; 1936 v E (3)

Reid, W. (Hearts), 1931 v E (1)

Reilly, J. (Portsmouth), 1900 v E; 1902 v E (2)

Renneville, W. T. (Leyton), 1910 v S, E, W; (with Aston Villa), 1911 v W (4)

Reynolds, J. (Distillery), 1890 v E, W; (with Ulster), 1891 v E, S, W (5)

Reynolds, R. (Bohemians), 1905 v W (1)

Rice, P. J. (Arsenal), 1969 v Is; 1970 v USSR; 1971 v E, S, W; 1972 v USSR, Sp, E, S, W; 1973 v Bul, Cy, E, S, W; 1974 v Bul, P, S, E, W; 1975 v N, Y, E, S, W; 1976 v Se, N, Y, Is, S, E, W; 1977 v Ho, Bel, WG, E, S, Ic;

1978 v Ic, Ho, Bel; 1979 v Ei, D, E (2), S, W, D; 1980 v E (49)

Roberts, F. C. (Glentoran), 1931 v S (1)

Robinson, P. (Distillery), 1920 v S; (with Blackburn R), 1921 v W (2)

Rogan, A. (Celtic), 1988 v Y (sub), Gr, Pol (sub); 1989 v Ei (sub), H, Sp, Sp, Ma (sub), Ch; 1990 v H, N (sub), U (12)

Rollo, D. (Linfield), 1912 v W; 1913 v W; 1914 v W, E; (with Blackburn R), 1920 v S, W; 1921 v E, S, W; 1922 v E; 1923 v E; 1924 v S, W; 1925 v W; 1926 v E; 1927 v E (16)

Rosbotham, A. (Cliftonville), 1887 v E, S, W; 1888 v E, S, W; 1889 v E (7)

Ross, W. E. (Newcastle U), 1969 v Is (1)

Rowley, R. W. M. (Southampton), 1929 v S, W; 1930 v W, E; (with Tottenham H), 1931 v W; 1932 v S (6)

Russell, A. (Linfield), 1947 v E (1)

Russell, S. R. (Bradford C), 1930 v E, S; (with Derry C), 1932 v E (3)

Ryan, R. A. (WBA), 1950 v W (1)

Sanchez, L. P. (Wimbledon), 1987 v T (sub); 1989 v Sp, Ma (3)

Scott, E. (Liverpool), 1920 v S; 1921 v E, S, W; 1922 v E; 1925 v W; 1926 v E, S, W; 1927 v E, S, W; 1928 v E, S, W; 1929 v E, S, W; 1930 v E; 1931 v E; 1932 v W; 1933 v E, S, W; 1934 v E, S, W; (with Belfast C), 1935 v S; 1936 v E, S, W (31)

Scott, J. (Grimsby), 1958 v Cz, F (2)

Scott, J. E. (Cliftonville), 1901 v S (1)

Scott, L. J. (Dublin University), 1895 v S, W (2)

Scott, P. W. (Everton), 1975 v W; 1976 v Y; (with York C), Is, S, E (sub), W; 1978 v S, E, W; (with Aldershot), 1979 v S (sub) (10)

Scott, T. (Cliftonville), 1894 v E, S; 1895 v S, W; 1896 v S, E, W; 1897 v E, W; 1898 v E, S, W; 1900 v W (13)

Scott, W. (Linfield), 1903 v E, S, W; 1904 v E, S, W; (with Everton), 1905 v E, S; 1907 v E, S; 1908 v E, S, W; 1909 v E, S, W; 1910 v E, S; 1911 v E, S, W; 1912 v E; (with Leeds City), 1913 v E, S, W (25)

Scraggs, M. J. (Glentoran), 1921 v W; 1922 v E (2)

Seymour, H. C. (Bohemians), 1914 v W (1)

Seymour, J. (Cliftonville), 1907 v W; 1909 v W (2)

Shanks, T. (Woolwich Arsenal), 1903 v S; 1904 v W; (with Brentford), 1905 v E (3)

Sharkey, P. (Ipswich T), 1976 v S (1)

Sheehan, Dr G. (Bohemians), 1899 v S; 1900 v E, W (3)

Sheridan, J. (Everton), 1903 v W, E, S; 1904 v E, S; (with Stoke C), 1905 v E (6)

Sherrard, J. (Limavady), 1885 v S; 1887 v W; 1888 v W (3)

Sherrard, W. (Cliftonville), 1895 v E, W, S (3)

Sherry, J. J. (Bohemians), 1906 v E; 1907 v W (2)

Shields, J. (Southampton), 1957 v S (1)

Silo, M. (Belfast YMCA), 1888 v E (1)

Simpson, W. J. (Glasgow R), 1951 v W, F; 1954 v E, S; 1955 v E; 1957 v I, P; 1958 v S, E, W, I; 1959 v S (12)

Sinclair, J. (Knock), 1882 v E, W (2)

Slemin, J. C. (Bohemians), 1909 v W (1)

Sloan, A. S. (London Caledonians), 1925 v W (1)

Sloan, D. (Oxford U), 1969 v Is; 1971 v Sp (2)

Sloan, H. A. de B. (Bohemians), 1903 v E; 1904 v S; 1905 v E; 1906 v W; 1907 v E, W; 1908 v W; 1909 v S (8)

Sloan, J. W. (Arsenal), 1947 v W (1)

Sloan, T. (Cardiff C), 1926 v S, W, E; 1927 v W, S; 1928 v E, W; 1929 v E; (with Linfield), 1930 v W, S; 1931 v S (11)

Sloan, T. (Manchester U), 1979 v S, W (sub), D (sub) (3)

Small, J. (Clarence), 1887 v E (1)

Small, J. M. (Cliftonville), 1893 v E, S, W (3)

Smith, E. E. (Cardiff C), 1921 v S; 1923 v W, E; 1924 v E (4)

Smith, J. (Distillery), 1901 v S, W (2)

Smyth, R. H. (Dublin University), 1886 v W (1)

Smyth, S. (Wolverhampton W), 1948 v E, S, W; 1949 v S, W; 1950 v E, S, W; (with Stoke C), 1952 v E (9)

Smyth, W. (Distillery), 1949 v E, S; 1954 v S, E (4)

Snape, A. (Airdrie), 1920 v E (1)

Spence, D. W. (Bury), 1975 v Y, E, S, W; 1976 v Se, Is, E, W, S (sub); (with Blackpool), 1977 v Ho (sub), WG (sub), E (sub), S (sub), W (sub), Ic (sub); 1979 v Ei, D (sub), E (sub), Bul (sub), E (sub), S, W, D; 1980 v Ei; (with Southend U), Is (sub), Aus (sub); 1981 v S (sub), Se (sub); 1982 v F (sub) (29)

Spencer, S. (Distillery), 1890 v E, S; 1892 v E, S, W; 1893 v E (6)

Spiller, E. A. (Cliftonville), 1883 v E, W; 1884 v E, W, S (5)

Stanfield, O. M. (Distillery), 1887 v E, S, W; 1888 v E, S, W; 1889 v E, S, W; 1890 v E, S; 1891 v E, S, W; 1892 v E, S, W; 1893 v E, S, W; 1894 v E, S, W; 1895 v E, S; 1896 v E, S, W; 1897 v E, S, W (30)

Steele, A. (Charlton Ath), 1926 v W, S; (with Fulham), 1929 v W, S (4)

Stevenson, A. E. (Rangers), 1934 v E, S, W; (with Everton), 1935 v E, S; 1936 v S, W; 1937 v E, W; 1938 v E, W; 1939 v E, S, W; 1947 v S, W; 1948 v S (17)

Stewart, A. (Glentoran), 1967 v W; 1968 v S, E; (with Derby Co), 1968 v W; 1969 v Is, T (1+1 sub) (7)

Stewart, D. C. (Hull C), 1978 v Bel (1)

Stewart, I. (QPR), 1982 v F (sub); 1983 v A, WG, Alb, T, Alb, S, E, W; 1984 v A, T, WG, S, E, W, Fi; 1985 v R, Fi, Is, E, Sp, T; (with Newcastle U), 1986 v R, E, D, Mor, Alg (sub), Sp (sub), Br; 1987 v E, Is (sub) (31)

Stewart, R. H. (St Columb's Court), 1890 v E, S, W; (with Cliftonville), 1892 v E, S, W; 1893 v E, W; 1894 v E, S, W (11)

Stewart, T. C. (Linfield), 1961 v W (1)

Swan, S. (Linfield), 1899 v S (1)

Taggart, G. P. (Barnsley), 1990 v N, U (2)

Taggart, J. (Walsall), 1899 v W (1)

Thompson, F. W. (Cliftonville), 1910 v E, S, W; (with Bradford C), 1911 v E; (with Linfield), v W; 1912 v E, W; 1913 v E, S, W; (with Clyde), 1914 v E, S (12)

Thompson, J. (Distillery), 1897 v S (1)

Thompson, J. (Belfast Ath), 1889 v S (1)

Thunder, P. J. (Bohemians), 1911 v W (1)

Todd, S. J. (Burnley), 1966 v M (sub); 1967 v E; 1968 v W; 1969 v E, S, W; 1970 v S, USSR; (with Sheffield W), 1971 v Cy (2), Sp (sub) (11)

Toner, J. (Arsenal), 1922 v W; 1923 v W; 1924 v W, E; 1925 v E, S; (with St Johnstone), 1927 v E, S (8)

Torrans, R. (Linfield), 1893 v S (1)

Torrans, S. (Linfield), 1889 v S; 1890 v S, W; 1891 v S, W; 1892 v E, S, W; 1893 v E, S; 1894 v E, S, W; 1895 v E; 1896 v E, S, W; 1897 v E, S, W; 1898 v E, S; 1899 v E, W; 1901 v S, W (26)

Trainor, D. (Crusaders), 1967 v W (1)

Tully, C. P. (Glasgow C), 1949 v E; 1950 v E; 1952 v S; 1953 v E, S, W, F; 1954 v S; 1956 v E; 1959 v Sp (10)

Turner, E. (Cliftonville), 1896 v E, W (2)

Turner, W. (Cliftonville), 1886 v E; 1886 v S; 1888 v S (3)

Twoomey, J. F. (Leeds U), 1938 v W; 1939 v E (2)

Uprichard, W. N. M. C. (Swindon T), 1952 v E, S, W; 1953 v E, S; (with Portsmouth), 1953 v W, F; 1955 v E, S, W; 1956 v E, S, W; 1958 v S, I, Cz; 1959 v S, Sp (18)

Vernon, J. (Belfast C), 1947 v E, S; (with WBA), 1947 v W; 1948 v E, S, W; 1949 v E, S, W; 1950 v E, S; 1951 v E, S, W, F; 1952 v S, E (17)

Waddell, T. M. R. (Cliftonville), 1906 v S (1)

Walker, J. (Doncaster R), 1955 v W (1)

Walker, T. (Bury), 1911 v S (1)

Walsh, D. J. (WBA), 1947 v S, W; 1948 v E, S, W; 1949 v E, S, W; 1950 v W (9)
Walsh, W. (Manchester C), 1948 v E, S, W; 1949 v E, S (5)
Waring, R. (Distillery), 1899 v E (1)
Warren, P. (Shelbourne), 1913 v E, S (2)
Watson, J. (Ulster), 1883 v E, W; 1886 v E, S, W; 1887 v S, W; 1889 v E, W (9)
Watson, P. (Distillery), 1971 v Cy (sub) (1)
Watson, T. (Cardiff C), 1926 v S (1)
Wattle, J. (Distillery), 1899 v E (1)
Webb, C. G. (Brighton), 1909 v S, W; 1911 v S (3)
Weir, E. (Clyde), 1939 v W (1)
Welsh, E. (Carlisle U), 1966 v W, WG, M; 1967 v W (4)
Whiteside, N. (Manchester U), 1982 v Y, Hon, Sp, A, F; 1983 v WG, Alb, T; 1984 v A, T, WG, S, E, W, Fi; 1985 v R, Fi, Is, E, Sp, T; 1986 v R, E, F, D, Mor, Alg, Sp, Br; 1987 v E (2), Is, Y; 1988 v T, Pol, F; (with Everton), 1990 v H, Ei (38)
Whiteside, T. (Distillery), 1891 v E (1)
Whitfield, E. R. (Dublin University), 1886 v W (1)
Williams, J. R. (Ulster), 1886 v E, S (2)
Williamson, J. (Cliftonville), 1890 v E; 1892 v S; 1893 v S (3)
Willigham, T. (Burnley), 1933 v W; 1934 v S (2)
Willis, G. (Linfield), 1906 v S, W; 1907 v S; 1912 v S (4)

Wilson, D. J. (Brighton & HA), 1987 v T, Is, E (sub); (with Luton T), 1988 v Y, T, Gr, Pol, F, Ma; 1989 v Ei, H, Sp, Ma, Ch; 1990 v H, Ei, N, U (18)
Wilson, H. (Linfield), 1925 v W (1)
Wilson, K. J. (Ipswich T), 1987 v Is, E, Y; (with Chelsea), 1988 v Y, T, Gr (sub), Pol (sub), F (sub); 1989 v H (sub), Sp, Sp, Ma, Ch; 1990 v Ei (sub), N, U (16)
Wilson, M. (Distillery), 1884 v E, S, W (3)
Wilson, R. (Cliftonville), 1888 v S (1)
Wilson, S. J. (Glenavon), 1962 v S; 1964 v S; (with Falkirk), 1964 v E, W, U, Sp; 1965 v E, Sw; (with Dundee), 1966 v W, WG; 1967 v S; 1968 v E (12)
Wilton, J. M. (St Columb's Court), 1888 v E, W; 1889 v S, E; (with Cliftonville), 1890 v E; (with St Columb's Court), 1892 v W; 1893 v S (7)
Worthington, N. (Sheffield W), 1984 v W, Fi (sub); 1985 v Is, Sp (sub); 1986 v T, R (sub), E (sub), D, Alg, Sp; 1987 v E (2), T, Is, Y; 1988 v Y, T, Gr, Pol, F, Ma; 1989 v Ei, H, Sp, Ma; 1990 v H, Ei, U (28)
Wright, J. (Cliftonville), 1906 v E, S, W; 1907 v E, S, W (6)
Wright, T. J. (Newcastle U), 1989 v Ma, Ch; 1990 v H, U (4)
Young, S. (Linfield), 1907 v E, S; 1908 v E, S; (with Airdrie), 1909 v E; 1912 v S; (with Linfield), 1914 v E, S, W (9)

SCOTLAND

Adams, J. (Hearts), 1889 v Ni; 1892 v W; 1893 v Ni (3)
Agnew, W. B. (Kilmarnock), 1907 v Ni; 1908 v W, Ni (3) ,
Aird, J. (Burnley), 1954 v N (2), A, U (4)
Aitken, A. (Newcastle U), 1901 v E; 1902 v E; 1903 v E, W; 1904 v E; 1905 v E, W; 1906 v E; (with Middlesbrough), 1907 v E, W; 1908 v E; (with Leicester Fosse), 1910 v E; 1911 v E, Ni (14)
Aitken, G. G. (East Fife), 1949 v E, F; 1950 v W, Ni, Sw; (with Sunderland), 1953 v W, Ni; 1954 v E (8)
Aitken, R. (Dumbarton), 1886 v E; 1888 v Ni (2)
Aitken, R. (Celtic), 1980 v Pe (sub), Bel, W (sub), E, Pol; 1983 v Bel, Ca (1+1 sub); 1984 v Bel (sub), Ni, W (sub); 1985 v E, Ic; 1986 v W, EG, Aus (2), Is, R, E, D, WG, U; 1987 v Bul, Ei (2), L, Bel, E, Br; 1988 v H, Bel, Bul, L, S, Ar, Ma, Sp, Co, E; 1989 v N, Y, I, Cy, F, Cy, E, Ch; 1990 v Y, F, N; (with Newcastle U), Arg (sub), Pol, Ma, Cr, Se, Br (56)
Aitkenhead, W. A. C. (Blackburn R), 1912 v Ni (1)
Albiston, A. (Manchester U), 1982 v Ni; 1984 v U, Bel, EG, W, E; 1985 v Y, Ic, Sp (2), W; 1986 v EG, Ho, U (14)
Alexander, D. (East Stirlingshire), 1894 v W, Ni (2)
Allan, D. S. (Queen's Park), 1885 v E, W; 1886 v W (3)
Allan, G. (Liverpool), 1897 v E (1)
Allan, H. (Hearts), 1902 v W (1)
Allan, J. (Queen's Park), 1887 v E, W (2)
Allan, T. (Dundee), 1974 v WG, N (2)
Ancell, R. F. D. (Newcastle U), 1937 v W, Ni (2)
Anderson, A. (Hearts), 1933 v E; 1934 v A, E, W, Ni; 1935 v E, W, Ni; 1936 v E, W, Ni; 1937 v G, E, W, Ni, A; 1938 v E, W, Ni, Cz, Ho; 1939 v W, H (23)
Anderson, F. (Clydesdale), 1874 v E (1)
Anderson, G. (Kilmarnock), 1901 v Ni (1)
Anderson, H. A. (Raith R), 1914 v W (1)
Anderson, J. (Leicester C), 1954 v Fi (1)
Anderson, K. (Queen's Park), 1896 v Ni; 1898 v E, Ni (3)
Anderson, W. (Queen's Park), 1882 v E; 1883 v E, W; 1884 v E; 1885 v E, W (6)
Andrews, P. (Eastern), 1875 v E (1)
Archibald, A. (Rangers), 1921 v W; 1922 v W, E; 1923 v Ni; 1924 v E, W; 1931 v E; 1932 v E (8)
Archibald, S. (Aberdeen), 1980 v P (sub); (with Totten-

ham H), Ni, Pol, H; 1981 v Se (sub), Is, Ní, Is, Ni, E; 1982 v Ni, P, Sp (sub), Ho, Nz (sub), Br, USSR; 1983 v EG, Sw (sub), Bel; 1984 v EG, E, F; (with Barcelona), 1985 v Sp, E, Ic (sub); 1986 v WG (27)
Armstrong, M. W. (Aberdeen), 1936 v W, Ni; 1937 v G (3)
Arnott, W. (Queen's Park), 1883 v W; 1884 v E, Ni; 1885 v E, W; 1886 v E; 1887 v E, W; 1888 v E; 1889 v E; 1890 v E; 1891 v E; 1892 v E; 1893 v E (14)
Auld, J. R. (Third Lanark), 1887 v E, W; 1889 v W (3)
Auld, R. (Celtic), 1959 v H, P; 1960 v W (3)
Baird, A. (Queen's Park), 1892 v Ni; 1894 v W (2)
Baird, D. (Hearts), 1890 v Ni; 1891 v E; 1892 v W (3)
Baird, H. (Airdrie), 1956 v A (1)
Baird, J. C. (Vale of Leven), 1876 v E; 1878 v W; 1880 v E (3)
Baird, S. (Rangers), 1957 v Y, Sp (2), Sw, WG; 1958 v F, Ni (7)
Baird, W. U. (St Bernard), 1897 v Ni (1)
Bannon, E. (Dundee U), 1980 v Bel; 1983 v Ni, W, E, Ca; 1984 v EG; 1986 v Is, R, E, D (sub), WG (11)
Barbour, A. (Renton), 1885 v Ni (1)
Barker, J. B. (Rangers), 1893 v W; 1894 v W (2)
Barrett, F. (Dundee), 1894 v Ni; 1895 v W (2)
Battles, B. (Celtic), 1901 v E, W, Ni (3)
Battles, B. jun. (Hearts), 1931 v W (1)
Bauld, W. (Hearts), 1950 v E, Sw, P (3)
Baxter, J. C. (Rangers), 1961 v Ni, Ei (2), Cz; 1962 v Ni, W, E, Cz (2), U; 1963 v W, Ni, E, A, N, Ei, Sp; 1964 v W, E, N, WG; 1965 v W, Ni, Fi; (with Sunderland), 1966 v P, Br, Ni, W, E, I; 1967 v W, E, USSR; 1968 v W (34)
Baxter, R. D. (Middlesbrough), 1939 v E, W, H (3)
Beattie, A. (Preston NE), 1937 v E, A, Cz; 1938 v E; 1939 v W, Ni, H (7)
Beattie, R. (Preston NE), 1939 v W (1)
Begbie, I. (Hearts), 1890 v Ni; 1891 v E; 1892 v W; 1894 v E (4)
Bell, A. (Manchester U), 1912 v Ni (1)
Bell, J. (Dumbarton), 1890 v Ni; 1892 v E; (with Everton), 1896 v E; 1897 v E; 1898 v E; (with Celtic), 1899 v E, W, Ni; 1900 v E, W (10)

Bell, M. (Hearts), 1901 v W (1)

Bell, W. J. (Leeds U), 1966 v P, Br (2)

Bennett, A. (Celtic), 1904 v W; 1907 v Ni; 1908 v W; (with Rangers), 1909 v W, Ni, E; 1910 v E, W; 1911 v E, W; 1913 v Ni (11)

Bennie, R. (Airdrieonians), 1925 v W, Ni; 1926 v Ni (3)

Berry, D. (Queen's Park), 1894 v W; 1899 v W, Ni (3)

Berry, W. H. (Queen's Park), 1888 v E; 1889 v E; 1890 v E; 1891 v E (4)

Bett, J. (Rangers), 1982 v Ho; 1983 v Bel; (with Lokeren), 1984 v Bel, W, E, F; 1985 v Y, Ic, Sp (2), W, E, Ic; (with Aberdeen), 1986 v W, Is, Ho; 1987 v Bel; 1988 v H '(sub); 1989 v Y; 1990 v F (sub), N, Arg, Eg, Ma, Cr (25)

Beveridge, W. W. (Glasgow University), 1879 v E, W; 1880 v W (3)

Black, A. (Hearts), 1938 v Cz, Ho; 1939 v H (3)

Black, D. (Hurlford), 1889 v Ni (1)

Black, E. (Metz), 1988 v H (sub), L (sub) (2)

Black, I. H. (Southampton), 1948 v E (1)

Blackburn, J. E. (Royal Engineers), 1873 v E (1)

Blacklaw, A. S. (Burnley), 1963 v N, Sp; 1966 v I (3)

Blackley, J. (Hibernian), 1974 v Cz, E, Bel, Z; 1976 v Sw; 1977 v W, Se (7)

Blair, D. (Clyde), 1929 v W, Ni; 1931 v E, A, I; 1932 v W, Ni; (with Aston Villa), 1933 v W (8)

Blair, J. (Sheffield W), 1920 v E, Ni; (with Cardiff C), 1921 v E; 1922 v E; 1923 v E, Ni; 1924 v W (8)

Blair, J. (Motherwell), 1934 v W (1)

Blair, J. A. (Blackpool), 1947 v W (1)

Blair, W. (Third Lanark), 1896 v W (1)

Blessington J. (Celtic), 1894 v E, Ni; 1896 v E, Ni (4)

Blyth, J. A. (Coventry), 1978 v Bul, W (2)

Bone, J. (Norwich C), 1972 v Y (sub); 1973 v D (2)

Bowie, J. (Rangers), 1920 v E, Ni (2)

Bowie, W. (Linthouse), 1891 v Ni (1)

Bowman, G. A. (Montrose), 1892 v Ni (1)

Boyd, J. M. (Newcastle U), 1934 v Ni (1)

Boyd, R. (Mossend Swifts), 1889 v Ni; 1891 v W (2)

Boyd, W. G. (Clyde), 1931 v I, Sw (2)

Brackenbridge, T. (Hearts), 1888 v Ni (1)

Bradshaw, T. (Bury), 1928 v E (1)

Brand, R. (Rangers), 1961 v Ni, Cz, Ei (2); 1962 v Ni, W, Cz, U (8)

Branden, T. (Blackburn R), 1896 v E (1)

Brazil, A. (Ipswich T), 1980 v Pol (sub), H; 1982 v Sp, Ho (sub), Ni, W, E, Nz, USSR (sub); 1983 v EG, Sw, W, E (sub) (13)

Bremner, D. (Hibernian), 1976 v Sw (sub) (1)

Bremner, W. J. (Leeds U), 1965 v Sp; 1966 v E, Pol, P, Br, I (2); 1967 v W, Ni, E; 1968 v W, E; 1969 v W, E, Ni, D, A, WG, Cy (2); 1970 v Ei, WG, A; 1971 v W, E; 1972 v P, Bel, Ho, Ni, W, E, Y, Cz, Br; 1973 v D (2), E (2), Ni (sub), Sw, Br; 1974 v Cz, WG, Ni, W, E, Bel, N, Z, Br, Y; 1975 v Sp (2); 1976 v D (54)

Brennan, F. (Newcastle U), 1947 v W, Ni; 1953 v W, Ni, E; 1954 v Ni, E (7)

Breslin, B. (Hibernian), 1897 v W (1)

Brewster, G. (Everton), 1921 v E (1)

Brogan, J. (Celtic), 1971 v W, Ni, P, E (4)

Brown, A. (Middlesbrough), 1904 v E (1)

Brown, A. (St Mirren), 1890 v W; 1891 v W (2)

Brown, A. D. (East Fife), 1950 v Sw, P, F; (with Blackpool), 1952 v USA, D, Se; 1953 v W; 1954 v W, E, N (2), Fi, A, U (14)

Brown, G. C. P. (Rangers), 1931 v W; 1932 v E, W, Ni; 1933 v W; 1935 v A, E, W; 1936 v E, W; 1937 v G, E, W, Ni, Cz; 1938 v E, W, Cz, Ho (19)

Brown, H. (Partick T), 1947 v W, Bel, L (3)

Brown, J. (Cambuslang), 1890 v W (1)

Brown, J. B. (Clyde), 1939 v W (1)

Brown, J. G. (Sheffield U), 1975 v R (1)

Brown, R. (Dumbarton), 1884 v W, Ni (2)

Brown, R. (Rangers), 1947 v Ni; 1949 v Ni; 1952 v E (3)

Brown, R. jun. (Dumbarton), 1885 v W (1)

Brown, W. D. F. (Dundee), 1958 v F; 1959 v E, W, Ni; (with Tottenham H), 1960 v W, Ni, Pol, A, H, T; 1962 v Ni, W, E, Cz; 1963 v W, Ni, E, A; 1964 v Ni, W, N; 1965 v E, Fi, Pol, Sp; 1966 v Ni, Pol, I (28)

Browning, J. (Celtic), 1914 v W (1)

Brownlie, J. (Hibernian), 1971 v USSR; 1972 v Pe, Ni, E; 1973 v D (2); 1976 v R (7)

Brownlie, J. (Third Lanark), 1909 v E, Ni; 1910 v E, W, Ni; 1911 v W, Ni; 1912 v W, Ni, E; 1913 v W, Ni, E; 1914 v W, Ni, E (16)

Bruce, D. (Vale of Leven), 1890 v W (1)

Bruce, R. F. (Middlesbrough), 1934 v A (1)

Buchan, M. M. (Aberdeen), 1972 v P (sub), Bel; (with Manchester U), W, Y, Cz, Br; 1973 v D (2), E; 1974 v WG, Ni, W, N, Br, Y; 1975 v EG, Sp, P; 1976 v D, R; 1977 v Fi, Cz, Ch, Arg, Br; 1978 v EG, W (sub), Ni, Pe, Ir, Ho; 1979 v A, N, P (34)

Buchanan, J. (Cambuslang), 1889 v Ni (1)

Buchanan, J. (Rangers), 1929 v E; 1930 v E (2)

Buchanan, P. S. (Chelsea), 1938 v Cz (1)

Buchanan, R. (Abercorn), 1891 v W (1)

Buckley, P. (Aberdeen), 1954 v N; 1955 v W, Ni (3)

Buick, A. (Hearts), 1902 v W, Ni (2)

Burley, G. (Ipswich T), 1979 v W, Ni, E, Arg, N; 1980 v P, Ni, E (sub), Pol; 1982 v W (sub), E (11)

Burns, F. (Manchester U), 1970 v A (1)

Burns, K. (Birmingham C), 1974 v WG; 1975 v EG (sub), Sp (2); 1977 v Cz (sub), W, Se, W (sub); (with Nottingham F), 1978 v Ni (sub), W, E, Pe, Ir; 1979 v N; 1980 v Pe, A, Bel; 1981 v Is, Ni, W (20)

Burns, T. (Celtic), 1981 v Ni; 1982 v Ho (sub), W; 1983 v Bel (sub), Ni, Ca (1 + 1 sub); 1988 v E (sub) (8)

Busby, M. W. (Manchester C), 1934 v W (1)

Cairns, T. (Rangers), 1920 v W; 1922 v E; 1923 v E, W; 1924 v Ni; 1925 v W, E, Ni (8)

Calderhead, D. (Queen of the South), 1889 v Ni (1)

Calderwood, R. (Cartvale), 1885 v Ni, E, W (3)

Caldow, E. (Rangers), 1957 v Sp (2), Sw, WG, E; 1958 v Ni, W, Sw, Par, H, Pol, Y, F; 1959 v E, W, Ni, WG, Ho, P; 1960 v E, W, Ni, A, H, T; 1961 v E, W, Ni, Ei (2), Cz; 1962 v Ni, W, E, Cz (2), U; 1963 v W, Ni, E (40)

Callaghan, P. (Hibernian), 1900 v Ni (1)

Callaghan, W. (Dunfermline Ath), 1970 v Ei (sub), W (2)

Cameron, J. (St Mirren), 1904 v Ni; (with Chelsea), 1909 v E (2)

Cameron, J. (Queen's Park), 1896 v Ni (1)

Cameron, J. (Rangers), 1886 v Ni (1)

Campbell, C. (Queen's Park), 1874 v E; 1876 v W; 1877 v E, W; 1878 v E; 1879 v E; 1880 v E; 1881 v E; 1882 v E, W; 1884 v E; 1885 v E; 1886 v E (13)

Campbell, H. (Renton), 1889 v W (1)

Campbell, Jas. (Sheffield W), 1913 v W (1)

Campbell, J. (South Western), 1880 v W (1)

Campbell, J. (Kilmarnock), 1891 v Ni; 1892 v W (2)

Campbell, John (Celtic), 1893 v E, Ni; 1898 v E, Ni; 1900 v E, Ni; 1901 v E, W, Ni; 1902 v W, Ni; 1903 v W (12)

Campbell, John (Rangers), 1899 v E, W, Ni; 1901 v Ni (4)

Campbell, K. (Liverpool), 1920 v E, W, Ni; (with Partick T), 1921 v W, Ni; 1922 v W, Ni, E (8)

Campbell, P. (Rangers), 1878 v W; 1879 v W (2)

Campbell, P. (Morton), 1898 v W (1)

Campbell, R. (Falkirk), 1947 v Bel, L; (with Chelsea), 1950 v Sw, P, F (5)

Campbell, W. (Morton), 1947 v Ni; 1948 v E, Bel, Sw, F (5)

Carabine, J. (Third Lanark), 1938 v Ho; 1939 v E, Ni (3)

Carr, W. M. (Coventry C), 1970 v Ni, W, E; 1971 v D; 1972 v Pe; 1973 v D (sub) (6)

Cassidy, J. (Celtic), 1921 v W, Ni; 1923 v Ni; 1924 v W (4)

Chalmers, S. (Celtic), 1965 v W, Fi; 1966 v P (sub), Br; 1967 v Ni (5)

Chalmers, W. (Rangers), 1885 v Ni (1)

Chalmers, W. S. (Queen's Park), 1929 v Ni (1)

Chambers, T. (Hearts), 1894 v W (1)

Chaplin, G. D. (Dundee), 1908 v W (1)

Cheyne, A. G. (Aberdeen), 1929 v E, N, G, Ho; 1930 v F (5)

Christie, A. J. (Queen's Park), 1898 v W; 1899 v E, Ni (3)

Christie, R. M. (Queen's Park), 1884 v E (1)

Clark, J. (Celtic), 1966 v Br; 1967 v W, Ni, USSR (4)

Clark, R. B. (Aberdeen), 1968 v W, Ho; 1970 v Ni; 1971 v W, Ni, E, D, P, USSR; 1972 v Bel, Ni, W, E, Cz, Br; 1973 v D, E (17)

Clarke, S. (Chelsea), 1988 v H, Bel, Bul, S.Ar, Ma (5)

Cleland, J. (Royal Albert), 1891 v Ni (1)

Clements, R. (Leith Ath), 1891 v Ni (1)

Clunas, W. L. (Sunderland), 1924 v E; 1926 v W (2)

Collier, W. (Raith R), 1922 v W (1)

Collins, J. (Hibernian), 1988 v S.Ar; 1990 v EG, Pol (sub), Ma (sub) (4)

Collins, R. Y. (Celtic), 1951 v W, Ni, A; 1955 v Y, A, H; 1956 v Ni, W; 1957 v E, W, Sp (2), Sw, WG; 1958 v Ni, W, Sw, H, Pol, Y, F, Par; (with Everton), 1959 v E, W, Ni, WG, Ho, P; (with Leeds U), 1965 v E, Pol, Sp (31)

Collins, T. (Hearts), 1909 v W (1)

Colman, D. (Aberdeen), 1911 v E, W, Ni; 1913 v Ni (4)

Colquhoun, E. P. (Sheffield U), 1972 v P, Ho, Pe, Y, Cz, Br; 1973 v D (2), E (9)

Colquhoun, J. (Hearts), 1988 v S.Ar (sub) (1)

Combe, J. R. (Hibernian), 1948 v E, Bel, Sw (3)

Conn, A. (Hearts), 1956 v A (1)

Conn, A. (Tottenham H), 1975 v Ni (sub), E (2)

Connachan, E. D. (Dunfermline Ath), 1962 v Cz, U (2)

Connelly, G. (Celtic), 1974 v Cz, WG (2)

Connolly, J. (Everton), 1973 v Sw (1)

Connor, J. (Airdrieonians), 1886 v Ni (1)

Connor, J. (Sunderland), 1930 v F; 1932 v Ni; 1934 v E; 1935 v Ni (4)

Connor, R. (Dundee), 1986 v Ho; (with Aberdeen), 1988 v S.Ar (sub); 1989 v E (3)

Cook, W. L. (Bolton W), 1934 v E; 1935 v W, Ni (3)

Cooke, C. (Dundee), 1966 v W, I; (with Chelsea), P, Br; 1968 v E, Ho; 1969 v W, Ni, A, WG (sub), Cy (2); 1970 v A; 1971 v Bel; 1975 v Sp, P (16)

Cooper, D. (Rangers), 1980 v Pe, A (sub); 1984 v W, E; 1985 v Y, Ic, Sp (2), W; 1986 v W (sub), EG, Aus (2), Ho, WG (sub), U (sub); 1987 v Bul, L, Ei, Br; (with Motherwell), 1990 v N, Eg (22)

Cormack, P. B. (Hibernian), 1966 v Br; 1969 v D (sub); 1970 v Ei, WG; (with Nottingham F), 1971 v D (sub), W, P, E; 1972 v Ho (sub) (9)

Cowan, J. (Aston Villa), 1896 v E; 1897 v E; 1898 v E (3)

Cowan, J. (Morton), 1948 v Bel, Sw; F; 1949 v E, W, F; 1950 v E, W, Ni, Sw, P, F; 1951 v E, W, Ni, A (2), D, F, Bel; 1952 v Ni, W, USA, D, Se (25)

Cowan, W. D. (Newcastle U), 1924 v E (1)

Cowie, D. (Dundee), 1953 v E, Se; 1954 v Ni, W, Fi, N, A, U; 1955 v W, Ni, A, H; 1956 v W, A; 1957 v Ni, W; 1958 v H, Pol, Y, Par (20)

Cox, C. J. (Hearts), 1948 v F (1)

Cox, S. (Rangers), 1948 v F; 1949 v E, F; 1950 v E, F, W, Ni, Sw, P; 1951 v E, D, F, Bel, A; 1952 v Ni, W, USA, D, Se; 1953 v W, Ni, E; 1954 v W, Ni, E (25)

Craig, A. (Motherwell), 1929 v N, Ho; 1932 v E (3)

Craig, J. (Celtic), 1977 v Se (sub) (1)

Craig, J. P. (Celtic), 1968 v W (1)

Craig, T. (Rangers), 1927 v Ni; 1928 v Ni; 1929 v N, G, Ho; 1930 v Ni, E, W (8)

Craig, T. B. (Newcastle U), 1976 v Sw (1)

Crapnell, J. (Airdrieonians), 1929 v E, N, G; 1930 v F; 1931 v Ni, Sw; 1932 v E, F; 1933 v Ni (9)

Crawford, D. (St Mirren), 1894 v W, Ni; 1900 v W (3)

Crawford, J. (Queen's Park), 1932 v F, Ni; 1933 v E, W, Ni (5)

Crerand, P. T. (Celtic), 1961 v Ei (2), Cz; 1962 v Ni, W, E, Cz (2), U; 1963 v W, Ni; (with Manchester U), 1964 v Ni; 1965 v E, Pol, Fi; 1966 v Pol (16)

Cringan, W. (Celtic), 1920 v W; 1922 v E, Ni; 1923 v W, E (5)

Crosbie, J. A. (Ayr U), 1920 v W; (with Birmingham), 1922 v E (2)

Croal, J. A. (Falkirk), 1913 v Ni; 1914 v E, W (3)

Cropley, A. J. (Hibernian), 1972 v P, Bel (2)

Cross, J. H. (Third Lanark), 1903 v Ni (1)

Cruickshank, J. (Hearts), 1964 v WG; 1970 v W, E; 1971 v D, Bel; 1976 v R (6)

Crum, J. (Celtic), 1936 v E; 1939 v Ni (2)

Cullen, M. J. (Luton T), 1956 v A (1)

Cumming, D. S. (Middlesbrough), 1938 v E (1)

Cumming, J. (Hearts), 1955 v E, H, P, Y; 1960 v E, Pol, A, H, T (9)

Cummings, G. (Partick T), 1935 v E; 1936 v W, Ni; (with Aston Villa), E; 1937 v G; 1938 v W, Ni, Cz; 1939 v E (9)

Cunningham, A. N. (Rangers), 1920 v Ni; 1921 v W, E; 1922 v Ni; 1923 v E, W; 1924 v E, Ni; 1926 v E, Ni; 1927 v E, W (12)

Cunningham, W. C. (Preston NE), 1954 v N (2), U, Fi, A; 1955 v W, E, H (8)

Curran, H. P. (Wolverhampton W), 1970 v A; 1971 v Ni, E, D, USSR (sub) (5)

Dalglish, K. (Celtic), 1972 v Bel (sub), Ho; 1973 v D (1+1 sub), E (2), W, Ni, Sw, Br; 1974 v Cz (2), WG (2), Ni, W, E, Bel, N (sub), Z, Br, Y; 1975 v EG, Sp (sub+1), Se, P, W, Ni, E, R; 1976 v D (2), R, Sw, Ni, E; 1977 v Fi, Cz, W (2), Se, Ni, E, Ch, Arg, Br; (with Liverpool), 1978 v EG, Cz, W, Bul, Ni (sub), W, E, Pe, Ir, Ho; 1979 v A, N, P, W, Ni, E, Arg, N; 1980 v Pe, A, Bel (2), P, Ni, W, E, Pol, H; 1981 v Se, P, Is; 1982 v Se, Ni, P (sub), Sp, Ho, Ni, W, E, Nz, Br (sub); 1983 v Bel, Sw; 1984 v U, Bel, EG; 1985 v Y, Ic, Sp, W; 1986 v EG, Aus, R; 1987 v Bul (sub), L (102)

Davidson, D. (Queen's Park), 1878 v W; 1879 v W; 1880 v W; 1881 v E, W (5)

Davidson, J. A. (Partick T), 1954 v N (2), A, U; 1955 v W, Ni, E, H (8)

Davidson, S. (Middlesbrough), 1921 v E (1)

Dawson, A. (Rangers), 1980 v Pol (sub), H; 1983 v Ni, Ca (2) (5)

Dawson, J. (Rangers), 1935 v Ni; 1936 v E; 1937 v G, E, W, Ni, A, Cz; 1938 v W, Ho, Ni; 1939 v E, Ni, H (14)

Deans, J. (Celtic), 1975 v EG, Sp (2)

Delaney, J. (Celtic), 1936 v W, Ni; 1937 v G, E, A, Cz; 1938 v Ni; 1939 v W, Ni; (with Manchester U), 1947 v E; 1948 v E, W, Ni (13)

Devine, A. (Falkirk), 1910 v W (1)

Dewar, G. (Dumbarton), 1888 v Ni; 1889 v E (2)

Dewar, N. (Third Lanark), 1932 v E, F; 1933 v W (3)

Dick, J. (West Ham U), 1959 v E (1)

Dickie, M. (Rangers), 1897 v Ni; 1899 v Ni; 1900 v W (3)

Dickson, W. (Kilmarnock), 1970 v Ni, W, E; 1971 v D, USSR (5)

Dickson, W. (Dumbarton), 1888 v Ni (1)

Divers, J. (Celtic), 1895 v W (1)

Divers, J. (Celtic), 1939 v Ni (1)

Docherty, T. H. (Preston NE), 1952 v W; 1953 v E, Se; 1954 v N (2), A, U; 1955 v W, E, H (2), A; 1957 v E, Y, Sp (2), Sw, WG; 1958 v Ni, W, E, Sw; (with Arsenal), 1959 v W, E, Ni (25)

Dodds, D. (Dundee U), 1984 v U (sub), Ni (2)

Dodds, J. (Celtic), 1914 v E, W, Ni (3)

Doig, J. E. (Arbroath), 1887 v Ni; 1889 v Ni; (with Sunderland), 1896 v E; 1899 v E; 1903 v E (5)

Donachie, W. (Manchester C), 1972 v Pe, Ni, E, Y, Cz,

Br; 1973 v D, E, W, Ni; 1974 v Ni; 1976 v R, Ni, W, E; 1977 v Fi, Cz, W (2), Se, Ni, E, Ch, Arg, Br; 1978 v EG, W, Bul, W, E, Ir, Ho; 1979 v A, N, P (sub) (35)

Donaldson, A. (Bolton W), 1914 v E, Ni, W; 1920 v E, Ni; 1922 v Ni (6)

Donnachie, J. (Oldham Ath), 1913 v E; 1914 v E, Ni (3)

Dougall, C. (Birmingham C), 1947 v W (1)

Dougall, J. (Preston NE), 1939 v E (1)

Dougan, R. (Hearts), 1950 v Sw (1)

Douglas, A. (Chelsea), 1911 v Ni (1)

Douglas, J. (Renfrew), 1880 v W (1)

Dowds, P. (Celtic), 1892 v Ni (1)

Downie, R. (Third Lanark), 1892 v W (1)

Doyle, D. (Celtic), 1892 v E; 1893 v W; 1894 v E; 1895 v E, Ni; 1897 v E; 1898 v E, Ni (8)

Doyle, J. (Ayr U), 1976 v R (1)

Drummond, J. (Falkirk), 1892 v Ni; (with Rangers), 1894 v Ni; 1895 v Ni, E; 1896 v E, Ni; 1897 v Ni; 1898 v E; 1900 v E; 1901 v E; 1902 v E, W, Ni; 1903 v Ni (14)

Dunbar, M. (Cartvale), 1886 v Ni (1)

Duncan, A. (Hibernian), 1975 v P (sub), W, Ni, E, R; 1976 v D (6)

Duncan, D. (Derby Co), 1933 v E, W; 1934 v A, W; 1935 v E, W; 1936 v E, W, Ni; 1937 v G, E, W, Ni; 1938 v W (14)

Duncan, D. M. (East Fife), 1948 v Bel, Sw, F (3)

Duncan, J. (Alexandra Ath), 1878 v W; 1882 v W (2)

Duncan, J. (Leicester C), 1926 v W (1)

Duncanson, J. (Rangers), 1947 v Ni (1)

Dunlop, J. (St Mirren), 1890 v W (1)

Dunlop, W. (Liverpool), 1906 v E (1)

Dunn, J. (Hibernian), 1925 v W, Ni; 1927 v Ni; 1928 v Ni, E; (with Everton), 1929 v W (6)

Durie, G. S. (Chelsea), 1988 v Bul (sub); 1989 v I (sub), Cy; 1990 v Y, EG, Eg, Se (7)

Durrant, I. (Rangers), 1988 v H, Bel, Ma, Sp; 1989 v N (sub) (5)

Dykes, J. (Hearts), 1938 v Ho; 1939 v Ni (2)

Easson, J. F. (Portsmouth), 1931 v A, Sw; 1934 v W (3)

Ellis, J. (Mossend Swifts), 1892 v Ni (1)

Evans, A. (Aston Villa), 1982 v Ho, Ni, E, Nz (4)

Evans, R. (Celtic), 1949 v E, W, Ni, F; 1950 v W, Ni, Sw, P; 1951 v E, A; 1952 v Ni; 1953 v Se; 1954 v Ni, W, E, N, Fi; 1955 v Ni, P, Y, A, H; 1956 v E, Ni, W, A; 1957 v WG, Sp; 1958 v Ni, W, E, Sw, H, Pol, Y, Par, F; 1959 v E, WG, Ho, P; 1960 v E, Ni, W, Pol; (with Chelsea), 1960 v A, H, T (48)

Ewart, J. (Bradford C), 1921 v E (1)

Ewing, T. (Partick T), 1958 v W, E (2)

Farm, G. N. (Blackpool), 1953 v W, Ni, E, Se; 1954 v Ni, W, E; 1959 v WG, Ho, P (10)

Ferguson, D. (Rangers), 1988 v Ma, Co (sub) (2)

Ferguson, I. (Rangers), 1989 v I, Cy (sub), F (3)

Ferguson, J. (Vale of Leven), 1874 v E; 1876 v E, W; 1877 v E, W; 1878 v W (6)

Ferguson, R. (Kilmarnock), 1966 v W, E, Ho, P, Br; 1967 v W, Ni (7)

Fernie, W. (Celtic), 1954 v Fi, A, U; 1955 v W, Ni; 1957 v E, Ni, W, Y; 1958 v W, Sw, Par (12)

Findlay, R. (Kilmarnock), 1898 v W (1)

Fitchie, T. T. (Woolwich Arsenal), 1905 v W; 1906 v W, Ni; (with Queen's Park), 1907 v W (4)

Flavell, R. (Airdrieonians), 1947 v Bel, L (2)

Fleck, R. (Norwich C), 1990 v Arg, Se, Br (sub) (3)

Fleming, C. (East Fife), 1954 v Ni (1)

Fleming, J. W. (Rangers), 1929 v G, Ho; 1930 v E (3)

Fleming, R. (Morton), 1886 v Ni (1)

Forbes, A. R. (Sheffield U), 1947 v Bel, L, E; 1948 v W, Ni; (with Arsenal), 1950 v E, P, F; 1951 v W, Ni, A; 1952 v W, D, Se (14)

Forbes, J. (Vale of Leven), 1884 v E, W, Ni; 1887 v W, E (5)

Ford, D. (Hearts), 1974 v Cz (sub), WG (sub), W (3)

Forrest, J. (Rangers), 1966 v W, I; (with Aberdeen), 1971 v Bel (sub), D, USSR (5)

Forrest, J. (Motherwell), 1958 v E (1)

Forsyth, A. (Partick T), 1972 v Y, Cz, Br; 1973 v D; (with Manchester U), E; 1975 v Sp, Ni (sub), R, EG; 1976 v D (10)

Forsyth, C. (Kilmarnock), 1964 v E; 1965 v W, Ni, Fi (4)

Forsyth, T. (Motherwell), 1971 v D; (with Rangers), 1974 v Cz; 1976 v Sw, Ni, W, E; 1977 v Fi, Se, W, Ni, E, Ch, Arg, Br; 1978 v Cz, W, Ni, W (sub), E, Pe, Ir (sub), Ho (22)

Foyers, R. (St Bernards), 1893 v W; 1894 v W (2)

Fraser, D. M. (WBA), 1968 v Ho; 1969 v Cy (2)

Fraser, J. (Moffat), 1891 v Ni (1)

Fraser, M. J. E. (Queen's Park), 1880 v W; 1882 v W, E; 1883 v W, E (5)

Fraser, J. (Dundee), 1907 v Ni (1)

Fraser, W. (Sunderland), 1955 v W, Ni (2)

Fulton, W. (Abercorn), 1884 v Ni (1)

Fyfe, J. H. (Third Lanark), 1895 v W (1)

Gabriel, J. (Everton), 1961 v W; 1964 v N (sub) (2)

Gallacher, H. K. (Airdrieonians), 1924 v Ni; 1925 v E, W, Ni; 1926 v W; (with Newcastle U), 1926 v E, Ni; 1927 v E, W, Ni; 1928 v E, W; 1929 v E, W, Ni; 1930 v W, Ni, F; (with Chelsea), 1934 v E; (with Derby Co), 1935 v E (20)

Gallacher, K. W. (Dundee U), 1988 v Co, E (sub); 1989 v N, I (4)

Gallacher, P. (Sunderland), 1935 v Ni (1)

Galt, J. H. (Rangers), 1908 v W, Ni (2)

Gardiner, I. (Motherwell), 1958 v W (1)

Gardner, D. R. (Third Lanark), 1897 v W (1)

Gardner, R. (Queen's Park), 1872 v E; 1873 v E; (with Clydesdale), 1874 v E; 1875 v E; 1878 v E (5)

Gemmell, T. (St Mirren), 1955 v P, Y (2)

Gemmell, T. (Celtic), 1966 v E; 1967 v W, Ni, E, USSR; 1968 v Ni, E; 1969 v W, Ni, E, D, A, WG, Cy; 1970 v E, Ei, WG; 1971 v Bel (18)

Gemmill, A. (Derby Co), 1971 v Bel; 1972 v P, Ho, Pe, Ni, W, E; 1976 v D, R, Ni, W, E; 1977 v Fi, Cz, W (2), Ni (sub), E (sub), Ch (sub), Arg, Br; 1978 v EG (sub); (with Nottingham F), Bul, Ni, W, E (sub), Pe (sub), Ir, Ho; 1979 v A, N, P, N; (with Birmingham C), 1980 v A, P, Ni, W, E, H; 1981 v Se, P, Is, Ni (43)

Gibb, W. (Clydesdale), 1873 v E (1)

Gibson, D. W. (Leicester C), 1963 v A, N, Ei, Sp; 1964 v Ni; 1965 v W, Fi (7)

Gibson, J. D. (Partick T), 1926 v E; 1927 v E, W, Ni; (with Aston Villa), 1928 v E, W; 1930 v W, Ni (8)

Gibson, N. (Rangers), 1895 v E, Ni; 1896 v E, Ni; 1897 v E, Ni; 1898 v E; 1899 v E, W, Ni; 1900 v E, Ni; 1901 v W; (with Partick T), 1905 v Ni (14)

Gilchrist, J. E. (Celtic), 1922 v E (1)

Gilhooley, M. (Hull C), 1922 v W (1)

Gillespie, G. (Rangers), 1880 v W; 1881 v E, W; 1882 v E; (with Queen's Park), 1886 v W; 1890 v W; 1891 v Ni (7)

Gillespie, G. T. (Liverpool), 1988 v Bel, Bul, Sp; 1989 v N, F, Ch; 1990 v Y, EG, Eg, Pol, Ma, Br (sub) (12)

Gillespie, Jas. (Third Lanark), 1898 v W (1)

Gillespie, John. (Queen's Park), 1896 v W (1)

Gillespie, R. (Queen's Park), 1927 v W; 1931 v W; 1932 v F; 1933 v E (4)

Gillick, T. (Everton), 1937 v A, Cz; 1939 v W, Ni, H (5)

Gilmour, J. (Dundee), 1931 v W (1)

Gilzean, A. J. (Dundee), 1964 v W, E, N, WG; 1965 v Ni, (with Tottenham H), Sp; 1966 v Ni, W, Pol, I; 1968 v W; 1969 v W, E, WG, Cy (2), A (sub); 1970 v Ni, E (sub), WG, A; 1971 v P (22)

Glavin, R. (Celtic), 1977 v Se (1)

Glen, A. (Aberdeen), 1956 v E, Ni (2)

Glen, R. (Renton), 1895 v W; 1896 v W; (with Hibernian), 1900 v Ni (3)

Goram, A. L. (Oldham Ath), 1986 v EG (sub), R, Ho; 1987 v Br; (with Hibernian) 1989 v Y,I; 1990 v EG, Pol, Ma (9)

Gordon, J. E. (Rangers), 1912 v E, Ni; 1913 v E, Ni, W; 1914 v E, Ni; 1920 v W, E, Ni (10)

Gossland, J. (Rangers), 1884 v Ni (1)

Goudle, J. (Abercorn), 1884 v Ni (1)

Gough, C. R. (Dundee U), 1983 v Sw, Ni, W, E, Ca (3); 1984 v U, Bel, EG, Ni, W, E, F; 1985 v Sp, E, Ic; 1986 v W, EG, Aus, Is, R, E, D, WG, U; (with Tottenham H), 1987, Bul, L, Ei (2), Bel, E, Br; 1988 v H (with Rangers), S.Ar, Sp, Co, E; 1989 v Y, I, Cy, F, Cy; 1990 v F, Arg, EG, Eg, Pol, Ma, Cr (50)

Gourlay, J. (Cambuslang), 1886 v Ni; 1888 v W (2)

Govan, J. (Hibernian), 1948 v E, W, Bel, Sw, F; 1949 v Ni (6)

Gow, D. R. (Rangers), 1888 v E (1)

Gow, J. J. (Queen's Park), 1885 v E (1)

Gow, J. R. (Rangers), 1888 v Ni (1)

Graham, A. (Leeds U), 1978 v EG (sub); 1979 v A (sub), N, W, Ni, E, Arg, N; 1980 v A; 1981 v W (10)

Graham, G. (Arsenal), 1972 v P, SW (sub), Ho, Ni, Y, Cz, Br; 1973 v D (2); (with Manchester U), E, W, Ni, Br (sub) (13)

Graham, J. (Annbank), 1884 v Ni (1)

Graham, J. A. (Arsenal), 1921 v Ni (1)

Grant, J. (Hibernian), 1959 v W, Ni (2)

Grant, P. (Celtic), 1989 v E (sub), Ch (2)

Gray, A. (Hibernian), 1903 v Ni (1)

Gray, A. M. (Aston Villa), 1976 v R, Sw; 1977 v Fi, Cz; 1979 v A, N; (with Wolverhampton W), 1980 v P, E (sub); 1981 v Se, P, Is (sub), Ni; 1982 v Se (sub), Ni (sub); 1983 v Ni, W, E, Ca (1+1); (with Everton), 1985 v Ic (20)

Gray, D. (Rangers), 1929 v W, Ni, G, Ho; 1930 v W, E, Ni; 1931 v W; 1933 v W, Ni (10)

Gray, E. (Leeds U), 1969 v E, Cy; 1970 v WG, A; 1971 v W, Ni; 1972 v Bel, Ho; 1976 v W, E; 1977 v Fi, W (12)

Gray, F. T. (Leeds U), 1976 v Sw; 1979 v N, P, W, Ni, E, Arg (sub); (with Nottingham F) 1980 v Bel (sub); 1981 v Se, P, Is, Ni, Is, W, (with Leeds U) Ni, E; 1982 v Se, Ni, P, Sp, Ho, W, Nz, Br, USSR; 1983 v EG, Sw, Bel, Sw, W, E, Ca (32)

Gray, W. (Pollokshields Ath), 1886 v E (1)

Green, A. (Blackpool), 1971 v Bel (sub), P (sub), Ni, E; 1972 v W, E (sub) (6)

Greig, J. (Rangers), 1964 v E, WG; 1965 v W, Ni, E, Fi (2), Sp, Pol; 1966 v Ni, W, E, Pol, I (2), P, Ho, Br; 1967 v W, Ni, E; 1968 v Ni, W, E, Ho; 1969 v W, Ni, E, D, A, WG, Cy (2); 1970 v W, E, Ei, WG, A; 1971 v D, Bel, W (sub), Ni, E; 1976 v D (44)

Groves, W. (Hibernian), 1888 v W; (with Celtic), 1889 v Ni; 1890 v E (3)

Guilliland, W. (Queen's Park), 1891 v W; 1892 v Ni; 1894 v E; 1895 v E (4)

Gunn, B. (Norwich C), 1990 v Eg (1)

Haddock, H. (Clyde), 1955 v E, H (2), P, Y; 1958 v E (6)

Haddow, D. (Rangers), 1894 v E (1)

Haffey, F. (Celtic), 1960 v E; 1961 v E (2)

Hamilton, A. (Queen's Park), 1885 v E, W; 1886 v E; 1888 v E (4)

Hamilton, A. W. (Dundee), 1962 v Cz, U, W, E; 1963 v W, Ni, E, A, N, Ei; 1964 v Ni, W, E, N, WG; 1965 v Ni, W, E, Fi (2), Pol, Sp; 1966 v Pol, Ni (24)

Hamilton, G. (Aberdeen), 1947 v Ni; 1951 v Bel, A; 1954 v N (2) (5)

Hamilton, G. (Port Glasgow Ath), 1906 v Ni (1)

Hamilton, J. (Queen's Park), 1892 v W; 1893 v E, Ni (3)

Hamilton, J. (St Mirren), 1924 v Ni (1)

Hamilton, R. C. (Rangers), 1899 v E, W, Ni; 1900 v W; 1901 v E, Ni; 1902 v W, Ni; 1903 v E; 1904 v Ni; (with Dundee), 1911 v W (11)

Hamilton, T. (Hurlford), 1891 v Ni (1)

Hamilton, T. (Rangers), 1932 v E (1)

Hamilton, W. M. (Hibernian), 1965 v Fi (1)

Hannah, A. B. (Renton), 1888 v W (1)

Hannah, J. (Third Lanark), 1889 v W (1)

Hansen, A. D. (Liverpool), 1979 v W, Arg; 1980 v Bel, P; 1981 v Se, P, Is; 1982 v Se, Ni, P, Sp, Ni (sub), W, E, Nz, Br, USSR; 1983 v EG, Sw, Bel, Sw; 1985 v W (sub); 1986 v R (sub); 1987 v Ei (2), L (26)

Hansen, J. (Partick K), 1972 v Bel (sub), Y (sub) (2)

Harkness, J. D. (Queen's Park), 1927 v E, Ni; 1928 v E; (with Hearts), 1929 v W, E, Ni; 1930 v E, W; 1932 v W, F; 1934 v Ni, W (12)

Harper, J. M. (Aberdeen), 1973 v D (1+1 sub); (with Hibernian), 1976 v D; (with Aberdeen), 1978 v Ir (sub) (4)

Harper, W. (Hibernian), 1923 v E, Ni, W; 1924 v E, Ni, W; 1925 v E, Ni, W; (with Arsenal), 1926 v E, Ni (11)

Harris, J. (Partick T), 1921 v W, Ni (2)

Harris, N. (Newcastle U), 1924 v E (1)

Harrower, W. (Queen's Park), 1882 v E; 1884 v Ni; 1886 v W (3)

Hartford, R. A. (WBA), 1972 v Pe, W (sub), E, Y, Cz, Br; (with Manchester C), 1976 v D, R, Ni (sub); 1977 v Cz (sub), W (sub), Se, W, Ni, E, Ch, Arg, Br; 1978 v EG, Cz, W, Bul, W, E, Pe, Ir, Ho; 1979 v A, N, P, W, Ni, E, Arg, N; (with Everton), 1980 v Pe, Bel; 1981 v Ni (sub), Is, W, Ni, E; 1982 v Se; (with Manchester C), Ni, P, Sp, Ni, W, E, Br (50)

Harvey, D. (Leeds U), 1973 v D; 1974 v Cz, WG, Ni, W, E, Bel, Z, Br, Y; 1975 v EG, Sp (2); 1976 v D (2); 1977 v Fi (sub) (16)

Hastings, A. C. (Sunderland), 1936 v Ni; 1938 v Ni (2)

Haughney, M. (Celtic), 1954 v E (1)

Hay, D. (Celtic), 1970 v Ni, W, E; 1971 v D, Bel, W, P, Ni; 1972 v P, Bel, Ho; 1973 v W, Ni, E, Sw, Br; 1974 v Cz (2), WG, Ni, W, E, Bel, N, Z, Br, Y (27)

Hay, J. (Celtic), 1905 v Ni; 1909 v Ni; 1910 v W, Ni, E; 1911 v Ni, E; (with Newcastle U), 1912 v E, W; 1914 v E, Ni (11)

Hegarty, P. (Dundee U), 1979 v W, Ni, E, Arg, N (sub); 1980 v W, E; 1983 v Ni (8)

Heggie, C. (Rangers), 1886 v Ni (1)

Henderson, G. H. (Rangers), 1904 v Ni (1)

Henderson, J. G. (Portsmouth), 1953 v Se; 1954 v Ni, E, N; 1956 v W; (with Arsenal), 1959 v W, Ni (7)

Henderson, W. (Rangers), 1963 v W, Ni, E, A, N, Ei, Sp; 1964 v W, Ni, E, N, WG; 1965 v Fi, Pol, E, Sp; 1966 v Ni, W, Pol, I, Ho; 1967 v W, Ni; 1968 v Ho; 1969 v Ni, E, Cy; 1970 v Ei; 1971 v P (29)

Hepburn, J. (Alloa Ath), 1891 v W (1)

Hepburn, R. (Ayr U), 1932 v Ni (1)

Herd, A. C. (Hearts), 1935 v Ni (1)

Herd, D. G. (Arsenal), 1959 v E, W, Ni; 1961 v E, Cz (5)

Herd, G. (Clyde), 1958 v E; 1960 v H, T; 1961 v W, Ni (5)

Herriot, J. (Birmingham C), 1969 v Ni, E, D, Cy (2), W (sub); 1970 v Ei (sub), WG (8)

Hewie, J. D. (Charlton Ath), 1956 v E, A; 1957 v E, Ni, W, Y, Sp (2), Sw, WG; 1958 v H, Pol, Y, F; 1959 v Ho, P; 1960 v Ni, W, Pol (19)

Higgins, A. (Kilmarnock), 1885 v Ni (1)

Higgins, A. (Newcastle U), 1910 v E, Ni; 1911 v E, Ni (4)

Highet, T. C. (Queen's Park), 1875 v E; 1876 v E, W; 1878 v E (4)

Hill, D. (Rangers), 1881 v E, W; 1882 v W (3)

Hill, D. A. (Third Lanark), 1906 v Ni (1)

Hill, F. R. (Aberdeen), 1930 v F; 1931 v W, Ni (3)

Hill, J. (Hearts), 1891 v E; 1892 v W (2)

Hogg, G (Hearts), 1896 v E, Ni (2)

Hogg, J. (Ayr U), 1922 v Ni (1)
Hogg, R. M. (Celtic), 1937 v Cz (1)
Holm, A. H. (Queen's Park), 1882 v W; 1883 v E, W (3)
Holt, D. D. (Hearts), 1963 v A, N, Ei, Sp; 1964 v WG (sub) (5)
Holton, J. A. (Manchester U), 1973 v W, Ni, E, Sw, Br; 1974 v Cz, WG, Ni, W, E, N, Z, Br, Y; 1975 v EG (15)
Hope, R. (WBA), 1968 v Ho; 1969 v D (2)
Houliston, W. (Queen of the South), 1949 v E, Ni, F (3)
Houston, S. M. (Manchester U), 1976 v D (1)
Howden, W. (Partick T), 1905 v Ni (1)
Howe, R. (Hamilton A), 1929 v N, Ho (2)
Howie, J. (Newcastle U), 1905 v E; 1906 v E; 1908 v E (3)
Howie, H. (Hibernian), 1949 v W (1)
Howieson, J. (St Mirren), 1927 v Ni (1)
Hughes, J. (Celtic), 1965 v Pol, Sp; 1966 v Ni, I (2); 1968 v E; 1969 v A; 1970 v Ei (8)
Hughes, W. (Sunderland), 1975 v Se (sub) (1)
Humphries, W. (Motherwell), 1952 v Se (1)
Hunter, A. (Kilmarnock), 1972 v Pe, Y; (with Celtic), 1973 v E; 1974 v Cz (4)
Hunter, J. (Dundee), 1909 v W (1)
Hunter, J. (Third Lanark), 1874 v E; (with Eastern), 1875 v E; (with Third Lanark), 1876 v E; 1877 v W (4)
Hunter, R. (St Mirren), 1890 v Ni (1)
Hunter, W. (Motherwell), 1960 v H, T; 1961 v W (3)
Husband, J. (Partick T), 1947 v W (1)
Hutchison, T. (Coventry C), 1974 v Cz (2), WG (2), Ni, W, Bel (sub), N, Z (sub), Y (sub); 1975 v EG, Sp (2), P, E (sub), R (sub); 1976 v D (17)
Hutton, J. (Aberdeen), 1923 v E, W, Ni; 1924 v Ni; 1926 v W, E, Ni; (with Blackburn R), 1927 v Ni; 1928 v W, Ni (10)
Hutton, J. (St Bernards), 1887 v Ni (1)
Hyslop, T. (Stoke C), 1896 v E; (with Rangers), 1897 v E (2)

Imlach, J. J. S. (Nottingham F), 1958 v H, Pol, Y, F (4)
Imrie, W. N. (St Johnstone), 1929 v N, G (2)
Inglis, J. (Kilmarnock Ath), 1884 v Ni (1)
Inglis, J. (Rangers), 1883 v E, W (2)
Irons, J. H. (Queen's Park), 1900 v W (1)

Jackson, A. (Cambuslang), 1886 v W; 1888 v Ni (2)
Jackson, A. (Aberdeen), 1925 v E, W, Ni; (with Huddersfield T), 1926 v E, W, Ni; 1927 v W, Ni; 1928 v E, W; 1929 v E, W, Ni; 1930 v E, W, Ni, F (17)
Jackson, C. (Rangers), 1975 v Se, P (sub); W; 1976 v D, R, Ni, W, E (8)
Jackson, J. (Partick T), 1931 v A, I, Sw; 1933 v E; (with Chelsea), 1934 v E; 1935 v E; 1936 v W, Ni (8)
Jackson, T. A. (St Mirren), 1904 v W, E, Ni; 1905 v W; 1907 v W, Ni (6)
James, A. W. (Preston NE), 1926 v W; 1928 v E; 1929 v E, Ni; (with Arsenal), 1930 v E, W, Ni; 1933 v W (8)
Jardine, A. (Rangers), 1971 v D (sub); 1972 v P, Bel, Ho; 1973 v E, Sw, Br; 1974 v Cz (2), WG (2), Ni, W, E, Bel, N, Z, Br, Y; 1975 v EG, Sp (2), Se, P, W, Ni, E; 1977 v Se (sub), Ch (sub), Br (sub); 1978 v Cz, W, Ni, Ir; 1980 v Pe, A, Bel (2) (38)
Jarvie, A. (Airdrieonians), 1971 v P (sub), Ni (sub), E (sub) (3)
Jenkinson, T. (Hearts), 1887 v Ni (1)
Johnston, L. H. (Clyde), 1948 v Bel, Sw (2)
Johnston, M. (Watford), 1984 v W (sub), E (sub), F; (with Celtic), 1985 v Y, Ic, Sp (2), W; 1986 v EG; 1987 v Bul, Ei (2), L; (with Nantes), 1988 v H, Bel, L, S.Ar, Sp, Co, E; 1989 v N, Y, I, Cy, F, Cy, E, Ch (sub); (with Rangers), 1990 v N, EG, Pol, Ma, Cr, Se, Br (36)
Johnston, R. (Sunderland), 1938 v Cz (1)
Johnston, W. (Rangers), 1966 v W, E, Pol, Ho; 1968 v W, E; 1969 v Ni (sub); 1970 v Ni; 1971 v D; (with WBA),

1977 v Se, W (sub), Ni, E, Ch, Arg, Br; 1978 v EG, Cz, W, W, E, Pe (22)
Johnstone, D. (Rangers), 1973 v W, Ni, E, Sw, Br; 1975 v EG (sub), Se (sub); 1976 v Sw, Ni (sub), E (sub); 1978 v Bul (sub), Ni, W; 1980 v Bel (14)
Johnstone, J. (Abercorn), 1888 v W (1)
Johnstone, J. (Celtic), 1965 v W, Fi; 1966 v E; 1967 v W, USSR; 1968 v W; 1969 v A, WG; 1970 v E, WG; 1971 v D, E; 1972 v P, Bel, Ho, Ni, E (sub); 1974 v W, E, Bel, N; 1975 v EG, Sp (23)
Johnstone, Jas (Kilmarnock), 1894 v W (1)
Johnstone, J. A. (Hearts), 1930 v W; 1933 v W, Ni (3)
Johnstone, R. (Hibernian), 1951 v E, D, F; 1952 v Ni, E; 1953 v E, Se; 1954 v E, N, Fi; 1955 v Ni, H; (with Manchester C), 1955 v E; 1956 v E, Ni, W (17)
Johnstone, W. (Third Lanark), 1887 v Ni; 1889 v W; 1890 v E (3)
Jordan, J. (Leeds U), 1973 v E (sub), Sw (sub), Br; 1974 v Cz (sub+1), WG (sub), Ni (sub), W, E, Bel, N, Z, Br, Y; 1975 v EG, Sp (2); 1976 v Ni, W, E; 1977 v Cz, W, Ni, E; 1978 v EG, Cz, W; (with Manchester U), Bul, Ni, E, Pe, Ir, Ho; 1979 v A, P, W (sub), Ni, E, N; 1980 v Bel, Ni (sub), W, E, Pol; 1981 v Is, W, E; (with AC Milan), 1982 v Se, Ho, W, E, USSR (52)

Kay, J. L. (Queen's Park), 1880 v E; 1882 v E, W; 1883 v E, W; 1884 v W (6)
Keillor, A. (Montrose), 1891 v W; 1892 v Ni; (with Dundee), 1894 v Ni; 1895 v W; 1896 v W; 1897 v W (6)
Keir, L. (Dumbarton), 1885 v W; 1886 v Ni; 1887 v E, W; 1888 v E (5)
Kelly, H. T. (Blackpool), 1952 v USA (1)
Kelly, J. (Renton), 1888 v E; (with Celtic), 1889 v E; 1890 v E; 1892 v E; 1893 v E, Ni; 1894 v W; 1896 v Ni (8)
Kelly, J. C. (Barnsley), 1949 v W, Ni (2)
Kelso, R. (Renton), 1885 v W, Ni; 1886 v W; 1887 v E, W; 1888 v E, Ni; (with Dundee), 1898 v Ni (8)
Kelso, T. (Dundee), 1914 v W (1)
Kennaway, J. (Celtic), 1934 v A (1)
Kennedy, A. (Eastern), 1875 v E; 1876 v E, W; (with Third Lanark), 1878 v E; 1882 v W; 1884 v W (6)
Kennedy, J. (Celtic), 1964 v W, E, WG; 1965 v W, Ni, Fi (6)
Kennedy, J. (Hibernian), 1897 v W (1)
Kennedy, S. (Aberdeen), 1978 v Bul, W, E, Pe, Ho; 1979 v A, P; 1982 v P (sub) (8)
Kennedy, S. (Partick T), 1905 v W (1)
Kennedy, S. (Rangers), 1975 v Se, P, W, Ni, E (5)
Ker, G. (Queen's Park), 1880 v E; 1881 v E, W; 1882 v W, E (5)
Ker, W. (Granville), 1872 v E; (with Queen's Park), 1873 v E (2)
Kerr, A. (Partick T), 1955 v A, H (2)
Kerr, P. (Hibernian), 1924 v Ni (1)
Key, G. (Hearts), 1902 v Ni (1)
Key, W. (Queen's Park), 1907 v Ni (1)
King, A. (Hearts), 1896 v E, W; (with Celtic), 1897 v Ni; 1898 v Ni; 1899 v Ni, W (6)
King, J. (Hamilton A), 1933 v Ni; 1934 v Ni (2)
King, W. S. (Queen's Park), 1929 v W (1)
Kinloch, J. D. (Partick T), 1922 v Ni (1)
Kinnaird, A. F. (Wanderers), 1873 v E (1)
Kinnear, D. (Rangers), 1938 v Cz (1)

Lambie, J. A. (Queen's Park), 1886 v Ni; 1887 v Ni; 1888 v E (3)
Lambie, W. A. (Queen's Park), 1892 v Ni; 1893 v W; 1894 v E; 1895 v E, Ni; 1896 v E, Ni; 1897 v E, Ni (9)
Lamont, D. (Pilgrims), 1885 v Ni (1)
Lang, A. (Dumbarton), 1880 v W (1)
Lang, J. J. (Clydesdale), 1876 v W; (with Third Lanark), 1878 v W (2)
Latta, A. (Dumbarton), 1888 v W; 1889 v E (2)

Law, D. (Huddersfield T), 1959 v W, Ni, Ho, P; 1960 v Ni, W; (with Manchester C), 1960 v E, Pol, A; 1961 v E, Ni; (with Torino), 1962 v Cz (2) E; (with Manchester U), 1963 v W, Ni, E, A, N, Ei, Sp; 1964 v W, E, N, WG; 1965 v W, Ni, E, Fi (2), Pol, Sp; 1966 v Ni, E, Pol; 1967 v W, E, USSR; 1968 v Ni; 1969 v Ni, A, WG; 1972 v Pe, Ni, W, E, Y, Cz, Br; (with Manchester C), 1974 v Cz (2), WG (2), Ni, Z (55)

Law, G. (Rangers), 1910 v E, Ni, W (3)

Law, T. (Chelsea), 1928 v E; 1930 v E (2)

Lawrence, J. (Newcastle U), 1911 v E (1)

Lawrence, T. (Liverpool), 1963 v Ei; 1969 v W, WG (3)

Lawson, D. (St Mirren), 1923 v E (1)

Leckie, R. (Queen's Park), 1872 v E (1)

Leggat, G. (Aberdeen), 1956 v E; 1957 v W; 1958 v Ni, H, Pol, Y, Par; (with Fulham), 1959 v E, W, Ni, WG, Ho; 1960 v E, Ni, W, Pol, A, H (18)

Leighton, J. (Aberdeen), 1983 v EG, Sw, Bel, Sw, W, E, Ca (2); 1984 v U, Bel, Ni, W, E, F; 1985 v Y, Ic, Sp (2), W, E, Ic; 1986 v W, EG, Aus (2), Is, D, WG, U; 1987 v Bul, Ei (2), L, Bel, E; 1988 v H, Bel, Bul, L, S.Ar, Ma, Sp, (with Manchester U), Co, E; 1989 v N, Cy, F, Cy, E, Ch; 1990 v Y, F, N, Arg, Ma (sub), Cr, Se, Br (58)

Lennie, W. (Aberdeen), 1908 v W, Ni (2)

Lennox, R. (Celtic), 1967 v Ni, E, USSR; 1968 v W, L; 1969 v D, A, WG, Cy (sub); 1970 v W (sub) (10)

Leslie, L. G. (Airdrieonians), 1961 v W, Ni, Ei (2), Cz (5)

Levein, C. (Hearts), 1990 v Arg, EG, Eg (sub), Pol, Ma (sub), Se (6)

Liddell, W. (Liverpool), 1947 v W, Ni; 1948 v E, W, Ni; 1950 v E, W, P, F; 1951 v W, Ni, E, A; 1952 v W, Ni, E, USA, D, Se; 1953 v W, Ni, E; 1954 v W; 1955 v P, Y, A, H; 1956 v Ni (28)

Liddle, D. (East Fife), 1931 v A, I, Sw (3)

Lindsay, D. (St Mirren), 1903 v Ni (1)

Lindsay, J. (Dumbarton), 1880 v W; 1881 v W, E; 1884 v W, E; 1885 v W, E; 1886 v E (8)

Lindsay, J. (Renton), 1888 v E; 1893 v E, Ni (3)

Linwood, A. B. (Clyde), 1950 v W (1)

Little, R. J. (Rangers), 1953 v Se (1)

Livingstone, G. T. (Manchester C), 1906 v E; (with Rangers), 1907 v W (2)

Lochhead, A. (Third Lanark), 1889 v W (1)

Logan, J. (Ayr U), 1891 v W (1)

Logan, T. (Falkirk), 1913 v Ni (1)

Logie, J. T. (Arsenal), 1953 v Ni (1)

Loney, W. (Celtic), 1910 v W, Ni (2)

Long, H. (Clyde), 1947 v Ni (1)

Longair, W. (Dundee), 1894 v Ni (1)

Lorimer, P. (Leeds U), 1970 v A (sub); 1971 v W, Ni; 1972 v Ni (sub), W, E; 1973 v D (2), E (2); 1974 v WG (sub), E, Bel, N, Z, Br, Y; 1975 v Sp (sub); 1976 v D (2), R (sub) (21)

Love, A. (Aberdeen), 1931 v A, I, Sw (3)

Low, A. (Falkirk), 1934 v Ni (1)

Low, T. P. (Rangers), 1897 v Ni (1)

Low, W. L. (Newcastle U), 1911 v E, W; 1912 v Ni; 1920 v E, Ni (5)

Lowe, J. (Cambuslang), 1891 v Ni (1)

Lowe, J. (St Bernards), 1887 v Ni (1)

Lundie, J. (Hibernian), 1886 v W (1)

Lyall, J. (Sheffield W), 1905 v E (1)

McAdam, J. (Third Lanark), 1880 v W (1)

McAllister, G. (Leicester C), 1990 v EG, Pol, Ma (sub) (3)

McArthur, D. (Celtic), 1895 v E, Ni; 1899 v W (3)

McAtee, A. (Celtic), 1913 v W (1)

McAulay, J. (Dumbarton), 1882 v W; (with Arthurlie), 1884 v Ni (2)

McAulay, J. (Dumbarton), 1883 v E, W; 1884 v E; 1885 v E, W; 1886 v E; 1887 v E, W (8)

McAuley, R. (Rangers), 1932 v Ni, W (2)

McAvennie, F. (West Ham U), 1986 v Aus (2), D (sub), WG (sub); (with Celtic), 1988 v S.Ar (5)

McBain, E. (St Mirren), 1894 v W (1)

McBain, N. (Manchester U), 1922 v E; (with Everton), 1923 v Ni; 1924 v W (3)

McBride, J. (Celtic), 1967 v W, Ni (2)

McBride, P. (Preston NE), 1904 v E; 1906 v E; 1907 v E, W; 1908 v E; 1909 v W (6)

McCall, J. (Renton), 1886 v W; 1887 v E, W; 1888 v E; 1890 v E (5)

McCall, S. M. (Everton), 1990 v Arg, EG, Eg (sub), Pol, Ma, Cr, Se, Br (8)

McCalliog, J. (Sheffield W), 1967 v E, USSR; 1968 v Ni; 1969 v D; (with Wolverhampton W), 1971 v P (5)

McCallum, N. (Renton), 1888 v Ni (1)

McCann, R. J. (Motherwell), 1959 v WG; 1960 v E, Ni, W; 1961 v E (5)

McCartney, W. (Hibernian), 1902 v Ni (1)

McClair, B. (Celtic), 1987 v L, Ei, E, Br (sub); (with Manchester U), 1988 v Bul, Ma (sub), Sp (sub); 1989 v N, Y, I (sub), Cy, F (sub); 1990 v N (sub), Arg (sub) (14)

McClory, A. (Motherwell), 1927 v W; 1928 v Ni; 1935 v W (3)

McCloy, P. (Ayr U), 1924 v E; 1925 v E (2)

McCloy, P. (Rangers), 1973 v W, Ni, Sw, Br (4)

McCoist, A. (Rangers), 1986 v Ho; 1987 v L (sub), Ei (sub), Bel, E, Br; 1988 v H, Bel, Ma, Sp, Co, E; 1989 v Y (sub), F, Cy, E; 1990 v Y, F, N, EG (sub), Eg, Pol, Ma (sub), Cr (sub), Se (sub), Br (26)

McColl, A. (Renton), 1888 v Ni (1)

McColl, I. M. (Rangers), 1950 v E, F; 1951 v W, Ni, Bel; 1957 v E, Ni, W, Y, Sp, Sw, WG; 1958 v Ni, E (14)

McColl, R. S. (Queen's Park), 1896 v W, Ni; 1897 v Ni; 1898 v Ni; 1899 v Ni, E, W; 1900 v E, W; 1901 v E, W; (with Newcastle U), 1902 v E; (with Queen's Park), 1908 v Ni (13)

McColl, W. (Renton), 1895 v W (1)

McCombie, A. (Sunderland), 1903 v E, W; (with Newcastle U), 1905 v E, W (4)

McCorkindale, J. (Partick T), 1891 v W (1)

McCormick, R. (Abercorn), 1886 v W (1)

McCrae, D. (St Mirren), 1929 v N, G (2)

McCreadie, A. (Rangers), 1893 v W; 1894 v E (2)

McCreadie, E. G. (Chelsea), 1965 v E, Sp, Fi, Pol; 1966 v P, Ni, W, Pol, I; 1967 v E, USSR; 1968 v Ni, W, E, Ho; 1969 v W, Ni, E, D, A, WG, Cy (2) (23)

McCulloch, D. (Hearts), 1935 v W; (with Brentford), 1936 v E; 1937 v W, Ni; 1938 v Cz; (with Derby Co), 1939 v H, W (7)

MacDonald, A. (Rangers), 1976 v Sw (1)

McDonald, J. (Edinburgh University), 1886 v E (1)

McDonald, J. (Sunderland), 1956 v W, Ni (2)

MacDougall, E. J. (Norwich C) 1975 v Se, P, W, Ni, E; 1976 v D, R (7)

McDougall, J. (Liverpool), 1931 v I, A (2)

McDougall, J. (Airdrieonians), 1926 v Ni (1)

McDougall, J. (Vale of Leven), 1877 v E, W; 1878 v E; 1879 v E, W (5)

McFadyen, W. (Motherwell), 1934 v A, W (2)

Macfarlane, A. (Dundee), 1904 v W; 1906 v W; 1908 v W; 1909 v Ni; 1911 v W (5)

McFarlane, R. (Greenock Morton), 1896 v W (1)

Macfarlane, W. (Hearts), 1947 v L (1)

McGarr, E. (Aberdeen), 1970 v Ei, A (2)

McGarvey, F. P. (Liverpool), 1979 v Ni (sub), Arg; (with Celtic), 1984 v U, Bel (sub), EG (sub), Ni, W (7)

McGeoch, A. (Dumbreck), 1876 v E, W; 1877 v E, W (4)

McGhee, J. (Hibernian), 1886 v W (1)

McGhee, M. (Aberdeen), 1983 v Ca (1+1 sub); 1984 v Ni (sub), E (4)

McGonagle, W. (Celtic), 1933 v E; 1934 v A, E, Ni; 1935 v Ni, W (6)

McGrain, D. (Celtic), 1973 v W, Ni, E, Sw, Br; 1974 v Cz (2), WG, W (sub), E, Bel, N, Z, Br, Y; 1975 v Sp, Se, P, W, Ni, E, R; 1976 v D (2), Sw, Ni, W, E; 1977 v Fi, Cz, W (2), Se, Ni, E, Ch, Arg, Br; 1978 v EG, Cz; 1980 v Bel, P, Ni, W, E, Pol, H; 1981 v Se, P, Is, Ni, Is, W (sub), Ni, E; 1982 v Se, Sp, Ho, Ni, E, Nz, USSR (sub) (62)

McGregor, J. C. (Vale of Leven), 1877 v E, W; 1878 v E; 1880 v E (4)

McGrory, J. E. (Kilmarnock), 1965 v Ni, Fi; 1966 v P (3)

McGrory, J. (Celtic), 1928 v Ni; 1931 v E; 1932 v Ni, W; 1933 v E, Ni; 1934 v Ni (7)

McGuire, W. (Beith), 1881 v E, W (2)

McGurk, F. (Birmingham), 1934 v W (1)

McHardy, H. (Rangers), 1885 v Ni (1)

McInally, A. (Aston Villa), 1989 v Cy (sub), Ch; (with Bayern Munich), 1990 v Y (sub), F (sub), Arg, Pol (sub), Ma, Cr (8)

McInally, J. (Dundee U), 1987 v Bel, Br; 1988 v Ma (sub) (3)

McInally, T. B. (Celtic), 1926 v Ni; 1927 v W (2)

McInnes, T. (Cowlairs), 1889 v Ni (1)

McIntosh, W. (Third Lanark), 1905 v Ni (1)

McIntyre, A. (Vale of Leven), 1878 v E; 1882 v E (2)

McIntyre, H. (Rangers), 1880 v W (1)

McIntyre, J. (Rangers), 1884 v W (1)

McKay, D. (Celtic), 1959 v E, WG, Ho, P; 1960 v E, Pol, A, H, T; 1961 v W, Ni; 1962 v Ni, Cz, U (sub) (14)

Mackay, D. C. (Hearts), 1957 v Sp; 1958 v F; 1959 v W, Ni; (with Tottenham H), 1959 v WG, E; 1960 v W, Ni, A, Pol, H, T; 1961 v W, Ni, E; 1963 v E, A, N; 1964 v Ni, W, N; 1966 v Ni (22)

Mackay, G. (Hearts), 1988 v Bul (sub), L (sub), S.Ar (sub), Ma (4)

McKay, J. (Blackburn R), 1924 v W (1)

McKay, R. (Newcastle U), 1928 v W (1)

McKean, R. (Rangers), 1976 v Sw (1)

McKenzie, D. (Brentford), 1938 v Ni (1)

Mackenzie, J. A. (Partick T), 1954 v W, E, N, Fi, A, U; 1955 v E, H; 1956 v A (9)

McKeown, M. (Celtic), 1889 v Ni; 1890 v E (2)

McKie, J. (East Stirling), 1898 v W (1)

McKillop, T. R. (Rangers), 1938 v Ho (1)

McKimmie, S. (Aberdeen), 1989 v E, Ch; 1990 v Arg, Eg, Cr (sub), Br (6)

McKinlay, D. (Liverpool), 1922 v W, Ni (2)

McKinnon, A. (Queen's Park), 1874 v E (1)

McKinnon, R. (Rangers), 1966 v W, E, I (2), Ho, Br; 1967 v W, Ni, E; 1968 v Ni, W, E, Ho; 1969 v D, A, WG, Cy; 1970 v Ni, W, E, Ei, WG, A; 1971 v D, Bel, P, USSR, D (28)

MacKinnon, W. (Dumbarton), 1883 v E, W; 1884 v E, W (4)

McKinnon, W. W. (Queen's Park), 1872 v E; 1873 v E; 1874 v E; 1875 v E; 1876 v E, W; 1877 v E; 1878 v E; 1879 v E (9)

McLaren, A. (St Johnstone), 1929 v N, G, Ho; 1933 v W, Ni (5)

McLaren, A. (Preston NE), 1947 v E, Bel, L; 1948 v W (4)

McLaren, J. (Hibernian), 1888 v W; (with Celtic), 1889 v E; 1890 v E (3)

McLean, A. (Celtic), 1926 v W, Ni; 1927 v W, E (4)

McLean, D. (St Bernards), 1896 v W; 1897 v Ni (2)

McLean, G. (Sheffield W), 1912 v E (1)

McLean, G. (Dundee), 1968 v Ho (1)

McLean, T. (Kilmarnock), 1969 v D, Cy, W; 1970 v Ni, W; 1971 v D (6)

McLeish, A. (Aberdeen), 1980 v F, Ni, W, E, Pol, H; 1981 v Se, Is, Is, Ni, E; 1982 v Se, Sp, Ni, Br (sub); 1983 v Bel, Sw (sub), W, E, Ca (3); 1984 v U, Bel, EG, Ni,

W, E, F; 1985 v Y, Ic, Sp (2), W, E, Ic; 1986 v W, EG, Aus (2), E, Ho, D; 1987 v Bel, E, Br; 1988 v Bel, Bul, L, S.Ar (sub), Ma, Sp, Co, E; 1989 v N, Y, I, Cy, Fr, Cy, E, Ch; 1990 v Y, F, N, Arg, EG, Eg, Cr, Se, Br (72)

McLeod, D. (Celtic), 1905 v Ni; 1906 v E, W, Ni (4)

McLeod, J. (Dumbarton), 1888 v Ni; 1889 v W; 1890 v Ni; 1892 v E; 1893 v W (5)

MacLeod, J. M. (Hibernian), 1961 v E, Ei (2), Cz (4)

MacLeod, M. (Celtic), 1985 v E (sub); 1987 v Ei, L, E, Br; (with Borussia Dortmund), 1988 v Co, E; 1989 v I, Ch; 1990 v Y, F, N (sub), Arg, EG, Pol, Se, Br (17)

McLeod, W. (Cowlairs), 1886 v Ni (1)

McLintock, A. (Vale of Leven), 1875 v E; 1876 v E; 1880 v E (3)

McLintock, F. (Leicester C), 1963 v N (sub), Ei, Sp; (with Arsenal), 1965 v Ni; 1967 v USSR; 1970 v Ni; 1971 v W, Ni, E (9)

McLuckie, J. S. (Manchester C), 1934 v W (1)

McMahon, A. (Celtic), 1892 v E; 1893 v E, Ni; 1894 v E; 1901 v Ni; 1902 v W (6)

McMenemy, J. (Celtic), 1905 v Ni; 1909 v Ni; 1910 v E, W; 1911 v Ni, W, E; 1912 v W; 1914 v W, Ni, E; 1920 v Ni (12)

McMenemy, J. (Motherwell), 1934 v W (1)

McMillan, J. (St Bernards), 1897 v W (1)

McMillan, I. L. (Airdrieonians), 1952 v E, USA, D; 1955 v E; 1956 v E; (with Rangers), 1961 v Cz (6)

McMillan, T. (Dumbarton), 1887 v Ni (1)

McMullan, J. (Partick T), 1920 v W; 1921 v W, Ni, E; 1924 v E, Ni; 1925 v E; 1926 v W; (with Manchester C), 1926 v E; 1927 v E, W; 1928 v E, W; 1929 v W, E, Ni (16)

McNab, A. (Morton), 1921 v E, Ni (2)

McNab, A. (Sunderland), 1937 v A; (with WBA), 1939 v E (2)

McNab, C. D. (Dundee), 1931 v E, W, A, I, Sw; 1932 v E (6)

McNab, J. S. (Liverpool), 1923 v W (1)

McNair, A. (Celtic), 1906 v W; 1907 v Ni; 1908 v E, W; 1909 v E; 1910 v W; 1912 v E, W, Ni; 1913 v E; 1914 v E, Ni; 1920 v E, W, Ni (15)

McNaught, W. (Raith R), 1951 v A, W, Ni; 1952 v E; 1955 v Ni (5)

McNeil, H. (Queen's Park), 1874 v E; 1875 v E; 1876 v E, W; 1877 v W; 1878 v E; 1879 v E, W; 1881 v E, W (10)

McNeil, M. (Rangers), 1876 v W; 1880 v E (2)

McNeill, W. (Celtic), 1961 v E, Ei (2), Cz; 1962 v Ni, E, Cz, U; 1963 v Ei, Sp; 1964 v W, E, WG; 1965 v E, Fi, Pol, Sp; 1966 v Ni, Pol; 1967 v USSR; 1968 v E; 1969 v Cy, W, E, Cy (sub); 1970 v WG; 1972 v Ni, W, E (29)

McPhail, J. (Celtic), 1950 v W; 1951 v W, Ni, A; 1954 v Ni (5)

McPhail, R. (Airdrieonians), 1927 v E; (with Rangers), 1929 v W; 1931 v E, Ni; 1932 v W, Ni, F; 1933 v E, Ni; 1934 v A, Ni; 1935 v E; 1937 v G, E, Cz; 1938 v W, Ni (17)

McPherson, D. (Kilmarnock), 1892 v Ni (1)

McPherson, D. (Hearts), 1989 v Cy, E; 1990 v N, Ma, Cr, Se, Br (7)

McPherson, J. (Kilmarnock), 1888 v W; (with Cowlairs), 1889 v E; 1890 v Ni, E; (with Rangers), 1892 v W; 1894 v E; 1895 v E, Ni; 1897 v Ni (9)

McPherson, J. (Clydesdale), 1875 v E (1)

McPherson, J. (Vale of Leven), 1879 v E, W; 1880 v E; 1881 v W; 1883 v E, W; 1884 v E; 1885 v N (8)

McPherson, J. (Hearts), 1891 v E (1)

McPherson, R. (Arthurlie), 1882 v E (1)

McQueen, G. (Leeds U), 1974 v Bel; 1975 v Sp (2), P, W, Ni, E, R; 1976 v D; 1977 v Cz (2), Ni, E; 1978 v EG, Cz, W; (with Manchester U), Bul, Ni, W; 1979 v A, N, P, Ni, E, N; 1980 v Pe, A, Bel; 1981 v W (30)

McQueen, M. (Leith Ath), 1890 v W; 1891 v W (2)

McRorie, D. M. (Morton), 1931 v W (1)

McSpadyen, A. (Partick T), 1939 v E, H (2)

McStay, P. (Celtic), 1984 v U, Bel, EG, Ni, W, E (sub); 1985 v Ic, Sp (2), W; 1986 v EG (sub), Aus, Is, U; 1987 v Bul, Ei (2, 1 sub), L (sub), Bel, E, Br; 1988 v H, Bel, Bul, L, S.Ar, Sp, Co, E; 1989 v N, Y, I, Cy, F, Cy, E, Ch; 1990 v Y, F, N, Arg, EG (sub), Eg, Pol (sub), Ma, Cr, Se (sub), Br (48)

McStay, W. (Celtic), 1921 v W, Ni; 1925 v E, Ni, W; 1926 v E, Ni, W; 1927 v E, Ni, W; 1928 v W, Ni (13)

McTavish, J. (Falkirk), 1910 v Ni (1)

McWhattie, G. C. (Queen's Park), 1901 v W, Ni (2)

McWilliam, P. (Newcastle U) 1905 v E; 1906 v E; 1907 v E, W; 1909 v E, W; 1910 v E; 1911 v W (8)

Macari, L. (Celtic), 1972 v W (sub), E, Y, Cz, Br; 1973 v D; (with Manchester U), E (2), W (sub), Ni (sub); 1975 v Se, P (sub), W, E (sub), R; 1977 v Ni (sub), E (sub), Ch, Arg; 1978 v EG, W, Bul, Pe (sub), Ir (24)

Macauley, A. R. (Brentford), 1947 v E; (with Arsenal), 1948 v E, W, Ni, Bel, Sw, F (7)

Madden, J. (Celtic), 1893 v W; 1895 v W (2)

Main, F. R. (Rangers), 1938 v W (1)

Main, J. (Hibernian), 1909 v Ni (1)

Maley, W. (Celtic), 1893 v E, Ni (2)

Malpas, M. (Dundee U), 1984 v F; 1985 v E, Ic; 1986 v W, Aus (2), Is, R, E, Ho, D, WG; 1987 v Bul, Ei, Bel; 1988 v Bel, Bul, L, S.Ar, Ma; 1989 v N, Y, I, Cy, F, Cy, E, Ch; 1990 v Y, F, N, Eg, Pol, Ma, Cr, Se, Br (37)

Marshall, H. (Celtic), 1899 v W; 1900 v Ni (2)

Marshall, J. (Rangers), 1932 v E; 1933 v E; 1934 v E (3)

Marshall, J. (Middlesbrough), 1921 v E, W, Ni; 1922 v E, W, Ni; (with Llanelly), 1924 v W (7)

Marshall, J. (Third Lanark), 1885 v Ni; 1886 v W; 1887 v E, W (4)

Marshall, R. W. (Rangers), 1892 v Ni; 1894 v Ni (2)

Martin, F. (Aberdeen), 1954 v N (2), A, U; 1955 v E, H (6)

Martin, N. (Hibernian), 1965 v Fi, Pol; (with Sunderland), 1966 v I (3)

Martis, J. (Motherwell), 1961 v W (1)

Mason, J. (Third Lanark), 1949 v E, W, Ni; 1950 v Ni; 1951 v Ni, Bel, A (7)

Massie, A. (Hearts), 1932 v Ni, W, F; 1933 v Ni; 1934 v E, Ni; 1935 v E, Ni, W; 1936 v W, Ni; (with Aston Villa), 1936 v E; 1937 v G, E, W, Ni, A; 1938 v W (18)

Masson, D. S. (QPR), 1976 v Ni, W, E; 1977 v Fi, Cz, W, Ni, E, Ch, Arg, Br; 1978 v EG, Cz, W; (with Derby Co), Ni, E, Pe (17)

Mathers, D. (Partick T), 1954 v Fi (1)

Maxwell, W. S. (Stoke C), 1898 v E (1)

May, J. (Rangers), 1906 v W, Ni; 1908 v E, Ni; 1909 v W (5)

Meechan, P. (Celtic), 1896 v Ni (1)

Meiklejohn, D. D. (Rangers), 1922 v W; 1924 v W; 1925 v W, Ni, E; 1928 v W, Ni; 1929 v E, Ni; 1930 v E, Ni; 1931 v E; 1932 v W, Ni; 1934 v A (15)

Menzies, A. (Hearts), 1906 v E (1)

Mercer, R. (Hearts), 1912 v W; 1913 v Ni (2)

Middleton, R. (Cowdenbeath), 1930 v Ni (1)

Millar, J. (Rangers), 1897 v E; 1898 v E, W (3)

Millar, J. (Rangers), 1963 v A, Ei (2)

Millar, A. (Hearts), 1939 v W (1)

Miller, J. (St Mirren), 4931 v E, I, Sw; 1932 v F; 1934 v E (5)

Miller, P. (Dumbarton), 1882 v E; 1883 v E, W (3)

Miller, T. (Liverpool) 1920 v E; (with Manchester U), 1921 v E, Ni (3)

Miller, W. (Third Lanark), 1876 v E (1)

Miller, W. (Celtic), 1947 v E, W, Bel, I.; 1948 v W, Ni (6)

Miller, W. (Aberdeen), 1975 v R; 1978 v Bul; 1980 v Bel, W, E, Pol, H; 1981 v Se, P, Is (sub), Ni, W, Ni, E; 1982 v Ni, P, Ho, Br, USSR; 1983 v EG, Sw, Sw, W, E, Ca (3); 1984 v U, Bel, EG, W, E, F; 1985 v Y, Ic, Sp (2), W, E, Ic; 1986 v W, EG, Aus (2), Is, R, E, Ho, D, WG,

U; 1987 v Bul, E, Br; 1988 v H, L, S.Ar, Ma, Sp, Co, E; 1989 v N, Y; 1990 v Y, N (65)

Mills, W. (Aberdeen), 1936 v W, Ni; 1937 v W (3)

Milne, J. V. (Middlesbrough), 1938 v E; 1939 v E (2)

Mitchell, D. (Rangers), 1890 v Ni; 1892 v E; 1893 v E, Ni; 1894 v E (5)

Mitchell, J. (Kilmarnock), 1908 v Ni; 1910 v Ni, W (3)

Mitchell, R. C. (Newcastle U), 1951 v D, F (2)

Mochan, N. (Celtic), 1954 v N, A, U (3)

Moir, W. (Bolton W), 1950 v E (1)

Moncur, R. (Newcastle U), 1968 v Ho; 1970 v Ni, W, E, Ei; 1971 v D, Bel, W, P, Ni, E, D; 1972 v Pe, Ni, W, E (16)

Morgan, H. (St Mirren), 1898 v W; (with Liverpool), 1899 v E (2)

Morgan, W. (Burnley), 1968 v Ni; (with Manchester U) 1972 v Pe, Y, Cz, Br; 1973 v D (2), E (2), W, Ni, Sw, Br; 1974 v Cz (2), WG (2), Ni, Bel (sub), Br, Y (21)

Morris, D. (Raith R), 1923 v Ni; 1924 v E, Ni; 1925 v E, W, Ni (6)

Morris, H. (East Fife), 1950 v Ni (1)

Morrison, T. (St Mirren), 1927 v E (1)

Morton, A. L. (Queen's Park), 1920 v W, Ni; (with Rangers), 1921 v E; 1922 v E, W; 1923 v E, W, Ni; 1924 v E, W, Ni; 1925 v E, W, Ni; 1927 v E, Ni; 1928 v E, W, Ni; 1929 v E, W, Ni; 1930 v E, W, Ni; 1931 v E, W, Ni; 1932 v E, W, F (31)

Morton, H. A. (Kilmarnock), 1929 v G, Ho (2)

Mudie, J. K. (Blackpool), 1957 v W, Ni, E, Y, Sw, Sp (2), WG; 1958 v Ni, E, W, Sw, H, Pol, Y, Par, F (17)

Muir, W. (Dundee), 1907 v Ni (1)

Muirhead, T. A. (Rangers), 1922 v Ni; 1923 v E; 1924 v W; 1927 v Ni; 1928 v Ni; 1929 v W, Ni; 1930 v W (8)

Mulhall, G. (Aberdeen), 1960 v Ni; (with Sunderland), 1963 v Ni; 1964 v Ni (3)

Munro, A. D. (Hearts), 1937 v W, Ni; (with Blackpool), 1938 v Ho (3)

Munro, F. M. (Wolverhampton W), 1971 v Ni (sub), E (sub), D, USSR; 1975 v Se, W (sub), Ni, E, R (9)

Munro, I. (St Mirren), 1979 v Arg, N; 1980 v Pe, A, Bel, W, E (7)

Munro, N. (Abercorn), 1888 v W; 1889 v E (2)

Murdoch, J. (Motherwell), 1931 v Ni (1)

Murdoch, R. (Celtic), 1966 v W, E, I (2); 1967 v Ni; 1968 v Ni; 1969 v W, Ni, E, WG, Cy; 1970 v A (12)

Murphy, F. (Celtic), 1938 v Ho (1)

Murray, J. (Renton), 1895 v W (1)

Murray, J. (Hearts), 1958 v E, H, Pol, Y, F (5)

Murray, J. W. (Vale of Leven), 1890 v W (1)

Murray, P. (Hibernian), 1896 v Ni; 1897 v W (2)

Murray, S. (Aberdeen), 1972 v Bel (1)

Mutch, G. (Preston NE), 1938 v E (1)

Napier, C. E. (Celtic), 1932 v E; 1935 v E, W; (with Derby Co), 1937 v Ni, A (5)

Narey, D. (Dundee U), 1977 v Se (sub); 1979 v P, Ni (sub), Arg; 1980 v P, Ni, Pol, H; 1981 v W, E (sub); 1982 v Ho, W, E, Nz (sub), Br, USSR; 1983 v EG, Sw, Bel, Ni, W, E, Ca (3); 1986 v Is, R, Ho, WG, U; 1987 v Bul, E; Bel; 1989 v I, Cy (35)

Neil, R. G. (Hibernian), 1896 v W; (with Rangers), 1900 v W (2)

Neill, R. W. (Queen's Park), 1876 v W; 1877 v E, W; 1878 v W; 1880 v E (5)

Neilles, P. (Hearts), 1914 v W, Ni (2)

Nelson, J. (Cardiff C), 1925 v W, Ni; 1928 v E; 1930 v F (4)

Nevin, P. K. F. (Chelsea), 1986 v R (sub), E (sub); 1987 v L. Ei, Bel (sub); 1988 v L; (with Everton), 1989 v Cy, E (7)

Niblo, T. D. (Aston Villa), 1904 v E (1)

Nibloe, J. (Kilmarnock), 1929 v E, N, Ho; 1930 v W; 1931 v E, Ni, A, I, Sw; 1932 v E, F (11)

Nicholas, C. (Celtic), 1983 v Sw, Ni, E, Ca (3); (with Arsenal), 1984 v Bel, F (sub); 1985 v Y (sub), Ic (sub), Sp (sub), W (sub); 1986 v Is, R (sub), E, D, U (sub); 1987 v Bul, E (sub); (with Aberdeen), 1989 v Cy (sub) (20)

Nicol, S. (Liverpool), 1985 v Y, Ic, Sp, W; 1986 v W, EG, Aus, E, D, WG, U; 1988 v H, Bul, S.Ar, Sp, Co, E; 1989 v N, Y, Cy, F; 1990 v Y, F (23)

Nisbet, J. (Ayr U), 1929 v N, G, Ho (3)

Niven, J. B. (Moffatt), 1885 v Ni (1)

O'Donnell, F. (Preston NE), 1937 v E, A, Cz; 1938 v E, W; (with Blackpool), Ho (6)

Ogilvie, D. H. (Motherwell), 1934 v A (1)

O'Hare, J. (Derby Co), 1970 v W, Ni, E; 1971 v D, Bel, W, Ni; 1972 v P, Bel, Ho (sub), Pe, Ni, W (13)

Ormond, W. E. (Hibernian), 1954 v E, N, Fi, A, U; 1959 v E (6)

O'Rourke, F. (Airdrieonians), 1907 v Ni (1)

Orr, J. (Kilmarnock), 1892 v W (1)

Orr, R. (Newcastle U), 1902 v E; 1904 v E (2)

Orr, T. (Morton), 1952 v Ni, W (2)

Orr, W. (Celtic), 1900 v Ni; 1903 v Ni; 1904 v W (3)

Orrock, R. (Falkirk), 1913 v W (1)

Oswald, J. (Third Lanark), 1889 v E; (with St Bernards), 1895 v E; (with Rangers), 1897 v W (3)

Parker, A. H. (Falkirk), 1955 v P, Y, A; 1956 v E, Ni, W, A; 1957 v Ni, W, Y; 1958 v Ni, W, E, Sw; (with Everton), Par (15)

Parlane, D. (Rangers), 1973 v W, Sw, Br; 1975 v Sp (sub), Se, P, W, Ni, E, R; 1976 v D (sub); 1977 v W (12)

Parlane, R. (Vale of Leven), 1878 v W; 1879 v E, W (3)

Paterson, G. D. (Celtic), 1939 v Ni (1)

Paterson, J. (Leicester C), 1920 v E (1)

Paterson, J. (Cowdenbeath), 1931 v A, I, Sw (3)

Paton, A. (Motherwell), 1952 v D, Se (2)

Paton, D. (St Bernards), 1896 v W (1)

Paton, M. (Dumbarton), 1883 v E; 1884 v W; 1885 v W, E; 1886 v E (5)

Paton, R. (Vale of Leven), 1879 v E, W (2)

Patrick, J. (St Mirren), 1897 v E, W (2)

Paul, H. McD. (Queen's Park), 1909 v E, W, Ni (3)

Paul, W. (Partick T), 1888 v W; 1889 v W; 1890 v W (3)

Paul, W. (Dykebar), 1891 v Ni (1)

Pearson, T. (Newcastle U), 1947 v E, Bel (2)

Penman, A. (Dundee), 1966 v Ho (1)

Pettigrew, W. (Motherwell), 1976 v Sw, Ni, W; 1977 v W (sub), Se (5)

Phillips, J. (Queen's Park), 1877 v E, W; 1878 v W (3)

Plenderleith, J. B. (Manchester C), 1961 v Ni (1)

Porteous, W. (Hearts), 1903 v Ni (1)

Pringle, C. (St Mirren), 1921 v W (1)

Provan, D. (Rangers), 1964 v Ni, N; 1966 v I (2), Ho (5)

Provan, D. (Celtic), 1980 v Bel (2 sub), P (sub), Ni (sub); 1981 v Is, W, E; 1982 v Se, P, Ni (10)

Pursell, P. (Queen's Park), 1914 v W (1)

Quinn, J. (Celtic), 1905 v Ni; 1906 v Ni, W; 1908 v Ni, E; 1909 v E; 1910 v E, Ni, W; 1912 v E, W (11)

Quinn, P. (Motherwell), 1961 v E, Ei (2); 1962 v U (4)

Rae, J. (Third Lanark), 1889 v W; 1890 v Ni (2)

Raeside, J. S. (Third Lanark), 1906 v W (1)

Raisbeck, A. G. (Liverpool), 1900 v E; 1901 v E; 1902 v E; 1903 v E, W; 1904 v E; 1906 v E; 1907 v E (8)

Rankin, G. (Vale of Leven), 1890 v Ni; 1891 v E (2)

Rankin, R. (St Mirren), 1929 v N, G, Ho (3)

Redpath, W. (Motherwell), 1949 v W, Ni; 1951 v E, D, F, Bel, A; 1952 v Ni, E (9)

Reid, J. G. (Airdrieonians), 1914 v W; 1920 v W; 1924 v Ni (3)

Reid, R. (Brentford), 1938 v E, Ni (2)

Reid, W. (Rangers), 1911 v E, W, Ni; 1912 v Ni; 1913 v E, W, Ni; 1914 v E, Ni (9)

Reilly, L. (Hibernian), 1949 v E, W, F; 1950 v W, Ni, Sw, F; 1951 v W, E, D, F, Bel, A; 1952 v Ni, W, E, USA, D, Se; 1953 v Ni, W, E, Se; 1954 v W; 1955 v H (2), P, Y, A, E; 1956 v E, W, Ni, A; 1957 v E, Ni, W, Y (38)

Rennie, H. G. (Hearts), 1900 v E, Ni; (with Hibernian), 1901 v E; 1902 v E, Ni, W; 1903 v Ni, W; 1904 v Ni; 1905 v W; 1906 v Ni; 1908 v Ni, W (13)

Renny-Tailyour, H. W. (Royal Engineers), 1873 v E (1)

Rhind, A. (Queen's Park), 1872 v E (1)

Richmond, A. (Queen's Park), 1906 v W (1)

Richmond, J. T. (Clydesdale), 1877 v E; (with Queen's Park), 1878 v E; 1882 v W (3)

Ring, T. (Clyde), 1953 v Se; 1955 v W, Ni, E, H; 1957 v E, Sp (2), Sw, WG; 1958 v Ni, Sw (12)

Rioch, B. D. (Derby Co), 1975 v P, W, Ni, E, R; 1976 v D (2), R, Ni, W, E; 1977 v Fi, Cz, W; (with Everton), W, Ni, E, Ch, Br; 1978 v Cz; (with Derby Co), Ni, E, Pe, Ho (24)

Ritchie, A. (East Stirlingshire), 1891 v W (1)

Ritchie, H. (Hibernian), 1923 v W; 1928 v Ni (2)

Ritchie, J. (Queen's Park), 1897 v W (1)

Ritchie, W. (Rangers), 1962 v U (sub) (1)

Robb, D. T. (Aberdeen), 1971 v W, E, P, D (sub), USSR (5)

Robb, W. (Rangers), 1926 v W; (with Hibernian), 1928 v W (2)

Robertson, A. (Clyde), 1955 v P, A, H; 1958 v Sw, Par (5)

Robertson, G. (Motherwell), 1910 v W; (with Sheffield W), 1912 v W; 1913 v E, Ni (4)

Robertson, G. (Kilmarnock), 1938 v Cz (1)

Robertson, H. (Dundee), 1962 v Cz (1)

Robertson, J. (Dundee), 1931 v A, I (2)

Robertson, J. N. (Nottingham F), 1978 v Ni, W (sub), Ir; 1979 v P, N; 1980 v Pe, A, Bel (2), P; 1981 v Se, P, Is, Ni, Is, Ni, E; 1982 v Se, Ni (2), E (sub), Nz, Br, USSR; 1983 v EG, Sw; (with Derby Co), 1984 v U, Bel (28)

Robertson, J. G. (Tottenham H), 1965 v W (1)

Robertson, J. T. (Everton), 1898 v E; (with Southampton), 1899 v E; (with Rangers), 1900 v E, W; 1901 v W, Ni, E; 1902 v W, Ni, E; 1903 v E, W; 1904 v E, W, Ni; 1905 v W (16)

Robertson, P. (Dundee), 1903 v Ni (1)

Robertson, T. (Queen's Park), 1889 v Ni; 1890 v E; 1891 v W; 1892 v Ni (4)

Robertson, T. (Hearts), 1898 v Ni (1)

Robertson, W. (Dumbarton), 1887 v E, W (2)

Robinson, R. (Dundee), 1974 v WG (sub); 1975 v Se, Ni, R (sub) (4)

Rough, A. (Partick T), 1976 v Sw, Ni, W, E; 1977 v Fi, Cz, W (2), Se, Ni, E, Ch, Arg, Br; 1978 v Cz, W, Ni, E, Pe, Ir, Ho; 1979 v A, P, W, Arg, N; 1980 v Pe, A, Bel (2), P, W, E, Pol, H; 1981 v Se, P, Is, Ni, Is, W, E; 1982 v Se, Ni, Sp, Ho, W, E, Nz, Br, USSR; (with Hibernian), 1986 v W (sub), E (53)

Rougvie, D. (Aberdeen), 1984 v Ni (1)

Rowan, A. (Caledonian), 1880 v E; (with Queen's Park), 1882 v W (2)

Russell, D. (Hearts), 1895 v E, Ni; (with Celtic), 1897 v W; 1898 v Ni; 1901 v W, Ni (6)

Russell, J. (Cambuslang), 1890 v Ni (1)

Russell, W. F. (Airdrieonians), 1924 v W; 1925 v E (2)

Rutherford, E. (Rangers), 1948 v F (1)

St John, I. (Motherwell), 1959 v WG; 1960 v E, Ni, W, Pol, A; 1961 v E; (with Liverpool), 1962 v Ni, W, E, Cz (2), U; 1963 v W, Ni, E, N, Ei (sub), Sp; 1964 v Ni; 1965 v E (21)

Sawers, W. (Dundee), 1895 v W (1)

Scarff, P. (Celtic), 1931 v Ni (1)

Schaedler, E. (Hibernian), 1974 v WG (1)

Scott, A. S. (Rangers), 1957 v Ni, Y, WG; 1958 v W, Sw;

1959 v P; 1962 v Ni, W, E, Cz, U; (with Everton), 1964 v W, N; 1965 v Fi; 1966 v P, Br (16)

Scott, J. (Hibernian), 1966 v Ho (1)

Scott, J. (Dundee), 1971 v D (sub), USSR (2)

Scott, M. (Airdrieonians), 1898 v W (1)

Scott, R. (Airdrieonians), 1894 v Ni (1)

Scoular, J. (Portsmouth), 1951 v D, F, A; 1952 v E, USA, D, Se; 1953 v W, Ni (9)

Sellar, W. (Battlefield), 1885 v E; 1886 v E; 1887 v E, W; 1888 v E; (with Queen's Park), 1891 v E; 1892 v E; 1893 v E, Ni (9)

Semple, W. (Cambuslang), 1886 v W (1)

Shankly, W. (Preston NE), 1938 v E; 1939 v E, W, Ni, H (5)

Sharp, G. M. (Everton), 1985 v Ic; 1986 v W, Aus (sub + sub), Is, R, U; 1987 v Ei; 1988 v Bel (sub), Bul, L, Ma (12)

Sharp, J. (Dundee), 1904 v W; (with Woolwich Arsenal), 1907 v W, E; 1908 v E; (with Fulham), 1909 v W (5)

Shaw, D. (Hibernian), 1947 v W, Ni; 1948 v E, Bel, Sw, F; 1949 v W, Ni (8)

Shaw, F. W. (Pollokshields Ath), 1884 v E, W (2)

Shaw, J. (Rangers), 1947 v E, Bel, L; 1948 v Ni (4)

Shearer, R. (Rangers), 1961 v E, Ei (2), Cz (4)

Sillars, D. C. (Queen's Park), 1891 v Ni; 1892 v E; 1893 v W; 1894 v E; 1895 v W (5)

Simpson, J. (Third Lanark), 1895 v E, W, Ni (3)

Simpson, J. (Rangers), 1935 v E, W, Ni; 1936 v E, W, Ni; 1937 v G, E, W, Ni, A, Cz; 1938 v W, Ni (14)

Simpson, N. (Aberdeen), 1983 v Ni; 1984 v F (sub); 1987 v E; 1988 v E (4)

Simpson, R. C. (Celtic), 1967 v E, USSR; 1968 v Ni, E; 1969 v A (5)

Sinclair, G. L. (Hearts), 1910 v Ni; 1912 v W, Ni (3)

Sinclair, J. W. E. (Leicester C), 1966 v P (1)

Skene, L. H. (Queen's Park), 1904 v W (1)

Sloan, T. (Third Lanark), 1904 v W (1)

Smellie, R. (Queen's Park), 1887 v Ni; 1888 v W; 1889 v E; 1891 v E; 1893 v E, Ni (6)

Smith, A. (Rangers), 1898 v E; 1900 v E, Ni, W; 1901 v E, Ni, W; 1902 v E, Ni, W; 1903 v E, Ni, W; 1904 v Ni; 1905 v W; 1906 v E, Ni; 1907 v W; 1911 v E, Ni (20)

Smith, D. (Aberdeen), 1966 v Ho (sub); (with Rangers), 1968 v Ho (2)

Smith, G. (Hibernian), 1947 v E, Ni; 1948 v W, Bel, Sw, F; 1952 v E, USA; 1955 v P, Y, A, H; 1956 v E, Ni, W; 1957 v Sp (2), Sw (18)

Smith, H. G. (Hearts), 1988 v S.Ar (sub) (1)

Smith, J. (Rangers), 1935 v Ni; 1938 v Ni (2)

Smith, J. (Ayr U), 1924 v E (1)

Smith, J. (Aberdeen), 1968 v Ho (sub); (with Newcastle U), 1974 v WG, Ni (sub), W (sub) (4)

Smith, J. E. (Celtic), 1959 v H, P (2)

Smith, Jas. (Queen's Park), 1872 v E (1)

Smith, John. (Mauchline), 1877 v E, W; 1879 v E, W; (with Edinburgh University), 1880 v E; (with Queen's Park), 1881 v W, E; 1883 v E, W; 1884 v E (10)

Smith, N. (Rangers), 1897 v E; 1898 v W; 1899 v E, W, Ni; 1900 v E, W, Ni; 1901 v Ni, W; 1902 v E, Ni (12)

Smith, R. (Queen's Park), 1872 v E; 1873 v E (2)

Smith, T. M. (Kilmarnock), 1934 v E; (with Preston NE), 1938 v E (2)

Somers, P. (Celtic), 1905 v E, Ni; 1907 v Ni; 1909 v W (4)

Somers, W. S. (Third Lanark), 1879 v E, W; (with Queen's Park), 1880 v W (3)

Somerville, G. (Queen's Park), 1886 v E (1)

Souness, G. J. (Middlesbrough), 1975 v EG, Sp, Se; (with Liverpool), 1978 v Bul, W, E (sub), Ho; 1979 v A, N, W, Ni, E; 1980 v Pe, A, Bel, P, Ni; 1981 v P, Is (2); 1982 v Ni, P, Sp, W, E, Nz, Br, USSR; 1983 v EG, Sw, Bel, Sw, W, E, Ca (2 + 1 sub); 1984 v U, Ni, W; (with Sampdoria), 1985 v Y, Ic, Sp (2), W, E, Ic; 1986 v EG, Aus (2), R, E, D, WG (54)

Speedie, D. R. (Chelsea), 1985 v E; 1986 v W, EG (sub), Aus, E; (with Coventry), 1989 v Y (sub), I (sub), Cy, Cy (sub), Ch (10)

Speedie, F. (Rangers), 1903 v E, W, Ni (3)

Speirs, J. H. (Rangers), 1908 v W (1)

Stanton, P. (Hibernian), 1966 v Ho; 1969 v Ni; 1970 v Ei, A; 1971 v D, Bel, P, USSR, D; 1972 v P, Bel, Ho, W; 1973 v W, Ni; 1974 v WG (16)

Stark, J. (Rangers), 1909 v E, Ni (2)

Steel, W. (Morton), 1947 v E, Bel, L; (with Derby Co), 1948 v F, E, W, Ni; 1949 v E, W, Ni, F; 1950 v E, W, Ni, Sw, P, F; (with Dundee), 1951 v W, Ni, E, A (2), D, F, Bel; 1952 v W; 1953 v W, E, Ni, Se (30)

Steele, D. M. (Huddersfield), 1923 v E, W, Ni (3)

Stein, C. (Rangers), 1969 v W, Ni, D, E, Cy (2); 1970 v A (sub), Ni (sub), W, E, Ei, WG; 1971 v D, USSR, Bel, D; 1972 v Cz (sub); (with Coventry C), 1973 v E (2 sub), W (sub), Ni (21)

Stephen, J. F. (Bradford), 1947 v W; 1948 v W (2)

Stevenson, G. (Motherwell), 1928 v W, Ni; 1930 v Ni, E, F; 1931 v E, W; 1932 v W, Ni; 1933 v Ni; 1934 v E; 1935 v Ni (12)

Stewart, A. (Queen's Park), 1888 v Ni; 1889 v W (2)

Stewart, A. (Third Lanark), 1894 v W (1)

Stewart, D. (Dumbarton), 1888 v Ni (1)

Stewart, D. (Queen's Park), 1893 v W; 1894 v Ni; 1897 v Ni (3)

Stewart, D. S. (Leeds U), 1978 v EG (1)

Stewart, G. (Hibernian), 1906 v W, E; (with Manchester C), 1907 v E, W (4)

Stewart, J. (Kilmarnock), 1977 v Ch (sub); (with Middlesbrough), 1979 v N (2)

Stewart, R. (West Ham U), 1981 v W, Ni, E; 1982 v Ni, P, W; 1984 v F; 1987 v Ei (2), L (10)

Stewart, W. E. (Queen's Park), 1898 v Ni; 1900 v Ni (2)

Storrier, D. (Celtic), 1899 v E, W, Ni (3)

Strachan, G. (Aberdeen), 1980 v Ni, W, E, Pol, H (sub); 1981 v Se, P; 1982 v Ni, P, Sp, Ho (sub), Nz, Br, USSR; 1983 v EG, Sw, Bel, Sw, Ni (sub), W, E, Ca (2+1 sub); 1984 v EG, Ni, E, F; (with Manchester U), 1985 v Sp (sub), E, Ic; 1986 v W, Aus, R, D, WG, U; 1987 v Bul, Ei (2); 1988 v H; 1989 v F (sub); (with Leeds U), 1990 v F (43)

Sturrock, P. (Dundee U), 1981 v W (sub), Ni, E (sub); 1982 v P, Ni (sub), W (sub), E (sub); 1983 v EG (sub), Sw, Bel (sub), Ca (3); 1984 v Y; 1985 v Y (sub); 1986 v Is (sub), Ho, D, U; 1987 v Bel (20)

Summers, W. (St Mirren), 1926 v E (1)

Symon, J. S. (Rangers), 1939 v H (1)

Tait, T. S. (Sunderland), 1911 v W (1)

Taylor, J. (Queen's Park), 1872 v E; 1873 v E; 1874 v E; 1875 v E; 1876 v E, W (6)

Taylor, J. D. (Dumbarton), 1892 v W; 1893 v W; 1894 v Ni; (with St Mirren), 1895 v Ni (4)

Taylor, W. (Hearts), 1892 v E (1)

Telfer, W. (Motherwell), 1933 v Ni; 1934 v Ni (2)

Telfer, W. D. (St Mirren), 1954 v W (1)

Templeton, R. (Aston Villa), 1902 v E; (with Newcastle U), 1903 v E, W; 1904 v E; (with Woolwich Arsenal), 1905 v W; (with Kilmarnock), 1908 v Ni; 1910 v E, Ni; 1912 v E, Ni; 1913 v W (11)

Thomson, A. (Arthurlie), 1886 v Ni (1)

Thomson, A. (Airdrieonians), 1909 v Ni (1)

Thomson, A. (Celtic), 1926 v E; 1932 v F; 1933 v W (3)

Thomson, A. (Third Lanark), 1889 v W (1)

Thomson, C. (Hearts), 1904 v Ni; 1905 v E, Ni, W; 1906 v W, Ni; 1907 v E, W, Ni; 1908 v E, W, Ni; (with Sunderland), 1909 v W; 1910 v E; 1911 v Ni; 1912 v E, W; 1913 v E, W; 1914 v E, Ni (21)

Thomson, C. (Sunderland), 1937 v Cz (1)

Thomson, D. (Dundee), 1920 v W (1)

Thomson, J. (Celtic), 1930 v F; 1931 v E, W, Ni (4)

Thomson, J. J. (Queen's Park), 1872 v E; 1873 v E; 1874 v E (3)

Thomson, J. R. (Everton), 1933 v W (1)

Thomson, R. (Celtic), 1932 v W (1)

Thomson, R. W. (Falkirk), 1927 v E (1)

Thomson, S. (Rangers), 1884 v W, Ni (2)

Thomson, W. (Dumbarton), 1892 v W; 1893 v W; 1898 v Ni, W (4)

Thomson, W. (Dundee), 1896 v W (1)

Thornton, W. (Rangers), 1947 v W, Ni; 1948 v E, Ni; 1949 v F; 1952 v D, Se (7)

Thomson, W. (St Mirren), 1980 v Ni; 1981 v Ni (sub), Ni; 1982 v P; 1983 v Ni, Ca; 1984 v EG (7)

Toner, W. (Kilmarnock), 1959 v W, Ni (2)

Townsley, T. (Falkirk), 1926 v W (1)

Troup, A. (Dundee), 1920 v E; 1921 v W, Ni; 1922 v Ni; (with Everton), 1926 v E (5)

Turnbull, E. (Hibernian), 1948 v Bel, Sw; 1951 v A; 1958 v H, Pol, Y, Par, F (8)

Turner, T. (Arthurlie), 1884 v W (1)

Turner, W. (Pollokshields), 1885 v Ni; 1886 v Ni (2)

Ure, J. F. (Dundee), 1962 v W, Cz; 1963 v W, Ni, E, A, N, Sp; (with Arsenal), 1964 v Ni, N; 1968 v Ni (11)

Urquhart, D. (Hibernian), 1934 v W (1)

Vallance, T. (Rangers), 1877 v E, W; 1878 v E; 1879 v E, W; 1881 v E, W (7)

Venters, A. (Cowdenbeath), 1934 v Ni; (with Rangers), 1936 v E; 1939 v E (3)

Waddell, T. S. (Queen's Park), 1891 v Ni; 1892 v E; 1893 v E, Ni; 1895 v E, Ni (6)

Waddell, W. (Rangers), 1947 v W; 1949 v E, W, Ni, F; 1950 v E, Ni; 1951 v E, D, F, Bel, A; 1952 v Ni, W; 1954 v Ni; 1955 v W, Ni (17)

Wales, H. M. (Motherwell), 1933 v W (1)

Walker, A. (Celtic), 1988 v Co (sub) (1)

Walker, F. (Third Lanark), 1922 v W (1)

Walker, G. (St Mirren), 1930 v F; 1931 v Ni, A, Sw (4)

Walker, J. (Hearts), 1895 v Ni; 1897 v W; 1898 v Ni; (with Rangers), 1904 v W, Ni (5)

Walker, J. (Swindon T), 1911 v E, W, Ni; 1912 v E, W, Ni; 1913 v E, W, Ni (9)

Walker, R. (Hearts), 1900 v E, Ni; 1901 v E, W; 1902 v E, W, Ni; 1903 v E, W, Ni; 1904 v E, W, Ni; 1905 v E, W, Ni; 1906 v Ni; 1907 v E, Ni; 1908 v E, W, Ni; 1909 v E, W; 1912 v E, W, Ni; 1913 v E, W (29)

Walker, T. (Hearts), 1935 v E, W; 1936 v E, W, Ni; 1937 v G, E, W, Ni, A, Cz; 1938 v E, W, Ni, Cz, Ho; 1939 v E, W, Ni, H (20)

Walker, W. (Clyde), 1909 v Ni; 1910 v Ni (2)

Wallace, I. A. (Coventry C), 1978 v Bul (sub); 1979 v P (sub), W (3)

Wallace, W. S. B. (Hearts), 1965 v Ni; 1966 v E, Ho; (with Celtic), 1967 v E, USSR (sub); 1968 v Ni; 1969 v E (sub) (7)

Wardhaugh, J. (Hearts), 1955 v H; 1957 v Ni (2)

Wark, J. (Ipswich T), 1979 v W, Ni, E, Arg, N (sub); 1980 v Pe, A, Bel (2); 1981 v Is, Ni; 1982 v Se, Sp, Ho, Ni, Nz, Br, USSR; 1983 v EG, Sw, Sw, Ni, E (sub); 1984 v U, Bel, EG; (with Liverpool), E, F; 1985 v Y (29)

Watson, A. (Queen's Park), 1881 v E, W; 1882 v E (3)

Watson, J. (Sunderland), 1903 v E, W; 1904 v E; 1905 v E; (with Middlesbrough), 1909 v E, Ni (6)

Watson, J. (Motherwell), 1948 v Ni; (with Huddersfield T), 1954 v Ni (2)

Watson, J. A. K. (Rangers), 1878 v W (1)

Watson, P. R. (Blackpool), 1934 v A (1)

Watson, R. (Motherwell), 1971 v USSR (1)

Watson, W. (Falkirk), 1898 v W (1)

Watt, F. (Kilbirnie), 1889 v W, Ni; 1890 v W; 1891 v E (4)

Watt, W. W. (Queen's Park), 1887 v Ni (1)

Waugh, W. (Hearts), 1938 v Cz (1)

Weir, A. (Motherwell), 1959 v WG; 1960 v E, P, A, H, T (6)

Weir, J. (Third Lanark), 1887 v Ni (1)

Weir, J. B. (Queen's Park), 1872 v E; 1874 v E; 1875 v E; 1878 v W (4)

Weir, P. (St Mirren), 1980 v N (sub), W, Pol (sub), H; (with Aberdeen), 1983 v Sw; 1984 v Ni (6)

White, John (Albion R), 1922 v W; (with Hearts), 1923 v Ni (2)

White, J. A. (Falkirk), 1959 v WG, Ho, P; 1960 v Ni; (with Tottenham H), 1960 v W, Pol, A, T; 1961 v W; 1962 v Ni, W, E, Cz (2); 1963 v W, Ni, E; 1964 v Ni, W, E, N, WG (22)

White, W. (Bolton W), 1907 v E; 1908 v E (2)

Whitelaw, A. (Vale of Leven), 1887 v Ni; 1890 v W (2)

Whyte, D. (Celtic), 1988 v Bel (sub), L; 1989 v Ch (sub) (3)

Wilson, A. (Sheffield W), 1907 v E; 1908 v E; 1912 v E; 1913 v E, W; 1914 v Ni (6)

Wilson, A. (Portsmouth), 1954 v Fi (1)

Wilson, A. N. (Dunfermline), 1920 v E, W, Ni; 1921 v E, W, Ni; (with Middlesbrough), 1922 v E, W, Ni; 1923 v E, W, Ni (12)

Wilson, D. (Queen's Park), 1900 v W (1)

Wilson, D. (Oldham Ath), 1913 v E (1)

Wilson, D. (Rangers), 1961 v E, W, Ni, Ei (2), Cz; 1962 v Ni, W, E, Cz, U; 1963 v W, E, A, N, Ei, Sp; 1964 v E, WG; 1965 v Ni, E, Fi (22)

Wilson, G. W. (Hearts), 1904 v W; 1905 v E, Ni; 1906 v W; (with Everton), 1907 v E; (with Newcastle U), 1909 v E (6)

Wilson, Hugh, (Newmilns), 1890 v W; (with Sunderland), 1897 v E; (with Third Lanark), 1902 v W; 1904 v Ni (4)

Wilson, I. A. (Leicester C), 1987 v E, Br; (with Everton), 1988 v Bel, Bul, L (5)

Wilson, J. (Vale of Leven), 1888 v W; 1889 v E; 1890 v E; 1891 v E (4)

Wilson, P. (Celtic), 1926 v Ni; 1930 v F; 1931 v Ni; 1933 v E (4)

Wilson, P. (Celtic), 1975 v Sp (sub) (1)

Wilson, R. P. (Arsenal), 1972 v P, Ho (2)

Wiseman, W. (Queen's Park), 1927 v W; 1930 v Ni (2)

Wood, G. (Everton), 1979 v Ni, E, Arg (sub); (with Arsenal), 1982 v Ni (4)

Woodburn, W. A. (Rangers), 1947 v E, Bel, L; 1948 v W, Ni; 1949 v E, F; 1950 v E, W, Ni, F; 1951 v E, W, Ni, A (2), D, F, Bel; 1952 v E, W, Ni, USA (24)

Wotherspoon, D. N. (Queen's Park), 1872 v E; 1873 v E (2)

Wright, T. (Sunderland), 1953 v W, Ni, E (3)

Wylie, T. G. (Rangers), 1890 v Ni (1)

Yeats, R. (Liverpool), 1965 v W; 1966 v I (2)

Yorston, B. C. (Aberdeen), 1931 v Ni (1)

Yorston, H. (Aberdeen), 1955 v W (1)

Young, A. (Hearts), 1960 v E, A (sub), H, T; 1961 v W, Ni; (with Everton), Ei; 1966 v P (8)

Young, A. (Everton), 1905 v E; 1907 v W (2)

Young, G. L. (Rangers), 1947 v E, Ni, Bel, L; 1948 v E, Ni, Bel, Sw, F; 1949 v E, W, Ni, F; 1950 v E, W, Ni, Sw, P, F; 1951 v E, W, Ni, A (2), D, F, Bel; 1952 v E, W, Ni, USA, D, Se; 1953 v W, E, Ni, Se; 1954 v Ni, W; 1955 v W, Ni, P, Y; 1956 v Ni, W, E, A; 1957 v E, Ni, W, Y, Sp, Sw (53)

Young, J. (Celtic), 1906 v Ni (1)

Younger, T. (Hibernian), 1955 v P, Y, A, H; 1956 v E, Ni, W, A; (with Liverpool), 1957 v E, Ni, W, Y, Sp (2), Sw, WG; 1958 v Ni, W, E, Sw, H, Pol, Y, Par (24)

WALES

Adams, H. (Berwyn R), 1882 v Ni, E; (with Druids), 1883 v Ni, E (4)

Aizlewood, M. (Charlton Ath), 1986 v S.Ar, Ca (2); 1987 v Fi (with Leeds U), USSR, Fi (sub); 1988 v D (sub), Se, Ma, I; 1989 v Ho, Se (sub); WG; (with Bradford C), 1990 v Fi, WG, Ei, Cr (17)

Allchurch, I. J. (Swansea T), 1951 v E, Ni, P, Sw; 1952 v E, S, Ni, R of UK; 1953 v S, E, Ni, F, Y; 1954 v S, E, Ni, A; 1955 v S, E, Ni, Y; 1956 v E, S, Ni, A; 1957 v E, S; 1958 v Ni, Is (2), H (2), M, Sw, Br; (with Newcastle U), 1959 v E, S, Ni; 1960 v E, S; 1961 v Ni, H, Sp (2); 1962 v E, S, Br (2), M; (with Cardiff C), 1963 v S, E, Ni, H (2); 1964 v E; 1965 v S, E, Ni, Gr, I, USSR; 1966 (with Swansea T), v USSR, E, S, D, Br (2), Ch (68)

Allchurch, L. (Swansea T), 1955 v Ni; 1956 v A; 1958 v S, Ni, EG, Is; 1959 v S; (with Sheffield U), 1962 v S, Ni, Br; 1964 v E (11)

Allen, B. W. (Coventry C), 1951 v S, E (2)

Allen, M. (Watford), 1986 v S.Ar (sub), Ca (1 + sub) (with Norwich C);1989 v Is (sub); 1990 v Ho, WG (with Millwall), Ei, Se, Cr (sub) (9)

Arridge, S. (Bootle), 1892 v S, Ni; (with Everton), 1894 v Ni; 1895 v Ni; 1896 v E; (with New Brighton Tower), 1898 v E, Ni; 1899 v E (8)

Astley, D. J. (Charlton Ath), 1931 v Ni; (with Aston Villa), 1932 v E; 1933 v E, S, Ni; 1934 v E, S; 1935 v S; 1936 v E, Ni; (with Derby Co), 1939 v E, S; (with Blackpool), F (13)

Atherton, R. W. (Hibernian), 1899 v E, Ni; 1903 v E, S, Ni; (with Middlesbrough), 1904 v E, S, Ni; 1905 v Ni (9)

Bailiff, W. E. (Llanelly), 1913 v E, S, Ni; 1920 v Ni (4)

Baker, C. W. (Cardiff C), 1958 v M; 1960 v S, Ni; 1961 v S, E, Ei; 1962 v S (7)

Baker, W. G. (Cardiff C), 1948 v Ni (1)

Bamford, T. (Wrexham), 1931 v E, S, Ni; 1932 v Ni; 1933 v F (5)

Barnes, W. (Arsenal), 1948 v E, S, Ni; 1949 v E, S, Ni; 1950 v E, S, Ni, Bel; 1951 v E, S, Ni, P; 1952 v E, S, Ni, R of UK; 1954 v E, S; 1955 v S, Y (22)

Bartley, T. (Glossop NE), 1898 v E (1)

Beadles, G. H. (Cardiff C), 1925 v E, S (2)

Bell, W. S. (Shrewsbury Engineers), 1881 v E, S; (with Crewe Alex), 1886 v E, S, Ni (5)

Bennion, S. R. (Manchester U), 1926 v S; 1927 v S; 1928 v S, E, Ni; 1929 v S, E, Ni; 1930 v S; 1932 v Ni (10)

Berry, G. F. (Wolverhampton W), 1979 v WG; 1980 v Ei, WG (sub), T; (with Stoke C), 1983 v E (sub) (5)

Blackmore, C. G. (Manchester U), 1985 v N (sub); 1986 v S (sub), H (sub), S.Ar, Ei, U; 1987 v Fi (2), USSR, Cz; 1988 v D (2), Cz, Y, Se, Ma, I; 1989 v Ho, Fi, Is, WG; 1990 v Fi, Ho,WG, Cr (25)

Blew, H. (Wrexham), 1899 v E, S, Ni; 1902 v S, Ni; 1903 v E, S; 1904 v E, S, Ni; 1905 v S, Ni; 1906 v E, S, Ni; 1907 v S; 1908 v E, S, Ni; 1909 v E, S; 1910 v E (22)

Boden, T. (Wrexham), 1880 v E (1)

Bodin, P. J. (Swindon T), 1990 v Cr (1)

Bostock, A. M. (Shrewsbury), 1892 v Ni (1)

Boulter, L. M. (Brentford), 1939 v Ni (1)

Bowdler, H. E. (Shrewsbury), 1893 v S (1)

Bowdler, J. C. H. (Shrewsbury), 1890 v Ni; (with Wolverhampton W), 1891 v S; 1892 v Ni; (with Shrewsbury), 1894 v E (4)

Bowen, D. L. (Arsenal), 1955 v S, Y; 1957 v Ni, Cz, EG; 1958 v S, Ni, EG, Is (2), H (2), M, Se, Br; 1959 v E, S, Ni (19)

Bowen, E. (Druids), 1880 v S; 1883 v S (2)

Bowen, M. R. (Tottenham H), 1986 v Ca (sub + sub); (with Norwich C), 1988 v Y (sub); 1989 v Fi (sub), Is, Se, WG (sub); 1990 v Fi (sub), Ho, WG, Se (11)

Bowsher, S. J. (Burnley), 1929 v Ni (1)

Boyle, T. (C Palace), 1981 v Ei, S (sub) (2)

Britten, T. J. (Parkgrove), 1878 v S; (with Presteigne), 1880 v S (2)

Brookes, S. J. (Llandudno), 1900 v E, Ni (2)

Brown, A. I. (Aberdare Ath), 1926 v Ni (1)

Bryan, T. (Oswestry), 1886 v E, Ni (2)

Buckland, T. (Bangor), 1899 v E (1)

Burgess, W. A. R. (Tottenham H), 1947 v E, S, Ni; 1948 v E, S; 1949 v E, S, Ni, P, Bel, Sw; 1950 v E, S, Ni, Bel; 1951 v S, Ni, P, Sw; 1952 v E, S, Ni, R of UK; 1953 v S, E, Ni, F, Y; 1954 v S, E, Ni, A (32)

Burke, T. (Wrexham), 1883 v E; 1884 v S; 1885 v E, S, Ni; (with Newton Heath), 1887 v E, S; 1888 v S (8)

Burnett, T. B. (Ruabon), 1877 v S (1)

Burton, A. D. (Norwich C), 1963 v Ni, H; (with Newcastle U), 1964 v E; 1969 v S, E, Ni, I, EG; 1972 v Cz (9)

Butler, A. (Druids), 1900 v S, Ni (2)

Butler, J. (Chirk), 1893 v E, S, Ni (3)

Cartwright, L. (Coventry C), 1974 v E (sub), S, Ni; 1976 v S (sub); 1977 v WG (sub); (with Wrexham), 1978 v Ir (sub); 1979 v Ma (7)

Carty, T. (Wrexham), 1889 v Ni (1)

Challen, J. B. (Corinthians), 1887 v E, S; 1888 v E; (with Wellingborough GS), 1890 v E (4)

Chapman, T. (Newtown), 1894 v E, S, Ni; 1895 v S, Ni; (with Manchester C), 1896 v E; 1897 v E (7)

Charles, J. M. (Swansea C), 1981 v Cz, T (sub), S (sub), USSR (sub); 1982 v Ic; 1983 v N (sub), Y (sub), Bul (sub), S, Ni, Br; 1984 v Bul (sub), (with QPR), Y (sub), S; (with Oxford U), 1985 v Ic (sub), Sp, Ic; 1986 v Ei; 1987 v Fi (19)

Charles, M. (Swansea T), 1955 v Ni; 1956 v E, S, A; 1957 v E, Ni, Cz (2), EG; 1958 v E, S, EG, Is (2), H (2), M, Se, Br; 1959 v E, S; (with Arsenal), 1961 v Ni, H, Sp (2); 1962 v E, S; (with Cardiff C), 1962 v Br, Ni; 1963 v S, H (31)

Charles, W. J. (Leeds U), 1950 v Ni; 1951 v Sw; 1953 v Ni, F, Y; 1954 v E, S, Ni, A; 1955 v S, E, Ni, Y; 1956 v E, S, A, Ni; 1957 v S, Ni, Cz (2), EG; (with Juventus), 1958 v Is (2), H (2) M, Se; 1960 v S; 1962 v E, Br (2), M; (with Leeds U), 1963 v S; (with Cardiff C), 1964 v S; 1965 v S, USSR (38)

Clarke, R. J. (Manchester C), 1949 v E; 1950 v S, Ni, Bel; 1951 v E, S, Ni, P, Sw; 1952 v S, E, Ni, R of UK; 1953 v S, E; 1954 v E, S, Ni; 1955 v Y, S, E; 1956 v Ni (22)

Collier, D. J. (Grimsby T), 1921 v S (1)

Collins, W. S. (Llanelly), 1931 v S (1)

Conde, C. (Chirk), 1884 v E, S, Ni (3)

Cook, F. C. (Newport Co), 1925 v E, S; (with Portsmouth), 1928 v E, S; 1930 v E, S, Ni; 1932 v E (8)

Crompton, W. (Wrexham), 1931 v E, S, Ni (3)

Cross, E. A. (Wrexham), 1876 v S; 1877 v S (2)

Cross, K. (Druids), 1879 v S; 1881 v E, S (3)

Crowe, V. H. (Aston Villa), 1959 v E, Ni; 1960 v E, Ni; 1961 v S, E, Ni, Ei, H, Sp (2); 1962 v E, S, Br, M; 1963 v H (16)

Cumner, R. H. (Arsenal), 1939 v E, S, Ni (3)

Curtis, A. (Swansea C), 1976 v E, Y (sub), S, Ni, Y (sub), E; 1977 v WG, S (sub), Ni (sub); 1978 v WG, E, S; 1979 v WG, S; (with Leeds U), E, Ni, Ma; 1980 v Ei, WG, T; (with Swansea C), 1982 v Cz, Ic, USSR, Sp, E, S, Ni; 1983 v N; 1984 v R (sub), (with Southampton), S; 1985 v Sp, N (1 + 1 sub); 1986 v H; 1987 (with Cardiff C) v USSR (35)

Curtis, E. R. (Cardiff C), 1928 v S; (with Birmingham), 1932 v S; 1934 v Ni (3)

Daniel, R. W. (Arsenal), 1951 v E, Ni, P; 1952 v E, S, Ni, R of UK; 1953 v S, E, Ni, F, Y; (with Sunderland), 1954 v E, S, Ni; 1955 v E, Ni; 1957 v S, E, Ni, Cz (21)

Darvell, S. (Oxford University), 1897 v S, Ni (2)

Davies, A. (Manchester U), 1983 v Ni, Br; 1984 v E, Ni; 1985 v Ic; (with Newcastle U), 1986 v H; (with Swansea C), 1988 v Ma, I; 1989 v Ho; (with Bradford C), 1990 v Fi, Ei (11)

Davies, A. (Wrexham), 1876 v S; 1877 v S (2)

Davies, A. (Shrewsbury), 1891 v Ni (1)

Davies, A. (Druids), 1904 v S; (with Middlesbrough), 1905 v S (2)

Davies, A. O. (Barmouth), 1885 v Ni; 1886 v E, S; (with Swifts), 1887 v E, S; 1888 v E, Ni; (with Wrexham), 1889 v S; (with Crewe Alex), 1890 v E (9)

Davies, C. (Brecon), 1899 v Ni; (with Hereford), 1900 v Ni (2)

Davies, C. (Charlton Ath), 1972 v R (sub) (1)

Davies, D. (Bolton W), 1904 v S, Ni; 1908 v E (sub) (3)

Davies, D. W. (Treharris), 1912 v Ni; (with Oldham Ath), 1913 v Ni (2)

Davies, E. Lloyd, (Stoke C), 1904 v E; 1907 v E, S, Ni; (with Northampton T), 1908 v S; 1909 v Ni; 1910 v Ni; 1911 v E, S; 1912 v E, S; 1913 v E, S; 1914 v Ni, E, S (16)

Davies, E. R. (Newcastle U), 1953 v S, E; 1954 v E, S; 1958 v E, EG (6)

Davies, G. (Fulham), 1980 v T, Ic; 1982 v Sp (sub), F (sub); 1983 v E, Bul, S, Ni, Br; 1984 v R (sub), S (sub), E, Ni; 1985 v Ic (2) (with Chelsea), N; (with Manchester C), 1986 v S.Ar, Ei (18)

Davies, Rev. H. (Wrexham), 1928 v Ni (1)

Davies, Idwal (Liverpool Marine), 1923 v S (1)

Davies, J. E. (Oswestry), 1885 v E (1)

Davies, Jas. (Wrexham), 1878 v S (1)

Davies, John. (Wrexham), 1879 v S (1)

Davies, Jos. (Everton), 1889 v S, Ni; (with Chirk), 1891 v Ni; (with Ardwick), 1893 v S; (with Sheffield U), 1895 v E, S, Ni; (with Manchester C), 1896 v E; (with Millwall), 1897 v E; (with Reading), 1900 v E (11)

Davies, Jos. (Newton Heath), 1888 v E, S, Ni; 1889 v S; 1890 v E; (with Wolverhampton W), 1892 v E; 1893 v E (7)

Davies, J. P. (Druids), 1883 v E, Ni (2)

Davies, Ll. (Wrexham), 1907 v Ni; 1910 v Ni, S, E; (with Everton), 1911 v S, Ni; 1912 v Ni, S, E; 1913 v Ni, S, E; 1914 v Ni (13)

Davies, L. S. (Cardiff C), 1922 v E, S, Ni; 1923 v E, S, Ni; 1924 v E, S, Ni; 1925 v S, Ni; 1926 v E, Ni; 1927 v E, Ni; 1928 v S, Ni, E; 1929 v S, Ni, E; 1930 v E, S (23)

Davies, O. (Wrexham), 1890 v S (1)

Davies, R. (Wrexham), 1883 v Ni; 1884 v Ni; 1885 v Ni (3)

Davies, R. (Druids), 1885 v E (1)

Davies, R. O. (Wrexham), 1892 v Ni, E (2)

Davies, R. T. (Norwich C), 1964 v Ni; 1965 v E; 1966 v Br (2), Ch; (with Southampton), 1967 v S, E, Ni; 1968 v S, Ni, WG; 1969 v S, E, Ni, I, WG, R of UK; 1970 v E, S, Ni; 1971 v Cz, S, E, Ni; 1972 v R, E, S, N; (with Portsmouth), 1974 v E (29)

Davies, R. W. (Bolton W), 1964 v E; 1965 v E, S, Ni, D, Gr, USSR; 1966 v E, S, Ni, USSR, D, Br (2), Ch (sub); 1967 v S; (with Newcastle U), E; 1968 v S, Ni, WG; 1969 v S, E, Ni, I; 1970 v EG; 1971 v R, Cz; (with Manchester C), 1972 v E, S, Ni; (with Manchester U), 1973 v E, S (sub), Ni; (with Blackpool), 1974 v Pol (34)

Davies, Stanley (Preston NE), 1920 v E, S, Ni; (with Everton), 1921 v E, S, Ni; (with WBA), 1922 v E, S, Ni; 1923 v S; 1925 v S, Ni; 1926 v S, E, Ni; 1927 v S; 1928 v S; (with Rotherham U), 1930 v Ni (18)

Davies, T. (Oswestry), 1886 v E (1)

Davies, T. (Druids), 1903 v E, Ni, S; 1904 v S (4)

Davies, W. (Swansea T), 1924 v E, S, Ni; (with Cardiff

C), 1925 v E, S, Ni; 1926 v E, S, Ni; 1927 v S; 1928 v Ni; (with Notts Co), 1929 v E, S, Ni; 1930 v E, S, Ni (17)

Davies, W. (Wrexham), 1884 v Ni (1)

Davies, William (Wrexham), 1903 v Ni; 1905 v Ni; (with Blackburn R), 1908 v E, S; 1909 v E, S, Ni; 1911 v E, S, Ni; 1912 v Ni (11)

Davies, W. C. (C Palace), 1908 v S; (with WBA), 1909 v E; 1910 v S; (with C Palace), 1914 v E (4)

Davies, W. D. (Everton), 1975 v H, L, S, E, Ni; 1976 v Y (2), E, Ni; 1977 v WG, S (2), Cz, E, Ni; 1978 v K; (with Wrexham), S, Cz, WG, Ir, E, S, Ni; 1979 v Ma, T, WG S, E, Ni, Ma; 1980 v Ei, WG, T, E, S, Ni, Ic; 1981 v T, Cz, Ei, T, S, E, USSR; (with Swansea C), 1982 v Cz, Ic, USSR, Sp, E, S, F; 1983 v Y (52)

Davies, W. H. (Oswestry), 1876 v S; 1877 v S; 1879 v E; 1880 v E (4)

Davies, W. O. (Millwall Ath), 1913 v E, S, Ni; 1914 v S, Ni (5)

Davis, G. (Wrexham), 1978 v Ir, E (sub), Ni (3)

Day, A. (Tottenham H), 1934 v Ni (1)

Deacy, N. (PSV Eindhoven), 1977 v Cz, S, E, Ni; 1978 v K (sub), S (sub), Cz (sub), WG, Ir, S (sub), Ni; (with Beringen), 1979 v T (12)

Dearson, D. J. (Birmingham), 1939 v S, Ni, F (3)

Derrett, S. C. (Cardiff C), 1969 v S, WG; 1970 v I; 1971 v Fi (4)

Dewey, F. T. (Cardiff Corinthians), 1931 v E, S (2)

Dibble, A. (Luton T), 1986 v Ca (1 + sub); (with Manchester C) 1989 v Is (3)

Doughty, J. (Druids), 1886 v S; (with Newton Heath), 1887 v S, Ni; 1888 v E, S, Ni; 1889 v S; 1890 v E (8)

Doughty, R. (Newton Heath and Druids), 1888 v S, Ni (2)

Durban, A. (Derby Co), 1966 v Br (sub); 1967 v Ni; 1968 v E, S, Ni, WG; 1969 v EG, S, E, Ni, WG; 1970 v E, S, Ni, EG, I; 1971 v R, S, E, Ni, Cz, Fi; 1972 v Fi, Cz, E, S, Ni (27)

Dwyer, P. (Cardiff C), 1978 v Ir, E, S, Ni; 1979 v T, S, E, Ni, Ma (sub); 1980 v WG (10)

Edwards, C. (Wrexham), 1878 v S (1)

Edwards, G. (Birmingham C), 1947 v E, S, Ni; 1948 v E, S, Ni; (with Cardiff C), 1949 v Ni, P, Bel, Sw; 1950 v E, S (12)

Edwards, H. (Wrexham Civil Service), 1878 v S; 1880 v E; 1882 v E, S; 1883 v S; 1884 v Ni; 1887 v Ni (7)

Edwards, R. I. (Chester), 1978 v K (sub); 1979 v Ma, WG; (with Wrexham), 1980 v T (sub) (4)

Edwards, J. H. (Oswestry), 1895 v Ni; 1897 v E, Ni; (with Aberystwyth), 1898 v Ni (4)

Edwards, J. H. (Wanderers), 1876 v S (1)

Edwards, L. T. (Charlton Ath), 1957 v Ni, EG (2)

Edwards, T. (Linfield), 1932 v S (1)

Egan, W. (Chirk), 1892 v S (1)

Ellis, B. (Motherwell), 1932 v E; 1933 v E, S; 1934 v S; 1936 v E; 1937 v S (6)

Ellis, E. (Nunhead), 1931 v E; (with Oswestry), S; 1932 v Ni (3)

Emanuel, W. J. (Bristol C), 1973 v E (sub), Ni (sub) (2)

England, H. M. (Blackburn R), 1962 v Ni, Br, M; 1963 v Ni, H; 1964 v E, S, Ni; 1965 v E, D, Gr (2), USSR, Ni, I; 1966 v E, S, Ni, USSR, D; (with Tottenham H), 1967 v S, E; 1968 v E, Ni, WG; 1969 v EG; 1970 v R of UK, EG, E, S, Ni, I; 1971 v R; 1972 v Fi, E, S, Ni; 1973 v E (3), S; 1974 v Pol; 1975 v H, L (44)

Evans, B. C. (Swansea C), 1972 v Fi, Cz; 1973 v E (2), Pol, S; (with Hereford U), 1974 v Pol (7)

Evans, D. G. (Reading), 1926 v Ni; 1927 v Ni, E; (with Huddersfield T), 1929 v S (4)

Evans, H. P. (Cardiff C), 1922 v E, S, Ni; 1924 v E, S, Ni (6)

Evans, I. (Crystal Palace), 1976 v A, E, Y (2), E, Ni; 1977 v WG, S (2), Cz, E, Ni; 1978 v K (13)

Evans, J. (Cardiff C), 1912 v Ni; 1913 v Ni; 1914 v S; 1920 v S, Ni; 1922 v Ni; 1923 v E, Ni (8)

Evans, J. (Oswestry), 1893 v Ni; 1894 v E, Ni (3)

Evans, J. H. (Southend U), 1922 v E, S, Ni; 1923 v S (4)

Evans, Len (Cardiff C), 1931 v E, S; (with Birmingham), 1934 v Ni (3)

Evans, L. H. (Aberdare Ath), 1927 v Ni (1)

Evans, M. (Oswestry), 1884 v E (1)

Evans, R. (Clapton), 1902 v Ni (1)

Evans, R. E. (Wrexham), 1906 v E, S; (with Aston Villa), Ni; 1907 v E; 1908 v E, S; (with Sheffield U), 1909 v S; 1910 v E, S, Ni (10)

Evans, R. O. (Wrexham), 1902 v Ni; 1903 v E, S, Ni; (with Blackburn R), 1908 v Ni; (with Coventry C), 1911 v E, Ni; 1912 v E, S, Ni (10)

Evans, R. S. (Swansea T), 1964 v Ni (1)

Evans T. J. (Clapton Orient), 1927 v S; 1928 v E, S; (with Newcastle U), Ni (4)

Evans, W. (Tottenham H), 1933 v Ni; 1934 v E, S; 1935 v E; 1936 v E, Ni (6)

Evans, W. A. W. (Oxford University), 1876 v S; 1877 v S (2)

Evans, W. G. (Bootle), 1890 v E; 1891 v E; (with Aston Villa), 1892 v E (3)

Evelyn, E. C. (Crusaders), 1887 v E (1)

Eyton-Jones, J. A. (Wrexham), 1883 v Ni; 1884 v Ni, E, S (4)

Farmer, G. (Oswestry), 1885 v E, S (2)

Felgate, D. (Lincoln C), 1984 v R (sub) (1)

Finnigan, R. J. (Wrexham), 1930 v Ni (1)

Flynn, B. (Burnley), 1975 v L (2 sub), H (sub), S, E, Ni; 1976 v A, E, Y (2), E, Ni; 1977 v WG (sub), S (2), Cz, E, Ni; 1978 v K (2), S; (with Leeds U), Cz, WG, Ir (sub), E, S, Ni; 1979 v Ma, T, S, E, Ni, Ma; 1980 v Ei, WG, E, S, Ni, Ic; 1981 v T, Cz, Ei, T, S, E, USSR; 1982 v Cz, USSR, E, S, Ni, F; 1983 v N, (with Burnley), v Y, E, Bul, S, Ni, Br; 1984 v N, R, Bul, Y, S, N, Is (66)

Ford, T. (Swansea T), 1947 v S; (with Aston Villa), 1947 v Ni; 1948 v S, Ni; 1949 v E, S, Ni, P, Bel, Sw; 1950 v E, S, Ni, Bel; 1951 v S; (with Sunderland), 1951 v E, Ni, P, Sw; 1952 v E, S, Ni, R of UK; 1953 v S, E, Ni, F, Y; (with Cardiff C), 1954 v A; 1955 v S, E, Ni, Y; 1956 v S, Ni, E, A; 1957 v S (38)

Foulkes, H. E. (WBA), 1932 v Ni (1)

Foulkes, W. I. (Newcastle U), 1952 v E, S, Ni, R of UK; 1953 v E, S, F, Y; 1954 v E, S, Ni (11)

Foulkes, W. T. (Oswestry), 1884 v Ni; 1885 v S (2)

Fowler, J. (Swansea T), 1925 v E; 1926 v E, Ni; 1927 v S; 1928 v S; 1929 v E (6)

Garner, J. (Aberystwyth), 1896 v S (1)

Giles, D. (Swansea C), 1980 v E, S, Ni, Ic; 1981 v T, Cz, T (sub), E (sub), USSR (sub); (with C Palace), 1982 v Sp (sub); 1983 v Ni (sub), Br (12)

Gillam, S. G. (Wrexham), 1889 v S, Ni; (with Shrewsbury), 1890 v E, Ni; (with Clapton), 1894 v S (5)

Glascodine, G. (Wrexham), 1879 v E (1)

Glover, E. M. (Grimsby T), 1932 v S; 1934 v Ni; 1936 v S; 1937 v E, S, Ni; 1939 v Ni (7)

Godding, G. (Wrexham), 1923 v S, Ni (2)

Godfrey, B. C. (Preston NE), 1964 v Ni; 1965 v D, I (3)

Goodwin, U. (Ruthin), 1881 v E (1)

Gough, R. T. (Oswestry White Star), 1883 v S (1)

Gray, A. (Oldham Ath), 1924 v E, S, Ni; 1925 v E, S, Ni; 1926 v E, S; 1927 v S; (with Manchester C), 1928 v E, S; 1929 v E, S, Ni; (with Manchester Central), 1930 v S; (with Tranmere R), 1932 v E, S, Ni; (with Chester), 1937 v E, S, Ni; 1938 v E, S, Ni (24)

Green, A. W. (Aston Villa), 1901 v Ni; (with Notts Co), 1903 v E; 1904 v S, Ni; 1906 v Ni, E; (with Nottingham F), 1907 v E; 1908 v S (8)

Green, C. R. (Birmingham C), 1965 v USSR, I; 1966 v E, S, USSR, Br (2); 1967 v E; 1968 v E, S, Ni, WG; 1969 v S, I, Ni (sub) (15)

Green, G. H. (Charlton Ath), 1938 v Ni; 1939 v E, Ni, F (4)

Grey, Dr W. (Druids), 1876 v S; 1878 v S (2)

Griffiths, A. T. (Wrexham), 1971 v Cz (sub); 1975 v A, H (2), L (2), E, Ni; 1976 v A, E, S, E (sub), Ni, Y (2); 1977 v WG, S (17)

Griffiths, F. J. (Blackpool), 1900 v E, S (2)

Griffiths, G. (Chirk), 1887 v Ni (1)

Griffiths, J. H. (Swansea T), 1953 v Ni (1)

Griffiths, M. W. (Leicester C), 1947 v Ni; 1949 v P, Bel; 1950 v E, S, Bel; 1951 v E, Ni, P, Sw; 1954 v A (11)

Griffiths, P. (Chirk), 1884 v E, Ni; 1888 v E; 1890 v S, Ni; 1891 v Ni (6)

Griffiths, S. (Wrexham), 1902 v S (1)

Griffiths, T. P. (Everton), 1927 v E, Ni; 1929 v E; 1930 v E; 1931 v Ni; 1932 v Ni, S, E; (with Bolton W), 1933 v F, E, S, Ni; (with Middlesbrough), 1934 v E, S; 1935 v E, Ni; 1936 v S; (with Aston Villa), Ni; 1937 v E, S, Ni (21)

Hall, G. D. (Chelsea), 1988 v Y (sub), Ma, I; 1989 v Ho, Fi, Is; 1990 v Ei (7)

Hallam, J. (Oswestry), 1889 v E (1)

Hanford, H. (Swansea T), 1934 v Ni; 1935 v S; 1936 v E; (with Sheffield W), 1936 v Ni; 1938 v E, S; 1939 v F (7)

Harrington, A. C. (Cardiff C), 1956 v Ni; 1957 v E, S; 1958 v S, Ni, Is (2); 1961 v S, E; 1962 v E, S (11)

Harris, C. S. (Leeds U), 1976 v E, S; 1978 v WG, Ir, E, S, Ni; 1979 v Ma, T, WG, E (sub), Ma; 1980 v Ni (sub), Ic (sub); 1981 v T, Cz (sub), Ei, T, S, E, USSR; 1982 v Cz, Ic, E (sub) (24)

Harris, W. C. (Middlesbrough), 1954 v A; 1957 v EG, Cz; 1958 v E, S, EG (6)

Harrison, W. C. (Wrexham), 1899 v E; 1900 v E, S, Ni; 1901 v Ni (5)

Hayes, A. (Wrexham), 1890 v Ni; 1894 v Ni (2)

Hennessey, W. T. (Birmingham C), 1962 v Ni, Br (2); 1963 v S, E, H (2); 1964 v E, S; 1965 v S, E, D, Gr, USSR; 1966 v E, USSR; (with Nottingham F), 1966 v S, Ni, D, Br (2), Ch; 1967 v S, E; 1968 v E, S, Ni; 1969 v WG, EG, R of UK, EG; (with Derby Co) 1970 v E, S, Ni; 1972 v Fi, Cz, E, S; 1973 v E (39)

Hersee, A. M. (Bangor), 1886 v S, Ni (2)

Hersee, R. (Llandudno), 1886 v Ni (1)

Hewitt, R. (Cardiff C), 1958 v Ni, Is, Se, H, Br (5)

Hewitt, T. J. (Wrexham), 1911 v E, S, Ni; (with Chelsea), 1913 v E, S, Ni; (with South Liverpool), 1914 v E, S (8)

Heywood, D. (Druids), 1879 v E (1)

Hibbott, H. (Newtown Excelsior), 1880 v E, S (2)

Hibbott, R. (Newtown), 1885 v S (1)

Higham, G. G. (Oswestry), 1878 v S; 1879 v E (2)

Hill, M. R. (Ipswich T), 1972 v Cz, R (2)

Hockey, T. (Sheffield U), 1972 v Fi, R; 1973 v E (2); (with Norwich C), Pol, S, E, Ni; (with Aston Villa), 1974 v Pol (9)

Hoddinott, T. F. (Watford), 1921 v E, S (2)

Hodges, G. (Wimbledon), 1984 v N (sub), Is (sub); 1987 v USSR, Fi, Cz; (with Newcastle U), 1988 v D (with Watford), D (sub), Cz (sub), Se, Ma (sub), I (sub); 1990 v Se, Cr (13)

Hodgkinson, A. V. (Southampton), 1908 v Ni (1)

Holden, A. (Chester C), 1984 v Is (sub) (1)

Hole, B. G. (Cardiff C), 1963 v Ni; 1964 v Ni; 1965 v S, E, Ni, D, Gr (2), USSR, I; 1966 v E, S, Ni, USSR, D, Br (2), Ch; (with Blackburn R), 1967 v S, E, Ni; 1968 v E, S, Ni, WG; (with Aston Villa), 1969 v I, WG, EG; 1970 v I; (with Swansea C), 1971 v R (30)

Hole, W. J. (Swansea T), 1921 v Ni; 1922 v E; 1923 v E, Ni; 1928 v E, S, Ni; 1929 v E, S (9)

Hollins, D. M. (Newcastle U); 1962 v Br (sub), M; 1963 v Ni, H; 1964 v E; 1965 v Ni, Gr, I; 1966 v S, D, Br (11)

Hopkins, I. J. (Brentford), 1935 v S, Ni; 1936 v E, Ni; 1937 v E, S, Ni; 1938 v E, Ni; 1939 v E, S, Ni (12)

Hopkins, J. (Fulham), 1983 v Ni, Br; 1984 v N, R, Bul, Y, S, E, Ni, N, Is; 1985 v Ic (1 + 1 sub), N; (with Crystal Palace), 1990 v Ho, Cr (16)

Hopkins, M. (Tottenham H), 1956 v Ni; 1957 v Ni, S, E, Cz (2), EG; 1958 v E, S, Ni, EG, Is (2), H (2), M, Se, Br; 1959 v E, S, Ni; 1960 v E, S; 1961 v Ni, H, Sp (2); 1962 v Ni, Br (2), M; 1963 v S, Ni, H (34)

Horne, B. (Portsmouth), 1988 v D (sub), Y, Se (sub), Ma, I; 1989 v Ho, Fi, Is (with Southampton), Se,WG; 1990 v WG (sub), Ei, Se, Cr (14)

Howell, E. G. (Builth), 1888 v Ni; 1890 v E; 1891 v E (3)

Howells, R. G. (Cardiff C), 1954 v E, S (2)

Hugh, A. R. (Newport Co), 1930 v Ni (1)

Hughes, A. (Rhos), 1894 v E, S (2)

Hughes, A. (Chirk), 1907 v Ni (1)

Hughes, A. J. (Aberystwyth), 1879 v S (1)

Hughes, E. (Everton), 1899 v S, Ni; (with Tottenham H), 1901 v S; 1902 v Ni; 1904 v Ni, S; 1905 v E, Ni, S; 1906 v E, Ni; 1907 v E (14)

Hughes, E. (Wrexham), 1906 v S; (with Nottingham F), 1906 v Ni; 1908 v S, E; 1910 v Ni, E, S; 1911 v Ni, E, S; (with Wrexham), 1912 v Ni, E, S; (with Manchester C), 1913 v E, S; 1914 v N (16)

Hughes, F. W. (Northwich Victoria), 1882 v E, Ni; 1883 v E, Ni, S; 1884 v S (6)

Hughes, I. (Luton T), 1951 v E, Ni, P, Sw (4)

Hughes, J. (Cambridge University), 1877 v S (1)

Hughes, J. (Liverpool), 1905 v E, S, Ni (3)

Hughes, J. I. (Blackburn R), 1935 v S (1)

Hughes, L. M. (Manchester U), 1984 v E, Ni; 1985 v Ic, Sp, Ic, N, S, Sp, N; 1986 v S, H, U; (with Barcelona), 1987 v USSR, Cz; 1988 v D (2), Cz, Se, Ma, I; (with Manchester U) 1989 v Ho, Fi, Is, Se, WG; 1990 v Fi, WG, Cr (28)

Hughes, P. W. (Bangor), 1887 v Ni; 1889 v Ni, E (3)

Hughes, W. (Bootle), 1891 v E; 1892 v S, Ni (3)

Hughes, W. A. (Blackburn R), 1949 v E, Ni, P, Bel, Sw (5)

Hughes, W. M. (Birmingham), 1938 v E, Ni, S; 1939 v E, Ni, S, F; 1947 v E, S, Ni (10)

Humphreys, J. V. (Everton), 1947 v Ni (1)

Humphreys, R. (Druids), 1888 v Ni (1)

Hunter, W. H. (North End, Belfast), 1887 v Ni (1)

Jackett, K. (Watford), 1983 v N, Y, E, Bul, S; 1984 v N, R, Y, S, Ni, N, Is; 1985 v Ic, Sp, Ic, N, S, Sp, N; 1986 v S, H, S.Ar, Ei, Ca (2); 1987 v Fi (2); 1988 v D, Cz, Y, Se (31)

Jackson, W. (St Helens Rec), 1899 v Ni (1)

James, E. (Chirk), 1893 v Ni; 1894 v E, S, Ni; 1898 v E; 1899 v Ni (7)

James, E. G. (Blackpool), 1966 v Br (2), Ch; 1967 v Ni; 1968 v S; 1971 v Cz, S, E, Ni (9)

James, L. (Burnley), 1972 v Cz, R, S (sub); 1973 v E (3), Pol, S, Ni; 1974 v Pol, E, S, Ni; 1975 v A, H (2), L (2), S, E, Ni; 1976 v A; (with Derby Co), S, E, Y (2), Ni; 1977 v WG, S (2), Cz, E, Ni; 1978 v K (2); (with QPR), WG; (with Burnley) 1979 v T; 1980 (with Swansea C), v E, S, Ni, Ic; 1981 v T, Ei, T, S, E; 1982 v Cz, Ic, USSR, E (sub), S, Ni, F; (with Sunderland), 1983 v E (sub) (54)

James, R. M. (Swansea C), 1979 v Ma, WG (sub), S, E, Ni, Ma; 1980 v WG; 1982 v Cz (sub), Ic, Sp, E, S, Ni, F; 1983 v N, Y, E, Bul; (with Stoke C), 1984 v N, R, Bul, Y, S, E, Ni, N, Is; 1985 v Ic, Sp, Ic, (with QPR), N, S, Sp, N; 1986 v S, S.Ar, Ei, U, Ca (2); 1987 v Fi (2), USSR, Cz; (with Leicester C), 1988 v D (2), (with Swansea C), Y (47)

James, W. (West Ham U), 1931 v Ni; 1932 v Ni (2)

Jarrett, R. H. (Ruthin), 1889 v Ni; 1890 v S (2)

Jarvis, A. L. (Hull C), 1967 v S, E, Ni (3)

Jenkins, E. (Lovell's Ath), 1925 v E (1)

Jenkins, J. (Brighton), 1924 v Ni, E, S; 1925 v S, Ni; 1926 v E, S; 1927 v S (8)

Jenkins, R. W. (Rhyl), 1902 v Ni (1)

Jenkyns, C. A. L. (Small Heath), 1892 v E, S, Ni; 1895 v E; (with Woolwich Arsenal), 1896 v S; (with Newton Heath), 1897 v Ni; (with Walsall), 1898 v S, E (8)

Jennings, W. (Bolton W), 1914 v E, S; 1920 v S; 1923 v Ni, E; 1924 v E, S, Ni; 1927 v S, Ni; 1929 v S (11)

John, R. F. (Arsenal), 1923 v S, Ni; 1925 v Ni; 1926 v E; 1927 v E; 1928 v E, Ni; 1930 v E, S; 1932 v E; 1933 v F, Ni; 1935 v Ni; 1936 v S; 1937 v E (15)

John, W. R. (Walsall), 1931 v Ni; (with Stoke C), 1933 v E, S, Ni, F; 1934 v E, S; (with Preston NE), 1935 v E, S; (with Sheffield U), 1936 v E, S, Ni; (with Swansea T), 1939 v E, S (14)

Johnson, M. G. (Swansea T), 1964 v Ni (1)

Jones, A. (Port Vale), 1987 v Fi, Cz (sub); 1988 v D, (with Charlton Ath), D (sub), Cz (sub); 1990 v Hol (sub) (6)

Jones, A. F. (Oxford University), 1877 v S (1)

Jones, A. T. (Nottingham F), 1905 v E; (with Notts Co), 1906 v E (2)

Jones, Bryn (Wolverhampton W), 1935 v Ni; 1936 v E, S, Ni; 1937 v E, S, Ni; 1938 v E, S, Ni; (with Arsenal), 1939 v E, S, Ni; 1947 v S, Ni; 1948 v E; 1949 v S (17)

Jones, B. S. (Swansea T), 1963 v S, E, Ni, H (2); 1964 v S, Ni; (with Plymouth Arg), 1965 v D; (with Cardiff C), 1969 v S, E, Ni, I (sub), WG, EG, R of UK (15)

Jones, Charlie (Nottingham F), 1926 v E; 1927 v S, Ni; 1928 v E; (with Arsenal), 1930 v E, S; 1932 v E; 1933 v F (8)

Jones, Cliff (Swansea T), 1954 v A; 1956 v E, Ni, S, A; 1957 v E, S, Ni, Cz (2), EG; 1958 v EG, E, S, Is (2); (with Tottenham H), 1958 v Ni, H (2), M, Se, Br; 1959 v Ni; 1960 v E, S; 1961 v S, E, Ni, Sp, H, Ei; 1962 v E, Ni, S, Br (2), M; 1963 v S, Ni, H; 1964 v E, S, Ni; 1965 v E, S, Ni, D, Gr (2), USSR, I; 1967 v S, E; 1968 v E, S, WG; (with Fulham), 1969 v I, R of UK (59)

Jones, C. W. (Birmingham), 1935 v Ni; 1939 v F (2)

Jones, D. (Chirk), 1888 v S, Ni; (with Bolton W), 1889 v E, S, Ni; 1890 v E, Ni; 1891 v S; 1892 v Ni; 1893 v G; 1894 v E; 1895 v E; 1898 v S; (with Manchester C), 1900 v E, Ni (15)

Jones, D. E. (Norwich C), 1976 v S, E (sub); 1978 v S, Cz, WG, Ir, E; 1980 v E (8)

Jones, D. O. (Leicester C), 1934 v E, Ni; 1935 v E, S; 1936 v E, Ni; 1937 v Ni (7)

Jones, Evan (Chelsea), 1910 v S, Ni; (with Oldham Ath), 1911 v E, S; 1912 v E, S; (with Bolton W), 1914 v Ni (7)

Jones, F. R. (Bangor), 1885 v E, Ni; 1886 v S (3)

Jones, F. W. (Small Heath), 1893 v S (1)

Jones, G. P. (Wrexham), 1907 v S, Ni (2)

Jones, H. (Aberaman), 1902 v Ni (1)

Jones, Humphrey (Bangor), 1885 v E, Ni, S; 1886 v E, Ni, S; (with Queen's Park), 1887 v E; (with East Stirlingshire), 1889 v E, Ni; 1890 v E, S, Ni; (with Queen's Park), 1891 v E, S (14)

Jones, Ivor (Swansea T), 1920 v S, Ni; 1921 v Ni, E; 1922 v S, Ni; (with WBA), 1923 v E, Ni; 1924 v S; 1926 v Ni (10)

Jones, J. (Druids), 1876 v S (1)

Jones, J. (Berwyn Rangers), 1883 v S, Ni; 1884 v S (3)

Jones, J. (Wrexham), 1925 v Ni (1)

Jones, Jeffrey (Llandrindod Wells), 1908 v Ni; 1909 v Ni; 1910 v S (3)

Jones, J. L. (Sheffield U), 1895 v E, S, Ni; 1896 v Ni, S, E; 1897 v Ni, S, E; (with Tottenham H), 1898 v Ni, E, S; 1899 v S, Ni; 1900 v S; 1902 v E, S, Ni; 1904 v E, S, Ni (21)

Jones, J. Love (Stoke C), 1906 v S; (with Middlesbrough), 1910 v Ni (2)

Jones, J. O. (Bangor), 1901 v S, Ni (2)

Jones, J. P. (Liverpool), 1976 v A, E, S; 1977 v WG, S (2), Cz, E, Ni; 1978 v K (2), S, Cz, WG, Ir, E, S, Ni;

(with Wrexham), 1979 v Ma, T, WG, S, E, Ni, Ma; 1980 v Ei, WG, T, E, S, Ni, Ic; 1981 v T, Ei, T, S, E, USSR; 1982 v Cz, Ic, USSR, Sp, E, S, Ni, F; 1983 v N, (with Chelsea), v Y, E, Bul, S, Ni, Br; 1984 v N, R, Bul, Y, S, E, Ni, N, Is; 1985 v Ic, N, S, N; (with Huddersfield T), 1986 v S, H, Ei, U, Ca (2) (72)

Jones, J. T. (Stoke C), 1912 v E, S, Ni; 1913 v E, Ni; 1914 v S, Ni; 1920 v E, S, Ni; (with C Palace), 1921 v E, S; 1922 v E, S, Ni (15)

Jones, K. (Aston Villa), 1950 v S (1)

Jones, Leslie J. (Cardiff C), 1933 v F; (with Coventry C), 1935 v Ni; 1936 v S; 1937 v E, S, Ni; (with Arsenal), 1938 v E, S, Ni; 1939 v E, S (11)

Jones, P. W. (Bristol R), 1971 v Fi (1)

Jones, R. (Bangor), 1887 v S; 1889 v E; (with Crewe Alex), 1890 v E (3)

Jones, R. (Bangor), 1900 v S, Ni (2)

Jones, R. (Druids), 1899 v S; (with Millwall), 1906 v S, Ni (3)

Jones, R. A. (Druids), 1884 v E, Ni, S; 1885 v S (4)

Jones, R. S. (Everton), 1894 v Ni; (with Leicester Fosse), 1898 v S (2)

Jones, S. (Wrexham), 1887 v Ni; (with Chester), 1890 v S (2)

Jones, S. (Wrexham), 1893 v S, Ni; (with Burton Swifts), 1895 v S; 1896 v E, Ni (5)

Jones, T. (Manchester U), 1926 v Ni; 1927 v E, Ni; 1930 v Ni (4)

Jones, T. D. (Aberdare), 1908 v Ni (1)

Jones, T. G. (Everton), 1938 v Ni; 1939 v E, S, Ni; 1947 v E, S; 1948 v E, S, Ni; 1949 v E, Ni, P, Bel, Sw; 1950 v E, S, Bel (17)

Jones, T. J. Sheffield W), 1932 v Ni; 1933 v F (2)

Jones, W. (Druids), 1899 v E (1)

Jones, W. E. A. (Swansea T), 1947 v E, S; (with Tottenham H), 1949 v E, S (4)

Jones, W. J. (Aberdare), 1901 v E, S; (with West Ham U), 1902 v E, S (4)

Jones, W. Lot (Manchester C), 1905 v E, Ni; 1906 v E, S, Ni; 1907 v E, S, Ni; 1908 v S; 1909 v E, S, Ni; 1910 v E; 1911 v E; 1913 v E, S; 1914 v S, Ni; (with Southend U), 1920 v E, Ni (20)

Jones, W. P. (Druids), 1889 v E, Ni; (with Wynstay), 1890 v S, Ni (4)

Jones, W. R. (Aberystwyth), 1897 v S (1)

Keenor, F. C. (Cardiff C), 1920 v E, Ni; 1921 v E, Ni, S; 1922 v Ni; 1923 v E, Ni, S; 1924 v E, Ni, S; 1925 v E, Ni, S; 1926 v S; 1927 v E, Ni, S; 1928 v E, Ni, S; 1929 v E, Ni, S; 1930 v E, Ni, S; 1931 v E, Ni, S; (with Crewe Alex), 1933 v S (32)

Kelly, F. C. (Wrexham), 1899 v S, Ni; (with Druids), 1902 v Ni (3)

Kelsey, A. J. (Arsenal), 1954 v Ni, A; 1955 v S, Ni, Y; 1956 v E, Ni, S, A; 1957 v E, Ni, S, Cz (2), EG; 1958 v E, S, Ni, Is (2), H (2), M, Se, Br; 1959 v E, S; 1960 v E, Ni, S; 1961 v E, Ni, S, H, Sp (2); 1962 v E, S, Ni, Br (2) (41)

Kenrick, S. L. (Druids), 1876 v S; 1877 v S; (with Oswestry), 1879 v E, S; (with Shropshire Wanderers), 1881 v E (5)

Ketley, C. F. (Druids), 1882 v Ni (1)

King, J. (Swansea T), 1955 v E (1)

Kinsey, N. (Norwich C), 1951 v Ni, P, Sw; 1952 v E; (with Birmingham C), 1954 v Ni; 1956 v E, S (7)

Knill, A. R. (Swansea C), 1989 v Ho (1)

Krzywicki, R. L. (Huddersfield T), 1970 v E, S; (with WBA), Ni, EG, I; 1971 v R, Fi; 1972 v Cz (sub) (8)

Lambert, R. (Liverpool), 1947 v S; 1948 v E; 1949 v P, Bel, Sw (5)

Lathom, G. (Liverpool), 1905 v E, S; 1906 v S; 1907 v E,

S, Ni; 1908 v E; 1909 v Ni; (with Southport Central), 1910 v E; (with Cardiff C), 1913 v Ni (10)

Law, B. J. (QPR), 1990 v Se (1)

Lawrence, E. (Clapton Orient), 1930 v Ni; (with Notts Co), 1932 v S (2)

Lawrence, S. (Swansea T), 1932 v Ni; 1933 v F; 1934 v S, E, Ni; 1935 v E, S; 1936 v S (8)

Lea, A. (Wrexham), 1889 v E; 1891 v S, Ni; 1893 v Ni (4)

Lea, C. (Ipswich T), 1965 v Ni, I (2)

Leary, P. (Bangor), 1889 v Ni (1)

Leek, K. (Leicester C), 1961 v S, E, Ni, H, Sp (2); (with Newcastle C), 1962 v S; (with Birmingham C), v Br (sub), M; 1963 v E; 1965 v S, Gr; (with Northampton T), 1965 v Gr (13)

Lever, A. R. (Leicester C), 1953 v S (1)

Lewis, B. (Wrexham), 1891 v Ni; 1892 v S, E, Ni; (with Middlesbrough), 1893 v S, E; (with Wrexham), 1894 v S, E, Ni; 1895 v S (10)

Lewis, D. (Arsenal), 1927 v E; 1928 v Ni; 1930 v E (3)

Lewis, D. J. (Swansea T), 1933 v E, S (2)

Lewis, D. (Swansea C), 1983 v Br (sub) (1)

Lewis, J. (Bristol R), 1906 v E (1)

Lewis, J. (Cardiff C), 1926 v S (1)

Lewis, T. (Wrexham), 1881 v E, S (2)

Lewis, W. L. (Swansea T), 1927 v E, Ni; 1928 v E, Ni; 1929 v S; (with Huddersfield T), 1930 v E (6)

Lewis, W. (Bangor), 1885 v E; 1886 v E, S; 1887 v E, S; 1888 v E; 1889 v E, Ni, S; (with Crewe Alex), 1890 v E, Ni, S; 1891 v E, Ni, S; 1892 v E, S, Ni; 1894 v E, S, Ni; (with Chester), 1895 v S, Ni, E; 1896 v E, S, Ni; (with Manchester C), 1897 v E, S; (with Chester), 1898 v Ni (30)

Lloyd, B. W. (Wrexham), 1976 v A, E, S (3)

Lloyd, J. W. (Wrexham), 1879 v S; (with Newtown), 1885 v S (2)

Lloyd, R. A. (Ruthin), 1891 v Ni; 1895 v S (2)

Lockley, A. (Chirk), 1898 v Ni (1)

Lovell, S. (C Palace), 1982 v USSR (sub); (with Millwall), 1985 v N; 1986 v S (sub), H (sub), Ca (1 + sub) (6)

Lowrie, G. (Coventry C), 1948 v E, S, Ni; (with Newcastle U), 1949 v P (4)

Lowndes, S. (Newport Co), 1983 v S (sub), Br (sub); (with Millwall), 1985 v N (sub); 1986 v S.Ar (sub), Ei, U, Ca (2); (with Barnsley), 1987 v Fi (sub); 1988 v Se (sub) (10)

Lucas, P. M. (Leyton Orient), 1962 v Ni, M; 1963 v S, E (4)

Lucas, W. H. (Swansea T), 1949 v S, Ni, P, Bel, Sw; 1950 v E; 1951 v E (7)

Lumberg, A. (Wrexham), 1929 v Ni; 1930 v E, S; (with Wolverhampton W), 1932 v S (4)

McMillan, R. (Shrewsbury Engineers), 1881 v E, S (2)

Maguire, G. T. (Portsmouth), 1990 v Fi (sub), Ho, WG, Ei, Se (5)

Mahoney, J. F. (Stoke C), 1968 v E; 1969 v EG; 1971 v Cz; 1973 v E (3), Pol, S, Ni; 1974 v Pol, E, S, Ni; 1975 v A, H (2), L (2), S, E, Ni; 1976 v A, Y (2), E, Ni; 1977 v WG, Cz, S, E, Ni; (with Middlesbrough), 1978 v K (2), S, Cz, Ir, E (sub), S, Ni; 1979 v WG, S, E, Ni, Ma; (with Swansea C), 1980 v Ei, WG, T (sub); 1982 v Ic, USSR; 1983 v Y, E (51)

Martin, J. (Newport Co), 1930 v Ni (1)

Marustik, C. (Swansea C), 1982 v Sp, E, S, Ni, F; 1983 v N (6)

Mates, J. (Chirk), 1891 v Ni; 1897 v E, S (3)

Mathews, R. W. (Liverpool), 1921 v Ni; (with Bristol C), 1923 v E; (with Bradford), 1926 v Ni (3)

Matthews, W. (Chester), 1905 v Ni; 1908 v E (2)

Matthias, J. S. (Brymbo), 1896 v S, Ni; (with Shrewsbury), 1897 v E, S; (with Wolverhampton W), 1899 v S (5)

Matthias, T. J. (Wrexham), 1914 v S, E; 1920 v Ni, S, E; 1921 v S, E, Ni; 1922 v S, E, Ni; 1923 v S (12)

Mays, A. W. (Wrexham), 1929 v Ni (1)

Medwin, T. C. (Swansea T), 1953 v Ni, F, Y; (with Tottenham H), 1957 v E, S, Ni, Cz (2), EG; 1958 v E, S, Ni, Is (2), H (2), M, Br; 1959 v E, S, Ni; 1960 v E, S, Ni; 1961 v S, Ei, Sp; 1963 v E, H (29)

Melville, A. K. (Swansea C), 1990 v WG, Ei, Se, Cr (Sub) (4)

Meredith, S. (Chirk), 1900 v S; 1901 v S, E, Ni; (with Stoke C), 1902 v E; 1903 v Ni; 1904 v E; (with Leyton), 1907 v E (8)

Meredith, W. H. (Manchester C), 1895 v E, Ni; 1896 v E, Ni; 1897 v E, Ni, S; 1898 v E, Ni; 1899 v E; 1900 v E, Ni; 1901 v E, Ni; 1902 v E, S; 1903 v E, S, Ni; 1904 v E; 1905 v E, S; (with Manchester U), 1907 v E, S, Ni; 1908 v E, Ni; 1909 v E, S, Ni; 1910 v E, S, Ni; 1911 v E, S, Ni; 1912 v E, S, Ni; 1913 v E, S, Ni; 1914 v E, S, Ni; 1920 v E, S, Ni (48)

Mielczarek, R. (Rotherham U), 1971 v Fi (1)

Millership, H. (Rotherham Co), 1920 v E, S, Ni; 1921 v E, S, Ni (6)

Millington, A. H. (WBA), 1963 v S, E, H; (with C Palace), 1965 v E, USSR; (with Peterborough U), 1966 v Ch, Br; 1967 v E, Ni; 1968 v Ni, WG; 1969 v I, EG; (with Swansea) 1970 v E, S, Ni; 1971 v Cz, Fi; 1972 v Fi (sub), Cz, R (21)

Mills, T. J. (Clapton Orient), 1934 v E, Ni; (with Leicester C), 1935 v E, S (4)

Mills-Roberts, R. H. (St Thomas' Hospital), 1885 v E, S, Ni; 1886 v E; 1887 v E; (with Preston NE), 1888 v E, Ni; (with Llanberis), 1892 v E (8)

Moore, G. (Cardiff C), 1960 v E, S, Ni; 1961 v Ei, Sp; (with Chelsea), 1962 v Br; 1963 v Ni, H; (with Manchester U), 1964 v S, Ni; (with Northampton T), 1966 v Ni, Ch; (with Charlton Ath), 1969 v S, E, Ni, R of UK; 1970 v E, S, Ni, I; 1971 v R (21)

Morgan, J. R. (Cambridge University), 1877 v S; (with Swansea), 1879 v S; (with Derby School Staff), 1880 v E, S; 1881 v E, S; 1882 v E, S, Ni; (with Swansea), 1883 v E (10)

Morgan, J. T. (Wrexham), 1905 v Ni (1)

Morgan-Owen, H. (Oxford University), 1901 v E, S; 1902 v S; 1906 v E, Ni; (with Welshpool), 1907 v S (6)

Morgan-Owen, M. M. (Oxford University), 1897 v S, Ni; 1898 v E, S; 1899 v S; 1900 v E; (with Corinthians), 1903 v S; 1906 v S, E, Ni; 1907 v E (11)

Morley, E. J. (Swansea T), 1925 v E; (with Clapton Orient), 1929 v E, S, Ni (4)

Morris, A. G. (Aberystwyth), 1896 v E, Ni, S; (with Swindon T), 1897 v E; 1898 v S; (with Nottingham F), 1899 v E, S; 1903 v E, S; 1905 v E, S; 1907 v E, S; 1908 v E; 1910 v E, S, Ni; 1911 v E, S, Ni; 1912 v E (21)

Morris, C. (Chirk), 1900 v E, S, Ni; (with Derby Co), 1901 v E, S, Ni; 1902 v E, S; 1903 v E, S, Ni; 1904 v Ni; 1905 v E, S, NI; 1906 v S; 1907 v S; 1908 v E, S; 1909 v E, S, Ni; 1910 v E, S, Ni; (with Huddersfield T), 1911 v E, S, Ni (28)

Morris, E. (Chirk), 1893 v E, S, Ni (3)

Morris, H. (Sheffield U), 1894 v S; (with Manchester C), 1896 v E; (with Grimsby T), 1897 v E (3)

Morris, J. (Oswestry), 1887 v S (1)

Morris, J. (Chirk), 1898 v Ni (1)

Morris, R. (Chirk), 1900 v E, Ni; 1901 v Ni; 1902 v S; (with Shrewsbury T), 1903 v E, Ni (6)

Morris, R. (Druids), 1902 v E, S; (with Newtown), 1902 v Ni; (with Liverpool), 1903 v S, Ni; 1904 v E, S, Ni; (with Leeds C), 1906 v S; (with Grimsby T), 1907 v Ni; (with Plymouth Arg), 1908 v Ni (11)

Morris, S. (Birmingham), 1937 v E, S; 1938 v E, S; 1939 v F (5)

Morris, W. (Burnley), 1947 v Ni; 1949 v E; 1952 v S, Ni, R of UK (5)

Moulsdale, J. R. B. (Corinthians), 1925 v Ni (1)

Murphy, J. P. (WBA), 1933 v F, E, Ni; 1934 v E, S; 1935

v E, S, Ni; 1936 v E, S, Ni; 1937 v S, Ni; 1938 v E, S (15)

Nardiello, D. (Coventry C), 1978 v Cz, WG (sub) (2)

Neal, J. E. (Colwyn Bay), 1931 v E, S (2)

Newnes, J. (Nelson), 1926 v Ni (1)

Newton, L. F. (Cardiff Corinthians), 1912 v Ni (1)

Nicholas, D. S. (Stoke C), 1923 v S; (with Swansea T), 1927 v E, Ni (3)

Nicholas, P. (C Palace), 1979 v S (sub), Ni (sub), Ma; 1980 v Ei, WG, T, E, S, Ni, Ic; 1981 v T, Cz, E; (with Arsenal), T, S, E, USSR; 1982 v Cz, Ic, USSR, Sp, E, S, Ni, F; 1983 v Y, Bul, S (sub), Ni; 1984 v N, Bul, N, Is; (with C Palace), 1985 v Sp; (with Luton T), N, S, Sp, N; 1986 v S, H, S.Ar, Ei, U, Ca (2); 1987 v Fi (2) USSR, Cz; (with Aberdeen), 1988 v D (2), Cz, Y, Se; (with Chelsea), 1989 v Ho, Fi, Is, Se, WG; 1990 v Fi, Ho, WG, Ei, Se, Cr (65)

Nicholls, J. (Newport Co), 1924 v E, Ni; (with Cardiff C), 1925 v E, S (4)

Niedzwiecki, E. A. (Chelsea), 1985 v N (sub); 1988 v D (2)

Nock, W. (Newtown), 1897 v Ni (1)

Norman, A. J. (Hull C), 1986 v Ei (sub), U, Ca; 1988 v Ma, I (5)

Nurse, M. T. G. (Swansea T), 1960 v E, Ni; 1961 v S, E, H, Ni, Ei, Sp (2); (with Middlesbrough), 1963 v E, H; 1964 v S (12)

O'Callaghan, E. (Tottenham H), 1929 v Ni; 1930 v S; 1932 v S, E; 1933 v Ni, S, E; 1934 v Ni, S, E; 1935 v E (11)

Oliver, A. (Blackburn R), 1905 v E; (with Bangor), S (2)

O'Sullivan, P. A. (Brighton), 1973 v S (sub); 1976 v S; 1979 v Ma (sub) (3)

Owen, D. (Oswestry), 1879 v E (1)

Owen, E. (Ruthin Grammar School), 1884 v E, Ni, S (3)

Owen, G. (Chirk), 1888 v S; (with Newton Heath), 1889 v S, Ni; 1892 v E; 1893 v Ni (5)

Owen, T (Oswestry), 1879 v E (1)

Owen, Trevor (Crewe Alex), 1899 v E, S (2)

Owen, W. (Chirk), 1884 v E; 1885 v Ni; 1887 v E; 1888 v E; 1889 v E, Ni, S; 1890 v S, Ni; 1891 v E, S, Ni; 1892 v E, S; 1893 v S, Ni (16)

Owen, W. P. (Ruthin), 1880 v E, S; 1881 v E, S; 1882 v E, S, Ni; 1883 v E, S; 1884 v E, S, Ni (12)

Owens, J. (Wrexham), 1902 v S (1)

Page, M. E. (Birmingham C), 1971 v Fi; 1972 v S, Ni; 1973 v E (1+1 sub), Ni; 1974 v S, Ni; 1975 v H, L, S, E, Ni; 1976 v K, Y (2), E, Ni; 1977 v WG, S; 1978 v K (sub+1), WG, Ir, E, S; 1979 v Ma, WG (28)

Palmer, D. (Swansea T), 1957 v Cz; 1958 v E, EG (3)

Parris, J. E. (Bradford), 1932 v Ni (1)

Parry, B. J. (Swansea T), 1951 v S (1)

Parry, C. (Everton), 1891 v E, S; 1893 v E; 1894 v E; 1895 v E, S; (with Newtown), 1896 v E, S, Ni; 1897 v Ni; 1898 v E, S, Ni (13)

Parry, E. (Liverpool), 1922 v S; 1923 v E, Ni; 1925 v Ni; 1926 v Ni (5)

Parry, H. (Newtown), 1895 v Ni (1)

Parry, M. (Liverpool), 1901 v E, S, Ni; 1902 v E, S, Ni; 1903 v E, S; 1904 v E, Ni; 1906 v E; 1908 v E, S, Ni; 1909 v E, S (16)

Parry, T. D. (Oswestry), 1900 v E, S, Ni; 1901 v E, S, Ni; 1902 v E (7)

Pascoe, C. (Swansea C), 1984 v N, Is; (with Sunderland) 1989 v Fi, Is, WG (sub); 1990 v Ho (sub), WG (sub) (7)

Paul, R. (Swansea T), 1949 v E, S, Ni, P, Sw; 1950 v E, S, Ni, Bel; (with Manchester C), 1951 v S, E, Ni, P, Sw; 1952 v E, S, Ni, R of UK; 1953 v S, E, Ni, F, Y; 1954 v E, S, Ni; 1955 v S, E, Y; 1956 v E, Ni, S, A (33)

Peake, E. (Aberystwyth), 1908 v Ni; (with Liverpool), 1909 v Ni, S, E; 1910 v S, Ni; 1911 v Ni; 1912 v E; 1913 v E, Ni; 1914 v Ni (11)

Peers, E. J. (Wolverhampton W), 1914 v Ni, S, E; 1920 v E, S; 1921 v S, Ni, E; (with Port Vale), 1922 v E, S, Ni; 1923 v E (12)

Perry, E. (Doncaster R), 1938 v E, S, Ni (3)

Phennah, E. (Civil Service), 1878 v S (1)

Phillips, C. (Wolverhampton W), 1931 v Ni; 1932 v E; 1933 v S; 1934 v E, S, Ni; 1935 v E, S, Ni; 1936 v S; (with Aston Villa), 1936 v E, Ni; 1938 v S (13)

Phillips, D. (Plymouth Arg), 1984 v E, Ni, N; (with Manchester C), 1985 v Sp, Ic, S, Sp, N; 1986 v S, H, S.Ar, Ei, U; (with Coventry C) 1987 v Fi, Cz; 1988 v D (2), Cz, Y, Se; 1989 v Se, WG; (with Norwich C), 1990 v Fi, Ho, WG, Ei, Se (27)

Phillips, L. (Cardiff C), 1971 v Cz, S, E, Ni; 1972 v Cz, R, S, Ni; 1973 v E; 1974 v Pol (sub), Ni; 1975 v A; (with Aston Villa), H (2), L (2), S, E, Ni; 1976 v A, E, Y (2), E, Ni; 1977 v WG, S (2), Cz, E; 1978 v K (2), S, Cz, WG, E, S; 1979 v Ma; (Swansea C), T, WG, S, E, Ni, Ma; 1980 v Ei, WG, T, S (sub), Ni, Ic; 1981 v T, Cz, T, S, E, USSR; (with Charlton Ath), 1982 v Cz, USSR (58)

Phillips, T. J. S. (Chelsea), 1973 v E; 1974 v E; 1975 v H (sub); 1978 v K (4)

Phoenix, H. (Wrexham), 1882 v S (1)

Poland, G. (Wrexham), 1939 v Ni, F (2)

Pontin, K. (Cardiff C), 1980 v E (sub), S (2)

Powell, A. (Leeds U), 1947 v E, S; 1948 v E, S, Ni; (with Everton), 1949 v E; 1950 v Bel; (with Birmingham C), 1951 v S (8)

Powell, D. (Wrexham), 1968 v WG; (with Sheffield U), 1969 v S, E, Ni, I, WG; 1970 v E, S, Ni, EG; 1971 v R (11)

Powell, I. V. (QPR), 1947 v E; 1948 v E, S, Ni; (with Aston Villa), 1949 v Bel; 1950 v S, Bel; 1951 v S (8)

Powell, J. (Druids), 1878 v S; 1880 v E, S; 1882 v E, S, Ni; 1883 v E, S, Ni; (with Bolton W), 1884 v E; (with Newton Heath), 1887 v E, S; 1888 v E, S, Ni (15)

Powell, Seth (WBA), 1885 v S; 1886 v E, Ni; 1891 v E, S; 1892 v E, S (7)

Price, H. (Aston Villa), 1907 v S; (with Burton U), 1908 v Ni; (with Wrexham), 1909 v S, E, Ni (5)

Price, J. (Wrexham), 1877 v S; 1878 v S; 1879 v E; 1880 v E, S; 1881 v E, S; (with Druids), 1882 v S, E, Ni; 1883 v S, Ni (12)

Price, P. (Luton T), 1980 v E, S, Ni, Ic; 1981 v T, Cz, Ei, T, S, E, USSR; (with Tottenham H), 1982 v USSR, Sp, F; 1983 v N, Y, E, Bul, S, Ni; 1984 v N, R, Bul, Y, S (sub) (25)

Pring, K. D. (Rotherham U), 1966 v Ch, D; 1967 v Ni (3)

Pritchard, H. K. (Bristol C), 1985 v N (sub) (1)

Pryce-Jones, A. W. (Newtown), 1895 v E (1)

Pryce-Jones, W. E. (Cambridge University), 1887 v S; 1888 v S, E, Ni; 1890 v Ni (5)

Pugh, A. (Rhostyllen), 1889 v S (sub) (1)

Pugh, D. H. (Wrexham), 1896 v S, Ni; 1897 v S, Ni; (with Lincoln C), 1900 v S; 1901 v S, E (7)

Pugsley, J. (Charlton Ath), 1930 v Ni (1)

Pullen, W. J. (Plymouth Arg), 1926 v E (1)

Rankmore, F. E. J. (Peterborough), 1966 v Ch (sub) (1)

Ratcliffe, K. (Everton), 1981 v Cz, Ei, T, S, E, USSR; 1982 v Cz, Ic, USSR, Sp, E; 1983 v Y, E, Bul, S, Ni, Br; 1984 v N, R, Bul, Y, S, E, Ni, N, Is; 1985 v Ic, Sp, Ic, N, S, Sp; 1986 v S, H, S.Ar, U; 1987 v Fi (2), USSR, Cz; 1988 v D (2), Cz; 1989 v Fi, Is, Se, WG; 1990 v Fi (48)

Rea, J. C. (Aberystwyth), 1894 v Ni, S, E; 1895 v S; 1896 v S, Ni; 1897 v S, Ni; 1898 v Ni (9)

Reece, G. I. (Sheffield U), 1966 v E, S, Ni, USSR; 1967 v S; 1969 v R of UK (sub); 1970 v I (sub); 1971 v S, E, Ni, Fi; 1972 v Fi, R, E (sub), S, Ni; (with Cardiff C), 1973 v E (sub), Ni; 1974 v Pol (sub), E, S, Ni; 1975 v A, H (2), L (2), S, Ni (29)

Reed, W. G. (Ipswich T), 1955 v S, Y (2)

Rees, A. (Birmingham C), 1984 v N (sub) (1)

Rees, R. R. (Coventry C), 1965 v S, E, Ni, D, Gr (2), I, R; 1966 v E, S, Ni, R, D, Br (2), Ch; 1967 v E, Ni; 1968 v E, S, Ni; (with WBA), WG; 1969 v I; (with Nottingham F), 1969 v WG, EG, S (sub), R of UK; 1970 v E, S, Ni, EG, I; 1971 v Cz, R, E (sub), Ni (sub), Fi; 1972 v Cz (sub), R (39)

Rees, W. (Cardiff C), 1949 v Ni, Bel, Sw; (with Tottenham H), 1950 v Ni (4)

Richards, A. (Barnsley), 1932 v S (1)

Richards, D. (Wolverhampton W), 1931 v Ni; 1933 v E, S, Ni; 1934 v E, S, Ni; 1935 v E, S, Ni; 1936 v S; (with Brentford), 1936 v E, Ni; 1937 v S, E; (with Birmingham), 1937 v Ni; 1938 v E, S, Ni; 1939 v E, S (21)

Richards, G. (Druids), 1899 v E, S, Ni; (with Oswestry), 1903 v Ni; (with Shrewsbury), 1904 v S; 1905 v Ni (6)

Richards, R. W. (Wolverhampton W), 1920 v E, S; 1921 v Ni; 1922 v E, S; (with West Ham U), 1924 v E, S, Ni; (with Mold), 1926 v S (9)

Richards, S. V. (Cardiff C), 1947 v E (1)

Richards, W. E. (Fulham), 1933 v Ni (1)

Roach, J. (Oswestry), 1885 v Ni (1)

Robbins, W. W. (Cardiff C), 1931 v E, S; 1932 v Ni, E, S; (with WBA), 1933 v F, E, S, Ni; 1934 v S; 1936 v S (11)

Roberts, D. F. (Oxford U), 1973 v Pol, E (sub), Ni; 1974 v E, S; 1975 v A; (with Hull C), L, Ni; 1976 v S, Ni, Y; 1977 v E (sub), Ni; 1978 v K (1+sub), S, Ni (17)

Roberts, I. W. (Watford), 1990 v Ho (1)

Roberts, J. G. (Arsenal), 1971 v S, E, Ni, Fi; 1972 v Fi, E, Ni; (with Birmingham C), 1973 v E (2), Pol, S, Ni; 1974 v Pol, E, S, Ni; 1975 v A, H, S, E; 1976 v E, S (22)

Roberts, J. H. (Bolton), 1949 v Bel (1)

Roberts, J. (Corwen), 1879 v S; 1880 v E, S; 1882 v E, S, Ni; (with Berwyn R), 1883 v E (7)

Roberts, J. (Ruthin), 1881 v S; 1882 v S (2)

Roberts, J. (Bradford C), 1906 v Ni; 1907 v Ni (2)

Roberts, Jas. (Chirk), 1898 v S (1)

Roberts, Jas (Wrexham), 1913 v S, Ni (2)

Roberts, P. S. (Portsmouth), 1974 v E; 1975 v A, H, L (4)

Roberts, R. (Rhos), 1891 v Ni; (with Crewe Alex), 1893 v E (2)

Roberts, R. (Druids), 1884 v S; (with Bolton W), 1887 v S; 1888 v S, E; 1889 v S, E; 1890 v S; 1892 v Ni; (with PNE), S (9)

Roberts, R. (Wrexham), 1886 v Ni; 1887 v Ni; 1891 v Ni (3)

Roberts, W. (Llangollen), 1879 v E, S; 1880 v E, S; (with Berwyn R), 1881 v S; 1883 v E, S (7)

Roberts, W. (Wrexham), 1886 v E, S, Ni; 1887 v Ni (4)

Roberts, W. H. (Ruthin), 1882 v E, S; 1883 v E, S, Ni; (with Rhyl), 1884 v S (6)

Rodrigues, P. J. (Cardiff C), 1965 v Ni, Gr (2); 1966 v USSR, S, D; (with Leicester C), v Ni, Br (2), Ch; 1967 v S; 1968 v E, S, Ni; 1969 v E, Ni, EG, R of UK; 1970 v E, S, Ni, EG; (with Sheffield W), 1971 v R, E, S, Cz, Ni; 1972 v Fi, Cz, R, E, Ni (sub); 1973 v E (3), Pol, S, Ni; 1974 v Pol (40)

Rogers, J. P. (Wrexham), 1896 v E, S, Ni (3)

Rogers, W. (Wrexham), 1931 v E, S (2)

Roose, L. R. (Aberystwyth), 1900 v Ni; (with London Welsh), 1901 v E, S, Ni; (with Stoke C), 1902 v E, S; 1904 v E; (with Everton), 1905 v S, E; (with Stoke C), 1906 v E, S, Ni; 1907 v E, S, Ni; (with Sunderland), 1908 v E, S, Ni; 1909 v E, S, Ni; 1910 v E, S, Ni; 1911 v S (24)

Rouse, R. V. (C Palace), 1959 v Ni (1)

Rowlands, A. C. (Tranmere R), 1914 v E (1)

Rowley, T. (Tranmere R), 1959 v Ni (1)

Rush, I. (Liverpool), 1980 v S (sub), Ni; 1981 v E (sub); 1982 v Ic (sub), USSR, E, S, Ni, F; 1983 v N, Y, E, Bul; 1984 v N, R, Bul, Y, S, Ni; 1985 v Ic, N, S, Sp; 1986 v S, S.Ar, Ei, U; 1987 v Fi (2), USSR, Cz; (with Juventus), 1988 v D, Cz, Y, Se, Ma, I; (with Liverpool) 1989 v Ho, Fi, Se, WG; 1990 v Fi, Ei (44)

Russell, M. R. (Merthyr T), 1912 v S, Ni; 1914 v E; (with Plymouth Arg), 1920 v E, S, Ni; 1921 v E, S, Ni; 1922 v E, Ni; 1923 v E, S, Ni; 1924 v E, S, Ni; 1925 v E, S; 1926 v E, S; 1928 v S; 1929 v E (23)

Sabine, H. W. (Oswestry), 1887 v Ni (1)

Saunders, D. (Brighton & HA), 1986 v Ei (sub), Ca (2); 1987 v Fi, USSR (sub); (with Oxford U), 1988 v Y, Se, Ma, I (sub); 1989 v Ho (sub),Fi, Is (with Derby Co) Se, WG; 1990 v Fi, Ho, WG, Se, Cr (19)

Savin, G. (Oswestry), 1878 v S (1)

Sayer, P. (Cardiff C), 1977 v Cz, S, E, Ni; 1978 v K (2), S (7)

Scrine, F. H. (Swansea T), 1950 v E, Ni (2)

Sear, C. R. (Manchester C), 1963 v E (1)

Shaw, E. G. (Oswestry), 1882 v Ni; 1884 v S, Ni (3)

Sherwood, A. T. (Cardiff C), 1947 v E, Ni; 1948 v S, Ni; 1949 v E, S, Ni, P, Sw; 1950 v E, S, Ni, Bel; 1951 v E, S, Ni, P, Sw; 1952 v E, S, Ni, R of UK; 1953 v S, E, Ni, F, Y; 1954 v E, S, Ni, A; 1955 v S, E, Y, Ni; 1956 v E, S, Ni, A; (with Newport Co), 1957 v E, S (41)

Shone, W. W. (Oswestry), 1879 v E (1)

Shortt, W. W. (Plymouth Arg), 1947 v Ni; 1950 v Ni, Bel; 1952 v E, S, Ni, R of UK; 1953 v S, E, Ni, F, Y (12)

Showers, D. (Cardiff C), 1975 v E (sub), Ni (2)

Sidlow, C. (Liverpool), 1947 v E, S; 1948 v E, S, Ni; 1949 v S; 1950 v E (7)

Sisson, H. (Wrexham Olympic), 1885 v Ni; 1886 v S, Ni (3)

Slatter, N. (Bristol R), 1983 v S; 1984 v N (sub), Is; 1985 v Ic, Sp, Ic, N, S, Sp, N; (with Oxford U), 1986 v H (sub), S.Ar, Ca (2); 1987 v Fi (sub), Cz; 1988 v D (2), Cz, Ma, I; 1989 v Is (sub) (22)

Smallman, D. P. (Wrexham), 1974 v E (sub), S (sub), Ni; (with Everton), 1975 v H (sub), E, Ni (sub); 1976 v A (7)

Southall, N. (Everton), 1982 v Ni; 1983 v N, E, Bul, S, Ni, Br; 1984 v N, R, Bul, Y, S, E, Ni, N, Is; 1985 v Ic, Sp, Ic, N, S, Sp, N; 1986 v S, H, S.Ar, Ei; 1987 v USSR, Fi, Cz; 1988 v D, Cz, Y, Se; 1989 v Ho, Fi, Se, WG; 1990 v Fi, Ho, WG, Ei, Se, Cr (44)

Speed, G. A. (Leeds U), 1990 v Cr (sub) (1)

Sprake, G. (Leeds U), 1964 v S, Ni; 1965 v S, D, Gr; 1966 v E, Ni, USSR; 1967 v S; 1968 v E, S; 1969 v S, E, Ni, WG, R of UK; 1970 v EG, I; 1971 v R, S, E, Ni; 1972 v Fi, E, S, Ni; 1973 v E (2), Pol, S, Ni; 1974 v Pol; (with Birmingham C), S, Ni; 1975 v A, H, L (37)

Stansfield, F. (Cardiff C), 1949 v S (1)

Stevenson, B. (Leeds U), 1978 v Ni; 1979 v Ma, T, S, E, Ni, Ma; 1980 v WG, T, Ic (sub); 1982 v Cz; (with Birmingham C), Sp, S, Ni, F (15)

Stevenson, N. (Swansea C), 1982 v E, S, Ni; 1983 v N (4)

Stitfall, R. F. (Cardiff C), 1953 v E; 1957 v Cz(2)

Sullivan, D. (Cardiff C), 1953 v Ni, F, Y; 1954 v Ni; 1955 v E, Ni; 1957 v E, S; 1958 v Ni, H (2), Se, Br; 1959 v S, Ni; 1960 v E, S (17)

Tapscott, D. R. (Arsenal), 1954 v A; 1955 v S, E, Ni, Y; 1956 v E, Ni, S, A; 1957 v Ni, Cz, EG; (with Cardiff C), 1959 v E, Ni (14)

Taylor, J. (Wrexham), 1898 v E (1)

Taylor, O. D. S. (Newtown), 1893 v S, Ni; 1894 v S, Ni (4)

Thomas, C. (Druids), 1899 v Ni; 1900 v S (2)

Thomas, D. A. (Swansea T), 1957 v Cz; 1958 v EG (2)

Thomas, D. S. (Fulham), 1948 v E, S, Ni; 1949 v S (4)

Thomas, E. (Cardiff Corinthians), 1925 v E (1)

Thomas, G. (Wrexham), 1885 v E, S (2)

Thomas, H. (Manchester U), 1927 v E (1)

Thomas, M. (Wrexham), 1977 v WG, S (1+1 sub), Ni (sub); 1978 v K (sub), S, Cz, Ir, E, Ni (sub); 1979 v Ma; (with Manchester U), T, WG, Ma (sub); 1980 v Ei, WG (sub), T, E, S, Ni; 1981 v Cz, S, E, USSR; (with Ever-

ton), 1982 v Cz; (with Brighton & HA), USSR (sub), Sp, E, S (sub), Ni (sub); 1983 (with Stoke C), v N, Y, E, Bul, S, Ni, Br; 1984 v R, Bul, Y; (with Chelsea), S, E; 1985 v Ic, Sp, Ic, S, Sp, N; 1986 v S; (with WBA), H, S.Ar (sub) (51)

Thomas, M. R. (Newcastle U), 1987 v Fi (1)

Thomas, R. J. (Swindon T), 1967 v Ni; 1968 v WG; 1969 v E, Ni, I, WG, R of UK; 1970 v E, S, Ni, EG, I; 1971 v S, E, Ni, R, Cz; 1972 v Fi, Cz, R, E, S, Ni; 1973 v E (3), Pol, S, Ni; 1974 v Pol; (with Derby Co), E, S, Ni; 1975 v H (2), L (2), S, E, Ni; 1976 v A, Y, E; 1977 v Cz, S, E, Ni; 1978 v K, S; (with Cardiff C), Cz (50)

Thomas, T. (Bangor), 1898 v S, Ni (2)

Thomas, W. R. (Newport Co), 1931 v E, S (2)

Thomson, D. (Druids), 1876 v S (1)

Thomson, G. F. (Druids), 1876 v S; 1877 v S (2)

Toshack, J. B. (Cardiff C), 1969 v S, E, Ni, WG, EG, R of UK; 1970 v EG, I; (with Liverpool), 1971 v S, E, Ni, Fi; 1972 v Fi, E; 1973 v E (3), Pol, S; 1975 v A, H (2), L (2), S, E; 1976 v Y (2), E; 1977 v S; 1978 v K (2), S, Cz; (Swansea C), 1979 v WG (sub), S, E, Ni, Ma; 1980 v WG (40)

Townsend, W. (Newtown), 1887 v Ni; 1893 v Ni (2)

Trainer, H. (Wrexham), 1895 v E, S, Ni (3)

Trainer, J. (Bolton W), 1887 v S; (with Preston NE), 1888 v S; 1889 v E; 1890 v S; 1891 v S; 1892 v Ni, S; 1893 v E; 1894 v Ni, E; 1895 v Ni, E; 1896 v S; 1897 v Ni, S, E; 1898 v S, E; 1899 v Ni, S (20)

Turner, H. G. (Charlton Ath), 1937 v E, S, Ni; 1938 v E, S, Ni; 1939 v Ni, F (8)

Turner, J. (Wrexham), 1892 v E (1)

Turner, R. E. (Wrexham), 1891 v E, Ni (2)

Turner, W. H. (Wrexham), 1887 v E, Ni; 1890 v S; 1891 v E, S (5)

Van Den Hauwe, P. W. R. (Everton), 1985 v Sp; 1986 v S, H; 1987 v USSR, Fi, Cz; 1988 v D (2), Cz, Y, I; 1989 v Fi, Se (13)

Vaughan, Jas (Druids), 1893 v E, S, Ni; 1899 v E (4)

Vaughan, John (Oswestry), 1879 v S; 1880 v S; 1881 v E, S; 1882 v E, S, Ni; 1883 v E, S, Ni; (with Bolton W), 1884 v E (11)

Vaughan, J. O. (Rhyl), 1885 v Ni; 1886 v Ni, E, S (4)

Vaughan, N. (Newport Co), 1983 v Y (sub), Br; 1984 v N; (with Cardiff C), R, Bul, Y, Ni (sub), N, Is; 1985 v Sp (sub) (10)

Vaughan, T. (Rhyl), 1885 v E (1)

Vearncombe, G. (Cardiff C), 1958 v EG; 1961 v Ei (2)

Vernon, T. R. (Blackburn R), 1957 v Ni, Cz (2), EG; 1958 v E, S, EG, Se; 1959 v S; (with Everton), 1960 v Ni; 1961 v S, E, Ei; 1962 v Ni, Br (2), M; 1963 v S, E, H; 1964 v S; (with Stoke C), 1965 v Ni, Gr, I; 1966 v E, S, Ni, USSR, D; 1967 v Ni; 1968 v E (32)

Villars, A. K. (Cardiff C), 1974 v E, S, Ni (sub) (3)

Vizard, E. T. (Bolton W), 1911 v E, S, Ni; 1912 v E, S; 1913 v S; 1914 v E, Ni; 1920 v E; 1921 v E, S, Ni; 1922 v E, S; 1923 v E, Ni; 1924 v E, S, Ni; 1926 v E, S; 1927 v S (22)

Walley, J. T. (Watford), 1971 v Cz (1)

Walsh, I. (C Palace), 1980 v Ei, T, E, S, Ic; 1981 v T, Cz, Ei, T, S, E, USSR; 1982 v Cz (sub), Ic; (with Swansea C), Sp, S (sub), Ni (sub), F (18)

Ward, D. (Bristol R), 1959 v E; (with Cardiff C), 1962 v E (2)

Warner, J. (Swansea T), 1937 v E; (with Manchester U), 1939 v F (2)

Warren, F. W. (Cardiff C), 1929 v Ni; (with Middlesbrough), 1931 v Ni; 1933 v F, E; (with Hearts), 1937 v Ni; 1938 v Ni (6)

Watkins, A. E. (Leicester Fosse), 1898 v E, S; (with Aston Villa), 1900 v E, S; (with Millwall), 1904 v Ni (5)

Watkins, W. M. (Stoke C), 1902 v E; 1903 v E, S; (with

Aston Villa); 1904 v E, S, Ni; (with Sunderland), 1905 v E, S, Ni; (with Stoke C), 1908 v Ni (10)
Webster, C (Manchester U), 1957 v Cz; 1958 v H, M, Br (4)
Whatley, W. J. (Tottenham H), 1939 v E, S (2)
White, P. F. (London Welsh), 1896 v Ni (1)
Wilcocks, A. R. (Oswestry), 1890 v Ni (1)
Wilding, J. (Wrexham O), 1885 v E, S, Ni; 1886 v E, Ni; (with Bootle), 1887 v E; 1888 v S, Ni; (with Wrexham), 1892 v S (9)
Williams, A. L. (Wrexham), 1931 v E (1)
Williams, B. (Bristol C), 1930 v Ni (1)
Williams, B. D. (Swansea T), 1928 v Ni, E; 1930 v E, S; (with Everton), 1931 v Ni; 1932 v E; 1933 v E, S, Ni; 1935 v Ni (10)
Williams, D. G. (Derby Co), 1988 v Cz, Y, Se, Ma, I; 1989 v Ho, Is, Se, WG; 1990 v Fi, Ho (11)
Williams, D. M. (Norwich C), 1986 v S.Ar (sub), U, Ca (2); 1987 v Fi (5)
Williams, D. R. (Merthyr T), 1921 v E, S; (with Sheffield W), 1923 v S; 1926 v S; 1927 v E, Ni; (with Manchester U), 1929 v E, S (8)
Williams, E. (Crewe Alex), 1893 v E, S (2)
Williams, E. (Druids), 1901 v E, Ni, S; 1902 v E, Ni (5)
Williams, G. (Chirk), 1893 v S; 1894 v S; 1895 v E, S, Ni; 1898 v Ni (6)
Williams, G. E. (WBA), 1960 v Ni; 1961 v S, E, Ei; 1963 v Ni, H; 1964 v E, S, Ni; 1965 v S, E, Ni, D, Gr (2), USSR, I; 1966 v Ni, Br (2), Ch; 1967 v S, E, Ni; 1968 v Ni; 1969 v I (26)
Williams, G. G. (Swansea T), 1961 v Ni, H, Sp (2); 1962 v E (5)
Williams, G. J. J. (Cardiff C), 1951 v Sw (1)
Williams, G. O. (Wrexham), 1907 v Ni (1)
Williams, H. J. (Swansea), 1965 v Gr (2); 1972 v R (3)
Williams, H. T. (Newport Co), 1949 v Ni, Sw; (with Leeds U), 1950 v Ni; 1951 v S (4)

Williams, J. H. (Oswestry), 1884 v E (1)
Williams, J. T. (Wrexham), 1939 v F (1)
Williams, J. T. (Middlesbrough), 1925 v Ni (1)
Williams, J. W. (C Palace), 1912 v S, Ni (2)
Williams, R. (Newcastle U), 1935 v S, E (2)
Williams, R. P. (Caernarvon), 1886 v S (1)
Williams, S. G. (WBA), 1954 v A; 1955 v E, Ni; 1956 v E, S, A; 1958 v E, S, Ni, Is (2), H (2), M, Se, Br; 1959 v E, S, Ni; 1960 v S, Ni; 1961 v Ni, Ei, H, Sp (2); 1962 v E, S, Ni, Br (2), M; (with Southampton), 1963 v S, E, H (2); 1964 v E, S; 1965 v S, E, D; 1966 v D (43)
Williams, W. (Druids), 1876 v S; 1878 v S; (with Oswestry), 1879 v E, S; (with Druids), 1880 v E, S; 1881 v E, S; 1882 v E, S, Ni; 1883 v Ni (12)
Williams, W. (Northampton T), 1925 v S (1)
Witcomb, D. F. (WBA), 1947 v E, S; (with Sheffield W), 1947 v Ni (3)
Woosnam, A. P. (Leyton Orient), 1959 v S; (with West Ham U), v E; 1960 v E, S, Ni; 1961 v S, E, Ni, Ei, Sp, H; 1962 v E, S, Ni, Br; (with Aston Villa), 1963 v Ni, H (17)
Woosnam, G. (Newton White Star), 1879 v S (1)
Worthington, T. (Newtown), 1894 v S (1)
Wynn, G. A. (Chirk), 1903 v Ni; (with Wrexham), 1909 v E, S, Ni; (with Manchester C), 1910 v E; 1911 v Ni; 1912 v E, S; 1913 v E, S; 1914 v E, S (12)

Yorath, T. C. (Leeds U), 1970 v I; 1971 v S, E, Ni; 1972 v Cz, E, S, Ni; 1973 v E, Pol, S; 1974 v Pol, E, Ni; 1975 v A, H (2), L (2), S; 1976 v A, E, S, Y (2), E, Ni; (with Coventry C), 1977 v WG, S (2), Cz, E, Ni; 1978 v K (2), S, Cz, WG, Ir, E, S, Ni; 1979 v T, WG, S, E, Ni; (with Tottenham H), 1980 v Ei, T, E, S, Ni, Ic; 1981 v T, Cz; (with Vancouver W), Ei, T, USSR (59)

Young, E. (Wimbledon), 1990 v Cr (1)

REPUBLIC OF IRELAND

Aherne, T. (Belfast Celtic), 1946 v P, Sp; (with Luton T), 1950 v Fi, E, Fi, Se, Bel; 1951 v N, Arg, N; 1952 v WG (2), A, Sp; 1953 v F; 1954 v F (16)
Aldridge, J. W. (Oxford U), 1986 v W, U, Ic, Cz; 1987 v Bel, S, Pol (with Liverpool), S, Bul, Bel, Br, L; 1988 v Bul, Pol, N, E, USSR, Ho; 1989 v Ni, Tun, Sp, F, H, Ma (sub), H; 1990 v WG (with Real Sociedad), Ni, Ma, Fi (sub), T. E, Eg, Ho, R, I (35)
Ambrose, P. (Shamrock R), 1955 v N, Ho; 1964 v Pol, N, E (5)
Anderson, J. (Preston NE), 1980 v Cz (sub), US (sub); 1982 v Ch, Br, Tr; (with Newcastle U), 1984 v Chn; 1986 v W, Ic, Cz; 1987 v Bul, Bel, Br, L; 1988 v R (sub), Y (sub); 1989 v Tun (16)
Andrews, P. (Bohemians), 1936 v Ho (1)
Arrigan, T. (Waterford), 1938 v N (1)

Bailham, E. (Shamrock R), 1964 v E (1)
Barber, E. (Shelbourne), 1966 v Sp; (with Birmingham C), 1966 v Bel (2)
Barry, P. (Fordsons), 1928 v Bel; 1929 v Bel (2)
Beglin, J. (Liverpool), 1984 v Chn; 1985 v M, D, I, Is, E, N, Sw; 1986 v Sw, USSR, D, W; 1987 v Bel (sub), S, Pol (15)
Bermingham, J. (Bohemians), 1929 v Bel (1)
Bermingham, P. (St James' Gate), 1935 v H (1)
Braddish, S. (Dundalk), 1978 v Pol (1)
Bonner, P. (Celtic), 1981 v Pol; 1982 v Alg; 1984 v Ma, Is, Chn; 1985 v I, Is, E, N; 1986 v U, Ic; 1987 v Bel (2), S (2), Pol, Bul, Br, L; 1988 v Bul, R, Y, N, E, USSR, Ho;

1989 v Sp, F, H, Sp, Ma, H; 1990 v WG, Ni, Ma, W, Fi, T, E, Eg, Ho, R, I (43)
Bradshaw, P. (St James' Gate), 1939 v Sw, Pol, H (2), G (5)
Brady, F. (Fordsons), 1926 v I; 1927 v I (2)
Brady, T. R. (QPR), 1964 v A (2), Sp (2), Pol, N (6)
Brady, W. L. (Arsenal), 1975 v USSR, T, Sw, USSR, Sw, WG; 1976 v T, N, Pol; 1977 v E, T, F (2), Sp, Bul; 1978 v Bul, N; 1979 v Ni, E, D, Bul, WG; 1980 v W, Bul, E, Cy; (with Juventus), 1981 v Ho, Bel, F, Cy, Bel; 1982 v Ho, F, Ch, Br, Tr; 1983 (with Sampdoria), v Ho, Sp, Ic, Ma; 1984 v Ic, Ho, Ma, Pol, Is; (with Internazionale), 1985 v USSR, N, D, I, E, N, Sp, Sw; 1986 v Sw, USSR, D, W; (with Ascoli), 1987 v Bel S (2), Pol, (with West Ham U), Bul, Bel, Br, L; 1988 v L, Bul (67); 1989 v F, H (sub), H (sub); 1990 v WG, Fi (72)
Breen, T. (Manchester U), 1937 v Sw, F; (with Shamrock R), 1947 v E, Sp, P (5)
Brennan, F. (Drumcondra), 1965 v Bel (1)
Brennan, S. A. (Manchester U), 1965 v Sp; 1966 v Sp, A, Bel; 1967 v Sp, T, Sp; 1969 v Cz, D, H; 1970 v S, Cz, D, H, Pol (sub), WG; (with Waterford), 1971 v Pol, Sc, I (19)
Brown, J. (Coventry C), 1937 v Sw, F (2)
Browne, W. (Bohemians), 1964 v A, Sp, E (3)
Buckley, L. (Shamrock R), 1984 v Pol (sub); (with Waregem), 1985 v M (2)
Burke, F. (Cork), 1934 v Bel (1)
Burke, F. (Cork Ath), 1952 v WG (1)
Burke, J. (Shamrock R), 1929 v Bel (1)

Byrne, A. B. (Southampton), 1970 v D, Pol, WG; 1971 v Pol, Se (2), I (2), A; 1973 v F, USSR (sub), F, N; 1974 v Pol (14)

Byrne, D. (Shelbourne), 1929 v Bel; (with Shamrock R), 1932 v Sp; (with Coleraine), 1934 v Bel (3)

Byrne, J. (Bray Unknowns), 1928 v Bel (1)

Byrne, J. (QPR), 1985 v I, Is (sub), E (sub), Sp (sub); 1987 v S (sub), Bel (sub), Br, L (sub); 1988 v L, Bul (sub), Is, R, Y (sub), Pol (sub); (with Le Havre), 1990 v WG (sub), W, Fi, T (sub), Ma (19)

Byrne, P. (Shamrock R), 1984 v Pol, Chn; 1985 v M, I; 1986 v D (sub), W (sub), U (sub), Ic (sub), Cz (9)

Byrne, P. (Shelbourne), 1931 v Sp; 1932 v Ho; (with Drumcondra), 1934 v Ho (3)

Byrne, S. (Bohemians), 1931 v Sp (1)

Campbell, A. (Santander), 1985 v I (sub), Is, Sp (3)

Campbell, N. (St Patrick's Ath), 1971 v A (sub); (with Fortuna, Cologne), 1972 v Ir, Ec, Ch, P; 1973 v USSR, F (sub); 1975 v WG; 1976 v N; 1977 v Sp, Bul (sub) (11)

Cannon, H. (Bohemians), 1926 v I; 1928 v Bel (2)

Cantwell, N. (West Ham U), 1954 v L; 1956 v Sp, Ho; 1957 v D, WG, E (2); 1958 v D, Pol, A; 1959 v Pol, Cz (2); 1960 v Se, Ch, Se; 1961 v N; (with Manchester U), 1961 v S (2); 1962 v Cz (2), A; 1963 v Ic (2), S; 1964 v A, Sp, E; 1965 v Pol, Sp; 1966 v Sp (2), A, Bel; 1967 v Sp, T (36)

Carey, J. J. (Manchester U), 1938 v N, Cz, Pol; 1939 v Sw, Pol, H (2), G; 1946 v P, Sp; 1947 v E, Sp, P; 1948 v P, Sp; 1949 v Sw, Bel, P, Se, Sp; 1950 v Fi, E, Fi, Se; 1951 v N, Arg, N; 1953 v F, A (29)

Carolan, J. (Manchester U), 1960 v Se, Ch (2)

Carroll, B. (Shelbourne), 1949 v Bel; 1950 v Fi (2)

Carroll, T. R. (Ipswich T), 1968 v Pol; 1969 v Pol, A, D; 1970 v Cz, Pol, WG; 1971 v Se; (with Birmingham C), 1972 v Ir, Ec, Ch, P; 1973 v USSR (2), Pol, F, N (17)

Cascarino, A. G. (Gillingham), 1986 v Sw, USSR, D; (with Millwall), 1988 v Pol, N (sub), USSR (sub), Ho (sub); 1989 v Ni, Tun, Sp, F, H, Sp, Ma, H; 1990 v WG (sub), Ni, Ma, (with Aston Villa), W, Fi, T, E, Eg, Ho (sub), R (sub), I (sub) (26)

Chandler, J. (Leeds U), 1980 v Cz (sub), US (2)

Chatton, H. A. (Shelbourne), 1931 v Sp; (with Dumbarton), 1932 v Sp; (with Cork), 1934 v Ho (3)

Clarke, J. (Drogheda U), 1978 v Pol (sub) (1)

Clarke, K. (Drumcondra), 1948 v P, Sp (2)

Clarke, M. (Shamrock R), 1950 v Bel (1)

Clinton, T. J. (Everton), 1951 v N; 1954 v F, L (3)

Coad, P. (Shamrock R), 1947 v E, Sp, P; 1948 v P, Sp; 1949 v Sw, Bel, P, Se; 1951 v N (sub); 1952 v Sp (11)

Coffey, T. (Drumcondra), 1950 v Fi (1)

Colfer, M. D. (Shelbourne), 1950 v Bel; 1951 v N (2)

Collins, F. (Jacobs), 1927 v I (1)

Conmy, O. M. (Peterborough U), 1965 v Bel; 1967 v Cz; 1968 v Cz, Pol; 1970 v Cz (5)

Connolly, J. (Fordsons), 1926 v I (1)

Connolly, N. (Cork), 1937 v G (1)

Conroy, G. A. (Stoke C), 1970 v Cz, D, H, Pol, WG; 1971 v Pol, Se (2), I; 1973 v USSR, F, USSR, N; 1974 v Pol, Br, U, Ch; 1975 v T, Sw, USSR, Sw, WG; 1976 v T (sub), Pol; 1977 v E, T, Pol (27)

Conway, J. P. (Fulham), 1967 v Sp, T, Sp; 1968 v Cz; 1969 v A (sub), H; 1970 v S, Cz, D, H, Pol, WG; 1971 v I, A; 1974 v U, Ch; 1975 v WG (sub); 1976 v N, Pol; (with Manchester C), 1977 v Pol (20)

Corr, P. J. (Everton), 1949 v P, Sp; 1950 v E, Se (4)

Courtney, E. (Cork U), 1946 v P (1)

Cummins, G. P. (Luton U), 1954 v L (2); 1955 v N (2), WG; 1956 v Y, Sp; 1958 v D, Pol, A; 1959 v Pol, Cz (2); 1960 v Se, Ch, WG, Se; 1961 v S (2) (19)

Cuneen, T. (Limerick), 1951 v N (1)

Curtis, D. P. (Shelbourne), 1957 v D, WG; (with Bristol C), 1957 v E (2); 1958 v D, Pol, A; (with Ipswich T),

1959 v Pol; 1960 v Se, Ch, WG, Se; 1961 v N, S; 1962 v A; 1963 v Ic (with Exeter C), 1964 v A (17)

Cusack, S. (Limerick), 1953 v F (1)

Daly, G. A. (Manchester U), 1973 v Pol (sub), N; 1974 v Br (sub), U (sub); 1975 v Sw (sub), WG; 1977 v E, T, F; (with Derby Co), F, Bul; 1978 v Bul, T, D; 1979 v Ni, E, D, Bul; 1980 v Ni, E, Cy, Sw, Arg; (with Coventry C), 1981 v Ho, Bel, Cy, W, Bel, Cz, Pol (sub); 1982 v Alg, Ch, Br, Tr; 1983 v Ho, Sp (sub), Ma; 1984 v Is (sub); (with Birmingham C), 1985 v M (sub), N, Sp, Sw; 1986 v Sw; (with Shrewsbury T), U, Ic (sub), Cz (sub); 1987 v S (sub) (47)

Daly, J. (Shamrock R), 1932 v Ho; 1935 v Sw (2)

Daly, M. (Wolverhampton W), 1978 v T, Pol (2)

Daly, P. (Shamrock R), 1950 v Fi (sub) (1)

Davis, T. L. (Oldham Ath), 1937 v G, H; (with Tranmere R), 1938 v Cz, Pol (4)

Deacy, E. (Aston Villa), 1982 v Alg (sub), Ch, Br, Tr (4)

De Mange, K. J. P. P. (Liverpool), 1987 v Br (sub); (with Hull C) 1989 v Tun (sub) (2)

Dempsey, J. T. (Fulham), 1967 v Sp, Cz; 1968 v Cz, Pol; 1969 v Pol, A, D; (with Chelsea), 1969 v Cz, D; 1970 v H, WG; 1971 v Pol, Se (2), I; 1972 v Ir, Ec, Ch, P (19)

Dennehy, J. (Cork Hibernians), 1972 v Ec (sub), Ch; (with Nottingham F), 1973 v USSR (sub), Pol, F, N; 1974 v Pol (sub); 1975 v T (sub), WG (sub); (with Walsall), 1976 v Pol (sub); 1977 v Pol (sub) (11)

Desmond, P. (Middlesbrough), 1950 v Fi, E, Fi, Se (4)

Devine, J. (Arsenal), 1980 v Cz, Ni; 1981 v Cz; 1982 v Ho, Alg; 1983 v Sp, Ma; (with Norwich C), 1984 v Ic, Ho, Is; 1985 v USSR, N (12)

Donnelly, J. (Dundalk), 1935 v H, Sw, G; 1936 v Ho, Sw, H, L; 1937 v G, H; 1938 v N (10)

Donnelly, T. (Drumcondra), 1938 v N; (Shamrock R), 1939 v Sw (2)

Donovan, D. C. (Everton), 1955 v N, Ho, N, WG; 1957 v E (5)

Donovan, T. (Aston Villa), 1980 v Cz (1)

Dowdall, C. (Fordsons), 1928 v Bel; (with Barnsley), 1929 v Bel; (with Cork), 1931 v Sp (3)

Doyle, C. (Shelbourne), 1959 v Cz (1)

Doyle, D. (Shamrock R), 1926 v I (1)

Doyle, L. (Dolphin), 1932 v Sp (1)

Duffy, B. (Shamrock R), 1950 v Bel (1)

Duggan, H. A. (Leeds U), 1927 v I; 1930 v Bel; 1936 v H, L; (with Newport Co), 1938 v N (5)

Dunne, A. P. (Manchester U), 1962 v A; 1963 v Ic, S; 1964 v A, Sp, Pol, N, E; 1965 v Pol, Sp; 1966 v Sp (2), A, Bel; 1967 v Sp, T, Sp; 1969 v Pol, D, H; 1970 v H; 1971 v Se, I, A; (with Bolton W), 1974 v Br (sub), U, Ch; 1975 v T, Sw, USSR, Sw, WG; 1976 v T (33)

Dunne, J. (Sheffield U), 1930 v Bel; (with Arsenal), 1936 v Sw, H, L; (with Southampton), 1937 v Sw, F; (with Shamrock R), 1938 v N (2), Cz, Pol; 1939 v Sw, Pol, H (2), G (15)

Dunne, J. C. (Fulham), 1971 v A (1)

Dunne, L. (Manchester C), 1935 v Sw, G (2)

Dunne, P. A. J. (Manchester U), 1965 v Sp; 1966 v Sp (2), WG; 1967 v T (5)

Dunne, S. (Luton T), 1953 v F, A; 1954 v F, L; 1956 v Sp, Ho; 1957 v D, WG, E; 1958 v D, Pol, A; 1959 v Pol; 1960 v WG, Se (15)

Dunne, T. (St Patrick's Ath), 1956 v Ho; 1957 v D, WG (3)

Dunning, P. (Shelbourne), 1971 v Se, I (2)

Dunphy, E. M. (York C), 1966 v Sp; (with Millwall), 1966 v WG; 1967 v T, Sp, T, Cz; 1968 v Cz, Pol; 1969 v Pol, A, D (2), H; 1970 v D, H, Pol, WG (sub); 1971 v Pol, Se (2), I (2), A (23)

Dwyer, N. M. (West Ham U), 1960 v Se, Ch, WG, Se; (with Swansea T), 1961 v W, N, S (2); 1962 v Cz (2); 1964 v Pol (sub), N, E; 1965 v Pol (14)

Eccles, P. (Shamrock R), 1986 v U (sub) (1)

Egan, R. (Dundalk), 1929 v Bel (1)

Eglington, T. J. (Shamrock R), 1946 v P, Sp; (with Everton), 1947 v E, Sp, P; 1948 v P; 1949 v Sw, P, Se; 1951 v N, Arg; 1952 v WG (2), A, Sp; 1953 v F, A; 1954 v F, L, F; 1955 v N, Ho, WG; 1956 v Sp (24)

Ellis, P. (Bohemians), 1935 v Sw, G; 1936 v Ho, Sw, L; 1937 v G, H (7)

Fagan, E. (Shamrock R), 1973 v N (sub) (1)

Fagan, F. (Manchester C), 1955 v N; 1960 v Se; (with Derby Co), 1960 v Ch, WG, Se; 1961 v W, N, S (8)

Fagan, K. (Shamrock R), 1926 v I (1)

Fairclough, M. (Dundalk), 1982 v Ch (sub), Tr (sub) (2)

Fallon, S. (Celtic), 1951 v N; 1952 v WG (2), A, Sp; 1953 v F; 1955 v N, WG (8)

Fallon, W. J. (Notts Co), 1935 v H; 1936 v H; 1937 v H, Sw, F; 1939 v Sw, Pol; (with Sheffield W), 1939 v H, G (9)

Farquharson, T. G. (Cardiff C), 1929 v Bel; 1930 v Bel; 1931 v Sp; 1932 v Sp (4)

Farrell, P. (Hibernian), 1937 v Sw, F (2)

Farrell, P. D. (Shamrock R), 1946 v P, Sp; (with Everton), 1947 v Sp, P; 1948 v P, Sp; 1949 v Sw, P (sub), Sp; 1950 v E, Fi, Se; 1951 v Arg, N; 1952 v WG (2), A, Sp; 1953 v F, A; 1954 v F (2); 1955 v N, Ho, WG; 1956 v Y, Sp; 1957 v E (28)

Feenan, J. J. (Sunderland), 1937 v Sw, F (2)

Finucane, A. (Limerick), 1967 v T, Cz; 1969 v Cz, D, H; 1970 v S, Cz; 1971 v Se, I, I (sub); 1972 v A (11)

Fitzgerald, F. J. (Waterford), 1955 v Ho; 1956 v Ho (2)

Fitzgerald, P. J. (Leeds U), 1961 v W, N, S; 1962 v Cz (2) (5)

Fitzpatrick, K. (Limerick), 1970 v Cz (1)

Fitzsimons, A. G. (Middlesbrough), 1950 v Fi, Bel; 1952 v WG (2), A, Sp; 1953 v F, A; 1954 v F, L, F; 1955 v Ho, N, WG; 1956 v Y, Sp, Ho; 1957 v D, WG, E (2); 1958 v D, Pol, A; 1959 v Pol; (with Lincoln C), 1959 v Cz (26)

Flood, J. J. (Shamrock R), 1926 v I; 1929 v Bel; 1930 v Bel; 1931 v Sp; 1932 v Sp (5)

Fogarty, A. (Sunderland), 1960 v WG, Se; 1961 v S; 1962 v Cz (2); 1963 v Ic (2), S (sub); 1964 v A (2); (with Hartlepools U), Sp (11)

Foley, J. (Cork), 1934 v Bel, Ho; (with Celtic), 1935 v H, Sw, G; 1937 v G, H (7)

Foley, M. (Shelbourne), 1926 v I (1)

Foley, T. C. (Northampton T), 1964 v Sp, Pol, N; 1965 v Pol, Bel; 1966 v Sp (2), WG; 1967 v Cz (9)

Foy, T. (Shamrock R), 1938 v N; 1939 v H (2)

Fullam, J. (Preston NE), 1961 v N; (with Shamrock R), 1964 v Sp, Pol, N; 1966 v A, Bel; 1968 v Pol; 1969 v Pol, A, D; 1970 v Cz (sub) (11)

Fullam, R. (Shamrock R), 1926 v I; 1927 v I (2)

Gallagher, C. (Celtic), 1967 v T, Cz (2)

Gallagher, M. (Hibernian), 1954 v L (1)

Gallagher, P. (Falkirk), 1932 v Sp (1)

Galvin, A. (Tottenham H), 1983 v Ho, Ma; 1984 v Ho (sub), Is (sub); 1985 v M, USSR, N, D, I, N, Sp; 1986 v U, Ic, Cz; 1987 v Bel (2), S, Bul, L; (with Sheffield W), 1988 v L, Bul, R, Pol, N, E, USSR, Ho; 1989 v Sp; (with Swindon T), 1990 v WG (29)

Gannon, E. (Notts Co), 1949 v Sw; (with Sheffield W), 1949 v Bel, P, Se, Sp; 1950 v Fi; 1951 v N; 1952 v G, A, 1954 v L, F; 1955 v N; (with Shelbourne), 1955 v N, WG (14)

Gannon, M. (Shelbourne), 1972 v A (1)

Gaskins, P. (Shamrock R), 1934 v Bel, Ho; 1935 v H, Sw, G; (with St James' Gate), 1938 v Cz, Pol (7)

Gavin, J. T. (Norwich C), 1950 v Fi (2); 1953 v F; 1954 v L; (with Tottenham H), 1955 v Ho, WG; (with Norwich C), 1957 v D (7)

Geoghegan, M. (St James' Gate), 1937 v G; 1938 v N (2)

Gibbons, A. (St Patrick's Ath), 1952 v WG; 1954 v L; 1956 v Y, Sp (4)

Gilbert, R. (Shamrock R), 1966 v WG (1)

Giles, C. (Doncaster R), 1951 v N (1)

Giles, M. J. (Manchester U), 1960 v Se, Ch; 1961 v W, N, S (2); 1962 v Cz (2), A; 1963 v Ic, S; (with Leeds U), 1964 v A (2), Sp (2), Pol, N, E; 1965 v Sp; 1966 v Sp (2), A, Bel; 1967 v Sp, T (2); 1969 v A, D, Cz; 1970 v S, Pol, WG; 1971 v I; 1973 v F, USSR; 1974 v Br, U, Ch; 1975 v USSR, T, Sw, USSR, Sw; (with WBA), 1976 v T; 1977 v E, T, F (2), Pol, Bul; (with Shamrock R), 1978 v Bul, T, Pol, N, D; 1979 v Ni, D, Bul, WG, (60)

Givens, D. J. (Manchester U), 1969 v D, H; 1970 v S, Cz, D, H; (with Luton T), 1970 v Pol, WG; 1971 v Se, I (2), A; 1972 v Ir, Ec, P; (with QPR), 1973 v F, USSR, Pol, F, N; 1974 v Pol, Br, U, Ch; 1975 v USSR, T, Sw, USSR, Sw, WG; 1976 v T, N, Pol; 1977 v E, T, F (2), Sp, Bul; 1978 v Bul, N, D; (with Birmingham C), 1979 v Ni (sub), E, D, Bul, WG; 1980 v US (sub), Ni (sub), Sw, Arg; 1981 v Ho, Bel, Cy (sub), W; (with Neuchatel X), 1982 v F (sub) (56)

Glen, W. (Shamrock R), 1927 v I; 1929 v Bel; 1930 v Bel; 1932 v Sp; 1936 v Ho, Sw, H, L (8)

Glynn, D. (Drumcondra), 1952 v WG; 1955 v N (2)

Godwin, T. F. (Shamrock R), 1949 v P, Se, Sp; 1950 v Fi, E; (with Leicester C), 1950 v Fi, Se, Bel; 1951 v N; (with Bournemouth), 1956 v Ho; 1957 v E; 1958 v D, Pol (13)

Golding, L. (Shamrock R), 1928 v Bel; 1930 v Bel (2)

Gorman, W. C. (Bury), 1936 v Sw, H, L; 1937 v G, H; 1938 v N, Cz, Pol; 1939 v Sw, Pol, H; (with Brentford), 1947 v E, P (13)

Grace, J. (Drumcondra), 1926 v I (1)

Grealish, A. (Orient), 1976 v N, Pol, D; 1979 v Ni, E, WG; (with Luton T), 1980 v W, Cz, Bul, US, Ni, E, Cy, Sw, Arg; 1981 v Ho, Bel, F, Cy, W, Bel, Pol; (with Brighton & HA), 1982 v Ho, Alg, Ch, Br, Tr; 1983 v Ho, Sp, Ic, Sp; 1984 v Ic, Ho (with WBA), Pol, Chn; 1985 v M, USSR, N, D, Sp (sub), Sw; 1986 v USSR, D (44)

Gregg, E. (Bohemians), 1978 v Pol, D (sub); 1979 v E (sub), D, Bul, WG; 1980 v W, Cz (9)

Griffith, R. (Walsall), 1935 v H (1)

Grimes, A. A. (Manchester U), 1978 v T, Pol, N (sub); 1980 v Bul, US, Ni, E, Cy; 1981 v Cz, Pol; 1982 v Alg; 1983 v Sp, Sp; (with Coventry C), 1984 v Pol, Is; (with Luton T), 1988 v L, R (17)

Hale, A. (Aston Villa), 1962 v A; (with Doncaster R), 1963 v Ic; 1964 v Sp (2); (with Waterford), 1967 v Sp; 1968 v Pol (sub); 1969 v Pol, A, D; 1970 v S, Cz; 1971 v Pol (sub); 1972 v A (sub) (13)

Hamilton, T. (Shamrock R), 1959 v Cz (2) (2)

Hand, E. K. (Portsmouth), 1969 v Cz (sub); 1970 v Pol, WG; 1971 v Pol, A; 1973 v USSR, F, USSR, Pol, F; 1974 v Pol, Br, U, Ch; 1975 v T, Sw, USSR, Sw, WG; 1976 v T (20)

Harrington, W. (Cork), 1936 v Ho, Sw, H, L (4)

Hartnett, J. B. (Middlesbrough), 1949 v Sp; 1954 v L (2)

Haverty, J. (Arsenal), 1956 v Ho; 1957 v D, WG, E (2); 1958 v D, Pol, A; 1959 v Pol; 1960 v Se, Ch; 1961 v W, N, S (2); (with Blackburn R), 1962 v Cz (2); (with Millwall), 1963 v S; 1964 v A, Sp, Pol, N, E; (with Celtic), 1965 v Pol; (with Bristol R), 1965 v Sp; (with Shelbourne), 1966 v Sp (2), WG, A, Bel; 1967 v T, Sp (32)

Hayes, A. W. P. (Southampton), 1979 v D (1)

Hayes, W. E. (Huddersfield T), 1947 v E, P (2)

Hayes, W. J. (Limerick), 1949 v Bel (1)

Healey, R. (Cardiff C), 1977 v Pol; 1980 v E (sub) (2)

Heighway, S. D. (Liverpool), 1971 v Pol, Se (2), I, A; 1973 v USSR; 1975 v USSR, T, USSR, WG; 1976 v T, N; 1977 v E, F (2), Sp, Bul; 1978 v Bul, N, D; 1979 v

Ni, Bul; 1980 v Bul, US, Ni, E, Cy, Arg; 1981 v Bel, F, Cy, W, Bel; (with Minnesota K), 1982 v Ho (34)

Henderson, B. (Drumcondra), 1948 v P, Sp (2)

Hennessy, J. (Shelbourne), 1956 v Pol, B, Sp; 1966 v WG; (with St Patrick's Ath), 1969 v A (5)

Herrick, J. (Cork Hibernians), 1972 v A, Ch (sub); (with Shamrock R), 1973 v F (sub) (3)

Higgins, J. (Birmingham C), 1951 v Arg (1)

Holmes, J. (Coventry C), 1971 v A (sub); 1973 v F, USSR, Pol, F, N; 1974 v Pol, Br; 1975 v USSR, Sw; 1976 v T, N, Pol; 197⁻ v E, T, F, Sp; (with Tottenham H), F, Pol, Bul; 1978 v Bul, T, Pol, N, D; 1979 v Ni, E, D, Bul; 1981 (with Vancouver W), v W (30)

Horlecher, A. F. (Bohemians), 1930 v Bel; 1932 v Sp, Ho; 1935 v H; 1936 v Ho, Sw (6)

Houghton, R. J. (Oxford U), 1986 v W, U, Ic, Cz; 1987 v Bel (2), Pol, L; 1988 v L, Bul, (with Liverpool), Is, Y, N, E, USSR, Ho; 1989 v Ni, Tun, Sp, F, H, Sp, Ma, H; 1990 v Ni, Ma, Fi, E, Eg, Ho, R, I (34)

Howlett, G. (Brighton & HA), 1984 v Chn (sub) (1)

Hoy, M. (Dundalk), 1938 v N; 1939 v Sw, Pol, H (2), G (6)

Hughton, C. (Tottenham H), 1980 v US, E, Sw, Arg; 1981 v Ho, Bel, F, Cy, W, Bel, Pol; 1982 v F; 1983 v Ho, Sp, Ma, Sp; 1984 v Ic, Ho, Ma; 1985 v M (sub), USSR, N, I, Is, E, Sp; 1986 v Sw, USSR, U, Ic; 1987 v Bel, Bul; 1988 v Is, Y, Pol, N, E, USSR, Ho; 1989 v Ni, F, H, Sp, Ma, H; 1990 v W (sub), USSR (sub), Fi, T (sub), Ma (sub) (50)

Hurley, C. J. (Millwall), 1957 v E; 1958 v D, Pol, A; (with Sunderland), 1959 v Cz (2); 1960 v Se, Ch,WG, Se; 1961 v W, N, S (2); 1962 v Cz (2), A; 1963 v Ic (2), S; 1964 v A (2), Sp (2), Pol, N; 1965 v Sp; 1966 v WG, A, Bel; 1967 v T, Sp, T, Cz; 1968 v Cz, Pol (2); (with Bolton W), 1969 v D, Cz, H (40)

Hutchinson, F. (Drumcondra), 1935 v Sw, G (2)

Jordan, D. (Wolverhampton W), 1937 v Sw, F (2)

Jordan, W. (Bohemians), 1934 v Ho; 1938 v N (2)

Kavanagh, P. J. (Celtic), 1931 v Sp; 1932 v Sp (2)

Keane, T. R. (Swansea T), 1949 v Sw, P, Se, Sp (4)

Kearin, M. (Shamrock R), 1972 v A (1)

Kearns, F. T. (West Ham U), 1954 v L (1)

Kearns, M. (Oxford U), 1970 v Pol (sub); (with Walsall), 1974 v Pol (sub), U, Ch; 1976 v N, Pol; 1977 v E, T, F (2), Sp, Bul; 1978 v N, D; 1979 v Ni, E; (with Wolverhampton W), 1980 v US, Ni (18)

Kelly, D. T. (Walsall), 1988 v Is, R, Y; (with West Ham U), 1989 v Tun (sub); (with Leicester C), 1990 v USSR, Ma (5)

Kelly, J. (Derry C), 1932 v Ho; 1934 v Bel; 1936 v Sw, L (4)

Kelly, J. A. (Drumcondra), 1957 v WG, E; (with Preston NE), 1962 v A; 1963 v Ic (2), S; 1964 v A (2), Sp (2), Pol; 1965 v Bel; 1966 v A, Bel; 1967 v Sp (2), T, Cz (2), Pol; 1968 v Pol, A, D, Cz, D, H; 1970 v S, D, H, Pol, WG; 1971 v Pol, Se (2), I (2), A; 1972 v Ir, Ec, Ch, P; 1973 v USSR, F, USSR, Pol, F, N (47)

Kelly, J. P. V. (Wolverhampton W), 1961 v W, N, S; 1962 v Cz (2) (5)

Kelly, M. J. (Portsmouth), 1988 v Y, Pol (sub); 1989 v Tun (32)

Kelly, N. (Nottingham F), 1954 v L (1)

Kendrick, J. (Everton), 1927 v I; 1934 v Bel, Ho; 1936 v Ho (4)

Kennedy, M. F. (Portsmouth), 1986 v Ic, Cz (sub) (2)

Kennedy, W. (St James' Gate), 1932 v Ho; 1934 v Bel, Ho (3)

Keogh, J. (Shamrock R), 1966 v WG (sub) (1)

Keogh, S. (Shamrock R), 1959 v Pol (1)

Kiernan, F. W. (Shamrock R), 1951 v Arg, N; (with Southampton), 1952 v WG (2), A (5)

Kinnear, J. P. (Tottenham H), 1967 v T; 1968 v Cz, Pol; 1969 v A; 1970 v Cz, D, H, Pol; 1971 v Se (sub), I; 1972 v Ir, Ec, Ch, P; 1973 v USSR, F; 1974 v Pol, Br, U, Ch; 1975 v USSR, T, Sw, USSR, WG; (with Brighton), 1976 v T (sub) (26)

Kinsella, J. (Shelbourne), 1928 v Bel (1)

Kinsella, P. (Shamrock R), 1932 v Ho; 1938 v N (2)

Kirkland, A. (Shamrock R), 1927 v I (1)

Lacey, W. (Shelbourne), 1927 v I; 1928 v Bel; 1930 v Bel (3)

Langan, D. (Derby Co), 1978 v T, N; 1980 v Sw, Arg; (with Birmingham C), 1981 v Ho, Bel, F, Cy, W, Bel, Cz, Pol; 1982 v Ho, F; (with Oxford U), 1985 v N, Sp, Sw; 1986 v W, U; 1987 v Bel, S, Pol, Br (sub), L (sub); 1988 v L (25)

Lawler, J. F. (Fulham), 1953 v A; 1954 v L, F; 1955 v N, H, N, WG; 1956 v Y (8)

Lawlor, J. C. (Drumcondra), 1949 v Bel; (with Doncaster R), 1951 v N, Arg (3)

Lawlor, M. (Shamrock R), 1971 v Pol, Se (2), I (sub); 1973 v Pol (5)

Lawrenson, M. (Preston NE), 1977 v Pol; (with Brighton), 1978 v Bul, Pol, N (sub); 1979 v Ni, E; 1980 v E, Cy, Sw; 1981 v Ho, Bel, F, Cy, Pol; (with Liverpool), 1982 v Ho, F; 1983 v Ho, Sp, Ic, Ma, Sp; 1984 v Ic, Ho, Ma, Is; 1985 v USSR, N, D, I, E, N; 1986 v Sw, USSR, D; 1987 v Bel, S; 1988 v Bul, Is (38)

Leech, M. (Shamrock R), 1969 v Cz, D, H; 1972 v A, Ir, Ec, P; 1973 v USSR (sub) (8)

Lennon, C. (St James' Gate), 1935 v H, Sw, G (3)

Lennox, G. (Dolphin), 1931 v Sp; 1932 v Sp (2)

Lowry, D. (St Patrick's Ath), 1962 v A (sub) (1)

Lunn, R. (Dundalk), 1939 v Sw, Pol (2)

Lynch, J. (Cork Bohemians), 1934 v Bel (1)

McAlinden, J. (Portsmouth), 1946 v P, Sp (2)

McCann, J. (Shamrock R), 1957 v WG (1)

McCarthy, J. (Bohemians), 1926 v I; 1928 v Bel; 1930 v Bel (3)

McCarthy, M. (Manchester C), 1984 v Pol, Chn; 1985 v M, D, I, Is, E, Sp, Sw; 1986 v Sw, USSR, W (sub), U, Ic, Cz; 1987 v S (2), Pol, Bul, Bel, Br, L; (with Celtic) 1988 v Bul, Is, R, Y, N, E, USSR, Ho; 1989 v Ni, Tun, Sp, F, H, Sp; (with Lyon), 1990 v WG, Ni, W, USSR, Fi, T, E, Eg, Ho, R, I (47)

McCarthy, M. (Shamrock R), 1932 v Ho (1)

McConville, T. (Dundalk), 1972 v A; (with Waterford), 1973 v USSR, F, USSR, Pol, F (6)

McDonagh, J. (Everton), 1981 v W, Bel, Cz; (with Bolton W), 1982 v Ho, F, Ch, Br; 1983 v Ho, Sp, Ic, Ma, Sp; (with Notts Co), 1984 v Ic, Ho, Pol; 1985 v M, USSR, N, D, Sp, Sw; 1986 v Sw, USSR, D (24)

McDonagh, Joe (Shamrock R), 1984 v Pol (sub), Ma; 1985 v M (sub) (3)

McEvoy, M. A. (Blackburn R), 1961 v S (2); 1963 v S; 1964 v A, Sp (2), Pol, N, E; 1965 v Pol, Bel, Sp; 1966 v Sp (2); 1967 v Sp, T, Cz (17)

McGee, P. (QPR), 1978 v T, N (sub), D (sub); 1979 v Ni, E, D (sub), Bul (sub); 1980 v Cz, Bul; (with Preston NE), US, Ni, Cy, Sw, Arg; 1981 v Bel (sub) (15)

McGowan, D. (West Ham U), 1949 v P, Se, Sp (3)

McGowan, J. (Cork U), 1947 v Sp (1)

McGrath, M. (Blackburn R), 1958 v A; 1959 v Pol, Cz (2); 1960 v Se, WG, Se; 1961 v W; 1962 v C (2); 1963 v S; 1964 v A (2), E; 1965 v Pol, Bel, Sp; 1966 v Sp; (with Bradford), 1966 v WG, A, Bel; 1967 v T (22)

McGrath, P. (Manchester U), 1985 v I (sub), Is, E, N (sub), Sw (sub); 1986 v Sw (sub), D, W, Ic, Cz; 1987 v Bel (2), S (2), Pol, Bul, Br, L; 1988 v L, Bul, Y, Pol, N, E, Ho; 1989 v Ni, F, H, Sp, Ma, H; (with Aston Villa), 1990 v WG, Ma, USSR, Fi, T, E, Eg, Ho, R, I (41)

McGuire, W. (Bohemians), 1936 v Ho (1)

McKenzie, G. (Southend U), 1938 v N (2), Cz, Pol; 1939 v Sw, Pol, H (2), G (9)

Mackey, G. (Shamrock R), 1957 v D, WG, E (3)

McLoughlin, A. F. (Swindon T), 1990 v Ma, E (sub), Eg (sub (3)

McLoughlin, F. (Fordsons), 1930 v Bel; (with Cork), 1932 v Sp (2)

McMillan, W. (Belfast Celtic), 1946 v P, Sp (2)

McNally, J. B. (Luton T), 1959 v Cz; 1961 v Sp; 1963 v Ic (3)

Macken, A. (Derby Co), 1977 v Sp (1)

Madden, O. (Cork), 1936 v H (1)

Maguire, J. (Shamrock R), 1929 v Bel (1)

Malone, G. (Shelbourne), 1949 v Bel (1)

Mancini, T. J. (QPR), 1974 v Pol, Br, U, Ch; (with Arsenal), 1975 v USSR (5)

Martin, C. (Bo'ness), 1927 v I (1)

Martin, C. J. (Glentoran), 1946 v P (sub), Sp; 1947 v E; (with Leeds U), 1947 v Sp; 1948 v P, Sp; (with Aston Villa), 1949 v Sw, Bel, P, Se, Sp; 1950 v Fi, E, Fi, Se, Bel; 1951 v Arg; 1952 v WG, A, Sp; 1954 v F (2), L; 1955 v N, Ho, N, WG; 1956 v Y, Sp, Ho (30)

Martin, M. P. (Bohemians), 1972 v A, Ir, Ec, Ch, P; 1973 v USSR; (with Manchester U), 1973 v USSR, Pol, F, N; 1974 v Pol, Br, U, Ch; 1975 v USSR, T, Sw, USSR, Sw, WG; (with WBA), 1976 v T, N, Pol; 1977 v E, T, F (2), Sp, Pol, Bul; (with Newcastle U), 1979 v D, Bul, WG; 1980 v W, Cz, Bul, US, Ni; 1981 v F, Bel, Cz; 1982 v Ho, F, Alg, Ch, Br, Tr; 1983 v Ho, Sp, Ma, Sp (51)

Meagan, M. K. (Everton), 1961 v S; 1962 v A; 1963 v Ic; 1964 v Sp; (with Huddersfield T), 1965 v Bel; 1966 v Sp (2), A, Bel; 1967 v Sp, T, Sp, T, Cz; 1968 v Cz, Pol; (with Drogheda), 1970 v S (17)

Meehan, P. (Drumcondra), 1934 v Ho (1)

Monahan, P. (Sligo R), 1935 v Sw, G (2)

Mooney, J. (Shamrock R), 1965 v Pol, Bel (2)

Moore, P. (Shamrock R), 1931 v Sp; 1932 v Ho; (with Aberdeen), 1934 v Bel, Ho; 1935 v H, G; (with Shamrock R), 1936 v Ho; 1937 v G, H (9)

Moran, K. (Manchester U), 1980 v Sw, Arg; 1981 v Bel, F, Cy, W (sub), Bel, Cz, Pol; 1982 v F, Alg; 1983 v Ic; 1984 v Ic, Ho, Ma, Is; 1985 v M; 1986 v D, Ic, Cz; 1987 v Bel (2), S (2), Pol, Bul, Br, L; 1988 v L, Bul, Is, R, Y, Pol, N, E, USSR, Ho; (with Sporting Gijon) 1989 v Ni, Sp, H, Sp, Ma, H; (with Blackburn R), 1990 v Ni, Ma, W, USSR (sub), Ma, E, Eg, Ho, R, I (54)

Moroney, T. (West Ham U), 1948 v Sp; 1949 v P, Se, Sp; 19.0 v Fi, E, Fi, Bel; 1951 v N (2); 1952 v WG; 1954 v F (12)

Morris, C. B. (Celtic), 1988 v Is, R, Y, Pol, N, E, USSR, Ho; 1989 v Ni, Tun, Sp, F, H, H (sub); 1990 v WG, Ni, Ma (sub), W, USSR, Fi (sub),T, E, Eg, Ho, R, I (26)

Moulson, C. (Lincoln C), 1936 v H, L; (with Notts Co), 1937 v H, Sw, F (5)

Moulson, G. B. (Lincoln C), 1948 v P, Sp; 1949 v Sw (3)

Mucklan, C. (Drogheda U), 1978 v Pol (1)

Muldoon, T. (Aston Villa), 1927 v I (1)

Mulligan, P. M. (Shamrock R), 1969 v Cz, D, H; 1970 v S, Cz, D; (with Chelsea), 1970 v H, Pol, WG; 1971 v Pol, Se, I; 1972 v A, Ir, Ec, Ch, P; (with Crystal Palace), 1973 v F, USSR, Pol, F, N; 1974 v Pol, Br, U, Ch; 1975 v USSR, T, Sw, USSR, Sw; (with WBA), 1976 v T, Pol; 1977 v E, T, F (2), Pol, Bul; 1978 v Bul, N, D; 1979 v E, D, Bul (sub), WG; (with Shamrock R) 1980 v W, Cz, Bul, US (sub) (50)

Munroe, L. (Shamrock R), 1954 v L (1)

Murphy, A. (Clyde), 1956 v Y (1)

Murphy, B. (Bohemians), 1986 v U (1)

Murphy, J. (C. Palace), 1980 v W, US, Cy (3)

Murray, T. (Dundalk), 1950 v Bel (1)

Newman, W. (Shelbourne), 1969 v D (1)

Nolan, R. (Shamrock R), 1957 v D, WG, E; 1958 v Pol; 1960 v Ch, WG, Se; 1962 v Cz (2); 1963 v Ic (10)

O'Brien, F. (Philadelphia F), 1980 v Cz, E, Cy (sub), Arg (4)

O'Brien, L. (Shamrock R), 1986 v U; (with Manchester U), 1987 v Br; 1988 v Is (sub), R (sub), Y (sub), Pol (sub); 1989 v Tun (with Newcastle U), Sp (sub) (8)

O'Brien, M. T. (Derby Co), 1927 v I; (with Walsall), 1929 v Bel; (with Norwich C), 1930 v Bel; (with Watford), 1932 v Ho (4)

O'Brien, R. (Notts Co), 1976 v N, Pol; 1977 v Sp, Pol (4)

O'Byrne, L. B. (Shamrock R), 1949 v Bel (1)

O'Callaghan, B. R. (Stoke C), 1979 v WG (sub); 1980 v W, US; 1981 v W; 1982 v Br, Tr (6)

O'Callaghan, K. (Ipswich T), 1981 v Cz, Pol; 1982 v Alg, Ch, Br, Tr (sub); 1983 v Sp, Ic (sub), Ma (sub), Sp (sub); 1984 v Ic, Ho, Ma; 1985 v M (sub), N (sub), D (sub), E (sub); (with Portsmouth), 1986 v Sw (sub), USSR (sub); 1987 v Br (20)

O'Connell, A. (Dundalk), 1967 v Sp; (with Bohemians), 1971 v Pol (sub) (2)

O'Connor, T. (Shamrock R), 1950 v Fi, E, Fi, Se (4)

O'Connor, T. (Fulham), 1968 v Cz; (with Dundalk), 1972 v A, Ir (sub), Ec (sub), Ch; (with Bohemians), 1973 v F (sub), Pol (sub) (7)

O'Driscoll, J. F. (Swansea T), 1949 v Sw, Bel, Se (3)

O'Driscoll, S. (Fulham), 1982 v Ch, Br, Tr (sub) (3)

O'Farrell, F. (West Ham U), 1952 v A; 1953 v A; 1954 v F; 1955 v Ho, N; 1956 v Y, Ho; (with Preston NE), 1958 v D; 1959 v Cz (9)

O'Flanagan, K. P. (Bohemians), 1938 v N, Cz, Pol (2), H (2), G; (with Arsenal), 1947 v E, Sp, P (10)

O'Flanagan, M. (Bohemians), 1947 v E (1)

O'Hanlon, K. G. (Rotherham U), 1988 v Is (1)

O'Kane, P. (Bohemians), 1935 v H, Sw, G (3)

O'Keefe, E. (Everton), 1981 v W; (with Port Vale), 1984 v Chn; 1985 v M, USSR (sub), E (5)

O'Keefe, T. (Cork), 1934 v Bel; (with Waterford), 1938 v Cz, Pol (3)

O'Leary, D. (Arsenal), 1977 v E, F (2), Sp, Bul; 1978 v Bul, N, D; 1979 v E, Bul, WG; 1980 v W, Bul, Ni, E, Cy; 1981 v Ho, Cz, Pol; 1982 v Ho, F; 1983 v Ho, Ic, Sp; 1984 v Pol, Is, Chn; 1985 v USSR, N, D, Is, E (sub), N, Sp, Sw; 1986 v Sw, USSR, D, W; 1989 v Sp, Ma, H; 1990 v WG, Ni (sub), Ma, W (sub), USSR, Fi, T, Ma, R (sub) (51)

O'Leary, P. (Shamrock R), 1980 v Bul, US, NI, E (sub), Cz, Arg; 1981 v Ho (7)

O'Mahoney, M. T. (Bristol R), 1938 v Cz, Pol; 1939 v Sw, Pol, H, G (6)

O'Neill, F. S. (Shamrock R), 1962 v Cz (2); 1965 v Pol, Bel, Sp; 1966 v Sp (2), WG, A; 1967 v Sp, T, Sp, T; 1969 v Pol, A, D, Cz, D (sub), H (sub); 1972 v A (20)

O'Neill, J. (Everton), 1952 v Sp; 1953 v F, A; 1954 v F, L, F; 1955 v N, Ho, N, WG; 1956 v Y, Sp; 1957 v D; 1958 v M; 1959 v Pol, Cz (2) (17)

O'Neill, J. (Preston NE), 1961 v W (1)

O'Neill, W. (Dundalk), 1936 v Ho, Sw, H, L; 1937 v G, H, Sw, F; 1938 v N; 1939 v H, G (11)

O'Regan, K. (Brighton & HA), 1984 v Ma, Pol; 1985 v M, Sp (sub) (4)

O'Reilly, J. (Brideville), 1932 v Ho; (with Aberdeen), 1934 v Bel, Ho; (with Brideville), 1936 v Ho; Sw, H, L; (with St James' Gate), 1937 v G, H, Sw, F; 1938 v N (2), Cz, Pol; 1939 v Sw, Pol, H (2), G (20)

O'Reilly, J. (Cork U), 1946 v P, Sp (2)

Peyton, G. (Fulham), 1977 v Sp (sub); 1978 v Bul, T, Pol; 1979 v D, Bul, WG; 1980 v W, Cz, Bul, E, Cy, Sw, Arg; 1981 v Ho, Bel, F, Cy; 1982 v Tr; 1985 v M (sub); 1986 v W, Cz; (with Bournemouth), 1988 v L, Pol; 1989 v Ni, Tun; 1990 v USSR, Ma (28)

Peyton, N. (Shamrock R), 1957 v WG; (with Leeds U), 1960 v WG, Se (sub); 1961 v W; 1963 v Ic, S (6)

Quinn, N. J. (Arsenal), 1986 v Ic (sub), Cz; 1987 v Bul (sub); 1988 v L (sub), Bul (sub), Is, R (sub), Pol (sub), E (sub); 1989 v Tun (sub), Sp (sub), H (sub); (with Manchester C), 1990 v USSR, Ma, Eg (sub), Ho, R, I (18)

Reid, C. (Brideville), 1931 v Sp (1)

Richardson, D. J. (Shamrock R), 1972 v A (sub); (with Gillingham), 1973 v N (sub); 1980 v Cz (3)

Rigby, A. (St James' Gate), 1935 v H, Sw, G (3)

Ringstead, A. (Sheffield U), 1951 v Arg, N; 1952 v WG (2), A, Sp; 1953 v A; 1954 v F; 1955 v N; 1956 v Y, Sp, Ho; 1957 v E (2); 1958 v D, Pol, A; 1959 v Pol, Cz (2) (20)

Robinson, J. (Bohemians), 1928 v Bel; (with Dolphin), 1931 v Sp (2)

Robinson, M. (Brighton & HA), 1981 v F, Cy, Bel, Pol; 1982 v Ho, F, Alg, Ch; 1983 v Ho, Sp, Ic, Ma; (with Liverpool), 1984 v Ic, Ho, Is; 1985 v USSR, N, (with QPR), N, Sp, Sw; 1986 v D (sub), W, Cz (23)

Roche, P. J. (Shelbourne), 1972 v A; (with Manchester U), 1975 v USSR, T, Sw, USSR, Sw, WG; 1976 v T (8)

Rogers, E. (Blackburn R), 1968 v Cz, Pol; 1969 v Pol, A, D, Cz, D, H; 1970 v S, D, H; 1971 v I (2), A; (with Charlton Ath), 1972 v Ir, Ec, Ch, P; 1973 v USSR (19)

Ryan, G. (Derby Co), 1978 v T; (with Brighton), 1979 v E, WG; 1980 v W, Cy (sub), Sw, Arg (sub); 1981 v F (sub), Pol (sub); 1982 v Ho (sub), Alg (sub), Ch (sub), Tr; 1984 v Pol, Chn; 1985 v M (16)

Ryan, R. A. (WBA), 1950 v Se, Bel; 1951 v N, Arg, N; 1952 v WG (2), A, Sp; 1953 v F, A; 1954 v F, L, F; 1955 v N; (with Derby Co), 1956 v Sp (16)

Saward, P. (Millwall), 1954 v L; (with Aston Villa), 1957 v E (2); 1958 v D, Pol, A; 1959 v Pol, Cz; 1960 v Se, Ch, WG, Se; 1961 v W, N; (with Huddersfield T), 1961 v S; 1962 v A; 1963 v Ic (2) (18)

Scannell, T. (Southend U), 1954 v L (1)

Scully, P. J. (Arsenal), 1989 v Tun (sub) (1)

Sheedy, K. (Everton), 1984 v Ho (sub), Ma; 1985 v D, I, Is, Sw; 1986 v Sw, D; 1987 v S, Pol; 1988 v Is, R, Pol, E (sub), USSR; 1989 v Ni, Tun, H, Sp, Ma, H; 1990 v Ni, Ma, W (sub), USSR, Fi (sub), T, E, Eg, Ho, R, I (32)

Sheridan, J. J. (Leeds U), 1988 v R, Y, Pol, N (sub); 1989 v Sp; (with Sheffield W), 1990 v W, T (sub), Ma, I (sub) (9)

Slaven, B. (Middlesbrough), 1990 v W, Fi, T (sub), Ma (4)

Sloan, J. W. (Arsenal), 1946 v P, Sp (2)

Smyth, M. (Shamrock R), 1969 v Pol (sub) (1)

Squires, J. (Shelbourne), 1934 v Ho (1)

Stapleton, F. (Arsenal), 1977 v T, F, Sp, Bul; 1978 v Bul, N, D; 1979 v Ni, E (sub), D, WG; 1980 v W, Bul, Ni, E, Cy; 1981 v Ho, Bel, F, Cy, Bel, Cz, Pol; (with Manchester U), 1982 v Ho, F, Alg; 1983 v Ho, Sp, Ic, Ma, Sp; 1984 v Ic, Ho, Ma, Pol, Is, Chn; 1985 v N, D, I, Is, E, N, Sw; 1986 v Sw, USSR, D, U, Ic, Cz (sub); 1987 v Bel (2), S (2), Pol, Bul, L; (with Ajax), 1988 v L, Bul, R, (with Derby Co), Y, N, E, USSR, Ho; 1989 (with Le Havre) v F, Sp, Ma; (with Blackburn R), 1990 v WG, Ma (sub) (70)

Staunton, S. (Liverpool), 1989 v Tun, Sp, Sp, Ma, H; 1990 v WG, Ni, Ma, W, USSR, Fi, T, Ma, E, Eg, Ho, R, I (18)

Stevenson, A. E. (Dolphin), 1932 v Ho; (with Everton), 1947 v E, Sp, P; 1948 v P; 1949 v Sw (7)

Strahan, F. (Shelbourne), 1964 v Pol, N, E; 1965 v Pol; 1966 v WG (5)

Sullivan, J. (Fordsons), 1928 v Bel (1)

Swan, M. M. G. (Drumcondra), 1960 v Se (sub) (1)

Synnott, N. (Shamrock R), 1978 v T, Pol; 1979 v Ni (3)

Thomas, P. (Waterford), 1974 v Pol, Br (2)

Townsend, A. D. (Norwich C) 1989 v F, Sp (sub), Ma (sub), H; 1990 v WG (sub), Ni, Ma, W, USSR, Fi (sub), T, Ma (sub), E, Eg, Ho, R, I (17)

Traynor, T. J. (Southampton), 1954 v L; 1962 v A; 1963 v Ic (2), S; 1964 v A (2), Sp (8)

Treacy, R. C. P. (WBA), 1966 v WG; 1967 v Sp, Cz; 1968 v Cz; (with Charlton Ath), 1968 v Pol; 1969 v Pol, Cz, D; 1970 v S, D, H (sub), Pol (sub), WG (sub); 1971 v Pol, Se (sub), Se, I, A; (with Swindon T), 1972 v Ir, Ec, Ch, P; 1973 v USSR, F, USSR, Pol, F, N; 1974 v Pol; (with Preston NE), 1974 v Br; 1975 v USSR, Sw (2), WG; 1976 v T, N (sub), Pol (sub); (with WBA), 1977 v F, Pol; 1978 (with Shamrock R), v T, Pol (2); 1980 v Cz (sub) (43)

Tuohy, L. (Shamrock R), 1956 v Y; 1959 v Cz (2); (with Newcastle U), 1962 v A; 1963 v Ic (2); (with Shamrock R), 1964 v A; 1965 v Bel (8)

Turner, A. (Celtic), 1963 v S; 1964 v Sp (2)

Turner, C. J. (Southend U), 1936 v Sw; 1937 v G, H, Sw, F; (with West Ham U), 1938 v N (2), Cz, Pol; 1939 v H (10)

Vernon, J. (Belfast Celtic), 1946 v P, Sp (2)

Waddock, G. (QPR), 1980 v Sw, Arg; 1981 v W, Pol (sub); 1982 v Alg; 1983 v Ic, Ma, Sp, Ho (sub); 1984 v Ic, Ho, Is; 1985 v I, Is, E, N, Sp; 1986 v USSR; (with Millwall), 1990 v USSR, T (20)

Walsh, D. J. (WBA), 1946 v P, Sp; 1947 v Sp, P; 1948 v P, Sp; 1949 v Sw, P, Se, Sp; 1950 v E, Fi, Se; 1951 v N; (with Aston Villa), v Arg, N; 1952 v Sp; 1953 v A; 1954 v F (2) (20)

Walsh, J. (Limerick), 1982 v Tr (1)

Walsh, M. (Blackpool), 1976 v N, Pol; 1977 v F (sub), Pol; (with Everton), 1979 v Ni (sub); (with QPR), D (sub), Bul, WG (sub); (with Porto), 1981 v Bel (sub), Cz; 1982 v Alg (sub); 1983 v Sp, Ho (sub); 1984 v Ic (sub), Ma, Pol, Chn; 1985 v USSR, N (sub), D (22)

Walsh, M. (Everton), 1982 v Ch, Br, Tr; 1983 v Sp, (with Norwich C), Ic (5)

Walsh, W. (Manchester C), 1947 v E, Sp, P; 1948 v P, Sp; 1949 v Bel; 1950 v E, Se, Bel (9)

Waters, J. (Grimsby T), 1977 v T; 1980 v Ni (sub) (2)

Watters, F. (Shelbourne), 1926 v I (1)

Weir, E. (Clyde), 1939 v H (2), G (3)

Whelan, R. (St Patrick's Ath), 1964 v A, E (sub) (2)

Whelan, R. (Liverpool), 1981 v Cz (sub); 1982 v Ho (sub), F; 1983 v Ic, Ma, Sp; 1984 v Is; 1985 v USSR, N, I (sub), Is, E, N (sub), Sw (sub); 1986 v USSR (sub), W; 1987 v Bel (sub), S, Bul, Bel, Br, L; 1988 v L, Bul, Pol, N, E, USSR, Ho; 1989 v Ni,F, H, Sp, Ma; 1990 v WG, Ni, Ma, W, Ho (sub) (39)

Whelan, W. (Manchester U), 1956 v Ho; 1957 v D, E (2) (4)

White, J. J. (Bohemians), 1928 v Bel (1)

Whittaker, R. (Chelsea), 1959 v Cz (1)

Williams, J. (Shamrock R), 1938 v N (1)

BRITISH INTERNATIONAL GOALSCORERS SINCE 1872

Where two players with the same surname and initials have appeared for the same country, and one or both have scored, they have been distinguished by reference to the club which appears *first* against their name in the international appearances section (pages 643–687). Unfortunately, four of the scorers in Scotland's 10-2 victory v Ireland in 1888 are unknown, as is the scorer of one of their nine goals v Wales in March 1878.

ENGLAND

A'Court, A.	1	Carter, J. H.	4	Grosvenor, A. T.	2	Marsh, R. W.	1
Adams, T. A.	4	Chadwick, E.	3	Gunn, W.	1	Matthews, S.	11
Adcock, H.	1	Chamberlain, M.	1			Matthews, V.	1
Alcock, C. W.	1	Chambers, H.	5	Haines, J. T. W.	2	McCall, J.	1
Allen, A.	3	Channon, M. R.	21	Hall, G. W.	9	McDermott, T.	3
Allen, R.	2	Charlton, J.	6	Halse, H. J.	2	Medley, L. D.	1
Anderson, V.	2	Charlton, R.	49	Hampson, J.	5	Melia, J.	1
Astall, G.	1	Chenery, C. J.	1	Hampton, H.	2	Mercer, D. W.	1
Athersmith, W. C.	3	Chivers, M.	13	Hancocks, J.	2	Milburn, J. E. T.	10
Atyeo, P. J. W.	5	Clarke, A. J.	10	Hardman, H. P.	1	Miller, H. S.	1
		Cobbold, W. N.	7	Harris, S. S.	2	Mills, G. R.	3
Bache, J. W.	4	Cock, J. G.	2	Hassall, H. W.	4	Milward, A.	3
Bailey, N. C.	2	Common, A.	2	Hateley, M.	9	Mitchell, C.	5
Baily, E. F.	5	Connelly, J. M.	7	Haynes, J. N.	18	Moore, J.	1
Baker, J. H.	3	Coppell, S. J.	7	Hegan, K. E.	4	Moore, R. F.	2
Ball, A. J.	8	Cotterill, G. H.	2	Henfrey, A. G.	2	Moore, W. G. B.	2
Bambridge, A. L.	1	Cowans, G.	2	Hilsdon, G. R.	14	Morren, T.	1
Bambridge, E. C.	12	Crawford, R.	1	Hine, E. W.	4	Morris, F.	1
Barclay, R.	2	Crawshaw, T. H.	1	Hitchens, G. A.	5	Morris, J.	3
Barnes, J.	10	Crayston, W. J.	1	Hobbis, H. H. F.	1	Mortensen, S. H.	23
Barnes, P. S.	4	Creek, F. N. S.	1	Hoddle, G.	8	Morton, J. R.	1
Barton, J.	1	Crooks, S. D.	7	Hodgetts, D.	1	Mosforth, W.	3
Bassett, W. I.	7	Currey, E. S.	2	Hodgson, G.	1	Mullen, J.	6
Bastin, C. S.	12	Currie, A. W.	3	Holley, G. H.	8	Mullery, A. P.	1
Beardsley, P. A.	7	Cursham, A. W.	2	Houghton, W. E.	5		
Beasley, A.	1	Cursham, H. A.	5	Howell, R.	1		
Beattie, T. K.	1			Hughes, E. W.	1	Neal, P. G.	5
Becton, F.	2	Daft, H. B.	3	Hulme, J. H. A.	4	Needham, E.	3
Bedford, H.	1	Davenport, J. K.	2	Hunt, G. S.	1	Nicholls, J.	1
Bell, C.	9	Davis, G.	1	Hunt, R.	18	Nicholson, W. E.	1
Bentley, R. T. F.	9	Davis, H.	1	Hunter, N.	2		
Bishop, S. M.	1	Day, S. H.	2	Hurst, G. C.	24		
Blackburn, F.	1	Dean, W. R.	18			O'Grady, M.	3
Blissett, L.	3	Devey, J. H. G.	1	Jack, D. N. B.	3	Osborne, F. R.	3
Bloomer, S.	28	Dewhurst, F.	11	Johnson, D. E.	6		
Bond, R.	2	Dix, W. R.	1	Johnson, E.	2	Own goals	22
Bonsor, A. G.	1	Dixon, K. M.	4	Johnson, J. A.	2		
Bowden, E. R.	1	Douglas, B.	11	Johnson, T. C. F.	5		
Bowers, J. W.	2	Drake, E. J.	6	Johnson, W. H.	1	Page, L. A.	1
Bowles, S.	1	Ducat, A.	1			Paine, T. L.	7
Bradford, G. R. W.	1	Dunn, A. T. B.	2	Kail, E. I. L.	2	Parry, E. H.	1
Bradford, J.	7			Kay, A. H.	1	Parry, R. A.	1
Bradley, W.	2	Eastham, G.	2	Keegan, J. K.	21	Pawson, F. W.	1
Bradshaw, F.	3	Edwards, D.	5	Kelly, R.	8	Payne, J.	2
Bridges, B. J.	1	Elliott, W. H.	3	Kennedy, R.	3	Peacock, A.	3
Bridgett, A.	3	Evans, R. E.	1	Kenyon-Slaney, W. S.	2	Pearce, S.	1
Brindle, T.	1			Kevan, D. T.	8	Pearson, J. S.	5
Britton, C. S.	1	Finney, T.	30	Kidd, B.	1	Pearson, S. C.	5
Broadbent, P. F.	2	Fleming, H. J.	9	Kingsford, R. K.	1	Perry, W.	2
Broadis, I. A.	8	Flowers, R.	10	Kirchen, A. J.	2	Peters, M.	20
Brodie, J. B.	1	Forman, Frank	1	Kirton, W. J.	1	Pickering, F.	5
Bromley-Davenport,	2	Forman, Fred	3			Platt, D.	3
Brook, E. F.	10	Foster, R. E.	3	Langton, R.	1	Pointer, R.	2
Brooking, T. D.	5	Francis, G. C. J.	3	Latchford, R. D.	5		
Brooks, J.	2	Francis, T.	12	Latheron, E. G.	1	Quantrill, A.	1
Broome, F. H.	3	Freeman, P. C.	3	Lawler, C.	1		
Brown, A.	4	Froggatt, J.	2	Lawton, T.	22		
Brown, A. S.	1	Froggatt, R.	2	Lee, F.	10	Ramsey, A. E.	3
Brown, G.	5			Lee, J.	1	Revie, D. G.	4
Brown, J.	3	Galley, T.	1	Lee, S.	2	Reynolds, J.	3
Brown, W.	1	Gascoigne, P. J.	2	Lindley, T.	15	Richardson, J. R.	2
Buchan, C. M.	4	Geary, F.	3	Lineker, G.	35	Rigby, A.	3
Bull, S. G.	4	Gibbins, W. V. T.	3	Lofthouse, J. M.	3	Rimmer, E. J.	2
Bullock, N.	2	Gilliatt, W. E.	3	Lofthouse, N.	30	Roberts, H.	1
Burgess, H.	4	Goddard, P.	1	Hon. A. Lyttelton	1	Roberts, W. T.	4
Butcher, T.	3	Goodall, J.	12			Robinson, J.	3
Byrne, J. J.	8	Goodyer, A. C.	1			Robson, B.	26
		Gosling, R. C.	2	Mabbutt, G	1	Robson, R.	4
Camsell, G. H.	18	Goulden, L. A.	4	Macdonald, M.	6	Rowley, J. F.	6
Carter, H. S.	7	Grainger, C.	3	Mannion, W. J.	11	Royle, J.	2
		Greaves, J.	44	Mariner, P.	13	Rutherford, J.	3

Sagar, C.	1
Sandilands, R. R.	2
Sansom, K.	1
Schofield, J.	1
Seed, J. M.	1
Settle, J.	6
Sewell, J.	3
Shackleton, L. F.	1
Sharp, J.	1
Shepherd, A.	2
Simpson, J.	1
Smith, G. O.	12
Smith, Joe	1
Smith, J. R.	2
Smith, J. W.	4
Smith, R.	13
Smith, S.	1
Sorby, T. H.	1
Southworth, J.	3
Sparks, F. J.	3
Spence, J. W.	1
Spiksley, F.	5
Spilsbury, B. W.	5
Steele, F. C.	8
Stephenson, G. T.	2
Steven, T. M.	3
Stewart, J	2
Stiles, N. P.	1
Storer, H.	1
Summerbee, M.G.	1
Tambling, R. V.	1
Taylor, P. J.	2
Taylor, T.	16
Thompson, P. B.	1
Thornewell, G.	1
Tilson, S. F.	6
Townley, W. J.	2
Tueart, D.	2
Vaughton, O. H.	6
Veitch, J. G.	3
Viollet, D. S.	1
Waddle, C. R.	6
Walker, W. H.	9
Wall, G.	2
Wallace, D.	1
Walsh, P.	1
Waring, T.	4
Warren, B.	2
Watson, D. V.	4
Watson, V. M.	4
Webb, G. W.	1
Webb, N.	3
Wedlock, W. J.	2
Weir, D.	2
Weller, K.	1
Welsh, D.	1
Whateley, O.	2
Wheldon, G. F.	6
Whitfield, H.	1
Wignall, F.	2
Wilkes, A.	1
Wilkins, R. G.	3
Willingham, C. K.	1
Wilshaw, D. J.	10
Wilson, D.	1
Wilson, G. P.	1
Winckworth, W. N.	1
Windridge, J. E.	7
Withe, P.	1
Wollaston, C. H. R.	1
Wood, H.	1
Woodcock, T.	16
Woodhall, G.	1
Woodward, V. J.	29
Worrall, F.	1
Worthington, F. S.	2
Wright, M.	1
Wright, W. A.	3
Wylie, J. G.	1
Yates, J.	3

NORTHERN IRELAND

Anderson, T.	3
Armstrong, G.	12
Bambrick, J.	12
Barr, H. H.	1
Barron, H.	3
Best, G.	9
Bingham, W. L.	10
Blanchflower, D.	2
Blanchflower, J.	1
Brennan, B.	1
Brennan, R. A.	1
Brotherston, N.	3
Brown, J.	1
Browne, F.	2
Campbell, J.	1
Campbell, W. G.	1
Casey, T.	2
Caskey, W.	1
Cassidy, T.	1
Chambers, J.	3
Clarke, C. J.	6
Clements, D.	2
Cochrane, T.	1
Condy, J.	1
Connor, M. J.	1
Coulter, J.	1
Croft, T.	1
Crone, W.	1
Crossan, E.	1
Crossan, J. A.	10
Curran, S.	2
Cush, W. W.	5
Dalton, W.	6
D'Arcy, S. D.	1
Darling, J.	1
Davey, H. H.	1
Davis, T. L.	1
Dill, A. H.	1
Doherty, L.	1
Doherty, P. D.	3
Dougan, A. D.	8
Dunne, J.	4
Elder, A. R.	1
Emerson, W.	1
English, S.	1
Ferguson, W.	1
Ferris, J.	1
Ferris, R. O.	1
Finney, T.	2
Gaffikin, J.	1
Gara, A.	3
Gawkrodger, G.	1
Gibb, J. T.	2
Gibb, T. J.	1
Gibson, W. K.	1
Gillespie, W.	12
Goodall, A. L.	2
Halligan, W.	1
Hamill, M.	1
Hamilton, B.	4
Hamilton, W.	5
Hannon, D. J.	1
Harkin, J. T.	2
Harvey, M.	3
Humphries, W.	1
Hunter, A. (Distillery)	1
Hunter, A. (Blackburn R)	
Irvine, R. W.	3
Irvine, W. J.	8
Johnston, H.	2
Johnston, S.	2
Johnston, W. C.	1
Jones, S.	1
Jones, J.	1

Kelly, J.	4
Kernaghan, N.	2
Kirwan, J.	2
Lacey, W.	3
Lemon, J.	2
Lockhart, N.	3
Mahood, J.	2
Martin, D. K.	3
Maxwell, J.	2
McAdams, W. J.	7
McAllen, J.	1
McAuley, J. L.	1
McCandless, J.	3
McCaw, J. H.	1
McClelland, J.	1
McCluggage, A.	2
McCracken, W.	1
McCrory, S.	1
McCurdy, C.	1
McDonald, A.	1
McGarry, J. K.	1
McGrath, R. C.	4
McIlroy, J.	10
McIlroy, S. B.	5
McKnight, J.	2
McLaughlin, J. C.	6
McMordie, A. S.	3
McMorran, E. J.	4
McPharland, P. J.	10
McWha, W. B. R.	1
Meldon, J.	1
Mercer, J. T.	1
Millar, W.	1
Milligan, D.	1
Milne, R. G.	2
Molyneux, T. B.	1
Moreland, V.	1
Morgan, S.	3
Morrow, W. J.	1
Murphy, N.	1
Neill, W. J. T.	2
Nelson, S.	1
Nicholl, C. J.	3
Nicholl, J. M.	2
Nicholson, J. J.	6
O'Hagan, C.	1
O'Kane, W. J.	1
O'Neill, J.	1
O Neill, M. A.	1
O'Neill, M. H.	8
Own goals	5
Peacock, R.	2
Peden, J.	7
Penney, S.	2
Pyper, James	2
Pyper, John	1
Quinn, J. M.	6
Reynolds, J.	1
Rowley, R. W. M.	2
Sheridan, J.	2
Sherrard, J.	1
Simpson, W. J.	5
Sloan, H. A. de B.	4
Smyth, S.	5
Spence, D. W.	3
Stanfield, O. M.	9
Stevenson, A. E.	2
Stewart, I.	2
Thompson, F. W.	2
Tully, C. P.	3
Turner, E.	1
Walker, J.	1
Walsh, D. J.	5
Welsh, E.	1

Whiteside, N.	9
Whiteside, T.	1
Williams, J. R.	1
Williamson, J.	1
Wilson, K. J.	2
Wilson, S. J.	7
Wilton, J. M.	2
Young, S.	2

SCOTLAND

Aitken, R.	1
Aitkenhead, W. A. C.	2
Alexander, D.	1
Allan, D. S.	4
Allan, J.	2
Anderson, F.	1
Anderson W.	4
Andrews, P.	1
Archibald, A.	1
Archibald, S.	4
Baird, D.	2
Baird, J. C.	2
Baird, S.	2
Bannon, E.	1
Barbour, A.	1
Barker, J. B.	4
Battles, B. Jr	1
Bauld, W.	2
Baxter, J. C.	3
Bell, J.	5
Bennett, A.	2
Berry, D.	1
Bett, J.	1
Beveridge, W. W.	1
Black, A.	3
Black, D.	1
Bone, J.	1
Boyd, R.	2
Boyd, W. G.	1
Brackenridge, T.	1
Brand, R.	8
Brazil, A.	1
Bremner, W. J.	3
Brown, A. D.	6
Buchanan, P. S.	1
Buchanan, R.	1
Buckley, P.	1
Buick, A.	2
Burns, K.	1
Cairns, T.	1
Calderwood, R.	2
Caldow, E.	4
Campbell, C.	1
Campbell, John (Celtic)	5
Campbell, John (Rangers)	4
Campbell, P.	2
Campbell, R.	1
Cassidy, J.	1
Chalmers, S.	3
Chambers, T.	1
Cheyne, A. G.	4
Christie, A. J.	1
Clunas, W. L.	1
Collins, J.	1
Collins, R. Y.	10
Combe, J. R.	1
Conn, A.	1
Cooper, D.	6
Craig, J.	1
Craig, T.	1
Cunningham, A. N.	5
Curran, H. P.	1
Dalglish, K.	30
Davidson, D.	1
Davidson, J. A.	1
Delaney, J.	3
Devine, A.	1
Dewar, G.	1
Dewar, N.	4
Dickson, W.	4
Divers, J.	1
Docherty, T. H.	1
Dodds, D.	1

Donaldson, A.	1	Johnstone, R.	9	Morris, H.	3	Wallace, I. A.	1
Donnachie, J.	1	Johnstone, W.	1	Morton, A. L.	5	Wark, J.	7
Dougall, J.	1	Jordan, J.	11	Mudie, J. K.	9	Watson, J. A. K.	1
Drummond, J.	2	Kay, J. L.	5	Mulhall, G.	1	Watt, F.	2
Dunbar, M.	1	Keillor, A.	3	Munro, A. D.	1	Watt, W. W.	1
Duncan, D.	7	Kelly, J.	1	Munro, N.	1	Weir, A.	1
Duncan, D. M.	1	Kelso, R.	1	Murdoch, R.	5	Weir, J. B.	2
Duncan, J.	1	Ker, G.	10	Murphy, F.	1	White, J. A.	3
Dunn, J.	2	King, A.	1	Murray, J.	1	Wilson, A.	2
Durie, G. S.	1	King, J.	1			Wilson, A. N.	13
		Kinnear, D.	1	Napier, C. E.	3	Wilson, D.	2
Easson, J. F.	1			Narey, D.	1	(Queen's Park)	
Ellis, J.	1	Lambie, W. A.	5	Neil, R. G.	2	Wilson, D. (Rangers)	9
		Lang, J. J.	1	Nicholas, C.	5	Wilson, H.	1
Ferguson, J.	6	Law, D.	30	Nisbet, J.	2	Wylie, T. G.	1
Fernie, W.	1	Leggat, G.	8				
Fitchie, T. T.	1	Lennie, W.	1	O'Donnell, F.	2	Young, A.	5
Flavell, R.	2	Lennox R.	3	O'Hare, J.	5		
Fleming, C.	2	Liddell, W.	6	Ormond, W. E.	1	**WALES**	
Fleming, J. W.	3	Lindsay, J.	6	O'Rourke, F.	1	Allchurch, I. J.	23
Fraser, M. J. E.	4	Linwood, A. B.	1	Orr, R.	1	Allen, M.	3
		Logan, J.	1	Orr, T.	1	Astley, D. J.	12
Gallacher, H. K.	23	Lorimer, P.	4	Oswald, J.	1	Atherton, R. W.	2
Gallacher, P.	1	Love, A.	1				
Galt, J. H.	1	Lowe, J. (Cambuslang)	1	Own goals	14	Bamford, T.	1
Gemmell, T. (St Mirren)	1	Lowe, J. (St Bernards)	1			Barnes, W.	1
Gemmell, T. (Celtic)	1	Macari, L.	5	Parlane, D.	1	Boulter, L. M.	1
Gemmill, A.	8	MacDougall, E. J.	3	Paul, H. McD.	2	Bowdler, J. C. H.	3
Gibb, W.	1	MacLeod, M.	1	Paul, W.	6	Bowen, D. L.	1
Gibson, D. W.	3	Mackay, D. C.	4	Pettigrew, W.	2	Bowen, M.	1
Gibson, J. D.	2	Mackay, G.	1	Provan, D.	1	Boyle, T.	1
Gibson, N.	1	MacKenzie, J. A.	1			Bryan, T.	1
Gillespie, Jas.	3	Madden, J.	5	Quinn, J.	7	Burgess, W. A. R.	1
Gillick, T.	3	Marshall, H.	1	Quinn, P.	1	Burke, T.	1
Gilzean, A. J.	10	Marshall, J.	1			Butler, A.	1
Gossland, J.	2	Mason, J.	4	Rankin, G.	2		
Goudie, J.	1	Massie, A.	1	Rankin, R.	2	Chapman, T.	2
Gough, C. R.	5	Masson, D. S.	5	Reid, W.	4	Charles, J.	1
Gourlay, J.	1	McAdam, J.	1	Reilly, L.	22	Charles, M.	6
Graham, A.	2	McAulay, J.	1	Renny-Tailyour, H. W.	1	Charles, W. J.	15
Graham, G.	3	McAvennie, F.	1	Richmond, J. T.	1	Clarke, R. J.	5
Gray, A.	7	McCall, J.	1	Ring, T.	2	Collier, D. J.	1
Gray, E.	3	McCall, S. M.	1	Rioch, B. D.	6	Cross, K.	1
Gray, F.	1	McCalliog, J.	1	Ritchie, J.	1	Cumner, R. H.	1
Greig, J.	3	McCallum, N.	1	Robertson, A.	2	Curtis, A.	6
Groves, W.	5	McCoist, A.	6	Robertson, J.	8	Curtis, E. R.	3
		McColl, R. S.	13	Robertson, J. T.	2		
Hamilton, G.	4	McCulloch, D.	3	Robertson, T.	1	Davies, D. W.	1
Hamilton, J.	3	McDougall, J.	4	Robertson, W.	1	Davies, E. Lloyd	1
(Queen's Park)		McFarlane, J.	1	Russell, D.	1	Davies, G.	2
Hamilton, R. C.	14	McFayden, W.	2			Davies, L. S.	6
Harper, J. M.	2	McGhee, M.	2	Scott, A. S.	5	Davies, R. T.	8
Harrower, W.	5	McGregor, J. C.	1	Sellar, W.	4	Davies, R. W.	7
Hartford, R. A.	3	McGrory, J.	6	Sharp, G.	1	Davies, S.	5
Heggie, C.	5	McGuire, W.	1	Shaw, F. W.	1	Davies, W.	6
Henderson, J. G.	1	McInally, A.	3	Simpson, J.	1	Davies, W. H.	1
Henderson, W.	1	McInnes, T.	2	Smith, A.	5	Davies, William	5
Herd, D. G.	4	McKie, J.	2	Smith, G.	4	Davies, W. O.	1
Hewie, J. D.	2	McKimmie, S.	1	Smith, J.	1	Deacy, N.	4
Higgins, A.	1	McKinnon, A.	1	Smith, John	12	Doughty, J.	6
(Newcastle U)		McKinnon, R.	1	Somerville, G.	1	Doughty, R.	2
Higgins, A. (Kilmarnock)	4	McKinnon, W. W.	5	Souness, G. J.	3	Durban, A.	2
Highet, T. C.	1	McLaren, A.	4	Speedie, F.	2	Dwyer, P.	2
Holton, J. A.	2	McLaren, J.	1	St John, I.	9		
Houliston, W.	2	McLean, A.	1	Steel, W.	12	Edwards, G.	2
Howie, H.	1	McLean, T.	1	Stein, C.	10	Edwards, R. I.	5
Howie, J.	1	McLintock, F.	1	Stevenson, G.	4	England, H. M.	3
Hughes, J.	1	McMahon, A.	6	Stewart, R.	1	Evans, I.	1
Hunter, W.	1	McMenemy, J.	5	Stewart, W. E.	1	Evans, J.	1
Hutchison, T.	1	McMillan, I. L.	2	Strachan, G.	4	Evans, R. E.	2
Hutton, J.	1	McNeil, H.	5	Sturrock, P.	3	Evans, W.	1
Hyslop, T.	1	McNeill, W.	3			Eyton-Jones, J. A.	1
		McPhail, J.	3	Taylor, J. D.	1		
Imrie, W. N.	1	McPhail, R.	7	Templeton, R.	1	Flynn, B.	6
		McPherson, J.	8	Thomson, A.	1	Ford, T.	23
Jackson, A.	8	McPherson, R.	1	Thomson, C.	4	Foulkes, W. I.	1
Jackson, C.	1	McQueen, G.	5	Thomson, R.	1	Fowler, J.	3
James, A. W.	3	McStay, P.	6	Thomson, W.	1		
Jardine, A.	1	Meiklejohn, D. D.	3	Thornton, W.	1	Giles, D.	2
Jenkinson, T.	1	Millar, J.	2			Glover, E. M.	7
Johnston, L. H.	1	Miller, T.	2	Waddell, T. S.	1	Godfrey, B. C.	2
Johnston, M.	14	Miller, W.	1	Waddell, W.	6	Green, A. W.	3
Johnstone, D.	2	Mitchell, R. C.	1	Walker, A.	2	Griffiths, A. T.	6
Johnstone, J.	4	Morgan, W.	1	Walker, R.	7	Griffiths, M. W.	2
Johnstone, Jas.	1	Morris, D.	1	Walker, T.	9	Griffiths, T. P.	3

Harris, C. S.	1	Own goals	12	Bermingham, P.	1	Kelly, D.	4
Hersee, R.	1			Bradshaw, P.	4	Kelly, J.	2
Hewitt, R.	1	Palmer, D.	3	Brady, L.	9		
Hockey, T.	1	Parry, T. D.	3	Brown, D.	1	Lacey, W.	1
Hodges G.	2	Paul, R.	1	Byrne, J. (Bray)	1	Lawrenson, M.	5
Hole, W. J.	1	Peake, E.	1	Byrne, J. (QPR)	2	Leech, M.	2
Hopkins, I. J.	2	Perry, E.	1				
Horne, B.	2	Phillips, C.	5	Cantwell, J.	14	McCann, J.	1
Howell, E. G.	3	Phillips, D.	1	Carey, J.	3	McCarthy, M.	1
Hughes, M.	8	Powell, A.	1	Carroll, T.	1	McEvoy, A.	6
		Powell, D.	1	Cascarino, A.	5	McGee, P.	4
James, E.	2	Price, J.	4	Coad, P.	3	McGrath, P.	4
James, L.	10	Price, P.	1	Conroy, T.	2	Madden, O.	1
James, R.	7	Pryce-Jones, W. E.	3	Conway, J.	3	Mancini, T.	1
Jarrett, R. H.	3	Pugh, D. H.	2	Cummings, G.	5	Martin, C.	6
Jenkyns, C. A.	1			Curtis, D.	8	Martin, M.	4
Jones, A.	1	Reece, G. I.	2			Mooney, J.	1
Jones, Bryn	6	Rees, R. R.	3	Daly, G.	13	Moore, P.	7
Jones, B. S.	2	Richards, R. W.	1	Davis, T.	4	Moran, K.	6
Jones, Cliff	15	Roach, J.	2	Dempsey, J.	1	Moroney, T.	1
Jones, C. W.	1	Robbins, W. W.	4	Dennehy, M.	2	Mulligan, P.	1
Jones, D. E.	1	Roberts, J. (*Corwen*)	1	Donnelly, J.	3		
Jones, Evan	1	Roberts, Jas.	1	Donnelly, T.	1	O'Callaghan, K.	1
Jones, H.	1	Roberts, P. S.	1	Duffy, B.	1	O'Connor, T.	2
Jones, I.	1	Roberts, R. (*Druids*)	1	Duggan, H.	1	O'Farrell, F.	2
Jones, J. O.	1	Roberts, W. (*Llangollen*)	2	Dunne, J.	12	O'Flannagan, A.	3
Jones, J. P.	1	Roberts, W. (*Wrexham*)	1	Dunne, L.	1	O'Keefe, E.	1
Jones, Leslic J.	1	Roberts, W. H.	1			O'Neill, F.	1
Jones, R. A.	2	Rush, I.	16	Eglinton, T.	2	O'Reilly, J.	2
Jones, W. L.	6	Russell, M. R.	1	Ellis, P.	1	O'Reilly, J	1
						own goals	5
Keenor, F. C.	2	Sabine, H. W.	1	Fagan, F.	5		
Krzywicki, R. L.	1	Saunders, D.	7	Fallon, S.	2	Quinn, N.	3
		Shaw, E. G.	2	Fallon, W.	2		
Leek, K.	5	Sisson, H.	4	Farrell, P.	3	Ringstead, A.	7
Lewis, B.	3	Slatter, N.	2	Fitzgerald, P.	2	Robinson, M.	4
Lewis, J.	1	Smallman, D. P.	1	Fitzgerald, J.	1	Rogers, E.	5
Lewis, W.	10			Fitzsimmons, A.	7	Ryan, G.	1
Lewis, W. L.	2	Tapscott, D. R.	4	Flood, J. J.	4	Ryan, R.	3
Lovell, S.	1	Thomas, M.	4	Fogarty, A.	3		
Lowrie, G.	2	Thomas, T.	1	Fullam, J.	1	Sheedy, K.	6
		Toshack, J. B.	13	Fullam, R.	1	Sheridan, J.	1
Mahoney, J. F.	1	Trainer, H.	2			Slaven, B.	1
Mays, A. W.	1			Galvin, A.	1	Sloan, W.	1
Medwin, T. C.	6	Vaughan, John	2	Gavin, J.	2	Squires, J.	1
Meredith, W. H.	11	Vernon, T. R.	8	Geoghegan, M.	2	Stapleton, F.	20
Mills, T. J.	1	Vizard, E. T.	1	Giles, J.	5	Sheridan, J.	
Moore, G.	1			Givens, D.	19	Strahan, J.	1
Morgan, J. R.	2	Walsh, I.	7	Glynn, D.	1	Sullivan, J.	1
Morgan-Owen, H.	1	Warren, F. W.	3	Grealish, T.	8		
Morgan-Owen, M. M.	2	Watkins, W. M.	4	Grimes, A. A.	1	Townsend, A. D.	1
Morris, A. G.	9	Wilding, J.	4			Treacy, R.	5
Morris, H.	2	Williams, G. E.	2	Hale, A.	2	Tuohy, L.	4
Morris, R.	1	Williams, W.	1	Hand, E.	2		
		Woosnam, A. P.	4	Haverty, J.	3	Waddock, G.	3
Nicholas, P.		Wynn, G. A.	1	Holmes, J.	1	Walsh, D.	5
				Horlacher, A.	2	Walsh, M.	3
O'Callaghan, E.	3	Yorath, T. C.	2	Houghton, R.	2	Waters, J.	1
O'Sullivan, P. A.	1	**EIRE**		Hughton, C.	1	White, J. J.	2
Owen, G.	2	Aldridge, J.	3	Hurley, C.	2	Whelan, R.	3
Owen, W.	4	Ambrose, P.	1				
Owen, W. P.	6	Anderson, J.	1	Jordan, D.	1		

4th WOMEN'S EUROPEAN TOURNAMENT

Group 1
Holland, Rep of Ireland, Northern Ireland.

Group 2
Poland 1, France 3; Sweden 4, Poland 1.

Group 3
Finland 0, Norway 1; England 0, Finland 0; Norway 4, Belgium 0.

Group 4
West Germany 0, Hungary 0; Czechoslovakia 2, Bulgaria 0.

Group 5
Switzerland 0, Denmark 4; Spain 0, Switzerland 0.

WOMEN'S FA CUP

Quarter-finals
St Helens 2, District Line 1
Arsenal 0, Friends of Fulham 4
Preston Rangers 2, Ipswich Town 1
Doncaster Belles 5, Leasowe Pacific 0

Semi-finals
Doncaster Belles 7, St Helens 0
Preston Rangers 0, Friends of Fulham 3

Final
Doncaster Belles 1, Friends of Fulham 0 (at Derby County)

ENGLAND WOMEN'S INTERNATIONALS 1989–90

England 0, Finland 0
England 1, Italy 1
Belgium 0, England 3
England 1, Belgium 0
Scotland 0, England 4
England 4, Scotland 0
Norway 0, England 0

7th UEFA UNDER-21 TOURNAMENT 1988–90

Group 1 *(Bulgaria, Denmark, Greece, Rumania)*

Greece (1) 2, Denmark (1) 2	Viareggio, 18 October 1988
Bulgaria (1) 2, Rumania (1) 1	Sofia, 18 October 1988
Denmark (0) 1, Bulgaria (0) 3	Slagelse, 1 November 1988
Rumania (1) 2, Greece (0) 0	1 November, 1988
Bulgaria (2) 6, Denmark (0) 0	25 April 1989
Greece (0) 1, Rumania (0) 0	25 April 1989
Denmark (0) 3, Greece (0) 0	16 May 1989
Rumania (2) 2, Bulgaria (1) 1	16 May 1989
Denmark (0) 1, Rumania (0) 2	Holbaek, 10 October 1989
Bulgaria (2) 2, Greece (0) 0	Tolbukhin, 10 October 1989
Greece (0) 0, Bulgaria (0) 2	Athens, 14 November 1989
Rumania (0) 1, Denmark (0) 2	Bucuresti, 14 November 1989

Group 2 *(Albania, England, Poland, Sweden)*

England (1) 1, Sweden (0) 1	Coventry, 18 October 1988
Poland (0) 0, Albania (0) 0	Opole, 18 October 1988
Albania (0) 0, Sweden (1) 2	Berat, 4 November 1988
Albania (1) 1, England (0) 2	7 March 1989
England (1) 2, Albania (0) 0	25 April 1989
Sweden (1) 4, Poland (0) 0	6 May 1989
England (2) 2, Poland (0) 1	2 June 1989
Sweden (1) 1, England (0) 0	Uppsala, 5 September 1989
Sweden (1) 1, Albania (0) 0	Eskilstun, 7 October 1989
Poland (0) 1, England (2) 3	Jastrzebi, 10 October 1989
Poland (1) 1, Sweden (0) 1	Opole, 24 October 1989
Albania (0) 0, Poland (1) 1	Vlora, 14 November 1989

Group 3 *(Austria, East Germany, Turkey, USSR)*

USSR (1) 2, Austria (2) 2	Kiev, 18 October 1988
Austria (2) 3, Turkey (0) 0	St Polten, 1 November 1988
Turkey (2) 3, East Germany (2) 2	Istanbul, 29 November 1988
East Germany (0) 0, Turkey (0) 0	11 April 1989
USSR (0) 1, East Germany (0) 0	25 April 1989
Turkey (0) 0, USSR (2) 3	9 May 1989
East Germany (0) 2, Austria (0) 0	16 May 1989
Austria (0) 0, USSR (0) 2	Amstetten, 5 September 1989
East Germany (1) 3, USSR (1) 2	Grimma, 7 October 1989
Turkey (0) 1, Austria (1) 1	Istanbul, 24 October 1989
Austria (0) 0, East Germany (0) 1	Stockerau, 14 November 1989
USSR (2) 2, Turkey (0) 0	Sevastopo, 14 November 1989

Group 4 *(Finland, Holland, Iceland, West Germany)*

Finland (0) 0, West Germany (2) 3	Kouvola, 30 August 1988
Iceland (0) 1, Holland (1) 1	Reykjavik, 13 September 1988
Finland (0) 2, Iceland (1) 1	Oulu, 28 September 1988
West Germany (0) 2, Holland (0) 0	Augsburg, 18 October 1988
Holland (0) 0, West Germany (1) 1	25 April 1989
Finland (1) 1, Holland (1) 1	30 May 1989
Iceland (0) 1, West Germany (0) 1	30 May 1989
Iceland (1) 4, Finland (0) 0	Akurlyri, 5 September 1989
West Germany (2) 2, Finland (0) 0	Arnsberg, 3 October 1989
Holland (0) 2, Iceland (1) 3	Schiedam, 10 October 1989
West Germany (0 1, Iceland (1) 1	Saarbruck, 25 October 1989
Holland (1) 2, Finland (1) 1	Heerenvee, 14 November 1989

Group 5 *(France, Norway, Scotland, Yugoslavia)*

Norway (0) 1, Scotland (1) 1	Drammen, 13 September 1988
France (1) 2, Norway (0) 0	Tours, 27 September 1988
Scotland (0) 0, Yugoslavia (0) 2	Edinburgh, 18 October 1988
Yugoslavia (1) 2, France (1) 2	Titov Vrbas, 18 November 1988
Scotland (1) 2, France (0) 3	Dundee, 7 March 1989
France (0) 0, Yugoslavia (0) 1	Le Havre, 28 April 1989
Norway (0) 0, Yugoslavia (0) 1	13 June 1989
Norway (1) 1, France (1) 1	Raufoss, 5 September 1989
Yugoslavia (2) 4, Scotland (0) 1	Slavonski, 5 September 1989
France (1) 3, Scotland (0) 1	Rennes, 10 October 1989
Yugoslavia (0) 0, Norway (0) 1	Zenica, 10 October 1989
Scotland (1) 2, Norway (0) 0	Perth, 14 November 1989

Group 6 *(Cyprus, Hungary, Spain)*

Cyprus (0) 0, Hungary (0) 0	Larnaca, 11 December 1988
Cyprus (0) 0, Spain (0) 1	22 March 1989
Hungary (1) 1, Cyprus (0) 0	?2 April 1989
Spain (0) 1, Cyprus (0) 0	31 May 1989
Hungary (1) 1, Spain (0) 0	Szekesfeh, 10 October 1989
Spain (1) 1, Hungary (0) 0	Benidorm, 14 November 1989

Group 7 *(Belgium, Czechoslovakia, Luxembourg, Portugal)*

Czechoslovakia (0) 0, Belgium (2) 3	Nitra, 15 November 1988
Portugal (0) 1, Belgium (1) 1	14 February 1989
Czechoslovakia (2) 4, Luxembourg (0) 0	5 April 1989
Portugal (0) 1, Luxembourg (0) 0	25 April 1989
Belgium (1) 1, Czechoslovakia (0) 1	29 April 1989
Luxembourg (0) 0, Belgium (0) 0	26 May 1989
Belgium (0) 1, Portugal (0) 1	Beveren, 5 September 1989
Czechoslovakia (0) 1, Portugal (0) 0	Chrudim, 5 October 1989
Luxembourg (0) 0, Portugal (1) 3	Ettelbruc, 9 October 1989
Belgium (1) 1, Luxembourg (0) 0	Liege, 24 October 1989
Portugal (0) 0, Czechoslovakia (2) 3	Lisbon, 14 November 1989
Luxembourg (0) 1, Czechoslovakia (0) 1	Lux.-Verl, 29 November 1989

Group 8 *(Italy, San Marino, Switzerland)*

Switzerland (0) 0, Italy (0) 0	26 April 1989
San Marino (0) 0, Switzerland (2) 5	6 June 1989
San Marino (0) 0, Italy (0) 2	San Marin, 4 October 1989
Italy (0) 1, Switzerland (0) 0	Padova, 25 October 1989
Switzerland (2) 3, San Marino (0) 0	Lugano, 14 November 1989
Italy (1) 2, San Marino (0) 0	Ravenna, 29 November 1989

Quarter-finals

Italy (1) 3, Spain (0) 1	Ancona, 21 February 1990
Czechoslovakia (0) 1, Sweden (0) 2	Praha, 14 March 1990
USSR (0) 1, West Germany (1) 1	Simferopo, 14 March 1990
Yugoslavia (1) 2, Bulgaria (0) 0	Zagreb, 14 March 1990
Bulgaria (0) 0, Yugoslavia (1) 1	Sofia, 28 March 1990
West Germany (1) 1, USSR (1) 2	Augsburg, 28 March 1990
Sweden (1) 4, Czechoslovakia (0) 0	Vaxjo, 28 March 1990
Spain (0) 1, Italy (0) 0	Logrono, 29 March 1990

Semi-finals

Yugoslavia (0) 0, Italy (0) 0	Zagreb, 11 April 1990
Sweden (0) 1, USSR (0) 1	Vaxjo, 25 April 1990
Italy (1) 2, Yugoslavia (1) 2	Parma, 9 May 1990
USSR (1) 2, Sweden (0) 0	Simferopo, 9 May 1990

Final to be arranged

WELSH FOOTBALL continued from Page 779 continued from Page 779

Division 2

	P	W	D	L	F	A	Pts
AFC Porth	34	23	7	4	105	33	76
Caerau	34	22	4	8	71	49	70
Goytre United	34	21	5	8	77	39	68
Penrhiwceiber Rngrs	34	20	5	9	92	52	65
Ely Rangers	34	19	8	7	63	38	65
Cambr. & Cl. BC***	34	20	5	9	74	43	62
Taffs Well	34	17	4	13	61	62	55
Cardiff Corinthans	34	16	6	12	52	41	54
Cardiff Cosmos	34	15	9	10	74	65	54
Dinas Powys	34	11	12	11	66	57	45
Llwydcoed Welfare	34	11	7	16	51	70	40
Pencoed Athletic	34	11	5	18	62	92	38
Llangeinor	34	10	6	18	54	80	36
FC Cwmaman	34	8	11	15	50	59	35
BA Campaign	34	8	6	20	52	83	30
Treorchy Athletic	34	6	6	22	42	88	24
Afan Lido	34	4	5	23	37	80	23
Bargoed United	34	4	5	25	40	92	17

***3 pts deducted.

Division 2

	P	W	D	L	F	A	Pts
Cafn Fforest	30	21	4	5	104	39	46
Undy United	30	19	7	4	84	45	45
Treowen Stars	30	19	2	9	99	50	40
Christchurch	30	16	8	6	86	37	40
Monmouth Town	30	15	9	6	106	52	39
Chepstow Town	30	15	7	8	74	55	37
Abertillery Town	30	16	4	10	95	60	36
Pontnewydd United	30	16	4	10	73	50	36
Cwmbran Town	30	14	6	10	67	77	34
Rangers	30	13	5	12	72	72	31
Tredegar Town**	30	10	6	14	60	78	24
Race	30	9	4	17	60	69	22
Cwmffrwdoer	30	7	5	18	47	74	19
Llanfrechfa Grange	30	7	5	18	53	90	19
Caerleon	30	2	1	27	32	149	5
Trethomas Rangers	30	1	3	26	32	149	5

GWENT COUNTY LEAGUE

Division One

	P	W	D	L	F	A	Pts
Albion Rovers	30	25	4	1	78	18	54
Civil Service	30	19	6	5	54	25	44
Risca United	30	17	7	6	66	50	41
Lliswerry	30	14	7	9	51	38	35
Fields Park Athletic	30	15	3	12	42	43	33
Pill AFC	30	11	9	10	42	32	31
Trinant	30	10	10	10	52	48	30
Cwmtillery	30	11	8	11	49	52	30
Cwmbran Celtic	30	9	9	12	43	49	27
Croesyceiliog	30	11	5	14	49	62	27
Aberbargoed Buds	30	10	5	15	38	70	25
Rogerstone	30	7	9	14	42	54	23
Newport Corinthians	30	7	7	16	42	60	21
Caldicot Town	30	7	6	17	41	50	20
RTB Ebbw Vale	30	7	6	17	49	69	20
Ringland Youth	30	5	9	16	48	66	19

Division 3

	P	W	D	L	F	A	Pts
Abergavenny Thur.	30	23	4	3	94	25	50
Fairfield United	30	21	4	5	81	40	46
Llanwern	30	16	11·	3	76	40	43
Tranch	30	18	4	8	89	50	40
AC Pontymister	30	15	9	6	58	44	39
S. Wales Switchg'r	30	14	8	8	72	60	36
New Inn	30	15	6	9	60	48	36
Brynmawr	30	14	3	13	77	69	31
Portsk'tt & Sudbr'k	30	12	4	14	80	68	28
Gilwern & District	30	12	3	15	63	69	27
Fleur de Lys	30	10	4	16	69	71	24
Lucas Girling	30	9	4	17	31	70	22
Abercarn Rangers	30	8	2	20	37	55	18
Newport YMCA	30	7	2	21	49	96	16
Newbridge Town	30	7	0	23	37	111	14
Llanhilleth	30	3	4	23	36	93	10

7th UEFA UNDER-18 CHAMPIONSHIP 1988-90

Group 1 *(Poland, Scotland, Sweden, West Germany)*
Scotland (0) 0, Sweden (0) 0	Ayr, 21 September 1988
Scotland (0) 1, Poland (2) 2	Hampden Park, 23 November 1988
West Germany (0) 0, Poland (0) 0	Heilbronn, 19 April 1989
West Germany (1) 1, Scotland (0) 0	Frankfurt, 3 May 1989
Sweden (1) 4, West Germany (0) 0	Lomma, 24 May 1989
Sweden (2) 4, Poland (0) 0	Ljungby, 7 June 1989
Poland (0) 2, Scotland (0) 1	Debica, 30 August 1989
Sweden (0) 4, Scotland (0) 0	Vaesteraa, 20 September 1989
Poland (1) 1, West Germany (0) 0	Jaworzno, 27 September 1989
Poland (1) 2, Sweden (0) 2	Debica, 17 October 1989
Scotland (1) 1, West Germany (1) 2	Motherwell, 18 October 1989
West Germany (1) 2, Sweden (0) 1	Kassel, 1 November 1989

Group 2 *(Cyprus, Holland, Norway, USSR)*
Norway (1) 2, Holland (0) 2	Stavanger, 12 October 1988
Cyprus (0) 0, Norway (0) 0	Paralimni, 1 November 1988
Holland (2) 2, Cyprus (0) 1	Roosendaal, 12 April 1989
USSR (0) 2, Cyprus (0) 0	Kishinev, 23 April 1989
Norway (0) 1, Cyprus (0) 0	Oslo, 21 May 1989
Norway (0) 0, USSR (0) 1	Fredrikst, 14 June 1989
USSR (1) 3, Norway (0) 0	Kishinev, 6 September 1989
Holland (1) 1, Norway (3) 5	Oss, 4 October 1989
Holland (0) 0, USSR (0) 3	Almelo, 25 October 1989
Cyprus (1) 1, USSR (2) 2	Larnaca, 19 November 1989
USSR (1) 2, Holland (0) 1	Baku, 29 November 1989
Cyprus (0) 0, Holland (0) 0	Aradippou, 6 December 1989

Group 3 *(Czechoslovakia, England, France, Greece)*
England (1) 5, Greece (0) 0	Birkenhead, 20 October 1988
England (0) 1, France (1) 1	Bradford, 15 November 1988
Greece (1) 2, France (3) 3	Indrama, 14 December 1988
Greece (0) 0, England (2) 3	Xanthi, 8 March 1989
Czechoslovakia (0) 0, Greece (0) 0	Trebechovicen, 12 April 1989
Czechoslovakia (0) 1, England (0) 0	Piovazska B, 26 April 1989
France (1) 1, Czechoslovakia (0) 0	Orleans, 10 May 1989
France (0) 0, England (0) 0	Martigues, 11 October 1989
Greece (1) 1, Czechoslovakia (2) 3	Aigio, 11 October 1989
Czechoslovakia (0) 0, France (0) 0	Senec, 28 October 1989
England (0) 1, Czechoslovakia (0) 0	Portsmouth, 14 November 1989
France (1) 1, Greece (0) 2	Gueugnon, 29 November 1989

Group 4 *(Albania, Italy, Portugal, Switzerland)*
Albania (0) 4, Switzerland (0) 0	Shkodra, 12 October 1988
Portugal (2) 2, Albania (0) 1	Lisbon, 15 March 1989
Albania (0) 1, Italy (2) 2	Elbasan, 12 April 1989
Switzerland (0) 0, Portugal (3) 3	Chatel-St. Denis, 19 April 1989
Albania (0) 0, Portugal (1) 2	Tirana, 23 April 1989
Switzerland (0) 0, Italy (1) 2	Moutier, 24 May 1989
Italy (0) 1, Albania (0) 0	Bisceglie, 11 October 1989
Portugal (2) 2, Switzerland (0) 0	Lisbon, 11 October 1989
Italy (0) 0, Portugal (0) 2	Manziana, 1 November 1989
Switzerland (1) 1, Albania (0) 0	Muri/AG, 7 November 1989
Italy (1) 5, Switzerland (0) 0	Cremona, 22 November 1989
Portugal (0) 0, Italy (0) 0	Lisbon, 6 December 1989

Group 5 *(Belgium, Wales, East Germany, Yugoslavia)*
East Germany (0) 0, Yugoslavia (1) 1	Soemmerda, 12 October 1988
Belgium (1) 1, East Germany (1) 1	Seraing, 2 November 1988
Yugoslavia (2) 4, Wales (1) 1	Bijeljina, 9 November 1988
Wales (0) 2, Belgium (0) 0	Newtown, 30 November 1988
Belgium (2) 2, Yugoslavia (0) 1	Roeselare, 29 March 1989
Wales (0) 0, East Germany (0) 0	Aberystwyth, 12 April 1989
East Germany (0) 0, Belgium (1) 2	Hettstedt, 3 May 1989
Yugoslavia (1) 1, East Germany (0) 2	Zavidovic, 20 September 1989
Yugoslavia (0) 1, Belgium (0) 0	Bosanksi, 4 October 1989
Belgium (1) 5, Wales (1) 1	Charleroi, 17 October 1989
East Germany (0) 1, Wales (1) 1	Neustreli, 19 October 1989
Wales (1) 2, Yugoslavia (0) 0	Newtown, 8 November 1989

Group 6 *(Bulgaria, Eire, Malta, Iceland (withdrew))*
Malta (1) 1, Bulgaria (1) 2	Ta'qali, 12 April 1989
Eire (1) 2, Malta (0) 0	Dublin, 27 May 1989
Bulgaria (1) 1, Malta (0) 0	Pazardjik, 4 October 1989
Eire (1) 3, Iceland (0) 0	Dublin, 12 October 1989
Eire (1) 3, Bulgaria (0) 0	Dublin, 31 October 1989
Malta (0) 0, Eire (1) 3	Corradino, 14 November 1989
Bulgaria (0) 1, Eire (0) 0	Blagoevgr, 28 November 1989

Group 7 *(Austria, Denmark, Rumania, Spain)*

Spain (1) 4, Denmark (0) 2	Las Palmas, 16 November 1988
Austria (0) 1, Spain (0) 2	Lanzendorf, 19 April 1989
Austria (1) 1, Rumania (0) 1	Kirchschl, 10 May 1989
Denmark (1) 2, Spain (0) 0	Ronne, 31 May 1989
Rumania (0) 1, Spain (1) 3	Ploiesti, 14 June 1989
Denmark (2) 2, Rumania (0) 2	Roskilde, 5 September 1989
Denmark (3) 4, Austria (1) 1	Nykobing, 20 September 1989
Spain (0) 0, Rumania (0) 0	Talavera 4 October 1989
Austria (0) 0, Denmark (0) 0	Ried im I 18 October 1989
Rumania (0) 0, Austria (0) 0	Sibiu, 1 November 1989
Rumania (1) 3, Denmark (1) 1	Ploiesti, 14 November 1989
Spain (3) 3, Austria (1) 1	Badajoz, 22 November 1989

Group 8 *(Finland, Hungary, Luxembourg, Turkey)*

Finland (0) 0, Hungary (0) 1	Toijala, 21 September 1988
Luxembourg (0) 0, Finland (3) 5	Esch sur Alzette, 26 October 1988
Turkey (2) 3, Luxembourg (0) 1	Izmir, 29 March 1989
Hungary (2) 6, Luxembourg (0) 0	Budapest, 3 May 1989
Hungary (1) 3, Finland (0) 0	Budapest, 10 May 1989
Finland (1) 2, Turkey (1) 2	Uusikaarl, 7 June 1989
Turkey (1) 1, Finland (0) 0	Kocaeli, 3 September 1989
Finland (3) 5, Luxembourg (0) 1	Raisio, 4 October 1989
Hungary (1) 2, Turkey (0) 2	Miske, 7 October 1989
Luxembourg (0) 0, Hungary (0) 2	Esch, 18 October 1989
Turkey (0) 0, Hungary (0) 0	Istanbul, 5 November 1989
Luxembourg (1) 1, Turkey (3) 4	Lux.-Bonn, 29 November 1989

Final competition held in Hungary in July 1990
Draw: England v Belgium (Nyiregyhaza); Sweden v USSR (Debrecen); Portugal v Hungary (Bekescsaba); Republic of Ireland v Spain (Gyula).

UEFA YOUTH TOURNAMENT FINALS 1948–90

Year	Winners		Runners-up		Venue
1948	England	3	Netherlands	2	London
1949	France	4	Netherlands	1	Rotterdam
1950	Austria	3	France	2	Vienna
1951	Yugoslavia	3	Austria	2	Cannes
1952	Spain*	0	Belgium	0	Barcelona
1953	Hungary	2	Yugoslavia	0	Brussels
1954	Spain*	2	West Germany	2	Cologne
1955–56 Played in groups only					
1957	Austria	3	Spain	2	Madrid
1958	Italy	1	England	0	Luxembourg
1959	Bulgaria	1	Italy	0	Sofia
1960	Hungary	2	Rumania	1	Vienna
1961	Portugal	4	Poland	0	Lisbon
1962	Rumania	4	Yugoslavia	1	Bucharest
1963	England	4	Northern Ireland	0	London
1964	England	4	Spain	0	Amsterdam
1965	East Germany	3	England	2	Essen
1966	Italy†	0	USSR	0	Belgrade
1967	USSR	1	England	0	Istanbul
1968	Czechoslovakia	2	France	1	Cannes
1969	Bulgaria*	1	East Germany	1	Leipzig
1970	East Germany*	1	Netherlands	1	Glasgow
1971	England	3	Portugal	0	Prague
1972	England	2	West Germany	0	Barcelona
1973	England	3	East Germany	2	Florence
1974	Bulgaria	1	Yugoslavia	0	Malmo
1975	England	1	Finland	0	Berne
1976	USSR	1	Hungary	0	Budapest
1977	Belgium	2	Bulgaria	1	Brussels
1978	USSR	3	Yugoslavia	0	Krakow
1979	Yugoslavia	1	Bulgaria	0	Vienna
1980	England	2	Poland	1	Leipzig

UEFA YOUTH CHAMPIONSHIPS

1981	West Germany	1	Poland	0	Dusseldorf
1982	Scotland	3	Czechoslovakia	1	Helsinki
1983	France	1	Czechoslovakia	0	London
1984	Hungary**	0	USSR	0	Moscow
1986	East Germany	3	Italy	1	Subotica
1988	USSR	3	Portugal	1	

---

*Won on toss of a coin.   † Joint holders.   ** Won on penalty kicks.*

8th UEFA UNDER-16 CHAMPIONSHIP 1990

Group 1: Iceland 0, Sweden 2; Sweden 5, Iceland 3. Sweden qualified.
Group 2: Finland 1, Denmark 3; Denmark 1, Finland 1. Denmark qualified.
Group 3: Wales 2, Northern Ireland 3; Northern Ireland 1, Wales 1. Northern Ireland qualified.
Group 4: Luxembourg 1, West Germany 5; West Germany 3, Luxembourg 0. West Germany qualified.
Group 5: Liechtenstein 0, Spain 3; Spain 7, Liechtenstein 0. Spain qualified.
Group 6: Czechoslovakia 9, Malta 0; Malta 0, Czechoslovakia 5. Czechoslovakia qualified.
Group 7: Turkey 0, Austria 1; Austria 1, Turkey 2. Turkey qualified.
Group 8: Cyprus 2, Greece 1; Greece 1, Cyprus 2. Cyprus qualified.
Group 9: Poland 1, Holland 2; Holland 0, Poland 4; Italy 1, Poland 1; Holland 1, Italy 0; Poland 1, Italy 0; Italy 6, Holland 1. Poland qualified.
Group 10: Bulgaria 0, Hungary 3; Hungary 3, Bulgaria 0. Hungary qualified.
Group 11: France 2, Switzerland 0; Switzerland 1, France 0. France qualified.
Group 12: San Marino 0, Portugal 3; Portugal 4, San Marino 0. Portugal qualified.
Group 13: Norway 1, Rumania 1; Norway 2, Scotland 0; Rumania 3, Norway 1; Rumania 2, Scotland 2; Scotland 2, Norway 0; Scotland 1, Rumania 0. Scotland qualified.
Group 14: Belgium 2, Eire 1; Eire 0, Belgium 0. Belgium qualified.
Group 15: Yugoslavia 2, USSR 0; USSR 1, Yugoslavia 0. Yugoslavia qualified.

FINAL TOURNAMENT IN EAST GERMANY

GROUP A

Denmark (2) 3, Turkey (0) 0	Leinefeld, 17 May 1990
Northern Ireland (0) 1, Portugal (1) 2	Arnstadt, 17 May 1990
Northern Ireland (0) 0, Denmark (4) 6	Eisenach, 19 May 1990
Portugal (2) 2, Turkey (0) 2	Sondersha, 19 May 1990
Northern Ireland (1) 2, Turkey (0) 0	Weimar, 21 May 1990
Portugal (2) 3, Denmark (0) 1	Muhlhause, 21 May 1990

	P	W	D	L	F	A	Pts
Portugal	3	2	1	0	7	4	5
Denmark	3	2	0	1	10	3	4
Northern Ireland	3	1	0	2	3	8	2
Turkey	3	0	1	2	2	7	1

GROUP B

Poland (2) 3, Cyprus (0) 0	Kolleda, 17 May 1990
Sweden (1) 2, Hungary (1) 2	Tambach, 17 May 1990
Cyprus (1) 2, Hungary (0) 0	Erfurt, 19 May 1990
Poland (1) 1, Sweden (0) 1	Nordhause, 19 May 1990
Cyprus (0) 0, Sweden (0) 3	Heiligens, 21 May 1990

	P	W	D	L	F	A	Pts
Poland	3	2	1	0	6	1	5
Sweden	3	1	2	0	6	3	4
Cyprus	3	1	0	2	2	6	2
Hungary	3	0	1	2	2	6	1

GROUP C

Czechoslovakia (0) 0, West Germany (0) 0	Ruhla, 17 May 1990
France (0) 1, Scotland (0) 1	Bad Lange, 17 May 1990
Czechoslovakia (1) 2, France (0) 0	Apolda, 19 May 1990
West Germany (1) 5, Scotland (0) 1	Sommerda, 19 May 1990
Czechoslovakia (2) 3, Scotland (0) 0	Ilmenau, 21 May 1990
West Germany (0) 1, France (1) 1	Sondersha, 21 May 1990

	P	W	D	L	F	A	Pts
Czechoslovakia	3	2	1	0	5	0	5
West Germany	3	1	2	0	6	2	4
France	3	0	2	1	2	4	2
Scotland	3	0	1	2	2	9	1

GROUP D

Belgium (0) 0, Yugoslavia (0) 2	Gera, 17 May 1990
Spain (2) 3, East Germany (0) 1	Elsterber, 17 May 1990
East Germany (0) 0, Yugoslavia (0) 1	Weida, 19 May 1990
Spain (0) 1, Belgium (0) 0	Lobenstei, 19 May 1990
East Germany (1) 1, Belgium (1) 1	Rudolstad, 21 May 1990
Spain (0) 0, Yugoslavia (0) 1	Zeulenrod, 21 May 1990

	P	W	D	L	F	A	Pts
Yugoslavia	3	3	0	0	4	0	6
Spain	3	2	0	1	4	2	4
East Germany	3	0	1	2	2	5	1
Belgium	3	0	1	2	1	4	1

Semi-finals

Poland (1) 1, Yugoslavia (2) 4	Sommerda, 24 May 1990
Portugal (0) 0, Czechoslovakia (0) 0	Nordhause, 24 May 1990
Czechoslovakia won on penalty-kicks aet	

Third-place match

Portugal (1) 2, Poland (1) 3	Erfurt, 27 May 1990

Final

Czechoslovakia (0) 3, Yugoslavia (1) 2 *(aet)*	Erfurt, 27 May 1990

England Under-21 Results 1976–90

EC UEFA Competition for Under-21 Teams

v ALBANIA

				Eng	Alb
EC1989	Mar	7	Shkroda	2	1
EC1989	April	25	Ipswich	2	0

v BULGARIA

Year	Date		Venue	Eng	Bulg
EC1979	June	5	Pernik	3	1
EC1979	Nov	20	Leicester	5	0
1989	June	5	Toulon	2	3

v CZECHOSLOVAKIA

				Eng	Cz
1990	May	28	Toulon	2	1

v DENMARK

				Eng	Den
EC1978	Sept	19	Hvidovre	2	1
EC1979	Sept	11	Watford	1	0
EC1982	Sept	21	Hvidovre	4	1
EC1983	Sept	20	Norwich	4	1
EC1986	Mar	12	Copenhagen	1	0
EC1986	Mar	26	Manchester	1	1
1988	Sept	13	Watford	0	0

v EAST GERMANY

				Eng	EG
EC1980	April	16	Sheffield	1	2
EC1980	April	23	Jena	0	1

v FINLAND

				Eng	Fin
EC1977	May	26	Helsinki	1	0
EC1977	Oct	12	Hull	8	1
EC1984	Oct	16	Southampton	2	0
EC1985	May	21	Mikkeli	1	3

v FRANCE

				Eng	Fra
EC1984	Feb	28	Sheffield	6	1
EC1984	Mar	28	Rouen	1	0
1987	June	11	Toulon	0	2
EC1988	April	13	Besancon	2	4
EC1988	April	27	Highbury	2	2
1988	June	12	Toulon	2	4
1990	May	23	Toulon	7	3

v GREECE

				Eng	Gre
EC1982	Nov	16	Piraeus	0	1
EC1983	Mar	29	Portsmouth	2	1
1989	Feb	7	Patras	0	1

v HUNGARY

				Eng	Hun
EC1981	June	5	Keszthely	2	1
EC1981	Nov	17	Nottingham	2	0
EC1983	April	26	Newcastle	1	0
EC1983	Oct	11	Nyiregyhaza	2	0

v ITALY

				Eng	Italy
EC1978	Mar	8	Manchester	2	1
EC1978	April	5	Rome	0	0
EC1984	April	18	Manchester	3	1
EC1984	May	2	Florence	0	1
EC1986	April	9	Pisa	0	2
EC1986	April	23	Swindon	1	1

v ISRAEL

				Eng	Isr
1985	Feb	27	Tel Aviv	2	1

v MEXICO

				Eng	Mex
1988	June	5	Toulon	2	1

v MOROCCO

				Eng	Mor
1987	June	7	Toulon	2	0
1988	June	9	Toulon	1	0

v NORWAY

				Eng	Nor
EC1977	June	1	Bergen	2	1
EC1977	Sept	6	Brighton	6	0
1980	Sept	9	Southampton	3	0
1981	Sept	8	Drammen	0	0

v POLAND

Year	Date		Venue	Eng	Pol
EC1982	Mar	17	Warsaw	2	1
EC1982	April	7	West Ham	2	2
EC1989	June	2	Plymouth	2	1
EC1989	Oct	10	Jastrzebie	3	1

v PORTUGAL

				Eng	Por
1987	June	13	Toulon	0	0
1990	May	21	Toulon	0	1

v REPUBLIC OF IRELAND

				Eng	Rep of Ire
1981	Feb	25	Liverpool	1	0
1985	Mar	25	Portsmouth	3	2
1989	June	9	Toulon	0	0

v RUMANIA

				Eng	Rum
EC1980	Oct	14	Ploesti	0	4
EC1981	April	28	Swindon	3	0
EC1985	April	30	Brasov	0	0
EC1985	Sept	10	Ipswich	3	0

v SENEGAL

				Eng	Sen
1989	June	7	Toulon	6	1

v SCOTLAND

				Eng	Scot
1977	April	27	Sheffield	1	0
EC1980	Feb	12	Coventry	2	1
EC1980	Mar	4	Aberdeen	0	0
EC1982	April	19	Glasgow	1	0
EC1982	April	28	Manchester	1	1
EC1988	Feb	16	Aberdeen	1	0
EC1988	Mar	22	Nottingham	1	0

v SPAIN

				Eng	Spa
EC1984	May	17	Seville	1	0
EC1984	May	24	Sheffield	2	0
1987	Feb	18	Burgos	2	1

v SWEDEN

				Eng	Swe
1979	June	9	Vasteras	2	1
1986	Sept	9	Ostersund	1	1
EC1988	Oct	18	Coventry	1	1
EC1989	Sept	5	Uppsala	0	1

v SWITZERLAND

				Eng	Swit
EC1980	Nov	18	Ipswich	5	0
EC1981	May	31	Neuenburg	0	0
1988	May	28	Lausanne	1	1

v USA

				Eng	USA
1989	June	11	Toulon	0	2

v TURKEY

				Eng	Tur
EC1984	Nov	13	Bursa	0	0
EC1985	Oct	15	Bristol	3	0
EC1987	April	28	Izmir	0	0
EC1987	Oct	13	Sheffield	1	1

v USSR

				Eng	USSR
1987	June	9	Toulon	0	0
1988	June	7	Toulon	1	0
1990	May	25	Toulon	2	1

v WALES

				Eng	Wales
1976	Dec	15	Wolverhampton	0	0
1979	Feb	6	Swansea	1	0

v WEST GERMANY

				Eng	WG
EC1982	Sept	21	Sheffield	3	1
EC1982	Oct	12	Bremen	2	3
1987	Sept	8	Ludenscheid	0	2

v YUGOSLAVIA

				Eng	Yugo
EC1978	April	19	Novi Sad	1	2
EC1978	May	2	Manchester	1	1
EC1986	Nov	11	Peterborough	1	1
EC1987	Nov	10	Zemun	5	1

ENGLAND UNDER-21 CAPS 1989–90

	Sweden 5.9.89	Poland 10.10.89	Portugal 21.5.90	France 23.5.90	USSR 25.5.90	Czechoslovakia 27.5.90
N. Martyn (Bristol Rovers)	1					1 o.g.
R. Wallace (Southampton)	2					
D. Burrows (Liverpool)	3	3				
M. Thomas (Arsenal)	4					
S. Redmond (Manchester City)	5	5				
S. Chettle (Nottingham Forest)	6	6				
S. Ripley (Middlesbrough)	7					
P. Ince (West Ham United)	8					
S. Bull (Wolverhampton Wanderers)	9	9[2]				
S. Sedgley (Tottenham Hotspur)	10					
D. Smith (Coventry City)	11	11				
J. Dozzell (Ipswich Town)	7*					
I. Brightwell (Manchester City)	8*	8[1]				
F. Digby (Swindon Town)		1				
P. Lake (Manchester City)		2				
D. Batty (Leeds United)		4				
D. White (Manchester City)		7				
P. Merson (Arsenal)		10				
M. Crossley (Nottingham Forest)			1		1	1
T. Sherwood (Norwich City)			2	8	8	2
G. Le Saux (Chelsea)			3	3	3	3
J. Ebbrell (Everton)			4	4	4	4
E. Barrett (Oldham Athletic)			5	5	5	5
C. Tiler (Barnsley)			6		6	6
R. Thomas (Watford)			7			
D. Matthew (Chelsea)			8		2*	8
M. Robins (Manchester United)			9	9[5]	9[1]	9
I. Olney (Aston Villa)			10	10	10[1]	10[1]
S. Slater (West Ham United)			11		11*	7
G. Stuart (Chelsea)			7*	7[2]	7	7
L. Sharpe (Manchester United)			11*	11	11	11
G. Muggleton (Leicester City)				1		
J. James (Luton Town)				2	2	
D. Lee (Chelsea)				6		
M. Blake (Aston Villa)				2*		2*

* Substitute

Scotland Under-21 internationals

5 Sept

Yugoslavia 4

Scotland 1 *(Gallacher)* — 9000

Scotland: Fridge; McLaren (Wright), Robertson D, McKinlay, Nisbet, Whyte, Kirkwood, Ferguson D, Gallacher, Collins, Glover (Crabbe).

11 Oct

France 3

Scotland 1 *(Wilson)* — 8000

Scotland: Gunn; Cleland, Wilson, Nisbet, Hamilton, McKinlay, Collins (Jess), McCall, McLeod, Miller (Hunter), Crabbe.

14 Nov

Scotland 2 *(Galloway, McKinlay)*

Norway 0 — 6137

Scotland: Main; Cleland, Robertson D (Sharp), McKinlay, Whyte, McLaren, Hamilton (Jess), McAllister, Galloway, Collins, Miller.

Wales Under-21 internationals

19 May

Wales 2 *(Coleman, Nogan)*

Poland 0 — 1785

Wales: Freestone; Hall, Coleman, Melville, Law, Perry, Griffith, Rees, Nogan, Ebdon, Speed.

England B internationals

14 Nov

England 1 *(Adams)*

Italy 1 — 16,125

England: Martyn (Beasant); Parker (Dixon), Dorigo, Thomas, Adams, Pallister (Linighan), Wise (Beagrie), Gascoigne, Bull, Batty, Newell (Williams).

12 Dec

England 2 *(Wise, Newell)*

Yugoslavia 1 — 8231

England: Woods (Martyn); Dixon (Sterland), Forsyth, Batty, Adams, Linighan (Pallister), Wright (Newell), Gascoigne, Williams, Beagrie (Parker), Wise.

27 March

Republic of Ireland 4 *(McLoughlin, Kelly (pen), Quinn 2)*

England 1 *(Atkinson)* — 10,000

Republic of Ireland: Kelly G; Irwin (Phelan), Beglin, Brazil, Scully, McLoughlin (De Mange), Mooney, Milligan (Waddock), Quinn, Kelly D (Coyle), Kelly M.
England: Beasant (Seaman); Dixon (Snodin), Winterburn, Palmer, Linighan, Adams, Le Tissier (Daley), Batty, Williams (Clough), Atkinson, Sinton (Lake).

24 April

England 2 *(Smith 2)*

Czechoslovakia 0 — 15,080

England: Seaman (Beasant); Borrows, Winterburn (Burrows), Webb (Thomas), Adams, Pallister (Linighan), Wise, Cowans, Smith, Gabbiadini, Wallace Rod (Le Tissier).

Scotland B internationals
27 March
Scotland 0
Yugoslavia 0   8288
Scotland: Gunn (Money); Clarke, Munro, McPherson,
Boyd, Whyte, Ferguson I (McKinlay), Grant, Stephen
(Gallacher), McAllister, Durie.

24 April
Scotland 1 *(Stephen)*
East Germany 2 *(Whyte (og), Weidermann)*   5042
Scotland: Gunn; Boyd, Munro, McPherson, Hendry,
Whyte (Gallacher), Black (Stephen), Grant, McClair,
Connor, Robertson (Nevin).

Republic of Ireland Under-21 international
24 April
Republic of Ireland 1 *(Cousins)*
Malta 1   2000

Gary Pallister the Manchester United and England international central defender who played in several B matches
for his country last season after becoming the country's most expensive player at £2.3 million. (Associated Sports
Photography)

UNDER-21 APPEARANCES 1976–1990

ENGLAND

Ablett, G. (Liverpool), 1988 v Fr (1)
Adams, A. (Arsenal), 1985 v Ei, Fi; 1986 v D; 1987 v Se, Y (5)
Adams, N. (Everton), 1987 v Se (1)
Allen, C. (QPR), 1980 v EG (sub); 1981 (C Palace) v N, R (3)
Allen, M. (QPR), 1987 v Se (sub); 1988 v Y (sub) (2)
Allen, P. (West Ham U), 1985 v Ei, R; (with Tottenham H) 1986 v R (3)
Anderson, V. A. (Nottingham F), 1978 v I (1)
Andrews, I. (Leicester C), 1987 v Se (1)
Bailey, G. R. (Manchester U), 1979 v W, Bul; 1980 v D, S (2), EG; 1982 v N; 1983 v D, Gr; 1984 v H, F (2), I, Sp (14)
Baker, G. E. (Southampton), 1981 v N, R (2)
Bannister, G. (Sheffield W), 1982 v Pol (1)
Barker, S. (Blackburn R), 1985 v Is (sub), Ei, R; 1986 v I (4)
Barnes, J. (Watford), 1983 v D, Gr (2)
Barnes, P. S. (Manchester C), 1977 v W (sub), S, Fi, N; 1978 v N, Fi, I (2), Y (9)
Barrett, E. D. (Oldham Ath), 1990 v P, F, USSR, Cz (4)
Batty, D. (Leeds U), 1988 v Sw (sub); 1989 v Gr (sub), Bul, Sen, Ei, USA; 1990 v Pol (6)
Beagrie, P. (Sheffield U), 1988 v WG, T (2)
Beardsmore, R. (Manchester U), 1989 v Gr, Alb (sub), Pol, Bul, USA (5)
Beeston, C (Stoke C), 1988 v USSR (1)
Bertschin, K. E. (Birmingham C), 1977 v S; 1978 v Y (2) (3)
Birtles, G. (Nottingham F), 1980 v Bul, EG (sub) (2)
Blake, M. A. (Aston Villa), 1990 v F (sub), Cz (sub) (2)
Blissett, L. L. (Watford), 1979 v W, Bul (sub), Se; 1980 v D (4)
Bracewell, P. (Stoke C), 1983 v D, Gr (2, one sub), H; 1984 v D, H, F (2), I (2), Sp (2); 1985 v T (13)
Bradshaw, P. W. (Wolverhampton W), 1977 v W, S; 1978 v Fi, Y (4)
Breaker, T. (Luton T), 1986 v I (2) (2)
Brennan, M. (Ipswich T), 1987 v Y, Sp, T, Mo, F (5)
Brightwell, I. (Manchester C), 1989 v D, Alb; 1990 v Se (sub), Pol (4)
Brock, K. (Oxford U), 1984 v I, Sp (2); 1986 v I (4)
Bull, S. G. (Wolverhampton W), 1989 v Alb (2) Pol; 1990 v Se, Pol (4)
Burrows, D. (WBA), 1989 v Se (sub) (with Liverpool), Gr, Alb (2) Pol; 1990 v Se, Pol (7)
Butcher, T. I. (Ipswich T), 1979 v Se; 1980 v D, Bul, S (2), EG (2) (7)
Butters, G. (Tottenham H), 1989 v Bul, Sen (sub), Ei (sub) (3)
Butterworth, I. (Coventry C), 1985 v T, R; 1986 (with Nottingham F) v R, T, D (2), I (2) (8)
Caesar, G. (Arsenal), 1987 v Mo, USSR (sub), F (3)
Callaghan, N. (Watford), 1983 v D, Gr (sub), H (sub); 1984 v D, H, F(2), I, Sp (9)
Carr, C. (Fulham), 1985 v Ei (sub) (1)
Carr, F. (Nottingham F), 1987 v Se, Y, Sp (sub), Mo, USSR; 1988 v WG (sub), T, Y, Fr (9)
Caton, T. (Manchester C), 1982 v N, H (sub), Pol (2), S; 1983 v WG (2), Gr; 1984 v D, H, F (2), I (2) (14)
Chamberlain, M. (Stoke C), 1983 v Gr; 1984 v F (sub), I, Sp (4)
Chapman, L. (Stoke C), 1981 v Ei (1)
Chettle, S. (Nottingham F), 1988 v M, USSR, Mor, Fr; 1989 v D, Se, Gr, Alb (2), Bul; 1990 v Se, Pol (12)
Clough, N. (Nottingham F), 1986 v D (sub); 1987 v Se, Y, T, USSR, F (sub), P; 1988 v WG, T, Y, S (2), M, Mor, Fr (15)
Coney, D. (Fulham), 1985 v T (sub); 1986 v R; 1988 v T, WG (8)
Connor, T. (Brighton & H A), 1987 v Y (1)
Cooke, R. (Tottenham H), 1986 v D (sub) (1)
Cooper, C. (Middlesbrough), 1988 v Fr (2), M, USSR, Mor; 1989 v D, Se, Gr (8)
Corrigan, J. T. (Manchester C), 1978 v I (2), Y (3)
Cottee, A. (West Ham U), 1985 v Fi (sub), Is (sub), Ei, R, Fi; 1987 v Sp, P; 1988 v WG (8)

Cowans, G. S. (Aston Villa), 1979 v W, Se; 1980 v Bul, EG; 1981 v R (5)
Cranson, I. (Ipswich T), 1985 v Fi, Is, R; 1986 v R, I (5)
Crooks, G. (Stoke C), 1980 v Bul, S (2), EG (sub) (4)
Crossley, M. G. (Nottingham F), 1990 v P, USSR, Cz (3)
Cunningham, L. (WBA), 1977 v S, Fi, N (sub); 1978 v N, Fi, I (6)
Curbishley, L. C. (Birmingham C), 1981 v Sw (1)
Daniel, P. W. (Hull C), 1977 v S, Fi, N; 1978 v Fi, I, Y (2) (7)
Davis, P. (Arsenal), 1982 v Pol, S; 1983 v D, Gr (2, one sub), H (sub); 1987 v T; 1988 v WG, T, Y, Fr (11)
D'Avray, M. (Ipswich T), 1984 v I, Sp (sub) (2)
Deehan, J. M. (Aston Villa), 1977 v N; 1978 v N, Fi, I; 1979 v Bul Se (sub); 1980 v D (7)
Dennis, M. E. (Birmingham C), 1980 v Bul; 1981 v N, R (3)
Dickens, A. (West Ham U), 1985 v Fi (sub) (1)
Dicks, J. (West Ham U), 1988 v Sw (sub), M, Mor, Fr (4)
Digby, F. (Swindon T), 1987 v Sp (sub), USSR, P; 1988 v T; 1990 v Pol (5)
Dillon, K. P. (Birmingham C), 1981 v R (1)
Dixon, K. (Chelsea), 1985 v Fi (1)
Dobson, A. (Coventry C), 1989 v Bul, Sen, Ei, USA (4)
Donowa, L. (Norwich C), 1985 v Is, R (sub), Fi (sub) (3)
Dorigo, A. (Aston Villa), 1987 v Se, Sp, T, Mo, USSR, F, P; 1988 v WG, Y, S (2) (11)
Dozzell, J. (Ipswich T), 1987 v Se, Y (sub), Sp, USSR, F, P; 1989 v Se, Gr (sub); 1990 v Se (sub) (9)
Duxbury, M. (Manchester U), 1981 v Sw (sub), Ei (sub), R (sub), Se; 1982 v N; 1983 v WG (2) (7)
Dyson, P. I. (Coventry C), 1981 v N, R, Sw, Ei (4)
Ebbrell, J. (Everton), 1989 v Sen, Ei, USA (sub); 1990 v P, F, USSR, Cz (7)
Elliott, P. (Luton T), 1985 v Fi; 1986 v T, D (3)
Fairclough, C. (with Nottingham F), 1985 v T, Is, Ei; 1987 v Sp, T; 1988 (with Tottenham H) v Y, F (7)
Fairclough, D. (Liverpool), 1977 v W (1)
Fashanu, J. (Norwich C), 1980 v EG; 1981 v N (sub), R, Sw, Ei (sub), H; (Nottingham F), 1982 v N, H, Pol, S; 1983 v WG (sub) (11)
Fenwick, T. W. (C Palace), 1981 v N, R, Sw, Ei, (QPR), R; 1982 v N, H, S (2); 1983 v WG (2) (11)
Fereday, W. (QPR), 1985 v T, Ei (sub), Fi; 1986 v T (sub), I (5)
Flowers, T. (Southampton), 1987 v Mo, F; 1988 v WG (sub) (3)
Forsyth, M. (Derby Co), 1988 v Sw (1)
Foster, S. (Brighton & HA), 1980 v EG (sub) (1)
Futcher, P. (Luton T), 1977 v W, S, Fi, N; (with Manchester C), 1978 v N, Fi, I (2), Y (2); 1979 v D (11)
Gabbiadini, M. (Sunderland), 1989 v Bul, USA (2)
Gale, A. (Fulham), 1982 v Pol (1)
Gascoigne, P. (Newcastle U), 1987 v Mo, USSR, P; 1988 v WG, Y, S (2), F (2), Sw, M, USSR (sub), Mor (13)
Gayle, H. (Birmingham C), 1984 v I, Sp (2) (3)
Gernon, T. (Ipswich T), 1983 v Gr (1)
Gibbs, N. (Watford), 1987 v Mo, USSR, F, P; 1988 v T (5)
Gibson, C. (Aston Villa), 1982 v N (1)
Gilbert, W. A. (C Palace), 1979 v W, Bul; 1980 v Bul; 1981 v N, R, Sw, R, Sw, H; 1982 v N (sub), H (11)
Goddard, P. (West Ham U), 1981 v N, Sw, Ei (sub); 1982 v N (sub), Pol, S; 1983 v WG (2) (8)
Gordon, D. (Norwich C), 1987 v T (sub), Mo (sub), F, P (4)
Gray, A. (Aston Villa), 1988 v S, F (2)
Haigh, P. (Hull C), 1977 v N (sub) (1)
Hardyman, P. (Portsmouth), 1985 v Ei; 1986 v D (2)
Hateley, M. (Coventry C), 1982 v Pol, S; 1983 v Gr (2), H; (with Portsmouth) 1984 v F (2), I, Sp (2) (10)
Hayes, M. (Arsenal), 1987 v Sp, T; 1988 v F (sub) (3)
Hazell, R. J. (Wolverhampton W), 1979 v D (1)
Heath, A. (Stoke C), 1981 v R, Sw, H; 1982 v N, H, (with Everton), Pol, S; 1983 v WG (8)
Hesford, I. (Blackpool), 1981 v Ei (sub), Pol (2), S (2); 1983 v WG (2) (7)

Slater, S. I. (West Ham U), 1990 v P, USSR (sub), Cz (sub) (3)

Smith, D. (Coventry C), 1988 v M, USSR (sub), Mor; 1989 v D, Se, Alb (2), Pol; 1990 v Se, Pol (10)

Smith, M. (Sheffield W), 1981 v Ei, R, Sw, H; 1982 v Pol (sub) (5)

Snodin, I. (Doncaster R), 1985 v T, Is, R, Fi (4)

Statham, B (Tottenham H), 1988 v Sw; 1989 v D (sub), Se (3)

Statham, D. J. (WBA), 1978 v Fi, 1979 v W, Bul, Se; 1980 v D; 1983 v D (6)

Stein, B. (Luton T), 1984 v D, H, I (3)

Sterland, M. (Sheffield W), 1984 v D, H, F (2), I, Sp (2) (7)

Steven, T. (Everton), 1985 v Fi, T (2)

Stewart, P. (Manchester C), 1988 v F (1)

Stuart, G. C. (Chelsea), 1990 v P (sub), F, USSR, Cz (4)

Suckling, P. (Coventry C), 1986 v D; (with Manchester C), 1987 v Se (sub), Y, Sp, T; (with Crystal Palace), 1988 v S (2), F (2), Sw (5)

Sunderland, A. (Wolverhampton W), 1977 v W (1)

Swindlehurst, D. (C Palace), 1977 v W (1)

Stevens, G. (Brighton & HA), 1983 v H; (with Tottenham H), 1984 v H, F (1 + sub), I (sub), Sp (1 + sub); 1986 v I (8)

Talbot, B. (Ipswich T), 1977 v W (1)

Thomas, D. (Coventry C), 1981 v Ei; 1983 v WG (2), Gr, H; (with Tottenham H), v I, Sp (7)

Thomas, M. (Arsenal), 1988 v Y, S, F (2), M, USSR, Mor; 1989 v Gr, Alb (2), Pol; 1990 v Se (12)

Thomas, M. (Luton T), 1986 v T, D, I (3)

Thomas, R. E. (Watford), 1990 v P (1)

Thompson, G. L. (Coventry C), 1981 v R, Sw, H; 1982 v N, H, S (6)

Thorn, A. (Wimbledon), 1988 v WG (sub), Y, S, F, Sw (5)

Tiler, C. (Barnsley), 1990 v P, USSR, Cz (3)

Venison, B. (Sunderland), 1983 v D, Gr; 1985 v Fi, T, Is, Fi; 1986 v R, T, D (2) (10)

Waddle, C. (Newcastle U), 1985 v Fi (1)

Wallace, D. (Southampton), 1983 v Gr, H; 1984 v D, H, F (2), I, Sp (sub); 1985 v Fi, T, Is; 1986 v R, D, I (14)

Wallace, Ray (Southampton), 1989 v Bul, Sen (sub), Ei; 1990 v Se (4)

Wallace, Rod (Southampton), 1989 v Bul, Ei (sub), USA (3)

Walker, D. (Nottingham F), 1985 v Fi; 1987 v Se, T; 1988 v WG, T, S (2) (7)

Walsh, G. (Manchester U), 1988 v WG, Y (2)

Walsh, P. (Luton T), 1983 v D (sub), Gr (2), H (4)

Walters, K. (Aston Villa), 1984 v D (sub), H (sub); 1985 v Is, Ei, R; 1986 v R, T, D, I (sub) (9)

Ward, P. D. (Brighton & HA), 1978 v N; 1980 v EG (2)

Watson, D. (Norwich C), 1984 v D, F (2), I (2), Sp (2) (7)

Webb, N. (Portsmouth), 1985 v Ei; (with Nottinham F), 1986 v D (2) (3)

White, D. (Manchester C), 1988 v S (2), F, USSR; 1989 v Se; 1990 v Pol (6)

Whyte, C. (Arsenal), 1982 v S (1 + sub); 1983 v D, Gr (4)

Wicks, S. (QPR), 1982 v S (1)

Wilkins, R. C. (Chelsea), 1977 v W (1)

Wilkinson, P. (Grimsby T), 1985 v Ei, R (sub); (with Everton), 1986 v R (sub), I (4)

Williams, P. (Charlton Ath), 1989 v Bul, Sen, Ei, USA (sub) (4)

Williams, S. C. (Southampton), 1977 v S, Fi, N; 1978 v N, I (1 + sub), Y (2); 1979 v D, Bul, Se (sub); 1980 v D, EG (2) (15)

Winterburn, N. (Wimbledon), 1986 v I (1)

Wise, D. (Wimbledon), 1988 v Sw (1)

Woodcock, A. S. (Nottingham F), 1978 v Fi, I (2)

Woods, C. C. E. (Nottingham F), 1979 v W (sub), Se; (with QPR), 1980 v Bul, EG; 1981 v Sw; (with Norwich C), 1984 v D (6)

Wright, M. (Southampton), 1983 v Gr, H; 1984 v D, H (4)

Wright, W. (Everton), 1979 v D, W, Bul; 1980 v D, S (2) (6)

Yates, D. (Notts Co), 1989 v D (sub), Bul, Sen, Ei, USA (4)

SCOTLAND

Aitken, R. (Celtic), 1977 v Cz, W, Sw; 1978 v Cz, W; 1979 v P, N (2); 1980 v B, E; 1984 v EG, Y (2); 1985 v WG, Ic, Sp (16)

Albiston A. (Manchester U), 1977 v Cz, W, Sw; 1978 v Sw, Cz (5)

Archdeacon, O. (Celtic), 1987 v WG (sub) (1)

Archibald, S. (Aberdeen), 1980 v B, E (2), WG; (with Tottenham H), 1981 v D (5)

Bannon, E. J. P. (Hearts), 1979 v US, (with Chelsea), P, N (2); (with Dundee U), 1980 v B, WG, E (7)

Beaumont, D. (Dundee U), 1985 v Ic (1)

Bell, D. (Aberdeen), 1981 v D; 1984 v Y (2)

Bett, J. (Rangers), 1981 v Se, D; 1982 v Se, D, I, E (2) (7)

Black, E. (Aberdeen), 1983 v EG, Sw (2), Bel; 1985 v Ic, Sp (2), Ic (8)

Blair, A. (Coventry C), 1980 v E; 1981 v Se; (with Aston Villa), 1982 v Se, D, I (5)

Bowman, D. (Hearts), 1985 v WG (sub) (1)

Boyd, T. (Motherwell), 1987 v WG. Ei (2), Bel; 1988 v Bel (5)

Brazil, A. (Hibernian), 1978 v W (1)

Brazil, A. (Ipswich T), 1979 v N; 1980 v B (2), E (2), WG; 1981 v Se; 1982 v Se (8)

Brough, J. (Hearts), 1981 v D (1)

Burley, G. E. (Ipswich T), 1977 v Cz, W, Sw; 1978 v Sw, Cz (5)

Burns, H. (Rangers), 1985 v Sp, Ic (sub) (2)

Burns, J. (Celtic), 1977 v Cz, W, E; 1978 v Sw; 1982 v E (5)

Campbell, S. (Dundee), 1989 v N (sub), Y, F (3)

Casey, J. (Celtic), 1978 v W (1)

Clark, R. (Aberdeen), 1977 v Cz, W, Sw (3)

Clarke, S. (St Mirren), 1984 v Bel, EG, Y; 1985 v WG, Ic, Sp (2), Ic (8)

Cleland, A. (Dundee U), 1990 v F, N (2)

Collins, J. (Hibernian), 1988 v Bel, E; 1989 v N, Y, F; 1990 v Y, F, N (8)

Connor, R. (Ayr U), 1981 v Se; 1982 v Se (2)

Cooper, D. (Clyde), 1977 v Cz, W, Sw, E; (with Rangers), 1978 v Sw, Cz (6)

Cooper, N. (Aberdeen), 1982 v D, E (2); 1983 v Bel, EG, Sw (2); 1984 v Bel, EG, Y; 1985 v Ic, Sp, Ic (13)

Crabbe, S. (Hearts), 1990 v Y (sub), F (2)

Craig, T. (Newcastle U), 1977 v E (1)

Crainie, D. (Celtic), 1983 v Sw (sub) (1)

Dawson, A. (Rangers), 1979 v P, N (2); 1980 v B (2), E (2) WG (8)

Dodds, D. (Dundee U), 1978 v W (1)

Duffy, J. (Dundee), 1987 v Ei (1)

Durie, D. (Chelsea), 1987 v WG, Ei Bel; 1988 v Bel (4)

Durrant, I. (Rangers), 1987 v WG, Ei, Bel; 1988 v E (4)

Doyle, J. (Partick Th), 1981 v D, I (sub) (2)

Ferguson, D. (Rangers), 1987 v WG, Ei, Bel; 1988 v E; 1990 v Y (5)

Ferguson, I. (Clyde), 1987 v WG (sub), Ei (with St. Mirren), Ei, Bel; 1988 v Bel (with Rangers), E (sub) (6)

Ferguson, I. (Dundee), 1983 v EG (sub), Sw (sub); 1984 v Bel (sub) EG (4)

Ferguson, R. (Hamilton A), 1977 v E (1)

Fitzpatrick, A. (St Mirren), 1977 v W (sub), Sw (sub), E; 1978 v Sw, Cz (5)

Fleck, R. (Rangers), 1987 v WG (sub), Ei, Bel; (with Norwich C), 1988 v E (2); 1989 v Y (6)

Fridge, L. (St Mirren), 1989 v F; 1990 v Y (2)

Fulton, M. (St Mirren), 1980 v B, WG, E; 1981 v Se, D (sub) (5)

Gallacher, K. (Dundee U), 1987 v WG, Ei (2), Bel (sub); 1988 v E (2); 1990 v Y (7)

Galloway, M. (Hearts), 1989 v F; (with Celtic), 1990 v N (2)

Geddes, R. (Dundee), 1982 v Se, D, E (2); 1988 v E (5)

Gillespie, G. (Coventry C), 1979 v US; 1980 v E; 1981 v D; 1982 v Se, D, I (2), E (8)

Glover, L. (Nottingham F), 1988 v Bel (sub); 1989 v N; 1990 v Y (3)

Goram, A. (Oldham Ath), 1987 v Ei (1)

Gough, C. R. (Dundee U), 1983 v EG, Sw, Bel; 1984 v Y (2) (5)

Grant, P. (Celtic), 1985 v WG, Ic, Sp; 1987 v WG, Ei (2), Bel; 1988 v Bel, E (2) (10)

Gunn, B. (Aberdeen), 1984 v EG, Y (2); 1985 v WG, Ic, Sp (2), Ic; 1990 v F (9)

Gray, S. (Aberdeen), 1987 v WG (1)

Hamilton, B. (St Mirren), 1989 v Y, F (sub); 1990 v F, N (4)

Hartford, R. A. (Manchester C), 1977 v Sw (1)

Hegarty, P. (Dundee U), 1987 v WG, Bel; 1988 v E (2); 1990 v F, N,(4)

Hewitt, J. (Aberdeen), 1982 v I; 1983 v EG, Sw (2); 1984 v Bel, Y (sub) (6)

Hogg, G. (Manchester U), 1984 v Y; 1985 v WG, Ic, Sp (4)

Hunter, G. (Hibernian), 1987 v Ei (sub); 1988 v Bel, E (3)

Hunter, P. (East Fife), 1989 v N (sub), F (sub); 1990 v F (sub) (3)

Jardine, I. (Kilmarnock), 1979 v US (1)

Jess, E. (Aberdeen), 1990 v F (sub), N (sub) (2)

Johnston, M. (Partick Th), 1984 v EG (sub); (with Watford), v Y (2) (3)

Kirkwood, D. (Hearts), 1990 v Y (1)

Leighton, J. (Aberdeen), 1982 v I (1)

Levein, C. (Hearts), 1985 v Sp, Ic (2)

Lindsey, J. (Motherwell), 1979 v US (1)

McAllister, G. (Leicester C), 1990 v N (1)

McAlpine, H. (Dundee U), 1983 v EG, Sw (2), Bel; 1984 v Bel (5)

McAvennie, F. (St Mirren), 1982 v I, E; 1985 v Is, Ei, R (5)

McBride, J. (Everton), 1981 v D (1)

McCall, S. (Bradford C), 1988 v E; (with Everton), 1990 v F (2)

McClair, B. (Celtic), 1984 v Bel (sub), EG, Y (1 + sub); 1985 v WG, Ic, Sp, Ic (8)

McCluskey, G. (Celtic), 1979 v US, P; 1980 v B (2); 1982 v D, I (6)

McCoist, A. (Rangers), 1984 v Bel (1)

McCulloch, A. (Kilmarnock), 1981 v Se (1)

McCulloch, I. (Notts Co), 1982 v E (2)

MacDonald, J. (Rangers), 1980 v WG (sub); 1981 v Se; 1982 v Se (sub), L, I (2), E (2 sub) (8)

McGarvey, F. (St Mirren), 1977 v E; 1978 v Cz; (with Celtic), 1982 v D (3)

McGarvey, S. (Manchester U), 1982 v E (sub); 1983 v Bel, Sw; 1984 v Bel (4)

McGhee, M. (Aberdeen), 1981 v D (1)

McGinnis, G. (Dundee U), 1985 v Sp (1)

McInally, J. (Dundee U), 1989 v F (1)

McKimmie, S. (Aberdeen), 1985 v WG, Ic (2) (3)

McKinlay, T. (Dundee), 1984 v EG (sub); 1985 v WG, Ic, Sp (2), Ic (6)

McKinlay, W. (Dundee U), 1989 v N, Y (sub); 1990 v Y, F, N (6)

McLaren, A. (Hearts), 1989 v F; 1990 v Y, N (3)

McLaughlin, J. (Morton), 1980 v I; 1982 v Se, D, I, E (2); 1983 v EG, Sw (2), Bel (10)

McLeish, A. (Aberdeen), 1978 v W; 1979 v US; 1980 v B, E (2); 1987 v Ei (6)

MacLeod, A. (Hibernian), 1979 v P, N (2) (3)

McLeod, J. (Dundee U), 1989 v N; 1990 v F (2)

MacLeod, M. (Dumbarton), 1979 v US; (with Celtic), P (sub), N (2); 1980 v B (5)

McNab, N. (Tottenham H), 1978 v W (1)

McNichol, J. (Brentford), 1979 v P, N (2); 1980 v B (2), WG, E (7)

McNiven, D. (Leeds U), 1977 v Cz, W (sub), Sw (sub) (3)

McPherson, D. (Rangers), 1984 v Bel; 1985 v Sp; (with Hearts), 1989 v N, Y (4)

McStay, P. (Celtic), 1983 v EG, Sw (2); 1984 v Y (2) (5)

Main, A. (Dundee U), 1988 v E; 1989 v Y; 1990 v N (3)

Malpas, M. (Dundee U), 1983 v Bel, Sw (1 + sub); 1984 v Bel, EG, Y (2); 1985 v Sp (8)

May, E. (Hibernian), 1989 v Y (sub), F (2)

Melrose, J. (Partick Th), 1977 v Sw; 1979 v US, P, N (2); 1980 v B (sub), WG, E (8)

Miller, J. (Aberdeen), 1987 v Ei (sub); 1988 v Bel (with Celtic) E; 1989 v N, Y; 1990 v F, N (7)

Miller, W. (Aberdeen), 1978 v Sw, Cz (2)

Milne, R. (Dundee U), 1982 v Se (sub); 1984 v Bel, EG (3)

Money, I. C. (St Mirren), 1987 v Ei; 1988 v Bel; 1989 v N (3)

Muir, L. (Hibernian), 1977 v Cz (sub) (1)

Narey, D. (Dundee U), 1977 v Cz, Sw; 1978 v Sw, Cz (4)

Nevin, P. (Chelsea), 1985 v WG, Ic, Sp (2), Ic (5)

Nicholas, C. (Celtic), 1981 v Se; 1982 v Se; 1983 v EG, Sw, Bel; (with Arsenal), 1984 v Y (6)

Nicol, S. (Ayr U), 1981 v Se; 1982 v Se, D; (with Liverpool), 1982 v I (2), E (2); 1983 v EG, Sw (2), Bel; 1984 v Bel, EG, Y (14)

Nisbet, S, (Rangers), 1989 v N, Y, F; 1990 v Y, F (5)

Orr, N. (Morton), 1978 v W (sub); 1979 v US, P, N (2); 1980 v B, E (7)

Parlane, D. (Rangers), 1977 v W (1)

Paterson, C. (Hibernian), 1981 v Se; 1982 v I (2)

Payne, G. (Dundee U), 1978 v Sw, Cz, W (3)

Provan, D. (Kilmarnock), 1977 v Cz (sub) (1)

Redford, I. (Rangers), 1981 v Se (sub); 1982 v Se, D, I (2), E (6)

Reid, M. (Celtic), 1982 v E; 1984 v Y (2)

Reid, R. (St Mirren), 1977 v W, Sw, E (3)

Rice, B. (Hibernian), 1985 v WG (1)

Richardson, L. (St Mirren), 1980 v WG, E (sub) (2)

Ritchie, A. (Morton), 1980 v B (1)

Robertson, C. (Rangers), 1977 v E (sub) (1)

Robertson, D. (Aberdeen), 1987 v Ei (sub); 1988 v E (2); 1989 v N, Y; 1990 v Y, N (7)

Robertson, J. (Hearts), 1985 v WG, Ic (sub) (2)

Ross, T. W. (Arsenal), 1977 v W (1)

Russell, R. (Rangers), 1978 v W; 1980 v B; 1984 v Y (3)

Shannon, R. (Dundee), 1987 v WG, Ei (2), Bel; 1988 v Bel, E (2) (6)

Sharp, G. (Everton), 1982 v E (1)

Sharp, R. (Dunfermline Ath), 1990 v N (sub) (1)

Simpson, N. (Aberdeen), 1982 v I (2), E; 1983 v EG, Sw (2), Bel; 1984 v Bel, EG, Y; 1985 v Sp (11)

Sinclair, G. (Dumbarton), 1977 v E (1)

Smith, G. (Rangers), 1978 v W (1)

Smith, H. G. (Hearts), 1987 v WG, Bel (2)

Sneddon, A. (Celtic), 1979 v US (1)

Speedie, D. (Chelsea), 1985 v Sp (1)

Stanton, P. (Hibernian), 1977 v Cz (1)

Stark, W. (Aberdeen), 1985 v Ic (1)

Stephen, R. (Dundee), 1983 v Bel (sub) (1)

Stevens, G. (Motherwell), 1977 v E (1)

Stewart, J. (Kilmarnock), 1978 v Sw, Cz; (with Middlesbrough), 1979 v P (3)

Stewart, R. (Dundee U), 1979 v P, N (2); (with West Ham U), 1980 v B (2), E (2), WG; 1981 v D; 1982 v I (2), E (12)

Strachan, G. (Aberdeen), 1980 v B (1)

Sturrock, P. (Dundee U), 1977 v Cz, W, Sw, E; 1978 v Sw, Cz; 1982 v Se, I, E (9)

Thomson, W. (Partick Th), 1977 v E (sub); 1978 v W; (with St Mirren), 1979 v US, N (2); 1980 v B (2), E (2), WG (10)

Tolmie, J. (Morton), 1980 v B (sub) (1)

Tortolano, J. (Hibernian), 1987 v WG, Ei (2)

Walker, A. (Celtic), 1988 v Bel (1)

Wallace, I. (Coventry C), 1978 v Sw (1)

Walsh, C. (Nottingham F), 1984 v EG, Sw (2), Bel; 1984 v EG (5)

Wark, J. (Ipswich T), 1977 v Cz, W, Sw; 1978 v W; 1979 v P; 1980 v Z (2), WG (8)

Watson, A. (Aberdeen), 1981 v Se, D; 1982 v D, I (sub) (4)

Watson, K. (Rangers), 1977 v E; 1978 v Sw (sub) (2)

Winnie, D. (St Mirren), 1988 v Bel (1)

Whyte, D. (Celtic), 1987 v Ei (2), Bel; 1988 v E (2); 1989 v N, Y; 1990 v Y, N (9)

Wilson, T. (St Mirren), 1983 v Sw (sub) (1)

Wilson, T. (Nottingham F), 1988 v E; 1989 v N, Y; 1990 v F (4)

Wright, P. (Aberdeen), 1989 v Y, F; (with QPR), 1990 v Y (sub) (3)

Wright, T. (Oldham Ath), 1987 v Bel (sub) (1)

WALES

Aizlewood, M. (Luton T), 1979 v E; 1981 v Ho (2)

Balcombe, S. (Leeds U), 1982 v F (sub) (1)

Bater, P. T. (Bristol R), 1977 v E, S (2)

Blackmore, C. (Manchester U), 1984 v N, Bul, Y (3)

Bodin, P. (Cardiff C), 1983 v Y (1)

Bowen, M. (Tottenham H), 1983 v N; 1984 v Bul, Y (3)

Boyle, T. (C Palace), 1982 v F (1)

Cegielski, W. (Wrexham), 1977 v E (sub), S (2)

Charles, J. M. (Swansea C), 1979 v E; 1981 v Ho (2)

Clark, J. (Manchester U), 1978 v S; (with Derby Co), 1979 v E (2)

Coleman, C. (Swansea C), 1990 v Pol (1)

Curtis, A. T. (Swansea C), 1977 v E (1)

Davies, A. (Manchester U), 1982 v F (2) Ho; 1983 v N, Y, Bul (6)
Davies, I. C. (Norwich C), 1978 v S (sub) (1)
Deacy, N. (PSV Eindhoven), 1977 v S (1)
Dibble, A. (Cardiff C), 1983 v Bul; 1984 v N, Bul (3)
Doyle, S. C. (Preston NE), 1979 v E (sub); 1984 (with Huddersfield T), v N (2)
Dwyer, P. J. (Cardiff C), 1979 v E (1)
Ebdon, M. (Everton), 1990 v Pol (1)
Edwards, R. I. (Chester), 1977 v S; 1978 v W (2)
Evans, A. (Bristol R), 1977 v E (1)
Freestone, R. (Chelsea), 1990 v Pol (1)
Gale, D. (Swansea C), 1983 v Bul; 1984 v N (sub) (2)
Giles, D. C. (Cardiff C), 1977 v S; 1978 v S; 1981 (with Swansea C), v Ho; 1983 (with C. Palace), v Y (4)
Giles, P. (Cardiff C), 1982 v F (2) Ho (3)
Griffith, C. (Cardiff C), 1990 v Pol (1)
Hall, G. D. (Chelsea), 1990 v Pol (1)
Hodges, G. (Wimbledon), 1983 v Y (sub), Bul (sub); 1984 v N, Bul, Y (6)
Holden, A. (Chester C), 1984 v Y (sub) (1)
Hopkins, J. (Fulham), 1982 v F (sub), Ho; 1983 v N, Y, Bul (5)
Hughes, M. (Manchester U), 1983 v N, Y; 1984 v N. Bul, Y (5)
Hughes, W. (WBA), 1977 v E, S; 1978 v S (3)
Jackett, K. (Watford), 1981 v Ho; 1982 v F (2)
James, R. M. (Swansea C), 1977 v E, S; 1978 v S (3)
Jones, F. (Wrexham), 1981 v Ho (1)
Jones, L. (Cardiff C), 1982 v F (2), Ho (3)
Jones, V. (Bristol R), 1979 v E; 1981 v Ho (2)
Kendall, M. (Tottenham H), 1978 v S (1)
Law, B. J. (QPR), 1990 v Pol (1)
Letheran, G. (Leeds U), 1977 v E, S (2)
Lewis, D. (Swansea C), 1982 v F (2), Ho; 1983 v N, Y, Bul; 1984 v N, Bul, Y (9)
Lewis, J. (Cardiff C), 1983 v N (1)
Loveridge, J. (Swansea C), 1982 v Ho; 1983 v N, Bul (3)
Lowndes, S. R. (Newport Co), 1979 v E; 1981 v Ho; 1984 (with Millwall), Bul, Y (4)
Maddy, P. (Cardiff C), 1982 v Ho; 1983 v N (sub) (2)

Marustik, C. (Swansea C), 1982 v F (2); 1983 v Y, Bul; 1984 v N, Bul, Y (7)
Melville, A. K. (Swansea C), 1990 v Pol (1)
Micallef, C. (Cardiff C), 1982 v F, Ho; 1983 v N (3)
Nardiello, D. (Coventry C), 1978 v S (1)
Nicholas, P. (C Palace), 1978 v S; 1979 v E; (with Arsenal), 1982 v F (3)
Nogan, K. (Luton T), 1990 v Pol (1)
Pascoe, C. (Swansea C), 1983 v Bul (sub); 1984 v N (sub), Bul, Y (4)
Perry, J. (Cardiff C), 1990 v Pol (1)
Phillips, D. (Plymouth Arg), 1984 v N, Bul, Y (3)
Phillips, L. (Swansea C), 1979 v E; (with Charlton Ath), 1983 v N (2)
Pontin, K. (Cardiff C), 1978 v S (1)
Price, P. (Luton T), 1981 v Ho (1)
Pugh, D. (Doncaster R), 1982 v F (2) (2)
Ratcliffe, K. (Everton), 1981 v Ho; 1982 v F (2)
Rees, A. (Birmingham C), 1984 v N (1)
Rees, J. (Luton T), 1990 v Pol (1)
Roberts, G. (Hull C), 1983 v Bul (1)
Roberts, J. G. (Wrexham), 1977 v E (1)
Rush, I. (Liverpool), 1981 v Ho; 1982 v F (2)
Sayer, P. A. (Cardiff C), 1977 v E, S (2)
Slatter, N. (Bristol R), 1983 v N, Y, Bul; 1984 v N, Bul, Y (6)
Speed, G. A. (Leeds U), 1990 v Pol (1)
Stevenson, N. (Swansea C), 1982 v F, Ho (2)
Stevenson, W. B. (Leeds U), 1977 v E, S; 1978 v S (3)
Thomas, Martin R. (Bristol R), 1979 v E; 1981 v Ho (2)
Thomas, Mickey R. (Wrexham), 1977 v E; 1978 v S (2)
Thomas, D. G. (Leeds U), 1977 v E; 1979 v E; 1984 v N (3)
Tibbott, L. (Ipswich T), 1977 v E, S (2)
Vaughan, N. (Newport Co), 1982 v F, Ho (2)
Walsh, I. P. (C Palace), 1979 v E; (with Swansea C), 1983 v Bul (2)
Williams, D. (Bristol R), 1983 v Y (1)
Williams, G. (Bristol R), 1983 v Y, Bul (2)
Wilmot, R. (Arsenal), 1982 v F (2), Ho; 1983 v N, Y; 1984 v Y (6)

FA Schools and Youth Games 1989–90

Under-16 Nordic Championships
5 Aug 1989 (at Stafford)
England 2 *(Lee, Berry)*

Norway 1   400
England: Foster (Stephenson); Fancutt (Jackson), Hughes (Everingham), Basham, Harriott, Caskey, Myers (Newcombe), Burke, Barmby, Nguyen (Berry), Lee

7 Aug 1989 (at Lilleshall)
England 2 *(Newcombe, Lee)*

Iceland 3   200
England: Stephenson (Foster); Harriott, Everingham (Hughes), Basham, Jackson (Fancutt), Caskey, Lee, Newcombe (Burke), Barmby, Berry (Nguyen), Myers.

8 Aug 1989 (at Sutton Coldfield)
England 2 *(Berry, Myers)*

Denmark 1   800
England: Foster (Stephenson); Fancutt (Jackson), Hughes, Basham (Everingham), Harriott, Newcombe, Lee, Burke (Barmby), Berry, Nguyen, Myers.

9 Aug 1989 (at Crewe)
England 3 *(Nguyen 2, Caskey)*

Sweden 2   1200

England: Stephenson (Foster); Harriott, Everingham (Hughes), Basham, Jackson (Fancutt), Caskey, Lee, Berry, Nguyen (Burke), Barmby, Myers (Newcombe).

11 Aug 1989 (at Burslem)
England 1 *(Nguyen)*

Finland 1   1500
England: Foster (Stephenson); Harriott, Hughes (Everingham), Basham, Jackson (Fancutt), Caskey, Lee, Berry (Burke), Barmby, Nguyen, Myers (Newcombe).

12 Aug 1989
England 2 *(Newcombe, Nguyen)*

Scandinavian Select 1   63,149
England: Foster (Stephenson); Fancutt (Jackson), Hughes (Everingham), Basham, Harriott, Caskey, Newcombe, Berry (Burke), Nguyen, Barmby, Myers (Lee).

UEFA Youth Championship
11 Oct 1989 (at Martigues)
France 0

England 0   8000
England: Walker; Kavanagh, Wright, Tuttle, Hendon, Hayward, Houghton, Rouse, Cole, Harkness, Small.

14 Nov 1989 (at Portsmouth)

England 1 *(Hayward)*

Czechoslovakia 0 5500

England: Walker; Kavanagh, Awford, Tuttle, Hendon, Hayward, Houghton, Rouse, Cole, Harkness, Small.

Under-16 tour to Italy

17 Oct 1989 (at Alassio)

Italy 1

England 1 *(Berry)* 500

England: Stephenson; Fancutt, Hughes, Harriott, Basham, Newcomhe, Burke, Berry, Barmby, Nguyen, Myers.

18 Oct 1989 (at Cairo, Italy)

USSR 0

England 0 150

England: Foster; Fancutt, Everingham, Newcombe (Berry), Basham, Jackson, Burke, Selley, Barmby, Nguyen, Lee (Myers).

19 Oct 1989 (at Alassio)

Turkey 1

England 3 *(Hughes, Barmby, og)* 150

England: Stephenson, Harriott, Hughes, Nguyen, Basham, Jackson, Selley, Myers, Barmby, Berry, Burke.

21 Oct 1989 (at Savona) Semi-Final

Scotland 1

England 1 *(Basham)*

Scotland won 10-9 on penalties

England: Foster; Harriott, Hughes, Myers, Basham, Jackson, Selley (Lee), Nguyen, Barmby, Berry, Burke.

23 Oct 1989 (at Genoa) Third place match

West Germany 2

England 1 *(Berry)*

England: Stephenson; Fancutt, Everingham (Lee), Newcombe (Selley), Basham, Harriott, Berry, Myers, Barmby, Nguyen, Burke.

Under-16 International

3 March 1990 (at Airdrie)

Scotland 4

England 1 *(Caskey)* 200

England: Foster; Fancutt, Hughes (Everingham), Caskey (Turner), Basham, Harriott, Burke (Bayley), Newcombe, Barmby, Nguyen (Forrester), Myers.

Under-17 International

22 May 1990 (at Wembley)

England 1 *(Clark (pen))*

France 3 38,751

England: Livingstone (Stanger); Hancock, Fowler, Makin, Webster (Burton), Flitcroft (Williams) (Redknapp), Flatts, Sinclair, Morah (Thompson), Clark, Doling.

Under-18 Internationals

28 Mar 1990 (at Wembley)

England 0

Denmark 0 80,000

England: Walker; Hendon, Minto, Hayward (Clark), Tuttle, Awford, Houghton, Rouse, Cole (Newhouse), Harkness, Small.

25 April 1990 (at Wembley)

England 1 *(Cole)*

Czechoslovakia 1 21,000

England: Walker; Hendon, Ullathorne (Taylor), Hayward, Tuttle, Awford, Houghton, Rouse, Cole, Harkness, Small.

15 May 1990 (at Wembley)

England 3 *(Harkness, Houghton, Newhouse)*

Poland 0 27,643

England: Walker (Livingstone); Hendon (Honeywood), Titterton, Hayward, Tuttle, Awford, Houghton (Small), Rouse (Burnett), Cole (Taylor), Newhouse, Harkness.

890

ENGLAND YOUTH INTERNATIONAL MATCHES 1947–90

Professionals. † *Abandoned.* UYT *UEFA Youth Tournament.* WYT *World Youth Tournament.*

v SCOTLAND

			E	S
1947	25 Oct	Doncaster	4	2
1948	30 Oct	Aberdeen	1	3
UYT1949	21 Apr	Utrecht	0	1
1950	4 Feb	Carlisle	7	1
1951	3 Feb	Kilmarnock	6	1
1952	15 Mar	Sunderland	3	1
1953	7 Feb	Glasgow	4	3
1954	6 Feb	Middlesbrough	2	1
1955	5 Mar	Kilmarnock	3	4
1956	3 Mar	Preston	2	2
1957	9 Mar	Aberdeen	3	1
1958	1 Mar	Hull	2	0
1959	28 Feb	Aberdeen	1	1
1960	27 Feb	Newcastle	1	1
1961	25 Feb	Elgin	3	2
1962	24 Feb	Peterborough	4	2
UYT1963	19 Apr	White City	1	0
1963	18 May	Dumfries	3	1
1964	22 Feb	Middlesbrough	1	1
1965	27 Feb	Inverness	1	2
1966	5 Feb	Hereford	5	3
1967	4 Feb	Aberdeen	0	1
UYT1967	1 Mar	Southampton	1	0
UYT1967	15 Mar	Dundee	0	0
1968	3 Feb	Walsall	0	5
1969	1 Feb	Stranraer	1	1
1970	31 Jan	Derby	1	2
1971	30 Jan	Greenock	1	2
1972	30 Jan	Bournemouth	2	0
1973	20 Jan	Kilmarnock	3	2
1974	26 Jan	Brighton	2	2
UYT1981	27 May	Aachen	0	1
UYT1982	23 Feb	Glasgow	0	1
UYT1982	23 Mar	Coventry	2	2
UYT1983	15 May	Birmingham	4	2
UI61983	5 Oct	Middlesbrough	3	1
UI61983	19 Oct	Motherwell	4	0
UYT1984	27 Nov	Craven Cottage	1	2
1985	8 Apr	Cannes	1	0
1986	25 Mar	Aberdeen	1	4

v WALES

			E	W
1948	28 Feb	High Wycombe	4	2
UYT1948	15 Apr	Shepherds Bush	4	0
1949	26 Feb	Swansea	0	0
1950	25 Feb	Worcester	1	0
1951	17 Feb	Wrexham	1	1
1952	23 Feb	Plymouth	6	0
1953	21 Feb	Swansea	4	2
1954	20 Feb	Derby	2	1
1955	19 Feb	Milford Haven	7	2
1956	18 Feb	Shrewsbury	5	1
1957	9 Feb	Cardiff	7	1
1958	15 Feb	Reading	8	2
1959	14 Feb	Portmadoc	3	0
1960	19 Mar	Canterbury	1	1
1961	18 Mar	Newtown	4	0
1962	17 Mar	Swindon	4	0
1963	16 Mar	Haverfordwest	1	0
1964	15 Mar	Leeds	2	1
1965	20 Mar	Newport	2	2
1966	19 Mar	Northampton	4	1
1967	18 Mar	Cwmbran	3	3
1968	16 Mar	Watford	2	3
1969	15 Mar	Haverfordwest	3	1
UYT1970	25 Feb	Newport	0	0
UYT1970	18 Mar	Leyton	1	2
1970	20 Apr	Reading	0	0
1971	20 Feb	Aberystwyth	1	2
1972	19 Feb	Swindon	4	0
1973	24 Feb	Portmadoc	4	1
UYT1974	9 Jan	West Bromwich	1	0
1974	2 Mar	Shrewsbury	2	1
UYT1974	13 Mar	Cardiff	0	1
UYT1976	11 Feb	Cardiff	1	0
UYT1976	3 Mar	Maine Rd	2	3
UYT1977	9 Mar	West Bromwich	3	0
UYT1977	23 Mar	Cardiff	1	1

v NORTHERN IRELAND

			E	NI
1948	15 May	Belfast	2	2
UYT1949	18 Apr	Haarlem	3	3
1949	14 May	Hull	4	2
1950	6 May	Belfast	0	1
1951	5 May	Liverpool	5	2
1952	19 Apr	Belfast	0	2
1953	11 Apr	Wolverhampton	0	0
UYT1954	10 Apr	Bruehl	5	0
1954	8 May	Newtownards	2	2
1955	14 May	Watford	3	0
1956	12 May	Belfast	0	1
1957	11 May	Leyton	6	2
1958	10 May	Bangor	2	4
1959	9 May	Liverpool	5	0
1960	14 May	Portadown	5	2
1961	13 May	Manchester	2	0
1962	12 May	Londonderry	1	2
UYT1963	23 Apr	Wembley	4	0
1963	11 May	Oldham	1	1
1964	25 Jan	Belfast	3	1
1965	22 Jan	Birkenhead	2	3
1966	26 Feb	Belfast	4	0
1967	25 Feb	Stockport	3	0
1968	23 Feb	Belfast	0	2
1969	28 Feb	Birkenhead	0	2
1970	28 Feb	Lurgan	1	3
1971	6 Mar	Blackpool	1	1
1972	11 Mar	Chester	1	1
UYT1972	17 May	Sabadell	4	0
1973	24 Mar	Telford	3	0
1974	19 Apr	Birkenhead	1	2
UYT1975	13 May	Kriens	3	0
UYT1980	16 May	Arnstadt	1	0
UYT1981	11 Feb	Walsall	1	0
UYT1981	11 Mar	Belfast	3	0

v ALGERIA

			E	A
1984	22 Apr	Cannes	3	0

v ARGENTINA

			E	A
*WYT1981	5 Oct	Sydney	1	1

v AUSTRIA

			E	A
UYT1949	19 Apr	Zeist	4	2
UYT1952	17 Apr	Barcelona	5	5
UYT1957	16 Apr	Barcelona	0	3
1958	4 Mar	Highbury	3	2
1958	1 June	Graz	4	3
UYT1960	20 Apr	Vienna	0	1
UYT1964	1 Apr	Rotterdam	2	1
1980	6 Sept	Pazin	0	1
UYT1981	29 May	Bonn	7	0
1981	3 Sept	Umag	3	0
1984	6 Sept	Izola	2	2

v AUSTRALIA

			E	A
*WYT1981	8 Oct	Sydney	1	1

v BELGIUM

			E	B
UYT1948	16 Apr	West Ham	3	1
UYT1951	22 Mar	Cannes	1	1
UYT1953	31 Mar	Brussels	2	0
†1956	7 Nov	Brussels	3	2
1957	13 Nov	Sheffield	2	0
UYT1965	15 Apr	Ludwigshafen	3	0
UYT1969	11 Mar	West Ham	1	0
UYT1969	26 Mar	Waregem	?	0
UYT1972	13 May	Palma	0	0
UYT1973	4 June	Viareggio	0	0
UYT1977	19 May	Lokeren	1	0
1979	17 Jan	Brussels	4	0
1980	8 Sept	Labia	6	1
1983	13 Apr	Birmingham	1	1
1988	20 May	Chatel	0	0

v BRAZIL

			E	B
1986	29 mar	Cannes	0	0
1986	13 may	Peking	1	2

v BULGARIA

			E	B
UYT1956	28 Mar	Salgotarjan	1	2
UYT1960	16 Apr	Graz	0	1
UYT1962	24 Apr	Ploesti	0	0
UYT1968	7 Apr	Nimes	0	0
UYT1979	31 May	Vienna	0	1

v CAMEROON

			E	C
*WYT1981	3 Oct	Sydney	2	0

v CHINA

			E	C
1983	31 Mar	Cannes	5	1
1985	26 Aug	Baku	0	2
1986	5 May	Peking	1	0

v CZECHOSLOVAKIA

			E	C
UYT1955	7 Apr	Lucca	0	1
UYT1966	21 May	Rijeka	2	3
UYT1969	20 May	Leipzig	3	1
UYT1979	24 May	Bischofshofen	3	0
1979	8 Sept	Pula	1	2
1982	11 Apr	Cannes	0	1
UYT1983	20 May	Highbury	1	1
UYT1989	26 Apr	Bystrica	0	0
UYT1989	14 Nov	Portsmouth	1	0
1989	25 Apr	Wembley	1	1

v DENMARK

			E	D
*1955	1 Oct	Plymouth	9	2
1956	20 May	Esbjerg	2	1
UYT1979	31 Oct	Esbjerg	3	1
UYT1980	26 Mar	Coventry	4	0
*1982	15 July	Stjordal	5	2
1983	16 July	Holbeck	0	1
1987	16 Feb	Maine Road	2	1
1990	28 Mar	Wembley	0	0

v EGYPT

			E	Eg
*WYT1981	11 Oct	Sydney	4	2

v FINLAND

			E	F
UYT1975	19 May	Berne	1	1

v FRANCE

			E	F
1957	24 Mar	Fontainebleau	1	0
1958	22 Mar	Eastbourne	0	1
UYT1966	23 May	Rijeka	1	2
UYT1967	11 May	Istanbul	2	0
*1968	25 Jan	Paris	0	1
UYT1978	8 Feb	Selhurst Park	3	1
UYT1978	1 Mar	Paris	0	0
UYT1979	2 June	Vienna	0	0
1982	12 Apr	Cannes	0	1
1983	2 Apr	Cannes	0	2
U161984	1 Mar	Watford	4	0
U161984	21 Mar	Bourg en Bresse	1	1
1984	23 Apr	Cannes	1	1
1986	31 Mar	Cannes	1	2
1986	11 May	Peking	1	1
1988	22 May	Monthey	1	2
UYT1988	15 Nov	Bradford	1	1
UYT1989	11 Oct	Martigues	0	0

v EAST GERMANY

			E	EG
UYT1958	7 Apr	Neunkirchen	1	0
1959	8 Mar	Zwickau	3	4
1960	2 Apr	Portsmouth	1	1
UYT1965	25 Apr	Essen	2	3
UYT1969	22 May	Magdeburg	0	4
UYT1973	10 June	Florence	3	2
UYT1984	25 May	Moscow	1	1
1988	21 May	Monthey	1	0

v WEST GERMANY

			E	WG
UYT1953	4 Apr	Boom	3	1
UYT1954	15 Apr	Gelsenkirchen	2	2
UYT1956	1 Apr	Sztalinvaros	2	1
1957	31 Mar	Oberhausen	4	1
1958	12 Mar	Bolton	1	2
1961	12 Mar	Flensberg	0	2

*1962	31 Mar	Northampton	1	0
*1967	14 Feb	Moenchengladbach	1	0
1975	25 Jan	Las Palmas	4	2
1976	14 Nov	Monte Carlo	1	1
UYT1979	28 May	Salzburg	2	0
1979	1 Sept	Pula	1	1
1983	5 Sept	Pazin	2	0

v GREECE

			E	G
UYT1957	18 Apr	Barcelona	2	3
UYT1959	2 Apr	Dimitrovo	4	0
UYT1977	23 May	Beveren	1	1
U161983	28 July	Puspokladany	1	0
UYT1988	26 Oct	Tranmere	5	0
UYT1989	8 Mar	Xanthi	3	0

v HOLLAND

			E	N
UYT1948	17 Apr	Tottenham	3	2
UYT1951	26 Mar	Cannes	2	1
*1954	21 Nov	Arnhem	2	3
*1955	5 Nov	Norwich	3	1
1957	2 Mar	Brentford	5	5
UYT1957	14 Apr	Barcelona	1	2
1957	2 Oct	Amsterdam	3	2
1961	9 Mar	Utrecht	0	1
*1962	31 Jan	Brighton	4	0
UYT1962	22 Apr	Ploesti	0	3
UYT1963	13 Apr	Wimbledon	5	0
UYT1968	9 Apr	Nimes	1	0
UYT1974	13 Feb	West Bromwich	1	1
UYT1974	27 Feb	The Hague	1	0
UYT1979	23 May	Halle	1	0
1982	9 Apr	Cannes	1	0
1985	7 Apr	Cannes	1	3
1987	1 Aug	Wembley	3	1

v HUNGARY

			E	H
UYT1954	11 Apr	Dusseldorf	1	3
UYT1956	31 Mar	Tatabanya	2	4
*1956	23 Oct	Tottenham	2	1
*1956	25 Oct	Sunderland	2	1
UYT1965	21 Apr	Wuppertal	5	0
UYT1975	16 May	Olten	3	1
UYT1977	10 Oct	Las Palmas	3	0
1979	5 Sept	Pula	2	0
1980	11 Sept	Pula	1	2
1981	7 Sept	Porec	4	0
U161983	29 July	Debrecen	1	2
1983	3 Sept	Umag	3	2
1986	30 Mar	Cannes	2	0

v ICELAND

			E	I
UYT1973	31 May	Viareggio	2	0
UYT1977	21 May	Turnhout	0	0
U161983	7 Sept	Reykjavik	2	1
U161983	19 Sept	Blackburn	4	0
1983	12 Oct	Reykjavik	3	0
1983	1 Nov	Selhurst Park	3	0
UYT1984	16 Oct	Maine Road	5	3
1985	11 Sept	Reykjevik	5	0

v REPUBLIC OF IRELAND

			E	RI
UYT1953	5 Apr	Leuven	2	0
UYT1964	30 Mar	Middleburg	6	0
UYT1968	7 Feb	Dublin	0	0
UYT1968	28 Feb	Portsmouth	4	1
UYT1970	14 Jan	Dublin	4	0
UYT1970	4 Feb	Luton	10	0
UYT1975	9 May	Brunnen	1	0
UYT1985	26 Feb	Dublin	1	0
1986	25 Feb	Leeds	2	0
1987	17 Feb	Stoke	2	0
1988	20 Sept	Dublin	2	0

v ISRAEL

			E	I
*1962	20 May	Tel Aviv	3	1
*1962	22 May	Haifa	1	2

v ITALY

			E	I
UYT1958	13 Apr	Luxembourg	0	1
UYT1959	25 Mar	Sofia	0	3
UYT1961	4 Apr	Braga	2	3

			E	
UYT1965	23 Apr	Marl-Huels	3	1
UYT1966	25 May	Rijeka	1	1
UYT1967	5 May	Izmir	1	0
1973	14 Feb	Cava dei Tirreni	0	1
1973	14 Mar	Highbury	1	0
UYT1973	6 June	Viareggio	1	0
1978	19 Nov	Monte Carlo	1	2
UYT1979	28 Feb	Rome	1	0
UYT1979	4 Apr	Villa Park	2	0
UYT1983	22 May	Watford	1	1
1983	20 Apr	Cannes	1	0
1985	5 Apr	Cannes	2	2

v LUXEMBOURG

			E	L
UYT1950	25 May	Vienna	1	2
UYT1954	17 Apr	Bad Neuenahr	0	2
1957	2 Feb	West Ham	7	1
1957	17 Nov	Luxembourg	3	0
UYT1958	9 Apr	Eschsalzette	5	0
UYT1984	29 May	Moscow	2	0

v MALTA

			E	M
UYT1969	18 May	Wolfen	6	0
UYT1979	26 May	Salzburg	3	0

v MEXICO

			E	M
1983	18 Apr	Cannes	4	0
1985	29 Aug	Baku	0	1

v NORWAY

			E	N
*1982	13 July	Levanger	1	4
1983	14 July	Korsor	1	0

v PARAGUAY

			E	P
1985	24 Aug	Baku	2	2

v POLAND

			E	P
UYT1960	18 Apr	Graz	4	2
UYT1964	26 Mar	Breda	1	1
UYT1971	26 May	Presov	0	0
UYT1972	20 May	Valencia	1	0
1975	21 Jan	Las Palmas	1	1
UYT1978	9 May	Chorzow	0	2
1979	3 Sept	Porac	0	1
UYT1980	25 May	Leipzig	2	1
*1982	17 July	Steinkver	3	2
1983	12 July	Slagelse	1	0
1990	15 May	Wembley	3	0

v PORTUGAL

			E	P
UYT1954	18 Apr	Bonn	0	2
UYT1961	2 Apr	Lisbon	0	4
UYT1964	3 Apr	The Hague	4	0
UYT1971	30 May	Prague	3	0
1978	13 Nov	Monte Carlo	2	0
UYT1980	18 May	Rosslau	1	1
1982	7 Apr	Cannes	3	0

v QATAR

			E	Q
*WYT1981	14 Oct	Sydney	1	2
1983	4 Apr	Cannes	1	1

v RUMANIA

			E	R
1957	15 Oct	Tottenham	4	2
UYT1958	11 Apr	Luxembourg	1	0
UYT1959	31 Mar	Pazardjic	1	2
UYT1963	15 Apr	Highbury	3	0
*WYT1981	17 Oct	Adelaide	0	1

v SAAR

			E	SAAR
UYT1954	13 Apr	Dortmund	1	1
UYT1955	9 Apr	Prato	3	1

v SPAIN

			E	S
UYT1952	15 Apr	Barcelona	1	4
1957	26 Sept	Birmingham	4	4
UYT1958	5 Apr	Saarbrucken	2	2
*1958	8 Oct	Madrid	4	2
UYT1961	30 Mar	Lisbon	0	0
*1964	27 Feb	Murcia	2	1

			E	
UYT1964	5 Apr	Amsterdam	4	0
UYT1965	17 Apr	Heilbronn	0	0
*1966	30 Mar	Swindon	3	0
UYT1967	7 May	Manisa	2	1
*1971	31 Mar	Pamplona	2	3
*1971	20 Apr	Luton	1	1
1972	9 Feb	Alicante	0	0
1972	15 Mar	Sheffield	4	1
UYT1975	25 Feb	Bristol	1	1
UYT1975	18 Mar	Madrid	1	0
1976	12 Nov	Monte Carlo	3	0
UYT1978	7 May	Bukowno	1	0
1978	17 Nov	Monte Carlo	1	1
UYT1981	25 May	Siegen	1	2
UYT1983	13 Mav	Stoke	1	0

v SWEDEN

			E	S
UYT1971	24 May	Poprad	1	0
1981	5 Sept	Pazin	3	2
1984	10 Sept	Rovinj	1	1
1986	10 Nov	West Bromwich	3	3

v SWITZERLAND

			E	S
UYT1950	26 May	Stockerau	2	1
UYT1951	27 Mar	Nice	3	1
UYT1952	13 Apr	Barcelona	4	0
UYT1955	11 Apr	Florence	0	0
1956	11 Mar	Schaffhausen	2	0
1956	13 Oct	Brighton	2	2
1958	26 May	Zurich	3	0
*1960	8 Oct	Leyton	4	3
*†1962	22 Nov	Coventry	1	0
*1963	21 Mar	Bienne	7	1
UYT1973	2 June	Forte dei Marim	2	0
UYT1975	11 May	Buochs	4	0
1980	4 Sept	Rovinj	3	0
*1982	6 Sept	Porec	2	0
U161983	26 July	Hajduboszormeny	4	0
1983	1 Sept	Porec	4	2
1988	19 May	Sion	2	0

v THAILAND

			E	T
1986	7 May	Peking	1	2

v TURKEY

			E	T
UYT1959	29 Mar	Dimitrovo	1	1
UYT1978	5 May	Wodzislaw	1	1

v URUGUAY

			E	U
1977	9 Oct	Las Palmas	1	1

v USSR

			E	USSR
UYT1963	17 Apr	Tottenham	2	0
UYT1967	13 May	Istanbul	0	1
UYT1968	11 Apr	Nimes	1	1
UYT1971	28 May	Prague	1	1
1978	10 Oct	Las Palmas	1	0
*1982	4 Sept	Umag	1	0
1983	29 Mar	Cannes	0	0
UYT1983	17 May	Aston Villa	0	2
U161984	3 May	Ludwigsburg	0	1
UYT1984	27 May	Moscow	1	1
1984	8 Sept	Porec	1	0
1985	3 Apr	Cannes	2	1

v YUGOSLAVIA

			E	Y
UYT1953	2 April	Liège	1	1
1958	4 Feb	Chelsea	2	2
UYT1962	20 Apr	Ploesti	0	5
UYT1967	9 May	Izmir	1	1
UYT1971	22 May	Bardejor	1	0
UYT1972	18 May	Barcelona	1	0
1976	16 Nov	Monte Carlo	0	3
1978	15 Nov	Monte Carlo	1	1
UYT1980	20 May	Altenburg	2	0
1981	10 Sept	Pula	5	0
*1982	9 Sept	Pula	1	0
U161983	25 July	Debrecen	4	4
**1983	8 Sept	Pula	2	2
U161984	5 May	Boblingen	1	0
1984	12 Sept	Buje	1	4

SCHOOLS FOOTBALL 1989–90

ESFA INTER-ASSOCIATION TROPHY 1989–90

Fourth Round

Barnsley v Salford	1-2
Walsall v Sheffield	2-3
North Hertfordshire v West Suffolk	0-2
West London v South East Sussex	1-1, 6-1
Liverpool v Coventry	1-1, 2-0
Blackpool v Nuneaton	2-3
Redbridge v Worksop	3-2
Havant v North Avon	4-2
Manchester v Rotherham	3-0
Cambridge v Sunderland	2-3
West Cornwall v Cheltenham	1-1, 3-2
Aldershot v Waltham Forest	0-1
Vale White Horse v Southampton	1-2
Ipswich v Norwich	2-0
Halton v Hull	1-3
Doncaster v Derby	1-1, 1-0

Fifth Round

Salford v Sheffield	1-3
West Suffolk v West London	0-0, 4-1

Liverpool v Nuneaton	0-0, 4-1
Redbridge v Havant	1-0
Manchester v Sunderland	2-2, 0-2
West Cornwall v Waltham Forest	0-2
Southampton v Ipswich	2-0
Hull v Doncaster	1-1, 2-1

Sixth Round

Sheffield v West Suffolk	3-1
Liverpool v Redbridge	3-1
Sunderland v Waltham Forest	2-0
Southampton v Hull	1-1, 1-3

Semi-Finals

Sheffield v Liverpool	2-2, 2-1
Sunderland v Hull	2-0

Final

Sheffield v Sunderland	2-1, 4-3

E.S.F.A. MITRE SPORTS INTER COUNTY COMPETITION 1989/90

Round 1:

Lincolnshire (Reg. III) v Gt Manchester (Reg. II)	0-5

Round 2:

Berkshire (Reg. V) v Gt Manchester (Reg. II)	1-3
Northumberland (Reg. I) v Essex (Reg. IV)	4-1

Final:

Gt Manchester (Reg. II) v Northumberland (Reg. I) 3-1
*(at Stockport County F.C. Ground
on Monday, 7th May, 1990)*

E.S.F.A. MITRE SPORTS INTER COUNTY COMPETITION-HONOURS LIST

	Winners	*Runners-up*
1978	Devon and South Yorkshire	Joint Holders
1979	Berkshire	Essex
1980	Berkshire	Durham
1981	Merseyside	Middlesex
1982	Humberside	Merseyside
1983	Greater Manchester	Humberside
1984	Hampshire	Durham
1985	Middlesex	Hampshire
1986	Merseyside	Bedfordshire
1987	Northumberland	Hertfordshire
1988	Northumberland	Avon
1989	West Midlands	Lincolnshire
1990	Greater Manchester	Northumberland

ESFA NABISCO GROUP TROPHY 1989–90

Second Round

Lancashire A v Merseyside A	1-4
Lancashire B v Cheshire A	4-3
Durham A v South Yorkshire	2-2, 3-1
Cleveland v Durham B	2-0
South Yorkshire B v Humberside A	1-0
Nottinghamshire B v Leicestershire	0-2
Greater Manchester B v Cheshire B	1-4
Derbyshire v West Midlands B	3-1
Kent v Berkshire	2-2, 1-5
Hampshire A v Kent B	3-1
Norfolk v Essex A	1-1, 3-2
Herfordshire v Essex B	4-0
Devon v Dorset	6-0
Avon v Hampshire B	2-4
Hereford & Worcester v West Midlands A	3-3, 0-1
Buckinghamshire v Shropshire A	4-3

Third Round

Merseyside A v Lancashire B	5-2
Durham A v Cleveland	1-1, 1-3
South Yorkshire B v Leicestershire	2-0

Cheshire B v Derbyshire	0-2
Berkshire v Hampshire A	3-4
Norfolk v Herfordshire	1-0
Devon v Hampshire B	0-2
West Midlands A v Buckinghamshire	3-2

Fourth Round

Merseyside A v Cleveland	2-2, 2-1
South Yorkshire B v Derbyshire	3-0
Hampshire A v Norfolk	2-0
Hampshire B v West Midlands A	1-0

Semi-Finals

Merseyside A (Campion School, Liverpool) v South Yorkshire (Brinsworth School, Rotherham)	2-1
Hampshire A (Cowes High School, Isle of Wight) v Hampshire B (West Park School, Southampton)	2-1

Final

Merseyside A v Hampshire A	3-0

VICTORY SHIELD 1989–90 (Under-15)

Wales), Northern Ireland 3 – February, Cwmbran
England 2, Northern 1 – 26 February, Sheffield
Northern Ireland 2, Scotland 1 – 16 March, Coleraine
England 3, Wales 2 – 31 March, Leicester
Wales 1, Scotland 1 – 6 April, Cardiff
Scotland 0, England 0 – 21 April, Dingwall

	P	W	D	L	F	A	Pts
England	3	2	1	0	5	2	5
Northern Ireland	3	2	0	1	5	3	4
Scotland	3	0	2	1	2	3	2
Wales	3	0	1	2	3	7	1

CENTENARY SHIELD 1989–90 (Under-18)

Wales 0, England 1 – 17 March, Abergavenny
Switzerland 3, England 2 – 15 May, Kreuzlingen
Switzerland 5, Wales 0 – 29 May, Menmenziken

	P	W	D	L	F	A	Pts
Switzerland	2	2	0	0	8	2	4
England	2	1	0	1	3	3	2
Wales	2	0	0	2	0	6	0

ESFA BARCLAYS BANK COMPETITION 1989/90

Second Round

Surrey A v Hampshire A	1-1, 2-1
Hampshire B v Middlesex A	5-2
Dorset v Avon A	7-1
Devon v Somerset	2-2, 1-2
Leicestershire B v Northamptonshire	3-0
Norfolk W/O Suffolk Scr.	
Hertfordshire A v Inner London B	4-1
Hertfordshire B v Kent B	1-2
West Midlands A v Hereford & Worcs	5-0
West Midlands B v Gloucestershire	7-1
Greater Manchester A v Clwyd	1-1, 2-1
Greater Manchester B v Merseyside B	2-1
Northumberland A v North Yorkshire A	0-4
Durham v Lancashire	3-0
North Yorkshire B v South Yorkshire A	2-2, 2-4
Humberside v South Yorkshire B	0-0, 0-5

Third Round

Surrey A v Hampshire B	3-0
Dorset v Somerset	0-2
Leicestershire B v Norfolk	1-0

Hertfordshire A v Kent B	2-3
West Midlands A v West Midlands B	3-4
Greater Manchester A v Greater Manchester B	1-0
North Yorkshire A v Durham	3-3, 0-3
South Yorkshire A v South Yorkshire B	0-6

Quarter-Finals

Surrey A v Somerset	3-1
Leicestershire B v Kent B	0-2
West Midlands B v Greater Manchester A	0-1
Durham v South Yorkshire B	1-2

Semi-Finals

Surrey A (Wilson's School, Wallington) v Kent B (Harvey Grammar, Folkestone)	0-1
Greater Manchester A (Xaverian Coll. Manchester v South Yorkshire B (Barnsley Sixth Form College)	0-1

Final

Kent B v South Yorkshire	0-1

ENGLAND'S INTERNATIONAL PROGRAMME 1990

U15
England 2 *(Smith, Boachie)*, Northern Ireland 1, Sheffield F.C. – 26 February

U18
England 0, Holland 0, Sunderland F.C. – 5 March

U15
England 1 *(Forrester)*, France 1, Wembley Stadium – 10 March

U18
Wales 0, England 1 *(Price)*, Abergavenny – 17 March

U15
England 3 *(Forrester, Thornley, Thomson*, Wales 2, Leicester F.C. – 31 March

U15
Scotland 0, England 0, Dingwall – 21 April

Italy 2, England 2 *(Clarke, Binks)*, Cortefranca Iseo – 1 May

U15
West Germany 2, England 0, Munich – 8 May

U15
West Germany 0, England 4 *(Sharp, Binks, Smith, Tinkler)*, Berlin – 10 May

U18
Switzerland 3, England 2, Kreuzlingen – 15 May

U18
Switzerland 1, England 1, Neuhausen – 17 May

U15
England 1, Holland 0, Wembley Stadium – 2 June

SOUTH AMERICA

COPA LIBERTADORES
(South American Cup) 1990

Group 1

	P	W	D	L	F	A	Pts
Emelec (Ecu)	6	2	2	2	9	8	6
The Strongest (Bol)	6	3	0	3	8	7	6
Oriente (Bol)	6	2	2	2	6	7	6
Barcelona (Ecu)	6	2	2	2	6	7	6

Play-off third place: Oriente v Barcelona 3-2, 1-3; Barcelona won on penalties.

Group 2

	P	W	D	L	F	A	Pts
Independiente (Arg)	2	1	1	0	1	0	3
River Plate (Arg)	2	0	1	1	0	1	1

(Colombian clubs not represented because championship abandoned).

Group 3

	P	W	D	L	F	A	Pts
Colo Colo (Chi)	6	3	2	1	9	5	8
Univ Catolica (Chi)	6	2	3	1	6	4	7
Union Huaral (Per)	6	1	3	2	5	9	5
Sporting Cristal (Per)	6	1	2	3	4	6	4

Group 4

	P	W	D	L	F	A	Pts
Progreso (Uru)*	7	3	3	1	11	4	9
Defensor (Uru)*	7	2	3	2	5	7	7
Pepeganga (Ven)	6	3	0	3	4	5	6
Mineros (Ven)	6	1	2	3	5	9	4

Progreso and Defensor played extra game to decide group winners.

Group 5

	P	W	D	L	F	A	Pts
Olimpia (Para)	6	3	1	2	9	8	7
Cerro Porteno (Para)	6	2	2	2	8	8	6
Vasco da Gama (Br)	6	2	2	2	5	5	6
Gremio (Br)	6	1	3	2	5	6	5

Tournament not completed at time of going to press.

South American Super Cup

First Round First Leg
Flamengo 0, Argentinos Juniors 1
Estudiantes 3, Penarol 0
Olimpia 2, Cruzeiro 0
Nacional (Uru) 2, Nacional (Col) 1
Santos 1, Independiente 2
River Plate 2, Gremio 1

First Round Second Leg
Argentinos Juniors 2, Flamengo 1
Argentinos Juniors won on aggregate: 4 pts, goals 3-1
Penarol 2, Estudiantes 0
Estudiantes won on aggregate: 2-2 pts, goals 3-2
Independiente 2, Santos 0
Independiente won on aggregate: 4 pts, goals 4-1
Gremio 2, River Plate 1
Gremio won 4-1 on penalties after 2-2 pts, goals 3-3
Nacional (Col) 2, Nacional (Uru) 0
Nacional (Colombia) won on aggregate: 2-2 pts, goals 3-2
Cruzeiro 3, Olimpia 0
Cruzeiro won on aggregate: 2-2 pts, goals 3-2

Second Round First Leg
Nacional (Col) 2, Independiente 2
Boca Juniors 0, Racing 0
Gremio 0, Estudiantes 1
Cruzeiro 1, Argentinos Juniors 1

Second Round Second Leg
Racing 1, Boca Juniors 2
Boca Juniors won on aggregate: 3-1 pts, 2-1 goals
Independiente 2, Nacional (Col) 0
Independiente won on aggregate: 3-1 pts, goals 4-2
Estudiantes 0, Gremio 3
Gremio won on aggregate: 2-2 pts, 3-1 goals
Argentinos Juniors 2, Cruzeiro 0
Argentinos Juniors won on aggregate: 3-1 pts, goals 3-1

Semi-finals First Leg
Argentinos Juniors 0, Independiente 1
Gremio 0, Boca Juniors 0

Semi-finals Second Leg
Independiente 2, Agentinos Juniors 1
Independiente won on aggregate: 4 pts, goals 3-1
Boca Juniors 2, Gremio 0
Boca Juniors won on aggregate: 3-1 pts, goals 2-0

Final First Leg
Boca Juniors 0, Independiente 0

Final Second Leg
Independiente 0, Boca Juniors 0
Boca Juniors won 5-3 on penalties

SOUTH AMERICA
League Champions

Argentina: Independiente
Bolivia: The Strongest
Brazil: Vasco da Gama
Chile: Colo Colo
Colombia: championship abandoned
Ecuador: Barcelona
Paraguay: Olimpia
Peru: Sporting Cristal
Uruguay: Progreso
Venezuela: Mineros

CONCACAF Champions Cup Final
UNAM (Mexico) v Pinar del Rio (Cuba) 1-1, 3-1

OTHER INTERNATIONAL RESULTS 1989

January
Iran 2, Japan 2
Iran 3, Japan 1
Senegal 1, Zaire 1
Senegal 2, Zaire 1

March
Guatemala 3, El Salvador 0
Tunisia 0, Egypt 0
Algeria 1, Morocco 1
Ethiopia 1, Malawi 1
Qatar 1, Malaysia 0
Ethiopia 1, Malawi 0
Ivory Coast 0, Guinea 0
Ethiopia 0, Zambia 1
Senegal 2, Morocco 1

April
Ethiopia 2, Zambia 2
Algeria 2, Tunisia 0
Angola 1, Mozambique 1
Faroe Islands 1, Canada 0
Trinidad & Tobago 1, Bermuda 1
Faroe Islands 0, Canada 1
Trinidad & Tobago 0, Bermuda 1

May
South Korea 1, Japan 0
Singapore 1, Indonesia 2
Morocco 1, Algeria 0

June
Ivory Coast 1, Zaire 1
Malawi 1, Tunisia 0
Gabon 0, Zaire 0
Zimbabwe 0, Zambia 0
Canada 0, Costa Rica 1

July
Mozambique 0, Gabon 1
Malawi 0, Mozambique 1
Kenya 0, Zaire 1
Malawi 0, Mozambique 2

August
Tunisia 3, Malawi 0
North Korea 1, Atletico Mineiro 0*
South Korea 1, Egypt 0
North Korea 2, Atletico Mineiro 0*

November
Tunisia 0, Algeria 0
Tunisia 0, Egypt 4
Senegal 3, Central Africa 0
Mexico 2, Ararat 0*

December
Senegal 1, Sierra Leone 0
*listed by FIFA as a full international!

World Military Championships
Italy 3, Morocco 1

Arab Champions Cup
Widad Casablanca 3, Hilal (Saudi Arabia) 1

African Champions Cup
Raja Casablanca 1, 0, Mouloudia Oran 0, 1
(Raja won 4-2 on penalties)

African Cup Winners' Cup
Al Merreikh (Sudan) 1, 0, Bendel United (Nigeria) 0, 0

East and Central African Challenge Cup
Final: Malawi 3, Uganda 3
Uganda won 2-1 on penalties)

African Cup

Group A
Algeria 5, Nigeria 1
Ivory Coast 3, Egypt 1
Algeria 3, Ivory Coast 0
Nigeria 1, Egypt 0
Algeria 2, Egypt 0
Nigeria 1, Ivory Coast 0

Group B
Cameroon 0, Zambia 1
Senegal 0, Kenya 0
Cameroon 0, Senegal 2
Zambia 1, Kenya 0
Cameroon 2, Kenya 0
Zambia 1, Senegal 1

Semi-finals
Algeria 2, Senegal 1
Nigeria 2, Zambia 0

Match for Third Place
Senegal 0, Zambia 1

Final in Algiers
Algeria 1, Nigeria 0

OLYMPIC FOOTBALL

Previous medallists

1896 Athens*	1 Denmark	1928 Amsterdam	1 Uruguay	1964 Tokyo	1 Hungary		
	2 Greece		2 Argentina		2 Czechoslovakia		
1900 Paris*	1 Great Britain		3 Italy		3 East Germany		
	2 France	1932 Los Angeles no tournament		1968 Mexico City	1 Hungary		
1904 St Louis**	1 Canada	1936 Berlin	1 Italy		2 Bulgaria		
	2 USA		2 Austria		3 Japan		
1908 London	1 Great Britain		3 Norway	1972 Munich	1 Poland		
	2 Denmark	1948 London	1 Sweden		2 Hungary		
	3 Holland		2 Yugoslavia		3 E Germany/USSR		
1912 Stockholm	1 England		3 Denmark	1976 Montreal	1 East Germany		
	2 Denmark	1952 Helsinki	1 Hungary		2 Poland		
	3 Holland		2 Yugoslavia		3 USSR		
1920 Antwerp	1 Belgium		3 Sweden	1980 Moscow	1 Czechoslovakia		
	2 Spain	1956 Melbourne	1 USSR		2 East Germany		
	3 Holland		2 Yugoslavia		3 USSR		
1924 Paris	1 Uruguay		3 Bulgaria	1984 Los Angeles	1 France		
	2 Switzerland	1960 Rome	1 Yugoslavia		2 Brazil		
	3 Sweden		2 Denmark		3 Yugoslavia		
			3 Hungary	1988 Seoul	1 USSR		
* No official tournament					2 Brazil		
** No official tournament but gold medal later awarded by IOC					3 West Germany		

EUROPEAN
CLUB
FOOTBALL

EUROPEAN CHAMPION CLUBS CUP

EUROPEAN CUP-WINNERS' CUP

FAIRS CUP AND UEFA CUP

BRITISH AND IRISH CLUBS IN EUROPE

EUROPEAN CLUB DIRECTORY

EUROPEAN NATIONS SECTION

WORLD CLUB CHAMPIONSHIP

EUROPEAN SUPER CUP

EUROPEAN CUP

EUROPEAN CUP FINALS 1956–89

Year	Winners		Runners-up		Venue	Attendance	Referee
1956	Real Madrid	4	Reims	3	Paris	38,000	Ellis (E)
1957	Real Madrid	2	Fiorentina	0	Madrid	124,000	Horn (Ho)
1958	Real Madrid	3	AC Milan	2 *(aet)*	Brussels	67,000	Alsteen (Bel)
1959	Real Madrid	2	Reims	0	Stuttgart	80,000	Dutsch (WG)
1960	Real Madrid	7	Eintracht Frankfurt	3	Glasgow	135,000	Mowat (S)
1961	Benfica	3	Barcelona	2	Berne	28,000	Dienst (Sw)
1962	Benfica	5	Real Madrid	3	Amsterdam	65,000	Horn (Ho)
1963	AC Milan	2	Benfica	1	Wembley	45,000	Holland (E)
1964	Internazionale	3	Real Madrid	1	Vienna	74,000	Stoll (A)
1965	Internazionale	1	Benfica	0	Milan	80,000	Dienst (Sw)
1966	Real Madrid	2	Partizan Belgrade	1	Brussels	55,000	Kreitlein (WG)
1967	Celtic	2	Internazionale	1	Lisbon	56,000	Tschenscher (WG)
1968	Manchester U	4	Benfica	1 *(aet)*	Wembley	100,000	Lo Bello (I)
1969	AC Milan	4	Ajax	1	Madrid	50,000	Ortiz (Sp)
1970	Feyenoord	2	Celtic	1 *(aet)*	Milan	50,000	Lo Bello (I)
1971	Ajax	2	Panathinaikos	0	Wembley	90,000	Taylor (E)
1972	Ajax	2	Internazionale	0	Rotterdam	67,000	Helies (F)
1973	Ajax	1	Juventus	0	Belgrade	93,500	Guglovic (Y)
1974	Bayern Munich	1	Atletico Madrid	1	Brussels	65,000	Loraux (Bel)
Replay	Bayern Munich	4	Atletico Madrid	0	Brussels	65,000	Delcourt (Bel)
1975	Bayern Munich	2	Leeds U	0	Paris	50,000	Kitabdjian (F)
1976	Bayern Munich	1	St Etienne	0	Glasgow	54,864	Palotai (H)
1977	Liverpool	3	Moenchengladbach	1	Rome	57,000	Wurtz (F)
1978	Liverpool	1	FC Brugge	0	Wembley	92,000	Corver (Ho)
1979	Nottingham F	1	Malmo	0	Munich	57,500	Linemayr (A)
1980	Nottingham F	1	Hamburg	0	Madrid	50,000	Garrido (P)
1981	Liverpool	1	Real Madrid	0	Paris	48,360	Palotai (H)
1982	Aston Villa	1	Bayern Munich	0	Rotterdam	46,000	Konrath (F)
1983	Hamburg	1	Juventus	0	Athens	75,000	Rainea (R)
1984	Liverpool	1	Roma	1	Rome	69,693	Fredriksson (Se)
	(aet; Liverpool won 4-2 on penalties)						
1985	Juventus	1	Liverpool	0	Brussels	58,000	Daina (SW)
1986	Steaua Bucharest	0	Barcelona	0	Seville	70,000	Vautrot (F)
	(aet; Steaua won 2-0 on penalties)						
1987	Porto	2	Bayern Munich	1	Vienna	59,000	Ponnet (Bel)
1988	PSV Eindhoven	0	Benfica	0	Stuttgart	70,000	Agnolin (I)
	(aet; PSV won 6-5 on penalties)						
1989	AC Milan	4	Steaua Bucharest	0	Barcelona	97,000	Tritschler (WG)

Frank Rijkaard (white shirt) powers through for AC Milan's goal in the European Cup Final against Benfica.
(Colorsport)

EUROPEAN CUP 1989–90

First Round, First Leg

Derry (0) 1 (*Carlyle 74*), Benfica (0) 2 (*Thern 59, Ricardo 64*) 12,500

Dynamo Dresden (0) 1 (*Lieberam 75*), AEK Athens (0) 0 33,000

Honved (0) 1 (*Fodor 55*), Vojvodina (0) 0 10,000

Linfield (0) 1 (*Mooney 88 pen*), Dnepr (1) 2 (*Kudritski 9, 53*) 1235

Malmo (0) 1 (*Lindman 75*), Internazionale (0) 0 20,023

Marseille (0) 3 (*Sauzee 62, Papin 67, Vercruysse 81*), Brondby (0) 0 33,000

AC Milan (2) 4 (*Stroppa 7, Massaro 39, 69, Evani 80*), HJK Helsinki (0) 0 41,205

PSV Eindhoven (3) 3 (*Kieft 2, Ellerman 9, Romario 35*), Lucerne (0) 0 18,900

Rangers (1) 1 (*Walters 27 pen*), Bayern Munich (1) 3 (*Kogl 29, Thon 46, Augenthaler 64*) 42,000

Rosenborg (0) 0, Mechelen (0) 0 10,400

Ruch Chorzow (1) 1 (*Szewczyk 43*), CSKA Sofia (1) 1 (*Penev 18*) 25,000

Sliema Wanderers (0) 1 (*Walker 57*), 17 Nentori (0) 0 2000

Sparta Prague (0) 3 (*Cabala 57, Bilek 74, 78*), Fenerbahce (1) 1 (*Hakan 19*) 16,050

Spora (0) 0, Real Madrid (1) 3 (*Butragueno 26, Michel 67 pen, 70*) 6500 *in Saarbrucken*

Steaua (2) 4 (*Petrescu 30, Hagi 41 pen, Balint 83, Mujnai 85*), Fram (0) 0 10,000

Tirol (2) 6 (*Peischl 7, Muller 10 pen, Westerthaler 57, Pacult 72, 74, Hartnagl 80*), Omonia (0) 0 13,000

First Round, Second Leg

AEK Athens (3) 5 (*Manolas 27, Okonski 34 pen, Savidis 38, 60, Savavski 81*), Dynamo Dresden (1) 3 (*Gutschov 9, Lieberam 63, Minge 84*) 32,000

Bayern Munich (0) 0, Rangers (0) 0 34,000

Benfica (1) 4 (*Magnusson 32, Garcia 61, Ricardo 69, Aldair 80*), Derry (0) 0 30,000

Brondby (0) 1 (*Olsen 54*), Marseille (0) 1 (*Papin 64*) 10,300

CSKA Sofia (2) 5 (*Georgiev 20, 48, Bakalov 25, Penez 75, Vitanov 89*), Ruch Chorzow (0) 1 (*Warzycha 83*) 16,000

Dnepr (1) 1 (*Sohn 7*), Linfield (0) 0 30,000

Fenerbahce (0) 1 (*Oguz 82*), Sparta Prague (1) 2 (*Hasek 38, Novak 89*) 35,000

Fram (0) 0, Steaua (0) 1 (*Negrau 58*) 700

HJK Helsinki (0) 0, AC Milan (1) 1 (*Borgonovo 30*) 17,664

Internazionale (0) 1 (*Serena 68*), Malmo (0) 1 (*Enqvist 80*) 70,000

Lucerne (0) 0, PSV Eindhoven (2) 2 (*Romario 25, 32*) 3000

Mechelen (1) 5 (*Bosman 16, 53, Ohana 54, 76, Severeyns 87*), Rosenborg (0) 0 6000

17 Nentori (3) 5 (*Kola 29, 34, Bardhi 39, Hodja 51, Riza 56*), Sliema Wanderers (0) 0 20,000

Omonia (1) 2 (*Xiuruppas 11, Yiatru 59*), Tirol (0) 3 (*Baur 48, Westerthaler 85, Pacult 89*) 10,000

Real Madrid (3) 6 (*Sanchez 31, Esteban 35, Kremer og 46, Losada 54, Julio Llorente 71, Tendillo 88*), Spora (0) 0 16,000

Vojvodina (1) 2 (*Mihajlovic 26, Tanjga 50*), Honved (0) 1 (*Gacesa og 74*) 12,000

Second Round, First Leg

Bayern Munich (2) 3 (*Kogl 16 pen, Mihajlovic 26, 64*), 17 Nentori (1) 1 (*Minga 30*) 11,000

Dnepr (1) 2 (*Yudin 36, Son 66*), Tirol (0) 0 27,500

Honved (0) 0, Benfica (1) 2 (*Pacecho 33 pen, Valdo 68*) 9000

Malmo (0) 0, Mechelen (0) 0 19,015

Marseille (0) 2 (*Papin 56, Manolas og 81*), AEK Athens (0) 0 40,000

AC Milan (2) 2 (*Rijkaard 8, Van Basten 13 pen*), Real Madrid (0) 0 68,000

Sparta Prague (0) 2 (*Bilek 75 pen, Skuhravy 85*), CSKA Sofia (1) 2 (*Stoichkov 13, Kostadinov 57*) 7690 *in Trnava*

Steaua (1) 1 (*Lacatus 17*), PSV Eindhoven (0) 0 27,500

Second Round, Second Leg

AEK Athens (0) 1 (*Savidis 78 pen*), Marseille (0) 1 (*Papin 85*) 35,000

Benfica (3) 7 (*Brito 20, 42, Abel 36, Vata 64, 66, Magnusson 88, 89*), Honved (0) 0 50,000

CSKA Sofia (1) 3 (*Stoichkov 44, 89, Kostadinov 84*), Sparta Prague (0) 0 30,000

Mechelen (2) 4 (*De Wilde 18, 20, Bosman 48, Versavel 55*), Malmo (0) 1 (*Lindman 58*) 8000

17 Nentori (0) 0, Bayern Munich (1) 3 (*Strunz 44, Grahammer 47, Dorfner 89*) 33,000

PSV Eindhoven (1) 5 (*Ellerman 22, 64, Romario 46, 48, 81*), Steaua (1) 1 (*Lacatus 16*) 28,000

Real Madrid (1) 1 (*Butragueno 44*), AC Milan (0) 0 90,000

Tirol (1) 2 (*Westerthaler 30, Pacult 76*), Dnepr (1) 2 (*Son 5, Liuty 80*) 17,000

Quarter-Finals, First Leg

Bayern Munich (0) 2 (*Wohlfarth 74, Grahammer 80*), PSV Eindhoven (0) 1 (*Povlsen 77*) 35,000

Benfica (1) 1 (*Magnusson 9 pen*), Dnepr (0) 0 70,000

CSKA Sofia (0) 0, Marseille (0) 1 (*Thys 85*) 58,000

Mechelen (0) 0, AC Milan (0) 0 33,000

Quarter-Finals, Second Leg

AC Milan (0) 2 (*Van Basten 94, Simone 116*), Mechelen (0) 0 *aet* 65,000

PSV Eindhoven (0) 0, Bayern Munich (0) 1 (*Augenthaler 89*) 30,000

Marseille (2) 3 (*Waddle 25, Papin 28, Sauzee 72*), CSKA Sofia (0) 1 (*Urukov 84*) 35,000

Dnepr (0) 0, Benfica (3) 3 (*Lima 55, 60, Ricardo 86*) 30,000

Semi-Finals, First Leg

Marseille (2) 2 (*Sauzee 13, Papin 44*), Benfica (1) 1 (*Lima 10*) 41,000

AC Milan (0) 1 (*Van Basten 77 pen*), Bayern Munich (0) 0 65,000

Semi-Finals, Second Leg

Bayern Munich (0) 2 (*Strunz 60, McInally 107*), AC Milan (0) 1 (*Borgonovo 101*) *aet* 73,000

Benfica (0) 1 (*Vata*), Marseille (0) 0 110,000

Final: AC Milan (0) 1, Benfica (0) 0
(in Vienna, 23 May 1990, 57,500)

AC Milan: Galli G; Tassotti, Costacurta, Baresi, Maldini, Colombo (Galli F 89), Evani, Gullit, Van Basten. *Scorer:* Rijkaard 68.

Benfica: Silvino; Jose Carlos, Aldair, Ricardo, Samuel, Vitor Paneira (Vata 76), Valdo, Thern, Hernani, Magnusson, Paceco (Brito 66).

Referee: Kohl (Austria).

EUROPEAN CUP 1989–90 – BRITISH AND IRISH CLUBS

FIRST ROUND, FIRST LEG

13 SEPT

Derry (0) 1 *(Carlyle)*

Benfica (0) 2 *(Thern, Ricardo)*   12,500

Derry: Dalton; Vaudequin, Brady, Curran, Neville, Doolin, Carlyle, Coyle, Krstic, Gauld, Healy.
Benfica: Silvio; Veloso, Ricardo, Fonseca, Aidair, Thern, Paneira, Abel (Chalana), Brito (Vata), Valdo, Magnusson.

Linfield (0) 1 *(Mooney [pen])*

Dnepr (1) 2 *(Kudritski 2)*   1235

Linfield: Dunlop; Dorman, Coyle D, Doherty, Jeffrey, Deahnoun, Grattan (Baxter), Mooney, McGaughey, McKeown, Bailley.
Dnepr: Gorodov; Yudin, Geraschenko, Sadeinikov, Tischenko, Kudritski, Bagmut, Kulishnov, Sohn, Lyuty, Shervny.

Rangers (1) 1 *(Walters [pen])*

Bayern Munich (1) 3 *(Kogl, Thon [pen], Augenthaler)*
40,135

Rangers: Woods; Stevens, Munro, Nisbet, Wilkins, Butcher, Steven, Ferguson I, Ferguson D, Johnston, Walters.
Bayern Munich: Scheuer; Grahammer, Pflugler, Johnsen, Augenthaler, Schwabi, Kogl, Reuter, Wohlfarth (Mihajlovic), Thon, McInally (Kastenmaier).

FIRST ROUND, SECOND LEG

27 SEPT

Bayern Munich (0) 0

Rangers (0) 0   43,000

Bayern Munich: Aumann; Grahammer, Pflugler, Johnsen (Schwabi), Augenthaler, Strunz, Kogl, Reuter, Mihajlovic (Wohlfarth), Thon, McInally.
Rangers: Ginzburg; Stevens, Munro, Gough, Wilkins, Butcher, Steven, Ferguson I, Cowan (Drinkell), Johnston, Walters.
(Bayern Munich won 3-1 on aggregate)

Benfica (1) 4 *(Magnusson, Vata, Ricardo, Aidair)*

Derry (0) 0   50,000

Benfica: Silvino; Veloso, Aidair, Ricardo (Paulinho), Fonseca, Thern, Valdo, Abel (Chalana), Pacheco, Magnusson, Vata.
Derry: Dalton; Vaudequin, Neville, Brady, Curran, Doolin, Carlyle, Coyle (Gaudy), Krstic, Gauld, Healy.
(Benfica won 6-1 on aggregate)

Denepr (1) 1 *(Sohn)*

Linfield (0) 0   30,000

Dnepr: Gorodov; Yudin (Shakhov), Geraschenko, Sadeinikov, Tischenko, Kudritski (Chervoni), Bagmut, Cherednik, Yakovenko, Sohn, Lyuty.
Linfield: Dunlop; Dornan, Coyle D, Doherty, Jeffrey, Deahnoun, Baxter, Mooney, McGaughey, McKeown, Baillie.
(Dnepr won 3-1 on aggregate)

EUROPEAN CUPS DRAW 1990–91

EUROPEAN CUP 1989–90
First Round: AC Milan bye; Red Star Belgrade v Grasshoppers; Marseille v Dinamo Tiranan; Tirol v Kuusysi; Lillestrom v FC Brugge; Sparta Prague v Spartak Moscow; Napoli v Ujpest Dozsa; Malmo v Besiktas; Dinamo Bucharest v St Patrick's; Union Luxembourg v Dynamo Dresden; Porto v Portadown; Real Madrid v Odense; Lech Poznan v Panathinaikos; Rangers v Valetta; Bayern Munich v Apoel; Akureyri v CSKA Sofia.

EUROPEAN CUP WINNERS CUP 1989–90
Preliminary Round: Bray Wanderers v Trabzonspor.
First Round: Legia v Hesperange; Bray or Tranzonspor v Barcelona; Viking v Liege; Sliven v Juventus; Manchester U v Pecs; Dynamo Kiev v KuPS; Schwerin v FK Austria; Sliema Wanderers v Dukla Prague; Salmina v Aberdeen; Montpellier v PSV Eindhoven; Olympiakos v Flamurtari; Glentoran v Steaue; Wrexham v Lyngby; Amadora v Neuchatel; Fram v Djurgaarden; Kaiserslautern v Sampdoria.

UEFA CUP 1989–90
First Round: Brondby v Eintracht Frankfurt; Dnepr v Hearts; Vitesse v Derry C; MTK VM v Lucerne; Sporting Lisbon v Mechelen; Lausanne v Real Sociedad; Avenir Beggen v Inter Bratislava; Borussia Dortmund v Chemnitz; Norrkoping v Cologne; Dundee U v FH; Antwerp v Ferencvaros; Zaglebie Lubin v Bologna; Glenavon v Bordeaux; Torpedo Moscow v GAIS Gothenburg; Aston Villa v Banik Ostrava; Magdeburg v Rovaniemen; Vejle v Admira Wacker; Bayer Leverkusen v Twente; Chernomoretz Odessa v Rosenborg; Katowice v Turun; Iraklis v Valencia; Anderlecht v Petrolul; Atlanta v Dinamo Zagreb; Slavia Sovia v Omonia; Roma v Benfica; Roda v Monaco; Seville v PAOK; Partizani Tirana v Uni Craiova; Timisoara v Atletico Madrid; Rapid Vienna v Internazionale; Fenerbahce v Guimaraes; Hibernians (Malta) v Partizan Belgrade.

EUROPEAN CUP-WINNERS' CUP

EUROPEAN CUP-WINNERS' CUP FINALS 1961–89

Year	Winners		Runners-up		Venue	Attendance	Referee
1961	Fiorentina	2	Rangers	0 *(1st Leg)*	Glasgow	80,000	Steiner (A)
	Fiorentina	2	Rangers	1 *(2nd Leg)*	Florence	50,000	Hernadi (H)
1962	Atletico Madrid	1	Fiorentina	1	Glasgow	27,389	Wharton (S)
Replay	Atletico Madrid	3	Fiorentina	0	Stuttgart	45,000	Tschenscher (WG)
1963	Tottenham Hotspur	5	Atletico Madrid	1	Rotterdam	25,000	Van Leuwen (Ho)
1964	Sporting Lisbon	3	MTK Budapest	3 *(aet)*	Brussels	9000	Van Nuffel (Bel)
Replay	Sporting Lisbon	1	MTK Budapest	0	Antwerp	18,000	Versyp (Bel)
1965	West Ham U	2	Munich 1860	0	Wembley	100,000	Szolt (H)
1966	Borussia Dortmund	2	Liverpool	1 *(aet)*	Glasgow	41,657	Schwinte (F)
1967	Bayern Munich	1	Rangers	0 *(aet)*	Nuremberg	69,480	Lo Bello (I)
1968	AC Milan	2	Hamburg	0	Rotterdam	60,000	Ortiz (Sp)
1969	Slovan Bratislava	3	Barcelona	2	Basle	40,000	Van Ravens (Ho)
1970	Manchester C	2	Gornik Zabrze	1	Vienna	10,000	Schiller (A)
1971	Chelsea	1	Real Madrid	1 *(aet)*	Athens	42,000	Scheurer (Sw)
Replay	Chelsea	2	Real Madrid	1 *(aet)*	Athens	24,000	Bucheli (Sw)
1972	Rangers	3	Moscow Dynamo	2	Barcelona	35,000	Ortiz (Sp)
1973	AC Milan	1	Leeds U	0	Salonika	45,000	Mihas (Gr)
1974	Magdeburg	2	AC Milan	0	Rotterdam	5000	Van Gemert (Ho)
1975	Dynamo Kiev	3	Ferencvaros	0	Basle	13,000	Davidson (S)
1976	Anderlecht	4	West Ham U	2	Brussels	58,000	Wurtz(F)
1977	Hamburg	2	Anderlecht	0	Amsterdam	65,000	Partridge (E)
1978	Anderlecht	4	Austria/WAC	0	Amsterdam	48,679	Adlinger (WG)
1979	Barcelona	4	Fortuna Dusseldorf	3 *(aet)*	Basle	58,000	Palotai (H)
1980	Valencia	0	Arsenal	0	Brussels	40,000	Christov (Cz)
	(aet; Valencia won 5-4 on penalties)						
1981	Dynamo Tbilisi	2	Carl Zeiss Jena	1	Dusseldorf	9000	Lattanzi (I)
1982	Barcelona	2	Standard Liege	1	Barcelona	100,000	Eschweiler (WG)
1983	Aberdeen	2	Real Madrid	1 *(aet)*	Gothenburg	17,804	Menegali (I)
1984	Juventus	2	Porto	1	Basle	60,000	Prokop (EG)
1985	Everton	3	Rapid Vienna	1	Rotterdam	30,000	Casarin (I)
1986	Dynamo Kiev	3	Atletico Madrid	0	Lyon	39,300	Wohrer (A)
1987	Ajax	1	Lokomotive Leipzig	0	Athens	35,000	Agnolin (I)
1988	Mechelen	1	Ajax	0	Strasbourg	39,446	Pauly (WG)
1989	Barcelona	2	Sampdoria	0	Berne	45,000	Courtney (E)

Sampdoria players and officials celebrate after the Italian club's success in the Cup Winners' Cup Final in Gothenburg when they defeated Anderlecht 2-0. (Bob Thomas)

EUROPEAN CUP-WINNERS' CUP 1989-90

Preliminary Round, First Leg
Chernomoretz (1) 3 (*Petkov 25, Stoyanov V 53, Kumpanov 77 pen*), Dinamo Tirana (0) 1 (*Demollari 69*) 11,000

Preliminary Round, Second Leg
Dinamo Tirana (0) 4 (*Camaj 46, Abazi 62, Jance 68, Demollari 71*), Chernomoretz (0) 0 8000

First Round, First Leg
Belenenses (0) 1 (*Chiquinho 55*), Monaco (0) 1 (*Diaz 70*) 10,000
Ferencvaros (3) 5 (*Kincses 1, Limperger 10, Szeibert 29, 64, Dzurjak 80*), Valkeakosken Haka (1) 1 (*Paavola 4*) 22,000
Partizan (1) 2 (*Milojevic 21, Djurdjevic 55*), Celtic (1) 1 (*Galloway 41*) in Mostar 15,000
Slovan Bratislava (1) 3 (*Timko 35, Vankovic 53 pen, Tittel 88 pen*), Grasshoppers (0) 0 12,817
Union Luxembourg (0) 0, Djurgaarden (0) 0 479
Valladolid (2) 5 (*Albis 22, 70, Roberto 38, 46, Ayarza 59*), Hamrun Spartans (0) 0 10,000
Anderlecht (3) 6 (*Ukkonen 11, Nilis 16, 35, Van der Linden 47, 52, Gudjohnsen 85*), Ballymena (0) 0 10,000
Admira Wacker (0) 3 (*Schaub 80, Knaller 88, Rodax 89*), AEL Limassol (0) 0 3900
Barcelona (0) 1 (*Koeman 85 pen*), Legia Warsaw (1) 1 (*Latka 25*) 34,500
Besiktas (0) 0, Borussia Dortmund (1) 1 (*Mill 13*) 35,000
Brann Bergen (0) 0, Sampdoria (1) 2 (*Vialli 40, Mancini 55*) 16,789
Dinamo Tirana (0) 1 (*Canaj 53*), Dinamo Bucharest (0) 0 18,000
Groningen (0) 1 (*Koevermans 48*), Ikast (0) 0 13,000
Panathinaikos (1) 3 (*Vlachos 4, 53, Saravakos 38*), Swansea C (0) 2 (*Raynor 63, Salako 80*) 45,000
Torpedo Moscow (4) 5 (*Grechnev 24, 40 pen, Yuri Savichev 27, Chugunov 34, Adanasiev 72*), Cork C (0) 0 20,000
Valur (1) 1 (*Askelsson 37*), Dynamo Berlin (0) 2 (*Bonan, 70, Thom 74*) 510

First Round, Second Leg
Dinamo Bucharest (2) 2 (*Mateut 8, Mihaescu 13*), Dinamo Tirana (0) 0 16,000
Grasshoppers (1) 4 (*Gren 16, 115, Egli 60 pen, Studal 83*), Slovan Bratislava (0) 0 aet 3400
Monaco (3) 3 (*Weah 30, 35, Mege 40*), Belenenses (0) 0 10,000
Hamrun Spartans (0) 0, Valladolid (1) 1 (*Hidalgo 37*) 3000
AEL Limassol (1) 1 (*Sophocleus 43*), Admira Wacker (0) 0 5000
Ballymena (0) 0, Anderlecht (1) 4 (*Vervoort 27, 87, Degryse 53, Gudjohnsen 85*) 5000
Borussia Dortmund (1) 2 (*Driller 16, Wegmann 86*), Besiktas (0) 1 (*Ali 82*) 43,800
Celtic (1) 5 (*Dziekanowski 25, 46, 56, 80, Walker 65*), Partizan (1) 4 (*Vujacic 8, Djordjevic 50, Djurovski 61, Scepovic 87*), 45,000
Cork C (0) 0, Torpedo Moscow (1) 1 (*Yuri Savichev 12*) 6000
Djurgaarden (0) 5 (*Martinsson 53, 84, Nilsson 60, Galloway 80, 89*), Union Luxembourg (0) 0 1180
Dynamo Berlin (1) 2 (*Ernst 23, Lenz 83*), Valur (0) 1 (*Kristjansson 53*) 15,000
Valkeakosken Haka (0) 1 (*Paavola 74*), Ferencvaros (0) 1 (*Keller 48*) 503
Ikast (0) 1 (*Kristensen 83 pen*), Groningen (1) 2 (*Meijer 35, Eykelkemp 69*) 3639
Legia Warsaw (0) 0, Barcelona (1) 1 (*Laudrup 11*) 25,000
Sampdoria (0) 1 (*Katanec 63*), Bran Bergen (0) 0 20,000
Swansea C (1) 3 (*James 31 pen, Melville 46, 67*), Panathinaikos (0) 3 (*Dimopoulos 59, Saravakos 73 pen, 89*) 8276

Second Round, First Leg
Borussia Dortmund (0) 1 (*Wegmann 64*), Sampdoria (0) 1 (*Mancini 88*) 45,560
Monaco (0) 0, Dynamo Berlin (0) 0 6500
Admira Wacker (0) 1 (*Rodax 88*), Ferencvaros (0) 0 8000
Anderlecht (1) 2 (*Jankovic 12, Degryse 46*), Barcelona (0) 0 30,000
Groningen (2) 4 (*Meijer 18, Ten Caat 38, Roossien 49, Koevermans 74*), Partizan (2) 3 (*Bajevic 34, Djurovski 45, 83*) 17,250
Panathinaikos (0) 0, Dinamo Bucharest (0) 2 (*Raducioiu 58, Mateut 66*) 45,000
Torpedo Moscow (1) 1 (*Yuri Savichev 29*), Grasshoppers (0) 1 (*Strudal 88*) 22,000
Valladolid (2) 2 (*Kullberg og 30, Moya 33*), Djurgaarden (0) 0 28,400

Second Round, Second Leg
Barcelona (0) 2 (*Salinas 50, Beguiristain 56*), Anderlecht (0) 1 (*Van der Linden 97*) aet 105,000
Dinamo Bucharest (3) 6 (*Mateut 32, 48, Sabau 41, 51, Rednic 23, Klein 89*), Panathinaikos (1) 1 (*Samaras 35*) 10,000
Djurgaarden (1) 2 (*Skoog 41, Martinsson 55*), Valladolid (0) 2 (*Moreno 65, 72*) 3166
Dynamo Berlin (0) 1 (*Kuttner 110*), Monaco (0) 1 (*Diaz 118*) aet 17,000
Ferencvaros (0) 0, Admira Wacker (0) 1 (*Oberhofer 48*) 20,000 in Szeged
Grasshoppers (2) 3 (*Egli 32, Wiederkehr 34, Gren 79*), Torpedo Moscow (0) 0 15,000
Partizan (1) 3 (*Djurovski 15, Milojevic 83, Djurdjevic 89*), Groningen (0) 1 (*Ten Caat 80*) 30,000
Sampdoria (0) 2 (*Vialli 74 pen, 88*), Borussia Dortmund (0) 0 38,000

Quarter-Finals, First Leg
Dinamo Bucharest (1) 2 (*Raducioiu 18, 58*), Partizan (0) 1 (*Spasic 70*) 20,000
Sampdoria (2) 4 (*Vierchowod 12, Meier og 84*), Grasshoppers (0) 0 50,000
Valladolid (0) 0, Monaco (0) 0 17,000
Anderlecht (1) 2 (*Degryse 32, 38*), Admira Wacker (0) 0 15,000

Quarter-Finals, Second Leg
Grasshoppers (0) 1 (*Wyss 69*), Sampdoria (1) 2 (*Cerezo 44, Lombardo 81*) 18,000
Partizan (0) 0, Dinamo Bucharest (0) 2 (*Lupescu 52, Radicioiu 70*) 10,000 in Titograd
Admira Wacker (0) 1 (*Rodax 65*), Anderlecht (0) 1 (*Nilis 57*) 6000
Monaco (0) 0, Valladolid (0) 0 Monaco won 3-1 on penalties aet 13,500

Semi-Finals, First Leg
Anderlecht (0) 1 (*Nilis 65*), Dinamo Bucharest (0) 0 16,000
Monaco (1) 2 (*Weah 43, Mege 79*), Sampdoria (0) 2 (*Vialli 74 pen, 78*) 20,000

Semi-Finals, Second Leg
Dinamo Bucharest (0) 0, Anderlecht (0) 1 (*Van der Linden 59*) 60,000
Sampdoria (0) 2 (*Vierchowod 8, Lombardo 11*), Monaco (0) 0 39,000

Final: Sampdoria (0) 2, Anderlecht (0) 0 aet
(in Gothenburg, 9 May 1990, 20,103)

Sampdoria: Pagliuca; Pellegrini, Mannini, Vierchowod, Carboni, Pari, Katanec (Salsano 93), Invernizzi (Lombardo 53), Dossena, Vialli, Mancini. *Scorer:* Vialli 105, 107.

Anderlecht: De Wilde; Grun, Marchoul, Keshi, Kooiman, Vervoort, Musonda, Gudjohnsen, Jankovic (Oliveira 112), Degryse (Nilis 103), Van der Linden.

Referee: Galler (Switzerland).

EUROPEAN CUP-WINNERS' CUP 1989–90 – BRITISH AND IRISH CLUBS

FIRST ROUND, FIRST LEG

12 SEPT

Partizan (1) 2 *(Milojevic, Djordjevic)*

Celtic (1) 1 *(Galloway)*   15,000

Partizan: Omerovic (Panourivic); Milanic, Spasic, Zupic, Petric, Vujacic, Dorjevic, Milojevic, Djordjevic, Djurovski, Bogdanovic (Pantic).
Celtic: Bonner; Morris, Rogan, Aitken, Whyte, Grant, Galloway, McStay, Dziekanowski (Walker), Coyne, Burns.

13 SEPT

Anderlecht (3) 6 *(Ukkonen, Nilis 2, Van der Linden 2, Gudjohnsen)*

Ballymena (0) 0   10,000

Anderlecht: De Wilde; Gudjohnsen, Marchoul, Van Tiggelen, Andersen, Vervoort, Jankovic, Ukkonen, Nilis, Degryse, Van der Linden.
Ballymena: Grant; Hamilton, Smyth M, Garrett, Heron, Young, McKee, Sloan, Hardy, Smyth D, Curry.

Panathinaikos (2) 3 *(Vlahos 2, Saravakos)*

Swansea C (0) 2 *(Raynor, Salako)*   45,000

Panathinaikos: Abadiocakis; Hatziathanasiou, Kolev, Kalitzakis, Kalantsis, Mavridis, Saravakos, Antoniou, Dimopoulos (Hristodoulu), Vlahos (Polak), Georgamlis.
Swansea C: Bracey; Hough, Coleman, Melville, Boyle, James (Davey), Cobb, D'Auria (Legg), Hutchison, Salako, Raynor.

Torpedo Moscow (4) 5 *(Grechnev 2 [1 pen], Savichev Y, Chugunov, Afanasiev)*

Cork C (0) 0   20,000

Torpedo Moscow: Sarichev; Polukarov, Soloviev, Chugunov, Afanasiev, Grechnev, Savichev Y, Geetzyelov (Rudakov), Savichev N, Shirinbekov (Zhukov), Grishin.
Cork C: Donnegan; Bowdren, Long, Healy, Murphy, Freyne, Cotter, Conroy, Bannon, Duggan (Hoare), Caulfield.

FIRST ROUND, SECOND LEG

27 SEPT

Ballymena (0) 0

Anderlecht (1) 4 *(Vervoort 2, Degryse, Gudjohnsen)*   2500

Ballymena: McErlean; Hamilton, Smyth M, Garrett, Heron, Young, McKee, Loughery, Pyper, Hardy, Simpson.
Anderlecht: De Wilde; Gudjohnsen, Marchoul, Van Tiggelen, Andersen, Ukkonen, Vervoort, Nilis, Degryse, Jankovic, Van der Linden.
(Anderlecht won 10-0 on aggregate)

Celtic (1) 5 *(Dziekanowski 4, Walker)*

Partizan (1) 4 *(Vujacic, Djordjevic B, Djurovski, Scepovic)*   49,500

Celtic: Bonner; Grant, Rogan, Aitken, Elliott, Whyte, Galloway, McStay, Dziekanowski, Walker, Miller.
Partizan: Panourivic; Stanojkovic, Spasic, Milanic, Petric, Vujacic, Djordjevic B, Milojevic, Scepovic, Djurovski, Bogdanovic (Djordjevic).
(Partizan won on away goals)

Cork C (0) 0

Torpedo Moscow (1) 1 *(Savichev Y)*   2500

Cork C: Harrington; Bowdren, Conroy, Murphy, Long, Freyne, Barry, Cotter, Nagle, Bannon, Caulfield.
Torpedo Moscow: Sarichev; Polukarov, Kovach, Chugunov, Rogovski, Grechnev, Savichev Y, Rudakov, Savichev N, Shirinbekov (Soloviev), Grishin (Zhukov).
(Torpedo Moscow won 6-0 on aggregate)

Swansea C (1) 3 *(James [pen], Melville 2)*

Panathinaikos (0) 3 *(Dimopoulos, Saravakos 2, [1 pen])*   8276

Swansea C: Bracey; Hough, Coleman, Melville, Boyle, James, Phillips, Legg (D'Auria), Hutchison, Salako, Raynor.
Panathinaikos: Abadiocakis; Hatziathanasiou, Kubanos, Kalantsis, Kalitzakis, Mavridis, Saravakos, Polak (Antoniou), Dimopoulos, Kolev, Georgamlis.
(Panathinaikos won 6-5 on aggregate)

INTER-CITIES FAIRS & UEFA CUP

FAIRS CUP FINALS 1958–71
(Winners in italics)

Year	First Leg	Attendance	Second Leg	Attendance
1958	London 2 Barcelona 2	45,466	*Barcelona* 6 London 0	62,000
1960	Birmingham C 0 Barcelona 0	40,500	*Barcelona* 4 Birmingham C 1	70,000
1961	Birmingham C 2 Roma 2	21,005	*Roma* 2 Birmingham C 0	60,000
1962	Valencia 6 Barcelona 2	65,000	Barcelona 1 *Valencia* 1	60,000
1963	Dynamo Zagreb 1 Valencia 2	40,000	*Valencia* 2 Dynamo Zagreb 0	55,000
1964	*Zaragoza* 2 Valencia 1	50,000	(in Barcelona)	
1965	*Ferencvaros* 1 Juventus 0	25,000	(in Turin)	
1966	Barcelona 0 Zaragoza 1	70,000	Zaragoza 2 *Barcelona* 4	70,000
1967	Dynamo Zagreb 2 Leeds U 0	40,000	Leeds U 0 *Dynamo Zagreb* 0	35,604
1968	Leeds U 1 Ferencvaros 0	25,368	Ferencvaros 0 *Leeds U* 0	70,000
1969	Newcastle U 3 Ujpest Dozsa 0	60,000	Ujpest Dozsa 2 *Newcastle U* 3	37,000
1970	Anderlecht 3 Arsenal 1	37,000	*Arsenal* 3 Anderlecht 0	51,612
1971	Juventus 0 Leeds U 0 *(abandoned 51 minutes)*			65,000
	Juventus 2 Leeds U 2	65,000	*Leeds U* 1* Juventus 1	42,483

UEFA CUP FINALS 1972–89
(Winners in italics)

Year	First Leg	Attendance	Second Leg	Attendance
1972	Wolverhampton W 1 Tottenham H 2	45,000	*Tottenham H* 1 Wolverhampton W 1	48,000
1973	Liverpool 3 Moenchengladbach 0	41,169	Moenchengladbach 0 *Liverpool* 2	35,000
1974	Tottenham H 2 Feyenoord 2	46,281	*Feyenoord* 2 Tottenham 0	68,000
1975	Moenchengladbach 0 Twente 0	45,000	Twente 1 *Moenchengladbach* 5	24,500
1976	Liverpool 3 FC Brugge 2	56,000	FC Brugge 1 *Liverpool* 1	32,000
1977	Juventus 1 Athletic Bilbao 0	75,000	Athletic Bilbao 2 *Juventus* 1*	43,000
1978	Bastia 0 PSV Eindhoven 0	15,000	*PSV Eindhoven* 3 Bastia 0	27,000
1979	Red Star Belgrade 1 Moenchengladbach 1	87,500	*Moenchengladbach* 1 Red Star Belgrade 0	45,000
1980	Moenchengladbach 3 Eintracht Frankfurt 2	25,000	Eintracht Frankfurt 1* Moenchengladbach 0	60,000
1981	Ipswich T 3 AZ 67 0	27,532	AZ 67 4 *Ipswich T* 2	28,500
1982	Gothenburg 1 Hamburg 0	42,548	Hamburg 0 *Gothenburg* 3	60,000
1983	Anderlecht 1 Benfica 0	45,000	Benfica 1 *Anderlecht* 1	80,000
1984	Anderlecht 1 Tottenham H 1	40,000	*Tottenham H* 1[1] Anderlecht 1	46,258
1985	Videoton 0 Real Madrid 3	30,000	*Real Madrid* 0 Videoton 1	98,300
1986	Real Madrid 5 Cologne 1	80,000	Cologne 2 *Real Madrid* 0	15,000
1987	Gothenburg 1 Dundee U 0	50,023	Dundee U 1 *Gothenburg* 1	20,911
1988	Espanol 3 Bayer Leverkusen 0	42,000	*Bayer Leverkusen* 3[2] Espanol 0	22,000
1989	Napoli 2 Stuttgart 1	83,000	Stuttgart 3 *Napoli* 3	67,000

* won on away goals
[1] Tottenham H won 4-3 on penalties aet
[2] Bayer Leverkusen won 3-2 on penalties aet

Pierluigi Casiraghi (left) of Fiorentina prepares to tackle the Juventus midfield player Carlos Dunga during the UEFA Cup Final second leg. (Allsport)

UEFA CUP 1989–90

Preliminary Round, First Leg
Auxerre (0) 0, Dinamo Zagreb (0) 1 (*Suker 80*) 11,000

Preliminary Round, Second Leg
Dinamo Zagreb (0) 1 (*Panadic 53*), Auxerre (2) 3 (*Kovacs 33, Otokore 36, 56*) 55,000

First Round, First Leg
Akranes (0) 0, Liege (1) 2 (*Ernes 7, Waseige 81*) 700
Gornik Zabrze (0) 0, Juventus (0) 1 (*Zavarov 73*) 35,000
Hibernian (1) 1 (*Mitchell 25*), Videoton (0) 0 14,000
Sochaux (3) 7 (*Lada 6, 24, Silvestre 22, Oudjani 46, 73, Carrasco 86, Petry og 89*), Jeunesse Esch (0) 0 8000
Valletta (0) 1 (*Zarb 63*), Vienna (2) 4 (*Camilleri og 17, Balzis 42, 86, Vidreis 56*) 11,000
Vitosha (0) 0, Antwerp (0) 0 10,000
Aberdeen (0) 2 (*Robertson C 80, Grant 89*), Rapid Vienna (1) 1 (*Kranjcar 7*) 16,800
Atalanta (0) 0, Spartak Moscow (0) 0 20,000
Atletico Madrid (0) 1 (*Baltazar 77*), Fiorentina (0) 0 46,000
Auxerre (1) 5 (*Boli 19, Vahirua 50, 56, Pogace og 65, Guerreiro 75*), Apolonia (0) 0 18,000
Glentoran (0) 1 (*Jameson 68*), Dundee U (1) 3 (*Cleland 31, McInally 71, Hinds 85*) 20,000
Hansa Rostock (2) 2 (*Wahl 26, 38 pen*), Banik Ostrava (0) 3 (*Kula 57, Hyravy 66, Horvath 75*) 20,000
Iraklis (1) 1 (*Toutziaris 29*), Sion (0) 0 10,000
Karl-Marx-Stadt (1) 1 (*Kohler 17*), Boavista (0) 0 20,000
Kiev Dynamo (3) 4 (*Protasov 12, Rats 23, 33, Yakovenko 55*), MTK Budapest (0) 0 35,000
Cologne (1) 4 (*Gotz 6, 56, 61, Littbarski 73 pen*), Plastika Nitra (1) 1 (*Hipp 20*) 7000
Kuusysi Lahti (0) 0, Paris St Germain (0) 0 3882
Lillestrom (0) 1 (*Pedersen 87*), Werder Bremen (2) 3 (*Eilts 10, Bude 15, 71*) 6970
Orgryte (0) 1 (*Roth 71*), Hamburg (1) 2 (*Furtok 8, Jensen 80*) 3450
Porto (1) 2 (*Jose Carlos 36, Branco 56*), Flacari Moreni (0) 0 50,000
Rad Belgrade (1) 2 (*Nestorovic 37, Djoincevic 53*), Olympiakos (0) 1 (*Tsaluhidis 89*) 5000
RoPs Rovaniemi (1) 1 (*Tiainen 43*), Katowice (1) 1 (*Kubisztal 1*) 3500
Stuttgart (1) 2 (*Walter 21, Allgower 48*), Feyenoord (0) 0 22,500
Twente (0) 0, FC Brugge (0) 0 15,000
Valencia (0) 3 (*Toni 36, Fenol 48, Sanchez 71*), Victoria Bucharest (1) 1 (*Coras 61*) 21,000
Wettingen (2) 3 (*Cleary og 42, Corneliusson 66, Loebmann 69*), Dundalk (0) 0 5000
Zenit Leningrad (1) 3 (*Chukhlov 22, Stepanov 59, Popyelnukha 72*), Naestved (0) 1 (*Argenesen 9*) 8200
Zhalgiris Vilnius (1) 2 (*Fridrikas 36, 88*), IFK Gothenburg (0) 0 20,000
Apollon Limassol (0), Zaragoza (1) 3 (*Rodriguez 44 pen, Pardeza 53, Alsaro 84*) 15,000
FK Austria (1) 1 (*Degiorgi 18*), Ajax (0) 0 12,000
Galatasaray (1) 1 (*Vezir 31*), Red Star Belgrade (1) 1 (*Mrkela 11* 30,500
Sporting Lisbon (0) 0, Napoli (0) 0 75,000

First Round, Second Leg
Antwerp (0) 4 (*Geilenkirchen 83, Claesen 87, 90, Quaranta 96*), Vitosha (1) 3 (*Slavchev 6, Donkov 82, Mikhtarski 84*) aet 8000
Jeunesse Esch (0) 0, Sochaux (4) 5 (*Carrasco 8, Thomas 28, 29, 53, Silvestre 38*) 1000
Videoton (0) 0, Hibernian (1) 3 (*Houchen 9, Evans 60, Collins 80*) 18,000
Vienna (1) 3 (*Jenisch 20, Balzis 53, 80*), Valletta (0) 0 1500
Zaragoza (1) 1 (*Pardeza 39*), Apollon Limassol (0) 1 (*Pyttas 89 pen*) 11,000
Olympiakos (1) 2 (*Detari 34, Anastopoulos 76*), Rad Belgrade (0) 0 32,000
Ajax (1) 1 (*Wouters 44*), FK Austria (0) 1 (*Pleva 98*) aet; match abandoned 104 minutes after missiles thrown at Austrian goalkeeper. 25,000

Apolonia (0) 0, Auxerre (2) 3 (*Scifo 25, 31, Cocard 72*) 12,000
Banik Ostrava (2) 4 (*Necas 28, Chylek 43, Zelski 69, Pechacek 77*), Hansa Rostock (0) 0 8000
Boavista (1) 2 (*Joao Pinto 40, 91*), Karl-Marx-Stadt (0) 2 (*Heidrich 104, Melhorn 119*), aet 18,000
FC Brugge (4) 4 (*Booy 6, Disztl 18, Staelens 20, Farina 32*), Twente (1) 1 (*Paus 24*) 19,000
Dundalk (0) 0, Wettingen (1) 2 (*Loebmann 40, 54*) 2000
Dundee U (1) 2 (*Clark 25, Gallacher 47*), Glentoran (0) 0 9340
Feyenoord (1) 2 (*Keur 24, Van Geel 55 pen*), Stuttgart (0) 1 (*Sigurvinsson 64*) 18,000
Fiorentina (0) 1 (*Buso 25*), Atletico Madrid (0) 0 25,000 in Perugia
Flacara Moreni (0) 1 (*Beldie 52*), Porto (1) 2 (*Magalhaes 21, Rui Aguas 89*) 11,000
Katowice (0) 0, RoPs Rovaniemi (0) 1 (*Karilla 61*) 3948
Hamburg (2) 5 (*Von Heesen 25, Beiersdorfer 35, Furtok 79, Eck 88, Fischer 89*), Orgryte (0) 1 (*Grandelius 76*) 9000
IFK Gothenburg (0) 1 (*Nilsson 53*), Zhalgiris Vilnius (0) 0 4676
Juventus (4) 4 (*Schillaci 2, 25, Fortunato 4, Marocchi 6*), Gornik Zabrze (1) 2 (*Kosela 44, Lissek 83*) 40,000
Liege (3) 4 (*Ernes 8, 19, Wegria 40, Boffin 81*), Akranes (1) 1 (*Petursson 22*) 2000
MTK Budapest (0) 1 (*Jovan 87*), Kiev Dynamo (1) 2 (*Zayets 10, Soleiko 88*) 2500
Naestved (0) 0, Zenit Leningrad (0) 0 4184
Napoli (0) 0, Sporting Lisbon (0) 0 70,000
Paris St Germain (1) 3 (*Susic 17, Zlatko Vujovic 56, Calderon 69 pen*), Kuusysi Lahti (1 2 (*Remes 15, Lius 89*) 8000
Plastika Nitra (0) 0, Cologne (1) 1 (*Higel 33*) 12,000
Rapid Vienna (1) 1 (*Fjortoft 18*), Aberdeen (0) 0 20,000
Red Star Belgrade (1) 2 (*Lukic 3, Pancev 67*), Galatasaray (0) 0 65,000
Sion (0) 2 (*Baljic 75, Lopez 79*), Iraklis (0) 0 8000
Spartak Moscow (1) 2 (*Cherenkov 29, Rodionov 89*), Atalanta (0) 0 10,000
Victoria Bucharest (0) 1 (*Haganu 50*), Valencia (1) 1 (*Toni 39*) 10,000
Werder Bremen (0) 2 (*Neubarth 66, Sauer 89*), Lillestrom (0) 0 6000

Second Round, First Leg
Antwerp (3) 4 (*Geilenkirchen 22, Van Rooij 23, 31, Claesen 47*), Dundee U (0) 0 8000
Vienna (1) 2 (*Niederstrasser 29, Haiden 84*), Olympiakos (1) 2 (*Tsaluhidis 35, Alexiou 69*) 5000
FC Brugge (1) 1 (*Christiaens 20*), Rapid Vienna (0) 2 (*Keglevits 63, Pfeiffenberger 89*) 20,000
Fiorentina (0) 0, Sochaux (0) 0 19,000 in Perugia
Hibernian (0) 0, Liege (0) 0, 21,000
Kiev Dynamo (1) 3 (*Mikhailichenko 33, Bessonov 54, Litovchenko 79*), Banik Ostrava (0) 0 45,000
Cologne (2) 3 (*Sturm 33, Gotz 40, Ordenewitz 71*), Spartak Moscow (1) 1 (*Cherenkov 31*) 20,000
Paris St Germain (0) 0, Juventus (0) 1 (*Rui Barros 66*) 29,000
Porto (1) 3 (*Rui Aguas 7, 48, Madjer 69*), Valencia (0) 1 (*Arroyo 60*) 45,000
Red Star Belgrade (3) 4 (*Savicevic 30, Kanatiarovski 31, Pancev 33, Drzic 56*), Zhalgiris Vilnius (0) 1 (*Narbekovas 70*) 65,000
RoPs Rovaniemi (0) 0, Auxerre (1) 5 (*Otokore 1, Scifo 65, 71, Guerreiro 86, Cocard 89*) 4036
Sion (0) 2 (*Brigger 88, Piffaretti 66*), Karl-Marx-Stadt (1) 1 (*Laudeley 24*) 12,000
Werder Bremen (2) 5 (*Neubarth 14, Hermann 23, Riedle 58, Rufer 72, Kutzop 75 pen*), FK Austria (0) 0 15,178
Wettingen (0) 0, Napoli (0) 0 24,000 in Zurich
Zaragoza (0) 1 (*Sirakov 88*), Hamburg (0) 0 15,000
Zenit Leningrad (0) 0, Stuttgart (0) 1 (*Allgower 87*) 40,000

Second Round, Second Leg

Auxerre (1) 3 (*Scifo 3 pen, Dutuel 65, Darras 70*), RoPs Rovaniemi (0) 0 12,000

Dundee U (1) 3 (*Paatelainen 43, O'Neill 61, Clark 89*), Antwerp (2) 2 (*Lehnoff 18, Claesen 20*) 8994

FK Austria (1) 2 (*Hasenhuttl 9, 79*), Werder Bremen (0) 0 2500

Hamburg (0) 2 (*Merkle 69, 96*), Zaragoza (0) 0 *aet* 21,000

Liege (0) 1 (De Saart 105), Hibernian (0) 0 *aet* 14,000

Banik Ostrava (1) 1 (*Chylek 35*), Kiev Dynamo (1) 1 (*Bessonov 2*) 15,000

Juventus (1) 2 (*Galia 26, De Agostini 83*), Paris St Germain (1) 1 (*Bravo*) 50,000

Karl-Marx-Stadt (3) 4 (*Ziffert 11, Steinmann 28 pen, Wienhold 41, Laudeley 65*), Sion (0) 1 (Cina 77) 20,800

Napoli (0) 2 (*Baroni 47, Mauro 74 pen*), Wettingen (1) 1 (*Bertelsen 16*) 50,000

Rapid Vienna (0) 4 (Fjortoft 55, Keglevits 71, 88, Pfeiffenberg 86), FC Brugge (1) 3 (*Farina 18, Ceulemans 84 pen, Booy 89*) 18,000

Sochaux (1) 1 (*Laurey 35*), Fiorentina (1) 1 (*Buso 33*) 13,000

Spartak Moscow (0) 0, Cologne (0) 0 65,000

Stuttgart (4) 5 (*Walter 27, Sigurvinsson 41, 44, Allgower 43, Buchwald 49*), Zenit Leningrad (0) 0 15,000

Valencia (1) 3 (*Fenoll 38, 61, 89*), Porto (1) 2 (*Madjer 42, Couto 80*) 45,000

Zhalgiris Vilnius (0) 0, Red Star Belgrade (0) 1 (*Prosinecki 70*) 27,500

Olympiakos (0) 1, Vienna (0) 1 45,000

Third Round, First Leg

Antwerp (1) 1 (*Lehnhoff 9*), Stuttgart (0) 0 10,000

Fiorentina (0) 1 (*Baggio 78 pen*), Kiev Dynamo (0) 0 38,000 *in Perugia*

Hamburg (0) 1 (*Von Heesen 48*), Porto (0) 0 20,000

Juventus (0) 2 (*Schillaci 81, Casiraghi 87*), Karl-Marx-Stadt (0) 1 (*Weinhold 68*) 25,000

Napoli (0) 2 (*Alemao 51, Careca 64*), Werder Bremen (1) 3 (*Neubarth 41, Riedle 47, Rufer 89*) 37,500

Olympiakos (1) 1 (*Anastopoulos 29*), Auxerre (1) 1 (*Kovacs 19*) 35,000

Rapid Vienna (0) 1 (*Kranjcar 47*), Liege (0) 0 15,500

Red Star Belgrade (0) 2 (*Savicevic 76, 80*), Cologne (0) 0 79,750

Third Round, Second Leg

Stuttgart (0) 1 (*Frontzeck 51*), Antwerp (0) 1 ((*Brockaert 60*) 15,000

Auxerre (0) 0, Olympiakos (0) 0 18,000

Karl-Marx-Stadt (0) 0, Juventus (1) 1 (*De Agostini 21*) 27,800

Kiev Dynamo (0) 0, Fiorentina (0) 0 80,000

Cologne (0) 3 (*Gotz 59, 83, Ordenewitz 89*), Red Star Belgrade (0) 0 45,000

Liege (3) 3 (*Waseige 4, Ernes 30, Boffin 44*), Rapid Vienna (0) 1 (*Fjortoft 78*) 10,000

Porto (1) 2 (*Nascimento 44, Couto 64*), Hamburg (1) 1 (*Eck 42*) 60,000

Werder Bremen (1) 5 (*Riedle 25, 61, Rufer 55, Sauer 89, Eilts 90*), Napoli (0) 1 (*Careca 71*) 38,500

Quarter-Finals, First Leg

Cologne (1) 2 (Littbarski 2, Giske 53), Antwerp (0) 0 20,000

Fiorentina (1) 1 (*Volpecina 71*), Auxerre (0) 0 25,000

Liege (1) 1 (*Varga 40*), Werder Bremen (3) 4 (*Bockenfeld 32, Riedle 35, 68, Rufer 39*) 15,000

Hamburg (0) 0 Juventus (0) 2 (*Schillaci 50, Casiraghi 57*) 42,900

Quarter-Finals, Second Leg

Auxerre (0) 0, Fiorentina (0) 1 (*Nappi 79*) 15,000 *in Perugia*

Juventus (1) 1 (*Galia 35*), Hamburg (0) 2 (*Furtok 72, Merkle 79*) 42,977

Werder Bremen (0) 0, Liege (1) 2 (*De Sart 25, Milosevic 80 pen*) 15,000

Antwerp (0) 0, Cologne (0) 0 20,000

Semi-Finals, First Leg

Werder Bremen (0) 1 (*Landucci og 89*), Fiorentina (0) 1 (*Nappi 79*) 28,000

Juventus (3) 3 (*Rui Barros 21, Casiraghi 44, Marocchi 53*), Cologne (0) 2 (*Gotz 79, Sturm 89*) 42,000

Semi-Finals, Second Leg

Fiorentina (0) 0, Werder Bremen (0) 0 40,000 *in Perugia*

Cologne (0) 0 Juventus (0) 0 55,000

Final
First Leg: Juventus (1) 3, Fiorentina (1) 1
(in Turin, 2 May 1990, 45,000)

Juventus: Tacconi; Napoli, De Agostini, Galia, Brio (Alessio 46), Bonetti, Aleinikov, Rui Barros, Casiraghi, Marocchi, Schillaci. *Scorers:* Galia 3, Casiraghi 59, De Agostini 73.

Fiorentina: Landucci; Dell'Oglio, Volpecina, Dunga, Pin, Battistini, Nappi, Kubik (Malusci 87), Buso, Baggio, Di Chiara. *Scorer:* Buso 10.

Referee: Soriano (Spain).

Final
Second Leg: Fiorentina (0) 0, Juventus (0) 0
(in Avellino, 16 May 1990, 32,000)

Fiorentina: Landucci; Dell'Oglio, Volpecina, Dunga, Pin, Battistini, Nappi, (Zironelli 71), Kubik, Buso, Baggio, Di Chiara.

Juventus: Tacconi; Napoli, De Agostini, Galia, Bruno, Alessio, Aleinikov, Rui Barros (Avallone 72), Casiraghi (Rosa 79), Marocchi, Schillaci.

Referee: Schmidhuber (West Germany).

UEFA CUP 1989–90 – BRITISH AND IRISH CLUBS

FIRST ROUND, FIRST LEG
12 SEPT

Hibernian (1) 1 *(Mitchell)*

Videoton (0) 0   14,000

Hibernian: Goram; Kane, Sneddon, Cooper, Mitchell, Hunter, Weir, Orr (Hamilton), Houchen, Collins, Evans.
Videoton: Petry; Kuttor, Horvath, Laszlo, Emmer, Takacs, Jonas, Mariasi, Sprecksak (Quiriko), Csucsanszky (Gyenti), Petres.

13 SEPT

Aberdeen (0) 2 *(Robertson C, Grant)*

Rapid Vienna (1) 1 *(Kranjcar)*   16,800

Aberdeen: Snelders; McKimmie, Robertson C (Grant), Simpson, McLeish, Miller, Nicholas, Bett, Mason, Connor, Jess (Van der Ark).
Rapid Vienna: Konsel; Reisinger, Blizenec, Peci, Schottel, Kienast, Keglevits, Pfeifenberger, Kranjcjar (Weber), Herzog, Fjortoft (Polger).

Glentoran (0) 1 *(Jameson)*

Dundee U (1) 3 *(Cleland, McInally, Hinds)*   8000

Glentoran: Smyth; Devine (Neill), McCaffrey, Bowers, Moore, McCreery, Caskey, McCartney, Jameson, Campbell, Douglas (Craig).
Dundee U: Thomson; Cleland, Malpas, Van der Hoorn, Hegarty, Narey, Gallacher, Bowman, O'Neill (Hinds), McInally, Paatelainen (French).

Wettingen (1) 3 *(Cleary (og), Corneliusson, Loebmann)*

Dundalk (0) 0   4700

Wettingen: Stiel; Germann, Rueda, Schepull, Kundert, Svensson, Heldmann, Jacobacci, Bertelsen, Loebmann, Corneliusson (Stutz).
Dundalk: O'Neill; Lawless, Cleary, Coll, Malone, Lawlor, McNulty, Wyse, Shelly, Cousins, Collins.

FIRST ROUND, SECOND LEG
26 SEPT

Videoton (0) 0

Hibernian (1) 3 *(Houchen, Evans, Collins)*   18,000

Videoton: Petry; Nemeth (Sprecksak), Horvath, Laszlo, Takacs, Mariasi, Kuttor, Csucsanszky, Quiriko (Babai), Jonas, Petres.
Hibernian: Goram; Kane, Sneddon, Cooper, Mitchell (McGinlay), Hunter, Hamilton, Orr, Houchen (Archibald), Collins, Evans.
Hibernian won 4-0 on aggregate)

27 SEPT

Dundalk (0) 0

Wettingen (1) 2 *(Loebmann 2)*   2000

Dundalk: O'Neill; Lawless (Eccles), Lawlor, Coll, Malone, McNulty, Wyse (Cleary), Newe, Cousins, Collins, Shelly.
Wettingen: Stiel; Germann, Rueda, Heldmann, Schepull, Kundert, Svensson (Hausermann), Bertelsen (Baumgartner), Corneliusson, Jacobacci, Loebmann.
(Wettingen won 5-0 on aggregate)

Dundee U (1) 2 *(Clark, Gallacher)*

Glentoran (0) 0   9340

Dundee U: Thomson; Cleland, Malpas, Van den Hoorn (Krivokapic), Clark, Narey, Gallacher, Bowman, Hinds (O'Neill), McInally, Preston.
Glentoran: Smyth; Neill, McCaffrey, Campbell, Moore, Bowers, Devine, Caskey (Mathieson), McCartney, Jameson, Totten (Douglas).
(Dundee U won 5-1 on aggregate)

Rapid Vienna (1) 1 *(Fjortoft)*

Aberdeen (0) 0   19,000

Rapid Vienna: Konsel; Reisinger, Blizenec, Brauneder, Schottel, Kienast, Keglevits, Pfeifenberger, Kranjcar (Weber), Herzog (Polger), Fjortoft.
Aberdeen: Snelders; McKimmie, Robertson C (Grant), Irvine, McLeish, Miller, Nicholas, Bett, Mason, Connor, Cameron (Van der Ark).
(Rapid Vienna won on away goals)

SECOND ROUND, FIRST LEG
17 OCT

Antwerp (3) 4 *(Geilenkirchen, Van Rooy 2, Claesen)*

Dundee U (0) 0   8000

Antwerp: De Coninck; Kiekens, Broeckaert, Quaranta, Smidts, Lehnhoff (Czerniatynski), Van Rooy, Schrooten, Emmerechts, Claesen, Geilenkirchen.
Dundee U: Thomson; Clark, Malpas, McInally, Hegarty (Van der Hoorn), Narey, McKinlay, Bowman, Paatelainen, Jackson (O'Neill), Gallacher.

18 OCT

Hibernian (0) 0

FC Liege (0) 0   18,000

Hibernian: Goram; Kane, Sneddon (Orr), Cooper, Hunter, Mitchell, Weir (Archibald), Hamilton, Houchen, Collins, Evans.
FC Liege: Munaron; Wegria, Waseige, Habrant, De Sart, Giusto, Boffin, Houben, Varga (Nijskens), Bosman, Ernes.

SECOND ROUND, SECOND LEG
31 OCT

Dundee U (1) 3 *(Paatelainen, O'Neill, Clark)*

Antwerp (2) 2 *(Lehnhoff, Claesen)*   8994

Dundee U: Main; Van der Hoorn, Malpas, McInally, Krivokapic, Clark, McKinlay, Bowman, O'Neill, Paatelainen, Gallacher (Hinds).
Antwerp: Svilar; Kiekens, Broeckaert, Czerniatynski, Smidts, Lehnhoff, Van Rooy, Schrooten, Emmerechts (Taeymans), Claesen, Geilenkirchen.
(Antwerp won 6-3 on aggregate)

FC Liege (0) 1 *(De Sart)*

Hibernian (0) 0   13,000

FC Liege: Munaron; Wegria, Waseige, Habrant, De Sart, Giusto, Boffin, Houben, Varga, Nijskens (Malbas), Ernes.
Hibernian: Goram; Kane, Sneddon, Cooper, Mitchell, Hunter, Hamilton, Orr, Houchen (McGinlay), Collins, Evans (Fellinger).
(aet; Liege won 1-0 on aggregate)

Summary of Appearances

EUROPEAN CUP (1955–90)

English clubs
12 Liverpool
5 Manchester U
3 Nottingham F
2 Derby Co, Wolverhampton W, Everton, Leeds U, Aston Villa
1 Burnley, Tottenham H, Ipswich T, Manchester C, Arsenal

Scottish clubs
15 Celtic
11 Rangers
3 Aberdeen
2 Hearts
1 Dundee, Dundee U, Kilmarnock, Hibernian

Clubs from Northern Ireland
17 Linfield
7 Glentoran
2 Crusaders
1 Glenavon, Ards, Distillery, Derry C, Coleraine

Clubs from Eire
7 Shamrock R
6 Waterford
6 Dundalk
3 Drumcondra
2 Bohemians, Limerick, Athlone T
1 Shelbourne, Cork Hibs, Cork Celtic, Derry C*, Sligo Rovers

Winners: Celtic 1966–67; Manchester U 1967–68; Liverpool 1976–77, 1977–78, 1980–81, 1983–84; Nottingham F 1978–79, 1979–80; Aston Villa 1981–82

Finalists: Celtic 1969–70; Leeds U 1974–75; Liverpool 1984–85

EUROPEAN CUP-WINNERS' CUP (1960–90)

English clubs
5 Tottenham H
4 West Ham U
3 Liverpool, Manchester U
2 Chelsea, Everton, Manchester C
1 Wolverhampton W, Leicester C, WBA, Leeds U, Sunderland, Southampton, Ipswich T, Arsenal

Scottish clubs
10 Rangers
7 Celtic
6 Aberdeen
2 Dunfermline Ath, Dundee U
1 Dundee, Hibernian, Hearts, St Mirren

Welsh clubs
12 Cardiff C
6 Swansea C, Wrexham
2 Bangor C
1 Borough U, Newport Co, Merthyr Tydfil

Clubs from Northern Ireland
6 Glentoran
4 Ballymena U, Coleraine
3 Crusaders,
2 Ards, Glenavon, Linfield
1 Derry C, Distillery, Portadown, Carrick Rangers, Cliftonville

Clubs from Eire
6 Shamrock R
3 Limerick, Waterford, Dundalk
2 Cork Hibs, Bohemians
1 Shelbourne, Cork Celtic, St Patrick's Ath, Finn Harps, Home Farm, Sligo Rovers, University College Dublin, Galway U, Derry C*, Cork City

Winners: Tottenham H 1962–63; West Ham U 1964–65; Manchester C 1969–70; Chelsea 1970–71; Rangers 1971–72; Aberdeen 1982–83; Everton 1984–85

Finalists: Liverpool 1965–66; Rangers 1960–61, 1966–67; Leeds U 1972–73; West Ham U 1975–76; Arsenal 1979–80

EUROPEAN FAIRS CUP & UEFA CUP (1955–90)

English clubs
8 Leeds U, Ipswich T
6 Liverpool, Everton, Arsenal
5 Manchester U, Southampton, Tottenham H
4 Manchester C, Birmingham C, Newcastle U, Nottingham F, Wolverhampton W, WBA
3 Aston Villa, Chelsea
2 Sheffield W, Stoke C, Derby Co, QPR
1 Burnley, Coventry C, London Rep XI, Watford

Scottish clubs
15 Dundee U
13 Hibernian
10 Aberdeen
8 Rangers
6 Hearts
5 Dunfermline Ath, Celtic
4 Dundee
3 St Mirren, Kilmarnock
2 Partick Th
1 Morton, St Johnstone

Clubs from Northern Ireland
11 Glentoran
6 Coleraine
4 Linfield
2 Glenavon
1 Ards, Portadown, Ballymena U

Clubs from Eire
7 Bohemians
4 Dundalk
3 Finn Harps, Shamrock R
2 Shelbourne, Drumcondra, St Patrick's Ath
1 Cork Hibs, Athlone T, Limerick, Drogheda U, Galway U

Winners: Leeds U 1967–68, 1970–71; Newcastle U 1968–69; Arsenal 1969–70; Tottenham H 1971–72, 1983–84; Liverpool 1972–73, 1975–76; Ipswich T 1980–81

Finalists: Birmingham C 1958–60, 1960–61; Leeds U 1966–67; Wolverhampton W 1971–72; Tottenham H 1973–74; Dundee U 1986–87

* Now playing in League of Ireland.

WORLD CLUB CHAMPIONSHIP

Played annually up to 1974 and intermittently since then between the winners of the European Cup and the winners of the South American Champions Cup – known as the Copa Libertadores. In 1980 the winners were decided by one match arranged in Tokyo in February 1981 and the venue has been the same since.

1960 Real Madrid beat Penarol 0-0, 5-1	1976 Bayern Munich beat Cruzeiro 2-0, 0-0
1961 Penarol beat Benfica 0-1, 5-0, 2-1	1977 Boca Juniors beat Borussia Moenchengladbach
1962 Santos beat Benfica 3-2, 5-2	2-2, 3-0
1963 Santos beat AC Milan 2-4, 4-2, 1-0	1978 Not played
1964 Inter-Milan beat Independiente 0-1, 2-0, 1-0	1979 Olimpia beat Malmö 1-0, 2-1
1965 Inter-Milan beat Independiente 3-0, 0-0	1980 Nacional beat Nottingham Forest 1-0
1966 Penarol beat Real Madrid 2-0, 2-0	1981 Flamenco beat Liverpool 3-0
1967 Racing Club beat Celtic 0-1, 2-1, 1-0	1982 Penarol beat Aston Villa 2-0
1968 Estudiantes beat Manchester United 1-0, 1-1	1983 Gremio Porto Alegre beat SV Hamburg 2-1
1969 AC Milan beat Estudiantes 3-0, 1-2	1984 Independiente beat Liverpool 1-0
1970 Feyenoord beat Estudiantes 2-2, 1-0	1985 Juventus beat Argentinos Juniors 4-2 on penalties
1971 Nacional beat Panathinaikos 1-1, 2-1	after a 2-2 draw
1972 Ajax beat Independiente 1-1, 3-0	1986 River Plate beat Steaua Bucharest 1-0
1973 Independiente beat Juventus 1-0	1987 FC Porto beat Penarol 2-1 after extra time
1974 Atlético Madrid beat Independiente 0-1, 2-0	**1988 Nacional (Uru) beat PSV Eindhoven 7-6 on**
1975 Independiente and Bayern Munich could not agree dates; no matches.	**penalties after 1-1 draw**

1989

17 December in Tokyo

AC Milan (0) 1 *(Evani 118)*

Atletico Nacional (0) 0 *aet*   62,000

AC Milan: Galli; Tassotti, Maldini, Fuser (Evani 65), Costacurta, Baresi, Donadini, Rijkaard, Van Basten, Ancelotti, Massaro (Simone 69).
Nacional: Higuita; Escobar, Gildardo Gomez, Herrera, Cassiani, Ricardo Perez, Arango (Restrepo 91), Alvarez, Arboleda (Uzurriaga 46), Garcia, Trellez.
Referee: Fredriksson (Sweden).

EUROPEAN SUPER CUP

Played annually between the winners of the European Champions' Cup and the European Cup-Winners' Cup.

Previous Matches

1972 Ajax beat Rangers 3-1, 3-2
1973 Ajax beat AC Milan 0-1, 6-0
1974 Not contested
1975 Dynamo Kiev beat Bayern Munich 1-0, 2-0
1976 Anderlecht beat Bayern Munich 4-1, 1-2
1977 Liverpool beat Hamburg 1-1, 6-0
1978 Anderlecht beat Liverpool 3-1, 1-2
1979 Nottingham F beat Barcelona 1-0, 1-1
1980 Valencia beat Nottingham F 1-0, 1-2
1981 Not contested
1982 Aston Villa beat Barcelona 0-1, 3-0
1983 Aberdeen beat Hamburg 0-0, 2-0
1984 Juventus beat Liverpool 2-0
1985 Juventus v Everton not contested due to UEFA ban on English clubs
1986 Steaua Bucharest beat Dynamo Kiev 1-0
1987 FC Porto beat Ajax 1-0, 1-0
1988 KV Mechelen beat PSV Eindhoven 3-0, 0-1

1989

First Leg, 23 November 1989, Barcelona

Barcelona (0) 1 *(Amor 67)*

AC Milan (1) 1 *(Van Basten 44 pen)*   50,000

Barcelona: Zubizarreta; Aloisio, Koeman, Serna, Eusebio, Milia, Baquero, Amor, Laudrup, Salinas (Roberto 65), Beguiristain.
AC Milan: Galli; Salvatore, Maldini, Fuser, Tassotti, Costacurta, Donadoni (Stroppa 84), Rijkaard, Van Basten, Evani, Massaro (Simone 88).
Referee: Quiniou (France).

Second Leg, 7 December 1989, Milan

AC Milan (0) 1 *(Evani 55)*

Barcelona (0) 0   50,000

AC Milan: Galli; Carobbi, Maldini, Fuser, Tassotti, Costacurta, Donadoni, Rijkaard, Van Basten, Evani, Massaro (Simone 65).
Barcelona: Zubizarreta; Lopez Recarte (Onesimo 74), Alesanco, Milia, Serena, Roberto, Baquero, Jordi Roura (Soler 10), Eusebio, Salinas, Beguiristain.
Referee: Kohl (Austria).

HARTLEPOOL UNITED *(continued from page 275)*

Player and Position	Ht	Wt	Birth Date	Place	Source	Clubs	League App	Gls
Wayne Entwistle‡	5 11	11 08	6 8 58		Apprentice	Bury	31	7
						Sunderland	45	12
						Leeds U	11	2
						Blackpool	32	6
						Crewe Alex	11	—
						Wimbledon	9	3
					Grays Ath	Bury	83	32
						Carlisle U	9	2
						Bolton W	8	—
						Burnley (loan)	8	2
						Stockport Co	49	8
						Bury	2	—
						Wigan Ath	29	6
						Hartlepool U	2	—
Simon Grayson	6 1	12 00	21 10 68	Sheffield		Sheffield U	—	—
						Chesterfield (loan)	8	—
						Hartlepool U	44	12
Don Hutchison	6 2	11 04	9 5 71	Gateshead	Trainee	Hartlepool U	13	2
Alan Lamb	5 10	11 12	30 10 70	Gateshead		Nottingham F	—	—
						Hereford U (loan)	10	2
						Hartlepool U	10	—
Gary MacDonald	6 0	12 01	26 3 62	Middlesbrough	Apprentice	Middlesbrough	53	5
						Carlisle U	9	—
						Darlington	162	35
						Stockport Co	1	—
						Hartlepool U	16	1
Gardner Speirs‡	5 8	10 00	14 4 63	Airdrie	St Mirren BC	St Mirren	90	15
						Kilmarnock	5	—
						Dunfermline Ath	4	—
						Hartlepool U	1	—

LEEDS UNITED *(continued from page 305)*

Player and Position	Ht	Wt	Birth Date	Place	Source	Clubs	League App	Gls
Vince Hilaire	5 6	10 00	10 10 59	Forest Hill	Apprentice	Crystal Palace	255	29
						Luton T	6	—
						Portsmouth	146	26
						Leeds U	44	6
						Stoke C (loan)	5	1
						Charlton Ath (loan)	—	—
Alessandro Nista*			10 7 65	Livorno	Pisa	Leeds U	—	—
John Pearson	6 2	13 02	1 9 63	Sheffield	Apprentice	Sheffield W	105	24
						Charlton Ath	61	15
						Leeds U	86	11
Carl Shutt	5 10	11 10	10 10 61	Sheffield	Spalding U	Sheffield W	40	16
						Bristol C	46	10
						Leeds U	23	6
Imre Varadi	5 8	11 01	8 7 59	Paddington	Letchworth GC	Sheffield U	10	4
						Everton	26	6
						Newcastle U	81	39
						Sheffield W	76	33
						WBA	32	9
						Manchester C	65	26
						Sheffield W	22	3
						Leeds U	13	2

NON-LEAGUE FOOTBALL

FA CHALLENGE TROPHY

FA CHALLENGE VASE

FA SUNDAY CUP

FA YOUTH CUP AND COUNTY YOUTH CUP

GM VAUXHALL CONFERENCE

HFS LOANS LEAGUE

BEAZER HOMES LEAGUE

VAUXHALL OPEL LEAGUE

AFA, SCHOOLS AND UNIVERSITIES

GM VAUXHALL CONFERENCE 1989–90

The championship was not decided until the last day of the season when Darlington needing only a draw at Welling to be certain of the title won with an 87th minute goal, leaving Barnet's 4-1 victory at Chorley of little title significance.

Barnet thus finished runners-up for the third time in four years and Darlington emulated the feat of Lincoln City in returning to the Football League at the first time of asking.

Overall attendances again rose to a record 1429 per game and Darlington had the best support with 3588 at Feethams, which compared with 2314 during their last season in the Fourth Division.

Barnet attracted 2,869 per game and 12 clubs in the League reported increased crowds over the previous season.

GM VAUXHALL CONFERENCE TABLE 1989–90

| | | | Home | | Goals | | Away | | | Goals | | |
	P	W	D	L	F	A	W	D	L	F	A	Pts
Darlington	42	13	6	2	43	12	13	3	5	33	13	87
Barnet	42	15	4	2	46	14	11	3	7	35	27	85
Runcorn	42	16	3	2	52	20	3	10	8	27	42	70
Macclesfield Town	42	11	6	4	35	16	6	9	6	21	25	66
Kettering Town	42	13	5	3	35	15	5	7	9	31	38	66
Welling United	42	11	6	4	36	16	7	4	10	26	34	65
Yeovil Town	42	9	8	4	32	25	8	4	9	30	29	63
Sutton United	42	14	2	5	42	24	5	4	12	26	40	63
Merthyr Tydfil	42	9	9	3	41	30	7	5	9	26	33	62
Wycombe Wanderers	42	11	6	4	42	24	6	4	11	22	32	61
Cheltenham Town	42	9	6	6	30	22	7	5	9	28	38	59
Telford United	42	8	7	6	31	29	7	6	8	25	34	58
Kidderminster Harriers	42	7	6	8	37	33	8	3	10	27	34	54
Barrow	42	11	8	2	33	25	1	8	12	18	42	52
Northwich Victoria	42	9	3	9	29	30	6	2	13	22	37	50
Altrincham	42	8	5	8	31	20	4	8	9	18	28	49
Stafford Rangers	42	9	6	6	25	23	3	6	12	25	39	48
Boston United	42	10	3	8	36	30	3	5	13	12	37	47
Fisher Athletic	42	9	1	11	34	34	4	6	11	21	44	46
Chorley	42	9	5	7	26	26	4	1	16	16	41	45
Farnborough Town	42	7	5	9	33	30	3	7	11	27	43	42
Enfield	42	9	3	9	36	34	1	3	17	16	55	36

GM VAUXHALL CONFERENCE ATTENDANCES 1989–1990

Aggregate 1989–90	Average Gate	% Inc	Gates over 1000	Gates over 2000	Clubs with % Inc
660,181	1429	+ 9	63%	21%	12

GM VAUXHALL CONFERENCE ATTENDANCES BY CLUB 1989–1990

Club	Aggregate Attendance 1989/90	Average Gate 1989/90	% Inc or Dec	Average Gate 1988/89	Gates over 1000
Darlington	75,343	3588	+ 55	2314	21
Barnet	60,244	2869	+ 18	2431	21
Yeovil Town	47,319	2253	− 6	2395	21
Kettering Town	46,359	2208	− 12	2506	21
Wycombe Wanderers	39,684	1890	− 16	2248	21
Merthyr Tydfil	34,554	1645	+ 16	1417	20
Boston United	33,160	1579	− 13	1826	21
Cheltenham Town	29,875	1423	+ 14	1245	19
Macclesfield Town	29,856	1422	0	1433	17
Kidderminster Harriers	29,712	1415	− 6	1504	17
Barrow	27,129	1292	+ 24	1042	19
Telford United	25,607	1219	− 1	1235	16
Stafford Rangers	24,946	1188	+ 6	1118	17
Welling United	23,238	1108	+ 9	1017	12
Farnborough Town	19,670	937	+ 65	567	8
Sutton United	19,208	915	+ 7	857	5
Enfield	17,642	840	+ 8	780	3
Runcorn	16,987	809	+ 3	785	4
Altrincham	16,578	789	− 15	930	3
Chorley	16,036	764	− 14	891	3
Northwich Victoria	15,242	726	− 3	753	1
Fisher Athletic	11,792	562	+ 6	529	2

HIGHEST ATTENDANCES 1989–90

5880	Barnet v Darlington	31.3.90	4297	Darlington v Wycombe Wanderers	14.4.90
5525	Darlington v Cheltenham Town	28.4.90	4244	Barrow v Darlington	1.1.90
4741	Darlington v Barrow	26.12.89	4237	Yeovil Town v Telford United	5.5.90
4546	Darlington v Macclesfield Town	3.4.90	3886	Darlington v Barnet	4.10.89
4481	Barnet v Enfield	26.12.89	3880	Darlington v Kettering Town	30.9.89

GM VAUXHALL CONFERENCE LEADING GOALSCORERS

Conf.			FA	BL	FT
28	Robbie Cooke (Kettering Town)	+	—	—	—
25	Efan Ekoku (Sutton United)	+	—	—	—
23	Simon Read (Farnborough Town)	+	2	1	—
21	Ian Thompson (Merthyr Tydfil)	+	3	—	—
19	John Borthwick (Darlington)	+	2	1	—
	Mark Carter (Runcorn)	+	—	1	2
18	Mick Doherty (Runcorn)	+	1	—	—
17	Gary Bull (Barnet)	+	5	3	—
	Andrew Clarke (Barnet)	+	2	—	—
	Paul Furlong (Enfield)	+	—	1	1
	Paul Gorman (Fisher Athletic)	+	—	—	—
	Terry Robbins (Welling United)	+	2	2	1
	Dave Webley (Merthyr Tydfil)	+	2	—	—
16	Steve Burr (Macclesfield Town)	+	3	—	2
	Kim Casey (Kidderminster Harriers)	+	—	6	3
15	Paul McKinnon (Sutton United)	+	1	3	—
	Mark West (Wycombe Wanderers)	+	1	2	1
14	Martin Hanchard (Northwich Victoria)	+	2	—	—
	Mark Whitehouse (Kidderminster Harriers)	+	2	2	3
12	David Cork (Darlington)	+	1	1	3
	Colin Cowperthwaite (Barrow)	+	2	1	—
	Ken McKenna (Telford United)	+	—	—	2
	Mickey Spencer (Yeovil Town)	+	1	3	1

GM VAUXHALL CONFERENCE SPONSORSHIP AWARDS 1989–90

	GM Vauxhall Sponsorship	GM Vauxhall Jackpot	Title Award	PPA	Total
Darlington	3000	250	8000	2500	13,750
Barnet	3000	750	4000	2500	10,000
Runcorn	3000	750	3000	2500	9250
Farnborough Town	3000	500	—	2500	6000
Kidderminster H.	3000	500	—	2500	6000
Macclesfield Town	3000	500	—	2500	6000
Merthyr Tydfil	3000	500	—	2500	6000
Welling United	3000	250	—	2500	5750
Altrincham	3000	—	—	2500	5500
Barrow	3000	—	—	2500	5500
Boston United	3000	—	—	2500	5500
Cheltenham Town	3000	—	—	2500	5500
Chorley	3000	—	—	2500	5500
Enfield	3000	—	—	2500	5500
Fisher Athletic	3000	—	—	2500	5500
Kettering Town	3000	—	—	2500	5500
Northwich Victoria	3000	—	—	2500	5500
Stafford Rangers	3000	—	—	2500	5500
Sutton United	3000	—	—	2500	5500
Telford United	3000	—	—	2500	5500
Wycombe Wanderers	3000	—	—	2500	5500
Yeovil Town	3000	—	—	2500	5500

HIGHEST SCORERS

5 Mick Doherty *RUNCORN* v Enfield
(GM Vauxhall Conference 3.3.90)
4 David Cork *DARLINGTON* v Boston United
(GM Vauxhall Conference 13.2.90)
Hughie Mann *FISHER ATHLETIC* v Merthyr Tydfil
(GM Vauxhall Conference 5.5.90)

HIGHEST AGGREGATE SCORES

Runcorn 9-0 Enfield 3.3.90
Farnborough Town 6-3 Runcorn 11.11.89
Enfield 3-5 Wycombe Wanderers 19.9.89

LARGEST HOME WINS

Runcorn 9-0 Enfield 3.3.90
Welling United 6-0 Boston United 29.11.89
Darlington 6-1 Boston United 13.2.90
Sutton United 6-1 Telford United 28.10.89
Wycombe Wanderers 6-1 Fisher Athletic 26.9.89

LARGEST AWAY WINS

Barrow 1-5 Merthyr Tydfil 18.4.90
Stafford Rangers 0-4 Darlington 21.4.90
Telford United 0-4 Chorley 9.12.89
Wycombe Wanderers 0-4 Cheltenham Town 30.12.89
Yeovil Town 0-4 Welling United 13.9.89

MATCHES WITHOUT DEFEAT

13 Darlington
10 Runcorn
8 Barnet, Barrow, Welling United
7 Barrow, Darlington (twice), Kidderminster Harriers, Sutton United, Yeovil Town

MATCHES WITHOUT A WIN

12 Enfield
10 Stafford Rangers
9 Fisher Athletic, Stafford Rangers
8 Barrow, Farnborough Town, Macclesfield Town, Northwich Victoria

CONSECUTIVE CONFERENCE VICTORIES

8 Barnet
7 Welling United
5 Darlington, Sutton United
4 Darlington (twice), Fisher Athletic, Kettering Town, Macclesfield Town

CONSECUTIVE CONFERENCE DEFEATS

6 Northwich Victoria
5 Enfield (twice), Northwich Victoria
4 Altrincham, Barrow, Chorley, Enfield, Fisher Athletic (twice), Kidderminster Harriers, Northwich Victoria, Yeovil Town

GM VAUXHALL CONFERENCE 1989–90

APPEARANCES AND GOALSCORERS

Altrincham
Baker, M. 41; Byrne, P. 9(13); Cook, C. 5; Crompton, J. 8(6); Davies, S. 1(1); Daws, N. 27(3); Diamond, B. 8(1); Easter, G. 3; Ellis, R. 9(3); Entwistle, W. 12; Farrelly, M. 8(4); Gamble, D. 8(4); Greenough, R. 6; Haw, S. 11(1); Heesom, D. 16(2); Hughes, M. 26; Knowles, B. 12; Lewis, M. 6; McMahon, J. 28(4); Mellish, S. 3(2); Murray, E. 16(6); Page, D. 4; Reid, A. 33(2); Roberts, S. 1; Rooney, A. 19; Rowlands, P. 39; Shaw, N. 33(2); Simpson, G. 22(2); Stewart, G. 5; Wealands, J. 41; Wood, N. 2.
Goals (49): Hughes 8, McMahon 5, Baker 4, Haw 4, Shaw 4, Easter 3, Ellis 3, Murray 3, Rowlands 3, Byrne 2, Diamond 2, Entwistle 2, Greenough 2, Daws 1, Knowles 1, Wood 1, own goal 1.

Barnet
Beattie, A. 29(1); Bodley, M. 7; Bull, G. 40; Clarke, A. 35(1); Cooper, G. 31(5); Cosby, A. (1); Gipp, D. (12); Gridelet, P. 37(2); Guthrie, P. 18; Harding, P. 12(2); Hayrettin, H. 4(2); Ironton, N. 2(1); Mehmet, D. 2; Murphy, F. 14(16); Payne, D. 25(7); Phillips, G. 24; Poole, G. 28(1); Regis, D. 16(6); Reilly, G. 16(2); Ryan, L. (1); Stacey, P. 31(3); Stein, E. 38(2); Turner, W. 1; Welsh, S. 6(3); Wilson, P. 41(1).
Goals (81): Bull 17, Clarke 17, Murphy 9, Regis 9, Gridelet 5, Cooper 4, Gipp 3, Harding 3, Poole 3, Reilly 3, Payne 2, Stacey 2, Stein 2, Beattie 1, own goal 1.

Barrow
Burgess, I. 24(7); Capstick, J. 14(1); Chilton, T. 31; Copeland, L. 2; Cowperthwaite, C. 34; Doherty, N. 41(1); Farrell, P. 32(2); Ferris, P. 21; Gilmour, B. 31(3); Gordon, K. 36; Hampson, P. (3); Higgins, S. 34; Jackson, M. 6(3); Lowe, K. 38; Mason S. 2 (6); McDonnell, P. 40; Messenger, G. 6(6); Proctor, K. 19; Skivington, G. 31; Todhunter, S. 20(8).
Goals (51): Cowperthwaite 12, Farrell 8, Gilmour 8, Doherty 5, Burgess 3, Capstick 3, Gordon 3, Proctor 3, Lowe 2, Messenger 2, Ferris 1, Higgins 1.

Boston United
Brogan, M. 2; Buckley, S. 25(7); Campbell, W. 19; Cook, C. 5(3); Cook, M. 28(4); Crombie, A. 11; Cusack, D. 28(1); Danzey, M. 3(1); Deane, A. 4(3); Gallagher, J. 14(5); Gamble, M. 17(5); Grant, D. 19(6); Grocock, C. 11; Hamill, S. 34(4); Hardy, M. 39(1); Hawkey, S. 1(1); Marshall, G. 1; McEwan, S. 14(1); McGinley, J. 17;McKenna, J. 40; McLaughlin, S. 10(6); Moore, D. 1(1); Morris, C. 9; Mossman, D. 2(1); Rawcliff, P. 4(3); Searchwell, N. (2); Shirtliff, P. 39; Simpson, G. 5; Stoutt, S. 7; Vaughan, D. 28; Waitt, M. 2; Wharton, D. 13; Willis, R. 10.
Goals (48): McGinley 10, Hamill 6, Willis 5, Cook 3, Deane 3, Hardy 3, Morris 3, Stoutt 3, Gamble 2, Grocock 2, McEwan 2, McLaughlin 2, Campbell 1, Grant 1, Rawcliff 1, own goal 1.

Cheltenham Town
Baverstock, R. 24(3); Beasley, A. 7; Boyland, M. 17(5); Brain, S. 13(5); Brooks, S. 35; Buckland, M. 41; Burns, C. 19(5); Churchward, A. 26; Craig, D. 7; Crawly, R. 35(3); Crouch, S. 11(4); Gray, A. 19; Jordan, N. 29(5); Lissaman, G. 2(2); Mardenborough, S. 9(3); Mogg, D. 9; Nuttell, M. 22(5); Purdie, J. 5(4); Sanderson, J. 4(8); Vircavs, A. 31; Whealan, S. 26(2); Willetts, K. 31; Williams, P. 40.
Goals (58): Buckland 11, Jordan 7, Brooks 5, Gray 5, Nuttell 5, Willetts 5, Brain 4, Boyland 3, Crawly 3, Williams 3, Mardenborough 2, Burns 1, Craig 1, Vircavs 1, own goals 2.

Chorley
Allan, S. 33; Brady, I. 41; Caldwell, R. 18(1); Clegg, T. 1(1); Cooper, C. 35; Dawson, R. 17; Diamond, B. 7; Edey, C. 10; Glendon, K. 23(2); Griffin, P. 11(5); Hughes, J. 3; Jackson, C. 38; Jones, G. 8; Keeley, G. 21; Lester, M. 14; Lomax, G. 7(2); Mellor, P. 1(1); Moss, P. 23(6); Neenan, J. 42; Peters, N. 26(2); Power, P. 20(5); Ross, B. 16(9); Sayer, P. 2(1); Smith, B. 9(2); Stimpson, B. 4; Walker, G. 2(1); Wardle, C. 26; Wright, N. 3(1); Yates, S. 1.
Goals (42): Power 11, Caldwell 5, Brady 4, Moss 4, Dawson 3, Diamond 3, Ross 3, Cooper 2, Glendon 2, Keeley 2, Griffin 1, Smith 1, Wardle 1.

Darlington
Anderson, D. 1(2); Batch, N. 8; Borthwick J. 41(1); Coatsworth. G. 3; Cork, D. 41; Corner, D. 41; Coverdale, D. 12(7); Emson, P. 28(6); Geddis, D. 9; Gill, G. 6(2); Gray, F. 36; Hine, M. 21; Hyde, G. 1(7); Kasule, V. 2; Linacre, P. 1(1); Mardenborough, S. 9(8); McJannet, L. 40; Prudhoe, M. 34; Robinson, N. 8; Smith, K. 39; Stephens, A. 4(19); Toman, A. 39(1); Willis, J. 38; Willis, P. (3).
Goals (76): Borthwick 19, Cork 12, Corner 9, Emson, 7, Toman 7, Hine 6, Geddis 3, Smith 3, Stephens 2, Willis 2, Coatsworth 1, Coverdale 1, Gray 1, Kasule 1, Mardenborough 1, McJannet 1.

Enfield
Abbott, G. 20(6); Atkin, P. 2; Benstock, D. 10(6); Campbell, A. 8(1); Coles, F. 4(5); Cooper, J. 7(5); Cottington, B. 14(2); Dalorto, G. 3(4); Docker, J. 2; Donnellan, G. 8; Edmunds, A. 17(4); Fergusson, I. 4; Francis, N. 22(2); Furlong, P. 36(1); Harding, P. 22; Hayrettin, H. 7(2); Hayzelden, K. 7; Holsgrove, P. 1(2); Howell, D. 25; Howells, G. 3; Hughton, H. 8(2); Ironton, N. 19(1); Keen, N. 19; Kemplen, C. 1; Kennedy, A. 2; Mehmet, D. 4; Mudd, K. 20(3); Pape, A. 39; Parkin, R. 22; Quinn, J. 12; Sim, P. (1); Smart, E. 22; Smart, S. 1; Smith, G. 9(5); Sparrow, B. 10(1); Stone, P. (1); Turner, P. 16; Waite, D. 9; Warmington, C. 11; Wilkinson, T. 17(1).
Goals (52): Furlong 17, Abbott 9, Francis 5, Harding 4, Benstock 3, Wilkinson 3, Turner 2, Cottington 1, Docker 1, Donnellan 1, Fergusson 1, Howell 1, Keen 1, Mehmet 1, Smart E. 1, own goal 1.

Farnborough Town
Banks, N. (2); Batty, L. 4; Braithwaite, R. 33(6); Bye, A. 40; Caldicott, M. (1); Calvert, T. (3); Donnellan, L. 10; Fielder, C. 34(3); Flanagan, T. 12(6); Frampton, M. 9(2); Gray, J. 23; Guthrie, P. 14; Hicks, J. 3(1); Holsgrove, P. 14(5); Horton, J. 27(2); Hughes, D. 12(3); Kerrins, W. 1(1); Link, D. 5; Mason, T. 42; McDonald, I. 15(2); Morris, D. 2(1); Osgood, D. 1(1); Parsons, F. 1; Powell, D. 13; Read, S. 40; Redknapp, M. 5; Rogers, A. 42; Smith, D. 1(1); Turkington, M. 31(1); Turner, P. 13; Wigmore, J. 15.
Goals (60): Read 23, Horton 6, Braithwaite 5, Bye 5, Frampton 3, Holsgrove 3, Rogers 3, Link 2, Turkington 2, Fielder 1, Hughes 1, Kerrins 1, Mason 1, McDonald 1, own goals 3.

Fisher Athletic
Ambrose, L. 15(6); Angell, D. 2; Blackford, G. 22(1); Boys, S. (1); Butler, G. 3(6); Carey, N. 1(2); Clark, F. 10(2); Collins, P. 31; Docker, J. 25(1); Dodds, A. (1); Donnelly, J. 3(2); Edwards, B. 5; England, S. 2(2); Ford, C. 3(2); Friar, P. 25(1); Gipp, D. 2; Gorman, P. 37(4); Hammond, P. 1; Hayrattin, S. 1; Hiscock, C. 3(2); Kennedy, M. 7(3); Keys, R. 1; Lee, J. 7; Little, B. 37; Malcolm, P. 1; Mann, H. 12; Marks, M. 6; Martin, D. 1(2); Massey, A. 38; Mehmet, D. 24; Mitchell, J. (1); Murray, S. 2; Neal, D. 7; Norman, N. 11; Nugent, K. 7; Nunes, S. 3(2); Nutton, M. 6; Palmer, L. 3; Rocadas, G. 5; Roles, J. 15(4); Scotting, A. 2; Shinners, R. 1; Stead, M. 37(2); Tivey, M. 2; Vogt, M. 1; Welch, R. (1); Wells, P. 36.
Goals (55): Gorman 17, Mann 9, Mehmet 6, Little 4, Lee 3, Massey 3, Ambrose 2, Blackford 2, Ford 1, Friar 1, Gipp 1, Malcolm 1, Marks 1, Neal 1, Norman 1, Nugent 1, Rocadas 1.

Kettering Town
Bastock, P. 2; Beech, G. 27(5); Boon, R. (1); Bowling, I. 2; Brown, R. 25(1); Collins, S. 38; Cooke, R. 39; Edwards, N. 5(7); Genovese, D. 7(4); Graham, J. (11); Griffith, C. 10; Horwood, N. 9(3); Jones, G. 12; Keast, D. 41; Lewis, R. 31; Mays, B. 1(1); Moss, E. 33(3); Nightingale, M. 34(2); Richardson, P. 33; Scope, D. 5(1); Shoemake, K. 38; Slack, T. 36(1); Wright, A. 34(5).
Goals (66): Cooke 28, Moss 8, Slack 5, Wright 4, Collins 3, Griffiths 3, Jones 3, Richardson 3, Beech 2, Keast 2, Lewis 2, Edwards 1, Genovese 1, Graham 1.

Kidderminster Harriers
Attwood, A. 1; Bancroft, P. 39; Barton, J. 24; Benton, D. 9(2); Blair, A. 10; Boxall, C. 15(1); Brazier, C. 14; Burton, C. 11; Casey, K. 36(1); Davies, P. 1; Dearlove, M. 15; Forsyth, R. 38; Howell, P. 23(4); Jones, P. 41; Jones, R. 7; Joseph, A. 17(4); Latchford, O. (1); Lilwall, S. 1; Lowe, J. 21; Mackenzie, G. 34(1); Mulders, J. 4(2); Pearson, J. 1(2); Shilvock, R. 6(2); Steadman, D. 1; Sugrue, P. 12(5); Tuohy, M. 13(7); Weir, M. 38; Whitehouse, M. 30(7).
Goals (64): Casey, 16, Whitehouse, 14, Forsyth 10, Howell 5, Sugrue 5, Burton 4, Barton 2, Attwood 1, Benton 1, Blair 1, Joseph 1, Mackenzie 1, Tuohy 1, Weir 1, own goal 1.

Macclesfield Town
Askey, J. 32(1); Askey, R. 5(3); Burr, S. 34; Connor, J. 19(3); Coyne, P. 3; Derbyshire, P. 10(4); Edwards, E. 37(1); Ellis, R. 19(1); Farrelly, H. 19(3); Glendon, K. 1; Hanlon, S. 42; Hardman, M. 12(9); Imrie, J. 32(3); Johnson, P. 32(1); Kendall, P. 24(1); Kirkham, P. 1; Lake, M. 11; Lyons, D. 1(3); Parlane, D. 1(1); Roberts, M. (1); Shepherd, G. 5; Timmons, J. 25(17); Tobin, G. 37; Wilson, P. 15; Worral, G. 3(17); Zelem, A. 42.
Goals (56): Burr 16, Askey 9, Hanlon 5, Edwards 4, Derbyshire 4, Imrie 3, Timmons 3, Ellis 2, Kendall 2, Lake 2, Askey 1, Hardman 1, Wilson 1, Worral 1, own goals 2.

Merthyr Tydfil
Beattie, A. 38(1); Evans, P. 37(4); French, N. 1(2); Giles, P. 34(6); Green, P. 16(23); Holby, C. 9(3); Homer, K. 1(5); Jones, P. 5(6); Lissaman, T. 24; Mullen, Roger 10(20); Mullen, Richard 3; Preece, R. (1); Rogers, K. 15; Sanderson, P. 20; Stephenson, N. 36(2); Thompson, I. 40; Tong, D. 21; Tucker, M. 20; Tupling, S. 2; Wager, G. 39; Webley, D. 37(1); Williams, Ceri 16(8); Williams, Chris (1); Williams, M. 1; Williams, S. 37(1).
Goals (67): Thompson 21, Webley 17, Green 7, Rogers 5, Beattie 2, Giles 2, Lissaman 2, Sanderson 2, Stephenson 2, Tucker 2, Mullen 1, Williams, Ceri, 1, Williams, S. 1, own goals 2.

Northwich Victoria
Aspin, J. 5; Blain, C. 34(2); Callaghan, I. 18(8); Carroll, M. (2); Coyle, T. 9(6); Crompton, A. 10; Crossley, R. 2; Edwards, P. 15; Edwards, R. 1; Fraser, R. 7(1); Hanchard, M. 31(6); Hancock, M. 12; Hollis, C. 1; Howard, M. 5; Jones, M. 37; Macowat, I. 15(1); Maguire, P. 39; McAughtrie, D. 32(1); McKearney, D. 3; Morton, N. 38(1); Nolan, I. 18(3); O'Connor, M. 27(4); Parker, D. 20(10); Roche, P. 1; Ryan, D. 25; Smith, O. 9(2); Smith, S. 5; Stringer, J. 8(1); Wintersgill, D. 6; Wrench, M. 3(1); Young, D. 26.
Goals (51): Hanchard 14, Morton 10, O'Connor 7, Maguire 6, Parker 4, Blain 3, Callaghan 1, Coyle 1, Howard 1, McAughtrie 1, Smith 1, Young 1, own goal 1.

Runcorn
Anderson, G. 28; Carroll, J. 37; Carter, M. 34; Densmore, P. 12; Doherty, M. 33(3); Edwards, T. 26; Ferguson, M. (5); Galloway, D. 24(2); Harold, I. 39; Highdale, D. 10(7); King, T. (1); Lomax, S. (10); McBride, R. 19; McNally, P. 12(5); Miller, T. 31(4); Murphy, C. 1(2); Rodwell, T. 12; Rudge, S. 23; Seasman, J. 26(1); Williams, A. 23; Williams, D. 21(5); Withers, P. 25(4); Woan, I. 26(3).
Goals (79): Carter 19, Doherty 18, Woan 11, Withers 9, Anderson 4, Seasman 4, Carroll 2, Rodwell 2, Rudge 2, Williams 2, Ferguson 1, Galloway 1, Highdale 1, McNally 1, Miller 1, own goal 1.

Stafford Rangers
Adams, K. 5(1); Atkinson, P. 7; Brown, I. 11; Camden, C. 38(2); Campbell, W. 8(2); Cavell, P. 31(2); Collymore, S. 11(5); Essex, S. 40; Gill, M. 26; Griffiths, A. 15(1); Heywood, D. 5(1); Johnson, C. (1); Jones, M. (5); King, P. 19; Knight, T. 1(2); Kurila, A. 40; Lundon, S. 4(1); Mossman, D. 2(1); Price, R. 42; O'Connor, J. 7(5); Reid,

J. 12; Simpson, W. 37; Turley, R. 16(5); Tyrell, A. 1; Upton, P. 36; Wassell, K. 2; Wharton, D. 20; Wood, F. 24(2); Wood, R. 2(5).
Goals (50): Cavell 12, Camden, 9, Gill 7, Collymore 4, Essex 4, Wood, F. 4, Turley 2, Atkinson 1, Campbell 1, Griffiths 1, Johnson 1, O'Connor 1, Reid 1, Upton 1, Wood, R. 1.

Sutton United
Adam, P. 6(2); Anderson, C. 12(7); Barwick, S. (3); Berry, G. 30; Cornwell, M. (1); Costello, M. (1); Dawson, P. 15; Dennis, L. 1; Dobinson, R. 3(1); Ekoku, E. 39; Fenton, J. 4(4); Flanagan, T. 8; Fowler, S. 5(1); Gates, P. 36; Golley, N. 23; Hanlan, M. 31(3); Hawkins, J. 18(3); Hemsley, S. 27; Massey, S. 30(1); McKinnon, P. 38; Morris, G. 1(4); Pratt, V. 7; Rains, T. 42; Robson, N. 2(1); Rogers, P. 29(1); Rondeau, I. 6; Seagroatt, R. 7(6); Stephens, M. (1); Sullivan, N. 42; Webb, S. (1).
Goals (68): Ekoku 25, McKinnon 15, Seagroatt 6, Hallan 5, Massey 5, Fowler 3, Anderson 2, Rains 2, Dawson 1, Golley 1, Hemsley 1, Rogers 1, own goal 1.

Telford United
Blackwell, K. 3; Brindley, C. 40; Brown, I. 15(1); Charlton, K. 38; Clarke, S. (2); Crawley, I. 14(3); Daly, G. 19(1); Davidson, M. 10; Eves, M. 18(3); Grainger, P. 35; Griffiths, A. 18(1); Hancock, M. 15; Harris, A. 5(1); Hunt, D. 7; Joseph, A. 14; Lloyd, T. 1(7); Lynex, S. 3; McGinty, J. 25; McKenna, K. 26(3); Mulliner, A. 1; Nelson, A. 29(8); Oakley, A. 2(3); Osbourne, G. 19(3); Roberts, M. (2); Sankey, I. 13(4); Stephens, G. 21; Storton, T. 2; Stringer, J. 15; Thompson, K. (1); Wiggins, H. 41(1); Williams, W. 13.
Goals (56): McKenna 12, Stringer 7, Crawley 6, Grainger 5, McGinty 4, Stephens 4, Brindley 3, Brown 3, Eves 3, Daly 2, Griffiths 1, Harris 1, Hunt 1, Lloyd 1, Oakley 1, own goals 2.

Welling United
Barron, P. 36; Booker, T. 30(2); Brown, W. 3(7); Buglione, M. 7(11); Burgess, R. 18(6); Clemmence, N. 37(2); Francis, J. 5(8); Glover, J. 41; Hales, R. 17(10); Handford, P. 34(3); Hone, M. 30; Horton, D. 38; Parsons, J. 5; Ransom, N. 41; Reynolds, T. 41; Robbins, T. 37; Shed, I. 1; Whited, S. 41.
Goals (62): Robbins 17, Booker 7, Glover 7, Reynolds 7, Hone 5, Whited 5, Hales 4, Burgess 3, Buglione 2, Clemmence 2, Ransom 2, Handford 1.

Wycombe Wanderers
Abbley, S. 23; Blackler, M. 4(3); Butler, M. (1); Carroll, D. 41(1); Creaser, G. 29; Crossley, M. 33(2); Durham, K. 34(4); Evans, N. 10; Franklin, P. 17(3); Gipp, D. 2(3); Granville, J. 42; Gumbs, D. 1; Guppy, S. 22(8); Kerr, A. 42; Kerr, J. 5; Lambert, M. 19; Pearson, R. 10(1); Piper, C. (1); Robinson, A. 31(1); Sanderson, P. 5; Smith, G. 9(6); Stapleton, S. 41(1); Thorpe, R. (10); West, M. 35(2); Wicks, S. 7.
Goals (64): West 15, Carroll 10, Durham 7, Lambert 5, Stapleton 5, Evans 4, Gipp 4, Guppy 4, Robinson 3, Butler 1, Creaser 1, Crossley 1, Franklin 1, Kerr, A. 1, Kerr, J. 1, Thorpe 1.

Yeovil Town
Blackman, B. 19(6); Bond, L. 10; Carroll, R. 36(1); Copeland, P. (1); Cordice, N. 26(7); Cunning, P. 33(4); Dawkins, D. 25(5); Dent, N. 6(13); Donnellan, G. 19(1); Ferns, P. 3(2); Fry, D. 32; Gill, C. 8(6); Gowans, S. 16(1); Lowe, T. 41; Pearson, G. 6(4); Quinn, J. 15(1); Rice, C. (1); Rutter, S. 17(1); Shail, M. 42; Sherewood, J. 24; Spencer, M. 39; Thomson, R. 5(3); Thorpe, P. 6(1); Wallace, A. 24(1); Wilson, P. 10(3).
Goals (62): Spencer 12, Carroll 11, Wallace 10, Cunning 6, Blackman 4, Dent 4, Wilson 3, Cordice 2, Gill 2, Lowe 2, Shail 2, Donnellan 1, Sherewood 1, own goals 2.

GM VAUXHALL CONFERENCE: MEMBER CLUBS SEASON 1990–1991

Club: ALTRINCHAM
Colours: Red and black striped shirts, black shorts
Ground: Moss Lane, Altrincham, Cheshire, WA15 8AP
Tel: 061 928 1045
Year Formed: 1903
Record Gate: 10,275 (1925 v Sunderland Boys)
Nickname: The Robins
Manager: John King
Secretary: Jean Baldwin

Club: BARNET
Colours: Amber shirts, black shorts
Ground: Underhill Stadium, Barnet Lane, Herts, EN5 2BE
Tel: 081 440 0277
Year Formed: 1888
Record Gate: 11,026 (1952 v Wycombe Wanderers)
Nickname: The Bees
Manager: Barry Fry
Secretary: Brian Ayres

Club: BARROW
Colours: White shirts, blue shorts
Ground: Holker Street, Barrow-in-Furness, Cumbria
Tel: 0229 23061
Year Formed: 1901
Record Gate: 16,840 (1954 v Swansea City)
Nickname: The Bluebirds
Manager: Ray Wilkie
Secretary: Cyril Whiteside

Club: BATH CITY
Colours: Black and white striped shirts, black shorts
Ground: Twerton Park, Bath BA2 1DB
Telephone: 0225 423087
Year Formed: 1889
Record Gate: 18,020 (1960 v Brighton)
Nickname: City
Manager: George Rooney
Secretary: Paul Britton

Club: BOSTON UNITED
Colours: Wolves gold shirts, black shorts
Ground: York Street Ground, York Street, Boston, Lincs
Tel: 0205 365524/5
Year Formed: 1934
Record Gate: 10,086 (v Corby Town)
Nickname: The Pilgrims
Manager: Dave Cusack
Secretary: John Blackwell

Club: CHELTENHAM TOWN
Colours: Red and white shirts, white shorts
Ground: Whaddon Road, Cheltenham, Glocs, GL52 5NA

Tel: 0242 513397
Year Formed: 1892
Record Gate: 8326 (1956 v Reading)
Nickname: The Robins
Manager: Jim Barron
Secretary: Reg Woodward

Club: COLCHESTER UNITED
Colours: Sky blue and white shirts, sky blue shorts
Ground: Layer Road, Colchester
Tel: 0206 574042
Year Formed: 1937
Record Gate: 19,072 (1948 v Reading)
Nickname: The U's
Manager: Ian Atkins
Secretary: Dee Ellwood

Club: FISHER ATHLETIC
Colours: Black and white shirts, black shorts
Ground: Surrey Docks Stadium, Salter Road, London, SE16
Tel: 071 231 5144
Year Formed: 1908
Record Gate: 2000 (1984 v Bristol City)
Nickname: The Fish
Manager: Mike Bailey
Secretary: Keith Wenham

Club: GATESHEAD
Colours: White shirts, black shorts
Ground: International Stadium, Neilson Road, Gateshead NE10 0EF
Telephone: 091 478 3883
Year Formed: 1977 (Reformed)
Record Gate: 20,752 (1937 v Lincoln City)
Nickname: Tynesiders
Manager: David Parnaby
Secretary: Jim Battla

Club: KETTERING TOWN
Colours: All red
Ground: Rockingham Road, Kettering, Northants, NN16 9AW
Tel: 0536 83028
Year Formed: 1875
Record Gate: 11,536 (1947 v Peterborough)
Nickname: The Poppies
Manager: Peter Morris
Secretary: George Ellitson

Club: KIDDERMINSTER HARRIERS
Colours: Red/white halves shirts, white shorts
Ground: Aggborough, Hoo Road, Kidderminster
Tel: 0562 823931
Year Formed: 1886
Record Gate: 9155 (1948 v Hereford)
Nickname: The Harriers
Manager: Graham Allner
Secretary: Ray Mercer

Club: MACCLESFIELD TOWN
Colours: Royal blue shirts, white shorts
Ground: Moss Rose Ground, London
  Road, Macclesfield, Cheshire, SK11 7SP
Tel: 0625 24324
Year Formed: 1875
Record Gate: 8900 (1968 v Stockport
  County)
Nickname: The Silkmen
Manager: Peter Wragg
Secretary: Barry Lingard

Club: MERTHYR TYDFIL
Colours: White shirts, black shorts
Ground: Penydarren Park, Merthyr Tydfil
Tel: 0685 4102
Year Formed: 1945
Record Gate: 21,000 (1949 v Reading)
Nickname: The Martyrs
Manager: Lyn Jones

Club: NORTHWICH VICTORIA
Colours: Green and white shirts, white
  shorts
Ground: The Drill Field, Northwich,
  Cheshire, CW9 5HN
Tel: 0606 41450
Year Formed: 1874
Record Gate: 11,290 (1949 v Witton
  Albion)
Nickname: The Vics
Manager: Cliff Roberts
Secretary: Derek Nuttall

Club: RUNCORN
Colours: Yellow shirts, green shorts
Ground: Canal Street, Runcorn, Cheshire
Tel: 09285 60076
Year Formed: 1919
Record Gate: 10,011 (1939 v Preston NE)
Nickname: The Linnets
Manager: Barry Whitehead
Secretary: Dave Bignall

Club: SLOUGH TOWN
Colours: Amber and navy broad hoops,
  navy blue shorts
Ground: Wexham Park Stadium, Wexham
  Road, Slough SL2 5QR
Tel: 0753 23358
Year Formed: 1890
Record Gate: 8940 (1953 v Pegasus at
  Dolphin Stadium); 5000 (1982 v Millwall
  at Wexham Stadium)
Nickname: The Rebels
Manager: Alan Davies
Secretary: Tony Abbott

Club: STAFFORD RANGERS
Colours: Black and white shirts, white
  shorts
Ground: Marston Road, Stafford, ST16
  3BX
Tel: 0785 42750

Year Formed: 1876
Record Gate: 8536 (1975 v Rotherham)
Nickname: The Boro
Manager:
Secretary: Angela Meddings

Club: SUTTON UNITED
Colours: Amber shirts, amber shorts
Ground: Boro Sports Ground, Gander
  Green Lane, Sutton, Surrey
Tel: 081 644 5120
Year Formed: 1898
Record Gate: 14,000 (1970 v Leeds United)
Nickname: The U's
Manager: Keith Blunt
Secretary: Brian Williams

Club: TELFORD UNITED
Colours: White shirts, blue shorts
Ground: Bucks Head, Watling Street,
  Telford, TF1 2NJ
Tel: 0952 223838
Year Formed: 1877
Record Gate: 13,000 (1935 v Shrewsbury)
Nickname: The Lillywhites
Manager: Derek Mann
Secretary: Mike Ferriday

Club: WELLING UNITED
Colours: Red shirts, red shorts
Ground: Park View Road Ground,
  Welling, Kent
Tel: 081 301 1196
Year Formed: 1963
Record Gate: 4020 (1989 v Gillingham)
Nickname: The Wings
Manager: Nicky Brigden
Secretary: Barrie Hobbins

Club: WYCOMBE WANDERERS
Colours: Light blue and dark blue quarters,
  navy blue shorts
Ground: Adams Park, Hillbottom Road,
  Sands, High Wycombe HP12 4HJ
Tel: 0494 26567
Year Formed: 1884
Record Gate: 16,000 (1950 v St Albans)
Nickname: The Blues
Manager: Martin O'Neill
Secretary: Alan Hutchinson

Club: YEOVIL TOWN
Colours: White shirts, green shorts
Ground: Huish Park, Boundary Road,
  Yeovil, BA22 9LL
Tel: 0935 23662
Year Formed: 1923
Record Gate: 17,200 (1949 v Sunderland)
Nickname: The Glovers
Manager: Brian Hall
Secretary: Roger Brinsford

GM VAUXHALL CONFERENCE RESULTS 1989-90

	Altrincham	Barnet	Barrow	Boston U	Cheltenham T	Chorley	Darlington	Enfield	Farnborough T	Fisher Ath	Kettering T	Kidderminster H	Macclesfield T	Merthyr Tydfil	Northwich Vic	Runcorn	Stafford R	Sutton U	Telford U	Welling U	Wycombe W	Yeovil Town
Altrincham	—	2-1	1-1	0-0	5-0	3-0	0-1	3-0	2-3	1-1	0-1	0-1	0-1	4-1	0-2	1-2	3-1	0-0	0-1	4-0	1-2	2-1
Barnet	1-0	—	1-0	1-2	4-0	5-0	0-2	2-0	4-1	4-1	4-1	2-1	0-0	4-0	1-0	2-2	1-1	4-1	2-1	1-1	2-0	1-0
Barrow	1-1	1-1	—	2-1	2-1	3-1	1-1	2-2	3-1	1-1	1-0	2-1	1-1	1-5	1-0	2-2	2-1	1-0	3-0	1-1	0-3	2-1
Boston U	2-3	1-2	2-1	—	2-1	0-1	1-3	3-1	2-2	2-0	1-2	2-3	2-1	0-2	2-3	3-2	3-0	3-1	2-2	2-1	2-0	0-1
Cheltenham T	0-0	2-0	1-0	0-0	—	0-1	0-1	2-1	1-0	0-0	1-2	2-1	0-0	1-0	1-2	0-2	1-3	2-0	1-2	3-2	1-1	2-1
Chorley	2-1	1-4	0-1	0-0	0-2	—	0-3	1-3	2-1	2-0	2-2	2-1	1-1	0-0	0-1	1-1	1-1	3-2	1-2	4-0	1-0	3-2
Darlington	2-0	1-2	0-0	6-1	5-1	3-0	—	2-1	1-1	2-0	1-1	1-0	1-1	0-1	4-0	1-1	2-1	2-3	1-1	1-0	0-1	1-0
Enfield	2-1	1-3	3-0	0-1	4-2	1-3	0-3	—	0-0	5-0	3-1	3-0	1-2	9-0	2-0	0-1	4-1	1-3	2-1	1-0	2-3	1-1
Farnborough T	0-0	0-1	4-0	1-0	4-0	2-0	1-0	0-0	—	1-2	1-1	2-1	1-3	0-1	0-1	0-0	3-3	1-2	1-3	2-3	3-5	2-4
Fisher Ath	3-0	1-2	2-0	5-0	2-5	2-1	0-2	3-2	4-2	—	3-0	0-1	2-2	1-2	3-1	3-0	0-2	2-0	3-0	3-1	1-1	1-0
Kettering T	3-0	3-2	2-0	1-3	1-2	3-1	1-3	3-2	1-1	1-1	—	1-1	2-2	2-0	4-0	4-0	0-0	2-0	3-1	0-1	3-1	1-2
Kidderminster H	1-2	0-1	2-1	0-0	3-0	1-0	3-2	4-0	3-1	3-0	3-1	—	2-3	1-2	3-1	3-2	3-0	2-2	2-2	1-3	0-2	1-0
Macclesfield T	1-0	0-1	3-3	1-0	1-1	0-1	0-0	5-1	2-0	1-1	3-2	2-3	—	2-2	1-1	4-3	2-2	2-0	1-2	3-2	1-0	3-1
Merthyr Tydfil	0-0	2-1	1-0	0-1	1-1	1-0	1-0	2-3	3-2	1-4	2-3	1-2	2-3	—	2-0	4-0	4-3	1-0	0-1	4-0	1-1	1-0
Northwich Vic	2-3	0-2	1-0	1-0	2-4	1-0	1-0	1-0	3-2	2-1	3-1	2-1	2-0	3-1	—	3-0	1-0	3-0	3-0	2-3	2-0	3-1
Runcorn	0-0	2-2	4-3	3-1	0-1	1-0	6-3	1-0	3-2	4-0	3-2	2-1	2-0	3-1	2-1	—	3-0	1-0	3-0	5-0	1-0	1-1
Stafford R	3-1	1-1	1-1	0-0	1-0	1-0	2-1	1-0	3-3	1-3	1-1	0-1	4-2	1-1	1-0	1-1	—	3-1	0-2	3-0	1-0	0-0
Sutton U	2-1	1-3	3-3	2-0	0-2	3-0	0-4	1-1	2-3	2-1	1-3	1-2	2-1	1-1	2-1	3-0	1-0	—	6-1	1-0	4-1	3-1
Telford U	1-3	1-3	3-0	4-2	0-0	0-1	0-1	3-0	4-2	3-1	3-0	1-1	1-0	0-3	2-1	1-0	0-2	1-1	—	2-0	0-0	0-1
Welling U	1-1	3-1	0-0	6-0	1-1	3-1	0-1	1-0	4-3	2-0	2-2	4-1	0-1	1-2	2-0	5-0	1-0	1-0	1-1	—	1-0	0-4
Wycombe Wanderers	1-1	1-0	4-0	1-0	0-4	4-0	0-1	1-0	1-0	6-1	1-0	3-3	1-1	1-1	3-3	1-1	2-1	1-0	1-0	1-0	—	4-2
Yeovil Town	0-0	3-2	2-2	2-1	1-1	2-1	0-2	3-1	0-0	2-2	0-2	3-1	0-0	4-0	1-2	1-1	0-0	3-1	1-0	0-4	1-2	—

THE BOB LORD CHALLENGE TROPHY 1989–90

First Round (2 legs)

Cheltenham Town 1 (Brooks)	
Telford United 0	851
Telford United 3 (Grainger, Eves, Osborne)	
Cheltenham Town 1 (Sanderson)	773
Chorley 0	
Barrow 1 (Burgess)	508
Barrow 2 (Doherty, Cowperthwaite)	
Chorley 0	806
Enfield 2 (Furlong, Edmunds)	
Fisher Athletic 3 (Clark, Marks 2)	464
Fisher Athletic 1 (Ambrose)	
Enfield 0	434
Farnborough Town 1 (Read)	
Merthyr Tydfil 2 (Beattie, og)	592
Merthyr Tydfil 0	
Farnborough Town 0	1017
Stafford Rangers 1 (Brown)	
Altrincham 1 (Shaw)	599
Altrincham 2 (Byrne, Hughes)	
Stafford Rangers 0	585
Sutton United 3 (Massey, McKinnon 2 (1 pen)	
Welling United 2 (Clemmence, og)	606
Welling United 4 (Robbins 2, Booker, Glover)	
Sutton United 2 (Massey, McKinnon) aet	716

Byes to Second Round

Barnet, Boston United, Darlington, Kettering Town, Kidderminster Harriers, Macclesfield Town, Northwich Victoria, Runcorn, Wycombe Wanderers, Yeovil Town.

Second Round

Barnet 3 (Stein, Bull, Regis)	
Kettering Town 2 (Genovese, Graham)	786
Boston United 3 (Willis, Searchwell, McGinlay)	
Fisher Athletic 0	646
Darlington 5 (Corner 2, Borthwick, Cork, Willis)	
Macclesfield Town 2 (Johnson, Butler)	2125
Kidderminster Harriers 3 (Casey, Sugrue, Whitehouse)	
Runcorn 3 (Withers 2, Carter) aet	925
Runcorn 1 (Withers)	
Kidderminster Harriers 3 (Forsyth 2, Weir)	772
Telford United 3 (Daly, Grainger, Osborne)	
Altrincham 2 (Hughes 2)	621
Welling United 1 (Glover) .	
Yeovil Town 2 (Carroll, Quinn)	810
Wycombe Wanderers 2 (Crossley, West)	
Merthyr Tydfil 0	703
Northwich Victoria 3 (Parker, O'Connor 2)	
Barrow 1 (Farrell)	344

Third Round

Kidderminster Harriers 3 (Forsyth, Casey, Burton)	
Darlington 1 (Hyde)	1473
Telford United 0	
Northwich Victoria 1 (Parker)	661
Boston United 0	
Wycombe Wanderers 2 (Lambert, West) aet	1425
Yeovil Town 3 (Dent 2, Spencer)	
Barnet 2 (Bull 2)	1252

Semi-Finals (2 legs)

Yeovil Town 2 (Wallace, Carroll)	
Wycombe Wanderers 1 (og)	1403
Wycombe Wanderers 3 (Carroll 2, Lambert)	
Yeovil Town 2 (Gill, Dent)	1556
(Yeovil Town won on away goals)	
Northwich Victoria 1 (Callaghan)	
Kidderminster Harriers 1 (Casey)	383
Kidderminster Harriers 6 (Casey 3, Mackenzie, Howell, Burton)	
Northwich Victoria 1 (Parker) aet	855

Final: First Leg Yeovil Town 3, Kidderminster Harriers 0, attendance 1609

Yeovil Town: Bond; Sherwood, Lowe, Shail (Dent), Rutter, Gowans, Carroll, Wallace, Wilson, Spencer (Dawkins), Conning. *Scorers:* Wallace, Wilson, Spencer.

Kidderminster Harriers: Jones; Burton, Bancroft, Boxall, Benton, Forsyth, Shilvock, Casey, Whitehouse, Howell, MacKenzie.

Second Leg Kidderminster Harriers 1, Yeovil Town 1, attendance 1009

Kidderminster Harriers: Jones; Lowe, Bancroft, Weir, Benton, Forsyth, Shilvock, Casey, Whitehouse, Tuohy, MacKenzie. *Scorer:* Forsyth.

Yeovil Town: Bond; Sherwood, Lowe, Shail (Conning), Rutter, Gowans, Carroll, Wallace, Wilson, Spencer (Dawkins), Cordice. *Scorer:* Conning.

HFS LOANS LEAGUE 1989–90

HFS LOANS LEAGUE – PREMIER DIVISION

		Home			Goals		Away			Goals		
	P	W	D	L	F	A	W	D	L	F	A	Pts
Colne Dynamoes	42	17	2	2	46	24	15	4	2	40	16	102
Gateshead	42	13	4	4	41	28	9	6	6	37	30	76
Witton Albion	42	14	3	4	39	10	8	4	9	28	29	73
Hyde United	42	13	2	6	43	24	8	6	7	30	26	71
South Liverpool	42	11	4	6	43	32	9	5	7	46	47	69
Matlock Town	42	13	3	5	39	17	5	9	7	22	25	66
Southport	42	10	7	4	27	17	7	7	7	27	31	65
Fleetwood Town	42	10	5	6	39	35	7	7	7	34	31	63
Marine	42	8	9	4	31	27	8	5	8	28	28	62
Bangor City	42	11	7	3	38	22	4	8	9	26	36	60
Bishop Auckland	42	9	4	9	46	34	8	4	9	26	30	59
Gainsborough Trinity	42	11	4	6	34	20	5	4	12	25	35	56
Frickley Ath	42	10	4	7	32	29	6	4	11	24	32	56
Horwich*[3]	42	8	7	6	38	33	7	6	8	28	36	55
Morecambe	42	11	5	5	39	30	4	4	13	19	40	54
Buxton	42	9	6	6	31	28	6	2	13	28	44	53
Stalybridge Celtic	42	8	4	9	31	30	4	5	12	17	31	45
Mossley	42	3	8	10	27	42	8	2	11	34	40	43
Goole Town	42	5	1	15	26	46	7	4	10	28	31	41
Shepshed Charterhouse	42	5	4	12	26	38	6	3	12	29	44	40
Caernarfon Town	42	5	6	10	25	30	5	2	14	31	56	38
Rhyl*[1]	42	4	6	11	21	33	3	4	14	22	44	30

* – pts deducted for breaches of rule   Goals scored – 1391 in 462 matches (average 3.010)

Leading scorers *(HFS Loans League and HFS cups only)*

Premier Division
26 Keith McNall (Gateshead)
25 Andy Green (South Liverpool)
24 Rod McDonald (Colne Dynamoes, inc 13 with South Liverpool)
22 Dave Lancaster (Colne Dynamoes)
21 Jim McCluskie (Hyde United, inc 11 with Mossley)
20 Steven Holden (Southport, inc 8 with Morecambe)
   Graham Hoyland (Matlock Town)
19 John Coleman (Witton Albion)
   Joe Olabode (Gateshead)
18 Tony Livens (Bangor City)
17 Ian Howat (Caernarfon Town)
   Mark Edwards (Witton Albion)
16 Trenton Wiggan (Gainsborough Trinity)
   Phil Clarkson (Fleetwood Town)

First Division
30 Ian Chandler (Whitley Bay)
29 Paul Beck (Rossendale United)

26 Darren Morris (Emley)
25 Peter McCrae (Lancaster City)
   Bernie Hughes (Droylsden)
   Mike Biddle (Congleton Town)
   Ian Blackstone (Harrogate Town, inc 13 with Accrington Stanley)
22 Billy Roberts (Farsley Celtic)
21 Dave Conlin (Netherfield)
19 Tony McDonald (Radcliffe Borough)
   Gary Haire (Whitley Bay)
18 Graham Nicholson (Workington)
   Bevan Blackwood (Lancaster City)
   Steve Parry (Rossendale United)
   Mark Richardson (Eastwood Town)
17 Kevin Todd (Whitley Bay)
   Alan Woan (Newtown)
16 Steve Curley (Accrington Stanley)
   Colin McCrory (Curzon Ashton)
   Dave Sutton (Leek Town)
   Simon Gate (Penrith)

HFS LOANS LEAGUE – FIRST DIVISION

		Home			Goals		Away			Goals		
	P	W	D	L	F	A	W	D	L	F	A	Pts
Leek Town	42	14	6	1	45	13	12	2	7	25	18	86
Droylsden*[7]	42	19	1	1	57	23	8	5	8	24	23	80
Accrington Stanley	42	14	4	3	46	19	8	6	7	34	34	76
Whitley Bay	42	10	4	7	46	32	11	7	3	47	27	74
Emley	42	14	3	4	45	17	6	6	9	25	25	69
Congleton Town*[3]	42	12	4	5	34	19	8	8	5	31	34	69
Winsford United	42	12	5	4	39	20	6	5	10	26	33	64
Curzon Ashton	42	9	5	7	30	24	8	6	7	36	36	62
Harrogate Town	42	10	4	7	40	29	7	5	9	28	33	60
Lancaster City	42	11	8	2	39	17	4	6	11	34	37	59
Eastwood Town	42	8	7	6	37	35	8	4	9	24	29	59
Farsley Celtic	42	10	4	7	33	29	7	2	12	39	47	57
Rossendale United	42	10	5	6	43	28	5	4	12	30	41	54
Newtown	42	7	7	7	25	26	7	5	9	24	36	54
Irlam Town	42	9	5	7	31	24	5	6	10	30	42	53
Workington	42	7	8	8	32	31	7	2	12	24	33	50
Radcliffe Borough	42	8	5	8	27	27	6	2	13	20	35	49
Alfreton Town	42	9	5	7	38	39	4	3	14	21	46	47
Worksop Town	42	9	3	9	37	33	4	2	15	19	62	44
Netherfield	42	9	1	11	32	34	2	5	14	24	55	39
Eastwood Hanley	42	8	4	9	31	32	2	2	17	14	44	36
Penrith	42	6	3	12	26	45	3	6	12	18	43	36

* – pts deducted for breaches of rule   Goals scored – 1409 in 462 matches (average 3.049)

HFS LOANS LEAGUE PREMIER DIVISION RESULTS 1989–90

	Bangor C	Bishop Auckland	Buxton	Caernarfon T	Colne Dynamoes	Fleetwood T	Frickley Ath	Gainsborough Tr	Gateshead	Goole T	Horwich	Hyde U	Marine	Matlock T	Morecambe	Mossley	Rhyl	Shepshed Ch	S Liverpool	Southport	Stalybridge	Witton Alb
Bangor C	—	5-0	2-2	1-2	2-1	0-0	2-2	1-1	2-1	1-4	1-2	2-1	3-0	0-0	1-1	1-0	4-3	2-1	2-1	2-2	3-1	2-0
Bishop Auckland	6-2	—	3-0	3-1	0-3	2-1	3-0	1-2	2-2	1-2	5-0	3-3	1-2	2-2	1-0	1-2	1-2	5-2	1-5	1-1	2-0	1-2
Buxton	2-2	3-0	—	1-1	1-2	1-3	1-0	2-1	0-4	1-0	2-0	1-2	1-4	1-0	4-0	0-3	3-0	1-1	3-3	0-1	2-1	2-2
Caernarfon T	1-2	0-2	1-1	—	1-0	0-4	1-3	1-2	1-1	0-0	1-0	1-1	0-2	1-0	3-0	3-3	3-1	3-0	2-3	0-1	0-1	1-1
Colne Dynamoes	2-1	2-2	0-0	1-2	—	2-2	2-1	4-1	2-1	2-1	4-2	1-3	3-1	3-3	3-1	3-2	2-1	2-1	6-1	1-0	1-0	1-1
Fleetwood T	2-0	0-2	3-1	4-3	2-2	—	1-3	3-1	0-2	2-1	2-2	3-2	0-0	2-1	1-2	2-1	4-2	1-0	6-0	1-1	1-0	3-2
Frickley Ath	1-1	2-1	4-3	0-2	1-3	1-3	—	3-1	0-1	2-4	2-0	1-1	1-1	2-1	1-0	1-3	3-1	2-0	2-2	1-0	1-0	1-6
Gainsborough Tr	4-2	1-0	3-0	4-1	3-2	0-1	0-1	—	1-0	1-0	1-1	3-1	1-0	1-3	1-1	2-0	1-2	0-1	2-2	1-2	1-0	2-1
Gateshead	2-1	1-0	3-1	2-1	1-0	1-3	1-0	2-1	—	2-2	3-2	2-1	0-1	1-1	5-1	4-2	1-1	3-1	0-2	3-3	3-1	1-2
Goole T	0-2	1-3	1-3	1-2	1-5	2-4	1-0	2-2	2-2	—	1-1	1-0	1-3	3-0	0-5	7-2	1-0	1-3	2-1	0-1	3-3	0-1
Horwich	2-2	1-2	1-1	5-1	1-3	3-2	0-1	1-1	4-1	1-0	—	1-1	1-3	2-0	1-0	2-3	1-2	4-2	2-2	5-4	1-1	0-2
Hyde U	1-0	1-2	1-0	3-0	2-2	3-1	1-0	3-1	4-0	0-2	0-2	—	0-2	0-2	2-0	0-1	3-1	1-1	1-2	1-3	2-0	1-0
Marine	3-3	0-0	3-1	3-2	1-0	1-1	2-1	0-3	2-3	6-0	1-3	1-0	—	1-1	2-0	1-1	3-1	5-1	4-3	1-2	1-1	2-0
Matlock T	3-0	3-1	1-0	3-0	2-0	2-0	0-2	0-1	1-1	0-3	3-3	2-0	2-1	—	2-0	2-1	1-0	1-2	1-2	3-2	2-0	0-2
Morecambe	2-1	2-2	4-4	4-4	1-3	2-2	1-0	2-1	1-3	0-0	1-2	0-0	1-3	2-0	—	0-2	3-1	1-2	2-0	3-1	3-2	5-0
Mossley	1-1	1-3	1-3	2-4	1-3	1-1	1-1	0-3	2-2	1-1	1-2	1-3	2-3	0-3	2-0	—	0-2	1-2	3-2	1-1	0-1	3-2
Rhyl	0-1	0-0	1-3	1-2	0-2	1-0	1-1	1-1	1-1	0-2	1-2	2-0	1-0	1-1	2-0	3-1	—	0-4	3-3	1-1	2-2	2-1
Shepshed Charterhouse	1-3	0-1	1-3	4-2	0-2	2-1	0-2	1-1	1-5	3-1	0-2	0-2	1-0	0-1	4-1	1-2	3-0	—	3-1	0-0	2-3	0-1
S Liverpool	2-1	3-1	4-2	4-2	1-2	1-3	5-3	3-2	1-3	3-2	2-2	1-2	4-3	1-1	2-1	2-1	2-1	1-2	—	1-1	0-1	1-2
Southport	1-1	2-1	4-0	4-0	0-0	0-0	2-0	2-0	2-2	1-3	0-1	0-1	1-0	1-1	4-1	2-4	1-0	0-0	1-3	—	2-0	1-1
Stalybridge	0-0	1-3	4-1	2-3	2-3	4-5	2-0	2-0	2-2	2-0	2-0	0-3	2-0	1-2	1-1	1-0	0-0	2-3	1-3	1-0	—	0-0
Witton Alb	0-0	1-0	3-0	2-0	3-0	3-0	3-0	1-1	0-1	0-1	2-0	2-2	2-0	2-0	2-0	2-1	2-0	3-1	0-2	5-0	4-0	—

HFS LOANS LEAGUE – FIRST DIVISION RESULTS 1989–90

(home \ away)	Accrington S	Alfreton T	Congleton T	Curzon Ashton	Droylsden	Eastwood Han	Eastwood T	Emley	Farsley Celtic	Harrogate T	Irlam T	Lancaster C	Leek T	Netherfield	Newtown	Penrith	Radcliffe Bor	Rossendale U	Whitley Bay	Winsford U	Workington	Worksop T
Accrington S	—	2-3	2-2	0-0	2-0	2-0	2-2	1-0	4-2	2-1	2-0	2-1	2-0	4-1	1-1	2-1	1-1	0-1	1-1	2-1	4-2	6-0
Alfreton T	1-0	—	1-2	3-0	4-1	4-1	3-2	0-3	3-5	1-2	1-2	2-6	0-1	1-0	3-1	0-0	1-0	5-3	2-5	1-1	2-0	4-1
Congleton T	2-3	1-2	—	0-2	5-1	5-1	1-1	1-0	4-3	2-4	1-0	4-1	0-1	3-1	0-0	5-0	1-0	1-0	1-1	0-0	1-0	2-0
Curzon Ashton	2-0	3-0	2-0	—	2-0	1-0	5-4	1-1	0-2	1-2	0-2	2-2	0-2	5-1	2-2	2-0	1-0	3-1	2-7	3-0	1-2	1-2
Droylsden	2-1	4-1	5-1	1-0	—	3-1	0-3	1-0	4-2	3-1	4-2	1-6	4-1	2-1	2-2	2-0	3-2	4-1	2-1	1-0	2-1	5-0
Eastwood Han	2-0	4-1	5-1	1-0	3-1	—	2-1	0-3	0-3	1-2	4-1	1-0	1-0	1-4	1-0	1-1	1-3	0-0	1-1	3-2	0-1	1-1
Eastwood T	2-2	1-1	1-1	5-4	0-3	2-0	—	2-1	6-2	1-2	3-3	0-0	0-3	3-2	1-2	3-1	1-2	1-0	2-3	0-1	1-0	3-3
Emley	1-2	0-3	1-0	1-1	4-2	0-3	3-2	—	2-1	2-1	2-1	2-1	2-0	6-1	0-1	1-1	4-1	1-0	0-3	2-0	0-1	4-0
Farsley Celtic	4-2	3-5	4-3	0-2	0-3	4-1	1-2	2-1	—	1-0	4-1	2-1	0-3	1-5	1-1	5-3	0-1	0-0	1-1	0-2	0-1	5-1
Harrogate T	2-1	1-2	2-4	1-2	3-0	3-1	0-0	1-0	1-2	—	5-2	7-2	0-3	3-1	0-0	4-1	3-2	3-1	2-1	0-1	2-1	2-1
Irlam T	2-0	1-2	1-0	1-4	2-0	4-1	3-3	2-0	1-0	1-1	—	2-2	0-0	3-1	3-0	2-0	2-0	3-2	0-0	2-2	0-2	3-0
Lancaster C	2-1	2-6	4-1	2-2	2-0	1-0	1-4	0-1	4-1	0-0	0-0	—	0-2	1-1	1-0	1-0	0-0	1-0	1-3	1-0	0-0	5-1
Leek T	2-0	0-1	0-1	0-2	4-1	4-1	0-3	2-2	4-0	2-0	0-0	0-0	—	4-0	2-2	4-1	3-0	1-1	2-2	0-0	1-0	1-2
Netherfield	4-1	1-0	3-1	5-1	2-1	1-4	3-2	2-0	1-2	7-1	4-0	3-2	0-2	—	4-0	1-1	0-1	0-2	1-1	4-0	1-3	1-0
Newtown	0-1	3-1	0-0	2-2	2-2	1-0	1-2	2-2	1-0	0-0	2-2	1-0	0-1	0-0	—	0-3	1-2	1-3	3-4	0-3	0-0	1-0
Penrith	2-1	0-0	5-0	2-0	2-0	1-1	3-1	5-3	0-3	0-3	0-0	3-1	2-2	3-1	1-3	—	1-2	1-1	0-2	1-1	4-3	2-1
Radcliffe Bor	1-1	1-0	1-0	1-0	1-0	1-3	1-2	1-5	0-1	1-3	2-2	3-1	0-1	4-0	3-0	1-1	—	1-2	2-3	3-0	2-0	1-2
Rossendale U	0-3	5-3	1-0	3-1	4-1	0-0	1-2	3-0	1-3	0-0	1-1	1-1	2-0	5-1	0-1	4-2	4-2	—	1-3	1-2	4-2	5-0
Whitley Bay	1-2	2-5	1-1	2-7	2-1	1-1	2-3	2-1	1-1	2-3	1-1	1-1	0-0	0-0	3-4	2-4	1-0	3-6	—	4-3	1-2	3-0
Winsford U	2-1	1-1	0-0	3-0	1-0	3-2	0-1	3-1	1-2	1-0	0-0	1-3	1-0	0-0	0-3	5-1	3-2	2-1	2-4	—	4-1	4-1
Workington	1-2	2-0	1-0	1-2	2-1	0-1	1-0	0-1	0-1	0-1	1-2	1-0	1-0	2-2	1-3	2-0	2-1	1-0	1-1	2-3	—	3-1
Worksop T	1-2	4-1	2-0	1-2	1-2	1-1	3-3	1-0	4-2	2-1	1-1	1-0	1-0	1-0	1-1	0-1	2-1	6-3	1-2	0-4	3-1	—

CUP HONOURS – 1989–90

HFS Challenge Cup – Winners: Hyde United; Runners-up: Gateshead.
HFS President's Cup – Winners: Fleetwood Town; Runners-up: Witton Albion.
HFS First Division Cup – Winners: Harrogate Town; Runners-up: Congleton Town.

THE BEAZER HOMES LEAGUE 1989–90

PREMIER DIVISION

	P	W	D	L	F	A	Pts
Dover Athletic	42	32	6	4	87	27	102
Bath City	42	30	8	4	81	28	98
Dartford	42	26	9	7	80	35	87
Burton Albion	42	20	12	10	64	40	72
VS Rugby	42	19	12	11	51	35	69
Atherstone United	42	19	10	13	60	52	67
Gravesend & Northfleet	42	18	12	12	44	50	66
Cambridge City	42	17	11	14	76	56	62
Gloucester City	42	17	11	14	80	68	62
Bromsgrove Rovers	42	17	10	15	56	48	61
Moor Green	42	18	7	17	62	59	61
Wealdstone	42	16	9	17	55	54	57
Dorchester Town	42	16	7	19	52	67	55
Worcester City	42	15	10	17	62	63	*54
Crawley Town	42	13	12	17	53	57	51
Waterlooville	42	13	10	19	63	81	49
Weymouth	42	11	13	18	50	70	46
Chelmsford City	42	11	10	21	52	72	43
Ashford Town	42	10	7	25	43	75	37
Corby Town	42	10	6	26	57	77	36
Alvechurch	42	7	5	30	46	95	26
Gosport Borough	42	6	5	31	28	93	23

* Denotes one point deducted

MIDLAND DIVISION

	P	W	D	L	F	A	Pts
Halesowen Town	42	28	8	6	100	49	92
Rushden Town	42	28	5	9	82	39	89
Nuneaton Borough	42	26	7	9	81	47	85
Tamworth	42	22	8	12	82	70	74
Barry Town	42	21	8	13	67	53	71
Spalding United	42	20	7	15	73	63	67
Sutton Coldfield Town	42	18	10	14	72	69	64
Stourbridge	42	17	12	13	73	61	63
Dudley Town	42	18	9	15	69	64	63
Stroud	42	16	13	13	75	62	61
Leicester United	42	17	5	20	66	77	56
Bridgnorth Town	42	13	14	15	68	73	53
King's Lynn	42	16	5	21	57	69	53
Grantham Town	42	14	10	18	57	63	52
Bedworth United	42	14	9	19	50	60	51
Hednesford Town	42	11	14	17	50	62	47
Bilston Town	42	11	14	17	40	54	47
Redditch United	42	11	13	18	57	64	46
Racing Club Warwick	42	11	11	20	45	66	44
Willenhall Town	42	9	9	24	37	66	36
Banbury United	42	9	9	24	46	83	*34
Sandwell Borough	42	6	12	24	46	79	30

* Denotes two points deducted

SOUTHERN DIVISION

	P	W	D	L	F	A	Pts
Bashley	42	25	7	10	80	47	82
Poole Town	42	23	8	11	85	60	77
Buckingham Town	42	22	10	10	67	46	76
Dunstable	42	20	14	8	56	38	74
Salisbury	42	21	9	12	72	50	72
Hythe Town	42	20	12	10	69	48	72
Trowbridge Town	42	20	9	13	79	64	69
Hastings Town	42	20	9	13	64	54	69
Bury Town	42	18	12	12	76	62	66
Baldock Town	42	18	11	13	69	52	65
Burnham	42	17	11	14	77	52	62
Fareham Town	42	14	14	14	49	53	56
Yate Town	42	16	6	20	53	52	54
Witney Town	42	16	6	20	54	56	54
Canterbury City	42	14	10	18	52	52	52
Margate	42	12	15	15	46	45	51
Folkestone	42	14	9	19	61	83	51
Andover	42	13	11	18	54	70	50
Hounslow	42	11	5	26	39	82	38
Erith & Belvedere	42	8	11	23	34	73	35
Corinthian	42	6	10	26	44	93	28
Sheppey United	42	6	7	29	35	83	25

Westgate Insurance Cup
Final: Dartford 0, VS Rugby 2; VS Rugby 0, Dartford 1
(VS Rugby won 2-1 on aggregate)

LEADING GOALSCORERS
(League and Cup)

Premier Division

P. Randall (Bath City)	40
K. Wilkin (Cambridge City)	29
P. Moody (Waterlooville)	28
D. Hedley (Moor Green)	26
L. Lee (Dover Athletic)	25

Midland Division

P. Joinson (Halesowen Town)	41
M. Twigger (Nuneaton)	28
F. Belfon (Rushden Town)	25
S. Doughty (Stroud)	24
P. Evans (Barry Town)	22
J. Muir (Dudley Town)	22

Southern Division

J. Lovell (Bashley)	41
J. Meacham (Trowbridge)	25
G. Manson (Poole Town)	24
I. Chalk (Salisbury)	23

Advance Sports Manager of the Season
Premier Division: Chris Kinnear (Dover Athletic)
Midland Division: John Morris (Halesowen Town)
Southern Division: Trevor Parker (Bashley)

BEAZER HOMES SOUTHERN LEAGUE PREMIER DIVISION RESULTS 1989-90

Home \ Away	Alvechurch	Ashford Town	Atherstone United	Bath City	Bromsgrove Rovers	Burton Albion	Cambridge City	Chelmsford City	Corby Town	Crawley Town	Dartford	Dorchester Town	Dover Athletic	Gloucester City	Gosport Borough	Gravesend & Northfleet	Moor Green	VS Rugby	Waterlooville	Wealdstone	Weymouth	Worcester City
Alvechurch	—	1-2	1-0	2-0	2-1	2-0	2-0	3-0	3-1	0-1	0-4	2-0	1-6	2-2	0-1	1-2	1-2	3-5	0-0	0-2	2-3	2-0
Ashford Town	1-2	—	0-5	0-0	0-3	1-1	0-2	1-2	5-0	0-3	4-0	1-3	0-2	1-2	1-0	0-1	4-0	1-1	1-7	0-1	0-0	1-2
Atherstone United	1-0	3-2	—	2-2	1-0	2-0	1-1	1-3	0-1	2-2	1-4	0-1	0-2	2-1	2-1	2-0	3-1	0-2	0-1	2-0	1-0	4-1
Bath City	2-0	4-0	2-2	—	0-0	0-2	1-2	1-2	1-2	0-3	2-3	6-0	1-0	2-1	5-0	1-0	2-1	1-0	3-2	1-0	3-3	3-1
Bromsgrove Rovers	2-1	0-3	1-0	0-0	—	0-1	2-1	0-1	1-0	2-3	1-1	3-3	0-2	0-2	5-0	1-0	0-0	2-0	2-4	4-0	3-1	1-3
Burton Albion	2-0	1-1	2-0	1-2	0-1	—	1-2	2-2	4-1	1-1	1-1	1-1	0-1	0-0	1-0	2-2	5-2	1-1	1-0	3-1	1-0	5-4
Cambridge City	2-0	2-1	0-2	2-1	2-1	5-0	—	0-1	5-0	1-1	1-2	6-0	0-1	0-2	2-3	1-1	2-2	0-0	2-4	2-4	3-0	0-1
Chelmsford City	3-0	2-1	1-2	1-2	2-1	0-1	0-1	—	0-1	1-1	2-2	0-2	1-3	3-1	2-0	2-0	1-2	2-2	2-2	1-3	2-1	1-3
Corby Town	3-1	2-0	0-1	1-2	0-1	1-1	5-0	0-1	—	1-2	1-2	3-3	0-2	3-1	2-1	2-1	2-1	0-0	2-2	0-0	8-0	1-3
Crawley Town	0-1	5-0	1-0	0-1	4-0	1-2	0-1	1-1	4-3	—	2-1	0-1	3-1	1-4	2-0	3-1	0-1	1-3	5-0	0-0	1-1	0-6
Dartford	1-0	0-1	2-2	0-1	1-0	2-1	1-2	2-2	1-0	2-1	—	2-0	2-2	2-3	5-1	1-1	2-0	1-0	3-0	1-1	6-2	2-1
Dorchester Town	3-1	3-1	2-0	0-1	1-0	0-1	6-0	0-2	5-0	2-0	2-0	—	0-1	6-2	4-1	5-0	0-1	3-0	2-1	2-0	0-1	3-0
Dover Athletic	3-0	5-2	3-1	2-2	2-0	3-1	0-1	1-3	0-1	1-0	1-1	5-0	—	3-2	3-0	0-2	2-3	2-3	3-2	2-2	7-0	5-3
Gloucester City	5-2	1-0	2-0	0-0	1-1	0-0	0-2	3-1	2-1	2-0	0-4	0-0	2-3	—	9-0	2-0	0-3	0-1	0-1	1-0	1-1	3-1
Gosport Borough	2-1	1-1	1-1	0-0	0-0	2-3	2-3	2-0	3-2	1-0	1-1	0-2	1-2	1-0	—	3-0	1-0	0-0	0-0	2-0	1-0	0-1
Gravesend & Northfleet	2-1	1-0	1-1	0-2	3-3	2-0	1-1	2-1	4-1	0-3	0-1	2-1	0-0	2-3	3-0	—	1-0	1-0	0-0	0-3	1-0	2-0
Moor Green	1-3	1-0	1-1	1-2	2-0	3-1	2-2	2-1	2-3	0-2	2-3	3-0	1-2	4-1	0-3	1-0	—	1-0	2-0	2-2	0-0	3-0
VS Rugby	2-0	0-5	0-3	0-1	2-0	1-1	1-2	2-3	1-0	4-3	2-1	2-0	0-1	3-0	2-2	0-1	2-1	—	2-2	2-0	0-3	0-0
Waterlooville	3-1	3-2	2-0	0-1	0-3	2-0	2-4	2-2	0-0	1-0	0-1	3-0	0-1	2-4	4-0	4-0	1-3	5-1	—	4-1	1-4	1-1
Wealdstone	1-0	0-4	2-0	0-1	0-0	4-0	3-1	1-3	2-0	0-1	1-1	2-0	1-3	2-3	1-1	2-3	2-1	1-0	1-0	—	2-1	4-1
Weymouth	3-0	0-5	0-1	1-2	1-1	1-0	3-0	2-1	1-0	1-0	0-2	1-2	0-3	1-1	2-0	4-2	2-1	1-0	1-1	1-0	—	2-2
Worcester City	4-0	0-2	2-1	2-0	0-3	5-4	0-1	1-3	1-0	1-0	0-0	3-0	0-1	2-0	5-1	0-1	2-4	1-2	0-0	1-0	4-2	—

BEAZER HOMES SOUTHERN LEAGUE SOUTHERN DIVISION RESULTS 1989–90

	Andover	Baldock Town	Bashley	Buckingham Town	Burnham	Bury Town	Canterbury City	Corinthian	Dunstable	Erith & Belvedere	Fareham Town	Folkestone	Hastings Town	Hounslow	Hythe Town	Margate	Poole Town	Salisbury	Sheppey United	Trowbridge Town	Witney Town	Yate Town
Andover	—	0-0	0-3	2-2	0-3	1-1	2-2	1-1	0-1	2-2	2-1	3-2	3-2	4-3	1-3	1-1	0-3	0-2	4-0	1-3	3-2	3-1
Baldock Town	2-1	—	0-1	0-7	1-0	2-2	2-2	5-1	2-2	2-1	1-1	3-0	0-0	1-0	2-3	5-0	1-2	1-2	0-2	2-0	0-2	1-0
Bashley	2-0	2-1	—	1-1	2-3	0-0	1-0	0-3	0-1	3-0	1-1	5-0	2-2	3-0	6-2	0-0	1-2	2-1	4-1	4-1	2-0	1-0
Buckingham Town	3-2	1-1	3-2	—	0-5	3-1	2-1	2-1	0-1	0-1	1-0	0-2	2-1	2-0	0-0	3-1	2-0	1-1	1-0	2-2	4-1	0-0
Burnham	1-2	1-2	4-0	0-0	—	1-4	3-1	3-1	0-3	0-1	0-2	1-2	2-2	3-1	0-0	0-0	1-1	0-0	1-0	2-3	4-1	2-0
Bury Town	0-0	1-0	1-2	3-0	5-1	—	0-0	2-2	0-1	2-0	0-2	1-2	2-2	5-2	3-1	3-1	1-1	0-0	2-1	2-3	2-1	2-0
Canterbury City	1-2	2-2	1-2	1-0	1-1	1-3	—	2-2	0-1	1-1	0-0	3-4	1-1	3-0	0-2	3-1	1-2	0-1	1-0	2-1	1-1	1-2
Corinthian	1-3	2-4	1-4	1-0	1-7	1-4	1-3	—	3-3	1-1	1-1	1-2	1-1	3-0	0-2	0-1	0-2	2-0	1-3	2-3	2-0	1-0
Dunstable	0-0	1-0	2-3	0-0	1-1	2-1	1-4	1-1	—	0-1	3-1	1-2	0-2	3-0	2-2	0-0	0-2	1-2	1-3	3-0	1-2	1-0
Erith & Belvedere	2-1	1-3	0-4	0-0	0-2	1-1	0-2	1-1	0-2	—	1-0	0-1	1-2	0-1	1-1	2-2	3-0	0-4	1-1	2-4	3-4	1-1
Fareham Town	0-0	2-3	3-0	2-1	1-1	1-1	0-2	2-0	2-1	1-0	—	1-1	1-2	2-1	1-1	2-1	3-0	1-6	1-1	2-4	0-2	2-0
Folkestone	1-0	3-2	3-1	1-2	1-5	2-4	1-2	3-1	2-1	2-1	1-0	—	1-2	1-2	0-3	1-1	1-5	3-0	3-3	2-2	2-1	1-3
Hastings Town	2-1	3-2	2-2	0-1	0-3	5-0	1-0	3-1	2-2	1-1	1-0	2-0	—	2-1	0-2	1-3	2-2	0-2	0-2	1-0	1-0	1-2
Hounslow	2-0	1-6	0-3	0-3	0-2	1-2	0-2	2-1	0-1	3-1	2-3	1-1	0-2	—	0-2	1-1	0-0	0-4	2-1	0-3	1-0	0-3
Hythe Town	0-1	0-0	1-1	1-2	4-3	4-3	4-1	2-1	0-2	4-0	1-1	3-1	0-1	1-1	—	1-1	1-1	5-1	4-1	3-1	2-0	1-0
Margate	3-0	1-1	2-1	1-1	1-1	0-0	1-1	2-0	1-1	1-2	0-0	0-1	3-1	1-0	0-1	—	1-2	1-2	5-0	2-1	0-1	1-0
Poole Town	5-0	0-2	2-0	4-2	5-4	2-1	2-5	5-1	2-1	4-1	2-0	4-0	1-1	3-1	0-1	0-2	—	2-2	3-2	2-0	2-0	3-2
Salisbury	3-0	2-2	0-1	1-3	1-5	1-1	2-1	2-0	1-1	0-1	1-1	3-4	2-0	0-1	2-0	1-2	2-0	—	2-0	3-0	3-0	2-1
Sheppey United	0-4	0-3	2-3	1-3	0-1	0-2	0-2	0-1	0-0	0-0	1-2	3-2	1-3	1-2	1-0	0-0	0-2	2-4	—	4-2	0-0	0-1
Trowbridge Town	1-1	1-2	1-2	2-1	0-3	5-1	0-2	5-1	4-0	4-0	0-0	2-2	4-0	2-2	3-2	1-0	1-4	1-1	3-0	—	0-0	3-0
Witney Town	1-2	2-0	0-2	2-3	0-0	1-1	0-2	3-1	2-2	2-1	2-1	1-2	2-1	4-0	2-1	1-0	3-1	2-0	4-0	1-2	—	0-1
Yate Town	2-1	0-2	0-1	1-3	1-0	3-1	2-1	4-0	2-2	3-0	2-3	1-1	1-3	3-0	1-2	0-1	6-1	1-2	2-1	0-3	1-0	—

BEAZER HOMES SOUTHERN LEAGUE MIDLAND DIVISION RESULTS 1989-90

Home \ Away	Banbury United	Barry Town	Bedworth United	Bilston Town	Bridgnorth Town	Dudley Town	Grantham Town	Halesowen Town	Hednesford Town	King's Lynn	Leicester United	Nuneaton Borough	Racing Club Warwick	Redditch United	Rushden Town	Sandwell Borough	Spalding United	Stourbridge	Stroud	Sutton Coldfield Town	Tamworth	Willenhall Town
Banbury United	—	0-1	1-3	1-0	4-2	2-1	3-2	1-2	0-0	2-3	2-0	1-7	0-2	2-2	1-3	1-1	1-1	3-2	2-2	1-2	2-3	1-0
Barry Town	3-0	—	1-0	0-1	2-0	1-3	4-1	1-0	3-1	1-0	2-0	3-1	1-0	0-0	1-3	1-0	2-3	2-2	2-2	4-0	2-1	1-2
Bedworth United	1-0	3-0	—	0-0	2-1	0-1	1-1	2-4	1-1	0-1	1-2	0-1	1-0	2-1	2-3	3-2	2-2	1-3	1-1	0-2	1-1	1-1
Bilston Town	1-1	2-2	1-1	—	1-2	1-0	2-0	0-4	1-1	2-0	2-3	1-3	1-3	1-1	3-2	1-0	0-2	1-3	0-1	2-2	1-2	1-0
Bridgnorth Town	6-0	1-1	0-1	1-1	—	1-0	4-2	3-1	6-1	5-2	1-3	0-4	1-4	2-1	3-2	1-0	0-2	3-5	3-1	2-2	2-2	2-2
Dudley Town	3-0	0-0	0-1	0-0	0-2	—	4-2	0-0	2-1	2-2	4-1	1-0	2-0	0-0	1-2	1-2	1-0	1-2	2-1	3-2	1-4	3-0
Grantham Town	1-1	0-3	1-1	0-1	1-1	2-2	—	0-0	1-1	1-0	0-3	1-0	3-1	0-0	0-0	4-2	1-0	1-3	2-1	0-1	3-1	4-1
Halesowen Town	7-2	3-3	2-1	0-2	1-1	6-4	3-2	—	1-1	5-1	3-1	2-0	3-0	1-2	1-0	4-2	1-0	0-0	3-0	3-2	5-1	2-0
Hednesford Town	1-0	3-1	1-1	1-1	2-2	1-1	1-2	1-1	—	1-4	4-0	0-1	1-1	1-1	0-1	1-2	3-1	1-1	2-3	1-1	0-3	1-1
King's Lynn	1-0	3-2	5-2	1-0	0-2	4-0	4-0	0-0	1-0	—	4-0	0-4	1-0	1-0	0-2	4-0	1-2	3-0	1-0	3-1	1-0	4-1
Leicester United	3-1	2-3	2-2	1-0	1-3	3-2	4-0	1-3	1-0	2-1	—	3-1	1-2	1-0	0-2	1-1	1-2	1-2	1-3	1-2	2-4	4-1
Nuneaton Borough	3-0	0-0	2-1	1-1	1-1	2-4	2-0	1-0	3-0	3-0	2-0	—	1-0	3-2	1-0	2-0	3-2	0-5	1-3	3-1	7-0	1-0
Racing Club Warwick	3-2	0-0	0-1	0-1	1-2	1-0	2-1	3-4	0-0	2-0	1-0	2-2	—	0-3	1-2	3-1	1-1	0-1	1-3	2-4	1-2	1-1
Redditch United	1-1	3-0	1-0	7-1	7-1	4-0	1-1	2-1	1-0	3-0	1-0	1-2	0-0	—	0-1	1-1	4-0	0-1	1-3	2-4	0-5	1-1
Rushden Town	1-2	3-0	4-0	2-0	0-2	0-2	1-1	2-1	2-1	5-2	2-1	1-2	2-0	5-0	—	4-2	1-3	2-1	2-2	1-3	0-2	2-0
Sandwell Borough	1-2	0-2	0-2	0-0	3-1	5-1	1-1	2-1	3-1	2-2	1-2	2-1	4-1	1-2	1-1	—	1-3	0-3	2-2	1-1	0-2	0-1
Spalding United	2-1	1-2	3-0	1-0	2-2	5-1	1-0	2-3	4-1	2-1	1-2	2-1	4-1	1-2	1-0	0-0	—	4-2	0-1	1-1	2-3	2-1
Stourbridge	1-0	1-0	2-2	0-0	1-1	1-4	1-5	0-1	2-3	4-1	3-3	1-1	6-0	4-1	1-0	2-2	1-1	—	0-1	1-3	0-3	5-3
Stroud	1-1	4-0	2-1	1-1	1-0	1-1	1-5	1-2	0-0	2-1	1-3	2-2	0-0	1-1	1-2	3-2	4-1	3-1	—	2-1	3-3	1-0
Sutton Coldfield Town	0-2	4-0	0-3	2-1	2-1	3-1	2-1	0-5	1-2	2-1	3-3	4-1	6-0	4-1	2-1	3-0	0-1	2-0	0-4	—	2-0	4-3
Tamworth	2-0	2-5	1-0	2-1	1-1	2-2	1-0	2-3	3-1	3-1	1-2	1-3	1-1	2-2	3-3	2-1	1-3	2-1	3-1	3-2	—	1-0
Willenhall Town	1-0	0-1	1-0	1-0	1-0	1-2	1-2	0-3	0-1	0-2	0-1	2-2	3-0	1-0	1-0	2-2	1-3	0-2	2-2	0-0	0-3	—

VAUXHALL LEAGUE 1989–90

Premier Division

	P	W	D	L	W	D	L	F	A	GD	Pts
		Home			*Away*						
Slough	42	15	4	2	12	7	2	85	38	47	92
Wokingham	42	13	7	1	13	4	4	67	34	33	89
Aylesbury Utd	42	14	3	4	11	6	4	86	30	56	84
Kingstonian	42	17	2	2	7	7	7	87	51	36	81
Grays Ath	42	13	4	4	6	9	6	59	44	15	70
Dagenham	42	9	8	4	8	7	6	54	43	11	66
Leyton-Wingate	42	9	4	8	11	2	8	54	48	6	66
Basingstoke	42	13	5	3	5	4	12	65	55	10	63
Bishops Stortford	42	9	1	11	10	5	6	60	59	1	63
Carshalton*	42	11	4	6	8	1	12	63	59	4	59
Redbridge F	42	9	6	6	7	5	9	65	62	3	59
Hendon	42	8	6	7	7	4	10	54	63	–9	55
Windsor & Eton	42	7	6	8	6	9	6	51	47	4	54
Hayes	42	9	6	6	5	5	11	61	59	2	53
St. Albans	42	8	5	8	5	5	11	49	59	–10	49
Staines	42	6	3	12	8	3	10	53	69	–16	48
Marlow	42	7	7	7	4	6	11	42	59	–17	46
Harrow Borough	42	9	2	10	2	8	11	51	79	–28	43
Bognor Regis	42	4	7	10	5	7	9	37	67	–30	41
Barking	42	5	9	7	2	2	17	53	86	–33	32
Bromley	42	4	8	9	3	3	15	32	69	–37	32
Dulwich Hamlet	42	2	5	14	4	3	14	32	80	–48	26

*Carshalton –3 points by order of the League

Division One

	P	W	D	L	W	D	L	F	A	GD	Pts
		Home			*Away*						
Wivenhoe Town	42	15	4	2	16	3	2	94	36	58	100
Woking	42	18	0	3	12	8	1	102	29	73	98
Southwick	42	13	7	1	10	8	3	68	30	38	84
Hitchin Town	42	13	4	4	9	9	3	60	30	30	79
Walton & Hersh	42	11	6	4	9	4	8	68	50	18	70
Dorking	42	9	8	4	10	4	7	66	41	25	69
Boreham Wood	42	9	7	5	8	6	7	60	59	1	64
Harlow Town	42	7	7	7	9	6	6	60	53	7	61
Met Police	42	9	5	7	7	6	8	54	59	–5	59
Chesham Utd	42	9	5	7	6	7	8	46	49	–3	57
Chalfont St. Peter	42	9	6	6	5	7	9	50	59	–9	55
Tooting & Mitcham	42	9	8	4	5	5	11	42	51	–9	55
Worthing	42	9	3	9	6	5	10	56	63	–7	53
Whyteleafe	42	4	8	9	7	8	6	50	65	–15	49
Lewes	42	5	5	9	7	4	10	55	65	–10	47
Wembley	42	5	7	9	6	3	12	57	68	–11	43
Croydon	42	5	9	7	4	7	10	43	57	–14	43
Uxbridge	42	4	6	11	7	4	10	52	75	–23	43
Hampton	42	5	5	11	3	8	10	28	51	–23	37
Leatherhead	42	4	3	14	3	7	11	34	77	–43	31
Purfleet	42	4	5	12	3	3	15	33	78	–45	29
Kingsbury*	42	6	6	9	2	4	15	45	78	–33	25

*Kingsbury –9 points by order of the League

Division Two (North)

	P	W	D	L	W	D	L	F	A	GD	Pts
		Home			*Away*						
Heybridge Swifts	42	12	5	4	14	4	3	79	29	50	87
Aveley	42	9	11	1	14	5	2	68	24	44	85
Hertford Town	42	14	4	3	10	7	4	92	51	41	83
Stevenage Boro	42	11	8	2	10	8	3	70	31	39	79
Barton Rovers	42	12	4	5	10	2	9	60	45	15	72
Tilbury	42	10	5	6	10	4	7	68	54	14	69
Basildon Utd	42	4	11	6	9	9	3	50	44	6	59
Collier Row	42	6	6	9	9	7	5	43	45	–2	58
Royston Town	42	3	8	10	12	3	6	63	72	–9	56
Saffron Walden	42	11	3	7	4	8	9	60	73	–13	56
Vauxhall Motors	42	7	4	10	7	9	5	55	54	1	55
Clapton*	42	9	5	7	4	11	6	50	46	4	54
Ware	42	3	9	9	11	2	8	53	59	–6	53
Hemel Hempstead	42	8	7	6	4	8	9	58	70	–12	51
Billericay	42	7	5	9	6	6	9	49	58	–9	50
Hornchurch	42	5	6	10	7	6	8	49	64	–15	48
Berkhamsted	42	5	7	9	4	9	8	44	68	–24	43
Finchley	42	7	3	11	4	7	10	50	75	–25	43
Tring Town	42	3	6	12	7	3	11	48	70	–22	39
Witham Town	42	6	7	8	2	7	12	44	56	–12	38
Rainham Town	42	5	6	10	4	5	12	48	75	–27	38
Letchworth G.C.	42	3	6	12	4	6	11	30	68	–38	33

*Clapton –1 point by order of the League

Division Two (South)

	P		Home			Away		F	A	GD	Pts
		W	D	L	W	D	L				
Yeading	40	14	3	3	15	1	4	86	37	49	91
Molesey	40	13	6	1	11	5	4	76	30	46	83
Abingdon Town	40	14	4	2	8	5	7	64	39	25	75
Ruislip Manor	40	11	6	3	9	6	5	60	32	28	72
Maidenhead Utd	40	9	9	2	11	3	6	66	39	27	72
Southall	40	12	1	7	10	4	6	56	33	23	71
Newbury	40	12	3	5	9	4	7	50	36	14	70
Flackwell Heath	40	10	6	4	6	5	9	69	65	4	59
Hungerford	40	10	7	3	4	9	7	54	51	3	58
Egham Town	40	7	7	6	5	7	8	39	38	1	50
Banstead Athletic	40	7	4	9	7	4	9	46	47	−1	50
Harefield	40	6	6	8	7	3	10	44	46	−2	48
Chertsey Town	40	7	5	8	6	4	10	53	58	−5	48
Epsom & Ewell	40	6	4	10	7	5	8	49	54	−5	48
Malden Vale	40	6	3	11	7	4	9	36	67	−31	46
Eastbourne Utd	40	7	5	8	4	5	11	47	65	−18	43
Camberley	40	8	4	8	3	5	12	44	66	−22	42
Feltham	40	8	3	9	3	4	13	47	80	−33	40
Bracknell	40	5	3	12	5	6	9	40	57	−17	39
Petersfield	40	6	5	9	4	3	13	48	93	−45	38
Horsham	40	1	3	16	3	5	12	29	70	−41	20

LEADING GOALSCORERS

Premier Division

		Lge	AC	CC
20	John Neal (B Stortford)	18	1	1
	Includes 9, 1, 1 for Barking)			
19	Devon Gayle (B Stortford)	15	4	0
18	Cliff Hercules (Aylesbury Utd)	17	1	0
	Dave Pearce (Wokingham T)	15	3	0
	Neal Stanley (Slough T)	16	1	1
17	Conrad Kane (Carshalton Ath)	16	1	0
	Francis Vines (Kingstonian)	17	0	0
	Leroy Whale (Basingstoke T)	16	1	0
16	Uche Egbe (Hendon)	15	1	0
	Paul Clarkson (Basingstoke T)	16	0	0
	Scott Young (B Stortford)	13	2	0
	Jim Bolton (Carshalton Ath)	16	0	0
	Neil Fraser (Hayes)	15	1	0
	Robin Lewis (Kingstonian)	16	0	0
	Tommy Langley (Sough T)	15	1	0

Division One

		Lge	AC
39	Tim Buzaglo (Woking)	33	6
26	Steve Clark (Wivenhoe T)	26	
22	Phil Coleman (Wivenhoe T)	22	
21	Terry Worsfold (Dorking)	21	
	(Includes 1 for Woking)		
	Paul Mulvaney (Woking)	18	3
19	Jeff Wood (Harlow)	18	1

Division Two North

		Lge	AC
30	Paddy Butcher (Royston T)	30	
	Kevin Newbury (Heybridge Swifts)	28	2
29	Micky Fredericks (Hertford T)	29	
23	Robert McComb (Stevenage Bor.)	23	
	(Includes 5 for Hertford T)		
21	Robert Smith (Barton Rovers)	20	1

Division Two South

		Lge	AC
23	Michael Rose (Moseley)	21	2
	Paul Sweales (Yeading)	23	
21	Tony Wood (Flackwell H)	21	
19	Victor Schwartz (Yeading)	18	1

VAUXHALL FOOTBALL LEAGUE PREMIER DIVISION RESULTS 1989–90

	Aylesbury Utd	Barking	Basingstoke	Bishops Stortford	Bognor Regis	Bromley	Carshalton Ath	Dagenham	Dulwich Hamlet	Grays Ath	Harrow Bor	Hayes	Hendon	Kingstonian	Leyton-Wingate	Marlow	Redbridge F	St Albans C	Slough T	Staines	Windsor & Eton	Wokingham T
Aylesbury	—	3-0	2-1	5-0	1-2	4-1	4-0	3-1	0-0	3-0	4-0	4-0	1-1	1-2	1-1	1-1	3-1	0-1	3-1	3-0	3-1	1-3
Barking	0-0	—	1-1	1-2	2-2	1-0	2-1	0-4	0-3	1-2	1-1	2-1	0-0	1-1	0-3	4-1	1-3	2-0	3-1	3-3	1-1	2-3
Basingstoke Town	0-0	2-1	—	0-0	2-1	2-0	2-0	3-1	3-1	1-1	1-0	3-1	3-2	1-2	1-1	3-0	4-0	3-1	1-3	3-1	0-0	1-2
Bishops Stortford	0-3	0-4	1-0	—	0-1	2-0	3-1	1-0	7-0	0-2	1-1	3-5	5-0	0-1	2-1	2-1	3-4	3-2	0-1	1-0	0-2	1-2
Bognor Regis T	0-2	3-2	1-0	2-3	—	2-2	2-0	1-1	1-2	0-0	0-0	1-1	0-3	0-0	0-1	0-2	1-6	3-1	1-3	1-3	0-4	0-2
Bromley	0-4	0-2	1-1	2-2	0-0	—	1-0	2-5	2-0	0-1	3-3	2-0	1-4	0-2	0-2	0-1	1-1	1-1	4-4	3-0	1-1	1-5
Carshalton Ath	1-0	4-2	2-2	1-2	3-1	1-0	—	2-0	0-1	1-2	3-3	3-0	3-1	2-0	2-0	6-1	5-1	1-2	0-3	3-1	1-1	2-2
Dagenham	1-0	1-1	3-2	1-0	0-1	1-0	0-2	—	1-1	0-0	3-0	2-1	1-1	2-0	1-0	0-1	2-2	1-3	0-3	1-1	0-0	2-2
Dulwich Hamlet	0-2	2-1	2-3	0-3	0-1	3-0	0-1	0-0	—	2-2	3-6	0-4	1-1	2-0	1-3	6-1	0-3	2-1	2-3	1-3	0-0	0-2
Grays Ath	2-1	2-1	3-1	1-1	2-0	3-0	0-1	0-0	2-1	—	4-0	2-1	3-0	3-1	1-0	2-0	1-1	0-1	1-5	4-3	3-0	0-2
Harrow Bor	1-5	3-1	1-0	2-3	1-0	2-1	0-1	1-2	4-1	4-2	—	2-0	0-2	1-3	0-2	1-1	0-0	3-2	1-5	3-2	1-3	1-4
Hayes	1-1	6-1	1-0	0-0	2-0	4-1	0-1	0-1	4-1	2-2	4-0	—	3-1	0-1	1-3	4-1	0-2	2-0	1-1	0-1	3-1	2-3
Hendon	1-1	1-0	5-0	0-1	0-1	2-1	3-1	2-1	1-0	3-0	1-1	0-2	—	3-0	0-1	0-0	2-2	1-0	2-0	1-4	2-2	0-0
Kingstonian	1-3	3-2	4-1	6-0	3-3	4-2	3-2	4-3	1-0	4-2	2-1	1-0	3-0	—	2-3	4-2	3-1	4-2	1-2	3-0	2-0	4-2
Leyton-Wingate	1-3	2-1	4-1	0-3	1-1	3-1	1-0	0-1	1-0	1-1	1-0	2-2	2-3	1-0	—	0-0	2-1	0-1	1-2	2-4	1-3	2-1
Marlow	0-3	4-1	3-1	1-3	2-0	0-0	3-0	0-1	2-1	3-1	3-1	2-2	2-3	1-1	0-1	—	0-2	1-1	2-0	1-3	1-0	0-0
Redbridge F.	1-2	3-1	4-0	3-1	0-2	0-0	3-1	1-1	2-1	2-1	3-0	1-2	1-1	0-1	0-1	2-1	—	1-1	2-0	1-1	1-0	1-1
St Albans C	0-1	3-1	1-1	2-1	3-1	2-0	1-2	0-1	2-1	1-2	4-0	3-0	2-1	0-0	2-0	1-1	1-0	—	0-3	0-2	2-4	1-2
Slough T	1-2	4-2	2-1	1-1	0-0	1-0	3-2	2-0	2-3	3-2	1-5	1-0	3-1	2-1	3-2	3-0	5-0	3-3	—	1-0	1-1	2-0
Staines	0-3	4-1	0-2	0-2	1-2	2-3	2-3	1-0	1-0	1-0	3-0	2-2	0-2	1-0	1-0	0-1	0-1	1-1	0-4	—	0-1	0-1
Windsor & Eton	2-1	1-1	0-2	0-2	2-1	4-0	0-0	1-2	0-0	0-0	1-1	0-1	3-0	1-1	0-0	0-2	4-1	1-0	0-3	0-3	—	3-0
Wokingham T	1-1	2-1	1-0	2-0	2-0	1-0	0-1	0-0	2-0	2-0	1-1	1-1	1-1	2-0	1-0	1-0	1-0	2-0	1-1	2-0	3-1	—

VAUXHALL FOOTBALL LEAGUE DIVISION ONE RESULTS 1989–90

	Boreham Wood	Chalfont St Peter	Chesham Utd	Croydon	Dorking	Hampton	Harlow Town	Hitchin	Kingsbury	Leatherhead	Lewes	Metropolitan Police	Purfleet	Southwick	Tooting & Mitcham	Uxbridge	Walton & Hersham	Wembley	Whyteleafe	Wivenhoe Town	Woking	Worthing
Boreham Wood	—	2-1	2-0	2-1	0-2	1-1	1-3	0-1	3-2	3-0	1-5	1-1	1-1	0-0	0-0	1-0	3-1	3-2	2-2	1-1	0-4	2-1
Chalfont St Peter	1-0	—	0-0	1-1	0-2	3-1	4-1	0-5	3-1	2-2	2-1	1-0	3-0	0-0	1-0	2-2	0-2	0-4	1-2	2-1	1-1	0-2
Chesham Utd	2-2	2-1	—	1-1	0-1	0-1	1-0	1-1	2-2	1-0	4-1	2-1	2-0	2-0	0-0	1-5	0-1	1-0	0-1	0-1	2-4	2-1
Croydon	0-0	2-1	2-0	—	0-1	1-1	0-1	1-1	3-0	3-3	0-3	1-1	3-1	0-0	1-0	1-2	1-1	0-2	0-0	1-2	0-2	0-0
Dorking	2-0	2-3	2-1	2-0	—	3-0	1-1	0-0	2-1	1-1	2-2	0-1	5-1	0-0	3-0	1-1	1-1	1-2	3-2	1-2	0-2	1-1
Hampton	0-1	2-0	1-2	1-0	3-0	—	0-2	0-1	1-0	0-0	0-1	1-2	0-1	1-2	4-2	3-1	0-0	0-1	3-2	1-2	0-1	0-1
Harlow Town	1-1	1-2	5-1	0-0	0-0	1-1	—	0-1	4-0	0-2	3-1	2-2	0-1	0-3	0-1	3-1	3-2	3-2	2-2	1-2	2-2	4-1
Hitchin Town	2-2	2-0	1-0	2-1	3-1	2-1	1-1	—	1-1	2-0	1-0	2-0	1-0	2-3	3-0	3-0	1-0	2-1	3-1	1-3	1-3	2-1
Kingsbury	0-1	0-0	0-1	4-1	1-4	4-1	0-3	1-1	—	2-0	1-0	2-2	1-0	2-3	3-0	3-0	1-0	2-1	3-1	0-1	1-3	2-1
Leatherhead	2-3	1-0	0-1	0-1	0-2	4-1	0-2	0-3	2-0	—	1-1	1-0	2-1	1-4	2-3	0-2	1-1	1-2	3-1	0-1	0-2	1-3
Lewes	2-1	0-1	0-1	1-3	2-2	0-0	0-2	1-2	3-3	0-0	—	0-1	2-2	0-0	3-1	3-1	2-4	3-1	4-1	0-0	0-3	0-1
Metropolitan Police	3-1	1-1	1-5	2-1	2-1	1-0	0-1	1-1	1-0	1-1	3-0	—	1-0	0-4	1-2	4-2	0-4	2-0	0-0	1-3	3-3	2-1
Purfleet	1-2	2-2	0-0	3-0	0-4	0-1	2-3	1-1	0-5	2-0	1-3	1-2	—	2-3	0-0	0-0	1-2	1-0	1-2	1-2	0-1	0-0
Southwick	1-0	0-2	1-1	3-1	2-0	3-1	0-0	0-0	6-0	3-0	1-0	2-0	2-1	—	1-0	0-0	3-2	1-0	4-0	1-1	1-1	1-1
Tooting & Mitcham	0-1	0-0	2-0	0-0	2-1	0-0	0-1	0-4	1-1	0-0	3-1	1-1	4-0	5-1	—	0-3	2-1	2-1	0-0	2-1	2-2	2-1
Uxbridge	2-2	0-0	1-2	1-2	0-3	0-0	2-2	0-2	1-0	3-0	2-0	2-0	3-1	0-4	1-0	—	0-1	2-6	0-1	0-3	2-3	1-1
Walton & Hersham	1-4	1-1	0-0	1-5	2-1	0-0	1-0	0-0	1-2	3-1	0-1	2-1	3-0	2-1	4-0	2-1	—	4-1	0-0	1-3	1-1	3-0
Wembley	1-2	1-1	1-1	1-1	1-3	3-1	5-2	0-0	3-0	3-1	2-2	1-3	1-2	1-1	2-2	2-1	1-0	—	1-1	1-5	0-3	1-2
Whyteleafe	3-2	2-3	2-2	1-1	1-1	0-1	0-0	1-1	3-0	2-3	2-2	2-2	1-2	1-1	1-0	5-2	0-3	1-1	—	0-4	0-0	1-2
Wivenhoe Town	3-2	3-1	3-1	3-2	1-1	2-1	0-0	2-1	3-0	4-0	2-1	2-2	3-0	1-1	0-1	2-1	4-1	4-1	4-1	—	1-2	3-1
Woking	1-2	4-1	1-0	5-0	3-0	2-0	4-0	3-0	3-0	6-0	6-0	1-0	4-0	1-0	2-0	6-1	3-1	2-1	2-1	1-2	—	2-1
Worthing	2-2	3-2	0-2	2-2	0-2	2-0	2-0	0-2	3-0	1-2	3-2	2-4	2-0	0-1	3-1	1-2	0-2	2-2	2-1	1-3	2-1	—

VAUXHALL FOOTBALL LEAGUE DIVISION TWO NORTH RESULTS 1989–90

	Aveley	Barton Rovers	Basildon Utd	Berkhamsted Town	Billericay Town	Clapton	Collier Row	Finchley	Hemel Hempstead	Hertford Town	Heybridge Swifts	Hornchurch	Letchworth Garden City	Rainham Town	Royston Town	Saffron Walden Town	Stevenage Borough	Tilbury	Tring Town	Vauxhall Motors	Ware	Witham Town
Aveley	—	3-0	0-1	3-1	0-0	0-0	0-0	1-1	1-1	1-1	0-0	0-3	0-0	0-0	3-0	2-2	1-1	3-2	4-1	0-0	0-0	1-0
Barton Rovers	3-1	—	0-0	1-3	2-2	1-0	0-4	0-3	1-0	1-1	2-1	2-3	1-2	1-1	2-0	2-1	0-4	4-1	2-2	1-0	2-0	1-0
Basildon Utd	1-2	0-1	—	2-3	1-1	0-0	0-2	2-1	3-1	0-0	0-0	0-3	1-2	2-0	0-1	1-1	1-3	0-2	1-0	1-1	0-2	1-1
Berkhamsted Town	2-1	1-3	2-3	—	1-4	0-2	0-1	1-0	2-1	0-0	5-0	0-3	0-0	2-1	0-2	3-0	2-2	0-1	1-0	0-3	2-2	1-1
Billericay Town	0-3	4-2	1-1	1-4	—	0-4	2-1	1-0	1-1	4-0	0-1	0-3	1-2	5-0	1-1	2-1	3-0	0-2	0-1	1-2	5-0	2-2
Clapton	1-2	0-2	0-0	1-1	0-4	—	0-2	1-1	1-1	3-2	0-2	0-3	3-1	2-1	0-2	3-0	4-0	3-0	0-1	3-0	2-0	3-0
Collier Row	0-3	1-3	0-2	1-3	2-1	0-2	—	1-1	1-0	1-1	2-3	0-1	4-0	0-3	1-4	0-0	0-4	1-3	2-1	1-1	1-0	0-3
Finchley	0-1	0-3	2-1	2-1	1-0	0-2	1-1	—	1-0	0-3	2-3	0-0	2-0	1-0	5-1	1-1	0-0	3-1	1-1	1-1	2-3	1-0
Hemel Hempstead	1-1	1-0	3-1	2-1	1-1	4-0	1-1	1-0	—	1-4	1-4	3-2	4-0	0-0	2-2	0-0	0-4	0-1	4-1	1-1	0-3	5-1
Hertford Town	1-1	1-0	0-0	1-0	2-1	4-2	4-1	1-0	1-0	—	3-1	2-0	1-1	0-1	5-1	5-2	0-4	3-1	4-1	1-1	1-0	1-0
Heybridge Swifts	1-1	2-1	0-0	0-0	1-1	4-2	0-3	4-1	3-2	3-1	—	0-1	0-0	1-0	0-1	6-0	1-0	6-1	4-1	4-3	0-2	2-0
Hornchurch	0-0	2-4	1-1	1-1	1-0	4-2	0-2	3-0	4-0	0-0	1-4	—	1-1	4-3	3-4	1-2	0-2	2-3	0-2	1-2	1-4	3-1
Letchworth Garden City	0-3	2-3	0-1	2-2	0-0	0-0	3-0	0-2	0-1	1-1	0-2	0-3	—	1-1	0-2	2-3	0-0	1-2	1-3	0-1	0-2	1-0
Rainham Town	0-0	2-1	1-2	1-1	1-2	1-1	2-1	2-2	2-4	1-1	2-2	1-0	0-2	—	0-2	1-2	1-0	0-1	2-1	0-3	2-4	1-0
Royston Town	0-1	0-4	2-0	2-0	2-2	3-0	1-0	2-3	3-3	2-2	1-2	2-2	1-3	0-2	—	1-2	0-2	0-0	1-1	2-2	1-2	2-2
Saffron Walden Town	1-4	2-0	2-2	2-0	5-0	0-2	1-0	1-0	2-0	2-0	2-0	3-1	3-2	2-0	4-0	—	1-2	1-1	3-3	1-1	0-5	2-1
Stevenage Town	0-3	2-0	3-3	0-0	0-1	0-2	3-0	2-0	2-1	1-1	2-2	1-0	0-0	1-1	4-0	4-1	—	1-2	1-3	3-1	4-1	0-0
Tilbury	0-2	1-2	4-1	0-1	2-0	0-0	0-0	1-3	3-3	3-1	1-3	2-0	0-0	3-1	3-0	3-3	0-1	—	1-1	0-1	5-0	1-0
Tring Town	0-4	0-1	2-3	0-0	2-3	2-3	2-3	1-2	2-2	1-2	0-1	1-1	5-0	3-0	0-5	1-3	1-3	0-2	—	1-3	1-2	1-1
Vauxhall Motors	0-2	3-1	1-2	4-1	3-1	1-0	0-1	3-1	1-2	3-3	0-1	0-2	1-1	2-1	1-2	2-1	1-3	0-1	3-0	—	0-2	0-0
Ware	1-2	1-1	1-1	0-0	1-0	1-0	1-0	1-1	2-3	1-3	0-2	1-1	3-1	1-3	0-1	2-1	2-1	1-2	0-1	0-0	—	2-2
Witham Town	0-1	1-2	1-2	1-1	2-1	1-1	1-1	0-1	3-0	2-2	0-1	4-1	0-1	2-2	1-1	4-1	1-0	2-2	2-1	1-1	1-2	—

VAUXHALL FOOTBALL LEAGUE DIVISION TWO SOUTH RESULTS 1989–90

	Abingdon Town	Banstead Athletic	Bracknell Town	Camberley Town	Chertsey Town	Eastbourne United	Egham Town	Epsom & Ewell	Feltham	Flackwell Heath	Harefield United	Horsham	Hungerford Town	Maidenhead United	Maiden Vale	Molesey	Newbury Town	Petersfield	Ruislip Manor	Southall	Yeading
Abingdon Town	—	5-3	2-0	1-0	1-0	4-0	2-1	2-1	4-2	3-2	2-0	1-1	2-2	1-0	1-0	0-0	2-0	7-0	1-1	0-1	2-3
Banstead Athletic	0-1	—	1-1	7-1	0-2	0-0	1-0	0-1	4-1	2-2	1-0	1-0	1-0	3-0	0-1	0-2	1-3	0-1	1-2	0-0	0-1
Bracknell Town	0-3	1-1	—	0-0	0-0	1-2	0-2	0-3	3-1	7-0	1-0	1-0	0-1	2-3	3-1	0-1	0-2	1-1	0-0	0-2	2-3
Camberley Town	2-1	1-0	7-1	—	1-0	1-1	1-2	0-0	4-0	3-2	0-1	1-3	4-1	0-3	0-1	0-7	2-0	3-3	0-1	2-0	0-2
Chertsey Town	1-2	3-1	0-0	0-0	—	1-2	2-0	1-1	4-1	1-3	1-3	1-1	2-2	2-6	2-2	2-1	1-0	2-0	0-1	1-2	2-3
Eastbourne Utd	0-0	1-2	1-2	1-1	1-2	—	1-1	1-0	0-1	1-3	1-3	2-1	0-0	1-1	4-1	3-5	0-1	3-1	1-1	2-0	0-2
Egham Town	0-1	0-0	4-0	1-1	3-2	3-2	—	1-1	1-0	0-2	0-1	3-0	1-0	0-1	1-0	0-0	1-0	2-2	0-5	2-2	0-1
Epsom & Ewell	3-0	1-1	2-3	1-0	1-2	3-1	0-0	—	0-2	0-2	0-2	4-1	1-0	0-1	4-1	1-4	0-1	2-1	0-5	0-1	1-2
Feltham	1-3	2-1	1-0	2-2	1-0	2-1	1-0	0-3	—	3-4	2-0	3-1	0-0	0-1	3-1	1-1	1-0	4-0	2-1	0-2	0-1
Flackwell Heath	2-1	1-1	3-1	1-0	4-2	1-1	1-1	1-1	0-2	—	2-0	3-0	1-1	3-0	0-1	3-2	0-3	3-2	0-0	3-5	1-2
Harefield United	1-1	0-1	1-1	2-0	0-3	3-0	0-1	0-3	1-1	3-3	—	1-0	2-2	0-1	2-4	1-2	1-1	1-2	0-1	0-1	2-1
Horsham	0-2	3-2	1-0	2-0	0-1	1-4	1-0	2-3	3-0	0-0	0-4	—	2-2	1-3	1-3	2-1	0-0	1-2	2-3	0-2	1-1
Hungerford Town	1-0	1-0	2-0	3-3	3-2	1-1	0-1	0-3	2-0	0-0	2-0	2-1	—	1-3	2-3	2-1	1-1	0-0	0-0	2-1	2-2
Maidenhead United	0-0	1-2	0-0	1-0	1-3	1-0	0-1	1-0	5-2	1-2	0-0	1-3	2-0	—	3-0	1-1	2-0	3-0	0-6	1-0	5-2
Maiden Vale	0-0	0-2	2-3	1-3	1-2	0-3	0-0	0-5	2-0	4-3	1-1	0-1	1-1	0-6	—	0-2	2-0	5-2	0-2	0-1	4-0
Molesey	2-0	0-2	0-1	2-0	3-0	1-1	1-0	3-1	4-1	1-2	1-0	2-1	1-1	1-3	3-0	—	2-0	3-0	2-2	0-0	1-0
Newbury Town	1-2	1-0	1-0	3-1	3-1	5-1	1-1	3-0	3-2	2-0	1-0	0-1	2-4	0-0	1-1	1-1	—	2-1	3-1	1-1	2-0
Petersfield	1-1	1-3	2-4	2-0	2-2	2-1	0-1	3-2	2-2	3-2	3-2	1-1	0-0	2-1	2-2	0-3	1-1	—	0-2	0-2	1-3
Ruislip Manor	4-1	2-0	0-0	2-2	1-1	1-0	1-0	0-0	3-1	1-0	2-1	1-1	0-1	0-4	0-1	2-2	1-2	0-1	—	1-0	2-3
Southall	0-1	1-2	2-0	4-1	2-0	2-0	1-0	4-0	2-2	1-3	3-0	2-1	2-1	1-0	4-0	0-3	0-1	0-2	2-0	—	1-2
Yeading	3-1	3-0	1-0	2-0	2-0	3-0	4-1	1-2	0-0	1-2	3-2	1-1	2-2	5-2	4-0	1-2	2-0	7-1	2-3	1-0	—

AC DELCO CUP 1989–90

Preliminary Round

Abindon Town 0, Purfleet 1	309
Basildon United 2, Hemel Hempstead 3	64
Billericay Town 1, Saffron Walden Town 0	233
Camberley Town 1, Ware 2	48
Egham Town 3, Ruislip Manor 1	121
Epsom & Ewell 1, Collier Row 1 *(aet)*	80
Feltham 1, Bracknell Town 2 *(aet)*	80
Finchley 1, Banstead Athletic 0	69
Flackwell Heath 1, Barton Rovers 2	112
Harlow Town 2, Hertford Town 1	86
(At Hertford Town FC)	
Hornchurch 1, Clapton 1 *(aet)*	78
Letchworth Garden City 1, Witham Town 2	74
Maidenhead United 1, Whyteleafe 2	101
Malden Vale 1, Aveley 3	70
Molesey 3, Tilbury 2	61
Newbury Town 1, Berkhamsted Town 0	101
Petersfield United 3, Eastbourne United 1	125
Rainham Town 2, Harefield United 1	42
Royston Town 0, Stevenage Borough 1	268
Southall 0, Hungerford Town 4	71
Tring Town 2, Chertsey Town 4 *(aet)*	74
Vauxhall Motors 3, Horsham 0	80
Yeading 2, Heybridge Swifts 3	122

Dorking received a walkover against Newport County

Replays

Clapton 1, Hornchurch 0	74
Collier Row 4, Epsom & Ewell 3	120

First Round

Aveley 1, Chertsey Town 0	90
Aylesbury United 3, Croydon 0	620
Basingstoke Town 2, Rainham Town 0	321
Bognor Regis Town 0, Bromley 1	364
Borehamwood 1, Barton Rovers 0	102
Bracknell Town 1, Dorking 2	84
Chalfont St. Peter 3, Harrow Borough 2	208
Chesham United 4, Egham Town 1	247
Clapton 2, Heybridge Swifts 0	130
Collier Row 1, Bishops Stortford 2	146
Dulwich Hamlet 0, Molesey 1	122
Finchley 1, Grays Athletic 0	64
Hampton 1, Barking 2	161
Harlow Town, Ware 2	141
Hayes 0, Wokingham Town 0 *(aet)*	141
Hendon 3, Metropolitan Police 2	147
Hungerford Town 1, Vauxhall Motors 2	92
Kingsbury Town 3, Hemel Hempstead 0	36
Leyton Wingate 3, Hitchin Town 2	105
Newbury Town 0, Uxbridge 1	105
Petersfield United 3, Leatherhead 5 *(aet)*	150
Purfleet 2, Billericay Town 0	120
Redbridge Forest 2, Dagenham 3	411
St Albans City 2, Witham Town 0	284
Slough Town 2, Lewes 1	416
Staines Town 2, Kingstonian 3	559
Stevenage Borough 0, Carshalton Athletic 1	267
Tooting & Mitcham United 1, Woking 5	273
Walton & Hersham 0, Windsor & Eton 0 *(aet)*	184
Whyteleafe 2, Marlow 1	146
Wivenhoe Town 2, Southwick 1	281
Worthing 2, Wembley 3 *(aet)*	212

Replays

Windsor & Eton 2, Walton & Hersham 1	230
Wokingham Town 2, Hayes 0	400

Second Round

Aveley 1, Windsor & Eton 0	110
Aylesbury United 6, Leyton Wingate 2	510
Barking 2, Borehamwood 1	99
Bishops Stortford 2, Slough Town 0	313
Bromley 0, St Albans City 3	181
Chesham United 2, Basingstoke Town 1	289
Dagenham 0, Uxbridge 1	206
Dorking 0, Carshalton Athletic 1	373
Finchley 2, Leatherhead 1	64
Kingsbury Town 2, Chalfont St. Peter 1	42
Purfleet 0, Molesey 0 *(aet)*	68
Wembley 4, Ware 1	98
Whyteleafe 0, Vauxhall Motors 1	93
Wivenhoe Town 0, Hendon 2	260
Woking 8, Clapton 1	492
Wokingham Town 2, Kingstonian 1	182
Molesey 2, Purfleet 0	82

Third Round

Aveley 1, Hendon 1 *(aet)*	175
Barking 1, Woking 1 *(aet)*	221
Bishops Stortford 0, Wokingham Town 1	353
Carshalton Athletic 3, Wembley 0	161
Chesham United 3, Vauxhall Motors 1	250
Molesey 0, Kingsbury Town 2	57
St Albans City 2, Aylesbury United 0	425
Uxbridge 3, Finchley 2	121

Replays

Hendon 1, Aveley 2	183
Woking 3, Barking 0	342

Fourth Round

Chesham United 1, St Albans City 2	425
Kingsbury Town 0, Woking 0 *(aet)*	240
Uxbridge 0, Aveley 3	144
Wokingham Town 0, Carshalton Athletic 0 *(aet)*	414

Replays

Carshalton Athletic 0, Wokingham Town 3	321
Woking 2, Kingsbury Town 1	599

Semi-Finals First Leg

Aveley 2, Wokingham Town 1	307
St Albans City 1, Woking 1	610

Semi-Finals Second Leg

Woking 1, St Albans City 2	1168
(St Albans City won 3-2 on agg.)	
Wokingham Town 0, Aveley 0	406
(Aveley won 2-1 on agg.)	

Final

Aveley 3, St Albans City 0 *(At Dagenham FC)*	1036

FA CHALLENGE TROPHY 1989–90

The following 32 clubs were exempted to the First Round Proper: Altrincham, Aylesbury United, Barnet, Barrow, Billingham Synthonia, Bishop Auckland, Boston United, Burton Albion, Cheltenham Town, Darlington, Dartford, Enfield, Farnborough Town, Fisher Athletic, Hyde United, Kettering Town, Kidderminster Harriers, Macclesfield Town, Myrthyr Tydfil, Newcastle Blue Star, Northwich Victoria, Redbridge Forest, Runcorn, Sutton United, Telford United, Tow Law Town, Wealdstone, Welling United, Windsor & Eton, Wokingham Town, Wycombe Wanderers, Yeovil Town.

The following 32 clubs were exempted to the Third Round Qualifying: Bangor City, Bath City, Blyth Spartans, Bromley, Bromsgrove Rovers, Buxton, Cambridge City, Carshalton Athletic, Chorley, Crawley Town, Dagenham, Dover Athletic, Fareham Town, Frickley Athletic, Gravesend & Northfleet, Gretna, Guisborough Town, Hendon, Leicester United, Leyton-Wingate, Marine, Rhyl, Slough Town, South Bank, South Liverpool, Spennymoor United, Stafford Rangers, VS Rugby, Weymouth, Witton Albion, Woking, Worcester City.

First Round Qualifying

Ferryhill Athletic v Morecambe	2-0
Fleetwood Town v Seaham Red Star	0-2
Workington v North Shields	0-1
Colne Dynamoes v Accrington Stanley	3-2
Brandon United v Easington Collieries	2-0
Gateshead v Shildon	3-3, 6-0
Billingham Town v Stockton	0-0, 1-3
Penrith v Whitby Town	1-2
Southport v Whitley Bay	2-3
Dudley Town v Moor Green	2-2, 2-3
Gainsborough Trinity v Caernarfon Town	2-2, 1-3
Atherstone United v Alfreton Town	1-2
Redditch United v Eastwood Town	4-1
Willenhall Town v Winsford United	1-2
Coventry Sporting v Nuneaton Borough	
(walkover for Nuneaton Borough)	
Goole Town v Colwyn Bay	5-2
Matlock Town v Stalybridge Celtic	0-1
Newtown v Grantham	3-2
Halesowen Town v Shepshed Charterhouse	0-3
Worksop Town v Bedworth United	1-1, 0-2
Leek Town v Hednesford Town	3-1
Mossley v Horwich RMI	4-0
Hayes v Sutton Coldfield Town	0-2
Banbury United v Barking	4-2
Dunstable v Corby Town	2-2, 4-1
Grays Athletic v Tamworth	0-3
Burnham v Chesham United	1-0
Boreham Wood v Kingsbury Town	1-2
Wivenhoe Town v Chelmsford City	3-0
Baldock Town v Chalfont St Peter	0-3
Purfleet v Uxbridge	0-2
Bishops Stortford v Harrow Borough	0-0, 1-2
Witney Town v Bury Town	1-0
Wembley v St Albans City	1-0
Canterbury City v Tooting & Mitcham United	2-1
Croydon v Bognor Regis Town	0-1
Salisbury v Lewes	4-4, 1-1, 4-2
Leatherhead v Marlow	1-1, 0-2
Margate v Andover	3-0
Tonbridge AFC v Folkestone	1-1, 0-4
Dulwich Hamlet v Staines Town	0-1
Walton & Hersham v Waterlooville	2-0
Erith & Belvedere v Gosport Borough	2-0
Dorking v Kingstonian	0-0, 2-7
Sheppey United v Ashford Town	2-2, 0-5
Hampton v Basingstoke Town	1-0
Maesteg Park v Cwmbran Town	2-1
Barry Town v Bridgend Town	2-0
Frome Town v Poole Town	0-0, 0-4
Gloucester City v Dorchester Town	4-0
Stroud v Bideford	3-0
Ton Pentre v Taunton Town	0-1

Second Round Qualifying

Gateshead v North Shields	1-2
Whitley Bay v Durham City	1-2
Stockton v Colne Dynamoes	0-5
Brandon United v Whitby Town	2-2, 2-0
Seaham Red Star v Ferryhill Athletic	2-2, 3-1
Winsford United v Bedworth United	1 1, 1 2
Nuneaton Borough v Alvechurch	1-1, 2-1
Goole Town v Alfreton Town	4-4, 1-3
Newtown v Radcliffe Borough	1-0
Congleton Town v Mossley	3-2
Redditch United v Caernarfon Town	2-3
Matlock Town v Shepshed Charterhouse	1-1, 1-2
Moor Green v Leek Town	1-3
Harrow Borough v Kingsbury Town	4-1
Dunstable v Burnham	1-3

Chalfont St Peter v Banbury United	3-0
Uxbridge v Sutton Coldfield Town	2-4
Wivenhoe Town v Tamworth	2-2, 4-1
Hitchin Town v Wembley	1-0
Witney Town v Stourbridge	3-0
Margate v Ashford Town	1-1, 2-3
Folkestone v Metropolitan Police	1-2
Staines Town v Salisbury	3-2
Erith & Belvedere v Southwick	4-2
Whyteleafe v Worthing	4-0
Marlow v Bognor Regis Town	0-0, 1-1, 1-6
Walton & Hersham v Kingstonian	0-1
Canterbury City v Hampton	0-3
Gloucester City v Barry Town	2-1
Stroud v Taunton Town	2-0
Weston-Super-Mare v Poole Town	2-0
Maesteg Park v Saltash United	2-2, 0-2

Third Round Qualifying

Chorley v Blyth Spartans	1-3
South Liverpool v Gretna	0-2
Seaham Red Star v Durham City	4-1
Brandon United v Marine	0-2
Frickley Athletic v Guisborough Town	0-1
North Shields v Colne Dynamoes	0-3
Spennymoor United v South Bank	4-0
Buxton v Shepshed Charterhouse	0-0, 0-1
Bromsgrove Rovers v Leicester United	4-2
Caernarfon v Bangor City	1-2
Sutton Coldfield Town v Congleton Town	2-1
Newtown v Leek Town	0-1
Witton Albion v Alfreton Town	3-0
Rhyl v Stafford Rangers	0-0, 1-2
Bedworth United v Nuneaton Borough	1-4
Hampton v Staines Town	1-2
Metropolitan Police v Whyteleafe	2-1
Gravesend & Northfleet v Carshalton Athletic	2-0
Burnham v Hendon	0-0, 2-3
Dover Athletic v Crawley Town	2-0
Chalfont St Peter v Ashford Town	1-3
VS Rugby v Wivenhoe Town	1-1, 0-1
Dagenham v Cambridge City	2-1
Leyton-Wingate v Bromley	1-0
Erith & Belvedere v Harrow Borough	1-1, 0-0, 0-2
Hitchin Town v Kingstonian	1-1, 1-2
Stroud v Slough Town	1-10
Weymouth v Saltash United	1-0
Bognor Regis Town v Weston-Super-Mare	2-4
Bath City v Witney Town	2-0
Woking v Fareham Town	5-1
Gloucester City v Worcester City	0-1

First Round Proper

Colne Dynamoes v Altrincham	5-0
Spennymoor United v Leek Town	1-2
Shepshed Charterhouse v Nuneaton Borough	1-1, 0-1
Billingham Synthonia v Darlington	2-2, 1-3
Stafford Rangers v Guisborough Town	2-1
Telford United v Burton Albion	2-1
Gretna v Hyde United	2-2, 1-1, 1-2
Northwich Victoria v Bishop Auckland	1-1, 3-2
Sutton Coldfield Town v Tow Law Town	2-2, 1-3
Barrow v Bangor City	1-0
Witton Albion v Blyth Spartans	2-0
(at Northwich Victoria FC)	
Seaham Red Star v Marine	2-0
Newcastle Blue Star v Runcorn	0-0, 1-4
Boston United v Macclesfield Town	0-0, 0-3
Welling United v Fisher Athletic	2-0
Wivenhoe Town v Hendon	2-1
Kettering Town v Wokingham Town	0-2

Slough Town v Redbridge Forest	1-1, 0-3
Wycombe Wanderers v Metropolitan Police	1-3
Leyton-Wingate v Kidderminster Harriers	0-3
Weston-Super-Mare v Windsor & Eton	2-3
Enfield v Merthyr Tydfil	3-2
Sutton United v Dover Athletic	0-1
Dartford v Yeovil Town	1-2
Farnborough Town v Staines Town	1-0
Ashford Town v Bath City	0-4
Weymouth v Barnet	2-0
Aylesbury United v Worcester City	2-2, 1-0
Cheltenham Town v Gravesend & Northfleet	5-1
Wealdstone v Harrow Borough	1-1, 0-1
Dagenham v Kingstonian	2-5
Woking v Bromsgrove Rovers	3-0

Second Round

Woking v Seaham Red Star	3-1
Leek Town v Nuneaton Borough	1-1, 1-0
Kingstonian v Hyde United	2-1
Wokingham Town v Stafford Rangers	0-0, 1-3
Darlington v Macclesfield Town	1-0
Barrow v Metropolitan Police	1-0
Harrow Borough v Redbridge Forest	0-0, 0-2
Witton Albion v Kidderminster Harriers	0-0, 1-2
Bath City v Tow Law Town	2-0
Cheltenham Town v Enfield	3-1
Farnborough Town v Windsor & Eton	2-1
Dover Athletic v Weymouth	2-1
Wivenhoe Town v Runcorn	1-1, 2-3
Telford United v Welling United	0-0, 2-0
Colne Dynamoes v Northwich Victoria	1-0
Yeovil Town v Aylesbury United	2-0

Third Round

Colne Dynamoes v Farnborough Town	2-1
Kingstonian v Cheltenham Town	3-3, 3-0
Yeovil Town v Barrow	1-1, 1-2
Stafford Rangers v Redbridge Forest	1-1, 2-1
Telford United v Leek Town	0-0, 0-3
Kidderminster Harriers v Dover Athletic	3-0
Darlington v Runcorn	1-0
Woking v Bath City	1-1, 1-2

Fourth Round

Kingstonian v Barrow	2-2, 0-1
Leek Town v Darlington	1-0
Kidderminster Harriers v Colne Dynamoes	0-0, 1-2
Bath City v Stafford Rangers	0-2

Semi-Finals *(2 legs)*

Stafford Rangers v Leek Town	0-0, 0-1
Colne Dynamoes v Barrow	0-1, 1-2

FINAL at Wembley

19 MAY

Barrow (1) 3 *(Gordon 2, Cowperthwaite)*

Leek Town (0) 0 19,011

Barrow: McDonald; Higgins, Chilton, Skivington, Gordon, Proctor, Doherty (Burgess), Farrell (Gilmour), Cowperthwaite, Lowe, Ferris.
Leek Town: Simpson; Elsby (Smith), Pearce, McMullen, Clowes, Coleman (Russell), Mellor, Somerville, Sutton, Millington, Norris.
Referee: T. Simpson.

FA COUNTY YOUTH CUP 1989–90

First Round

Cumberland v Durham	2-1
Lancashire v West Riding	2-0
Derbyshire v Nottinghamshire	1-2
East Riding v Sheffield & Hallamshire	3-2
Norfolk v Huntingdonshire	6-1
Staffordshire v Leicestershire & Rutland	2-1
Worcestershire v Herefordshire	4-1
Bedfordshire v Cambridgeshire	1-3
Essex v London	1-0
Middlesex v Berks & Bucks	3-1
Army v Hampshire	1-2
Oxfordshire v Wiltshire	1-2
Somerset & Avon (South) v Dorset	3-1

Second Round

Northumberland v Cumberland	2-0
Westmorland v Lancashire	0-5
Cheshire v Liverpool	1-4
Manchester v Nottinghamshire	2-1
North Riding v East Riding	0-2
Lincolnshire v Norfolk	0-3
Shropshire v Staffordshire	1-4
Birmingham v Worcestershire	3-1
Northamptonshire v Cambridgeshire	1-1, 2-1
Suffolk v Essex	1-3
Kent v Hertfordshire	1-3
Surrey v Middlesex	4-1
Sussex v Hampshire	0-3
Royal Navy v Wiltshire	1-2
Gloucestershire v Somerset & Avon (South)	2-1
Cornwall v Devon	1-2

Third Round

East Riding v Northumberland	0-2
Lancashire v Manchester	3-1
Liverpool v Staffordshire	0-0, 1-2
Northamptonshire v Norfolk	3-1
Gloucestershire v Birmingham	3-0
Hertfordshire v Essex	1-0
Hampshire v Surrey	3-1
Devon v Wiltshire	5-1

Fourth Round

Staffordshire v Northumberland	4-1
Northamptonshire v Lancashire	3-2
Hampshire v Gloucestershire	4-2
Devon v Hertfordshire	2-3

Semi-Finals

Northamptonshire v Hampshire	3-3, 0-1
Staffordshire v Hertfordshire	1-0

Final

Hampshire v Staffordshire	1-1
(at Aldershot FC, 28 April)	

Replay

Hampshire v Staffordshire	1-2
(at Port Vale FC, 5 May)	

936

FA CHALLENGE VASE 1989–90

The following 32 clubs were exempted to the Second Round: Bashley, Berkhamsted Town, Braintree Town, Bridgnorth Town, Bridlington Town, Bridport, Burnham Ramblers, Chertsey Town, Clevedon Town, Corinthian, East Thurrock United, Eastwood Hanley, Emley, Falmouth Town, Farsley Celtic, Garforth Town, Great Yarmouth Town, Gresley Rovers, Guiseley, Hailsham Town, Havant Town, Haverhill Rovers, Holbeach United, Hounslow, Hungerford Town, March Town United, North Ferriby United, Ossett Town, Rossendale United, Sudbury Town, Thatcham Town, Wisbech Town.

The following 32 clubs were exempted to the First Round: Abingdon Town, Borrowash Victoria, Brigg Town, Camberley Town, Dawlish Town, Epsom & Ewell, Exmouth Town, Harefield United, Harrogate RA, Hatfield Main, Heanor Town, Horsham, Ilkeston Town, Mangotsfield United, Murton, Newport IOW, Old Georgians, Paget Rangers, Paulton Rovers, Rainworth MW, St Helens Town, Sholing Sports, Stamford, Tilbury, Tiverton Town, Warrington Town, Welton Rovers, West Allotment Celtic, Whickham, Witham Town, Wythenshawe Amateurs, Yeading.

Extra Preliminary Round

Sunderland Roker v Horden CW	2-0
Boldon CA v Seaton Deleval Amateurs	1-1, 0-2
South Shields v Sunderland Vaux Ryhope CW	1-0
Coundon TT v Ponteland United	4-1
Darlington RA v Hebburn	1-3
Marchon v Eppleton CW	0-4
Prudhoe East End v Langley Park Welfare	4-2
Annfield Plain v Seaton Deleval ST	3-1
Marske United v Dunston FB	1-2
Whitehaven MS v Cleator Moor Celtic	0-1
Salford v Ford Motors	2-1
Prestwich Heys v St Dominics	2-4
Newcastle Town v Rocester	0-1
Heswall v Rylands	2-2, 1-0
Poulton Victoria v Nelson	13-0
General Chemicals v Hanley Town	5-0
Atherton LR v Atherton Collieries	1-2
Great Harwood Town v Redgate Clayton	3-1
Knowsley United v Ayone	2-0
Westhoughton Town v Cheadle Town	1-3
Waterloo Dock v Merseyside Police	1-2
Linotype v Vauxhall GM	1-2
Maghull v Flixton	1-4
Newton v Knypersly Victoria	0-4
Gainsborough Town v Radford	4-3
Derby Prims v Pickering Town	1-7
Lincoln United v Hallam	2-2, 2-1
Hucknall Town v Glasshoughton Welfare	2-0
Grimethorpe MW v Keyworth United	4-2
Frechville Community v Collingham	2-0
Pontefract Collieries v Mickleover RBL	5-0
Clipstone Welfare v Skegness Town	3-0
Kimberley Town v Bradley Rangers	0-1
Maltby MW v Worsbro Bridge MW	5-0
Rossington Main v Eccleshill United	2-4
Hall Road Rangers v Yorkshire Amateurs	0-3
Long Eaton United v Selby Town	2-4
Armthorpe Welfare v Liversedge	1-1, 1-0
Immingham Town v Blidworth MW	3-0
Hinckley Town v Blakenall	2-0
Wolverhampton Casuals v Mile Oak Rovers	2-2, 3-1
Long Buckby v Solihull Borough	1-1, 0-1
Hinckley v Meir KA	1-3
Oakham United v Knowle	0-2
Baker Perkins v Princes End United	2-0
Stratford Town v Chelmsley Town	2-0
Raunds Town v Friar Lane Old Boys	3-0
Pegasus Juniors v Anstey Nomads	0-1
(at Hereford United)	
Holwell Sports v Wigston Fields	4-1
Wednesfield v Lutterworth Town	1-0
(at Lutterworth Town FC)	
Stapenhill v Westfields	4-4, 0-4
Melton Town v St Andrews	4-2
Northfield v Burton Park Wanderers	4-1
Cogenhoe United v Kings Heath	0-3
West Midlands Police v Boldmere St Michaels	1-6
Ramsey Town v Long Sutton Athletic	0-1
Stansted v Halstead Town	1-3
Huntingdon United v Chatteris Town	3-2
Great Shelford v Hadleigh United	0-0, 1-0
Somersham Town v Bowers United	0-1
LBC Ortonians v Downham Town	1-2
St Ives Town v Coalite Yaxley	4-0
Norwich United v Clacton Town	1-0
Ely City v Wroxham	1-2
Brightlingsea United v Sawbridgeworth Town	4-0
Wingate v Electrolux	5-2
Walthamstow Pennant v Viking Sports	2-1
Southall v Stotfold	1-4

Southgate Athletic v Woodford Town	3-3, 0-1
East Ham United v Biggleswade Town	0-1
(at East Thurrock United)	
London Colney v Kempston Rovers	2-6
MK Wolverton Town v Norsemen	3-0
The 61 v Waltham Abbey	0-2
Amersham Town v Pirton	2-0
Hanwell Town v Beaconsfield United	0-2
Cockfosters v Mount Grace (Potters Bar)	3-2
Sun Sports v Barkingside	1-0
Beckton United v Totternhoe	3-3, 2-0
Sandridge Rovers v Rayners Lane	1-2
Shillington v Park Street	2-0
Langford v Winslow United	1-3
Elliott Star v Ford United	2-1
Herne Bay v Crockenhill	0-1
Old Salesians v Horley Town	1-2
Slade Green v Danson (Bexley Boro)	1-3
Alma Swanley v Selsey	6-1
Bedfont v Bosham	6-1
Wandsworth & Norwood v Cove	2-0
Midland Bank v Eastbourne Town	3-1
Godalming Town v Hartley Wintney	1-4
Chobham v Farleigh Rovers	0-5
Greenwich Borough v Ash United	4-0
West Wickham v Bexhill Town	3-1
Farnham Town v Thamesmead Town	3-1
Oakwood v Thames Polytechnic	4-0
Christchurch v Bishops Cleeve	0-0, 1-2
Flight Refuelling v Headington Amateurs	2-2, 2-3
AFC Lymington v Easington Sports	4-0
Kintbury Rangers v Bicester Town	0-1
Sherborne Town v Swindon Athletic	0-1
Larkhall Athletic v Brislington	2-3
DRG (FP) v Lawrence Weston Hallen	4-2
Ellwood v Almondsbury Picksons	0-2
Patchway v Cinderford Town	3-2
Clanfield v Harrow Hill	1-0
Cirencester Town v Backwell United	0-1
Highworth Town v Keynsham Town	3-0
Clandown v Odd Down	4-2
Newquay v Ottery St Mary	1-0
Westland Sports v Liskeard Athletic	
(walkover for Liskeard Athletic)	

Preliminary Round

Esh Winning v Hebburn	1-2
Consett v South Shields	3-1
Washington v Newton Aycliffe	0-1
Norton & Stockton Ancients v Evenwood Town	0-0, 1-2
Netherfield v Ryhope CA	4-3
Darlington CB v Chester-le-Street Town	1-2
Coundon TT v Seaton Deleval Amateurs	3-5
Bridlington Trinity v Annfield Plain	5-3
Shotton Comrades v Bedlington Terriers	0-2
Eppleton CW v Crook Town	3-1
Sunderland Roker v Dunston FB	0-3
Northallerton Town v Cleator Moor Celtic	2-0
West Auckland Town v Prudhoe East End	0-1
Alnwick Town v Willington	1-0
Peterlee Newtown v Ashington	3-2
Heswall v Salford	1-0
Lancaster City v Skelmersdale United	3-1
Knowsley United v Vauxhall GM	1-0
Flixton v Merseyside Police	0-2
Prescot Cables v Ashton United	0-2
Great Harwood Town v Curzon Ashton	1-1, 0-1
Burscough v Rocester	0-2
Darwen v Knypersley Victoria	2-1
Oldham Town v Atherton LR	0-4
Chadderton v Poulton Victoria	3-2

Leyland Motors v Cheadle Town	1-3
Blackpool Mechanics v Droylsden	0-6
General Chemicals v Maine Road	0-1
St Dominics v Formby	5-2
Blackpool Wren Rovers v Douglas High School OB	1-2
Clitheroe v Bootle	2-1
Glossop v Irlam Town	1-2
Armthorpe Welfare v Sheffield	0-2
Clipstone Welfare v Grimethorpe MW	2-1
Eccleshill United v Staveley Works	
(walkover for Eccleshill United)	
Arnold Town v Bradley Rangers	3-1
Denaby United v Harworth CI	3-0
Immingham Town v Ossett Albion	4-2
Frecheville Community v Sutton Town	1-4
Pickering Town v Hucknall Town	0-4
Louth United v Thackley	1-2
Lincoln United v Belper Town	1-2
Selby Town v Harrogate Town	1-3
Gainsborough Town v Maltby MW	1-4
(at Maltby MW)	
Pontefract Collieries v Yorkshire Amateurs	3-1
Walsall Wood v Boldmere St Michaels	0-0, 1-3
Westfields v Boston	3-3, 0-3
Raunds Town v Wellingborough Town	3-2
Wolverhampton Casuals v Melton Town	2-2, 2-0
Anstey Nomads v Racing Club Warwick	2-1
Baker Perkins v Sandwell Borough	2-3
Rushall Olympic v Holwell Sports	2-3
Rushden Town v Chasetown	3-0
Halesowen Harriers v Kings Heath	1-0
Northampton Spencer v Evesham United	2-4
Highgate United v Meir KA	3-2
Harrisons v Stratford Town	3-0
Lye Town v Malvern Town	1-1, 1-1, 2-1
Oldbury United v Hinckley Athletic	1-2
Spalding United v Knowle	3-0
Wednesfield v Irthlingborough Diamonds	0-1
Northfield Town v Rothwell Town	5-1
Desborough Town v Solihull Borough	1-5
Hinckley Town v Brackley Town	4-0
Bilston Town v Tividale	1-2
RSSC Ransomes v Billericay Town	0-1
Great Shelford v Newmarket Town	1-3
Histon v Long Sutton Athletic	2-1
Felixstowe Town v Lowestoft Town	5-2
Saffron Walden Town v Heybridge Swifts	3-0
Brantham Athletic v Soham Town Rangers	2-3
St Ives Town v Eynesbury Rovers	1-0
Tiptree United v Downham Town	0-0, 4-0
Wroxham v Basildon United	1-0
Gorleston v Bowers United	1-2
Norwich United v Kings Lynn	2-1
Halstead Town v Diss Town	1-2
Mirrlees Blackstone v Stowmarket Town	0-3
Royston Town v Canvey Island	1-0
Brightlingsea United v Harwich & Parkeston	2-1
Huntingdon United v Bourne Town	1-9
Edgware Town v Aveley	2-3
Ruislip Manor v Amersham Town	5-1
Rayners Lane v Biggleswade Town	1-0
Rainham Town v Elliott Star	3-3, 2-3
Kempston Rovers v Wootton Blue Cross	2-2, 2-1
Welwyn Garden City v Beckenham Town	1-2
Flackwell Heath v Northwood	4-3
Woodford Town v Beaconsfield United	2-1
Stotfold v Winslow United	1-0
Tring Town v Arlesey Town	1-0
Letchworth Garden City v Ware	2-0
Sun Sports v Vauxhall Motors	2-0
Eton Manor v Molesey	1-3
Finchley v Hoddesdon Town	3-1
Buckingham Town v Collier Row	3-4
MK Wolverton Town v Hertford Town	4-4, 1-1, 3-1
Cheshunt v Potton United	0-3
Feltham v Beckton United	2-4
Stevenage Borough v Waltham Abbey	3-1
Brimsdown Rovers v Leighton Town	0-1
Clapton v Shillington	3-0
Hornchurch v Wingate	2-3
Cockfosters v Barton Rovers	0-2
Hemel Hempstead v Walthamstow Pennant	0-1
Cray Wanderers v Ringmer	3-1
Darenth Heathside v Tunbridge Wells	2-1
Hartley Wintney v Banstead Athletic	2-3

Hythe Town v Malden Vale	3-1
Chichester City v Chatham Town	3-1
Danson (Bexley Boro) v Littlehampton Town	0-3
Portfield v Steyning Town	2-3
Oakwood v Egham Town	2-1
Redhill v Midland Bank	1-2
Peacehaven & Telscombe v Farnham Town	3-2
Wandsworth & Norwood v Crockenhill	2-0
Bracknell Town v Ramsgate	0-2
Wick v Lancing	5-0
Langney Sports v Sittingbourne	0-2
Horley Town v Deal Town	1-5
Merstham v Pagham	1-0
Maidenhead United v West Wickham	1-0
Eastbourne United v Corinthian Casuals	1-3
Shoreham v Farleigh Rovers	2-1
Haywards Heath v Hastings Town	1-2
Horsham YMCA v Whitstable Town	3-3, 0-1
Arundel v Burgess Hill Town	0-2
Alma Swanley v Greenwich Borough	1-2
Three Bridges v Whitehawk	1-0
Chipstead v Bedfont	2-1
Bicester Town v Newbury Town	1-3
Supermarine v Wimborne Town	0-1
Wantage Town v Petersfield United	3-1
Abingdon United v Wallingford Town	0-0, 3-1
Brockenhurst v Eastleigh	0-4
Swindon Athletic v Horndean	4-3
Warminster Town v Romsey Town	0-1
AFC Totton v Vale Recreation	2-2, 2-6
First Tower United v Swanage Town & Herston	2-1
Westbury United v Bournemouth	0-6
AFC Lymington v Didcot Town	3-1
Thame United v Bishops Cleeve	2-0
East Cowes VA v Headington Amateurs	1-3
Wotton Rovers v Radstock Town	3-1
Clanfield v Yate Town	2-7
Portishead v Clandown	0-2
Sharpness v Trowbridge Town	3-2
Patchway v Bristol Manor Farm	0-2
Port of Bristol v Melksham Town	1-2
DRG (FP) v Fairford Town	1-0
Shortwood United v Devizes Town	4-1
Moreton Town v Backwell United	1-0
Chippenham Town v Almondsbury Picksons	2-1
Highworth Town v Calne Town	2-1
Glastonbury v Brislington	1-4
Barnstaple Town v St Austell	2-1
Torrington v Chard Town	0-3
Wellington v St Blazey	1-0
Minehead v Ilfracombe Town	3-2
Liskeard Athletic v Newquay	1-0

First Round

Seaton Deleval Amateurs v Netherfield	1-5
Northallerton Town v Alnwick Town	2-1
Consett v Murton	1-0
Bridlington Trinity v Dunston FB	0-1
Eppleton CW v Hebburn	4-1
Bedlington Terriers v Whickham	
(tie awarded to Whickham as Bedlington Terriers withdrew)	
Prudhoe East End v Peterlee Newtown	1-3
Newton Aycliffe v West Allotment Celtic	5-2
Chester-le-Street Town v Evenwood Town	2-1
Droylsden v Clitheroe	5-0
Warrington Town v Atherton LR	2-0
Cheadle Town v Maine Road	1-2
Wythenshawe Amateurs v Rocester	0-2
Heswall v Merseyside Police	3-1
Ashton United v Knowsley United	3-2
Darwen v Irlam Town	2-1
St Helens Town v Chadderton	4-2
Curzon Ashton v Lancaster City	2-0
St Dominics v Douglas High School OB	2-2, 4-4, 5-5, 4-1
Hucknall Town v Maltby MW	3-0
Brigg Town v Denaby United	1-2
Sutton Town v Thackley	1-0
Harrogate RA v Eccleshill United	2-0
Hatfield Main v Rainworth MW	0-2
Sheffield v Ilkeston Town	2-0
Arnold Town v Pontefract Collieries	2-0
Borrowash Victoria v Immingham Town	2-2, 2-1
Clipstone Welfare v Heanor Town	2-5
Belper Town v Harrogate Town	0-0, 1-2

938

Highgate United v Sandwell Borough	0-0, 2-4
Harrisons v Tividale	2-0
Stamford v Spalding United	2-2, 0-9
Northfield v Paget Rangers	0-1
Rushden Town v Wolverhampton Casuals	6-1
Raunds Town v Solihull Borough	1-0
Halesowen Harriers v Hinckley Town	1-2
Evesham United v Lye Town	0-2
Hinckley Athletic v Holwell Sports	3-0
Irthlingborough Diamonds v Anstey Nomads	1-0
Boldmere St Michaels v Boston	5-1
Tiptree United v Soham Town Rangers	3-2
Stowmarket Town v Brightlingsea United	0-1
Histon v Witham Town	2-1
Wroxham v Diss Town	0-3
Norwich United v Newmarket Town	3-1
Bowers United v Billericay Town	0-1
Royston Town v Bourne Town	0-1
Felixstowe Town v Tilbury	6-3
St Ives Town v Saffron Walden Town	3-1
Barton Rovers v Beckenham Town	1-1, 0-3
Potton United v Finchley	2-1
Stevenage Borough v Flackwell Heath	2-1
Yeading v Beckton United	2-0
Aveley v Rayners Lane	2-1
Walthamstow Pennant v Kempston Rovers	1-0
Collier Row v Woodford Town	2-0
Letchworth Garden City v Molesey	0-1
Elliott Star v Stotfold	1-2
Sun Sports v Harefield United	0-4
Wingate v Ruislip Manor	2-1
Tring Town v Leighton Town	2-1
MK Wolverton Town v Clapton	1-2
Hastings Town v Banstead Athletic	5-1
Merstham v Shoreham	4-3
Wick v Chipstead	2-3
Steyning Town v Corinthian Casuals	0-1
Deal Town v Three Bridges	3-2
Hythe Town v Littlehampton Town	3-1
Epsom & Ewell v Camberley Town	1-3
Chichester City v Maidenhead United	2-5
Oakwood v Horsham	0-1
Greenwich Borough v Cray Wanderers	3-2
Burgess Hill Town v Bracknell Town	1-2
Peacehaven & Telscombe v Whitstable Town	1-3
Wandsworth & Norwood v Darenth Heathside	1-0
Sittingbourne v Midland Bank	3-0
Bournemouth v Sholing Sports	1-3
Eastleigh v AFC Lymington	1-3
Swindon Athletic v Abingdon Town	1-3
Headington Amateurs v Newbury Town	1-1, 0-1
Abingdon United v Romsey Town	0-2
Wimborne Town v Newport IOW	2-1
Vale Recreation v First Tower United	2-1
Wantage Town v Thame United	1-2
Moreton Town v Paulton Rovers	1-3
Sharpness v Chippenham Town	4-1
(at Gloucester City FC)	
Bristol Manor Farm v Mangotsfield United	3-2
Brislington v Welton Rovers	3-0
Clandown v Melksham Town	2-1
Wotton Rovers v Old Georgians	0-4
DRG (FP) v Shortwood United	1-4
Yate Town v Highworth Town	5-0
Dawlish Town v Tiverton Town	3-1
Wellington v Barnstaple Town	4-1
Minehead v Chard Town	1-4
Liskeard Athletic v Exmouth Town	0-2

Second Round

Chester-le-Street v Sheffield	4-2
Bridlington Town v Newton Aycliffe	1-0
Northallerton Town v Consett	1-0
Farsley Celtic v Borrowash Victoria	6-2
Darwen v North Ferriby United	2-1
Emley v Dunston FB	4-1
Eppleton CW v Netherfield	1-2
Guiseley v Whickham	3-1
Harrogate RA v Peterlee Newtown	1-3
Arnold Town v Heanor Town	1-2
Ossett Town v Denaby United	2-4
St Dominics v Curzon Ashton	1-2
Ashton United v Eastwood Hanley	1-2
St Helens Town v Heswall	2-0
Harrogate Town v Rainworth MW	4-2

Warrington Town v Garforth Town	2-0
Rossendale United v Maine Road	6-2
Rocester v Hucknall Town	1-2
Droylsden v Sutton Town	4-0
Hinckley Athletic v Histon	4-1
Bridgnorth Town v Lye Town	0-1
Harrisons v Spalding United	1-3
Holbeach United v Bourne Town	1-2
Irthlingborough Diamonds v Wisbech Town	1-3
Gresley Rovers v Paget Rangers	4-4, 2-3
Rushden Town v Sandwell Borough	5-1
March Town United v Raunds Town	1-2
Boldmere St Michaels v Hinckley Town	2-1
Billericay Town v Wingate	2-1
Collier Row v Berkhamsted Town	1-0
Stotfold v Tring Town	3-1
Brightlingsea United v Stevenage Borough	0-2
East Thurrock United v Felixstowe Town	2-1
Braintree Town v Yeading	0-0, 2-5
Diss Town v Walthamstow Pennant	0-1
Beckenham Town v Haverhill Rovers	0-2
Burnham Ramblers v Aveley	1-2
Clapton v Sudbury Town	1-6
Norwich United v Potton United	0-2
Harefield United v Tiptree United	2-0
Great Yarmouth Town v St Ives Town	3-0
Whitstable Town v Wandsworth & Norwood	3-2
Hailsham Town v Horsham	3-1
Camberley Town v Hythe Town	0-1
Corinthian Casuals v Chertsey Town	2-2, 1-4
Deal Town v Chipstead	1-0
Sittingbourne v Bracknell Town	1-2
Molesey v Corinthians	2-0
Havant Town v Hastings Town	1-6
Merstham v Maidenhead United	3-1
Hounslow v Greenwich Borough	1-2
Thame United v Eastleigh	0-1
Vale Recreation v Sholing Sports	1-0
Bashley v Hungerford Town	3-2
Abingdon Town v Romsey Town	2-0
Wimborne Town v Newbury Town	0-2
Bridport v Thatcham Town	2-3
Clevedon Town v Yate Town	0-4
Bristol Manor Farm v Brislington	1-4
Exmouth Town v Wellington	3-2
Chard Town v Sharpness	3-1
Dawlish Town v Old Georgians	2-1
Paulton Rovers v Clandown	1-1, 3-0
Falmouth Town v Shortwood United	2-0

Third Round

Droylsden v Rossendale United	3-3
(tie awarded to Rossendale United as Droylsden played a suspended player)	
Harrogate Town v Chester-le-Street Town	3-0
Warrington Town v Netherfield	3-1
Guiseley v Northallerton Town	4-2
Emley v Denaby United	3-1
Curzon Ashton v Bridlington Town	1-2
Darwen v St Helens Town	1-2
Peterlee Newtown v Farsley Celtic	1-0
Spalding United v Lye Town	1-0
Heanor Town v Paget Rangers	3-2
Hucknall Town v Boldmere St Michaels	2-1
Bourne Town v Eastwood Hanley	1-0
Raunds Town v Hinckley Athletic	1-0
Rushden Town v Wisbech Town	3-0
Yeading v East Thurrock United	1-0
Billericay Town v Aveley	3-1
Stotfold v Great Yarmouth Town	0-2
Walthamstow Pennant v Collier Row	1-2
Potton United v Stevenage Borough	2-0
Sudbury Town v Haverhill Rovers	4-1
Whitstable Town v Greenwich Borough	1-2
Bracknell Town v Harefield United	0-2
Eastleigh v Thatcham Town	1-2
Deal Town v Hythe Town	1-0
Hailsham Town v Hastings Town	1-1, 2-5
Vale Recreation v Merstham	0-1
Chertsey Town v Molesey	0-2
Chard Town v Dawlish Town	2-1
Exmouth Town v Bashley	0-4
Abingdon Town v Brislington	3-2
Paulton Rovers v Yate Town	2-1
Falmouth Town v Newbury Town	2-1

Fourth Round

Guiseley v Rossendale United	3-1
Harrogate Town v Bridlington Town	1-3
Emley v Warrington Town	2-2, 3-0
Farsley Celtic v St Helens Town	1-1, 0-0, 1-0
Bourne Town v Spalding United	1-1, 1-3
Heanor Town v Rushden Town	1-2
Raunds Town v Hucknall Town	1-4
Sudbury Town v Great Yarmouth Town	3-4
Potton United v Hastings Town	2-2, 3-1
Harefield United v Greenwich Borough	1-1, 5-4
Yeading v Molesey	1-0
Merstham v Billericay Town	2-3
Hythe Town v Collier Row	1-1, 3-1
Falmouth Town v Paulton Rovers	0-2
Bashley v Chard Town	1-0
Thatcham Town v Abingdon Town	0-1

Fifth Round

Farsley Celtic v Guiseley	1-3
Rushden Town v Emley	2-0
Great Yarmouth Town v Spalding United	0-2
Bridlington Town v Hucknall Town	5-2
Billericay Town v Potton United	2-1
Paulton Rovers v Yeading	1-1, 1-2
Abingdon Town v Hythe Town	1-1, 1-3
Harefield United v Bashley	2-1

Sixth Round

Rushden Town v Hythe Town	0-1
Yeading v Harefield United	2-0
Spalding United v Guiseley	1-3
Billericay Town v Bridlington Town	0-1

Semi-Finals *(2 legs)*

Hythe Town v Yeading	3-2, 0-2
Guiseley v Bridlington Town	0-3, 0-1

FINAL at Wembley

5 MAY

Bridlington Town (0) 0

Yeading (0) 0   7932

Bridlington Town: Taylor; Pugh, Freeman, McNeil, Warburton, Brentano, Wilkes, Noteman, Gauden, Whiteman, Bratton (Brown).
Yeading: McKenzie; Wickens, Turner, Whiskey (McCarthy), Croad, Denton, Matthews, James, Sweales, Impey, Cordery.
Referee: R. Groves.

14 MAY

REPLAY at Leeds

Yeading (1) 1 *(Sweales)*

Bridlington Town (0) 0   5000

Yeading: MacKenzie; Wickens, Turner, Whiskey, Croad (McCarthy), Impey (Welsh), Matthews, James, Sweales, Schwartz, Cordery.
Bridlington Town: Taylor; Pugh, Freeman, McNeil, Warburton, Brentano, Wilkes (Brown), Noteman, Gauden (Downing), Whiteman, Brattan.
Referee: R. Groves.

FA SUNDAY CUP 1989–90

First Round

Lynemouth v Blyth Waterloo SC	1-4
Nicosia v Airedale Magnet	2-0
Deborah United v Sir Robert Peel	0-2
Gibraltar v Dudley & Weetslade	2-1
Eagle v Clubmoor Nalgo	1-3
Baildon Athletic v Cleator Moor Celtic	
(walkover for Baildon Athletic)	
Royal Oak v West Wideopen Social	4-2
Town Mouse v Iron Bridge	5-6
East Bowling Unity v Boundary	5-0
FC Coachman v Stanton Vale	1-0
Green Man 88 v Northwood	1-3
Broadoak Hotel v Kebroyd Rovers	2-1
Sandwell v Toshiva Sharples	1-1, 2-1
Carnforth v Oakenshaw	0-2
Bolton Woods v Railway Hotel	
(walkover for Railway Hotel)	
Overpool United v Instones United	1-1, 3-2
Goodwin Lock v Hope Crime Metro	5-0
Grosvenor Park v Whetley Lane	3-1
Sarton United v Hallen Sunday	0-1
Marston Sports v Bulmers	4-0
Oakhill United v Swaffam United	2-1
Sheffield House Rangers v St Josephs	1-3
Brookvale Athletic v Mackintosh	4-4, 3-1
St Josephs v Cork & Bottle	1-2
Leggatts Athletic v Chequers	0-1
Shakespeare v Poringland Wanderers	0-1
Concord Rangers v Colne Hammers	5-0
Leyton Argyle v Brimsdown Rovers	6-1
Santogee 66 v Nicholas Colts	
(walkover for Santogee 66)	
Inter Royalle v Winged Horse	1-0
Whittingham v Verulam Arms Athletic	2-0
Welwyn Youth v Trinity	1-0
Lebeq Tavern Easton v Watford LC	1-0
Elliott Star v Bedfont	1-5
ABP v Oxford Road Social	3-1

Second Round

Annfield Plain Morrison S v Framwellgate Moor	3-1
Humbledon Plains Farm v Queens Arms	2-0
Sir Robert Peel v Gibraltar	0-3
Blyth Waterloo SC v Nicosia	2-3

Northwood v Almithak	4-1
Royal Oak v Overpool United	4-1
Clubmoor Nalgo v East Levenshulme	2-5
Lobster v Baildon Athletic	1-0
East Bowling Unity v Blue Union	3-3, 1-3
Iron Bridge v East & West Toxteth	1-2
Broadoak Hotel v Avenue Victoria Lodge	1-4
Sandwell v Railway Hotel	1-0
Woodpecker v Oakenshaw	2-1
Marston Sports v Inter Volante	4-2
Brereton Town v Cork & Bottle	1-0
Hallen Sunday v FC Coachman	1-4
Brookdale Athletic v Goodwin Lock	1-0
Shouldham Sunday v Grosvenor Park	1-3
Lodge Cottrell v Welwyn Youth	3-1
Kettering Odyssey v Newey Goodman	2-1
Olympic Star v Chequers	4-2
Hazel Tennants v Poringland Wanderers	3-5
Girton Eagles v Ford Basildon	0-2
Slade Celtic v Norbridge	4-1
Oak Hill United v Ranelagh Sports	1-0
Concord Rangers v Lee Chapel North	0-1
Santogee 66 v Whittingham	2-1
St Josephs (Sth Oxley) v Leyton Argyle	1-3
Merton Admiral v Broad Plain House	5-0
Lebeq Tavern Easton v ABP	3-1
AFC Bishopstoke v Artois United	0-2
Bedfont v Inter Royalle	4-1

Third Round

Royal Oak v Lobster	1-2
East Levenshulme v Humbledon Plains Farm	0-1
Blue Union v Nicosia	0-3
Northwood v Annfield Plain Morrison Sports	2-3
East & West Toxteth v Gibraltar	3-0
Lebeq Tavern v Olympic Star	2-3
Slade Celtic v Brookvale Athletic	0-1
Sandwell v Woodpecker	2-1
Avenue Victoria Lodge v FC Coachman	3-1
Kettering Odyssey v Marston Sports	1-3
Grosvenor Park v Brereton Town	1-5
Leyton Argyle v Artois United	5-0
Merton Admiral v Ford Basildon	2-3
Bedfont v Lee Chapel North	0-1
Santogee 66 v Poringland Wanderers	1-3
Lodge Cottrell v Oak Hill United	4-2

Fourth Round

Sandwell v Annfield Plain Morrison Sports	2-0
Nicosia v Lobster	2-0
East & West Toxteth v Brereton Town	3-1
Avenue Victoria Lodge v Humbledon Plains Farm	2-2, 0-3
Lee Chapel North v Leyton Argyle	2-2, 3-1
Marston Sports v Olympic Star	3-1
Ford Basildon v Lodge Cottrell	2-2, 1-1, 0-2
Poringland Wanderers v Brookvale Athletic	3-1

Fifth Round

Sandwell v East & West Toxteth	2-3
Nicosia v Humbledon Plains Farm	0-1

Lee Chapel North v Lodge Cottrell	2-0
Marston Sports v Poringland Wanderers	3-2

Semi-Finals

East & West Toxteth v Humbledon Plains Farm	0-2
Marston Sports v Lee Chapel North	1-0

Final

Marston Sports v Humbledon Plains Farm	1-2
(at West Bromwich Albion FC, 6 May)	

FA YOUTH CUP 1989-90

The following 30 clubs were exempted to the Second Round: Arsenal, Birmingham City, Charlton Athletic, Chelsea, Coventry City, Crystal Palace, Doncaster Rovers, Everton, Ipswich Town, Leeds United, Leicester City, Leyton Orient, Liverpool, Luton Town, Manchester City, Manchester United, Middlesbrough, Newcastle United, Nottingham Forest, Plymouth Argyle, Reading, Sheffield United, Sheffield Wednesday, Southampton, Southend United, Stoke City, Tottenham Hotspur, Watford, West Bromwich Albion.

The following 50 clubs were exempted to the First Round: Aston Villa, Barnsley, Blackburn Rovers, Blackpool, AFC Bournemouth, Bradford City, Brighton & Hove Albion, Bristol City, Bristol Rovers, Burnley, Cambridge United, Cardiff City, Carlisle United, Colchester United, Crewe Alexandra, Darlington, Derby County, Epsom & Ewell, Fulham, Gillingham, Grimsby Town, Hartlepool United, Hednesford Town, Hendon, Hereford United, Horndean, Hull City, Mansfield Town, Millwall, Newbury, Northampton Town, Notts County, Oldham Athletic, Peterborough United, Portsmouth, Port Vale, Queen's Park Rangers, Staines Town, Sunderland, Sutton United, Swansea City, Swindon Town, Tranmere Rovers, Walsall, West Ham United, Whyteleafe, Wigan Athletic, Wimbledon, Wokingham Town, Wolverhampton Wanderers.

Preliminary Round

Guisborough Town v Chester-le-Street Town	1-2
Billingham Synthonia v Marske United	3-1
Marine v Bootle	3-0
Huddersfield Town v Chadderton	11-0
Halifax Town v Atherton Collieries	7-1
Scarborough v Horwich RMI	4-1
Rotherham United v York City	2-2, 4-3
Preston North End v Scunthorpe United	2-5
Lincoln City v Shrewsbury Town	2-0
Radford v Wrexham	0-8
Stockport County v Chesterfield	2-2, 1-1, 3-2
Hinckley Town v Burton Albion	1-1, 0-3
Alvechurch v Lye Town	3-2
Rothwell Town v Corby Town	2-1
Wellingborough Town v Mile Oak Rovers	0-5
Kidderminster Harriers v Willenhall Town	4-3
Leicester United v Hinckley Athletic	
(walkover for Hinckley Athletic)	
Brackley Town v Nuneaton Borough	2-4
(match awarded to Brackley Town as Nuneaton Borough	
played an ineligible player)	
Chelmsford City v Bury Town	
(walkover for Chelmsford City)	
Billericay Town v Wivenhoe Town	
(walkover for Wivenhoe Town)	
Bishops Stortford v Collier Row	0-1
St Albans City v Berkhamsted Town	3-2
Stevenage Borough v Rushden Town	4-0
Enfield v Welwyn Garden City	3-2
Kingsbury Town v Letchworth Garden City	4-0
Boreham Wood v Canvey Island	2-3
Clapton v Ruislip Manor	
(walkover for Clapton)	
Burnham v Hounslow	2-5
Slough Town v Chertsey Town	2-3
Uxbridge v Walton & Hersham	11-0
Thamesmead Town v Dover Athletic	3-2
Whitehawk v Sheppey United	0-0, 1-1, 0-2
Ramsgate v Erith & Belvedere	0-2
Horley Town v Southwick	0-5
Croydon v Horsham	
(walkover for Croydon)	
Worthing United v Banstead Athletic	4-0
Farnborough Town v Dorking	6-0
Egham Town v Windsor & Eton	1-1, 3-1
Malden Vale v Aldershot	0-7

Marlow v Chichester City	2-1
Gosport Borough v Maidenhead United	1-3
Havant Town v Romsey Town	3-1
Basingstoke Town v Witney Town	2-3
Bicester Town v Oxford United	0-5
(at Oxford United)	
Thatcham Town v Hungerford Town	5-1
Keynsham Town v Exeter City	1-2
Dorchester Town v Torquay United	0-10
Wotton Rovers v Worcester City	0-3
Cwmbran Town v Yate Town	2-3
(at Yate Town)	

First Round Qualifying

Billingham Synthonia v Chester-le-Street Town	1-1, 2-0
Shildon v South Bank	1-1, 4-4, 1-0
Huddersfield Town v Marine	4-1
Halifax Town v Bolton Wanderers	2-0
Rotherham United v Scarborough	7-2
Scunthorpe United v Bury	4-1
Wrexham v Lincoln City	6-2
Stockport County v Chester City	4-2
Alvechurch v Burton Albion	0-0, 0-0, 1-0
Paget Rangers v Walsall Wood	1-2
Mile Oak Rovers v Rothwell Town	1-1, 0-2
Kidderminster Harriers v Bilston Town	3-1
Brackley Town v Hinckley Athletic	0-3
Tamworth v Wisbech Town	4-2
Wivenhoe Town v Chelmsford City	2-5
Collier Row v Norwich City	0-9
Stevenage Borough v St Albans City	3-2
Enfield v Dunstable	
(walkover for Enfield)	
Canvey Island v Kingsbury Town	2-4
Clapton v Royston Town	3-3, 0-2
Chertsey Town v Hounslow	7-1
Uxbridge v Feltham	5-0
Sheppey United v Thamesmead Town	1-3
Erith & Belvedere v Herne Bay	8-0
Croydon v Southwick	0-3
Worthing United v Worthing	3-1
Egham Town v Farnborough Town	2-2, 0-2
Aldershot v Carshalton Athletic	0-2
Maidenhead United v Marlow	3-1
Havant Town v Bracknell Town	1-3
Oxford United v Witney Town	4-1
Thatcham Town v Banbury United	1-0

Torquay United v Exeter City	1-1, 0-1
Trowbridge Town v Weston-Super-Mare	2-0
Yate Town v Worcester City	0-1
Gloucester City v Cheltenham Town	2-1

Second Round Qualifying

Billingham Synthonia v Shildon	0-1
Huddersfield Town v Halifax Town	0-0, 1-2
Rotherham United v Scunthorpe United	0-1
Wrexham v Stockport County	10-1
Alvechurch v Walsall Wood	2-3
Rothwell Town v Kidderminster Harriers	3-0
Hinckley Athletic v Tamworth	2-6
Chelmsford City v Norwich City	1-0
Stevenage Borough v Enfield	7-4
Kingsbury Town v Royston Town	3-1
Chertsey Town v Uxbridge	1-4
Thamesmead Town v Erith & Belvedere	0-1
Southwick v Worthing United	0-2
Farnborough Town v Carshalton Athletic	0-4
Maidenhead United v Bracknell Town	5-2
Oxford United v Thatcham Town	7-2
Exeter City v Trowbridge Town	4-0
Worcester City v Gloucester City	4-1

First Round Proper

Carlisle United v Blackpool	4-1
Wigan Athletic v Shildon	2-1
Scunthorpe United v Bradford City	2-2, 2-0
Halifax Town v Tranmere Rovers	0-1
Darlington v Sunderland	2-0
Blackburn Rovers v Hull City	3-2
Barnsley v Burnley	1-1, 1-3
Hartlepool United v Oldham Athletic	0-0, 2-5
Mansfield Town v Derby County	1-3
Walsall Wood v Rothwell Town	0-1
Hereford United v Grimsby Town	1-1, 1-2
Tamworth v Wrexham	2-6
Northampton Town v Wolverhampton Wanderers	0-0, 1-3
Crewe Alexandra v Port Vale	1-1, 1-2
Aston Villa v Hednesford Town	9-0
Notts County v Walsall	4-0
Uxbridge v Wokingham Town	0-4
Millwall v Stevenage Borough	2-1
Colchester United v Chelmsford City	1-1, 2-1
Hendon v Wimbledon	0-4
Epsom & Ewell v Cambridge United	1-7
Kingsbury Town v Peterborough United	1-0
West Ham United v Queen's Park Rangers	1-1, 0-3
Whyteleafe v Worthing United	4-1
Brighton & Hove Albion v Erith & Belvedere	4-0
Carshalton Athletic v Staines Town	4-0
Fulham v Gillingham	1-2
Sutton United v Maidenhead United	1-4
Exeter City v Bristol Rovers	1-0
Oxford United v Cardiff City	4-0
Swansea City v Worcester City	6-2
Newbury Town v AFC Bournemouth	0-6
Bristol City v Horndean	10-0
Swindon Town v Portsmouth	2-3

Second Round

Everton v Doncaster Rovers	0-2
Port Vale v Blackburn Rovers	4-0
Newcastle United v Tranmere Rovers	1-1, 2-0
Oldham Athletic v Liverpool	0-1
Leeds United v Carlisle United	4-1
Sheffield Wednesday v Sheffield United	5-1
Wigan Athletic v Darlington	4-0
Scunthorpe United v Middlesbrough	1-1, 0-2
Burnley v Manchester United	0-2
Wrexham v Manchester United	1-6
Coventry City v Birmingham City	2-0
Watford v Aston Villa	2-1
Cambridge United v Wolverhampton Wanderers	1-2
Kingsbury Town v Leicester City	1-1, 0-8
Ipswich Town v Rothwell Town	11-1
Derby County v West Bromwich Albion	1-2
Grimsby Town v Colchester United	1-2
Stoke City v Southend United	1-2
Notts County v Nottingham Forest	3-0
Arsenal v Luton Town	2-2, 4-2
Bristol City v Plymouth Argyle	0-4

Whyteleafe v Wokingham Town	2-3
Chelsea v Maidenhead United	5-1
Portsmouth v Millwall	3-1
Southampton v Crystal Palace	0-2
Swansea City v Carshalton Athletic	6-1
Queen's Park Rangers v Reading	3-1
Exeter City v Gillingham	1-2
Leyton Orient v Brighton & Hove Albion	2-2, 2-1
Tottenham Hotspur v AFC Bournemouth	
(tie awarded to Tottenham Hotspur FC as AFC Bournemouth failed to fulfil fixture)	
Oxford United v Charlton Athletic	4-0
Brentford v Wimbledon	1-0

Third Round

Liverpool v Newcastle United	5-0
Wolverhampton Wanderers v Leeds United	3-2
Doncaster Rovers v West Bromwich Albion	2-4
Notts County v Middlesbrough	0-2
Sheffield Wednesday v Wigan Athletic	2-0
Port Vale v Manchester United	0-3
Manchester City v Coventry City	0-0, 6-1
Colchester United v Tottenham Hotspur	0-3
Oxford United v Arsenal	1-5
Ipswich Town v Chelsea	1-0
Wokingham Town v Swansea City	2-2, 1-3
Crystal Palace v Brentford	1-1, 1-0
Watford v Southend United	3-0
Portsmouth v Queen's Park Rangers	1-1, 3-2
Leyton Orient v Gillingham	1-1, 1-2
Leicester City v Plymouth Argyle	5-0

Fourth Round

Tottenham Hotspur v Wolverhampton Wanderers	4-1
Watford v Leicester City	1-5
Manchester City v Crystal Palace	3-0
Manchester United v Sheffield Wednesday	3-1
Arsenal v Portsmouth	0-1
West Bromwich Albion v Gillingham	3-0
Middlesbrough v Ipswich Town	2-0
Swansea City v Liverpool	0-1

Fifth Round

Middlesbrough v West Bromwich Albion	2-0
Manchester City v Tottenham Hotspur	1-2
Manchester United v Leicester City	2-0
Liverpool v Portsmouth	2-2, 1-2

Semi-finals *(2 legs)*

Portsmouth v Middlesbrough	0-1, 1-3
Tottenham Hotspur v Manchester United	2-0, 1-1

FINAL – FIRST LEG

7 MAY

Middlesbrough (0) 1 *(Tucker)*

Tottenham H (1) 2 *(Houghton, Potts)* 8000

Middlesbrough: Devine; Nesbitt, Green (Melling), Sunley, Crosby, Lake, Keavney (Ferguson), Holmes, Arnold, Fletcher, Tucker.
Tottenham H: Walker; Hendon, Hackett, Smith N, Tuttle, Hardwicke, Howell (Nettercott), Smith K, Morah, Potts, Houghton (Fulling).
Referee: G. Ashby.

SECOND LEG

13 MAY

Tottenham H (1) 1 *(Morah)*

Middlesbrough (0) 1 *(Fletcher)* 5579

Tottenham H; Walker; Hendon, Hackett, Smith N, Tuttle, Hardwicke, Fulling (Howell), Smith K, Morah (Nettercott), Potts, Halton.
Middlesbrough: Devine; Nesbitt, Roxby (Melling), Sunley, Crosby, Lake, Keavney (Ferguson), Holmes, Arnold, Fletcher, Tucker.
Referee: G. Ashby.

942

FA CHALLENGE TROPHY FINALS 1970–89

Year	Winner		Runner-up	
1970	Macclesfield T	2	Telford U	0
1971	Telford U	3	Hillingdon B	2
1972	Stafford R	3	Barnet	0
1973	Scarborough	2	Wigan Ath	aet 1
1974	Morecambe	2	Dartford	1
1975	Matlock	4	Scarborough	0
1976	Scarborough	3	Stafford R	aet 2
1977	Scarborough	2	Dagenham	1
1978	Altrincham	3	Leatherhead	1
1979	Stafford R	2	Kettering T	0
1980	Dagenham	2	Mossley	1
1981	Bishop's Stortford	1	Sutton U	0
1982	Enfield	1	Altrincham	aet 0
1983	Telford U	2	Northwich V	1
1984	Northwich V	2	Bangor C	1
			(after 1-1 draw)	
1985	Wealdstone	2	Boston U	1
1986	Altrincham	1	Runcorn	0
1987	Kidderminster H	2	Burton A	1
			(after 0-0 draw)	
1988	Enfield	3	Telford U (after 0-0 draw)	2
1989	Telford U	1	Macclesfield T	aet 0

FA CHALLENGE VASE FINALS 1975–89

Year	Winner		Runner-up	
1975	Hoddesdon T	2	Epsom & Ewell	1
1976	Billericay T	1	Stamford	aet 0
1977	Billericay T	2	Sheffield	1
			(after 1-1 draw)	
1978	Blue Star	2	Barton R	1
1979	Billericay T	4	Almondsbury G	1
1980	Stamford	2	Guisborough	0
1981	Whickham	3	Willenhall T	aet 2
1982	Forest Green R	3	Rainworth MW	0
1983	VS Rugby	1	Halesowen T	0
1984	Stansted	3	Stamford	2
1985	Halesowen T	3	Fleetwood T	1
1986	Halesowen T	3	Southall	0
1987	St Helens T	3	Warrington T	2
1988	Colne D	1	Emley	0
1989	Tamworth	3	Sudbury T (after 1-1 draw)	0

FA YOUTH CHALLENGE CUP FINALS 1953–89 (aggregate scores)

Year	Winner		Runner-up	
1953	Manchester U	9	Wolverhampton W	3
1954	Manchester U	5	Wolverhampton W	4
1955	Manchester U	7	WBA	1
1956	Manchester U	4	Chesterfield	3
1957	Manchester U	8	West Ham U	2
1958	Wolverhampton W	7	Chelsea	6
1959	Blackburn R	2	West Ham U	1
1960	Chelsea	5	Preston N E	2
1961	Chelsea	5	Everton	3
1962	Newcastle U	2	Wolverhampton W	1
1963	West Ham U	6	Liverpool	5
1964	Manchester U	5	West Ham U	2
1965	Everton	3	Arsenal	2
1966	Arsenal	5	Sunderland	3
1967	Sunderland	2	Birmingham C	0
1968	Burnley	3	Coventry C	2
1969	Sunderland	6	WBA	3
1970	Tottenham H	4	Coventry C	3
1971	Arsenal	2	Cardiff C	0
1972	Aston Villa	5	Liverpool	2
1973	Ipswich T	4	Bristol C	1
1974	Tottenham H	2	Huddersfield T	1
1975	Ipswich T	5	West Ham U	1
1976	WBA	5	Wolverhampton W	0
1977	C Palace	1	Everton	0
1978	C Palace	1	Aston Villa	0
			(one game only)	
1979	Millwall	2	Manchester C	0
1980	Aston Villa	3	Manchester C	2
1981	West Ham U	2	Tottenham H	1
1982	Watford	7	Manchester U	6
1983	Norwich C	6	Everton (inc replay)	5
1984	Everton	4	Stoke C	2
1985	Newcastle U	4	Watford	1
1986	Manchester C	3	Manchester U	1
1987	Coventry C	2	Charlton Ath	1
1988	Arsenal	6	Doncaster R	1
1989	Watford	2	Manchester C	1

FA COUNTY YOUTH CHALLENGE CUP FINALS 1945–89 (aggregate scores)

Year	Winner		Runner-up	
1945	Staffordshire	3	Wiltshire	2
1946	Berks & Bucks	4	Durham	3
1947	Durham	4	Essex	2
1948	Essex	5	Liverpool	3
1949	Liverpool	4	Middlesex	3
1950	Essex	3	Middlesex	3
1951	Middlesex	3	Leics. & Rutland	1
1952	Sussex	4	Liverpool	3
1953	Sheffield & Hallam	5	Hampshire	3
1954	Liverpool	4	Gloucestershire	1
1955	Bedfordshire	2	Sheffield & Hallam	1
1956	Middlesex	3	Staffordshire	2
1957	Hampshire	4	Cheshire	3
1958	Staffordshire	8	London	0
1959	Birmingham	7	London	5
1960	London	6	Birmingham	4
1961	Lancashire	6	Nottinghamshire	3
1962	Middlesex	6	Nottinghamshire	3
1963	Durham	3	Essex	2
1964	Sheffield & Hallam	1	Birmingham	0
1965	Northumberland	7	Middlesex	4
1966	Leics. & Rutland	6	London	5
1967	Northamptonshire	5	Hertfordshire	4
1968	North Riding	7	Devon	4
1969	Northumberland	1	Sussex	0
	(one game only from here)			
1970	Hertfordshire	2	Cheshire	1
1971	Lancashire	2	Gloucestershire	0
1972	Middlesex	2	Liverpool	0
1973	Hertfordshire	3	Northumberland	0
1974	Nottinghamshire	2	London	0
1975	Durham	2	Bedfordshire	1
1976	Northamptonshire	7	Surrey	1
1977	Liverpool	3	Surrey	0
1978	Liverpool	3	Kent	1
1979	Hertfordshire	4	Liverpool	1
1980	Liverpool	2	Lancashire	0
1981	Lancashire	3	East Riding	2
1982	Devon	2	Kent	2
			(after 0-0 draw)	
1983	London	3	Gloucestershire	0
1984	Cheshire	2	Manchester	1
1985	East Riding	2	Middlesex	1
1986	Hertfordshire	4	Manchester	0
1987	North Riding	3	Gloucestershire	1
1988	East Riding	2	Middlesex	3
			(after 0-0 draw)	
1989	Liverpool	2	Hertfordshire	1

FA SUNDAY CUP FINALS 1965–89

Year	Winner		Runner-up	
1965	London	6	Staffordshire	2
			(aggregate scores)	
1966	Unique U	1	Aldridge F	0
1967	Carlton U	2	Stoke W	0
1968	Drovers	2	Brook U	0
1969	Leigh Park	3	Loke U	1
1970	Vention U	1	Unique U	0
1971	Beacontree R	2	Saltley U	0
1972	Newton Unity	4	Springfield C	0
1973	Carlton U	2	Wear Valley	aet 1
1974	Newtown Unity	2	Brentford E	0
1975	Fareham T Cent	1	Players Ath E	0
1976	Brandon U	2	Evergreen	1
1977	Langley Park RH	2	Newtown Unity	0
1978	Arras	2	Lion R (after 2-2 draw)	1
1979	Lobster	3	Carlton U	2
1980	Fantail	1	Twin Foxes	0
1981	Fantail	1	Mackintosh	0
1982	Dingle Rail	2	Twin Foxes	1
1983	Eagle	2	Lee Chapel N	1
			(after 1-1 draw)	
1984	Lee Chapel North	4	Eagle	3
1985	Hobbies	2	Avenue	1
			(after 1-1 and 2-2 draws)	
1986	Avenue	1	Glenn Sports	0
1987	Lodge Cottrell	1	Avenue	0
1988	Nexday	2	Sunderland HP	0
1989	Almethak	3	East Levenshulme	1

OVENDEN PAPERS FOOTBALL COMBINATION

	P	W	D	L	F	A	Pts
Arsenal	38	26	6	6	84	51	84
Tottenham Hotspur	38	25	6	7	93	47	81
Chelsea	38	22	6	10	78	47	72
Millwall	38	20	11	7	58	36	71
Norwich City	38	20	7	11	66	41	67
Wimbledon	38	18	9	11	69	46	63
West Ham Utd	38	18	7	13	83	59	61
Oxford Utd	38	16	9	13	73	58	57
Brighton & HA	38	15	6	17	52	66	51
Portsmouth	38	12	13	13	47	57	49
Swindon Town	38	15	3	20	58	68	48
Luton Town	38	13	8	17	68	70	47
Q.P.R.	38	14	5	19	65	93	47
Crystal Palace	38	11	10	17	56	50	43
Southampton	38	10	12	16	45	58	42
Ipswich Town	38	12	5	21	60	75	41
Watford	38	11	8	19	59	79	41
Reading	38	11	8	19	64	86	41
Charlton Athletic	38	11	6	21	49	70	39
Fulham	38	4	7	27	25	95	19

CENTRAL LEAGUE

Division One

	P	W	D	L	F	A	Pts
Liverpool	34	24	4	6	74	42	76
Nottingham Forest	34	19	6	9	79	48	63
Aston Villa	34	17	7	10	84	42	58
Manchester United	34	17	7	10	54	39	58
Manchester City	34	18	3	13	64	51	57
Leicester City	34	16	8	10	51	48	56
Derby County	34	16	7	11	64	47	55
Everton	34	16	5	13	58	53	53
Leeds United	34	14	8	12	62	49	50
Blackburn Rovers	34	14	8	12	69	59	50
Newcastle United	34	15	5	14	42	50	50
Sheffield United	34	14	5	15	47	46	47
Coventry City	34	12	5	17	50	64	41
Huddersfield Town	34	11	5	18	40	64	38
Notts County	34	8	9	17	44	90	33
Bradford City	34	8	6	20	41	64	30
Hull City	34	6	6	22	47	74	24
Oldham Athletic	34	6	6	22	34	74	24

Division Two

	P	W	D	L	F	A	Pts
Sunderland	34	20	8	6	68	32	68
Rotherham United	34	20	6	8	61	31	66
Sheffield Wednesday	34	19	6	9	69	36	63
Wolverhampton Wanderers	34	17	10	7	91	43	61
West Bromwich Albion	34	16	10	8	64	36	58
Stoke City	34	14	8	12	50	44	50
Middlesbrough	34	12	13	9	48	34	49
Barnsley	34	15	4	15	54	50	49
Scunthorpe United	34	14	7	13	48	47	49
Port Vale	34	13	9	12	58	63	48
York City	34	13	5	16	43	53	44
Bolton Wanderers	34	10	11	13	47	55	41
Mansfield Town	34	12	5	17	36	55	41
Wigan Athletic	34	11	7	16	41	49	40
Blackpool	34	10	9	15	40	60	39
Preston North End	34	10	5	19	30	71	35
Grimsby Town	34	6	8	20	35	65	26
Burnley	34	7	3	24	30	69	24

SKOL NORTHERN LEAGUE

Division One

	P	W	D	L	F	A	Pts
Billingham Synthonia	38	29	4	5	87	35	91
Gretna	38	23	6	9	79	44	75
Tow Law Town	38	22	7	9	78	57	73
Newcastle Blue Star	38	19	10	9	77	48	67
Stockton	38	18	8	12	73	64	62
Consett	38	16	9	13	57	61	57
Guisborough Town	38	16	8	14	59	46	56
Alnwick Town	38	16	6	16	59	54	54
Blyth Spartans	38	15	8	15	58	58	53
Seaham Red Star	38	15	7	16	62	66	52
Spennymoor United	38	14	8	16	58	53	50
Whitby Town*	38	15	8	15	74	73	50
Ferryhill Athletic	38	14	4	20	63	79	46
Shildon	38	12	10	16	58	75	46
Whickham	38	11	7	20	48	69	40
South Bank	38	10	10	18	40	65	40
Durham City	38	9	12	17	64	77	39
Brandon United	38	9	12	17	46	60	39
Billingham Town	38	10	9	19	52	67	39
Easington Colliery	38	6	9	23	29	70	27

Division Two

	P	W	D	L	F	A	Pts
Murton	38	27	8	3	86	33	89
Northallerton Town	38	26	9	3	82	32	87
Peterlee Newtown	38	24	10	4	71	24	82
Langley Park Welfare	38	24	8	6	67	35	80
Chester-le-Street Town	38	23	8	7	62	34	77
Crook Town	38	20	7	11	70	45	67
Evenwood Town	38	19	8	11	77	52	65
Prudhoe East End	38	17	10	11	63	49	61
Bedlington Terriers	38	17	5	16	67	72	56
Washington	38	16	4	18	50	58	52
Ryhope Community	38	14	6	18	68	67	48
DarlingCleveland Bridge*	38	13	7	18	45	72	43
Ashington	38	10	6	22	62	85	36
Willington	38	10	5	23	51	86	35
Hebburn	38	8	8	22	56	76	32
Horden Colliery Welfare	38	8	8	22	34	66	32
Shotton Comrades*	38	8	10	20	51	69	31
Norton & Stockton Ancients*	38	7	9	22	43	71	30
West Auckland Town	38	5	13	20	43	72	28
Esh Winning*	38	7	5	26	41	91	23

*Denotes three points deducted.

League Challenge Cup Winners: Billingham Synthonia.
League Challenge Cup Finalists: Whitby Town.
J. R. Cleator Cup Winners: Billingham Synthonia.
Craven Cup Winners: Billingham Synthonia.
North Riding Senior Cup Winners: Whitby Town.

T.S.W. PRINTERS (SCUNTHORPE) LINCOLNSHIRE FOOTBALL LEAGUE

	P	W	D	L	F	A	Pts
Bottesford Town	22	14	4	4	51	19	46
Sleaford Town	22	13	5	4	57	24	44
Skegness Town	22	11	5	6	38	31	38
Ruston Sports	22	10	7	5	46	27	37
Cleethorpes Amateurs	22	10	5	7	35	26	35
Louth Park Avenue	22	9	6	7	30	26	33
BRSA Immingham	22	9	5	8	34	38	32
Louth Old Boys	22	7	7	8	31	32	28
Nettleham (Mulsanne)*	22	6	3	13	34	52	20
Eaton Hall College	22	5	4	13	22	48	19
Grimsby Athletic	22	4	7	11	26	54	19
Barton Town	22	4	3	15	28	56	15

*Point deducted for playing ineligible player.

KEY CONSULTANTS SOUTH MIDLANDS LEAGUE

Premier Division

	P	W	D	L	F	A	Pts
Pitstone & Ivinghoe	36	22	8	6	72	33	74
Thame United	36	20	8	8	70	43	68
Leighton Town	36	19	9	8	67	34	66
Hoddesdon T	36	18	10	8	74	41	64
Biggleswade T	36	20	4	12	64	42	64
Totternhoe	36	18	9	9	72	47	63
Shillington	36	17	7	12	59	43	58
Electrolux	36	16	9	11	72	49	57
MK Wolv. Town	36	16	7	13	67	55	55
Welwyn G City	36	15	10	11	59	48	55
New Bradwell St. Peter	36	13	7	16	57	57	46
MK Borough	36	14	3	19	51	66	45
Pirton	36	13	5	18	44	48	44
Brache Sparta	36	9	13	14	47	68	40
The 61 FC	36	9	10	17	53	72	37
Langford	36	9	10	17	37	59	37
Winslow Utd	36	10	7	19	53	92	37
Welwyn Garden United	36	8	8	20	45	96	32
Shefford Town	36	2	4	30	34	104	10

Division One

	P	W	D	L	F	A	Pts
Harpenden Town	30	21	7	2	74	19	70
Wingate	30	20	6	4	96	37	66
Caddington	30	18	5	7	52	31	59
Buckingham A	30	16	3	11	59	38	51
Ashcroft	30	13	7	10	55	49	46
Cranfield Utd	30	13	6	11	53	46	45
Stony Stratford Town	30	10	11	9	40	30	41
Shenley & L	30	11	8	11	38	49	41
Tring Athletic	30	10	9	11	42	56	39
Bedford Utd	30	11	4	15	49	57	37
Walden Rangers	30	9	9	12	41	44	36
Toddington R	30	8	9	13	41	60	33
Delco Products	30	8	7	15	46	55	31
Ickleford	30	8	7	15	33	62	31
Risborough R	30	4	9	17	32	64	21
Sandy Albion	30	4	5	21	41	55	17

VAUX WEARSIDE LEAGUE

Division One

	P	W	D	L	F	A	Pts
Dunston FB	28	21	5	2	60	14	68
Eppleton CW	28	18	8	2	77	25	62
Newton Aycliffe	28	14	9	5	59	32	51
Boldon CA*	28	13	9	6	46	38	45
South Shields	28	11	10	7	68	46	43
Coundon TT	28	12	4	12	61	60	40
Annfield Plain	28	12	4	12	42	51	40
Marske Utd	28	11	5	12	50	57	38
Hartlepool BWOB	28	8	9	11	52	50	33
Roker	28	10	2	16	45	61	32
Vaux Ryhope	28	8	6	14	43	54	30
Cleator Moor	28	7	8	13	36	53	29
Dawdon CW*	28	8	7	13	39	43	28
Herrington CW	28	8	1	19	37	89	25
NEI Parsons	28	3	5	20	30	72	14

*3 points deducted.

Division Two

	P	W	D	L	F	A	Pts
Wolviston	22	16	4	2	54	22	52
Nissan	22	12	4	6	48	31	40
Greatham	22	10	8	4	45	25	38
Wingate	22	11	4	7	45	34	37
Thornley	22	10	4	8	48	42	34
Silksworth	22	9	5	8	42	32	32
Lambton St	22	7	9	6	36	31	30
Stanley Utd	22	9	2	11	51	47	29
Leam Lane	22	7	5	10	41	47	26
Blackhall CW	22	7	3	12	33	40	24
Winlaton YD	22	5	5	12	37	63	20
Wingate Parish	22	1	3	18	18	84	6

JEWSON SOUTH-WESTERN LEAGUE

	P	W	D	L	F	A	Pts
Falmouth Town	32	26	2	4	99	29	54
St. Blazey	32	21	8	3	84	40	50
Bodmin Town	32	18	8	6	73	28	44
Newquay	32	17	10	5	66	32	44
Bugle	32	16	7	9	55	44	39
Millbrook	32	16	4	12	61	42	36
Launceston	32	14	7	11	55	45	35
Clyst Rovers	32	14	5	13	42	56	33
Tavistock	32	14	4	14	53	57	32
Truro	32	11	9	12	55	52	31
Appledore/BAAC	32	13	4	15	43	53	30
Wadebridge Town	32	10	9	13	49	53	29
St Austell	32	8	6	18	39	71	22
Torpoint Athletic	32	6	7	19	35	69	19
Penzance	32	5	8	19	37	79	23
Porthleven	32	5	7	20	53	91	17
Holsworthy	32	4	3	25	27	85	11

BASS NORTH WEST COUNTIES LEAGUE

Division 1

	P	W	D	L	F	A	Pts
Warrington Town	34	22	6	6	69	31	72
Knowsley United	34	21	6	7	68	45	69
Colwyn Bay	34	16	12	6	79	50	60
Vauxhall G.M.	34	16	9	9	50	42	57
Clitheroe	34	17	6	11	48	47	57
Darwen	34	15	9	10	40	34	54
Nantwich Town	34	13	5	16	50	52	44
St. Helens Town	34	10	13	11	50	48	43
Ashton United	34	11	10	13	39	45	43
Prescot Cables	34	10	11	13	49	54	41
Bootle	34	11	8	15	44	58	41
Flixton	34	11	7	16	37	47	40
Leyland Motors	34	10	7	17	55	64	37
Atherton L.R.	34	8	13	13	43	58	37
Skelmersdale United	34	8	11	15	48	59	35
Salford	34	8	11	15	31	47	35
Burscough	34	8	12	14	38	41	*33
Chadderton	34	7	12	15	39	55	33

*Denotes points deducted for breach of rule.

Division 2

	P	W	D	L	F	A	Pts
Maine Road	30	22	4	4	84	35	70
Bacup Borough	34	21	5	4	76	30	68
Blackpool Mechanics	30	17	6	7	59	30	57
Wren Rovers	30	16	7	7	72	38	55
Great Harwood Town	30	16	6	8	52	29	54
Cheadle Town	30	13	8	9	54	45	47
Maghull	30	13	6	11	40	43	45
Atherton Collieries	30	12	7	11	34	38	43
Oldham Town	30	11	5	14	47	51	38
Ashton Town	30	9	7	14	42	57	34
Padiham	30	9	6	15	44	53	33
Formby	30	7	7	16	33	57	28
Newcastle Town	30	8	4	18	38	65	28
Glossop	30	8	3	19	34	58	27
Westhoughton Town	30	8	3	19	36	62	27
Newton	30	5	6	19	29	83	21

THE SCORELINE COMBINATION

Premier Division

	P	W	D	L	F	A	Pts
Boldmere St. Michaels	38	24	9	5	72	24	81
Northfield Town	38	22	8	8	79	32	74
Evesham United	38	22	7	9	79	44	73
Stapenhill	38	21	7	10	77	35	70
Stratford Town	38	18	9	11	77	50	63
West Midlands Police	38	18	8	12	80	66	62
Bloxwich Town	38	17	9	12	65	62	60
Bolehall Swifts	38	16	6	16	70	58	54
Princes End Utd	38	14	11	13	68	55	53
Solihull Borough	38	16	3	19	53	52	51
Highgate Utd	38	12	13	13	46	50	49
Hinckley F.C.	38	13	9	16	39	69	48
Chelmsley Town	38	13	6	19	46	66	45
Polesworth North	38	11	10	17	51	72	43
Kings Heath	38	10	12	16	55	74	42
Coleshill Town	38	11	8	19	58	73	41
Walsall Wood	38	9	12	17	50	73	39
Knowle	38	10	9	19	50	81	39
Mile Oak Rovers	38	8	14	16	47	74	38
Streetly Celtic	38	7	6	25	38	89	27

NENE GROUP UNITED COUNTIES LEAGUE

Premier Division

	P	W	D	L	F	A	Pts
Holbeach	42	29	5	8	94	46	92
Rothwell	42	27	8	7	72	38	89
Raunds	42	20	10	12	67	42	70
Bourne	42	19	13	10	71	47	70
Cogenhoe	42	20	10	12	57	46	70
Stotfold	42	19	9	14	66	52	66
N'ton Spencer	42	19	9	14	63	51	66
M. Blackstone	42	18	12	12	73	63	66
Arlesey	42	17	10	15	55	60	61
Long Buckby	42	16	9	17	58	61	57
Hamlet S & L	42	12	17	13	46	42	53
Irthlingborough	42	14	10	18	64	66	52
Baker Perkins	42	14	9	19	50	63	51
Potton	42	12	14	16	54	48	50
Stamford	42	13	11	18	55	63	50
Desborough	42	13	11	18	65	77	50
Burton PW	42	12	12	18	48	67	48
M Wootton	42	12	11	19	52	71	47
Wellingborough	42	13	7	22	59	70	46
Brackley	42	12	10	20	46	67	46
Eynesbury	42	8	14	20	30	68	38
Kempston	42	8	9	25	41	78	33

Division One

	P	W	D	L	F	A	Pts
Daventry	36	26	3	7	102	43	81
Higham	36	24	8	4	85	37	80
Ramsey	36	22	6	8	91	33	72
St. Ives	36	20	9	7	74	40	69
Bugbrooke	36	20	7	9	71	43	67
Newport Pagnell	36	15	16	5	65	36	61
Sharnbrook	36	17	8	11	65	61	59
Thrapston	36	15	10	11	70	52	55
Olney	36	15	10	11	58	47	55
Ampthill	36	15	10	11	56	53	55
Timken Athletic	36	14	7	15	76	71	49
Cottingham	36	11	10	15	56	58	43
Irchester	36	12	7	17	52	71	43
Blisworth	36	8	9	19	45	64	33
O N Chenecks	36	9	5	22	39	52	32
Whitworths	36	8	7	21	46	91	31
Timken Duston	36	8	5	23	34	87	29
Ford Sports	36	5	6	25	33	101	21
Towcester	36	4	5	27	47	116	17

NORTHERN COUNTIES EAST LEAGUE

Premier Division

	P	W	D	L	F	A	Pts
Bridlington Town	34	22	9	3	72	24	75
North Shields	34	21	6	7	63	31	69
Denaby United	34	19	5	10	55	40	62
Bridlington Trinity	34	18	6	10	82	44	60
Harrogate Railway	34	17	9	8	59	50	60
North Ferriby United	34	18	5	11	66	43	59
Armthorpe Welfare	34	18	4	12	53	39	58
Sutton Town	34	16	9	9	52	38	57
Sheffield	34	15	10	9	44	33	55
Brigg Town	34	13	7	14	57	50	46
Guiseley	34	12	7	15	54	46	43
Belper Town	34	11	6	17	39	50	39
Pontefract Colls	34	10	7	17	43	67	37
Hallam	34	9	8	17	45	64	35
Thackley	34	7	9	18	43	64	30
Ossett Albion	34	6	7	21	27	69	25
Grimethorpe MW	34	7	3	24	40	90	24
Hatfield Main	34	6	5	23	27	79	23

Division 1

	P	W	D	L	F	A	Pts
Rowntree Mackintosh	28	18	7	3	63	23	61
Liversedge	28	17	3	8	57	29	54
Ossett Town	28	15	9	4	49	22	54
Woolley MW	28	15	5	8	51	33	50
Maltby MW	28	12	11	5	51	29	47
Garforth Town	28	13	7	8	42	23	46
Eccleshill United	28	11	9	8	50	45	42
Kiveton Park	28	13	2	13	35	31	41
Immingham Town	28	10	7	11	28	37	37
Collingham	28	10	3	15	29	41	33
Frecheville CA	28	8	7	13	41	45	31
Parkgate	28	7	10	11	33	42	31
York RI	28	9	3	16	34	66	30
Pickering Town	28	6	5	17	39	64	23
Mexborough Town	28	1	2	25	17	89	5

WINSTON LEAD KENT LEAGUE

Division One

	P	W	D	L	F	A	Pts
Faversham	38	28	4	6	101	30	88
Sittingbourne	38	27	5	6	85	39	86
Tonbridge AVC	38	26	6	6	87	42	84
Deal Town	38	21	11	6	88	48	74
Alma Swanley	38	22	8	8	80	41	74
Greenwich Boro'	38	20	6	12	66	55	65
Tunbridge Wells	38	17	9	12	85	66	60
Whitstable Town	38	17	5	16	51	57	56
Slade Green	38	14	8	16	54	61	50
Darenth Heathside	38	12	12	14	61	64	48
Kent Police	38	13	9	16	60	84	48
Beckenham Town	38	12	10	16	54	60	46
Thames Poly	38	11	11	16	49	61	44
Herne Bay	38	12	7	19	64	62	43
Crockenhill	38	12	6	20	52	75	39
Chatham Town	38	9	8	21	38	84	35
Danson	38	8	9	21	42	58	33
Cray Wanderers	38	7	11	20	48	74	32
Met. Police (Hayes)	38	8	6	24	36	87	28
Ramsgate	38	6	7	25	25	39	25

Deducted: Chatham Town 1 goal; Crockenhill 4 goals and 3 points; Greenwich B. 1 goal and 1 point; Met. Police 2 goals. For playing unregistered players.

Division Two

	P	W	D	L	F	A	Pts
Margate	32	23	3	6	72	34	72
Hastings Town	32	21	3	8	73	43	66
Canterbury City	32	20	5	7	73	46	62
Dover Athletic	32	18	7	7	84	40	61
Sittingbourne	32	18	3	11	65	35	57
Fisher Athletic	32	18	6	8	74	39	56
Folkestone	32	16	7	9	55	47	55
Ashford Town	32	13	7	12	40	43	46
Greenwich Boro'	32	14	4	14	60	64	46
Beckenham Town	32	12	5	15	49	47	41
Thames Poly	32	10	8	14	41	50	38
Whitstable Town	32	9	6	17	39	61	30
Cray Wanderers	32	8	6	18	34	66	30
Faversham	32	8	4	20	39	90	28
Sheppey United	32	8	5	19	35	63	26
Ramsgate	32	7	3	22	43	79	24
Herne Bay	32	5	6	21	30	70	21

Deducted: Beckenham Town 2 goals; Canterbury City 1 goal and 3 points; Fisher Athletic 5 goals and 4 points; Sheppey United 2 goals and 3 points; Whitstable Town 1 goal and 3 points. For playing unregistered players.

McEWAN'S NORTHERN ALLIANCE

Premier Division

	P	W	D	L	F	A	Pts
Seaton Delaval	28	18	5	5	63	39	59
West Allotment	28	17	7	4	72	34	58
Forest Hall	28	17	6	5	70	28	57
Newbiggin	28	17	3	8	70	43	54
Ponteland	28	17	3	8	62	35	54
Percy Main	28	14	3	11	53	39	45
Wigton	28	12	5	11	56	56	41
Heaton Stannington	28	11	7	10	39	41	40
Seaton Terrace	28	9	8	11	46	44	35
Morpeth	28	11	2	15	55	70	35
Swalwell	28	9	5	14	50	52	32
Haltwhistle	28	6	7	15	27	51	25
Dunston*	28	9	1	18	45	74	25
Wark*	28	8	1	19	44	72	22
Dudley	28	1	5	22	32	107	8

* 3 points deducted

BANKS'S BREWERY LEAGUE

Premier Division

	P	W	D	L	F	A	Pts
Hinckley Town	40	24	10	6	87	30	82
Rocester	40	25	7	8	85	44	82
Gresley Rovers	40	24	8	8	89	42	80
Blakenall	40	24	5	11	78	52	77
Lye Town	40	22	10	8	68	35	76
Hinckley Athletic	40	18	10	12	58	47	64
Wednesfield	40	16	14	10	60	44	62
Oldbury United	40	18	8	14	62	60	62
Halesowen Harriers	40	17	10	13	79	55	61
Chasetown	40	16	12	12	57	36	60
Paget Rangers	40	18	6	16	74	63	60
Harrisons STS	40	15	11	14	55	54	56
Malvern Town	40	15	10	15	62	62	55
Rushall Olympic	40	15	5	20	65	56	50
Stourport Swifts	40	12	10	18	40	59	46
Wolverhampton Casuals	40	10	9	21	41	80	39
Westfields	40	10	7	23	44	84	37
Oldswinford	40	10	5	25	39	82	35
Tividale	40	8	8	24	42	80	32
Millfields	40	6	9	25	39	90	27
Tipton Town	40	4	12	24	30	99	24

League Cup: Chasetown 5 v 2 Halesowen Harriers

Division 1

	P	W	D	L	F	A	Pts
Darlaston	30	23	4	3	81	35	73
Springvale-Tranco	30	19	6	5	82	41	63
Pelsall Villa	30	20	3	7	73	34	63
Newport Town	30	19	3	8	73	46	60
Ludlow Town	30	14	7	9	80	47	49
Donnington Wood	30	13	8	9	57	56	47
Ettingshall HT	30	13	6	11	55	47	45
Gornal Athletic	30	12	6	12	60	51	42
Brewood	30	11	8	11	31	38	41
Cannock Chase	30	9	7	14	52	64	34
Great Wyrley	30	9	6	15	52	64	33
Nuneaton Bor Res	30	7	8	15	41	69	29
Wolverhampton United	30	7	7	16	37	71	28
Chasetown Reserves	30	7	6	17	43	60	27
Hinton	30	6	8	16	37	59	26
Cradley Town	30	2	5	23	21	93	11

League Cup: Darlaston 1 v 0 Pelsall Villa

GREAT MILLS LEAGUE

Premier Division

	P	W	D	L	F	A	Pts
Taunton Town	40	28	8	4	80	41	92
Liskeard Athletic	40	28	7	5	91	30	91
Mangotsfield United	40	27	7	6	96	42	88
Tiverton Town	40	26	6	8	92	51	84
Exmouth Town	40	24	5	11	74	37	77
Weston Super Mare	40	20	8	12	86	56	68
Plymouth Argyle	40	19	10	11	75	47	67
Saltash United	40	19	9	12	62	41	.66
Swanage & Herston	40	18	7	15	77	67	61
Clevedon Town	40	16	8	16	58	60	56
Paulton Rovers	40	16	7	17	51	52	55
Bristol Manor Farm	40	13	12	15	49	59	51
Chippenham Town	40	14	7	19	36	46	49
Dawlish Town	40	12	7	21	55	78	43
Chard Town	40	8	14	18	50	74	38
Bideford	40	8	14	18	37	76	38
Torrington	40	8	11	21	48	74	35
Barnstaple Town	40	8	10	22	38	75	34
Radstock Town	40	7	12	21	43	82	33
Frome Town	40	4	14	22	43	77	26
Welton Rovers	40	3	5	32	30	106	14

First Division

	P	W	D	L	F	A	Pts
Ottery St Mary	38	27	4	7	72	36	85
Backwell United	38	21	10	7	63	32	73
Ilfracombe Town	38	20	11	7	67	38	71
Bridport	38	20	8	10	69	46	68
Odd Down	38	20	6	12	53	44	66
Larkhall Athletic	38	19	8	11	73	57	65
Westbury United	38	17	8	13	66	55	59
Keynsham Town	38	15	11	12	57	46	56
Melksham Town	38	16	7	15	46	41	55
Devizes Town	38	14	12	12	38	44	54
Heavitree United	38	15	8	15	53	44	53
Calne Town	38	14	11	13	52	45	53
Clandown	38	14	8	16	45	45	50
Elmore	38	14	5	19	46	60	47
Warminster Town	38	10	12	16	43	54	42
Yeovil Town	38	9	9	20	46	67	36
Wellington	38	7	13	18	40	60	34
Bath City	38	9	4	25	37	82	31
Glastonbury	38	7	7	24	35	72	28
Minehead	38	5	12	21	29	62	27

JEWSON LEAGUE

Premier Division

	P	W	D	L	F	A	Pts
Sudbury Town	40	28	4	8	130	52	88
Thetford Town	40	23	7	10	86	56	76
Braintree Town	40	22	9	9	94	49	75
Harwich & Parkeston	40	20	13	7	77	42	73
Gorleston	40	20	9	11	61	46	69
Great Yarmouth Town	40	19	10	11	80	62	67
Histon	40	19	8	13	85	60	65
Brantham Athletic	40	19	8	13	78	63	65
March Town United	40	18	11	11	68	58	65
Wisbech Town	40	18	9	13	73	46	63
Stowmarket Town	40	17	9	14	54	51	60
Wroxham	40	16	9	15	71	76	57
Felixstowe Town	40	13	12	15	59	61	51
Halstead Town	40	14	7	19	82	99	49
Haverhill Rovers	40	12	8	20	64	69	44
Watton United	40	8	19	13	62	61	43
Newmarket Town	40	10	13	17	42	54	43
Lowestoft Town	40	11	8	21	65	77	41
Tiptree United	40	9	10	21	46	68	37
Clacton Town	40	7	8	25	48	89	29
Chatteris Town	40	0	3	37	22	208	3

First Division

	P	W	D	L	F	A	Pts
Cornard United	32	22	5	5	88	32	71
Norwich United	32	21	6	5	91	26	69
Soham Town Rangers	32	21	5	6	58	28	68
Fakenham Town	32	18	9	5	60	30	63
Ely City	32	17	6	9	59	44	57
Diss Town	32	16	7	9	63	37	55
King's Lynn Reserves	32	16	7	9	50	40	55
Downham Town	32	16	4	12	64	46	52
Woodbridge Town	32	12	7	13	53	43	43
Mildenhall Town	32	12	7	13	48	55	43
Long Sutton Athletic	32	11	4	17	43	49	37
Ipswich Wanderers	32	9	8	15	53	72	35
Somersham Town	32	9	3	20	36	67	30
Huntingdon United	32	7	8	17	36	57	29
Coalite Yaxley	32	7	6	19	29	66	27
Bury Town Reserves	32	6	4	22	36	82	22
Warboys Town	32	3	2	27	20	113	11

FEDERATED HOMES LEAGUE

Premier Division

	P	W	D	L	F	A	Pts
Newport AFC	34	23	6	5	70	28	75
Shortwood United	34	20	7	7	81	39	67
Abingdon United	33	19	7	7	65	33	64
Sharpness Town	33	16	9	8	75	56	57
Fairford Town	34	17	6	11	59	42	57
Bicester Town	34	15	11	8	43	30	56
Almondsbury Picksons	34	15	9	10	60	41	54
Kintbury Rangers	34	14	8	12	37	45	50
Swindon Athletic	33	11	11	11	47	36	44
Rayners Lane	34	12	6	16	43	44	42
Pegasus Juniors	32	12	6	14	42	60	42
Headington Amateurs	34	9	14	11	43	44	41
Moreton Town	32	11	8	13	54	62	41
Wantage Town	34	10	10	14	52	58	40
Didcot Town	34	11	6	17	54	48	39
Bishops Cleeve	34	7	9	18	33	61	30
Supermarine	33	6	5	22	25	71	23
Ruislip Park	34	2	6	26	32	117	12

Division One

	P	W	D	L	F	A	Pts
Carterton Town	30	24	4	2	72	16	76
Milton United	30	21	3	6	77	21	66
Cheltenham Town Res.	30	19	2	9	78	55	59
Kidlington	30	18	3	9	52	34	57
Chipping Norton	30	15	8	7	44	26	53
Purton	30	14	8	8	55	36	50
Wootton Bassett	30	13	8	9	52	34	47
Wallingford Town	30	9	12	9	37	37	39
Viking Sports	30	11	5	14	30	43	38
Highworth Town	30	9	7	14	43	50	34
Cirencester Town	30	8	10	12	38	53	34
Clanfield	30	7	9	14	31	57	30
Lambourne Sports	30	5	7	18	27	60	22
Easington Sports	29	6	4	19	31	67	22
The Herd	29	4	9	16	26	60	21
Cheltenham Saracens	30	3	7	20	36	76	16

CENTRAL MIDLANDS LEAGUE

Supreme Division

	P	W	D	L	F	A	Pts
Hucknall Town	38	30	3	5	102	39	93
Heanor Town	38	25	6	7	108	49	81
Arnold Town	38	23	7	8	76	32	76
Harworth CI	38	21	6	11	77	55	69
Long Eaton Utd	38	19	10	9	69	46	67
Ilkeston Town	38	17	15	6	56	31	66
Boston FC	38	19	7	12	67	42	64
Crookes FC	38	16	12	10	62	45	60
Lincoln Utd	38	18	6	14	57	62	60
Gainsborough Town	38	17	5	16	51	51	56
Borrowash Victoria	38	14	10	14	63	62	52
Louth Utd	38	14	9	15	52	50	51
Oakham Utd	38	14	5	19	54	66	47
Priory FC	38	12	7	19	54	69	43
Melton Town	38	11	10	17	58	74	43
Bradford Park Avenue	38	11	8	19	59	83	41
Stanton FC	38	7	9	22	33	69	30
Kimberley Town	38	8	4	26	48	110	28
Rossington Main	38	5	7	26	46	105	22
Grimsby Borough	38	4	4	30	32	84	16

Premier Division

	P	W	D	L	F	A	Pts
Mickleover RBL	38	28	6	3	122	29	91
Highfield Rangers	38	25	5	7	85	33	81
Nettleham	38	22	8	8	89	33	74
Lincoln Moorlands	38	20	12	6	76	49	72
Blackwell MW	38	19	12	7	79	46	69
Rossington Haslam	38	18	8	12	77	48	62
Derby Prims	38	18	6	14	44	50	60
Radford FC	38	16	11	11	61	45	59
Derby Rolls Royce	38	16	9	13	71	51	57
West Hallam	38	17	6	15	57	67	57
Blidworth	38	14	8	16	72	75	50
Newhall Utd	38	11	13	14	76	76	47
Kilburn MW	38	14	4	20	43	64	46
Swanwick PR	38	13	5	20	59	101	44
Shirebrook Coll	38	12	7	19	62	89	43
Brailsford	38	11	8	19	66	78	41
Sandiacre Town	38	11	4	23	60	90	37
Slack & Parr	38	9	4	25	57	106	31
Wombwell SA	38	8	6	24	52	103	30
Retford Rail	38	4	5	29	34	116	17

GREENE KING SPARTAN LEAGUE

Premier Division

	P	W	D	L	F	A	Pts
Edgware Town	36	27	5	4	96	29	86
Northwood	36	26	6	4	97	36	84
Southgate Athletic	36	20	10	6	72	40	70
Cheshunt	36	20	8	8	83	41	68
Corinthian Casuals	36	20	8	8	76	39	68
Haringey Borough	36	20	6	10	65	53	66
Walthamstow Pennant	36	17	11	8	56	34	62
Barkingside	36	16	10	10	74	51	58
Waltham Abbey	36	13	10	13	56	58	49
Beckton United**	36	12	9	15	57	68	42
Brook House	36	10	8	18	47	72	38
Hanwell Town	36	10	17	17	44	64	37
Wandsworth & Norwood*	36	9	10	17	51	69	36
Brimsdown Rovers	36	8	11	17	41	52	35
North Greenford U	36	7	11	18	47	72	32
Thamesmead Town	36	7	7	22	50	106	28
Beaconsfield United	36	5	12	19	34	78	27
Eltham Town	36	7	6	23	38	91	27
Amersham Town	36	5	10	21	42	73	25

** 3 points deducted ineligible player
* 1 point deducted ineligible player

Division One

	P	W	D	L	F	A	Pts
K.P.G. Tipples	29	20	6	3	89	27	66
Royal George	30	20	4	6	83	41	64
Newmont Travel**	29	19	6	4	76	25	60
Metrogas	30	16	7	7	61	34	55
AFC Millwall	30	16	4	10	66	42	52
Walthamstow Trojans	30	14	9	7	64	48	51
Hackney Downs	30	14	7	9	57	42	49
Old Roan	30	13	5	12	50	51	44
Catford Wanderers	30	12	7	11	55	42	43
Rema/Charlton**	30	13	7	10	51	47	43
Ulysses	30	9	5	16	46	63	32
Swanley Town	30	7	6	17	43	74	27
Met Police (Chigwell)	30	6	5	19	46	77	23
Phoenix Sports	30	6	4	20	38	101	22
Penhill Standard	30	5	4	21	27	80	19
Ilford	30	4	4	22	32	90	16

** 3 points deducted ineligible player

ESSEX SENIOR LEAGUE

Senior Section

	P	W	D	L	F	A	Pts
Brightlingsea United	30	21	5	4	70	22	68
Woodford Town	30	19	7	4	64	35	64
East Thurrock United	30	16	8	6	64	29	56
Canvey Island	30	15	10	5	76	34	55
Sawbridgeworth Town	30	15	7	8	67	46	52
Stambridge	30	14	8	8	66	37	50
Brentwood	30	14	7	9	55	40	49
Burnham Ramblers	30	12	8	10	62	45	44
Ford Utd	30	13	5	12	48	50	44
Southend Manor	30	12	6	12	52	42	42
Bowers United	30	12	5	13	42	40	41
Eton Manor	30	8	4	18	34	56	28
Stansted	30	8	3	19	31	77	27
Chelmsford City Res.	30	7	5	18	38	57	26
Maldon Town	30	6	4	20	32	84	22
East Ham United	30	1	2	27	17	124	5

LEICESTERSHIRE SENIOR LEAGUE

Premier Division

	P	W	D	L	F	A	Pts
St. Andrews S.C.	30	20	7	3	69	28	67
Syston St. Peters	30	18	10	2	59	20	64
Lutterworth Town	30	16	7	7	61	39	55
Friar Lane O.B.	30	16	7	7	56	36	55
Anstey Nomads	30	14	9	7	63	42	51
Oadby Town	30	12	9	9	58	32	45
Pedigree Petfoods	30	13	6	11	57	46	45
Newfoundpool WMC	30	11	11	8	33	39	44
Holwell Sports	30	12	5	13	49	40	41
Wigston Town	30	11	5	14	36	44	38
Narborough & Litt.*	30	11	5	14	37	43	36
Birstall United	30	9	7	14	38	43	34
Thringstone	30	9	7	14	43	54	34
Hillcroft	30	7	5	18	28	52	26
Wigston Fields	30	3	9	18	32	77	18
Earl Shilton Albion	30	1	5	24	24	108	8

*2 points deducted.

Wigston Town FC resigned.

Division One

	P	W	D	L	F	A	Pts
Barlestone St. Giles	34	21	8	5	83	35	71
Rolls Royce (Mouts)	34	19	11	4	61	28	68
Barwell Athletic	34	21	4	9	88	47	67
Kirby Muxloe S.C.	34	19	7	8	66	45	64
Anstey Town	34	18	7	9	65	49	61
Leics. Constabulary	34	16	9	9	62	51	57
Barrow Town	34	18	3	13	62	57	57
Downes Sports	34	16	7	11	66	55	55
Ibstock Welfare	34	12	11	11	65	62	47
Whetstone Athletic	34	14	5	15	45	52	47
Houghton Rangers	34	11	10	13	51	59	43
North Kilworth	34	11	7	16	57	67	40
Quorn	34	10	9	15	43	47	39
Aylestone Park O.B.	34	9	7	18	49	66	34
Loughborough Dynamo	34	8	9	17	46	66	33
Leicester YMCA	34	6	6	22	32	79	24
Sileby Town	34	4	11	19	32	56	23
Harborough Town	34	3	9	22	33	85	18

SOUTH EAST COUNTIES LEAGUE

Division One

	P	W	D	L	F	A	Pts
Tottenham Hotspur	30	19	7	4	76	29	45
Chelsea	30	17	8	5	59	22	42
Arsenal	30	17	6	7	66	35	40
Watford	30	15	5	10	53	44	35
West Ham United	30	15	4	11	62	52	34
Charlton Athletic	30	15	4	11	48	42	34
Queens Park Rangers	30	12	7	11	44	45	31
Ipswich Town	30	13	4	13	54	57	30
Gillingham	30	11	6	13	62	63	28
Millwall	30	9	10	11	42	45	28
Norwich City	30	10	8	12	33	42	28
Leyton Orient	30	10	6	14	47	57	26
Portsmouth	30	10	6	14	41	55	26
Cambridge United	30	7	9	14	43	66	23
Southend United	30	7	6	17	44	66	20
Fulham	30	2	6	22	20	74	10

Division Two

	P	W	D	L	F	A	Pts
Crystal Palace	30	23	5	2	74	23	51
Oxford United	30	19	4	7	69	34	42
Northampton Town	30	14	7	9	48	37	35
Southampton	30	13	8	9	41	37	34
Wimbledon	30	13	7	10	54	32	33
Luton Town	30	11	10	9	42	47	32
Brighton & HA	30	13	4	13	45	39	30
Colchester United	30	14	2	14	48	48	30
Bristol Rovers	30	14	2	14	51	60	30
Reading	30	12	5	13	43	38	29
Bristol City	30	13	3	14	43	40	29
A.F.C. Bournemouth	30	10	7	13	45	47	27
Brentford	30	10	6	14	47	51	26
Tottenham Hotspur	30	10	2	18	38	57	22
Swindon	30	9	4	17	37	57	22
Aldershot	30	3	2	25	26	104	8

HIGHLAND LEAGUE

	P	W	D	L	F	A	Pts
Elgin City	34	26	3	5	103	33	81
Caledonian	34	23	7	4	103	35	76
Peterhead	34	23	4	7	77	35	73
Inverness Thistle	34	23	4	7	69	31	73
Forres Mechanics	34	20	5	9	79	53	65
Cove Rangers	34	17	8	9	72	59	59
Fraserburgh	34	17	6	11	58	51	57
Huntly	34	17	5	12	72	46	56
Lossiemouth	34	15	5	14	77	67	50
Buckie Thistle	34	14	7	13	63	53	49
Ross County	34	13	5	16	54	54	44
Keith	34	11	8	15	49	45	41
Fort William	34	12	4	18	59	73	40
Brora Rangers	34	9	6	19	52	80	33
Nairn County	34	9	6	19	51	90	33
Deveronvale	34	6	2	26	42	102	20
Rothes	34	4	6	24	36	84	18
Clachnacuddin	34	0	3	31	26	151	3

AMATEUR FOOTBALL ALLIANCE
SEASON 1989–90

CUP COMPETITION FINALS

Senior
Old Salesians v West Wickham — 2-1

Greenland Memorial
Royal Bank of Scotland v Sedgwick — 4-1

Essex Senior
Old Parkonians v Old Fairlopians — 3-1

Middlesex Senior
Mill Hill Village v Polytechnic — 1-3

Surrey Senior
Royal Bank of Scotland v Old Tiffinians — 0-1

Intermediate
National Westminster Bank 2nd v Parkfield 2nd — 5-1

Essex Intermediate
Old Parkonians 2nd v Old Fairlopians 2nd — *1-1, 1-2

Kent Intermediate
British Petroleum 2nd v Coutts Bank 1st — 3-1

Middlesex Intermediate
Crouch End Vampires 2nd v Southgate Olympic 2nd — 2-1

Surrey Intermediate
Bank of England 2nd v Old Tenisonians 2nd — 1-4

Junior
Crouch End Vampires 3rd v Winchmore Hill 3rd — 2-2, 0-0, 2-0

Minor
Albanian 4th v Southgate Olympic 4th — 0-0

Senior Novets
Carshalton 5th v National Westminster Bank 5th — 1-4

Intermediate Novets
Old Meadonians 6th v West Wickham 6th — 4-0

Junior Novets
Old Parmiterians 8th v Old Parmiterians 9th — 2-1

Veterans
Harrodian Exiles v Metropolitan Police (Chigwell) — 1-0

Open Veterans
Port of London Authority v Ulysses — 3-0

* after extra time

AMATEUR FOOTBALL ALLIANCE SENIOR CUP 1989–90

1st Round Proper
O. Westhamians v O. Bromleians — 4-3
Ulysses v O. Malvernian — 4-1
Civil Service v O. Ignatians — 1-5
O. Vaughanians v O. Stationers — 2-8
Mill Hill Village v Wake Green — 2-0
Norsemen v O. Actonians Assn. — 1-2
Broomfield v Ibis — *4-3
O. Danes v O. Hamptonians — 4-3
Polytechnic v O. Greenfordians — 2-1
O. Manorians v Crouch End Vampires — 0-3
O. Southallians v Finchleians — 2-1
Southgate Olympic v Nat. Westminster Bank — 0-1
Nottsborough v O. Meadonians — 4-2
O. Esthameians v Derbyshire Amateurs — *3-2
Hassocks v Carshalton — 3-2
O. Salesians v O. Tiffinians — 6-0
Albanian v O. Sinjuns — 5-0
O. Parmiterians v Midland Bank — *3-3, 1-2
O. Josephians v Parkfield — *3-2
Merton v St. Mary's College — 3-2
Lloyds Bank v O. Parkonians — 0-1
Cardinal Manning OB v Birkbeck College — 6-0
Hale End v O. Tollingtonians — 4-5
O. Chigwellians v O. Minchendenians — 1-0
O. Aloysians v West Wickham — 1-2
British Petroleum v Alleyn O.B. — 5-2
O. Grammarians v Mill Hill County OB — 6-1
South Bank Polytechnic v O. Monovians — 5-0
Liverpool Victoria v Hadley — *1-1, 1-5
O. Kingsburians v Barclays Bank — 0-7
Pollygons v Kew Association — 1-4
Colposa v Lensbury — 5-1

2nd Round Proper
O. Westhamians v Ulysses — 3-2
O. Ignatians v O. Stationers — 3-0
Mill Hill Village v O. Actonians Assn. — 3-1
Broomfield v Old Danes — *2-2, 0-1

Polytechnic v Crouch End Vampires — 0-1
O. Southallians v Nat. Westminster Bank — 1-4
Nottsborough v O. Esthameians — 0-5
Hassocks v O. Salesians — 0-1
Albanian v Midland Bank — 0-5
O. Josephians v Merton — 2-1
O. Parkonians v Cardinal Manning OB — 3-2
O. Tollingtonians v O. Chigwellians — 1-5
West Wickham v British Petroleum — 2-0
O. Grammarians v South Bank Polytechnic — 1-3
Hadley v Barclays Bank — *2-3
Kew Association v Colposa — 0-3

3rd Round Proper
O. Westhamians v O. Ignatians — 1-3
Mill Hill Village v O. Danes — 5-4
Crouch End Vampires v Nat. Westminster Bank — 1-2
O. Esthameians v O. Salesians — 1-2
Midland Bank v O. Josephians — 3-0
O. Parkonians v O. Chigwellians — *2-2, 3-0
West Wickham v South Bank Polytechnic — 2-0
Barclays Bank v Colposa — 2-1

4th Round Proper
O. Ignatians v Mill Hill Village — 3-1
Nat. Westminster Bank v O. Salesians — 2-3
Midland Bank v O. Parkonians — 4-0
West Wickham v Barclays Bank — 2-0

Semi-Finals
O. Ignatians v O. Salesians — 1-3
Midland Bank v West Wickham — 0-5

Final
O. Salesians v West Wickham — 2-1

* after extra time

REPRESENTATIVE MATCHES

v Army FA — Won 4-1
v Cambridge University — Won 5-4
v Kent County FA — Won 1-0
v Oxford University — Cancelled

v Royal Navy FA — Won 2-1
v Royal Air Force FA — Won 3-0
v Sussex County FA — Lost 0-3
v London University — Won 3-1

ARTHUR DUNN CUP

Final Tie: Old Chigwellians v Old Reptonians *1-1, 3-2

ARTHURIAN LEAGUE

Premier Division	P	W	D	L	F	A	Pts
Old Chigwellians	16	10	3	3	45	22	23
Old Reptonians	16	6	6	4	30	22	18
Old Foresters	16	8	2	6	22	30	18
Old Salopians	16	7	3	6	37	29	17
Old Malvernians	16	7	2	7	23	33	16
Old Brentwoods	16	5	5	6	27	24	15
Old Carthusians	16	5	5	6	20	24	15
Old Cholmeleians	16	4	3	9	28	31	11
Old Etonians	16	4	3	9	21	38	11

Division One	P	W	D	L	F	A	Pts
Lancing Old Boys	16	13	2	1	57	25	28
Old Wellingburians	16	12	1	3	52	21	25
Old Haileyburians	16	10	4	2	35	30	24
Old Harrovians	16	8	2	6	33	30	18
Old Aldenhamians	16	5	2	9	31	38	12
Old Bradfieldians	16	5	2	9	24	32	12
Old Wykehamists	16	3	4	9	18	30	10
Old Westminsters	16	3	4	9	24	47	10
Old Ardinians	16	2	3	13	27	58	7

Division Two – 9 Teams – won by Old Malvernians 2nd
Division Three – 9 Teams – won by Old Chigwellians 3rd
Division Four – 9 Teams – won by Old Etonians 2nd
Division Five – 7 Teams – won by Old Brentwoods 4th

Junior League Cup O. Chigwellians 2nd v O. Salopians 2nd *3-2
Jim Dixon VI-a-Side O. Aldenhamians v O. Ardinians 2-0

LONDON LEGAL LEAGUE 1989–90

Division One	P	W	D	L	F	A	Pts
Gray's Inn	22	17	3	2	86	22	37
Clifford Chance Royex	22	13	7	2	60	16	33
Slaughter & May	22	14	4	4	61	27	32
Freshfields	22	14	3	5	65	31	31
Nabarro Nathanson	22	9	6	7	38	45	24
Linklaters & Paines	22	9	4	9	39	39	22
Wilde Sapte	22	9	3	10	56	59	21
Titmuss Sainer & Webb	22	9	2	11	32	49	20
Boodle Hatfield	22	5	6	10	20	34	18
Taylor Joynson Garret	22	5	2	15	24	69	12
Norton Rose	22	4	3	15	18	49	11
Baker McKenzie	22	0	3	19	27	86	3

Division Two	P	W	D	L	F	A	Pts
Pegasus	26	19	4	3	86	20	42
Cameron Markby Hewitt	26	18	4	4	60	25	40
D. J. Freeman & Co	26	16	3	7	71	35	35
Allen & Overy	26	13	6	7	85	44	32
Gouldens	26	12	7	7	59	46	31
Macfarlanes	26	14	3	9	48	40	31
Beachcroft Stanleys	26	12	4	10	45	47	28
Lovell White Durrant (Holborn)	26	9	4	13	50	59	22
Bristows	26	7	8	11	28	42	22
McKenna & Co	26	9	3	14	42	60	21
Ashurst Goddard	26	6	7	13	43	59	19
Lovell White Durrant (Cheapside)	26	7	2	17	37	76	16
Denton Hall Burgin & Warrens	26	5	4	17	24	68	14
Clifford Chance Blackfriars	26	4	3	19	29	86	11

League Challenge Cup
Slaughter & May v Clifford Chance Royex — 4-1

Weavers Arms Cup
Pegasus v Lovell White & Durrant (Holborn) — 2-1

LONDON INSURANCE FA 1989–90

Division One	P	W	D	L	F	A	Pts
Liverpool Victoria	16	13	2	1	65	20	28
Gaflac	16	8	5	3	41	34	21
Sun Alliance	16	7	4	5	36	34	18
Granby	16	8	1	7	57	40	17
Temple Bar	16	6	3	7	40	41	15
Bardhill	16	7	1	8	44	51	15
Eagle Star	16	6	1	9	37	38	13
Sedgwick	16	5	3	8	30	41	13
Hill Samuel IS	16	1	2	13	22	73	4

Division Two	P	W	D	L	F	A	Pts
Bowring	16	11	2	3	62	24	24
Sedgwick 2nd	16	11	2	3	53	32	24
Sun Alliance 2nd	16	10	3	3	72	16	23
Liverpool Victoria 2nd	16	8	4	4	44	25	20
Beaumont	15	6	3	6	33	33	15
Eagle Star 2nd	16	4	6	6	34	42	14
Granby 2nd	16	4	3	9	34	42	11
Medical Sickness	15	1	6	8	23	41	8
Hill Samuel IS 2nd	14	0	1	13	20	122	1

Division Three	P	W	D	L	F	A	Pts
Temple Bar 2nd	17	12	1	4	70	27	25
Guardian Royal Exchange	17	11	3	3	53	24	25
Colonial Mutual	18	10	2	6	55	26	22
Gaflac 2nd	17	8	4	5	38	27	20
Norwich Union	18	6	2	10	33	45	14
Sedgwick 3rd	14	3	2	9	26	53	8
Eagle Star 3rd	17	1	2	14	19	89	4

Division Four	P	W	D	L	F	A	Pts
Asphalia	14	11	1	2	48	21	23
Temple Bar 3rd	13	8	1	4	43	23	17
Bowring 2nd	14	8	1	5	49	42	17
Sun Alliance 3rd	14	7	1	6	49	36	15
Liverpool Victoria 3rd	14	6	3	5	31	36	12
Gaflac 3rd	14	3	3	8	33	48	9
Medical Sickness 2nd	12	2	3	7	36	49	7
Colonial Mutual 2nd	13	2	1	10	36	49	5

Charity Cup – Cuaco 4 Gaflac 1
Challenge Cup – Granby 1 Bardhill 0
Junior Cup – Sedgwick 2nd 6 Cuaco 3rd 0
Minor Cup – Eagle Star 3rd 3 Gaflac 0
Novets Cup – Liverpool Victoria 3rd 1 Asphalia 0
Sportsmanship Trophy – Asphalia
W. A. Jewell Memorial Trophy
Granby (5-a-Side); Runners-up – Eagle Star
Sportsmanship Trophy – Bardhill

LONDON BANKS FA 1989–90

Division One	P	W	D	L	F	A	Pts
Royal Bank of Scotland	16	16	0	0	74	14	32
Royal Bank of Scotland 2nd	16	10	2	4	52	26	22
Coutts & Co	16	7	5	4	47	32	19
Bankers Trust Co	16	6	3	7	26	31	15
Midland Montagu	16	6	3	7	27	40	15
Bank of America	16	6	2	8	30	44	14
Allied Irish Banks	16	3	5	8	23	39	11
Bank Credit & Commerce Intl	16	4	1	11	29	49	9
Citibank	16	3	1	12	19	52	7

Division Two	P	W	D	L	F	A	Pts
Hill Samuel & Co	18	14	2	2	62	28	30
Chase Manhattan Bank	18	13	3	2	59	26	29
Kleinwort Benson	18	9	1	8	42	43	19
Standard Chartered Bank	18	9	1	8	37	39	19
Royal Bank of Scotland 3rd	18	7	4	7	43	45	18
Hong Kong & Shanghai Bank	18	7	2	9	30	33	16
Banque Nationale de Paris	18	6	3	9	31	51	15
National Westminster Bank 'A'	18	5	3	10	26	39	13
Credit Suisse	18	4	4	10	28	43	12
Bank of Scotland	18	4	1	13	38	49	9

Division Three	P	W	D	L	F	A	Pts
Austral & N.Z.							
Banking Corpn	16	11	2	3	47	18	24
Morgan Guaranty Trust							
Co.	16	9	4	3	44	23	22
Coutts & Co 2nd	16	7	4	5	44	28	18
Westpac	16	7	4	5	42	28	18
Royal Bank of Scotland							
3rd	16	5	7	4	35	27	17
Polytechnic	16	5	4	7	24	37	14
Manufacturers Hanover							
Trust	16	6	1	9	39	45	13
National Westminster							
Bank 'B'	16	5	3	8	35	43	13
Citibank 2nd	16	2	1	13	12	73	5

Division Four	P	W	D	L	F	A	Pts
Union Bank of							
Switzerland	18	12	3	3	48	32	27
Midland Montague 2nd	18	12	1	3	48	32	25
Bank of Ireland	18	10	2	6	37	33	22
Bank of America 2nd	18	9	3	6	58	38	21
National Westminster							
Bank 'C'	18	9	3	6	51	33	21
C. Hoare & Co	18	9	2	7	46	38	20
Trustee Savings Bank	18	8	3	7	37	41	19
National Westminster							
Bank 'D'	18	3	3	12	22	51	9
Swiss Bank Corpn.	18	3	2	13	23	48	8
Austral & N.Z. Bank 2nd	18	4	0	14	22	56	8

Division Five – 10 Teams – won by Chase Manhattan Bank
Division Six – 11 Teams – won by Morgan Stanley
Challenge Cup – 16 entries
National Westminster v Polytechnic   2-0
Senior Cup – 27 entries
R. Bank of Scotland v Bankers Trust   5-1
Senior Plate – 11 entries
Royal Bank of Scotland 2nd v Allied Irish   2-0
Minor Cup – 40 entries
Royal Bank of Scotland 3rd v N. Westminster 4th   2-0
Junior Cup – 50 entries
Midland Montagu 2nd v Midland Bank 5th   4-0
Veterans' Cup – 13 entries
Royal Bank of Scotland Vets v Bank of America   4-1
Sportsmans Cup – 4 entries
Morgan Guaranty U. v Bank of Switzerland   *2-2, 5p-3p

LONDON OLD BOYS' CUP

Senior Cup (68 Entries)
O. Meadonians v O. Wokingians   *0-0, 2-0
Intermediate Cup (75)
Latymer Old Boys 2nd v O. Ignatians 2nd   *0-2
Junior Cup (70)
O. Tenisonians 3rd v Albanian 3rd   *1-2
Minor Cup (61)
O. Greenfordians 4th v O. Meadonians 4th   *1-1, 2-1
Novets Cup (53)
E. Barnet OG 5th v O. Parmiterians 5th   0-3
Drummond Cup (32)
O. Salvatorians 6th v Latymer OB 6th   *2-1
Nemean Cup (39)
O. Wokingians 7th v O. Parmiterians 7th   1-4
Veterans' Cup (29)
Shene OG Vets v Wm Fitt OB Vets   1-2

THE OLD BOYS' FOOTBALL LEAGUE 1989–90

Premier Division	P	W	D	L	F	A	Pts
Old Ignatians	20	16	3	1	59	14	35
Old Aloysians	20	14	3	3	51	17	31
Old Meadonians	20	13	4	3	45	21	30
Cardinal Manning OB	20	12	5	3	34	21	29
Enfield Old							
Grammarians	20	5	11	4	29	26	21
Old Danes	20	7	4	9	35	41	18
Latymer OB	20	3	7	10	27	43	13
Old Suttonians	20	5	3	12	33	51	13
Old Kingsburians	20	2	7	11	15	46	11
Mill Hill County OB	20	3	4	13	26	41	10
Old Isleworthians	20	3	3	14	26	59	9

Senior Division One	P	W	D	L	F	A	Pts
Chertsey O. Salesians	20	16	3	1	54	14	35
Glyn OB	20	15	3	2	53	18	33
Old Tenisonians	20	10	7	3	37	22	27
Old Minchendenians	20	8	6	6	27	24	22
Old Wokingians	20	6	7	7	40	37	19
Old Josephians	20	7	5	8	32	32	19
Old Greenfordians	20	6	6	8	23	33	19
Phoenix OB	20	6	3	11	20	31	15
Old Salvatorians	20	3	8	9	34	48	14
Old Sinjuns	20	3	3	14	24	49	9
Clapham O. Xaverians	20	3	3	14	26	62	9

Senior Division Two	P	W	D	L	F	A	Pts
Old Wilsonians	22	17	2	3	42	15	36
Old Westhamians	22	15	4	3	48	29	34
Old Vaughanians	22	14	5	3	49	33	33
Old Southallians	22	10	5	7	42	32	25
Shene Old Grammarians	22	7	7	8	33	24	21
Strand Hollingtonian OB	22	7	5	10	38	36	19
Old Tollingtonians	22	6	7	9	34	32	19
Old Alpertonians	22	6	7	9	32	38	19
Old Tiffinians	22	7	4	11	36	41	18
Old Edmontonians	22	7	2	13	42	53	16
Enfield Old Grammarians							
2nd	22	7	2	13	34	50	16
Old Sedcopians	22	3	2	17	23	60	8

Senior Division 3 (A) – 12 Teams – won by O. Ignatians 2nd
Senior Division 3 (B) – 11 Teams – won by John Fisher OB
Senior Division 4 (North) – 11 Teams – won by Latymer Old Boys
Senior Division 4 (South) – 11 Teams – won by Old Tenisonians 2nd
Senior Division 4 (West) – 11 Teams – won by Old Greenfordians 2nd

SOUTHERN AMATEUR LEAGUE 1989–90

SENIOR SECTION

Division One	P	W	D	L	F	A	Pts
West Wickham	22	16	4	2	45	18	36
Old Esthameians	22	13	3	6	40	27	29
Old Salesians	22	11	5	6	40	36	27
Winchmore Hill	22	9	6	7	40	32	24
Norsemen	22	8	5	9	26	27	21
Old Parkonians	22	7	7	8	29	33	21
National Westminster							
Bank	22	7	5	10	31	34	19
Midland Bank	22	6	7	9	26	32	19
Old Actonians Asso.	22	5	9	8	38	46	19
Old Stationers	22	5	8	9	25	31	18
Crouch End Vampires	22	6	6	10	23	29	18
South Bank Polytechnic	22	5	3	14	27	45	13

Division Two	P	W	D	L	F	A	Pts
Carshalton	22	13	6	3	45	24	32
Civil Service	22	13	3	6	54	33	29
Broomfield	22	11	5	6	36	23	27
Merton	22	9	7	6	35	33	25
British Petroleum	22	9	3	10	40	38	21
Old Bromleians	22	8	4	11	30	27	20
Barclays Bank	22	7	6	9	31	40	20
Polytechnic	22	7	5	10	30	32	19
East Barnet Old							
Grammarians	22	7	5	10	38	43	19
Old Lyonians	22	8	3	11	23	36	19
Lensbury	22	6	5	11	22	37	17
Lloyds Bank	22	7	2	13	30	48	16

Division Three	P	W	D	L	F	A	Pts
Southgate Olympic	20	14	4	2	53	21	32
Ibis	20	13	3	4	62	21	29
Alleyn Old Boys	20	12	5	3	47	29	29
Bank of England	20	9	5	6	48	38	23
Alexandra Park	20	9	5	6	44	35	23
Kew Association	20	7	5	8	31	41	19
Old Westminster							
Citizens	20	6	4	10	27	39	16
Cuaco	20	6	3	11	33	48	15
Old Latymerians	20	5	5	10	28	43	15
Brentham	20	4	6	10	26	37	11
Reigate Priory	20	1	3	16	17	64	5

RESERVE TEAM SECTION
Division One – 12 Teams – won by West Wickham 2nd
Division Two – 12 Teams – won by Southgate Olympic 2nd
Division Three – 11 Teams – won by Merton 2nd

THIRD TEAM SECTION
Division One – 12 Teams – won by Southgate Olympic 3rd
Division Two – 12 Teams – won by Crouch End Vampires 3rd
Division Three – 11 Teams – won by Merton 3rd

FOURTH TEAM SECTION
Division One – 12 Teams – won by Old Stationers 4th
Division Two – 12 Teams – won by Civil Service 4th
Division Three – 11 Teams – won by Kew Association 4th

FIFTH TEAM SECTION
Division One – 12 Teams – won by Winchmore Hill 5th
Division Two – 11 Teams – won by National Westminster Bank 5th
Division Three – 10 Teams – won by Civil Service 5th

SIXTH TEAM SECTION
Division One – 11 Teams – won by Polytechnic 6th
Division Two – 9 Teams – won by Old Salesians 6th
Division Three – 9 Teams – won by Old Latymerians 6th

SEVENTH TEAM SECTION
Division One – 11 Teams – won by Winchmore Hill 7th
Division Two – 10 Teams – won by Norsemen 7th

EIGHTH TEAM SECTION
Division One – 11 Teams – won by Midland Bank 8th
Division Two – 10 Teams – won by National Westminster Bank 9th

SOUTHERN OLYMPIAN LEAGUE 1989–90

SENIOR SECTION

Division One	P	W	D	L	F	A	Pts
Old Parmiterians	18	12	1	5	42	19	25
Old Grammarians	18	9	7	2	41	21	25
St Mary's College	18	9	6	3	31	18	24
Parkfield	18	8	4	6	36	38	20
Mill Hill Village	18	7	3	8	37	44	17
Southgate County	18	6	4	8	34	31	16
Old Bealonians	18	6	3	9	28	37	15
Old Finchleians	18	5	2	11	38	41	14
Albanian	18	5	2	11	20	38	12
Fulham Compton OB	18	4	4	10	25	45	12

Division Two	P	W	D	L	F	A	Pts
Colposa	18	14	4	1	53	16	31
Witan	18	9	4	5	34	25	22
Old Fairlopians	18	8	4	8	39	38	20
Old Monovians	18	7	6	5	29	29	20
Hadley	18	7	5	6	27	22	19
Hale End Athletic	18	8	3	7	31	31	19
Inland Revenue	18	7	3	8	26	27	17
Old Colfeians	18	6	5	7	30	34	17
Academicals	18	2	6	10	24	42	10
Wandsworth Borough	18	1	3	14	26	55	5

Division Three	P	W	D	L	F	A	Pts
Old Owens	16	12	3	1	56	18	27
Pollygons	16	12	0	4	55	28	24
Birkbeck College	16	10	1	5	33	24	21
Hampstead Heathens	16	6	2	8	27	31	14
Old Woodhouseans	16	5	3	8	27	36	13
Mayfield Athletic	16	5	3	8	29	46	13
Cent YMCA	16	4	3	9	18	28	11
Ealing Association	16	4	3	9	34	48	11
Tansley	16	3	4	9	17	37	10

Division Four	P	W	D	L	F	A	Pts
Nottsborough	18	17	0	1	87	20	34
Electrosport	18	10	4	4	46	33	24
BBC	18	9	5	4	44	25	23
Westerns	18	11	1	6	48	30	23
London Welsh	18	11	1	6	48	30	16
London Airways	18	4	8	6	21	25	16
Economicals	18	6	2	10	31	59	14
Brent	18	3	7	8	30	38	13
Distillers	18	3	4	11	21	60	10
Bourneside	18	2	3	13	19	54	7

Intermediate Division One – 10 Teams – won by Old Fairlopians 2nd
Intermediate Division Two – 10 Teams – won by Old Finchleians 2nd
Intermediate Division Three – 10 Teams – won by Fulham Compton OB 2nd
Intermediate Division Four – 10 Teams – won by Duncombe Sports
Junior Division One – 10 Teams – won by Albanian 3rd
Junior Division Two – 10 Teams – won by Old Parmiterians 4th
Junior Division Three – 10 Teams – won by Old Parmiterians 5th
Junior Division Four – 10 Teams – won by Old Monovians 4th
Minor Division 'A' – 10 Teams – won by BBC 3rd
Minor Division 'B' – 10 Teams – won by Old Parmiterians 8th
Minor Division 'C' – 10 Teams – won by Parkfield 6th
Minor Division 'D' – 10 Teams – won by Old Bealonians 5th
Minor Division 'E' – 10 Teams – won by Fulham Compton OB 4th
Minor Division 'F' – 10 Teams – won by Albanian 9th
Veterans' Section – 7 Teams – won by LNER & Belstone Vets

Challenge Bowl – won by Old Parmiterians
Challenge Shield – won by Nottsborough
Intermediate Challenge Cup – won by Old Parmiterians 2nd
Intermediate Challenge Shield – won by Duncombe Sports
Junior Challenge Cup – won by Parkfield 3rd
Junior Challenge Shield – won by Colposa 3rd
Mander Challenge Cup – won by Old Parmiterians 4th
Mander Challenge Shield – won by Old Monovians 4th
Burntwood Trophy – won by Old Parmiterians 5th
Burntwood Challenge Shield – won by Parkfield 5th
Thomas Parmiter Cup – won by Old Parmiterians 6th
Thomas Parmiter Challenge Shield – won by Parkfield 6th
Veterans' Cup – won by Old Finchleians Vets
Veterans' Challenge Shield – won by Old Fairlopians Vets
Ken Elbourne Memorial Award – Not awarded

MIDLAND AMATEUR ALLIANCE

Division One	P	W	D	L	F	A	Pts
Wollaton	22	19	3	0	84	25	41
Bassingfield	22	16	1	5	65	38	33
Old Elizabethans	22	13	5	4	50	25	31
Kirton BW	22	9	6	7	42	35	24
Nottinghamshire	22	10	3	9	44	46	23
Beeston OBA	22	9	5	8	43	49	23
Derbyshire Amateurs	22	7	7	8	44	39	21
Brunts Old Boys	22	7	5	10	37	42	19
Magdala Amateurs	22	7	3	12	47	57	17
Tibshelf Old Boys	22	4	5	13	32	65	13
Lady Bay	22	4	3	15	32	63	11
Peoples College	22	3	2	17	28	64	8

Division Two	P	W	D	L	F	A	Pts
Sherwood Amateurs	22	19	2	1	98	18	40
Wollaton 2nd	22	15	5	2	68	22	35
FC Toton	22	12	5	5	62	46	29
Old Elizabethans 2nd	22	13	2	7	50	30	28
Heanor Amateurs	22	12	4	6	48	37	28
Old Bemrosians	22	10	4	8	43	29	24
Nottingham Spartan	22	5	8	9	39	59	18
Nottinghamshire 2nd	22	7	3	12	44	53	17
Nottingham Univ PG's	22	5	5	12	42	62	15
Mapperley Park	22	5	3	14	34	61	13
Chilwell	22	4	4	14	31	73	12
W. Bridgford Casuals	22	1	3	18	20	89	5

Division Three	P	W	D	L	F	A	Pts
Old Elizabethans 3rd	26	15	8	3	63	26	38
Brunts OB 2nd	26	14	8	4	64	37	36
Wollaton 3rd	26	12	6	8	62	51	30
Derbyshire Amateurs 2nd	26	12	5	9	66	57	29
Old Bemrosians 2nd	26	12	5	9	56	49	29
Lady Bay 2nd	26	11	5	10	56	52	27
Tibshelf Old Boys 2nd	25	11	5	10	50	48	27
Magdala Amateurs 2nd	26	11	3	12	56	57	25
Sherwood Amateurs 2nd	26	9	7	10	43	52	25
People's College 2nd	26	9	5	12	47	66	23
Nottingham Cougars	26	9	4	13	47	42	22
Heanor Amateurs 2nd	26	8	6	12	45	54	22
County Nalgo	26	6	7	13	33	51	19
Charnos	26	5	2	19	40	86	12

Division Four	P	W	D	L	F	A	Pts
Beeston OB Assn 2nd	24	19	3	2	90	27	41
Bassingfield 2nd	24	19	3	2	85	23	41
Woodborough United	24	17	1	6	76	36	35
Derbyshire Amateurs 3rd	24	15	2	7	66	51	32
Nottinghamshire 3rd	24	13	0	11	74	59	26
Brunts OB 3rd	24	11	2	11	53	64	24
Tibsheld Old Boys 3rd	24	8	7	9	65	59	23
Old Elizabethans 4th	24	8	5	11	40	49	21
Old Bemrosians 3rd	24	8	1	15	45	70	17
Mapperley Park 2nd	24	4	5	15	27	54	13
Lady Bay 3rd	24	4	1	19	29	95	9
Peoples College 3rd	24	3	1	20	29	98	7

Senior Cup – O Elizabethans 0 Wollaton 4
Intermediate Cup – Brunts OB 2nd 0 Wollaton 2nd 3
Minor Cup – O Elizabethans 3rd 1 Wollaton 3rd 0
1st Division Challenge Trophy – O Elizabethans 5 Wollaton 3
2nd Division Challenge Cup – O Elizabethans 2nd 1 S'wood Amateurs 2
3rd Division Challenge Cup – Wollaton 3rd 3 S'wood Amateurs 2nd 2
4th Division Challenge Cup – Beeston OBA 2nd 1 Brunts OB 3rd 2

THE OLD BOYS' INVITATION CUP 1989–90

Senior Cup O. Parkonians v O. Salesians — 3-2
Junior Cup
Minor Cup
E. Barnet O. Grammarians 2nd v O. Tenisonians 2nd — 1-2
O. Stationers 3rd v E. Barnet O. Grammarians 3rd — 0-1
4th XI Cup O. Minchendenians 4th v O.Stationers 4th — 0-1
5th XI Cup O. Salesians 5th v O. Finchleians 5th — 2-3
6th XI Cup
O. Minchendenians 6th v E. Barnet O. Grammarians 6th 3-0
7th XI Cup
O. Salesians 7th v O. Stationers 7th — 3:pw-3:pl
Veterans' Cup
O. Stationers Veterans v O. Colfians Vets — 1-2

UNIVERSITY FOOTBALL 1989–90

UNIVERSITY OF LONDON INTER-COLLEGIATE LEAGUE

Premier Division

	P	W	D	L	F	A	Pts
Guy's Hospital	16	10	3	3	38	20	23
Goldsmiths' College	16	9	4	3	31	20	22
Imperial College	16	8	3	5	27	20	19
London School of Economics	16	8	1	7	40	27	17
King's College	16	8	1	7	34	41	17
Queen Mary College	16	7	1	8	20	29	15
University College	16	5	1	7	24	34	14
R. Holloway & Bedford New College	16	5	1	10	31	41	11
St. George's Hospital Med. Sch.	16	2	2	12	19	42	6

Division One

	P	W	D	L	F	A	Pts
Imperial College 2nd	18	12	3	3	34	23	27
King's College M.S.	18	11	3	4	49	26	25
Queen Mary College	18	8	6	4	38	28	22
The London Hospital Med. College	18	7	6	5	42	32	20
Middlesex & Univ. Coll. Hospitals M.S.	18	8	3	7	32	34	19
University College 2nd	18	9	1	8	32	35	19
Royal Free Hospital Sch. Medicine	18	4	6	8	29	33	14
St. Thomas's Hospital Med. Sch.	18	5	3	10	26	29	13
Royal School of Mines (Imperial Coll.)	18	4	5	9	29	35	13
R. Holloway & Bedford N. Coll. 2nd	18	2	4	12	31	68	8

Division Two

	P	W	D	L	F	A	Pts
School of Pharmacy	18	14	3	1	67	27	31
King's College 2nd	18	14	2	2	54	26	30
London Sch .Econ. 2nd	18	10	3	5	41	27	23
University College 3rd	19	8	4	6	35	30	20
Charing Cross & W'min Hospital M.S.	18	8	3	7	45	33	19
St. Bartholomew's Hosp. Med. Coll.	18	6	3	9	25	26	15
Imperial College 3rd	18	5	3	10	27	43	13
St. Mary's Hospital Med. School	18	5	2	1	31	49	12
Guy's Hospital 2nd	18	3	3	12	10	34	9
Goldsmiths' College 2nd	18	3	2	13	22	62	8

Division 1 – 10 Teams – won by Imperial College 2nd
Division 2 – 10 Teams – won by School of Pharmacy
Division 4 – 9 Teams – won by University College 4th
Division 5 – 8 Teams – won by Westfield College
Division 6 – 9 Teams – won by London School of Economics 5th

Challenge Cup – Goldsmiths' College 2 King's College 0

Upper Reserves Cup – King's College 2nd 0*: 14p L.S.E. 2nd 0*: 13p

Lower Reserves Cup – King's College M.S. 2nd 3 L.S.E. 4th 1

UNIVERSITY MATCH

(6 December 1989, at Abbey Stadium, Cambridge)

Oxford 0, Cambridge 0 (h-t 0-0)

Oxford: A. Sainsbury (Plymouth and Exeter); M. Ramsey (Warwick and St Peter's), N. Glenn (Hartlepool Sixth Form College and Christchurch), S. Moorey (Beaumont Leys, Leicester and Queen's); B. Rodger (Hamilton GS, Strathclyde Univ and Worcester), M. Crawley (Manchester GS and Keble), R. Morris (Ysgol Dyffryn Conway, Llanrwst and Oriel), D. Westgate (Varndean College, Brighton and St Edmund Hall), I. Falshaw (St. Francis Xavier's, Liverpool and Pembroke), D. Goldie (John Nielson HS, Paisley and Wadham), (sub: M. Evans (Park View Sixth Form College, Nottingham and St Edmund Hall), K. Campbell (Manchester GS and Oriel) (sub: I. Schongwe (Welyan College, US and Christchurch)).

Cambridge: J. Hergenrother (Princeton, US and Trinity); G. Lough (Latymer and Downing), M. Bowden (Bolton School and Jesus) (sub: S. Hudson (King's School, Chester and Christ's)), R. Devey (Salts GS, Bradford and Emmanuel), P. Hales (St Bede's, Manchester and Christ's), S. Finnigan (Maricourt Comp School, Maghull and St John's), B. Auchlineck (Monifieth HS, Dundee and Churchill), J. Beeby (Pudsey Grangefield School and Trinity), M. Morris (Cherwell School, Oxford and Pembroke), K. Julien (King's College, London and Churchill), (sub: C. Jones (Nabwood GS, Shipley and Fitzwilliam)), J. Curwen (Tupton and St Catherine's).

COMMERCIAL UNION/UAU 1989–90
DIVISIONAL MATCHES

NORTH EAST GROUP

Hull, 1, Leeds 4
Newcastle 3, York 0
York 1, Durham 1
Newcastle 5, Hull 0
Durham 0, Leeds 4

York 1, Hull 3
Hull 1, Durham 2
Leeds 1, Newcastle 2
Leeds 3, York 2
Durham 1, Newcastle 4

	P	W	D	L	F	A	Pts
Newcastle	4	4	0	0	14	2	8
Leeds	4	3	0	1	12	4	6
Durham	4	1	1	2	4	10	3
Hull	4	1	0	3	5	13	2
York	4	0	0	4	4	10	0

WEST MIDLANDS GROUP

Aston 1, Birmingham 1
Leicester 1, Keele 0
Keele 1, Warwick 2
Aston 0, Leicester 2
Warwick 1, Birmingham 2

Keele 1, Aston 2
Warwick 6, Aston 2
Birmingham 5, Leicester 2
Birmingham 4, Keele 0
Leicester 0, Warwick 0

	P	W	D	L	F	A	Pts
Birmingham	4	3	1	0	12	7	7
Warwick	4	2	1	1	9	5	5
Leicester	4	2	1	1	5	5	5
Aston	4	1	1	2	5	10	3
Keele	4	0	0	4	2	9	0

EAST MIDLANDS GROUP
Loughborough 3, Bradford 0
Sheffield 2, Nottingham 0
Loughborough 7, Sheffield 2
Nottingham 2, Bradford 2
Bradford 4, Sheffield 0
Nottingham 0, Loughborough 8

	P	W	D	L	F	A	Pts
Loughborough	3	3	0	0	18	2	6
Bradford	3	1	1	1	6	5	3
Sheffield	3	1	0	2	4	11	2
Nottingham	3	0	1	2	2	12	1

NORTH WEST GROUP
Liverpool 0, Salford 1
Manchester 1, Lancaster 3
Lancaster 2, Liverpool 2
Manchester 0, U.M.I.S.T. 1
Salford 1, Manchester 3
U.M.I.S.T. 1, Lancaster 1
Liverpool 3, Manchester 1
Salford 1, U.M.I.S.T. 1
Lancaster 4, Salford 2
U.M.I.S.T. 1, Liverpool 2

	P	W	D	L	F	A	Pts
Lancaster	4	2	2	0	10	6	6
Liverpool	4	2	1	1	7	5	5
U.M.I.S.T.	4	1	2	1	4	4	4
Salford	4	1	1	2	5	8	3
Manchester	4	1	0	3	5	8	2

SOUTH EAST (NORTH) GROUP
City 3, Buckingham 5
East Anglia 3, Brunel 1
U.C.L. 0, Essex 3
Buckingham 1, East Anglia 5
Brunel 3, U.C.L. 2
City 1, Essex 6
Brunel 0, Essex 2
City 1, East Anglia 8
U.C.L. 13, Buckingham 0
Brunel 8, City 0
East Anglia 0, U.C.L. 0
Essex 6, Buckingham 1
Buckingham 2, Brunel 10
Essex 0, East Anglia 2
U.C.L. 1, City 0

	P	W	D	L	F	A	Pts
East Anglia	5	4	1	0	18	3	9
Essex	5	4	0	1	17	4	8
Brunel	5	3	0	2	22	7	6
U.C.L.	5	2	1	2	14	6	5
Buckingham	5	1	0	4	9	37	2
City	5	0	0	5	6	28	0

SOUTH EAST (SOUTH) GROUP
Kent 2, Surrey 1
Imperial 2, L.S.E. 1
R.H.B.N.C. 0, Sussex 1
Sussex 2, L.S.E. 1
Surrey 1, Imperial 1
R.H.B.N.C. 0, Kent 2
Kent 7, Sussex 0
Surrey 4, L.S.E. 0
R.H.B.N.C. 4, Imperial 0
Sussex 1, Surrey 2
Kent, 2 Imperial 1
L.S.E. 2, R.H.B.N.C. 1
L.S.E. 1, Kent 5
Imperial 3, Sussex 4
Surrey 8, R.H.B.N.C. 1

	P	W	D	L	F	A	Pts
Kent	5	5	0	0	18	3	10
Surrey	5	3	1	1	16	5	7
Sussex	5	3	0	2	8	13	6
Imperial	5	1	1	3	7	12	3
R.H.B.N.C.	5	1	0	4	6	13	2
L.S.E.	5	1	0	4	5	14	2

SOUTH WEST GROUP
Bristol 3, Reading 0
Bath 1, Exeter 5
Bath 0, Southampton 1
Reading 2, Exeter 0
Southampton 0, Bristol 0
Reading 6, Bath 1
Southampton 3, Reading 1
Exeter SC, Bristol WO
Bristol 3, Bath 1
Exeter 3, Southampton 0

	P	W	D	L	F	A	Pts
Bristol	4	3	1	0	6	1	7
Southampton	4	2	1	1	4	4	5
Exeter	4	2	0	2	8	3	4
Reading	4	2	0	2	9	7	4
Bath	4	0	0	4	3	15	0

WELSH GROUP
Aberystwyth 1, U.C.N.W. (Bangor) 0
Swansea 1, Aberystwyth 0
U.C.N.W. 0, U.W.C.C. 1
U.W.C.C. 1, Swansea 1
U.W.C.C. 3, Aberystwyth 1
Swansea WO, U.C.N.W. SC

	P	W	D	L	F	A	Pts
U.W.C.C.	3	2	1	0	5	2	5
Swansea	3	2	1	0	2	1	5
Aberystwyth	3	1	0	2	2	4	2
U.C.N.W.	3	0	0	3	0	2	0

Play-offs (Eastern Division)
Sheffield 3, Hull 1
Durham 0, Nottingham 4

Play-off Round
Bradford 0, Nottingham 2
Warwick 0, Aberystwyth 1
Essex 1, Exeter 2
Liverpool 1, Sheffield 2
Southampton 2, Sussex 3
Surrey 1, Brunel 2
Leeds 2, U.M.I.S.T. 0
Swansea 3, Leicester 1

Challenge Round
Newcastle 0, Nottingham 1
Kent 2, Aberystwyth 1
U.W.C.C. 0, Exeter 1
Bristol 1, Sheffield 6
Loughborough 11, Sussex 0
Birmingham 2, Brunel 1
Lancaster 2, Leeds 1
East Anglia 2, Swansea 0

Quarter-finals
Nottingham 2, Kent 3
Exeter 2, Sheffield 1
Loughborough 3, Birmingham 1
Leeds 4, East Anglia 0

Semi-finals
Kent 0, Exeter 1
Loughborough 5, Leeds 0

Final at Worcester City FC
Exeter 0, Loughborough 5

2nd XI CHAMPIONSHIP

Quarter-finals
Liverpool 0, Essex 1
Hull 2, Kent 4
Swansea 1, Reading 2
Warwick 2, Birmingham 1

Semi-finals
Liverpool 2, Kent 0
Reading 1, Warwick 2

Final at Willenhall F.C.
Liverpool 2, Warwick 1

3rd XI CHAMPIONSHIP

Final
Reading 0, Loughborough 3

956

REPRESENTATIVE MATCHES

Commercial Union/U.A.U.:
Lost to Leicester City F.C.   1-3
Beat B.P.S.A.   6-0
Beat B.C.S.A.   4-1
Drew with Stoke City F.C.   2-2
Lost to English Schools F.A. 1-2
Beat Millwall F.C.   2-1

Tour to Dublin and Galway:
Lost to University College, Dublin   1-2
Drew with Irish Universities   1-1
Drew with Irish Technical Colleges   1-1

BRITISH UNIVERSITIES SPORTS FEDERATION TOURNAMENT

at Liverpool University
U.A.U. results in group games
U.A.U. I 2, London University 1
U.A.U. I 2, Northern Ireland 0
U.A.U. I 3, Oxford University 2
U.A.U. II 1, Wales 0
U.A.U. II 0, Scotland 4
U.A.U. II 2, Cambridge University 1

Tournament placings
For 1st and 2nd:
U.A.U. I 1, Scottish Universities 0

For 3rd and 4th:
U.A.U. II 5, Oxford University 4

For 5th and 6th:
University of Wales 4, University of London 1

For Equal 7th:
Cambridge University 2, N. Ireland Universities 2

UNIVERSITY OF LONDON FA – 1989–90
("Chiasmus Tournament" in Bologna)*

v Coimbra Univ (Portugal)*	Won	1-0
v Budapest University*	Won	7-0
v Vilnus Univ (Lithuania)*	Won	6-0
v Amsterdam University*	Lost	0-2
v Ulysses	Won	6-0
v Arthurian League	Drawn	3-3
v Old Boys' League	Lost	0-2
v Southern Amateur League	Lost	0-2
v Cambridge University	Lost	0-1
v Oxford University	Won	1-0
v Royal Air Force	Lost	2-5
v Royal Navy	Lost	1-3
v London Legal League	Lost	2-3
v United Banks	Lost	1-2
v The Army	Lost	0-3
v Crystal Palace XI	Lost	1-3
v Middlesex County FA	Lost	0-1
v British Colleges	Lost	0-1
v Aldershot XI	Lost	0-4
v Mississippi St. Univ.	Won	5-0
v Amateur Football Alli.	Lost	1-3
v Windsor & Eton	Lost	0-2

(London British Universities Tournament - Liverpool)

v U.A.U. I	Lost	1-2
v Oxford University	Lost	0-2
v N. Ireland	Won	2-1
v University of Wales	Lost	1-4

INFORMATION
AND
RECORDS

ALL-TIME FOOTBALL LEAGUE TABLES

OBITUARIES

REFEREES

FOOTBALL AWARDS

RECORDS

THE CHAPLAIN

IMPORTANT ADDRESSES

FOOTBALL LEAGUE FIXTURES

INTERNATIONAL AND CUP DATES

OBITUARIES

Astley, David (b. Dowlais, S. Wales 11.10.1909; d. November 1989). A prolific goalscorer at either centre or inside-forward he was capped 17 times by Wales including 13 full internationals. One of the stars of the great Welsh side that won the International championship two seasons in succession 1932–34. Beginning with Merthyr Town he subsequently served Charlton Athletic, Aston Villa, Derby County and Blackpool before retiring during the war.

Blackmore, Harold (b. Silverton, nr. Exeter 10.5.1904; d. Exeter 28.12.89). When he was at his peak with Bolton Wanderers around 1930 there was no harder left-foot shot in the First Division than this centre-forward. Bolton signed him from Exeter City and he helped them win the FA Cup in 1929. Also played for Middlesbrough, Bradford P.A. and Bury before returning to Exeter where he went into business as a butcher.

Dawes, Fred (b. Frimley Green 2.5.1911; d. Croydon August 1989). Played full-back for Crystal Palace from 1936 to 1949 and was the only man at Selhurst Park to register over a hundred League appearances on both sides of the war. He was formerly with Northampton Town and was Palace's captain for much of the above period, following this with a spell as the club's manager in 1950–51.

Delaney, Jimmy (b. Cleland, Lanarks 3.9.14; d. 27.9.89). This outside-right created a record by winning Scottish, English, N. Ireland and Eire cup medals. The first three were winners' medals with Celtic 1937, Manchester United 1948, Derry City 1954, and the last with Cork Athletic was a runners-up medal in 1956. He began his professional career with Celtic in 1933 and apart from the other clubs just mentioned he also appeared with Aberdeen, Falkirk and Elgin City before retiring in 1957. 13 Scottish caps.

Doherty, Peter (b. Magherafelt 5.6.13; d. Blackpool 6.4.90). One of the cleverest inside-forwards of the 1930s he joined Blackpool from Glentoran in 1933 and moved to Manchester City for a £10,000 fee in 1936. Helped City win the League championship in 1936–37 when he was top scorer with 30 goals and after transferring to Derby County at the end of the war he was in their FA Cup-winning side of 1945–46. Because of the war he made only 16 international appearances for Northern Ireland. A soccer genius, Peter Doherty finished his playing career with Huddersfield Town and Doncaster Rovers and managed N. Ireland when they reached the quarter-finals of the World Cup in 1958.

Duncan, Douglas "Dally" (b. Aberdeen 14.10.1909; d. Brighton January 1990). A clever goalscoring outside-left who was another of that generation whose playing career was interrupted by World War 2. Hull City brought him into the Football League from Aberdeen Richmond in 1928 before selling him to Derby County four years later. He stayed long enough to help them win the FA Cup in 1945–46 and went to Luton Town as player-coach and then as manager, a position he held for 11 years, steering them into the First Division before taking over at Blackburn Rovers in 1958. 14 Scottish caps.

Dunlop, Albert (b. Liverpool 21.4.32; d. March 1990). Signed professional with Everton in 1949 but owing to the brilliance of Eire international Jimmy O'Neill he had to wait seven years before getting his first team place. He then became highly regarded as a safe goalkeeper over the next six years before ending his career with Wrexham in 1963–64.

Fox, Oscar (b. Clowne 1.1.21; d. 15.1.90). Son of an old Bradford City player Oscar Jnr had nearly seven years with Sheffield Wednesday where he was generally regarded as an outside-right before transferring to Mansfield Town in June 1950. Over six seasons he gave the Field Mill club grand service as a utility player appearing in every position except goal.

Gannon, Eddie (b. Dublin 3.1.21; d. Dublin 31.7.89). An attacking right-half who joined Notts County from Shelborne in 1946 and cost Sheffield Wednesday £15,000 when they signed him in March 1949. Made over 200 appearances for the Wednesday helping them to regain First Division status in 1950 and again in 1952. In 1955 he returned to Shelbourne as player-manager. 14 Eire caps.

Hodgson, Tommy (b. Hetton-le-Hole, County Durham 1902, d. Hampshire December 1989). Involved in first-class football for over 40 years he began as a full-back with West Ham United in 1901 and had nine seasons with them before joining Luton Town where a leg injury ended his playing career. However, he became a director of that club in the 1950s and was chairman 1964–69 and president until 1983. In 1959 he led Luton out at Wembley in the FA Cup Final when he was acting as manager for a short period.

Hunter, George (b. Troon 29.8.30; d. Nottingham May 1990). A goalkeeper who won a Scottish Cup medal with Celtic at the age of 19 and had a season with Derby County before joining Exeter City in 1955. Had five good seasons with them until a broken leg put him out of action for a year and he was given a free transfer. A small number of games with Yiewsley, Darlington, Burton Albion and Lincoln City brought his career to a close.

Horrix, Dean b. Taplow 21.11.61); d. 11.3.90). Tragically met his death in a motor accident only eight days after making his debut for Bristol City following his transfer from Millwall. A forward who had been in his second spell with the London club where he began as an apprentice in 1978. Also appeared with Gillingham, Reading and Cardiff City.

Peter Doherty, one of the finest inside-forwards to wear the green shirt of Northern Ireland.

Moulson, Cornelious "Con" (b. Tipperary 1906; d. Lincoln 2.11.89). A half-back who played for the Royal Military College, Dublin, before moving to England where he appeared with Cleethorpes, Grimsby Town (reserves), Bristol City, Lincoln City and then Notts County until the war. Capped five times by Eire.

Murphy, Jimmy (b. Pentre, S. Wales October 1910; d. November 1989). Best remembered as the man who led Manchester United to Wembley after the Munich disaster when he stood in for injured manager Matt Busby. However, he was a fine right-half with West Bromwich Albion 1928–39 before serving United as coach 1945–55 and assistant manager 1955–71. Was also Welsh team manager 1957–63 guiding them to the World Cup finals in Sweden in 1958.

Pace, Derek (b. Bloxwich 11.3.32; d. Birmingham 18.10.89). Although small for a centre-forward he proved himself a real opportunist especially with Sheffield United with whom he had seven seasons as top scorer netting a total of 140 League goals 1957– 67. Had begun his career with Aston Villa in 1949 and after United he was with Notts County and Walsall.

Paterson, Andy (b. Leeholm, Durham 1909, d. Chadderton, Lancashire 11.12.1989). Made a number of Football League appearances with Gateshead 1931–34 and with Oldham Athletic 1937 until the outbreak of war. Had a good run with Wigan Athletic 1934–37 in the Cheshire County League.

Ruffell, Jimmy (b. Doncaster 8.8.1900; d. Bury St. Edmunds 6.9.89). One of the outstanding personalities in West Ham's history, making well over 500 appearances as a goalscoring outside-left over a period of 16 seasons 1921–37. Played in the first Wembley Final in 1923 and was capped six times by England. Ended his career with Aldershot in 1938–39.

Sherwood, Alf (b. Aberaman 13.11.23; d. Cardiff March 1990). Capped 41 times by Wales he joined Cardiff City at the age of 17 and became the club's finest-ever full-back. He remained with City until 1956 making 353 League appearances; and when he went to Newport in 1956 at the age of 32 he played over 200 more first-team games before retiring in 1960.

Shipman, Len M.B.E. (b. Leicester 1903, d. March 1990). Joined Leicester City board 1939, becoming chairman 1947. He was elected to the Football League management committee in 1955 and also served on various FA committees. League President 1966–74.

Sleeuwenhoek, John (b. Wednesfield 26.2.44; d. August 1989). Turned professional with Aston Villa in 1961 after gaining England Schoolboy and Youth international honours and was their regular centre-half for six seasons before transferring to Birmingham City in 1967. Also had a spell on loan to Torquay before ending his League career with Oldham Athletic. Won two U-23 caps.

Welsh, Don (b. Manchester, 25.2.1911; d. Stevenage, Herts 1989). Began professional career as a centre-half with Torquay United in 1933 and Charlton Athletic paid £3,250 for his transfer in February 1935. Played in several positions for the Londoners helping them win promotion to the First Division and captaining their FA Cup winning team in 1947. Capped three times for England as well as nine war-time games. After retiring in 1947 he managed Brighton 1947–51, Liverpool 1951–56, and Bournemouth 1958–61.

Yashin, Lev (b. Moscow 12.10.1929; d. Moscow 21.3.90). Usually clad in black he earned his reputation as one of the finest goalkeepers of all-time. Played in 78 internationals for Russia and in well over 600 games for Moscow Dynamo 1949–71. Won Olympic gold medal in 1956 and appeared in World Cup final tournaments in 1958, 1962 and 1966. Played for Rest of Europe and Rest of World teams.

LIST OF REFEREES FOR SEASON 1990–91

ALCOCK, P. E. (S. Merstham, Surrey)
ALLISON, D. B. (Lancaster)
APLIN, G. (Kendal)
ASHBY, G. R. (Worcester)
ASHWORTH, J. (Luffenham, Leics.)
AXCELL, D. J. (Southend)
BAILEY, M. C. (Impington, Cambridge)
BARRATT, K. P. (Coventry)
BELL, S. D. (Huddersfield)
BENNETT, A. (Sheffield)
BIGGER, R. L. (Croydon)
BODENHAM, M. J. (Looe, Cornwall)
BORRETT, I. J. (Harleston, Norfolk)
BRANDWOOD, M. J. (Lichfield, Staffs.)
BREEN, K. J. (Liverpool)
BUKSH, A. N. (London)
BURGE, W. K. (Tonypandy)
BURNS, W. C. (Scarborough)
CALLOW, V. G. (Solihull)
CARTER, J. M. (Christchurch)
COOPER, K. (Pontypridd)
COOPER, K. A. (Swindon)
COURTNEY, G. (Spennymoor)
CRUIKSHANKS, I. G. (Hartlepool)
DANSON, P. S. (Leicester)
DAWSON, A. (Jarrow)
DEAKIN, J. C. (Llantwit Major, S. Glam.)
DILKES, L. R. (Mossley, Lancs)
DON, P. (Hanworth Park, Middlesex)
DURKIN, P. A. (Portland, Dorset)
ELLERAY, D. R. (Harrow)
FITZHARRIS, T. (Bolton)
FLOOD, W. A. (Stockport)
FOAKES, P. L. (Clacton-on-Sea)
FRAMPTON, D. G. (Poole, Dorset)
GALLAGHER, D. J. (Banbury, Oxon)
GIFFORD, R. B. (Llanbradach, Mid. Glam.)
GROVES, R. G. (Weston-Super-Mare)
GUNN, A. (South Chailey, Sussex)
HACKETT, K. S. (Sheffield)
HAMER, R. L. (Bristol)
HARRISON, P. W. (Oldham, Lancs.)
HART, R. A. (Darlington)
HEMLEY, I. S. (Ampthill, Beds.)
HENDRICK, I. A. (Preston)
HILL, B. (Kettering)
HOLBROOK, T. J. (Walsall)

HUTCHINSON, D. (Marcham, Oxford)
JAMES, M. L. (Horsham)
JONES, P. (Loughborough)
KEY, J. M. (Sheffield)
KING, H. W. (Merthyr Tydfil)
KIRKBY, J. A. (Sheffield)
LEWIS, R. S. (Gt. Bookham, Surrey)
LLOYD, J. W. (Wrexham)
LODGE S. J. (Barnsley)
LUNT, T. (Ashton-in-Makerfield, Lancs)
LUPTON, K. A. (Stockton-on-Tees)
MARTIN, J. E. (Nr. Alton, Hants.)
MIDGLEY, N. (Bolton)
MILFORD, R. G. (Bristol)
MORTON, K. (Bury St. Edmunds)
MOULES, J. A. (Erith, Kent)
NIXON, R. F. (West Kirkby, Wirral)
PARKER, E. J. (Preston)
PAWLEY, R. K. (Cambridge)
PECK, M. G. (Kendal)
PHILLIPS, D. T. (Barnsley)
PIERCE, M. E. (Portsmouth)
POOLEY, G. R. (Bishop's Stortford)
REDFERN, K. A. (Whitley Bay)
REED, M. D. (Birmingham)
RUSHTON, J. (Stoke-on-Trent)
SEVILLE, A. (Birmingham)
SHAPTER, L. C. (Torquay)
SHEPHERD, R. (Leeds)
SIMMONS, A. F. (Cheadle Hulme, Cheshire)
SIMPSON, T. (Sowerby Bridge, W. Yorks.)
SINGH, G. (Wolverhampton)
SMITH, A. W. (Rubery, Birmingham)
STEVENS, B. T. (Stonehouse. Glos.)
TAYLOR, P. (Waltham Cross, Herts)
TRUSSELL, C. C. (Liverpool)
TYLDESLEY, P. A. (Stockport)
VANES, P. W. (Warley, West Midlands)
WARD, A. W. (London)
WATSON, J. L. (Whitley Bay)
WEST, T. E. (Hull)
WILKES, C. R. (Gloucester)
WILLARD, G. S. (Worthing, W. Sussex)
WILKIE, A. B. (Chester-le-Street)
WISEMAN, R. M. (Borehamwood, Herts.)
WORRALL, J. B. (Warrington)
WRIGHT, P. L. (Northwich)

LAWS OF THE GAME – Amendments

Law IV Players' Equipment

(1) (a) The basic compulsory equipment of a player shall consist of a jersey or shirt, shorts, stockings, shinguards and footwear.
(b) A player shall not wear anything which is dangerous to another player.

(2) Shinguards, which must be covered entirely by the stockings, shall be made of a suitable material (rubber, plastic, polyurethane or similar substance) and shall afford a reasonable degree of protection.

Decisions of the International FA Board

(1) In international matches, international competitions, international club competitions and friendly matches between clubs of different National Associations, the referee, prior to the start of the game, shall inspect *the players'* equipment and prevent any player whose equipment does not conform to the requirements of this Law from playing until such time as it does comply. The rules of any competition may include a similar provision.

N.B. the present points (3) become (2), (4) becomes (3) and (5) becomes (4).

Law XI Off-side – (1)

(1) A player is in an off-side position if he is nearer to his opponents' goal-line than the ball, unless:
(a) he is in his own half of the field of play, or
(b) *he is not nearer to his opponents' goal-line than at least two of his opponents.*

Law XI Off-side – (3)

(3) A player shall not be declared offside by the referee
(a) merely because of his being in an off-side position, or
(b) if he receives the ball, direct from a goal-kick, a corner-kick *or* a throw-in.

Decisions of the International FA Board

(2) A player who is level with the second last opponent or with the last two opponents is not in an offside position.

ADDRESSES

The Football Association: R. H. G. Kelly, F.C.I.S., 16 Lancaster Gate, London W2 3LW

Scotland: J. Farry, 6 Park Gardens, Glasgow G3 7YE. *041-332 6372*

Northern Ireland (Irish FA): D. I. Bowen, 20 Windsor Avenue, Belfast BT9 6EG. *0232-669458*

Wales: A. Evans, 3 Westgate Street, Cardiff, South Glamorgan CF1 1JF. *0222-372325*

Republic of Ireland (FA of Ireland): 80 Merrion Square South, Dublin 2. *0001-766864*

International Federation (FIFA): S. Blatter, FIFA House, Hitzigweg 11, CH-8032 Zurich, Switzerland

Union of European Football Associations: G. Aigner, PO Box 16, CH-3000 Berne 15, Switzerland

THE LEAGUES

The Football League: J. D. Dent, F.C.I.S., The Football League, Lytham St Annes, Lancs FY8 1JG. *0253-729421. Telex 67675*

The Scottish League: P. Donald, 188 West Regent Street, Glasgow G2 4RY. *041-248 384415*

The Irish League: M. Brown, 87 University Street, Belfast BT7 1HP. *0232-242888*

Football League of Ireland: E. Morris, 80 Merrion Square South, Dublin. *0001-765120*

GM Vauxhall Conference: P. D. Hunter, 24 Barnehurst Road, Bexleyheath, Kent DA7 6EZ. *0322-521116*

Central League: D. J. Grimshaw, 118 St Stephens Road, Deepdale, Preston, Lancs PR1 6TD. *Preston 55898*

North West Counties League: N. A. Rowles, 845 Liverpool Road, Peel Green, Eccles, Manchester, M3O 7LJ. *061 962 4623*

Eastern Counties League: A. C. Dockerill, 10 Church Leys, Fenstanton, Huntingdon, Cambs, PE18 9QD

Football Combination: N. Chamberlain, 2 Vicarage Close, Old Costessey, Norwich, NR8 5DL *0603 743998*

Hellenic League: T. Cuss, 7 Blenheim Road, Kidlington, Oxford OX5 2HP. *08675 5920*

Kent League: R. Vintner, The Smithy, The Square, Chilham, Canterbury, Kent, CT4 8BY

Lancashire Amateur League: R. G. Bowker, 13 Shores Green Drive, Wincham, Northwich, Cheshire CW9 6EE. *061-480 7723*

Lancashire Football League: J. W. Howarth, 465 Whalley Road, Clapton-le-Moors, Accrington, Lancs BB5 5RP. *0704-79523*

Leicestershire Senior League: P. Henwood, 450 London Road, Leicester LE2 2PP. *Leicester 704121*

London Spartan: D. Cordell, 44 Greenleas, Waltham Abbey, Essex. *Lea Valley 712428*

Manchester League: F. J. Fitzpatrick, 102 Victoria Road, Stretford, Manchester. *061-865 2726*

Midland Combination: L. W. James, 175 Barnet Lane, Kingswinford, Brierley Hill, West Midlands. *Kingswinford 3459*

Mid-Week Football League: N. A. S. Matthews, Cedar Court, Steeple Aston, Oxford. *0869-40347*

Northern Premier: R. D. Bayley, 22 Woburn Drive, Hale, Altrincham, Cheshire WA15. *061-980 7007*

Northern Intermediate League: G. Thompson, Clegg House, 253 Pitsmoor Road, Sheffield, S3 9AQ. *9742-27817*

Northern League: G. Nicholson, 99 Watling Road, Bishop Auckland, Co. Durham. *Bishop Auckland 2167*

North Midlands League: G. Thompson, 7 Wren Park Close, Ridgway, Sheffield

Peterborough and District League: M. J. Croson, 44 Storrington Way, Werrington, Peterborough, Cambs. PE4 6QP.

Vauxhall League: N. Robinson, 226 Rye Lane, Peckham SE15. *081-653 3903*

Southern Amateur League: S. J. Lucas, 23 Beaufort Close, North Weald Bassett, Epping, Essex CM16 6JZ. *037882-3932*

South-East Counties League: R. A. Bailey, 10 Highlands Road, New Barnet, Herts. EN5 5AB. *081-449 5131*

Southern League: D. J. Strudwick, 11 Welland Close, Durrington, Worthing, West Sussex BN13 3NR. *0903-67788*

South Midlands League: M. Mitchell, 26 Leighton Court, Dunstable, Beds LU6 1EW. *0582-67291*

South Western League: R. Lowe, Panorama, Lamerton, Tavistock, Devon PL19 8SD. *0822 61376*

United Counties League: R. Gamble, 8 Bostock Avenue, Northampton. *0604 37766*

Wearside: B. Robson, 12 Deneside Howdon Lewear, Crook, Co. Durham, DL15 8JR. *0388 762034*

Western League: M. E. Washer, 126 Chessel Street, Bristol BS3 3DQ. *0272-638308*

The Welsh League: K. J. Tucker, 16 The Parade, Merthyr Tydfil, Mid Glamorgan, CF47 0ET. *0685 723884*

West Midlands Regional League: K. H. Goodfellow, 11 Emsworth Grove, Kings Heath, Birmingham B14 6HY. *021 444 3056*

West Yorkshire League: W. Keyworth, 2 Hill Court Grove, Branley, Yorks L13 2AP. *Pudsey 74465*

Northern Counties (East): B. Wood, 6 Restmore Avenue, Guiseley, Nr Leeds LS20 9DG. *Guiseley 4558 (home); Bradford 29595 (9 a.m. to 5 p.m.)*

COUNTY FOOTBALL ASSOCIATIONS

Bedfordshire: R. G. Berridge, The Limes, 14 Bedford Road, Sandy, Beds SG19 1EL. *0767-80417*

Berks and Bucks: W. S. Gosling, 15a London Street, Faringdon, Oxon SN7 8AG. *0367 22099*

Birmingham County: M. Pennick, County FA Offices, Rayhall Lane, Great Barr, Birmingham B43 6JE. *021-357 4278*

Cambridgeshire: R. E. Rogers, 20 Aingers Road, Histon, Cambridge CB4 4JP. *022023 2803*

Cheshire: A. Collins, 50 Ash Grove, Timperley, Altrincham WA15 6JX. *061-980 4706*

Cornwall: J. M. Ryder, Penare, 16 Gloweth View, Truro, Cornwall, TR1 3JZ

Cumberland: R. Johnson, 72 Victoria Road, Workington, Cumbria CA14 2QT. *0900-3979*

Derbyshire: K. Compton, King's Chambers, 35 Ocean Street, Derby DE1 3DS. *0332-361422*

Devon County: C. Squirrel, 51A Wolborough Street, Newton Abbott, Devon TQ12 1JQ. *0626 332077*

Dorset County: P. Hough, 110 Dorchester Road, Oakdale, Poole, Dorset BH15 3SD. *0202 746244*

Durham: J. R. Walsh, 'Codeslaw', Ferens Park, Durham DH1 1JZ. *0385-48653*

East Riding County: C. Branton, 83 Belvedere Road, Hessel, Hull HU13 9JH. *0482-649294*

Essex County: T. Alexander, 31 Mildmay Road, Chelmsford, Essex CM2 0DN. *0245-357727*

Gloucestershire: E. J. Marsh, 46 Douglas Road, Horfield, Bristol BS7 0JD. *0272-519435*

Guernsey: G. R. Skuse, Ar-Hyd-Y-Nos, Courtil Olivier Castel, Guernsey CI. *0481-26241*

Hampshire: R. G. Barnes, 8 Ashwood Gardens, off Winchester Road, Southampton SO9 2UA. *0703-766884*

Herefordshire: E. R. Prescott, 7 Kirkland Close, Hampton Park, Hereford HR1 1XP. *0432-51134*

Hertfordshire: C. R. Brown, 21 Hawthorn Crescent, Caddington, Luton, Beds LU1 4EQ. *082-423094*

Huntingdonshire: M. M. Armstrong, 1 Chapel End, Great Giddings, Huntingdon. Cambs PE17 5NP. *08323-262*

Isle of Man: Mrs J. F. Shaw, 120 Bucks Road, Douglas, IOM. *0624-6349*

Jersey: B. Ahier, Sunbrayton, Route Orange, St Brelade, Jersey, CI

Kent County: K. T. Masters, 69 Maidstone Road, Chatham, Kent ME4 6DT. *0634-43824*

Lancashire: J. Kenyon, 31a Wellington St, St John's, Blackburn, Lancs BB1 8AU. *0254-64333*
Leicestershire and Rutland: R. E. Barston, Holmes Park, Dog and Gun Lane, Whetstone, Leicester LE8 3LJ. *0533-867828*
Lincolnshire: F. S. Richardson, PO Box 26, 12 Dean Road, Lincoln LN2 4DP. *0522-24917*
Liverpool County: S. A. Rudd, 23 Greenfield Road, Old Swann, Liverpool L13 3EN. *051-526 9515*
London: R. S. Ashford, 4 Aldworth Grove, London SE13 6HY. *081-690-9626*
Manchester County: F. Brocklehurst, Sports Complex, Brantingham Road, Chorlton, Manchester, M21 1TG. *061 881 0299*
Middlesex County: P. J. Clayton, 30 Rowland Avenue, Kenton, Harrow, Middx HA3 9AF.
Norfolk County: R. Kiddell, 39 Beaumont Road, Costessey, Norwich NR5 0HG. *0603-742421*
Northamptonshire: B. Walden, 37 Harding Terrace, Northampton NN1 2PF. *0604-39584*
North Riding County: P. Kirby, 284 Linthorpe Road, Middlesbrough TS1 3QU. *0642-224585*
Northumberland: J. A. Forster, 30 St Mary's Place, Newcastle upon Tyne NE1 7PG. *0632-261 0779*
Nottinghamshire: W. T. Annable, 7 Clarendon Street, Nottingham NG1 5HS. *0602-418954*

Oxfordshire: P. J. Ladbrook, 3 Wilkins Road, Cowley, Oxford OX4 2HY. *0865-775432*
Sheffield and Hallamshire: G. Thompson, Clegg House, 5 Onslow Road, Sheffield S11 7AF. *0742-670068*
Shropshire: A. W. Brett, High Street Chambers, 10–11 High Street, Shrewsbury SY1 1SG. *0743-56066*
Somerset & Avon (South): L. G. Webb, 32 North Road, Midsomer Norton, Bath BA3 2QQ. *0761-413176*
Staffordshire: G. S. Brookes, 2 Miller Street, Newcastle, Staffs ST5 1HB. *0782-622585*
Suffolk County: W. M. Steward, 2 Millfields, Haughley, Suffolk IP14 3PU. *0449-673481*
Surrey County: L. F. J. Smith, 2 Fairfield Avenue, Horley, Surrey RH6 7PD. *0293-784945*
Sussex County: D. M. Worsfold, County Office, Culver Road, Lancing, Sussex BN15 9AX. *0903-753547*
Westmorland: J. B. Fleming, 101, Burneside Road, Kendal, Cumbria LA9 4RZ *0539 722915*
West Riding County: R. M. Robin, 77 Great George Street, Leeds LS1 3DR. *0532-452444*
Wiltshire: E. M. Parry, 44 Kennet Avenue, Swindon SN2 3LG. *0793-29036*
Worcestershire: P. Rushton, 84 Windermere Drive, Warndon, Worcester WR4 9IB. *0905-51166*

OTHER USEFUL ADDRESSES

Amateur Football Alliance: W. P. Goss, 55 Islington Park Street, London N1 1QB. *071-359 3493*
English Schools FA: C. S. Allatt, 4a Eastgate Street, Stafford ST16 2NN. *0785-51142*
Oxford University: S. Morley, The Queen's College, Oxford OX1 4AW.
Cambridge University: Dr A. J. Little, St Catherine's College, Cambridge CB2 1RL.
Army: Major T. C. Knight, Clayton Barracks, Aldershot, Hants GU11 2BG. *0252-24431 Ext 3571*
Royal Air Force: Group Capt P. W. Hilton, DDSM 5 (RAF) Block 3, Room E21, Ministry of Defence, St Georges Road, Harrogate, N. Yorks HG2 9DB. *0423-793 295*
Royal Navy: Lt-Cdr J. Danks, R.N. Sports Office, H.M.S. Temeraire, Portsmouth, Hants PO1 4QS. *0705-822351 Ext 22671*
Universities Athletic Union: I. Grant, U.A.U., 28 Woburn Square, London WC1 0AA. *071-637 4828*
Central Council of Physical Recreation: General Secretary, 70 Brompton Road, London SW3 1HE. *071-584 6651*
British Olympic Association: 6 John Prince's Street, London W1,M 0DH. *071-408 2029*
National Federation of Football Supporters' Clubs: Lottery Office: 1 Saville Row, Bath, Avon BA1 2QP. *0224-312247*. General Secretary: Malcolm Gamlen, 69 Fourth Avenue, Chelmsford, Essex. *0245-263305*
National Playing Fields Association: Col R. Satterthwaite, O.B.E., 578b Catherine Place, London, SW1.
The Scottish Football Commercial Managers Association: J. E. Hillier (Chairman), c/o Keith FC Promotions Office, 60 Union Street, Keith, Banffshire, Scotland.

Professional Footballers' Association: G. Taylor, 2 Oxford Couret, Bishopsgate, Off Lower Mosley Street, Manchester M2 3W2. *061-236 0575*
Referees' Association: W. J. Taylor, Cross Offices, Summerhill, Kingswinford, West Midlands DY6 9JE. *0384 288386*
Women's Football Association: Miss L. Whitehead, 448/450 Hanging Ditch, The Corn Exchange, Manchester M4 3ES. *061-832 5911*
The Association of Football League Commercial Managers: G. H. Dimbleby, Secretary WBA FC, The Hawthorns, Halford Lane, West Bromwich B71 4LF
The Association of Football Statisticians: R. J. Spiller, 22 Bretons, Basildon, Essex SS15 5BY. *0268 416020*
The Football Programme Directory: David Stacey, 'The Beeches', 66 Southend Road, Wickford, Essex SS11 8EN.
England Football Supporters Association: Publicity Officer, David Stacey, 66 Southend Road, Wickford, Essex SS11 8EN.
The Football League Executive Staffs Association: PO Box 52, Leamington Spa, Warwickshire.
The Ninety-Two Club: 104 Gilda Crescent, Whitchurch, Bristol BS14 9LD.
The Football Trust: Second Floor, Walkden House, 10 Melton Stree, London NW1 2EJ. *01-388 4504.*
Association of Provincial Football Supporters' Clubs in London: Miss Sallyann Watson, Secretary APFSCIL. 6 Bradshaws Close, Kings Road, London SE25 4ES. *081-676 8390 (home).*

AWARDS 1989–90

FOOTBALLER OF THE YEAR

The Football Writers' Association Award for the Footballer of the Year went to John Barnes of Liverpol and England. It was his second such award, having achieved the honour originally in 1987–88.

Past Winners
1947–48 Stanley Matthews (Blackpool), 1948–49 Johnny Carey (Manchester U), 1949–50 Joe Mercer (Arsenal), 1950–51 Harry Johnston (Blackpool), 1951–52 Billy Wright (Wolverhampton W), 1952–53 Nat Lofthouse (Bolton W), 1953–54 Tom Finney (Preston NE), 1954–55 Don Revie (Manchester C), 1955–56 Bert Trautmann (Manchester C), 1956–57 Tom Finney (Preston NE), 1957–58 Danny Blanchflower (Tottenham H), 1958–59 Syd Owen (Luton T), 1959–60 Bill Slater (Wolverhampton W), 1960–61 Danny Blanchflower (Tottenham H), 1961–62 Jimmy Adamson (Burnley), 1962–63 Stanley Matthews (Stoke C), 1963–64 Bobby Moore (West Ham U), 1964–65 Bobby Collins (Leeds U), 1965–66 Bobby Charlton (Manchester U), 1966–67 Jackie Charlton (Leeds U), 1967–68 George Best (Manchester U), 1968–69 Dave Mackay (Derby Co) shared with Tony Book (Manchester C), 1969–70 Billy Bremner (Leeds U), 1970–71 Frank McLintock (Arsenal), 1971–72 Gordon Banks (Stoke C), 1972–73 Pat Jennings (Tottenham H), 1973–74 Ian Callaghan (Liverpool), 1974–75 Alan Mullery (Fulham), 1975–76 Kevin Keegan (Liverpool), 1976–77 Emlyn Hughes (Liverpool), 1977–78 Kenny Burns (Nottingham F), 1978–79 Kenny Dalglish (Liverpool), 1979–80 Terry McDermott (Liverpool), 1980–81 Frans Thijssen (Ipswich T), 1981–82 Steve Perryman (Tottenham H), 1982–83 Kenny Dalglish (Liverpool), 1983–84 Ian Rush (Liverpool), 1984–85 Neville Southall (Everton), 1985–86 Gary Lineker (Everton), 1986–87 Clive Allen (Tottenham H), 1987–88 John Barnes (Liverpool), 1988–89 Steve Nicol (Liverpool).

THE PFA AWARDS 1990

Player of the Year: David Platt (Aston Villa).
Previous Winners: 1974 Norman Hunter (Leeds U); 1975 Colin Todd (Derby Co); 1976 Pat Jennings (Tottenham H); 1977 Andy Gray (Aston Villa); 1978 Peter Shilton (Nottingham F) 1979 Liam Brady (Arsenal); 1980 Terry McDermott (Liverpool); 1981 John Wark (Ipswich T); 1982 Kevin Keegan (Southampton); 1983 Kenny Dalglish (Liverpool); 1984 Ian Rush (Liverpool); 1985 Peter Reid (Everton); 1986 Gary Lineker (Everton); 1987 Clive Allen (Tottenham H); 1988 John Barnes (Liverpool); 1989 Mark Hughes (Manchester U).
Young Player of the Year: Matthew Le Tissier (Southampton).
Previous Winners: 1974 Kevin Beattie (Ipswich T); 1975 Mervyn Day (West Ham U); 1976 Peter Barnes (Manchester C); 1977 Andy Gray (Aston Villa); 1978 Tony Woodcock (Nottingham F); 1979 Cyrille Regis (WBA); 1980 Glenn Hoddle (Tottenham H); 1981 Gary Shaw (Aston Villa); 1982 Steve Moran (Southampton); 1983 Ian Rush (Liverpool); 1984 Paul Walsh (Luton T); 1985 Mark Hughes (Manchester U); 1986 Tony Cottee (West Ham U); 1987 Tony Adams (Arsenal); 1988 Paul Gascoigne (Tottenham H); 1989 Paul Merson (Arsenal).
Merit Award: Peter Shilton.
Previous Winners: 1974 Bobby Charlton CBE, Cliff Lloyd OBE; 1975 Denis Law; 1976 George Eastham OBE; 1977 Jack Taylor OBE; 1978 Bill Shankley OBE; 1979 Tom Finney OBE; 1980 Sir Matt Busby CBE; 1981 John Trollope MBE; 1982 Joe Mercer OBE; 1983 Bob Paisley OBE; 1984 Bill Nicholson; 1985 Ron Greenwood; 1986 The 1966 England World Cup team, Sir Alf Ramsey, Harold Shepherdson; 1987 Sir Stanley Matthews; 1988 Billy Bonds MBE; 1989 Nat Lofthouse.

BARCLAYS BANK MANAGER OF THE YEAR 1989-90

Kenny Dalglish of Liverpool, the Barclays League Champions, named the Barclays Bank Manager of the Year at the Football Managers' Awards Luncheon at Barclays Head Office in the City – his third Manager of the Year title in his five years in charge at Anfield. Dalglish received the Barclays Bank Manager of the Year trophy, a replica and a Barclays Higher Rate Interest Deposit account cheque for £5,000. The presentation was made by Mr Alastair Robinson, Barclays UK Executive Director.

It was Dalglish's twelfth managerial award: including nine overall Manager of the Month awards – three in the course of the past season (September, March and April). This is the 11th time in the last 18 seasons that a Liverpool F.C. manager has picked up the top boss trophy from 1973 with Bill Shankly and including Bob Paisley (1976, '77, '79, '80, '82 and '83), Joe Fagan (1984) and Dalglish ('86 and '88).

Voting for the 25th annual award among the thirty-strong panel of football journalists was keen between Dalglish and Joe Royle of Oldham Athletic whose highly-featured Cup exploits brightened the 1989/90 season. Royle was named for a Barclays Bank Special Award and received a Silver Eagle trophy and a cheque for £1,000.

BARCLAYS BANK DIVISIONAL MANAGERS OF THE SEASON 1989/90

Barclays Bank Divisional Managers of the Season – each of whom received a Barclays Silver Eagle and a Barclays Higher Rate Interest Deposit Account cheque for £1,000 – named by the Football League, and presented by Bill Fox, the League president, were: Division Two: Howard Wilkinson (Leeds United); Division Three: Gerry Francis (Bristol Rovers) and Division Four: Terry Cooper (Exeter City).

THE SCOTTISH PFA AWARDS 1989

Player of the Year: Jim Bett (Aberdeen).
Previous Winners: 1978 Derek Johnstone (Rangers); 1979 Paul Hegarty (Dundee U); 1980 Davie Provan (Celtic); 1981 Sandy Clark (Airdrieonians); 1982 Mark McGhee (Aberdeen); 1983 Charlie Nicholas (Celtic); 1984 Willie Miller (Aberdeen); 1985 Jim Duffy (Morton); 1986 Richard Gough (Dundee U); 1987 Brian McClair (Celtic); 1988 Paul McStay (Celtic); 1989 Theo Snelders (Aberdeen).
Young Player of the Year: Scott Crabbe (Hearts).
Previous Winners: 1978 Graeme Payne (Dundee U); 1979 Graham Stewart (Dundee U); 1980 John MacDonald (Rangers); 1981 Francis McAvennie (St Mirren); 1982 Charlie Nicholas (Celtic); 1983 Pat Nevin (Clyde); 1984 John Robertson (Hearts); 1985 Craig Levein (Hearts); 1986 Craig Levein (Hearts); 1987 Robert Fleck (Rangers); 1988 John Collins (Hibernian); 1989 Bill McKinlay (Dundee U).

BARCLAYS YOUNG EAGLE OF THE YEAR 1990

Matthew Le Tissier of Southampton completed the 1990 Young Player of the Year double when he collected the Barclays Young Eagle of the Year accolade from England team manager Bobby Robson who chairs the Barclays Young Eagle panel (including Ron Greenwood, Bill Nicholson, Bob Paisley, Jack Charlton, Trevor Cherry, Stan Cullis and Terry Yorath). His prize was a Barclays Silver Eagle trophy, a replica and a £5,000 Barclays Higher Rate Interest Deposit Account cheque (presented by Alastair Robinson).

The previous month Le Tissier was named the PFA Young Player of the Year by his fellow professionals. (The PFA Awards Dinner was sponsored by Barclays – an association which will continue for the next three seasons through the extension of the Barclays League sponsorship).

BARCLAYS YOUNG EAGLES AWARDS 1989–90

August	**Paul Mortimer** (Charlton Ath.)
September	**David White** (Manchester City)
October	**David Batty** (Leeds United)
November	**Michael Thomas** (Arsenal)
December	**Matthew Le Tissier** (Southampton)
January	**Nigel Jemson** (Nottingham Forest)
February	**Tony Daley** (Aston Villa)
March	**Steve Staunton** (Liverpool)

SCOTTISH FOOTBALL WRITERS' ASSOCIATION
Player of the Year 1990 – Alex McLeish (Aberdeen)

1965 **Billy McNeill** (Celtic)
1966 **John Greig** (Rangers)
1967 **Ronnie Simpson** (Celtic)
1968 **Gordon Wallace** (Raith R)
1969 **Bobby Murdoch** (Celtic)
1970 **Pat Stanton** (Hibernian)
1971 **Martin Buchan** (Aberdeen)
1972 **Dave Smith** (Rangers)
1973 **George Connelly** (Celtic)
1974 **Scotland's World Cup Squad**
1975 **Sandy Jardine** (Rangers)
1976 **John Greig** (Rangers)
1977 **Danny McGrain** (Celtic)

1978 **Derek Johnstone** (Rangers)
1979 **Andy Ritchie** (Morton)
1980 **Gordon Strachan** (Aberdeen)
1981 **Alan Rough** (Partick Th)
1982 **Paul Sturrock** (Dundee U)
1983 **Charlie Nicholas** (Celtic)
1984 **Willie Miller** (Aberdeen)
1985 **Hamish McAlpine** (Dundee U)
1986 **Sandy Jardine** (Hearts)
1987 **Brian McClair** (Celtic)
1988 **Paul McStay** (Celtic)
1989 **Richard Gough** (Rangers)

EUROPEAN FOOTBALLER OF THE YEAR 1989

Marco Van Basten was voted European Footballer of the Year for 1989 in the poll carried out by *France Football* magazine. It was his second successive award and came after outstanding displays for AC Milan. The Italian club won the European Cup and Van Basten scored twice as did his Dutch colleague Ruud Gullit, the European Footballer of the Year in 1987.

There was considerable expectation that Van Basten would dominate the World Cup in Italy during the summer of 1990. Unfortunately it proved to be a disastrous tournament for Van Basten and the Dutch team as a whole.

Born on 31 October 1964 in Utrecht, he joined Ajax from Elinkwijk as a 17-year-old in 1981 and made his debut as substitute for the legendary Johan Cruyff, twice winner of Europe's top award himself. Two years later he broke into the international scene in the World Youth Cup finals in Mexico.

His zenith was reached during the 1988 European Championship and he scored a hat-trick against England. A world class striker his overall work as a target man in attack, able to hold on to the ball by sheer ease of control, raised him above the normal sharp-shooter's ability.

Past winners

1956 **Stanley Matthews** (Blackpool)
1957 **Alfredo Di Stefano** (Real Madrid)
1958 **Raymond Kopa** (Real Madrid)
1959 **Alfredo Di Stefano** (Real Madrid)
1960 **Luis Suarez** (Barcelona)
1961 **Omar Sivori** (Juventus)
1962 **Josef Masopust** (Dukla Prague)
1963 **Lev Yashin** (Moscow Dynamo)
1964 **Denis Law** (Manchester United)
1965 **Eusebio** (Benfica)
1966 **Bobby Charlton** (Manchester United)
1967 **Florian Albert** (Ferencvaros)
1968 **George Best** (Manchester United)
1969 **Gianni Rivera** (AC Milan)
1970 **Gerd Muller** (Bayern Munich)
1971 **Johan Cruyff** (Ajax)
1972 **Franz Beckenbauer** (Bayern Munich)
1973 **Johan Cruyff** (Barcelona)

1974 **Johan Cruyff** (Barcelona)
1975 **Oleg Blokhin** (Dynamo Kiev)
1976 **Franz Beckenbauer** (Bayern Munich)
1977 **Allan Simonsen** (Borussia Moenchengladbach)
1978 **Kevin Keegan** (SV Hamburg)
1979 **Kevin Keegan** (SV Hamburg)
1980 **Karl-Heinz Rummenigge** (Bayern Munich)
1981 **Karl-Heinz Rummenigge** (Bayern Munich)
1982 **Paolo Rossi** (Juventus)
1983 **Michel Platini** (Juventus)
1984 **Michel Platini** (Juventus)
1985 **Michel Platini** (Juventus)
1986 **Igor Belanov** (Dynamo Kiev)
1987 **Ruud Gullit** (AC Milan)
1988 **Marco Van Basten** (AC Milan)

BARCLAYS BANK MANAGER AWARDS 1989–90

AUGUST

Division 1 – **Lennie Lawrence** (Charlton Athletic); *Division 2* – **Don Mackay** (Blackburn Rovers); *Division 3* – **Billy McEwan** (Rotherham United); *Division 4* – **Terry Cooper** (Exeter City).

SEPTEMBER

Kenny Dalglish (Liverpool); *Division 2* – **Dave Bassett** (Sheffield Utd); *Division 3* – **John King** (Tranmere Rovers); *Division 4* – **David Webb** (Southend Utd).

OCTOBER

Division 1 – **Chris Nicholl** (Southampton); *Division 2* – **Howard Wilkinson** (Leeds United); *Division 3* – **Phil Neal** (Bolton Wanderers); *Division 4* – **Mark Lawrenson** (Peterborough Utd).

NOVEMBER

Division 1 – **Graham Taylor** (Aston Villa); *Division 2* – **Joe Royle** (Oldham Athletic); *Division 3* – **Billy McEwan** (Rotherham Utd); *Division 4* – **Clive Middlemass** (Carlisle United).

DECEMBER

Division 1 – **Graham Taylor** (Aston Villa); *Division 2* – **Steve Harrison** (Watford); *Division 3* – **Neil Warnock** (Notts County); *Division 4* – **Terry Cooper** (Exeter City).

JANUARY

Division 1 – **Graham Taylor** (Aston Villa); *Division 2* – **Joe Royle** (Oldham Athletic); *Division 3* – **Joe Jordan** (Bristol City); *Division 4* – **John Beck** (Cambridge Utd).

FEBRUARY

Division 1 – **Brian Clough** (Nottingham Forest); *Division 2* – **Joe Royle** (Oldham Athletic); *Division 3* – **John King** (Tranmere Rovers); *Division 4* – **John Beck** (Cambridge Utd).

MARCH

Division 1 – **Kenny Dalglish** (Liverpool); *Division 2* – **Don Mackay** (Blackburn Rovers); *Division 3* – **Gerry Francis** (Bristol Rovers); *Division 4* – **Alan Buckley** (Grimsby Town).

APRIL

Division 1 – **Kenny Dalglish** (Liverpool); *Division 2* – **Jim Smith** (Newcastle Utd); *Division 3* – **Neil Warnock** (Notts County); *Division 4* – **Terry Cooper** (Exeter City).

Barclays Bank Manager of the Year 1989/90: Kenny Dalglish (Liverpool).

Barclays Bank Division Two Manager of the Season: Howard Wilkinson (Leeds Utd).
Barclays Bank Division Three Manager of the Season: Gerry Francis (Bristol Rovers).
Barclays Bank Division Four Manager of the Season: Terry Cooper (Exeter City).
Barclays Bank Special Award: Joe Royle (Oldham Athletic).

The formidable "Front Five" of the country's top managers: Barclays Bank Manager of the Year, Kenny Dalglish (Liverpool); Special Award winner, Joe Royle (Oldham Athletic); and Divisional Managers of the Season – Howard Wilkinson (Leeds United), Division 2, Gerry Francis (Bristol Rovers), Division 3, and Terry Cooper (Exeter City). Left to right: Wilkinson, Royle, Dalglish, Cooper, Francis.

FOOTBALL LEAGUE MATCHES
1889–1990

	P	W	D	L	Goals F	A
Aberdare Athletic	252	78	59	115	334	413
Accrington Stanley*	1542	544	298	700	2441	2954
Aldershot	2300	779	594	927	3156	3531
Arsenal	3444	1494	842	1108	5690	4663
Ashington	328	109	71	148	489	650
Aston Villa	3580	1531	802	1247	6153	5354
Barnsley	3412	1237	863	1312	4886	5171
Barrow	1924	624	414	886	2606	3349
Birmingham City	3486	1301	837	1348	5182	5173
Blackburn Rovers	3608	1407	869	1332	5691	5552
Blackpool	3380	1244	835	1301	4941	5040
Bolton Wanderers	3614	1404	835	1375	5484	5310
Bootle	22	8	3	11	49	63
AFC Bournemouth	2678	1007	700	971	3735	3625
Bradford (Park Avenue)	2190	837	476	877	3516	3582
Bradford City	3284	1219	835	1230	4782	4730
Brentford	2790	1064	699	1027	4096	3990
Brighton & Hove Albion	2746	1104	691	951	4130	3774
Bristol City	3280	1281	825	1174	4816	4571
Bristol Rovers	2742	1035	687	1020	4125	4101
Burnley	3614	1403	856	1355	5479	5457
Burton United[1]	484	147	80	257	657	994
Burton Wanderers	90	42	13	35	167	146
Bury	3530	1325	822	1383	5255	5291
Cambridge United	896	312	244	340	1142	1238
Cardiff City	2674	968	661	1045	3720	4053
Carlisle United	2402	880	569	953	3524	3737
Charlton Athletic	2610	943	643	1024	3905	4165
Chelsea	3066	1185	797	1084	4654	4512
Chester City	2340	825	592	923	3352	3495
Chesterfield	3106	1208	727	1171	4567	4406
Colchester United	1838	675	485	678	2647	2679
Coventry City	2726	1003	690	1033	4028	4048
Crewe Alexandra	2862	956	675	1231	3928	4711
Crystal Palace	2716	996	722	998	3870	3883
Darlington	2706	925	643	1138	3902	4412
Darwen	232	75	27	130	401	619
Derby County	3584	1426	852	1306	5768	5402
Doncaster Rovers	2746	992	677	1077	3929	4251
Durham City	286	95	54	137	394	529
Everton	3568	1511	858	1199	5916	5104
Exeter City	2803	957	718	1128	3876	4323
Fulham	3024	1126	736	1162	4552	4499
Gainsborough Trinity	564	175	118	271	718	1029
Gateshead	1466	559	361	546	2292	2335
Gillingham	2594	913	669	1012	3471	3818
Glossop North End	618	197	136	285	829	1026
Grimsby Town	3538	1373	776	1389	5336	5433
Halifax Town	2754	884	716	1154	3556	4330
Hartlepool United	2752	913	609	1230	3709	4626
Hereford United	824	273	233	318	1001	1085
Huddersfield Town	2928	1134	749	1045	4264	4007
Hull City	3140	1218	815	1107	4664	4357
Ipswich Town	1924	794	459	671	2933	2697
Leeds United[2]	3044	1243	763	1038	4622	4204
Leicester City	3436	1276	868	1292	5323	5402
Leyton Orient	3140	1051	804	1285	4043	4621
Lincoln City	3426	1253	791	1382	5192	5439
Liverpool	3444	1611	828	1005	5947	4447
Loughborough Town	158	34	20	104	170	410
Luton Town	2762	1081	685	996	4372	4054
Maidstone United	46	22	7	17	77	61
Manchester City	3478	1426	829	1223	5804	5213
Manchester United	3476	1531	845	1100	5835	4763
Mansfield Town	2338	863	597	878	3531	3505

	P	W	D	L	Goals F	A
Merthyr Town	420	115	106	199	524	779
Middlesbrough	3282	1244	785	1253	5064	4937
Middlesbrough Ironopolis	28	8	4	16	37	72
Millwall	2730	1077	709	944	4001	3717
Nelson	412	154	73	185	668	796
New Brighton	884	287	187	410	1191	1527
New Brighton Tower	102	48	24	30	194	148
Newcastle United	3452	1416	785	1251	5546	5034
Newport County	2672	888	625	1159	3700	4557
Northampton Town	2790	1090	633	1067	4330	4203
Northwich Victoria	50	12	5	33	72	156
Norwich City	2676	988	718	970	3900	3899
Nottingham Forest	3480	1308	856	1316	5150	5117
Notts County	3656	1369	886	1401	5389	5491
Oldham Athletic	3092	1152	777	1163	4525	4594
Oxford United	1238	427	357	454	1573	1608
Peterborough United	1380	543	383	454	2063	1820
Plymouth Argyle	2740	1071	699	970	4192	3878
Portsmouth	2684	995	695	994	4018	4008
Port Vale[3]	3252	1163	838	1251	4497	4740
Preston North End	3634	1401	900	1333	5514	5270
Queen's Park Rangers	2696	1081	671	944	4084	3743
Reading	2800	1125	689	986	4327	4001
Rochdale	2752	903	679	1170	3763	4447
Rotherham United[4]	2858	1079	653	1126	4305	4474
Scarborough	138	53	38	47	183	173
Scunthorpe United	1815	637	510	668	2490	2566
Sheffield United	3508	1414	833	1261	5576	5267
Sheffield Wednesday	3496	1379	852	1265	5415	5134
Shrewsbury Town	1806	636	494	676	2496	2573
Southampton	2664	1040	685	939	4150	3881
Southend United	2806	1058	687	1061	4144	4114
Southport	2200	723	568	909	2961	3488
Stalybridge Celtic	76	33	11	32	104	110
Stockport County	3356	1222	799	1335	4718	4962
Stoke City	3300	1186	803	1311	4591	4866
Sunderland	3546	1467	849	1230	1826	5211
Swansea City	2726	1008	648	1070	3972	4216
Swindon Town	2776	1059	715	1002	4152	4007
Thames	84	20	17	47	107	202
Torquay United	2512	890	632	990	3535	3899
Tottenham Hotspur	2944	1249	712	983	4956	4179
Tranmere Rovers	2752	1049	649	1054	4207	4125
Walsall	2988	1050	709	1229	4450	4774
Watford	2756	1043	703	1010	4034	3896
West Bromwich Albion	3588	1411	858	1319	5728	5410
West Ham United	2686	1027	652	1007	4207	4102
Wigan Athletic	552	227	150	175	774	688
Wigan Borough[5]	412	145	94	173	635	706
Wimbledon	564	238	153	173	855	731
Wolverhampton W	3598	1473	795	1330	6031	5552
Workington	1194	385	310	499	1525	1810
Wrexham	2736	1036	668	1032	4160	4039
York City	2416	859	591	966	3585	3709

The above figures do not include games played at the start of season 1939–40 before the competition was abandoned because of the outbreak of World War II, nor do they include the old end-of-season Test matches or the modern Play-offs.

* Includes the original club known simply as Accrington but none of the games played during season 1961–62 when they resigned from the League.

[1] Includes Burton Swifts who amalgamated with Burton Wanderers to form Burton United in 1901.

[2] Includes Leeds City and the eight games played 1919–20.

[3] Includes only 34 games played 1919–20 when took over from Leeds City.

[4] Including Rotherham County who amalgamated with Rotherham Town to form Rotherham United in 1925.

[5] Games played in season 1931–32 prior to their resignation on 26 October were expunged from the record and therefore not included in these figures.

RECORDS

Major British Records

HIGHEST WINS

First-Class Match	Arbroath *(Scottish Cup 1st Round)*	36	Bon Accord	0	12 Sept 1885
International Match	England	13	Ireland	0	18 Feb 1882
FA Cup	Preston NE *(1st Round)*	26	Hyde U	0	15 Oct 1887
League Cup	West Ham U *(2nd Round, 2nd Leg)*	10	Bury	0	25 Oct 1983
	Liverpool *(2nd Round, 1st Leg)*	10	Fulham	0	23 Sept 1986

FOOTBALL LEAGUE

Division 1	*(Home)*	WBA	12	Darwen	0	4 April 1892
		Nottingham F	12	Leicester Fosse	0	21 April 1909
	(Away)	Newcastle U	1	Sunderland	9	5 Dec 1908
		Cardiff C	1	Wolverhampton W	9	3 Sept 1955
Division 2	*(Home)*	Newcastle U	13	Newport Co	0	5 Oct 1946
	(Away)	Burslem PV	0	Sheffield U	10	10 Dec 1892
Division 3	*(Home)*	Gillingham	10	Chesterfield	0	5 Sept 1987
	(Away)	Halifax T	0	Fulham	8	16 Sept 1969
Division 3(S)	*(Home)*	Luton T	12	Bristol R	0	13 April 1936
	(Away)	Northampton T	0	Walsall	8	2 Feb 1947
Division 3(N)	*(Home)*	Stockport Co	13	Halifax T	0	6 Jan 1934
	(Away)	Accrington S	0	Barnsley	9	3 Feb 1934
Division 4	*(Home)*	Oldham Ath	11	Southport	0	26 Dec 1962
	(Away)	Crewe Alex	1	Rotherham U	8	8 Sept 1973
Aggregate Division 3(N)		Tranmere R	13	Oldham Ath	4	26 Dec 1935

SCOTTISH LEAGUE

Premier Division	*(Home)*	Aberdeen	8	Motherwell	0	26 March 1979
	(Away)	Hamilton A	0	Celtic	8	5 Nov 1988
Division 1	*(Home)*	Celtic	11	Dundee	0	26 Oct 1895
	(Away)	Airdrieonians	1	Hibernian	11	24 Oct 1950
Division 2	*(Home)*	Airdrieonians	15	Dundee Wanderers	1	1 Dec 1894
	(Away)	Alloa Ath	0	Dundee	10	8 March 1947

LEAGUE CHAMPIONSHIP HAT-TRICKS

Huddersfield T	1923–24 to 1925–26
Arsenal	1932–33 to 1934–35
Liverpool	1981–82 to 1983–84

MOST GOALS FOR IN A SEASON

FOOTBALL LEAGUE		*Goals*	*Games*	*Season*
Division 1	Aston V	128	42	1930–31
Division 2	Middlesbrough	122	42	1926–27
Division 3(S)	Millwall	127	42	1927–28
Division 3(N)	Bradford C	128	42	1928–29
Division 3	QPR	111	46	1961–62
Division 4	Peterborough U	134	46	1960–61
SCOTTISH LEAGUE				
Premier Division	Dundee U	90	36	1982–83
	Celtic	90	36	1982–83
	Celtic	90	44	1986–87
Division 1	Hearts	132	34	1957–58
Division 2	Raith R	142	34	1937–38

FEWEST GOALS FOR IN A SEASON

FOOTBALL LEAGUE	(minimum 42 games)	*Goals*	*Games*	*Season*
Division 1	Stoke C	24	42	1984–85
Division 2	Watford	24	42	1971–72
Division 3(S)	Crystal Palace	33	42	1950–51
Division 3(N)	Crewe Alex	32	42	1923–24
Division 3	Stockport Co	27	46	1969–70
Division 4	Crewe Alex	29	46	1981–82

SCOTTISH LEAGUE	(minimum 30 games)			
Premier Division	Hamilton A	19	36	1988–89
Division 1	Stirling Albion	18	39	1980–81
Division 2	Lochgelly U	20	38	1923–24

MOST GOALS AGAINST IN A SEASON

FOOTBALL LEAGUE		Goals	Games	Season
Division 1	Blackpool	125	42	1930–31
Division 2	Darwen	141	34	1898–99
Division 3(S)	Merthyr T	135	42	1929–30
Division 3(N)	Nelson	136	42	1927–28
Division 3	Accrington S	123	46	1959–60
Division 4	Hartlepools U	109	46	1959–60
SCOTTISH LEAGUE				
Premier Division	Morton	100	36	1984–85
	Morton	100	44	1987–88
Division 1	Leith Ath	137	38	1931–32
Division 2	Edinburgh C	146	38	1931–32

FEWEST GOALS AGAINST IN A SEASON

FOOTBALL LEAGUE	(minimum 42 games)	Goals	Games	Season
Division 1	Liverpool	16	42	1978–79
Division 2	Manchester U	23	42	1924–25
Division 3(S)	Southampton	21	42	1921–22
Division 3(N)	Port Vale	21	46	1953–54
Division 3	Middlesbrough	30	46	1986–87
Division 4	Lincoln C	25	46	1980–81
SCOTTISH LEAGUE	(minimum 30 games)			
Premier Division	Rangers	19	36	1989–90
Division 1	Celtic	14	38	1913–14
Division 2	Morton	20	38	1966–67

MOST POINTS IN A SEASON

FOOTBALL LEAGUE	(under old system)	Points	Games	Season
Division 1	Liverpool	68	42	1978–79
Division 2	Tottenham H	70	42	1919–20
Division 3	Aston V	70	46	1971–72
Division 3(S)	Nottingham F	70	46	1950–51
	Bristol C	70	46	1954–55
Division 3(N)	Doncaster R	72	42	1946–47
Division 4	Lincoln C	74	46	1975–76
FOOTBALL LEAGUE	(three points for a win)			
Division 1	Everton	90	42	1984–85
	Liverpool	90	40	1987–88
Division 2	Chelsea	99	46	1988–89
Division 3	Bournemouth	97	46	1986–87
Division 4	Swindon T	102	46	1985–86
SCOTTISH LEAGUE				
Premier Division	Celtic	72	44	1987–88
Division 1	Rangers	76	42	1920–21
Division 2	Morton	69	38	1966–67

FEWEST POINTS IN A SEASON

FOOTBALL LEAGUE	(minimum 34 games)	Points	Games	Season
Division 1	Stoke C	17	42	1984–85
Division 2	Doncaster R	8	34	1904–05
	Loughborough T	8	34	1899–1900
Division 3	Rochdale	21	46	1973–74
	Cambridge U	21	46	1984–85
Division 3(S)	Merthyr T	21	42	1924–25 & 1929–30
	QPR	21	42	1925–26
Division 3(N)	Rochdale	11	40	1931–32
Division 4	Workington	19	46	1976–77
SCOTTISH LEAGUE	(minimum 30 games)			
Premier Division	St Johnstone	11	36	1975–76
Division 1	Stirling Albion	6	30	1954–55
Division 2	Edinburgh C	7	34	1936–37

MOST WINS IN A SEASON

FOOTBALL LEAGUE		Wins	Games	Season
Division 1	Tottenham H	31	42	1960–61
Division 2	Tottenham H	32	42	1919–20
Division 3(S)	Millwall	30	42	1927–28
	Plymouth Arg	30	42	1929–30
	Cardiff C	30	42	1946–47
	Nottingham F	30	46	1950–51
	Bristol C	30	46	1954–55
Division 3(N)	Doncaster R	33	42	1946–47
Division 3	Aston Villa	32	46	1971–72
Division 4	Lincoln C	32	46	1975–76
	Swindon T	32	46	1985–86
SCOTTISH LEAGUE				
Premier Division	Aberdeen	27	36	1984–85
	Rangers	31	44	1986–87
	Celtic	31	44	1987–88
Division 1	Rangers	35	42	1920–21
Division 2	Morton	33	38	1966–67

RECORD HOME WINS IN A SEASON

Brentford won all 21 games in Division 3(S), 1929–30

UNDEFEATED AT HOME

Liverpool 85 games (63 League, 9 League Cup, 7 European, 6 FA Cup), Jan 1978–Jan 1981

RECORD AWAY WINS IN A SEASON

Doncaster R won 18 of 21 games in Division 3(N), 1946–47

FEWEST WINS IN A SEASON

FOOTBALL LEAGUE		Wins	Games	Season
Division 1	Stoke	3	22	1889–90
	Woolwich Arsenal	3	38	1912–13
	Stoke C	3	42	1984–85
Division 2	Loughborough T	1	34	1899–1900
Division 3(S)	Merthyr T	6	42	1929–30
	QPR	6	42	1925–26
Division 3(N)	Rochdale	4	40	1931–32
Division 3	Rochdale	2	46	1973–74
Division 4	Southport	3	46	1976–77
SCOTTISH LEAGUE				
Premier Division	St Johnstone	3	36	1975–76
	Kilmarnock	3	36	1982–83
Division 1	Vale of Leven	0	22	1891–92
Division 2	East Stirlingshire	1	22	1905–06
	Forfar Ath	1	38	1974–75

MOST DEFEATS IN A SEASON

FOOTBALL LEAGUE		Defeats	Games	Season
Division 1	Stoke C	31	42	1984–85
Division 2	Tranmere R	31	42	1938–39
Division 3	Cambridge U	33	46	1984–85
Division 3(S)	Merthyr T	29	42	1924–25
	Walsall	29	46	1952–53
	Walsall	29	46	1953–54
Division 3(N)	Rochdale	33	40	1931–32
Division 4	Newport Co	33	46	1987–88
SCOTTISH LEAGUE				
Premier Division	Morton	29	36	1984–85
Division 1	St Mirren	31	42	1920–21
Division 2	Brechin C	30	36	1962–63
	Lochgelly	30	38	1923–24

HAT-TRICKS

Career   37 Dixie Dean (Tranmere R, Everton, Notts Co, England)
Division 1 (one season post-war)   6 Jimmy Greaves (Chelsea), 1960–61
Three for one team one match
West, Spouncer, Hooper, Nottingham F v Leicester Fosse, Division 1, 21 April 1909
Barnes, Ambler, Davies, Wrexham v Hartlepools U, Division 4, 3 March 1962
Adcock, Stewart, White, Manchester C v Huddersfield T, Division 2, 7 Nov 1987
Loasby, Smith, Wells, Northampton T v Walsall, Division 3S, 5 Nov 1927.
Bowater, Hoyland, Readman, Mansfield T v Rotherham U, Division 3N, 27 Dec 1932.

FEWEST DEFEATS IN A SEASON
(Minimum 20 games)

FOOTBALL LEAGUE		Defeats	Games	Season
Division 1	Preston NE	0	22	1888–89
	Leeds U	2	42	1968–69
Division 2	Liverpool	0	28	1893–94
	Burnley	2	30	1897–98
	Bristol C	2	38	1905–06
	Leeds U	3	42	1963–64
Division 3	QPR	5	46	1966–67
Division 3(S)	Southampton	4	42	1921–22
	Plymouth Arg	4	42	1929–30
Division 3(N)	Port Vale	3	46	1953–54
	Doncaster R	3	42	1946–47
	Wolverhampton W	3	42	1923–24
Division 4	Lincoln C	4	46	1975–76
	Sheffield U	4	46	1981–82
	Bournemouth	4	46	1981–82
SCOTTISH LEAGUE				
Premier Division	Celtic	3	44	1987–88
Division 1	Rangers	1	42	1920–21
Division 2	Clyde	1	36	1956–57
	Morton	1	36	1962–63
	St Mirren	1	36	1967–68

MOST DRAWN GAMES IN A SEASON

FOOTBALL LEAGUE		Draws	Games	Season
Division 1	Norwich C	23	42	1978–79
Division 4	Exeter C	23	46	1986–87
SCOTTISH LEAGUE				
Premier Division	Hibernian	19	44	1987–88

MOST GOALS IN A GAME

FOOTBALL LEAGUE		
Division 1	Ted Drake (Arsenal) 7 goals v Aston Villa	14 Dec 1935
	James Ross (Preston NE) 7 goals v Stoke	6 Oct 1888
Division 2	Tommy Briggs (Blackburn R) 7 goals v Bristol R	5 Feb 1955
	Neville Coleman (Stoke C) 7 goals v Lincoln C (away)	23 Feb 1957
Division 3(S)	Joe Payne (Luton T) 10 goals v Bristol R	13 April 1936
Division 3(N)	Bunny Bell (Tranmere R) 9 goals v Oldham Ath	26 Dec 1935
Division 3	Steve Earle (Fulham) 5 goals v Halifax T	16 Sept 1969
	Barrie Thomas (Scunthorpe U) 5 goals v Luton T	24 April 1965
	Keith East (Swindon T) 5 goals v Mansfield T	20 Nov 1965
	Alf Wood (Shrewsbury T) 5 goals v Blackburn R	2 Oct 1971
	Tony Caldwell (Bolton W) 5 goals v Walsall	10 Sept 1983
	Andy Jones (Port Vale) 5 goals v Newport Co	4 May 1987
Division 4	Bert Lister (Oldham Ath) 6 goals v Southport	26 Dec 1962
FA CUP	Ted MacDougall (Bournemouth) 9 goals v Margate (1st Round)	20 Nov 1971
LEAGUE CUP	Derek Reeves (Southampton) 5 goals v Leeds U	5 Dec 1960
	Alan Wilks (QPR) 5 goals v Oxford U	10 Oct 1967
	Bob Latchford (Everton) 5 goals v Wimbledon	28 Aug 1978
	Cyrille Regis (Coventry C) 5 goals v Chester C	9 Oct 1985
SCOTTISH LEAGUE CUP	Jim Fraser (Ayr U) 5 goals v Dumbarton	13 Aug 1952
SCOTTISH LEAGUE		
Premier Division	Paul Sturrock (Dundee U) 5 goals v Morton	17 Nov 1984
Division 1	Jimmy McGrory (Celtic) 8 goals v Dunfermline Ath	14 Sept 1928
Division 2	Owen McNally (Arthurlie) 8 goals v Armadale	1 Oct 1927
	Jim Dyet (King's Park) 8 goals v Forfar Ath	2 Jan 1930
	John Calder (Morton) 8 goals v Raith R	18 April 1936
	Norman Hayward (Raith R) 8 goals v Brechin C	20 Aug 1937
SCOTTISH CUP	John Petrie (Arbroath) 13 goals v Bon Accord (1st Round)	12 Sept 1885

MOST LEAGUE GOALS IN A SEASON

FOOTBALL LEAGUE		Goals	Games	Season
Division 1	Dixie Dean (Everton)	60	39	1927–28
Division 2	George Camsell (Middlesbrough)	59	37	1926–27
Division 3(S)	Joe Payne (Luton T)	55	39	1936–37
Division 3(N)	Ted Harston (Mansfield T)	55	41	1936–37
Division 3	Derek Reeves (Southampton)	39	46	1959–60
Division 4	Terry Bly (Peterborough U)	52	46	1960–61

FA CUP	Albert Brown (Tottenham H)	15		1900–01
LEAGUE CUP	Clive Allen (Tottenham H)	12		1986–87

SCOTTISH LEAGUE

Division 1	William McFadyen (Motherwell)	52	34	1931–32
Division 2	Jim Smith (Ayr U)	66	38	1927–28

MOST LEAGUE GOALS IN A CAREER

		Goals	Games	Season
FOOTBALL LEAGUE				
Arthur Rowley	WBA	4	24	1946–48
	Fulham	27	56	1948–50
	Leicester C	251	303	1950–58
	Shrewsbury T	152	236	1958–65
		434	619	
SCOTTISH LEAGUE				
Jimmy McGrory	Celtic	1	3	1922–23
	Clydebank	13	30	1923–24
	Celtic	396	375	1924–38
		410	408	

MOST CUP GOALS IN A CAREER

FA CUP
Denis Law 41 (Huddersfield T, Manchester C, Manchester U)

A CENTURY OF LEAGUE AND CUP GOALS IN CONSECUTIVE SEASONS

George Camsell	Middlesbrough	59 Lge	5 Cup	1926–27
(101 goals)		33	4	1927–28
Steve Bull	Wolverhampton W	34 Lge	18 Cup	1987–88
(102 goals)		37	13	1988–89

(Camsell's cup goals were all scored in the FA Cup; Bull had 12 in the Sherpa Van Trophy, 3 Littlewoods Cup, 3 FA Cup in 1987–88; 11 Sherpa Van Trophy, 2 Littlewoods Cup in 1988–89).

LONGEST WINNING SEQUENCE

		Games		Season
FOOTBALL LEAGUE				
Division 1	Everton	12		1893–94 (4)
			and	1894–95 (8)
Division 2	Manchester U	14		1904–05
	Bristol C	14		1905–06
	Preston NE	14		1950–51
Division 3	Reading	13		1985–86
From season's start				
Division 1	Tottenham H	11		1960–61

LONGEST SEQUENCE WITHOUT A WIN FROM SEASON'S START

Division 1	Manchester U	12		1930–31

LONGEST SEQUENCE OF CONSECUTIVE SCORING (Individual)

John Aldridge (Liverpool)	10		1986–87 (1)
		and	1987–88 (9)

LONGEST WINNING SEQUENCE IN A SEASON

		Games	Season
FOOTBALL LEAGUE			
Division 1	Tottenham H	11	1960–61
Division 2	Manchester U	14	1904–05
Division 2	Bristol C	14	1905–06
Division 2	Preston NE	14	1950–51
SCOTTISH LEAGUE			
Division 2	Morton	23	1963–64

LONGEST UNBEATEN SEQUENCE

		Games	Seasons
FOOTBALL LEAGUE			
Division 1	Nottingham F	42	Nov 1977– Dec 1978

LONGEST UNBEATEN CUP SEQUENCE

Liverpool   25 rounds   League/Milk Cup   1980–1984

LONGEST UNBEATEN SEQUENCE IN A SEASON

FOOTBALL LEAGUE		Games	Season
Division 1	Burnley	30	1920–21

LONGEST UNBEATEN START TO A SEASON

FOOTBALL LEAGUE		Games	Season
Division 1	Leeds U	29	1973–74
Division 1	Liverpool	29	1987–88

LONGEST SEQUENCE WITHOUT A WIN IN A SEASON

FOOTBALL LEAGUE		Games	Season
Division 2	Cambridge U	31	1983–84

LONGEST SEQUENCE OF CONSECUTIVE DEFEATS

FOOTBALL LEAGUE		Games	Season
Division 3N	Rochdale	17	1931–32

GOALKEEPING RECORDS (Without conceding a goal)

British record *(all competitive games)*
Chris Woods, Rangers, in 1196 minutes from 26 November 1986 to 31 January 1987.
Football League
Steve Death, Reading, 1103 minutes from 24 March to 18 August 1979.

PENALTIES

Most in a season (individual)		Goals	Season
Division 1	Francis Lee (Manchester C)	13	1971–72
Most awarded in one game			
Five	Crystal Palace (4 – 1 scored, three missed) v Brighton & HA (1 scored), Div 2		1988–89
Most saved in a season			
Division 1	Paul Cooper (Ipswich T)	8 (of 10)	1979–80

MOST LEAGUE APPEARANCES

FOOTBALL LEAGUE
899 Peter Shilton (286 Leicester City, 110 Stoke City, 202 Nottingham Forest, 188 Southampton, 113 Derby County) 1966–90
824 Terry Paine (713 Southampton, 111 Hereford United) 1957–77
786 Tommy Hutchison (165 Blackpool, 314 Coventry City, 46 Manchester City, 92 Burnley 169 Swansea City, also 68 Alloa 1965–68) 1968–90
777 Alan Oakes (565 Manchester City, 211 Chester City, 1 Port Vale) 1959–84
770 John Trollope (all for Swindon Town) 1960–80†
764 Jimmy Dickinson (all for Portsmouth) 1946–65
761 Roy Sproson (all for Port Vale) 1950–72
758 Ray Clemence (48 Scunthorpe United, 470 Liverpool, 240 Tottenham Hotspur) 1966–87
757 Pat Jennings (48 Watford, 472 Tottenham Hotspur, 237 Arsenal) 1963–86
†record for one club
Consecutive
401 Harold Bell (401 Tranmere R; 459 in all games) 1946–55
FA CUP
  88 Ian Callaghan (79 Liverpool, 7 Swansea C, 2 Crewe Alex)

Most Senior Matches
1263 Peter Shilton (899 League, 81 FA Cup, 88 League Cup, 125 Internationals, 13 Under-23, 4 Football League XI, 53 others including European Cup, UEFA Cup, World Club Championship, various domestic cup competitions)

MOST CUP WINNERS' MEDALS

FA CUP – 5 medals each
James Forrest (Blackburn R) 1884, 1885, 1886, 1890, 1891.
Hon. A. F. Kinnaird (Wanderers) 1873, 1877, 1878, (Old Etonians) 1879, 1882.
C. H. R. Wollaston (Wanderers) 1872, 1873, 1876, 1877, 1878.

SCOTTISH CUP – 7 medals each
Jimmy McMenemy (Celtic) 1904, 1907, 1908, 1911, 1912, 1914, (Partick Th) 1921.
Bob McPhail (Airdieonians) 1924, (Rangers) 1928, 1930, 1932, 1934, 1935, 1936.
Billy McNeill (Celtic) 1965, 1967, 1969, 1971, 1972, 1974, 1975.

MOST LEAGUE MEDALS

Phil Neal (Liverpool) 8: 1976, 1977, 1979, 1980, 1982, 1983, 1984, 1986

RECORD ATTENDANCES

Football League	83,260	Manchester U v Arsenal, Maine Road	17.1.1948
Scottish League	118,567	Rangers v Celtic, Ibrox Stadium	2.1.1939
FA Cup Final	126,047*	Bolton W v West Ham U, Wembley	28.4.1923
European Cup	135,826	Celtic v Leeds U, semi-final at Hampden Park	15.4.1970
Scottish Cup	146,433	Celtic v Aberdeen, Hampden Park	24.4.37
World Cup	199,854†	Brazil v Uruguay, Maracana, Rio	16.7.50

* It has been estimated that as many as 70,000 more broke in without paying.
† 173,830 paid.

OTHER RECORDS

YOUNGEST PLAYERS
Football League   Albert Geldard, 15 years 158 days, Bradford Park Avenue v Millwall, Division 2, 16.9.29; and Ken Roberts, 15 years 158 days, Wrexham v Bradford Park Avenue, Division 3N, 1.9.51
Football League scorer
  Ronnie Dix, 15 years 180 days, Bristol Rovers v Norwich City, Division 3S, 3.3.28.
Division 1
  Derek Forster, 15 years 185 days, Sunderland v Leicester City, 22.8.84.
Division 1 scorer
  Jason Dozzell, 16 years 57 days as substitute Ipswich Town v Coventry City, 4.2.84
Division 1 hat-tricks
  Alan Shearer, 17 years 240 days, Southampton v Arsenal, 9.4.88
  Jimmy Greaves, 17 years 10 months, Chelsea v Portsmouth, 25.12.57
FA Cup (any round)
  Andy Awford, 15 years 88 days as substitute Worcester City v Borehamwood, 3rd Qual. rd, 10.10.87
FA Cup proper
  Scott Endersby, 15 years 288 days, Kettering v Tilbury, 1st rd, 26.11.77
FA Cup Final
  Paul Allen, 17 years 256 days, West Ham United v Arsenal, 1980
FA Cup Final scorer
  Norman Whiteside, 18 years 18 days, Manchester United v Brighton & Hove Albion, 1983
FA Cup Final captain
  David Nish, 21 years 212 days, Leicester City v Manchester City, 1969
League Cup Final scorer
  Norman Whiteside, 17 years 324 days, Manchester U v Liverpool, 1983
League Cup Final captain
  Barry Venison, 20 years, 7 months, 8 days, Sunderland v Norwich C, 1985

INTERNATIONALS
England
  Pre-war: James Prinsep (Clapham Rovers) 17 years 252 days, v Scotland, 5.4.1879
  Post-war: Duncan Edwards (Manchester United), 18 years 183 days, v Scotland, 2.4.55.
Northern Ireland
  Norman Whiteside (Manchester United), 17 years 42 days, v Yugoslavia, 17.6.82
Scotland
  Johnny Lambie (Queen's Park), 17 years 92 days, v Ireland, 20.3.1886
Wales
  John Charles (Leeds United), 18 years 71 days, v Ireland, 8.3.50
Republic of Ireland
  Jimmy Holmes, 17 years 200 days, v Austria, 30.5.71

OLDEST PLAYERS
Football League
  Neil McBain, 52 years 4 months, New Brighton v Hartlepools United, Div 3N, 15.3.47 (McBain was New Brighton's manager and had to play in an emergency)
Division 1
  Stanley Matthews, 50 years 5 days, Stoke City v Fulham, 6.2.65
FA Cup Final
  Walter Hampson, 41 years 8 months, Newcastle United v Aston Villa, 1924
FA Cup
  Billy Meredith, 49 years 8 months, Manchester City v Newcastle United, 29.3.24
International debutant
  Leslie Compton, 38 years 2 months, England v Wales, 15.11.50
International
  Billy Meredith, 45 years 229 days, Wales v England, 15.3.20

SENDINGS-OFF

Season	242 (211 League, 19 FA Cup, 12 Milk Cup)	1982–83
Day	15 (3 League, 12 FA Cup*)	20 Nov 1982
	worst overall FA Cup total	
League	13	14 Dec 1985
FA Cup Final	Kevin Moran, Manchester U v Everton	1985
Wembley	Boris Stankovic, Yugoslavia v Sweden (Olympics)	1948
	Antonio Rattin, Argentina v England (World Cup)	1966
	Billy Bremner (Leeds U) and Kevin Keegan (Liverpool), Charity Shield	1974
	Gilbert Dresch, Luxembourg v England (World Cup)	1977
	Mike Henry, Sudbury T v Tamworth (FA Vase)	1989
Quickest	Ambrose Brown, Wrexham v Hull C (away) Div 3N: 20 secs	25 Dec 1936
Division 1	Liam O'Brien, Manchester U v Southampton (away): 85 secs	3 Jan 1987
World Cup	Jose Batista, Uruguay v Scotland, Neza, Mexico (World Cup): 55 secs	13 June 1986
Most one game	Four: Crewe Alex (2) v Bradford PA (2) Div 3N	8 Jan 1955
	Four: Sheffield U (1) v Portsmouth (3) Div 2	13 Dec 1986
	Four: Port Vale (2) v Northampton T (2) Littlewoods Cup	18 Aug 1987
	Four: Brentford (2) v Mansfield T (2) Div 3	12 Dec 1987

FROM THE CHAPLAIN

The Rothmans Football Yearbook is the Bible of Football, so this year's Chaplains' page builds an identikit of the ideal Club Chaplain.

About one-third of the 92 League clubs now have the benefit of honorary Chaplains, most of them appointed in the last four or five seasons. Some of the Chaplains have been 'in football for years', and most of them watch between twenty and forty League and Cup matches every season, as well as Reserve and Junior games, so they are usually pretty knowledgeable about our sport.

The first national residential conference for Football Chaplains was convened by Christians In Sport in October 1988. It gathered 25 chaplains to scrutinise their role and maximise the support they can offer to their clubs. Professionals present included a club manager, several players and a TV commentator, while the FA graciously invited the chaplains to England's international against Sweden at Wembley. A second conference is scheduled for later this year.

Ten Commandments for the Ideal Chaplain

1 Thou shalt live football and want to help.
2 Thou shalt work under the manager's direction.
3 Thou shalt attend training sessions and home matches regularly, as well as occasional away games.
4 Thou shalt help to welcome visiting teams, supporters and officials.
5 Thou shalt concentrate on youth and reserve teams, on players injured, out of favour or transfer listed, and make pastoral visits to hospitals and players' homes.
6 Thou shalt help new players settle happily.
7 Thou shalt maintain contact with directors and all non-playing staff.
8 Thou shalt be seen regularly among the loyal supporters of thy club.
9 Thou shalt know when to keep a low profile and always keep out of club politics.
10 Thou shalt be a good ambassador for thy club and for football at all times.

Appreciated

The role of the club chaplain (whether he keeps all of the 'ten commandments' or not!) is becoming increasingly appreciated within our sport. The FA's kindness referred to above is a public indication of that, and, year by year, new clubs join the list below of those who have chaplains ministering within them.

Should any reader be interested in serving in such a capacity, or in making contact with a potential chaplain on behalf of his club, he is invited to write, in complete confidence of course, to Christians In Sport, PO Box 93, Oxford.

CHAPLAINS TO FOOTBALL LEAGUE CLUBS

Rev Ernie Hume — Sheffield U
Rev John Bingham — Chesterfield
Rev Richard Chewter — Exeter C
Rev Alan Fisher — Bournemouth
Rev Andrew Taggart — Torquay U
Rev David Jeans — Sheffield W
Rev Nigel Sands — Swindon T, Crystal Palace
Very Rev Alan Warren — Leicester C
Rev Phillip Miller — Ipswich T
Rev Allen Bagshawe — Hull C
Rev Tony Adamson — Newcastle U
Rev Derek Cleave — Bristol C
Rev Brian Rice — Hartlepool U
Rev John Boyers — Watford
Rev Michael Chantry — Oxford U

Rev Dennis Hall — Wigan Ath
Rev William Hall — Middlesbrough
Rev Canon John Hestor — Brighton & HA
Rev Mervyn Terrett — Luton T
Rev Jim Rushton — Carlisle U
Rev Robert de Berry — Queen's Park Rangers
Rev Gary Piper — Fulham
Rev Tony Horsfall — Barnsley
Rev Barry Kirk — Reading
Rev Martin Short — Bradford City
Rev Justin Dennison — Manchester United
Rev Martin Butt — Walsall
Rev Kevin Tugwell — Cardiff City
Rev Steve Riley — Leeds United
Revs Alan Poulter and Robin Sutton — Tranmere Rovers

BARCLAYS LEAGUE FIXTURES 1990–91

Saturday 25 August
Division One
Aston Villa v Southampton
Chelsea v Derby Co
Everton v Leeds U
Luton T v Crystal Palace
Manchester U v Coventry C
Norwich C v Sunderland
Nottingham F v QPR
Sheffield U v Liverpool
Tottenham H v Manchester C
Wimbledon v Arsenal

Division Two
Barnsley v Brighton & HA
Bristol C v Blackburn R
Charlton Ath v Swindon T
Hull C v Notts Co
Ipswich T v Sheffield W
Leicester C v Bristol R
Middlesbrough v West Ham U
Newcastle U v Plymouth Arg
Oxford U v Port Vale
Portsmouth v WBA
Watford v Millwall
Wolverhampton W v Oldham Ath

Division Three
Bradford C v Tranmere R
Brentford v AFC Bournemouth
Bury v Chester C
Cambridge U v Birmingham C
Crewe Alex v Fulham
Exeter C v Reading
Huddersfield T v Southend U
Leyton O v Swansea C
Preston NE v Grimsby T
Shrewsbury T v Bolton W
Stoke C v Rotherham U
Wigan Ath v Mansfield T

Division Four
Burnley v Lincoln C
Cardiff C v Scarborough
Carlisle U v Doncaster R
Chesterfield v Hartlepool U
Gillingham v Darlington
Halifax T v Stockport Co
Hereford U v Northampton T
Rochdale v Aldershot
Scunthorpe U v Blackpool
Walsall v Torquay U
Wrexham v Peterborough U
York C v Maidstone U

Tuesday 28 August
Division One
Crystal Palace v Chelsea (7.45)
Leeds U v Manchester U
Liverpool v Nottingham F
Southampton v Norwich C
Sunderland v Tottenham H

Division Two
Blackburn R v Hull C (7.45)
Oldham Ath v Leicester C
Plymouth Arg v Watford
Port Vale v Wolverhampton W
Swindon T v Ipswich T (7.45)

Wednesday 29 August
Division One
Arsenal v Luton T (7.45)
Coventry C v Everton (7.45)
Derby Co v Sheffield U
QPR v Wimbledon (7.45)

Divisioin Two
West Ham U v Portsmouth (7.45)

Friday 31 August
Division Three
Tranmere R v Stoke C

Division Four
Torquay United v Gillingham

Saturday 1 September
Division One
Arsenal v Tottenham H
Coventry C v Nottingham F
Crystal Palace v Sheffield U
Derby Co v Wimbledon
Leeds U v Norwich C
Liverpool v Aston Villa
Manchester C v Everton
QPR v Chelsea
Southampton v Luton T
Sunderland v Manchester U

Division Two
Blackburn R v Newcastle U
Brighton & HA v Wolverhampton W
Bristol R v Charlton Ath
Millwall v Barnsley
Notts Co v Oxford U
Oldham Ath v Portsmouth
Plymouth Arg v Middlesbrough
Port Vale v Leicester C
Sheffield W v Hull City
WBA v Ipswich T
West Ham U v Watford

Division Three
AFC Bournemouth v Bury
Birmingham C v Leyton O
Bolton W v Bradford C
Chester C v Exeter C
Fulham v Cambridge U
Grimsby T v Wigan Ath
Mansfield T v Brentford
Reading v Preston NE
Rotherham U v Shrewsbury T
Southend U v Crewe Alex
Swansea C v Huddersfield T

Division Four
Aldershot v Scunthorpe U
Blackpool v Rochdale
Darlington v Burnley
Doncaster R v Wrexham
Hartlepool U v Cardiff C
Hereford U v York C
Lincoln C v Halifax
Maidstone U v Northampton T
Peterborough U v Carlisle U
Scarborough v Chesterfield
Stockport Co v Walsall

Sunday 2 September
Division Two
Swindon T v Bristol C

Tuesday 4 September
Division One
Luton T v Manchester U (7.45)

Wednesday 5 September
Division One
Manchester C v Aston Villa (7.45)

Saturday 8 September
Division One
Aston Villa v Coventry C
Chelsea v Sunderland

Everton v Arsenal
Luton T v Leeds U
Manchester U v QPR
Norwich C v Crystal Palace
Nottingham F v Southampton
Sheffield U v Manchester C
Tottenham H v Derby Co
Wimbledon v Liverpool

Division Two
Barnsley v Olham Ath
Bristol C v Plymouth Arg
Charlton Ath v Sheffield W
Hull C v Swindon T
Ipswich T v Blackburn R
Leicester C v West Ham U
Middlesbrough v Notts Co
Newcastle U v Millwall
Oxford U v WBA
Portsmouth v Port Vale
Watford v Brighton & HA
Wolverhampton W v Bristol R

Division Three
Bradford C v Reading
Brentford v Chester C
Bury v Rotherham U
Crewe Alex v Grimsby T
Exeter C v Swansea C
Huddersfield T v Bolton W
Leyton O v Mansfield T
Preston NE v Tranmere R
Shrewsbury T v Fulham
Stoke C v Birmingham C
Wigan Ath v AFC Bournemouth

Division Four
Burnley v Scarborough
Cardiff C v Torquay U
Carlisle U v Maidstone U (3.30)
Chesterfield v Hereford U
Gillingham v Hartlepool U
Halifax T v Doncaster R
Northampton T v Blackpool
Rochdale v Stockport Co
Scunthorpe U v Peterborough U
Walsall v Darlington
Wrexham v Aldershot
York C v Lincoln C

Sunday 9 September
Division Three
Cambridge U v Southend U

Tuesday 11 September
Division Two
Notts Co v Charlton Ath (7.45)

Friday 14 September
Division Three
Tranmere R v Shrewsbury T

Division Four
Aldershot v Northampton T
Hartlepool U v York C
Stockport Co v Burnley

Saturday 15 September
Division One
Arsenal v Chelsea
Coventry C v Wimbledon
Crystal Palace v Nottingham F
Derby Co v Aston Villa
Leeds U v Tottenham H
Liverpool v Manchester U

Manchester C v Norwich C
QPR v Luton T
Southampton v Sheffield U
Sunderland v Everton

Division Two
Blackburn R v Barnsley
Brighton & HA v Charlton Ath
Bristol R v Hull C
Millwall v Ipswich T
Notts Co v Portsmouth
Oldham Ath v Oxford U
Plymouth Arg v Leicester C
Port Vale v Newcastle U
Sheffield W v Watford
Swindon T v Middlebrough
WBA v Bristol C
West Ham U v Wolverhampton W

Division Three
AFC Bournemouth v Stoke C
Birmingham C v Bury
Bolton W v Crewe Alex
Chester C v Leyton O
Fulham v Huddersfield T
Grimsby T v Bradford C
Mansfield T v Exeter C
Reading v Cambridge U
Rotherham U v Wigan Ath
Southend U v Preston NE
Swansea C v Brentford

Division Four
Blackpool v Wrexham
Darlington v Halifax T
Hereford U v Carlisle U
Lincoln C v Cardiff C
Maidstone U v Scunthorpe U
Peterborough U v Walsall
Rochdale v Doncaster R
Scarborough v Gillingham
Torquay U v Chesterfield

Monday, 17 September
Division Three
Port Vale v Middlesbrough
Tranmere R v Leyton O
Stockport Co v Carlisle U

Tuesday 18 September
Division Two
Blackburn R v Leicester C (7.45)
Notts Co v Barnsley (7.45)
Oldham Ath v Charlton Ath
Plymouth Arg v Oxford U
Swindon T v Wolverhampton W
(7.45)

Division Three
AFC Bournemouth v Bradford C
(7.45)
Birmingham C v Exeter C (7.45)
Bolton W v Preston NE
Chester C v Stoke C
Fulham v Wigan Ath
Grimsby T v Huddersfield T
Mansfield T v Cambridge U
Reading v Crewe Alex
Rotherham U v Shrewsbury T
Southend U v Shrewsbury T
Swansea C v Bury

Division Four
Aldershot v Cardiff C
Blackpool v Burnley
Darlington v York C
Doncaster R v Walsall
Harlepool U v Rochdale
Peterborough U v Halifax T
Torquay U v Scunthorpe U

Wednesday 19 September
Division Two
Brighton & HA v Portsmouth
Bristol R v Bristol C (8.00)

Millwall v Hull C
Sheffield W v Newcastle U
West Ham U v Ipswich T (7.45)

Division Four
Hereford U v Gillingham
Lincoln C v Chesterfield (7.45)
Maidstone U v Wrexham (8.00)
Scarborough v Northampton T

Friday 21 September
Division Three
Cambridge U v Chester C
Crewe Alex v Tranmere R

Division Four
Halifax T v Torquay U

Saturday 22 September
Division One
Aston Villa v QPR
Chelsea v Manchester C
Everton v Liverpool
Luton T v Coventry C
Manchester U v Southampton
Norwich C v Derby Co
Nottingham F v Arsenal
Tottenham H v Crystal Palace
Wimbledon v Sunderland

Division Two
Barnsley v Port Vale
Bristol C v Brighton & HA
Charlton Ath v Millwall
Hull City v WBA
Ipswich T v Bristol R
Leicester C v Sheffield W
Middlesbrough v Oldham Ath
Newcastle U v West Ham U
Oxford U v Swindon T
Portsmouth v Blackburn R
Watford v Notts Co
Wolverhampton W v Plymouth Arg

Division Three
Bradford C v Swansea C
Brentford v Bolton W
Bury v Mansfield T
Exeter C v AFC Bournemouth
Huddersfield T v Reading
Leyton O v Rotherham U
Preston NE v Fulham
Shrewsbury T v Grimsby T
Stoke C v Southend U
Wigan Ath v Birmingham C

Division Four
Burnley v Aldershot
Cardiff C v Stockport Co
Carlisle U v Hartlepool U
Chesterfield v Blackpool
Gillingham v Maidstone U
Northampton T v Peterborough U
Rochdale v Scarborough
Scunthorpe U v Lincoln C (11.00)
Walsall v Hereford U
Wrexham v Darlington
York C v Doncaster R

Sunday 23 September
Division One
Sheffield U v Leeds U (12.00 noon)

Friday 28 September
Division Three
Swansea C v Tranmere R
Wigan Ath v Bolton W

Division Four
Carlisle U v Burnley

Saturday 29 September
Division One
Chelsea v Sheffield U

Coventry C v QPR
Derby Co v Crystal Palace
Everton v Southampton
Leeds U v Arsenal
Manchester U v Nottingham F
Norwich C v Luton T
Sunderland v Liverpool
Tottenham H v Aston Villa
Wimbledon v Manchester C

Division Two
Blackburn R v Brighton HA
Bristol C v Newcastle U
Charlton Ath v Barnsley
Hull C v Port Vale
Ipswich T v Watford
Middlesbrough v Leicester C
Notts C v Bristol C
Oxford U v Wolverhampton W
Portsmouth v Plymouth Arg
Sheffield W v West Ham U
WBA v Oldham Ath

Division Three
AFC Bournemouth v Fulham
Birmingham C v Preston NE
Brentford v Grimsby T
Bury v Crewe Alex
Chester C v Huddersfield T
Exeter C v Cambridge U
Leyton O v Bradford C
Mansfield T v Southend U
Rotherham U v Reading
Stoke C v Shrewsbury T

Division Four
Aldershot v Scarborough
Blackpool v Hartlepool U
Doncaster R v Darlington
Hereford U v Stockport C
Maidstone U v Lincoln C
Northampton T v Halifax T
Peterborough U v Torquay U
Rochdale v Walsall
Scunthorpe U v Cardiff C
Wrexham v Chesterfield
York C v Gillingham

Sunday, 30 September
Division Two
Swindon T v Millwall

Monday, 1 October
Division Two
Port Vale v Notts Co

Division Three
Tranmere R v Wigan Ath

Division Four
Stockport Co v Maidstone U

Tuesday 2 October
Division Two
Barnsley v Ipswich T (7.45)
Oldham Ath v Swindon T
Plymouth Arg v WBA (7.45)
Watford v Hull C (7.45)
Wolverhampton W v Charlton Ath

Division Three
Bolton W v Mansfield T
Cambridge U v Leyton O
Crewe Alex v Stoke C
Fulham v Birmingham C
Grimsby T v Rotherham U
Huddersfield T v Exeter C
Preston NE v Brentford
Reading v AFC Bournemouth
Shrewsbury T v Bury
Southend U v Swansea C

Division Four
Burnley v Northampton T
Cardiff C v Rochdale

Chesterfield v York C
Darlington v Peterborough U
Gillingham v Carlisle U
Halifax T v Wrexham
Hartlepool U v Aldershot
Torquay U v Doncaster R
Walsall v Scunthorpe U

Wednesday 3 October
Division Two
Brighton & HA v Sheffield W
Bristol R v Blackburn R (8.00)
Leicester C v Bristol C (7.45)
Millwall v Portsmouth
Newcastle U v Middlesbrough (7.45)
West Ham U v Oxford U (7.45)

Division Three
Bradford C v Chester C (7.45)

Division Four
Lincoln C v Hereford U
Scarborough v Blackpool

Friday 29 October
Division Three
Southend U v AFC Bournemouth

Division Four
Cardiff C v Wrexham

Saturday 6 October
Division One
Arsenal v Norwich C
Aston Villa v Sunderland
Crystal Palace v Leeds U
Liverpool v Derby Co
Manchester C v Coventry C
QPR v Tottenham H
Sheffield U v Wimbledon
Southampton v Chelsea

Division Two
Barnsley v Oxford U
Brighton & HA v Swindon T
Bristol R v Sheffield W
Leicester C v Notts C
Millwall v WBA
Newcastle U v Portsmouth
Oldham Ath v Blackburn R
Plymouth Arg v Ipswich T
Port Vale v Charlton Ath
Watford v Middlesbrough
West Ham U v Hull C
Wolverhampton W v Bristol C

Division Three
Bolton W v Stoke C
Bradford C v Brentford
Cambridge U v Bury
Crewe Alex v Wigan Ath
Fulham v Rotherham U
Grimsby T v Swansea C
Huddersfield T v Leyton O
Preston NE v Exeter C
Reading v Birmingham C
Shrewsbury T v Mansfield T
Tranmere R v Chester C

Division Four
Burnley v York C
Chesterfield v Northampton T
Darlington v Hereford U
Gillingham v Rochdale
Halifax T v Scunthorpe U
Hartlepool U v Maidstone U (3.15)
Lincoln C v Aldershot
Stockport Co v Peterborough U
Torquay U v Blackpool
Walsall v Carlisle U

Sunday 7 October
Division One
Nottingham F v Everton

Division Four
Scarborough v Doncaster R

Friday 12 October
Division Four
Aldershot v Torquay U

Saturday 13 October
Division Two
Blackburn R v Watford
Bristol C v West Ham U
Charlton Ath v Leicester C
Hull C v Oldham Ath
Ipswich T v Port Vale
Middlesbrough v Millwall
Notts Co v Wolverhampton W
Oxford U v Newcastle U
Portsmouth v Barnsley
Sheffield W v Plymouth Arg
Swindon T v Bristol R
WBA v Brighton & HA

Division Three
Birmingham C v Southend U
Bury v Bolton W
Chester C v Grimsby T
Exeter C v Bradford C
Leyton O v Shrewsbury T
Mansfield T v Preston NE
Rotherham U v Huddersfield T
Stoke C v Fulham
Swansea C v Crewe Alex
Wigan Ath v Reading

Division Four
Blackpool v Darlington
Carlisle U v Halifax T
Doncaster R v Hartlepool U
Hereford U v Burnley
Maidstone U v Walsall
Northampton T v Stockport Co
Peterborough U v Lincoln C
Rochdale v Chesterfield
Scunthorpe U v Gillingham
Wrexham v Scarborough
York C v Cardiff C

Sunday 14 October
Division Three
Brentford v Cambridge U (12.00 noon)

Tuesday 16 October
Division Three
AFC Bournemouth v Tranmere R (7.45)

Friday 19 October
Division Four
Aldershot v Stockport Co
Northampton T v Walsall

Saturday 20 October
Division One
Chelsea v Nottingham F
Coventry C v Southampton
Derby Co v Manchester C
Everton v Crystal Palace
Leeds U v QPR
Manchester U v Arsenal
Norwich C v Liverpool
Sunderland v Luton T
Tottenham H v Sheffield U
Wimbledon v Aston Villa

Division Two
Blackburn R v Plymouth Arg
Bristol C v Oldham Ath
Charlton Ath v Watford
Hull C v Wolverhampton W
Ipswich T v Newcastle U
Middlesbrough v Bristol R
Notts Co v Millwall

Oxford U v Brighton & HA
Portsmouth v Leicester C
Sheffield W v Port Vale
Swindon T v West Ham U
WBA v Barnsley

Division Three
AFC Bournemouth v Crewe Alex
Birmingham C v Grimsby T
Brentford v Huddersfield T
Bury v Reading
Chester C v Shrewsbury T
Exeter C v Tranmere R
Leyton O v Bolton W
Mansfield T v Bradford C
Rotherham U v Preston NE
Stoke C v Cambridge U
Swansea C v Fulham
Wigan Ath v Southend U

Division Four
Blackpool v Gillingham
Carlisle U Chesterfield
Doncaster R v Lincoln C
Hereford U v Cardiff C
Maidstone U v Darlington
Peterborough U v Burnley
Rochdale v Torquay U
Scunthorpe U v Scarborough
Wrexham v Hartlepool U
York C v Halifax T

Monday 22 October
Division Two
Port Vale v WBA

Division Three
Tranmere Rovers v Mansfield T

Division Four
Stockport Co v Blackpool

Tuesday 23 October
Division Two
Barnsley v Sheffield W (7.45)
Oldham Ath v Ipswich T
Plymouth Arg v Notts Co (7.45)
Watford v Portsmouth
Wolverhampton W v Middlesbrough

Division Three
Bolton W v Rotherham
Cambridge U v Wigan Ath
Crewe Alex v Birmingham C
Fulham v Bury
Grimsby T v Leyton O
Huddersfield T v AFC Bournemouth
Preston NE v Chester C
Reading v Brentford
Shrewsbury T v Swansea C
Southend U v Exeter C

Division Four
Burnley v Maidstone U
Cardiff C v Doncaster R
Chesterfield v Scunthorpe U
Darlington v Northampton T
Gillingham v Aldershot
Halifax T v Hereford U
Hartlepool U v Peterborough U
Torquay U v Wrexham
Walsall v York C

Wednesday 24 October
Division Two
Brighton & HA v Hull C
Bristol R v Oxford U (8.00)
Leicester C v Swindon T (7.45)
Millwall v Bristol C
Newcastle U v Charlton Ath (7.45)
West Ham U v Blackburn R (7.45)

Division Three
Bradford C v Stoke C (7.45)

Division Four
Lincoln C v Rochdale
Scarborough v Carlisle U

Friday 26 October
Division Three
Tranmere R v Brentford

Division Four
Stockport Co v York C

Saturday 27 October
Division One
Arsenal v Sunderland
Aston Villa v Leeds U
Crystal Palace v Wimbledon
Liverpool v Chelsea
Luton T v Everton
Manchester C v Manchester U
Nottingham F v Tottenham H
QPR v Norwich C
Sheffield U v Coventry C
Southampton v Derby Co

Division Two
Barnsley v Swindon T
Brighton & HA v Middlesbrough
Bristol R v Portsmouth
Leicester C v Ipswich T
Millwall v Sheffield W
Newcastle U v WBA
Oldham Ath v Notts Co
Plymouth Arg v Hull C
Port Vale v Bristol C
Watford v Oxford U
West Ham U v Charlton Ath
Wolverhampton W v Blackburn R

Division Three
Bolton Wanderers v Swansea C
Bradford C v Wigan Ath
Cambridge U v Rotherham U
Crewe Alex v Chester C
Fulham v Exeter C
Grimsby T v Stoke C
Huddersfield T v Mansfield T
Preston NE v AFC Bournemouth
Reading v Leyton O
Shrewsbury T v Birmingham C
Southend U v Bury

Division Four
Burnley v Rochdale
Cardiff C v Peterborough U
Chesterfield v Doncaster R
Darlington v Scunthorpe U
Gillingham v Wrexham
Halifax T v Blackpool
Hartlepool U v Hereford U
Lincoln C v Northampton T
Scarborough v Maidstone U
Torquay U v Carlisle U
Walsall v Aldershot

Friday 2 November
Division Four
Aldershot v Halifax T

Saturday 3 November
Division One
Chelsea v Aston Villa
Coventry C v Arsenal
Derby C v Luton T
Everton v QPR
Leeds U v Nottingham F
Manchester U v Crystal Palace
Norwich C v Sheffield U
Sunderland v Manchester C
Tottenham H v Liverpool
Wimbledon v Southampton

Division Two
Blackburn R v Millwall
Bristol C v Watford

Charlton Ath v Plymouth Arg
Hull C v Newcastle U
Ipswich T v Brighton & HA
Middlesbrough v Barnsley
Notts Co v West Ham U
Oxford U v Leicester C
Portsmouth v Wolverhampton W
Sheffield W v Oldham Ath
Swindon T v Port Vale
WBA v Bristol R

Division Three
AFC Bournemouth v Shrewsbury T
Birmingham C v Huddersfield T
Bury v Tranmere R
Chester C v Bolton W
Exeter C v Grimsby T
Mansfield T v Crewe Alex
Rotherham U v Bradford C
Stoke C v Reading
Swansea C v Cambridge U
Wigan Ath v Preston NE

Division Four
Blackpool v Walsall
Carlisle U v Lincoln C
Doncaster R v Gillingham
Hereford U v Scarborough
Maidstone U v Cardiff C
Northampton T v Hartlepool U
Peterborough U v Chesterfield
Rochdale v Darlington
Scunthorpe U v Stockport Co
Wrexham v Burnley
York C v Torquay U

Sunday 4 November
Division Three
Brentford v Southend U (11.30)
Leyton O v Fulham (12.00 noon)

Wednesday 7 November
Division Two
Brighton & HA v Newcastle U
Bristol R v Barnsley (8.00)
Millwall v Oxford U
Sheffield W v Bristol C (7.45)
WBA v Middlesbrough

Friday 9 November
Division Three
Shrewsbury T v Crewe Alex

Division Four
Halifax T v Gillingham
Northampton T v Wrexham
Scarborough v Torquay U

Saturday 10 November
Division One
Aston Villa v Nottingham F
Chelsea v Norwich C
Crystal Palace v Arsenal
Derby Co v Manchester U
Liverpool v Luton T
Manchester C v Leeds U
Sheffield U v Everton
Southampton v QPR
Sunderland v Coventry C
Tottenham Hotspur v Wimbledon

Division Two
Barnsley v Leicester C
Blackburn R v Sheffield W
Brighton & HA v Plymouth Arg
Bristol R v Port Vale
Hull C v Ipswich T
Middlesbrough v Charlton Ath
Millwall v West Ham U
Notts Co v WBA
Oldham Ath v Watford
Oxford U v Bristol C
Swindon T v Portsmouth
Wolverhampton W v Newcastle U

Division Three
AFC Bournemouth v Rotherham U
Bolton W v Reading
Bradford C v Preston NE
Brentford v Bury
Chester C v Birmingham C
Huddersfield T v Cambridge U
Leyton O v Exeter C
Mansfield T v Swansea C
Southend U v Fulham
Stoke C v Wigan Ath
Tranmere R v Grimsby T

Division Four
Blackpool v Aldershot
Cardiff C v Chesterfield
Carlisle U v York C
Darlington v Hartlepool U
Maidstone U v Hereford U
Peterborough U v Doncaster R
Scunthorpe U v Rochdale
Stockport Co v Lincoln C
Walsall v Burnley

Saturday 17 November
Division One
Arsenal v Southampton
Coventry C v Liverpool
Everton v Tottenham H
Leeds U v Derby Co
Luton T v Manchester C
Manchester U v Sheffield U
Norwich C v Aston Villa
Nottingham F v Sunderland
QPR v Crystal Palace
Wimbledon v Chelsea

Division Two
Bristol C v Hull C
Charlton Ath v Oxford U
Ipswich T v Notts Co
Leicester C v Wolverhampton W
Newcastle U v Barnsley
Plymouth Arg v Millwall
Port Vale v Oldham Ath
Portsmouth v Middlesbrough
Sheffield Wednesday v Swindon T
Watford v Bristol R
WBA v Blackburn R
West Ham U v Brighton & HA

Friday 23 November
Division Two
Blackburn R v Port Vale
Hull C v Leicester C

Division Four
Torquay U v Stockport Co

Saturday 24 November
Division One
Coventry C v Leeds U
Derby Co v Nottingham F
Liverpool v Manchester C
Luton T v Aston Villa
Manchester U v Chelsea
QPR v Arsenal
Sheffield U v Sunderland
Southampton v Crystal Palace
Tottenham H v Norwich C
Wimbledon v Everton

Division Two
Barnsley v Wolverhampton W
Brighton & HA v Millwall
Bristol R v Oldham Ath
Charlton Ath v Portsmouth
Ipswich T v Bristol C
Newcastle U v Watford
Notts Co v Swindon T
Oxford U v Middlesbrough
Plymouth Arg v West Ham U
WBA v Sheffield W

Division Three
Birmingham C v AFC Bournemouth
Bury v Stoke City
Cambridge U v Shrewsbury T
Crewe Alex v Bradford C
Exeter C v Brentford
Fulham v Tranmere R
Grimsby T v Bolton W
Preston NE v Huddersfield T
Reading v Southend U
Rotherham U v Mansfield T
Swansea C v Chester C
Wigan Ath v Leyton O

Division Four
Aldershot v Maidstone U
Burnley v Halifax T
Chesterfield v Walsall
Doncaster R v Blackpool
Gillingham v Cardiff C
Hartlepool U v Scarborough
Hereford U v Peterborough U
Lincoln C v Darlington
Rochdale v Carlisle U
Wrexham v Scunthorpe U
York C v Northampton T

Friday 30 November
Division Three
Cambridge U v Crewe Alex

Saturday 1 December
Division One
Arsenal v Liverpool
Aston Villa v Sheffield U
Chelsea v Tottenham H
Crystal Palace v Coventry C
Everton v Manchester U
Leeds U v Southampton
Manchester C v QPR
Norwich C v Wimbledon
Nottingham F v Luton T
Sunderland v Derby Co

Division Two
Bristol C v Charlton Ath
Leicester C v Newcastle U
Middlesbrough v Hull C
Millwall v Bristol R
Oldham Ath v Brighton & HA
Port Vale v Plymouth Arg
Portsmouth v Oxford U
Sheffield W v Notts Co
Swindon T v Blackburn R
Watford v Barnsley
West Ham U v WBA
Wolverhampton W v Ipswich T

Division Three
Bolton W v Tranmere R
Chester C v AFC Bournemouth
Exeter C v Stoke C
Grimsby T v Mansfield T
Huddersfield T v Bradford C
Preston NE v Shrewsbury T
Reading v Fulham
Rotherham U v Southend U
Swansea C v Birmingham C
Wigan Ath v Bury

Division Four
Burnley v Cardiff C
Chesterfield v Gillingham
Doncaster R v Aldershot
Hereford U v Blackpool
Lincoln C v Scarborough
Maidstone U v Peterborough U
Northampton T v Rochdale
Stockport Co v Darlington
Torquay v Hartlepool U
Walsall v Halifax T
Wrexham v Carlisle U
York C v Scunthorpe U

Sunday 2 December
Division Three
Brentford v Leyton O

Wednesday 5 December
Division Two
WBA v Watford

Saturday 8 December
Division One
Aston Villa v Manchester C
Chelsea v Crystal Palace
Everton v Coventry C
Luton T v Arsenal
Manchester U v Leeds U
Norwich C v Southampton
Nottingham F v Liverpool
Sheffield U v Derby Co
Tottenham H v Sunderland
Wimbledon v QPR

Division Two
Barnsley v Bristol R
Bristol C v Sheffield W
Charlton Ath v Notts Co
Hull C v Blackburn R
Ipswich T v Swindon T
Leicester C v Oldham Ath
Middlesbrough v WBA
Newcastle U v Brighton & HA
Oxford U v Millwall
Portsmouth v West Man U
Watford v Plymouth Arg
Wolverhampton W v Port Vale

Friday 14 December
Division Three
AFC Bournemouth v Swansea C (7.45)
Tranmere R v Reading

Saturday 15 December
Division One
Arsenal v Wimbledon
Coventry C v Manchester U
Derby Co v Chelsea
Leeds U v Everton
Liverpool v Sheffield U
Manchester C v Tottenham H
QPR v Nottingham F
Southampton v Aston Villa
Sunderland v Norwich C

Division Two
Blackburn R v Bristol C
Brighton & HA v Barnsley
Bristol R v Leicester C
Millwall v Watford
Notts Co v Hull C
Oldham Ath v Wolverhampton W
Port Vale v Oxford U
Sheffield W v Ipswich T
Swindon T v Charlton Ath
WBA v Portsmouth
West Ham U v Middlesbrough

Division Three
Birmingham C v Rotherham U
Bradford C v Cambridge U
Bury v Exeter C
Crewe Alex v Huddersfield T
Fulham v Bolton W
Leyton O v Preston NE
Mansfield T v Chester C
Shrewsbury T v Wigan Ath
Southend U v Grimsby T

Division Four
Aldershot v Hereford U
Blackpool v Maidstone U
Cardiff C v Walsall
Carlisle U v Northampton T
Darlington v Torquay U
Gillingham v Burnley

Halifax T v Chesterfield
Hartlepool U v Lincoln C
Peterborough U v York C
Rochdale v Wrexham
Scarborough v Stockport Co
Scunthorpe U v Doncaster R

Sunday 16 December
Division One
Crystal Palace v Luton T

Division Two
Plymouth Arg v Newcastle U

Division Three
Stoke C v Brentford (2.00)

Friday 21 December
Division Two
Oldham Ath v Plymouth Arg
Portsmouth v Ipswich T (7.45)

Division Three
Tranmere R v Birmingham C

Division Four
Halifax T v Rochdale
Northampton T v Cardiff C
Stockport Co v Doncaster R
Walsall v Wrexham
York C v Aldershot

Saturday 22 December
Division One
Aston Villa v Arsenal
Chelsea v Coventry C
Liverpool v Southampton
Manchester C v Crystal Palace
Norwich C v Everton
Sheffield U v Nottingham F
Tottenham H v Luton T
Wimbledon v Manchester U

Division Two
Barnsley v West Ham U
Bristol R v Newcastle U
Charlton Ath v Hull C
Middlesbrough v Blackburn R
Notts Co v Bristol C
Oxford U v Sheffield W
Port Vale v Brighton & HA
Swindon T v WBA
Wolverhampton W v Millwall

Division Three
Bolton W v Cambridge U
Bradford C v Shrewsbury T
Chester C v Southend U
Exeter C v Rotherham U
Grimsby T v AFC Bournemouth
Huddersfield T v Bury
Leyton O v Crewe Alex
Mansfield T v Fulham
Preston NE v Stoke C
Swansea C v Reading

Division Four
Burnley v Hartlepool U
Darlington v Chesterfield
Hereford U v Scunthorpe U
Lincoln C v Gillingham
Maidstone U v Torquay U
Peterborough U v Scarborough

Sunday 23 December
Division One
Derby Co v QPR (12.00 noon)
Sunderland v Leeds U

Division Two
Leicester C v Watford

Division Three
Brentford v Wigan Ath (11.30)

Division Four
Carlisle U v Blackpool

Wednesday 26 December
Division One
Arsenal v Derby Co (12.00 noon)
Coventry C v Tottenham H (12 noon)
Crystal Palace v Sunderland (12.00 noon)
Everton v Aston Villa
Leeds U v Chelsea (12.00 noon)
Luton T v Sheffield United (11.30)
Manchester U v Norwich C
Nottingham F v Wimbledon
QPR v Liverpool (12.00 noon)
Southampton v Manchester C

Division Two
Blackburn R v Notts Co
Brighton & HA v Bristol R
Bristol C v Portsmouth
Hull C v Oxford U
Ipswich T v Middlesbrough
Millwall v Leicester C (11.30)
Newcastle U v Swindon T
Plymouth Arg v Barnsley
Sheffield W v Wolverhampton W (12.00 noon)
Watford v Port Vale (12.00 noon)
WBA v Charlton Ath
West Ham U v Oldham Ath

Division Three
AFC Bournemouth v Mansfield T
Birmingham C v Brentford
Bury v Leyton Orient
Cambridge U v Tranmere R
Crewe Alex v Preston NE
Fulham v Bradford C (12.00 noon)
Reading v Grimsby Town
Rotherham U v Chester C
Shrewsbury T v Huddersfield T
Southend U v Bolton W (11.30)
Stoke C v Swansea C
Wigan Ath v Exeter C

Division Four
Aldershot v Darlington
Blackpool v Peterborough U
Cardiff C v Carlisle U
Chesterfield v Burnley
Doncaster R v Maidstone U
Gillingham v Walsall
Hartlepool U v Stockport Co
Rochdale v York C
Scarborough v Halifax T
Scunthorpe U v Northampton T
Torquay U v Lincoln C
Wrexham v Hereford U (12.00 noon)

Friday, 28 December
Division Three
Southend U v Bradford C

Saturday 29 December
Division One
Arsenal v Sheffield U
Coventry C v Norwich C
Crystal Palace v Liverpool
Everton v Derby Co
Leeds U v Wimbledon
Luton T v Chelsea
Manchester U v Aston Villa
Nottingham F v Manchester C
QPR v Sunderland
Southampton v Tottenham H

Division Two
Blackburn R v Oxford U
Brighton & HA v Leicester C
Bristol C v Middlesbrough
Hull C v Barnsley
Ipswich T v Charlton Ath
Millwall v Oldham Ath
Newcastle U v Notts Co
Plymouth Arg v Bristol R
Sheffield W v Portsmouth
Watford v Swindon T

WBA v Wolverhampton W
West Ham U v Port Vale

Division Three
AFC Bournemouth v Leyton O
Birmingham C v Bolton W
Bury v Preston NE
Cambridge U v Grimsby T
Crewe Alex v Brentford
Fulham v Chester C
Reading v Mansfield T
Rotherham U v Tranmere R
Shrewsbury T v Exeter C
Stoke C v Huddersfield T
Wigan Ath v Swansea C

Division Four
Aldershot v Peterborough U
Blackpool v Lincoln C
Cardiff C v Halifax T
Chesterfield v Stockport Co
Doncaster R v Hereford U
Gillingham v Northampton T
Hartlepool U v Walsall
Rochdale v Maidstone U
Scarborough v Darlington
Scunthorpe U v Carlisle U
Torquay U v Burnley
Wrexham v York C

Tuesday 1 January 1991
Division One
Aston Villa v Crystal Palace
Chelsea v Everton
Derby Co v Coventry C
Liverpool v Leeds U (12.00 noon)
Manchester C v Arsenal
Sheffield U v QPR
Sunderland v Southampton
Tottenham H v Manchester U
Wimbledon v Luton T

Division Two
Barnsley v Bristol C
Bristol R v West Ham U
Charlton Ath v Blackburn R
Leicester C v WBA
Middlesbrough v Sheffield W
Notts Co v Brighton & HA
Oldham Ath v Newcastle U (1.00)
Oxford U v Ipswich T (7.30)
Port Vale v Millwall
Portsmouth v Hull C
Swindon T v Plymouth Arg
Wolverhampton W v Watford

Division Three
Bolton W v AFC Bournemouth
Bradford C v Bury (12.00 noon)
Brentford v Shrewsbury T
Chester C v Reading
Exeter C v Crewe Alex
Grimsby T v Fulham
Huddersfield T v Wigan Ath
Leyton O v Stoke C
Mansfield T v Birmingham C (11.30)
Preston NE v Cambridge U
Swansea C v Rotherham U
Tranmere R v Southend U

Division Four
Burnley v Scunthorpe U
Carlisle U v Aldershot
Darlington v Cardiff C
Halifax T v Hartlepool U
Hereford U v Torquay U
Lincoln C v Wrexham
Maidstone U v Chesterfield
Northampton T v Doncaster R
Peterborough U v Rochdale
Stockport Co v Gillingham
Walsall v Scarborough
York C v Blackpool

Wednesday 2 January
Norwich C v Nottingham F (7.45)

Friday 4 January
Division Three
Southend U v Leyton O

Division Four
Stockport Co v Wrexham
Torquay U v Northampton T

Saturday 5 January
Division Three
AFC Bournemouth v Cambridge U
Birmingham C v Bradford C
Bolton W v Exeter C
Chester C v Wigan Ath
Fulham v Brentford
Grimsby v Bury
Mansfield T v Stoke C
Reading v Shrewsbury T
Rotherham U v Crewe Alex
Swansea C v Preston NE
Tranmere R v Huddersfield T

Division Four
Aldershot v Chesterfield
Blackpool v Cardiff C
Darlington v Carlisle U
Doncaster R v Burnley
Hartlepool U v Scunthorpe U
Hereford U v Rochdale
Lincoln C v Walsall
Maidstone U v Halifax T
Peterborough U v Gillingham
Scarborough v York C

Friday 11 January
Division Four
Gillingham v Torquay U

Saturday 12 January
Division One
Aston Villa v Liverpool
Chelsea v QPR
Everton v Manchester C
Luton T v Southampton
Manchester U v Sunderland
Norwich C v Leeds U
Nottingham F v Coventry C
Sheffield U v Crystal P
Tottenham H v Arsenal
Wimbledon v Derby Co

Division Two
Barnsley v Millwall
Bristol C v Swindon T
Charlton Ath v Bristol R
Hull City v Sheffield W
Ipswich T v WBA
Leicester C v Port Vale
Middlesbrough v Plymouth Arg
Newcastle U v Blackburn R
Oxford U v Notts Co
Portsmouth v Oldham Ath
Watford v West Ham U
Wolverhampton W v Brighton & H

Division Three
Bradford C v Bolton W
Brentford v Mansfield Town
Bury v AFC Bournemouth
Cambridge U v Fulham
Crewe Alex v Southend U
Exeter C v Chester C
Huddersfield T v Swansea C
Leyton O v Birmingham C
Preston NE v Reading
Shrewsbury T v Rotherham U
Stoke C v Tranmere R
Wigan Ath v Grimsby T

Division Four
Burnley v Darlington
Cardiff C v Hartlepool U
Carlisle U v Peterborough U
Chesterfield v Scarborough
Halifax T v Lincoln C

Northampton T v Maidstone U
Rochdale v Blackpool
Scunthorpe U v Aldershot
Walsall v Stockport Co
Wrexham v Doncaster R
York C v Hereford U

Friday 18 January
Division Three
Tranmere R v Bradford C

Division Four
Stockport Co v Halifax T

Saturday 19 January
Division One
Arsenal v Everton
Coventry C v Aston Villa
Crystal Palace v Norwich C
Derby Co v Tottenham H
Leeds U v Luton T
Liverpool v Wimbledon
Manchester C v Sheffield U
QPR v Manchester U
Southampton v Nottingham F
Sunderland v Chelsea

Division Two
Blackburn R v Ipswich T
Brighton & HA v Watford
Bristol R v Wolverhampton W
Millwall v Newcastle U
Notts Co v Middlesbrough
Oldham Ath v Barnsley
Plymouth Arg v Bristol C
Port Vale v Portsmouth
Sheffield W v Charlton Ath
Swindon T v Hull C
WBA v Oxford U
West Ham U v Leicester C

Division Three
AFC Bournemouth v Brentford
Birmingham C v Cambridge U
Bolton W v Shrewsbury T
Chester C v Bury
Fulham v Crewe Alex
Grimsby T v Preston NE
Mansfield T v Wigan Ath
Reading v Exeter C
Rotherham U v Stoke C
Southend U v Huddersfield T
Swansea C v Leyton O

Division Four
Aldershot v Rochdale
Blackpool v Scunthorpe U
Darlington v Gillingham
Doncaster Rovers v Carlisle U
Hartlepool U v Chesterfield
Lincoln C v Burnley
Maidstone U v York C
Northampton T v Hereford U
Peterborough U v Wrexham
Scarborough v Cardiff C
Torquay U v Walsall

Friday 25 January
Division Three
Crewe Alex v Bolton W
Shrewsbury T v Tranmere R

Division Four
Gillingham v Scarborough

Saturday 26 January
Division Three
Bradford C v Grimsby T
Brentford v Swansea C
Bury v Birmingham C
Cambridge U v Reading
Exeter C v Mansfield T
Huddersfield T v Fulham
Leyton O v Chester C

Preston NE v Southend U
Stoke C v AFC Bournemouth
Wigan Ath v Rotherham U

Division Four
Burnley v Stockport Co
Cardiff C v Lincoln C
Carlisle U v Hereford U
Chesterfield v Torquay U
Doncaster R v Rochdale
Halifax T v Darlington
Northampton T v Aldershot
Scunthorpe U v Maidstone U
Walsall v Peterborough U
Wrexham v Blackpool
York C v Hartlepool U

Friday, 1 February
Division Three
Cambridge U v Mansfield T
Crewe Alex v Reading

Division Four
Cardiff C v Aldershot
Halifax T v Peterborough U
Northampton T v Scarborough

Saturday 2 February
Division One
Aston Villa v Derby Co
Chelsea v Arsenal
Everton v Sunderland
Luton T v QPR
Manchester U v Liverpool
Norwich C v Manchester C
Nottingham F v Crystal Palace
Sheffield U v Southampton
Tottenham H v Leeds U
Wimbledon v Coventry C

Division Two
Barnsley v Blackburn R
Bristol C v WBA
Charlton Ath v Brighton & HA
Hull C v Bristol R
Ipswich T v Millwall
Leicester C v Plymouth Arg
Middlesbrough v Swindon T
Newcastle U v Port Vale
Oxford U v Oldham Ath
Portsmouth v Notts Co
Watford v Sheffield W
Wolverhampton W v West Ham U

Division Three
Bradford C v AFC Bournemouth
Brentford v Rotherham U
Bury v Swansea C
Exeter C v Birmingham C
Huddersfield T v Grimsby T
Leyton O v Tranmere R
Preston NE v Bolton W
Shrewsbury T v Southend U
Stoke C v Chester C
Wigan Ath v Fulham

Division Four
Burnley v Blackpool
Carlisle U v Stockport Co
Chesterfield v Lincoln C
Gillingham v Hereford U
Rochdale v Hartlepool U
Scunthorpe U v Torquay U
Walsall v Doncaster R
Wrexham v Maidstone U
York C v Darlington

Monday 4 February
Division Two
Tranmere R v Crewe Alex

Division Four
Stockport Co v Cardiff C

Tuesday 5 February
Division Three
AFC Bournemouth v Exeter C (7.45)
Birmingham C v Wigan Ath (7.45)
Bolton W v Brentford
Chester C v Cambridge U
Fulham v Preston NE
Grimsby T v Shrewsbury T
Mansfield T v Bury
Reading v Huddersfield T
Rotherham U v Leyton O
Southend U v Stoke C
Swansea C v Bradford C

Division Four
Aldershot v Burnley
Blackpool v Chesterfield
Darlington v Wrexham
Doncaster R v York C
Hartlepool U v Carlisle U
Peterborough U v Northampton T
Torquay U v Halifax T

Wednesday 6 February
Division Four
Hereford U v Walsall
Lincoln C v Scunthorpe U (7.45)
Maidstone U v Gillingham (8.00)
Scarborough v Rochdale

Friday 8 February
Division Three
AFC Bournemouth v Wigan Ath (7.45)
Southend U v Cambridge U
Swansea C v Exeter C
Tranmere R v Preston NE

Division Four
Torquay U v Cardiff C

Saturday 9 February
Division One
Arsenal v Nottingham F
Coventry C v Luton T
Crystal Palace v Tottenham H
Derby Co v Norwich C
Leeds U v Sheffield U
Liverpool v Everton
Manchester C v Chelsea
QPR v Aston Villa
Southampton v Manchester U
Sunderland v Wimbledon

Division Two
Blackburn R v Portsmouth
Brighton & HA v Bristol C
Bristol R v Ipswich T
Millwall v Charlton Ath
Notts Co v Watford
Oldham Ath v Middlesbrough
Plymouth Arg v Wolverhampton W
Port Vale v Barnsley
Sheffield W v Leicester C
Swindon T v Oxford U
WBA v Hull C
West Ham U v Newcastle U

Division Three
Birmingham C v Stoke C
Bolton W v Huddersfield T
Chester C v Brentford
Fulham v Shrewsbury T
Grimsby T v Crewe Alex
Mansfield T v Leyton O
Reading v Bradford C
Rotherham U v Bury

Division Four
Aldershot v Wrexham
Blackpool v Northampton T
Darlington v Walsall
Doncaster R v Halifax T
Hartlepool U v Gillingham

Hereford U v Chesterfield
Lincoln C v York C
Maidstone U v Carlisle U
Peterborough U v Scunthorpe U
Scarborough v Burnley
Stockport Co v Rochdale

Tuesday 12 February
Division Two
Barnsley v Notts Co (7.45)
Bristol C v Bristol R (7.45)
Charlton Ath v Oldham Ath (7.45)
Hull C v Millwall
Ipswich T v West Ham U (7.45)
Middlesbrough v Port Vale
Portsmouth v Brighton & HA (7.45)
Watford v WBA (7.45)
Wolverhampton W v Swindon T

Division Three
Brentford v Fulham (7.45)
Bury v Grimsby T
Cambridge U v AFC Bournemouth
Crewe Alex v Rotherham U
Huddersfield T v Tranmere R
Leyton O v Southend U (7.45)
Preston NE v Swansea C
Shrewsbury T v Reading
Wigan Ath v Chester C

Division Four
Burnley v Doncaster R
Cardiff C v Blackpool
Carlisle U v Darlington
Chesterfield v Aldershot
Gillingham v Peterborough U
Halifax T v Maidstone U
Northampton T v Torquay U
Rochdale v Hereford U
Scunthorpe U v Hartlepool U
Walsall v Lincoln C
Wrexham v Stockport Co
York C v Scarborough

Wednesday 13 February
Division Two
Leicester C v Blackburn R (7.45)
Newcastle U v Sheffield W (7.45)
Oxford U v Plymouth Arg

Division Three
Bradford C v Birmingham C (7.45)
Exeter C v Bolton W
Stoke C v Mansfield T

Friday 15 February
Division Three
Southend U v Reading

Division Four
Cardiff C v Gillingham
Northampton T v York C
Stockport Co v Torquay U

Saturday 16 February
Division One
Aston Villa v Norwich C
Chelsea v Wimbledon
Crystal Palace v QPR
Derby Co v Leeds U
Liverpool v Coventry C
Manchester C v Luton T
Sheffield U v Manchester U
Southampton v Arsenal
Sunderland v Nottingham F
Tottenham H v Everton

Division Two
Barnsley v Newcastle U
Blackburn R v WBA
Brighton & HA v West Ham U
Bristol R v Watford
Hull C v Bristol C
Middlesbrough v Portsmouth

Millwall v Plymouth Arg
Notts Co v Ipswich T
Oldham Ath v Port Vale
Oxford U v Charlton Ath
Swindon T v Sheffield W
Wolverhampton W v Leicester C

Division Three
AFC Bournemouth v Birmingham C
Bolton Wanderers v Grimsby T
Bradford C v Crewe Alex
Brentford v Exeter C
Chester C v Swansea C
Huddersfield T v Preston NE
Leyton O v Wigan Ath
Mansfield Town v Rotherham U
Shrewsbury T v Cambridge U
Stoke C v Bury
Tranmere R v Fulham

Division Four
Blackpool v Doncaster R
Carlisle U v Rochdale
Darlington v Lincoln C
Halifax T v Burnley
Maidstone U v Aldershot
Peterborough U v Hereford U
Scarborough v Hartlepool U
Scunthorpe U v Wrexham
Walsall v Chesterfield

Friday 22 February
Division Three
Crewe Alexandra v Shrewsbury T

Division Four
Doncaster R v Peterborough U (7.45)
Gillingham v Halifax T
Torquay U v Scarborough

Saturday 23 February
Division One
Arsenal v Crystal Palace
Coventry C v Sunderland
Everton v Sheffield U
Leeds U v Manchester C
Luton T v Liverpool
Manchester U v Derby Co
Norwich C v Chelsea
Nottingham F v Aston Villa
QPR v Southampton
Wimbledon v Tottenham H

Division Two
Bristol C v Oxford U
Charlton Ath v Middlesbrough
Ipswich T v Hull C
Leicester C v Barnsley
Newcastle U v Wolverhampton W
Plymouth Arg v Brighon & HA
Port Vale v Bristol R
Portsmouth v Swindon T
Sheffield W v Blackburn R
Watford v Oldham Ath
WBA v Notts Co
West Ham U v Millwall

Division Three
Birmingham C v Chester C
Bury v Brentford
Cambridge U v Huddersfield T
Exeter C v Leyton O
Fulham v Southend U
Grimsby T v Tranmere R
Preston NE v Bradford C
Reading v Bolton W
Rotherham U v AFC Bournemouth
Swansea C v Mansfield T
Wigan Ath v Stoke C

Division Four
Aldershot v Blackpool
Burnley v Walsall
Chesterfield v Cardiff C

Hartlepool U v Darlington
Hereford U v Maidstone U
Lincoln C v Stockport Co
Rochdale v Scunthorpe U
Wrexham v Northampton T
York C v Carlisle U

Friday 1 March
Division Three
Crewe Alexandra v Cambridge U
Southend U v Rotherham U
Tranmere R v Bolton W

Division Four
Cardiff C v Burnley

Saturday 2 March
Division One
Coventry C v Crystal Palace
Derby Co v Sunderland
Liverpool v Arsenal
Luton T v Nottingham F
Manchester U v Everton
QPR v Manchester C
Sheffield U v Aston Villa
Southampton v Leeds U
Tottenham H v Chelsea
Wimbledon v Norwich C

Division Two
Barnsley v Watford
Blackburn R v Swindon T
Brighton & HA v Oldham Ath
Bristol R v Millwall
Charlton Ath v Bristol C
Hull C v Middlesbrough
Ipswich T v Wolverhampton W
Newcastle U v Leicester C
Notts Co v Sheffield W
Oxford U v Portsmouth
Plymouth Arg v Port Vale
WBA v West Ham U

Division Three
AFC Bournemouth v Chester C
Birmingham C v Swansea C
Bradford C v Huddersfield T
Bury v Wigan Ath
Fulham v Reading
Mansfield C v Grimsby T
Shrewsbury T v Preston NE
Stoke C v Exeter C

Division Four
Aldershot v Doncaster R
Blackpool v Hereford U
Carlisle U v Wrexham
Darlington v Stockport Co
Gillingham v Chesterfield
Halifax T v Walsall
Hartlepool U v Torquay U
Peterborough U v Maidstone U
Rochdale v Northampton T
Scarborough v Lincoln C
Scunthorpe U v York C

Sunday 3 March
Division Three
Leyton O v Brentford (12.00)

Friday 8 March
Division Three
Cambridge U v Bradford C

Division Four
Doncaster R v Scunthorpe U
Stockport Co v Scarborough (8.00)

Saturday 9 March
Division One
Arsenal v QPR
Aston Villa v Luton T
Chelsea v Manchester U
Crystal Palace v Southampton

Everton v Wimbledon
Leeds U v Coventry C
Manchester C v Liverpool
Norwich C v Tottenham H
Nottingham F v Derby Co
Sunderland v Sheffield U

Division Two
Bristol C v Ipswich T
Leicester C v Hull C
Middlesbrough v Oxford U
Millwall v Brighton & HA
Oldham Ath v Bristol R
Port Vale v Blackburn R
Portsmouth v Charlton Ath
Sheffield W v WBA
Swindon T v Notts Co
Watford v Newcastle U
West Ham U v Plymouth Arg
Wolverhampton W v Barnsley

Division Three
Bolton W v Fulham
Brentford v Stoke C
Chester C v Mansfield T
Exeter C v Bury
Grimsby T v Southend U
Huddersfield T v Crewe Alex
Preston NE v Leyton O
Reading v Tranmere R
Rotherham U v Birmingham C
Swansea C v AFC Bournemouth
Wigan Ath v Shrewsbury T

Division Four
Burnley v Gillingham
Chesterfield v Halifax T
Hereford U v Aldershot
Lincoln C v Hartlepool U
Maidstone U v Blackpool
Northampton T v Carlisle U
Torquay U v Darlington
Walsall v Cardiff C
Wrexham v Rochdale
York C v Peterborough U

Tuesday 12 March
Division Two
Blackburn R v Bristol R (7.45)
Bristol C v Leicester C (7.45)
Charlton Ath v Wolverhampton W (7.45)
Hull C v Watford
Ipswich T v Barnsley (7.45)
Middlesbrough v Newcastle U
Notts Co v Port Vale (7.45)
Portsmouth v Millwall (7.45)
Swindon T v Oldham Ath (7.45)

Division Three
AFC Bournemouth v Reading (7.45)
Birmingham C v Fulham (7.45)
Brentford v Preston NE (7.45)
Bury v Shrewsbury T
Chester C v Bradford C
Leyton O v Cambridge U (7.45)
Mansfield T v Bolton W
Rotherham U v Grimsby T
Swansea C v Southend U
Wigan Ath v Tranmere R

Division Four
Aldershot v Hartlepool U
Blackpool v Scarborough
Carlisle U v Gillingham
Doncaster R v Torquay U (7.45)
Northampton T v Burnley
Peterborough U v Darlington
Rochdale v Cardiff C
Scunthorpe U v Walsall
Wrexham v Halifax T
York C v Chesterfield

Wednesday 13 March
Division Two
Oxford U v West Ham U

Sheffield W v Brighton & HA (7.45)
WBA v Plymouth Arg

Division Three
Exeter C v Huddersfield T
Stoke C v Crewe Alex

Division Four
Hereford U v Lincoln C
Maidstone U v Stockport C (8.00)

Friday 15 March
Division Three
Southend U v Mansfield T
Tranmere R v Swansea C

Division Four
Halifax T v Northampton T
Torquay U v Peterborough U

Saturday 16 March
Division One
Arsenal v Leeds U
Aston Villa v Tottehnham H
Crystal Palace v Derby Co
Liverpool v Sunderland
Luton T v Norwich C
Manchester C v Wimbledon
Nottingham F v Manchester U
QPR v Coventry C
Sheffield U v Chelsea
Southampton v Everton

Division Two
Barnsley v Charlton Ath
Brighton & HA v Blackburn R
Bristol R v Notts Co
Leicester C v Middlesbrough
Millwall v Swindon T
Newcastle U v Bristol C
Oldham Ath v WBA
Plymouth Arg v Portsmouth
Port Vale v Hull C
Watford v Ipswich T
West Ham U v Sheffield W
Wolverhampton W v Oxford U

Division Three
Bolton W v Wigan Ath
Bradford C v Leyton O
Cambridge U v Exeter C
Crewe Alex v Bury
Fulham v AFC Bournemouth
Grimsby T v Brentford
Huddersfield T v Chester C
Preston NE v Birmingham C
Reading v Rotherham U
Shrewsbury T v Stoke C

Division Four
Burnley v Carlisle U
Cardiff C v Scunthorpe U
Chesterfield v Wrexham
Darlington v Doncaster R
Gillingham v York C
Hartlepool U v Blackpool
Lincoln C v Maidstone U
Scarborough v Aldershot
Stockport Co v Hereford U
Walsall v Rochdale

Monday 18 March
Division Two
Port Vale v Ipswich T

Division Three
Tranmere R v AFC Bournemouth

Division Four
Stockport Co v Northampton T

Tuesday 19 March
Division Two
Barnsley v Portsmouth (7.45)

Oldham Ath v Hull C
Plymouth Arg v Sheffield W (7.45)
Watford v Blackburn R (7.45)
Wolverhampton W v Notts Co

Division Three
Bolton W v Bury
Cambridge U v Brentford
Crewe Alexandra v Swansea C
Fulham v Stoke C
Grimsby T v Chester C
Huddersfield T v Rotherham U
Preston NE v Mansfield T
Reading v Wigan Ath
Shrewsbury T v Leyton O
Southend U v Birmingham C

Division Four
Burnley v Hereford U
Cardiff C v York C
Chesterfield v Rochdale
Darlington v Blackpool
Gillingham v Scunthorpe U
Halifax Town v Carlisle U
Hartlepool U v Doncaster R
Torquay U v Aldershot
Walsall v Maidstone U

Wednesday 20 March
Division One
Chelsea v Leeds U

Division Two
Brighton & HA v WBA
Bristol R v Swindon T (8.00)
Leicester C v Charlton Ath (7.45)
Millwall v Middlesbrough
Newcastle U v Oxford U
West Ham U v Bristol C (7.45)

Division Three
Bradford C v Exeter City (7.45)

Division Four
Lincoln C v Peterborough U (7.45)
Scarborough v Wrexham

Friday 22 March
Division Three
Ipswich T v Plymouth Arg

Division Four
Wrexham v Cardiff C

Saturday 23 March
Division One
Chelsea v Southampton
Coventry C v Manchester C
Derby Co v Liverpool
Everton v Nottingham F
Leeds U v Crystal Palace
Manchester U v Luton T
Norwich C v Arsenal
Sunderland v Aston Villa
Tottenham H v QPR
Wimbledon v Sheffield U

Division Two
Blackburn R v Oldham Ath
Bristol C v Wolverhampton W
Charlton Ath v Port Vale
Hull C v West Ham U
Middlesbrough v Watford
Notts Co v Leicester C
Oxford U v Barnsley
Portsmouth v Newcastle U
Sheffield W v Bristol R
Swindon T v Brighton & HA
WBA v Millwall

Division Three
AFC Bournemouth v Southend U
Birmingham C v Reading
Brentford v Bradford C
Bury v Cambridge U

Chester C v Tranmere R
Exeter C v Preston NE
Leyton Orient v Huddersfield T
Mansfield T v Shrewsbury T
Rotherham U v Fulham
Stoke C v Bolton W
Swansea C v Grimsby T
Wigan Athletic v Crew Alex

Division Four
Aldershot v Lincoln C
Blackpool v Torquay U
Carlisle U v Walsall
Hereford U v Darlington
Maidstone U v Hartlepool U
Northampton T v Chesterfield
Peterborough v Stockport Co
Rochdale v Gillingham
Scunthorpe U v Halifax T
York City v Burnley

Sunday 24 March
Division Four
Doncaster R v Scarborough (12.00 noon)

Friday 29 March
Division Two
Oldham Ath v West Ham U

Division Three
Brentford v Birmingham C
Tranmere R v Cambridge U (7.30)

Division Four
Stockport Co v Hartlepool U

Saturday 30 March
Division One
Aston Villa v Everton
Derby Co v Arsenal
Liverpool v QPR
Manchester C v Southampton
Norwich C v Manchester U
Sheffield U v Luton T
Sunderland v Crystal Palace
Tottenham H v Coventry C
Wimbledon v Nottingham F

Division Two
Barnsley v Plymouth Arg
Bristol R v Brighton & HA
Charlton Ath v WBA
Leicester C v Millwall
Middlesbrough v Ipswich T
Notts Co v Blackburn R
Oxford U v Hull C
Port Vale v Watford
Portsmouth v Bristol C
Swindon T v Newcastle U
Wolverhampton W v Sheffield W

Division Three
Bolton W v Southend U
Bradford C v Fulham
Chester C v Rotherham U
Exeter C v Wigan Ath
Grimsby T v Reading
Huddersfield T v Shrewsbury T
Leyton O v Bury
Mansfield T v Crewe Alex
Preston NE v Crewe Alex
Swansea C v Stoke C

Division Four
Burnley v Chesterfield
Carlisle U v Cardiff C
Darlington v Aldershot
Halifax T v Scarborough
Hereford U v Wrexham
Lincoln C v Torquay U
Maidstone U v Doncaster R
Northampton T v Scunthorpe U
Peterborough U v Blackpool
Walsall v Gillingham

York C v Rochdale

Monday 1 April
Coventry C v Chelsea
Crystal Palace v Manchester C
Everton v Norwich C
Luton T v Tottenham H
Nottingham F v Sheffield U
QPR v Derby Co
Southampton v Liverpool

Division Two
Blackburn R v Middlesbrough
Bristol C v Notts Co
Hull C v Charlton Ath
Newcastle U v Bristol R
Plymouth Arg v Oldham Ath
Sheffield W v Oxford U
Watford v Leicester C
WBA v Swindon T
West Ham U v Barnsley

Division Three
Birmingham C v Tranmere R
Bury v Huddersfield T
Cambridge U v Bolton W
Crewe Alex v Leyton O
Fulham v Mansfield T
Reading v Swansea C
Rotherham U v Exeter C
Stoke C v Preston NE
Wigan Ath v Brentford

Division Four
Aldershot v York C
Cardiff C v Northampton T
Chesterfield v Darlington
Doncaster R v Stockport Co
Gillingham v Lincoln C
Hartlepool U v Burnley
Rochdale v Halifax T (7.30)
Scunthorpe U v Hereford U
Wrexham v Walsall

Tuesday 2 April
Division One
Arsenal v Aston Villa (7.45)
Leeds U v Sunderland (7.45)
Manchester U v Wimbledon (7.45)

Division Two
Ipswich T v Portsmouth (7.45)

Division Three
AFC Bournemouth v Grimsby T (7.45)
Shrewsbury T v Bradford C
Southend U v Chester C

Division Four
Blackpool v Carlisle U
Torquay U v Maidstone U

Wednesday 3 April
Division Two
Brighton & HA v Port Vale
Millwall v Wolverhampton W

Division Four
Scarborough v Peterborough U

Friday 5 April
Division Three
Tranmere R v Rotherham U

Saturday 6 April
Division One
Aston Villa v Manchester U
Chelsea v Luton T
Derby Co v Everton
Liverpool v Crystal Palace
Manchester C v Nottingham F
Norwich C v Coventry C
Sheffield U v Arsenal
Sunderland v QPR

Tottenham H v Southampton
Wimbledon v Leeds U

Division Two
Barnsley v Hull C
Bristol R v Plymouth Arg
Charlton Ath v Ipswich T
Leicester C v Brighton & HA
Middlesbrough v Bristol C
Notts C v Newcastle U
Oldham Ath v Millwall
Oxford U v Blackburn R
Port Vale v West Ham U
Portsmouth v Sheffield W
Swindon T v Watford
Wolverhampton W v WBA

Division Three
Bolton W v Birmingham C
Bradford C v Southend U
Brentford v Crewe Alex
Chester C v Fulham
Exeter C v Shrewsbury T
Grimsby T v Cambridge U
Huddersfield T v Stoke C
Leyton O v AFC Bournemouth
Mansfield T v Reading
Preston NE v Bury
Swansea C v Wigan Ath

Division Four
Burnley v Torquay U
Carlisle U v Scunthorpe U
Darlington v Scarborough
Halifax T v Cardiff C
Hereford U v Doncaster R
Lincoln C v Blackpool
Maidstone U v Rochdale
Northampton T v Gillingham
Peterborough U v Aldershot
Stockport Co v Chesterfield
Walsall v Hartlepool U
York C v Wrexham

Friday 12 April
Division Three
Southend U v Tranmere R

Saturday 13 April
Division One
Arsenal v Manchester C
Coventry C v Derby Co
Crystal Palace v Aston Villa
Everton v Chelsea
Leeds U v Liverpool
Luton T v Wimbledon
Manchester U v Tottenham H
Nottingham F v Norwich C
QPR v Sheffield U
Southampton v Sunderland

Division Two
Blackburn R v Charlton Ath
Brighton & HA v Notts Co
Bristol C v Barnsley
Hull C v Portsmouth
Ipswich T v Oxford U
Millwall v Port Vale
Newcastle U v Oldham Ath
Plymouth Argyle v Swindon T
Sheffield Wednesday v Middlesbrough
Watford v Wolverhampton W
WBA v Leicester C
West Ham U v Bristol R

Division Three
AFC Bournemouth v Bolton W
Birmingham C v Mansfield T
Bury v Bradford C
Cambridge U v Preston NE
Crewe Alex v Exeter C
Fulham v Grimsby T
Reading v Chester C
Rotherham U v Swansea C

Shrewsbury T v Brentford
Stoke C v Leyton O
Wigan Ath v Huddersfield T

Division Four
Aldershot v Carlisle U
Blackpool v York C
Cardiff City v Darlington
Chesterfield v Maidstone U
Doncaster R v Northampton T
Gillingham v Stockport Co
Hartlepool U v Halifax T
Rochdale v Peterborough U
Scarborough v Walsall
Scunthorpe U v Burnley (11.00)
Torquay U v Hereford U
Wrexham v Lincoln C

Wednesday 17 April
Division One
QPR v Leeds U

Friday 19 April
Division Three
Southend U v Wigan Ath

Division Four
Halifax T v York C
Stockport Co v Aldershot

Saturday 20 April
Arsenal v Manchester U
Aston Villa v Wimbledon
Crystal Palace v Everton
Liverpool v Norwich C
Luton T v Sunderland
Manchester C v Derby Co
Nottingham F v Chelsea
Sheffield U v Tottenham H
Southampton v Coventry C

Division Two
Barnsley v WBA
Brighton & HA v Oxford U
Bristol R v Middlesbrough
Leicester C v Portsmouth
Millwall v Notts Co
Newcastle U v Ipswich T
Oldham Ath v Bristol C
Plymouth Argyle v Blackburn R
Port Vale v Sheffield W
Watford v Charlton Ath
West Ham U v Swindon T
Wolverhampton W v Hull C

Division Three
Bolton W v Leyton O
Bradford C v Mansfield T
Cambridge U v Stoke C
Crew Alex v AFC Bournemouth
Fulham v Swansea C
Grimsby T v Birmingham C
Huddersfield T v Brentford
Preston NE v Rotherham U
Reading v Bury
Shrewsbury T v Chester C
Tranmere R v Exeter C

Division Four
Burnley v Peterborogh U
Cardiff C v Hereford U
Chesterfield v Carlisle U
Darlington v Maidstone U
Gillingham v Blackpool
Hartlepool U v Wrexham
Lincoln C v Doncaster R
Scarborough v Scunthorpe U
Torquay U v Rochdale
Walsall v Northampton T

Saturday 28 April
Division Two
Blackburn R v West Ham U
Bristol C v Millwall
Charlton Ath v Newcastle U

Hull C v Brighton & HA
Ipswich T v Oldham Ath
Middlesbrough v Wolverhampton W
Notts Co v Plymouth Arg
Oxford U v Bristol R
Portsmouth v Watford
Sheffield W v Barnsley
Swindon T v Leicester C
WBA v Port Vale

Division Three
AFC Bournemouth v Huddersfield T
Birmingham C v Crewe Alex
Brentford v Reading
Bury v Fulham
Chester C v Preston NE
Exeter C v Southend U
Leyton Orient v Grimsby T
Mansfield T v Tranmere R
Rotherham U v Bolton W
Stoke C v Bradford C
Swansea C v Shrewsbury T
Wigan Ath v Cambridge U

Division Four
Aldershot v Gillingham
Blackpool v Stockport Co
Carlisle U v Scarborough
Doncaster R v Cardiff C
Hereford U v Halifax T
Maidstone U v Burnley
Northampton T v Darlington
Peterborough U v Harlepool U
Rochdale v Lincoln C
Scunthorpe U v Chesterfield
Wrexham v Torquay U
York C v Walsall

Tuesday 30 April
Division Three
AFC Bournemouth v Preston NE
(7.45)

Division Four
Blackpool v Halifax T
Northampton T v Lincoln C

Friday 3 May
Division Four
York C v Stockport Co

Saturday 4 May
Division One
Chelsea v Liverpool
Coventry C v Sheffield U
Derby Co v Southampton
Everton v Luton T
Leeds U v Aston Villa
Manchester U v Manchester C
Norwich C v QPR
Sunderland v Arsenal
Tottenham H v Nottingham F
Wimbledon v Crystal Palace

Division Two
Blackburn R v Wolverhampton W
Bristol C v Port Vale
Charlton Ath v West Ham U
Hull C v Plymouth Arg
Ipswich T v Leicester C
Middlesbrough v Brighton & HA
Notts Co v Oldham Ath
Oxford U v Watford
Portsmouth v Bristol R
Sheffield W v Millwall
Swindon T v Barnsley
WBA v Newcastle U

Division Three
Birmingham C v Shrewsbury T
Brentford v Tranmere R
Bury v Southend U
Chester C v Crewe Alex
Exeter C v Fulham
Leyton O v Reading

Mansfield T v Huddersfield T
Rotherham U v Cambridge U
Stoke C v Grimsby T
Swansea C v Bolton W
Wigan Ath v Bradford C

Division Four
Aldershot v Walsall
Carlisle U v Torquay U
Doncaster R v Chesterfield
Hereford U v Hartlepool U
Maidstone U v Scarborough
Peterborough U v Cardiff C
Rochdale v Burnley
Scunthorpe U v Darlington
Wrexham v Gillingham

Saturday 11 May
Division One
Arsenal v Coventry C
Aston Villa v Chelsea
Crystal Palace v Manchester U
Liverpool v Tottenham H
Luton T v Derby Co
Manchester C v Sunderland
Nottingham F v Leeds U
QPR v Everton
Sheffield U v Norwich C
Southampton v Wimbledon

Division Two
Barnsley v Middlesbrough
Brighton & HA v Ipswich T
Bristol R v WBA
Leicester C v Oxford U
Millwall v Blackburn R
Newcastle U v Hull C
Oldham Ath v Sheffield W
Plymouth Arg v Charlton Ath
Port Vale v Swindon T
Watford v Bristol C
West Ham U v Notts Co
Wolverhampton W v Portsmouth

Division Three
Bolton W v Chester C
Bradford C v Rotherham U
Cambridge U v Swansea C
Crewe Alex v Mansfield T
Fulham v Leyton O
Grimsby T v Exeter C
Huddersfield T v Birmingham C
Preston NE v Wigan Ath
Reading v Stoke C
Shrewsbury T v AFC Bournemouth
Southend U v Brentford
Tranmere R v Bury

Division Four
Burnley v Wrexham
Cardiff C v Maidstone U
Chesterfield v Peterborough U
Darlington v Rochdale
Gillingham v Doncaster R
Halifax T v Aldershot
Hartlepool U v Northampton T
Lincoln C v Carlisle U
Scarborough v Hereford U
Stockport Co v Scunthorpe U
Torquay U v York C
Walsall v Blackpool

BARCLAYS LEAGUE FIXTURES 1990–91

The copyrights in the League Fixtures Lists are owned by The Football League Limited and have been reproduced with their permission under Licence. © The Football League Limited 1990. Subject to alteration.

DIVISION ONE

	Arsenal	Aston Villa	Chelsea	Coventry C	Crystal Palace	Derby C	Everton	Leeds U	Liverpool	Luton T	Manchester C	Manchester U	Norwich C	Nottingham F	QPR	Sheffield U	Southampton	Sunderland	Tottenham H	Wimbledon
Arsenal	—	2.4	15.9	11.5	23.2	26.12	19.1	16.3	1.12	29.8	13.4	20.4	6.10	9.2	9.3	29.12	17.11	27.10	1.9	15.12
Aston Villa	22.12	—	11.5	8.9	1.1	2.2	30.3	27.10	12.1	9.3	8.12	6.4	16.2	10.11	22.9	1.12	25.8	6.10	16.3	20.4
Chelsea	2.2	3.11	—	22.12	8.12	25.8	1.1	20.3	4.5	6.4	22.9	9.3	10.11	20.10	12.1	29.9	23.3	8.9	1.12	16.2
Coventry C	3.11	19.1	1.4	—	2.3	13.4	29.8	24.11	17.11	9.2	23.3	15.12	29.12	1.9	29.9	4.5	20.10	23.2	26.12	15.9
Crystal Palace	10.11	13.4	28.8	1.12	—	16.3	20.4	6.10	29.12	16.12	1.4	11.5	19.1	15.9	16.2	1.9	4.5	26.12	9.2	27.10
Derby Co	30.3	15.9	15.12	1.1	16.3	—	6.4	16.2	22.9	3.11	20.10	10.11	9.2	24.11	23.12	29.8	29.9	2.3	19.1	1.9
Everton	8.9	26.12	13.4	8.12	29.12	6.4	—	25.8	22.9	4.5	12.1	15.9	1.4	23.3	31.1	23.2	29.9	2.2	17.11	9.3
Leeds U	29.9	4.5	26.12	9.3	20.10	16.2	25.8	—	13.4	8.9	8.12	17.4	11.5	23.9	17.4	13.4	23.12	2.4	23.9	6.4
Liverpool	2.3	1.9	27.10	16.2	23.3	22.9	13.4	8.9	—	23.2	2.2	8.12	20.10	26.12	25.8	23.9	1.4	29.9	3.11	8.9
Luton T	8.12	24.11	29.12	22.9	6.4	3.11	4.5	23.9	29.9	—	23.2	30.3	20.10	1.12	23.2	30.3	20.10	20.10	22.12	1.1
Manchester C	1.1	5.9	9.2	6.10	25.8	20.10	2.3	8.12	2.2	23.2	—	30.3	26.12	29.9	1.12	8.9	26.12	3.11	25.8	29.9
Manchester U	20.10	29.12	24.11	25.8	22.12	10.11	7.10	17.4	8.12	30.3	4.5	—	13.4	19.1	8.9	16.2	1.9	1.1	9.3	1.12
Norwich C	23.3	17.11	23.2	6.4	3.11	9.2	22.12	11.5	20.10	29.9	29.12	13.4	—	27.10	11.5	15.9	28.8	1.12	15.12	24.11
Nottingham F	22.9	23.2	20.4	12.1	8.9	24.11	11.5	23.9	26.12	1.12	29.9	19.1	23.3	—	22.12	1.4	22.12	19.1	16.2	4.5
QPR	24.11	9.2	1.9	16.3	2.2	23.12	31.1	17.4	25.8	23.2	1.12	16.2	11.5	22.12	—	13.4	2.2	1.1	6.10	8.12
Sheffield U	6.4	2.3	16.3	27.10	12.1	8.12	10.11	13.4	23.9	24.11	8.9	22.12	27.10	15.12	22.12	—	2.2	13.4	6.10	11.5
Southampton	16.2	15.12	6.10	20.4	30.3	1.12	16.3	23.12	1.4	1.9	26.12	9.2	11.5	28.8	9.3	15.9	—	1.1	29.12	9.2
Sunderland	4.5	23.3	19.1	10.11	1.12	2.3	1.4	2.3	29.9	20.10	3.11	1.1	15.12	19.1	6.4	9.3	1.1	—	28.8	10.11
Tottenham H	12.1	29.9	2.3	30.3	22.9	8.9	16.2	2.2	3.11	22.12	25.8	9.3	24.11	16.2	23.3	20.10	6.4	8.12	—	23.2
Wimbledon	25.8	20.10	17.11	2.2	4.5	12.1	24.11	6.4	8.9	1.1	29.9	1.12	2.3	30.3	8.12	11.5	3.11	10.11	23.2	—

DIVISION TWO

	Barnsley	Blackburn R	Brighton & HA	Bristol C	Bristol R	Charlton Ath	Hull C	Ipswich T	Leicester C	Middlesbrough	Millwall	Newcastle U	Notts Co	Oldham Ath	Oxford U	Plymouth Arg	Portsmouth	Port Vale	Sheffield W	Swindon T	Watford	WBA	West Ham U	Wolverhampton W
Barnsley	—	2.2	25.8	1.1	8.12	16.3	6.4	2.10	10.11	11.5	12.1	16.2	12.2	8.9	6.10	30.3	19.3	22.9	23.10	27.10	2.3	20.4	22.12	24.11
Blackburn R	15.9	—	29.9	15.12	12.3	13.4	28.8	19.1	18.9	1.4	3.11	1.9	26.12	23.3	29.12	10.10	9.2	23.11	10.11	2.3	13.10	16.2	27.4	4.5
Brighton & HA	15.12	16.3	—	9.2	26.12	15.9	24.10	11.5	29.12	27.10	24.0	7.11	13.4	2.3	20.4	10.11	19.9	3.4	3.10	6.10	19.1	20.3	16.2	1.9
Bristol C	13.4	25.8	22.9	—	12.2	1.12	17.11	9.3	29.12	20.4	27.4	29.9	1.4	20.10	23.2	8.9	19.9	4.5	8.12	12.1	3.11	2.2	16.2	23.3
Bristol R	7.11	3.10	30.3	19.9	—	1.9	15.9	9.2	15.12	20.4	23.2	22.12	16.3	23.2	24.10	6.4	27.10	10.11	26.12	20.3	16.2	11.5	13.10	19.1
Charlton Ath	29.9	1.1	30.3	19.9	1.9	—	22.12	6.4	13.10	23.2	22.9	27.4	8.12	12.2	17.11	6.4	24.11	23.3	8.9	25.8	20.10	20.10	27.4	12.3
Hull C	29.12	8.12	27.4	16.2	2.2	1.4	—	10.11	23.11	23.2	2.3	3.11	25.8	13.10	26.12	21.12	24.11	19.3	11.5	6.4	20.10	12.3	23.3	22.12
Ipswich T	12.3	8.9	3.11	16.2	2.2	10.11	10.11	—	4.5	26.12	2.2	2.10	12.1	3.11	15.9	21.12	18.3	1.1	11.5	2.10	9.2	1.9	22.9	2.3
Leicester C	23.2	13.2	6.4	3.10	15.12	4.5	26.12	4.5	—	16.3	30.3	2.2	6.10	8.12	11.5	2.2	20.4	2.4	25.8	24.10	23.12	1.1	12.1	17.11
Middlesbrough	3.11	22.12	27.10	29.12	20.3	10.11	16.3	30.3	16.3	—	13.10	1.12	8.9	22.9	13.10	2.2	16.2	12.2	1.1	2.3	23.3	6.10	20.10	18.9
Millwall	1.9	11.5	9.3	24.10	1.12	9.2	20.3	15.9	29.9	13.10	—	19.1	20.4	29.12	7.11	16.2	3.10	13.4	1.1	2.3	23.3	6.10	10.11	3.4
Newcastle U	17.11	12.1	8.12	16.3	1.1	22.12	20.4	16.2	23.3	20.3	8.9	—	29.12	13.4	1.9	27.4	15.9	13.4	2.3	26.12	24.11	27.10	22.9	23.2
Notts Co	18.9	30.3	1.1	22.12	23.3	28.8	23.3	16.2	28.8	19.1	20.10	19.1	—	4.5	1.9	27.4	15.9	16.2	2.10	24.11	10.11	10.11	3.11	16.2
Oldham Ath	19.1	6.10	1.12	20.4	9.3	18.9	19.3	23.10	28.8	9.2	6.4	1.1	27.0	—	15.9	21.12	1.9	16.2	11.5	2.10	10.11	16.3	29.3	15.12
Oxford U	23.3	6.4	20.10	10.11	27.4	16.2	1.1	1.1	3.11	24.11	8.12	13.10	12.1	2.2	—	13.2	2.3	2.3	22.12	22.9	4.5	8.9	13.3	29.9
Plymouth Arg	26.12	20.4	23.2	19.1	29.12	11.5	1.9	21.12	1.9	23.3	2.2	16.12	23.10	1.4	18.9	—	16.3	2.3	19.3	13.4	28.8	2.10	24.11	9.2
Portsmouth	13.10	9.3	12.2	30.3	23.2	27.10	17.11	21.12	17.9	2.2	1.10	23.3	2.2	12.1	15.12	13.10	—	19.1	6.4	23.2	27.4	23.10	29.12	19.3
Port Vale	9.2	9.3	3.4	23.2	8.9	6.10	2.3	25.8	2.4	13.10	3.11	2.3	1.10	17.11	18.9	29.9	16.3	—	8.9	20.10	3.11	26.12	8.12	3.11
Sheffield W	27.4	23.2	13.2	7.11	23.3	19.1	15.12	15.12	9.2	20.4	4.5	19.9	9.3	17.11	15.12	1.12	19.1	20.4	—	17.11	30.5	22.10	9.3	20.3
Swindon T	4.5	1.12	2.3	2.9	7.11	23.3	28.8	16.3	27.4	15.9	30.9	25.8	9.3	12.3	9.2	13.3	29.12	3.11	20.4	—	6.4	17.11	17.11	29.12
Watford	1.12	19.3	8.9	11.5	19.1	13.4	1.4	16.3	1.4	6.10	25.8	9.3	22.9	23.2	27.10	8.12	23.10	26.12	2.2	29.12	—	12.2	12.1	13.3
WBA	20.10	17.11	13.10	15.9	3.11	26.12	9.2	1.9	13.4	23.2	23.2	4.5	22.9	29.9	19.1	13.3	15.12	27.4	24.11	1.4	5.12	—	12.2	29.12
West Ham U	1.4	24.10	17.11	20.3	13.4	27.10	19.9	19.1	23.2	9.2	11.5	9.2	11.5	29.8	3.10	9.3	29.8	29.12	16.3	20.4	1.9	1.12	—	15.9
Wolverhampton W	9.3	27.10	12.1	6.10	8.9	2.10	20.4	16.2	19.1	23.10	19.3	10.11	19.3	25.8	16.3	22.9	11.5	8.12	30.3	12.2	1.1	6.4	2.2	—

DIVISION THREE

	Birmingham C	Bolton W	Bournemouth	Bradford C	Brentford	Bury	Cambridge	Chester C	Crewe Alex	Exeter C	Fulham	Grimsby	Huddersfield T	Leyton O	Mansfield T	Preston NE	Reading	Rotherham U	Shrewsbury T	Southend u	Stoke C	Swansea C	Tranmere R	Wigan Ath
Birmingham C	—	29.12	24.11	5.1	26.12	15.9	19.1	23.2	27.4	18.9	12.3	20.10	3.11	1.9	13.4	29.9	23.3	15.12	4.5	13.10	9.2	2.3	1.4	5.2
Bolton W	6.4	—	1.1	1.9	5.2	19.3	22.12	11.5	15.9	5.1	29.9	16.2	9.2	20.4	2.10	18.9	10.11	23.10	19.1	30.3	6.10	27.10	1.12	16.3
Bournemouth	16.2	13.4	—	18.9	19.1	1.9	5.1	2.3	20.10	5.2	29.9	2.4	27.4	6.4	26.12	30.4	12.3	10.11	3.11	23.3	15.9	14.12	16.10	8.2
Bradford C	13.2	12.1	2.2	—	6.10	1.1	15.12	3.10	16.2	20.3	30.3	26.1	2.3	16.3	20.4	10.11	8.9	11.5	22.12	6.4	24.10	22.9	25.8	27.10
Brentford	29.3	22.9	25.8	23.3	—	10.11	14.10	8.9	6.4	16.2	12.2	29.9	16.3	2.12	12.1	29.12	27.4	2.2	1.1	4.1	9.3	26.1	4.5	23.12
Bury	26.1	13.10	12.1	13.4	23.2	—	23.3	25.8	29.9	15.12	27.4	12.2	1.4	6.10	22.9	29.12	26.1	8.9	24.11	4.5	24.11	2.2	3.11	2.3
Cambridge	25.8	1.4	8.3	12.3	19.3	6.10	—	21.9	30.11	16.3	12.1	29.12	23.2	2.10	1.2	3.4	1.1	30.3	20.10	22.12	20.4	11.5	26.12	23.10
Chester C	10.11	3.11	12.3	8.3	9.2	21.9	5.2	—	4.5	1.9	6.4	13.10	16.3	15.9	9.3	27.4	1.1	12.2	22.2	12.1	18.9	19.3	23.3	5.1
Crewe Alex	23.10	25.1	20.4	24.11	29.12	13.10	4.5	27.10	—	13.4	25.8	8.9	15.12	1.4	1.2	23.2	1.2	30.3	22.2	12.1	1.12	8.9	21.9	6.10
Exeter	2.2	13.2	22.9	13.10	5.1	20.3	4.5	12.1	1.1	—	25.8	3.11	13.3	23.2	1.4	5.2	25.8	6.10	6.4	27.4	1.12	8.9	20.10	30.3
Fulham	20.4	13.2	16.3	30.3	12.2	27.4	1.9	6.4	25.8	4.5	—	13.4	15.9	11.5	1.4	23.10	2.3	6.10	9.2	23.2	19.3	20.4	24.11	18.9
Grimsby T	11.5	8.9	22.12	1.12	16.3	5.1	6.4	16.3	6.10	3.11	1.1	—	18.9	6.10	1.12	16.2	30.3	19.3	30.3	9.3	27.10	6.10	23.2	1.9
Huddersfield T	12.1	8.9	6.4	1.12	20.4	22.12	10.11	16.3	29.9	23.3	4.11	2.2	—	6.10	27.10	16.2	22.9	22.9	13.10	25.8	1.1	12.1	12.2	1.1
Leyton O	1.1	20.10	6.4	29.9	1.9	5.2	12.3	26.1	1.9	23.3	22.12	2.2	23.3	—	8.9	15.12	12.1	22.9	13.10	12.2	5.1	25.8	2.2	24.11
Mansfield T	16.3	2.10	26.12	20.4	12.1	22.9	1.2	9.3	1.2	4.5	22.9	27.10	8.9	19.3	—	3.4	19.3	24.11	6.10	15.3	13.2	12.2	27.4	19.1
Preston NE	6.10	27.10	30.3	23.2	1.9	6.4	3.11	13.4	30.3	6.10	1.12	2.3	4.5	9.3	19.3	—	12.1	16.2	23.3	26.1	2.12	12.2	8.9	19.1
Reading	9.3	23.2	2.10	9.2	23.10	4.5	6.10	13.4	27.10	19.1	29.12	2.3	5.2	9.3	24.11	20.10	—	16.3	1.12	26.1	22.12	1.4	9.3	15.9
Rotherham U	27.10	27.4	23.2	3.11	18.9	9.2	4.5	26.12	5.1	1.4	8.9	12.3	13.10	20.10	24.11	6.10	29.9	—	1.9	2.2	19.1	13.4	29.12	15.9
Shrewsbury T	19.3	25.8	11.5	2.4	13.4	2.10	16.2	20.4	9.11	29.12	8.9	22.9	26.12	19.3	6.10	2.3	12.2	12.1	—	2.2	16.3	23.10	25.1	15.12
Southend U	8.9	26.12	5.10	28.12	11.5	27.10	8.2	2.4	1.9	2.3	10.11	15.12	19.1	4.1	15.3	15.9	15.2	1.3	18.9	—	5.2	2.10	12.4	19.4
Stoke C	1.12	23.3	26.1	27.4	16.12	16.2	20.10	2.2	13.3	2.3	13.10	4.5	29.12	13.4	13.2	1.4	3.11	25.8	29.9	22.9	—	26.12	12.1	10.11
Swansea C	21.12	4.5	9.3	5.2	15.9	18.9	3.11	24.11	13.10	8.2	16.2	23.3	1.9	19.1	23.2	5.1	22.12	1.1	27.4	12.3	30.3	—	28.9	6.4
Tranmere R	22.9	1.3	18.3	18.1	26.10	11.5	29.3	6.10	4.2	20.4	16.2	10.11	5.1	17.9	22.10	8.2	14.12	5.4	14.9	1.1	31.8	15.3	—	1.10
Wigan Ath	22.9	28.9	8.9	4.5	1.4	1.12	27.4	12.2	23.3	26.12	2.2	12.1	13.4	24.11	25.8	3.11	13.10	26.1	9.3	20.10	23.2	29.12	12.3	—

DIVISION FOUR

	Aldershot	Blackpool	Burnley	Cardiff C	Carlisle U	Chesterfield C	Darlington	Doncaster R	Gillingham	Halifax	Hartlepool U	Hereford U	Lincoln C	Maidstone U	Northampton T	Peterborough U	Rochdale	Scarborough	Scunthorpe U	Stockport Co	Torquay U	Walsall	Wrexham	York C
Aldershot	—	23.2	22.9	18.9	13.4	5.1	26.12	2.3	27.4	2.11	12.3	15.12	23.3	24.11	14.9	29.12	19.1	29.9	16.3	19.10	12.10	4.5	9.2	1.4
Blackpool	10.11	—	18.9	5.1	2.4	5.2	13.10	16.2	20.10	30.4	29.9	2.3	29.12	15.12	9.2	26.12	1.9	12.3	3.10	27.4	23.3	3.11	15.9	13.4
Burnley	22.9	2.2	—	1.12	16.3	30.3	12.1	12.2	9.3	24.11	22.12	19.3	21.12	25.8	19.1	20.4	27.0	8.9	13.4	26.1	6.4	23.2	11.5	6.10
Cardiff C	1.2	12.2	1.12	—	26.12	10.11	12.1	23.10	9.11	13.4	1.9	27.10	13.10	23.10	21.12	4.5	12.3	19.1	29.9	4.2	8.2	15.12	5.10	19.3
Carlisle U	1.1	23.12	28.9	23.2	—	20.10	5.1	25.8	2.10	19.3	4.5	3.10	29.12	24.10	24.10	1.2	2.10	27.4	29.12	2.2	4.5	23.3	2.3	10.11
Chesterfield	12.2	22.9	26.12	10.11	20.4	—	1.4	27.10	2.3	9.3	12.1	8.9	2.2	13.4	6.10	12.1	16.2	27.4	4.5	2.2	26.1	24.11	16.3	2.10
Darlington	30.3	19.3	1.9	1.1	5.1	22.12	—	16.3	3.11	15.9	10.11	8.9	2.2	13.4	6.10	8.9	19.3	12.1	20.4	9.3	15.12	9.2	5.2	18.9
Doncaster R	1.12	24.11	5.1	27.4	19.1	4.5	16.3	—	3.11	15.9	26.1	6.10	5.1	26.12	23.10	2.10	26.1	24.3	27.10	2.3	12.3	18.9	1.9	5.2
Gillingham	23.10	20.4	15.12	24.11	2.10	2.3	1.4	5.1	—	22.2	29.12	29.12	20.10	22.9	29.12	22.2	26.1	24.3	27.10	1.4	11.1	18.9	27.10	16.3
Halifax T	11.5	27.10	16.2	6.4	19.3	15.12	15.9	15.9	22.2	—	1.1	2.2	9.2	22.9	29.12	1.2	6.10	25.1	6.10	13.4	11.1	26.1	2.10	19.4
Hartlepool U	2.10	16.3	1.4	1.9	5.2	19.1	10.11	26.1	29.12	1.1	—	27.10	13.3	6.10	11.5	23.10	18.9	30.3	5.1	23.3	21.9	2.3	2.10	14.9
Hereford U	9.3	1.12	13.10	20.10	15.9	9.2	8.9	6.10	29.12	2.2	27.10	—	13.3	23.2	11.5	24.11	5.1	3.11	29.9	2.3	1.1	6.2	30.3	1.9
Lincoln C	6.10	6.4	19.1	15.9	11.5	19.9	2.2	5.1	20.10	9.2	13.3	13.3	—	16.3	27.10	20.3	24.10	3.11	6.2	23.2	30.3	5.1	1.1	9.2
Maidstone	16.2	9.3	27.4	3.11	24.11	1.1	13.4	26.12	22.9	22.9	6.10	23.2	16.3	—	1.9	1.12	6.4	4.5	15.9	13.3	22.12	13.10	19.9	19.1
Northampton T	26.1	8.9	12.3	21.12	24.10	3.11	6.10	23.10	29.12	29.12	11.5	11.5	27.10	1.9	—	22.9	6.4	4.5	15.9	13.10	22.12	19.10	9.11	15.2
Peterborough U	6.4	30.3	20.4	12.1	2.3	23.3	3.11	1.1	5.1	18.9	18.3	16.2	19.1	16.2	1.9	—	1.1	1.2	23.3	8.9	29.9	15.9	19.1	15.12
Rochdale	25.8	12.1	4.5	12.3	2.10	16.2	19.3	26.1	6.10	6.10	18.9	5.1	24.10	6.4	1.12	22.9	—	1.2	6.2	10.11	20.4	29.9	15.12	26.12
Scarborough	16.3	3.10	9.2	19.1	13.10	27.4	12.1	24.3	24.3	25.1	30.3	3.11	3.11	4.5	4.5	1.2	1.2	—	2.2	8.9	20.10	13.4	20.3	5.1
Scunthorpe U	12.1	25.8	13.4	29.9	19.1	24.10	4.5	29.12	1.4	26.1	26.12	1.4	22.9	27.10	1.10	8.9	20.4	2.11	—	3.11	20.10	12.3	16.2	2.3
Stockport Co	19.4	22.10	14.9	4.2	17.9	15.9	9.3	2.2	1.1	5.2	18.3	16.3	10.11	2.4	4.1	15.3	9.2	22.2	20.4	—	2.2	1.9	4.1	26.10
Torquay U	19.3	6.10	29.12	8.2	17.9	16.2	15.12	12.3	12.3	11.1	18.3	1.1	30.3	15.2	12.2	29.9	20.4	8.3	20.4	15.2	—	19.1	23.10	11.5
Walsall	27.10	11.5	3.11	9.3	27.10	16.2	8.9	2.2	30.3	6.4	20.4	26.1	12.2	19.3	20.4	25.8	16.3	22.2	23.2	12.1	25.8	—	21.12	23.10
Wrexham	8.9	26.1	23.3	22.3	1.12	29.9	22.9	12.1	24.11	9.3	2.3	26.12	13.4	19.3	20.4	25.8	9.3	1.1	23.2	12.2	12.2	1.4	—	29.12
York C	21.12	1.1	5.2	13.10	23.2	12.3	22.9	2.2	29.9	30.3	24.11	8.9	8.9	25.8	24.11	9.3	30.3	12.2	29.9	3.5	3.11	27.4	6.4	—

THE FOOTBALL ASSOCIATION
FIXTURE PROGRAMME – SEASON 1990–91

August
11 Sat Official Opening of Season
18 Sat Tennent's FA Charity Shield
25 Sat Football League Season starts
29 Wed Littlewoods Cup 1st Round (1st Leg)

September
1 Sat FA Cup Preliminary Round
5 Wed Littlewoods Cup 1st Round (2nd Leg)
8 Sat FA Vase Extra Preliminary Round
       FA Youth Cup Preliminary Round*
11 Tue Hungary v England (U21)
12 Wed Hungary v England (F)
        Scotland v Romania (EC)
        N.Ireland v Yugoslavia (EC)
        Iceland v England (U17)
15 Sat FA Cup 1st Round Qualifying
19 Wed European Cups 1st Round (1st Leg)
22 Sat FA Trophy 1st Round Qualifying
26 Wed Littlewoods Cup 2nd Round (1st Leg)
29 Sat FA Cup 2nd Round Qualifying
        FA Youth Cup 1st Round Qualifying*

October
3 Wed European Cups 1st Round (2nd Leg)
6 Sat FA Vase Preliminary Round
10 Wed Littlewoods Cup 2nd Round (2nd Leg)
13 Sat FA Cup 3rd Round Qualifying
        FA Youth Cup 2nd Round Qualifying*
14 Sun FA Sunday Cup 1st Round
16 Tue England v Poland (U21)
        England v Belgium (U17)
17 Wed England v Poland (EC)
        Scotland v Switzerland (EC)
        N. Ireland v Denmark (EC)
        Wales v Belgium (EC)
20 Sat FA Trophy 2nd Round Qualifying
        FA County Youth Cup 1st Round*
24 Wed European Cups 2nd Round (1st Leg)
27 Sat FA Cup 4th Round Qualifying
31 Wed Littlewoods Cup 3rd Round

November
3 Sat FA Vase 1st Round
7 Wed European Cups 2nd Round (2nd Leg)
10 Sat FA Youth Cup 1st Round Proper*
11 Sun FA Sunday Cup 2nd Round
13 Tue Rep of Ireland v England (U21)
14 Wed Rep of Ireland v England (EC)
        Bulgaria v Scotland (EC)
        Austria v N. Ireland (EC)
        Luxembourg v Wales (EC)
17 Sat FA Cup 1st Round Proper
24 Sat FA Vase 2nd Round
28 Wed UEFA Cup 3rd Round (1st Leg)
        Littlewoods Cup 4th Round

December
1 Sat FA Trophy 3rd Round Qualifying
       FA County Youth Cup 2nd Round*
8 Sat FA Cup 2nd Round Proper
       FA Youth Cup 2nd Round Proper*
9 Sun FA Sunday Cup 3rd Round
12 Wed UEFA Cup 3rd Round (2nd Leg)
15 Sat FA Vase 3rd Round
22 Sat
29 Sat

January
5 Sat FA Cup 3rd Round Proper
12 Sat FA Trophy 1st Round Proper
        FA Youth Cup 3rd Round Proper*

16 Wed Littlewoods Cup 5th Round
19 Sat FA Vase 4th Round
        FA County Youth Cup 3rd Round*
20 Sun FA Sunday Cup 4th Round
26 Sat FA Cup 4th Round Proper

February
2 Sat FA Trophy 2nd Round Proper
6 International Date
9 Sat FA Vase 5th Round
       FA Youth Cup 4th Round Proper*
13 Wed Littlewoods Cup Semi-Finals (1st Leg)
16 Sat FA Cup 5th Round Proper
17 Sun FA Sunday Cup 5th Round
23 Sat FA Trophy 3rd Round Proper
        FA County Youth Cup 4th Round*
27 Wed Littlewoods Cup Semi-Finals (2nd Leg)

March
2 Sat FA Vase 6th Round
       FA Youth Cup 5th Round Proper*
6 Wed European Cups Quarter Finals (1st Leg)
9 Sat FA Cup 6th Round Proper
       England v Scotland (Schoolboys)
16 Sat FA Trophy 4th Round Proper
20 Wed European Cups Quarter Finals (2nd Leg)
23 Sat FA Vase Semi-Finals (1st Leg)
        FA County Youth Cup Semi-Final*
24 Sun FA Sunday Cup Semi-Finals
26 Tue England v Rep of Ireland (U21)
27 Wed England v Rep of Ireland (EC)
        Scotland v Bulgaria (EC)
        Yugoslavia v N. Ireland (EC)
        Belgium v Wales (EC)
30 Sat FA Vase Semi-Finals (2nd Leg)
        FA Youth Cup Semi-Final*

April
6 Sat FA Trophy Semi-Finals (1st Leg)
10 Wed European Cups Semi-Finals (1st Leg)
13 Sat FA Trophy Semi-Finals (2nd Leg)
14 Sun FA Cup Semi-Finals
20 Sat
21 Sun Littlewoods Cup Final
24 Wed European Cups Semi-Finals (2nd Leg)
27 Sat FA County Youth Cup Final
        Rugby League Final
30 Tue Turkey v England (U21)
        Wales v England (U17)

May
1 Wed Turkey v England (EC)
       San Marino v Scotland (EC)
       East Germany v Wales (EC)
4 Sat FA Vase Final
       FA Youth Cup Final*
5 Sun FA Sunday Cup Final
8 Wed UEFA Cup Final (1st Leg)
11 Sat FA Trophy Final
15 Wed European Cup Winners' Cup Final
18 Sat FA Cup Final
22 Wed UEFA Cup Final (2nd Leg)
        England v Wales (U17)
29 Wed European Champion Clubs' Cup Final

June
5 Wed Wales v West Germany (EC)
8 Sat England v West Germany (Schoolboys)
* Closing date for Rounds